The Who, What, and Where of America

The Who, What, *and* Where *of* America

Understanding the American Community Survey

edited by
Deirdre A. Gaquin
Gwenavere W. Dunn

 **Bernan** Press

Lanham • Boulder • New York • Toronto • Plymouth, UK

Published by Bernan Press
A wholly owned subsidary of
The Rowman & Littlefield Publishing Group, Inc.
4501 Forbes Boulevard, Suite 200
Lanham, Maryland 20706

800-865-3457; info@bernan.com

10 Thornbury Road, Plymouth PL6 7PP, United Kingdom

ISBN 13: 978-1-59888-709-9
e-ISBN: 978-1-59888-710-5

⊗ ™ The paper used in this publication meets the minimum requirements of
American National Standard for Information Sciences—Permanence of
Paper for Printed Library Materials, ANSI/NISO Z39.48-1992.
Manufactured in the United States of America.

Contents

Contents

v

Page

Preface

The 2010 census was different from any census in recent memory. All American households answered a simple questionnaire with ten questions. No longer did some people get the "long form" with dozens of detailed questions about employment, education, income, previous residence, housing characteristics, and more. The data gleaned from these important questions have long been used by federal, state, and local governments to evaluate their populations and program needs; by large and small businesses and nonprofit organizations for a variety of planning and location purposes; and by academic researchers to study trends in social and economic conditions. The "long form" has been replaced by the American Community Survey (ACS). Under development for more than a decade, the ACS is an ongoing survey of the American people that is ushering in a new era in social and economic data analysis. The census "long form" provided detailed estimates of social and economic characteristics every ten years. The ACS collects this same information on a rolling basis. It takes 5 years of ACS responses to accumulate a sample almost as large as the census "long form" collected at a single point in time. But data users now have the ability to study these characteristics and trends throughout the decade.

Because the ACS is a sample survey, large numbers of sample cases are needed before reliable estimates can be made for small populations. Each year's sample is large enough to produce estimates for the nation, all the states, all metropolitan areas, and many counties and cities. The state and metropolitan area tables in this book include 1-year estimates for 2012. The county and city tables contain a selection of data from the ACS 3-year estimates for all states, and for counties and cities with populations of 20,000 or more. Five-year estimates are now being released for all geographic entities in the United States.

The richness of the ACS data can be accessed in varying degrees. Much more subject matter detail is available for large geographic areas partly because reliable estimates for large areas can be produced with smaller samples, and partly because more data must be suppressed for the smaller areas to protect the confidentiality of the respondents.

This book is designed to include a sampling of key information, but also to guide users through the process of using the Census Bureau's website to expand on the information included here. The state tables in this book

include more than 300 data items. The metropolitan area, county, and city tables include 48 data items. The data in the tables are a small selection that show what is available for the smaller counties and cities in the book. Every column includes an ACS Table Number that enables users to find the original data on the Census Bureau's website. The selection in this book is limited because there is a great deal of suppression in the county and city data. Much more information is likely to be available for analysis of larger cities and counties or for analysis of specific racial or ethnic groups if those groups have large populations in a particular city or county. Furthermore, as the 5-year data are also available, most of the same information can be found for all cities and counties in the nation, no matter how small.

One of the most notable differences between the census "long form" and the ACS is the time frame of the estimates. We are accustomed to the census data that give us specific information every ten years, a snapshot of the country on April 1. The ACS multiyear estimates are different. The data in this book are from the ACS 2012 estimates and the 3-year, 2010–2012 estimates. They are not averages, nor do they represent 2011, the midpoint of the 3-year estimates. They are period estimates with data spread evenly throughout the survey time period—1 year or 3 years. To help in the understanding of these estimates, we have included a measure of population change for each geographic area. These are from the Census Bureau's Population Estimates Program, showing the estimated population growth or decline in each geographic area. Each table shows a total population as estimated for the ACS period represented (either 2012 or the 3-year period, 2010–2012), but the decennial censuses and the Census Bureau's Population Estimates Program provide the official population counts that underlie the ACS sample. If an area experienced unusually large population growth or decline, we should recognize the variations that may be hidden in the ACS estimates—perhaps a city annexing a large tract of land, many people moving into a new development, or many people leaving the area because of a plant closing.

An earlier edition of this book included data from 2008 through 2010, years with increases in unemployment and decreases in housing values. The data in this book generally represent the social and economic picture of the recovery years 2010 through 2012, with lower unemployment rates and increasing housing values. The annual estimates let us include more timely information for the larger areas with populations of 65,000 or more.

Finally, it is always critical to remember that all estimates are subject to sampling error. On the Census Bureau's website, every ACS number is accompanied by its margin of error. In the interests of space and simplicity, this book does not include the margins of error, but all users are **encouraged to consult the Census Bureau's website** and to understand some basics: **small differences are very likely to represent no difference at all**; **do not draw conclusions from small numbers**; use these numbers as a starting point to explore the wealth of information from the ACS.

Introduction

The American Community Survey (ACS) has ushered in the most substantial change in the decennial census in more than 60 years. It replaced the decennial census long form in 2010, providing more current data throughout the decade by collecting long-form-type information annually rather than only once every 10 years. The ACS provides annual data for states, metropolitan areas, and large cities and counties, and combines 3 years of survey responses (in this book, 2010–2012) to produce data for midsize communities.

The ACS, part of the 2010 Decennial Census Program, gathers demographic, social, economic, housing, and financial information about the nation's people and communities on a continuous basis. The ACS is an ongoing survey conducted by the U.S. Census Bureau in every county, American Indian and Alaska Native Area, and Hawaiian Home Land in the United States. The ACS is also conducted as the Puerto Rico Community Survey in every municipality in Puerto Rico. As the largest survey in the United States, it is the only source of small-area data on a wide range of important social and economic characteristics for all communities in the country. After years of planning, development, and a demonstration period, the ACS began nationwide full implementation in 2005.

Data from the ACS are available on the Census Bureau's website. The ACS main page is www.census.gov/acs/www .

A vast amount of information is collected in the ACS. In this publication, selections of these data have been assembled in various tables by subject and geographic type.

Volume Organization

The data tables in this book contain a representative selection of information from the ACS.

Part A: Who contains the following subjects: age, race/ethnicity, and household structure, among others.
Part B: What contains the following subject areas: education, employment, and income.
Part C: Where comprises data on: migration, housing, and transportation.

Within each part are four tables. Table 1 has 2012 data for the 50 states and the District of Columbia; Table 2 has 2010–2012 data for all counties with populations of 20,000 or more; Table 3 has 2012 data for all the nation's metropolitan statistical areas; and Table 4 has 2010–2012 data

for all cities with populations of 20,000 or more. Counties and cities are listed alphabetically by state. Metropolitan areas are listed alphabetically, except that Metropolitan divisions are listed alphabetically within the metropolitan statistical area of which they are components.

In addition, each part is preceded by highlights and ranking tables that show how areas diverge from the national norm, as well as the differences among small areas. These research aids are invaluable for helping people understand what the census data tell us about who we are, what we do, and where we live.

In the following sections, information about the ACS and how to use the data is included, much of it excerpted from the wealth of information available on the Census Bureau's website. Especially helpful are the instructions, definitions, and guidelines on using the data in the section on "Guidance for Data Users." Readers are encouraged to explore the Census Bureau's website to expand on the information contained here and to keep up to date with this constantly changing dataset.

Deirdre A. Gaquin has been a data use consultant to private organizations, government agencies, and universities for more than 30 years. Prior to that, she was Director of Data Access Services at Data Use & Access Laboratories, a pioneer in private sector distribution of federal statistical data. A former President of the Association of Public Data Users, Ms. Gaquin has served on numerous boards, panels, and task forces concerned with federal statistical data and has worked on five decennial censuses. She holds a Master of Urban Planning (MUP) degree from Hunter College. Ms. Gaquin is also an editor of Bernan Press's *County and City Extra; The Who, What, and Where of America: Understanding the Census Results*; *Places, Towns and Townships*; *The Congressional District Atlas*; *The Almanac of American Education; State and Metropolitan Area Data Book;* and *Race and Employment in America.*

Gwenavere W. Dunn is a research editor for Bernan Press. She holds a Master of Science degree in Human Resource Management from Trinity Washington University and is a former senior editor with the Board of Governors of the Federal Reserve System and managing editor of the Board's *Federal Reserve Bulletin*. At Bernan, she is the editor of *Crime in the United States* and *Employment, Hours, and Earnings*; and assistant editor of the *State and Metropolitan Area Data Book*; *Race and Employment in America*, and the *Almanac of American Education.*

Understanding the American Community Survey

Every 10 years since 1790, the Congress has authorized funds to conduct a national census of the U.S. population, as required by the U.S. Constitution. From 1960 through 2000, censuses have consisted of:

- a "short form," which included basic questions about age, sex, race, Hispanic origin, household relationship, and owner/renter status, and

- a "long form" used for only a sample of households that included not only the basic short-form questions, but also detailed questions about socioeconomic and housing characteristics.

Beginning with the 2010 census, the American Community Survey (ACS) has replaced the decennial census long form by collecting long-form-type information annually rather than only once every 10 years, providing more current data throughout the decade. The 2010 Census counted the population to support the constitutional mandate—to provide population counts needed to apportion the seats in the U.S. House of Representatives. The ACS data now provide, for the first time, a regular stream of updated information for states and local areas, revolutionizing the way we use data to understand our communities. It produces social, housing, and economic characteristics for demographic groups, even for geographic areas as small as census tracts and block groups.

Some Key Facts about the ACS:

- The ACS annually provides the same kind of detailed information previously available only every 10 years from the census. The ACS is conducted under the authority of Title 13, United States Code, Sections 141 and 193.

- All answers are confidential. Any Census Bureau employee who violates that confidentiality is subject to a jail term, a fine, or both.

- The Census Bureau may use the information it collects only for statistical purposes.

- Addresses are selected at random to represent similar households in the area. The survey is conducted by mail, telephone, and personal visit. Response to this survey is required by Section 221 of Title 13.

- Approximately 2.5 percent of U.S. households are surveyed each year. A sample of group quarters (nursing homes, college dormitories, etc.) is included in the ACS as well.

Data from the ACS can be extremely valuable for a variety of purposes that include: to monitor the well-being of America's children and families, to investigate the characteristics of the U.S. workforce, to determine the economic well-being of working-poor families, or to track social, economic, and demographic changes in the general U.S. population. Many people are being cautious in their approach to the ACS, and rightly so. This is a relatively new survey with a new approach to measuring change in our communities. The ACS has great potential, particularly as a source of annual data for local areas. By providing data each year, the ACS will provide critical information for communities when they need it most.

New Opportunities

The main benefits of the ACS are timeliness and access to annual data for states, local areas, and small population subgroups. The ACS will deliver useful, relevant data, similar to data from previous census long forms, but updated every year rather than every 10 years. The ACS provides comparable information across and within states for program evaluation and use in funding formulas.

- ACS information is often used to determine the placement of new schools, hospitals, and highways.

- ACS provides information for tracking the well-being of children, families, and the elderly.

- The data will aid federal, state, and local governments in distributing benefits fairly. About $300 billion in federal program funds are distributed each year based, in whole or in part, on census and ACS data.

- The data are used by community programs, such as those for the elderly, libraries, hospitals, banks, and other organizations.

- The data are used by transportation planners to evaluate peak volumes of traffic in order to reduce congestion, plan for parking, and develop plans for carpooling and flexible work schedules.

- Corporations, small businesses, and individuals can use these data to develop business plans, to set strategies for expansion or starting a business, and to determine trends in their service areas to meet current and future needs.

- Small towns and rural communities have much to gain from the ACS. Lacking the staff and resources to conduct their own research, many local communities have relied on decennial census information that became increasingly outdated throughout the decade, or used local administrative records that are not comparable with information collected in neighboring areas.

- The ACS also provides tools for those who want to conduct their own research. The ACS includes a Public Use Microdata Sample (PUMS) file each year that enables researchers to create custom universes and tabulations from individual ACS records that have been stripped of personally identifiable information.

- The use of professional, highly trained, permanent interviewers has improved the accuracy of ACS data compared with those from the decennial census long-form sample. This strategy has effectively reduced the number of refusals to complete the ACS questionnaire. ACS interviewers also obtain more complete information than decennial census interviewers.

New Challenges

The main challenges for ACS data users are understanding and using multiyear estimates and the relatively large confidence intervals associated with ACS data for smaller geographic areas and subgroups of the population.

- ACS data will be produced every year, but the sample size of the ACS is smaller than that of the Census 2000 long form sample. Data users need to pay more attention to the margin of error.

- Data users have access to 5-year estimates of ACS data. The sample size based on 5-year period estimates of ACS data is still smaller than the long-form sample in the decennial census, resulting in larger standard errors in the ACS 5-year estimates.

- Because the ACS will produce 1-year, 3-year, and 5-year estimates, data users will have to decide which datasets are appropriate for their needs.

- Data users will need to be aware of the implications of multiyear estimates, particularly in analyzing employment and income data that will span a full year or even a 5-year period.

The ACS includes several questions that are very similar to those collected in other federal surveys—especially the Current Population Survey (CPS), the American Housing Survey, and the Survey of Income and Program Participation. In some cases, there are clear guidelines about which data to use. For example, the CPS is the official source of income and poverty data. It includes detailed questions on these topics and should be used in reporting national trends in these subject areas. The Census Bureau recommends that ACS information on income and poverty be used to supplement CPS data for areas below the state level and for population subgroups (such as age, sex, race, Hispanic origin, and type of household) at the state level. For an explanation of various income and poverty data sources, see the Census Bureau's guidelines at www.census.gov/hhes/www/poverty/about/datasources/ description.html . For states, generally the Census Bureau recommends using the ACS, though the CPS is still valuable as a source for examining historical state income and poverty trends.

The ACS Sample

The ACS is sent each month to a sample of roughly 250,000 addresses in the United States and Puerto Rico, or 3 million a year, resulting in nearly 2 million final interviews. The sample represents all housing units and group quarters in the United States and Puerto Rico. (Group quarters include places such as college dormitories, prisons, military barracks, and nursing homes.) The addresses are selected from the Census Bureau's Master Address File (MAF), which is also the basis for the decennial census.

The annual ACS sample is smaller than that of the Census 2000 long-form sample, which included about 18 million housing units. As a result, the ACS needs to combine population or housing data from multiple years to produce reliable numbers for small counties, neighborhoods, and other local areas. To provide information for communities each year, the ACS provides 1-, 3-, and 5-year estimates.

The ACS sample is not spread evenly across all areas but includes a larger proportion of addresses in sparsely populated rural communities and American Indian reservations and a lower proportion in densely populated areas. Over a 5-year period, the ACS will sample about 15 million addresses and complete interviews for about 11 million. This sample is sufficient to produce estimates for small geographic areas, such as neighborhoods and sparsely-populated rural counties. In a 5-year period no address will be selected for the ACS more than once, and many addresses will never be selected for the survey.

Geography

The ACS data are tabulated for a variety of geographic areas ranging in size from broad geographic regions (Northeast, Midwest, South, and West) to cities, towns, neighborhoods, and census block groups. Before December 2008, the ACS data were only available for geographic areas with at least 65,000 people, including regions, divisions, states, the District of Columbia, Puerto Rico, congressional districts, Public Use Microdata Areas (PUMAs)—census-constructed geographic areas, each with approximately a population of 100,000—and many large counties, metropolitan areas, cities, school districts, and American Indian areas. Starting in December 2008, 3-year estimates became available for all areas with at least 20,000 residents, and in 2010, 5-year estimates for geographic areas down to the block group level became available. One-, three-, and five-year estimates—three sets of numbers—are now available. Less populous areas will receive only 5-year estimates. The vast majority of areas will receive only 5-year estimates.

The state and Metropolitan Area tables in this book contain data from the one-year 2012 estimates. The county and city tables contain data from the 3-year estimates, 2010–2012. The population cutoff of 20,000 yields data for 1,846 of the 3,141 counties in the United States, and for 2,143 cities, as well as all states and metropolitan areas. More information about geography can be found in Appendix C.

Data Comparability

Since the ACS data are collected continuously, they are not always comparable with data collected from the decennial census. For example, both surveys ask about employment status during the week prior to the survey. However, data from the decennial census are typically collected between March and August, whereas data from the ACS are collected nearly every day and reflect employment throughout the year. Other factors that may also have an impact on the data include seasonal variation in population and minor differences in question wording and question order. In 2006, the ACS began including samples of the population living in group quarters (e.g., jails, college dormitories, and nursing homes) for the first time. As a result, the ACS data from 2010 through 2012 may not be comparable with data from earlier ACS surveys. This is especially true for estimates of young adults and the elderly, who are more likely than other groups to be living in group quarters facilities.

One of the most important uses of the ACS estimates is to make comparisons between estimates. Several key types of comparisons are of general interest to users:

- Comparisons of estimates from different geographic areas within the same time period (e.g., comparing the proportion of people below the poverty level in two counties).

- Comparisons of estimates for the same geographic area across time periods (e.g., comparing the proportion of people below the poverty level in a metropolitan area for 2010 and 2012).

- Comparisons of ACS estimates with the corresponding estimates from past decennial census samples (e.g., comparing the proportion of people below the poverty level in a county for 2010–2012 and 2000).

A number of conditions must be met when comparing survey estimates. Of primary importance is that the comparison takes into account the sampling error associated with each estimate, thus determining whether the observed differences between estimates are statistically significant. Statistical significance means that there is statistical evidence that a true difference exists within the full population, and that the observed difference is unlikely to have occurred by chance due to sampling. A method for determining statistical significance when making comparisons, as well as considerations associated with the various types of comparisons, can be found in Appendix 4 of the *ACS General Handbook*: www.census.gov/acs/www/Downloads/handbooks/ACSGeneralHandbook.pdf .

Subjects Covered

The topics covered by the ACS focus on demographic, social, economic, and housing characteristics. These topics are virtually the same as those covered by the 2000 census long-form sample data.

Demographic Characteristics

Age, Sex, Hispanic Origin, Race, and Relationship to Householder (e.g., spouse)

Social Characteristics

Marital Status and Marital History; Fertility; Grandparents as Caregivers; Ancestry; Place of Birth; Citizenship and Year of Entry; Language Spoken at Home; Educational Attainment and School Enrollment; Residence One Year Ago; Veteran Status, Period of Military Service, and VA Service-Connected Disability Rating; and Disability

Economic Characteristics

Income, Food Stamps Benefit, Labor Force Status, Industry, Occupation, Class of Worker, Place of Work and

Journey to Work, Work Status Last Year, Vehicles Available, and Health Insurance Coverage

Housing Characteristics

Year Structure Built, Units in Structure, Year Moved Into Unit, Rooms, Bedrooms, Kitchen Facilities, Plumbing Facilities, House Heating Fuel, Telephone Service Available, and Farm Residence

Financial Characteristics

Tenure (Owner/Renter), Housing Value, Rent, and Selected Monthly Owner Costs

Availability of ACS Estimates

The ACS began in 1996 and has expanded each subsequent year. From 2000 through 2004, the sample included between 740,000 and 900,000 addresses annually. In 2005, the ACS shifted from a demonstration program to the full sample size and design. It became the largest household survey in the United States, with an annual sample size of about 3 million addresses. Beginning with 2005, the ACS single-year estimates are available for geographic areas with a population of 65,000 or more. Three-year period estimates for areas of 20,000 or more were first released for the 2005–2007 time period. The ACS will continue to accumulate samples over 3-year and 5-year intervals to produce estimates for smaller geographic areas, including census tracts and block groups. For small areas with populations less than 20,000, it takes 5 years to accumulate a large enough sample to provide estimates with accuracy similar to the decennial census. Beginning in 2010, and every year thereafter, the nation will have this five-year period estimate available, a resource that will show the most up-to-date estimates annually for neighborhoods and rural areas. Even with the accumulated 5-year averages of 15 million sample households, the ACS will not achieve the sample size of the decennial census long form, which included about 18 million households in 2000.

Annually, the ACS produces updated, single-year estimates of demographic, housing, social, and economic characteristics for all states, as well as for larger counties, cities, metropolitan and urban areas, and congressional districts. Geographic areas must have a minimum population of 65,000 to qualify for estimates based on a single year's sample. Every congressional district meets this threshold and therefore new single year estimates are released each year for every congressional district. Some school districts, townships, and American Indian and Alaska Native areas also meet this population threshold.

For areas with populations of at least 20,000, the Census Bureau produces estimates using data collected over a 3-year period. For rural areas and city neighborhoods (including census tracts and block groups) with fewer than 20,000 people, the Census Bureau produces estimates using data collected over a 5-year period, with plans to update these multiyear estimates every year. ACS data are released annually, about 8 months after the end of each calendar year of data collection.

For some geographic areas—including three-quarters of all counties, most school districts, and most cities, towns, and American Indian reservations—only 3-year or 5-year estimates are available because of their population size. Because some federal grant programs allocate funds directly to these areas, the Congress can use the 3- and 5-year estimates to evaluate needs at the relevant geographic level, compare characteristics between areas within and among states, and analyze how various formulas distribute funds. The vast majority of areas will receive only 5-year estimates. In partnership with the states, the Census Bureau created *Public Use Microdata Areas (PUMAs)*, which are special, non-overlapping areas within a state, each with a population of about 100,000.

Definitions of these geographic areas are at www.census .gov/acs/www/UseData/geo.htm .

Using the ACS

Differences between the ACS and the Decennial Census

While the main function of the decennial census is to provide *counts* of people for the purpose of congressional apportionment and legislative redistricting, the primary purpose of the ACS is to measure the changing social and economic *characteristics* of the U.S. population. As a result, the ACS does not provide official counts of the population. In nondecennial census years, the Census Bureau's Population Estimates Program continues to be the official source for annual population totals, by age, race, Hispanic origin, and sex. ACS estimates are controlled to match the decennial census and the Census Bureau's annual population estimates, by age, sex, race, and Hispanic origin. For more information about population estimates, visit the Census Bureau's website at http://www.census.gov/popest/ .

There are many similarities between the methods used in the past decennial census sample and the ACS. Both the ACS and the decennial census sample data are based on information from a sample of the population. The data from the Census 2000 sample of about one-sixth of the population were collected using a "long-form" questionnaire whose content was the model for the ACS. While some differences exist in the specific Census 2000 question wording and that of the ACS, most questions are identical or nearly identical. Differences in the design and implementation of the two surveys are noted below with references provided to a series of evaluation studies that assess the degree to which these differences are likely to impact the estimates. The ACS produces period estimates and these estimates do not measure characteristics for the same time frame as the decennial census estimates, which are interpreted to be a snapshot of April 1 of the census year.

Some data items were collected by both the ACS and the Census 2000 long form with slightly different definitions that could affect the comparability of the estimates for these items. One example is annual costs for a mobile home. Census 2000 included installment loan costs in the total annual costs but the ACS does not. In this example, the ACS could be expected to yield smaller estimates than Census 2000.

While some differences were a part of the census and survey design objectives, other differences observed between ACS and census results were not by design, but due to nonsampling error—differences related to how well the surveys were conducted. The ACS and the census experience different levels and types of coverage error, different levels and treatment of unit and item nonresponse, and different instances of measurement and processing error. Both Census 2000 and the ACS had similar high levels of survey coverage and low levels of unit nonresponse. Higher levels of unit nonresponse were found in the nonresponse follow-up stage of Census 2000. Higher item nonresponse rates were also found in Census 2000.

Census Bureau analysts have compared sample estimates from Census 2000 with 1-year ACS estimates based on data collected in 2000 and 3-year ACS estimates based on data collected in 1999–2001 in selected counties. In general, ACS estimates were found to be quite similar to those produced from decennial census data.

Detailed information about the ACS methodology can be found at: www.census.gov/acs/www/methodology/methodology_main/ .

Residence Rules

The fundamentally different purposes of the ACS and the census, and their timing, led to important differences in the choice of data collection methods. For example, the residence rules for a census or survey determine the sample unit's occupancy status and household membership. Defining the rules in a dissimilar way can affect those two very important estimates. The 2010 census residence rules, which determined where people should be counted, were based on the principle of "usual residence" on April 1, 2010, in keeping with the focus of the census on the requirements of congressional apportionment and state redistricting. To accomplish this, the decennial census attempts to restrict and determine a principal place of residence on one specific date for everyone enumerated. The ACS residence rules are based on a "current residence" concept since data are collected continuously throughout the entire year with responses provided relative to the continuously changing survey interview dates. This method is consistent with the goal that the ACS produce estimates that reflect annual averages of the characteristics of all areas.

Residence rules determine which individuals are considered to be residents of a particular housing unit or group quarters. While many people have definite ties to a single housing unit or group quarters, some people may stay in different places for significant periods of time over the course of the year. For example, migrant workers move with crop seasons and do not live in any one location for the entire year. Differences in treatment of these populations in the census and ACS can lead to differences in estimates of the characteristics of some areas.

For the past several censuses, decennial census residence rules were designed to produce an accurate count of the population as of Census Day, April 1, while the ACS residence rules were designed to collect representative information to produce annual average estimates of the characteristics of all types of areas. When interviewing the population living in housing units, the decennial census uses a "usual residence" rule to enumerate people at the place where they live or stay most of the time as of April 1. The ACS uses a "current residence" rule to interview people who are currently living or staying in the sample housing unit as long as their stay at that address will exceed 2 months. The residence rules governing the census enumerations of people in group quarters depend on the type of group quarter and, where permitted, whether people claim a "usual residence" elsewhere. The ACS applies a straight de facto residence rule to every type of group quarter. Everyone living or staying in a group quarter on the day it is visited by an ACS interviewer is eligible to be sampled and interviewed for the survey.

Further information on residence rules can be found at www.census.gov/acs/www/Downloads/survey_methodology/acs_design_methodology_ch06.pdf .

The differences in the ACS and census data as a consequence of the different residence rules are most likely minimal for most areas and most characteristics. However, for certain segments of the population the usual and current residence concepts could result in different residence decisions. Appreciable differences may occur in areas where large proportions of the total population spend several months of the year in what would not be considered their residence under decennial census rules. In particular, data for areas that include large beach, lake, or mountain vacation areas may differ appreciably between the census and the ACS if populations live there for more than 2 months.

Reference Periods

Estimates produced by the ACS are not measuring exactly what decennial samples have been measuring. The ACS yearly samples, spread over 12 months, collect information that is anchored to the day on which the sampled unit was interviewed, whether it is the day that a mail questionnaire is completed or the day that an interview is conducted by telephone or personal visit. Individual questions with time references such as "last week" or "the last 12 months" all

begin the reference period as of this interview date. Even the information on types and amounts of income refers to the 12 months prior to the day the question is answered. ACS interviews are conducted just about every day of the year, and all of the estimates that the survey releases are considered to be averages for a specific time period. The 1-year estimates reflect the full calendar year; 3-year and 5-year estimates reflect the full 36- or 60-month period.

Most decennial census sample estimates are anchored in this same way to the date of enumeration. The most obvious difference between the ACS and the census is the overall time frame in which they are conducted. The census enumeration time period is less than half the time period used to collect data for each single-year ACS estimate. But a more important difference is that the distribution of census enumeration dates are highly clustered in March and April (when most census mail returns were received) with additional, smaller clusters seen in May and June (when nonresponse follow-up activities took place).

This means that the data from the decennial census tend to describe the characteristics of the population and housing in the March through June time period (with an overrepresentation of March/April), while the ACS characteristics describe the characteristics nearly every day over the full calendar year. For employment and income estimates, the decennial census referred to the prior calendar year for all respondents, while the ACS asks about the 12 months preceding the interview.

Those who are interested in more information about differences in reference periods should refer to the Census Bureau's guidance on comparisons that contrasts for each question the specific reference periods used in Census 2000 with those used in the ACS: www.census.gov/acs/www/guidance_for_data_users/table_comparisons/ .

Some specific differences in reference periods between the ACS and the decennial census are described below. Users should consider the potential impact these different reference periods could have on distributions when comparing ACS estimates with Census 2000.

Income Data
To estimate annual income, the Census 2000 longform sample used the calendar year prior to Census Day as the reference period, and the ACS uses the 12 months prior to the interview date as the reference period. Thus, while Census 2000 collected income information for calendar year 1999, the ACS collects income information for the 12 months preceding the interview date. The responses are a mixture of 12 reference periods ranging from, in the case of the 2010 ACS single-year estimates, the full calendar year 2009 through November 2010. The ACS income responses

for each of these reference periods are individually inflation-adjusted to represent dollar values for the ACS collection year. Further inflation adjustments are made to the 3- and 5-year estimates to reflect dollar values of the final year of the estimate.

School Enrollment

The school enrollment question on the ACS asks if a person had "at any time in the last 3 months attended a school or college." A consistent 3-month reference period is used for all interviews. In contrast, Census 2000 asked if a person had "at any time since February 1 attended a school or college." Since Census 2000 data were collected from mid-March to late-August, the reference period could have been as short as about 6 weeks or as long as 7 months.

Utility Costs

The reference periods for two utility cost questions—gas and electricity—differ between Census 2000 and the ACS. The census asked for annual costs, while the ACS asks for the utility costs in the previous month.

Period Estimates

The ACS produces period estimates of socioeconomic and housing characteristics. It is designed to provide estimates that describe the average characteristics of an area over a specific time period. In the case of ACS single-year estimates, the period is the calendar year (e.g., the 2012 ACS covers January through December 2012). In the case of ACS multiyear estimates, the period is either 3 or 5 calendar years (e.g., the 2010–2012 ACS estimates cover January 2010 through December 2012, and the 2008–2012 ACS estimates cover January 2008 through December 2012). The ACS multiyear estimates are similar in many ways to the ACS single-year estimates, but they encompass a longer time period. The differences in time periods between single-year and multiyear ACS estimates affect decisions about which set of estimates should be used for a particular analysis. While one may think of these estimates as representing average characteristics over a single calendar year or multiple calendar years, it must be remembered that the 1-year estimates are not calculated as an average of 12 monthly values and the multiyear estimates are not calculated as the average of either 36 or 60 monthly values, nor are the multiyear estimates calculated as the average of 3 or 5 single-year estimates. Rather, the ACS collects survey information continuously nearly every day of the year and then aggregates the results over a specific time period—1 year, 3 years, or 5 years. The data collection is spread evenly across the entire period represented so as not to over-represent any particular month or year within the period.

Because ACS estimates provide information about the characteristics of the population and housing for areas over an entire time frame, ACS single-year and multiyear estimates contrast with "point-in-time" estimates, such as those from the decennial census long-form samples or monthly employment estimates from the Current Population Survey (CPS), which are designed to measure characteristics as of a certain date or narrow time period. For example, Census 2000 was designed to measure the characteristics of the population and housing in the United States based upon data collected around April 1, 2000, and thus its data reflect a narrower time frame than ACS data. The monthly CPS collects data for an even narrower time frame, the week containing the 12th of each month.

Most areas have consistent population characteristics throughout the calendar year, and their period estimates may not look much different from estimates that would be obtained from a "point-in-time" survey design. However, some areas may experience changes in the estimated characteristics of the population, depending on when in the calendar year the measurement occurred. For these areas, the ACS period estimates (even for a single-year) may noticeably differ from "point-in-time" estimates. The impact will be more noticeable in smaller areas where changes such as a factory closing can have a large impact on population characteristics, and in areas with a large physical event such as Hurricane Katrina's impact on the New Orleans area. This logic can be extended to better interpret 3- and 5-year estimates where the periods involved are much longer. If, over the full period of time (for example, 36 months) there have been major or consistent changes in certain population or housing characteristics for an area, a period estimate for that area could differ markedly from estimates based on a "point-in-time" survey. For example, the 5-year estimates for 2008–2012 will be affected by the volatility in the economy and the housing market during those years.

The tables in this book include 1-year estimates from 2012 and 3-year estimates from 2010 through 2012. The Cape Coral figure illustrates some of the issues involved in using the different estimates. Cape Coral, Florida, is a city that experienced great fluctuation in housing prices. A median value of $219,600 was estimated in the 2007–2009 3-year data, while the 2010–2012 estimate was $130,000. This shows a decline of more than 40 percent, comparing two 3-year files with no overlapping years. Because Cape Coral's population is large enough to allow 1-year ACS data, we can also look at the single-year changes, showing that the 2007–2009 value masks a 3-year drop from $259,100 in 2007 to $164.700 in 2009, and further declines in 2010 and 2011 to $121,900, with the 2012 value rising to $137,100. But, because of the margin of error, the 2010–2012 value actually represents a rather stable value during the 3-year period.

The important thing to keep in mind is that ACS single-year estimates describe the population and characteristics of an area for the full year, not for any specific day or period within the year, while ACS multiyear estimates describe the population and characteristics of an area for the full 3- or 5-year period, not for any specific day, period, or year within the multiyear time period.

Deciding Which ACS Estimate to Use

Three primary uses of ACS estimates are:

- to understand the characteristics of the population of an area for local planning needs,

- to make comparisons across areas, and

- to assess change over time in an area.

Local planning could include making local decisions such as where to place schools or hospitals, determining the need for services or new businesses, and carrying out transportation or other infrastructure analysis. In the past, decennial census sample data provided the most comprehensive information. However, the currency of those data suffered through the intercensal period, and the ability to assess change over time was limited. ACS estimates greatly improve the currency of data for understanding the characteristics of housing and population and enhance the ability to assess change over time.

Several key factors can help users decide whether to use single-year or multiyear ACS estimates for areas where both are available:

- intended use of the estimates

- precision of the estimates

- currency of the estimates

All of these factors, along with an understanding of the differences between single-year and multiyear ACS estimates, should be taken into consideration when deciding which set of estimates to use.

For users interested in obtaining estimates for small geographic areas, multiyear ACS estimates are the only option. For the very smallest of these areas (less than 20,000 population), the only option is to use the 5-year ACS estimates. Users have a choice of two sets of multiyear estimates when analyzing data for small geographic areas with populations of at least 20,000. Both 3- and 5-year ACS estimates are available. Only the largest areas with populations of 65,000 and more receive all three data series.

The key trade-off to be made in deciding whether to use single-year or multiyear estimates is between currency and precision. In general, the single-year estimates are

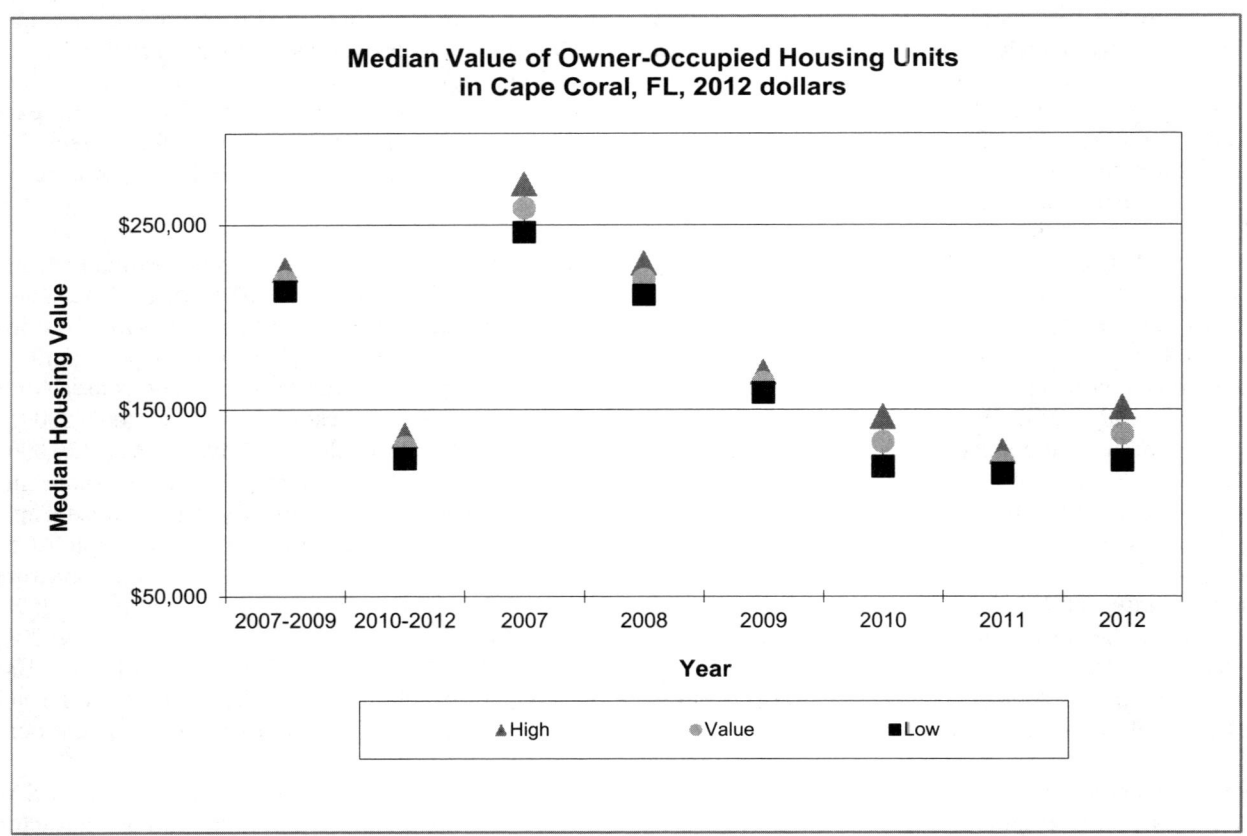

Single-year estimates provide more current information

Single-year estimates provide more current information about areas that have changing population and/or housing characteristics because they are based on the most current data—data from the past year. In contrast, multiyear estimates provide less current information because they are based on both data from the previous year and data that are 2 and 3 years old. As noted earlier, for many areas with minimal change taking place, using the "less current" sample used to produce the multiyear estimates may not have a substantial influence on the estimates. However, in areas experiencing major changes over a given time period, the multiyear estimates may be quite different from the single-year estimates for any of the individual years. Single-year and multiyear estimates are not expected to be the same because they are based on data from two different time periods. This will be true even if the ACS single year is the midyear of the ACS multiyear period (for example, 2011 single year, 2010–2012 multiyear).

Multiyear estimates are based on larger sample sizes and are therefore more reliable

The 3-year estimates are based on three times as many sample cases as the 1-year estimates. For some characteristics this increased sample is needed for the estimates to be reliable enough for use in certain applications. For other characteristics the increased sample may not be necessary.

Multiyear estimates are the only type of estimates available for geographic areas with populations of less than 65,000. Users may think that they only need to use multiyear estimates when they are working with small areas, but this isn't the case. Estimates for large geographic areas benefit from the increased sample, resulting in more precise estimates of population and housing characteristics, especially for subpopulations within those areas. In addition, users may determine that they want to use single-year estimates, despite their reduced reliability, as building blocks to produce estimates for meaningful higher levels of geography. These aggregations will similarly benefit from the increased sample sizes and gain reliability.

preferred, as they will be more relevant to the current conditions. However, the user must take into account the level of uncertainty present in the single-year estimates, which may be large for small subpopulation groups and rare characteristics. While single-year estimates offer more current estimates, they also have higher sampling variability. One measure, the coefficient of variation (CV) can help you determine the fitness for use of a single-year estimate in order to assess if you should opt instead to use the multiyear estimate (or if you should use a 5-year estimate rather than a 3-year estimate). The CV is calculated as the ratio of the standard error of the estimate to the estimate, times 100. A single-year estimate with a small CV is usually preferable to a multiyear estimate as it is more up to date. However, multiyear estimates are an alternative option when a single-year estimate has an unacceptably high CV. Single-year estimates for small subpopulations (e.g., families with a female householder, no husband, and related children less than 18 years) will typically have larger CVs. In general, multiyear estimates are preferable to single-year estimates when looking at estimates for small subpopulations.

For the complete discussion on deciding which estimates to use and on calculating the CV, see Appendix 1 of the *ACS General Handbook*: www.census.gov/acs/www/Downloads/handbooks/ACSGeneralHandbook.pdf .

Often users want to compare the characteristics of one area to those of another area. These comparisons can be in the form of rankings or of specific pairs of comparisons. Whenever you want to make a comparison between two different geographic areas you need to take the type of estimate into account. It is important that comparisons be made within the same estimate type. That is, 1-year estimates should only be compared with other 1-year estimates, 3-year estimates should only be compared with other 3-year estimates, and 5-year estimates should only be compared with other 5-year estimates.

You certainly can compare characteristics for areas with populations of 30,000 to areas with populations of 100,000 but you should use the data set that they have in common. In this example you could use the 3- or the 5-year estimates because they are available for areas of 30,000 and areas of 100,000. This book includes both the 1-year estimates for 2012 and the 3-year estimates for 2010 through 2012, but users should not compare data from the two different time periods.

Users are encouraged to make comparisons between sequential single-year estimates. In American FactFinder (AFF), comparison profiles are available beginning with the 2007 single-year data. These profiles identify statistically significant differences between each year from 2007 through the most recently released year.

Caution is needed when using multiyear estimates for estimating year-to-year change in a particular characteristic. This is because roughly two-thirds of the data in a 3-year estimate overlap with the data in the next year's 3-year estimate (the overlap is roughly four-fifths for 5-year estimates). When comparing 3-year estimates from 2009–2011 with those from 2010–2012, the differences in overlapping multiyear estimates are driven by differences in the non-overlapping years. A data user interested in comparing 2012 with 2011 will not be able to isolate those differences using these two successive 3-year estimates. While the interpretation of this difference is difficult, these comparisons can be made with caution.

Users who are interested in comparing overlapping multiyear period estimates should refer to Appendix 4 of the *ACS General Handbook* for more information: www.census.gov/acs/www/Downloads/handbooks/ACS-GeneralHandbook.pdf.

Multiyear estimates are likely to confuse some data users, in part because of their statistical properties, and in part because this is a new product from the Census Bureau. The ACS will provide all states and communities that have at least 65,000 residents with single-year estimates of demographic, housing, social, and economic characteristics—a boon to government agencies that need to budget and plan for public services like transportation, medical care, and schools. For geographic areas with smaller populations, the ACS samples too few households to provide reliable single-year estimates. For these communities, several years of data will be pooled together to create reliable 3- or 5-year estimates.

Single-year, 3- and 5-year estimates from the ACS are all "period" estimates that represent data collected over a period of time (as opposed to "point-in-time" estimates, such as the decennial census, that approximate the characteristics of an area on a specific date). While a single-year estimate includes information collected over a 12-month period, a 3-year estimate represents data collected over a 36-month period, and a 5-year estimate includes data collected over a 60-month period. Therefore, ACS estimates based on data collected from 2010–2012 should not be called "2011" or "2012" estimates. Nor should 2008–2012 period estimates be labeled "2010" estimates, even though that is the midpoint of the 5-year period. Multiyear estimates should be labeled to indicate clearly the full period of time (e.g., "The child poverty rate in 2010–2012 was X percent"). The primary advantage of using multiyear estimates is the increased statistical reliability of the data for less populated areas and small population subgroups.

Multiyear estimates should, in general, be used when single-year estimates have large CVs or when the precision of the estimates is more important than the currency of the data. Multiyear estimates should also be used when analyzing data for smaller geographies and smaller populations in larger geographies. Multiyear estimates are also of value when examining change over non-overlapping time periods and for smoothing data trends over time.

Single-year estimates should, in general, be used for larger geographies and populations when currency is more important than the precision of the estimates. Single-year estimates should be used to examine year-to-year change for estimates with small CVs. Given the availability of a single-year estimate, calculating the CV provides useful information to determine if the single-year estimate should be used. For areas believed to be experiencing rapid changes in a characteristic, single-year estimates should generally be used rather than multiyear estimates as long as the CV for the single-year estimate is reasonable for the specific usage.

Local area variations may occur due to rapidly occurring changes. Multiyear estimates will tend to be insensitive to such changes when they first occur. Single-year estimates, if associated with sufficiently small CVs, can be very valuable in identifying and studying such phenomena.

Data users also need to use caution in looking at trends involving income or other measures that are adjusted for inflation, such as rental costs, home values, and energy costs. Note that inflation adjustment is based on a national-level consumer price index: it does not adjust for differences in costs of living across different geographic areas.

Appendix 5 of the *ACS General Handbook* provides information on the adjustment of single-year and multiyear ACS estimates for inflation: www.census.gov/acs/www/Downloads/handbooks/ACSGeneralHandbook.pdf .

Margin of Error

All data that are based on samples, such as the ACS and the census long-form samples, include a range of uncertainty. Two broad types of error can occur: sampling error and nonsampling error. Nonsampling errors can result from mistakes in how the data are reported or coded, problems in the sampling frame or survey questionnaires, or problems related to nonresponse or interviewer bias. The Census Bureau tries to minimize nonsampling errors by using trained interviewers and by carefully reviewing the survey's sampling methods, data processing techniques, and questionnaire design.

Appendix 6 of the *ACS General Handbook* includes a more detailed description of different types of errors in the ACS and other measures of ACS quality: www.census

.gov/acs/www/Downloads/handbooks/ACSGeneralHand-book.pdf .

Sampling error occurs when data are based on a sample of a population rather than the full population. Sampling error is easier to measure than nonsampling error and can be used to assess the statistical reliability of survey data. For any given area, the larger the sample and the more months included in the data, the greater the confidence in the estimate. The Census Bureau reported the 90-percent confidence interval on all ACS estimates produced for 2005 and earlier. Beginning with the release of the 2006 ACS data, *margins of error* are now provided for every ACS estimate. Ninety percent confidence intervals define a range expected to contain the *true* value of an estimate with a level of confidence of 90 percent. Margins of error are easily converted into these confidence ranges. By adding and subtracting the margin of error from the point estimate, we can calculate the 90-percent confidence interval for an estimate. Therefore, we can be 90 percent confident that the true number falls between the lower-bound interval and the upper-bound interval.

Detailed information about sampling error and instructions for calculating confidence intervals and margins of error are included in Appendix 3 of the *ACS General Hand-book*: www.census.gov/acs/www/Downloads/handbooks/ACSGeneralHandbook.pdf .

The margin of error around an estimate is important because it helps one draw conclusions about the data. Small differences between two estimates may not be statistically significant if the confidence intervals of those estimates overlap. However, the Census Bureau cautions data users not to rely on overlapping confidence intervals as a test for statistical significance, because this method will not always produce accurate results. Instead, the Census Bureau recommends following the detailed instructions for conducting statistical significance tests in Appendix 4 of the *ACS General Handbook*.

In some cases, data users will need to construct custom ACS estimates by combining data across multiple geographic areas or population subgroups or it may be necessary to derive a new percentage, proportion, or ratio from published ACS data. In such cases, additional calculations are needed to produce confidence intervals and margins of error for the derived estimates. Appendix 3 of the *ACS General Handbook* provides detailed instructions on how to make these calculations. Note that these error measures do not tell us about the magnitude of nonsampling errors.

Some advanced data users will also want to construct custom ACS estimates from the Census Bureau's Public Use Microdata Samples (PUMS). There are separate instructions for conducting significance tests for PUMS estimates, available on the Census Bureau's American FactFinder (AFF) website at: www.census.gov/acs/www/Downloads/data_documentation/pums/Accuracy/2012AccuracyPUMS.pdf and http://www.census.gov/acs/www/Downloads/data_documentation/Accuracy/MultiyearACSAccuracyofData2012.pdf.

Accessing ACS Data Online

All ACS data are available through the Census Bureau's American FactFinder (AFF) website at factfinder2.census .gov . From the AFF home page, click on the Topics button to view and select the desired dataset. For the 2012 ACS, three datasets are shown—the 1-year estimates (based on the 2012 ACS), the 3-year estimates (based on the 2010–2012 ACS), and the 5-year estimates (based on the 2008–2012 ACS). The tables in this book were produced from the 1-year estimates for 2012 and the 3-year estimates for 2010–2012. It is important for all users to understand that once a data set is selected, the accessed tables will all correspond to this specific data set. All tables are clearly labeled, identifying the data set.

Basic information using American FactFinder can be found at factfinder2.census.gov . The *American FactFinder* main page provides information about available data and guidance on using FactFinder, under the tabs *What We Provide* and *Using FactFinder*. Additional assistance can be found at FactFinder Help (online help, census data information, glossary, and tutorial): factfinder2.census.gov/ help/en/american_factfinder_help.htm .

The various ACS data products are described below.

• **Data profiles and ranking tables.** The *data profiles* and *ranking tables* are good places to start for novice data users. *Data profiles* provide separate fact sheets on the social, economic, demographic, and housing characteristics for different geographic areas, while *ranking tables* provide state-level rankings of key ACS variables.

• **Geographic comparison tables.** Those interested in geographic comparisons for areas other than states may be interested in the *geographic comparison tables*, which allow comparison of ACS data across a variety of geographic areas, including metropolitan areas, cities, counties, and congressional districts.

• **Subject tables.** For information about a particular topic (for example, employment, education, and income), start with the *subject tables*, which provide pretabulated numbers and percentages for a wide variety of topics, often available separately by age, gender, or race/ethnicity.

• **Selected population profiles.** The most detailed race/ethnic data are available through the *selected population profiles*, which provide summary tables separately for more than 400 detailed race, ethnic, tribal, ancestry, and country of birth groups.

• **Comparison profiles.** The *comparison profiles* show data side-by-side from multiple years, indicating where there is a statistically significant difference between the two sets of estimates. Comparison profiles are only available for 1-year estimates.

• **Detailed tables and summary files.** The *detailed tables* are the best source for advanced data users or those who want access to the most comprehensive ACS tables. The tables in this book were developed through this option. For more advanced users, *detailed tables* are also available for download through the ACS *Summary File*: www.census .gov/acs/www/data_documentation/summary_file .

• **Thematic maps.** The *thematic maps* provide graphic displays of the data available through the various tables. Different shades of color are used to display variations in the data across geographic areas. Data users can also highlight areas with statistically different values from a selected state, county, or metropolitan area of interest. If a mapping option is available, it will display as an option when you view a table.

• **Public Use Microdata Sample files.** Those with expertise in using SAS, SPSS, or STATA may also be interested in the *Public Use Microdata Sample (PUMS) files*, which contain a sample of individual records of people and households that responded to the survey (stripped of all identifying information). The PUMS files permit analysis of specific population groups and custom variables that are not available through the American FactFinder. For example, PUMS data users can look at the proportion of children ages 5 to 11 living in low-income working families, or the number of scientists and engineers earning more than $75,000. Data users can also combine multiple years of PUMS data to produce data for relatively small population subgroups (for example, American Indian physicians). More information about the PUMS is available at www .census.gov/acs/www/data_documentation/public_use_ microdata_sample .

The ACS data are complex and cover a broad range of topics and geographic areas. Because this is a relatively new survey, many people do not fully understand how to interpret and use the ACS data. The key points are summarized below.

• Use caution in comparing ACS data with data from the decennial census or other sources. Every survey uses different methods, which could affect the comparability of the numbers.

• The ACS was designed to provide estimates of the characteristics of the population, not to provide counts of the population in different geographic areas or population subgroups.

• Be careful in drawing conclusions about small differences between two estimates because they may not be statistically different.

• Data users need to be careful not to interpret annual fluctuations in the data as long-term trends.

• Use caution in comparing data from 2006 and later surveys with data from the 2000–2005 surveys. Unlike earlier surveys, the 2006 and later ACS surveys include samples of the population living in group quarters (for example, college dorms and nursing homes), so the data may not be comparable, especially for young adults and the elderly, who are more likely than other age groups to be living in group quarters facilities.

• Data users should not interpret or refer to 3-year or 5-year period estimates as estimates of the middle year or last year in the series. For example, a 2010–2012 estimate is not a "2011 average."

• Data users should *not* rely on overlapping confidence intervals as a test for statistical significance because this method will not always provide an accurate result.

More ACS Resources

There is a wealth of information about the ACS on the Web, and new information becomes available on a regular basis. Each year, the ACS data release represents a new stage in a new process. Consequently, many new documents are required to explain the survey and how to use it. These resources cover many of the topics discussed in this book, but in greater detail.

The best place to start is the Census Bureau's ACS main page:

www.census.gov/acs/www

Background and Overview Information

The American Community Survey Web page site map provides an overview of the links and materials that are available online, including numerous reference documents.

www.census.gov/acs/www/utilities/sitemap.php

Basic information and links to a variety of information about using the ACS.

www.census.gov/acs/www/guidance_for_data_users/guidance_main

Information about the ACS methodology, with links to detailed descriptions of key topics.

www.census.gov/acs/www/methodology/methodology_main

PUMS Accuracy of the Data (2010)

Provides a basic understanding of the sample design, estimation methodology, and accuracy of the 2010 ACS data.

www.census.gov/acs/www/Downloads/data_documentation/pums/Accuracy/2012AccuracyPUMS.pdf

ACS Sample Size

Provides sample size information for each state for each year of the ACS. The initial sample size and the final completed interviews are provided. Sample sizes for all published geographic entities starting with the 2007 ACS are available in the B98 series of detailed tables on American FactFinder.

www.census.gov/acs/www/methodology/sample_size_data

ACS Quality Measures

Multi-Year Estimate Study Quality Measures Definitions:

Includes information about the steps taken by the Census Bureau to improve the accuracy of ACS data. Four indicators of survey quality are described and measures are provided at the national and state level.

www.census.gov/acs/www/Downloads/methodology/special_data_studies/multiyear_estimates/Quality_Measures_Documentation_MYE.pdf

Guidance on Data Products and Using the Data

How to Use the Data:

Includes links to many documents and materials that explain the ACS data products.

www.census.gov/acs/www/guidance_for_data_users/guidance_main

Comparing ACS Data to other sources:

Guidance on comparing the ACS data products to other years of ACS data and to Census 2000 long-form data.

www.census.gov/acs/www/guidance_for_data_users/comparing_data .

Information on Using Different Sources of Data for Income and Poverty:

Highlights the sources that should be used for data on income and poverty, focusing on comparing the ACS and the Current Population Survey (CPS).

www.census.gov/hhes/www/poverty/about/datasources/description.html

Poverty: 2000 to 2012. American Community Survey Brief on poverty.

www.census.gov/prod/2013pubs/acsbr12-01.pdf

Public Use Microdata Sample (PUMS):

Provides guidance on accessing ACS microdata.

www.census.gov/acs/www/data_documentation/public _use_microdata_sample

Other Data Resources:

• FactFinder Help (online help, census data information, glossary, and tutorial)

factfinder2.census.gov/help/en/american_factfinder_help .htm

• Guide to the Data Products (Web page)

www.census.gov/acs/www/data_documentation/ product_descriptions

• *A Compass for Understanding and Using American Community Survey Data: What General Data Users Need to Know* provides a complete overview:

www.census.gov/acs/www/Downloads/handbooks/ACS-GeneralHandbook.pdf

• *Using the American Community Survey: Benefits and Challenges*, edited by Constance F. Citro and Graham Kalton (The National Academies Press, 2007). An excellent overview of the ACS, complete with several chapters of useful information for data users. The book is available for purchase and is also available to read online at no charge.

www.nap.edu/openbook.php?record_id=11901

• *Benefits, Burdens, and Prospects of the American Community Survey: Summary of a Workshop* (2013), Daniel L. Cork, Rapporteur; Committee on National Statistics; Division on Behavioral and Social Sciences and Education; National Research Council.

www.nap.edu/openbook.php?record_id=18259

• *Small Populations, Large Effects: Improving the Measurement of the Group Quarters Population in the American Community Survey* (2012), Paul R. Voss and Krisztina Marton, Editors; Panel on Statistical Methods for Measuring the Group Quarters Population in the American Community Survey; Committee on National Statistics; Division of Behavioral and Social Sciences and Education; National Research Council.

www.nap.edu/openbook.php?record_id=13387

• *Measuring the Group Quarters Population in the American Community Survey: Interim Report* (2010), Kristina Marton and Paul R. Voss, Editors; Panel on Statistical Methods for Measuring the Group Quarters Population in the American Community Survey; National Research Council.

www.nap.edu/openbook.php?record_id=13075

Who
Age, Race/Ethnicity, and Households

Who: Age, Race/Ethnicity, and Household Structure

The 2010 census has recently documented changes in the American population: shifts in race and ethnic groups, changing age patterns, and changes in the predominant household structures. The American Community Survey is now being used to discover the details of these changes and the changes that are occurring in the new decade. The ACS provides annual detailed information about states, metropolitan areas, and other geographic entities with at least 65,000 people. Three years of survey responses are used to produce data for communities with populations of 20,000 or more, and 5-year estimates are available for even the smallest cities and towns, providing a regular stream of updated social, housing, and economic characteristics for demographic groups.

In earlier decades, these detailed characteristics could not be updated until the next decennial census. The American Community Survey permits ongoing analysis and measurement of changes that have occurred in the years since the 2010 census. One of this survey's most valuable aspects is that it allows users to compare their city or town against other local areas or against the United States. It highlights the differences among small areas within the United States. National trends are not mirrored in every community. Some places are changing even faster than the national picture; others are lagging or even going in a different direction. It is important for people to know how their locality fits into the national picture. These tables offer Americans information needed to compare various areas to see how they differ and how they are similar. In the discussion that follows, and in the tables in this book, the state and metropolitan area data are for the single year 2012, while the city and county data are for the 3-year period, 2010–2012.

Population

Although the ACS has replaced the census long form as the key source of detailed social and economic characteristics, the official population estimates are still developed through the Census Bureau's Population Estimates Program. After the 2010 census, all ACS estimates were adjusted to reflect the new population count. The ACS single-year estimates use the official total population estimates from the Population Estimates Program, but the population totals in the 3-year ACS files are adjusted for the 3-year time period.

Seven states had populations of 10 million or more, led by California, with 38 million, and Texas, with 26 million. Nearly 45 percent of the nation's population lived in these seven states. Another six states and the District of Columbia had populations of less than 1 million, representing 1.6 percent of the nation's population. Between 2010 and 2012, the United States' population increased 1.5 percent. The District of Columbia grew 4.6 percent during that two-year period, a growth rate exceeding all the states. North Dakota and Texas each grew more than 3 percent. Overall, 21 states and the District of Columbia had population growth above the national average. Ten states had population growth less than 0.5 percent, Vermont remained unchanged and Rhode Island lost population.

More than one-third of the U.S. population resided in the 75 most populous counties. Thirty-nine of these counties had populations exceeding 1 million. Los Angeles County was, by far, the most populous county in the nation, with nearly 10 million residents. Four counties had population growth exceeding 10 percent from 2010 to 2012. Two of these counties were in North Dakota, which is experiencing an oil boom. Another was St. Bernard Parish in Louisiana, still regaining population lost during Hurricane Katrina, and the other was Fredericksburg city in Virginia, near Washington DC. Another 22 counties grew 5 percent or more, 12 of them in Texas, and 4 each in Virginia, Georgia, and Florida. Between 2010 and 2012, 735 of the medium to large counties included in this book experienced population losses. Four counties had population losses of 4 percent or more. Wayne County, Michigan, was the only county with more than a million people that experienced a population loss. Since the ACS includes only counties with populations of 20,000 or more, gains and losses in smaller counties are not included in this discussion.

More than 260 million people, or about 84 percent of the population, lived in the nation's 366 metropolitan statistical areas. More than 26 percent of the U.S. population resided in the 10 most populous metropolitan areas. Fifty-one metropolitan areas had populations of 1 million or more. Eighteen metropolitan areas had growth rates exceeding 4 percent between 2010 and 2012. The highest growth rate was 12.6 percent in Hinesville-Fort Stewart, Georgia, a relatively small metropolitan area with a large military population. Among metropolitan areas of more than 1 million people, the largest growth was 6.1 percent

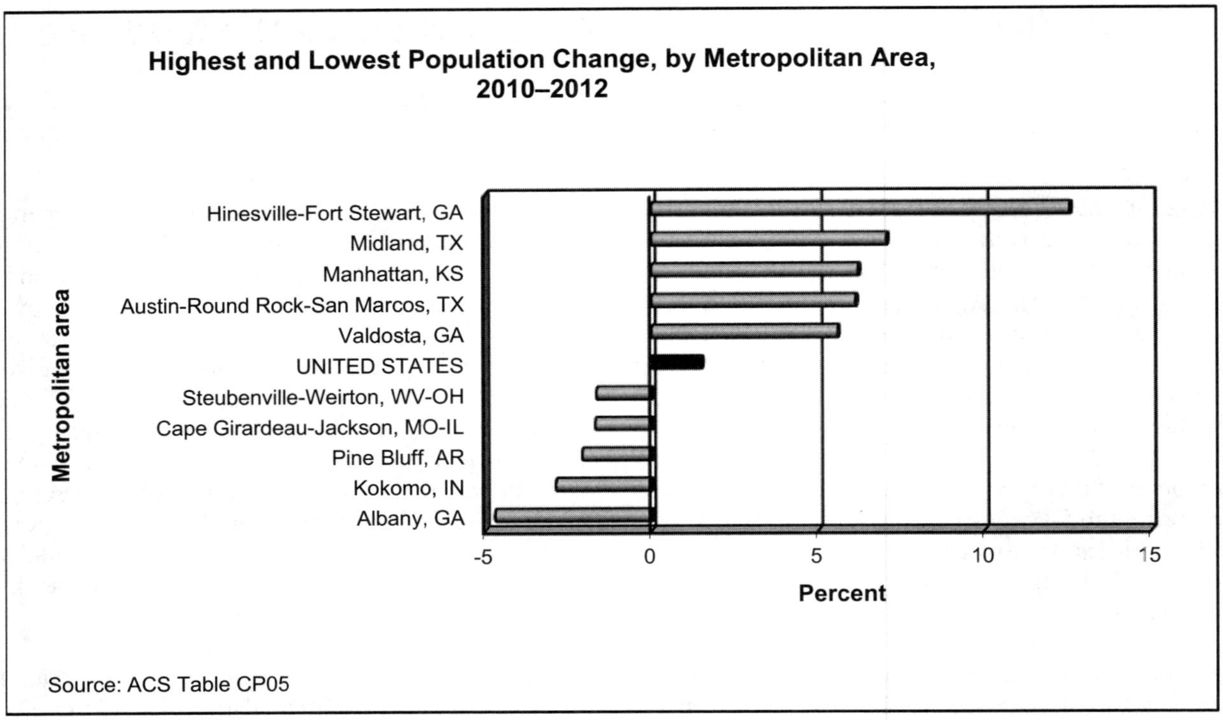
Highest and Lowest Population Change, by Metropolitan Area, 2010–2012
Metropolitan area
Hinesville-Fort Stewart, GA
Midland, TX
Manhattan, KS
Austin-Round Rock-San Marcos, TX
Valdosta, GA
UNITED STATES
Steubenville-Weirton, WV-OH
Cape Girardeau-Jackson, MO-IL
Pine Bluff, AR
Kokomo, IN
Albany, GA
-5
0
5
10
15
Percent
Source: ACS Table CP05

in Austin–Round Rock–San Marcos, Texas, followed by Raleigh–Carey, North Carolina, which grew 4.5 percent. About 40 percent of the metropolitan areas had growth rates exceeding the national rate of 1.5 percent and 65 areas lost population, with Albany, Georgia, losing 4.7 percent of its population.

Thirty-four cities have populations of 500,000 or more, including nine with populations of 1 million or more. With more than 8 million people, New York is, by far, the largest city. Los Angeles is second, with 3.8 million people, and Chicago's 2.7 million people still outnumber the fast-growing Houston's 2.1 million. Of the 2,143 cities with populations of 20,000 or more, 297 have populations exceeding 100,000, representing about 28 percent of the nation's population.[1] From 2010 to 2012, 181 of these more populous cities had growth rates exceeding the national rate of 1.5 percent. Frisco, Texas had the highest growth rate of these cities, at 8.6 percent, while Irvine, California and McKinney, Texas, both grew 7.8 percent during the three-year period.

Age

In 2012, the United States' median age was 37.4 years. Eight states had median ages of 40 or higher, topped by Maine, at 43.5 years. Utah had the lowest median age, at 29.9 years, the only state with a median age lower than 30. Only two more states and the District of Columbia had median ages lower than 35. Thirty-one percent of Utah's population was under age 18. At the other extreme, 17.3 percent of DC's population was under 18, despite its relatively low median age. Florida, Maine, West Virginia, and Pennsylvania had the highest proportions of population 65 years and over. In four states, 2.5 percent or more of the population was 85 years old and over, while only Alaska had fewer than 1 percent in that age group.

Three metropolitan areas had more than 1 in 3 residents under the age of 18. Two were located in Texas, and one in Utah. Ten metropolitan areas had at least 1 in 4 residents who were over age 65. Seven of the ten areas were in Florida, with the highest population, 36.2 percent, in Punta Gorda, Florida.

Twenty-three counties had median ages over 50. The most populous were Sarasota County, Florida; Barnstable County, Massachusetts; and Yavapai County, Arizona, all with more than 200,000 residents. About two-thirds of the more than 1,800 counties included in this book had median ages that exceeded the U.S. average of 37.3 years. Thirty counties had at least 1 in 4 residents age 65 years or over. Eleven of these were in Florida, topped by Sumter County, where 46 percent of the residents were 65 or older. Six counties, all with universities, had median ages

1. Official population estimates are not developed for Census Designated Places (CDPs) so they are not included in this discussion. See Appendix A for more information.

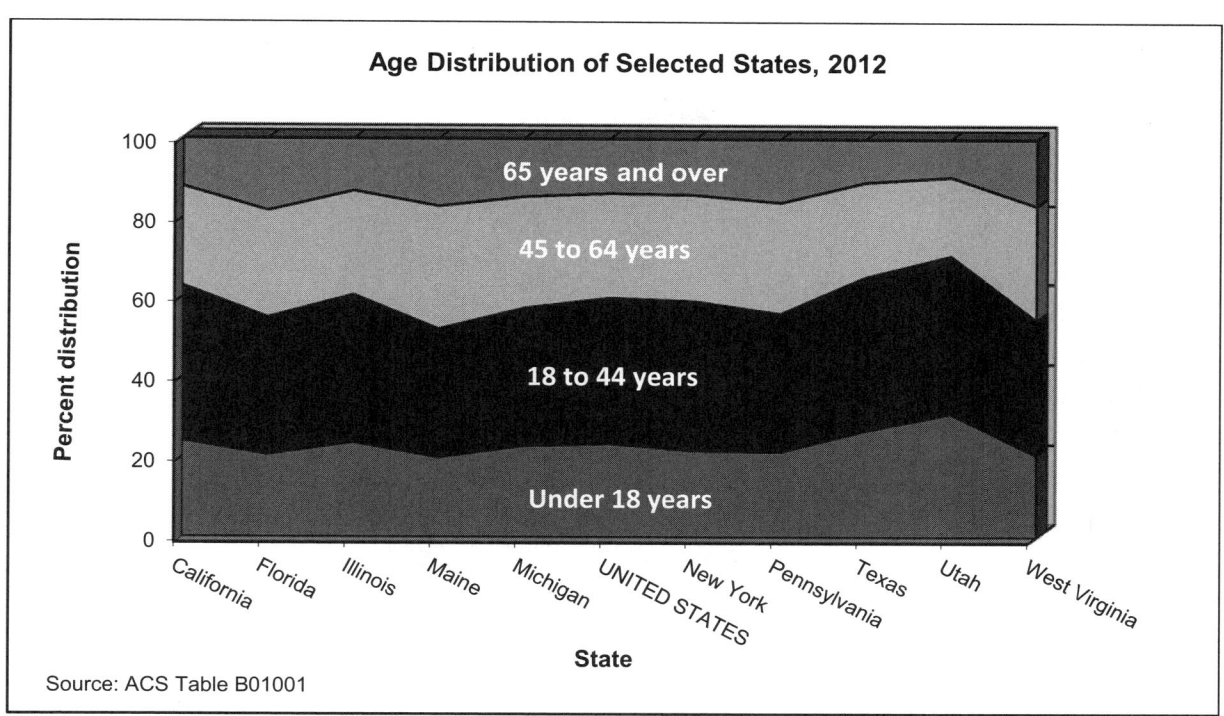

Age Distribution of Selected States, 2012

Source: ACS Table B01001

under 25. In thirteen counties, at least one-third of the population was under age 18; five of these counties were in Utah and three were in Texas.

The median age in eight cities was 60 years or more. All of these cities were located in Florida and Arizona. Four age-restricted communities had median ages over 70. Forty-four cities had 25 percent or more of their populations consisting of people 65 years and older. Nationally, this age group accounted for 13.4 percent of the population. In eight cities, more than 40 percent of the population was under 18 years old. The highest proportions—62 and 50 percent—were in Kiryas Joel Village, New York, and Lakewood CDP, New Jersey. The other six were in Utah. Fifty-six cities, predominantly college towns, had median ages of 25 years or less.

The working-age population is generally considered to include people between the ages of 25 and 64. Nationally, 53 percent of the population was in this category. Fifty-four cities had proportions of working-age population that exceeded 60 percent. Three of these cities were among the 75 most populous—San Francisco, Seattle, and Portland. Many others were suburban communities and a few had large prison populations.

Race/Ethnicity

Probably the most visible place-based demographic difference is in racial and ethnic composition. Seen from afar, the U.S. population may be a melting pot, but at close range

it varies widely. Among the states, Illinois came the closest to matching the national portrait of race and Hispanic origin, followed by New Jersey and New York, though each state differed along one or more dimensions. The other states showed a wide range of racial and ethnic composition. For example, about 94 percent of the population of Vermont and Maine was non-Hispanic White. In contrast, Hawaii, the District of Columbia, California, New Mexico, and Texas are all "majority minority" states, with non-Hispanic Whites making up less that 50 percent of their populations. About 51 percent of the District of Columbia's population was Black. About 20 percent of Alaska residents were American Indian or Alaska Native alone or in combination. Close to four in five Hawaiian residents were Asian, Native Hawaiian, or Pacific Islander. In New Mexico, 47 percent of the population was Hispanic.

Twenty-eight metropolitan areas—all relatively small—had populations consisting of 95 percent or more of Whites alone or in combination. In the Honolulu metropolitan area, about 85 percent of the population identified as Asian, Native Hawaiian, or Pacific Islander.[2] Fifty-three percent of the population of Albany, Georgia, was Black, the only majority Black metropolitan area. In another ten metropolitan areas—all in the South—more than 40 percent of the residents were Black. The Memphis TN–MS–AR metropolitan area was the only one of these with

2. There is some double-counting of persons who identified with both groups ("Asian alone or in combination" and "Native Hawaiian or Pacific Islander alone or in combination").

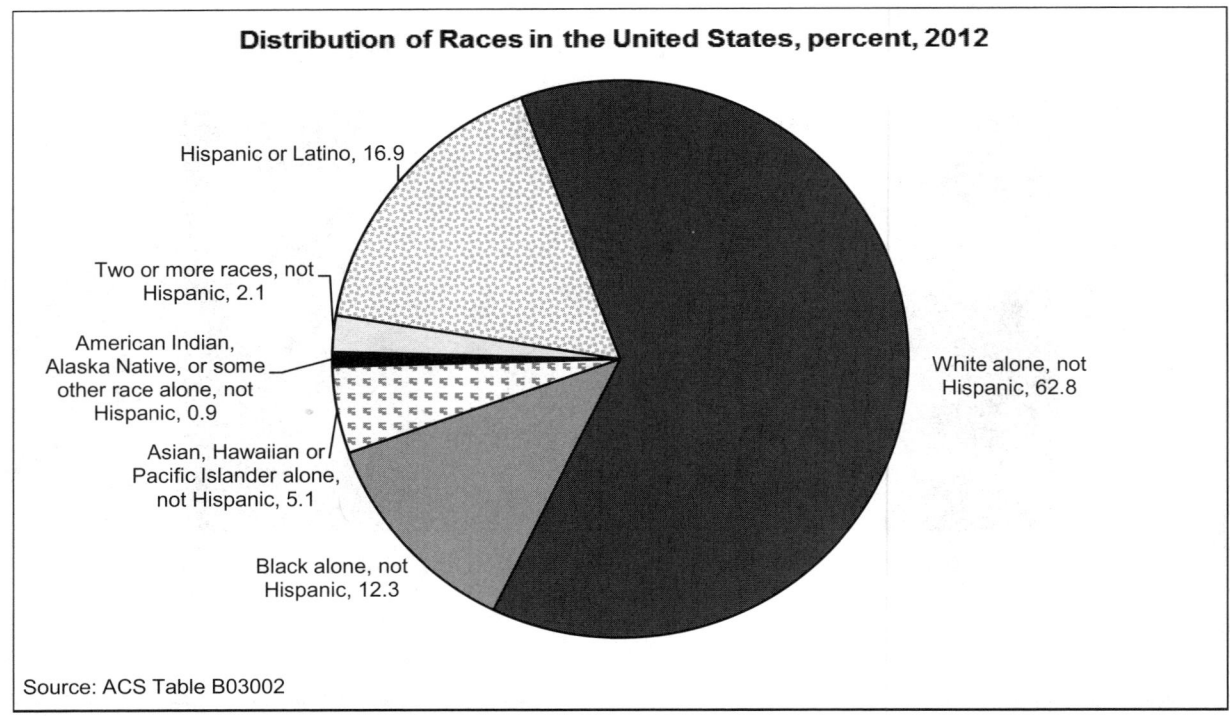

Distribution of Races in the United States, percent, 2012

Hispanic or Latino, 16.9

Two or more races, not Hispanic, 2.1

American Indian, Alaska Native, or some other race alone, not Hispanic, 0.9

Asian, Hawaiian or Pacific Islander alone, not Hispanic, 5.1

Black alone, not Hispanic, 12.3

White alone, not Hispanic, 62.8

Source: ACS Table B03002

more than 1 million residents. Hispanic or Latino residents make up a majority in 18 metropolitan areas, the largest of which is San Antonio, Texas, with more than 2 million residents.[3] In another ten metropolitan areas, the proportion of Hispanic or Latino residents is between 40 percent and 50 percent. These include three of the largest metropolitan areas: Los Angeles, with 13 million residents; Miami, with nearly 6 million; and Riverside–San Bernardino, California, with more than 4 million.

Among smaller geography types, the racial and ethnic characteristics of a population varied even more widely. More than 95 percent of the 1,846 counties or county equivalents included in the American Community Survey 2010–2012 estimates were majority White. Of these counties, 538 had White populations of 95 percent or more. However, many counties had a majority population that was some other race or ethnic group. Among the 55 counties with majority Black populations, the largest are Shelby County, Tennessee (Memphis), and Prince George's County, Maryland (near Washington DC), both with about 900,000 residents. Four U.S. counties had majority Asian, Native Hawaiian, or Pacific Islander populations. All were located in Hawaii. Four large California counties had populations that surpassed 30 percent of this race group, all in the San Francisco and San Jose metropolitan areas. Four counties had majority Native American,

Alaska Native, or some other race populations. They were located in Arizona, New Mexico, and Oklahoma. Some of these counties contained (or were contained in) tribal reservations. Forty-five counties had populations that were majority Hispanic (of any race). Counties in the Southwest that were originally settled by the Spanish had populations with higher proportions of Hispanic residents. In four Texas counties along the Mexican border, more than 90 percent of the residents were Hispanic or Latino.

More than 500 cities had White populations of 90 percent or higher. The most populous of these cities was Lincoln, Nebraska, with more than a quarter of a million people. More than 100 cities were majority Black, with 30 having Black populations of three-quarters or more. Six of these cities were in Maryland, and 4 were in Illinois. Detroit, Michigan (83 percent Black) was, by far, the most populous, with more than 700,000 residents. Twenty-six cities were majority Asian, Native Hawaiian, and Pacific Islander.[4] All were located in either California or Hawaii. Honolulu was the most populous of these cities. In the city table in this book, the American Indian or Alaska Native population is combined with those who answered "some other race" because most cities had too few respondents in either category. In eight cities, the majority of people

3. Hispanic or Latino persons may be of any race. Most self-identify as "White" or "some other race."

4. Some Hawaiian cities show more than 100 percent in this category because the categories "Asian alone or in combination" with "Native Hawaiian or Pacific Islander alone or in combination" have been combined in this book.

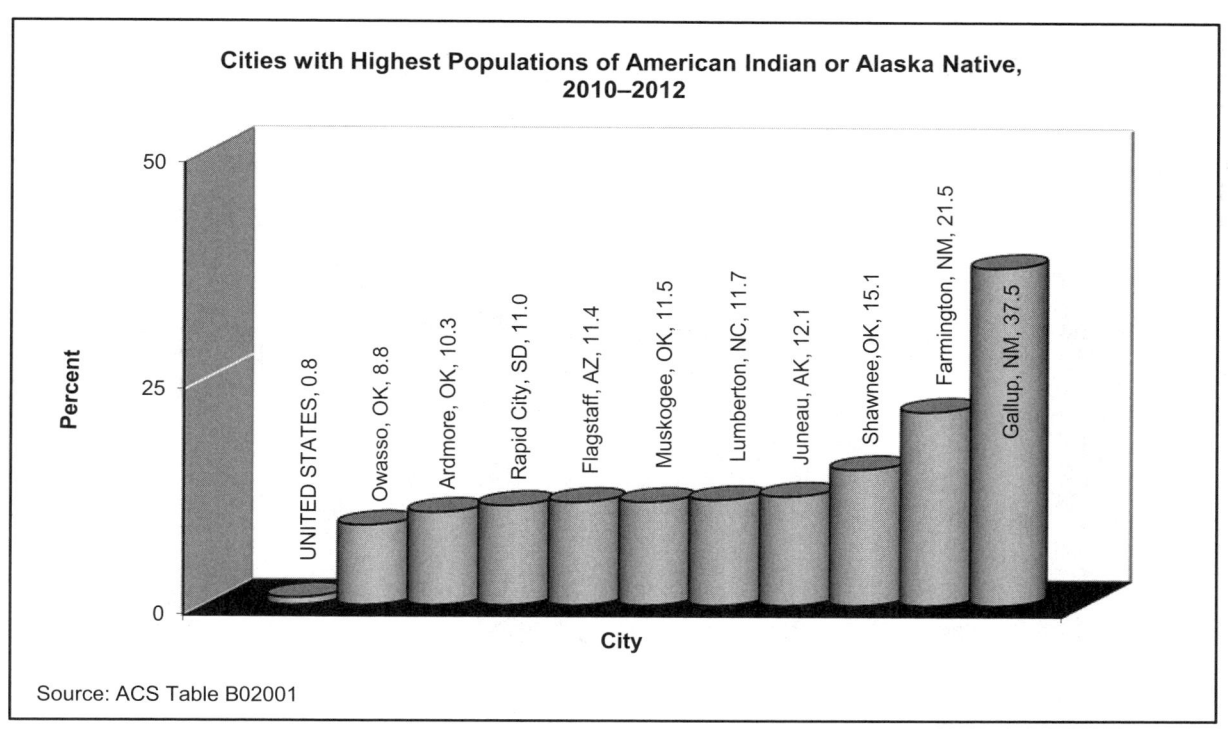

Cities with Highest Populations of American Indian or Alaska Native, 2010–2012

Source: ACS Table B02001

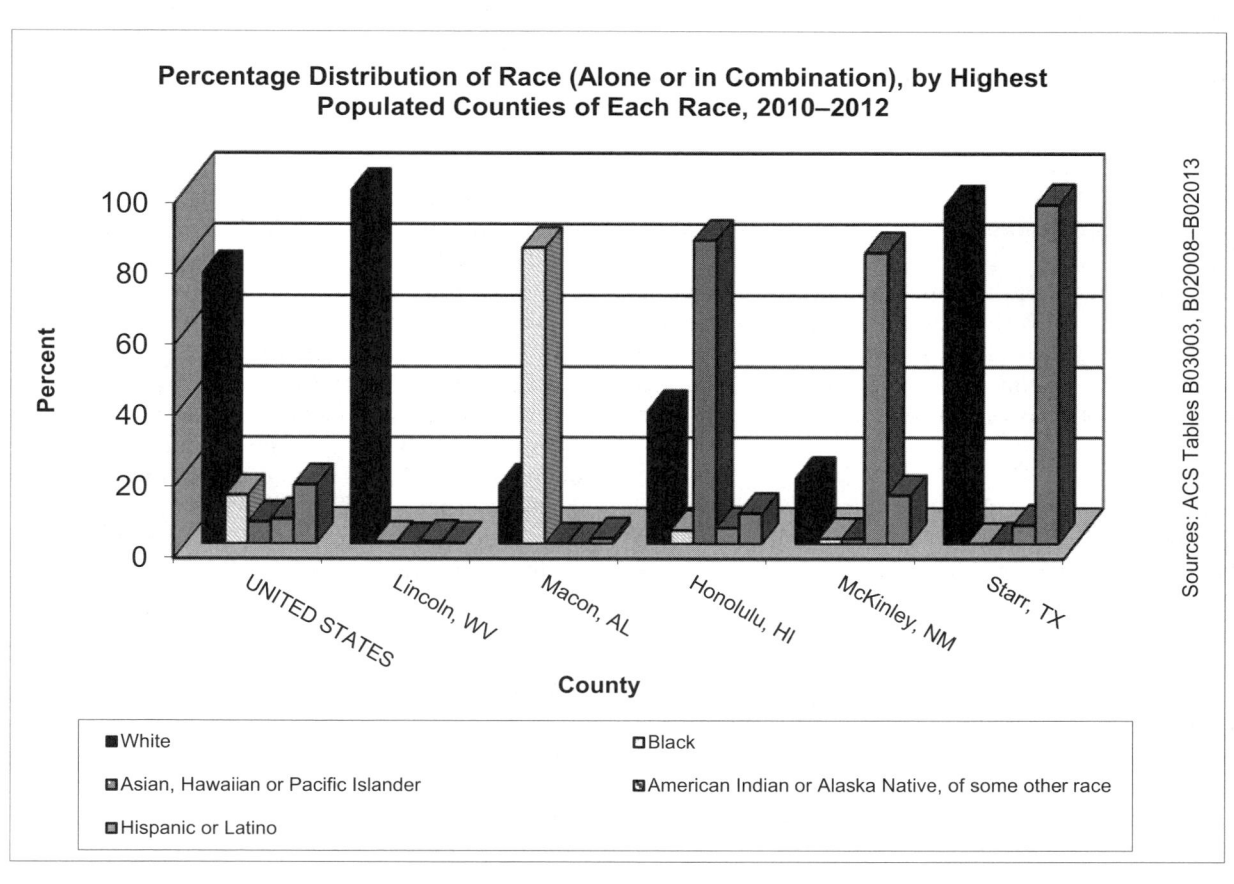

Percentage Distribution of Race (Alone or in Combination), by Highest Populated Counties of Each Race, 2010–2012

Sources: ACS Tables B03003, B02008–B02013

Legend:
- White
- Black
- Asian, Hawaiian or Pacific Islander
- American Indian or Alaska Native, of some other race
- Hispanic or Latino

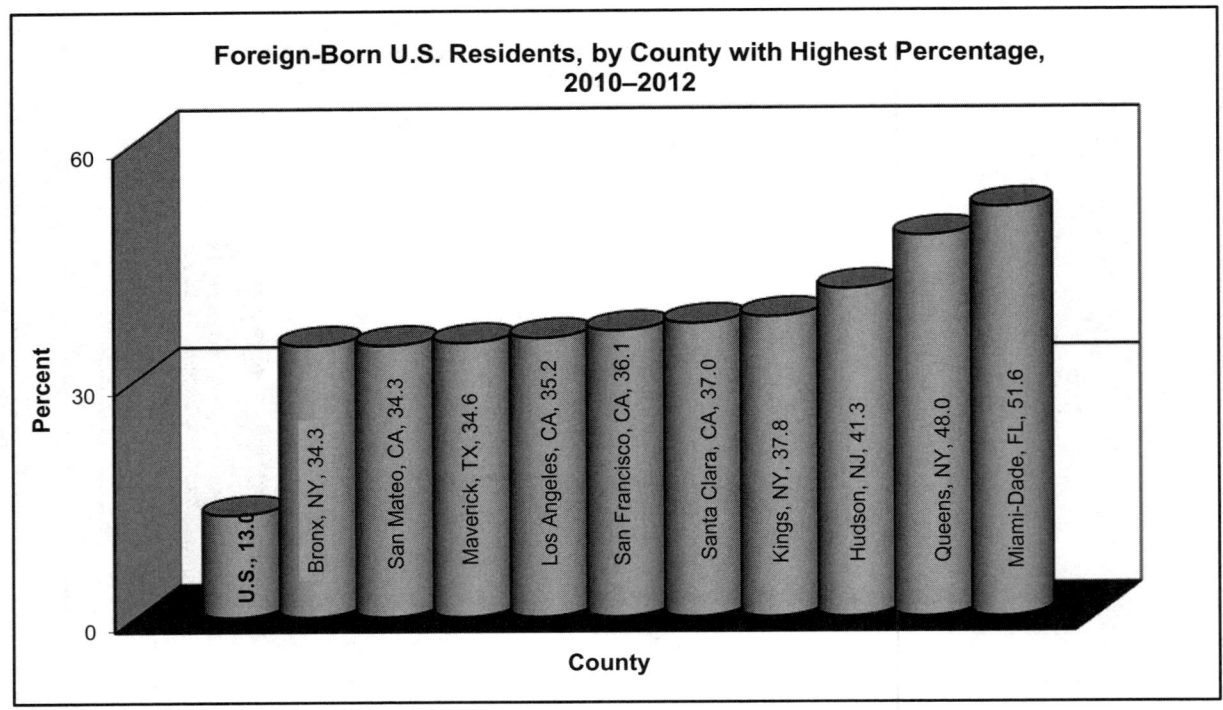

Foreign-Born U.S. Residents, by County with Highest Percentage, 2010–2012

x-axis: County; y-axis: Percent

- U.S., 13.0
- Bronx, NY, 34.3
- San Mateo, CA, 34.3
- Maverick, TX, 34.6
- Los Angeles, CA, 35.2
- San Francisco, CA, 36.1
- Santa Clara, CA, 37.0
- Kings, NY, 37.8
- Hudson, NJ, 41.3
- Queens, NY, 48.0
- Miami-Dade, FL, 51.6

were in this group, some cities with large Native American populations and others who indicated "some other race," often largely Latino populations. In 185 cities, a majority of the population identified themselves as Hispanic or Latino. Ninety-two of these cities are in California and 25 are in Texas. Most are small cities, but there are seven with populations greater than 250,000. San Antonio, Texas, with 1.4 million residents, is the largest.

Foreign-Born Populations and Foreign Languages

Nationally, 13 percent of the population was foreign born. More than 27 percent of California's population was foreign born, and both New York and New Jersey exceeded 20 percent. West Virginia (1.4 percent) and Montana (1.8 percent) had the lowest proportions of foreign-born residents.

In eleven counties, more than one-third of the residents were foreign born. Six of these counties had more than a million residents, led by Miami-Dade County, Florida, with 51.6 percent and Queens County, New York, with 48 percent. More than 90 percent of the counties included in this publication had foreign-born proportions less than the U.S. average of 13 percent, including eight counties with more than 1 million people. Thirty metropolitan areas had foreign-born populations of 20 percent or more. Miami–Fort Lauderdale–Pompano Beach, Florida, and San Jose–Sunnyvale–Santa Clara, California, had the highest proportions, both more than 36 percent.

Of the 2,143 cities, 915 had foreign-born proportions that exceeded the U.S. average. Thirty-five cities had majority foreign-born residents. Florida had the most with 19 such cities, followed by California with 11 cities. More than 70 percent of the residents of Sweetwater and Hialeah, Florida, were foreign-born. Among the most populous cities, Miami, Florida, had the highest proportion at 58.2 percent.

About 20 percent of American households spoke a language other than English at home (in addition to or instead of English). States with the highest proportions were California and New Mexico, both over 40 percent. Spanish-speaking households were most prevalent in New Mexico (32.5 percent), Texas (28.8 percent), and California (25.2 percent). In nearly 10 percent of California households and 8 percent of New York households, no adult spoke English well. In New York, Spanish-speaking households were slightly outnumbered by households that spoke a different language other than English. West Virginia and Mississippi had the lowest proportions of households speaking a language other than English, both under 5 percent.

Household Structure

Places that differ from the national age portrait also differ from the nation's household portrait. Two-thirds of the nation's households were family households (people related by birth, marriage, or adoption). Nonfamily households included people living alone or with unrelated people. Just under half of all households were married-couple family

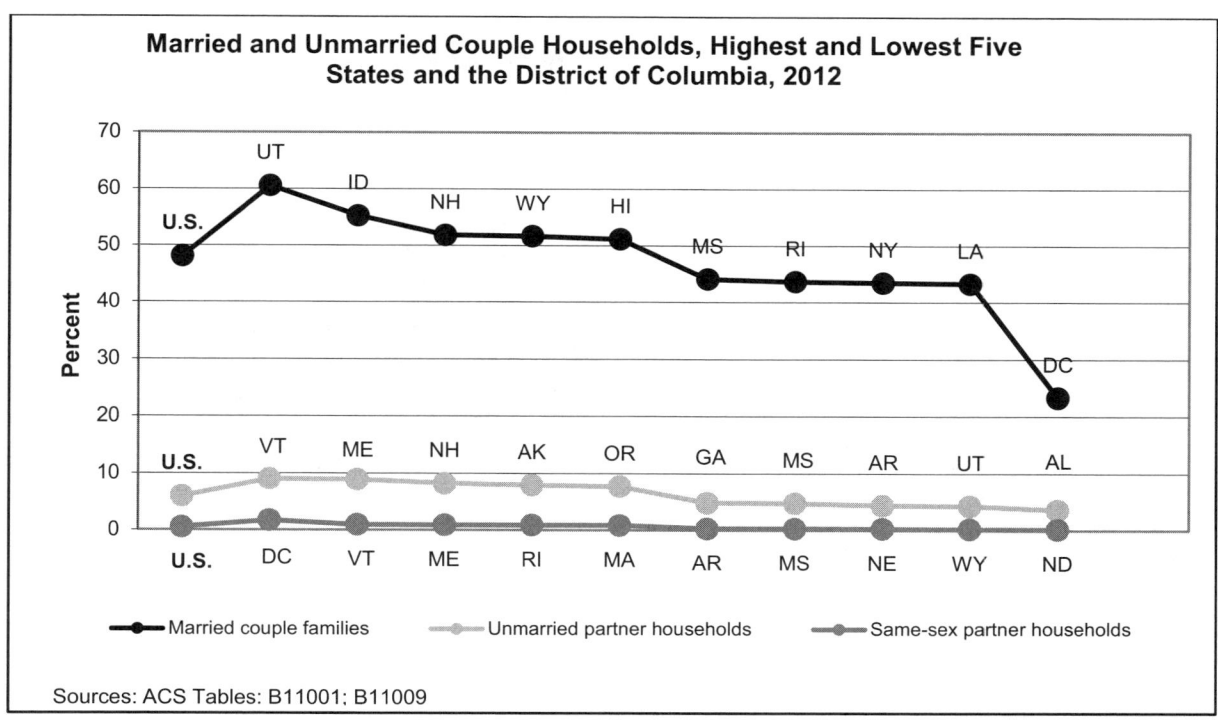

Married and Unmarried Couple Households, Highest and Lowest Five States and the District of Columbia, 2012

Sources: ACS Tables: B11001; B11009

households. In some areas, people lived predominantly in married-couple households, while others were dominated by male- and female-headed family households (no spouse present) or by nonfamily households.

About one third of the nation's households are made up of nonfamily households—people living alone, or with other, unrelated adults. Twenty-nine states and the District of Columbia had proportions of nonfamily households that exceeded this national level of 34 percent. More than 57 percent of the District of Columbia's households were nonfamily households, many of them one-person households (45.8 percent). Nationally, 27.8 percent of households consisted of a person living alone.

Although there were large numbers of single-person households in every age group, West Virginia and Rhode Island had the highest proportion of persons over 65 years old living alone, both above 12 percent. Among all ages, Utah had the lowest proportion of single-person households, at 19.8 percent. About 6 percent of householders were unmarried partner couples, ranging from 3.6 percent in Alabama to 9 percent in Vermont. Less than one percent of all householders were same-gender couples.

The District of Columbia had the highest proportion of never married residents at 57.5 percent. In New York, California, Massachusetts, and Rhode Island, more than 35 percent of the population had never married. Utah and Idaho had the highest percentages of currently married

residents, both about 57 percent. Nationally, half of all persons are currently married, but 19 states have lower proportions. Nevada and Maine had the highest proportions of divorced residents, both over 14 percent, while more than 13 percent were divorced in seven more states. New York and New Jersey had the lowest proportions of divorced individuals, both under 9 percent.

In eight metropolitan areas, 20 percent or more of households were female-headed families, compared with 13 percent for the nation as a whole. Four of these metropolitan areas were in Texas. Nationally, 48 percent of households were married-couple families. In four metropolitan areas in Utah, married-couple families exceeded 60 percent of households. The proportion was less than 40 percent in the New Orleans, Louisiana; and Gainesville, Florida; metropolitan areas.

Among the cities covered in this book, nearly 1,000 had proportions of married-couple families that exceeded the national level of 48 percent. Among the 75 most populous cities, 9 exceeded this level, 5 of them in California. Plano, Texas, had the highest proportion, 56.9 percent. Sixty of these most populous cities had above average rates of nonfamily households, including one-person households. In ten of these large cities, more than half of all households were nonfamily households. Two cities—Washington, DC and Atlanta, Georgia—had rates exceeding 45 percent of householders living alone. Many smaller cities have higher proportions of married-couple families and one-person households.

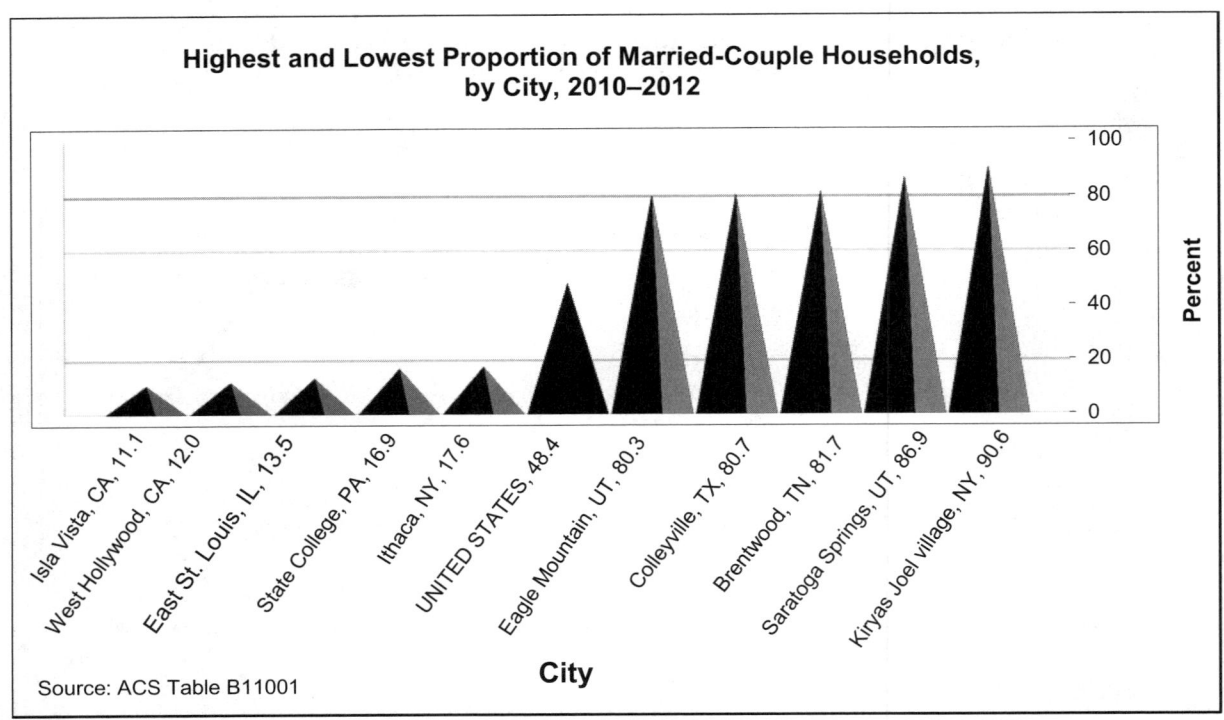

Highest and Lowest Proportion of Married-Couple Households, by City, 2010–2012

Source: ACS Table B11001

Among the states, Utah had the highest average household size—3.14 persons per household, followed by Hawaii with 3.01 and California with 2.97. The District of Columbia (2.22 persons), Vermont and North Dakota (2.32 persons), and Maine (2.33 persons) had the lowest average household sizes. The national average was 2.64 persons per household.

Sixty-four percent of households with children were married-couple family households. Utah had the highest proportion—77 percent—and the District of Columbia had the lowest proportion, where 45.7 percent of households with children were married-couple family households.

About one-third of American households include children under 18 years old. Four metropolitan areas—two in Texas, one in California, and one in Utah—had someone under age 18 in more than half of their households. About 60 percent of metropolitan areas had a lower proportion than the U.S. average.

In five counties, 50 percent or more of households included children under age 18. Among the 75 most populous counties, Kern County, California, and El Paso County, Texas, had the highest proportion of households with children, both above 45 percent. Among the 75 most populous counties, New York and San Francisco had the lowest proportions of households with children, both under 19 percent.

Nationally, about 35 percent of households included someone 60 years old or older. About half of the states had higher proportions, led by Hawaii, Florida, and West Virginia, all with more than 40 percent. In 50 counties—13 of them in Florida—more than half of the households included someone age 60 or over. Among the 75 largest cities, 43.5 percent of households in Urban Honolulu CDP, Hawaii, 38.3 percent of households in Henderson, Nevada, and 37.3 percent of households in Miami, Florida, included someone age 60 years or over.

State Rankings, 2012
Selected Rankings

Population rank	State	Total population [A-1, col. 1]	Percent change rank	State	Percent change 2010–2012 [A-1, col. 2]	Percent Non-Hispanic White rank	State	Percent Non-Hispanic White alone [A-1, col. 11]
	United States	313,914,040		United States	1.5		United States	62.8
1	California.............................	38,041,430	1	District of Columbia	4.6	1	Maine	94.1
2	Texas....................................	26,059,203	2	North Dakota.............................	3.7	2	Vermont	94.0
3	New York	19,570,261	3	Texas.....................................	3.2	3	West Virginia	92.8
4	Florida	19,317,568	4	Utah	2.8	4	New Hampshire	91.8
5	Illinois	12,875,255	5	Colorado	2.7	5	North Dakota	88.1
6	Pennsylvania	12,763,536	6	Florida	2.5	6	Iowa	88.0
7	Ohio	11,544,225	7	Alaska....................................	2.4	7	Montana	87.2
8	Georgia	9,919,945	8	Washington	2.3	8	Kentucky	85.8
9	Michigan	9,883,360	9	Arizona	2.2	9	Wyoming	84.6
10	North Carolina	9,752,073	10	Georgia	2.1	10	South Dakota	83.8
11	New Jersey............................	8,864,590	10	Wyoming	2.1	11	Idaho	83.4
12	Virginia	8,185,867	10	Hawaii	2.1	12	Wisconsin	82.8
13	Washington	6,897,012	10	South Dakota..........................	2.1	13	Minnesota	82.3
14	Massachusetts	6,646,144	14	Virginia	2.0	14	Nebraska	81.3
15	Arizona	6,553,255	14	Nevada	2.0	15	Indiana	80.9
16	Indiana	6,537,334	14	North Carolina	2.0	16	Ohio	80.6
17	Tennessee	6,456,243	17	Delaware	1.9	17	Missouri	80.5
18	Missouri	6,021,988	17	South Carolina.........................	1.9	18	Utah	79.8
19	Maryland	5,884,563	17	California................................	1.9	19	Pennsylvania	78.6
20	Wisconsin	5,726,398	20	Maryland	1.7	20	Oregon	77.6
21	Minnesota	5,379,139	21	Oregon	1.6	21	Kansas	77.4
22	Colorado	5,187,582	21	Tennessee	1.6	22	Michigan	76.1
23	Alabama...............................	4,822,023	23	Idaho	1.5	23	Rhode Island	75.4
24	South Carolina	4,723,723	24	Oklahoma	1.4	24	Massachusetts	75.3
25	Louisiana	4,601,893	24	Montana	1.4	25	Tennessee	75.0
26	Kentucky	4,380,415	24	Nebraska	1.4	26	Arkansas	73.9
27	Oregon	3,899,353	24	Massachusetts	1.4	27	Washington	71.4
28	Oklahoma	3,814,820	28	Minnesota	1.3	28	Connecticut	70.0
29	Connecticut	3,590,347	28	Louisiana	1.3	29	Colorado	69.4
30	Iowa	3,074,186	30	New Mexico............................	0.9	30	Oklahoma	67.8
31	Mississippi............................	2,984,926	30	Arkansas	0.9	31	Alabama	66.6
32	Arkansas...............................	2,949,131	30	Kansas	0.9	32	North Carolina	64.5
33	Kansas..................................	2,885,905	30	New York	0.9	33	Delaware	64.3
34	Utah	2,855,287	34	Iowa	0.8	34	Virginia	63.9
35	Nevada	2,758,931	34	Kentucky	0.8	34	South Carolina	63.9
36	New Mexico..........................	2,085,538	34	Alabama	0.8	36	Alaska	63.0
37	Nebraska	1,855,525	37	Indiana	0.7	37	Illinois	62.9
38	West Virginia	1,855,413	37	New Jersey.............................	0.7	38	Louisiana	59.7
39	Idaho	1,595,728	39	Wisconsin	0.6	39	New Jersey............................	57.9
40	Hawaii	1,392,313	40	Mississippi..............................	0.5	40	Mississippi............................	57.5
41	Maine	1,329,192	41	Missouri	0.4	41	New York	57.4
42	New Hampshire	1,320,718	41	Pennsylvania	0.4	42	Arizona	56.9
43	Rhode Island	1,050,292	41	Connecticut	0.4	43	Florida	56.8
44	Montana	1,005,141	44	New Hampshire	0.3	44	Georgia	55.0
45	Delaware	917,092	45	Illinois	0.2	45	Maryland	53.8
46	South Dakota........................	833,354	46	Maine	0.1	46	Nevada	52.7
47	Alaska..................................	731,449	46	West Virginia	0.1	47	Texas....................................	44.3
48	North Dakota........................	699,628	46	Ohio	0.1	48	New Mexico..........................	39.7
49	District of Columbia	632,323	46	Michigan	0.1	49	California...............................	39.2
50	Vermont	626,011	50	Vermont	0.0	50	District of Columbia	35.3
51	Wyoming..............................	576,412	51	Rhode Island	-0.2	51	Hawaii	22.8

State Rankings, 2012
Selected Rankings

Percent Black rank	State	Percent Black alone or in combination [A-1, col. 4]	Percent American Indian or Alaska Native rank	State	Percent American Indian or Alaska Native alone or in combination [A-1, col. 5]	Percent Asian and Native Hawaiian or Pacific Islander rank	State	Percent Asian and Native Hawaiian or Pacific Islander alone or in combination [A-1, cols. 6 + 7]
	United States	13.7		United States	1.7		United States	6.2
1	District of Columbia	50.8	1	Alaska............................	19.6	1	Hawaii	82.5
2	Mississippi	38.2	2	Oklahoma......................	13.4	2	California.......................	16.1
3	Louisiana	33.1	3	New Mexico...................	10.4	3	Washington	10.6
4	Georgia	32.0	4	South Dakota.................	10.0	4	Nevada	10.5
5	Maryland	30.9	5	Montana........................	8.1	5	New Jersey.....................	9.6
6	South Carolina...............	28.8	6	North Dakota.................	6.4	6	Alaska............................	9.1
7	Alabama	27.2	7	Arizona..........................	5.4	7	New York	8.6
8	Delaware	23.1	8	Wyoming.......................	3.9	8	Virginia..........................	7.1
9	North Carolina	22.9	9	Oregon	3.0	9	Maryland	6.9
10	Virginia	20.8	9	Washington	3.0	10	Massachusetts	6.5
11	Tennessee	17.7	11	Idaho.............................	2.4	11	Oregon	5.9
12	Florida	17.3	12	Kansas...........................	2.1	12	Illinois	5.5
13	New York	16.9	12	Hawaii	2.1	13	Minnesota	5.0
14	Arkansas........................	16.3	14	Nevada	2.0	14	Connecticut	4.9
15	Illinois	15.4	14	Colorado	2.0	15	Texas.............................	4.8
16	Michigan	15.3	16	North Carolina	1.9	15	District of Columbia	4.8
17	New Jersey.....................	14.9	16	Minnesota	1.9	17	Utah	4.4
18	Ohio	13.6	16	California.......................	1.9	17	Arizona..........................	4.2
19	Texas.............................	12.7	19	Utah	1.7	19	Colorado	4.1
20	Missouri.........................	12.6	19	Arkansas........................	1.7	19	Georgia	4.1
21	Pennsylvania	12.2	19	Maine	1.7	21	Delaware	4.0
22	Connecticut....................	11.6	22	Wisconsin	1.6	22	Rhode Island	3.9
23	Indiana	10.3	22	Nebraska	1.6	23	Pennsylvania	3.5
24	Nevada	9.7	24	Michigan	1.4	23	Florida	3.4
25	Kentucky	9.0	24	Missouri.........................	1.4	25	Kansas...........................	3.3
26	Oklahoma......................	8.9	26	Vermont	1.3	26	Michigan	3.2
27	Massachusetts	8.6	26	West Virginia	1.3	27	North Carolina	2.9
28	Rhode Island	8.1	26	Rhode Island	1.3	27	New Hampshire	2.9
29	Kansas...........................	7.3	26	Louisiana	1.3	29	Wisconsin	2.8
30	Wisconsin	7.2	30	Texas.............................	1.2	30	Nebraska	2.6
31	California.......................	7.1	30	Alabama	1.2	31	Oklahoma......................	2.5
32	Minnesota	6.4	32	Virginia	1.1	32	Idaho.............................	2.4
33	Nebraska	5.5	32	Maryland	1.1	32	Iowa	2.3
34	Arizona..........................	5.2	34	New York	1.0	32	Missouri.........................	2.3
35	Alaska............................	5.1	35	New Hampshire	0.9	35	Ohio	2.3
35	Colorado	5.1	35	Tennessee	0.9	36	Indiana	2.2
37	Washington	5.0	35	Iowa	0.9	36	New Mexico...................	2.1
38	West Virginia	4.1	35	South Carolina...............	0.9	38	Louisiana	2.0
39	Iowa	3.9	39	Connecticut....................	0.8	38	Tennessee	2.0
40	Hawaii	3.2	39	Indiana	0.8	40	Arkansas........................	1.9
41	New Mexico...................	2.8	39	Ohio	0.8	40	South Carolina...............	1.8
42	Oregon	2.6	39	Delaware	0.8	42	Vermont	1.8
43	South Dakota.................	2.2	39	Mississippi.....................	0.8	43	Kentucky	1.7
44	North Dakota.................	2.0	39	Kentucky	0.8	44	Alabama	1.6
44	Wyoming.......................	2.0	39	District of Columbia	0.8	44	North Dakota.................	1.5
46	New Hampshire	1.9	39	Florida	0.8	46	Maine	1.5
47	Utah	1.6	47	Georgia	0.7	46	South Dakota.................	1.5
47	Maine	1.6	47	New Jersey.....................	0.7	48	Wyoming.......................	1.4
47	Vermont	1.6	47	Massachusetts	0.7	49	Montana........................	1.4
50	Idaho.............................	1.0	47	Illinois	0.7	49	Mississippi.....................	1.1
51	Montana........................	0.8	51	Pennsylvania	0.6	51	West Virginia	0.9

State Rankings, 2012
Selected Rankings

Percent Hispanic or Latino rank rank	State	Percent Hispanic or Latino [A-1. col. 9]	Median age rank	State	Median age (years) [A-1, col. 23]	Average household size rank	State	Average household size [A-1, col. 43]
	United States	16.9		United States	37.4		United States	2.64
1	New Mexico	47.0	1	Maine	43.5	1	Utah	3.14
2	Texas	38.2	2	Vermont	42.4	2	Hawaii	3.01
2	California	38.2	3	New Hampshire	41.9	3	California	2.97
4	Arizona	30.2	4	West Virginia	41.5	4	Texas	2.84
5	Nevada	27.3	5	Florida	41.1	5	Alaska	2.80
6	Florida	23.2	6	Pennsylvania	40.5	6	Georgia	2.73
7	Colorado	21.0	7	Connecticut	40.4	7	New Jersey	2.71
8	New Jersey	18.5	8	Montana	40.2	8	Nevada	2.70
9	New York	18.2	9	Rhode Island	39.8	9	Idaho	2.69
10	Illinois	16.3	10	Massachusetts	39.5	10	Arizona	2.68
11	Connecticut	14.2	10	Michigan	39.5	11	New Mexico	2.67
12	Utah	13.3	12	New Jersey	39.4	12	Maryland	2.66
13	Rhode Island	13.2	13	Ohio	39.3	13	Mississippi	2.65
14	Oregon	12.2	14	Delaware	39.2	14	Illinois	2.64
15	Washington	11.7	15	Oregon	38.9	15	Delaware	2.62
16	Idaho	11.6	16	Wisconsin	38.8	15	Florida	2.62
17	Kansas	10.9	17	Kentucky	38.4	15	New York	2.62
18	Massachusetts	10.1	18	Hawaii	38.3	18	Virginia	2.61
19	District of Columbia	9.9	18	South Carolina	38.3	19	Louisiana	2.60
20	Nebraska	9.6	20	Alabama	38.2	20	South Carolina	2.57
21	Hawaii	9.5	20	Missouri	38.2	21	Connecticut	2.56
22	Wyoming	9.4	20	Tennessee	38.2	21	Indiana	2.56
23	Oklahoma	9.3	23	Maryland	38.1	21	Oklahoma	2.56
24	Georgia	9.1	23	New York	38.1	21	Washington	2.56
25	Maryland	8.7	25	Iowa	38.0	25	Alabama	2.55
25	North Carolina	8.7	26	North Carolina	37.8	25	North Carolina	2.55
27	Delaware	8.6	27	Arkansas	37.6	27	Colorado	2.54
28	Virginia	8.4	27	Minnesota	37.6	27	Massachusetts	2.54
29	Arkansas	6.7	29	Virginia	37.5	27	Tennessee	2.54
30	Indiana	6.3	29	Washington	37.5	30	Michigan	2.53
31	Wisconsin	6.2	31	Indiana	37.3	31	Kansas	2.52
32	Pennsylvania	6.1	32	Illinois	37.0	31	Wyoming	2.52
33	Alaska	6.0	33	Wyoming	36.9	33	Arkansas	2.51
34	South Carolina	5.3	34	Nevada	36.8	33	Oregon	2.51
35	Iowa	5.2	34	New Mexico	36.8	35	Kentucky	2.49
36	Minnesota	4.9	36	South Dakota	36.7	35	Pennsylvania	2.49
37	Tennessee	4.8	37	Arizona	36.6	37	Minnesota	2.48
38	Michigan	4.6	38	Nebraska	36.3	37	Missouri	2.48
39	Louisiana	4.5	38	Oklahoma	36.3	39	New Hampshire	2.47
40	Alabama	3.8	40	Colorado	36.2	39	Ohio	2.47
41	Missouri	3.7	40	Mississippi	36.2	39	South Dakota	2.47
42	Ohio	3.2	40	North Dakota	36.2	42	Nebraska	2.46
43	Montana	3.1	43	Kansas	36.0	43	Rhode Island	2.44
43	Kentucky	3.1	43	Louisiana	36.0	43	West Virginia	2.44
45	New Hampshire	3.0	45	Georgia	35.7	43	Wisconsin	2.44
45	South Dakota	3.0	46	California	35.5	46	Iowa	2.42
47	Mississippi	2.7	47	Idaho	35.2	47	Montana	2.39
48	North Dakota	2.4	48	Texas	33.9	48	Maine	2.33
49	Vermont	1.6	49	Alaska	33.8	49	North Dakota	2.32
50	Maine	1.4	50	District of Columbia	33.7	49	Vermont	2.32
51	West Virginia	1.3	51	Utah	29.9	51	District of Columbia	2.22

State Rankings, 2012
Selected Rankings

Never married rank	State	Percent never married [A-1, col.33]	Now married rank	State	Percent now married [A-1, col. 34]	Divorced rank	State	Percent divorced [A-1, col. 36]
	United States	32.7		United States	50.2		United States	11.1
1	District of Columbia	57.5	1	Utah	57.3	1	Nevada	14.6
2	New York	38.0	2	Idaho	56.3	2	Maine	14.2
3	California	36.6	3	Wyoming	54.7	3	Oklahoma	13.5
4	Massachusetts	36.0	4	Iowa	54.0	4	Oregon	13.4
5	Rhode Island	35.6	4	Nebraska	54.0	5	Arkansas	13.3
6	Maryland	34.9	4	Montana	54.0	6	West Virginia	13.3
7	Illinois	34.6	7	Kansas	53.8	7	Florida	13.2
8	Louisiana	34.5	8	Minnesota	53.5	7	Kentucky	13.2
9	Alaska	34.1	9	Arkansas	52.9	9	New Mexico	13.1
10	New Jersey	34.0	10	North Dakota	52.8	10	Tennessee	13.0
11	Connecticut	33.8	11	New Hampshire	52.6	11	Wyoming	12.8
12	Mississippi	33.4	11	Virginia	52.6	12	Alabama	12.7
12	Hawaii	33.4	13	Kentucky	52.3	12	Indiana	12.7
14	Georgia	33.2	13	Oklahoma	52.3	14	Missouri	12.5
14	Pennsylvania	33.2	13	Colorado	52.3	14	Arizona	12.5
16	New Mexico	33.1	13	South Dakota	52.3	14	Idaho	12.5
17	Arizona	32.7	17	North Carolina	52.2	14	Ohio	12.5
17	Delaware	32.7	17	Texas	52.2	18	Alaska	12.4
19	Michigan	32.6	17	Washington	52.2	18	Colorado	12.4
20	Nevada	32.3	20	Wisconsin	52.0	20	Montana	12.3
21	South Carolina	31.9	20	Maine	52.0	20	New Hampshire	12.3
22	Virginia	31.8	22	West Virginia	51.5	20	Louisiana	12.3
23	Texas	31.6	23	Tennessee	51.4	20	Washington	12.3
24	North Dakota	31.5	24	Vermont	51.3	24	Kansas	12.2
25	Minnesota	31.3	25	New Jersey	51.2	25	Vermont	12.1
26	Wisconsin	31.2	25	Indiana	51.2	26	Mississippi	11.9
26	Ohio	31.2	27	Missouri	51.0	27	Michigan	11.8
28	Florida	31.1	27	Alabama	51.0	27	Delaware	11.8
29	Colorado	30.9	29	Hawaii	50.9	29	Rhode Island	11.5
30	Vermont	30.8	29	Oregon	50.9	30	Georgia	11.4
31	North Carolina	30.7	31	South Carolina	50.6	30	Iowa	11.4
31	Washington	30.7	32	Pennsylvania	50.2	32	Texas	11.0
33	South Dakota	30.5	33	Ohio	49.9	32	South Dakota	11.0
34	Oregon	30.2	34	Georgia	49.7	32	Wisconsin	11.0
35	Indiana	30.1	34	Alaska	49.7	35	North Carolina	10.8
36	Missouri	29.9	36	Connecticut	49.6	36	South Carolina	10.7
37	New Hampshire	29.6	37	Michigan	49.5	37	Connecticut	10.6
38	Utah	29.5	38	Illinois	49.4	38	Nebraska	10.4
38	Nebraska	29.5	39	Delaware	49.3	39	Minnesota	10.2
40	Alabama	29.3	40	Arizona	49.2	39	Virginia	10.2
41	Tennessee	29.2	40	Maryland	49.2	41	Massachusetts	10.1
42	Iowa	28.3	42	California	48.5	41	Maryland	10.1
43	Kansas	28.2	42	Florida	48.5	43	Illinois	10.0
44	Kentucky	27.8	44	Massachusetts	48.0	44	California	9.8
45	Montana	27.6	44	Nevada	48.0	45	North Dakota	9.7
46	Oklahoma	27.5	46	New Mexico	47.9	46	Hawaii	9.5
47	Maine	27.4	47	Mississippi	47.5	46	Pennsylvania	9.5
47	West Virginia	27.4	48	New York	46.9	46	Utah	9.5
49	Wyoming	27.2	49	Louisiana	46.6	49	District of Columbia	9.2
50	Arkansas	26.9	49	Rhode Island	46.6	50	New York	8.8
51	Idaho	26.0	51	District of Columbia	28.8	51	New Jersey	8.6

State Rankings, 2012
Selected Rankings

Foreign born rank	State	Percent foreign-born population [A-1, col. 37]	Spanish-speaking households rank	State	Percent of households speaking Spanish with or without English [A-1, col. 39]	Households where no adult speaks English well rank	State	Percent of households where no adult speaks English well [A-1, col. 41]
	United States	13.0		United States	11.9		United States	4.5
1	California	27.1	1	New Mexico	32.5	1	California	9.6
2	New York	22.6	2	Texas	28.8	2	New York	8.1
3	New Jersey	21.2	3	California	25.2	3	Texas	7.9
4	Florida	19.4	4	Arizona	19.5	4	New Jersey	7.3
5	Nevada	19.2	5	Florida	19.2	5	Hawaii	6.9
6	Hawaii	18.1	6	Nevada	18.7	6	Florida	6.8
7	Texas	16.4	7	New Jersey	15.0	7	Nevada	6.1
8	Massachusetts	15.0	8	New York	14.5	8	Massachusetts	5.8
9	District of Columbia	14.3	9	Connecticut	11.6	9	Connecticut	5.3
9	Maryland	14.3	9	Colorado	11.6	10	Rhode Island	5.2
11	Illinois	13.9	11	Illinois	11.1	11	New Mexico	5.1
12	Connecticut	13.8	12	Utah	10.7	12	Illinois	4.9
13	Arizona	13.4	13	Rhode Island	9.6	13	Arizona	4.7
14	Rhode Island	13.3	14	Massachusetts	8.5	14	Washington	3.9
14	Washington	13.3	15	District of Columbia	7.8	15	District of Columbia	3.2
16	Virginia	11.6	15	Washington	7.8	16	Georgia	3.0
17	Colorado	9.8	17	Idaho	7.6	16	Utah	3.0
18	Oregon	9.6	17	Oregon	7.6	16	Maryland	3.0
19	Georgia	9.5	19	Georgia	7.4	19	Colorado	2.9
20	New Mexico	9.2	20	Delaware	7.0	20	Oregon	2.7
21	Delaware	8.5	21	Kansas	6.9	21	Nebraska	2.6
22	Utah	8.4	22	Nebraska	6.8	21	Virginia	2.6
23	North Carolina	7.7	23	Maryland	6.5	23	North Carolina	2.5
24	Minnesota	7.2	23	North Carolina	6.5	24	Delaware	2.4
24	Alaska	7.2	25	Virginia	6.3	25	Pennsylvania	2.3
26	Kansas	6.5	26	Wyoming	6.2	26	Oklahoma	2.2
27	Nebraska	6.4	27	Oklahoma	6.1	26	Kansas	2.2
28	Michigan	6.1	28	Alaska	4.9	26	Minnesota	2.2
28	Idaho	6.1	29	Indiana	4.8	29	Alaska	2.1
30	Pennsylvania	6.0	29	Pennsylvania	4.8	30	Idaho	2.1
31	Oklahoma	5.6	31	Wisconsin	4.7	31	Indiana	1.8
32	New Hampshire	5.4	31	Arkansas	4.7	32	Michigan	1.7
33	Wisconsin	4.8	33	South Carolina	4.4	32	Louisiana	1.7
34	South Carolina	4.7	34	Minnesota	4.1	34	Wisconsin	1.6
35	Indiana	4.6	34	Louisiana	4.1	34	Arkansas	1.6
36	Tennessee	4.5	34	Iowa	4.1	36	South Carolina	1.5
36	Iowa	4.5	37	Tennessee	3.7	37	New Hampshire	1.4
38	Arkansas	4.4	38	Michigan	3.5	37	Tennessee	1.4
39	Vermont	4.1	39	Alabama	3.4	37	Iowa	1.4
40	Ohio	3.9	40	Hawaii	2.9	37	South Dakota	1.4
41	Missouri	3.8	40	Kentucky	2.9	41	Ohio	1.3
42	Louisiana	3.7	40	Ohio	2.9	41	Alabama	1.3
43	Maine	3.5	43	Missouri	2.8	43	Missouri	1.1
44	Alabama	3.4	44	Montana	2.6	43	Kentucky	1.1
44	Wyoming	3.4	45	Mississippi	2.4	45	Maine	1.0
46	Kentucky	3.1	45	New Hampshire	2.4	45	North Dakota	1.0
47	North Dakota	2.8	47	North Dakota	2.3	47	Wyoming	0.9
48	South Carolina	2.7	48	South Dakota	2.1	48	Vermont	0.7
49	Mississippi	2.0	49	Vermont	1.6	48	Mississippi	0.7
50	Montana	1.8	50	West Virginia	1.5	50	Montana	0.6
51	West Virginia	1.4	51	Maine	1.4	51	West Virginia	0.3

State Rankings, 2012
Selected Rankings

Married-couple family households rank	State	Percent of households married-couple family [A-1, col. 45]	Female family householder rank	State	Percent of households female householder families [A-1, col. 47]
	United States	48.1		United States	13.1
1	Utah	60.6	1	Mississippi..	19.2
2	Idaho	55.3	2	Louisiana	16.9
3	New Hampshire	51.8	3	South Carolina	15.6
4	Wyoming	51.6	4	Georgia	15.5
5	Hawaii	51.2	5	District of Columbia	15.4
6	Minnesota	51.1	6	Alabama	15.0
7	Iowa	51.0	7	New York	14.8
8	New Jersey	50.8	8	Maryland	14.5
9	Virginia	50.7	8	New Mexico	14.5
10	Kansas	50.6	10	Texas	14.3
11	Nebraska	50.3	11	Rhode Island	14.0
11	Montana..	50.3	12	Nevada	13.9
13	Texas	50.1	13	California	13.7
14	Indiana	49.6	14	North Carolina	13.5
15	Washington	49.4	14	New Jersey	13.5
16	South Dakota	49.3	14	Delaware	13.5
17	Wisconsin	49.2	17	Tennessee	13.3
18	Alaska..	49.0	17	Florida	13.3
19	Vermont	48.9	19	Kentucky	13.2
19	Kentucky	48.9	20	Arkansas	13.1
21	Colorado	48.8	20	Connecticut.......................................	13.1
21	Maine	48.8	22	Michigan	12.9
21	Arkansas	48.8	22	Arizona	12.9
24	Connecticut	48.7	24	Illinois..	12.8
25	California...	48.6	24	Massachusetts	12.8
26	Oklahoma	48.5	26	Ohio	12.7
27	Tennessee	48.4	27	Hawaii	12.6
27	West Virginia	48.4	28	Oklahoma	12.5
29	North Carolina	48.1	29	Missouri	12.4
29	Pennsylvania	48.1	29	Virginia	12.4
29	North Dakota	48.1	31	Indiana	12.3
29	Oregon..	48.1	32	Pennsylvania	12.1
33	Delaware	48.0	33	Alaska..	11.8
33	Illinois	48.0	34	Oregon..	11.0
35	Georgia	47.9	35	West Virginia	10.9
35	Alabama	47.9	36	Colorado	10.6
37	Michigan	47.7	37	South Dakota	10.2
37	Missouri	47.7	37	Washington	10.2
39	Maryland	47.2	37	Wisconsin	10.2
40	South Carolina	47.0	37	Kansas	10.2
41	Arizona..	46.9	37	Idaho	10.2
42	Ohio	46.8	42	Nebraska	10.0
43	Massachusetts	46.5	43	Iowa	9.9
44	Florida	46.1	44	New Hampshire	9.8
45	New Mexico.......................................	45.4	45	Minnesota	9.7
46	Nevada	44.2	46	Utah	9.6
47	Mississippi...	44.1	46	Maine	9.6
48	Rhode Island	43.7	48	Wyoming	9.4
49	New York	43.5	48	Vermont	9.4
50	Louisiana	43.3	50	Montana..	8.5
51	District of Columbia..........................	23.3	51	North Dakota	8.1

County Rankings, 2010–2012
Selected Rankings

Population rank	County	Total population [A-2, col.1]	Percent change rank	County	Percent change 2010–2012 [A-2, col. 2]	Foreign born rank	County	Percent foreign-born population [A-2, col. 15]
	United States	311,609,369		United States	1.5		United States	13.0
1	Los Angeles County, CA	9,892,525	1	Williams County, ND	18.3	1	Miami-Dade County, FL	51.6
2	Cook County, IL	5,214,942	2	St. Bernard Parish, LA	13.2	2	Queens County, NY	48.0
3	Harris County, TX	4,178,437	3	Fredericksburg city, VA	11.7	3	Hudson County, NJ	41.3
4	Maricopa County, AZ	3,878,086	4	Stark County, ND	10.0	4	Kings County, NY	37.8
5	San Diego County, CA	3,139,726	5	Russell County, AL	8.6	5	Santa Clara County, CA	37.0
6	Orange County, CA	3,054,809	6	Franklin County, WA	8.5	6	San Francisco County, CA	36.1
7	Miami-Dade County, FL	2,553,696	7	Dallas County, IA	7.9	7	Los Angeles County, CA	35.2
8	Kings County, NY	2,538,529	8	Sumter County, FL	7.8	8	Maverick County, TX	34.6
9	Dallas County, TX	2,411,891	9	Geary County, KS	7.6	9	San Mateo County, CA	34.3
10	Queens County, NY	2,254,750	10	Midland County, TX	7.1	9	Bronx County, NY	34.3
11	Riverside County, CA	2,236,158	11	Williamson County, TX	6.9	11	Santa Cruz County, AZ	34.0
12	San Bernardino County, CA	2,062,483	11	Lincoln County, SD	6.9	12	Starr County, TX	32.6
13	Clark County, NV	1,974,036	13	Loudoun County, VA	6.8	13	Imperial County, CA	32.4
14	King County, WA	1,972,284	13	Hays County, TX	6.8	14	Montgomery County, MD	32.2
15	Tarrant County, TX	1,847,884	15	Kendall County, TX	6.7	15	Broward County, FL	31.7
16	Santa Clara County, CA	1,811,955	15	Wasatch County, UT	6.7	16	Seward County, KS	31.1
17	Wayne County, MI	1,803,251	17	Osceola County, FL	6.6	17	Middlesex County, NJ	30.9
18	Broward County, FL	1,784,340	18	Uintah County, UT	6.5	18	Monterey County, CA	30.8
19	Bexar County, TX	1,754,058	19	Montgomery County, TN	6.4	19	Alameda County, CA	30.7
20	New York County, NY	1,604,407	19	Hoke County, NC	6.4	20	Orange County, CA	30.6
21	Philadelphia County, PA	1,538,211	21	Travis County, TX	6.3	21	Fairfax County, VA	29.7
22	Alameda County, CA	1,533,311	21	Forsyth County, GA	6.3	21	Bergen County, NJ	29.7
23	Middlesex County, MA	1,521,993	23	Orleans Parish, LA	6.2	23	Hidalgo County, TX	29.4
24	Suffolk County, NY	1,498,125	23	Berkeley County, SC	6.2	24	Union County, NJ	29.2
25	Sacramento County, CA	1,436,233	25	Fort Bend County, TX	6.1	25	Moore County, TX	29.0
26	Bronx County, NY	1,397,357	25	Manassas city, VA	6.1	26	Webb County, TX	28.9
27	Nassau County, NY	1,345,448	27	Denton County, TX	6.0	27	Passaic County, NJ	28.8
28	Palm Beach County, FL	1,339,372	28	Collin County, TX	5.9	28	New York County, NY	28.7
29	Cuyahoga County, OH	1,271,187	28	Bryan County, GA	5.9	29	Suffolk County, MA	27.5
30	Hillsborough County, FL	1,260,333	30	Prince William County, VA	5.8	30	Alexandria city, VA	26.6
31	Allegheny County, PA	1,226,873	31	St. Johns County, FL	5.7	31	Manassas city, VA	25.9
32	Oakland County, MI	1,211,683	32	Fulton County, GA	5.6	32	El Paso County, TX	25.7
33	Franklin County, OH	1,180,276	32	Montgomery County, TX	5.6	33	Franklin County, WA	25.5
34	Orange County, FL	1,174,032	32	Arlington County, VA	5.6	33	Fort Bend County, TX	25.5
35	Hennepin County, MN	1,169,434	32	Guadalupe County, TX	5.6	33	Merced County, CA	25.5
36	Fairfax County, VA	1,103,177	32	Riley County, KS	5.6	36	Westchester County, NY	25.1
37	Contra Costa County, CA	1,066,333	37	Harnett County, NC	5.5	36	Essex County, NJ	25.1
38	Travis County, TX	1,062,335	38	Canadian County, OK	5.4	38	Harris County, TX	25.0
39	Salt Lake County, UT	1,048,261	39	Ector County, TX	5.3	39	Cameron County, TX	24.7
40	St. Louis County, MO	999,595	39	Columbia County, GA	5.3	40	Ford County, KS	24.6
41	Montgomery County, MD	990,787	39	Limestone County, AL	5.3	40	Yuma County, AZ	24.6
42	Pima County, AZ	987,294	42	Okaloosa County, FL	5.2	40	Hendry County, FL	24.6
43	Honolulu County, HI	966,405	43	Denver County, CO	5.1	43	Gwinnett County, GA	24.5
44	Westchester County, NY	956,494	43	Rockwall County, TX	5.1	44	Napa County, CA	24.2
45	Milwaukee County, WI	951,833	45	Wake County, NC	5.0	45	Colusa County, CA	24.0
46	Fulton County, GA	951,157	45	Burleigh County, ND	5.0	46	Fairfax city, VA	23.9
47	Mecklenburg County, NC	945,889	47	Mecklenburg County, NC	4.9	47	Arlington County, VA	23.5
48	Fresno County, CA	940,493	48	Williamson County, TN	4.8	47	Santa Barbara County, CA	23.5
49	Shelby County, TN	934,654	48	Beckham County, OK	4.8	49	Contra Costa County, CA	23.4
50	Wake County, NC	929,250	50	Hamilton County, IN	4.7	49	San Diego County, CA	23.4
51	Fairfield County, CT	926,739	50	Elko County, NV	4.7	51	Dallas County, TX	23.2
52	DuPage County, IL	923,503	52	Orange County, FL	4.6	51	Somerset County, NJ	23.2
53	Erie County, NY	919,268	52	Lee County, AL	4.6	51	Val Verde County, TX	23.2
54	Pinellas County, FL	918,385	52	Washington County, UT	4.6	54	Collier County, FL	23.1
55	Bergen County, NJ	912,753	52	Comal County, TX	4.6	55	San Joaquin County, CA	23.0
56	Marion County, IN	911,593	52	Matanuska-Susitna Borough, AK	4.6	56	Texas County, OK	22.9
57	Hartford County, CT	895,987	57	District of Columbia	4.5	56	Tulare County, CA	22.9
58	Prince George's County, MD	873,629	58	Lowndes County, GA	4.4	56	Sutter County, CA	22.9
59	Duval County, FL	872,307	58	Ward County, ND	4.4	59	Loudoun County, VA	22.8
60	New Haven County, CT	862,776	60	Horry County, SC	4.3	59	Ventura County, CA	22.8
61	Kern County, CA	849,101	60	Liberty County, GA	4.3	61	Palm Beach County, FL	22.5
62	Macomb County, MI	843,852	62	Gwinnett County, GA	4.2	62	Fresno County, CA	22.3
63	Ventura County, CA	830,828	62	Durham County, NC	4.2	63	Rockland County, NY	22.0
64	Gwinnett County, GA	825,375	62	Benton County, AR	4.2	64	Riverside County, CA	21.9
65	Middlesex County, NJ	816,975	62	Muscogee County, GA	4.2	65	Clark County, NV	21.7
66	El Paso County, TX	816,295	62	Natrona County, WY	4.2	65	Nassau County, NY	21.7
67	San Francisco County, CA	815,234	62	Lafayette County, MS	4.2	67	Richmond County, NY	21.5
68	Baltimore County, MD	812,043	68	Baldwin County, AL	4.1	68	San Bernardino County, CA	21.3
69	Collin County, TX	811,948	68	Ascension Parish, LA	4.1	69	Madera County, CA	21.2
70	Montgomery County, PA	804,896	68	Walton County, FL	4.1	69	Cook County, IL	21.2
71	Pierce County, WA	803,585	68	Summit County, UT	4.1	71	Prince William County, VA	21.1
72	Worcester County, MA	803,429	72	Lee County, FL	4.0	71	Yolo County, CA	21.1
73	Hamilton County, OH	801,587	72	Utah County, UT	4.0	73	San Benito County, CA	21.0
74	Hidalgo County, TX	793,312	72	Ada County, ID	4.0	74	King County, WA	20.8
75	Essex County, NJ	786,363	72	Charleston County, SC	4.0	75	Mercer County, NJ	20.6
			72	Rutherford County, TN	4.0			
			72	Faulkner County, AR	4.0			
			72	Whitman County, WA	4.0			

County Rankings, 2010–2012
Selected Rankings

Married-couple family households rank	County	Percent of households married-couple family [A-2, col. 18]	Female family householder rank	County	Percent of households female family householder [A-2, col. 20]	One-person households	County	Percent one-person households [A-2, col. 22]
	United States	48.4		United States	13.1		United States	27.6
1	Goochland County, VA	72.5	1	Coahoma County, MS	32.4	1	Hampshire County, WV	54.2
2	Holmes County, OH	72.0	2	Bronx County, NY	31.4	2	New York County, NY	47.7
3	Madison County, ID	71.3	3	Leflore County, MS	31.3	3	District of Columbia	46.9
4	Utah County, UT	70.7	4	Washington County, MS	30.5	4	Mineral County, WV	44.1
5	Jefferson County, ID	70.6	5	Sunflower County, MS	30.4	5	St. Louis city, MO	43.6
6	Forsyth County, GA	70.1	6	Bolivar County, MS	28.5	6	Alexandria city, VA	42.9
7	Botetourt County, VA	69.6	7	Petersburg city, VA	28.0	7	Richmond city, VA	41.8
8	Oconee County, GA	68.7	8	Yazoo County, MS	26.9	8	Denver County, CO	40.4
9	Williamson County, TN	68.6	9	Phillips County, AR	26.3	9	Arlington County, VA	40.2
10	Oldham County, KY	68.2	10	Crittenden County, AR	26.2	10	Philadelphia County, PA	39.6
11	Davis County, UT	68.0	11	Clay County, MS	25.9	11	Baltimore city, MD	39.4
11	Elbert County, CO	68.0	11	Macon County, AL	25.9	12	Orleans Parish, LA	39.1
13	Box Elder County, UT	67.8	13	Concordia Parish, LA	25.3	13	San Francisco County, CA	39.0
14	Chambers County, TX	67.7	14	Marion County, SC	25.2	14	Roanoke city, VA	38.6
15	Sioux County, IA	67.4	14	St. Francis County, AR	25.2	15	Charlottesville city, VA	37.8
16	Rockwall County, TX	67.3	14	Dallas County, AL	25.2	16	Suffolk County, MA	37.5
17	Wilson County, TX	66.7	17	St. James Parish, LA	24.9	17	Ohio County, WV	37.3
18	Woodford County, IL	66.4	18	Dougherty County, GA	24.8	18	Pinellas County, FL	37.2
19	Kendall County, IL	66.3	19	Dillon County, SC	24.6	19	Cuyahoga County, OH	36.7
20	Fort Bend County, TX	66.2	20	Crisp County, GA	24.0	19	Staunton city, VA	36.7
20	Pickens County, GA	66.2	20	Hinds County, MS	24.0	21	Fulton County, GA	36.6
20	Washington County, NE	66.2	22	Northampton County, NC	23.8	22	Fredericksburg city, VA	36.4
23	Lincoln County, SD	65.8	23	Robeson County, NC	23.7	23	Adams County, MS	36.1
24	Wasatch County, UT	65.7	23	Iberville Parish, LA	23.7	23	Silver Bow County, MT	36.1
24	Douglas County, CO	65.7	25	Marshall County, MS	23.6	23	Jackson County, IL	36.1
24	Carver County, MN	65.7	26	Baltimore city, MD	23.4	23	Monongalia County, WV	36.1
27	Loudoun County, VA	65.6	27	Halifax County, NC	23.3	23	Brown County, SD	36.1
27	Stafford County, VA	65.6	28	Willacy County, TX	23.2	28	Dallas County, AL	36.0
29	Union County, NC	65.4	29	Edgecombe County, NC	23.0	28	Jefferson County, WA	36.0
29	Fayette County, GA	65.4	30	Starr County, TX	22.9	30	Lynchburg city, VA	35.9
31	Delaware County, OH	65.3	31	McKinley County, NM	22.8	31	Davidson County, TN	35.8
31	LaGrange County, IN	65.3	32	Orangeburg County, SC	22.7	32	Berkshire County, MA	35.7
33	Powhatan County, VA	65.1	33	Webb County, TX	22.5	33	Danville city, VA	35.4
34	Wise County, TX	65.0	33	Vance County, NC	22.5	33	Milwaukee County, WI	35.4
35	Warrick County, IN	64.8	35	Clayton County, GA	22.4	33	Allegheny County, PA	35.4
36	Cache County, UT	64.5	36	Williamsburg County, SC	22.3	33	Adair County, MO	35.4
36	Tooele County, UT	64.5	36	Portsmouth city, VA	22.3	37	San Miguel County, NM	34.9
38	Scott County, MN	64.4	38	Muscogee County, GA	22.2	37	Taos County, NM	34.9
38	Marion County, IA	64.4	39	Scotland County, NC	21.9	37	Knox County, TN	34.9
40	Kendall County, TX	64.3	39	Sumter County, GA	21.9	40	Rock Island County, IL	34.8
41	Washington County, UT	64.2	41	Maverick County, TX	21.6	40	Plumas County, CA	34.8
41	Jasper County, IN	64.2	41	Lauderdale County, MS	21.6	42	Petersburg city, VA	34.7
43	Warren County, OH	64.1	43	Richmond County, GA	21.4	42	Thomas County, GA	34.7
43	Isle of Wight County, VA	64.1	44	Hampton County, SC	21.3	42	Cerro Gordo County, IA	34.7
45	Calumet County, WI	64.0	44	Morehouse Parish, LA	21.3	45	Montgomery County, OH	34.6
46	Bingham County, ID	63.9	44	Bibb County, GA	21.3	45	Mecklenburg County, VA	34.6
47	Summit County, UT	63.8	44	Danville city, VA	21.3	47	Houston County, TX	34.5
47	Harris County, GA	63.8	48	Hertford County, NC	21.2	47	Schenectady County, NY	34.5
49	Sanpete County, UT	63.6	48	Shelby County, TN	21.2	47	Webster County, IA	34.5
49	Monroe County, IL	63.6	50	Mississippi County, AR	21.1	47	Iosco County, MI	34.5
51	Hanover County, VA	63.5	50	Prince George's County, MD	21.1	47	Monroe County, IN	34.5
51	Benton County, IA	63.5	50	Adams County, MS	21.1	52	Hopewell city, VA	34.4
53	York County, VA	63.4	53	Chester County, SC	21.0	52	Kent County, MD	34.4
53	Queen Anne's County, MD	63.4	54	Cameron County, TX	20.9	52	Knox County, IL	34.4
55	King George County, VA	63.2	54	De Soto Parish, LA	20.9	52	Marinette County, WI	34.4
55	Barry County, MI	63.2	54	Decatur County, GA	20.9	52	Cass County, ND	34.4
57	Putnam County, NY	63.0	54	Florence County, SC	20.9	52	Grand Forks County, ND	34.4
58	Union County, OH	62.9	54	Warren County, MS	20.9	58	DeKalb County, GA	34.3
59	Paulding County, GA	62.8	54	Montgomery County, AL	20.9	58	Coles County, IL	34.3
60	Livingston County, MI	62.7	54	Philadelphia County, PA	20.9	60	Marion County, IN	34.0
60	Christian County, MO	62.7	61	McDuffie County, GA	20.8	60	Hamilton County, OH	34.0
62	Dawson County, GA	62.6	61	Spalding County, GA	20.8	60	Santa Fe County, NM	34.0
63	Boone County, IL	62.5	61	Lauderdale County, TN	20.8	63	Macon County, AL	33.9
64	Hunterdon County, NJ	62.4	61	Mitchell County, GA	20.8	63	Chambers County, AL	33.9
64	Plymouth County, IA	62.4	65	Gadsden County, FL	20.7	63	Grant County, NM	33.9
66	Hamilton County, IN	62.3	65	Apache County, AZ	20.7	66	Halifax County, VA	33.8
66	Sumter County, FL	62.3	67	St. Charles Parish, LA	20.6	67	Jefferson County, AR	33.7
66	Rogers County, OK	62.3	68	Peach County, GA	20.5	67	Oktibbeha County, MS	33.7
69	McHenry County, IL	62.1	68	Panola County, MS	20.5	67	Albany County, NY	33.7
69	Putnam County, OH	62.1	68	Fairfield County, SC	20.5	70	Winchester city, VA	33.5
71	Moore County, TX	62.0	71	El Paso County, TX	20.3	70	Ramsey County, MN	33.5
71	Geauga County, OH	62.0	71	Evangeline Parish, LA	20.3	70	Multnomah County, OR	33.5
71	Prince George County, VA	62.0	71	Essex County, NJ	20.3	70	Coos County, NH	33.5
71	Wright County, MN	62.0	71	Caddo Parish, LA	20.3	70	Winston County, AL	33.5
75	Spotsylvania County, VA	61.9	75	Neshoba County, MS	20.2	75	Kanawha County, WV	33.4
75	Ottawa County, MI	61.9	75	Leake County, MS	20.2	75	Ellis County, KS	33.4
75	Fauquier County, VA	61.9	75	Franklin Parish, LA	20.2			
75	Spencer County, IN	61.9	75	Orleans Parish, LA	20.2			

Metropolitan Area Rankings, 2012
Selected Rankings

Population rank	Area name	Total population [A-3, col.1]	Percent change rank	Area name	Percent change 2010–2012 [A-3, col. 2]
	United States	313,914,040		United States	1.5
1	New York-Northern New Jersey-Long Island, NY-NJ-PA	19,160,024	1	Hinesville-Fort Stewart, GA	12.6
2	Los Angeles-Long Beach-Santa Ana, CA...........	13,052,921	2	Midland, TX	7.1
3	Chicago-Joliet-Naperville, IL-IN-WI..........	9,522,446	3	Manhattan, KS	6.2
4	Dallas-Fort Worth-Arlington, TX................	6,647,496	4	Austin-Round Rock-San Marcos, TX	6.1
5	Houston-Sugar Land-Baytown, TX...............	6,204,161	5	Valdosta, GA	5.6
6	Philadelphia-Camden-Wilmington, PA-NJ-DE-MD	6,018,800	6	Odessa, TX	5.2
7	Washington-Arlington-Alexandria, DC-VA-MD-WV	5,804,333	6	Crestview-Fort Walton Beach-Destin, FL	5.2
8	Miami-Fort Lauderdale-Pompano Beach, FL...............	5,762,717	8	Kennewick-Pasco-Richland, WA	4.9
9	Atlanta-Sandy Springs-Marietta, GA..........	5,442,113	8	Columbus, GA-AL..........	4.9
10	Boston-Cambridge-Quincy, MA-NH..........	4,640,802	10	Auburn-Opelika, AL	4.6
11	San Francisco-Oakland-Fremont, CA	4,455,560	10	St. George, UT...........................	4.6
12	Riverside-San Bernardino-Ontario, CA	4,350,096	12	Raleigh-Cary, NC...........................	4.5
13	Phoenix-Mesa-Glendale, AZ..........	4,329,534	12	Clarksville, TN-KY...........................	4.5
14	Detroit-Warren-Livonia, MI..........	4,292,060	14	Charleston-North Charleston-Summerville, SC	4.4
15	Seattle-Tacoma-Bellevue, WA..........	3,552,157	14	Myrtle Beach-North Myrtle Beach-Conway, SC	4.4
16	Minneapolis-St. Paul-Bloomington, MN-WI	3,353,724	16	Bismarck, ND	4.2
17	San Diego-Carlsbad-San Marcos, CA	3,177,063	17	Casper, WY...........................	4.1
18	Tampa-St. Petersburg-Clearwater, FL..........	2,842,878	17	Cape Coral-Fort Myers, FL..........	4.1
19	St. Louis, MO-IL..........	2,819,381	19	Orlando-Kissimmee-Sanford, FL..........	3.9
20	Baltimore-Towson, MD	2,753,149	19	Provo-Orem, UT...........................	3.9
21	Denver-Aurora-Broomfield, CO	2,645,209	19	Warner Robins, GA...........................	3.9
22	Pittsburgh, PA	2,360,733	22	Rapid City, SD...........................	3.8
23	Portland-Vancouver-Hillsboro, OR-WA..........	2,289,651	22	Dallas-Fort Worth-Arlington, TX..........	3.8
24	San Antonio-New Braunfels, TX..........	2,234,003	22	Savannah, GA...........................	3.8
25	Orlando-Kissimmee-Sanford, FL..........	2,223,674	22	Houston-Sugar Land-Baytown, TX..........	3.8
26	Sacramento--Arden-Arcade--Roseville, CA..........	2,196,482	22	Charlotte-Gastonia-Rock Hill, NC-SC..........	3.8
27	Cincinnati-Middletown, OH-KY-IN..........	2,146,560	27	Greeley, CO...........................	3.7
28	Kansas City, MO-KS..........	2,064,296	28	Sioux Falls, SD...........................	3.6
29	Cleveland-Elyria-Mentor, OH	2,063,535	29	San Antonio-New Braunfels, TX..........	3.5
30	Las Vegas-Paradise, NV..........	2,000,759	29	Fayetteville-Springdale-Rogers, AR-MO..........	3.5
31	San Jose-Sunnyvale-Santa Clara, CA	1,894,388	29	Iowa City, IA...........................	3.5
32	Columbus, OH..........	1,878,714	29	Washington-Arlington-Alexandria, DC-VA-MD-WV	3.5
33	Austin-Round Rock-San Marcos, TX..........	1,834,303	33	Boulder, CO...........................	3.4
34	Charlotte-Gastonia-Rock Hill, NC-SC..........	1,831,084	33	Fargo, ND-MN...........................	3.4
35	Indianapolis-Carmel, IN..........	1,798,786	33	McAllen-Edinburg-Mission, TX..........	3.4
36	Virginia Beach-Norfolk-Newport News, VA-NC..........	1,693,567	33	Columbia, MO...........................	3.4
37	Nashville-Davidson--Murfreesboro--Franklin, TN	1,645,638	37	Durham-Chapel Hill, NC...........................	3.3
38	Providence-New Bedford-Fall River, RI-MA..........	1,601,374	37	Charlottesville, VA...........................	3.3
39	Milwaukee-Waukesha-West Allis, WI..........	1,566,981	37	Denver-Aurora-Broomfield, CO..........	3.3
40	Jacksonville, FL..........	1,377,850	37	Nashville-Davidson--Murfreesboro--Franklin, TN	3.3
41	Memphis, TN-MS-AR	1,333,315	37	Wilmington, NC...........................	3.3
42	Louisville-Jefferson County, KY-IN..........	1,302,451	37	Fort Collins-Loveland, CO...........................	3.3
43	Oklahoma City, OK..........	1,296,565	37	Des Moines-West Des Moines, IA..........	3.3
44	Richmond, VA..........	1,280,678	44	Miami-Fort Lauderdale-Pompano Beach, FL..........	3.2
45	Hartford-West Hartford-East Hartford, CT	1,214,400	44	Cleveland, TN...........................	3.2
46	New Orleans-Metairie-Kenner, LA	1,205,374	46	Naples-Marco Island, FL..........	3.1
47	Raleigh-Cary, NC..........	1,188,564	46	Oklahoma City, OK...........................	3.1
48	Salt Lake City, UT..........	1,161,715	46	Jonesboro, AR...........................	3.1
49	Birmingham-Hoover, AL..........	1,136,650	49	Laredo, TX...........................	3.0
50	Buffalo-Niagara Falls, NY..........	1,134,210	49	Colorado Springs, CO...........................	3.0
51	Rochester, NY..........	1,056,940	49	Seattle-Tacoma-Bellevue, WA..........	3.0
52	Tucson, AZ..........	992,394	49	Morgantown, WV...........................	3.0
53	Honolulu, HI..........	976,372	49	Brunswick, GA...........................	3.0
54	Tulsa, OK..........	951,514	49	Columbus, IN...........................	3.0
55	Fresno, CA..........	947,895	55	Atlanta-Sandy Springs-Marietta, GA..........	2.9
56	Bridgeport-Stamford-Norwalk, CT	933,835	55	Salt Lake City, UT...........................	2.9
57	Albuquerque, NM..........	902,794	55	Dover, DE...........................	2.9
58	Omaha-Council Bluffs, NE-IA..........	886,348	55	Killeen-Temple-Fort Hood, TX..........	2.9
59	Albany-Schenectady-Troy, NY..........	874,646	55	El Paso, TX...........................	2.9
60	New Haven-Milford, CT..........	862,813	55	Gainesville, GA...........................	2.9
61	Bakersfield-Delano, CA..........	856,158	61	Gulfport-Biloxi, MS...........................	2.8
62	Dayton, OH..........	842,858	61	Phoenix-Mesa-Glendale, AZ..........	2.8
63	Oxnard-Thousand Oaks-Ventura, CA..........	835,981	61	Bend, OR...........................	2.8
64	El Paso, TX..........	827,398	61	San Jose-Sunnyvale-Santa Clara, CA..........	2.8
65	Allentown-Bethlehem-Easton, PA-NJ..........	827,171	61	Huntsville, AL...........................	2.8
66	Baton Rouge, LA..........	815,298	66	New Orleans-Metairie-Kenner, LA..........	2.7
67	McAllen-Edinburg-Mission, TX..........	806,552	67	Victoria, TX...........................	2.6
68	Worcester, MA..........	806,163	67	Boise City-Nampa, ID...........................	2.6
69	Columbia, SC..........	785,641	67	Billings, MT...........................	2.6
70	Grand Rapids-Wyoming, MI..........	785,352	67	Blacksburg-Christiansburg-Radford, VA..........	2.6
71	Greensboro-High Point, NC..........	736,065	67	Portland-Vancouver-Hillsboro, OR-WA..........	2.6
72	North Port-Bradenton-Sarasota, FL..........	720,042	67	Cheyenne, WY...........................	2.6
73	Little Rock-North Little Rock-Conway, AR	715,210	73	San Francisco-Oakland-Fremont, CA..........	2.5
74	Knoxville, TN..........	709,492	73	Palm Coast, FL...........................	2.5
75	Stockton, CA..........	702,612	73	Anchorage, AK...........................	2.5
			73	Pensacola-Ferry Pass-Brent, FL...........................	2.5
			73	Coeur d'Alene, ID...........................	2.5
			73	Riverside-San Bernardino-Ontario, CA..........	2.5

Metropolitan Area Rankings, 2012
Selected Rankings

Foreign born rank	Area name	Percent foreign-born population [A-3, col. 15]	One-person households	Area name	Percent one-person households [A-3, col. 22]
	United States	13.0		United States	27.8
1	Miami-Fort Lauderdale-Pompano Beach, FL	38.2	1	Cumberland, MD-WV	40.0
2	San Jose-Sunnyvale-Santa Clara, CA	36.7	2	Sebastian-Vero Beach, FL	37.8
3	Los Angeles-Long Beach-Santa Ana, CA	33.9	3	Morgantown, WV	37.0
4	El Centro, CA	31.5	4	Pittsfield, MA	35.7
5	Salinas, CA	30.6	5	Grand Forks, ND-MN	35.0
6	San Francisco-Oakland-Fremont, CA	30.1	6	Santa Fe, NM	34.8
7	New York-Northern New Jersey-Long Island, NY-NJ-PA	29.3	7	Pine Bluff, AR	34.5
8	McAllen-Edinburg-Mission, TX	28.9	8	Cleveland-Elyria-Mentor, OH	34.0
9	Laredo, TX	27.3	9	Elmira, NY	33.4
10	Yuma, AZ	26.7	10	La Crosse, WI-MN	33.3
11	Napa, CA	25.9	11	Buffalo-Niagara Falls, NY	33.2
12	El Paso, TX	25.2	12	Wheeling, WV-OH	33.1
13	Merced, CA	25.0	13	Johnson City, TN	33.0
14	Brownsville-Harlingen, TX	24.5	14	Bloomington, IN	32.9
15	Stockton, CA	23.3	14	Scranton--Wilkes-Barre, PA	32.9
15	Naples-Marco Island, FL	23.3	16	Gainesville, FL	32.8
17	San Diego-Carlsbad-San Marcos, CA	23.2	16	Sandusky, OH	32.8
18	Santa Barbara-Santa Maria-Goleta, CA	23.0	16	Fargo, ND-MN	32.8
19	Oxnard-Thousand Oaks-Ventura, CA	22.8	19	Duluth, MN-WI	32.7
20	Visalia-Porterville, CA	22.6	20	Jackson, TN	32.6
21	Fresno, CA	22.3	21	Dayton, OH	32.5
21	Houston-Sugar Land-Baytown, TX	22.3	21	Pittsburgh, PA	32.5
23	Washington-Arlington-Alexandria, DC-VA-MD-WV	22.2	21	Albany-Schenectady-Troy, NY	32.5
24	Madera-Chowchilla, CA	21.8	24	Great Falls, MT	32.4
24	Las Vegas-Paradise, NV	21.8	24	Columbia, MO	32.4
26	Riverside-San Bernardino-Ontario, CA	21.7	26	Toledo, OH	32.3
27	Bakersfield-Delano, CA	20.8	26	Springfield, IL	32.3
28	Vallejo-Fairfield, CA	20.6	26	Oshkosh-Neenah, WI	32.3
29	Bridgeport-Stamford-Norwalk, CT	20.5	29	Utica-Rome, NY	32.2
30	Trenton-Ewing, NJ	20.2	29	Danville, IL	32.2
31	Modesto, CA	19.9	29	Ithaca, NY	32.2
32	Honolulu, HI	19.5	29	Lewiston-Auburn, ME	32.2
33	Hanford-Corcoran, CA	18.6	33	Ocean City, NJ	32.1
34	Santa Cruz-Watsonville, CA	18.1	34	Tampa-St. Petersburg-Clearwater, FL	32.0
35	Yakima, WA	17.9	34	Winchester, VA-WV	32.0
36	Sacramento--Arden-Arcade--Roseville, CA	17.8	34	Champaign-Urbana, IL	32.0
36	Atlantic City-Hammonton, NJ	17.8	34	Cape Girardeau-Jackson, MO-IL	32.0
36	Yuba City, CA	17.8	34	Lawrence, KS	32.0
39	Chicago-Joliet-Naperville, IL-IN-WI	17.7	34	New Orleans-Metairie-Kenner, LA	32.0
39	Dallas-Fort Worth-Arlington, TX	17.7	40	Huntington-Ashland, WV-KY-OH	31.9
41	Seattle-Tacoma-Bellevue, WA	17.1	40	North Port-Bradenton-Sarasota, FL	31.9
42	Santa Rosa-Petaluma, CA	16.9	42	Texarkana, TX-Texarkana, AR	31.8
43	Boston-Cambridge-Quincy, MA-NH	16.7	42	Anderson, IN	31.8
44	Orlando-Kissimmee-Sanford, FL	16.2	42	Johnstown, PA	31.8
45	Gainesville, GA	16.1	42	Pueblo, CO	31.8
46	Las Cruces, NM	15.5	42	Palm Bay-Melbourne-Titusville, FL	31.8
46	Reno-Sparks, NV	15.5	47	Deltona-Daytona Beach-Ormond Beach, FL	31.7
48	Palm Coast, FL	14.7	48	Beaumont-Port Arthur, TX	31.6
49	Cape Coral-Fort Myers, FL	14.6	48	Kalamazoo-Portage, MI	31.6
49	Wenatchee-East Wenatchee, WA	14.6	48	Battle Creek, MI	31.6
51	Austin-Round Rock-San Marcos, TX	14.4	48	Saginaw-Saginaw Township North, MI	31.6
52	Phoenix-Mesa-Glendale, AZ	14.3	52	Decatur, IL	31.5
52	Dalton, GA	14.3	52	Steubenville-Weirton, WV-OH	31.5
54	Port St. Lucie, FL	14.1	54	Rochester, NY	31.4
55	Odessa, TX	13.3	54	Springfield, OH	31.4
56	Atlanta-Sandy Springs-Marietta, GA	13.2	54	Topeka, KS	31.4
56	Kennewick-Pasco-Richland, WA	13.2	57	Carson City, NV	31.3
58	Tampa-St. Petersburg-Clearwater, FL	13.0	57	Kokomo, IN	31.3
59	Providence-New Bedford-Fall River, RI-MA	12.9	57	Little Rock-North Little Rock-Conway, AR	31.3
60	Carson City, NV	12.8	60	Altoona, PA	31.2
60	Santa Fe, NM	12.8	60	Youngstown-Warren-Boardman, OH-PA	31.2
62	New Haven-Milford, CT	12.7	62	Knoxville, TN	31.0
63	Hartford-West Hartford-East Hartford, CT	12.6	62	Akron, OH	31.0
64	Salem, OR	12.5	64	Binghamton, NY	30.9
65	Tucson, AZ	12.4	64	Barnstable Town, MA	30.9
66	Denver-Aurora-Broomfield, CO	12.2	64	Lynchburg, VA	30.9
66	Portland-Vancouver-Hillsboro, OR-WA	12.2	64	Fairbanks, AK	30.9
68	Ithaca, NY	12.1	64	Madison, WI	30.9
68	North Port-Bradenton-Sarasota, FL	12.1	64	Syracuse, NY	30.9
70	San Antonio-New Braunfels, TX	12.0	64	Danville, VA	30.9
70	College Station-Bryan, TX	12.0	71	Davenport-Moline-Rock Island, IA-IL	30.8
70	Salt Lake City, UT	12.0	71	Milwaukee-Waukesha-West Allis, WI	30.8
73	Durham-Chapel Hill, NC	11.9	71	Columbus, GA-AL	30.8
74	Poughkeepsie-Newburgh-Middletown, NY	11.7	71	Roanoke, VA	30.8
75	Raleigh-Cary, NC	11.6	75	Tucson, AZ	30.7

City Rankings, 2010–2012
Selected Rankings

Population rank	City	Total population [A-4, col.1]	Percent change rank	City	Percent change 2010–2012 [A-4, col. 2]	Foreign born rank	City	Percent foreign-born population [A-4, col. 15]
	United States	311,609,369		United States	1.5		United States	13.0
1	New York city, NY	8,265,445	1	Saratoga Springs city, UT	17.1	1	Sweetwater city, FL	73.2
2	Los Angeles city, CA	3,825,653	2	Cooper City city, FL	13.0	2	Hialeah city, FL	72.2
3	Chicago city, IL	2,705,981	3	Farmington city, UT	12.4	3	Fountainebleau CDP, FL	69.7
4	Houston city, TX	2,130,116	4	Fredericksburg city, VA	11.7	4	Hialeah Gardens city, FL	68.6
5	Philadelphia city, PA	1,538,211	5	San Marcos city, TX	11.0	5	Langley Park CDP, MD	68.4
6	Phoenix city, AZ	1,467,400	6	Leander city, TX	10.8	6	Tamiami CDP, FL	67.6
7	San Antonio city, TX	1,358,143	7	Washington city, UT	10.7	7	Coral Terrace CDP, FL	65.4
8	San Diego city, CA	1,321,545	8	Cedar Park city, TX	10.6	8	University Park CDP, FL	64.4
9	Dallas city, TX	1,219,879	9	Little Elm city, TX	10.5	9	Kendale Lakes CDP, FL	63.0
10	San Jose city, CA	969,324	10	Morrisville town, NC	9.5	10	Kendall West CDP, FL	62.9
11	Jacksonville city, FL	829,535	11	Phenix City city, AL	9.2	11	Doral city, FL	62.0
12	Indianapolis city (balance), IN	827,639	12	South Jordan city, UT	9.1	12	West New York town, NJ	60.3
13	Austin city, TX	818,236	13	Georgetown city, TX	9.0	13	Westchester CDP, FL	59.1
14	San Francisco city, CA	815,234	14	Schertz city, TX	8.8	14	Miami city, FL	58.3
15	Columbus city, OH	799,357	15	Frisco city, TX	8.6	15	Sunny Isles Beach city, FL	57.7
16	Fort Worth city, TX	761,862	16	Wake Forest town, NC	8.5	15	Rosemead city, CA	57.7
17	Charlotte city, NC	756,725	16	Kyle city, TX	8.5	17	Union City city, NJ	56.6
18	Detroit city, MI	706,522	18	Herriman city, UT	8.4	18	San Gabriel city, CA	56.2
19	El Paso city, TX	662,707	19	St. Cloud city, FL	8.1	19	Glendale city, CA	56.0
20	Memphis city, TN	651,363	20	Pasco city, WA	8.0	19	Rowland Heights CDP, CA	56.0
21	Boston city, MA	628,365	21	Hilliard city, OH	7.9	21	Bailey's Crossroads CDP, VA	55.0
22	Seattle city, WA	622,273	21	Holly Springs town, NC	7.9	22	Monterey Park city, CA	54.4
23	Baltimore city, MD	620,843	21	Junction City city, KS	7.9	23	Country Club CDP, FL	53.6
24	Denver city, CO	619,016	24	Irvine city, CA	7.8	24	North Miami Beach city, FL	52.9
25	Washington city, DC	618,777	24	McKinney city, TX	7.8	25	Miami Beach city, FL	52.7
26	Nashville-Davidson metro gov, TN	613,829	26	Mount Juliet city, TN	7.6	26	Daly City city, CA	52.4
27	Louisville/Jefferson County metro gov, KY	601,670	27	Midland city, TX	7.3	27	Alhambra city, CA	52.0
28	Milwaukee city, WI	597,247	27	Bixby city, OK	7.3	28	The Hammocks CDP, FL	51.8
29	Portland city, OR	594,524	29	Alpharetta city, GA	7.2	29	Huntington Park city, CA	51.7
30	Oklahoma City city, OK	590,292	29	Papillion city, NE	7.2	30	Miami Lakes town, FL	51.2
31	Las Vegas city, NV	589,541	31	Conroe city, TX	7.1	30	Richmond West CDP, FL	51.2
32	Albuquerque city, NM	551,597	31	Apex town, NC	7.1	32	Milpitas city, CA	51.1
33	Tucson city, AZ	522,770	33	Pooler city, GA	7.0	33	El Monte city, CA	50.9
34	Fresno city, CA	501,350	34	Lehi city, UT	6.9	34	South Miami Heights CDP, FL	50.5
35	Sacramento city, CA	471,552	34	Ankeny city, IA	6.9	35	Cupertino city, CA	50.1
36	Long Beach city, CA	465,125	34	Midvale city, UT	6.9	36	Fort Lee borough, NJ	49.5
37	Kansas City city, MO	462,292	34	Eagle Mountain city, UT	6.9	37	Aventura city, FL	49.1
38	Mesa city, AZ	445,671	38	The Colony city, TX	6.8	37	North Miami city, FL	49.1
39	Virginia Beach city, VA	443,102	38	Bentonville city, AR	6.8	39	Walnut city, CA	48.9
40	Atlanta city, GA	432,752	38	Issaquah city, WA	6.8	40	Lennox CDP, CA	48.7
41	Colorado Springs city, CO	425,725	41	Cary town, NC	6.7	41	Santa Ana city, CA	48.3
42	Omaha city, NE	416,374	41	Leesburg town, VA	6.7	42	Arvin city, CA	48.2
43	Raleigh city, NC	414,373	41	Goose Creek city, SC	6.7	43	Arcadia city, CA	48.1
44	Miami city, FL	408,322	41	Ocoee city, FL	6.7	44	Lauderdale Lakes city, FL	47.8
45	Oakland city, CA	396,030	41	Parkland city, FL	6.7	45	Temple City city, CA	47.7
46	Cleveland city, OH	393,288	46	Clarksville city, TN	6.6	46	Cudahy city, CA	47.6
47	Tulsa city, OK	393,124	46	Johns Creek city, GA	6.6	47	Garfield city, NJ	47.5
48	Minneapolis city, MN	388,054	48	Manhattan city, KS	6.5	47	Elizabeth city, NJ	47.5
49	Wichita city, KS	384,025	48	Buckeye town, AZ	6.5	47	Maywood city, CA	47.5
50	Arlington city, TX	370,854	48	Pflugerville city, TX	6.5	50	Calexico city, CA	46.8
51	New Orleans city, LA	359,130	48	Spring Hill city, TN	6.5	51	Union City city, CA	46.5
52	Bakersfield city, CA	353,780	48	Athens city, AL	6.5	52	Golden Gate CDP, FL	46.4
53	Tampa city, FL	343,677	53	Meridian city, ID	6.4	52	Lincolnia CDP, VA	46.4
54	Urban Honolulu CDP, HI	342,190	53	Milton city, GA	6.4	54	The Crossings CDP, FL	46.3
55	Anaheim city, CA	340,306	53	Dinuba city, CA	6.4	55	Kendall CDP, FL	46.2
56	Aurora city, CO	332,532	56	Dublin city, CA	6.3	56	Chelsea city, MA	46.1
57	Santa Ana city, CA	328,180	56	Apopka city, FL	6.3	57	Golden Glades CDP, FL	46.0
58	St. Louis city, MO	318,612	56	Crestview city, FL	6.3	58	Baldwin Park city, CA	45.9
59	Riverside city, CA	309,793	59	New Orleans city, LA	6.2	58	Port Chester village, NY	45.9
60	Corpus Christi city, TX	308,497	59	Odessa city, TX	6.2	60	Chillum CDP, MD	45.7
61	Pittsburgh city, PA	306,006	59	Minot city, ND	6.2	61	Bell Gardens city, CA	45.4
62	Lexington-Fayette urban county, KY	301,211	59	Winter Garden city, FL	6.2	62	Spring Valley village, NY	45.3
63	Cincinnati city, OH	296,443	63	Goodyear city, AZ	6.1	63	Wheaton CDP, MD	45.1
64	Anchorage municipality, AK	296,039	63	Richland city, WA	6.1	64	Miramar city, FL	44.8
65	Stockton city, CA	295,354	63	Manassas city, VA	6.1	64	Westminster city, CA	44.8
66	St. Paul city, MN	288,347	66	Austin city, TX	6.0	66	San Luis city, AZ	44.6
67	Toledo city, OH	285,532	66	Pearland city, TX	6.0	66	Elmont CDP, NY	44.6
68	Newark city, NJ	277,627	66	Kissimmee city, FL	6.0	68	Passaic city, NJ	44.5
69	Greensboro city, NC	273,641	66	Wylie city, TX	6.0	68	Annandale CDP, VA	44.5
70	Plano city, TX	266,857	66	Westfield city, IN	6.0	70	Cerritos city, CA	44.3
71	Lincoln city, NE	262,214	66	West Fargo city, ND	6.0	70	South El Monte city, CA	44.3
72	Henderson city, NV	261,370	66	Maple Valley city, WA	6.0	72	Sunnyvale city, CA	44.0
73	Buffalo city, NY	260,321	73	Marana town, AZ	5.9	72	Diamond Bar city, CA	44.0
74	Fort Wayne city, IN	253,795	73	Wentzville city, MO	5.9	72	Hamtramck city, MI	44.0
75	Jersey City city, NJ	251,485	73	Beaumont city, CA	5.8	75	Springfield CDP, VA	43.9
			73	Gardner city, KS	5.8			
			73	Oxford city, MS	5.8			

Table A-1. States — Who: Age, Race/Ethnicity, and Household Structure, 2012

State code	STATE	Total population	Percent change 2010–2012	Race alone or in combination (percent)						Percent Hispanic or Latino	Percent two or more races	Percent White alone, not Hispanic or Latino
				White	Black	American Indian or Alaska Native	Asian	Native Hawaiian or Pacific Islander	Some other race			
	ACS table number:	B01003	B01003	B02008	B02009	B02010	B02011	B02012	B02013	C03002	B02001	B01001H
	Column number:	1	2	3	4	5	6	7	8	9	10	11

Table A-1. States — Who: Age, Race/Ethnicity, and Household Structure, 2012—*Continued*

State code	STATE	Total population	Population by age (percent)								+/- U.S. percent under 18 years	+/- U.S. percent 65 years and over	Percent female
			Under 5 years	5 to 17 years	18 to 24 years	25 to 44 years	45 to 64 years	65 to 84 years	85 years and over			
	ACS table number:	B01001	B01001	B01001	B01001	B01001	B01001	B01001	B01001	B01001	B01001	B01001
	Column number:	12	13	14	15	16	17	18	19	20	21	22

Table A-1. States — Who: Age, Race/Ethnicity, and Household Structure, 2012—*Continued*

State code	STATE	Median age								
		Total population	White alone, not Hispanic or Latino	Black	American Indian or Alaska Native	Asian	Native Hawaiian or Pacific Islander	Some other race	Two or more races	Hispanic or Latino
	ACS table number:	B01002	B01002H	B01002B	B01002C	B01002D	B01002E	B01002F	B01002G	B01002I
	Column number:	23	24	25	26	27	28	29	30	31

Table A-1. States — Who: Age, Race/Ethnicity, and Household Structure, 2012—*Continued*

State code	STATE	Total population 15 years and over	Marital status of population 15 years and over (percent)				Percent foreign born	Languages spoken (percent of households)			
			Never married	Now married	Widowed	Divorced		English only	Spanish, with or without English	Other languages, with or without English	No adult speaks English well
	ACS table number:	B12001	B12001	B12001	B12001	B12001	C05002	B16002	B16002	B16002	B16002
	Column number:	32	33	34	35	36	37	38	39	40	41

Table A-1. States — Who: Age, Race/Ethnicity, and Household Structure, 2012—*Continued*

State code	STATE	Total households	Average household size	Household type (percent of all households)									
				Family households				Nonfamily households			Unmarried partner households	
				Total family households	Married-couple families	Male householder families	Female householder families	Total	Total one-person households	One person households age 65 or over	Total unmarried partner households	Same-sex partner households
	ACS table number:	B11001	B25010	B11001	B11001	B11001	B11001	B11001	B11001	B11010	B11009	B11009
	Column number:	42	43	44	45	46	47	48	49	50	51	52

Table A-1. States — Who: Age, Race/Ethnicity, and Household Structure, 2012—*Continued*

State code	STATE	Households with people under 18 years old				Households with people 60 years and over					
		Total households with children	Household type (percent)			Total households with people 60 years and over	Household type (percent)			
			Married-couple families	Male householder families	Female householder families		Married-couple families	Male householder families	Female householder families	Nonfamily households
	ACS table number:	C11005	C11005	C11005	C11005	B11006	B11006	B11006	B11006	B11006
	Column number:	53	54	55	56	57	58	59	60	61

Table A-2. Counties — Who: Age, Race/Ethnicity, and Household Structure, 2010–2012

STATE and County code	STATE County	Total population	Percent change 2010–2012	Population by age (percent)							Race alone or in combination (percent)			
				Under 5 years	5 to 17 years	18 to 24 years	25 to 44 years	45 to 64 years	65 years and over	Median age	White	Black	Asian Hawaiian or Pacific Islander	American Indian, Alaska Native, or some other race
	ACS table number:	B01003	Population estimates	B01001	B01001	B01001	B01001	B01001	B01001	B01002	B02008	B02009	B02011 + B02012	B02010 + B02013
	Column number:	1	2	3	4	5	6	7	8	9	10	11	12	13

Table A-2. Counties — Who: Age, Race/Ethnicity, and Household Structure, 2010–2012—*Continued*

State and County code	State and County	Percent Hispanic or Latino	Percent foreign born	Total households	Household type (percent)						Percent of households with people under 18 years	Percent of households with people 60 years and over
					Family households				Nonfamily households			
					Total family households	Married-couple families	Male householder families	Female householder families	Total nonfamily households	One-person households		
	ACS table number:	B03003	C05003	B11001	B11001	B11001	B11001	B11001	B11001	B11001	B11005	B11006
	Column number:	14	15	16	17	18	19	20	21	22	23	24

Table A-3. Metropolitan Areas — Who: Age, Race/Ethnicity, and Household Structure, 2012

Metro area or division code	Area name	Total population	Percent change 2010–2012	Population by age (percent)						Median age	Race alone or in combination (percent)			
				Under 5 years	5 to 17 years	18 to 24 years	25 to 44 years	45 to 64 years	65 years and over		White	Black	Asian, Hawaiian, or Pacific Islander	American Indian, Alaska Native, or some other race
	ACS table number:	B01003	CP05	B01001	B01001	B01001	B01001	B01001	B01001	B01002	B02008	B02009	B02011 + B02012	B02010 + B02013
	Column number:	1	2	3	4	5	6	7	8	9	10	11	12	13

Table A-3. Metropolitan Areas — Who: Age, Race/Ethnicity, and Household Structure, 2012—*Continued*

Metro area or division code	Area name	Percent Hispanic or Latino	Percent foreign born	Household type (percent)								Percent of households with people under 18 years	Percent of households with people 60 years and over
				Total households	Family households				Nonfamily households				
					Total family households	Married-couple families	Male household families	Female household families	Total nonfamily households	One-person households			
	ACS table number:	B03003	B05012	B11001	B11001	B11001	B11001	B11001	B11001	B11001	C11005	B11006
	Column number:	14	15	16	17	18	19	20	21	22	23	24

Table A-4. Cities — Who: Age, Race/Ethnicity, and Household Structure, 2010–2012

STATE and Place code	STATE or City	Total population	Percent change 2010–2012	Population by age (percent)						Median age	Race alone or in combination (percent)			
				Under 5 years	5 to 17 years	18 to 24 years	25 to 44 years	45 to 64 years	65 years and over		White	Black	Asian, Hawaiian, or Pacific Islander	American Indian, Alaska Native, or some other race
	ACS table number:	B01003	Population estimates	B01001	B01001	B01001	B01001	B01001	B01001	B01002	B02008	B02009	B02011 + B02012	B02010 + B02013
	Column number:	1	2	3	4	5	6	7	8	9	10	11	12	13

Table A-4. Cities — Who: Age, Race/Ethnicity, and Household Structure, 2010–2012—*Continued*

STATE and Place code	STATE or City	Percent Hispanic or Latino	Percent foreign born	Household type (percent)								Percent of households with people under 18 years	Percent of households with people 60 years and over
				Total households	Family households				Nonfamily households				
					Total family households	Married-couple families	Male household families	Female household families	Total nonfamily households	One-person households			
	ACS table number:	B03003	C05003	B11001	B11001	B11001	B11001	B11001	B11001	B11001	B11005	B11006
	Column number:	14	15	16	17	18	19	20	21	22	23	24

Table A-1. States — Who: Age, Race/Ethnicity, and Household Structure, 2012

State code	STATE	Total population	Percent change 2010–2012	Race alone or in combination (percent)						Percent Hispanic or Latino	Percent two or more races	Percent White alone, not Hispanic or Latino
				White	Black	American Indian or Alaska Native	Asian	Native Hawaiian or Pacific Islander	Some other race			
	ACS table number:	B01003	B01003	B02008	B02009	B02010	B02011	B02012	B02013	C03002	B02001	B01001H
	Column number:	1	2	3	4	5	6	7	8	9	10	11
00	United States	313,914,040	1.5	76.3	13.7	1.7	5.8	0.4	5.2	16.9	2.9	62.8
01	Alabama.................	4,822,023	0.8	70.5	27.2	1.2	1.5	0.1	1.2	3.8	1.6	66.6
02	Alaska....................	731,449	2.4	73.6	5.1	19.6	7.6	1.6	1.3	6.0	8.0	63.0
04	Arizona..................	6,553,255	2.2	81.2	5.2	5.4	3.7	0.5	7.1	30.2	2.9	56.9
05	Arkansas................	2,949,131	0.9	80.1	16.3	1.7	1.6	0.2	2.2	6.7	2.0	73.9
06	California...............	38,041,430	1.9	65.7	7.1	1.9	15.3	0.8	14.1	38.2	4.4	39.2
08	Colorado	5,187,582	2.7	87.3	5.1	2.0	3.9	0.3	5.1	21.0	3.3	69.4
09	Connecticut............	3,590,347	0.4	80.3	11.6	0.8	4.7	0.1	5.2	14.2	2.6	70.0
10	Delaware	917,092	1.9	72.0	23.1	0.8	3.9	0.1	2.9	8.6	2.6	64.3
11	District of Columbia .	632,323	4.6	41.5	50.8	0.8	4.6	0.2	4.9	9.9	2.5	35.3
12	Florida	19,317,568	2.5	78.3	17.3	0.8	3.2	0.2	2.9	23.2	2.4	56.8
13	Georgia	9,919,945	2.1	62.1	32.0	0.7	4.0	0.1	3.3	9.1	2.0	55.0
15	Hawaii...................	1,392,313	2.1	42.3	3.2	2.1	56.4	26.1	2.6	9.5	23.3	22.8
16	Idaho....................	1,595,728	1.5	93.8	1.0	2.4	2.1	0.3	3.1	11.6	2.5	83.4
17	Illinois	12,875,255	0.2	74.5	15.4	0.7	5.4	0.1	6.2	16.3	2.2	62.9
18	Indiana..................	6,537,334	0.7	86.3	10.3	0.8	2.1	0.1	2.7	6.3	2.2	80.9
19	Iowa	3,074,186	0.8	93.6	3.9	0.9	2.2	0.1	1.4	5.2	2.0	88.0
20	Kansas...................	2,885,905	0.9	88.4	7.3	2.1	3.1	0.2	2.4	10.9	3.2	77.4
21	Kentucky	4,380,415	0.8	89.6	9.0	0.8	1.6	0.1	1.1	3.1	2.0	85.8
22	Louisiana	4,601,893	1.3	64.3	33.1	1.3	1.9	0.1	1.2	4.5	1.7	59.7
23	Maine	1,329,192	0.1	97.0	1.6	1.7	1.5	0.0	0.3	1.4	2.0	94.1
24	Maryland	5,884,563	1.7	60.6	30.9	1.1	6.8	0.2	3.9	8.7	3.1	53.8
25	Massachusetts	6,646,144	1.4	82.5	8.6	0.7	6.4	0.1	4.6	10.1	2.8	75.3
26	Michigan	9,883,360	0.1	81.6	15.3	1.4	3.1	0.1	1.2	4.6	2.6	76.1
27	Minnesota	5,379,139	1.3	87.8	6.4	1.9	4.9	0.2	1.6	4.9	2.5	82.3
28	Mississippi..............	2,984,926	0.5	60.3	38.2	0.8	1.0	0.0	0.8	2.7	1.1	57.5
29	Missouri	6,021,988	0.4	84.8	12.6	1.4	2.1	0.1	1.4	3.7	2.4	80.5
30	Montana................	1,005,141	1.4	91.6	0.8	8.1	1.1	0.2	0.8	3.1	2.6	87.2
31	Nebraska	1,855,525	1.4	90.1	5.5	1.6	2.5	0.2	2.5	9.6	2.1	81.3
32	Nevada	2,758,931	2.0	73.0	9.7	2.0	9.3	1.2	9.4	27.3	4.1	52.7
33	New Hampshire	1,320,718	0.3	95.7	1.9	0.9	2.8	0.1	0.7	3.0	1.8	91.8
34	New Jersey..............	8,864,590	0.7	70.9	14.9	0.7	9.5	0.1	6.6	18.5	2.5	57.9
35	New Mexico.............	2,085,538	0.9	74.5	2.8	10.4	1.9	0.2	13.5	47.0	3.2	39.7
36	New York................	19,570,261	0.9	67.3	16.9	1.0	8.5	0.1	9.3	18.2	2.7	57.4
37	North Carolina	9,752,073	2.0	71.8	22.9	1.9	2.8	0.1	3.0	8.7	2.3	64.5
38	North Dakota..........	699,628	3.7	91.4	2.0	6.4	1.3	0.2	0.8	2.4	2.0	88.1
39	Ohio	11,544,225	0.1	84.8	13.6	0.8	2.2	0.1	1.0	3.2	2.3	80.6
40	Oklahoma...............	3,814,820	1.4	80.5	8.9	13.4	2.3	0.2	2.7	9.3	7.7	67.8
41	Oregon	3,899,353	1.6	88.9	2.6	3.0	5.1	0.8	4.0	12.2	4.0	77.6
42	Pennsylvania	12,763,536	0.4	83.7	12.2	0.6	3.3	0.2	2.2	6.1	2.1	78.6
44	Rhode Island...........	1,050,292	-0.2	83.8	8.1	1.3	3.7	0.2	5.0	13.2	2.8	75.4
45	South Carolina.........	4,723,723	1.9	68.7	28.8	0.9	1.7	0.1	1.9	5.3	2.0	63.9
46	South Dakota..........	833,354	2.1	87.4	2.2	10.0	1.4	0.1	1.1	3.0	2.1	83.8
47	Tennessee	6,456,243	1.6	79.7	17.7	0.9	1.9	0.1	1.6	4.8	1.8	75.0
48	Texas.....................	26,059,203	3.2	77.0	12.7	1.2	4.6	0.2	5.7	38.2	2.4	44.3
49	Utah	2,855,287	2.8	90.4	1.6	1.7	3.0	1.4	4.6	13.3	2.4	79.8
50	Vermont	626,011	0.0	97.0	1.6	1.3	1.8	0.0	0.4	1.6	2.0	94.0
51	Virginia..................	8,185,867	2.0	71.8	20.8	1.1	6.9	0.2	2.7	8.4	3.2	63.9
53	Washington	6,897,012	2.3	82.7	5.0	3.0	9.5	1.2	4.3	11.7	5.0	71.4
54	West Virginia	1,855,413	0.1	95.4	4.1	1.3	0.8	0.1	0.3	1.3	1.9	92.8
55	Wisconsin	5,726,398	0.6	88.6	7.2	1.6	2.8	0.1	2.0	6.2	2.0	82.8
56	Wyoming................	576,412	2.1	93.8	2.0	3.9	1.2	0.2	2.2	9.4	3.1	84.6

Table A-1. States — Who: Age, Race/Ethnicity, and Household Structure, 2012—*Continued*

State code	STATE	Total population	Population by age (percent) Under 5 years	5 to 17 years	18 to 24 years	25 to 44 years	45 to 64 years	65 to 84 years	85 years and over	+/- U.S. percent under 18 years	+/- U.S. percent 65 years and over	Percent female
	ACS table number:	B01001	B01001	B01001	B01001	B01001	B01001	B01001	B01001	B01001	B01001	B01001
	Column number:	12	13	14	15	16	17	18	19	20	21	22
00	United States	313,914,040	6.3	17.1	10.0	26.4	26.4	11.9	1.9	0.0	0.0	50.8
01	Alabama	4,822,023	6.3	17.1	10.1	25.4	26.6	12.9	1.7	-0.2	0.8	51.5
02	Alaska	731,449	7.4	18.2	10.9	28.0	27.0	7.7	0.8	2.1	-5.3	47.9
04	Arizona	6,553,255	6.7	18.0	10.0	26.0	24.5	13.1	1.7	1.2	1.1	50.2
05	Arkansas	2,949,131	6.5	17.6	9.8	25.4	25.8	13.2	1.7	0.6	1.2	50.9
06	California	38,041,430	6.7	17.6	10.6	28.0	25.1	10.4	1.7	0.8	-1.7	50.3
08	Colorado	5,187,582	6.5	17.2	9.9	28.2	26.4	10.4	1.4	0.3	-2.0	49.9
09	Connecticut	3,590,347	5.4	16.7	9.5	24.8	28.8	12.4	2.4	-1.4	1.1	51.3
10	Delaware	917,092	6.1	16.2	10.2	24.7	27.4	13.5	1.9	-1.1	1.6	51.5
11	District of Columbia .	632,323	6.2	11.1	13.2	35.5	22.6	9.9	1.5	-6.2	-2.4	52.7
12	Florida	19,317,568	5.5	15.2	9.4	24.8	26.9	15.6	2.5	-2.8	4.4	51.1
13	Georgia	9,919,945	6.8	18.4	10.3	27.6	25.4	10.3	1.2	1.7	-2.3	51.1
15	Hawaii	1,392,313	6.4	15.4	9.9	26.9	26.4	12.5	2.7	-1.7	1.4	49.6
16	Idaho	1,595,728	7.1	19.5	9.9	25.5	24.7	11.6	1.7	3.1	-0.5	49.9
17	Illinois	12,875,255	6.3	17.5	9.7	27.0	26.3	11.3	1.9	0.3	-0.6	50.9
18	Indiana	6,537,334	6.5	17.8	10.2	25.3	26.6	11.8	1.8	0.8	-0.1	50.8
19	Iowa	3,074,186	6.4	17.1	10.2	24.4	26.6	12.9	2.4	0.0	1.5	50.4
20	Kansas	2,885,905	7.0	18.0	10.4	25.2	25.7	11.6	2.1	1.5	-0.1	50.3
21	Kentucky	4,380,415	6.3	16.9	9.7	25.8	27.2	12.4	1.6	-0.2	0.3	50.8
22	Louisiana	4,601,893	6.7	17.6	10.3	26.3	26.0	11.5	1.5	0.8	-0.8	51.1
23	Maine	1,329,192	5.0	15.0	8.7	23.3	31.0	14.8	2.2	-3.5	3.3	51.0
24	Maryland	5,884,563	6.2	16.6	9.7	26.8	27.7	11.2	1.8	-0.7	-0.8	51.6
25	Massachusetts	6,646,144	5.5	15.6	10.4	26.2	27.9	12.1	2.4	-2.4	0.7	51.6
26	Michigan	9,883,360	5.8	17.2	10.1	24.3	28.1	12.5	2.1	-0.5	0.9	50.9
27	Minnesota	5,379,139	6.5	17.3	9.3	26.2	27.2	11.5	2.1	0.3	-0.2	50.4
28	Mississippi	2,984,926	6.8	18.3	10.9	25.1	25.5	11.9	1.6	1.6	-0.3	51.7
29	Missouri	6,021,988	6.2	17.1	9.9	25.3	26.9	12.7	1.9	-0.2	0.9	51.0
30	Montana	1,005,141	5.9	16.0	9.8	23.7	28.8	13.6	2.1	-1.6	2.0	49.9
31	Nebraska	1,855,525	7.1	17.8	10.0	25.5	25.7	11.7	2.1	1.5	0.1	50.3
32	Nevada	2,758,931	6.6	17.5	9.2	28.1	25.6	11.8	1.2	0.6	-0.7	49.6
33	New Hampshire	1,320,718	5.0	15.9	9.5	24.0	31.0	12.8	1.9	-2.7	1.0	50.9
34	New Jersey	8,864,590	5.9	16.9	8.9	26.3	27.9	12.0	2.1	-0.6	0.4	51.3
35	New Mexico	2,085,538	6.9	17.9	10.0	25.1	26.0	12.4	1.7	1.3	0.4	50.4
36	New York	19,570,261	5.9	15.8	10.2	27.0	26.9	12.0	2.1	-1.7	0.4	51.5
37	North Carolina	9,752,073	6.3	17.1	10.0	26.5	26.3	12.2	1.6	-0.1	0.1	51.3
38	North Dakota	699,628	6.4	15.6	12.5	25.2	25.8	12.1	2.3	-1.5	0.7	48.9
39	Ohio	11,544,225	6.0	17.1	9.6	24.8	27.8	12.7	2.1	-0.4	1.0	51.1
40	Oklahoma	3,814,820	6.9	17.7	10.3	25.8	25.4	12.3	1.7	1.1	0.3	50.5
41	Oregon	3,899,353	6.0	16.1	9.4	26.6	27.0	12.8	2.1	-1.4	1.2	50.4
42	Pennsylvania	12,763,536	5.6	15.8	9.9	24.5	28.1	13.5	2.5	-2.0	2.3	51.2
44	Rhode Island	1,050,292	5.3	15.3	11.5	24.6	28.1	12.5	2.7	-2.8	1.4	51.7
45	South Carolina	4,723,723	6.2	16.6	10.4	25.4	26.6	13.1	1.6	-0.6	1.0	51.4
46	South Dakota	833,354	7.0	17.5	10.2	24.5	26.2	12.1	2.4	1.0	0.8	49.9
47	Tennessee	6,456,243	6.2	16.9	9.7	26.2	26.7	12.7	1.6	-0.3	0.5	51.3
48	Texas	26,059,203	7.4	19.4	10.3	28.1	24.0	9.6	1.3	3.3	-2.9	50.3
49	Utah	2,855,287	9.0	22.0	11.4	28.1	19.9	8.4	1.1	7.6	-4.2	49.7
50	Vermont	626,011	5.0	14.8	10.7	23.0	30.8	13.6	2.2	-3.7	2.0	50.6
51	Virginia	8,185,867	6.2	16.5	10.1	27.4	26.9	11.4	1.6	-0.8	-0.8	51.0
53	Washington	6,897,012	6.4	16.6	9.7	27.3	26.9	11.4	1.7	-0.5	-0.6	50.1
54	West Virginia	1,855,413	5.7	15.0	9.4	24.2	28.9	14.7	2.0	-2.8	3.0	50.9
55	Wisconsin	5,726,398	6.1	16.9	9.7	25.0	27.9	12.3	2.1	-0.5	0.6	50.4
56	Wyoming	576,412	6.6	17.1	10.2	25.8	27.2	11.4	1.6	0.2	-0.7	49.2

Table A-1. States — Who: Age, Race/Ethnicity, and Household Structure, 2012—*Continued*

State code	STATE	Median age								
		Total population	White alone, not Hispanic or Latino	Black	American Indian or Alaska Native	Asian	Native Hawaiian or Pacific Islander	Some other race	Two or more races	Hispanic or Latino
	ACS table number:	B01002	B01002H	B01002B	B01002C	B01002D	B01002E	B01002F	B01002G	B01002I
	Column number:	23	24	25	26	27	28	29	30	31
00	United States	37.4	42.6	32.9	31.9	36.0	30.4	28.1	19.6	27.7
01	Alabama........................	38.2	41.9	32.8	42.0	34.7	37.2	22.5	18.8	24.4
02	Alaska...........................	33.8	38.5	30.0	29.8	34.9	22.9	29.6	19.0	25.0
04	Arizona.........................	36.6	45.5	30.2	27.8	35.1	29.7	27.4	18.3	26.0
05	Arkansas.......................	37.6	41.6	30.8	38.1	31.4	21.6	23.6	19.3	23.3
06	California.......................	35.5	45.1	35.4	34.1	38.4	32.8	27.7	21.6	27.6
08	Colorado.......................	36.2	40.7	31.1	33.5	34.8	30.5	29.1	20.5	26.8
09	Connecticut..................	40.4	45.4	33.0	28.2	33.3	17.8	30.1	18.7	27.6
10	Delaware	39.2	44.9	33.5	51.7	34.4	48.6	26.9	14.7	25.3
11	District of Columbia	33.7	32.2	37.2	41.1	32.3	. . .	29.6	26.6	30.5
12	Florida	41.1	48.3	31.6	37.7	36.8	32.5	30.2	21.2	34.2
13	Georgia	35.7	41.0	32.1	30.7	34.1	33.2	25.9	17.7	25.6
15	Hawaii	38.3	43.3	28.7	40.1	48.0	30.7	29.6	24.7	25.4
16	Idaho	35.2	37.7	26.1	29.9	33.3	24.3	24.5	19.8	23.1
17	Illinois	37.0	42.1	33.5	35.0	35.3	37.4	28.0	16.8	27.1
18	Indiana	37.3	40.2	31.7	36.0	31.7	30.5	25.4	15.9	24.1
19	Iowa	38.0	40.8	27.3	28.5	29.3	32.1	25.2	15.0	22.3
20	Kansas	36.0	40.2	31.5	29.2	31.3	26.5	28.1	18.1	22.8
21	Kentucky	38.4	40.3	32.2	46.0	31.5	21.9	26.8	17.0	25.5
22	Louisiana	36.0	40.3	31.4	38.6	32.3	41.0	30.4	18.3	29.9
23	Maine	43.5	44.6	27.3	38.5	31.2	42.3	18.6	20.3	24.0
24	Maryland	38.1	43.4	35.3	38.3	36.7	26.9	28.1	18.8	28.3
25	Massachusetts	39.5	43.3	31.3	34.6	32.6	. . .	28.4	22.4	26.9
26	Michigan	39.5	42.5	33.6	35.5	32.7	30.4	29.0	17.4	24.6
27	Minnesota	37.6	41.5	27.5	29.2	28.9	28.9	26.4	14.7	23.7
28	Mississippi....................	36.2	41.3	31.0	25.8	34.4	63.9	26.2	16.8	24.5
29	Missouri	38.2	40.8	32.0	34.1	32.9	34.1	26.1	18.2	25.1
30	Montana.......................	40.2	42.3	34.9	27.2	34.8	33.1	31.8	21.7	26.2
31	Nebraska	36.3	39.8	28.3	25.8	30.8	32.3	24.8	15.4	22.9
32	Nevada	36.8	44.7	33.0	33.8	39.0	31.6	26.6	18.7	26.6
33	New Hampshire	41.9	43.4	26.5	49.2	34.9	61.5	26.3	17.5	24.7
34	New Jersey....................	39.4	44.9	35.3	33.0	35.9	31.6	29.3	21.3	30.6
35	New Mexico..................	36.8	48.2	26.5	29.3	36.1	21.4	32.1	21.5	30.3
36	New York......................	38.1	42.8	34.9	36.9	35.8	39.3	30.4	23.0	30.7
37	North Carolina..............	37.8	42.3	34.5	34.9	32.6	27.5	23.8	16.5	24.7
38	North Dakota................	36.2	38.8	25.7	25.7	31.1	14.4	28.3	18.6	22.9
39	Ohio	39.3	41.6	32.9	43.7	32.9	33.4	26.6	16.5	25.0
40	Oklahoma.....................	36.3	41.6	32.1	30.0	32.1	29.3	27.4	22.0	23.7
41	Oregon	38.9	43.0	30.4	32.7	36.1	27.4	26.1	20.8	23.9
42	Pennsylvania	40.5	43.7	32.8	34.1	32.8	21.1	26.1	18.2	25.6
44	Rhode Island.................	39.8	44.5	30.1	38.4	29.6	. . .	26.8	20.1	25.5
45	South Carolina..............	38.3	42.4	33.8	33.1	34.2	32.7	25.9	16.9	25.7
46	South Dakota................	36.7	40.4	23.4	24.5	27.4	30.0	28.5	13.6	22.2
47	Tennessee	38.2	41.5	31.9	32.2	33.7	25.7	26.3	18.3	24.8
48	Texas............................	33.9	41.8	32.1	35.6	34.4	29.8	28.5	19.6	27.3
49	Utah	29.9	31.4	25.3	30.0	33.0	24.6	24.1	15.8	23.4
50	Vermont	42.4	43.3	22.1	47.2	33.4	. . .	23.0	19.9	23.3
51	Virginia	37.5	41.5	34.6	40.3	35.4	34.4	30.1	18.3	27.8
53	Washington	37.5	42.2	32.2	33.6	36.3	29.1	25.6	19.5	24.0
54	West Virginia	41.5	42.4	32.4	37.8	32.6	. . .	26.4	22.4	25.2
55	Wisconsin	38.8	42.3	28.2	33.2	27.9	22.7	25.7	16.0	23.7
56	Wyoming......................	36.9	39.5	27.3	28.4	31.3	46.5	25.7	21.2	26.4

Table A-1. States — Who: Age, Race/Ethnicity, and Household Structure, 2012—*Continued*

			Marital status of population 15 years and over (percent)					Languages spoken (percent of households)			
State code	STATE	Total population 15 years and over	Never married	Now married	Widowed	Divorced	Percent foreign born	English only	Spanish, with or without English	Other languages, with or without English	No adult speaks English well
	ACS table number:	B12001	B12001	B12001	B12001	B12001	C05002	B16002	B16002	B16002	B16002
	Column number:	32	33	34	35	36	37	38	39	40	41
00	United States	252,745,149	32.7	50.2	5.9	11.1	13.0	79.2	11.9	9.0	4.5
01	Alabama	3,886,060	29.3	51.0	7.0	12.7	3.4	94.1	3.4	2.5	1.3
02	Alaska.....................	574,398	34.1	49.7	3.8	12.4	7.2	82.0	4.9	13.1	2.1
04	Arizona....................	5,203,019	32.7	49.2	5.5	12.5	13.4	72.8	19.5	7.7	4.7
05	Arkansas..................	2,353,968	26.9	52.9	6.9	13.3	4.4	93.1	4.7	2.3	1.6
06	California.................	30,416,010	36.6	48.5	5.1	9.8	27.1	57.3	25.2	17.6	9.6
08	Colorado	4,152,392	30.9	52.3	4.4	12.4	9.8	82.1	11.6	6.3	2.9
09	Connecticut.............	2,945,674	33.8	49.6	6.0	10.6	13.8	75.4	11.6	13.0	5.3
10	Delaware	746,748	32.7	49.3	6.2	11.8	8.5	85.8	7.0	7.1	2.4
11	District of Columbia...	539,055	57.5	28.8	4.5	9.2	14.3	81.4	7.8	10.8	3.2
12	Florida	16,016,557	31.1	48.5	7.1	13.2	19.4	72.5	19.2	8.3	6.8
13	Georgia	7,830,116	33.2	49.7	5.7	11.4	9.5	86.4	7.4	6.2	3.0
15	Hawaii	1,137,619	33.4	50.9	6.2	9.5	18.1	69.2	2.9	27.9	6.9
16	Idaho	1,239,521	26.0	56.3	5.2	12.5	6.1	88.3	7.6	4.1	2.1
17	Illinois	10,344,646	34.6	49.4	5.9	10.0	13.9	78.1	11.1	10.8	4.9
18	Indiana	5,218,923	30.1	51.2	6.0	12.7	4.6	90.8	4.8	4.4	1.8
19	Iowa	2,472,319	28.3	54.0	6.3	11.4	4.5	92.3	4.1	3.6	1.4
20	Kansas.....................	2,281,272	28.2	53.8	5.8	12.2	6.5	88.7	6.9	4.5	2.2
21	Kentucky..................	3,530,921	27.8	52.3	6.7	13.2	3.1	94.5	2.9	2.7	1.1
22	Louisiana	3,663,532	34.5	46.6	6.6	12.3	3.7	88.6	4.1	7.3	1.7
23	Maine	1,111,822	27.4	52.0	6.4	14.2	3.5	90.2	1.4	8.4	1.0
24	Maryland	4,773,742	34.9	49.2	5.8	10.1	14.3	82.2	6.5	11.3	3.0
25	Massachusetts	5,498,140	36.0	48.0	5.9	10.1	15.0	75.8	8.5	15.8	5.8
26	Michigan	8,030,918	32.6	49.5	6.1	11.8	6.1	89.7	3.5	6.8	1.7
27	Minnesota	4,315,429	31.3	53.5	5.0	10.2	7.2	88.5	4.1	7.4	2.2
28	Mississippi................	2,359,979	33.4	47.5	7.2	11.9	2.0	95.8	2.4	1.8	0.7
29	Missouri...................	4,856,639	29.9	51.0	6.6	12.5	3.8	93.0	2.8	4.1	1.1
30	Montana...................	821,687	27.6	54.0	6.1	12.3	1.8	93.8	2.6	3.7	0.6
31	Nebraska	1,465,286	29.5	54.0	6.1	10.4	6.4	88.8	6.8	4.3	2.6
32	Nevada	2,204,567	32.3	48.0	5.1	14.6	19.2	70.0	18.7	11.3	6.1
33	New Hampshire	1,098,030	29.6	52.6	5.5	12.3	5.4	89.6	2.4	8.0	1.4
34	New Jersey...............	7,196,853	34.0	51.2	6.2	8.6	21.2	68.8	15.0	16.3	7.3
35	New Mexico..............	1,654,214	33.1	47.9	5.8	13.1	9.2	59.1	32.5	8.3	5.1
36	New York..................	16,062,969	38.0	46.9	6.2	8.8	22.6	69.3	14.5	16.2	8.1
37	North Carolina	7,840,375	30.7	52.2	6.2	10.8	7.7	89.2	6.5	4.3	2.5
38	North Dakota............	569,837	31.5	52.8	6.1	9.7	2.8	92.0	2.3	5.7	1.0
39	Ohio	9,351,828	31.2	49.9	6.4	12.5	3.9	92.0	2.9	5.2	1.3
40	Oklahoma.................	3,026,600	27.5	52.3	6.7	13.5	5.6	90.0	6.1	3.9	2.2
41	Oregon	3,185,235	30.2	50.9	5.5	13.4	9.6	85.5	7.6	6.9	2.7
42	Pennsylvania	10,519,780	33.2	50.2	7.1	9.5	6.0	88.3	4.8	6.9	2.3
44	Rhode Island	872,769	35.6	46.6	6.3	11.5	13.3	78.3	9.6	12.0	5.2
45	South Carolina..........	3,818,052	31.9	50.6	6.8	10.7	4.7	92.4	4.4	3.3	1.5
46	South Dakota............	662,015	30.5	52.3	6.2	11.0	2.7	92.3	2.1	5.6	1.4
47	Tennessee	5,216,402	29.2	51.4	6.4	13.0	4.5	92.9	3.7	3.4	1.4
48	Texas.......................	20,202,653	31.6	52.2	5.1	11.0	16.4	64.8	28.8	6.4	7.9
49	Utah	2,100,869	29.5	57.3	3.7	9.5	8.4	82.4	10.7	6.9	3.0
50	Vermont...................	525,211	30.8	51.3	5.9	12.1	4.1	92.5	1.6	5.9	0.7
51	Virginia	6,642,567	31.8	52.6	5.5	10.2	11.6	84.3	6.3	9.4	2.6
53	Washington	5,576,731	30.7	52.2	4.9	12.3	13.3	80.5	7.8	11.7	3.9
54	West Virginia	1,535,612	27.4	51.5	7.9	13.3	1.4	96.5	1.5	2.0	0.3
55	Wisconsin	4,634,334	31.2	52.0	5.8	11.0	4.8	90.5	4.7	4.8	1.6
56	Wyoming..................	461,254	27.2	54.7	5.4	12.8	3.4	90.7	6.2	3.2	0.9

State code	STATE	Total households	Average household size	Household type (percent of all households)								
				Family households				Nonfamily households			Unmarried partner households	
				Total family households	Married-couple families	Male householder families	Female householder families	Total	Total one-person households	One-person households age 65 or over	Total unmarried partner households	Same-sex partner households
	ACS table number:	B11001	B25010	B11001	B11001	B11001	B11001	B11001	B11001	B11010	B11009	B11009
	Column number:	42	43	44	45	46	47	48	49	50	51	52
00	United States	115,969,540	2.64	66.0	48.1	4.8	13.1	34.0	27.8	9.9	6.0	0.6
01	Alabama	1,845,169	2.55	66.9	47.9	4.0	15.0	33.1	28.9	10.4	3.6	0.3
02	Alaska	251,651	2.80	66.1	49.0	5.4	11.8	33.9	26.7	6.0	7.9	0.4
04	Arizona	2,392,168	2.68	65.2	46.9	5.4	12.9	34.8	27.5	9.6	7.0	0.7
05	Arkansas	1,143,859	2.51	66.3	48.8	4.4	13.1	33.7	29.0	10.6	4.4	0.3
06	California	12,552,658	2.97	68.4	48.6	6.0	13.7	31.6	24.4	8.6	6.9	0.7
08	Colorado	1,996,088	2.54	64.0	48.8	4.6	10.6	36.0	28.2	8.1	6.1	0.6
09	Connecticut	1,357,812	2.56	66.5	48.7	4.7	13.1	33.5	27.8	11.0	6.0	0.6
10	Delaware	340,308	2.62	66.3	48.0	4.8	13.5	33.7	27.1	10.6	7.0	0.6
11	District of Columbia	266,662	2.22	42.2	23.3	3.5	15.4	57.8	45.8	10.0	6.3	1.7
12	Florida	7,197,943	2.62	63.9	46.1	4.5	13.3	36.1	29.6	12.2	6.2	0.6
13	Georgia	3,532,908	2.73	68.1	47.9	4.7	15.5	31.9	26.8	8.0	4.8	0.6
15	Hawaii	447,748	3.01	69.0	51.2	5.3	12.6	31.0	24.0	8.2	6.8	0.6
16	Idaho	583,106	2.69	69.6	55.3	4.2	10.2	30.4	24.0	9.1	5.8	0.4
17	Illinois	4,770,194	2.64	65.4	48.0	4.6	12.8	34.6	28.8	10.1	5.8	0.5
18	Indiana	2,480,077	2.56	66.5	49.6	4.6	12.3	33.5	27.9	9.8	6.0	0.5
19	Iowa	1,227,048	2.42	64.9	51.0	4.1	9.9	35.1	28.6	10.8	6.3	0.4
20	Kansas	1,113,911	2.52	65.3	50.6	4.5	10.2	34.7	28.9	10.0	5.2	0.4
21	Kentucky	1,707,004	2.49	66.8	48.9	4.8	13.2	33.2	27.9	10.2	5.7	0.4
22	Louisiana	1,719,473	2.60	65.5	43.3	5.3	16.9	34.5	29.3	9.6	5.8	0.4
23	Maine	554,543	2.33	62.6	48.8	4.2	9.6	37.4	29.5	11.8	8.9	0.9
24	Maryland	2,157,717	2.66	66.6	47.2	4.9	14.5	33.4	27.5	9.5	5.9	0.6
25	Massachusetts	2,522,394	2.54	63.4	46.5	4.1	12.8	36.6	28.9	11.2	6.4	0.9
26	Michigan	3,819,068	2.53	65.0	47.7	4.4	12.9	35.0	29.2	10.8	5.7	0.4
27	Minnesota	2,111,943	2.48	65.1	51.1	4.3	9.7	34.9	28.0	9.8	6.6	0.6
28	Mississippi	1,090,521	2.65	68.6	44.1	5.2	19.2	31.4	27.5	10.3	4.8	0.3
29	Missouri	2,359,135	2.48	64.3	47.7	4.3	12.4	35.7	29.5	10.6	6.1	0.4
30	Montana	408,938	2.39	63.5	50.3	4.7	8.5	36.5	29.7	10.5	5.7	0.3
31	Nebraska	733,570	2.46	64.7	50.3	4.3	10.0	35.3	29.3	10.5	5.8	0.3
32	Nevada	1,006,605	2.70	64.7	44.2	6.5	13.9	35.3	27.4	8.7	7.3	0.5
33	New Hampshire	519,137	2.47	65.8	51.8	4.2	9.8	34.2	26.1	9.3	8.2	0.5
34	New Jersey	3,198,799	2.71	69.1	50.8	4.8	13.5	30.9	25.8	10.5	5.3	0.5
35	New Mexico	764,996	2.67	65.5	45.4	5.7	14.5	34.5	28.6	10.1	6.9	0.7
36	New York	7,238,922	2.62	63.4	43.5	5.1	14.8	36.6	30.0	11.0	6.2	0.7
37	North Carolina	3,731,325	2.55	66.3	48.1	4.6	13.5	33.7	27.9	9.8	5.4	0.5
38	North Dakota	290,944	2.32	60.3	48.1	4.1	8.1	39.7	32.3	10.8	6.9	0.2
39	Ohio	4,554,672	2.47	64.0	46.8	4.5	12.7	36.0	30.3	11.0	6.0	0.4
40	Oklahoma	1,446,667	2.56	66.2	48.5	5.1	12.5	33.8	28.2	10.3	5.3	0.4
41	Oregon	1,516,957	2.51	63.6	48.1	4.6	11.0	36.4	27.7	10.4	7.7	0.7
42	Pennsylvania	4,958,249	2.49	64.6	48.1	4.3	12.1	35.4	29.6	11.8	6.0	0.5
44	Rhode Island	413,083	2.44	62.3	43.7	4.6	14.0	37.7	30.0	11.3	6.8	0.9
45	South Carolina	1,787,340	2.57	67.4	47.0	4.8	15.6	32.6	27.6	9.7	4.9	0.4
46	South Dakota	323,765	2.47	63.8	49.3	4.3	10.2	36.2	30.3	10.8	6.1	0.4
47	Tennessee	2,480,090	2.54	66.2	48.4	4.5	13.3	33.8	28.5	9.8	5.2	0.4
48	Texas	8,970,959	2.84	69.5	50.1	5.2	14.3	30.5	25.2	7.6	5.2	0.5
49	Utah	895,691	3.14	74.4	60.6	4.2	9.6	25.6	19.8	7.0	4.3	0.4
50	Vermont	258,520	2.32	62.2	48.9	3.9	9.4	37.8	27.9	11.5	9.0	1.0
51	Virginia	3,038,967	2.61	67.3	50.7	4.2	12.4	32.7	26.6	9.1	5.2	0.5
53	Washington	2,636,817	2.56	64.0	49.4	4.4	10.2	36.0	28.2	9.4	7.1	0.8
54	West Virginia	741,544	2.44	63.6	48.4	4.3	10.9	36.4	31.1	12.5	5.8	0.3
55	Wisconsin	2,288,362	2.44	63.9	49.2	4.4	10.2	36.1	29.2	10.3	6.7	0.4
56	Wyoming	223,513	2.52	65.7	51.6	4.6	9.4	34.3	28.1	9.5	6.6	0.2

Table A-1. States — Who: Age, Race/Ethnicity, and Household Structure, 2012—*Continued*

		Households with people under 18 years old				Households with people 60 years and over				
			Household type (percent)					Household type (percent)			
State code	STATE	Total households with children	Married-couple families	Male householder families	Female householder families	Total households with people 60 years and over	Married-couple families	Male householder families	Female householder families	Nonfamily households
	ACS table number:	C11005	C11005	C11005	C11005	B11006	B11006	B11006	B11006	B11006
	Column number:	53	54	55	56	57	58	59	60	61
00	United States	37,555,698	64.0	8.5	26.7	41,299,245	48.5	3.5	9.0	39.1
01	Alabama	578,661	61.2	6.4	31.8	677,624	47.5	3.3	10.2	39.0
02	Alaska	89,989	64.0	9.7	25.5	70,457	50.6	4.9	8.7	35.8
04	Arizona	760,499	61.0	10.7	27.4	893,390	51.1	3.3	8.2	37.4
05	Arkansas	360,141	62.6	8.1	28.0	416,397	49.2	2.9	8.9	38.9
06	California	4,554,047	65.9	9.4	23.9	4,396,832	47.9	4.9	11.0	36.2
08	Colorado	640,681	67.7	8.8	22.6	619,488	50.8	2.7	6.9	39.6
09	Connecticut	435,474	65.6	7.4	26.5	503,280	47.7	3.5	8.5	40.3
10	Delaware	108,926	61.0	10.0	28.2	129,370	50.2	2.8	7.7	39.3
11	District of Columbia	54,105	45.7	7.9	45.9	77,163	25.9	4.0	16.0	54.1
12	Florida	2,015,178	60.1	8.8	30.2	3,057,298	48.4	3.2	8.6	39.8
13	Georgia	1,252,827	61.9	7.5	30.0	1,126,910	48.6	3.8	10.9	36.7
15	Hawaii	148,666	69.4	7.6	22.5	190,542	50.3	6.3	13.1	30.3
16	Idaho	198,607	70.8	8.1	20.4	205,890	54.5	2.2	6.7	36.6
17	Illinois	1,546,781	65.7	7.7	25.7	1,640,898	47.6	3.3	9.1	39.9
18	Indiana	801,536	63.8	9.0	26.1	856,183	49.7	2.7	7.9	39.6
19	Iowa	374,050	66.9	8.8	23.2	438,083	51.5	2.0	5.4	41.1
20	Kansas	365,102	67.2	9.0	22.5	372,229	50.9	2.3	6.0	40.8
21	Kentucky	542,160	62.3	8.6	28.3	603,471	48.1	3.4	9.0	39.5
22	Louisiana	569,610	54.5	9.4	35.1	590,194	45.4	3.9	11.2	39.4
23	Maine	147,943	63.6	9.9	24.9	218,818	49.7	2.3	5.6	42.5
24	Maryland	714,950	62.9	8.4	28.0	760,571	47.1	3.6	10.8	38.5
25	Massachusetts	762,069	66.4	6.6	26.3	922,085	46.1	3.4	8.1	42.4
26	Michigan	1,155,699	62.9	8.2	27.7	1,406,734	48.1	2.7	8.3	40.8
27	Minnesota	660,056	68.5	8.2	22.3	694,993	51.7	2.6	5.1	40.6
28	Mississippi	383,093	52.8	8.6	37.9	397,669	44.4	4.2	12.4	39.0
29	Missouri	713,827	62.6	8.5	27.8	838,619	48.4	2.7	8.0	41.0
30	Montana	114,621	67.2	10.7	21.0	154,445	52.0	2.4	4.7	40.9
31	Nebraska	233,885	67.1	9.1	22.5	244,862	50.8	2.0	5.2	42.0
32	Nevada	333,697	58.7	11.6	28.5	347,748	47.5	4.1	8.8	39.6
33	New Hampshire	152,899	67.6	8.5	22.6	189,060	53.6	2.5	6.0	37.9
34	New Jersey	1,099,126	68.7	6.8	24.1	1,198,195	48.3	4.0	10.0	37.8
35	New Mexico	245,054	57.2	11.2	31.0	288,104	47.6	3.5	9.4	39.5
36	New York	2,241,126	61.9	8.3	29.2	2,672,673	43.3	4.3	11.0	41.4
37	North Carolina	1,205,732	62.1	8.3	28.6	1,296,080	49.1	3.1	8.6	39.2
38	North Dakota	80,191	67.2	9.1	21.7	95,886	51.5	2.7	3.5	42.4
39	Ohio	1,372,623	61.6	8.8	28.4	1,657,268	47.5	2.9	7.9	41.7
40	Oklahoma	470,194	62.6	9.6	26.6	507,801	48.6	3.0	8.2	40.2
41	Oregon	447,248	64.2	9.8	24.9	569,100	49.5	2.8	6.7	40.9
42	Pennsylvania	1,427,978	64.4	8.2	26.4	1,911,018	47.3	3.2	8.3	41.2
44	Rhode Island	118,381	59.8	8.3	30.8	153,587	46.6	2.9	8.4	42.1
45	South Carolina	570,320	57.9	8.1	33.2	664,741	49.4	3.7	10.5	36.5
46	South Dakota	96,230	63.8	9.0	26.4	111,692	51.4	2.1	4.8	41.7
47	Tennessee	778,851	62.7	8.3	27.9	891,777	49.3	2.9	9.5	38.4
48	Texas	3,422,277	64.9	8.0	26.4	2,767,321	50.6	4.0	10.4	35.1
49	Utah	378,034	77.0	6.4	15.7	254,318	57.7	2.9	7.1	32.3
50	Vermont	71,482	65.6	9.0	23.7	99,455	49.5	2.4	4.8	43.4
51	Virginia	995,173	67.8	7.3	24.0	1,044,654	50.5	3.2	9.3	37.0
53	Washington	820,803	68.1	8.6	22.0	901,567	51.0	2.8	6.3	40.0
54	West Virginia	199,097	64.2	8.9	25.3	307,576	47.9	3.2	7.2	41.7
55	Wisconsin	677,124	65.5	9.0	24.2	789,827	50.5	2.6	5.4	41.5
56	Wyoming	68,875	66.6	10.3	21.6	75,302	54.0	2.3	4.8	38.9

Page intentionally left blank

Table A-2. Counties — Who: Age, Race/Ethnicity, and Household Structure, 2010–2012

STATE and County code	STATE or County	Total population	Percent change 2010–2012	Population by age (percent)						Median age	Race alone or in combination (percent)			
				Under 5 years	5 to 17 years	18 to 24 years	25 to 44 years	45 to 64 years	65 years and over		White	Black	Asian, Hawaiian, or Pacific Islander	American Indian, Alaska Native, or some other race
	ACS table number:	B01003	Population estimates	B01001	B01001	B01001	B01001	B01001	B01001	B01002	B02008	B02009	B02011 + B02012	B02010 + B02013
	Column number:	1	2	3	4	5	6	7	8	9	10	11	12	13
00 000	**United States**............	311,609,369	1.5	6.4	17.3	10.0	26.5	26.5	13.4	37.3	76.4	13.6	6.1	6.9
01 000	**Alabama**....................	4,803,488	0.8	6.4	17.1	10.1	25.5	26.9	14.1	38.0	70.5	27.0	1.5	2.5
01 001	Autauga	55,180	1.6	6.4	19.8	8.7	26.2	26.0	12.8	37.9	80.1	18.7	1.3	0.9
01 003	Baldwin	186,965	4.1	6.2	16.6	7.4	24.3	28.3	17.1	41.6	88.4	10.0	1.1	2.3
01 005	Barbour	27,293	-0.6	5.5	16.0	8.9	27.1	27.6	14.9	38.9	49.5	47.6	1.1	4.3
01 007	Bibb............................	22,733	-1.2	5.1	17.7	9.6	26.9	26.8	13.9	39.0	77.9	22.3	0.3	0.9
01 009	Blount.........................	57,644	0.8	6.2	18.0	7.7	25.7	27.2	15.3	40.0	96.9	1.9	0.3	2.4
01 013	Butler..........................	20,611	-3.0	6.2	17.4	8.2	23.1	27.9	17.1	40.6	55.1	44.4	0.5	0.3
01 015	Calhoun.......................	117,845	-1.0	6.0	16.7	10.8	24.6	27.1	14.8	38.8	76.5	21.7	1.3	2.5
01 017	Chambers.....................	34,065	-0.2	6.0	16.8	8.1	23.7	28.4	17.1	42.2	59.9	39.7	0.6	0.2
01 019	Cherokee.....................	26,032	0.2	5.5	15.1	7.6	21.9	30.9	18.9	44.9	94.0	5.0	0.9	1.1
01 021	Chilton	43,778	0.3	6.8	17.9	8.5	26.6	26.2	13.9	37.3	86.0	10.2	0.4	4.1
01 025	Clarke	25,506	-2.3	5.7	18.6	8.2	23.3	27.7	16.6	40.5	54.1	45.4	0.0	0.0
01 031	Coffee.........................	50,624	2.2	6.7	17.4	8.3	27.2	25.8	14.6	38.0	79.2	18.0	1.9	3.1
01 033	Colbert	54,451	-0.1	5.5	16.5	8.4	23.7	28.3	17.6	41.9	81.4	17.2	0.7	2.6
01 039	Covington....................	37,941	0.5	6.0	16.6	8.1	22.7	27.8	18.8	42.2	85.8	13.1	0.6	2.1
01 043	Cullman	80,463	0.0	6.1	16.9	8.8	23.9	27.9	16.5	40.5	96.7	1.7	0.5	2.4
01 045	Dale............................	50,306	0.2	7.1	17.4	9.5	26.5	25.7	13.8	36.2	77.6	20.6	2.0	2.8
01 047	Dallas..........................	43,278	-2.1	7.4	18.9	9.1	22.7	27.5	14.4	37.6	29.5	70.8	0.0	0.5
01 049	DeKalb.........................	71,217	0.0	6.9	18.7	8.8	25.0	26.6	14.0	38.7	93.6	2.7	0.4	6.0
01 051	Elmore.........................	80,107	1.4	6.3	16.8	9.9	27.7	27.1	12.2	37.5	77.6	21.5	1.1	1.7
01 053	Escambia......................	38,145	-0.8	6.2	16.4	8.8	26.1	27.2	15.3	39.2	62.3	34.3	0.0	4.1
01 055	Etowah........................	104,381	-0.1	5.9	16.9	8.7	24.9	27.6	16.1	40.4	82.7	15.9	0.9	1.7
01 059	Franklin.......................	31,757	0.1	7.0	17.6	8.9	24.9	26.4	15.2	38.5	89.5	5.3	0.0	5.6
01 061	Geneva........................	26,849	0.4	5.8	16.4	7.6	24.4	27.8	18.1	41.6	87.4	10.1	0.0	4.0
01 069	Houston.......................	102,538	1.6	6.6	17.7	8.2	25.7	26.9	14.8	38.4	71.4	26.9	1.2	2.3
01 071	Jackson........................	53,136	-0.3	5.7	16.5	7.8	24.1	29.0	16.9	41.5	93.2	3.9	0.8	3.7
01 073	Jefferson......................	659,122	0.2	6.8	16.7	9.7	26.8	26.8	13.3	37.1	53.7	42.8	1.7	2.6
01 077	Lauderdale...................	92,638	-0.2	5.6	15.7	11.0	23.5	27.2	17.1	40.6	88.2	10.7	0.9	1.3
01 079	Lawrence.....................	34,077	-1.4	6.2	17.1	8.3	24.0	29.5	14.8	41.3	81.9	12.4	0.5	10.3
01 081	Lee	143,866	4.6	5.9	16.1	20.4	26.7	21.5	9.3	30.0	72.3	23.7	3.4	2.2
01 083	Limestone....................	85,469	5.3	6.4	17.4	7.9	28.1	27.7	12.6	39.0	82.7	13.6	1.3	3.9
01 087	Macon	21,094	-4.6	5.2	14.4	19.1	20.4	26.3	14.6	36.6	16.6	83.3	0.0	0.0
01 089	Madison	339,640	2.1	6.2	17.2	10.1	26.3	27.7	12.5	37.4	71.4	25.4	3.4	2.8
01 091	Marengo......................	20,681	-2.6	6.0	17.8	8.7	22.0	28.2	17.3	41.6	47.3	52.3	0.0	0.3
01 093	Marion.........................	30,547	-1.5	5.5	15.6	7.9	23.4	28.8	18.9	43.9	95.1	4.0	0.0	0.7
01 095	Marshall.......................	94,021	1.7	7.0	18.1	8.9	25.2	25.7	15.1	38.3	93.7	2.3	0.7	4.6
01 097	Mobile.........................	413,432	0.2	6.8	18.0	10.0	25.3	26.5	13.3	36.7	61.6	35.5	2.2	2.0
01 099	Monroe........................	22,785	-1.6	6.1	18.5	9.1	21.6	28.3	16.4	40.4	55.5	41.9	0.7	1.7
01 101	Montgomery.................	230,604	0.2	6.9	17.6	11.6	26.9	24.7	12.2	34.7	41.1	55.9	2.5	1.9
01 103	Morgan........................	120,001	0.7	6.4	17.5	8.5	25.5	27.6	14.5	38.9	85.0	12.8	0.8	3.7
01 109	Pike	33,013	0.7	5.5	14.6	21.9	22.2	22.7	13.0	31.1	59.7	38.1	2.3	2.6
01 111	Randolph......................	22,802	-0.9	5.6	17.3	9.8	20.5	28.8	18.1	41.2	78.3	21.1	0.6	0.3
01 113	Russell	55,364	8.6	7.9	17.4	9.6	27.2	25.4	12.5	35.1	56.1	43.2	0.9	1.5
01 115	St. Clair.......................	84,473	1.7	6.5	17.1	7.6	28.1	27.4	13.4	39.0	89.3	9.3	0.8	1.1
01 117	Shelby.........................	198,314	2.6	6.5	18.7	7.8	28.7	27.0	11.3	37.0	83.2	11.5	2.3	4.1
01 121	Talladega.....................	81,853	-0.3	5.9	17.3	8.6	25.5	28.1	14.6	40.0	66.6	33.0	0.1	1.4
01 123	Tallapoosa...................	41,390	-0.8	6.0	16.3	7.8	23.1	29.1	17.7	42.1	71.2	28.1	0.0	0.8
01 125	Tuscaloosa...................	196,794	1.9	6.0	15.3	19.6	25.0	23.0	11.0	31.5	67.9	30.4	1.5	1.0
01 127	Walker.........................	66,632	-1.2	5.7	16.5	8.5	23.8	28.8	16.7	42.0	93.0	6.7	0.6	2.3
01 133	Winston.......................	24,258	-1.1	5.4	15.8	7.4	22.9	30.1	18.3	43.8	98.1	0.8	0.2	2.9
02 000	**Alaska**	723,120	2.4	7.5	18.5	10.8	27.6	27.5	8.1	33.7	73.7	5.0	8.9	20.9
02 020	Anchorage....................	296,039	1.8	7.5	18.0	11.4	29.0	26.4	7.7	32.8	73.8	8.6	13.5	14.4
02 090	Fairbanks North Star	99,275	2.0	8.0	17.2	14.0	29.5	24.6	6.7	30.8	83.8	6.1	5.1	12.4
02 110	Juneau........................	32,071	3.6	6.2	16.8	8.8	28.1	31.7	8.5	37.8	78.1	1.8	10.0	20.9
02 122	Kenai Peninsula.............	56,307	2.3	6.1	17.2	8.4	23.7	32.7	11.9	40.9	89.2	0.9	2.6	12.7
02 170	Matanuska-Susitna	91,877	4.6	7.5	20.8	8.5	26.7	28.1	8.3	35.0	91.3	1.8	3.3	10.7
04 000	**Arizona**	6,477,128	2.2	6.9	18.2	9.9	26.1	24.6	14.3	36.2	81.6	5.0	4.1	12.3
04 001	Apache........................	72,399	2.1	8.2	22.9	10.4	22.1	24.1	12.2	32.2	25.1	0.6	0.8	75.0
04 003	Cochise........................	132,162	0.4	6.4	16.4	9.5	23.8	26.1	17.8	39.7	82.8	5.6	3.6	13.7
04 005	Coconino.....................	134,909	1.0	6.5	16.6	18.4	24.7	24.3	9.4	31.1	64.8	1.9	2.9	34.0
04 007	Gila.............................	53,394	-0.7	5.8	15.2	7.3	18.3	29.5	23.9	48.1	82.0	1.0	0.8	18.9
04 009	Graham	37,138	1.5	8.3	19.8	12.1	26.6	21.3	11.9	31.8	78.0	2.4	1.1	21.6
04 012	La Paz	20,410	-0.9	4.8	13.0	6.0	16.1	26.3	33.8	54.2	72.6	0.4	0.4	27.5
04 013	Maricopa	3,878,086	3.1	7.2	18.8	9.9	27.8	23.8	12.6	35.0	83.3	6.1	4.9	8.7
04 015	Mohave........................	202,102	1.5	5.3	14.9	7.1	19.0	29.7	24.0	48.0	92.8	1.5	2.4	8.2
04 017	Navajo.........................	107,292	-0.5	7.8	21.4	9.6	21.3	25.8	14.1	35.5	52.0	1.4	1.3	48.7
04 019	Pima	987,294	1.1	6.2	16.4	10.9	24.7	25.8	16.0	37.9	82.0	4.6	4.0	12.7
04 021	Pinal	385,577	0.4	7.5	18.5	8.1	27.8	23.4	14.7	35.9	80.2	5.5	3.1	14.2
04 023	Santa Cruz	47,377	-0.2	7.6	22.5	9.0	22.0	25.0	14.0	36.1	69.6	0.8	0.8	31.1
04 025	Yavapai........................	211,339	1.1	4.8	13.8	6.9	18.2	31.1	25.2	50.2	93.9	1.0	1.4	5.9
04 027	Yuma...........................	199,061	1.6	7.6	20.1	11.4	24.0	21.0	16.0	33.5	78.1	2.7	2.0	19.7

Table A-2. Counties — Who: Age, Race/Ethnicity, and Household Structure, 2010–2012—*Continued*

STATE and County code	STATE or County	Percent Hispanic or Latino	Percent foreign born	Total households	Household type (percent) Family households				Nonfamily households		Percent of households with people under 18 years	Percent of households with people 60 years and over
					Total family households	Married-couple families	Male household families	Female household families	Total nonfamily households	One-person households		
	ACS table number:	B03003	C05003	B11001	B11001	B11001	B11001	B11001	B11001	B11001	B11005	B11006
	Column number:	14	15	16	17	18	19	20	21	22	23	24
00 000	**United States**.............	16.6	13.0	115,241,776	66.2	48.4	4.8	13.1	33.8	27.6	32.8	34.8
01 000	**Alabama**..................	4.0	3.5	1,837,823	67.5	48.1	4.2	15.3	32.5	28.4	32.2	36.0
01 001	Autauga....................	2.5	1.4	20,001	70.9	55.4	3.5	12.0	29.1	24.7	36.7	32.1
01 003	Baldwin	4.5	4.0	73,210	71.4	56.5	3.6	11.2	28.6	25.2	29.8	40.1
01 005	Barbour	5.0	3.1	9,292	66.2	44.6	2.9	18.7	33.8	30.9	32.1	41.6
01 007	Bibb........................	1.9	0.9	7,107	71.8	50.2	6.0	15.6	28.2	25.0	34.3	41.5
01 009	Blount......................	8.4	4.3	21,192	74.2	59.5	5.3	9.4	25.8	23.2	37.4	40.7
01 013	Butler......................	1.1	0.7	8,177	67.6	41.9	5.7	20.0	32.4	30.8	30.0	41.4
01 015	Calhoun....................	3.4	2.3	45,553	67.0	48.0	4.4	14.6	33.0	27.8	29.9	37.4
01 017	Chambers..................	1.7	1.0	13,688	63.3	43.0	4.3	16.1	36.7	33.9	26.0	41.3
01 019	Cherokee..................	1.3	1.5	11,999	72.2	56.1	3.2	12.9	27.8	25.6	31.4	40.1
01 021	Chilton	7.7	5.6	16,262	73.8	55.3	4.6	14.0	26.2	23.8	37.0	36.3
01 025	Clarke	0.8	0.5	9,840	66.8	45.5	4.5	16.9	33.2	31.6	30.4	38.2
01 031	Coffee	6.3	5.0	19,108	67.3	49.4	4.1	13.8	32.7	28.6	32.6	36.0
01 033	Colbert	2.2	1.9	22,302	70.0	51.5	4.7	13.8	30.0	26.8	31.7	40.2
01 039	Covington..................	1.4	1.1	14,934	68.3	46.4	4.1	17.8	31.7	28.9	31.6	43.2
01 043	Cullman....................	4.3	2.8	31,222	70.1	54.0	3.4	12.8	29.9	26.7	30.2	40.8
01 045	Dale........................	5.7	3.6	19,732	65.8	46.4	4.3	15.2	34.2	29.8	33.1	33.2
01 047	Dallas......................	0.4	0.4	16,153	61.4	29.7	6.5	25.2	38.6	36.0	33.2	40.3
01 049	DeKalb.....................	13.9	7.2	25,160	73.6	58.5	5.0	10.2	26.4	23.9	34.9	37.9
01 051	Elmore	2.7	1.9	28,370	73.9	56.0	3.3	14.6	26.1	23.4	35.8	32.0
01 053	Escambia	0.7	0.5	13,787	68.6	40.3	9.4	18.9	31.4	29.8	34.0	39.0
01 055	Etowah.....................	3.5	1.9	39,881	69.3	48.2	5.2	15.9	30.7	28.0	31.6	41.4
01 059	Franklin....................	15.1	9.5	12,417	68.7	51.3	5.9	11.5	31.3	28.7	31.0	37.7
01 061	Geneva.....................	3.4	2.4	11,004	71.5	48.2	5.4	17.9	28.5	24.7	30.5	40.9
01 069	Houston....................	3.1	2.3	39,172	67.5	48.0	3.1	16.4	32.5	28.6	32.4	36.3
01 071	Jackson....................	2.6	2.5	21,097	70.6	55.4	4.9	10.3	29.4	26.7	30.1	41.2
01 073	Jefferson...................	3.9	4.3	257,586	64.1	42.6	3.7	17.8	35.9	31.1	30.9	34.0
01 077	Lauderdale.................	2.3	2.2	38,524	65.8	51.4	3.0	11.4	34.2	29.6	29.3	39.2
01 079	Lawrence...................	1.8	1.3	13,325	72.2	52.5	4.6	15.1	27.8	25.0	32.0	36.2
01 081	Lee.........................	3.4	5.3	55,655	60.3	45.4	3.3	11.6	39.7	28.8	30.8	25.3
01 083	Limestone..................	5.6	4.7	31,807	73.0	58.1	3.9	11.0	27.0	24.5	32.0	34.6
01 087	Macon......................	1.5	0.7	8,055	63.1	30.9	6.3	25.9	36.9	33.9	32.1	41.8
01 089	Madison....................	4.7	5.2	132,631	65.2	48.6	4.4	12.2	34.8	30.5	31.2	31.3
01 091	Marengo...................	1.8	0.8	8,536	66.8	45.7	4.0	17.1	33.2	31.8	36.6	43.5
01 093	Marion.....................	2.2	2.1	12,538	71.5	56.1	3.2	12.2	28.5	25.2	30.2	44.1
01 095	Marshall....................	12.5	8.0	34,253	71.4	54.2	4.9	12.2	28.6	25.4	34.5	39.6
01 097	Mobile.....................	2.5	3.3	156,085	66.6	44.0	4.0	18.6	33.4	28.9	33.8	35.6
01 099	Monroe....................	1.0	1.3	8,487	67.5	45.5	3.6	18.4	32.5	32.0	29.2	41.1
01 101	Montgomery...............	3.5	4.5	88,569	64.4	38.3	5.1	20.9	35.6	30.4	33.6	32.7
01 103	Morgan....................	7.8	4.9	45,753	68.9	52.2	3.9	12.8	31.1	27.4	31.2	35.9
01 109	Pike	2.3	3.0	13,053	61.4	41.8	4.7	14.9	38.6	28.6	27.6	33.3
01 111	Randolph..................	2.9	1.5	9,173	68.6	47.8	4.8	16.0	31.4	29.2	34.3	39.9
01 113	Russell	4.2	1.9	21,376	64.4	41.5	4.9	17.9	35.6	32.2	34.8	32.9
01 115	St. Clair...................	2.1	1.9	31,323	73.1	56.4	4.2	12.5	26.9	22.9	37.0	36.5
01 117	Shelby.....................	5.9	5.8	74,187	71.3	57.7	3.0	10.6	28.7	24.7	36.3	29.6
01 121	Talladega...................	2.1	1.4	31,346	71.3	46.4	5.3	19.5	28.7	25.6	35.6	38.1
01 123	Tallapoosa.................	2.5	2.3	16,172	71.2	50.2	4.0	17.0	28.8	25.0	29.3	42.0
01 125	Tuscaloosa.................	3.1	3.4	67,244	65.3	47.3	3.7	14.2	34.7	28.2	31.0	31.4
01 127	Walker.....................	2.1	1.1	25,624	71.4	50.7	4.3	16.4	28.6	25.2	32.7	42.8
01 133	Winston....................	2.7	0.8	9,686	65.4	53.5	3.7	8.2	34.6	33.5	30.6	43.7
02 000	**Alaska**	5.8	7.0	253,718	66.8	49.4	5.7	11.6	33.2	25.7	36.6	26.6
02 020	Anchorage.................	7.9	9.4	105,688	65.4	47.7	5.4	12.3	34.6	26.2	37.3	24.7
02 090	Fairbanks North Star	6.3	5.5	36,499	65.4	51.0	3.6	10.9	34.6	26.3	35.1	22.8
02 110	Juneau.....................	5.4	6.1	12,314	64.8	47.0	5.7	12.1	35.2	25.3	31.8	27.4
02 122	Kenai Peninsula...........	3.1	2.4	21,561	66.8	54.0	4.2	8.6	33.2	27.4	29.7	34.6
02 170	Matanuska-Susitna	3.9	3.8	31,383	72.0	55.4	6.1	10.5	28.0	21.5	37.5	27.2
04 000	**Arizona**	29.9	13.4	2,357,799	65.7	47.5	5.4	12.8	34.3	27.3	32.3	36.5
04 001	Apache.....................	6.0	1.7	19,445	67.9	40.8	6.4	20.7	32.1	28.2	35.5	43.0
04 003	Cochise....................	32.8	11.8	49,533	66.4	49.4	4.5	12.5	33.6	28.9	31.0	45.4
04 005	Coconino..................	13.6	5.5	44,949	64.6	45.1	5.7	13.8	35.4	24.7	33.0	29.1
04 007	Gila........................	18.2	3.8	19,980	63.4	48.9	4.9	9.5	36.6	32.0	22.2	53.6
04 009	Graham	30.9	5.4	10,563	73.4	53.4	5.9	14.1	26.6	22.7	38.0	38.1
04 012	La Paz	24.3	11.0	9,913	60.7	46.8	4.7	9.2	39.3	32.6	21.2	58.9
04 013	Maricopa...................	29.8	14.8	1,404,105	65.6	47.0	5.6	12.9	34.4	27.0	33.9	32.5
04 015	Mohave....................	15.1	6.7	80,346	63.6	49.0	3.6	10.9	36.4	28.8	21.2	54.2
04 017	Navajo.....................	10.8	2.4	34,107	71.1	46.7	5.9	18.5	28.9	25.5	36.3	43.1
04 019	Pima.......................	35.0	12.8	381,827	61.9	44.1	4.9	12.8	38.1	30.8	28.5	38.9
04 021	Pinal.......................	28.8	10.3	122,490	72.1	54.9	5.9	11.3	27.9	22.8	35.7	40.8
04 023	Santa Cruz.................	82.8	34.0	15,371	77.1	56.5	4.2	16.4	22.9	20.0	44.9	40.6
04 025	Yavapai.....................	13.8	6.4	91,813	62.4	49.7	3.5	9.2	37.6	30.8	20.6	53.4
04 027	Yuma.......................	60.1	24.6	70,062	78.0	56.5	6.9	14.6	22.0	17.5	42.0	38.8

STATE and County code	STATE or County	Total population	Percent change 2010–2012	Population by age (percent)						Median age	Race alone or in combination (percent)			
				Under 5 years	5 to 17 years	18 to 24 years	25 to 44 years	45 to 64 years	65 years and over		White	Black	Asian, Hawaiian, or Pacific Islander	American Indian, Alaska Native, or some other race
	ACS table number:	B01003	Population estimates	B01001	B01001	B01001	B01001	B01001	B01001	B01002	B02008	B02009	B02011 + B02012	B02010 + B02013
	Column number:	1	2	3	4	5	6	7	8	9	10	11	12	13
05 000	**Arkansas**	2,936,822	0.9	6.7	17.5	9.8	25.4	25.9	14.6	37.5	80.1	16.2	1.8	3.9
05 003	Ashley	21,663	-1.4	6.6	17.6	7.0	24.7	27.4	16.7	40.5	70.8	26.3	0.0	3.6
05 005	Baxter	41,285	-1.2	4.4	13.5	6.2	18.4	29.1	28.5	51.1	98.7	0.5	0.4	2.0
05 007	Benton	227,570	4.2	7.8	19.9	8.2	28.5	23.4	12.1	34.6	90.3	1.9	3.8	7.0
05 009	Boone	37,114	1.1	5.9	17.1	7.6	23.9	26.9	18.5	41.6	98.4	0.5	0.7	2.5
05 015	Carroll	27,542	0.2	6.2	16.5	6.8	21.0	30.1	19.3	44.5	95.7	1.0	0.5	5.1
05 019	Clark	22,959	-0.1	5.7	13.8	22.0	19.8	23.2	15.4	34.1	73.6	25.6	0.8	0.3
05 023	Cleburne	25,918	-0.7	5.5	14.2	6.9	20.8	28.7	24.0	46.5	99.2	0.2	0.5	1.7
05 027	Columbia	24,643	-1.2	5.8	16.4	16.5	21.1	24.2	16.0	35.5	60.2	38.9	0.6	2.8
05 029	Conway	21,244	0.2	5.8	17.6	8.4	23.6	27.2	17.3	40.4	87.3	12.6	0.0	1.4
05 031	Craighead	98,249	3.1	7.2	17.7	12.6	27.3	23.2	12.0	33.3	84.3	14.0	1.6	1.4
05 033	Crawford	61,941	-0.1	6.5	19.4	8.4	25.3	26.7	13.8	38.3	94.6	1.8	1.8	5.2
05 035	Crittenden	50,488	-1.8	8.2	20.3	9.3	25.6	25.5	11.1	33.9	46.7	52.3	0.2	2.4
05 045	Faulkner	116,454	4.0	7.0	17.2	15.6	27.3	22.6	10.2	31.4	87.0	11.2	1.6	2.0
05 051	Garland	96,590	0.7	5.5	15.4	8.1	21.7	28.4	20.8	44.3	86.5	9.1	1.1	5.1
05 055	Greene	42,703	2.3	6.7	18.5	8.9	25.6	26.0	14.2	37.9	98.4	0.9	0.0	2.3
05 057	Hempstead	22,500	-1.0	7.6	18.7	8.6	22.2	27.6	15.3	39.1	68.5	30.8	0.0	3.2
05 059	Hot Spring	33,173	0.8	5.9	16.8	8.2	24.8	28.0	16.4	40.1	87.5	12.0	0.0	1.6
05 063	Independence	36,914	0.5	7.1	17.0	8.7	25.3	26.0	15.9	37.9	95.7	3.5	0.0	2.1
05 069	Jefferson	76,023	-3.4	6.2	17.4	10.9	24.1	27.7	13.7	37.5	42.9	55.8	1.1	1.2
05 071	Johnson	25,720	1.3	7.0	17.6	10.2	23.6	26.5	15.1	38.8	95.0	1.9	0.5	4.9
05 083	Logan	22,210	-1.5	6.5	17.4	8.6	21.4	28.2	17.9	42.2	94.8	1.8	2.0	1.9
05 085	Lonoke	69,267	1.7	6.9	20.3	8.2	28.5	24.6	11.4	35.3	90.7	6.5	1.3	2.7
05 091	Miller	43,639	0.2	7.2	17.0	9.0	26.5	26.0	14.2	37.7	74.1	25.3	0.0	2.0
05 093	Mississippi	46,016	-1.8	7.5	20.3	9.4	24.9	25.5	12.4	34.9	64.2	34.9	0.7	1.8
05 103	Ouachita	25,749	-2.7	6.8	16.4	7.4	22.6	29.6	17.1	42.6	59.3	41.7	0.3	0.8
05 107	Phillips	21,280	-4.1	7.8	20.2	8.5	22.0	26.3	15.1	36.9	37.6	63.1	0.0	0.6
05 111	Poinsett	24,433	-1.0	6.5	17.8	8.5	23.9	27.0	16.3	39.9	91.8	8.3	0.0	0.7
05 113	Polk	20,569	-0.9	5.9	17.5	6.8	21.1	28.4	20.3	44.1	95.4	0.0	0.7	5.9
05 115	Pope	62,478	1.1	6.9	16.2	14.5	24.6	24.7	13.2	35.1	92.9	3.9	1.3	4.5
05 119	Pulaski	386,435	1.4	7.0	16.9	9.4	28.1	26.3	12.3	36.0	60.9	36.3	2.5	1.8
05 123	St. Francis	27,999	-1.1	6.6	16.9	8.6	28.2	27.2	12.6	36.8	45.9	53.0	0.0	2.4
05 125	Saline	109,842	3.9	6.3	18.0	7.4	26.5	26.2	15.6	38.7	93.0	5.5	1.2	2.0
05 131	Sebastian	126,700	1.2	7.1	18.1	9.6	25.9	26.3	13.1	36.6	86.8	7.8	4.7	4.8
05 139	Union	41,268	-1.7	6.6	17.4	8.3	24.0	27.8	15.8	39.6	66.0	33.5	0.8	1.3
05 143	Washington	207,763	3.6	7.5	17.9	14.5	28.8	21.5	9.9	31.3	80.9	4.0	4.9	12.5
05 145	White	77,967	1.5	6.5	17.1	12.4	25.3	24.2	14.4	36.1	93.7	5.0	0.8	3.0
05 149	Yell	22,029	-1.1	7.0	18.9	8.2	24.5	25.4	16.0	38.3	82.6	1.5	1.5	15.9
06 000	**California**	37,686,586	1.9	6.7	17.9	10.6	28.1	25.1	11.7	35.4	66.0	7.1	15.9	15.8
06 001	Alameda	1,533,311	2.7	6.4	15.9	9.8	30.1	26.3	11.5	36.7	50.4	13.8	31.0	11.2
06 005	Amador	37,445	-2.1	3.2	13.0	6.3	21.0	34.9	21.5	49.1	90.5	2.6	2.5	6.9
06 007	Butte	220,565	0.7	5.6	15.1	15.1	22.6	26.0	15.7	37.1	89.8	2.6	6.3	7.9
06 009	Calaveras	45,124	-1.6	3.7	15.4	6.6	17.3	34.8	22.2	50.1	95.4	0.6	2.0	6.4
06 011	Colusa	21,421	-0.2	9.0	21.0	9.4	24.5	23.9	12.2	33.3	82.1	1.3	2.6	19.4
06 013	Contra Costa	1,066,333	2.5	6.2	18.2	8.4	26.3	28.0	12.9	38.6	67.9	10.7	18.7	8.7
06 015	Del Norte	28,462	-1.0	6.7	14.3	9.0	26.5	28.8	14.7	39.5	82.2	3.7	6.5	15.6
06 017	El Dorado	180,866	-0.3	5.0	17.2	7.6	21.3	33.6	15.4	44.1	90.7	1.6	5.4	6.2
06 019	Fresno	940,493	1.6	8.4	21.1	11.6	26.5	22.0	10.3	30.9	59.9	6.0	11.4	27.1
06 021	Glenn	28,090	-0.4	7.5	20.2	9.4	23.4	26.3	13.3	36.4	87.4	1.6	3.1	11.5
06 023	Humboldt	135,061	-0.2	5.6	14.2	12.8	25.8	28.0	13.6	37.4	87.8	1.8	4.0	11.6
06 025	Imperial	175,837	1.3	8.0	20.9	11.3	26.6	22.4	10.7	31.7	70.9	3.5	2.3	27.2
06 029	Kern	849,101	1.7	8.6	21.4	11.2	27.4	22.2	9.2	30.8	75.9	6.7	5.6	15.7
06 031	Kings	151,869	-0.6	8.4	19.4	11.6	30.7	21.7	8.1	31.2	77.3	7.7	5.6	13.7
06 033	Lake	64,331	-1.2	5.4	15.4	7.8	21.2	32.1	18.1	45.1	84.6	3.2	2.5	13.0
06 035	Lassen	34,253	-3.3	4.2	11.0	12.0	34.5	27.9	10.3	37.3	73.0	9.5	2.6	19.5
06 037	Los Angeles	9,892,525	1.4	6.6	17.5	10.8	29.5	24.5	11.2	35.0	56.5	9.5	15.8	22.4
06 039	Madera	151,827	0.7	7.9	20.5	10.3	26.2	23.4	11.8	33.1	85.0	4.4	3.2	10.7
06 041	Marin	254,844	1.2	5.3	15.2	5.8	23.8	32.4	17.5	44.9	82.8	3.7	8.0	9.9
06 045	Mendocino	87,564	-0.4	5.9	16.2	8.1	23.4	30.2	16.3	41.9	86.1	1.5	3.0	13.4
06 047	Merced	259,716	2.1	8.5	22.6	12.0	26.1	21.1	9.7	29.9	70.5	4.4	9.0	19.5
06 053	Monterey	421,570	2.5	7.9	18.8	11.1	28.1	23.2	10.9	32.9	77.5	3.7	8.9	13.9
06 055	Napa	137,949	1.6	5.9	16.9	8.9	25.1	27.6	15.5	40.1	83.2	2.5	8.7	9.0
06 057	Nevada	98,605	-0.5	4.3	14.5	6.8	20.1	34.0	20.4	48.5	95.0	0.8	2.6	4.3
06 059	Orange	3,054,809	2.4	6.3	17.8	10.2	28.1	25.7	12.0	36.4	65.8	2.2	20.7	14.9
06 061	Placer	356,331	3.3	5.8	18.2	7.7	24.4	28.0	15.9	40.3	87.8	2.0	8.6	6.0
06 063	Plumas	19,684	-2.7	4.8	12.9	7.1	19.0	33.9	22.3	50.0	92.8	1.4	2.6	6.5
06 065	Riverside	2,236,158	3.0	7.3	20.5	10.6	26.2	23.3	12.1	33.9	69.8	7.5	8.1	18.9
06 067	Sacramento	1,436,233	2.0	7.0	18.2	10.1	28.0	25.2	11.5	35.0	64.9	12.5	19.1	10.8
06 069	San Benito	56,210	2.3	7.2	20.8	9.6	26.0	26.1	10.3	34.7	87.9	1.3	5.1	10.0
06 071	San Bernardino	2,062,483	1.9	7.7	21.0	11.4	27.2	23.5	9.2	31.9	66.7	10.0	8.5	19.6
06 073	San Diego	3,139,726	2.4	6.6	16.5	11.8	28.8	24.6	11.7	34.8	75.0	6.3	14.2	9.6
06 075	San Francisco	815,234	2.5	4.4	9.0	9.0	37.8	25.9	13.8	38.5	53.7	6.9	36.8	7.1
06 077	San Joaquin	695,251	2.2	7.8	21.1	10.5	26.3	23.6	10.7	32.8	64.9	8.9	18.8	14.8
06 079	San Luis Obispo	272,034	1.8	4.9	13.6	15.0	22.8	28.0	15.7	39.8	86.0	2.7	5.2	9.6
06 081	San Mateo	729,489	2.7	6.3	15.7	7.6	28.8	27.9	13.7	39.4	62.3	3.5	30.1	9.5

Table A-2. Counties — Who: Age, Race/Ethnicity, and Household Structure, 2010–2012—*Continued*

STATE and County code	STATE or County	Percent Hispanic or Latino	Percent foreign born	Total households	Household type (percent)							Percent of households with people under 18 years	Percent of households with people 60 years and over
					Family households				Nonfamily households				
					Total family households	Married-couple families	Male household families	Female household families	Total nonfamily households	One-person households			
ACS table number:		B03003	C05003	B11001	B11001	B11001	B11001	B11001	B11001	B11001	B11005	B11006
Column number:		14	15	16	17	18	19	20	21	22	23	24
05 000	**Arkansas**	6.6	4.5	1,129,845	67.5	49.4	4.5	13.6	32.5	27.8	32.3	36.0
05 003	Ashley	5.0	1.8	8,684	72.4	52.4	5.5	14.5	27.6	27.0	33.8	40.1
05 005	Baxter	1.8	1.7	17,741	65.8	52.6	3.9	9.3	34.2	29.3	21.4	56.0
05 007	Benton	15.7	11.4	81,141	73.6	60.7	2.9	10.0	26.4	21.5	37.4	32.4
05 009	Boone	2.0	1.4	15,163	71.9	56.9	3.1	11.8	28.1	24.9	31.3	38.7
05 015	Carroll	13.4	6.3	11,372	68.7	56.9	2.6	9.2	31.3	25.7	30.8	45.9
05 019	Clark	4.2	2.6	8,079	65.0	46.4	3.1	15.5	35.0	30.5	31.8	38.7
05 023	Cleburne	2.1	2.1	10,018	68.4	55.8	3.9	8.6	31.6	29.1	23.3	51.0
05 027	Columbia	2.3	2.9	9,526	69.2	47.2	4.2	17.9	30.8	26.0	34.6	37.5
05 029	Conway	3.7	2.7	8,331	70.3	49.2	7.4	13.7	29.7	27.5	30.9	40.3
05 031	Craighead	4.5	3.4	37,834	67.6	47.9	4.8	14.9	32.4	24.8	35.4	31.7
05 033	Crawford	6.2	4.3	23,333	76.3	57.5	5.9	12.9	23.7	21.3	38.4	36.2
05 035	Crittenden	2.1	1.7	18,302	70.6	39.2	5.2	26.2	29.4	26.4	38.2	31.8
05 045	Faulkner	3.9	2.9	43,040	67.2	51.2	4.4	11.5	32.8	24.5	35.1	25.7
05 051	Garland	5.0	3.6	38,910	64.9	48.7	4.6	11.5	35.1	29.6	27.8	45.9
05 055	Greene	2.3	1.2	16,660	66.8	50.2	5.2	11.4	33.2	27.3	33.4	35.7
05 057	Hempstead	12.1	6.0	8,513	66.9	43.7	4.2	19.0	33.1	30.3	36.3	41.2
05 059	Hot Spring	2.9	1.2	12,291	69.3	51.2	5.9	12.2	30.7	25.2	31.1	40.6
05 063	Independence	6.0	3.9	14,425	67.0	50.0	5.2	11.8	33.0	27.1	30.4	37.4
05 069	Jefferson	1.7	1.2	28,592	63.2	38.6	5.3	19.3	36.8	33.7	31.4	36.5
05 071	Johnson	12.6	8.2	10,051	69.5	52.8	3.8	12.9	30.5	26.7	34.1	35.7
05 083	Logan	2.4	1.0	8,442	70.4	52.1	5.7	12.5	29.6	26.8	33.7	42.0
05 085	Lonoke	3.4	1.9	25,274	74.3	56.7	4.7	12.9	25.7	21.9	39.7	30.2
05 091	Miller	2.6	0.8	16,746	65.9	43.0	5.6	17.3	34.1	31.2	34.0	32.1
05 093	Mississippi	3.7	1.8	16,962	71.8	45.6	5.2	21.1	28.2	24.1	39.1	34.1
05 103	Ouachita	1.7	0.9	10,745	68.6	46.7	3.6	18.3	31.4	29.3	32.1	41.2
05 107	Phillips	1.4	0.7	8,396	65.8	33.8	5.7	26.3	34.2	30.8	36.5	41.4
05 111	Poinsett	2.4	0.9	9,056	66.6	47.2	5.6	13.8	33.4	30.3	32.0	40.5
05 113	Polk	6.0	2.9	8,118	68.2	48.3	8.0	11.8	31.8	28.1	27.9	45.8
05 115	Pope	7.1	3.2	22,558	71.5	54.0	5.2	12.4	28.5	25.1	32.2	34.3
05 119	Pulaski	5.9	5.3	154,268	61.4	40.1	4.2	17.1	38.6	33.0	29.0	30.6
05 123	St. Francis	4.2	2.2	9,528	70.1	39.7	5.1	25.2	29.9	26.3	36.7	36.3
05 125	Saline	4.0	2.3	41,717	72.9	57.4	4.6	10.9	27.1	23.3	32.6	36.7
05 131	Sebastian	12.5	9.4	49,165	65.2	47.1	5.4	12.7	34.8	30.2	31.7	32.7
05 139	Union	3.5	2.1	16,706	69.7	49.6	3.8	16.2	30.3	27.2	32.6	36.8
05 143	Washington	15.8	11.4	79,464	63.0	46.6	5.0	11.4	37.0	29.0	34.6	26.0
05 145	White	3.9	2.1	29,702	71.0	55.7	4.2	11.1	29.0	25.8	34.3	35.2
05 149	Yell	19.2	13.1	7,739	70.4	56.5	5.9	8.1	29.6	25.4	31.0	41.2
06 000	**California**	38.0	27.1	12,474,950	68.5	48.8	6.0	13.7	31.5	24.3	36.7	34.3
06 001	Alameda	22.6	30.7	543,175	65.2	47.1	5.2	12.9	34.8	26.7	34.4	32.5
06 005	Amador	12.5	6.2	14,146	66.5	52.6	3.4	10.5	33.5	25.9	22.3	52.4
06 007	Butte	14.5	7.7	84,421	60.6	43.3	5.8	11.6	39.4	29.1	27.2	40.3
06 009	Calaveras	10.6	4.3	18,819	68.7	55.4	4.4	9.0	31.3	25.9	23.4	51.6
06 011	Colusa	55.9	24.0	6,882	74.3	55.0	8.2	11.1	25.7	22.2	40.7	37.7
06 013	Contra Costa	24.6	23.4	374,552	70.4	53.4	5.1	11.9	29.6	23.7	36.7	36.3
06 015	Del Norte	18.2	7.1	9,474	62.9	43.6	6.0	13.3	37.1	31.7	29.7	43.1
06 017	El Dorado	12.2	8.9	67,209	72.0	59.5	3.5	9.0	28.0	22.1	30.8	41.4
06 019	Fresno	50.8	22.3	288,016	73.0	48.1	7.6	17.2	27.0	21.2	43.3	32.7
06 021	Glenn	38.1	16.2	9,577	69.1	50.5	7.3	11.3	30.9	24.5	36.4	38.5
06 023	Humboldt	10.1	5.7	52,621	58.0	41.0	4.7	12.3	42.0	32.5	27.7	35.3
06 025	Imperial	80.9	32.4	47,828	78.4	51.9	6.7	19.8	21.6	18.4	47.6	34.8
06 029	Kern	49.8	20.5	254,255	75.4	50.7	8.1	16.6	24.6	19.8	45.4	30.9
06 031	Kings	51.6	20.2	40,684	78.5	54.3	8.6	15.5	21.5	17.4	49.6	28.1
06 033	Lake	17.6	7.9	26,261	59.8	42.1	5.6	12.1	40.2	30.8	26.6	45.2
06 035	Lassen	17.9	6.1	10,206	65.3	50.7	5.7	8.9	34.7	26.4	30.0	35.2
06 037	Los Angeles	48.0	35.2	3,211,482	67.0	44.3	6.9	15.9	33.0	25.7	36.6	33.2
06 039	Madera	54.5	21.2	41,702	78.4	57.0	6.6	14.7	21.6	17.8	42.2	38.5
06 041	Marin	15.6	19.5	102,286	62.7	50.1	3.5	9.1	37.3	29.9	30.4	42.8
06 045	Mendocino	22.7	12.6	33,791	59.9	43.5	4.5	11.9	40.1	33.2	29.4	42.9
06 047	Merced	55.6	25.5	74,958	77.6	53.7	6.7	17.2	22.4	18.2	47.5	31.4
06 053	Monterey	56.0	30.8	124,727	72.5	52.2	7.3	13.0	27.5	21.5	41.9	35.2
06 055	Napa	32.7	24.2	49,517	68.4	51.7	5.3	11.4	31.6	24.6	33.4	41.5
06 057	Nevada	8.7	5.7	41,707	65.1	51.8	5.0	8.2	34.9	27.0	23.9	47.1
06 059	Orange	33.9	30.6	992,242	71.6	54.1	5.5	12.0	28.4	21.6	37.2	34.6
06 061	Placer	13.1	10.6	132,525	70.0	56.3	3.7	10.0	30.0	23.8	33.0	39.4
06 063	Plumas	8.2	5.2	8,412	59.4	45.6	4.1	9.7	40.6	34.8	21.4	45.5
06 065	Riverside	46.0	21.9	679,014	73.5	53.8	6.1	13.5	26.5	20.6	41.6	36.8
06 067	Sacramento	21.8	19.9	513,594	64.5	43.6	5.9	15.0	35.5	27.9	35.0	32.5
06 069	San Benito	56.9	21.0	16,893	77.6	59.1	5.8	12.7	22.4	18.8	44.6	33.7
06 071	San Bernardino	49.9	21.3	601,327	75.9	51.8	7.4	16.7	24.1	19.3	44.6	31.9
06 073	San Diego	32.4	23.4	1,067,043	66.2	49.0	4.9	12.3	33.8	25.1	34.3	32.7
06 075	San Francisco	15.3	36.1	341,721	45.2	32.8	3.6	8.7	54.8	39.0	18.9	33.0
06 077	San Joaquin	39.3	23.0	214,808	74.1	51.1	7.1	15.9	25.9	20.4	43.7	33.5
06 079	San Luis Obispo	21.1	10.6	100,767	63.9	50.2	4.1	9.6	36.1	26.1	27.3	39.9
06 081	San Mateo	25.4	34.3	257,529	67.2	52.1	4.6	10.5	32.8	26.0	33.5	37.0

Table A-2. Counties — Who: Age, Race/Ethnicity, and Household Structure, 2010–2012—*Continued*

STATE and County code	STATE or County	Total population	Percent change 2010–2012	Population by age (percent) Under 5 years	5 to 17 years	18 to 24 years	25 to 44 years	45 to 64 years	65 years and over	Median age	Race alone or in combination (percent) White	Black	Asian, Hawaiian, cr Pacific Islander	American Indian, Alaska Native, or some other race
	ACS table number:	B01003	Population estimates	B01001	B01001	B01001	B01001	B01001	B01001	B01002	B02008	B02009	B02011 + B02012	B02010 + B02013
	Column number:	1	2	3	4	5	6	7	8	9	10	11	12	13
	California—Cont.													
06 083	Santa Barbara	427,251	1.6	6.5	16.4	15.3	25.2	23.5	13.1	33.5	79.6	2.7	7.1	14.7
06 085	Santa Clara	1,811,955	2.9	6.9	17.0	8.8	30.6	25.4	11.4	36.4	53.9	3.4	36.0	11.4
06 087	Santa Cruz	265,057	1.3	5.7	15.1	14.5	24.9	28.2	11.6	36.9	84.9	1.7	6.5	11.0
06 089	Shasta	177,980	0.7	5.8	16.3	8.9	22.3	29.2	17.5	42.1	91.5	1.9	4.0	7.2
06 093	Siskiyou	44,599	-1.8	5.3	15.1	7.5	20.1	31.7	20.4	47.0	92.4	2.5	3.0	8.5
06 095	Solano	417,261	1.6	6.4	17.6	9.9	26.3	27.9	11.8	37.0	58.8	16.6	20.0	12.3
06 097	Sonoma	488,237	1.4	5.8	15.9	9.5	25.0	29.3	14.5	40.1	83.4	2.4	6.1	12.0
06 099	Stanislaus	518,336	1.2	7.7	20.6	10.6	26.5	23.8	11.0	33.0	81.0	3.8	8.0	12.4
06 101	Sutter	94,951	0.2	7.3	19.9	10.0	25.7	24.1	13.1	34.8	72.1	3.2	18.0	13.6
06 103	Tehama	63,488	-0.4	6.7	18.1	8.4	23.0	27.6	16.3	39.6	92.3	1.2	2.7	8.4
06 107	Tulare	447,704	2.0	9.2	23.0	10.8	26.3	21.0	9.6	29.8	83.2	2.2	4.9	13.8
06 109	Tuolumne	54,621	-2.1	4.1	12.8	8.0	21.5	31.8	21.9	47.9	90.4	2.5	2.3	7.7
06 111	Ventura	830,828	1.3	6.6	18.7	10.0	26.1	26.5	12.1	36.5	79.9	2.5	9.2	12.8
06 113	Yolo	202,473	1.5	6.0	16.3	19.4	25.4	22.6	10.2	30.9	71.4	3.7	17.5	14.3
06 115	Yuba	72,613	0.8	8.3	20.4	10.3	26.4	24.4	10.2	32.2	75.9	4.4	9.4	18.2
08 000	**Colorado**	5,117,453	2.8	6.7	17.4	9.8	28.3	26.5	11.4	36.2	86.9	5.0	4.1	7.7
08 001	Adams	451,455	3.6	8.3	20.1	9.3	30.9	22.9	8.7	32.6	83.5	3.9	4.8	11.6
08 005	Arapahoe	585,388	3.6	6.9	18.4	8.5	29.1	26.5	10.6	35.9	78.5	11.8	6.7	7.8
08 013	Boulder	300,681	3.0	5.4	15.4	15.0	26.8	26.8	10.5	35.7	90.9	1.6	5.4	5.2
08 014	Broomfield	57,198	3.9	6.6	18.8	8.0	30.7	25.5	10.4	36.2	91.1	1.7	7.2	3.8
08 029	Delta	30,561	-1.5	5.2	15.8	6.9	20.1	30.5	21.5	47.2	96.3	1.2	0.8	3.7
08 031	Denver	619,016	5.1	7.3	14.3	9.8	36.0	22.2	10.4	33.7	75.0	11.2	4.6	12.9
08 035	Douglas	292,509	3.9	7.2	22.6	5.8	28.9	27.7	7.8	37.1	93.8	2.0	5.2	2.0
08 037	Eagle	51,896	-0.4	6.9	17.3	8.2	36.0	25.2	6.3	34.6	90.0	1.3	1.1	9.2
08 039	Elbert	23,231	1.3	4.6	20.7	6.7	20.2	37.2	10.5	42.8	98.7	1.0	1.4	1.5
08 041	El Paso	636,034	2.9	7.1	18.6	11.0	27.3	25.7	10.3	33.9	86.2	8.1	5.5	6.3
08 043	Fremont	46,997	-0.2	4.3	12.9	6.7	28.4	29.6	18.0	42.6	87.4	6.7	2.1	6.5
08 045	Garfield	56,370	1.5	7.7	19.1	8.2	30.0	26.0	9.1	35.0	90.0	1.7	1.0	9.4
08 059	Jefferson	539,836	1.9	5.5	16.3	8.4	25.8	30.9	13.1	40.6	93.5	1.7	3.8	3.9
08 067	La Plata	51,940	1.8	5.6	14.5	11.6	26.5	29.6	12.3	38.1	89.2	0.8	1.2	10.8
08 069	Larimer	305,335	3.3	5.7	15.3	14.3	26.0	26.4	12.4	35.6	93.4	1.6	3.1	5.0
08 075	Logan	22,708	-0.6	5.7	13.9	14.5	25.3	25.5	15.0	37.3	93.9	2.5	2.4	4.3
08 077	Mesa	147,268	0.9	6.5	16.7	10.1	24.4	26.8	15.4	37.8	93.6	1.2	1.6	6.9
08 083	Montezuma	25,464	-0.4	6.2	16.7	6.5	22.9	30.5	17.1	43.0	85.6	0.0	0.9	15.5
08 085	Montrose	40,926	-1.1	6.2	17.7	6.7	22.7	28.4	18.4	42.5	95.0	1.1	0.0	5.9
08 087	Morgan	28,400	1.1	7.5	19.9	8.8	24.6	25.1	14.1	36.4	92.7	3.6	0.0	5.5
08 101	Pueblo	160,256	0.8	6.4	17.6	9.5	23.9	27.0	15.6	39.0	83.1	2.5	1.6	17.1
08 107	Routt	23,368	-0.6	5.0	15.3	9.5	28.2	32.9	9.1	39.9	97.6	0.0	0.0	4.0
08 117	Summit	27,982	0.0	5.3	12.2	9.6	36.1	28.2	8.6	36.0	89.9	1.3	1.3	8.1
08 119	Teller	23,385	-0.3	4.4	15.5	5.8	19.8	40.3	14.2	47.9	95.6	1.6	1.4	3.2
08 123	Weld	258,708	3.8	7.7	19.9	10.8	27.4	24.2	10.0	33.4	90.4	1.3	2.1	8.9
09 000	**Connecticut**	3,584,561	0.4	5.5	16.9	9.3	25.0	28.7	14.5	40.2	80.1	11.4	4.6	6.6
09 001	Fairfield	926,739	1.6	6.0	18.4	8.1	25.6	28.2	13.7	39.7	76.8	12.0	5.6	8.0
09 003	Hartford	895,987	0.3	5.6	16.9	8.9	25.4	28.4	14.8	40.1	75.7	14.9	5.1	7.5
09 005	Litchfield	188,731	-1.2	4.6	16.4	7.1	22.0	33.4	16.5	45.0	95.5	1.9	2.1	2.1
09 007	Middlesex	165,876	0.0	4.8	15.8	8.2	23.5	31.7	16.0	43.5	91.2	5.9	3.3	2.0
09 009	New Haven	862,776	0.0	5.5	16.5	10.0	25.5	27.8	14.6	39.4	77.0	14.0	4.3	7.3
09 011	New London	274,118	0.0	5.3	15.9	10.1	24.8	29.3	14.6	40.6	85.4	7.5	5.4	5.9
09 013	Tolland	152,257	-0.8	4.3	15.4	16.6	22.4	28.8	12.4	38.5	92.3	4.6	4.1	1.9
09 015	Windham	118,077	-0.7	5.3	16.6	10.7	25.2	28.9	13.3	39.6	94.6	3.3	1.6	3.2
10 000	**Delaware**	908,351	1.9	6.2	16.4	10.2	25.0	27.4	14.8	39.0	72.3	23.0	3.9	3.6
10 001	Kent	165,306	2.9	6.8	17.7	11.1	24.6	25.9	14.0	36.8	71.8	26.5	3.1	3.0
10 003	New Castle	542,490	1.3	6.1	16.8	11.0	26.6	27.0	12.6	37.1	68.6	25.3	5.1	3.4
10 005	Sussex	200,555	2.8	5.8	14.5	7.3	21.2	29.7	21.6	45.9	82.5	14.0	1.4	4.4
11 000	**District of Columbia**	618,777	4.5	5.8	11.2	13.7	34.9	23.0	11.4	33.7	41.6	51.4	4.6	4.9
11 001	District of Columbia	618,777	4.5	5.8	11.2	13.7	34.9	23.0	11.4	33.7	41.6	51.4	4.6	4.9
12 000	**Florida**	19,081,930	2.5	5.6	15.3	9.3	24.9	27.1	17.7	41.0	78.2	17.1	3.3	3.9
12 001	Alachua	249,440	1.6	5.3	12.4	23.1	25.2	22.9	11.0	30.3	72.3	21.8	6.5	2.5
12 003	Baker	27,067	0.1	6.7	19.1	10.2	26.4	26.1	11.4	35.6	84.9	13.4	2.3	0.0
12 005	Bay	170,351	1.5	6.2	15.6	9.5	25.7	28.1	14.9	39.7	86.1	12.5	3.4	2.7
12 007	Bradford	28,027	-5.3	5.6	13.3	8.8	28.9	27.2	16.1	38.9	77.6	22.6	0.3	1.8
12 009	Brevard	545,202	0.6	4.8	14.6	8.0	21.2	30.5	20.9	45.9	85.8	11.3	3.1	2.6
12 011	Broward	1,784,340	3.5	5.8	16.1	8.6	27.1	27.9	14.4	39.8	65.6	28.4	4.4	4.4
12 015	Charlotte	160,602	1.6	3.3	10.6	5.6	15.6	29.6	35.3	56.5	92.5	6.3	1.6	1.1
12 017	Citrus	140,174	-1.4	3.7	11.8	5.7	15.7	30.4	32.7	54.6	94.7	3.3	1.7	1.5
12 019	Clay	192,689	1.5	5.8	19.7	8.8	25.3	27.9	12.3	38.9	85.0	11.1	4.4	2.9
12 021	Collier	327,537	3.0	5.2	14.0	6.9	20.8	25.7	27.3	47.6	88.3	7.2	1.5	4.5
12 023	Columbia	67,666	0.5	5.9	16.3	9.8	24.4	27.9	15.8	39.8	79.5	18.8	1.3	2.9
12 027	DeSoto	34,725	-0.5	6.4	16.0	11.5	23.2	24.6	18.3	39.0	83.5	13.1	0.7	4.2
12 031	Duval	872,307	1.6	6.9	16.4	10.4	28.4	26.4	11.5	35.8	64.5	30.9	5.6	2.3
12 033	Escambia	300,150	1.5	6.2	15.1	13.0	24.2	26.8	14.7	37.6	73.3	24.1	4.3	3.0

STATE and County code	STATE or County	Percent Hispanic or Latino	Percent foreign born	Total households	Household type (percent)							Percent of households with people under 18 years	Percent of households with people 60 years and over
					Family households				Nonfamily households				
					Total family households	Married-couple families	Male household families	Female household families	Total nonfamily households	One-person households		
	ACS table number:	B03003	C05003	B11001	B11001	B11001	B11001	B11001	B11001	B11001	B11005	B11006
	Column number:	14	15	16	17	18	19	20	21	22	23	24
	California—Cont.											
06 083	Santa Barbara	43.4	23.5	141,196	65.3	49.0	5.0	11.4	34.7	25.0	33.3	36.3
06 085	Santa Clara..................	26.9	37.0	607,217	71.4	55.5	5.1	10.7	28.6	21.8	38.6	32.1
06 087	Santa Cruz..................	32.4	18.3	92,834	62.7	46.4	5.3	11.1	37.3	26.5	31.4	36.3
06 089	Shasta.....................	8.6	4.7	68,408	65.9	49.1	4.7	12.1	34.1	27.6	28.7	43.3
06 093	Siskiyou	10.7	5.5	19,500	62.2	47.5	4.9	9.7	37.8	30.5	25.4	46.5
06 095	Solano	24.4	20.2	140,669	71.3	50.5	5.8	15.0	28.7	22.8	36.6	35.7
06 097	Sonoma.....................	25.2	16.4	183,773	63.3	47.6	5.4	10.3	36.7	28.0	30.5	39.3
06 099	Stanislaus...................	42.5	20.4	166,948	74.6	52.1	6.9	15.5	25.4	20.5	43.0	32.9
06 101	Sutter	29.1	22.9	31,620	72.2	53.7	5.5	13.0	27.8	22.6	39.1	38.7
06 103	Tehama	22.4	8.6	23,441	68.0	50.4	4.8	12.8	32.0	26.1	34.7	41.2
06 107	Tulare......................	61.3	22.9	131,426	78.0	53.4	8.5	16.1	22.0	17.6	49.4	32.1
06 109	Tuolumne	10.9	5.1	21,733	65.8	50.0	4.9	10.8	34.2	30.1	21.7	51.6
06 111	Ventura	40.8	22.8	266,414	73.3	55.2	5.6	12.5	26.7	20.8	38.7	36.6
06 113	Yolo.......................	30.7	21.1	70,114	62.6	46.9	4.7	11.0	37.4	24.3	33.3	30.1
06 115	Yuba.......................	25.7	12.3	24,060	73.0	50.4	8.2	14.4	27.0	20.2	42.1	32.4
08 000	**Colorado**	20.9	9.7	1,977,737	64.0	49.1	4.6	10.3	36.0	28.4	32.3	30.1
08 001	Adams......................	38.3	15.1	152,332	70.7	50.9	6.3	13.4	29.3	23.3	41.1	26.2
08 005	Arapahoe...................	18.6	15.3	225,471	65.5	47.8	5.3	12.4	34.5	28.9	34.6	28.5
08 013	Boulder	13.5	10.5	120,203	59.2	47.1	3.8	8.3	40.8	28.2	29.4	27.1
08 014	Broomfield	11.7	8.1	21,553	67.6	54.7	4.2	8.7	32.4	26.2	34.8	26.6
08 029	Delta	14.2	3.3	12,424	65.8	52.1	4.4	9.4	34.2	29.4	24.1	49.0
08 031	Denver	31.7	16.0	266,248	47.9	32.8	4.4	10.8	52.1	40.4	25.1	26.1
08 035	Douglas	7.7	6.7	103,574	77.4	65.7	4.0	7.8	22.6	17.5	44.7	23.6
08 037	Eagle	30.2	19.2	18,390	63.4	51.0	4.4	8.0	36.6	25.3	34.1	18.2
08 039	Elbert......................	5.7	3.5	8,180	75.6	68.0	3.1	4.4	24.4	19.8	33.6	32.1
08 041	El Paso.....................	15.4	7.4	237,258	68.0	52.5	3.9	11.5	32.0	26.4	35.4	28.6
08 043	Fremont....................	12.6	4.7	16,909	63.8	52.3	2.7	8.9	36.2	30.3	27.0	47.1
08 045	Garfield	28.4	14.4	20,188	69.4	55.3	4.6	9.5	30.6	23.8	37.5	28.7
08 059	Jefferson...................	14.6	6.2	218,728	65.6	50.7	4.7	10.3	34.4	27.5	30.2	33.4
08 067	La Plata....................	12.0	2.8	20,956	60.3	48.8	3.5	8.0	39.7	29.5	27.0	33.0
08 069	Larimer	10.7	5.0	121,183	63.5	51.2	3.9	8.4	36.5	25.3	29.3	30.8
08 075	Logan	15.9	7.5	7,845	67.2	52.8	3.7	10.8	32.8	29.1	28.8	36.8
08 077	Mesa	13.5	4.0	58,652	65.5	50.8	5.4	9.3	34.5	27.9	29.5	37.1
08 083	Montezuma.................	11.5	2.2	11,040	67.6	51.0	5.6	11.0	32.4	27.3	28.1	38.8
08 085	Montrose...................	19.9	7.0	16,977	69.6	56.6	4.5	8.5	30.4	25.2	30.3	42.0
08 087	Morgan	34.1	13.7	10,467	70.8	51.2	5.9	13.7	29.2	25.1	35.8	34.5
08 101	Pueblo.....................	41.8	3.7	62,260	62.4	44.0	5.3	13.1	37.6	31.3	30.2	38.3
08 107	Routt......................	6.8	2.6	9,705	67.3	53.1	5.0	9.3	32.7	25.5	32.8	28.3
08 117	Summit.....................	14.2	11.8	12,103	54.2	45.7	3.7	4.9	45.8	28.1	23.4	23.0
08 119	Teller......................	5.6	2.5	9,493	70.3	58.9	3.7	7.6	29.7	25.7	26.4	41.0
08 123	Weld.......................	28.4	8.5	90,830	71.6	56.5	5.2	9.9	28.4	22.1	38.7	28.5
09 000	**Connecticut**.................	13.8	13.6	1,355,973	66.2	48.8	4.3	13.1	33.8	28.1	32.4	36.4
09 001	Fairfield....................	17.4	20.1	331,766	68.7	52.8	3.9	12.0	31.3	26.5	35.1	35.8
09 003	Hartford....................	15.8	14.8	348,446	64.9	45.1	4.6	15.2	35.1	29.2	32.3	36.1
09 005	Litchfield	4.7	7.0	75,801	67.1	53.7	3.8	9.5	32.9	27.7	29.1	39.1
09 007	Middlesex	5.0	7.4	65,962	66.9	53.3	4.3	9.3	33.1	27.0	29.6	38.6
09 009	New Haven	15.5	11.9	328,434	64.8	45.3	4.4	15.1	35.2	29.2	31.8	36.7
09 011	New London................	8.9	8.6	106,959	64.4	48.2	4.9	11.3	35.6	29.1	30.3	37.0
09 013	Tolland	4.5	6.9	54,537	68.5	55.7	3.9	8.9	31.5	24.9	33.0	34.1
09 015	Windham	9.9	4.7	44,068	67.3	50.9	4.8	11.6	32.7	26.0	31.6	34.8
10 000	**Delaware**	8.4	8.3	334,228	67.1	48.5	4.9	13.7	32.9	26.4	32.0	37.6
10 001	Kent	6.1	4.5	57,023	69.0	49.7	5.2	14.1	31.0	25.0	34.4	37.2
10 003	New Castle	8.9	10.0	201,107	66.4	47.5	4.6	14.3	33.6	26.7	33.9	33.1
10 005	Sussex......................	8.9	6.8	76,098	67.4	50.2	5.4	11.8	32.6	26.7	25.4	50.0
11 000	**District of Columbia**	9.5	13.8	261,567	41.0	21.9	3.6	15.5	59.0	46.9	19.6	29.0
11 001	District of Columbia	9.5	13.8	261,567	41.0	21.9	3.6	15.5	59.0	46.9	19.6	29.0
12 000	**Florida**......................	22.9	19.5	7,120,273	64.3	46.5	4.5	13.3	35.7	29.1	28.4	41.7
12 001	Alachua....................	8.6	10.8	94,455	53.9	38.2	3.5	12.3	46.1	32.2	24.0	29.3
12 003	Baker......................	2.1	2.1	8,596	74.7	56.0	4.4	14.3	25.3	20.6	40.2	34.2
12 005	Bay	5.0	5.2	68,622	63.3	46.7	4.4	12.2	36.7	29.4	27.7	35.7
12 007	Bradford	3.7	2.3	8,828	70.8	48.8	4.5	17.4	29.2	25.1	33.9	43.5
12 009	Brevard	8.4	9.1	219,293	64.0	48.2	4.1	11.6	35.0	29.8	25.2	45.5
12 011	Broward.....................	25.8	31.7	664,337	62.4	42.2	4.8	15.4	37.6	30.7	31.9	37.0
12 015	Charlotte	6.1	10.0	70,035	65.4	53.1	3.9	8.3	34.6	29.3	18.2	63.6
12 017	Citrus	4.8	4.8	59,783	61.9	50.2	3.8	7.9	33.1	31.4	17.8	62.0
12 019	Clay.......................	8.0	5.7	66,626	75.4	57.9	3.9	13.6	24.6	19.1	38.3	32.7
12 021	Collier.....................	26.1	23.1	121,788	66.5	53.9	3.3	9.3	33.5	28.6	22.0	57.0
12 023	Columbia...................	5.0	3.6	23,472	63.5	43.9	4.8	14.8	35.5	31.6	28.8	41.9
12 027	DeSoto	30.1	18.2	10,595	68.3	45.8	5.9	16.6	31.7	26.2	31.1	47.9
12 031	Duval	7.9	9.4	329,194	62.8	42.6	4.5	15.7	37.2	30.7	30.9	31.0
12 033	Escambia	4.9	5.8	110,981	62.0	42.7	4.3	15.0	33.0	31.4	28.1	38.0

Table A-2. Counties — Who: Age, Race/Ethnicity, and Household Structure, 2010–2012—*Continued*

STATE and County code	STATE or County	Total population	Percent change 2010–2012	Population by age (percent)						Median age	Race alone or in combination (percent)			
				Under 5 years	5 to 17 years	18 to 24 years	25 to 44 years	45 to 64 years	65 years and over		White	Black	Asian, Hawaiian, or Pacific Islander	American Indian, Alaska Native, or some other race
	ACS table number:	B01003	Population estimates	B01001	B01001	B01001	B01001	B01001	B01001	B01002	B02008	B02009	B02011 + B02012	B02010 + B02013
	Column number:	1	2	3	4	5	6	7	8	9	10	11	12	13
	Florida—Cont.													
12 035	Flagler	97,229	2.4	4.7	14.6	6.7	20.0	28.3	25.7	48.4	82.5	12.4	2.7	4.5
12 039	Gadsden	47,177	-2.6	6.7	16.5	8.3	25.9	28.8	13.8	39.0	38.0	56.3	0.4	6.9
12 049	Hardee	27,158	0.9	7.8	19.6	11.2	25.9	22.1	13.5	33.8	83.5	8.1	1.6	8.3
12 051	Hendry	38,387	-4.0	8.0	20.0	11.2	26.8	22.4	11.6	33.1	69.9	14.1	0.6	17.2
12 053	Hernando	173,178	0.2	4.6	14.9	6.9	19.6	27.7	26.2	48.0	91.4	5.9	1.7	3.0
12 055	Highlands	98,382	-0.6	5.0	13.3	6.5	17.7	25.0	32.5	51.7	86.3	10.0	2.1	3.3
12 057	Hillsborough	1,260,333	3.6	6.5	17.0	10.3	28.2	25.9	12.0	36.3	74.8	18.1	4.5	5.6
12 061	Indian River	139,241	1.7	4.6	14.0	6.6	18.8	28.0	28.1	49.5	88.9	9.6	1.6	1.6
12 063	Jackson	49,203	-1.2	5.0	14.4	9.2	27.4	27.9	16.1	40.4	70.6	27.8	0.8	4.0
12 069	Lake	300,270	1.8	5.3	15.2	7.0	21.3	26.5	24.7	45.9	85.5	10.7	2.5	3.8
12 071	Lee	632,499	4.0	5.2	14.1	7.6	21.7	27.0	24.3	46.0	85.4	9.0	2.0	5.3
12 073	Leon	279,378	2.8	5.4	13.7	23.0	25.3	22.8	9.8	29.9	64.6	31.7	3.8	2.4
12 075	Levy	40,339	-1.7	5.4	15.3	7.4	20.5	31.7	19.7	46.1	88.6	10.3	0.8	2.4
12 081	Manatee	328,231	3.2	5.5	14.8	7.1	21.3	27.4	23.9	45.9	84.7	9.7	2.3	5.1
12 083	Marion	333,001	1.1	5.1	14.0	7.3	20.2	27.1	26.3	47.7	82.8	13.4	2.1	3.7
12 085	Martin	147,536	1.6	4.2	13.2	6.4	19.0	29.4	27.8	50.1	88.0	6.3	1.4	5.9
12 086	Miami-Dade	2,553,696	3.5	5.9	15.5	9.9	28.4	26.0	14.3	38.5	76.2	19.5	2.0	3.7
12 087	Monroe	74,007	2.2	4.7	10.4	7.0	24.8	35.2	17.9	47.0	91.2	6.6	1.5	1.9
12 089	Nassau	74,096	1.5	5.2	16.0	8.0	23.1	30.5	17.2	43.3	92.1	6.9	1.2	1.3
12 091	Okaloosa	184,699	5.2	6.6	15.6	10.2	26.3	27.2	14.0	37.5	84.1	11.1	5.4	5.0
12 093	Okeechobee	39,676	-1.4	6.2	17.8	9.1	24.1	25.6	17.2	39.5	85.1	10.0	0.0	5.4
12 095	Orange	1,174,032	4.6	6.4	16.9	12.5	29.9	24.3	9.9	34.0	67.8	22.2	6.1	7.1
12 097	Osceola	278,254	6.6	6.5	19.3	10.1	27.6	24.9	11.5	35.7	78.6	13.0	4.0	8.5
12 099	Palm Beach	1,339,372	2.5	5.3	14.9	8.1	23.4	26.5	21.8	43.6	77.7	18.4	3.1	2.8
12 101	Pasco	467,486	1.1	5.4	15.5	7.1	23.3	27.5	21.2	44.0	91.6	5.4	2.9	2.6
12 103	Pinellas	918,385	0.5	4.6	12.9	7.4	22.8	30.7	21.6	46.6	85.3	11.3	3.8	1.8
12 105	Polk	609,775	2.1	6.3	16.9	9.0	23.9	25.5	18.3	40.1	80.6	15.9	2.2	3.4
12 107	Putnam	73,858	-1.4	6.2	16.2	8.1	21.0	29.0	19.5	43.7	78.9	17.5	1.0	4.8
12 109	St. Johns	196,491	5.7	5.1	17.5	7.9	23.0	30.2	16.3	42.4	91.5	6.2	3.0	1.5
12 111	St. Lucie	281,245	1.8	5.7	16.2	7.7	23.0	26.8	20.7	42.8	75.4	20.6	2.3	5.1
12 113	Santa Rosa	155,782	3.6	5.9	17.4	8.7	26.1	28.9	13.0	39.5	90.4	7.1	3.5	3.1
12 115	Sarasota	382,652	1.6	3.8	11.7	6.0	18.0	28.8	31.8	53.1	92.5	5.4	1.8	1.9
12 117	Seminole	426,864	1.8	5.3	17.1	10.0	26.8	28.2	12.6	38.7	82.9	12.2	5.1	2.5
12 119	Sumter	98,042	7.8	2.2	6.4	3.7	14.0	27.2	46.4	63.7	88.8	9.5	1.0	1.7
12 121	Suwannee	43,133	3.2	6.0	15.9	8.1	24.1	27.6	18.4	42.1	84.6	13.9	0.9	3.0
12 123	Taylor	22,655	0.8	5.7	13.7	8.5	27.1	28.9	16.1	41.1	76.2	22.8	0.0	1.3
12 127	Volusia	495,284	0.5	4.9	13.7	9.1	21.4	29.3	21.6	45.7	83.0	11.5	2.1	5.6
12 129	Wakulla	30,868	-0.1	5.7	16.1	9.4	28.2	29.6	11.0	39.3	83.8	15.3	0.8	1.8
12 131	Walton	56,216	4.1	5.8	14.2	7.8	24.3	30.9	17.1	43.5	89.0	6.5	1.6	5.0
12 133	Washington	24,754	0.5	5.9	15.1	8.2	27.3	27.7	15.9	40.6	82.8	16.5	0.5	4.1
13 000	**Georgia**	9,815,725	2.1	6.9	18.4	10.2	27.9	25.5	11.0	35.6	62.2	31.8	4.0	4.2
13 009	Baldwin	45,649	1.7	5.9	14.4	19.6	22.5	25.2	12.5	34.0	55.8	41.8	1.7	1.3
13 013	Barrow	69,923	0.6	7.9	19.9	8.0	30.2	24.4	9.6	34.1	82.1	13.2	3.7	3.1
13 015	Bartow	100,380	0.5	6.8	19.4	8.8	27.9	26.0	11.2	36.6	85.2	11.5	1.1	4.4
13 021	Bibb	156,088	0.5	7.4	18.2	10.5	25.3	25.7	12.8	35.4	45.3	52.7	2.6	1.6
13 029	Bryan	31,306	5.9	6.7	22.2	7.5	28.4	26.3	8.8	35.7	82.9	16.8	2.4	0.7
13 031	Bulloch	72,037	2.9	5.6	14.5	28.0	23.1	19.7	9.1	25.7	67.3	29.1	2.0	3.2
13 033	Burke	23,336	-1.0	7.3	20.7	9.5	23.1	27.0	12.3	35.8	47.5	51.3	0.0	1.5
13 035	Butts	23,626	-1.0	5.7	16.0	10.5	28.0	26.9	12.8	38.2	71.0	28.9	0.0	0.2
13 039	Camden	50,813	1.4	7.8	18.4	12.7	27.4	24.2	9.6	31.9	76.9	20.8	3.0	1.7
13 045	Carroll	111,024	0.8	7.0	18.3	12.9	26.7	23.9	11.3	33.8	78.7	19.5	1.2	2.6
13 047	Catoosa	64,661	1.6	6.0	18.7	8.2	26.4	26.4	14.3	38.9	94.8	3.1	1.6	2.2
13 051	Chatham	271,443	3.9	7.0	15.4	13.1	27.9	24.0	12.6	34.0	55.8	40.9	3.1	2.0
13 055	Chattooga	25,829	-1.1	5.8	16.5	7.9	27.4	27.6	14.7	40.5	86.2	12.6	0.6	2.0
13 057	Cherokee	218,189	2.8	7.0	20.0	7.9	28.7	26.6	9.7	36.7	88.6	6.8	2.6	4.6
13 059	Clarke	118,734	2.4	5.9	11.5	30.3	26.8	16.6	8.8	26.0	67.9	27.4	5.0	2.1
13 063	Clayton	262,721	2.3	8.3	20.4	10.8	30.1	23.4	7.1	32.1	23.0	68.0	5.7	6.2
13 067	Cobb	698,168	2.6	6.9	18.4	9.2	30.1	26.2	9.2	35.6	64.5	26.6	5.3	5.7
13 069	Coffee	42,976	1.0	7.1	18.4	10.6	28.5	23.9	11.5	34.9	65.1	27.5	0.0	7.1
13 071	Colquitt	45,878	1.0	8.3	19.3	10.0	26.1	23.2	13.1	34.8	71.6	23.9	0.0	4.7
13 073	Columbia	128,257	5.3	6.6	20.2	8.4	26.9	27.4	10.5	36.8	78.1	16.8	4.9	2.3
13 077	Coweta	129,426	2.4	6.9	19.9	7.9	27.7	26.8	10.7	37.3	79.6	18.5	2.0	1.7
13 081	Crisp	23,559	1.0	7.2	18.5	10.3	22.8	27.0	14.3	37.9	54.9	40.2	4.3	0.8
13 085	Dawson	22,317	0.5	5.3	16.8	8.4	24.2	30.2	15.1	40.7	95.7	0.9	0.8	4.3
13 087	Decatur	27,669	-1.1	6.3	19.0	8.8	24.8	26.7	14.4	38.1	53.2	41.9	0.6	4.6
13 089	DeKalb	699,017	2.1	7.3	16.5	9.9	32.3	24.7	9.3	34.5	36.1	55.3	6.0	4.8
13 091	Dodge	21,495	-1.9	6.3	16.7	10.1	26.2	26.7	14.1	39.5	67.1	32.5	0.4	0.8
13 095	Dougherty	94,634	-0.3	7.5	18.1	12.7	24.8	24.4	12.4	33.6	30.1	68.1	1.2	1.9
13 097	Douglas	133,274	1.0	7.1	20.7	8.8	28.9	25.3	9.1	35.5	55.7	41.6	1.9	3.2
13 103	Effingham	52,790	1.7	6.7	21.5	8.2	27.4	26.3	9.9	35.9	83.4	14.5	1.1	2.0
13 105	Elbert	19,900	-2.2	6.4	16.5	8.8	24.0	27.1	17.3	40.9	65.9	30.6	0.0	3.3
13 107	Emanuel	22,708	1.2	7.2	17.5	9.3	25.9	25.7	14.4	36.8	62.4	33.5	0.0	4.6
13 111	Fannin	23,564	-0.9	4.4	14.3	6.2	19.4	33.1	22.6	49.2	98.4	0.2	0.0	1.5
13 113	Fayette	107,314	0.4	4.2	21.0	7.6	20.7	32.9	13.6	42.9	74.1	21.4	5.0	2.4
13 115	Floyd	96,238	-0.2	6.5	17.5	10.6	25.2	25.7	14.4	38.2	79.9	15.4	1.5	5.2

STATE and County code	STATE or County	Percent Hispanic or Latino	Percent foreign born	Total households	Household type (percent)						Percent of households with people under 18 years	Percent of households with people 60 years and over
					Family households				Nonfamily households			
					Total family households	Married-couple families	Male household families	Female household families	Total nonfamily households	One-person households		
ACS table number:		B03003	C05003	B11001	B11001	B11001	B11001	B11001	B11001	B11001	B11005	B11006
Column number:		14	15	16	17	18	19	20	21	22	23	24
	Florida—Cont.											
12 035	Flagler	9.0	14.8	35,363	70.1	58.1	3.3	8.7	29.9	24.2	21.7	56.0
12 039	Gadsden	10.0	6.0	16,847	66.9	41.5	4.7	20.7	33.1	29.0	32.4	39.6
12 049	Hardee	43.1	20.1	7,687	77.7	54.7	6.8	16.2	22.3	17.4	41.1	41.0
12 051	Hendry	49.4	24.6	10,809	73.1	48.3	8.3	16.4	26.9	22.6	39.5	37.8
12 053	Hernando	10.7	6.2	70,046	67.3	51.5	3.7	12.1	32.7	28.5	24.2	54.1
12 055	Highlands	17.8	9.9	39,466	63.1	50.8	3.3	9.0	36.9	31.9	19.6	61.9
12 057	Hillsborough	25.3	15.7	467,397	63.0	43.8	4.8	14.4	37.0	29.6	32.3	31.4
12 061	Indian River	11.5	10.9	57,183	61.9	48.8	3.6	9.5	38.1	33.1	21.8	55.2
12 063	Jackson	4.5	2.7	15,148	64.0	48.5	4.1	11.4	36.0	32.6	26.5	44.8
12 069	Lake	12.6	7.8	114,640	69.8	56.4	3.6	9.8	30.2	24.8	26.2	51.9
12 071	Lee	18.6	14.9	238,476	65.3	50.6	4.3	10.4	34.7	28.4	24.3	51.2
12 073	Leon	5.9	6.8	109,003	55.1	37.7	4.4	13.0	44.9	30.2	27.1	26.7
12 075	Levy	7.6	2.6	16,180	65.4	48.7	3.4	13.4	34.6	27.8	28.8	46.8
12 081	Manatee	15.1	12.5	131,255	64.2	50.5	3.2	10.4	35.8	29.2	23.1	49.9
12 083	Marion	11.2	8.2	132,975	66.0	50.5	4.1	11.4	34.0	28.0	23.5	54.3
12 085	Martin	12.5	9.8	59,741	62.6	51.5	3.5	7.6	37.4	33.0	22.0	54.3
12 086	Miami-Dade	64.7	51.6	822,746	68.2	43.7	6.3	18.2	31.8	26.1	34.0	38.2
12 087	Monroe	21.1	17.6	28,341	57.2	45.6	5.2	6.4	42.8	31.7	19.4	45.4
12 089	Nassau	3.4	2.6	27,937	74.5	58.4	4.2	11.9	25.5	21.8	29.8	43.4
12 091	Okaloosa	7.4	6.5	72,695	66.2	49.1	4.4	12.7	33.8	27.7	30.9	32.9
12 093	Okeechobee	24.5	11.1	13,413	68.0	48.6	5.9	13.4	32.0	26.0	33.4	40.8
12 095	Orange	27.6	19.1	414,460	64.1	44.0	4.7	15.5	35.9	27.3	32.5	27.3
12 097	Osceola	46.7	19.3	90,945	74.5	51.3	5.7	17.5	25.5	19.9	40.7	34.1
12 099	Palm Beach	19.6	22.5	520,971	61.8	45.6	4.2	12.1	38.2	31.5	26.2	46.8
12 101	Pasco	12.2	9.2	181,324	65.9	51.8	4.2	9.9	34.1	28.3	27.5	47.5
12 103	Pinellas	8.3	11.6	399,785	55.5	40.0	4.0	11.5	44.5	37.2	21.4	45.5
12 105	Polk	18.2	10.3	220,874	69.1	50.3	4.8	13.9	30.9	25.6	31.2	44.1
12 107	Putnam	9.3	4.9	28,634	67.0	46.5	5.4	15.1	33.0	27.6	27.6	47.4
12 109	St. Johns	5.5	6.3	75,762	68.3	55.3	3.4	9.6	31.7	24.6	33.2	38.5
12 111	St. Lucie	16.9	14.9	106,641	68.0	50.0	5.3	12.8	32.0	26.3	28.8	46.0
12 113	Santa Rosa	4.6	3.7	57,180	73.1	58.6	3.7	10.7	26.9	20.6	33.3	34.0
12 115	Sarasota	8.2	11.8	169,819	60.8	48.5	3.5	8.9	39.2	32.7	19.7	57.7
12 117	Seminole	17.7	11.9	145,481	67.8	50.6	3.8	13.4	32.2	26.3	31.4	34.3
12 119	Sumter	5.9	5.9	43,178	69.9	62.3	1.8	5.8	30.1	26.2	9.4	81.3
12 121	Suwannee	8.9	6.0	15,697	70.6	51.8	4.6	14.2	29.4	26.5	33.1	46.5
12 123	Taylor	3.7	2.5	7,776	68.8	46.7	5.6	16.5	31.2	23.9	26.5	41.5
12 127	Volusia	11.5	7.2	193,177	61.7	47.4	4.0	10.4	38.3	31.9	22.8	47.7
12 129	Wakulla	3.4	2.9	10,577	73.7	57.6	3.9	12.2	26.3	23.0	33.2	34.8
12 131	Walton	5.6	4.6	22,138	64.5	50.6	3.9	10.0	35.5	30.9	27.2	40.2
12 133	Washington	3.1	2.7	8,310	64.6	49.1	4.5	11.0	35.4	30.7	27.7	43.6
13 000	**Georgia**	9.0	9.6	3,504,888	68.1	48.0	4.7	15.4	31.9	26.6	35.7	31.2
13 009	Baldwin	2.1	2.6	16,159	60.5	38.9	3.5	18.1	39.5	28.5	27.9	31.4
13 013	Barrow	9.1	6.9	23,190	77.6	57.8	6.3	13.5	22.4	18.3	42.7	29.0
13 015	Bartow	7.8	4.9	34,714	74.4	56.7	5.2	12.4	25.6	20.6	38.1	31.6
13 021	Bibb	3.0	3.6	56,393	64.4	39.1	4.1	21.3	35.6	30.7	32.7	35.3
13 029	Bryan	5.1	4.3	10,956	76.9	59.1	5.7	12.1	23.1	19.1	40.8	29.0
13 031	Bulloch	3.5	4.3	25,786	60.0	40.6	4.5	14.9	40.0	22.9	31.9	25.9
13 033	Burke	2.7	1.4	7,892	68.8	41.2	7.7	19.9	31.2	26.1	33.5	38.1
13 035	Butts	2.7	2.9	7,785	70.3	51.7	4.6	14.0	29.7	26.8	39.0	37.0
13 039	Camden	5.4	2.5	18,998	75.7	57.9	3.6	14.2	24.3	18.1	40.8	28.3
13 045	Carroll	6.3	4.4	39,392	71.9	50.3	5.4	16.2	28.1	22.8	37.7	32.4
13 047	Catoosa	2.4	2.2	23,630	73.0	54.7	6.3	11.9	27.0	23.3	37.0	37.9
13 051	Chatham	5.7	6.8	102,502	60.0	39.6	4.1	16.2	40.0	32.6	29.4	32.7
13 055	Chattooga	4.3	3.0	9,510	69.4	47.3	7.6	14.4	30.6	26.5	32.7	39.6
13 057	Cherokee	9.8	8.9	76,576	76.7	60.4	4.8	11.4	23.3	19.5	41.0	28.7
13 059	Clarke	10.6	10.3	40,529	51.6	34.3	3.4	13.9	48.4	32.7	25.7	24.8
13 063	Clayton	13.5	15.5	85,801	63.5	34.3	6.8	22.4	36.5	31.5	38.0	24.1
13 067	Cobb	12.5	15.1	260,646	67.6	50.2	4.5	12.9	32.4	25.5	36.3	26.4
13 069	Coffee	10.4	5.5	14,748	71.5	48.9	6.2	16.4	28.5	24.7	35.9	33.8
13 071	Colquitt	17.5	10.0	15,874	71.1	50.5	4.4	16.2	28.9	26.4	38.7	36.1
13 073	Columbia	5.3	7.2	45,271	76.5	59.4	4.4	12.8	23.5	19.7	39.9	30.8
13 077	Coweta	6.8	6.1	46,706	71.9	56.3	4.0	11.6	28.1	23.3	36.2	31.8
13 081	Crisp	3.3	3.6	8,792	70.3	41.5	4.8	24.0	29.7	26.1	36.4	39.4
13 085	Dawson	3.9	3.9	8,138	79.2	62.6	7.2	9.4	20.8	17.2	32.7	41.2
13 087	Decatur	5.3	2.9	10,458	68.0	42.4	4.7	20.9	32.0	29.6	31.7	37.0
13 089	DeKalb	9.7	16.6	260,968	58.7	36.2	5.0	17.4	41.3	34.3	31.1	26.4
13 091	Dodge	1.3	1.9	8,097	68.1	44.2	5.5	18.4	31.9	29.3	37.3	36.6
13 095	Dougherty	2.4	2.0	36,084	63.0	33.4	4.9	24.8	37.0	31.9	32.0	34.3
13 097	Douglas	8.6	7.7	46,335	74.8	51.6	5.8	17.3	25.2	21.4	41.9	28.6
13 103	Effingham	3.0	2.1	17,871	76.6	59.2	6.2	11.3	23.4	20.1	43.8	31.4
13 105	Elbert	5.1	2.5	7,784	71.2	46.4	5.8	19.0	28.8	24.9	33.1	43.5
13 107	Emanuel	4.3	1.2	7,863	69.9	44.9	7.1	17.9	30.1	27.0	36.7	39.3
13 111	Fannin	1.9	0.5	9,683	69.9	57.2	2.2	10.5	30.1	26.1	23.2	53.7
13 113	Fayette	6.5	8.8	37,817	79.1	65.4	3.9	9.8	20.9	19.0	37.9	37.8
13 115	Floyd	9.6	6.4	34,961	66.7	50.4	4.2	12.1	33.3	27.6	32.8	39.3

STATE and County code	STATE or County	Total population	Percent change 2010–2012	Under 5 years	5 to 17 years	18 to 24 years	25 to 44 years	45 to 64 years	65 years and over	Median age	White	Black	Asian, Hawaiian, or Pacific Islander	American Indian, Alaska Native, or some other race
	ACS table number:	B01003	Population estimates	B01001	B01001	B01001	B01001	B01001	B01001	B01002	B02008	B02009	B02011 + B02012	B02010 + B02013
	Column number:	1	2	3	4	5	6	7	8	9	10	11	12	13
	Georgia—Cont.													
13 117	Forsyth	182,395	6.3	7.3	22.7	6.3	28.4	25.6	9.8	37.0	87.6	3.2	7.4	3.5
13 119	Franklin	21,981	-0.9	5.5	16.9	9.4	23.5	27.2	17.5	40.4	87.1	9.2	1.0	4.1
13 121	Fulton	951,157	5.6	6.7	16.9	10.8	31.9	24.4	9.3	34.3	47.2	45.4	6.6	3.0
13 123	Gilmer	28,258	-0.4	5.6	16.1	7.2	21.3	30.7	19.1	44.8	96.2	1.0	0.0	4.0
13 127	Glynn	80,394	1.5	6.6	17.3	8.4	24.6	27.6	15.6	40.3	68.7	27.3	1.6	5.3
13 129	Gordon	55,483	1.0	7.4	19.0	9.2	26.8	25.8	11.8	36.3	87.3	4.5	1.2	8.7
13 131	Grady	25,240	1.5	6.9	18.6	8.1	25.0	26.6	14.8	38.5	63.7	29.8	0.0	8.6
13 135	Gwinnett	825,375	4.2	7.5	21.1	8.7	30.4	25.0	7.3	34.0	54.7	25.5	11.8	11.0
13 137	Habersham	43,231	1.0	6.1	17.4	9.4	25.1	26.4	15.6	38.7	90.1	4.4	2.6	4.1
13 139	Hall	182,791	3.0	7.6	20.0	9.5	27.0	24.1	11.8	34.9	83.8	8.2	2.1	7.7
13 143	Haralson	28,572	-1.3	6.8	18.2	8.7	24.8	27.2	14.2	39.8	93.4	5.9	1.0	1.1
13 145	Harris	32,349	1.3	5.1	18.0	7.3	23.7	32.4	13.4	42.4	81.0	18.2	1.2	1.7
13 147	Hart	25,379	1.3	5.9	16.1	7.5	22.9	28.4	19.2	43.3	77.5	21.3	0.0	1.9
13 151	Henry	207,215	1.8	6.5	21.8	8.8	28.4	25.7	8.8	35.7	57.4	38.6	3.9	3.5
13 153	Houston	143,718	3.8	7.1	19.2	9.7	28.0	25.5	10.5	34.6	64.3	30.1	3.7	5.0
13 157	Jackson	60,623	-0.3	7.0	19.4	8.5	26.8	26.3	12.1	37.4	89.4	7.4	2.4	2.1
13 169	Jones	28,642	-0.2	6.3	19.2	8.0	26.2	27.0	13.4	38.4	73.0	26.1	0.9	0.0
13 175	Laurens	48,176	-0.8	6.9	18.4	8.5	24.9	26.3	14.9	38.0	62.3	36.7	1.3	0.7
13 177	Lee	28,602	1.1	6.3	20.7	7.9	28.5	27.2	9.3	36.8	77.6	20.1	2.5	0.0
13 179	Liberty	64,540	4.3	10.5	19.2	14.6	29.4	20.0	6.3	27.9	51.3	43.5	4.0	6.0
13 185	Lowndes	112,050	4.4	7.4	16.8	18.4	25.6	22.0	9.8	29.7	59.2	37.8	2.3	3.4
13 187	Lumpkin	30,450	1.0	5.4	15.0	16.4	22.4	27.4	13.4	36.2	95.8	2.6	0.8	2.1
13 189	McDuffie	21,729	-0.9	7.2	18.7	9.6	23.3	27.1	14.2	38.3	58.0	41.9	0.0	0.3
13 195	Madison	28,038	-1.0	6.7	17.2	8.0	25.1	28.8	14.2	38.8	88.4	9.2	0.9	2.6
13 199	Meriwether	21,583	-2.6	6.6	16.7	8.9	21.8	29.6	16.5	42.6	59.0	40.3	0.0	1.0
13 205	Mitchell	23,373	-1.6	7.0	17.6	8.4	27.0	26.5	13.6	36.8	49.7	49.1	0.0	2.4
13 207	Monroe	26,559	0.9	5.6	16.5	8.9	23.4	31.0	14.6	40.9	73.7	24.3	1.3	1.3
13 213	Murray	39,472	-0.4	6.8	19.5	8.7	28.5	25.2	11.3	36.4	95.9	1.9	0.5	3.2
13 215	Muscogee	194,276	4.2	7.5	17.9	12.5	26.7	24.0	11.5	33.2	49.3	47.5	3.5	4.0
13 217	Newton	100,833	1.4	7.3	20.9	9.1	27.6	24.8	10.4	35.2	55.9	42.9	1.3	1.7
13 219	Oconee	33,330	1.7	6.1	21.4	7.2	24.2	29.3	11.8	39.0	90.0	6.7	3.9	1.0
13 223	Paulding	143,802	1.4	7.5	22.0	8.3	30.4	24.0	7.8	34.6	80.8	18.1	1.3	1.3
13 225	Peach	27,652	-0.5	6.3	16.1	18.0	21.7	26.3	11.4	35.1	48.2	47.2	1.0	4.8
13 227	Pickens	29,384	-0.6	5.4	16.1	7.6	23.1	30.1	17.6	42.9	95.9	2.0	2.0	1.1
13 233	Polk	41,319	-0.8	7.0	19.4	9.2	25.3	25.9	13.2	36.9	80.0	13.6	0.9	6.3
13 237	Putnam	21,222	0.0	5.3	16.5	6.3	22.8	30.1	19.0	44.0	73.0	27.7	0.0	0.0
13 245	Richmond	201,592	0.8	7.4	17.0	12.4	26.9	24.6	11.7	33.3	41.6	56.5	2.8	2.3
13 247	Rockdale	85,619	0.5	6.6	19.7	9.4	25.1	27.9	11.2	37.5	46.9	48.1	2.4	4.0
13 255	Spalding	64,036	-0.4	7.1	18.0	9.2	25.8	26.0	13.9	37.4	64.6	33.8	1.1	2.0
13 257	Stephens	25,980	-1.1	5.0	17.4	11.0	22.1	27.9	16.6	40.5	85.9	13.8	0.6	1.1
13 261	Sumter	32,130	-3.6	7.0	18.7	12.5	23.7	24.8	13.2	34.4	45.1	52.4	1.4	2.8
13 267	Tattnall	25,415	-0.5	6.4	15.0	10.9	31.3	24.7	11.7	35.8	65.0	29.6	0.0	7.4
13 275	Thomas	44,753	-0.2	6.4	18.3	8.3	23.8	27.7	15.4	39.2	59.4	38.0	1.1	2.2
13 277	Tift	40,865	2.1	6.7	18.5	12.6	24.9	24.2	13.1	34.1	62.8	30.8	1.5	5.8
13 279	Toombs	27,309	0.0	8.1	19.8	8.8	24.5	24.8	14.0	35.7	72.9	26.9	0.0	2.9
13 285	Troup	67,816	1.9	7.0	19.2	10.0	24.8	26.2	12.7	36.4	63.2	34.7	2.0	2.0
13 291	Union	21,366	0.7	3.7	14.2	5.9	17.9	30.5	27.8	51.2	97.3	0.7	1.5	0.0
13 293	Upson	26,875	-1.5	6.0	17.0	9.0	22.8	28.9	16.3	42.1	71.5	29.0	0.0	0.0
13 295	Walker	68,533	-1.2	5.9	17.4	7.8	25.3	28.3	15.3	40.1	93.6	5.1	0.6	2.1
13 297	Walton	84,299	0.6	6.5	20.0	8.1	26.2	26.8	12.5	37.8	81.0	16.5	1.5	3.4
13 299	Ware	36,149	-1.7	7.0	16.6	10.0	24.8	26.3	15.3	38.6	67.0	30.7	1.0	1.7
13 303	Washington	21,006	-1.1	6.5	17.2	9.1	24.5	28.7	14.0	39.5	46.8	53.1	0.3	0.3
13 305	Wayne	30,243	0.7	6.7	18.0	7.7	28.0	26.2	13.4	37.3	75.1	22.2	0.0	3.2
13 311	White	27,377	1.3	5.2	16.3	8.4	23.1	28.6	18.4	43.0	95.6	3.1	0.0	1.0
13 313	Whitfield	103,068	0.5	7.7	20.3	9.6	27.1	23.9	11.4	34.2	89.7	5.0	1.6	6.4
13 321	Worth	21,743	0.5	6.3	17.7	9.4	23.4	28.4	14.9	39.3	70.9	29.6	0.0	0.0
15 000	**Hawaii**	1,378,239	2.1	6.4	15.6	9.7	26.7	26.9	14.7	38.5	42.4	3.1	83.0	5.0
15 001	Hawaii	187,286	2.0	6.3	16.2	8.5	23.4	30.3	15.3	40.7	54.4	1.6	77.3	8.9
15 003	Honolulu	966,405	2.1	6.4	15.4	10.4	27.4	25.5	14.8	37.6	37.5	3.7	85.4	4.4
15 007	Kauai	67,815	1.8	6.5	15.7	7.2	24.6	30.5	15.5	41.8	49.4	1.2	73.8	3.6
15 009	Maui	156,670	2.1	6.4	16.4	7.5	26.7	29.6	13.4	39.9	55.7	1.7	78.8	4.8
16 000	**Idaho**	1,583,422	1.6	7.4	19.6	9.9	25.4	24.8	12.8	34.9	94.4	1.0	2.2	5.0
16 001	Ada	401,204	4.0	6.9	19.1	9.1	28.8	25.2	10.9	35.1	94.5	1.6	3.9	3.0
16 005	Bannock	83,439	1.0	7.9	19.2	12.6	26.0	22.9	11.3	31.6	92.9	1.2	2.4	5.9
16 011	Bingham	45,686	-0.6	9.2	23.4	8.6	23.8	23.2	11.7	32.2	91.6	0.6	1.0	8.7
16 013	Blaine	21,183	-0.7	6.3	17.4	5.8	25.8	31.9	12.8	41.4	89.2	0.0	1.4	8.7
16 017	Bonner	40,751	-1.1	5.1	16.0	6.0	21.4	33.3	18.2	45.9	97.7	0.4	0.9	2.5
16 019	Bonneville	105,686	1.9	9.2	22.0	8.6	26.0	23.1	11.1	32.1	94.2	1.1	1.7	5.9
16 027	Canyon	191,542	2.4	8.7	22.4	9.4	26.3	21.9	11.3	32.1	94.3	0.9	2.0	6.0
16 031	Cassia	23,152	0.8	8.9	23.6	8.9	23.8	22.5	12.4	31.8	93.5	0.8	0.7	6.7
16 039	Elmore	26,525	-3.2	8.5	19.0	13.0	27.1	21.4	11.0	30.7	89.1	3.3	4.6	8.7

Table A-2. Counties — Who: Age, Race/Ethnicity, and Household Structure, 2010–2012—*Continued*

STATE and County code	STATE or County	Percent Hispanic or Latino	Percent foreign born	Total households	Household type (percent)							Percent of households with people under 18 years	Percent of households with people 60 years and over
					Family households				Nonfamily households				
					Total family households	Married-couple families	Male household families	Female household families	Total nonfamily households	One-person households		
ACS table number:		B03003	C05003	B11001	B11001	B11001	B11001	B11001	B11001	B11001	B11005	B11006
Column number:		14	15	16	17	18	19	20	21	22	23	24
	Georgia—Cont.											
13 117	Forsyth	9.5	13.5	54,017	79.8	70.1	2.1	7.6	20.2	16.8	47.0	28.4
13 119	Franklin	4.1	3.1	8,766	67.5	51.7	3.0	12.8	32.5	28.7	30.2	42.0
13 121	Fulton	7.9	12.7	365,494	55.8	36.6	3.6	15.6	44.2	36.6	30.6	26.2
13 123	Gilmer	10.0	5.6	10,768	69.6	58.8	3.6	7.2	30.4	24.7	25.5	44.6
13 127	Glynn	6.5	5.2	31,392	69.7	48.2	4.5	17.0	30.3	26.6	32.2	40.7
13 129	Gordon	14.3	9.8	19,128	68.6	53.2	3.6	11.8	31.4	26.2	32.7	33.5
13 131	Grady	10.4	5.7	9,614	67.5	50.8	4.3	12.5	32.5	29.1	29.1	38.5
13 135	Gwinnett	20.4	24.5	267,526	76.1	57.2	5.1	13.8	23.9	19.5	44.5	23.4
13 137	Habersham	12.8	8.2	14,317	74.5	58.0	5.8	10.7	25.5	22.1	30.9	43.4
13 139	Hall	26.5	15.4	60,520	75.0	56.8	6.5	11.6	25.0	20.9	39.6	34.2
13 143	Haralson	1.2	1.4	10,711	71.6	52.0	6.2	13.3	28.4	25.6	36.4	38.3
13 145	Harris	2.8	2.3	11,570	79.6	63.8	7.3	8.6	20.4	17.7	32.5	36.6
13 147	Hart	3.3	1.6	10,508	65.5	46.1	5.6	13.8	34.5	30.2	29.1	46.8
13 151	Henry	6.0	7.0	69,233	75.3	53.8	5.1	16.4	24.7	20.9	42.7	25.8
13 153	Houston	6.2	5.7	52,077	70.6	52.2	3.6	14.8	29.4	26.6	39.5	28.7
13 157	Jackson	6.4	3.6	21,146	77.1	59.5	4.8	12.8	22.9	17.9	40.3	34.2
13 169	Jones	0.4	1.5	10,494	74.9	53.6	3.4	18.0	25.1	21.3	35.4	35.4
13 175	Laurens	2.4	2.0	17,667	70.0	46.7	4.5	18.8	30.0	27.3	33.1	39.3
13 177	Lee	2.2	3.7	9,873	77.1	58.4	7.1	11.6	22.9	18.9	39.7	30.1
13 179	Liberty	10.7	5.7	22,967	76.2	53.4	4.4	18.5	23.8	19.8	43.8	19.5
13 185	Lowndes	5.0	3.9	39,481	63.9	42.5	4.3	17.0	36.1	26.4	34.4	28.3
13 187	Lumpkin	4.5	3.4	10,406	68.8	56.5	4.0	8.3	31.2	26.3	28.9	37.6
13 189	McDuffie	2.3	1.2	8,403	74.9	50.2	3.8	20.8	25.1	22.1	33.8	37.4
13 195	Madison	4.2	2.5	9,515	70.3	53.6	5.4	11.3	29.7	26.5	31.4	41.7
13 199	Meriwether	1.7	0.6	7,792	72.0	47.7	5.1	19.2	28.0	27.1	29.3	43.4
13 205	Mitchell	4.4	2.0	8,291	63.5	39.0	3.6	20.8	36.5	32.9	31.8	37.6
13 207	Monroe	2.2	1.8	9,551	72.0	51.5	3.7	16.7	28.0	25.2	27.8	41.3
13 213	Murray	13.4	7.9	13,923	76.4	54.9	7.5	13.9	23.6	20.7	39.2	33.5
13 215	Muscogee	6.8	5.2	71,509	64.6	38.4	4.0	22.2	35.4	31.1	35.1	32.4
13 217	Newton	4.7	6.0	34,208	73.9	49.3	5.8	18.8	26.1	22.2	41.1	29.4
13 219	Oconee	4.5	5.1	11,268	82.0	68.7	3.6	9.8	18.0	15.7	43.9	31.8
13 223	Paulding	5.2	4.3	47,751	81.0	62.8	4.4	13.8	19.0	15.5	46.5	24.9
13 225	Peach	7.0	6.6	9,700	73.1	49.4	3.2	20.5	26.9	21.6	34.6	30.4
13 227	Pickens	0.9	2.7	10,993	77.8	66.2	4.1	7.5	22.2	20.5	31.8	45.1
13 233	Polk	12.3	8.2	14,711	72.4	52.8	7.7	11.9	27.6	25.8	37.1	37.8
13 237	Putnam	6.5	2.1	8,814	75.2	54.0	2.9	18.3	24.8	18.2	33.0	42.6
13 245	R chmond	4.3	3.4	71,826	62.3	35.4	5.5	21.4	37.7	32.6	32.2	31.3
13 247	Rockdale	9.8	10.4	29,104	74.2	49.2	5.4	19.6	25.8	22.6	41.4	33.5
13 255	Spalding	4.0	3.5	22,519	71.2	45.4	5.0	20.8	28.8	25.4	35.2	40.1
13 257	Stephens	1.2	1.7	9,112	70.9	54.4	5.2	11.3	29.1	25.3	29.4	46.0
13 261	Sumter	5.4	3.2	11,384	66.2	40.6	3.7	21.9	33.8	31.5	34.4	34.5
13 267	Tattnall	10.3	5.6	8,090	66.6	46.9	5.7	14.1	33.4	27.5	34.1	34.4
13 275	Thomas	3.1	2.4	17,256	61.9	42.2	3.3	16.4	38.1	34.7	29.1	37.7
13 277	Tift	10.3	4.6	13,492	65.0	44.8	5.8	14.4	35.0	31.4	34.1	34.5
13 279	Toombs	11.3	4.7	10,368	65.2	50.0	4.4	10.8	34.8	32.4	36.7	39.8
13 285	Troup	3.4	4.4	24,738	71.7	46.3	5.3	20.1	28.3	24.0	36.2	34.9
13 291	Union	2.6	2.3	8,926	69.7	60.0	3.7	6.1	30.3	25.7	19.3	56.4
13 293	Upson	2.3	0.9	9,992	70.3	50.9	2.4	17.0	29.7	27.1	30.9	42.7
13 295	Walker	1.7	1.2	26,323	70.6	53.2	5.1	12.3	29.4	25.7	36.0	37.4
13 297	Walton	3.5	4.1	29,261	78.2	59.8	4.7	13.7	21.8	19.3	38.1	33.6
13 299	Ware	3.4	3.3	13,271	64.6	45.9	4.3	14.4	35.4	31.8	34.2	40.6
13 303	Washington	2.0	0.8	6,809	69.1	48.2	3.6	17.4	30.9	28.4	29.1	40.4
13 305	Wayne	5.9	3.6	10,133	72.8	53.8	4.4	14.6	27.2	24.2	37.0	39.3
13 311	White	2.5	1.7	11,402	72.4	60.4	4.8	7.2	27.6	22.3	26.5	38.5
13 313	Whitfield	32.3	17.7	34,409	74.4	55.3	6.1	13.1	25.6	20.4	43.1	31.6
13 321	Worth	1.8	1.5	8,089	69.7	47.4	7.3	15.1	30.3	27.5	35.3	38.5
15 000	**Hawaii**	9.2	18.1	447,566	68.7	50.8	5.4	12.5	31.3	24.2	33.1	41.7
15 001	Hawaii	11.8	11.6	63,897	66.2	46.9	5.8	13.5	33.8	26.5	30.2	44.6
15 003	Honolulu	8.5	19.7	308,906	69.4	51.4	5.5	12.5	30.6	23.9	33.7	41.4
15 007	Kauai	9.7	15.3	22,565	68.9	53.1	4.9	10.9	31.1	22.3	32.3	43.6
15 009	Maui	10.3	17.0	52,158	67.8	50.7	5.0	12.1	32.2	24.4	33.2	39.5
16 000	**Idaho**	11.4	5.9	580,280	69.4	55.5	4.2	9.8	30.6	24.2	34.9	34.0
16 001	Ada	7.3	5.8	151,822	67.8	53.1	5.0	9.6	32.2	25.1	35.1	29.8
16 005	Bannock	7.0	3.0	30,098	65.3	50.4	4.7	10.2	34.7	28.4	32.7	29.5
16 011	Bingham	17.4	7.4	14,885	76.4	63.9	3.8	8.8	23.6	19.3	40.0	32.9
16 013	Blaine	20.2	14.2	9,290	65.3	53.1	3.4	8.8	34.7	27.1	34.7	32.1
16 017	Bonner	2.3	1.7	17,643	64.4	53.9	2.4	8.1	35.6	27.1	27.5	43.9
16 019	Bonneville	11.8	5.5	36,010	75.4	59.8	3.8	11.8	24.6	21.2	41.5	32.4
16 027	Canyon	24.1	8.5	63,130	74.1	56.9	4.0	13.2	25.9	21.3	41.0	31.8
16 031	Cassia	25.4	9.3	7,637	70.3	59.7	3.5	7.1	29.7	26.3	38.5	34.9
16 039	Elmore	15.6	9.2	9,847	69.8	58.6	2.8	8.4	30.2	25.5	38.6	29.2

STATE and County code	STATE or County	Total population	Percent change 2010–2012	Population by age (percent)						Median age	Race alone or in combination (percent)			
				Under 5 years	5 to 17 years	18 to 24 years	25 to 44 years	45 to 64 years	65 years and over		White	Black	Asian, Hawaiian, or Pacific Islander	American Indian, Alaska Native, or some other race
	ACS table number:	B01003	Population estimates	B01001	B01001	B01001	B01001	B01001	B01001	B01002	B02008	B02009	B02011 + B02012	B02010 + B02013
	Column number:	1	2	3	4	5	6	7	8	9	10	11	12	13
	Idaho—Cont.													
16 051	Jefferson	26,412	1.7	10.2	25.4	7.5	25.6	21.3	10.1	30.3	97.2	0.0	0.8	3.1
16 053	Jerome	22,481	0.2	9.5	21.5	9.1	25.3	23.7	11.0	31.1	86.1	0.3	0.0	14.2
16 055	Kootenai	140,793	2.5	6.4	18.0	8.7	24.4	27.5	15.0	39.1	96.7	0.7	1.7	3.1
16 057	Latah	37,788	2.4	5.8	12.8	25.6	23.7	21.6	10.5	28.3	96.2	1.5	3.4	2.6
16 065	Madison	37,623	-0.3	9.4	16.8	34.8	21.8	11.5	5.8	22.7	97.6	0.6	2.2	1.4
16 067	Minidoka	20,089	-0.3	8.2	21.0	9.6	21.6	24.8	14.9	35.3	90.0	0.0	2.4	11.2
16 069	Nez Perce	39,424	0.6	5.8	15.8	9.9	23.3	27.2	17.9	40.7	92.2	0.9	1.2	8.0
16 075	Payette	22,595	0.0	6.8	21.5	8.5	21.8	25.5	15.9	38.1	97.5	0.0	1.5	4.5
16 083	Twin Falls	78,066	1.4	8.0	19.3	9.6	25.1	23.8	14.2	34.7	93.5	1.0	1.5	5.9
17 000	**Illinois**	12,858,490	0.3	6.4	17.6	9.7	27.1	26.2	12.8	36.8	74.3	15.4	5.4	7.1
17 001	Adams	67,169	0.1	6.0	16.6	9.0	23.5	27.2	17.7	40.0	94.3	4.6	1.0	1.7
17 007	Boone	54,114	-0.4	6.8	21.4	8.6	25.0	26.0	12.2	37.2	90.5	3.0	1.9	6.1
17 011	Bureau	34,618	-1.6	5.6	17.1	7.2	22.4	29.2	18.5	42.9	97.3	0.9	1.0	1.7
17 019	Champaign	202,373	0.9	5.7	13.6	23.8	25.6	21.1	10.3	29.1	76.8	13.8	10.2	1.5
17 021	Christian	34,748	-0.5	6.2	16.1	8.0	23.7	28.4	17.6	41.8	97.3	2.0	0.7	1.0
17 027	Clinton	38,011	0.6	5.9	16.4	8.3	26.4	27.9	15.1	40.1	95.9	4.1	0.7	0.6
17 029	Coles	53,782	-0.5	5.0	13.4	23.3	21.1	23.1	14.0	32.0	94.8	4.6	1.4	1.0
17 031	Cook	5,214,942	0.6	6.6	16.9	9.8	29.7	24.9	12.1	35.4	58.4	25.3	7.2	11.3
17 037	DeKalb	104,785	-0.4	6.1	15.8	20.9	25.0	22.1	10.0	29.6	85.2	7.6	2.9	6.6
17 043	DuPage	923,503	1.1	6.1	18.3	8.5	26.4	28.1	12.0	38.4	82.2	5.3	11.3	3.5
17 049	Effingham	34,280	0.4	6.3	18.0	8.4	23.6	28.1	15.6	40.0	98.5	0.4	0.6	1.4
17 051	Fayette	22,105	-0.5	5.6	16.6	9.0	25.5	27.0	16.2	39.8	97.1	2.4	0.0	0.8
17 055	Franklin	39,520	-0.4	6.0	16.8	8.0	23.4	27.4	18.6	41.8	99.1	0.7	0.7	0.9
17 057	Fulton	36,876	-1.1	5.2	15.5	8.2	24.8	28.0	18.3	42.5	97.2	2.7	0.3	2.4
17 063	Grundy	50,160	0.4	7.2	20.0	7.7	28.0	25.6	11.5	36.6	97.1	1.5	1.1	1.6
17 073	Henry	50,288	-0.5	5.9	17.7	8.1	22.0	28.9	17.4	41.7	96.4	2.4	0.7	2.4
17 075	Iroquois	29,451	-1.3	5.6	17.6	7.3	21.4	28.6	19.5	43.4	97.0	1.5	0.6	2.0
17 077	Jackson	60,230	-0.5	5.3	12.4	25.3	24.1	21.3	11.7	29.3	81.7	15.5	4.2	1.7
17 081	Jefferson	38,764	-0.2	6.3	15.6	8.5	24.9	28.3	16.5	40.5	90.3	9.2	1.2	2.1
17 083	Jersey	22,850	-0.9	5.2	17.0	9.5	23.1	29.1	16.2	42.2	98.8	0.5	1.5	0.0
17 085	Jo Daviess	22,639	-0.5	5.2	15.2	6.3	20.0	31.3	22.0	47.3	98.5	0.8	0.6	0.0
17 089	Kane	519,581	1.3	7.5	21.0	8.5	27.6	25.2	10.2	34.9	75.2	6.4	4.1	16.5
17 091	Kankakee	113,361	-0.4	6.6	18.4	10.4	24.8	26.3	13.6	36.9	81.2	16.1	1.4	3.5
17 093	Kendall	116,693	2.5	8.3	22.6	6.9	32.7	22.2	7.4	33.6	85.8	7.0	3.6	6.0
17 095	Knox	52,612	-1.3	5.1	15.3	9.9	23.1	27.9	18.7	41.3	89.2	8.8	1.1	2.3
17 097	Lake	702,666	-0.3	6.5	20.4	9.1	25.2	27.9	10.8	37.0	81.2	7.9	7.5	6.1
17 099	LaSalle	113,423	-0.7	5.7	16.9	8.6	23.5	28.6	16.6	41.4	96.1	3.2	0.4	1.7
17 103	Lee	35,476	-2.5	5.7	15.6	8.7	24.4	29.5	16.0	41.4	93.9	5.6	1.2	1.8
17 105	Livingston	38,796	-0.6	5.6	16.6	8.3	25.0	28.5	15.9	40.4	90.6	7.7	0.9	1.9
17 107	Logan	30,178	-0.8	5.1	14.5	10.6	26.7	26.9	16.1	39.2	82.8	14.2	1.9	2.5
17 109	McDonough	32,539	-0.1	4.4	11.3	29.2	19.3	21.5	14.2	29.7	91.8	5.8	2.5	0.7
17 111	McHenry	308,501	-0.3	6.2	20.5	7.9	25.8	29.0	10.6	38.4	91.8	1.6	3.4	5.1
17 113	McLean	170,964	1.4	6.1	16.2	17.6	25.9	23.6	10.5	32.5	86.6	8.6	5.0	2.1
17 115	Macon	110,491	-0.6	6.4	16.2	9.4	23.2	28.2	16.6	40.3	81.7	18.2	1.5	1.3
17 117	Macoupin	47,613	-1.2	5.6	16.8	8.1	23.2	29.1	17.2	42.3	98.9	0.8	0.6	1.4
17 119	Madison	268,573	-0.5	6.0	16.5	10.0	25.3	27.5	14.7	38.8	90.5	8.9	1.4	1.4
17 121	Marion	39,112	-1.4	6.4	16.8	8.3	22.6	28.4	17.6	41.6	95.2	4.9	0.8	1.5
17 133	Monroe	33,211	1.1	5.6	18.4	7.0	24.4	29.9	14.7	41.4	99.5	0.0	0.9	0.9
17 135	Montgomery	29,829	-1.5	5.4	15.1	8.5	25.0	28.5	17.5	41.9	89.8	9.4	1.0	0.6
17 137	Morgan	35,452	-0.7	5.5	15.8	10.6	23.2	27.8	17.1	40.8	93.6	7.6	0.2	0.7
17 141	Ogle	53,156	-1.1	5.5	18.8	8.4	23.1	28.3	15.9	40.8	97.6	1.6	0.9	1.4
17 143	Peoria	186,755	0.5	6.8	17.2	10.1	25.7	26.0	14.1	36.8	77.4	19.7	3.9	1.6
17 145	Perry	22,208	-1.2	4.9	15.1	9.8	26.4	27.4	16.4	40.6	88.9	8.8	0.7	2.9
17 157	Randolph	33,218	-1.4	4.9	14.7	7.9	26.9	29.0	16.6	41.6	89.0	10.4	0.5	0.7
17 161	Rock Island	147,489	-0.1	6.4	16.0	9.2	24.2	27.7	16.5	40.2	84.5	10.6	2.5	5.7
17 163	St. Clair	269,786	-0.6	6.8	18.3	9.2	26.0	27.0	12.8	37.3	66.9	31.7	2.1	1.7
17 165	Saline	24,942	0.0	6.0	17.1	8.4	22.3	27.6	18.6	42.0	94.7	5.3	0.8	0.8
17 167	Sangamon	198,698	0.7	6.2	17.2	8.5	25.4	28.6	14.1	39.5	85.2	13.3	2.2	1.3
17 173	Shelby	22,266	-0.6	5.6	16.4	7.2	22.1	29.4	19.4	44.3	99.2	0.3	0.0	0.6
17 177	Stephenson	47,355	-1.5	5.7	16.7	7.8	21.7	28.9	19.2	43.8	89.3	11.4	1.1	0.4
17 179	Tazewell	135,685	0.4	6.2	17.1	7.3	25.7	27.9	15.8	40.2	97.7	1.6	1.1	1.3
17 183	Vermilion	81,225	-1.0	6.6	17.7	8.5	23.0	27.8	16.3	40.0	84.5	14.2	0.9	2.2
17 195	Whiteside	58,184	-1.1	5.8	17.3	7.7	22.7	28.7	17.8	42.3	94.8	1.8	0.7	4.6
17 197	Will	680,662	0.5	6.9	21.5	8.4	27.5	25.9	9.7	35.8	78.4	12.1	5.6	6.6
17 199	Williamson	66,590	0.4	6.1	15.7	8.5	25.3	27.6	16.7	40.7	94.1	5.1	1.3	0.8
17 201	Winnebago	293,608	-1.0	6.6	18.0	8.5	25.2	27.4	14.2	38.7	82.3	13.9	3.0	3.5
17 203	Woodford	38,851	0.9	6.5	18.9	8.5	22.6	28.4	15.1	40.5	97.5	1.2	0.8	1.2
18 000	**Indiana**	6,514,516	0.7	6.6	17.9	10.1	25.5	26.6	13.2	37.1	86.6	10.1	2.1	3.4
18 001	Adams	34,383	-0.2	9.4	21.5	8.5	22.5	24.2	13.8	34.3	98.3	0.4	0.7	1.3
18 003	Allen	358,248	1.3	7.4	19.4	9.4	26.0	25.6	12.1	35.5	82.8	13.6	3.4	3.3
18 005	Bartholomew	77,946	2.9	6.7	18.2	8.1	26.6	26.1	14.3	38.1	90.0	2.6	4.6	4.4
18 011	Boone	57,851	3.8	6.8	20.8	6.6	25.2	28.3	12.3	39.0	96.6	1.6	2.2	1.1
18 015	Carroll	20,102	-0.3	5.6	18.4	7.4	23.1	29.1	16.4	41.5	99.5	0.4	0.0	0.0
18 017	Cass	38,780	-0.9	7.0	18.5	7.9	24.5	27.1	15.1	39.2	90.7	2.6	1.3	7.2
18 019	Clark	111,342	1.3	6.7	16.9	8.2	28.0	27.1	13.1	38.1	91.0	8.4	1.1	1.6
18 021	Clay	26,861	-0.1	6.2	17.7	8.4	24.1	28.1	15.6	41.0	99.2	1.1	0.0	1.0

STATE and County code	STATE or County	Percent Hispanic or Latino	Percent foreign born	Total households	Household type (percent)							Percent of households with people under 18 years	Percent of households with people 60 years and over
					Family households				Nonfamily households				
					Total family households	Married-couple families	Male household families	Female household families	Total nonfamily households	One-person households			
	ACS table number:	B03003	C05003	B11001	B11001	B11001	B11001	B11001	B11001	B11001		B11005	B11006
	Column number:	14	15	16	17	18	19	20	21	22		23	24
	Idaho—Cont.												
16 051	Jefferson	10.3	4.5	8,143	83.4	70.6	4.0	8.7	16.6	13.8		47.4	30.1
16 053	Jerome	31.9	16.9	7,856	73.8	59.1	5.0	9.7	26.2	22.2		43.6	30.5
16 055	Kootenai	4.0	2.3	55,713	68.6	54.1	3.8	10.7	31.4	23.0		32.6	37.5
16 057	Latah	3.7	3.8	14,871	54.9	46.6	1.9	6.3	45.1	26.4		25.6	27.1
16 065	Madison	6.1	4.5	9,982	78.6	71.3	1.6	5.7	21.4	11.2		39.1	18.7
16 067	Minidoka	32.6	12.6	6,989	74.3	60.5	4.0	9.8	25.7	22.7		36.3	40.4
16 069	Nez Perce	2.9	1.4	16,050	64.1	50.1	4.6	9.4	35.9	29.0		24.6	39.9
16 075	Payette	15.2	5.0	8,172	70.5	52.5	5.5	12.4	29.5	26.4		34.4	39.5
16 083	Twin Falls	14.1	8.4	28,129	70.6	54.9	4.5	11.3	29.4	22.9		37.6	35.6
17 000	**Illinois**	16.1	13.9	4,759,131	65.7	48.2	4.6	12.9	34.3	28.6		32.9	33.7
17 001	Adams	1.3	1.5	26,517	66.1	52.3	3.1	10.6	33.9	28.7		29.6	38.6
17 007	Boone	20.2	11.5	17,755	79.3	62.5	4.1	12.7	20.7	16.6		41.3	33.2
17 011	Bureau	7.9	4.3	14,181	64.3	52.3	3.2	8.7	35.7	29.7		27.2	41.2
17 019	Champaign	5.4	11.9	79,246	53.5	39.4	3.7	10.5	46.5	33.3		25.1	26.3
17 021	Christian	1.4	1.0	14,333	65.2	47.9	6.2	11.1	34.8	29.0		28.3	40.9
17 027	Clinton	2.8	0.8	14,048	68.4	56.5	2.7	9.1	31.6	26.6		30.8	36.1
17 029	Coles	2.2	1.8	20,932	53.9	39.9	3.1	10.9	46.1	34.3		24.8	32.6
17 031	Cook	24.3	21.2	1,927,303	61.2	40.8	5.0	15.4	38.8	32.1		31.5	32.6
17 037	DeKalb	10.4	6.8	37,386	60.5	46.3	4.3	9.9	39.5	28.4		30.2	28.0
17 043	DuPage	13.6	18.5	334,764	71.2	57.6	3.8	9.8	28.8	24.4		35.3	32.8
17 049	Effingham	1.8	0.8	13,761	68.3	54.4	4.8	9.1	31.7	27.4		33.1	36.3
17 051	Fayette	1.5	1.4	8,156	68.7	55.0	6.0	7.8	31.3	27.5		31.0	35.8
17 055	Franklin	1.3	0.8	16,112	64.8	48.6	4.7	11.6	35.2	30.0		30.4	42.9
17 057	Fulton	2.5	1.7	14,557	65.9	51.8	4.4	9.7	34.1	27.9		28.4	41.8
17 063	Grundy	8.4	3.4	18,051	70.7	54.3	5.0	11.4	29.3	24.7		37.5	31.5
17 073	Henry	5.0	2.6	20,143	68.2	53.0	3.8	11.4	31.8	27.2		29.3	38.8
17 075	Iroquois	5.7	3.2	11,889	67.7	54.1	4.6	9.0	32.3	27.0		29.6	42.4
17 077	Jackson	4.1	5.7	23,189	50.6	36.7	4.0	9.8	49.4	36.1		24.0	28.4
17 081	Jefferson	2.2	1.5	15,185	65.0	50.5	4.6	9.9	35.0	29.9		28.6	38.4
17 083	Jersey	1.0	0.7	8,742	73.9	59.0	4.6	10.3	26.1	22.8		28.6	37.6
17 085	Jo Daviess	2.9	3.3	9,532	66.2	54.3	4.6	7.3	33.8	28.3		26.7	44.1
17 089	Kane	31.0	18.5	169,535	75.9	59.3	4.9	11.7	24.1	19.8		41.0	31.2
17 091	Kankakee	9.1	4.7	41,515	67.9	48.3	4.4	15.2	32.1	26.7		34.9	35.2
17 093	Kendall	15.9	8.8	38,486	79.0	66.3	4.3	8.3	21.0	17.2		47.3	24.0
17 095	Knox	5.0	2.4	21,592	59.9	43.9	3.7	12.3	40.1	34.4		25.5	42.4
17 097	Lake	20.2	18.4	240,273	74.8	59.5	4.1	11.2	25.2	21.4		40.8	32.0
17 099	LaSalle	8.3	2.9	44,023	66.5	51.0	4.4	11.1	33.5	29.1		29.3	38.4
17 103	Lee	5.2	2.0	13,591	68.3	54.3	3.3	10.6	31.7	26.6		30.0	36.8
17 105	Livingston	4.1	1.8	14,351	66.6	51.3	5.9	9.4	33.4	28.8		29.4	38.4
17 107	Logan	3.6	2.4	10,338	64.3	47.3	2.9	14.1	35.7	29.8		24.3	43.3
17 109	McDonough	2.7	3.6	12,697	54.3	41.5	2.6	10.2	45.7	33.2		25.0	34.3
17 111	McHenry	11.7	9.5	108,995	75.4	62.1	4.1	9.2	24.6	19.9		39.4	30.5
17 113	McLean	4.5	6.0	63,314	61.8	48.7	3.6	9.5	38.2	28.1		30.1	27.6
17 115	Macon	1.9	2.2	45,580	61.8	45.2	4.3	12.3	38.2	32.8		28.1	38.4
17 117	Macoupin	0.9	1.0	19,647	69.0	53.6	4.7	10.7	31.0	24.6		32.5	38.0
17 119	Madison	2.8	2.2	107,047	65.8	49.3	4.8	11.7	34.2	27.6		29.8	34.7
17 121	Marion	1.5	0.8	15,748	64.6	47.8	4.0	12.7	35.4	30.3		31.8	41.3
17 133	Monroe	1.4	0.8	12,443	76.2	63.6	4.0	8.6	23.8	20.5		34.1	33.4
17 135	Montgomery	1.6	1.6	10,750	68.7	53.3	3.5	11.9	31.3	27.8		28.4	44.3
17 137	Morgan	2.1	1.6	13,738	63.2	48.2	3.1	11.9	36.8	31.4		28.0	37.6
17 141	Ogle	9.0	4.8	20,812	66.6	54.6	3.6	8.4	33.4	27.3		30.8	37.2
17 143	Peoria	4.0	5.0	76,007	62.5	44.1	4.0	14.4	37.5	31.6		30.4	33.8
17 145	Perry	2.8	2.1	8,030	65.1	51.7	4.8	8.7	34.9	30.8		26.5	40.6
17 157	Randolph	2.6	1.3	12,072	69.6	52.5	4.4	12.7	30.4	27.5		31.2	39.8
17 161	Rock Island	11.8	7.3	60,758	60.9	44.5	3.9	12.5	39.1	34.8		28.7	39.6
17 163	St. Clair	3.4	2.7	101,778	65.5	44.6	4.1	16.9	34.5	30.1		33.5	33.3
17 165	Saline	1.4	1.3	10,170	64.4	47.5	3.8	13.1	35.6	31.5		27.5	42.2
17 167	Sangamon	1.9	3.5	82,927	61.8	43.5	5.6	12.7	38.2	32.1		29.8	34.6
17 173	Shelby	0.9	0.9	8,915	70.7	59.8	3.0	7.9	29.3	25.9		29.0	43.3
17 177	Stephenson	3.0	2.2	19,420	65.1	49.0	4.0	12.0	34.9	30.3		25.4	41.3
17 179	Tazewell	2.0	1.3	54,302	68.4	54.3	3.3	10.8	31.6	27.3		31.4	36.6
17 183	Vermilion	4.4	2.1	31,486	64.0	45.0	4.6	14.4	36.0	31.1		29.3	40.5
17 195	Whiteside	11.3	3.3	22,878	67.9	52.4	4.2	11.3	32.1	28.1		29.5	40.6
17 197	Will	15.9	11.6	222,401	77.1	61.4	5.0	10.7	22.9	19.2		43.7	29.7
17 199	Williamson	2.0	2.1	26,383	66.5	51.4	3.2	11.9	33.5	29.1		30.6	39.3
17 201	Winnebago	11.2	7.6	112,594	66.1	47.1	4.5	14.5	33.9	28.6		32.5	35.5
17 203	Woodford	1.5	1.0	14,276	77.7	66.4	3.2	8.1	22.3	19.5		34.8	34.5
18 000	**Indiana**	6.2	4.7	2,474,926	66.6	49.8	4.5	12.4	33.4	27.8		32.7	33.6
18 001	Adams	4.2	0.8	12,097	70.0	57.4	3.7	8.9	30.0	27.0		35.0	36.5
18 003	Allen	6.7	6.0	137,586	65.4	48.0	4.2	13.2	34.6	28.7		33.5	31.4
18 005	Bartholomew	6.3	7.0	29,929	69.6	52.6	5.3	11.7	30.4	26.8		33.8	35.5
18 011	Boone	2.4	3.5	21,799	72.9	61.2	3.7	8.1	27.1	22.3		38.8	30.0
18 015	Carroll	3.7	3.0	7,990	67.7	55.9	4.3	7.5	32.3	28.5		31.8	40.4
18 017	Cass	13.0	8.6	14,857	67.9	51.5	4.5	12.0	32.1	26.8		32.6	37.1
18 019	Clark	4.9	3.7	42,689	66.6	49.1	5.1	12.3	33.4	27.6		31.2	33.5
18 021	Clay	1.2	0.4	9,919	72.6	59.9	2.7	10.0	27.4	23.4		32.5	38.1

Table A-2. Counties — Who: Age, Race/Ethnicity, and Household Structure, 2010–2012—*Continued*

STATE and County code	STATE or County	Total population	Percent change 2010–2012	Under 5 years	5 to 17 years	18 to 24 years	25 to 44 years	45 to 64 years	65 years and over	Median age	White	Black	Asian, Hawaiian, or Pacific Is lander	American Indian, Alaska Native, or some other race
	ACS table number:	B01003	Population estimates	B01001	B01001	B01001	B01001	B01001	B01001	B01002	B02008	B02009	B02011 + B02012	B02010 + B02013
	Column number:	1	2	3	4	5	6	7	8	9	10	11	12	13
	Indiana—Cont.													
18 023	Clinton	33,088	-0.5	7.2	19.2	8.5	23.8	26.7	14.5	37.8	93.6	1.3	0.0	6.2
18 027	Daviess	31,895	1.1	8.2	20.3	9.3	22.8	25.2	14.2	35.4	97.3	1.1	0.6	1.7
18 029	Dearborn	49,982	-0.5	5.9	18.7	7.7	24.2	30.0	13.6	40.1	98.1	1.0	0.6	0.8
18 031	Decatur	25,889	1.0	6.3	18.5	7.7	25.1	27.8	14.6	39.8	97.9	1.0	1.1	0.5
18 033	DeKalb	42,335	0.2	6.4	19.5	8.0	24.8	27.9	13.5	38.1	98.4	0.5	0.6	2.0
18 035	Delaware	117,599	-0.2	5.3	14.4	19.9	21.4	23.9	15.0	34.6	92.5	6.1	1.5	4.1
18 037	Dubois	42,041	0.5	6.4	19.1	6.6	23.8	28.9	15.2	41.0	98.5	0.6	0.2	0.7
18 039	Elkhart	198,598	1.1	8.0	20.3	9.1	25.6	24.8	12.3	34.9	87.8	7.1	1.3	6.2
18 041	Fayette	24,156	-1.1	5.6	17.5	7.6	24.0	28.4	16.9	41.0	98.1	1.9	0.4	0.7
18 043	Floyd	74,982	0.8	5.9	17.6	9.0	25.1	29.0	13.4	39.3	93.4	6.4	1.3	1.6
18 047	Franklin	23,006	-0.4	6.0	19.3	7.4	23.4	29.3	14.7	40.0	99.1	0.0	0.0	0.9
18 049	Fulton	20,789	-0.4	6.3	18.0	7.5	23.8	27.9	16.4	40.7	96.4	1.5	0.0	2.6
18 051	Gibson	33,503	-0.3	6.5	17.4	8.6	23.8	28.1	15.7	40.0	96.5	4.1	0.7	0.0
18 053	Grant	69,661	-0.9	5.7	15.8	13.5	21.2	27.3	16.5	39.9	92.5	8.3	1.0	1.5
18 055	Greene	33,062	-0.7	5.7	17.5	7.4	23.8	29.0	16.6	41.9	98.8	1.1	0.0	0.0
18 057	Hamilton	283,040	4.7	7.5	22.1	6.0	29.5	25.9	9.0	35.9	90.5	4.6	5.7	1.8
18 059	Hancock	70,534	1.1	6.2	19.5	7.4	25.5	28.3	13.1	39.2	96.6	2.5	1.2	1.2
18 061	Harrison	39,245	-0.6	5.9	17.6	7.8	24.3	30.0	14.3	41.0	98.8	0.8	0.7	0.5
18 063	Hendricks	148,249	3.1	6.7	20.1	7.5	27.7	26.9	11.2	37.2	92.0	5.6	2.8	1.6
18 065	Henry	49,394	-0.2	5.0	16.2	8.2	25.0	29.1	16.5	41.8	97.4	1.9	0.5	2.4
18 067	Howard	82,799	0.1	6.0	17.3	8.1	23.4	28.4	16.8	41.1	90.7	8.2	1.6	1.9
18 069	Huntington	37,090	-0.3	5.8	17.4	10.2	23.7	28.0	14.9	39.9	98.2	0.9	0.8	1.2
18 071	Jackson	42,856	1.2	6.5	18.0	7.9	25.7	27.1	14.8	39.1	94.5	1.1	1.6	4.1
18 073	Jasper	33,470	-0.2	6.2	19.1	9.4	24.1	26.9	14.3	38.6	98.5	1.5	0.6	0.4
18 075	Jay	21,300	0.9	7.0	19.0	8.3	23.7	26.3	15.7	39.2	99.4	0.6	0.0	1.0
18 077	Jefferson	32,454	0.3	5.8	16.6	10.4	23.9	28.3	14.9	41.1	95.8	2.8	0.9	1.5
18 079	Jennings	28,279	-1.1	6.4	19.8	8.3	25.2	27.2	13.1	38.0	99.0	0.0	0.9	0.8
18 081	Johnson	141,550	2.3	6.7	19.4	8.2	26.6	26.3	12.7	37.1	94.9	2.1	2.8	2.5
18 083	Knox	38,322	-0.7	6.2	15.0	13.3	22.3	27.3	15.9	39.6	95.7	3.4	0.7	1.3
18 085	Kosciusko	77,429	0.4	6.8	18.5	9.2	24.5	27.2	13.8	38.1	93.8	1.4	1.2	4.7
18 087	LaGrange	37,374	1.0	9.7	24.6	9.3	22.7	22.0	11.7	31.0	99.6	0.2	0.0	2.0
18 089	Lake	494,961	-0.5	6.6	18.7	8.8	25.1	27.2	13.5	37.5	64.0	26.6	1.7	10.4
18 091	LaPorte	111,314	-0.2	5.9	16.6	8.8	25.6	28.6	14.5	39.6	88.1	12.1	0.7	1.6
18 093	Lawrence	46,095	-0.1	5.9	17.2	7.2	23.9	29.0	16.8	41.5	98.4	0.7	0.7	1.5
18 095	Madison	131,028	-1.0	6.1	16.7	9.4	25.0	27.0	15.8	39.4	91.1	7.8	0.7	3.4
18 097	Marion	911,593	1.6	7.6	17.5	10.3	29.1	24.8	10.7	33.9	66.2	28.5	2.6	5.8
18 099	Marshall	47,028	0.0	6.7	19.6	8.2	23.3	27.2	15.0	39.2	94.5	1.3	0.8	4.8
18 103	Miami	36,614	-0.8	5.6	16.9	8.7	25.5	28.9	14.3	40.2	93.3	5.3	0.6	2.5
18 105	Monroe	139,880	1.8	4.6	11.6	29.0	24.3	20.1	10.4	27.9	89.8	4.3	6.5	2.3
18 107	Montgomery	38,218	0.5	6.3	17.1	10.3	23.3	27.2	15.8	39.7	97.5	1.7	0.5	0.5
18 109	Morgan	69,206	0.4	5.9	18.7	7.6	24.2	29.8	13.7	40.7	98.7	0.6	0.6	1.1
18 113	Noble	47,534	0.2	6.9	19.4	8.3	25.1	27.3	13.0	37.1	98.2	0.8	0.6	2.0
18 119	Owen	21,503	-0.9	5.4	16.9	8.1	24.2	31.6	15.3	42.7	98.4	0.7	0.5	0.7
18 127	Porter	165,274	0.7	5.8	18.0	9.2	25.6	28.5	12.8	38.5	93.9	3.8	1.6	2.0
18 129	Posey	25,727	-1.1	5.7	17.5	8.0	22.8	31.4	14.6	41.8	97.8	0.8	0.0	1.6
18 133	Putnam	37,866	-0.5	4.8	15.9	14.2	24.2	27.0	13.8	38.7	94.2	4.3	1.3	0.8
18 135	Randolph	25,987	-1.3	5.2	19.0	7.6	22.9	27.9	17.5	41.7	98.7	0.4	0.0	2.3
18 137	Ripley	28,730	-0.8	6.7	19.6	7.3	23.5	27.4	15.4	39.9	98.1	0.6	0.9	1.1
18 141	St. Joseph	266,605	-0.2	6.6	17.8	11.4	24.7	26.0	13.5	36.3	82.5	14.5	2.5	3.6
18 143	Scott	23,989	-1.7	5.8	18.3	8.6	25.1	28.3	13.9	39.4	98.1	1.3	0.0	0.8
18 145	Shelby	44,426	0.2	6.1	18.0	8.1	24.3	29.3	14.2	39.9	94.8	1.4	0.7	3.5
18 147	Spencer	20,924	-0.2	5.7	17.7	7.2	23.1	30.5	15.8	42.4	96.3	0.3	1.4	1.9
18 149	Starke	23,276	-0.7	6.0	18.0	8.2	22.9	29.1	15.8	40.7	97.9	1.4	0.3	1.5
18 151	Steuben	34,110	0.0	5.4	16.7	10.8	22.6	28.9	15.5	40.7	99.2	0.6	0.4	1.3
18 153	Sullivan	21,287	-1.1	5.2	15.4	8.8	26.8	28.6	15.1	40.4	94.4	5.1	0.0	0.0
18 157	Tippecanoe	175,204	2.7	6.3	14.3	24.6	25.1	20.1	9.6	27.8	87.9	5.1	7.2	2.3
18 163	Vanderburgh	180,334	0.6	6.4	15.7	11.6	24.8	27.0	14.5	37.4	88.7	10.6	1.6	1.8
18 167	Vigo	108,209	0.5	5.7	15.4	14.5	25.6	25.2	13.5	36.1	90.4	8.3	2.3	1.8
18 169	Wabash	32,581	-1.4	5.9	16.6	10.1	21.6	27.3	18.5	41.9	96.1	0.9	0.4	3.2
18 173	Warrick	60,195	1.0	6.3	19.1	7.1	24.2	29.2	14.0	39.8	97.0	1.9	2.0	1.0
18 175	Washington	28,123	-1.2	5.9	19.3	7.9	24.2	28.6	14.0	39.3	98.9	1.0	0.0	0.8
18 177	Wayne	68,636	-0.8	6.3	16.6	9.2	23.5	27.7	16.6	40.4	94.4	5.2	1.2	3.5
18 179	Wells	27,671	0.0	6.4	18.1	7.8	22.7	28.5	16.4	41.1	99.2	1.2	0.0	0.7
18 181	White	24,538	-0.9	6.1	17.7	7.4	22.1	29.4	17.3	42.4	98.7	0.6	0.3	2.3
18 183	Whitley	33,333	0.0	6.4	17.9	7.8	23.7	29.8	14.4	40.3	97.8	1.0	0.5	2.0
19 000	**Iowa**	3,062,869	0.8	6.5	17.2	10.1	24.5	26.7	15.0	38.0	93.3	3.9	2.3	2.6
19 011	Benton	26,001	-0.9	6.0	18.8	7.0	23.6	28.8	15.7	40.6	98.6	0.4	0.0	2.2
19 013	Black Hawk	131,472	0.5	6.3	15.1	15.9	23.9	24.8	13.9	34.6	88.0	10.4	1.9	1.7
19 015	Boone	26,268	-0.3	5.3	18.5	7.5	23.6	29.0	16.1	40.5	97.9	1.5	0.0	0.7
19 017	Bremer	24,375	0.8	5.7	16.5	12.9	21.6	26.0	17.4	38.6	97.9	1.2	0.6	0.9
19 019	Buchanan	20,923	0.0	7.1	19.4	7.2	23.1	27.5	15.6	39.4	98.0	0.0	0.9	1.1
19 021	Buena Vista	20,406	1.3	7.5	17.5	12.0	23.2	24.8	15.1	35.9	82.1	2.9	7.0	11.1
19 027	Carroll	20,757	-0.9	7.3	17.6	6.8	21.5	28.2	18.6	41.9	97.7	1.1	0.0	0.9
19 033	Cerro Gordo	43,963	-0.7	5.6	15.6	8.0	22.7	30.0	18.2	43.6	97.2	2.4	1.3	1.1
19 045	Clinton	48,974	-0.8	5.9	17.2	8.2	22.8	28.9	17.0	41.9	95.3	3.8	0.7	1.7

Table A-2. Counties — Who: Age, Race/Ethnicity, and Household Structure, 2010–2012—*Continued*

STATE and County code	STATE or County	Percent Hispanic or Latino	Percent foreign born	Total households	Household type (percent) Family households				Nonfamily households		Percent of households with people under 18 years	Percent of households with people 60 years and over
					Total family households	Married-couple families	Male household families	Female household families	Total nonfamily households	One-person households		
	ACS table number:	B03003	C05003	B11001	B11001	B11001	B11001	B11001	B11001	B11001	B11005	B11006
	Column number:	14	15	16	17	18	19	20	21	22	23	24
	Indiana—Cont.											
18 023	Clinton	13.7	6.1	11,724	71.3	52.8	6.9	11.6	28.7	23.2	35.2	35.8
18 027	Daviess	4.2	2.3	11,258	72.2	58.9	3.9	9.4	27.8	25.0	37.5	36.8
18 029	Dearborn	1.0	1.3	18,454	71.4	56.7	5.8	8.9	28.6	23.4	33.6	35.9
18 031	Decatur	1.7	2.3	9,655	72.4	54.4	4.1	14.0	27.6	24.5	34.2	37.1
18 033	DeKalb	2.4	1.5	16,343	71.9	56.0	5.5	10.5	28.1	24.2	33.1	32.7
18 035	Delaware	1.9	2.0	46,179	59.8	42.7	4.4	12.7	40.2	29.9	26.5	35.4
18 037	Dubois	6.2	3.9	15,854	72.0	59.8	3.6	8.5	28.0	25.4	32.0	35.4
18 039	Elkhart	14.4	8.5	69,984	72.0	54.1	5.2	12.7	28.0	24.0	38.6	33.2
18 041	Fayette	1.0	0.7	9,466	68.2	48.8	6.6	12.8	31.8	28.8	30.8	39.6
18 043	Floyd	2.8	2.8	28,844	67.5	50.2	4.0	13.3	32.5	28.0	31.1	33.4
18 047	Franklin	1.0	0.6	8,491	75.5	61.8	5.2	8.5	24.5	19.0	35.6	34.6
18 049	Fulton	4.4	3.1	8,248	71.9	59.7	3.2	9.0	28.1	26.0	29.4	39.0
18 051	Gibson	0.3	0.6	12,949	70.2	56.4	4.9	8.9	29.8	25.4	31.2	36.2
18 053	Grant	3.7	1.8	27,158	65.7	48.2	3.8	13.6	34.3	29.7	28.1	39.5
18 055	Greene	1.0	0.6	13,065	71.9	56.7	5.6	9.6	28.1	25.7	32.7	39.5
18 057	Hamilton	3.6	7.0	103,033	74.5	62.3	3.4	8.8	25.5	21.3	43.0	25.1
18 059	Hancock	1.8	1.7	25,968	74.6	58.3	4.8	11.5	25.4	20.9	37.2	34.2
18 061	Harrison	1.6	1.3	14,487	71.3	58.3	4.9	8.2	28.7	23.7	34.1	38.8
18 063	Hendricks	3.1	4.3	52,743	74.7	61.8	3.6	9.3	25.3	21.9	38.4	30.7
18 065	Henry	1.5	0.8	18,164	67.3	50.7	4.1	12.5	32.7	29.9	29.3	40.2
18 067	Howard	2.8	2.3	34,446	63.5	47.8	4.1	11.6	36.5	32.2	29.9	38.0
18 069	Huntington	1.8	1.7	14,269	68.3	54.8	4.1	9.5	31.7	24.4	31.1	34.4
18 071	Jackson	5.9	4.2	16,374	70.2	51.5	6.3	12.4	29.8	24.6	33.8	35.3
18 073	Jasper	5.5	2.6	12,131	76.0	64.2	4.5	7.4	24.0	21.1	37.5	34.3
18 075	Jay	2.8	1.5	8,131	71.3	55.2	5.6	10.5	28.7	23.7	32.6	38.4
18 077	Jefferson	2.3	1.5	12,664	67.6	50.3	5.1	12.2	32.4	28.3	33.0	35.9
18 079	Jennings	2.1	0.9	10,534	70.0	54.4	3.9	11.6	30.0	25.0	37.4	35.1
18 081	Johnson	3.2	3.2	52,464	71.8	58.0	4.1	9.7	28.2	23.6	37.0	32.7
18 083	Knox	1.6	1.5	14,591	62.1	46.9	5.3	9.9	37.9	32.4	28.0	37.8
18 085	Kosciusko	7.5	3.8	29,284	71.2	58.1	5.0	8.1	28.8	25.1	33.2	35.1
18 087	LaGrange	3.6	1.7	11,713	76.7	65.3	2.9	8.5	23.3	21.1	39.5	34.3
18 089	Lake	17.1	6.9	181,174	67.2	45.4	5.1	16.7	32.8	28.2	33.8	36.3
18 091	LaPorte	5.6	2.8	42,715	65.5	49.1	3.4	13.1	34.5	29.4	29.6	37.5
18 093	Lawrence	1.3	1.1	18,974	71.5	55.2	4.8	11.5	28.5	25.2	33.3	38.7
18 095	Madison	3.3	1.9	49,973	64.3	46.8	4.4	13.1	35.7	30.6	30.6	39.3
18 097	Marion	9.6	8.3	358,923	58.8	37.2	4.7	16.9	41.2	34.0	31.4	27.8
18 099	Marshall	8.7	4.7	17,788	68.4	55.6	4.6	8.2	31.6	28.1	34.4	38.6
18 103	Miami	2.5	1.0	13,160	70.7	55.1	6.2	9.4	29.3	25.5	31.9	37.0
18 105	Monroe	3.0	8.0	53,551	51.1	38.6	3.7	8.8	48.9	34.5	22.0	27.0
18 107	Montgomery	4.6	2.5	14,667	69.7	53.8	5.2	10.6	30.3	25.3	32.2	37.1
18 109	Morgan	1.2	1.5	25,501	74.2	60.4	3.6	10.2	25.8	20.4	34.9	37.2
18 113	Noble	9.7	4.6	17,522	73.6	56.4	5.1	12.0	26.4	22.6	35.4	35.6
18 119	Owen	1.0	0.9	8,738	70.8	55.2	4.9	10.7	29.2	23.2	32.0	40.7
18 127	Porter	8.7	4.1	61,297	70.8	55.0	3.6	12.1	29.2	24.4	34.4	33.8
18 129	Posey	1.6	0.9	10,201	72.6	59.0	3.9	9.7	27.4	24.4	32.6	35.7
18 133	Putnam	1.6	2.3	12,484	72.6	58.0	5.2	9.5	27.4	22.4	31.2	35.9
18 135	Randolph	3.1	0.6	10,497	66.1	53.1	4.6	8.4	33.9	28.7	31.8	39.9
18 137	Ripley	1.6	1.3	10,643	71.9	59.4	3.4	9.1	28.1	24.3	33.4	39.5
18 141	St. Joseph	7.5	5.4	101,171	64.4	46.9	4.1	13.4	35.6	29.2	31.3	34.0
18 143	Scott	1.5	1.2	8,932	68.6	49.7	6.4	12.4	31.4	27.9	35.2	37.8
18 145	Shelby	3.8	2.5	17,104	69.7	51.0	5.9	12.8	30.3	23.8	36.4	34.2
18 147	Spencer	2.5	3.1	7,945	74.5	61.9	5.5	7.1	25.5	21.1	33.0	38.3
18 149	Starke	3.4	1.3	9,087	71.5	54.1	5.7	11.8	28.5	24.9	31.1	37.2
18 151	Steuben	3.0	1.3	13,317	72.4	57.0	5.3	10.1	27.6	22.9	30.3	37.8
18 153	Sullivan	2.0	1.2	7,728	72.2	56.0	5.3	11.0	27.8	21.5	30.6	38.7
18 157	Tippecanoe	7.7	10.5	66,464	56.7	43.6	3.6	9.5	43.3	29.9	28.1	25.1
18 163	Vanderburgh	2.3	2.4	74,271	61.0	41.8	4.9	14.3	39.0	33.1	29.4	33.3
18 167	Vigo	2.4	3.0	39,326	62.4	45.2	5.3	11.9	37.6	30.9	29.8	34.1
18 169	Wabash	2.2	1.6	12,584	73.7	59.1	5.3	9.3	26.3	22.7	30.7	39.7
18 173	Warrick	1.6	2.6	22,380	76.4	64.8	2.7	9.0	23.6	18.7	36.3	34.9
18 175	Washington	1.2	0.5	10,591	68.4	53.4	4.5	10.5	31.6	27.8	31.2	36.6
18 177	Wayne	2.6	2.2	28,230	65.9	46.9	4.1	14.8	34.1	29.1	30.0	37.9
18 179	Wells	2.2	0.7	10,888	72.7	56.8	4.2	11.6	27.3	25.4	32.5	37.8
18 181	White	7.1	2.7	9,441	72.6	57.8	5.7	9.2	27.4	24.9	30.6	42.3
18 183	Whitley	1.6	0.7	13,136	70.6	56.5	4.0	10.0	29.4	25.3	31.5	35.3
19 000	**Iowa**	5.1	4.5	1,224,399	64.8	51.5	3.9	9.4	35.2	28.7	30.3	35.0
19 011	Benton	1.1	1.2	10,204	75.5	63.5	2.9	9.0	24.5	22.3	33.2	36.4
19 013	Black Hawk	3.8	4.8	51,852	59.8	46.1	3.4	10.4	40.2	30.9	27.5	33.9
19 015	Boone	2.0	0.4	10,328	65.1	53.0	3.6	8.5	34.9	30.1	29.1	36.8
19 017	Bremer	1.1	0.8	9,232	70.8	59.8	3.7	7.3	29.2	25.7	30.1	40.3
19 019	Buchanan	1.3	1.0	8,225	72.6	60.5	4.6	7.6	27.4	23.1	32.1	37.4
19 021	Buena Vista	23.7	18.9	7,638	67.5	53.1	7.4	7.0	32.5	28.1	34.1	38.8
19 027	Carroll	1.8	1.0	8,470	65.4	52.9	4.1	8.4	34.6	31.6	28.4	39.3
19 033	Cerro Gordo	3.9	1.7	20,034	59.3	47.2	4.5	7.7	40.7	34.7	26.4	37.3
19 045	Clinton	2.6	1.9	19,677	64.7	51.4	4.3	9.0	35.3	29.5	29.3	39.1

Part A — Who   45

Table A-2. Counties — Who: Age, Race/Ethnicity, and Household Structure, 2010–2012—*Continued*

STATE and County code	STATE or County	Total population	Percent change 2010–2012	\<\<Population by age (percent)\>\> Under 5 years	5 to 17 years	18 to 24 years	25 to 44 years	45 to 64 years	65 years and over	Median age	\<\<Race alone or in combination (percent)\>\> White	Black	Asian, Hawaiian, or Pacific Islander	American Indian, Alaska Native, or some other race
	ACS table number:	B01003	Population estimates	B01001	B01001	B01001	B01001	B01001	B01001	B01002	B02008	B02009	B02011 + B02012	B02010 + B02013
	Column number:	1	2	3	4	5	6	7	8	9	10	11	12	13
	Iowa—Cont.													
19 049	Dallas	69,451	7.9	8.6	20.2	6.0	31.9	23.3	10.0	34.1	93.7	2.1	3.2	3.4
19 057	Des Moines	40,242	0.2	6.4	16.8	7.3	23.1	28.6	17.8	41.7	93.6	7.1	0.5	1.0
19 061	Dubuque	94,471	1.3	6.3	17.2	10.4	23.5	27.4	15.3	39.0	96.7	2.6	1.8	2.1
19 065	Fayette	20,874	-0.3	5.9	16.0	10.3	20.2	28.2	19.4	42.6	98.1	1.2	0.7	1.0
19 087	Henry	20,233	0.6	6.6	16.7	9.0	24.0	28.0	15.8	40.7	94.9	3.0	3.0	0.6
19 097	Jackson	19,758	-0.6	5.4	17.5	7.1	21.3	29.9	18.8	44.2	96.4	2.3	2.4	4.7
19 099	Jasper	36,709	-0.6	5.6	16.7	7.1	25.0	28.8	16.9	42.1	97.6	1.7	0.7	1.2
19 103	Johnson	133,719	3.8	6.1	13.6	21.6	28.5	21.5	8.8	29.6	87.4	5.9	6.3	2.8
19 105	Jones	20,673	-0.1	5.4	16.6	6.8	23.9	29.9	17.4	42.7	96.2	2.0	0.5	2.0
19 111	Lee	35,676	-0.6	5.8	15.9	8.2	23.2	29.5	17.4	41.9	95.4	4.5	0.7	1.4
19 113	Linn	213,666	1.7	6.6	17.7	10.0	26.4	26.0	13.3	36.8	92.8	5.6	2.5	1.6
19 123	Mahaska	22,437	0.3	6.6	17.4	9.4	23.5	26.6	16.5	39.3	97.7	1.3	1.9	0.8
19 125	Marion	33,318	0.5	6.6	17.9	10.4	23.0	26.2	15.9	38.8	97.9	1.2	1.7	0.2
19 127	Marshall	40,803	0.4	7.1	17.9	8.7	22.7	27.1	16.5	38.9	89.0	2.5	2.0	8.2
19 139	Muscatine	42,783	0.4	7.1	18.8	8.0	24.7	27.2	14.3	38.4	94.5	1.6	1.8	4.0
19 149	Plymouth	24,917	-0.2	6.4	19.0	6.1	22.6	28.8	17.0	42.2	97.1	0.0	1.6	2.4
19 153	Polk	437,941	2.6	7.5	17.9	9.2	29.5	25.0	11.0	34.7	87.6	7.4	4.3	3.4
19 155	Pottawattamie	93,262	-0.5	6.5	17.3	9.4	24.5	27.9	14.4	38.4	96.5	2.0	1.1	2.3
19 163	Scott	167,251	1.8	6.7	17.7	8.9	26.1	27.3	13.4	37.4	89.0	9.1	2.5	2.4
19 167	Sioux	33,977	1.7	7.7	19.0	13.9	22.0	23.1	14.2	33.1	94.0	0.9	0.9	5.2
19 169	Story	90,519	1.7	5.0	12.5	29.9	23.2	19.4	10.0	26.7	90.2	3.4	6.8	1.0
19 179	Wapello	35,461	-0.7	6.5	16.1	9.9	23.9	27.2	16.4	40.0	94.9	2.0	1.0	3.5
19 181	Warren	46,606	1.3	6.5	19.1	9.7	23.9	27.0	13.8	38.4	98.7	1.0	0.8	0.8
19 183	Washington	21,815	1.0	6.0	18.4	7.2	22.3	28.7	17.4	42.1	96.1	1.2	0.0	3.5
19 187	Webster	37,629	-1.6	6.0	15.8	10.8	22.9	27.7	16.7	39.6	94.2	5.7	0.9	1.5
19 191	Winneshiek	21,054	0.0	4.8	15.6	15.8	19.2	27.7	16.9	40.3	97.5	1.0	1.0	1.5
19 193	Woodbury	102,416	0.0	7.6	18.8	10.4	24.8	25.2	13.0	35.0	85.9	4.1	3.0	10.5
20 000	**Kansas**	2,871,709	0.9	7.1	18.1	10.2	25.3	25.9	13.4	36.1	88.2	7.2	3.2	4.9
20 009	Barton	27,646	-0.5	7.1	17.5	8.7	22.2	27.2	17.4	40.0	93.4	3.0	0.2	5.1
20 015	Butler	65,893	-0.2	6.5	20.0	9.4	23.6	27.7	12.9	37.7	96.1	2.2	1.1	3.3
20 021	Cherokee	21,409	-1.6	5.5	19.3	7.2	22.8	28.7	16.5	41.4	95.0	1.1	0.0	7.4
20 035	Cowley	36,273	0.0	7.2	17.1	10.9	22.8	25.9	16.1	38.4	89.4	3.9	2.1	7.6
20 037	Crawford	39,234	0.5	6.0	15.9	17.0	23.3	23.7	14.2	33.4	94.9	3.1	1.8	3.1
20 045	Douglas	112,105	1.5	5.4	13.4	25.0	26.4	20.6	9.2	28.5	89.4	5.8	5.1	5.0
20 051	Ellis	28,754	2.1	6.6	14.4	17.8	23.8	23.9	13.5	31.5	95.3	1.6	1.6	2.8
20 055	Finney	37,094	0.6	9.7	22.3	10.7	25.9	22.8	8.6	30.3	88.6	3.7	4.1	6.7
20 057	Ford	34,426	2.0	10.3	20.6	10.6	27.0	22.1	9.3	31.0	89.4	3.0	1.9	8.2
20 059	Franklin	25,953	-0.4	7.3	18.3	8.7	23.8	27.6	14.3	38.4	96.2	2.2	0.5	3.9
20 061	Geary	36,246	7.6	11.2	19.8	14.6	30.1	17.4	6.9	26.6	75.4	22.8	7.2	4.6
20 079	Harvey	34,772	0.3	6.4	18.5	8.9	21.9	27.3	17.0	39.7	94.7	2.6	1.2	4.6
20 091	Johnson	552,886	2.6	7.0	19.0	7.3	28.7	26.7	11.3	36.5	89.8	5.5	5.2	2.5
20 099	Labette	21,442	-1.3	6.6	17.5	9.1	22.1	27.9	16.8	40.3	93.7	6.2	0.9	7.4
20 103	Leavenworth	77,137	1.6	6.6	18.0	8.0	28.6	27.4	11.3	37.3	86.9	10.4	2.6	3.7
20 111	Lyon	33,716	0.3	6.9	16.2	17.3	22.9	24.1	12.6	32.4	92.9	3.5	2.9	5.0
20 113	McPherson	29,241	0.7	5.9	17.2	9.0	21.6	28.1	18.2	41.8	96.9	1.8	0.8	1.6
20 121	Miami	32,719	-0.7	6.1	20.4	7.2	22.9	29.7	13.7	40.3	98.3	1.8	0.7	1.6
20 125	Montgomery	34,902	-2.7	6.8	16.8	10.2	21.8	26.8	17.7	39.7	90.1	7.3	1.3	7.4
20 149	Pottawatomie	22,004	2.7	8.5	20.8	7.8	24.9	25.6	12.3	34.7	96.6	2.4	0.6	2.9
20 155	Reno	64,521	-0.2	6.4	17.1	9.3	23.1	27.1	17.0	40.1	92.8	4.4	0.9	5.0
20 161	Riley	73,398	5.6	6.8	11.6	33.1	26.4	14.9	7.2	24.5	87.3	8.0	5.9	3.0
20 169	Saline	55,829	0.4	7.2	17.5	9.5	23.9	26.8	15.2	38.1	91.5	5.1	2.6	4.5
20 173	Sedgwick	501,408	0.9	7.8	19.1	9.6	26.4	25.3	11.7	34.4	82.3	11.0	5.0	6.2
20 175	Seward	23,271	2.4	10.8	21.2	12.2	27.6	19.9	8.4	29.1	63.2	6.0	4.5	30.7
20 177	Shawnee	178,736	0.4	6.9	17.8	8.6	24.7	27.3	14.7	38.6	85.5	10.7	2.1	6.7
20 191	Sumner	23,867	-1.7	6.9	18.9	7.9	21.3	29.3	15.7	40.3	97.5	1.4	0.0	3.4
20 209	Wyandotte	158,287	0.9	8.7	19.7	9.5	27.5	23.8	10.8	33.0	64.1	26.8	3.2	9.0
21 000	**Kentucky**	4,364,627	0.8	6.4	17.0	9.6	26.0	27.3	13.6	38.2	89.6	8.9	1.6	1.9
21 003	Allen	20,128	0.9	6.2	17.3	9.2	25.0	27.2	15.1	40.3	97.6	1.9	0.0	0.0
21 005	Anderson	21,598	1.2	6.7	18.8	7.2	26.7	28.1	12.5	38.8	97.2	3.0	0.6	0.9
21 009	Barren	42,392	1.1	6.0	18.0	7.8	24.7	27.7	15.7	39.9	94.3	5.1	0.6	0.9
21 013	Bell	28,520	-1.8	5.8	16.1	9.0	24.5	28.4	16.2	40.9	96.4	3.1	0.0	1.0
21 015	Boone	121,435	3.4	7.3	20.7	7.4	28.6	26.0	9.9	36.1	93.4	3.6	2.6	1.7
21 019	Boyd	49,395	-0.9	5.6	15.9	7.5	25.1	29.0	16.9	41.7	96.3	3.5	0.6	1.0
21 021	Boyle	28,547	0.7	5.3	16.1	10.8	22.9	28.1	16.8	41.7	92.4	7.6	1.1	2.1
21 027	Breckinridge	20,114	0.0	5.9	18.3	7.1	22.6	30.1	16.0	41.8	96.5	3.2	0.3	0.7
21 029	Bullitt	75,225	1.9	5.9	18.8	8.3	26.7	28.4	11.9	38.4	98.6	1.1	0.8	0.9
21 035	Calloway	37,473	1.0	5.3	12.7	21.5	22.1	23.2	15.3	33.7	93.4	4.5	2.2	1.3
21 037	Campbell	90,794	0.4	6.4	16.2	11.4	25.9	27.2	12.9	36.7	95.8	3.4	1.2	1.5
21 043	Carter	27,478	-1.3	6.4	16.6	9.8	24.4	27.7	15.1	38.9	98.7	1.6	0.0	0.7
21 047	Christian	74,373	1.7	9.6	18.5	14.2	27.8	19.6	10.4	28.9	75.7	23.0	2.6	2.3
21 049	Clark	35,637	0.5	6.4	16.8	7.2	25.4	29.3	14.9	40.7	93.9	5.7	0.6	0.5
21 051	Clay	21,642	-0.8	6.8	15.1	9.0	30.1	26.8	12.2	37.9	94.4	5.3	0.0	1.7
21 059	Daviess	97,294	1.1	6.5	17.8	8.6	24.7	27.5	14.9	39.0	93.4	6.1	1.0	1.2
21 067	Fayette	301,211	3.0	6.4	14.7	14.2	29.8	24.2	10.7	33.8	78.9	16.1	4.0	4.3
21 071	Floyd	39,222	-1.2	6.2	16.1	8.5	25.9	29.4	13.9	40.3	98.8	1.1	0.2	0.7
21 073	Franklin	49,480	1.1	5.9	15.5	9.7	26.0	28.7	14.2	40.0	85.3	12.4	1.6	3.1
21 081	Grant	24,621	-0.8	7.0	20.8	8.4	27.0	25.6	11.1	36.5	97.7	1.2	0.0	2.4

Table A-2. Counties — Who: Age, Race/Ethnicity, and Household Structure, 2010–2012—*Continued*

STATE and County code	STATE or County	Percent Hispanic or Latino	Percent foreign born	Total households	Household type (percent)						Percent of households with people under 18 years	Percent of households with people 60 years and over
					Family households				Nonfamily households			
					Total family households	Married-couple families	Male household families	Female household families	Total nonfamily households	One-person households		
ACS table number:		B03003	C05003	B11001	B11001	B11001	B11001	B11001	B11001	B11001	B11005	B11006
Column number:		14	15	16	17	18	19	20	21	22	23	24
	Iowa—Cont.											
19 049	Dallas	6.2	7.4	26,221	72.0	59.3	2.7	10.0	28.0	22.4	37.4	27.0
19 057	Des Moines	2.7	1.3	16,934	65.8	49.2	3.1	13.5	34.2	29.4	29.1	40.0
19 061	Dubuque	2.0	2.1	37,548	64.3	52.0	3.6	8.8	35.7	29.2	29.7	34.6
19 065	Fayette	1.9	0.8	8,601	63.7	53.7	2.9	7.1	35.3	29.6	26.2	38.0
19 087	Henry	4.0	2.2	7,497	69.3	54.8	3.4	11.1	30.7	26.7	29.5	38.3
19 097	Jackson	1.2	1.4	8,368	69.2	56.5	4.9	7.7	30.8	24.7	29.6	40.1
19 099	Jasper	1.5	1.2	14,781	67.4	53.2	4.3	9.9	32.6	27.9	31.1	38.0
19 103	Johnson	4.9	9.9	54,073	53.8	42.2	3.2	8.3	45.2	30.8	25.5	23.6
19 105	Jones	1.4	1.2	8,265	68.4	54.5	5.4	8.5	31.6	26.1	29.6	41.3
19 111	Lee	3.2	2.2	14,194	65.8	50.4	5.3	10.1	34.2	29.1	28.2	40.1
19 113	Linn	2.8	2.9	85,889	62.7	48.6	4.4	9.8	37.3	29.6	31.6	31.6
19 123	Mahaska	1.7	1.1	9,030	63.6	53.7	2.7	7.2	36.4	32.0	29.0	39.0
19 125	Marion	1.7	2.7	12,780	74.0	64.4	3.5	6.2	26.0	23.3	33.8	37.2
19 127	Marshall	17.9	12.1	15,316	66.8	55.3	2.4	9.0	33.2	27.3	30.1	39.2
19 139	Muscatine	16.2	5.9	16,445	69.0	54.2	3.5	11.3	31.0	25.5	33.9	36.2
19 149	Plymouth	3.1	2.4	10,008	71.8	62.4	3.3	6.1	28.2	23.7	31.7	37.2
19 153	Polk	7.7	8.4	171,697	65.2	48.8	4.7	11.6	34.8	28.1	35.2	28.9
19 155	Pottawattamie	6.7	3.3	36,440	67.3	49.2	5.0	13.1	32.7	27.1	31.1	36.2
19 163	Scott	5.8	3.4	66,945	62.9	48.0	3.5	11.3	37.1	30.4	30.3	33.6
19 167	Sioux	9.1	7.0	11,614	75.5	67.4	1.4	6.7	24.5	21.4	36.3	35.0
19 169	Story	3.1	8.6	35,314	54.0	46.0	2.8	5.2	46.0	28.1	23.2	24.6
19 179	Wapello	9.2	7.3	14,572	65.7	49.2	4.5	12.0	34.3	28.4	31.3	37.2
19 181	Warren	2.0	1.1	17,335	74.1	58.5	5.0	10.5	25.9	22.3	34.9	33.9
19 183	Washington	5.3	2.3	9,213	67.3	55.4	3.5	8.4	32.7	27.1	30.8	37.5
19 187	Webster	3.9	2.0	15,483	58.9	42.0	4.9	12.0	41.1	34.5	27.4	37.4
19 191	Winneshiek	2.0	1.5	8,078	66.9	56.9	4.0	6.0	33.1	28.0	26.7	38.4
19 193	Woodbury	14.0	8.7	38,737	65.3	47.0	5.2	13.1	34.7	29.0	33.5	33.4
20 000	**Kansas**	10.8	6.7	1,106,960	65.5	50.7	4.4	10.4	34.5	28.5	32.7	33.0
20 009	Barton	13.6	6.9	11,293	64.6	52.2	4.6	7.8	35.4	31.2	29.2	39.1
20 015	Butler	4.0	1.7	23,995	69.6	56.1	5.1	8.5	30.4	26.9	34.7	32.7
20 021	Cherokee	2.1	1.0	8,166	72.4	56.4	5.3	10.7	27.6	25.6	28.8	40.3
20 035	Cowley	9.4	3.4	13,804	65.4	51.7	4.5	9.1	34.6	29.4	30.5	38.3
20 037	Crawford	4.7	3.7	15,490	58.8	43.9	4.5	10.4	41.2	31.7	27.6	31.4
20 045	Douglas	5.3	7.0	43,566	54.3	40.9	4.5	8.9	45.7	28.0	27.4	24.0
20 051	Ellis	4.9	3.2	11,941	55.3	45.5	2.0	7.7	44.7	33.4	26.4	29.6
20 055	Finney	47.3	20.5	12,521	69.0	54.6	4.0	10.4	31.0	24.9	43.1	26.7
20 057	Ford	51.8	24.6	10,976	73.3	54.3	5.4	13.6	26.7	21.8	42.5	27.8
20 059	Franklin	3.7	0.9	10,047	71.2	56.9	4.9	9.4	28.8	23.9	32.3	32.8
20 061	Geary	13.1	8.0	12,775	67.3	53.0	2.4	11.9	32.7	26.2	40.6	20.9
20 079	Harvey	10.8	5.3	13,089	69.2	56.6	3.1	9.5	30.8	27.2	30.9	37.8
20 091	Johnson	7.3	8.2	215,199	67.5	54.9	3.5	9.0	32.5	26.9	35.6	29.0
20 099	Labette	4.1	1.5	8,639	66.8	51.1	6.4	9.3	33.2	29.2	30.4	39.0
20 103	Leavenworth	6.0	3.4	26,103	71.6	57.5	3.4	10.8	28.4	23.2	36.9	32.5
20 111	Lyon	20.3	9.2	12,984	59.4	47.0	3.4	9.0	40.6	30.5	30.0	32.2
20 113	McPherson	3.6	1.8	11,567	69.8	59.4	3.9	6.6	30.2	25.2	31.5	38.7
20 121	Miami	2.7	0.7	12,033	73.1	59.7	4.6	8.9	26.9	22.3	35.8	33.9
20 125	Montgomery	5.5	2.8	13,876	65.8	47.4	6.1	12.3	34.2	30.3	30.1	40.5
20 149	Pottawatomie	4.7	1.3	8,000	69.9	61.2	1.9	6.8	30.1	24.9	33.3	33.9
20 155	Reno	8.3	2.5	25,770	65.4	51.4	2.9	11.0	34.6	30.5	29.7	37.4
20 161	Riley	7.0	6.6	25,831	52.9	41.9	3.5	7.5	47.1	29.5	28.2	19.8
20 169	Saline	10.0	5.5	22,480	63.3	47.2	3.8	12.3	36.7	30.3	30.4	34.9
20 173	Sedgwick	13.2	8.5	191,191	64.6	47.2	5.0	12.4	35.4	29.8	34.0	30.5
20 175	Seward	57.3	31.1	7,367	71.9	51.1	7.3	13.5	28.1	21.5	47.7	26.7
20 177	Shawnee	11.1	4.8	72,189	63.5	46.5	4.9	12.1	36.5	30.9	31.2	35.3
20 191	Sumner	4.8	0.1	9,241	70.1	55.2	4.9	10.1	29.9	26.7	33.9	37.2
20 209	Wyandotte	26.7	14.3	56,817	64.4	39.1	6.7	18.7	35.6	29.7	36.2	30.9
21 000	**Kentucky**	3.1	3.2	1,690,132	66.9	49.3	4.7	12.9	33.1	28.0	32.2	34.7
21 003	Allen	1.5	1.0	8,144	67.0	48.5	5.9	12.6	33.0	28.4	29.6	36.6
21 005	Anderson	1.4	0.6	8,446	69.3	52.9	5.3	11.1	30.7	24.3	38.6	33.1
21 009	Barren	2.7	1.2	16,616	70.9	53.5	5.5	11.9	29.1	26.8	34.6	36.5
21 013	Bell	0.6	0.2	11,056	68.1	47.3	6.2	14.6	31.9	29.7	32.0	41.2
21 015	Boone	3.6	4.5	42,680	74.0	59.2	5.1	9.7	26.0	22.0	40.8	29.9
21 019	Boyd	1.5	1.3	19,097	67.6	50.9	6.0	10.6	32.4	28.0	30.4	41.5
21 021	Boyle	3.0	2.5	11,190	66.2	47.8	4.3	14.1	33.8	29.3	29.7	39.7
21 027	Breckinridge	1.0	0.5	7,510	72.4	56.6	6.2	9.6	27.6	24.0	29.8	42.1
21 029	Bullitt	1.4	0.9	28,109	75.9	57.1	5.6	13.1	24.1	19.7	36.4	32.2
21 035	Calloway	2.4	4.1	14,656	60.1	49.2	3.8	7.1	39.9	31.2	26.8	37.4
21 037	Campbell	1.7	2.2	35,254	63.5	46.6	4.2	12.7	36.5	31.3	29.3	32.9
21 043	Carter	0.7	0.4	10,398	69.7	57.4	3.3	8.9	30.3	25.9	28.6	41.5
21 047	Christian	6.4	3.0	25,828	70.8	52.2	3.3	15.3	29.2	25.6	41.9	27.9
21 049	Clark	2.6	1.3	14,559	70.7	54.8	4.1	11.9	29.3	24.9	32.1	36.5
21 051	Clay	1.2	0.7	7,479	69.0	50.7	5.4	13.0	31.0	28.3	29.6	36.3
21 059	Daviess	2.7	2.1	37,435	66.8	50.7	3.9	12.2	33.2	28.3	30.7	36.3
21 067	Fayette	6.9	8.9	122,046	57.7	40.8	4.5	12.3	42.3	33.2	28.9	27.7
21 071	Floyd	0.6	0.4	15,522	69.4	49.7	6.6	13.1	30.6	26.5	30.3	37.0
21 073	Franklin	2.8	2.9	21,237	63.4	42.8	6.3	14.3	36.6	31.1	30.8	33.8
21 081	Grant	2.4	1.2	8,506	76.0	61.5	3.9	10.6	24.0	20.0	41.8	30.9

Table A-2. Counties — Who: Age, Race/Ethnicity, and Household Structure, 2010–2012—*Continued*

STATE and County code	STATE or County	Total population	Percent change 2010–2012	Population by age (percent)						Median age	Race alone or in combination (percent)			
				Under 5 years	5 to 17 years	18 to 24 years	25 to 44 years	45 to 64 years	65 years and over		White	Black	Asian, Hawaiian, or Pacific Islander	American Indian, Alaska Native, or some other race
	ACS table number:	B01003	Population estimates	B01001	B01001	B01001	B01001	B01001	B01001	B01002	B02008	B02009	B02011 + 302012	B02010 + B02013
	Column number:	1	2	3	4	5	6	7	8	9	10	11	12	13
	Kentucky—Cont.													
21 083	Graves	37,402	1.0	6.7	17.8	7.6	23.9	27.7	16.3	40.2	94.4	5.5	0.6	1.8
21 085	Grayson	25,894	0.6	7.3	17.2	8.3	24.3	27.7	15.2	39.0	97.7	1.6	0.0	1.5
21 089	Greenup	36,818	-0.5	5.5	16.7	7.2	23.9	29.4	17.3	42.7	98.4	1.4	0.4	0.9
21 093	Hardin	107,129	0.0	7.3	18.4	10.0	27.1	26.3	11.0	35.4	83.3	14.8	3.5	2.5
21 095	Harlan	28,975	-2.4	6.4	16.5	8.5	24.3	29.5	14.8	40.6	96.3	2.7	0.4	1.1
21 101	Henderson	46,395	0.5	6.6	16.8	8.0	25.4	28.8	14.3	39.3	90.7	9.6	0.3	1.3
21 107	Hopkins	46,828	-0.3	6.3	16.9	7.3	25.6	28.5	15.4	39.8	92.3	7.7	0.7	1.0
21 111	Jefferson	746,508	1.1	6.6	16.5	9.1	27.0	27.3	13.5	37.9	75.7	22.3	2.8	2.0
21 113	Jessamine	49,125	1.9	6.9	18.7	10.0	26.4	26.0	12.0	35.9	94.0	3.9	1.3	2.2
21 115	Johnson	23,406	-0.1	5.8	17.2	8.0	25.3	29.3	14.4	39.8	99.0	0.0	1.1	0.0
21 117	Kenton	160,710	1.1	7.3	17.6	8.7	28.2	26.9	11.3	36.2	92.4	5.8	1.3	2.3
21 121	Knox	31,901	-0.4	6.6	17.8	9.4	24.0	26.9	15.2	38.7	98.2	1.4	0.0	1.8
21 125	Laurel	59,266	0.8	6.5	17.8	7.9	27.0	27.5	13.2	37.9	98.6	1.1	0.6	0.8
21 133	Letcher	24,318	-2.5	6.1	16.2	7.6	25.2	30.3	14.5	41.1	98.8	0.6	0.5	0.4
21 137	Lincoln	24,638	-1.2	7.1	17.7	7.6	25.2	27.0	15.4	39.0	96.4	3.2	0.0	0.6
21 141	Logan	26,753	-0.7	6.3	17.6	7.9	24.1	28.4	15.7	40.7	91.8	8.4	0.0	0.6
21 145	McCracken	65,616	0.0	5.8	16.3	7.5	24.1	29.2	17.0	42.4	88.1	12.0	1.2	1.6
21 151	Madison	84,016	2.0	5.9	15.3	17.2	25.7	24.3	11.5	33.5	93.5	5.4	1.5	1.5
21 155	Marion	19,981	1.4	6.6	17.8	7.4	26.7	27.8	13.6	38.1	89.1	10.3	0.0	1.0
21 157	Marshall	31,378	-0.4	5.5	15.1	7.3	22.9	29.4	19.8	44.2	99.4	0.7	0.4	0.6
21 163	Meade	29,177	1.9	7.0	19.9	8.8	27.6	26.1	10.6	35.8	93.9	5.7	1.2	1.4
21 167	Mercer	21,285	-0.4	5.9	17.4	7.5	22.4	30.1	16.7	42.5	96.1	4.3	0.8	0.0
21 173	Montgomery	26,733	1.4	7.0	17.7	7.8	26.9	26.7	13.9	38.0	95.2	3.9	0.0	1.9
21 177	Muhlenberg	31,335	-1.0	5.2	16.0	8.6	25.0	28.7	16.6	41.2	93.9	4.8	0.0	1.6
21 179	Nelson	43,980	1.7	6.9	18.8	8.0	25.9	28.3	12.1	38.3	94.3	5.9	0.6	0.5
21 183	Ohio	23,987	0.9	6.6	18.4	7.8	24.2	27.5	15.5	40.0	96.4	3.9	0.0	0.5
21 185	Oldham	60,878	1.6	4.8	22.3	6.5	26.1	30.1	10.0	39.8	92.3	5.0	1.6	2.8
21 193	Perry	28,562	-1.6	6.1	15.8	8.9	26.2	29.6	13.5	41.9	97.5	2.1	1.2	0.0
21 195	Pike	64,635	-1.3	5.7	16.2	8.2	26.0	29.6	14.3	40.6	98.3	0.8	0.6	0.9
21 199	Pulaski	63,415	0.6	6.1	16.6	7.7	24.2	28.6	16.8	41.6	97.6	1.6	0.6	1.3
21 205	Rowan	23,439	0.4	5.4	14.0	21.9	23.1	22.8	12.7	33.1	97.8	1.7	0.9	2.2
21 209	Scott	48,190	3.4	7.0	19.5	9.3	29.0	25.5	9.6	35.4	91.0	6.4	1.2	2.9
21 211	Shelby	42,936	3.1	6.6	18.2	8.0	27.2	27.5	12.5	38.2	87.7	9.2	1.1	4.0
21 217	Taylor	24,648	0.5	5.8	16.4	12.3	22.4	26.7	16.3	39.6	93.8	6.2	0.8	0.7
21 227	Warren	115,586	2.6	6.5	16.2	16.6	25.9	23.7	11.1	32.7	84.1	10.2	3.4	4.7
21 231	Wayne	20,848	0.0	6.3	16.7	7.9	23.9	28.1	17.1	40.8	95.7	2.6	0.0	2.1
21 235	Whitley	35,542	-0.5	6.4	17.9	11.1	24.1	26.5	14.0	37.6	98.7	1.0	0.7	0.9
21 239	Woodford	24,997	0.3	5.4	18.1	7.3	23.6	31.8	13.8	41.5	90.7	7.0	0.9	3.1
22 000	**Louisiana**	4,573,595	1.3	6.9	17.5	10.4	26.3	26.2	12.6	36.0	64.3	32.9	2.0	2.7
22 001	Acadia	61,830	0.2	7.5	19.3	9.4	25.0	26.0	12.8	35.5	80.8	18.5	0.6	2.0
22 003	Allen	25,661	-0.8	6.2	14.9	8.3	29.6	28.4	12.6	39.2	74.7	20.9	1.4	6.3
22 005	Ascension	110,057	4.1	7.7	20.6	8.5	29.1	24.8	9.2	34.7	75.5	22.9	1.2	1.7
22 007	Assumption	23,187	-1.4	5.8	18.3	10.0	23.6	28.1	14.2	38.5	68.3	30.5	0.0	1.0
22 009	Avoyelles	41,850	-1.0	6.8	17.4	8.7	25.8	26.8	14.5	38.5	69.0	30.1	0.5	2.2
22 011	Beauregard	36,091	1.2	7.0	18.9	8.5	26.4	26.2	13.1	37.2	84.8	14.4	1.0	2.8
22 015	Bossier	119,899	3.9	7.4	18.2	9.8	28.1	24.7	11.9	34.6	74.1	21.9	2.3	3.9
22 017	Caddo	256,551	0.6	7.1	17.4	9.8	25.7	26.2	13.7	36.2	49.7	48.1	1.5	2.3
22 019	Calcasieu	193,842	0.6	7.0	18.1	10.3	25.3	26.3	12.9	36.0	72.6	25.9	1.4	1.9
22 029	Concordia	20,659	-2.1	6.7	18.0	8.5	25.3	26.7	14.7	37.9	58.6	40.9	0.0	0.8
22 031	De Soto	26,823	0.9	6.7	17.8	8.3	23.6	28.9	14.7	39.8	58.6	39.4	0.5	2.8
22 033	East Baton Rouge	442,322	0.8	6.6	16.5	14.4	26.8	24.4	11.2	32.8	50.4	46.1	3.5	1.7
22 037	East Feliciana	20,120	-0.8	5.6	14.9	9.0	25.3	31.4	13.8	40.8	54.2	45.6	0.0	0.6
22 039	Evangeline	33,850	-0.8	7.4	19.4	9.9	24.7	25.4	13.3	35.5	70.1	29.3	0.0	1.9
22 041	Franklin	20,712	-1.2	7.4	18.2	8.1	23.7	26.2	16.4	38.6	67.2	32.8	0.0	0.0
22 043	Grant	22,172	-1.2	6.1	16.3	8.4	30.6	26.2	12.4	37.8	81.5	16.7	0.0	3.3
22 045	Iberia	73,580	1.1	7.7	19.4	9.5	24.7	26.3	12.5	35.7	64.4	32.9	2.7	1.4
22 047	Iberville	33,284	-0.3	6.0	16.1	9.7	27.5	28.1	12.6	38.4	51.1	49.4	0.0	1.8
22 051	Jefferson	433,283	0.2	6.5	15.8	9.0	26.8	28.0	14.0	38.5	64.7	27.4	4.6	5.3
22 053	Jefferson Davis	31,540	-0.5	7.3	19.2	8.3	24.7	25.8	14.7	37.5	80.6	18.5	0.6	1.9
22 055	Lafayette	224,469	2.2	7.1	17.2	12.2	28.0	25.1	10.5	33.8	72.1	26.6	1.9	2.0
22 057	Lafourche	96,860	0.4	6.8	17.3	10.5	25.4	27.1	12.8	37.3	82.0	14.0	0.9	5.0
22 061	Lincoln	46,907	0.3	6.0	14.4	25.1	22.5	20.4	11.5	27.7	56.3	41.8	1.9	1.1
22 063	Livingston	130,255	2.6	7.3	19.8	8.4	28.9	25.3	10.4	35.1	92.9	5.7	0.6	1.8
22 067	Morehouse	27,668	-1.2	7.0	17.4	9.2	23.4	27.3	15.7	37.9	52.6	48.4	0.0	0.0
22 069	Natchitoches	39,500	-0.2	6.5	17.5	15.8	22.7	23.5	13.9	33.6	57.1	42.4	0.7	2.3
22 071	Orleans	359,130	6.2	6.6	14.8	12.0	29.4	26.2	11.2	34.7	34.7	60.9	3.3	2.9
22 073	Ouachita	154,658	0.9	7.2	19.0	10.9	26.0	24.3	12.6	34.3	61.4	37.3	1.3	1.5
22 075	Plaquemines	23,564	3.5	7.0	19.9	8.4	26.8	26.8	11.1	36.9	72.5	21.8	3.6	4.4
22 077	Pointe Coupee	22,764	-0.1	6.3	17.6	7.6	22.6	29.6	16.3	42.7	62.8	36.7	0.0	0.9
22 079	Rapides	132,132	0.5	7.0	18.7	8.9	25.3	26.1	14.0	37.2	65.1	32.7	1.4	1.8
22 083	Richland	20,844	1.0	6.8	18.7	9.5	22.9	27.6	14.4	38.9	63.9	36.4	0.0	0.0
22 085	Sabine	24,335	0.4	6.7	17.8	8.4	22.5	27.5	17.1	41.0	74.6	17.7	0.6	12.0
22 087	St. Bernard	39,326	13.2	8.1	17.8	10.4	29.2	25.4	9.0	32.7	77.7	20.4	2.6	2.4
22 089	St. Charles	52,693	-0.3	6.7	19.7	8.9	25.9	28.4	10.4	37.3	72.0	26.6	1.2	1.7
22 093	St. James	21,855	-1.2	6.8	18.4	9.4	23.5	28.4	13.5	38.6	48.1	51.4	0.0	0.0
22 095	St. John the Baptist	45,186	-2.0	7.0	19.5	9.6	26.0	27.0	10.8	35.5	44.3	54.6	0.9	0.9
22 097	St. Landry	83,540	0.2	7.9	19.2	9.0	23.3	26.8	13.8	36.7	58.0	42.2	0.5	1.6
22 099	St. Martin	52,592	1.0	7.3	18.7	9.0	25.8	27.1	12.1	36.1	67.1	31.4	0.9	1.1

Table A-2. Counties — Who: Age, Race/Ethnicity, and Household Structure, 2010–2012—*Continued*

STATE and County code	STATE or County	Percent Hispanic or Latino	Percent foreign born	Total households	Household type (percent)							Percent of households with people under 18 years	Percent of households with people 60 years and over
					Family households				Nonfamily households				
					Total family households	Married-couple families	Male household families	Female household families	Total nonfamily households	One-person households			
	ACS table number:	B03003	C05003	B11001	B11001	B11001	B11001	B11001	B11001	B11001		B11005	B11006
	Column number:	14	15	16	17	18	19	20	21	22		23	24
	Kentucky—Cont.												
21 083	Graves	5.8	3.9	14,517	71.4	58.0	3.2	10.2	28.6	26.8		32.5	37.9
21 085	Grayson	1.5	0.8	9,944	68.1	57.4	3.4	7.3	31.9	27.8		30.4	38.6
21 089	Greenup	0.9	0.9	14,208	70.6	54.2	4.3	12.1	29.4	25.9		31.6	42.2
21 093	Hardin	5.2	4.7	39,246	73.2	54.2	3.9	15.1	26.8	22.4		38.1	30.0
21 095	Harlan	0.8	0.4	11,066	70.4	48.7	7.0	14.8	29.6	26.5		33.5	41.0
21 101	Henderson	1.9	0.8	18,826	64.3	47.9	4.4	12.0	35.7	32.2		29.8	37.2
21 107	Hopkins	1.6	0.9	18,257	67.3	50.3	3.9	13.1	32.7	29.3		32.3	38.4
21 111	Jefferson	4.5	6.6	303,988	61.2	41.4	4.7	15.1	38.8	32.6		30.3	33.4
21 113	Jessamine	2.7	3.0	18,112	73.5	55.6	4.6	13.3	26.5	20.7		38.0	31.7
21 115	Johnson	0.5	0.5	9,263	71.5	55.8	4.9	10.8	28.5	25.5		33.2	37.7
21 117	Kenton	2.8	2.3	61,671	63.8	45.2	5.3	13.3	36.2	29.7		32.4	30.3
21 121	Knox	0.1	0.5	12,762	67.2	50.4	4.1	12.7	32.8	30.3		27.2	38.4
21 125	Laurel	1.3	1.1	23,280	71.5	52.7	4.7	14.1	28.5	23.4		35.3	34.0
21 133	Letcher	0.6	0.4	9,157	70.2	56.6	3.6	10.0	29.8	26.8		30.2	40.8
21 137	Lincoln	1.6	0.3	9,602	71.6	50.0	7.4	14.3	28.4	24.8		35.3	39.8
21 141	Logan	2.5	1.0	10,801	66.4	47.9	5.9	12.6	33.6	31.7		28.3	40.5
21 145	McCracken	2.2	2.3	27,159	64.8	48.4	4.3	12.1	35.2	30.6		29.1	37.6
21 151	Madison	2.2	1.9	31,085	64.4	47.3	4.4	12.6	35.6	27.9		32.1	30.0
21 155	Marion	2.6	1.1	7,369	67.8	51.0	6.4	10.4	32.2	28.4		34.0	37.9
21 157	Marshall	1.2	1.2	12,119	72.7	57.6	4.3	10.8	27.3	24.6		28.8	44.9
21 163	Meade	3.3	1.4	10,282	78.2	60.1	4.5	13.6	21.8	18.3		37.2	31.8
21 167	Mercer	2.3	1.5	8,647	67.1	50.4	3.4	13.3	32.9	28.4		28.3	39.3
21 173	Montgomery	2.6	0.7	10,131	67.9	46.7	6.7	14.6	32.1	27.0		35.4	35.5
21 177	Muhlenberg	1.2	1.1	11,839	72.6	56.6	4.9	11.0	27.4	25.3		30.4	42.7
21 179	Nelson	2.0	1.6	16,470	75.5	56.0	6.5	13.0	24.5	20.8		36.6	30.4
21 183	Ohio	1.1	0.4	8,439	73.9	58.2	3.1	12.6	26.1	23.4		31.6	38.2
21 185	Oldham	3.5	3.2	19,533	82.5	68.2	4.4	10.0	17.5	14.2		42.5	31.4
21 193	Perry	0.3	1.0	11,176	70.6	45.9	7.6	17.1	29.4	22.8		34.2	36.1
21 195	Pike	0.7	0.7	26,492	68.4	50.5	5.0	12.8	31.6	28.6		32.3	37.8
21 199	Pulaski	2.2	1.1	26,135	68.2	52.8	2.6	12.8	31.8	27.0		30.8	37.7
21 205	Rowan	0.8	1.0	8,143	64.6	47.6	4.9	12.1	35.4	27.2		30.5	35.6
21 209	Scott	4.2	2.5	17,881	71.3	53.7	4.8	12.9	28.7	25.2		38.2	26.7
21 211	Shelby	9.0	6.0	15,394	75.7	58.5	5.7	11.6	24.3	20.4		36.7	36.4
21 217	Taylor	1.3	0.9	9,439	66.7	52.1	2.6	12.1	33.3	28.6		30.3	38.8
21 227	Warren	4.7	7.3	44,378	62.2	45.2	4.2	12.9	37.8	29.1		31.5	27.8
21 231	Wayne	2.9	0.8	8,176	71.5	52.3	4.3	14.9	28.5	25.9		31.4	40.7
21 235	Whitley	0.9	0.8	13,308	72.4	50.1	7.9	14.5	27.6	23.6		37.4	36.1
21 239	Woodford	6.7	6.3	9,506	65.3	51.8	4.4	9.1	34.7	29.0		30.2	36.0
22 000	**Louisiana**	4.4	3.8	1,706,091	66.2	44.0	5.0	17.2	33.8	28.5		33.8	33.6
22 001	Acadia	1.8	1.5	22,508	69.2	48.1	4.2	16.9	30.8	25.5		35.3	33.9
22 003	Allen	4.9	5.0	8,205	68.7	45.3	6.3	17.1	31.3	28.5		41.6	34.0
22 005	Ascension	4.8	3.2	37,877	74.9	56.7	4.2	13.9	25.1	21.0		43.3	27.6
22 007	Assumption	2.1	1.6	8,857	73.7	52.3	6.4	15.0	26.3	21.7		35.4	36.6
22 009	Avoyelles	1.5	1.2	15,277	69.3	47.2	4.7	17.3	30.7	27.1		33.3	38.2
22 011	Beauregard	3.0	2.0	13,040	74.7	55.8	5.6	13.3	25.3	22.1		39.5	35.3
22 015	Bossier	6.1	4.5	45,632	67.0	46.7	4.6	15.6	33.0	29.2		36.3	30.1
22 017	Caddo	2.5	2.3	98,582	63.1	37.2	5.6	20.3	36.9	32.4		31.3	34.8
22 019	Calcasieu	2.7	2.4	73,614	69.2	47.2	5.3	16.7	30.8	25.8		35.8	34.0
22 029	Concordia	1.1	1.3	7,940	70.1	40.7	4.2	25.3	29.9	27.7		37.6	39.9
22 031	De Soto	2.6	1.2	10,254	69.2	44.9	3.4	20.9	30.8	27.2		34.0	41.9
22 033	East Baton Rouge	3.8	4.8	167,220	61.2	39.1	4.9	17.2	38.8	31.2		30.7	30.2
22 037	East Feliciana	1.0	0.8	6,901	71.5	49.3	5.8	16.4	28.5	26.6		29.5	39.6
22 039	Evangeline	2.3	1.3	12,172	71.7	46.3	5.1	20.3	28.3	26.3		37.8	35.8
22 041	Franklin	0.4	0.3	7,692	67.0	41.8	5.0	20.2	33.0	30.5		34.1	37.8
22 043	Grant	4.3	3.3	7,199	64.8	47.2	3.7	13.9	35.2	28.8		32.4	35.9
22 045	Iberia	3.3	3.7	26,463	72.3	46.3	7.2	18.8	27.7	23.4		40.4	33.6
22 047	Iberville	2.1	0.7	11,101	71.0	38.9	8.3	23.7	29.0	25.3		34.4	37.0
22 051	Jefferson	12.8	11.2	166,467	64.2	42.6	5.0	16.7	35.8	30.6		31.4	36.5
22 053	Jefferson Davis	1.8	1.0	11,816	71.3	48.6	5.7	17.0	28.7	26.5		36.9	36.6
22 055	Lafayette	4.0	4.3	86,632	62.3	43.1	4.2	14.9	37.7	30.9		33.4	26.8
22 057	Lafourche	3.9	3.0	35,360	71.5	51.3	5.2	14.9	28.5	22.9		36.4	33.6
22 061	Lincoln	2.6	5.6	16,886	60.5	38.2	3.8	18.6	39.5	30.1		30.9	30.3
22 063	Livingston	3.1	1.8	46,185	74.7	54.8	6.6	13.2	25.3	21.7		40.9	30.5
22 067	Morehouse	1.0	0.7	10,559	68.5	44.9	2.3	21.3	31.5	29.1		33.3	37.5
22 069	Natchitoches	1.9	1.1	15,013	63.6	41.8	3.8	17.9	36.4	29.7		33.7	36.8
22 071	Orleans	5.3	5.8	146,018	52.0	26.7	5.1	20.2	48.0	39.1		26.6	30.7
22 073	Ouachita	1.9	1.9	57,825	65.0	40.6	4.8	19.6	35.0	30.3		35.3	32.1
22 075	Plaquemines	5.1	4.2	8,823	75.4	52.8	5.6	17.0	24.6	19.9		41.4	29.6
22 077	Pointe Coupee	2.2	1.6	9,121	64.8	47.1	6.1	11.6	35.2	30.9		29.2	41.7
22 079	Rapides	2.7	2.4	47,148	64.9	44.0	3.9	17.0	35.1	31.1		32.2	36.7
22 083	Richland	1.8	0.4	7,566	75.6	51.2	5.3	19.2	24.4	22.2		38.9	36.6
22 085	Sabine	3.5	1.1	9,246	69.0	48.3	4.4	16.3	31.0	26.8		32.2	42.0
22 087	St. Bernard	9.5	4.6	13,694	71.7	46.2	5.4	20.1	28.3	22.3		38.0	26.6
22 089	St. Charles	5.2	3.8	18,267	75.0	49.8	4.6	20.6	25.0	19.5		40.8	32.1
22 093	St. James	0.5	0.7	7,710	78.8	50.9	3.0	24.9	21.2	20.3		39.5	35.9
22 095	St. John the Baptist	4.9	2.7	15,467	71.7	47.4	5.1	19.3	28.3	24.4		36.8	32.3
22 097	St. Landry	1.7	0.7	30,940	69.6	45.8	4.9	19.0	30.4	27.2		34.5	37.7
22 099	St. Martin	2.2	1.6	18,672	69.7	48.4	3.5	17.9	30.3	27.3		34.7	34.7

Table A-2. Counties — Who: Age, Race/Ethnicity, and Household Structure, 2010–2012—*Continued*

STATE and County code	STATE or County	Total population	Percent change 2010–2012	Population by age (percent)						Median age	White	Black	Asian, Hawaiian, or Pacific Islander	American Indian, Alaska Native, or some other race
				Under 5 years	5 to 17 years	18 to 24 years	25 to 44 years	45 to 64 years	65 years and over					
	ACS table number:	B01003	Population estimates	B01001	B01001	B01001	B01001	B01001	B01001	B01002	B02008	B02009	B02011 + B02012	B02010 + B02013
	Column number:	1	2	3	4	5	6	7	8	9	10	11	12	13
	Louisiana—Cont.													
22 101	St. Mary............	54,174	-1.6	7.0	18.2	9.3	24.9	27.5	13.3	37.5	62.4	33.3	2.2	5.5
22 103	St. Tammany.............	236,980	2.1	6.2	19.1	7.5	24.8	29.2	13.2	39.6	85.2	12.2	2.0	2.4
22 105	Tangipahoa.............	122,471	1.6	7.1	17.9	12.5	25.5	25.2	11.8	33.7	67.9	30.9	0.8	1.6
22 109	Terrebonne............	111,730	0.3	7.3	18.5	10.0	26.9	25.8	11.4	35.1	72.9	19.4	1.4	8.9
22 111	Union...............	22,620	-1.4	6.1	16.7	9.3	22.1	28.6	17.1	40.8	71.8	27.1	0.2	2.2
22 113	Vermilion............	58,367	1.1	7.3	19.3	8.6	25.7	25.9	13.1	36.4	82.2	15.1	2.3	1.4
22 115	Vernon..............	52,934	2.1	9.1	18.3	13.4	29.8	19.8	9.6	29.9	80.9	16.7	3.8	3.8
22 117	Washington............	46,954	-0.8	6.6	18.3	8.2	24.2	28.0	14.7	39.0	68.7	31.4	0.0	1.2
22 119	Webster.............	41,136	-0.7	6.3	17.1	8.6	23.5	27.4	17.1	40.9	65.0	34.1	0.5	1.7
22 121	West Baton Rouge.........	24,046	0.7	6.9	17.9	10.2	26.5	27.3	11.3	36.3	62.4	36.8	2.1	0.5
23 000	**Maine**	1,328,440	0.1	5.1	15.2	8.8	23.5	31.0	16.4	43.2	96.9	1.6	1.5	1.9
23 001	Androscoggin	107,571	-0.1	6.2	16.1	9.3	25.2	28.7	14.5	40.2	96.6	2.5	1.3	3.9
23 003	Aroostook.............	71,328	-1.2	4.9	14.8	8.1	21.2	31.4	19.6	45.7	97.2	0.9	0.8	3.0
23 005	Cumberland.............	282,689	0.9	5.1	15.4	9.1	25.6	30.0	14.8	41.5	94.6	3.1	2.7	1.3
23 007	Franklin...............	30,696	-0.3	4.7	14.4	11.7	20.7	31.3	17.3	44.0	98.8	0.5	0.8	1.3
23 009	Hancock..............	54,493	0.3	4.7	13.2	7.8	21.8	33.5	19.0	46.6	98.4	0.7	1.2	1.1
23 011	Kennebec.............	121,959	-0.2	5.0	15.4	8.8	23.3	31.5	16.0	43.3	97.4	1.1	1.1	1.7
23 013	Knox...............	39,697	-0.1	4.6	14.5	6.4	22.0	32.6	19.9	46.9	98.2	1.0	0.8	1.6
23 015	Lincoln..............	34,269	-0.6	4.6	13.6	6.1	20.2	33.0	22.5	48.7	98.6	0.7	0.8	1.3
23 017	Oxford..............	57,670	-0.5	5.0	16.0	7.0	22.0	32.5	17.5	45.0	98.4	0.7	1.1	1.3
23 019	Penobscot.............	153,856	-0.1	4.9	14.6	13.0	23.5	29.2	14.9	40.5	96.9	1.2	1.5	2.3
23 023	Sagadahoc.............	35,181	-0.1	5.0	15.4	6.6	23.4	32.4	17.1	44.6	98.0	1.5	1.2	1.6
23 025	Somerset	52,024	-0.6	4.9	16.1	6.9	23.3	31.8	17.0	44.2	98.2	0.7	0.8	1.5
23 027	Waldo...............	38,806	0.0	5.4	15.3	7.6	22.5	32.3	16.8	44.5	98.6	0.8	0.6	1.8
23 029	Washington	32,648	-1.0	5.0	14.2	7.7	21.3	31.7	20.1	46.1	94.1	0.9	0.9	6.1
23 031	York...............	198,155	0.9	5.1	15.8	7.7	23.7	31.7	16.0	43.3	97.6	1.2	1.6	1.2
24 000	**Maryland**	5,837,378	1.7	6.3	16.8	9.7	26.9	27.8	12.6	38.0	60.7	31.0	6.7	4.6
24 001	Allegany.............	74,495	-1.3	4.5	13.3	12.4	24.4	27.2	18.2	41.6	90.3	9.2	1.2	0.8
24 003	Anne Arundel	544,889	2.1	6.4	16.6	9.1	27.3	28.4	12.3	38.5	77.8	17.2	4.7	3.7
24 005	Baltimore.............	812,043	1.4	6.0	15.8	10.1	25.6	27.6	14.8	39.2	66.3	27.6	6.1	2.3
24 009	Calvert..............	89,279	0.8	5.3	20.2	8.4	23.5	31.3	11.4	40.1	84.1	14.5	2.2	2.3
24 011	Caroline.............	32,913	-1.1	6.7	18.0	8.9	24.5	28.1	13.8	39.2	81.8	15.3	1.0	3.8
24 013	Carroll	167,261	0.0	5.1	18.8	8.8	22.7	30.8	13.8	41.6	94.5	4.1	2.0	1.1
24 015	Cecil...............	101,500	0.5	6.2	18.3	9.3	24.9	29.1	12.2	39.6	90.9	7.3	1.5	2.1
24 017	Charles..............	148,982	2.4	6.2	19.6	9.0	27.1	28.2	9.9	37.5	53.1	43.7	4.5	2.8
24 019	Dorchester.............	32,638	-0.3	6.1	15.2	7.9	23.0	29.8	17.9	43.2	68.9	28.8	1.2	2.7
24 021	Frederick............	237,037	2.3	6.2	18.6	8.6	26.3	28.8	11.5	38.8	84.5	10.1	5.3	3.3
24 023	Garrett..............	30,009	-0.7	5.0	16.4	8.4	22.6	29.5	18.1	43.3	98.1	1.3	0.5	0.8
24 025	Harford.............	246,839	1.4	5.9	18.1	8.4	25.3	29.3	13.0	39.7	83.1	14.1	3.4	1.7
24 027	Howard	293,972	3.8	6.0	19.4	7.5	27.1	29.4	10.7	38.8	64.3	19.7	16.2	3.6
24 029	Kent...............	20,213	0.0	5.4	11.3	13.3	19.0	28.8	22.3	46.2	81.8	16.0	1.1	1.4
24 031	Montgomery.............	990,787	2.9	6.5	17.2	7.6	28.0	28.0	12.6	38.5	60.2	18.9	15.9	9.3
24 033	Prince George's.............	873,629	1.8	6.8	16.7	11.6	28.7	26.3	9.9	35.1	23.2	65.9	4.9	8.8
24 035	Queen Anne's.............	48,291	1.5	5.5	17.8	7.7	22.9	30.6	15.5	42.4	90.5	7.6	1.5	1.4
24 037	St. Mary's.............	107,482	3.0	7.1	18.7	10.1	26.5	27.0	10.6	35.9	82.5	15.9	3.7	1.8
24 039	Somerset	26,371	-0.9	4.8	11.4	19.3	24.6	25.6	14.2	36.4	55.9	43.7	0.9	2.6
24 041	Talbot	37,976	0.6	5.0	14.2	7.1	19.5	29.5	24.7	47.7	83.6	15.6	1.5	0.7
24 043	Washington	148,595	0.9	5.9	16.6	8.5	26.5	28.0	14.5	40.1	87.2	12.0	2.1	1.4
24 045	Wicomico	99,840	1.8	6.3	15.9	14.9	24.0	25.7	13.3	35.5	71.5	25.8	3.3	2.6
24 047	Worcester	51,494	0.2	4.5	13.6	7.5	20.0	30.9	23.5	48.2	84.3	14.9	1.4	1.1
24 510	Baltimore city.............	620,843	0.1	6.7	14.7	12.3	29.2	25.3	11.8	34.3	31.8	65.0	3.0	2.8
25 000	**Massachusetts**	6,605,468	1.3	5.5	15.8	10.4	26.3	27.9	14.1	39.3	82.9	8.4	6.3	5.3
25 001	Barnstable.............	215,681	-0.2	4.1	12.8	6.9	18.3	32.2	25.7	50.4	94.8	3.0	1.6	2.4
25 003	Berkshire.............	130,565	-0.9	4.5	14.6	9.5	21.3	30.9	19.2	45.1	94.4	4.0	1.9	2.0
25 005	Bristol.............	549,972	0.3	5.6	16.4	9.6	25.6	28.3	14.5	40.2	90.9	4.8	2.5	4.3
25 009	Essex.............	750,452	1.4	5.8	17.0	8.9	24.5	29.3	14.4	40.7	82.7	4.9	3.6	10.9
25 011	Franklin.............	71,495	0.3	4.6	14.6	8.1	22.9	34.1	15.7	44.9	96.4	1.9	2.0	2.3
25 013	Hampden.............	465,177	0.4	5.9	17.4	10.7	24.1	27.4	14.4	38.8	79.8	10.0	2.4	10.1
25 015	Hampshire.............	159,575	0.4	3.7	12.5	22.4	20.7	27.6	13.2	36.3	91.6	3.3	5.7	1.6
25 017	Middlesex.............	1,521,993	2.0	5.7	15.4	9.5	28.6	27.5	13.3	38.6	82.8	5.9	10.8	3.4
25 021	Norfolk.............	677,462	1.3	5.5	16.8	8.2	25.6	29.1	14.8	40.8	83.3	6.6	10.0	1.9
25 023	Plymouth.............	497,975	0.8	5.6	18.0	8.3	23.5	30.2	14.5	41.4	87.2	9.5	1.9	3.6
25 025	Suffolk.............	734,699	2.7	5.6	12.0	17.1	33.6	21.2	10.6	31.6	61.2	27.2	9.2	8.7
25 027	Worcester.............	803,429	0.7	5.8	17.3	9.7	25.4	28.7	13.0	39.4	88.1	5.4	4.9	4.4
26 000	**Michigan**	9,879,277	0.1	5.9	17.4	10.0	24.5	28.1	14.2	39.2	81.5	15.3	3.1	2.8
26 005	Allegan.............	111,701	0.5	6.5	19.2	7.8	23.9	29.0	13.6	39.6	96.2	1.9	0.8	2.9
26 007	Alpena.............	29,379	-1.1	5.0	15.4	7.4	20.7	31.4	20.0	46.2	98.1	0.7	0.0	2.2
26 009	Antrim.............	23,442	-0.4	4.6	15.6	6.1	19.1	31.5	23.0	48.6	97.9	0.7	0.0	2.6
26 015	Barry.............	58,996	-0.1	5.7	18.2	7.6	22.7	30.5	15.3	41.8	97.9	0.8	0.5	1.9
26 017	Bay.............	107,310	-0.7	5.6	16.2	8.5	23.2	29.7	16.7	42.0	96.8	2.4	0.8	2.6
26 021	Berrien.............	156,452	-0.5	6.2	17.0	8.5	23.2	28.6	16.5	40.9	80.0	16.6	2.2	3.6
26 023	Branch.............	44,306	-2.8	6.4	17.5	8.0	24.4	28.3	15.4	40.3	95.8	2.8	0.8	1.6
26 025	Calhoun.............	135,568	-0.7	6.3	17.7	9.0	24.3	27.7	15.0	39.6	85.7	12.8	2.0	2.6

Table A-2. Counties — Who: Age, Race/Ethnicity, and Household Structure, 2010–2012—*Continued*

STATE and County code	STATE or County	Percent Hispanic or Latino	Percent foreign born	Total households	Household type (percent)						Percent of households with people under 18 years	Percent of households with people 60 years and over
					Family households				Nonfamily households			
					Total family households	Married-couple families	Male household families	Female household families	Total nonfamily households	One-person households		
ACS table number:		B03003	C05003	B11001	B11001	B11001	B11001	B11001	B11001	B11001	B11005	B11006
Column number:		14	15	16	17	18	19	20	21	22	23	24
	Louisiana—Cont.											
22 101	St. Mary	5.5	4.4	20,095	69.7	44.5	6.4	18.8	30.3	25.3	36.1	35.3
22 103	St. Tammany	4.9	3.4	87,583	72.4	54.7	4.5	13.1	27.6	22.7	33.8	36.0
22 105	Tangipahoa	3.6	2.1	44,111	68.4	45.0	5.1	18.2	31.6	25.9	35.2	33.7
22 109	Terrebonne	4.1	3.5	39,436	71.4	49.0	7.1	15.2	28.6	22.3	38.3	31.8
22 111	Union	4.2	2.5	8,376	72.2	55.1	3.6	13.4	27.8	25.6	32.4	42.2
22 113	Vermilion	2.6	2.5	21,659	71.8	53.4	4.7	13.7	28.2	23.3	37.9	32.9
22 115	Vernon	7.8	3.7	18,437	75.9	58.8	3.6	13.5	24.1	21.3	41.4	28.4
22 117	Washington	2.0	1.0	17,756	66.3	44.6	3.1	18.6	33.7	31.5	31.5	38.8
22 119	Webster	1.7	0.4	16,226	67.0	42.6	6.4	18.1	33.0	29.1	31.9	41.6
22 121	West Baton Rouge	2.6	2.0	9,016	70.3	46.2	7.5	16.6	29.7	25.8	39.4	31.9
23 000	**Maine**	1.3	3.5	552,963	62.9	48.9	4.2	9.7	37.1	28.9	27.0	38.5
23 001	Androscoggin	1.6	3.2	44,502	63.3	46.7	4.8	11.8	36.7	28.2	30.7	34.8
23 003	Aroostook	1.0	4.8	30,763	63.2	50.9	3.8	8.5	36.8	31.7	25.1	42.0
23 005	Cumberland	1.9	5.8	117,068	60.3	47.2	3.7	9.4	39.7	30.3	27.6	35.2
23 007	Franklin	1.0	1.7	12,198	63.9	50.6	4.7	8.6	36.1	28.0	24.6	40.1
23 009	Hancock	1.2	2.6	24,248	61.8	50.4	3.1	8.3	38.2	31.0	23.9	42.0
23 011	Kennebec	1.3	2.1	51,509	62.7	47.1	4.7	10.8	37.3	29.1	27.6	37.0
23 013	Knox	0.9	2.7	17,060	62.8	48.0	5.5	9.3	37.2	31.4	23.0	45.3
23 015	Lincoln	0.9	2.9	14,846	64.9	50.5	4.0	10.4	35.1	27.7	23.9	48.1
23 017	Oxford	1.0	1.7	23,321	64.7	49.8	5.1	9.8	35.3	28.0	23.8	40.2
23 019	Penobscot	1.1	2.9	62,186	61.3	48.1	4.0	9.2	38.7	27.7	26.9	36.0
23 023	Sagadahoc	1.4	2.6	14,854	65.4	51.6	4.3	9.6	34.6	27.2	25.5	39.1
23 025	Somerset	0.8	1.7	21,860	65.4	50.4	4.0	11.0	34.6	27.5	28.0	39.5
23 027	Waldo	1.0	2.1	16,604	64.4	49.8	4.3	10.3	35.6	28.5	27.7	42.0
23 029	Washington	1.5	3.6	14,115	62.2	47.9	4.1	10.3	37.8	31.9	28.2	45.7
23 031	York	1.3	3.4	80,414	65.2	51.3	4.7	9.2	34.8	26.9	27.9	38.7
24 000	**Maryland**	8.4	14.0	2,141,086	66.9	47.4	4.9	14.7	33.1	27.2	33.7	34.2
24 001	Allegany	1.5	1.5	28,829	59.6	44.2	3.1	12.3	40.4	32.8	25.1	42.5
24 003	Anne Arundel	6.4	7.8	199,577	69.6	53.5	4.9	11.2	30.4	24.4	34.1	33.4
24 005	Baltimore	4.4	11.3	313,195	64.5	45.8	4.6	14.1	35.5	29.4	31.3	37.2
24 009	Calvert	2.9	3.1	30,780	75.9	58.3	5.2	12.4	24.1	20.3	39.4	33.9
24 011	Caroline	5.5	4.2	11,983	71.1	53.2	4.4	13.5	28.9	22.9	34.4	36.9
24 013	Carroll	2.7	3.5	59,373	73.6	61.1	3.9	8.7	26.4	21.9	35.3	37.6
24 015	Cecil	3.6	3.1	35,997	72.8	56.3	5.1	11.4	27.2	22.6	36.0	35.0
24 017	Charles	4.5	5.8	51,274	74.0	52.1	5.2	16.7	26.0	21.7	39.0	28.9
24 019	Dorchester	3.8	4.2	13,827	68.0	46.7	3.9	17.3	32.0	27.9	28.8	39.8
24 021	Frederick	7.6	9.7	85,862	72.3	57.7	4.1	10.5	27.7	22.4	36.4	32.1
24 023	Garrett	0.8	1.8	12,144	68.2	55.7	3.3	9.1	31.8	28.8	26.9	39.9
24 025	Harford	3.7	5.3	90,302	73.8	57.1	4.5	12.1	26.2	21.4	36.2	34.6
24 027	Howard	6.0	18.4	106,284	73.8	59.1	3.8	10.9	26.2	21.4	39.2	29.5
24 029	Kent	4.5	4.0	7,779	62.5	47.4	2.6	12.5	37.5	34.4	23.1	52.2
24 031	Montgomery	17.5	32.2	359,995	68.4	52.7	4.4	11.3	31.6	25.9	35.3	34.4
24 033	Prince George's	15.3	20.4	302,436	65.9	38.2	6.6	21.1	34.1	27.8	35.8	30.7
24 035	Queen Anne's	3.2	3.5	17,107	77.8	63.4	5.5	8.8	22.2	18.2	33.6	39.7
24 037	St. Mary's	4.0	4.4	37,772	75.5	61.2	4.7	9.6	24.5	19.5	38.9	28.7
24 039	Somerset	3.4	3.2	8,470	59.9	41.6	5.7	12.6	40.1	31.3	25.7	40.9
24 041	Talbot	5.6	5.3	16,033	67.8	52.7	3.9	11.2	32.2	30.1	26.4	50.3
24 043	Washington	3.6	4.9	55,790	68.1	50.3	4.6	13.3	31.9	26.4	32.9	36.6
24 045	Wicomico	4.7	7.4	36,019	68.0	45.2	4.7	18.1	32.0	25.2	36.3	34.4
24 047	Worcester	3.2	4.5	19,683	66.4	53.8	4.2	8.5	33.6	28.3	24.2	49.5
24 510	Baltimore city	4.3	7.3	240,575	52.3	23.6	5.2	23.4	47.7	39.4	27.3	33.2
25 000	**Massachusetts**	9.9	15.0	2,524,028	63.3	46.5	4.0	12.7	36.7	29.1	30.8	35.7
25 001	Barnstable	2.3	7.0	93,426	61.8	49.1	3.2	9.5	38.2	32.1	21.4	51.9
25 003	Berkshire	3.6	5.0	55,573	58.7	42.4	4.3	12.1	41.3	35.7	25.0	43.8
25 005	Bristol	6.2	11.9	209,314	65.7	46.6	4.3	14.8	34.3	28.0	31.7	36.1
25 009	Essex	17.0	15.1	285,412	66.2	47.7	4.5	13.9	33.8	28.0	33.0	37.3
25 011	Franklin	3.3	4.7	30,159	60.8	44.3	5.4	11.2	39.2	28.8	28.1	38.6
25 013	Hampden	21.5	9.1	177,900	65.3	42.0	5.3	18.0	34.7	28.8	33.3	36.2
25 015	Hampshire	4.9	8.3	58,670	58.8	44.8	3.0	10.9	41.2	30.6	26.1	37.0
25 017	Middlesex	6.8	19.4	580,358	63.7	50.4	3.3	10.0	36.3	28.0	31.0	34.0
25 021	Norfolk	3.4	15.3	257,153	65.4	52.5	3.1	9.9	34.6	28.1	31.9	37.0
25 023	Plymouth	3.3	8.0	179,835	70.9	53.7	4.2	13.0	29.1	23.7	35.4	38.8
25 025	Suffolk	20.4	27.5	288,162	48.9	27.5	4.5	16.9	51.1	37.5	24.6	27.9
25 027	Worcester	9.7	11.1	298,224	66.6	49.8	4.5	12.3	33.4	27.0	33.8	33.9
26 000	**Michigan**	4.5	6.1	3,805,261	65.6	48.2	4.5	12.9	34.4	28.9	30.9	35.9
26 005	Allegan	6.8	3.1	41,881	73.3	58.7	3.8	10.9	26.7	21.7	33.7	34.3
26 007	Alpena	1.1	1.0	12,862	65.2	51.8	4.6	8.9	34.8	29.2	26.2	41.6
26 009	Antrim	1.8	2.4	9,536	71.1	60.9	3.6	6.5	28.9	24.4	25.2	46.0
26 015	Barry	2.4	1.4	22,355	73.3	63.2	3.0	7.1	26.7	22.2	31.6	38.6
26 017	Bay	4.8	1.2	43,793	65.5	50.4	3.7	11.5	34.5	28.7	28.3	38.9
26 021	Berrien	4.7	6.0	59,373	66.7	49.8	3.8	13.1	33.3	29.4	29.5	39.9
26 023	Branch	4.1	2.1	15,640	70.4	55.2	4.3	10.9	29.6	24.1	31.8	40.2
26 025	Calhoun	4.6	3.7	52,569	65.6	45.8	5.3	14.5	34.4	29.5	31.6	37.8

STATE and County code	STATE or County	Total population	Percent change 2010–2012	Population by age (percent)						Median age	Race alone or in combination (percent)			
				Under 5 years	5 to 17 years	18 to 24 years	25 to 44 years	45 to 64 years	65 years and over		White	Black	Asian, Hawaiian, or Pacific Islander	American Indian, Alaska Native, or some other race
	ACS table number:	B01003	Population estimates	B01001	B01001	B01001	B01001	B01001	B01001	B01002	B02008	B02009	B02011 + B02012	B02010 + B02013
	Column number:	1	2	3	4	5	6	7	8	9	10	11	12	13
	Michigan—Cont.													
26 027	Cass....................	52,338	0.1	5.5	17.4	7.6	21.7	30.8	17.0	43.1	92.1	7.0	1.1	3.8
26 029	Charlevoix.............	25,978	0.4	4.9	16.4	6.7	20.7	32.0	19.3	46.0	96.1	1.2	0.7	3.4
26 031	Cheboygan.............	25,968	-1.0	4.5	15.6	6.3	20.0	31.5	22.1	47.7	97.0	1.0	0.6	5.3
26 033	Chippewa..............	38,725	1.1	5.2	14.6	10.7	26.9	27.8	14.9	39.4	76.4	6.3	1.4	21.6
26 035	Clare....................	30,900	-0.8	5.7	15.1	7.9	20.3	30.8	20.1	45.6	98.3	1.1	0.4	1.5
26 037	Clinton.................	75,746	0.8	5.3	18.8	10.8	23.1	28.4	13.6	38.2	96.2	2.6	1.9	1.7
26 041	Delta...................	36,969	-0.5	5.3	15.3	7.4	20.9	31.6	19.5	46.1	97.5	1.5	0.1	4.0
26 043	Dickinson..............	26,150	0.3	5.1	15.8	6.8	21.2	32.1	19.0	46.0	98.3	0.6	0.8	2.0
26 045	Eaton...................	107,952	0.1	5.6	17.2	9.1	23.7	29.9	14.5	40.7	90.7	7.7	2.2	2.5
26 047	Emmet..................	32,793	0.8	5.0	17.0	7.9	22.1	30.8	17.3	43.3	95.5	1.2	1.2	5.1
26 049	Genesee................	421,871	-1.6	6.3	18.3	9.1	24.4	27.8	14.2	38.7	77.3	22.2	1.4	2.1
26 051	Gladwin................	25,662	-0.8	4.6	15.1	6.8	19.4	30.9	23.2	48.2	98.4	0.7	0.4	1.6
26 055	Grand Traverse........	88,147	2.4	5.3	16.0	8.1	25.0	30.3	15.2	41.1	95.9	1.9	1.2	2.5
26 057	Gratiot.................	42,214	-0.9	5.4	15.9	11.2	25.4	27.0	15.1	39.1	92.8	6.2	0.4	2.5
26 059	Hillsdale...............	46,466	-0.8	5.8	17.5	9.7	22.0	28.8	16.1	41.4	98.2	0.8	0.6	1.2
26 061	Houghton..............	36,642	-0.5	5.9	14.9	20.0	20.1	24.0	15.1	33.3	95.4	1.3	3.3	2.0
26 063	Huron..................	32,743	-1.8	4.6	15.6	6.5	20.1	31.1	22.1	47.4	98.3	0.7	0.7	1.2
26 065	Ingham.................	281,470	0.3	5.7	14.9	19.8	25.0	23.8	10.8	31.4	80.8	14.2	6.3	4.3
26 067	Ionia...................	63,907	0.1	6.2	18.4	8.9	27.5	27.2	11.7	36.8	93.8	5.5	0.6	3.3
26 069	Iosco...................	25,562	-1.7	3.7	13.4	6.4	17.4	32.5	26.6	51.4	97.3	0.9	0.9	2.1
26 073	Isabella................	70,525	0.4	5.1	12.7	31.7	20.5	20.2	9.9	25.4	91.4	4.0	2.2	5.9
26 075	Jackson................	160,115	0.1	5.8	17.0	9.3	24.8	28.7	14.5	39.7	89.7	9.6	1.1	2.0
26 077	Kalamazoo.............	252,546	1.5	6.1	16.3	15.5	24.9	24.8	12.5	34.1	84.7	13.0	3.0	2.4
26 081	Kent....................	608,517	1.9	7.2	18.7	10.4	26.8	25.5	11.4	34.5	85.2	11.5	3.0	3.8
26 087	Lapeer.................	88,147	0.0	5.1	18.5	7.8	22.9	31.7	14.0	42.2	97.4	1.4	0.6	2.0
26 089	Leelanau...............	21,643	-0.3	3.4	14.8	5.8	16.8	34.0	25.2	51.2	94.5	1.0	0.8	5.3
26 091	Lenawee................	99,324	-0.7	5.5	17.2	9.7	23.4	29.0	15.2	40.5	94.9	3.6	0.9	3.2
26 093	Livingston	182,045	1.0	5.2	19.5	7.3	23.6	31.6	12.7	41.3	98.3	0.8	1.2	1.4
26 099	Macomb................	843,852	0.7	5.7	17.0	8.4	25.8	28.5	14.6	40.3	86.4	10.0	3.8	2.0
26 101	Manistee...............	24,662	0.4	4.4	14.2	7.5	20.3	32.4	21.3	47.7	94.0	3.9	0.7	3.6
26 103	Marquette..............	67,528	1.2	5.2	13.2	14.8	23.1	28.7	15.0	39.6	95.5	2.3	0.9	3.4
26 105	Mason..................	28,679	-0.1	5.4	15.8	7.5	20.9	30.9	19.5	45.2	96.9	1.4	0.9	3.0
26 107	Mecosta................	43,143	1.2	5.0	14.6	21.1	19.4	24.5	15.4	34.0	95.8	4.0	1.2	1.7
26 109	Menominee.............	23,923	-0.7	4.5	16.0	6.5	20.4	32.8	19.9	46.6	98.0	0.4	0.5	4.0
26 111	Midland................	83,825	0.2	5.4	17.7	9.3	23.6	29.0	15.0	40.5	95.4	1.7	2.5	1.7
26 115	Monroe.................	151,539	-0.6	5.7	18.0	8.5	23.8	30.0	13.9	40.9	96.1	2.9	0.8	1.7
26 117	Montcalm..............	63,218	-0.4	5.9	17.8	8.4	25.3	28.0	14.6	39.5	96.0	3.3	0.8	2.4
26 121	Muskegon..............	170,724	-1.0	6.5	18.1	9.1	24.4	28.0	13.9	39.1	84.2	15.7	1.0	2.8
26 123	Newaygo...............	48,262	-0.9	6.1	18.3	7.9	22.2	29.5	16.0	41.4	96.3	1.6	0.6	3.0
26 125	Oakland................	1,211,683	1.5	5.6	17.4	7.8	25.8	29.7	13.7	40.6	79.3	14.8	6.7	2.0
26 127	Oceana.................	26,426	-0.8	6.4	18.0	7.6	21.2	29.7	17.2	42.5	97.0	0.8	0.8	3.0
26 129	Ogemaw................	21,544	-1.0	4.6	15.2	6.8	19.3	31.4	22.7	48.1	98.8	1.1	0.5	1.3
26 133	Osceola.................	23,415	-1.0	6.0	18.3	7.7	21.2	29.4	17.4	42.2	98.5	1.2	0.4	1.6
26 137	Otsego..................	24,103	-0.6	5.5	16.9	7.5	21.8	30.7	17.5	43.1	98.1	0.8	0.0	2.4
26 139	Ottawa.................	266,464	1.9	6.6	19.1	12.7	24.2	25.4	12.0	34.8	92.1	2.4	3.2	4.6
26 143	Roscommon............	24,293	-1.5	3.8	11.6	5.8	16.0	34.4	28.3	53.9	98.0	0.5	0.8	1.3
26 145	Saginaw................	199,094	-0.8	5.9	17.2	10.6	22.8	27.9	15.6	39.7	78.4	20.1	1.5	3.4
26 147	St. Clair................	161,640	-1.3	5.5	17.7	8.1	23.3	30.5	15.0	42.1	96.0	3.3	0.8	2.3
26 149	St. Joseph..............	61,024	-0.8	6.8	18.7	8.1	23.7	27.5	15.1	38.8	96.0	3.5	1.0	1.9
26 151	Sanilac.................	42,661	-1.8	5.7	17.7	7.3	21.5	29.7	18.1	43.4	98.4	0.8	0.5	2.0
26 155	Shiawassee.............	69,925	-2.0	5.3	18.2	8.6	23.4	29.6	14.9	40.9	98.1	0.9	0.8	1.3
26 157	Tuscola.................	55,223	-1.8	5.4	17.5	8.0	22.7	29.9	16.6	42.3	97.6	1.5	0.5	1.8
26 159	Van Buren..............	75,887	-1.0	6.4	18.7	7.7	23.3	29.6	14.3	40.4	90.6	5.2	0.8	5.7
26 161	Washtenaw.............	348,311	1.6	5.4	15.0	17.4	26.6	24.9	10.6	33.2	78.0	14.5	9.4	2.7
26 163	Wayne..................	1,803,251	-1.3	6.5	18.4	9.9	25.2	27.1	12.9	37.6	54.8	41.5	3.3	3.0
26 165	Wexford................	32,683	-0.5	6.5	17.3	7.3	23.4	29.1	16.3	41.6	98.3	0.9	0.9	1.6
27 000	**Minnesota**..............	5,345,721	1.3	6.6	17.3	9.4	26.2	27.2	13.2	37.5	87.9	6.3	4.9	3.5
27 003	Anoka..................	333,728	1.5	6.6	18.9	8.1	27.3	28.8	10.2	37.3	89.1	5.6	4.8	3.2
27 005	Becker..................	32,780	1.4	6.6	17.8	6.8	21.4	29.6	17.8	43.0	91.6	0.9	0.8	10.6
27 007	Beltrami................	45,072	1.8	7.4	17.8	14.1	22.4	25.1	13.2	33.5	77.3	1.5	1.2	22.8
27 009	Benton..................	38,727	1.0	7.2	17.1	10.2	28.9	24.3	12.4	34.7	95.5	2.8	1.5	1.1
27 013	Blue Earth..............	64,510	1.6	5.7	13.6	22.5	24.2	22.2	11.9	30.1	94.1	3.7	2.6	1.5
27 015	Brown..................	25,659	-1.7	5.9	15.9	9.5	20.9	28.5	19.3	43.5	98.5	0.4	0.6	1.2
27 017	Carlton.................	35,421	-0.2	6.2	17.3	7.6	24.8	28.8	15.2	40.9	91.4	2.2	1.0	7.6
27 019	Carver..................	92,574	2.6	7.0	22.4	6.6	27.3	27.9	8.9	36.8	94.7	1.8	3.2	2.4
27 021	Cass....................	28,459	-1.0	5.8	15.4	6.4	19.4	31.2	21.9	47.6	88.3	0.8	1.1	12.9
27 025	Chisago	53,697	-0.8	5.7	19.3	7.6	26.2	29.0	12.2	39.4	97.0	1.6	1.2	1.7
27 027	Clay....................	59,759	1.7	7.0	16.1	16.9	25.2	22.9	12.0	32.2	94.9	2.0	2.4	3.4
27 035	Crow Wing.............	62,707	0.4	6.2	16.5	7.5	22.2	28.5	19.1	43.2	97.5	0.9	0.7	1.6
27 037	Dakota.................	402,136	1.5	6.8	19.0	7.7	27.6	28.3	10.5	37.0	87.6	6.3	5.5	3.9
27 039	Dodge..................	20,185	0.4	7.2	21.3	7.5	25.1	26.2	12.6	37.4	97.7	1.1	0.6	1.2
27 041	Douglas................	36,217	1.1	5.5	15.6	8.0	22.1	28.6	20.2	44.2	98.7	0.9	0.7	0.8
27 045	Fillmore................	20,830	0.0	6.5	17.3	6.7	21.7	28.3	19.4	42.9	99.1	0.4	0.7	0.7
27 047	Freeborn...............	31,119	-0.5	6.0	15.9	7.3	21.3	29.1	20.4	44.7	96.4	1.1	1.2	2.4
27 049	Goodhue................	46,256	0.3	5.8	17.8	6.9	22.9	29.7	16.9	42.5	96.8	1.5	1.0	2.3

Table A-2. Counties — Who: Age, Race/Ethnicity, and Household Structure, 2010–2012—*Continued*

STATE and County code	STATE or County	Percent Hispanic or Latino	Percent foreign born	Total households	Household type (percent)						Percent of households with people under 18 years	Percent of households with people 60 years and over
					Family households				Nonfamily households			
					Total family households	Married-couple families	Male household families	Female household families	Total nonfamily households	One-person households		
	ACS table number:	B03003	C05003	B11001	B11001	B11001	B11001	B11001	B11001	B11001	B11005	B11006
	Column number:	14	15	16	17	18	19	20	21	22	23	24
	Michigan—Cont.											
26 027	Cass	3.0	2.1	19,742	71.3	55.3	5.6	10.4	28.7	25.7	28.6	41.3
26 029	Charlevoix	1.4	2.0	10,191	68.0	54.4	5.3	8.3	32.0	27.6	25.7	44.1
26 031	Cheboygan	1.0	0.9	11,201	66.9	52.4	5.1	9.3	33.1	28.1	25.1	46.5
26 033	Chippewa	1.5	3.2	14,597	63.1	48.9	5.8	8.4	36.9	30.6	29.7	35.8
26 035	Clare	1.6	1.1	13,436	63.1	47.5	4.6	11.0	36.9	31.8	26.4	45.1
26 037	Clinton	4.1	2.7	28,521	68.8	55.6	3.5	9.8	31.2	23.5	31.7	34.0
26 041	Delta	0.9	1.0	15,973	63.9	50.0	4.7	9.2	36.1	30.8	24.4	41.9
26 043	Dickinson	1.1	1.1	11,405	66.7	53.8	3.2	9.6	33.3	30.0	29.4	41.6
26 045	Eaton	4.9	3.8	42,981	66.2	51.8	3.5	10.8	33.8	29.0	29.5	34.9
26 047	Emmet	1.3	2.1	13,140	69.4	55.8	4.6	9.0	30.6	24.8	29.9	41.9
26 049	Genesee	3.1	2.3	165,651	65.1	43.3	4.9	16.9	34.9	29.7	32.0	36.0
26 051	Gladwin	1.3	1.1	10,721	68.4	56.4	4.5	7.5	31.6	27.6	24.7	48.2
26 055	Grand Traverse	2.3	2.1	34,555	64.5	50.8	3.5	10.2	35.5	29.3	27.8	37.3
26 057	Gratiot	5.4	1.3	14,754	68.7	54.0	4.6	10.1	31.3	26.6	30.8	36.6
26 059	Hillsdale	1.9	0.6	17,784	70.9	56.2	4.4	10.3	29.1	24.2	30.6	39.8
26 061	Houghton	1.3	4.5	13,987	58.8	45.2	5.0	8.5	41.2	30.9	24.9	39.4
26 063	Huron	2.0	1.6	13,957	65.2	53.8	4.0	7.3	34.8	30.7	23.7	45.5
26 065	Ingham	7.4	8.5	108,326	56.4	40.0	4.1	12.3	43.6	32.7	27.8	29.6
26 067	Ionia	4.5	1.5	22,464	72.4	55.9	4.7	11.8	27.6	23.8	35.6	33.1
26 069	Iosco	1.7	2.7	11,256	60.7	49.0	2.3	9.4	39.3	34.5	19.7	52.2
26 073	Isabella	3.4	2.8	24,456	54.9	40.6	4.4	9.9	45.1	28.6	26.4	26.8
26 075	Jackson	3.1	1.8	59,781	66.2	48.2	5.1	12.8	33.8	28.1	30.1	37.6
26 077	Kalamazoo	4.1	4.9	99,085	59.9	44.3	4.0	11.5	40.1	30.9	30.0	31.4
26 081	Kent	9.8	7.4	229,328	66.7	49.8	4.0	12.9	33.3	26.6	34.4	29.8
26 087	Lapeer	4.2	2.9	32,426	74.0	61.7	3.9	8.4	26.0	22.1	33.3	36.5
26 089	Leelanau	3.7	3.6	9,267	70.5	61.6	2.5	6.4	29.5	24.4	23.3	52.1
26 091	Lenawee	7.6	2.2	37,498	67.3	51.8	4.2	11.3	32.7	27.8	30.0	38.5
26 093	Livingston	2.0	2.9	67,112	75.4	62.7	3.9	8.8	24.6	20.5	35.6	33.4
26 099	Macomb	2.3	10.4	331,023	67.0	50.1	4.4	12.6	33.0	28.8	31.5	36.7
26 101	Manistee	2.7	1.6	10,729	63.6	48.5	5.4	9.7	36.4	30.7	23.4	47.3
26 103	Marquette	1.2	1.4	27,180	58.7	48.6	3.2	6.9	41.3	31.9	22.4	35.6
26 105	Mason	4.0	2.1	12,242	66.7	52.6	3.7	10.3	33.3	29.8	25.8	42.9
26 107	Mecosta	1.8	2.4	15,376	66.0	53.0	4.6	8.4	34.0	24.3	28.4	40.3
26 109	Menominee	1.3	1.3	10,622	64.7	50.0	4.4	10.3	35.3	31.6	25.2	42.2
26 111	Midland	2.1	4.1	33,552	68.8	56.8	3.3	8.7	31.2	25.8	30.9	35.0
26 115	Monroe	3.2	2.2	57,876	71.4	55.5	4.5	11.4	28.6	24.7	32.9	36.8
26 117	Montcalm	3.1	1.3	23,285	72.3	54.8	5.3	12.2	27.7	24.1	33.3	37.5
26 121	Muskegon	4.9	1.9	64,394	68.7	47.1	5.7	15.9	31.3	26.6	33.8	35.8
26 123	Newaygo	5.6	2.1	18,074	71.7	56.4	4.8	10.5	28.3	23.5	31.4	39.6
26 125	Oakland	3.6	11.1	485,367	65.6	50.4	4.0	11.2	34.4	29.5	31.2	34.4
26 127	Oceana	14.0	6.4	9,466	71.8	58.4	4.2	9.2	28.2	24.0	28.2	42.1
26 129	Ogemaw	1.6	1.4	9,031	64.3	51.1	3.7	9.5	35.7	30.1	23.8	48.9
26 133	Osceola	1.6	0.6	8,877	69.7	53.8	4.7	11.2	30.3	24.7	29.8	42.1
26 137	Otsego	1.4	3.2	9,803	67.7	55.0	4.7	7.9	32.3	24.4	30.0	38.7
26 139	Ottawa	8.9	5.8	94,154	74.2	61.9	3.8	8.5	25.8	20.2	36.5	31.5
26 143	Roscommon	1.2	2.2	11,723	60.3	46.4	3.6	10.3	39.7	32.7	19.3	52.7
26 145	Saginaw	7.9	2.4	77,081	65.0	46.7	4.1	14.2	35.0	30.4	29.8	38.1
26 147	St. Clair	2.9	2.6	64,291	68.2	52.2	4.8	11.2	31.8	25.8	30.3	37.7
26 149	St. Joseph	6.7	3.1	22,577	69.7	53.3	4.5	11.8	30.3	26.3	31.8	38.0
26 151	Sanilac	3.5	1.0	16,011	66.3	54.4	3.7	8.2	33.7	29.4	25.0	42.9
26 155	Shiawassee	2.5	1.2	27,183	71.7	54.0	6.3	11.4	28.3	24.1	32.6	35.9
26 157	Tuscola	2.9	1.0	21,180	70.2	56.0	4.3	10.0	29.8	25.8	29.8	39.6
26 159	Van Buren	10.4	4.4	27,952	71.2	54.0	5.3	11.9	28.8	24.8	32.7	38.4
26 161	Washtenaw	4.2	11.2	134,570	57.1	44.3	3.1	9.7	42.9	32.2	27.8	28.7
26 163	Wayne	5.4	7.8	667,145	62.6	37.2	5.6	19.7	37.4	32.9	32.4	35.9
26 165	Wexford	1.6	1.2	12,271	67.5	52.6	4.7	10.2	32.5	28.9	28.1	40.1
27 000	**Minnesota**	4.8	7.3	2,102,761	64.9	51.1	4.3	9.6	35.1	28.2	31.6	32.2
27 003	Anoka	3.7	6.9	122,793	70.9	56.1	4.7	10.0	29.1	23.2	36.9	29.2
27 005	Becker	1.4	1.5	13,347	68.4	53.4	5.1	9.9	31.6	26.2	31.0	40.6
27 007	Beltrami	1.6	1.8	16,677	67.0	47.2	6.5	13.3	33.0	25.9	33.0	34.5
27 009	Benton	1.7	2.1	15,390	64.1	50.4	5.1	8.7	35.9	26.8	34.4	27.9
27 013	Blue Earth	2.6	3.7	24,573	57.2	48.1	3.4	5.7	42.8	28.8	25.9	29.6
27 015	Brown	3.4	1.4	10,688	62.3	51.2	5.6	5.5	37.7	33.2	24.9	41.0
27 017	Carlton	1.4	0.9	13,621	66.6	52.1	6.6	7.9	33.4	28.8	33.3	39.0
27 019	Carver	4.0	5.5	33,166	75.8	65.7	3.6	6.4	24.2	20.6	43.7	25.1
27 021	Cass	1.3	0.9	13,009	67.6	53.4	4.8	9.4	32.4	26.7	26.1	45.2
27 025	Chisago	1.6	1.8	19,807	71.8	59.2	4.4	8.2	28.2	22.1	36.0	30.5
27 027	Clay	3.6	2.4	22,352	65.0	51.1	4.2	9.7	35.0	28.5	32.7	30.6
27 035	Crow Wing	1.1	1.6	26,793	67.1	53.3	5.0	8.9	32.9	26.2	28.9	41.4
27 037	Dakota	6.2	8.2	153,554	69.5	54.7	4.3	10.5	30.5	24.8	35.7	28.3
27 039	Dodge	4.6	2.0	7,414	72.5	59.2	3.8	9.5	27.5	23.9	38.5	31.0
27 041	Douglas	1.1	1.2	15,609	66.9	57.0	5.1	4.8	33.1	27.7	26.4	40.0
27 045	Fillmore	1.0	0.9	8,349	67.2	57.2	3.2	6.8	32.8	28.6	28.9	42.4
27 047	Freeborn	8.9	2.5	13,249	64.9	48.9	4.7	11.4	35.1	30.9	27.9	40.9
27 049	Goodhue	3.0	2.2	18,623	67.9	54.9	4.4	8.7	32.1	27.7	30.9	37.4

Table A-2. Counties — Who: Age, Race/Ethnicity, and Household Structure, 2010–2012—*Continued*

STATE and County code	STATE or County	Total population	Percent change 2010–2012	Population by age (percent)						Median age	Race alone or in combination (percent)			
				Under 5 years	5 to 17 years	18 to 24 years	25 to 44 years	45 to 64 years	65 years and over		White	Black	Asian, Hawaiian, or Pacific Islander	American Indian, Alaska Native, or some other race
	ACS table number:	B01003	Population estimates	B01001	B01001	B01001	B01001	B01001	B01001	B01002	B02008	B02009	B02011 + B02012	B02010 + B02013
	Column number:	1	2	3	4	5	6	7	8	9	10	11	12	13
	Minnesota—Cont.													
27 053	Hennepin	1,169,434	2.6	6.6	16.0	9.6	29.8	26.5	11.6	36.0	78.6	13.7	7.4	4.0
27 057	Hubbard	20,376	-0.4	5.6	15.9	5.9	19.5	31.6	21.6	47.3	96.5	0.7	0.7	4.1
27 059	Isanti	38,120	0.9	6.9	18.6	7.8	25.6	27.9	13.2	38.5	98.1	1.0	1.2	1.4
27 061	Itasca	45,114	0.5	5.3	16.2	7.0	20.8	31.3	19.5	45.6	95.6	0.7	0.8	5.3
27 067	Kandiyohi	42,284	0.3	6.7	17.0	9.5	22.3	27.9	16.6	40.3	95.5	3.1	0.7	2.2
27 079	Le Sueur	27,725	0.0	6.5	18.5	7.1	24.1	28.8	15.0	40.5	96.6	0.7	0.9	3.1
27 083	Lyon	25,719	-1.2	7.3	17.4	12.7	24.4	24.6	13.7	34.3	90.8	2.9	3.1	4.4
27 085	McLeod	36,353	-1.5	6.4	18.4	7.4	24.5	27.5	15.8	39.3	96.8	1.4	1.2	2.1
27 091	Martin	20,643	-1.7	5.3	16.5	6.5	20.7	29.8	21.2	44.1	98.9	0.6	0.9	1.1
27 093	Meeker	23,186	-1.0	6.8	18.2	6.8	22.4	28.8	16.9	41.5	98.7	0.6	0.4	1.3
27 095	Mille Lacs	25,907	-1.3	6.7	18.1	7.1	24.4	27.4	16.3	39.8	92.3	1.1	0.7	7.5
27 097	Morrison	33,148	-0.5	6.5	17.6	7.4	23.2	29.0	16.3	40.8	98.4	0.7	0.6	1.4
27 099	Mower	39,286	0.5	7.1	18.1	8.8	23.1	25.8	17.1	38.6	94.1	3.3	2.4	2.2
27 103	Nicollet	32,879	0.6	6.1	15.7	15.3	24.9	25.5	12.6	33.9	94.8	2.9	2.1	1.5
27 105	Nobles	21,433	0.6	7.9	17.9	9.0	23.9	25.7	15.6	36.7	85.9	4.2	6.3	6.3
27 109	Olmsted	145,828	1.8	7.3	17.7	7.7	27.9	26.5	12.9	36.2	88.9	5.7	6.5	1.6
27 111	Otter Tail	57,294	0.0	5.7	15.7	6.8	19.9	30.7	21.3	46.5	97.3	1.2	0.7	2.0
27 115	Pine	29,517	-1.7	5.6	15.8	6.8	25.0	29.9	16.9	42.7	93.4	2.9	0.9	4.8
27 119	Polk	31,510	-0.6	6.3	17.0	10.1	21.9	28.0	16.7	40.5	94.7	1.6	1.0	4.6
27 123	Ramsey	514,982	2.1	7.0	16.3	11.8	27.4	25.4	12.2	34.5	74.2	12.8	13.1	3.8
27 131	Rice	64,645	1.0	5.8	16.8	15.6	23.9	25.2	12.7	34.9	92.2	3.8	2.7	2.9
27 137	St. Louis	200,269	0.1	5.3	14.2	12.7	22.4	29.3	16.1	40.7	94.9	2.2	1.4	3.7
27 139	Scott	132,768	3.6	7.9	21.8	6.6	30.3	25.0	8.3	35.2	89.2	3.6	6.6	3.4
27 141	Sherburne	89,139	0.8	7.3	21.2	8.6	28.9	25.4	8.6	34.7	95.4	2.5	1.7	1.5
27 145	Stearns	151,178	0.6	6.4	16.5	15.7	24.0	25.0	12.4	33.6	93.6	3.9	2.6	1.7
27 147	Steele	36,459	-0.5	7.5	18.7	7.3	24.6	26.9	15.0	39.6	94.4	3.3	1.2	3.4
27 153	Todd	24,739	-1.5	6.7	17.8	7.6	20.5	29.5	17.9	42.7	95.8	0.6	0.8	3.9
27 157	Wabasha	21,553	-0.8	5.7	18.2	6.7	21.8	29.8	17.7	43.3	98.7	0.6	0.7	0.5
27 163	Washington	241,538	2.1	6.3	19.8	7.4	26.0	29.4	11.1	38.4	90.0	4.6	6.0	1.7
27 169	Winona	51,508	0.5	4.9	14.0	21.5	21.1	24.7	13.8	33.5	95.4	1.7	3.1	0.8
27 171	Wright	126,271	1.7	8.3	21.2	6.8	29.0	24.7	10.0	34.9	96.4	1.6	1.9	2.2
28 000	**Mississippi**	2,977,179	0.5	6.9	18.3	10.5	25.4	25.8	13.1	36.1	60.4	38.0	1.1	1.7
28 001	Adams	32,340	-1.3	6.1	15.7	8.2	24.6	29.4	15.9	40.6	39.8	57.5	0.5	2.8
28 003	Alcorn	37,157	0.2	7.3	17.1	8.5	25.1	25.9	16.1	40.2	86.7	12.4	0.0	2.1
28 011	Bolivar	33,904	-0.5	7.5	17.9	12.3	24.5	25.3	12.5	34.3	33.6	66.2	0.2	0.4
28 025	Clay	20,495	-0.6	6.8	18.6	9.5	23.7	26.8	14.7	38.5	40.1	59.8	0.0	0.4
28 027	Coahoma	25,896	-1.6	8.4	20.7	10.9	23.4	24.3	12.3	33.0	23.1	76.0	0.7	0.0
28 029	Copiah	29,184	-1.5	7.3	17.6	11.1	23.2	26.9	14.0	37.4	46.7	52.0	0.4	1.5
28 031	Covington	19,582	0.0	6.6	16.8	9.3	23.1	27.3	16.8	40.5	61.1	39.0	0.0	0.0
28 033	DeSoto	163,919	2.8	7.0	20.9	8.2	28.7	24.8	10.5	35.3	75.0	23.4	1.6	2.6
28 035	Forrest	75,944	2.5	7.2	16.5	16.2	26.4	22.0	11.7	31.2	61.3	37.2	1.0	2.1
28 039	George	22,808	1.1	7.3	19.2	9.4	25.4	25.5	13.2	35.8	89.9	8.7	0.0	1.7
28 043	Grenada	21,734	-0.9	6.7	17.9	10.7	22.8	26.5	15.3	39.6	56.3	42.5	0.0	0.7
28 045	Hancock	44,661	2.8	5.6	17.8	8.3	23.1	29.0	16.1	41.0	89.0	9.0	1.2	2.0
28 047	Harrison	190,962	3.3	7.3	17.1	10.6	26.8	26.0	12.1	35.3	73.3	24.1	3.7	1.9
28 049	Hinds	247,502	1.2	7.2	18.7	12.1	26.3	24.7	11.0	33.2	28.7	70.0	0.9	1.2
28 057	Itawamba	23,356	-0.2	5.9	17.0	10.8	24.7	25.4	16.2	40.1	93.4	6.7	0.0	0.3
28 059	Jackson	140,062	0.4	6.7	18.5	9.0	25.9	27.0	12.8	37.1	75.0	22.6	2.6	2.1
28 067	Jones	68,192	1.1	7.4	18.1	9.9	24.4	25.7	14.5	36.6	69.6	29.5	0.0	0.1
28 071	Lafayette	48,480	4.2	5.1	13.6	27.0	24.7	19.3	10.4	27.8	72.5	25.4	2.6	1.0
28 073	Lamar	56,978	3.1	7.2	18.7	11.2	28.9	23.1	10.9	33.2	77.4	20.8	1.4	1.8
28 075	Lauderdale	80,361	-0.1	6.8	18.0	10.0	25.3	25.8	14.1	36.6	56.5	43.3	0.9	0.9
28 079	Leake	23,462	-2.0	8.0	22.3	10.2	23.0	23.3	13.2	32.8	52.4	41.2	0.0	6.2
28 081	Lee	84,080	2.5	7.3	19.1	8.6	26.4	25.4	13.3	35.9	70.8	28.6	0.8	1.0
28 083	Leflore	31,715	-4.2	8.1	19.1	12.1	24.9	23.8	12.0	32.4	25.8	72.2	0.8	0.8
28 085	Lincoln	34,883	0.1	7.1	19.0	9.4	23.9	26.3	14.4	37.5	68.9	30.5	0.0	0.9
28 087	Lowndes	59,699	-0.2	6.8	17.9	10.9	25.0	26.1	13.2	36.2	54.6	44.5	0.9	0.7
28 089	Madison	97,020	3.1	6.8	19.7	8.6	26.9	27.1	10.9	36.3	57.5	38.7	2.3	2.1
28 091	Marion	26,748	-2.3	7.2	18.2	8.5	25.0	26.0	15.1	37.6	67.1	33.5	0.0	0.0
28 093	Marshall	36,838	-1.3	6.6	16.4	9.8	25.2	28.7	13.3	39.1	50.9	47.5	0.0	2.7
28 095	Monroe	36,616	-1.2	6.2	17.6	9.2	23.2	27.6	16.2	39.9	68.4	31.5	0.3	0.3
28 099	Neshoba	29,718	0.5	8.0	21.1	8.2	24.4	24.7	13.6	35.2	61.6	21.9	0.6	17.2
28 101	Newton	21,599	-0.4	6.7	19.2	9.7	24.0	25.2	15.2	37.7	63.1	31.9	0.0	5.2
28 105	Oktibbeha	47,853	1.1	5.4	12.2	31.9	22.4	18.7	9.5	25.2	59.7	37.1	3.2	0.9
28 107	Panola	34,561	-0.6	7.5	19.3	9.5	24.1	26.6	13.1	36.0	48.8	51.3	0.0	0.0
28 109	Pearl River	55,603	-0.9	6.5	18.1	9.1	24.0	26.8	15.4	39.9	85.1	14.3	0.3	0.9
28 113	Pike	40,293	-0.8	7.6	19.2	9.1	23.7	26.1	14.3	37.3	46.4	52.7	0.0	1.0
28 115	Pontotoc	30,188	2.0	6.3	20.2	8.2	25.5	26.7	13.1	36.1	80.0	18.1	0.0	2.7
28 117	Prentiss	25,296	0.8	6.6	16.8	11.3	23.6	25.7	15.9	38.6	84.6	14.9	0.0	0.9
28 121	Rankin	143,637	2.2	6.8	18.1	7.9	29.4	25.9	11.9	36.5	78.9	19.7	1.3	1.1
28 123	Scott	28,279	-0.1	7.9	19.2	10.2	25.0	25.1	12.6	35.1	59.1	38.1	0.0	2.0
28 127	Simpson	27,396	-0.4	7.2	19.2	8.7	23.3	27.3	14.4	37.9	63.5	35.5	0.0	0.0
28 133	Sunflower	28,654	-1.9	7.1	17.1	12.3	28.5	24.4	10.6	33.4	25.7	73.0	0.3	1.1

Table A-2. Counties — Who: Age, Race/Ethnicity, and Household Structure, 2010–2012—*Continued*

STATE and County code	STATE or County	Percent Hispanic or Latino	Percent foreign born	Total households	Household type (percent)							Percent of households with people under 18 years	Percent of households with people 60 years and over
					Family households				Nonfamily households				
					Total family households	Married-couple families	Male household families	Female household families	Total nonfamily households	One-person households			
ACS table number:		B03003	C05003	B11001	B11001	B11001	B11001	B11001	B11001	B11001	B11005	B11006
Column number:		14	15	16	17	18	19	20	21	22	23	24
	Minnesota—Cont.											
27 053	Hennepin	6.8	12.7	478,538	57.9	43.3	4.1	10.4	42.1	32.9	28.9	28.9
27 057	Hubbard	1.6	1.4	8,506	67.9	59.0	3.2	5.8	32.1	27.2	25.7	45.3
27 059	Isanti	1.6	1.0	13,771	74.9	61.3	4.1	9.5	25.1	21.6	36.2	31.2
27 061	Itasca	1.0	1.0	18,341	69.2	56.6	4.1	8.4	30.8	25.1	26.3	44.4
27 067	Kandiyohi	11.2	5.6	17,154	67.1	54.1	3.5	9.6	32.9	27.5	28.4	35.8
27 079	Le Sueur	5.3	2.2	11,098	70.7	58.0	5.1	7.5	29.3	25.0	33.7	35.3
27 083	Lyon	6.0	5.2	10,030	63.2	49.6	5.0	8.6	36.8	30.6	31.0	33.6
27 085	McLeod	5.1	3.8	14,802	68.1	55.1	5.4	7.7	31.9	26.2	31.3	34.3
27 091	Martin	3.7	2.0	8,884	66.4	55.8	4.3	6.3	33.6	30.1	25.9	41.7
27 093	Meeker	3.3	2.1	9,493	71.4	58.6	5.2	7.6	28.6	25.6	30.2	37.2
27 095	Mille Lacs	1.5	1.1	10,356	67.5	50.9	5.6	10.9	32.5	27.6	34.6	36.3
27 097	Morrison	1.3	1.0	13,496	66.1	53.6	4.6	7.9	33.9	27.9	29.9	36.4
27 099	Mower	10.8	6.9	15,748	63.5	49.0	4.8	9.7	36.5	31.7	31.4	38.4
27 103	Nicollet	3.8	2.5	12,240	67.3	53.8	4.3	9.2	32.7	24.7	35.4	31.5
27 105	Nobles	23.2	17.9	7,877	71.0	55.5	6.4	9.2	29.0	27.0	35.0	37.5
27 109	Olmsted	4.3	9.8	57,073	65.3	53.5	3.4	8.4	34.7	28.6	33.0	29.9
27 111	Otter Tail	2.7	2.5	24,350	68.4	58.0	3.8	6.6	31.6	26.8	25.4	43.1
27 115	Pine	2.5	2.1	12,008	66.7	52.6	5.6	8.5	33.3	26.9	30.4	38.3
27 119	Polk	5.6	2.3	12,682	66.5	51.9	3.5	11.0	33.5	28.0	32.8	37.2
27 123	Ramsey	7.2	14.4	204,535	58.3	41.1	4.7	12.6	41.7	33.5	28.9	31.2
27 131	Rice	7.9	6.7	22,321	69.7	56.2	3.7	9.8	30.3	24.6	33.5	32.7
27 137	St. Louis	1.3	2.2	84,519	59.0	45.0	4.3	9.6	41.0	32.7	25.4	36.8
27 139	Scott	4.5	9.0	45,770	76.8	64.4	4.1	8.4	23.2	18.1	43.7	24.4
27 141	Sherburne	2.2	3.1	30,356	74.8	61.7	4.4	8.7	25.2	18.8	41.5	24.3
27 145	Stearns	2.9	4.5	56,182	65.8	54.3	4.2	7.3	34.2	24.0	30.3	31.0
27 147	Steele	6.5	4.3	14,448	66.3	54.1	4.5	7.7	33.7	29.8	32.6	35.1
27 153	Todd	5.3	3.8	10,118	68.8	57.5	4.5	6.8	31.2	27.7	28.8	39.7
27 157	Wabasha	2.8	1.0	8,845	71.1	59.2	3.8	8.1	28.9	24.5	29.3	37.5
27 163	Washington	3.5	5.9	89,096	74.2	60.6	3.5	10.2	25.8	20.7	39.0	30.7
27 169	Winona	2.5	3.8	18,998	59.5	50.9	2.3	6.3	40.5	31.5	24.4	34.8
27 171	Wright	2.6	2.4	45,213	75.3	62.0	4.4	8.8	24.7	20.5	41.1	26.1
28 000	**Mississippi**	2.7	2.2	1,085,563	68.9	45.3	4.9	18.7	31.1	27.3	35.1	35.5
28 001	Adams	4.2	4.5	12,237	62.5	35.7	5.7	21.1	37.5	36.1	28.6	40.5
28 003	Alcorn	2.8	0.9	14,389	67.9	51.3	5.1	11.5	32.1	29.9	31.1	40.1
28 011	Bolivar	0.5	0.4	12,257	64.9	32.7	3.7	28.5	35.1	30.3	35.7	35.2
28 025	Clay	0.8	0.3	7,947	75.3	44.9	4.5	25.9	24.7	23.9	36.4	33.9
28 027	Coahoma	0.6	1.1	9,396	65.9	27.8	5.6	32.4	34.1	29.8	39.7	34.8
28 029	Copiah	2.7	2.0	10,027	68.5	47.6	4.3	16.6	31.5	30.3	33.4	39.8
28 031	Covington	1.6	0.4	7,267	70.0	50.2	2.1	17.7	30.0	28.3	31.8	41.1
28 033	DeSoto	5.0	3.3	57,912	75.4	55.3	4.5	15.6	24.6	21.2	41.4	29.3
28 035	Forrest	3.5	2.7	27,608	60.0	37.8	4.8	17.4	40.0	31.7	33.3	31.3
28 039	George	2.0	2.1	7,740	75.6	56.3	5.9	13.3	24.4	23.3	40.0	36.5
28 043	Grenada	0.1	0.7	8,102	67.6	47.1	2.3	18.3	32.4	30.2	28.8	40.8
28 045	Hancock	3.4	3.2	18,131	70.3	49.7	6.7	14.0	29.7	26.7	32.6	40.6
28 047	Harrison	5.3	4.4	72,134	65.5	43.6	5.2	16.7	34.5	28.7	33.4	32.6
28 049	Hinds	1.5	2.0	87,736	65.6	34.8	6.9	24.0	34.4	29.5	35.5	31.3
28 057	Itawamba	1.3	0.3	8,945	73.1	55.9	4.8	12.4	26.9	25.3	33.7	39.5
28 059	Jackson	4.8	3.5	50,558	69.1	48.5	5.0	15.5	30.9	25.8	33.5	34.1
28 067	Jones	4.6	3.4	24,560	71.3	48.5	6.6	16.3	28.7	25.1	35.7	38.2
28 071	Lafayette	2.2	2.5	14,428	60.3	43.7	3.6	13.0	39.7	33.2	30.1	33.4
28 073	Lamar	2.2	2.5	21,665	68.7	51.6	4.3	12.8	31.3	25.1	37.7	27.8
28 075	Lauderdale	1.9	1.8	29,458	67.8	43.1	3.2	21.6	32.2	28.3	35.1	35.9
28 079	Leake	4.3	2.5	8,175	70.0	45.2	4.6	20.2	30.0	27.3	39.8	37.6
28 081	Lee	2.4	2.1	31,534	71.4	47.9	4.8	18.7	28.6	24.8	37.6	34.8
28 083	Leflore	2.3	3.7	10,896	65.2	29.0	4.8	31.3	34.8	32.2	37.0	32.0
28 085	Lincoln	1.0	0.8	13,170	74.6	49.5	5.8	19.2	25.4	23.7	35.0	39.8
28 087	Lowndes	1.6	1.7	23,518	64.6	42.7	3.5	18.5	35.4	30.8	34.4	34.2
28 089	Madison	2.9	3.9	36,617	69.3	50.4	4.7	14.3	30.7	26.4	37.1	29.2
28 091	Marion	1.3	0.1	9,902	73.3	45.6	9.8	17.9	26.7	25.0	35.8	41.4
28 093	Marshall	3.3	1.3	13,041	74.8	42.7	8.5	23.6	25.2	23.3	33.1	40.1
28 095	Monroe	1.0	0.3	13,790	74.6	52.4	4.2	18.0	25.4	24.1	34.8	41.0
28 099	Neshoba	1.8	1.0	10,587	71.9	46.9	4.9	20.2	28.1	25.9	40.3	37.1
28 101	Newton	0.6	1.0	8,053	73.4	48.3	6.4	18.7	26.6	24.5	34.6	40.7
28 105	Oktibbeha	1.5	2.9	18,499	54.7	34.7	3.6	16.3	45.3	33.7	28.2	24.8
28 107	Panola	0.2	0.2	11,525	67.3	42.8	4.0	20.5	32.7	30.4	33.0	38.3
28 109	Pearl River	3.0	1.2	20,344	71.3	52.2	3.8	15.2	28.7	25.6	35.0	38.7
28 113	Pike	1.3	0.9	14,686	65.6	42.1	3.6	19.8	34.4	29.7	33.8	42.6
28 115	Pontotoc	2.8	1.0	9,769	73.7	52.6	4.1	17.0	26.3	23.5	33.6	39.5
28 117	Prentiss	1.2	0.3	9,711	71.8	51.3	4.8	15.7	28.2	25.3	31.4	40.5
28 121	Rankin	2.6	2.1	52,875	74.1	54.3	4.1	15.7	25.9	21.9	38.6	31.9
28 123	Scott	10.6	7.4	9,753	73.6	45.7	8.6	19.3	26.4	23.8	38.8	34.3
28 127	Simpson	1.6	1.8	9,883	68.0	49.7	5.5	12.8	32.0	29.1	33.1	38.7
28 133	Sunflower	1.4	0.1	8,285	71.7	33.5	7.8	30.4	28.3	24.3	37.1	37.2

Part A — Who 55

Table A-2. Counties — Who: Age, Race/Ethnicity, and Household Structure, 2010–2012—*Continued*

STATE and County code	STATE or County	Total population	Percent change 2010–2012	Population by age (percent) Under 5 years	5 to 17 years	18 to 24 years	25 to 44 years	45 to 64 years	65 years and over	Median age	Race alone or in combination (percent) White	Black	Asian, Hawaiian, or Pacific Islander	American Indian, Alaska Native, or some other race
ACS table number:		B01003	Population estimates	B01001	B01001	B01001	B01001	B01001	B01001	B01002	B02008	B02009	B02011 + B02012	B02010 + B02013
Column number:		1	2	3	4	5	6	7	8	9	10	11	12	13
	Mississippi—Cont.													
28 137	Tate	28,722	-1.7	6.6	19.2	11.4	23.3	26.3	13.2	36.4	67.3	31.0	0.5	1.7
28 139	Tippah	22,107	-0.8	5.6	19.0	9.5	25.0	26.3	14.7	37.7	82.1	14.3	0.0	5.0
28 145	Union	27,292	1.0	7.0	18.6	8.4	24.9	26.3	14.8	37.5	83.4	15.2	0.0	2.8
28 149	Warren	48,363	-1.4	6.7	18.8	8.4	24.5	28.2	13.4	38.0	50.7	47.8	1.1	1.0
28 151	Washington	50,416	-2.5	7.9	20.1	9.7	23.3	26.5	12.5	35.3	27.4	71.4	0.7	1.1
28 153	Wayne	20,681	-0.5	7.0	19.0	9.4	24.1	26.4	14.2	38.4	60.2	39.8	0.0	0.9
28 163	Yazoo	28,153	0.4	7.1	17.6	9.4	29.7	24.2	12.0	35.8	39.7	56.7	0.0	4.0
29 000	**Missouri**	6,009,025	0.4	6.4	17.1	9.8	25.4	27.0	14.3	38.0	85.0	12.6	2.3	2.6
29 001	Adair	25,578	-0.1	4.9	13.9	26.3	20.0	21.4	13.4	29.4	95.1	2.1	2.4	1.2
29 007	Audrain	25,561	0.6	6.3	18.3	7.7	25.5	26.3	16.0	38.9	91.4	7.1	1.0	2.6
29 009	Barry	35,609	-0.6	6.3	17.4	7.3	22.0	28.1	18.8	42.5	93.4	0.2	1.4	7.2
29 019	Boone	165,893	3.3	6.2	14.6	21.3	26.2	22.2	9.5	29.7	85.2	10.7	4.7	2.6
29 021	Buchanan	89,420	0.7	6.8	16.5	11.3	25.3	26.3	13.8	36.6	92.3	6.5	1.8	3.4
29 023	Butler	42,976	0.5	6.2	17.0	8.1	24.3	27.6	16.9	41.2	93.5	6.3	0.9	1.7
29 027	Callaway	44,296	-0.1	5.7	16.3	11.3	25.6	28.3	12.7	38.8	94.1	5.3	1.0	1.8
29 029	Camden	43,811	-0.4	5.0	13.9	6.4	19.4	32.8	22.5	49.2	98.3	0.6	0.0	1.6
29 031	Cape Girardeau	76,460	1.5	6.0	15.6	13.4	24.8	25.7	14.4	35.9	91.0	7.8	1.5	1.3
29 037	Cass	100,013	0.6	6.3	19.7	7.5	25.5	26.9	14.1	38.8	94.2	4.3	1.0	2.3
29 043	Christian	78,786	2.5	7.3	19.8	7.7	26.9	25.5	12.8	37.0	98.5	1.1	1.1	1.5
29 047	Clay	225,142	2.2	7.1	18.5	8.1	28.5	26.2	11.6	36.4	90.6	6.6	3.3	3.4
29 049	Clinton	20,630	-1.1	6.3	17.9	7.2	23.4	29.2	15.9	40.9	96.6	2.0	0.0	1.4
29 051	Cole	76,299	0.3	6.2	17.1	9.1	27.1	27.5	12.9	37.8	85.1	12.1	2.0	2.7
29 055	Crawford	24,755	0.8	6.4	17.8	7.7	23.1	28.4	16.6	41.0	98.7	0.2	0.4	1.5
29 069	Dunklin	31,905	-0.3	7.1	18.5	8.5	23.2	26.4	16.3	39.8	87.9	11.1	0.3	1.9
29 071	Franklin	101,543	-0.1	6.2	18.2	8.3	24.1	29.1	14.1	39.9	97.8	1.3	0.7	1.2
29 077	Greene	277,813	1.9	6.2	14.9	13.8	25.9	24.9	14.3	35.6	94.0	4.0	2.4	2.4
29 083	Henry	22,201	-0.5	5.9	16.4	7.3	22.1	28.7	19.6	43.7	97.4	1.5	0.0	1.2
29 091	Howell	40,608	0.1	6.6	18.1	8.4	23.1	26.5	17.3	39.8	98.7	0.4	0.0	2.6
29 095	Jackson	675,911	0.3	7.0	17.4	9.2	27.5	26.3	12.7	36.2	69.4	25.5	2.6	5.9
29 097	Jasper	116,957	-2.1	7.5	18.2	10.2	26.1	24.6	13.4	35.3	94.3	3.2	1.6	4.5
29 099	Jefferson	219,655	0.5	6.6	18.1	8.4	26.4	28.7	11.7	38.0	98.1	1.3	1.1	1.2
29 101	Johnson	53,527	3.2	6.6	15.8	20.2	24.7	21.6	11.1	29.3	93.5	5.9	3.0	1.6
29 105	Laclede	35,554	-0.6	6.6	18.3	7.9	23.9	27.5	15.7	39.2	98.1	1.6	0.6	1.1
29 107	Lafayette	33,237	-1.0	6.3	18.0	8.1	22.8	28.1	16.7	40.0	96.8	3.7	0.4	1.3
29 109	Lawrence	38,545	-0.3	6.8	19.3	8.0	23.5	26.0	16.4	39.6	96.9	0.3	0.6	3.7
29 113	Lincoln	53,032	1.3	6.9	20.7	8.0	26.6	26.8	11.0	35.6	96.0	2.8	0.6	1.7
29 119	McDonald	22,943	-0.9	7.8	20.1	8.4	24.6	26.2	13.0	36.8	94.4	1.6	0.0	8.6
29 127	Marion	28,749	-0.1	6.9	16.9	9.3	24.0	26.7	16.2	39.7	93.2	6.6	0.7	0.7
29 131	Miller	24,802	0.4	6.6	18.0	7.3	24.0	27.9	16.1	40.2	98.7	0.7	0.7	1.7
29 141	Morgan	20,362	-2.2	5.6	16.2	6.6	19.1	29.6	22.9	47.0	98.1	2.5	0.0	1.2
29 145	Newton	58,674	1.6	6.5	18.6	8.8	23.4	26.6	16.1	39.4	93.8	1.5	2.0	5.6
29 147	Nodaway	23,419	0.2	5.1	12.8	28.2	20.0	20.8	13.2	28.3	96.0	3.1	1.2	1.0
29 159	Pettis	42,249	0.1	7.3	18.0	9.1	24.7	26.0	14.9	37.5	92.3	4.3	1.1	4.9
29 161	Phelps	45,128	-0.7	5.8	15.8	17.3	22.4	24.6	14.1	33.9	93.6	3.5	3.6	1.6
29 165	Platte	90,871	2.6	6.2	18.0	7.7	27.3	29.1	11.7	38.5	89.2	7.1	3.3	2.6
29 167	Polk	31,100	-0.4	6.2	18.0	11.4	21.9	25.8	16.8	38.5	97.7	1.2	0.2	1.9
29 169	Pulaski	53,056	0.8	7.6	16.5	22.7	28.8	17.5	6.9	26.8	80.7	14.3	5.1	5.3
29 175	Randolph	25,326	-0.4	6.4	16.8	9.1	26.7	26.7	14.4	37.8	92.6	7.4	0.7	0.7
29 177	Ray	23,268	-1.7	6.6	18.0	7.2	23.5	28.9	15.8	39.9	98.1	2.1	0.0	2.3
29 183	St. Charles	365,131	1.9	6.6	18.7	8.6	27.0	27.4	11.7	37.2	92.1	5.3	2.9	1.5
29 187	St. Francois	65,696	0.5	5.6	15.5	9.5	28.0	27.1	14.3	38.9	94.3	5.2	0.2	1.5
29 189	St. Louis	999,595	0.1	5.8	17.3	8.7	24.4	28.5	15.3	40.1	72.1	24.4	4.3	1.7
29 195	Saline	23,324	-0.2	5.9	17.1	11.7	22.2	26.9	16.4	38.3	87.1	6.8	0.5	7.1
29 201	Scott	39,161	-0.2	6.9	17.7	8.2	24.9	27.0	15.3	39.1	88.3	12.0	0.5	1.3
29 207	Stoddard	29,876	-0.7	5.5	16.8	8.1	23.9	27.5	18.2	41.8	98.0	1.5	0.0	0.8
29 209	Stone	31,836	-1.5	4.2	14.2	5.9	18.2	32.6	24.9	50.4	99.2	1.0	0.0	7.1
29 213	Taney	52,492	2.0	6.0	16.1	10.1	22.7	26.9	18.3	40.2	97.5	0.4	0.7	5.1
29 215	Texas	25,937	-0.9	6.5	16.4	8.8	22.0	28.2	18.1	41.7	95.6	3.9	0.5	2.3
29 217	Vernon	20,943	-1.7	6.3	18.5	8.6	22.1	27.9	16.6	40.9	98.0	0.5	0.7	1.9
29 219	Warren	32,635	0.6	6.7	17.7	7.1	24.5	28.5	15.4	40.1	96.8	2.8	0.0	1.7
29 221	Washington	25,125	-0.3	6.4	17.4	8.1	25.6	28.5	14.0	40.2	96.6	2.9	0.5	1.0
29 225	Webster	36,327	0.1	6.9	20.3	7.8	24.7	26.8	13.6	38.3	97.7	1.3	0.4	2.2
29 510	St. Louis city	318,612	-0.3	6.8	14.4	11.8	30.9	25.0	11.1	33.9	47.4	50.2	3.5	2.0
30 000	**Montana**	997,852	1.5	6.1	16.2	9.7	23.8	29.0	15.2	39.9	91.9	0.9	1.3	8.6
30 013	Cascade	81,677	0.2	6.7	16.0	10.2	24.2	27.1	15.8	38.9	93.2	2.0	1.8	7.1
30 029	Flathead	91,221	0.8	5.9	17.2	7.8	23.0	31.1	15.0	41.4	97.2	0.5	1.1	3.0
30 031	Gallatin	91,193	3.4	6.3	14.4	16.1	29.4	24.0	9.9	32.8	97.3	0.6	2.2	2.4
30 047	Lake	28,929	0.7	7.0	18.1	8.0	20.5	28.8	17.6	41.1	76.6	0.7	0.5	29.2
30 049	Lewis and Clark	64,247	2.0	6.1	16.4	8.7	23.6	31.0	14.3	40.4	96.2	1.1	1.1	4.3
30 063	Missoula	110,183	1.4	5.5	14.1	15.2	27.3	26.1	11.7	34.4	95.6	0.8	2.0	4.4
30 081	Ravalli	40,459	0.7	5.1	16.4	6.2	20.1	32.2	20.1	46.5	97.9	1.1	0.9	1.8
30 093	Silver Bow	34,334	0.5	5.3	15.6	10.6	22.5	29.7	16.3	41.7	96.9	1.0	0.8	3.0
30 111	Yellowstone	150,078	2.3	6.7	16.9	8.8	25.7	27.6	14.3	38.3	92.6	1.3	1.4	7.2

Table A-2. Counties — Who: Age, Race/Ethnicity, and Household Structure, 2010–2012—*Continued*

STATE and County code	STATE or County	Percent Hispanic or Latino	Percent foreign born	Total households	Household type (percent)							Percent of households with people under 18 years	Percent of households with people 60 years and over
					Family households				Nonfamily households				
					Total family households	Married-couple families	Male household families	Female household families	Total nonfamily households	One-person households			
	ACS table number:	B03003	C05003	B11001	B11001	B11001	B11001	B11001	B11001	B11001	B11005	B11006
	Column number:	14	15	16	17	18	19	20	21	22	23	24
	Mississippi—Cont.											
28 137	Tate	2.3	1.0	9,967	69.8	51.1	4.6	14.1	30.2	24.8	33.0	40.3
28 139	Tippah	4.7	2.3	8,318	73.2	51.3	6.1	15.7	26.8	25.1	38.0	38.5
28 145	Union	4.4	2.8	10,234	73.3	54.0	4.1	15.2	26.7	22.9	35.3	35.8
28 149	Warren	1.9	1.8	18,508	65.0	40.6	3.6	20.9	35.0	31.5	32.2	34.3
28 151	Washington	1.2	1.5	18,301	69.8	34.4	4.8	30.5	30.2	26.4	38.6	37.2
28 153	Wayne	1.3	0.2	8,192	67.9	50.4	1.5	15.9	32.1	29.4	36.7	36.4
28 163	Yazoo	5.4	5.0	8,515	66.6	34.9	4.8	26.9	33.4	30.5	39.6	39.1
29 000	**Missouri**	3.6	3.9	2,354,106	65.1	48.6	4.3	12.2	34.9	28.9	31.1	34.8
29 001	Adair	2.2	3.5	9,512	56.2	43.3	2.7	10.2	43.8	35.4	27.1	31.6
29 007	Audrain	2.7	1.4	9,337	71.2	56.0	5.0	10.1	28.8	23.9	33.0	39.6
29 009	Barry	7.9	3.6	13,477	69.5	56.3	4.7	8.4	30.5	26.0	29.6	43.5
29 019	Boone	3.1	5.9	64,944	56.3	43.7	3.1	9.5	43.7	30.7	28.7	24.1
29 021	Buchanan	5.5	3.7	33,578	62.5	44.9	5.5	12.1	37.5	31.0	29.6	35.2
29 023	Butler	1.6	0.9	16,894	66.8	51.5	3.2	12.1	33.2	28.6	31.1	40.8
29 027	Callaway	1.6	2.2	16,904	65.7	49.9	3.9	12.0	34.3	28.3	33.7	34.4
29 029	Camden	2.4	2.4	17,642	68.9	56.8	2.8	9.4	31.1	26.7	22.7	49.8
29 031	Cape Girardeau	2.0	2.4	29,489	65.4	50.9	3.8	10.7	34.6	27.2	31.7	32.5
29 037	Cass	4.0	1.9	37,183	72.8	57.5	3.9	11.5	27.2	22.5	36.6	33.4
29 043	Christian	2.6	2.3	29,537	75.6	62.7	3.7	9.2	24.4	20.2	38.1	32.6
29 047	Clay	6.1	4.7	86,466	68.7	51.7	4.9	12.1	31.3	26.0	34.4	29.8
29 049	Clinton	1.7	0.8	8,059	73.7	59.2	2.8	11.8	26.3	20.6	34.0	36.9
29 051	Cole	2.5	2.9	29,288	67.0	48.5	4.7	13.8	33.0	27.6	34.4	33.7
29 055	Crawford	1.5	0.8	9,580	69.9	52.6	6.8	10.5	30.1	25.1	29.8	41.3
29 069	Dunklin	5.7	2.5	12,635	64.5	45.0	3.7	15.8	35.5	30.5	32.7	39.7
29 071	Franklin	1.4	1.3	39,448	70.0	54.2	5.5	10.3	30.0	26.0	32.5	34.0
29 077	Greene	3.1	3.1	115,196	60.4	45.0	4.9	10.5	39.6	30.9	28.7	32.8
29 083	Henry	1.8	1.0	9,500	64.8	50.3	4.5	9.9	35.2	29.9	30.1	41.4
29 091	Howell	1.7	1.5	15,921	67.7	55.5	2.3	10.0	32.3	28.8	29.5	37.6
29 095	Jackson	8.4	5.6	269,581	60.1	40.4	4.6	15.1	39.9	33.0	30.2	31.9
29 097	Jasper	6.9	4.0	45,262	65.8	47.6	4.8	13.4	34.2	26.9	35.7	32.8
29 099	Jefferson	1.6	1.6	81,076	73.2	55.8	5.0	12.3	26.8	21.5	35.8	31.4
29 101	Johnson	3.3	2.1	20,139	65.8	54.6	3.2	8.1	34.2	22.0	32.1	26.3
29 105	Laclede	2.0	1.1	14,064	74.5	58.0	3.4	13.0	25.5	21.1	34.9	39.7
29 107	Lafayette	2.3	1.3	13,050	69.5	56.3	3.5	9.7	30.5	26.7	31.3	40.1
29 109	Lawrence	6.5	2.6	14,665	70.0	55.1	5.5	9.4	30.0	25.2	33.3	37.6
29 113	Lincoln	2.0	1.9	19,009	72.6	58.1	4.5	10.1	27.4	23.2	39.2	29.5
29 119	McDonald	11.2	6.9	8,249	66.6	49.9	2.9	13.9	33.4	30.9	33.2	36.5
29 127	Marion	1.4	1.1	11,206	66.1	47.0	4.3	14.7	33.9	27.9	31.0	38.7
29 131	Miller	1.5	0.8	9,891	69.8	51.8	6.9	11.1	30.2	25.9	34.4	39.9
29 141	Morgan	1.8	0.9	7,945	67.1	55.3	3.5	8.3	32.9	27.4	25.3	50.8
29 145	Newton	4.6	3.3	22,205	71.2	57.5	3.6	10.0	28.8	23.7	30.2	38.5
29 147	Nodaway	2.3	1.1	8,563	55.2	45.3	3.2	6.7	44.8	31.1	23.1	30.7
29 159	Pettis	7.5	6.2	16,256	67.8	53.4	4.0	10.4	32.2	28.2	32.0	35.4
29 161	Phelps	2.1	3.6	16,861	63.7	48.9	4.4	10.4	36.3	29.0	29.2	35.7
29 165	Platte	5.2	5.9	36,355	67.2	53.4	4.2	9.7	32.8	27.1	34.3	29.5
29 167	Polk	2.0	1.3	11,727	69.9	56.7	5.4	7.9	30.1	25.0	33.1	39.2
29 169	Pulaski	9.3	5.4	15,610	65.7	52.3	3.3	10.1	34.3	26.4	36.8	22.8
29 175	Randolph	1.7	0.5	8,767	65.5	49.8	4.0	11.6	34.5	28.1	29.4	36.0
29 177	Ray	1.9	1.0	9,040	70.9	57.5	3.7	9.6	29.1	24.7	32.4	38.8
29 183	St. Charles	2.9	3.8	135,386	72.8	59.4	3.7	9.8	27.2	22.5	36.7	31.1
29 187	St. Francois	1.3	0.6	24,934	64.4	47.8	4.8	11.9	35.6	29.7	31.6	34.8
29 189	St. Louis	2.6	7.0	402,680	64.9	46.8	4.1	14.1	35.1	30.2	30.7	36.1
29 195	Saline	8.6	6.2	8,848	63.9	44.4	5.5	14.0	36.1	28.3	29.6	38.7
29 201	Scott	1.9	0.9	15,335	70.4	49.6	4.5	16.4	29.6	23.8	34.3	37.2
29 207	Stoddard	1.3	0.5	12,179	68.4	54.2	4.7	9.5	31.6	27.3	29.4	41.1
29 209	Stone	1.8	0.9	12,934	72.0	60.3	4.1	7.7	28.0	23.3	23.6	54.1
29 213	Taney	5.0	4.6	19,933	64.8	47.3	4.7	12.7	35.2	30.0	26.7	43.7
29 215	Texas	1.8	0.9	9,564	70.8	56.4	4.3	10.2	29.2	25.0	28.8	42.8
29 217	Vernon	1.7	2.1	8,078	65.5	48.1	5.3	12.1	34.5	29.2	29.1	40.5
29 219	Warren	3.0	2.1	12,766	70.5	56.4	3.9	10.2	29.5	23.3	32.4	35.7
29 221	Washington	0.7	0.7	9,114	71.2	53.8	6.6	10.8	28.8	25.5	32.1	37.1
29 225	Webster	1.8	0.9	12,481	73.3	59.4	4.2	9.6	26.7	23.3	37.0	37.8
29 510	St. Louis city	3.6	6.9	138,981	46.6	24.4	4.0	18.2	53.4	43.6	23.8	28.8
30 000	**Montana**	3.0	2.0	404,990	63.1	49.9	4.3	8.8	36.9	30.1	27.8	36.9
30 013	Cascade	3.5	2.7	32,982	64.1	49.6	4.8	9.7	35.9	31.3	28.2	37.0
30 029	Flathead	2.4	2.1	36,950	65.2	53.5	4.3	7.4	34.8	28.5	27.0	36.9
30 031	Gallatin	2.8	2.6	36,704	61.1	50.2	4.6	6.3	38.9	26.4	28.1	25.1
30 047	Lake	3.6	1.3	12,094	66.9	48.8	4.8	13.3	33.1	27.2	31.9	41.3
30 049	Lewis and Clark	2.6	1.6	26,502	61.4	49.3	3.9	8.2	38.6	31.2	27.2	36.4
30 063	Missoula	2.7	2.8	45,413	58.5	43.9	5.4	9.2	41.5	29.0	25.6	28.9
30 081	Ravalli	3.0	2.5	17,026	66.0	54.8	2.6	8.6	34.0	28.3	28.7	48.2
30 093	Silver Bow	3.8	1.3	14,874	56.9	42.2	4.0	10.7	43.1	36.1	25.5	35.4
30 111	Yellowstone	4.8	1.7	60,814	63.0	47.2	4.8	11.1	37.0	29.9	31.1	34.5

Table A-2. Counties — Who: Age, Race/Ethnicity, and Household Structure, 2010–2012—*Continued*

STATE and County code	STATE or County	Total population	Percent change 2010–2012	Population by age (percent)						Median age	Race alone or in combination (percent)			
				Under 5 years	5 to 17 years	18 to 24 years	25 to 44 years	45 to 64 years	65 years and over		White	Black	Asian, Hawaiian, or Pacific Islander	American Indian, Alaska Native, or some other race
	ACS table number:	B01003	Population estimates	B01001	B01001	B01001	B01001	B01001	B01001	B01002	B02008	B02009	302011 + B02012	B02010 + B02013
	Column number:	1	2	3	4	5	6	7	8	9	10	11	12	13
31 000	**Nebraska**............	1,842,480	1.4	7.2	17.8	10.0	25.4	25.9	13.6	36.3	90.3	5.5	2.4	4.1
31 001	Adams.................	31,351	0.3	6.8	17.1	11.7	22.7	26.4	15.3	38.3	96.3	1.1	1.7	2.9
31 019	Buffalo...............	46,779	2.8	7.1	16.7	16.4	24.6	22.8	12.3	32.1	94.8	1.2	1.9	3.7
31 025	Cass...................	25,208	-0.5	6.2	18.7	7.0	22.8	30.5	14.8	41.2	97.5	1.5	1.0	1.5
31 043	Dakota................	20,954	-0.6	8.8	20.6	10.7	24.3	24.3	11.3	33.0	72.4	3.8	3.7	20.9
31 047	Dawson...............	24,320	-0.6	7.9	20.5	8.9	23.6	25.5	13.5	37.1	85.5	4.1	0.0	10.9
31 053	Dodge.................	36,599	-0.6	6.7	17.1	7.8	24.2	25.7	18.5	40.2	97.4	0.8	1.1	2.5
31 055	Douglas...............	524,969	2.4	7.8	18.3	10.0	28.7	24.5	10.7	33.6	80.7	12.9	3.5	6.0
31 067	Gage..................	22,035	-2.2	6.5	16.3	7.2	20.9	29.6	19.5	44.3	99.4	0.7	0.0	1.7
31 079	Hall...................	59,552	2.7	7.9	19.3	8.5	25.5	25.8	13.0	35.7	94.1	2.4	1.3	3.5
31 109	Lancaster.............	289,807	2.5	7.0	16.1	14.8	27.1	23.9	11.1	32.7	91.2	5.0	4.3	2.2
31 111	Lincoln...............	36,160	-0.5	6.9	17.7	7.5	24.1	27.9	15.8	39.4	96.1	1.3	0.8	3.6
31 119	Madison...............	34,967	0.3	8.1	17.3	10.0	22.9	26.7	15.0	37.2	95.1	2.5	0.6	3.1
31 141	Platte................	32,477	1.3	7.4	18.9	8.5	22.6	27.9	14.6	39.2	97.4	0.5	0.8	3.0
31 153	Sarpy.................	162,718	3.9	8.3	20.2	8.7	29.6	24.3	8.8	33.1	91.9	5.4	3.6	2.5
31 155	Saunders..............	20,839	-0.1	6.5	18.9	6.5	22.1	30.1	15.9	41.5	98.2	0.5	0.6	1.5
31 157	Scotts Bluff..........	36,987	-0.3	7.0	17.6	9.3	23.1	26.4	16.6	38.8	94.3	0.9	0.8	5.3
31 177	Washington............	20,260	-0.1	5.7	18.9	8.3	21.9	30.7	14.5	41.0	99.1	1.1	0.5	0.3
32 000	**Nevada**.............	2,727,571	2.0	6.8	17.5	9.2	28.2	25.7	12.6	36.6	74.5	9.4	10.4	10.0
32 001	Churchill.............	24,593	-1.7	5.6	18.3	9.0	23.5	27.6	16.1	39.5	83.5	2.5	4.3	13.1
32 003	Clark.................	1,974,036	2.4	7.0	17.8	9.2	29.5	24.8	11.8	35.7	70.0	12.0	12.2	10.6
32 005	Douglas...............	47,014	-0.1	4.6	15.1	6.1	20.4	32.5	21.4	47.8	92.5	1.1	3.3	6.0
32 007	Elko..................	49,861	4.7	8.1	20.6	9.7	26.8	26.5	8.4	33.3	89.6	1.7	1.9	8.5
32 019	Lyon..................	51,670	-1.5	5.9	18.3	7.4	22.2	29.4	16.7	41.4	90.3	1.8	2.6	8.3
32 023	Nye...................	43,397	-2.1	4.4	15.5	6.2	17.7	31.0	25.2	49.6	89.8	2.8	2.5	6.4
32 031	Washoe................	425,845	1.8	6.5	16.7	10.4	26.5	27.1	12.7	37.4	84.2	3.2	7.9	8.4
32 510	Carson City...........	54,989	-0.8	5.8	15.4	8.5	25.1	28.1	17.1	41.7	86.7	1.2	4.7	10.0
33 000	**New Hampshire**.......	1,318,455	0.3	5.1	16.1	9.4	24.3	30.9	14.1	41.5	95.6	1.7	2.8	1.6
33 001	Belknap...............	60,206	0.4	5.0	15.6	7.0	22.3	32.8	17.4	45.2	97.5	0.9	1.5	1.5
33 003	Carroll...............	47,677	-0.5	4.2	13.7	6.0	19.3	35.4	21.5	49.2	99.1	0.6	0.8	1.3
33 005	Cheshire..............	76,919	-0.3	4.9	14.3	13.4	22.3	30.0	15.2	41.4	97.4	1.1	1.8	1.3
33 007	Coos..................	32,549	-2.6	4.1	14.2	6.6	22.0	33.1	19.9	47.2	98.1	0.8	0.8	1.6
33 009	Grafton...............	89,085	0.1	4.5	13.4	14.1	22.0	29.9	16.0	41.2	95.7	1.5	3.6	1.5
33 011	Hillsborough..........	401,933	0.5	5.8	17.2	8.7	26.4	29.7	12.3	39.6	92.9	2.8	4.1	2.4
33 013	Merrimack.............	146,606	0.2	5.0	16.2	9.0	24.2	31.4	14.2	42.0	96.7	1.6	2.0	1.2
33 015	Rockingham............	296,427	0.8	4.8	17.3	7.3	24.3	32.9	13.3	42.7	97.0	1.2	2.3	0.9
33 017	Strafford.............	123,661	0.8	5.4	14.7	15.6	24.6	27.3	12.3	36.9	95.4	1.6	3.6	1.9
33 019	Sullivan..............	43,392	-1.5	5.0	15.5	7.0	23.1	32.4	17.0	44.6	97.6	0.7	1.0	2.1
34 000	**New Jersey**.........	8,834,249	0.7	6.0	17.1	8.8	26.5	27.8	13.8	39.1	71.1	14.7	9.4	7.5
34 001	Atlantic..............	274,982	0.3	6.0	17.0	9.4	24.3	28.8	14.6	40.3	68.3	17.4	8.8	8.8
34 003	Bergen................	912,753	1.4	5.4	16.8	7.6	25.7	29.2	15.3	41.4	73.9	6.3	15.9	6.2
34 005	Burlington............	450,454	0.4	5.6	17.1	8.5	25.2	29.4	14.2	40.7	76.2	18.1	5.7	3.5
34 007	Camden................	513,593	0.0	6.4	17.6	9.0	26.5	27.4	13.1	38.0	66.1	20.9	6.1	10.4
34 009	Cape May..............	96,716	-1.0	4.7	13.8	7.8	19.8	31.6	22.3	47.9	92.4	5.5	1.4	2.5
34 011	Cumberland............	157,351	0.5	6.7	17.2	9.6	28.3	25.5	12.8	36.7	64.8	22.9	1.8	14.8
34 013	Essex.................	786,363	0.4	6.8	17.8	9.5	28.3	25.8	11.7	36.5	46.0	42.4	5.6	10.0
34 015	Gloucester............	289,167	0.3	5.9	18.0	9.3	25.4	28.6	12.8	39.0	84.5	11.4	3.5	3.0
34 017	Hudson................	644,288	2.6	6.7	13.8	9.8	36.3	23.0	10.5	34.3	56.3	14.2	15.0	17.8
34 019	Hunterdon.............	127,722	-1.0	4.4	18.4	7.3	21.7	34.8	13.4	43.8	92.2	3.0	4.1	2.2
34 021	Mercer................	367,567	0.3	5.8	16.5	11.0	26.6	27.1	12.9	38.1	63.8	21.1	10.0	7.2
34 023	Middlesex.............	816,975	1.5	6.1	16.5	10.2	28.1	26.5	12.5	37.4	64.5	10.4	23.2	4.4
34 025	Monmouth..............	630,099	-0.2	5.3	18.0	8.0	23.6	30.9	14.2	41.6	85.1	8.3	5.9	3.1
34 027	Morris................	495,613	1.0	5.3	18.0	7.3	24.8	30.3	14.3	41.5	83.5	3.7	10.3	4.5
34 029	Ocean.................	579,066	0.5	6.7	16.6	7.5	21.9	26.0	21.2	42.7	93.2	3.6	2.4	2.8
34 031	Passaic...............	502,431	0.2	6.8	17.8	10.4	26.8	25.9	12.3	36.3	71.5	15.0	5.9	11.4
34 033	Salem.................	65,960	-0.4	5.7	17.3	8.7	23.2	29.6	15.4	41.6	80.9	16.0	1.2	3.5
34 035	Somerset..............	325,944	1.1	5.8	18.7	6.8	25.8	30.1	12.9	40.4	71.5	9.7	15.8	5.3
34 037	Sussex................	148,393	-1.2	4.9	18.2	7.7	23.4	33.3	12.5	42.4	94.7	2.5	2.3	2.0
34 039	Union.................	540,650	1.1	6.6	17.7	8.6	27.3	27.1	12.7	38.0	60.0	22.5	5.4	14.2
34 041	Warren................	108,162	-1.0	5.3	17.6	8.0	24.0	30.8	14.3	41.5	90.9	4.1	3.1	3.4
35 000	**New Mexico**.........	2,076,325	1.0	6.9	17.9	10.0	25.0	26.5	13.7	36.8	74.9	2.8	2.0	23.5
35 001	Bernalillo............	669,153	1.4	6.7	17.0	10.3	27.2	26.2	12.6	36.1	72.4	3.9	3.4	24.5
35 005	Chaves................	65,742	0.0	7.9	19.8	10.3	23.5	24.5	14.1	34.8	84.7	2.4	1.0	14.8
35 006	Cibola................	27,370	0.2	7.0	17.9	8.2	27.0	26.9	13.0	36.6	48.9	1.2	0.0	53.4
35 009	Curry.................	49,480	2.1	8.7	19.1	11.4	27.3	22.2	11.2	31.0	74.6	7.7	2.2	18.5
35 013	Dona Ana..............	212,571	2.0	7.6	18.8	13.0	24.5	23.3	12.7	32.5	91.4	2.0	1.5	7.1
35 015	Eddy..................	54,107	1.0	6.9	18.8	8.8	24.3	27.2	14.0	37.2	89.6	1.6	0.0	10.8
35 017	Grant.................	29,408	-0.1	5.8	15.8	7.6	19.2	29.3	22.3	46.7	82.1	0.6	0.6	19.5
35 025	Lea...................	65,377	2.6	9.1	20.2	10.2	26.8	22.8	11.0	31.7	90.4	4.7	0.4	6.4
35 027	Lincoln...............	20,407	-0.8	4.8	14.0	5.6	19.2	33.0	23.5	49.9	85.3	0.0	0.0	15.8
35 029	Luna..................	25,106	-0.3	7.3	19.5	8.5	21.1	24.1	19.5	38.5	89.9	1.8	0.0	9.2
35 031	McKinley..............	72,807	1.7	8.8	22.3	12.0	23.9	23.2	9.7	30.5	18.6	1.4	1.4	81.9
35 035	Otero.................	65,306	2.7	7.6	17.2	10.8	24.5	25.1	14.8	35.5	78.9	5.0	2.0	17.0
35 039	Rio Arriba............	40,325	0.0	6.8	17.4	8.6	24.2	28.3	14.7	39.3	69.0	1.0	0.5	31.4

STATE and County code	STATE or County	Percent Hispanic or Latino	Percent foreign born	Total households	Household type (percent)							Percent of households with people under 18 years	Percent of households with people 60 years and over
					Family households				Nonfamily households				
					Total family households	Married-couple families	Male household families	Female household families	Total nonfamily households	One-person households			
	ACS table number:	B03003	C05003	B11001	B11001	B11001	B11001	B11001	B11001	B11001		B11005	B11006
	Column number:	14	15	16	17	18	19	20	21	22		23	24
31 000	**Nebraska**	9.5	6.3	726,422	64.9	50.8	4.2	9.9	35.1	28.9		31.9	32.8
31 001	Adams	8.1	4.8	12,721	61.9	51.6	3.5	6.8	38.1	30.2		29.1	36.0
31 019	Buffalo	7.7	4.4	17,615	65.0	53.7	3.4	7.9	35.0	25.5		31.8	29.4
31 025	Cass	2.6	1.4	9,689	72.7	61.6	5.2	5.8	27.3	24.3		32.1	38.1
31 043	Dakota	35.8	20.0	7,308	74.4	53.1	9.3	12.0	25.6	20.4		44.1	29.2
31 047	Dawson	32.0	18.2	8,706	71.2	54.2	5.6	11.4	28.8	26.3		36.2	35.3
31 053	Dodge	10.3	5.6	15,282	66.3	53.5	4.0	8.7	33.7	28.7		31.7	38.4
31 055	Douglas	11.4	8.8	203,592	61.6	44.1	4.7	12.8	38.4	31.2		32.8	28.8
31 067	Gage	1.8	0.4	9,028	62.0	51.8	2.6	7.6	38.0	31.1		26.5	41.1
31 079	Hall	24.2	12.8	22,366	65.8	49.1	4.2	12.5	34.2	27.5		37.2	32.9
31 109	Lancaster	6.0	7.2	114,964	61.0	47.3	3.9	9.8	39.0	29.2		30.3	27.9
31 111	Lincoln	7.5	2.1	15,104	63.9	49.9	3.7	10.3	36.1	31.3		31.0	34.6
31 119	Madison	13.2	7.3	14,050	65.5	49.8	4.4	11.4	34.5	29.3		30.1	32.9
31 141	Platte	14.6	7.3	12,547	67.8	56.6	4.2	7.0	32.2	28.3		31.9	33.6
31 153	Sarpy	7.5	5.6	59,930	73.8	59.4	4.0	10.5	26.2	21.5		40.6	24.7
31 155	Saunders	2.0	1.5	8,282	68.7	59.3	3.1	6.3	31.3	27.6		32.3	37.8
31 157	Scotts Bluff	21.5	4.5	14,906	64.3	45.8	6.5	12.0	35.7	30.7		30.8	39.8
31 177	Washington	2.1	0.5	7,721	73.9	66.2	2.9	4.8	26.1	23.1		33.6	37.9
32 000	**Nevada**	26.9	19.1	992,757	64.7	45.2	6.4	13.1	35.3	27.3		33.5	34.3
32 001	Churchill	12.5	6.5	9,597	70.2	51.5	6.6	12.1	29.8	23.9		29.4	40.8
32 003	Clark	29.5	21.7	703,972	64.7	43.8	6.8	14.1	35.3	27.2		34.6	32.8
32 005	Douglas	11.2	6.6	19,429	65.7	53.4	3.9	8.4	34.3	27.7		24.3	49.1
32 007	Elko	23.3	10.3	17,425	73.4	58.5	7.1	7.8	26.6	20.3		37.8	27.8
32 019	Lyon	15.1	7.7	19,504	69.0	52.4	5.7	10.9	31.0	23.4		32.6	44.2
32 023	Nye	13.8	9.2	18,431	68.6	52.6	6.1	9.9	31.4	24.0		26.5	53.3
32 031	Washoe	22.7	14.8	162,452	62.5	45.6	5.1	11.7	37.5	29.0		31.3	34.2
32 510	Carson City	22.0	12.0	21,212	62.4	46.1	4.1	12.3	37.6	30.7		29.5	43.0
33 000	**New Hampshire**	2.9	5.4	518,009	66.9	53.0	4.1	9.7	33.1	25.5		30.3	35.3
33 001	Belknap	1.3	3.8	25,422	68.0	53.1	4.2	10.6	32.0	26.3		27.8	41.6
33 003	Carroll	1.1	2.8	21,192	66.0	54.6	3.3	8.1	34.0	27.3		22.7	46.1
33 005	Cheshire	1.5	2.7	30,405	62.8	48.3	5.0	9.5	37.2	27.9		26.1	39.4
33 007	Coos	1.3	2.8	14,515	60.6	46.8	4.2	9.6	39.4	33.5		23.1	43.4
33 009	Grafton	1.9	5.7	35,102	62.5	49.6	3.7	9.2	37.5	29.1		25.3	38.0
33 011	Hillsborough	5.5	8.5	153,838	67.5	52.7	4.4	10.3	32.5	25.1		33.5	31.8
33 013	Merrimack	1.7	3.8	57,387	65.9	52.3	3.6	10.1	34.1	26.5		29.7	35.8
33 015	Rockingham	2.2	4.4	116,143	70.3	58.2	3.6	8.4	29.7	22.5		32.2	34.2
33 017	Strafford	1.9	4.6	46,300	64.4	48.2	4.7	11.5	35.6	25.4		30.6	31.9
33 019	Sullivan	1.2	2.8	17,705	68.6	54.5	4.5	9.5	31.4	24.3		27.3	39.7
34 000	**New Jersey**	18.1	21.3	3,181,881	69.1	50.9	4.8	13.4	30.9	26.0		34.6	36.6
34 001	Atlantic	17.3	16.7	99,782	66.2	45.3	4.8	16.2	33.8	28.6		32.9	39.1
34 003	Bergen	16.7	29.7	333,711	71.5	56.3	4.1	11.1	28.5	24.8		33.8	38.9
34 005	Burlington	6.8	9.8	164,889	69.8	53.5	4.5	11.8	30.2	25.6		34.0	37.5
34 007	Camden	14.7	10.5	187,178	66.8	45.9	5.1	15.8	33.2	27.7		34.2	35.3
34 009	Cape May	6.4	5.5	41,459	65.1	51.4	4.3	9.3	34.9	30.2		24.9	48.4
34 011	Cumberland	27.6	10.9	49,981	69.3	44.6	6.2	18.5	30.7	25.5		35.8	38.8
34 013	Essex	20.9	25.1	276,592	64.9	38.7	5.9	20.3	35.1	30.2		36.6	32.4
34 015	Gloucester	5.0	5.2	104,568	72.5	55.8	4.4	12.4	27.5	22.8		36.0	35.7
34 017	Hudson	42.5	41.3	243,675	62.0	38.1	6.6	17.4	38.0	28.8		32.1	28.6
34 019	Hunterdon	5.5	8.5	47,306	73.4	62.4	2.4	8.6	26.6	21.9		34.8	35.6
34 021	Mercer	15.5	20.6	131,315	66.8	48.9	4.9	13.1	33.2	27.5		33.0	35.7
34 023	Middlesex	18.8	30.9	280,599	72.6	55.3	5.2	12.0	27.4	22.6		37.4	34.6
34 025	Monmouth	9.9	13.0	234,366	69.4	55.2	3.9	10.3	30.6	26.0		34.4	37.9
34 027	Morris	11.8	19.0	179,946	71.7	59.9	3.3	8.5	28.3	23.9		35.2	37.0
34 029	Ocean	8.5	7.9	222,796	67.3	53.5	4.0	9.7	32.7	28.5		28.6	48.9
34 031	Passaic	37.7	28.8	162,615	71.7	47.2	6.2	18.3	28.3	24.8		38.1	35.8
34 033	Salem	7.1	4.5	24,817	68.9	49.1	5.2	14.5	31.1	27.1		33.8	39.5
34 035	Somerset	13.3	23.2	115,709	72.9	60.2	2.9	9.8	27.1	23.0		38.5	34.5
34 037	Sussex	6.7	7.2	54,274	74.2	61.0	3.8	9.4	25.8	21.7		34.6	34.1
34 039	Union	28.1	29.2	184,721	71.1	49.2	6.0	16.0	28.9	24.6		38.4	35.3
34 041	Warren	7.4	9.0	41,582	70.1	55.2	4.2	10.7	29.9	24.7		33.3	36.5
35 000	**New Mexico**	46.7	9.8	765,306	65.4	45.4	6.0	14.0	34.6	28.7		32.5	36.7
35 001	Bernalillo	48.2	10.8	264,592	61.2	41.2	6.2	13.9	38.8	31.5		31.4	33.0
35 005	Chaves	52.7	15.3	23,386	69.8	48.6	4.9	16.4	30.2	25.8		37.3	37.6
35 006	Cibola	36.9	3.7	8,056	69.8	41.8	8.8	19.3	30.2	25.9		37.1	39.7
35 009	Curry	39.7	8.5	18,058	69.0	50.1	5.2	13.7	31.0	28.2		36.9	30.0
35 013	Dona Ana	66.1	17.1	73,889	71.1	49.0	5.2	16.9	28.9	22.9		37.1	34.4
35 015	Eddy	44.7	4.9	19,860	68.1	48.7	6.5	13.0	31.9	27.5		32.6	37.7
35 017	Grant	48.7	4.8	12,226	61.9	46.3	3.4	12.2	38.1	33.9		25.9	48.2
35 025	Lea	52.2	15.7	20,396	76.1	55.2	7.8	13.1	23.9	19.8		41.9	33.1
35 027	Lincoln	30.5	6.7	8,644	61.9	46.5	3.6	11.9	38.1	31.8		24.2	48.9
35 029	Luna	62.4	14.8	9,329	64.8	47.2	3.5	14.1	35.2	30.5		29.7	47.1
35 031	McKinley	13.6	2.5	17,642	70.3	41.8	5.7	22.8	29.7	26.9		39.3	39.9
35 035	Otero	34.9	10.8	24,463	69.8	50.4	6.1	13.4	30.2	25.9		32.8	39.9
35 039	Rio Arriba	71.3	7.2	15,029	68.0	42.4	8.1	17.5	32.0	26.8		32.8	39.2

Table A-2. Counties — Who: Age, Race/Ethnicity, and Household Structure, 2010–2012—*Continued*

STATE and County code	STATE or County	Total population	Percent change 2010–2012	Population by age (percent)						Median age	Race alone or in combination (percent)			
				Under 5 years	5 to 17 years	18 to 24 years	25 to 44 years	45 to 64 years	65 years and over		White	Black	Asian, Hawaiian, or Pacific Islander	American Indian, Alaska Native, or some other race
	ACS table number:	B01003	Population estimates	B01001	B01001	B01001	B01001	B01001	B01001	B01002	B02008	B02009	B02011 + B02012	B02010 + B02013
	Column number:	1	2	3	4	5	6	7	8	9	10	11	12	13
	New Mexico—Cont.													
35 041	Roosevelt	20,311	2.0	7.6	18.7	19.6	21.8	20.5	11.8	28.8	78.1	2.3	1.6	19.0
35 043	Sandoval	134,053	2.5	6.5	19.5	8.1	25.0	28.2	12.7	38.3	76.1	3.6	2.3	21.5
35 045	San Juan	128,912	-1.2	8.1	20.4	9.9	25.4	25.0	11.2	33.1	55.9	1.4	1.0	45.0
35 047	San Miguel	29,185	-1.6	5.6	16.0	11.0	21.1	30.3	16.0	41.2	73.6	2.4	0.5	27.7
35 049	Santa Fe	145,378	1.3	5.4	15.1	7.7	23.7	31.8	16.2	43.5	87.6	1.2	1.8	12.2
35 055	Taos	32,872	-0.4	5.4	14.8	6.9	21.9	32.7	18.4	45.8	61.4	0.9	2.6	39.3
35 061	Valencia	76,738	-0.1	6.8	19.0	8.9	24.1	27.8	13.4	38.0	66.1	1.6	0.8	34.4
36 000	**New York**	19,490,373	0.9	6.0	16.1	10.2	27.1	26.9	13.8	38.0	67.5	16.9	8.4	10.1
36 001	Albany	304,694	0.5	4.9	14.5	13.6	25.0	27.7	14.2	38.2	79.9	14.4	5.9	2.8
36 003	Allegany	48,680	-1.2	5.2	16.0	16.0	20.3	27.0	15.5	38.1	96.6	1.7	1.4	1.1
36 005	Bronx	1,397,357	1.5	7.6	18.8	11.7	27.9	23.3	10.7	32.9	24.1	36.3	4.3	39.3
36 007	Broome	199,225	-1.2	5.1	14.8	12.9	22.5	28.0	16.7	40.3	90.6	5.8	4.5	1.8
36 009	Cattaraugus	79,859	-1.0	6.0	17.1	9.6	22.1	29.5	15.6	41.3	94.4	2.1	1.0	4.2
36 011	Cayuga	79,775	-0.5	5.1	16.1	9.0	23.9	30.3	15.7	42.2	94.2	5.1	0.8	1.6
36 013	Chautauqua	134,190	-0.9	5.5	16.0	11.4	21.7	28.6	16.8	40.9	94.1	3.3	1.0	3.2
36 015	Chemung	88,848	0.1	5.9	16.3	9.3	24.0	29.2	15.4	40.6	92.2	8.0	1.7	1.4
36 017	Chenango	50,162	-0.8	5.3	16.8	7.6	22.4	30.6	17.3	43.5	98.3	1.2	0.9	1.6
36 019	Clinton	81,862	-0.6	4.8	14.1	12.9	25.4	29.1	13.7	39.4	93.0	4.6	1.6	1.7
36 021	Columbia	62,709	-0.8	4.5	15.3	7.7	20.7	33.0	18.7	46.3	93.4	5.2	2.1	2.3
36 023	Cortland	49,456	0.4	5.3	15.6	17.8	21.6	26.2	13.6	36.1	96.1	2.8	1.3	2.1
36 025	Delaware	47,570	-1.2	5.0	14.2	10.3	19.4	31.1	19.9	45.8	96.0	2.2	1.1	2.1
36 027	Dutchess	297,768	-0.2	5.0	16.7	11.1	23.6	29.7	14.0	40.5	81.4	11.4	4.4	5.6
36 029	Erie	919,268	0.0	5.3	16.0	10.6	24.0	28.3	15.8	40.5	81.5	14.3	3.3	3.3
36 031	Essex	39,211	-0.8	4.5	14.2	7.5	23.6	31.1	19.0	45.1	91.9	4.5	1.8	5.9
36 033	Franklin	51,626	0.5	5.3	15.0	10.3	26.9	28.6	13.8	39.5	85.5	6.6	2.2	7.9
36 035	Fulton	55,216	-1.0	5.4	16.4	8.0	24.3	29.5	16.5	41.9	97.0	2.3	0.9	1.4
36 037	Genesee	60,044	-0.2	5.5	16.0	9.0	24.0	29.4	16.0	42.1	94.3	3.9	0.9	2.6
36 039	Greene	48,924	-0.9	4.3	14.2	9.7	22.6	30.8	18.3	44.0	92.2	6.8	1.5	2.3
36 043	Herkimer	64,530	0.1	5.3	16.3	9.0	22.5	29.5	17.3	42.6	97.7	1.4	0.7	1.3
36 045	Jefferson	118,332	3.2	8.3	16.9	12.7	28.2	22.6	11.3	32.3	90.4	6.8	2.7	3.8
36 047	Kings	2,538,529	2.2	7.2	16.4	10.4	30.9	23.6	11.6	34.2	45.7	35.0	11.6	9.9
36 049	Lewis	27,128	0.6	6.3	17.9	7.9	23.2	29.3	15.4	40.6	97.8	1.7	0.1	0.7
36 051	Livingston	65,007	-0.8	4.6	15.1	14.9	21.7	29.3	14.5	40.3	95.2	3.4	1.7	1.5
36 053	Madison	72,881	-1.4	5.0	16.2	13.4	21.6	29.3	14.5	39.7	96.5	2.5	1.4	1.4
36 055	Monroe	746,442	0.4	5.7	16.5	11.3	24.7	27.5	14.3	38.4	78.5	16.5	3.9	3.6
36 057	Montgomery	50,058	-0.6	6.0	17.0	8.1	24.1	28.1	16.7	41.1	92.3	3.0	1.1	6.1
36 059	Nassau	1,345,448	0.6	5.4	17.4	8.6	23.7	29.3	15.5	41.2	73.5	12.0	8.8	8.4
36 061	New York	1,604,407	2.0	5.0	9.8	10.8	36.7	24.0	13.7	36.4	60.0	17.5	12.6	14.3
36 063	Niagara	215,837	-0.6	5.3	15.8	9.4	23.3	30.0	16.1	42.2	90.0	7.9	1.3	2.2
36 065	Oneida	234,193	-0.6	5.6	16.0	10.0	23.7	28.2	16.5	41.1	89.0	7.3	3.5	3.1
36 067	Onondaga	467,263	-0.1	5.8	16.8	11.2	24.2	27.8	14.3	38.8	83.7	12.4	3.9	3.1
36 069	Ontario	108,374	0.4	5.1	16.8	9.1	22.4	30.5	16.0	42.6	95.7	3.2	1.4	1.8
36 071	Orange	374,158	0.3	6.9	19.8	10.1	24.7	27.1	11.3	36.9	78.4	11.7	3.4	10.0
36 073	Orleans	42,916	-0.1	5.4	16.2	9.6	24.3	29.7	14.8	41.0	91.1	7.1	0.8	2.7
36 075	Oswego	121,951	-0.4	5.7	16.9	12.4	23.1	29.0	12.9	38.8	97.4	1.5	1.0	1.8
36 077	Otsego	61,965	-0.8	4.3	13.5	16.9	19.7	28.5	17.1	40.7	95.9	2.9	1.2	1.9
36 079	Putnam	99,791	-0.2	4.6	18.4	7.7	23.5	32.8	13.1	42.3	91.3	2.9	2.7	5.9
36 081	Queens	2,254,750	1.7	6.0	14.6	9.6	30.7	26.1	13.0	37.4	43.8	19.9	25.1	14.8
36 083	Rensselaer	159,719	0.2	5.5	15.4	11.8	24.5	28.8	13.8	39.9	90.9	7.7	3.0	2.0
36 085	Richmond	470,402	0.3	6.0	16.9	9.5	26.5	28.0	13.1	38.7	77.0	11.6	8.4	5.0
36 087	Rockland	315,331	1.7	7.6	20.3	9.0	23.3	26.1	13.8	36.7	73.1	13.2	7.2	8.5
36 089	St. Lawrence	112,150	0.3	5.6	15.3	15.2	22.7	27.0	14.2	37.6	95.1	2.8	1.7	2.4
36 091	Saratoga	221,076	1.0	5.3	16.8	8.1	25.5	30.1	14.1	41.2	96.0	2.3	2.6	1.5
36 093	Schenectady	154,973	0.1	5.8	16.7	9.8	24.5	28.3	14.9	40.1	82.8	11.3	4.9	4.3
36 095	Schoharie	32,473	-1.8	4.7	14.9	11.4	21.8	30.7	16.5	43.1	96.7	1.9	1.0	1.9
36 099	Seneca	35,291	0.2	5.3	14.9	9.4	25.3	29.0	16.0	41.5	94.2	4.0	2.0	1.6
36 101	Steuben	99,095	0.1	5.7	17.3	8.0	23.2	29.6	16.2	41.7	96.1	2.2	1.6	1.2
36 103	Suffolk	1,498,125	0.3	5.6	17.8	8.9	24.9	28.7	14.0	40.1	83.2	8.1	4.2	6.8
36 105	Sullivan	77,100	-0.8	5.7	16.4	8.8	23.4	30.3	15.5	41.8	83.8	11.2	1.9	7.0
36 107	Tioga	50,867	-1.2	5.3	17.4	7.4	22.3	31.0	16.5	43.2	98.0	1.1	1.0	0.6
36 109	Tompkins	101,989	0.9	4.3	11.6	27.1	23.1	22.8	11.1	30.0	84.6	5.3	10.6	2.0
36 111	Ulster	182,256	-0.3	4.8	14.8	10.2	23.8	30.9	15.5	42.6	90.5	7.7	2.8	3.1
36 113	Warren	65,653	-0.2	5.0	14.9	7.9	22.6	31.8	17.8	44.6	97.2	1.5	1.0	1.3
36 115	Washington	63,071	-0.5	5.1	15.4	8.6	25.0	30.0	15.8	42.5	95.4	3.5	0.7	1.7
36 117	Wayne	93,333	-0.8	5.8	17.4	7.8	23.2	31.0	14.8	42.1	94.9	4.1	0.9	1.5
36 119	Westchester	956,494	1.2	5.9	17.8	8.3	25.1	28.0	14.9	40.2	69.1	16.0	6.6	11.8
36 121	Wyoming	41,980	-0.5	4.8	14.8	8.8	27.5	30.2	14.3	40.9	92.9	5.6	0.7	2.2
36 123	Yates	25,366	0.0	6.1	17.9	11.0	19.5	28.7	16.8	40.5	98.3	1.4	0.8	0.7
37 000	**North Carolina**	9,654,079	2.0	6.5	17.2	10.0	26.7	26.3	13.4	37.6	71.8	22.7	2.9	5.1
37 001	Alamance	152,730	1.6	6.1	17.0	10.7	24.7	26.5	14.9	38.7	73.0	19.5	1.5	9.1
37 003	Alexander	37,060	-1.0	5.8	16.5	7.7	25.5	28.4	16.1	41.3	90.8	6.2	0.0	5.2
37 007	Anson	26,581	-2.0	5.9	15.7	9.2	26.8	27.8	14.6	40.3	48.3	49.6	1.2	0.5
37 009	Ashe	27,165	-0.6	5.2	13.9	7.0	22.8	30.2	20.9	46.1	95.4	1.0	0.5	4.3
37 013	Beaufort	47,643	-0.5	5.5	16.2	7.6	21.6	29.7	19.3	44.1	70.6	26.8	0.2	4.0

Table A-2. Counties — Who: Age, Race/Ethnicity, and Household Structure, 2010–2012—*Continued*

STATE and County code	STATE or County	Percent Hispanic or Latino	Percent foreign born	Total households	Household type (percent)							Percent of households with people under 18 years	Percent of households with people 60 years and over
					Family households				Nonfamily households				
					Total family households	Married-couple families	Male household families	Female household families	Total nonfamily households	One-person households			
	ACS table number:	B03003	C05003	B11001	B11001	B11001	B11001	B11001	B11001	B11001		B11005	B11006
	Column number:	14	15	16	17	18	19	20	21	22		23	24
	New Mexico—Cont.												
35 041	Roosevelt	40.1	8.2	7,188	65.0	45.6	6.1	13.3	35.0	26.9		36.3	29.0
35 043	Sandoval	35.8	5.4	47,339	70.6	51.3	7.3	12.0	29.4	23.1		35.3	36.2
35 045	San Juan	19.3	4.0	41,128	73.9	49.9	8.3	15.7	26.1	22.0		39.1	34.1
35 047	San Miguel	76.9	3.4	11,614	57.6	34.8	8.7	14.2	42.4	34.9		27.4	42.6
35 049	Santa Fe	50.8	13.6	61,371	57.2	41.3	4.6	11.2	42.8	34.0		24.8	41.6
35 055	Taos	56.1	6.0	13,534	60.8	43.6	4.0	13.2	39.2	34.9		24.8	45.9
35 061	Valencia	58.6	7.3	27,290	72.6	50.8	7.3	14.5	27.4	23.6		37.7	37.4
36 000	**New York**	17.9	22.3	7,210,095	64.0	44.1	5.0	14.9	36.0	29.5		31.6	36.2
36 001	Albany	5.1	8.7	121,548	56.9	40.7	3.7	12.4	43.1	33.7		26.5	34.4
36 003	Allegany	1.4	2.1	18,572	64.3	50.0	5.4	8.8	35.7	29.0		29.6	39.6
36 005	Bronx	53.9	34.3	471,665	66.0	27.1	7.6	31.4	34.0	29.8		40.1	32.0
36 007	Broome	3.5	5.6	80,214	60.1	44.2	4.5	11.4	39.9	32.6		26.6	38.4
36 009	Cattaraugus	1.8	1.9	32,114	62.7	47.5	5.1	10.1	37.3	30.8		27.0	37.9
36 011	Cayuga	2.4	2.4	30,819	65.6	48.1	6.6	10.8	34.4	28.4		29.6	40.7
36 013	Chautauqua	6.3	2.1	54,688	62.9	45.9	4.0	13.0	37.1	30.3		28.1	39.9
36 015	Chemung	2.7	2.9	35,240	62.9	46.2	4.7	12.1	37.1	30.3		30.3	38.1
36 017	Chenango	1.9	1.9	19,371	66.8	51.6	4.3	10.9	33.2	27.2		28.3	40.3
36 019	Clinton	2.5	4.8	31,901	63.3	47.5	4.9	10.9	36.7	27.6		28.7	33.7
36 021	Columbia	4.0	5.8	24,953	65.1	48.9	4.8	11.4	34.9	28.1		27.8	42.6
36 023	Cortland	2.4	1.8	17,923	61.2	45.0	5.2	11.1	38.8	31.6		29.3	38.5
36 025	Delaware	3.3	3.4	19,887	61.7	46.3	6.0	9.4	38.3	33.1		24.3	45.5
36 027	Dutchess	10.8	12.1	107,134	67.6	52.4	4.1	11.0	32.4	26.8		31.9	37.0
36 029	Erie	4.7	6.4	379,140	60.6	42.0	4.5	14.2	39.4	32.7		28.4	36.6
36 031	Essex	4.2	5.5	16,523	62.3	48.9	4.4	9.0	37.7	31.0		25.8	41.4
36 033	Franklin	3.1	5.4	19,184	64.2	48.0	6.0	10.3	35.8	29.2		28.8	37.2
36 035	Fulton	2.4	2.4	22,665	66.1	45.9	6.5	13.8	33.9	26.3		31.5	37.1
36 037	Genesee	2.7	2.9	23,840	67.3	52.4	4.6	10.3	32.7	26.3		29.1	35.6
36 039	Greene	5.0	5.3	18,569	64.0	49.2	4.5	10.4	36.0	30.9		27.4	43.0
36 043	Herkimer	1.7	4.0	26,951	64.3	47.8	4.4	12.1	35.7	29.7		29.2	40.2
36 045	Jefferson	6.0	4.4	45,679	67.4	51.4	4.2	11.8	32.6	26.6		36.8	29.8
36 047	Kings	19.9	37.8	908,959	63.2	37.3	5.8	20.1	36.8	29.1		33.5	33.7
36 049	Lewis	1.4	1.7	10,885	70.5	56.2	4.3	10.0	29.5	24.2		32.2	35.1
36 051	Livingston	2.9	2.9	24,065	68.1	52.4	4.0	11.6	31.9	24.9		31.5	36.5
36 053	Madison	1.8	2.0	26,523	66.6	51.5	4.6	10.4	33.4	28.4		29.7	37.9
36 055	Monroe	7.5	8.3	296,800	61.1	42.7	3.9	14.6	38.9	31.6		29.9	34.3
36 057	Montgomery	11.7	3.8	19,701	64.4	45.9	6.7	11.8	35.6	30.0		30.6	38.2
36 059	Nassau	15.0	21.7	441,906	76.6	60.4	4.3	12.0	23.4	19.8		36.7	43.3
36 061	New York	25.7	28.7	733,765	41.0	26.0	3.4	11.6	59.0	47.7		18.4	31.1
36 063	Niagara	2.3	3.7	88,432	62.9	45.8	4.9	12.2	37.1	31.9		27.1	37.9
36 065	Oneida	4.8	7.5	90,538	62.6	45.8	4.5	12.3	37.4	31.0		29.5	40.5
36 067	Onondaga	4.2	7.3	184,224	61.2	43.6	4.0	13.6	38.8	31.4		29.5	34.6
36 069	Ontario	3.6	3.6	44,113	64.6	48.6	5.5	10.4	35.4	28.1		29.6	39.0
36 071	Orange	18.4	11.4	125,338	72.3	55.5	4.7	12.1	27.7	23.2		38.7	33.4
36 073	Orleans	4.2	3.1	15,849	70.1	50.7	5.2	14.2	29.9	25.2		33.7	38.0
36 075	Oswego	2.2	2.0	44,893	67.4	48.5	5.3	13.6	32.6	24.3		31.6	34.4
36 077	Otsego	3.2	3.9	23,875	62.7	48.6	4.3	9.9	37.3	29.0		27.2	40.7
36 079	Putnam	12.0	11.9	34,855	76.0	63.0	3.7	9.3	24.0	20.9		35.9	35.6
36 081	Queens	27.7	48.0	773,822	67.4	44.2	6.9	16.3	32.6	26.5		33.1	36.8
36 083	Rensselaer	4.0	5.0	63,991	60.7	44.5	3.8	12.3	39.3	30.9		27.8	35.0
36 085	Richmond	17.5	21.5	162,916	74.0	55.0	4.8	14.2	26.0	23.0		36.9	38.0
36 087	Rockland	16.0	22.0	97,943	75.8	60.9	4.4	10.5	24.2	20.8		40.6	39.4
36 089	St. Lawrence	2.0	4.3	42,055	64.9	47.5	5.3	12.1	35.1	27.3		29.9	36.4
36 091	Saratoga	2.6	4.7	89,371	64.6	52.6	3.9	8.1	35.4	28.4		29.2	34.3
36 093	Schenectady	5.9	8.1	58,120	60.4	44.8	3.6	12.0	39.6	34.5		28.1	36.1
36 095	Schoharie	2.9	2.5	12,942	63.3	50.6	3.3	9.4	36.7	29.8		27.9	44.0
36 099	Seneca	2.9	1.8	13,321	62.8	49.2	4.8	8.8	37.2	28.6		29.0	40.0
36 101	Steuben	1.4	2.4	41,422	62.1	47.6	4.1	10.4	37.9	30.9		29.4	38.2
36 103	Suffolk	17.0	14.5	496,396	75.2	58.0	4.7	12.6	24.8	20.2		37.5	39.1
36 105	Sullivan	13.9	9.9	29,768	64.4	44.6	5.5	14.4	35.6	29.3		31.0	38.6
36 107	Tioga	1.4	2.3	20,135	70.0	56.5	3.9	9.7	30.0	25.6		29.5	40.4
36 109	Tompkins	4.5	12.7	38,530	52.2	42.5	2.2	7.6	47.8	32.4		23.6	30.8
36 111	Ulster	9.0	6.8	69,477	63.4	46.9	4.9	11.5	36.6	29.3		29.2	40.9
36 113	Warren	1.9	3.0	28,195	65.0	50.0	3.4	11.5	35.0	27.8		26.8	40.6
36 115	Washington	2.3	2.3	24,242	69.1	53.1	5.1	10.9	30.9	25.1		30.4	40.3
36 117	Wayne	3.8	2.9	36,872	70.5	54.9	5.0	10.7	29.5	23.5		32.8	36.6
36 119	Westchester	22.4	25.1	342,568	69.2	51.7	4.2	13.2	30.8	27.2		35.7	38.4
36 121	Wyoming	3.0	2.4	15,716	66.1	52.1	5.2	8.8	33.9	27.7		28.7	36.1
36 123	Yates	1.8	2.0	9,466	69.4	54.8	4.1	10.5	30.6	23.9		29.7	40.2
37 000	**North Carolina**	8.5	7.6	3,699,308	66.5	48.3	4.4	13.8	33.5	27.9		32.6	33.9
37 001	Alamance	11.3	7.5	60,459	66.8	47.3	5.1	14.4	33.2	28.9		31.5	36.1
37 003	Alexander	4.3	2.0	13,949	68.7	54.1	5.5	9.1	31.3	27.9		30.8	40.0
37 007	Anson	3.1	3.1	9,592	65.5	39.2	7.7	18.6	34.5	31.3		31.3	40.0
37 009	Ashe	4.8	4.2	11,646	69.9	54.7	3.8	11.3	30.1	25.5		27.2	44.3
37 013	Beaufort	6.9	4.7	19,218	65.5	49.8	3.2	12.6	34.5	31.8		27.2	45.0

STATE and County code	STATE or County	Total population	Percent change 2010– 2012	Under 5 years	5 to 17 years	18 to 24 years	25 to 44 years	45 to 64 years	65 years and over	Median age	White	Black	Asian, Hawaiian, or Pacific Islander	American Indian, Alaska Native, or some other race
				Population by age (percent)							Race alone or in combination (percent)			
ACS table number:		B01003	Population estimates	B01001	B01001	B01001	B01001	B01001	B01001	B01002	B02008	B02009	B02011 + B02012	B02010 + B02013
Column number:		1	2	3	4	5	6	7	8	9	10	11	12	13
	North Carolina—Cont.													
37 015	Bertie	20,946	-2.7	5.2	15.0	8.7	23.1	30.0	18.0	42.0	35.9	63.4	0.6	0.3
37 017	Bladen	35,030	-0.8	5.6	17.0	8.5	22.4	30.2	16.3	41.6	60.1	35.8	0.0	5.4
37 019	Brunswick	110,196	3.9	5.2	13.1	5.9	21.7	31.3	22.8	48.3	86.1	12.2	1.2	3.6
37 021	Buncombe	241,626	2.4	5.5	14.8	8.6	26.6	28.1	16.4	40.6	91.0	7.5	1.8	2.6
37 023	Burke	90,713	-0.3	5.4	16.4	9.4	23.7	28.5	16.5	41.7	87.4	7.5	3.8	3.3
37 025	Cabarrus	181,358	3.4	7.0	20.1	7.8	28.0	25.6	11.4	36.8	79.7	16.5	2.6	3.3
37 027	Caldwell	82,380	-1.2	5.0	16.9	8.5	24.2	29.2	16.2	41.5	91.3	7.4	0.7	2.0
37 031	Carteret	67,235	1.4	4.8	14.1	7.3	23.0	31.4	19.5	45.6	90.3	7.1	1.5	2.7
37 033	Caswell	23,480	-1.9	5.0	14.8	7.7	23.6	31.7	17.2	44.0	64.0	35.2	0.0	3.2
37 035	Catawba	154,182	0.1	6.1	17.4	8.3	25.4	27.9	14.9	40.2	84.3	9.5	3.9	4.0
37 037	Chatham	65,001	3.5	5.7	15.4	6.4	22.9	29.8	19.8	44.8	79.8	14.1	1.3	6.2
37 039	Cherokee	27,199	-1.6	4.4	14.4	6.4	19.4	31.2	24.2	49.1	95.3	1.2	1.0	4.2
37 045	Cleveland	97,695	-0.6	5.9	17.2	9.3	23.6	28.4	15.6	40.8	77.5	21.6	1.0	1.1
37 047	Columbus	57,799	-0.5	5.6	17.4	8.9	24.3	28.0	15.8	40.5	62.7	31.4	0.4	7.4
37 049	Craven	104,392	0.8	7.3	15.6	12.5	24.1	24.8	15.8	36.4	72.7	23.2	3.1	4.4
37 051	Cumberland	322,532	1.2	8.4	18.2	12.7	28.5	22.6	9.7	30.9	56.2	39.1	4.2	6.6
37 053	Currituck	23,890	1.8	5.6	17.6	7.3	25.0	31.5	13.0	41.4	92.7	5.2	3.0	2.3
37 055	Dare	34,288	1.7	5.4	14.4	6.2	25.7	32.5	15.8	43.8	92.0	4.4	0.0	2.7
37 057	Davidson	163,071	0.2	5.9	17.5	7.5	25.3	28.6	15.1	40.9	87.8	9.5	1.6	2.4
37 059	Davie	41,377	0.3	5.2	18.1	6.8	22.9	30.2	16.8	42.7	88.6	7.2	0.8	4.2
37 061	Duplin	59,435	2.3	7.2	18.1	8.8	25.0	26.5	14.3	37.3	57.9	26.3	0.0	17.4
37 063	Durham	273,900	4.2	7.4	15.1	11.6	32.4	23.4	10.1	33.6	52.2	39.1	5.3	6.2
37 065	Edgecombe	56,203	-1.1	6.7	17.4	8.9	23.2	28.7	15.1	40.1	39.1	57.9	0.4	3.7
37 067	Forsyth	354,659	1.9	6.7	17.4	10.1	26.2	26.4	13.2	37.4	68.5	27.2	2.3	3.9
37 069	Franklin	61,156	1.1	6.2	17.7	8.5	25.7	28.7	13.2	39.8	69.5	27.5	0.5	5.2
37 071	Gaston	207,039	0.9	6.3	17.4	8.6	26.4	27.7	13.6	39.2	79.5	16.2	1.5	4.8
37 077	Granville	60,188	0.7	5.3	16.6	9.6	26.3	29.0	13.2	40.7	63.5	34.2	0.8	4.1
37 079	Greene	21,482	0.3	6.4	16.4	9.5	27.9	26.9	12.9	38.6	51.9	37.2	0.0	13.0
37 081	Guilford	495,297	2.3	6.2	17.0	11.6	26.8	25.8	12.6	36.6	59.3	34.4	4.7	4.0
37 083	Halifax	54,288	-1.0	5.8	16.8	8.8	22.4	29.5	16.8	42.2	43.3	54.0	0.8	7.4
37 085	Harnett	119,058	5.5	7.9	19.8	10.4	28.4	23.0	10.5	33.4	72.4	22.6	1.7	6.6
37 087	Haywood	58,871	-0.1	4.8	14.4	7.4	22.1	29.6	21.7	45.9	97.6	1.2	0.9	1.9
37 089	Henderson	107,594	1.2	5.3	14.9	6.4	22.4	27.9	23.0	45.7	93.9	4.0	1.2	2.4
37 091	Hertford	24,522	-0.7	5.4	14.9	10.6	23.5	29.4	16.2	41.7	35.9	61.3	0.8	3.0
37 093	Hoke	49,174	6.4	9.7	20.2	9.5	31.6	22.0	6.9	31.0	52.2	36.6	2.8	15.2
37 097	Iredell	161,160	1.8	5.9	19.0	8.3	25.7	27.9	13.2	39.4	83.5	13.0	2.3	2.7
37 099	Jackson	40,359	0.3	4.4	12.9	19.7	21.6	25.7	15.8	35.8	86.3	2.5	1.5	12.3
37 101	Johnston	172,463	3.1	7.3	20.2	7.9	28.3	25.5	10.8	36.7	81.8	16.2	1.0	3.8
37 105	Lee	58,732	3.2	7.1	18.6	8.7	26.1	25.6	13.9	37.4	70.0	20.4	1.7	10.1
37 107	Lenoir	59,347	-0.3	6.2	17.5	8.3	22.7	28.9	16.5	42.0	55.7	41.8	0.9	3.5
37 109	Lincoln	78,848	1.2	5.8	17.3	7.6	25.5	29.9	13.9	41.1	91.9	6.2	0.8	2.9
37 111	McDowell	44,999	-0.1	5.5	16.2	7.0	25.3	28.9	17.1	42.6	92.6	4.6	1.0	4.5
37 113	Macon	33,883	-0.2	5.0	14.1	6.4	20.2	29.9	24.4	48.6	95.0	0.5	1.9	3.6
37 115	Madison	20,783	-0.1	4.3	15.3	9.9	21.7	30.6	18.2	44.3	96.9	1.1	0.7	2.2
37 117	Martin	24,227	-2.0	5.2	16.5	8.1	20.4	31.2	18.6	44.8	53.9	43.7	0.0	2.6
37 119	Mecklenburg	945,889	4.9	7.3	17.8	9.6	32.4	23.8	9.1	34.1	60.1	32.3	5.6	5.1
37 123	Montgomery	27,760	-0.3	6.1	18.0	7.9	24.2	27.6	16.2	39.4	77.7	17.5	1.7	4.3
37 125	Moore	89,402	2.0	5.8	15.6	6.5	21.8	27.3	22.9	45.2	85.1	14.1	1.1	2.2
37 127	Nash	95,838	-0.2	6.1	17.4	8.6	24.4	29.0	14.6	40.4	58.0	38.7	1.0	4.9
37 129	New Hanover	206,165	2.9	5.5	14.2	12.8	27.2	26.0	14.3	37.6	82.2	15.4	1.8	2.3
37 131	Northampton	21,812	-2.6	5.0	15.3	8.3	20.1	30.7	20.5	46.0	42.5	58.8	0.0	1.8
37 133	Onslow	180,060	2.1	9.7	15.5	22.1	27.8	17.2	7.7	26.0	77.7	17.9	3.5	4.3
37 135	Orange	135,886	2.7	5.0	15.6	18.5	25.3	25.5	10.1	33.2	78.7	13.0	8.0	3.8
37 139	Pasquotank	40,553	-0.3	6.9	15.4	12.9	24.5	26.2	14.1	37.3	59.4	39.6	1.5	1.0
37 141	Pender	53,350	3.5	5.1	17.3	8.2	24.2	29.6	15.6	41.7	78.2	18.4	0.6	4.2
37 145	Person	39,419	-0.4	6.0	16.7	8.2	22.9	30.5	15.6	41.4	69.4	27.9	0.4	3.3
37 147	Pitt	170,685	2.2	6.4	15.9	18.8	26.1	22.7	10.2	31.2	61.0	35.4	2.2	3.7
37 149	Polk	20,336	-0.8	3.5	14.9	7.0	17.8	31.3	25.5	50.2	91.9	5.0	0.0	3.8
37 151	Randolph	142,122	0.4	6.2	18.0	8.1	25.4	27.7	14.5	39.9	90.9	6.4	1.2	3.4
37 153	Richmond	46,655	-0.1	6.1	18.5	9.1	23.9	27.8	14.6	39.4	64.2	31.4	1.2	5.7
37 155	Robeson	134,961	0.8	7.6	19.1	11.1	25.6	24.9	11.7	34.5	33.1	25.7	1.3	43.0
37 157	Rockingham	93,158	-0.9	5.4	16.3	7.8	23.6	30.0	16.8	42.7	77.5	20.1	0.8	4.1
37 159	Rowan	138,221	-0.1	6.4	17.0	9.1	24.9	27.8	14.9	39.5	78.6	17.1	1.3	4.6
37 161	Rutherford	67,508	-0.7	5.5	16.5	7.4	24.3	28.4	17.8	42.0	87.6	11.6	0.6	1.6
37 163	Sampson	63,693	0.7	6.7	18.6	8.1	25.2	26.8	14.5	38.5	59.0	28.0	0.6	14.5
37 165	Scotland	36,185	0.0	6.6	17.8	9.8	24.0	27.3	14.4	38.3	49.4	39.9	1.0	13.2
37 167	Stanly	60,511	0.1	5.8	16.6	9.4	24.5	27.8	15.9	40.9	85.7	12.7	2.1	1.1
37 169	Stokes	47,112	-1.2	5.0	16.6	7.6	23.2	30.7	16.9	44.0	94.3	5.0	0.4	1.0
37 171	Surry	73,615	-0.2	5.8	17.2	7.6	24.1	28.3	17.0	41.2	93.4	4.8	0.8	3.1
37 175	Transylvania	32,909	-0.7	4.3	12.1	8.2	18.5	30.0	26.8	49.9	93.7	5.0	0.6	2.4
37 179	Union	205,292	3.1	6.9	22.9	7.7	26.9	25.6	10.0	36.4	83.5	12.6	2.1	3.7
37 181	Vance	45,238	-0.5	6.8	18.3	9.6	23.8	26.9	14.6	38.9	43.0	50.7	0.5	7.2
37 183	Wake	929,250	5.0	7.0	18.7	9.6	31.1	24.7	8.8	34.7	70.1	21.9	6.3	4.0
37 185	Warren	20,806	-1.7	5.7	14.2	8.8	20.8	31.2	19.4	45.2	41.0	54.0	0.0	8.4
37 189	Watauga	51,514	1.7	3.6	10.0	31.6	19.6	22.4	12.7	28.6	96.7	1.5	1.3	2.9
37 191	Wayne	123,656	1.1	7.0	17.7	10.2	25.7	26.2	13.3	36.7	58.7	33.0	1.7	9.4
37 193	Wilkes	69,250	0.1	5.5	16.5	7.3	23.7	29.2	17.8	43.0	91.6	4.9	0.5	4.4

Table A-2. Counties — Who: Age, Race/Ethnicity, and Household Structure, 2010–2012—*Continued*

STATE and County code	STATE or County	Percent Hispanic or Latino	Percent foreign born	Total households	Household type (percent)							Percent of households with people under 18 years	Percent of households with people 60 years and over
					Family households				Nonfamily households				
					Total family households	Married-couple families	Male household families	Female household families	Total nonfamily households	One-person households			
ACS table number:		B03003	C05003	B11001	B11001	B11001	B11001	B11001	B11001	B11001		B11005	B11006
Column number:		14	15	16	17	18	19	20	21	22		23	24
	North Carolina—Cont.												
37 015	Bertie	0.9	0.5	7,661	67.1	43.2	6.1	17.8	32.9	30.0		27.9	43.5
37 017	Bladen	7.2	5.1	14,362	63.9	42.7	4.2	17.0	36.1	32.3		29.8	42.3
37 019	Brunswick	5.1	4.1	47,114	71.2	55.7	4.6	10.9	28.8	24.0		25.9	49.8
37 021	Buncombe	6.2	5.1	100,782	59.9	44.6	3.8	11.4	40.1	32.1		26.5	37.7
37 023	Burke	5.4	5.5	34,563	68.3	51.1	4.5	12.7	31.7	26.8		30.0	41.1
37 025	Cabarrus	9.6	7.4	64,386	70.8	56.1	4.0	10.7	29.2	24.9		38.1	30.7
37 027	Caldwell	2.8	2.2	31,899	64.3	48.5	3.9	11.9	35.7	32.5		27.7	42.3
37 031	Carteret	3.6	3.5	28,481	65.0	49.2	4.0	11.7	35.0	30.6		25.6	43.3
37 033	Caswell	3.2	1.8	8,623	71.3	50.0	5.6	15.7	28.7	25.6		26.4	43.1
37 035	Catawba	8.4	7.0	58,281	68.1	51.0	5.4	11.7	31.9	26.1		31.5	37.4
37 037	Chatham	12.9	10.0	25,834	69.7	56.6	2.5	10.5	30.3	26.4		25.4	45.9
37 039	Cherokee	2.6	2.8	10,916	69.7	57.5	2.6	9.6	30.3	26.3		24.3	52.1
37 045	Cleveland	2.9	2.2	36,958	66.1	48.5	4.7	12.9	33.9	29.8		27.5	39.4
37 047	Columbus	4.6	3.1	21,790	66.1	45.3	4.5	16.4	33.9	30.5		29.3	41.9
37 049	Craven	6.4	4.6	39,932	70.9	54.2	3.2	13.5	29.1	25.0		32.1	39.0
37 051	Cumberland	9.9	6.1	120,577	66.7	43.0	4.6	19.1	33.3	28.1		37.5	27.4
37 053	Currituck	3.2	3.0	9,093	72.0	56.1	5.2	10.7	28.0	20.0		34.7	37.5
37 055	Dare	6.6	5.3	14,722	65.4	50.6	5.3	9.6	34.6	26.2		30.2	41.2
37 057	Davidson	6.4	4.8	64,482	69.5	53.1	3.7	12.7	30.5	26.3		32.0	36.7
37 059	Davie	6.2	4.5	16,750	70.3	54.1	2.8	13.3	29.7	25.9		32.0	40.1
37 061	Duplin	20.9	11.8	22,586	69.0	48.4	6.6	14.0	31.0	25.7		35.3	36.1
37 063	Durham	13.4	14.0	110,642	59.8	38.8	4.9	16.0	40.2	31.0		30.9	26.0
37 065	Edgecombe	3.8	2.3	20,673	67.9	39.7	5.3	23.0	32.1	28.0		31.4	39.9
37 067	Forsyth	12.1	9.2	139,085	63.1	44.4	4.7	14.0	36.9	31.8		31.2	33.2
37 069	Franklin	7.8	4.7	23,417	68.7	53.5	3.5	11.7	31.3	27.2		33.4	33.6
37 071	Gaston	6.0	5.0	79,259	68.1	48.3	5.3	14.5	31.9	28.0		31.5	34.9
37 077	Granville	7.6	4.1	19,493	70.7	50.6	5.4	14.6	29.3	26.6		33.4	34.7
37 079	Greene	14.4	7.8	7,039	68.8	48.9	2.9	17.0	31.2	29.9		36.1	38.1
37 081	Guilford	7.3	9.8	196,171	63.0	42.7	4.5	15.7	37.0	30.3		31.9	31.5
37 083	Halifax	2.3	1.7	21,914	65.6	37.2	5.2	23.3	34.4	31.1		30.2	40.9
37 085	Harnett	11.1	5.6	40,352	71.0	52.4	4.3	14.3	29.0	24.4		36.7	29.9
37 087	Haywood	3.4	2.6	26,240	65.9	51.1	4.5	10.2	34.1	29.0		27.3	43.5
37 089	Henderson	9.9	8.3	44,465	67.3	55.5	3.5	8.3	32.7	28.0		25.3	47.6
37 091	Hertford	2.9	4.0	8,637	66.3	40.2	4.9	21.2	33.7	29.5		27.9	42.8
37 093	Hoke	12.4	4.6	15,958	74.9	50.6	5.8	18.6	25.1	21.0		44.1	23.5
37 097	Iredell	6.9	5.4	59,408	73.0	56.9	4.1	12.1	27.0	23.6		34.7	34.5
37 099	Jackson	5.1	4.5	15,620	62.1	45.9	6.1	10.0	37.9	32.4		23.2	36.9
37 101	Johnston	13.0	7.8	60,552	75.2	56.4	5.5	13.2	24.8	21.0		40.3	30.4
37 105	Lee	18.8	11.8	21,191	70.5	51.0	6.1	13.4	29.5	25.0		35.5	36.6
37 107	Lenoir	6.7	3.3	24,032	66.7	41.0	6.6	19.0	33.3	28.7		32.4	39.9
37 109	Lincoln	6.8	4.8	29,724	72.0	57.1	4.1	10.9	28.0	23.1		34.3	35.0
37 111	McDowell	5.4	2.8	16,791	64.9	50.2	3.6	11.0	35.1	31.0		25.1	41.0
37 113	Macon	6.6	6.8	15,750	63.7	51.1	3.1	9.5	36.3	30.2		23.3	49.0
37 115	Madison	2.1	2.1	8,511	70.0	56.0	3.8	10.2	30.0	24.6		29.2	44.1
37 117	Martin	3.3	2.4	9,562	66.7	45.8	5.5	15.4	33.3	29.9		27.7	47.0
37 119	Mecklenburg	12.4	13.6	362,469	62.5	43.3	4.7	14.5	37.5	30.1		34.8	24.7
37 123	Montgomery	14.4	7.9	10,315	65.5	47.0	4.1	14.4	34.5	28.6		30.3	45.9
37 125	Moore	6.0	5.7	37,021	66.5	52.9	2.8	10.8	33.5	29.7		25.0	46.9
37 127	Nash	6.4	4.7	37,210	66.2	46.7	4.3	15.3	33.8	29.6		32.3	38.6
37 129	New Hanover	5.3	5.7	85,918	58.7	43.0	4.3	11.4	41.3	31.4		26.9	33.0
37 131	Northampton	1.5	1.4	8,738	64.0	35.7	4.5	23.8	36.0	32.0		24.4	46.7
37 133	Onslow	10.6	4.2	60,656	72.2	54.9	3.2	14.1	27.8	22.2		41.4	22.9
37 135	Orange	8.2	12.7	51,372	60.0	46.5	3.1	10.4	40.0	30.2		31.1	26.7
37 139	Pasquotank	4.2	2.4	14,416	70.2	49.9	4.5	15.8	29.8	25.0		33.1	36.3
37 141	Pender	6.2	4.0	19,598	69.8	54.1	5.7	10.1	30.2	24.3		30.0	40.7
37 145	Person	4.1	2.6	15,228	69.9	47.7	6.6	15.7	30.1	24.9		30.0	38.6
37 147	Pitt	5.6	5.2	65,837	59.8	39.9	3.2	16.8	40.2	29.2		32.6	26.8
37 149	Polk	5.6	3.7	8,871	67.1	52.4	3.4	11.4	32.9	27 4		24.2	49.9
37 151	Randolph	10.6	6.5	54,744	70.8	53.2	4.2	13.4	29.2	25 7		33.5	37.2
37 153	Richmond	6.1	4.2	18,304	63.1	40.9	4.3	17.8	36.9	30 6		31.4	38.8
37 155	Robeson	8.2	5.8	44,706	72.4	42.3	6.5	23.7	27.6	23 4		39.7	35.8
37 157	Rockingham	5.6	3.8	37,496	68.3	49.0	5.1	14.2	31.7	28 2		31.0	39.8
37 159	Rowan	7.8	5.5	52,290	68.5	49.6	4.8	14.1	31.5	26 3		30.2	37.6
37 161	Rutherford	3.7	2.7	27,024	71.2	52.0	5.4	13.9	28.8	25 8		32.4	43.3
37 163	Sampson	17.0	8.8	23,504	69.3	46.0	5.9	17.4	30.7	26 4		34.1	38.1
37 165	Scotland	2.3	2.1	12,934	68.0	40.8	5.2	21.9	32.0	28 6		35.6	40.1
37 167	Stanly	3.7	3.0	23,246	68.8	53.2	4.4	11.3	31.2	27 6		31.8	41.4
37 169	Stokes	2.7	1.5	19,141	72.7	56.5	3.7	12.5	27.3	24.8		31.1	38.6
37 171	Surry	9.9	5.4	30,026	68.3	51.7	4.2	12.5	31.7	28.8		30.1	41.2
37 175	Transylvania	2.9	1.9	13,790	67.1	56.0	2.9	8.3	32.9	28.9		22.3	55.2
37 179	Union	10.7	9.1	67,769	80.4	65.4	4.7	10.3	19.6	16.2		44.9	29.3
37 181	Vance	6.8	3.9	15,934	67.1	40.1	4.5	22.5	32.9	30.2		32.0	39.2
37 183	Wake	9.9	13.0	346,096	66.3	51.1	3.6	11.5	33.7	27.1		37.3	24.7
37 185	Warren	3.5	2.1	7,426	67.5	46.0	4.4	17.1	32.5	28.7		25.2	49.2
37 189	Watauga	3.4	3.8	20,354	52.4	43.0	1.9	7.5	47.6	28.2		19.2	31.3
37 191	Wayne	10.1	7.1	48,016	66.8	44.6	4.4	17.9	33.2	28.0		33.9	34.2
37 193	Wilkes	5.6	3.9	27,575	70.1	55.6	3.2	11.3	29.9	26.0		30.2	41.9

STATE and County code	STATE or County	Total population	Percent change 2010–2012	Population by age (percent)						Median age	Race alone or in combination (percent)			
				Under 5 years	5 to 17 years	18 to 24 years	25 to 44 years	45 to 64 years	65 years and over		White	Black	Asian, Hawaiian, or Pacific Islander	American Indian, Alaska Native, or some other race
	ACS table number:	B01003	Population estimates	B01001	B01001	B01001	B01001	B01001	B01001	B01002	B02008	B02009	B02011 + B02012	B02010 + B02013
	Column number:	1	2	3	4	5	6	7	8	9	10	11	12	13
	North Carolina—Cont													
37 195	Wilson	81,549	0.7	6.5	17.8	8.9	24.4	27.7	14.7	39.0	53.0	39.7	1.2	8.3
37 197	Yadkin	38,251	-0.8	5.7	17.1	7.8	24.5	28.0	16.8	41.7	91.3	4.8	0.0	5.4
38 000	**North Dakota**	686,244	3.7	6.5	15.7	12.3	24.9	26.2	14.4	36.6	91.6	1.7	1.6	7.1
38 015	Burleigh	83,635	5.0	6.5	15.8	10.5	26.6	26.8	13.7	37.1	94.8	1.0	1.3	4.8
38 017	Cass	153,012	3.9	6.8	14.8	16.0	29.4	23.0	10.0	31.8	93.3	3.2	2.9	3.0
38 035	Grand Forks	67,006	0.7	6.2	13.5	22.5	24.6	22.4	10.8	29.3	92.3	3.1	2.5	3.9
38 059	Morton	27,819	1.9	6.5	16.7	8.0	25.6	28.5	14.6	39.4	95.1	0.0	0.0	5.2
38 089	Stark	25,417	10.0	6.4	16.1	11.6	24.6	26.2	15.2	37.0	95.6	1.1	1.4	2.7
38 093	Stutsman	21,001	-0.8	5.5	15.1	9.9	23.0	29.5	16.9	41.8	97.3	0.8	0.7	3.0
38 101	Ward	63,727	4.4	7.6	15.9	14.8	26.4	22.8	12.6	32.0	93.5	3.2	2.4	4.9
38 105	Williams	24,563	18.3	6.7	16.6	9.6	26.3	27.6	13.1	36.0	92.7	0.6	0.6	7.4
39 000	**Ohio**	11,541,175	0.1	6.1	17.2	9.6	24.9	27.4	14.4	39.0	84.9	13.5	2.2	1.8
39 001	Adams	28,477	-0.8	6.3	18.3	7.8	24.4	27.7	15.4	40.3	99.7	0.0	0.0	1.8
39 003	Allen	105,701	-1.0	6.4	17.4	11.2	22.9	27.3	14.8	38.1	86.0	14.0	1.0	1.9
39 005	Ashland	53,070	-0.4	5.7	17.7	10.7	22.8	27.1	16.1	39.7	98.1	1.5	0.7	0.8
39 007	Ashtabula	100,967	-1.0	5.9	17.2	7.9	23.8	29.3	15.9	41.5	95.2	4.9	0.7	1.3
39 009	Athens	64,598	-0.8	4.0	11.5	32.0	21.2	20.9	10.4	26.8	93.9	3.6	3.5	1.8
39 011	Auglaize	45,836	-0.2	6.4	18.4	7.5	23.3	28.6	15.8	40.5	98.6	0.5	0.6	0.8
39 013	Belmont	70,039	-1.0	4.8	14.4	8.1	24.4	30.4	17.8	43.7	95.1	4.9	0.6	1.2
39 015	Brown	44,641	-1.1	6.6	18.0	7.7	24.2	28.6	14.8	39.8	98.9	1.4	0.3	0.6
39 017	Butler	369,778	0.5	6.6	18.3	11.2	25.3	26.7	11.9	36.3	87.9	8.7	3.1	2.3
39 019	Carroll	28,741	-0.7	5.3	17.0	7.1	22.5	30.8	17.3	43.5	98.5	1.7	0.0	0.2
39 021	Champaign	39,794	-1.1	6.2	18.5	8.1	24.0	28.1	15.1	40.0	96.9	3.5	0.6	1.5
39 023	Clark	137,735	-0.7	6.1	17.2	9.1	23.1	28.1	16.4	41.0	88.5	10.5	1.0	2.8
39 025	Clermont	198,437	0.7	6.5	18.6	8.0	25.5	29.1	12.3	38.8	97.0	1.8	1.4	1.2
39 027	Clinton	41,910	0.0	6.0	18.4	9.5	23.5	28.5	14.0	38.7	96.3	3.3	0.7	1.2
39 029	Columbiana	107,190	-1.2	5.3	16.2	7.5	24.1	30.0	16.9	42.5	96.8	2.9	0.5	1.0
39 031	Coshocton	36,856	-0.3	6.1	17.7	7.8	23.2	28.7	16.6	41.6	98.4	1.8	0.3	0.8
39 033	Crawford	43,301	-2.1	5.4	17.4	7.7	22.9	28.4	18.1	42.5	98.8	1.7	0.5	0.8
39 035	Cuyahoga	1,271,187	-1.0	5.8	16.5	8.9	24.7	28.4	15.7	40.4	66.1	31.1	3.2	2.1
39 037	Darke	52,715	-0.9	6.6	18.1	7.5	22.6	28.0	17.3	41.1	99.0	1.2	0.3	0.8
39 039	Defiance	38,856	-0.8	6.2	18.0	8.9	23.7	27.5	15.7	39.3	94.5	2.9	0.3	4.4
39 041	Delaware	178,314	3.3	7.0	21.5	6.6	27.4	27.4	10.1	37.7	91.1	4.2	5.1	1.2
39 043	Erie	76,700	-0.8	5.3	16.4	7.5	22.1	30.8	17.9	43.5	89.5	10.3	0.8	1.7
39 045	Fairfield	147,071	0.7	6.1	19.5	8.2	25.6	28.0	12.7	39.2	92.3	7.0	2.2	1.4
39 047	Fayette	28,944	-0.5	6.6	18.0	7.6	24.5	28.2	15.2	40.2	96.5	3.3	0.8	1.1
39 049	Franklin	1,180,276	2.5	7.1	16.7	11.6	30.1	24.3	10.1	33.6	72.3	23.3	4.9	3.1
39 051	Fulton	42,550	-0.3	6.2	19.1	7.6	23.2	29.2	14.8	39.9	96.5	1.2	0.6	3.0
39 053	Gallia	30,844	-0.8	6.1	17.9	8.7	23.4	27.8	16.2	40.3	96.7	3.4	0.6	1.3
39 055	Geauga	93,465	0.3	5.3	19.8	7.1	19.9	31.8	16.1	43.7	98.0	1.6	1.0	0.7
39 057	Greene	162,830	1.2	5.5	15.7	14.7	23.3	26.7	14.1	36.9	88.5	9.1	4.0	1.3
39 059	Guernsey	39,897	-0.5	5.9	17.2	8.3	23.4	28.6	16.5	41.4	97.3	2.7	0.5	0.9
39 061	Hamilton	801,587	0.0	6.7	16.8	10.4	25.7	27.0	13.4	37.2	71.2	27.1	2.8	1.6
39 063	Hancock	75,156	1.3	6.1	17.1	10.4	24.5	27.0	14.9	38.6	95.6	2.2	2.2	1.4
39 065	Hardin	31,849	-1.4	6.2	17.4	14.9	22.6	25.0	13.8	35.4	98.1	2.1	0.9	0.4
39 069	Henry	28,128	-0.2	6.4	18.3	7.5	23.8	28.0	16.0	39.8	96.6	0.8	0.7	3.6
39 071	Highland	43,331	-1.3	6.4	18.4	8.1	24.4	27.2	15.5	39.5	98.8	2.7	0.0	0.7
39 073	Hocking	29,353	-0.4	5.7	17.9	7.7	23.3	29.6	15.8	42.4	98.3	1.2	0.6	0.9
39 075	Holmes	42,733	1.4	9.6	24.3	9.9	23.0	21.5	11.7	30.1	99.1	1.0	0.0	0.0
39 077	Huron	59,421	-0.5	6.6	19.3	7.8	24.7	27.8	13.8	38.1	96.1	1.9	0.5	3.4
39 079	Jackson	33,130	-0.9	6.5	18.0	8.3	24.8	27.8	14.6	39.2	98.5	1.3	0.0	1.6
39 081	Jefferson	68,965	-1.7	4.8	15.2	9.7	21.3	30.4	18.5	44.2	93.9	6.7	0.7	0.9
39 083	Knox	60,992	-0.5	6.0	17.8	11.8	22.3	27.1	15.1	39.1	98.2	1.4	1.3	1.0
39 085	Lake	229,836	-0.2	5.3	16.5	7.5	24.1	30.1	16.6	42.6	94.1	4.2	1.6	1.4
39 087	Lawrence	62,299	-0.5	5.9	17.3	8.2	24.8	27.7	16.1	40.9	96.8	3.0	0.0	1.3
39 089	Licking	167,159	0.5	6.1	18.3	8.7	24.8	28.5	13.7	39.3	95.3	4.7	1.1	1.3
39 091	Logan	45,636	-0.7	6.1	19.0	7.3	23.8	28.6	15.3	39.9	97.0	2.9	0.9	1.0
39 093	Lorain	301,611	0.0	5.9	17.6	8.6	24.1	29.0	14.8	40.4	87.8	10.4	1.7	3.7
39 095	Lucas	439,826	-0.8	6.6	17.1	10.9	25.0	27.0	13.4	37.3	77.0	21.1	2.2	3.5
39 097	Madison	43,184	-0.8	5.4	16.8	8.7	28.3	28.0	12.8	39.4	92.6	7.4	0.9	1.1
39 099	Mahoning	236,713	-1.3	5.3	15.9	8.5	22.5	29.8	18.0	43.3	82.1	17.1	1.1	1.8
39 101	Marion	66,411	-0.3	5.7	15.4	8.9	26.1	29.4	14.4	40.5	92.1	7.1	0.8	1.7
39 103	Medina	173,217	0.6	5.7	19.0	7.0	24.5	30.1	13.6	40.9	97.3	1.8	1.3	1.0
39 105	Meigs	23,672	-0.6	5.6	16.8	7.7	24.2	29.7	15.9	41.5	98.8	1.2	0.0	0.3
39 107	Mercer	40,818	0.2	6.8	19.1	7.7	22.7	28.0	15.7	40.1	98.7	0.5	0.5	1.1
39 109	Miami	102,777	0.6	6.0	17.8	7.5	24.2	28.7	15.8	41.0	96.0	3.1	1.6	0.9
39 113	Montgomery	535,057	-0.3	6.2	16.6	9.6	24.7	27.5	15.5	39.5	76.1	22.4	2.4	1.7
39 117	Morrow	34,896	0.3	6.3	19.1	7.4	24.3	29.1	13.9	40.0	98.9	0.8	0.0	1.2
39 119	Muskingum	86,109	-0.3	6.0	17.5	9.3	23.9	27.8	15.4	39.8	95.6	5.6	0.6	1.3
39 123	Ottawa	41,390	-0.1	4.6	15.5	6.2	20.8	33.0	19.7	46.9	98.0	1.5	0.4	1.6
39 127	Perry	36,095	-0.1	6.4	19.0	8.6	24.2	28.6	13.2	38.9	99.0	1.2	0.0	1.2
39 129	Pickaway	56,093	1.0	5.6	17.5	9.3	27.1	27.3	13.3	38.8	95.8	4.2	0.7	0.9
39 131	Pike	28,606	-0.8	6.1	18.6	8.1	24.5	28.0	14.7	39.9	98.7	1.6	0.0	1.7
39 133	Portage	161,494	0.0	4.8	15.5	16.0	22.9	27.6	13.3	37.3	94.0	5.3	2.0	1.1

Table A-2. Counties — Who: Age, Race/Ethnicity, and Household Structure, 2010–2012—*Continued*

STATE and County code	STATE or County	Percent Hispanic or Latino	Percent foreign born	Total households	Household type (percent) Family households — Total family households	Married-couple families	Male household families	Female household families	Nonfamily households — Total nonfamily households	One-person households	Percent of households with people under 18 years	Percent of households with people 60 years and over
	ACS table number:	B03003	C05003	B11001	B11001	B11001	B11001	B11001	B11001	B11001	B11005	B11006
	Column number:	14	15	16	17	18	19	20	21	22	23	24
	North Carolina—Cont											
37 195	Wilson	9.6	7.1	31,853	65.8	43.5	5.7	16.6	34.2	29.4	30.7	36.5
37 197	Yadkin	10.0	6.1	14,847	70.5	53.9	6.2	10.4	29.5	27.1	31.3	40.4
38 000	**North Dakota**	2.2	2.6	285,639	60.6	49.1	3.7	7.9	39.4	31.9	27.7	32.4
38 015	Burleigh	1.3	1.3	34,391	62.8	51.1	3.3	8.4	37.2	30.3	29.4	32.1
38 017	Cass	2.2	5.5	65,568	54.2	43.2	3.9	7.1	45.8	34.4	27.2	24.0
38 035	Grand Forks	3.1	3.9	27,483	54.1	43.4	3.7	7.0	45.9	34.4	24.1	25.7
38 059	Morton	1.5	0.6	11,371	67.1	53.6	4.6	8.9	32.9	27.6	31.2	34.6
38 089	Stark	2.5	2.7	10,238	60.0	49.7	4.1	6.3	40.0	31.1	27.9	33.5
38 093	Stutsman	1.7	0.7	8,736	63.5	47.9	4.9	10.6	36.5	31.2	27.2	37.6
38 101	Ward	3.4	2.4	24,834	62.9	50.9	2.8	9.2	37.1	29.7	31.3	29.5
38 105	Williams	2.5	2.5	9,974	61.8	49.7	4.2	7.9	38.2	30.3	29.6	31.4
39 000	**Ohio**	3.2	4.0	4,542,141	64.6	47.4	4.3	12.9	35.4	29.8	30.7	35.5
39 001	Adams	0.8	0.1	10,870	70.6	53.9	5.0	11.8	29.4	25.3	34.5	39.5
39 003	Allen	2.5	1.4	40,398	67.3	47.2	5.5	14.7	32.7	28.0	33.2	36.3
39 005	Ashland	1.0	2.2	20,261	69.7	57.6	2.6	9.5	30.3	25.5	30.1	39.8
39 007	Ashtabula	3.5	1.2	39,103	65.2	47.6	6.0	11.6	34.8	29.1	31.5	39.4
39 009	Athens	1.7	4.0	22,023	55.4	41.6	5.3	8.5	44.6	30.0	24.7	29.7
39 011	Auglaize	1.2	1.1	18,418	68.9	55.9	4.6	8.4	31.1	26.8	30.6	36.5
39 013	Belmont	0.7	1.1	28,383	65.3	51.7	4.9	8.8	34.7	30.7	26.3	42.3
39 015	Brown	0.7	0.6	16,501	73.7	58.0	4.1	11.7	26.3	22.4	33.6	35.0
39 017	Butler	4.1	4.8	134,423	70.0	53.2	4.6	12.1	30.0	24.2	34.4	32.6
39 019	Carroll	0.9	0.9	11,226	70.7	59.2	3.8	7.7	29.3	23.5	29.7	39.3
39 021	Champaign	1.2	0.9	15,075	72.6	57.1	4.0	11.5	27.4	23.8	34.6	36.1
39 023	Clark	2.8	2.3	54,969	64.4	46.2	3.9	14.4	35.6	29.6	30.8	39.9
39 025	Clermont	1.6	2.6	74,067	71.8	55.8	5.8	10.2	28.2	23.8	35.0	33.0
39 027	Clinton	1.5	1.0	16,000	68.7	50.7	6.8	11.2	31.3	26.9	33.7	38.1
39 029	Columbiana	1.3	1.3	42,471	66.9	51.2	4.7	11.1	33.1	27.3	29.9	40.1
39 031	Coshocton	0.8	0.4	14,568	70.1	54.3	3.9	11.9	29.9	26.1	29.8	39.3
39 033	Crawford	1.2	0.7	17,367	67.3	54.3	3.4	9.6	32.7	27.5	26.4	41.2
39 035	Cuyahoga	5.0	7.1	531,045	58.0	37.7	4.1	16.2	42.0	36.7	27.8	37.1
39 037	Darke	1.3	0.7	21,016	68.9	55.7	3.5	9.8	31.1	27.5	29.9	38.9
39 039	Defiance	9.0	1.9	15,322	70.8	52.3	5.9	12.7	29.2	24.5	29.9	34.5
39 041	Delaware	2.2	5.9	64,360	76.6	65.3	3.1	8.1	23.4	19.8	42.7	28.6
39 043	Erie	3.5	1.7	31,908	65.7	50.2	5.1	10.4	34.3	29.9	27.8	40.4
39 045	Fairfield	1.8	2.8	54,138	73.1	57.8	4.1	11.2	26.9	22.7	37.0	33.6
39 047	Fayette	1.8	0.8	11,451	64.8	48.3	4.4	12.1	35.2	29.3	31.3	35.8
39 049	Franklin	4.9	9.3	467,314	58.1	39.7	4.3	14.1	41.9	32.9	31.3	26.7
39 051	Fulton	7.9	1.6	16,272	74.7	60.7	5.9	8.1	25.3	22.5	33.0	36.2
39 053	Gallia	0.9	1.1	11,497	70.2	53.3	5.9	11.0	29.8	26.0	30.8	41.3
39 055	Geauga	1.1	3.3	34,527	73.8	62.0	3.1	8.7	26.2	22.3	32.4	41.3
39 057	Greene	2.3	4.3	62,924	66.2	51.5	3.6	11.1	33.8	28.4	30.1	34.7
39 059	Guernsey	0.9	0.8	15,348	68.9	53.5	5.4	10.0	31.1	27.1	30.5	40.0
39 061	Hamilton	2.7	4.9	323,398	59.7	40.6	3.9	15.2	40.3	34.0	29.6	32.8
39 063	Hancock	4.7	2.2	29,974	67.1	50.2	5.2	11.8	32.9	28.3	29.9	34.0
39 065	Hardin	1.4	1.3	11,655	68.4	51.1	5.9	11.4	31.6	26.2	32.6	36.3
39 069	Henry	6.7	1.5	11,163	69.4	56.5	4.2	8.7	30.6	25.0	31.3	36.0
39 071	Highland	0.4	0.6	17,062	70.4	50.9	7.0	12.5	29.6	24.6	34.1	38.6
39 073	Hocking	0.7	1.2	11,413	71.6	56.7	3.8	11.1	28.4	24.8	32.1	40.3
39 075	Holmes	0.6	0.9	12,392	80.1	72.0	2.5	5.5	19.9	18.1	43.8	32.0
39 077	Huron	5.7	3.1	22,350	70.9	55.0	4.7	11.3	29.1	23.0	35.2	36.0
39 079	Jackson	0.8	0.7	13,421	69.2	50.3	5.6	13.3	30.8	26.7	34.6	37.4
39 081	Jefferson	1.2	1.2	28,224	64.9	49.2	4.4	11.3	35.1	30.5	26.1	42.7
39 083	Knox	1.3	1.4	22,311	71.3	57.5	4.1	9.7	28.7	22.9	32.6	39.0
39 085	Lake	3.5	5.5	94,137	65.1	50.3	3.8	11.1	34.9	29.7	28.2	38.1
39 087	Lawrence	0.8	0.3	23,408	67.0	48.5	4.9	13.6	33.0	28.9	29.0	43.3
39 089	Licking	1.5	1.7	63,875	70.2	55.1	4.6	10.5	29.8	24.9	33.7	35.1
39 091	Logan	1.2	1.4	18,377	69.2	52.6	6.6	9.9	30.8	25.2	29.2	37.2
39 093	Lorain	8.5	3.0	116,604	68.2	50.2	4.6	13.4	31.8	26.9	31.8	37.0
39 095	Lucas	6.3	3.5	177,384	61.0	39.6	4.9	16.6	39.0	32.4	30.3	32.6
39 097	Madison	1.5	1.7	14,720	70.0	55.3	4.2	10.5	30.0	25.7	34.7	36.4
39 099	Mahoning	4.8	3.1	97,457	62.2	42.5	4.5	15.2	37.8	33.1	26.3	42.8
39 101	Marion	2.3	1.0	24,839	69.0	50.3	5.8	12.9	31.0	25.7	31.5	37.9
39 103	Medina	1.7	3.0	65,591	72.8	59.9	3.8	9.2	27.2	22.5	34.5	34.9
39 105	Meigs	1.1	0.7	9,469	68.5	53.0	4.7	10.8	31.5	27.2	27.6	40.2
39 107	Mercer	1.5	0.8	15,910	71.3	58.4	4.3	8.5	28.7	24.0	32.1	36.6
39 109	Miami	1.4	1.6	40,994	67.0	51.1	4.7	11.2	33.0	27.2	30.6	37.4
39 113	Montgomery	2.4	3.8	222,279	60.0	40.8	4.3	14.9	40.0	34.6	28.7	37.2
39 117	Morrow	1.2	0.6	12,629	76.1	59.2	5.7	11.3	23.9	20.2	35.5	38.2
39 119	Muskingum	0.8	0.9	33,947	67.4	48.5	5.1	13.8	32.6	27.2	32.2	38.3
39 123	Ottawa	4.4	1.2	17,495	70.0	58.0	4.5	7.4	30.0	25.2	25.4	43.8
39 127	Perry	0.6	0.4	13,656	72.0	54.7	4.5	12.9	28.0	24.5	35.4	32.5
39 129	Pickaway	1.1	0.5	19,307	73.2	57.7	4.5	11.1	26.8	22.8	35.3	35.3
39 131	Pike	0.5	0.6	10,865	68.7	46.9	5.3	16.5	31.3	26.8	35.0	38.7
39 133	Portage	1.4	2.9	60,143	66.0	50.3	3.7	12.0	34.0	26.0	29.7	34.1

Part A — Who 65

Table A-2. Counties — Who: Age, Race/Ethnicity, and Household Structure, 2010–2012—*Continued*

STATE and County code	STATE or County	Total population	Percent change 2010–2012	Population by age (percent)						Median age	Race alone or in combination (percent)			
				Under 5 years	5 to 17 years	18 to 24 years	25 to 44 years	45 to 64 years	65 years and over		White	Black	Asian, Hawaiian, or Pacific Islander	American Indian, Alaska Native, or some other race
	ACS table number:	B01003	Population estimates	B01001	B01001	B01001	B01001	B01001	B01001	B01002	B02008	B02009	B02011 + B02012	B02010 + B02013
	Column number:	1	2	3	4	5	6	7	8	9	10	11	12	13
	Ohio—Cont.													
39 135	Preble	42,029	-0.7	5.8	18.2	7.6	23.2	29.6	15.6	41.6	98.8	0.9	0.6	0.9
39 137	Putnam	34,328	-0.7	7.1	19.1	7.5	23.1	28.6	14.6	39.8	97.6	1.2	0.1	2.6
39 139	Richland	123,331	-1.2	5.7	16.4	8.2	24.5	28.2	16.8	41.3	89.5	10.6	0.9	1.9
39 141	Ross	77,723	-0.9	5.7	16.6	7.7	26.8	29.3	13.8	40.4	94.6	6.1	0.7	2.8
39 143	Sandusky	60,663	-0.6	6.1	17.8	8.1	23.4	28.9	15.7	41.2	94.5	5.1	0.5	2.3
39 145	Scioto	79,079	-1.3	5.6	16.7	10.0	25.1	26.9	15.6	38.9	96.3	3.4	0.7	2.2
39 147	Seneca	56,351	-1.1	5.8	17.4	11.1	22.8	28.0	14.9	38.8	95.9	3.4	0.7	1.7
39 149	Shelby	49,268	-0.4	6.4	20.4	7.5	24.3	28.1	13.3	39.3	97.3	3.8	0.6	0.5
39 151	Stark	374,871	-0.1	5.7	16.9	8.8	23.2	28.9	16.5	41.7	91.6	9.1	1.2	1.2
39 153	Summit	541,230	-0.2	5.8	16.7	9.2	24.6	28.9	14.9	40.5	83.0	15.9	2.7	1.3
39 155	Trumbull	208,743	-1.2	5.5	16.3	8.0	22.6	29.8	17.8	43.1	90.9	9.4	0.7	0.9
39 157	Tuscarawas	92,481	-0.2	5.9	17.6	7.8	23.5	28.7	16.6	40.9	98.2	1.3	0.5	1.0
39 159	Union	52,704	0.7	6.5	20.3	7.4	29.3	26.6	9.9	36.9	94.6	3.0	3.1	1.4
39 161	Van Wert	28,706	0.3	6.1	18.4	7.4	23.0	28.1	17.0	40.8	97.6	2.0	0.0	1.2
39 165	Warren	215,286	1.9	6.4	20.5	6.8	27.3	27.8	11.2	37.8	91.6	3.9	4.7	1.2
39 167	Washington	61,583	-0.4	5.3	15.3	8.9	22.5	30.1	17.9	43.3	98.1	1.8	0.8	1.3
39 169	Wayne	114,674	0.3	6.6	18.4	10.2	22.6	27.1	15.0	38.6	97.0	2.3	1.0	1.1
39 171	Williams	37,549	-0.1	5.8	17.5	7.6	23.8	28.8	16.5	41.1	97.2	1.6	0.7	1.8
39 173	Wood	126,871	2.1	5.4	15.9	16.9	23.2	26.0	12.6	35.5	94.4	3.0	2.0	3.0
39 175	Wyandot	22,615	0.1	6.0	17.9	7.2	24.1	28.2	16.7	41.7	97.9	0.4	1.2	0.5
40 000	**Oklahoma**	3,786,152	1.5	6.9	17.7	10.2	25.8	25.6	13.7	36.3	80.7	8.8	2.5	16.1
40 001	Adair	22,509	-1.9	6.9	20.7	8.4	24.9	25.8	13.3	36.7	62.5	0.6	0.0	53.7
40 009	Beckham	22,470	4.8	8.1	16.3	11.1	27.4	24.7	12.4	34.3	93.0	4.8	0.4	9.3
40 013	Bryan	43,053	1.8	6.8	16.6	11.5	24.5	24.5	16.1	36.7	84.4	2.1	0.6	22.9
40 015	Caddo	29,649	0.0	7.0	18.3	8.6	25.2	26.1	14.9	38.1	69.7	4.1	0.2	34.3
40 017	Canadian	119,446	5.4	7.2	19.5	7.9	28.6	25.6	11.3	35.5	87.5	3.4	3.6	10.9
40 019	Carter	47,894	0.9	7.0	18.6	7.9	25.0	26.2	15.3	38.5	80.0	8.8	1.8	15.3
40 021	Cherokee	47,706	2.1	7.0	17.2	13.9	23.4	24.4	14.1	34.3	67.1	2.3	0.8	44.4
40 027	Cleveland	261,386	3.4	6.3	16.4	14.7	27.9	24.1	10.6	33.0	85.9	5.8	5.0	10.5
40 031	Comanche	125,850	0.8	7.6	17.3	13.5	29.0	22.3	10.3	31.4	72.3	20.3	4.8	12.1
40 037	Creek	70,439	0.7	6.1	18.5	7.9	23.8	28.3	15.4	40.2	88.2	3.5	0.6	17.4
40 039	Custer	27,938	3.7	7.3	16.1	17.2	24.0	22.2	13.3	31.0	88.6	3.6	1.4	11.7
40 041	Delaware	41,451	-0.2	5.2	16.9	7.1	20.5	29.2	21.2	45.2	75.0	0.5	1.5	30.8
40 047	Garfield	60,843	0.7	7.4	17.4	9.2	24.3	26.3	15.5	37.4	86.3	4.0	3.6	9.5
40 049	Garvin	27,414	-0.9	6.6	17.9	7.9	23.6	27.3	16.7	39.7	88.9	3.1	0.3	14.5
40 051	Grady	52,802	1.2	6.5	18.3	9.2	24.6	27.2	14.2	38.3	90.3	3.5	1.1	10.7
40 065	Jackson	26,360	-0.8	8.1	18.0	10.7	26.1	24.1	13.0	34.1	84.2	9.2	2.1	12.3
40 071	Kay	46,072	-1.3	7.1	17.9	8.4	22.8	26.5	17.2	39.2	86.3	2.9	0.9	17.1
40 079	Le Flore	50,162	-1.2	6.6	17.7	9.1	24.1	26.8	15.6	39.2	83.0	2.9	0.9	21.8
40 081	Lincoln	34,264	-0.4	6.4	18.7	7.1	23.1	28.7	16.0	40.7	91.5	2.5	0.5	11.4
40 083	Logan	42,944	3.8	6.4	18.3	9.5	24.4	27.8	13.6	38.0	86.1	10.2	0.7	7.4
40 087	McClain	35,142	2.6	6.7	19.8	7.2	24.6	28.2	13.5	38.6	91.5	1.1	1.4	12.0
40 089	McCurtain	33,202	0.1	7.0	18.9	8.2	23.4	26.6	15.9	39.4	72.0	10.3	0.0	23.9
40 091	McIntosh	20,406	1.4	5.0	15.7	6.8	19.9	29.7	22.9	46.9	81.9	4.6	0.0	25.5
40 097	Mayes	41,244	-0.3	6.8	18.6	8.3	23.1	27.4	15.8	38.9	91.2	1.2	0.5	31.0
40 101	Muskogee	70,815	-0.7	6.9	17.7	9.4	24.7	26.5	14.9	38.1	72.9	13.2	0.9	25.6
40 109	Oklahoma	730,787	2.9	7.7	17.6	10.2	27.8	24.7	12.0	34.1	74.0	17.4	3.9	11.8
40 111	Okmulgee	39,884	-1.3	6.3	18.0	9.7	23.5	26.5	16.0	38.9	77.0	10.5	0.5	24.4
40 113	Osage	47,824	1.0	5.5	18.3	7.8	21.7	29.9	16.8	42.0	72.2	13.1	0.8	21.9
40 115	Ottawa	31,992	1.2	6.7	17.9	9.9	22.6	25.6	17.3	38.7	80.4	1.6	1.8	27.3
40 119	Payne	77,921	1.2	5.7	13.1	27.4	23.5	20.0	10.4	27.1	88.5	4.8	4.7	9.7
40 121	Pittsburg	45,504	-1.7	6.2	15.9	8.0	24.8	27.7	17.4	41.3	85.8	4.4	0.9	22.5
40 123	Pontotoc	37,740	1.0	6.7	16.8	12.7	24.2	24.5	15.0	35.4	88.4	4.1	1.5	24.1
40 125	Pottawatomie	70,209	1.6	6.9	18.0	9.9	24.8	25.8	14.6	37.4	83.5	4.1	0.9	19.2
40 131	Rogers	87,729	1.5	6.0	19.5	8.8	24.3	27.4	14.0	38.8	84.0	1.5	1.3	21.8
40 133	Seminole	25,448	0.0	6.7	18.9	8.9	22.2	26.9	16.4	38.9	74.8	6.5	0.5	26.0
40 135	Sequoyah	41,897	-2.3	5.9	19.4	7.8	24.5	26.9	15.5	39.2	85.0	2.8	0.9	30.3
40 137	Stephens	44,978	-0.7	6.0	17.6	8.1	23.6	27.0	17.7	39.8	88.0	3.0	0.9	11.1
40 139	Texas	21,144	3.4	8.8	20.0	11.1	27.7	22.2	10.2	30.8	67.8	2.1	4.0	29.4
40 143	Tulsa	609,067	1.4	7.4	18.1	9.7	27.5	25.2	12.3	35.3	78.2	12.3	3.1	13.6
40 145	Wagoner	74,182	2.2	6.8	19.1	8.0	25.9	26.8	13.4	38.3	85.4	4.7	1.9	17.7
40 147	Washington	51,388	1.1	6.5	16.9	8.3	23.3	27.1	17.9	40.6	85.8	3.3	1.6	16.1
40 153	Woodward	20,191	2.9	6.6	17.7	8.7	27.6	25.3	14.2	37.2	93.7	1.6	0.0	6.8
41 000	**Oregon**	3,868,598	1.6	6.1	16.2	9.4	26.7	27.3	14.4	38.7	88.2	2.6	5.7	7.4
41 003	Benton	85,989	1.1	4.5	12.8	23.2	22.2	24.8	12.5	32.3	90.6	1.7	7.7	3.1
41 005	Clackamas	380,281	1.8	5.5	17.6	7.8	24.6	30.1	14.3	40.8	92.8	1.5	5.6	3.9
41 007	Clatsop	37,182	0.6	5.2	14.9	8.4	22.7	31.4	17.5	43.7	96.3	1.1	2.7	4.3
41 009	Columbia	49,327	-0.1	5.6	17.7	7.5	23.7	30.8	14.7	41.9	95.3	0.7	2.3	4.7
41 011	Coos	62,794	-0.8	5.1	13.7	7.6	20.0	31.4	22.2	47.8	93.6	1.0	2.1	6.7
41 013	Crook	20,762	-0.8	4.9	16.1	6.0	20.4	30.6	21.9	47.2	95.6	0.0	0.8	5.4
41 015	Curry	22,358	-0.5	4.7	11.0	6.3	16.6	32.6	28.8	53.6	96.9	0.0	0.3	5.8
41 017	Deschutes	160,085	2.8	6.0	16.5	7.3	25.7	28.6	15.8	40.7	95.0	0.6	2.4	4.8
41 019	Douglas	107,420	-0.5	5.1	14.9	7.5	20.4	30.6	21.6	46.5	96.5	0.5	1.9	4.7
41 027	Hood River	22,478	0.7	5.7	20.1	7.0	27.5	26.7	12.9	37.9	94.0	1.2	1.9	5.9
41 029	Jackson	204,868	1.4	5.8	15.8	8.5	23.1	28.7	18.2	42.2	95.5	1.4	3.0	4.7
41 031	Jefferson	21,705	0.3	7.0	17.9	9.1	22.2	27.9	15.9	40.2	70.5	1.0	1.2	29.3

Table A-2. Counties — Who: Age, Race/Ethnicity, and Household Structure, 2010–2012—*Continued*

STATE and County code	STATE or County	Percent Hispanic or Latino	Percent foreign born	Total households	Household type (percent) Family households				Nonfamily households		Percent of households with people under 18 years	Percent of households with people 60 years and over
					Total family households	Married-couple families	Male household families	Female household families	Total nonfamily households	One-person households		
ACS table number:		B03003	C05003	B11001	B11001	B11001	B11001	B11001	B11001	B11001	B11005	B11006
Column number:		14	15	16	17	18	19	20	21	22	23	24
	Ohio—Cont.											
39 135	Preble	0.6	1.1	16,360	70.9	55.6	3.6	11.6	29.1	24.3	31.0	41.0
39 137	Putnam	5.6	0.9	12,982	72.6	62.1	3.8	6.7	27.4	23.0	32.7	36.0
39 139	Richland	1.5	1.3	48,336	64.8	49.4	3.4	12.1	35.2	31.0	28.6	41.2
39 141	Ross	1.0	0.7	28,074	67.4	51.9	4.0	11.5	32.6	26.9	32.7	34.9
39 143	Sandusky	9.1	1.3	23,907	68.1	52.3	4.4	11.4	31.9	27.7	29.3	38.5
39 145	Scioto	1.1	1.1	29,339	64.4	48.2	5.0	11.2	35.6	30.2	31.3	40.8
39 147	Seneca	4.5	1.3	21,792	67.7	50.4	5.2	12.1	32.3	26.6	31.3	38.7
39 149	Shelby	1.4	1.1	18,508	74.0	58.2	6.1	9.8	26.0	20.5	34.2	32.8
39 151	Stark	1.7	1.9	149,275	65.9	48.4	4.9	12.6	34.1	29.2	28.9	38.5
39 153	Summit	1.7	4.3	219,302	62.6	45.3	4.0	13.3	37.4	31.5	29.3	36.2
39 155	Trumbull	1.4	1.6	86,233	64.1	46.1	4.7	13.3	35.9	31.2	27.1	42.6
39 157	Tuscarawas	2.0	1.2	36,140	70.2	55.5	4.3	10.4	29.8	25.8	30.5	39.1
39 159	Union	1.3	2.7	18,208	75.4	62.9	4.0	8.5	24.6	20.2	41.9	29.8
39 161	Van Wert	2.7	0.9	11,331	68.7	56.9	3.9	8.0	31.3	28.1	29.8	39.1
39 165	Warren	2.3	5.4	76,331	75.8	64.1	3.2	8.5	24.2	19.8	39.3	31.2
39 167	Washington	0.8	1.1	24,652	65.4	54.6	2.4	8.4	34.6	29.3	26.7	39.0
39 169	Wayne	1.6	1.7	42,023	71.2	57.2	4.2	9.8	28.8	24.8	31.2	38.5
39 171	Williams	3.8	1.6	14,741	68.4	51.4	5.8	11.2	31.6	26.5	31.7	39.1
39 173	Wood	4.7	3.2	48,870	62.0	48.7	3.4	9.8	38.0	29.3	28.3	32.3
39 175	Wyandot	2.3	1.1	9,408	68.0	55.2	4.3	8.5	32.0	27.1	31.3	39.1
40 000	**Oklahoma**	9.1	5.5	1,441,163	66.6	49.3	4.7	12.5	33.4	28.0	32.9	34.5
40 001	Adair	5.4	2.4	7,863	76.5	53.6	6.9	16.1	23.5	21.4	39.6	38.1
40 009	Beckham	12.4	2.8	7,727	65.4	49.1	3.8	12.5	34.6	29.8	32.4	33.5
40 013	Bryan	5.1	2.2	16,563	63.7	48.0	4.3	11.3	35.3	29.7	31.3	36.2
40 015	Caddo	10.3	3.0	10,215	68.9	50.8	5.2	12.9	31.1	25.8	33.9	41.8
40 017	Canadian	7.2	4.6	42,386	75.3	60.0	4.6	10.7	24.7	20.3	39.2	30.3
40 019	Carter	5.6	2.7	17,125	66.7	51.1	4.5	11.1	33.3	28.9	31.7	39.1
40 021	Cherokee	6.4	3.2	17,256	66.1	47.8	5.2	13.2	33.9	29.0	30.6	35.6
40 027	Cleveland	7.3	5.6	96,150	67.5	51.8	4.7	11.0	32.5	24.7	33.8	28.4
40 031	Comanche	11.6	6.1	44,614	66.2	46.1	4.8	15.3	33.8	28.5	37.1	28.4
40 037	Creek	3.3	1.5	26,476	71.1	54.6	5.8	10.7	28.9	25.0	32.8	38.8
40 039	Custer	14.8	7.2	10,369	64.5	45.8	10.5	8.2	35.5	26.5	28.6	31.1
40 041	Delaware	3.0	2.0	16,891	69.5	55.3	4.3	9.9	30.5	25.9	28.1	48.6
40 047	Garfield	9.4	6.6	23,745	67.9	50.8	3.9	13.3	32.1	28.0	31.7	35.8
40 049	Garvin	6.5	2.8	10,294	65.7	50.4	4.7	10.7	34.3	30.1	29.3	41.8
40 051	Grady	4.8	2.1	19,711	74.0	58.3	5.8	9.9	26.0	23.1	35.0	37.0
40 065	Jackson	21.6	6.4	10,503	65.5	50.4	5.2	9.9	34.5	27.8	32.9	32.7
40 071	Kay	6.8	3.5	18,387	63.9	46.6	5.4	11.9	36.1	31.3	29.9	40.4
40 079	Le Flore	6.9	3.4	18,255	69.1	51.1	6.0	11.9	30.9	26.6	31.5	39.2
40 081	Lincoln	2.5	0.9	13,234	69.9	55.2	3.1	11.6	30.1	26.1	32.3	39.5
40 083	Logan	5.3	1.7	14,997	73.2	58.7	3.1	11.4	26.8	24.0	34.9	34.8
40 087	McClain	7.2	3.1	12,863	75.6	61.8	5.0	8.8	24.4	21.3	39.6	36.2
40 089	McCurtain	4.8	1.4	12,849	71.8	50.6	5.1	16.1	28.2	25.7	36.4	37.7
40 091	McIntosh	2.1	0.7	8,078	67.7	54.5	3.6	9.6	32.3	28.3	24.6	51.3
40 097	Mayes	2.8	1.0	16,036	71.0	54.6	5.0	11.4	29.0	26.0	34.4	38.7
40 101	Muskogee	5.4	2.9	26,604	67.0	47.7	5.4	13.9	33.0	28.8	33.6	37.2
40 109	Oklahoma	15.5	10.6	282,883	62.2	43.3	4.8	14.1	37.8	31.3	32.8	31.3
40 111	Okmulgee	3.4	0.7	15,000	65.8	46.4	4.7	14.6	34.2	30.7	31.7	40.1
40 113	Osage	3.0	1.2	18,507	67.8	51.3	4.5	11.9	32.2	28.4	28.6	40.9
40 115	Ottawa	4.8	1.9	12,050	69.4	51.5	4.8	13.2	30.6	26.7	32.5	41.4
40 119	Payne	4.0	6.0	30,218	55.2	43.1	2.7	9.5	44.8	29.9	27.3	25.6
40 121	Pittsburg	4.1	1.3	19,100	66.2	49.3	4.1	12.8	33.8	28.5	31.7	40.2
40 123	Pontotoc	4.1	1.6	14,680	64.7	46.0	4.4	14.3	35.3	29.4	33.8	36.5
40 125	Pottawatomie	4.3	1.7	26,043	69.3	52.1	4.6	12.5	30.7	27.0	33.8	36.1
40 131	Rogers	3.9	2.3	32,902	77.2	62.3	5.3	9.6	22.8	19.6	37.0	34.6
40 133	Seminole	3.8	1.4	9,501	70.9	49.8	6.4	14.7	29.1	25.7	34.8	41.2
40 135	Sequoyah	3.5	1.1	15,542	71.9	54.2	4.5	13.2	28.1	24.0	33.8	37.8
40 137	Stephens	6.4	2.3	17,875	66.2	52.0	3.8	10.5	33.8	30.4	29.4	40.0
40 139	Texas	43.7	22.9	7,177	72.4	58.9	5.1	8.4	27.6	23.6	39.7	30.7
40 143	Tulsa	11.3	7.9	240,665	63.7	45.1	4.6	14.1	36.3	30.3	33.2	31.0
40 145	Wagoner	4.9	3.4	26,749	76.7	60.8	5.0	10.9	23.3	19.6	36.2	36.8
40 147	Washington	5.2	3.4	21,242	66.0	50.9	4.5	10.7	34.0	29.2	29.8	40.1
40 153	Woodward	10.7	4.0	7,203	67.4	58.0	2.0	7.4	32.6	29.2	29.5	38.2
41 000	**Oregon**	12.0	9.8	1,513,005	63.4	48.3	4.6	10.6	36.6	28.0	29.6	36.5
41 003	Benton	6.6	8.5	32,925	56.3	46.0	2.2	8.2	43.7	29.3	23.6	32.1
41 005	Clackamas	7.9	8.4	145,555	69.4	55.1	4.6	9.6	30.6	24.2	32.5	37.9
41 007	Clatsop	7.8	5.7	15,357	62.2	48.3	3.0	10.9	37.8	30.4	25.3	42.3
41 009	Columbia	4.2	3.5	18,901	71.7	56.9	3.6	11.3	28.3	23.5	29.5	38.5
41 011	Coos	5.6	3.3	25,910	60.2	47.3	4.4	8.4	39.8	31.2	23.0	50.6
41 013	Crook	7.3	3.1	8,923	67.4	55.2	3.8	8.3	32.6	26.4	27.6	49.6
41 015	Curry	5.7	2.0	10,132	59.4	47.9	4.6	7.0	40.6	32.4	18.0	58.7
41 017	Deschutes	7.6	4.8	64,982	66.7	53.1	4.7	8.9	33.3	25.2	29.8	37.8
41 019	Douglas	4.8	2.8	43,654	67.2	51.7	4.3	11.2	32.8	25.4	24.6	49.2
41 027	Hood River	29.8	16.2	7,802	65.8	55.9	3.2	6.8	34.2	26.1	33.8	37.7
41 029	Jackson	11.1	5.6	82,524	64.2	48.2	4.8	11.1	35.8	28.8	27.5	42.5
41 031	Jefferson	19.6	6.3	8,032	71.7	45.8	10.7	15.2	28.3	22.4	30.4	38.5

Table A-2. Counties — Who: Age, Race/Ethnicity, and Household Structure, 2010–2012—*Continued*

STATE and County code	STATE or County	Total population	Percent change 2010–2012	Population by age (percent)						Median age	Race alone or in combination (percent)			
				Under 5 years	5 to 17 years	18 to 24 years	25 to 44 years	45 to 64 years	65 years and over		White	Black	Asian, Hawaiian, or Pacific Islander	American Indian, Alaska Native, or some other race
	ACS table number:	B01003	Population estimates	B01001	B01001	B01001	B01001	B01001	B01001	B01002	B02008	B02009	B02011 + B02012	B02010 + B02013
	Column number:	1	2	3	4	5	6	7	8	9	10	11	12	13
	Oregon—Cont.													
41 033	Josephine	82,825	0.1	5.1	15.0	7.3	19.4	30.4	22.8	47.9	96.1	0.6	2.2	3.9
41 035	Klamath	66,186	-0.7	5.8	16.3	9.2	22.2	28.7	17.9	41.8	91.2	1.4	2.2	8.8
41 039	Lane	353,315	0.7	5.1	14.4	13.1	24.2	27.6	15.6	38.9	92.9	1.8	4.3	5.6
41 041	Lincoln	46,019	0.3	5.0	12.2	6.6	19.9	34.0	22.5	49.9	92.0	1.0	2.2	9.4
41 043	Linn	117,796	1.3	6.6	17.3	8.4	24.7	27.1	16.0	39.0	94.1	1.0	1.9	5.5
41 045	Malheur	30,903	-2.2	7.0	17.7	10.1	25.5	24.4	15.2	37.0	89.9	1.9	1.9	11.4
41 047	Marion	317,945	1.3	7.3	18.9	9.7	26.3	24.6	13.2	35.3	82.4	1.7	3.8	16.4
41 051	Multnomah	748,280	3.0	6.2	14.1	9.4	34.0	25.4	10.8	36.0	81.8	7.0	9.2	6.2
41 053	Polk	75,987	1.0	6.3	17.7	12.5	22.5	25.5	15.5	37.2	90.9	1.3	3.9	8.8
41 057	Tillamook	25,314	0.1	5.0	14.6	6.6	20.4	32.2	21.2	48.2	95.6	0.5	1.8	5.0
41 059	Umatilla	76,514	1.0	7.2	19.2	9.4	25.8	25.6	12.8	35.7	92.0	1.3	2.1	9.6
41 061	Union	25,765	0.0	6.7	15.8	11.2	21.4	27.5	17.3	40.7	96.5	0.9	3.2	3.2
41 065	Wasco	25,323	0.9	6.3	16.5	8.4	21.6	29.0	18.3	42.0	86.7	0.7	2.0	12.1
41 067	Washington	539,525	3.1	7.0	18.3	8.3	30.8	25.2	10.5	35.6	79.6	2.6	11.9	10.2
41 071	Yamhill	99,803	0.9	6.1	18.4	10.5	24.9	26.0	13.9	37.6	89.3	1.7	2.9	9.9
42 000	**Pennsylvania**	12,739,595	0.4	5.7	16.0	10.0	24.5	28.2	15.7	40.3	83.9	12.0	3.4	2.8
42 001	Adams	101,485	0.1	5.4	16.3	9.9	22.7	29.3	16.4	42.0	94.4	2.2	1.0	4.5
42 003	Allegheny	1,226,873	0.4	5.2	14.3	10.0	25.1	28.6	16.8	41.1	83.2	14.5	3.6	1.2
42 005	Armstrong	68,659	-0.7	5.0	15.2	7.0	22.9	31.1	18.8	45.0	98.6	1.2	0.4	0.6
42 007	Beaver	170,404	-0.2	5.2	15.0	8.0	22.3	30.8	18.7	44.5	92.9	7.6	0.7	0.9
42 009	Bedford	49,486	-0.8	5.0	16.2	7.2	22.7	29.5	19.4	44.3	98.6	1.0	0.4	0.7
42 011	Berks	412,610	0.4	6.1	17.5	10.1	24.0	27.6	14.7	39.5	86.3	6.1	1.7	8.1
42 013	Blair	127,131	0.1	5.8	15.2	9.3	23.1	28.7	18.0	42.3	97.3	2.3	0.9	0.7
42 015	Bradford	62,801	0.3	5.9	16.6	7.4	22.2	30.0	18.0	43.2	98.7	0.8	0.8	0.8
42 017	Bucks	626,494	0.2	5.3	17.2	7.7	23.7	31.1	15.1	42.2	90.9	4.3	4.6	1.8
42 019	Butler	184,574	0.5	5.3	16.7	9.3	23.3	29.9	15.6	41.7	97.5	1.6	1.4	0.5
42 021	Cambria	142,564	-1.3	5.0	14.5	9.5	22.3	29.8	19.1	43.9	95.3	4.4	0.8	1.1
42 025	Carbon	65,118	-0.3	5.1	15.2	7.5	22.9	31.2	18.1	44.5	97.2	2.0	0.8	1.5
42 027	Centre	154,698	0.6	4.3	11.5	28.7	22.4	21.7	11.5	29.2	90.6	3.9	6.2	1.2
42 029	Chester	503,325	1.4	6.1	18.4	9.0	24.4	28.9	13.3	39.6	88.9	7.0	4.6	1.6
42 031	Clarion	39,808	-0.7	5.2	14.0	15.9	21.1	27.3	16.6	40.0	97.8	1.5	0.7	0.7
42 033	Clearfield	81,422	-0.5	4.8	14.7	8.0	25.0	29.7	17.7	43.1	96.6	2.7	0.7	1.2
42 035	Clinton	39,425	0.7	5.4	15.2	15.5	21.4	26.1	16.4	38.5	97.8	2.2	0.7	0.5
42 037	Columbia	67,018	-0.6	4.7	13.7	16.4	21.4	27.6	16.2	40.0	96.5	2.3	1.2	0.8
42 039	Crawford	88,132	-1.2	5.5	16.6	9.9	22.0	29.1	17.0	42.0	97.6	2.5	0.9	0.9
42 041	Cumberland	237,100	1.1	5.3	15.1	10.8	24.9	28.0	15.9	40.7	92.3	4.3	4.0	1.9
42 043	Dauphin	268,990	0.5	6.2	16.7	8.6	25.7	28.8	14.0	39.5	75.9	20.0	3.8	3.7
42 045	Delaware	560,011	0.3	6.0	17.0	10.6	24.3	27.7	14.4	38.9	73.9	21.1	5.6	1.6
42 047	Elk	31,730	-1.0	4.4	15.5	6.2	22.5	32.0	19.4	45.7	98.3	0.6	0.7	0.1
42 049	Erie	280,794	0.0	5.9	16.5	11.7	23.6	27.5	14.7	38.7	90.3	8.7	1.6	1.8
42 051	Fayette	136,102	-0.6	4.9	15.0	7.9	23.8	30.3	18.1	43.6	95.0	6.0	0.2	0.9
42 055	Franklin	150,691	0.9	6.5	17.1	8.1	24.4	27.0	16.9	40.4	94.6	4.1	1.5	1.5
42 059	Greene	38,377	-1.4	4.9	14.5	10.1	25.3	29.4	15.8	41.5	92.0	7.2	0.8	1.9
42 061	Huntingdon	45,968	0.1	5.2	14.4	9.7	25.0	28.9	16.8	41.7	94.0	5.8	0.6	1.1
42 063	Indiana	88,532	-0.7	5.0	13.7	17.4	21.2	26.9	15.8	38.8	95.4	3.1	1.4	1.1
42 065	Jefferson	44,974	-1.0	5.7	15.6	8.2	22.7	29.3	18.4	43.2	99.1	0.7	0.3	0.8
42 067	Juniata	24,787	1.5	5.9	17.5	7.7	23.4	27.8	17.8	41.9	98.2	1.0	0.5	1.0
42 069	Lackawanna	214,528	0.0	5.4	14.9	10.1	23.6	28.1	17.9	42.1	94.3	3.4	2.2	1.6
42 071	Lancaster	523,676	1.2	6.7	17.8	9.8	23.9	26.5	15.3	38.3	91.4	4.8	2.3	3.7
42 073	Lawrence	90,411	-1.2	5.3	15.6	8.2	22.5	29.4	19.1	44.0	94.9	4.9	0.7	0.8
42 075	Lebanon	134,452	1.1	6.2	16.6	8.7	23.8	27.6	17.1	41.0	91.2	2.7	1.4	6.9
42 077	Lehigh	352,948	1.5	6.1	17.2	8.9	25.3	27.6	14.9	39.3	83.8	8.0	3.8	7.6
42 079	Luzerne	321,013	0.0	5.1	14.9	9.4	23.8	28.7	18.1	42.9	92.8	4.3	1.4	2.9
42 081	Lycoming	116,668	0.9	5.5	15.1	10.9	23.2	28.8	16.5	41.5	94.1	5.7	1.1	1.2
42 083	McKean	43,233	-0.6	5.3	15.4	9.3	24.1	28.6	17.2	42.4	96.3	2.8	0.7	1.2
42 085	Mercer	116,122	-0.8	5.0	16.3	9.5	21.7	28.7	18.7	43.1	93.0	6.7	0.9	0.9
42 087	Mifflin	46,736	0.2	6.1	16.6	7.3	22.8	28.2	19.0	43.2	98.6	1.1	0.6	0.5
42 089	Monroe	169,588	-0.7	4.9	18.0	10.6	22.6	30.7	13.2	40.7	81.7	14.7	2.9	3.8
42 091	Montgomery	804,896	0.9	5.8	16.8	7.8	25.5	28.7	15.4	40.8	83.5	9.8	7.4	1.4
42 095	Northampton	298,618	0.4	5.3	16.2	10.1	23.7	28.8	16.0	41.3	89.5	6.9	2.9	3.5
42 097	Northumberland	94,427	0.1	5.3	14.5	7.9	24.2	29.5	18.6	43.6	96.1	2.8	0.6	1.3
42 099	Perry	45,844	-0.6	5.9	16.9	7.9	24.4	30.7	14.1	41.2	98.4	1.2	0.5	1.1
42 101	Philadelphia	1,538,211	1.3	6.8	15.7	13.0	28.8	23.6	12.1	33.4	43.3	44.9	7.3	7.4
42 103	Pike	57,258	-0.7	4.5	17.7	7.4	20.9	31.8	17.8	44.8	92.7	6.4	1.4	3.7
42 107	Schuylkill	147,618	-0.8	5.0	14.8	7.2	25.3	29.5	18.3	43.5	95.6	3.5	0.8	1.4
42 109	Snyder	39,690	-0.2	5.6	16.3	12.5	22.6	27.2	15.9	39.8	97.7	1.3	0.8	0.7
42 111	Somerset	77,348	-1.0	4.6	14.3	7.6	23.9	30.6	19.0	44.7	96.8	2.8	0.5	1.0
42 115	Susquehanna	43,035	-1.5	4.9	15.8	7.4	21.4	32.3	18.3	45.5	98.9	0.9	0.5	0.5
42 117	Tioga	42,326	1.4	5.4	14.9	11.1	21.7	28.7	18.3	42.6	98.5	1.4	0.6	0.8
42 119	Union	44,957	0.0	4.8	13.5	14.0	27.3	25.3	15.2	38.3	88.7	8.1	1.8	3.4
42 121	Venango	54,640	-1.2	5.5	15.7	7.5	21.8	31.3	18.3	44.7	98.7	1.0	0.5	1.5
42 123	Warren	41,461	-1.5	4.9	15.4	7.0	22.1	31.5	19.3	45.6	98.7	0.8	0.5	0.8
42 125	Washington	208,256	0.4	5.0	15.3	9.0	22.4	30.4	17.8	43.7	95.7	4.3	0.9	0.9
42 127	Wayne	52,417	-1.9	4.2	14.5	7.3	22.8	32.2	19.0	45.7	95.3	3.7	0.7	1.5

Table A-2. Counties — Who: Age, Race/Ethnicity, and Household Structure, 2010–2012—*Continued*

STATE and County code	STATE or County	Percent Hispanic or Latino	Percent foreign born	Total households	Household type (percent)						Percent of households with people under 18 years	Percent of households with people 60 years and over
					Family households				Nonfamily households			
					Total family households	Married-couple families	Male household families	Female household families	Total nonfamily households	One-person households		
	ACS table number:	B03003	C05003	B11001	B11001	B11001	B11001	B11001	B11001	B11001	B11005	B11006
	Column number:	14	15	16	17	18	19	20	21	22	23	24
	Oregon—Cont.											
41 033	Josephine	6.5	2.8	34,151	63.6	49.8	4.9	8.9	36.4	30.6	23.6	51.4
41 035	Klamath	10.8	5.0	27,789	66.8	48.3	6.4	12.2	33.2	26.9	29.9	41.9
41 039	Lane	7.6	5.9	145,265	59.4	43.6	4.9	10.9	40.6	28.7	26.3	37.9
41 041	Lincoln	8.1	5.9	20,979	61.0	50.2	3.7	7.1	39.0	32.7	21.0	49.0
41 043	Linn	8.0	4.7	44,926	67.4	51.8	4.6	11.0	32.6	25.1	29.7	40.5
41 045	Malheur	32.1	11.3	10,125	68.9	54.2	5.0	9.6	31.1	28.2	35.3	39.9
41 047	Marion	24.7	13.4	113,116	69.4	50.2	5.9	13.2	30.6	25.8	36.5	35.2
41 051	Multnomah	11.0	13.9	305,069	53.7	38.6	4.0	11.1	46.3	33.5	26.6	28.9
41 053	Polk	12.4	6.3	28,501	69.2	54.2	5.0	10.0	30.8	23.5	31.5	38.7
41 057	Tillamook	9.2	5.6	10,367	62.6	49.2	5.6	7.8	37.4	30.2	24.1	48.0
41 059	Umatilla	24.3	10.6	26,867	68.2	47.6	6.3	14.3	31.8	26.2	36.0	37.2
41 061	Union	4.1	3.2	10,185	65.4	52.9	4.6	7.9	34.6	26.3	27.6	39.3
41 065	Wasco	15.5	9.6	9,693	66.7	51.0	3.8	11.9	33.3	28.6	27.4	42.8
41 067	Washington	15.9	16.8	201,111	66.9	52.8	4.1	10.0	33.1	25.4	35.7	29.3
41 071	Yamhill	15.0	8.3	33,574	72.5	54.3	6.3	11.9	27.5	22.2	35.2	36.9
42 000	**Pennsylvania**	5.9	5.9	4,949,494	64.7	48.3	4.4	12.1	35.3	29.5	29.3	37.9
42 001	Adams	6.2	3.8	37,919	70.7	56.3	4.2	10.1	29.3	24.5	30.3	39.9
42 003	Allegheny	1.7	4.9	522,238	58.0	42.4	3.6	11.9	42.0	35.4	25.1	37.8
42 005	Armstrong	0.6	0.4	28,735	68.1	53.1	5.7	9.3	31.9	28.2	26.8	42.3
42 007	Beaver	1.2	1.8	70,787	66.0	49.7	4.5	11.7	34.0	29.8	26.0	42.3
42 009	Bedford	0.9	0.8	20,570	68.8	53.5	4.7	10.6	31.2	28.0	27.8	42.7
42 011	Berks	16.9	7.1	154,092	68.8	51.2	5.2	12.4	31.2	25.1	33.2	36.3
42 013	Blair	1.0	1.3	50,990	65.5	49.0	4.6	11.9	34.5	29.5	28.1	41.4
42 015	Bradford	1.2	1.7	24,103	67.3	54.1	4.3	8.9	32.7	27.0	27.8	43.8
42 017	Bucks	4.4	8.2	230,384	71.6	58.4	3.7	9.5	28.4	24.0	32.3	38.5
42 019	Butler	1.1	1.9	73,147	68.2	56.7	3.1	8.4	31.8	26.3	30.6	36.1
42 021	Cambria	1.5	1.3	58,197	63.3	48.0	4.5	10.8	36.7	32.3	24.9	43.6
42 025	Carbon	3.5	3.0	25,919	67.4	53.3	3.6	10.5	32.6	26.2	26.3	40.8
42 027	Centre	2.5	6.9	57,266	55.1	45.1	3.6	6.4	44.9	29.1	22.6	29.5
42 029	Chester	6.7	8.7	184,364	70.3	58.9	3.4	8.0	29.7	24.1	35.0	34.2
42 031	Clarion	0.7	1.2	16,027	62.6	49.7	4.2	8.7	37.4	28.0	27.3	38.5
42 033	Clearfield	2.4	2.1	32,158	66.6	53.6	4.4	8.5	33.4	29.1	28.1	41.0
42 035	Clinton	1.2	1.3	15,287	62.7	48.4	4.2	10.1	37.3	29.4	27.2	39.5
42 037	Columbia	2.2	2.2	26,188	63.9	49.7	4.3	9.9	36.1	27.6	27.4	39.3
42 039	Crawford	1.0	1.1	35,042	66.3	51.9	4.3	10.0	33.7	28.4	27.2	40.6
42 041	Cumberland	2.9	5.3	95,126	65.5	52.1	3.9	9.4	34.5	28.9	29.1	36.9
42 043	Dauphin	7.3	5.9	107,891	64.1	44.6	5.1	14.3	35.9	30.5	30.6	35.2
42 045	Delaware	3.1	9.4	205,185	66.5	47.3	5.0	14.3	33.5	28.6	32.1	37.1
42 047	Elk	0.6	1.1	13,596	67.2	51.3	5.7	10.2	32.8	29.7	26.1	42.6
42 049	Erie	3.5	4.1	109,522	63.2	45.9	4.5	12.8	36.8	30.5	28.8	36.1
42 051	Fayette	0.9	0.8	54,372	65.0	47.1	5.2	12.6	35.0	30.2	27.2	43.1
42 055	Franklin	4.5	3.3	57,739	70.2	56.6	4.6	9.0	29.8	25.4	31.1	38.7
42 059	Greene	2.2	0.5	14,222	66.4	51.4	4.0	10.9	33.6	28.6	27.7	42.2
42 061	Huntingdon	1.7	1.2	16,992	69.2	55.7	4.6	8.9	30.8	27.2	29.9	42.0
42 063	Indiana	1.2	1.8	34,652	63.5	51.4	3.8	8.3	36.5	27.8	25.5	36.6
42 065	Jefferson	0.7	0.7	18,637	66.1	52.5	4.2	9.3	33.9	29.6	27.4	40.3
42 067	Juniata	2.6	1.5	9,321	71.2	60.1	3.3	7.8	28.8	23.8	27.6	41.2
42 069	Lackawanna	5.2	4.9	85,721	63.1	45.8	4.7	12.6	36.9	31.4	27.7	40.6
42 071	Lancaster	9.0	4.2	193,931	70.3	57.6	3.6	9.1	29.7	24.5	32.2	36.9
42 073	Lawrence	1.1	1.5	36,752	67.2	51.2	4.0	12.1	32.8	29.4	28.9	43.1
42 075	Lebanon	9.9	3.7	51,807	69.8	55.0	4.4	10.5	30.2	25.8	31.1	39.6
42 077	Lehigh	19.6	10.3	133,322	67.2	49.3	4.7	13.2	32.8	27.2	32.7	36.0
42 079	Luzerne	7.3	5.0	130,097	63.2	44.6	4.9	13.7	36.8	31.8	27.2	41.4
42 081	Lycoming	1.5	1.3	45,933	64.8	49.3	4.6	10.9	35.2	28.0	27.7	38.7
42 083	McKean	1.8	1.5	17,373	66.1	47.3	6.0	12.9	33.9	29.0	31.3	39.4
42 085	Mercer	1.1	1.2	46,345	66.2	49.6	3.6	13.0	33.8	30.1	27.9	42.8
42 087	Mifflin	1.2	0.8	18,947	66.0	52.3	4.1	9.7	34.0	28.8	28.8	42.1
42 089	Monroe	13.6	10.6	58,173	73.6	55.3	5.4	12.9	26.4	20.4	35.6	36.9
42 091	Montgomery	4.4	9.7	307,618	68.2	55.3	3.6	9.3	31.8	26.5	32.4	37.0
42 095	Northampton	10.9	6.8	112,120	69.1	53.2	4.8	11.2	30.9	25.1	32.0	38.9
42 097	Northumberland	2.5	1.4	39,109	65.7	50.7	4.2	10.8	34.3	29.2	26.3	42.8
42 099	Perry	1.4	1.0	18,231	70.8	56.7	4.5	9.7	29.2	22.8	31.2	35.7
42 101	Philadelphia	12.7	12.0	576,889	53.3	27.0	5.5	20.9	46.7	39.6	27.4	33.3
42 103	Pike	9.3	7.7	21,759	71.6	57.4	3.9	10.4	28.4	24.3	30.8	42.7
42 107	Schuylkill	2.9	2.0	59,689	66.6	48.5	5.8	12.3	33.4	28.1	27.9	42.1
42 109	Snyder	1.7	1.6	14,481	72.4	60.0	5.1	7.3	27.6	22.4	32.0	39.6
42 111	Somerset	1.1	0.6	29,626	67.6	56.7	3.7	7.2	32.4	28.8	25.4	43.7
42 115	Susquehanna	1.4	1.6	17,001	68.8	54.8	4.6	9.4	31.2	26.1	26.8	42.8
42 117	Tioga	1.1	1.0	17,039	67.9	52.6	5.8	9.6	32.1	26.5	28.3	41.6
42 119	Union	5.4	3.9	15,295	67.1	54.3	4.6	9.1	32.9	24.6	31.0	36.8
42 121	Venango	0.9	0.5	22,956	66.6	50.8	4.8	10.9	33.4	29.7	28.1	41.4
42 123	Warren	0.8	1.3	17,046	66.1	53.2	4.1	8.7	33.9	29.2	24.1	43.0
42 125	Washington	1.2	1.8	83,920	65.6	51.9	3.6	10.1	34.4	29.5	27.8	42.3
42 127	Wayne	3.6	3.7	19,521	68.1	55.5	4.2	8.3	31.9	27.3	26.1	45.9

STATE and County code	STATE or County	Total population	Percent change 2010–2012	Population by age (percent)						Median age	Race alone or in combination (percent)			
				Under 5 years	5 to 17 years	18 to 24 years	25 to 44 years	45 to 64 years	65 years and over		White	Black	Asian, Hawaiian, or Pacific Islander	American Indian, Alaska Native, or some other race
	ACS table number:	B01003	Population estimates	B01001	B01001	B01001	B01001	B01001	B01001	B01002	B02008	B02009	E02011 + B02012	B02010 + B02013
	Column number:	1	2	3	4	5	6	7	8	9	10	11	12	13
	Pennsylvania—Cont.													
42 129	Westmoreland	364,357	-0.5	4.7	14.8	7.7	22.1	31.5	19.1	45.4	96.4	3.3	1.1	0.7
42 131	Wyoming	28,181	-0.5	5.2	15.9	9.3	23.0	30.1	16.5	42.0	98.5	1.2	0.5	0.9
42 133	York	436,824	0.5	6.0	17.1	8.4	25.1	28.9	14.5	40.4	90.7	6.9	1.7	3.1
44 000	**Rhode Island**	1,051,236	-0.2	5.3	15.6	11.5	24.9	28.0	14.7	39.7	83.6	7.7	3.8	7.9
44 001	Bristol	49,413	-1.4	4.2	16.0	11.4	20.3	30.8	17.2	43.5	97.6	1.3	2.2	1.4
44 003	Kent	165,432	-0.7	4.8	15.3	7.6	25.0	31.1	16.1	43.0	94.7	2.1	2.8	2.4
44 005	Newport	82,372	-1.0	4.5	14.7	9.7	23.0	30.5	17.6	43.7	93.0	5.0	2.9	3.0
44 007	Providence	627,625	0.2	5.9	15.8	12.2	26.4	26.1	13.6	37.0	76.1	11.2	4.5	11.7
44 009	Washington	126,394	-0.8	4.0	15.4	13.7	20.0	31.2	15.7	42.3	94.9	1.9	2.3	2.3
45 000	**South Carolina**	4,677,636	1.9	6.4	16.7	10.3	25.6	26.9	14.2	38.1	68.7	28.8	1.8	2.8
45 001	Abbeville	25,207	-1.0	5.9	16.6	10.3	21.6	28.4	17.1	42.6	71.2	29.7	0.0	0.6
45 003	Aiken	161,817	1.4	5.9	16.6	9.1	24.2	28.1	15.9	40.5	71.2	25.5	1.1	3.7
45 007	Anderson	188,359	1.1	6.2	17.5	8.5	24.4	27.7	15.7	40.2	82.0	17.2	1.2	1.4
45 011	Barnwell	22,414	-1.8	6.4	19.5	9.5	21.9	28.3	14.4	39.4	52.2	45.8	0.0	2.3
45 013	Beaufort	165,149	3.1	6.5	14.2	10.2	22.8	24.8	21.5	41.4	74.3	20.0	1.8	6.1
45 015	Berkeley	184,225	6.2	7.2	17.6	10.6	28.5	25.4	10.6	34.6	69.4	26.3	3.6	3.5
45 019	Charleston	358,009	4.0	6.4	14.2	11.8	28.5	26.0	13.2	35.9	67.5	30.3	2.0	1.9
45 021	Cherokee	55,542	0.4	6.7	17.7	10.5	24.5	26.8	13.8	38.1	78.0	21.1	0.8	2.1
45 023	Chester	32,825	-1.7	6.3	17.4	8.7	23.2	29.1	15.4	40.7	60.5	39.2	0.0	0.8
45 025	Chesterfield	46,451	-1.2	6.1	17.9	9.0	25.3	27.5	14.2	39.5	65.8	34.0	0.5	0.9
45 027	Clarendon	34,637	-1.6	5.8	16.0	10.3	21.1	29.4	17.5	42.2	48.3	50.7	0.0	2.2
45 029	Colleton	38,483	-1.8	6.3	17.6	9.3	21.5	28.9	16.4	41.5	58.2	40.1	0.0	1.9
45 031	Darlington	68,341	-0.7	6.2	17.6	9.5	23.2	28.7	14.9	39.7	58.0	41.9	0.5	1.1
45 033	Dillon	31,754	-2.0	7.2	18.5	9.3	25.0	26.5	13.5	37.4	48.3	47.4	0.2	5.2
45 035	Dorchester	140,010	3.6	7.0	19.7	8.6	28.0	26.2	10.5	35.7	71.5	27.3	2.6	2.4
45 037	Edgefield	26,670	-2.3	4.9	15.8	8.3	27.3	30.1	13.6	40.9	60.9	37.5	0.0	2.9
45 039	Fairfield	23,602	-2.1	5.6	16.4	8.9	21.4	31.9	15.7	42.7	38.9	60.9	0.0	0.6
45 041	Florence	137,473	0.7	6.7	17.8	9.9	25.2	26.9	13.5	37.3	57.1	42.4	1.5	0.6
45 043	Georgetown	60,145	0.1	5.4	15.7	7.4	20.3	30.3	21.0	45.8	63.7	34.0	0.4	2.0
45 045	Greenville	459,753	3.3	6.8	17.1	9.5	27.2	26.3	13.1	37.4	78.0	19.2	2.6	2.5
45 047	Greenwood	69,731	0.1	6.7	16.8	10.5	24.7	25.8	15.5	38.7	66.4	30.5	1.0	5.5
45 049	Hampton	20,839	-1.5	6.0	17.5	9.5	25.3	27.5	14.1	39.1	43.3	54.1	0.0	2.8
45 051	Horry	276,156	4.3	5.6	14.4	9.5	24.6	28.1	17.8	41.9	81.8	14.4	1.6	4.3
45 053	Jasper	25,369	3.6	7.3	17.0	10.9	28.1	24.5	12.2	35.4	46.1	46.5	1.1	7.2
45 055	Kershaw	62,126	0.8	6.5	17.6	8.1	23.7	29.2	14.9	41.1	72.4	26.2	0.3	2.4
45 057	Lancaster	77,898	2.8	6.6	16.4	8.0	25.4	27.2	16.4	40.4	74.2	24.2	0.6	2.0
45 059	Laurens	66,349	-0.4	6.4	16.5	10.2	23.1	28.5	15.4	40.5	73.1	26.2	0.5	2.0
45 063	Lexington	266,797	2.7	6.6	17.6	8.7	26.7	27.8	12.7	37.9	82.6	15.2	2.0	2.6
45 067	Marion	32,730	-1.6	6.9	17.1	8.5	23.4	28.8	15.2	39.1	41.8	57.6	0.6	1.7
45 069	Marlboro	28,495	-2.5	5.4	15.7	9.7	27.0	28.5	13.7	39.7	42.6	51.8	0.5	7.0
45 071	Newberry	37,518	0.1	6.2	16.5	10.4	23.5	27.2	16.2	39.9	62.6	31.2	0.8	7.8
45 073	Oconee	74,425	0.3	5.6	15.3	8.4	22.2	28.8	19.7	43.5	90.8	8.3	0.9	2.0
45 075	Orangeburg	91,835	-0.9	6.6	16.3	12.2	22.2	27.2	15.4	38.6	35.3	63.1	0.9	1.5
45 077	Pickens	119,440	0.4	5.2	15.0	18.5	22.9	24.6	13.8	34.9	90.2	7.3	2.1	2.2
45 079	Richland	389,648	2.1	6.3	16.3	15.0	28.0	24.3	10.1	32.8	49.2	47.4	3.0	3.0
45 083	Spartanburg	286,563	1.4	6.6	17.5	9.9	25.2	26.9	13.8	38.0	74.6	21.9	2.5	3.1
45 085	Sumter	107,642	0.5	7.3	17.9	10.8	25.2	25.7	13.1	35.5	50.5	47.8	1.6	2.3
45 087	Union	28,583	-2.1	5.7	16.9	8.1	22.7	29.5	17.1	42.9	68.1	32.3	0.0	0.9
45 089	Williamsburg	34,031	-2.1	5.8	17.2	8.6	23.9	29.0	15.5	40.4	32.5	66.7	0.3	1.2
45 091	York	230,600	3.4	6.7	18.5	9.1	26.9	27.0	11.7	37.4	78.0	20.0	2.0	2.6
46 000	**South Dakota**	824,391	2.1	7.1	17.5	10.0	24.5	26.4	14.5	37.0	87.6	1.9	1.4	11.3
46 011	Brookings	32,258	1.9	5.6	12.7	29.1	22.9	19.7	10.0	26.5	94.5	1.2	3.1	2.3
46 013	Brown	36,922	2.0	6.7	16.8	10.3	23.8	26.6	15.8	38.9	93.6	1.3	0.7	5.0
46 029	Codington	27,414	1.4	7.0	17.7	9.3	24.5	26.6	14.9	38.2	96.0	0.0	0.7	3.7
46 081	Lawrence	24,292	0.9	5.2	14.3	12.9	21.3	29.0	17.3	41.7	93.8	0.0	0.9	5.3
46 083	Lincoln	46,722	6.9	8.9	20.2	6.6	32.0	23.3	9.1	33.5	97.3	1.3	1.4	1.2
46 093	Meade	25,679	2.4	7.0	17.4	11.3	24.4	27.5	12.4	35.7	93.1	1.9	1.4	6.3
46 099	Minnehaha	172,303	3.0	7.6	17.3	9.8	28.3	25.7	11.3	34.8	89.1	4.9	1.9	5.7
46 103	Pennington	102,742	2.9	7.2	17.2	9.5	25.7	26.7	13.8	36.9	88.0	2.4	1.5	13.0
46 135	Yankton	22,523	0.7	6.0	15.8	8.0	25.2	28.9	16.1	40.8	92.6	2.2	2.0	3.5
47 000	**Tennessee**	6,404,240	1.6	6.3	17.0	9.6	26.3	26.9	13.8	38.2	79.8	17.5	1.9	2.7
47 001	Anderson	75,255	0.4	5.4	16.2	7.9	23.4	29.4	17.6	43.2	94.1	5.3	1.4	1.0
47 003	Bedford	45,354	1.0	7.4	19.3	8.8	25.6	25.1	13.8	36.6	90.4	9.0	0.9	2.6
47 009	Blount	123,676	0.8	5.3	16.6	8.1	24.4	29.0	16.6	41.9	95.4	3.4	1.0	1.4
47 011	Bradley	100,080	2.0	5.9	16.9	10.6	25.7	26.3	14.7	39.0	93.8	4.8	1.1	2.0
47 013	Campbell	40,561	-0.7	5.6	15.8	8.0	24.2	28.6	17.8	42.3	98.1	0.6	0.5	1.7
47 017	Carroll	28,438	-0.4	5.7	16.0	9.6	22.7	27.8	18.2	42.4	88.7	11.1	0.5	1.9
47 019	Carter	57,374	0.0	5.2	14.3	9.5	24.0	28.9	18.1	42.6	97.6	2.0	0.7	1.6
47 021	Cheatham	39,133	0.4	6.2	18.3	7.9	25.5	30.5	11.6	40.1	96.6	2.0	0.6	2.0
47 025	Claiborne	32,021	-1.6	5.0	15.5	9.6	24.8	28.6	16.5	41.2	98.4	1.2	0.0	0.7
47 029	Cocke	35,560	-0.2	5.4	15.8	7.6	23.6	30.3	17.3	42.8	96.8	2.8	0.0	1.3
47 031	Coffee	52,997	0.8	6.2	17.8	8.1	24.4	27.4	16.1	39.0	94.4	3.2	1.3	4.2

Table A-2. Counties — Who: Age, Race/Ethnicity, and Household Structure, 2010–2012—*Continued*

STATE and County code	STATE or County	Percent Hispanic or Latino	Percent foreign born	Total households	Household type (percent)							Percent of households with people under 18 years	Percent of households with people 60 years and over
					Family households				Nonfamily households				
					Total family households	Married-couple families	Male household families	Female household families	Total nonfamily households	One-person households			
ACS table number:		B03003	C05003	B11001	B11001	B11001	B11001	B11001	B11001	B11001		B11005	B11006
Column number:		14	15	16	17	18	19	20	21	22		23	24
	Pennsylvania—Cont.												
42 129	Westmoreland	0.9	1.4	152,022	66.5	51.0	4.3	11.2	33.5	28.9		26.2	42.9
42 131	Wyoming	1.6	1.4	10,852	69.4	54.3	5.3	9.9	30.6	24.1		28.9	41.5
42 133	York	5.9	3.5	168,566	70.4	54.6	4.5	11.3	29.6	24.5		32.6	36.5
44 000	**Rhode Island**	12.8	13.2	409,308	61.9	43.6	4.6	13.7	38.1	30.5		29.2	36.6
44 001	Bristol	2.1	8.8	19,241	68.5	53.3	3.2	12.0	31.5	26.0		30.4	39.1
44 003	Kent	3.4	6.4	68,271	61.9	45.9	4.7	11.3	38.1	31.6		27.8	37.9
44 005	Newport	4.4	6.7	34,364	61.3	48.3	2.5	10.5	38.7	32.0		26.2	39.9
44 007	Providence	19.3	18.0	237,634	60.7	39.7	5.2	15.8	39.3	31.2		30.6	34.7
44 009	Washington	2.5	4.2	49,798	65.8	52.1	3.6	10.1	34.2	26.8		26.4	40.3
45 000	**South Carolina**	5.2	4.8	1,774,128	67.4	47.4	4.6	15.4	32.6	27.5		32.0	36.5
45 001	Abbeville	0.7	1.4	9,716	68.3	49.5	4.9	13.9	31.7	26.8		31.9	44.5
45 003	Aiken	5.0	3.5	63,373	67.1	47.7	4.6	14.8	32.9	28.8		29.8	38.1
45 007	Anderson	3.0	2.5	72,891	69.6	50.9	5.1	13.6	30.4	27.3		32.8	38.9
45 011	Barnwell	2.0	0.9	8,284	67.8	42.4	7.0	18.4	32.2	26.8		37.6	38.2
45 013	Beaufort	11.9	10.0	63,600	69.9	56.1	3.6	10.2	30.1	25.0		27.0	48.7
45 015	Berkeley	6.0	5.8	65,396	71.8	53.8	4.1	13.9	28.2	24.2		36.0	30.1
45 019	Charleston	5.3	5.3	142,536	58.7	40.1	4.0	14.7	41.3	31.8		27.1	33.6
45 021	Cherokee	3.8	2.0	21,096	69.4	46.8	5.3	17.2	30.6	26.7		34.1	35.8
45 023	Chester	1.5	1.1	12,348	70.8	43.2	6.7	21.0	29.2	26.0		32.3	40.6
45 025	Chesterfield	3.7	2.0	17,471	67.3	46.9	5.0	15.4	32.7	28.9		30.6	37.7
45 027	Clarendon	2.7	1.7	12,044	71.4	46.1	5.3	20.0	28.6	25.4		30.7	45.5
45 029	Colleton	2.8	2.2	14,808	68.4	41.8	6.8	19.9	31.6	27.5		29.9	42.0
45 031	Darlington	1.7	1.6	26,568	70.3	44.7	5.6	20.0	29.7	27.1		34.3	39.5
45 033	Dillon	2.6	3.1	11,875	68.7	37.5	6.5	24.6	31.3	28.2		34.6	38.2
45 035	Dorchester	4.5	4.1	50,323	73.1	53.4	5.0	14.7	26.9	23.9		40.5	29.7
45 037	Edgefield	5.5	4.9	8,908	72.6	50.9	7.5	14.2	27.4	25.8		32.7	39.5
45 039	Fairfield	0.4	0.8	9,869	66.1	39.0	6.7	20.5	33.9	31.8		30.3	36.4
45 041	Florence	2.3	2.4	51,477	69.5	42.1	6.4	20.9	30.5	26.2		36.1	34.8
45 043	Georgetown	3.1	2.4	23,229	67.3	49.1	4.0	14.2	32.7	28.2		26.3	50.6
45 045	Greenville	8.3	8.0	175,023	66.8	49.6	3.8	13.4	33.2	28.6		32.8	33.0
45 047	Greenwood	5.6	4.1	26,354	65.9	43.3	6.2	16.4	34.1	29.9		30.8	40.3
45 049	Hampton	3.6	1.9	7,507	71.3	45.6	4.4	21.3	28.7	25.4		34.3	40.9
45 051	Horry	6.2	6.8	113,314	63.7	47.2	4.3	12.2	36.3	28.8		27.1	43.0
45 053	Jasper	14.7	9.0	8,537	66.8	47.8	5.2	13.8	33.2	29.3		32.6	33.4
45 055	Kershaw	3.9	2.6	24,020	70.9	51.7	4.1	15.1	29.1	25.1		31.6	39.4
45 057	Lancaster	4.6	2.5	29,268	71.6	49.7	4.2	17.7	28.4	25.7		33.2	39.4
45 059	Laurens	4.2	2.5	24,783	72.3	46.5	7.6	18.2	27.7	24.3		30.9	38.9
45 063	Lexington	5.6	5.0	103,724	69.0	50.9	4.1	14.0	31.0	25.9		34.1	32.3
45 067	Marion	2.6	1.9	12,010	71.2	40.4	5.6	25.2	23.8	25.3		35.2	42.0
45 069	Marlboro	2.9	1.6	9,697	68.1	39.1	9.8	19.1	31.9	28.9		31.6	42.5
45 071	Newberry	7.4	5.6	13,875	69.8	46.8	4.7	18.3	30.2	26.8		31.5	43.2
45 073	Oconee	4.6	3.1	30,082	68.8	51.5	3.9	13.4	31.2	25.6		28.0	44.5
45 075	Orangeburg	2.0	2.0	34,266	67.5	39.6	5.2	22.7	32.5	29.2		31.8	40.5
45 077	Pickens	3.2	3.6	43,553	66.5	51.2	5.0	10.3	33.5	25.8		29.3	34.7
45 079	Richland	4.9	5.2	142,881	61.4	39.7	3.7	17.9	33.6	31.6		31.9	28.5
45 083	Spartanburg	6.0	6.6	106,734	70.9	51.0	4.5	15.4	29.1	24.8		34.5	36.8
45 085	Sumter	3.4	3.5	39,766	69.8	46.0	4.8	19.1	30.2	26.6		36.1	36.1
45 087	Union	1.0	0.8	11,734	68.7	44.4	6.3	18.0	31.3	28.7		33.6	42.4
45 089	Williamsburg	2.0	0.9	11,823	65.3	37.5	5.5	22.3	34.7	31.0		30.6	46.2
45 091	York	4.6	4.7	86,271	71.9	54.9	3.9	13.2	28.1	23.6		36.7	31.0
46 000	**South Dakota**	2.9	2.8	322,005	64.2	50.2	4.3	9.7	35.8	29.7		30.2	33.9
46 011	Brookings	2.1	4.8	12,275	58.8	44.4	7.2	7.2	41.2	28.6		25.5	24.8
46 013	Brown	1.6	1.8	15,593	58.8	48.2	3.3	7.3	41.2	36.1		27.3	34.1
46 029	Codington	1.6	1.3	11,519	60.7	46.4	5.0	9.3	39.3	32.7		26.9	33.7
46 081	Lawrence	2.8	2.3	10,445	60.0	48.7	3.6	7.7	40.0	32.9		24.9	38.7
46 083	Lincoln	1.4	2.5	17,269	76.8	65.8	2.3	8.7	23.2	18.5		41.7	22.9
46 093	Meade	3.4	1.5	9,911	71.6	60.2	4.3	7.1	28.4	23.6		33.9	31.5
46 099	Minnehaha	4.3	6.5	67,205	63.6	47.5	4.5	11.7	36.4	29.1		32.7	27.7
46 103	Pennington	4.1	1.8	40,606	62.7	46.3	4.9	11.4	37.3	30.4		29.8	33.3
46 135	Yankton	2.9	2.8	8,512	64.8	53.3	3.3	8.2	35.2	28.0		26.3	36.8
47 000	**Tennessee**	4.7	4.6	2,466,659	66.7	48.7	4.4	13.6	33.3	28.2		31.7	35.2
47 001	Anderson	2.4	3.1	30,638	66.5	49.5	4.9	12.1	33.5	30.3		28.8	41.4
47 003	Bedford	11.3	7.8	16,290	73.2	55.0	5.4	12.9	26.8	22.3		34.6	35.7
47 009	Blount	2.9	2.5	48,349	70.7	55.9	3.2	11.6	29.3	25.6		31.5	40.2
47 011	Bradley	4.9	4.3	37,747	68.9	51.3	4.7	12.9	31.1	26.5		31.7	37.8
47 013	Campbell	1.2	0.6	15,880	66.4	50.4	3.2	14.0	33.6	30.3		30.5	41.6
47 017	Carroll	2.2	0.7	10,705	65.5	50.9	4.6	10.0	34.5	31.8		28.7	44.3
47 019	Carter	1.6	1.3	23,940	67.3	51.4	4.1	11.8	32.7	28.4		30.2	41.2
47 021	Cheatham	2.5	1.3	14,476	75.8	58.6	5.5	11.7	24.2	18.3		35.2	31.6
47 025	Claiborne	1.4	1.0	12,679	67.9	51.7	3.3	12.8	32.1	28.6		27.4	40.4
47 029	Cocke	1.9	1.4	14,680	69.5	51.1	3.1	15.3	30.5	26.7		31.3	41.1
47 031	Coffee	3.9	3.1	21,064	69.7	48.6	5.1	16.0	30.3	26.9		32.8	38.4

Table A-2. Counties — Who: Age, Race/Ethnicity, and Household Structure, 2010–2012—*Continued*

STATE and County code	STATE or County	Total population	Percent change 2010–2012	Population by age (percent)							Race alone or in combination (percent)			
				Under 5 years	5 to 17 years	18 to 24 years	25 to 44 years	45 to 64 years	65 years and over	Median age	White	Black	Asian, Hawaiian, or Pacific Islander	American Indian, Alaska Native, or some other race
	ACS table number:	B01003	Population estimates	B01001	B01001	B01001	B01001	B01001	B01001	B01002	B02008	B02009	B02011 + B02012	B02010 + B02013
	Column number:	1	2	3	4	5	6	7	8	9	10	11	12	13
	Tennessee—Cont.													
47 035	Cumberland................	56,621	1.4	5.1	14.0	6.7	19.5	27.9	26.8	48.6	98.4	0.5	0.6	2.6
47 037	Davidson....................	637,303	3.2	7.1	14.7	11.3	32.0	24.3	10.5	33.9	64.0	28.8	3.9	5.9
47 043	Dickson.....................	50,071	1.3	6.5	18.2	7.8	26.2	27.3	14.0	39.0	94.2	5.0	0.7	1.8
47 045	Dyer.........................	38,255	-0.2	6.3	18.4	7.6	25.0	28.1	14.6	39.6	83.8	15.8	0.7	1.4
47 047	Fayette......................	38,537	0.6	6.3	16.4	6.8	23.8	30.9	15.8	42.1	70.0	28.4	0.8	1.9
47 051	Franklin.....................	40,875	-0.5	5.6	16.0	10.7	22.1	28.0	17.7	41.8	93.4	6.0	1.4	2.8
47 053	Gibson.......................	49,729	-0.1	6.2	18.6	7.2	24.5	26.8	16.7	39.9	80.0	19.3	0.4	1.5
47 055	Giles.........................	29,265	-1.1	5.8	16.0	8.8	22.4	29.7	17.3	42.7	87.7	11.3	0.6	1.6
47 057	Grainger....................	22,724	0.0	5.6	16.3	7.6	24.0	30.0	16.4	42.7	98.7	0.7	0.0	2.3
47 059	Greene	68,901	0.0	5.2	15.8	8.2	23.5	29.3	18.0	43.0	97.0	2.6	0.5	0.7
47 063	Hamblen....................	62,736	0.2	5.9	17.6	7.9	26.4	25.8	16.4	39.1	92.8	5.0	1.0	3.4
47 065	Hamilton....................	341,248	2.4	6.1	15.4	10.0	25.9	27.6	15.0	39.3	76.2	20.9	2.2	2.5
47 069	Hardeman...................	26,839	-2.3	5.1	15.9	9.6	26.8	28.0	14.7	39.6	57.1	41.7	0.8	1.2
47 071	Hardin.......................	25,944	-0.3	5.9	15.7	8.2	22.1	29.1	19.1	43.5	95.6	4.5	0.6	0.8
47 073	Hawkins.....................	56,691	-0.4	5.3	16.6	6.9	24.2	29.7	17.3	42.8	97.3	1.6	0.6	0.7
47 077	Henderson..................	27,925	1.0	6.2	18.0	8.0	25.0	27.6	15.2	39.3	91.2	8.4	0.8	1.5
47 079	Henry........................	32,339	0.0	5.4	16.1	7.4	21.5	29.7	20.0	44.8	91.2	9.6	0.0	0.6
47 081	Hickman.....................	24,395	-2.0	5.1	17.2	8.2	26.0	29.1	14.5	40.7	94.3	5.5	0.0	1.7
47 089	Jefferson....................	51,801	1.5	5.4	16.3	10.3	22.8	28.4	16.9	41.0	96.7	3.5	0.0	1.8
47 093	Knox.........................	437,095	1.9	6.0	15.7	11.9	26.6	26.5	13.4	37.2	87.6	9.9	2.4	1.8
47 097	Lauderdale.................	27,720	-0.1	6.2	17.7	9.3	28.1	26.0	12.6	36.9	63.3	34.4	1.4	2.2
47 099	Lawrence...................	42,046	0.2	7.3	17.9	8.0	24.2	26.5	16.2	40.0	96.6	1.6	1.1	2.5
47 103	Lincoln......................	33,454	0.2	6.1	16.9	7.9	22.8	29.1	17.2	42.9	93.5	4.9	0.0	6.4
47 105	Loudon......................	49,217	2.1	5.0	15.0	6.5	21.8	29.2	22.3	46.0	96.9	1.5	0.8	2.3
47 107	McMinn.....................	52,337	0.4	5.7	16.6	8.6	23.3	28.3	17.5	41.2	94.2	4.8	0.9	1.8
47 109	McNairy....................	26,099	0.4	5.5	17.6	7.3	23.3	28.3	18.1	41.5	92.6	7.2	0.0	1.5
47 111	Macon.......................	22,399	1.1	7.0	18.0	8.2	25.3	27.2	14.3	39.4	96.3	0.7	0.7	3.3
47 113	Madison.....................	98,364	0.3	6.7	17.0	11.6	24.4	26.8	13.5	37.3	61.7	37.4	1.5	1.0
47 115	Marion......................	28,213	0.2	5.4	16.9	7.6	23.3	30.5	16.4	42.6	98.0	1.5	0.6	4.4
47 117	Marshall.....................	30,805	0.7	5.9	18.3	8.1	25.5	28.3	13.8	39.8	93.1	6.0	0.6	3.3
47 119	Maury.......................	81,491	1.0	7.0	17.1	8.4	25.8	28.2	13.5	37.8	86.2	13.6	0.8	2.0
47 123	Monroe......................	44,874	1.2	6.1	15.7	8.0	23.3	29.8	17.2	42.7	96.5	2.7	0.6	1.3
47 125	Montgomery...............	178,227	6.4	8.7	18.8	12.3	31.4	20.8	8.0	30.1	75.5	21.1	3.8	4.0
47 129	Morgan......................	21,948	-0.2	4.8	15.8	8.7	27.2	28.7	14.8	39.8	95.7	3.6	0.8	1.4
47 131	Obion........................	31,614	-1.5	5.1	17.8	8.3	23.9	27.8	17.1	41.3	88.0	11.6	0.0	1.0
47 133	Overton.....................	22,151	0.4	6.4	17.2	7.6	23.7	27.8	17.4	41.3	98.8	0.0	0.0	0.0
47 141	Putnam......................	72,845	1.0	6.1	15.4	15.1	24.2	24.3	14.9	36.3	95.2	2.7	1.6	1.7
47 143	Rhea.........................	32,020	1.2	5.7	17.7	9.4	23.7	27.2	16.2	39.9	95.9	3.7	0.0	1.0
47 145	Roane........................	53,799	-1.2	5.0	15.2	7.2	21.8	31.4	19.5	45.5	96.4	3.4	0.8	1.4
47 147	Robertson..................	66,714	0.8	6.8	18.7	7.8	26.5	28.0	12.2	38.5	89.4	8.3	0.8	3.1
47 149	Rutherford.................	269,144	4.0	7.2	18.7	12.1	30.3	23.1	8.6	32.7	82.3	13.9	3.8	2.0
47 151	Scott.........................	22,191	-0.3	6.6	18.3	8.5	25.7	26.7	14.2	38.1	99.5	0.7	0.0	0.6
47 155	Sevier........................	91,338	2.6	5.7	16.3	8.1	24.9	29.1	15.9	41.5	96.9	1.2	1.1	2.1
47 157	Shelby.......................	934,654	1.3	7.2	18.8	10.4	27.3	25.8	10.5	34.6	42.1	53.1	2.9	3.7
47 163	Sullivan.....................	156,895	-0.1	5.1	15.2	7.6	23.6	29.3	19.1	43.9	96.4	2.8	1.0	1.7
47 165	Sumner......................	163,737	3.0	6.3	18.5	8.0	26.1	27.7	13.3	39.2	90.6	7.3	1.4	1.9
47 167	Tipton.......................	61,399	0.9	6.9	20.1	9.4	25.2	27.0	11.4	37.0	79.9	18.8	2.1	1.2
47 177	Warren......................	39,865	0.0	6.4	17.8	7.3	26.9	26.1	15.5	38.8	92.6	3.5	0.7	5.9
47 179	Washington................	124,150	1.4	5.0	15.0	11.5	25.9	27.1	15.6	39.9	94.3	4.8	1.4	1.0
47 183	Weakley....................	34,931	-0.6	6.1	13.7	17.6	22.2	25.1	15.2	36.6	89.5	10.0	0.3	1.5
47 185	White........................	25,993	0.9	5.5	16.8	8.2	23.0	28.4	17.9	41.5	97.6	3.4	0.0	0.7
47 187	Williamson.................	188,432	4.8	6.4	22.3	6.1	25.7	29.4	10.1	38.6	91.3	5.0	3.8	1.8
47 189	Wilson.......................	116,756	3.8	6.0	18.7	7.6	26.0	28.8	12.9	39.6	90.8	7.3	1.4	2.0
48 000	**Texas**	25,644,550	3.2	7.5	19.5	10.3	28.0	24.0	10.6	33.8	76.5	12.6	4.7	8.6
48 001	Anderson...................	58,325	-0.4	5.3	14.2	9.0	31.4	27.3	12.8	39.0	76.2	21.7	0.7	2.7
48 005	Angelina....................	87,254	0.8	7.4	19.1	9.3	25.1	25.2	14.0	36.5	80.8	15.6	1.0	4.2
48 007	Aransas.....................	23,479	2.9	4.7	14.3	7.2	17.2	31.1	25.4	49.4	96.4	1.9	2.5	3.9
48 013	Atascosa....................	45,628	3.3	7.5	20.9	8.8	23.9	25.8	13.1	35.8	84.2	1.2	0.3	18.5
48 015	Austin.......................	28,558	0.7	6.5	18.5	8.6	22.5	28.2	15.8	40.6	87.8	10.2	0.0	4.9
48 019	Bandera.....................	20,537	0.0	4.6	14.1	4.8	19.7	35.6	21.2	49.4	96.7	0.5	0.7	4.2
48 021	Bastrop.....................	74,713	0.6	6.3	19.6	7.6	25.1	29.5	11.9	38.2	85.7	8.5	1.0	6.3
48 025	Bee..........................	32,245	2.1	5.9	15.6	11.6	32.0	24.3	10.6	36.0	76.3	9.3	0.5	16.4
48 027	Bell..........................	317,284	3.2	9.0	19.1	12.5	29.7	20.7	8.9	29.9	70.3	23.9	5.4	5.5
48 029	Bexar........................	1,754,058	3.6	7.5	19.3	11.0	28.3	23.4	10.5	33.0	77.4	8.3	3.6	13.9
48 037	Bowie.......................	92,907	0.5	6.4	17.7	8.9	26.0	26.5	14.5	37.7	72.0	25.1	1.1	3.8
48 039	Brazoria....................	319,498	3.3	7.7	19.8	8.3	28.8	25.5	9.9	35.3	77.1	13.1	6.1	5.6
48 041	Brazos......................	197,968	2.5	6.4	14.1	30.3	25.2	16.5	7.5	24.7	76.5	12.0	6.0	7.9
48 049	Brown.......................	37,985	-0.8	6.3	17.7	10.0	22.1	26.5	17.5	39.3	92.7	4.3	0.6	3.9
48 053	Burnet......................	43,214	1.5	5.4	17.2	6.6	22.8	28.5	19.4	43.8	94.9	2.5	0.0	3.4
48 055	Caldwell....................	38,419	1.7	6.9	19.3	11.8	25.1	24.6	12.4	34.7	72.7	8.0	0.0	21.6
48 057	Calhoun.....................	21,438	1.3	7.1	18.6	7.5	24.0	27.3	15.4	38.6	93.4	3.5	3.3	4.9
48 061	Cameron....................	411,930	1.9	8.8	23.9	10.2	25.2	20.6	11.3	30.7	91.8	0.7	0.8	7.7
48 067	Cass.........................	30,369	-0.9	5.9	16.9	7.4	21.8	28.2	19.8	44.0	81.4	17.9	0.5	1.6

STATE and County code	STATE or County	Percent Hispanic or Latino	Percent foreign born	Total households	Household type (percent) Family households				Nonfamily households		Percent of households with people under 18 years	Percent of households with people 60 years and over
					Total family households	Married-couple families	Male household families	Female household families	Total nonfamily households	One-person households		
	ACS table number:	B03003	C05003	B11001	B11001	B11001	B11001	B11001	B11001	B11001	B11005	B11006
	Column number:	14	15	16	17	18	19	20	21	22	23	24
	Tennessee—Cont.											
47 035	Cumberland	2.5	2.0	23,243	65.4	53.9	3.2	8.3	34.6	30.2	19.9	54.5
47 037	Davidson	9.8	11.7	254,917	55.4	36.6	4.3	14.5	44.6	35.8	27.2	27.3
47 043	Dickson	3.1	2.4	18,526	74.6	56.3	3.6	14.7	25.4	22.2	37.0	36.9
47 045	Dyer	2.7	1.9	14,825	73.8	50.5	5.3	18.0	26.2	23.0	36.7	38.8
47 047	Fayette	2.4	2.0	14,578	75.2	58.7	4.2	12.2	24.8	22.3	31.6	41.0
47 051	Franklin	2.6	1.7	15,927	71.3	55.5	3.7	12.1	28.7	23.5	29.0	42.7
47 053	Gibson	2.1	1.2	19,064	67.6	50.1	3.1	14.4	32.4	29.3	34.7	40.7
47 055	Giles	1.7	1.8	11,541	68.4	51.1	4.4	12.9	31.6	27.3	30.0	40.6
47 057	Grainger	2.4	0.8	8,831	72.0	57.5	5.8	8.7	28.0	25.0	32.5	42.7
47 059	Greene	2.6	1.7	29,192	69.5	51.9	4.4	13.3	30.5	26.2	28.3	41.5
47 063	Hamblen	10.8	7.3	24,200	69.2	51.5	3.1	14.5	30.8	26.6	34.1	39.9
47 065	Hamilton	4.6	4.9	135,018	64.7	46.9	4.4	13.4	35.3	30.0	29.0	36.9
47 069	Hardeman	1.4	0.8	8,762	67.6	42.3	6.4	18.9	32.4	29.5	26.4	43.6
47 071	Hardin	1.9	0.8	9,817	66.2	50.1	2.8	13.4	33.8	30.3	27.7	44.7
47 073	Hawkins	1.3	1.0	23,495	69.9	55.8	4.3	9.8	30.1	26.5	30.0	40.1
47 077	Henderson	2.1	0.8	11,073	70.8	51.9	6.6	12.3	29.2	27.3	36.2	38.0
47 079	Henry	1.9	1.2	13,298	67.6	52.7	4.6	10.3	32.4	28.8	28.6	43.5
47 081	Hickman	1.9	0.9	8,741	69.5	54.8	5.9	8.8	30.5	25.5	28.2	44.0
47 089	Jefferson	3.3	1.8	19,742	68.5	54.0	3.8	10.7	31.5	25.6	29.8	41.8
47 093	Knox	3.6	4.9	181,578	59.3	45.5	3.8	9.9	40.7	34.9	27.4	32.3
47 097	Lauderdale	2.2	1.9	9,932	68.9	42.1	6.1	20.8	31.1	27.7	35.1	36.9
47 099	Lawrence	1.7	2.0	15,953	70.9	58.2	3.6	9.1	29.1	26.0	34.2	39.6
47 103	Lincoln	2.7	1.2	13,517	67.1	48.9	5.4	12.8	32.9	27.8	27.8	43.4
47 105	Loudon	7.2	4.6	19,921	73.3	61.1	4.2	8.0	26.7	23.9	26.4	47.5
47 107	McMinn	2.9	2.4	20,418	70.6	55.5	4.4	10.7	29.4	26.0	29.7	42.1
47 109	McNairy	1.6	0.5	9,736	66.3	53.2	3.7	9.3	33.7	30.6	28.3	43.5
47 111	Macon	4.4	4.2	8,319	72.2	57.1	3.2	11.9	27.8	22.7	32.0	36.0
47 113	Madison	3.4	3.5	35,185	64.9	45.6	3.4	15.9	35.1	31.7	30.5	34.9
47 115	Marion	1.3	0.8	11,078	71.0	53.4	4.6	13.0	29.0	25.4	30.7	41.7
47 117	Marshall	4.6	2.9	11,857	71.7	50.4	7.0	14.3	28.3	23.5	33.7	35.3
47 119	Maury	5.0	3.2	31,800	68.1	49.1	4.8	14.2	31.9	27.5	32.5	35.1
47 123	Monroe	3.4	2.2	17,767	72.1	60.2	3.6	8.3	27.9	23.8	32.5	40.6
47 125	Montgomery	8.4	5.9	64,010	73.5	54.0	4.0	15.6	26.5	21.3	42.5	22.2
47 129	Morgan	0.6	1.1	7,416	72.1	56.8	3.7	11.6	27.9	23.5	34.3	42.5
47 131	Obion	3.2	1.6	12,205	71.9	52.2	3.8	15.8	28.1	24.5	34.2	40.4
47 133	Overton	1.6	0.7	8,826	68.8	58.0	3.5	7.3	31.2	28.9	30.4	43.5
47 141	Putnam	5.4	4.5	28,829	64.4	47.8	3.6	13.0	35.6	28.0	29.7	36.0
47 143	Rhea	3.9	2.1	12,051	66.4	49.8	3.0	13.7	33.6	26.9	30.2	40.4
47 145	Roane	1.4	2.0	22,041	66.7	52.8	3.9	9.9	33.3	28.2	26.5	43.4
47 147	Robertson	5.9	3.5	24,302	74.7	56.3	4.9	13.4	25.3	21.4	34.8	32.7
47 149	Rutherford	6.8	6.4	95,363	69.9	52.5	4.6	12.7	30.1	22.9	37.7	25.1
47 151	Scott	0.7	0.4	8,226	65.7	49.3	4.6	11.8	34.3	27.7	33.2	39.0
47 155	Sevier	5.4	5.4	36,333	71.8	56.2	4.1	11.4	28.2	22.8	32.7	38.8
47 157	Shelby	5.8	6.2	342,124	64.9	38.2	5.5	21.2	35.1	30.2	34.1	30.6
47 163	Sullivan	1.5	1.5	66,038	66.4	51.3	3.5	11.6	33.6	29.0	28.9	43.3
47 165	Sumner	4.0	3.6	60,301	74.6	57.8	4.2	12.6	25.4	21.7	37.4	33.9
47 167	Tipton	2.2	1.8	21,350	75.3	53.2	5.2	16.8	24.7	21.5	40.5	32.2
47 177	Warren	8.2	4.4	15,223	69.1	49.4	7.8	11.9	30.9	28.6	34.3	38.3
47 179	Washington	3.0	3.5	52,066	64.0	48.4	4.9	10.7	36.0	28.5	26.7	35.9
47 183	Weakley	2.1	1.0	13,741	64.8	48.4	4.0	12.4	35.2	26.8	28.8	35.7
47 185	White	1.3	0.8	9,907	70.0	54.7	3.1	12.1	30.0	28.1	31.7	43.8
47 187	Williamson	4.6	6.1	66,153	78.5	68.6	2.5	7.5	21.5	19.2	42.9	30.6
47 189	Wilson	3.4	4.0	42,697	75.0	58.7	4.2	12.1	25.0	21.6	36.4	34.9
48 000	**Texas**	38.0	16.4	8,852,441	69.7	50.1	5.1	14.4	30.3	24.9	38.3	30.2
48 001	Anderson	16.2	5.9	16,738	69.9	52.5	5.1	12.2	30.1	27.4	34.0	40.9
48 005	Angelina	20.2	7.8	31,055	73.6	51.6	7.4	14.6	26.4	22.7	36.5	37.0
48 007	Aransas	25.2	6.6	9,516	68.4	54.3	4.2	9.8	31.6	26.6	23.7	50.2
48 013	Atascosa	62.3	6.9	15,107	77.0	57.2	4.8	15.0	23.0	19.4	43.0	39.8
48 015	Austin	24.2	9.5	10,855	71.2	57.9	2.5	10.9	28.8	26.6	29.3	40.3
48 019	Bandera	16.9	3.9	8,687	70.4	60.7	3.8	6.0	29.6	26.4	23.6	46.2
48 021	Bastrop	33.2	10.9	25,097	72.6	57.5	4.5	10.6	27.4	24.2	35.8	34.4
48 025	Bee	56.6	4.8	8,940	68.1	47.7	3.3	17.2	31.9	27.9	35.9	39.9
48 027	Bell	22.2	7.9	103,230	72.6	52.5	4.1	16.0	27.4	23.0	42.4	25.5
48 029	Bexar	59.0	13.4	602,654	68.0	46.1	5.5	16.4	32.0	26.4	38.1	30.1
48 037	Bowie	6.7	2.9	34,013	66.9	45.7	4.8	16.5	33.1	29.3	33.9	38.4
48 039	Brazoria	28.2	12.4	107,526	73.7	55.8	4.7	13.2	26.3	22.0	40.6	28.6
48 041	Brazos	23.8	12.7	69,824	55.2	39.2	4.6	11.4	44.8	27.4	29.5	22.0
48 049	Brown	20.1	4.7	13,004	71.6	55.5	5.3	10.8	28.4	24.2	31.4	43.6
48 053	Burnet	20.5	6.2	16,567	70.0	55.8	2.6	11.6	30.0	26.2	29.7	45.5
48 055	Caldwell	47.9	5.6	11,766	68.6	46.0	6.2	16.4	31.4	25.5	34.7	37.0
48 057	Calhoun	47.1	11.0	7,906	74.1	57.1	4.0	13.0	25.9	21.6	34.4	37.6
48 061	Cameron	88.3	24.7	118,445	80.0	53.4	5.7	20.9	20.0	17.5	48.9	35.4
48 067	Cass	3.7	0.9	11,776	67.0	48.9	3.5	14.6	33.0	29.1	27.1	44.2

Table A-2. Counties — Who: Age, Race/Ethnicity, and Household Structure, 2010–2012—*Continued*

STATE and County code	STATE or County	Total population	Percent change 2010–2012	Under 5 years	5 to 17 years	18 to 24 years	25 to 44 years	45 to 64 years	65 years and over	Median age	White	Black	Asian, Hawaiian, or Pacific Islander	American Indian, Alaska Native, or some other race
	ACS table number:	B01003	Population estimates	B01001	B01001	B01001	B01001	B01001	B01001	B01002	B02008	B02009	B02011 + B02012	B02010 + B02013
	Column number:	1	2	3	4	5	6	7	8	9	10	11	12	13
	Texas—Cont.													
48 071	Chambers	35,654	2.6	6.5	21.6	7.8	26.8	27.7	9.6	36.2	85.8	8.6	1.5	8.1
48 073	Cherokee	51,009	0.7	7.0	18.8	9.9	23.6	25.9	14.9	37.7	82.9	15.7	0.7	2.4
48 085	Collin	811,948	5.9	7.2	21.0	7.4	30.9	25.3	8.2	35.4	76.3	9.5	13.0	4.4
48 089	Colorado	20,772	-0.9	5.8	17.6	7.6	21.3	28.0	19.7	43.2	82.6	13.2	0.0	3.7
48 091	Comal	111,768	4.6	5.5	17.6	7.3	22.5	31.0	16.1	42.8	94.4	2.2	1.3	4.8
48 097	Cooke	38,500	0.6	6.8	18.4	9.0	22.1	27.5	16.3	38.9	94.0	4.1	0.4	4.0
48 099	Coryell	76,471	2.1	8.3	19.0	12.7	33.0	19.1	8.0	30.1	75.9	17.7	5.0	7.1
48 113	Dallas	2,411,891	3.4	8.1	19.4	9.9	30.6	23.1	9.0	32.6	59.6	23.1	5.9	14.2
48 121	Denton	686,622	6.0	7.2	19.9	10.3	31.2	24.0	7.4	33.3	81.7	9.8	8.0	4.5
48 123	DeWitt	20,277	2.0	6.1	16.3	7.4	22.9	28.4	18.9	41.5	70.6	10.7	0.3	21.1
48 135	Ector	140,323	5.3	8.7	20.2	11.3	26.6	23.1	10.0	31.2	89.3	5.3	1.2	7.6
48 139	Ellis	152,258	2.4	7.0	21.4	9.1	26.0	26.0	10.5	35.2	85.4	9.7	1.0	6.3
48 141	El Paso	816,295	3.0	8.1	21.6	11.4	26.6	21.9	10.4	31.2	82.3	3.8	1.8	14.4
48 143	Erath	38,743	3.7	6.6	15.3	20.6	22.4	22.2	12.8	30.8	91.0	2.2	0.8	7.6
48 147	Fannin	33,867	-0.2	5.6	16.3	8.8	23.7	28.1	17.5	40.7	89.9	7.5	0.4	4.1
48 149	Fayette	24,657	0.7	5.5	16.2	6.4	18.9	30.7	22.3	47.5	91.2	7.4	0.0	1.4
48 157	Fort Bend	608,747	6.1	7.2	21.8	8.1	28.1	26.9	7.9	35.3	55.6	22.0	18.8	6.2
48 167	Galveston	296,100	2.7	6.8	18.4	8.8	26.2	28.1	11.6	37.3	80.7	14.5	3.7	3.4
48 171	Gillespie	25,023	1.1	5.0	14.9	6.8	17.6	28.2	27.5	49.7	96.7	0.0	0.0	3.1
48 177	Gonzales	19,900	1.2	7.4	19.8	8.6	23.7	24.8	15.7	38.3	61.6	7.6	0.0	32.2
48 179	Gray	22,721	2.3	7.4	17.5	7.3	27.1	25.0	15.7	38.0	90.5	5.5	0.6	6.3
48 181	Grayson	121,434	0.7	6.3	17.6	9.4	23.4	27.5	15.8	39.5	87.9	6.8	1.5	7.1
48 183	Gregg	122,287	0.6	7.4	17.9	10.5	25.7	25.0	13.6	35.6	75.1	20.7	1.4	3.9
48 185	Grimes	26,708	0.7	5.5	16.9	8.0	25.8	28.7	14.9	39.8	75.3	17.3	0.0	9.5
48 187	Guadalupe	136,021	5.6	6.7	20.4	8.7	26.3	26.0	11.9	36.6	87.2	7.5	2.9	5.8
48 189	Hale	36,393	0.1	8.2	20.4	11.5	25.4	22.6	11.9	32.3	88.7	5.5	0.7	11.3
48 199	Hardin	55,017	0.7	6.6	18.8	7.8	25.5	27.4	13.8	38.9	90.6	6.1	0.7	3.3
48 201	Harris	4,178,437	3.5	8.1	19.7	10.1	30.4	23.3	8.4	32.3	64.2	19.5	7.1	11.2
48 203	Harrison	66,832	2.6	6.9	18.6	10.2	24.3	26.3	13.7	36.7	74.3	23.4	0.9	2.5
48 209	Hays	163,675	6.8	6.6	17.7	17.7	26.4	22.7	8.8	30.7	82.6	4.2	2.2	13.6
48 213	Henderson	78,843	0.5	5.7	16.8	8.2	21.7	28.1	19.5	42.8	91.0	7.0	0.8	2.9
48 215	Hidalgo	793,312	3.5	9.6	24.7	10.9	26.8	18.3	9.6	28.5	91.5	0.7	1.2	7.5
48 217	Hill	35,131	0.0	6.3	17.7	8.3	21.4	27.5	18.8	42.2	90.2	7.6	0.3	2.9
48 219	Hockley	22,965	1.0	7.2	19.0	12.8	23.1	24.8	13.2	32.7	80.7	3.9	0.4	18.1
48 221	Hood	51,617	1.4	5.3	15.4	6.6	21.1	29.3	22.3	46.8	92.8	0.7	0.8	6.7
48 223	Hopkins	35,349	0.7	6.8	18.5	7.9	24.4	26.2	16.1	38.8	87.3	8.1	0.6	4.6
48 225	Houston	23,421	-2.3	5.2	14.9	6.8	24.8	28.5	19.8	43.9	67.7	27.4	0.0	5.8
48 227	Howard	35,119	1.2	6.6	15.9	9.9	28.7	25.6	13.1	37.3	83.3	7.7	0.7	12.4
48 231	Hunt	86,689	0.9	6.4	18.3	10.4	23.9	27.1	14.0	37.7	81.5	9.3	1.4	9.6
48 233	Hutchinson	21,975	-0.7	6.8	19.5	7.5	24.8	26.6	14.7	37.3	92.8	3.0	0.6	6.3
48 241	Jasper	36,005	0.3	6.8	18.0	7.7	23.3	27.3	16.8	40.4	80.3	16.9	0.6	2.9
48 245	Jefferson	252,457	-0.2	6.8	17.0	10.7	26.6	26.1	12.8	36.0	58.3	34.4	4.0	5.6
48 249	Jim Wells	41,294	2.1	8.0	20.4	9.6	23.9	24.8	13.4	34.3	92.2	1.3	0.5	7.6
48 251	Johnson	152,218	1.4	6.9	20.0	8.6	26.0	26.5	12.0	36.3	94.6	3.2	1.5	2.8
48 253	Jones	20,154	-1.2	4.1	13.1	9.9	32.2	26.7	13.9	39.9	79.4	16.5	0.8	5.0
48 257	Kaufman	105,310	2.8	7.3	21.2	8.1	27.0	25.8	10.6	35.5	86.4	10.8	1.3	4.4
48 259	Kendall	34,772	6.7	5.0	18.6	6.6	21.9	30.4	17.4	43.4	96.0	0.7	1.5	2.4
48 265	Kerr	49,689	0.3	5.1	14.6	8.3	18.9	27.7	25.5	48.0	94.1	2.1	1.1	3.8
48 273	Kleberg	32,065	-0.2	7.3	16.9	18.4	25.1	20.5	11.8	28.9	87.1	4.5	3.1	7.7
48 277	Lamar	49,877	0.0	6.4	17.4	9.6	23.3	26.3	17.0	40.2	82.5	14.6	0.9	4.7
48 281	Lampasas	19,907	2.0	5.0	18.1	7.7	23.3	29.2	16.7	41.6	89.8	6.8	1.1	4.3
48 291	Liberty	76,119	1.0	6.9	18.6	9.3	27.2	26.5	11.5	36.4	81.4	11.6	0.4	8.1
48 293	Limestone	23,504	0.7	6.5	17.3	8.4	24.9	26.7	16.4	38.4	80.3	18.0	0.2	2.7
48 303	Lubbock	283,082	2.0	7.1	17.1	17.0	25.6	22.0	11.1	30.5	81.6	8.4	2.8	10.5
48 309	McLennan	237,471	1.2	7.2	18.1	14.3	24.2	23.6	12.6	32.8	80.1	15.5	1.9	4.3
48 321	Matagorda	36,659	-0.5	7.0	18.8	10.6	21.1	27.8	14.6	38.6	82.3	12.5	2.1	5.1
48 323	Maverick	54,970	1.7	8.7	24.2	10.7	24.4	21.2	10.7	30.2	93.4	0.3	0.2	7.5
48 325	Medina	46,436	1.4	6.2	18.8	9.3	23.8	27.9	13.9	37.9	92.2	3.0	0.6	7.3
48 329	Midland	141,207	7.1	8.2	19.2	10.1	27.1	24.5	10.8	33.1	86.3	7.5	1.7	6.0
48 331	Milam	24,508	-2.2	6.9	19.3	7.5	21.6	27.6	17.1	39.7	86.1	10.8	0.0	4.7
48 339	Montgomery	472,014	5.6	7.2	20.3	8.1	27.0	26.6	10.8	36.2	89.6	4.9	3.2	4.9
48 341	Moore	22,110	1.5	8.9	23.2	9.8	27.3	21.1	9.8	30.8	84.7	3.2	7.4	7.9
48 347	Nacogdoches	65,421	2.2	6.9	16.4	20.2	22.5	22.1	11.8	29.8	77.1	19.0	1.5	3.3
48 349	Navarro	47,901	0.5	7.3	19.6	9.1	24.0	25.5	14.4	37.2	79.8	14.9	0.7	7.3
48 355	Nueces	343,697	2.2	6.9	18.7	10.5	25.8	25.8	12.3	35.2	88.0	4.7	2.3	7.4
48 361	Orange	82,444	1.2	6.4	18.4	8.7	24.5	27.8	14.1	38.5	87.6	9.0	1.3	3.0
48 363	Palo Pinto	28,020	-0.8	6.7	17.8	7.8	23.2	27.4	17.0	40.7	89.9	2.6	0.6	8.6
48 365	Panola	23,951	0.9	6.7	17.8	7.2	24.4	28.1	15.8	39.3	78.8	17.9	0.0	2.9
48 367	Parker	118,462	2.0	6.0	18.9	8.5	24.5	29.2	13.0	39.5	95.3	2.0	0.9	3.1
48 373	Polk	45,587	0.5	5.7	15.2	8.1	23.5	28.2	19.4	43.0	84.5	12.0	0.6	5.0
48 375	Potter	121,878	0.8	8.4	19.3	10.1	27.7	23.4	11.0	32.9	81.2	11.2	4.9	5.8
48 381	Randall	123,283	3.2	6.7	17.9	11.3	26.1	25.4	12.6	35.2	92.3	3.1	2.5	5.2
48 397	Rockwall	81,054	5.1	6.7	22.5	6.7	27.8	26.2	10.1	36.1	89.5	5.9	4.0	4.0
48 401	Rusk	53,688	1.3	6.4	16.7	9.7	25.7	27.3	14.3	39.1	79.9	18.3	0.6	2.2
48 407	San Jacinto	26,812	2.6	6.4	17.4	7.7	20.4	30.3	17.9	43.6	86.1	11.4	0.6	1.9
48 409	San Patricio	64,863	1.6	7.2	20.4	9.1	24.3	25.9	13.1	36.1	93.5	2.8	1.4	4.1
48 419	Shelby	25,703	2.3	7.5	19.2	10.0	21.3	26.8	15.3	38.5	79.7	18.0	0.0	2.3

Table A-2. Counties — Who: Age, Race/Ethnicity, and Household Structure, 2010–2012—*Continued*

STATE and County code	STATE or County	Percent Hispanic or Latino	Percent foreign born	Total households	Household type (percent) Family households — Total family households	Married-couple families	Male household families	Female household families	Nonfamily households — Total nonfamily households	One-person households	Percent of households with people under 18 years	Percent of households with people 60 years and over
ACS table number:		B03003	C05003	B11001	B11001	B11001	B11001	B11001	B11001	B11001	B11005	B11006
Column number:		14	15	16	17	18	19	20	21	22	23	24
	Texas—Cont.											
48 071	Chambers	19.7	8.5	12,115	81.4	67.7	7.1	6.7	18.6	15.0	42.4	28.1
48 073	Cherokee	21.2	9.5	17,455	72.4	52.9	5.4	14.1	27.6	24.1	35.1	40.0
48 085	Collin	14.9	17.7	287,166	74.2	60.3	3.8	10.1	25.8	21.2	43.5	23.6
48 089	Colorado	26.7	8.2	7,883	71.5	56.2	6.4	8.9	28.5	28.0	29.7	44.9
48 091	Comal	25.4	6.2	42,043	74.0	60.7	3.5	9.8	26.0	22.4	33.4	40.2
48 097	Cooke	16.1	7.4	14,409	71.3	54.7	4.9	11.7	28.7	25.8	30.3	40.6
48 099	Coryell	16.5	5.7	19,793	78.9	60.7	3.4	14.7	21.1	18.9	47.3	26.7
48 113	Dallas	38.6	23.2	854,403	65.3	43.4	5.8	16.0	34.7	28.7	37.3	26.4
48 121	Denton	18.5	13.7	242,679	70.7	56.0	3.8	10.9	29.3	22.3	40.9	21.6
48 123	DeWitt	32.8	2.5	6,840	66.9	48.8	4.7	13.4	33.1	31.1	30.1	43.2
48 135	Ector	54.0	13.2	49,495	69.5	48.0	6.2	15.4	30.5	24.8	40.6	28.8
48 139	Ellis	24.0	8.2	50,850	78.2	60.0	5.7	12.5	21.8	18.2	44.1	31.2
48 141	El Paso	81.7	25.7	256,148	76.0	50.2	5.5	20.3	24.0	20.5	45.3	32.0
48 143	Erath	19.5	8.5	14,340	60.3	46.9	3.5	9.9	39.7	29.0	28.2	33.8
48 147	Fannin	9.9	5.4	11,943	72.0	56.4	4.7	11.0	28.0	25.0	32.2	40.8
48 149	Fayette	19.0	8.0	10,079	65.9	56.4	2.9	6.6	34.1	31.7	28.4	47.0
48 157	Fort Bend	23.9	25.5	189,865	83.2	66.2	4.3	12.7	16.8	14.5	48.4	26.8
48 167	Galveston	22.8	9.4	109,510	68.3	51.2	4.0	13.1	31.7	26.0	35.0	32.6
48 171	Gillespie	20.5	7.4	10,496	68.3	56.4	2.8	9.1	31.7	28.8	25.5	53.9
48 177	Gonzales	48.1	12.3	6,453	71.7	51.5	4.5	15.7	28.3	25.5	36.4	40.7
48 179	Gray	24.7	7.4	8,398	67.4	53.1	3.7	10.6	32.6	29.7	34.7	41.0
48 181	Grayson	11.6	5.1	46,349	68.6	50.0	4.9	13.8	31.4	25.7	32.8	38.6
48 183	Gregg	16.9	9.7	44,819	67.7	46.2	5.4	16.1	32.3	28.0	35.0	35.4
48 185	Grimes	21.8	8.8	8,816	71.0	51.6	5.8	13.6	29.0	26.1	34.0	42.2
48 187	Guadalupe	36.0	7.0	46,485	76.5	61.0	2.9	12.5	23.5	19.9	40.4	34.9
48 189	Hale	56.9	9.6	11,616	73.2	53.6	3.6	16.0	26.8	24.1	44.4	31.2
48 199	Hardin	4.7	0.9	20,608	73.5	57.8	4.8	11.0	26.5	22.3	35.6	37.8
48 201	Harris	41.2	25.0	1,419,274	68.2	46.7	6.0	15.5	31.8	26.2	39.5	26.0
48 203	Harrison	11.5	5.6	23,670	73.0	51.9	5.7	15.4	27.0	22.3	36.1	39.8
48 209	Hays	35.9	7.1	56,282	65.2	51.0	4.7	9.5	34.8	23.2	36.3	26.7
48 213	Henderson	11.2	5.3	29,673	66.2	51.5	3.6	11.2	33.8	28.3	28.3	46.4
48 215	Hidalgo	90.8	29.4	217,706	81.9	57.4	4.8	19.6	18.1	15.4	52.6	31.6
48 217	Hill	18.7	6.9	13,501	70.0	52.8	5.0	12.3	30.0	26.0	31.0	42.3
48 219	Hockley	44.7	5.7	8,033	74.7	59.9	3.7	11.1	25.3	21.3	36.0	35.8
48 221	Hood	10.6	6.2	20,783	68.7	57.8	2.3	8.7	31.3	26.4	26.6	47.4
48 223	Hopkins	15.5	8.3	13,468	74.5	58.3	4.1	12.1	25.5	21.7	33.4	38.7
48 225	Houston	10.3	3.7	7,847	63.4	43.8	4.9	14.7	36.6	34.5	26.7	49.2
48 227	Howard	38.6	10.8	10,869	64.1	44.1	4.6	15.5	35.9	31.2	31.0	37.3
48 231	Hunt	14.1	7.0	30,939	68.8	51.9	4.5	12.4	31.2	26.5	32.9	38.2
48 233	Hutchinson	20.7	6.9	8,336	68.5	48.5	5.8	14.2	31.5	29.5	34.6	34.5
48 241	Jasper	5.9	3.7	13,369	69.6	53.3	3.2	13.2	30.4	27.1	31.0	41.4
48 245	Jefferson	17.6	10.2	92,508	64.5	40.8	6.0	17.7	35.5	30.8	32.8	35.1
48 249	Jim Wells	79.1	5.8	13,118	76.8	54.9	5.0	16.9	23.2	20.2	41.3	38.5
48 251	Johnson	18.6	7.4	52,243	77.2	59.9	5.9	11.4	22.8	18.7	41.6	32.7
48 253	Jones	25.5	4.4	5,436	64.0	50.7	2.5	10.8	36.0	31.3	28.7	50.5
48 257	Kaufman	17.7	7.2	35,181	78.3	58.8	5.1	14.3	21.7	17.7	45.6	32.7
48 259	Kendall	20.9	9.3	12,987	77.9	64.3	4.4	9.2	22.1	18.3	35.5	44.0
48 265	Kerr	24.5	7.4	20,656	65.3	51.0	3.1	11.1	34.7	30.5	23.7	51.8
48 273	Kleberg	70.4	7.4	11,081	70.8	43.9	6.8	20.0	29.2	19.3	38.2	31.8
48 277	Lamar	6.7	4.8	19,008	69.9	50.7	5.1	14.2	30.1	27.2	31.8	40.8
48 281	Lampasas	17.1	8.0	7,639	73.6	58.9	6.0	8.7	26.4	21.1	29.3	39.9
48 291	Liberty	18.7	7.7	24,813	74.5	56.0	5.2	13.3	25.5	21.7	39.1	36.0
48 293	Limestone	19.5	9.3	8,245	70.6	57.0	2.8	10.8	29.4	27.1	31.8	38.5
48 303	Lubbock	32.5	5.8	105,477	62.6	43.9	4.7	14.0	37.4	28.2	32.5	29.1
48 309	McLennan	24.1	7.9	84,399	67.6	47.3	4.5	15.8	32.4	25.4	34.9	32.6
48 321	Matagorda	38.9	11.4	13,278	72.5	52.5	3.6	16.4	27.5	24.5	35.1	41.0
48 323	Maverick	95.5	34.6	15,843	81.1	56.5	3.0	21.6	18.9	17.2	50.4	35.7
48 325	Medina	50.2	5.2	15,349	80.4	60.6	5.5	14.4	19.6	16.6	39.7	37.5
48 329	Midland	38.8	9.2	50,251	71.3	52.9	5.4	13.0	28.7	24.5	37.9	29.9
48 331	Milam	24.0	4.9	9,304	68.0	49.4	5.4	13.2	32.0	28.8	31.4	42.1
48 339	Montgomery	21.3	13.0	163,842	73.2	56.9	5.1	11.1	26.8	21.9	37.4	31.2
48 341	Moore	52.8	29.0	6,797	77.7	62.0	3.1	12.6	22.3	17.4	44.9	30.5
48 347	Nacogdoches	18.0	9.3	23,627	63.2	43.8	4.5	15.0	36.8	30.5	32.3	31.4
48 349	Navarro	24.4	11.0	17,627	70.5	49.9	5.0	15.5	29.5	24.5	35.4	36.8
48 355	Nueces	61.2	7.5	122,839	68.7	44.2	6.4	18.0	31.3	25.1	36.1	34.2
48 361	Orange	6.1	2.4	30,401	71.0	53.0	4.9	13.1	29.0	25.1	34.2	36.4
48 363	Palo Pinto	18.4	6.4	10,385	68.1	50.6	4.2	13.2	31.9	27.2	31.8	42.3
48 365	Panola	8.5	4.2	8,965	70.2	51.7	4.1	14.4	29.8	25.6	31.9	42.2
48 367	Parker	10.9	3.9	42,457	74.7	61.4	4.5	8.8	25.3	21.2	35.1	35.8
48 373	Polk	13.4	6.4	17,292	73.4	51.6	6.5	15.3	26.6	24.1	33.5	47.9
48 375	Potter	35.9	13.7	42,670	63.0	41.5	5.5	15.9	37.0	31.5	35.7	30.9
48 381	Randall	17.2	3.9	48,617	67.4	53.3	4.1	10.0	32.6	26.5	32.9	31.3
48 397	Rockwall	16.2	9.7	27,108	81.1	67.3	4.5	9.3	18.9	15.9	45.3	29.9
48 401	Rusk	14.8	6.5	17,780	69.0	51.7	4.8	12.6	31.0	27.3	32.4	40.1
48 407	San Jacinto	11.2	3.7	9,300	80.7	60.7	6.2	13.8	19.3	15.9	27.2	46.0
48 409	San Patricio	54.8	5.4	22,121	75.4	52.4	8.0	15.0	24.6	21.2	39.7	36.6
48 419	Shelby	16.8	10.9	9,884	68.5	49.1	6.1	13.3	31.5	27.4	33.8	39.2

Table A-2. Counties — Who: Age, Race/Ethnicity, and Household Structure, 2010–2012—*Continued*

STATE and County code	STATE or County	Total population	Percent change 2010–2012	Population by age (percent)						Median age	Race alone or in combination (percent)			
				Under 5 years	5 to 17 years	18 to 24 years	25 to 44 years	45 to 64 years	65 years and over		White	Black	Asian, Hawaiian, or Pacific Islander	American Indian, Alaska Native, or some other race
	ACS table number:	B01003	Population estimates	B01001	B01001	B01001	B01001	B01001	B01001	B01002	B02008	B02009	B02011 + B02012	B02010 + B02013
	Column number:	1	2	3	4	5	6	7	8	9	10	11	12	13
	Texas—Cont.													
48 423	Smith	212,694	2.1	7.0	18.5	10.8	24.9	24.3	14.6	35.7	77.6	18.8	2.0	3.2
48 427	Starr	61,421	0.8	9.5	24.0	11.0	25.7	19.2	10.7	29.1	95.3	0.0	0.2	5.2
48 439	Tarrant	1,847,884	3.5	7.7	20.0	9.5	29.1	24.4	9.2	33.5	73.2	15.8	5.7	7.8
48 441	Taylor	132,658	1.2	7.4	16.9	14.2	24.9	23.3	13.3	32.7	85.9	8.7	2.2	6.1
48 449	Titus	32,504	0.8	8.8	21.3	10.9	24.6	22.6	11.8	32.8	82.5	10.9	0.8	8.1
48 451	Tom Green	111,883	2.4	6.9	16.5	13.7	24.5	24.6	13.9	34.0	89.7	4.8	1.9	6.2
48 453	Travis	1,062,335	6.3	7.3	16.5	12.0	34.3	22.4	7.6	32.2	76.4	9.4	7.0	10.2
48 457	Tyler	21,628	-1.3	4.7	15.3	8.6	24.9	27.0	19.6	42.2	85.1	11.8	0.0	3.5
48 459	Upshur	39,713	1.6	6.5	18.2	8.0	22.9	28.5	15.9	40.3	87.4	10.2	0.0	5.0
48 463	Uvalde	26,580	1.1	7.5	21.0	10.5	22.3	23.5	15.2	35.3	96.2	0.6	0.8	2.8
48 465	Val Verde	48,848	-0.6	8.5	21.5	11.2	25.3	21.0	12.4	32.2	93.3	1.8	1.0	5.4
48 467	Van Zandt	52,569	-0.4	5.6	18.2	7.5	21.8	28.5	18.3	42.9	95.4	2.9	0.2	2.7
48 469	Victoria	87,847	2.8	7.4	19.0	9.0	24.6	26.3	13.6	36.2	86.6	7.7	1.4	9.2
48 471	Walker	68,254	0.4	4.6	11.6	19.2	28.5	25.6	10.5	35.4	74.0	23.1	1.1	3.0
48 473	Waller	43,934	2.2	7.1	17.4	17.8	22.0	24.9	10.9	32.5	73.3	25.2	0.4	4.4
48 477	Washington	33,938	1.1	5.9	15.7	11.5	20.5	27.7	18.7	41.7	79.4	17.9	1.5	2.0
48 479	Webb	255,135	3.1	9.8	25.1	11.1	27.4	18.7	7.9	28.0	94.2	0.3	0.9	5.2
48 481	Wharton	41,292	-0.1	7.2	19.3	8.7	24.0	26.1	14.9	37.2	82.8	15.2	0.2	2.8
48 485	Wichita	131,281	-0.1	6.7	16.2	13.9	25.5	24.5	13.1	34.0	84.9	11.5	2.8	3.7
48 489	Willacy	22,096	-0.5	6.7	19.6	12.1	28.2	21.4	12.1	32.4	95.9	2.0	0.0	2.7
48 491	Williamson	441,748	6.9	7.6	20.6	7.6	31.4	23.4	9.4	34.6	85.9	7.3	6.2	3.7
48 493	Wilson	43,719	3.0	5.7	19.5	7.9	23.4	30.2	13.3	40.1	92.1	2.4	0.6	7.3
48 497	Wise	59,813	2.2	6.6	19.2	8.3	24.7	28.3	13.0	39.2	96.1	1.5	0.7	3.3
48 499	Wood	42,015	0.0	5.0	15.3	7.3	18.6	29.5	24.4	48.4	91.7	5.3	0.6	3.3
49 000	**Utah**	2,814,910	2.9	9.3	22.0	11.4	28.1	19.9	9.3	29.6	90.6	1.6	4.2	6.2
49 003	Box Elder	50,163	0.1	9.6	23.7	8.2	25.4	21.7	11.4	31.5	94.7	0.5	1.8	4.7
49 005	Cache	114,454	2.0	9.8	21.5	17.6	26.6	16.7	7.9	25.7	93.3	1.0	3.2	4.7
49 007	Carbon	21,342	-0.9	8.5	18.8	10.3	23.3	25.0	14.2	34.0	94.0	1.2	1.1	5.4
49 011	Davis	311,852	2.6	9.8	24.2	9.3	28.2	20.0	8.4	29.6	92.7	1.8	3.8	4.6
49 021	Iron	46,560	1.0	8.7	21.2	17.0	23.5	19.4	10.2	27.0	94.2	0.7	2.4	5.8
49 035	Salt Lake	1,048,261	3.0	8.6	20.4	10.4	30.5	21.4	8.9	31.1	87.2	2.3	6.4	7.1
49 039	Sanpete	27,918	0.1	7.5	22.2	15.5	23.1	19.6	12.1	29.2	92.2	1.2	1.5	6.4
49 041	Sevier	20,834	-0.1	8.5	23.1	8.0	23.8	22.0	14.7	33.1	96.8	0.6	0.6	3.3
49 043	Summit	37,307	4.1	6.7	20.7	6.9	27.2	30.2	8.3	37.1	94.7	0.8	1.9	3.3
49 045	Tooele	59,221	2.3	9.6	26.4	7.8	28.5	20.3	7.3	29.9	95.1	1.1	1.9	3.2
49 047	Uintah	33,369	6.5	10.4	22.9	9.7	27.6	20.5	9.0	29.6	89.1	0.0	1.3	13.6
49 049	Utah	530,147	4.0	10.9	24.0	16.1	27.6	14.6	6.7	24.6	93.8	1.0	3.8	4.1
49 051	Wasatch	24,433	6.7	9.5	24.0	7.4	28.2	22.2	8.7	31.9	98.1	0.3	1.3	2.0
49 053	Washington	141,594	4.6	8.7	21.3	9.4	22.9	19.8	18.0	32.8	95.0	0.9	2.4	3.6
49 057	Weber	234,303	1.9	8.8	21.0	10.3	28.0	21.6	10.4	31.1	87.7	1.9	2.7	10.5
50 000	**Vermont**	626,172	0.0	5.0	15.2	10.5	23.4	30.8	15.1	42.0	97.1	1.5	1.8	1.6
50 001	Addison	36,773	-0.1	4.4	15.4	12.8	21.5	31.2	14.7	42.0	96.8	1.3	1.9	1.2
50 003	Bennington	36,877	-1.1	5.0	14.9	9.1	20.4	31.3	19.3	45.4	98.4	0.7	1.0	1.8
50 005	Caledonia	31,157	-0.2	5.3	16.2	9.5	22.3	30.7	16.0	42.1	98.0	0.9	1.0	1.7
50 007	Chittenden	157,675	1.1	4.9	14.6	15.8	25.6	27.3	11.7	36.4	94.4	2.8	3.8	1.4
50 011	Franklin	48,061	0.9	6.0	18.0	7.4	26.3	29.7	12.6	39.6	98.1	1.4	0.7	3.0
50 015	Lamoille	24,731	1.7	6.3	15.6	9.6	25.0	29.7	13.9	40.5	98.0	1.1	0.4	2.2
50 017	Orange	28,967	-0.1	4.9	15.9	8.1	22.3	33.4	15.4	43.7	98.6	0.8	0.9	1.2
50 019	Orleans	27,162	-0.4	5.3	15.4	7.7	22.6	30.5	18.4	44.2	98.5	0.9	0.5	1.6
50 021	Rutland	61,226	-1.1	4.4	14.4	10.2	21.3	32.6	17.2	44.8	98.4	0.8	0.8	1.2
50 023	Washington	59,560	-0.2	5.0	15.1	9.2	23.7	32.1	14.8	42.7	97.7	1.2	1.3	1.2
50 025	Windham	44,234	-1.1	4.7	14.7	8.3	21.8	33.6	16.9	45.3	97.4	1.6	1.7	1.8
50 027	Windsor	56,492	-0.7	4.8	14.7	6.2	22.6	33.2	18.4	45.9	98.0	1.0	1.9	1.4
51 000	**Virginia**	8,105,120	2.0	6.3	16.6	10.1	27.4	27.1	12.6	37.5	71.8	20.8	6.9	3.7
51 001	Accomack	33,294	0.4	6.1	14.9	7.4	22.2	30.0	19.3	44.4	68.7	29.3	0.0	2.6
51 003	Albemarle	100,757	3.1	5.6	15.7	12.5	24.4	26.9	14.9	38.6	84.3	11.1	5.6	1.9
51 009	Amherst	32,183	1.0	5.4	15.4	9.9	22.0	30.0	17.3	43.0	78.9	19.9	0.8	1.6
51 013	Arlington	215,481	5.6	5.7	10.2	9.0	44.0	22.3	8.7	33.7	74.1	9.5	11.5	8.4
51 015	Augusta	73,638	0.2	4.8	15.6	7.4	23.9	31.3	16.8	43.8	93.5	4.6	0.9	1.8
51 019	Bedford	69,252	1.2	4.6	17.0	6.8	22.2	32.2	17.2	44.5	92.5	6.3	1.4	0.6
51 023	Botetourt	33,124	-0.1	4.6	17.1	6.6	20.5	33.6	17.6	45.6	95.8	4.6	0.0	0.7
51 027	Buchanan	23,917	-0.7	4.5	13.9	7.7	25.0	31.7	17.2	44.2	97.4	2.2	0.0	0.0
51 031	Campbell	55,093	0.5	5.2	16.3	9.5	23.2	29.2	16.5	42.1	84.2	15.5	1.2	1.1
51 033	Caroline	28,759	1.2	6.3	16.7	8.6	26.5	28.3	13.6	39.1	68.1	31.0	1.2	2.5
51 035	Carroll	29,959	-0.6	4.8	15.6	6.8	22.3	30.4	20.1	44.3	98.6	1.4	0.0	1.2
51 041	Chesterfield	320,514	2.1	6.1	19.4	8.8	26.1	28.6	11.0	37.8	72.2	23.6	4.3	2.6
51 047	Culpeper	47,392	2.2	6.7	18.9	7.6	26.8	27.6	12.4	38.3	79.8	17.2	1.7	4.0
51 053	Dinwiddie	28,015	0.0	5.4	16.5	9.4	23.9	30.3	14.6	42.0	65.9	33.5	0.5	0.5
51 059	Fairfax	1,103,177	2.9	6.7	17.3	7.8	29.7	28.2	10.2	37.5	66.7	10.4	20.3	7.3
51 061	Fauquier	66,003	1.8	5.7	19.0	7.6	23.0	31.0	13.7	41.3	90.7	9.3	2.0	1.2
51 065	Fluvanna	25,903	0.8	5.8	16.6	5.4	26.9	28.9	16.4	42.1	83.8	16.4	1.2	1.6
51 067	Franklin	56,348	0.3	5.3	15.0	8.4	21.9	31.0	18.4	44.6	91.0	8.9	0.8	0.6
51 069	Frederick	79,483	2.3	6.0	18.5	8.0	26.2	28.2	13.0	39.3	93.5	5.3	1.7	1.6

STATE and County code	STATE or County	Percent Hispanic or Latino	Percent foreign born	Total households	Household type (percent)							Percent of households with people under 18 years	Percent of households with people 60 years and over
					Family households				Nonfamily households				
					Total family households	Married-couple families	Male household families	Female household families	Total nonfamily households	One-person households			
ACS table number:		B03003	C05003	B11001	B11001	B11001	B11001	B11001	B11001	B11001		B11005	B11006
Column number:		14	15	16	17	18	19	20	21	22		23	24
	Texas—Cont.												
48 423	Smith	17.6	8.7	79,299	67.9	49.7	4.9	13.2	32.1	26.5		34.0	36.2
48 427	Starr	95.7	32.6	15,783	83.7	55.2	5.6	22.9	16.3	14.7		53.8	35.1
48 439	Tarrant	27.1	15.8	657,094	69.0	49.4	5.2	14.4	31.0	25.9		39.3	27.2
48 441	Taylor	22.5	5.8	49,159	65.1	47.2	4.0	14.0	34.9	27.9		32.8	32.7
48 449	Titus	40.1	19.4	10,474	74.1	57.4	4.9	11.8	25.9	22.2		39.3	34.6
48 451	Tom Green	36.3	6.6	41,907	67.0	47.4	5.0	14.6	33.0	28.0		32.3	34.6
48 453	Travis	33.7	17.7	409,351	57.4	40.9	4.8	11.8	42.6	30.8		31.4	21.4
48 457	Tyler	7.1	2.2	8,249	69.5	52.2	4.9	12.3	30.5	26.8		26.7	47.6
48 459	Upshur	6.9	3.2	14,387	72.8	59.4	4.2	9.2	27.2	24.2		34.4	40.1
48 463	Uvalde	69.7	9.5	8,503	72.3	48.6	5.4	18.4	27.7	21.7		38.3	43.8
48 465	Val Verde	80.4	23.2	14,960	76.1	58.1	5.4	12.6	23.9	21.4		41.9	36.6
48 467	Van Zandt	9.5	4.3	19,093	71.2	55.6	4.2	11.4	28.8	25.5		31.2	44.7
48 469	Victoria	44.3	5.3	31,967	71.4	49.4	5.3	16.6	28.6	25.1		36.7	35.4
48 471	Walker	17.2	6.8	20,601	60.2	42.1	3.4	14.7	39.8	30.0		31.6	30.8
48 473	Waller	29.6	14.0	13,482	73.1	55.5	3.5	14.1	26.9	21.2		36.1	34.8
48 477	Washington	14.0	5.9	11,718	70.3	54.4	4.3	11.7	29.7	26.2		29.4	45.8
48 479	Webb	95.6	28.9	67,572	82.0	53.7	5.8	22.5	18.0	15.0		55.6	29.6
48 481	Wharton	38.1	8.7	14,653	67.3	43.1	7.0	17.2	32.7	30.5		33.6	39.9
48 485	Wichita	17.1	6.8	47,266	65.2	47.6	4.3	13.3	34.8	30.1		32.5	34.0
48 489	Willacy	87.2	16.2	5,396	79.5	49.9	6.4	23.2	20.5	18.1		47.1	43.8
48 491	Williamson	23.5	11.3	154,373	72.6	57.6	3.9	11.0	27.4	22.2		41.2	25.8
48 493	Wilson	38.6	5.2	15,593	81.3	66.7	3.9	10.8	18.7	14.5		39.7	36.6
48 497	Wise	17.5	6.8	20,404	78.5	65.0	2.9	10.6	21.5	18.1		38.6	35.6
48 499	Wood	8.8	3.6	16,015	70.5	56.2	4.2	10.1	29.5	24.8		23.1	53.7
49 000	**Utah**	13.2	8.3	886,032	75.0	60.9	4.2	9.9	25.0	19.6		42.5	28.0
49 003	Box Elder	8.5	3.2	16,012	81.4	67.8	4.4	9.2	18.6	16.9		42.9	33.0
49 005	Cache	10.1	7.5	35,449	75.7	64.5	2.6	8.6	24.3	16.6		42.2	23.6
49 007	Carbon	12.5	2.8	7,625	69.1	55.6	5.2	8.3	30.9	26.8		32.0	37.3
49 011	Davis	8.6	4.9	95,457	81.1	68.0	3.8	9.4	18.9	15.4		47.9	25.8
49 021	Iron	7.9	2.9	15,500	73.2	59.0	5.2	9.0	26.8	20.4		40.3	28.8
49 035	Salt Lake	17.3	12.2	344,187	70.2	54.4	4.7	11.1	29.8	23.3		39.5	27.2
49 039	Sanpete	9.4	4.7	7,933	75.7	63.6	4.2	7.9	24.3	18.8		37.4	37.2
49 041	Sevier	4.6	2.4	7,060	74.7	61.3	4.8	8.6	25.3	24.5		40.0	36.5
49 043	Summit	11.6	10.9	12,367	73.9	63.8	3.2	7.0	26.1	19.1		39.6	30.5
49 045	Tooele	11.7	3.5	18,102	80.7	64.5	5.4	10.8	19.3	15.9		49.4	26.9
49 047	Uintah	7.4	2.2	10,829	77.1	60.9	6.5	9.7	22.9	19.1		46.0	26.5
49 049	Utah	10.9	7.3	142,724	82.0	70.7	3.3	8.0	18.0	12.4		51.6	22.6
49 051	Wasatch	13.2	10.3	7,515	78.5	65.7	5.2	7.6	21.5	18.5		48.3	27.0
49 053	Washington	9.9	5.6	47,115	75.6	64.2	2.7	8.8	24.4	20.3		34.0	43.0
49 057	Weber	17.0	7.4	79,718	73.1	56.8	4.9	11.5	26.9	21.6		39.8	29.4
50 000	**Vermont**	1.5	4.1	257,887	62.5	49.2	4.2	9.0	37.5	28.2		27.7	36.7
50 001	Addison	1.8	4.2	14,106	67.5	52.7	3.6	11.1	32.5	24.6		29.4	37.5
50 003	Bennington	1.5	2.3	15,389	65.1	51.4	4.1	9.6	34.9	29.2		27.6	41.7
50 005	Caledonia	1.2	2.3	12,635	64.2	50.2	4.3	9.7	35.8	29.4		28.6	39.1
50 007	Chittenden	1.9	7.1	62,699	58.4	46.3	3.8	8.3	41.6	27.9		27.7	30.3
50 011	Franklin	1.3	2.7	18,800	69.7	53.7	6.2	9.7	30.3	23.1		34.4	32.4
50 015	Lamoille	1.4	3.9	9,889	60.9	50.6	3.6	6.8	39.1	27.4		27.6	33.3
50 017	Orange	1.1	1.8	11,794	67.2	54.3	3.7	9.1	32.8	24.9		27.5	39.7
50 019	Orleans	1.2	4.6	11,342	61.5	48.1	3.9	9.5	38.5	31.1		26.0	41.3
50 021	Rutland	1.2	2.1	26,070	63.9	50.0	5.1	8.9	36.1	27.6		26.8	40.6
50 023	Washington	1.7	3.5	24,956	61.2	46.7	4.1	10.3	38.8	29.7		27.7	36.4
50 025	Windham	1.9	3.6	19,142	60.2	47.5	4.1	8.6	39.8	30.8		26.7	40.8
50 027	Windsor	1.3	3.6	25,171	61.5	48.8	4.0	8.6	38.5	31.0		23.8	40.4
51 000	**Virginia**	8.1	11.4	3,007,690	67.3	50.8	4.2	12.3	32.7	26.5		33.0	33.7
51 001	Accomack	8.9	8.1	14,483	62.9	44.3	5.1	13.6	37.1	32.4		26.3	43.6
51 003	Albemarle	5.6	10.5	37,788	63.6	52.9	2.5	8.2	36.4	30.2		29.6	36.9
51 009	Amherst	2.0	1.8	12,624	66.5	48.4	3.7	14.4	33.5	28.8		28.0	40.8
51 013	Arlington	15.2	23.5	93,236	46.1	36.5	3.1	6.5	53.9	40.2		20.0	21.9
51 015	Augusta	2.2	1.8	28,281	74.0	59.7	4.9	9.5	26.0	22.6		30.2	41.9
51 019	Bedford	1.7	1.7	27,146	71.4	60.1	4.3	7.0	28.6	23.8		28.4	41.4
51 023	Botetourt	1.2	2.0	12,663	79.4	69.6	2.4	7.4	20.6	18.0		29.6	43.0
51 027	Buchanan	0.5	0.5	9,411	70.1	54.9	4.0	11.2	29.9	25.0		28.3	40.6
51 031	Campbell	1.8	1.7	21,452	71.6	53.1	3.9	14.6	28.4	23.9		31.0	39.4
51 033	Caroline	3.5	3.4	10,686	75.0	52.6	7.1	15.3	25.0	20.0		34.8	38.8
51 035	Carroll	2.8	1.5	12,720	68.0	54.5	4.4	9.1	32.0	28.8		26.7	44.7
51 041	Chesterfield	7.4	8.2	112,630	72.6	55.8	4.0	12.8	27.4	23.1		38.0	32.1
51 047	Culpeper	8.8	6.3	16,175	72.4	56.0	4.6	11.9	27.6	22.1		38.2	35.7
51 053	Dinwiddie	2.5	1.9	9,736	73.0	52.4	3.8	16.7	27.0	22.5		32.9	38.3
51 059	Fairfax	15.9	29.7	390,130	71.1	57.7	3.9	9.4	28.9	22.9		37.0	30.9
51 061	Fauquier	6.5	5.4	22,768	74.4	61.9	3.7	8.9	25.6	21.0		34.2	37.3
51 065	Fluvanna	3.1	3.9	9,582	73.3	60.9	3.0	9.4	26.7	22.3		30.0	41.6
51 067	Franklin	2.6	2.5	23,022	71.2	58.5	2.8	10.0	28.8	24.6		29.9	43.4
51 069	Frederick	6.8	5.3	28,866	74.3	60.2	4.2	9.9	25.7	18.2		37.0	36.4

Table A-2. Counties — Who: Age, Race/Ethnicity, and Household Structure, 2010–2012—*Continued*

STATE and County code	STATE or County	Total population	Percent change 2010–2012	Population by age (percent) Under 5 years	5 to 17 years	18 to 24 years	25 to 44 years	45 to 64 years	65 years and over	Median age	Race alone or in combination (percent) White	Black	Asian, Hawaiian, or Pacific Islander	American Indian, Alaska Native, or some other race
ACS table number:		B01003	Population estimates	B01001	B01001	B01001	B01001	B01001	B01001	B01002	B02008	B02009	B02011 + B02012	B02010 + B02013
Column number:		1	2	3	4	5	6	7	8	9	10	11	12	13
	Virginia—Cont.													
51 073	Gloucester	36,896	-0.1	4.9	16.7	7.8	23.4	31.2	16.0	42.2	89.8	9.8	1.6	1.0
51 075	Goochland	21,530	-2.0	4.0	16.0	4.9	22.9	35.7	16.5	46.0	78.6	20.9	0.0	0.3
51 083	Halifax	36,020	-0.8	5.8	16.3	7.5	20.5	29.9	20.0	44.9	60.9	37.7	0.0	1.5
51 085	Hanover	100,255	0.7	5.2	19.0	8.2	23.2	30.7	13.6	41.3	87.9	10.1	1.8	2.3
51 087	Henrico	310,972	2.4	6.5	17.3	8.3	28.4	26.8	12.7	37.6	61.7	30.9	7.9	2.3
51 089	Henry	53,460	-2.1	5.4	15.0	7.7	21.9	29.9	20.1	45.0	76.3	22.9	0.7	2.1
51 093	Isle of Wight	35,326	0.3	4.8	17.1	7.9	20.9	33.8	15.5	44.5	73.1	25.4	1.6	2.4
51 095	James City	68,048	2.4	4.9	16.2	6.9	21.3	29.5	21.3	45.7	82.4	14.3	3.3	1.5
51 099	King George	24,122	3.6	7.2	19.9	8.6	26.0	27.9	10.4	36.4	78.3	20.5	1.9	0.5
51 105	Lee	25,534	-0.2	5.1	14.7	7.8	27.1	28.6	16.8	41.2	96.2	2.6	0.6	1.7
51 107	Loudoun	326,222	6.8	8.5	21.7	6.2	32.1	24.6	7.0	35.0	72.3	9.0	17.4	5.9
51 109	Louisa	33,367	0.5	5.8	15.6	7.1	23.8	32.3	15.4	43.6	80.2	18.6	0.8	1.8
51 117	Mecklenburg	32,335	-2.8	4.7	14.7	7.5	21.2	30.6	21.3	46.4	61.3	37.4	1.0	1.8
51 121	Montgomery	94,800	0.6	4.4	11.5	31.1	23.2	19.8	10.1	26.7	89.1	4.6	6.7	1.5
51 137	Orange	33,907	2.1	5.7	16.5	7.1	22.7	30.1	17.9	43.3	83.5	15.1	0.6	2.7
51 139	Page	23,969	-0.6	5.4	15.6	7.8	23.6	29.3	18.3	44.6	97.5	2.8	0.9	0.8
51 143	Pittsylvania	63,244	-1.3	4.8	15.9	7.2	22.5	31.6	17.9	44.7	76.9	22.7	0.9	1.6
51 145	Powhatan	28,095	0.2	4.6	16.9	7.4	25.6	32.5	13.1	42.2	85.6	13.9	0.7	1.0
51 147	Prince Edward	22,955	-0.5	4.4	13.0	25.8	18.9	23.6	14.3	34.4	63.7	34.7	1.4	1.2
51 149	Prince George	36,393	3.8	5.2	17.1	10.4	29.0	27.3	11.0	38.0	62.1	33.0	2.9	4.1
51 153	Prince William	418,759	5.8	8.1	20.4	8.7	30.7	25.0	7.1	33.6	65.7	22.6	10.0	7.3
51 155	Pulaski	34,768	-0.2	4.9	13.9	7.0	24.9	30.3	19.0	44.6	93.5	7.0	0.2	0.0
51 161	Roanoke	92,748	0.5	4.9	16.4	7.2	23.7	29.9	17.9	43.5	91.0	6.0	3.4	1.2
51 163	Rockbridge	22,384	0.6	5.0	14.1	7.6	20.5	31.1	21.7	47.3	95.9	3.9	0.7	1.1
51 165	Rockingham	76,946	1.4	6.0	17.3	9.3	22.8	28.3	16.3	40.7	96.2	2.3	0.9	1.9
51 167	Russell	28,673	-1.4	5.6	14.3	7.8	24.0	31.0	17.2	43.0	98.0	2.0	0.0	0.0
51 169	Scott	22,952	-1.4	4.8	14.1	7.3	23.8	29.8	20.1	45.0	98.5	1.5	0.0	0.0
51 171	Shenandoah	42,306	1.2	5.7	15.9	7.1	23.3	29.1	18.9	43.3	95.8	2.8	0.8	2.1
51 173	Smyth	31,949	-1.4	5.6	14.7	7.9	23.9	29.2	18.7	43.7	97.2	2.7	0.5	0.4
51 177	Spotsylvania	124,345	2.3	6.5	20.5	8.4	26.7	27.5	10.4	36.7	76.4	16.6	3.3	6.2
51 179	Stafford	132,152	3.5	6.6	21.4	9.9	27.4	27.0	7.7	34.6	73.3	18.6	4.8	7.0
51 185	Tazewell	44,714	-2.0	5.3	14.7	7.7	24.9	30.0	17.4	43.0	97.0	3.6	0.9	0.5
51 187	Warren	37,778	1.4	6.3	17.1	8.4	25.1	29.7	13.3	40.1	94.6	5.5	2.3	0.8
51 191	Washington	54,752	0.6	4.9	14.6	8.2	23.8	30.2	18.2	44.3	97.6	1.8	0.5	1.0
51 195	Wise	41,287	-1.6	5.4	15.1	10.4	27.3	27.7	14.2	39.3	93.6	5.8	0.6	1.0
51 197	Wythe	29,226	0.1	5.1	15.4	7.4	24.3	29.8	17.9	43.3	95.5	3.8	0.0	0.0
51 199	York	65,791	1.5	5.6	19.8	9.1	23.0	30.1	12.5	39.8	79.9	15.0	6.7	1.9
51 510	Alexandria city	143,737	3.9	7.3	10.0	6.8	42.2	24.4	9.3	35.6	67.2	23.2	8.1	5.7
51 540	Charlottesville city	43,644	0.9	5.4	9.8	26.8	30.2	18.7	9.1	28.5	71.6	21.0	8.0	1.4
51 550	Chesapeake city	225,844	2.1	6.4	19.0	9.4	26.5	28.0	10.8	36.8	64.8	31.4	4.4	2.5
51 590	Danville city	42,888	0.3	6.6	15.1	9.8	21.6	27.9	19.0	42.3	48.9	49.5	1.2	2.0
51 600	Fairfax city	23,010	3.7	6.3	13.9	9.7	29.1	26.5	14.5	39.1	73.9	6.3	17.4	6.2
51 630	Fredericksburg city	25,869	11.7	7.4	13.0	21.5	27.5	20.9	9.7	28.3	69.2	24.7	3.8	6.1
51 650	Hampton city	136,855	-0.5	6.4	16.1	12.7	25.5	26.7	12.6	35.7	45.1	52.1	3.3	2.6
51 660	Harrisonburg city	49,878	3.9	5.0	10.5	40.0	22.6	14.2	7.7	22.7	87.5	8.8	4.7	1.8
51 670	Hopewell city	22,492	-1.3	9.3	17.1	11.1	23.1	24.3	15.1	35.8	59.1	42.2	0.0	0.0
51 680	Lynchburg city	76,377	1.8	6.1	13.6	22.5	22.3	21.8	13.7	30.2	67.2	30.9	3.0	2.5
51 683	Manassas city	39,394	6.1	8.3	19.6	10.1	29.9	24.8	7.3	32.4	77.7	16.2	5.9	4.1
51 700	Newport News city	180,623	-0.1	7.5	16.6	13.5	27.7	24.0	10.8	32.4	54.0	42.9	4.7	3.7
51 710	Norfolk city	244,118	1.2	6.9	13.9	19.7	28.7	21.3	9.4	29.6	50.8	45.0	5.1	3.3
51 730	Petersburg city	32,213	-1.9	7.2	14.1	11.7	23.8	28.2	15.0	36.0	19.0	80.8	0.5	0.4
51 740	Portsmouth city	95,915	1.0	7.5	16.3	10.8	26.8	25.3	13.3	35.1	43.0	55.0	1.7	3.1
51 760	Richmond city	206,936	2.9	6.5	12.5	16.7	29.6	23.5	11.2	32.3	45.9	51.5	2.9	3.7
51 770	Roanoke city	96,958	0.7	7.3	14.4	8.7	28.4	27.1	14.2	38.3	68.6	30.6	2.2	3.0
51 775	Salem city	24,868	0.5	5.5	14.4	13.5	22.9	27.5	16.3	40.1	88.0	8.4	2.0	2.3
51 790	Staunton city	23,941	0.4	5.6	13.3	10.4	24.3	26.4	20.0	42.7	86.4	14.3	1.1	1.7
51 800	Suffolk city	84,942	0.3	6.8	18.8	8.6	26.2	27.9	11.8	38.4	54.9	44.4	2.4	2.5
51 810	Virginia Beach city	443,102	1.8	6.6	17.0	10.8	29.1	25.6	10.9	34.8	72.1	21.7	8.3	2.8
51 820	Waynesboro city	21,082	0.3	6.7	18.5	7.4	25.6	25.1	16.7	38.1	83.7	15.4	1.2	2.1
51 840	Winchester city	26,537	2.5	6.4	16.2	11.8	27.3	24.9	13.5	35.1	82.9	11.5	2.6	5.0
53 000	**Washington**	6,821,303	2.3	6.5	16.7	9.7	27.4	27.0	12.7	37.3	82.6	4.9	10.3	7.4
53 003	Asotin	21,828	0.9	5.9	15.5	8.0	21.9	28.7	19.9	43.6	96.9	0.7	1.0	3.8
53 005	Benton	179,809	3.3	7.4	19.5	9.2	25.5	26.4	12.1	35.6	84.4	1.9	3.9	13.0
53 007	Chelan	73,221	1.3	6.7	18.1	8.6	23.0	28.2	15.4	38.8	91.2	0.6	2.4	8.3
53 009	Clallam	71,737	0.5	4.8	13.3	7.0	20.1	30.3	24.5	49.4	91.4	1.4	3.0	8.2
53 011	Clark	432,801	2.6	6.7	19.3	8.4	26.7	26.8	12.1	37.0	89.1	3.2	6.9	5.3
53 015	Cowlitz	102,291	-0.4	6.4	17.5	8.1	23.3	28.4	16.2	40.5	94.5	1.3	2.9	6.2
53 017	Douglas	38,897	2.1	7.1	19.6	8.4	24.2	26.4	14.2	36.9	77.6	0.8	1.1	23.7
53 021	Franklin	82,715	8.5	10.5	23.4	10.2	29.7	19.1	7.2	28.5	59.7	2.6	2.7	38.0
53 025	Grant	90,714	2.3	8.9	21.7	9.9	25.0	22.4	12.1	32.0	70.7	1.8	2.3	28.3
53 027	Grays Harbor	72,289	-1.6	5.7	15.7	8.7	23.4	29.8	16.7	42.2	89.1	1.8	2.7	10.3
53 029	Island	78,970	0.6	5.7	14.4	8.8	22.3	29.6	19.1	43.9	89.7	3.4	7.8	4.7

STATE and County code	STATE or County	Percent Hispanic or Latino	Percent foreign born	Total households	Household type (percent)							Percent of households with people under 18 years	Percent of households with people 60 years and over
					Family households				Nonfamily households				
					Total family households	Married-couple families	Male household families	Female household families	Total nonfamily households	One-person households			
	ACS table number:	B03003	C05003	B11001	B11001	B11001	B11001	B11001	B11001	B11001		B11005	B11006
	Column number:	14	15	16	17	18	19	20	21	22		23	24
	Virginia—Cont.												
51 073	Gloucester	2.6	1.5	13,685	74.9	58.8	4.0	12.1	25.1	21.7		32.2	40.3
51 075	Goochland	2.1	2.6	8,037	81.4	72.5	2.0	6.9	18.6	16.9		28.1	41.0
51 083	Halifax	1.7	0.4	14,558	64.4	46.2	1.9	16.3	35.6	33.8		26.8	45.2
51 085	Hanover	2.2	3.2	36,329	76.6	63.5	4.5	8.6	23.4	19.6		35.8	35.5
51 087	Henrico	5.0	11.8	123,131	64.7	46.3	4.1	14.3	35.3	29.3		33.8	32.6
51 089	Henry	4.9	3.3	22,522	66.0	48.2	4.0	13.8	34.0	30.9		25.3	43.7
51 093	Isle of Wight	2.0	2.4	13,353	78.0	64.1	3.3	10.6	22.0	19.0		32.0	39.5
51 095	James City	4.8	7.8	26,836	71.1	58.5	2.9	9.6	28.9	23.9		26.4	47.2
51 099	King George	3.7	1.7	8,023	75.0	63.2	3.2	8.7	25.0	19.9		38.6	29.3
51 105	Lee	1.7	1.1	9,799	65.9	49.9	8.5	7.6	34.1	30.9		29.5	42.1
51 107	Loudoun	12.6	22.8	106,027	78.4	65.6	4.0	8.9	21.6	16.7		49.8	22.2
51 109	Louisa	2.4	3.2	12,728	71.6	57.7	4.5	9.4	28.4	23.2		28.7	38.9
51 117	Mecklenburg	2.5	3.1	13,132	62.0	44.9	2.9	14.2	38.0	34.6		24.9	48.6
51 121	Montgomery	2.8	9.1	34,718	55.6	44.8	2.9	7.9	44.4	26.3		24.2	26.9
51 137	Orange	3.6	4.0	12,239	75.2	59.5	3.9	11.7	24.8	20.8		31.5	44.7
51 139	Page	1.7	1.8	9,584	70.7	55.1	4.4	11.2	29.3	23.7		29.2	43.1
51 143	Pittsylvania	2.2	2.1	25,845	71.2	53.0	5.3	12.9	28.8	24.9		29.4	43.3
51 145	Powhatan	1.8	2.8	9,405	78.3	65.1	3.3	9.9	21.7	18.3		35.8	39.5
51 147	Prince Edward	1.7	1.6	7,238	64.0	45.2	4.5	14.3	36.0	30.9		27.3	43.0
51 149	Prince George	6.3	3.2	10,595	79.9	62.0	6.7	11.2	20.1	18.5		38.7	33.9
51 153	Prince William	20.6	21.1	132,261	77.2	59.1	5.7	12.4	22.8	17.8		46.3	24.7
51 155	Pulaski	1.3	1.1	15,275	65.6	48.3	3.9	13.5	34.4	30.1		23.7	41.7
51 161	Roanoke	2.2	5.0	38,024	67.7	54.2	4.0	9.5	32.3	28.3		29.7	40.5
51 163	Rockbridge	1.4	1.9	9,181	69.7	56.5	4.2	9.0	30.3	26.7		23.6	49.4
51 165	Rockingham	5.5	4.5	29,063	71.9	57.4	4.0	10.6	28.1	23.3		31.1	40.1
51 167	Russell	0.4	0.9	10,824	66.2	51.1	5.7	9.4	33.8	30.5		23.8	42.0
51 169	Scott	0.5	0.7	9,392	69.3	56.9	4.0	8.3	30.7	28.4		26.6	45.2
51 171	Shenandoah	6.2	4.1	16,780	68.1	52.4	5.7	10.0	31.9	26.1		28.6	42.9
51 173	Smyth	1.7	1.4	12,550	69.8	50.0	6.0	13.8	30.2	27.0		28.0	42.6
51 177	Spotsylvania	7.8	6.9	41,892	80.2	61.9	5.2	13.1	19.8	15.4		42.1	32.1
51 179	Stafford	9.6	8.7	41,760	79.9	65.6	4.0	10.3	20.1	16.3		44.7	24.6
51 185	Tazewell	0.7	0.4	18,308	69.2	53.1	4.7	11.5	30.8	26.6		29.2	41.4
51 187	Warren	3.6	3.7	14,334	70.2	53.7	6.4	10.1	29.8	24.7		34.9	34.9
51 191	Washington	1.3	1.1	22,879	68.5	53.1	4.6	10.8	31.5	27.1		29.6	43.2
51 195	Wise	1.2	1.9	15,539	66.1	48.1	5.1	12.9	33.9	28.8		29.8	41.5
51 197	Wythe	1.0	1.0	11,807	67.7	50.6	4.9	12.2	32.3	28.8		26.0	44.2
51 199	York	4.8	7.0	23,983	79.3	63.4	2.7	13.2	20.7	17.8		39.2	33.3
51 510	Alexandria city	16.4	26.6	64,754	47.6	35.8	3.5	8.3	52.4	42.9		21.5	23.0
51 540	Charlottesville city	5.0	12.7	17,142	41.9	29.0	3.5	9.5	58.1	37.8		20.5	25.3
51 550	Chesapeake city	4.6	5.1	78,867	74.4	54.9	4.8	14.7	25.6	21.2		38.9	31.3
51 590	Danville city	3.0	3.3	18,481	61.3	35.6	4.3	21.3	38.7	35.4		28.7	42.2
51 600	Fairfax city	16.0	23.9	8,358	67.1	55.3	4.2	7.7	32.9	21.4		29.8	35.1
51 630	Fredericksburg city	10.9	8.1	9,629	54.3	33.9	3.7	16.7	45.7	36.4		29.9	27.9
51 650	Hampton city	4.8	4.6	51,699	64.4	42.7	4.1	17.6	35.6	29.7		30.9	32.3
51 660	Harrisonburg city	16.6	15.8	15,268	49.8	38.1	5.6	6.1	50.2	24.8		25.1	21.6
51 670	Hopewell city	6.5	3.3	8,593	61.3	35.9	5.5	19.9	38.7	34.4		32.9	40.1
51 680	Lynchburg city	3.1	4.5	28,363	56.2	38.5	3.1	14.6	43.8	35.9		29.0	35.4
51 683	Manassas city	31.9	25.9	12,204	75.8	53.9	5.9	15.9	24.2	19.4		42.9	23.5
51 700	Newport News city	7.7	7.2	69,003	63.1	40.1	5.3	17.7	36.9	30.8		32.7	29.2
51 710	Norfolk city	6.9	6.5	85,626	57.3	34.1	5.4	17.8	42.7	32.8		31.0	27.9
51 730	Petersburg city	3.8	3.2	12,031	58.6	27.4	3.3	28.0	41.4	34.7		24.2	40.1
51 740	Portsmouth city	3.2	2.4	36,752	64.7	36.6	5.8	22.3	35.3	30.7		32.3	35.2
51 760	Richmond city	6.3	7.5	83,747	46.5	23.5	4.5	18.4	53.5	41.8		23.8	29.5
51 770	Roanoke city	5.6	7.0	41,819	55.0	33.3	4.3	17.4	45.0	38.6		25.8	35.5
51 775	Salem city	2.6	6.6	9,820	61.5	45.4	3.1	13.1	38.5	33.0		29.4	36.0
51 790	Staunton city	2.4	3.5	10,809	58.1	41.2	3.6	13.3	41.9	36.7		26.3	39.3
51 800	Suffolk city	3.0	2.7	30,657	74.4	53.8	4.3	16.3	25.6	21.5		38.4	33.8
51 810	Virginia Beach city	6.9	8.8	164,066	68.4	51.0	3.5	14.0	31.6	23.7		35.3	29.7
51 820	Waynesboro city	6.5	3.7	8,592	65.3	44.4	4.2	16.8	34.7	30.4		32.5	40.7
51 840	Winchester city	15.7	11.6	10,668	55.4	37.7	4.5	13.2	44.6	33.5		28.6	33.4
53 000	**Washington**	11.5	13.3	2,624,689	64.2	49.4	4.4	10.4	35.8	28.0		31.4	33.1
53 003	Asotin	3.2	1.5	9,298	62.2	47.2	4.4	10.6	37.8	33.2		26.4	45.7
53 005	Benton	18.9	9.7	65,278	68.2	54.0	4.4	9.7	31.8	26.7		33.8	33.2
53 007	Chelan	26.4	12.0	26,915	69.3	53.5	4.7	11.1	30.7	24.7		31.2	40.5
53 009	Clallam	5.2	5.3	30,750	59.9	49.3	3.0	7.6	40.1	30.9		20.3	49.5
53 011	Clark	7.8	10.0	158,539	68.8	52.9	4.5	11.4	31.2	24.1		35.8	33.6
53 015	Cowlitz	8.0	4.4	39,823	67.1	50.2	5.3	11.6	32.9	26.7		30.2	40.0
53 017	Douglas	29.0	16.1	14,207	76.6	59.2	6.6	10.8	23.4	17.1		36.4	36.2
53 021	Franklin	51.0	25.5	23,466	76.1	55.5	6.8	13.8	23.9	17.9		49.9	27.2
53 025	Grant	38.8	18.4	30,367	72.8	53.9	5.8	13.2	27.2	23.4		39.9	33.6
53 027	Grays Harbor	8.9	6.1	27,582	64.0	46.2	7.2	10.6	36.0	29.2		26.6	43.6
53 029	Island	5.8	7.6	32,698	68.5	58.0	2.6	7.9	31.5	26.3		26.9	42.9

STATE and County code	STATE or County	Total population	Percent change 2010–2012	Population by age (percent)						Median age	Race alone or in combination (percent)			
				Under 5 years	5 to 17 years	18 to 24 years	25 to 44 years	45 to 64 years	65 years and over		White	Black	Asian, Hawaiian, or Pacific Islander	American Indian, Alaska Native, or some other race
ACS table number:		B01003	Population estimates	B01001	B01001	B01001	B01001	B01001	B01001	B01002	B02008	B02009	B02011 + B02012	B02010 + B02013
Column number:		1	2	3	4	5	6	7	8	9	10	11	12	13
	Washington—Cont.													
53 031	Jefferson	29,883	-0.2	3.6	10.8	5.3	17.4	35.4	27.6	54.1	93.8	1.3	5.4	5.2
53 033	King	1,972,284	3.6	6.2	15.0	9.1	31.6	26.8	11.2	37.1	73.7	7.7	18.7	5.7
53 035	Kitsap	253,763	1.3	5.8	16.1	10.6	24.7	29.1	13.8	39.3	87.5	4.1	9.4	6.1
53 037	Kittitas	41,430	1.6	4.8	13.9	21.6	21.9	24.7	13.1	33.4	91.3	1.5	3.8	5.8
53 039	Klickitat	20,602	1.5	5.9	16.3	6.2	22.2	30.9	18.6	44.0	92.6	1.1	1.5	6.5
53 041	Lewis	75,594	0.2	5.9	16.9	8.6	22.3	28.6	17.7	42.3	95.4	1.2	1.3	6.1
53 045	Mason	60,869	0.1	5.4	14.9	7.5	22.8	30.5	19.1	44.7	91.0	2.4	2.5	9.9
53 047	Okanogan	41,288	0.0	6.6	16.6	7.5	21.6	30.2	17.6	42.4	80.1	0.9	2.7	21.1
53 049	Pacific	20,798	-1.6	4.7	13.3	6.4	17.8	32.7	25.2	50.7	91.9	1.0	3.0	8.4
53 053	Pierce	803,585	2.0	7.0	17.6	10.0	27.6	26.3	11.4	35.8	81.4	9.4	11.0	5.8
53 057	Skagit	117,691	1.0	6.4	17.0	8.4	23.8	27.7	16.7	40.2	90.7	1.2	3.3	8.1
53 061	Snohomish	723,763	2.4	6.5	17.4	8.8	28.4	28.1	10.8	37.4	84.2	3.7	12.1	5.3
53 063	Spokane	473,793	0.8	6.3	16.6	11.3	25.5	26.9	13.4	37.0	92.5	3.0	4.2	4.4
53 065	Stevens	43,515	0.1	5.0	18.2	6.2	19.8	32.6	18.1	45.5	93.8	0.2	1.6	8.1
53 067	Thurston	255,927	2.1	6.1	16.5	9.4	26.6	27.9	13.5	38.3	87.8	4.2	8.5	4.7
53 071	Walla Walla	59,266	0.8	6.3	16.0	13.2	23.9	25.7	15.0	36.8	91.6	2.5	2.7	6.4
53 073	Whatcom	203,482	1.8	5.4	15.1	14.5	24.8	26.4	13.7	36.6	90.3	1.6	5.7	6.2
53 075	Whitman	45,492	4.0	4.6	10.2	37.5	20.8	17.5	9.5	24.1	88.6	2.9	10.5	2.7
53 077	Yakima	245,797	1.1	8.8	21.4	10.0	25.2	22.7	11.8	32.3	79.7	1.4	1.9	20.4
54 000	**West Virginia**	1,854,775	0.1	5.5	15.2	9.3	24.5	29.1	16.4	41.4	95.6	4.0	1.0	1.6
54 003	Berkeley	105,863	2.3	6.7	18.1	7.8	28.2	27.5	11.8	38.0	90.2	8.7	1.5	2.7
54 005	Boone	24,509	-0.5	6.1	16.6	7.5	24.9	30.4	14.6	41.3	99.0	1.5	0.0	0.0
54 009	Brooke	23,928	-0.6	4.5	14.2	9.8	21.3	30.9	19.3	45.1	97.3	1.5	1.0	0.0
54 011	Cabell	96,651	0.6	5.8	14.0	12.9	25.3	26.0	16.0	38.7	94.1	6.3	1.4	1.1
54 019	Fayette	45,932	-0.3	5.5	15.0	7.7	24.5	29.8	17.3	42.5	94.6	5.5	0.1	1.0
54 025	Greenbrier	35,684	0.8	5.1	14.6	7.9	22.6	30.3	19.5	44.8	97.2	3.2	0.8	0.9
54 027	Hampshire	23,823	-1.0	2.8	19.0	7.1	23.5	30.7	16.8	43.3	98.4	1.6	0.0	0.6
54 029	Hancock	30,474	-1.1	5.1	15.0	6.3	23.5	31.4	18.8	45.1	98.1	1.7	0.0	2.2
54 033	Harrison	69,220	-0.1	5.8	15.9	7.2	25.2	29.1	16.8	41.7	97.1	2.5	0.7	1.0
54 035	Jackson	29,258	-0.1	6.0	16.3	7.5	23.5	28.6	18.1	41.9	99.3	1.0	0.0	1.3
54 037	Jefferson	54,162	1.6	5.9	17.6	10.4	25.2	28.6	12.3	38.8	90.5	8.5	1.7	2.9
54 039	Kanawha	192,432	-0.4	5.6	14.9	8.0	24.6	29.9	17.0	42.2	94.3	5.3	1.6	5.5
54 043	Lincoln	21,632	-0.2	5.8	16.7	7.3	25.0	29.8	15.4	42.1	99.8	0.4	0.0	0.7
54 045	Logan	36,449	-1.5	5.1	15.4	7.4	25.7	30.7	15.7	42.4	97.0	2.6	0.4	0.3
54 047	McDowell	21,686	-3.3	5.7	14.4	7.7	23.7	31.9	16.7	44.2	89.5	10.4	0.5	0.0
54 049	Marion	56,577	0.3	5.3	14.8	10.4	24.5	28.1	17.0	41.4	96.1	4.2	0.7	0.7
54 051	Marshall	32,867	-1.2	5.2	15.2	7.5	22.9	31.2	17.9	44.1	98.4	1.1	0.4	0.3
54 053	Mason	27,268	-0.5	6.0	16.2	6.9	23.8	29.6	17.4	42.3	99.3	2.0	0.0	0.8
54 055	Mercer	62,411	0.4	6.0	14.7	8.8	23.6	28.7	18.1	42.0	92.9	6.8	0.7	1.1
54 057	Mineral	28,114	-1.1	5.5	15.0	9.8	23.1	28.9	17.7	42.0	96.4	5.2	0.0	0.0
54 059	Mingo	26,503	-2.5	6.1	15.9	7.5	25.5	30.9	14.0	41.5	97.3	2.6	0.0	0.7
54 061	Monongalia	98,573	3.7	4.6	11.3	26.5	25.8	21.6	10.1	29.3	92.7	4.7	3.6	1.0
54 067	Nicholas	26,205	0.0	5.8	15.1	7.4	23.5	30.7	17.4	43.6	99.2	0.0	0.0	0.0
54 069	Ohio	44,236	-0.8	5.3	13.9	11.4	21.5	29.7	18.3	43.0	94.8	4.9	1.1	0.8
54 077	Preston	33,651	0.9	5.2	14.2	7.3	27.3	29.9	16.0	41.9	96.3	3.2	0.3	1.3
54 079	Putnam	56,024	1.5	5.7	17.5	6.4	25.8	29.8	14.9	41.4	97.7	0.9	1.5	0.6
54 081	Raleigh	79,033	0.2	6.1	14.6	8.3	25.7	29.0	16.4	40.9	89.4	9.0	1.3	1.5
54 083	Randolph	29,397	0.0	5.2	14.4	8.5	24.2	29.4	18.3	44.0	98.7	1.2	0.0	1.1
54 097	Upshur	24,332	0.9	6.0	14.6	11.9	22.5	28.0	17.0	42.1	98.5	1.3	0.0	0.7
54 099	Wayne	41,986	-1.8	5.4	16.6	7.9	24.5	28.7	16.9	42.0	99.3	0.5	0.5	0.8
54 107	Wood	86,851	-0.4	5.8	15.9	7.7	24.2	29.3	17.2	42.0	97.7	1.9	0.7	1.1
54 109	Wyoming	23,495	-1.9	5.4	16.0	7.6	23.9	31.8	15.4	42.2	98.7	1.4	0.0	0.0
55 000	**Wisconsin**	5,708,612	0.6	6.2	17.1	9.7	25.2	27.9	14.0	38.7	88.8	7.1	2.8	3.5
55 001	Adams	20,819	-0.8	4.1	12.1	5.9	21.3	32.1	24.5	49.7	94.7	3.5	0.9	2.4
55 005	Barron	45,842	-0.3	5.8	16.1	7.6	22.5	29.4	18.7	43.3	97.6	0.6	0.8	2.5
55 009	Brown	250,712	1.8	6.9	17.8	9.7	26.9	26.8	11.8	36.4	91.5	3.4	3.3	4.7
55 015	Calumet	49,444	1.3	6.5	19.7	7.0	26.1	28.8	11.9	38.7	96.3	0.9	2.5	1.6
55 017	Chippewa	62,763	0.7	6.2	17.3	7.4	25.5	29.0	14.7	40.1	96.9	1.9	1.6	1.2
55 019	Clark	34,606	-0.7	8.1	21.0	7.6	22.0	25.7	15.6	36.8	98.3	0.5	0.6	1.6
55 021	Columbia	56,716	-0.6	5.8	17.2	6.9	25.2	30.0	15.0	41.6	97.1	1.7	0.9	1.4
55 025	Dane	496,374	2.9	6.1	15.4	13.1	29.2	25.6	10.6	34.5	87.9	6.6	5.6	2.6
55 027	Dodge	88,596	-0.3	5.4	16.2	7.7	26.2	29.3	15.2	41.0	95.8	3.2	0.8	1.6
55 029	Door	27,807	0.4	4.6	13.0	5.7	19.4	33.6	23.6	50.2	97.8	1.4	0.7	1.4
55 031	Douglas	43,995	-0.9	5.9	15.4	9.9	24.5	29.7	14.7	40.3	95.3	1.9	1.3	3.7
55 033	Dunn	43,997	0.4	5.2	15.0	19.5	22.6	25.0	12.7	33.8	96.5	0.9	2.9	1.0
55 035	Eau Claire	99,769	1.8	5.9	14.9	17.6	24.3	24.5	12.8	33.2	94.8	1.5	4.0	1.4
55 039	Fond du Lac	101,798	0.1	5.8	16.6	8.9	24.3	29.0	15.3	40.7	95.8	1.8	1.4	2.9
55 043	Grant	51,174	-0.2	5.6	15.4	17.2	20.4	25.7	15.7	36.4	97.8	1.5	1.0	0.6
55 045	Green	36,910	0.2	6.2	17.6	6.7	23.8	30.3	15.4	41.6	98.9	0.8	0.7	0.4
55 049	Iowa	23,755	0.6	6.3	17.6	6.2	23.6	31.5	14.8	42.4	98.5	0.9	0.8	0.5
55 053	Jackson	20,486	0.1	6.1	16.4	7.4	24.4	29.2	16.4	42.4	91.3	2.7	0.4	8.0
55 055	Jefferson	84,046	1.0	6.1	17.4	10.4	24.9	27.8	13.5	38.1	96.4	1.1	1.1	3.0
55 057	Juneau	26,651	-0.1	5.6	15.9	7.2	23.1	30.3	17.8	43.5	95.6	2.4	0.3	2.7

Table A-2. Counties — Who: Age, Race/Ethnicity, and Household Structure, 2010–2012—*Continued*

STATE and County code	STATE or County	Percent Hispanic or Latino	Percent foreign born	Total households	Household type (percent)							Percent of households with people under 18 years	Percent of households with people 60 years and over
					Family households				Nonfamily households				
					Total family households	Married-couple families	Male household families	Female household families	Total nonfamily households	One-person households			
	ACS table number:	B03003	C05003	B11001	B11001	B11001	B11001	B11001	B11001	B11001		B11005	B11006
	Column number:	14	15	16	17	18	19	20	21	22		23	24
	Washington—Cont.												
53 031	Jefferson	3.0	2.6	13,826	56.9	50.1	1.4	5.4	43.1	36.0		16.7	57.4
53 033	King	9.1	20.8	796,640	58.6	45.6	3.9	9.1	41.4	31.8		29.2	28.8
53 035	Kitsap	6.5	6.5	98,682	66.2	51.5	4.4	10.2	33.8	26.8		31.0	36.2
53 037	Kittitas	8.0	6.1	16,490	57.0	45.7	4.0	7.3	43.0	30.8		26.7	32.9
53 039	Klickitat	11.1	5.2	8,209	68.5	53.2	6.1	9.3	31.5	25.5		27.8	42.6
53 041	Lewis	8.9	5.0	29,391	67.0	52.4	5.1	9.5	33.0	27.9		28.1	43.5
53 045	Mason	8.2	5.5	23,565	64.6	51.4	5.4	7.8	35.4	27.6		25.4	45.5
53 047	Okanogan	18.0	11.5	16,415	66.0	50.7	5.0	10.2	34.0	28.8		30.8	41.3
53 049	Pacific	8.3	5.8	9,358	62.7	48.7	4.7	9.2	37.3	32.1		22.8	55.3
53 053	Pierce	9.4	9.9	299,514	66.6	49.5	4.7	12.4	33.4	26.6		34.4	31.0
53 057	Skagit	17.1	9.6	45,207	68.6	52.0	4.6	12.0	31.4	25.0		31.2	41.2
53 061	Snohomish	9.1	14.5	268,565	67.6	52.2	5.2	10.2	32.4	25.3		34.2	30.2
53 063	Spokane	4.7	5.7	187,863	63.7	48.2	4.4	11.1	36.3	28.9		30.5	33.9
53 065	Stevens	2.9	3.1	17,858	69.1	55.2	4.6	9.3	30.9	25.2		30.3	44.6
53 067	Thurston	7.4	7.8	101,296	66.8	50.7	4.7	11.4	33.2	26.1		30.2	34.7
53 071	Walla Walla	20.2	10.4	21,572	63.2	48.9	4.3	10.0	36.8	32.0		28.6	40.0
53 073	Whatcom	8.1	11.9	79,643	62.4	49.6	2.9	9.9	37.6	27.4		29.0	34.8
53 075	Whitman	4.9	9.3	16,865	49.2	41.6	1.5	6.1	50.8	29.9		21.6	24.2
53 077	Yakima	45.7	17.9	79,396	72.6	51.7	6.2	14.6	27.4	22.1		40.9	33.9
54 000	**West Virginia**	1.2	1.4	741,661	64.8	49.2	4.2	11.3	35.2	30.2		27.5	40.5
54 003	Berkeley	3.8	3.6	40,297	71.4	52.1	5.6	13.6	28.6	24.1		34.3	33.4
54 005	Boone	0.1	0.2	9,506	72.3	55.6	4.3	12.4	27.7	24.8		35.8	39.9
54 009	Brooke	0.7	1.0	10,008	66.2	46.9	7.1	12.2	33.8	30.9		24.3	46.8
54 011	Cabell	1.2	2.0	39,766	60.4	42.2	3.8	14.4	39.6	33.1		25.2	37.3
54 019	Fayette	0.9	0.5	17,267	65.2	46.8	3.9	14.5	34.8	29.7		28.4	46.0
54 025	Greenbrier	1.3	1.0	15,206	65.3	48.6	5.0	11.7	34.7	29.0		26.3	44.8
54 027	Hampshire	1.1	0.5	10,829	43.1	33.6	1.9	7.5	56.9	54.2		17.8	40.1
54 029	Hancock	1.1	0.7	12,978	65.9	49.6	5.4	10.9	34.1	31.0		27.8	42.3
54 033	Harrison	1.3	0.8	27,904	65.8	49.3	3.5	12.9	34.2	29.8		28.9	40.2
54 035	Jackson	0.0	0.6	11,428	68.1	51.8	4.7	11.6	31.9	27.3		29.7	40.5
54 037	Jefferson	4.8	4.7	19,681	72.7	57.4	4.7	10.6	27.3	20.8		33.1	33.7
54 039	Kanawha	1.1	1.6	83,146	60.7	43.9	4.2	12.5	39.3	33.4		25.2	39.6
54 043	Lincoln	0.2	0.2	8,298	70.8	56.5	4.7	9.7	29.2	26.7		33.2	40.9
54 045	Logan	0.8	0.5	14,656	70.8	52.2	6.1	12.4	29.2	24.3		30.4	43.9
54 047	McDowell	0.1	0.3	8,489	66.3	45.4	6.5	14.3	33.7	29.1		28.0	45.2
54 049	Marion	1.0	0.9	22,750	65.0	49.8	3.9	11.3	35.0	29.6		26.4	41.9
54 051	Marshall	0.8	0.7	14,113	66.4	52.0	5.1	9.3	33.6	28.5		27.7	42.8
54 053	Mason	0.9	0.6	10,304	69.6	51.4	3.8	14.4	30.4	25.9		28.5	40.8
54 055	Mercer	0.8	1.2	26,117	63.4	49.5	3.2	10.7	36.6	31.9		28.0	44.0
54 057	Mineral	0.2	0.3	11,053	53.0	41.3	2.8	8.9	47.0	44.1		21.8	48.7
54 059	Mingo	0.3	0.5	10,751	68.4	50.0	4.6	13.9	31.6	27.8		28.3	39.9
54 061	Monongalia	1.8	4.4	36,183	51.3	40.3	3.2	7.8	48.7	36.1		21.6	26.4
54 067	Nicholas	0.0	0.8	10,398	72.8	56.9	6.5	9.4	27.2	24.0		28.3	43.7
54 069	Ohio	0.9	1.2	18,437	58.3	42.9	3.1	12.3	41.7	37.3		24.8	42.0
54 077	Preston	1.2	0.8	12,652	69.1	56.2	5.2	7.6	30.9	25.7		29.4	41.9
54 079	Putnam	0.9	1.8	21,176	74.1	60.0	2.7	11.4	25.9	21.0		34.9	38.3
54 081	Raleigh	1.3	1.7	31,384	66.5	51.6	5.1	9.8	33.5	28.2		30.0	41.8
54 083	Randolph	0.7	0.3	11,129	66.7	52.4	4.0	10.3	33.3	31.1		26.9	42.6
54 097	Upshur	1.0	0.5	8,990	69.3	55.5	3.3	10.5	30.7	26.2		30.8	44.8
54 099	Wayne	0.3	0.4	16,708	63.4	46.5	3.5	13.4	36.6	32.5		27.3	43.9
54 107	Wood	0.9	0.7	35,302	64.6	49.8	3.7	11.1	35.4	30.5		28.1	40.5
54 109	Wyoming	0.2	0.1	9,068	71.8	57.3	5.4	9.1	28.2	25.5		31.1	41.2
55 000	**Wisconsin**	6.1	4.7	2,282,454	64.0	49.6	4.3	10.2	36.0	29.0		30.1	33.6
55 001	Adams	3.8	3.2	8,244	65.0	53.6	4.5	6.9	35.0	29.5		19.7	54.7
55 005	Barron	2.0	1.2	18,660	66.9	52.8	5.3	8.8	33.1	27.6		27.0	40.9
55 009	Brown	7.5	5.1	98,677	64.9	50.5	4.1	10.2	35.1	28.5		33.6	29.2
55 015	Calumet	3.6	3.3	18,211	73.9	64.0	5.2	4.7	26.1	21.3		37.4	30.0
55 017	Chippewa	1.3	1.2	24,398	66.8	54.0	3.8	8.9	33.2	27.4		31.9	35.3
55 019	Clark	3.8	2.9	12,990	69.8	58.5	3.6	7.6	30.2	25.8		33.0	35.8
55 021	Columbia	2.6	1.9	22,743	67.2	53.6	4.8	8.7	32.8	26.8		30.3	35.3
55 025	Dane	6.0	8.0	205,451	58.5	45.7	4.0	8.8	41.5	30.7		28.5	26.8
55 027	Dodge	4.1	2.3	33,293	67.4	54.6	4.3	8.5	32.6	27.8		30.3	35.8
55 029	Door	2.5	2.4	13,345	62.3	52.2	4.2	5.9	37.7	31.1		21.0	45.3
55 031	Douglas	1.2	2.2	18,955	61.0	44.9	5.9	10.2	39.0	32.3		29.0	34.7
55 033	Dunn	1.5	2.2	16,457	63.7	50.9	3.9	8.9	36.3	26.7		30.9	32.4
55 035	Eau Claire	2.0	3.2	39,957	58.3	45.5	3.9	9.0	41.7	30.9		26.4	32.1
55 039	Fond du Lac	4.4	2.8	41,025	67.1	52.6	4.6	9.9	32.9	28.1		30.7	36.3
55 043	Grant	1.3	1.4	19,538	62.7	51.4	5.0	6.2	37.3	26.5		26.5	34.8
55 045	Green	2.8	2.3	14,674	67.5	55.8	3.8	7.9	32.5	26.4		30.3	37.4
55 049	Iowa	1.5	1.6	9,630	67.4	59.0	3.7	4.7	32.6	26.9		30.7	35.5
55 053	Jackson	2.7	1.4	8,133	63.7	48.7	5.0	10.1	36.3	30.3		29.5	39.8
55 055	Jefferson	6.8	4.1	32,115	67.6	54.7	3.6	9.3	32.4	26.6		32.0	33.7
55 057	Juneau	2.7	1.3	10,658	65.8	50.4	5.6	9.7	34.2	29.5		27.1	41.6

STATE and County code	STATE or County	Total population	Percent change 2010–2012	Population by age (percent)						Median age	Race alone or in combination (percent)			
				Under 5 years	5 to 17 years	18 to 24 years	25 to 44 years	45 to 64 years	65 years and over		White	Black	Asian, Hawaiian, or Pacific Islander	American Indian, Alaska Native, or some other race
	ACS table number:	B01003	Population estimates	B01001	B01001	B01001	B01001	B01001	B01001	B01002	B02008	B02009	B02011 + B02012	B02010 + B02013
	Column number:	1	2	3	4	5	6	7	8	9	10	11	12	13
	Wisconsin—Cont.													
55 059	Kenosha	167,242	0.8	6.5	18.9	10.1	26.0	27.2	11.4	36.6	89.4	7.9	2.0	2.9
55 061	Kewaunee	20,602	0.3	5.6	17.6	7.0	22.7	30.2	17.0	43.0	98.0	0.6	0.0	1.7
55 063	La Crosse	115,603	1.4	5.8	15.2	15.8	23.9	25.7	13.6	35.4	93.0	2.2	4.8	1.4
55 067	Langlade	19,807	-1.5	4.8	15.4	7.0	20.7	31.7	20.4	46.3	96.8	0.5	0.6	3.2
55 069	Lincoln	28,541	-1.2	4.9	16.4	6.4	21.6	31.9	18.7	45.4	97.6	1.4	0.6	1.1
55 071	Manitowoc	81,011	-0.7	5.5	16.5	7.5	22.7	30.5	17.4	43.5	95.4	1.0	2.8	2.1
55 073	Marathon	134,459	0.5	6.5	17.7	7.9	25.0	28.3	14.7	39.6	93.5	1.2	5.9	1.3
55 075	Marinette	41,570	-0.3	4.8	15.1	7.9	20.6	31.3	20.4	46.3	98.1	0.7	0.8	2.0
55 079	Milwaukee	951,833	0.7	7.4	17.5	11.2	28.2	24.2	11.6	33.7	64.7	28.3	4.1	6.7
55 081	Monroe	44,993	0.8	7.3	18.4	7.3	24.3	28.3	14.4	39.1	96.3	1.5	1.2	2.8
55 083	Oconto	37,564	-0.6	5.4	16.3	6.5	22.4	32.5	16.8	44.4	97.4	0.4	0.5	2.7
55 085	Oneida	35,823	-0.6	4.4	13.6	6.3	20.1	33.2	22.3	48.5	97.4	0.7	1.0	1.6
55 087	Outagamie	177,774	1.1	6.5	18.2	8.7	26.8	27.7	12.1	37.6	93.4	1.5	3.7	3.4
55 089	Ozaukee	86,581	0.6	5.1	17.9	7.7	21.7	31.9	15.8	43.5	95.9	1.8	2.3	1.1
55 093	Pierce	40,947	-0.7	5.6	16.3	16.9	23.2	27.0	10.9	34.8	97.4	1.0	1.2	1.2
55 095	Polk	43,920	-1.3	5.9	17.3	6.5	22.8	30.8	16.6	43.3	97.3	0.6	0.6	2.3
55 097	Portage	70,206	0.6	5.7	15.0	16.5	22.9	26.7	13.2	35.8	95.9	1.1	3.2	1.2
55 101	Racine	195,086	-0.3	6.5	18.1	8.2	24.9	28.9	13.5	39.4	83.4	12.3	1.6	5.2
55 105	Rock	160,240	0.1	6.4	18.3	8.7	25.6	27.3	13.9	38.5	93.7	4.9	1.5	3.7
55 109	St. Croix	84,856	1.0	6.9	19.9	6.8	28.0	27.8	10.5	36.8	97.3	1.1	1.5	1.5
55 111	Sauk	62,324	1.0	6.1	17.4	7.4	25.1	28.4	15.5	39.7	95.4	1.2	1.0	3.9
55 115	Shawano	41,773	-0.8	5.4	16.9	7.2	22.4	29.3	18.8	43.7	90.5	0.8	0.6	9.7
55 117	Sheboygan	115,224	-0.4	6.0	17.6	8.0	24.5	29.1	14.9	40.4	92.6	2.0	5.1	1.8
55 119	Taylor	20,627	-0.7	6.6	17.6	7.0	22.4	29.8	16.6	42.4	98.8	0.7	0.5	0.8
55 121	Trempealeau	29,062	1.6	6.8	17.2	6.8	24.5	28.4	16.3	40.7	95.7	0.4	0.6	4.5
55 123	Vernon	30,016	1.7	6.9	19.1	6.6	21.0	29.1	17.2	41.8	98.4	0.7	0.5	1.4
55 125	Vilas	21,385	-0.5	4.2	13.0	4.8	18.0	33.2	26.8	51.6	89.6	2.0	0.5	10.8
55 127	Walworth	102,519	0.7	5.8	17.3	11.7	23.6	27.9	13.8	38.3	94.9	1.3	1.3	4.4
55 131	Washington	132,276	0.5	5.9	18.2	6.8	24.7	30.6	13.9	41.4	97.5	1.3	1.4	1.4
55 133	Waukesha	391,017	0.6	5.3	18.2	7.1	23.3	31.3	14.8	42.5	94.8	1.8	3.4	1.8
55 135	Waupaca	52,300	-0.5	5.5	16.7	6.7	22.7	30.0	18.4	43.9	97.7	0.8	0.6	1.4
55 137	Waushara	24,504	-0.1	4.8	14.3	6.8	21.2	32.2	20.6	47.2	95.7	2.1	0.5	2.5
55 139	Winnebago	167,860	1.0	5.8	15.6	11.5	26.2	27.3	13.6	37.9	94.4	2.3	2.9	2.1
55 141	Wood	74,604	-0.5	5.9	16.5	7.4	22.6	30.2	17.4	42.9	96.1	0.4	2.5	1.7
56 000	**Wyoming**	569,380	2.1	6.9	16.9	10.1	25.8	27.7	12.7	36.8	93.6	1.5	1.3	6.5
56 001	Albany	36,849	2.3	5.1	11.3	29.2	26.4	19.2	8.8	27.0	91.2	1.7	3.8	5.5
56 005	Campbell	46,902	3.5	8.5	19.3	9.3	30.0	27.0	5.9	32.1	93.8	0.7	0.8	5.9
56 013	Fremont	40,641	2.2	7.8	17.4	8.7	23.5	28.0	14.7	38.3	76.3	0.7	0.8	24.6
56 021	Laramie	93,030	2.6	6.9	17.1	9.8	26.2	27.1	13.0	37.1	90.7	3.5	2.2	7.2
56 025	Natrona	76,821	4.2	7.0	16.7	9.6	26.9	27.4	12.5	36.2	96.0	2.0	1.1	4.3
56 029	Park	28,470	1.5	5.9	15.0	8.7	21.9	30.5	18.0	43.3	97.8	0.4	0.9	2.0
56 033	Sheridan	29,334	1.5	6.2	15.8	8.0	23.2	30.8	16.0	42.3	95.2	0.6	1.0	4.8
56 037	Sweetwater	44,320	3.8	8.1	19.1	9.7	28.2	26.3	8.6	32.9	95.9	1.8	1.1	5.3
56 039	Teton	21,470	1.8	5.9	13.3	8.2	34.0	28.3	10.2	37.2	97.6	0.0	0.0	1.0
56 041	Uinta	21,015	-0.4	7.9	21.9	7.8	26.0	27.3	9.1	34.7	98.1	0.0	0.0	6.6

Table A-2. Counties — Who: Age, Race/Ethnicity, and Household Structure, 2010–2012—*Continued*

STATE and County code	STATE or County	Percent Hispanic or Latino	Percent foreign born	Total households	Household type (percent)							Percent of households with people under 18 years	Percent of households with people 60 years and over
					Family households				Nonfamily households				
					Total family households	Married-couple families	Male household families	Female household families	Total nonfamily households	One-person households			
	ACS table number:	B03003	C05003	B11001	B11001	B11001	B11001	B11001	B11001	B11001	B11005	B11006
	Column number:	14	15	16	17	18	19	20	21	22	23	24
	Wisconsin—Cont.											
55 059	Kenosha	12.0	6.4	62,408	66.6	47.4	5.4	13.8	33.4	26.8	36.2	30.3
55 061	Kewaunee	2.3	1.5	7,984	68.0	59.0	3.7	5.4	32.0	26.6	28.6	39.0
55 063	La Crosse	1.6	3.3	46,174	60.7	48.3	4.0	8.4	39.3	29.4	27.9	32.0
55 067	Langlade	1.8	2.1	8,727	62.5	50.3	5.0	7.2	37.5	29.5	24.8	43.0
55 069	Lincoln	1.2	1.3	12,474	67.6	57.7	3.6	6.2	32.4	26.3	26.2	39.0
55 071	Manitowoc	3.2	2.4	34,062	64.3	53.2	3.5	7.6	35.7	30.5	26.9	37.5
55 073	Marathon	2.3	3.8	52,515	68.1	55.6	4.1	8.4	31.9	25.8	30.6	35.0
55 075	Marinette	1.4	1.5	18,386	61.0	50.1	3.8	7.1	39.0	34.4	24.1	42.6
55 079	Milwaukee	13.6	8.8	379,601	56.7	34.8	5.0	16.9	43.3	35.4	30.7	29.5
55 081	Monroe	3.8	2.1	17,450	67.5	53.8	5.3	8.5	32.5	27.1	32.1	33.9
55 083	Oconto	1.5	1.2	15,641	69.3	59.2	4.0	6.0	30.7	25.2	27.5	37.8
55 085	Oneida	1.1	1.8	15,884	62.8	53.5	2.8	6.5	37.2	32.7	20.0	46.0
55 087	Outagamie	3.7	3.8	69,255	68.0	54.6	4.8	8.7	32.0	26.3	33.0	30.2
55 089	Ozaukee	2.4	4.5	34,281	70.6	60.5	3.1	7.0	29.4	25.0	30.2	37.5
55 093	Pierce	1.6	1.5	15,190	65.4	55.0	3.6	6.8	34.6	24.3	30.1	29.3
55 095	Polk	1.5	1.4	18,239	68.7	54.0	5.8	8.9	31.3	25.6	29.4	37.2
55 097	Portage	2.8	2.9	28,189	63.2	50.8	4.3	8.1	36.8	27.6	27.1	34.1
55 101	Racine	11.8	5.1	75,450	64.8	48.8	4.1	11.9	35.2	29.1	31.5	34.7
55 105	Rock	7.7	4.5	63,114	67.0	49.1	5.4	12.5	33.0	26.2	33.9	33.3
55 109	St. Croix	2.1	1.7	32,023	72.9	58.9	4.6	9.4	27.1	21.5	38.6	27.2
55 111	Sauk	4.4	3.7	25,547	64.4	52.3	3.6	8.5	35.6	28.6	29.4	35.4
55 115	Shawano	2.2	0.8	17,007	69.1	55.0	5.3	8.8	30.9	25.6	30.3	38.2
55 117	Sheboygan	5.6	5.4	46,072	65.6	53.6	3.5	8.5	34.4	27.7	28.7	34.0
55 119	Taylor	1.6	1.5	8,788	67.6	56.6	3.3	7.7	32.4	26.4	27.6	36.3
55 121	Trempealeau	6.0	3.6	11,802	67.7	53.5	6.3	7.9	32.3	27.4	32.4	36.8
55 123	Vernon	1.4	1.1	11,657	66.4	54.8	4.0	7.7	33.6	28.5	29.3	40.0
55 125	Vilas	1.3	2.2	10,589	62.4	50.2	3.9	8.3	37.6	31.8	19.1	51.3
55 127	Walworth	10.5	6.3	39,455	66.4	50.9	5.3	10.1	33.6	25.3	32.3	34.4
55 131	Washington	2.7	2.7	51,759	72.9	59.7	4.7	8.5	27.1	22.9	32.8	33.9
55 133	Waukesha	4.3	4.6	152,574	70.9	60.8	2.8	7.3	29.1	24.2	31.6	36.2
55 135	Waupaca	2.6	1.9	21,218	67.5	54.9	3.7	8.9	32.5	26.9	28.3	37.5
55 137	Waushara	5.8	2.1	9,759	67.4	56.2	3.8	7.3	32.6	28.7	25.0	44.5
55 139	Winnebago	3.6	3.1	67,750	60.1	47.9	3.8	8.3	39.9	31.5	28.2	32.0
55 141	Wood	2.3	2.2	31,949	63.6	52.0	4.0	7.6	36.4	30.9	27.4	36.7
56 000	**Wyoming**	9.2	3.2	222,558	65.4	52.3	4.1	9.0	34.6	27.6	30.6	32.3
56 001	Albany	9.0	5.4	15,246	47.4	38.3	3.3	5.8	52.6	32.6	21.5	22.8
56 005	Campbell	7.8	3.8	17,240	69.2	55.9	4.5	8.7	30.8	22.3	34.5	19.2
56 013	Fremont	5.9	0.9	15,375	67.8	51.1	4.9	11.8	32.2	26.0	31.1	38.4
56 021	Laramie	13.5	2.5	37,119	65.2	50.1	4.1	11.1	34.8	29.0	30.7	31.2
56 025	Natrona	7.3	2.1	31,080	65.8	48.3	6.2	11.2	34.2	27.2	32.0	31.8
56 029	Park	5.1	3.3	11,909	62.6	53.3	2.3	6.9	37.4	30.7	23.1	42.7
56 033	Sheridan	3.8	2.4	12,247	64.1	53.6	3.2	7.3	35.9	29.2	27.1	39.1
56 037	Sweetwater	15.6	5.7	16,480	68.7	55.8	4.2	8.7	31.3	24.9	36.0	26.3
56 039	Teton	15.2	10.9	7,224	61.5	52.4	2.3	6.8	38.5	24.9	28.6	29.4
56 041	Uinta	8.8	2.5	7,263	73.1	57.8	1.9	13.5	26.9	22.3	38.5	27.2

Table A-3. Metropolitan Areas — Who: Age, Race/Ethnicity, and Household Structure, 2012

Metro area or division code	Area name	Total population	Percent change 2010–2012	Under 5 years	5 to 17 years	18 to 24 years	25 to 44 years	45 to 64 years	65 years and over	Median age	White	Black	Asian, Hawaiian, or Pacific Islander	American Indian, Alaska Native, or some other race
	ACS table number:	B01003	CP05	B01001	B01001	B01001	B01001	B01001	B01001	B01002	B02008	B02009	B02011 + B02012	B02010 + B02013
	Column number:	1	2	3	4	5	6	7	8	9	10	11	12	13
10180	Abilene, TX	167,800	1.7	7.0	16.6	13.4	25.7	23.4	13.9	33.7	85.0	8.8	1.9	6.4
10420	Akron, OH	702,262	-0.1	5.4	16.2	10.9	24.1	28.5	15.0	40.1	85.5	13.5	2.7	1.4
10500	Albany, GA	155,019	-4.7	7.1	18.0	11.4	24.4	26.0	13.0	35.8	45.0	53.1	1.2	1.5
10580	Albany-Schenectady-Troy, NY	874,646	0.4	5.2	15.4	11.3	24.6	28.7	14.8	39.9	87.3	9.1	4.4	2.8
10740	Albuquerque, NM	902,794	1.2	6.6	17.5	9.8	26.5	26.4	13.3	37.0	73.3	3.5	3.0	24.2
10780	Alexandria, LA	154,441	0.2	6.8	18.9	9.0	25.4	26.1	13.8	37.3	67.7	30.4	1.3	1.9
10900	Allentown-Bethlehem-Easton, PA-NJ	827,171	0.6	5.4	16.6	9.3	24.2	28.6	16.0	41.2	86.9	6.7	3.1	5.8
11020	Altoona, PA	127,121	0.1	5.6	15.1	9.2	23.3	28.4	18.4	42.6	97.7	2.4	1.2	0.7
11100	Amarillo, TX	254,579	1.1	7.4	18.5	11.0	26.9	24.0	12.3	34.1	87.1	6.9	3.7	5.2
11180	Ames, IA	91,140	1.7	5.1	12.1	29.9	23.7	18.8	10.3	26.9	90.8	3.7	6.9	0.7
11260	Anchorage, AK	392,535	2.5	7.3	18.5	10.9	28.9	26.3	8.1	33.5	77.8	7.3	11.2	13.2
11300	Anderson, IN	130,348	-1.0	5.9	16.8	9.2	24.9	27.0	16.2	39.6	89.3	9.0	0.7	2.6
11340	Anderson, SC	189,355	1.1	6.3	17.3	8.8	23.7	27.9	16.1	40.1	81.1	17.5	1.1	1.6
11460	Ann Arbor, MI	350,946	1.6	5.2	14.7	17.8	26.3	24.9	11.1	33.5	77.5	14.5	9.4	2.6
11500	Anniston-Oxford, AL	117,296	-1.0	6.1	16.4	11.1	24.7	26.8	15.0	38.8	76.8	22.1	1.1	0.9
11540	Appleton, WI	228,450	1.1	6.4	18.4	8.2	26.4	28.2	12.4	38.0	93.4	1.3	3.5	3.4
11700	Asheville, NC	432,406	2.3	5.3	14.5	8.0	24.5	28.4	19.3	43.1	93.3	5.6	1.4	2.1
12020	Athens-Clarke County, GA	194,337	0.8	6.3	14.2	21.6	25.3	20.9	11.6	29.9	74.9	21.0	3.8	2.2
12060	Atlanta-Sandy Springs-Marietta, GA	5,442,113	2.9	6.9	19.0	9.4	29.4	25.4	9.9	35.4	57.8	34.0	5.9	4.7
12100	Atlantic City-Hammonton, NJ	275,422	0.3	6.1	16.8	9.5	23.9	28.7	15.0	40.7	68.6	17.5	8.9	8.4
12220	Auburn-Opelika, AL	147,257	4.6	6.0	15.8	21.1	26.1	21.6	9.5	29.8	71.5	23.4	3.3	2.9
12260	Augusta-Richmond County, GA-SC	568,161	1.4	6.7	17.5	10.1	26.4	26.2	13.0	36.6	59.7	37.4	2.3	2.8
12420	Austin-Round Rock-San Marcos, TX	1,834,303	6.1	7.1	17.8	10.9	32.3	23.1	8.7	33.1	82.9	8.5	6.1	5.7
12540	Bakersfield-Delano, CA	856,158	1.7	8.6	21.2	11.3	27.3	22.1	9.4	30.8	73.9	6.7	5.7	17.1
12580	Baltimore-Towson, MD	2,753,149	1.4	6.1	16.3	9.8	26.7	27.7	13.3	38.2	64.1	30.2	5.8	2.7
12620	Bangor, ME	153,746	-0.1	4.9	14.1	12.9	23.2	29.4	15.4	41.2	96.6	1.2	1.3	1.9
12700	Barnstable Town, MA	215,423	-0.2	3.8	12.7	7.1	17.7	31.9	26.7	50.9	94.3	3.1	1.6	2.9
12940	Baton Rouge, LA	815,298	1.4	6.5	17.7	11.8	27.4	25.0	11.6	34.3	61.1	36.6	2.2	1.6
12980	Battle Creek, MI	135,099	-0.7	6.1	17.5	8.8	24.6	27.4	15.4	39.9	85.6	12.7	2.2	2.1
13020	Bay City, MI	106,935	-0.7	5.6	16.1	8.3	23.1	29.5	17.4	42.9	97.2	2.3	0.7	2.1
13140	Beaumont-Port Arthur, TX	389,980	0.2	6.8	17.4	10.1	25.9	26.4	13.4	37.0	71.1	24.8	3.2	2.9
13380	Bellingham, WA	205,262	1.8	5.2	15.0	14.6	23.8	27.2	14.1	37.0	89.3	1.7	6.1	6.8
13460	Bend, OR	162,277	2.8	5.4	16.8	7.2	25.6	28.2	16.9	41.7	96.9	0.0	2.4	3.8
13740	Billings, MT	161,487	2.6	6.3	17.1	8.6	25.2	27.8	15.0	38.9	92.4	1.2	1.2	7.7
13780	Binghamton, NY	248,538	-1.1	4.9	15.2	11.4	22.5	28.8	17.1	41.8	91.3	5.1	3.8	1.8
13820	Birmingham-Hoover, AL	1,136,650	0.7	6.6	17.1	8.9	26.9	26.8	13.7	38.1	67.9	29.1	1.6	2.8
13900	Bismarck, ND	113,875	4.2	6.5	16.1	10.1	26.4	26.8	14.1	36.8	94.3	1.2	0.6	5.0
13980	Blacksburg-Christiansburg-Radford, VA	165,969	2.6	4.1	12.5	23.9	23.6	22.9	13.0	32.3	90.9	5.3	4.3	0.9
14020	Bloomington, IN	195,339	1.4	5.3	14.2	23.1	23.4	23.2	12.4	32.0	91.6	3.3	5.3	1.6
14060	Bloomington-Normal, IL	172,281	1.4	6.0	16.1	18.0	25.6	23.5	10.8	32.7	86.8	8.9	5.2	1.5
14260	Boise City-Nampa, ID	635,964	2.6	6.9	20.1	8.8	27.8	24.5	11.8	34.9	94.2	1.4	3.3	4.3
14460	Boston-Cambridge-Quincy, MA-NH	4,640,802	1.8	5.5	15.5	10.2	27.4	27.6	13.7	38.8	80.7	9.4	7.8	5.2
1446014484	•Boston-Quincy, MA Division	1,926,030	1.8	5.5	15.1	11.3	28.3	26.3	13.5	37.4	75.6	15.6	7.7	4.8
1446015764	•Cambridge-Newton-Framingham, MA Division	1,537,215	2.1	5.6	15.2	9.5	28.6	27.5	13.5	38.7	82.2	6.0	11.2	3.6
1446037764	•Peabody, MA Division	755,618	1.5	5.7	16.8	9.1	24.3	29.2	14.8	40.7	81.7	5.2	3.8	11.4
1446040484	•Rockingham County-Strafford County, NH Division	421,939	0.8	4.8	16.3	9.9	24.2	31.2	13.6	41.6	96.4	1.4	2.6	1.3
14500	Boulder, CO	305,318	3.4	5.2	15.2	15.3	26.8	26.5	11.0	35.7	90.7	1.7	5.5	4.4
14540	Bowling Green, KY	128,016	0.6	6.1	16.6	15.7	25.6	24.5	11.5	33.6	83.9	10.0	3.0	4.6
14740	Bremerton-Silverdale, WA	254,991	1.3	5.6	15.7	10.4	25.1	28.6	14.5	39.1	88.7	4.1	10.0	5.2
14860	Bridgeport-Stamford-Norwalk, CT	933,835	1.6	5.9	18.2	8.2	25.3	28.4	14.0	39.8	76.5	12.5	5.8	8.0
15180	Brownsville-Harlingen, TX	415,557	1.8	8.7	23.6	10.5	24.9	20.7	11.6	31.0	89.7	0.8	0.8	9.4
15260	Brunswick, GA	111,088	3.0	6.8	17.0	9.3	23.0	27.9	16.0	40.3	74.6	22.1	2.2	4.4
15380	Buffalo-Niagara Falls, NY	1,134,210	-0.1	5.3	15.6	10.4	23.9	28.6	16.2	41.0	82.6	13.2	3.1	3.3
15500	Burlington, NC	153,920	1.6	5.8	17.0	11.0	24.4	26.7	15.1	39.2	73.8	19.4	1.6	8.0
15540	Burlington-South Burlington, VT	213,280	1.1	5.0	14.9	14.0	25.0	28.6	12.6	38.0	94.9	2.4	3.2	1.8
15940	Canton-Massillon, OH	403,455	0.1	5.5	16.8	9.0	23.2	28.4	17.1	41.8	92.3	8.6	1.2	1.4
15980	Cape Coral-Fort Myers, FL	645,293	4.1	5.1	14.0	7.6	21.5	26.7	25.0	46.5	86.2	9.2	2.1	4.4
16020	Cape Girardeau-Jackson, MO-IL	96,410	-1.7	5.6	15.9	13.0	23.7	26.1	15.7	37.5	89.5	9.2	1.5	1.8
16180	Carson City, NV	54,838	-0.7	5.4	16.5	7.6	26.4	27.2	16.9	41.4	85.0	0.8	5.1	12.2
16220	Casper, WY	78,621	4.1	7.4	16.6	9.4	27.5	26.5	12.6	35.7	96.7	2.8	0.0	5.0
16300	Cedar Rapids, IA	261,761	1.4	6.4	17.6	9.5	25.8	26.5	14.2	37.9	93.8	5.0	2.3	1.3
16580	Champaign-Urbana, IL	234,072	-0.2	5.5	14.4	21.7	24.6	22.2	11.6	30.7	79.8	12.2	9.2	1.4
16620	Charleston, WV	305,091	0.2	5.9	15.7	7.7	24.6	29.2	16.9	41.7	95.7	3.8	1.2	4.0
16700	Charleston-North Charleston-Summerville, SC	697,439	4.4	6.7	16.1	10.7	28.4	25.7	12.4	35.7	69.4	28.1	2.8	2.2
16740	Charlotte-Gastonia-Rock Hill, NC-SC	1,831,084	3.8	6.9	18.6	9.0	29.6	25.2	10.7	35.9	69.0	25.4	4.1	4.1
16820	Charlottesville, VA	206,414	3.3	5.3	14.8	13.4	26.3	25.4	14.8	37.5	81.4	14.2	5.3	2.1
16860	Chattanooga, TN-GA	539,094	1.7	5.7	16.3	9.2	25.7	27.6	15.5	39.5	83.4	14.5	2.1	1.9
16940	Cheyenne, WY	94,483	2.6	6.4	17.0	10.8	25.9	26.4	13.6	37.1	92.0	4.2	2.2	5.7

Metro area or division code	Area name	Percent Hispanic or Latino	Percent foreign born	Total households	Household type (percent)						Percent of households with people under 18 years	Percent of households with people 60 years and over
					Family households				Nonfamily households			
					Total family households	Married-couple families	Male household families	Female household families	Total nonfamily households	One-person households		
	ACS table number:	B03003	B05012	B11001	B11001	B11001	B11001	B11001	B11001	B110C1	C11005	B11006
	Column number:	14	15	16	17	18	19	20	21	22	23	24
10180	Abilene, TX	21.3	5.2	60,066	65.4	48.7	5.0	11.7	34.6	29.5	33.4	34.2
10420	Akron, OH	1.7	4.3	280,887	62.4	45.7	3.9	12.7	37.6	31.0	29.1	36.0
10500	Albany, GA	2.3	2.3	57,699	66.3	41.8	4.6	20.0	33.7	30.6	32.6	35.7
10580	Albany-Schenectady-Troy, NY	4.5	6.9	342,705	59.4	44.5	4.1	10.7	40.6	32.5	26.0	36.3
10740	Albuquerque, NM	47.4	9.4	344,869	64.2	44.4	5.9	13.9	35.8	29.3	33.0	34.9
10780	Alexandria, LA	3.0	1.9	57,277	66.9	45.5	4.2	17.2	33.1	27.8	32.3	34.9
10900	Allentown-Bethlehem-Easton, PA-NJ	14.1	8.7	314,173	67.9	50.8	4.7	12.4	32.1	25.8	31.6	38.4
11020	Altoona, PA	1.0	1.2	50,098	64.0	48.6	5.1	10.4	36.0	31.2	27.5	42.6
11100	Amarillo, TX	26.4	8.6	94,559	64.7	46.5	4.7	13.5	35.3	28.3	33.5	31.2
11180	Ames, IA	3.1	9.1	35,541	56.0	48.1	3.1	4.8	44.0	25.8	26.0	24.8
11260	Anchorage, AK	7.2	8.4	137,052	66.9	49.4	5.3	12.2	33.1	25.9	35.9	27.2
11300	Anderson, IN	3.4	1.6	49,124	63.9	47.7	2.9	13.3	36.1	31.8	30.8	39.9
11340	Anderson, SC	3.2	3.0	72,363	69.7	49.2	5.8	14.7	30.3	27.2	33.0	38.4
11460	Ann Arbor, MI	4.3	11.0	137,565	58.4	44.6	3.7	10.1	41.6	29.9	28.4	29.5
11500	Anniston-Oxford, AL	3.5	2.1	45,986	67.9	48.4	5.8	13.7	32.1	26.1	31.7	37.6
11540	Appleton, WI	3.8	3.6	87,010	70.4	56.3	4.7	9.3	29.6	23.3	34.3	30.4
11700	Asheville, NC	6.6	5.1	178,131	63.4	48.6	4.2	10.6	36.6	29.4	25.8	43.4
12020	Athens-Clarke County, GA	8.4	7.3	67,610	60.9	44.9	4.5	11.5	39.1	28.2	30.6	31.4
12060	Atlanta-Sandy Springs-Marietta, GA	10.6	13.2	1,923,727	68.1	48.4	4.7	15.0	31.9	26.3	37.0	28.6
12100	Atlantic City-Hammonton, NJ	17.7	17.8	100,065	68.0	45.5	5.1	17.4	32.0	27.0	32.8	40.7
12220	Auburn-Opelika, AL	3.6	4.2	55,520	61.3	45.1	2.8	13.4	38.7	27.9	30.6	27.5
12260	Augusta-Richmond County, GA-SC	4.8	4.2	204,147	68.4	47.0	4.3	17.1	31.6	27.6	33.1	34.6
12420	Austin-Round Rock-San Marcos, TX	31.9	14.4	665,027	62.1	46.2	4.6	11.2	37.9	27.9	33.7	24.2
12540	Bakersfield-Delano, CA	50.3	20.8	255,967	75.7	51.6	7.8	16.4	24.3	19.7	46.2	31.8
12580	Baltimore-Towson, MD	4.9	9.5	1,034,914	64.7	45.7	4.7	14.3	35.3	29.2	31.7	35.6
12620	Bangor, ME	1.2	3.6	63,171	60.1	47.2	4.2	8.8	39.9	29.2	26.5	37.5
12700	Barnstable Town, MA	2.4	6.2	89,766	63.2	52.1	2.5	8.6	36.8	30.9	21.2	53.7
12940	Baton Rouge, LA	3.6	3.1	298,690	64.8	43.4	5.6	15.8	35.2	28.8	33.5	31.0
12980	Battle Creek, MI	4.6	4.0	53,182	63.9	43.6	5.5	14.8	36.1	31.6	30.7	36.7
13020	Bay City, MI	4.9	1.1	43,967	64.3	50.8	3.3	10.2	35.7	30.3	26.4	39.5
13140	Beaumont-Port Arthur, TX	13.8	8.3	143,663	64.4	44.0	5.2	15.2	35.6	31.6	31.2	35.8
13380	Bellingham, WA	8.4	11.3	79,029	62.0	49.1	2.1	10.8	38.0	27.7	28.4	37.3
13460	Bend, OR	7.6	5.2	66,086	66.0	54.1	3.3	8.6	34.0	25.8	27.5	39.2
13740	Billings, MT	4.8	1.5	65,215	65.0	49.9	5.5	9.5	35.0	28.6	30.0	36.9
13780	Binghamton, NY	3.1	5.6	101,258	62.2	46.8	5.5	9.8	37.8	30.9	25.2	38.8
13820	Birmingham-Hoover, AL	4.3	4.2	437,667	66.9	48.2	3.6	15.1	33.1	29.0	32.8	35.0
13900	Bismarck, ND	1.3	1.7	46,991	66.0	53.0	3.3	9.7	34.0	27.7	31.2	32.9
13980	Blacksburg-Christiansburg-Radford, VA	2.4	5.6	63,346	59.4	47.2	2.9	9.2	40.6	27.1	25.0	33.5
14020	Bloomington, IN	2.7	6.1	76,163	55.4	40.5	4.8	10.1	44.6	32.9	24.6	30.5
14060	Bloomington-Normal, IL	4.6	6.1	65,744	62.7	49.4	3.1	10.3	37.3	25.5	29.3	28.5
14260	Boise City-Nampa, ID	12.7	6.8	231,388	69.6	53.7	4.9	11.0	30.4	23.7	35.1	33.0
14460	Boston-Cambridge-Quincy, MA-NH	9.6	16.7	1,757,711	63.4	47.3	3.9	12.2	36.6	28.3	30.4	35.2
1446014484	•Boston-Quincy, MA Division	10.2	18.2	728,639	60.6	42.8	4.1	13.7	39.4	30.4	29.4	34.5
1446015764	•Cambridge-Newton-Framingham, MA Division	7.0	18.9	582,405	64.2	50.7	3.4	10.1	35.8	27.2	30.6	34.8
1446037764	•Peabody, MA Division	17.4	15.2	283,543	66.6	48.1	4.3	14.1	33.4	27.4	32.2	37.9
1446040484	•Rockingham County-Strafford County, NH Division	2.2	4.5	163,124	67.3	53.7	4.1	9.6	32.7	24.4	31.2	35.0
14500	Boulder, CO	13.5	10.9	121,743	59.8	48.4	3.4	8.0	40.2	27.1	29.8	28.6
14540	Bowling Green, KY	4.5	6.7	50,137	62.5	46.4	4.0	12.0	37.5	29.2	29.6	29.6
14740	Bremerton-Silverdale, WA	6.8	5.7	97,027	65.6	51.3	4.7	9.6	34.4	26.8	30.8	37.6
14860	Bridgeport-Stamford-Norwalk, CT	17.8	20.5	334,255	70.1	53.1	4.2	12.9	29.9	25.1	35.6	36.2
15180	Brownsville-Harlingen, TX	88.4	24.5	121,179	79.2	50.2	6.7	22.4	20.8	18.5	49.6	36.3
15260	Brunswick, GA	5.1	4.5	41,858	72.2	48.6	6.9	16.6	27.8	24.7	35.6	41.1
15380	Buffalo-Niagara Falls, NY	4.3	5.7	468,089	60.7	42.1	4.7	13.8	39.3	33.2	27.7	37.4
15500	Burlington, NC	11.6	8.3	59,520	66.5	48.4	5.2	12.9	33.5	29.6	32.6	37.3
15540	Burlington-South Burlington, VT	1.8	5.9	84,977	60.8	47.9	4.0	8.9	39.2	25.4	29.3	32.0
15940	Canton-Massillon, OH	1.6	1.9	161,763	65.9	49.6	5.5	10.7	34.1	28.4	28.5	39.3
15980	Cape Coral-Fort Myers, FL	18.9	14.6	245,100	66.7	51.1	4.5	11.1	33.3	27.1	24.4	51.5
16020	Cape Girardeau-Jackson, MO-IL	2.0	2.2	37,612	61.7	47.7	4.7	9.3	38.3	32.0	26.5	36.3
16180	Carson City, NV	22.5	12.8	21,494	60.3	45.7	2.9	11.8	39.7	31.3	25.8	42.5
16220	Casper, WY	7.6	2.2	32,065	67.3	50.2	8.5	8.6	32.7	27.3	34.5	32.4
16300	Cedar Rapids, IA	2.5	2.7	102,818	64.1	51.1	3.3	9.7	35.9	27.7	31.9	34.1
16580	Champaign-Urbana, IL	5.0	9.8	92,013	57.0	43.2	3.5	10.4	43.0	32.0	25.6	28.4
16620	Charleston, WV	1.1	1.2	127,153	63.8	49.1	3.8	11.0	36.2	30.6	27.8	41.4
16700	Charleston-North Charleston-Summerville, SC	5.4	4.8	262,131	65.1	45.3	4.7	15.1	34.9	28.5	31.7	32.7
16740	Charlotte-Gastonia-Rock Hill, NC-SC	10.2	10.5	675,362	66.6	48.3	4.7	13.6	33.4	27.1	35.7	28.6
16820	Charlottesville, VA	4.5	9.4	77,795	64.8	52.5	3.1	9.2	35.2	26.7	29.4	35.8
16860	Chattanooga, TN-GA	3.6	3.8	207,794	66.0	48.2	4.6	13.2	34.0	28.8	30.9	37.8
16940	Cheyenne, WY	14.0	1.6	35,245	67.0	50.2	3.4	13.4	33.0	28.5	30.8	33.6

Metro area or division code	Area name	Total population	Percent change 2010–2012	Population by age (percent)						Median age	Race alone or in combination (percent)				
				Under 5 years	5 to 17 years	18 to 24 years	25 to 44 years	45 to 64 years	65 years and over		White	Black	Asian, Hawaiian, or Pacific Islander	American Indian, Alaska Native, or some other race	
	ACS table number:	B01003	CP05	B01001	B01001	B01001	B01001	B01001	B01001	B01002	B02008	B02009	B02011 + B02012	B02010 + B02013	
	Column number:	1	2	3	4	5	6	7	8	9	10	11	12	13	
16980	Chicago-Joliet-Naperville, IL-IN-WI..................	9,522,446	0.5	6.5	18.0	9.4	28.1	26.0	12.0	36.2	68.7	18.0	6.7	8.9
1698016974	•Chicago-Joliet-Naperville, IL Division.............	7,945,578	0.6	6.5	17.7	9.5	28.7	25.6	12.0	35.9	66.5	18.9	7.2	9.7
1698023844	•Gary, IN Division...............	706,812	-0.2	6.2	18.4	9.1	24.9	27.6	13.8	38.3	73.2	19.4	1.7	7.9
1698029404	•Lake County-Kenosha County, IL-WI Division	870,056	-0.1	6.4	19.7	9.6	25.0	28.0	11.4	37.3	84.8	8.0	6.5	3.1
17020	Chico, CA..................	221,539	0.7	5.3	15.2	15.2	22.3	26.0	15.9	37.1	90.7	2.8	6.4	6.8
17140	Cincinnati-Middletown, OH-KY-IN..................	2,146,560	0.6	6.5	17.9	9.5	25.8	27.5	12.8	37.6	84.7	13.1	2.6	1.6
17300	Clarksville, TN-KY...........	286,973	4.5	8.6	18.5	12.3	30.4	20.7	9.4	30.5	77.2	19.9	3.7	3.7
17420	Cleveland, TN	119,445	3.2	6.1	16.4	9.9	24.9	27.0	15.7	40.3	95.0	4.8	0.7	1.4
17460	Cleveland-Elyria-Mentor, OH	2,063,535	-0.6	5.6	16.8	8.5	24.3	28.9	15.9	41.2	76.3	21.3	2.6	1.9
17660	Coeur d'Alene, ID	142,357	2.5	6.3	17.6	9.1	24.4	27.2	15.4	39.5	96.9	0.6	2.5	3.3
17780	College Station-Bryan, TX	233,135	1.3	6.2	14.7	26.5	25.3	17.9	9.4	26.3	75.7	13.0	5.3	8.1
17820	Colorado Springs, CO	668,353	3.0	6.9	18.3	11.1	27.0	25.8	10.9	34.4	86.5	8.0	5.1	5.7
17860	Columbia, MO	178,101	3.4	6.5	14.3	21.3	25.8	22.1	10.1	30.2	87.9	8.6	4.2	4.5
17900	Columbia, SC	785,641	2.0	6.2	17.0	11.7	26.7	26.2	12.3	36.1	62.5	34.6	2.2	3.2
17980	Columbus, GA-AL.............	306,326	4.9	7.5	18.2	11.3	27.0	24.4	11.7	33.6	55.0	42.7	2.9	3.3
18020	Columbus, IN	79,129	3.0	6.6	18.0	8.3	26.8	25.7	14.6	37.9	88.4	2.7	5.1	4.5
18140	Columbus, OH	1,878,714	2.1	6.7	17.7	10.2	28.7	25.5	11.2	35.4	79.9	16.7	4.2	2.4
18580	Corpus Christi, TX............	435,596	1.7	6.6	18.2	10.2	25.4	25.8	13.8	36.2	87.4	4.2	2.2	7.9
18700	Corvallis, OR	86,430	1.0	5.4	11.8	22.7	22.7	24.2	13.2	31.8	89.8	1.8	8.4	3.8
18880	Crestview-Fort Walton Beach-Destin, FL	190,083	5.2	6.7	15.5	10.4	27.5	25.8	14.1	36.3	83.2	10.9	5.9	5.8
19060	Cumberland, MD-WV	101,968	-1.2	4.7	13.6	12.0	23.5	27.5	18.6	42.0	91.1	8.3	1.0	0.3
19100	Dallas-Fort Worth-Arlington, TX..........	6,647,496	3.8	7.4	19.9	9.4	29.5	24.4	9.4	34.0	72.0	16.1	6.6	8.0
1910019124	•Dallas-Plano-Irving, TX Division.........	4,433,758	4.1	7.5	19.9	9.3	30.1	24.1	9.1	33.8	69.3	17.2	7.3	9.1
1910023104	•Fort Worth-Arlington, TX Division..............	2,213,738	3.2	7.3	19.9	9.5	28.3	25.0	10.1	34.3	77.5	14.0	5.0	5.8
19140	Dalton, GA	142,751	0.2	7.5	19.8	9.5	26.9	24.2	12.1	34.8	93.6	4.6	0.3	3.2
19180	Danville, IL	80,727	-1.0	6.6	17.8	7.9	23.8	27.6	16.4	39.6	86.1	14.7	1.0	2.0
19260	Danville, VA	105,803	-0.6	5.3	15.7	7.3	22.8	30.0	18.9	43.7	65.4	33.6	1.4	2.0
19340	Davenport-Moline-Rock Island, IA-IL..............	381,928	-0.1	6.2	17.0	9.0	24.2	27.7	15.9	39.4	89.4	8.5	2.3	2.8
19380	Dayton, OH	842,858	0.2	5.9	16.5	10.3	24.1	27.4	15.7	39.5	82.4	16.5	2.6	1.3
19460	Decatur, AL	154,233	0.2	6.0	17.4	9.0	24.8	28.1	14.7	39.8	83.8	13.2	0.9	5.3
19500	Decatur, IL	110,122	-0.5	6.3	16.1	9.1	23.8	27.8	16.9	40.5	82.4	18.4	1.4	1.5
19660	Deltona-Daytona Beach-Ormond Beach, FL.....	496,950	0.5	4.8	13.6	9.1	21.1	29.2	22.2	46.0	84.6	11.6	2.2	3.5
19740	Denver-Aurora-Broomfield, CO	2,645,209	3.3	6.7	17.7	8.5	30.2	26.1	10.8	36.0	85.2	6.7	5.1	6.7
19780	Des Moines-West Des Moines, IA..................	588,999	3.3	7.4	18.5	8.6	28.9	25.0	11.6	35.2	90.0	6.0	3.9	2.9
19820	Detroit-Warren-Livonia, MI	4,292,060	0.0	5.8	17.6	9.0	25.1	28.6	13.9	39.8	72.3	23.7	4.2	2.4
1982019804	•Detroit-Livonia-Dearborn, MI Division.........	1,792,365	-1.3	6.5	18.0	10.1	25.1	27.2	13.2	37.9	55.3	41.1	3.4	2.8
1982047644	•Warren-Troy-Farmington Hills, MI Division	2,499,695	1.0	5.4	17.3	8.2	25.1	29.6	14.5	41.0	84.4	11.3	4.8	2.0
20020	Dothan, AL	147,620	1.1	6.5	17.1	8.0	24.6	27.2	16.5	40.3	74.2	24.5	0.8	2.0
20100	Dover, DE	167,626	2.9	6.7	17.3	10.9	24.7	25.8	14.6	37.8	71.3	26.4	2.8	2.7
20220	Dubuque, IA	95,097	1.3	6.2	17.1	10.4	23.8	27.0	15.4	38.9	97.2	2.1	1.4	2.8
20260	Duluth, MN-WI...............	279,452	-0.2	5.4	14.7	11.6	23.1	29.1	16.1	41.0	94.7	2.0	1.6	4.4
20500	Durham-Chapel Hill, NC............	522,826	3.3	6.2	15.5	12.2	28.8	24.9	12.3	35.7	65.6	28.2	5.6	3.6
20740	Eau Claire, WI...............	163,599	1.3	5.6	15.8	13.1	25.6	25.9	13.9	36.2	95.3	1.6	3.2	1.5
20940	El Centro, CA................	176,948	1.0	8.1	20.4	11.6	26.5	22.6	10.8	32.0	83.3	3.6	2.4	14.4
21060	Elizabethtown, KY............	121,165	-1.0	6.9	18.3	9.8	26.6	27.0	11.5	36.6	84.3	14.5	3.0	2.7
21140	Elkhart-Goshen, IN...........	199,619	1.0	7.7	20.2	9.3	25.2	24.8	12.7	35.3	88.6	7.5	1.3	5.7
21300	Elmira, NY.................	88,911	0.1	5.3	17.0	9.5	23.3	29.1	15.7	40.1	92.0	8.3	1.7	1.8
21340	El Paso, TX.................	827,398	2.9	8.1	21.2	11.7	26.7	21.7	10.6	31.1	84.5	4.1	1.9	11.8
21500	Erie, PA...................	280,646	0.0	5.9	16.4	11.6	23.7	27.5	14.9	38.5	90.0	9.0	1.5	2.2
21660	Eugene-Springfield, OR............	354,542	0.7	4.9	14.3	13.3	24.0	27.2	16.2	38.8	92.2	1.8	4.8	6.2
21780	Evansville, IN-KY	358,960	0.3	6.1	16.4	9.7	24.3	28.5	15.0	39.1	92.0	7.4	1.5	1.3
21820	Fairbanks, AK...............	100,272	2.0	7.5	17.2	13.9	30.1	24.1	7.2	30.9	84.4	6.1	5.9	11.5
22020	Fargo, ND-MN...............	216,312	3.4	6.4	15.4	16.2	28.2	22.8	11.0	32.1	93.9	2.8	3.0	3.1
22140	Farmington, NM	128,529	-1.2	7.9	20.4	10.0	25.3	24.9	11.6	33.3	53.8	1.6	0.8	47.5
22180	Fayetteville, NC	374,585	1.9	8.5	18.3	12.1	29.2	22.3	9.7	31.0	55.9	39.6	3.9	7.6
22220	Fayetteville-Springdale-Rogers, AR-MO	482,013	3.5	7.3	19.5	11.1	28.3	22.4	11.4	33.3	86.7	2.9	4.3	9.1
22380	Flagstaff, AZ	136,011	1.0	6.1	16.3	19.6	24.6	23.8	9.6	31.0	65.5	2.0	3.7	32.2
22420	Flint, MI	418,408	-1.5	6.1	18.1	9.2	24.0	28.0	14.7	39.8	76.6	22.2	1.6	2.1
22500	Florence, SC	206,087	0.2	6.5	17.7	9.8	24.5	27.0	14.5	38.6	56.6	42.9	1.1	1.2
22520	Florence-Muscle Shoals, AL............	146,988	-0.1	5.6	16.1	9.5	23.6	27.8	17.4	41.2	86.6	13.1	0.9	1.7
22540	Fond du Lac, WI.............	101,843	0.2	6.6	15.7	9.1	24.1	28.8	15.7	40.2	95.3	2.2	0.9	3.5
22660	Fort Collins-Loveland, CO............	310,487	3.3	5.4	15.2	14.5	25.8	26.4	12.8	35.8	93.8	1.8	3.0	4.9
22900	Fort Smith, AR-OK............	298,110	-0.5	6.4	18.2	8.6	25.2	26.6	15.0	38.2	86.1	4.5	2.6	11.7
23060	Fort Wayne, IN	421,406	1.5	7.1	19.1	9.3	25.7	25.9	13.0	36.6	84.6	12.0	3.0	3.1
23420	Fresno, CA.................	947,895	1.6	8.4	20.9	11.5	26.5	22.0	10.6	31.0	58.7	5.9	11.8	28.1
23460	Gadsden, AL................	104,392	-0.1	5.7	16.7	8.9	25.2	26.7	16.9	40.8	82.7	16.1	1.0	1.8
23540	Gainesville, FL	268,698	0.9	5.3	12.8	22.7	24.6	23.1	11.6	30.9	73.7	20.9	6.1	2.9
23580	Gainesville, GA	185,416	2.9	7.4	20.0	9.8	26.6	24.0	12.2	35.1	81.1	8.0	2.0	10.3
24020	Glens Falls, NY..............	128,472	-0.4	4.8	15.2	8.2	23.5	30.6	17.6	43.9	96.1	3.4	0.9	1.3
24140	Goldsboro, NC	124,246	1.1	6.2	18.2	10.0	25.7	26.6	13.4	37.1	59.5	32.8	1.8	9.9

Table A-3. Metropolitan Areas — Who: Age, Race/Ethnicity, and Household Structure, 2012—*Continued*

Metro area or division code	Area name	Percent Hispanic or Latino	Percent foreign born	Total households	Total family households	Married-couple families	Male household families	Female household families	Total nonfamily households	One-person households	Percent of households with people under 18 years	Percent of households with people 60 years and over
	ACS table number:	B03003	B05012	B11001	B11001	B11001	B11001	B11001	B11001	B11001	C11005	B11006
	Column number:	14	15	16	17	18	19	20	21	22	23	24
16980	Chicago-Joliet-Naperville, IL-IN-WI.........	21.3	17.7	3,426,426	66.0	47.6	4.8	13.6	34.0	28.3	34.2	33.2
1698016974	•Chicago-Joliet-Naperville, IL Division...	22.1	19.0	2,864,963	65.0	46.4	4.9	13.7	35.0	29.1	33.7	33.0
1698023844	•Gary, IN Division	14.6	5.8	256,947	69.6	49.8	5.1	14.7	30.4	25.6	34.7	37.0
1698029404	•Lake County-Kenosha County, IL-WI Division	18.9	15.9	304,516	72.0	56.6	3.9	11.5	28.0	23.2	38.6	32.4
17020	Chico, CA	14.8	8.3	85,388	61.7	43.7	6.4	11.5	38.3	27.2	27.8	40.2
17140	Cincinnati-Middletown, OH-KY-IN.........	2.7	3.8	825,221	65.1	48.0	4.5	12.7	34.9	28.9	32.0	33.7
17300	Clarksville, TN-KY..................	7.7	4.4	101,067	74.6	53.7	5.2	15.7	25.4	19.4	44.0	25.2
17420	Cleveland, TN	4.5	3.6	46,079	69.1	49.9	5.9	13.3	30.9	26.4	33.6	37.7
17460	Cleveland-Elyria-Mentor, OH	5.0	5.5	839,838	61.2	43.0	4.3	13.9	38.8	34.0	28.7	38.2
17660	Coeur d'Alene, ID	4.1	2.0	55,848	68.7	54.4	3.2	11.1	31.3	24.0	31.0	37.5
17780	College Station-Bryan, TX	23.4	12.0	82,134	58.0	42.5	4.5	11.0	42.0	26.7	29.1	25.3
17820	Colorado Springs, CO	15.2	7.9	247,950	68.0	52.3	4.2	11.6	32.0	27.0	35.4	29.3
17860	Columbia, MO	3.0	5.8	69,963	55.1	43.4	3.6	8.1	44.9	32.4	26.4	24.0
17900	Columbia, SC	5.4	4.6	294,039	65.4	45.4	4.5	15.5	34.6	28.8	32.3	31.7
17980	Columbus, GA-AL	6.1	3.6	110,334	64.9	43.2	4.0	17.7	35.1	30.8	34.7	32.3
18020	Columbus, IN	6.5	8.6	29,640	69.5	54.3	5.0	10.1	30.5	26.2	33.8	37.1
18140	Columbus, OH	3.8	7.1	719,081	63.9	46.3	4.6	12.9	36.1	29.0	33.7	29.3
18580	Corpus Christi, TX	58.3	7.1	156,182	70.1	46.7	7.0	16.3	29.9	24.7	35.0	36.7
18700	Corvallis, OR	6.7	8.0	33,395	55.8	44.5	2.1	9.2	44.2	29.7	20.9	33.3
18880	Crestview-Fort Walton Beach-Destin, FL..	8.1	6.4	75,099	66.2	49.5	4.7	12.0	33.8	27.2	32.7	33.4
19060	Cumberland, MD-WV	1.2	1.2	39,475	54.5	41.8	3.1	9.6	45.5	40.0	20.8	45.7
19100	Dallas-Fort Worth-Arlington, TX	28.0	17.7	2,337,076	69.2	50.7	5.0	13.6	30.8	25.4	39.3	27.3
1910019124	•Dallas-Plano-Irving, TX Division..........	29.2	19.0	1,555,596	68.7	50.2	5.0	13.5	31.3	25.8	39.5	26.5
1910023104	•Fort Worth-Arlington, TX Division.......	25.7	14.9	781,480	70.1	51.5	5.0	13.6	29.9	24.8	39.0	29.0
19140	Dalton, GA	27.5	14.3	48,205	72.9	53.7	5.3	14.0	27.1	23.8	43.3	32.9
19180	Danville, IL	4.5	1.8	31,714	60.9	43.1	5.0	12.7	39.1	32.2	28.8	41.6
19260	Danville, VA	2.6	2.5	45,216	65.7	48.0	4.5	13.3	34.3	30.9	28.2	44.4
19340	Davenport-Moline-Rock Island, IA-IL......	8.0	5.0	155,726	63.6	48.6	3.7	11.4	36.4	30.8	29.8	37.4
19380	Dayton, OH.....................	2.2	3.4	341,240	61.7	43.7	4.1	13.8	38.3	32.5	28.8	38.3
19460	Decatur, AL.....................	6.1	3.2	59,790	69.3	50.9	4.0	14.4	30.7	27.5	33.7	36.6
19500	Decatur, IL.....................	2.0	2.6	46,336	62.4	43.9	5.0	13.5	37.6	31.5	28.7	37.0
19660	Deltona-Daytona Beach-Ormond Beach, FL ...	11.8	7.2	197,599	61.8	46.4	4.4	10.9	38.2	31.7	23.1	48.7
19740	Denver-Aurora-Broomfield, CO	22.8	12.2	1,021,036	62.7	46.7	4.8	11.2	37.3	29.5	32.6	29.0
19780	Des Moines-West Des Moines, IA..........	6.9	6.9	230,228	67.3	51.1	4.7	11.5	32.7	26.6	35.7	30.1
19820	Detroit-Warren-Livonia, MI.................	4.1	8.9	1,645,835	64.9	45.5	4.7	14.7	35.1	30.3	31.4	36.5
1982019804	•Detroit-Livonia-Dearborn, MI Division .	5.5	7.8	660,724	62.3	37.0	5.3	20.1	37.7	32.8	31.4	36.6
1982047644	•Warren-Troy-Farmington Hills, MI Division	3.1	9.7	985,111	66.7	51.2	4.3	11.2	33.3	28.6	31.4	36.3
20020	Dothan, AL	3.2	2.2	56,259	66.6	47.3	3.5	15.7	33.4	29.5	28.8	39.2
20100	Dover, DE	6.4	5.5	59,499	68.6	51.7	4.8	12.1	31.4	23.9	35.3	37.8
20220	Dubuque, IA	2.1	2.4	37,726	64.9	50.1	2.9	12.0	35.1	29.8	30.5	35.6
20260	Duluth, MN-WI	1.3	1.6	116,531	60.0	44.9	4.5	10.6	40.0	32.7	25.9	38.3
20500	Durham-Chapel Hill, NC.....................	11.3	11.9	207,572	61.8	44.6	4.5	12.7	38.2	29.8	29.9	30.9
20740	Eau Claire, WI	1.8	3.0	64,765	64.2	51.3	4.4	8.5	35.8	27.4	29.1	33.6
20940	El Centro, CA	81.2	31.5	46,747	78.2	49.5	7.7	21.1	21.8	18.7	47.3	36.5
21060	Elizabethtown, KY	4.8	4.7	44,998	72.4	55.2	3.5	13.7	27.6	21.6	36.0	31.6
21140	Elkhart-Goshen, IN	14.7	8.3	70,857	72.5	51.9	7.5	13.1	27.5	23.7	40.3	34.7
21300	Elmira, NY.....................	2.8	2.5	34,867	61.6	44.4	5.5	11.6	38.4	33.4	28.4	38.4
21340	El Paso, TX.....................	81.2	25.2	260,645	76.9	51.6	5.2	20.1	23.1	19.5	45.3	31.8
21500	Erie, PA	3.6	4.5	109,973	64.7	47.1	4.3	13.3	35.3	28.3	29.1	36.6
21660	Eugene-Springfield, OR.....................	7.8	5.9	146,327	58.9	42.3	4.4	12.2	41.1	28.2	26.2	38.9
21780	Evansville, IN-KY	1.9	1.7	145,212	66.0	49.5	4.7	11.8	34.0	29.5	31.3	35.3
21820	Fairbanks, AK	6.8	4.8	35,944	61.5	47.4	3.6	10.4	38.5	30.9	34.8	23.8
22020	Fargo, ND-MN	2.7	4.9	89,002	57.0	44.5	4.4	8.2	43.0	32.8	28.6	27.0
22140	Farmington, NM	19.3	2.8	40,025	73.0	51.1	5.8	16.1	27.0	22.0	34.9	34.7
22180	Fayetteville, NC	10.5	5.4	139,404	67.8	44.9	4.9	18.1	32.2	27.7	37.6	27.8
22220	Fayetteville-Springdale-Rogers, AR-MO .	15.5	10.4	179,264	68.4	54.6	3.7	10.2	31.6	25.7	34.9	29.6
22380	Flagstaff, AZ	13.7	4.4	46,366	63.9	44.5	6.1	13.3	36.1	23.9	32.9	28.9
22420	Flint, MI	3.1	2.6	166,225	63.4	42.6	4.7	16.0	36.6	30.5	29.8	37.2
22500	Florence, SC	2.2	2.1	77,878	70.3	45.6	5.1	19.6	29.7	26.5	35.3	36.4
22520	Florence-Muscle Shoals, AL..................	2.4	1.7	58,960	67.3	52.8	3.8	10.7	32.7	28.2	27.9	40.3
22540	Fond du Lac, WI	4.5	2.5	41,191	66.8	50.8	5.4	10.5	33.2	29.0	29.7	38.1
22660	Fort Collins-Loveland, CO	10.8	4.6	124,031	62.9	50.3	3.9	8.7	37.1	24.5	28.8	32.3
22900	Fort Smith, AR-OK	8.6	5.7	116,089	67.8	49.4	6.3	12.1	32.2	28.6	32.5	36.1
23060	Fort Wayne, IN	6.0	5.7	162,645	64.9	47.3	5.0	12.5	35.1	29.8	31.1	33.9
23420	Fresno, CA	51.2	22.3	292,280	72.3	45.7	8.7	17.9	27.7	21.2	42.5	32.9
23460	Gadsden, AL.....................	3.6	2.5	39,031	66.8	44.8	5.8	16.3	33.2	29.3	29.0	41.5
23540	Gainesville, FL	8.6	10.0	99,542	54.9	38.9	3.6	12.4	45.1	32.8	24.4	31.0
23580	Gainesville, GA	26.9	16.1	60,500	75.8	57.5	5.9	12.4	24.2	20.5	38.7	36.0
24020	Glens Falls, NY	1.7	3.0	51,781	64.9	49.5	3.9	11.5	35.1	27.8	27.7	41.6
24140	Goldsboro, NC	10.4	7.6	47,554	65.6	43.9	5.9	15.9	34.4	29.5	33.4	36.3

Metro area or division code	Area name	Total population	Percent change 2010–2012	Population by age (percent)						Median age	Race alone or in combination (percent)				
				Under 5 years	5 to 17 years	18 to 24 years	25 to 44 years	45 to 64 years	65 years and over		White	Black	Asian, Hawaiian, or Pacific Islander	American Indian, Alaska Native, or some other race	
	ACS table number:	B01003	CP05	B01001	B01001	B01001	B01001	B01001	B01001	B01002	B02008	B02009	B02011 + B02012	B02010 + B02013	
	Column number:	1	2	3	4	5	6	7	8	9	10	11	12	13
24220	Grand Forks, ND-MN	98,888	-0.7	6.2	14.5	19.1	23.6	23.9	12.6	32.0	93.6	2.7	2.2	4.0
24300	Grand Junction, CO	147,848	1.0	6.3	16.5	10.1	24.6	27.1	15.5	38.6	95.1	1.2	1.7	5.2
24340	Grand Rapids-Wyoming, MI	785,352	1.4	6.9	18.5	9.9	26.2	26.2	12.3	35.7	88.0	9.6	2.5	3.5
24500	Great Falls, MT	81,723	0.3	6.9	15.5	10.3	24.0	26.4	16.9	37.8	92.8	2.5	1.5	8.0
24540	Greeley, CO	263,691	3.7	7.7	19.5	10.7	27.3	24.2	10.5	33.5	86.8	1.5	2.0	12.4
24580	Green Bay, WI	311,098	1.4	6.5	17.4	9.3	25.3	28.1	13.3	38.1	92.0	2.8	2.8	4.4
24660	Greensboro-High Point, NC	736,065	1.5	6.0	17.0	10.3	26.1	26.5	14.0	38.1	67.3	27.5	3.6	3.6
24780	Greenville, NC	194,252	2.1	6.1	15.8	18.2	25.8	23.1	10.9	32.2	60.3	36.5	1.8	3.9
24860	Greenville-Mauldin-Easley, SC	653,498	2.3	6.4	16.7	11.3	25.7	26.0	13.9	37.2	79.8	17.6	2.4	1.9
25060	Gulfport-Biloxi, MS	257,312	2.8	6.8	17.4	9.9	26.7	26.1	13.0	35.9	76.3	21.5	3.0	1.7
25180	Hagerstown-Martinsburg, MD-WV	273,604	2.4	6.5	16.7	7.8	26.6	28.3	14.2	40.2	88.8	10.7	1.4	2.2
25260	Hanford-Corcoran, CA	151,364	-1.2	8.0	19.5	10.7	31.5	21.8	8.5	31.7	72.7	7.5	6.0	18.6
25420	Harrisburg-Carlisle, PA	553,980	0.7	5.7	16.0	9.3	25.3	28.4	15.3	40.6	84.3	12.0	3.7	3.0
25500	Harrisonburg, VA	128,372	2.3	5.5	14.5	21.0	22.9	22.9	13.2	32.1	93.0	4.9	2.4	2.0
25540	Hartford-West Hartford-East Hartford, CT	1,214,400	0.1	5.2	16.3	9.9	24.7	28.8	15.0	40.6	80.4	12.6	5.0	5.0
25620	Hattiesburg, MS	147,408	0.8	6.8	17.9	15.4	26.5	21.8	11.7	31.8	67.8	30.2	1.1	2.0
25860	Hickory-Lenoir-Morganton, NC	363,627	-0.5	5.5	16.7	8.6	24.1	28.9	16.3	41.9	86.8	8.4	2.8	3.3
25980	Hinesville-Fort Stewart, GA	84,165	12.6	10.9	18.3	14.4	28.5	20.0	7.9	27.9	51.2	44.2	4.6	6.2
26100	Holland-Grand Haven, MI	269,099	1.9	6.3	19.1	12.3	24.3	25.3	12.6	35.4	93.4	2.3	3.2	3.0
26180	Honolulu, HI	976,372	2.2	6.4	15.1	10.6	27.7	25.1	15.1	37.2	37.9	4.0	85.0	4.3
26300	Hot Springs, AR	96,903	0.8	4.6	16.0	8.1	21.5	28.7	21.2	44.7	85.5	9.2	1.1	5.8
26380	Houma-Bayou Cane-Thibodaux, LA	208,922	0.4	7.1	17.8	10.1	25.7	26.0	13.2	36.1	78.5	17.1	1.3	6.7
26420	Houston-Sugar Land-Baytown, TX	6,204,161	3.8	7.7	19.7	9.6	29.4	24.4	9.2	33.5	68.0	17.9	7.7	8.8
26580	Huntington-Ashland, WV-KY-OH	286,603	-0.4	5.7	15.9	9.6	24.4	27.7	16.8	41.2	96.1	3.9	0.6	0.9
26620	Huntsville, AL	430,734	2.8	6.0	17.3	9.5	26.5	27.6	13.0	38.1	73.6	23.4	3.0	3.1
26820	Idaho Falls, ID	133,368	0.6	9.2	22.8	8.7	26.1	22.2	10.9	31.9	93.1	0.8	1.5	6.4
26900	Indianapolis-Carmel, IN	1,798,786	2.2	7.1	18.7	8.8	27.9	26.1	11.4	35.7	78.9	16.5	3.0	4.2
26980	Iowa City, IA	158,231	3.5	5.7	14.5	19.5	27.8	22.2	10.2	30.8	87.4	5.8	5.3	2.9
27060	Ithaca, NY	102,554	0.9	4.5	11.3	26.7	23.7	22.3	11.4	29.7	85.7	4.9	10.8	1.2
27100	Jackson, MI	160,309	0.1	5.7	17.1	9.0	24.3	28.9	15.1	39.9	89.4	9.6	1.0	1.9
27140	Jackson, MS	548,945	1.6	6.8	18.8	10.4	26.6	25.5	11.9	35.0	49.5	48.9	1.3	1.1
27180	Jackson, TN	115,257	0.9	6.6	16.6	12.0	23.6	26.8	14.3	38.2	65.0	34.6	0.5	0.8
27260	Jacksonville, FL	1,377,850	2.0	6.3	16.9	9.6	26.8	27.2	13.1	37.8	73.6	22.9	4.9	2.2
27340	Jacksonville, NC	183,263	2.1	9.5	15.5	21.7	28.8	16.9	7.7	26.1	76.5	18.4	3.2	5.1
27500	Janesville, WI	160,418	0.1	6.2	18.1	8.8	25.1	27.4	14.5	38.4	94.3	4.8	1.5	4.4
27620	Jefferson City, MO	149,889	0.0	5.7	17.3	10.2	25.6	27.0	14.2	38.1	90.4	8.8	1.6	1.0
27740	Johnson City, TN	200,684	0.9	4.9	15.4	10.3	25.1	27.0	17.3	41.1	95.8	4.1	1.0	0.8
27780	Johnstown, PA	141,584	-1.3	4.9	14.4	9.5	22.3	29.5	19.4	44.1	95.7	3.8	1.1	1.8
27860	Jonesboro, AR	124,042	3.1	7.3	17.2	11.7	26.1	24.5	13.1	35.0	85.3	13.3	1.1	1.5
27900	Joplin, MO	174,327	-0.9	6.6	18.2	10.0	25.3	25.2	14.7	36.8	94.3	2.7	1.7	4.5
28020	Kalamazoo-Portage, MI	330,034	1.0	6.0	16.6	13.9	24.0	26.0	13.4	35.7	86.2	11.4	2.5	3.4
28100	Kankakee-Bradley, IL	113,040	-0.4	6.3	18.1	10.4	25.5	25.7	13.9	37.0	82.5	16.1	1.3	2.0
28140	Kansas City, MO-KS	2,064,296	1.4	6.8	18.3	8.3	27.3	26.7	12.7	37.0	81.6	13.7	3.3	4.4
28420	Kennewick-Pasco-Richland, WA	268,243	4.9	8.1	20.9	9.5	26.4	24.3	10.8	33.0	78.8	1.9	4.3	18.6
28660	Killeen-Temple-Fort Hood, TX	420,133	2.9	8.3	19.0	12.5	29.9	21.0	9.3	30.5	71.1	22.1	5.1	7.1
28700	Kingsport-Bristol-Bristol, TN-VA	309,654	-0.3	4.9	15.4	7.9	23.5	29.1	19.2	43.7	97.0	2.5	0.7	1.5
28740	Kingston, NY	181,791	-0.4	4.7	14.6	9.9	24.0	30.9	15.9	43.0	91.0	8.2	2.6	3.3
28940	Knoxville, TN	709,492	1.5	5.6	15.8	10.4	25.5	27.1	15.5	39.6	90.5	7.4	1.9	1.9
29020	Kokomo, IN	97,599	-2.9	5.7	16.6	8.3	22.8	28.6	18.1	42.1	91.9	7.3	1.2	1.1
29100	La Crosse, WI-MN	135,298	1.0	5.8	15.3	14.8	23.7	25.9	14.6	36.7	94.1	2.0	4.2	1.7
29140	Lafayette, IN	205,917	1.5	5.8	15.3	22.3	24.8	21.1	10.7	29.4	89.6	4.7	6.1	1.3
29180	Lafayette, LA	279,781	2.0	7.2	17.3	11.4	27.6	25.5	11.0	34.1	71.6	27.4	1.6	3.1
29340	Lake Charles, LA	200,509	0.9	6.9	17.9	10.4	25.0	26.6	13.1	36.7	73.9	24.8	1.3	1.7
29420	Lake Havasu City-Kingman, AZ	203,334	1.6	5.0	14.5	6.7	20.1	28.9	24.9	48.7	90.3	1.4	1.9	11.0
29460	Lakeland-Winter Haven, FL	616,158	2.2	6.1	16.9	9.1	23.8	25.2	18.8	40.2	81.1	16.5	2.3	2.6
29540	Lancaster, PA	526,823	1.3	6.7	17.6	9.8	23.8	26.5	15.6	38.5	90.4	5.2	2.3	4.4
29620	Lansing-East Lansing, MI	465,732	0.4	5.5	15.8	16.3	23.8	26.0	12.6	35.1	86.1	11.1	4.9	2.8
29700	Laredo, TX	259,172	3.0	10.0	24.7	11.2	27.3	18.7	8.1	28.2	94.7	0.2	1.0	4.6
29740	Las Cruces, NM	214,445	1.9	7.9	18.5	12.9	24.7	22.9	13.1	32.4	90.9	2.1	1.8	7.3
29820	Las Vegas-Paradise, NV	2,000,759	2.4	6.8	17.7	9.2	29.3	24.8	12.3	36.0	68.0	12.3	12.4	12.4
29940	Lawrence, KS	112,864	1.6	5.4	13.2	24.7	26.4	20.5	9.7	29.1	88.9	5.5	5.3	5.0
30020	Lawton, OK	126,390	0.8	7.7	17.0	14.1	27.8	23.2	10.3	32.0	71.4	20.2	5.2	11.8
30140	Lebanon, PA	135,251	1.2	6.3	16.5	8.6	24.1	27.1	17.4	41.0	89.7	2.8	1.4	7.8
30300	Lewiston, ID-WA	61,419	0.8	5.6	15.6	8.9	23.1	27.9	18.9	42.1	93.7	0.4	1.4	7.2
30340	Lewiston-Auburn, ME	107,609	0.0	6.4	15.6	9.6	24.6	28.8	14.9	40.7	97.5	2.8	1.1	4.3
30460	Lexington-Fayette, KY	485,023	2.4	6.3	16.0	12.7	28.1	25.1	11.8	35.3	84.3	12.0	3.0	3.3
30620	Lima, OH	105,141	-1.0	5.9	17.7	10.6	23.0	27.3	15.6	38.2	86.2	13.8	1.0	1.2
30700	Lincoln, NE	309,387	2.1	6.9	16.2	14.8	26.6	23.9	11.6	33.2	91.4	4.8	4.2	2.7
30780	Little Rock-North Little Rock-Conway, AR	715,210	1.9	6.8	17.5	10.2	27.5	25.3	12.8	35.9	74.3	23.6	2.1	1.7

Metro area or division code	Area name	Percent Hispanic or Latino	Percent foreign born	Total households	Household type (percent)							Percent of households with people under 18 years	Percent of households with people 60 years and over
					Family households				Nonfamily households				
					Total family households	Married-couple families	Male household families	Female household families	Total nonfamily households	One-person households			
	ACS table number:	B03003	B05012	B11001	B11001	B11001	B11001	B11001	B11001	B11001		C11005	B11006
	Column number:	14	15	16	17	18	19	20	21	22		23	24
24220	Grand Forks, ND-MN	4.1	3.2	40,954	57.1	45.7	4.1	7.3	42.9	35.0		25.6	29.2
24300	Grand Junction, CO	13.7	4.3	58,779	68.0	50.7	6.0	11.3	32.0	27.3		29.8	38.9
24340	Grand Rapids-Wyoming, MI	8.7	6.4	294,081	68.1	51.4	4.1	12.6	31.9	25.1		34.4	31.6
24500	Great Falls, MT	3.8	1.9	33,471	62.0	47.2	5.0	9.7	38.0	32.4		28.6	38.4
24540	Greeley, CO	28.4	8.7	92,447	73.6	58.0	5.5	10.2	26.4	19.7		39.8	29.6
24580	Green Bay, WI	6.6	4.2	122,718	65.2	51.0	5.0	9.2	34.8	28.8		32.2	33.2
24660	Greensboro-High Point, NC	7.8	9.2	292,421	65.4	44.5	4.8	16.1	34.6	29.3		32.3	34.4
24780	Greenville, NC	7.0	5.5	76,461	61.1	41.6	2.9	16.6	38.9	28.0		32.3	28.2
24860	Greenville-Mauldin-Easley, SC	7.1	6.7	245,906	68.5	50.2	5.4	13.0	31.5	26.3		32.9	34.1
25060	Gulfport-Biloxi, MS	4.8	3.4	100,195	67.0	44.4	6.5	16.1	33.0	28.0		34.7	34.1
25180	Hagerstown-Martinsburg, MD-WV	3.6	3.8	104,765	68.2	47.8	6.4	14.0	31.8	26.3		30.9	36.8
25260	Hanford-Corcoran, CA	52.0	18.6	40,376	77.1	50.9	8.9	17.3	22.9	18.3		48.7	29.1
25420	Harrisburg-Carlisle, PA	5.1	5.6	220,146	65.7	49.2	4.5	12.0	34.3	28.9		29.4	37.0
25500	Harrisonburg, VA	10.3	9.3	45,298	63.9	52.0	3.4	8.5	36.1	24.6		30.0	33.8
25540	Hartford-West Hartford-East Hartford, CT	13.2	12.6	468,942	64.9	46.7	4.7	13.4	35.1	28.9		30.8	36.9
25620	Hattiesburg, MS	2.7	3.1	53,480	65.6	42.9	5.6	17.2	34.4	29.0		34.3	31.3
25860	Hickory-Lenoir-Morganton, NC	6.0	4.8	140,419	64.3	48.5	5.4	10.4	35.7	30.3		29.1	41.6
25980	Hinesville-Fort Stewart, GA	11.1	4.2	28,309	71.4	50.2	5.0	16.2	28.6	24.3		38.6	19.6
26100	Holland-Grand Haven, MI	9.0	6.1	95,048	72.2	59.5	3.8	8.8	27.8	22.3		35.2	32.6
26180	Honolulu, HI	8.8	19.5	308,072	69.9	51.9	5.4	12.6	30.1	23.3		33.8	41.9
26300	Hot Springs, AR	5.1	3.6	40,656	67.5	52.0	3.9	11.6	32.5	28.2		30.0	43.4
26380	Houma-Bayou Cane-Thibodaux, LA	4.2	3.3	74,435	71.3	49.6	7.6	14.1	28.7	24.0		34.8	34.0
26420	Houston-Sugar Land-Baytown, TX	35.9	22.3	2,099,897	70.4	50.7	5.5	14.2	29.6	24.8		39.7	28.0
26580	Huntington-Ashland, WV-KY-OH	1.0	0.9	112,510	63.4	48.1	4.4	10.8	36.6	31.9		26.1	41.8
26620	Huntsville, AL	4.9	5.4	167,556	66.3	50.7	4.3	11.3	33.7	29.8		30.9	32.1
26820	Idaho Falls, ID	11.8	5.4	43,620	74.9	58.8	3.9	12.2	25.1	22.1		40.5	32.1
26900	Indianapolis-Carmel, IN	6.4	6.0	682,276	65.6	47.8	4.3	13.4	34.4	28.5		34.0	29.7
26980	Iowa City, IA	5.2	9.2	64,540	57.9	44.1	4.3	9.5	42.1	29.9		26.8	26.4
27060	Ithaca, NY	4.6	12.1	38,269	50.9	42.0	1.8	7.1	49.1	32.2		22.6	31.5
27100	Jackson, MI	3.1	1.3	60,420	65.0	46.3	5.1	13.6	35.0	29.5		29.6	40.3
27140	Jackson, MS	2.2	2.1	196,282	68.5	43.0	5.9	19.6	31.5	26.7		36.6	33.6
27180	Jackson, TN	3.0	1.7	43,040	63.4	46.2	3.7	13.5	36.6	32.6		27.1	38.0
27260	Jacksonville, FL	7.4	7.9	508,977	64.9	46.6	4.0	14.3	35.1	29.4		31.2	34.4
27340	Jacksonville, NC	11.1	4.1	61,842	74.3	57.3	3.9	13.1	25.7	20.2		42.5	23.5
27500	Janesville, WI	7.9	4.3	63,287	65.7	47.0	4.4	14.3	34.3	27.8		33.4	34.7
27620	Jefferson City, MO	1.8	2.0	57,934	65.3	49.2	3.2	12.9	34.7	28.5		33.6	35.5
27740	Johnson City, TN	2.6	2.5	83,530	61.3	45.8	4.2	11.3	38.7	33.0		25.6	39.8
27780	Johnstown, PA	1.5	1.0	58,228	64.0	47.1	4.9	12.0	36.0	31.8		24.3	44.8
27860	Jonesboro, AR	4.2	3.1	47,481	68.7	48.9	4.9	14.8	31.3	24.5		35.5	32.5
27900	Joplin, MO	6.3	4.0	68,745	66.0	50.2	4.7	11.1	34.0	27.8		32.8	33.6
28020	Kalamazoo-Portage, MI	5.7	4.8	128,529	60.9	44.7	4.5	11.7	39.1	31.6		29.0	33.7
28100	Kankakee-Bradley, IL	9.3	5.5	41,267	67.3	46.8	4.7	15.8	32.7	27.1		34.9	34.9
28140	Kansas City, MO-KS	8.4	5.8	801,060	65.2	48.6	4.3	12.3	34.8	28.7		32.8	32.0
28420	Kennewick-Pasco-Richland, WA	29.3	13.2	90,215	69.7	54.4	4.1	11.2	30.3	26.0		38.0	32.2
28660	Killeen-Temple-Fort Hood, TX	21.2	6.8	133,995	74.2	54.8	4.7	14.6	25.8	22.7		40.4	27.8
28700	Kingsport-Bristol-Bristol, TN-VA	1.5	1.1	127,704	65.5	51.0	3.9	10.6	34.5	30.3		27.9	43.0
28740	Kingston, NY	9.3	7.4	70,353	62.6	45.9	4.5	12.1	37.4	30.0		26.8	42.3
28940	Knoxville, TN	3.8	4.3	290,393	63.8	49.9	3.8	10.0	36.2	31.0		29.3	36.7
29020	Kokomo, IN	2.9	2.1	40,571	64.0	47.0	5.9	11.2	36.0	31.3		29.1	40.7
29100	La Crosse, WI-MN	1.5	2.8	54,799	58.4	47.3	3.6	7.4	41.6	33.3		25.2	34.3
29140	Lafayette, IN	7.3	9.3	79,034	58.6	44.0	3.4	11.2	41.4	29.3		27.9	28.1
29180	Lafayette, LA	3.8	3.4	106,842	64.8	43.8	5.3	15.7	35.2	29.6		35.7	28.6
29340	Lake Charles, LA	2.8	2.0	77,201	68.8	47.0	6.0	15.8	31.2	27.4		36.1	35.1
29420	Lake Havasu City-Kingman, AZ	15.4	7.9	79,239	61.1	46.2	2.8	12.0	38.9	28.9		19.6	56.4
29460	Lakeland-Winter Haven, FL	18.6	10.0	223,507	68.9	49.9	5.2	13.8	31.1	25.6		30.3	44.9
29540	Lancaster, PA	9.3	3.9	194,198	71.3	57.8	4.3	9.2	28.7	23.7		32.3	38.0
29620	Lansing-East Lansing, MI	6.4	5.8	181,262	59.8	43.6	4.2	12.0	40.2	30.3		27.6	32.5
29700	Laredo, TX	95.4	27.3	68,980	81.8	53.3	6.2	22.3	18.2	15.4		55.2	30.6
29740	Las Cruces, NM	66.4	15.5	73,717	73.7	49.8	4.6	19.3	26.3	21.8		37.0	34.3
29820	Las Vegas-Paradise, NV	29.8	21.8	715,837	64.5	42.6	7.1	14.7	35.5	27.5		34.2	33.2
29940	Lawrence, KS	5.5	7.4	43,992	54.4	40.1	5.2	9.2	45.6	32.0		28.4	25.2
30020	Lawton, OK	12.0	6.9	43,470	64.7	45.7	4.3	14.6	35.3	30.6		33.6	29.7
30140	Lebanon, PA	10.4	5.3	52,424	66.7	51.5	3.9	11.2	33.3	29.5		29.3	39.7
30300	Lewiston, ID-WA	4.0	1.2	25,325	63.8	49.3	4.1	10.4	36.2	29.3		27.2	41.6
30340	Lewiston-Auburn, ME	1.7	3.1	44,641	62.6	47.8	3.9	10.8	37.4	32.2		29.1	36.0
30460	Lexington-Fayette, KY	5.9	6.7	191,487	62.5	45.3	4.3	12.9	37.5	30.2		30.2	30.8
30620	Lima, OH	2.5	1.2	40,366	63.5	45.1	4.6	13.8	36.5	29.1		32.5	36.4
30700	Lincoln, NE	6.0	6.3	121,906	61.0	48.5	3.3	9.3	39.0	30.2		30.3	29.3
30780	Little Rock-North Little Rock-Conway, AR	5.0	3.8	277,026	63.8	46.4	4.6	12.8	36.2	31.3		29.7	32.1

Metro area or division code	Area name	Total population	Percent change 2010–2012	Population by age (percent)						Median age	Race alone or in combination (percent)				
				Under 5 years	5 to 17 years	18 to 24 years	25 to 44 years	45 to 64 years	65 years and over		White	Black	Asian, Hawaiian, or Pacific Islander	American Indian, Alaska Native, or some other race	
	ACS table number:	B01003	CP05	B01001	B01001	B01001	B01001	B01001	B01001	B01002	B02008	B02009	B02011 + B02012	B02010 + B02013
	Column number:	1	2	3	4	5	6	7	8	9	10	11	12	13
30860	Logan, UT-ID	128,374	2.1	9.4	21.8	16.8	26.0	17.2	8.8	26.1	95.0	0.6	3.2	3.3
30980	Longview, TX	216,679	1.0	6.9	17.8	10.1	24.9	25.6	14.7	37.4	79.6	17.4	1.1	3.7
31020	Longview, WA	101,996	-0.5	6.0	17.0	8.1	23.4	28.5	16.8	41.4	94.5	1.3	3.2	6.2
31100	Los Angeles-Long Beach-Santa Ana, CA	13,052,921	1.6	6.5	17.2	10.7	29.0	24.9	11.7	35.5	59.1	7.8	17.2	20.3
3110031084	•Los Angeles-Long Beach-Glendale, CA Division	9,962,789	1.3	6.5	17.2	10.8	29.4	24.6	11.5	35.2	56.6	9.5	16.0	22.3
3110042044	•Santa Ana-Anaheim-Irvine, CA Division	3,090,132	2.4	6.3	17.5	10.3	27.8	25.8	12.3	36.7	67.1	2.2	21.1	13.6
31140	Louisville-Jefferson County, KY-IN	1,302,457	1.2	6.4	17.2	8.9	26.3	27.8	13.5	38.5	83.3	15.0	2.2	2.0
31180	Lubbock, TX	291,548	1.1	6.9	17.2	17.2	25.4	21.8	11.5	31.1	82.1	8.0	3.1	10.0
31340	Lynchburg, VA	256,934	2.4	5.6	15.1	13.1	22.5	27.2	16.6	40.7	79.4	19.7	1.9	2.1
31420	Macon, GA	232,398	2.0	6.8	17.6	9.8	25.0	27.1	13.7	37.6	52.9	44.7	1.9	1.5
31460	Madera-Chowchilla, CA	152,218	0.5	7.9	20.5	10.2	26.2	23.1	12.0	32.3	83.0	5.6	2.5	12.2
31540	Madison, WI	583,869	2.4	6.0	15.4	12.4	28.4	26.2	11.5	35.4	88.4	6.2	5.1	2.7
31700	Manchester-Nashua, NH	402,922	0.5	5.6	16.9	8.7	26.2	29.9	12.8	40.0	93.4	3.2	4.2	1.9
31740	Manhattan, KS	135,823	6.2	7.8	15.3	23.9	28.6	16.2	8.1	26.1	85.2	12.1	4.4	2.1
31860	Mankato-North Mankato, MN	98,020	1.2	5.6	14.4	19.8	24.6	23.2	12.4	31.7	94.1	3.8	2.3	1.3
31900	Mansfield, OH	122,673	-1.2	6.1	16.1	8.5	24.3	28.0	17.1	41.1	89.8	10.6	0.6	3.4
32580	McAllen-Edinburg-Mission, TX	806,552	3.4	9.6	24.6	11.0	26.6	18.5	9.8	28.6	92.8	0.7	1.2	5.8
32780	Medford, OR	206,412	1.4	6.1	15.5	8.8	22.4	28.6	18.7	42.7	95.5	1.1	2.7	5.3
32820	Memphis, TN-MS-AR	1,333,315	1.3	7.1	18.9	10.0	26.9	25.9	11.1	35.2	49.6	47.0	2.4	2.8
32900	Merced, CA	262,305	2.2	8.3	22.5	12.4	25.9	21.0	10.0	30.0	64.1	4.9	8.6	26.5
33100	Miami-Fort Lauderdale-Pompano Beach, FL	5,762,717	3.2	5.7	15.3	9.1	26.7	26.8	16.4	40.2	73.3	22.3	3.1	3.4
3310022744	•Fort Lauderdale-Pompano Beach-Deerfield Beach, FL Division	1,815,137	3.5	5.7	15.9	8.7	27.1	28.0	14.7	40.0	65.0	28.9	4.4	4.7
3310033124	•Miami-Miami Beach-Kendall, FL Division	2,591,035	3.4	5.9	15.2	9.8	28.3	26.3	14.5	38.6	77.0	19.5	2.1	2.9
3310048424	•West Palm Beach-Boca Raton-Boynton Beach, FL Division	1,356,545	2.5	5.2	14.9	8.2	23.3	26.3	22.1	43.6	77.4	18.8	3.4	2.7
33140	Michigan City-La Porte, IN	111,246	-0.2	6.0	16.3	8.7	25.6	28.3	15.1	39.9	87.5	12.5	0.7	1.5
33260	Midland, TX	146,645	7.1	8.3	19.0	9.8	28.3	23.6	10.9	32.3	85.6	7.6	1.6	6.6
33340	Milwaukee-Waukesha-West Allis, WI	1,566,981	0.6	6.6	17.6	9.5	26.2	26.9	13.1	37.1	76.4	17.9	3.6	4.7
33460	Minneapolis-St. Paul-Bloomington, MN-WI	3,353,724	2.1	6.7	17.8	8.9	28.2	26.9	11.4	36.3	84.0	9.0	6.9	3.4
33540	Missoula, MT	110,977	1.4	5.2	13.5	15.6	27.4	25.9	12.4	34.7	95.9	0.5	2.8	4.7
33660	Mobile, AL	413,936	0.2	6.8	17.8	9.9	25.4	26.4	13.8	37.1	61.6	35.7	2.2	1.8
33700	Modesto, CA	521,726	1.2	7.6	20.4	10.4	26.3	24.0	11.4	33.3	79.4	3.7	7.9	14.0
33740	Monroe, LA	177,781	0.6	7.1	18.7	10.5	25.1	25.1	13.5	35.2	61.5	36.7	1.1	1.2
33780	Monroe, MI	151,048	-0.6	5.4	17.9	8.5	23.4	30.4	14.4	41.3	96.2	3.0	0.9	0.9
33860	Montgomery, AL	377,844	0.4	6.8	17.6	10.6	27.0	25.3	12.7	36.3	53.5	43.9	2.2	2.0
34060	Morgantown, WV	134,164	3.0	4.9	12.2	21.3	26.2	23.5	11.9	32.3	93.2	4.0	2.7	1.9
34100	Morristown, TN	137,643	0.6	5.2	17.0	9.2	24.0	27.1	17.5	40.8	95.4	3.4	0.5	2.8
34580	Mount Vernon-Anacortes, WA	118,222	1.0	6.5	16.7	9.0	22.9	27.7	17.2	40.7	90.9	1.4	3.3	8.2
34620	Muncie, IN	117,364	-0.3	5.4	14.2	20.0	21.3	23.6	15.4	34.8	93.4	5.1	1.5	5.5
34740	Muskegon-Norton Shores, MI	170,182	-1.1	6.3	18.1	8.8	24.5	28.0	14.3	38.6	84.2	15.6	1.1	2.6
34820	Myrtle Beach-North Myrtle Beach-Conway, SC	282,285	4.4	5.5	14.4	9.4	24.4	27.7	18.6	41.8	83.1	14.8	1.5	3.1
34900	Napa, CA	139,045	1.6	5.7	16.9	9.1	24.7	27.5	15.9	40.7	78.8	2.5	8.7	13.0
34940	Naples-Marco Island, FL	332,427	3.1	5.1	13.9	7.1	20.3	25.4	28.2	48.0	89.3	7.2	1.5	3.0
34980	Nashville-Davidson--Murfreesboro--Franklin, TN	1,645,638	3.3	6.6	17.4	9.7	29.0	25.8	11.5	36.0	79.0	16.4	3.1	3.6
35300	New Haven-Milford, CT	862,813	0.0	5.4	16.2	10.1	25.4	27.9	15.0	39.7	77.2	13.9	4.5	6.8
35380	New Orleans-Metairie-Kenner, LA	1,205,374	2.7	6.4	16.6	9.5	27.2	27.4	12.8	37.2	59.9	35.4	3.4	3.3
35620	New York-Northern New Jersey-Long Island, NY-NJ-PA	19,160,024	1.3	6.1	16.2	9.4	28.1	26.6	13.6	37.8	61.1	18.7	11.4	11.8
3562020764	•Edison, NJ Division	2,360,602	0.7	5.9	17.1	8.6	24.8	28.1	15.6	40.4	77.5	8.1	12.7	3.6
3562035004	•Nassau-Suffolk, NY Division	2,848,506	0.5	5.5	17.3	9.0	24.0	29.1	15.1	40.9	79.1	10.1	6.5	6.9
3562035084	•Newark-Union, NJ-PA Division	2,161,110	0.5	5.9	17.7	8.6	26.0	28.5	13.2	39.4	64.7	22.4	6.4	9.0
3562035644	•New York-White Plains-Wayne, NY-NJ Division	11,789,806	1.7	6.4	15.5	9.8	30.1	25.3	12.9	36.4	52.8	22.1	13.2	15.2
35660	Niles-Benton Harbor, MI	156,067	-0.5	5.7	17.3	8.2	23.3	28.5	17.0	41.4	79.5	16.5	2.6	4.0
35840	North Port-Bradenton-Sarasota, FL	720,042	2.4	4.5	13.0	6.7	19.1	27.8	28.8	50.3	89.7	7.5	2.2	2.2
35980	Norwich-New London, CT	274,170	0.0	5.1	15.6	10.5	24.3	29.4	15.0	40.8	85.4	7.4	5.3	5.7
36100	Ocala, FL	335,125	1.2	5.0	13.9	8.1	19.5	26.7	26.8	48.2	84.8	13.1	2.5	3.9
36140	Ocean City, NJ	96,304	-1.0	4.5	13.6	7.8	19.6	31.8	22.6	48.2	92.9	4.9	1.3	4.1
36220	Odessa, TX	144,325	5.2	8.4	20.3	11.0	27.4	22.8	10.1	31.6	89.8	5.0	1.0	7.0
36260	Ogden-Clearfield, UT	562,356	2.0	9.2	22.9	9.5	28.1	20.7	9.6	30.7	91.0	1.8	3.3	6.7
36420	Oklahoma City, OK	1,296,565	3.1	7.2	17.7	10.7	27.4	24.7	12.3	34.7	80.1	11.9	3.8	11.0
36500	Olympia, WA	258,332	2.1	5.9	16.5	9.4	26.5	27.4	14.4	38.0	88.0	4.3	8.5	4.4
36540	Omaha-Council Bluffs, NE-IA	886,348	2.1	7.5	18.6	9.1	27.8	25.3	11.7	34.9	85.9	9.1	3.2	4.6
36740	Orlando-Kissimmee-Sanford, FL	2,223,674	3.9	5.9	16.9	11.0	27.8	25.4	13.0	36.4	73.8	17.8	5.1	6.3
36780	Oshkosh-Neenah, WI	168,794	1.0	6.0	15.3	11.0	26.4	27.3	13.9	38.0	94.4	2.7	2.9	1.8
36980	Owensboro, KY	117,609	1.5	6.5	18.2	7.6	24.8	27.5	15.3	39.3	94.3	5.3	0.8	1.4

Metro area or division code	Area name	Percent Hispanic or Latino	Percent foreign born	Total households	Household type (percent)							Percent of households with people under 18 years	Percent of households with people 60 years and over
					Family households				Nonfamily households				
					Total family households	Married-couple families	Male household families	Female household families	Total nonfamily households	One-person households			
ACS table number:		B03003	B05012	B11001	B11001	B11001	B11001	B11001	B11001	B11001		C11005	B11006
Column number:		14	15	16	17	18	19	20	21	22		23	24
30860	Logan, UT-ID	9.8	7.1	39,798	73.3	63.5	2.3	7.6	26.7	19.9		38.9	26.6
30980	Longview, TX	14.9	7.2	75,316	67.5	47.5	5.5	14.5	32.5	29.1		34.1	38.2
31020	Longview, WA	8.0	4.0	38,834	66.1	48.7	6.2	11.1	33.9	27.3		30.5	41.2
31100	Los Angeles-Long Beach-Santa Ana, CA..	44.9	33.9	4,227,028	67.9	46.5	6.5	14.9	32.1	24.9		36.0	34.1
3110031084	•Los Angeles-Long Beach-Glendale, CA Division	48.2	34.9	3,231,660	66.7	44.1	6.9	15.7	33.3	26.0		35.9	33.8
3110042044	•Santa Ana-Anaheim-Irvine, CA Division	34.1	30.8	995,368	71.7	54.2	5.4	12.2	28.3	21.6		36.5	35.3
31140	Louisville-Jefferson County, KY-IN	4.2	5.0	510,269	65.6	46.7	4.7	14.1	34.4	28.5		31.8	34.3
31180	Lubbock, TX	33.3	5.2	108,426	64.2	44.7	5.3	14.2	35.8	28.1		32.9	29.5
31340	Lynchburg, VA	2.1	3.1	99,273	63.8	48.6	3.0	12.1	36.2	30.9		25.9	39.6
31420	Macon, GA	2.8	2.7	84,022	68.1	42.6	5.2	20.3	31.9	28.4		32.0	36.4
31460	Madera-Chowchilla, CA	55.2	21.8	41,035	75.7	54.9	5.6	15.1	24.3	20.5		39.9	39.4
31540	Madison, WI	5.6	7.1	239,964	59.0	46.5	3.7	8.7	41.0	30.9		28.0	29.6
31700	Manchester-Nashua, NH	5.6	8.4	155,260	65.6	51.1	4.2	10.3	34.4	25.0		32.0	32.5
31740	Manhattan, KS	8.8	6.7	47,675	60.3	49.9	2.2	8.1	39.7	27.9		31.7	22.7
31860	Mankato-North Mankato, MN	3.1	3.6	36,476	59.7	50.3	3.8	5.7	40.3	29.1		26.5	32.2
31900	Mansfield, OH	1.5	1.2	48,529	66.2	48.9	2.6	14.7	33.8	29.7		28.5	42.3
32580	McAllen-Edinburg-Mission, TX	90.9	28.9	222,849	80.7	55.2	4.8	20.7	19.3	16.5		50.5	32.1
32780	Medford, OR	11.4	5.7	80,957	64.8	49.2	4.5	11.1	35.2	28.5		28.3	44.5
32820	Memphis, TN-MS-AR	5.2	4.8	484,923	66.4	41.4	5.0	20.0	33.6	28.8		35.3	31.7
32900	Merced, CA	56.1	25.0	76,451	78.3	51.3	8.0	19.0	21.7	17.4		48.4	33.5
33100	Miami-Fort Lauderdale-Pompano Beach, FL	42.0	38.2	2,024,878	64.6	43.4	5.3	15.8	35.4	28.9		31.2	41.1
3310022744	•Fort Lauderdale-Pompano Beach-Deerfield Beach, FL Division	26.5	31.6	663,905	61.9	42.1	4.5	15.3	38.1	30.7		31.6	38.0
3310033124	•Miami-Miami Beach-Kendall, FL Division	64.3	51.0	838,772	68.2	43.4	6.4	18.3	31.8	26.1		34.1	39.1
3310048424	•West Palm Beach-Boca Raton-Boynton Beach, FL Division	20.1	22.5	522,201	62.2	45.2	4.5	12.6	37.8	31.1		25.9	48.3
33140	Michigan City-La Porte, IN	5.7	2.7	43,468	67.1	49.3	3.5	14.3	32.9	26.9		28.5	38.6
33260	Midland, TX	39.8	9.7	51,216	73.3	54.8	7.0	11.5	26.7	23.0		40.1	32.0
33340	Milwaukee-Waukesha-West Allis, WI	9.9	7.4	623,682	62.5	44.8	4.5	13.2	37.5	30.8		30.9	32.5
33460	Minneapolis-St. Paul-Bloomington, MN-WI	5.5	9.5	1,296,603	65.0	50.2	4.2	10.6	35.0	27.6		33.1	29.6
33540	Missoula, MT	2.8	2.4	46,384	57.9	46.1	4.3	7.5	42.1	30.2		24.8	28.7
33660	Mobile, AL	2.5	3.3	156,755	65.8	43.4	3.5	18.9	34.2	30.3		33.1	36.9
33700	Modesto, CA	43.0	19.9	167,497	74.4	52.1	7.0	15.2	25.6	20.4		42.0	33.7
33740	Monroe, LA	2.2	1.6	67,742	64.1	42.1	3.0	18.9	35.9	30.1		33.7	33.9
33780	Monroe, MI	3.2	2.2	57,506	66.9	51.2	4.1	11.6	33.1	28.0		31.0	38.1
33860	Montgomery, AL	3.0	3.5	142,926	66.4	44.0	4.4	18.0	33.6	28.6		33.7	32.3
34060	Morgantown, WV	1.8	3.8	49,069	52.9	43.8	2.7	6.4	47.1	37.0		20.2	32.3
34100	Morristown, TN	6.3	4.2	52,341	71.7	51.2	5.4	15.0	28.3	24.8		33.4	42.7
34580	Mount Vernon-Anacortes, WA	17.3	9.9	44,671	68.2	51.5	5.3	11.4	31.8	25.2		29.7	42.8
34620	Muncie, IN	1.9	1.8	46,572	60.5	43.6	3.9	13.0	39.5	29.7		26.7	36.4
34740	Muskegon-Norton Shores, MI	5.1	1.6	63,860	69.0	47.8	4.4	16.8	31.0	27.7		34.4	37.0
34820	Myrtle Beach-North Myrtle Beach-Conway, SC	6.2	6.8	118,092	63.1	46.5	4.0	12.6	36.9	29.8		27.2	44.2
34900	Napa, CA	33.1	25.9	48,224	67.6	50.9	6.2	10.5	32.4	26.3		31.7	43.7
34940	Naples-Marco Island, FL	26.2	23.3	123,714	65.6	53.7	3.3	8.6	34.4	29.3		21.9	59.0
34980	Nashville-Davidson--Murfreesboro--Franklin, TN	6.8	7.0	616,606	65.4	49.1	4.1	12.2	34.6	27.9		32.5	30.9
35300	New Haven-Milford, CT	15.9	12.7	330,054	64.8	45.8	4.5	14.4	35.2	29.4		31.8	37.3
35380	New Orleans-Metairie-Kenner, LA	8.2	6.8	463,402	61.5	39.9	5.2	16.5	38.5	32.0		30.1	34.5
35620	New York-Northern New Jersey-Long Island, NY-NJ-PA	23.5	29.3	6,872,526	65.8	45.3	5.2	15.3	34.2	28.3		33.2	36.7
3562020764	•Edison, NJ Division	13.4	19.4	860,223	70.1	55.0	4.5	10.6	29.9	25.3		33.6	40.1
3562035004	•Nassau-Suffolk, NY Division	16.4	18.4	938,085	76.0	58.7	4.7	12.6	24.0	19.9		37.0	42.2
3562035084	•Newark-Union, NJ-PA Division	18.8	21.4	766,727	69.2	49.6	4.5	15.1	30.8	26.0		36.0	35.6
3562035644	•New York-White Plains-Wayne, NY-NJ Division	28.2	35.3	4,307,491	62.1	39.6	5.5	16.9	37.9	31.2		31.7	35.1
35660	Niles-Benton Harbor, MI	4.8	7.0	60,223	66.8	49.4	4.0	13.4	33.2	29.7		29.2	40.9
35840	North Port-Bradenton-Sarasota, FL	11.6	12.1	303,355	60.9	49.5	2.6	8.8	39.1	31.9		19.9	54.9
35980	Norwich-New London, CT	9.2	8.4	105,801	66.8	48.6	6.1	12.0	33.2	27.5		31.3	37.8
36100	Ocala, FL	11.4	8.0	133,910	65.2	50.2	4.8	10.2	34.8	28.8		23.1	55.1
36140	Ocean City, NJ	6.6	4.9	40,470	63.1	50.2	2.9	9.3	36.9	32.1		23.4	49.4
36220	Odessa, TX	55.1	13.3	49,382	68.4	47.7	5.6	15.1	31.6	26.2		36.8	29.8
36260	Ogden-Clearfield, UT	12.2	6.4	179,915	77.1	62.8	4.4	9.8	22.9	18.6		43.7	27.5
36420	Oklahoma City, OK	11.9	7.8	484,733	64.8	47.5	5.0	12.3	35.2	28.8		32.4	32.5
36500	Olympia, WA	7.7	8.0	102,335	66.6	49.1	4.9	12.7	33.4	25.7		30.9	36.8
36540	Omaha-Council Bluffs, NE-IA	9.3	6.9	341,740	65.4	47.7	5.0	12.6	34.6	28.7		34.1	30.5
36740	Orlando-Kissimmee-Sanford, FL	26.7	16.2	778,693	65.6	46.8	4.4	14.4	34.4	27.4		31.3	33.4
36780	Oshkosh-Neenah, WI	3.7	3.0	67,627	59.3	48.6	3.4	7.3	40.7	32.3		28.3	33.6
36980	Owensboro, KY	2.3	1.9	46,026	68.2	50.3	4.6	13.3	31.8	27.6		32.3	35.1

Table A-3. Metropolitan Areas — Who: Age, Race/Ethnicity, and Household Structure, 2012—*Continued*

Metro area or division code	Area name	Total population	Percent change 2010–2012	Population by age (percent): Under 5 years	5 to 17 years	18 to 24 years	25 to 44 years	45 to 64 years	65 years and over	Median age	Race alone or in combination (percent): White	Black	Asian, Hawaiian, or Pacific Islander	American Indian, Alaska Native, or some other race
	ACS table number:	B01003	CP05	B01001	B01001	B01001	B01001	B01001	B01001	B01002	B02008	B02009	B02011 + B02012	B02010 + B02013
	Column number:	1	2	3	4	5	6	7	8	9	10	11	12	13
37100	Oxnard-Thousand Oaks-Ventura, CA	835,981	1.2	6.6	18.4	10.1	25.8	26.5	12.6	36.5	81.7	2.6	9.3	11.1
37340	Palm Bay-Melbourne-Titusville, FL	547,307	0.7	4.7	14.3	8.1	20.9	30.4	21.6	46.3	85.7	11.3	3.5	2.1
37380	Palm Coast, FL	98,359	2.5	4.0	15.0	7.1	18.8	29.1	26.1	49.7	81.0	13.1	3.0	5.3
37460	Panama City-Lynn Haven-Panama City Beach, FL	171,903	1.6	6.0	15.6	9.2	26.1	27.7	15.4	39.8	86.1	12.5	3.7	2.3
37620	Parkersburg-Marietta-Vienna, WV-OH	163,853	0.7	5.3	15.9	8.3	23.7	29.3	17.5	42.2	97.5	2.6	0.7	1.0
37700	Pascagoula, MS	163,228	0.5	7.2	17.5	9.8	24.3	27.4	13.8	37.8	76.8	20.7	2.1	3.0
37860	Pensacola-Ferry Pass-Brent, FL	461,227	2.5	6.0	15.6	11.5	24.6	27.6	14.6	38.4	79.6	18.4	4.1	3.0
37900	Peoria, IL	380,558	0.5	6.4	17.3	9.0	25.0	26.9	15.5	38.8	87.6	10.5	2.7	1.5
37980	Philadelphia-Camden-Wilmington, PA-NJ-DE-MD	6,018,800	0.8	6.1	16.7	10.0	26.0	27.4	13.9	38.3	70.0	22.3	6.1	4.2
3798015804	•Camden, NJ Division	1,254,461	0.2	5.9	17.3	9.0	25.5	28.4	13.9	39.6	73.4	18.1	5.4	6.4
3798037964	•Philadelphia, PA Division	4,050,793	0.9	6.2	16.5	10.2	26.2	27.0	14.0	37.9	68.5	23.7	6.6	3.7
3798048864	•Wilmington, DE-MD-NJ Division	713,546	1.0	6.0	16.9	10.6	25.6	27.7	13.2	38.0	72.5	22.0	4.4	3.6
38060	Phoenix-Mesa-Glendale, AZ	4,329,534	2.8	6.9	18.7	9.7	27.6	23.8	13.2	35.4	82.7	6.1	4.8	9.3
38220	Pine Bluff, AR	97,798	-2.1	5.6	17.0	10.1	25.4	27.4	14.5	38.9	50.7	48.6	0.9	1.6
38300	Pittsburgh, PA	2,360,733	0.2	5.1	14.6	9.1	24.0	29.5	17.7	42.8	89.2	9.5	2.4	1.0
38340	Pittsfield, MA	130,016	-0.9	4.2	14.4	10.0	20.6	31.2	19.6	45.5	94.3	4.0	1.9	2.3
38540	Pocatello, ID	91,096	0.7	8.0	18.9	12.3	25.3	23.6	12.0	31.7	92.8	1.1	2.0	6.6
38860	Portland-South Portland-Biddeford, ME	518,117	0.8	4.9	15.4	8.3	24.6	30.9	15.9	42.8	96.2	2.3	2.1	1.4
38900	Portland-Vancouver-Hillsboro, OR-WA	2,289,651	2.6	6.2	16.8	8.6	29.5	26.6	12.3	37.4	85.9	3.9	8.5	6.3
38940	Port St. Lucie, FL	432,683	1.8	5.2	14.8	7.6	21.3	27.1	24.0	46.1	79.3	15.7	2.2	5.0
39100	Poughkeepsie-Newburgh-Middletown, NY	671,834	0.1	5.9	18.1	11.0	23.7	28.4	13.0	38.9	80.8	11.8	4.1	7.0
39140	Prescott, AZ	212,637	0.7	4.5	13.4	7.3	17.9	30.8	26.1	51.0	93.3	0.9	1.3	6.2
39300	Providence-New Bedford-Fall River, RI-MA	1,601,374	0.0	5.4	15.6	10.9	24.9	28.1	15.1	40.0	86.2	7.0	3.4	6.3
39340	Provo-Orem, UT	550,461	3.9	10.5	24.3	16.2	27.1	14.9	6.9	24.6	94.7	1.0	4.0	3.4
39380	Pueblo, CO	160,852	0.9	6.4	17.4	9.7	23.8	26.8	15.9	38.9	83.7	2.7	1.4	17.0
39460	Punta Gorda, FL	162,449	1.5	3.2	10.3	5.6	16.0	28.7	36.2	56.8	93.3	4.5	1.6	3.5
39540	Racine, WI	194,797	-0.4	6.6	17.9	8.1	24.3	29.1	14.0	39.5	84.3	12.3	1.6	4.6
39580	Raleigh-Cary, NC	1,188,564	4.5	6.8	18.9	9.4	29.9	25.2	9.8	35.5	72.1	21.4	5.4	3.8
39660	Rapid City, SD	131,668	3.8	7.2	17.4	9.9	25.8	26.3	13.4	35.5	89.3	2.6	1.8	10.6
39740	Reading, PA	413,491	0.4	6.0	17.3	10.3	23.5	27.8	15.1	39.7	87.5	6.1	2.1	6.7
39820	Redding, CA	178,586	0.7	5.5	16.5	8.5	22.4	28.8	18.3	42.7	90.2	2.0	3.5	7.6
39900	Reno-Sparks, NV	433,612	1.7	6.3	16.5	10.5	26.0	27.4	13.3	37.9	84.6	3.3	7.7	8.0
40060	Richmond, VA	1,280,678	1.5	6.0	16.8	10.0	26.7	27.5	13.0	38.2	64.6	31.2	4.1	2.9
40140	Riverside-San Bernardino-Ontario, CA	4,350,096	2.5	7.4	20.4	11.1	26.6	23.5	11.0	33.1	67.5	8.7	8.3	20.0
40220	Roanoke, VA	309,408	0.2	5.3	15.8	8.3	24.2	29.5	17.0	42.2	84.7	13.6	2.2	2.7
40340	Rochester, MN	188,773	1.3	7.1	17.9	7.8	26.5	26.9	13.8	36.9	90.4	4.8	5.5	1.3
40380	Rochester, NY	1,056,940	0.2	5.5	16.0	11.1	24.0	28.3	15.0	39.6	83.2	13.1	3.2	2.9
40420	Rockford, IL	346,009	-0.9	6.5	18.3	8.5	25.5	26.8	14.4	38.6	81.6	12.4	2.8	6.6
40580	Rocky Mount, NC	151,662	-0.5	6.0	17.7	9.8	22.8	28.6	15.2	40.5	50.6	46.7	0.0	5.6
40660	Rome, GA	96,177	-0.1	6.5	17.5	10.6	25.2	25.7	14.4	38.2	75.7	15.2	1.3	9.5
40900	Sacramento--Arden-Arcade--Roseville, CA	2,196,482	2.0	6.4	17.8	10.4	26.5	26.0	13.0	36.4	71.2	9.0	16.5	9.8
40980	Saginaw-Saginaw Township North, MI	198,353	-0.8	5.7	16.9	10.9	22.5	27.8	16.2	40.1	78.0	20.4	1.5	2.9
41060	St. Cloud, MN	190,471	0.6	6.2	16.7	13.8	25.1	25.5	12.8	34.9	94.3	3.8	2.4	1.7
41100	St. George, UT	144,809	4.6	8.4	21.1	9.9	22.4	19.7	18.5	33.7	95.0	0.8	2.5	4.0
41140	St. Joseph, MO-KS	128,278	-1.1	6.1	16.0	11.5	25.0	26.8	14.6	38.4	93.6	6.2	1.5	2.9
41180	St. Louis, MO-IL	2,819,381	0.1	6.2	17.1	9.1	25.8	27.7	14.1	38.6	78.5	19.4	2.8	1.7
41420	Salem, OR	396,338	1.2	6.6	19.0	10.0	25.5	24.8	14.0	35.9	85.5	1.5	4.0	13.6
41500	Salinas, CA	426,762	2.4	7.9	18.8	11.1	27.9	23.1	11.2	33.0	76.5	3.7	8.6	15.3
41540	Salisbury, MD	126,900	1.3	6.0	14.7	15.0	24.1	26.4	13.7	36.9	68.9	29.3	2.8	3.5
41620	Salt Lake City, UT	1,161,715	2.9	8.4	20.7	10.0	30.3	21.6	9.0	31.4	86.4	2.3	6.2	7.8
41660	San Angelo, TX	114,946	2.2	6.4	16.2	13.3	25.2	24.0	14.8	34.6	90.2	5.5	1.7	4.8
41700	San Antonio-New Braunfels, TX	2,234,003	3.5	7.0	19.1	10.4	27.6	24.3	11.6	34.4	80.0	7.5	3.2	12.5
41740	San Diego-Carlsbad-San Marcos, CA	3,177,063	2.3	6.6	16.3	11.7	28.9	24.6	12.0	34.9	74.2	6.4	14.5	9.9
41780	Sandusky, OH	76,398	-0.9	5.3	16.0	8.5	21.2	31.0	18.1	44.2	89.9	9.8	0.8	2.1
41860	San Francisco-Oakland-Fremont, CA	4,455,560	2.5	5.9	15.0	8.6	30.0	27.2	13.3	38.5	58.7	9.4	28.0	9.8
4186036084	•Oakland-Fremont-Hayward, CA Division	2,634,317	2.6	6.3	16.6	9.2	28.5	27.0	12.4	37.6	57.3	12.5	26.5	10.4
4186041884	•San Francisco-San Mateo-Redwood City, CA Division	1,821,243	2.4	5.3	12.5	7.8	32.3	27.5	14.6	39.8	60.7	4.9	30.1	9.0
41940	San Jose-Sunnyvale-Santa Clara, CA	1,894,388	2.8	6.7	17.0	8.9	30.2	25.6	11.6	36.6	54.8	3.3	35.5	10.9
42020	San Luis Obispo-Paso Robles, CA	274,804	1.7	4.8	13.9	15.6	22.3	27.1	16.3	39.2	86.9	2.7	5.1	9.0
42060	Santa Barbara-Santa Maria-Goleta, CA	431,249	1.5	6.5	16.1	15.6	25.0	23.4	13.3	33.8	77.6	2.7	7.4	16.6
42100	Santa Cruz-Watsonville, CA	266,776	1.4	5.6	15.1	14.8	24.5	27.8	12.2	37.0	87.0	1.8	6.9	9.3
42140	Santa Fe, NM	146,375	1.2	5.2	15.1	7.5	23.6	31.4	17.2	44.1	87.6	1.2	1.5	12.2
42220	Santa Rosa-Petaluma, CA	491,829	1.4	5.6	15.7	9.6	24.9	29.0	15.2	40.3	80.0	2.6	6.1	15.5
42340	Savannah, GA	361,941	3.8	6.9	16.9	11.9	27.9	24.5	12.0	34.3	62.6	35.0	3.0	1.5
42540	Scranton--Wilkes-Barre, PA	563,629	-0.1	5.1	14.8	9.8	23.3	28.7	18.2	42.8	93.0	3.9	1.7	2.8
42660	Seattle-Tacoma-Bellevue, WA	3,552,157	3.0	6.4	15.9	9.2	30.1	26.8	11.6	37.0	77.5	7.4	16.0	5.7
4266042644	•Seattle-Bellevue-Everett, WA Division	2,740,476	3.3	6.2	15.5	9.0	30.8	27.1	11.5	37.3	76.6	6.8	17.4	5.6
4266045104	•Tacoma, WA Division	811,681	2.0	6.9	17.4	10.0	27.7	26.1	11.8	35.7	80.7	9.3	11.2	6.2
42680	Sebastian-Vero Beach, FL	140,567	1.7	5.0	13.4	7.2	18.2	27.7	28.6	50.1	87.4	10.3	1.6	2.2
43100	Sheboygan, WI	115,009	-0.4	5.6	17.6	7.4	24.8	29.2	15.4	41.4	91.9	2.1	5.4	2.4
43300	Sherman-Denison, TX	121,935	0.7	6.1	17.4	9.6	23.3	27.5	16.1	40.0	87.6	7.0	1.4	6.6
43340	Shreveport-Bossier City, LA	406,253	1.6	7.2	17.6	9.6	26.5	25.4	13.5	36.0	57.7	39.9	1.7	2.2
43580	Sioux City, IA-NE-SD	144,243	0.3	7.8	18.3	10.4	24.4	25.8	13.2	35.9	87.5	3.2	3.5	8.4

Metro area or division code	Area name	Percent Hispanic or Latino	Percent foreign born	Total households	Household type (percent)							Percent of households with people under 18 years	Percent of households with people 60 years and over
					Family households				Nonfamily households				
					Total family households	Married-couple families	Male household families	Female household families	Total nonfamily households	One-person households			
	ACS table number:	B03003	B05012	B11001	B11001	B11001	B11001	B11001	B11001	B11001		C11005	B11006
	Column number:	14	15	16	17	18	19	20	21	22		23	24
37100	Oxnard-Thousand Oaks-Ventura, CA.....	41.2	22.8	267,877	73.2	54.8	5.3	13.1	26.8	21.3		37.8	37.4
37340	Palm Bay-Melbourne-Titusville, FL	8.8	9.0	218,094	63.0	46.5	4.0	12.4	37.0	31.8		25.5	46.3
37380	Palm Coast, FL	9.2	14.7	36,358	64.7	53.1	3.2	8.4	35.3	27.1		22.1	58.2
37460	Panama City-Lynn Haven-Panama City Beach, FL	5.2	4.4	68,653	63.0	46.4	3.5	13.1	37.0	29.0		28.8	35.2
37620	Parkersburg-Marietta-Vienna, WV-OH...	0.4	0.8	66,271	67.5	51.3	3.9	12.3	32.5	27.1		29.3	41.0
37700	Pascagoula, MS.....................................	4.2	3.0	58,424	68.7	47.9	5.5	15.3	31.3	25.6		33.3	36.4
37860	Pensacola-Ferry Pass-Brent, FL	5.0	4.3	172,413	65.2	47.9	4.5	12.8	34.8	28.2		27.5	36.4
37900	Peoria, IL	3.0	3.2	152,743	65.7	50.8	3.9	11.0	34.3	29.3		29.9	35.4
37980	Philadelphia-Camden-Wilmington, PA-NJ-DE-MD..........	8.3	9.8	2,227,140	64.7	45.8	4.5	14.3	35.3	29.6		31.4	36.0
3798015804	•Camden, NJ Division	9.9	8.9	454,987	69.5	50.9	4.7	13.9	30.5	25.4		34.3	37.2
3798037964	•Philadelphia, PA Division	7.9	10.2	1,508,981	62.9	44.2	4.3	14.4	37.1	31.2		30.3	35.8
3798048864	•Wilmington, DE-MD-NJ Division	8.2	8.7	263,172	66.3	46.9	5.0	14.4	33.7	27.5		32.9	34.8
38060	Phoenix-Mesa-Glendale, AZ	29.9	14.3	1,551,267	65.7	46.8	5.8	13.1	34.3	27.0		33.5	33.8
38220	Pine Bluff, AR.......................................	1.7	1.1	35,581	61.9	40.7	4.6	16.6	38.1	34.5		28.8	38.2
38300	Pittsburgh, PA	1.4	3.3	990,931	61.5	46.9	3.9	10.8	38.5	32.5		25.8	40.0
38340	Pittsfield, MA	3.7	6.0	55,420	59.1	42.8	4.1	12.2	40.9	35.7		25.2	44.6
38540	Pocatello, ID	8.0	3.8	33,239	65.6	50.0	5.4	10.3	34.4	28.3		33.1	32.2
38860	Portland-South Portland-Biddeford, ME..	1.7	4.5	213,459	62.4	49.1	4.0	9.3	37.6	29.0		27.3	37.2
38900	Portland-Vancouver-Hillsboro, OR-WA...	11.2	12.2	872,878	63.4	48.2	4.4	10.8	36.6	27.6		31.5	32.9
38940	Port St. Lucie, FL	15.6	14.1	170,309	66.4	51.0	4.2	11.1	33.6	28.4		25.5	50.5
39100	Poughkeepsie-Newburgh-Middletown, NY	15.3	11.7	232,334	69.8	53.8	4.5	11.5	30.2	24.8		34.5	36.4
39140	Prescott, AZ	13.9	6.9	93,697	63.7	51.7	3.2	8.8	36.3	29.9		21.0	55.2
39300	Providence-New Bedford-Fall River, RI-MA	10.9	12.9	622,066	63.4	44.7	4.7	14.1	36.6	29.4		29.6	37.1
39340	Provo-Orem, UT	10.9	6.6	147,329	81.8	71.4	3.3	7.1	18.2	12.4		51.7	22.6
39380	Pueblo, CO	42.0	3.3	62,388	63.7	45.1	5.9	12.7	36.3	31.8		30.2	37.8
39460	Punta Gorda, FL	6.5	9.4	71,811	66.5	54.3	3.4	8.8	33.5	28.4		18.8	64.4
39540	Racine, WI	12.0	4.8	75,752	66.2	48.2	4.7	13.3	33.8	28.8		31.6	34.7
39580	Raleigh-Cary, NC	10.3	11.6	441,987	67.6	51.8	4.2	11.6	32.4	26.1		37.1	26.5
39660	Rapid City, SD	4.3	1.7	50,646	64.0	48.4	4.7	10.9	36.0	29.1		29.2	34.3
39740	Reading, PA	17.5	7.6	151,291	68.3	50.3	5.4	12.5	31.7	25.8		32.3	37.6
39820	Redding, CA	8.9	4.0	68,165	67.0	52.0	4.8	10.3	33.0	26.4		26.0	44.8
39900	Reno-Sparks, NV	22.8	15.5	165,964	62.2	44.5	4.9	12.8	37.8	29.3		31.4	34.7
40060	Richmond, VA	5.3	7.0	476,759	65.7	47.2	4.6	13.9	34.3	28.6		32.2	35.1
40140	Riverside-San Bernardino-Ontario, CA...	48.4	21.7	1,285,948	74.6	52.6	7.0	15.0	25.4	20.1		42.8	35.6
40220	Roanoke, VA	3.5	4.6	129,023	64.4	48.3	4.1	12.0	35.6	30.8		29.1	40.5
40340	Rochester, MN	4.2	8.9	73,900	68.1	54.3	4.4	9.5	31.9	26.5		32.2	31.4
40380	Rochester, NY	6.5	6.7	419,798	61.3	43.3	4.4	13.7	38.7	31.4		28.8	35.7
40420	Rockford, IL	12.8	8.2	130,401	70.2	49.2	4.9	16.1	29.8	25.9		35.1	35.7
40580	Rocky Mount, NC	5.5	3.5	55,868	66.2	43.9	3.8	18.5	33.8	28.8		30.1	42.7
40660	Rome, GA	9.9	6.7	34,373	65.2	47.4	4.3	13.5	34.8	28.4		31.9	38.4
40900	Sacramento–Arden-Arcade– Roseville, CA...........	20.6	17.8	786,864	66.4	47.0	5.2	14.2	33.6	26.0		34.2	35.5
40980	Saginaw-Saginaw Township North, MI ..	7.9	2.4	78,010	64.3	44.7	4.4	15.3	35.7	31.6		28.0	40.1
41060	St. Cloud, MN	2.7	3.4	71,971	66.0	54.3	4.3	7.4	34.0	24.4		31.3	29.7
41100	St. George, UT	9.9	5.0	48,186	73.5	60.6	3.3	9.7	26.5	21.5		32.7	44.9
41140	St. Joseph, MO-KS	4.5	3.1	47,656	65.4	48.4	5.9	11.1	34.6	29.4		30.8	37.3
41180	St. Louis, MO-IL	2.7	4.4	1,108,723	64.8	47.1	4.3	13.5	35.2	29.5		30.7	34.6
41420	Salem, OR	22.7	12.5	142,746	71.0	51.1	5.8	14.2	29.0	24.2		36.1	36.5
41500	Salinas, CA	56.4	30.6	124,171	71.9	51.2	6.9	13.8	28.1	21.7		40.4	36.2
41540	Salisbury, MD	4.3	7.3	44,623	67.0	45.4	4.1	17.5	33.0	27.4		34.8	38.0
41620	Salt Lake City, UT	17.0	12.0	380,362	70.3	54.6	4.8	10.9	29.7	22.6		40.0	27.7
41660	San Angelo, TX	36.5	5.3	43,104	64.8	46.4	5.6	12.7	35.2	30.6		31.9	36.2
41700	San Antonio-New Braunfels, TX	54.4	12.0	766,963	69.9	48.7	5.8	15.4	30.1	24.7		38.4	32.8
41740	San Diego-Carlsbad-San Marcos, CA.....	32.7	23.2	1,079,653	66.3	48.9	5.2	12.3	33.7	24.8		33.7	33.3
41780	Sandusky, OH.......................................	3.6	1.3	31,739	64.2	47.7	4.5	12.0	35.8	32.8		24.9	43.5
41860	San Francisco-Oakland-Fremont, CA	21.9	30.1	1,636,828	61.9	46.4	4.5	11.0	38.1	29.1		30.8	35.2
4186036084	•Oakland-Fremont-Hayward, CA Division	23.5	28.0	928,671	67.3	49.7	5.2	12.3	32.7	25.7		35.3	34.4
4186041884	•San Francisco-San Mateo-Redwood City, CA Division	19.5	33.0	708,157	54.8	42.1	3.6	9.1	45.2	33.6		25.0	36.2
41940	San Jose-Sunnyvale-Santa Clara, CA	27.8	36.7	630,849	72.0	56.1	5.1	10.8	28.0	21.5		39.0	32.1
42020	San Luis Obispo-Paso Robles, CA	21.5	10.5	101,897	63.9	49.7	4.5	9.7	36.1	25.3		28.0	41.2
42060	Santa Barbara-Santa Maria-Goleta, CA .	43.8	23.0	141,639	65.7	48.9	5.2	11.5	34.3	25.5		33.8	37.7
42100	Santa Cruz-Watsonville, CA	32.7	18.1	93,253	62.0	47.0	5.0	10.0	38.0	27.0		30.1	36.8
42140	Santa Fe, NM	50.9	12.8	62,311	56.0	40.4	5.0	10.6	44.0	34.8		23.0	43.9
42220	Santa Rosa-Petaluma, CA......................	25.5	16.9	184,348	63.9	48.1	5.1	10.7	36.1	27.4		30.4	41.0
42340	Savannah, GA	5.5	5.0	132,868	64.4	44.6	4.7	15.1	35.6	29.3		32.2	32.6
42540	Scranton--Wilkes-Barre, PA	6.8	5.1	225,527	62.1	44.8	4.1	13.2	37.9	32.9		27.1	41.7
42660	Seattle-Tacoma-Bellevue, WA...............	9.3	17.1	1,375,184	61.7	47.6	4.3	9.8	38.3	29.5		30.8	30.3
4266042644	•Seattle-Bellevue-Everett, WA Division .	9.2	19.4	1,074,630	60.5	47.0	4.2	9.3	39.5	30.2		29.8	29.9
4266045104	•Tacoma, WA Division.........................	9.6	9.6	300,554	66.2	49.8	4.9	11.6	33.8	26.8		34.2	31.9
42680	Sebastian-Vero Beach, FL	11.7	10.4	58,950	57.6	46.7	2.4	8.4	42.4	37.8		19.4	53.9
43100	Sheboygan, WI	5.7	5.9	46,653	66.2	52.6	3.4	10.2	33.8	28.2		29.2	34.3
43300	Sherman-Denison, TX	11.9	5.3	47,770	68.6	49.7	5.0	13.9	31.4	26.1		33.1	38.3
43340	Shreveport-Bossier City, LA...................	3.7	3.4	153,275	65.9	40.3	5.9	19.7	34.1	30.5		34.1	34.3
43580	Sioux City, IA-NE-SD............................	16.1	9.1	53,573	64.7	46.3	5.2	13.1	35.3	29.6		34.5	34.9

Metro area or division code	Area name	Total population	Percent change 2010–2012	Population by age (percent)						Median age	Race alone or in combination (percent)			
				Under 5 years	5 to 17 years	18 to 24 years	25 to 44 years	45 to 64 years	65 years and over		White	Black	Asian, Hawaiian, or Pacific Islander	American Indian, Alaska Native, or some other race
	ACS table number:	B01003	CP05	B01001	B01001	B01001	B01001	B01001	B01001	B01002	B02008	B02009	B02011 + B02012	B02010 + B02013
	Column number:	1	2	3	4	5	6	7	8	9	10	11	12	13
43620	Sioux Falls, SD	237,597	3.6	7.7	17.9	9.0	28.7	25.2	11.4	34.7	90.6	4.3	1.8	4.8
43780	South Bend-Mishawaka, IN-MI	318,586	-0.2	6.3	17.6	10.8	24.0	26.7	14.6	37.9	84.0	13.2	2.2	4.0
43900	Spartanburg, SC	288,745	1.4	6.6	17.6	9.9	25.1	26.7	14.2	38.1	73.3	21.7	2.7	4.4
44060	Spokane, WA	475,735	0.8	6.3	16.5	11.1	25.7	26.6	13.7	37.1	92.3	3.1	4.3	4.5
44100	Springfield, IL	211,610	0.6	6.1	17.1	8.4	25.7	28.2	14.5	39.9	86.0	12.7	2.2	1.3
44140	Springfield, MA	697,258	0.6	5.2	15.7	13.2	23.1	28.0	14.8	39.1	84.4	7.6	3.1	7.3
44180	Springfield, MO	444,407	2.1	6.2	16.7	11.7	25.7	25.3	14.4	36.7	94.8	2.9	1.9	2.8
44220	Springfield, OH	137,206	-0.7	5.9	17.2	9.4	22.3	28.3	16.9	41.5	89.4	10.9	1.1	2.3
44300	State College, PA	155,171	0.7	4.2	11.4	28.0	22.8	21.6	12.0	29.3	90.7	4.4	6.1	1.4
44600	Steubenville-Weirton, WV-OH	122,207	-1.6	5.4	14.8	8.9	22.0	29.8	19.0	43.8	95.6	5.1	0.3	0.7
44700	Stockton, CA	702,612	2.2	7.7	21.0	10.5	26.3	23.5	11.0	33.0	62.6	9.0	19.4	17.8
44940	Sumter, SC	108,052	0.4	6.7	17.6	11.1	25.7	25.4	13.6	35.4	50.2	47.5	1.8	4.2
45060	Syracuse, NY	660,934	-0.3	5.7	16.5	11.8	23.4	28.2	14.5	39.0	87.3	9.6	3.2	2.9
45220	Tallahassee, FL	376,331	2.2	5.2	14.0	20.1	25.4	23.8	11.5	32.6	62.7	33.6	2.9	2.8
45300	Tampa-St. Petersburg-Clearwater, FL	2,842,878	1.9	5.5	15.2	8.6	25.0	27.7	18.0	41.8	82.0	13.1	4.0	3.8
45460	Terre Haute, IN	173,704	0.4	5.8	16.4	12.4	24.7	26.2	14.6	38.0	92.9	6.4	1.5	1.5
45500	Texarkana, TX-Texarkana, AR	136,782	0.4	6.6	17.7	9.0	26.6	25.4	14.7	36.9	73.3	24.6	0.8	4.6
45780	Toledo, OH	650,050	-0.1	6.0	16.7	11.9	24.0	27.2	14.3	38.1	82.5	15.3	1.9	3.7
45820	Topeka, KS	234,566	-0.7	6.4	18.1	8.3	23.6	27.9	15.6	39.9	89.5	8.2	1.5	5.4
45940	Trenton-Ewing, NJ	368,303	0.4	5.8	16.4	11.4	25.9	27.3	13.2	38.5	65.2	21.0	10.1	5.7
46060	Tucson, AZ	992,394	1.0	6.1	16.3	10.8	24.8	25.5	16.5	38.0	80.4	5.0	4.4	14.1
46140	Tulsa, OK	951,514	1.3	6.9	18.3	9.1	26.2	26.0	13.6	36.9	79.8	9.9	2.4	16.1
46220	Tuscaloosa, AL	223,468	1.7	6.1	15.6	18.2	24.8	23.5	11.8	32.6	63.9	34.6	1.4	0.4
46340	Tyler, TX	214,821	2.0	7.1	18.4	11.1	24.5	24.1	14.9	36.0	77.9	19.0	1.5	3.3
46540	Utica-Rome, NY	298,064	-0.4	5.5	15.8	9.6	23.4	28.4	17.2	41.6	90.9	5.9	3.1	2.6
46660	Valdosta, GA	145,348	5.6	7.0	17.3	17.9	25.1	22.1	10.6	30.2	61.3	34.7	1.7	4.2
46700	Vallejo-Fairfield, CA	420,757	1.6	6.3	17.3	10.1	26.3	27.9	12.3	37.2	60.1	16.5	19.9	11.7
47020	Victoria, TX	118,429	2.6	6.6	19.1	8.7	24.7	26.5	14.5	37.2	88.4	6.7	1.6	9.0
47220	Vineland-Millville-Bridgeton, NJ	157,785	0.4	6.8	16.9	9.4	28.1	26.1	12.6	36.8	63.3	23.0	2.0	16.3
47260	Virginia Beach-Norfolk-Newport News, VA-NC	1,693,567	1.1	6.3	16.6	12.0	27.0	25.8	12.2	35.2	63.1	33.0	5.2	2.8
47300	Visalia-Porterville, CA	451,977	1.9	9.1	23.1	10.9	26.4	20.7	9.9	30.0	84.2	2.2	5.6	13.0
47380	Waco, TX	238,707	1.1	7.0	17.9	14.7	23.8	23.7	13.0	33.2	78.6	15.5	2.1	6.0
47580	Warner Robins, GA	146,136	3.9	6.7	19.3	9.7	29.2	24.2	11.0	34.0	64.6	30.2	3.4	4.4
47900	Washington-Arlington-Alexandria, DC-VA-MD-WV	5,804,333	3.5	6.7	16.7	9.2	30.3	26.5	10.6	36.1	58.7	27.1	11.3	7.1
4790013644	•Bethesda-Rockville-Frederick, MD Division	1,244,291	2.8	6.4	17.3	7.9	27.6	28.1	12.8	38.7	65.0	17.2	14.2	8.2
4790047894	•Washington-Arlington-Alexandria, DC-VA-MD-WV Division	4,560,042	3.6	6.8	16.5	9.5	31.1	26.1	10.0	35.5	56.9	29.8	10.5	6.8
47940	Waterloo-Cedar Falls, IA	168,747	2.2	5.9	15.6	14.8	23.5	25.3	15.0	35.7	90.9	8.4	1.7	0.8
48140	Wausau, WI	134,735	0.5	6.4	17.5	7.8	24.7	28.6	15.1	39.8	93.2	1.1	6.0	1.1
48300	Wenatchee-East Wenatchee, WA	113,037	1.5	7.0	18.2	9.1	22.6	27.7	15.5	38.8	87.0	0.8	0.9	13.2
48540	Wheeling, WV-OH	146,420	-1.0	5.1	14.3	9.1	23.1	30.2	18.2	43.5	95.9	4.0	0.6	1.0
48620	Wichita, KS	628,242	0.9	7.5	19.1	9.6	25.6	25.6	12.7	35.3	85.9	9.2	4.2	4.2
48660	Wichita Falls, TX	150,829	-0.9	6.0	16.7	13.2	25.4	24.7	14.2	34.9	86.9	10.3	2.6	3.6
48700	Williamsport, PA	117,168	0.9	5.8	14.7	10.9	23.5	28.2	16.8	41.3	94.0	6.1	1.0	1.2
48900	Wilmington, NC	375,686	3.3	5.1	14.3	10.3	24.6	27.9	17.8	41.6	82.7	14.9	1.3	2.9
49020	Winchester, VA-WV	131,052	1.8	5.2	17.7	9.7	24.3	28.6	14.5	39.9	92.2	6.3	1.6	2.3
49180	Winston-Salem, NC	484,437	1.3	6.1	17.2	9.6	25.1	27.4	14.6	39.4	75.3	21.7	1.8	2.8
49340	Worcester, MA	806,163	0.8	5.7	16.9	9.9	25.1	28.9	13.4	39.7	87.6	6.1	4.9	4.3
49420	Yakima, WA	246,977	1.0	8.8	21.4	10.0	25.1	22.4	12.2	32.3	82.3	1.4	2.0	17.3
49620	York-Hanover, PA	437,846	0.5	5.9	16.9	8.5	24.9	28.9	15.0	40.6	91.1	7.1	1.7	2.2
49660	Youngstown-Warren-Boardman, OH-PA	558,206	-1.2	5.1	15.9	8.6	22.1	29.6	18.6	43.5	87.6	12.3	0.8	1.4
49700	Yuba City, CA	167,948	0.5	7.8	19.8	10.7	26.2	23.4	12.2	33.4	76.2	3.3	14.8	12.9
49740	Yuma, AZ	200,022	1.8	7.5	19.7	11.9	23.8	20.7	16.4	33.6	78.3	2.5	2.4	18.9

Table A-3. Metropolitan Areas — Who: Age, Race/Ethnicity, and Household Structure, 2012—*Continued*

Metro area or division code	Area name	Percent Hispanic or Latino	Percent foreign born	Total households	Family households				Nonfamily households		Percent of households with people under 18 years	Percent of households with people 60 years and over
					Total family households	Married-couple families	Male household families	Female household families	Total nonfamily households	One-person households		
	ACS table number:	B03003	B05012	B11001	B11001	B11001	B11001	B11001	B11001	B11001	C11005	B11006
	Column number:	14	15	16	17	18	19	20	21	22	23	24
43620	Sioux Falls, SD	3.6	4.9	90,466	65.4	48.9	4.2	12.2	34.6	28.7	33.6	28.1
43780	South Bend-Mishawaka, IN-MI	7.0	5.4	121,241	65.3	48.8	4.8	11.7	34.7	28.1	29.5	35.4
43900	Spartanburg, SC	6.1	7.0	108,569	68.7	47.1	5.3	16.3	31.3	25.3	34.2	38.4
44060	Spokane, WA	4.9	5.2	189,004	62.5	47.7	4.1	10.8	37.5	30.0	30.2	35.3
44100	Springfield, IL	1.9	3.1	87,490	61.2	44.6	5.0	11.6	38.8	32.3	28.1	34.8
44140	Springfield, MA	16.2	8.7	263,453	62.6	42.5	4.8	15.3	37.4	30.2	30.6	38.1
44180	Springfield, MO	2.9	2.5	176,987	63.3	48.1	4.0	11.3	36.7	28.2	29.7	33.9
44220	Springfield, OH	2.9	1.9	54,288	62.7	44.7	3.4	14.7	37.3	31.4	28.2	39.9
44300	State College, PA	2.6	6.6	56,980	59.0	47.7	2.7	8.7	41.0	24.2	24.7	30.8
44600	Steubenville-Weirton, WV-OH	0.9	1.0	50,663	64.8	48.8	5.4	10.6	35.2	31.5	24.7	45.0
44700	Stockton, CA	39.7	23.3	215,761	75.3	51.2	7.5	16.5	24.7	20.2	42.9	35.6
44940	Sumter, SC	3.6	3.9	40,321	70.1	46.0	4.9	19.2	29.9	24.1	36.1	38.2
45060	Syracuse, NY	3.7	5.6	257,456	61.9	44.1	4.9	12.8	38.1	30.9	28.7	35.6
45220	Tallahassee, FL	6.6	6.3	140,759	58.1	40.5	3.7	13.9	41.9	30.3	27.5	31.0
45300	Tampa-St. Petersburg-Clearwater, FL	17.0	13.0	1,131,949	61.3	44.0	4.7	12.6	38.7	32.0	27.2	40.8
45460	Terre Haute, IN	1.9	2.2	65,165	65.3	47.9	6.3	11.1	34.7	27.9	31.3	35.5
45500	Texarkana, TX-Texarkana, AR	5.6	3.2	53,337	63.8	43.0	4.1	16.7	36.2	31.8	34.7	34.9
45780	Toledo, OH	6.1	2.9	260,332	60.3	43.1	4.6	12.6	39.7	32.3	29.4	34.5
45820	Topeka, KS	9.3	3.5	93,196	62.8	47.4	5.6	9.8	37.2	31.4	30.1	39.0
45940	Trenton-Ewing, NJ	15.9	20.2	132,004	67.6	51.1	4.7	11.8	32.4	27.3	34.0	36.9
46060	Tucson, AZ	35.4	12.4	386,104	61.5	44.7	4.9	11.9	38.5	30.7	27.8	39.9
46140	Tulsa, OK	8.7	6.1	369,404	66.6	48.2	5.3	13.1	33.4	28.0	33.6	33.8
46220	Tuscaloosa, AL	2.8	2.8	77,713	64.7	45.4	3.7	15.6	35.3	29.8	31.4	34.6
46340	Tyler, TX	17.9	8.7	78,290	69.1	51.1	6.2	11.8	30.9	25.8	34.2	37.2
46540	Utica-Rome, NY	4.2	7.3	118,135	61.7	44.6	4.0	13.0	38.3	32.2	27.9	40.9
46660	Valdosta, GA	5.8	4.1	51,065	65.8	45.1	3.8	16.9	34.2	26.2	35.4	30.0
46700	Vallejo-Fairfield, CA	24.8	20.6	141,139	70.6	49.5	5.7	15.4	29.4	23.4	35.9	36.7
47020	Victoria, TX	43.8	6.4	42,565	70.5	50.3	6.2	14.0	29.5	24.8	33.3	36.4
47220	Vineland-Millville-Bridgeton, NJ	28.1	10.0	50,068	67.3	42.3	6.2	18.8	32.7	28.0	35.1	39.5
47260	Virginia Beach-Norfolk-Newport News, VA-NC	5.8	6.1	623,964	68.0	47.1	4.5	16.4	32.0	25.8	33.7	32.5
47300	Visalia-Porterville, CA	61.8	22.6	132,614	77.8	52.5	9.0	16.2	22.2	17.6	50.9	32.8
47380	Waco, TX	24.4	7.0	85,171	67.6	48.2	5.3	14.2	32.4	25.1	34.5	34.3
47580	Warner Robins, GA	6.3	5.4	52,832	69.5	47.3	2.9	19.3	30.5	27.8	39.9	28.8
47900	Washington-Arlington-Alexandria, DC-VA-MD-WV	14.5	22.2	2,085,494	65.5	48.4	4.4	12.6	34.5	27.5	34.5	30.4
4790013644	•Bethesda-Rockville-Frederick, MD Division	16.0	28.2	447,608	69.9	54.3	4.6	11.1	30.1	24.1	36.1	34.8
4790047894	•Washington-Arlington-Alexandria, DC-VA-MD-WV Division	14.1	20.6	1,637,886	64.2	46.9	4.4	13.0	35.8	28.4	34.1	29.2
47940	Waterloo-Cedar Falls, IA	3.2	3.8	66,320	62.0	48.8	3.7	9.6	38.0	29.4	28.0	35.9
48140	Wausau, WI	2.4	3.8	52,147	68.4	54.5	5.4	8.4	31.6	25.3	30.3	36.5
48300	Wenatchee-East Wenatchee, WA	27.7	14.6	41,750	71.8	57.8	3.8	10.3	28.2	22.7	33.3	40.9
48540	Wheeling, WV-OH	0.8	1.1	61,627	62.8	49.5	3.1	10.2	37.2	33.1	25.3	42.0
48620	Wichita, KS	12.0	7.2	239,925	66.7	49.9	5.1	11.6	33.3	28.6	33.9	32.0
48660	Wichita Falls, TX	16.1	6.0	56,261	67.8	50.8	4.7	12.2	32.2	27.9	33.0	34.7
48700	Williamsport, PA	1.6	0.9	45,595	65.4	49.0	4.0	12.4	34.6	28.3	27.7	39.7
48900	Wilmington, NC	5.4	5.3	152,292	65.0	48.6	4.4	12.0	35.0	26.9	27.0	40.3
49020	Winchester, VA-WV	8.8	7.6	50,815	61.6	48.6	5.2	7.9	38.4	32.0	27.7	38.5
49180	Winston-Salem, NC	10.6	7.6	193,105	65.2	46.4	4.5	14.3	34.8	29.8	31.7	35.4
49340	Worcester, MA	9.8	11.1	300,308	65.5	48.1	4.8	12.6	34.5	27.4	32.1	35.2
49420	Yakima, WA	46.3	17.9	78,472	71.4	52.1	5.3	14.0	28.6	23.9	39.8	35.1
49620	York-Hanover, PA	6.1	3.2	168,508	70.1	54.3	5.1	10.7	29.9	24.8	31.1	36.9
49660	Youngstown-Warren-Boardman, OH-PA	2.9	2.0	229,328	64.6	46.0	4.3	14.2	35.4	31.2	26.9	43.0
49700	Yuba City, CA	28.0	17.8	56,101	72.1	51.8	6.7	13.6	27.9	20.1	40.7	34.7
49740	Yuma, AZ	60.5	26.7	70,895	77.4	57.2	5.5	14.7	22.6	17.7	41.8	39.6

Table A-4. Cities — Who: Age, Race/Ethnicity, and Household Structure, 2010–2012

STATE and Place code	STATE or City	Total population	Percent change 2010–2012	Population by age (percent)						Median age	Race alone or in combination (percent)			
				Under 5 years	5 to 17 years	18 to 24 years	25 to 44 years	45 to 64 years	65 years and over		White	Black	Asian, Hawaiian, or Pacific Islander	American Indian, Alaska Native, or some other race
	ACS table number:	B01003	Population estimates	B01001	B01001	B01001	B01001	B01001	B01001	B01002	B02008	B02009	B02011 + B02012	B02010 + B02013
	Column number:	1	2	3	4	5	6	7	8	9	10	11	12	13
00 00000	**United States**	311,609,369	1.5	6.4	17.3	10.0	26.5	26.5	13.4	37.3	76.4	13.6	6.1	6.9
01 00000	**Alabama**	4,803,488	0.8	6.4	17.1	10.1	25.5	26.9	14.1	38.0	70.5	27.0	1.5	2.5
01 00820	Alabaster city	30,706	1.7	7.3	19.7	6.6	31.9	25.0	9.6	36.3	78.8	13.6	0.6	8.5
01 00988	Albertville city	21,346	1.7	9.0	21.0	7.2	30.1	20.2	12.5	33.5	90.9	2.7	...	7.5
01 01852	Anniston city	22,897	-1.3	6.0	14.0	9.8	23.1	29.1	18.0	41.2	43.8	56.4	0.4	0.8
01 02956	Athens city	22,749	6.5	5.5	20.1	8.7	26.0	24.8	14.9	36.9	76.6	19.9	0.4	5.1
01 03076	Auburn city	55,207	5.7	5.2	12.7	38.4	23.4	13.9	6.3	23.0	76.1	17.3	6.9	1.2
01 05980	Bessemer city	27,361	-0.5	7.3	18.8	9.6	22.4	26.6	15.3	38.2	25.2	73.8	...	1.6
01 07000	Birmingham city	211,827	-0.1	7.3	14.6	11.7	27.2	26.4	12.8	35.8	23.0	74.9	1.1	1.6
01 19648	Daphne city	22,314	4.8	7.3	18.7	6.9	25.7	27.4	14.0	39.9	85.8	12.2	2.6	...
01 20104	Decatur city	55,774	0.5	6.1	16.8	9.2	26.7	25.9	15.3	38.5	73.7	22.2	1.3	5.3
01 21184	Dothan city	67,269	1.9	7.2	17.4	8.9	25.5	26.5	14.6	37.8	64.1	34.1	1.6	2.1
01 24184	Enterprise city	27,412	3.9	6.3	18.8	9.2	29.2	22.9	13.6	36.1	74.6	22.1	2.8	2.4
01 26896	Florence city	39,388	0.3	6.1	13.6	15.3	22.7	24.4	18.0	37.4	76.2	22.1	1.5	1.7
01 28696	Gadsden city	36,760	-0.5	7.2	15.3	9.3	24.8	26.6	16.8	39.2	60.2	38.6	1.1	1.0
01 35800	Homewood city	25,174	0.4	7.4	15.8	18.3	31.5	18.2	8.7	28.9	77.4	18.2	3.2	2.3
01 35896	Hoover city	82,214	2.6	7.5	18.9	6.3	29.4	25.8	12.1	36.3	74.5	13.5	5.8	7.2
01 37000	Huntsville city	181,734	1.6	6.1	15.2	12.0	26.7	26.0	14.0	36.6	64.8	32.3	3.6	2.8
01 45784	Madison city	44,402	3.8	5.9	22.5	8.3	26.2	29.1	8.0	36.3	78.9	14.3	6.8	2.7
01 50000	Mobile city	194,829	-0.1	7.0	16.4	11.9	25.0	25.9	13.9	35.8	46.6	51.4	1.7	1.5
01 51000	Montgomery city	206,346	-0.3	7.3	17.8	12.0	27.0	24.0	11.9	34.0	39.0	57.7	2.7	2.1
01 51696	Mountain Brook city	20,393	-0.2	7.1	23.3	3.8	21.6	28.7	15.5	40.6	85.8	...	2.0	...
01 55200	Northport city	23,753	2.8	7.7	17.7	9.4	29.1	22.7	13.3	32.8	71.7	25.5	1.6	...
01 57048	Opelika city	27,203	5.2	6.6	16.5	9.5	26.0	27.6	13.8	37.7	52.5	42.9	1.1	4.5
01 57576	Oxford city	22,052	-0.2	7.5	19.9	7.6	27.9	25.2	11.9	36.5	82.3	14.5	1.2	4.4
01 58848	Pelham city	21,714	2.6	4.1	18.8	9.4	29.9	27.4	10.3	37.5	84.9	6.5	1.1	7.7
01 59472	Phenix City city	36,115	9.2	8.4	20.3	10.2	27.8	21.8	11.5	32.3	51.3	47.9	0.9	...
01 62328	Prattville city	34,462	2.4	7.9	18.8	11.5	26.0	23.8	12.1	34.5	78.1	19.5	2.1	1.6
01 62496	Prichard city	22,514	-0.9	6.6	18.2	10.7	22.1	29.1	13.3	38.4	16.7	81.9	...	0.9
01 69120	Selma city	20,482	-2.3	9.6	18.3	10.1	23.3	24.7	13.9	33.2	20.3	79.4	...	0.6
01 76944	Trussville city	20,031	0.8	4.7	21.6	4.9	25.2	31.7	11.9	42.2	93.6	5.4	1.0	...
01 77256	Tuscaloosa city	92,217	2.5	5.6	12.7	28.2	23.4	19.8	10.3	26.9	54.4	43.1	2.3	0.8
01 78552	Vestavia Hills city	34,039	0.1	6.0	19.2	5.5	25.7	27.4	16.3	40.6	92.7	2.9	4.7	0.4
02 00000	**Alaska**	723,120	2.4	7.5	18.5	10.8	27.6	27.5	8.1	33.7	73.7	5.0	8.9	20.9
02 03000	Anchorage municipality	296,039	1.8	7.5	18.0	11.4	29.0	26.4	7.7	32.8	73.8	8.6	13.5	14.4
02 05000	Badger CDP	20,892	...	10.2	22.1	12.7	25.6	25.4	4.1	28.0	89.2	4.8	2.9	10.1
02 24230	Fairbanks city	32,021	1.8	9.4	17.2	16.3	30.9	18.9	7.3	28.1	73.7	11.7	8.3	14.3
02 36400	Juneau city and borough	32,071	3.6	6.2	16.8	8.8	28.1	31.7	8.5	37.8	78.1	1.8	10.0	20.9
04 00000	**Arizona**	6,477,128	2.2	6.9	18.2	9.9	26.1	24.6	14.3	36.2	81.6	5.0	4.1	12.3
04 02430	Anthem CDP	23,285	...	11.0	28.1	3.9	25.8	21.5	9.7	33.6	90.5	...	4.3	3.4
04 02830	Apache Junction city	36,421	0.1	5.6	14.8	6.0	19.7	27.3	26.5	47.5	94.4	1.8	3.3	5.7
04 04720	Avondale city	77,270	2.5	10.7	22.3	10.6	31.2	19.5	5.8	28.4	79.5	10.9	3.7	8.5
04 07940	Buckeye town	52,722	6.5	10.6	21.6	8.5	30.9	20.8	7.5	30.2	80.7	7.5	1.9	12.6
04 08220	Bullhead City city	39,577	0.0	6.6	14.1	7.4	17.2	27.6	27.0	48.5	93.9	2.2	2.2	7.4
04 10530	Casa Grande city	49,720	0.5	7.7	19.7	8.9	22.6	24.9	16.2	38.1	78.7	5.0	3.4	15.0
04 10670	Casas Adobes CDP	68,644	...	5.6	16.4	7.3	24.9	27.8	18.0	41.2	89.7	2.2	4.9	5.7
04 11230	Catalina Foothills CDP	51,623	...	2.8	12.6	5.7	17.9	36.6	24.4	52.3	91.1	3.2	6.5	2.1
04 12000	Chandler city	240,626	3.8	7.2	19.7	9.2	30.5	25.0	8.5	34.5	81.5	6.5	11.0	5.3
04 20540	Drexel Heights CDP	28,594	...	10.3	20.2	8.4	25.2	25.7	10.2	32.5	80.6	1.3	1.1	19.1
04 22220	El Mirage city	32,151	2.4	9.5	22.8	10.5	31.9	17.5	7.7	30.1	83.4	5.0	3.3	13.0
04 23620	Flagstaff city	66,400	2.2	6.0	14.4	27.1	26.5	19.2	6.7	26.0	76.4	2.7	3.6	20.9
04 23760	Florence town	26,832	-0.8	2.8	7.9	10.9	40.6	21.8	16.0	38.6	82.0	6.4	1.1	11.7
04 25030	Fortuna Foothills CDP	28,362	...	5.6	9.8	5.3	17.3	22.8	39.2	57.6	91.2	...	0.8	8.6
04 25300	Fountain Hills town	22,749	2.3	3.2	10.5	5.7	17.6	35.3	27.7	54.2	94.7	...	2.2	2.1
04 27400	Gilbert town	214,757	5.6	7.8	24.4	7.6	31.4	22.0	6.7	32.3	87.4	4.6	7.6	3.8
04 27820	Glendale city	229,166	2.4	7.3	19.8	12.0	27.4	24.4	9.1	32.5	76.6	8.4	4.6	13.9
04 28380	Goodyear city	67,545	6.1	6.9	19.4	7.6	31.2	23.6	11.3	35.9	86.8	5.9	5.6	5.1
04 29710	Green Valley CDP	22,602	...	1.2	1.8	0.9	3.8	21.0	71.4	71.1	98.0	...	0.7	0.5
04 37620	Kingman city	28,250	0.7	6.1	15.4	7.5	21.6	28.4	20.9	44.6	95.7	1.1	4.6	7.0
04 39370	Lake Havasu City city	52,745	0.4	4.0	14.6	6.3	16.4	30.5	28.2	51.7	95.5	1.3	1.9	3.7
04 44270	Marana town	35,808	5.9	7.2	18.3	6.1	27.2	26.3	14.9	39.5	84.2	6.5	5.7	6.8
04 44410	Maricopa city	44,582	0.5	12.0	18.1	5.6	35.4	23.3	5.5	32.4	75.7	14.7	5.6	8.2
04 46000	Mesa city	445,671	2.7	7.1	17.7	10.4	25.6	23.9	15.3	35.5	85.1	4.6	3.2	10.1
04 49640	Nogales city	20,775	-0.2	7.6	23.8	12.0	19.8	22.5	14.3	31.3	64.4	...	0.4	35.7
04 51600	Oro Valley town	41,237	0.8	4.3	16.7	6.8	17.8	29.2	25.3	48.2	91.4	1.6	5.0	5.2
04 54050	Peoria city	156,920	3.5	5.9	20.0	8.0	26.1	25.8	14.2	38.3	89.1	5.3	5.4	3.9
04 55000	Phoenix city	1,467,400	2.7	7.9	19.8	10.4	29.9	23.3	8.8	32.7	79.9	7.7	4.4	10.9
04 57380	Prescott city	39,763	3.3	3.0	9.5	8.2	16.8	31.2	31.3	55.2	94.1	1.2	2.2	4.3
04 57450	Prescott Valley town	38,922	0.7	6.7	17.5	9.3	22.3	24.4	19.7	38.5	94.7	1.2	2.0	5.1
04 58150	Queen Creek town	27,011	5.3	9.1	30.0	5.2	29.4	19.9	6.5	32.0	84.9	2.9	2.8	10.1
04 62140	Sahuarita town	25,877	2.8	9.9	20.0	4.5	26.6	21.0	18.0	36.5	90.0	3.9	4.5	4.8
04 63470	San Luis city	26,103	2.6	8.2	26.0	12.1	26.7	19.3	7.6	27.5	93.6	1.0	...	5.3
04 64210	San Tan Valley CDP	83,015	...	10.3	26.8	7.2	32.9	17.2	5.6	28.7	79.3	5.5	4.1	14.6
04 65000	Scottsdale city	220,293	2.7	4.5	13.4	7.0	24.6	29.9	20.6	45.4	92.0	2.3	4.5	2.8
04 66820	Sierra Vista city	45,918	2.4	7.6	15.9	13.6	25.8	21.5	15.5	33.6	79.5	10.9	7.0	10.5
04 70320	Sun City CDP	37,915	...	0.0	0.4	0.7	2.2	23.1	73.7	73.0	96.3	2.0	1.0	1.3
04 70355	Sun City West CDP	25,407	...	...	...	...	...	...	...	75.7	96.7	0.3	2.5	0.5
04 71510	Surprise city	119,378	3.0	7.7	22.3	5.3	26.2	18.9	19.6	36.3	90.1	6.1	2.3	3.5
04 73000	Tempe city	164,186	3.0	5.8	11.4	25.1	30.1	19.3	8.4	28.1	80.2	6.3	9.7	8.1
04 77000	Tucson city	522,770	0.7	6.4	16.1	14.8	26.9	23.5	12.4	33.3	78.5	6.2	4.1	15.1
04 85540	Yuma city	95,130	1.8	7.3	20.9	13.6	26.1	19.2	12.9	30.0	71.4	4.2	3.2	24.9

Table A-4. Cities — Who: Age, Race/Ethnicity, and Household Structure, 2010–2012—*Continued*

STATE and Place code	STATE or City	Percent Hispanic or Latino	Percent foreign born	Total households	Household type (percent)						Percent of households with people under 18 years	Percent of households with people 60 years and over
					Family households				Nonfamily households			
					Total family households	Married-couple families	Male household families	Female household families	Total nonfamily households	One-person households		
ACS table number:		B03003	C05003	B11001	B11001	B11001	B11001	B11001	B11001	B11001	B11005	B11006
Column number:		14	15	16	17	18	19	20	21	22	23	24
00 00000	**United States**...............	16.6	13.0	115,241,776	66.2	48.4	4.8	13.1	33.8	27.6	32.8	34.8
01 00000	**Alabama**......................	4.0	3.5	1,837,823	67.5	48.1	4.2	15.3	32.5	28.4	32.2	36.0
01 00820	Alabaster city...............	10.1	8.4	10,708	76.7	60.8	3.6	12.3	23.3	21.0	42.3	25.3
01 00988	Albertville city.............	27.9	17.3	7,297	69.4	53.1	4.9	11.3	30.6	27.9	39.9	37.1
01 01852	Anniston city...............	2.5	1.2	9,561	57.6	35.3	4.3	18.1	42.4	38.9	23.1	42.2
01 02956	Athens city.................	8.3	6.0	8,914	65.3	48.0	3.4	13.8	34.7	30.6	32.0	37.8
01 03076	Auburn city.................	2.7	9.4	20,700	47.8	36.3	3.0	8.5	52.2	31.0	25.0	16.2
01 05980	Bessemer city..............	2.1	2.2	10,378	62.7	31.9	4.4	26.4	37.3	34.4	30.7	39.9
01 07000	Birmingham city...........	3.4	3.4	87,407	54.9	25.7	4.3	25.0	45.1	38.6	26.5	31.8
01 19648	Daphne city.................	5.3	2.9	8,403	68.8	55.3	3.0	10.5	31.2	28.3	35.3	33.9
01 20104	Decatur city................	13.1	8.0	22,076	62.3	44.9	3.8	13.5	37.7	33.3	28.7	35.8
01 21184	Dothan city.................	2.7	2.5	25,799	66.6	45.1	3.0	18.4	33.4	29.4	32.6	35.3
01 24184	Enterprise city.............	7.6	6.3	10,075	67.6	49.0	4.4	14.3	32.4	26.7	35.5	33.2
01 26896	Florence city...............	1.9	2.8	17,508	55.8	39.9	2.5	13.5	44.2	38.3	26.6	37.9
01 28696	Gadsden city...............	5.1	3.2	14,823	60.9	32.5	5.7	22.7	39.1	35.9	29.2	41.4
01 35800	Homewood city............	8.4	9.2	9,144	58.8	40.4	8.3	10.1	41.2	31.6	33.2	26.7
01 35896	Hoover city.................	8.3	9.9	31,316	69.9	58.7	2.8	8.4	30.1	25.9	35.5	31.4
01 37000	Huntsville city.............	6.0	6.5	75,373	58.4	39.7	4.5	14.2	41.6	36.7	26.9	32.3
01 45784	Madison city...............	3.5	7.7	15,986	72.6	60.2	4.5	7.9	27.4	22.8	40.2	22.3
01 50000	Mobile city.................	2.3	3.4	76,621	59.7	34.3	4.0	21.4	40.3	34.6	30.6	35.3
01 51000	Montgomery city...........	3.7	4.7	79,764	63.0	36.4	5.1	21.6	37.0	31.5	33.7	31.5
01 51696	Mountain Brook city.......	1.9	2.9	7,294	77.6	73.4	1.1	3.1	22.4	20.6	41.7	36.8
01 55200	Northport city..............	3.8	3.6	8,758	64.2	49.1	3.4	11.7	35.8	32.7	31.3	34.1
01 57048	Opelika city.................	5.6	5.3	11,055	62.9	41.6	3.3	18.1	37.1	32.2	30.4	34.6
01 57576	Oxford city.................	6.6	3.9	7,564	77.7	58.9	6.0	12.8	22.3	20.2	35.8	32.5
01 58848	Pelham city.................	13.5	11.0	8,466	65.2	49.2	4.8	11.2	34.8	29.4	32.4	27.7
01 59472	Phenix City city...........	5.2	1.8	14,105	63.4	38.0	5.1	20.3	36.6	34.3	38.9	29.2
01 62328	Prattville city..............	3.0	1.3	12,092	69.1	53.2	3.5	12.4	30.9	25.4	37.3	29.5
01 62496	Prichard city...............	1.1	1.9	8,650	59.5	25.9	4.5	29.2	40.5	35.4	31.3	37.0
01 69120	Selma city..................	0.5	0.6	7,743	54.9	20.8	5.2	28.9	45.1	43.3	32.2	40.1
01 76944	Trussville city..............	0.0	1.4	7,116	79.7	69.8	1.3	8.6	20.3	18.0	39.8	35.3
01 77256	Tuscaloosa city............	3.8	4.7	30,979	56.5	35.8	3.6	17.1	43.5	33.3	27.7	28.9
01 78552	Vestavia Hills city.........	0.5	4.5	13,797	66.1	57.0	1.6	7.5	33.9	31.2	32.9	38.3
02 00000	**Alaska**.......................	5.8	7.0	253,718	66.8	49.4	5.7	11.6	33.2	25.7	36.6	26.6
02 03000	Anchorage municipality ...	7.9	9.4	105,688	65.4	47.7	5.4	12.3	34.6	26.2	37.3	24.7
02 05000	Badger CDP.................	3.9	3.2	6,988	69.8	55.7	1.9	12.2	30.2	22.4	41.6	21.9
02 24230	Fairbanks city..............	8.5	6.5	11,811	62.9	42.5	6.6	13.8	37.1	28.8	37.3	20.0
02 36400	Juneau city and borough....	5.4	6.1	12,314	64.8	47.0	5.7	12.1	35.2	25.3	31.8	27.4
04 00000	**Arizona**......................	29.9	13.4	2,357,799	65.7	47.5	5.4	12.8	34.3	27.3	32.3	36.5
04 02430	Anthem CDP................	18.4	4.2	7,652	79.2	60.4	3.2	15.6	20.8	19.6	50.7	31.9
04 02830	Apache Junction city.......	14.5	6.3	14,525	61.3	46.3	4.3	10.7	38.7	31.2	21.8	55.4
04 04720	Avondale city..............	54.4	15.6	22,330	77.6	48.4	8.7	20.6	22.4	15.4	50.6	21.9
04 07940	Buckeye town..............	39.2	9.3	14,454	80.6	63.0	5.7	11.9	19.4	15.4	48.4	29.0
04 08220	Bullhead City city.........	19.7	7.8	16,569	63.7	46.7	4.0	12.9	36.3	28.9	21.1	54.7
04 10530	Casa Grande city...........	36.3	12.0	16,716	71.9	52.8	6.8	12.3	28.1	23.7	35.8	46.1
04 10670	Casas Adobes CDP.........	18.9	8.5	27,904	62.5	47.4	3.7	11.4	37.5	31.4	27.8	39.2
04 11230	Catalina Foothills CDP.....	8.8	12.9	24,046	60.0	52.5	2.0	5.5	40.0	33.8	18.9	50.4
04 12000	Chandler city..............	23.4	14.7	86,507	69.1	51.9	5.9	11.3	30.9	23.2	38.4	24.9
04 20540	Drexel Heights CDP........	69.1	19.4	8,663	77.3	50.7	7.6	18.9	22.7	19.0	42.1	36.4
04 22220	El Mirage city..............	49.8	16.9	10,005	74.7	50.4	6.6	17.8	25.3	18.9	47.3	24.1
04 23620	Flagstaff city...............	18.3	7.9	22,385	58.2	38.5	7.0	12.7	41.8	25.6	31.9	21.2
04 23760	Florence town..............	42.5	24.0	5,273	66.2	57.2	4.2	4.9	33.8	29.0	22.9	56.3
04 25030	Fortuna Foothills CDP.....	19.3	10.4	12,932	73.4	64.8	4.2	4.5	26.6	20.2	18.3	62.6
04 25300	Fountain Hills town........	3.7	6.9	10,215	66.8	57.6	3.3	5.9	33.2	27.5	18.6	55.0
04 27400	Gilbert town...............	17.1	8.9	69,703	76.8	62.2	3.9	10.8	23.2	16.3	46.7	21.3
04 27820	Glendale city..............	37.0	16.8	78,437	68.2	45.3	6.2	16.8	31.8	25.2	36.9	27.5
04 28380	Goodyear city..............	31.5	10.7	22,141	79.5	62.5	7.2	9.8	20.5	16.7	40.3	28.2
04 29710	Green Valley CDP..........	7.0	8.1	13,144	56.5	52.4	0.6	3.5	43.5	38.7	2.0	90.2
04 37620	Kingman city...............	16.8	4.8	10,880	59.8	43.2	3.3	13.3	40.2	29.6	23.5	45.6
04 39370	Lake Havasu City city	10.3	4.9	22,977	65.8	52.6	2.5	10.8	34.2	27.0	19.5	54.1
04 44270	Marana town...............	20.3	9.1	13,128	76.6	62.6	4.7	9.4	23.4	18.3	36.5	38.8
04 44410	Maricopa city..............	20.6	10.1	14,469	74.6	60.7	4.3	9.7	25.4	18.3	45.3	24.2
04 46000	Mesa city..................	26.6	12.5	165,344	65.0	46.1	6.3	12.7	35.0	27.6	31.2	37.0
04 49640	Nogales city...............	93.2	41.2	6,332	76.9	45.7	6.6	24.6	23.1	21.0	48.3	45.0
04 51600	Oro Valley town............	10.7	7.4	16,684	72.6	59.4	3.3	10.0	27.4	22.9	27.3	51.4
04 54050	Peoria city.................	18.7	8.8	56,220	71.3	53.5	5.7	12.1	28.7	23.7	36.4	35.7
04 55000	Phoenix city...............	39.9	20.1	516,383	63.3	41.3	6.5	15.6	36.7	28.8	36.7	26.3
04 57380	Prescott city...............	7.0	6.8	19,284	51.2	40.3	1.5	9.4	48.8	39.2	12.5	56.6
04 57450	Prescott Valley town.......	19.0	7.1	15,177	68.2	51.7	6.3	10.2	31.8	25.2	29.4	43.6
04 58150	Queen Creek town.........	16.1	4.3	7,982	82.3	67.6	5.2	9.5	17.7	14.9	57.3	22.1
04 62140	Sahuarita town.............	28.2	9.6	9,417	77.4	67.5	1.3	8.5	22.6	18.7	41.8	38.7
04 63470	San Luis city...............	95.6	44.6	6,866	91.3	63.7	8.7	18.9	8.7	6.0	67.5	26.6
04 64210	San Tan Valley CDP........	22.1	7.1	23,627	81.0	62.4	6.4	12.2	19.0	15.0	54.0	21.4
04 65000	Scottsdale city.............	9.2	10.1	99,734	57.7	46.4	3.4	8.0	42.3	33.9	21.6	40.3
04 66820	Sierra Vista city...........	21.9	9.3	17,691	67.8	50.9	5.1	11.8	32.2	27.9	33.4	37.6
04 70320	Sun City CDP...............	3.8	5.1	22,943	49.6	42.9	2.3	4.4	50.4	45.4	0.5	93.5
04 70355	Sun City West CDP.........	0.8	6.3	14,922	58.7	55.8	0.3	2.6	41.3	37.7	...	98.0
04 71510	Surprise city...............	17.5	10.1	42,029	76.3	60.3	4.4	11.6	23.7	19.9	37.3	42.3
04 73000	Tempe city.................	21.9	13.3	63,328	47.6	29.8	5.5	12.3	52.4	34.4	22.5	23.0
04 77000	Tucson city................	42.7	15.1	200,627	55.9	34.5	5.8	15.5	44.1	35.0	28.7	32.1
04 85540	Yuma city..................	57.3	20.3	33,492	74.4	51.8	6.6	16.0	25.6	20.3	43.3	32.0

Table A-4. Cities — Who: Age, Race/Ethnicity, and Household Structure, 2010–2012—*Continued*

STATE and Place code	STATE or City	Total population	Percent change 2010–2012	Under 5 years	5 to 17 years	18 to 24 years	25 to 44 years	45 to 64 years	65 years and over	Median age	White	Black	Asian, Hawaiian, or Pacific Islander	American Indian, Alaska Native, or some other race
	ACS table number:	B01003	Population estimates	B01001	B01001	B01001	B01001	B01001	B01001	B01002	B02008	B02009	B02011 + B02012	B02010 + B02013
	Column number:	1	2	3	4	5	6	7	8	9	10	11	12	13
05 00000	**Arkansas**	2,936,822	0.9	6.7	17.5	9.8	25.4	25.9	14.6	37.5	80.1	16.2	1.8	3.9
05 04840	Bella Vista town	26,967	2.9	5.7	12.5	4.0	21.7	24.0	32.2	50.6	97.0	...	1.9	1.4
05 05290	Benton city	31,484	4.1	7.0	19.3	8.3	26.7	24.5	14.2	36.3	91.7	7.1	...	1.4
05 05320	Bentonville city	37,033	6.8	8.1	20.3	8.6	33.3	22.2	7.5	32.2	85.6	2.5	9.3	4.1
05 10300	Cabot city	24,210	2.4	7.4	21.3	8.7	30.5	22.3	9.8	32.8	95.6	1.6	2.8	1.9
05 15190	Conway city	61,461	5.4	6.1	16.2	22.6	28.1	18.8	8.2	27.8	80.7	16.5	2.8	1.8
05 23290	Fayetteville city	75,473	3.9	5.8	12.5	25.4	29.6	18.3	8.3	27.7	85.7	7.0	3.6	5.8
05 24550	Fort Smith city	86,981	1.3	7.5	18.2	9.6	27.2	25.1	12.4	35.1	82.7	11.1	5.9	5.0
05 33400	Hot Springs city	35,381	0.6	6.2	14.3	9.5	21.8	27.2	21.1	43.1	72.3	19.9	1.5	8.1
05 34750	Jacksonville city	28,615	0.9	6.4	20.4	12.8	26.9	23.6	10.0	32.4	59.9	36.9	4.2	3.4
05 35710	Jonesboro city	68,844	4.0	7.9	17.3	14.9	27.9	21.0	11.0	30.7	78.6	19.4	1.9	1.4
05 41000	Little Rock city	195,242	1.3	7.4	16.8	10.0	28.6	25.4	11.7	35.1	52.5	43.8	3.6	1.4
05 50450	North Little Rock city	63,492	3.6	7.2	17.7	8.1	30.3	23.9	12.8	34.8	58.5	39.8	0.8	2.1
05 53390	Paragould city	26,620	3.1	6.6	18.3	9.9	27.1	24.2	13.9	36.4	97.9	1.4	...	1.5
05 55310	Pine Bluff city	48,054	-4.0	6.9	18.0	13.0	23.8	25.6	12.7	33.9	21.1	77.2	1.3	0.9
05 60410	Rogers city	57,636	4.6	9.5	20.9	10.1	29.4	21.0	9.3	31.2	86.4	1.7	2.9	11.3
05 61670	Russellville city	28,434	1.5	7.4	16.3	19.3	24.9	19.7	12.4	29.6	87.3	7.7	2.1	7.3
05 63020	Searcy city	23,216	2.5	7.1	13.1	24.0	23.3	18.0	14.5	28.2	91.4	7.9	0.4	...
05 63800	Sherwood city	29,780	0.8	7.8	14.7	7.8	29.2	28.0	12.5	37.9	82.1	16.5	1.7	2.2
05 66080	Springdale city	74,156	3.4	10.4	23.8	9.0	30.6	17.9	8.3	29.4	67.3	2.9	8.2	23.7
05 68810	Texarkana city	30,052	0.2	7.7	16.5	8.3	28.3	25.8	13.4	36.8	66.0	33.7	...	1.8
05 71480	Van Buren city	22,914	0.7	8.4	21.4	9.2	28.2	21.9	10.9	32.6	92.3	3.1	2.2	7.4
05 74540	West Memphis city	25,957	-2.2	8.9	20.5	9.6	23.2	25.8	12.0	33.7	35.0	65.0	0.3	0.3
06 00000	**California**	37,686,586	1.9	6.7	17.9	10.6	28.1	25.1	11.7	35.4	66.0	7.1	15.9	15.8
06 00296	Adelanto city	31,541	-0.7	11.6	27.2	12.8	29.6	14.4	4.3	24.0	59.8	28.0	3.1	15.6
06 00394	Agoura Hills city	20,516	1.5	4.5	19.8	7.0	22.3	34.0	12.3	43.0	86.0	3.1	8.7	5.7
06 00562	Alameda city	74,760	2.3	5.5	15.5	7.8	29.2	29.2	12.6	39.6	53.7	9.7	37.9	6.6
06 00884	Alhambra city	83,722	1.4	4.8	13.2	8.8	30.0	28.4	14.8	40.3	27.8	2.0	54.4	18.5
06 00947	Aliso Viejo city	48,746	3.1	9.6	17.1	7.4	33.4	26.4	6.1	35.8	76.0	3.1	18.1	7.6
06 01290	Altadena CDP	44,118	...	5.9	15.3	7.9	26.6	29.8	14.5	41.2	67.3	23.8	7.1	6.4
06 02000	Anaheim city	340,306	1.8	7.7	19.1	11.0	29.8	22.7	9.7	32.6	65.8	3.0	16.8	17.7
06 02210	Antelope CDP	48,621	...	8.0	21.7	13.5	27.3	23.6	5.9	29.6	73.3	12.7	12.9	10.1
06 02252	Antioch city	104,041	2.7	6.6	20.0	10.9	25.3	27.9	9.3	34.9	57.5	18.4	15.9	16.2
06 02364	Apple Valley town	70,083	2.0	6.7	20.3	10.2	21.6	25.7	15.5	36.2	84.8	9.2	3.0	6.5
06 02462	Arcadia city	56,930	1.9	4.7	18.5	7.2	24.3	29.6	15.7	42.7	34.4	1.6	59.2	7.8
06 02553	Arden-Arcade CDP	90,054	...	6.8	14.3	9.6	27.0	26.8	15.6	38.8	77.1	10.7	9.3	10.3
06 02924	Arvin city	19,729	4.0	10.3	25.7	14.7	27.8	16.9	4.5	24.5	85.1	1.5	1.6	11.6
06 02980	Ashland CDP	22,984	...	8.4	21.3	10.3	31.6	21.4	7.1	31.7	49.6	23.3	21.3	11.1
06 03064	Atascadero city	28,634	1.3	5.2	15.3	8.7	23.9	32.1	14.8	42.8	89.9	2.6	2.8	9.0
06 03162	Atwater city	28,520	1.7	8.5	23.3	9.8	26.5	21.1	10.8	30.9	74.2	4.3	8.8	16.5
06 03386	Azusa city	46,822	2.2	6.1	18.6	21.3	27.4	19.4	7.2	27.5	43.2	3.3	10.3	46.7
06 03526	Bakersfield city	353,780	2.7	8.8	22.1	11.3	27.3	21.7	8.8	30.2	69.9	9.8	8.6	16.8
06 03666	Baldwin Park city	75,914	1.3	7.1	20.8	12.2	28.8	22.0	9.1	31.0	37.3	1.9	16.4	46.8
06 03820	Banning city	30,029	1.9	6.1	13.8	8.2	19.4	22.5	30.0	46.8	75.9	10.0	6.1	13.0
06 04030	Barstow city	22,884	1.4	10.6	18.9	11.8	24.1	24.7	10.0	31.6	64.4	16.7	10.5	15.2
06 04415	Bay Point CDP	23,791	...	9.2	23.3	10.5	31.2	19.6	6.1	29.7	57.3	13.3	10.4	25.7
06 04758	Beaumont city	38,445	5.8	9.3	20.4	7.3	30.7	21.9	10.4	34.0	72.3	10.9	10.7	11.5
06 04870	Bell city	35,652	0.9	9.4	22.2	12.5	28.6	20.5	6.7	29.6	65.7	1.6	0.6	33.1
06 04982	Bellflower city	77,006	0.9	8.2	21.7	10.8	28.9	21.7	8.7	31.0	45.6	15.6	12.4	29.5
06 04996	Bell Gardens city	42,380	1.6	9.4	24.8	10.8	31.3	17.8	6.0	27.6	65.8	1.7	0.5	34.4
06 05108	Belmont city	26,183	2.3	7.3	14.6	6.5	28.4	28.0	15.2	40.4	69.8	3.5	28.5	5.3
06 05290	Benicia city	27,231	1.4	3.7	20.5	6.1	21.1	35.4	13.1	43.9	82.6	6.3	15.0	5.7
06 06000	Berkeley city	114,156	2.1	3.8	9.0	26.1	27.0	21.6	12.5	31.1	66.3	10.8	23.3	5.4
06 06308	Beverly Hills city	34,370	1.4	4.6	15.4	8.3	24.4	27.6	19.7	42.7	85.3	3.7	9.0	4.1
06 07064	Bloomington CDP	23,474	...	6.5	26.3	12.7	26.1	22.0	6.3	29.2	67.5	2.5	1.4	33.1
06 07218	Blythe city	20,436	0.5	3.9	14.9	9.6	32.9	30.0	8.7	37.5	65.8	12.1	2.9	22.4
06 08058	Brawley city	25,271	2.2	9.5	24.7	11.4	22.4	21.5	10.6	28.9	86.8	2.3	0.7	12.2
06 08100	Brea city	39,928	2.0	4.5	18.8	9.8	27.0	27.0	12.9	39.0	77.5	1.8	19.4	4.1
06 08142	Brentwood city	52,769	3.5	6.1	24.0	7.4	26.2	23.9	12.3	36.2	80.3	6.1	12.5	6.3
06 08786	Buena Park city	81,471	1.8	6.5	18.6	10.6	27.4	25.5	11.4	35.5	61.6	4.8	30.8	6.5
06 08954	Burbank city	103,900	1.0	5.3	14.6	7.3	32.4	26.1	14.2	39.0	79.6	2.9	15.5	7.0
06 09066	Burlingame city	29,270	2.8	8.2	14.0	5.2	30.6	28.7	13.3	40.6	74.1	1.6	24.0	5.0
06 09598	Calabasas city	23,748	2.0	3.4	23.4	5.9	19.8	34.6	12.9	44.0	87.9	4.5	13.5	0.6
06 09710	Calexico city	38,992	1.7	7.8	22.9	11.7	24.1	22.4	11.2	32.0	60.2	...	1.0	38.4
06 10046	Camarillo city	65,671	0.9	6.1	16.5	8.3	24.1	27.3	17.6	40.8	80.6	3.5	12.9	9.2
06 10345	Campbell city	39,852	2.1	6.4	13.7	8.5	34.3	25.8	11.3	36.9	77.9	2.1	20.5	5.2
06 11194	Carlsbad city	107,615	3.3	5.6	16.5	6.7	26.8	29.3	15.0	41.2	87.3	2.2	10.2	4.2
06 11390	Carmichael CDP	61,565	...	6.0	14.3	8.9	23.4	29.3	17.9	42.7	85.9	8.1	7.4	4.1
06 11530	Carson city	92,358	1.3	5.6	16.8	11.6	25.2	27.1	13.7	37.4	43.5	25.2	31.2	18.4
06 11964	Castro Valley CDP	60,847	...	6.2	16.4	7.6	24.5	31.9	13.4	41.1	64.1	6.7	29.3	5.5
06 12048	Cathedral City city	52,108	2.3	7.2	21.8	10.4	25.2	22.8	12.6	33.8	73.9	3.3	5.6	18.2
06 12524	Ceres city	45,471	1.0	7.7	21.2	12.1	28.5	21.5	9.1	30.8	73.6	1.9	10.0	19.5
06 12552	Cerritos city	49,357	1.1	3.6	17.4	9.0	22.6	29.8	17.6	43.5	25.2	8.3	63.9	6.2
06 13014	Chico city	86,920	1.8	5.9	13.7	23.6	25.2	20.9	10.8	29.6	88.9	3.7	5.0	7.9
06 13210	Chino city	79,441	2.0	6.3	17.2	11.1	31.7	24.8	8.8	33.9	61.8	5.8	14.4	22.4
06 13214	Chino Hills city	75,762	1.9	5.5	20.5	11.1	24.8	30.8	7.3	36.9	58.7	5.2	31.3	9.6
06 13392	Chula Vista city	248,425	3.2	7.1	19.7	11.0	28.2	23.7	10.3	33.8	71.9	6.3	17.8	9.8

Table A-4. Cities — Who: Age, Race/Ethnicity, and Household Structure, 2010–2012—*Continued*

STATE and Place code	STATE or City	Percent Hispanic or Latino	Percent foreign born	Total households	Household type (percent)							Percent of households with people under 18 years	Percent of households with people 60 years and over
					Family households				Nonfamily households				
					Total family households	Married-couple families	Male household families	Female household families	Total nonfamily households	One-person households			
ACS table number:		B03003	C05003	B11001	B11001	B11001	B11001	B11001	B11001	B11001		B11005	B11006
Column number:		14	15	16	17	18	19	20	21	22		23	24
05 00000	**Arkansas**	6.6	4.5	1,129,845	67.5	49.4	4.5	13.6	32.5	27.8		32.3	36.0
05 04840	Bella Vista town	2.1	4.4	11,423	75.6	70.0	0.7	4.8	24.4	19.1		22.3	57.4
05 05290	Benton city	4.9	2.0	11,794	69.2	50.0	5.0	14.2	30.8	26.3		35.2	35.1
05 05320	Bentonville city	9.4	13.8	13,779	67.6	55.1	2.8	9.7	32.4	25.4		39.8	23.0
05 10300	Cabot city	4.4	2.9	9,043	72.0	56.9	2.6	12.5	28.0	23.5		42.7	26.8
05 15190	Conway city	5.4	4.6	23,046	59.0	43.1	4.1	11.8	41.0	29.0		31.8	20.0
05 23290	Fayetteville city	6.3	6.2	32,050	47.9	34.7	3.3	9.8	52.1	38.4		25.3	20.8
05 24550	Fort Smith city	16.5	11.9	34,062	61.7	41.9	5.6	14.2	38.3	33.0		30.5	31.3
05 33400	Hot Springs city	9.1	6.0	14,791	56.4	38.4	3.5	14.4	43.6	37.5		25.7	45.8
05 34750	Jacksonville city	6.0	5.4	10,734	68.6	40.8	6.1	21.8	31.4	26.7		34.1	26.0
05 35710	Jonesboro city	5.2	4.4	26,359	64.4	43.3	4.8	16.3	35.6	27.0		35.1	29.8
05 41000	Little Rock city	5.9	6.6	79,047	58.5	35.6	4.6	18.3	41.5	36.0		28.7	28.9
05 50450	North Little Rock city	9.5	5.6	25,763	56.9	36.4	3.1	17.5	43.1	35.7		27.7	30.5
05 53390	Paragould city	3.1	1.6	10,627	62.2	44.9	5.5	11.8	37.8	31.4		32.1	35.1
05 55310	Pine Bluff city	1.5	1.5	18,107	58.6	29.2	4.7	24.7	41.4	37.9		31.8	34.5
05 60410	Rogers city	30.9	19.1	19,280	70.6	53.7	4.2	12.7	29.4	25.2		41.7	27.8
05 61670	Russellville city	13.0	5.6	9,723	65.6	44.4	4.8	16.4	34.4	30.2		33.3	32.0
05 63020	Searcy city	3.1	2.5	8,348	64.5	48.6	2.9	13.0	35.5	31.1		32.2	35.9
05 63800	Sherwood city	5.8	5.1	12,006	65.7	47.0	3.0	15.7	34.3	29.8		30.3	32.2
05 66080	Springdale city	35.3	23.6	24,286	74.2	51.5	7.3	15.4	25.8	22.6		49.1	23.0
05 68810	Texarkana city	2.8	0.9	11,887	63.9	40.6	4.7	18.6	36.1	33.1		32.9	31.3
05 71480	Van Buren city	11.1	7.1	8,549	70.9	50.6	4.1	16.2	29.1	24.5		41.9	28.8
05 74540	West Memphis city	0.8	0.6	9,505	68.7	31.2	3.4	34.1	31.3	27.9		39.0	32.9
06 00000	**California**	38.0	27.1	12,474,950	68.5	48.8	6.0	13.7	31.5	24.3		36.7	34.3
06 00296	Adelanto city	46.9	18.3	7,371	86.2	55.2	5.9	25.2	13.8	9.2		64.8	23.8
06 00394	Agoura Hills city	11.4	19.8	7,086	74.1	59.2	1.8	13.1	25.9	18.8		39.7	34.4
06 00562	Alameda city	12.7	26.9	29,709	61.7	45.4	4.2	12.1	38.3	30.8		31.1	32.6
06 00884	Alhambra city	33.2	52.0	29,065	68.9	47.6	6.5	14.9	31.1	25.4		29.9	37.5
06 00947	Aliso Viejo city	15.3	21.9	18,269	66.7	53.3	3.5	9.9	33.3	25.8		40.7	17.2
06 01290	Altadena CDP	31.1	22.0	15,025	70.2	52.1	5.4	12.7	29.8	22.4		31.3	41.8
06 02000	Anaheim city	53.5	38.0	98,137	75.8	52.9	7.2	15.7	24.2	18.0		44.1	32.0
06 02210	Antelope CDP	13.8	25.1	14,369	78.8	56.8	5.3	16.7	21.2	17.3		47.2	24.9
06 02252	Antioch city	34.5	20.9	32,064	76.8	53.4	6.7	16.7	23.2	18.0		41.9	32.6
06 02364	Apple Valley town	28.6	7.4	23,656	78.9	54.1	7.6	17.2	21.1	18.6		37.9	42.1
06 02462	Arcadia city	13.1	48.1	19,036	77.5	61.4	5.3	10.9	22.5	18.7		39.5	39.4
06 02553	Arden-Arcade CDP	19.7	14.7	40,088	50.6	33.3	5.4	11.9	49.4	42.0		24.1	33.4
06 02924	Arvin city	91.9	48.2	4,555	85.8	60.5	6.3	18.9	14.2	11.3		67.7	23.1
06 02980	Ashland CDP	44.9	33.7	7,606	64.9	37.7	3.7	23.5	35.1	29.6		44.2	25.5
06 03064	Atascadero city	14.9	6.8	11,077	70.9	55.2	4.4	11.2	29.1	21.2		33.7	34.8
06 03162	Atwater city	48.2	20.1	8,643	75.5	50.9	5.6	19.0	24.5	19.6		46.2	33.6
06 03386	Azusa city	66.6	32.9	11,286	77.7	50.2	8.1	19.4	22.3	16.7		47.5	30.6
06 03526	Bakersfield city	46.0	18.8	110,198	74.7	50.4	7.0	17.2	25.3	19.7		46.3	27.8
06 03666	Baldwin Park city	78.9	45.9	16,846	89.2	54.7	8.9	25.5	10.8	8.5		55.8	38.0
06 03820	Banning city	37.9	18.4	12,272	58.9	43.8	4.0	11.1	41.1	35.7		21.1	57.9
06 04030	Barstow city	42.5	11.9	8,094	67.8	41.8	7.1	18.9	32.2	25.2		38.3	29.8
06 04415	Bay Point CDP	58.7	34.1	6,695	73.7	43.3	6.6	23.8	26.3	21.9		53.2	26.5
06 04758	Beaumont city	34.3	18.1	12,821	74.8	59.4	5.0	10.4	25.2	21.2		44.0	31.2
06 04870	Bell city	92.2	41.7	8,844	85.3	52.7	10.8	21.7	14.7	12.3		59.3	26.5
06 04982	Bellflower city	52.4	28.8	23,088	74.7	44.7	7.6	22.3	25.3	21.0		46.9	29.6
06 04996	Bell Gardens city	97.4	45.4	9,868	85.4	52.3	8.7	24.3	14.6	12.0		62.0	25.0
06 05108	Belmont city	12.5	28.9	10,349	64.1	55.3	2.3	6.5	35.9	30.0		33.4	36.2
06 05290	Benicia city	13.6	11.7	10,412	67.3	50.3	5.0	11.9	32.7	25.5		33.5	39.5
06 06000	Berkeley city	11.5	21.1	44,826	42.7	32.5	2.3	7.9	57.3	35.9		18.6	33.3
06 06308	Beverly Hills city	5.0	36.5	14,252	58.4	45.7	3.8	8.9	41.6	35.0		25.4	42.1
06 07064	Bloomington CDP	87.4	35.7	5,007	89.1	61.4	8.7	18.9	10.9	9.7		58.9	29.5
06 07218	Blythe city	55.2	17.0	5,316	73.1	45.0	12.1	16.0	26.9	20.6		35.5	30.2
06 08058	Brawley city	83.1	22.3	7,307	78.4	46.7	9.1	22.7	21.6	17.8		48.5	29.7
06 08100	Brea city	26.9	22.4	13,856	71.8	57.3	1.9	12.5	28.2	22.0		36.9	39.3
06 08142	Brentwood city	26.1	14.7	16,342	82.9	65.8	6.5	10.6	17.1	13.7		48.4	34.0
06 08786	Buena Park city	38.8	38.5	22,947	81.3	55.8	9.5	16.0	13.7	14.0		44.1	35.0
06 08954	Burbank city	25.8	34.6	40,962	62.0	44.8	4.9	12.3	33.0	30.7		29.6	34.4
06 09066	Burlingame city	14.7	24.9	12,677	53.7	40.6	4.9	8.2	45.3	38.9		27.9	30.6
06 09598	Calabasas city	7.2	25.2	8,751	77.9	59.6	4.0	14.2	22.1	16.3		41.5	34.5
06 09710	Calexico city	97.6	46.8	9,139	88.5	56.8	6.1	25.6	11.5	9.8		58.5	39.8
06 10046	Camarillo city	26.3	14.6	23,854	68.7	55.3	4.5	8.9	31.3	25.3		33.4	44.1
06 10345	Campbell city	18.7	24.3	16,017	60.7	43.7	4.4	12.6	33.3	29.7		30.6	27.2
06 11194	Carlsbad city	13.3	14.6	42,299	66.2	53.1	4.1	8.9	33.8	26.9		30.2	35.2
06 11390	Carmichael CDP	9.5	10.5	25,430	61.0	39.8	6.3	14.9	39.0	31.6		26.4	41.3
06 11530	Carson city	41.1	33.9	24,849	80.8	54.1	6.6	20.0	19.2	15.2		40.4	47.4
06 11964	Castro Valley CDP	15.4	24.2	22,055	74.0	55.5	5.2	13.3	25.0	20.9		35.4	37.5
06 12048	Cathedral City city	63.5	35.1	16,141	65.8	46.1	4.0	15.6	34.2	25.0		42.2	40.0
06 12524	Ceres city	56.8	28.3	13,145	79.5	52.6	8.2	18.7	20.5	15.9		51.9	31.8
06 12552	Cerritos city	11.5	44.3	14,954	85.1	68.5	5.0	11.5	14.9	11.8		37.0	50.9
06 13014	Chico city	15.9	7.7	33,516	52.5	34.5	5.9	12.1	47.5	32.4		27.7	28.8
06 13210	Chino city	52.5	24.0	21,625	75.7	56.0	6.6	13.0	24.3	20.7		42.8	31.6
06 13214	Chino Hills city	31.3	28.7	22,897	81.9	64.5	6.3	11.1	18.1	15.1		44.6	29.0
06 13392	Chula Vista city	57.3	30.4	76,159	77.4	55.2	6.3	15.9	22.6	19.0		44.9	32.1

STATE and Place code	STATE or City	Total population	Percent change 2010–2012	Population by age (percent)						Median age	Race alone or in combination (percent)			
				Under 5 years	5 to 17 years	18 to 24 years	25 to 44 years	45 to 64 years	65 years and over		White	Black	Asian, Hawaiian, or Pacific Islander	American Indian, Alaska Native, or some other race
	ACS table number:	B01003	Population estimates	B01001	B01001	B01001	B01001	B01001	B01001	B01002	B02008	B02009	B02011 + B02012	B02010 + B02013
	Column number:	1	2	3	4	5	6	7	8	9	10	11	12	13
	California—Cont.													
06 13588	Citrus Heights city	84,192	1.7	6.2	15.8	10.0	27.4	26.7	13.9	37.5	85.2	3.8	5.4	11.3
06 13756	Claremont city	35,227	1.4	3.0	16.2	17.7	19.2	27.1	16.7	40.4	75.9	6.0	16.3	5.2
06 14218	Clovis city	97,434	2.6	6.7	22.1	10.2	26.0	23.9	11.1	33.0	74.4	3.2	12.7	13.6
06 14260	Coachella city	41,891	4.2	9.8	28.9	10.0	30.2	16.2	4.8	25.6	39.8	2.4	...	58.6
06 14890	Colton city	52,735	1.6	9.6	22.6	14.5	27.0	20.2	6.1	27.2	56.8	9.2	4.4	31.8
06 15044	Compton city	97,054	1.1	9.7	23.0	12.9	27.3	19.6	7.6	27.7	36.9	32.9	1.3	32.0
06 16000	Concord city	123,571	1.8	7.4	15.5	8.4	29.6	27.0	12.1	37.2	74.3	5.6	16.2	9.9
06 16224	Corcoran city	23,952	-3.3	5.6	11.9	9.6	39.5	27.3	6.1	36.5	70.1	15.4	2.3	16.9
06 16350	Corona city	155,603	3.4	7.1	22.0	10.4	28.5	24.3	7.6	32.9	74.2	6.6	14.0	9.6
06 16378	Coronado city	23,660	-2.7	4.5	15.5	13.5	22.8	27.0	16.7	40.7	93.5	1.9	5.5	2.4
06 16532	Costa Mesa city	111,034	1.7	6.8	15.1	10.2	34.8	24.2	8.9	33.8	68.8	1.8	11.2	22.0
06 16742	Covina city	48,077	1.1	7.9	19.1	9.8	27.1	25.8	10.4	33.6	59.4	5.2	12.4	27.8
06 17498	Cudahy city	23,919	0.9	8.9	26.6	12.8	28.7	18.3	4.6	25.7	63.2	1.6	1.8	36.3
06 17568	Culver City city	39,105	1.1	4.6	14.2	7.0	32.2	26.9	15.0	40.5	71.2	10.3	17.2	7.1
06 17610	Cupertino city	59,341	2.2	5.7	21.9	4.3	26.7	28.6	12.7	40.4	35.1	0.2	65.8	1.1
06 17750	Cypress city	48,380	1.8	5.1	17.5	10.4	23.9	29.9	13.3	40.4	61.6	3.5	36.0	3.8
06 17918	Daly City city	102,417	2.5	5.8	13.7	9.4	30.2	27.2	13.6	38.7	27.3	3.4	61.8	11.8
06 17946	Dana Point city	33,745	1.9	5.7	12.2	6.2	27.9	30.9	17.1	43.6	87.7	1.0	4.9	9.1
06 17988	Danville town	42,616	2.3	5.9	20.8	4.6	17.0	35.3	16.4	45.9	86.3	1.1	15.3	1.3
06 18100	Davis city	65,800	0.6	4.4	12.9	31.9	21.9	20.6	8.2	25.4	69.0	4.1	28.4	7.3
06 18394	Delano city	53,023	-1.3	9.4	21.1	12.8	31.6	18.7	6.4	28.6	68.0	5.8	13.7	15.7
06 18996	Desert Hot Springs city	27,474	2.1	8.5	22.2	10.6	27.6	20.1	10.8	31.2	54.3	8.4	5.7	35.1
06 19192	Diamond Bar city	55,972	1.4	4.3	16.8	9.5	25.5	31.5	12.4	41.3	34.4	4.1	55.5	9.0
06 19318	Dinuba city	22,401	6.4	13.9	19.6	11.5	29.0	17.9	8.0	27.5	75.8	...	2.5	27.7
06 19766	Downey city	112,341	0.9	6.6	19.8	10.0	30.4	22.8	10.4	34.1	60.0	4.4	7.7	30.8
06 19990	Duarte city	21,493	1.4	5.4	15.8	9.1	25.2	28.7	15.8	40.6	53.1	7.7	15.5	26.5
06 20018	Dublin city	47,156	6.3	7.2	15.8	7.1	36.9	25.2	7.8	36.1	56.9	7.7	34.0	6.6
06 20802	East Los Angeles CDP	127,448	...	7.5	22.3	12.9	30.1	18.5	8.6	29.4	56.8	1.2	1.0	42.7
06 20956	East Palo Alto city	28,542	2.3	9.4	22.6	13.1	32.1	17.3	5.5	28.1	53.7	16.4	14.6	18.1
06 21230	Eastvale CDP	54,261	1.4	10.7	22.5	9.1	32.9	18.8	6.1	30.9	55.6	8.6	25.3	13.4
06 21712	El Cajon city	100,631	1.7	7.7	18.0	12.6	27.2	23.7	10.8	32.3	82.0	7.7	3.9	8.5
06 21782	El Centro city	42,933	1.0	7.6	21.8	11.1	26.7	22.8	10.0	30.9	67.6	3.0	3.7	30.4
06 21796	El Cerrito city	23,830	1.7	4.5	10.3	6.6	27.2	31.7	19.7	46.0	64.0	9.3	29.9	4.1
06 21880	El Dorado Hills CDP	43,807	...	5.6	22.3	7.7	20.4	31.2	12.7	41.1	88.9	3.4	12.4	1.3
06 22020	Elk Grove city	156,190	3.6	6.4	23.2	8.7	26.9	25.5	9.3	34.3	51.5	13.1	35.2	10.2
06 22230	El Monte city	114,338	1.3	7.6	18.5	10.6	29.7	23.3	10.3	33.4	47.6	0.8	28.0	25.2
06 22300	El Paso de Robles (Paso Robles)	30,203	2.4	7.5	17.6	6.8	28.6	25.9	13.5	35.6	77.2	3.9	2.9	17.9
06 22678	Encinitas city	60,321	2.2	6.4	14.6	6.0	29.1	30.7	13.3	41.2	90.5	0.6	7.6	4.1
06 22804	Escondido city	145,990	2.2	8.1	18.9	10.8	29.4	22.6	10.2	32.7	85.1	2.4	5.6	8.4
06 23042	Eureka city	27,117	-0.9	5.4	12.3	13.0	26.2	29.4	13.7	37.6	86.9	3.0	7.5	8.8
06 23182	Fairfield city	106,469	2.1	7.2	18.6	11.9	27.7	24.1	10.6	33.2	53.1	17.0	21.7	15.3
06 23294	Fair Oaks CDP	32,110	...	5.0	15.6	7.9	20.5	31.9	19.1	45.6	89.4	3.2	6.3	5.4
06 23462	Fallbrook CDP	32,910	...	7.3	17.3	11.9	24.5	22.7	16.2	32.6	81.4	2.1	2.7	16.7
06 24477	Florence-Graham CDP	64,867	...	10.7	24.0	13.5	30.1	16.3	5.3	25.8	70.5	8.1	0.1	22.6
06 24498	Florin CDP	50,237	...	8.8	20.3	10.8	25.6	23.7	10.8	32.3	44.5	16.8	36.7	9.0
06 24638	Folsom city	72,779	1.6	6.3	18.1	8.4	31.2	26.6	9.4	37.1	75.9	6.3	15.7	6.1
06 24680	Fontana city	199,630	2.4	8.1	23.1	11.5	30.4	20.9	6.1	29.5	63.3	10.9	8.8	21.9
06 24722	Foothill Farms CDP	34,467	...	9.8	18.4	9.5	31.5	22.3	8.5	31.3	69.9	15.6	7.8	14.3
06 25338	Foster City city	31,247	4.9	6.5	15.2	5.0	31.4	26.4	15.6	40.2	51.1	3.7	49.8	2.4
06 25380	Fountain Valley city	55,970	1.8	4.3	15.0	8.7	24.7	28.4	19.0	43.1	55.8	2.8	38.4	6.7
06 26000	Fremont city	218,160	3.4	7.0	17.4	7.1	31.3	26.2	11.0	37.2	35.5	5.0	55.2	10.9
06 26067	French Valley CDP	25,861	...	10.1	23.0	8.3	33.0	20.1	5.6	32.1	78.8	3.1	13.7	7.2
06 27000	Fresno city	501,350	1.8	8.8	21.1	12.4	27.6	20.9	9.3	29.5	54.7	9.0	15.2	26.5
06 28000	Fullerton city	136,886	2.4	6.4	16.4	12.4	28.6	24.1	12.1	34.8	58.0	3.0	27.0	16.3
06 28112	Galt city	24,059	2.7	7.9	21.5	9.4	29.4	21.0	10.9	32.1	72.0	4.4	3.4	24.8
06 28168	Gardena city	59,179	1.1	6.1	15.6	8.1	28.3	26.9	14.9	38.8	26.0	25.9	30.6	22.0
06 29000	Garden Grove city	172,868	1.9	5.9	18.8	10.9	28.0	25.2	11.2	35.8	48.8	1.7	40.9	11.7
06 29504	Gilroy city	49,735	3.5	7.9	22.2	9.0	27.6	23.6	9.7	33.0	73.9	2.5	8.4	18.9
06 30000	Glendale city	193,099	1.4	5.0	14.4	8.5	28.0	28.4	15.8	41.1	78.3	1.5	18.6	4.7
06 30014	Glendora city	50,486	1.0	4.7	19.1	11.2	22.0	29.8	13.3	39.4	82.8	3.2	8.4	8.9
06 30378	Goleta city	30,101	1.1	4.5	14.9	14.5	22.9	27.4	15.7	39.0	79.1	1.1	10.8	14.0
06 30693	Granite Bay CDP	22,636	...	5.2	22.1	7.1	18.7	32.5	14.4	43.2	91.3	1.8	8.4	4.9
06 31596	Hacienda Heights CDP	57,294	...	5.2	17.0	8.3	26.4	27.4	15.7	40.0	50.9	1.6	38.6	10.8
06 31960	Hanford city	54,205	0.6	7.7	21.8	11.2	27.8	21.4	10.2	31.1	82.4	5.1	5.1	10.6
06 32548	Hawthorne city	85,016	1.6	7.6	20.7	11.0	32.1	21.2	7.5	30.6	53.5	29.0	8.3	13.2
06 33000	Hayward city	147,038	3.2	7.1	16.9	11.0	29.8	24.8	10.4	33.7	44.3	13.3	28.8	20.9
06 33182	Hemet city	80,140	2.4	7.0	19.1	8.1	21.0	22.2	22.7	40.0	75.2	10.1	3.8	16.3
06 33308	Hercules city	24,402	2.1	4.8	20.3	8.1	26.7	29.3	10.8	37.1	33.2	24.4	46.2	5.2
06 33434	Hesperia city	91,307	1.8	7.9	21.9	11.2	25.0	23.9	9.9	31.9	73.7	8.2	2.9	18.4
06 33588	Highland city	53,725	1.7	7.8	24.7	10.7	26.1	23.0	7.7	30.2	62.3	13.7	8.3	22.0
06 34120	Hollister city	35,625	2.7	8.0	22.6	9.7	28.6	23.3	7.9	31.4	85.6	1.5	4.9	11.6
06 36000	Huntington Beach city	193,074	1.8	5.2	14.6	9.1	27.5	29.1	14.5	40.5	80.5	1.5	12.9	9.0
06 36056	Huntington Park city	58,414	0.9	9.4	21.3	12.3	30.7	19.7	6.6	29.6	82.2	0.5	0.7	17.7
06 36294	Imperial Beach city	26,611	1.7	7.9	19.8	12.8	27.8	23.4	8.2	29.9	73.2	6.2	15.2	12.1
06 36448	Indio city	77,953	3.6	7.8	23.0	8.8	26.2	20.6	13.6	33.1	59.6	3.5	3.2	36.4
06 36546	Inglewood city	110,528	1.3	7.9	18.7	10.1	29.5	24.4	9.4	33.4	29.6	45.8	2.9	25.1

Table A-4. Cities — Who: Age, Race/Ethnicity, and Household Structure, 2010–2012—Continued

STATE and Place code	STATE or City	Percent Hispanic or Latino	Percent foreign born	Total households	Total family households	Married-couple families	Male household families	Female household families	Total nonfamily households	One-person households	Percent of households with people under 18 years	Percent of households with people 60 years and over
ACS table number:		B03003	C05003	B11001	B11001	B11001	B11001	B11001	B11001	B11001	B11005	B11006
Column number:		14	15	16	17	18	19	20	21	22	23	24
	California—Cont.											
06 13588	Citrus Heights city	18.6	13.0	32,472	62.6	43.6	5.6	13.4	37.4	28.5	30.9	35.5
06 13756	Claremont city	21.4	17.7	11,865	66.9	57.8	1.2	7.9	33.1	28.3	30.1	47.7
06 14218	Clovis city	26.2	11.5	33,284	71.5	53.2	5.1	13.2	28.5	23.3	40.5	31.9
06 14260	Coachella city	97.0	43.2	9,000	93.8	60.8	8.8	24.2	6.2	4.4	72.8	21.9
06 14890	Colton city	72.9	26.1	14,485	78.3	44.4	12.1	21.8	21.7	17.0	52.1	24.1
06 15044	Compton city	66.0	29.9	23,387	81.8	45.2	10.1	26.6	18.2	15.3	56.1	32.1
06 16000	Concord city	29.2	25.5	44,492	68.8	51.0	6.5	11.3	31.2	24.3	34.7	32.1
06 16224	Corcoran city	62.5	22.2	3,610	77.3	54.1	6.5	16.7	22.7	18.1	53.6	27.8
06 16350	Corona city	42.4	25.4	44,071	80.0	60.2	6.7	13.1	20.0	14.7	50.2	27.0
06 16378	Coronado city	12.8	10.3	8,983	65.0	53.8	3.8	7.3	35.0	30.8	28.7	40.9
06 16532	Costa Mesa city	35.9	25.1	40,576	59.3	41.6	6.3	11.4	40.7	27.7	30.6	25.6
06 16742	Covina city	56.6	21.0	15,418	70.8	46.1	6.1	18.6	29.2	22.9	41.3	30.9
06 17498	Cudahy city	97.1	47.6	5,671	89.1	49.4	12.7	26.9	10.9	8.0	66.7	20.1
06 17568	Culver City city	23.9	22.2	16,613	55.9	40.2	4.5	11.1	44.1	35.3	25.5	34.9
06 17610	Cupertino city	4.3	50.1	20,868	76.3	65.9	2.6	7.7	23.7	20.3	46.7	33.0
06 17750	Cypress city	18.3	28.3	15,633	79.7	58.3	5.8	15.5	20.3	16.5	40.4	37.1
06 17918	Daly City city	21.7	52.4	30,731	72.7	52.8	5.7	14.2	27.3	20.4	36.6	41.6
06 17946	Dana Point city	18.8	14.1	14,521	60.1	47.2	4.8	8.1	39.9	29.9	24.4	38.0
06 17988	Danville town	4.8	12.5	15,796	76.9	68.2	3.0	5.7	23.1	20.2	37.4	43.4
06 18100	Davis city	13.0	19.0	23,693	50.4	39.9	2.6	7.9	49.6	24.7	26.9	23.9
06 18394	Delano city	73.8	38.2	10,335	89.0	55.9	10.7	22.4	11.0	9.3	60.5	29.2
06 18996	Desert Hot Springs city	54.9	24.2	8,799	66.2	43.1	7.8	15.2	33.8	24.7	42.2	31.7
06 19192	Diamond Bar city	20.0	44.0	17,275	83.0	63.5	6.0	13.5	17.0	13.1	39.3	39.3
06 19318	Dinuba city	85.9	34.9	5,864	82.1	50.8	10.5	20.9	17.9	13.5	58.1	28.9
06 19766	Downey city	71.2	34.9	33,044	80.0	52.1	8.9	19.0	20.0	16.1	46.2	33.3
06 19990	Duarte city	45.3	33.9	7,058	67.7	49.3	5.3	13.1	32.3	30.2	35.3	45.6
06 20018	Dublin city	14.8	27.3	15,349	72.4	59.9	4.1	8.4	27.6	21.4	39.5	24.2
06 20802	East Los Angeles CDP	97.4	42.3	30,816	80.6	45.0	12.1	23.6	19.4	15.4	52.8	34.5
06 20956	East Palo Alto city	63.7	39.0	6,808	74.5	51.2	8.7	14.7	25.5	18.9	54.3	23.2
06 21230	Eastvale CDP	40.1	29.1	12,454	91.9	75.7	4.6	11.5	8.1	5.0	65.6	24.1
06 21712	El Cajon city	28.9	29.9	31,995	70.0	45.7	6.9	17.4	30.0	24.0	39.6	30.4
06 21782	El Centro city	81.2	32.4	12,774	76.1	48.5	7.4	20.3	23.9	20.3	44.5	30.8
06 21796	El Cerrito city	11.0	30.0	10,210	60.4	47.8	4.7	8.0	39.6	29.3	21.8	43.8
06 21880	El Dorado Hills CDP	6.8	13.0	14,122	86.2	77.3	2.7	6.2	13.8	11.6	42.5	37.7
06 22020	Elk Grove city	19.1	23.0	47,132	79.5	59.1	7.7	12.7	20.5	15.1	47.4	29.2
06 22230	El Monte city	67.1	50.9	28,955	84.8	50.9	11.9	22.0	15.2	11.6	49.5	37.2
06 22300	El Paso de Robles (Paso Robles)	34.8	16.8	11,445	70.6	53.1	4.2	13.3	29.4	22.7	35.0	35.7
06 22678	Encinitas city	15.6	13.3	22,544	65.8	55.3	3.6	6.9	34.2	24.3	30.9	35.5
06 22804	Escondido city	47.9	27.8	44,581	73.0	53.1	6.9	13.0	27.0	20.6	41.9	30.9
06 23042	Eureka city	9.2	6.9	10,914	49.8	32.4	3.4	14.0	50.2	39.0	22.5	35.1
06 23182	Fairfield city	25.5	21.4	34,199	75.3	54.9	6.5	13.9	24.7	19.1	42.2	31.2
06 23294	Fair Oaks CDP	11.3	11.0	13,021	66.2	50.9	4.5	10.8	33.8	28.4	27.4	42.4
06 23462	Fallbrook CDP	43.0	24.4	10,885	76.0	56.9	6.6	12.5	24.0	18.2	34.0	41.3
06 24477	Florence-Graham CDP	91.5	43.0	14,181	89.0	45.6	15.3	28.1	11.0	8.3	65.0	26.0
06 24498	Florin CDP	29.1	31.2	14,986	72.4	41.9	8.8	21.7	27.6	23.5	44.6	37.9
06 24638	Folsom city	12.4	14.6	24,700	67.9	56.0	3.2	8.7	32.1	26.5	39.9	28.5
06 24680	Fontana city	66.7	30.0	48,176	86.3	61.2	7.5	17.6	13.7	9.7	57.0	25.4
06 24722	Foothill Farms CDP	22.9	19.2	12,189	70.1	37.9	6.5	25.7	29.9	20.8	39.7	25.6
06 25338	Foster City city	7.1	42.4	12,012	69.8	59.1	2.0	8.7	30.2	24.5	35.6	37.5
06 25380	Fountain Valley city	15.5	31.6	18,581	75.5	57.3	5.5	12.6	24.5	20.7	31.6	49.1
06 26000	Fremont city	14.7	42.8	70,645	78.4	63.7	4.3	10.5	21.6	17.2	44.2	30.5
06 26067	French Valley CDP	22.3	13.5	7,247	85.6	64.1	11.4	10.1	14.4	11.8	53.8	22.5
06 27000	Fresno city	47.8	21.8	157,154	70.1	42.0	8.4	19.6	29.9	22.7	42.8	30.0
06 28000	Fullerton city	33.6	31.5	43,938	72.1	54.0	4.6	13.5	27.9	19.6	35.6	32.9
06 28112	Galt city	41.4	18.7	7,447	76.5	54.3	5.3	16.9	23.5	19.9	46.6	34.2
06 28168	Gardena city	36.0	34.7	21,004	65.3	41.4	6.5	17.4	34.7	28.5	31.4	39.2
06 29000	Garden Grove city	36.5	43.6	46,227	80.2	55.9	7.5	16.8	19.8	14.4	44.6	37.3
06 29504	Gilroy city	57.3	24.2	14,694	80.3	60.2	6.3	13.8	19.7	16.1	47.4	33.5
06 30000	Glendale city	17.0	56.0	69,678	69.9	51.2	5.7	12.9	30.1	25.8	31.3	39.7
06 30014	Glendora city	29.9	15.1	16,358	76.6	55.5	6.2	14.9	23.4	18.9	38.3	39.7
06 30378	Goleta city	34.7	23.1	11,056	60.7	46.2	3.5	11.0	39.3	29.6	31.3	37.5
06 30693	Granite Bay CDP	5.6	5.9	7,529	85.3	72.1	4.0	9.2	14.7	12.0	42.8	40.3
06 31596	Hacienda Heights CDP	47.1	42.8	16,243	82.4	61.3	5.9	15.2	17.6	14.3	36.3	51.2
06 31960	Hanford city	48.3	18.0	16,812	77.0	53.5	10.2	13.2	23.0	19.3	46.6	32.3
06 32548	Hawthorne city	53.2	32.4	28,451	67.0	35.7	8.2	23.2	33.0	28.1	43.5	23.6
06 33000	Hayward city	41.5	37.9	44,815	73.0	48.7	7.6	16.7	27.0	20.9	39.3	32.0
06 33182	Hemet city	35.7	14.0	30,500	61.8	40.0	6.5	15.3	38.2	32.9	32.3	53.3
06 33308	Hercules city	14.9	30.1	8,013	76.1	55.0	4.5	16.6	23.9	18.2	42.3	37.2
06 33434	Hesperia city	46.3	14.4	26,419	78.0	52.7	9.2	16.0	22.0	18.2	44.8	34.0
06 33588	Highland city	50.9	20.8	14,716	79.6	53.3	7.4	18.9	20.4	16.4	51.7	28.8
06 34120	Hollister city	68.7	25.4	10,036	79.6	58.4	6.3	14.8	20.4	17.1	49.2	27.1
06 36000	Huntington Beach city	18.4	16.3	73,787	66.3	49.8	5.5	10.9	33.7	24.9	28.0	36.6
06 36056	Huntington Park city	98.4	51.7	14,668	84.4	45.0	13.7	25.7	15.6	11.3	56.6	27.0
06 36294	Imperial Beach city	47.5	21.9	8,571	67.4	40.0	8.0	19.4	32.6	25.9	41.7	27.5
06 36448	Indio city	67.7	26.8	23,282	76.6	52.3	9.3	14.9	23.4	18.8	43.3	41.7
06 36546	Inglewood city	49.2	27.8	36,350	67.5	36.2	7.1	24.2	32.5	27.5	42.2	30.7

Table A-4. Cities — Who: Age, Race/Ethnicity, and Household Structure, 2010–2012—*Continued*

STATE and Place code	STATE or City	Total population	Percent change 2010–2012	Population by age (percent)						Median age	Race alone or in combination (percent)			
				Under 5 years	5 to 17 years	18 to 24 years	25 to 44 years	45 to 64 years	65 years and over		White	Black	Asian, Hawaiian, or Pacific Islander	American Indian, Alaska Native, or some other race
	ACS table number:	B01003	Population estimates	B01001	B01001	B01001	B01001	B01001	B01001	B01002	B02008	B02009	B02011 + B02012	B02010 + B02013
	Column number:	1	2	3	4	5	6	7	8	9	10	11	12	13
	California—Cont.													
06 36770	Irvine city	221,358	7.8	5.2	17.2	14.1	31.9	23.0	8.6	33.3	55.5	2.9	42.7	3.7
06 36868	Isla Vista CDP	24,379	…	0.8	2.7	84.1	8.2	2.1	2.1	20.7	72.0	3.0	17.7	12.7
06 37692	Jurupa Valley city	96,465	2.1	8.5	20.4	12.9	27.7	22.9	7.6	30.3	56.6	4.1	4.6	37.9
06 39003	La Cañada Flintridge city	20,381	1.2	2.7	23.1	9.2	12.4	36.3	16.3	46.5	70.1	0.7	30.7	0.6
06 39045	La Crescenta-Montrose CDP	19,995	…	5.8	15.6	8.8	23.6	33.4	12.9	41.9	66.5	1.2	31.0	5.5
06 39114	Ladera Ranch CDP	23,588	…	10.6	25.3	3.6	36.2	19.9	4.4	34.5	79.8	…	20.9	2.8
06 39122	Lafayette city	24,251	2.9	4.1	19.1	6.6	20.4	32.5	17.4	44.9	89.1	1.3	12.1	1.0
06 39178	Laguna Beach city	22,992	1.8	3.3	13.5	3.4	21.4	37.6	20.8	50.2	94.6	1.4	3.8	1.9
06 39220	Laguna Hills city	30,682	1.8	4.3	15.1	8.1	25.9	31.7	14.8	42.3	74.3	2.4	17.5	12.3
06 39248	Laguna Niguel city	63,834	2.1	5.3	17.4	7.6	23.0	33.6	13.1	43.0	82.1	2.7	11.8	7.9
06 39290	La Habra city	60,929	1.7	7.3	19.0	10.1	29.3	23.4	10.9	33.6	60.2	2.0	9.7	32.6
06 39486	Lake Elsinore city	54,015	5.2	8.8	24.2	11.7	30.1	19.8	5.5	28.3	63.7	7.1	9.7	23.7
06 39496	Lake Forest city	78,188	1.8	5.9	18.3	8.1	27.5	30.0	10.2	38.6	73.7	2.1	13.0	10.3
06 39766	Lakeside CDP	21,803	…	5.4	23.1	9.6	22.5	26.7	12.6	37.1	94.0	1.5	3.8	5.2
06 39892	Lakewood city	80,475	0.9	6.6	17.2	9.3	26.3	28.6	12.0	38.3	57.6	8.8	21.3	18.9
06 40004	La Mesa city	57,673	1.7	7.3	12.6	11.9	30.5	24.7	13.1	34.8	78.1	11.8	9.9	8.2
06 40032	La Mirada city	48,784	0.9	5.4	15.8	14.1	22.8	25.1	16.8	39.2	57.4	2.9	21.5	21.9
06 40130	Lancaster city	158,108	1.4	8.2	21.4	11.1	26.9	23.9	8.5	31.7	67.4	22.2	5.5	8.6
06 40326	La Presa CDP	34,522	…	5.9	21.4	13.0	27.5	22.3	9.8	30.5	68.5	15.6	11.7	8.6
06 40340	La Puente city	40,069	1.1	7.7	19.2	12.1	30.4	21.0	9.7	32.0	66.8	1.9	9.2	24.6
06 40354	La Quinta city	38,241	2.9	6.3	16.3	6.3	21.3	27.2	22.7	44.9	85.5	3.3	4.1	11.2
06 40830	La Verne city	31,214	0.9	4.2	16.3	10.9	21.4	29.7	17.5	43.0	80.7	4.4	11.4	8.2
06 40886	Lawndale city	32,958	1.0	9.0	20.2	12.0	30.8	20.9	7.0	31.7	58.1	10.5	14.5	24.1
06 41124	Lemon Grove city	25,672	2.3	6.8	20.1	11.5	24.3	25.7	11.6	34.1	56.2	11.9	10.2	26.2
06 41152	Lemoore city	24,592	0.8	11.0	19.0	11.5	31.4	19.9	7.1	29.1	70.2	10.1	12.9	11.4
06 41180	Lennox CDP	22,160	…	8.4	24.5	11.7	30.1	20.3	5.1	27.8	34.3	7.0	1.5	57.8
06 41474	Lincoln city	43,781	3.0	7.8	15.6	5.2	25.6	21.1	24.7	40.4	85.9	1.2	8.7	7.3
06 41992	Livermore city	82,326	2.9	6.5	17.7	8.5	27.1	29.7	10.5	38.4	84.5	3.3	12.6	4.1
06 42202	Lodi city	62,825	1.6	7.4	20.4	10.6	24.2	23.7	13.7	34.9	83.7	1.5	9.6	9.8
06 42370	Loma Linda city	23,434	1.3	5.9	14.1	9.4	31.8	25.1	13.7	34.9	46.6	12.9	33.5	10.9
06 42468	Lomita city	20,411	1.3	8.2	15.3	8.5	27.1	29.3	11.6	39.7	74.8	3.4	22.6	15.1
06 42524	Lompoc city	42,586	2.2	8.4	20.7	10.0	29.1	22.4	9.4	32.0	74.0	7.1	5.3	19.5
06 43000	Long Beach city	465,125	1.1	7.0	17.7	11.7	30.0	24.0	9.5	33.8	59.8	15.7	15.0	17.0
06 43280	Los Altos city	29,496	3.0	6.0	19.4	2.9	19.4	31.6	20.7	46.3	72.4	2.1	29.3	0.4
06 44000	Los Angeles city	3,825,653	1.6	6.6	16.0	11.4	31.8	23.5	10.7	34.3	55.4	10.3	13.2	24.9
06 44028	Los Banos city	36,453	1.8	8.0	25.5	11.7	25.4	20.3	9.1	29.6	80.6	5.9	3.5	14.8
06 44112	Los Gatos town	29,816	2.1	5.5	17.3	5.0	22.3	31.4	18.5	44.9	86.0	1.2	12.4	3.1
06 44574	Lynwood city	70,014	1.6	8.2	24.3	13.1	29.5	18.2	6.5	28.2	30.4	8.6	0.6	61.6
06 45022	Madera city	62,065	1.7	10.4	24.2	12.1	27.8	17.0	8.4	26.8	83.8	4.5	3.6	10.7
06 45400	Manhattan Beach city	35,439	1.6	4.6	19.7	3.5	27.8	29.1	15.1	41.2	88.7	1.9	11.3	4.0
06 45484	Manteca city	69,309	5.1	8.3	21.4	9.3	26.6	24.3	10.1	32.8	75.0	4.5	11.9	14.8
06 45778	Marina city	19,982	2.6	6.3	15.3	13.5	25.6	27.0	12.3	35.6	63.2	8.5	25.2	13.2
06 46114	Martinez city	36,316	1.9	3.7	15.3	8.8	25.5	34.0	12.8	42.7	82.6	4.4	12.8	6.0
06 46492	Maywood city	27,530	0.9	9.3	23.4	13.8	29.4	18.5	5.7	27.3	80.4	0.5	…	19.3
06 46646	Mead Valley CDP	20,118	…	8.8	22.2	14.0	23.4	24.5	7.1	27.5	55.3	5.9	2.1	39.6
06 46842	Menifee city	79,843	4.3	7.1	18.9	8.0	24.8	23.1	18.1	37.8	80.6	6.1	8.0	9.1
06 46870	Menlo Park city	32,493	2.4	6.4	16.3	5.9	31.0	26.8	13.6	39.1	77.0	6.3	15.4	4.9
06 46898	Merced city	79,987	2.0	9.4	21.6	12.8	27.6	19.4	9.1	28.7	64.0	6.4	14.4	18.5
06 47486	Millbrae city	21,847	2.4	5.1	15.0	7.3	23.8	30.9	18.0	43.8	55.4	0.7	42.8	4.7
06 47766	Milpitas city	67,530	3.2	6.4	15.6	7.4	32.7	27.9	10.0	37.1	23.0	3.8	67.0	11.6
06 48256	Mission Viejo city	94,434	1.9	5.5	16.0	8.7	23.4	31.3	15.0	42.8	85.2	2.4	11.5	5.0
06 48354	Modesto city	202,400	1.0	7.5	19.1	10.8	26.3	24.7	11.6	33.7	77.3	5.5	10.6	12.9
06 48648	Monrovia city	36,800	0.9	7.3	15.2	7.7	29.7	28.7	11.3	37.9	56.5	7.6	15.7	24.6
06 48788	Montclair city	37,208	2.1	7.8	19.6	11.6	28.4	23.1	9.6	33.2	45.3	6.5	10.2	41.0
06 48816	Montebello city	62,941	1.2	8.2	16.4	10.3	27.6	22.8	14.8	34.8	70.4	2.0	12.4	17.1
06 48872	Monterey city	28,492	3.5	5.4	11.3	14.5	29.7	22.9	16.3	35.7	82.2	4.5	11.7	6.7
06 48914	Monterey Park city	60,630	1.1	5.3	13.2	9.8	26.1	27.2	18.4	41.4	21.0	0.7	64.5	16.6
06 49138	Moorpark city	34,858	1.5	6.0	19.5	10.8	26.1	29.2	8.4	36.2	80.5	1.7	8.0	12.5
06 49270	Moreno Valley city	197,068	2.6	8.2	23.5	12.6	27.5	21.5	6.7	28.6	64.1	19.3	7.2	13.8
06 49278	Morgan Hill city	38,741	3.7	7.3	19.7	8.7	26.2	28.1	10.1	37.7	71.7	3.9	14.6	14.9
06 49670	Mountain View city	75,381	3.1	6.9	14.5	7.0	37.9	22.9	10.8	36.1	65.0	2.9	23.4	7.6
06 50076	Murrieta city	105,369	2.7	6.9	22.4	9.9	27.0	23.8	10.0	32.8	72.1	9.3	13.0	11.8
06 50258	Napa city	77,714	1.6	7.0	18.0	8.2	27.2	25.9	13.7	37.0	88.6	1.0	3.1	10.1
06 50398	National City city	59,021	1.3	6.1	18.2	14.0	28.1	22.3	11.4	33.4	58.4	5.9	19.3	19.5
06 50916	Newark city	43,111	2.3	5.7	16.2	8.7	30.5	27.4	11.3	37.6	42.6	4.6	32.7	27.2
06 51182	Newport Beach city	86,259	2.0	3.6	14.2	8.1	26.4	29.0	18.7	43.5	88.2	0.7	9.5	5.0
06 51560	Norco city	27,263	1.1	5.1	16.8	9.1	28.1	29.7	11.2	39.4	78.6	7.1	5.3	14.0
06 51924	North Highlands CDP	45,215	…	7.4	20.1	12.6	24.8	23.5	11.6	31.8	73.0	12.0	7.8	12.5
06 52379	North Tustin CDP	25,986	…	3.2	18.5	7.2	19.7	31.6	19.8	45.9	87.2	1.1	13.3	2.8
06 52526	Norwalk city	105,961	0.7	6.3	20.6	11.4	28.7	23.0	10.0	33.2	48.3	5.8	14.5	35.0
06 52582	Novato city	52,721	2.5	6.5	15.2	5.6	24.8	32.1	15.8	43.6	80.5	3.5	8.9	12.8
06 52694	Oakdale city	20,939	2.1	7.6	21.9	9.2	25.8	23.2	12.3	33.3	92.5	1.1	5.8	4.9
06 53000	Oakland city	396,030	2.4	6.7	14.7	9.1	32.9	25.0	11.6	36.3	45.0	29.2	19.7	12.2
06 53070	Oakley city	36,552	4.4	6.5	23.1	9.6	28.1	24.2	8.6	33.6	75.7	9.0	10.9	11.2
06 53322	Oceanside city	169,530	2.2	6.5	17.3	11.4	28.1	24.4	12.3	34.7	70.3	6.5	11.4	18.4
06 53448	Oildale CDP	31,400	…	8.9	20.0	9.1	28.9	23.3	9.9	32.7	91.6	3.0	…	9.1
06 53896	Ontario city	165,909	1.7	7.2	20.8	12.4	30.0	22.1	7.4	31.1	65.2	6.9	5.2	26.4
06 53980	Orange city	138,220	1.9	6.0	16.5	12.3	28.9	25.3	11.0	35.6	64.9	1.8	14.6	21.7
06 54094	Orangevale CDP	32,878	…	5.5	15.7	8.5	26.1	30.5	13.6	41.2	91.3	3.1	5.0	5.8
06 54120	Orcutt CDP	30,578	…	5.9	19.7	6.0	20.8	29.5	18.2	43.2	92.0	2.6	4.9	4.6
06 54652	Oxnard city	200,015	1.6	8.7	20.5	11.7	29.5	21.2	8.3	30.2	76.4	3.2	10.2	14.1
06 54806	Pacifica city	37,732	2.4	4.4	15.9	6.8	25.9	33.9	13.1	42.7	71.9	3.7	25.5	7.4

Table A-4. Cities — Who: Age, Race/Ethnicity, and Household Structure, 2010–2012—*Continued*

STATE and Place code	STATE or City	Percent Hispanic or Latino	Percent foreign born	Total households	Family households: Total family households	Married-couple families	Male household families	Female household families	Nonfamily households: Total nonfamily households	One-person households	Percent of households with people under 18 years	Percent of households with people 60 years and over
	ACS table number:	B03003	C05003	B11001	B11001	B11001	B11001	B11001	B11001	B11001	B11005	B11006
	Column number:	14	15	16	17	18	19	20	21	22	23	24
	California—Cont.											
06 36770	Irvine city	9.7	36.2	79,235	66.7	53.1	4.3	9.3	33.3	23.4	34.6	24.2
06 36868	Isla Vista CDP	23.7	14.7	5,186	15.6	10.8	0.8	4.0	84.4	24.2	8.2	9.1
06 37692	Jurupa Valley city	69.1	29.5	24,054	80.1	59.3	7.7	13.1	19.9	14.8	51.1	31.4
06 39003	La Cañada Flintridge city	6.8	26.1	6,746	85.7	75.9	2.7	7.1	14.3	13.7	43.0	40.9
06 39045	La Crescenta-Montrose CDP	9.0	36.6	7,071	72.7	60.8	2.1	9.7	27.3	22.7	35.9	31.8
06 39114	Ladera Ranch CDP	15.6	19.8	7,445	79.8	72.8	2.0	5.0	20.2	15.1	56.7	14.0
06 39122	Lafayette city	7.9	13.5	9,315	72.2	63.0	3.9	5.3	27.8	20.8	34.8	42.2
06 39178	Laguna Beach city	5.4	11.1	11,289	52.3	42.1	3.1	7.1	47.7	36.7	22.2	41.8
06 39220	Laguna Hills city	21.2	25.5	10,808	72.8	60.3	3.9	8.5	27.2	22.5	31.6	39.2
06 39248	Laguna Niguel city	15.0	20.9	23,951	68.8	57.8	2.8	8.2	31.2	24.8	32.5	37.3
06 39290	La Habra city	60.3	27.0	18,677	75.0	54.1	7.3	13.6	25.0	20.5	41.0	32.8
06 39486	Lake Elsinore city	51.2	21.6	13,959	80.3	60.1	6.5	13.7	19.7	13.6	55.5	22.2
06 39496	Lake Forest city	23.0	22.6	27,440	73.7	59.7	3.6	10.5	26.3	22.6	38.5	28.7
06 39766	Lakeside CDP	21.3	8.8	7,144	76.3	57.3	6.1	12.9	23.7	18.7	41.9	37.8
06 39892	Lakewood city	31.5	21.7	26,665	74.9	52.5	6.3	16.0	25.1	20.5	38.2	36.5
06 40004	La Mesa city	22.6	13.1	23,220	57.6	41.7	4.6	11.3	42.4	31.9	26.3	31.8
06 40032	La Mirada city	40.8	26.3	14,042	79.9	63.2	4.7	12.0	20.1	18.5	36.0	46.4
06 40130	Lancaster city	37.7	13.3	47,311	73.5	49.3	6.4	17.7	26.5	21.1	43.5	30.0
06 40326	La Presa CDP	46.1	25.2	10,118	75.1	49.4	7.3	18.5	24.9	17.8	43.9	33.2
06 40340	La Puente city	85.7	42.3	9,206	84.2	54.6	10.7	18.9	15.8	12.1	51.6	36.1
06 40354	La Quinta city	33.1	14.4	15,157	70.6	58.3	3.6	8.7	29.4	23.2	28.8	52.9
06 40830	La Verne city	31.5	15.1	10,876	70.6	53.2	5.2	12.2	29.4	22.8	30.2	51.1
06 40886	Lawndale city	65.0	41.0	9,496	76.2	42.7	12.0	21.5	23.8	17.7	49.9	27.6
06 41124	Lemon Grove city	44.7	18.5	7,959	66.5	42.8	6.6	17.0	33.5	26.2	37.4	35.9
06 41152	Lemoore city	39.1	15.2	8,020	74.8	44.6	8.4	21.9	25.2	19.4	45.7	23.5
06 41180	Lennox CDP	91.2	48.7	5,259	86.9	58.4	10.5	18.0	13.1	8.1	61.4	20.6
06 41474	Lincoln city	18.9	13.4	16,683	69.9	60.6	2.5	6.8	30.1	22.8	27.1	50.9
06 41992	Livermore city	18.8	16.8	28,999	74.0	58.0	5.7	10.2	26.0	20.0	36.9	30.8
06 42202	Lodi city	37.0	19.9	21,871	68.1	45.9	8.3	13.9	31.9	25.0	38.1	35.0
06 42370	Loma Linda city	23.1	33.6	8,657	62.5	43.9	6.3	12.3	37.5	30.6	26.6	36.9
06 42468	Lomita city	42.1	27.1	7,763	62.5	47.0	6.1	9.4	37.5	31.7	30.5	32.3
06 42524	Lompoc city	53.7	23.3	13,375	68.2	46.8	7.0	14.3	31.8	26.2	41.6	29.1
06 43000	Long Beach city	41.3	25.9	159,984	61.6	36.8	7.2	17.6	38.4	29.2	35.5	28.8
06 43280	Los Altos city	4.2	23.8	11,250	74.8	66.8	2.8	5.3	25.2	22.7	35.7	48.1
06 44000	Los Angeles city	48.5	38.9	1,317,210	60.0	37.7	6.8	15.5	40.0	30.4	32.6	30.5
06 44028	Los Banos city	67.8	26.0	10,098	83.8	57.8	7.3	18.7	16.2	13.0	55.2	29.4
06 44112	Los Gatos town	5.3	16.9	12,148	64.9	54.2	4.1	6.6	35.1	29.3	31.7	38.0
06 44574	Lynwood city	88.9	40.6	14,836	86.1	51.6	10.4	24.1	13.9	11.1	62.7	26.9
06 45022	Madera city	77.6	31.5	16,067	80.5	49.4	8.0	23.0	19.5	16.6	52.2	30.6
06 45400	Manhattan Beach city	7.6	10.7	14,463	62.3	53.4	2.9	6.0	37.7	30.1	30.1	35.3
06 45484	Manteca city	39.5	15.4	22,128	75.6	55.2	5.4	15.0	24.4	18.2	43.3	32.5
06 45778	Marina city	28.0	20.9	6,612	64.6	43.3	4.7	16.5	35.4	24.3	35.6	39.3
06 46114	Martinez city	14.5	12.0	13,791	64.1	47.7	3.2	13.2	35.9	27.0	29.0	37.2
06 46492	Maywood city	98.2	47.5	6,283	88.7	53.0	12.7	23.1	11.3	8.8	63.8	25.6
06 46646	Mead Valley CDP	72.1	29.3	4,433	83.8	61.4	10.7	11.7	16.2	12.3	57.6	36.7
06 46842	Menifee city	31.2	12.5	26,686	71.4	55.3	6.4	9.7	28.6	23.1	35.9	45.8
06 46870	Menlo Park city	16.4	24.0	12,483	57.1	46.6	2.8	7.7	42.9	31.8	30.3	31.8
06 46898	Merced city	48.7	21.1	24,542	71.0	44.3	7.8	18.9	29.0	22.6	43.5	30.1
06 47486	Millbrae city	16.7	37.3	7,863	72.9	57.9	3.6	11.4	27.1	23.5	31.7	46.7
06 47766	Milpitas city	16.7	51.1	19,280	79.9	63.6	6.2	10.1	20.1	15.6	41.9	33.8
06 48256	Mission Viejo city	14.8	19.4	33,255	75.3	63.1	5.0	7.2	24.7	19.7	33.1	42.0
06 48354	Modesto city	37.2	17.3	68,814	71.2	47.2	6.7	17.4	28.8	23.8	38.8	33.7
06 48648	Monrovia city	36.0	26.1	13,318	66.5	47.1	7.5	11.9	33.5	26.6	34.3	32.8
06 48788	Montclair city	68.9	35.9	9,980	80.3	49.5	11.4	19.4	19.7	15.6	51.2	31.2
06 48816	Montebello city	76.1	37.3	19,133	75.3	44.0	8.0	23.4	24.7	20.2	38.0	42.5
06 48872	Monterey city	17.6	19.8	11,812	54.6	42.0	6.5	6.1	45.4	37.8	22.6	36.8
06 48914	Monterey Park city	31.7	54.4	18,426	79.4	51.4	8.5	19.6	20.6	16.0	32.8	47.5
06 49138	Moorpark city	30.5	16.9	10,475	81.2	65.0	5.8	10.3	18.8	12.2	43.5	28.7
06 49270	Moreno Valley city	55.1	24.8	50,180	84.2	53.9	7.0	23.3	15.8	11.9	53.6	26.8
06 49278	Morgan Hill city	33.4	19.3	12,455	81.5	60.3	5.7	15.5	18.5	14.5	42.6	33.2
06 49670	Mountain View city	22.6	37.5	31,736	55.9	44.4	3.3	8.2	44.1	34.4	28.5	26.0
06 50076	Murrieta city	26.9	13.7	32,215	76.5	61.0	4.8	10.7	23.5	19.0	44.1	32.6
06 50258	Napa city	39.3	24.6	28,315	67.0	49.9	5.0	12.0	33.0	25.3	34.6	38.7
06 50398	National City city	65.8	41.4	16,004	75.5	46.2	7.2	22.1	24.5	20.1	42.4	37.4
06 50916	Newark city	36.0	35.6	13,086	77.8	58.7	5.6	13.4	22.2	16.2	37.2	34.1
06 51182	Newport Beach city	8.9	13.6	38,093	55.7	46.2	2.5	6.9	44.3	33.5	22.5	39.4
06 51560	Norco city	28.8	12.1	7,127	77.2	61.9	2.6	12.7	22.8	16.5	41.3	39.6
06 51924	North Highlands CDP	22.2	24.5	14,772	70.4	44.0	7.9	18.5	29.6	23.0	39.1	33.2
06 52379	North Tustin CDP	9.6	13.0	8,937	81.5	71.2	3.4	6.9	18.5	15.0	32.0	52.4
06 52526	Norwalk city	69.1	35.5	26,703	82.6	53.5	9.4	19.7	17.4	13.0	48.2	35.6
06 52582	Novato city	20.6	21.5	20,743	68.0	52.8	5.1	10.2	32.0	25.8	33.4	41.1
06 52694	Oakdale city	29.0	11.9	7,130	72.5	48.5	9.0	15.0	27.5	22.4	42.6	33.0
06 53000	Oakland city	25.2	26.8	154,737	53.9	32.6	5.8	15.5	46.1	35.9	29.0	31.9
06 53070	Oakley city	37.9	15.6	11,089	79.2	60.7	7.9	10.5	20.8	16.9	48.4	30.6
06 53322	Oceanside city	37.3	21.2	57,210	67.7	51.1	5.2	11.5	32.3	24.8	34.6	35.1
06 53448	Oildale CDP	19.9	4.9	11,507	71.0	38.0	10.0	23.0	29.0	22.9	43.2	28.9
06 53896	Ontario city	71.2	31.0	44,255	77.2	50.5	7.8	18.8	22.8	17.9	48.4	29.0
06 53980	Orange city	37.5	26.7	43,294	71.8	53.8	5.7	12.3	28.2	20.4	36.8	32.8
06 54092	Orangevale CDP	9.6	8.2	12,607	65.0	48.2	5.7	11.1	35.0	26.8	30.4	36.1
06 54120	Orcutt CDP	23.1	7.2	10,973	75.7	62.2	3.7	9.9	24.3	20.8	36.5	42.4
06 54652	Oxnard city	73.5	36.8	50,022	81.1	55.4	8.0	17.7	18.9	14.7	51.1	31.6
06 54806	Pacifica city	14.4	21.4	14,169	67.7	51.8	4.7	11.2	32.3	26.4	30.9	37.8

Table A-4. Cities — Who: Age, Race/Ethnicity, and Household Structure, 2010–2012—*Continued*

STATE and Place code	STATE or City	Total population	Percent change 2010–2012	Under 5 years	5 to 17 years	18 to 24 years	25 to 44 years	45 to 64 years	65 years and over	Median age	White	Black	Asian, Hawaiian, or Pacific Islander	American Indian, Alaska Native, or some other race
	ACS table number:	B01003	Population estimates	B01001	B01001	B01001	B01001	B01001	B01001	B01002	B02008	B02009	B02011 + B02012	B02010 + B02013
	Column number:	1	2	3	4	5	6	7	8	9	10	11	12	13
	California—Cont.													
06 55156	Palmdale city	154,383	1.7	9.0	24.0	12.5	25.4	22.1	7.0	28.3	44.9	16.2	6.0	38.0
06 55184	Palm Desert city	49,369	2.7	3.3	13.2	6.7	17.3	26.4	33.1	52.2	87.3	1.7	5.8	7.0
06 55254	Palm Springs city	45,306	2.5	3.7	8.7	6.2	19.5	35.8	26.1	52.1	80.2	5.6	7.5	10.1
06 55282	Palo Alto city	65,498	2.7	5.0	17.6	6.0	27.3	26.8	17.2	41.2	67.6	2.4	30.9	2.9
06 55520	Paradise town	26,176	0.1	4.1	11.3	8.3	18.5	33.0	24.8	50.4	95.4	1.6	3.7	3.5
06 55618	Paramount city	54,377	1.0	8.2	23.7	11.8	30.1	20.0	6.1	29.1	39.3	11.5	4.7	47.0
06 56000	Pasadena city	137,900	1.0	6.0	12.5	9.6	32.5	25.4	14.0	37.0	68.9	12.0	17.5	5.5
06 56112	Patterson city	20,541	1.1	9.7	24.6	8.2	26.6	22.6	8.3	31.3	73.1	10.7	10.4	12.5
06 56700	Perris city	70,174	3.6	9.5	28.4	11.0	29.6	17.1	4.5	26.0	48.1	11.9	3.6	38.9
06 56784	Petaluma city	58,420	1.5	6.6	17.3	6.9	25.1	30.6	13.5	41.0	84.9	1.9	7.1	9.8
06 56924	Pico Rivera city	63,238	0.9	6.8	19.6	11.5	26.6	22.4	13.1	34.7	49.1	1.0	3.7	48.6
06 57456	Pittsburg city	64,609	3.3	6.9	18.3	12.0	29.2	24.6	9.0	33.0	42.4	21.4	20.9	21.2
06 57526	Placentia city	51,210	1.9	6.5	18.6	10.5	26.6	25.0	12.7	36.2	79.0	2.5	16.5	5.9
06 57764	Pleasant Hill city	33,494	1.9	4.8	14.1	10.2	26.6	30.2	14.1	40.9	81.8	2.7	17.0	4.7
06 57792	Pleasanton city	71,366	2.7	5.6	20.1	7.7	24.3	31.1	11.3	40.2	71.7	2.6	26.6	2.8
06 58072	Pomona city	149,961	1.1	7.9	20.8	13.9	28.2	21.2	8.0	29.6	64.9	8.4	10.6	20.1
06 58240	Porterville city	54,691	1.3	9.8	24.0	10.6	25.9	19.3	10.4	28.7	81.2	1.8	8.8	14.3
06 58296	Port Hueneme city	21,772	0.7	9.4	17.0	13.6	27.3	21.8	10.9	30.6	76.3	6.7	9.3	13.8
06 58520	Poway city	48,575	2.3	5.8	18.0	8.6	24.5	30.1	13.1	40.1	83.4	2.5	14.9	5.8
06 59346	Ramona CDP	21,708	...	7.8	18.5	9.5	22.7	29.2	12.4	36.7	92.1	0.7	0.6	10.5
06 59444	Rancho Cordova city	66,066	2.9	8.2	17.6	8.9	31.1	23.5	10.8	34.3	67.4	13.1	16.5	11.5
06 59451	Rancho Cucamonga city	168,448	2.7	6.7	18.7	9.7	30.4	26.2	8.3	34.9	71.4	10.4	15.9	10.0
06 59514	Rancho Palos Verdes city	42,002	1.6	4.0	18.9	3.7	16.4	32.7	24.3	49.6	64.3	4.7	31.2	4.6
06 59550	Rancho San Diego CDP	22,531	...	4.6	16.4	8.8	25.5	29.3	15.4	41.0	84.0	8.7	8.1	9.2
06 59587	Rancho Santa Margarita city	48,430	1.9	5.9	22.7	8.4	27.9	28.5	6.6	35.9	81.8	1.7	13.8	6.2
06 59920	Redding city	90,351	0.9	6.2	16.5	10.5	25.2	24.9	16.6	37.0	90.6	2.3	4.9	7.1
06 59962	Redlands city	69,395	1.6	6.1	18.1	11.3	25.7	25.9	13.0	35.9	76.8	4.5	9.8	12.5
06 60018	Redondo Beach city	67,256	1.3	7.6	13.4	4.3	35.4	27.9	11.3	39.7	77.8	4.3	18.5	6.4
06 60102	Redwood City city	77,945	2.7	7.7	17.9	7.2	31.3	24.7	11.1	36.1	77.6	2.8	14.3	9.9
06 60242	Reedley city	24,629	2.1	9.9	23.4	11.2	26.5	19.0	10.0	28.4	51.7	1.2	3.3	48.1
06 60466	Rialto city	100,663	2.3	8.9	24.4	12.4	27.4	19.5	7.4	27.7	64.1	16.7	3.3	19.3
06 60620	Richmond city	105,304	2.3	8.1	17.2	9.8	30.4	24.8	9.7	34.3	51.0	26.7	17.5	11.1
06 60704	Ridgecrest city	28,002	2.3	6.9	19.1	10.1	26.4	24.9	12.5	35.1	82.7	7.1	7.0	8.9
06 61068	Riverbank city	23,076	2.3	9.5	22.9	10.7	28.9	20.0	8.1	30.2	82.9	3.6	5.2	13.9
06 62000	Riverside city	309,793	2.6	7.2	19.1	15.0	27.4	21.9	9.3	30.5	70.6	7.7	8.6	17.9
06 62364	Rocklin city	58,219	3.0	6.0	20.5	8.5	28.1	26.0	10.8	36.0	86.3	2.9	10.9	5.2
06 62546	Rohnert Park city	41,085	0.7	6.1	13.3	15.6	26.5	28.7	9.8	34.9	82.4	3.7	9.8	10.5
06 62896	Rosemead city	54,109	1.1	5.2	16.3	9.0	27.8	28.4	13.3	39.4	27.0	0.2	64.3	10.2
06 62910	Rosemont CDP	22,158	...	6.0	17.8	10.0	29.8	26.6	9.7	35.3	71.7	16.1	14.7	6.7
06 62938	Roseville city	122,221	4.2	5.9	20.1	8.3	27.1	25.3	13.4	36.9	83.8	2.2	12.0	7.0
06 63218	Rowland Heights CDP	52,087	...	6.2	14.6	10.3	27.8	27.2	14.0	38.4	24.1	1.2	57.4	20.1
06 64000	Sacramento city	471,552	1.7	7.2	17.1	11.2	29.5	23.7	11.2	33.6	55.3	16.8	23.8	12.0
06 64224	Salinas city	152,650	2.5	9.3	22.4	10.9	30.7	19.1	7.6	29.3	75.1	2.4	8.8	17.2
06 65000	San Bernardino city	211,847	1.4	8.6	23.4	12.2	26.5	21.2	8.1	28.8	55.1	16.0	6.2	29.3
06 65028	San Bruno city	41,666	2.4	5.8	13.8	7.8	31.0	28.2	13.4	38.7	57.0	4.2	34.0	14.5
06 65042	San Buenaventura (Ventura) city	106,994	1.3	6.2	15.3	9.2	27.1	27.9	14.4	39.6	82.4	2.6	5.5	13.9
06 65070	San Carlos city	28,769	2.3	6.0	17.8	4.5	26.5	31.5	13.7	42.6	85.7	2.4	13.9	3.5
06 65084	San Clemente city	64,336	1.9	6.2	19.0	7.9	25.1	27.6	14.2	40.0	88.8	1.0	4.7	9.8
06 66000	San Diego city	1,321,545	2.5	6.3	15.2	12.9	31.2	23.5	11.0	33.9	68.0	8.1	19.6	9.6
06 66070	San Dimas city	33,570	1.0	4.2	15.6	10.6	21.3	32.8	15.5	43.5	73.7	5.8	16.4	11.4
06 66140	San Fernando city	23,767	0.9	7.5	22.1	10.9	29.7	20.4	9.4	32.2	76.2	...	0.7	21.6
06 67000	San Francisco city	815,234	2.5	4.4	9.0	9.0	37.8	25.9	13.8	38.5	53.7	6.9	36.8	7.1
06 67042	San Gabriel city	39,958	1.0	4.0	14.6	8.5	28.2	30.6	14.1	41.9	24.1	1.3	62.0	15.2
06 67056	Sanger city	24,450	1.0	9.5	21.4	10.4	28.3	19.5	10.9	30.4	55.5	1.6	3.7	40.2
06 67112	San Jacinto city	44,910	2.2	9.5	22.2	10.9	26.2	20.4	10.7	30.3	66.8	8.2	6.3	24.7
06 68000	San Jose city	969,324	2.9	7.1	17.2	9.5	30.8	25.0	10.5	35.6	50.3	4.0	36.4	14.4
06 68028	San Juan Capistrano city	35,058	1.9	8.1	18.2	6.3	22.2	29.2	16.1	41.3	73.2	0.4	4.1	23.9
06 68084	San Leandro city	85,958	2.1	5.4	15.7	8.2	28.6	28.5	13.4	39.6	48.2	14.5	34.9	9.7
06 68112	San Lorenzo CDP	24,290	...	4.8	17.2	9.1	25.3	29.0	14.5	40.9	53.8	6.8	30.3	16.1
06 68154	San Luis Obispo city	45,527	1.4	3.2	8.7	37.0	22.9	17.7	10.5	25.5	85.8	3.0	9.2	5.5
06 68196	San Marcos city	85,213	3.3	7.4	18.9	9.9	30.8	21.9	11.2	35.1	83.7	2.5	10.8	7.1
06 68252	San Mateo city	98,499	2.3	6.7	13.5	8.2	31.2	25.8	14.6	39.3	69.2	3.2	24.4	9.2
06 68294	San Pablo city	29,466	1.7	7.4	18.7	12.0	29.8	21.7	10.3	32.0	55.7	19.5	16.6	12.3
06 68364	San Rafael city	58,206	1.1	6.3	13.6	8.0	27.5	28.0	16.4	41.4	73.4	3.2	7.6	18.3
06 68378	San Ramon city	73,160	2.1	6.7	24.0	5.1	30.6	26.3	7.4	37.0	55.6	3.6	42.6	3.6
06 69000	Santa Ana city	328,180	1.8	8.8	21.8	12.3	31.3	19.1	6.7	29.0	48.5	1.5	10.9	40.7
06 69070	Santa Barbara city	88,996	1.2	6.2	13.3	12.5	29.8	24.1	14.0	35.4	77.4	2.2	4.6	19.2
06 69084	Santa Clara city	118,010	2.1	8.3	15.1	10.1	35.9	21.2	9.2	34.1	50.2	4.4	41.0	8.8
06 69088	Santa Clarita city	177,748	1.4	6.1	19.9	9.8	26.5	27.7	10.0	36.9	79.2	3.8	11.8	11.6
06 69112	Santa Cruz city	61,372	2.3	3.9	10.8	29.9	24.1	22.6	8.7	28.8	83.3	3.3	10.7	7.2
06 69196	Santa Maria city	100,529	1.8	8.8	21.5	11.8	29.3	18.9	9.6	29.6	77.6	2.2	7.2	15.4
06 70000	Santa Monica city	90,780	2.2	3.9	10.4	9.0	34.0	27.7	14.9	40.3	82.8	5.8	12.3	4.2
06 70042	Santa Paula city	29,732	2.0	8.7	21.9	13.2	24.5	21.1	10.6	30.6	65.0	0.4	2.2	36.2

STATE and Place code	STATE or City	Percent Hispanic or Latino	Percent foreign born	Total households	Household type (percent)						Percent of households with people under 18 years	Percent of households with people 60 years and over
					Family households				Nonfamily households			
					Total family households	Married-couple families	Male household families	Female household families	Total nonfamily households	One-person households		
ACS table number:		B03003	C05003	B11001	B11001	B11001	B11001	B11001	B11001	B11001	B11005	B11006
Column number:		14	15	16	17	18	19	20	21	22	23	24
	California—Cont.											
06 55156	Palmdale city	56.0	25.7	40,762	82.0	53.6	9.0	19.3	18.0	13.4	55.2	26.5
06 55184	Palm Desert city	22.6	16.3	23,489	54.9	43.3	2.8	8.8	45.1	38.7	17.7	57.8
06 55254	Palm Springs city	24.7	20.8	22,648	36.6	25.1	3.9	7.6	63.4	44.3	13.1	53.1
06 55282	Palo Alto city	7.4	31.2	26,426	63.6	53.7	2.8	7.2	36.4	29.6	34.1	37.7
06 55520	Paradise town	8.5	5.3	11,657	55.6	42.6	3.9	9.1	44.4	36.8	19.7	52.0
06 55618	Paramount city	78.2	38.1	13,378	81.0	49.6	8.6	22.8	19.0	14.5	57.1	25.8
06 56000	Pasadena city	32.3	31.1	54,371	55.0	40.2	4.2	10.6	45.0	34.4	25.4	32.3
06 56112	Patterson city	55.4	24.3	5,624	82.7	64.1	7.2	11.3	17.3	15.2	55.6	26.3
06 56700	Perris city	73.5	25.4	15,842	88.2	54.0	8.1	26.1	11.8	7.9	65.1	18.9
06 56784	Petaluma city	21.9	17.7	21,318	66.7	53.5	4.0	9.1	33.3	26.3	34.7	37.7
06 56924	Pico Rivera city	91.8	34.4	16,262	80.8	52.9	9.3	18.6	19.2	15.2	47.3	42.4
06 57456	Pittsburg city	39.8	30.0	19,267	74.7	48.3	7.9	18.5	25.3	17.9	44.2	32.6
06 57526	Placentia city	38.8	27.4	15,579	76.9	57.5	4.9	14.4	23.1	15.7	38.7	37.9
06 57764	Pleasant Hill city	13.9	21.2	13,712	57.9	46.9	3.6	7.4	42.1	32.6	27.7	34.5
06 57792	Pleasanton city	13.0	24.9	24,715	79.5	66.3	4.2	8.9	20.5	16.8	44.1	32.3
06 58072	Pomona city	69.4	34.4	37,883	78.5	49.7	9.2	19.6	21.5	16.2	50.8	31.1
06 58240	Porterville city	63.7	19.3	15,749	78.6	50.7	8.9	18.9	21.4	16.6	53.6	31.5
06 58296	Port Hueneme city	55.1	22.9	7,032	67.1	38.4	6.9	21.8	32.9	27.3	39.7	37.4
06 58520	Poway city	16.0	17.2	15,675	80.7	66.7	2.7	11.3	19.3	14.4	42.4	34.9
06 59346	Ramona CDP	31.8	18.6	6,387	76.1	57.1	5.7	13.4	23.9	19.3	36.2	42.9
06 59444	Rancho Cordova city	19.7	24.3	23,679	65.8	43.2	6.1	16.5	34.2	25.8	35.5	31.2
06 59451	Rancho Cucamonga city	35.5	19.4	54,680	74.9	56.0	5.3	13.6	25.1	19.7	40.9	27.6
06 59514	Rancho Palos Verdes city	5.8	25.7	15,535	76.9	66.0	3.2	7.7	23.1	20.4	31.1	55.7
06 59550	Rancho San Diego CDP	18.7	15.6	8,358	75.9	59.0	4.6	12.3	24.1	20.9	31.5	39.5
06 59587	Rancho Santa Margarita city	18.6	17.9	16,759	77.3	62.0	4.0	11.3	22.7	19.9	46.0	20.0
06 59920	Redding city	8.8	4.8	34,623	63.3	45.1	4.8	13.4	36.7	28.3	30.1	40.1
06 59962	Redlands city	29.9	14.3	24,485	66.6	50.8	5.1	10.7	33.4	28.1	32.6	34.2
06 60018	Redondo Beach city	17.2	17.9	28,696	58.6	45.1	4.6	8.9	41.4	33.0	28.0	27.0
06 60102	Redwood City city	40.8	32.1	27,731	65.5	49.1	5.1	11.3	34.5	27.6	36.3	30.5
06 60242	Reedley city	79.6	30.5	6,291	85.6	66.1	6.6	12.9	14.4	13.6	55.0	34.6
06 60466	Rialto city	69.8	26.2	24,269	81.4	52.7	8.0	20.7	18.6	14.9	56.6	30.6
06 60620	Richmond city	39.8	31.5	36,317	66.4	39.8	5.8	20.8	33.6	28.7	37.5	32.6
06 60704	Ridgecrest city	15.0	8.9	10,856	59.9	42.4	8.0	9.4	40.1	33.0	28.3	35.9
06 61068	Riverbank city	54.3	21.5	6,526	82.2	59.4	8.9	13.9	17.8	12.8	57.7	25.8
06 62000	Riverside city	51.0	23.4	89,588	70.3	49.3	5.6	15.4	29.7	22.2	41.5	30.4
06 62364	Rocklin city	13.2	10.5	21,467	70.6	53.8	3.8	13.0	29.4	23.8	38.9	31.0
06 62546	Rohnert Park city	24.4	15.9	15,875	56.8	40.3	4.3	12.2	43.2	31.9	28.4	29.2
06 62896	Rosemead city	31.2	57.7	14,271	82.4	57.0	10.8	14.6	17.6	13.6	42.7	43.5
06 62910	Rosemont CDP	18.9	20.0	8,610	62.9	38.4	4.7	19.8	37.1	29.9	33.6	33.0
06 62938	Roseville city	14.2	12.6	45,049	67.4	52.4	3.8	11.3	32.6	25.5	35.8	33.9
06 63218	Rowland Heights CDP	33.3	56.0	14,408	84.8	60.1	10.2	14.5	15.2	11.9	39.7	45.4
06 64000	Sacramento city	27.3	22.0	175,723	57.9	36.4	5.9	15.7	42.1	33.0	31.9	30.9
06 64224	Salinas city	74.6	37.2	40,959	77.8	50.0	9.9	17.9	22.2	17.7	52.3	27.2
06 65000	San Bernardino city	60.5	22.3	57,865	74.6	41.5	9.0	24.1	25.4	20.3	49.1	29.7
06 65028	San Bruno city	27.0	35.5	14,672	66.2	49.1	5.3	11.9	33.8	26.3	30.2	36.5
06 65042	San Buenaventura (Ventura) city	32.2	14.7	41,174	61.8	44.4	4.1	13.3	38.2	29.6	30.0	37.1
06 65070	San Carlos city	11.3	18.0	11,413	65.9	55.0	2.1	8.8	34.1	27.7	31.9	34.4
06 65084	San Clemente city	18.0	10.2	24,286	69.3	56.8	3.1	9.4	30.7	24.3	34.3	35.5
06 66000	San Diego city	29.5	26.3	469,700	59.1	42.9	4.5	11.8	40.9	29.2	30.8	30.0
06 66070	San Dimas city	29.1	21.9	11,698	69.0	52.4	5.1	11.5	31.0	25.7	32.6	46.0
06 66140	San Fernando city	88.0	36.1	6,187	81.0	55.3	9.1	16.5	19.0	12.1	56.3	35.1
06 67000	San Francisco city	15.3	36.1	341,721	45.2	32.8	3.6	8.7	54.8	39.0	18.9	33.0
06 67042	San Gabriel city	27.0	56.2	12,174	74.1	49.1	11.4	13.6	25.9	20.8	33.6	38.5
06 67056	Sanger city	78.1	25.2	6,998	76.9	51.5	9.7	15.7	23.1	18.9	49.4	36.3
06 67112	San Jacinto city	53.8	22.0	13,113	76.0	52.4	9.5	14.1	24.0	19.2	48.0	34.6
06 68000	San Jose city	33.3	38.5	305,787	73.4	54.7	6.0	12.6	26.6	19.6	40.6	32.0
06 68028	San Juan Capistrano city	36.4	25.0	11,538	76.3	60.3	8.4	7.5	23.7	20.2	36.6	47.7
06 68084	San Leandro city	27.4	33.8	30,496	67.8	48.7	6.4	12.6	32.2	26.8	32.3	38.1
06 68112	San Lorenzo CDP	35.7	33.1	7,362	76.7	50.9	7.1	18.7	23.3	19.3	39.2	46.0
06 68154	San Luis Obispo city	16.8	10.6	17,774	41.2	31.4	3.6	6.3	58.8	32.0	18.7	25.7
06 68196	San Marcos city	33.9	22.5	27,752	70.7	52.9	4.4	13.4	29.3	20.5	39.0	30.6
06 68252	San Mateo city	27.2	33.4	37,364	62.1	47.1	5.0	10.1	37.9	30.3	29.3	36.0
06 68294	San Pablo city	52.4	40.7	8,875	74.8	45.1	7.8	21.9	25.2	19.4	46.9	33.2
06 68364	San Rafael city	29.6	29.3	22,782	61.0	45.5	4.1	11.4	39.0	30.0	29.6	38.8
06 68378	San Ramon city	9.5	29.7	25,013	75.4	66.2	2.9	6.3	24.6	19.3	49.6	22.3
06 69000	Santa Ana city	79.1	48.3	71,546	81.6	54.4	8.8	18.4	18.4	13.5	56.2	28.3
06 69070	Santa Barbara city	40.7	25.5	33,667	55.2	39.9	4.1	11.1	44.8	32.2	26.8	34.8
06 69084	Santa Clara city	19.9	39.5	41,942	67.0	52.5	4.8	9.8	33.0	25.3	36.9	25.1
06 69088	Santa Clarita city	31.5	19.9	58,865	74.9	56.7	5.8	12.5	25.1	20.0	40.1	31.1
06 69112	Santa Cruz city	20.0	12.9	20,865	48.8	35.3	5.5	8.0	51.2	32.0	25.8	27.9
06 69196	Santa Maria city	69.7	35.0	27,417	75.7	51.4	8.2	16.1	24.3	19.7	46.3	31.2
06 70000	Santa Monica city	14.2	23.4	45,805	38.9	27.6	3.3	8.0	61.1	48.4	17.6	30.6
06 70042	Santa Paula city	77.6	30.5	8,411	77.4	53.6	8.8	15.0	22.6	19.0	49.6	33.0

Table A-4. Cities — Who: Age, Race/Ethnicity, and Household Structure, 2010–2012—Continued

STATE and Place code	STATE or City	Total population	Percent change 2010–2012 (Population estimates)	Population by age (percent) Under 5 years	5 to 17 years	18 to 24 years	25 to 44 years	45 to 64 years	65 years and over	Median age	Race alone or in combination (percent) White	Black	Asian Hawaiian, or Pacific Islander	American Indian, Alaska Native, or some other race
ACS table number:		B01003	Population estimates	B01001	B01001	B01001	B01001	B01001	B01001	B01002	B02008	B02009	B02011 + B02012	B02010 + B02013
Column number:		1	2	3	4	5	6	7	8	9	10	11	12	13
	California—Cont.													
06 70098	Santa Rosa city	169,376	1.6	6.6	17.3	9.4	26.8	26.7	13.2	36.9	81.9	3.3	7.3	11.4
06 70224	Santee city	54,492	3.2	6.8	18.3	9.8	26.6	27.8	10.7	37.1	91.6	4.1	7.7	5.1
06 70280	Saratoga city	30,347	2.2	3.1	20.4	3.8	17.6	35.1	20.1	47.8	54.7	...	48.1	0.6
06 70686	Seal Beach city	24,476	1.6	2.9	10.6	3.6	15.7	27.5	39.7	58.6	85.6	1.3	10.7	6.5
06 70742	Seaside city	33,454	2.4	8.8	18.1	11.7	33.0	20.6	7.9	31.8	63.1	10.4	13.1	18.8
06 70882	Selma city	23,507	2.0	7.5	23.4	10.4	28.0	20.1	10.6	31.2	49.4	3.1	7.4	46.6
06 72016	Simi Valley city	125,188	1.0	6.0	18.4	8.8	27.4	28.5	10.9	37.5	80.1	1.9	12.0	11.1
06 72520	Soledad city	26,296	1.8	6.3	13.9	10.0	38.5	26.7	4.7	35.4	72.9	12.5	3.4	14.7
06 72996	South El Monte city	20,219	0.9	7.7	20.6	9.3	30.5	22.5	9.4	32.8	72.2	0.3	9.9	18.4
06 73080	South Gate city	94,875	0.9	7.9	21.4	12.1	29.6	21.3	7.8	30.2	41.4	1.1	1.2	57.6
06 73108	South Lake Tahoe city	21,359	-0.6	6.4	14.9	11.8	26.4	29.9	10.6	38.4	72.0	1.2	9.5	21.6
06 73220	South Pasadena city	25,742	0.9	5.6	19.6	4.7	32.1	27.4	10.6	38.7	60.3	3.4	34.6	6.8
06 73262	South San Francisco city	64,602	2.8	5.7	15.7	8.4	29.7	26.6	13.9	38.4	44.2	3.4	42.3	15.3
06 73290	South San Jose Hills CDP	21,531	...	8.2	20.3	14.3	27.0	19.6	10.6	29.5	75.8	1.7	9.2	15.5
06 73430	South Whittier CDP	57,412	...	7.0	20.7	10.0	29.4	23.0	9.9	32.8	58.7	1.8	4.9	38.7
06 73696	Spring Valley CDP (San Diego County)	30,103	...	6.8	18.8	10.0	27.0	26.0	11.4	35.3	79.4	11.2	9.4	5.8
06 73962	Stanton city	38,633	1.6	7.1	19.5	10.7	28.1	24.9	9.7	34.2	48.0	3.8	26.3	27.1
06 75000	Stockton city	295,354	1.8	8.2	21.9	11.6	26.6	21.8	10.0	30.6	50.6	14.2	26.1	17.0
06 75630	Suisun City city	28,398	1.7	5.9	22.2	9.6	27.4	26.3	8.6	34.3	43.4	23.5	25.5	17.8
06 77000	Sunnyvale city	143,443	4.1	8.0	14.5	7.0	35.8	23.7	11.0	35.0	51.8	2.4	43.8	6.2
06 78120	Temecula city	103,101	4.2	6.7	24.2	9.9	26.3	25.5	7.5	33.0	77.2	4.3	13.1	11.8
06 78138	Temescal Valley CDP	23,721	...	7.3	18.6	7.9	27.3	26.8	12.0	38.9	78.9	6.6	10.2	8.7
06 78148	Temple City city	35,856	1.4	4.8	16.4	7.8	24.0	31.7	15.4	42.9	28.7	0.7	58.6	14.7
06 78582	Thousand Oaks city	127,762	1.1	4.7	19.8	8.3	22.6	29.7	14.9	41.5	82.7	1.9	11.9	7.2
06 80000	Torrance city	146,284	1.0	5.4	16.1	8.0	26.5	28.2	15.8	41.4	56.0	3.8	38.2	8.0
06 80238	Tracy city	83,957	1.8	8.2	23.1	8.4	28.5	24.1	7.7	33.4	67.5	7.8	21.0	14.0
06 80644	Tulare city	60,127	2.4	8.8	23.9	10.4	26.7	21.0	9.2	29.9	83.5	5.7	3.6	10.3
06 80812	Turlock city	69,201	1.5	7.4	19.8	11.1	28.6	21.4	11.7	32.6	84.5	2.5	8.7	8.4
06 80854	Tustin city	76,823	3.0	7.7	19.2	10.5	32.6	21.7	8.3	32.8	61.0	2.6	22.8	16.1
06 80994	Twentynine Palms city	25,427	2.4	13.6	11.6	29.6	27.0	12.3	5.8	23.6	78.5	8.0	4.9	11.6
06 81204	Union City city	70,700	3.0	7.4	17.8	8.6	29.7	25.1	11.5	36.0	26.6	6.3	60.1	15.0
06 81344	Upland city	74,570	1.7	5.8	18.3	9.5	27.1	26.2	13.1	37.4	65.5	7.8	10.6	23.1
06 81554	Vacaville city	93,276	1.4	5.7	16.7	10.2	29.3	27.3	10.7	38.0	70.3	11.6	11.1	14.1
06 81638	Valinda CDP	20,419	...	6.5	23.0	10.0	30.1	20.2	10.3	31.6	67.8	2.5	11.9	21.9
06 81666	Vallejo city	116,927	1.4	6.9	16.5	9.9	25.5	29.0	12.2	37.2	44.5	25.4	30.1	8.0
06 82590	Victorville city	118,277	3.4	8.3	25.1	11.9	27.6	19.7	7.4	29.0	60.7	19.4	6.8	16.9
06 82852	Vineyard CDP	26,509	...	8.1	24.8	8.2	29.0	24.8	5.1	32.4	49.1	12.4	37.5	6.4
06 82954	Visalia city	125,986	1.8	8.0	21.3	9.5	28.0	22.4	10.8	31.8	84.1	2.8	7.4	10.2
06 82996	Vista city	95,053	2.1	7.7	18.2	10.6	32.0	21.8	9.8	33.3	84.0	3.9	6.8	9.1
06 83332	Walnut city	29,591	2.7	2.5	17.7	10.5	22.2	33.7	13.4	43.2	24.0	4.1	67.6	8.0
06 83346	Walnut Creek city	64,987	2.1	4.5	12.4	5.7	24.3	26.5	26.6	47.2	83.1	3.5	14.2	2.4
06 83542	Wasco city	25,667	-0.7	7.0	19.6	12.5	34.4	20.5	5.9	30.3	81.6	7.6	1.3	10.9
06 83668	Watsonville city	51,595	1.1	9.1	22.2	12.4	28.0	19.3	9.0	29.4	72.3	0.3	5.3	25.1
06 84144	West Carson CDP	20,476	...	5.4	15.0	8.3	24.1	29.3	17.9	42.7	44.8	12.2	32.7	17.3
06 84200	West Covina city	106,829	1.2	6.9	18.3	10.7	27.3	24.5	12.2	35.3	40.4	5.8	27.3	30.8
06 84410	West Hollywood city	34,607	1.0	1.7	2.5	6.7	46.1	26.7	16.2	40.5	85.1	3.8	7.5	9.0
06 84550	Westminster city	90,669	1.7	5.8	17.2	9.8	25.5	26.5	15.1	38.8	37.9	1.3	49.9	13.9
06 84592	Westmont CDP	29,817	...	9.8	19.3	12.1	26.3	22.4	10.2	31.1	18.0	56.8	...	26.2
06 84774	West Puente Valley CDP	23,824	...	5.4	22.2	12.5	27.6	22.0	10.3	32.4	58.1	1.6	7.1	37.8
06 84780	West Rancho Dominguez CDP	21,613	...	8.2	22.0	10.3	23.5	23.5	12.5	34.3	29.7	55.9	1.4	18.9
06 84816	West Sacramento city	49,148	1.4	7.5	19.1	9.8	31.1	22.1	10.4	33.3	67.9	7.4	15.0	17.7
06 84921	West Whittier-Los Nietos CDP	25,858	...	4.7	18.3	11.9	28.8	26.1	10.2	34.2	50.8	0.8	2.1	49.0
06 85292	Whittier city	85,766	1.0	6.6	17.5	11.8	27.5	24.8	11.8	34.5	58.9	1.6	5.4	37.4
06 85446	Wildomar city	32,840	2.4	6.6	21.1	10.4	24.9	27.0	10.0	34.8	71.7	4.7	5.8	21.5
06 85614	Willowbrook CDP	19,945	...	10.7	25.3	13.5	26.2	18.6	5.7	25.6	44.7	24.7	...	31.2
06 85922	Windsor town	26,982	1.2	6.6	19.4	9.2	25.7	25.7	13.4	37.5	80.8	1.1	4.8	16.8
06 85992	Winter Gardens CDP	21,662	...	7.5	17.4	8.9	28.7	27.5	10.0	34.2	95.0	0.3	1.5	5.7
06 86328	Woodland city	55,853	1.3	7.2	17.9	11.1	27.3	25.1	11.5	35.0	76.5	1.1	8.9	17.8
06 86832	Yorba Linda city	65,698	3.4	6.0	17.3	9.0	22.6	32.5	12.6	41.6	78.8	1.0	21.2	3.7
06 86972	Yuba City city	65,005	0.1	7.1	20.1	10.6	26.5	23.0	12.7	33.8	68.6	4.0	22.3	12.3
06 87042	Yucaipa city	51,887	1.5	5.8	19.9	9.0	25.1	25.8	14.5	37.7	83.6	2.6	3.9	13.0
06 87056	Yucca Valley town	20,936	1.7	8.4	19.1	8.0	23.3	22.4	18.9	36.6	83.0	5.2	3.2	14.8
08 00000	**Colorado**	5,117,453	2.8	6.7	17.4	9.8	28.3	26.5	11.4	36.2	86.9	5.0	4.1	7.7
08 03455	Arvada city	107,960	2.9	5.6	16.5	8.0	25.1	30.1	14.6	41.0	93.2	1.1	3.0	5.1
08 04000	Aurora city	332,532	4.0	8.4	18.7	9.6	30.3	23.7	9.3	33.2	70.0	18.4	6.6	10.8
08 07850	Boulder city	100,403	3.0	4.2	10.1	29.2	27.4	19.8	9.2	28.3	91.5	2.0	6.1	3.9
08 08675	Brighton city	34,100	3.4	8.5	22.5	7.6	30.7	21.7	9.0	32.4	84.8	2.7	2.4	13.3
08 09280	Broomfield city	57,198	3.9	6.6	18.8	8.0	30.7	25.5	10.4	36.2	91.1	1.7	7.2	3.8
08 12415	Castle Rock town	50,016	5.7	8.8	21.9	6.4	31.4	24.9	6.6	35.2	95.6	1.8	2.5	3.0
08 12815	Centennial city	102,215	3.0	5.1	19.8	6.5	24.6	31.5	12.5	40.8	89.7	3.5	5.5	4.2
08 15165	Clifton CDP	21,470	...	9.4	18.7	12.0	29.6	21.4	8.9	30.0	94.1	1.5	0.6	7.8
08 16000	Colorado Springs city	425,725	3.0	7.1	17.6	10.6	27.9	25.8	11.0	34.6	84.7	8.0	5.7	7.2
08 16110	Columbine CDP	24,280	...	5.0	18.4	6.8	20.9	33.2	15.6	43.2	95.2	2.9	2.5	2.0
08 16495	Commerce City city	47,353	4.9	11.6	21.5	7.0	34.3	19.6	6.0	30.6	78.8	4.1	5.1	16.7
08 19150	Dakota Ridge CDP	33,006	...	5.5	20.2	7.6	27.0	32.2	7.5	37.9	94.1	0.9	4.0	3.2
08 20000	Denver city	619,016	5.1	7.3	14.3	9.8	36.0	22.2	10.4	33.7	75.0	11.2	4.6	12.9
08 24785	Englewood city	30,763	2.7	6.4	12.6	8.9	31.9	27.7	12.6	37.7	88.5	2.8	2.1	10.3

STATE and Place code	STATE or City	Percent Hispanic or Latino	Percent foreign born	Total households	Household type (percent)						Percent of households with people under 18 years	Percent of households with people 60 years and over
					Family households				Nonfamily households			
					Total family households	Married-couple families	Male household families	Female household families	Total nonfamily households	One-person households		
ACS table number:		B03003	C05003	B11001	B11001	B11001	B11001	B11001	B11001	B11001	B11005	B11006
Column number:		14	15	16	17	18	19	20	21	22	23	24
	California—Cont.											
06 70098	Santa Rosa city	28.7	18.0	62,249	62.6	44.8	6.8	11.1	37.4	28.5	33.3	36.4
06 70224	Santee city	16.5	7.6	18,790	72.0	52.3	4.8	14.9	28.0	20.8	38.2	31.1
06 70280	Saratoga city	2.3	37.6	10,823	82.9	75.0	2.6	5.3	17.1	15.2	37.5	47.1
06 70686	Seal Beach city	14.7	12.5	12,704	47.9	41.6	1.8	4.6	52.1	46.0	13.7	66.3
06 70742	Seaside city	41.6	32.1	10,318	69.4	46.9	7.4	15.1	30.6	21.9	42.4	28.9
06 70882	Selma city	75.6	30.1	6,595	81.0	51.9	11.1	18.1	19.0	16.3	46.3	39.0
06 72016	Simi Valley city	24.2	19.7	41,388	75.4	59.2	4.8	11.5	24.6	17.9	39.5	33.2
06 72520	Soledad city	72.7	32.5	3,759	91.6	62.2	10.1	19.3	8.4	5.4	64.0	24.4
06 72996	South El Monte city	87.7	44.3	4,585	88.8	51.8	13.6	23.4	11.2	5.6	53.9	38.0
06 73080	South Gate city	95.8	43.2	23,294	84.8	53.6	9.1	22.1	15.2	12.4	55.4	31.0
06 73108	South Lake Tahoe city	36.8	22.7	8,580	56.1	39.9	4.8	11.4	43.9	35.1	29.4	33.1
06 73220	South Pasadena city	24.7	29.4	10,245	65.9	47.3	5.2	13.4	34.1	29.3	37.8	29.0
06 73262	South San Francisco city	35.1	42.8	21,631	71.5	54.1	4.9	12.6	28.5	22.7	35.6	38.2
06 73290	South San Jose Hills CDP	83.7	39.4	4,183	86.7	52.3	11.1	23.3	13.3	9.3	52.9	43.3
06 73430	South Whittier CDP	75.7	25.4	15,398	83.4	55.6	8.7	19.2	16.6	12.8	48.0	37.8
06 73696	Spring Valley CDP (San Diego County)	31.9	18.6	9,440	75.7	51.7	6.3	17.7	24.3	17.4	39.6	37.7
06 73962	Stanton city	47.9	43.3	12,032	69.7	48.1	6.6	15.0	30.3	24.2	43.5	32.1
06 75000	Stockton city	40.0	25.5	90,318	73.2	45.4	7.1	20.7	26.8	21.6	46.1	32.4
06 75600	Suisun City city	26.6	20.8	8,450	78.7	54.3	8.4	16.0	21.3	15.2	45.8	32.4
06 77000	Sunnyvale city	19.2	44.0	54,071	66.2	54.3	4.6	7.4	33.8	25.3	35.4	26.9
06 78120	Temecula city	26.6	15.1	31,409	78.2	61.7	4.9	11.6	21.8	15.5	48.7	25.9
06 78138	Temescal Valley CDP	29.0	17.5	7,641	80.8	67.5	4.1	9.2	19.2	14.0	42.1	33.1
06 78148	Temple City city	20.3	47.7	11,683	79.3	60.8	4.5	14.0	20.7	18.3	38.1	40.8
06 78582	Thousand Oaks city	17.7	18.4	44,969	73.1	60.0	4.6	8.5	26.9	22.0	34.5	40.8
06 80000	Torrance city	17.8	29.5	54,894	68.6	52.6	3.9	12.2	31.4	26.4	31.5	37.7
06 80238	Tracy city	39.4	26.4	24,014	80.9	63.3	6.4	11.2	19.1	14.3	50.9	27.8
06 80644	Tulare city	56.9	19.7	17,865	78.9	53.9	8.5	16.4	21.1	16.8	48.5	32.1
06 80812	Turlock city	35.0	24.4	23,266	73.8	55.1	5.0	13.6	26.2	20.7	41.1	31.2
06 80854	Tustin city	40.0	36.2	24,902	72.7	51.0	6.9	14.8	27.3	21.2	43.2	26.1
06 80994	Twentynine Palms city	23.5	6.2	8,057	71.5	51.3	7.3	13.0	28.5	24.8	40.7	21.2
06 81204	Union City city	21.5	46.5	20,574	82.1	63.8	5.5	12.7	17.9	15.2	45.9	37.3
06 81344	Upland city	38.3	19.0	26,009	71.3	48.6	4.3	18.4	28.7	22.4	36.5	34.9
06 81554	Vacaville city	24.3	13.6	30,946	68.7	49.7	4.9	14.1	31.3	26.2	33.8	31.5
06 81638	Valinda CDP	78.4	34.7	4,447	88.5	62.0	8.3	18.2	11.5	10.2	57.8	41.4
06 81666	Vallejo city	24.7	28.4	39,574	68.2	42.5	6.4	19.3	31.8	25.4	34.8	39.1
06 82590	Victorville city	47.3	17.7	30,780	79.6	48.5	10.0	21.0	20.4	14.6	53.1	29.1
06 82852	Vineyard CDP	14.7	24.8	7,630	80.9	63.2	3.9	13.8	19.1	9.9	54.1	21.1
06 82954	Visalia city	46.1	13.8	41,823	72.0	50.2	7.2	14.6	28.0	22.6	42.9	32.8
06 82996	Vista city	49.8	25.9	30,058	68.7	50.6	5.1	13.1	31.3	22.1	37.1	27.5
06 83332	Walnut city	18.5	48.9	8,115	91.8	76.6	5.2	10.0	8.2	5.4	43.7	45.8
06 83346	Walnut Creek city	9.6	23.2	29,685	55.4	45.4	3.6	6.4	44.6	37.3	21.4	49.7
06 83542	Wasco city	76.0	28.6	5,239	84.1	52.2	11.5	20.4	15.9	11.0	58.3	30.3
06 83668	Watsonville city	81.5	39.5	13,587	80.6	53.0	7.9	19.7	19.4	17.3	51.8	31.2
06 84144	West Carson CDP	36.0	35.6	7,083	66.2	44.7	6.9	14.5	33.8	30.4	34.2	42.5
06 84200	West Covina city	55.2	33.7	30,643	80.4	55.0	6.5	18.9	19.6	15.3	44.7	39.1
06 84410	West Hollywood city	12.4	27.9	22,070	18.7	12.0	2.6	4.1	81.3	63.8	4.3	26.4
06 84550	Westminster city	22.9	44.8	27,123	78.1	54.9	8.6	14.5	21.9	17.4	39.0	44.4
06 84592	Westmont CDP	42.4	21.7	9,888	66.6	24.8	10.1	31.7	33.4	30.6	40.5	30.7
06 84774	West Puente Valley CDP	86.5	37.7	5,059	89.9	56.2	8.8	24.9	10.1	8.4	56.3	43.2
06 84780	West Rancho Dominguez CDP	40.5	23.0	6,246	75.9	36.1	8.1	31.7	24.1	21.8	48.1	38.3
06 84816	West Sacramento city	32.9	23.8	17,184	67.2	46.2	6.6	14.4	32.8	25.2	36.6	31.0
06 84921	West Whittier-Los Nietos CDP	88.4	29.6	6,484	82.0	52.1	10.4	19.5	18.0	13.8	46.4	44.8
06 85292	Whittier city	66.2	19.2	27,212	73.2	49.0	7.4	16.8	26.8	21.4	40.4	33.5
06 85446	Wildomar city	37.9	18.2	9,909	80.5	61.8	7.2	11.6	19.5	15.8	44.7	34.5
06 85614	Willowbrook CDP	72.8	31.4	4,672	84.7	43.2	12.0	29.6	15.3	12.0	61.6	25.9
06 85922	Windsor town	28.1	12.9	9,333	72.6	57.5	5.8	9.3	27.4	23.4	41.7	39.2
06 85992	Winter Gardens CDP	20.0	10.6	7,093	71.0	53.4	3.1	14.5	29.0	21.9	36.1	33.6
06 86328	Woodland city	46.9	21.6	19,363	70.0	51.4	5.5	13.1	30.0	24.1	38.7	33.0
06 86832	Yorba Linda city	16.8	18.8	21,943	80.8	70.7	2.9	7.3	19.2	16.1	37.6	36.6
06 86972	Yuba City city	27.7	24.9	21,679	70.5	51.8	4.9	13.7	29.5	23.0	39.2	38.3
06 87042	Yucaipa city	29.6	12.2	17,478	73.1	56.9	4.4	11.8	26.9	21.8	38.2	37.7
06 87056	Yucca Valley town	16.9	6.5	7,498	63.9	42.8	9.3	11.8	36.1	32.0	34.2	46.0
08 00000	**Colorado**	20.9	9.7	1,977,737	64.0	49.1	4.6	10.3	36.0	28.4	32.3	30.1
08 03455	Arvada city	13.6	4.9	43,522	67.5	51.1	6.1	10.3	32.5	27.0	30.3	36.0
08 04000	Aurora city	29.4	21.0	121,540	65.2	43.2	6.7	15.4	34.8	28.7	37.1	27.3
08 07850	Boulder city	9.1	10.0	40,913	43.7	34.4	3.0	6.3	56.3	32.9	20.9	22.1
08 08675	Brighton city	41.6	13.3	10,520	76.7	58.8	5.0	12.9	23.3	21.1	48.6	27.2
08 09280	Broomfield city	11.7	8.1	21,553	67.6	54.7	4.2	8.7	32.4	26.2	34.8	26.6
08 12415	Castle Rock town	12.6	7.2	17,449	77.7	62.0	4.5	11.3	22.3	17.2	44.7	19.5
08 12815	Centennial city	7.4	8.8	37,985	75.0	61.8	3.4	9.8	25.0	20.9	35.8	34.3
08 15165	Clifton CDP	21.1	5.1	7,799	71.7	49.4	8.6	13.6	28.3	20.3	39.0	26.1
08 16000	Colorado Springs city	16.5	8.4	167,862	63.6	47.9	4.2	11.5	36.4	30.0	32.5	28.6
08 16110	Columbine CDP	8.3	5.0	9,671	72.6	57.7	3.6	11.3	27.4	24.4	31.2	40.9
08 16495	Commerce City city	47.3	16.6	14,634	77.0	56.7	5.8	14.4	23.0	18.7	49.8	22.5
08 19150	Dakota Ridge CDP	12.5	4.8	12,588	74.5	59.2	5.1	10.3	25.5	21.3	38.3	25.9
08 20000	Denver city	31.7	16.0	266,248	47.9	32.8	4.4	10.8	52.1	40.4	25.1	26.1
08 24785	Englewood city	17.6	9.0	14,288	46.9	29.1	6.4	11.5	53.1	43.8	21.9	27.8

Table A-4. Cities — Who: Age, Race/Ethnicity, and Household Structure, 2010–2012—*Continued*

STATE and Place code	STATE or City	Total population	Percent change 2010–2012 / Population estimates	Under 5 years	5 to 17 years	18 to 24 years	25 to 44 years	45 to 64 years	65 years and over	Median age	White	Black	Asian, Hawaiian, or Pacific Islander	American Indian, Alaska Native, or some other race
	ACS table number:	B01003		B01001	B01001	B01001	B01001	B01001	B01001	B01002	B02008	B02009	B02011 + B02012	B02010 + B02013
	Column number:	1	2	3	4	5	6	7	8	9	10	11	12	13
	Colorado—Cont.													
08 27425	Fort Collins city	146,235	3.0	6.0	14.2	21.5	28.4	21.3	8.6	29.6	92.9	2.3	4.7	4.2
08 27865	Fountain city	26,509	3.1	8.0	25.2	7.6	33.0	20.5	5.8	30.1	83.5	15.2	7.3	4.5
08 31660	Grand Junction city	59,586	1.3	6.5	15.1	11.8	25.9	24.4	16.4	36.6	92.2	1.6	2.1	7.9
08 32155	Greeley city	94,217	2.4	7.1	17.5	17.0	26.3	21.1	10.9	31.1	85.5	2.2	2.8	12.7
08 36410	Highlands Ranch CDP	100,896	...	7.4	24.3	5.7	29.3	26.1	7.2	36.2	92.4	2.5	7.2	1.4
08 40377	Ken Caryl CDP	31,219	...	5.3	17.3	8.3	25.4	34.3	9.3	40.9	95.5	2.4	2.9	2.2
08 41835	Lafayette city	25,028	4.8	7.0	16.0	8.6	29.2	29.9	9.3	37.9	89.1	2.0	6.8	6.3
08 43000	Lakewood city	144,282	1.6	6.1	14.6	9.4	28.4	27.0	14.5	38.3	91.3	2.8	4.8	4.8
08 45255	Littleton city	43,276	4.2	6.3	15.8	8.3	26.4	27.4	15.8	40.1	91.8	1.4	3.4	5.7
08 45970	Longmont city	87,474	2.6	6.9	18.8	9.5	27.6	26.0	11.3	36.0	87.8	1.8	4.1	9.2
08 46465	Loveland city	68,815	4.8	6.2	16.9	8.7	27.0	26.9	14.3	37.7	91.8	1.1	2.4	7.5
08 54330	Northglenn city	36,366	2.8	6.1	16.9	12.6	30.2	22.7	11.6	33.5	89.2	2.4	3.9	7.9
08 57630	Parker town	46,300	3.7	8.1	23.7	6.1	33.9	22.8	5.3	34.1	95.3	2.3	3.6	3.0
08 62000	Pueblo city	107,364	0.8	7.1	16.6	10.2	24.8	25.7	15.6	37.8	79.1	3.1	1.8	21.1
08 62220	Pueblo West CDP	29,635	...	5.4	21.7	7.5	23.5	28.7	13.1	39.1	90.4	1.9	1.1	9.5
08 68847	Security-Widefield CDP	32,505	...	6.1	20.6	8.1	26.2	26.5	12.5	36.8	83.9	12.0	5.5	6.8
08 77290	Thornton city	121,742	4.0	8.1	21.7	9.3	31.5	22.3	7.1	31.6	87.5	1.9	5.5	8.2
08 83835	Westminster city	107,778	2.6	7.0	16.6	8.8	30.7	27.1	9.8	35.8	87.1	2.5	7.2	7.6
08 84440	Wheat Ridge city	30,431	1.6	4.7	14.8	7.4	26.7	29.2	17.2	42.2	94.7	0.7	2.0	4.2
09 00000	**Connecticut**	3,584,561	0.4	5.5	16.9	9.3	25.0	28.7	14.5	40.2	80.1	11.4	4.6	6.6
09 08000	Bridgeport city	145,555	1.3	7.1	18.4	12.0	30.3	22.3	9.9	32.7	46.5	37.5	4.6	13.7
09 08420	Bristol city	60,560	0.2	5.5	15.6	8.0	27.1	28.4	15.4	41.1	91.5	5.2	2.1	4.3
09 18430	Danbury city	82,007	2.0	6.0	13.7	10.6	32.4	25.5	11.8	36.3	67.8	10.3	6.4	19.6
09 18920	Darien CDP	20,948	...	6.6	29.0	3.8	19.8	28.3	12.5	39.6	96.2	1.0	4.0	0.6
09 22700	East Hartford CDP	51,284	...	5.6	16.3	9.6	26.5	29.2	12.9	39.3	57.6	28.0	6.9	11.0
09 22980	East Haven CDP	29,215	...	4.7	15.1	7.4	26.2	29.0	17.6	42.7	89.3	5.4	2.9	4.1
09 37000	Hartford city	124,894	0.1	6.9	18.8	15.6	28.2	21.0	9.4	30.1	40.0	40.8	3.0	21.2
09 44690	Manchester CDP	30,994	...	8.4	12.8	10.7	29.0	26.0	13.0	35.8	78.4	13.9	5.1	6.2
09 46450	Meriden city	60,733	-0.4	6.7	15.7	8.8	28.1	26.6	14.2	38.0	74.3	12.1	2.4	13.9
09 47290	Middletown city	47,583	-0.7	4.9	13.7	13.4	28.3	27.0	12.6	37.1	80.2	16.2	5.2	2.8
09 47515	Milford city (balance)	51,541	0.3	5.4	14.8	6.4	26.5	30.6	16.3	42.6	89.6	2.8	6.8	2.6
09 49880	Naugatuck borough	31,830	-0.3	7.2	15.2	8.4	25.9	30.5	12.9	39.7	89.5	5.6	4.8	3.0
09 50370	New Britain city	73,200	-0.1	6.4	17.0	13.4	27.5	23.4	12.2	33.2	65.7	14.0	2.9	21.9
09 52000	New Haven city	130,378	0.8	6.1	16.3	15.8	32.3	19.8	9.8	30.6	47.0	36.4	5.3	13.9
09 52210	Newington CDP	30,576	...	4.6	14.7	6.7	25.0	30.2	18.8	44.4	86.1	6.2	6.0	3.7
09 52280	New London city	27,668	0.3	5.6	12.5	20.4	28.7	23.2	9.6	31.9	63.2	19.2	3.7	18.9
09 54940	North Haven CDP	24,055	...	4.7	15.1	6.1	21.9	32.0	20.2	46.5	92.7	3.4	4.0	...
09 55990	Norwalk city	86,632	1.4	5.9	11.7	5.9	31.5	29.8	15.2	42.1	75.6	15.2	7.0	5.0
09 56200	Norwich city	40,528	-0.1	6.1	16.6	8.4	26.6	28.4	14.0	39.3	74.9	14.5	8.8	7.4
09 68100	Shelton city	39,953	1.6	3.9	15.8	7.6	22.8	31.6	18.3	44.9	92.9	1.3	3.9	1.9
09 73000	Stamford city	123,995	1.8	7.4	15.5	7.8	33.0	23.6	12.6	35.8	61.6	15.1	8.8	16.9
09 74260	Stratford CDP	51,797	...	5.0	16.1	7.2	25.2	29.2	17.3	42.5	78.9	15.9	2.9	3.8
09 76500	Torrington city	36,085	-1.5	5.1	15.4	7.1	24.5	30.1	17.8	43.6	92.6	3.0	3.4	3.8
09 77270	Trumbull CDP	36,297	...	5.7	20.5	7.1	20.6	28.5	17.6	42.4	92.1	2.3	5.3	2.7
09 80000	Waterbury city	110,089	-0.4	7.6	17.6	10.7	27.2	24.9	12.0	34.7	62.2	23.3	1.9	18.8
09 82660	West Hartford CDP	63,243	...	5.6	17.1	6.9	25.2	28.2	17.0	41.5	83.7	8.2	8.6	3.6
09 82800	West Haven city	55,475	-0.3	6.1	15.3	12.0	26.8	27.5	12.3	37.8	69.8	23.7	4.4	5.6
09 83570	Westport CDP	26,777	...	4.6	24.0	4.9	15.1	34.6	16.8	45.5	92.8	1.1	6.3	1.8
09 84970	Wethersfield CDP	26,707	...	4.2	16.6	6.0	23.1	29.1	21.0	45.0	90.4	5.1	4.3	2.7
10 00000	**Delaware**	908,351	1.9	6.2	16.4	10.2	25.0	27.4	14.8	39.0	72.3	23.0	3.9	3.6
10 04130	Bear CDP	20,149	...	6.1	19.5	11.0	31.6	26.3	5.5	33.2	57.4	32.0	5.8	6.7
10 21200	Dover city	36,643	2.5	6.5	15.6	20.0	23.5	20.6	13.9	30.5	50.7	45.3	3.3	4.2
10 50670	Newark city	31,910	2.9	2.7	7.0	46.4	17.0	16.0	10.8	22.2	83.8	8.6	7.6	1.8
10 77580	Wilmington city	71,005	0.7	7.7	16.7	9.1	29.8	24.6	12.1	34.4	37.8	58.6	1.0	5.2
11 00000	**District of Columbia**	618,777	4.5	5.8	11.2	13.7	34.9	23.0	11.4	33.7	41.6	51.4	4.6	4.9
11 50000	Washington city	618,777	4.5	5.8	11.2	13.7	34.9	23.0	11.4	33.7	41.6	51.4	4.6	4.9
12 00000	**Florida**	19,081,930	2.5	5.6	15.3	9.3	24.9	27.1	17.7	41.0	78.2	17.1	3.3	3.9
12 00410	Alafaya CDP	79,423	...	6.8	20.5	13.6	31.6	21.5	6.0	30.9	80.5	8.5	7.7	4.9
12 00950	Altamonte Springs city	41,729	0.9	5.3	13.4	8.3	33.9	25.4	13.7	38.1	79.3	18.4	2.6	1.4
12 01700	Apopka city	43,160	6.3	7.2	19.6	9.5	28.1	25.2	10.4	36.0	67.2	20.9	6.7	11.3
12 02681	Aventura city	36,525	3.1	5.3	13.6	4.6	26.3	22.8	27.4	45.1	91.6	4.9	2.4	2.4
12 04162	Bayonet Point CDP	23,891	...	3.2	14.3	7.1	20.0	26.4	28.9	49.6	96.1	2.2	0.6	2.5
12 05462	Bellview CDP	19,954	...	8.3	12.9	8.2	25.8	31.5	13.3	40.5	72.9	21.2	7.8	1.9
12 06875	Bloomingdale CDP	21,179	...	4.6	19.2	5.9	26.9	31.3	12.1	41.7	87.5	9.6	5.7	3.4
12 07300	Boca Raton city	86,489	3.1	4.3	13.5	11.6	20.4	29.1	21.1	45.2	90.0	6.1	2.9	2.6
12 07525	Bonita Springs city	45,146	5.2	4.3	9.9	6.6	22.7	25.3	31.0	51.4	88.0	1.5	3.2	8.6
12 07875	Boynton Beach city	69,093	2.5	5.4	13.5	9.2	25.7	24.4	21.8	42.4	63.7	31.1	3.9	3.1
12 07950	Bradenton city	50,085	2.1	6.1	13.4	7.9	24.7	25.0	23.0	43.8	78.5	15.5	0.8	6.7
12 08150	Brandon CDP	104,183	...	6.1	16.3	11.6	30.0	26.2	9.8	34.8	78.4	17.5	4.1	4.3
12 08300	Brent CDP	22,190	...	5.0	14.9	24.9	20.6	22.2	12.4	29.4	57.0	36.5	6.2	4.2
12 09415	Buenaventura Lakes CDP	30,657	...	5.0	20.0	12.4	27.3	23.8	11.6	34.5	71.7	16.4	2.6	12.4
12 10275	Cape Coral city	157,933	4.2	5.9	17.5	6.6	23.5	28.6	18.0	42.2	92.4	4.1	2.0	2.9
12 10825	Carrollwood CDP	35,881	...	6.2	14.6	10.3	27.4	26.9	14.6	40.0	80.7	11.0	4.9	5.3
12 11050	Casselberry city	26,360	0.8	7.8	14.1	9.3	26.8	28.3	13.7	37.6	85.4	9.3	2.6	5.4
12 12425	Citrus Park CDP	24,086	...	5.6	20.3	8.7	25.8	29.0	10.6	37.0	85.1	9.0	6.3	3.4

Table A-4. Cities — Who: Age, Race/Ethnicity, and Household Structure, 2010–2012—*Continued*

STATE and Place code	STATE or City	Percent Hispanic or Latino	Percent foreign born	Total households	Household type (percent) — Family households — Total family households	Married-couple families	Male household families	Female household families	Nonfamily households — Total nonfamily households	One-person households	Percent of households with people under 18 years	Percent of households with people 60 years and over
	ACS table number:	B03003	C05003	B11001	B11001	B11001	B11001	B11001	B11001	B11001	B11005	B11006
	Column number:	14	15	16	17	18	19	20	21	22	23	24
	Colorado—Cont.											
08 27425	Fort Collins city	10.5	6.0	56,319	56.1	45.0	3.1	8.0	43.9	26.7	29.0	23.7
08 27865	Fountain city	14.3	6.4	9,100	77.2	55.5	4.1	17.6	22.8	18.9	50.4	17.8
08 31660	Grand Junction city	13.6	4.4	24,778	58.0	44.3	5.0	8.7	42.0	33.2	26.8	37.1
08 32155	Greeley city	34.6	11.2	33,494	65.6	46.8	6.3	12.6	34.4	25.9	34.2	29.2
08 36410	Highlands Ranch CDP	6.8	7.3	34,763	78.6	67.0	4.0	7.7	21.4	16.9	48.7	23.2
08 40377	Ken Caryl CDP	10.2	4.1	12,620	68.8	56.0	4.3	8.5	31.2	26.5	33.3	27.6
08 41835	Lafayette city	15.5	12.1	10,228	61.5	45.3	3.7	12.5	38.5	31.3	30.8	27.7
08 43000	Lakewood city	22.3	8.8	60,712	59.4	41.8	5.5	12.1	40.6	33.0	27.5	33.6
08 45255	Littleton city	14.1	8.2	18,420	59.9	46.5	3.9	9.5	40.1	35.2	30.4	35.0
08 45970	Longmont city	25.2	13.9	33,527	67.2	49.4	5.8	12.0	32.8	25.7	36.7	28.6
08 46465	Loveland city	11.9	4.0	28,384	65.8	49.6	6.2	10.1	34.2	27.4	31.7	32.5
08 54330	Northglenn city	29.3	9.3	13,715	62.4	42.6	7.6	12.2	37.6	30.7	31.8	29.1
08 57630	Parker town	7.1	4.2	16,372	74.9	65.2	3.2	6.5	25.1	20.2	48.8	14.8
08 62000	Pueblo city	50.2	4.0	42,981	57.6	37.2	5.4	14.9	42.4	36.0	29.0	37.4
08 62220	Pueblo West CDP	24.7	3.0	10,508	73.7	59.5	3.8	10.4	26.3	20.3	36.9	37.4
08 68847	Security-Widefield CDP	20.3	5.9	11,570	78.6	62.7	4.3	13.6	21.4	17.7	37.5	32.8
08 77290	Thornton city	31.3	10.4	40,547	73.4	56.1	6.0	11.3	26.6	21.0	45.3	21.5
08 83835	Westminster city	21.7	10.8	41,399	65.4	47.9	5.6	11.9	34.6	26.7	34.3	27.0
08 84440	Wheat Ridge city	23.2	6.2	13,243	56.4	39.4	5.3	11.7	43.6	33.8	26.0	37.9
09 00000	**Connecticut**	13.8	13.6	1,355,973	66.2	48.8	4.3	13.1	33.8	28.1	32.4	36.4
09 08000	Bridgeport city	38.9	27.1	49,928	62.0	30.3	6.3	25.4	38.0	31.1	36.8	30.4
09 08420	Bristol city	11.0	10.4	25,087	59.6	43.0	4.9	11.7	40.4	33.4	29.1	35.0
09 18430	Danbury city	25.8	33.0	29,268	63.0	46.5	4.8	11.7	37.0	28.3	30.8	31.6
09 18920	Darien CDP	2.6	10.7	6,553	81.2	76.8	1.1	3.3	18.8	17.9	48.6	36.2
09 22700	East Hartford CDP	26.2	21.4	20,085	64.5	35.9	6.8	21.8	35.5	30.1	33.5	33.9
09 22980	East Haven CDP	10.4	9.9	11,300	67.1	46.7	6.0	14.4	32.9	25.9	28.5	37.5
09 37000	Hartford city	43.9	22.7	45,739	58.2	20.8	5.9	31.5	41.8	34.6	37.2	28.5
09 44690	Manchester CDP	16.2	9.9	12,864	60.6	38.3	6.6	15.7	39.4	32.7	29.3	31.1
09 46450	Meriden city	28.6	11.2	23,361	66.5	43.9	5.5	17.1	33.5	26.7	32.5	33.4
09 47290	Middletown city	8.9	10.9	19,065	55.0	35.8	5.3	13.9	45.0	35.4	26.5	31.0
09 47515	Milford city (balance)	4.8	10.5	20,427	65.1	50.7	4.5	9.9	34.9	27.8	30.3	38.0
09 49880	Naugatuck borough	10.0	13.7	12,588	64.8	46.6	5.5	12.7	35.2	29.9	31.3	33.6
09 50370	New Britain city	36.8	20.9	27,540	60.3	29.3	7.4	23.7	39.7	32.3	33.3	30.7
09 52000	New Haven city	27.8	16.5	49,680	53.4	25.8	5.6	22.0	46.6	37.4	31.5	26.4
09 52210	Newington CDP	6.6	17.2	12,818	63.6	50.0	3.0	10.6	36.4	30.6	28.3	41.4
09 52280	New London city	30.8	18.0	10,293	50.5	28.2	7.3	15.0	49.5	38.6	28.0	27.6
09 54940	North Haven CDP	3.6	8.5	8,838	74.7	63.7	4.2	6.8	25.3	22.8	30.9	50.2
09 55990	Norwalk city	18.5	22.4	37,882	56.7	43.9	3.4	9.5	43.3	38.1	22.8	35.8
09 56200	Norwich city	10.8	13.4	16,930	57.2	37.7	5.6	13.9	42.8	35.5	29.4	35.5
09 68100	Shelton city	6.4	11.9	14,878	73.3	60.3	3.5	9.5	26.7	24.0	29.7	43.3
09 73000	Stamford city	26.8	34.8	44,854	65.2	47.5	4.5	13.2	34.8	28.6	35.2	31.5
09 74260	Stratford CDP	14.8	12.1	19,942	68.0	49.8	4.2	14.1	32.0	27.4	30.5	40.8
09 76500	Torrington city	8.5	9.2	15,067	60.9	44.1	4.0	12.7	39.1	34.2	27.6	36.6
09 77270	Trumbull CDP	6.8	10.9	11,821	78.7	67.0	3.2	8.4	21.3	19.6	43.8	43.4
09 80000	Waterbury city	33.0	14.1	41,419	64.8	35.0	5.8	24.0	35.2	29.7	36.5	32.8
09 82660	West Hartford CDP	9.8	18.0	24,960	66.5	52.8	3.4	10.3	33.5	27.8	32.8	38.1
09 82800	West Haven city	17.3	14.9	21,341	62.1	40.7	2.9	18.5	37.9	32.6	31.1	36.3
09 83570	Westport CDP	4.8	12.2	9,309	78.3	68.4	3.5	6.5	21.7	18.7	40.9	44.0
09 84970	Wethersfield CDP	9.7	15.6	10,919	63.9	51.4	2.8	9.7	36.1	32.5	28.7	47.7
10 00000	**Delaware**	8.4	8.3	334,228	67.1	48.5	4.9	13.7	32.9	26.4	32.0	37.6
10 04130	Bear CDP	14.7	12.9	6,862	73.8	48.3	7.5	18.0	26.2	18.4	40.0	22.6
10 21200	Dover city	6.8	6.0	12,398	57.0	33.9	5.2	18.0	43.0	34.9	28.9	37.1
10 50670	Newark city	4.1	10.1	10,039	46.4	38.9	2.0	5.5	53.6	30.9	15.7	30.9
10 77580	Wilmington city	12.9	7.1	29,045	54.1	23.5	5.8	24.8	45.9	37.5	32.7	32.1
11 00000	**District of Columbia**	9.5	13.8	261,567	41.0	21.9	3.6	15.5	59.0	46.9	19.6	29.0
11 50000	Washington city	9.5	13.8	261,567	41.0	21.9	3.6	15.5	59.0	46.9	19.6	29.0
12 00000	**Florida**	22.9	19.5	7,120,273	64.3	46.5	4.5	13.3	35.7	29.1	28.4	41.7
12 00410	Alafaya CDP	38.5	18.7	26,938	71.8	52.7	4.4	14.8	28.2	18.8	41.1	19.3
12 00950	Altamonte Springs city	22.8	14.7	15,734	53.6	34.9	3.6	15.1	46.4	38.9	23.5	31.9
12 01700	Apopka city	22.1	19.7	14,071	77.2	55.1	5.0	17.0	22.8	18.3	40.0	29.1
12 02681	Aventura city	37.5	49.1	17,266	56.0	43.8	3.4	8.8	44.0	37.7	21.3	46.9
12 04162	Bayonet Point CDP	12.9	6.5	10,287	57.0	40.7	3.4	12.9	43.0	38.5	21.6	56.3
12 05462	Bellview CDP	4.0	7.3	7,955	64.2	48.6	3.7	12.0	35.8	30.7	26.2	35.9
12 06875	Bloomingdale CDP	13.9	10.5	7,159	77.7	64.7	4.2	8.9	22.3	14.9	35.3	33.1
12 07300	Boca Raton city	12.8	18.5	35,304	59.6	48.1	3.1	8.3	40.4	32.2	23.4	45.3
12 07525	Bonita Springs city	29.5	26.9	17,871	64.2	54.7	4.1	5.4	35.8	29.0	14.6	61.2
12 07875	Boynton Beach city	11.3	24.1	27,852	54.3	37.6	3.8	13.0	45.7	36.6	25.0	44.0
12 07950	Bradenton city	20.3	14.9	20,698	55.5	38.1	4.0	13.3	44.5	36.3	22.6	45.3
12 08150	Brandon CDP	23.2	10.9	38,860	63.4	43.8	4.0	15.6	36.6	28.6	32.4	27.0
12 08300	Brent CDP	4.4	7.3	6,553	65.1	39.0	4.4	21.7	34.9	28.6	31.1	37.3
12 09415	Buenaventura Lakes CDP	66.6	22.9	8,992	77.0	46.1	8.9	21.9	23.0	17.8	44.0	34.1
12 10275	Cape Coral city	18.2	13.6	55,406	71.9	54.0	6.1	11.8	28.1	22.5	33.1	42.6
12 10825	Carrollwood CDP	28.8	18.4	14,316	67.9	46.5	6.3	15.0	32.1	27.1	31.2	34.1
12 11050	Casselberry city	25.8	10.0	9,737	58.4	38.1	5.8	14.5	41.6	35.6	27.2	37.0
12 12425	Citrus Park CDP	31.4	17.9	8,571	69.9	48.7	6.6	14.6	30.1	23.6	39.7	30.4

Table A-4. Cities — Who: Age, Race/Ethnicity, and Household Structure, 2010–2012—*Continued*

STATE and Place code	STATE or City	Total population	Percent change 2010–2012	Population by age (percent) Under 5 years	5 to 17 years	18 to 24 years	25 to 44 years	45 to 64 years	65 years and over	Median age	Race alone or in comb nation (percent) White	Black	Asian, Hawaiian, or Pacific Islander	American Indian, Alaska Native, or some other race
ACS table number:		B01003	Population estimates	B01001	B01001	B01001	B01001	B01001	B01001	B01002	B02008	B02009	B02011 + B02012	B02010 + B02013
Column number:		1	2	3	4	5	6	7	8	9	10	11	12	13
	Florida—Cont.													
12 12875	Clearwater city	108,403	0.5	5.4	12.9	8.2	23.4	29.1	20.9	45.1	86.2	11.1	3.2	2.0
12 12925	Clermont city	29,107	2.0	6.8	17.1	8.7	23.0	24.6	19.8	41.5	75.8	17.2	5.0	7.7
12 13275	Coconut Creek city	54,077	3.6	5.3	17.0	7.4	28.2	23.6	18.4	39.5	80.8	12.2	5.8	3.4
12 14125	Cooper City city	30,335	13.0	4.2	19.8	9.8	22.9	33.2	10.1	40.2	83.5	8.6	8.3	3.2
12 14250	Coral Gables city	48,137	5.2	4.4	11.6	16.8	23.3	27.4	16.5	41.4	93.7	3.3	3.1	0.9
12 14400	Coral Springs city	123,406	3.2	6.3	20.3	9.7	25.8	28.8	9.1	37.0	72.7	20.1	5.5	4.2
12 14412	Coral Terrace CDP	24,536	...	5.0	12.7	9.0	26.7	25.7	20.9	42.1	98.7	0.6	...	0.6
12 14895	Country Club CDP	46,518	...	8.6	17.1	10.2	28.8	25.7	9.7	33.9	80.9	14.3	2.8	2.8
12 15475	Crestview city	21,606	6.3	10.0	19.1	9.8	31.0	22.4	7.8	31.3	78.8	24.4	3.2	2.8
12 15968	Cutler Bay town	41,448	4.4	7.9	18.4	8.7	28.2	25.8	11.1	35.1	78.7	16.8	1.7	4.9
12 16335	Dania Beach city	30,150	2.9	7.3	13.1	10.3	26.0	29.2	14.1	40.0	71.9	23.8	2.5	4.2
12 16475	Davie town	93,973	3.5	5.8	17.6	11.4	26.1	28.4	10.7	37.2	81.0	9.7	5.4	6.3
12 16525	Daytona Beach city	61,376	1.7	5.5	10.3	17.1	21.4	26.8	18.8	40.9	59.8	36.2	3.1	3.1
12 16725	Deerfield Beach city	76,352	3.0	4.3	14.2	8.1	26.0	26.2	21.2	43.0	71.2	26.4	1.5	2.5
12 16875	DeLand city	27,239	1.4	5.5	17.9	14.0	19.9	22.6	20.1	38.8	73.7	17.0	5.2	8.0
12 17100	Delray Beach city	61,553	2.6	4.7	11.5	8.2	24.3	28.4	22.9	45.9	66.8	26.9	2.8	5.3
12 17200	Deltona city	85,255	0.3	6.0	18.0	9.6	25.7	26.8	13.9	38.3	77.0	12.6	1.3	13.5
12 17935	Doral city	47,156	4.8	10.3	20.8	8.0	34.7	21.1	5.2	32.4	92.0	2.6	4.5	2.6
12 18575	Dunedin city	35,328	0.4	5.2	11.7	5.0	21.0	30.3	26.8	50.6	95.9	2.6	1.6	1.0
12 19206	East Lake CDP	33,239	...	4.1	16.8	6.4	17.8	35.7	19.3	48.1	94.1	2.6	4.0	0.9
12 19212	East Lake-Orient Park CDP	23,315	...	9.0	19.6	11.2	26.9	26.6	6.7	31.6	54.4	38.5	4.1	6.4
12 19825	Edgewater city	20,755	0.3	4.6	11.8	6.9	21.7	31.8	23.2	48.2	94.2	5.4	1.5	2.0
12 20108	Egypt Lake-Leto CDP	40,468	...	6.7	15.7	10.7	32.3	22.6	12.0	34.7	80.2	9.0	5.9	6.3
12 20925	Ensley CDP	21,320	...	5.8	17.9	10.0	26.8	24.0	15.5	34.2	70.0	28.0	2.8	1.0
12 21150	Estero CDP	23,070	...	4.0	9.7	7.2	14.8	27.1	37.3	59.9	91.7	...	4.0	...
12 22275	Ferry Pass CDP	29,687	...	6.3	12.5	13.9	24.4	25.3	17.5	39.1	79.0	20.4	3.0	2.8
12 22660	Fleming Island CDP	33,556	...	4.7	26.6	9.7	22.4	28.1	8.5	38.1	90.1	6.0	4.3	3.4
12 24000	Fort Lauderdale city	168,405	2.9	5.2	12.4	7.7	27.8	30.9	16.0	42.6	64.7	31.6	2.3	3.4
12 24125	Fort Myers city	64,070	5.1	5.8	15.6	9.3	26.6	24.5	18.1	39.9	59.0	33.7	1.6	7.7
12 24300	Fort Pierce city	42,328	1.6	7.5	18.2	9.3	26.6	23.3	15.1	34.8	54.3	40.9	0.4	5.2
12 24475	Fort Walton Beach city	19,822	4.1	6.1	15.0	11.3	23.7	27.0	17.0	40.8	79.2	14.2	5.1	5.5
12 24562	Fountainebleau CDP	53,580	...	5.5	11.3	10.1	30.6	25.7	16.8	40.5	96.6	1.7	1.0	2.3
12 24581	Four Corners CDP	30,437	...	5.1	21.0	8.0	27.7	24.8	13.4	34.1	89.4	6.2	4.1	4.0
12 24925	Fruit Cove CDP	28,509	...	3.2	22.4	8.5	21.3	30.3	14.3	41.1	94.6	2.4	3.7	...
12 25175	Gainesville city	125,273	1.3	4.3	8.3	37.6	24.4	17.1	8.3	24.9	68.4	24.3	8.1	2.4
12 26300	Golden Gate CDP	28,490	...	8.6	21.8	9.8	31.5	21.7	6.7	30.4	74.4	14.9	...	10.5
12 26375	Golden Glades CDP	33,365	...	6.0	18.2	11.4	28.6	25.6	10.2	34.0	23.1	72.2	2.8	5.1
12 27322	Greenacres city	38,046	2.1	5.9	16.9	8.3	31.4	23.1	14.5	36.9	78.1	21.8	2.1	3.6
12 28400	Haines City city	20,802	2.1	10.8	19.2	8.6	27.6	19.4	14.3	32.9	69.3	23.3	2.4	6.0
12 28452	Hallandale Beach city	37,798	3.0	3.6	9.4	6.3	25.6	28.0	27.1	49.2	74.4	20.5	3.1	3.1
12 30000	Hialeah city	229,152	2.9	4.9	13.4	9.8	26.8	25.8	19.2	41.8	94.7	2.9	0.5	2.7
12 30025	Hialeah Gardens city	22,203	3.1	6.3	15.6	10.3	27.7	26.5	13.6	39.6	96.1	2.2	...	1.0
12 31075	Holiday CDP	20,568	...	6.2	11.9	7.1	22.7	28.3	23.8	46.4	91.4	4.9	1.8	3.3
12 32000	Hollywood city	143,222	2.9	5.8	15.3	8.0	27.2	28.6	15.1	41.2	75.7	20.0	3.6	5.3
12 32275	Homestead city	62,129	4.0	10.8	20.5	9.7	32.5	18.5	8.0	30.4	76.8	19.0	3.3	2.3
12 32967	Hunters Creek CDP	20,132	...	6.9	15.0	9.1	31.9	29.4	7.7	36.9	77.2	11.4	9.8	3.7
12 33250	Immokalee CDP	22,760	...	11.5	22.8	17.0	28.0	15.0	5.7	24.4	65.9	18.7	...	17.0
12 35000	Jacksonville city	829,535	1.6	7.0	16.5	10.5	28.5	26.1	11.3	35.5	63.2	32.0	5.7	2.4
12 35050	Jacksonville Beach city	21,518	1.4	4.5	13.0	8.4	26.3	32.7	15.1	43.2	91.8	7.2	1.9	0.3
12 35875	Jupiter town	56,294	3.2	5.3	15.2	4.2	23.0	30.4	21.9	46.2	94.7	1.1	2.5	2.5
12 36062	Kendale Lakes CDP	59,230	...	4.2	13.5	9.3	29.5	28.0	15.6	40.8	93.8	2.8	2.2	2.4
12 36100	Kendall CDP	77,366	...	5.1	13.9	8.4	27.1	28.3	17.3	41.6	91.5	4.4	4.2	1.4
12 36121	Kendall West CDP	38,288	...	4.4	16.0	11.3	25.0	30.4	12.9	40.2	93.0	3.3	2.4	1.8
12 36462	Keystone CDP	23,555	...	4.3	21.0	6.9	17.8	37.2	12.8	45.0	89.5	...	5.6	1.1
12 36550	Key West city	24,870	1.5	5.4	9.3	9.4	31.7	32.1	12.1	40.2	87.3	9.6	2.2	1.8
12 36950	Kissimmee city	61,484	6.0	8.2	18.5	12.2	28.5	22.7	9.9	31.9	72.8	15.9	3.3	11.6
12 38250	Lakeland city	98,968	2.2	5.9	15.6	11.7	23.4	22.9	20.4	39.5	74.7	21.8	2.2	3.2
12 38350	Lake Magdalene CDP	28,783	...	3.3	14.2	8.3	23.8	31.6	18.8	45.2	80.5	10.9	3.9	6.3
12 38813	Lakeside CDP	31,438	...	4.8	17.2	11.3	24.4	29.3	12.9	40.3	83.8	11.2	4.6	3.8
12 39075	Lake Worth city	35,324	2.3	7.0	15.7	11.1	30.9	24.6	10.7	34.4	76.4	21.1	1.3	3.6
12 39200	Land O' Lakes CDP	33,621	...	5.1	19.3	7.4	24.0	31.1	13.1	40.8	93.3	4.5	1.7	3.0
12 39425	Largo city	77,769	0.1	3.9	11.3	7.5	24.4	28.1	24.9	47.4	88.5	8.6	4.4	1.8
12 39525	Lauderdale Lakes city	33,262	3.2	6.8	17.9	9.9	25.0	26.3	14.1	37.3	13.1	84.9	2.0	2.0
12 39550	Lauderhill city	68,110	3.1	7.6	16.5	11.0	25.8	26.8	12.3	37.1	17.4	79.2	3.1	2.5
12 39775	Lealman CDP	21,366	...	5.4	14.3	7.6	24.5	32.2	16.1	42.6	83.8	10.2	6.1	3.3
12 39875	Leesburg city	20,614	1.7	3.8	18.4	10.5	19.9	23.3	24.0	41.0	68.1	30.8	3.0	2.4
12 39925	Lehigh Acres CDP	97,531	...	7.9	20.7	9.4	26.8	23.0	12.2	33.2	69.5	21.1	1.5	11.4
12 39950	Leisure City CDP	22,880	...	6.9	19.4	13.5	23.6	25.8	10.7	33.7	76.0	22.1	1.4	2.0
12 43125	Margate city	54,266	3.0	4.9	13.3	9.1	25.2	28.6	18.9	43.1	65.7	27.5	5.4	5.0
12 43800	Meadow Woods CDP	23,464	...	3.9	19.5	9.6	31.5	28.9	6.6	35.4	74.9	12.3	7.7	7.9
12 43975	Melbourne city	76,656	0.9	4.6	13.6	10.2	22.1	28.7	20.8	44.5	86.5	11.2	4.1	1.9
12 44275	Merritt Island CDP	34,880	...	3.9	13.7	7.7	18.5	32.2	23.9	48.6	89.3	8.1	2.1	2.8
12 45000	Miami city	408,322	3.3	6.1	12.5	8.6	31.6	25.6	15.6	39.0	75.7	20.2	1.1	4.1
12 45025	Miami Beach city	89,541	2.8	6.0	9.8	6.7	37.1	25.0	15.2	39.7	74.5	5.8	2.3	18.8
12 45060	Miami Gardens city	109,331	3.0	6.2	18.4	11.9	27.5	24.8	11.2	34.3	18.8	78.8	0.6	2.9
12 45100	Miami Lakes town	30,016	3.1	6.2	17.0	9.1	28.2	26.7	12.7	38.4	93.5	3.5	2.6	...
12 45975	Miramar city	125,351	5.2	6.6	19.9	10.0	30.9	25.3	7.4	34.1	43.7	46.7	7.6	5.8
12 47625	Naples city	19,841	2.7	2.1	8.2	3.0	10.4	29.6	46.7	63.4	94.9	4.6	0.6	0.3
12 48050	Navarre CDP	31,500	...	6.2	20.4	9.5	28.0	27.4	8.7	36.1	89.4	8.1	3.1	3.5
12 48625	New Smyrna Beach city	22,715	1.4	5.1	10.5	4.1	17.3	33.3	29.7	54.5	92.2	6.1	...	...
12 49260	Northdale CDP	19,735	...	4.5	16.2	10.1	25.2	30.9	13.0	41.4	87.8	5.6	5.3	0.8
12 49350	North Fort Myers CDP	39,628	...	2.2	7.1	4.6	12.5	27.3	46.3	63.0	97.2	2.4	0.5	1.0
12 49425	North Lauderdale city	41,789	3.0	10.2	19.4	12.5	30.4	21.9	5.7	29.8	37.3	56.4	3.5	4.5

Table A-4. Cities — Who: Age, Race/Ethnicity, and Household Structure, 2010–2012—*Continued*

STATE and Place code	STATE or City	Percent Hispanic or Latino	Percent foreign born	Total households	Household type (percent)						Percent of households with people under 18 years	Percent of households with people 60 years and over
					Family households				Nonfamily households			
					Total family households	Married-couple families	Male household families	Female household families	Total nonfamily households	One-person households		
ACS table number:		B03003	C05003	B11001	B11001	B11001	B11001	B11001	B11001	B11001	B11005	B11006
Column number:		14	15	16	17	18	19	20	21	22	23	24
	Florida—Cont.											
12 12875	Clearwater city	12.1	14.2	47,178	53.9	35.8	4.1	14.0	46.1	39.4	22.6	45.2
12 12925	Clermont city	20.6	14.0	10,362	77.1	62.5	4.3	10.4	22.9	19.1	32.5	49.1
12 13275	Coconut Creek city	21.3	26.3	22,223	57.7	40.6	4.5	12.6	42.3	34.5	33.2	38.5
12 14125	Cooper City city	26.9	23.6	9,868	81.9	63.4	5.2	13.4	18.1	15.5	43.0	32.6
12 14250	Coral Gables city	53.4	38.0	17,731	60.6	52.2	2.2	6.2	39.4	33.8	21.3	40.5
12 14400	Coral Springs city	23.4	27.7	40,511	79.5	55.3	5.4	18.8	20.5	17.5	45.1	29.2
12 14412	Coral Terrace CDP	89.8	65.4	7,334	78.6	51.2	7.0	20.4	21.4	17.5	32.0	50.3
12 14895	Country Club CDP	77.1	53.6	14,987	75.8	43.0	7.3	25.5	24.2	17.8	44.9	28.6
12 15475	Crestview city	5.9	3.0	7,489	68.3	43.3	5.1	19.9	31.7	24.2	42.0	24.6
12 15968	Cutler Bay town	48.3	35.5	12,811	73.3	54.3	4.5	14.5	26.7	21.7	39.4	35.5
12 16335	Dania Beach city	25.5	30.1	12,040	55.9	33.3	3.8	18.8	44.1	36.5	27.2	34.8
12 16475	Davie town	32.3	25.5	32,146	69.2	48.2	4.8	16.1	30.8	22.3	39.3	31.5
12 16525	Daytona Beach city	7.9	9.0	25,186	46.9	28.6	4.0	14.3	53.1	43.3	18.1	39.4
12 16725	Deerfield Beach city	15.4	31.5	31,277	54.7	36.2	5.5	13.0	45.3	37.3	24.5	45.2
12 16875	DeLand city	11.2	7.4	9,475	61.2	41.8	5.2	14.2	38.8	36.5	30.5	50.9
12 17100	Delray Beach city	10.9	22.6	26,128	50.9	35.4	4.6	10.9	49.1	40.1	19.4	48.4
12 17200	Deltona city	31.1	8.4	27,727	74.6	57.8	5.3	11.5	25.4	21.0	33.3	38.8
12 17935	Doral city	79.9	62.0	13,682	82.0	65.0	3.7	13.3	18.0	13.2	56.2	19.3
12 18575	Dunedin city	6.8	10.1	15,803	54.1	41.7	3.0	9.4	45.9	38.2	19.3	51.8
12 19206	East Lake CDP	6.8	10.6	13,544	67.3	55.8	3.0	8.6	32.7	27.3	27.7	46.2
12 19212	East Lake-Orient Park CDP	20.7	13.2	8,801	61.1	32.5	5.1	23.5	38.9	32.8	37.8	23.9
12 19825	Edgewater city	1.9	3.1	8,545	67.1	52.2	4.3	10.5	32.9	26.4	20.9	47.4
12 20108	Egypt Lake-Leto CDP	64.1	37.8	13,770	61.8	39.0	6.3	16.5	38.2	29.6	35.0	27.7
12 20925	Ensley CDP	3.5	5.7	8,130	53.4	34.0	3.8	15.6	46.6	33.5	29.2	38.8
12 21150	Estero CDP	7.0	12.1	10,244	72.5	66.2	2.0	4.4	27.5	23.6	15.8	69.8
12 22275	Ferry Pass CDP	5.4	6.3	12,369	52.0	36.3	2.1	13.6	48.0	40.3	22.5	35.3
12 22660	Fleming Island CDP	8.1	6.6	10,645	82.3	68.8	1.5	12.0	17.7	14.1	46.8	22.8
12 24000	Fort Lauderdale city	14.4	21.9	72,479	44.4	29.4	4.4	10.5	55.6	43.3	20.0	37.1
12 24125	Fort Myers city	20.1	14.5	22,967	58.4	36.2	3.2	19.0	41.6	35.0	28.0	41.4
12 24300	Fort Pierce city	23.3	21.2	15,765	60.8	34.2	6.6	20.0	39.2	32.6	33.1	38.1
12 24475	Fort Walton Beach city	9.7	6.5	7,957	61.2	42.3	5.3	13.6	38.8	31.5	26.5	37.2
12 24562	Fountainebleau CDP	93.5	69.7	17,780	72.6	44.9	9.6	18.1	27.4	19.5	31.3	40.3
12 24581	Four Corners CDP	34.5	11.0	10,225	73.8	53.2	4.1	16.5	26.2	20.9	36.9	35.2
12 24925	Fruit Cove CDP	5.5	6.5	9,702	83.6	69.2	4.9	9.5	16.4	13.8	43.5	38.0
12 25175	Gainesville city	10.2	12.7	46,374	41.2	25.6	3.7	11.9	58.8	37.0	17.7	23.3
12 26300	Golden Gate CDP	63.7	46.4	6,734	78.9	45.0	9.3	24.6	21.1	16.2	52.5	25.6
12 26375	Golden Glades CDP	21.3	46.0	9,222	72.7	37.8	6.8	28.2	27.3	22.2	41.7	34.7
12 27322	Greenacres city	45.5	37.1	12,971	67.9	39.2	8.3	20.4	32.1	26.4	35.8	36.5
12 28400	Haines City city	38.1	23.9	6,948	69.8	41.1	6.3	22.5	30.2	25.1	42.5	38.2
12 28452	Hallandale Beach city	28.9	43.2	18,047	51.1	35.6	5.4	10.0	48.9	42.5	15.5	52.9
12 30000	Hialeah city	94.4	72.2	68,760	75.1	47.3	8.0	19.8	24.9	20.3	36.3	48.0
12 30025	Hialeah Gardens city	95.4	68.6	5,933	81.8	57.4	7.6	16.8	18.2	17.4	46.0	41.9
12 31075	Holiday CDP	9.5	7.7	8,602	57.5	42.9	5.0	9.6	42.5	37.6	23.0	51.4
12 32000	Hollywood city	32.2	32.8	54,825	58.8	40.4	4.6	13.8	41.2	33.3	28.2	37.4
12 32275	Homestead city	57.6	37.9	19,165	67.5	39.3	8.3	19.9	32.5	24.2	43.8	21.8
12 32967	Hunters Creek CDP	36.1	23.6	7,251	72.0	56.9	1.1	14.1	28.0	19.6	34.7	24.0
12 33250	Immokalee CDP	76.7	40.5	4,081	79.1	40.7	10.7	27.7	20.9	15.9	54.7	30.7
12 35000	Jacksonville city	8.1	9.6	310,528	63.3	42.6	4.5	16.1	36.7	30.6	31.4	30.8
12 35050	Jacksonville Beach city	3.0	5.5	9,616	52.5	38.7	3.4	10.4	47.5	35.4	21.2	34.5
12 35875	Jupiter town	12.4	12.2	24,036	62.6	53.0	2.5	7.2	37.4	31.6	26.1	43.4
12 36062	Kendale Lakes CDP	87.5	63.0	17,903	80.3	52.9	7.1	20.2	19.7	15.4	34.9	41.9
12 36100	Kendall CDP	64.2	46.2	28,328	65.9	47.5	3.9	14.5	34.1	29.1	27.4	40.0
12 36121	Kendall West CDP	89.3	62.9	11,184	79.0	51.6	4.5	22.9	21.0	16.9	39.0	36.0
12 36462	Keystone CDP	9.4	8.9	8,098	84.5	75.5	4.1	4.9	15.5	12.8	42.5	34.6
12 36550	Key West city	18.6	18.5	9,412	49.6	37.1	4.8	7.6	50.4	35.6	18.9	35.4
12 36950	Kissimmee city	60.6	25.8	20,514	70.8	42.9	5.1	22.7	29.2	22.1	41.7	30.0
12 38250	Lakeland city	13.0	9.0	39,776	58.6	40.0	4.4	14.2	41.4	35.0	26.1	44.5
12 38350	Lake Magdalene CDP	24.3	13.6	11,715	56.8	40.2	2.9	13.8	43.2	35.1	23.9	40.3
12 38813	Lakeside CDP	11.4	6.2	11,066	76.6	52.3	6.7	17.6	23.4	19.9	34.3	34.8
12 39075	Lake Worth city	44.0	39.1	11,363	57.3	32.9	9.0	15.4	42.7	29.6	32.6	30.8
12 39200	Land O' Lakes CDP	19.7	11.4	11,544	76.4	63.0	4.7	8.7	23.6	16.3	36.7	33.9
12 39425	Largo city	10.9	12.3	35,622	52.0	37.4	4.5	10.1	48.0	39.4	18.7	46.5
12 39525	Lauderdale Lakes city	7.3	47.8	11,309	66.7	31.4	9.0	26.3	33.3	29.9	36.5	40.8
12 39550	Lauderhill city	7.0	36.5	23,973	64.7	32.1	6.4	26.3	35.3	29.8	35.3	36.6
12 39775	Lealman CDP	8.5	10.9	8,894	50.2	27.7	5.0	17.4	49.8	38.8	21.2	45.2
12 39875	Leesburg city	8.8	6.3	8,280	60.8	41.2	3.9	15.7	39.2	34.1	25.7	49.1
12 39925	Lehigh Acres CDP	33.7	22.2	29,024	73.7	48.5	7.0	18.2	26.3	20.5	41.1	33.7
12 39950	Leisure City CDP	65.7	42.7	6,073	82.4	44.5	9.0	29.0	17.6	11.6	44.4	39.5
12 43125	Margate city	22.8	32.6	21,026	61.1	42.6	4.0	14.6	38.9	33.7	26.6	45.3
12 43800	Meadow Woods CDP	63.8	30.0	7,440	87.1	61.3	6.0	19.8	12.9	10.9	40.3	25.0
12 43975	Melbourne city	8.4	11.2	32,235	54.1	37.9	4.3	11.9	45.9	39.6	23.7	42.1
12 44275	Merritt Island CDP	7.3	8.3	14,127	65.8	46.6	5.7	13.4	34.2	28.3	24.6	47.4
12 45000	Miami city	70.4	58.3	149,591	55.4	31.1	6.6	17.7	44.6	36.5	26.3	37.3
12 45025	Miami Beach city	53.5	52.7	42,859	42.0	28.5	4.9	8.6	58.0	47.5	17.8	31.1
12 45060	Miami Gardens city	21.4	28.4	30,757	76.2	38.8	7.3	30.1	23.8	20.9	38.3	39.4
12 45100	Miami Lakes town	80.4	51.2	9,906	70.9	53.5	6.1	11.2	29.1	21.3	37.9	32.8
12 45975	Miramar city	37.4	44.8	37,820	78.4	49.7	5.0	23.7	21.6	18.5	50.0	23.9
12 47625	Naples city	6.1	14.8	9,712	58.6	53.8	1.2	3.6	41.4	37.4	10.0	74.9
12 48050	Navarre CDP	7.4	4.5	11,523	74.4	57.7	4.6	12.0	25.6	18.9	37.6	22.8
12 48625	New Smyrna Beach city	3.3	5.0	10,443	59.7	50.9	2.6	6.2	40.3	35.9	17.1	54.9
12 49260	Northdale CDP	25.5	17.5	7,665	66.8	50.6	4.7	11.4	33.2	25.1	29.9	34.5
12 49350	North Fort Myers CDP	6.6	7.6	18,810	54.6	47.3	2.6	4.7	45.4	39.8	10.5	74.3
12 49425	North Lauderdale city	22.9	41.0	11,607	75.2	44.6	5.4	25.2	24.8	16.5	50.3	24.7

Table A-4. Cities — Who: Age, Race/Ethnicity, and Household Structure, 2010–2012—*Continued*

STATE and Place code	STATE or City	Total population	Percent change 2010–2012	Population by age (percent) Under 5 years	5 to 17 years	18 to 24 years	25 to 44 years	45 to 64 years	65 years and over	Median age	Race alone or in combination (percent) White	Black	Asian, Hawaiian, or Pacific Islander	American Indian, Alaska Native, or some other race
	ACS table number:	B01003	Population estimates	B01001	B01001	B01001	B01001	B01001	B01001	B01002	B02008	B02009	B02011 + B02012	B02010 + B02013
	Column number:	1	2	3	4	5	6	7	8	9	10	11	12	13
	Florida—Cont.													
12 49450	North Miami city	59,860	2.8	6.9	16.3	12.4	26.9	26.7	10.8	35.9	34.5	58.9	2.3	5.0
12 49475	North Miami Beach city	42,422	3.1	4.8	17.3	10.2	29.6	26.7	11.4	36.6	51.0	45.0	3.6	1.2
12 49675	North Port city	57,831	1.7	5.6	17.5	7.7	23.2	26.4	19.6	41.9	88.3	9.9	1.3	3.0
12 50575	Oakland Park city	42,191	3.2	7.8	13.1	8.4	31.2	28.9	10.6	38.4	68.3	26.0	3.4	5.3
12 50638	Oak Ridge CDP	19,946	...	9.0	11.0	11.7	34.4	25.3	8.5	35.3	52.9	38.9	6.1	6.5
12 50750	Ocala city	56,616	1.0	7.2	16.3	10.8	26.0	22.8	17.0	35.9	71.0	23.3	4.0	4.7
12 51075	Ocoee city	37,127	6.7	7.4	20.1	11.1	28.3	24.7	8.4	34.4	66.2	24.3	4.3	9.3
12 53000	Orlando city	243,895	4.5	7.3	14.6	12.2	34.8	21.6	9.4	32.4	60.2	30.3	4.5	7.8
12 53150	Ormond Beach city	38,251	0.5	3.3	12.7	7.5	20.3	28.5	27.6	49.8	88.9	6.3	3.6	1.8
12 53575	Oviedo city	34,426	5.1	7.0	20.8	9.1	28.7	27.1	7.3	35.0	85.7	6.8	7.5	2.3
12 53725	Pace CDP	19,356	...	6.8	18.9	6.6	24.1	30.2	13.4	39.9	91.3	5.2	3.9	4.5
12 54000	Palm Bay city	103,606	0.8	6.0	17.3	8.7	22.8	28.7	16.4	40.6	78.5	19.1	2.7	3.5
12 54075	Palm Beach Gardens city	49,200	2.7	4.3	12.6	6.5	23.1	27.9	25.8	47.0	91.8	5.1	2.9	0.8
12 54175	Palm City CDP	22,911	...	3.3	17.6	6.6	16.0	31.6	25.0	48.6	97.5	1.2	1.5	0.4
12 54200	Palm Coast city	76,474	2.5	4.9	16.0	6.7	21.0	27.2	24.2	45.9	79.8	14.0	3.1	5.7
12 54275	Palmetto Bay village	23,873	3.0	4.5	22.4	8.2	20.7	30.6	13.6	41.2	87.6	6.2	6.4	1.2
12 54350	Palm Harbor CDP	58,688	...	3.4	13.1	6.4	18.5	32.8	25.8	50.0	96.0	1.6	2.0	0.2
12 54387	Palm River-Clair Mel CDP	21,438	...	6.7	18.0	8.2	28.3	27.3	11.5	38.5	64.8	30.8	1.6	5.0
12 54450	Palm Springs village	20,124	2.2	7.8	17.6	8.0	29.7	25.6	11.2	35.2	79.2	17.1	3.0	1.3
12 54525	Palm Valley CDP	20,698	...	3.1	18.5	6.7	19.5	36.9	15.4	46.2	94.1	2.8	4.8	...
12 54700	Panama City city	35,829	1.6	5.7	15.3	10.6	24.4	26.9	17.1	40.0	78.4	20.0	4.4	3.2
12 55125	Parkland city	24,891	6.7	6.7	23.3	7.8	26.0	29.4	6.7	38.1	85.0	6.2	7.4	...
12 55775	Pembroke Pines city	157,847	3.3	5.2	16.8	8.3	27.2	27.5	15.0	39.9	70.6	20.9	6.0	5.8
12 55925	Pensacola city	52,083	0.6	4.9	13.8	9.7	24.4	29.4	17.8	42.6	72.3	25.7	3.3	1.9
12 56825	Pine Hills CDP	64,798	...	7.0	23.2	8.8	27.5	23.3	10.1	33.1	15.3	75.6	4.0	7.9
12 56975	Pinellas Park city	49,411	1.2	5.7	12.7	8.6	25.4	27.9	19.7	43.1	86.2	5.9	7.4	3.2
12 57425	Plantation city	86,708	3.1	5.6	15.5	6.6	28.6	29.3	14.4	40.5	70.5	23.8	4.6	4.1
12 57550	Plant City city	35,443	3.2	8.3	20.6	8.5	28.3	23.3	10.8	31.8	80.1	14.1	1.2	7.5
12 57900	Poinciana CDP	53,561	...	5.8	21.1	8.7	23.8	26.6	14.1	38.3	66.0	27.3	3.8	7.1
12 58050	Pompano Beach city	101,596	2.9	6.1	12.6	8.1	27.2	27.4	18.6	42.1	66.2	30.8	1.4	2.6
12 58350	Port Charlotte CDP	54,790	...	3.6	12.8	6.8	18.0	30.4	28.4	51.6	87.7	10.0	2.9	1.5
12 58575	Port Orange city	56,612	0.4	3.7	14.5	7.7	20.3	30.6	23.2	47.9	93.0	3.8	2.3	2.5
12 58715	Port St. Lucie city	166,927	2.1	6.4	18.2	8.3	24.7	26.2	16.3	39.5	77.2	18.1	3.0	6.5
12 58975	Princeton CDP	23,529	...	7.7	22.2	11.9	29.0	21.8	7.4	30.9	67.2	32.3	1.8	1.2
12 60230	Richmond West CDP	36,064	...	4.1	19.9	10.4	28.3	26.0	11.3	38.7	82.5	10.5	2.4	6.1
12 60950	Riverview CDP	70,107	...	8.1	18.5	8.0	31.2	25.2	8.9	35.5	75.1	17.7	4.6	6.2
12 60975	Riviera Beach city	32,822	1.8	9.5	17.1	10.6	25.8	24.5	12.5	35.5	28.2	68.9	3.0	1.4
12 61500	Rockledge city	25,206	1.7	5.4	15.8	8.3	19.7	32.4	18.4	45.3	77.2	19.9	2.4	2.0
12 62100	Royal Palm Beach village	34,656	2.7	4.5	22.7	8.5	25.0	27.6	11.7	37.7	71.9	21.1	6.9	1.8
12 62625	St. Cloud city	37,671	8.1	7.9	16.5	9.3	28.1	26.4	11.9	36.1	88.9	6.8	2.7	2.6
12 63000	St. Petersburg city	245,623	0.7	5.3	13.8	8.7	26.3	29.8	16.0	41.9	70.8	25.6	4.4	1.7
12 63650	Sanford city	54,146	1.8	7.1	21.0	9.3	29.7	22.9	10.0	33.2	68.5	27.3	5.0	2.9
12 64175	Sarasota city	52,420	1.3	4.7	12.2	9.3	23.8	27.4	22.6	45.0	82.1	16.0	1.8	2.7
12 64825	Sebastian city	22,124	1.9	4.0	15.4	5.9	16.5	31.3	26.9	50.4	93.2	6.7	1.8	1.0
12 67258	South Bradenton CDP	22,603	...	6.3	12.7	9.3	21.0	26.6	24.0	45.7	79.8	16.1	2.0	5.9
12 67575	South Miami Heights CDP	36,700	...	5.1	18.9	8.3	26.8	27.4	13.5	38.3	73.2	22.9	2.0	3.1
12 68350	Spring Hill CDP	101,103	...	5.2	16.4	7.3	21.0	26.8	23.3	45.1	90.8	5.6	2.1	4.1
12 69250	Sun City Center CDP	19,014	...	1.1	1.1	1.2	3.7	18.8	74.1	73.4	92.1	7.8	...	...
12 69555	Sunny Isles Beach city	21,263	3.0	1.9	11.5	5.7	24.3	28.6	28.0	48.0	91.7	6.2	0.9	1.5
12 69700	Sunrise city	86,648	4.9	6.2	15.2	8.1	29.0	26.3	15.1	38.6	58.6	33.4	5.9	4.6
12 70345	Sweetwater city	20,329	2.7	6.1	14.2	12.0	28.5	26.0	13.2	38.3	95.5	0.9	...	2.6
12 70600	Tallahassee city	184,079	2.8	5.1	11.8	30.4	26.7	17.9	8.2	26.1	59.2	36.4	4.6	2.6
12 70675	Tamarac city	61,657	3.1	4.5	12.2	5.7	25.6	24.8	27.2	46.7	69.3	25.9	2.9	4.5
12 70700	Tamiami CDP	55,567	...	4.1	13.9	10.8	25.3	28.6	17.3	42.2	97.5	1.5	0.3	0.8
12 71000	Tampa city	343,677	3.2	6.4	15.9	12.2	29.8	24.8	10.9	34.5	65.8	27.9	4.5	4.8
12 71150	Tarpon Springs city	23,544	0.8	3.3	12.4	5.1	20.2	31.4	27.7	50.7	92.2	6.5	2.0	0.4
12 71400	Temple Terrace city	25,004	2.3	6.5	15.7	13.1	26.8	24.5	13.4	35.0	77.0	16.7	5.2	4.4
12 71564	The Acreage CDP	40,372	...	4.6	18.5	8.8	26.3	31.4	10.4	40.3	83.6	14.3	2.6	1.1
12 71567	The Crossings CDP	25,431	...	6.9	17.2	8.2	29.5	27.7	10.5	37.1	87.8	4.3	2.2	5.9
12 71569	The Hammocks CDP	54,791	...	5.7	16.6	14.0	25.9	27.1	10.6	35.2	88.9	6.9	3.0	1.8
12 71625	The Villages CDP	54,036	...	0.0	0.0	0.2	2.4	25.1	72.2	69.3	98.9	0.3	0.6	0.3
12 71900	Titusville city	43,803	0.3	5.3	14.3	9.1	22.1	28.0	21.3	44.5	81.1	16.7	2.2	2.6
12 72145	Town 'n' Country CDP	80,664	...	4.8	15.8	9.5	30.4	27.1	12.3	38.5	81.8	9.7	4.8	6.2
12 73163	University CDP (Hillsborough County)	40,398	...	9.3	12.0	21.9	30.9	17.3	8.6	28.0	54.9	31.6	6.1	10.5
12 73172	University CDP (Orange County)	27,999	...	4.4	10.1	53.1	17.1	11.2	4.1	20.7	79.9	14.2	6.1	2.3
12 73287	University Park CDP	27,458	...	3.4	13.3	12.9	24.7	25.2	20.5	41.1	91.8	5.7	0.6	2.1
12 73700	Valrico CDP	36,170	...	6.8	18.8	7.4	24.7	27.9	14.5	39.3	81.8	13.5	5.0	4.9
12 73900	Venice city	20,885	1.4	2.3	4.7	2.7	10.5	26.1	53.7	66.7	98.2	0.8	1.2	0.3
12 74200	Vero Beach South CDP	21,979	...	6.2	14.6	5.7	20.4	27.8	25.4	47.0	94.2	5.6	...	0.3
12 75725	Wekiwa Springs CDP	24,198	...	2.4	17.6	8.9	20.3	33.3	17.5	45.5	92.8	2.8	4.7	0.5
12 75812	Wellington village	57,712	3.2	4.8	21.2	8.1	23.3	30.4	12.2	40.6	81.4	14.0	5.0	2.1
12 75875	Wesley Chapel CDP	43,129	...	6.9	20.9	6.4	33.0	24.9	7.9	34.2	79.9	11.4	6.4	5.4
12 76062	Westchase CDP	22,308	...	8.1	20.5	4.0	31.4	26.4	9.6	37.9	80.8	12.6	7.6	2.4
12 76075	Westchester CDP	30,308	...	4.9	12.2	9.7	24.0	28.2	21.1	44.2	97.1	2.0	0.4	1.2
12 76487	West Little River CDP	31,381	...	5.9	16.3	9.4	26.4	28.0	14.0	39.9	45.8	52.1	0.6	3.5
12 76582	Weston city	66,603	3.3	4.8	26.5	7.7	24.1	29.3	7.7	38.4	88.2	5.4	5.1	4.1
12 76600	West Palm Beach city	100,940	1.8	5.9	12.6	10.0	28.1	26.1	17.3	39.7	64.2	31.0	2.2	3.8
12 76675	West Pensacola CDP	20,920	...	5.7	17.1	11.6	25.6	27.1	13.0	35.7	52.5	46.3	4.8	2.3
12 78250	Winter Garden city	35,951	6.2	8.1	20.2	7.2	31.9	23.4	9.3	35.0	66.6	19.8	4.4	11.8

STATE and Place code	STATE or City	Percent Hispanic or Latino	Percent foreign born	Total households	Household type (percent)							Percent of households with people under 18 years	Percent of households with people 60 years and over
					Family households				Nonfamily households				
					Total family households	Married-couple families	Male household families	Female household families	Total nonfamily households	One-person households			
ACS table number:		B03003	C05003	B11001	B11001	B11001	B11001	B11001	B11001	B11001		B11005	B11006
Column number:		14	15	16	17	18	19	20	21	22		23	24
	Florida—Cont.												
12 49450	North Miami city	26.7	49.1	17,550	65.9	36.7	6.0	23.2	34.1	27.9		36.9	36.1
12 49475	North Miami Beach city	33.4	52.9	13,829	64.9	39.3	8.0	17.5	35.1	29.0		34.9	34.0
12 49675	North Port city	8.6	12.5	21,768	71.8	55.8	5.3	10.7	28.2	21.3		33.1	43.8
12 50575	Oakland Park city	26.7	30.4	17,469	49.2	26.9	5.8	16.6	50.8	39.5		27.6	28.9
12 50638	Oak Ridge CDP	43.8	38.9	7,213	63.6	31.6	6.7	25.3	36.4	27.9		32.4	24.2
12 50750	Ocala city	12.0	7.3	21,767	59.4	37.6	4.0	17.8	40.6	33.9		28.3	37.7
12 51075	Ocoee city	20.8	18.8	11,188	79.9	58.2	6.4	15.4	20.1	16.6		42.7	26.2
12 53000	Orlando city	26.7	18.9	98,916	53.0	30.4	4.6	18.0	47.0	36.3		27.3	23.2
12 53150	Ormond Beach city	3.9	8.6	15,829	63.6	50.1	4.6	8.9	36.4	31.0		19.7	55.4
12 53575	Oviedo city	14.4	12.2	9,982	83.4	71.0	3.9	8.5	16.6	13.1		44.0	26.3
12 53725	Pace CDP	5.3	2.7	7,049	75.6	64.6	3.0	8.1	24.4	20.3		36.2	35.6
12 54000	Palm Bay city	14.1	12.8	36,939	70.1	49.5	5.2	15.4	29.9	24.5		32.8	41.1
12 54075	Palm Beach Gardens city	9.6	14.1	21,936	59.6	47.5	2.3	9.8	40.4	33.6		21.7	48.4
12 54175	Palm City CDP	5.6	5.7	8,799	71.9	63.2	1.6	7.2	28.1	26.7		29.3	50.9
12 54200	Palm Coast city	10.5	16.4	27,054	70.9	58.6	3.5	8.8	29.1	23.2		23.7	54.0
12 54275	Palmetto Bay village	35.7	26.8	7,444	82.1	65.8	5.2	11.0	17.9	15.6		40.7	39.3
12 54350	Palm Harbor CDP	6.1	10.7	26,189	61.3	49.4	2.3	9.6	38.7	33.4		20.7	50.2
12 54387	Palm River-Clair Mel CDP	39.9	21.3	7,265	71.0	47.1	7.4	16.6	29.0	23.6		37.0	34.6
12 54450	Palm Springs village	47.9	40.3	7,169	62.5	36.1	5.6	20.8	37.5	30.0		38.7	34.6
12 54525	Palm Valley CDP	6.0	6.5	8,080	68.8	60.7	0.4	7.6	31.2	23.2		28.5	38.6
12 54700	Panama City city	8.1	5.9	15,219	55.7	35.5	4.7	15.5	44.3	35.5		26.4	35.3
12 55125	Parkland city	15.9	20.0	7,486	86.1	72.0	3.3	10.9	13.9	10.6		50.3	25.4
12 55775	Pembroke Pines city	44.3	35.9	56,871	69.4	51.4	3.6	14.4	30.6	27.4		35.1	37.6
12 55925	Pensacola city	4.5	6.3	22,416	55.8	35.7	5.5	14.6	44.2	37.1		23.3	39.7
12 56825	Pine Hills CDP	11.4	28.0	19,833	70.4	39.2	5.4	25.8	29.6	24.4		39.4	31.8
12 56975	Pinellas Park city	11.8	14.8	20,236	58.1	41.0	6.2	10.9	41.9	35.3		24.9	42.4
12 57425	Plantation city	19.6	26.2	33,427	64.3	46.4	3.9	14.0	35.7	27.7		29.7	34.6
12 57550	Plant City city	30.0	15.7	12,147	69.0	45.6	4.6	18.9	31.0	26.9		39.1	34.5
12 57900	Poinciana CDP	51.1	18.3	17,236	81.9	62.4	4.0	15.5	18.1	14.9		39.8	43.7
12 58050	Pompano Beach city	16.8	24.9	41,231	52.6	33.0	5.6	14.0	47.4	38.5		23.6	42.1
12 58350	Port Charlotte CDP	8.8	12.8	22,864	61.9	46.2	4.6	11.1	38.1	33.6		22.0	58.5
12 58575	Port Orange city	3.4	7.3	22,707	63.1	51.3	2.3	9.5	36.9	30.6		22.6	49.7
12 58715	Port St. Lucie city	18.7	16.3	58,095	74.5	55.2	5.8	13.5	25.5	20.2		34.7	40.1
12 58975	Princeton CDP	57.9	37.3	5,888	87.0	49.7	10.7	26.6	13.0	10.8		52.2	28.2
12 60230	Richmond West CDP	75.4	51.2	9,073	93.4	68.8	5.5	19.1	6.6	4.9		51.5	37.1
12 60950	Riverview CDP	19.3	11.4	23,683	73.2	55.7	5.4	12.1	26.8	19.3		39.4	25.9
12 60975	Riviera Beach city	6.8	15.3	11,602	60.9	31.6	6.0	23.3	39.1	34.0		32.1	35.0
12 61500	Rockledge city	8.1	8.7	9,841	70.8	54.7	2.7	13.5	29.2	22.8		29.8	43.6
12 62100	Royal Palm Beach village	22.8	18.7	11,246	77.6	59.1	3.5	15.0	22.4	18.8		40.7	34.7
12 62625	St. Cloud city	31.3	10.4	13,323	71.8	47.0	6.0	18.7	28.2	22.7		39.4	32.3
12 63000	St. Petersburg city	7.1	10.8	104,131	53.6	35.2	4.7	13.6	46.4	38.1		23.7	36.7
12 63650	Sanford city	21.0	10.8	17,693	63.1	40.9	3.1	19.1	36.9	31.0		37.4	30.3
12 64175	Sarasota city	16.5	16.4	22,018	52.4	34.3	4.7	13.5	47.6	37.4		21.9	45.5
12 64825	Sebastian city	6.5	6.8	9,205	64.7	48.2	3.5	12.9	35.3	31.0		24.7	55.2
12 67258	South Bradenton CDP	17.1	15.8	10,188	54.4	35.7	5.5	13.2	45.6	38.8		21.0	44.2
12 67575	South Miami Heights CDP	69.9	50.5	10,400	73.9	42.9	8.4	22.6	26.1	23.4		41.1	42.5
12 68350	Spring Hill CDP	14.2	7.3	38,976	69.5	52.5	3.8	13.2	30.5	26.0		27.3	51.1
12 69250	Sun City Center CDP	2.8	7.4	11,215	50.3	46.6	0.3	3.4	49.7	47.4		2.6	91.5
12 69555	Sunny Isles Beach city	38.2	57.7	11,352	45.0	33.1	5.2	6.7	55.0	48.7		14.8	45.5
12 69700	Sunrise city	27.0	36.2	31,170	66.8	45.6	4.7	16.4	33.2	27.2		32.1	38.7
12 70345	Sweetwater city	95.6	73.2	5,646	78.1	46.2	5.7	26.1	21.9	15.2		38.7	39.4
12 70600	Tallahassee city	6.4	7.9	72,525	46.6	29.1	3.8	13.8	53.4	33.9		23.9	21.7
12 70675	Tamarac city	25.7	31.1	27,172	55.6	36.0	4.7	14.9	44.4	38.8		23.5	54.0
12 70700	Tamiami CDP	93.6	67.6	15,503	84.4	59.5	8.2	16.6	15.6	12.1		38.7	46.3
12 71000	Tampa city	22.7	15.6	135,990	54.6	33.7	4.6	16.4	45.4	36.6		29.0	28.5
12 71150	Tarpon Springs city	5.1	11.4	9,862	61.1	46.3	1.9	12.9	38.9	34.6		22.0	52.4
12 71400	Temple Terrace city	13.5	12.3	10,337	51.7	34.6	3.5	13.6	48.3	42.8		28.7	30.9
12 71564	The Acreage CDP	16.4	15.4	11,969	82.8	70.2	5.4	7.2	17.2	11.9		40.9	29.0
12 71567	The Crossings CDP	67.3	46.3	8,195	72.4	52.6	5.4	14.5	27.6	23.0		37.5	31.3
12 71569	The Hammocks CDP	76.2	51.8	16,375	78.0	54.7	4.0	19.2	22.0	18.9		41.2	30.7
12 71625	The Villages CDP	1.7	...	29,690	73.5	69.9	0.8	2.7	26.5	24.0		0.1	97.6
12 71900	Titusville city	5.2	4.7	17,742	64.5	45.3	5.1	14.1	35.5	29.1		26.4	45.1
12 72145	Town 'n' Country CDP	43.9	26.2	29,746	63.4	43.2	5.1	15.1	36.6	26.5		31.3	32.3
12 73163	University CDP (Hillsborough County)	32.4	21.6	16,096	44.7	19.9	5.8	19.0	55.3	42.2		27.7	19.5
12 73172	University CDP (Orange County)	25.0	12.7	5,958	49.6	33.2	3.4	13.0	50.4	30.4		30.0	17.0
12 73287	University Park CDP	89.9	64.4	8,181	73.6	52.5	3.1	18.0	26.4	20.1		32.4	56.3
12 73700	Valrico CDP	15.5	7.3	12,320	77.5	64.8	3.0	9.7	22.5	19.2		36.3	38.8
12 73900	Venice city	3.4	6.8	11,177	53.0	46.5	0.5	5.9	47.0	42.7		8.4	75.7
12 74200	Vero Beach South CDP	9.6	7.5	9,045	61.2	45.3	4.0	11.9	38.8	34.5		25.2	51.4
12 75725	Wekiwa Springs CDP	9.4	10.4	8,647	73.1	57.3	4.2	11.6	26.9	22.8		29.2	40.0
12 75812	Wellington village	16.7	20.8	19,195	79.9	66.5	2.5	10.9	20.1	16.7		40.5	31.6
12 75875	Wesley Chapel CDP	19.1	13.8	15,129	73.1	58.0	4.8	10.3	26.9	20.5		41.8	27.3
12 76062	Westchase CDP	13.9	13.2	8,165	69.3	58.7	3.5	7.1	30.7	24.0		40.4	27.3
12 76075	Westchester CDP	91.9	59.1	9,141	78.9	58.1	3.3	17.5	21.1	17.7		33.6	53.3
12 76487	West Little River CDP	49.7	40.2	9,306	69.9	33.7	8.2	28.0	30.1	27.3		37.7	44.0
12 76582	Weston city	47.6	41.2	20,818	81.9	66.6	4.4	10.9	18.1	14.4		52.8	26.2
12 76600	West Palm Beach city	22.1	25.7	41,680	51.3	31.6	4.7	15.0	48.7	38.9		23.2	38.3
12 76675	West Pensacola CDP	4.8	6.9	7,796	60.1	29.3	6.6	24.2	39.9	33.0		30.4	33.8
12 78250	Winter Garden city	22.3	14.9	11,891	75.6	62.2	3.5	9.9	24.4	19.4		42.6	21.8

Table A-4. Cities — Who: Age, Race/Ethnicity, and Household Structure, 2010–2012—*Continued*

STATE and Place code	STATE or City	Total population	Percent change 2010–2012	Population by age (percent)						Median age	Race alone or in combination (percent)		Asian, Hawaiian, or Pacific Islander	American Indian, Alaska Native, or some other race
				Under 5 years	5 to 17 years	18 to 24 years	25 to 44 years	45 to 64 years	65 years and over		White	Black		
	ACS table number:	B01003	Population estimates	B01001	B01001	B01001	B01001	B01001	B01001	B01002	B02008	B02009	B02011 + B02012	B02010 + B02013
	Column number:	1	2	3	4	5	6	7	8	9	10	11	12	13
	Florida—Cont.													
12 78275	Winter Haven city	34,509	3.0	6.1	16.8	7.5	22.0	25.7	21.8	42.3	67.3	29.7	2.7	1.4
12 78300	Winter Park city	28,408	3.5	4.7	14.0	14.6	20.6	27.5	18.6	40.7	88.0	7.6	3.8	2.9
12 78325	Winter Springs city	33,413	0.8	4.2	17.3	10.5	25.4	29.4	13.3	38.7	91.6	5.9	2.3	2.9
12 78800	Wright CDP	25,774	...	8.6	15.0	12.8	29.1	25.2	9.3	31.7	68.5	19.4	7.5	12.5
13 00000	**Georgia**	9,815,725	2.1	6.9	18.4	10.2	27.9	25.5	11.0	35.6	62.2	31.8	4.0	4.2
13 00408	Acworth city	20,811	3.5	7.6	21.8	7.6	30.6	22.4	10.0	35.6	61.5	29.3	4.1	4.4
13 01052	Albany city	77,546	-0.3	7.9	18.2	13.1	26.1	23.0	11.7	31.9	25.6	72.4	1.4	2.0
13 01696	Alpharetta city	59,751	7.2	8.6	21.9	5.7	30.1	25.9	7.9	35.8	73.9	11.3	5.3	3.0
13 03440	Athens-Clarke County unified government	117,331	2.5	5.9	11.5	30.6	26.8	16.5	8.7	25.9	67.8	27.5	5.1	2.1
13 04000	Atlanta city	432,752	5.0	6.4	12.3	14.6	34.9	22.0	9.7	33.2	40.7	54.5	4.3	2.6
13 04204	Augusta-Richmond County, consolidated	196,200	0.8	7.3	17.1	12.4	26.9	24.6	11.7	33.3	41.2	56.8	2.8	2.3
13 12834	Candler-McAfee CDP	21,731	...	7.3	11.3	8.1	26.7	29.8	16.7	42.2	9.5	90.2	...	0.8
13 12988	Canton city	23,410	3.2	8.0	21.6	6.6	33.0	21.6	9.2	32.5	76.0	11.0	2.0	12.3
13 13492	Carrollton city	24,568	2.5	7.2	16.6	23.9	25.9	17.4	9.1	26.3	64.1	31.5	2.6	2.6
13 19000	Columbus city	194,276	4.2	7.5	17.9	12.5	26.7	24.0	11.5	33.2	49.3	47.5	3.5	4.0
13 21380	Dalton city	33,314	0.6	9.2	19.7	9.1	29.7	21.9	10.4	32.0	82.6	9.6	3.7	6.8
13 23900	Douglasville city	31,144	0.8	8.8	20.0	9.3	31.2	22.9	7.7	33.6	39.1	59.7	1.6	1.1
13 24600	Duluth city	27,307	4.6	6.0	18.2	7.7	31.8	28.1	8.3	36.8	47.3	21.3	26.0	7.7
13 24768	Dunwoody city	46,730	2.0	6.8	16.8	7.4	34.2	22.3	12.6	36.4	70.8	11.8	15.3	4.4
13 25720	East Point city	34,732	5.0	7.6	16.4	11.7	27.3	27.4	9.6	35.9	15.9	76.4	2.0	5.8
13 28044	Evans CDP	31,768	...	6.2	21.4	8.2	23.5	29.1	11.6	39.7	78.1	13.5	8.3	2.2
13 31908	Gainesville city	34,331	2.8	10.6	19.6	13.2	28.3	17.2	11.1	28.9	65.0	17.4	3.1	15.7
13 35324	Griffin city	23,523	-1.0	8.2	17.9	10.5	25.8	24.1	13.4	34.8	42.6	54.8	1.6	3.1
13 38964	Hinesville city	34,161	4.9	10.7	18.7	14.7	30.5	20.7	4.7	27.5	43.5	49.7	5.5	6.7
13 42425	Johns Creek city	79,649	6.6	5.9	24.4	6.4	24.9	30.8	7.6	38.3	65.9	12.3	22.0	2.0
13 43192	Kennesaw city	30,503	2.9	7.0	19.5	10.2	32.9	22.2	8.3	34.0	64.9	26.6	6.0	6.1
13 44340	LaGrange city	30,107	2.4	7.9	20.3	12.9	22.5	23.0	13.3	33.0	46.0	50.0	2.6	2.8
13 45488	Lawrenceville city	28,975	3.5	8.7	23.1	10.3	27.1	21.6	9.3	32.0	36.3	38.2	10.1	16.4
13 48288	Mableton CDP	40,122	...	10.8	17.8	8.8	31.1	23.7	7.9	33.9	50.7	38.3	3.1	9.3
13 48624	McDonough city	22,479	1.5	8.1	21.7	6.9	32.2	22.7	8.4	32.4	43.0	54.4	4.0	...
13 49000	Macon city	91,675	-0.2	8.7	18.7	12.4	24.5	23.8	11.9	32.7	31.0	68.0	1.1	1.7
13 49756	Marietta city	57,564	2.8	8.1	14.2	11.4	33.8	22.5	10.0	34.3	57.1	32.2	3.3	9.0
13 50036	Martinez CDP	36,632	...	6.2	19.3	8.4	27.2	28.9	9.9	37.4	80.5	14.4	6.2	0.3
13 51670	Milton city	33,953	6.4	5.7	24.9	5.3	28.2	28.5	7.3	36.8	75.4	13.4	11.7	1.8
13 55020	Newnan city	33,754	2.5	9.2	20.7	8.6	29.5	21.7	10.2	34.2	65.3	32.1	2.3	1.8
13 56000	North Atlanta CDP	38,671	...	8.6	11.8	10.8	45.1	17.8	5.8	30.7	70.4	11.0	4.6	14.8
13 59724	Peachtree City city	34,576	0.4	3.6	22.3	7.8	21.1	32.8	12.4	42.2	84.3	9.3	7.0	2.3
13 62104	Pooler city	19,924	7.0	10.3	19.0	9.1	34.5	20.3	6.8	32.2	65.5	28.4	6.0	...
13 63952	Redan CDP	34,999	...	7.0	23.1	10.8	28.3	25.0	5.9	29.8	4.1	94.0	1.7	2.2
13 66668	Rome city	36,260	-0.5	9.6	16.4	11.3	25.9	22.3	14.5	32.8	60.4	27.9	2.2	11.9
13 67284	Roswell city	91,213	5.5	5.4	18.1	6.9	28.1	29.7	11.8	39.3	82.0	12.0	5.0	2.9
13 68516	Sandy Springs city	96,890	5.4	6.8	14.9	8.6	34.9	23.7	11.0	34.8	70.3	21.1	7.7	3.5
13 69000	Savannah city	139,667	3.7	7.1	15.2	16.2	27.3	22.4	11.8	31.2	42.0	55.2	2.9	1.7
13 71492	Smyrna city	51,990	2.5	8.8	13.4	8.3	40.0	21.4	8.1	34.2	55.3	32.6	6.6	7.0
13 73256	Statesboro city	29,239	4.3	3.1	9.1	51.3	17.7	11.9	6.9	21.9	55.4	41.1	3.8	2.0
13 73704	Stockbridge city	26,050	1.8	5.7	25.1	10.2	30.0	22.0	7.0	34.2	29.0	59.4	9.9	5.9
13 77652	Tucker CDP	27,470	...	6.7	15.7	3.8	32.3	26.1	15.4	40.0	69.3	17.3	12.1	2.6
13 78324	Union City city	20,027	4.8	11.5	22.3	8.4	30.2	20.0	7.6	29.0	10.3	86.3	...	3.5
13 78800	Valdosta city	56,216	4.7	7.8	14.3	23.8	24.3	19.6	10.3	27.3	44.5	52.4	2.9	3.8
13 80508	Warner Robins city	69,489	3.9	8.4	19.0	10.0	31.1	21.8	9.8	31.3	55.1	39.9	3.5	5.8
13 84176	Woodstock city	24,590	4.6	9.8	18.8	7.6	35.5	19.9	8.4	33.1	84.8	9.3	8.0	3.2
15 00000	**Hawaii**	1,378,239	2.1	6.4	15.6	9.7	26.7	26.9	14.7	38.5	42.4	3.1	83.0	5.0
15 06290	East Honolulu CDP	48,315	...	3.9	15.1	5.4	21.7	30.8	23.1	48.2	44.2	1.2	77.7	2.9
15 07470	Ewa Gentry CDP	21,935	...	8.5	17.1	11.9	32.7	23.2	6.5	32.6	39.1	4.8	91.4	3.2
15 14650	Hilo CDP	41,705	...	5.0	14.9	11.1	21.5	28.4	19.2	42.3	43.2	1.1	100.4	5.0
15 22700	Kahului CDP	27,312	...	6.3	17.5	9.5	26.3	23.6	16.8	38.3	26.4	1.3	103.9	6.8
15 23150	Kailua CDP (Honolulu County)	39,227	...	4.7	15.8	7.0	26.2	30.7	15.6	42.1	64.5	2.3	62.5	5.0
15 28250	Kaneohe CDP	33,234	...	5.3	13.4	8.7	25.8	27.8	19.1	42.4	46.2	1.8	91.5	5.4
15 51000	Mililani Mauka CDP	21,065	...	8.5	23.0	5.4	32.0	24.0	7.1	34.4	34.0	...	87.7	2.8
15 51050	Mililani Town CDP	29,969	...	5.4	17.2	9.1	23.8	30.8	13.7	40.2	44.0	4.7	92.3	4.0
15 62600	Pearl City CDP	49,316	...	7.5	14.3	8.8	25.7	24.5	19.2	40.4	32.9	3.7	94.2	5.5
15 71550	Urban Honolulu CDP	342,190	2.0	5.2	12.2	10.7	27.1	26.8	18.0	40.6	29.9	3.0	86.7	3.4
15 79700	Waipahu CDP	38,399	...	6.0	16.1	10.6	25.0	25.7	16.5	39.0	15.1	1.5	101.9	4.5
16 00000	**Idaho**	1,583,422	1.6	7.4	19.6	9.9	25.4	24.8	12.8	34.9	94.4	1.0	2.2	5.0
16 08830	Boise City city	209,292	2.9	6.3	15.3	11.3	28.7	26.3	12.0	36.1	92.7	2.0	5.4	3.3
16 12250	Caldwell city	47,130	2.5	10.4	20.6	12.3	27.9	18.7	10.1	29.0	93.3	0.8	3.2	5.7
16 16750	Coeur d'Alene city	44,973	2.9	6.1	16.3	12.2	25.5	25.3	14.6	35.3	96.2	0.3	2.2	3.0
16 23410	Eagle city	20,474	5.4	3.4	25.0	6.2	20.1	32.0	13.3	41.8	96.9	0.7	2.2	1.8
16 39700	Idaho Falls city	57,478	1.5	8.8	19.6	8.9	26.4	24.1	12.3	33.4	93.7	1.6	1.2	6.8
16 46540	Lewiston city	32,204	0.4	5.8	15.4	10.9	22.8	26.6	18.6	40.3	96.3	0.7	1.3	3.6
16 52120	Meridian city	77,936	6.4	8.0	24.6	6.4	29.8	21.9	9.2	33.2	97.0	1.7	2.2	1.7

Table A-4. Cities — Who: Age, Race/Ethnicity, and Household Structure, 2010–2012—*Continued*

STATE and Place code	STATE or City	Percent Hispanic or Latino	Percent foreign born	Total households	Household type (percent)						Percent of households with people under 18 years	Percent of households with people 60 years and over
					Family households				Nonfamily households			
					Total family households	Married-couple families	Male household families	Female household families	Total nonfamily households	One-person households		
ACS table number:		B03003	C05003	B11001	B11001	B11001	B11001	B11001	B11001	B11001	B11005	B11006
Column number:		14	15	16	17	18	19	20	21	22	23	24
	Florida—Cont.											
12 78275	Winter Haven city	12.5	12.3	13,501	63.8	44.1	4.8	14.9	36.2	32.2	29.2	49.1
12 78300	Winter Park city	8.6	7.6	11,331	55.9	44.9	3.2	7.9	44.1	34.6	22.1	40.7
12 78325	Winter Springs city	17.7	11.1	11,301	72.7	55.3	3.0	14.4	27.3	22.4	31.8	38.7
12 78800	Wright CDP	14.6	10.7	10,563	57.6	38.9	3.8	14.9	42.4	35.3	30.6	21.3
13 00000	**Georgia**	9.0	9.6	3,504,888	68.1	48.0	4.7	15.4	31.9	26.6	35.7	31.2
13 00408	Acworth city	8.0	19.3	7,908	66.8	46.2	7.3	13.3	33.2	25.6	44.1	25.8
13 01052	Albany city	2.6	2.2	29,538	60.5	29.2	5.0	26.4	39.5	33.9	32.3	32.3
13 01696	Alpharetta city	9.5	21.2	22,175	69.7	58.7	3.0	8.1	30.3	27.2	44.5	23.2
13 03440	Athens-Clarke County unified government	10.6	10.3	40,003	51.3	34.0	3.5	13.9	48.7	32.8	25.6	24.6
13 04000	Atlanta city	5.7	8.2	177,215	43.3	24.1	3.6	15.6	56.7	45.6	22.1	26.0
13 04204	Augusta-Richmond County, consolidated	4.4	3.4	70,152	62.0	34.9	5.4	21.6	38.0	32.9	32.0	31.2
13 12834	Candler-McAfee CDP	0.8	2.5	7,563	61.2	31.9	6.3	23.0	38.8	33.9	25.2	46.3
13 12988	Canton city	26.0	17.5	8,031	72.6	46.6	7.0	19.1	27.4	23.5	45.1	26.6
13 13492	Carrollton city	13.4	10.9	8,257	59.1	34.3	4.5	20.3	40.9	28.8	36.0	27.8
13 19000	Columbus city	6.8	5.2	71,509	64.6	38.4	4.0	22.2	35.4	31.1	35.1	32.4
13 21380	Dalton city	44.7	25.3	11,464	66.7	44.2	6.5	16.0	33.3	25.4	43.3	25.3
13 23900	Douglasville city	7.5	8.0	11,446	64.6	38.1	2.5	24.0	35.4	29.1	40.7	27.0
13 24600	Duluth city	10.0	29.8	10,470	67.5	49.8	4.4	13.3	32.5	27.4	36.4	23.4
13 24768	Dunwoody city	8.9	21.5	19,066	57.0	48.1	3.3	5.6	43.0	37.5	28.7	28.1
13 25720	East Point city	12.2	8.8	12,578	59.6	23.5	7.4	28.6	40.4	33.5	31.1	31.0
13 28044	Evans CDP	2.8	8.7	10,253	83.3	72.1	1.6	9.5	16.7	14.2	42.0	31.8
13 31908	Gainesville city	42.9	26.0	11,118	65.0	37.2	9.7	18.1	35.0	28.1	40.0	33.3
13 35324	Griffin city	5.0	4.7	8,557	65.2	35.8	5.5	23.9	34.8	29.9	35.5	36.5
13 38964	Hinesville city	12.5	7.9	12,581	76.9	51.9	6.0	19.0	23.1	19.8	45.2	16.3
13 42425	Johns Creek city	5.8	24.1	25,886	79.6	70.3	2.8	6.4	20.4	18.0	50.1	26.1
13 43192	Kennesaw city	12.9	19.0	11,515	61.7	43.8	3.3	14.7	38.3	30.2	39.3	20.5
13 44340	LaGrange city	5.0	7.0	11,395	65.3	32.8	5.9	26.6	34.7	29.4	35.8	33.4
13 45488	Lawrenceville city	25.3	29.0	9,475	70.1	42.0	3.6	24.4	29.9	25.4	46.7	26.6
13 48288	Mableton CDP	20.7	16.6	14,001	72.7	46.6	6.6	19.5	27.3	21.1	41.0	23.2
13 48624	McDonough city	3.3	8.3	7,775	63.2	42.1	3.8	17.3	36.8	30.7	37.9	18.9
13 49000	Macon city	2.6	2.6	33,184	59.6	27.6	4.0	28.0	40.4	34.7	32.0	33.8
13 49756	Marietta city	21.3	21.3	23,034	57.1	37.8	5.6	13.7	42.9	34.6	30.6	25.6
13 50036	Martinez CDP	3.3	7.6	13,522	71.7	53.9	4.1	13.6	28.3	22.2	35.4	32.1
13 51670	Milton city	4.9	16.1	11,813	83.0	71.7	1.9	9.4	17.0	15.2	46.2	21.2
13 55020	Newnan city	12.8	10.5	12,424	65.4	42.5	6.8	16.1	34.6	28.8	36.0	26.5
13 56000	North Atlanta CDP	34.3	31.6	15,514	47.4	36.4	4.7	6.3	52.6	39.9	23.6	16.0
13 59724	Peachtree City city	7.3	11.8	12,443	77.2	64.5	4.0	8.6	22.8	20.8	39.5	34.5
13 62104	Pooler city	4.9	14.9	7,169	68.4	55.8	3.4	9.2	31.6	26.9	41.3	19.5
13 63952	Redan CDP	1.8	7.6	11,080	72.4	29.9	7.3	35.2	27.6	23.4	44.2	23.1
13 66668	Rome city	19.4	12.7	13,400	58.5	39.5	3.2	15.8	41.5	32.7	35.0	38.4
13 67284	Roswell city	13.4	17.6	34,440	68.0	54.9	3.3	9.8	32.0	28.0	32.9	30.4
13 68516	Sandy Springs city	14.4	18.5	40,833	55.1	42.1	3.1	9.9	44.9	36.7	26.4	26.1
13 69000	Savannah city	5.2	6.2	51,445	54.8	29.3	5.3	20.2	45.2	36.1	28.3	32.1
13 71492	Smyrna city	13.7	14.8	22,946	54.5	36.4	3.8	14.3	45.5	38.1	30.4	21.2
13 73256	Statesboro city	2.1	4.9	9,985	42.0	20.8	3.6	17.6	58.0	26.4	20.1	20.3
13 73704	Stockbridge city	7.0	14.4	9,413	72.8	42.7	6.1	24.1	27.2	24.0	42.7	22.1
13 77652	Tucker CDP	11.5	23.0	10,631	63.5	49.9	3.6	10.0	36.5	30.4	30.3	33.7
13 78324	Union City city	6.7	8.8	7,748	55.7	17.9	2.1	35.7	44.3	38.3	40.9	22.8
13 78800	Valdosta city	4.6	5.3	21,259	55.6	30.7	4.2	20.7	44.4	31.4	30.8	27.5
13 80508	Warner Robins city	7.0	5.9	26,128	63.3	42.4	3.9	17.0	36.7	32.9	37.5	27.0
13 84176	Woodstock city	6.1	12.7	9,611	68.5	53.4	2.1	13.1	31.5	27.3	39.3	22.0
15 00000	**Hawaii**	9.2	18.1	447,566	68.7	50.8	5.4	12.5	31.3	24.2	33.1	41.7
15 06290	East Honolulu CDP	4.0	14.2	17,069	76.8	62.6	5.8	8.4	23.2	17.6	30.8	55.9
15 07470	Ewa Gentry CDP	8.3	20.6	6,561	75.7	59.4	7.4	8.9	24.3	17.2	45.9	22.2
15 14650	Hilo CDP	9.9	7.5	14,352	66.3	46.0	5.7	14.5	33.7	28.3	26.3	51.4
15 22700	Kahului CDP	8.9	32.1	6,730	77.5	55.6	5.5	16.4	22.5	17.4	43.0	43.9
15 23150	Kailua CDP (Honolulu County)	6.0	9.1	12,949	76.2	59.3	4.4	12.5	23.8	18.6	32.5	44.9
15 28250	Kaneohe CDP	8.0	7.7	10,905	75.4	53.2	8.5	13.7	24.6	19.4	28.2	46.6
15 51000	Mililani Mauka CDP	9.5	10.2	6,770	77.7	67.8	4.1	5.7	22.3	13.9	48.5	21.8
15 51050	Mililani Town CDP	8.7	12.3	9,316	83.0	65.8	6.0	11.2	17.0	14.2	37.0	45.4
15 62600	Pearl City CDP	11.0	12.9	14,410	78.4	58.2	5.7	14.5	21.6	18.4	34.4	54.4
15 71550	Urban Honolulu CDP	5.6	28.6	127,145	57.3	40.1	5.0	12.2	42.7	33.8	24.4	43.5
15 79700	Waipahu CDP	8.9	36.2	8,273	80.5	53.1	9.6	17.8	19.5	14.4	46.3	51.9
16 00000	**Idaho**	11.4	5.9	580,280	69.4	55.5	4.2	9.8	30.6	24.2	34.9	34.0
16 08830	Boise City city	7.5	7.2	86,763	59.3	44.1	5.4	9.8	40.7	31.2	28.7	30.5
16 12250	Caldwell city	35.0	9.8	15,979	69.3	48.6	4.6	16.1	30.7	25.0	42.1	28.0
16 16750	Coeur d'Alene city	4.0	3.2	19,137	56.8	41.1	3.8	11.9	43.2	31.5	28.8	35.4
16 23410	Eagle city	4.1	4.1	7,408	80.0	67.7	4.8	7.5	20.0	15.3	36.4	38.0
16 39700	Idaho Falls city	11.9	5.9	20,948	70.3	51.9	4.9	13.6	29.7	25.7	38.0	35.0
16 46540	Lewiston city	3.0	1.7	13,279	62.8	49.1	4.5	9.3	37.2	30.0	23.8	39.3
16 52120	Meridian city	6.4	4.6	26,876	78.5	63.5	4.5	10.5	21.5	18.1	44.6	27.0

Table A-4. Cities — Who: Age, Race/Ethnicity, and Household Structure, 2010–2012—*Continued*

STATE and Place code	STATE or City	Total population	Percent change 2010–2012	Population by age (percent)							Race alone or in combination (percent)			
				Under 5 years	5 to 17 years	18 to 24 years	25 to 44 years	45 to 64 years	65 years and over	Median age	White	Black	Asian, Hawaiian, or Pacific Islander	American Indian, Alaska Native, or some other race
	ACS table number:	B01003	Population estimates	B01001	B01001	B01001	B01001	B01001	B01001	B01002	B02008	B02009	B0201* + B02012	B02010 + B02013
	Column number:	1	2	3	4	5	6	7	8	9	10	11	12	13
	Idaho—Cont.													
16 54550	Moscow city...............	24,221	2.7	5.5	9.6	36.3	25.0	16.2	7.5	24.7	94.9	1.4	4.6	2.2
16 56260	Nampa city.................	82,786	2.5	9.3	23.2	9.7	27.8	19.1	11.0	30.3	92.6	1.2	1.7	6.9
16 64090	Pocatello city.............	54,549	0.9	7.3	17.9	15.3	26.5	22.6	10.4	30.6	94.1	1.4	2.9	4.1
16 64810	Post Falls city............	28,246	3.2	9.8	19.1	7.2	29.4	23.3	11.3	33.3	97.3	1.6	2.3	2.7
16 67420	Rexburg city..............	25,749	0.7	8.9	12.4	46.0	21.4	7.4	3.9	22.3	96.6	0.9	2.9	1.9
16 82810	Twin Falls city...........	44,845	1.5	8.6	18.6	12.3	27.1	20.4	13.0	32.1	92.3	1.3	2.4	6.5
17 00000	**Illinois**..................	12,858,490	0.3	6.4	17.6	9.7	27.1	26.2	12.8	36.8	74.3	15.4	5.4	7.1
17 00243	Addison village...........	36,784	0.7	6.7	19.5	8.7	27.5	26.8	10.8	33.8	84.7	3.3	7.5	6.2
17 00685	Algonquin village.........	29,461	-0.2	6.0	20.7	7.3	25.1	31.7	9.2	40.6	90.5	2.2	6.4	...
17 01114	Alton city.................	27,619	-1.5	6.8	18.7	9.2	27.7	24.0	13.6	34.2	73.4	25.9	1.3	2.7
17 02154	Arlington Heights village..........	75,337	0.8	6.3	15.4	7.3	24.5	28.8	17.7	41.9	88.0	2.2	8.5	2.5
17 03012	Aurora city................	196,491	0.9	8.7	22.3	9.4	32.4	20.4	6.8	31.0	58.8	11.2	7.5	25.8
17 04013	Bartlett village..........	41,459	0.8	5.9	20.3	7.2	27.5	29.6	9.5	36.8	77.5	4.2	15.1	4.3
17 04078	Batavia city...............	25,939	0.9	5.6	23.1	6.6	22.4	32.5	9.9	40.1	93.5	2.9	2.1	2.7
17 04845	Belleville city............	44,132	-1.6	5.6	16.0	7.6	29.4	28.8	12.5	38.4	74.2	23.7	3.5	2.0
17 05092	Belvidere city............	25,746	-0.7	6.3	22.8	10.7	26.5	22.4	11.4	34.3	85.8	3.9	1.6	10.5
17 05573	Berwyn city................	56,749	0.2	8.2	19.3	8.2	30.9	22.9	10.5	34.4	69.4	8.1	2.8	23.0
17 06587	Bloomingdale village..............	22,158	0.9	5.6	13.1	7.5	28.4	30.5	14.9	41.9	81.2	4.2	14.0	2.1
17 06613	Bloomington city..........	77,196	1.3	6.9	17.8	11.0	29.7	24.3	10.2	33.8	79.6	12.8	7.8	2.2
17 06704	Blue Island city..........	23,880	0.4	6.8	22.3	9.6	26.8	23.9	10.7	34.1	51.6	32.0	0.5	16.7
17 07133	Bolingbrook village........	72,849	0.7	7.5	21.1	9.7	29.8	24.9	7.1	34.2	60.2	23.1	12.0	7.9
17 09447	Buffalo Grove village......	41,879	0.4	4.9	17.9	6.1	24.8	34.0	12.3	42.9	82.2	2.3	15.2	1.3
17 09642	Burbank city..............	29,036	0.6	4.0	19.3	10.0	25.4	28.0	13.4	39.0	83.5	0.8	4.7	12.2
17 10487	Calumet City city.........	37,155	0.4	5.2	24.5	7.9	24.9	24.3	13.2	35.8	26.6	68.8	...	5.2
17 11163	Carbondale city...........	25,583	0.1	4.9	8.0	44.7	23.1	12.6	6.7	23.1	68.2	26.9	7.2	2.6
17 11332	Carol Stream village.......	39,613	1.2	5.4	17.2	11.0	26.7	31.0	8.7	36.6	77.9	5.1	14.8	3.2
17 11358	Carpentersville village...........	38,020	1.1	7.9	26.1	9.3	31.2	20.8	4.7	29.9	67.4	9.2	4.7	20.4
17 12385	Champaign city............	81,852	1.6	4.8	11.9	29.1	27.1	18.8	8.4	27.2	71.1	16.2	12.7	1.8
17 12567	Charleston city...........	21,994	0.2	3.1	10.1	44.4	17.4	15.8	9.2	23.1	89.5	8.5	2.4	1.5
17 14000	Chicago city..............	2,705,981	0.6	7.0	15.9	11.1	33.0	22.6	10.5	33.1	49.3	33.4	6.4	13.1
17 14026	Chicago Heights city.......	30,348	0.3	7.8	21.2	10.4	25.8	23.2	11.6	31.8	46.3	40.2	...	16.7
17 14351	Cicero town...............	84,035	0.2	9.3	24.7	10.9	33.5	16.2	5.4	28.3	39.4	4.3	0.6	57.6
17 15599	Collinsville city..........	25,778	-1.2	8.3	15.9	9.0	28.3	26.1	12.4	37.8	88.3	12.6	...	0.9
17 17458	Crest Hill city...........	21,043	0.0	6.8	14.0	6.6	33.4	25.1	14.1	37.2	70.4	19.6	3.5	9.8
17 17887	Crystal Lake city.........	40,269	-0.7	6.2	21.0	8.1	26.0	27.9	10.9	36.8	92.0	2.4	3.2	3.8
17 18563	Danville city.............	32,941	-1.1	7.5	18.7	10.0	24.3	24.6	14.9	37.0	65.6	32.0	1.9	3.2
17 18628	Darien city...............	22,216	0.9	4.8	16.3	7.2	19.5	33.6	18.6	46.7	86.4	4.2	10.0	...
17 18823	Decatur city..............	76,080	-0.9	6.9	15.7	10.1	23.5	27.1	16.7	39.1	74.7	25.9	1.7	1.3
17 19161	DeKalb city...............	44,778	-0.5	5.7	12.9	35.3	22.0	15.2	8.8	23.6	75.6	14.8	3.9	8.0
17 19642	Des Plaines city..........	58,499	0.7	6.0	13.2	7.4	27.0	29.8	16.6	42.4	80.8	1.1	13.2	6.1
17 20292	Dolton village............	23,221	0.4	4.7	20.0	11.5	25.6	27.3	10.8	35.4	7.0	92.7	...	1.1
17 20591	Downers Grove village......	49,857	1.0	5.9	17.5	7.5	23.7	30.9	14.6	41.7	88.4	3.4	6.7	2.3
17 22073	East Moline city..........	20,360	0.4	8.0	14.1	8.3	26.7	24.3	18.7	38.5	74.5	16.3	2.8	9.5
17 22164	East Peoria city..........	22,618	0.2	5.0	17.3	7.1	25.2	27.6	17.8	41.4	98.2	1.2	1.3	1.6
17 22255	East St. Louis city.......	26,830	-1.0	8.4	19.9	11.5	21.2	25.4	13.6	33.0	1.3	97.6	0.4	0.4
17 22697	Edwardsville city.........	24,250	0.7	4.8	15.4	23.0	22.5	22.7	11.7	31.7	90.3	7.7	2.8	...
17 23074	Elgin city................	110,400	1.4	10.3	19.4	8.7	30.0	22.6	9.0	32.6	69.4	7.3	6.0	20.0
17 23256	Elk Grove Village village..	33,260	0.6	5.7	14.0	8.3	24.5	32.5	15.0	43.3	84.6	1.3	10.1	5.7
17 23620	Elmhurst city.............	44,770	2.2	5.2	21.8	9.1	22.5	27.1	14.4	39.8	92.1	1.6	5.4	1.9
17 23724	Elmwood Park village.......	24,939	0.3	5.3	14.9	9.1	28.3	28.0	14.3	39.8	81.9	2.8	3.4	13.7
17 24582	Evanston city.............	75,018	1.1	5.8	15.0	16.7	27.5	23.8	11.3	33.5	71.0	19.3	10.1	2.9
17 27884	Freeport city.............	25,418	-1.7	6.0	16.4	8.3	22.8	27.3	19.2	42.9	82.6	19.3	1.2	0.3
17 28326	Galesburg city............	31,979	-1.3	5.6	13.8	12.2	24.5	25.2	18.7	38.0	83.3	13.4	1.7	3.1
17 28872	Geneva city...............	21,016	0.9	6.2	20.0	8.3	20.2	32.6	12.8	42.2	92.9	1.4	2.3	3.1
17 29730	Glendale Heights village...........	34,091	0.8	9.2	16.6	11.7	31.7	23.1	7.7	32.1	63.6	7.5	25.9	5.7
17 29756	Glen Ellyn village........	27,376	0.9	6.7	20.4	7.1	23.7	29.5	12.6	40.3	89.0	4.7	7.0	0.8
17 29938	Glenview village..........	46,005	0.6	6.1	18.5	5.0	20.8	28.8	20.7	44.5	85.1	1.6	13.5	1.3
17 30926	Granite City city.........	29,978	-1.0	6.0	16.8	9.6	24.8	27.5	15.2	37.7	94.1	6.3	0.8	1.6
17 31121	Grayslake village.........	20,507	0.6	6.8	22.1	9.3	25.8	28.3	7.7	37.6	88.7	5.1	7.1	2.7
17 32018	Gurnee village............	31,303	-0.2	4.6	21.8	7.5	26.0	30.8	9.3	39.2	75.6	12.0	12.2	3.5
17 32746	Hanover Park village.......	38,636	1.0	7.4	21.2	8.8	30.4	25.9	6.3	33.4	57.8	8.9	14.8	20.6
17 33383	Harvey city...............	24,306	0.3	11.9	17.7	10.2	25.9	24.3	10.0	31.7	12.8	78.3	...	9.8
17 34722	Highland Park city........	30,200	0.2	4.3	20.5	6.7	18.6	30.2	19.8	45.0	94.2	2.9	3.4	0.7
17 35411	Hoffman Estates village....	52,339	0.7	6.2	19.1	8.2	27.9	28.5	10.0	36.5	61.6	4.7	25.6	10.5
17 35835	Homer Glen village........	24,330	0.4	4.5	19.5	7.6	21.5	33.1	13.8	43.3	95.5	1.2	1.7	...
17 36750	Huntley village...........	24,445	1.9	6.3	17.6	4.2	23.7	20.8	27.4	42.9	92.2	0.9	8.1	...
17 38570	Joliet city...............	147,151	0.4	8.9	21.5	9.5	30.6	20.7	8.8	31.9	71.7	16.7	2.4	11.7
17 38934	Kankakee city.............	27,397	-0.7	9.1	20.4	8.9	27.1	21.5	13.1	33.4	55.9	39.8	...	6.7
17 41105	Lake Forest city..........	19,075	-0.2	4.0	20.5	8.6	14.0	33.5	19.3	46.7	93.2	1.2	6.0	0.9
17 41183	Lake in the Hills village..	28,980	0.4	6.7	22.2	8.4	30.7	25.3	6.7	35.8	88.5	2.6	8.1	2.7
17 41742	Lake Zurich village.......	19,758	1.2	7.2	21.5	7.7	23.1	32.5	8.0	37.8	92.0	...	8.2	...
17 42028	Lansing village...........	28,947	0.4	6.0	18.3	8.1	24.2	29.0	14.4	39.5	62.5	32.4	1.3	5.5
17 43250	Libertyville village......	20,352	0.1	5.8	19.0	5.8	20.5	32.2	16.7	44.4	92.6	1.4	6.1	0.8

STATE and Place code	STATE or City	Percent Hispanic or Latino	Percent foreign born	Total households	Household type (percent)						Percent of households with people under 18 years	Percent of households with people 60 years and over
					Family households				Nonfamily households			
					Total family households	Married-couple families	Male household families	Female household families	Total nonfamily households	One-person households		
ACS table number:		B03003	C05003	B11001	B11001	B11001	B11001	B11001	B11001	B11001	B11005	B11006
Column number:		14	15	16	17	18	19	20	21	22	23	24
	Idaho—Cont.											
16 54550	Moscow city	4.2	5.4	9,596	43.7	36.7	1.2	5.7	56.3	29.7	21.4	19.8
16 56260	Nampa city	22.1	8.5	27,068	72.6	53.6	4.0	15.0	27.4	22.8	42.6	30.6
16 64090	Pocatello city	7.0	3.7	20,539	60.5	45.2	5.7	9.6	39.5	31.8	30.6	26.4
16 64810	Post Falls city	5.0	1.6	10,941	73.5	53.5	1.7	18.3	26.5	21.6	41.2	29.4
16 67420	Rexburg city	4.2	4.7	6,726	74.2	68.5	1.1	4.5	25.8	11.3	33.2	12.2
16 82810	Twin Falls city	15.3	10.0	16,037	67.1	51.1	3.5	12.6	32.9	24.7	38.8	33.7
17 00000	**Illinois**	16.1	13.9	4,759,131	65.7	48.2	4.6	12.9	34.3	28.6	32.9	33.7
17 00243	Addison village	36.5	33.8	12,062	79.7	57.6	5.7	16.5	20.3	17.8	42.0	33.4
17 00685	Algonquin village	7.3	11.3	10,467	76.3	65.9	3.8	6.6	23.7	19.5	38.3	31.8
17 01114	Alton city	2.0	1.4	11,609	57.0	33.0	5.7	18.3	43.0	35.7	30.2	31.8
17 02154	Arlington Heights village	6.2	17.9	30,140	65.8	56.6	2.7	6.6	34.2	29.5	29.5	38.1
17 03012	Aurora city	42.3	25.9	61,135	74.4	55.7	5.5	13.2	25.6	20.6	47.6	22.2
17 04013	Bartlett village	10.2	18.7	13,937	79.1	68.9	2.6	7.5	20.9	17.6	40.8	31.0
17 04078	Batavia city	6.9	4.7	9,278	73.8	61.7	2.2	9.9	26.2	22.9	38.8	30.7
17 04845	Belleville city	3.5	2.8	18,473	55.0	37.6	3.7	13.8	45.0	38.1	28.0	30.7
17 05092	Belvidere city	34.3	17.2	8,437	75.0	53.3	4.7	17.0	25.0	21.4	41.9	31.8
17 05573	Berwyn city	57.6	25.9	18,734	69.7	45.8	6.7	17.2	30.3	24.8	40.2	32.6
17 06587	Bloomingdale village	6.7	21.0	8,682	64.3	52.5	3.0	8.7	35.7	32.8	24.8	37.2
17 06613	Bloomington city	5.1	9.3	30,397	59.2	45.4	3.8	10.0	40.8	32.4	30.6	26.9
17 06704	Blue Island city	45.2	21.3	7,917	64.8	37.8	8.3	18.7	35.2	29.7	42.4	33.6
17 07133	Bolingbrook village	22.1	19.9	21,861	80.8	62.4	4.8	13.6	19.2	15.9	46.2	26.8
17 09447	Buffalo Grove village	4.8	25.2	16,511	71.8	61.3	2.8	7.7	28.2	24.8	34.8	34.4
17 09642	Burbank city	28.6	31.8	9,023	75.7	59.0	5.8	10.9	24.3	21.0	37.5	41.7
17 10487	Calumet City city	16.8	8.1	14,352	57.5	27.4	7.8	22.3	42.5	39.5	34.7	35.2
17 11163	Carbondale city	5.8	9.6	9,137	32.6	18.6	3.2	10.7	67.4	44.5	17.0	16.2
17 11332	Carol Stream village	12.9	20.6	14,478	69.6	58.5	3.8	7.4	30.4	26.4	33.8	26.6
17 11358	Carpentersville village	49.2	28.3	10,854	81.3	55.9	8.6	16.8	18.7	13.6	54.9	19.9
17 12385	Champaign city	6.0	14.4	32,331	47.1	34.3	3.8	9.0	52.9	37.6	21.0	22.8
17 12567	Charleston city	3.2	3.3	7,616	41.4	30.2	2.3	8.9	58.6	36.6	19.8	23.3
17 14000	Chicago city	28.8	21.1	1,023,839	54.9	32.0	5.4	17.6	45.1	36.2	29.3	28.7
17 14026	Chicago Heights city	36.8	13.9	9,893	72.7	40.8	9.0	22.9	27.3	25.9	42.5	32.6
17 14351	Cicero town	87.6	41.5	21,284	81.7	52.8	8.8	20.1	18.3	14.6	57.7	24.4
17 15599	Collinsville city	4.6	1.6	10,995	61.5	40.2	6.5	14.9	38.5	32.3	28.3	29.3
17 17458	Crest Hill city	21.7	9.8	8,097	60.7	43.2	2.8	14.7	39.3	34.3	27.5	37.7
17 17887	Crystal Lake city	10.9	10.3	14,216	73.0	56.6	4.5	11.9	27.0	22.1	39.7	29.2
17 18563	Danville city	5.4	3.8	12,488	58.2	32.9	5.2	20.0	41.8	36.4	29.8	38.7
17 18628	Darien city	4.3	18.5	8,681	71.0	59.2	3.4	8.4	29.0	25.0	30.6	47.0
17 18823	Decatur city	2.3	2.2	31,973	56.7	37.4	4.3	15.0	43.3	37.2	27.1	38.0
17 19161	DeKalb city	13.6	8.1	15,029	50.6	36.1	3.6	10.8	49.4	32.0	25.7	23.9
17 19642	Des Plaines city	18.0	29.6	22,763	63.9	52.3	2.8	8.8	36.1	31.6	26.1	40.8
17 20292	Dolton village	4.0	1.8	7,821	70.8	32.5	6.0	32.3	29.2	23.0	38.6	33.1
17 20591	Downers Grove village	5.9	10.1	18,951	70.6	57.0	3.3	10.3	29.4	25.6	32.7	35.3
17 22073	East Moline city	19.0	12.3	8,119	59.2	41.1	2.6	15.4	40.8	36.0	28.0	41.3
17 22164	East Peoria city	2.3	1.6	9,356	63.3	49.6	3.1	10.6	36.7	31.5	27.4	39.6
17 22255	East St. Louis city	0.1	0.2	9,997	57.9	13.5	4.6	39.9	42.1	38.8	33.5	36.2
17 22697	Edwardsville city	1.1	3.4	8,675	62.5	54.3	1.2	7.1	37.5	24.6	29.1	28.0
17 23074	Elgin city	46.9	26.6	34,322	71.2	51.7	6.5	13.0	28.8	24.6	41.2	29.7
17 23256	Elk Grove Village village	10.2	17.4	13,406	62.2	52.7	2.8	6.7	37.8	33.6	26.5	37.7
17 23620	Elmhurst city	6.3	8.0	15,425	71.0	59.8	1.5	9.7	29.0	25.0	37.7	38.6
17 23724	Elmwood Park village	24.5	27.6	9,005	66.2	47.8	3.9	14.6	33.8	28.9	31.8	37.0
17 24582	Evanston city	10.6	18.9	28,790	53.5	39.9	3.6	10.1	46.5	37.5	27.8	31.0
17 27884	Freeport city	4.0	1.9	10,705	58.4	39.3	3.7	15.4	41.6	36.5	25.1	41.5
17 28326	Galesburg city	7.6	3.8	13,036	52.9	35.2	3.8	13.9	47.1	40.0	24.0	43.3
17 28872	Geneva city	6.0	5.5	7,750	76.5	64.7	3.9	7.9	23.5	21.2	35.8	34.4
17 29730	Glendale Heights village	30.4	37.4	11,295	71.1	54.1	6.0	11.0	28.9	24.6	38.5	25.4
17 29756	Glen Ellyn village	3.2	9.8	10,370	68.7	55.8	3.2	9.7	31.3	28.5	35.8	33.8
17 29938	Glenview village	7.7	21.0	16,916	71.2	63.0	2.2	5.9	28.8	27.2	33.1	51.1
17 30926	Granite City city	4.4	1.6	11,959	63.2	42.0	5.2	16.0	36.8	31.6	30.0	36.1
17 31121	Grayslake village	6.0	9.8	7,351	73.7	59.1	5.0	9.6	26.3	21.1	44.0	23.8
17 32018	Gurnee village	10.6	15.7	11,354	68.6	53.0	3.6	12.1	31.4	26.5	41.1	26.9
17 32746	Hanover Park village	37.7	36.1	11,001	85.2	65.7	6.2	13.2	14.8	12.0	48.9	27.7
17 33383	Harvey city	17.6	7.1	7,416	70.6	28.5	6.9	35.3	29.4	26.1	42.2	31.5
17 34722	Highland Park city	5.9	12.0	11,618	73.4	63.0	3.2	7.1	26.6	23.8	33.8	44.7
17 35411	Hoffman Estates village	15.3	30.2	17,880	76.8	62.3	3.4	11.1	23.2	18.4	37.6	31.7
17 35835	Homer Glen village	7.7	11.2	7,958	85.5	75.4	5.4	4.6	14.5	13.2	34.7	38.8
17 36750	Huntley village	7.2	8.5	9,832	75.0	70.2	1.6	3.2	25.0	22.9	30.2	54.6
17 38570	Joliet city	26.8	15.3	46,586	72.5	53.0	6.3	13.2	27.5	22.6	46.0	26.6
17 38934	Kankakee city	18.9	9.4	9,426	60.7	32.5	5.5	22.7	39.3	34.0	37.9	34.1
17 41105	Lake Forest city	1.8	8.6	6,592	79.9	72.1	2.3	5.5	20.1	18.3	35.3	49.9
17 41183	Lake in the Hills village	10.1	10.8	9,632	77.6	64.8	1.5	11.3	22.4	18.1	44.5	23.0
17 41742	Lake Zurich village	9.1	18.1	6,405	83.4	69.7	4.6	9.1	16.6	14.9	44.7	25.9
17 42028	Lansing village	13.2	6.2	11,158	63.6	42.9	4.2	16.5	36.4	32.1	31.3	35.9
17 43250	Libertyville village	5.2	10.8	7,602	73.3	61.1	3.3	9.0	26.7	24.4	35.7	40.6

Table A-4. Cities — Who: Age, Race/Ethnicity, and Household Structure, 2010–2012—*Continued*

STATE and Place code	STATE or City	Total population	Percent change 2010–2012	Population by age (percent)							Race alone or in combination (percent)			
				Under 5 years	5 to 17 years	18 to 24 years	25 to 44 years	45 to 64 years	65 years and over	Median age	White	Black	Asian, Hawaiian, or Pacfic Islander	American Indian, Alaska Native, or some other race
	ACS table number:	B01003	Population estimates	B01001	B01001	B01001	B01001	B01001	B01001	B01002	B02008	B02009	B02011 + B02012	B02010 + B02013
	Column number:	1	2	3	4	5	6	7	8	9	10	11	12	13
	Illinois—Cont.													
17 43939	Lisle village	22,522	0.9	5.5	16.5	9.7	29.4	27.8	11.2	36.8	81.0	6.6	10.8	4.8
17 44225	Lockport city	24,991	0.6	6.8	21.9	6.9	31.2	23.9	9.3	34.3	96.5	1.5	1.5	1.8
17 44407	Lombard village	43,616	0.8	3.9	15.0	10.0	26.7	29.1	15.4	41.2	85.1	5.3	9.4	3.0
17 45031	Loves Park city	23,373	-0.8	6.3	17.2	8.6	28.5	26.5	13.0	37.9	92.8	4.0	3.6	1.6
17 45694	McHenry city	26,808	-0.7	7.2	18.1	8.5	27.4	27.0	11.8	37.1	90.1	1.0	2.4	8.9
17 45726	Machesney Park village	23,226	-0.9	6.7	17.6	9.4	25.5	28.0	12.7	38.8	95.4	2.7	2.5	0.9
17 47774	Maywood village	24,125	0.2	5.4	18.3	8.9	28.3	26.0	13.2	36.4	13.7	73.5	...	12.6
17 48242	Melrose Park village	25,681	0.4	9.0	21.4	11.3	29.5	19.3	9.5	30.4	51.0	6.0	2.1	43.2
17 49867	Moline city	43,398	-0.6	5.6	17.0	9.0	26.0	27.4	15.0	39.0	85.3	6.4	3.3	7.4
17 50647	Morton Grove village	23,033	0.7	4.5	13.7	5.6	23.9	29.6	22.8	46.5	69.0	2.8	28.8	3.3
17 51089	Mount Prospect village	54,352	0.5	5.7	17.4	7.3	28.6	26.5	14.5	39.0	74.5	2.7	11.4	13.3
17 51349	Mundelein village	31,314	0.4	7.7	19.1	7.9	27.9	28.9	8.5	36.2	86.5	1.1	8.5	5.0
17 51622	Naperville city	143,310	1.1	5.3	22.5	8.4	24.2	29.8	9.7	38.7	76.4	5.6	18.3	2.2
17 52584	New Lenox village	24,501	1.1	8.5	21.3	7.5	26.2	27.8	8.7	35.7	92.0	1.2	...	4.7
17 53000	Niles village	29,274	0.5	4.3	13.3	5.1	22.2	28.5	26.5	49.2	79.0	1.6	17.8	2.2
17 53234	Normal town	53,712	2.3	5.2	12.2	34.7	22.0	17.6	8.2	23.8	87.8	8.4	4.0	2.6
17 53481	Northbrook village	33,236	0.8	4.6	19.2	5.6	17.1	30.9	22.5	47.3	86.6	1.4	12.3	0.9
17 53559	North Chicago city	31,359	-9.0	7.6	14.9	31.2	29.0	12.7	4.7	24.0	50.5	34.6	6.1	13.9
17 54638	Oak Forest city	28,076	0.6	6.2	18.2	9.9	27.5	26.8	11.4	35.8	87.2	7.8	3.7	4.5
17 54820	Oak Lawn village	56,861	0.5	6.0	15.6	8.0	24.9	27.0	18.7	40.6	88.8	6.1	1.6	5.1
17 54885	Oak Park village	51,949	0.2	6.9	18.0	5.6	28.7	30.0	10.9	39.6	69.8	23.9	6.7	3.3
17 55249	O'Fallon city	28,921	2.0	7.7	21.5	8.8	27.8	25.2	9.1	35.0	79.4	18.6	4.4	1.8
17 56640	Orland Park village	57,110	1.0	5.1	15.8	8.7	20.2	30.8	19.3	45.1	91.0	2.9	5.9	1.4
17 56887	Oswego village	31,332	3.7	7.6	24.1	6.3	32.5	23.4	6.2	35.1	90.3	7.4	4.1	1.7
17 57225	Palatine village	68,886	0.8	7.0	18.2	6.7	28.7	28.4	11.0	37.7	78.8	4.6	12.9	5.3
17 57732	Park Forest village	22,673	0.2	5.6	20.1	8.2	27.4	27.8	10.9	35.4	33.0	66.6	1.0	2.8
17 57875	Park Ridge city	37,699	0.5	4.0	19.9	7.3	18.3	32.5	18.1	45.4	94.5	1.3	4.5	0.2
17 58447	Pekin city	34,071	0.0	6.9	15.3	8.8	26.8	26.2	16.1	38.7	96.9	2.9	0.2	1.2
17 59000	Peoria city	114,398	0.7	7.1	17.6	12.2	26.7	23.2	13.2	33.6	65.8	29.8	5.4	2.0
17 60287	Plainfield village	40,044	1.3	7.7	28.6	5.6	32.1	21.2	4.8	33.5	83.1	7.9	9.1	3.2
17 62367	Quincy city	40,745	0.3	6.5	15.6	10.1	24.1	25.6	18.2	38.6	91.3	7.0	1.6	2.6
17 65000	Rockford city	152,235	-1.3	7.7	18.9	8.8	26.1	24.5	13.9	35.3	71.5	23.5	3.4	5.1
17 65078	Rock Island city	38,741	-0.2	6.7	16.7	13.5	22.3	24.9	15.9	36.2	77.2	19.8	2.0	5.7
17 65338	Rolling Meadows city	24,391	0.5	7.1	15.6	8.4	30.7	26.4	11.8	36.2	71.9	3.3	7.5	18.6
17 65442	Romeoville village	39,710	0.2	7.2	24.2	10.1	30.7	19.4	8.5	32.0	72.2	10.8	9.2	12.8
17 65806	Roselle village	23,245	0.8	5.5	18.5	8.4	26.2	30.0	11.4	39.4	82.6	7.3	9.7	2.0
17 66040	Round Lake Beach village	28,328	-0.3	10.4	20.6	10.8	31.0	21.1	6.2	31.3	87.1	4.2	3.0	6.0
17 66703	St. Charles city	33,405	1.0	5.1	19.8	6.2	27.4	28.6	13.0	40.2	93.5	1.7	2.9	3.2
17 68003	Schaumburg village	74,384	0.6	7.3	13.5	7.8	33.3	26.4	11.5	36.7	73.0	4.4	19.8	4.5
17 70122	Skokie village	64,962	0.4	4.6	15.3	7.7	22.6	31.2	18.6	44.6	64.9	7.8	27.2	1.9
17 70720	South Elgin village	20,739	1.0	7.0	23.6	5.6	31.9	24.3	7.6	36.0	85.6	4.4	9.7	0.8
17 70850	South Holland village	22,092	0.4	3.8	19.8	9.8	22.3	28.2	16.2	40.4	20.3	78.4	0.9	0.9
17 72000	Springfield city	116,824	0.6	6.5	15.7	9.7	25.2	28.1	14.8	39.0	77.6	20.6	2.7	1.3
17 73157	Streamwood village	40,166	0.8	7.5	20.5	7.5	30.0	26.5	8.0	34.1	62.8	4.7	16.0	18.2
17 75484	Tinley Park village	57,973	0.7	6.4	17.9	6.4	27.1	29.5	12.7	39.0	91.2	4.2	4.6	2.0
17 77005	Urbana city	41,553	0.1	5.0	6.5	42.8	23.8	13.8	8.1	23.8	64.5	19.0	18.0	1.6
17 77694	Vernon Hills village	25,474	2.1	6.5	20.8	7.1	28.0	28.3	9.3	37.5	79.0	1.9	21.1	1.8
17 77993	Villa Park village	21,965	0.6	7.6	17.2	8.2	29.1	27.5	10.4	35.3	86.4	4.4	5.4	4.5
17 79293	Waukegan city	88,637	-0.3	7.8	21.7	11.1	28.8	22.7	7.7	31.1	56.8	19.9	5.2	21.0
17 80060	West Chicago city	27,428	0.9	10.1	22.6	10.0	29.1	20.6	7.6	30.1	86.6	2.7	5.0	6.6
17 80645	Westmont village	25,011	0.8	5.3	13.1	7.1	29.9	28.5	16.1	40.6	73.3	8.0	15.2	6.3
17 81048	Wheaton city	53,276	0.8	5.7	17.6	11.0	24.3	29.2	12.2	37.7	88.5	4.8	7.7	1.3
17 81087	Wheeling village	37,850	0.6	7.8	14.6	7.6	33.5	24.2	12.4	35.6	73.2	1.8	14.8	11.0
17 82075	Wilmette village	27,298	0.7	5.1	23.9	5.9	17.7	29.9	17.4	43.3	84.1	1.3	14.6	0.9
17 83245	Woodridge village	33,029	0.9	6.7	14.6	9.8	31.1	27.5	10.2	37.5	74.4	10.9	12.1	6.5
17 83349	Woodstock city	24,949	1.0	7.8	18.5	8.6	30.0	25.1	9.9	35.6	87.2	2.2	4.5	7.3
17 84220	Zion city	24,409	-0.3	7.5	22.5	11.3	27.0	23.0	8.7	31.4	54.5	36.7	5.0	9.7
18 00000	**Indiana**	6,514,516	0.7	6.6	17.9	10.1	25.5	26.6	13.2	37.1	86.6	10.1	2.1	3.4
18 01468	Anderson city	55,500	-1.0	6.5	15.6	11.7	24.2	25.6	16.5	38.3	84.7	14.4	0.7	3.4
18 05860	Bloomington city	80,127	1.7	4.0	7.3	43.9	23.1	13.5	8.2	22.3	84.9	5.6	9.9	2.9
18 08416	Brownsburg town	21,503	4.1	7.3	18.9	7.1	29.0	24.1	13.7	36.9	93.3	4.2	2.2	1.2
18 10342	Carmel city	82,485	4.8	6.6	22.6	5.3	25.9	29.0	10.6	38.8	86.5	4.1	10.9	1.5
18 12934	Clarksville town	22,341	0.4	8.7	17.5	8.3	28.9	21.6	15.0	34.9	94.6	4.3	0.7	...
18 14734	Columbus city	45,106	3.0	6.6	19.2	7.7	29.0	22.9	14.7	36.1	87.3	4.0	7.4	3.1
18 16138	Crown Point city	28,595	1.1	5.2	15.6	8.2	27.5	27.0	16.6	39.2	88.4	8.6	1.6	3.0
18 19486	East Chicago city	29,585	-0.8	9.7	22.9	11.1	23.7	22.3	10.3	29.9	28.5	44.4	...	30.7
18 20728	Elkhart city	51,421	0.6	9.7	20.3	9.4	27.0	22.7	11.0	33.3	75.4	16.4	1.2	11.6
18 22000	Evansville city	120,386	0.1	7.0	15.7	11.5	26.0	25.3	14.5	35.5	85.6	14.2	1.2	2.3
18 23278	Fishers town	79,903	5.7	8.3	23.7	5.7	32.9	23.7	5.6	33.3	89.6	5.7	5.7	1.9
18 25000	Fort Wayne city	253,795	0.3	7.7	18.8	10.0	26.4	24.7	12.4	34.8	77.5	18.3	3.8	3.9
18 25450	Franklin city	24,007	1.0	5.2	23.3	11.6	26.1	19.3	14.4	33.2	95.0	1.7	0.9	3.4
18 27000	Gary city	79,849	-1.3	7.0	20.1	8.9	22.0	27.0	14.9	37.3	12.2	85.6	0.9	3.0
18 28386	Goshen city	31,989	1.2	9.9	16.4	11.5	27.6	19.3	15.2	31.9	83.4	6.2	2.2	10.3
18 28800	Granger CDP	27,656	...	4.9	21.1	6.8	22.4	32.7	12.1	42.2	91.1	4.6	5.5	0.5
18 29520	Greenfield city	21,642	1.7	7.1	19.4	8.5	29.0	22.3	13.6	34.9	97.0	1.4	...	2.3
18 29898	Greenwood city	52,174	3.2	8.6	17.1	7.8	29.3	25.1	12.2	34.7	91.2	3.6	5.2	3.5

Table A-4. Cities — Who: Age, Race/Ethnicity, and Household Structure, 2010–2012—*Continued*

STATE and Place code	STATE or City	Percent Hispanic or Latino	Percent foreign born	Total households	Household type (percent) Family households Total family households	Married-couple families	Male household families	Female household families	Nonfamily households Total nonfamily households	One-person households	Percent of households with people under 18 years	Percent of households with people 60 years and over
	ACS table number:	B03003	C05003	B11001	B11001	B11001	B11001	B11001	B11001	B11001	B11005	B11006
	Column number:	14	15	16	17	18	19	20	21	22	23	24
	Illinois—Cont.											
17 43939	Lisle village	9.7	12.8	9,165	62.4	49.0	4.9	8.6	37.6	31.6	31.4	28.1
17 44225	Lockport city	8.2	8.2	9,107	71.6	60.9	3.4	7.3	28.4	25.3	41.4	24.8
17 44407	Lombard village	7.8	12.6	17,610	63.1	48.6	3.9	10.6	36.9	32.1	26.5	36.6
17 45031	Loves Park city	5.9	4.8	9,192	64.0	48.5	3.5	12.0	36.0	30.7	33.3	34.1
17 45694	McHenry city	13.1	8.1	9,800	69.0	55.2	5.3	8.6	31.0	25.1	35.9	32.1
17 45726	Machesney Park village	4.6	4.1	8,425	72.6	52.1	5.1	15.4	27.4	21.5	35.3	32.9
17 47774	Maywood village	22.8	10.6	7,772	74.6	41.4	5.1	28.0	25.4	21.9	38.6	41.5
17 48242	Melrose Park village	73.3	39.3	7,539	73.9	45.8	10.5	17.6	26.1	22.7	48.2	32.7
17 49867	Moline city	16.5	9.8	18,300	59.8	43.5	3.8	12.5	40.2	36.1	29.2	37.3
17 50647	Morton Grove village	7.9	39.1	8,512	74.7	60.5	3.8	10.4	25.3	22.9	24.0	53.8
17 51089	Mount Prospect village	17.1	32.1	19,911	70.4	59.6	4.6	6.2	29.6	24.0	33.5	36.5
17 51349	Mundelein village	30.6	29.2	10,521	77.1	62.3	6.6	8.2	22.9	20.6	40.8	30.7
17 51622	Naperville city	6.1	18.1	48,897	77.9	66.8	2.7	8.4	22.1	18.3	44.0	27.6
17 52584	New Lenox village	7.6	3.6	7,990	81.7	69.6	3.4	8.6	18.3	16.2	47.4	26.1
17 53000	Niles village	8.5	41.6	11,385	66.2	50.4	5.2	10.6	33.8	31.6	26.2	53.9
17 53234	Normal town	5.2	4.4	18,039	54.1	41.1	3.6	9.4	45.9	27.8	27.1	21.8
17 53481	Northbrook village	2.6	18.9	12,246	75.1	66.3	2.9	6.0	24.9	22.2	32.9	48.4
17 53559	North Chicago city	27.7	16.4	6,771	72.6	41.1	6.1	25.3	27.4	22.3	46.0	24.3
17 54638	Oak Forest city	13.4	7.1	9,766	74.4	57.0	3.9	13.5	25.6	21.0	38.8	32.8
17 54820	Oak Lawn village	15.2	14.3	21,794	63.5	47.2	5.6	10.8	36.5	32.9	27.9	42.2
17 54885	Oak Park village	6.9	10.6	21,605	61.0	47.5	2.5	11.1	39.0	33.7	33.6	30.9
17 55249	O'Fallon city	4.0	3.5	10,456	70.3	54.4	5.0	10.9	29.7	25.7	41.2	24.7
17 56640	Orland Park village	5.1	13.5	21,451	71.0	59.0	2.7	9.3	29.0	25.9	28.5	44.0
17 56887	Oswego village	11.4	4.7	10,310	83.0	70.2	3.0	9.8	17.0	14.0	49.8	21.0
17 57225	Palatine village	17.3	23.2	25,646	67.9	52.9	3.9	11.1	32.1	26.7	36.2	29.8
17 57732	Park Forest village	6.5	2.6	8,556	62.6	35.5	6.1	20.9	37.4	33.8	35.1	33.5
17 57875	Park Ridge city	5.0	13.8	14,182	72.8	58.8	4.1	9.9	27.2	25.0	33.4	41.7
17 58447	Pekin city	3.1	1.1	13,939	62.6	44.2	3.9	14.4	37.4	31.9	28.5	37.0
17 59000	Peoria city	5.3	7.0	47,114	58.1	36.6	4.4	17.1	41.9	35.9	30.5	31.6
17 60287	Plainfield village	8.3	10.3	11,459	86.4	72.6	5.2	8.6	13.6	10.8	58.3	16.2
17 62367	Quincy city	1.7	2.0	16,650	60.3	44.0	2.8	13.5	39.7	34.1	29.0	39.2
17 65000	Rockford city	17.2	10.7	58,379	61.2	38.2	4.9	18.1	38.8	33.2	33.1	34.3
17 65078	Rock Island city	10.2	6.2	15,531	55.7	36.2	4.4	15.2	44.3	39.0	29.9	37.6
17 65338	Rolling Meadows city	32.9	30.6	8,931	70.8	51.7	8.3	10.8	29.2	26.5	36.4	32.8
17 65442	Romeoville village	33.3	20.5	12,022	80.5	58.1	9.5	13.0	19.5	16.2	52.1	26.1
17 65806	Roselle village	8.5	15.8	8,834	69.6	54.6	5.2	9.8	30.4	26.1	33.1	29.0
17 66040	Round Lake Beach village	50.3	30.5	8,203	79.3	58.0	6.9	14.4	20.7	18.0	52.4	21.6
17 66703	St. Charles city	8.2	9.1	12,503	72.7	62.0	2.2	8.6	27.3	22.4	34.4	33.9
17 68003	Schaumburg village	9.2	25.1	29,885	61.8	49.3	3.9	8.7	38.2	32.1	30.9	29.0
17 70122	Skokie village	9.5	43.1	23,176	71.6	54.8	4.6	12.2	28.4	25.7	29.3	47.7
17 70720	South Elgin village	10.6	11.3	6,739	77.9	64.9	2.6	10.4	22.1	18.3	44.2	24.5
17 70850	South Holland village	4.1	4.6	7,150	75.9	48.4	7.4	20.0	24.1	21.6	35.1	39.8
17 72000	Springfield city	2.2	4.4	51,264	55.5	35.7	5.8	14.0	44.5	37.7	26.3	34.9
17 73157	Streamwood village	29.0	31.1	12,802	78.8	65.7	3.0	10.1	21.2	18.2	40.5	25.1
17 75484	Tinley Park village	7.6	7.0	21,517	70.8	57.6	3.1	10.1	29.2	24.8	35.9	34.8
17 77005	Urbana city	5.0	19.2	16,068	36.4	23.9	2.6	9.9	63.6	38.9	16.0	22.1
17 77694	Vernon Hills village	9.9	29.1	9,415	70.7	58.1	3.7	8.8	29.3	25.6	41.6	28.9
17 77993	Villa Park village	22.5	16.2	7,608	74.1	55.6	4.8	13.7	25.9	20.3	38.5	31.5
17 79293	Waukegan city	53.2	30.3	28,829	71.6	46.8	5.5	19.3	28.4	23.2	46.4	26.1
17 80060	West Chicago city	51.6	31.7	7,595	78.4	60.7	6.7	10.9	21.6	14.8	50.7	25.3
17 80645	Westmont village	8.3	21.2	10,810	56.6	43.8	2.4	10.4	43.4	36.1	24.7	34.1
17 81048	Wheaton city	4.7	11.8	18,973	70.3	59.3	3.9	7.1	29.7	24.8	34.1	32.2
17 81087	Wheeling village	34.0	41.3	14,163	65.9	51.9	4.9	9.1	34.1	28.1	31.4	32.7
17 82075	Wilmette village	5.0	19.6	9,479	76.8	64.1	3.1	9.7	23.2	21.1	41.0	44.6
17 83245	Woodridge village	13.2	21.4	12,793	69.0	54.9	4.0	10.1	31.0	25.4	31.4	28.7
17 83349	Woodstock city	20.1	14.7	9,470	66.4	47.6	5.9	12.8	33.6	28.5	38.6	24.6
17 84220	Zion city	26.1	13.6	8,099	66.3	43.4	4.5	18.3	33.7	28.9	43.4	26.0
18 00000	**Indiana**	6.2	4.7	2,474,926	66.6	49.8	4.5	12.4	33.4	27.8	32.7	33.6
18 01468	Anderson city	4.4	2.6	22,481	57.5	35.0	4.7	17.8	42.5	36.4	28.7	40.2
18 05860	Bloomington city	4.2	11.9	29,534	37.7	25.9	3.4	8.4	62.3	40.2	16.7	22.0
18 08416	Brownsburg town	2.8	3.8	8,510	70.2	58.4	2.5	9.4	29.8	27.8	34.5	31.1
18 10342	Carmel city	3.7	11.7	29,769	77.5	68.3	2.4	6.7	22.5	18.7	43.0	28.6
18 12934	Clarksville town	12.6	6.4	8,868	59.7	39.9	6.2	13.6	40.3	32.9	31.3	37.0
18 14734	Columbus city	5.7	10.0	17,840	64.9	46.1	5.3	13.5	35.1	30.7	33.6	34.0
18 16138	Crown Point city	5.8	8.4	10,746	68.5	54.4	4.7	9.3	31.5	28.0	30.9	38.9
18 19486	East Chicago city	47.6	14.4	9,660	66.5	30.7	4.1	31.7	33.5	28.6	44.1	33.9
18 20728	Elkhart city	23.0	12.9	19,025	61.3	37.5	6.8	17.0	38.7	32.1	37.2	28.8
18 22000	Evansville city	3.0	2.1	51,410	56.6	33.8	5.1	17.8	43.4	37.0	29.0	32.0
18 23278	Fishers town	3.3	7.1	27,620	76.0	63.8	2.6	9.6	24.0	19.4	47.8	18.2
18 25000	Fort Wayne city	7.9	7.3	100,418	61.6	41.6	4.8	15.1	38.4	32.2	32.0	31.5
18 25450	Franklin city	3.1	2.0	8,333	67.5	49.3	4.8	13.5	32.5	28.5	40.3	33.8
18 27000	Gary city	5.3	1.6	30,229	60.0	23.7	6.7	29.6	40.0	34.9	31.9	41.3
18 28386	Goshen city	28.2	18.3	11,413	69.3	46.3	4.5	18.4	30.7	26.9	36.4	38.5
18 28800	Granger CDP	2.2	6.5	9,676	82.6	74.6	2.7	5.3	17.4	13.6	37.3	33.8
18 29520	Greenfield city	2.3	1.1	7,927	70.9	46.5	8.8	15.6	29.1	24.3	38.8	32.7
18 29898	Greenwood city	4.6	5.8	20,736	63.4	49.4	3.3	10.8	36.6	31.3	33.5	30.4

Table A-4. Cities — Who: Age, Race/Ethnicity, and Household Structure, 2010–2012—*Continued*

STATE and Place code	STATE or City	Total population	Percent change 2010–2012	Population by age (percent)						Median age	Race alone or in combination (percent)			
				Under 5 years	5 to 17 years	18 to 24 years	25 to 44 years	45 to 64 years	65 years and over		White	Black	Asian, Hawaiian, or Pacific Islander	American Indian, Alaska Native, or some other race
	ACS table number:	B01003	Population estimates	B01001	B01001	B01001	B01001	B01001	B01001	B01002	B02008	B02009	B02011 + B02012	B02010 + B02013
	Column number:	1	2	3	4	5	6	7	8	9	10	11	12	13
	Indiana—Cont.													
18 31000	Hammond city	80,218	-1.3	7.6	19.4	10.0	27.5	25.0	10.6	34.2	54.6	23.7	1.7	24.0
18 33466	Highland town	23,587	-1.1	4.8	17.0	7.9	25.0	28.1	17.2	41.9	87.0	4.9	2.5	10.0
18 34114	Hobart city	28,552	-1.1	6.2	16.0	8.4	26.2	28.4	14.7	38.3	87.2	7.4	0.9	6.7
18 36003	Indianapolis city (balance)	827,639	1.6	7.6	17.4	10.5	29.3	24.6	10.5	33.7	65.0	29.4	2.7	5.9
18 38358	Jeffersonville city	46,115	1.1	6.8	16.2	8.8	29.9	26.3	12.0	36.2	84.4	15.0	2.0	1.0
18 40392	Kokomo city	56,431	0.1	7.0	16.0	8.5	24.4	27.2	16.9	39.9	87.1	11.5	1.9	2.2
18 40788	Lafayette city	66,822	1.1	7.5	15.6	14.2	29.0	22.2	11.5	31.7	88.9	7.5	2.0	3.3
18 42246	La Porte city	21,696	0.2	7.6	15.2	8.2	27.2	26.8	15.0	37.7	95.3	2.5	...	2.4
18 42426	Lawrence city	46,383	1.5	8.0	20.9	7.4	27.8	26.3	9.7	33.5	71.2	26.2	1.9	5.6
18 46908	Marion city	28,052	-0.9	5.6	13.4	16.8	21.7	25.4	17.2	37.5	84.9	16.9	0.9	1.0
18 48528	Merrillville town	35,482	1.1	7.3	20.0	8.1	26.7	25.5	12.4	35.9	46.9	47.4	1.2	7.9
18 48798	Michigan City city	30,614	-0.9	6.8	15.7	11.6	24.9	26.4	14.7	37.1	71.1	29.9	1.5	2.3
18 49932	Mishawaka city	48,921	-0.4	7.3	16.2	12.4	28.0	23.8	12.2	33.0	87.8	8.2	3.8	3.1
18 51876	Muncie city	69,830	-0.1	5.5	11.4	29.1	20.4	20.3	13.2	27.6	88.6	9.6	1.8	5.8
18 51912	Munster town	24,359	-0.8	4.9	18.5	6.8	21.2	28.5	20.1	44.2	86.8	4.0	5.6	7.3
18 52326	New Albany city	36,425	0.2	6.6	17.0	10.3	26.6	25.6	13.9	36.9	90.3	9.4	1.1	2.3
18 54180	Noblesville city	56,501	4.9	8.1	21.6	6.1	32.1	22.3	9.8	34.4	92.6	6.2	1.5	1.0
18 60246	Plainfield town	27,169	5.1	5.5	17.5	8.6	30.6	24.9	12.9	37.4	87.1	6.1	6.1	1.0
18 61092	Portage city	37,020	0.0	5.9	18.9	9.0	26.8	27.1	12.4	37.2	90.5	8.2	0.7	2.1
18 64260	Richmond city	36,587	-0.5	6.9	15.5	11.6	24.0	25.7	16.2	38.2	90.5	8.2	1.8	5.5
18 68220	Schererville town	29,177	-0.5	5.3	15.5	7.1	26.7	30.4	15.1	41.1	86.7	5.3	3.7	5.9
18 71000	South Bend city	99,803	-0.3	8.2	19.2	9.2	27.4	22.9	13.1	34.2	66.6	30.4	1.5	5.9
18 75428	Terre Haute city	61,181	0.5	5.8	14.4	18.2	26.7	22.5	12.3	32.8	86.8	12.4	1.6	2.3
18 78326	Valparaiso city	31,558	0.7	5.2	16.4	15.5	26.2	23.4	13.3	33.9	92.7	5.1	2.2	1.7
18 82700	Westfield city	30,551	6.0	9.0	22.4	7.4	31.6	23.7	5.9	31.9	94.3	3.3	3.3	2.9
18 82862	West Lafayette city	30,238	2.7	3.8	8.8	47.7	18.2	12.6	8.9	22.9	78.0	4.6	18.7	1.8
18 86372	Zionsville town	23,649	3.4	7.1	25.5	5.1	24.8	27.6	9.9	37.8	94.0	1.8	4.7	...
19 00000	**Iowa**	3,062,869	0.8	6.5	17.2	10.1	24.5	26.7	15.0	38.0	93.3	3.9	2.3	2.6
19 01855	Ames city	59,941	2.8	4.1	10.0	41.9	22.5	13.9	7.5	23.5	86.1	4.5	9.8	1.2
19 02305	Ankeny city	47,397	6.9	9.3	18.9	8.6	34.2	20.1	8.9	32.8	95.7	1.3	3.1	2.6
19 06355	Bettendorf city	33,814	2.6	7.3	17.7	6.4	25.2	28.6	14.9	39.8	91.8	4.0	4.3	1.2
19 09550	Burlington city	25,621	0.1	6.5	16.8	7.9	23.7	27.5	17.5	40.1	90.5	10.2	0.5	1.0
19 11755	Cedar Falls city	39,628	1.7	5.0	10.9	30.9	20.3	19.7	13.2	27.0	94.2	3.7	2.2	1.0
19 12000	Cedar Rapids city	127,503	1.2	7.1	15.9	12.1	27.3	24.7	12.9	35.2	90.5	8.1	2.5	2.0
19 14430	Clinton city	26,801	-0.8	6.0	16.3	8.4	24.2	26.9	18.2	41.1	92.2	6.5	1.3	1.9
19 16860	Council Bluffs city	62,329	-0.5	6.6	17.2	10.8	26.0	26.0	13.4	36.0	96.0	2.9	0.8	2.3
19 19000	Davenport city	100,643	1.4	6.9	17.4	10.5	27.5	25.2	12.5	35.0	85.0	13.4	2.7	3.4
19 21000	Des Moines city	205,622	1.0	8.0	17.0	10.7	29.7	23.8	10.9	33.5	80.7	12.3	5.4	4.8
19 22395	Dubuque city	57,908	0.8	5.8	14.7	12.7	23.6	26.7	16.6	39.2	95.8	3.5	2.3	3.2
19 28515	Fort Dodge city	24,966	-1.4	5.8	15.5	11.2	25.7	25.1	16.8	37.8	91.8	8.0	1.2	2.1
19 38595	Iowa City city	69,103	3.1	4.5	10.6	32.9	25.4	18.1	8.3	25.7	84.0	6.8	8.0	3.6
19 49485	Marion city	35,374	2.8	6.0	20.9	6.5	27.9	24.7	14.0	37.8	95.8	1.8	2.9	1.2
19 49755	Marshalltown city	27,648	0.4	8.1	18.1	8.7	24.3	24.4	16.4	35.7	84.9	2.9	2.8	11.1
19 50160	Mason City city	27,959	-0.8	5.8	16.3	9.5	23.2	27.7	17.5	41.7	96.6	3.4	1.2	1.2
19 55110	Muscatine city	22,900	0.5	7.5	18.3	7.1	26.3	25.8	14.9	37.5	91.8	2.2	0.9	6.1
19 60465	Ottumwa city	24,887	-0.8	6.2	16.1	11.3	24.9	25.4	16.1	38.5	93.5	2.6	1.0	4.8
19 73335	Sioux City city	82,828	-0.2	7.8	18.2	11.4	25.3	24.5	12.9	34.1	83.1	5.0	3.5	12.6
19 79950	Urbandale city	41,036	3.5	5.9	20.2	7.1	26.9	28.0	12.0	39.1	92.7	3.9	4.4	0.6
19 82425	Waterloo city	68,361	-0.2	7.3	16.9	10.5	25.9	25.5	14.0	35.5	81.6	16.9	2.2	2.3
19 83910	West Des Moines city	58,185	3.9	7.5	16.5	9.8	32.5	23.4	10.3	33.2	88.8	4.5	6.2	2.9
20 00000	**Kansas**	2,871,709	0.9	7.1	18.1	10.2	25.3	25.9	13.4	36.1	88.2	7.2	3.2	4.9
20 17800	Derby city	24,645	2.1	6.7	24.3	9.2	27.0	23.2	9.5	31.6	93.9	5.6	1.9	2.6
20 18250	Dodge City city	28,064	2.0	10.3	20.9	11.5	28.5	20.9	8.0	29.4	88.3	3.1	2.1	8.6
20 21275	Emporia city	24,939	0.3	7.4	14.9	20.6	24.3	20.7	12.1	29.5	91.2	4.4	3.7	5.2
20 25325	Garden City city	26,905	0.7	10.0	21.4	11.7	25.6	21.9	9.4	29.9	87.7	4.9	4.8	5.2
20 25425	Gardner city	19,830	5.8	11.0	23.1	6.7	35.3	17.0	6.9	30.1	94.2	3.0	2.3	2.2
20 31100	Hays city	20,754	2.3	7.1	13.4	21.9	23.0	22.3	12.2	29.3	95.2	1.8	2.0	2.4
20 33625	Hutchinson city	42,063	-0.4	6.9	16.4	9.9	24.7	25.9	16.2	38.3	90.0	6.1	0.9	6.7
20 35750	Junction City city	24,597	7.9	8.7	18.8	13.5	31.2	19.7	8.0	29.1	70.5	26.2	8.4	5.2
20 36000	Kansas City city	146,502	0.9	8.6	19.8	9.7	27.5	23.6	10.7	32.8	61.8	28.5	3.3	9.5
20 38900	Lawrence city	88,791	1.8	5.3	12.3	29.6	27.3	17.8	7.7	26.1	87.5	6.7	6.2	5.4
20 39000	Leavenworth city	35,620	1.3	8.7	17.4	9.1	31.1	23.7	10.0	34.2	79.8	17.3	3.4	4.1
20 39075	Leawood city	32,233	1.9	5.4	22.2	4.9	18.1	32.9	16.5	44.7	94.2	1.9	4.4	0.6
20 39350	Lenexa city	48,843	2.3	7.0	17.9	7.9	28.5	27.9	10.8	36.6	89.0	6.4	4.9	2.4
20 39825	Liberal city	20,647	2.5	11.0	21.1	12.8	27.1	19.5	8.6	28.5	60.8	6.7	5.0	32.1
20 44250	Manhattan city	54,162	6.5	5.4	9.7	37.8	26.3	13.9	6.9	24.2	86.2	8.4	6.7	3.1
20 52575	Olathe city	128,195	3.0	8.5	20.8	8.0	31.0	24.3	7.3	33.8	88.5	6.4	5.6	2.2
20 53775	Overland Park city	176,376	2.8	6.8	17.6	6.9	28.4	27.4	12.9	37.3	87.1	6.2	7.6	2.4
20 56025	Pittsburg city	20,290	0.5	6.6	13.5	27.9	23.1	17.7	11.1	26.1	92.7	4.6	3.0	3.4
20 57575	Prairie Village city	21,621	1.4	5.0	15.9	4.8	28.4	27.1	18.8	42.3	95.9	2.8	1.8	0.8
20 62700	Salina city	48,637	0.5	7.7	17.4	10.1	24.7	25.1	15.0	36.7	90.5	5.7	2.9	5.0
20 64500	Shawnee city	63,000	2.1	5.9	20.9	7.3	28.8	26.5	10.6	36.8	91.1	5.7	3.1	3.8
20 71000	Topeka city	127,895	0.2	7.5	17.2	9.8	26.4	25.0	14.1	35.5	80.7	14.2	2.6	8.6
20 79000	Wichita city	384,025	0.7	8.1	18.1	10.3	26.9	25.0	11.6	34.2	78.6	13.2	6.0	7.2

Table A-4. Cities — Who: Age, Race/Ethnicity, and Household Structure, 2010–2012—*Continued*

STATE and Place code	STATE or City	Percent Hispanic or Latino	Percent foreign born	Total households	Household type (percent)							Percent of households with people under 18 years	Percent of households with people 60 years and over
					Family households				Nonfamily households				
					Total family households	Married-couple families	Male household families	Female household families	Total nonfamily households	One-person households			
ACS table number:		B03003	C05003	B11001	B11001	B11001	B11001	B11001	B11001	B11001		B11005	B11006
Column number:		14	15	16	17	18	19	20	21	22		23	24
	Indiana—Cont.												
18 31000	Hammond city	35.1	11.8	28,565	65.2	39.3	6.9	18.9	34.8	30.5		37.0	31.0
18 33466	Highland town	16.7	5.5	9,565	65.0	50.2	3.4	11.4	35.0	29.7		27.8	37.6
18 34114	Hobart city	14.5	5.8	11,124	66.3	48.5	7.5	10.3	33.7	29.8		30.7	37.3
18 36003	Indianapolis city (balance)	9.6	8.4	325,624	58.3	36.6	4.7	17.0	41.7	34.3		31.4	27.6
18 38358	Jeffersonville city	3.6	4.0	17,660	63.3	44.7	5.2	13.4	36.7	29.8		30.5	31.6
18 40392	Kokomo city	3.5	2.7	24,785	57.4	39.6	4.2	13.7	42.6	37.6		28.3	37.8
18 40788	Lafayette city	13.1	8.4	28,474	56.0	40.0	4.2	11.7	44.0	35.5		26.9	26.7
18 42246	La Porte city	8.3	4.4	9,016	61.7	44.0	4.4	13.3	38.3	31.3		29.5	36.7
18 42426	Lawrence city	13.0	8.0	16,994	69.0	45.1	4.7	19.1	31.0	25.9		37.5	25.9
18 46908	Marion city	5.6	2.1	11,402	56.3	35.9	4.0	16.4	43.7	38.1		25.8	38.7
18 48528	Merrillville town	14.2	7.4	12,789	62.5	42.7	3.9	15.9	37.5	32.4		33.7	33.4
18 48798	Michigan City city	6.9	3.3	12,309	57.3	34.8	4.5	18.0	42.7	36.3		28.3	34.2
18 49932	Mishawaka city	4.4	5.6	20,738	55.6	35.5	5.3	14.9	44.4	36.2		28.0	28.7
18 51876	Muncie city	2.4	2.7	27,611	48.9	30.6	4.0	14.2	51.1	36.2		22.2	32.4
18 51912	Munster town	8.9	10.9	8,588	74.7	59.5	5.1	10.0	25.3	24.2		33.9	48.7
18 52326	New Albany city	4.6	3.0	14,931	58.7	35.3	4.7	18.7	41.3	35.5		29.1	32.5
18 54180	Noblesville city	4.9	4.2	21,030	71.7	58.0	4.1	9.6	28.3	24.6		40.1	25.5
18 60246	Plainfield town	2.8	6.7	9,559	67.7	51.8	5.0	11.0	32.3	28.2		33.3	33.9
18 61092	Portage city	18.5	4.9	13,731	68.4	48.8	4.7	15.0	31.6	26.9		35.4	34.4
18 64260	Richmond city	4.2	3.7	15,489	60.1	38.0	4.1	18.0	39.9	34.4		29.8	36.0
18 68220	Schererville town	12.6	9.3	11,759	66.0	53.2	3.6	9.1	34.0	27.2		26.6	37.0
18 71000	South Bend city	13.0	7.0	39,167	57.8	35.4	3.8	18.5	42.2	34.9		31.9	33.2
18 75428	Terre Haute city	3.1	3.2	21,585	54.7	35.5	5.6	13.7	45.3	38.2		28.4	31.7
18 78326	Valparaiso city	8.1	5.8	11,897	58.6	43.0	3.2	12.4	41.4	34.1		31.1	32.8
18 82700	Westfield town	3.0	3.4	11,083	74.3	62.4	2.9	9.0	25.7	20.9		48.4	17.2
18 82862	West Lafayette city	3.5	20.7	12,073	34.3	26.9	2.2	5.2	65.7	38.5		17.4	20.9
18 86372	Zionsville town	2.1	6.3	8,224	77.9	71.4	2.0	4.5	22.1	19.6		46.2	26.5
19 00000	**Iowa**	5.1	4.5	1,224,399	64.8	51.5	3.9	9.4	35.2	28.7		30.3	35.0
19 01855	Ames city	3.7	11.6	22,838	44.2	37.3	2.9	4.0	55.8	31.3		19.1	19.1
19 02305	Ankeny city	2.4	2.7	18,328	70.6	57.5	5.1	8.1	29.4	22.5		39.1	23.6
19 06355	Bettendorf city	3.0	4.8	13,221	67.6	58.0	2.2	7.5	32.4	28.1		32.7	38.1
19 09550	Burlington city	3.7	1.4	10,909	64.0	44.2	3.0	16.8	36.0	30.1		29.9	39.3
19 11755	Cedar Falls city	1.3	3.3	14,369	56.8	48.0	2.2	6.7	43.2	27.4		22.9	30.6
19 12000	Cedar Rapids city	3.6	3.1	52,438	58.7	43.2	4.5	11.0	41.3	32.3		29.4	30.6
19 14430	Clinton city	3.2	3.0	11,107	59.6	44.2	4.5	10.9	40.4	33.0		27.9	40.4
19 16860	Council Bluffs city	8.1	3.6	24,673	62.8	42.0	5.4	15.4	37.2	30.6		31.2	34.3
19 19000	Davenport city	7.9	3.8	40,894	57.9	40.4	3.6	14.0	42.1	34.0		29.2	30.7
19 21000	Des Moines city	11.9	10.9	81,018	60.1	39.4	5.3	15.4	39.9	32.2		32.9	29.2
19 22395	Dubuque city	2.5	2.8	24,051	56.5	42.3	3.6	10.7	43.5	35.0		26.0	35.2
19 28515	Fort Dodge city	5.1	2.7	10,429	53.6	35.2	4.0	14.4	46.4	38.8		27.5	35.6
19 38595	Iowa City city	5.2	12.8	28,050	44.1	32.9	3.1	8.1	55.9	35.5		19.9	21.9
19 49485	Marion city	1.8	3.2	14,235	65.0	52.2	3.2	9.7	35.0	29.0		35.5	32.2
19 49755	Marshalltown city	24.5	16.8	9,963	64.9	52.5	1.9	10.5	35.1	28.3		32.0	36.7
19 50160	Mason City city	4.7	1.6	13,015	54.9	40.3	5.6	9.1	45.1	39.6		27.4	35.7
19 55110	Muscatine city	15.3	5.2	9,303	63.7	48.2	4.1	11.3	36.3	30.0		32.1	35.5
19 60465	Ottumwa city	10.0	8.2	10,379	62.1	42.9	4.8	14.4	37.9	31.0		31.8	35.7
19 73335	Sioux City city	16.8	10.4	31,350	63.7	43.7	5.4	14.6	36.3	30.0		32.8	32.5
19 79950	Urbandale city	1.9	8.6	16,355	71.0	61.3	2.0	7.7	29.0	24.2		36.0	29.0
19 82425	Waterloo city	6.1	7.1	28,283	57.9	40.4	4.2	13.3	42.1	34.9		28.5	34.5
19 83910	West Des Moines city	5.9	11.7	24,068	63.9	51.6	4.1	8.1	36.1	28.5		34.3	25.6
20 00000	**Kansas**	10.8	6.7	1,106,960	65.5	50.7	4.4	10.4	34.5	28.5		32.7	33.0
20 17800	Derby city	6.2	2.7	9,155	72.7	54.0	6.4	12.3	27.3	22.3		40.2	23.8
20 18250	Dodge City city	57.9	28.4	8,784	74.1	53.2	6.2	14.7	25.9	21.3		45.3	25.5
20 21275	Emporia city	25.9	12.1	9,594	54.8	40.7	4.0	10.0	45.2	32.7		29.8	29.6
20 25325	Garden City city	49.7	20.4	9,257	66.8	49.9	4.8	12.1	33.2	26.5		43.3	28.7
20 25425	Gardner city	6.8	4.0	6,841	75.0	56.4	9.0	9.6	25.0	20.4		52.7	19.5
20 31100	Hays city	4.7	3.3	8,569	51.8	41.4	1.7	8.8	48.2	34.9		25.2	27.7
20 33625	Hutchinson city	11.2	3.4	17,286	61.0	45.4	3.0	12.6	39.0	34.3		29.8	35.1
20 35750	Junction City city	13.4	10.2	9,456	62.9	47.0	2.7	13.2	37.1	29.3		34.4	22.7
20 36000	Kansas City city	28.2	15.0	52,447	63.6	38.0	6.7	18.9	36.4	30.2		36.2	30.6
20 38900	Lawrence city	6.5	8.5	34,574	49.9	36.5	4.5	9.0	50.1	29.3		25.8	20.6
20 39000	Leavenworth city	7.9	4.9	12,184	65.0	46.5	3.6	14.9	35.0	27.9		38.2	28.6
20 39075	Leawood city	1.5	4.7	12,044	78.9	72.1	1.1	5.7	21.1	18.6		36.0	38.4
20 39350	Lenexa city	8.3	8.9	19,563	63.8	49.3	5.1	9.4	36.2	27.2		33.1	30.0
20 39825	Liberal city	58.9	31.7	6,577	70.1	48.6	6.9	14.5	29.9	22.9		46.7	27.0
20 44250	Manhattan city	5.8	8.3	20,118	46.9	36.4	3.3	7.1	53.1	32.2		24.3	17.7
20 52575	Olathe city	10.4	10.4	45,072	73.8	60.1	4.2	9.4	26.2	21.2		43.3	22.5
20 53775	Overland Park city	6.8	10.1	72,431	64.2	51.9	2.6	9.8	35.3	30.7		32.8	31.0
20 56025	Pittsburg city	6.0	6.0	7,945	50.5	33.6	4.8	12.0	49.5	35.0		27.2	23.6
20 57575	Prairie Village city	2.7	3.4	9,724	58.3	48.9	2.6	6.8	41.7	35.3		24.3	37.4
20 62700	Salina city	11.1	5.9	19,503	61.5	44.5	4.0	13.0	38.5	32.1		30.7	34.2
20 64500	Shawnee city	7.4	5.9	23,731	70.4	57.8	4.0	8.6	29.6	23.6		39.0	27.1
20 71000	Topeka city	13.9	5.9	53,366	57.2	38.5	5.1	13.6	42.8	36.3		29.7	33.7
20 79000	Wichita city	15.5	10.4	149,703	61.7	43.7	5.1	12.9	38.3	32.2		32.5	30.2

Table A-4. Cities — Who: Age, Race/Ethnicity, and Household Structure, 2010–2012—*Continued*

STATE and Place code	STATE or City	Total population	Percent change 2010–2012	Population by age (percent)						Median age	Race alone or in combination (percent)			
				Under 5 years	5 to 17 years	18 to 24 years	25 to 44 years	45 to 64 years	65 years and over		White	Black	Asian, Hawaiian, or Pacific Islander	American Indian, Alaska Native, or some other race
	ACS table number:	B01003	Population estimates	B01001	B01001	B01001	B01001	B01001	B01001	B01002	B02008	B02009	B02011 + B02012	B02010 + B02013
	Column number:	1	2	3	4	5	6	7	8	9	10	11	12	13
21 00000	**Kentucky**	4,364,627	0.8	6.4	17.0	9.6	26.0	27.3	13.6	38.2	89.6	8.9	1.6	1.9
21 02368	Ashland city	21,619	-1.0	6.4	13.8	8.1	23.7	29.4	18.5	43.5	96.0	4.0	1.3	0.5
21 08902	Bowling Green city	59,707	2.6	6.5	13.7	24.9	25.5	18.8	10.5	27.4	75.4	15.8	5.0	6.4
21 17848	Covington city	40,622	0.4	7.3	15.8	10.6	30.7	25.5	10.2	34.8	85.3	13.8	0.5	3.3
21 24274	Elizabethtown city	29,154	1.4	7.4	16.8	11.8	25.9	26.0	12.2	35.2	84.4	14.1	3.6	2.0
21 27982	Florence city	30,635	3.4	8.4	17.9	8.4	28.1	22.0	15.2	36.0	89.4	6.6	3.6	0.6
21 28900	Frankfort city	27,420	1.0	6.2	13.3	12.7	28.6	25.3	13.8	37.3	77.4	19.4	1.9	5.3
21 30700	Georgetown city	29,734	3.4	8.0	18.4	11.8	31.6	21.8	8.5	32.7	89.2	9.2	1.2	2.3
21 35866	Henderson city	28,849	0.4	7.1	14.6	8.7	26.7	27.8	15.1	38.7	86.6	13.9	0.3	1.9
21 37918	Hopkinsville city	32,365	2.6	8.1	14.9	10.8	26.5	25.5	14.1	35.6	66.9	31.8	1.3	2.4
21 39142	Independence city	25,260	3.2	9.6	21.4	6.9	31.6	23.4	7.0	32.8	96.8	2.9	1.0	...
21 40222	Jeffersontown city	26,797	1.0	5.1	17.3	7.9	29.9	26.0	13.7	38.5	84.7	12.2	2.3	...
21 46027	Lexington-Fayette urban county	301,211	3.0	6.4	14.7	14.2	29.8	24.2	10.7	33.8	78.9	16.1	4.0	4.3
21 48006	Louisville/Jefferson County metro	601,670	1.1	6.8	16.7	9.5	27.0	27.2	12.8	37.2	73.8	24.4	2.8	1.9
21 56136	Nicholasville city	28,226	1.0	8.4	19.7	7.6	32.4	21.5	10.4	33.4	93.6	4.4	...	3.1
21 58620	Owensboro city	57,763	1.1	7.0	17.0	9.2	24.6	26.2	16.0	38.9	90.4	9.3	0.8	1.7
21 58836	Paducah city	25,040	0.2	7.1	12.9	7.2	24.2	28.8	19.8	43.3	77.3	24.0	1.2	1.8
21 63912	Radcliff city	22,886	1.8	9.6	18.8	9.9	28.9	22.4	10.4	32.6	63.9	33.4	6.7	4.4
21 65226	Richmond city	31,805	2.1	6.5	12.1	27.9	25.3	18.9	9.3	26.7	87.0	10.3	2.8	1.7
22 00000	**Louisiana**	4,573,595	1.3	6.9	17.5	10.4	26.3	26.2	12.6	36.0	64.3	32.9	2.0	2.7
22 00975	Alexandria city	48,217	0.8	7.8	21.1	7.8	23.9	25.0	14.3	34.8	36.5	61.3	1.8	1.4
22 05000	Baton Rouge city	229,572	0.2	6.5	15.2	18.6	25.8	22.6	11.3	30.4	40.8	55.4	3.7	1.9
22 05210	Bayou Cane CDP	20,399	...	5.5	18.4	9.2	31.3	21.6	13.9	35.0	80.5	11.7	2.2	9.1
22 08920	Bossier City city	63,345	4.3	8.1	16.6	11.6	27.8	23.3	12.6	33.5	67.0	29.2	2.7	4.0
22 13960	Central city	27,208	2.3	6.4	15.2	9.6	23.7	29.3	15.8	40.4	89.3	10.7	...	0.4
22 32755	Hammond city	20,047	0.6	5.9	13.0	25.7	20.8	22.2	12.4	30.0	49.9	49.2	1.2	1.3
22 33245	Harvey CDP	21,685	...	6.2	17.2	11.3	27.3	26.0	12.0	35.1	44.8	40.7	7.5	7.5
22 36255	Houma city	33,700	0.1	7.5	18.3	9.2	26.0	26.7	12.2	36.2	68.1	25.6	1.6	7.6
22 39475	Kenner city	66,786	0.2	6.5	15.0	10.3	26.1	28.6	13.5	37.7	67.8	23.6	3.6	6.5
22 40735	Lafayette city	121,744	1.6	5.3	16.1	15.3	26.4	24.5	12.4	34.5	66.3	31.7	2.4	1.7
22 41155	Lake Charles city	72,741	1.7	7.5	15.4	13.1	23.9	26.3	13.9	35.2	49.5	48.8	2.1	1.8
22 42030	Laplace CDP	30,185	...	6.8	19.3	10.6	25.7	27.7	10.0	35.0	47.8	50.7	1.4	0.9
22 48785	Marrero CDP	34,947	...	7.0	19.4	8.8	22.1	28.3	14.4	37.7	41.0	51.3	5.4	4.1
22 50115	Metairie CDP	135,326	...	6.2	13.0	8.5	28.2	26.7	17.3	40.2	81.6	11.7	4.4	4.4
22 51410	Monroe city	49,013	0.6	7.2	19.5	13.3	23.7	22.8	13.4	32.6	33.5	65.2	0.7	2.5
22 54035	New Iberia city	30,735	0.8	8.5	19.7	9.8	22.3	25.9	13.9	36.8	57.7	40.0	3.0	0.8
22 55000	New Orleans city	359,130	6.2	6.6	14.8	12.0	29.4	26.2	11.2	34.7	34.7	60.9	3.3	2.9
22 62385	Prairieville CDP	25,220	...	5.3	21.2	10.5	27.8	26.5	8.7	38.2	84.6	13.2	1.1	1.6
22 66655	Ruston city	21,941	0.2	5.9	12.6	34.1	22.0	15.0	10.3	24.4	51.7	44.4	3.2	1.2
22 70000	Shreveport city	201,332	0.5	7.3	17.8	10.3	26.5	25.3	12.9	34.3	42.4	55.3	1.8	2.2
22 70805	Slidell city	27,274	0.9	5.8	18.3	7.8	25.4	27.7	15.1	38.8	77.6	19.6	0.8	3.4
22 73640	Sulphur city	20,308	-1.4	7.6	19.1	6.5	26.7	25.6	14.5	37.4	91.0	7.4	1.4	...
22 75180	Terrytown CDP	24,243	...	11.0	18.9	11.0	29.4	22.8	6.9	30.6	41.2	42.2	8.8	10.8
23 00000	**Maine**	1,328,440	0.1	5.1	15.2	8.8	23.5	31.0	16.4	43.2	96.9	1.6	1.5	1.9
23 02060	Auburn city	23,004	-0.3	5.2	18.6	8.2	24.5	26.8	16.6	40.5	96.1	2.7	1.1	3.7
23 02795	Bangor city	32,933	-0.7	4.8	12.8	16.7	24.7	26.1	14.9	37.1	94.6	2.2	2.3	1.7
23 04860	Biddeford city	21,294	0.2	7.4	13.4	13.7	26.6	24.6	14.4	35.3	96.5	0.6	3.4	0.4
23 38740	Lewiston city	36,498	-0.3	6.2	14.3	12.9	24.0	26.8	15.9	38.9	93.7	4.9	2.6	3.7
23 60545	Portland city	66,159	0.2	4.8	11.8	11.1	34.2	26.2	11.9	36.5	88.4	7.6	4.6	1.7
23 71990	South Portland city	25,029	0.5	6.3	14.1	8.0	28.6	27.8	15.2	40.7	92.5	3.3	5.0	0.8
24 00000	**Maryland**	5,837,378	1.7	6.3	16.8	9.7	26.9	27.8	12.6	38.0	60.7	31.0	6.7	4.6
24 01600	Annapolis city	38,577	0.2	8.0	11.9	9.7	31.0	26.3	13.2	36.9	62.3	27.7	2.5	8.8
24 02275	Arnold CDP	22,204	...	4.6	20.4	7.0	23.5	31.0	13.5	41.2	93.1	3.7	3.4	2.5
24 02825	Aspen Hill CDP	49,398	...	7.2	16.8	7.2	28.6	26.4	13.7	38.1	48.2	24.3	11.9	19.2
24 04000	Baltimore city	620,843	0.1	6.7	14.7	12.3	29.2	25.3	11.8	34.3	31.8	65.0	3.0	2.8
24 05825	Bel Air North CDP	29,801	...	5.7	18.9	9.1	24.1	29.9	12.3	40.4	93.9	4.3	2.6	0.6
24 05950	Bel Air South CDP	45,068	...	6.2	20.0	6.2	27.3	27.7	12.7	37.8	87.7	7.7	5.2	1.2
24 07125	Bethesda CDP	61,560	...	5.8	17.3	6.4	25.2	29.1	16.3	41.7	87.0	3.3	11.7	0.9
24 08775	Bowie city	55,602	1.9	7.0	18.2	8.2	26.5	29.3	10.8	39.1	46.2	48.0	5.5	4.8
24 13325	Carney CDP	25,997	...	5.9	11.9	7.8	29.4	26.1	18.9	40.1	81.6	12.5	4.5	4.0
24 14125	Catonsville CDP	41,723	...	5.0	14.9	14.6	22.8	25.9	16.9	39.5	75.7	19.0	4.4	2.8
24 16875	Chillum CDP	39,191	...	7.6	14.7	13.9	36.8	18.3	8.6	31.1	14.4	54.2	2.4	31.0
24 17900	Clinton CDP	37,925	...	5.2	17.7	9.2	23.7	32.2	11.9	41.1	15.1	82.2	3.8	1.5
24 18250	Cockeysville CDP	19,246	...	5.2	13.6	11.2	30.4	26.0	13.6	38.4	66.9	19.1	14.5	2.3
24 18750	College Park city	30,921	2.5	2.6	7.3	58.3	17.1	10.1	4.7	21.0	65.5	19.7	14.3	3.0
24 19125	Columbia CDP	103,512	...	6.7	17.2	7.7	30.8	26.7	10.9	37.4	57.9	27.4	13.9	5.0
24 20875	Crofton CDP	30,016	...	7.4	22.4	6.5	29.1	25.5	9.1	34.4	78.6	19.1	2.9	2.6
24 21325	Cumberland city	20,708	-1.1	6.0	16.5	8.6	23.9	25.5	19.4	41.7	90.0	10.0	1.8	0.8
24 23975	Dundalk CDP	61,087	...	6.6	16.0	9.0	24.9	26.5	16.9	40.0	87.1	10.0	2.5	3.7
24 25150	Edgewood CDP	27,754	...	7.1	23.2	8.5	29.5	23.7	8.0	32.1	53.5	44.5	3.6	1.7
24 25575	Eldersburg CDP	30,727	...	4.7	21.3	7.5	21.8	30.9	13.8	41.6	93.3	3.4	4.2	1.3
24 26000	Ellicott City CDP	68,883	...	5.6	21.2	6.9	24.8	28.7	12.7	40.0	66.4	10.8	24.4	1.3
24 26600	Essex CDP	35,980	...	6.9	13.2	10.1	27.2	30.0	12.7	38.9	70.1	26.3	2.0	4.1
24 27250	Fairland CDP	22,463	...	10.0	15.2	9.4	29.3	27.2	8.9	34.6	22.4	53.2	18.6	10.0

Table A-4. Cities — Who: Age, Race/Ethnicity, and Household Structure, 2010–2012—*Continued*

STATE and Place code	STATE or City	Percent Hispanic or Latino	Percent foreign born	Total households	Household type (percent)						Percent of households with people under 18 years	Percent of households with people 60 years and over
					Family households				Nonfamily households			
					Total family households	Married-couple families	Male household families	Female household families	Total nonfamily households	One-person households		
ACS table number:		B03003	C05003	B11001	B11001	B11001	B11001	B11001	B11001	B11001	B11005	B11006
Column number:		14	15	16	17	18	19	20	21	22	23	24
21 00000	**Kentucky**..........	3.1	3.2	1,690,132	66.9	49.3	4.7	12.9	33.1	28.0	32.2	34.7
21 02368	Ashland city........	1.5	1.9	9,299	61.0	41.1	6.9	13.1	39.0	33.9	27.6	40.8
21 08902	Bowling Green city.......	6.8	11.3	23,219	49.6	29.4	4.4	15.8	50.4	37.3	25.3	25.4
21 17848	Covington city.......	3.9	2.0	16,696	51.5	28.3	6.9	16.3	48.5	39.1	27.5	25.9
21 24274	Elizabethtown city......	3.3	5.3	11,458	64.1	42.6	3.9	17.6	35.9	30.8	34.9	30.2
21 27982	Florence city........	1.1	6.8	12,415	61.7	44.5	6.7	10.5	38.3	34.8	32.6	36.3
21 28900	Frankfort city.......	4.7	4.3	12,233	57.3	33.3	6.8	17.2	42.7	36.5	28.5	32.0
21 30700	Georgetown city.......	4.1	2.5	10,997	69.8	47.5	6.2	16.0	30.2	26.8	40.1	22.5
21 35866	Henderson city.......	2.3	0.7	12,310	59.4	40.5	3.4	15.5	40.6	36.4	27.6	36.6
21 37918	Hopkinsville city.......	5.6	2.7	12,969	62.0	40.0	4.1	17.9	38.0	32.5	33.5	33.4
21 39142	Independence city.......	2.6	1.9	8,690	77.7	55.4	4.6	17.7	22.3	16.9	46.2	23.7
21 40222	Jeffersontown city.......	4.5	8.7	10,363	68.5	51.9	6.0	10.5	31.5	25.8	31.1	30.6
21 46027	Lexington-Fayette urban county...	6.9	8.9	122,046	57.7	40.8	4.5	12.3	42.3	33.2	28.9	27.7
21 48006	Louisville/Jefferson County me	4.6	6.7	242,395	61.0	39.8	4.9	16.3	39.0	32.7	31.0	32.8
21 56136	Nicholasville city.......	4.0	2.2	10,669	71.1	48.6	5.9	16.7	28.9	21.9	42.3	26.8
21 58620	Owensboro city.......	3.0	2.4	23,387	59.9	41.8	3.8	14.4	40.1	34.1	29.2	36.2
21 58836	Paducah city........	2.1	2.2	11,429	53.7	35.0	5.1	13.5	46.3	41.0	25.2	39.6
21 63912	Radcliff city........	9.8	7.4	8,536	72.5	48.5	4.6	19.3	27.5	23.3	40.8	26.0
21 65226	Richmond city........	2.7	2.2	12,385	48.7	29.5	5.4	13.8	51.3	39.0	26.7	26.2
22 00000	**Louisiana**........	4.4	3.8	1,706,091	66.2	44.0	5.0	17.2	33.8	28.5	33.8	33.6
22 00975	Alexandria city.........	0.8	2.2	16,587	60.2	31.2	4.6	24.4	39.8	35.8	33.1	38.5
22 05000	Baton Rouge city.......	3.3	5.0	87,336	54.5	28.9	5.7	19.9	45.5	35.0	28.1	29.6
22 05210	Bayou Cane CDP........	7.9	4.9	7,616	66.2	48.2	4.0	14.0	33.8	23.8	36.0	29.6
22 08920	Bossier City city........	6.5	4.9	25,021	61.3	39.9	3.7	17.6	38.7	34.0	34.1	29.8
22 13960	Central city........	1.7	1.4	10,278	79.2	61.2	5.9	12.1	20.8	19.3	31.4	38.9
22 32755	Hammond city........	5.2	3.1	6,885	62.2	32.9	6.6	22.6	37.8	28.9	27.8	31.2
22 33245	Harvey CDP........	17.0	13.8	7,900	66.8	36.4	4.0	26.4	33.2	28.4	37.1	32.8
22 36255	Houma city........	5.2	4.7	12,750	65.0	40.1	7.0	18.0	35.0	28.5	32.9	34.4
22 39475	Kenner city........	20.6	17.2	24,270	67.5	46.6	5.4	15.5	32.5	28.3	31.2	37.0
22 40735	Lafayette city........	4.4	5.2	49,438	55.5	36.4	4.0	15.1	44.5	35.4	27.6	29.1
22 41155	Lake Charles city.......	3.3	3.7	29,568	61.1	35.9	4.5	20.8	38.9	33.8	32.2	34.9
22 42030	Laplace CDP........	6.6	4.0	10,274	74.8	50.4	5.0	19.4	25.2	21.8	38.4	30.5
22 48785	Marrero CDP........	6.6	6.6	12,597	66.2	34.3	4.6	27.3	33.8	30.5	34.5	40.3
22 50115	Metairie CDP........	13.8	12.4	57,040	57.9	41.8	4.6	11.5	42.1	35.1	26.0	39.5
22 51410	Monroe city........	1.9	2.6	18,695	56.2	26.3	3.1	26.9	43.8	39.0	31.5	33.0
22 54035	New Iberia city.......	4.7	4.8	11,391	66.1	38.1	7.4	20.6	33.9	28.5	35.7	35.2
22 55000	New Orleans city.......	5.3	5.8	146,018	52.0	26.7	5.1	20.2	43.0	39.1	26.6	30.7
22 62385	Prairieville CDP........	5.3	3.4	8,808	74.0	60.7	3.1	10.3	25.0	21.8	43.3	27.0
22 66655	Ruston city........	1.7	6.8	8,282	50.2	30.7	2.9	16.5	49.8	36.7	26.5	26.4
22 70000	Shreveport city.......	2.7	2.7	78,212	60.6	32.7	5.7	22.2	39.4	34.5	31.2	32.3
22 70805	Slidell city........	5.7	3.6	9,979	71.0	51.2	4.7	15.1	29.0	21.8	32.9	39.3
22 73640	Sulphur city........	1.5	2.7	7,832	70.3	46.8	4.2	19.2	29.7	23.9	38.5	34.3
22 75180	Terrytown CDP........	17.9	17.5	8,225	72.6	41.2	7.6	23.8	27.4	24.4	45.0	27.4
23 00000	**Maine**........	1.3	3.5	552,963	62.9	48.9	4.2	9.7	37.1	28.9	27.0	38.5
23 02060	Auburn city........	2.2	3.6	9,798	59.0	41.5	6.6	10.8	41.0	31.1	30.7	35.6
23 02795	Bangor city........	1.8	4.4	14,258	46.5	33.0	4.5	9.1	53.5	38.1	22.3	33.2
23 04860	Biddeford city........	0.7	3.7	8,987	55.1	38.5	4.7	12.0	44.9	35.3	28.8	34.8
23 38740	Lewiston city........	2.6	5.2	15,535	58.0	38.5	3.4	16.2	42.0	33.1	28.2	34.6
23 60545	Portland city........	3.3	11.7	30,846	43.1	30.6	3.2	9.3	56.9	40.3	19.9	27.8
23 71990	South Portland city.......	1.9	8.0	10,994	56.6	40.7	2.6	13.3	43.4	32.7	26.2	35.4
24 00000	**Maryland**........	8.4	14.0	2,141,086	66.9	47.4	4.9	14.7	33.1	27.2	33.7	34.2
24 01600	Annapolis city........	16.7	17.1	16,136	54.2	37.3	3.8	13.1	45.8	37.0	26.3	34.9
24 02275	Arnold CDP........	4.9	5.3	8,131	71.3	58.7	4.6	8.0	28.7	23.7	35.0	37.1
24 02825	Aspen Hill CDP........	27.5	38.3	17,050	68.8	46.0	9.0	13.7	31.2	25.7	36.0	36.7
24 04000	Baltimore city........	4.3	7.3	240,575	52.3	23.6	5.2	23.4	47.7	39.4	27.3	33.2
24 05825	Bel Air North CDP.......	2.4	3.3	10,175	81.1	68.1	2.5	10.6	18.9	14.5	40.4	34.7
24 05950	Bel Air South CDP.......	3.7	6.4	17,035	69.2	53.4	6.3	9.6	30.8	25.4	38.9	33.3
24 07125	Bethesda CDP........	8.2	21.5	25,000	64.5	54.9	2.1	7.5	35.5	29.1	31.3	37.7
24 08775	Bowie city........	7.2	13.8	19,068	73.7	56.2	5.0	12.5	26.3	21.3	37.4	31.6
24 13325	Carney CDP........	3.9	9.9	11,903	55.0	41.1	3.1	10.8	45.0	37.8	21.9	40.5
24 14125	Catonsville CDP........	3.9	6.6	14,999	61.0	48.0	2.8	10.2	39.0	31.5	30.0	40.8
24 16875	Chillum CDP........	43.5	45.7	11,593	67.0	30.4	12.0	24.6	33.0	21.6	40.7	24.9
24 17900	Clinton CDP........	5.8	7.9	12,629	73.2	49.0	4.2	20.1	26.8	25.0	36.5	36.6
24 18250	Cockeysville CDP........	5.7	20.6	8,817	50.5	37.3	3.7	9.5	49.5	42.5	24.4	27.5
24 18750	College Park city.......	10.5	18.9	6,307	40.7	31.9	3.5	5.4	59.3	30.4	18.3	24.2
24 19125	Columbia CDP........	8.2	19.8	40,526	67.6	52.2	4.4	11.0	32.4	26.9	33.9	29.0
24 20875	Crofton CDP........	4.7	4.4	10,988	71.0	55.3	5.9	9.7	29.0	22.7	43.9	22.7
24 21325	Cumberland city........	0.8	1.9	8,956	53.7	33.0	3.4	17.3	46.3	40.0	29.5	43.3
24 23975	Dundalk CDP........	4.8	6.5	23,501	63.9	40.1	6.8	17.0	36.1	30.1	31.0	40.6
24 25150	Edgewood CDP........	6.1	6.8	9,705	75.7	46.9	3.1	25.7	24.3	16.5	43.4	25.9
24 25575	Eldersburg CDP........	2.4	4.0	10,274	77.6	67.8	2.6	7.2	22.4	20.3	40.3	37.1
24 26000	Ellicott City CDP........	4.3	22.1	24,413	79.4	68.6	2.1	8.7	20.6	17.7	43.0	32.4
24 26600	Essex CDP........	6.0	9.2	14,486	62.2	38.7	6.8	16.7	37.8	31.8	30.3	32.6
24 27250	Fairland CDP........	11.7	35.1	8,434	66.8	44.1	2.8	19.9	33.2	27.9	36.8	28.2

Table A-4. Cities — Who: Age, Race/Ethnicity, and Household Structure, 2010–2012—*Continued*

STATE and Place code	STATE or City	Total population	Percent change 2010–2012	Population by age (percent)						Median age	Race alone or in combination (percent)			
				Under 5 years	5 to 17 years	18 to 24 years	25 to 44 years	45 to 64 years	65 years and over		White	Black	Asian, Hawaiian, or Pacific Islander	American Indian, Alaska Native, or some other race
	ACS table number:	B01003	Population estimates	B01001	B01001	B01001	B01001	B01001	B01001	B01002	B02008	B02009	B02011 + B02012	B02010 + B02013
	Column number:	1	2	3	4	5	6	7	8	9	10	11	12	13
	Maryland—Cont.													
24 29525	Fort Washington CDP..............	25,638	...	5.2	16.1	8.4	20.7	32.5	17.1	44.5	18.6	71.7	9.4	5.2
24 30325	Frederick city......................	65,905	1.5	7.1	15.4	9.7	32.1	24.6	11.1	35.5	69.9	19.5	6.8	7.2
24 31175	Gaithersburg city..................	61,413	4.4	8.9	15.8	6.6	34.9	24.3	9.6	34.2	59.1	18.6	20.4	7.8
24 32025	Germantown CDP..................	86,574	...	6.4	19.5	8.0	33.5	26.6	5.9	35.2	51.6	25.0	22.6	6.3
24 32650	Glen Burnie CDP...................	67,649	...	6.9	13.1	10.5	29.5	29.3	10.6	37.1	70.8	25.1	6.1	2.9
24 34775	Greenbelt city......................	23,340	1.8	5.8	17.1	11.6	32.2	25.3	8.0	32.8	37.8	52.5	7.4	5.8
24 36075	Hagerstown city...................	40,393	1.7	7.4	17.3	8.7	29.8	24.5	12.3	34.8	78.2	21.8	2.4	1.8
24 41475	Ilchester CDP......................	24,521	...	5.6	21.2	7.4	26.9	31.1	7.7	37.7	60.2	19.5	17.9	7.1
24 45325	Landover CDP......................	22,211	...	7.8	18.1	11.1	27.8	25.4	9.7	32.2	6.2	87.6	1.5	6.3
24 45525	Langley Park CDP..................	21,657	...	8.4	13.8	14.0	47.9	13.9	2.0	29.5	20.0	9.7	2.4	69.8
24 45900	Laurel city.........................	25,366	1.4	9.5	14.4	7.7	37.7	23.4	7.3	34.1	29.8	53.2	7.6	13.1
24 47450	Lochearn CDP......................	25,148	...	5.1	16.4	8.4	24.3	30.1	15.6	40.8	14.2	82.4	1.9	0.2
24 52300	Middle River CDP..................	27,642	...	7.1	20.0	9.8	30.8	22.2	10.1	32.7	67.1	30.3	3.2	1.4
24 52562	Milford Mill CDP...................	31,468	...	5.8	14.7	10.5	31.8	27.8	9.4	37.4	11.7	84.8	2.2	3.3
24 53325	Montgomery Village CDP.........	32,823	...	8.6	16.4	7.6	33.4	25.0	8.9	34.9	57.5	21.1	13.2	12.7
24 56337	North Bethesda CDP..............	45,862	...	4.9	13.6	7.9	31.1	27.3	15.1	39.0	75.9	9.3	15.8	3.7
24 56875	North Potomac CDP...............	23,800	...	4.5	23.2	7.4	21.5	34.8	8.6	41.4	55.2	5.1	40.9	1.4
24 58300	Odenton CDP......................	36,416	...	7.7	16.4	9.1	34.0	22.3	10.5	35.0	68.8	23.6	7.8	4.0
24 58900	Olney CDP..........................	35,953	...	4.8	22.5	7.2	22.2	32.8	10.4	40.7	72.1	16.1	11.6	4.7
24 59425	Owings Mills CDP..................	34,346	...	8.1	16.5	12.7	33.8	21.6	7.3	30.9	36.0	53.0	10.0	2.8
24 60275	Parkville CDP.......................	32,367	...	7.1	15.5	10.6	29.4	26.5	11.0	35.2	61.1	33.9	3.1	3.2
24 60475	Pasadena CDP......................	24,193	...	5.6	19.9	8.9	31.0	24.8	9.7	33.5	90.5	5.7	1.8	1.3
24 60975	Perry Hall CDP.....................	29,784	...	6.8	17.0	7.9	25.7	29.9	12.7	39.2	78.4	8.5	13.7	2.2
24 61400	Pikesville CDP......................	32,546	...	6.6	13.2	5.5	23.8	25.9	25.0	45.9	78.0	14.1	8.7	...
24 63300	Potomac CDP.......................	46,353	...	5.0	19.3	5.9	17.9	33.4	18.6	46.1	75.5	5.5	19.9	1.7
24 64950	Randallstown CDP.................	30,035	...	5.2	17.0	8.4	21.4	32.3	15.7	43.5	15.9	79.3	2.2	...
24 65600	Reisterstown CDP..................	27,488	...	7.1	17.1	11.1	29.6	24.9	10.3	34.2	58.5	30.0	8.7	5.8
24 67675	Rockville city......................	62,299	2.8	7.0	14.1	6.6	30.4	27.0	15.0	39.6	66.7	9.7	21.2	5.7
24 69925	Salisbury city......................	30,913	2.6	8.2	13.3	21.8	23.7	21.7	11.3	29.6	60.9	36.2	3.6	0.7
24 71150	Severn CDP.........................	43,718	...	6.8	17.5	7.8	29.6	29.5	8.7	37.0	50.9	39.9	11.8	3.5
24 71200	Severna Park CDP..................	37,047	...	5.7	19.5	7.3	21.7	31.6	14.2	42.8	91.7	3.8	5.2	...
24 72450	Silver Spring CDP..................	76,520	...	7.8	14.0	9.2	38.1	22.6	8.2	33.4	46.6	30.7	3.9	18.1
24 73650	South Laurel CDP..................	26,110	...	8.5	19.9	8.1	32.1	22.1	9.4	33.0	27.7	62.5	5.5	7.6
24 75725	Suitland CDP.......................	24,644	...	9.1	19.6	12.3	29.2	22.1	7.8	30.2	4.6	95.0	0.6	0.7
24 78425	Towson CDP........................	57,143	...	4.7	13.3	20.8	22.6	22.3	16.3	35.1	80.4	12.2	3.0	1.4
24 81175	Waldorf CDP.......................	71,987	...	7.5	21.1	9.2	30.3	25.5	6.4	33.7	38.5	58.3	5.8	3.0
24 83775	Wheaton CDP......................	50,126	...	9.0	16.0	9.0	34.2	23.2	8.6	33.4	37.9	19.6	12.4	33.8
24 86475	Woodlawn CDP (Baltimore County).................	40,307	...	7.6	21.2	7.3	30.0	22.7	11.1	33.0	30.4	59.9	10.4	2.9
25 00000	**Massachusetts**..................	6,605,468	1.3	5.5	15.8	10.4	26.3	27.9	14.1	39.3	82.9	8.4	6.3	5.3
25 00840	Agawam Town city................	28,542	0.5	4.7	16.2	8.2	23.4	30.4	17.0	43.7	94.2	1.8	2.2	2.5
25 01640	Arlington CDP......................	43,305	...	6.4	15.2	3.8	29.7	29.7	15.1	42.0	88.9	3.6	8.8	1.6
25 02690	Attleboro city.....................	43,727	0.5	7.9	14.2	8.4	27.7	28.9	13.0	40.0	87.8	6.1	5.4	2.5
25 03690	Barnstable Town city.............	44,969	-0.8	4.9	13.5	5.7	21.3	33.1	21.5	47.7	93.6	3.1	1.5	4.0
25 05105	Belmont CDP.......................	24,962	...	6.3	18.6	5.6	27.9	26.6	14.9	39.9	84.4	2.7	13.2	1.6
25 05595	Beverly city........................	40,027	1.5	6.0	12.6	13.7	25.8	27.3	14.6	38.8	95.5	2.3	2.4	1.5
25 07000	Boston city.........................	628,365	2.6	5.3	11.5	18.6	33.6	20.6	10.3	30.9	57.4	28.6	10.1	8.6
25 07740	Braintree Town city...............	36,026	1.2	6.0	16.4	8.2	26.4	26.6	16.4	40.1	86.1	5.0	8.5	1.8
25 09000	Brockton city......................	94,031	0.3	7.3	18.9	10.4	24.9	25.7	12.8	36.1	48.9	41.3	3.4	10.6
25 09210	Brookline CDP......................	58,948	...	5.1	13.3	12.8	31.9	22.4	14.7	35.1	76.9	3.4	19.3	1.9
25 09875	Burlington CDP.....................	24,882	...	4.8	16.4	6.4	27.8	27.4	17.1	41.5	81.2	4.7	16.2	...
25 11000	Cambridge city....................	105,733	1.5	4.3	7.2	19.7	39.4	18.5	10.9	30.9	72.0	12.3	16.9	3.6
25 13205	Chelsea city.......................	36,057	4.3	10.3	15.6	9.7	36.7	18.8	9.0	31.1	81.2	38.5	3.1	10.6
25 13660	Chicopee city......................	55,430	0.4	5.5	15.5	9.3	25.4	27.5	16.9	40.6	87.1	4.5	1.4	9.0
25 16285	Danvers CDP.......................	26,808	...	4.5	16.9	7.2	21.5	31.5	18.4	44.9	94.1	1.9	2.8	...
25 16530	Dedham CDP.......................	24,897	...	5.9	15.0	7.2	25.2	28.8	18.0	43.2	90.6	4.8	4.8	1.5
25 21990	Everett city........................	42,140	2.0	5.8	13.8	9.9	33.1	25.5	11.9	36.5	73.3	20.1	4.6	8.2
25 23000	Fall River city.....................	88,885	0.1	6.2	15.3	9.0	28.2	26.0	15.3	38.3	90.6	4.3	2.5	5.5
25 23875	Fitchburg city.....................	40,403	0.0	5.1	16.8	13.6	27.0	24.3	13.2	35.0	80.7	6.1	4.2	12.5
25 24960	Framingham CDP...................	69,409	...	6.9	14.2	8.6	30.3	26.5	13.4	37.7	78.0	10.3	8.4	6.1
25 25172	Franklin Town city................	32,148	1.6	6.1	21.7	9.3	23.5	28.3	11.1	39.0	93.2	1.8	5.4	0.2
25 25485	Gardner city.......................	20,204	0.5	5.3	15.0	8.5	27.9	28.6	14.6	40.9	91.7	2.3	2.3	5.7
25 26150	Gloucester city....................	29,023	1.1	4.0	14.4	6.6	20.5	34.7	19.7	47.6	97.2	2.2	0.6	2.1
25 29405	Haverhill city......................	61,399	1.4	7.6	15.0	8.4	28.2	27.8	12.9	38.8	87.7	3.3	1.8	8.9
25 30840	Holyoke city.......................	40,063	0.6	8.0	18.2	9.3	27.9	22.7	13.9	35.1	85.3	5.0	1.2	10.2
25 34550	Lawrence city.....................	76,928	1.1	9.1	20.4	12.2	27.9	22.3	8.2	30.7	37.1	9.7	2.7	54.3
25 35075	Leominster city....................	40,888	0.5	4.8	14.4	8.6	26.1	31.4	14.7	42.5	83.4	7.9	2.9	9.7
25 35250	Lexington CDP.....................	31,874	...	5.0	21.6	4.3	16.7	33.2	19.2	46.5	78.0	1.5	22.0	0.7
25 37000	Lowell city.........................	107,616	1.7	7.2	15.4	12.0	30.3	24.4	10.7	33.5	60.2	7.8	22.3	13.2

Table A-4. Cities — Who: Age, Race/Ethnicity, and Household Structure, 2010–2012—*Continued*

STATE and Place code	STATE or City	Percent Hispanic or Latino	Percent foreign born	Total households	Household type (percent)							Percent of households with people under 18 years	Percent of households with people 60 years and over
					Family households				Nonfamily households				
					Total family households	Married-couple families	Male household families	Female household families	Total nonfamily households	One-person households			
	ACS table number:	B03003	C05003	B11001	B11001	B11001	B11001	B11001	B11001	B11001		B11005	B11006
	Column number:	14	15	16	17	18	19	20	21	22		23	24
	Maryland—Cont.												
24 29525	Fort Washington CDP.................	4.8	12.7	8,672	80.5	59.6	3.3	17.6	19.5	17.3		33.3	47.0
24 30325	Frederick city.........................	16.3	19.4	26,038	59.9	41.4	5.1	13.4	40.1	32.0		29.6	29.8
24 31175	Gaithersburg city	21.1	39.6	22,526	68.4	49.0	4.3	15.1	31.6	25.7		39.4	27.7
24 32025	Germantown CDP.....................	19.2	38.2	30,942	70.8	50.2	6.1	14.5	29.2	25.4		41.9	20.7
24 32650	Glen Burnie CDP......................	7.3	9.3	26,283	64.8	40.4	6.2	18.2	35.2	28.5		31.4	28.5
24 34775	Greenbelt city.........................	13.9	27.1	9,317	55.2	29.1	7.3	18.8	44.8	35.9		31.5	24.4
24 36075	Hagerstown city	5.0	7.1	16,293	59.7	36.2	4.7	18.8	40.3	33.0		33.9	30.6
24 41475	Ilchester CDP..........................	6.9	18.5	9,047	71.3	49.6	6.4	15.3	28.7	22.8		41.9	24.7
24 45325	Landover CDP..........................	11.5	18.4	7,907	61.6	27.6	8.2	25.7	38.4	30.5		36.8	27.3
24 45525	Langley Park CDP.....................	83.2	68.4	5,188	67.1	31.6	22.4	13.0	32.9	15.9		44.7	10.9
24 45900	Laurel city.............................	22.0	26.5	9,639	55.9	31.7	5.2	19.1	44.1	37.2		34.7	23.1
24 47450	Lochearn CDP.........................	4.6	11.9	9,526	66.7	42.7	2.9	21.1	33.3	30.5		31.8	41.3
24 52300	Middle River CDP	7.5	11.0	9,931	67.0	40.6	8.1	18.4	33.0	27.1		39.1	31.2
24 52562	Milford Mill CDP......................	6.0	14.8	12,339	66.3	35.1	4.9	26.3	33.7	27.7		32.2	27.0
24 53325	Montgomery Village CDP............	30.1	37.9	11,871	65.8	45.6	5.4	14.8	34.2	27.8		37.8	26.5
24 56337	North Bethesda CDP..................	12.4	34.0	20,448	53.4	38.9	4.5	10.0	46.6	36.2		24.3	31.1
24 56875	North Potomac CDP..................	3.3	36.2	7,701	86.4	76.7	0.6	9.1	13.6	12.5		48.3	33.0
24 58300	Odenton CDP..........................	5.0	6.2	14,296	64.7	51.8	1.9	11.0	35.3	25.9		34.5	26.9
24 58900	Olney CDP	8.7	20.2	11,881	82.1	66.8	3.8	11.6	17.9	14.5		42.1	33.4
24 59425	Owings Mills CDP	7.3	18.0	13,305	60.0	38.8	3.3	17.9	40.0	31.2		37.2	20.2
24 60275	Parkville CDP...........................	5.2	10.8	12,894	59.7	34.1	7.2	18.3	40.3	33.3		32.8	26.9
24 60475	Pasadena CDP..........................	5.5	4.6	8,233	72.0	55.0	6.8	10.2	28.0	22.0		38.9	28.5
24 60975	Perry Hall CDP.........................	2.8	13.3	11,472	69.2	55.0	2.7	11.5	30.8	26.9		35.0	34.3
24 61400	Pikesville CDP..........................	2.9	21.6	14,127	59.9	48.7	1.6	9.6	40.1	33.8		24.7	49.7
24 63300	Potomac CDP..........................	8.9	30.7	15,991	81.8	73.2	1.4	7.1	18.2	16.1		38.5	46.8
24 64950	Randallstown CDP	2.4	9.2	11,277	65.1	41.0	7.0	17.1	34.9	31.8		32.1	43.4
24 65600	Reisterstown CDP	12.0	22.6	10,413	71.2	43.3	4.7	23.2	28.8	22.4		39.3	30.3
24 67675	Rockville city..........................	16.1	33.2	24,375	65.7	52.7	4.5	8.5	34.3	27.5		31.6	35.7
24 69925	Salisbury city..........................	5.6	9.6	11,541	53.6	29.2	3.8	20.6	46.4	34.1		32.9	30.1
24 71150	Severn CDP.............................	6.5	13.6	15,909	73.7	51.3	6.7	15.6	26.3	21.9		36.4	27.3
24 71200	Severna Park CDP	2.9	5.7	12,730	81.4	69.8	4.6	7.0	18.6	16.1		38.1	41.8
24 72450	Silver Spring CDP	25.7	36.8	30,566	53.8	37.3	5.2	11.4	46.2	36.3		28.7	24.4
24 73650	South Laurel CDP.....................	12.1	24.1	9,551	63.6	37.9	6.8	18.9	36.4	32.1		38.6	23.2
24 75725	Suitland CDP...........................	5.1	5.7	9,699	64.2	22.1	8.7	33.5	35.8	31.5		40.5	23.4
24 78425	Towson CDP............................	3.9	10.7	20,991	56.5	45.2	3.7	7.6	43.5	34.8		26.6	37.9
24 81175	Waldorf CDP...........................	5.5	8.2	24,821	71.4	45.0	5.2	21.2	28.6	23.3		43.1	22.5
24 83775	Wheaton CDP..........................	45.3	45.1	14,708	73.2	46.6	9.0	17.6	26.8	19.2		42.9	33.1
24 86475	Woodlawn CDP (Baltimore County)	5.0	13.9	14,960	62.4	38.8	3.8	19.7	37.6	31.0		36.6	32.2
25 00000	**Massachusetts**	9.9	15.0	2,524,028	63.3	46.5	4.0	12.7	36.7	29.1		30.8	35.7
25 00840	Agawam Town city	2.8	8.6	11,253	68.0	50.7	6.0	11.4	32.0	29.3		28.9	40.6
25 01640	Arlington CDP..........................	3.6	17.1	18,915	57.2	47.4	1.8	8.0	42.8	34.7		28.8	35.4
25 02690	Attleboro city.........................	7.7	9.3	16,580	67.0	51.6	4.6	10.8	33.0	25.3		31.8	32.1
25 03690	Barnstable Town city	4.1	10.9	19,369	60.2	47.6	4.5	8.1	39.8	31.8		22.8	47.0
25 05105	Belmont CDP	4.1	22.9	9,016	74.2	62.4	2.2	9.7	25.8	20.7		39.3	37.4
25 05595	Beverly city............................	3.1	6.3	15,406	58.3	46.5	2.6	9.2	41.7	31.2		27.4	36.2
25 07000	Boston city.............................	17.7	26.6	248,738	47.2	26.1	4.4	16.6	52.8	38.2		23.5	27.1
25 07740	Braintree Town city	2.7	12.1	12,955	71.0	54.4	3.9	12.7	29.0	23.0		34.3	39.0
25 09000	Brockton city..........................	10.1	25.4	33,057	68.3	37.0	7.2	24.1	31.7	27.3		40.9	34.3
25 09210	Brookline CDP.........................	5.5	25.1	25,897	50.3	41.3	1.7	7.3	49.7	37.6		23.9	33.7
25 09875	Burlington CDP........................	2.4	20.0	9,434	70.6	59.9	2.3	8.5	29.4	23.1		33.0	38.9
25 11000	Cambridge city	6.7	28.1	44,598	39.9	29.5	2.1	8.4	60.1	41.9		16.6	27.1
25 13205	Chelsea city	62.4	46.1	11,927	60.3	28.7	7.1	24.5	39.7	32.8		39.0	27.0
25 13660	Chicopee city..........................	16.1	9.3	23,123	57.9	39.5	5.4	13.0	42.1	35.2		28.0	37.8
25 16285	Danvers CDP...........................	3.9	7.4	10,314	67.3	55.7	3.5	8.1	32.7	28.7		30.1	40.0
25 16530	Dedham CDP...........................	4.5	12.3	9,580	67.8	54.3	4.2	9.4	32.2	26.9		31.0	39.7
25 21990	Everett city.............................	20.5	43.6	15,611	65.9	38.9	6.8	20.3	34.1	26.2		33.5	33.1
25 23000	Fall River city..........................	7.8	18.8	38,292	56.6	32.6	4.3	19.6	43.4	35.7		28.4	33.0
25 23875	Fitchburg city..........................	22.3	11.5	14,680	63.3	39.9	6.6	16.9	36.7	28.6		32.8	33.7
25 24960	Framingham CDP......................	12.3	25.4	26,682	62.8	46.8	4.0	12.1	37.2	30.4		31.7	32.7
25 25172	Franklin Town city	2.6	6.4	11,063	75.1	64.7	2.5	7.9	24.9	21.8		43.1	30.1
25 25485	Gardner city	7.7	9.4	7,913	61.5	42.4	5.4	13.7	38.5	31.9		31.0	37.4
25 26150	Gloucester city........................	3.5	8.6	12,099	65.0	48.9	4.8	11.4	35.0	29.6		24.6	49.8
25 29405	Haverhill city...........................	13.6	8.6	23,923	62.6	40.9	6.2	15.5	37.4	30.2		33.1	34.1
25 30840	Holyoke city............................	47.0	4.4	15,760	63.1	27.4	6.1	29.5	36.9	30.2		37.1	31.4
25 34550	Lawrence city..........................	76.5	37.7	26,606	69.0	29.9	6.2	32.9	31.0	26.0		45.3	27.3
25 35075	Leominster city........................	14.0	13.7	16,870	61.2	45.2	6.9	9.1	38.8	30.9		28.6	33.3
25 35250	Lexington CDP.........................	1.6	23.6	11,627	78.2	67.4	2.5	8.3	21.8	19.4		42.0	46.9
25 37000	Lowell city.............................	16.1	24.6	38,913	62.0	37.6	5.6	18.8	38.0	29.3		34.2	29.5

Table A-4. Cities — Who: Age, Race/Ethnicity, and Household Structure, 2010–2012—*Continued*

STATE and Place code	STATE or City	Total population	Percent change 2010–2012	Under 5 years	5 to 17 years	18 to 24 years	25 to 44 years	45 to 64 years	65 years and over	Median age	White	Black	Asian, Hawaiian, or Pacific Islander	American Indian, Alaska Native, or some other race
	ACS table number:	B01003	Population estimates	B01001	B01001	B01001	B01001	B01001	B01001	B01002	B02008	B02009	B02011 + B02012	B02010 + B02013
	Column number:	1	2	3	4	5	6	7	8	9	10	11	12	13
	Massachusetts—Cont.													
25 37490	Lynn city	90,885	0.8	7.3	17.6	10.5	28.9	24.3	11.4	34.0	62.5	15.2	8.2	19.5
25 37875	Malden city	59,969	1.4	6.3	14.1	10.6	33.3	24.4	11.3	35.9	58.0	16.6	25.0	5.3
25 38435	Marblehead CDP	19,959	...	4.4	22.3	4.0	19.1	33.2	17.0	45.1	98.5	...	1.0	0.6
25 38715	Marlborough city	38,875	1.7	5.4	15.0	9.9	29.1	27.9	12.8	39.6	89.7	11.0	5.3	4.9
25 39835	Medford city	56,673	1.2	4.7	10.4	11.9	32.5	25.6	14.8	36.9	82.0	10.9	8.6	1.2
25 40115	Melrose city	27,230	1.5	6.7	13.8	5.8	30.3	28.2	15.1	41.2	95.1	1.8	3.5	...
25 40710	Methuen Town city	47,683	1.4	6.3	16.5	8.3	25.3	29.3	14.3	40.4	81.5	3.0	4.5	12.3
25 41200	Milford CDP	25,495	...	7.3	16.3	7.7	28.8	26.3	13.6	38.1	88.5	2.9	3.6	7.2
25 41725	Milton CDP	27,106	...	5.3	19.2	12.9	20.0	28.2	14.4	39.4	80.7	14.4	5.4	1.2
25 44140	Needham CDP	29,218	...	7.2	19.5	5.6	20.8	29.8	17.1	42.9	91.1	2.5	7.1	0.9
25 45000	New Bedford city	94,946	-0.1	6.8	15.7	9.5	27.4	25.5	15.1	37.5	80.4	10.6	1.6	12.2
25 45560	Newton city	85,742	1.1	5.8	15.9	12.7	22.4	27.6	15.6	40.2	83.1	3.4	14.3	1.3
25 46330	Northampton city	28,613	-0.1	3.5	12.7	15.3	25.8	27.8	14.9	38.5	90.4	3.1	5.9	3.1
25 50285	Norwood CDP	28,705	...	6.9	15.0	6.6	27.1	27.8	16.5	40.9	90.3	2.3	4.1	4.0
25 52490	Peabody city	51,601	1.0	5.2	15.0	6.5	25.0	28.2	20.2	44.0	89.4	2.3	3.0	6.5
25 53960	Pittsfield city	44,409	-1.2	5.8	15.1	7.8	23.7	29.1	18.5	43.3	91.0	8.0	1.9	2.6
25 55745	Quincy city	92,720	0.6	5.0	11.2	8.6	33.9	26.8	14.5	38.0	67.7	6.4	26.0	2.3
25 55990	Randolph CDP	32,791	...	5.4	17.0	8.6	26.2	27.9	14.9	40.4	39.4	45.1	13.1	4.0
25 56165	Reading CDP	24,981	...	5.7	20.2	6.0	24.3	28.3	15.5	40.5	93.3	1.0	4.9	0.8
25 56585	Revere city	52,536	2.5	5.8	14.2	7.8	32.9	26.4	12.9	38.9	81.4	10.8	5.2	9.8
25 59105	Salem city	42,028	0.9	4.6	13.0	14.6	26.3	29.1	12.4	38.3	85.3	9.1	3.1	6.2
25 60050	Saugus CDP	27,019	...	3.7	14.2	5.8	24.3	32.9	19.1	46.2	92.7	2.9	3.0	2.5
25 62535	Somerville city	76,381	1.8	5.9	8.1	15.0	45.5	17.1	8.4	31.0	78.1	8.9	10.7	4.8
25 67000	Springfield city	153,531	0.1	7.3	19.4	13.5	25.3	23.5	11.1	32.1	55.9	24.2	2.6	21.2
25 67700	Stoneham CDP	21,457	...	4.5	14.7	7.3	25.5	30.8	17.3	43.8	91.3	2.3	5.3	2.4
25 69170	Taunton city	55,968	0.3	5.5	15.8	9.0	26.3	29.8	13.6	40.7	90.8	5.7	1.5	3.9
25 72250	Wakefield CDP	25,384	...	6.7	15.7	7.2	26.8	29.8	14.0	41.1	94.9	0.6	4.6	0.6
25 72600	Waltham city	61,411	1.7	5.3	9.8	17.0	33.1	22.8	12.1	33.7	76.3	6.6	14.2	6.0
25 73440	Watertown Town city	32,358	2.7	5.6	8.9	8.0	35.3	26.5	15.6	38.7	86.8	4.6	3.1	2.9
25 74210	Wellesley CDP	28,482	...	4.7	21.4	17.5	16.1	27.1	13.2	37.5	87.1	2.6	11.3	2.0
25 76030	Westfield city	41,301	0.7	4.8	15.2	16.0	22.3	27.7	14.0	38.9	91.5	2.1	3.1	4.8
25 77890	West Springfield Town city	28,490	0.8	5.5	16.1	9.2	27.1	27.1	15.0	39.5	89.3	3.2	4.6	5.0
25 78972	Weymouth Town city	54,285	2.1	5.1	15.5	6.3	25.3	31.9	15.8	43.3	91.9	3.8	4.1	0.7
25 80195	Wilmington CDP	22,655	...	6.7	19.2	7.1	23.4	30.9	12.7	41.8	93.9	1.5	5.7	...
25 80545	Winchester CDP	21,628	...	5.4	23.6	4.8	19.4	30.1	16.6	43.4	87.8	0.8	12.1	0.3
25 81035	Woburn city	38,606	1.7	6.7	12.9	6.1	30.3	28.4	15.7	40.8	86.9	5.4	7.7	1.6
25 82000	Worcester city	182,344	0.4	7.0	15.1	14.6	27.6	23.3	12.4	33.4	77.7	13.8	7.2	5.4
26 00000	**Michigan**	9,879,277	0.1	5.9	17.4	10.0	24.5	28.1	14.2	39.2	81.5	15.3	3.1	2.8
26 00440	Adrian city	20,953	-1.2	6.9	15.6	17.3	23.2	21.4	15.7	33.9	90.5	5.8	0.8	6.4
26 01380	Allen Park city	27,886	-1.4	4.6	16.9	9.1	24.3	28.9	16.3	41.8	95.6	3.6	...	2.5
26 03000	Ann Arbor city	115,124	1.8	4.1	9.9	29.0	28.1	18.9	10.0	28.1	77.4	8.1	16.4	2.5
26 04105	Auburn Hills city	21,506	0.9	7.6	13.3	14.9	31.2	23.0	10.0	31.7	74.7	13.5	10.1	4.2
26 05920	Battle Creek city	52,112	-0.8	7.7	18.2	8.4	26.0	25.3	14.5	36.2	76.4	21.8	2.7	3.9
26 06020	Bay City city	34,700	-1.1	7.0	17.1	10.0	27.0	26.6	12.3	36.5	95.1	3.8	0.7	3.9
26 08640	Birmingham city	20,279	1.6	6.5	19.0	4.3	27.3	29.2	13.8	41.2	92.0	5.8	3.7	0.5
26 12060	Burton city	29,706	-1.7	5.5	17.8	8.6	25.0	29.5	13.5	39.6	93.5	6.8	0.6	3.2
26 21000	Dearborn city	97,123	-1.4	8.4	21.4	9.4	26.2	23.3	11.3	32.4	93.2	4.4	4.5	1.7
26 21020	Dearborn Heights city	57,196	-1.3	6.9	18.2	8.4	25.9	25.0	15.6	37.8	88.7	9.2	3.8	1.9
26 22000	Detroit city	706,522	-1.4	7.0	18.9	11.8	24.6	25.7	11.9	35.1	13.6	83.2	1.5	4.1
26 24120	East Lansing city	48,582	-0.1	2.5	5.7	60.8	15.7	9.2	6.0	21.3	80.4	9.6	12.8	2.3
26 24290	Eastpointe city	32,412	-0.1	6.6	20.1	9.5	27.3	25.1	11.4	35.4	59.6	36.7	2.8	3.6
26 27440	Farmington Hills city	80,266	1.2	5.0	16.0	7.8	25.4	29.7	16.3	42.1	70.2	19.1	11.9	2.3
26 27880	Ferndale city	19,983	0.8	5.5	12.6	9.1	38.1	25.3	9.5	35.4	85.0	13.0	3.2	3.0
26 29000	Flint city	101,423	-1.7	8.2	18.4	11.4	25.5	25.0	11.5	33.9	42.4	58.1	0.6	2.8
26 29580	Forest Hills CDP	26,798	...	6.6	23.9	5.2	19.7	33.2	11.4	41.1	97.3	...	2.3	...
26 31420	Garden City city	27,415	-1.4	7.1	15.8	8.1	27.3	28.2	13.6	40.3	95.8	2.9	1.0	2.0
26 34000	Grand Rapids city	189,162	1.3	7.7	17.2	14.5	29.0	20.7	11.0	30.7	73.0	24.1	2.9	4.9
26 36280	Hamtramck city	22,209	-1.1	9.6	22.8	13.6	28.5	18.7	6.8	27.8	64.9	14.3	23.0	3.6
26 37100	Haslett CDP	20,562	...	3.9	15.1	13.7	25.7	26.9	14.7	37.5	89.2	8.5	3.5	2.9
26 38640	Holland city	33,134	0.7	7.8	16.2	19.2	24.3	19.2	13.3	30.1	83.3	5.4	5.2	10.2
26 38780	Holt CDP	24,205	...	6.8	20.0	5.7	28.2	28.2	11.2	37.8	89.9	6.4	4.5	1.5
26 40680	Inkster city	25,120	-1.3	10.1	20.5	10.8	24.9	23.4	10.3	31.6	17.5	81.0	2.1	2.3
26 41420	Jackson city	33,449	-0.3	8.8	20.7	10.1	28.0	22.0	10.4	31.4	74.9	25.8	1.0	2.3
26 42160	Kalamazoo city	74,689	1.0	5.4	14.7	27.7	24.3	18.4	9.4	26.2	73.3	23.6	2.8	3.4
26 42820	Kentwood city	49,213	2.0	7.2	16.7	10.8	28.5	24.7	12.1	34.4	74.2	18.9	8.6	4.7
26 46000	Lansing city	113,594	-0.2	7.7	15.2	13.7	29.6	23.5	10.2	32.1	68.5	27.6	5.4	7.5
26 47800	Lincoln Park city	37,752	-1.5	7.6	17.9	8.6	29.0	25.5	11.4	35.4	87.4	8.2	0.2	6.4
26 49000	Livonia city	96,101	-1.1	4.5	15.7	7.7	22.9	31.4	17.9	44.4	93.4	3.7	3.6	0.9
26 50560	Madison Heights city	29,841	1.0	6.9	12.3	9.1	31.7	25.2	14.8	38.9	87.5	7.6	5.2	2.7
26 51900	Marquette city	21,438	0.8	3.8	8.6	30.3	20.8	23.9	12.6	29.4	92.9	5.3	.2	3.2
26 53780	Midland city	42,149	0.4	6.2	16.3	10.7	24.3	26.5	15.9	37.8	92.5	2.1	4.4	1.8

Table A-4. Cities — Who: Age, Race/Ethnicity, and Household Structure, 2010–2012—*Continued*

STATE and Place code	STATE or City	Percent Hispanic or Latino	Percent foreign born	Total households	Total family households	Married-couple families	Male household families	Female household families	Total nonfamily households	One-person households	Percent of households with people under 18 years	Percent of households with people 60 years and over
					Family households				**Nonfamily households**			
ACS table number:		B03003	C05003	B11001	B11001	B11001	B11001	B11001	B11001	B11001	B11005	B11006
Column number:		14	15	16	17	18	19	20	21	22	23	24
	Massachusetts—Cont.											
25 37490	Lynn city	32.4	31.0	32,900	65.1	34.0	7.6	23.5	34.9	28.7	38.8	31.3
25 37875	Malden city	11.2	42.9	22,565	60.5	43.1	3.3	14.1	39.5	29.0	33.1	28.3
25 38435	Marblehead CDP	2.2	6.9	7,618	71.5	62.3	2.4	6.8	23.5	24.9	36.7	42.4
25 38715	Marlborough city	12.0	20.1	15,726	57.4	44.5	2.8	10.1	42.6	33.1	27.5	32.5
25 39835	Medford city	4.6	21.9	22,448	59.3	45.1	3.8	10.4	40.7	26.9	23.5	35.7
25 40115	Melrose city	3.8	9.3	11,422	63.7	53.5	3.8	6.4	35.3	30.9	26.5	36.0
25 40710	Methuen Town city	17.5	15.3	17,885	68.4	52.7	3.6	12.2	31.6	28.3	33.8	36.3
25 41200	Milford CDP	10.4	19.7	9,562	69.5	55.9	3.2	10.4	30.5	23.8	36.7	29.1
25 41725	Milton CDP	3.9	11.8	8,937	76.2	59.5	3.7	13.1	23.8	19.2	39.2	40.6
25 44140	Needham CDP	3.2	12.9	10,449	74.6	65.9	2.3	6.4	25.4	23.6	38.1	41.9
25 45000	New Bedford city	15.8	19.6	38,851	59.2	33.5	4.9	20.8	40.8	33.7	31.0	34.8
25 45560	Newton city	5.2	20.8	30,484	69.5	60.3	1.8	7.3	30.5	24.9	34.5	40.2
25 46330	Northampton city	8.3	8.9	11,628	49.0	34.9	2.6	11.5	51.0	36.8	23.6	36.3
25 50285	Norwood CDP	3.6	13.2	11,296	60.1	46.8	4.1	9.2	39.9	30.3	29.3	36.6
25 52490	Peabody city	8.2	15.4	21,564	61.5	47.2	3.5	10.8	33.5	33.5	27.9	45.1
25 53960	Pittsfield city	5.1	5.7	19,905	54.7	33.7	4.9	16.1	45.3	39.7	27.2	40.7
25 55745	Quincy city	3.7	29.1	39,414	54.2	39.7	3.9	10.6	45.8	36.1	22.4	33.8
25 55990	Randolph CDP	6.2	29.9	11,580	69.2	45.9	3.3	19.9	30.8	25.1	32.6	39.4
25 56165	Reading CDP	3.8	9.2	9,122	73.0	64.3	0.9	7.8	27.0	22.1	36.4	38.4
25 56585	Revere city	28.4	32.8	19,757	59.5	37.0	4.6	18.0	40.5	32.1	29.8	33.9
25 59105	Salem city	15.1	16.7	18,150	53.1	31.1	5.1	16.9	45.9	37.7	24.2	29.8
25 60050	Saugus CDP	5.0	9.2	10,433	70.3	54.0	4.6	11.7	29.7	25.5	26.2	49.3
25 62535	Somerville city	10.3	24.2	31,630	45.4	30.3	3.9	11.2	54.6	31.9	19.6	21.9
25 67000	Springfield city	40.8	10.8	55,911	64.5	30.5	6.7	27.3	35.5	29.3	38.3	31.2
25 67700	Stoneham CDP	3.1	11.9	8,899	60.4	46.3	2.0	12.1	39.6	30.8	24.9	44.6
25 69170	Taunton city	6.8	11.0	21,594	64.3	44.1	5.3	14.9	35.7	28.8	29.8	35.0
25 72250	Wakefield CDP	1.3	6.1	9,730	66.8	53.4	3.1	10.2	33.2	28.5	31.9	32.2
25 72600	Waltham city	14.1	27.2	23,488	55.4	41.8	4.5	9.2	44.6	33.2	22.9	32.1
25 73440	Watertown Town city	6.5	26.0	14,093	53.8	44.3	2.8	6.8	45.2	33.9	19.8	34.1
25 74210	Wellesley CDP	3.8	12.7	8,561	77.8	69.8	2.1	5.9	22.2	20.1	43.0	41.2
25 76030	Westfield city	6.9	8.9	15,299	64.2	46.4	4.9	12.9	35.8	29.7	28.8	36.8
25 77890	West Springfield Town city	9.2	13.8	11,585	62.8	42.9	4.3	15.6	37.2	31.0	30.1	39.1
25 78972	Weymouth Town city	2.6	9.5	22,672	57.2	44.6	2.5	10.1	42.8	34.5	27.7	38.6
25 80195	Wilmington CDP	1.7	7.1	7,555	80.9	67.1	4.0	9.8	19.1	15.0	41.6	34.0
25 80545	Winchester CDP	1.4	14.2	7,516	80.5	70.9	2.4	7.3	19.5	18.3	42.2	37.5
25 81035	Woburn city	3.9	17.6	15,140	63.1	48.0	5.0	10.0	36.9	30.7	29.8	39.9
25 82000	Worcester city	19.9	20.3	68,665	58.2	34.2	5.4	18.6	41.8	33.4	30.9	31.4
26 00000	**Michigan**	4.5	6.1	3,805,261	65.6	48.2	4.5	12.9	34.4	28.9	30.9	35.9
26 00440	Adrian city	17.9	3.1	7,836	54.8	30.9	5.0	18.9	45.2	37.9	29.4	34.5
26 01380	Allen Park city	9.8	5.4	10,858	67.4	47.9	5.7	13.9	32.6	28.5	33.0	39.0
26 03000	Ann Arbor city	4.8	17.6	45,974	43.0	34.1	2.6	6.3	57.0	38.9	19.5	26.2
26 04105	Auburn Hills city	13.3	17.5	8,746	60.1	43.2	1.9	15.0	39.9	30.2	28.6	26.4
26 05920	Battle Creek city	8.6	6.3	20,745	61.6	38.4	4.3	18.9	38.4	33.0	34.4	37.1
26 06020	Bay City city	8.0	1.4	14,339	56.8	37.7	4.2	14.9	43.2	34.7	29.9	32.1
26 08640	Birmingham city	2.6	9.3	8,658	64.6	54.2	1.4	8.9	35.4	31.9	33.0	32.7
26 12060	Burton city	2.8	1.1	11,404	69.2	47.9	5.3	16.0	30.8	25.9	33.4	34.5
26 21000	Dearborn city	3.7	26.5	31,824	65.4	49.4	5.8	10.3	34.6	30.2	38.1	36.0
26 21020	Dearborn Heights city	4.2	18.1	20,931	65.4	45.7	4.7	15.1	34.6	30.5	31.6	38.8
26 22000	Detroit city	7.3	5.1	253,968	57.6	21.2	6.9	29.5	42.4	37.9	32.5	36.1
26 24120	East Lansing city	3.1	15.2	13,473	33.0	24.5	1.9	6.6	67.0	39.2	14.0	21.8
26 24290	Eastpointe city	2.5	4.3	12,513	62.9	34.9	4.9	23.0	37.1	32.5	37.5	32.7
26 27440	Farmington Hills city	2.4	18.3	33,932	63.3	50.0	4.2	9.1	36.7	32.4	28.8	37.9
26 27880	Ferndale city	5.3	4.3	9,383	43.9	28.6	3.1	12.1	56.1	44.3	23.5	22.1
26 29000	Flint city	4.2	1.1	40,853	56.5	23.6	6.6	26.4	43.5	36.9	32.0	33.0
26 29580	Forest Hills CDP	1.8	6.9	9,028	85.1	79.0	1.7	4.5	14.9	13.6	44.7	36.2
26 31420	Garden City city	2.0	3.3	10,149	68.9	48.9	5.4	14.6	31.1	26.4	32.2	34.1
26 34000	Grand Rapids city	15.6	9.3	72,868	56.1	34.8	4.4	16.9	43.9	33.2	31.1	27.4
26 36280	Hamtramck city	0.9	44.0	6,046	69.6	47.3	6.6	15.7	30.4	25.8	45.2	27.3
26 37100	Haslett CDP	5.4	7.4	8,908	55.5	44.5	2.1	8.9	44.5	33.8	23.3	35.7
26 38640	Holland city	25.5	12.9	11,302	68.0	50.2	4.4	13.3	32.0	24.5	35.6	32.5
26 38780	Holt CDP	4.1	4.8	9,513	69.2	56.8	4.0	8.5	30.8	24.7	35.3	28.6
26 40680	Inkster city	2.3	2.9	9,272	58.7	22.7	4.4	31.6	41.3	37.1	34.5	29.1
26 41420	Jackson city	5.6	2.2	12,679	60.4	30.6	4.7	25.2	39.6	33.8	36.8	28.8
26 42160	Kalamazoo city	6.6	6.3	27,568	46.6	27.0	3.7	15.9	53.4	36.3	26.3	26.0
26 42820	Kentwood city	9.7	15.3	19,820	64.0	43.6	4.5	15.9	36.0	30.3	33.0	29.6
26 46000	Lansing city	12.7	8.3	47,522	54.0	30.2	5.3	18.4	46.0	35.3	29.2	27.7
26 47800	Lincoln Park city	14.3	6.1	14,252	65.4	38.2	9.0	18.2	34.6	30.5	34.4	32.9
26 49000	Livonia city	2.3	6.8	37,094	68.9	56.4	3.9	8.7	31.1	27.7	27.7	42.4
26 50560	Madison Heights city	2.1	14.2	12,751	56.7	38.8	5.4	12.6	43.3	38.0	28.1	34.2
26 51900	Marquette city	1.2	1.8	8,082	46.3	36.7	2.9	6.8	53.7	38.1	17.4	31.7
26 53780	Midland city	2.6	7.0	17,650	61.8	49.2	2.9	9.7	38.2	31.7	28.7	35.2

Table A-4. Cities — Who: Age, Race/Ethnicity, and Household Structure, 2010–2012—*Continued*

STATE and Place code	STATE or City	Total population	Percent change 2010–2012	Population by age (percent) Under 5 years	5 to 17 years	18 to 24 years	25 to 44 years	45 to 64 years	65 years and over	Median age	White	Black	Race alone or in combination (percent) Asian, Hawaiian, or Pacific Islander	American Indian, Alaska Native, or some other race
	ACS table number:	B01003	Population estimates	B01001	B01001	B01001	B01001	B01001	B01001	B01002	B02008	B02009	B02011 + B02012	B02010 + B02013
	Column number:	1	2	3	4	5	6	7	8	9	10	11	12	13
	Michigan—Cont.													
26 55020	Monroe city	20,631	-0.9	6.6	17.9	10.0	24.7	26.5	14.2	37.8	93.9	6.5	0.4	1.3
26 56020	Mount Pleasant city	26,129	0.6	3.5	8.5	52.0	15.4	13.3	7.3	21.8	89.0	5.1	4.7	4.3
26 56320	Muskegon city	37,431	-3.1	7.3	14.9	11.4	27.3	26.7	12.3	37.1	64.4	36.9	...	5.4
26 59140	Norton Shores city	23,887	-0.5	4.6	16.9	9.7	21.2	29.9	17.7	43.0	94.6	3.5	3.4	1.9
26 59440	Novi city	56,048	3.0	5.5	19.1	6.9	28.0	27.5	13.0	39.6	75.1	7.9	18.2	1.6
26 59920	Oak Park city	29,460	0.9	4.8	19.7	11.1	26.7	24.7	13.0	36.6	39.6	60.1	1.8	4.0
26 60340	Okemos CDP	20,597	...	4.5	16.6	13.7	22.8	29.4	13.0	38.7	81.4	4.6	14.5	1.9
26 65440	Pontiac city	59,872	1.1	7.6	19.6	11.5	27.4	23.9	10.0	33.3	42.4	54.3	5.2	4.0
26 65560	Portage city	46,701	1.7	7.2	17.1	8.9	27.2	26.2	13.4	38.0	89.7	6.9	4.4	2.1
26 65820	Port Huron city	29,893	-1.4	6.6	18.7	10.1	26.4	24.7	13.5	35.6	88.7	11.5	1.6	2.9
26 69035	Rochester Hills city	71,650	1.7	5.7	17.3	7.1	25.8	30.6	13.5	41.0	84.8	5.3	10.3	1.6
26 69420	Romulus city	23,742	-1.4	6.8	18.7	8.8	28.4	26.9	10.4	35.7	53.4	45.2	1.5	3.3
26 69800	Roseville city	47,277	0.0	5.9	17.0	8.1	28.2	27.6	13.1	39.1	84.3	11.8	2.3	4.4
26 70040	Royal Oak city	57,928	2.0	5.0	11.0	7.6	34.4	28.7	13.4	39.3	94.1	3.2	3.2	0.8
26 70520	Saginaw city	51,087	-1.2	7.3	19.5	12.2	24.1	25.7	11.1	33.9	50.6	47.9	0.9	4.8
26 70760	St. Clair Shores city	59,715	0.0	4.2	15.2	6.2	25.6	30.4	18.3	44.2	92.7	5.6	1.3	2.2
26 74900	Southfield city	72,131	1.0	5.3	15.3	8.3	24.0	29.4	17.8	43.0	27.0	71.3	2.9	2.5
26 74960	Southgate city	29,768	-1.3	3.5	15.5	10.3	26.3	27.8	16.6	42.2	91.3	6.4	1.7	2.2
26 76460	Sterling Heights city	130,037	0.5	5.0	16.2	8.9	25.9	28.2	15.7	40.7	87.0	6.0	8.3	1.1
26 79000	Taylor city	62,498	-1.3	7.0	16.9	9.8	26.0	26.6	13.8	37.6	79.1	18.5	1.3	3.8
26 80700	Troy city	81,616	1.4	5.3	18.0	7.5	24.3	30.8	14.2	41.7	74.6	5.0	21.2	1.4
26 82960	Walker city	23,768	1.9	5.3	17.6	10.1	28.5	26.3	12.2	33.9	93.6	3.8	2.7	0.6
26 84000	Warren city	134,055	0.1	6.4	16.5	9.7	25.3	26.6	15.6	39.3	79.5	15.1	6.1	1.7
26 84800	Waverly CDP	23,774	...	3.8	13.5	10.5	24.3	31.0	16.9	43.8	81.0	14.2	4.8	3.7
26 86000	Westland city	83,340	-1.2	6.2	15.5	9.7	26.5	27.5	14.8	38.6	75.1	20.4	4.3	2.7
26 88900	Wyandotte city	25,618	-1.3	4.9	15.6	7.8	28.2	30.4	13.0	40.7	96.0	1.9	0.6	2.1
26 88940	Wyoming city	72,741	1.7	8.9	16.7	11.1	30.6	24.0	8.8	32.6	86.4	6.8	3.3	6.8
26 89140	Ypsilanti city	19,542	0.9	5.3	10.2	34.4	24.1	17.0	9.1	25.0	65.1	34.1	3.7	2.5
27 00000	**Minnesota**	5,345,721	1.3	6.6	17.3	9.4	26.2	27.2	13.2	37.5	87.9	6.3	4.9	3.5
27 01486	Andover city	30,904	1.7	6.3	24.2	7.8	24.6	30.0	7.0	36.9	95.5	1.9	3.3	0.8
27 01900	Apple Valley city	49,630	1.7	7.5	17.9	8.1	26.8	29.6	10.2	37.5	87.9	9.4	5.7	2.6
27 02908	Austin city	24,763	0.3	7.6	17.2	10.9	23.6	23.2	17.5	37.1	92.0	4.2	3.2	2.9
27 06382	Blaine city	58,357	3.5	7.9	18.2	7.0	30.4	27.0	9.5	36.0	85.6	4.6	9.6	2.9
27 06616	Bloomington city	84,347	3.6	5.4	14.5	7.2	25.3	28.9	18.7	42.7	83.3	8.5	5.5	4.8
27 07948	Brooklyn Center city	30,392	1.7	8.3	18.0	9.1	30.2	22.6	11.9	33.1	50.0	31.6	17.4	5.2
27 07966	Brooklyn Park city	76,868	2.3	8.5	21.4	9.3	28.6	24.1	8.1	32.0	56.9	28.2	15.0	3.1
27 08794	Burnsville city	60,740	1.2	6.5	16.5	8.9	28.3	27.2	12.7	37.3	79.2	12.3	6.2	5.3
27 10846	Champlin city	23,428	2.4	4.5	20.3	6.5	28.3	33.1	7.3	39.9	92.1	5.9	2.5	...
27 10918	Chanhassen city	23,441	3.5	6.4	23.6	4.5	25.3	31.8	8.4	40.0	94.2	1.2	5.4	0.9
27 10972	Chaska city	23,945	1.0	7.3	21.8	6.2	30.0	27.0	7.7	35.0	91.4	2.8	3.8	3.7
27 13114	Coon Rapids city	61,669	0.6	7.1	17.2	9.6	27.3	27.6	11.1	35.9	89.9	7.4	3.5	2.9
27 13456	Cottage Grove city	34,928	1.4	8.0	21.3	7.8	28.6	25.9	8.4	35.2	90.8	3.4	5.9	1.4
27 14158	Crystal city	22,361	1.6	7.1	14.6	5.3	32.5	26.9	13.6	38.8	79.6	14.4	5.7	2.0
27 17000	Duluth city	86,221	0.0	5.6	12.9	19.8	23.8	23.9	14.1	32.8	93.9	3.5	2.4	3.3
27 17288	Eagan city	64,561	0.9	6.5	19.0	7.6	27.5	31.3	8.1	37.1	84.0	6.2	9.5	3.6
27 18116	Eden Prairie city	61,608	2.2	7.1	20.1	6.7	27.3	30.2	8.5	37.1	82.4	6.7	10.9	2.6
27 18188	Edina city	48,561	2.2	5.6	19.0	5.5	21.0	29.1	19.8	44.3	88.7	3.7	7.2	2.7
27 18674	Elk River city	23,191	1.0	8.7	19.2	8.9	27.5	25.1	10.7	34.8	92.9	1.4	5.4	2.3
27 20546	Faribault city	23,387	0.1	6.8	18.8	7.1	29.5	23.7	14.1	35.7	89.8	8.1	1.2	2.3
27 20618	Farmington city	21,523	3.6	10.0	22.5	5.6	36.8	20.1	5.0	33.0	93.7	2.5	2.9	0.6
27 22814	Fridley city	27,395	1.5	7.5	16.6	9.2	25.7	26.8	14.2	38.2	77.2	14.7	6.6	6.5
27 24308	Golden Valley city	20,595	1.9	7.2	12.7	5.1	25.1	29.8	20.0	44.7	87.8	10.0	4.8	1.2
27 27530	Hastings city	22,252	0.6	7.2	17.1	7.5	30.4	24.9	13.0	36.3	95.7	1.6	1.2	2.7
27 31076	Inver Grove Heights city	34,060	0.8	6.0	17.9	9.3	25.4	28.0	13.3	38.3	87.6	5.6	5.3	4.9
27 35180	Lakeville city	56,712	2.2	7.4	23.4	6.5	29.1	27.8	5.8	34.9	91.1	3.2	5.5	2.1
27 37322	Lino Lakes city	20,520	2.4	6.2	21.9	7.1	24.7	34.2	5.9	38.8	91.2	4.7	4.1	2.0
27 39878	Mankato city	39,707	1.8	5.7	10.1	32.2	23.7	17.2	11.1	26.0	91.8	5.6	3.7	1.5
27 40166	Maple Grove city	63,155	4.2	6.8	19.3	5.5	30.0	30.6	7.8	37.8	89.1	4.8	7.7	0.5
27 40382	Maplewood city	38,704	3.3	6.0	17.7	6.8	26.1	28.0	15.4	39.1	79.6	10.6	11.6	2.4
27 43000	Minneapolis city	388,054	2.6	7.0	13.3	14.6	34.4	22.2	8.5	31.6	71.3	20.3	6.8	6.4
27 43252	Minnetonka city	50,505	2.7	4.4	15.9	6.2	23.8	33.1	16.7	44.8	91.3	6.0	4.6	1.4
27 43864	Moorhead city	38,694	2.2	7.2	13.2	22.1	25.1	21.2	11.3	29.8	93.5	2.6	3.5	3.9
27 45430	New Brighton city	21,676	1.8	8.6	13.3	8.3	27.0	26.4	16.4	37.6	81.8	11.6	8.2	1.6
27 45628	New Hope city	20,543	1.8	6.4	15.7	7.0	27.3	25.0	18.5	40.6	77.6	17.8	6.3	1.7
27 46924	Northfield city	20,210	2.3	4.4	12.7	34.7	16.7	19.6	12.0	23.4	88.2	2.4	6.4	5.7
27 47680	Oakdale city	27,578	1.0	6.2	20.1	9.2	24.4	28.7	11.4	37.5	82.8	9.7	9.1	1.2
27 49300	Owatonna city	25,520	-0.5	8.4	17.9	7.6	25.7	25.7	14.8	38.1	92.7	4.4	1.4	4.1
27 51730	Plymouth city	71,771	3.1	5.8	17.3	6.9	27.3	30.1	12.5	40.1	87.3	5.8	8.0	1.9
27 52594	Prior Lake city	23,301	3.8	7.2	23.1	6.2	26.2	27.4	10.0	37.2	92.4	4.2	3.7	1.5
27 53026	Ramsey city	23,892	1.4	6.7	22.9	7.0	28.8	27.8	6.8	35.4	91.7	3.8	4.3	1.1
27 54214	Richfield city	35,657	2.3	8.0	11.8	8.6	33.6	24.4	13.5	35.8	75.3	13.8	7.1	7.3

Table A-4. Cities — Who: Age, Race/Ethnicity, and Household Structure, 2010–2012—*Continued*

STATE and Place code	STATE or City	Percent Hispanic or Latino	Percent foreign born	Total households	Household type (percent)							Percent of households with people under 18 years	Percent of households with people 60 years and over
					Family households				Nonfamily households				
					Total family households	Married-couple families	Male household families	Female household families	Total nonfamily households	One-person households			
	ACS table number:	B03003	C05003	B11001	B11001	B11001	B11001	B11001	B11001	B11001		B11005	B11006
	Column number:	14	15	16	17	18	19	20	21	22		23	24
	Michigan—Cont.												
26 55020	Monroe city	5.0	2.9	8,145	63.5	44.4	3.3	15.8	36.5	32.6		30.9	34.0
26 56020	Mount Pleasant city	2.7	4.7	8,217	38.6	27.4	3.7	7.5	61.4	34.8		18.0	21.7
26 56320	Muskegon city	6.3	2.5	14,207	55.2	27.7	5.4	22.1	44.8	38.4		30.6	32.2
26 59140	Norton Shores city	4.6	3.3	9,570	68.5	54.2	3.7	10.6	31.5	28.5		29.7	39.7
26 59440	Novi city	2.0	17.6	23,254	62.0	51.7	1.8	8.5	38.0	33.8		33.6	30.0
26 59920	Oak Park city	1.1	8.9	11,195	66.9	38.2	9.0	19.7	33.1	29.6		32.8	35.8
26 60340	Okemos CDP	3.3	15.3	8,399	62.7	50.6	3.3	8.8	37.3	30.0		30.0	28.1
26 65440	Pontiac city	15.8	7.0	23,223	59.4	25.5	8.7	25.1	40.6	34.6		35.0	28.9
26 65560	Portage city	3.1	5.0	19,348	63.3	48.7	4.4	10.2	36.7	31.8		32.9	33.1
26 65820	Port Huron city	4.4	3.5	12,072	60.7	35.8	6.4	18.4	39.3	33.0		31.9	33.1
26 69035	Rochester Hills city	3.1	14.9	27,546	69.6	58.6	3.3	7.7	30.4	25.3		32.4	34.6
26 69420	Romulus city	2.6	2.5	8,954	66.2	39.6	5.2	21.3	33.8	29.5		35.0	31.1
26 69800	Roseville city	2.2	3.9	19,990	60.3	36.7	5.1	18.5	39.7	34.9		29.3	33.7
26 70040	Royal Oak city	3.0	6.6	28,485	45.9	35.8	2.8	7.3	54.1	43.3		19.4	29.1
26 70520	Saginaw city	13.0	1.7	19,247	58.4	26.6	5.8	25.9	41.6	36.4		34.3	29.4
26 70760	St. Clair Shores city	2.3	4.7	26,492	59.4	44.2	3.6	11.6	40.6	35.7		25.8	40.5
26 74900	Southfield city	1.7	10.9	31,386	57.4	33.0	4.1	20.3	42.6	38.8		27.5	42.4
26 74960	Southgate city	6.7	4.7	12,772	56.6	39.2	5.3	12.1	43.4	36.3		24.0	37.7
26 76460	Sterling Heights city	1.6	24.1	49,577	70.2	54.6	5.1	10.5	29.8	26.8		30.9	38.9
26 79000	Taylor city	5.5	4.7	23,573	67.6	41.3	6.1	20.2	32.4	27.2		34.0	33.8
26 80700	Troy city	1.9	26.8	30,382	74.0	63.1	3.7	7.2	26.0	23.3		34.6	38.2
26 82960	Walker city	3.8	4.4	10,141	58.3	47.0	4.3	7.0	41.7	34.3		28.2	27.8
26 84000	Warren city	2.0	11.5	52,377	63.6	43.4	5.6	14.7	36.4	30.6		30.1	37.8
26 84800	Waverly CDP	6.7	7.0	11,130	51.2	40.0	1.7	9.4	48.8	42.9		20.4	35.1
26 86000	Westland city	2.9	7.1	33,798	60.2	38.8	4.4	17.0	39.8	34.4		28.4	35.1
26 88900	Wyandotte city	3.7	1.6	10,453	59.6	41.9	5.6	12.2	40.4	35.4		28.8	35.8
26 88940	Wyoming city	19.1	11.0	26,908	65.8	47.9	5.0	13.0	34.2	26.9		35.8	27.8
26 89140	Ypsilanti city	3.2	6.9	7,573	38.0	20.8	3.8	13.4	62.0	43.9		18.1	23.6
27 00000	**Minnesota**	4.8	7.3	2,102,761	64.9	51.1	4.3	9.6	35.1	28.2		31.6	32.2
27 01486	Andover city	1.8	4.4	10,095	82.1	66.9	7.6	7.6	17.9	15.2		47.1	24.6
27 01900	Apple Valley city	3.7	10.3	19,067	70.5	55.2	4.2	11.1	29.5	24.7		34.2	27.7
27 02908	Austin city	15.3	10.1	9,992	59.5	42.7	5.6	11.2	40.5	35.1		31.4	38.3
27 06382	Blaine city	2.2	10.4	21,737	73.4	58.5	4.4	10.5	26.6	21.0		38.6	28.5
27 06616	Bloomington city	7.3	11.5	35,940	60.1	47.2	3.7	9.2	39.9	33.0		24.9	40.8
27 07948	Brooklyn Center city	8.5	23.2	11,124	66.1	38.9	7.1	20.1	33.9	28.6		38.1	33.2
27 07966	Brooklyn Park city	6.8	20.9	26,100	72.5	48.1	7.5	17.0	27.5	22.7		42.3	25.1
27 08794	Burnsville city	7.6	12.7	24,737	62.0	47.6	3.5	10.9	38.0	31.0		29.5	30.0
27 10846	Champlin city	2.9	5.4	8,951	68.8	57.5	3.5	7.8	31.2	23.5		35.7	23.9
27 10918	Chanhassen city	1.9	6.4	8,408	76.3	69.4	2.4	4.5	23.7	20.4		44.6	27.1
27 10972	Chaska city	6.3	8.0	9,234	70.6	56.7	4.5	9.5	29.4	26.0		43.3	20.7
27 13114	Coon Rapids city	3.8	6.3	23,411	65.8	50.0	4.3	11.4	34.2	26.4		34.6	30.1
27 13456	Cottage Grove city	4.6	4.5	11,989	78.4	67.7	2.5	8.2	21.6	16.1		45.6	24.9
27 14158	Crystal city	3.8	9.0	9,212	60.6	46.0	3.2	11.4	39.4	30.1		28.9	29.5
27 17000	Duluth city	0.9	2.9	35,340	53.5	38.2	3.9	11.4	46.5	34.3		25.1	32.8
27 17288	Eagan city	5.0	11.1	25,433	68.0	54.7	3.4	9.8	32.0	26.8		34.9	25.4
27 18116	Eden Prairie city	3.9	14.0	23,427	70.7	58.3	3.9	8.6	29.3	24.7		38.6	25.9
27 18188	Edina city	3.2	9.8	20,398	63.3	55.3	2.3	5.7	36.7	32.9		30.8	44.6
27 18674	Elk River city	2.0	5.3	8,163	72.3	61.9	3.6	6.8	27.7	23.9		39.4	27.0
27 20546	Faribault city	15.6	10.7	8,200	67.8	48.8	5.1	13.8	32.2	25.8		36.1	33.9
27 20618	Farmington city	2.4	4.7	7,379	76.3	63.5	5.2	7.6	23.7	19.7		51.4	15.3
27 22814	Fridley city	7.3	10.3	11,083	60.4	42.9	5.3	12.1	39.6	32.5		29.3	34.0
27 24308	Golden Valley city	2.5	9.0	8,773	62.5	48.8	4.4	9.3	37.5	29.5		26.7	41.4
27 27530	Hastings city	3.8	1.5	8,538	68.7	52.2	6.5	10.0	31.3	23.3		34.6	32.3
27 31076	Inver Grove Heights city	9.9	5.4	13,549	67.7	48.2	5.2	14.3	32.3	26.4		32.1	33.2
27 35180	Lakeville city	3.5	6.5	18,816	80.6	67.8	3.6	9.2	19.4	14.0		47.8	20.0
27 37322	Lino Lakes city	2.3	2.3	6,400	83.0	73.3	2.4	7.4	17.0	12.7		46.0	24.4
27 39878	Mankato city	2.6	5.1	15,230	47.3	38.6	3.3	5.4	52.7	33.3		21.8	28.0
27 40166	Maple Grove city	2.0	8.8	23,778	74.6	63.7	3.7	7.3	25.4	19.1		37.2	25.4
27 40382	Maplewood city	5.1	9.6	15,278	60.7	43.7	3.8	13.2	39.3	32.4		30.4	36.9
27 43000	Minneapolis city	10.0	14.7	165,018	44.4	28.5	4.1	11.9	55.6	40.8		23.8	22.5
27 43252	Minnetonka city	1.8	8.0	21,880	63.4	52.5	2.7	8.1	36.6	31.0		24.2	37.7
27 43864	Moorhead city	4.3	3.3	14,567	59.4	44.8	4.4	10.1	40.6	32.1		29.8	28.8
27 45430	New Brighton city	4.7	11.0	8,977	63.1	45.3	4.4	13.4	36.9	28.8		30.1	38.1
27 45628	New Hope city	8.5	13.2	8,600	58.7	44.6	3.9	10.2	41.3	34.9		28.7	37.5
27 46924	Northfield city	5.6	6.9	6,207	62.5	49.1	2.2	11.2	37.5	30.8		29.1	32.0
27 47680	Oakdale city	2.5	7.9	10,551	65.4	47.5	5.0	12.9	34.6	28.1		36.2	33.2
27 49300	Owatonna city	7.9	5.6	10,366	63.2	50.6	4.4	8.2	36.8	33.1		32.3	33.5
27 51730	Plymouth city	4.3	11.4	28,748	69.2	58.6	3.5	7.2	30.8	25.0		32.8	29.8
27 52594	Prior Lake city	1.7	4.7	8,495	76.8	63.6	2.5	10.7	23.2	17.7		43.3	26.0
27 53026	Ramsey city	1.7	5.7	7,966	80.8	66.2	7.4	7.2	19.2	15.3		45.8	22.7
27 54214	Richfield city	19.6	21.5	14,566	56.8	39.5	5.4	12.0	43.2	33.8		27.0	32.9

Table A-4. Cities — Who: Age, Race/Ethnicity, and Household Structure, 2010–2012—*Continued*

STATE and Place code	STATE or City	Total population	Percent change 2010–2012	Population by age (percent)						Median age	Race alone or in combination (percent)			
				Under 5 years	5 to 17 years	18 to 24 years	25 to 44 years	45 to 64 years	65 years and over		White	Black	Asian, Hawaiian, or Pacific Islander	American Indian, Alaska Native, or some other race
	ACS table number:	B01003	Population estimates	B01001	B01001	B01001	B01001	B01001	B01001	B01002	B02008	B02009	B02011 + B02012	B02010 + B02013
	Column number:	1	2	3	4	5	6	7	8	9	10	11	12	13
	Minnesota—Cont.													
27 54880	Rochester city	108,024	1.9	7.4	17.4	8.1	29.6	24.6	13.0	35.1	85.6	7.4	8.5	1.7
27 55726	Rosemount city	22,205	2.1	6.9	24.8	6.8	27.1	26.1	8.4	35.6	88.1	5.5	5.0	2.9
27 55852	Roseville city	34,119	2.8	5.3	12.3	11.2	23.6	26.9	20.7	42.3	85.1	7.0	8.1	1.1
27 56896	St. Cloud city	65,838	0.0	5.6	13.3	22.8	24.8	22.7	10.8	29.0	86.8	10.5	4.0	1.9
27 57220	St. Louis Park city	45,814	2.4	5.6	13.6	8.9	35.6	23.2	13.1	34.5	87.1	9.8	4.3	2.7
27 58000	St. Paul city	288,347	1.8	7.6	17.4	14.0	29.5	22.6	9.0	30.9	65.3	17.8	16.5	5.5
27 58738	Savage city	27,444	3.5	7.7	23.6	6.2	28.0	27.8	6.6	35.0	86.8	5.2	8.6	3.1
27 59350	Shakopee city	38,026	3.7	9.5	19.3	7.4	37.6	19.4	6.8	32.7	80.6	5.1	11.5	6.9
27 59998	Shoreview city	25,370	2.1	5.6	15.5	6.1	22.7	34.7	15.5	45.1	90.4	3.3	8.0	0.3
27 61492	South St. Paul city	20,307	1.2	6.6	15.9	8.8	28.8	27.9	12.0	37.1	88.7	5.6	1.0	7.9
27 69970	White Bear Lake city	24,085	2.0	7.6	16.4	6.5	23.7	27.0	18.9	41.1	92.0	3.4	5.0	1.5
27 71032	Winona city	27,725	1.4	3.5	9.2	32.4	18.9	22.0	14.0	28.4	96.4	2.4	1.8	...
27 71428	Woodbury city	63,426	3.6	7.1	21.8	6.0	29.3	26.6	9.2	35.9	84.7	7.3	10.0	1.7
28 00000	**Mississippi**	2,977,179	0.5	6.9	18.3	10.5	25.4	25.8	13.1	36.1	60.4	38.0	1.1	1.7
28 06220	Biloxi city	44,288	1.1	6.1	15.1	14.5	26.4	25.6	12.3	34.8	74.5	20.7	6.4	2.5
28 08300	Brandon city	21,933	2.3	6.1	18.9	5.8	32.0	25.4	11.8	37.6	80.3	18.3	1.2	...
28 14420	Clinton city	25,571	1.9	6.2	16.5	14.9	24.0	24.9	13.4	34.6	54.8	39.8	5.4	...
28 15380	Columbus city	23,558	-1.0	6.1	16.4	11.6	25.6	23.8	16.6	38.2	36.9	61.9	...	0.8
28 29180	Greenville city	33,877	-2.7	7.9	20.1	9.2	24.4	26.4	12.0	35.3	22.2	76.5	0.9	1.2
28 29700	Gulfport city	68,979	3.2	8.4	16.3	10.4	28.0	24.8	12.1	35.0	60.5	38.0	1.8	1.8
28 31020	Hattiesburg city	47,239	2.4	7.1	13.9	23.4	27.1	17.8	10.7	27.1	43.0	53.9	2.1	1.4
28 33700	Horn Lake city	26,315	1.6	10.7	21.4	8.8	29.2	23.1	6.7	30.8	64.3	33.3	1.3	4.2
28 36000	Jackson city	174,706	1.0	7.5	19.8	12.5	26.9	23.1	10.3	31.2	18.9	80.2	0.4	1.2
28 44520	Madison city	24,557	2.5	5.3	25.0	5.2	23.0	29.8	11.7	40.4	87.1	10.0	3.6	0.6
28 46640	Meridian city	40,998	-0.6	7.5	19.0	9.9	25.7	24.4	13.4	34.4	37.2	62.8	1.2	0.3
28 54040	Olive Branch city	34,039	2.8	4.7	20.8	9.4	26.4	26.7	12.0	38.2	73.2	25.3	1.2	2.0
28 54840	Oxford city	19,519	5.8	4.5	13.4	33.7	22.7	16.1	9.5	24.6	73.7	22.2	3.2	2.0
28 55360	Pascagoula city	22,298	-0.4	7.3	17.0	11.0	27.2	24.5	13.0	36.0	65.2	32.3	1.3	2.2
28 55760	Pearl city	25,947	1.5	6.2	18.3	10.8	29.2	23.5	12.1	34.8	77.4	22.4	...	...
28 62520	Ridgeland city	24,161	0.8	6.8	14.8	10.0	31.0	27.4	10.0	35.7	57.0	36.2	4.3	3.0
28 69280	Southaven city	49,738	2.6	7.1	21.9	7.8	30.5	22.1	10.6	33.5	72.9	25.1	2.5	2.3
28 70240	Starkville city	24,111	2.0	6.0	11.4	29.5	25.2	18.2	9.7	25.8	61.7	34.3	4.4	0.7
28 74840	Tupelo city	35,085	2.5	8.2	19.6	7.5	26.9	23.1	14.6	35.5	59.8	39.6	1.2	1.2
28 76720	Vicksburg city	23,613	-1.7	6.5	19.2	9.6	23.2	26.7	14.9	36.8	29.9	68.0	1.5	0.6
29 00000	**Missouri**	6,009,025	0.4	6.4	17.1	9.8	25.4	27.0	14.3	38.0	85.0	12.6	2.3	2.6
29 01972	Arnold city	20,909	0.8	7.9	14.9	9.2	25.0	28.3	14.6	40.1	99.0	1.2	1.7	...
29 03160	Ballwin city	30,430	0.1	5.1	18.5	8.0	24.5	29.5	14.5	41.1	93.2	2.0	5.5	1.3
29 04384	Belton city	23,194	0.4	7.0	21.6	10.8	26.0	23.4	11.2	33.9	89.8	7.6	2.8	2.5
29 06652	Blue Springs city	52,794	0.7	5.9	20.5	8.6	26.8	28.3	9.9	36.3	91.4	7.2	2.8	2.5
29 11242	Cape Girardeau city	38,314	1.3	6.4	13.0	17.3	25.9	22.7	14.7	33.2	84.6	13.1	2.5	1.7
29 13600	Chesterfield city	47,600	0.4	4.5	18.1	6.4	18.1	32.6	20.4	46.5	87.6	4.2	9.4	0.2
29 15670	Columbia city	111,204	3.6	6.2	12.9	27.3	26.4	18.4	8.8	26.5	81.7	12.7	6.4	3.0
29 23986	Ferguson city	21,167	-0.3	8.9	17.6	9.7	26.3	26.3	11.3	33.7	33.7	66.6	1.1	...
29 24778	Florissant city	52,229	0.2	6.5	16.8	10.1	25.2	25.9	15.5	38.6	70.6	30.6	1.7	2.7
29 27190	Gladstone city	25,715	1.8	8.0	13.9	8.2	24.9	27.2	18.0	40.8	90.1	8.3	1.0	4.6
29 28324	Grandview city	24,571	0.4	7.3	16.5	11.3	29.0	24.2	11.7	33.8	61.2	34.6	0.7	8.3
29 31276	Hazelwood city	25,673	-0.1	4.9	19.4	9.6	28.4	25.8	11.9	35.4	63.5	33.7	4.3	1.9
29 35000	Independence city	117,028	0.3	6.9	15.9	8.4	25.8	26.6	16.3	39.3	86.6	8.5	1.8	6.0
29 37000	Jefferson City city	43,170	0.1	6.3	15.0	10.1	28.3	26.2	14.2	37.4	78.8	18.5	2.1	2.9
29 37592	Joplin city	51,822	-1.5	6.9	15.2	13.5	26.4	23.8	14.2	35.3	92.2	4.6	2.7	5.4
29 38000	Kansas City city	462,292	0.8	7.3	16.8	9.7	29.6	25.5	11.2	35.0	62.3	31.3	3.6	6.8
29 39044	Kirkwood city	27,542	0.0	5.2	16.4	6.4	24.4	30.0	17.6	43.4	90.6	8.1	1.8	0.5
29 41348	Lee's Summit city	91,979	1.0	7.3	20.4	7.4	26.5	26.5	11.9	36.7	87.4	10.7	2.8	2.0
29 42032	Liberty city	29,530	1.9	5.2	18.7	10.8	25.6	27.3	12.4	37.7	94.0	4.8	1.3	2.0
29 46586	Maryland Heights city	27,467	-0.1	7.4	12.9	8.8	34.1	25.4	11.5	34.5	71.9	13.1	11.2	7.9
29 47180	Mehlville CDP	31,091	...	4.7	15.3	9.9	24.2	26.3	19.6	41.5	94.1	4.2	4.2	0.9
29 53876	Oakville CDP	36,911	...	4.2	18.1	7.2	24.1	32.0	14.3	43.3	96.4	1.6	3.4	0.4
29 54074	O'Fallon city	80,986	2.6	7.7	22.3	7.9	29.2	23.7	9.3	34.2	90.2	6.3	4.3	1.4
29 54352	Old Jamestown CDP	19,716	...	3.0	22.1	6.3	16.7	37.3	14.6	45.8	45.5	54.4	...	1.6
29 60788	Raytown city	29,516	-0.1	7.8	17.8	7.6	24.1	26.7	16.0	39.4	66.5	30.1	1.6	3.2
29 64082	St. Charles city	66,173	0.7	5.6	14.2	14.5	26.3	26.1	13.3	35.8	89.5	7.2	2.6	2.8
29 64550	St. Joseph city	76,953	0.7	7.3	16.1	11.8	25.9	25.4	13.6	35.6	91.2	7.5	2.0	3.7
29 65000	St. Louis city	318,612	-0.3	6.8	14.4	11.8	30.9	25.0	11.1	33.9	47.4	50.2	3.5	2.0
29 65126	St. Peters city	53,421	2.4	6.3	17.1	8.0	27.6	29.8	11.2	37.8	92.9	4.5	2.5	0.8
29 66440	Sedalia city	21,431	0.3	7.6	17.5	10.2	25.9	23.6	15.1	34.8	91.4	6.5	0.2	4.6
29 69266	Spanish Lake CDP	19,874	...	11.4	21.3	8.1	25.8	20.8	12.6	30.6	22.2	77.0	0.8	2.4
29 70000	Springfield city	160,748	1.6	6.2	11.8	19.3	26.0	22.1	14.5	32.9	92.0	5.3	3.0	3.1
29 75220	University City city	35,279	-0.4	7.4	10.8	11.3	29.6	22.6	18.2	37.3	56.7	39.0	5.3	1.6
29 78154	Webster Groves city	23,008	0.3	5.8	18.8	7.4	23.5	30.0	14.5	40.2	92.1	7.9	1.1	1.2
29 78442	Wentzville city	30,409	5.9	8.7	23.5	5.6	34.6	19.0	8.4	32.9	94.7	5.9	0.6	1.2
29 79820	Wildwood city	35,619	0.5	5.1	24.7	5.2	19.8	35.8	9.4	42.3	94.2	2.0	3.8	0.6

Table A-4. Cities — Who: Age, Race/Ethnicity, and Household Structure, 2010–2012—*Continued*

STATE and Place code	STATE or City	Percent Hispanic or Latino	Percent foreign born	Total households	Household type (percent) Family households Total family households	Married-couple families	Male household families	Female household families	Nonfamily households Total nonfamily households	One-person households	Percent of households with people under 18 years	Percent of households with people 60 years and over
		ACS table number: B03003	C05003	B11001	B11001	B11001	B11001	B11001	B11001	B11001	B11005	B11006
		Column number: 14	15	16	17	18	19	20	21	22	23	24
	Minnesota—Cont.											
27 54880	Rochester city	5.3	12.7	43,055	61.9	49.6	3.4	8.8	38.1	31.2	32.3	29.1
27 55726	Rosemount city	5.6	9.8	7,405	78.7	61.8	4.7	12.2	21.3	18.4	47.4	26.4
27 55852	Roseville city	5.5	11.7	14,847	56.1	46.5	2.3	7.2	43.9	38.1	23.2	40.1
27 56896	St. Cloud city	2.4	7.1	25,211	53.5	39.3	4.7	9.5	46.5	29.5	23.4	25.8
27 57220	St. Louis Park city	4.3	9.2	21,411	49.6	36.6	4.2	8.8	50.4	40.3	23.1	26.1
27 58000	St. Paul city	9.6	18.1	111,521	55.1	34.8	5.6	14.6	44.9	35.2	30.5	25.5
27 58738	Savage city	2.7	10.5	9,066	78.2	65.4	5.7	7.2	21.8	15.9	47.3	20.0
27 59350	Shakopee city	9.8	16.7	13,285	71.5	58.8	3.5	9.2	28.5	22.9	43.1	20.7
27 59998	Shoreview city	1.5	8.5	10,663	66.9	55.2	3.1	8.6	33.1	29.9	27.3	39.3
27 61492	South St. Paul city	11.3	6.3	8,454	61.7	41.8	6.7	13.2	38.3	29.6	29.4	29.2
27 69970	White Bear Lake city	2.5	5.2	10,158	62.6	47.5	2.9	12.2	37.4	33.2	29.1	41.6
27 71032	Winona city	0.4	2.7	10,431	48.0	39.4	1.8	6.8	52.0	39.6	18.1	34.1
27 71428	Woodbury city	3.9	9.7	23,195	75.0	62.2	2.7	10.1	25.0	19.3	42.9	25.2
28 00000	**Mississippi**	2.7	2.2	1,085,563	68.9	45.3	4.9	18.7	31.1	27.3	35.1	35.5
28 06220	Biloxi city	7.9	7.8	17,821	58.7	38.4	6.2	14.1	41.3	34.4	26.8	31.4
28 08300	Brandon city	2.9	1.9	7,835	79.4	60.6	3.1	15.7	20.6	19.1	39.6	33.1
28 14420	Clinton city	1.7	5.6	9,123	70.2	52.8	3.9	13.5	29.8	24.9	36.7	32.4
28 15380	Columbus city	1.5	1.8	9,729	56.9	28.5	3.1	25.3	43.1	36.2	31.0	39.5
28 29180	Greenville city	1.4	2.1	12,168	68.7	35.0	4.2	29.5	31.3	27.0	38.5	36.4
28 29700	Gulfport city	6.3	3.8	26,288	62.5	37.4	5.6	19.6	37.5	31.4	33.0	32.3
28 31020	Hattiesburg city	3.2	4.0	18,225	48.1	24.4	5.4	18.3	51.9	41.0	28.1	25.5
28 33700	Horn Lake city	9.2	3.5	8,659	72.6	41.2	6.4	25.0	27.4	23.1	46.2	26.4
28 36000	Jackson city	1.7	1.8	61,612	62.9	27.9	7.6	27.4	37.1	31.6	35.8	29.8
28 44520	Madison city	0.8	3.3	8,473	80.3	70.3	4.2	5.8	19.7	18.6	41.2	33.4
28 46640	Meridian city	2.1	2.1	15,855	62.5	31.4	3.2	27.9	37.5	33.1	33.4	36.9
28 54040	Olive Branch city	4.4	4.1	12,548	73.6	55.4	4.9	13.4	26.4	22.2	37.4	29.1
28 54840	Oxford city	3.6	4.5	6,707	44.1	30.1	2.5	11.5	55.9	44.8	19.9	28.0
28 55360	Pascagoula city	10.4	5.6	8,342	63.5	41.5	4.1	17.9	36.5	30.7	29.0	32.8
28 55760	Pearl city	5.0	1.7	9,964	69.3	46.3	4.4	18.6	30.7	25.0	36.5	30.4
28 62520	Ridgeland city	2.3	6.0	10,969	52.4	36.2	3.6	12.6	47.6	38.1	27.1	22.6
28 69280	Southaven city	4.5	3.0	18,143	73.3	54.9	3.6	14.9	26.7	22.3	42.2	26.9
28 70240	Starkville city	1.5	3.1	10,402	49.6	31.1	3.8	14.7	50.4	38.3	26.4	21.1
28 74840	Tupelo city	4.9	3.6	13,438	66.2	40.7	2.9	22.6	33.8	30.1	38.1	35.8
28 76720	Vicksburg city	1.2	2.3	9,276	57.8	27.1	5.0	25.7	42.2	39.5	30.4	37.6
29 00000	**Missouri**	3.6	3.9	2,354,106	65.1	48.6	4.3	12.2	34.9	28.9	31.1	34.8
29 01972	Arnold city	3.0	5.3	8,127	69.0	56.3	3.1	9.6	31.0	25.8	33.7	36.9
29 03160	Ballwin city	1.9	8.2	11,328	78.7	64.0	3.2	11.4	21.3	17.4	35.9	36.8
29 04384	Belton city	6.8	4.7	8,417	66.7	46.8	3.2	16.7	33.3	26.5	37.3	28.1
29 06652	Blue Springs city	3.6	2.3	19,207	72.7	54.8	4.8	13.1	27.3	20.1	38.2	30.8
29 11242	Cape Girardeau city	2.5	4.2	15,062	58.2	41.4	3.4	13.5	41.8	31.1	28.4	29.0
29 13600	Chesterfield city	3.5	11.2	18,813	72.7	62.2	3.0	7.6	27.3	23.9	31.4	42.5
29 15670	Columbia city	3.6	7.8	43,348	49.3	37.1	3.2	9.1	50.7	33.5	26.9	20.8
29 23986	Ferguson city	0.8	0.9	8,863	66.4	29.8	5.1	31.5	33.6	30.8	35.6	31.0
29 24778	Florissant city	1.5	2.6	20,827	65.6	45.0	4.7	15.9	34.4	30.5	31.0	35.8
29 27190	Gladstone city	7.0	5.4	10,693	64.9	46.5	4.4	14.0	35.1	29.6	24.7	39.4
29 28324	Grandview city	14.1	11.2	9,603	58.1	40.4	6.2	11.5	41.9	34.6	28.3	30.2
29 31276	Hazelwood city	4.4	6.9	11,089	59.5	37.5	6.9	15.1	40.5	36.0	30.4	29.2
29 35000	Independence city	8.1	4.5	47,939	60.3	41.4	4.9	14.0	39.7	33.9	27.9	36.4
29 37000	Jefferson City city	1.5	3.3	17,033	61.0	41.5	4.6	14.9	39.0	33.4	32.1	33.1
29 37592	Joplin city	4.0	2.7	21,193	59.1	42.0	4.4	12.7	40.9	31.5	29.7	32.3
29 38000	Kansas City city	10.0	7.6	190,467	56.7	35.8	4.7	16.2	43.3	35.8	29.5	28.7
29 39044	Kirkwood city	1.5	3.2	11,866	60.4	52.0	2.1	6.3	39.6	34.9	26.5	41.9
29 41348	Lee's Summit city	3.7	3.1	33,846	71.6	58.9	2.5	10.3	28.4	23.4	38.5	31.4
29 42032	Liberty city	3.2	2.4	10,813	70.3	56.1	4.1	10.1	29.7	25.0	35.1	32.4
29 46586	Maryland Heights city	9.8	16.7	11,666	56.7	40.3	5.3	11.1	43.3	34.4	26.4	26.8
29 47180	Mehlville CDP	3.6	16.6	13,435	60.3	39.9	6.5	13.8	39.7	36.0	27.4	42.7
29 53876	Oakville CDP	1.5	3.9	13,783	79.3	66.7	2.5	10.1	20.7	16.6	30.8	35.8
29 54074	O'Fallon city	2.5	4.0	28,697	75.1	60.1	4.5	10.5	24.9	20.6	44.5	26.1
29 54352	Old Jamestown CDP	2.0	2.3	7,290	75.0	58.9	1.6	14.5	25.0	21.9	33.9	40.7
29 60788	Raytown city	6.0	2.4	11,730	63.5	44.9	4.2	14.4	36.5	31.5	30.9	37.3
29 64082	St. Charles city	4.8	6.2	26,344	62.7	45.0	2.7	15.0	37.3	31.0	29.1	31.3
29 64550	St. Joseph city	6.0	4.2	29,005	60.2	42.0	5.7	12.5	39.8	32.8	29.4	34.7
29 65000	St. Louis city	3.6	6.9	138,981	46.6	24.4	4.0	18.2	53.4	43.6	23.8	28.8
29 65126	St. Peters city	2.5	3.5	21,017	67.2	54.5	3.7	8.9	32.8	27.3	32.9	30.7
29 66440	Sedalia city	8.4	5.6	8,972	58.9	41.6	3.4	13.9	41.1	36.5	30.4	32.9
29 69266	Spanish Lake CDP	1.8	2.2	7,616	59.1	30.4	5.6	23.1	40.9	36.8	38.0	30.5
29 70000	Springfield city	3.9	4.0	70,120	50.8	33.9	5.1	11.8	49.2	37.7	24.0	31.5
29 75220	University City city	5.3	8.5	15,963	48.4	33.8	2.2	12.4	51.6	40.4	21.5	38.0
29 78154	Webster Groves city	1.3	3.2	9,241	65.3	56.8	2.3	6.3	34.7	28.3	33.1	37.5
29 78442	Wentzville city	2.7	1.1	10,305	81.6	69.2	2.9	9.5	18.4	15.4	49.2	22.7
29 79820	Wildwood city	1.7	6.8	12,185	84.9	74.5	3.6	6.8	15.1	13.0	45.6	29.1

Table A-4. Cities — Who: Age, Race/Ethnicity, and Household Structure, 2010–2012—*Continued*

STATE and Place code	STATE or City	Total population	Percent change 2010–2012	Population by age (percent) Under 5 years	5 to 17 years	18 to 24 years	25 to 44 years	45 to 64 years	65 years and over	Median age	Race alone or in combination (percent) White	Black	Asian, Hawaiian, or Pacific Islander	American Indian, Alaska Native, or some other race
	ACS table number:	B01003	Population estimates	B01001	B01001	B01001	B01001	B01001	B01001	E01002	B02008	B02009	B02011 + B02012	B02010 + B02013
	Column number:	1	2	3	4	5	6	7	8	9	10	11	12	13
30 00000	**Montana**	997,852	1.5	6.1	16.2	9.7	23.8	29.0	15.2	39.9	91.9	0.9	1.3	8.6
30 06550	Billings city	105,648	2.4	7.0	15.9	9.5	26.5	26.3	14.9	37.6	91.7	1.2	1.8	7.7
30 08950	Bozeman city	38,022	3.7	5.1	9.1	30.0	32.3	16.0	7.4	27.1	95.5	1.0	3.9	3.1
30 11397	Butte-Silver Bow (balance)	33,344	0.5	5.1	15.5	10.7	22.4	29.8	16.6	42.1	96.8	1.1	0.8	2.7
30 32800	Great Falls city	58,876	0.2	7.0	15.7	9.8	24.8	26.4	16.4	39.1	91.8	2.1	1.3	8.8
30 35600	Helena city	28,722	2.9	7.1	11.7	11.8	23.7	30.0	15.8	40.4	96.3	1.6	0.8	3.9
30 40075	Kalispell city	20,227	2.6	8.8	17.1	10.2	26.3	22.3	15.2	34.8	97.2	...	2.0	3.0
30 50200	Missoula city	67,643	2.1	5.1	13.1	19.1	29.6	21.9	11.2	31.5	95.1	0.9	2.2	4.8
31 00000	**Nebraska**	1,842,480	1.4	7.2	17.8	10.0	25.4	25.9	13.6	36.3	90.3	5.5	2.4	4.1
31 03950	Bellevue city	51,950	2.4	7.2	19.7	8.5	27.9	25.0	11.6	34.3	88.6	7.8	3.3	4.0
31 10110	Columbus city	22,339	1.5	7.7	18.1	8.1	24.0	26.9	15.2	38.4	97.0	0.5	1.0	3.4
31 17670	Fremont city	26,319	-0.8	7.1	16.7	9.1	27.0	23.7	16.4	37.4	96.6	0.8	1.5	2.8
31 19595	Grand Island city	49,317	2.7	7.5	19.6	8.7	26.4	25.1	12.7	35.2	93.2	2.8	1.6	4.0
31 21415	Hastings city	24,833	-0.6	7.5	15.7	11.9	23.0	27.0	14.9	38.1	95.9	0.8	2.2	3.6
31 25055	Kearney city	31,290	3.1	8.0	13.8	21.7	25.4	20.2	10.9	28.4	93.9	1.5	2.6	3.8
31 28000	Lincoln city	262,214	2.5	7.1	15.6	15.7	27.7	23.0	10.9	31.9	90.5	5.4	4.7	2.4
31 34615	Norfolk city	24,284	0.4	8.7	18.1	12.1	23.7	23.6	13.8	34.4	94.9	2.6	...	3.4
31 35000	North Platte city	24,642	-0.5	7.7	18.0	8.1	25.9	25.5	14.8	35.9	95.1	1.6	1.0	4.2
31 37000	Omaha city	416,374	2.5	7.5	17.5	10.9	28.1	24.7	11.4	33.6	78.1	14.9	3.4	7.2
31 38295	Papillion city	20,074	7.2	6.6	21.0	8.6	24.7	28.5	10.6	35.5	94.5	3.4	4.5	0.5
32 00000	**Nevada**	2,727,571	2.0	6.8	17.5	9.2	28.2	25.7	12.6	36.6	74.5	9.4	10.4	10.0
32 09700	Carson City	54,989	-0.8	5.8	15.4	8.5	25.1	28.1	17.1	41.7	86.7	1.2	4.7	10.0
32 23770	Enterprise CDP	120,483	...	7.0	17.9	8.2	38.6	22.0	6.3	32.6	62.1	12.5	26.3	5.5
32 31900	Henderson city	261,370	2.9	5.7	17.0	7.8	26.1	28.1	15.3	40.3	81.8	7.6	10.6	3.8
32 40000	Las Vegas city	589,541	2.1	7.0	17.8	9.1	28.3	24.8	12.9	36.4	71.4	12.4	9.5	11.7
32 51800	North Las Vegas city	219,976	2.9	8.2	23.5	9.8	30.6	20.6	7.3	30.6	56.6	22.3	9.3	17.2
32 53800	Pahrump CDP	34,569	...	3.6	15.7	5.7	16.0	31.2	27.9	51.9	90.3	3.4	2.4	4.9
32 54600	Paradise CDP	219,805	...	6.4	15.5	9.7	31.1	25.4	11.9	36.5	72.1	10.1	12.9	10.5
32 60600	Reno city	228,658	2.0	6.9	16.4	12.3	28.1	24.2	12.0	34.0	81.8	4.0	8.6	9.5
32 68400	Sparks city	91,242	1.9	7.5	16.9	8.6	28.4	26.5	12.1	37.8	82.1	2.5	10.8	9.3
32 68585	Spring Valley CDP	183,459	...	7.2	13.6	10.1	32.7	25.1	11.3	36.3	66.0	10.4	21.5	6.8
32 70900	Summerlin South CDP	23,640	...	5.5	14.1	4.3	28.0	29.2	18.8	43.8	84.4	5.1	10.8	3.0
32 71400	Sunrise Manor CDP	185,471	...	8.3	21.2	10.8	27.2	23.1	9.4	31.9	64.1	13.5	8.4	18.6
32 83800	Whitney CDP	38,677	...	7.5	16.9	9.0	34.0	23.0	9.7	33.7	66.1	11.7	17.7	9.7
32 84600	Winchester CDP	29,251	...	7.7	15.5	9.0	25.3	29.1	13.4	38.1	77.5	6.6	8.8	10.5
33 00000	**New Hampshire**	1,318,455	0.3	5.1	16.1	9.4	24.3	30.9	14.1	41.5	95.6	1.7	2.8	1.6
33 14200	Concord city	42,640	-0.1	5.6	15.2	8.3	28.4	28.8	13.7	40.6	94.0	3.4	2.5	1.7
33 17860	Derry CDP	21,721	...	4.6	17.5	8.4	31.7	26.2	11.6	38.4	93.3	3.2	3.5	0.5
33 18820	Dover city	30,139	0.7	6.0	13.6	13.3	28.7	25.8	12.7	36.3	94.8	2.9	4.1	1.7
33 39300	Keene city	23,315	-0.5	3.3	12.8	22.9	20.4	25.4	15.2	35.2	96.3	1.4	3.1	...
33 45140	Manchester city	109,879	0.5	6.3	15.0	10.1	30.6	25.9	12.2	36.6	88.0	5.4	5.1	4.2
33 50260	Nashua city	86,769	0.4	6.6	15.4	9.4	27.4	28.4	12.8	38.3	88.9	3.8	7.3	2.8
33 62900	Portsmouth city	21,293	0.7	5.2	11.5	6.5	32.3	28.3	16.2	41.4	94.1	2.1	4.2	0.8
33 65140	Rochester city	29,820	0.3	5.3	14.3	9.0	25.7	29.4	16.3	42.6	97.4	1.0	1.7	0.6
34 00000	**New Jersey**	8,834,249	0.7	6.0	17.1	8.8	26.5	27.8	13.8	39.1	71.1	14.7	9.4	7.5
34 02080	Atlantic City city	39,543	-0.2	8.3	17.6	8.7	25.0	26.8	13.6	36.5	37.1	41.0	15.5	9.2
34 03580	Bayonne city	63,826	2.0	6.1	14.7	8.5	30.4	27.4	13.0	38.6	77.0	11.2	9.1	5.4
34 05170	Bergenfield borough	26,911	0.7	4.7	17.4	7.8	27.5	27.9	14.7	40.5	52.9	6.2	24.6	20.2
34 07600	Bridgeton city	25,298	-0.1	8.3	17.2	12.1	36.0	19.1	7.3	30.6	44.8	36.0	...	22.4
34 10000	Camden city	77,398	-0.2	9.0	22.1	12.5	27.7	20.7	7.9	28.9	16.1	50.5	2.3	36.5
34 10750	Carteret borough	23,536	4.8	6.9	18.5	8.9	28.0	26.5	11.3	35.5	59.5	14.6	22.4	5.0
34 13570	Cliffside Park borough	23,752	1.0	6.2	10.6	6.2	28.1	29.2	19.6	43.8	78.1	7.0	14.1	4.1
34 13690	Clifton city	84,525	0.6	6.0	16.9	9.8	29.2	25.2	12.9	36.8	73.6	5.4	10.0	13.3
34 19390	East Orange city	64,213	0.3	6.7	16.8	10.4	27.7	25.1	13.2	36.7	5.0	91.2	0.8	4.6
34 21000	Elizabeth city	125,825	1.0	9.0	18.1	10.6	31.4	21.6	9.2	32.4	51.3	21.0	2.6	27.2
34 21480	Englewood city	27,428	1.5	6.9	14.4	7.7	30.0	26.4	14.6	39.1	42.5	36.7	9.8	13.7
34 22470	Fair Lawn borough	32,679	1.1	5.2	18.2	6.3	25.3	29.0	16.0	41.2	82.2	3.2	12.2	3.7
34 24420	Fort Lee borough	35,553	0.9	4.2	11.6	5.8	28.2	28.0	22.1	45.2	59.2	2.8	37.6	2.8
34 25770	Garfield city	30,697	1.1	6.3	15.4	10.7	30.5	26.4	10.7	35.9	89.9	6.3	1.9	3.5
34 28680	Hackensack city	43,374	1.8	6.6	11.4	9.0	32.4	27.3	13.3	39.1	43.9	22.9	10.9	24.8
34 32250	Hoboken city	51,116	3.8	7.0	6.7	11.4	55.1	13.7	6.2	31.0	88.2	4.6	8.2	1.7
34 34470	Iselin CDP	20,193	...	4.9	17.7	8.2	29.3	25.6	14.3	36.7	40.2	12.4	45.1	6.3
34 36000	Jersey City city	251,485	2.4	6.8	13.9	9.8	37.9	22.4	9.3	33.3	35.8	27.0	26.2	14.1
34 36510	Kearny town	41,098	1.6	6.9	16.5	9.9	30.8	25.4	10.6	36.4	61.0	3.6	4.7	32.5
34 38580	Lakewood CDP	51,425	...	17.8	31.9	11.5	24.3	10.1	4.5	18.5	92.0	4.6	0.5	3.4
34 40350	Linden city	40,693	0.7	5.8	14.1	9.8	28.8	28.3	13.1	39.2	58.9	28.5	3.4	12.5
34 41100	Lodi borough	24,277	0.8	5.5	16.8	9.1	30.7	25.3	12.5	36.5	79.6	7.3	7.1	8.1
34 41310	Long Branch city	30,734	-0.4	7.7	14.6	10.2	31.3	23.9	12.2	34.2	78.5	19.2	2.0	8.8

Table A-4. Cities — Who: Age, Race/Ethnicity, and Household Structure, 2010–2012—*Continued*

STATE and Place code	STATE or City	Percent Hispanic or Latino	Percent foreign born	Total households	Family households — Total family households	Married-couple families	Male household families	Female household families	Nonfamily households — Total nonfamily households	One-person households	Percent of households with people under 18 years	Percent of households with people 60 years and over
	ACS table number:	B03003	C05003	B11001	B11001	B11001	B11001	B11001	B11001	B11001	B11005	B11006
	Column number:	14	15	16	17	18	19	20	21	22	23	24
30 00000	**Montana**	3.0	2.0	404,990	63.1	49.9	4.3	8.8	36.9	30.1	27.8	36.9
30 06550	Billings city	5.2	1.8	43,926	59.4	43.2	4.6	11.7	40.6	32.5	29.7	34.9
30 08950	Bozeman city	3.2	3.9	15,360	46.5	35.6	4.2	6.7	53.5	32.0	21.7	18.0
30 11397	Butte-Silver Bow (balance)	3.7	1.4	14,500	56.7	42.1	3.9	10.7	43.3	36.3	25.4	35.6
30 32800	Great Falls city	3.9	2.8	24,535	60.6	43.9	5.7	11.0	39.4	34.5	27.6	36.8
30 35600	Helena city	2.7	1.6	12,799	52.0	40.1	3.0	8.8	48.0	40.9	22.7	37.8
30 40075	Kalispell city	2.6	2.2	8,388	55.4	39.6	4.6	11.2	44.6	36.8	27.5	34.3
30 50200	Missoula city	3.5	3.1	28,776	50.6	36.5	4.8	9.3	49.4	33.1	22.8	25.0
31 00000	**Nebraska**	9.5	6.3	726,422	64.9	50.8	4.2	9.9	35.1	28.9	31.9	32.8
31 03950	Bellevue city	12.9	8.4	19,517	72.9	52.6	4.5	15.9	27.1	22.8	38.7	31.1
31 10110	Columbus city	16.9	8.5	8,881	63.6	52.0	4.4	7.2	36.4	32.0	30.7	34.5
31 17670	Fremont city	12.6	7.1	10,829	65.6	51.1	3.6	10.9	34.4	28.7	33.1	34.7
31 19595	Grand Island city	26.8	14.8	18,702	63.4	46.0	4.0	13.3	36.6	29.3	37.7	31.9
31 21415	Hastings city	9.9	5.9	10,416	58.0	47.2	3.6	7.2	42.0	33.7	26.6	36.1
31 25055	Kearney city	8.0	4.7	11,999	61.1	48.6	3.7	8.8	38.9	26.8	30.8	25.1
31 28000	Lincoln city	6.4	7.8	105,019	59.2	44.9	3.9	10.4	40.8	30.4	29.6	27.3
31 34615	Norfolk city	12.2	6.8	9,833	63.1	44.2	5.2	13.8	36.9	31.4	31.7	29.7
31 35000	North Platte city	9.0	2.3	10,384	59.4	43.9	3.0	12.6	40.6	35.0	32.5	33.2
31 37000	Omaha city	13.4	9.7	164,695	58.7	39.8	5.0	13.9	41.3	33.8	30.9	29.7
31 38295	Papillion city	5.9	3.5	7,495	73.3	59.6	2.7	11.0	26.7	23.3	36.6	27.3
32 00000	**Nevada**	26.9	19.1	992,757	64.7	45.2	6.4	13.1	35.3	27.3	33.5	34.3
32 09700	Carson City	22.0	12.0	21,212	62.4	46.1	4.1	12.3	37.6	30.7	29.5	43.0
32 23770	Enterprise CDP	19.3	25.2	41,666	67.4	46.3	7.1	14.1	32.6	21.1	40.4	20.2
32 31900	Henderson city	14.6	11.5	98,623	68.5	50.0	6.1	12.4	31.5	24.5	31.2	38.3
32 40000	Las Vegas city	31.8	21.2	210,927	64.4	42.5	6.8	15.2	35.6	28.5	34.7	34.6
32 51800	North Las Vegas city	38.3	21.8	67,222	72.1	50.1	6.8	15.2	27.9	20.9	47.4	25.1
32 53800	Pahrump CDP	13.8	9.7	14,962	69.8	52.9	6.9	9.9	30.2	24.2	25.3	56.9
32 54600	Paradise CDP	31.6	24.5	87,162	54.8	34.1	7.5	13.2	45.2	35.1	28.6	30.4
32 60600	Reno city	25.4	16.3	89,155	57.4	39.0	5.6	12.8	42.6	33.2	30.7	31.8
32 68400	Sparks city	27.8	18.0	34,330	64.8	46.4	5.5	13.0	35.2	27.5	33.9	32.6
32 68585	Spring Valley CDP	21.8	30.0	69,215	59.5	40.7	6.8	12.1	40.5	29.4	29.2	31.5
32 70900	Summerlin South CDP	10.1	16.2	10,146	66.1	51.9	4.6	9.5	33.9	27.6	26.1	42.5
32 71400	Sunrise Manor CDP	49.6	26.7	58,720	69.5	42.6	7.9	19.0	30.5	23.7	42.2	30.3
32 83800	Whitney CDP	34.9	27.4	13,598	65.2	44.0	6.4	14.7	34.8	26.6	37.2	28.0
32 84600	Winchester CDP	50.3	33.7	10,793	55.5	30.5	9.7	15.3	44.5	33.7	30.5	39.5
33 00000	**New Hampshire**	2.9	5.4	518,009	66.9	53.0	4.1	9.7	33.1	25.5	30.3	35.3
33 14200	Concord city	2.1	5.6	17,318	56.3	41.0	3.7	11.6	43.7	34.2	28.1	32.1
33 17860	Derry CDP	1.4	6.8	9,059	63.6	45.2	4.5	13.9	36.4	28.1	33.5	28.4
33 18820	Dover city	1.6	6.0	12,484	57.3	40.5	5.4	11.5	42.7	30.3	26.7	28.3
33 39300	Keene city	1.3	3.7	9,080	52.4	38.4	4.0	10.0	47.6	32.9	22.1	37.5
33 45140	Manchester city	8.5	13.0	44,629	59.2	40.2	5.4	13.6	40.8	31.3	28.8	30.2
33 50260	Nashua city	9.4	12.8	34,600	63.4	46.8	4.3	12.2	36.6	28.5	30.9	30.5
33 62900	Portsmouth city	3.2	8.0	10,425	45.4	38.8	1.6	5.0	54.6	43.2	21.6	33.2
33 65140	Rochester city	1.9	2.1	12,782	60.1	39.5	5.5	15.0	39.9	30.7	27.7	37.7
34 00000	**New Jersey**	18.1	21.3	3,181,881	69.1	50.9	4.8	13.4	30.9	26.0	34.6	36.6
34 02080	Atlantic City city	24.0	28.8	15,721	53.2	23.6	6.9	22.7	46.8	40.8	31.5	35.5
34 03580	Bayonne city	18.8	28.3	25,933	62.4	37.9	5.3	19.2	37.6	31.8	32.2	34.2
34 05170	Bergenfield borough	29.3	37.4	9,219	74.1	55.7	5.8	12.6	25.9	21.0	34.9	41.0
34 07600	Bridgeton city	48.6	25.3	5,784	70.2	36.4	7.5	26.3	29.8	25.2	45.3	30.3
34 10000	Camden city	48.5	11.8	24,739	67.2	20.9	7.4	38.9	32.8	26.6	42.6	28.1
34 10750	Carteret borough	31.6	31.2	7,549	78.9	51.4	9.1	18.3	21.1	20.2	42.4	34.4
34 13570	Cliffside Park borough	31.9	41.9	10,174	64.2	44.0	6.6	13.7	35.8	32.6	23.5	41.3
34 13690	Clifton city	34.4	36.5	28,383	68.4	49.6	6.0	12.7	31.6	28.4	33.0	36.9
34 19390	East Orange city	7.4	24.2	25,239	55.7	21.9	6.5	27.3	44.3	40.2	32.8	31.3
34 21000	Elizabeth city	61.3	47.5	38,814	70.1	37.1	8.9	24.2	29.9	23.1	43.7	28.7
34 21480	Englewood city	19.0	32.0	10,602	60.7	39.4	5.5	15.8	39.3	34.1	26.9	39.5
34 22470	Fair Lawn borough	12.4	30.2	11,516	75.1	59.4	4.6	11.1	24.9	20.6	38.4	42.4
34 24420	Fort Lee borough	11.9	49.5	16,871	52.8	40.3	4.8	7.7	47.2	44.9	19.7	47.3
34 25770	Garfield city	35.0	47.5	10,763	71.1	46.1	4.4	20.6	28.9	23.2	35.7	31.0
34 28680	Hackensack city	36.4	39.6	17,644	56.4	34.1	6.2	16.1	43.6	35.3	26.9	33.3
34 32250	Hoboken city	17.3	16.1	24,487	40.4	29.8	1.6	8.9	59.6	39.0	18.9	14.6
34 34470	Iselin CDP	8.2	43.7	6,325	80.6	63.6	5.3	11.8	19.4	15.2	40.6	42.7
34 36000	Jersey City city	27.4	39.0	95,560	61.3	36.9	6.4	18.1	38.7	29.2	31.7	26.3
34 36510	Kearny town	44.4	40.2	13,373	79.4	55.1	8.8	15.6	20.6	17.4	41.4	32.6
34 38580	Lakewood CDP	12.8	13.1	9,956	86.0	70.9	4.2	10.9	14.0	12.3	67.2	22.2
34 40350	Linden city	27.6	34.5	14,698	67.8	42.8	6.4	18.5	32.2	28.5	32.9	38.3
34 41100	Lodi borough	40.9	38.0	9,262	61.7	35.5	5.1	21.1	38.3	34.0	30.9	34.0
34 41310	Long Branch city	25.1	27.6	12,157	57.3	38.8	5.0	13.4	42.7	35.1	28.8	31.1

Table A-4. Cities — Who: Age, Race/Ethnicity, and Household Structure, 2010–2012—*Continued*

STATE and Place code	STATE or City	Total population	Percent change 2010–2012	Population by age (percent) Under 5 years	5 to 17 years	18 to 24 years	25 to 44 years	45 to 64 years	65 years and over	Median age	Race alone or in combination (percent) White	Black	Asian, Hawaiian, or Pacific Islander	American Indian, Alaska Native, or some other race
	ACS table number:	B01003	Population estimates	B01001	B01001	B01001	B01001	B01001	B01001	B01002	B02008	B02009	B02011 + B02012	B02010 + B02013
	Column number:	1	2	3	4	5	6	7	8	9	10	11	12	13
	New Jersey—Cont.													
34 46680	Millville city	28,580	0.4	7.2	17.6	10.2	26.1	25.5	13.3	36.8	73.9	20.6	1.2	7.2
34 51000	Newark city	277,627	0.1	7.7	18.3	11.6	31.8	22.2	8.4	32.1	30.7	55.3	2.4	17.9
34 51210	New Brunswick city	55,684	1.6	7.8	13.6	33.0	28.1	12.5	5.1	23.0	72.2	14.6	8.6	6.0
34 53280	North Plainfield borough	21,992	0.2	4.8	20.5	8.8	33.0	25.9	7.1	35.2	48.7	17.8	5.9	28.5
34 54690	Old Bridge CDP	23,718	...	5.1	17.7	8.5	24.9	29.8	13.9	40.5	86.4	3.2	10.0	2.0
34 55950	Paramus borough	26,455	0.6	4.6	14.8	6.3	21.0	30.6	22.7	47.4	71.2	1.1	25.1	4.1
34 56550	Passaic city	70,066	0.5	10.1	21.6	11.1	29.4	19.8	7.9	29.5	47.6	11.4	2.6	41.4
34 57000	Paterson city	145,644	-0.8	8.3	19.3	11.6	28.7	22.8	9.3	32.2	57.9	37.9	4.4	7.8
34 58200	Perth Amboy city	51,388	1.6	8.0	18.8	10.6	30.5	22.8	9.3	32.9	80.2	10.3	2.5	10.3
34 59190	Plainfield city	50,052	0.7	7.5	15.9	11.3	31.3	24.5	9.5	33.4	16.2	46.1	2.5	37.1
34 59640	Pleasantville city	20,520	2.3	8.8	18.6	10.3	28.3	24.0	10.0	35.3	44.8	43.2	5.7	14.7
34 61530	Rahway city	27,614	1.1	5.8	16.0	7.8	28.7	28.5	13.2	39.3	51.5	31.4	6.3	13.3
34 63000	Ridgewood village	25,098	0.8	5.8	24.7	4.7	21.3	31.8	11.8	41.6	80.4	2.2	17.1	3.2
34 64620	Roselle borough	21,204	0.8	6.1	17.0	8.1	26.1	29.0	13.6	39.9	27.9	52.3	5.6	15.4
34 65790	Sayreville borough	43,270	2.4	6.2	15.9	8.7	28.0	28.1	13.2	39.1	69.2	12.5	17.5	2.7
34 68370	Somerset CDP	24,175	...	8.8	11.4	6.0	31.9	26.8	15.0	39.5	51.7	24.1	23.2	4.1
34 69390	South Plainfield borough	23,520	1.1	3.4	17.4	7.0	26.3	32.4	13.4	41.9	72.9	10.3	17.5	1.7
34 71430	Summit city	21,646	1.5	5.0	23.6	4.6	25.9	29.2	11.7	40.5	85.4	5.5	8.6	2.7
34 73110	Toms River CDP	89,105	...	4.8	16.3	8.4	24.4	29.3	16.7	42.4	92.4	2.6	4.8	1.3
34 74000	Trenton city	84,660	-0.6	7.4	18.8	10.9	30.9	23.2	8.8	33.2	33.2	53.3	1.2	15.0
34 74630	Union City city	67,193	1.8	6.9	17.0	10.4	32.5	23.5	9.7	33.7	65.8	4.9	3.2	28.9
34 76070	Vineland city	60,830	0.0	7.0	19.3	9.3	25.3	24.9	14.1	36.1	63.9	18.6	2.5	20.5
34 79040	Westfield town	30,504	0.8	6.0	22.2	6.5	23.3	29.3	12.7	40.9	88.0	5.3	7.1	0.5
34 79610	West New York town	50,591	3.3	7.4	13.3	8.8	36.9	21.6	12.1	35.7	60.2	5.3	5.5	32.7
34 81950	Woodbridge CDP	19,616	...	10.2	14.1	6.2	33.5	25.9	10.2	36.2	61.3	11.7	25.7	6.0
35 00000	**New Mexico**	2,076,325	1.0	6.9	17.9	10.0	25.0	26.5	13.7	36.8	74.9	2.8	2.0	23.5
35 01780	Alamogordo city	31,141	2.8	7.2	16.1	8.6	27.5	24.2	16.3	35.8	82.0	7.3	3.6	11.2
35 02000	Albuquerque city	551,597	1.5	6.9	16.8	10.4	28.2	25.4	12.4	35.5	72.9	4.4	3.7	23.5
35 12150	Carlsbad city	26,349	2.0	6.7	19.3	8.7	23.8	26.3	15.2	37.3	89.7	2.4	...	9.8
35 16420	Clovis city	38,752	2.5	8.9	18.9	10.1	27.7	22.8	11.6	32.0	73.0	8.0	2.4	19.9
35 25800	Farmington city	45,798	-0.2	8.5	19.8	9.2	26.8	24.0	11.6	32.8	69.8	2.1	1.0	30.8
35 28460	Gallup city	22,075	1.4	9.3	24.4	8.8	23.9	23.6	9.9	30.7	46.3	2.4	2.9	54.8
35 32520	Hobbs city	34,495	2.7	9.9	19.5	10.2	28.4	21.8	10.3	30.8	87.9	7.2	...	6.6
35 39380	Las Cruces city	99,754	2.9	7.6	17.1	13.9	26.9	21.6	13.0	31.7	90.5	2.3	2.2	7.1
35 63460	Rio Rancho city	89,499	3.2	6.9	21.2	7.7	26.7	26.2	11.4	36.2	86.0	5.2	2.8	10.1
35 64930	Roswell city	48,452	0.0	8.2	19.7	10.3	23.5	24.0	14.3	34.0	84.1	3.1	1.1	15.1
35 70500	Santa Fe city	68,677	1.6	5.4	13.5	7.7	23.9	30.4	19.1	44.6	89.3	1.8	2.7	9.7
35 74520	South Valley CDP	41,733	...	6.5	18.8	10.4	23.9	27.1	13.3	36.6	60.1	1.3	0.8	40.4
36 00000	**New York**	19,490,373	0.9	6.0	16.1	10.2	27.1	26.9	13.8	38.0	67.5	16.9	8.4	10.1
36 01000	Albany city	97,843	0.2	5.2	12.5	21.1	26.1	22.9	12.2	31.7	60.2	33.8	6.3	4.0
36 03078	Auburn city	27,526	-1.0	5.6	13.7	10.7	27.2	26.2	16.6	40.9	88.2	11.1	1.4	2.1
36 04143	Baldwin CDP	25,166	...	6.6	17.6	12.2	25.6	28.2	9.8	35.8	62.1	30.4	4.0	9.1
36 04935	Bay Shore CDP	27,327	...	7.3	15.6	9.9	29.8	26.9	10.6	36.0	55.8	20.4	7.6	17.9
36 06607	Binghamton city	46,917	-1.6	4.9	14.6	15.8	23.2	25.6	15.9	37.5	81.7	13.9	6.1	2.4
36 08026	Brentwood CDP	57,472	...	6.8	18.8	10.1	34.4	21.6	8.4	33.0	46.3	18.0	3.2	40.2
36 08257	Brighton CDP	36,635	...	4.9	14.1	10.9	26.3	25.4	18.4	39.4	82.3	6.3	13.1	1.2
36 11000	Buffalo city	260,321	-0.7	6.5	16.2	14.1	26.7	25.1	11.6	33.4	53.0	39.8	4.6	6.3
36 13376	Centereach CDP	33,430	...	6.2	18.5	9.6	26.4	27.5	11.8	38.6	86.0	4.4	5.8	4.7
36 13552	Central Islip CDP	38,029	...	7.7	17.7	11.6	30.7	23.0	9.1	33.5	52.5	23.4	3.5	25.2
36 15000	Cheektowaga CDP	75,427	...	4.9	13.9	9.7	24.5	28.0	19.0	43.0	87.7	10.4	1.5	2.3
36 17530	Commack CDP	35,153	...	5.4	20.6	6.0	21.4	29.7	16.8	43.1	90.8	1.7	7.5	1.6
36 18146	Copiague CDP	21,404	...	5.1	15.0	9.7	25.9	32.8	11.5	41.6	77.1	9.2	4.0	10.5
36 18157	Coram CDP	38,039	...	6.5	17.1	7.1	29.5	26.2	13.6	38.8	81.9	10.9	5.1	5.7
36 19972	Deer Park CDP	25,546	...	5.2	18.3	6.6	25.3	29.0	15.5	41.3	81.0	9.2	7.8	3.5
36 20687	Dix Hills CDP	26,752	...	3.4	19.5	8.1	20.5	34.2	14.3	43.5	83.4	6.0	9.8	1.7
36 22502	East Meadow CDP	39,073	...	5.5	15.3	9.4	23.0	30.5	16.2	41.8	82.4	4.7	9.4	4.4
36 22612	East Northport CDP	20,302	...	4.9	18.3	7.8	23.2	33.0	12.9	42.1	95.7	2.1	1.8	0.8
36 22733	East Patchogue CDP	23,701	...	6.1	14.2	7.4	28.1	27.4	16.9	41.6	92.5	4.7	2.6	1.4
36 24229	Elmira city	29,080	-0.7	7.1	17.0	14.0	27.1	24.0	10.8	33.6	84.6	17.9	0.8	2.2
36 24273	Elmont CDP	37,426	...	5.3	18.4	11.5	27.8	27.2	9.9	35.2	21.5	48.6	14.8	18.4
36 27309	Franklin Square CDP	29,395	...	5.3	16.2	7.2	24.6	30.3	16.4	42.5	80.6	6.1	9.9	7.4
36 27485	Freeport village	43,047	0.5	6.6	15.2	8.7	29.5	26.7	13.3	38.8	42.7	36.4	3.4	26.0
36 28178	Garden City village	22,496	0.7	7.8	18.1	9.4	18.0	30.3	16.4	43.1	95.7	0.6	4.9	1.2
36 29113	Glen Cove city	27,047	0.4	7.1	14.1	8.4	26.8	26.8	16.7	39.5	66.8	6.6	3.6	24.0
36 32402	Harrison CDP	27,666	1.0	4.2	19.1	18.4	22.8	22.4	13.1	35.0	82.1	4.1	7.6	7.7
36 32732	Hauppauge CDP	20,295	...	4.9	17.6	6.9	21.2	31.9	17.5	44.7	92.7	2.1	4.7	1.4
36 33139	Hempstead village	54,306	1.7	7.7	17.0	11.7	30.1	23.5	10.1	33.6	21.7	49.5	2.4	30.6

Table A-4. Cities — Who: Age, Race/Ethnicity, and Household Structure, 2010–2012—*Continued*

STATE and Place code	STATE or City	Percent Hispanic or Latino	Percent foreign born	Total households	Household type (percent) Family households Total family households	Married-couple families	Male household families	Female household families	Nonfamily households Total nonfamily households	One-person households	Percent of households with people under 18 years	Percent of households with people 60 years and over
ACS table number:		B03003	C05003	B11001	B11001	B11001	B11001	B11001	B11001	B11001	B11005	B11006
Column number:		14	15	16	17	18	19	20	21	22	23	24
	New Jersey—Cont.											
34 46680	Millville city...................	16.7	4.6	10,169	64.5	38.6	6.2	19.7	35.5	29.3	36.1	36.2
34 51000	Newark city....................	33.9	28.1	91,552	63.4	25.2	8.2	29.9	36.6	30.5	39.8	27.0
34 51210	New Brunswick city.........	54.0	39.4	14,153	59.2	27.0	9.1	23.1	40.8	24.8	37.4	20.2
34 53280	North Plainfield borough..............	44.5	40.2	7,190	70.8	49.0	6.1	15.7	29.2	20.3	41.9	24.7
34 54690	Old Bridge CDP...............	10.1	14.2	7,643	82.1	69.9	3.6	8.5	17.9	14.2	40.8	38.1
34 55950	Paramus borough	8.5	30.2	8,533	82.5	70.9	1.3	10.3	17.5	14.7	34.4	50.4
34 56550	Passaic city....................	71.8	44.5	20,530	70.2	33.5	8.8	27.9	29.8	26.2	45.5	26.7
34 57000	Paterson city..................	57.4	33.0	43,618	73.1	34.2	8.5	30.5	26.9	23.5	45.6	30.7
34 58200	Perth Amboy city............	78.7	38.1	16,750	73.9	38.6	12.2	23.2	26.1	22.1	44.5	28.8
34 59190	Plainfield city.................	38.9	38.3	14,096	71.7	33.7	11.3	26.7	28.3	22.3	43.2	32.8
34 59640	Pleasantville city............	37.4	27.0	6,248	70.6	28.3	10.4	31.9	29.4	25.3	43.0	34.4
34 61530	Rahway city	21.8	23.3	10,508	62.4	40.7	6.2	15.4	37.6	31.9	33.9	32.5
34 63000	Ridgewood village...........	8.2	19.5	8,223	77.6	69.1	1.6	6.8	22.4	18.3	46.6	32.9
34 64620	Roselle borough..............	28.8	28.7	8,439	65.0	38.0	4.4	22.5	35.0	33.0	32.5	38.8
34 65790	Sayreville borough..........	12.6	26.2	15,509	74.7	53.4	7.4	13.9	25.3	22.7	38.8	33.8
34 68370	Somerset CDP.................	12.3	25.7	8,816	67.4	53.9	3.5	10.0	32.6	25.2	30.6	39.8
34 69390	South Plainfield borough.............	13.4	22.6	8,113	77.3	60.0	4.4	12.9	22.7	16.4	35.6	38.3
34 71430	Summit city....................	11.0	17.0	7,871	72.2	62.9	2.2	7.1	27.8	23.2	40.1	33.7
34 73110	Toms River CDP...............	9.1	9.4	33,512	70.1	53.4	4.2	12.5	29.9	24.3	30.0	41.8
34 74000	Trenton city...................	33.3	21.6	28,218	61.6	25.5	9.0	27.1	38.4	31.7	37.5	29.0
34 74630	Union City city	83.6	56.6	22,440	70.2	34.5	9.8	25.8	29.8	23.5	41.6	31.6
34 76070	Vineland city..................	36.3	11.8	20,577	69.7	44.7	5.9	19.1	30.3	24.9	36.8	39.7
34 79040	Westfield town................	5.7	12.3	10,236	76.4	69.0	2.5	4.9	23.6	21.2	43.4	35.9
34 79610	West New York town.........	79.4	60.3	18,859	63.2	36.0	9.8	17.4	36.8	27.2	32.8	30.4
34 81950	Woodbridge CDP..............	18.0	31.3	6,933	74.4	57.4	6.9	10.1	25.6	22.3	39.6	31.0
35 00000	**New Mexico**...................	46.7	9.8	765,306	65.4	45.4	6.0	14.0	34.6	28.7	32.5	36.7
35 01780	Alamogordo city	32.6	7.7	12,398	67.1	45.8	6.4	15.0	32.9	28.0	31.2	38.4
35 02000	Albuquerque city.............	47.0	10.5	224,766	59.3	39.2	6.1	14.1	40.7	33.1	30.8	31.5
35 12150	Carlsbad city..................	42.3	4.0	10,019	65.1	42.8	7.2	15.1	34.9	31.6	33.4	39.7
35 16420	Clovis city......................	42.2	9.0	14,373	66.3	46.8	4.8	14.6	33.7	30.5	35.1	31.8
35 25800	Farmington city...............	22.8	5.5	15,696	72.1	53.1	5.9	13.1	27.9	24.1	36.9	32.7
35 28460	Gallup city.....................	34.5	6.5	6,108	69.0	44.3	4.7	20.0	31.0	26.0	40.4	36.1
35 32520	Hobbs city......................	52.8	15.6	10,621	74.3	52.6	6.4	15.3	25.7	22.2	42.6	29.3
35 39380	Las Cruces city................	57.3	10.8	37,828	62.0	41.1	5.2	15.7	38.0	29.7	32.2	33.1
35 63460	Rio Rancho city...............	38.5	5.2	32,137	69.8	51.2	7.4	11.2	30.2	23.9	37.9	31.2
35 64930	Roswell city....................	54.2	14.1	17,714	67.4	43.8	5.6	18.0	32.6	27.7	37.5	37.9
35 70500	Santa Fe city	47.9	13.9	31,570	49.6	33.7	4.2	11.7	50.4	40.2	21.6	43.5
35 74520	South Valley CDP..............	81.1	18.5	12,956	72.2	48.3	8.2	15.7	27.8	19.3	40.3	39.7
36 00000	**New York**	17.9	22.3	7,210,095	64.0	44.1	5.0	14.9	36.0	29.5	31.6	36.2
36 01000	Albany city.....................	8.1	11.6	38,841	45.2	25.5	3.7	15.9	54.8	41.7	22.0	29.6
36 03078	Auburn city....................	4.1	3.8	11,159	54.1	34.6	5.8	13.7	45.9	39.6	26.6	42.7
36 04143	Baldwin CDP...................	30.6	29.1	7,627	84.1	57.2	7.5	19.4	15.9	12.8	44.7	31.4
36 04935	Bay Shore CDP................	34.4	26.6	9,217	63.8	39.9	6.6	17.3	36.2	31.4	34.9	34.8
36 06607	Binghamton city..............	6.0	9.1	20,327	48.0	27.3	4.7	16.1	52.0	41.0	21.9	35.3
36 08026	Brentwood CDP...............	68.1	43.6	14,024	82.6	51.4	9.6	21.5	17.4	12.8	55.1	31.8
36 08257	Brighton CDP..................	3.3	16.3	15,535	53.8	43.2	2.8	7.9	46.2	36.0	27.8	36.4
36 11000	Buffalo city....................	9.6	8.2	111,275	52.2	23.5	5.5	23.2	47.8	38.9	28.9	29.0
36 13376	Centereach CDP...............	12.2	11.6	9,979	83.5	62.9	6.4	14.3	16.5	13.0	43.9	36.9
36 13552	Central Islip CDP..............	59.0	37.3	10,062	77.7	44.0	8.5	25.3	22.3	16.2	47.0	35.1
36 15000	Cheektowaga CDP............	2.7	4.8	32,306	60.3	41.7	4.8	13.9	39.7	33.3	25.8	40.7
36 17530	Commack CDP.................	6.2	11.6	11,685	82.2	74.0	2.2	6.1	17.8	16.1	42.3	41.7
36 18146	Copiague CDP.................	25.2	30.3	7,236	73.1	49.5	6.5	17.0	26.9	22.2	33.2	35.1
36 18157	Coram CDP.....................	11.4	16.1	14,007	69.4	52.2	3.4	13.8	30.6	22.3	35.7	34.5
36 19972	Deer Park CDP.................	12.9	13.2	8,969	72.9	56.5	3.0	13.4	27.1	23.4	36.9	38.3
36 20687	Dix Hills CDP..................	6.5	18.6	8,550	81.4	74.2	2.7	4.5	18.6	13.7	38.0	39.9
36 22502	East Meadow CDP............	9.0	14.6	12,640	76.6	63.8	4.5	8.3	23.4	21.5	36.1	49.4
36 22612	East Northport CDP...........	7.0	5.0	7,193	80.3	63.6	1.6	15.1	19.7	17.5	36.5	41.3
36 22733	East Patchogue CDP..........	19.9	10.0	8,696	67.7	50.2	4.9	12.6	32.3	27.4	30.5	41.2
36 24229	Elmira city.....................	4.1	2.3	10,569	55.4	32.5	5.1	17.9	44.6	35.6	33.1	32.4
36 24273	Elmont CDP....................	22.7	44.6	9,594	85.1	59.5	5.9	19.7	14.9	11.4	48.4	39.5
36 27309	Franklin Square CDP	13.7	19.7	9,829	79.0	62.2	3.6	13.2	21.0	19.1	35.0	44.3
36 27485	Freeport village..............	43.0	36.7	13,663	68.9	40.3	6.5	22.0	31.1	23.7	35.8	40.4
36 28178	Garden City village..........	4.8	6.8	7,489	83.1	73.0	2.1	7.9	16.9	16.5	38.6	44.5
36 29113	Glen Cove city................	31.5	36.3	9,431	68.4	50.7	7.4	10.4	31.6	24.7	33.6	45.0
36 32402	Harrison village	15.8	22.6	8,525	75.0	62.8	3.8	8.4	25.0	19.9	40.9	34.6
36 32732	Hauppauge CDP	7.2	8.2	7,045	75.9	59.5	5.7	10.8	24.1	19.6	31.8	46.4
36 33139	Hempstead village...........	41.0	37.3	16,240	67.9	34.6	7.8	25.5	32.1	24.6	43.3	31.8

Table A-4. Cities — Who: Age, Race/Ethnicity, and Household Structure, 2010–2012—*Continued*

STATE and Place code	STATE or City	Total population	Percent change 2010–2012	Population by age (percent)						Median age	Race alone or in combination (percent)			
				Under 5 years	5 to 17 years	18 to 24 years	25 to 44 years	45 to 64 years	65 years and over		White	Black	Asian, Hawaiian, or Pacific Islander	American Indian, Alaska Native, or some other race
	ACS table number:	B01003	Population estimates	B01001	B01001	B01001	B01001	B01001	B01001	B01002	B02008	B02009	B02011 + B02012	B02010 + B02013
	Column number:	1	2	3	4	5	6	7	8	9	10	11	12	13
	New York—Cont.													
36 34374	Hicksville CDP	42,780	...	4.9	15.0	8.9	24.8	30.3	16.1	41.9	73.3	3.1	21.2	5.2
36 35056	Holbrook CDP	27,140	...	4.5	20.8	6.5	28.2	27.1	12.9	40.4	93.5	1.1	3.3	4.4
36 35254	Holtsville CDP	20,793	...	5.8	20.9	9.9	24.6	27.1	11.7	38.4	88.3	6.4	3.4	...
36 37044	Huntington Station CDP	32,412	...	6.6	18.9	10.0	28.1	25.2	11.2	36.8	69.2	10.3	3.6	18.9
36 37737	Irondequoit CDP	51,624	...	5.0	15.9	7.6	24.3	29.0	18.2	42.9	86.3	9.6	2.7	3.3
36 38077	Ithaca city	30,160	1.0	1.9	5.5	56.9	18.4	11.6	5.7	22.2	73.5	8.4	18.7	2.5
36 38264	Jamestown city	30,916	-1.1	7.1	18.0	9.5	24.9	26.2	14.4	36.6	90.8	5.7	0.7	5.1
36 39727	Kingston city	23,783	-0.6	7.9	14.2	10.3	25.0	27.0	15.6	39.2	81.7	20.2	2.2	3.6
36 39853	Kiryas Joel village	20,670	5.6	23.6	38.5	10.4	21.5	5.2	0.9	12.2	99.5	...	...	...
36 40838	Lake Ronkonkoma CDP	19,743	...	6.5	16.2	8.9	27.1	27.0	14.3	39.7	91.8	3.7	3.3	2.6
36 42081	Levittown CDP	53,021	...	4.8	17.7	7.8	25.3	30.6	13.7	40.7	88.6	0.6	6.7	5.4
36 42554	Lindenhurst village	27,285	0.0	4.0	17.8	8.2	26.2	31.4	12.4	41.0	94.5	...	1.4	0.6
36 43082	Lockport city	21,055	-0.9	5.9	16.4	8.3	27.0	27.5	14.8	40.0	87.5	10.6	...	3.7
36 43335	Long Beach city	33,402	0.5	4.0	13.2	7.3	29.8	29.1	16.6	43.2	85.5	6.1	3.4	7.2
36 45986	Massapequa CDP	21,997	...	5.4	20.2	7.3	21.7	30.8	14.5	42.3	98.1	0.1	1.5	...
36 46404	Medford CDP	25,826	...	7.0	17.6	10.2	27.3	26.3	11.6	36.9	89.0	9.5	2.0	...
36 46514	Melville CDP	20,744	...	4.4	20.3	7.5	18.3	27.1	22.4	44.5	88.7	...	6.1	...
36 46668	Merrick CDP	21,446	...	4.1	19.9	8.3	16.3	36.2	15.2	45.8	94.3	...	3.5	2.3
36 47042	Middletown city	28,026	-0.8	7.8	19.2	11.2	29.6	21.1	11.2	32.5	50.5	26.6	4.3	24.0
36 49121	Mount Vernon city	67,684	0.8	7.3	16.1	9.0	28.4	25.8	13.4	37.8	28.6	64.5	3.1	8.3
36 50034	Newburgh city	28,791	-0.8	9.0	22.3	14.4	26.5	19.0	8.8	28.8	38.0	36.0	0.6	28.7
36 50100	New City CDP	34,845	...	4.2	19.4	8.0	22.2	29.7	16.3	43.4	78.6	8.9	12.0	3.2
36 50617	New Rochelle city	77,733	1.6	5.6	17.3	10.4	25.3	27.3	14.2	38.1	70.5	21.6	4.0	8.1
36 51000	New York city	8,265,445	1.8	6.4	15.1	10.4	31.2	24.5	12.3	35.5	46.1	26.4	14.1	16.8
36 51055	Niagara Falls city	49,934	-0.9	5.5	16.6	10.2	25.0	28.0	14.6	38.9	73.9	24.6	1.7	2.2
36 51495	North Bay Shore CDP	20,103	...	7.7	19.3	12.6	29.8	23.5	7.0	31.1	44.1	25.1	1.6	32.7
36 51517	North Bellmore CDP	20,515	...	4.6	17.6	6.7	21.8	34.5	14.8	44.5	87.3	1.4	5.7	4.8
36 53682	North Tonawanda city	31,410	-0.9	5.1	13.1	9.8	24.4	31.7	16.0	42.9	97.3	1.4	1.3	...
36 54441	Oceanside CDP	32,924	...	4.7	17.0	8.8	22.4	32.0	15.0	43.1	92.9	...	3.3	2.8
36 55530	Ossining village	25,230	0.6	6.5	14.8	8.0	34.4	26.4	9.8	36.7	51.9	15.3	4.2	31.1
36 56979	Peekskill city	23,732	0.9	7.7	13.2	9.1	34.5	23.3	12.2	37.1	46.7	25.3	5.3	26.6
36 58442	Plainview CDP	27,231	...	5.6	18.5	6.1	20.6	30.3	18.8	44.6	89.0	0.5	10.3	1.1
36 59223	Port Chester village	29,137	0.8	6.8	15.7	10.2	35.2	22.0	10.2	34.4	41.2	8.7	2.2	49.1
36 59641	Poughkeepsie city	30,976	-0.7	8.4	16.0	9.7	28.3	24.1	13.6	35.0	50.7	38.1	3.5	14.5
36 63000	Rochester city	210,548	0.0	7.3	16.9	13.9	29.5	23.1	9.2	30.9	48.0	43.9	4.1	8.7
36 63264	Rockville Centre village	24,083	0.2	5.0	19.1	8.2	19.0	31.4	17.3	44.1	90.5	6.6	1.4	2.9
36 63418	Rome city	33,346	-2.6	6.0	14.7	9.5	25.9	27.6	16.3	40.2	90.0	7.1	1.7	4.7
36 63473	Ronkonkoma CDP	19,322	...	4.6	17.0	8.3	28.8	29.2	12.2	41.0	91.6	2.0	6.4	1.8
36 63924	Rotterdam CDP	21,228	...	4.6	15.5	8.4	24.9	28.7	17.9	42.6	95.1	2.0	2.5	2.0
36 65255	Saratoga Springs city	26,751	1.3	5.0	11.2	13.0	27.6	26.6	16.6	39.5	94.0	3.7	3.1	4.4
36 65508	Schenectady city	66,124	-0.2	7.3	17.1	12.7	27.3	23.8	11.9	33.4	67.0	24.3	6.5	8.1
36 66212	Selden CDP	20,519	...	5.8	16.8	12.1	26.7	28.7	9.9	36.8	88.5	3.8	6.3	5.1
36 67070	Shirley CDP	26,140	...	7.2	16.7	8.5	28.4	33.0	6.4	38.0	82.0	7.0	9.5	5.3
36 67851	Smithtown CDP	26,884	...	5.8	19.8	8.2	20.6	30.7	14.8	42.2	95.1	2.2	2.8	0.8
36 70420	Spring Valley village	31,725	1.9	10.7	20.8	9.9	30.8	20.6	7.1	28.8	30.7	40.6	3.7	26.3
36 72554	Syosset CDP	19,167	...	4.0	21.9	6.5	20.6	31.7	15.3	42.6	76.0	...	22.4	...
36 73000	Syracuse city	144,575	-0.7	7.0	16.0	19.6	25.0	21.9	10.5	29.4	60.5	32.2	6.7	5.9
36 74183	Tonawanda CDP	58,179	...	3.6	15.5	8.9	24.5	28.5	19.0	43.1	93.5	3.9	3.2	1.4
36 75484	Troy city	50,034	-0.3	7.1	13.2	21.7	26.1	20.5	11.4	30.2	79.4	18.4	5.3	3.0
36 76089	Uniondale CDP	23,141	...	6.2	17.6	14.1	28.3	21.9	11.9	34.1	27.0	54.7	2.3	24.4
36 76540	Utica city	62,006	-0.7	7.8	17.6	12.3	24.0	23.6	14.8	34.8	73.7	18.2	8.6	5.7
36 76705	Valley Stream village	37,621	0.3	6.9	17.3	9.0	27.7	26.8	12.3	36.8	51.0	18.0	15.4	19.7
36 78608	Watertown city	27,454	3.0	10.4	13.6	13.2	28.8	21.1	12.9	31.3	88.5	7.9	3.3	3.2
36 79246	West Babylon CDP	44,516	...	4.5	17.8	9.4	25.6	28.6	14.0	40.1	81.2	10.7	3.3	7.2
36 80302	West Islip CDP	27,990	...	5.8	19.8	9.2	22.2	29.1	13.8	39.9	97.8	...	2.2	0.7
36 80907	West Seneca CDP	44,766	...	5.0	16.0	8.2	22.1	29.0	19.6	43.7	98.5	1.2	0.5	1.1
36 81677	White Plains city	57,176	0.8	6.2	13.3	8.2	30.9	25.2	16.2	39.0	68.6	17.6	7.6	14.1
36 84000	Yonkers city	197,514	1.0	6.9	15.8	8.8	27.6	26.2	14.7	37.8	56.5	19.6	7.8	20.0
37 00000	**North Carolina**	9,654,079	2.0	6.5	17.2	10.0	26.7	26.3	13.4	37.6	71.8	22.7	2.9	5.1
37 01520	Apex town	38,976	7.1	7.8	24.9	6.0	33.3	22.1	5.8	34.9	84.4	9.8	6.9	2.5
37 02080	Asheboro city	25,407	1.2	9.3	18.5	10.4	28.0	21.1	12.7	33.4	80.4	14.3	1.3	7.4
37 02140	Asheville city	84,661	2.6	5.7	13.4	9.8	30.4	24.9	15.8	38.2	84.6	12.7	2.2	2.4
37 09060	Burlington city	51,047	0.6	6.3	17.2	9.1	25.4	25.8	16.2	39.4	62.5	28.8	2.1	9.8
37 10620	Carrboro town	20,015	4.1	7.5	15.4	11.5	38.2	22.6	4.8	30.4	74.7	11.3	9.4	9.8
37 10740	Cary town	140,824	6.7	7.0	20.6	6.6	31.0	26.6	8.2	36.2	74.1	8.1	14.3	5.9
37 11800	Chapel Hill town	57,167	1.6	3.7	13.2	32.6	22.0	18.9	9.6	25.3	76.6	10.5	13.6	1.6
37 12000	Charlotte city	756,725	4.9	7.6	17.5	10.1	32.9	23.2	8.8	33.4	55.3	36.4	6.0	5.4
37 14100	Concord city	80,576	3.4	6.7	20.1	8.2	29.5	24.4	11.1	36.3	76.7	18.5	3.1	3.5
37 14700	Cornelius town	25,603	5.1	6.2	19.3	6.1	32.9	25.7	9.7	35.9	90.0	5.0	4.6	1.5
37 19000	Durham city	234,160	4.4	7.7	15.1	12.5	33.2	22.1	9.3	32.2	48.9	41.9	5.8	6.5
37 22920	Fayetteville city	201,334	0.6	8.6	16.7	14.2	29.0	21.4	10.0	30.1	51.1	43.6	5.0	6.3
37 25480	Garner town	26,316	3.3	7.1	18.5	7.8	28.2	26.4	11.9	38.3	56.1	39.4	1.6	5.1
37 25580	Gastonia city	72,151	1.3	7.8	19.6	9.8	25.5	25.6	11.8	36.0	64.1	28.9	1.5	8.6

Table A-4. Cities — Who: Age, Race/Ethnicity, and Household Structure, 2010–2012—*Continued*

STATE and Place code	STATE or City	Percent Hispanic or Latino	Percent foreign born	Total households	Total family households	Married-couple families	Male household families	Female household families	Total nonfamily households	One-person households	Percent of households with people under 18 years	Percent of households with people 60 years and over
	ACS table number:	B03003	C05003	B11001	B11001	B11001	B11001	B11001	B11001	B11001	B11005	B11006
	Column number:	14	15	16	17	18	19	20	21	22	23	24
	New York—Cont.											
36 34374	Hicksville CDP	10.0	25.9	13,665	82.2	66.8	4.4	11.0	17.8	13.9	32.5	44.1
36 35056	Holbrook CDP	14.8	6.4	8,902	78.4	57.5	4.2	16.8	21.6	17.4	42.0	36.4
36 35254	Holtsville CDP	13.6	9.8	6,641	79.1	60.7	2.5	15.9	20.9	15.9	42.2	34.9
36 37044	Huntington Station CDP	31.9	23.1	10,453	74.2	50.8	6.0	17.4	25.8	21.4	42.4	34.5
36 37737	Irondequoit CDP	6.1	7.9	22,050	60.5	43.5	3.8	13.3	39.5	33.7	27.3	40.6
36 38077	Ithaca city	7.8	18.6	9,910	26.2	17.6	1.6	7.0	73.8	42.9	12.4	19.7
36 38264	Jamestown city	9.0	1.8	13,476	57.8	33.9	5.4	18.5	42.2	36.1	29.2	34.3
36 39727	Kingston city	14.0	10.5	9,720	54.6	33.6	5.3	15.7	45.4	37.5	28.8	38.3
36 39853	Kiryas Joel village	1.5	6.5	3,726	93.6	90.6	0.9	2.1	6.4	5.3	87.5	9.4
36 40838	Lake Ronkonkoma CDP	10.3	9.3	6,782	71.4	57.8	4.2	9.3	28.6	24.7	41.3	37.8
36 42081	Levittown CDP	12.8	12.5	16,571	83.9	64.3	6.9	12.7	16.1	13.6	41.5	41.6
36 42554	Lindenhurst village	10.9	12.7	8,979	77.0	55.2	5.3	16.5	23.0	18.9	37.2	42.0
36 43082	Lockport city	4.0	2.4	8,928	60.2	37.4	5.1	17.7	39.8	32.1	26.9	35.1
36 43335	Long Beach city	16.5	17.3	14,477	52.6	36.2	4.4	12.1	47.4	38.7	23.4	35.0
36 45986	Massapequa CDP	4.9	5.5	7,086	80.6	68.0	3.5	9.1	19.4	16.8	43.2	40.4
36 46404	Medford CDP	15.6	10.4	7,766	78.9	59.8	6.2	13.0	21.1	15.0	44.4	40.2
36 46514	Melville CDP	4.3	10.0	7,141	80.2	65.3	3.7	11.2	19.8	17.5	35.1	46.6
36 46668	Merrick CDP	6.2	9.4	7,105	86.1	72.3	3.5	10.3	13.9	12.2	38.9	44.8
36 47042	Middletown city	38.0	21.5	9,453	64.4	36.4	5.3	22.7	35.6	29.8	40.0	30.7
36 49121	Mount Vernon city	14.8	33.0	26,283	61.0	34.8	4.8	21.4	39.0	34.5	33.1	34.1
36 50034	Newburgh city	49.1	22.6	8,907	64.9	34.5	7.7	22.7	35.1	28.7	45.1	27.8
36 50100	New City CDP	8.1	19.2	10,962	84.7	76.4	2.8	5.5	15.3	13.6	40.7	44.9
36 50617	New Rochelle city	27.3	27.2	27,785	67.4	47.5	5.0	14.9	32.6	28.8	34.1	35.4
36 51000	New York city	28.8	37.3	3,051,127	59.9	35.7	5.7	18.5	40.1	32.7	31.0	33.8
36 51055	Niagara Falls city	2.3	4.9	21,503	56.2	30.5	6.9	18.8	43.8	37.5	25.8	35.2
36 51495	North Bay Shore CDP	63.3	32.6	4,882	86.3	51.0	7.7	27.6	13.7	10.3	52.0	29.2
36 51517	North Bellmore CDP	12.5	10.9	6,723	80.0	68.5	3.7	7.7	20.0	16.9	38.4	43.7
36 53682	North Tonawanda city	1.5	3.2	13,946	58.3	43.3	5.3	9.6	41.7	35.8	24.3	36.2
36 54441	Oceanside CDP	11.7	12.5	11,240	78.0	64.2	4.9	8.9	22.0	19.1	35.0	43.8
36 55530	Ossining village	49.6	38.9	7,449	71.5	50.2	7.5	13.8	28.5	22.9	39.6	31.2
36 56979	Peekskill city	35.2	30.4	8,691	60.7	40.3	6.6	13.9	39.3	33.3	30.7	37.3
36 58442	Plainview CDP	4.0	14.1	9,330	81.8	72.6	2.6	6.5	18.2	16.6	39.6	47.0
36 59223	Port Chester village	59.0	45.9	9,536	70.1	41.1	9.6	19.4	29.9	23.0	39.0	29.1
36 59641	Poughkeepsie city	22.2	23.0	12,192	54.2	28.6	4.5	21.1	45.8	36.0	31.3	32.8
36 63000	Rochester city	16.9	9.9	86,273	49.8	21.4	4.7	23.6	50.2	40.3	29.7	24.8
36 63264	Rockville Centre village	9.4	8.7	9,100	68.8	57.5	2.1	9.2	31.2	28.4	30.9	42.2
36 63418	Rome city	5.9	3.6	13,002	57.2	38.3	6.2	12.7	42.8	35.2	26.8	39.7
36 63473	Ronkonkoma CDP	11.3	11.4	6,528	75.9	60.3	2.9	12.7	24.1	18.7	36.8	35.4
36 63924	Rotterdam CDP	2.0	4.5	7,942	64.7	47.7	5.2	11.7	35.3	31.2	27.5	42.3
36 65255	Saratoga Springs city	4.9	7.0	11,530	47.6	40.3	3.9	3.4	52.4	40.6	20.6	36.5
36 65508	Schenectady city	11.1	11.1	24,486	52.2	30.5	3.8	17.9	47.8	41.3	27.0	29.6
36 66212	Selden CDP	19.5	14.8	6,414	78.8	56.4	8.3	14.1	21.2	17.1	41.9	32.6
36 67070	Shirley CDP	17.4	14.8	7,973	81.2	65.1	4.0	12.1	18.8	13.4	41.9	28.5
36 67851	Smithtown CDP	4.6	5.8	8,561	78.5	67.6	3.4	7.5	21.5	17.9	40.9	41.3
36 70420	Spring Valley village	30.0	45.3	9,021	71.7	47.7	5.3	18.7	28.3	24.2	47.8	28.9
36 72554	Syosset CDP	5.6	21.7	6,445	85.4	72.4	0.5	12.4	14.6	13.6	40.8	41.7
36 73000	Syracuse city	8.1	11.4	54,577	49.7	23.7	4.6	21.4	50.3	39.0	28.5	27.8
36 74183	Tonawanda CDP	3.4	5.1	25,202	60.0	44.5	3.4	12.1	40.0	34.0	24.7	39.5
36 75484	Troy city	8.0	8.9	19,869	49.7	23.7	4.7	21.3	50.3	37.7	26.8	27.7
36 76089	Uniondale CDP	35.5	41.5	5,348	79.2	43.7	11.0	24.6	20.8	15.1	49.4	45.2
36 76540	Utica city	10.0	17.9	23,888	56.4	32.8	4.3	19.3	43.6	37.0	33.1	36.6
36 76705	Valley Stream village	28.2	34.0	11,197	77.7	59.3	6.7	11.6	22.3	17.7	39.1	41.3
36 78608	Watertown city	5.2	5.4	11,853	53.9	37.3	3.0	13.7	46.1	37.8	30.8	28.6
36 79246	West Babylon CDP	14.3	14.3	14,286	77.9	57.1	5.0	15.7	22.1	18.0	37.6	39.4
36 80302	West Islip CDP	3.9	5.2	8,899	81.8	68.9	3.1	9.8	18.2	15.5	43.3	34.9
36 80907	West Seneca CDP	1.0	2.7	18,518	65.4	51.5	3.3	10.7	34.6	30.9	27.6	42.7
36 81677	White Plains city	33.7	33.2	22,070	60.5	44.0	4.6	11.8	39.5	34.7	29.0	38.0
36 84000	Yonkers city	35.2	31.3	73,077	64.3	40.5	5.3	18.5	35.7	32.1	32.7	39.1
37 00000	**North Carolina**	8.5	7.6	3,699,308	66.5	48.3	4.4	13.8	33.5	27.9	32.6	33.9
37 01520	Apex town	8.7	9.6	13,193	76.6	63.4	3.2	10.1	23.4	18.4	51.6	15.1
37 02080	Asheboro city	22.8	14.4	9,729	62.8	39.0	3.4	20.4	37.2	32.6	36.4	34.2
37 02140	Asheville city	6.2	7.0	36,896	48.7	34.0	2.4	12.3	51.3	39.5	23.8	35.4
37 09060	Burlington city	12.5	8.9	21,922	61.3	39.1	5.4	16.8	38.7	34.0	29.1	38.0
37 10620	Carrboro town	18.2	19.9	8,980	46.5	34.5	3.8	8.2	53.5	40.5	30.3	12.9
37 10740	Cary town	9.8	20.7	51,021	71.9	61.3	3.1	7.4	28.1	22.3	40.6	23.8
37 11800	Chapel Hill town	4.9	16.6	19,756	51.8	42.9	1.9	7.0	48.2	34.3	28.2	25.3
37 12000	Charlotte city	13.2	14.7	292,501	60.8	40.3	4.7	15.8	39.2	31.4	34.2	23.9
37 14100	Concord city	12.4	9.5	29,364	68.2	52.7	3.7	11.7	31.8	27.2	38.8	27.8
37 14700	Cornelius town	9.7	9.4	10,130	64.3	49.2	6.3	8.8	35.7	26.8	36.9	26.1
37 19000	Durham city	13.6	14.5	95,863	57.8	35.8	5.0	17.0	42.2	32.2	31.1	24.3
37 22920	Fayetteville city	10.6	6.4	76,398	64.8	40.1	4.9	19.8	35.2	29.7	35.6	26.7
37 25480	Garner town	4.7	6.1	10,671	61.6	42.4	1.6	17.6	38.4	34.4	36.7	27.4
37 25580	Gastonia city	10.9	8.2	26,141	69.7	44.6	5.5	19.6	30.3	25.3	36.7	31.5

Table A-4. Cities — Who: Age, Race/Ethnicity, and Household Structure, 2010–2012—*Continued*

STATE and Place code	STATE or City	Total population	Percent change 2010–2012	Population by age (percent)						Median age	Race alone or in combination (percent)			
				Under 5 years	5 to 17 years	18 to 24 years	25 to 44 years	45 to 64 years	65 years and over		White	Black	Asian, Hawaiian, or Pacific Islander	American Indian, Alaska Native, or some other race
	ACS table number:	B01003	Population estimates	B01001	B01001	B01001	B01001	B01001	B01001	B01002	B02008	B02009	B02011 + B02012	B02010 + B02013
	Column number:	1	2	3	4	5	6	7	8	9	10	11	12	13
	North Carolina—Cont.													
37 26880	Goldsboro city	36,836	1.5	8.5	16.0	10.8	24.6	25.8	14.2	34.6	40.5	57.1	2.0	3.1
37 28000	Greensboro city	273,641	2.5	6.5	15.8	14.0	27.9	23.9	11.8	34.0	51.6	42.4	4.7	4.1
37 28080	Greenville city	86,115	2.7	5.8	13.4	28.5	27.9	16.9	7.6	25.8	59.0	37.3	3.7	2.4
37 30120	Havelock city	20,781	0.0	11.6	14.9	26.8	27.5	13.8	5.3	23.5	75.6	17.5	5.1	7.7
37 31060	Hickory city	40,126	0.1	6.7	16.2	10.7	27.2	23.8	15.5	38.2	76.8	13.7	3.6	7.3
37 31400	High Point city	106,164	1.9	7.3	18.4	10.0	27.9	24.6	11.8	35.6	57.3	34.0	7.2	3.4
37 32260	Holly Springs town	25,840	7.9	10.0	24.4	3.8	33.9	21.0	7.0	33.6	81.1	14.0	5.8	1.1
37 33120	Huntersville town	48,145	5.0	7.2	19.9	6.0	35.0	24.9	7.1	35.3	88.1	9.5	2.6	1.9
37 33560	Indian Trail town	34,210	3.3	6.0	25.9	7.9	29.8	22.4	7.9	34.6	82.8	13.6	2.1	3.3
37 34200	Jacksonville city	69,356	-2.3	10.1	14.0	31.1	26.3	12.0	6.4	23.4	69.8	24.5	4.8	4.6
37 35200	Kannapolis city	43,197	2.5	8.6	17.6	8.9	29.4	23.9	11.6	34.7	73.9	21.0	2.3	4.3
37 35600	Kernersville town	23,398	1.3	4.8	17.7	7.6	28.9	26.5	14.5	40.8	78.3	15.3	3.3	5.0
37 35920	Kinston city	21,634	-0.1	7.9	17.8	7.2	20.5	28.1	18.5	41.0	27.5	71.8	2.0	0.7
37 39700	Lumberton city	21,676	0.8	8.8	15.2	9.5	27.4	24.7	14.3	35.7	47.2	34.7	1.8	20.6
37 41960	Matthews town	27,987	5.1	4.9	20.0	8.4	23.6	28.4	14.8	40.3	82.6	12.5	4.5	1.0
37 43480	Mint Hill town	23,315	5.0	6.2	17.8	5.4	25.7	30.4	14.4	42.4	80.4	12.8	5.2	4.0
37 43920	Monroe city	33,286	2.3	7.9	21.3	7.9	30.5	22.2	10.2	33.9	66.4	23.7	1.4	10.2
37 44220	Mooresville town	33,096	2.0	5.3	22.9	8.4	30.0	23.6	9.7	34.7	84.8	12.1	4.0	0.4
37 44520	Morrisville town	19,642	9.5	8.4	19.4	4.5	43.9	19.6	4.1	32.8	51.4	18.1	33.0	2.4
37 46340	New Bern city	30,074	2.0	7.7	17.4	10.3	23.7	23.6	17.3	36.7	55.4	36.7	5.8	5.8
37 55000	Raleigh city	414,373	4.2	7.2	15.8	14.0	33.2	21.3	8.5	32.3	62.5	30.6	5.0	4.0
37 57500	Rocky Mount city	57,307	-0.6	6.0	17.8	9.0	23.2	28.4	15.6	40.4	35.5	62.3	1.7	2.1
37 58860	Salisbury city	33,596	0.0	6.8	17.1	12.2	25.6	21.8	16.5	35.5	56.1	40.2	1.6	5.4
37 59280	Sanford city	28,576	3.4	7.7	21.1	9.5	26.6	23.8	11.2	33.9	60.8	28.1	2.0	12.3
37 61200	Shelby city	20,270	-0.1	8.4	14.6	7.8	22.6	27.5	19.0	43.0	54.1	43.2	3.0	0.6
37 64740	Statesville city	24,807	1.9	6.2	20.1	10.0	25.2	23.9	14.5	36.5	55.0	38.6	2.9	5.3
37 67420	Thomasville city	26,823	0.3	9.4	18.4	8.6	25.7	23.1	14.8	34.6	72.9	22.7	0.9	6.1
37 70540	Wake Forest town	31,683	8.5	7.7	24.2	6.2	32.0	20.7	9.3	34.5	78.5	16.5	5.1	2.3
37 74440	Wilmington city	108,320	2.9	5.4	13.2	16.6	26.9	24.3	13.6	34.2	76.4	20.8	2.1	2.1
37 74540	Wilson city	49,394	0.8	7.0	18.8	9.9	23.1	26.4	14.7	37.5	43.8	48.5	1.8	8.4
37 75000	Winston-Salem city	232,090	1.9	7.4	17.2	12.0	27.1	23.6	12.7	34.2	59.9	35.7	2.5	4.1
38 00000	**North Dakota**	686,244	3.7	6.5	15.7	12.3	24.9	26.2	14.4	36.6	91.6	1.7	1.6	7.1
38 07200	Bismarck city	63,075	5.2	6.4	14.6	10.6	26.8	25.9	15.6	37.4	94.0	1.1	1.5	5.0
38 25700	Fargo city	107,752	3.6	6.1	12.9	19.5	29.3	21.9	10.2	30.3	92.6	3.1	3.4	3.7
38 32060	Grand Forks city	53,023	0.9	5.3	12.0	25.8	24.7	21.5	10.7	28.3	91.7	2.9	3.0	4.3
38 53380	Minot city	42,641	6.2	7.1	14.3	15.2	26.6	22.7	14.0	32.6	94.1	2.7	1.6	5.3
38 84780	West Fargo city	26,652	6.0	8.8	17.9	9.4	31.9	23.2	8.8	33.0	92.5	5.2	2.9	1.0
39 00000	**Ohio**	11,541,175	0.1	6.1	17.2	9.6	24.9	27.8	14.4	39.0	84.9	13.5	2.2	1.8
39 01000	Akron city	198,816	-0.2	7.0	15.9	12.7	25.2	26.3	12.7	35.6	66.6	33.6	2.7	1.9
39 01420	Alliance city	22,256	-0.5	5.8	14.8	17.0	21.4	25.3	15.6	37.6	87.4	13.5	0.6	...
39 02568	Ashland city	20,344	-0.2	6.7	12.7	15.6	23.9	23.8	17.4	36.0	96.8	2.0	1.5	0.9
39 02736	Athens city	23,623	-0.4	2.5	3.3	66.7	13.9	8.8	4.8	21.5	88.9	5.2	7.1	2.1
39 03184	Austintown CDP	29,601	...	5.7	13.6	7.8	24.5	29.2	19.3	43.2	91.6	6.8	...	0.9
39 03352	Avon city	21,531	2.4	5.5	23.8	3.3	25.8	25.4	16.2	41.1	94.0	4.2	2.1	...
39 03464	Avon Lake city	22,742	0.9	6.8	19.9	6.0	22.3	30.5	14.6	41.6	97.7	1.2	2.2	0.6
39 03828	Barberton city	26,419	-0.8	6.5	17.1	7.4	25.4	27.3	16.3	40.8	96.1	4.3	0.5	1.0
39 04720	Beavercreek city	45,310	1.3	4.1	16.7	10.2	25.4	28.2	15.4	40.1	90.9	3.6	6.6	1.4
39 07454	Boardman CDP	34,760	...	4.6	15.3	7.5	23.7	31.1	17.8	43.8	92.4	7.4	1.3	...
39 07972	Bowling Green city	30,711	4.4	4.2	8.0	43.5	19.2	16.6	8.5	22.9	88.8	7.0	2.0	4.1
39 09680	Brunswick city	34,350	0.3	5.6	17.5	9.5	26.7	28.7	12.0	39.1	98.0	2.2	0.4	0.8
39 12000	Canton city	72,778	-0.4	7.5	18.0	8.5	25.4	27.2	13.5	36.2	75.9	28.9	0.9	1.9
39 13190	Centerville city	23,984	-0.2	5.0	16.2	5.7	19.8	28.3	25.0	46.7	89.5	8.0	2.1	0.7
39 14184	Chillicothe city	21,596	-0.8	5.9	13.8	8.4	23.6	28.9	19.4	43.5	94.6	6.6	0.9	3.0
39 15000	Cincinnati city	296,443	-0.1	7.2	14.9	14.7	28.0	24.2	11.1	32.4	52.4	46.1	2.4	2.2
39 16000	Cleveland city	393,288	-1.3	6.7	16.9	11.0	25.9	27.2	12.4	36.6	42.8	54.7	2.1	3.9
39 16014	Cleveland Heights city	45,750	-1.2	6.4	17.4	10.9	27.0	25.1	13.2	34.6	50.9	45.4	5.3	1.3
39 18000	Columbus city	799,357	2.4	7.7	15.6	13.3	32.7	21.9	8.8	31.7	65.1	30.1	5.2	3.6
39 19778	Cuyahoga Falls city	49,409	-0.7	5.8	15.4	7.4	28.7	27.7	15.0	39.7	96.0	3.5	1.6	0.9
39 21000	Dayton city	141,690	-0.4	6.8	14.9	16.3	25.2	25.0	11.8	33.6	55.3	43.7	1.3	2.0
39 21434	Delaware city	35,693	2.8	7.5	16.8	12.7	28.9	22.7	11.5	33.6	94.9	5.4	0.6	2.0
39 22694	Dublin city	41,696	3.4	6.2	23.6	4.8	26.1	30.7	8.5	38.5	82.0	1.8	16.2	1.7
39 25256	Elyria city	54,296	-0.8	7.4	14.7	10.4	26.1	27.1	14.4	37.4	83.2	17.7	2.2	3.8
39 25704	Euclid city	48,545	-1.2	5.4	18.5	8.2	23.3	30.3	14.3	40.3	43.0	57.3	0.8	1.0
39 25914	Fairborn city	32,356	0.7	7.2	13.2	18.9	25.0	23.0	12.7	31.4	85.7	13.4	4.1	0.8
39 25970	Fairfield city	42,607	0.2	5.9	16.3	8.0	29.2	27.4	13.2	38.4	83.0	16.1	1.6	3.0
39 27048	Findlay city	41,305	1.0	6.2	14.2	13.1	25.4	26.1	15.1	37.7	94.3	3.3	2.6	1.3
39 29106	Gahanna city	33,714	1.6	4.5	18.3	10.9	22.9	31.7	11.8	39.7	83.1	13.2	3.5	1.3
39 29428	Garfield Heights city	28,607	-1.2	6.0	19.2	8.6	24.3	26.3	15.7	38.5	60.1	40.0	2.4	0.5
39 31860	Green city	25,756	0.1	4.3	16.2	9.6	21.7	32.2	16.1	44.1	96.8	2.5	1.4	...
39 32592	Grove City city	36,925	3.1	7.7	17.4	8.0	27.7	26.1	13.1	36.7	94.6	2.5	2.1	3.1
39 33012	Hamilton city	62,365	-0.1	7.8	16.9	8.4	27.1	26.7	13.0	36.4	87.8	10.2	0.7	3.4
39 35476	Hilliard city	29,043	7.9	5.5	25.5	6.7	26.6	26.9	8.8	36.1	92.0	4.5	3.9	0.8
39 36610	Huber Heights city	38,498	-0.1	6.5	18.3	8.7	25.0	27.4	14.1	37.3	83.1	16.9	3.7	2.7
39 36651	Hudson city	22,282	0.2	4.8	24.0	5.7	18.5	34.0	12.9	42.7	93.8	1.7	4.5	0.7
39 39872	Kent city	29,204	3.2	4.8	10.5	39.5	21.9	15.3	8.0	23.5	85.8	11.6	5.9	0.3
39 40040	Kettering city	56,391	-0.4	5.4	16.2	7.3	26.3	26.9	17.9	40.3	94.3	4.3	2.2	1.4

Table A-4. Cities — Who: Age, Race/Ethnicity, and Household Structure, 2010–2012—*Continued*

STATE and Place code	STATE or City	Percent Hispanic or Latino	Percent foreign born	Total households	Household type (percent)							Percent of households with people under 18 years	Percent of households with people 60 years and over
					Family households				Nonfamily households				
					Total family households	Married-couple families	Male household families	Female household families	Total nonfamily households	One-person households			
ACS table number:		B03003	C05003	B11001	B11001	B11001	B11001	B11001	B11001	B11001	B11005	B11006	
Column number:		14	15	16	17	18	19	20	21	22	23	24	
	North Carolina—Cont.												
37 26880	Goldsboro city	4.1	4.9	14,349	60.5	35.4	3.1	22.0	39.5	35.8	31.6	36.5
37 28000	Greensboro city	7.4	11.1	111,765	57.1	35.8	4.5	16.8	42.9	34.7	30.2	29.1
37 28080	Greenville city	3.6	5.3	34,263	49.0	29.8	1.6	17.5	51.0	34.2	27.4	19.4
37 30120	Havelock city	14.0	6.1	6,811	76.3	57.7	4.0	14.5	23.7	18.4	44.3	18.0
37 31060	Hickory city	12.9	9.9	16,140	59.3	40.4	3.1	15.8	40.7	32.6	30.0	34.4
37 31400	High Point city	8.7	11.4	40,848	65.4	41.1	4.7	19.6	34.6	29.0	35.8	29.5
37 32260	Holly Springs town	4.5	8.1	8,665	79.2	69.1	0.6	9.5	20.8	17.1	52.6	23.7
37 33120	Huntersville town	5.4	6.4	17,647	70.7	62.5	1.8	6.4	29.3	22.8	40.4	19.6
37 33560	Indian Trail town	10.8	8.7	11,119	83.2	70.5	2.5	10.2	16.8	13.4	51.1	20.3
37 34200	Jacksonville city	14.1	4.8	20,720	73.7	54.2	3.2	16.3	26.3	21.9	43.8	19.2
37 35200	Kannapolis city	10.7	7.1	15,666	65.3	46.2	3.4	15.7	34.7	28.6	35.9	33.0
37 35600	Kernersville town	6.7	6.5	9,904	62.0	47.9	3.7	10.3	38.0	34.3	30.3	31.4
37 35920	Kinston city	1.2	1.7	9,009	59.8	27.1	5.9	26.8	40.2	34.6	30.3	45.3
37 39700	Lumberton city	11.8	9.6	7,480	65.6	38.2	5.2	22.3	34.4	30.1	34.3	34.9
37 41960	Matthews town	5.2	9.2	10,614	71.1	59.5	4.6	6.9	28.9	25.1	32.3	34.1
37 43480	Mint Hill town	8.3	7.9	8,598	74.6	61.0	5.6	8.1	25.4	21.5	33.5	39.1
37 43920	Monroe city	31.0	22.3	10,932	76.8	47.5	10.6	18.7	23.2	18.5	42.2	30.0
37 44220	Mooresville town	4.0	6.3	11,899	72.3	57.7	3.7	10.8	27.7	24.4	39.3	25.4
37 44520	Morrisville town	3.6	27.1	7,598	69.6	55.9	2.3	11.4	30.4	26.0	43.8	14.4
37 46340	New Bern city	7.2	7.6	12,358	60.0	41.7	1.9	16.4	40.0	36.8	29.1	41.1
37 55000	Raleigh city	11.3	13.9	161,309	57.2	39.0	4.0	14.2	42.8	33.5	32.5	22.6
37 57500	Rocky Mount city	2.7	3.3	22,942	61.8	36.7	4.7	20.4	38.2	34.4	29.1	39.9
37 58860	Salisbury city	7.0	5.8	12,109	61.0	34.6	6.3	20.2	39.0	31.9	31.5	38.8
37 59280	Sanford city	23.3	15.0	9,980	67.6	43.8	7.4	16.4	32.4	26.9	40.8	31.7
37 61200	Shelby city	1.6	2.8	8,267	58.6	39.4	3.8	15.3	41.4	36.9	22.7	43.3
37 64740	Statesville city	12.4	10.0	9,663	62.4	36.7	5.1	20.6	37.6	32.2	35.2	33.8
37 67420	Thomasville city	16.1	9.7	10,804	61.7	40.9	5.6	15.2	38.3	33.0	37.1	34.5
37 70540	Wake Forest town	6.0	9.0	10,832	72.8	61.7	3.8	7.3	27.2	21.6	45.6	26.2
37 74440	Wilmington city	5.1	6.5	46,561	52.3	34.6	3.9	13.8	47.7	34.7	24.1	30.7
37 74540	Wilson city	9.2	7.5	19,168	63.4	39.0	6.2	18.2	36.6	31.8	32.8	35.6
37 75000	Winston-Salem city	15.4	11.4	90,752	58.9	36.9	5.7	16.3	41.1	35.3	30.5	31.9
38 00000	**North Dakota**	2.2	2.6	285,639	60.6	49.1	3.7	7.9	39.4	31.9	27.7	32.4
38 07200	Bismarck city	1.3	1.5	27,576	57.7	45.2	3.4	9.2	42.3	34.5	26.7	32.9
38 25200	Fargo city	2.8	6.2	47,991	47.9	37.1	3.3	7.6	52.1	37.9	23.9	23.3
38 32060	Grand Forks city	2.8	4.6	22,518	48.9	37.6	3.7	7.6	51.1	37.7	21.0	24.8
38 53380	Minot city	3.1	3.2	17,698	56.3	43.2	2.7	10.4	43.7	34.4	28.0	30.1
38 84780	West Fargo city	0.7	5.9	10,741	65.0	53.6	5.3	6.1	35.0	29.9	33.7	23.7
39 00000	**Ohio**	3.2	4.0	4,542,141	64.6	47.4	4.3	12.9	35.4	29.8	30.7	35.5
39 01000	Akron city	2.1	4.1	82,276	54.7	30.7	5.2	18.8	45.3	37.3	28.4	32.4
39 01420	Alliance city	2.6	1.3	8,633	57.0	34.0	5.9	17.1	43.0	38.4	27.3	36.0
39 02568	Ashland city	1.3	4.1	8,235	59.2	45.9	2.3	11.0	40.8	34.4	27.8	41.4
39 02736	Athens city	2.8	7.5	6,377	28.6	21.8	1.5	5.2	71.4	37.9	13.1	17.7
39 03184	Austintown CDP	2.2	1.8	12,888	61.7	44.1	4.0	13.5	38.3	35.5	23.9	43.9
39 03352	Avon city	3.5	5.6	7,829	68.4	60.3	1.4	6.6	31.6	26.5	40.9	36.5
39 03464	Avon Lake city	2.0	3.6	8,837	71.3	60.7	3.6	6.9	28.7	24.0	34.6	37.8
39 03828	Barberton city	1.3	2.8	10,920	60.7	39.5	4.2	17.1	39.3	35.1	30.6	39.0
39 04720	Beavercreek city	2.9	6.4	17,974	69.2	57.7	3.7	7.7	30.8	25.0	30.1	36.9
39 07454	Boardman CDP	3.6	3.0	15,760	58.0	39.5	4.3	14.2	42.0	38.0	23.6	40.9
39 07972	Bowling Green city	5.5	4.8	10,776	42.5	32.1	2.5	7.9	57.5	36.4	19.5	23.8
39 09680	Brunswick city	3.5	2.9	13,100	70.7	54.7	5.4	10.6	29.3	23.7	33.6	30.6
39 12000	Canton city	2.3	2.0	29,928	57.6	32.0	5.7	19.9	42.4	35.6	29.5	32.4
39 13190	Centerville city	3.0	4.2	10,829	59.2	48.1	3.0	8.1	40.8	35.1	24.5	46.7
39 14184	Chillicothe city	0.9	0.8	9,196	55.3	37.3	3.1	15.0	44.7	39.6	24.5	38.9
39 15000	Cincinnati city	2.9	5.3	127,708	47.5	23.9	3.8	19.8	52.5	43.4	26.0	27.5
39 16000	Cleveland city	9.9	4.7	165,887	51.5	21.7	5.4	24.4	48.5	41.7	28.4	31.9
39 16014	Cleveland Heights city	1.7	8.4	19,155	54.8	35.6	2.3	16.9	45.2	37.8	26.9	33.2
39 18000	Columbus city	5.6	10.9	324,641	53.2	32.9	4.4	15.9	46.8	36.4	29.5	23.8
39 19778	Cuyahoga Falls city	2.3	3.0	21,794	58.7	41.5	3.7	13.5	41.3	35.5	26.5	34.1
39 21000	Dayton city	3.2	3.8	56,385	50.9	24.6	4.6	21.7	49.1	41.6	26.7	32.7
39 21434	Delaware city	1.4	2.4	13,496	62.8	46.6	3.1	13.0	37.2	31.3	37.4	27.9
39 22694	Dublin city	2.9	14.9	14,908	78.4	70.5	1.9	6.0	21.6	18.3	46.0	25.4
39 25256	Elyria city	6.1	1.8	23,118	61.9	40.0	5.5	16.4	38.1	30.4	28.9	32.7
39 25704	Euclid city	1.5	3.2	21,550	54.3	29.3	4.4	20.6	45.7	41.2	29.4	35.7
39 25914	Fairborn city	3.4	4.5	14,138	55.6	35.1	4.2	16.3	44.4	36.0	26.0	28.3
39 25970	Fairfield city	4.0	6.0	17,187	66.4	47.4	4.4	14.7	33.6	27.0	31.1	30.5
39 27048	Findlay city	6.3	2.8	17,279	61.9	43.2	4.0	14.7	38.1	32.4	27.7	32.7
39 29106	Gahanna city	1.8	5.6	12,853	68.2	55.8	2.6	9.8	31.8	25.1	34.6	32.7
39 29428	Garfield Heights city	2.4	3.5	11,247	63.3	38.6	5.9	18.8	36.7	32.9	34.5	38.8
39 31860	Green city	0.5	2.7	10,421	66.6	55.1	1.7	9.7	33.4	26.4	27.2	38.0
39 32592	Grove City city	4.0	2.8	14,175	68.4	51.9	3.9	12.6	31.6	26.9	34.2	33.5
39 33012	Hamilton city	6.2	3.6	24,149	63.0	38.7	7.1	17.2	37.0	29.7	31.4	34.1
39 35476	Hilliard city	1.9	5.4	9,991	78.0	63.5	3.1	11.3	22.0	18.0	47.0	24.0
39 36610	Huber Heights city	2.6	4.0	15,071	68.4	50.9	2.7	14.8	31.6	27.5	34.2	36.0
39 36651	Hudson city	1.7	7.1	7,512	82.5	76.4	1.0	5.2	17.5	15.2	41.7	36.3
39 39872	Kent city	1.7	5.8	10,104	49.7	33.4	2.4	13.9	50.3	29.2	25.7	23.3
39 40040	Kettering city	1.9	3.6	25,560	57.0	41.3	5.4	10.3	43.0	37.6	26.2	36.2

Table A-4. Cities — Who: Age, Race/Ethnicity, and Household Structure, 2010–2012—*Continued*

STATE and Place code	STATE or City	Total population	Percent change 2010–2012	Population by age (percent) Under 5 years	5 to 17 years	18 to 24 years	25 to 44 years	45 to 64 years	65 years and over	Median age	Race alone or in combination (percent) White	Black	Asian, Hawaiian, or Pacific Islander	American Indian, Alaska Native, or some other race
	ACS table number:	B01003	Population estimates	B01001	B01001	B01001	B01001	B01001	B01001	B01002	B02008	B02009	B02011 + B02012	B02010 + B02013
	Column number:	1	2	3	4	5	6	7	8	9	10	11	12	13
	Ohio—Cont.													
39 41664	Lakewood city	51,698	-1.3	5.6	14.0	11.1	34.0	24.8	10.3	34.2	91.2	9.4	2.1	1.3
39 41720	Lancaster city	38,865	0.2	7.2	17.6	9.2	26.0	24.8	15.1	36.6	98.3	1.5	0.8	1.2
39 42364	Lebanon city	20,257	1.4	8.7	20.0	8.8	28.1	24.3	10.1	33.4	95.3	4.3	1.1	0.4
39 43554	Lima city	38,514	-1.0	8.2	18.5	13.7	24.9	23.3	11.4	32.0	70.7	30.7	1.1	2.4
39 44856	Lorain city	63,903	-0.6	6.7	20.1	8.4	23.6	27.3	13.8	37.7	72.5	21.9	1.6	9.9
39 47138	Mansfield city	47,337	-1.4	6.1	14.5	8.7	29.1	25.4	16.2	38.7	76.8	25.0	0.7	3.0
39 47306	Maple Heights city	22,960	-1.1	4.7	17.1	9.5	23.7	31.2	13.9	41.2	31.4	68.5	1.4	...
39 47754	Marion city	38,116	0.3	6.4	14.5	10.8	28.6	28.1	11.6	38.1	87.7	11.4	0.6	2.1
39 48160	Marysville city	22,808	-0.3	7.8	17.9	9.5	34.0	22.6	8.2	33.8	93.4	4.6	3.7	1.7
39 48188	Mason city	30,940	1.1	5.7	24.8	6.6	24.8	27.1	10.9	37.4	83.9	5.1	12.0	1.3
39 48244	Massillon city	32,113	0.0	6.2	16.4	8.8	24.2	28.2	16.2	40.2	92.4	9.4	...	0.5
39 48790	Medina city	26,588	-0.5	6.8	21.7	7.3	24.7	26.6	12.9	38.4	94.9	4.6	1.7	0.4
39 49056	Mentor city	47,095	-0.3	5.3	15.8	6.1	22.7	33.3	16.8	45.1	96.9	1.6	1.5	0.4
39 49434	Miamisburg city	20,193	-0.2	7.6	16.3	5.3	23.9	28.4	18.5	42.2	95.9	3.2	2.1	...
39 49840	Middletown city	48,133	-0.1	8.4	15.5	9.2	23.7	27.9	15.3	37.8	83.4	15.5	0.9	3.1
39 54040	Newark city	47,683	0.1	7.3	17.1	8.5	26.2	26.4	14.6	37.6	95.3	6.0	1.1	2.5
39 56882	North Olmsted city	32,498	-1.0	5.2	14.3	6.5	24.1	31.6	18.4	45.0	93.8	3.5	2.6	0.8
39 56966	North Ridgeville city	30,094	3.3	7.0	16.0	5.4	26.8	28.9	15.9	40.4	96.8	1.4	1.7	0.5
39 57008	North Royalton city	30,368	-0.3	4.3	15.3	6.7	23.6	33.7	16.3	45.0	94.4	1.8	4.1	0.5
39 57386	Norwood city	19,127	-0.5	6.3	14.4	15.1	29.0	24.9	10.3	32.6	87.8	10.3	0.6	2.5
39 58730	Oregon city	20,280	-0.5	5.0	15.5	9.0	21.6	29.7	19.2	44.2	95.1	3.2	...	2.7
39 59234	Oxford city	20,817	-0.2	1.7	4.3	66.2	10.5	10.3	7.0	21.2	90.4	4.6	5.3	1.5
39 61000	Parma city	80,997	-1.1	5.6	14.4	9.4	24.2	28.2	18.1	42.5	94.7	3.0	2.5	2.2
39 61028	Parma Heights city	20,569	-1.1	6.7	14.5	7.1	25.7	27.2	18.9	40.1	92.9	3.9	4.1	2.0
39 62148	Perrysburg city	20,999	1.7	4.6	20.2	6.8	26.4	28.7	13.4	38.8	94.5	2.2	4.2	0.8
39 62848	Piqua city	20,564	0.5	9.2	15.4	9.0	25.1	26.4	14.9	38.1	93.1	7.7	0.8	1.7
39 64304	Portsmouth city	20,308	0.3	4.0	14.2	13.7	24.2	27.7	16.3	39.0	92.6	7.5	1.1	3.2
39 66390	Reynoldsburg city	36,154	1.0	5.9	20.0	10.0	25.0	27.6	11.5	37.2	72.9	26.0	4.0	1.6
39 67468	Riverside city	25,173	-0.4	6.2	19.0	9.4	25.8	25.5	14.1	37.5	89.8	8.1	2.3	1.0
39 68056	Rocky River city	20,109	-0.9	5.0	17.3	4.7	21.9	27.7	23.3	46.2	97.4	1.1	1.8	...
39 70380	Sandusky city	25,630	-1.1	6.2	16.2	8.5	24.9	28.1	16.1	38.8	75.4	24.9	0.7	2.2
39 71682	Shaker Heights city	28,193	-1.3	5.4	19.8	5.6	23.7	29.0	16.5	42.0	57.3	37.4	6.5	1.5
39 72424	Sidney city	21,404	-0.7	5.5	19.7	7.7	25.3	28.5	13.4	39.4	94.8	7.4	0.9	0.5
39 72928	Solon city	23,242	-0.7	4.6	22.7	5.2	20.4	32.9	14.1	43.3	78.4	12.4	9.5	1.4
39 73264	South Euclid city	22,130	-1.1	5.1	16.5	12.1	24.7	27.9	13.6	37.3	56.9	41.2	1.9	1.3
39 74118	Springfield city	60,339	-0.7	7.5	16.8	11.6	24.3	24.7	15.0	35.4	77.5	21.5	1.4	3.9
39 74944	Stow city	34,744	-0.4	5.6	16.4	8.6	26.4	28.3	14.7	39.7	95.2	2.9	3.6	1.3
39 75098	Strongsville city	44,661	-0.2	5.1	17.8	6.8	21.6	31.5	17.2	44.0	90.8	3.4	5.1	1.6
39 77000	Toledo city	285,532	-1.0	7.1	16.6	12.7	26.1	25.4	12.0	34.5	68.9	29.6	1.9	4.4
39 77504	Trotwood city	24,391	-0.5	4.5	17.1	9.5	21.1	30.2	17.7	43.2	31.7	67.3	0.6	2.1
39 77588	Troy city	24,454	0.6	5.7	18.7	7.3	30.1	25.0	13.2	36.9	92.9	4.9	3.2	0.6
39 79002	Upper Arlington city	33,941	1.5	5.9	19.6	5.4	23.5	29.6	16.1	42.0	93.6	1.6	5.8	0.9
39 80304	Wadsworth city	21,685	0.4	5.2	21.0	6.8	27.7	23.5	15.8	37.8	96.9	0.9	2.4	1.9
39 80892	Warren city	41,077	-1.8	7.2	16.6	9.6	24.5	25.6	16.5	39.1	71.8	30.3	0.7	1.1
39 83342	Westerville city	37,108	2.4	5.5	17.2	11.8	23.9	28.4	13.1	39.4	88.2	9.5	4.5	1.3
39 83622	Westlake city	32,574	-0.6	4.3	17.9	5.0	23.6	29.7	19.5	44.4	91.3	2.9	7.6	...
39 84812	White Oak CDP	20,002	...	5.4	17.9	6.8	22.7	32.1	15.1	43.2	89.3	9.1	...	0.5
39 85484	Willoughby city	22,330	0.3	4.0	14.0	8.8	25.5	28.0	19.8	43.7	94.0	2.7	3.2	1.1
39 86548	Wooster city	26,262	1.1	6.7	12.7	17.8	24.2	22.0	16.6	34.7	93.3	5.7	2.0	1.7
39 86772	Xenia city	25,843	1.1	6.0	19.1	8.9	26.1	23.7	16.2	35.7	84.7	15.1	1.9	1.5
39 88000	Youngstown city	66,005	-2.1	6.2	16.2	10.9	23.2	27.9	15.7	39.6	50.5	48.4	1.3	3.6
39 88084	Zanesville city	25,471	-0.4	7.4	18.6	8.5	25.8	24.8	14.9	36.8	91.2	12.1	...	1.8
40 00000	**Oklahoma**	3,786,152	1.5	6.9	17.7	10.2	25.8	25.6	13.7	36.3	80.7	8.8	2.5	16.1
40 02600	Ardmore city	24,546	1.4	7.6	18.7	7.7	26.7	23.8	15.6	37.8	73.5	13.0	2.7	18.4
40 04450	Bartlesville city	36,040	1.2	7.0	15.7	9.0	24.1	25.9	18.2	39.8	86.3	4.4	2.3	13.5
40 06400	Bixby city	21,692	7.3	8.9	21.4	5.3	29.5	23.1	11.9	34.7	91.8	2.1	1.2	10.3
40 09050	Broken Arrow city	100,497	2.8	7.0	19.8	8.4	26.9	27.1	10.7	36.5	86.1	6.4	4.3	11.7
40 19900	Del City city	21,566	2.0	9.8	19.9	11.1	23.4	22.7	13.2	31.4	69.5	25.3	2.9	10.9
40 21900	Duncan city	23,395	-0.7	5.7	17.6	8.7	25.3	24.4	18.3	38.3	86.9	4.4	1.4	10.7
40 23200	Edmond city	83,197	3.9	5.6	18.8	13.3	23.2	27.7	11.4	35.5	85.9	6.4	5.6	5.5
40 23950	Enid city	49,596	0.7	7.8	16.5	9.7	24.9	25.5	15.6	37.0	85.3	4.8	3.8	9.9
40 41850	Lawton city	98,075	0.5	8.0	16.8	14.3	30.1	21.0	9.8	30.3	68.1	24.1	5.7	11.8
40 48350	Midwest City city	55,317	2.7	5.6	18.2	9.5	26.9	26.3	13.6	36.3	71.1	24.6	2.6	9.2
40 49200	Moore city	56,641	4.3	7.5	19.8	9.3	32.1	22.4	8.9	32.4	86.6	6.2	4.0	12.9
40 50050	Muskogee city	39,126	-0.7	7.8	18.4	10.2	24.8	24.2	14.7	35.8	70.3	18.7	1.4	19.0
40 52500	Norman city	113,599	3.7	5.5	13.5	21.8	25.8	22.4	10.9	30.6	87.0	5.8	5.0	8.9
40 55000	Oklahoma City city	590,292	2.9	8.0	17.5	9.7	29.2	24.4	11.2	33.6	72.8	16.8	4.8	13.0
40 56650	Owasso city	30,898	5.0	7.0	22.2	9.3	30.5	23.0	8.0	34.2	84.2	3.4	3.5	14.6
40 59850	Ponca City city	25,118	-1.4	8.0	18.3	7.7	23.6	25.0	17.4	37.4	85.5	4.4	1.3	16.0
40 65400	Sapulpa city	20,688	0.9	6.1	16.7	9.6	23.3	26.8	17.6	40.7	85.4	4.5	0.9	19.6
40 66800	Shawnee city	30,278	2.3	8.9	17.0	12.8	24.2	23.2	14.0	32.9	78.8	5.5	1.1	22.6
40 70300	Stillwater city	46,143	1.8	5.0	10.0	38.9	21.6	16.2	8.2	24.0	85.7	6.1	7.6	7.5
40 75000	Tulsa city	393,124	0.4	7.3	17.1	10.7	27.2	25.0	12.6	34.9	72.5	17.8	3.1	13.7
40 82950	Yukon city	23,495	5.6	7.0	18.2	7.6	27.2	25.5	14.5	37.5	93.3	1.6	2.3	6.4

Table A-4. Cities — Who: Age, Race/Ethnicity, and Household Structure, 2010–2012—*Continued*

STATE and Place code	STATE or City	Percent Hispanic or Latino	Percent foreign born	Total households	Household type (percent)							Percent of households with people under 18 years	Percent of households with people 60 years and over
					Family households				Nonfamily households				
					Total family households	Married-couple families	Male household families	Female household families	Total nonfamily households	One-person households			
	ACS table number:	B03003	C05003	B11001	B11001	B11001	B11001	B11001	B11001	B11001		B11005	B11006
	Column number:	14	15	16	17	18	19	20	21	22		23	24
	Ohio—Cont.												
39 41664	Lakewood city	3.6	8.9	24,362	46.2	29.7	4.2	12.2	53.8	44.4		22.2	26.0
39 41720	Lancaster city	0.9	1.3	15,919	60.1	40.9	5.3	14.0	39.9	33.8		32.1	36.3
39 42364	Lebanon city	1.8	2.9	7,146	73.5	54.0	6.2	13.3	26.5	23.4		42.2	30.1
39 43554	Lima city	2.3	1.3	14,460	59.4	29.1	7.3	22.9	40.6	34.9		35.2	31.1
39 44856	Lorain city	25.4	3.0	25,243	65.0	38.3	5.9	20.8	35.0	31.2		34.1	36.3
39 47138	Mansfield city	2.2	1.7	18,422	56.0	36.6	3.0	16.4	44.0	38.7		27.1	42.9
39 47306	Maple Heights city	1.6	3.4	9,510	62.2	32.5	3.4	26.4	37.8	35.6		29.3	36.8
39 47754	Marion city	3.0	1.1	13,154	63.6	40.8	5.9	16.8	36.4	30.0		32.5	34.5
39 48160	Marysville city	1.5	2.6	7,393	69.6	53.3	4.5	11.8	30.4	26.4		43.0	28.3
39 48188	Mason city	4.1	10.5	10,651	74.0	62.0	3.6	8.5	26.0	21.5		44.5	29.0
39 48244	Massillon city	2.0	1.0	13,108	60.3	40.9	4.3	15.1	39.7	34.1		29.1	38.7
39 48790	Medina city	1.4	2.7	10,328	66.9	53.2	4.1	9.6	33.1	28.3		36.5	34.3
39 49056	Mentor city	1.1	3.9	19,015	68.3	56.3	2.2	9.8	31.7	27.1		28.7	38.7
39 49434	Miamisburg city	0.9	1.5	8,205	65.8	52.3	2.8	10.7	34.2	30.0		31.8	39.2
39 49840	Middletown city	2.5	2.2	19,650	61.9	40.7	4.7	16.4	38.1	32.5		29.2	35.9
39 54040	Newark city	1.5	1.6	19,655	60.9	43.1	4.9	13.0	39.1	32.8		31.2	35.7
39 56882	North Olmsted city	3.7	8.2	13,667	62.3	50.6	2.6	9.1	37.7	32.1		25.3	43.1
39 56966	North Ridgeville city	3.1	5.7	12,031	70.2	57.9	2.9	9.5	29.8	27.4		30.3	35.6
39 57008	North Royalton city	1.6	9.2	12,275	66.9	54.5	3.9	8.5	33.1	28.0		28.8	38.9
39 57386	Norwood city	3.1	2.8	8,222	51.0	32.1	3.5	15.5	49.0	38.2		24.3	24.5
39 58730	Oregon city	7.4	2.3	8,406	65.9	50.4	4.8	10.8	34.1	31.0		30.8	41.1
39 59234	Oxford city	2.6	5.5	5,710	37.2	25.1	3.9	8.2	62.8	35.9		13.9	25.0
39 61000	Parma city	4.6	10.6	32,925	65.1	46.7	5.5	12.9	34.9	31.3		27.1	40.2
39 61028	Parma Heights city	4.1	13.2	8,922	56.0	41.2	3.2	11.5	44.0	39.6		25.3	43.5
39 62148	Perrysburg city	2.8	5.7	8,609	62.2	52.7	2.3	7.1	37.8	34.6		31.0	31.6
39 62848	Piqua city	0.5	1.2	8,604	60.7	39.7	5.5	15.5	39.3	33.0		31.2	36.2
39 64304	Portsmouth city	2.3	1.9	8,083	51.8	34.9	3.3	13.6	48.2	39.9		24.9	40.7
39 66390	Reynoldsburg city	4.6	6.7	13,889	64.6	44.0	6.7	13.9	35.4	28.3		36.7	29.2
39 67468	Riverside city	3.0	2.3	9,989	68.6	47.3	6.8	14.4	31.4	26.3		33.8	37.3
39 68056	Rocky River city	0.3	10.4	8,754	58.3	49.8	1.4	7.1	41.7	39.4		25.5	47.1
39 70380	Sandusky city	4.7	2.2	11,420	57.0	34.2	6.4	16.5	43.0	39.7		27.3	37.5
39 71682	Shaker Heights city	2.5	8.9	11,595	66.5	47.9	2.3	16.3	33.5	30.7		32.5	39.6
39 72424	Sidney city	2.6	1.2	8,581	67.7	46.0	7.9	13.8	32.3	25.0		31.5	32.7
39 72928	Solon city	3.1	12.6	8,289	80.6	70.2	3.3	7.1	19.4	18.8		38.8	37.0
39 73264	South Euclid city	3.0	6.3	8,918	63.1	38.5	5.0	19.6	36.9	32.9		29.7	36.3
39 74118	Springfield city	3.9	3.1	24,184	57.1	33.2	4.1	19.7	42.9	34.9		31.1	35.6
39 74944	Stow city	1.3	4.3	13,733	66.6	55.4	3.5	7.7	33.4	27.7		32.3	34.1
39 75098	Strongsville city	2.6	8.6	17,163	72.0	63.0	2.6	6.5	28.0	24.3		31.1	39.5
39 77000	Toledo city	7.6	3.2	117,071	56.7	31.4	5.3	20.0	43.3	35.7		29.5	30.1
39 77504	Trotwood city	0.6	2.1	10,280	59.0	32.4	4.2	22.4	41.0	38.2		27.0	42.2
39 77588	Troy city	1.9	2.7	10,058	61.1	42.5	4.2	14.3	38.9	30.6		31.4	32.6
39 79002	Upper Arlington city	2.7	7.4	13,326	70.0	60.6	3.4	6.0	30.0	25.3		33.1	36.8
39 80304	Wadsworth city	1.8	2.2	8,611	63.3	47.9	2.1	13.2	36.7	30.9		35.8	35.7
39 80892	Warren city	2.2	1.8	17,110	54.8	30.5	5.4	18.9	45.2	40.7		28.0	38.9
39 83342	Westerville city	1.8	6.3	13,291	72.2	62.8	2.6	6.8	27.8	23.5		33.6	35.2
39 83622	Westlake city	3.4	9.7	13,392	61.2	54.4	2.2	4.6	38.8	34.7		27.0	40.6
39 84812	White Oak CDP	1.3	4.4	7,871	69.3	56.2	3.6	9.5	30.7	26.8		30.0	37.4
39 85484	Willoughby city	1.8	7.3	10,398	57.2	41.9	4.2	11.2	42.8	37.2		21.3	38.9
39 86548	Wooster city	2.2	3.7	10,403	58.2	44.1	3.7	10.5	41.8	35.4		24.8	39.7
39 86772	Xenia city	0.7	2.0	10,539	59.1	40.2	4.4	14.5	40.9	38.6		29.6	37.2
39 88000	Youngstown city	9.7	4.7	26,165	55.3	25.0	6.0	24.3	44.7	39.3		26.6	40.3
39 88084	Zanesville city	1.2	1.0	10,535	59.3	33.9	5.3	20.1	40.7	35.3		33.5	36.6
40 00000	**Oklahoma**	9.1	5.5	1,441,163	66.6	49.3	4.7	12.5	33.4	28.0		32.9	34.5
40 02600	Ardmore city	9.2	4.8	8,918	63.2	43.6	5.7	13.9	36.8	32.6		32.0	38.2
40 04450	Bartlesville city	6.3	4.4	15,191	64.2	47.5	4.4	12.3	35.8	31.5		29.0	40.2
40 06400	Bixby city	3.8	4.9	7,660	77.6	66.3	3.1	8.1	22.4	18.2		42.8	31.8
40 09050	Broken Arrow city	7.4	5.5	36,180	75.7	60.3	4.0	11.4	24.3	20.6		38.9	30.1
40 19900	Del City city	10.0	3.9	8,280	60.4	34.8	7.3	18.2	39.6	33.2		36.0	35.7
40 21900	Duncan city	10.2	3.8	9,668	61.4	47.8	3.0	10.7	38.6	35.5		27.1	38.0
40 23200	Edmond city	4.7	6.9	30,704	70.0	56.3	3.9	9.8	30.0	23.1		34.6	30.6
40 23950	Enid city	10.7	7.6	19,457	65.9	47.5	3.9	14.5	34.1	29.8		31.6	35.3
40 41850	Lawton city	13.4	7.0	35,159	63.7	41.4	5.1	17.3	36.3	30.1		36.6	26.5
40 48350	Midwest City city	5.3	3.8	22,702	63.1	41.7	4.4	17.1	36.9	32.3		30.3	33.4
40 49200	Moore city	10.7	4.0	20,427	75.2	57.4	4.9	12.8	24.8	19.6		42.6	26.3
40 50050	Muskogee city	6.9	4.4	15,203	62.9	40.9	4.9	17.1	37.1	32.1		34.9	36.0
40 52500	Norman city	5.8	5.9	44,382	57.0	41.6	4.9	10.4	43.0	31.3		27.3	27.4
40 55000	Oklahoma City city	17.7	12.2	226,306	63.0	44.6	5.0	13.4	37.0	30.5		33.6	29.9
40 56650	Owasso city	7.4	4.1	10,979	74.0	59.0	5.8	9.2	26.0	20.7		42.8	22.1
40 59850	Ponca City city	5.9	2.4	10,230	61.1	45.0	4.0	12.0	38.9	34.3		30.7	39.0
40 65400	Sapulpa city	4.5	2.1	8,179	63.7	45.5	4.4	13.9	36.3	31.0		29.8	39.8
40 66800	Shawnee city	5.4	2.7	11,774	62.4	42.2	4.6	15.6	37.6	31.8		33.6	34.0
40 70300	Stillwater city	4.1	9.1	18,187	45.0	34.2	1.3	9.5	55.0	34.6		22.1	19.8
40 75000	Tulsa city	14.5	10.0	162,791	58.2	37.8	4.7	15.6	41.8	35.0		30.0	30.9
40 82950	Yukon city	6.0	4.3	8,709	73.7	60.1	2.9	10.8	26.3	19.9		34.3	36.8

Table A-4. Cities — Who: Age, Race/Ethnicity, and Household Structure, 2010–2012—*Continued*

STATE and Place code	STATE or City	Total population	Percent change 2010–2012	Population by age (percent) Under 5 years	5 to 17 years	18 to 24 years	25 to 44 years	45 to 64 years	65 years and over	Median age	Race alone or in combination (percent) White	Black	Asian, Hawaiian, or Pacific Islander	American Indian, Alaska Native, or some other race
ACS table number:		B01003	Population estimates	B01001	B01001	B01001	B01001	B01001	B01001	B01002	B02008	B02009	B02011 + B02012	B02010 + B02013
Column number:		1	2	3	4	5	6	7	8	9	10	11	12	13
41 00000	**Oregon**	3,868,598	1.6	6.1	16.2	9.4	26.7	27.3	14.4	38.7	88.2	2.6	5.7	7.4
41 01000	Albany city	50,784	1.9	7.2	17.7	9.1	28.4	25.0	12.6	35.2	91.0	0.9	3.0	8.1
41 01650	Aloha CDP	51,230	...	9.0	19.1	8.2	34.1	23.6	6.0	31.9	74.5	2.8	11.9	16.9
41 03050	Ashland city	20,230	1.3	3.3	13.5	14.0	20.0	30.9	18.3	43.8	93.9	3.1	5.3	2.1
41 05350	Beaverton city	91,414	2.8	6.8	16.8	9.5	32.4	23.8	10.7	34.7	74.9	3.5	15.4	9.9
41 05800	Bend city	77,887	3.1	6.4	16.7	7.1	29.9	25.3	14.5	38.4	94.4	1.0	3.2	3.8
41 05950	Bethany CDP	21,102	...	6.3	25.6	6.6	29.2	22.0	10.4	35.6	59.9	1.1	38.5	3.6
41 15800	Corvallis city	54,633	1.2	4.4	10.5	32.5	22.7	19.6	10.3	26.5	88.9	1.5	9.6	3.0
41 23850	Eugene city	157,196	1.0	4.8	12.6	19.7	25.8	23.7	13.3	34.0	91.2	2.4	6.7	5.0
41 26200	Forest Grove city	21,555	3.8	6.0	18.8	11.6	25.0	24.9	13.7	37.5	86.3	2.8	2.2	10.2
41 30550	Grants Pass city	34,699	0.5	6.8	17.0	9.1	20.9	25.4	20.8	40.8	95.5	0.5	2.3	4.6
41 31250	Gresham city	107,505	2.8	7.6	17.8	10.2	27.5	25.8	11.2	34.7	83.6	4.6	8.0	7.9
41 34100	Hillsboro city	93,876	3.1	8.5	19.2	9.1	34.6	20.9	7.8	32.0	73.6	2.6	11.7	16.6
41 38500	Keizer city	36,730	0.9	7.4	19.0	8.2	27.4	23.8	14.2	35.0	89.2	1.6	3.8	9.5
41 39700	Klamath Falls city	20,946	0.6	5.7	15.2	12.9	26.7	26.1	13.4	36.5	90.0	1.3	2.4	9.1
41 40550	Lake Oswego city	37,219	1.5	4.0	18.6	4.8	23.2	32.8	16.5	44.7	89.2	0.8	10.1	2.5
41 45000	McMinnville city	32,381	1.0	6.0	19.2	12.1	25.5	22.0	15.3	34.6	85.0	1.6	2.5	13.9
41 47000	Medford city	75,704	1.9	7.0	15.9	10.1	25.7	24.9	16.4	38.0	94.3	1.5	3.7	4.9
41 48650	Milwaukie city	20,378	0.6	5.2	15.3	9.0	28.6	28.6	13.3	39.3	91.8	4.8	4.3	4.9
41 52100	Newberg city	22,297	0.9	7.6	16.7	17.3	27.2	20.6	10.6	30.4	90.7	3.0	4.6	8.6
41 55200	Oregon City city	32,356	2.5	5.4	20.5	7.7	29.7	26.6	10.2	36.7	93.1	0.9	3.3	5.4
41 59000	Portland city	594,524	3.0	6.0	13.1	9.3	35.9	25.0	10.7	36.0	80.9	7.6	9.7	6.1
41 61200	Redmond city	26,592	2.6	7.1	19.9	10.8	26.8	23.2	12.2	33.3	94.3	0.8	2.7	6.1
41 63650	Roseburg city	21,850	0.1	5.8	13.4	6.5	23.0	28.1	23.2	46.3	96.8	1.4	3.8	3.6
41 64900	Salem city	156,155	1.5	7.7	17.4	10.1	27.1	24.8	12.9	35.0	83.2	2.0	5.7	13.8
41 69600	Springfield city	59,668	0.8	7.4	16.7	11.3	28.5	25.4	10.7	33.9	92.5	1.7	3.0	7.2
41 73650	Tigard city	48,977	3.3	5.1	16.9	8.7	28.5	28.4	12.4	39.6	84.6	1.5	10.0	8.2
41 74950	Tualatin city	26,776	2.4	6.4	19.8	9.4	30.3	26.1	8.0	35.5	91.9	3.1	3.3	5.4
41 80150	West Linn city	25,409	1.7	3.1	20.5	8.5	18.8	35.7	13.4	44.1	95.0	1.3	4.5	1.6
41 82800	Wilsonville city	19,622	4.8	6.1	16.0	8.4	32.7	22.8	14.1	35.2	91.4	1.2	7.4	4.9
41 83750	Woodburn city	24,151	0.5	8.0	20.9	10.5	28.5	16.4	15.7	32.3	65.3	0.9	1.7	37.0
42 00000	**Pennsylvania**	12,739,595	0.4	5.7	16.0	10.0	24.5	28.2	15.7	40.3	83.9	12.0	3.4	2.8
42 02000	Allentown city	118,587	0.8	7.9	18.2	12.5	26.7	23.0	11.8	32.9	70.2	15.6	2.6	16.6
42 02056	Allison Park CDP	21,823	...	4.2	16.6	9.6	19.3	32.3	18.1	45.2	94.2	1.2	4.7	...
42 02184	Altoona city	46,239	-0.3	7.5	15.6	9.1	24.8	26.9	16.1	39.2	95.0	4.9	1.3	1.1
42 06064	Bethel Park municipality	32,351	0.2	4.8	16.3	6.3	22.2	30.7	19.7	45.5	95.0	3.3	1.6	1.0
42 06088	Bethlehem city	75,057	0.1	5.4	14.8	16.0	25.6	23.4	14.7	34.3	82.6	10.5	3.4	8.0
42 12536	Chambersburg borough	20,330	0.3	7.5	17.1	10.8	22.3	24.0	18.4	37.2	85.6	11.2	1.5	4.7
42 13208	Chester city	34,027	0.1	6.4	15.8	16.7	23.9	25.0	12.1	33.2	20.7	75.6	0.8	4.8
42 19920	Drexel Hill CDP	29,351	...	7.4	16.7	8.0	30.0	24.7	13.3	36.4	84.5	11.8	5.6	1.7
42 21648	Easton city	26,873	0.6	7.1	13.2	18.0	26.3	24.7	10.7	33.5	73.6	22.3	3.6	8.8
42 24000	Erie city	101,419	-0.7	7.1	16.4	13.1	26.5	23.9	13.1	33.9	78.9	19.2	2.6	3.1
42 32800	Harrisburg city	49,381	-0.5	9.0	18.1	11.3	27.8	24.6	9.3	32.5	37.7	54.5	4.2	8.4
42 33408	Hazleton city	25,264	-0.4	6.5	18.4	11.5	23.3	24.6	15.7	37.3	81.6	5.5	0.8	13.6
42 38288	Johnstown city	20,755	-1.7	7.9	13.4	7.7	23.0	28.8	19.2	42.8	87.3	17.0	0.8	2.6
42 41216	Lancaster city	59,370	0.1	7.9	16.3	14.4	29.3	23.0	9.1	31.0	67.4	19.0	3.9	15.1
42 42168	Lebanon city	25,506	0.3	7.7	18.9	9.8	26.8	23.6	13.2	34.8	73.3	6.1	1.1	24.4
42 42928	Levittown CDP	52,480	...	5.2	17.2	8.1	25.5	30.3	13.7	40.7	93.6	4.3	2.4	1.5
42 46256	McKeesport city	19,706	-0.2	5.5	14.4	9.4	23.2	29.0	18.5	42.3	69.3	33.1	...	2.4
42 50528	Monroeville municipality	28,368	0.2	4.8	14.4	5.1	25.7	28.8	21.2	45.0	80.5	16.7	5.6	0.6
42 52432	Murrysville municipality	20,181	0.6	5.0	15.5	6.2	20.8	33.7	18.8	46.8	96.0	0.8	3.5	...
42 53368	New Castle city	23,025	-1.6	7.0	16.5	8.2	23.0	26.7	18.6	42.1	85.4	15.2	0.9	1.7
42 54656	Norristown borough	34,387	0.2	7.6	15.1	10.6	32.9	23.7	10.1	34.3	60.1	37.0	2.6	4.6
42 60000	Philadelphia city	1,538,211	1.3	6.8	15.7	13.0	28.8	23.6	12.1	33.4	43.3	44.9	7.3	7.4
42 61000	Pittsburgh city	306,006	0.2	5.0	11.4	18.0	28.2	23.4	14.1	33.1	68.7	27.2	5.6	1.9
42 61536	Plum borough	27,283	0.9	5.4	17.0	7.8	24.2	28.6	17.0	41.9	94.9	4.4	0.9	0.3
42 62416	Pottstown borough	22,437	0.4	6.9	17.4	7.4	27.8	27.6	12.8	38.1	75.4	24.5	0.6	2.4
42 63624	Reading city	88,098	0.0	9.2	21.9	12.1	26.6	20.7	9.5	29.4	58.6	16.8	1.6	28.5
42 69000	Scranton city	75,951	-0.3	5.7	14.2	15.4	22.4	25.6	16.8	38.0	88.2	7.4	3.7	3.0
42 73808	State College borough	42,026	-0.1	1.6	3.1	70.2	14.5	6.3	4.2	21.3	83.4	5.3	11.9	1.8
42 83512	West Mifflin borough	20,288	-0.1	4.1	14.0	9.0	22.6	30.6	19.7	45.3	90.2	9.8	...	0.8
42 85152	Wilkes-Barre city	41,329	-0.6	6.3	15.4	16.0	24.7	22.3	15.4	34.2	79.9	14.9	1.5	6.0
42 85312	Williamsport city	29,438	0.4	6.4	14.4	20.7	24.4	23.3	10.8	30.6	83.2	17.7	0.8	1.6
42 87048	York city	43,651	-0.5	8.8	19.5	12.2	28.3	22.4	8.8	30.4	56.9	33.2	1.1	15.4
44 00000	**Rhode Island**	1,051,236	-0.2	5.3	15.6	11.5	24.9	28.0	14.7	39.7	83.6	7.7	3.8	7.9
44 19180	Cranston city	80,465	0.1	5.5	14.1	10.5	24.9	29.9	15.2	41.5	84.5	6.6	5.8	5.8
44 22960	East Providence city	47,058	0.1	7.1	15.3	6.3	25.4	27.8	18.2	41.1	88.5	8.6	2.7	5.8
44 49960	Newport city	24,262	-2.5	3.8	11.9	14.3	28.2	25.8	16.0	37.7	89.7	8.5	2.3	4.1
44 54640	Pawtucket city	71,158	0.0	6.4	16.1	9.3	29.2	26.2	12.8	37.7	68.1	20.3	2.1	14.4
44 59000	Providence city	178,299	0.2	6.1	16.7	20.4	28.4	19.8	8.5	28.6	53.1	18.1	7.4	26.0
44 74300	Warwick city	82,222	-0.9	4.6	13.9	7.5	25.1	31.2	17.7	44.3	93.5	2.2	3.5	2.7
44 80780	Woonsocket city	41,082	-0.4	9.1	15.8	8.1	27.6	25.0	14.4	37.0	82.8	10.3	6.7	3.5

Table A-4. Cities — Who: Age, Race/Ethnicity, and Household Structure, 2010–2012—*Continued*

STATE and Place code	STATE or City	Percent Hispanic or Latino	Percent foreign born	Total households	Household type (percent)						Percent of households with people under 18 years	Percent of households with people 60 years and over
					Family households				Nonfamily households			
					Total family households	Married-couple families	Male household families	Female household families	Total nonfamily households	One-person households		
	ACS table number:	B03003	C05003	B11001	B11001	B11001	B11001	B11001	B11001	B11001	B11005	B11006
	Column number:	14	15	16	17	18	19	20	21	22	23	24
41 00000	**Oregon**	12.0	9.8	1,513,005	63.4	48.3	4.6	10.6	36.6	28.0	29.6	36.5
41 01000	Albany city	10.8	6.5	19,681	64.7	46.4	5.5	12.7	35.3	28.1	31.6	32.5
41 01650	Aloha CDP	24.5	18.2	16,733	74.1	56.0	6.4	11.6	25.9	17.7	42.3	22.5
41 03050	Ashland city	3.0	6.3	9,069	50.2	35.6	3.7	10.9	49.8	39.6	20.3	41.4
41 05350	Beaverton city	14.4	20.5	35,730	60.4	45.6	3.5	11.3	39.6	29.4	31.8	28.3
41 05800	Bend city	7.7	5.1	32,633	60.0	47.2	4.9	7.9	40.0	30.8	29.4	34.4
41 05950	Bethany CDP	5.3	27.6	7,468	80.3	68.0	2.6	9.7	19.7	16.2	48.5	24.7
41 15800	Corvallis city	8.0	10.7	20,821	47.9	36.8	1.9	9.1	52.1	32.8	20.9	27.5
41 23850	Eugene city	7.8	8.1	65,952	51.2	36.6	4.0	10.6	48.8	32.0	24.2	32.3
41 26200	Forest Grove city	20.8	12.2	7,819	65.7	45.7	7.7	12.3	34.3	25.7	36.9	37.8
41 30550	Grants Pass city	9.1	2.5	14,471	57.8	40.7	5.4	11.7	42.2	37.0	27.6	44.3
41 31250	Gresham city	18.7	17.2	39,011	66.5	44.4	6.0	16.1	33.5	26.4	36.6	30.6
41 34100	Hillsboro city	25.7	20.3	32,267	68.3	50.7	4.6	13.0	31.7	24.9	40.2	24.5
41 38500	Keizer city	20.6	8.3	13,919	72.4	52.3	6.3	13.8	27.6	23.7	36.5	34.4
41 39700	Klamath Falls city	10.5	3.7	9,377	57.6	37.0	5.5	15.1	42.4	34.4	28.6	32.6
41 40550	Lake Oswego city	4.5	12.0	16,039	62.8	53.9	3.0	5.9	37.2	31.9	29.6	43.6
41 45000	McMinnville city	22.5	9.8	11,550	66.9	48.3	5.6	13.0	33.1	26.4	33.5	36.1
41 47000	Medford city	13.0	7.0	29,771	63.7	45.7	4.7	13.3	36.3	30.5	30.3	37.6
41 48650	Milwaukie city	5.3	6.3	8,430	59.6	41.3	5.8	12.4	40.4	32.0	27.5	34.9
41 52100	Newberg city	13.1	9.2	7,165	69.9	46.8	9.9	13.2	30.1	22.3	38.9	32.2
41 55200	Oregon City city	11.3	6.1	12,216	68.5	48.6	7.0	12.9	31.5	25.1	40.3	29.5
41 59000	Portland city	9.9	13.8	248,701	50.5	36.7	3.6	10.2	49.5	35.4	24.6	28.1
41 61200	Redmond city	13.2	6.6	10,049	71.6	47.4	6.7	17.5	28.4	21.8	37.5	32.9
41 63650	Roseburg city	3.4	3.7	9,658	55.4	41.7	4.6	9.1	44.6	37.5	22.4	49.1
41 64900	Salem city	20.6	11.9	57,838	64.3	45.6	5.9	12.8	35.7	29.8	34.5	33.5
41 69600	Springfield city	12.6	5.4	23,495	61.0	40.2	7.1	13.6	39.0	28.4	33.9	29.6
41 73650	Tigard city	12.6	14.9	19,427	63.1	52.3	3.6	7.2	36.9	28.3	31.1	32.8
41 74950	Tualatin city	19.4	11.8	10,532	63.8	48.6	5.5	9.7	36.2	28.3	35.3	25.5
41 80150	West Linn city	3.3	8.6	9,448	77.6	68.3	1.9	7.4	22.4	19.0	36.2	33.5
41 82800	Wilsonville city	12.9	10.0	7,776	58.2	47.1	1.1	10.1	41.8	34.1	31.1	34.0
41 83750	Woodburn city	55.0	31.9	7,926	67.3	53.5	5.5	8.3	32.7	29.8	40.7	42.8
42 00000	**Pennsylvania**	5.9	5.9	4,949,494	64.7	48.3	4.4	12.1	35.3	29.5	29.3	37.9
42 02000	Allentown city	43.1	15.3	42,457	62.2	33.2	6.5	22.5	37.8	30.6	36.0	32.0
42 02056	Allison Park CDP	0.6	5.1	8,494	68.9	58.6	3.8	6.5	31.1	27.7	28.5	44.1
42 02184	Altoona city	1.2	1.5	18,954	61.2	41.1	5.6	14.5	38.8	33.5	30.3	37.7
42 06064	Bethel Park municipality	1.3	2.6	12,865	69.9	60.2	3.0	6.7	30.1	26.5	29.3	42.9
42 06088	Bethlehem city	23.9	7.7	29,528	57.2	36.0	5.3	15.9	42.8	34.9	29.4	35.5
42 12536	Chambersburg borough	19.5	9.8	7,985	59.7	39.1	5.3	15.3	40.3	35.5	30.4	41.6
42 13208	Chester city	9.7	4.3	12,131	57.0	20.9	5.4	30.6	43.0	36.6	29.9	36.3
42 19920	Drexel Hill CDP	1.7	8.5	11,455	64.4	46.8	5.9	11.7	35.6	32.0	32.7	34.1
42 21648	Easton city	22.5	13.6	9,294	62.1	33.8	7.2	21.1	37.9	31.7	36.2	32.6
42 24000	Erie city	6.7	6.4	41,214	55.4	33.3	4.4	17.7	44.6	36.9	27.5	31.0
42 32800	Harrisburg city	17.2	8.4	20,640	54.2	20.7	6.6	26.9	45.8	39.2	33.1	28.3
42 33408	Hazleton city	40.4	24.4	9,494	64.7	35.6	6.0	23.1	35.3	29.3	32.3	36.7
42 38288	Johnstown city	1.5	0.6	9,806	48.3	29.5	4.5	14.3	51.7	43.7	22.7	41.0
42 41216	Lancaster city	38.7	8.2	22,420	55.0	30.4	6.1	18.4	45.0	36.6	31.4	27.4
42 42168	Lebanon city	33.8	6.4	10,344	57.3	32.5	4.9	19.9	42.7	36.3	33.0	33.7
42 42928	Levittown CDP	5.7	4.3	18,312	75.0	54.4	5.3	15.2	25.0	21.2	34.5	38.1
42 46256	McKeesport city	3.1	2.8	8,763	51.3	25.5	5.1	20.7	48.7	42.1	25.6	39.1
42 50528	Monroeville municipality	1.5	7.1	12,229	63.0	50.0	3.1	10.0	37.0	33.9	25.7	42.8
42 52432	Murrysville municipality	1.0	4.3	7,877	75.8	65.9	2.4	7.5	24.2	20.6	29.2	44.5
42 53368	New Castle city	1.4	1.3	9,578	61.8	36.8	5.1	19.9	38.2	35.3	31.8	41.3
42 54656	Norristown borough	26.1	20.0	13,058	59.1	31.8	6.6	20.7	40.9	32.6	31.6	30.2
42 60000	Philadelphia city	12.7	12.0	576,889	53.3	27.0	5.5	20.9	46.7	39.6	27.4	33.3
42 61000	Pittsburgh city	2.6	7.2	131,719	47.0	28.5	3.8	14.7	53.0	41.7	20.9	32.7
42 61536	Plum borough	2.2	1.2	10,663	67.9	58.5	2.4	7.0	32.1	28.5	31.9	39.2
42 62416	Pottstown borough	6.5	2.1	9,612	54.1	34.4	3.5	16.1	45.9	39.3	27.9	33.1
42 63624	Reading city	58.9	18.7	30,896	63.4	28.8	6.6	28.0	36.6	30.0	42.6	28.9
42 69000	Scranton city	10.2	7.8	29,585	56.2	35.7	5.3	15.3	43.8	36.2	26.0	39.2
42 73808	State College borough	3.9	11.7	12,471	23.5	16.9	2.0	4.5	76.5	36.5	9.1	11.9
42 83512	West Mifflin borough	1.0	0.8	8,604	64.6	44.6	6.0	14.0	35.4	30.3	24.8	45.7
42 85152	Wilkes-Barre city	12.7	5.3	16,027	54.7	30.6	5.2	18.9	45.3	38.6	28.1	37.6
42 85312	Williamsport city	3.5	1.6	11,121	53.7	28.7	5.9	19.1	46.3	31.7	26.9	29.1
42 87048	York city	28.4	7.4	15,861	60.8	26.6	7.6	26.6	39.2	31.1	37.7	30.1
44 00000	**Rhode Island**	12.8	13.2	409,308	61.9	43.6	4.6	13.7	38.1	30.5	29.2	36.6
44 19180	Cranston city	10.4	12.9	30,200	63.6	48.7	4.3	10.5	36.4	30.2	27.9	39.0
44 22960	East Providence city	4.4	15.7	19,829	57.7	38.1	3.8	15.8	42.3	35.9	28.9	39.4
44 49960	Newport city	6.9	6.7	10,746	46.3	31.8	2.5	12.0	53.7	42.8	20.0	36.7
44 54640	Pawtucket city	19.5	23.7	29,164	59.2	33.8	6.0	19.4	40.8	34.5	30.1	32.1
44 59000	Providence city	40.2	29.8	60,526	56.1	27.9	6.2	22.0	43.9	30.5	33.9	26.6
44 74300	Warwick city	4.0	7.2	35,097	59.8	44.1	5.2	10.6	40.2	33.7	25.5	40.6
44 80780	Woonsocket city	13.1	10.1	16,714	57.3	35.6	4.1	17.6	42.7	34.2	31.2	32.5

Table A-4. Cities — Who: Age, Race/Ethnicity, and Household Structure, 2010–2012—*Continued*

STATE and Place code	STATE or City	Total population	Percent change 2010–2012	Population by age (percent) Under 5 years	5 to 17 years	18 to 24 years	25 to 44 years	45 to 64 years	65 years and over	Median age	Race alone or in combination (percent) White	Black	Asian, Hawaiian, or Pacific Islander	American Indian, Alaska Native, or some other race
	ACS table number:	B01003	Population estimates	B01001	B01001	B01001	B01001	B01001	B01001	B01002	B02008	B02009	B02011 + B02012	B02010 + B02013
	Column number:	1	2	3	4	5	6	7	8	9	10	11	12	13
45 00000	**South Carolina**	4,677,636	1.9	6.4	16.7	10.3	25.6	26.9	14.2	38.1	68.7	28.8	1.8	2.8
45 00550	Aiken city	29,779	0.8	5.2	14.7	12.4	18.2	27.6	21.9	44.5	67.0	30.6	2.1	…
45 01360	Anderson city	26,552	1.2	6.8	15.9	12.0	25.4	21.4	18.5	36.7	61.4	37.6	1.7	0.7
45 13330	Charleston city	123,226	3.9	5.7	11.7	16.3	31.0	23.0	12.2	33.2	72.2	26.3	2.1	0.9
45 16000	Columbia city	130,596	1.3	5.5	12.0	25.3	28.2	19.9	9.0	28.2	52.7	44.2	2.7	3.1
45 21985	Easley city	20,153	0.3	6.7	17.8	7.2	27.4	24.6	16.3	39.2	85.9	12.4	…	2.7
45 25810	Florence city	37,328	0.9	6.9	18.6	8.3	26.4	25.9	13.9	36.8	52.2	46.4	1.7	0.4
45 29815	Goose Creek city	37,385	6.7	8.0	17.4	16.4	28.3	22.2	7.7	29.9	72.0	20.5	7.5	4.2
45 30850	Greenville city	59,955	2.4	7.2	13.5	13.2	30.7	24.2	11.2	33.7	65.7	31.7	1.9	2.7
45 30895	Greenwood city	23,316	0.1	7.4	17.3	11.5	25.2	22.2	16.3	34.6	51.2	46.6	…	1.4
45 30985	Greer city	25,427	3.5	8.9	16.0	8.6	31.3	24.4	10.8	34.5	77.9	18.7	1.5	4.8
45 34045	Hilton Head Island town	37,752	3.0	4.6	11.1	6.1	21.4	26.1	30.7	52.6	82.7	8.2	1.0	8.6
45 45115	Mauldin city	23,350	3.7	7.3	18.6	7.0	29.8	25.4	12.0	36.6	68.2	27.7	2.5	5.2
45 48535	Mount Pleasant town	69,771	5.6	6.0	18.7	6.9	28.8	26.5	13.1	37.8	93.5	4.7	2.4	0.3
45 49075	Myrtle Beach city	27,708	4.0	6.2	12.5	9.3	29.3	26.0	16.7	38.5	79.1	10.6	1.3	10.4
45 50695	North Augusta city	21,535	2.2	5.4	16.4	8.2	25.3	28.6	16.1	41.3	78.5	21.0	2.4	1.0
45 50875	North Charleston city	99,999	4.0	9.0	16.0	12.8	31.1	22.5	8.6	30.8	47.0	48.2	2.7	4.6
45 61405	Rock Hill city	67,348	2.3	6.6	16.9	14.5	28.9	22.9	10.1	31.9	57.1	40.9	2.3	2.9
45 62395	St. Andrews CDP	20,099	…	9.2	15.7	12.2	29.7	24.4	8.8	30.8	28.8	71.6	2.3	…
45 67390	Socastee CDP	21,318	…	7.6	20.1	9.0	29.5	23.3	10.5	32.8	81.3	14.9	4.2	5.5
45 68290	Spartanburg city	37,238	1.0	7.9	13.8	14.3	23.0	24.8	16.1	37.4	49.7	48.5	2.3	1.1
45 70270	Summerville town	44,234	3.3	7.3	18.7	9.1	28.3	24.9	11.7	36.1	77.7	22.3	2.5	1.3
45 70405	Sumter city	40,628	0.7	7.1	17.4	11.8	25.4	24.2	14.1	34.8	47.5	50.3	2.0	2.0
45 71395	Taylors CDP	22,324	…	6.6	15.0	7.3	31.0	27.8	12.3	36.9	79.6	15.9	4.3	0.7
46 00000	**South Dakota**	824,391	2.1	7.1	17.5	10.0	24.5	26.4	14.5	37.0	87.6	1.9	1.4	11.3
46 00100	Aberdeen city	26,443	2.3	7.4	16.6	11.9	24.9	23.4	15.8	34.8	92.2	1.2	1.0	6.1
46 07580	Brookings city	22,320	2.0	4.8	10.9	37.0	22.7	15.9	8.7	23.2	93.5	1.1	4.1	2.2
46 52980	Rapid City city	68,912	2.4	7.7	16.4	9.9	26.0	25.5	14.6	36.0	85.7	2.8	1.4	15.6
46 59020	Sioux Falls city	156,997	3.5	8.4	15.9	10.1	29.7	24.6	11.3	34.0	87.8	5.3	2.3	6.1
46 69300	Watertown city	22,140	1.3	6.7	16.8	10.5	24.9	25.8	15.3	37.3	95.2	…	0.8	4.4
47 00000	**Tennessee**	6,404,240	1.6	6.3	17.0	9.6	26.3	26.9	13.8	38.2	79.8	17.5	1.9	2.7
47 03440	Bartlett city	55,247	2.2	5.2	20.1	7.6	25.2	28.7	13.1	38.8	80.9	16.2	3.6	0.8
47 08280	Brentwood city	38,118	4.8	5.9	25.3	5.6	20.8	32.0	10.4	40.7	92.6	3.1	5.4	0.5
47 08540	Bristol city	26,695	-0.2	5.6	14.4	11.0	23.7	27.5	17.8	41.1	95.6	2.6	0.5	1.7
47 14000	Chattanooga city	169,718	1.8	6.4	14.6	11.8	26.6	25.9	14.9	37.1	60.6	35.4	2.8	3.1
47 15160	Clarksville city	137,588	6.6	9.2	18.7	14.1	32.0	18.7	7.3	28.3	70.4	25.8	4.1	4.7
47 15400	Cleveland city	41,891	2.5	6.3	16.0	14.8	26.3	22.6	14.0	35.1	88.7	8.4	2.1	2.3
47 16420	Collierville town	46,046	1.7	5.6	23.4	8.3	22.9	30.3	9.4	38.6	78.9	13.5	7.1	1.9
47 16540	Columbia city	34,793	0.4	8.1	19.6	8.6	25.3	24.3	14.1	35.2	78.0	22.2	1.0	2.3
47 16920	Cookeville city	30,755	1.6	5.2	14.1	22.7	24.8	20.3	12.8	29.7	93.6	3.8	2.8	1.3
47 22720	East Ridge city	21,146	1.3	6.0	15.0	8.3	24.9	27.4	18.5	39.9	84.8	15.2	1.3	4.4
47 25760	Farragut town	20,888	2.0	3.7	23.2	7.9	18.9	29.7	16.5	42.0	90.1	2.7	6.8	…
47 27740	Franklin city	64,492	5.4	6.3	19.6	6.5	29.7	27.4	10.6	38.1	87.0	7.8	5.4	1.9
47 28540	Gallatin city	31,061	3.4	7.7	16.4	9.1	27.6	25.4	13.8	35.5	80.8	15.7	1.4	2.4
47 28960	Germantown city	39,182	1.4	6.2	18.2	5.6	20.3	33.3	16.4	44.7	87.5	6.4	6.3	0.3
47 33280	Hendersonville city	52,316	3.1	6.2	21.1	7.5	26.0	26.3	13.0	38.8	89.0	8.3	2.4	1.7
47 37640	Jackson city	67,009	0.5	7.4	17.5	13.3	24.1	24.3	13.4	33.9	52.6	46.3	2.0	1.1
47 38320	Johnson City city	63,581	1.9	4.7	14.3	15.5	25.2	24.9	15.4	37.8	90.2	8.6	2.3	1.0
47 39560	Kingsport city	51,206	0.0	5.3	15.5	7.0	23.5	27.8	21.0	44.2	93.5	4.9	1.8	2.6
47 40000	Knoxville city	180,714	1.7	6.2	11.6	16.4	28.0	23.5	14.3	34.6	79.2	18.7	1.9	2.3
47 41200	La Vergne city	33,260	3.3	8.8	22.9	6.7	35.5	20.0	6.2	31.9	75.0	21.4	2.8	2.4
47 41520	Lebanon city	27,070	5.5	6.5	17.6	9.2	27.6	24.3	14.9	36.9	81.7	13.6	2.1	3.2
47 46380	Maryville city	27,771	1.0	5.3	18.2	9.3	24.3	26.1	16.8	40.4	95.4	2.5	2.2	0.5
47 48000	Memphis city	651,363	1.2	7.5	17.8	11.7	27.8	24.8	10.5	33.2	31.2	64.1	2.2	4.4
47 50280	Morristown city	29,234	0.3	6.9	18.3	8.9	29.2	20.9	15.7	34.8	87.9	8.9	1.2	5.6
47 50780	Mount Juliet city	25,904	7.6	6.7	20.8	6.5	31.1	25.2	9.7	36.5	88.3	9.0	2.8	1.6
47 51560	Murfreesboro city	111,813	4.1	7.5	15.8	17.8	30.6	19.6	8.8	29.4	79.7	16.3	4.3	2.4
47 52006	Nashville-Davidson metropolitan government	613,829	3.3	7.1	14.6	11.4	32.4	24.1	10.3	33.7	63.1	29.5	4.0	6.1
47 55120	Oak Ridge city	29,426	0.0	6.0	15.9	7.7	22.8	29.5	18.1	43.4	86.7	11.5	3.1	1.6
47 67760	Shelbyville city	20,501	1.0	8.5	21.3	9.8	29.3	19.7	11.4	30.9	84.1	14.4	1.1	5.0
47 69420	Smyrna town	40,950	3.9	8.6	20.1	8.2	32.3	22.0	8.7	33.3	80.5	13.4	5.0	2.6
47 70580	Spring Hill city	30,770	6.5	11.7	22.1	4.9	36.4	20.8	4.1	32.0	90.2	5.9	1.2	3.8
48 00000	**Texas**	25,644,550	3.2	7.5	19.5	10.3	28.0	24.0	10.6	33.8	76.5	12.6	4.7	8.6
48 01000	Abilene city	120,027	1.3	7.4	15.1	15.7	26.8	22.5	12.5	31.9	82.7	11.5	2.4	6.5
48 01924	Allen city	87,343	5.6	8.4	22.8	6.4	30.1	26.0	6.2	35.4	75.6	10.7	13.1	4.5
48 02272	Alvin city	24,624	2.5	7.0	20.5	10.5	29.9	20.9	11.1	31.9	90.1	5.1	…	4.9
48 03000	Amarillo city	193,429	2.0	7.8	19.2	10.1	27.4	23.4	12.0	33.4	85.5	8.0	4.3	5.6
48 04000	Arlington city	370,854	2.5	7.5	19.5	11.8	29.4	23.6	8.2	32.1	68.6	19.9	7.7	6.0
48 04456	Atascocita CDP	70,851	…	6.6	23.6	8.1	33.9	21.4	6.4	32.4	67.0	26.4	2.9	5.4
48 05000	Austin city	818,236	6.0	7.1	15.0	13.7	36.1	21.0	7.1	31.4	75.2	9.1	7.6	11.3
48 05372	Balch Springs city	24,402	3.9	10.6	24.9	12.7	26.4	18.6	6.8	26.6	67.1	27.4	0.8	8.2
48 06128	Baytown city	71,567	1.9	9.1	19.7	10.2	26.9	24.6	9.5	32.0	68.6	17.1	1.5	14.2
48 07000	Beaumont city	118,440	-0.1	7.2	17.8	11.6	26.4	24.4	12.6	33.9	45.3	47.8	3.3	5.9

144   **The Who, What, and Where of America**

Table A-4. Cities — Who: Age, Race/Ethnicity, and Household Structure, 2010–2012—*Continued*

STATE and Place code	STATE or City	Percent Hispanic or Latino	Percent foreign born	Total households	Household type (percent)							Percent of households with people under 18 years	Percent of households with people 60 years and over
					Family households				Nonfamily households				
					Total family households	Married-couple families	Male household families	Female household families	Total nonfamily households	One-person households			
	ACS table number:	B03003	C05003	B11001	B11001	B11001	B11001	B11001	B11001	B11001		B11005	B11006
	Column number:	14	15	16	17	18	19	20	21	22		23	24
45 00000	**South Carolina**	5.2	4.8	1,774,128	67.4	47.4	4.6	15.4	32.6	27.5		32.0	36.5
45 00550	Aiken city	2.8	4.0	12,379	59.3	43.5	3.0	12.8	40.7	36.5		22.3	45.8
45 01360	Anderson city	4.0	4.8	10,609	57.6	34.3	2.0	21.2	42.4	38.5		28.1	38.4
45 13330	Charleston city	3.0	4.1	52,182	50.8	35.7	3.0	12.0	49.2	35.8		22.7	30.4
45 16000	Columbia city	4.9	5.0	44,324	50.9	30.4	2.6	17.9	49.1	38.3		25.7	26.0
45 21985	Easley city	5.8	5.3	7,961	69.4	50.4	4.1	14.9	30.6	28.0		34.6	37.7
45 25810	Florence city	1.1	1.7	14,680	65.6	37.0	4.8	23.7	34.4	30.3		34.6	34.2
45 29815	Goose Creek city	5.5	6.2	12,281	76.5	61.8	2.4	12.3	23.5	19.8		40.6	26.2
45 30850	Greenville city	6.1	7.3	25,539	49.1	32.1	3.5	13.5	50.9	43.1		24.6	29.2
45 30895	Greenwood city	7.6	4.2	8,659	59.2	28.2	9.8	21.2	40.8	35.7		32.3	39.9
45 30985	Greer city	18.5	12.1	9,622	65.3	43.7	6.4	15.2	34.7	28.2		32.5	28.9
45 34045	Hilton Head Island town	15.7	16.2	16,390	65.9	56.2	3.9	5.8	34.1	26.6		19.3	57.6
45 45115	Mauldin city	9.9	7.9	9,073	65.0	47.7	3.4	13.9	35.0	33.0		36.5	29.2
45 48535	Mount Pleasant town	3.2	4.6	27,718	66.2	52.9	2.8	10.5	33.8	26.6		33.0	31.2
45 49075	Myrtle Beach city	13.7	16.6	11,875	54.8	36.1	5.2	13.5	45.2	34.3		24.1	40.3
45 50695	North Augusta city	3.1	3.5	8,854	66.3	45.9	3.4	16.9	33.7	30.2		28.5	38.7
45 50875	North Charleston city	10.2	9.1	35,889	62.1	36.1	4.7	21.3	37.9	30.9		36.1	26.1
45 61405	Rock Hill city	5.3	5.0	26,257	62.9	39.5	3.8	19.5	37.1	30.0		34.4	26.8
45 62395	St. Andrews CDP	3.2	3.6	9,211	49.3	25.3	5.5	18.4	50.7	41.5		28.2	25.7
45 67390	Socastee CDP	8.3	8.0	7,632	65.1	46.8	4.7	13.6	34.9	22.8		40.6	32.6
45 68090	Spartanburg city	1.8	4.1	15,763	57.6	31.3	3.8	22.6	42.4	37.9		30.5	37.5
45 70270	Summerville town	3.9	3.4	17,022	66.0	49.2	2.9	14.0	34.0	29.7		36.6	30.6
45 70405	Sumter city	3.4	3.2	15,818	64.7	40.7	3.8	20.2	35.3	30.8		33.8	35.2
45 71395	Taylors CDP	6.2	9.4	8,471	69.9	49.6	3.1	17.1	30.1	25.8		33.2	32.6
46 00000	**South Dakota**	2.9	2.8	322,005	64.2	50.2	4.3	9.7	35.8	29.7		30.2	33.9
46 00100	Aberdeen city	1.7	1.9	11,130	56.1	44.2	2.8	9.2	43.9	38.2		28.5	34.3
46 07580	Brookings city	1.9	5.5	8,422	54.1	39.1	7.3	7.8	45.9	30.7		23.0	21.6
46 52980	Rapid City city	4.5	1.7	28,016	57.9	40.8	4.8	12.2	42.1	34.7		28.7	34.3
46 59020	Sioux Falls city	4.8	7.4	62,651	62.5	46.1	4.6	11.8	37.5	29.8		32.2	27.3
46 69300	Watertown city	1.5	1.3	9,442	59.1	43.5	5.1	10.5	40.9	34.0		24.8	33.7
47 00000	**Tennessee**	4.7	4.6	2,466,659	66.7	48.7	4.4	13.6	33.3	28.2		31.7	35.2
47 03440	Bartlett city	2.2	4.0	18,861	79.5	65.2	3.3	10.9	20.5	17.0		37.3	37.2
47 08280	Brentwood city	2.0	6.2	12,305	89.1	81.7	2.4	5.0	10.9	9.6		51.3	33.0
47 08540	Bristol city	2.0	2.1	11,426	59.6	42.0	3.8	13.8	40.4	34.0		28.0	40.9
47 14000	Chattanooga city	5.7	5.7	69,721	56.9	35.6	4.6	16.8	43.1	36.2		26.3	36.2
47 15160	Clarksville city	9.7	6.7	49,635	72.2	50.0	4.5	17.7	27.8	22.4		43.1	20.3
47 15400	Cleveland city	7.4	7.1	15,964	61.3	42.7	5.4	13.2	38.7	32.3		30.1	33.8
47 16420	Collierville town	2.0	6.5	14,590	85.3	72.8	2.0	10.6	14.7	13.5		48.0	29.8
47 16540	Columbia city	7.3	4.1	13,813	61.6	36.8	6.6	18.2	38.4	34.3		32.9	36.8
47 16920	Cookeville city	4.5	6.0	12,246	54.4	35.0	4.0	15.5	45.6	33.2		26.1	32.8
47 22720	East Ridge city	5.7	5.4	9,109	57.4	38.3	4.5	14.6	42.6	37.7		26.5	41.1
47 25760	Farragut town	1.3	7.2	7,140	79.8	71.4	2.8	5.7	20.2	18.5		40.4	44.0
47 27740	Franklin city	7.6	10.1	25,281	68.2	58.5	1.7	8.0	31.8	28.3		35.6	29.8
47 28540	Gallatin city	7.4	5.1	11,952	67.5	47.7	3.4	16.3	32.5	29.0		33.8	34.9
47 28960	Germantown city	1.8	8.0	14,138	78.7	70.7	3.2	4.8	21.3	18.3		35.2	44.8
47 33280	Hendersonville city	4.6	5.2	19,476	73.3	56.8	3.7	12.7	26.7	23.1		40.0	32.4
47 37640	Jackson city	4.4	4.5	23,764	60.1	39.1	2.8	18.3	39.9	36.1		30.6	33.3
47 38320	Johnson City city	4.2	5.1	27,008	55.2	40.6	4.6	10.1	44.8	34.4		24.6	33.1
47 39560	Kingsport city	2.1	2.3	22,462	63.6	48.1	2.8	12.7	36.4	33.2		27.7	42.7
47 40000	Knoxville city	4.0	4.8	84,221	45.4	30.4	3.8	11.2	54.6	46.6		20.8	30.9
47 41200	La Vergne city	17.4	10.7	10,636	75.0	51.8	7.9	15.3	25.0	19.9		45.5	19.0
47 41520	Lebanon city	6.2	6.2	10,191	66.7	46.5	5.4	14.8	33.3	29.6		33.3	36.9
47 46380	Maryville city	2.1	3.2	10,595	65.4	50.5	2.2	12.6	34.6	31.4		33.4	38.6
47 48000	Memphis city	6.7	6.4	244,775	60.0	29.0	6.0	24.9	40.0	34.3		31.4	30.2
47 50280	Morristown city	19.6	12.0	11,058	64.0	42.1	3.1	18.9	36.0	31.3		35.1	37.2
47 50780	Mount Juliet city	2.7	4.5	9,365	78.6	57.8	7.3	13.5	21.4	17.1		44.1	24.9
47 51560	Murfreesboro city	5.3	6.1	41,261	62.7	45.6	3.4	13.8	37.3	26.6		32.9	24.1
47 52006	Nashville-Davidson metropolitan government	10.1	12.0	246,103	54.9	36.0	4.3	14.5	45.1	36.2		27.1	27.0
47 55120	Oak Ridge city	5.0	6.9	12,571	60.4	46.1	5.1	9.2	39.6	35.7		26.4	40.4
47 67760	Shelbyville city	21.8	14.6	7,171	69.9	44.5	9.2	16.1	30.1	25.0		37.2	30.0
47 69420	Smyrna town	9.8	7.4	15,186	65.7	45.7	6.1	13.9	34.3	28.6		39.6	24.5
47 70580	Spring Hill city	7.6	3.9	9,743	79.4	67.6	4.5	7.3	20.6	18.3		54.3	13.3
48 00000	**Texas**	38.0	16.4	8,852,441	69.7	50.1	5.1	14.4	30.3	24.9		38.3	30.2
48 01000	Abilene city	25.1	6.2	42,110	63.3	44.7	3.9	14.8	36.7	29.2		32.7	32.4
48 01924	Allen city	9.8	16.1	28,556	79.9	67.1	3.0	9.8	20.1	15.4		53.1	18.9
48 02272	Alvin city	34.6	8.6	8,335	72.3	49.5	6.1	16.7	27.7	22.8		38.7	27.5
48 03000	Amarillo city	29.9	10.3	73,908	64.3	45.4	5.0	14.0	35.7	30.0		34.5	30.5
48 04000	Arlington city	28.7	20.2	132,177	68.6	46.7	5.8	16.1	31.4	25.4		40.2	24.7
48 04462	Atascocita CDP	22.0	9.0	21,985	80.5	62.7	3.9	13.9	19.5	16.1		48.5	22.6
48 05000	Austin city	35.0	18.5	327,971	52.5	35.3	4.8	12.4	47.5	34.0		28.5	19.9
48 05372	Balch Springs city	46.6	20.7	7,016	78.9	48.1	5.9	24.9	21.1	17.5		53.8	26.7
48 06128	Baytown city	44.3	18.2	23,866	71.7	46.2	7.3	18.3	28.3	24.2		44.3	30.9
48 07000	Beaumont city	14.1	9.2	45,417	61.3	35.6	6.2	19.5	38.7	33.3		32.2	35.1

Table A-4. Cities — Who: Age, Race/Ethnicity, and Household Structure, 2010–2012—*Continued*

STATE and Place code	STATE or City	Total population	Percent change 2010–2012	Under 5 years	5 to 17 years	18 to 24 years	25 to 44 years	45 to 64 years	65 years and over	Median age	White	Black	Asian, Hawaiian, or Pacific Islander	American Indian, Alaska Native, or some other race
	ACS table number:	B01003	Population estimates	B01001	B01001	B01001	B01001	B01001	B01001	B01002	B02008	B02009	B02011 + B02012	B02010 + B02013
	Column number:	1	2	3	4	5	6	7	8	9	10	11	12	13
	Texas—Cont.													
48 07132	Bedford city	47,617	2.3	5.8	14.5	7.9	27.6	29.6	14.5	40.3	81.9	7.8	7.1	5.8
48 07552	Benbrook city	21,618	3.0	6.5	14.1	7.8	24.9	28.7	18.0	42.6	91.2	8.2	2.3	1.4
48 08236	Big Spring city	27,763	1.0	7.1	16.0	10.2	30.6	24.4	11.7	35.5	80.9	9.3	0.9	14.0
48 10768	Brownsville city	178,045	2.5	9.1	25.0	10.2	26.2	19.7	9.8	29.7	92.0	0.4	1.0	7.4
48 10897	Brushy Creek CDP	23,650	...	8.1	27.3	4.9	29.4	25.3	5.0	33.8	80.0	7.7	12.0	3.9
48 10912	Bryan city	77,266	2.0	8.2	15.7	18.1	29.2	19.2	9.6	29.1	67.8	19.7	2.1	13.0
48 11428	Burleson city	38,048	5.7	8.5	22.0	7.3	29.5	22.3	10.4	34.1	95.1	3.6	0.7	1.8
48 12580	Canyon Lake CDP	19,719	...	2.4	14.9	5.5	22.0	33.9	21.3	48.8	97.0	1.6	...	3.4
48 13024	Carrollton city	122,468	5.0	6.7	18.9	8.4	29.0	28.5	8.5	35.8	73.2	9.9	14.2	6.0
48 13492	Cedar Hill city	45,719	3.0	7.3	22.8	8.7	29.0	25.6	6.6	33.8	40.7	54.3	3.3	4.6
48 13552	Cedar Park city	55,258	10.6	7.8	22.0	8.0	32.9	21.9	7.5	34.1	86.0	5.8	8.3	2.1
48 14236	Channelview CDP	37,477	...	7.7	25.6	12.6	27.2	22.0	5.0	28.9	64.3	14.7	0.7	21.1
48 15364	Cleburne city	29,321	-0.2	9.0	18.8	11.2	25.0	23.3	12.7	33.2	92.1	5.6	1.8	3.9
48 15628	Cloverleaf CDP	24,987	...	11.7	23.8	14.1	24.6	19.0	6.8	25.2	68.0	7.6	2.0	24.2
48 15976	College Station city	95,960	3.5	4.4	11.0	45.7	22.5	11.4	5.0	22.5	81.2	7.0	10.3	3.8
48 15988	Colleyville city	23,372	4.5	4.1	23.5	6.5	15.3	39.2	11.4	45.3	86.5	1.4	9.9	5.2
48 16432	Conroe city	59,376	7.1	9.9	18.4	9.6	32.0	19.3	10.7	31.8	84.6	10.4	1.2	4.8
48 16612	Coppell city	39,377	3.2	5.8	23.4	5.5	25.9	33.3	6.1	38.4	75.2	5.1	18.7	2.9
48 16624	Copperas Cove city	33,018	3.7	9.2	20.9	8.8	31.3	20.4	9.4	31.0	73.6	19.5	3.9	6.1
48 16696	Corinth city	20,203	3.1	9.0	20.4	8.3	27.6	26.2	8.5	35.2	90.3	7.0	2.8	4.0
48 17000	Corpus Christi city	308,497	2.2	6.9	18.8	10.7	26.3	25.4	11.9	34.5	87.4	5.1	2.5	7.5
48 17060	Corsicana city	23,878	0.5	9.5	17.8	10.9	27.5	21.7	12.6	33.0	69.7	22.9	0.7	10.7
48 19000	Dallas city	1,219,879	3.4	8.3	17.8	10.4	32.5	21.9	9.2	31.9	58.0	25.3	3.4	15.4
48 19624	Deer Park city	32,529	2.7	8.2	19.4	10.2	28.7	24.9	8.6	33.4	90.1	2.7	2.1	6.4
48 19792	Del Rio city	35,612	-0.4	8.7	21.4	9.4	25.1	21.9	13.4	33.5	92.6	1.2	0.5	7.2
48 19900	Denison city	22,662	-0.2	7.0	17.0	8.4	24.7	26.0	16.8	38.7	84.8	11.4	0.9	5.6
48 19972	Denton city	117,997	5.4	6.2	14.1	24.9	27.5	18.8	8.5	27.2	81.6	12.6	5.6	5.8
48 20092	DeSoto city	50,201	3.6	5.2	20.6	8.3	25.3	28.4	12.3	39.4	27.8	69.1	0.4	4.6
48 21628	Duncanville city	39,040	2.4	8.2	19.4	9.2	25.0	25.6	12.6	36.8	55.3	30.3	3.0	12.9
48 21892	Eagle Pass city	26,899	3.3	7.4	24.5	8.8	24.8	20.7	13.9	33.2	93.9	0.7	0.5	7.0
48 22660	Edinburg city	79,342	4.6	9.7	21.6	12.9	30.3	18.3	7.2	28.1	91.8	1.5	2.3	5.5
48 24000	El Paso city	662,707	3.2	7.8	20.6	11.3	26.2	22.7	11.3	32.4	83.6	3.9	2.0	12.7
48 24768	Euless city	52,121	2.6	6.5	19.1	8.7	34.0	24.0	7.6	33.9	66.5	13.2	12.8	10.6
48 25452	Farmers Branch city	29,011	2.5	7.2	18.9	9.3	28.7	23.9	12.1	35.9	86.6	4.9	5.4	4.4
48 26232	Flower Mound town	66,732	4.5	5.8	25.6	6.4	25.5	31.4	5.4	38.0	86.3	4.4	8.9	2.6
48 26736	Fort Hood CDP	33,688	...	14.5	20.2	29.5	31.8	3.9	0.1	22.0	67.4	25.7	6.4	6.7
48 27000	Fort Worth city	761,862	4.3	8.9	20.3	9.8	30.9	21.9	8.3	31.6	68.6	19.7	4.8	9.5
48 27648	Friendswood city	36,370	2.7	4.0	20.7	9.3	21.4	32.0	12.6	41.3	89.5	6.8	4.2	2.7
48 27684	Frisco city	123,175	8.6	8.9	24.3	6.2	34.9	19.4	6.2	34.2	79.3	8.8	12.4	3.9
48 28068	Galveston city	47,689	-0.1	5.7	14.6	13.6	24.6	27.5	14.0	37.9	74.7	19.7	4.6	3.1
48 29000	Garland city	230,317	2.7	8.2	21.0	9.7	27.8	24.2	9.1	33.3	48.3	16.3	11.2	30.9
48 29336	Georgetown city	50,145	9.0	6.5	18.5	6.9	20.7	22.6	24.7	42.3	92.2	4.5	1.0	4.6
48 30464	Grand Prairie city	178,835	3.3	8.3	22.6	9.6	29.9	22.5	7.0	31.4	65.1	20.4	7.3	9.0
48 30644	Grapevine city	47,408	3.9	6.7	19.4	7.9	28.2	29.5	8.4	36.7	83.7	2.1	5.0	11.6
48 30920	Greenville city	25,750	0.7	9.0	16.3	10.6	25.7	23.8	14.6	35.3	67.9	16.2	2.8	15.1
48 31928	Haltom City	42,938	2.1	8.7	18.3	11.2	27.6	22.5	11.7	32.8	71.6	7.4	6.9	15.4
48 32312	Harker Heights city	27,347	3.3	8.0	22.0	11.4	29.3	21.2	8.0	31.7	73.3	21.7	9.8	4.3
48 32372	Harlingen city	65,425	0.9	8.8	21.2	8.3	26.6	21.8	13.4	33.7	93.5	2.0	1.2	4.4
48 35000	Houston city	2,130,116	2.8	7.9	17.7	10.7	31.7	22.7	9.2	32.4	58.9	23.8	6.9	12.2
48 35528	Huntsville city	39,308	2.5	4.7	8.8	28.0	29.9	21.2	7.4	29.9	66.6	29.2	2.0	2.8
48 35576	Hurst city	37,823	2.1	5.9	17.5	9.0	24.6	26.2	16.8	38.1	87.1	6.5	2.5	5.7
48 37000	Irving city	220,677	3.9	8.9	18.3	9.0	36.4	20.8	6.6	31.4	58.6	13.4	15.7	14.9
48 38632	Keller city	40,864	5.2	4.7	25.0	6.4	23.6	30.4	9.9	40.0	92.8	2.1	4.8	1.8
48 39040	Kerrville city	22,405	0.4	5.2	14.2	9.7	19.6	25.3	26.0	46.5	91.4	3.9	1.5	4.5
48 39148	Killeen city	131,639	4.2	10.5	20.2	13.2	34.0	16.9	5.1	27.5	55.7	37.6	7.3	6.5
48 39352	Kingsville city	25,425	-0.1	8.0	16.5	19.3	26.4	18.6	11.2	28.0	86.2	5.3	3.5	7.8
48 39952	Kyle city	29,541	8.5	9.3	24.1	6.4	38.9	17.8	3.6	30.5	73.2	8.1	1.8	19.2
48 40588	Lake Jackson city	27,039	1.2	5.5	19.6	10.6	25.8	26.5	12.0	36.4	86.6	8.2	2.8	4.7
48 41212	Lancaster city	37,303	2.9	7.8	22.8	7.7	29.2	24.8	7.7	35.1	28.7	68.4	0.2	4.4
48 41440	La Porte city	34,170	1.8	6.8	19.1	10.0	27.5	27.3	9.2	35.8	83.4	8.1	1.7	8.8
48 41464	Laredo city	240,773	3.2	9.7	24.9	11.1	27.7	18.7	8.0	28.2	94.0	0.2	1.0	5.3
48 41980	League City city	86,105	4.8	7.2	20.1	6.9	30.7	26.6	8.5	35.4	84.7	8.3	5.9	3.2
48 42016	Leander city	28,081	10.8	8.6	26.0	4.8	34.9	19.9	5.8	32.7	90.6	6.8	4.2	4.0
48 42508	Lewisville city	97,421	3.8	7.8	17.9	9.3	36.1	21.7	7.3	32.2	78.9	11.0	9.9	5.7
48 43012	Little Elm city	27,622	10.5	10.5	26.1	3.8	39.4	16.7	3.5	29.9	75.7	16.7	3.6	6.3
48 43888	Longview city	81,021	0.7	7.3	18.3	10.2	26.6	23.8	13.7	34.5	73.2	22.1	1.6	4.2
48 45000	Lubbock city	233,475	2.3	7.4	16.0	19.0	25.7	20.9	11.1	29.5	79.8	9.2	3.3	11.1
48 45072	Lufkin city	35,492	2.6	8.2	17.1	12.0	24.0	22.7	16.0	35.2	68.3	27.9	1.7	3.9
48 45384	McAllen city	132,720	3.3	7.7	20.1	10.8	27.8	22.8	10.8	32.9	88.9	1.4	3.1	8.1
48 45744	McKinney city	137,971	7.8	8.6	23.0	7.3	32.2	21.6	7.3	32.9	82.4	10.4	6.4	2.9
48 46452	Mansfield city	57,690	4.4	7.0	24.8	7.5	28.1	25.3	7.4	34.3	76.2	18.5	5.1	4.4
48 46776	Marshall city	24,322	5.1	8.4	18.7	14.7	23.7	21.9	12.6	32.3	51.6	44.1	1.2	3.4
48 47892	Mesquite city	141,533	2.4	8.4	21.5	10.2	28.3	22.9	8.7	31.5	69.8	24.1	3.4	5.6
48 48072	Midland city	114,805	7.3	8.2	19.2	10.4	27.4	23.6	11.2	32.4	84.5	8.9	1.9	6.3
48 48768	Mission city	79,179	3.4	8.4	26.5	9.5	26.4	18.7	10.5	29.9	93.4	1.0	1.3	5.4

Table A-4. Cities — Who: Age, Race/Ethnicity, and Household Structure, 2010–2012—*Continued*

STATE and Place code	STATE or City	Percent Hispanic or Latino	Percent foreign born	Total households	Household type (percent)							Percent of households with people under 18 years	Percent of households with people 60 years and over
					Family households				Nonfamily households			
					Total family households	Married-couple families	Male household families	Female household families	Total nonfamily households	One-person households		
ACS table number:		B03003	C05003	B11001	B11001	B11001	B11001	B11001	B11001	B11001	B11005	B11006
Column number:		14	15	16	17	18	19	20	21	22	23	24
	Texas—Cont.											
48 07132	Bedford city	12.0	8.8	20,756	61.2	45.7	5.0	10.5	38.8	33.0	25.9	33.8
48 07552	Benbrook city	11.5	5.0	9,349	64.0	48.6	2.8	12.5	36.0	32.9	26.0	39.4
48 08236	Big Spring city	42.8	13.0	8,017	61.1	39.2	4.6	17.2	38.9	33.0	31.8	36.7
48 10768	Brownsville city	93.5	29.8	50,159	80.9	52.4	5.2	23.4	19.1	17.3	53.1	32.4
48 10897	Brushy Creek CDP	15.3	12.0	7,325	83.2	72.1	3.5	7.6	16.8	13.6	55.7	19.0
48 10912	Bryan city	36.6	13.3	27,502	59.7	38.8	6.1	14.7	40.3	30.7	31.8	27.6
48 11428	Burleson city	11.5	2.9	13,244	76.6	61.6	5.7	9.3	23.4	21.4	46.8	29.0
48 12580	Canyon Lake CDP	14.9	3.2	8,461	66.9	57.0	4.6	5.2	33.1	28.9	23.1	45.0
48 13024	Carrollton city	31.3	25.0	42,972	73.2	55.8	4.6	12.8	26.8	21.3	39.6	24.0
48 13492	Cedar Hill city	18.4	9.2	15,647	73.8	50.7	3.1	19.9	26.2	23.9	43.9	25.0
48 13552	Cedar Park city	16.1	10.2	18,499	75.5	59.2	3.2	13.1	24.5	19.2	46.8	21.2
48 14236	Channelview CDP	59.5	22.6	10,926	78.9	50.3	9.2	19.4	21.1	16.6	50.7	21.1
48 15364	Cleburne city	23.7	10.3	10,391	71.5	49.3	5.3	16.9	28.5	22.5	43.0	31.5
48 15628	Cloverleaf CDP	76.7	35.7	6,787	78.5	52.0	9.7	16.9	21.5	17.3	54.8	26.4
48 15976	College Station city	14.2	13.5	33,540	45.8	34.3	3.4	8.1	54.2	27.3	24.4	14.4
48 15988	Colleyville city	8.7	8.9	7,968	88.4	80.7	2.0	5.7	11.6	10.7	40.7	36.2
48 16432	Conroe city	39.3	23.4	20,149	65.1	42.3	5.2	17.5	34.9	27.5	38.8	29.8
48 16612	Coppell city	10.2	19.4	14,375	78.8	65.9	3.3	9.5	21.2	18.6	47.1	20.6
48 16624	Copperas Cove city	15.2	7.6	10,601	77.6	59.7	2.8	15.1	22.4	19.5	45.8	24.1
48 16696	Corinth city	10.1	8.4	7,108	78.3	67.6	1.4	9.3	21.7	19.4	42.3	25.5
48 17000	Corpus Christi city	60.4	7.7	110,803	68.2	43.6	6.5	18.1	31.8	25.6	36.2	33.0
48 17060	Corsicana city	31.1	15.5	8,765	67.5	44.4	5.1	18.0	32.5	25.9	36.9	34.2
48 19000	Dallas city	42.2	24.8	456,781	57.3	35.2	6.1	16.0	42.7	34.7	32.6	25.6
48 19624	Deer Park city	27.0	7.4	10,900	82.5	61.4	6.4	14.6	17.5	15.5	42.9	28.9
48 19792	Del Rio city	84.7	25.0	11,169	73.9	53.6	5.5	14.8	26.1	23.7	41.6	37.7
48 19900	Denison city	8.7	2.5	8,770	64.3	41.9	5.2	17.3	35.7	31.4	30.7	39.3
48 19972	Denton city	21.9	12.7	41,474	56.7	41.6	4.6	10.5	43.3	29.0	29.6	23.3
48 20092	DeSoto city	12.0	4.9	18,673	70.5	49.5	3.0	18.0	29.5	27.0	36.3	35.3
48 21628	Duncanville city	35.2	15.8	14,027	71.6	48.1	6.6	16.9	28.4	26.2	36.0	36.6
48 21892	Eagle Pass city	95.6	33.9	8,477	78.4	53.3	3.6	21.6	21.6	20.8	46.6	40.3
48 22660	Edinburg city	88.8	19.2	24,104	75.2	53.3	4.9	17.0	24.8	18.6	46.5	23.3
48 24000	El Paso city	80.0	24.6	216,792	73.9	48.8	5.1	20.1	26.1	22.4	42.5	33.0
48 24768	Euless city	20.3	18.8	20,862	61.6	41.0	7.2	13.5	38.4	31.0	34.4	21.1
48 25452	Farmers Branch city	39.3	24.1	10,643	65.6	48.2	4.2	13.2	34.4	29.6	34.5	34.8
48 26232	Flower Mound town	8.6	10.8	21,264	85.0	74.9	2.0	8.1	15.0	12.9	54.0	19.8
48 26736	Fort Hood CDP	21.2	5.0	5,913	96.9	76.5	4.8	15.6	3.1	2.6	79.2	1.6
48 27000	Fort Worth city	33.9	17.6	264,584	67.0	45.6	5.2	16.3	33.0	27.8	40.7	25.3
48 27648	Friendswood city	15.9	8.7	12,522	76.8	64.4	4.2	8.2	23.2	19.9	39.5	33.1
48 27684	Frisco city	12.7	14.3	41,055	81.8	67.8	4.5	9.5	18.2	15.5	53.0	18.9
48 28068	Galveston city	30.2	13.2	19,805	52.4	33.3	2.6	16.6	47.6	39.5	25.2	36.6
48 29000	Garland city	40.2	27.2	72,934	77.1	53.5	6.6	17.1	22.9	18.7	43.6	29.1
48 29336	Georgetown city	27.0	11.0	19,304	68.1	56.6	3.7	7.8	31.9	28.9	28.4	52.6
48 30464	Grand Prairie city	43.5	22.0	57,572	73.5	50.2	6.5	16.9	26.5	22.1	46.3	23.7
48 30644	Grapevine city	22.0	13.4	18,165	69.8	53.9	5.0	10.9	30.2	23.7	36.4	23.7
48 30920	Greenville city	23.0	13.1	9,957	58.7	41.0	3.5	14.2	41.3	36.1	30.3	36.2
48 31928	Haltom City city	41.7	25.7	14,892	64.9	45.3	6.3	13.3	35.1	30.1	36.8	31.2
48 32312	Harker Heights city	20.8	10.0	8,169	80.5	59.0	5.1	16.5	19.5	15.2	46.5	25.5
48 32372	Harlingen city	78.8	16.9	20,829	74.3	48.3	7.0	18.9	25.7	22.0	42.8	37.0
48 35000	Houston city	43.9	28.1	770,098	60.9	38.5	6.0	16.4	39.1	32.2	33.9	26.4
48 35528	Huntsville city	19.0	7.4	10,376	52.4	31.0	3.7	17.8	47.5	32.8	28.3	22.0
48 35576	Hurst city	22.3	13.3	14,714	66.4	47.9	4.7	13.8	33.5	28.6	30.9	39.5
48 37000	Irving city	41.0	33.6	82,382	63.2	44.1	5.3	13.7	36.3	30.9	36.8	19.0
48 38632	Keller city	5.8	5.8	13,876	81.1	71.9	3.3	6.0	18.9	16.0	45.3	27.4
48 39040	Kerrville city	25.5	7.4	9,596	58.9	42.7	4.1	12.1	41.1	37.0	22.8	49.2
48 39148	Killeen city	24.5	9.2	44,085	70.1	47.2	3.5	19.4	29.9	24.2	45.3	16.3
48 39352	Kingsville city	74.7	7.9	9,007	67.8	39.1	7.2	21.5	32.2	20.5	39.1	29.4
48 39952	Kyle city	47.1	9.0	9,090	80.2	65.3	5.5	9.4	19.8	14.8	56.1	16.9
48 40588	Lake Jackson city	20.7	5.9	9,781	68.1	52.8	4.1	11.2	31.9	25.8	32.6	31.5
48 41212	Lancaster city	19.3	7.1	13,277	69.8	44.0	7.1	18.6	30.2	27.3	40.5	23.8
48 41440	La Porte city	27.8	9.3	11,295	79.0	54.6	8.7	15.7	21.0	15.9	41.6	27.7
48 41464	Laredo city	95.4	28.6	64,115	82.0	53.9	5.7	22.4	18.0	14.9	55.3	29.9
48 41980	League City city	19.5	9.8	31,114	72.1	59.9	2.7	9.4	27.9	21.4	41.1	24.4
48 42016	Leander city	27.3	7.2	8,811	80.8	64.8	4.4	11.6	19.2	13.6	56.7	17.5
48 42508	Lewisville city	30.9	20.3	38,392	62.9	45.8	4.5	12.6	37.1	29.4	35.8	19.0
48 43012	Little Elm city	27.9	14.8	8,288	84.2	65.7	4.2	14.3	15.8	13.9	59.0	12.6
48 43888	Longview city	19.0	10.8	29,841	66.8	44.0	5.9	16.9	33.2	29.0	35.7	34.8
48 45000	Lubbock city	33.0	6.0	88,762	59.8	40.6	5.0	14.1	40.2	30.1	30.9	28.6
48 45072	Lufkin city	25.0	11.0	13,120	68.9	43.9	6.4	18.6	31.1	25.5	34.0	38.3
48 45384	McAllen city	85.1	30.0	42,241	74.2	51.0	5.3	17.9	25.8	22.0	43.0	32.4
48 45744	McKinney city	19.9	12.4	44,732	79.7	63.7	3.2	12.8	20.3	16.7	51.7	21.8
48 46452	Mansfield city	13.8	9.8	19,193	78.8	61.9	5.5	11.4	21.2	17.6	47.2	25.7
48 46776	Marshall city	16.0	8.5	8,202	68.8	38.1	4.7	25.9	31.2	27.4	37.6	37.7
48 47892	Mesquite city	34.7	15.3	48,321	74.2	48.7	6.0	19.5	25.8	22.5	43.6	25.1
48 48072	Midland city	39.6	9.6	40,862	70.5	50.5	4.9	15.0	29.5	24.7	37.6	30.3
48 48768	Mission city	85.4	25.0	22,664	82.4	62.1	3.7	16.6	17.6	15.0	51.4	33.3

STATE and Place code	STATE or City	Total population	Percent change 2010–2012	Population by age (percent)							Median age	Race alone or in combination (percent)				
				Under 5 years	5 to 17 years	18 to 24 years	25 to 44 years	45 to 64 years	65 years and over			White	Black	Asian, Hawaiian, or Pacific Islander	American Indian, Alaska Native, or some other race
	ACS table number:	B01003	Population estimates	B01001	B01001	B01001	B01001	B01001	B01001		B01002	B02008	B02009	B02011 + B02012	B02010 + B02013
	Column number:	1	2	3	4	5	6	7	8		9	10	11	12	13
	Texas—Cont.														
48 48772	Mission Bend CDP	35,466	...	7.5	21.8	11.0	27.1	26.4	6.2		32.6	40.0	32.4	12.6	17.2
48 48804	Missouri City city	68,004	2.0	5.4	20.5	8.9	24.6	30.2	10.4		37.4	37.6	42.0	16.9	6.3
48 50256	Nacogdoches city	33,604	3.2	6.3	14.1	29.9	21.5	17.9	10.3		24.9	64.3	30.1	2.0	4.3
48 50820	New Braunfels city	59,362	4.4	7.7	20.3	8.2	28.6	21.2	14.0		34.0	93.2	3.0	1.1	4.9
48 52356	North Richland Hills city	64,370	2.8	7.5	16.1	9.7	26.7	28.0	12.0		37.5	87.6	5.1	3.3	6.0
48 53388	Odessa city	103,063	6.2	8.5	19.9	11.6	27.3	22.5	10.2		30.9	87.9	7.0	1.2	7.5
48 55080	Paris city	25,159	-0.4	7.1	16.7	10.0	24.1	25.0	17.0		38.3	72.2	26.2	1.3	3.8
48 56000	Pasadena city	150,903	1.8	8.1	21.8	10.7	27.3	23.4	8.8		31.3	75.4	3.3	2.8	20.2
48 56348	Pearland city	93,887	6.0	8.3	21.0	7.8	31.3	23.8	7.8		34.7	66.3	16.3	14.1	5.8
48 57176	Pflugerville city	50,022	6.5	8.0	22.0	6.8	28.5	28.0	6.8		35.8	73.5	16.0	9.6	3.6
48 57200	Pharr city	72,008	3.3	9.6	25.7	10.3	27.7	15.7	11.0		28.4	94.5	...	...	5.3
48 57980	Plainview city	22,250	-0.1	9.3	21.4	12.3	24.2	20.7	12.1		30.0	87.8	4.4	0.7	12.6
48 58016	Plano city	266,857	4.2	6.5	19.0	7.3	29.1	28.4	9.7		37.5	71.9	8.7	19.4	3.4
48 58820	Port Arthur city	54,088	0.1	8.5	18.8	9.5	25.3	25.9	12.1		35.3	47.6	39.9	8.3	6.8
48 61796	Richardson city	101,483	3.8	5.6	16.1	11.7	27.3	26.8	12.4		37.0	67.8	7.9	17.8	10.0
48 62828	Rockwall city	39,035	5.1	5.9	22.5	6.5	28.0	26.0	11.1		35.8	88.5	7.1	4.7	3.9
48 63284	Rosenberg city	31,248	3.1	8.2	21.2	10.6	31.6	19.7	8.7		30.5	81.6	11.6	...	6.3
48 63500	Round Rock city	104,543	5.7	9.4	20.7	9.3	32.7	21.5	6.4		31.7	82.5	10.8	5.8	4.2
48 63572	Rowlett city	58,073	2.5	4.7	21.5	9.2	27.5	28.1	8.9		37.5	75.0	16.0	6.1	5.4
48 64064	Sachse city	21,797	5.5	7.5	21.3	6.0	33.1	26.0	6.2		36.8	73.6	9.7	13.5	4.2
48 64112	Saginaw city	20,395	4.8	7.8	19.1	9.4	28.3	29.4	6.0		35.7	86.6	5.1	4.0	8.0
48 64472	San Angelo city	94,684	2.4	7.2	16.0	15.1	24.6	23.3	13.7		32.2	88.6	5.4	1.8	6.6
48 65000	San Antonio city	1,358,143	3.7	7.4	19.0	11.3	28.2	23.3	10.8		32.8	77.3	7.6	3.2	14.7
48 65036	San Benito city	24,417	0.8	9.1	24.3	8.2	25.6	19.0	13.8		31.0	88.2	...	...	12.8
48 65516	San Juan city	34,635	3.3	10.2	25.9	9.9	26.1	20.2	7.8		27.2	96.5	...	...	3.4
48 65600	San Marcos city	47,577	11.0	5.1	10.6	42.4	24.3	10.7	6.9		23.3	80.0	5.7	2.9	14.5
48 66128	Schertz city	32,976	8.8	7.0	18.1	7.6	27.1	28.1	12.2		37.1	87.3	9.4	4.6	2.3
48 66644	Seguin city	25,776	4.2	6.8	19.0	11.3	23.8	23.1	16.0		35.8	83.7	9.4	1.4	7.5
48 67496	Sherman city	38,790	2.0	6.7	17.7	13.0	27.1	22.5	12.9		33.1	77.4	12.7	2.2	11.9
48 68636	Socorro city	32,402	1.8	7.4	25.0	11.4	26.0	22.4	7.7		30.2	70.9	...	...	30.1
48 69032	Southlake city	26,873	3.9	5.1	27.8	4.2	18.8	37.3	6.9		41.7	90.2	3.1	7.4	1.6
48 69596	Spring CDP	57,151	...	8.5	22.9	8.3	28.5	23.7	8.2		32.4	65.3	22.8	4.3	11.5
48 70808	Sugar Land city	81,092	3.6	5.3	17.8	9.1	23.0	33.9	10.9		41.6	54.7	7.6	37.0	3.1
48 72176	Temple city	67,809	3.4	7.6	17.5	7.2	27.5	25.4	14.9		36.4	78.2	16.0	3.5	4.1
48 72368	Texarkana city	36,856	2.0	7.4	16.6	11.0	26.0	25.2	13.9		35.2	58.6	39.3	1.8	3.1
48 72392	Texas City city	45,395	0.8	8.6	19.3	8.1	27.2	24.2	12.6		34.0	68.0	29.4	0.6	4.0
48 72530	The Colony city	37,553	6.8	6.3	21.1	8.8	33.4	25.0	5.4		32.7	83.0	6.7	9.5	6.8
48 72656	The Woodlands CDP	101,019	...	6.9	21.9	6.4	24.3	30.0	10.5		39.4	90.7	3.2	6.4	3.2
48 73057	Timberwood Park CDP	27,519	...	8.5	22.7	5.7	30.3	26.0	6.8		35.7	87.1	3.6	6.5	4.8
48 74144	Tyler city	98,296	2.2	6.1	17.2	14.3	25.5	22.0	14.8		33.8	71.3	23.7	2.5	4.0
48 74492	University Park city	23,434	3.0	4.3	24.2	19.7	17.6	27.2	7.0		29.2	95.7	1.4	4.0	0.8
48 75428	Victoria city	63,342	2.8	7.3	19.6	9.9	24.9	24.7	13.6		35.2	84.3	9.1	1.5	10.7
48 76000	Waco city	126,250	1.3	8.1	16.6	19.2	24.5	20.4	11.2		28.8	72.1	22.0	2.2	5.7
48 76672	Watauga city	23,790	2.1	7.8	20.0	7.9	30.9	24.9	8.4		32.9	81.9	4.9	5.3	11.6
48 76816	Waxahachie city	30,405	4.3	6.5	19.1	12.4	26.4	24.4	11.2		33.0	80.5	14.4	0.7	5.6
48 76864	Weatherford city	25,886	3.6	7.3	19.7	9.9	26.1	22.9	14.2		34.7	92.6	3.1	0.7	5.0
48 77272	Weslaco city	36,321	3.3	7.7	23.4	8.4	24.4	20.0	16.1		33.4	89.8	...	1.1	9.0
48 77728	West Odessa CDP	22,890	...	10.0	22.9	10.9	25.7	22.1	8.4		29.7	92.3	0.7	...	8.6
48 79000	Wichita Falls city	104,348	-0.1	6.7	16.3	15.5	25.7	23.7	12.1		32.4	81.6	13.8	3.4	4.3
48 80356	Wylie city	42,939	6.0	7.4	25.3	8.3	31.7	20.3	6.9		33.4	76.6	12.0	8.0	6.6
49 00000	**Utah**	2,814,910	2.9	9.3	22.0	11.4	28.1	19.9	9.3		29.6	90.6	1.6	4.2	6.2
49 01310	American Fork city	26,778	2.8	10.2	28.8	9.9	25.6	16.3	9.2		26.1	95.4	...	5.1	2.3
49 07690	Bountiful city	42,794	0.5	8.2	21.2	9.3	23.7	21.9	15.7		33.5	94.3	1.2	3.6	3.2
49 11320	Cedar City city	29,069	0.6	10.2	16.8	22.8	23.9	17.6	8.7		25.1	94.8	1.0	2.8	5.8
49 13850	Clearfield city	30,320	0.6	12.3	22.8	11.0	32.4	15.8	5.7		27.2	87.8	3.2	5.5	8.7
49 14290	Clinton city	20,676	1.4	11.2	25.5	8.2	31.8	17.8	5.3		28.6	88.7	2.9	4.6	8.5
49 16270	Cottonwood Heights city	33,715	1.7	6.5	16.4	10.1	25.3	27.5	14.2		36.1	92.5	1.3	5.7	1.9
49 20120	Draper city	44,053	4.0	9.7	24.1	7.6	32.5	20.7	5.4		30.8	93.6	1.4	3.5	4.2
49 20810	Eagle Mountain city	22,525	6.9	16.5	29.7	9.4	34.9	6.9	2.6		22.1	95.7	...	2.2	2.5
49 24740	Farmington city	19,504	12.4	11.2	25.4	8.1	29.1	18.8	7.4		28.6	96.6	1.0	...	2.1
49 34970	Herriman city	23,457	8.4	11.1	36.2	6.7	32.9	9.8	3.3		19.9	96.4	1.0	1.9	...
49 36070	Holladay city	26,699	1.7	6.2	18.3	8.0	24.0	25.8	17.7		39.3	95.5	0.4	4.1	0.9
49 40360	Kaysville city	27,890	3.1	9.2	27.8	9.3	26.5	20.2	7.0		28.0	96.4	0.8	1.4	1.6
49 40470	Kearns CDP	33,346	...	9.9	24.1	9.3	30.3	20.7	5.7		28.5	88.4	1.7	7.8	6.6
49 43660	Layton city	68,165	1.6	10.2	22.1	10.7	28.4	20.9	7.6		29.6	90.9	2.5	4.8	4.8
49 44320	Lehi city	49,482	6.9	13.3	31.4	7.3	30.7	13.0	4.2		23.3	94.9	0.6	3.1	3.1
49 45860	Logan city	48,733	1.0	9.9	14.8	29.8	28.0	11.0	6.5		24.0	89.6	2.0	3.7	6.6
49 47290	Magna CDP	28,403	...	9.8	24.7	9.4	31.0	19.0	6.1		28.8	90.4	1.2	6.3	6.5
49 49710	Midvale city	29,037	6.9	7.0	17.6	11.6	34.2	19.0	10.5		30.9	85.0	2.0	6.0	12.5
49 50150	Millcreek CDP	62,727	...	6.9	15.3	9.5	29.8	23.3	15.2		35.5	90.1	2.3	5.8	3.4
49 53230	Murray city	47,439	3.2	6.7	16.9	10.9	28.0	24.3	13.2		34.3	92.7	1.8	2.6	4.4
49 55980	Ogden city	83,375	0.9	9.5	19.5	12.5	29.8	19.5	9.3		29.4	77.8	2.9	2.7	19.9
49 57300	Orem city	89,712	2.3	10.8	19.4	16.3	27.8	17.4	8.4		26.7	92.3	1.3	4.3	5.9
49 60930	Pleasant Grove city	34,125	2.4	11.2	26.3	11.6	28.4	14.6	7.9		25.6	97.9	0.6	1.5	1.0
49 62470	Provo city	114,467	2.7	8.6	13.7	35.1	25.6	11.0	5.9		23.7	90.3	1.4	6.1	5.6
49 64340	Riverton city	39,615	3.9	10.8	26.6	7.8	30.8	18.4	5.6		28.8	96.7	...	3.3	0.6
49 65110	Roy city	37,271	1.6	9.3	22.8	8.6	29.3	20.3	9.7		30.3	90.4	2.1	3.4	6.3
49 65330	St. George city	74,225	3.5	7.9	21.2	10.4	23.9	18.8	17.7		32.6	93.5	1.4	2.6	4.8
49 67000	Salt Lake City city	187,964	1.5	7.7	15.0	13.4	34.3	20.1	9.5		31.1	78.0	3.8	8.0	12.9
49 67440	Sandy city	88,451	2.0	7.1	21.3	8.9	27.2	25.6	9.9		34.3	93.1	0.9	5.9	3.1
49 67825	Saratoga Springs city	19,414	17.1	17.2	30.7	5.6	33.8	9.6	3.1		19.4	92.9	2.9	4.5	...
49 70850	South Jordan city	53,520	9.1	10.0	23.7	9.8	27.9	21.2	7.3		29.0	95.2	1.0	5.1	1.5

Table A-4. Cities — Who: Age, Race/Ethnicity, and Household Structure, 2010–2012—*Continued*

STATE and Place code	STATE or City	Percent Hispanic or Latino	Percent foreign born	Total households	Family households				Nonfamily households		Percent of households with people under 18 years	Percent of households with people 60 years and over
					Total family households	Married-couple families	Male household families	Female household families	Total nonfamily households	One-person households		
	ACS table number:	B03003	C05003	B11001	B11001	B11001	B11001	B11001	B11001	B11001	B11005	B11006
	Column number:	14	15	16	17	18	19	20	21	22	23	24
	Texas—Cont.											
48 48772	Mission Bend CDP	45.8	37.8	10,093	83.2	57.8	6.8	18.6	16.8	14.3	49.0	23.7
48 48804	Missouri City city	18.0	22.6	22,382	80.9	60.9	3.8	16.2	19.1	17.4	40.8	34.2
48 50256	Nacogdoches city	18.8	10.3	12,039	53.7	30.3	4.6	18.8	46.3	36.5	29.2	26.4
48 50820	New Braunfels city	35.5	6.7	21,531	70.0	53.0	3.0	14.0	30.0	24.8	40.0	34.1
48 52356	North Richland Hills city	17.3	8.8	24,745	67.9	52.8	4.0	11.1	32.1	27.8	33.0	32.1
48 53388	Odessa city	52.2	12.1	37,223	67.9	46.1	6.1	15.7	32.1	26.2	39.4	29.0
48 55080	Paris city	5.0	3.6	10,026	63.7	37.8	6.7	19.2	36.3	33.7	32.2	38.8
48 56000	Pasadena city	62.3	25.4	48,255	71.3	50.0	6.3	15.1	28.7	24.7	44.1	29.3
48 56348	Pearland city	21.7	17.2	32,096	79.3	62.3	4.3	12.7	20.7	18.3	48.8	23.2
48 57176	Pflugerville city	25.9	13.0	17,303	74.2	57.8	2.9	13.6	25.8	21.4	44.6	24.2
48 57200	Pharr city	93.5	31.4	19,993	82.3	54.1	6.3	21.9	17.7	14.9	53.0	34.8
48 57980	Plainview city	60.3	11.1	7,424	73.5	53.5	3.1	16.9	26.5	23.4	46.2	29.3
48 58016	Plano city	15.0	24.3	99,888	71.2	56.9	4.2	10.1	28.8	24.2	39.0	27.0
48 58820	Port Arthur city	30.5	20.5	19,967	63.4	35.4	5.9	22.1	36.6	31.5	35.0	32.2
48 61796	Richardson city	16.4	23.7	38,786	67.1	51.5	4.0	11.6	32.9	25.3	32.1	30.1
48 62828	Rockwall city	16.5	10.0	13,409	78.9	64.9	3.5	10.5	21.1	16.8	42.3	33.0
48 63284	Rosenberg city	59.1	16.0	9,928	74.1	45.8	9.5	18.8	25.9	22.4	42.9	25.9
48 63500	Round Rock city	30.9	14.5	34,847	72.0	54.9	5.3	11.8	28.0	21.4	44.9	19.5
48 63572	Rowlett city	18.4	12.3	18,552	84.6	68.7	4.0	11.9	15.4	13.1	46.9	26.1
48 64064	Sachse city	18.4	19.2	7,181	84.3	64.6	8.0	11.8	15.7	12.5	52.9	24.3
48 64112	Saginaw city	22.1	7.2	7,031	79.4	62.0	3.9	13.4	20.6	18.7	42.4	28.0
48 64472	San Angelo city	39.6	6.6	35,375	64.7	43.7	5.3	15.7	35.3	29.5	32.0	34.0
48 65000	San Antonio city	63.3	14.3	476,131	65.8	42.4	5.8	17.6	34.2	28.4	36.8	30.3
48 65036	San Benito city	92.1	20.1	7,052	78.7	50.2	3.7	24.8	21.3	17.8	46.0	42.3
48 65516	San Juan city	98.1	30.7	9,017	84.3	59.7	3.6	20.9	15.7	14.5	57.4	30.1
48 65600	San Marcos city	39.8	5.1	17,030	39.6	25.0	4.3	10.3	60.4	32.8	21.4	17.4
48 66128	Schertz city	27.8	7.6	12,151	73.2	59.5	2.6	11.1	26.8	23.0	38.7	35.7
48 66644	Seguin city	50.7	8.3	8,733	67.1	43.3	4.8	19.0	32.9	28.1	36.1	41.2
48 67496	Sherman city	22.1	10.5	14,571	65.2	42.9	4.7	17.7	34.8	27.6	36.1	32.9
48 68636	Socorro city	97.2	35.5	8,812	87.4	52.0	10.5	25.0	12.6	10.7	56.4	33.0
48 69032	Southlake city	5.0	8.1	8,661	85.2	78.4	1.2	5.6	14.8	13.2	51.6	27.0
48 69596	Spring CDP	29.3	11.9	17,728	78.6	58.7	4.7	15.2	21.4	19.2	45.7	26.2
48 70808	Sugar Land city	11.2	34.1	26,237	84.3	72.6	3.2	8.6	15.7	14.3	41.7	36.1
48 72176	Temple city	22.4	7.9	24,155	67.2	50.1	4.5	12.6	32.8	29.1	35.7	35.8
48 72368	Texarkana city	7.3	4.0	13,925	59.6	36.3	4.5	18.7	40.4	36.7	30.2	37.8
48 72392	Texas City city	27.9	6.5	16,019	70.3	41.4	6.4	22.5	29.7	26.3	38.5	34.9
48 72530	The Colony city	19.5	14.8	13,572	64.7	48.0	4.3	12.4	35.3	26.6	38.9	20.2
48 72656	The Woodlands CDP	14.9	14.4	36,759	74.1	63.2	4.4	6.5	25.9	22.8	39.0	28.6
48 73057	Timberwood Park CDP	25.7	11.0	8,699	86.0	76.0	1.3	8.7	14.0	10.3	52.4	20.2
48 74144	Tyler city	22.6	12.0	38,832	60.0	41.0	4.1	14.8	40.0	32.8	30.1	34.4
48 74492	University Park city	3.7	5.1	7,144	78.9	65.7	2.7	10.5	21.1	15.0	49.1	28.6
48 75428	Victoria city	47.6	5.5	23,833	67.4	43.4	5.7	18.3	32.6	28.6	36.7	34.1
48 76000	Waco city	31.8	10.7	45,326	59.7	37.5	4.9	17.3	40.3	31.2	33.1	28.7
48 76672	Watauga city	23.1	11.6	8,070	75.5	56.4	5.4	13.7	24.5	18.9	41.0	25.1
48 76816	Waxahachie city	22.8	6.3	10,405	73.0	53.9	3.8	15.3	27.0	22.2	38.4	32.4
48 76864	Weatherford city	16.6	5.1	9,821	67.4	51.0	4.8	11.7	32.6	28.0	37.4	35.7
48 77272	Weslaco city	82.4	21.0	11,342	78.6	49.4	6.2	23.0	21.4	20.0	45.4	41.4
48 77728	West Odessa CDP	58.0	16.6	7,364	73.8	50.7	8.6	14.5	26.2	21.1	46.8	26.0
48 79000	Wichita Falls city	20.3	8.2	36,659	63.2	44.3	4.4	14.5	36.8	31.6	32.5	33.0
48 80356	Wylie city	18.9	10.5	13,645	80.2	65.9	2.2	12.1	19.8	17.9	53.5	17.2
49 00000	**Utah**	13.2	8.3	886,032	75.0	60.9	4.2	9.9	25.0	19.6	42.5	28.0
49 01310	American Fork city	5.9	4.7	7,185	80.7	70.5	2.1	8.1	19.3	16.9	51.7	28.8
49 07690	Bountiful city	6.5	3.9	13,871	78.8	67.2	3.6	8.0	21.2	17.9	40.8	35.8
49 11320	Cedar City city	7.1	3.6	9,933	69.6	55.7	5.3	8.6	30.4	21.6	38.5	24.4
49 13850	Clearfield city	15.9	6.2	9,648	74.3	55.3	4.8	14.2	25.7	20.8	49.3	18.5
49 14290	Clinton city	12.0	5.5	6,087	86.7	70.2	3.8	12.7	13.3	11.8	54.3	19.8
49 16270	Cottonwood Heights city	5.2	7.0	12,078	75.3	63.2	3.6	8.4	24.7	20.5	32.6	35.2
49 20120	Draper city	6.5	6.1	11,995	85.2	69.7	5.2	10.3	14.8	11.7	51.5	22.0
49 20810	Eagle Mountain city	5.9	4.1	5,319	92.4	80.3	6.0	6.1	7.6	5.7	73.5	9.7
49 24744	Farmington city	3.0	3.5	5,624	86.9	77.6	3.4	5.9	13.1	11.2	51.8	24.6
49 34970	Herriman city	10.7	6.2	5,809	89.5	74.3	3.7	11.4	10.5	9.0	72.7	10.6
49 36070	Holladay city	4.9	6.0	10,370	65.9	55.1	1.8	8.9	34.1	30.1	28.0	41.8
49 40360	Kaysville city	5.2	2.6	7,938	83.6	72.6	3.0	8.0	16.4	13.6	52.8	23.8
49 40470	Kearns CDP	32.3	15.5	9,274	81.2	61.8	5.3	14.2	18.8	14.7	50.4	25.3
49 43660	Layton city	10.3	7.0	21,561	78.7	63.1	4.6	11.0	21.3	16.3	46.5	24.9
49 44320	Lehi city	8.3	3.8	12,477	88.8	79.7	2.0	7.1	11.2	9.3	64.3	16.4
49 45860	Logan city	15.5	11.6	15,885	65.3	52.4	2.1	10.8	34.7	19.4	34.6	19.2
49 47290	Magna CDP	22.3	10.9	7,826	83.0	62.7	7.3	13.0	17.0	11.2	54.8	22.2
49 49710	Midvale city	28.1	15.1	10,958	62.5	42.6	5.3	14.6	37.5	30.5	32.0	25.2
49 50150	Millcreek CDP	6.0	10.4	24,499	59.0	45.4	4.2	9.4	41.0	30.2	28.2	33.7
49 53230	Murray city	10.5	6.5	18,413	62.6	47.7	4.7	10.2	37.4	28.8	29.0	31.6
49 55980	Ogden city	29.8	13.3	28,687	66.1	45.1	5.6	15.4	33.9	25.1	39.0	26.8
49 57300	Orem city	15.2	10.2	26,071	79.6	64.5	4.1	11.0	20.4	14.5	45.1	27.6
49 60930	Pleasant Grove city	10.2	4.8	9,617	82.2	70.7	1.4	10.1	17.8	14.6	52.9	24.2
49 62470	Provo city	17.2	12.1	31,937	69.8	57.3	4.6	7.9	30.2	14.9	36.0	19.3
49 64340	Riverton city	4.8	2.3	10,995	89.5	79.6	2.3	7.6	10.5	9.1	58.0	16.5
49 65110	Roy city	14.4	6.2	12,250	77.9	62.6	4.4	11.0	22.1	19.5	44.4	27.6
49 65330	St. George city	12.0	7.2	25,259	72.0	60.8	3.0	8.1	28.0	22.5	33.5	42.3
49 67000	Salt Lake City city	20.9	17.5	74,037	52.0	36.6	4.6	10.8	48.0	36.6	28.2	25.6
49 67440	Sandy city	6.8	6.9	28,158	78.8	66.0	4.7	8.1	21.2	16.6	41.9	30.9
49 67825	Saratoga Springs city	4.2	3.7	4,723	91.6	86.9	0.7	4.0	8.4	8.0	77.0	11.7
49 70850	South Jordan city	5.8	5.1	14,302	84.8	76.9	2.4	5.6	15.2	10.3	49.0	28.9

Table A-4. Cities — Who: Age, Race/Ethnicity, and Household Structure, 2010–2012—*Continued*

STATE and Place code	STATE or City	Total population	Percent change 2010–2012	Population by age (percent)						Median age	Race alone or in combination (percent)			
				Under 5 years	5 to 17 years	18 to 24 years	25 to 44 years	45 to 64 years	65 years and over		White	Black	Asian, Hawaiian, or Pacific Islander	American Indian, Alaska Native, or some other race
	ACS table number:	B01003	Population estimates	B01001	B01001	B01001	B01001	B01001	B01001	B01002	B02008	B02009	B02011 + B02012	B02010 + B02013
	Column number:	1	2	3	4	5	6	7	8	9	10	11	12	13
	Utah—Cont.													
49 71070	South Salt Lake city	24,023	2.8	9.7	16.2	12.2	36.3	19.4	6.1	29.2	71.4	4.5	10.9	15.4
49 71290	Spanish Fork city	35,718	3.4	11.7	28.5	10.2	30.6	14.0	5.1	24.8	96.5	0.3	...	3.8
49 72280	Springville city	30,180	3.1	13.0	23.9	11.7	27.9	15.3	8.2	25.9	93.6	0.4	1.5	6.6
49 74810	Syracuse city	24,810	2.6	9.6	32.3	6.7	28.1	17.6	5.6	27.1	95.2	2.1	2.9	0.9
49 75360	Taylorsville city	59,590	2.6	8.8	19.0	10.3	29.9	22.6	9.4	31.4	84.6	3.0	6.2	9.6
49 76680	Tooele city	31,986	1.2	9.6	25.3	8.0	29.4	19.8	7.9	29.9	94.0	1.1	2.3	4.4
49 81960	Washington city	19,922	10.7	11.2	17.9	9.3	26.6	17.4	17.6	30.7	94.3	0.7	4.6	1.5
49 82950	West Jordan city	106,387	4.0	9.5	23.9	10.7	30.7	20.3	4.9	29.0	91.3	2.2	4.8	5.0
49 83470	West Valley City city	130,981	2.1	10.1	22.4	10.3	30.3	19.7	7.2	29.7	78.3	3.4	10.3	11.8
50 00000	**Vermont**	626,172	0.0	5.0	15.2	10.5	23.4	30.8	15.1	42.0	97.1	1.5	1.8	1.6
50 10675	Burlington city	42,378	-0.3	3.1	9.1	33.2	25.3	19.6	9.8	27.2	91.2	4.9	4.8	2.3
51 00000	**Virginia**	8,105,120	2.0	6.3	16.6	10.1	27.4	27.1	12.6	37.5	71.8	20.8	6.9	3.7
51 01000	Alexandria city	143,737	3.9	7.3	10.0	6.8	42.2	24.4	9.3	35.6	67.2	23.2	8.1	5.7
51 01912	Annandale CDP	42,025	...	6.9	14.6	8.9	27.3	29.7	12.6	39.2	57.5	8.3	29.2	9.7
51 03000	Arlington CDP	215,481	...	5.7	10.2	9.0	44.0	22.3	8.7	33.7	74.1	9.5	11.5	8.4
51 03320	Ashburn CDP	46,673	...	9.0	20.6	5.9	32.9	23.3	8.3	34.8	71.0	10.6	20.2	5.9
51 04088	Bailey's Crossroads CDP	24,069	...	7.3	14.0	10.8	34.1	22.6	11.3	37.4	50.8	20.1	9.9	22.9
51 07784	Blacksburg town	42,683	-0.2	2.9	7.3	57.3	18.3	9.7	4.4	21.8	81.9	5.3	13.5	2.1
51 11464	Burke CDP	41,198	...	6.3	20.5	7.2	24.0	30.7	11.2	39.4	72.4	4.1	23.6	3.0
51 13720	Cave Spring CDP	26,251	...	4.7	15.4	8.2	24.5	29.0	18.1	42.8	89.7	5.1	5.3	0.6
51 14440	Centreville CDP	73,918	...	7.2	19.6	8.8	33.1	26.3	5.1	33.1	59.5	9.5	30.4	8.7
51 14744	Chantilly CDP	21,408	...	7.0	20.8	7.4	26.8	30.6	7.4	36.2	55.9	9.6	24.6	11.8
51 14968	Charlottesville city	43,644	0.9	5.4	9.8	26.8	30.2	18.7	9.1	28.5	71.6	21.0	8.0	1.4
51 16000	Chesapeake city	225,844	2.1	6.4	19.0	9.4	26.5	28.0	10.8	36.8	64.8	31.4	4.4	2.5
51 16096	Chester CDP	23,190	...	6.6	18.7	10.1	26.2	27.0	11.3	36.0	76.7	22.1	1.3	0.4
51 16608	Christiansburg town	21,251	1.7	8.4	15.4	9.8	32.4	22.2	11.8	32.9	91.5	7.6	1.7	...
51 21088	Dale City CDP	67,551	...	7.1	20.9	10.1	28.5	26.4	7.0	32.8	50.9	34.4	10.3	10.2
51 21344	Danville city	42,888	0.3	6.6	15.1	9.8	21.6	27.9	19.0	42.3	48.9	49.5	1.2	2.0
51 26496	Fairfax city	23,010	3.7	6.3	13.9	9.7	29.1	26.5	14.5	39.1	73.9	6.3	17.4	6.2
51 26875	Fair Oaks CDP	31,705	...	9.3	10.9	10.9	40.7	22.1	6.1	32.4	60.5	11.3	31.3	1.7
51 29628	Franklin Farm CDP	19,623	...	5.1	22.7	6.9	23.4	37.6	4.4	40.2	77.1	4.7	20.5	1.7
51 29744	Fredericksburg city	25,869	11.7	7.4	13.0	21.5	27.5	20.9	9.7	28.3	69.2	24.7	3.8	6.1
51 35000	Hampton city	136,855	-0.5	6.4	16.1	12.7	25.5	26.7	12.6	35.7	45.1	52.1	3.3	2.6
51 35624	Harrisonburg city	49,878	3.9	5.0	10.5	40.0	22.6	14.2	7.7	22.7	87.5	8.8	4.7	1.8
51 36648	Herndon town	23,852	3.7	7.2	17.7	7.2	37.2	24.1	6.6	33.4	56.6	12.1	17.5	16.9
51 38424	Hopewell city	22,492	-1.3	9.3	17.1	11.1	23.1	24.3	15.1	35.8	59.1	42.2	...	...
51 43432	Lake Ridge CDP	43,575	...	8.4	18.3	8.7	29.3	27.4	8.0	34.7	64.2	23.5	12.4	5.8
51 44984	Leesburg town	44,486	6.7	9.3	20.8	7.4	32.5	23.6	6.3	33.4	77.1	10.5	8.3	7.1
51 45784	Lincolnia CDP	23,592	...	8.1	16.0	9.0	33.5	25.4	7.9	33.0	49.8	21.0	17.0	15.4
51 45957	Linton Hall CDP	39,016	...	11.5	23.5	5.2	35.8	20.2	3.9	33.6	77.7	13.4	10.5	2.9
51 47672	Lynchburg city	76,377	1.8	6.1	13.6	22.5	22.3	21.8	13.7	30.2	67.2	30.9	3.0	2.5
51 48376	McLean CDP	48,051	...	4.6	22.0	5.7	16.9	33.9	16.9	45.4	79.4	1.3	20.8	2.1
51 48450	McNair CDP	20,352	...	11.2	10.4	9.9	50.8	14.5	3.2	31.1	38.2	18.3	37.8	9.2
51 48952	Manassas city	39,394	6.1	8.3	19.6	10.1	29.9	24.8	7.3	32.4	77.7	16.2	5.9	4.1
51 49792	Marumsco CDP	39,502	...	9.3	19.7	9.1	35.5	19.5	6.8	30.1	55.1	22.0	9.7	17.8
51 50856	Mechanicsville CDP	36,951	...	6.7	19.0	5.9	26.8	26.9	14.7	39.4	86.6	9.9	2.7	3.2
51 52658	Montclair CDP	19,944	...	5.4	22.5	8.3	26.0	27.7	10.2	38.0	66.4	26.5	5.9	6.6
51 56000	Newport News city	180,623	-0.1	7.5	16.6	13.5	27.7	24.0	10.8	32.4	54.0	42.9	4.7	3.7
51 57000	Norfolk city	244,118	1.2	6.9	13.9	19.7	28.7	21.3	9.4	29.6	50.8	45.0	5.1	3.3
51 58472	Oakton CDP	37,082	...	7.9	15.2	5.1	34.9	24.4	12.5	37.2	68.9	7.6	19.3	6.2
51 61832	Petersburg city	32,213	-1.9	7.2	14.1	11.7	23.8	28.2	15.0	40.6	19.0	80.8	0.5	0.4
51 64000	Portsmouth city	95,915	1.0	7.5	16.3	10.8	26.8	25.3	13.3	35.1	43.0	55.0	1.7	3.1
51 66672	Reston CDP	58,190	...	7.6	13.8	5.7	33.7	28.2	11.0	38.0	76.9	11.1	12.0	3.5
51 67000	Richmond city	206,936	2.9	6.5	12.5	16.7	29.6	23.5	11.2	32.3	45.9	51.5	2.9	3.7
51 68000	Roanoke city	96,958	0.7	7.3	14.4	8.7	28.4	27.1	14.2	38.3	68.6	30.6	2.2	3.0
51 70000	Salem city	24,868	0.5	5.5	14.4	13.5	22.9	27.5	16.3	40.1	88.0	8.4	2.0	2.3
51 72272	Short Pump CDP	26,753	...	6.9	23.6	6.4	30.3	24.4	8.3	35.1	78.9	4.8	17.0	...
51 74100	South Riding CDP	23,740	...	8.3	26.4	4.5	35.7	20.0	5.1	34.9	58.8	8.3	34.7	5.1
51 74592	Springfield CDP	31,063	...	6.5	13.3	7.6	30.7	25.8	16.1	38.1	61.2	9.9	26.6	6.1
51 75216	Staunton city	23,941	0.4	5.6	13.3	10.4	24.3	26.4	20.0	42.7	86.4	14.3	1.1	1.7
51 75376	Sterling CDP	26,241	...	8.7	15.1	10.3	35.3	22.1	8.5	32.3	63.1	11.0	12.8	17.1
51 76432	Suffolk city	84,942	0.3	6.8	18.8	8.6	26.2	27.9	11.8	38.4	54.9	44.4	2.4	2.5
51 79560	Tuckahoe CDP	44,890	...	6.0	18.2	7.6	24.7	27.1	16.4	40.1	83.3	10.4	6.1	1.8
51 79952	Tysons Corner CDP	21,799	...	5.5	15.9	4.7	40.4	23.9	9.7	35.4	68.1	8.7	26.8	3.8
51 82000	Virginia Beach city	443,102	1.8	6.6	17.0	10.8	29.1	25.6	10.9	34.8	72.1	21.7	8.3	2.8
51 83680	Waynesboro city	21,082	0.3	6.7	18.5	7.4	25.6	25.1	16.7	38.1	83.7	15.4	1.2	2.1
51 84368	West Falls Church CDP	27,775	...	7.6	15.2	6.4	32.8	27.0	11.1	37.4	60.0	6.3	22.6	17.4
51 84976	West Springfield CDP	24,344	...	6.3	17.3	7.3	26.8	29.5	12.9	40.6	73.7	8.6	18.5	2.1
51 86720	Winchester city	26,537	2.5	6.4	16.2	11.8	27.3	24.9	13.5	35.1	82.9	11.5	2.6	5.0
53 00000	**Washington**	6,821,303	2.3	6.5	16.7	9.7	27.4	27.0	12.7	37.3	82.6	4.9	10.8	7.4
53 03180	Auburn city	71,743	4.4	6.1	18.1	11.0	27.2	26.4	11.2	36.3	74.6	8.0	13.1	11.9
53 03736	Bainbridge Island city	23,174	0.8	3.5	19.2	4.1	18.3	36.4	18.5	47.9	93.4	...	7.0	3.2
53 05210	Bellevue city	124,646	3.0	5.4	14.6	8.4	31.1	26.8	13.7	37.6	65.6	3.2	31.9	4.0
53 05280	Bellingham city	81,647	1.5	5.0	10.7	24.2	25.7	21.5	12.9	30.9	90.2	1.9	6.4	5.4
53 07380	Bothell city	34,108	3.1	5.4	16.0	7.0	28.9	30.9	11.8	40.5	83.9	1.9	13.6	3.9
53 07695	Bremerton city	38,711	3.8	7.8	11.9	18.3	30.0	21.7	10.3	30.9	80.2	8.2	7.9	12.2
53 08850	Burien city	48,807	2.5	7.3	16.4	8.8	27.5	27.2	12.9	37.5	68.0	11.4	16.8	11.6

Table A-4. Cities — Who: Age, Race/Ethnicity, and Household Structure, 2010–2012—*Continued*

STATE and Place code	STATE or City	Percent Hispanic or Latino	Percent foreign born	Total households	Household type (percent) Family households Total family households	Married-couple families	Male household families	Female household families	Nonfamily households Total nonfamily households	One-person households	Percent of households with people under 18 years	Percent of households with people 60 years and over
	ACS table number:	B03003	C05003	B11001	B11001	B11001	B11001	B11001	B11001	B11001	B11005	B11006
	Column number:	14	15	16	17	18	19	20	21	22	23	24
	Utah—Cont.											
49 71070	South Salt Lake city	29.7	27.6	8,504	55.9	34.1	7.5	14.3	44.1	33.0	33.8	21.3
49 71290	Spanish Fork city	9.7	6.2	9,179	84.0	75.0	2.2	6.8	16.0	13.3	60.3	16.8
49 72280	Springville city	7.9	6.0	8,751	83.6	70.0	5.4	8.2	16.4	13.7	54.4	25.4
49 74810	Syracuse city	5.3	2.2	6,605	90.3	79.7	3.5	7.1	9.7	8.4	57.6	21.6
49 75360	Taylorsville city	21.6	13.3	19,633	71.4	54.7	3.3	13.4	28.6	23.3	38.1	30.4
49 76680	Tooele city	13.4	2.4	10,218	76.9	59.6	4.9	12.5	23.1	18.8	48.4	29.8
49 81960	Washington city	11.2	6.8	6,770	81.7	67.4	3.3	11.0	18.3	17.1	35.4	40.2
49 82950	West Jordan city	19.3	9.8	30,840	80.4	64.2	5.2	10.9	19.6	16.0	49.7	21.1
49 83470	West Valley City city	34.9	21.8	37,418	80.8	56.5	7.0	17.3	19.2	15.9	49.7	26.0
50 00000	**Vermont**	1.5	4.1	257,887	62.5	49.2	4.2	9.0	37.5	28.2	27.7	36.7
50 10675	Burlington city	2.4	8.2	16,744	38.9	27.5	4.1	7.3	61.1	37.1	17.7	25.3
51 00000	**Virginia**	8.1	11.4	3,007,690	67.3	50.8	4.2	12.3	32.7	26.5	33.0	33.7
51 01000	Alexandria city	16.4	26.6	64,754	47.6	35.8	3.5	8.3	52.4	42.9	21.5	23.0
51 01912	Annandale CDP	29.2	44.5	13,746	69.8	48.9	5.3	15.7	30.2	25.2	34.8	39.7
51 03000	Arlington CDP	15.2	23.5	93,236	46.1	36.5	3.1	6.5	53.9	40.2	20.0	21.9
51 03320	Ashburn CDP	11.7	24.8	15,475	79.0	63.4	4.0	11.6	21.0	16.8	48.7	24.6
51 04088	Bailey's Crossroads CDP	38.8	55.0	8,922	58.9	37.0	8.5	13.4	41.1	33.0	30.5	30.9
51 07784	Blacksburg town	3.3	16.5	13,327	34.9	28.5	1.7	4.7	65.1	28.5	18.2	13.2
51 11464	Burke CDP	9.9	23.2	13,207	85.5	73.9	4.1	7.5	14.5	11.5	43.5	37.9
51 13720	Cave Spring CDP	1.4	7.2	11,742	62.3	49.0	3.6	9.8	37.7	33.3	26.8	37.7
51 14440	Centreville CDP	15.4	33.9	24,536	72.1	57.6	4.6	9.9	27.9	20.0	43.6	20.3
51 14744	Chantilly CDP	20.6	31.0	6,795	84.2	62.6	5.4	16.2	15.8	11.3	47.2	32.5
51 14968	Charlottesville city	5.0	12.7	17,142	41.9	29.0	3.5	9.5	58.1	37.8	20.5	25.3
51 16000	Chesapeake city	4.6	5.1	78,867	74.4	54.9	4.8	14.7	25.6	21.2	38.9	31.3
51 16096	Chester CDP	11.4	8.4	8,461	69.2	41.1	7.2	21.0	30.8	25.2	38.7	30.0
51 16608	Christiansburg town	3.2	2.3	8,838	64.4	48.2	3.9	12.2	35.6	28.6	32.1	30.4
51 21088	Dale City CDP	25.3	24.9	20,269	80.3	56.9	8.0	15.4	19.7	15.4	47.7	25.7
51 21344	Danville city	3.0	3.3	18,481	61.3	35.6	4.3	21.3	38.7	35.4	28.7	42.2
51 26496	Fairfax city	16.0	23.9	8,358	67.1	55.3	4.2	7.7	32.9	21.4	29.8	35.1
51 26875	Fair Oaks CDP	8.8	32.7	13,939	52.1	39.1	4.1	8.9	47.9	33.7	28.0	16.4
51 29628	Franklin Farm CDP	5.6	16.6	6,260	91.2	79.9	0.9	10.4	8.8	7.0	49.7	25.4
51 29744	Fredericksburg city	10.9	8.1	9,629	54.3	33.9	3.7	16.7	45.7	36.4	29.9	27.9
51 35000	Hampton city	4.8	4.6	51,699	64.4	42.7	4.1	17.6	35.6	29.7	30.9	32.3
51 35624	Harrisonburg city	16.6	15.8	15,268	49.8	38.1	5.6	6.1	50.2	24.8	25.1	21.6
51 36648	Herndon town	35.1	43.1	7,575	71.7	56.6	6.7	8.5	28.3	19.6	42.8	25.5
51 38424	Hopewell city	6.5	3.3	8,593	61.3	35.9	5.5	19.9	38.7	34.4	32.9	40.1
51 43432	Lake Ridge CDP	16.6	21.5	14,319	75.2	59.4	4.3	11.6	24.8	20.3	42.7	31.3
51 44984	Leesburg town	20.9	23.6	14,162	75.2	60.0	4.9	10.3	24.8	17.9	48.8	20.8
51 45784	Lincolnia CDP	30.7	46.4	7,795	64.5	45.7	7.2	11.6	35.5	25.6	33.6	25.5
51 45957	Linton Hall CDP	11.8	14.0	11,306	88.5	74.3	4.7	9.5	11.5	8.4	60.4	14.4
51 47672	Lynchburg city	3.1	4.5	28,363	56.2	38.5	3.1	14.6	43.8	35.9	29.0	35.4
51 48376	McLean CDP	6.3	24.6	16,746	80.3	71.8	2.6	5.9	19.7	17.9	39.9	46.5
51 48450	McNair CDP	14.1	39.9	8,103	61.8	49.9	4.1	7.8	38.2	29.7	34.1	10.1
51 48952	Manassas city	31.9	25.9	12,204	75.8	53.9	5.9	15.9	24.2	19.4	42.9	23.5
51 49792	Marumsco CDP	40.4	35.3	11,812	71.2	41.9	10.5	18.8	28.8	22.0	47.8	21.7
51 50856	Mechanicsville CDP	2.6	4.5	13,627	74.7	61.2	4.6	9.0	25.3	21.0	38.1	36.1
51 52658	Montclair CDP	8.7	12.3	6,584	82.9	68.3	4.8	9.7	17.1	16.3	45.3	31.9
51 56000	Newport News city	7.7	7.2	69,003	63.1	40.1	5.3	17.7	36.9	30.8	32.7	29.2
51 57000	Norfolk city	6.9	6.5	85,626	57.3	34.1	5.4	17.8	42.7	32.8	31.0	27.9
51 58472	Oakton CDP	17.4	35.2	13,392	71.5	58.9	5.1	7.5	28.5	21.5	35.0	33.8
51 61832	Petersburg city	3.8	3.2	12,031	58.6	27.4	3.3	28.0	41.4	34.7	24.2	40.1
51 64000	Portsmouth city	3.2	2.4	36,752	64.7	36.6	5.8	22.3	35.3	30.7	32.3	35.2
51 66672	Reston CDP	13.8	22.2	25,214	58.2	47.9	1.8	8.6	41.8	34.7	27.5	27.5
51 67000	Richmond city	6.3	7.5	83,747	46.5	23.5	4.5	18.4	53.5	41.8	23.8	29.5
51 68000	Roanoke city	5.6	7.0	41,819	55.0	33.3	4.3	17.4	45.0	38.6	25.8	35.5
51 70000	Salem city	2.6	6.6	9,820	61.5	45.4	3.1	13.1	38.5	33.0	29.4	36.0
51 72272	Short Pump CDP	3.8	20.1	9,346	73.8	64.1	4.1	5.7	26.2	21.7	47.0	22.1
51 74100	South Riding CDP	8.3	30.0	7,037	86.7	76.4	4.6	5.7	13.3	9.9	65.4	18.6
51 74592	Springfield CDP	25.1	43.9	10,104	67.6	52.8	6.9	7.9	32.4	27.2	33.0	46.7
51 75216	Staunton city	2.4	3.5	10,809	58.1	41.2	3.6	13.3	41.9	36.7	26.3	39.3
51 75376	Sterling CDP	32.8	35.1	8,699	67.5	49.3	4.7	13.5	32.5	24.5	40.2	25.6
51 76432	Suffolk city	3.0	2.7	30,657	74.4	53.8	4.3	16.3	25.6	21.5	38.4	33.8
51 79560	Tuckahoe CDP	6.1	16.2	18,052	63.5	50.7	2.7	10.0	36.5	30.5	33.3	39.1
51 79952	Tysons Corner CDP	10.3	38.2	9,814	57.3	43.6	3.3	10.5	42.7	36.5	28.1	22.3
51 82000	Virginia Beach city	6.9	8.8	164,066	68.4	51.0	3.5	14.0	31.6	23.7	35.3	29.7
51 83680	Waynesboro city	6.5	3.7	8,592	65.3	44.4	4.2	16.8	34.7	30.4	32.5	40.7
51 84368	West Falls Church CDP	27.6	37.9	9,919	67.3	49.3	4.9	13.1	32.7	26.5	33.8	33.5
51 84976	West Springfield CDP	8.3	23.7	8,352	74.3	61.7	3.9	8.7	25.7	20.8	38.3	35.2
51 86720	Winchester city	15.7	11.6	10,668	55.4	37.7	4.5	13.2	44.6	33.5	28.6	33.4
53 00000	**Washington**	11.5	13.3	2,624,689	64.2	49.4	4.4	10.4	35.8	28.0	31.4	33.1
53 03180	Auburn city	15.1	18.8	27,345	65.5	44.0	5.9	15.6	34.5	27.3	35.6	30.3
53 03736	Bainbridge Island city	4.0	7.4	9,338	70.1	57.5	3.4	9.2	29.9	26.2	31.4	44.5
53 05210	Bellevue city	6.1	34.2	51,064	64.7	53.5	4.4	6.8	35.3	27.2	30.0	30.6
53 05280	Bellingham city	8.8	11.1	33,873	49.1	35.4	3.0	10.7	50.9	33.6	22.7	31.1
53 07380	Bothell city	6.7	14.5	13,884	62.6	51.0	4.8	6.8	37.4	28.5	30.2	31.5
53 07695	Bremerton city	13.3	7.5	14,677	54.5	33.7	6.0	14.9	45.5	34.4	29.1	29.1
53 08850	Burien city	22.8	25.4	18,199	63.8	44.1	5.5	14.2	36.2	29.3	30.9	31.3

Table A-4. Cities — Who: Age, Race/Ethnicity, and Household Structure, 2010–2012—*Continued*

STATE and Place code	STATE or City	Total population	Percent change 2010–2012	Population by age (percent)						Median age	Race alone or in combination (percent)		Asian, Hawaiian, or Pacific Islander	American Indian, Alaska Native, or some other race
				Under 5 years	5 to 17 years	18 to 24 years	25 to 44 years	45 to 64 years	65 years and over		White	Black		
	ACS table number:	B01003	Population estimates	B01001	B01001	B01001	B01001	B01001	B01001	B01002	B02008	B02009	B02011 + B02012	B02010 + B02013
	Column number:	1	2	3	4	5	6	7	8	9	10	11	12	13
	Washington—Cont.													
53 09480	Cottage Lake CDP..................	20,009	5.3	6.3	23.8	6.2	27.4	27.2	9.2	37.8	89.5	...	8.9	0.9
53 14940	Des Moines city..................	22,288	...	4.8	21.5	6.8	19.5	38.3	9.1	43.1	93.8	1.5	7.0	0.9
53 17635	East Hill-Meridian CDP	30,089	2.3	7.7	15.8	8.1	29.1	25.5	13.9	36.0	71.2	11.0	17.5	7.8
53 19630	Eastmont CDP..................	20,140	...	5.7	21.6	7.7	27.9	27.8	9.4	38.1	80.9	4.1	14.5	0.9
53 20750	Edmonds city..................	40,038	1.6	5.2	13.3	7.8	22.2	32.1	19.4	46.4	85.4	3.6	12.0	2.6
53 22640	Everett city..................	103,818	1.4	7.5	14.3	11.1	30.5	26.2	10.4	35.1	81.7	6.7	11.8	6.8
53 23160	Fairwood CDP (King County).....	19,902	...	6.3	16.9	9.4	26.6	29.5	11.3	39.5	69.4	10.7	20.4	7.0
53 23515	Federal Way city..................	90,709	2.7	7.3	17.5	10.5	26.8	27.1	10.7	35.8	67.3	12.5	18.7	8.2
53 24188	Five Corners CDP..................	20,214	...	6.9	23.1	9.5	29.7	23.8	7.0	31.2	87.6	3.7	7.0	5.8
53 27785	Graham CDP..................	24,677	...	8.4	20.3	7.4	31.3	25.9	6.5	33.2	91.3	5.9	5.0	2.4
53 33380	Inglewood-Finn Hill CDP	24,287	...	6.8	17.7	6.4	30.6	28.9	9.6	36.7	89.2	4.0	11.1	2.5
53 33805	Issaquah city..................	31,691	6.8	7.8	14.9	4.1	35.7	24.3	13.3	38.3	82.3	1.8	19.1	2.3
53 35170	Kenmore city..................	20,928	3.6	5.9	20.2	5.3	28.2	27.7	12.6	38.8	80.2	1.9	14.9	6.5
53 35275	Kennewick city..................	75,328	2.1	8.6	19.6	10.4	27.1	23.2	11.2	32.2	79.2	2.4	3.1	17.6
53 35415	Kent city..................	120,964	3.3	8.1	18.6	10.5	29.1	24.1	9.5	33.3	63.3	11.6	24.0	8.0
53 35940	Kirkland city..................	49,823	3.5	6.2	13.9	7.2	36.0	26.7	10.1	37.0	81.9	3.1	16.3	3.8
53 36745	Lacey city..................	43,252	3.0	7.3	17.5	8.5	31.0	20.7	14.9	35.1	77.5	8.3	15.0	3.2
53 37900	Lake Stevens city..................	28,677	2.9	8.4	21.0	7.7	31.1	23.6	8.2	32.9	92.3	1.8	4.9	5.2
53 38038	Lakewood city..................	58,569	1.0	6.9	14.0	10.4	27.3	27.1	14.2	37.0	69.4	13.9	17.2	8.2
53 40245	Longview city..................	36,592	-0.7	6.4	16.0	7.0	23.4	29.7	17.4	42.3	92.1	1.8	4.7	8.5
53 40840	Lynnwood city..................	36,097	1.0	4.2	15.6	11.2	28.5	26.8	13.7	37.4	72.8	5.7	19.2	8.8
53 43150	Maple Valley city..................	23,473	6.0	7.4	23.8	6.0	30.2	25.0	7.6	35.3	89.5	5.2	7.2	2.3
53 43955	Marysville city..................	61,313	3.6	7.9	19.0	9.2	28.5	25.3	10.1	35.0	86.3	3.8	10.0	5.9
53 45005	Mercer Island city..................	23,236	3.9	5.3	19.1	3.8	19.7	31.3	20.7	46.6	82.0	1.2	17.7	0.7
53 47245	Moses Lake city..................	20,869	3.3	8.2	22.9	7.7	26.9	21.4	12.9	32.0	82.0	3.4	1.6	17.0
53 47490	Mountlake Terrace city	20,055	1.3	6.6	11.2	8.3	34.2	27.8	12.0	38.9	79.6	4.6	15.8	6.0
53 47560	Mount Vernon city..................	32,064	1.5	9.0	20.7	10.9	26.7	19.9	12.7	32.3	87.4	1.3	4.5	10.0
53 47735	Mukilteo city..................	20,435	1.5	3.4	18.9	8.2	25.0	34.2	10.2	41.0	79.1	2.2	20.5	2.6
53 50360	Oak Harbor city..................	22,232	0.4	10.3	17.1	10.3	33.7	17.6	11.1	30.4	78.8	6.9	19.0	5.0
53 51300	Olympia city..................	47,250	2.2	5.8	13.5	11.5	29.6	25.9	13.7	37.1	88.3	2.1	9.1	4.4
53 51795	Orchards CDP..................	21,659	...	9.3	25.6	8.6	28.7	21.3	6.5	30.7	89.5	3.9	6.9	1.8
53 53335	Parkland CDP..................	36,514	...	7.8	17.6	16.0	24.9	23.7	9.9	31.5	71.5	14.1	15.8	7.9
53 53545	Pasco city..................	63,065	8.0	11.3	23.8	10.4	30.9	16.7	7.0	27.6	55.6	2.6	2.5	42.3
53 56625	Pullman city..................	30,388	5.1	3.7	7.7	53.4	20.3	10.7	4.1	21.9	84.6	4.0	14.5	3.0
53 56695	Puyallup city..................	37,562	3.0	5.8	15.7	11.8	26.7	27.9	12.1	38.9	91.1	5.4	6.2	3.2
53 57535	Redmond city..................	55,518	3.8	7.9	13.6	6.8	41.2	21.0	9.5	34.7	67.4	2.2	30.4	4.6
53 57745	Renton city..................	93,673	3.8	7.6	15.1	8.3	35.3	23.6	10.0	35.3	59.1	12.3	24.6	12.5
53 58235	Richland city..................	50,066	6.1	7.2	17.4	7.8	24.4	28.3	15.0	39.6	88.9	1.9	8.0	5.6
53 61000	Salmon Creek CDP..................	21,444	...	8.8	16.6	7.5	27.6	26.6	12.9	38.4	88.8	2.7	7.5	6.9
53 61115	Sammamish city..................	47,976	4.6	7.8	25.3	4.8	27.5	28.5	6.0	37.5	78.2	1.8	22.5	2.7
53 62288	SeaTac city..................	27,338	2.5	8.0	13.3	12.0	30.8	25.3	10.5	35.2	57.7	23.7	18.1	8.3
53 63000	Seattle city..................	622,273	4.0	5.3	10.2	11.3	37.3	24.8	11.1	36.0	74.3	9.3	18.0	4.2
53 63960	Shoreline city..................	53,726	2.3	5.2	13.6	9.2	26.4	29.4	16.3	41.8	76.4	6.3	18.0	5.3
53 64365	Silverdale CDP..................	20,302	...	6.7	14.5	13.9	29.1	22.8	13.0	33.4	80.0	5.3	17.4	6.3
53 64380	Silver Firs CDP..................	21,231	...	8.3	23.0	6.1	27.8	28.4	6.5	36.5	82.8	1.5	19.9	2.3
53 65922	South Hill CDP..................	55,271	...	7.2	22.9	8.9	28.5	22.6	9.9	33.3	85.3	6.1	12.5	7.1
53 66255	Spanaway CDP..................	27,704	...	8.3	20.5	8.8	30.5	22.1	9.8	33.2	78.1	11.5	14.7	4.7
53 67000	Spokane city..................	209,346	0.0	7.1	15.0	12.1	27.6	24.6	13.7	35.4	91.0	4.1	4.4	5.0
53 67167	Spokane Valley city..................	90,437	0.6	6.1	17.9	9.4	25.3	27.0	14.3	37.8	93.4	3.1	3.8	4.4
53 70000	Tacoma city..................	200,090	1.8	7.1	16.2	10.7	29.3	25.1	11.6	35.1	73.3	15.2	13.3	7.3
53 73465	University Place city..................	31,358	1.4	5.8	18.1	10.9	23.2	28.2	13.8	39.1	80.5	10.3	15.2	4.6
53 74060	Vancouver city..................	163,964	1.9	6.3	17.2	9.5	28.8	25.1	13.2	36.8	84.7	4.6	9.4	6.7
53 75775	Walla Walla city..................	31,882	0.2	5.4	14.2	13.8	26.0	26.2	14.5	37.5	88.4	3.6	3.7	8.5
53 77105	Wenatchee city..................	32,381	1.1	8.4	19.2	8.6	25.8	23.7	14.4	33.3	90.3	0.7	3.8	8.2
53 80010	Yakima city..................	92,506	1.6	9.2	18.1	9.9	27.3	21.7	13.8	32.9	74.8	2.1	2.4	25.0
54 00000	**West Virginia**..................	1,854,775	0.1	5.5	15.2	9.3	24.5	29.1	16.4	41.4	95.6	4.0	1.0	1.6
54 14600	Charleston city..................	51,153	-0.6	4.9	14.9	8.7	24.6	29.4	17.5	42.1	88.2	10.8	3.5	6.3
54 39460	Huntington city..................	49,309	0.1	4.8	12.2	17.0	27.0	24.7	14.2	35.4	90.9	10.6	0.9	1.0
54 55756	Morgantown city..................	30,480	4.0	2.4	5.5	44.8	23.7	15.5	8.2	23.8	89.5	8.2	3.8	1.7
54 62140	Parkersburg city..................	31,343	-0.5	5.9	14.7	8.8	24.5	28.3	17.8	41.5	97.0	3.0	0.5	1.9
54 86452	Wheeling city..................	28,333	-0.9	6.0	13.4	9.3	21.2	29.9	20.3	45.1	93.1	6.5	1.4	1.2
55 00000	**Wisconsin**..................	5,708,612	0.6	6.2	17.1	9.7	25.2	27.9	14.0	38.7	88.8	7.1	2.8	3.5
55 02375	Appleton city..................	72,689	0.5	7.0	18.0	9.5	26.6	27.7	11.2	36.7	90.9	2.4	5.9	3.3
55 06500	Beloit city..................	36,849	-0.2	6.8	18.4	13.2	24.4	24.3	13.0	34.8	83.7	13.6	1.7	7.8
55 10025	Brookfield city..................	37,934	0.2	3.9	19.1	6.7	17.0	32.5	20.9	47.5	93.5	2.2	5.2	0.7
55 11950	Caledonia village..................	24,692	-0.1	4.8	16.3	5.8	23.2	33.8	16.2	45.0	89.6	6.2	3.3	2.5
55 19775	De Pere city..................	24,054	1.3	6.3	18.9	15.3	24.5	23.9	11.1	33.2	94.1	3.1	2.4	1.5
55 22300	Eau Claire city..................	66,087	1.5	5.5	14.0	22.1	25.4	21.8	11.2	30.0	94.3	1.6	4.9	1.4
55 25950	Fitchburg city..................	25,552	2.6	6.7	18.2	8.6	34.8	23.2	8.5	34.1	71.7	13.5	6.4	12.3
55 26275	Fond du Lac city..................	43,076	0.0	6.4	16.2	9.6	27.0	25.6	15.2	38.5	92.4	3.3	2.3	4.7
55 27300	Franklin city..................	35,779	1.7	6.4	16.5	6.8	28.9	28.0	13.4	39.4	88.0	4.8	7.3	3.1
55 31000	Green Bay city..................	104,494	0.7	7.6	17.0	11.0	28.3	24.3	11.8	33.7	87.2	5.5	4.6	7.0
55 31175	Greenfield city..................	36,892	0.8	5.6	10.4	7.4	25.1	30.5	21.0	46.2	92.6	2.5	4.1	1.6
55 37825	Janesville city..................	63,551	0.1	7.1	18.6	8.0	28.3	24.6	13.4	35.9	95.2	3.3	2.0	3.0
55 39225	Kenosha city..................	99,743	0.8	7.3	19.0	10.7	27.9	24.1	10.9	33.9	85.9	11.2	2.1	3.1
55 40775	La Crosse city..................	51,478	0.5	4.4	12.0	26.9	22.6	21.0	13.2	29.2	90.7	3.4	5.2	2.1
55 48000	Madison city..................	237,136	2.8	6.0	12.0	20.0	31.2	21.1	9.5	30.6	82.7	9.3	8.7	2.8

STATE and Place code	STATE or City	Percent Hispanic or Latino	Percent foreign born	Total households	Household type (percent) Family households				Nonfamily households		Percent of households with people under 18 years	Percent of households with people 60 years and over
					Total family households	Married-couple families	Male household families	Female household families	Total nonfamily households	One-person households		
	ACS table number:	B03003	C05003	B11001	B11001	B11001	B11001	B11001	B11001	B11001	B11005	B11006
	Column number:	14	15	16	17	18	19	20	21	22	23	24
	Washington—Cont.											
53 09480	Cottage Lake CDP	3.5	9.6	6,741	76.4	65.0	2.0	9.4	23.6	19.4	46.8	27.5
53 14940	Des Moines city	2.8	10.9	7,750	84.7	75.2	3.0	6.5	15.3	12.3	41.8	31.8
53 17635	East Hill-Meridian CDP	15.2	23.4	11,161	63.8	45.3	5.2	13.4	36.2	29.5	34.4	35.0
53 19630	Eastmont CDP	6.3	18.7	6,820	77.9	62.7	6.2	9.1	22.1	16.9	41.6	27.2
53 20750	Edmonds city	4.6	15.1	17,263	62.9	49.1	4.2	9.6	37.1	31.8	24.5	43.9
53 22640	Everett city	15.8	18.2	41,699	53.2	36.6	4.7	11.9	46.8	36.9	28.3	29.1
53 23160	Fairwood CDP (King County)	7.2	14.7	7,301	71.8	52.6	5.2	14.0	28.2	20.5	37.3	29.3
53 23515	Federal Way city	16.4	22.8	33,638	67.1	45.0	6.6	15.5	32.9	26.2	35.4	30.0
53 24188	Five Corners CDP	7.2	15.7	5,808	75.6	56.0	3.7	16.0	24.4	16.2	44.8	27.6
53 27785	Graham CDP	5.5	3.1	8,304	75.5	61.2	4.3	10.0	24.5	20.1	44.0	21.6
53 33380	Inglewood-Finn Hill CDP	4.9	14.9	8,841	72.7	59.8	3.7	9.3	27.3	20.4	36.9	24.7
53 33805	Issaquah city	3.9	17.9	13,688	62.7	53.5	2.4	6.9	37.3	30.4	32.0	27.0
53 35170	Kenmore city	9.1	18.4	7,670	70.5	57.3	3.8	9.3	29.5	22.5	37.9	31.9
53 35275	Kennewick city	24.1	10.0	26,974	64.3	49.0	4.7	10.6	35.7	29.6	34.7	31.8
53 35415	Kent city	16.8	26.6	41,854	66.7	47.4	4.9	14.4	33.3	26.5	38.6	28.6
53 35940	Kirkland city	7.0	21.0	22,018	58.0	48.1	3.0	6.8	42.0	34.6	26.9	25.0
53 36745	Lacey city	7.8	11.7	16,724	67.6	51.0	3.7	13.0	32.4	28.1	33.3	32.2
53 37900	Lake Stevens city	7.8	6.3	9,942	70.2	56.2	4.0	10.0	29.8	20.8	44.2	23.6
53 38038	Lakewood city	17.4	16.3	24,085	56.3	39.7	3.9	12.7	43.7	36.5	25.9	34.5
53 40245	Longview city	9.2	5.8	15,149	60.5	43.3	4.3	13.0	39.5	32.7	27.6	42.5
53 40840	Lynnwood city	12.8	25.0	14,052	58.9	39.5	7.3	12.2	41.1	31.2	27.8	32.3
53 43150	Maple Valley city	5.4	6.7	8,125	76.5	60.6	3.6	12.4	23.5	18.5	49.4	22.1
53 43955	Marysville city	8.9	9.6	21,744	71.5	54.9	5.6	11.0	28.5	22.8	38.1	29.6
53 45005	Mercer Island city	2.7	18.9	9,427	71.8	63.7	1.6	6.5	28.2	25.6	31.1	46.5
53 47245	Moses Lake city	30.9	10.1	7,984	65.5	47.4	4.1	14.0	34.5	29.6	38.7	32.2
53 47490	Mountlake Terrace city	9.6	18.4	8,364	57.9	35.5	9.3	13.0	42.1	33.2	27.2	28.5
53 47560	Mount Vernon city	33.1	16.3	11,271	67.6	46.0	3.8	17.7	32.4	24.4	38.9	33.4
53 47735	Mukilteo city	1.6	19.6	7,934	71.1	56.0	5.6	9.5	28 9	22.8	33.8	27.9
53 50360	Oak Harbor city	9.7	14.2	8,881	64.8	53.3	3.3	8.2	35 2	29.6	36.9	26.0
53 51300	Olympia city	8.4	9.0	20,549	55.0	40.7	2.8	11.4	45 0	35.3	26.6	33.0
53 51795	Orchards CDP	7.5	11.6	6,865	77.1	58.5	5.2	13.3	22 9	17.7	49.1	21.1
53 53335	Parkland CDP	13.5	13.8	13,127	61.5	42.2	5.7	13.5	38 5	29.2	34.6	27.4
53 53545	Pasco city	56.5	28.3	17,711	77.1	54.3	7.3	15.5	22 9	17.5	52.5	25.7
53 56625	Pullman city	6.4	13.2	10,346	39.2	33.6	0.7	5.0	60 8	29.8	18.9	13.5
53 56695	Puyallup city	6.9	6.2	14,841	63.8	43.1	3.6	17.1	36 2	28.7	30.9	32.1
53 57535	Redmond city	8.1	34.8	23,650	59.7	50.7	3.5	5.5	40 3	31.6	31.1	23.0
53 57745	Renton city	14.0	28.3	36,182	58.2	40.8	6.5	10.8	41 8	31.7	31.7	27.2
53 58235	Richland city	7.5	9.1	19,964	66.1	52.4	3.3	10.5	33 9	29.3	30.6	32.8
53 61000	Salmon Creek CDP	9.7	7.1	7,569	73.2	54.3	5.9	13.0	26.8	20.7	38.8	35.9
53 61115	Sammamish city	3.7	23.8	15,581	87.7	79.3	3.4	5.0	12.3	9.0	56.3	21.5
53 62288	SeaTac city	18.5	32.8	10,022	60.1	37.1	8.7	14.3	39.9	33.0	31.9	31.0
53 63000	Seattle city	6.5	18.1	284,559	43.8	34.0	2.6	7.3	56.2	41.9	19.9	26.5
53 63960	Shoreline city	7.4	19.4	21,269	60.9	47.4	3.2	10.2	39.1	31.5	28.3	38.5
53 64365	Silverdale CDP	8.0	10.8	8,057	63.1	47.8	3.4	11.9	36.9	28.8	30.6	28.9
53 64380	Silver Firs CDP	4.0	15.9	6,677	84.4	75.6	2.9	5.9	15.6	11.4	54.0	21.3
53 65922	South Hill CDP	10.1	9.6	18,545	78.0	61.3	6.4	10.3	22.0	16.9	45.7	26.7
53 66255	Spanaway CDP	13.0	9.9	9,535	70.8	53.1	5.8	11.9	29.2	21.7	40.4	29.0
53 67000	Spokane city	5.3	7.2	88,184	57.1	40.2	4.1	12.8	42.9	34.4	28.9	32.4
53 67167	Spokane Valley city	4.8	4.9	36,143	64.8	48.2	4.5	12.1	35.2	28.3	31.5	36.0
53 70000	Tacoma city	11.2	13.4	77,704	57.8	39.2	4.2	14.3	42.2	33.3	30.6	30.9
53 73465	University Place city	6.4	12.2	12,665	67.3	47.5	7.2	12.6	32.7	29.1	34.5	33.8
53 74060	Vancouver city	10.4	13.1	65,449	60.5	42.5	4.3	13.8	39.5	30.1	31.8	33.3
53 75775	Walla Walla city	20.5	10.5	11,760	56.9	42.5	4.6	9.7	43.1	38.6	27.4	42.4
53 77105	Wenatchee city	32.7	14.5	11,596	66.2	48.3	6.2	11.7	33.8	27.5	34.0	38.2
53 80010	Yakima city	43.2	17.2	33,020	65.5	45.3	6.5	13.7	34.5	28.6	36.0	34.7
54 00000	**West Virginia**	1.2	1.4	741,661	64.8	49.2	4.2	11.3	35.2	30.2	27.5	40.5
54 14600	Charleston city	1.8	2.6	23,454	52.8	35.6	4.1	13.0	47.2	41.4	23.0	38.6
54 39460	Huntington city	1.0	2.2	21,353	50.4	31.3	3.3	15.8	49.6	40.8	20.7	33.7
54 55756	Morgantown city	2.7	5.1	10,200	34.3	25.6	2.3	6.4	65.7	48.0	12.2	24.3
54 62140	Parkersburg city	0.9	0.6	13,274	55.8	38.2	5.2	12.4	44.2	38.4	24.2	39.6
54 86452	Wheeling city	1.1	1.5	12,621	53.0	35.8	3.4	13.8	47.0	42.6	22.7	42.4
55 00000	**Wisconsin**	6.1	4.7	2,282,454	64.0	49.6	4.3	10.2	36.0	29.0	30.1	33.6
55 02375	Appleton city	4.4	5.6	28,620	63.5	46.5	5.8	11.2	36.5	29.7	33.9	31.1
55 06500	Beloit city	18.4	10.0	14,277	62.2	36.3	7.3	18.6	37.8	30.9	35.3	31.3
55 10025	Brookfield city	2.8	5.9	14,524	75.2	67.4	2.6	5.2	24.8	22.5	31.3	44.9
55 11950	Caledonia village	4.8	4.1	10,018	69.8	59.6	4.1	6.1	30.2	26.0	28.0	41.5
55 19775	De Pere city	2.3	2.8	9,197	60.6	45.5	4.1	11.0	39.4	32.7	35.4	26.6
55 22300	Eau Claire city	2.1	3.6	26,837	52.0	37.7	3.6	10.8	48.0	34.8	25.6	28.5
55 25950	Fitchburg city	20.4	16.5	10,109	64.2	48.3	3.1	12.8	35.8	29.5	34.4	24.5
55 26275	Fond du Lac city	6.6	4.6	17,982	59.5	40.9	4.5	14.0	40.5	34.2	30.3	33.8
55 27300	Franklin city	5.3	7.2	12,820	70.6	59.0	3.4	8.2	29.4	25.0	31.0	35.5
55 31000	Green Bay city	12.2	8.0	42,755	56.4	39.9	4.5	12.0	43.6	34.9	31.0	28.3
55 31175	Greenfield city	8.3	8.1	16,783	52.0	41.8	3.6	6.6	48.0	40.6	19.1	42.9
55 37825	Janesville city	5.2	3.1	25,325	65.2	46.5	5.3	13.4	34.8	27.0	34.6	32.4
55 39225	Kenosha city	16.0	8.2	37,653	63.5	40.2	6.4	16.8	36.5	29.0	37.5	28.4
55 40775	La Crosse city	2.4	3.7	20,740	47.2	33.3	4.9	8.9	52.8	37.1	22.5	30.1
55 48000	Madison city	6.9	11.0	101,354	49.2	35.8	4.5	8.9	50.3	35.6	23.9	23.5

Table A-4. Cities — Who: Age, Race/Ethnicity, and Household Structure, 2010–2012—*Continued*

STATE and Place code	STATE or City	Total population	Percent change 2010–2012	Under 5 years	5 to 17 years	18 to 24 years	25 to 44 years	45 to 64 years	65 years and over	Median age	White	Black	Asian, Hawaiian, or Pacific Islander	American Indian, Alaska Native, or some other race
													B02011 + B02012	B02010 + B02013
	ACS table number:	B01003	Population estimates	B01001	B01001	B01001	B01001	B01001	B01001	B01002	B02008	B02009		
	Column number:	1	2	3	4	5	6	7	8	9	10	11	12	13
	Wisconsin—Cont.													
55 48500	Manitowoc city	33,542	-0.8	5.6	15.8	7.6	23.7	28.3	18.9	43.2	92.7	1.0	5.5	2.9
55 51000	Menomonee Falls village	35,698	0.5	4.8	17.1	6.2	22.9	30.3	18.7	44.5	93.6	2.7	4.1	0.6
55 51150	Mequon city	23,164	0.5	3.4	18.8	6.0	17.5	35.2	19.2	47.8	94.8	3.7	2.0	0.6
55 53000	Milwaukee city	597,247	0.6	8.0	18.9	13.3	28.8	21.8	9.1	30.5	49.5	41.7	4.3	8.7
55 54875	Mount Pleasant village	26,199	-0.1	5.4	15.9	7.5	21.6	31.6	18.0	44.8	86.8	9.0	2.3	3.3
55 55275	Muskego city	24,274	1.0	4.5	20.4	6.1	22.9	32.6	13.5	42.6	97.2	...	2.4	...
55 55750	Neenah city	25,628	1.0	7.3	18.1	7.0	26.4	28.3	12.8	38.2	93.5	1.2	2.3	5.2
55 56375	New Berlin city	39,643	0.3	4.0	16.8	6.2	21.9	34.4	16.8	46.0	94.3	1.0	5.0	0.6
55 58800	Oak Creek city	34,704	1.2	7.3	16.1	8.0	30.1	27.9	10.7	36.6	89.8	2.1	4.9	4.4
55 60500	Oshkosh city	66,301	0.9	5.5	13.9	18.9	26.7	22.6	12.5	32.5	93.7	4.2	2.5	1.5
55 63300	Pleasant Prairie village	19,865	1.4	3.8	20.9	10.7	21.1	31.7	11.7	39.7	89.6	6.7	1.0	5.6
55 66000	Racine city	78,552	-0.6	8.0	20.2	9.5	27.2	24.1	11.0	33.6	70.4	23.1	1.3	9.3
55 72975	Sheboygan city	49,045	-0.6	7.5	17.2	9.1	26.5	25.3	14.4	36.7	87.0	2.5	9.7	2.8
55 75125	South Milwaukee city	21,189	0.3	6.7	16.5	9.2	27.0	26.6	14.0	39.2	96.8	2.7	0.5	3.0
55 77200	Stevens Point city	26,731	0.2	5.2	12.0	30.4	22.2	18.6	11.6	26.4	92.9	2.0	5.4	2.1
55 78600	Sun Prairie city	29,905	3.2	7.3	19.7	7.1	33.1	23.7	9.0	34.2	89.8	9.2	3.6	0.4
55 78650	Superior city	27,051	-1.4	5.8	15.0	12.9	25.8	27.5	13.1	36.0	94.8	2.2	1.7	3.4
55 83975	Watertown city	23,919	0.5	6.3	18.6	9.7	26.4	24.4	14.6	36.9	96.3	0.7	1.6	2.9
55 84250	Waukesha city	70,752	0.3	7.6	15.3	11.2	30.4	24.8	10.9	34.1	91.1	3.3	4.5	4.1
55 84475	Wausau city	39,122	0.1	7.6	15.9	8.8	25.2	25.9	16.7	37.5	84.1	2.5	14.7	1.8
55 84675	Wauwatosa city	46,683	1.3	7.1	15.8	6.1	28.4	26.8	15.9	38.7	92.2	6.1	3.3	1.6
55 85300	West Allis city	60,586	0.5	6.6	14.8	7.6	29.5	27.1	14.3	37.4	90.6	4.9	3.0	4.6
55 85350	West Bend city	31,380	1.2	6.6	17.6	7.0	29.1	25.3	14.3	36.7	96.6	1.3	1.5	1.9
56 00000	**Wyoming**	569,380	2.1	6.9	16.9	10.1	25.8	27.7	12.7	36.8	93.6	1.5	1.3	6.5
56 13150	Casper city	56,391	4.6	7.0	16.5	10.4	27.3	26.0	12.7	35.3	95.6	2.5	1.5	4.6
56 13900	Cheyenne city	60,497	3.0	7.0	17.1	9.9	27.3	24.8	13.9	35.7	88.8	4.3	2.7	8.3
56 31855	Gillette city	30,562	4.9	10.3	18.6	10.1	33.1	22.1	5.9	29.9	92.0	1.0	0.8	7.3
56 45050	Laramie city	32,074	2.5	5.5	11.2	32.0	28.4	16.1	6.8	25.5	90.7	1.8	4.4	5.2
56 67235	Rock Springs city	23,486	4.5	8.4	18.1	10.8	28.5	26.1	8.0	32.1	96.1	2.7	1.6	4.9

Table A-4. Cities — Who: Age, Race/Ethnicity, and Household Structure, 2010–2012—*Continued*

STATE and Place code	STATE or City	Percent Hispanic or Latino	Percent foreign born	Total households	Household type (percent)							Percent of households with people under 18 years	Percent of households with people 60 years and over
					Family households				Nonfamily households				
					Total family households	Married-couple families	Male household families	Female household families	Total nonfamily households	One-person households			
ACS table number:		B03003	C05003	B11001	B11001	B11001	B11001	B11001	B11001	B11001		B11005	B11006
Column number:		14	15	16	17	18	19	20	21	22		23	24
	Wisconsin—Cont.												
55 48500	Manitowoc city	4.4	3.5	15,018	56.9	44.0	3.5	9.3	43.1	36.6		24.7	35.9
55 51000	Menomonee Falls village	3.3	5.1	14,444	69.5	61.1	2.4	6.0	30.5	27.2		28.4	41.4
55 51150	Mequon city	1.3	7.1	9,164	72.0	65.0	2.2	4.8	28.0	23.1		27.5	47.0
55 53000	Milwaukee city	17.5	10.0	228,852	56.0	27.5	6.1	22.4	44.0	35.2		33.4	25.5
55 54875	Mount Pleasant village	10.7	6.1	10,762	62.8	50.4	3.7	8.7	37.2	29.0		26.2	42.0
55 55275	Muskego city	2.6	3.8	8,988	78.1	68.2	2.7	7.2	21.9	19.2		36.9	35.0
55 55750	Neenah city	5.0	3.3	10,619	60.3	46.8	4.1	9.4	39.7	32.5		31.7	30.4
55 56375	New Berlin city	2.3	4.7	16,384	68.2	59.7	1.5	6.9	31.8	27.2		27.8	40.0
55 58800	Oak Creek city	9.2	6.9	13,900	61.6	53.6	2.4	5.6	38.4	30.6		30.1	28.3
55 60500	Oshkosh city	3.4	2.7	25,344	51.9	36.9	3.9	11.1	48.1	35.6		27.3	30.1
55 63300	Pleasant Prairie village	7.0	1.9	7,031	71.6	59.6	4.8	7.2	28.4	22.4		35.8	35.8
55 66000	Racine city	20.3	7.2	30,358	59.3	37.5	4.4	17.4	40.7	33.8		34.5	29.9
55 72975	Sheboygan city	10.4	9.9	20,028	58.6	43.8	4.0	10.8	41.4	32.1		27.8	32.0
55 75125	South Milwaukee city	8.2	5.7	8,181	63.0	43.8	6.3	13.0	37.0	31.4		32.3	33.1
55 77200	Stevens Point city	2.3	3.9	10,611	49.4	36.0	3.4	10.0	50.6	33.9		21.8	29.7
55 78600	Sun Prairie city	4.0	4.5	11,628	66.9	51.0	4.9	11.0	33.1	23.7		36.6	24.9
55 78650	Superior city	0.9	2.9	11,960	54.6	35.9	6.4	12.3	45.4	37.6		29.3	32.0
55 83975	Watertown city	4.9	3.1	9,280	64.9	54.4	3.4	7.2	35.1	32.1		29.8	33.0
55 84250	Waukesha city	11.6	7.8	28,645	59.4	45.7	3.0	10.7	40.6	31.7		29.3	29.3
55 84475	Wausau city	3.1	7.5	16,353	56.4	39.5	5.2	11.6	43.6	35.1		28.2	36.4
55 84675	Wauwatosa city	2.2	3.7	20,283	58.8	45.5	3.8	9.4	41.2	35.3		28.7	34.8
55 85300	West Allis city	9.6	5.0	27,253	51.2	37.6	4.2	9.4	48.8	40.3		25.0	31.0
55 85350	West Bend city	3.5	2.5	12,810	65.3	49.6	5.9	9.7	34.7	29.0		32.3	34.5
56 00000	**Wyoming**	9.2	3.2	222,558	65.4	52.3	4.1	9.0	34.6	27.6		30.6	32.3
56 13150	Casper city	7.7	2.4	23,191	64.4	47.3	5.1	11.9	35.6	28.6		31.8	31.3
56 13900	Cheyenne city	14.0	2.2	24,849	60.7	43.8	4.5	12.4	39.3	32.7		29.2	32.6
56 31855	Gillette city	10.4	4.9	11,358	66.3	49.8	6.0	10.6	33.7	24.3		36.4	17.0
56 45050	Laramie city	9.0	5.9	13,081	44.8	34.8	3.4	6.7	55.2	33.7		22.3	18.7
56 67235	Rock Springs city	16.3	5.4	9,081	65.9	50.6	5.9	9.3	34.1	27.3		37.7	25.0

What

Education, Employment, and Income

What: Education, Employment, and Income

What do Americans do? During the years 2010 to 2012, more than 150 million Americans were in the labor force, and more than 80 million were enrolled in school. Many people were in both groups at the same time. Americans' employment and income potential are closely related to their educational attainment. Educational differences among states, cities, and metropolitan areas can influence location decisions of both workers and employers. Employers with low-wage jobs might seek locations with lower education levels, while locations with highly educated work forces might be sought out by other employers.

Education

About 29 percent of Americans (age 25 and over) held bachelor's degrees or advanced degrees, and another 29 percent had attended some college or held associate's degrees. In the District of Columbia, more than half of the population held bachelor's or advanced degrees. Massachusetts, Colorado, Connecticut, Maryland, New Jersey, Vermont, and Virginia, all had more than 35 percent of their residents in this group, while fewer than 22 percent of people in West Virginia, Mississippi, Arkansas, and Kentucky were college-educated. The five metropolitan areas with the highest proportions of college-educated

residents—about half of their populations—were Boulder, Colorado; Corvallis, Oregon; Ithaca, New York; Ames, Iowa, and Ann Arbor, Michigan—all relatively small metropolitan areas with large universities. Among metropolitan areas with more than 1 million people, there were five where more than 40 percent of the residents had college degrees: Washington, DC; San Jose and San Francisco, California; Boston, Massachusetts; and Austin–Round Rock, Texas. More than half of the people in 25 counties had bachelors or advanced degrees, with six of the top ten counties being suburbs of Washington, DC. More than three-quarters of the people in 15 cities were college-educated. Some were university cities; some were suburbs of large metropolitan areas; all had fewer than 100,000 people and most had closer to 20,000 people.

In the United States, 13.6 percent of adults had not graduated from high school. Another 28 percent had a high school diploma but no further education in regular 2-year or 4-year colleges. Vocational training for specific trades is not measured in the ACS. Thus, about 42 percent of the American people were in the group with a high school diploma or less. In eight cities, most of them in California, more than 80 percent of the people had a high school education or less. Statewide, 39.1 percent of California's

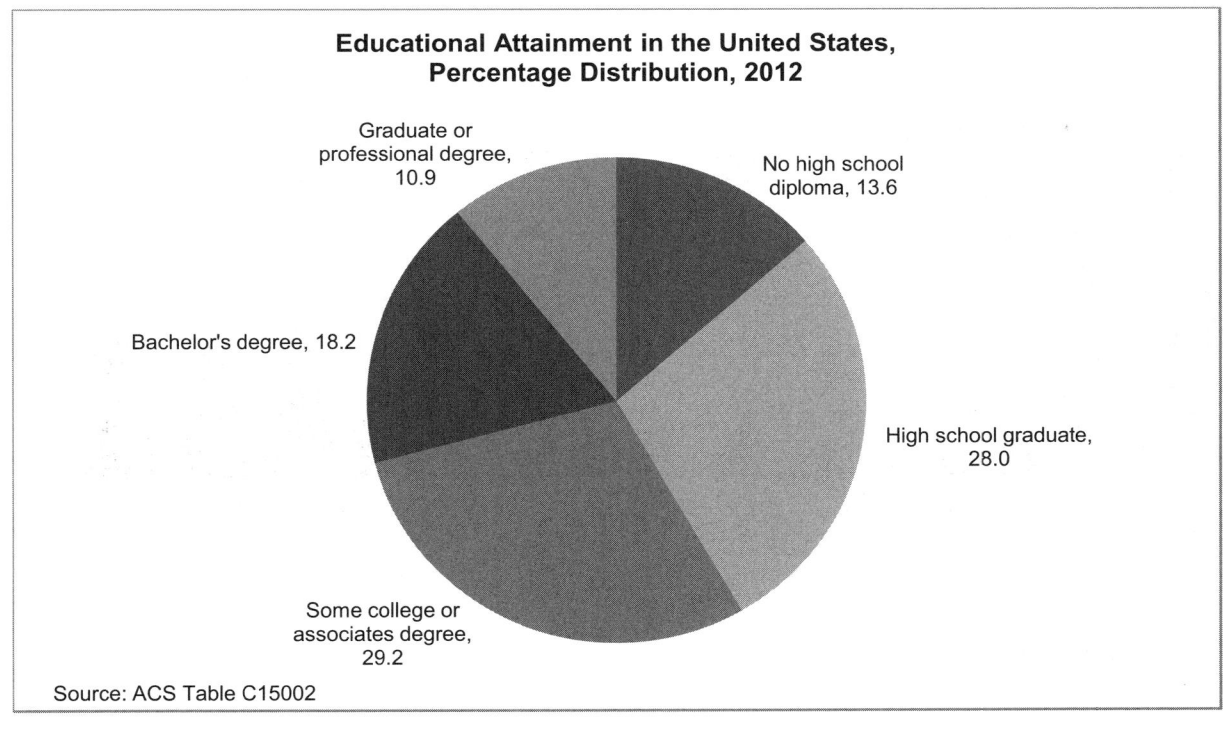

Educational Attainment in the United States, Percentage Distribution, 2012

Graduate or professional degree, 10.9

No high school diploma, 13.6

Bachelor's degree, 18.2

High school graduate, 28.0

Some college or associates degree, 29.2

Source: ACS Table C15002

residents were in this group with a high school education or less; lower than the national figure of 42 percent. In West Virginia, Louisiana, Arkansas, and Kentucky, more than 50 percent of the people had not attended college.

Among 16- to 19-year-olds in the United States, 2.4 percent were not enrolled in school, not high school graduates, and not in the labor force. This measure provides one way to use ACS data to identify unemployed high school dropouts. Twenty-one states exceeded the national level, led by Delaware and Mississippi, where 4 percent of 16- to 19-year-olds were in this high-risk category. South Dakota and New Hampshire had the lowest levels, at less than 1 percent.

Of the 83 million people enrolled in school in the United States in 2012, 65.2 percent were in kindergarten through 12th grade, 28.8 percent were in college or graduate school, and the remaining 6 percent were in preschool. Overall, 16.3 percent of the students were in private schools, but this varied by level of school and by location. More than 40 percent of preschoolers were in private schools, but the proportion decreased to less than 10 percent of high school students. The proportion of high school students in private schools ranged from below 5 percent in Wyoming, and Nevada to more than 15 percent in Hawaii and Louisiana. Just over 22 percent of undergraduates and 41.1 percent of professional and graduate students attended private schools. In some states with large numbers of private colleges, higher education attracts many students from other states. Nearly 70 percent of the college undergraduates in the District of Columbia were in private schools, as were 45 percent in Massachusetts and Rhode Island. Private school proportions were even higher for medical, law, and graduate school enrollment in these states.

Employment

Sixty-four percent of adults (age 16 and over) in the United States were in the labor force—the civilian labor force or the armed forces. Those who were not in the labor force might be retired, in school, disabled, homemakers, or formerly employed individuals who have become discouraged from seeking work. Labor force participation was highest in North Dakota, Nebraska, Alaska, and Minnesota, where at least 70 percent of adults were in the labor force. In West Virginia, Mississippi, Alabama, Arkansas, Florida, and Kentucky, labor force participation was below 60 percent. But labor force participation does not mean full-time permanent work. Only 40.2 percent of adults worked 35 hours or more per week for 50 to 52 weeks—full-year, full-time workers—in the past 12 months. North Dakota had the highest level of full-year, full-time workers, at 49 percent, while about 47 percent were full-year full-time workers in Nebraska, South Dakota, and the District of Columbia. Oregon, Michigan, and West Virginia, had the lowest levels of full-year, full-time workers—just over 35 percent.

In 2012, at least half of the adults in five metropolitan areas worked at full-year, full-time jobs (the Sioux Falls, South Dakota; Bismarck and Fargo, North Dakota; Midland, Texas; and Washington, DC). The rates were higher than 45 percent in 25 more metropolitan areas. In the 2010–2012 time period, Lincoln County, South Dakota, had the highest proportion of full-year, full-time workers—61.4

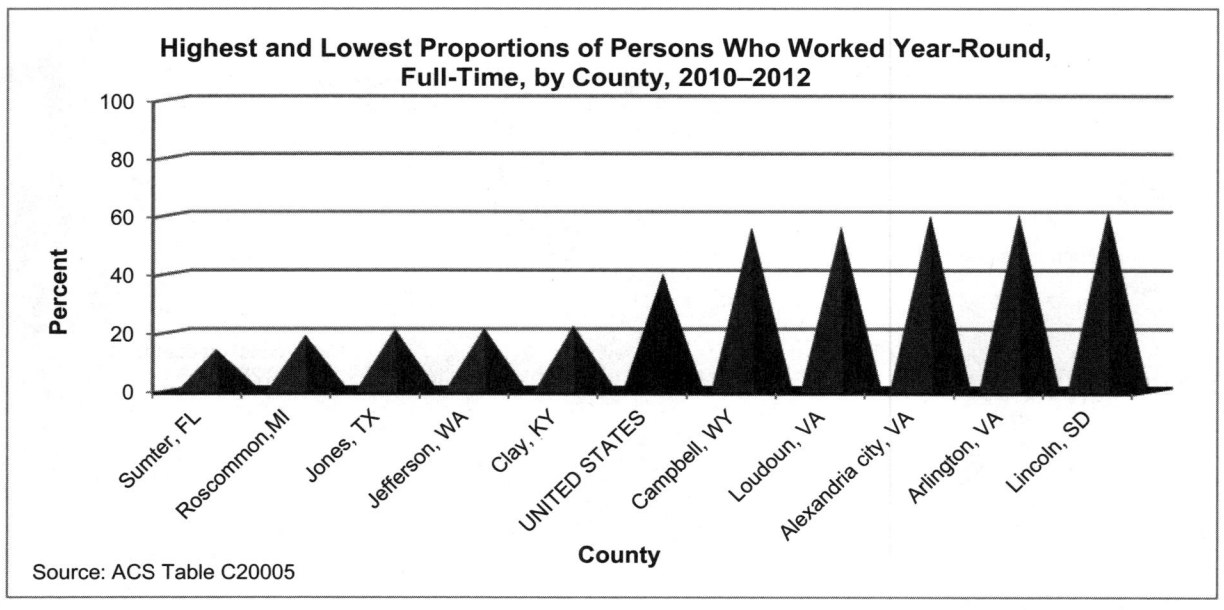

Highest and Lowest Proportions of Persons Who Worked Year-Round, Full-Time, by County, 2010–2012

Source: ACS Table C20005

percent—followed closely by three counties in the Virginia suburbs of Washington, DC. In Sumter County, Florida, only 14 percent of adults worked at full-year, full-time jobs and only 18.9 percent worked full-time all year in Roscommon County, Michigan.

In 2012, the national unemployment rate, as measured in the ACS, was 9.3 percent, but many states had higher levels. Nevada's rate was 12.2 percent. Florida, California, Michigan, Mississippi, South Carolina, and Oregon, all had rates at 11 percent or higher. In the 2010–2012 time period, the ACS unemployment rate for the nation was 10.1 percent. The difference between the 1-year and 3-year unemployment rates shows how the 3 years of data can mask the trend of declining unemployment. In that 3-year period, the cities of Detroit and Flint, Michigan; and Harvey, Illinois; had unemployment rates of 28 percent or higher; while Inkster, Michigan; Sun City Center, Florida; and York, Pennsylvania; were higher than 25 percent. Four metropolitan areas had unemployment rates of 17 percent or higher in 2012. None of these had a population of more than 1 million. The highest unemployment rate in a large metropolitan area was 14.1 percent in Riverside–San Bernardino, California. Eight metropolitan areas had unemployment rates below 4 percent, with Iowa City, Iowa, the lowest, at 2.6 percent.

Unemployment was higher among workers aged 16 to 24, whose 18.9 percent national rate compared with 7.8 percent for workers aged 25 to 64. Among workers in that 25- to 64-year-old group, 14.2 percent of those without a high school diploma were unemployed, while 4.1 percent of college-educated workers were unemployed. Among workers aged 16 to 24, unemployment rates were above the national level (18.9 percent) in 18 states. Mississippi's youth unemployment was 26.3 percent and both Georgia and New Mexico had rates of about 23 percent for that age group.

In the United States, about 65 percent of children under 18 lived in families with two parents. Around 41 percent of children lived with two parents, where both were in the labor force. Another 21 percent lived with both parents, but only their father was in the labor force. About 28 percent lived with a single parent who was in the labor force. In Minnesota, North Dakota, Iowa, Nebraska, South Dakota, and Vermont, at least half of the children had two parents in the labor force.

More than 79 percent of employed civilians age 16 and over worked for private employers. In 15 states, more than 80 percent of workers were private employees, led by Indiana, Pennsylvania, and Michigan, with more than 83 percent of employees. With the exceptions of Nevada and Florida, these 15 states were all in the Midwest and the Northeast. Alaska had the lowest level of private sector employment, with only 67.5 percent of its labor force employed in the private sector. Nationally, 14.5 percent worked for federal, state, or local government agencies, but in Alaska and the District of Columbia, government employment provided more than 25 percent of jobs. New Mexico, Maryland, Hawaii, and Virginia, also had high levels of government employment, all over 20 percent. Government employment was lowest—around 11 percent—in Indiana and Pennsylvania. At the national level, 6.3 percent of workers were self-employed or unpaid family workers. In Vermont and Montana, the proportion reached nearly 10 percent. Delaware and West Virginia had the lowest level of self-employment, at 4.5 percent.

Income

The median income for all American households in 2012 was $51,371, ranging from a high of $71,122 in Maryland to a low of $37,095 in Mississippi. Among metropolitan areas, San Jose, California, had the highest median income ($90,737), while Brownsville-Harlingen, Texas, had the lowest median income, just under $31,000. Because the national median income declined slightly between 2010 and 2012, the 3-year median income for 2010–2012 was $51,771, slightly higher than the 2012 median. Five counties had 2010–2012 median incomes over $100,000: Loudoun, Fairfax, and Arlington Counties in Virginia; Howard County, Maryland; and Hunterdon County, New Jersey, while four counties had median incomes under $25,000: Clay County, Kentucky; McDowell County, West Virginia; LeFlore County, Mississippi; and Starr County, Texas. One hundred thirty-five cities had median household incomes higher than $100,000, topped by Darien, Connecticut, with a median of $185,583. Cities at the lower end of the income spectrum included East St. Louis and Carbondale, Illinois; Athens, Ohio, and Isla Vista, California, all under $20,000.

In the United States, households headed by 45- to 64-year-olds had higher incomes than other households. Among households of different race and Hispanic origin groups, Asian-headed households had the highest median incomes, followed by non-Hispanic Whites. Among household types, married-couple families had the highest median incomes. Among individuals, the median income for men was more than $10,000 higher than the median income for women. Per capita income is the total aggregate income in the geographic area, divided by the population of the area, resulting in a measure of the income for every man, woman, and child. The 2012 per capita income for the United States was $27,319, essentially the same as the 2010 per capita income.[1] The District of Columbia had

---

1. Source: 2012 American Community Survey 1-year Estimates, Comparison Table CP03.

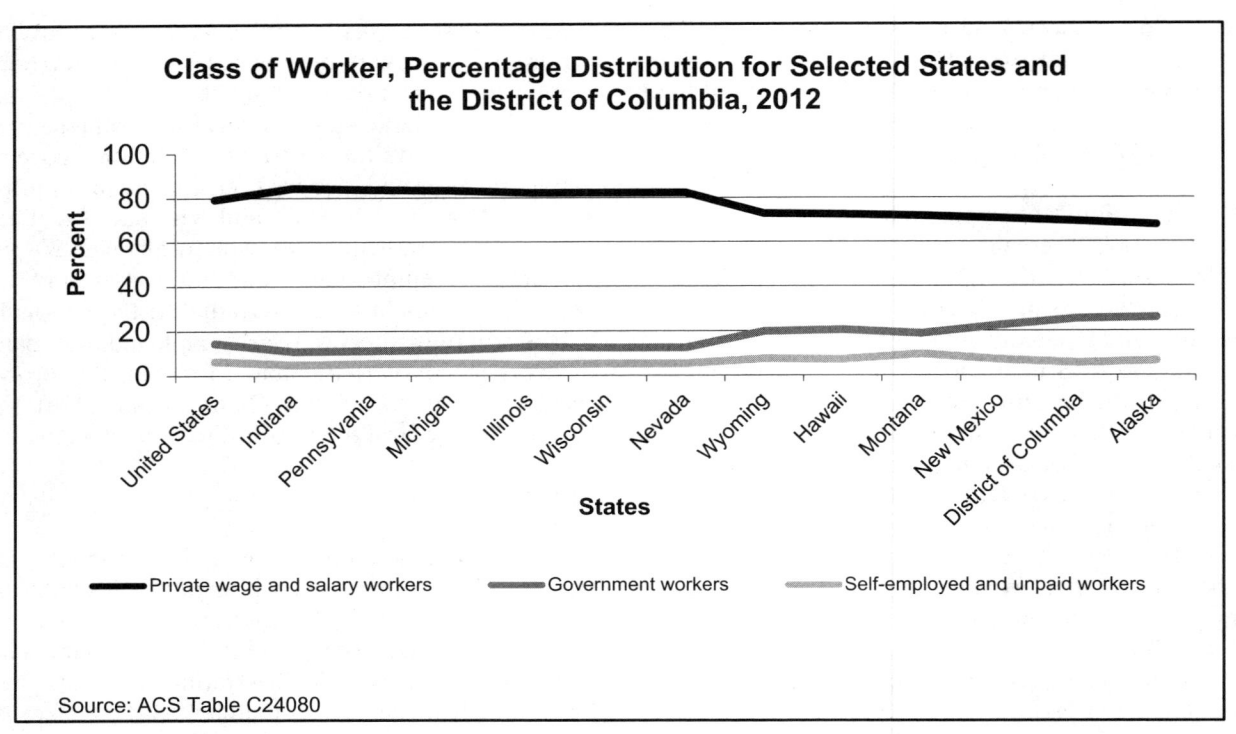

Class of Worker, Percentage Distribution for Selected States and the District of Columbia, 2012

States

— Private wage and salary workers — Government workers — Self-employed and unpaid workers

Source: ACS Table C24080

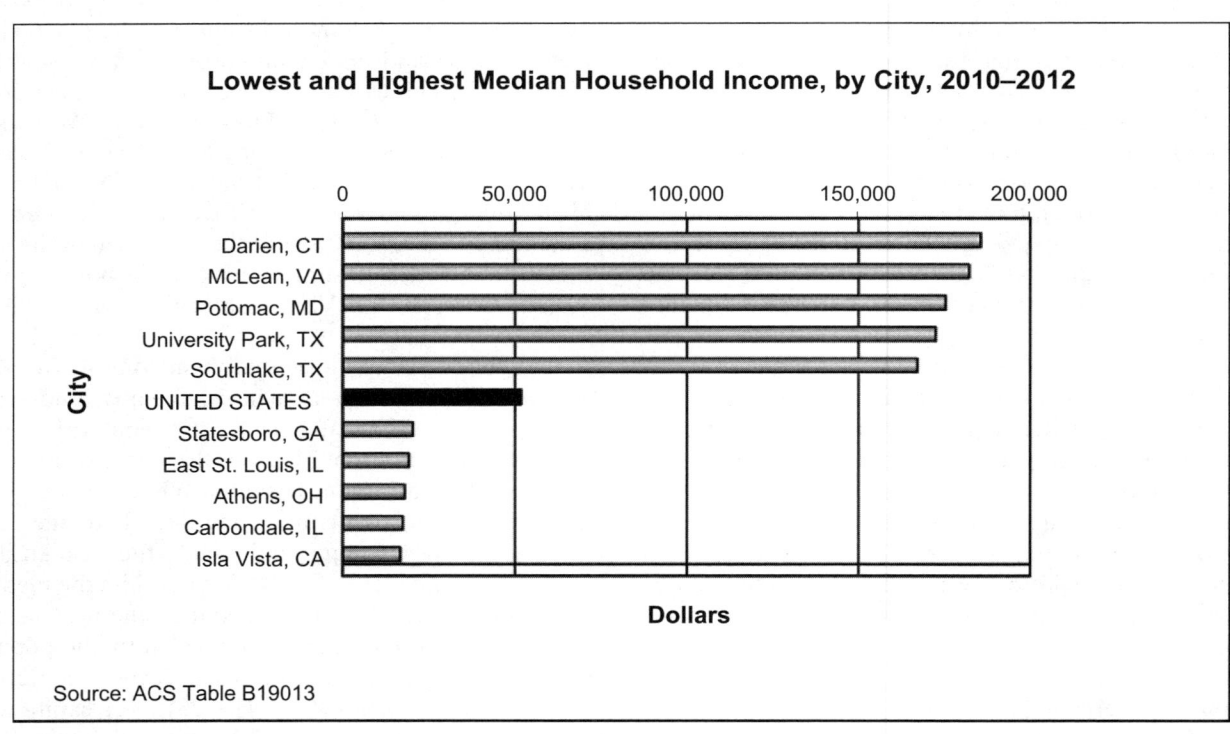

Lowest and Highest Median Household Income, by City, 2010–2012

Dollars

Source: ACS Table B19013

the highest per capita income, at $45,307 (partly because it has a very high proportion of one-person households), followed by Connecticut, Maryland, Massachusetts, and New Jersey, all over $34,000. The lowest per capita income—$20,119—was in Mississippi, while six other states had per capita income levels under $23,000.

Most American households (74.7 percent) had some wage and salary income in 2012, ranging from 82.9 percent of Alaska's households to 65.8 percent of West Virginia's households. Social Security income was reported by 28.4 percent of households. West Virginia had the highest level at 38.6 percent, and more than one-third of households in Florida, Maine, Arkansas, and Alabama collected Social Security. With younger populations, only 18.2 percent of the households in the District of Columbia and 20.4 percent of the households in Alaska had income from Social Security. In 2012, 14.3 percent of households reported income from cash public assistance or SNAP (Supplemental Assistance Nutrition Program, or Food Stamps.) Oregon had the highest proportion of households in this group—20.8 percent—and Mississippi, Kentucky, Maine, Michigan, and Tennessee, all had levels above 18 percent. The lowest levels were in Wyoming and North Dakota, at 7.6 and 8.1 percent. Interest, Dividend, and Net Rental Income were reported by 20.3 percent of households. The highest level was 42.3 percent of households in Alaska, where most residents receive an annual dividend payment from the state. Outside of Alaska, the highest level was 29 percent in Vermont. The lowest level was in Mississippi where only 12.1 percent of households had any income in this category.

About one in five American households had incomes over $100,000. In the District of Columbia, Maryland, and New Jersey, the proportion in this income bracket was more than one-third, and in West Virginia, Mississippi, and Arkansas, the proportion was below 13 percent. In ten metropolitan areas, more than one-third of households had incomes of $100,000 or more. In the Gadsden, Alabama, metropolitan area, only 7.4 percent of households had incomes in that range, and 13 metropolitan areas had levels below ten percent. In Loudon, Fairfax, and Arlington counties, Virginia; Howard County, Maryland; and Hunterdon County, New Jersey; more than half of all households had incomes of $100,000 or more in the 2010–2012 time period. In 39 additional counties, the proportion of $100,000 households was 40 percent or higher. In Hampshire County, West Virginia, and Lee County, Virginia, the proportion was below 4 percent. In Franklin Farm, Virginia, more than 80 percent of households had incomes of $100,000 or more. McLean, Linton Hall, and South Riding, Virginia; Potomac, Maryland; Southlake, Texas; Sammamish, Washington; and Saratoga, California; also had

$100,000 incomes in more than 70 percent of their households. Less than three percent of households in University (Hillsborough County), Florida; Prichard, Alabama; East St. Louis, Illinois; and Johnstown, Pennsylvania; had incomes higher than $100,000, and ten other cities had levels below 4 percent.

Poverty status is determined by a standard national definition that includes a household or family's income and number of household or family members. In the 2012 ACS, an estimated 14.7 percent of households were below the poverty level. The poverty measure does not vary from state to state, despite variations in the cost of living. In Mississippi, 22.4 percent of households had incomes below the poverty level, as did about 19 percent of households in New Mexico and Louisiana and less than 10 percent of households in Alaska, New Hampshire, and Maryland. In all states, poverty rates were higher for female-headed family households. The national rate for this group was 31.8 percent. In Mississippi, 44 percent of female-headed family households were below the poverty level, and Maryland's rate of 20.5 percent was the lowest in the nation.

In four metropolitan areas, more than 25 percent of families were below the poverty level— Brownsville, McAllen, and Laredo, Texas; and Porterville, California. At the other extreme, less than 5 percent of families in the Bismarck, North Dakota; Midland, Texas; Fairbanks, Alaska; Ithaca, New York; and Manhattan, Kansas; metropolitan areas had incomes below the poverty level. In 12 counties, most of them in Texas and Mississippi, more than 30 percent of families had incomes below the poverty level. Loudoun County, Virginia; and Hunterdon County, New Jersey; had poverty rates of less than 3 percent. Fifty-five cities, in 18 states, had family poverty rates over 30 percent. The highest level was in Kiryas Joel village, New York, where families below the poverty level were estimated at 51.6 percent. In eleven cities, less than 1 percent of families had incomes below the poverty level.

Nearly 25 percent of American households had incomes under $25,000, a few thousand dollars higher than the poverty level for a family of four. The proportion was more than 35 percent in Mississippi and less than 18 percent in New Hampshire, Maryland, Alaska, and Hawaii. In 20 cities more than half of all households had incomes below $25,000. The highest level was 62 percent in Isla Vista, California, primarily a student community near Santa Barbara. Both Carbondale and East St. Louis city, Illinois, had levels just below 60 percent. In eight cities, less than 4 percent of households had incomes below $25,000, with North Bellmore, New York, at only 2 percent.

Health Care Coverage

In 2012, about 85 percent of Americans had some type of health care coverage (public, private, or both), while 14.8 percent of all Americans had no health care coverage. Massachusetts had the highest percentage of residents with some type of health care coverage, at 96.1 percent and more than 90 percent of residents in nine other states had some health insurance coverage. Texas had the highest percentage of residents with no health care coverage, at 22.5 percent, while more than 20 percent of residents in Nevada, Alaska, and Florida also had no health insurance.

A little more than half of all Americans (54.1 percent) had only private health care coverage, while 20.1 percent had only public coverage, and 11 percent had both private and public health care coverage. Private insurance is most often employment-related, while public health insurance includes Medicare (primarily for persons age 65 and older), and Medicaid (mainly for low-income persons). With its low unemployment rate, North Dakota had the highest proportion of private health insurance at 66.6, while New Mexico with a low labor force participation rate, had the lowest proportion of private health insurance, at 43.7 percent. Mississippi and New Mexico had the highest proportion of public health care coverage, at almost 27 percent, reflecting their high unemployment and poverty levels—many low-income workers do not receive employment-based health insurance. Maine had the highest proportion of residents carrying both private and public health care coverage (14.7 percent), and five other states had levels at 14 percent or higher. Many Medicare recipients carry supplemental private insurance, and several states with large older populations have high proportions with both public and private insurance. The lowest proportion is shared by California and Texas, both just over 8 percent, and five other states with relatively young populations have less than 10 percent carrying both public and private insurance.

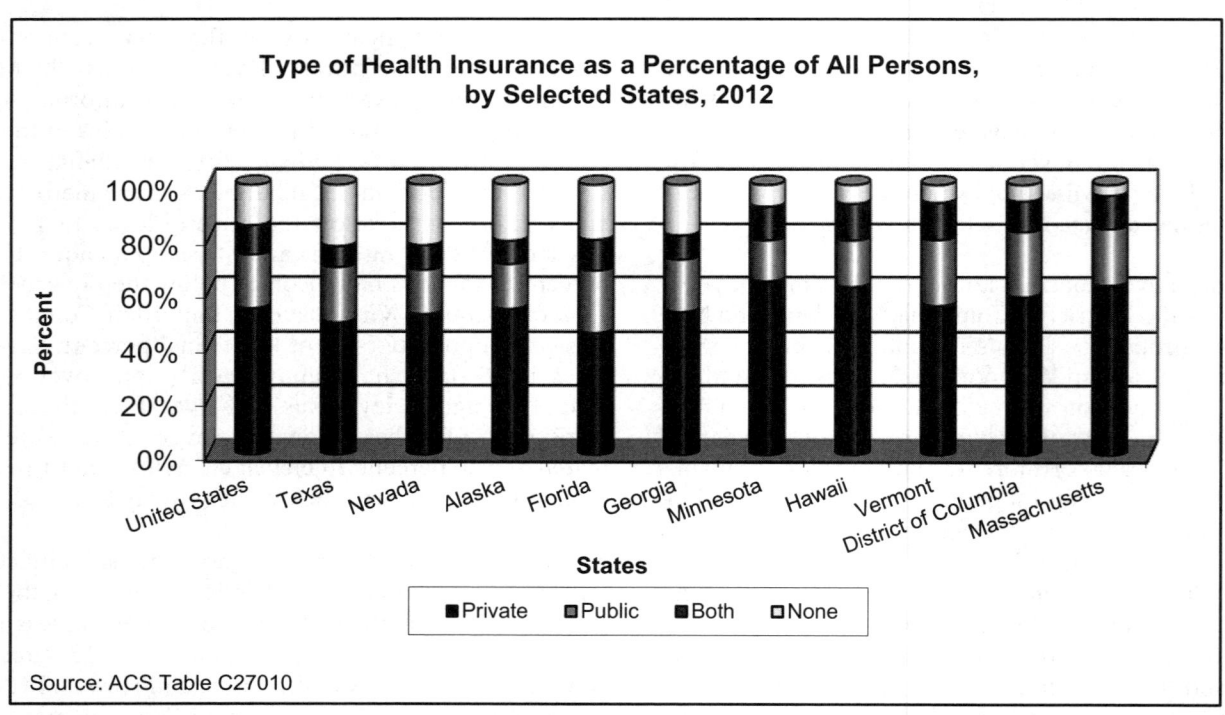

Source: ACS Table C27010

State Rankings, 2012
Selected Rankings

High school diploma or less rank	State	Percent with a high school diploma or less [B-1, cols. 2 + 3]	Bachelor's degree or more rank	State	Percent with a bachelor's degree or more [B-1, cols. 5 + 6]	Labor force participation rate rank	State	Labor force participation rate [B-1, col. 20]
	United States	41.7		United States	29.1		United States	63.8
1	West Virginia	56.1	1	District of Columbia	53.0	1	North Dakota	70.8
2	Louisiana	51.2	2	Massachusetts	39.3	2	Nebraska	70.4
3	Arkansas	50.4	3	Colorado	37.5	3	Alaska	70.4
4	Kentucky	50.3	4	Connecticut	37.1	4	Minnesota	70.1
5	Mississippi	48.2	5	Maryland	36.9	5	District of Columbia	69.0
6	Tennessee	47.9	6	New Jersey	36.2	6	South Dakota	68.9
6	Pennsylvania	47.9	7	Vermont	35.8	7	Maryland	68.8
8	Indiana	47.8	8	Virginia	35.5	8	Utah	68.8
9	Alabama	47.3	9	New Hampshire	34.6	9	Colorado	68.7
10	Ohio	45.8	10	New York	33.4	10	New Hampshire	68.7
11	Oklahoma	44.9	11	Minnesota	33.2	11	Wyoming	68.0
11	South Carolina	44.9	12	Washington	31.7	12	Iowa	67.7
13	Nevada	43.9	13	Illinois	31.6	13	Connecticut	67.7
14	Texas	43.7	14	Rhode Island	31.4	14	Kansas	67.4
14	Missouri	43.7	15	California	30.9	15	Massachusetts	67.3
16	Georgia	43.3	16	Utah	30.7	16	Vermont	67.3
16	Florida	43.3	17	Kansas	30.4	17	Wisconsin	67.3
18	Maine	43.2	18	Hawaii	30.1	18	Virginia	66.4
19	Delaware	43.0	19	Oregon	29.9	19	New Jersey	66.2
20	South Dakota	42.2	20	Delaware	29.5	20	Illinois	66.2
21	New Mexico	42.1	21	Montana	29.4	21	Rhode Island	66.1
22	North Carolina	42.0	22	Nebraska	29.0	22	Hawaii	65.5
23	Rhode Island	41.7	23	Georgia	28.2	23	Nevada	65.1
24	Wisconsin	41.6	24	Alaska	28.0	24	Washington	64.8
24	New York	41.6	24	Maine	28.0	25	Texas	64.8
26	Michigan	41.4	26	North Dakota	27.9	26	Montana	64.6
27	Iowa	40.7	27	Pennsylvania	27.8	27	Indiana	64.3
28	New Jersey	40.5	28	North Carolina	27.4	28	Delaware	64.1
29	Illinois	39.4	29	Arizona	27.3	29	Maine	63.9
30	California	39.1	30	Wisconsin	27.1	30	California	63.8
31	Vermont	38.8	31	Florida	26.8	31	Missouri	63.7
32	Wyoming	38.7	32	Texas	26.7	32	Idaho	63.7
33	Arizona	38.5	33	Missouri	26.4	33	New York	63.5
34	Idaho	37.9	34	Iowa	26.3	34	Ohio	63.3
34	Connecticut	37.9	34	South Dakota	26.3	35	North Carolina	63.1
34	Hawaii	37.9	36	New Mexico	26.1	36	Georgia	63.0
37	New Hampshire	37.6	37	Michigan	26.0	37	Pennsylvania	62.8
38	Virginia	37.4	38	Idaho	25.5	38	Oregon	62.4
39	Nebraska	37.2	39	Ohio	25.2	39	Oklahoma	61.8
40	Kansas	37.1	40	South Carolina	25.1	40	Louisiana	61.3
41	Maryland	37.0	41	Wyoming	24.7	41	Michigan	61.2
42	Montana	36.9	42	Tennessee	24.3	42	Tennessee	61.1
43	North Dakota	36.3	43	Oklahoma	23.8	43	South Carolina	61.0
43	Massachusetts	36.3	44	Indiana	23.4	44	Arizona	60.2
45	Alaska	36.0	45	Alabama	23.3	45	New Mexico	60.1
46	Oregon	35.2	46	Nevada	22.4	46	Kentucky	59.8
47	Minnesota	33.9	47	Louisiana	22.0	47	Florida	59.6
48	Washington	33.3	48	Kentucky	21.8	48	Arkansas	59.4
49	Utah	32.0	49	Arkansas	21.0	49	Alabama	58.5
50	Colorado	31.2	50	Mississippi	20.7	50	Mississippi	58.5
51	District of Columbia	29.9	51	West Virginia	18.6	51	West Virginia	54.1

State Rankings, 2012
Selected Rankings

Unemployment rate rank	State	Unemployment rate [B-1, col. 23]	Veterans rank	State	Veterans as a percent of population 18 years and over [B-1, col. 84]	Families with income below poverty rank	State	Percent of families with income below poverty [B-1, col. 139]
	United States	9.3		United States	8.9		United States	11.8
1	Nevada	12.2	1	Alaska	13.6	1	Mississippi	19.2
2	Florida	11.5	2	Montana	12.7	2	New Mexico	16.8
3	California	11.3	3	Virginia	11.7	3	Louisiana	15.5
3	Michigan	11.3	4	Maine	11.6	4	Georgia	15.0
5	Mississippi	11.2	5	New Mexico	11.4	5	Kentucky	14.8
6	South Carolina	11.1	6	Oklahoma	11.2	6	Alabama	14.7
7	Oregon	11.0	6	Washington	11.2	7	Arkansas	14.6
8	Georgia	10.9	8	Hawaii	11.1	8	South Carolina	14.1
9	North Carolina	10.6	8	West Virginia	11.1	9	Texas	14.0
10	District of Columbia	10.2	8	Wyoming	11.1	10	District of Columbia	13.9
10	New Mexico	10.2	11	Nevada	11.0	11	Tennessee	13.7
12	Illinois	10.1	11	South Dakota	11.0	12	Arizona	13.6
12	New Jersey	10.1	13	South Carolina	10.9	13	North Carolina	13.4
14	Alabama	9.9	14	Delaware	10.8	14	Oklahoma	13.1
15	Arizona	9.8	15	Oregon	10.7	15	California	12.9
16	Connecticut	9.7	15	Arizona	10.7	15	West Virginia	12.9
17	Tennessee	9.5	17	Idaho	10.6	17	Florida	12.6
18	Rhode Island	9.3	17	New Hampshire	10.6	17	Michigan	12.6
19	Kentucky	9.2	19	North Dakota	10.5	17	Nevada	12.6
19	New York	9.2	20	Alabama	10.4	20	New York	12.2
21	Ohio	9.1	20	Missouri	10.4	21	Oregon	12.1
22	Pennsylvania	8.8	20	Nebraska	10.4	22	Ohio	12.0
22	Indiana	8.8	20	Arkansas	10.4	23	Missouri	11.7
22	Louisiana	8.8	20	Colorado	10.4	23	Idaho	11.7
25	Delaware	8.7	25	Florida	10.2	25	Indiana	11.3
26	Washington	8.6	26	Kansas	10.0	26	Illinois	10.9
27	Missouri	8.5	27	North Carolina	9.8	27	Montana	10.2
27	Massachusetts	8.5	28	Maryland	9.7	28	Maine	9.8
29	Arkansas	8.4	28	Iowa	9.7	29	Utah	9.6
30	Maryland	8.2	30	Tennessee	9.6	30	Pennsylvania	9.5
31	West Virginia	8.0	30	Ohio	9.6	31	Kansas	9.3
31	Idaho	8.0	30	Vermont	9.6	31	Colorado	9.3
33	Texas	7.9	33	Georgia	9.5	31	Washington	9.3
34	Colorado	7.7	34	Kentucky	9.4	34	Rhode Island	9.2
35	Maine	7.6	35	Pennsylvania	9.3	35	Nebraska	9.1
36	Alaska	7.5	36	Wisconsin	9.2	36	Wisconsin	8.9
37	Wisconsin	7.3	36	Indiana	9.2	37	Iowa	8.8
38	Montana	7.1	38	Mississippi	9.1	38	South Dakota	8.6
39	Utah	6.8	39	Minnesota	9.0	38	Hawaii	8.6
39	Virginia	6.8	40	Louisiana	8.9	38	Virginia	8.6
41	Oklahoma	6.7	41	Michigan	8.7	41	Massachusetts	8.5
41	Hawaii	6.7	42	Rhode Island	8.5	41	Wyoming	8.5
43	New Hampshire	6.5	42	Texas	8.5	43	New Jersey	8.2
44	Kansas	6.4	44	Connecticut	7.7	43	Delaware	8.2
44	Vermont	6.4	45	Illinois	7.5	45	Connecticut	7.9
46	Minnesota	6.3	46	Utah	7.4	46	Minnesota	7.6
47	Wyoming	5.5	47	Massachusetts	7.3	47	Alaska	7.5
48	Iowa	5.3	48	California	6.5	48	Vermont	7.4
48	Nebraska	5.3	49	New Jersey	6.4	49	Maryland	7.3
50	South Dakota	4.7	50	District of Columbia	6.0	50	North Dakota	7.0
51	North Dakota	3.3	51	New York	5.8	51	New Hampshire	6.7

State Rankings, 2012
Selected Rankings

Median household income rank	State	Median household income (dollars) [B-1, col. 85]	Households with income of less than $25,000 rank	State	Percent of households with income of less than $25,000 [B-1, cols. 123 + 124 + 125]	Households with income of $100,000 or more rank	State	Percent of households with income of $100,000 or more [B-1, col. 133]
	United States	51,371		United States	24.4		United States	21.6
1	Maryland	71,122	1	Mississippi	35.6	1	District of Columbia	35.7
2	New Jersey	69,667	2	West Virginia	32.8	2	Maryland	34.5
3	Alaska	67,712	3	Arkansas	32.3	3	New Jersey	33.9
4	Connecticut	67,276	4	Alabama	31.3	4	Connecticut	32.5
5	District of Columbia	66,583	5	Louisiana	31.2	5	Massachusetts	31.6
6	Hawaii	66,259	6	Kentucky	31.1	6	Alaska	30.5
7	Massachusetts	65,339	7	New Mexico	29.9	7	Hawaii	29.1
8	New Hampshire	63,280	8	South Carolina	29.3	8	Virginia	28.8
9	Virginia	61,741	9	Tennessee	29.1	9	New Hampshire	27.6
10	Minnesota	58,906	10	Oklahoma	28.0	10	California	27.5
11	Delaware	58,415	11	North Carolina	27.7	11	New York	26.3
12	California	58,328	12	Montana	27.4	12	Washington	24.5
13	Washington	57,573	13	Missouri	27.2	13	Colorado	24.3
14	Utah	57,049	13	Georgia	27.2	14	Delaware	24.1
15	Colorado	56,765	15	Florida	27.1	14	Minnesota	24.1
16	New York	56,448	16	Ohio	26.9	16	Rhode Island	23.9
17	Illinois	55,137	17	Michigan	26.7	17	Illinois	23.7
18	Wyoming	54,901	18	Maine	25.7	18	Texas	21.4
19	Rhode Island	54,554	19	Oregon	25.5	19	Utah	21.1
20	North Dakota	53,585	20	Idaho	25.4	19	North Dakota	21.1
21	Vermont	52,977	21	Indiana	25.3	21	Wyoming	20.8
22	Pennsylvania	51,230	22	Arizona	25.2	22	Pennsylvania	20.3
23	Wisconsin	51,059	23	Texas	24.5	23	Vermont	19.3
24	Iowa	50,957	24	Rhode Island	24.3	24	Georgia	18.8
25	Texas	50,740	25	Pennsylvania	24.2	25	Kansas	18.6
26	Nebraska	50,723	26	New York	24.0	26	Oregon	18.5
27	Kansas	50,241	27	South Dakota	23.3	27	Arizona	18.4
28	Nevada	49,760	27	Kansas	23.3	28	Wisconsin	18.2
29	Oregon	49,161	29	Nevada	23.2	29	Nevada	17.8
30	South Dakota	48,362	30	Wisconsin	23.1	29	Nebraska	17.8
31	Arizona	47,826	30	Iowa	23.1	31	Iowa	17.5
32	Georgia	47,209	32	Illinois	22.8	32	Michigan	17.3
33	Indiana	46,974	33	Nebraska	22.7	33	Florida	17.1
34	Michigan	46,859	34	District of Columbia	22.4	34	Ohio	17.0
35	Ohio	46,829	35	Vermont	22.1	34	Louisiana	17.0
36	Maine	46,709	36	California	21.8	36	North Carolina	16.3
37	Idaho	45,489	37	Wyoming	21.2	37	New Mexico	16.2
38	Missouri	45,321	37	North Dakota	21.2	38	Missouri	16.0
39	North Carolina	45,150	39	Massachusetts	21.0	39	Indiana	15.9
40	Montana	45,076	40	Colorado	20.7	40	South Dakota	15.7
41	Florida	45,040	41	Washington	20.3	40	Maine	15.7
42	Oklahoma	44,312	42	Delaware	19.7	42	South Carolina	15.3
43	South Carolina	43,107	43	Minnesota	19.6	43	Montana	15.2
44	Louisiana	42,944	44	Virginia	19.3	44	Oklahoma	15.0
45	Tennessee	42,764	45	Connecticut	19.0	45	Alabama	14.9
46	New Mexico	42,558	45	Utah	19.0	46	Tennessee	14.8
47	Kentucky	41,724	47	New Jersey	18.0	47	Kentucky	14.4
48	Alabama	41,574	48	Hawaii	17.8	47	Idaho	14.4
49	West Virginia	40,196	49	New Hampshire	17.6	49	Arkansas	12.8
50	Arkansas	40,112	50	Maryland	16.4	50	Mississippi	12.3
51	Mississippi	37,095	51	Alaska	16.2	51	West Virginia	12.1

County Rankings, 2010–2012
Selected Rankings

High school diploma or less rank	County	Percent with a high school diploma or less [B-2, col. 2]	Bachelor's degree or more rank	County	Percent with a bachelor's degree or more [B-2, col. 3]	Unemployment rate rank	County	Unemployment rate [B-2, col. 6]
	United States	42.3		United States	28.6		United States	10.1
1	McDowell County, WV.............	78.2	1	Arlington County, VA...............	71.0	1	Washington County, MS	24.2
2	Hampshire County, WV...........	77.8	2	Alexandria city, VA.................	60.5	2	Clay County, KY..................	23.9
3	Holmes County, OH	77.3	3	Howard County, MD...............	59.7	3	Sunflower County, MS.........	23.2
4	Clay County, KY	76.2	4	New York County, NY	58.3	4	Yazoo County, MS	22.9
5	Starr County, TX.....................	74.7	5	Boulder County, CO	58.1	5	Hardeman County, TN..........	21.9
6	Knox County, KY.....................	72.3	6	Fairfax County, VA..................	57.8	6	Apache County, AZ..............	21.4
7	Willacy County, TX..................	72.1	7	Loudoun County, VA...............	57.0	7	Crook County, OR...............	20.5
8	Campbell County, TN	71.4	8	Montgomery County, MD	56.8	8	Clarendon County, SC..........	20.1
8	Cocke County, TN	71.4	9	Hamilton County, IN...............	55.2	8	Pike County, OH	20.1
10	Chattooga County, GA	71.1	10	Orange County, NC	55.0	10	Hertford County, NC	20.0
11	Morgan County, TN	70.9	11	Douglas County, CO	54.7	11	Plumas County, CA	19.9
12	Wyoming County, WV	70.8	12	Marin County, CA...................	54.3	11	Dallas County, AL................	19.9
13	Hardee County, FL..................	70.6	13	Fairfax city, VA.....................	53.1	11	Columbia County, FL............	19.9
13	Wayne County, KY..................	70.6	14	San Francisco County, CA	52.2	14	Navajo County, AZ	19.8
15	White County, TN	70.2	14	Albemarle County, VA.............	52.2	15	Leflore County, MS	19.7
16	Assumption Parish, LA	69.9	14	Williamson County, TN............	52.2	16	Coahoma County, MS...........	19.6
17	Avoyelles Parish, LA	69.8	17	Teton County, WY	51.8	17	Clarke County, AL................	19.5
17	Dunklin County, MO	69.8	18	District of Columbia	51.7	18	Edgecombe County, NC	19.1
19	Juniata County, PA	69.7	19	Johnson County, KS	51.5	19	Wayne County, MI	19.0
20	Lincoln County, WV	69.6	20	Johnson County, IA	51.4	19	Hardin County, TN	19.0
21	Hendry County, FL..................	69.5	21	Tompkins County, NY	51.3	21	Clay County, MS	18.9
21	Mifflin County, PA...................	69.5	22	Somerset County, NJ	51.0	21	Macon County, AL...............	18.9
21	Macon County, TN	69.5	23	Washtenaw County, MI............	50.4	21	Hernando County, FL	18.9
24	Scott County, TN	69.4	24	Middlesex County, MA.............	50.3	24	Tuolumne County, CA...........	18.7
25	Elbert County, GA...................	69.1	24	Delaware County, OH	50.3	24	Lyon County, NV	18.7
26	Pike County, OH	68.9	26	Summit County, CO	49.3	24	Imperial County, CA............	18.7
26	Hardeman County, TN.............	68.9	27	Albany County, WY	49.1	27	Dougherty County, GA..........	18.6
28	Bell County, KY	68.8	28	Morris County, NJ	49.0	27	Anson County, NC	18.6
29	Lauderdale County, TN	68.6	28	Boone County, MO	49.0	29	Petersburg city, VA.............	18.5
30	Murray County, GA.................	68.5	28	Benton County, OR	49.0	29	Halifax County, NC.............	18.5
30	Evangeline Parish, LA	68.5	31	Whitman County, WA..............	48.9	29	Adams County, OH	18.5
32	Grainger County, TN	68.4	32	Collin County, TX...................	48.8	29	Bradford County, FL	18.5
33	St. Martin Parish, LA	68.3	33	Norfolk County, MA................	48.6	33	Yuba County, CA	18.4
33	Boone County, WV	68.3	34	Charlottesville city, VA............	48.5	33	Wayne County, KY	18.4
35	Mitchell County, GA................	68.2	35	Eagle County, CO	48.4	35	Curry County, OR...............	18.3
35	St. Mary Parish, LA.................	68.2	36	Story County, IA	48.3	35	Martin County, NC..............	18.3
37	Poinsett County, AR	68.1	37	Fulton County, GA	48.2	35	Concordia Parish, LA	18.3
38	Lincoln County, KY..................	68.0	38	Chester County, PA	48.1	38	Barnwell County, SC	18.2
38	Acadia Parish, LA	68.0	39	Broomfield County, CO	48.0	39	Lake County, CA	18.1
40	Dillon County, SC...................	67.9	40	Summit County, UT	47.9	39	Marion County, SC..............	18.1
41	Claiborne County, TN	67.8	41	Douglas County, KS	47.8	39	Clare County, MI	18.1
41	Mingo County, WV	67.8	42	Hunterdon County, NJ.............	47.7	42	Amador County, CA.............	18.0
43	Grayson County, KY................	67.7	43	Chittenden County, VT.............	47.5	42	Jefferson County, OR	18.0
44	Yell County, AR......................	67.6	44	Wake County, NC	46.9	42	Richmond County, NC...........	18.0
44	Breckinridge County, KY	67.6	45	Madison County, MS................	46.6	42	Hendry County, FL...............	18.0
46	Warren County, TN	67.5	46	Santa Clara County, CA	46.5	46	Clayton County, GA.............	17.9
47	Jasper County, SC	67.4	46	Dane County, WI....................	46.5	47	Mecosta County, MI.............	17.8
48	Worth County, GA..................	67.2	48	Gallatin County, MT	46.4	47	Tehama County, CA	17.8
48	Hickman County, TN	67.2	49	Ozaukee County, WI...............	46.0	49	Merced County, CA	17.7
48	Jones County, TX	67.2	50	Bergen County, NJ	45.9	50	Bolivar County, MS..............	17.6
51	Washington County, MO	67.1	50	DuPage County, IL..................	45.9	50	Dillon County, SC	17.6
51	Marlboro County, SC...............	67.1	52	Hennepin County, MN.............	45.8	52	Genesee County, MI.............	17.5
51	Hardin County, TN	67.1	53	King County, WA	45.6	52	Stanislaus County, CA...........	17.5
54	Colquitt County, GA	67.0	54	Montgomery County, PA..........	45.5	54	Chester County, SC.............	17.3
55	Baker County, FL....................	66.8	54	James City County, VA.............	45.5	54	Northampton County, NC ...	17.3
55	Grady County, GA...................	66.8	56	Riley County, KS	45.3	56	San Joaquin County, CA......	17.2
55	Adams County, OH	66.8	56	Routt County, CO...................	45.3	57	Crisp County, GA	17.1
58	Okeechobee County, FL	66.7	58	Westchester County, NY	45.1	57	Nye County, NV	17.1
58	Whitley County, KY.................	66.7	59	Fairfield County, CT................	44.9	57	Escambia County, AL............	17.1
60	Meriwether County, GA...........	66.6	60	Leon County, FL.....................	44.6	57	Scott County, TN	17.1
61	DeSoto County, FL..................	66.5	61	Larimer County, CO	44.2	61	Cheboygan County, MI..........	16.8
61	Washington County, GA...........	66.5	62	Travis County, TX	44.1	61	Scotland County, NC............	16.8
61	Johnson County, KY................	66.5	62	Blaine County, ID	44.1	61	Phillips County, AR........	16.8
64	Overton County, TN	66.4	64	Durham County, NC................	44.0	61	Washington Parish, LA	16.8
65	Carroll County, OH.................	66.2	65	Montgomery County, VA..........	43.8	65	Danville city, VA.................	16.7
65	Buchanan County, VA	66.2	65	Oktibbeha County, MS.............	43.8	65	Citrus County, FL................	16.7
67	St. Landry Parish, LA	66.1	65	Cobb County, GA	43.8	65	Talladega County, AL............	16.7
67	McNairy County, TN	66.1	65	Oconee County, GA	43.8	65	Fayette County, IN..............	16.7
67	Maverick County, TX...............	66.1	69	Carver County, MN	43.7	69	Polk County, NC.................	16.6
70	Lafourche Parish, LA	66.0	70	San Mateo County, CA............	43.6	69	Iron County, UT.................	16.6
70	Brown County, OH..................	66.0	71	La Plata County, CO	43.5	69	Colleton County, SC.............	16.6
72	Burke County, GA...................	65.9	72	Newport County, RI.................	43.3	72	Carson City, NV..................	16.5
72	LaGrange County, IN...............	65.9	72	Washington County, RI.............	43.3	72	Hampton County, SC............	16.5
74	Northumberland County, PA	65.7	74	Bristol County, RI...................	43.2	74	Highlands County, FL...........	16.4
75	Vermilion Parish, LA	65.6	75	Hampshire County, MA............	43.1	74	Highland County, OH...........	16.4
75	Bedford County, TN	65.6				74	Knox County, KY.................	16.4
75	Page County, VA	65.6						
75	Mineral County, WV................	65.6						

County Rankings, 2010–2012
Selected Rankings

Families with income below poverty rank	County	Percent of families with income below poverty [B-2, col. 10]	Households with income of less than $25,000 rank	County	Percent of households with income of less than $25,000 [B-2, col. 11]	Households with income of $100,000 or more rank	County	Percent of households with income of $100,000 or more [B-2, col. 12]
	United States	11.6		United States	24.1		United States	
1	Starr County, TX......................	40.6	1	Clay County, KY......................	56.0	1	Loudoun County, VA...............	61.2
2	Sunflower County, MS	35.3	2	McDowell County, WV............	53.4	2	Fairfax County, VA	54.4
3	Washington County, MS	33.8	3	Leflore County, MS	51.1	3	Howard County, MD...............	53.7
4	Willacy County, TX..................	33.5	4	Starr County, TX......................	50.7	4	Hunterdon County, NJ............	51.4
5	Leflore County, MS	33.0	5	Bell County, KY	49.8	5	Arlington County, VA..............	50.7
6	Coahoma County, MS	32.9	5	Williamsburg County, SC	49.8	6	Somerset County, NJ	49.1
7	Hidalgo County, TX.................	31.1	7	Dallas County, AL	49.4	6	Douglas County, CO	49.1
8	Dallas County, AL	31.0	8	Coahoma County, MS	49.2	8	Fairfax city, VA.......................	49.0
9	Clay County, KY	30.9	9	Harlan County, KY	49.1	9	Montgomery County, MD	48.0
9	Yazoo County, MS	30.9	10	Yazoo County, MS	48.7	10	Stafford County, VA................	47.9
11	McKinley County, NM	30.7	10	Knox County, KY.....................	48.7	11	Nassau County, NY	47.5
12	Cameron County, TX................	30.3	12	Adams County, MS	48.6	12	Prince William County, VA.......	47.4
13	McDowell County, WV	29.8	13	Hampshire County, WV............	48.4	13	Morris County, NJ	47.1
14	Maverick County, TX...............	29.6	14	Dillon County, SC	48.0	14	Putnam County, NY	46.5
15	Bolivar County, MS.................	28.8	15	Willacy County, TX..................	47.8	15	Summit County, UT	46.0
16	Harlan County, KY	28.5	16	Washington County, MS	47.4	15	Calvert County, MD	46.0
17	Bell County, KY	28.3	17	Grady County, GA...................	46.9	17	Santa Clara County, CA	45.2
18	Bronx County, NY	28.0	17	Morehouse Parish, LA	46.9	18	Charles County, MD................	44.7
19	Dillon County, SC	27.8	19	Sunflower County, MS	46.6	19	Williamson County, TN...........	44.3
19	Webb County, TX....................	27.8	20	Marlboro County, SC	46.4	20	Fauquier County, VA...............	44.2
21	Apache County, AZ..................	27.5	21	Wayne County, MS	46.2	21	King George County, VA.........	44.1
22	Dougherty County, GA.............	27.1	22	Mineral County, WV................	46.0	22	Marin County, CA...................	43.9
23	Phillips County, AR	26.9	23	Phillips County, AR	45.9	23	San Mateo County, CA	43.2
24	Knox County, KY.....................	26.8	24	Wayne County, KY	45.6	24	Delaware County, OH	43.0
24	Hardee County, FL..................	26.8	24	Cocke County, TN...................	45.6	25	Suffolk County, NY	42.4
26	Marlboro County, SC	26.6	26	Bladen County, NC	45.5	25	Anne Arundel County, MD......	42.4
27	Crisp County, GA....................	26.5	27	Hardeman County, TN.............	45.4	27	Rockland County, NY	42.1
28	Decatur County, GA................	26.3	28	Escambia County, AL...............	45.1	27	Forsyth County, GA................	42.1
29	Lauderdale County, TN............	25.9	29	Floyd County, KY	45.0	29	Monmouth County, NJ............	41.8
30	Robeson County, NC	25.8	30	Clarke County, AL	44.6	30	Goochland County, VA............	41.7
31	Cibola County, NM	25.7	31	Decatur County, GA................	44.5	31	Norfolk County, MA................	41.6
32	Franklin Parish, LA..................	25.5	31	Marion County, SC..................	44.5	32	Chester County, PA.................	41.5
33	Scotland County, NC...............	25.4	33	Bolivar County, MS.................	44.4	32	Alexandria city, VA.................	41.5
34	Concordia Parish, LA	25.0	34	Evangeline Parish, LA	44.1	34	Westchester County, NY	41.2
34	Wayne County, MS	25.0	35	Monroe County, AL.................	44.0	34	Bergen County, NJ	41.2
36	Barnwell County, SC	24.9	36	Poinsett County, AR	43.9	36	Fairfield County, CT................	41.0
37	Escambia County, AL...............	24.8	37	Hertford County, NC	43.7	37	Queen Anne's County, MD......	40.9
37	Adams County, MS	24.8	37	Luna County, NM	43.7	38	St. Mary's County, MD	40.8
39	Madison County, ID	24.7	39	San Miguel County, NM...........	43.6	38	Sussex County, NJ	40.8
40	Navajo County, AZ..................	24.6	40	Maverick County, TX...............	43.4	40	Collin County, TX....................	40.6
41	Thomas County, GA................	24.5	41	Campbell County, TN..............	43.1	41	Frederick County, MD	40.5
41	Floyd County, KY	24.5	42	Concordia Parish, LA	43.0	42	Carroll County, MD.................	40.4
43	Wayne County, KY	24.4	43	Macon County, AL	42.8	43	Middlesex County, MA............	40.0
43	Hart County, GA	24.4	43	Mitchell County, GA................	42.8	43	Fort Bend County, TX.............	40.0
43	Union Parish, LA	24.4	45	Dougherty County, GA.............	42.7	45	Carver County, MN	39.9
46	Forrest County, MS	24.3	45	Hempstead County, AR	42.7	46	Rockwall County, TX...............	39.6
46	Williamsburg County, SC	24.3	47	Oktibbeha County, MS............	42.6	46	Hamilton County, IN	39.6
46	Grady County, GA	24.3	47	Marion County, MS.................	42.6	48	Scott County, MN	39.0
49	Hendry County, FL..................	24.1	49	Scotland County, NC...............	42.5	49	Contra Costa County, CA.........	38.5
49	Cocke County, TN...................	24.1	49	Thomas County, GA................	42.5	50	San Francisco County, CA	38.3
49	Tattnall County, GA.................	24.1	49	Scott County, TN....................	42.5	50	Fayette County, GA.................	38.3
49	Morehouse Parish, LA	24.1	52	Robeson County, NC	42.4	52	York County, VA	38.1
49	Burke County, GA	24.1	53	Marengo County, AL...............	42.3	53	Lake County, IL.......................	37.9
54	Poinsett County, AR	24.0	53	Whitley County, KY.................	42.3	54	Montgomery County, PA.........	37.8
54	Montgomery County, NC	24.0	53	Winston County, AL................	42.3	55	Elbert County, CO	37.7
54	Perry County, KY	24.0	56	McKinley County, NM	42.2	56	Kendall County, IL	37.6
57	DeSoto County, FL..................	23.6	56	Washington Parish, LA	42.2	57	Middlesex County, NJ.............	37.3
58	Clay County, MS	23.5	56	Pike County, AL......................	42.2	57	Tolland County, CT.................	37.3
59	Lowndes County, MS	23.4	59	Baldwin County, GA	42.1	59	Washington County, MN..........	37.2
59	Leake County, MS	23.4	60	Franklin Parish, LA	42.0	60	Oldham County, KY	37.1
61	Orleans Parish, LA	23.2	61	Clay County, MS	41.9	61	New York County, NY	36.7
62	Macon County, AL...................	23.1	61	Halifax County, NC.................	41.9	61	Broomfield County, CO	36.7
62	Mitchell County, GA................	23.1	61	Jackson County, IL..................	41.9	61	DuPage County, IL..................	36.7
64	Santa Cruz County, AZ............	23.0	61	Hardin County, TN	41.9	64	Spotsylvania County, VA.........	36.4
64	Colquitt County, GA................	23.0	61	Houston County, TX................	41.9	64	Rockingham County, NH..........	36.4
66	Baldwin County, GA	22.9	66	Hart County, GA	41.8	66	Middlesex County, CT	36.3
67	Doña Ana County, NM............	22.7	66	Covington County, MS	41.8	67	Burlington County, NJ.............	36.2
67	St. Francis County, AR	22.7	66	Butler County, AL...................	41.8	68	Orange County, CA.................	36.1
67	McCurtain County, OK.............	22.7	69	Dunklin County, MO	41.7	69	Mercer County, NJ	36.0
67	Hempstead County, AR	22.7	69	Bertie County, NC	41.7	69	Harford County, MD	36.0
71	Covington County, MS.............	22.6	71	Burke County, GA...................	41.6	71	Ventura County, CA................	35.8
71	Rowan County, KY	22.6	71	Lincoln County, KY.................	41.6	72	Powhatan County, VA.............	35.7
73	Chester County, SC	22.5	71	Whitman County, WA..............	41.6	72	Ozaukee County, WI...............	35.7
73	Danville city, VA	22.5	74	Forrest County, MS	41.5	74	Bucks County, PA...................	35.5
73	Lincoln County, KY.................	22.5	74	Chesterfield County, SC	41.5	74	Oconee County, GA................	35.5

Metropolitan Area Rankings, 2012
Selected Rankings

High school diploma or less rank	Area name	Percent with a high school diploma or less [B-3, col. 2]	Bachelor's degree or more rank	Area name	Percent with a bachelor's degree or more [B-3, col. 3]
	United States	41.6		United States	29.1
1	Vineland-Millville-Bridgeton, NJ	63.3	1	Boulder, CO	57.9
2	Houma-Bayou Cane-Thibodaux, LA	63.2	2	Corvallis, OR	53.1
3	Dalton, GA	61.9	3	Ithaca, NY	51.9
4	Brownsville-Harlingen, TX	61.2	4	Ames, IA	50.8
5	Altoona, PA	60.8	5	Ann Arbor, MI	49.7
5	McAllen-Edinburg-Mission, TX	60.8	6	Washington-Arlington-Alexandria, DC-VA-MD-WV	48.2
7	Morristown, TN	60.3	7	Lawrence, KS	48.0
8	Laredo, TX	59.7	8	Columbia, MO	47.8
9	Merced, CA	59.0	9	Iowa City, IA	47.6
10	El Centro, CA	58.9	10	San Jose-Sunnyvale-Santa Clara, CA	46.4
11	Lebanon, PA	58.8	11	Bridgeport-Stamford-Norwalk, CT	46.3
12	Pine Bluff, AR	57.9	12	San Francisco-Oakland-Fremont, CA	45.0
13	Johnstown, PA	57.3	13	Fort Collins-Loveland, CO	44.7
14	Elkhart-Goshen, IN	57.1	13	Durham, NC	44.7
15	Visalia-Porterville, CA	56.7	15	Bloomington-Normal, IL	43.6
16	Cumberland, MD-WV	56.6	16	Charlottesville, VA	43.1
17	Madera, CA	56.4	17	Boston-Cambridge-Quincy, MA-NH	42.9
18	Rocky Mount, NC	56.2	18	Missoula, MT	42.8
19	Yakima, WA	55.0	19	Madison, WI	42.6
20	Reading, PA	54.7	20	Raleigh-Cary, NC	42.0
21	Lake Havasu City-Kingman, AZ	54.5	20	Burlington-South Burlington, VT	42.0
21	Hanford-Corcoran, CA	54.5	22	Barnstable Town, MA	40.6
21	Mansfield, OH	54.5	23	Austin-Round Rock, TX	40.5
24	Gadsden, AL	54.4	24	Champaign-Urbana, IL	40.1
25	Lancaster, PA	54.3	25	Denver-Aurora, CO	39.9
26	Danville, VA	54.1	26	Santa Fe, NM	39.5
26	Youngstown-Warren-Boardman, OH-PA	54.1	26	Minneapolis-St. Paul-Bloomington, MN-WI	39.5
28	Fort Smith, AR-OK	54.0	28	State College, PA	39.4
28	Michigan City-La Porte, IN	54.0	29	Gainesville, FL	38.6
28	Williamsport, PA	54.0	30	Santa Cruz-Watsonville, CA	38.3
31	Odessa, TX	53.9	31	Trenton-Ewing, NJ	38.2
31	Wheeling, WV-OH	53.9	32	Seattle-Tacoma-Bellevue, WA	37.7
33	York-Hanover, PA	53.8	33	Manchester-Nashua, NH	37.3
33	Cleveland, TN	53.8	34	Fargo, ND-MN	37.1
33	Dothan, AL	53.8	34	Tallahassee, FL	37.1
36	Owensboro, KY	53.7	36	New York-Northern New Jersey-Long Island, NY-NJ-PA	37.0
37	Parkersburg-Marietta-Vienna, WV-OH	53.6	37	Huntsville, AL	36.9
38	Kingsport-Bristol-Bristol, TN-VA	53.5	38	Hartford-West Hartford-East Hartford, CT	36.6
38	Steubenville-Weirton, OH	53.5	39	Portland-South Portland-Biddeford, ME	36.5
40	Bakersfield, CA	53.4	40	Baltimore-Towson, MD	36.4
40	Hickory-Lenoir-Morganton, NC	53.4	41	Lincoln, NE	35.9
42	Anniston-Oxford, AL	53.3	41	Rochester, MN	35.9
43	Huntington-Ashland, WV-KY-OH	52.8	43	Provo-Orem, UT	35.8
43	Lake Charles, LA	52.8	44	College Station-Bryan, TX	35.7
45	Lakeland, FL	52.7	45	Athens-Clarke County, GA	35.5
45	Alexandria, LA	52.7	46	Atlanta-Sandy Springs-Marietta, GA	35.3
47	Hagerstown-Martinsburg, MD-WV	52.3	47	Lexington-Fayette, KY	35.2
48	Anderson, IN	52.2	48	Portland-Vancouver-Beaverton, OR-WA	35.1
48	Springfield, OH	52.2	49	Des Moines-West Des Moines, IA	35.0
50	Yuma, AZ	52.1	50	Chicago-Naperville-Joliet, IL-IN-WI	34.8
50	Danville, IL	52.1	50	Colorado Springs, CO	34.8
52	St. Joseph, MO-KS	51.8	50	San Diego-Carlsbad-San Marcos, CA	34.8
53	Gainesville, GA	51.7	53	Logan, UT-ID	34.6
54	Victoria, TX	51.6	54	Albany-Schenectady-Troy, NY	34.1
55	Terre Haute, IN	51.4	54	Columbus, OH	34.1
55	Decatur, AL	51.4	56	Philadelphia-Camden-Wilmington, PA-NJ-DE-MD	34.0
57	Johnson City, TN	51.1	57	Omaha-Council Bluffs, NE-IA	33.7
57	Florence-Muscle Shoals, AL	51.1	58	Worcester, MA	33.6
59	Modesto, CA	51.0	59	San Luis Obispo-Paso Robles, CA	33.5
59	Ocala, FL	51.0	59	Kansas City, MO-KS	33.5
61	Anderson, SC	50.9	61	Charlotte-Gastonia-Concord, NC-SC	33.4
62	Harrisonburg, VA	50.8	62	Mankato-North Mankato, MN	33.2
62	Jonesboro, AR	50.8	62	Manhattan, KS	33.2
62	Scranton–Wilkes-Barre, PA	50.8	64	Springfield, IL	33.1
62	Rome, GA	50.8	65	Auburn-Opelika, AL	32.9
66	Charleston, WV	50.7	66	New Haven-Milford, CT	32.7
67	Kokomo, IN	50.6	67	Nashville-Davidson–Murfreesboro–Franklin, TN	32.6
68	Macon, GA	50.4	67	Richmond, VA	32.6
69	Spartanburg, SC	50.3	67	Bloomington, IN	32.6
69	Lima, OH	50.3	70	Milwaukee-Waukesha-West Allis, WI	32.5
71	Monroe, LA	50.2	71	Salt Lake City, UT	32.4
72	Beaumont-Port Arthur, TX	50.1	72	Bend, OR	32.3
72	Fresno, CA	50.1	73	Honolulu, HI	32.2
74	Joplin, MO	49.9	73	Lansing-East Lansing, MI	32.2
75	Sioux City, IA-NE-SD	49.7	75	Indianapolis-Carmel, IN	32.1
75	Atlantic City, NJ	49.7			
75	Florence, SC	49.7			

Metropolitan Area Rankings, 2012
Selected Rankings

Families with income below poverty rank	Area name	Percent of families with income below poverty [B-3, col. 10]	Households with income of $100,000 or more rank	Area name	Percent of households with income of $100,000 or more [B-3, col. 12]
	United States	11.8		United States	21.6
1	Brownsville-Harlingen, TX	31.9	1	San Jose-Sunnyvale-Santa Clara, CA	45.4
2	McAllen-Edinburg-Mission, TX	30.2	2	Washington-Arlington-Alexandria, DC-VA-MD-WV	44.1
3	Laredo, TX	27.8	3	Bridgeport-Stamford-Norwalk, CT	41.8
4	Visalia-Porterville, CA	25.6	4	San Francisco-Oakland-Fremont, CA	38.5
5	Fresno, CA	24.1	5	Boston-Cambridge-Quincy, MA-NH	35.4
6	Monroe, LA	21.7	6	Trenton-Ewing, NJ	34.9
7	Albany, GA	21.6	7	Boulder, CO	34.4
7	Las Cruces, NM	21.6	8	Anchorage, AK	34.2
9	El Centro, CA	21.4	9	Oxnard-Thousand Oaks-Ventura, CA	33.6
10	Pine Bluff, AR	21.1	10	Santa Cruz-Watsonville, CA	33.3
11	Merced, CA	20.6	11	Baltimore-Towson, MD	32.5
11	El Paso, TX	20.6	12	Honolulu, HI	32.2
13	Bakersfield, CA	20.0	13	New York-Northern New Jersey-Long Island, NY-NJ-PA	32.0
14	Hattiesburg, MS	19.2	14	Napa, CA	31.7
15	Goldsboro, NC	19.1	15	Poughkeepsie-Newburgh-Middletown, NY	31.4
16	Rocky Mount, NC	19.0	16	Manchester-Nashua, NH	31.1
16	Madera, CA	19.0	17	Norwich-New London, CT	30.9
18	Yuma, AZ	18.7	18	Hartford-West Hartford-East Hartford, CT	30.8
18	Texarkana, TX-Texarkana, AR	18.7	19	Seattle-Tacoma-Bellevue, WA	30.4
20	Anniston-Oxford, AL	18.4	20	Minneapolis-St. Paul-Bloomington, MN-WI	29.5
21	Valdosta, GA	18.3	21	Worcester, MA	29.0
22	Rome, GA	18.2	21	Midland, TX	29.0
23	Flagstaff, AZ	18.1	23	Charlottesville, VA	28.9
23	Muskegon-Norton Shores, MI	18.1	24	Philadelphia-Camden-Wilmington, PA-NJ-DE-MD	28.0
25	Fort Smith, AR-OK	18.0	25	San Diego-Carlsbad-San Marcos, CA	27.8
25	Dalton, GA	18.0	26	Santa Barbara-Santa Maria-Goleta, CA	27.7
27	Macon, GA	17.8	26	Santa Rosa-Petaluma, CA	27.7
28	Yakima, WA	17.6	26	Vallejo-Fairfield, CA	27.7
28	Mobile, AL	17.6	29	New Haven-Milford, CT	27.6
30	Morristown, TN	17.5	30	Denver-Aurora, CO	27.4
31	Farmington, NM	17.4	31	Los Angeles-Long Beach-Santa Ana, CA	27.2
32	Hanford-Corcoran, CA	17.3	32	Fairbanks, AK	26.8
33	Decatur, IL	17.2	33	Chicago-Naperville-Joliet, IL-IN-WI	26.7
34	Florence, SC	17.0	34	Raleigh-Cary, NC	26.6
35	Gulfport-Biloxi, MS	16.8	34	San Luis Obispo-Paso Robles, CA	26.6
36	Alexandria, LA	16.7	36	Austin-Round Rock, TX	26.5
37	Michigan City-La Porte, IN	16.6	37	Houston-Sugar Land-Baytown, TX	26.3
37	Yuba City, CA	16.6	38	Ann Arbor, MI	26.1
39	Gadsden, AL	16.5	38	Barnstable Town, MA	26.1
40	Flint, MI	16.4	38	Bismarck, ND	26.1
40	Augusta-Richmond County, GA-SC	16.4	41	Rochester, MN	25.7
40	Jackson, MS	16.4	42	Bloomington-Normal, IL	25.3
43	Salem, OR	16.2	43	Albany-Schenectady-Troy, NY	25.1
43	Gainesville, GA	16.2	44	Dallas-Fort Worth-Arlington, TX	25.0
45	Modesto, CA	16.0	44	Sacramento–Arden-Arcade–Roseville, CA	25.0
46	Lake Havasu City-Kingman, AZ	15.8	46	Salinas, CA	24.6
47	Winston-Salem, NC	15.7	47	Burlington-South Burlington, VT	24.5
48	Vineland-Millville-Bridgeton, NJ	15.6	48	Portland-Vancouver-Beaverton, OR-WA	24.4
49	Memphis, TN-MS-AR	15.5	49	Richmond, VA	24.3
49	Springfield, OH	15.5	50	Kennewick-Richland-Pasco, WA	24.2
49	Tuscaloosa, AL	15.5	50	Huntsville, AL	24.2
49	Decatur, AL	15.5	50	Madison, WI	24.2
53	Anderson, SC	15.4	53	Corvallis, OR	23.9
54	Spartanburg, SC	15.3	53	Bremerton-Silverdale, WA	23.9
54	Albuquerque, NM	15.3	55	Atlanta-Sandy Springs-Marietta, GA	23.7
54	Riverside-San Bernardino-Ontario, CA	15.3	55	Des Moines-West Des Moines, IA	23.7
54	Dothan, AL	15.3	57	Salt Lake City, UT	23.6
58	Warner Robins, GA	15.2	57	Providence-New Bedford-Fall River, RI-MA	23.6
58	Lubbock, TX	15.2	59	Ocean City, NJ	23.5
60	Johnson City, TN	15.1	59	Naples-Marco Island, FL	23.5
61	Jackson, MI	15.0	59	Kingston, NY	23.5
61	Greenville, NC	15.0	62	Colorado Springs, CO	23.4
63	Niles-Benton Harbor, MI	14.9	62	Ithaca, NY	23.4
64	Burlington, NC	14.8	64	Virginia Beach-Norfolk-Newport News, VA-NC	22.8
64	Cleveland, TN	14.8	65	Fort Collins-Loveland, CO	22.7
64	Beaumont-Port Arthur, TX	14.8	66	Durham, NC	22.6
67	Mansfield, OH	14.7	67	Ogden-Clearfield, UT	22.4
67	Lima, OH	14.7	67	Iowa City, IA	22.4
67	Sumter, SC	14.7	67	Casper, WY	22.4
67	Stockton, CA	14.7	70	Olympia, WA	22.2
67	Gainesville, FL	14.7	70	Charlotte-Gastonia-Concord, NC-SC	22.2
72	New Orleans-Metairie-Kenner, LA	14.6	72	Cheyenne, WY	22.1
72	Shreveport-Bossier City, LA	14.6	73	Kansas City, MO-KS	22.0
72	Athens-Clarke County, GA	14.6	74	Columbus, OH	21.8
75	Bend, OR	14.5	75	Cincinnati-Middletown, OH-KY-IN	21.7
75	Toledo, OH	14.5	75	Cedar Rapids, IA	21.7

City Rankings, 2010–2012
Selected Rankings

High school diploma or less rank	City	Percent with a high school diploma or less [B-4, col. 2]	Bachelor's degree or more rank	City	Percent with a bachelor's degree or more [B-4, col. 3]	Unemployment rate rank	City	Unemployment rate [B-4, col. 6]
	United States	42.3		United States	28.0		United States	10.1
1	Immokalee CDP, FL...........	85.8	1	Bethesda CDP, MD............	83.2	1	Detroit city, MI................	29.8
2	Cudahy city, CA...............	82.2	2	Wellesley CDP, MA............	82.7	2	Flint city, MI...................	28.1
3	Florence-Graham CDP, CA	82.0	3	Wilmette village, IL............	81.8	3	Harvey city, IL.................	28.0
4	Bell Gardens city, CA........	81.2	4	McLean CDP, VA...............	80.5	4	Inkster city, MI...............	26.4
5	Arvin city, CA.................	81.0	5	Palo Alto city, CA.............	79.6	5	Sun City Center CDP, FL.....	26.3
6	Coachella city, CA............	80.6	6	Potomac CDP, MD.............	79.5	6	York city, PA..................	25.6
6	Maywood city, CA............	80.6	7	Brookline CDP, MA............	78.5	7	Camden city, NJ..............	24.8
8	Huntington Park city, CA....	80.5	8	Darien CDP, CT................	77.9	8	Selma city, AL.................	24.7
9	Langley Park CDP, MD........	79.6	9	Los Altos city, CA.............	77.0	8	Saginaw city, MI..............	24.7
10	Lennox CDP, CA...............	79.2	10	Saratoga city, CA.............	76.7	10	Muskegon city, MI............	24.5
11	Kiryas Joel village, NY.......	78.4	11	Lexington CDP, MA............	75.7	11	Mead Valley CDP, CA........	24.2
12	Wasco city, CA...............	78.3	12	Newton city, MA..............	75.5	12	Adelanto city, CA............	24.1
13	East Los Angeles CDP, CA ...	76.5	12	North Potomac CDP, MD......	75.5	13	Greenville city, MS...........	23.9
13	Bridgeton city, NJ...........	76.5	14	Westport CDP, CT.............	75.3	13	Dolton village, IL.............	23.9
15	South El Monte city, CA.....	76.3	15	Cupertino city, CA............	75.0	15	University CDP (Hillsborough County), FL.....	23.8
16	Shelbyville city, TN..........	75.7	16	Mercer Island city, WA.......	74.8	16	Coachella city, CA............	23.6
17	Lynwood city, CA............	75.1	17	Lafayette city, CA.............	74.7	17	Candler-McAfee CDP, GA....	23.3
18	South Gate city, CA..........	74.7	18	Cambridge city, MA..........	74.3	18	West Pensacola CDP, FL......	22.9
19	Delano city, CA..............	74.0	19	Ridgewood village, NJ.........	74.1	19	San Jacinto city, CA..........	22.8
20	Bell city, CA..................	73.6	20	Chapel Hill town, NC	74.0	20	Prichard city, AL..............	22.1
21	Cicero town, IL...............	73.2	20	Lake Forest city, IL	74.0	21	Maywood village, IL..........	22.0
21	York city, PA.................	73.2	22	Hoboken city, NJ..............	73.9	22	Pontiac city, MI...............	21.9
23	Reading city, PA..............	72.9	23	Tysons Corner CDP, VA..........	73.7	23	Hamtramck city, MI...........	21.8
24	Cloverleaf CDP, TX............	72.7	24	Needham CDP, MA...........	73.5	24	Apache Junction city, AZ.....	21.7
25	Lebanon city, PA.............	72.4	25	Leawood city, KS..............	73.3	24	Perris city, CA.................	21.7
25	San Juan city, TX.............	72.4	26	Manhattan Beach city, CA.....	73.2	26	Blythe city, CA................	21.5
27	La Puente city, CA...........	72.1	27	Dublin city, OH...............	73.1	27	East Point city, GA...........	21.4
28	Soledad city, CA.............	72.0	28	Sammamish city, WA..........	73.0	27	Hemet city, CA................	21.4
29	South San Jose Hills CDP, CA..........	71.9	29	Upper Arlington city, OH.......	72.8	27	Youngstown city, OH..........	21.4
30	West Puente Valley CDP, CA..........	71.6	30	Belmont CDP, MA.............	72.0	30	Jackson city, MI..............	21.2
31	Mead Valley CDP, CA.........	71.3	31	Boulder city, CO..............	71.3	30	Florin CDP, CA................	21.2
32	Leisure City CDP, FL..........	71.2	32	Arlington CDP, VA.............	71.0	32	Newark city, NJ...............	21.1
33	Passaic city, NJ..............	71.0	33	North Bethesda CDP, MD	70.9	33	Jurupa Valley city, CA........	20.8
34	Paramount city, CA...........	70.4	33	Davis city, CA.................	70.9	33	Reading city, PA..............	20.8
35	El Monte city, CA............	70.2	35	La Cañada Flintridge city, CA ...	70.8	35	Pleasantville city, NJ.........	20.7
36	Bloomington CDP, CA.........	69.8	36	Los Gatos town, CA...........	70.4	36	Calumet City city, IL..........	20.6
36	Lealman CDP, FL..............	69.8	37	Blacksburg town, VA..........	70.3	36	Pahrump CDP, NV.............	20.6
36	Newburgh city, NY...........	69.8	38	Summit city, NJ...............	70.1	38	Spanish Lake CDP, MO........	20.5
39	Sweetwater city, FL..........	69.7	38	Highland Park city, IL.........	70.1	38	Kinston city, NC..............	20.5
40	Corcoran city, CA............	69.6	40	Zionsville town, IN............	69.6	40	Redan CDP, GA...............	20.4
40	Socorro city, TX..............	69.6	41	Marblehead CDP, MA..........	69.5	40	Nogales city, AZ..............	20.4
42	Santa Ana city, CA...........	69.2	41	Bethany CDP, OR..............	69.5	42	Riviera Beach city, FL.........	20.3
43	Marrero CDP, LA..............	69.0	43	Ann Arbor city, MI............	69.3	42	East Orange city, NJ..........	20.3
44	Willowbrook CDP, CA.........	68.9	43	Short Pump CDP, VA..........	69.3	42	Calexico city, CA..............	20.3
45	Nogales city, AZ..............	68.8	45	West Lafayette city, IN.......	69.0	42	Yucca Valley town, CA........	20.3
45	Baldwin Park city, CA........	68.8	46	East Lansing city, MI.........	68.8	46	Lauderdale Lakes city, FL.....	20.2
47	Hamtramck city, MI..........	68.5	47	Hudson city, OH..............	68.7	46	Desert Hot Springs city, CA..	20.2
47	Paterson city, NJ.............	68.5	48	Southlake city, TX............	68.5	46	Brawley city, CA..............	20.2
49	Melrose Park village, IL......	68.3	49	Berkeley city, CA.............	68.4	46	Hesperia city, CA.............	20.2
50	Golden Gate CDP, FL.........	68.2	49	Northbrook village, IL..........	68.4	50	Redmond city, OR............	20.1
51	Chelsea city, MA.............	68.1	51	Winchester CDP, MA..........	68.3	50	Los Banos city, CA...........	20.1
51	Trenton city, NJ..............	68.1	51	Brentwood city, TN...........	68.3	52	Chicago Heights city, IL......	20.0
51	San Benito city, TX..........	68.1	51	Prairie Village city, KS	68.3	52	Trenton city, NJ..............	20.0
54	Camden city, NJ..............	68.0	54	Vestavia Hills city, AL.........	68.0	54	Hartford city, CT.............	19.9
55	San Luis city, AZ.............	67.4	55	Carmel city, IN...............	67.9	54	Cleveland city, OH............	19.9
56	Elizabeth city, NJ............	67.2	56	Menlo Park city, CA...........	67.8	56	Spring Hill CDP, FL...........	19.8
57	Watsonville city, CA..........	67.1	57	Ithaca city, NY...............	67.7	56	Taylor city, MI................	19.8
57	Hialeah city, FL..............	67.1	58	Okemos CDP, MI..............	67.5	58	Sun City CDP, AZ.............	19.7
59	Compton city, CA............	67.0	59	Pullman city, WA.............	67.4	58	Albany city, GA...............	19.7
60	Chester city, PA..............	66.9	60	Edina city, MN................	67.2	58	Eastpointe city, MI...........	19.7
61	Brentwood CDP, NY..........	66.6	61	Milton city, GA...............	66.8	58	Willowbrook CDP, CA.........	19.7
62	Dundalk CDP, MD............	66.5	62	Reston CDP, VA...............	66.7	62	Sebastian city, FL.............	19.6
63	Perth Amboy city, NJ........	66.4	63	Colleyville city, TX............	66.5	62	Lima city, OH.................	19.6
64	Pharr city, TX................	66.1	64	Oak Park village, IL...........	66.4	64	Lealman CDP, FL..............	19.5
65	San Fernando city, CA.......	65.9	65	South Riding CDP, VA..........	66.3	65	Port Huron city, MI..........	19.3
66	Hazleton city, PA............	65.7	66	Naperville city, IL.............	66.2	65	Gary city, IN.................	19.3
67	Liberal city, KS...............	65.6	67	Oakton CDP, VA..............	66.1	67	San Bernardino city, CA......	19.2
68	Perris city, CA................	65.5	67	Evanston city, IL..............	66.1	67	San Pablo city, CA............	19.2
68	Atlantic City city, NJ.........	65.5	69	Webster Groves city, MO.....	66.0	69	Thomasville city, NC..........	19.1
70	Dinuba city, CA..............	65.4	70	State College borough, PA	65.8	70	Greenwood city, SC...........	19.0
71	Alliance city, OH.............	65.3	71	Irvine city, CA................	65.7	70	Pine Bluff city, AR............	19.0
72	Madera city, CA..............	65.2	71	Lake Oswego city, OR..........	65.7	70	Maple Heights city, OH.......	19.0
73	Oak Ridge CDP, FL...........	64.9	73	Ellicott City CDP, MD..........	65.6	70	Holiday CDP, FL..............	19.0
73	West Little River CDP, FL.....	64.9	74	Fair Oaks CDP, VA............	65.5	74	Poinciana CDP, FL............	18.9
73	Barberton city, OH...........	64.9	74	Rancho Palos Verdes city, CA.	65.5	74	Galt city, CA.................	18.9
73	Rosenberg city, TX...........	64.9						

City Rankings, 2010–2012
Selected Rankings

Families with income below poverty rank	City	Percent of families with income below poverty [B-4, col. 10]	Households with income of $25,000 or less rank	City	Households with income of $25,000 or less [B-4, col.11]	Percent of households with income of $100,000 or more rank	City	Percent of households with income of $100,000 or more [B-4, col. 12]
	United States	11.6		United States	24.1		United States	21.6
1	Kiryas Joel village, NY	51.6	1	Isla Vista CDP, CA	62.0	1	Franklin Farm CDP, VA	82.1
2	Immokalee CDP, FL	50.2	2	Carbondale city, IL	59.6	2	McLean CDP, VA	76.2
3	University CDP (Hillsborough County), FL	46.2	3	East St. Louis city, IL	59.0	3	Potomac CDP, MD	73.5
4	East St. Louis city, IL	45.0	4	University CDP (Hillsborough County), FL	58.9	4	Southlake city, TX	72.7
5	Selma city, AL	39.7	5	Athens city, OH	57.4	5	Sammamish city, WA	72.1
6	Hamtramck city, MI	38.9	6	Statesboro city, GA	55.9	6	South Riding CDP, VA	71.9
7	Reading city, PA	38.1	7	Selma city, AL	54.9	6	Linton Hall CDP, VA	71.9
8	Nogales city, AZ	36.7	8	Immokalee CDP, FL	54.1	8	Saratoga city, CA	70.1
9	Camden city, NJ	36.6	9	Prichard city, AL	53.5	9	University Park city, TX	69.8
9	Columbus city, MS	36.6	9	Greenwood city, SC	53.5	9	North Potomac CDP, MD	69.8
11	Leisure City CDP, FL	36.1	11	Pullman city, WA	53.1	11	La Cañada Flintridge city, CA	69.0
12	Flint city, MI	35.6	12	Youngstown city, OH	52.7	12	Colleyville city, TX	68.4
13	Adelanto city, CA	35.5	13	State College borough, PA	52.4	13	Ladera Ranch CDP, CA	67.9
14	Detroit city, MI	35.0	14	Nogales city, AZ	52.0	14	Wellesley CDP, MA	67.5
14	York city, PA	35.0	15	Kiryas Joel village, NY	51.0	15	Cottage Lake CDP, WA	67.3
14	Westmont CDP, CA	35.0	16	Hattiesburg city, MS	50.9	16	Darien CDP, CT	67.0
17	Lennox CDP, CA	34.7	17	Flint city, MI	50.4	17	Garden City village, NY	66.4
18	Pharr city, TX	34.2	18	Columbus city, MS	50.3	18	Brentwood city, TN	65.7
19	Inkster city, MI	33.9	18	Macon city, GA	50.3	19	Burke CDP, VA	65.2
20	East Chicago city, IN	33.5	18	Vicksburg city, MS	50.3	20	Westport CDP, CT	64.9
21	Gary city, IN	33.4	21	Camden city, NJ	49.5	21	Cupertino city, CA	64.5
22	Lakewood CDP, NJ	33.2	22	Fort Pierce city, FL	49.4	22	Lake Forest city, IL	64.1
23	Saginaw city, MI	33.1	23	Muskegon city, MI	49.3	23	Merrick CDP, NY	64.0
23	Carbondale city, IL	33.1	24	Hamtramck city, MI	49.2	24	Dix Hills CDP, NY	63.7
25	Macon city, GA	33.0	24	Detroit city, MI	49.2	25	Bethesda CDP, MD	63.6
26	Jackson city, MI	32.9	24	East Chicago city, IN	49.2	25	Mountain Brook city, AL	63.6
27	Cudahy city, CA	32.7	27	Reading city, PA	48.8	27	San Ramon city, CA	63.4
28	San Benito city, TX	32.6	28	Cleveland city, OH	48.7	28	Lexington CDP, MA	63.2
28	Newburgh city, NY	32.6	28	Gadsden city, AL	48.7	29	Manhattan Beach city, CA	63.0
30	Bridgeton city, NJ	32.2	30	Zanesville city, OH	48.5	30	Los Altos city, CA	62.9
30	Arvin city, CA	32.2	31	Inkster city, MI	48.3	31	Danville town, CA	62.6
30	Hattiesburg city, MS	32.2	32	Mount Pleasant city, MI	48.0	32	Leawood city, KS	62.3
33	West Pensacola CDP, FL	32.0	33	Blacksburg town, VA	47.9	32	Ridgewood village, NJ	62.3
33	Pontiac city, MI	32.0	34	Pontiac city, MI	47.8	34	North Tustin CDP, CA	61.6
35	Hartford city, CT	31.9	34	Huntsville city, TX	47.8	35	Olney CDP, MD	61.5
36	Greenville city, MS	31.6	36	Oxford city, OH	47.7	36	Ashburn CDP, VA	61.4
36	Lima city, OH	31.6	37	Ithaca city, NY	47.6	37	Wildwood city, MO	61.2
38	Fort Pierce city, FL	31.5	38	Lima city, OH	47.5	38	Montclair CDP, VA	61.0
39	Brownsville city, TX	31.3	39	Gary city, IN	47.3	38	Flower Mound town, TX	61.0
39	Florence-Graham CDP, CA	31.3	40	Johnstown city, PA	47.2	40	Westfield town, NJ	60.7
41	Socorro city, TX	31.2	41	Bloomington city, IN	47.1	41	New City CDP, NY	60.3
42	Albany city, GA	31.1	42	Rexburg city, ID	47.0	42	Dublin city, OH	60.1
43	Monroe city, LA	30.9	42	Portsmouth city, OH	47.0	43	Parkland city, FL	59.9
43	Statesboro city, GA	30.9	44	Jackson city, MI	46.9	44	Plainview CDP, NY	59.8
45	Prichard city, AL	30.8	45	Charleston city, IL	46.8	45	Mercer Island city, WA	59.3
45	Holyoke city, MA	30.8	46	Dayton city, OH	46.7	46	Smithtown CDP, NY	59.2
47	Cleveland city, OH	30.7	47	Monroe city, LA	46.4	47	Needham CDP, MA	59.1
47	Vicksburg city, MS	30.7	47	Starkville city, MS	46.4	48	Lafayette city, CA	59.0
47	Rexburg city, ID	30.7	49	Saginaw city, MI	46.3	49	Winchester CDP, MA	58.9
50	San Luis city, AZ	30.4	49	Alliance city, OH	46.3	50	Granite Bay CDP, CA	58.7
50	Rochester city, NY	30.4	49	McKeesport city, PA	46.3	51	Pleasanton city, CA	58.4
52	Oildale CDP, CA	30.3	49	East Lansing city, MI	46.3	52	Severna Park CDP, MD	58.2
52	Sweetwater city, FL	30.3	53	San Benito city, TX	46.2	52	Hudson city, OH	58.2
54	Willowbrook CDP, CA	30.1	53	Albany city, GA	46.2	54	Summit city, NJ	57.9
55	Meridian city, MS	30.0	53	Bessemer city, AL	46.2	54	Syosset CDP, NY	57.9
56	Muskegon city, MI	29.9	53	Huntington city, West VA	46.2	54	Rancho Palos Verdes city, CA	57.9
57	Lawrence city, MA	29.6	57	Greenville city, MS	46.1	54	El Dorado Hills CDP, CA	57.9
58	Delano city, CA	29.5	58	Shelbyville city, TN	46.0	54	West Springfield CDP, VA	57.9
59	Youngstown city, OH	29.2	59	Westmont CDP, CA	45.9	59	Calabasas city, CA	57.5
59	Harrisburg city, PA	29.2	59	Meridian city, MS	45.9	60	Yorba Linda city, CA	57.4
61	Union City city, GA	29.0	61	Urbana city, IL	45.8	61	Dublin city, CA	57.3
61	Homestead city, FL	29.0	62	Cookeville city, TN	45.6	62	Palo Alto city, CA	57.1
63	Dayton city, OH	28.9	63	Morgantown city, West VA	45.5	63	Keystone CDP, FL	56.9
63	Selma city, CA	28.9	64	Hartford city, CT	45.4	64	Newton city, MA	56.8
65	Maywood city, CA	28.8	64	Ypsilanti city, MI	45.4	65	Wilmette village, IL	56.7
65	San Juan city, TX	28.8	64	San Marcos city, TX	45.4	66	Keller city, TX	56.6
67	Statesville city, NC	28.7	67	Richmond city, KY	45.3	67	Foster City city, CA	56.4
67	Atlantic City city, NJ	28.7	68	Kinston city, NC	45.2	67	Eastvale city, CA	56.4
69	West Memphis city, AR	28.4	68	Adrian city, MI	45.2	69	Germantown city, TN	56.3
70	Syracuse city, NY	28.3	70	Harvey city, IL	45.1	70	Ellicott City CDP, MD	56.2
71	Griffin city, GA	27.9	71	New Castle city, PA	44.9	71	Chantilly CDP, VA	56.1
71	Passaic city, NJ	27.9	72	Miami city, FL	44.7	72	Oakton CDP, VA	55.8
73	Coachella city, CA	27.8	72	Morristown city, TN	44.7	72	Massapequa CDP, NY	55.8
73	Danville city, IL	27.8	72	Anderson city, SC	44.7	74	Los Gatos town, CA	55.7
73	Huntsville city, TX	27.8	75	Pharr city, TX	44.6	75	Forest Hills CDP, MI	55.6
			75	Atlantic City city, NJ	44.6			
			75	Griffin city, GA	44.6			

Table B-1. States — What: Education, Employment, and Income, 2012

State code	STATE	Educational attainment (percent)						School enrollment by level of school			
		Total population 25 years and over	No high school diploma	High school graduate	Some college or associate's degree	Bachelor's degree	Graduate or professional degree	Total enrolled in school	Enrolled in preschool (percent)	Enrolled in grades K–12 (percent)	Enrolled in college or graduate school
	ACS table number:	C15002	C15002	C15002	C15002	C15002	C15002	C14002	C14002	C14002	C14002
	Column number:	1	2	3	4	5	6	7	8	9	10

Table B-1. States — What: Education, Employment, and Income, 2012—Continued

State code	STATE	Percent enrolled in private schools by level of school							Total population 16 years and over	Total labor force	Labor force participation (percent)		
		All levels	Preschool, nursery school	Kinder-garten	Grades 1–8	Grades 9–12	College, under-graduate	Graduate or professional school			Total	Men	Women
	ACS table number:	C14002	C14002	C14002	C14002	C14002	C14002	C14002	C23001	C23001	C23001	C23001	C23001
	Column number:	11	12	13	14	15	16	17	18	19	20	21	22

Table B-1. States — What: Education, Employment, and Income, 2012—Continued

State code	STATE	Unemployment rates by age (percent unemployed)				Total labor force 25 to 64 years	Unemployment rates for the labor force age 25 to 64 by educational attainment					
							Unemployment rate (percent unemployed)					
		Total labor force	16 to 24 years	25 to 64 years	65 years and over		Total 25 to 64 years	No high school diploma	High school graduate	Some college or associate's degree	Bachelor's degree or higher	
	ACS table number:	C23001	C23001	C23001	C23001	B23006	B23006	B23006	B23006	B23006	B23006	
	Column number:	23	24	25	26	27	28	29	30	31	32	

Table B-1. States — What: Education, Employment, and Income, 2012—Continued

State code	STATE	Total population 16 to 19 years	16 to 19 years, not enrolled in school, not high school graduate, not in labor force	Total population 16 years and over	Percent of population 16 years and over who worked full-time, year-round in the past 12 months			Total households	Percent of households with no workers	Family status of children under 18 years, by employment status of parents and age of children			
										Children under 18 years in families			
										Number	Percent living with two parents		Percent living with one parent who is in labor force
					Total	Male	Female				Both in labor force	Father only in labor force	
	ACS table number:	C14005	C14005	C20005	C20005	C20005	C20005	C08202	C08202	C23008	C23008	C23008	C23008
	Column number:	33	34	35	36	37	38	39	40	41	42	43	44

Table B-1. States — What: Education, Employment, and Income, 2012—Continued

State code	STATE	Family status of children under 18 years, by employment status of parents and age of children								Total families	Employment status of family householders			
		Children under 6 years in families				Children 6–17 years in families					Married-couple families		Other families	
		Number	Percent living with two parents		Percent living with one parent who is in labor force	Number	Percent living with two parents		Percent living with one parent who is in labor force		Total	Percent with both in labor force	Total	Percent with householder in labor force
			Both in labor force	Father only in labor force			Both in labor force	Father only in labor force						
	ACS table number:	C23008	C23008	C23008	C23008	C23008	C23008	C23008	C23008	C23007	C23007	C23007	C23007	C23007
	Column number:	45	46	47	48	49	50	51	52	53	54	55	56	57

Table B-1. States — What: Education, Employment, and Income, 2012—Continued

State code	STATE	Women 20 to 64 years in households, by presence of children and labor force status			Class of worker for employed civilians 16 years and over				Civilian employed population 16 years and over	Occupation (percent)				
		Total women 20 to 64 years in households	Percent with children under 18 years	Percent in labor force with children under 18 years	Civilian employed population 16 years and over	Percent private wage and salary workers	Percent government workers	Percent self-employed and unpaid workers		Management, business, science, and arts	Service	Sales and office	Natural resources, construction, and maintenance	Production, transportation, and material moving
	ACS table number:	B23003	B23003	B23003	C24080	C24080	C24080	C24080	B24060	B24060	B24060	B24060	B24060	B24060
	Column number:	58	59	60	61	62	63	64	65	66	67	68	69	70

Table B-1. States — What: Education, Employment, and Income, 2012—Continued

State code	STATE	Industry (percent)								Industry (percent)				
		Agriculture, forestry, fishing and hunting, and mining	Construction	Manufacturing	Wholesale trade	Retail trade	Transportation and warehousing, and utilities	Information	Finance and insurance, real estate, and rental and leasing	Professional, scientific, and management, and administrative and waste management services	Educational services, and health care and social assistance	Arts, entertainment, and recreation, and accommodation and food services	Other services, except public administration	Public administration
	ACS table number:	C24070	C24070	C24070	C24070	C24070	C24070	C24070	C24070	C24070	C24070	C24070	C24070	C24070
	Column number:	71	72	73	74	75	76	77	78	79	80	81	82	83

Table B-1. States — What: Education, Employment, and Income, 2012—Continued

State code	STATE	Veterans as a percent of the population 18 years and over	Median income in the past 12 months (in 2012 inflation-adjusted dollars)					Median income in the past 12 months (in 2012 inflation-adjusted dollars)								
			Median household income by age of householder					Median household income by race and Hispanic origin of householder								
			All households	Householder under 25 years	Householder 25 to 44 years	Householder 45 to 64 years	Householder 65 years and over	White alone	Black alone	American Indian, Alaska Native alone	Asian alone	Native Hawaiian and other Pacific Islander alone	Some other race alone	Two or more races	White alone, not Hispanic or Latino	Hispanic or Latino
	ACS table number:	B21001	B19049	B19049	B19049	B19049	B19049	B19013A	B19013B	B19013C	B19013D	B19013E	B19013F	B19013G	B19013H	B19013I
	Column number:	84	85	86	87	88	89	90	91	92	93	94	95	96	97	98

Table B-1. States — What: Education, Employment, and Income, 2012—Continued

State code	STATE	Median income in the past 12 months (in 2012 inflation-adjusted dollars)							Median nonfamily household income			Median individual income	
		Median family income by type of family							All nonfamily households	Living alone, 65 years and over		Persons 15 years and over who worked full-time, year-round	
		All families	Married-couple families with children	Married-couple families, no children	Male householder with children	Male householder, no children	Female householder with children	Female householder, no children		Male	Female	Male	Female
	ACS table number:	B19126	B19126	B19126	B19126	B19126	B19126	B19126	B19215	B19215	B19215	B19326	B19326
	Column number:	99	100	101	102	103	104	105	106	107	108	109	110

Table B-1. States — What: Education, Employment, and Income, 2012—Continued

State code	STATE	Per capita income in the past 12 months (in 2012 inflation-adjusted dollars)	Households, by type of income (percent)									
			Total number of households	With wage or salary income	With self-employment income	With interest, dividends, or net rental income	With Social Security	With Supplemental Security Income (SSI)	With public assistance income	With cash public assistance or Food Stamps	With retirement income	With other types of income
	ACS table number:	B19301	B19052	B19052	B19053	B19054	B19055	B19056	B19057	B19058	B19059	B19060
	Column number:	111	112	113	114	115	116	117	118	119	120	121

Table B-1. States — What: Education, Employment, and Income, 2012—*Continued*

State code	STATE	Household income in the past 12 months (in 2012 inflation-adjusted dollars)										
			Households by income group (percent)									
		Total number of households	Less than $10,000	$10,000 to $14,999	$15,000 to $24,999	$25,000 to $34,999	$35,000 to $49,999	$50,000 to $74,999	$75,000 to $99,999	$100,000 to $149,999	$150,000 to $199,999	$200,000 or more
	ACS table number:	C19001	C19001	C19001	C19001	C19001	C19001	C19001	C19001	C19001	C19001	C19001
	Column number:	122	123	124	125	126	127	128	129	130	131	132

Table B-1. States — What: Education, Employment, and Income, 2012—*Continued*

State code	STATE	Households with income over $100,000, by age of householder (as a percent of all households in age group)					Households with income below poverty (as a percent of all households in household-type group)						
		All households	Householder under 25 years	Householder 25 to 44 years	Householder 45 to 64 years	Householder 65 years and over	All households	Family households	Married-couple family households	Male householder family households	Female householder family households	Male householder nonfamily households	Female householder nonfamily households
	ACS table number:	C19001	C19037	C19037	C19037	C19037	C17017	C17017	C17017	C17017	C17017	C17017	C17017
	Column number:	133	134	135	136	137	138	139	140	141	142	143	144

Table B-1. States — What: Education, Employment, and Income, 2012—*Continued*

State code	STATE	Population for whom poverty status is determined	Persons with income below poverty by age (as a percent of all persons in age group)				Persons with income below poverty by selected race and Hispanic origin groups (as a percent of all persons in race/Hispanic group)				Total civilian non-institutionalized population	Type of health insurance (as a percent of all persons)			
			All ages	Under 18 years	18 to 64 years	65 years and over	White alone, not Hispanic or Latino	Black alone	Asian alone	Hispanic or Latino		Private	Public	Both	None
	ACS table number:	C17001	C17001	C17001	C17001	C17001	C17001H	C17001B	C17001D	C17001I	C27010	C27010	C27010	C27010	C27010
	Column number:	145	146	147	148	149	150	151	152	153	154	155	156	157	158

Table B-2. Counties — What: Education, Employment, and Income, 2008–2010

State or county code	State or county	Educational attainment			Employment status			Percent who worked full-time year-round	Percent of households with no workers	Median household income (dollars)	Percent of families with income below poverty	Percent of households with income less than $25,000	Percent of households with income of $100,000 or more
		Total population 25 years and over	Percent with a high school diploma or less	Percent with a bachelor's degree or more	Total population 16 years and over	Percent in the labor force	Unemployment rate						
	ACS table number:	C15002	C15002	C15002	B23025	B23025	B23025	C20005	C08202	B19013	C17013	C19001	C19001
	Column number:	1	2	3	4	5	6	7	8	9	10	11	12

Table B-3. Metropolitan Areas — What: Education, Employment, and Income, 2010

Metro area or division code	Area name	Educational attainment			Employment status			Percent who worked full-time year-round	Percent of households with no workers	Median household income (dollars)	Percent of families with income below poverty	Percent of households with income less than $25,000	Percent of households with income of $100,000 or more
		Total population 25 years and over	Percent with a high school diploma or less	Percent with a bachelor's degree or more	Total population 16 years and over	Percent in the labor force	Unemployment rate						
	ACS table number:	C15002	C15002	C15002	B23025	B23025	B23025	C20005	C08202	B19013	C17013	C19001	C19001
	Column number:	1	2	3	4	5	6	7	8	9	10	11	12

Table B-4. Cities — What: Education, Employment, and Income, 2008–2010

STATE and Place code	STATE city	Educational attainment			Employment status			Percent who worked full-time year-round	Percent of households with no workers	Median household income (dollars)	Percent of families with income below poverty	Percent of households with income less than $25,000	Percent of households with income of $100,000 or more
		Total population 25 years and over	Percent with a high school diploma or less	Percent with a bachelor's degree or more	Total population 16 years and over	Percent in the labor force	Unemployment rate						
	ACS table number:	C15002	C15002	C15002	B23025	B23025	B23025	C20005	C08202	B19013	C17013	C19001	C19001
	Column number:	1	2	3	4	5	6	7	8	9	10	11	12

Table B-1. States — What: Education, Employment, and Income, 2012

State code	STATE	Educational attainment (percent)						School enrollment by level of school (percent)			
		Total population 25 years and over	No high school diploma	High school graduate	Some college or associate's degree	Bachelor's degree	Graduate or professional degree	Total number enrolled in school	Enrolled in preschool	Enrolled in grades K–12	Enrolled in college or graduate school
	ACS table number:	C15002	C15002	C15002	C15002	C15002	C15002	C14002	C14002	C14002	C14002
	Column number:	1	2	3	4	5	6	7	8	9	10
00	United States	208,731,498	13.6	28.0	29.2	18.2	10.9	83,085,860	6.1	65.2	28.8
01	Alabama	3,209,646	16.0	31.3	29.4	14.7	8.6	1,220,639	5.6	67.4	27.0
02	Alaska	464,594	8.0	28.0	35.9	17.1	10.9	195,535	5.6	68.1	26.4
04	Arizona	4,280,464	14.3	24.3	34.1	17.2	10.2	1,753,081	4.3	67.5	28.2
05	Arkansas	1,949,382	15.2	35.2	28.6	13.8	7.2	752,357	6.6	67.6	25.8
06	California	24,779,784	18.5	20.6	30.0	19.6	11.3	10,678,252	5.5	64.0	30.5
08	Colorado	3,444,654	9.4	21.8	31.3	23.8	13.7	1,395,046	6.4	64.2	29.4
09	Connecticut	2,457,978	10.1	27.8	25.0	20.5	16.6	954,957	6.8	64.0	29.2
10	Delaware	618,612	11.5	31.5	27.4	18.1	11.4	236,066	6.0	63.2	30.8
11	District of Columbia ..	439,531	11.4	18.4	17.2	23.0	30.0	159,737	8.1	46.8	45.1
12	Florida	13,503,747	13.5	29.8	29.9	17.3	9.6	4,688,008	6.1	63.3	30.6
13	Georgia	6,403,838	15.0	28.3	28.5	17.8	10.4	2,797,844	6.9	65.5	27.6
15	Hawaii	952,281	9.6	28.3	32.1	19.6	10.5	336,071	6.4	63.8	29.8
16	Idaho	1,012,786	10.2	27.7	36.6	17.3	8.2	454,364	4.6	68.1	27.3
17	Illinois	8,558,895	12.4	27.0	28.9	19.7	12.0	3,478,102	6.8	65.1	28.1
18	Indiana	4,278,945	12.4	35.3	28.8	15.0	8.4	1,753,514	5.8	66.3	27.9
19	Iowa	2,036,993	8.4	32.3	33.0	18.1	8.2	809,898	6.7	64.7	28.5
20	Kansas	1,863,224	9.8	27.3	32.5	19.5	10.9	802,896	6.7	64.9	28.4
21	Kentucky	2,935,461	16.2	34.1	27.9	12.9	8.9	1,108,468	6.3	67.1	26.6
22	Louisiana	3,006,605	17.0	34.3	26.8	14.4	7.5	1,207,176	7.1	67.8	25.1
23	Maine	947,017	8.4	34.8	28.9	18.1	9.8	306,571	5.4	66.0	28.6
24	Maryland	3,972,135	10.9	26.1	26.1	20.0	16.9	1,580,906	6.4	61.4	32.2
25	Massachusetts	4,556,609	10.3	25.9	24.4	22.2	17.1	1,761,641	6.4	59.7	34.0
26	Michigan	6,621,018	10.8	30.6	32.6	16.0	10.0	2,652,338	5.5	64.6	29.9
27	Minnesota	3,600,744	7.5	26.4	32.9	22.4	10.8	1,414,524	7.0	65.3	27.7
28	Mississippi	1,911,968	17.7	30.6	31.1	13.0	7.6	830,938	6.4	66.6	27.0
29	Missouri	4,023,641	12.0	31.6	29.9	16.7	9.7	1,552,442	6.0	65.8	28.2
30	Montana	686,770	7.2	29.7	33.7	20.2	9.2	231,634	6.0	67.9	26.1
31	Nebraska	1,206,908	9.5	27.7	33.8	19.3	9.7	510,963	6.9	64.8	28.4
32	Nevada	1,840,642	15.1	28.8	33.7	14.8	7.5	680,801	4.4	71.0	24.6
33	New Hampshire	919,883	8.2	29.4	27.8	21.9	12.6	323,979	5.9	64.5	29.7
34	New Jersey	6,049,352	11.7	28.7	23.3	22.5	13.8	2,294,691	7.4	65.9	26.7
35	New Mexico	1,360,330	15.6	26.5	31.8	14.9	11.2	572,854	5.6	65.1	29.3
36	New York	13,309,761	14.7	26.9	25.0	19.0	14.4	5,029,814	6.1	62.6	31.2
37	North Carolina	6,489,883	14.8	27.1	30.7	18.0	9.3	2,550,114	5.7	65.6	28.7
38	North Dakota	457,904	8.3	28.0	35.8	19.6	8.4	177,584	6.2	61.0	32.8
39	Ohio	7,770,716	11.2	34.6	29.0	16.0	9.3	3,013,300	6.0	65.6	28.3
40	Oklahoma	2,487,456	13.3	31.6	31.3	15.8	7.9	985,249	6.5	68.1	25.4
41	Oregon	2,671,772	10.1	25.1	34.9	18.6	11.3	982,675	5.6	63.7	30.7
42	Pennsylvania	8,756,317	11.1	36.8	24.3	17.0	10.9	3,108,390	6.4	64.5	29.1
44	Rhode Island	712,271	13.9	27.9	26.8	18.7	12.8	275,680	5.9	58.2	35.9
45	South Carolina	3,151,616	15.1	29.8	30.0	16.0	9.1	1,201,763	5.4	66.5	28.1
46	South Dakota	544,292	9.5	32.7	31.6	18.1	8.1	217,047	6.3	66.9	26.8
47	Tennessee	4,336,473	14.9	33.1	27.8	15.7	8.6	1,605,001	5.8	67.7	26.5
48	Texas	16,390,379	18.6	25.2	29.5	17.7	9.0	7,389,940	6.1	68.9	25.0
49	Utah	1,641,335	9.0	23.1	37.2	20.3	10.4	932,634	6.4	66.6	27.0
50	Vermont	434,948	8.3	30.5	25.4	21.9	13.9	154,731	6.3	60.0	33.8
51	Virginia	5,504,766	12.1	25.3	27.2	20.6	14.9	2,173,528	5.9	62.4	31.7
53	Washington	4,645,859	9.6	23.7	35.0	20.3	11.3	1,718,203	5.9	66.5	27.6
54	West Virginia	1,296,201	15.5	40.6	25.3	11.4	7.3	419,145	5.5	65.9	28.6
55	Wisconsin	3,854,170	9.3	32.4	31.2	17.9	9.3	1,500,226	5.4	65.6	29.0
56	Wyoming	380,942	8.3	30.4	36.6	16.9	7.8	154,543	6.9	63.5	29.5

Table B-1. States — What: Education, Employment, and Income, 2012—*Continued*

State code	STATE	Percent enrolled in private schools by level of school							Total population 16 years and over	Total labor force	Labor force participation (percent)		
		All levels	Preschool, nursery school	Kindergarten	Grades 1–8	Grades 9–12	College, undergraduate	Graduate or professional school			Total	Men	Women
	ACS table number:	C14002	C14002	C14002	C14002	C14002	C14002	C14002	C23001	C23001	C23001	C23001	C23001
	Column number:	11	12	13	14	15	16	17	18	19	20	21	22
00	United States	16.3	42.8	12.1	10.0	9.3	21.8	41.1	248,601,283	158,729,043	63.8	69.2	58.8
01	Alabama	14.0	48.2	12.7	10.4	10.1	14.3	23.0	3,825,109	2,236,878	58.5	64.3	53.1
02	Alaska....................	13.0	39.3	12.7	9.6	9.2	14.0	22.4	564,238	397,115	70.4	74.7	65.7
04	Arizona..................	10.9	41.5	8.7	6.5	5.9	13.1	35.0	5,110,763	3,076,722	60.2	65.3	55.2
05	Arkansas.................	10.6	27.0	8.0	8.4	7.3	12.4	19.0	2,312,234	1,372,556	59.4	64.7	54.3
06	California................	14.2	43.1	10.6	8.3	7.6	16.9	45.5	29,884,983	19,068,155	63.8	70.3	57.5
08	Colorado	13.9	43.4	10.4	8.3	7.8	16.1	34.5	4,085,464	2,808,337	68.7	74.6	62.9
09	Connecticut............	20.4	46.0	14.3	8.6	10.3	34.3	53.8	2,893,530	1,958,032	67.7	72.5	63.2
10	Delaware	19.2	54.3	17.4	13.8	12.7	18.1	51.4	734,481	470,752	64.1	67.9	60.6
11	District of Columbia ..	42.4	28.6	16.1	20.5	14.6	69.6	71.2	533,647	368,070	69.0	71.3	66.9
12	Florida	17.0	45.3	12.8	11.0	9.6	21.3	42.1	15,784,363	9,409,668	59.6	64.3	55.2
13	Georgia	14.8	38.1	9.7	9.0	8.9	19.3	40.1	7,692,523	4,843,992	63.0	68.7	57.6
15	Hawaii	23.1	59.3	13.5	18.2	20.0	22.6	38.7	1,122,846	735,451	65.5	71.2	59.8
16	Idaho	13.1	56.3	8.8	5.6	5.9	23.1	27.5	1,216,830	774,831	63.7	69.2	58.2
17	Illinois	18.5	38.9	13.4	11.2	8.7	26.6	53.1	10,169,058	6,729,843	66.2	71.3	61.4
18	Indiana..................	16.0	47.4	14.7	11.5	8.9	20.7	26.1	5,126,773	3,295,395	64.3	69.3	59.5
19	Iowa	16.0	31.1	10.7	10.0	7.6	26.5	32.6	2,430,288	1,646,420	67.7	72.4	63.3
20	Kansas...................	14.0	35.4	11.9	10.8	9.6	15.3	23.7	2,242,491	1,510,382	67.4	73.0	61.8
21	Kentucky................	15.3	35.0	10.9	11.7	12.0	18.5	24.4	3,470,977	2,076,714	59.8	64.3	55.6
22	Louisiana	18.9	34.3	19.6	16.4	16.8	17.9	31.1	3,603,962	2,210,208	61.3	66.0	56.9
23	Maine	16.0	46.8	7.3	6.4	10.7	26.1	41.7	1,096,245	700,752	63.9	68.2	59.9
24	Maryland	19.9	53.0	14.8	13.5	12.8	20.8	42.2	4,697,087	3,229,761	68.8	73.1	64.8
25	Massachusetts	27.0	52.5	13.2	9.9	12.0	45.3	69.4	5,416,163	3,647,354	67.3	71.7	63.3
26	Michigan	13.6	31.1	12.3	10.8	8.3	15.9	27.0	7,897,753	4,832,544	61.2	65.5	57.1
27	Minnesota	17.5	38.2	12.8	11.7	8.5	25.3	42.0	4,242,762	2,975,845	70.1	74.2	66.2
28	Mississippi..............	12.9	23.0	11.3	10.8	11.4	13.5	24.6	2,320,405	1,356,521	58.5	63.1	54.3
29	Missouri.................	18.6	42.9	12.9	12.8	11.3	24.3	45.5	4,776,269	3,044,407	63.7	67.9	59.8
30	Montana.................	12.7	45.6	13.3	9.5	9.5	12.4	13.7	809,850	523,305	64.6	69.0	60.3
31	Nebraska	17.4	43.1	16.4	13.2	9.6	20.3	31.9	1,442,595	1,015,594	70.4	75.6	65.3
32	Nevada	11.2	42.7	11.1	7.3	4.4	15.6	33.9	2,167,405	1,411,331	65.1	70.0	60.2
33	New Hampshire	21.6	52.0	16.7	9.6	9.7	36.8	57.2	1,079,792	741,565	68.7	73.2	64.3
34	New Jersey..............	19.5	49.5	16.2	10.1	11.9	27.0	51.2	7,077,678	4,684,932	66.2	72.0	60.8
35	New Mexico	10.5	31.7	6.2	8.3	7.8	10.5	20.5	1,627,551	978,436	60.1	64.8	55.6
36	New York	23.4	47.8	15.6	12.7	12.4	35.0	59.3	15,822,629	10,052,158	63.5	68.6	58.8
37	North Carolina	14.1	46.4	10.0	9.0	7.6	17.8	32.8	7,720,907	4,869,338	63.1	68.4	58.1
38	North Dakota	13.1	34.6	15.8	11.5	6.4	13.0	21.4	561,051	397,411	70.8	75.6	65.9
39	Ohio	18.3	43.8	12.5	13.4	12.6	23.3	32.9	9,196,303	5,820,299	63.3	68.0	58.9
40	Oklahoma...............	10.8	21.4	7.5	7.2	7.4	16.0	26.0	2,975,401	1,837,468	61.8	67.7	56.0
41	Oregon	15.0	55.1	13.8	9.3	8.8	16.1	34.9	3,136,866	1,955,966	62.4	67.2	57.7
42	Pennsylvania	24.3	53.4	16.1	14.3	12.4	37.7	55.9	10,366,567	6,513,773	62.8	67.8	58.2
44	Rhode Island	26.7	58.1	13.6	10.3	12.9	45.1	53.5	860,108	568,402	66.1	70.9	61.8
45	South Carolina	14.0	47.0	12.0	7.5	8.4	19.7	29.8	3,761,993	2,295,100	61.0	65.6	56.7
46	South Dakota...........	12.3	33.2	9.4	9.3	7.0	16.9	16.8	652,501	449,465	68.9	73.0	64.8
47	Tennessee	17.0	39.2	11.4	11.0	12.2	24.3	35.6	5,131,838	3,137,337	61.1	66.6	56.0
48	Texas....................	10.5	35.6	8.6	6.1	6.0	14.2	27.1	19,828,118	12,841,906	64.8	72.0	57.8
49	Utah	13.9	48.0	8.0	4.8	5.5	27.0	28.3	2,054,876	1,412,812	68.8	76.5	61.0
50	Vermont	20.7	45.2	7.5	9.9	8.8	32.5	53.8	518,107	348,871	67.3	70.9	63.9
51	Virginia	17.0	58.5	12.7	9.9	8.0	20.5	36.8	6,541,339	4,342,319	66.4	71.5	61.5
53	Washington	15.5	55.7	15.5	10.1	7.2	17.9	38.3	5,486,401	3,556,836	64.8	70.7	59.1
54	West Virginia	10.5	19.6	7.8	7.0	7.8	14.9	21.4	1,513,215	818,616	54.1	58.9	49.5
55	Wisconsin	16.8	32.8	17.0	14.1	9.2	20.1	37.6	4,562,954	3,070,595	67.3	71.1	63.6
56	Wyoming................	8.6	31.3	6.3	5.7	4.9	9.0	16.0	453,994	308,503	68.0	72.9	62.9

Table B-1. States — What: Education, Employment, and Income, 2012—*Continued*

State code	STATE	Unemployment rates by age (percent unemployed)					Unemployment rates for the labor force age 25 to 64 by educational attainment					
							Unemployment rate (percent unemployed)					
		Total labor force	16 to 24 years	25 to 64 years	65 years and over	Total labor force 25 to 64 years	Total 25 to 64 years	No high school diploma	High school graduate	Some college or associate's degree	Bachelor's degree or higher
	ACS table number:	C23001	C23001	C23001	C23001	B23006	B23006	B23006	B23006	B23006	B23006
	Column number:	23	24	25	26	27	28	29	30	31	32
00	United States	9.3	18.9	7.8	6.4	128,412,653	7.8	14.2	10.0	7.9	4.1
01	Alabama..........................	9.9	21.4	8.0	5.3	1,790,775	8.0	17.0	9.5	7.9	3.7
02	Alaska.............................	7.5	13.0	6.5	3.2	316,186	6.5	16.5	11.1	5.6	2.3
04	Arizona...........................	9.8	18.8	8.1	7.3	2,465,538	8.1	14.1	10.8	8.0	4.2
05	Arkansas..........................	8.4	19.0	6.7	3.4	1,100,279	6.7	11.7	8.1	7.0	2.8
06	California.........................	11.3	22.1	9.5	8.4	15,565,118	9.5	13.2	12.8	10.1	5.7
08	Colorado	7.7	15.9	6.3	6.7	2,278,183	6.3	10.6	8.3	7.3	3.9
09	Connecticut......................	9.7	18.7	8.4	7.2	1,589,752	8.4	17.1	11.6	9.3	4.6
10	Delaware	8.7	17.6	7.3	7.2	379,766	7.3	15.0	10.3	6.2	3.9
11	District of Columbia...........	10.2	20.2	8.8	7.0	301,918	8.8	22.1	18.5	14.6	3.5
12	Florida	11.5	21.7	9.9	9.8	7,634,528	9.9	17.8	12.4	9.5	5.6
13	Georgia	10.9	23.0	9.0	7.2	3,975,734	9.0	15.7	11.0	9.4	5.1
15	Hawaii	6.7	12.9	5.8	4.3	589,160	5.8	9.7	8.4	5.8	3.1
16	Idaho	8.0	16.1	6.4	5.8	612,509	6.4	11.8	7.9	6.4	3.5
17	Illinois	10.1	20.7	8.5	5.8	5,490,850	8.5	15.4	11.6	8.9	4.8
18	Indiana	8.8	18.6	7.0	5.8	2,643,300	7.0	15.1	8.7	6.5	3.5
19	Iowa	5.3	11.2	4.3	3.1	1,296,109	4.3	11.3	5.8	4.0	2.0
20	Kansas	6.4	13.1	5.3	3.2	1,186,423	5.3	9.2	7.9	5.3	2.7
21	Kentucky	9.2	19.6	7.5	4.2	1,665,099	7.5	15.0	9.1	7.8	3.2
22	Louisiana	8.8	18.8	7.1	5.2	1,780,298	7.1	15.4	7.9	6.9	2.9
23	Maine	7.6	16.3	6.3	4.7	561,476	6.3	13.1	8.3	6.7	3.0
24	Maryland	8.2	18.4	6.7	5.3	2,637,959	6.7	14.0	9.9	7.1	3.4
25	Massachusetts	8.5	15.9	7.3	6.5	2,933,233	7.3	16.7	10.6	7.5	4.3
26	Michigan	11.3	21.4	9.4	7.8	3,870,370	9.4	22.5	13.0	9.0	4.4
27	Minnesota	6.3	13.0	5.2	3.3	2,412,102	5.2	12.5	7.4	5.3	2.9
28	Mississippi.......................	11.2	26.3	8.6	3.8	1,078,104	8.6	17.9	9.3	9.2	3.2
29	Missouri..........................	8.5	16.4	7.2	4.9	2,426,435	7.2	17.0	9.2	7.5	3.1
30	Montana	7.1	13.7	6.1	4.2	414,411	6.1	15.2	7.3	6.5	3.4
31	Nebraska	5.3	11.8	4.1	2.6	793,363	4.1	11.4	4.6	4.4	2.0
32	Nevada	12.2	19.8	10.9	12.9	1,153,361	10.9	15.6	14.6	10.0	5.3
33	New Hampshire	6.5	15.9	5.0	5.0	601,827	5.0	12.8	5.7	5.3	3.2
34	New Jersey.......................	10.1	20.0	8.7	9.2	3,875,529	8.7	15.7	11.5	9.7	5.1
35	New Mexico......................	10.2	22.9	7.9	6.9	779,954	7.9	14.4	9.8	7.8	4.0
36	New York.........................	9.2	19.5	7.7	7.4	8,261,782	7.7	13.7	9.8	8.2	4.6
37	North Carolina	10.6	22.3	8.8	5.4	3,941,014	8.8	16.9	11.7	8.7	4.1
38	North Dakota....................	3.3	7.3	2.3	2.9	301,916	2.3	7.7	3.9	1.9	1.0
39	Ohio	9.1	18.9	7.5	4.4	4,673,272	7.5	18.6	9.3	7.4	3.4
40	Oklahoma........................	6.7	14.3	5.4	3.8	1,449,345	5.4	10.3	6.6	5.5	2.4
41	Oregon	11.0	21.5	9.4	6.4	1,596,032	9.4	16.6	12.2	10.3	5.0
42	Pennsylvania....................	8.8	18.6	7.3	6.1	5,247,170	7.3	16.3	9.1	7.5	3.8
44	Rhode Island....................	9.3	15.3	8.2	7.5	444,879	8.2	14.9	11.7	7.4	4.9
45	South Carolina.................	11.1	22.1	9.1	7.7	1,832,732	9.1	20.3	11.9	8.6	3.5
46	South Dakota...................	4.7	10.8	3.7	1.2	353,871	3.7	12.2	4.1	3.8	1.7
47	Tennessee	9.5	19.8	7.8	5.7	2,531,223	7.8	15.1	10.3	7.7	3.2
48	Texas	7.9	16.9	6.4	5.3	10,389,061	6.4	9.4	8.1	6.5	3.5
49	Utah	6.8	12.9	5.3	3.7	1,082,531	5.3	11.4	7.1	5.3	2.9
50	Vermont	6.4	15.6	5.0	2.7	275,303	5.0	16.4	7.0	4.9	2.3
51	Virginia	6.8	16.2	5.4	3.4	3,545,899	5.4	12.0	7.5	5.9	2.6
53	Washington	8.6	18.4	7.0	7.1	2,907,691	7.0	11.4	9.6	7.7	3.8
54	West Virginia	8.0	16.5	6.8	3.6	663,599	6.8	16.0	7.9	6.6	2.9
55	Wisconsin	7.3	14.8	6.0	4.9	2,470,742	6.0	13.6	8.1	6.0	2.7
56	Wyoming.........................	5.5	12.0	4.6	1.1	244,942	4.6	11.5	6.3	3.6	2.7

Table B-1. States — What: Education, Employment, and Income, 2012—*Continued*

State code	STATE	Total population 16 to 19 years	16 to 19 years, not enrolled in school, not high school graduate, not in labor force	Total population 16 years and over	Percent of population 16 years and over who worked full-time, year-round in the past 12 months			Total households	Percent of households with no workers	Children under 18 years in families	Percent living with two parents		Percent living with one parent who is in labor force
					Total	Male	Female			Number	Both in labor force	Father only in labor force	
	ACS table number:	C14005	C14005	C20005	C20005	C20005	C20005	C08202	C08202	C23008	C23008	C23008	C23008
	Column number:	33	34	35	36	37	38	39	40	41	42	43	44
00	United States	17,406,603	2.4	248,601,283	40.2	47.3	33.5	115,969,540	27.3	70,152,775	40.6	20.7	28.1
01	Alabama......................	270,829	3.0	3,825,109	37.8	45.2	31.1	1,845,169	32.5	1,059,458	36.4	20.2	30.8
02	Alaska........................	39,882	2.1	564,238	42.5	46.9	37.7	251,651	20.2	177,876	40.0	21.1	25.9
04	Arizona......................	357,674	3.3	5,110,763	37.8	44.0	31.7	2,392,168	30.1	1,531,641	35.0	23.1	29.8
05	Arkansas....................	156,393	3.4	2,312,234	39.5	45.9	33.5	1,143,859	31.3	666,074	38.2	19.4	28.5
06	California...................	2,187,805	1.9	29,884,983	37.7	45.2	30.4	12,552,658	25.1	8,811,331	37.7	24.2	26.8
08	Colorado	275,489	2.0	4,085,464	43.7	51.4	36.0	1,996,088	22.6	1,176,281	42.7	23.6	24.8
09	Connecticut	205,157	1.3	2,893,530	41.3	48.9	34.2	1,357,812	25.6	764,160	45.9	18.6	28.1
10	Delaware	50,133	4.0	734,481	41.2	46.4	36.4	340,308	27.0	191,503	40.2	16.6	33.5
11	District of Columbia	34,407	3.0	533,647	46.6	50.4	43.3	266,662	24.7	101,051	33.4	9.1	43.5
12	Florida	960,979	2.8	15,784,363	36.8	41.9	31.9	7,197,943	33.0	3,795,358	38.2	18.2	32.4
13	Georgia	573,076	3.5	7,692,523	40.4	47.1	34.2	3,532,908	26.8	2,364,265	36.8	20.8	31.2
15	Hawaii........................	67,439	2.2	1,122,846	43.0	49.7	36.4	447,748	23.0	285,907	46.0	18.4	24.3
16	Idaho.........................	91,103	2.1	1,216,830	37.7	45.6	29.9	583,106	27.2	410,264	42.7	26.7	22.4
17	Illinois	717,636	1.9	10,169,058	41.5	48.4	35.0	4,770,194	25.8	2,943,497	43.0	20.6	28.3
18	Indiana......................	370,305	2.8	5,126,773	40.0	47.3	33.1	2,480,077	27.1	1,511,563	42.0	20.3	28.4
19	Iowa..........................	168,633	1.9	2,430,288	44.4	52.1	36.9	1,227,048	25.6	693,174	52.9	14.3	25.2
20	Kansas.......................	169,012	1.8	2,242,491	44.6	52.9	36.6	1,113,911	24.1	689,263	45.4	21.0	26.4
21	Kentucky	229,354	2.6	3,470,977	38.2	44.2	32.6	1,707,004	32.6	942,987	40.2	17.2	27.7
22	Louisiana	255,299	3.9	3,603,962	40.3	46.7	34.2	1,719,473	28.4	1,046,269	34.2	14.7	38.2
23	Maine........................	69,937	2.4	1,096,245	38.3	45.1	32.0	554,543	31.3	251,996	45.5	17.2	25.4
24	Maryland	317,897	2.2	4,697,087	46.3	53.0	40.2	2,157,717	22.2	1,281,406	45.3	16.3	30.0
25	Massachusetts	387,346	1.8	5,416,163	41.1	48.3	34.4	2,522,394	26.1	1,352,482	48.2	16.5	25.4
26	Michigan	567,764	2.6	7,897,753	35.3	41.7	29.3	3,819,068	32.4	2,163,729	41.2	19.3	28.0
27	Minnesota	288,309	1.6	4,242,762	44.2	51.5	37.1	2,111,943	24.0	1,235,902	53.5	15.2	24.0
28	Mississippi.................	185,344	4.0	2,320,405	37.1	42.6	32.0	1,090,521	32.0	694,285	32.2	15.2	36.4
29	Missouri	330,339	2.6	4,776,269	40.7	46.3	35.4	2,359,135	28.7	1,325,990	43.5	17.5	28.3
30	Montana.....................	51,368	3.1	809,850	39.4	46.1	32.8	408,938	28.2	205,930	46.0	20.0	25.2
31	Nebraska	103,261	1.9	1,442,595	47.4	55.7	39.4	733,570	22.7	442,956	51.2	16.5	25.5
32	Nevada	138,632	3.1	2,167,405	39.3	44.5	34.2	1,006,605	26.6	634,076	37.0	20.7	31.7
33	New Hampshire	74,893	0.5	1,079,792	43.7	51.2	36.5	519,137	24.1	263,652	47.6	18.5	24.7
34	New Jersey..................	468,739	1.4	7,077,678	42.2	50.2	34.8	3,198,799	25.0	1,960,687	45.7	20.8	24.9
35	New Mexico................	123,668	3.3	1,627,551	38.0	44.0	32.3	764,996	30.3	488,544	33.8	18.5	33.6
36	New York....................	1,073,785	2.6	15,822,629	40.7	47.4	34.5	7,238,922	27.4	4,082,490	39.6	20.0	28.6
37	North Carolina	540,547	2.7	7,720,907	39.4	46.4	32.9	3,731,325	28.8	2,168,092	39.0	19.8	30.0
38	North Dakota..............	40,176	1.3	561,051	49.1	57.8	39.9	290,944	22.0	147,988	53.2	17.3	23.5
39	Ohio..........................	637,449	1.9	9,196,303	39.4	46.3	32.9	4,554,672	29.8	2,520,666	42.0	18.1	29.1
40	Oklahoma...................	207,240	3.9	2,975,401	42.1	49.6	34.8	1,446,667	28.2	878,570	39.7	20.9	28.0
41	Oregon......................	198,801	1.8	3,136,866	35.2	41.8	28.8	1,516,957	31.0	819,094	40.3	22.4	26.3
42	Pennsylvania	720,700	2.0	10,366,567	39.7	46.9	33.1	4,958,249	29.7	2,613,007	43.3	18.8	26.8
44	Rhode Island...............	63,434	2.5	860,108	39.9	46.8	33.5	413,083	28.6	207,495	44.5	12.3	31.7
45	South Carolina.............	263,874	2.8	3,761,993	38.0	44.2	32.2	1,787,340	31.1	1,019,411	36.3	17.3	34.4
46	South Dakota..............	50,028	0.9	652,501	47.1	53.9	40.2	323,765	23.2	192,726	50.3	13.5	28.7
47	Tennessee	343,225	2.0	5,131,838	39.2	46.0	32.9	2,480,090	30.0	1,401,624	37.5	21.4	28.8
48	Texas.........................	1,514,381	2.8	19,828,118	43.6	52.1	35.4	8,970,959	22.2	6,630,350	36.7	24.8	28.0
49	Utah..........................	176,356	2.3	2,054,876	41.6	52.6	30.8	895,691	19.2	852,833	41.7	35.5	17.0
50	Vermont.....................	38,247	1.0	518,107	41.0	47.8	34.6	258,520	25.9	117,991	50.0	14.4	25.6
51	Virginia......................	453,014	1.8	6,541,339	45.1	52.4	38.2	3,038,967	23.3	1,770,830	44.5	21.3	25.6
53	Washington.................	356,338	2.2	5,486,401	40.0	48.2	32.1	2,636,817	26.4	1,515,522	40.4	25.4	24.0
54	West Virginia	89,574	2.7	1,513,215	35.5	41.7	29.6	741,544	37.4	360,444	36.6	21.9	24.4
55	Wisconsin	319,793	1.3	4,562,954	42.0	48.8	35.5	2,288,362	26.5	1,260,474	48.4	16.3	26.8
56	Wyoming....................	31,539	1.3	453,994	45.3	54.8	35.5	223,513	23.0	129,604	43.4	22.7	26.3

Table B-1. States — What: Education, Employment, and Income, 2012—*Continued*

State code	STATE	Family status of children under 18 years, by employment status of parents and age of children								Employment status of family householders				
		Children under 6 years in families				Children 6–17 years in families					Married-couple families		Other families	
			Percent living with two parents		Percent living with one parent who is in labor force		Percent living with two parents		Percent living with one parent who is in labor force			Percent with both in labor force		Percent with householder in labor force
		Number	Both in labor force	Father only in labor force		Number	Both in labor force	Father only in labor force		Total families	Total		Total	
	ACS table number:	C23008	C23008	C23008	C23008	C23008	C23008	C23008	C23008	C23007	C23007	C23007	C23007	C23007
	Column number:	45	46	47	48	49	50	51	52	53	54	55	56	57
00	United States	23,202,782	36.8	23.5	28.1	46,949,993	42.4	19.3	28.2	76,509,262	55,754,450	52.6	20,754,812	73.1
01	Alabama	349,442	32.8	23.7	30.3	710,016	38.1	18.6	31.0	1,233,937	883,291	47.2	350,646	66.3
02	Alaska....................	62,172	35.5	24.7	25.7	115,704	42.4	19.2	26.1	166,400	123,248	56.7	43,152	75.9
04	Arizona..................	506,765	30.7	25.5	30.7	1,024,876	37.1	22.0	29.4	1,560,687	1,122,884	45.6	437,803	73.7
05	Arkansas.................	219,939	35.6	22.4	29.0	446,135	39.5	17.9	28.3	758,601	557,982	48.0	200,619	69.6
06	California................	2,942,198	34.8	26.8	26.1	5,869,133	39.1	22.9	27.2	8,585,787	6,104,099	51.3	2,481,688	73.8
08	Colorado................	395,637	40.1	27.6	22.4	780,644	44.0	21.5	26.0	1,278,264	975,070	55.7	303,194	79.3
09	Connecticut.............	230,068	42.3	21.1	28.2	534,092	47.4	17.6	28.0	902,369	660,876	58.8	241,493	77.4
10	Delaware	62,709	35.8	20.6	32.6	128,794	42.3	14.6	34.0	225,593	163,460	53.3	62,133	77.1
11	District of Columbia..	43,938	37.6	12.6	38.3	57,113	30.2	6.5	47.5	112,493	62,149	62.2	50,344	68.7
12	Florida	1,244,863	33.6	20.5	33.6	2,550,495	40.4	17.1	31.8	4,598,222	3,319,620	46.3	1,278,602	73.5
13	Georgia	785,220	33.1	24.0	30.6	1,579,045	38.6	19.2	31.5	2,406,226	1,693,386	51.8	712,840	72.1
15	Hawaii	104,508	39.5	23.1	24.9	181,399	49.8	15.7	24.0	309,165	229,027	54.0	80,138	65.0
16	Idaho	133,775	39.2	30.8	21.0	276,489	44.3	24.7	23.0	405,908	322,225	49.7	83,683	74.4
17	Illinois	952,121	39.5	23.1	28.5	1,991,376	44.7	19.4	28.2	3,121,020	2,289,429	55.8	831,591	75.5
18	Indiana	495,233	37.0	22.9	30.1	1,016,330	44.5	19.0	27.5	1,648,172	1,229,106	53.5	419,066	74.8
19	Iowa	229,559	50.0	17.2	24.4	463,615	54.3	12.9	25.6	796,744	625,952	59.5	170,792	78.4
20	Kansas...................	235,904	40.9	24.7	26.2	453,359	47.8	19.0	26.5	727,171	563,407	56.6	163,764	78.3
21	Kentucky................	315,985	36.9	19.3	28.3	627,002	41.9	16.1	27.5	1,140,771	834,642	50.2	306,129	64.9
22	Louisiana	357,776	31.0	15.2	39.7	688,493	35.9	14.5	37.4	1,125,659	744,806	49.8	380,853	70.6
23	Maine	78,111	42.6	22.3	22.5	173,885	46.9	14.9	26.7	346,950	270,568	54.2	76,382	70.1
24	Maryland	431,149	41.7	18.9	30.0	850,257	47.1	14.9	30.0	1,437,113	1,018,129	60.1	418,984	78.1
25	Massachusetts	428,070	46.4	19.1	23.5	924,419	49.1	15.3	26.2	1,598,867	1,173,287	60.1	425,580	72.2
26	Michigan	664,684	37.2	21.3	29.5	1,499,045	43.0	18.4	27.3	2,482,612	1,821,915	50.1	660,697	69.7
27	Minnesota	414,355	50.8	17.6	24.0	821,547	54.9	14.0	24.0	1,374,436	1,079,809	62.0	294,627	79.8
28	Mississippi..............	231,540	29.0	16.8	38.9	462,745	33.9	14.4	35.2	747,620	481,032	49.1	266,588	66.0
29	Missouri.................	434,117	38.2	20.7	29.4	891,873	46.1	15.9	27.8	1,517,231	1,124,203	53.7	393,028	72.8
30	Montana.................	69,532	39.5	25.5	25.3	136,398	49.4	17.2	25.1	259,650	205,584	53.7	54,066	78.4
31	Nebraska................	154,605	48.1	20.2	24.5	288,351	52.8	14.5	26.0	474,564	369,338	61.9	105,226	82.4
32	Nevada	216,495	34.6	24.6	30.5	417,581	38.2	18.7	32.4	650,833	445,312	50.1	205,521	78.0
33	New Hampshire	77,491	43.3	21.7	24.6	186,161	49.4	17.1	24.7	341,718	269,048	59.3	72,670	78.4
34	New Jersey..............	620,856	42.8	23.6	23.6	1,339,831	47.1	19.5	25.5	2,211,642	1,626,018	56.4	585,624	74.6
35	New Mexico.............	166,590	29.9	21.7	32.8	321,954	35.8	16.8	34.0	501,421	347,070	46.5	154,351	71.2
36	New York................	1,344,060	36.7	22.6	27.9	2,738,430	41.0	18.8	29.0	4,587,857	3,147,912	53.5	1,439,945	71.7
37	North Carolina	719,530	34.7	22.9	30.5	1,448,562	41.1	18.2	29.8	2,472,230	1,795,932	51.5	676,298	72.1
38	North Dakota...........	53,735	50.6	18.3	23.2	94,253	54.8	16.7	23.6	175,380	139,907	61.4	35,473	82.3
39	Ohio	813,090	37.8	20.1	30.4	1,707,576	44.0	17.1	28.5	2,913,312	2,131,425	53.0	781,887	71.6
40	Oklahoma...............	299,184	37.2	23.6	27.4	579,386	41.0	19.5	28.3	957,067	702,265	49.4	254,802	70.9
41	Oregon	268,761	36.1	25.6	25.2	550,333	42.4	20.8	26.8	964,892	729,381	50.1	235,511	72.5
42	Pennsylvania	842,095	39.5	21.1	27.8	1,770,912	45.1	17.7	26.4	3,202,089	2,386,165	54.1	815,924	69.5
44	Rhode Island............	65,968	42.1	14.2	31.0	141,527	45.6	11.4	32.0	257,419	180,454	58.5	76,965	74.3
45	South Carolina..........	341,686	32.8	18.6	35.8	677,725	38.1	16.7	33.6	1,204,041	839,168	48.2	364,873	69.9
46	South Dakota...........	68,378	46.0	16.7	28.0	124,348	52.6	11.7	29.1	206,668	159,567	61.6	47,101	78.8
47	Tennessee	466,254	33.7	24.6	29.7	935,370	39.3	19.8	28.3	1,641,665	1,200,647	48.4	441,018	69.9
48	Texas.....................	2,241,190	32.2	27.8	27.6	4,389,160	39.0	23.3	28.2	6,239,195	4,492,603	51.2	1,746,592	74.7
49	Utah	305,249	36.8	41.6	15.0	547,584	44.4	32.1	18.0	666,661	542,587	52.4	124,074	75.7
50	Vermont	37,566	44.0	16.9	28.5	80,425	52.8	13.2	24.3	160,878	126,519	59.2	34,359	75.5
51	Virginia	593,623	39.9	24.6	26.3	1,177,207	46.8	19.6	25.3	2,044,422	1,541,185	55.6	503,237	75.1
53	Washington	507,994	35.4	31.1	22.8	1,007,528	42.9	22.5	24.6	1,687,786	1,301,823	51.9	385,963	75.3
54	West Virginia	121,845	31.8	26.0	24.4	238,599	39.0	19.7	24.4	471,536	358,666	41.0	112,870	59.4
55	Wisconsin	412,791	44.6	19.2	26.7	847,683	50.3	14.9	26.9	1,461,573	1,126,874	58.5	334,699	76.8
56	Wyoming.................	44,376	38.1	26.9	26.4	85,228	46.2	20.6	26.3	146,745	115,398	55.7	31,347	80.0

Table B-1. States — What: Education, Employment, and Income, 2012—*Continued*

State code	STATE	Women 20 to 64 years in households, by presence of children and labor force status			Class of worker for employed civilians 16 years and over					Occupation (percent)				
		Total women 20 to 64 years in households	Percent with children under 18 years	Percent in labor force with children under 18 years	Civilian employed population 16 years and over	Percent private wage and salary workers	Percent government workers	Percent self-employed and unpaid workers	Civilian employed population 16 years and over	Management, business, science, and arts	Service	Sales and office	Natural resources, construction, and maintenance	Production, transportation, and material moving
	ACS table number:	B23003	B23003	B23003	C24080	C24080	C24080	C24080	B24060	B24060	B24060	B24060	B24060	B24060
	Column number:	58	59	60	61	62	63	64	65	66	67	68	69	70
00	United States	93,557,152	36.2	26.4	142,921,687	79.2	14.5	6.3	142,921,687	36.1	18.3	24.5	9.0	12.2
01	Alabama....................	1,446,962	36.5	26.3	2,001,628	77.7	16.7	5.7	2,001,628	32.7	16.9	24.4	10.1	15.9
02	Alaska.......................	216,152	38.3	27.3	351,496	67.5	26.0	6.5	351,496	36.8	19.2	21.4	11.8	10.8
04	Arizona.....................	1,869,984	35.9	24.7	2,757,652	79.0	14.9	6.1	2,757,652	34.9	20.2	26.2	9.1	9.5
05	Arkansas...................	857,304	37.1	26.3	1,252,225	76.0	17.6	6.5	1,252,225	31.2	17.3	23.9	10.7	16.9
06	California..................	11,372,723	36.5	25.0	16,778,061	77.5	13.9	8.6	16,778,061	36.8	19.0	24.1	9.1	11.1
08	Colorado...................	1,563,900	36.6	26.4	2,559,194	79.2	14.2	6.6	2,559,194	40.0	17.6	24.2	9.5	8.8
09	Connecticut...............	1,074,260	37.0	28.9	1,760,162	80.3	13.3	6.4	1,760,162	41.5	18.1	23.7	7.0	9.7
10	Delaware...................	275,896	34.6	27.2	427,114	80.5	15.1	4.5	427,114	36.7	18.8	25.3	8.4	10.8
11	District of Columbia.....	213,518	22.7	18.3	326,957	69.1	25.3	5.6	326,957	59.9	15.4	17.8	3.1	3.8
12	Florida......................	5,679,324	32.7	24.3	8,277,586	80.9	13.0	6.1	8,277,586	33.7	20.5	28.0	8.9	8.9
13	Georgia	3,016,510	38.2	27.6	4,263,543	78.9	15.5	5.6	4,263,543	35.5	17.2	25.1	9.1	13.1
15	Hawaii	401,134	34.5	26.2	648,504	72.4	20.5	7.1	648,504	33.3	23.1	24.8	10.1	8.7
16	Idaho.......................	451,253	40.1	28.1	710,247	76.2	15.6	8.1	710,247	32.8	18.5	24.4	12.0	12.3
17	Illinois	3,865,109	36.6	27.4	6,030,591	82.3	12.8	4.9	6,030,591	36.1	17.6	24.9	7.3	14.1
18	Indiana	1,916,367	37.1	27.8	3,003,089	84.3	10.8	4.9	3,003,089	31.2	17.2	23.9	9.1	18.6
19	Iowa........................	870,562	37.8	30.8	1,556,772	79.5	13.7	6.8	1,556,772	34.1	16.3	23.7	9.6	16.3
20	Kansas......................	822,421	38.9	29.3	1,394,404	76.8	17.0	6.1	1,394,404	35.4	17.3	24.0	9.9	13.5
21	Kentucky	1,304,323	36.0	26.1	1,867,958	78.7	15.5	5.7	1,867,958	32.3	16.7	24.5	9.8	16.7
22	Louisiana	1,381,723	36.4	27.2	2,001,905	78.6	15.7	5.7	2,001,905	31.9	19.6	23.5	12.7	12.2
23	Maine	401,637	31.7	23.8	646,362	77.4	13.8	8.7	646,362	33.9	18.7	24.5	11.2	11.6
24	Maryland	1,839,837	35.2	27.9	2,937,440	73.0	22.0	5.0	2,937,440	44.2	17.0	23.2	7.8	7.8
25	Massachusetts	2,029,434	34.5	26.8	3,334,794	81.4	12.5	6.1	3,334,794	43.3	17.4	23.4	7.2	8.7
26	Michigan	2,947,287	35.5	26.2	4,285,132	83.2	11.5	5.3	4,285,132	34.1	19.0	24.2	7.7	15.0
27	Minnesota	1,580,911	37.5	30.5	2,786,812	82.0	12.1	6.0	2,786,812	39.1	16.3	23.6	8.0	13.0
28	Mississippi.................	880,962	38.4	28.0	1,193,047	75.0	19.3	5.7	1,193,047	30.8	18.1	24.0	11.3	15.9
29	Missouri....................	1,782,717	35.5	27.2	2,764,577	81.0	12.9	6.1	2,764,577	34.5	18.2	25.0	8.7	13.6
30	Montana	291,379	34.3	26.4	482,710	71.6	18.8	9.5	482,710	36.5	19.2	22.4	12.3	9.6
31	Nebraska	529,127	38.7	31.1	956,636	77.9	14.6	7.5	956,636	35.4	17.1	24.1	10.3	13.2
32	Nevada	820,930	36.0	26.0	1,230,084	82.2	12.4	5.3	1,230,084	27.1	28.1	26.1	8.8	9.9
33	New Hampshire	399,349	34.3	26.2	692,142	78.9	13.7	7.4	692,142	39.9	16.2	24.0	9.1	10.9
34	New Jersey.................	2,684,762	38.1	28.3	4,206,029	81.0	14.0	5.0	4,206,029	40.3	16.8	25.3	7.2	10.5
35	New Mexico...............	599,404	35.8	25.1	870,667	70.5	22.5	7.0	870,667	35.6	20.6	23.5	11.2	9.1
36	New York..................	6,012,895	34.1	24.8	9,099,766	78.1	15.8	6.1	9,099,766	38.5	20.3	24.2	7.3	9.7
37	North Carolina............	2,941,777	36.7	27.0	4,268,510	79.0	14.9	6.1	4,268,510	35.6	18.0	23.5	9.7	13.2
38	North Dakota.............	196,376	35.9	28.9	379,029	74.2	17.1	8.7	379,029	34.2	17.2	23.2	13.4	12.0
39	Ohio........................	3,425,869	35.4	26.7	5,285,177	81.9	12.8	5.2	5,285,177	34.0	18.0	24.5	7.8	15.8
40	Oklahoma.................	1,099,489	37.2	26.6	1,694,799	76.1	17.2	6.7	1,694,799	32.3	18.2	24.5	11.9	13.1
41	Oregon.....................	1,169,810	33.4	23.7	1,738,117	78.1	13.8	8.1	1,738,117	36.1	19.2	23.9	8.7	12.1
42	Pennsylvania	3,772,744	34.0	25.5	5,931,277	83.6	11.1	5.3	5,931,277	36.3	17.7	24.4	8.2	13.4
44	Rhode Island	318,406	33.6	27.1	512,801	81.4	13.2	5.4	512,801	35.8	20.6	24.3	7.7	11.5
45	South Carolina............	1,423,414	36.0	26.9	2,007,569	78.6	15.9	5.6	2,007,569	32.8	18.4	25.0	9.1	14.7
46	South Dakota.............	230,716	36.9	30.7	426,383	76.1	15.3	8.6	426,383	35.2	17.4	23.5	10.8	13.0
47	Tennessee	1,952,978	35.3	25.1	2,823,508	79.1	14.2	6.7	2,823,508	33.6	16.9	25.5	9.0	15.1
48	Texas.......................	7,669,260	40.5	27.8	11,731,417	78.9	14.2	6.9	11,731,417	34.2	18.1	24.6	11.1	11.9
49	Utah	789,501	44.4	28.5	1,312,966	79.8	15.5	4.8	1,312,966	36.8	15.6	26.5	9.1	12.0
50	Vermont	186,347	32.9	26.4	325,960	76.2	14.0	9.8	325,960	40.6	17.1	21.7	10.0	10.6
51	Virginia	2,507,448	36.1	26.9	3,938,818	74.2	20.5	5.4	3,938,818	41.9	16.9	23.1	8.5	9.5
53	Washington	2,076,309	35.2	24.4	3,204,090	77.3	16.3	6.4	3,204,090	38.1	18.0	22.8	9.7	11.4
54	West Virginia	551,742	32.2	21.6	752,314	76.6	18.8	4.5	752,314	31.5	18.7	24.8	12.2	12.9
55	Wisconsin	1,679,586	35.4	28.3	2,844,814	82.3	12.5	5.2	2,844,814	34.5	16.8	23.4	8.3	16.9
56	Wyoming...................	166,224	36.3	26.7	288,852	72.8	19.8	7.5	288,852	31.6	18.3	21.1	16.4	12.6

Table B-1. States — What: Education, Employment, and Income, 2012—Continued

State code	STATE	Industry (percent) Agriculture, forestry, fishing and hunting, and mining	Construc-tion	Manufac-turing	Wholesale trade	Retail trade	Transporta-tion and warehous-ing, and utilities	Information	Finance and insurance, real estate, and rental and leasing	Industry (percent) Professional, scientific, and manage-ment, and administrative and waste management services	Educational services, and health care and social assistance	Arts, enter-tainment, and recreation, and accom-modation and food services	Other services, except public administra-tion	Public adminis-tration
	ACS table number:	C24070	C24070	C24070	C24070	C24070	C24070	C24070	C24070	C24070	C24070	C24070	C24070	C24070
	Column number:	71	72	73	74	75	76	77	78	79	80	81	82	83
00	United States	2.0	6.2	10.5	2.6	11.6	4.9	2.1	6.6	10.9	23.2	9.6	5.0	4.9
01	Alabama.................	1.7	6.7	13.3	2.5	12.2	5.6	1.8	5.5	9.1	22.3	8.4	5.2	5.6
02	Alaska...................	5.5	7.3	3.8	1.6	10.7	7.4	1.9	4.2	8.1	24.4	9.3	4.2	11.7
04	Arizona..................	1.5	6.3	7.5	2.2	12.2	4.8	1.8	8.1	11.9	22.3	10.6	5.1	5.6
05	Arkansas................	3.2	6.7	14.0	2.6	13.0	5.3	1.7	4.8	6.6	24.2	8.0	4.9	5.0
06	California................	2.5	5.9	9.9	3.0	11.3	4.6	2.8	6.3	12.8	21.0	10.1	5.5	4.4
08	Colorado	2.6	7.2	7.1	2.6	10.9	4.6	2.8	6.8	13.6	20.6	11.0	5.1	5.0
09	Connecticut............	0.4	5.5	10.8	2.4	10.9	3.6	2.4	9.2	11.0	26.8	8.8	4.5	3.6
10	Delaware	1.2	6.1	9.4	2.0	12.3	4.8	1.7	9.9	10.3	23.4	8.4	4.6	6.0
11	District of Columbia .	0.1	3.3	1.3	0.5	4.7	3.3	4.4	5.1	21.6	20.3	9.8	9.3	16.5
12	Florida	1.1	6.2	5.3	2.9	13.8	4.9	1.9	7.7	12.6	21.5	12.0	5.3	4.9
13	Georgia	1.1	6.2	11.0	2.7	11.9	5.8	2.4	6.3	11.9	21.0	9.4	4.9	5.4
15	Hawaii...................	1.7	7.0	3.1	2.1	12.4	6.0	1.4	6.3	11.0	19.2	16.2	4.7	8.8
16	Idaho....................	5.6	7.5	9.6	3.0	12.2	4.4	1.8	5.1	8.9	23.3	9.4	4.3	4.8
17	Illinois	1.1	5.0	12.7	2.9	11.0	6.0	2.1	7.3	11.1	23.0	9.1	4.9	3.9
18	Indiana..................	1.3	5.8	19.0	2.5	11.7	5.2	1.3	5.1	7.9	22.8	9.1	4.8	3.3
19	Iowa.....................	4.0	6.2	15.1	2.7	11.6	4.8	1.9	7.7	7.0	24.5	7.2	4.3	3.1
20	Kansas...................	3.3	6.4	12.7	2.7	11.1	4.7	2.4	5.9	8.5	24.6	8.2	4.7	4.9
21	Kentucky	2.9	6.1	13.6	2.7	11.9	5.9	1.7	5.5	7.5	24.4	8.8	4.6	4.5
22	Louisiana	5.1	8.1	7.9	2.5	11.5	5.0	1.5	5.4	8.6	23.5	10.5	5.2	5.4
23	Maine	2.5	7.4	9.2	2.2	13.6	4.1	1.7	5.8	8.3	27.5	9.1	4.4	4.3
24	Maryland	0.6	6.6	4.9	1.9	10.1	4.4	2.1	6.2	15.5	23.4	8.2	5.3	10.9
25	Massachusetts	0.4	5.6	9.1	2.3	10.9	3.7	2.2	7.7	12.8	27.9	9.0	4.4	4.1
26	Michigan................	1.3	4.9	17.2	2.4	11.4	4.1	1.6	5.5	9.4	24.0	9.6	4.8	3.7
27	Minnesota..............	2.3	5.5	13.6	2.7	11.4	4.7	2.0	7.3	9.7	24.7	8.1	4.7	3.4
28	Mississippi..............	3.1	6.5	13.3	2.5	11.6	5.7	1.2	4.8	6.2	24.4	9.7	4.8	6.2
29	Missouri.................	1.7	5.9	11.6	2.6	12.1	4.9	2.0	6.9	9.3	24.3	9.3	4.8	4.5
30	Montana................	7.2	8.1	4.7	2.2	11.7	4.6	1.8	5.0	8.8	22.8	11.9	4.2	6.9
31	Nebraska................	4.7	6.6	11.1	2.7	11.6	5.6	2.0	7.2	8.2	23.3	8.1	4.5	4.4
32	Nevada	1.6	6.0	4.2	1.9	12.1	5.1	1.6	5.3	11.2	15.2	25.9	5.0	4.8
33	New Hampshire	0.7	7.1	12.5	3.0	12.4	4.0	2.0	6.7	10.3	24.5	8.9	4.3	3.7
34	New Jersey..............	0.3	5.6	8.7	3.4	11.4	5.6	2.8	8.6	12.8	23.7	8.3	4.5	4.1
35	New Mexico............	4.4	7.1	5.1	2.1	11.3	4.3	1.4	4.4	10.6	26.1	10.6	4.8	7.9
36	New York...............	0.6	5.6	6.7	2.5	11.2	5.0	2.8	8.0	11.2	27.3	9.4	5.0	4.7
37	North Carolina........	1.6	6.9	12.5	2.7	11.8	4.2	1.8	6.1	9.9	23.7	9.6	5.0	4.3
38	North Dakota..........	9.3	7.1	6.9	3.1	13.1	5.3	1.5	5.5	6.4	24.6	7.7	3.9	5.3
39	Ohio.....................	1.1	5.2	15.4	2.7	11.6	4.8	1.6	6.4	9.4	24.1	9.0	4.6	4.0
40	Oklahoma..............	5.2	7.1	9.7	2.4	11.4	5.2	1.8	5.8	8.2	22.8	9.1	5.2	6.2
41	Oregon..................	3.2	5.3	11.5	2.8	12.0	4.2	1.9	5.7	10.7	23.3	10.0	5.1	4.3
42	Pennsylvania	1.5	5.6	12.3	2.8	11.8	5.0	1.7	6.3	9.7	26.2	8.3	4.7	4.1
44	Rhode Island...........	0.4	5.1	11.4	2.1	11.9	4.0	1.7	6.9	9.6	27.0	10.6	4.6	4.7
45	South Carolina........	1.0	6.3	13.8	2.6	12.0	4.5	1.7	6.0	9.7	21.4	10.9	5.1	5.0
46	South Dakota..........	7.3	6.7	9.4	3.2	11.2	4.3	1.7	6.8	6.1	24.3	9.3	4.6	4.9
47	Tennessee	1.1	6.5	12.8	2.6	12.2	6.3	2.0	5.7	9.2	23.3	9.3	4.8	4.3
48	Texas....................	3.4	7.9	9.3	2.8	11.7	5.5	1.7	6.6	10.9	21.6	8.9	5.3	4.4
49	Utah.....................	2.1	6.3	10.7	2.3	12.2	4.4	2.3	6.7	12.1	22.3	8.8	4.7	5.2
50	Vermont	2.6	7.7	10.9	2.3	11.8	2.8	2.4	5.1	9.0	27.5	9.2	4.1	4.4
51	Virginia..................	1.0	6.6	7.4	1.8	11.1	3.9	2.1	6.3	14.8	21.4	8.9	5.4	9.3
53	Washington............	2.7	5.9	10.8	2.8	11.5	5.3	2.2	5.3	12.4	21.3	9.2	5.0	5.7
54	West Virginia	5.4	6.0	8.2	2.1	13.3	5.0	1.8	4.3	7.8	26.0	9.2	4.4	6.5
55	Wisconsin...............	2.4	5.1	18.4	2.7	11.2	4.2	1.6	6.4	7.9	23.7	8.7	4.2	3.5
56	Wyoming................	12.7	8.2	3.4	2.2	10.1	7.2	1.7	3.7	7.3	20.7	10.7	5.4	6.5

State code	STATE	Veterans as a percent of the population 18 years and over	Median income in the past 12 months (in 2012 inflation-adjusted dollars) — Median household income by age of householder					Median income in the past 12 months (in 2012 inflation-adjusted dollars) — Median household income by race and Hispanic origin of householder								
			All households	Householder under 25 years	Householder 25 to 44 years	Householder 45 to 64 years	Householder 65 years and over	White alone	Black alone	American Indian, Alaska Native alone	Asian alone	Native Hawaiian and other Pacific Islander alone	Some other race alone	Two or more races	White alone, not Hispanic or Latino	Hispanic or Latino
	ACS table number:	B21001	B19049	B19049	B19049	B19049	B19049	B19013A	B19013B	B19013C	B19013D	B19013E	B19013F	B19013G	B19013H	B19013I
	Column number:	84	85	86	87	88	89	90	91	92	93	94	95	96	97	98
00	United States	8.9	51,371	24,476	55,821	62,049	36,743	54,729	33,764	35,310	70,644	51,322	38,439	44,930	56,565	40,417
01	Alabama	10.4	41,574	18,760	45,956	50,583	32,287	48,649	27,493	35,000	55,055	41,500	31,664	30,323	49,159	31,937
02	Alaska	13.6	67,712	41,108	67,520	80,208	46,666	74,573	42,825	42,556	56,473	51,342	48,775	52,321	75,354	51,396
04	Arizona	10.7	47,826	23,819	51,431	56,242	39,083	50,071	38,426	31,014	62,633	48,304	35,258	40,139	53,277	36,828
05	Arkansas	10.4	40,112	20,456	44,745	46,767	30,891	42,740	25,256	33,419	53,099	28,495	33,332	37,381	43,443	33,131
06	California	6.5	58,328	27,561	61,004	70,182	42,406	61,419	41,275	40,116	74,715	57,184	41,755	54,464	68,530	44,401
08	Colorado	10.4	56,765	25,727	60,627	68,891	41,985	59,255	39,941	37,286	63,755	51,915	33,589	46,639	62,024	39,223
09	Connecticut	7.7	67,276	29,945	70,181	85,472	41,947	72,469	38,051	39,580	91,168	51,686	33,570	53,018	76,046	36,756
10	Delaware	10.8	58,415	29,749	64,021	67,439	42,211	61,824	45,453	32,218	83,656	...	53,653	42,479	62,669	45,690
11	District of Columbia	6.0	66,583	33,841	81,142	65,365	46,926	108,699	39,139	36,904	104,826	...	37,110	65,256	110,619	51,460
12	Florida	10.2	45,040	23,207	48,011	52,960	36,415	47,731	32,218	39,778	59,503	45,760	36,644	39,109	50,400	37,915
13	Georgia	9.5	47,209	21,855	50,242	56,749	35,371	54,595	34,717	31,383	65,321	...	30,288	40,237	55,831	35,951
15	Hawaii	11.1	66,259	44,762	63,843	75,924	59,378	66,286	58,478	30,728	71,946	59,935	42,904	60,826	67,731	50,276
16	Idaho	10.6	45,489	26,946	49,189	55,721	34,040	45,882	50,710	35,189	52,425	...	34,729	42,246	46,970	33,323
17	Illinois	7.5	55,137	22,263	60,798	67,510	37,161	60,343	32,090	42,213	73,690	63,587	43,911	46,472	61,887	45,188
18	Indiana	9.2	46,974	21,823	51,216	57,662	34,636	49,669	28,577	34,953	50,327	33,535	36,045	35,263	49,841	40,748
19	Iowa	9.7	50,957	24,583	57,916	61,484	34,731	51,670	27,373	20,000	56,397	39,686	37,716	38,784	51,995	36,642
20	Kansas	10.0	50,241	25,155	54,410	61,740	36,516	51,813	33,461	36,881	57,943	95,013	35,299	37,980	52,681	38,578
21	Kentucky	9.4	41,724	21,609	47,644	50,280	30,023	43,190	26,739	40,386	52,261	48,292	34,572	36,294	43,338	36,764
22	Louisiana	8.9	42,944	21,320	48,614	51,206	30,935	52,333	27,123	34,783	45,394	60,866	42,843	36,620	52,958	39,494
23	Maine	11.6	46,709	28,288	51,438	56,035	33,358	47,253	28,839	18,214	44,638	...	...	41,891	47,311	37,370
24	Maryland	9.7	71,122	30,422	72,761	87,178	47,949	80,097	54,887	61,344	91,327	...	55,729	70,006	80,908	58,756
25	Massachusetts	7.3	65,339	30,196	73,806	79,754	38,233	69,713	40,394	21,933	72,350	43,642	34,123	46,696	71,284	32,605
26	Michigan	8.7	46,859	20,316	50,328	57,665	35,504	50,385	27,986	38,691	71,563	45,985	31,963	34,574	50,715	37,087
27	Minnesota	9.0	58,906	27,635	65,976	71,902	37,428	61,220	28,136	32,153	65,959	...	47,324	44,520	61,667	41,718
28	Mississippi	9.1	37,095	17,302	40,587	43,250	28,388	46,174	24,414	40,390	48,607	...	27,757	38,448	46,524	30,912
29	Missouri	10.4	45,321	22,657	50,725	54,578	33,906	48,448	28,487	31,932	57,575	36,875	30,834	33,298	48,649	36,073
30	Montana	12.7	45,076	25,127	51,835	52,080	34,941	46,838	...	27,187	35,520	77,237	30,190	33,460	47,013	35,629
31	Nebraska	10.4	50,723	28,430	54,212	62,509	35,655	52,210	29,059	25,485	57,028	68,529	39,373	32,189	53,326	38,096
32	Nevada	11.0	49,760	29,713	51,281	56,218	40,181	51,422	36,479	39,621	58,973	40,009	41,761	46,694	54,341	40,601
33	New Hampshire	10.6	63,280	30,850	68,877	77,833	41,445	63,364	47,907	...	81,677	...	62,553	50,112	63,705	48,309
34	New Jersey	6.4	69,667	30,600	75,816	84,227	43,254	74,261	45,318	43,766	100,656	...	44,571	55,298	78,667	47,547
35	New Mexico	11.4	42,558	20,712	44,878	51,416	34,727	40,305	34,425	31,924	56,854	...	31,594	36,697	53,047	34,897
36	New York	5.8	56,448	25,435	62,282	66,980	37,246	63,078	40,955	34,830	59,340	98,659	34,619	45,923	65,385	38,089
37	North Carolina	9.8	45,150	22,996	48,377	53,487	33,749	50,476	31,650	26,752	62,579	33,167	33,194	36,648	51,306	33,940
38	North Dakota	10.5	53,585	30,655	62,267	67,356	34,462	55,230	31,283	34,121	66,435	81,683	46,739	38,378	55,450	43,307
39	Ohio	9.6	46,829	20,719	51,624	57,396	33,901	50,421	26,016	32,134	63,428	65,711	31,364	30,077	50,675	34,422
40	Oklahoma	11.2	44,312	24,509	49,043	52,881	33,397	47,052	30,005	36,095	52,366	46,240	34,549	38,569	48,057	34,320
41	Oregon	10.7	49,161	24,721	53,678	57,448	38,428	50,134	27,054	31,199	60,965	34,678	36,603	42,673	50,649	37,533
42	Pennsylvania	9.3	51,230	24,263	57,468	63,394	33,942	54,371	31,074	32,378	63,378	29,639	27,549	36,518	54,967	31,349
44	Rhode Island	8.5	54,554	25,542	59,881	68,994	35,510	58,234	34,591	34,214	52,129	...	36,866	30,466	60,156	30,329
45	South Carolina	10.9	43,107	21,096	46,675	50,521	34,541	50,111	29,043	31,334	53,691	31,474	41,259	40,162	50,469	38,524
46	South Dakota	11.0	48,362	26,882	52,346	60,247	34,913	50,479	31,111	25,846	52,588	38,569	42,398	34,718	50,600	45,138
47	Tennessee	9.6	42,764	22,441	46,058	51,040	32,963	45,923	30,474	37,750	62,330	...	33,463	28,870	46,254	33,487
48	Texas	8.5	50,740	24,794	52,899	61,330	36,675	53,501	37,018	43,389	71,469	55,809	37,234	43,676	62,053	38,863
49	Utah	7.4	57,049	30,329	58,420	72,437	42,491	58,880	47,242	29,859	52,050	55,723	33,611	41,205	60,476	37,502
50	Vermont	9.6	52,977	30,784	58,549	62,278	36,848	53,552	51,210	16,331	40,507	...	36,000	50,102	53,582	40,221
51	Virginia	11.7	61,741	28,154	66,185	75,977	41,982	66,441	42,187	54,176	90,048	93,036	51,750	59,912	66,784	57,874
53	Washington	11.2	57,573	26,771	62,092	70,251	41,474	59,527	40,084	37,472	68,863	45,245	40,152	49,835	60,716	40,858
54	West Virginia	11.1	40,196	21,864	48,163	46,865	29,897	40,645	22,470	...	75,529	22,002	45,385	31,714	40,643	40,299
55	Wisconsin	9.2	51,059	24,268	56,615	62,757	34,652	53,231	26,039	35,888	51,137	22,440	33,606	36,295	53,914	35,344
56	Wyoming	11.1	54,901	34,386	58,769	68,925	36,362	56,406	32,071	39,296	45,182	...	34,541	38,750	57,429	39,020

Table B-1. States — What: Education, Employment, and Income, 2012—*Continued*

State code	STATE	Median income in the past 12 months (in 2012 inflation-adjusted dollars)											
		Median family income by type of family							Median nonfamily household income			Median individual income	
		All families	Married-couple families with children	Married-couple families, no children	Male householder with children	Male householder, no children	Female householder with children	Female householder, no children	All nonfamily households	Living alone, 65 years and over		Persons 15 years and over who worked full-time, year-round	
										Male	Female	Male	Female
	ACS table number:	B19126	B19126	B19126	B19126	B19126	B19126	B19126	B19215	B19215	B19215	B19326	B19326
	Column number:	99	100	101	102	103	104	105	106	107	108	109	110
00	United States	62,527	81,222	72,469	36,253	50,142	23,151	41,184	31,231	24,730	19,884	49,510	38,877
01	Alabama....................	52,700	73,242	62,976	32,219	39,105	17,579	33,353	23,243	20,413	16,805	46,090	32,469
02	Alaska......................	80,219	90,981	93,745	50,667	65,949	30,293	59,727	41,357	25,371	23,032	60,602	44,771
04	Arizona....................	56,792	71,283	66,705	35,440	46,196	25,547	38,310	31,605	24,730	21,596	45,482	36,803
05	Arkansas..................	50,300	63,418	57,547	30,321	40,312	18,367	32,153	22,332	20,935	17,037	40,865	31,632
06	California.................	66,215	80,847	82,061	36,126	53,618	25,524	45,934	39,504	27,627	22,613	50,843	42,807
08	Colorado	71,083	84,153	80,414	40,477	55,145	27,989	46,376	35,841	27,060	22,493	51,346	41,378
09	Connecticut..............	85,254	111,336	95,795	51,924	64,938	30,047	52,988	37,836	27,460	22,312	61,870	49,621
10	Delaware.................	70,655	92,024	78,628	41,592	61,008	29,025	47,611	36,280	27,219	21,663	51,306	41,987
11	District of Columbia	82,268	151,107	130,966	32,301	61,716	28,733	51,724	55,639	29,627	28,178	67,958	60,995
12	Florida	54,777	70,330	63,607	33,288	44,323	23,618	38,999	29,072	24,588	19,887	41,681	35,375
13	Georgia	56,684	75,945	68,161	32,714	44,211	21,015	34,761	29,479	23,857	18,113	45,494	36,243
15	Hawaii	77,447	85,660	87,088	51,276	70,858	24,327	69,683	40,883	30,732	25,118	47,328	39,889
16	Idaho	54,483	63,601	60,859	35,097	36,988	19,597	38,555	27,027	19,040	18,830	42,543	31,885
17	Illinois	68,705	88,053	78,853	35,975	53,187	23,827	43,316	32,785	25,839	20,733	51,979	41,045
18	Indiana	58,596	75,899	64,660	33,468	47,631	21,425	39,301	27,484	24,161	19,941	46,538	34,993
19	Iowa........................	64,122	79,339	69,675	36,200	46,942	24,102	41,609	28,873	25,118	19,478	46,411	35,947
20	Kansas.....................	62,955	77,611	70,309	33,200	50,905	24,271	40,136	29,850	25,607	20,904	46,207	35,476
21	Kentucky	53,012	73,137	60,393	30,242	38,304	18,250	32,383	23,078	19,624	16,491	44,444	33,310
22	Louisiana..................	54,059	81,792	66,297	35,950	44,880	19,153	32,776	24,428	20,762	16,444	49,313	32,230
23	Maine	58,689	73,283	64,357	31,382	52,034	22,546	42,946	28,040	23,226	18,610	44,196	36,138
24	Maryland	85,985	111,818	100,398	46,396	66,556	35,289	57,921	43,675	29,697	23,826	60,192	50,286
25	Massachusetts	82,977	111,787	92,370	47,899	62,778	26,654	52,879	37,769	24,423	19,901	61,139	49,440
26	Michigan	59,295	79,245	66,565	35,022	46,145	20,036	37,923	27,575	25,674	20,668	50,659	37,730
27	Minnesota	73,511	92,972	78,261	41,221	56,850	26,751	47,402	34,549	25,506	20,284	51,643	41,237
28	Mississippi................	45,857	66,545	58,229	31,810	38,806	18,291	27,819	20,660	19,888	14,911	40,982	30,841
29	Missouri...................	57,274	74,764	64,614	33,130	44,887	21,460	38,975	26,849	24,790	18,880	45,219	34,324
30	Montana	59,706	71,987	64,704	32,682	55,440	20,626	37,028	25,951	23,789	19,581	43,383	32,705
31	Nebraska	63,442	77,680	71,025	36,382	48,477	23,883	40,965	30,438	25,395	19,470	45,186	35,051
32	Nevada	56,954	67,033	70,115	36,341	52,441	26,547	43,760	34,519	27,067	22,003	43,538	36,856
33	New Hampshire	78,524	99,818	82,256	42,215	53,298	28,643	52,251	38,070	30,383	21,688	55,815	42,395
34	New Jersey................	84,442	109,952	94,801	44,924	64,239	27,589	55,821	38,028	28,498	22,072	61,999	49,805
35	New Mexico..............	51,449	66,892	63,282	31,293	46,287	20,953	33,021	27,610	20,788	19,888	42,212	34,506
36	New York..................	68,395	90,634	82,373	39,233	55,091	25,834	47,947	35,873	25,676	19,752	51,996	44,793
37	North Carolina...........	54,995	72,764	65,326	30,189	40,832	21,527	34,031	27,468	21,502	18,554	43,129	35,410
38	North Dakota.............	70,573	88,399	73,498	45,323	54,414	24,621	46,177	33,000	26,605	18,709	47,655	35,261
39	Ohio........................	60,088	80,213	67,737	35,920	45,690	20,028	38,732	27,408	24,361	19,462	48,169	36,982
40	Oklahoma.................	54,988	68,708	64,449	35,999	43,730	20,740	37,387	26,166	22,490	18,889	42,328	32,190
41	Oregon	59,476	74,087	68,471	33,988	43,486	21,338	38,699	30,797	26,367	21,301	49,355	38,779
42	Pennsylvania.............	65,109	86,630	71,970	36,099	51,040	23,417	42,987	29,281	24,466	18,951	50,540	38,776
44	Rhode Island.............	71,293	93,473	83,053	40,653	58,149	30,102	47,506	30,843	22,069	17,060	51,896	41,829
45	South Carolina...........	52,763	73,377	62,963	31,477	42,091	19,484	32,388	26,070	22,518	17,798	42,496	34,123
46	South Dakota.............	61,505	77,217	68,130	40,301	45,966	22,793	37,811	30,301	24,390	19,476	41,855	32,907
47	Tennessee	53,342	70,718	61,411	31,101	41,260	19,379	34,172	25,686	20,408	17,973	42,935	33,804
48	Texas.......................	59,765	74,337	73,151	36,244	48,708	23,083	38,104	31,816	23,109	19,217	45,950	36,388
49	Utah........................	64,801	71,428	71,862	41,344	52,526	25,263	48,849	33,123	25,147	21,203	50,067	35,187
50	Vermont	66,047	80,736	72,435	36,135	42,664	24,965	43,050	31,803	22,161	19,465	46,214	39,563
51	Virginia....................	74,485	95,098	83,694	43,430	57,022	26,589	45,354	38,540	28,375	21,390	54,724	41,974
53	Washington	69,937	83,992	79,022	41,717	56,405	25,664	44,784	36,548	28,003	22,623	55,436	41,795
54	West Virginia	51,320	69,756	55,661	27,162	41,613	17,660	32,510	21,944	20,749	17,810	45,996	31,711
55	Wisconsin	65,154	83,173	70,738	36,347	50,082	24,375	41,471	29,986	24,873	19,397	47,930	37,296
56	Wyoming..................	68,827	77,502	78,228	45,192	59,239	22,006	45,468	29,627	22,859	19,901	53,776	35,371

Table B-1. States — What: Education, Employment, and Income, 2012—*Continued*

State code	STATE	Per capita income in the past 12 months (in 2012 inflation-adjusted dollars)	Total number of households	Households, by type of income (percent)								
				With wage or salary income	With self-employment income	With interest, dividends, or net rental income	With Social Security	With Supplemental Security Income (SSI)	With public assistance income	With cash public assistance or Food Stamps	With retirement income	With other types of income
	ACS table number:	B19301	B19052	B19052	B19053	B19054	B19055	B19056	B19057	B19058	B19059	B19060
	Column number:	111	112	113	114	115	116	117	118	119	120	121
00	United States............	27,319	115,969,540	74.7	10.6	20.3	29.3	5.4	2.9	14.3	18.0	13.4
01	Alabama..................	22,815	1,845,169	69.9	8.4	15.5	33.7	6.9	1.9	17.2	20.5	13.7
02	Alaska....................	31,890	251,651	82.9	14.2	42.3	20.4	4.6	6.6	14.0	18.8	48.5
04	Arizona...................	24,600	2,392,168	72.1	9.7	18.6	31.0	4.2	2.3	15.0	19.7	12.5
05	Arkansas.................	21,643	1,143,859	70.6	9.1	15.6	34.3	7.2	2.7	15.9	17.2	12.8
06	California................	28,341	12,552,658	75.8	13.6	20.2	25.7	6.1	4.1	10.2	15.7	14.2
08	Colorado	30,329	1,996,088	79.3	13.1	23.1	23.5	3.6	2.2	10.0	16.0	13.9
09	Connecticut.............	36,891	1,357,812	76.1	11.1	26.9	29.2	4.3	3.1	12.9	17.9	13.3
10	Delaware	28,705	340,308	75.6	7.9	21.2	32.3	4.5	2.6	14.8	22.8	13.9
11	District of Columbia..	45,307	266,662	77.7	10.7	24.9	18.2	6.2	3.9	16.1	14.3	9.5
12	Florida	25,428	7,197,943	68.9	9.1	20.0	35.6	4.9	2.3	15.8	19.5	12.3
13	Georgia	24,321	3,532,908	75.7	9.4	15.4	27.1	5.3	1.8	16.9	16.7	12.4
15	Hawaii	28,099	447,748	77.7	12.6	27.2	32.6	4.0	3.4	12.1	23.1	13.4
16	Idaho.....................	22,053	583,106	74.8	13.9	18.9	29.9	5.1	3.0	14.6	17.7	15.4
17	Illinois....................	28,741	4,770,194	76.7	9.2	21.3	27.0	4.5	2.5	13.6	16.8	11.8
18	Indiana	23,898	2,480,077	75.8	9.2	18.4	30.1	4.8	2.1	13.3	18.5	13.3
19	Iowa	26,436	1,227,048	76.1	13.2	24.9	29.9	4.2	2.6	13.0	16.7	13.6
20	Kansas....................	26,390	1,113,911	77.6	11.8	22.4	28.6	4.0	2.1	10.4	16.5	13.4
21	Kentucky	22,722	1,707,004	70.1	9.6	15.9	33.1	8.4	2.8	18.8	19.7	14.0
22	Louisiana	23,800	1,719,473	74.0	8.8	15.3	29.0	6.9	1.5	17.9	15.8	10.8
23	Maine.....................	26,020	554,543	70.4	14.7	24.1	34.5	6.4	5.2	18.7	19.1	15.3
24	Maryland	35,144	2,157,717	79.6	10.3	23.1	26.1	4.3	2.6	11.8	20.2	12.5
25	Massachusetts	34,907	2,522,394	75.6	11.1	24.8	28.8	6.5	3.2	13.7	16.1	12.9
26	Michigan	25,074	3,819,068	70.8	9.1	20.2	33.1	6.1	3.9	18.5	23.1	14.3
27	Minnesota	30,529	2,111,943	77.8	12.7	24.3	27.2	4.2	3.7	9.9	15.9	14.3
28	Mississippi...............	20,119	1,090,521	70.5	8.7	12.1	32.7	8.3	3.4	19.8	18.2	12.8
29	Missouri	24,697	2,359,135	73.4	10.5	19.9	31.7	5.5	2.6	15.2	19.0	13.5
30	Montana..................	25,148	408,938	72.9	16.1	24.2	31.7	4.9	2.5	12.5	18.4	14.2
31	Nebraska	26,245	733,570	78.3	14.6	22.9	27.3	3.6	2.1	9.8	13.6	14.4
32	Nevada	25,331	1,006,605	75.4	8.7	16.3	27.3	4.2	3.2	13.4	17.9	15.2
33	New Hampshire	32,201	519,137	77.1	13.2	23.9	30.0	4.7	3.0	9.1	17.9	12.1
34	New Jersey..............	34,885	3,198,799	77.1	9.1	23.9	29.1	4.4	3.0	10.2	17.7	13.6
35	New Mexico.............	22,874	764,996	71.2	10.2	17.5	31.0	5.9	2.8	17.1	19.5	13.2
36	New York................	31,290	7,238,922	74.3	10.1	20.4	29.2	6.4	3.4	16.3	17.8	11.7
37	North Carolina.........	24,435	3,731,325	73.7	10.0	18.2	30.4	4.9	2.0	15.8	18.6	13.8
38	North Dakota...........	30,796	290,944	79.1	15.5	25.4	26.5	2.5	1.5	8.1	11.8	12.1
39	Ohio......................	25,445	4,554,672	73.0	9.3	19.5	30.4	5.7	3.3	16.3	21.4	13.4
40	Oklahoma................	23,740	1,446,667	73.2	10.8	17.8	31.0	5.6	3.4	15.0	17.3	12.9
41	Oregon...................	26,011	1,516,957	71.3	13.6	23.7	31.5	4.6	4.2	20.8	18.7	17.6
42	Pennsylvania	27,774	4,958,249	73.0	8.8	23.1	33.0	6.0	3.7	14.0	20.3	13.5
44	Rhode Island............	29,389	413,083	73.3	9.2	21.2	30.3	7.9	3.1	16.2	16.6	14.2
45	South Carolina.........	23,396	1,787,340	71.5	8.8	17.2	33.1	5.4	1.6	16.7	20.1	13.7
46	South Dakota...........	25,275	323,765	77.6	16.1	23.4	29.1	3.5	2.9	11.1	14.7	14.5
47	Tennessee	23,692	2,480,090	72.0	10.6	16.7	32.2	5.6	3.4	18.3	18.6	12.7
48	Texas......................	25,359	8,970,959	78.7	11.6	16.3	24.5	4.9	1.8	14.7	13.9	12.6
49	Utah......................	23,213	895,691	82.5	11.5	19.9	23.1	3.8	2.4	10.6	15.5	13.3
50	Vermont	28,818	258,520	75.3	17.4	29.0	32.9	6.2	4.6	15.7	16.8	13.6
51	Virginia...................	32,517	3,038,967	78.6	10.3	23.7	27.2	4.0	2.0	10.2	20.9	12.6
53	Washington	29,861	2,636,817	75.6	11.5	25.1	27.3	4.7	4.0	15.9	18.3	15.2
54	West Virginia	22,410	741,544	65.8	6.8	15.9	38.6	7.3	2.2	16.2	23.8	13.6
55	Wisconsin	26,994	2,288,362	76.1	9.9	24.8	29.8	4.7	2.2	13.9	18.2	14.8
56	Wyoming.................	27,813	223,513	78.1	14.5	23.2	28.3	4.0	1.7	7.6	16.1	13.7

Table B-1. States — What: Education, Employment, and Income, 2012—*Continued*

State code	STATE	Household income in the past 12 months (in 2012 inflation-adjusted dollars)										
		Total number of households	Households by income group (percent)									
			Less than $10,000	$10,000 to $14,999	$15,000 to $24,999	$25,000 to $34,999	$35,000 to $49,999	$50,000 to $74,999	$75,000 to $99,999	$100,000 to $149,999	$150,000 to $199,999	$200,000 or more
	ACS table number:	C19001	C19001	C19001	C19001	C19001	C19001	C19001	C19001	C19001	C19001	C19001
	Column number:	122	123	124	125	126	127	128	129	130	131	132
00	United States	115,969,540	7.7	5.6	11.1	10.4	13.8	18.0	11.9	12.4	4.6	4.6
01	Alabama....................	1,845,169	10.5	7.7	13.0	11.5	14.3	17.2	10.7	9.7	3.0	2.3
02	Alaska......................	251,651	3.9	4.0	8.3	8.2	12.0	18.9	14.1	17.4	7.2	5.9
04	Arizona.....................	2,392,168	7.9	5.6	11.7	11.3	15.1	18.5	11.3	11.5	3.7	3.2
05	Arkansas...................	1,143,859	9.7	8.0	14.6	12.4	14.9	17.9	9.7	8.5	2.2	2.0
06	California..................	12,552,658	6.3	5.4	10.1	9.2	12.6	17.0	12.0	14.4	6.3	6.8
08	Colorado...................	1,996,088	6.4	4.5	9.8	9.7	13.7	18.6	13.1	13.9	5.4	5.0
09	Connecticut...............	1,357,812	5.9	4.6	8.5	8.0	10.9	16.9	12.7	16.7	7.2	8.6
10	Delaware	340,308	5.7	4.4	9.6	9.6	13.3	19.4	13.8	15.0	4.9	4.2
11	District of Columbia.....	266,662	10.4	4.4	7.7	7.3	10.9	13.5	10.1	15.7	7.9	12.1
12	Florida	7,197,943	8.2	6.1	12.8	12.1	15.2	17.9	10.6	10.2	3.3	3.6
13	Georgia	3,532,908	9.3	6.1	11.8	10.9	14.0	18.0	11.1	10.9	3.9	4.0
15	Hawaii	447,748	6.2	3.7	7.9	7.3	12.3	18.5	14.9	17.0	6.9	5.3
16	Idaho.......................	583,106	6.9	5.8	12.7	12.7	15.9	20.4	11.2	9.4	2.7	2.2
17	Illinois.....................	4,770,194	7.5	4.9	10.4	9.7	13.2	17.9	12.8	13.5	5.1	5.1
18	Indiana.....................	2,480,077	7.6	5.7	12.0	11.6	15.8	19.2	12.2	10.6	2.9	2.4
19	Iowa........................	1,227,048	6.5	5.6	11.0	11.2	14.5	20.5	13.1	11.6	3.1	2.7
20	Kansas.....................	1,113,911	6.5	5.4	11.4	11.2	15.2	19.7	12.0	11.9	3.3	3.4
21	Kentucky	1,707,004	10.6	7.3	13.2	11.9	14.4	17.4	10.8	9.6	2.5	2.2
22	Louisiana..................	1,719,473	10.3	7.7	13.1	11.1	13.5	16.4	10.8	10.5	3.4	3.1
23	Maine.......................	554,543	7.4	6.5	11.9	12.0	14.9	19.8	11.8	10.4	2.5	2.7
24	Maryland	2,157,717	5.3	3.7	7.4	7.2	11.3	17.5	13.1	17.9	8.5	8.1
25	Massachusetts	2,522,394	7.0	5.0	8.9	7.7	11.0	16.3	12.5	16.3	7.4	7.9
26	Michigan	3,819,068	8.7	5.9	12.1	11.3	14.7	18.4	11.5	10.9	3.5	3.0
27	Minnesota	2,111,943	5.8	4.6	9.2	9.3	13.7	19.2	14.1	14.4	5.0	4.7
28	Mississippi.................	1,090,521	12.2	8.4	15.0	11.9	14.6	16.8	8.8	7.9	2.3	2.1
29	Missouri...................	2,359,135	8.4	6.6	12.3	11.9	14.9	18.6	11.4	10.1	3.2	2.7
30	Montana...................	408,938	7.6	6.5	13.3	11.9	15.1	18.9	11.5	10.3	2.6	2.3
31	Nebraska	733,570	6.0	5.5	11.2	11.2	15.3	20.2	12.9	11.6	3.4	2.8
32	Nevada	1,006,605	6.7	5.1	11.4	11.5	15.5	19.9	12.1	11.2	3.5	3.1
33	New Hampshire	519,137	4.5	4.2	8.9	8.9	12.8	18.4	14.7	16.0	6.5	5.1
34	New Jersey.................	3,198,799	5.8	4.0	8.1	8.2	10.8	16.3	12.8	16.7	8.5	8.6
35	New Mexico...............	764,996	10.4	6.8	12.8	12.1	13.9	16.8	11.1	10.0	3.7	2.5
36	New York..................	7,238,922	8.3	5.4	10.3	8.9	12.0	17.0	11.8	13.8	5.9	6.6
37	North Carolina............	3,731,325	8.7	6.6	12.3	11.8	14.9	18.1	11.2	10.0	3.1	3.1
38	North Dakota.............	290,944	6.6	4.8	9.8	10.4	15.1	19.1	13.2	12.8	3.9	4.4
39	Ohio........................	4,554,672	8.5	6.2	12.3	11.0	14.7	18.7	11.6	10.6	3.4	3.0
40	Oklahoma.................	1,446,667	8.5	6.7	12.8	11.7	15.3	18.6	11.2	9.5	2.9	2.7
41	Oregon.....................	1,516,957	8.1	5.6	11.8	10.6	14.6	18.7	12.1	11.9	3.5	3.1
42	Pennsylvania..............	4,958,249	7.2	5.7	11.3	10.6	13.8	18.6	12.5	12.1	4.2	4.0
44	Rhode Island..............	413,083	8.1	6.1	10.1	9.1	13.0	17.4	12.2	14.2	5.2	4.6
45	South Carolina............	1,787,340	9.5	6.8	13.0	11.7	15.2	18.0	10.5	9.5	3.1	2.7
46	South Dakota.............	323,765	6.4	5.4	11.5	11.5	16.9	19.6	13.0	10.3	2.8	2.5
47	Tennessee	2,480,090	9.0	7.0	13.0	12.5	14.9	18.0	10.6	9.2	2.9	2.8
48	Texas.......................	8,970,959	7.8	5.5	11.2	10.7	14.0	17.8	11.6	12.3	4.6	4.5
49	Utah........................	895,691	5.4	4.0	9.5	9.4	14.8	21.6	14.1	13.5	4.2	3.4
50	Vermont	258,520	5.7	5.9	10.5	10.1	14.6	20.1	13.7	12.5	3.5	3.4
51	Virginia....................	3,038,967	6.1	4.3	9.0	8.8	12.6	17.9	12.6	14.9	6.8	7.1
53	Washington	2,636,817	6.6	4.4	9.3	9.4	13.7	19.1	13.0	14.5	5.3	4.7
54	West Virginia	741,544	10.7	7.3	14.8	12.0	14.4	17.6	11.1	8.1	2.1	1.9
55	Wisconsin	2,288,362	6.3	5.6	11.2	10.7	15.0	19.9	13.1	12.0	3.3	2.9
56	Wyoming..................	223,513	5.2	5.7	10.3	10.1	14.0	19.3	14.7	13.8	4.5	2.4

Table B-1. States — What: Education, Employment, and Income, 2012—*Continued*

State code	STATE	Households with income over $100,000, by age of householder (as a percent of all households in age group)					Households with income below poverty (as a percent of all households in household-type group)						
		All households	Householder under 25 years	Householder 25 to 44 years	Householder 45 to 64 years	Householder 65 years and over	All households	Family households	Married-couple family households	Male householder family households	Female householder family households	Male householder nonfamily households	Female householder nonfamily households
	ACS table number:	C19001	C19037	C19037	C19037	C19037	C17017	C17017	C17017	C17017	C17017	C17017	C17017
	Column number:	133	134	135	136	137	138	139	140	141	142	143	144
00	United States	21.6	3.1	22.1	28.2	12.4	14.7	11.8	5.8	17.7	31.8	18.2	21.9
01	Alabama....................	14.9	1.4	14.7	20.3	9.0	18.4	14.7	6.6	20.4	38.9	22.9	28.5
02	Alaska......................	30.5	8.4	30.0	37.3	19.0	8.5	7.5	2.9	14.4	23.7	9.9	11.1
04	Arizona.....................	18.4	2.5	18.7	24.8	11.6	15.7	13.6	7.6	21.2	32.5	18.2	21.1
05	Arkansas...................	12.8	2.3	12.8	17.1	8.1	18.2	14.6	7.2	22.3	39.4	22.6	27.7
06	California..................	27.5	5.8	27.9	34.0	18.1	15.0	12.9	7.7	18.0	29.2	17.3	21.3
08	Colorado	24.3	2.8	24.5	31.8	14.2	12.6	9.3	4.8	15.8	26.9	17.4	19.3
09	Connecticut...............	32.5	4.9	32.1	42.5	17.7	10.4	7.9	3.1	10.0	24.9	15.1	15.9
10	Delaware	24.1	6.8	26.2	30.5	13.8	11.0	8.2	3.7	12.5	22.6	12.5	19.9
11	District of Columbia	35.7	12.6	40.8	36.9	27.3	15.2	13.9	3.7	15.2	29.3	14.6	17.3
12	Florida	17.1	3.0	16.7	22.6	11.7	15.4	12.6	6.8	19.9	30.3	18.6	21.5
13	Georgia	18.8	1.7	18.6	24.6	11.1	17.4	15.0	7.1	21.5	37.6	20.1	24.6
15	Hawaii......................	29.1	9.2	23.9	36.6	26.5	11.2	8.6	4.9	11.6	22.3	13.0	20.8
16	Idaho	14.4	0.9	13.0	20.7	9.7	14.9	11.7	7.0	15.9	35.5	21.5	23.1
17	Illinois	23.7	3.0	24.9	31.0	12.2	13.8	10.9	4.9	16.7	31.2	17.6	20.6
18	Indiana.....................	15.9	1.7	16.3	21.8	7.9	14.2	11.3	4.9	19.9	33.7	18.2	21.4
19	Iowa........................	17.5	2.2	17.7	24.8	9.3	12.5	8.8	3.8	17.6	31.2	17.8	20.5
20	Kansas......................	18.6	1.9	18.8	25.7	10.3	12.8	9.3	4.2	19.2	30.4	17.2	21.5
21	Kentucky	14.4	0.8	15.3	19.4	6.9	18.9	14.8	7.2	22.5	40.2	25.2	28.8
22	Louisiana	17.0	2.9	17.9	22.3	9.1	19.1	15.5	5.9	19.4	38.9	21.6	29.7
23	Maine.......................	15.7	2.2	14.3	21.9	8.5	14.0	9.8	4.9	18.3	30.9	18.5	23.4
24	Maryland	34.5	4.7	33.9	43.8	21.1	9.7	7.3	2.9	10.3	20.5	12.6	16.1
25	Massachusetts	31.6	7.1	35.3	39.3	15.6	12.3	8.5	3.1	11.6	27.1	17.1	20.3
26	Michigan	17.3	1.4	18.0	23.7	8.4	15.8	12.6	5.6	20.1	35.9	21.2	22.4
27	Minnesota	24.1	3.7	26.0	32.3	10.4	10.9	7.6	3.1	13.1	29.0	15.2	18.6
28	Mississippi.................	12.3	1.1	11.6	16.2	8.6	22.4	19.2	7.8	24.5	44.0	26.5	31.8
29	Missouri	16.0	1.2	16.5	21.5	9.0	15.4	11.7	5.5	19.1	33.1	20.1	23.8
30	Montana....................	15.2	2.3	15.3	19.8	10.2	14.8	10.2	5.5	17.0	34.4	20.3	25.3
31	Nebraska	17.8	1.5	18.5	24.2	10.2	12.4	9.1	4.0	17.0	31.3	14.7	21.6
32	Nevada	17.8	4.7	17.0	22.5	13.3	14.3	12.6	7.2	16.3	28.0	15.9	19.4
33	New Hampshire	27.6	2.2	27.8	36.1	13.9	9.0	6.7	3.1	12.2	23.7	12.2	14.5
34	New Jersey.................	33.9	9.1	36.2	42.0	18.1	10.5	8.2	3.4	12.0	25.0	12.9	17.7
35	New Mexico...............	16.2	0.6	15.4	21.0	12.5	19.2	16.8	9.7	20.5	37.4	22.7	24.7
36	New York..................	26.3	5.9	28.5	32.0	15.5	14.9	12.2	6.3	15.8	28.4	17.3	21.5
37	North Carolina	16.3	1.5	16.3	22.1	9.3	16.4	13.4	6.3	22.0	36.0	20.4	23.8
38	North Dakota.............	21.1	4.5	22.4	29.7	11.1	11.6	7.0	2.8	13.7	28.8	13.5	24.2
39	Ohio........................	17.0	1.5	17.4	23.5	8.3	15.2	12.0	4.8	19.3	35.9	19.7	21.8
40	Oklahoma..................	15.0	2.5	15.2	20.7	8.8	16.2	13.1	6.7	19.1	35.4	20.4	23.8
41	Oregon	18.5	1.9	19.7	24.1	11.1	15.6	12.1	6.3	21.8	33.9	21.4	22.0
42	Pennsylvania	20.3	2.6	22.1	27.2	9.5	13.1	9.5	3.9	16.8	29.1	17.9	21.1
44	Rhode Island..............	23.9	6.1	25.2	30.7	13.4	14.1	9.2	3.8	11.7	25.4	20.4	23.5
45	South Carolina............	15.3	1.1	14.5	20.5	10.0	17.1	14.1	5.8	21.4	36.9	20.9	25.4
46	South Dakota.............	15.7	2.6	14.6	22.2	10.1	12.0	8.6	3.5	16.4	29.7	14.8	21.4
47	Tennessee	14.8	1.1	14.3	20.3	9.0	16.9	13.7	6.8	21.6	36.0	20.6	25.2
48	Texas	21.4	2.6	20.7	28.8	12.9	16.0	14.0	8.0	17.2	34.0	17.5	23.5
49	Utah	21.1	3.4	18.5	31.8	13.3	11.9	9.6	6.3	14.7	28.1	16.7	20.7
50	Vermont	19.3	2.4	19.5	25.3	11.1	11.7	7.4	2.8	16.6	27.3	18.5	19.2
51	Virginia	28.8	4.2	29.3	37.2	16.9	11.2	8.6	3.8	12.5	26.6	15.3	17.7
53	Washington	24.5	3.6	25.2	32.4	13.3	12.2	9.3	4.7	14.4	28.9	16.1	18.8
54	West Virginia	12.1	2.3	13.3	16.5	5.9	17.6	12.9	7.0	20.6	36.0	24.6	26.7
55	Wisconsin	18.2	1.6	19.0	25.1	8.4	12.4	8.9	3.7	16.3	31.0	16.7	20.4
56	Wyoming...................	20.8	4.3	20.6	28.7	10.8	11.4	8.5	3.8	8.3	34.0	16.5	17.5

Table B-1. States — What: Education, Employment, and Income, 2012—*Continued*

State code	STATE	Population for whom poverty status is determined	Persons with income below poverty by age (as a percent of all persons in age group)				Persons with income below poverty by selected race and Hispanic origin groups (as a percent of all persons in race/Hispanic group)				Total civilian non-institutionalized population	Type of health insurance (as a percent of all persons)			
			All ages	Under 18 years	18 to 64 years	65 years and over	White alone, not Hispanic or Latino	Black alone	Asian alone	Hispanic or Latino		Private	Public	Both	None
	ACS table number:	C17001	C17001	C17001	C17001	C17001	C17001H	C17001B	C17001D	C17001I	C27010	C27010	C27010	C27010	C27010
	Column number:	145	146	147	148	149	150	151	152	153	154	155	156	157	158
00	United States	306,086,063	15.9	22.6	14.8	9.5	11.0	28.1	13.0	25.4	308,896,460	54.1	20.1	11.0	14.8
01	Alabama	4,706,978	19.0	27.5	17.5	11.1	12.9	31.6	15.0	34.5	4,741,698	52.0	21.5	13.1	13.3
02	Alaska....................	715,608	10.1	13.9	9.4	4.4	6.5	15.9	10.5	11.8	708,946	53.9	16.7	9.0	20.5
04	Arizona...................	6,401,273	18.7	27.0	17.8	8.3	11.3	26.2	14.2	29.0	6,443,654	48.3	23.1	11.0	17.6
05	Arkansas..................	2,865,098	19.8	28.5	18.5	10.9	15.5	35.1	10.1	31.7	2,896,297	47.1	24.9	11.5	16.4
06	California.................	37,303,266	17.0	23.8	15.6	10.4	10.5	26.1	12.3	23.9	37,524,274	51.7	22.1	8.3	17.9
08	Colorado	5,069,071	13.7	18.5	13.0	7.8	9.4	29.7	11.6	24.8	5,094,766	58.9	16.6	9.8	14.7
09	Connecticut..............	3,484,178	10.7	14.8	10.1	6.9	5.8	24.0	5.6	27.6	3,534,619	60.5	18.9	11.5	9.1
10	Delaware	890,738	12.0	17.4	11.3	7.4	8.8	18.3	6.6	23.5	902,915	55.9	20.7	14.6	8.8
11	District of Columbia ...	598,151	18.2	26.5	17.1	11.9	7.4	25.7	12.0	22.1	621,380	58.3	24.5	11.2	5.9
12	Florida	18,912,479	17.1	25.4	16.4	10.2	11.9	29.0	12.8	22.4	19,011,070	45.3	22.7	11.9	20.1
13	Georgia	9,652,596	19.2	27.2	17.3	11.2	12.3	27.9	15.6	32.1	9,719,411	52.8	19.6	9.2	18.4
15	Hawaii	1,356,822	11.6	17.1	10.8	6.9	10.8	11.9	7.3	19.1	1,341,708	62.1	17.7	13.4	6.9
16	Idaho	1,565,511	15.9	20.7	15.1	9.7	13.9	. . .	15.5	28.6	1,575,682	54.2	17.6	12.0	16.2
17	Illinois	12,573,676	14.7	20.7	13.7	8.8	9.2	32.0	12.3	21.4	12,698,371	56.8	19.9	10.5	12.8
18	Indiana	6,342,423	15.6	22.4	14.8	7.2	12.3	32.9	21.7	28.7	6,437,142	56.4	17.9	11.4	14.3
19	Iowa	2,974,225	12.7	15.9	12.6	7.8	10.8	35.5	16.7	26.0	3,028,864	61.3	16.0	14.3	8.4
20	Kansas	2,802,207	14.0	19.0	13.5	6.7	11.1	24.8	14.6	26.0	2,825,416	60.5	15.1	11.9	12.6
21	Kentucky	4,247,103	19.4	26.5	18.3	12.3	17.3	36.3	12.7	31.1	4,292,718	52.7	21.6	11.8	13.9
22	Louisiana	4,471,142	19.9	28.1	18.2	12.6	12.4	33.5	23.0	22.8	4,498,884	48.3	24.2	10.6	16.9
23	Maine	1,293,457	14.7	20.9	14.4	8.2	13.7	39.1	29.4	29.3	1,315,703	50.6	24.5	14.7	10.2
24	Maryland	5,744,445	10.3	13.8	9.6	7.6	6.8	16.3	7.7	13.5	5,788,196	62.1	16.2	11.3	10.3
25	Massachusetts	6,414,762	11.9	15.4	11.3	9.3	8.0	23.4	16.0	30.9	6,566,851	62.6	21.3	12.2	3.9
26	Michigan	9,663,760	17.4	24.9	16.8	8.3	13.1	36.4	15.4	29.4	9,772,550	54.5	19.8	14.2	11.4
27	Minnesota	5,257,443	11.4	14.6	10.9	7.9	8.1	37.8	15.9	25.7	5,319,783	64.1	15.6	12.3	8.0
28	Mississippi................	2,890,890	24.2	34.7	21.7	15.1	15.0	37.7	18.6	34.5	2,918,405	45.3	26.8	10.8	17.0
29	Missouri..................	5,838,008	16.2	22.6	15.5	9.0	13.1	31.6	17.0	29.9	5,908,769	55.7	18.9	11.9	13.6
30	Montana	980,594	15.5	20.3	15.6	8.6	13.4	. . .	12.5	27.8	989,823	50.5	18.5	13.0	18.0
31	Nebraska	1,800,904	13.0	17.9	12.2	7.4	9.6	34.2	16.2	26.8	1,826,832	62.0	15.0	11.8	11.3
32	Nevada	2,718,565	16.4	24.0	15.3	8.1	11.4	27.5	8.8	24.8	2,723,965	51.9	16.4	9.5	22.2
33	New Hampshire	1,280,027	10.0	15.6	9.0	6.6	9.2	23.0	11.2	25.4	1,306,026	62.9	14.1	12.4	10.6
34	New Jersey................	8,691,673	10.8	15.4	9.7	7.9	6.2	20.7	6.5	19.8	8,756,542	60.3	16.5	10.5	12.7
35	New Mexico...............	2,044,778	20.8	29.3	19.5	11.9	12.0	30.8	12.1	25.6	2,051,805	43.7	26.7	11.2	18.4
36	New York.................	19,064,064	15.9	22.8	14.4	11.4	10.1	23.3	19.5	26.7	19,316,728	54.4	23.7	11.0	10.9
37	North Carolina	9,498,993	18.0	26.0	16.8	10.0	12.2	28.4	13.1	33.9	9,552,529	51.3	20.7	11.4	16.6
38	North Dakota............	674,852	11.2	13.2	10.7	10.6	8.8	45.0	25.2	20.1	684,776	66.6	10.3	13.1	10.0
39	Ohio	11,227,482	16.3	23.8	15.4	8.0	12.6	35.6	14.7	29.6	11,371,766	56.2	19.9	12.5	11.5
40	Oklahoma................	3,699,653	17.2	24.1	16.1	9.9	13.4	29.8	12.7	28.8	3,733,058	49.3	20.5	11.9	18.4
41	Oregon	3,826,398	17.2	23.0	17.5	7.5	14.5	40.8	12.4	30.2	3,860,452	52.7	19.4	13.0	14.9
42	Pennsylvania	12,353,867	13.7	19.7	13.0	8.3	9.9	29.5	16.5	33.4	12,559,315	58.1	18.1	14.0	9.8
44	Rhode Island	1,010,449	13.7	19.5	12.8	9.7	9.4	26.1	14.0	33.0	1,034,895	57.8	18.7	12.4	11.1
45	South Carolina..........	4,585,454	18.3	26.9	17.0	10.1	12.7	29.0	13.5	29.7	4,623,171	49.6	21.2	12.4	16.8
46	South Dakota............	804,310	13.4	17.5	12.5	10.0	8.9	41.8	10.3	27.2	816,425	59.3	16.4	12.7	11.5
47	Tennessee	6,295,994	17.9	25.8	16.8	10.0	14.1	29.2	16.8	35.2	6,354,629	52.6	21.6	11.9	13.9
48	Texas.....................	25,450,518	17.9	25.8	15.6	11.6	9.6	24.9	12.0	26.2	25,584,499	49.1	20.2	8.1	22.5
49	Utah	2,806,920	12.8	15.1	12.6	6.8	9.5	18.6	20.5	28.5	2,829,001	64.7	12.1	8.7	14.5
50	Vermont	601,611	11.8	15.5	11.7	7.5	11.3	23.2	14.6	16.7	619,928	55.1	24.9	13.6	6.5
51	Virginia...................	7,936,903	11.7	15.3	11.3	7.9	8.8	20.3	8.2	16.1	7,973,466	62.8	13.3	11.3	12.5
53	Washington	6,761,934	13.5	18.5	12.9	7.8	10.5	25.6	13.0	26.0	6,793,078	57.2	17.1	11.8	13.9
54	West Virginia	1,801,131	17.8	24.6	17.9	8.8	17.0	37.4	21.5	22.4	1,826,512	48.7	22.5	14.4	14.4
55	Wisconsin	5,573,134	13.2	18.2	12.7	7.5	9.8	38.2	20.5	28.3	5,652,085	59.9	18.6	12.5	9.0
56	Wyoming.................	561,445	12.6	16.9	12.7	4.8	11.2	. . .	. . .	19.0	567,082	57.2	15.6	11.8	15.4

Table B-2. Counties — What: Education, Employment, and Income, 2010–2012

State or county code	State or county	Educational attainment			Employment status				Percent of households with no workers	Median household income (dollars)	Percent of families with income below poverty	Percent of households with income less than $25,000	Percent of households with income of $100,000 or more
		Total population 25 years and over	Percent with a high school diploma or less	Percent with a bachelor's degree or more	Total population 16 years and over	Percent in the labor force	Unemployment rate	Percent who worked full-time year-round					
	ACS table number:	C15002	C15002	C15002	B23025	B23025	B23025	C20005	C08202	B19013	C17013	C19001	C19001
	Column number:	1	2	3	4	5	6	7	8	9	10	11	12
00 000	**United States**............	206,597,203	42.3	28.6	246,234,513	64.1	10.1	39.8	27.3	51,771	11.6	24.1	21.6
01 000	**Alabama**....................	3,192,004	48.2	22.5	3,806,456	59.3	11.0	37.7	32.4	42,054	14.8	30.7	15.3
01 001	Autauga	35,902	49.6	20.9	42,376	63.2	10.0	43.4	28.5	51,939	8.7	21.4	20.5
01 003	Baldwin	130,462	40.5	28.2	148,903	61.0	9.2	38.9	31.8	50,391	9.6	23.2	19.4
01 005	Barbour.....................	18,996	59.3	14.0	22,035	48.7	13.1	30.3	37.7	33,895	20.2	41.2	8.4
01 007	Bibb..........................	15,367	64.9	7.9	18,400	46.7	14.5	29.4	39.7	31,763	17.0	40.4	6.7
01 009	Blount........................	39,263	59.3	12.2	45,463	56.3	11.0	36.6	33.5	42,863	12.0	27.6	12.3
01 013	Butler.........................	14,047	61.3	14.6	16,367	54.9	13.0	35.3	38.0	30,915	20.9	41.8	7.8
01 015	Calhoun......................	78,319	54.4	16.1	93,922	57.2	14.1	34.0	35.3	39,972	16.6	33.6	11.7
01 017	Chambers...................	23,570	59.2	12.5	27,382	54.6	15.2	36.1	40.4	31,144	22.0	40.9	8.5
01 019	Cherokee....................	18,686	55.2	14.7	21,086	55.5	10.9	34.1	39.2	32,760	19.4	39.7	11.2
01 021	Chilton	29,243	64.8	12.3	34,306	57.1	11.7	37.7	34.0	39,553	16.1	30.1	12.3
01 025	Clarke........................	17,241	61.3	12.9	20,087	52.8	19.5	35.0	47.5	31,143	22.1	44.6	10.5
01 031	Coffee........................	34,224	46.9	23.1	39,745	57.9	7.6	40.0	32.4	42,480	14.2	29.7	16.6
01 033	Colbert.......................	37,886	52.0	17.3	44,079	53.4	9.4	34.7	39.1	37,687	15.4	33.6	10.0
01 039	Covington...................	26,296	56.3	14.2	30,470	53.6	11.0	32.1	39.0	34,194	19.3	37.6	10.0
01 043	Cullman.....................	54,916	51.8	14.0	64,220	57.2	10.4	34.1	35.9	37,939	14.8	34.2	10.0
01 045	Dale..........................	33,196	46.6	17.1	39,546	62.4	8.4	41.3	28.5	43,989	14.1	28.0	11.0
01 047	Dallas........................	27,964	60.2	13.9	32,879	51.8	19.9	29.2	47.3	25,387	31.0	49.4	7.8
01 049	DeKalb.......................	46,723	63.5	10.1	54,997	56.7	11.5	36.5	35.4	37,912	12.8	31.6	8.3
01 051	Elmore	53,712	46.9	21.3	63,817	61.1	8.6	41.2	24.7	54,213	11.2	20.1	19.5
01 053	Escambia	26,177	62.3	11.4	30,797	49.5	17.1	30.3	41.9	28,740	24.8	45.1	7.8
01 055	Etowah	71,570	52.2	14.0	83,368	53.1	11.8	31.1	40.9	35,655	15.9	36.4	9.3
01 059	Franklin......................	21,131	59.8	12.1	24,604	57.3	8.9	36.5	34.4	37,301	14.4	33.1	8.1
01 061	Geneva......................	18,881	62.9	11.5	21,608	56.4	11.6	34.3	37.4	34,216	20.9	37.7	8.9
01 069	Houston.....................	69,149	50.8	19.8	80,563	60.7	7.8	41.1	30.7	40,643	14.5	30.9	14.4
01 071	Jackson......................	37,187	61.6	13.1	42,756	55.3	9.6	36.3	37.6	37,047	14.5	34.0	9.9
01 073	Jefferson....................	440,861	39.3	29.7	522,494	61.8	10.8	39.7	30.2	43,809	14.4	29.0	18.0
01 077	Lauderdale.................	62,761	49.4	22.8	75,323	57.9	8.2	36.0	34.3	41,504	13.2	30.7	13.3
01 079	Lawrence	23,305	61.5	12.6	27,052	54.4	13.5	34.2	35.7	37,649	14.0	30.3	12.1
01 081	Lee	82,884	40.3	32.2	115,857	63.3	9.5	36.8	25.0	43,125	11.7	31.9	15.9
01 083	Limestone	58,396	49.2	22.7	67,663	58.4	9.2	39.1	28.9	48,956	10.4	24.4	19.5
01 087	Macon	12,935	46.7	19.8	17,500	54.1	18.9	30.7	41.7	29,191	23.1	42.8	6.9
01 089	Madison	225,884	31.8	37.9	269,825	66.5	10.3	43.3	24.2	56,311	9.6	22.5	26.4
01 091	Marengo.....................	13,956	59.0	16.5	16,425	51.0	11.6	34.2	43.8	32,212	20.1	42.3	12.2
01 093	Marion.......................	21,706	62.9	8.7	24,799	52.6	13.5	30.5	41.1	30,283	16.4	39.9	9.5
01 095	Marshall.....................	62,107	56.3	15.4	72,944	58.1	9.8	37.2	33.9	39,562	16.0	32.8	12.7
01 097	Mobile.......................	269,358	48.8	20.9	322,824	59.6	11.9	37.8	31.7	41,772	16.9	31.5	13.8
01 099	Monroe	15,112	64.1	11.1	17,991	50.2	14.7	33.2	43.2	29,750	20.6	44.0	7.0
01 101	Montgomery...............	147,161	41.1	31.1	180,084	61.1	9.3	40.0	28.8	43,580	17.8	30.2	16.7
01 103	Morgan	81,159	50.7	18.9	94,703	64.1	11.6	39.6	31.3	45,085	10.8	27.8	15.7
01 109	Pike	19,119	55.1	21.8	27,226	60.1	10.5	34.1	28.9	31,444	18.1	42.2	9.4
01 111	Randolph....................	15,355	64.7	11.0	18,202	52.7	11.6	35.4	39.8	34,569	18.6	36.4	8.1
01 113	Russell.......................	36,011	52.1	15.4	43,046	61.4	11.2	40.5	32.5	34,562	19.6	36.3	10.4
01 115	St. Clair......................	58,177	53.0	15.0	66,676	59.0	11.4	37.4	29.7	49,660	14.1	24.6	15.0
01 117	Shelby........................	132,870	30.2	39.4	153,636	69.5	7.3	46.1	20.4	66,861	6.8	16.6	28.2
01 121	Talladega....................	55,850	58.9	12.2	65,127	54.7	16.7	33.0	39.5	32,865	22.2	38.2	8.5
01 123	Tallapoosa..................	28,926	55.7	17.0	33,341	54.4	10.8	36.6	36.0	38,115	16.8	32.6	10.1
01 125	Tuscaloosa..................	116,186	44.4	27.3	159,412	59.0	8.6	37.8	28.9	43,340	14.2	29.5	16.0
01 127	Walker	46,180	59.7	9.8	53,420	51.5	15.5	30.9	41.4	35,493	18.3	36.6	10.9
01 133	Winston......................	17,312	59.7	9.9	19,704	51.7	11.3	29.9	40.7	32,467	15.3	42.3	7.4
02 000	**Alaska**....................	457,070	35.7	27.5	555,762	70.9	8.4	42.7	20.3	68,818	7.2	15.7	30.8
02 020	Anchorage.................	186,778	30.9	32.5	228,921	74.1	7.1	48.6	16.1	74,648	6.2	13.0	35.2
02 090	Fairbanks North Star ...	60,354	32.7	29.0	76,675	72.8	6.9	48.1	19.1	67,169	6.0	15.5	27.7
02 110	Juneau.......................	21,880	25.1	37.5	25,634	71.6	5.3	48.7	18.5	78,547	4.4	9.9	33.9
02 122	Kenai Peninsula..........	38,463	39.1	24.0	45,002	63.2	9.0	31.0	27.1	60,682	5.2	18.9	26.4
02 170	Matanuska-Susitna	57,953	39.0	21.5	68,485	64.9	10.7	36.1	25.6	69,822	7.6	17.3	30.8
04 000	**Arizona**..................	4,209,589	38.9	26.7	5,034,808	60.5	10.8	37.4	30.1	48,307	13.4	24.9	18.5
04 001	Apache......................	42,347	55.5	11.0	52,678	46.2	21.4	24.9	42.0	32,473	27.5	40.7	7.5
04 003	Cochise......................	89,452	39.3	22.4	105,588	52.7	9.1	34.2	37.0	44,446	12.4	27.6	14.7
04 005	Coconino...................	78,845	35.5	31.2	107,379	66.3	10.2	33.4	23.0	45,919	16.9	27.1	17.3
04 007	Gila...........................	38,276	47.4	17.3	43,356	46.3	10.3	26.8	45.6	38,847	13.6	33.6	9.9
04 009	Graham	22,215	48.7	13.5	27,644	49.7	12.5	28.5	29.6	46,129	17.0	28.1	13.6
04 012	La Paz	15,553	57.9	9.5	17,150	41.9	11.8	26.3	54.0	36,053	13.9	33.3	8.7
04 013	Maricopa	2,486,912	37.1	29.4	2,981,365	64.3	9.9	41.2	26.0	51,976	12.6	22.5	21.5
04 015	Mohave......................	147,062	50.1	11.9	166,457	48.1	15.1	26.5	46.7	36,976	13.8	32.6	8.9
04 017	Navajo.......................	65,618	48.0	14.6	79,652	50.4	19.8	25.2	39.1	36,047	24.6	36.8	9.6
04 019	Pima	655,979	35.5	29.8	790,246	59.3	11.2	34.9	32.2	45,133	13.6	27.7	16.8
04 021	Pinal	254,063	44.9	18.4	294,566	51.9	14.2	31.9	35.3	48,794	10.3	22.1	13.6
04 023	Santa Cruz..................	28,903	55.2	19.8	34,771	58.0	15.4	33.2	27.8	36,396	23.0	36.4	13.4
04 025	Yavapai......................	157,438	36.4	24.8	177,083	51.3	11.0	26.4	44.2	42,966	12.6	28.2	12.4
04 027	Yuma.........................	121,413	52.4	14.2	150,491	54.7	13.4	32.5	36.7	41,060	18.0	28.8	10.9

Table B-2. Counties — What: Education, Employment, and Income, 2010–2012—Continued

State or county code	State or county	Educational attainment			Employment status				Percent of households with no workers	Median household income (dollars)	Percent of families with income below poverty	Percent of households with income less than $25,000	Percent of households with income of $100,000 or more
		Total population 25 years and over	Percent with a high school diploma or less	Percent with a bachelor's degree or more	Total population 16 years and over	Percent in the labor force	Unemployment rate	Percent who worked full-time year-round					
	ACS table number:	C15002	C15002	C15002	B23025	B23025	B23025	C20005	C08202	B19013	C17013	C19001	C19001
	Column number:	1	2	3	4	5	6	7	8	9	10	11	12
05 000	**Arkansas**	1,938,675	51.3	20.2	2,302,696	59.8	9.1	38.9	31.5	40,104	14.5	31.8	13.0
05 003	Ashley	14,909	60.2	13.2	17,011	56.2	10.4	32.8	35.3	38,725	13.8	34.4	8.3
05 005	Baxter	31,370	50.2	16.3	34,822	46.4	10.3	26.9	50.7	34,256	10.9	36.3	6.7
05 007	Benton	145,741	44.8	29.1	170,496	64.3	5.3	47.2	23.1	53,964	8.5	19.5	21.1
05 009	Boone	25,735	52.4	14.3	29,524	55.8	8.7	35.8	34.4	36,800	14.0	33.5	11.6
05 015	Carroll	19,412	54.2	16.6	21,949	57.2	7.9	35.2	35.1	35,263	14.0	34.2	8.0
05 019	Clark	13,412	50.4	22.2	19,036	56.6	12.9	28.9	32.7	31,570	18.2	40.9	9.9
05 023	Cleburne	19,036	53.6	17.8	21,492	49.4	13.3	30.5	47.1	40,038	13.1	31.8	10.2
05 027	Columbia	15,096	49.9	20.2	19,875	55.4	11.6	30.4	38.3	33,796	20.5	39.1	15.0
05 029	Conway	14,486	57.3	15.8	16,872	56.5	10.6	36.7	35.6	33,037	19.8	38.8	11.5
05 031	Craighead	61,415	47.9	23.8	76,595	63.0	9.4	39.1	30.5	40,907	15.6	31.2	14.3
05 033	Crawford	40,717	55.3	13.9	47,579	57.5	8.8	37.4	30.7	38,495	15.0	32.6	7.9
05 035	Crittenden	31,397	55.4	14.8	37,334	63.3	13.6	39.4	27.8	36,398	19.6	34.6	11.7
05 045	Faulkner	70,028	42.8	26.9	90,685	66.8	7.1	43.4	22.9	50,066	9.1	25.6	17.1
05 051	Garland	68,533	46.3	20.7	78,819	55.4	10.3	32.4	37.6	38,201	15.9	33.2	12.5
05 055	Greene	28,127	61.6	13.0	33,331	56.6	12.2	36.7	38.8	37,009	12.2	34.3	9.5
05 057	Hempstead	14,651	53.6	15.5	17,215	61.1	10.6	39.4	32.0	29,849	22.7	42.7	8.5
05 059	Hot Spring	22,948	56.8	13.6	26,649	56.9	8.6	37.1	34.5	41,016	10.9	30.5	8.4
05 063	Independence	24,803	60.8	13.3	28,965	58.2	9.3	37.5	35.5	33,058	18.6	37.3	6.8
05 069	Jefferson	49,812	53.9	17.7	60,070	57.2	14.6	35.3	33.0	37,485	17.8	35.0	10.6
05 071	Johnson	16,761	61.4	16.6	20,002	57.3	6.2	38.6	30.9	32,389	16.2	37.6	9.1
05 083	Logan	14,976	59.0	12.1	17,608	55.3	7.5	35.4	36.9	36,113	12.1	32.7	9.4
05 085	Lonoke	44,703	48.8	18.9	52,170	66.7	7.7	46.4	22.2	50,730	9.8	21.7	15.8
05 091	Miller	29,117	58.5	11.7	34,165	59.6	10.4	39.6	32.3	38,380	16.5	32.3	9.5
05 093	Mississippi	28,892	58.7	14.2	34,566	57.7	13.8	34.3	35.1	36,226	21.8	36.5	12.3
05 103	Ouachita	17,855	56.1	15.2	20,512	57.3	12.6	37.2	37.1	32,668	17.6	36.6	8.7
05 107	Phillips	13,499	54.1	12.9	15,931	56.6	16.8	33.8	36.7	27,337	26.9	45.9	9.2
05 111	Poinsett	16,419	68.1	7.6	19,020	55.5	15.9	33.9	39.7	30,016	24.0	43.9	5.4
05 113	Polk	14,356	51.3	12.8	16,272	53.7	8.3	33.4	36.5	32,830	14.6	39.2	7.2
05 115	Pope	39,044	51.1	21.3	49,868	62.2	7.2	37.2	26.4	39,471	14.9	30.6	12.1
05 119	Pulaski	257,851	38.4	31.9	303,837	65.4	8.7	44.4	27.1	45,256	12.7	28.5	17.6
05 123	St. Francis	19,020	57.0	13.3	22,293	51.1	13.3	34.7	33.2	32,771	22.7	41.0	9.4
05 125	Saline	75,109	46.6	22.9	85,941	64.0	6.5	45.1	28.3	54,847	5.7	18.6	18.5
05 131	Sebastian	82,657	48.8	19.6	98,329	60.7	7.0	41.9	29.0	39,106	16.4	30.9	14.3
05 139	Union	27,917	53.9	17.0	32,593	56.4	9.1	33.9	33.7	39,300	18.1	35.1	11.4
05 143	Washington	124,966	45.4	27.9	160,230	67.0	8.4	42.2	23.1	40,511	13.7	30.2	16.0
05 145	White	49,850	53.3	18.4	61,574	57.4	7.2	37.3	31.9	41,839	14.5	31.5	14.0
05 149	Yell	14,508	67.6	12.3	16,895	55.3	6.7	39.6	35.1	38,130	16.9	36.0	9.3
06 000	**California**	24,444,584	39.7	30.5	29,523,512	64.0	12.1	37.5	25.2	59,368	12.3	21.2	27.9
06 001	Alameda	1,040,734	33.0	41.4	1,230,291	66.1	10.8	39.9	25.6	70,007	9.3	19.2	35.2
06 005	Amador	29,001	39.6	18.2	32,281	46.1	18.0	22.4	44.0	49,660	8.4	25.3	21.1
06 007	Butte	141,663	36.3	23.8	180,640	56.4	15.6	27.8	39.3	41,759	13.2	29.9	15.2
06 009	Calaveras	33,540	33.3	21.7	37,813	51.8	12.5	28.6	41.1	54,070	6.5	21.6	20.5
06 011	Colusa	12,982	55.8	12.4	15,749	64.7	13.9	32.5	28.0	51,016	12.1	21.3	16.1
06 013	Contra Costa	716,194	30.6	38.9	836,774	65.5	11.0	38.4	24.1	75,835	7.9	15.0	38.5
06 015	Del Norte	19,932	53.1	14.4	23,088	43.7	14.7	23.9	41.0	36,603	16.0	36.4	14.8
06 017	El Dorado	127,077	29.2	31.4	146,231	62.8	12.7	34.0	29.8	67,003	6.4	16.3	31.9
06 019	Fresno	553,556	49.9	19.2	695,787	61.7	15.7	32.7	28.9	44,312	22.0	29.2	17.3
06 021	Glenn	17,673	52.3	17.7	21,149	57.2	12.9	34.0	30.9	38,920	12.0	29.4	14.3
06 023	Humboldt	90,944	37.0	26.6	111,503	59.9	11.4	31.1	33.0	40,997	12.6	30.7	13.0
06 025	Imperial	105,081	57.9	13.3	130,907	54.4	18.7	28.3	30.5	40,735	21.5	33.9	15.0
06 029	Kern	498,849	53.9	15.0	623,060	59.5	14.5	33.7	28.0	46,694	19.1	27.0	18.5
06 031	Kings	91,964	55.2	12.6	113,873	56.0	13.8	36.4	24.4	47,112	17.8	24.9	18.0
06 033	Lake	45,927	41.3	16.8	52,668	53.2	18.1	24.6	42.3	35,325	15.2	36.4	11.7
06 035	Lassen	24,920	45.5	13.3	29,497	39.1	12.2	25.5	33.2	53,543	9.2	23.4	19.0
06 037	Los Angeles	6,444,066	44.2	29.5	7,807,908	64.7	12.0	38.5	23.1	54,188	14.5	23.7	25.0
06 039	Madera	93,128	55.0	13.8	113,479	51.6	10.2	27.3	42.0	46,192	17.5	26.4	16.1
06 041	Marin	187,692	20.0	54.3	208,320	65.1	8.4	37.0	26.5	85,523	5.5	14.7	43.9
06 045	Mendocino	61,192	40.9	21.4	70,162	61.7	13.3	29.4	36.1	41,535	13.8	30.8	13.4
06 047	Merced	147,934	58.2	12.5	188,415	61.1	17.7	31.9	28.1	42,337	21.0	29.4	14.8
06 053	Monterey	262,324	49.9	23.2	320,867	63.3	10.7	34.6	23.8	57,212	13.0	19.4	24.4
06 055	Napa	94,180	36.8	31.4	110,187	65.8	9.3	37.4	25.4	67,511	8.3	16.7	31.6
06 057	Nevada	73,426	27.1	31.9	82,568	58.1	11.9	29.8	36.9	54,765	9.7	20.8	23.3
06 059	Orange	2,007,451	34.2	36.9	2,409,592	66.7	9.9	40.8	20.7	73,648	9.0	15.4	36.1
06 061	Placer	243,345	26.5	34.8	281,247	62.1	10.7	36.6	30.2	70,030	6.4	16.3	33.3
06 063	Plumas	14,818	31.7	25.9	16,610	54.3	19.9	25.6	43.7	49,663	10.5	27.7	17.5
06 065	Riverside	1,377,752	46.1	20.4	1,688,926	61.0	15.6	34.0	28.8	54,808	13.1	21.9	22.8
06 067	Sacramento	929,391	36.3	27.6	1,114,644	63.8	14.6	35.8	28.4	53,970	13.8	22.6	22.2
06 069	San Benito	35,088	45.1	19.6	42,457	67.8	15.1	35.4	22.7	62,786	9.1	18.7	27.6
06 071	San Bernardino	1,235,997	48.3	18.4	1,545,553	61.5	15.1	35.3	24.9	52,980	15.2	23.0	20.9
06 073	San Diego	2,044,519	33.8	34.1	2,500,303	64.7	10.1	39.8	24.5	61,364	11.0	19.8	28.2
06 075	San Francisco	632,398	27.5	52.2	717,664	68.4	8.0	43.3	25.2	72,888	8.5	21.7	38.3
06 077	San Joaquin	421,423	48.7	18.3	517,604	62.2	17.2	32.9	27.6	51,685	14.7	23.1	21.3
06 079	San Luis Obispo	180,732	31.0	31.8	227,239	59.4	9.5	32.6	29.4	57,441	7.8	21.1	24.7
06 081	San Mateo	513,299	29.0	43.6	586,356	68.9	8.5	43.6	21.4	84,740	5.0	11.9	43.2

Table B-2. Counties — What: Education, Employment, and Income, 2010–2012—*Continued*

State or county code	State or county	Educational attainment			Employment status				Percent of households with no workers	Median household income (dollars)	Percent of families with income below poverty	Percent of households with income less than $25,000	Percent of households with income of $100,000 or more
		Total population 25 years and over	Percent with a high school diploma or less	Percent with a bachelor's degree or more	Total population 16 years and over	Percent in the labor force	Unemployment rate	Percent who worked full-time year-round					
	ACS table number:	C15002	C15002	C15002	B23025	B23025	B23025	C20005	C08202	B19013	C17013	C19001	C19001
	Column number:	1	2	3	4	5	6	7	8	9	10	11	12
	California—Cont.												
06 083	Santa Barbara	264,105	39.1	30.7	340,697	63.5	10.0	35.9	26.8	61,351	9.8	19.9	28.4
06 085	Santa Clara................	1,219,751	29.2	46.5	1,424,866	67.0	10.0	42.0	19.7	89,445	7.1	13.8	45.2
06 087	Santa Cruz.................	171,374	30.7	36.8	216,759	65.8	9.1	33.9	25.2	65,225	8.7	19.3	31.4
06 089	Shasta......................	122,809	38.4	18.7	143,782	54.2	13.8	27.4	40.2	43,627	12.7	29.0	14.7
06 093	Siskiyou	32,163	38.1	23.9	36,613	52.3	15.8	24.7	44.4	36,016	19.7	38.5	8.8
06 095	Solano	275,566	37.4	23.9	329,181	64.7	12.7	37.5	24.8	65,198	10.0	17.5	29.0
06 097	Sonoma	335,801	33.8	32.0	395,091	65.6	10.6	35.3	27.6	61,491	7.9	18.8	27.4
06 099	Stanislaus..................	317,273	52.2	16.2	389,759	62.2	17.5	32.5	28.6	46,879	17.4	26.0	17.7
06 101	Sutter	59,728	45.5	18.2	72,247	61.2	15.2	33.6	30.9	49,463	14.6	25.3	19.2
06 103	Tehama.....................	42,426	48.1	13.3	49,660	54.3	17.8	29.2	40.4	40,288	14.9	29.5	12.2
06 107	Tulare......................	254,868	55.9	13.7	318,824	62.9	15.4	34.6	25.9	42,462	22.0	29.2	15.5
06 109	Tuolumne	41,048	41.6	17.2	46,262	49.9	18.7	24.0	44.9	44,342	10.9	26.8	13.0
06 111	Ventura	537,622	36.1	31.3	645,926	67.9	10.3	39.7	22.6	74,458	8.2	15.1	35.8
06 113	Yolo........................	118,040	34.7	37.7	163,110	62.8	11.4	33.6	25.8	53,275	10.6	24.5	26.0
06 115	Yuba	44,271	46.3	13.7	54,141	60.1	18.4	31.0	32.2	44,117	15.7	26.2	12.0
08 000	**Colorado**	3,388,423	32.2	36.8	4,021,332	69.1	8.9	43.0	23.0	56,837	9.2	20.8	24.6
08 001	Adams	281,635	48.7	20.5	335,762	71.0	10.7	44.4	19.7	55,004	10.9	19.3	19.8
08 005	Arapahoe..................	387,672	29.7	38.3	453,596	72.0	9.0	46.0	19.8	59,978	8.9	17.9	26.6
08 013	Boulder	192,935	19.1	58.1	245,611	70.3	7.6	40.1	20.4	66,783	6.8	19.3	33.5
08 014	Broomfield.................	38,048	21.3	48.0	43,931	73.7	7.1	50.7	20.0	77,239	5.7	14.6	36.7
08 029	Delta.......................	22,031	48.5	19.6	24,862	55.3	15.1	31.0	40.3	40,756	12.5	31.8	12.3
08 031	Denver.....................	424,886	33.4	42.8	497,431	71.1	9.4	44.7	24.1	49,049	14.7	26.5	21.5
08 035	Douglas....................	188,498	16.9	54.7	214,536	75.1	5.7	50.9	14.0	98,327	3.1	7.2	49.1
08 037	Eagle.......................	35,032	29.0	48.4	40,779	82.2	6.2	51.6	10.5	68,105	7.1	12.2	34.0
08 039	Elbert......................	15,781	32.2	31.0	18,224	69.3	8.8	42.1	18.9	81,672	4.5	10.9	37.7
08 041	El Paso.....................	402,326	28.2	34.9	489,907	68.8	9.3	43.8	22.9	55,435	9.5	20.8	23.7
08 043	Fremont....................	35,735	53.0	16.2	40,053	38.7	9.5	24.8	40.8	39,426	13.1	29.6	10.4
08 045	Garfield	36,645	37.9	28.3	42,818	74.0	9.3	42.0	16.6	53,992	7.8	18.1	19.2
08 059	Jefferson...................	376,722	28.6	40.6	436,478	69.9	8.2	45.6	23.1	67,060	6.2	16.3	30.1
08 067	La Plata....................	35,507	24.3	43.5	42,704	66.2	6.8	39.2	23.9	54,648	6.4	20.5	22.3
08 069	Larimer....................	197,750	23.9	44.2	249,022	69.0	8.9	39.0	23.1	56,274	7.4	21.7	22.9
08 075	Logan	14,945	47.1	15.7	18,742	67.7	11.2	40.4	25.9	41,740	10.6	25.1	14.6
08 077	Mesa	98,101	39.8	24.5	116,669	63.7	9.4	37.1	30.7	47,531	10.2	24.6	18.2
08 083	Montezuma	17,982	39.7	25.4	20,412	62.0	12.3	35.5	30.6	41,539	14.8	28.7	10.1
08 085	Montrose	28,442	44.8	24.9	32,413	61.7	12.3	35.5	34.1	45,078	12.1	27.4	11.7
08 087	Morgan	18,108	52.9	13.1	21,467	66.3	7.1	44.8	25.3	42,996	10.4	29.1	10.3
08 101	Pueblo......................	106,557	42.7	20.7	125,842	58.9	12.0	34.8	34.8	40,617	14.2	31.0	11.9
08 107	Routt	16,406	20.2	45.3	19,160	76.2	8.0	45.1	18.5	60,965	7.5	18.2	23.9
08 117	Summit.....................	20,397	18.9	49.3	23,488	80.0	6.8	48.9	17.4	60,577	7.8	15.2	21.3
08 119	Teller.......................	17,374	32.2	31.1	19,506	65.1	10.7	39.9	25.2	58,570	4.9	20.4	27.1
08 123	Weld........................	159,465	41.4	25.6	194,723	67.5	7.9	43.4	21.7	54,459	10.1	21.4	21.4
09 000	**Connecticut**...............	2,446,413	38.6	36.3	2,878,893	68.0	10.2	41.1	25.3	67,544	7.7	18.6	32.4
09 001	Fairfield....................	626,098	33.7	44.9	727,129	68.4	10.2	41.5	22.9	79,705	6.6	16.3	41.0
09 003	Hartford....................	614,619	39.5	34.6	719,232	67.7	10.9	40.9	26.8	63,136	9.1	20.5	29.1
09 005	Litchfield...................	135,828	38.3	33.5	154,750	69.6	8.7	42.6	24.6	69,138	3.9	16.1	31.9
09 007	Middlesex	118,112	34.7	38.6	135,965	68.9	7.3	43.0	23.5	75,225	4.1	14.0	36.3
09 009	New Haven	586,913	42.3	32.5	696,852	67.2	11.4	39.9	27.2	60,105	10.0	21.7	28.0
09 011	New London	188,357	41.1	30.8	223,173	67.9	8.7	42.1	25.5	65,499	6.0	17.0	29.8
09 013	Tolland.....................	96,895	34.2	36.8	126,225	67.9	8.0	41.3	20.9	79,105	3.5	13.2	37.3
09 015	Windham	79,591	50.3	22.4	95,567	68.3	10.9	38.9	25.5	57,628	9.2	20.7	22.6
10 000	**Delaware**	610,658	44.3	28.6	726,185	64.0	9.0	41.1	26.9	59,144	8.0	19.4	25.0
10 001	Kent	106,510	48.6	21.0	129,116	63.7	10.8	40.2	27.7	54,413	8.9	21.5	18.8
10 003	New Castle	358,861	40.1	33.5	432,521	66.2	8.5	43.1	23.6	63,152	7.4	17.9	28.9
10 005	Sussex......................	145,287	51.3	22.2	164,548	58.2	8.9	36.4	35.1	52,338	8.9	22.0	19.4
11 000	**District of Columbia**...	428,597	31.2	51.7	524,752	67.8	11.3	46.0	25.7	64,610	14.6	22.9	33.8
11 001	District of Columbia	428,597	31.2	51.7	524,752	67.8	11.3	46.0	25.7	64,610	14.6	22.9	33.8
12 000	**Florida**......................	13,307,799	44.1	26.2	15,562,915	59.9	12.3	36.6	32.8	45,637	12.3	26.6	17.2
12 001	Alachua	147,457	30.3	40.3	209,898	60.0	8.9	35.1	27.8	41,545	12.7	32.7	17.7
12 003	Baker	17,330	66.8	10.6	20,742	53.6	12.7	34.7	30.6	46,992	13.9	25.4	13.6
12 005	Bay	117,097	42.7	22.2	137,179	64.0	10.5	39.2	29.1	45,979	11.3	25.2	14.5
12 007	Bradford	20,258	63.6	7.7	23,425	46.3	18.5	27.3	37.4	38,940	18.5	36.1	10.6
12 009	Brevard	395,752	40.4	25.9	453,533	57.5	13.1	34.2	37.0	47,495	9.5	24.3	18.0
12 011	Broward....................	1,239,840	40.4	29.7	1,439,582	67.5	12.6	40.9	26.0	50,101	11.2	24.4	21.1
12 015	Charlotte	129,244	45.4	20.9	141,149	44.6	13.2	24.1	53.0	44,047	8.6	26.2	11.5
12 017	Citrus......................	110,318	52.7	16.0	121,579	42.9	16.7	24.3	53.4	37,545	11.4	31.7	9.2
12 019	Clay	126,419	40.3	24.2	149,934	64.0	11.8	39.2	27.1	57,136	8.0	17.8	22.3
12 021	Collier......................	242,009	41.7	31.5	272,556	53.7	10.1	31.2	41.4	53,384	9.9	20.3	23.6
12 023	Columbia...................	46,063	53.9	11.8	54,349	55.3	19.9	31.7	36.4	35,929	15.0	32.1	8.9
12 027	DeSoto	22,962	66.5	10.6	27,789	49.8	13.0	28.8	44.0	32,575	23.6	38.3	7.3
12 031	Duval	578,460	41.4	25.7	690,917	66.4	12.1	41.9	26.1	46,353	13.6	26.9	16.9
12 033	Escambia	197,235	42.2	22.8	243,444	62.1	12.0	37.5	31.7	43,004	13.7	28.3	13.2
12 035	Flagler.....................	71,915	44.8	23.7	80,697	48.3	13.1	29.4	45.1	45,929	11.4	25.1	14.2
12 039	Gadsden....................	32,325	59.7	13.9	37,484	52.6	14.6	35.7	36.7	36,508	21.5	35.6	9.2

Table B-2. Counties — What: Education, Employment, and Income, 2010–2012—Continued

State or county code	State or county	Educational attainment			Employment status				Percent of households with no workers	Median household income (dollars)	Percent of families with income below poverty	Percent of households with income less than $25,000	Percent of households with income of $100,000 or more
		Total population 25 years and over	Percent with a high school diploma or less	Percent with a bachelor's degree or more	Total population 16 years and over	Percent in the labor force	Unemployment rate	Percent who worked full-time year-round					
	ACS table number:	C15002	C15002	C15002	B23025	B23025	B23025	C20005	C08202	B19013	C17013	C19001	C19001
	Column number:	1	2	3	4	5	6	7	8	9	10	11	12
	Florida—Cont.												
12 049	Hardee..............	16,694	70.6	9.7	20,626	53.7	14.9	31.6	32.4	33,255	26.8	37.1	7.2
12 051	Hendry................	23,337	69.5	9.6	28,744	57.4	18.0	33.4	34.5	34,821	24.1	37.2	10.4
12 053	Hernando...........	127,446	52.1	15.5	143,535	47.0	18.9	25.9	50.6	39,444	13.5	30.8	7.9
12 055	Highlands	73,952	55.7	15.6	82,481	44.0	16.4	24.4	53.8	35,197	13.3	33.6	7.9
12 057	Hillsborough	833,952	41.7	28.7	998,375	65.4	11.5	41.6	26.0	47,530	13.6	26.0	18.8
12 061	Indian River........	104,195	42.1	26.1	116,557	52.4	15.8	27.5	46.4	43,058	10.5	29.1	17.1
12 063	Jackson..............	35,150	58.9	13.5	40,741	45.9	11.2	32.2	38.6	36,487	11.4	35.6	11.4
12 069	Lake..................	217,757	47.9	21.1	245,882	53.9	12.1	31.5	41.8	43,931	10.0	25.9	13.4
12 071	Lee...................	462,065	46.2	24.1	524,310	53.8	14.3	30.3	40.9	46,022	11.1	24.4	16.9
12 073	Leon..................	161,952	27.7	44.6	232,335	65.8	11.2	38.4	24.1	45,500	12.6	29.3	19.1
12 075	Levy..................	28,992	59.4	10.5	33,047	49.9	14.8	27.5	41.7	34,152	20.1	37.3	8.3
12 081	Manatee.............	238,301	44.1	26.2	269,242	55.8	12.1	32.6	40.1	46,555	10.6	25.8	17.0
12 083	Marion...............	245,211	51.5	16.6	277,545	48.8	15.0	27.7	46.2	37,574	13.1	30.2	9.2
12 085	Martin	112,285	37.5	30.1	125,106	53.2	13.5	29.3	42.7	47,313	8.2	24.1	22.0
12 086	Miami-Dade.........	1,754,862	50.0	26.1	2,073,402	62.3	12.5	40.2	25.1	41,420	17.0	31.5	17.0
12 087	Monroe	57,681	39.3	28.3	64,267	63.7	8.2	41.1	29.2	52,407	8.4	21.8	21.6
12 089	Nassau	52,438	45.3	22.2	60,538	57.2	10.6	35.5	34.1	55,833	8.1	18.0	22.6
12 091	Okaloosa	124,758	35.6	27.6	148,498	66.8	8.7	42.4	25.4	53,008	11.2	20.4	19.9
12 093	Okeechobee........	26,547	66.7	9.1	31,167	51.3	15.5	31.7	37.3	32,025	21.9	36.7	9.5
12 095	Orange	752,829	39.7	29.9	932,954	68.7	11.8	41.7	21.3	46,172	13.4	25.7	17.7
12 097	Osceola..............	178,296	51.1	17.3	215,261	65.4	13.4	39.2	23.3	43,265	14.8	25.8	11.5
12 099	Palm Beach.........	960,151	39.0	32.5	1,102,205	60.3	12.3	36.0	35.4	51,405	10.6	23.4	22.7
12 101	Pasco................	336,597	47.2	20.4	380,731	53.6	12.9	32.2	41.1	42,601	10.4	27.6	13.5
12 103	Pinellas.............	689,889	41.7	27.4	777,478	59.3	11.3	37.5	36.1	44,614	9.6	27.3	16.6
12 105	Polk.................	413,212	53.9	18.1	484,796	56.1	13.8	33.6	36.4	41,788	13.8	27.8	11.5
12 107	Putnam	51,318	62.6	10.8	59,359	47.2	13.9	28.9	45.6	32,288	20.9	39.2	8.3
12 109	St. Johns............	136,383	29.1	40.9	158,008	63.6	8.0	40.1	28.5	61,939	7.7	18.5	28.1
12 111	St. Lucie	198,085	49.2	19.5	227,159	56.8	15.9	32.2	38.9	41,458	13.7	28.0	13.0
12 113	Santa Rosa.........	105,924	37.6	26.6	123,730	62.4	10.7	38.9	25.9	57,532	7.6	17.6	20.5
12 115	Sarasota............	300,494	39.7	30.1	331,168	51.6	12.1	29.9	46.1	47,905	8.0	23.5	17.8
12 117	Seminole............	288,586	33.3	34.1	343,505	66.1	11.0	41.1	22.5	57,164	8.2	18.6	23.6
12 119	Sumter..............	85,874	45.4	23.6	90,537	27.0	12.9	14.0	67.9	45,712	7.3	23.8	12.6
12 121	Suwannee...........	30,205	63.3	11.4	34,851	50.4	10.0	32.5	43.1	37,269	18.6	37.6	7.4
12 123	Taylor...............	16,325	63.6	9.9	18,861	47.5	13.6	28.2	34.5	34,102	10.4	34.7	10.4
12 127	Volusia..............	358,405	45.9	20.4	414,683	52.4	11.8	31.7	40.7	40,836	11.9	29.5	12.3
12 129	Wakulla	21,227	52.3	16.1	24,832	57.3	9.7	38.6	24.5	50,156	11.8	22.9	15.5
12 131	Walton..............	40,604	44.2	25.3	46,093	58.3	10.2	36.0	32.4	42,732	11.5	27.2	15.0
12 133	Washington	17,548	57.9	12.6	20,163	48.0	11.8	28.9	42.0	38,523	15.6	33.8	7.3
13 000	**Georgia**	6,326,651	44.3	27.7	7,600,267	63.6	11.8	40.1	26.4	47,642	14.4	26.8	18.9
13 009	Baldwin	27,472	55.2	19.1	37,436	47.8	11.7	29.3	37.4	30,695	22.9	42.1	10.8
13 013	Barrow..............	44,897	54.8	16.5	52,413	67.8	13.0	42.2	23.9	52,029	9.4	19.9	13.3
13 015	Bartow..............	65,244	58.5	15.4	76,635	62.1	12.4	40.0	25.7	46,014	13.4	25.7	12.7
13 021	Bibb.................	99,719	49.7	22.3	120,591	56.9	11.6	34.7	32.6	35,966	21.0	37.4	14.1
13 029	Bryan................	19,888	40.8	30.3	23,370	68.6	8.9	47.6	19.4	62,351	9.5	17.9	22.3
13 031	Bulloch	37,385	45.2	26.5	59,157	55.2	8.8	30.9	26.8	33,479	18.3	38.4	10.9
13 033	Burke................	14,582	65.9	8.5	17,398	54.8	10.2	34.4	34.4	31,877	24.1	41.6	8.9
13 035	Butts................	16,006	64.9	9.6	19,092	55.7	15.9	34.5	33.5	50,164	11.9	23.0	14.2
13 039	Camden..............	31,073	41.4	19.3	39,026	66.2	8.5	47.7	23.6	53,375	13.6	23.7	14.8
13 045	Carroll	68,679	55.4	19.5	86,179	62.2	13.8	37.6	27.8	45,740	15.6	28.3	14.9
13 047	Catoosa	43,413	47.3	18.6	51,032	64.1	11.4	41.5	27.3	47,676	9.6	24.4	15.6
13 051	Chatham	175,163	39.5	30.8	216,752	61.9	9.1	40.6	27.6	44,356	13.9	27.9	16.3
13 055	Chattooga	18,018	71.1	7.9	20,628	48.4	8.9	33.1	35.8	32,306	17.7	38.4	5.2
13 057	Cherokee...........	141,945	34.1	35.8	165,224	69.8	8.0	46.2	18.6	66,065	6.4	14.8	30.1
13 059	Clarke...............	61,987	36.7	40.4	99,660	56.1	9.2	29.1	30.1	33,044	21.5	41.2	12.9
13 063	Clayton..............	158,957	50.8	16.9	195,375	68.6	17.9	39.2	24.4	37,767	21.0	31.3	9.6
13 067	Cobb.................	457,541	28.6	43.8	541,456	72.0	10.5	45.8	18.1	61,791	10.1	18.0	28.7
13 069	Coffee	27,456	64.7	11.8	33,237	53.1	11.8	35.9	30.9	36,441	17.8	37.1	12.2
13 071	Colquitt.............	28,610	67.0	12.2	34,255	58.4	11.0	35.6	34.5	32,186	23.0	41.2	8.8
13 073	Columbia............	83,171	35.5	34.6	98,186	66.1	6.8	44.8	20.1	64,724	7.8	15.2	26.9
13 077	Coweta..............	84,478	45.4	24.9	98,676	64.9	9.1	44.3	23.1	58,831	10.6	19.6	22.5
13 081	Crisp................	15,091	57.9	14.4	18,200	57.2	17.1	32.6	39.1	35,635	26.5	38.8	8.5
13 085	Dawson..............	15,518	44.9	24.7	18,038	60.4	11.5	37.0	26.3	51,972	10.1	23.3	20.7
13 087	Decatur..............	18,217	55.0	13.8	21,603	51.5	9.3	35.9	35.5	28,755	26.3	44.5	9.0
13 089	DeKalb...............	463,126	33.7	39.1	548,854	69.5	15.0	42.5	23.8	48,841	15.5	25.4	21.0
13 091	Dodge...............	14,392	63.0	13.8	17,027	51.5	11.2	37.7	34.9	35,097	17.2	36.0	10.0
13 095	Dougherty	58,327	49.6	17.2	73,322	57.4	18.6	32.6	37.8	30,380	27.1	42.7	9.1
13 097	Douglas	84,349	43.7	25.1	100,429	67.2	13.0	43.1	23.2	51,154	12.7	20.3	17.2
13 103	Effingham...........	33,603	51.6	17.5	39,606	65.0	6.5	46.1	20.0	64,203	7.7	18.7	24.4
13 105	Elbert...............	13,609	69.1	12.2	15,757	53.3	15.5	32.3	37.0	34,624	16.0	37.0	6.5
13 107	Emanuel	14,978	64.0	9.4	17,731	56.2	14.0	33.7	35.5	33,750	19.6	39.1	7.4
13 111	Fannin...............	17,699	57.7	15.9	19,713	50.7	15.2	31.1	42.4	35,295	16.2	33.8	11.4
13 113	Fayette..............	72,097	28.5	41.6	84,292	64.8	9.0	41.3	25.1	80,025	6.7	12.0	38.3
13 115	Floyd................	62,861	52.1	18.5	75,786	58.6	14.3	33.4	34.8	39,933	15.2	32.1	13.9
13 117	Forsyth..............	116,427	32.7	41.2	133,393	68.5	9.6	44.0	17.3	84,494	5.4	13.5	42.1
13 119	Franklin.............	15,005	61.5	13.3	17,756	52.7	9.7	35.3	38.8	32,130	13.5	36.3	8.5
13 121	Fulton	624,361	28.2	48.2	750,671	67.9	12.3	43.1	24.3	55,491	13.9	24.9	28.0

Table B-2. Counties — What: Education, Employment, and Income, 2010–2012—Continued

State or county code	State or county	Educational attainment			Employment status				Percent of households with no workers	Median household income (dollars)	Percent of families with income below poverty	Percent of households with income less than $25,000	Percent of households with income of $100,000 or more
		Total population 25 years and over	Percent with a high school diploma or less	Percent with a bachelor's degree or more	Total population 16 years and over	Percent in the labor force	Unemployment rate	Percent who worked full-time year-round					
	ACS table number:	C15002	C15002	C15002	B23025	B23025	B23025	C20005	C08202	B19013	C17013	C19001	C19001
	Column number:	1	2	3	4	5	6	7	8	9	10	11	12
	Georgia—Cont.												
13 123	Gilmer	20,100	55.4	15.7	22,715	52.5	9.8	28.7	37.7	39,488	11.7	27.4	10.0
13 127	Glynn	54,529	43.6	24.4	62,907	64.6	12.5	40.1	29.3	44,497	14.8	27.7	18.8
13 129	Gordon	35,727	62.2	14.6	42,426	61.3	10.8	39.1	27.2	40,562	17.1	32.6	9.6
13 131	Grady	16,757	66.8	11.0	19,529	47.3	10.9	30.7	44.9	28,032	24.3	46.9	7.7
13 135	Gwinnett	517,222	36.8	34.0	614,519	70.5	10.9	45.3	15.7	58,611	11.6	18.3	25.2
13 137	Habersham	28,998	56.6	15.1	34,139	53.6	9.8	34.5	32.7	40,562	12.1	28.2	10.6
13 139	Hall	115,004	52.3	22.7	137,688	63.4	10.7	41.1	25.0	50,311	14.9	22.9	18.3
13 143	Haralson	18,929	62.6	13.5	22,349	57.4	14.0	34.3	37.6	39,635	16.0	31.9	12.1
13 145	Harris	22,512	36.6	29.3	25,989	62.6	7.6	44.9	25.1	73,514	5.2	16.2	32.8
13 147	Hart	17,904	59.6	14.1	20,515	49.7	11.1	34.3	41.0	31,848	24.4	41.8	10.9
13 151	Henry	130,265	42.7	25.2	155,383	67.8	13.1	43.5	21.9	57,720	11.5	18.7	20.4
13 153	Houston	91,911	39.3	23.9	110,539	67.2	11.5	43.1	23.2	55,184	13.1	21.8	19.4
13 157	Jackson	39,501	55.8	18.3	46,619	60.4	8.3	42.0	25.0	51,478	13.5	24.2	16.1
13 169	Jones	19,073	50.9	16.8	22,114	60.6	9.4	41.1	29.9	53,506	14.6	23.6	17.1
13 175	Laurens	31,880	64.2	13.6	37,254	48.5	7.4	34.5	39.8	33,368	22.0	40.2	9.8
13 177	Lee	18,606	45.1	21.8	21,609	65.0	8.5	44.4	23.5	59,119	9.0	19.6	24.5
13 179	Liberty	35,932	41.6	18.2	46,666	68.5	10.9	47.0	20.1	44,274	16.6	25.3	11.2
13 185	Lowndes	64,307	47.7	22.4	87,752	62.6	12.7	35.0	28.1	36,373	17.1	35.2	12.2
13 187	Lumpkin	19,234	45.3	26.0	25,187	63.5	14.9	32.4	28.2	43,551	10.8	30.5	13.6
13 189	McDuffie	14,030	60.9	15.5	16,672	53.0	10.5	32.9	34.5	37,972	20.7	36.2	9.8
13 195	Madison	19,093	62.1	13.7	22,149	58.6	8.5	36.9	28.3	40,699	11.7	26.9	10.5
13 199	Meriwether	14,641	66.6	8.8	17,171	53.7	15.5	32.2	40.6	36,850	15.0	32.5	9.2
13 205	Mitchell	15,678	68.2	10.1	18,260	47.9	11.7	32.9	41.1	29,903	23.1	42.8	5.6
13 207	Monroe	18,317	53.1	17.6	21,450	57.2	10.1	35.5	28.1	44,233	11.5	26.9	18.5
13 213	Murray	25,655	68.5	8.6	30,113	58.8	15.1	37.5	32.4	32,618	19.5	36.7	6.1
13 215	Muscogee	120,815	42.9	22.4	150,605	62.5	10.7	37.7	30.4	39,113	15.9	31.8	12.9
13 217	Newton	63,277	48.0	19.0	75,653	64.5	14.9	38.4	25.4	47,580	14.0	23.8	15.0
13 219	Oconee	21,754	28.3	43.8	25,522	65.2	5.3	45.0	20.8	77,794	5.7	12.7	35.5
13 223	Paulding	89,468	49.0	22.6	105,915	71.1	11.6	45.0	18.1	60,282	10.9	17.6	19.4
13 225	Peach	16,453	50.2	18.1	22,256	60.6	15.1	32.2	29.6	39,161	20.8	32.4	15.4
13 227	Pickens	20,826	50.9	24.9	23,770	59.4	11.0	36.9	31.5	48,010	8.3	22.6	17.3
13 233	Polk	26,601	64.1	12.6	31,521	57.4	15.4	34.8	33.7	37,288	17.3	34.4	9.2
13 237	Putnam	15,249	54.1	17.7	17,068	58.9	8.7	38.6	30.7	41,247	13.6	29.6	17.2
13 245	Richmond	127,386	46.8	20.2	157,517	60.6	11.6	37.2	30.4	38,990	20.0	34.1	11.3
13 247	Rockdale	55,016	43.5	24.2	65,499	66.5	14.3	40.9	24.2	52,510	13.1	20.4	18.7
13 255	Spalding	42,079	61.6	14.9	49,561	57.2	15.8	33.2	35.0	39,345	20.0	36.0	11.2
13 257	Stephens	17,289	61.5	13.6	20,775	57.0	12.8	35.7	33.5	38,291	13.2	31.2	10.7
13 261	Sumter	19,820	55.0	20.6	24,775	58.7	13.8	34.0	34.8	33,732	22.3	39.0	10.0
13 267	Tattnall	17,214	64.2	10.8	20,638	44.4	12.5	28.2	37.6	35,444	24.1	40.0	10.0
13 275	Thomas	29,961	54.5	16.3	34,961	50.8	14.0	33.3	40.4	30,813	24.5	42.5	8.9
13 277	Tift	25,417	53.1	18.5	31,920	57.0	9.7	34.6	32.4	36,131	19.4	36.2	13.5
13 279	Toombs	17,286	62.0	15.4	20,606	55.7	6.9	39.9	35.6	31,200	19.9	41.4	9.0
13 285	Troup	43,204	53.0	20.1	52,276	60.4	15.2	38.6	33.1	40,180	18.7	32.9	12.8
13 291	Union	16,287	50.5	18.0	17,976	47.4	14.8	27.5	45.2	40,956	14.8	34.2	9.5
13 293	Upson	18,272	60.8	10.7	21,470	53.7	13.6	31.8	37.6	33,923	17.5	37.8	7.2
13 295	Walker	47,188	57.5	14.5	53,935	58.8	12.5	36.3	33.8	37,750	13.8	32.7	11.4
13 297	Walton	55,144	48.6	18.4	64,442	62.6	8.9	39.8	26.0	50,923	12.8	23.6	19.3
13 299	Ware	24,009	59.5	15.4	28,639	51.3	9.8	31.8	36.3	34,594	19.4	37.8	9.1
13 303	Washington	14,115	66.5	10.3	16,527	46.5	13.6	32.1	39.5	31,293	19.1	41.1	9.2
13 305	Wayne	20,448	60.6	12.2	23,637	54.0	11.0	35.5	33.5	37,758	18.9	33.3	8.0
13 311	White	19,189	47.9	20.2	22,243	55.1	8.1	34.2	35.3	40,338	10.1	35.3	11.9
13 313	Whitfield	64,326	60.8	14.3	77,537	64.4	12.4	39.2	24.9	39,575	15.6	29.5	12.6
13 321	Worth	14,478	67.2	7.2	17,130	59.3	13.8	37.1	32.8	36,735	15.1	32.8	8.1
15 000	**Hawaii**	941,038	38.1	29.6	1,107,535	65.8	7.1	43.3	22.9	65,087	8.1	17.4	29.2
15 001	Hawaii	129,247	43.4	24.5	149,860	59.8	10.6	36.1	32.0	48,995	14.5	27.3	17.6
15 003	Honolulu	654,665	36.5	31.6	778,312	66.5	6.1	45.5	20.8	70,541	6.8	15.3	32.6
15 007	Kauai	47,863	38.4	25.3	54,395	64.1	6.7	39.0	25.5	60,332	8.7	17.7	22.7
15 009	Maui	109,201	41.6	25.2	124,905	69.1	9.8	40.6	23.5	61,383	8.4	17.6	26.1
16 000	**Idaho**	999,548	38.9	25.1	1,201,048	63.8	9.3	37.1	27.3	45,395	11.7	25.6	14.2
16 001	Ada	260,640	28.2	35.5	307,840	67.6	8.6	41.8	22.5	52,697	9.4	20.9	20.0
16 005	Bannock	50,269	36.2	27.0	62,985	65.0	8.2	36.1	27.5	42,276	10.5	27.9	12.6
16 011	Bingham	26,850	45.0	19.2	32,240	63.6	6.7	40.3	26.0	47,684	12.4	24.5	14.0
16 013	Blaine	14,919	23.4	44.1	16,736	73.7	6.6	44.6	21.7	57,955	6.9	18.5	23.3
16 017	Bonner	29,698	39.5	21.7	33,013	54.1	9.6	30.3	39.5	39,725	12.2	30.0	14.2
16 019	Bonneville	63,581	35.9	26.6	76,131	66.5	7.0	40.4	23.1	50,447	10.7	22.6	18.4
16 027	Canyon	113,921	48.8	17.9	137,734	63.3	12.5	34.5	27.5	41,569	16.7	28.7	10.3
16 031	Cassia	13,577	47.2	15.8	16,379	63.0	8.8	40.7	29.6	43,069	10.1	32.3	8.2
16 039	Elmore	15,784	44.7	16.6	20,056	66.1	9.1	44.9	23.3	41,077	12.1	24.1	7.1
16 051	Jefferson	15,047	40.7	22.0	17,743	67.1	6.9	39.6	21.3	50,022	9.8	21.5	15.2
16 053	Jerome	13,463	56.6	16.3	16,230	63.9	7.6	42.9	21.9	40,721	17.0	29.5	7.8
16 055	Kootenai	94,226	36.7	23.2	110,339	63.2	11.1	34.4	29.6	46,941	9.5	23.2	13.9
16 057	Latah	21,078	27.1	41.8	31,665	61.4	7.2	31.9	28.0	40,265	9.4	32.1	14.0
16 065	Madison	14,680	22.8	32.3	28,576	61.4	9.4	24.2	19.3	32,578	24.7	37.1	10.3
16 067	Minidoka	12,314	57.2	9.8	14,909	64.9	6.8	40.8	27.0	42,896	11.0	25.7	10.1
16 069	Nez Perce	26,998	42.1	21.4	31,820	63.0	6.6	36.0	31.6	45,819	6.3	25.5	13.3

Table B-2. Counties — What: Education, Employment, and Income, 2010–2012—*Continued*

State or county code	State or county	Educational attainment			Employment status				Percent of households with no workers	Median household income (dollars)	Percent of families with income below poverty	Percent of households with income less than $25,000	Percent of households with income of $100,000 or more
		Total population 25 years and over	Percent with a high school diploma or less	Percent with a bachelor's degree or more	Total population 16 years and over	Percent in the labor force	Unemployment rate	Percent who worked full-time year-round					
	ACS table number:	C15002	C15002	C15002	B23025	B23025	B23025	C20005	C08202	B19013	C17013	C19001	C19001
	Column number:	1	2	3	4	5	6	7	8	9	10	11	12
	Idaho—Cont.												
16 075	Payette	14,276	53.1	13.7	16,807	61.5	14.5	34.7	31.4	40,172	13.5	30.1	10.1
16 083	Twin Falls	49,253	45.1	16.6	59,077	62.4	8.0	38.5	24.3	41,778	13.6	25.2	10.7
17 000	**Illinois**..................	8,515,161	40.1	31.2	10,130,477	66.2	10.8	40.6	26.0	55,231	10.6	22.5	23.6
17 001	Adams	45,946	46.9	19.4	53,637	65.5	7.7	43.1	29.0	44,315	10.1	26.4	12.7
17 007	Boone	34,182	50.8	18.8	40,911	67.4	12.4	39.6	23.4	58,922	10.9	17.7	23.2
17 011	Bureau	24,273	48.3	18.4	27,725	64.5	9.1	38.7	30.9	47,348	7.8	25.1	14.5
17 019	Champaign..................	115,237	29.6	42.5	167,486	64.6	7.8	35.5	25.1	44,574	10.4	30.4	18.2
17 021	Christian	24,229	56.1	12.9	28,043	60.1	7.6	39.5	29.9	44,177	12.2	26.5	14.8
17 027	Clinton	26,410	43.4	19.7	30,527	67.8	5.2	44.5	25.2	60,424	6.2	19.5	23.0
17 029	Coles	31,304	43.8	23.0	44,926	62.3	11.9	31.8	34.1	36,725	12.5	34.6	11.9
17 031	Cook	3,481,359	40.1	34.3	4,134,566	66.3	12.7	40.4	26.2	52,754	13.5	24.5	23.2
17 037	DeKalb..................	59,912	36.4	29.2	84,292	68.5	11.0	35.4	25.2	51,624	9.9	27.4	19.5
17 043	DuPage..................	620,125	27.5	45.9	727,072	71.2	9.0	45.1	19.3	77,020	5.0	12.5	36.7
17 049	Effingham..................	23,065	45.1	19.1	26,865	69.0	5.7	46.9	27.1	51,273	5.3	23.0	17.0
17 051	Fayette..................	15,195	56.7	14.2	17,804	60.9	11.4	38.7	30.5	43,614	12.6	26.4	13.4
17 055	Franklin..................	27,401	49.9	12.4	31,815	54.4	10.9	31.9	37.3	37,296	13.8	31.8	8.7
17 057	Fulton..................	26,234	50.9	14.7	30,087	55.9	8.0	34.5	33.2	43,583	9.5	27.9	12.5
17 063	Grundy..................	32,673	47.4	18.3	37,941	66.2	10.9	38.0	26.8	60,711	7.0	18.6	24.5
17 073	Henry..................	34,305	48.0	17.9	39,996	63.6	6.3	42.4	28.8	51,243	7.7	20.3	16.8
17 075	Iroquois..................	20,489	52.4	15.3	23,499	63.8	9.3	40.9	31.3	46,794	9.0	23.5	14.4
17 077	Jackson..................	34,405	34.8	33.0	50,956	57.2	10.5	26.6	36.2	31,495	17.7	41.9	12.0
17 081	Jefferson..................	26,978	47.1	16.9	31,304	60.2	10.0	36.1	32.1	42,330	10.6	29.5	12.4
17 083	Jersey..................	15,613	46.5	16.1	18,489	62.3	9.2	38.7	31.0	55,737	4.8	19.2	18.7
17 085	Jo Daviess..................	16,599	45.0	25.1	18,611	63.2	5.8	37.2	31.9	50,000	5.9	20.7	15.5
17 089	Kane..................	327,260	40.6	31.7	388,036	70.4	10.3	43.3	19.7	67,042	9.2	15.7	31.4
17 091	Kankakee..................	73,292	48.2	17.3	88,417	63.0	11.3	37.4	29.4	47,360	13.2	25.0	17.3
17 093	Kendall..................	72,633	33.7	34.4	84,229	74.6	6.9	50.7	14.7	81,946	3.3	8.7	37.6
17 095	Knox..................	36,690	51.8	17.3	43,348	55.4	8.7	33.6	36.8	40,077	11.8	31.8	11.0
17 097	Lake..................	449,817	32.8	42.1	537,956	70.5	10.0	44.0	20.4	76,657	7.4	14.5	37.9
17 099	LaSalle..................	77,991	49.9	15.1	90,717	65.6	11.6	36.5	31.3	49,754	9.7	25.0	16.9
17 103	Lee..................	24,813	50.8	15.0	28,693	60.5	7.0	38.5	27.2	48,758	10.3	21.9	14.6
17 105	Livingston	26,927	53.6	14.6	31,224	54.7	8.3	35.1	30.2	54,818	7.5	22.9	15.5
17 107	Logan	21,052	50.5	15.3	24,995	43.0	7.0	28.7	34.4	46,102	12.4	28.6	14.3
17 109	McDonough	17,917	36.9	33.0	28,132	58.7	12.3	29.6	33.1	33,971	15.7	38.1	11.4
17 111	McHenry..................	201,708	35.0	32.0	236,657	72.6	11.1	44.2	18.7	74,008	5.9	13.6	33.3
17 113	McLean..................	102,656	31.3	41.5	136,807	69.9	6.8	42.2	21.4	60,954	6.4	21.3	26.3
17 115	Macon..................	75,129	45.4	23.0	88,183	62.4	12.1	37.1	32.4	45,275	12.6	27.6	15.7
17 117	Macoupin..................	33,096	49.8	16.8	38,286	62.2	8.1	37.8	30.9	48,086	11.6	23.7	14.9
17 119	Madison..................	181,304	43.2	23.9	215,132	63.4	9.1	38.8	29.5	51,947	10.2	24.3	19.5
17 121	Marion..................	26,816	49.9	13.7	31,202	61.2	11.2	37.1	33.5	39,924	12.8	34.2	11.7
17 133	Monroe..................	22,920	40.1	25.0	26,037	68.0	6.1	45.1	24.3	69,056	3.8	11.7	30.2
17 135	Montgomery..............	21,188	57.7	11.8	24,531	42.8	5.1	29.7	37.6	45,662	11.1	28.3	11.4
17 137	Morgan	24,155	50.1	21.6	28,911	62.3	10.1	37.7	28.9	45,602	7.9	25.3	15.1
17 141	Ogle	35,804	46.3	19.7	41,918	67.9	10.2	42.3	27.6	55,071	7.5	19.3	20.9
17 143	Peoria	122,992	40.3	28.2	146,521	64.3	9.9	39.6	29.1	50,102	13.0	25.3	18.7
17 145	Perry	15,591	48.8	14.9	18,298	53.4	8.9	32.6	36.2	40,674	10.8	30.1	10.5
17 157	Randolph	24,090	57.8	11.6	27,513	56.9	7.2	37.8	32.1	49,292	8.7	24.7	16.4
17 161	Rock Island	100,846	44.1	21.3	117,806	62.7	8.4	37.5	32.2	46,535	10.2	25.0	14.5
17 163	St. Clair..................	177,412	38.3	25.6	210,240	64.0	9.4	41.0	28.5	50,047	14.4	26.7	19.6
17 165	Saline..................	17,092	47.5	13.7	19,884	52.6	12.6	30.8	42.8	37,039	15.4	36.2	9.4
17 167	Sangamon	135,279	36.5	32.2	157,648	67.1	8.5	43.8	26.6	53,209	11.3	23.0	21.4
17 173	Shelby..................	15,791	53.5	13.6	17,951	58.4	8.2	40.2	33.4	45,217	7.8	24.1	12.0
17 177	Stephenson..................	33,088	47.4	18.9	37,850	65.0	12.5	36.9	33.3	44,786	10.7	28.3	12.5
17 179	Tazewell..................	94,112	42.2	23.4	107,492	64.3	6.9	42.1	27.5	53,763	6.9	19.7	19.1
17 183	Vermilion..................	54,584	53.3	13.9	63,694	57.7	12.2	36.8	36.3	40,796	15.5	30.3	10.5
17 195	Whiteside..................	40,248	49.4	16.1	46,243	63.4	9.7	38.4	31.8	46,137	8.5	23.8	12.9
17 197	Will..................	430,227	36.6	32.6	510,255	69.8	10.1	43.8	19.6	73,707	6.5	13.7	33.4
17 199	Williamson..................	46,357	41.2	22.4	53,611	57.9	8.3	35.7	33.4	41,746	11.5	29.8	13.1
17 201	Winnebago..................	196,239	48.0	21.1	229,422	65.1	13.2	36.6	29.8	46,747	13.3	27.6	15.0
17 203	Woodford..................	25,685	38.8	26.8	30,210	66.6	6.4	41.8	24.0	69,505	4.7	15.9	28.6
18 000	**Indiana**..................	4,256,342	48.2	23.1	5,099,178	64.2	9.8	39.3	27.6	47,185	11.2	25.2	15.9
18 001	Adams..................	20,817	59.2	14.9	24,875	67.5	7.8	39.7	24.1	45,796	11.8	24.1	12.0
18 003	Allen..................	228,609	41.1	26.2	272,764	66.0	9.7	42.2	25.8	49,088	11.6	22.8	15.6
18 005	Bartholomew............	52,275	45.5	26.9	60,966	65.5	5.9	42.0	26.3	53,072	9.9	23.0	19.7
18 011	Boone..................	38,107	35.2	41.6	43,685	67.6	4.9	46.1	20.8	65,956	5.8	14.8	30.0
18 015	Carroll..................	13,780	54.1	17.2	15,871	64.3	9.1	40.8	28.8	50,241	9.0	24.3	16.3
18 017	Cass..................	25,845	58.9	12.7	30,230	63.3	11.4	39.4	28.6	39,200	14.9	29.0	8.8
18 019	Clark..................	75,921	47.3	20.1	87,923	66.4	8.8	43.2	27.3	48,789	9.3	24.3	14.8
18 021	Clay..................	18,195	58.0	14.6	21,277	60.9	9.2	39.0	29.3	45,140	12.0	26.2	13.7
18 023	Clinton	21,515	60.5	14.3	25,155	66.4	10.1	41.4	27.7	48,251	11.1	24.2	12.2
18 027	Daviess	19,853	64.2	11.9	23,675	62.6	4.9	42.6	27.4	45,583	9.3	22.3	12.9
18 029	Dearborn..................	33,877	51.6	17.9	39,141	66.1	9.1	41.3	27.4	59,013	5.1	19.1	19.3
18 031	Decatur..................	17,461	62.1	11.9	20,264	65.3	10.5	40.3	26.1	49,407	13.0	21.5	10.7
18 033	DeKalb..................	27,985	54.1	15.9	32,593	63.2	11.5	37.9	31.2	46,565	11.6	25.2	12.6
18 035	Delaware..................	70,938	48.8	22.4	97,337	58.0	13.6	28.5	35.0	36,720	13.9	34.8	10.7

Table B-2. Counties — What: Education, Employment, and Income, 2010–2012—*Continued*

State or county code	State or county	Educational attainment			Employment status				Percent of households with no workers	Median household income (dollars)	Percent of families with income below poverty	Percent of households with income less than $25,000	Percent of households with income of $100,000 or more
		Total population 25 years and over	Percent with a high school diploma or less	Percent with a bachelor's degree or more	Total population 16 years and over	Percent in the labor force	Unemployment rate	Percent who worked full-time year-round					
	ACS table number:	C15002	C15002	C15002	B23025	B23025	B23025	C20005	C08202	B19013	C17013	C19001	C19001
	Column number:	1	2	3	4	5	6	7	8	9	10	11	12
	Indiana—Cont.												
18 037	Dubois	28,559	55.3	17.7	32,781	68.8	4.6	44.8	21.1	53,630	6.4	20.2	14.1
18 039	Elkhart	124,431	57.3	17.9	148,884	66.4	10.3	38.7	25.9	45,133	13.5	23.9	12.1
18 041	Fayette	16,752	63.0	9.6	19,229	57.0	16.7	31.0	39.6	35,622	16.8	37.6	7.1
18 043	Floyd	50,586	46.5	22.1	59,543	66.7	9.1	42.2	27.1	51,230	10.4	24.4	18.0
18 047	Franklin	15,492	59.1	15.7	17,893	64.4	6.3	40.9	24.6	46,291	11.2	19.6	13.0
18 049	Fulton	14,167	58.1	13.0	16,292	60.0	8.8	38.6	28.8	40,939	12.5	31.6	10.9
18 051	Gibson	22,636	50.0	13.7	26,339	66.0	6.9	43.9	25.0	47,687	9.3	21.8	15.5
18 053	Grant	45,302	56.2	17.4	56,751	56.9	10.7	31.8	37.0	38,033	14.3	32.0	9.2
18 055	Greene	22,941	57.0	12.1	26,372	60.6	9.9	38.6	31.8	42,402	11.7	29.9	11.2
18 057	Hamilton	182,185	20.1	55.2	208,155	73.5	5.4	51.3	14.3	82,404	3.6	9.8	39.6
18 059	Hancock	47,191	44.1	25.5	54,688	65.7	6.2	45.3	24.3	61,507	6.7	16.1	21.9
18 061	Harrison	26,926	54.3	15.6	31,119	63.7	9.8	39.4	31.3	51,765	8.6	23.4	17.0
18 063	Hendricks	97,503	37.3	32.2	113,487	68.0	6.0	47.6	19.7	68,043	3.1	12.2	28.9
18 065	Henry	34,862	61.3	13.9	40,135	53.4	13.3	30.3	37.5	37,282	14.9	29.1	8.2
18 067	Howard	56,823	49.6	19.2	66,008	58.2	11.2	34.1	37.5	40,087	12.4	30.6	13.3
18 069	Huntington	24,691	53.5	17.1	29,457	67.0	11.1	40.6	28.7	46,461	6.8	24.0	12.1
18 071	Jackson	28,987	61.4	13.3	33,514	64.2	10.0	40.1	26.9	46,236	10.0	23.5	10.5
18 073	Jasper	21,848	55.7	15.5	25,974	61.6	9.1	36.5	25.7	57,703	6.6	18.5	16.6
18 075	Jay	13,986	63.0	9.5	16,465	66.0	9.1	41.8	28.2	40,649	9.2	28.5	7.1
18 077	Jefferson	21,785	57.2	16.7	26,154	58.9	10.6	34.4	31.7	41,004	11.6	27.4	10.0
18 079	Jennings	18,532	61.0	10.8	21,842	63.3	13.3	37.4	31.2	45,051	10.1	23.2	12.5
18 081	Johnson	92,922	44.2	26.5	108,390	69.0	7.5	45.0	22.3	61,544	7.7	16.9	23.9
18 083	Knox	25,089	54.5	13.8	31,267	58.0	8.9	36.5	32.1	40,088	10.4	29.6	9.6
18 085	Kosciusko	50,686	52.5	20.7	60,074	68.2	9.5	41.6	25.0	50,867	7.9	20.6	16.1
18 087	LaGrange	21,087	65.9	11.1	25,925	63.1	9.6	35.2	25.7	45,294	11.8	23.6	12.4
18 089	Lake	325,834	49.4	20.2	384,160	62.0	12.0	36.7	30.4	48,069	13.9	27.1	16.8
18 091	LaPorte	76,445	52.7	16.3	89,204	59.0	11.8	35.0	30.3	46,944	13.8	27.4	14.4
18 093	Lawrence	32,117	59.3	13.2	36,660	59.3	9.6	36.2	31.1	42,678	13.7	30.5	11.9
18 095	Madison	88,870	52.3	17.6	104,482	58.5	12.2	34.5	36.0	42,187	12.9	28.2	10.9
18 097	Marion	589,035	45.0	27.0	706,387	67.7	12.0	40.4	26.3	40,655	16.5	29.8	13.6
18 099	Marshall	30,797	57.0	15.1	36,083	65.3	10.8	38.9	28.4	44,571	9.8	25.5	12.3
18 103	Miami	25,191	59.4	10.1	29,495	56.7	15.2	32.1	34.5	42,444	12.3	27.0	10.3
18 105	Monroe	76,608	31.8	42.5	119,562	60.7	8.3	31.1	28.9	39,332	12.2	35.1	13.7
18 107	Montgomery	25,307	59.6	14.9	30,314	62.6	11.0	38.0	28.6	42,419	15.0	25.1	10.1
18 109	Morgan	46,892	53.1	16.1	54,163	64.3	9.6	40.8	26.1	53,637	7.6	19.7	19.8
18 113	Noble	31,058	57.6	13.2	36,576	66.3	11.2	41.2	25.1	47,133	10.7	21.0	11.0
18 119	Owen	14,948	62.2	11.0	17,353	59.5	9.4	36.3	33.6	41,091	13.5	28.9	10.2
18 127	Porter	110,648	43.2	26.1	130,662	63.6	8.8	39.5	25.7	60,925	7.8	19.0	24.7
18 129	Posey	17,684	47.7	21.2	20,683	65.2	7.5	41.5	27.3	59,969	8.0	18.9	20.4
18 133	Putnam	24,644	56.5	15.8	31,080	52.4	9.2	32.3	29.5	47,029	7.5	20.6	14.4
18 135	Randolph	17,747	59.2	12.9	20,449	61.6	8.4	37.2	33.2	41,164	11.3	29.0	10.7
18 137	Ripley	19,066	60.9	15.0	22,058	62.2	7.8	40.1	31.7	46,566	7.8	24.7	14.3
18 141	St. Joseph	171,112	43.8	27.1	208,965	64.8	11.8	37.2	28.4	44,626	13.1	27.3	15.5
18 143	Scott	16,162	63.9	11.4	18,772	57.1	15.7	34.5	37.3	40,989	17.3	29.9	8.7
18 145	Shelby	30,116	57.3	15.3	35,053	67.2	10.6	41.8	27.2	50,354	8.2	22.4	13.8
18 147	Spencer	14,525	55.9	14.9	16,675	64.2	6.8	38.9	26.2	55,278	8.5	22.3	14.5
18 149	Starke	15,781	63.6	10.7	18,438	59.4	14.4	34.3	33.9	38,955	13.9	28.8	7.3
18 151	Steuben	22,846	50.5	20.4	27,613	64.3	10.1	38.1	27.7	47,513	7.9	21.7	13.2
18 153	Sullivan	15,009	56.0	12.8	17,323	51.7	9.1	32.7	32.4	45,392	12.0	26.5	12.6
18 157	Tippecanoe	95,957	38.3	35.0	143,001	63.6	7.6	35.9	24.6	42,660	10.4	29.6	15.2
18 163	Vanderburgh	119,561	45.0	22.3	144,708	64.8	7.5	41.9	27.6	42,623	10.8	27.3	12.9
18 167	Vigo	69,674	48.3	22.1	88,075	59.2	8.0	34.8	30.4	41,322	12.2	30.6	13.3
18 169	Wabash	21,929	57.7	16.4	26,350	59.7	8.9	36.6	31.0	45,205	9.9	26.2	9.3
18 173	Warrick	40,593	41.0	25.4	46,386	68.6	8.2	44.9	22.3	61,619	6.5	14.7	22.9
18 175	Washington	18,809	64.3	12.5	21,885	61.9	11.7	34.8	32.2	40,366	12.0	26.2	7.6
18 177	Wayne	46,604	56.6	16.5	54,842	58.3	12.1	34.0	34.1	35,925	17.5	34.8	8.7
18 179	Wells	18,724	54.0	15.3	21,797	63.9	6.8	41.4	28.6	47,254	7.1	23.0	12.7
18 181	White	16,896	55.9	14.2	19,341	64.0	7.9	41.3	28.2	48,626	8.2	22.8	12.7
18 183	Whitley	22,619	52.8	16.9	26,256	68.2	8.0	43.4	24.8	51,526	6.3	17.7	13.5
19 000	**Iowa**	2,027,762	42.0	25.8	2,420,545	68.0	6.0	44.0	25.5	50,773	8.4	22.9	17.3
19 011	Benton	17,715	47.9	18.4	20,319	67.8	4.9	45.7	25.4	56,397	6.6	15.7	20.2
19 013	Black Hawk	82,326	44.3	26.7	106,160	67.4	8.4	40.8	28.6	45,576	10.3	25.3	15.0
19 015	Boone	18,052	42.9	21.0	20,962	65.6	4.5	41.9	25.2	51,279	5.5	21.2	14.9
19 017	Bremer	15,847	41.5	27.8	19,606	66.9	5.4	41.5	27.4	59,104	5.1	19.6	19.9
19 019	Buchanan	13,870	51.8	17.3	15,980	68.4	4.7	47.5	24.4	54,645	7.2	17.8	17.4
19 021	Buena Vista	12,865	52.9	19.3	15,856	68.9	4.0	44.9	24.3	46,244	8.0	22.6	12.0
19 027	Carroll	14,169	51.6	17.0	16,213	70.0	2.9	47.5	24.8	50,460	5.1	23.2	14.0
19 033	Cerro Gordo	31,150	39.9	21.8	35,801	68.6	6.3	42.3	28.8	43,314	11.3	27.6	14.3
19 045	Clinton	33,615	48.7	17.7	38,998	64.7	6.7	41.8	30.2	48,541	10.7	25.2	16.0
19 049	Dallas	45,279	28.9	41.6	51,515	73.3	3.7	53.4	18.4	70,404	4.6	14.0	31.5
19 057	Des Moines	27,977	45.1	20.3	32,015	62.3	9.1	38.6	32.7	42,408	14.6	30.0	11.6
19 061	Dubuque	62,454	44.1	27.7	74,726	69.6	5.3	43.6	23.9	51,171	7.6	20.6	15.6
19 065	Fayette	14,152	51.9	19.0	16,849	62.3	6.7	39.2	31.6	44,472	5.1	23.9	11.1
19 087	Henry	13,709	43.2	21.0	15,990	60.7	5.4	41.8	28.4	44,937	13.4	26.9	11.5
19 097	Jackson	13,823	57.5	13.4	15,786	64.2	5.8	41.4	30.9	43,810	10.7	28.8	12.8
19 099	Jasper	25,956	49.6	16.7	29,742	61.8	6.0	41.0	28.3	48,116	7.9	23.5	14.7
19 103	Johnson	78,537	22.1	51.4	110,178	71.5	4.0	41.7	18.5	52,935	7.6	25.3	21.7

Table B-2. Counties — What: Education, Employment, and Income, 2010–2012—Continued

State or county code	State or county	Total population 25 years and over	Percent with a high school diploma or less	Percent with a bachelor's degree or more	Total population 16 years and over	Percent in the labor force	Unemployment rate	Percent who worked full-time year-round	Percent of households with no workers	Median household income (dollars)	Percent of families with income below poverty	Percent of households with income less than $25,000	Percent of households with income of $100,000 or more
	ACS table number:	C15002	C15002	C15002	B23025	B23025	B23025	C20005	C08202	B19013	C17013	C19001	C19001
	Column number:	1	2	3	4	5	6	7	8	9	10	11	12
	Iowa—Cont.												
19 105	Jones	14,715	49.4	16.1	16,744	64.1	6.4	41.8	26.1	53,145	6.4	19.7	14.5
19 111	Lee	25,008	52.9	15.7	28,752	62.3	8.6	40.5	32.4	41,405	11.1	26.0	10.8
19 113	Linn	140,312	33.3	31.8	167,717	70.9	5.5	46.3	22.4	57,173	5.6	19.6	22.0
19 123	Mahaska	14,922	48.2	20.9	17,587	67.9	9.5	39.1	29.5	48,420	8.5	26.8	11.4
19 125	Marion	21,702	41.3	24.0	26,080	67.4	4.5	43.4	25.2	53,588	8.5	19.7	17.9
19 127	Marshall	27,039	48.7	20.2	31,749	66.7	7.1	42.7	27.7	51,550	7.6	19.4	14.5
19 139	Muscatine	28,304	50.2	15.7	33,087	65.4	6.3	41.2	25.8	47,643	12.9	24.3	14.4
19 149	Plymouth	17,044	45.1	20.5	19,402	72.4	2.5	51.8	22.3	57,274	4.5	16.0	18.7
19 153	Polk	286,560	34.6	34.7	337,819	72.7	6.5	48.8	20.8	56,992	8.9	19.5	22.5
19 155	Pottawattamie	62,300	46.9	18.6	73,534	68.4	6.5	47.0	25.2	50,624	10.3	23.3	15.3
19 163	Scott	111,591	35.1	31.2	130,838	66.3	6.4	43.6	25.9	51,026	8.6	22.1	20.1
19 167	Sioux	20,169	45.0	23.9	25,921	73.1	2.2	42.6	20.3	57,408	4.8	17.7	17.2
19 169	Story	47,685	22.7	48.3	76,199	68.1	6.6	36.5	21.7	49,638	7.9	27.5	17.8
19 179	Wapello	23,936	53.9	14.9	28,320	62.7	9.7	37.2	29.1	39,778	13.7	31.5	10.4
19 181	Warren	30,156	38.9	27.3	35,870	73.1	6.1	48.5	22.3	62,066	6.4	14.8	26.0
19 183	Washington	14,929	45.7	22.8	17,015	71.0	5.3	45.9	24.1	52,116	5.2	19.8	16.2
19 187	Webster	25,345	43.6	18.6	30,598	62.2	11.2	37.6	31.9	40,146	12.0	30.2	13.8
19 191	Winneshiek	13,430	45.3	27.7	17,256	72.1	3.9	40.2	23.7	52,614	4.7	18.6	14.0
19 193	Woodbury	64,600	47.6	20.6	78,371	68.5	6.0	44.7	25.7	44,098	12.1	27.5	13.7
20 000	**Kansas**	1,854,150	37.8	30.1	2,225,644	67.9	7.2	44.3	24.0	50,346	9.4	23.2	18.5
20 009	Barton	18,452	46.3	18.0	21,845	66.7	6.6	46.5	25.2	45,781	8.7	24.6	13.9
20 015	Butler	42,259	33.8	27.3	50,284	66.2	7.5	43.9	25.4	55,189	5.1	18.5	21.8
20 021	Cherokee	14,557	47.0	14.0	16,728	61.0	6.2	41.1	30.5	40,533	12.8	26.6	7.6
20 035	Cowley	23,502	39.8	19.7	28,391	60.8	9.0	38.9	30.4	39,756	11.2	29.9	12.5
20 037	Crawford	23,997	41.0	28.3	31,500	62.1	6.9	38.7	28.8	36,125	13.2	35.3	10.0
20 045	Douglas	62,986	26.9	47.8	93,058	70.8	7.4	38.1	18.5	48,528	7.5	26.9	18.8
20 051	Ellis	17,573	38.4	31.7	23,275	75.5	5.5	46.5	20.6	42,651	8.1	29.4	13.9
20 055	Finney	21,274	55.3	17.6	26,302	73.9	3.9	51.8	13.4	47,215	12.5	19.8	15.9
20 057	Ford	20,127	52.7	18.2	24,942	69.9	8.4	47.1	19.2	50,021	14.5	19.6	12.7
20 059	Franklin	17,033	44.7	21.6	19,828	68.0	7.4	43.4	25.7	49,528	8.5	23.0	13.7
20 061	Geary	19,723	38.2	19.1	26,008	72.4	7.4	52.4	17.7	46,000	9.2	17.1	9.9
20 079	Harvey	23,035	43.0	25.8	27,308	64.4	7.7	38.1	28.9	46,899	9.3	25.2	15.0
20 091	Johnson	369,068	20.0	51.5	424,959	73.4	5.5	50.0	17.8	73,021	4.3	13.3	34.1
20 099	Labette	14,329	40.7	20.9	16,746	63.4	7.6	41.7	32.2	39,805	9.8	31.3	6.4
20 103	Leavenworth	51,931	40.4	29.2	60,206	61.6	8.2	42.0	25.0	61,709	8.3	19.2	25.4
20 111	Lyon	20,086	45.5	24.7	26,810	69.4	7.8	38.6	25.1	40,225	13.2	31.0	9.0
20 113	McPherson	19,859	40.4	26.1	23,296	67.2	3.9	45.1	22.1	53,851	4.3	18.0	20.5
20 121	Miami	21,691	38.0	23.2	25,109	67.2	8.6	43.7	24.8	60,018	6.1	17.0	26.9
20 125	Montgomery	23,111	45.0	16.8	27,590	61.3	12.8	36.9	32.4	39,322	14.3	33.1	9.0
20 149	Pottawatomie	13,826	37.8	29.5	16,220	70.5	3.3	49.8	21.6	55,244	5.2	20.0	16.8
20 155	Reno	43,364	39.7	18.7	50,989	62.1	6.5	42.2	28.9	42,496	8.7	26.4	12.2
20 161	Riley	35,585	23.3	45.3	61,145	68.2	3.7	41.5	19.0	44,414	6.6	27.5	15.0
20 169	Saline	36,745	44.2	24.1	43,285	69.8	5.9	45.5	23.5	45,164	13.4	27.0	13.5
20 173	Sedgwick	318,010	38.9	28.4	380,690	68.8	9.2	44.3	23.9	48,511	11.0	24.3	16.8
20 175	Seward	12,997	64.3	11.4	16,418	69.6	9.7	49.1	18.8	48,198	13.2	22.0	12.1
20 177	Shawnee	119,339	41.2	28.7	139,375	66.0	7.9	42.4	27.9	46,847	13.0	24.6	16.7
20 191	Sumner	15,811	46.5	19.7	18,518	64.1	8.1	43.0	28.4	47,729	10.6	23.3	13.0
20 209	Wyandotte	98,389	54.1	15.2	117,984	66.7	13.7	38.7	28.9	38,940	19.3	31.8	9.6
21 000	**Kentucky**	2,922,675	51.2	21.1	3,454,206	60.0	10.2	37.5	32.8	41,782	14.6	31.1	14.3
21 003	Allen	13,531	59.5	12.3	16,055	59.0	14.8	33.7	36.8	37,291	14.6	35.3	6.7
21 005	Anderson	14,552	55.2	18.5	16,791	67.3	8.4	41.7	25.6	54,347	9.0	20.6	11.6
21 009	Barren	28,878	64.6	12.7	33,259	60.5	8.3	37.2	33.7	38,603	17.8	35.5	9.1
21 013	Bell	19,711	68.8	10.2	23,068	43.1	14.4	24.8	48.6	25,209	28.3	49.8	4.5
21 015	Boone	78,400	37.6	29.1	90,694	70.9	6.6	46.6	20.1	65,042	7.6	16.3	25.5
21 019	Boyd	35,064	51.4	14.4	40,100	51.1	11.7	31.5	40.8	38,933	12.8	31.9	14.3
21 021	Boyle	19,350	50.5	22.1	23,194	57.4	11.0	30.5	33.7	39,101	12.8	31.4	10.3
21 027	Breckinridge	13,823	67.6	9.3	15,800	53.4	14.6	31.4	39.0	39,755	14.1	32.5	6.5
21 029	Bullitt	50,443	56.5	13.0	59,197	68.1	8.6	42.3	24.9	53,748	8.0	19.3	17.0
21 035	Calloway	22,663	45.5	25.8	31,264	62.7	10.3	34.2	30.6	40,304	8.5	32.4	11.1
21 037	Campbell	59,940	42.4	28.0	72,696	68.2	9.0	41.4	26.7	53,080	11.2	24.7	19.8
21 043	Carter	18,448	63.9	9.3	21,972	53.3	11.2	29.6	39.0	36,726	15.3	35.6	10.8
21 047	Christian	42,923	48.9	14.4	55,199	62.3	12.0	41.6	28.4	37,463	17.4	32.7	9.1
21 049	Clark	24,800	54.2	18.6	28,283	61.2	10.0	39.1	33.7	43,797	12.6	28.4	18.1
21 051	Clay	14,958	76.2	7.9	17,461	38.2	23.9	22.1	56.9	20,925	30.9	56.0	4.7
21 059	Daviess	65,254	52.3	19.0	76,150	61.2	7.6	40.1	31.4	44,858	13.0	29.0	12.7
21 067	Fayette	194,695	32.6	39.8	243,487	69.0	8.8	42.2	23.2	47,785	11.4	27.1	20.2
21 071	Floyd	27,133	62.1	11.9	31,362	41.9	9.5	27.6	51.4	27,788	24.5	45.0	10.5
21 073	Franklin	34,094	47.4	27.4	40,008	60.2	9.2	38.9	30.4	44,972	14.4	24.5	17.1
21 081	Grant	15,699	59.2	12.8	18,482	63.1	11.8	41.8	26.6	46,813	13.1	23.0	12.8
21 083	Graves	25,416	56.1	16.3	29,170	56.9	10.8	34.5	38.0	36,927	13.8	34.3	11.3
21 085	Grayson	17,427	67.7	8.0	20,333	55.3	12.1	34.0	37.6	34,020	17.4	38.4	9.0
21 089	Greenup	26,000	54.7	15.7	29,618	52.0	13.1	30.7	41.4	42,443	12.9	30.4	13.3
21 093	Hardin	68,878	45.6	20.2	82,648	65.6	9.3	44.6	24.7	47,469	12.7	25.4	15.7
21 095	Harlan	19,901	65.2	11.0	23,134	38.4	10.1	23.8	49.9	25,718	28.5	49.1	7.1
21 101	Henderson	31,807	53.5	17.8	36,720	60.3	11.9	36.8	34.6	39,947	13.2	31.3	11.2
21 107	Hopkins	32,557	55.0	13.8	37,020	58.5	9.6	37.7	36.9	40,979	15.7	31.3	13.0
21 111	Jefferson	506,637	39.9	30.2	592,964	65.8	11.0	40.5	29.4	45,482	13.0	27.7	17.9
21 113	Jessamine	31,673	45.1	26.6	38,083	65.3	8.4	39.6	24.7	46,522	15.9	26.9	18.4

Table B-2. Counties — What: Education, Employment, and Income, 2010–2012—Continued

State or county code	State or county	Educational attainment			Employment status				Percent of households with no workers	Median household income (dollars)	Percent of families with income below poverty	Percent of households with income less than $25,000	Percent of households with income of $100,000 or more
		Total population 25 years and over	Percent with a high school diploma or less	Percent with a bachelor's degree or more	Total population 16 years and over	Percent in the labor force	Unemployment rate	Percent who worked full-time year-round					
	ACS table number:	C15002	C15002	C15002	B23025	B23025	B23025	C20005	C08202	B19013	C17013	C19001	C19001
	Column number:	1	2	3	4	5	6	7	8	9	10	11	12
	Kentucky—Cont.												
21 115	Johnson	16,146	66.5	10.0	18,588	44.9	9.4	30.6	44.6	34,126	20.8	37.4	7.2
21 117	Kenton	106,725	42.0	28.7	124,979	67.7	9.4	43.1	24.7	52,555	11.3	23.1	18.8
21 121	Knox	21,113	72.3	11.1	25,047	44.2	16.4	26.8	51.8	26,047	26.8	48.7	7.7
21 125	Laurel	40,160	62.3	12.3	46,233	54.5	13.0	35.3	39.9	35,738	17.3	36.1	8.3
21 133	Letcher	17,033	59.9	10.8	19,546	45.7	11.2	30.7	47.2	33,447	17.5	41.4	13.8
21 137	Lincoln	16,653	68.0	10.2	19,210	53.8	14.3	33.2	42.3	33,164	22.5	41.6	8.6
21 141	Logan	18,249	65.5	11.9	21,117	56.3	10.2	35.8	35.5	35,588	15.2	33.4	8.8
21 145	McCracken	46,127	44.3	21.5	52,562	59.7	8.3	39.0	34.5	44,910	12.4	28.6	16.1
21 151	Madison	51,675	45.1	27.5	68,001	62.1	10.1	33.5	31.0	40,065	14.9	33.5	12.9
21 155	Marion	13,606	62.7	11.4	15,611	56.3	7.4	36.4	32.9	36,676	16.8	36.8	6.1
21 157	Marshall	22,625	55.2	16.6	25,720	55.5	8.5	37.7	37.1	44,123	7.9	25.8	12.1
21 163	Meade	18,760	51.3	14.0	22,012	61.2	11.9	39.1	27.9	48,529	14.9	24.2	13.8
21 167	Mercer	14,720	55.0	20.0	16,994	60.9	14.7	33.8	36.1	41,234	13.8	33.7	13.4
21 173	Montgomery	18,044	59.0	16.5	20,724	55.9	13.8	35.5	37.5	35,534	19.1	34.4	9.7
21 177	Muhlenberg	21,992	64.4	10.0	25,555	49.3	6.9	35.6	37.1	39,082	13.5	34.3	10.9
21 179	Nelson	29,168	57.6	16.0	34,111	63.2	12.9	40.7	25.9	41,976	13.5	26.0	13.4
21 183	Ohio	16,132	65.3	7.4	18,615	53.3	6.9	37.0	38.0	38,924	16.0	33.5	8.8
21 185	Oldham	40,380	31.4	38.8	46,189	64.4	6.2	42.4	18.3	77,659	6.8	12.3	37.1
21 193	Perry	19,760	64.9	13.2	23,106	49.9	13.4	33.1	42.9	31,250	24.0	40.1	8.9
21 195	Pike	45,164	65.2	11.8	51,902	43.7	9.5	29.4	47.4	31,110	19.2	41.4	9.5
21 199	Pulaski	44,147	58.4	15.6	50,865	55.5	9.3	33.9	36.2	32,805	17.2	39.2	9.7
21 205	Rowan	13,747	54.0	21.7	19,352	50.9	8.8	28.5	34.9	34,666	22.6	37.7	11.5
21 209	Scott	30,891	44.8	26.9	36,490	70.5	9.5	47.3	23.6	60,161	8.9	18.9	21.1
21 211	Shelby	28,850	46.1	24.3	33,419	64.8	9.5	41.7	23.0	54,016	7.4	19.2	22.5
21 217	Taylor	16,133	61.4	13.8	19,883	58.5	10.8	37.5	35.6	35,471	14.8	34.6	7.7
21 227	Warren	70,276	44.8	27.1	92,114	66.2	10.8	37.9	26.7	41,184	14.2	31.0	14.4
21 231	Wayne	14,418	70.6	8.0	16,621	49.3	18.4	25.8	47.2	27,165	24.4	45.6	4.7
21 235	Whitley	22,963	66.7	11.3	28,048	50.4	11.0	29.1	40.7	30,568	18.6	42.3	8.0
21 239	Woodford	17,306	45.6	28.5	19,904	66.9	8.2	43.5	25.2	56,407	8.0	21.0	20.8
22 000	**Louisiana**	2,980,393	51.9	21.5	3,580,858	61.5	9.2	40.0	28.4	43,484	15.3	30.5	17.1
22 001	Acadia	39,442	68.0	8.5	47,243	58.2	10.0	37.0	30.3	36,192	17.1	35.2	11.1
22 003	Allen	18,114	65.4	10.4	20,879	43.9	7.5	30.8	34.8	36,583	13.0	33.5	13.4
22 005	Ascension	69,479	48.4	23.2	82,043	68.6	6.9	46.6	21.9	66,575	10.3	18.9	27.9
22 007	Assumption	15,276	69.9	9.8	18,294	55.8	14.0	35.9	34.8	43,992	15.1	31.9	12.7
22 009	Avoyelles	28,099	69.8	8.9	32,761	51.8	12.5	32.1	36.1	33,197	16.9	39.2	9.7
22 011	Beauregard	23,693	57.8	16.5	27,979	56.3	7.4	35.7	27.9	44,807	13.9	30.1	16.8
22 015	Bossier	77,581	44.7	23.9	92,288	68.6	6.1	48.1	22.0	53,096	11.4	23.0	20.2
22 017	Caddo	168,404	47.6	23.2	200,615	61.3	8.1	41.0	28.4	40,546	15.9	32.1	16.6
22 019	Calcasieu	125,189	52.4	19.6	150,467	61.4	9.3	37.2	29.6	42,059	13.5	30.4	16.7
22 029	Concordia	13,787	65.0	11.0	16,034	52.3	18.3	30.6	40.4	29,990	25.0	43.0	9.9
22 031	De Soto	18,034	64.1	10.9	21,195	57.9	10.5	36.9	34.0	40,385	16.6	35.7	12.8
22 033	East Baton Rouge	276,213	37.5	34.4	351,723	67.3	8.6	42.0	23.1	47,640	12.8	27.3	20.1
22 037	East Feliciana	14,192	63.1	13.8	16,520	49.8	7.8	35.4	29.8	46,505	12.1	30.9	16.3
22 039	Evangeline	21,435	68.5	12.0	25,626	47.5	7.4	32.3	37.4	30,925	21.9	44.1	11.1
22 041	Franklin	13,740	64.1	13.4	15,853	54.0	11.4	30.6	34.1	30,728	25.5	42.0	13.0
22 043	Grant	15,345	65.3	9.6	17,816	46.1	10.2	32.4	38.1	35,383	12.6	34.8	8.9
22 045	Iberia	46,732	62.9	14.9	55,954	62.0	10.6	39.0	27.3	43,939	20.2	29.5	15.6
22 047	Iberville	22,695	62.5	12.6	26,627	53.0	10.3	34.7	31.3	41,912	15.4	34.0	13.7
22 051	Jefferson	297,658	48.8	23.0	348,092	64.9	8.1	44.2	25.8	46,511	13.2	26.6	18.2
22 053	Jefferson Davis	20,593	61.5	13.6	24,077	54.9	9.9	35.0	33.5	39,790	19.4	37.6	15.5
22 055	Lafayette	142,600	44.8	27.5	175,938	68.4	6.9	43.2	22.2	48,757	13.7	28.3	21.4
22 057	Lafourche	63,288	66.0	15.0	76,077	61.0	6.7	41.3	26.5	47,843	10.1	26.8	18.4
22 061	Lincoln	25,540	42.4	34.5	38,226	58.8	11.5	32.2	30.5	35,629	20.6	39.5	12.5
22 063	Livingston	84,096	56.4	17.9	98,613	65.9	8.1	45.4	24.1	55,479	10.7	22.7	20.3
22 067	Morehouse	18,367	63.0	12.2	21,671	50.8	10.8	37.4	36.0	26,865	24.1	46.9	7.3
22 069	Natchitoches	23,769	54.6	21.5	31,015	58.8	9.1	35.1	33.3	33,459	20.4	40.4	14.0
22 071	Orleans	239,521	40.3	33.0	290,873	62.0	12.8	38.2	31.9	36,004	23.2	37.8	15.6
22 073	Ouachita	97,342	49.6	22.1	118,729	60.4	8.1	41.1	28.2	36,951	19.8	34.5	14.9
22 075	Plaquemines	15,236	58.7	13.9	18,008	61.5	5.5	45.7	26.7	55,796	8.8	21.0	24.5
22 077	Pointe Coupee	15,600	61.5	11.9	17,831	57.4	6.8	39.0	32.5	45,438	13.0	30.0	13.9
22 079	Rapides	86,477	53.4	17.3	102,124	56.6	8.5	37.8	33.1	40,255	17.1	33.3	13.2
22 083	Richland	13,542	64.6	12.2	16,061	56.0	12.5	37.3	31.7	40,524	16.6	35.8	9.1
22 085	Sabine	16,334	59.1	13.6	19,110	54.3	12.9	33.5	37.8	36,634	16.1	37.2	14.4
22 087	St. Bernard	25,026	60.0	11.7	30,188	61.3	12.3	43.1	26.2	41,713	15.7	29.8	15.1
22 089	St. Charles	34,078	48.4	20.1	40,397	67.6	8.0	45.0	23.2	55,259	10.4	20.1	25.5
22 093	St. James	14,279	61.5	12.3	16,993	60.9	13.0	40.1	32.6	50,518	17.8	29.3	20.6
22 095	St. John the Baptist	28,866	56.0	15.4	34,679	65.2	11.8	40.1	27.5	53,458	13.1	22.5	17.9
22 097	St. Landry	53,398	66.1	13.9	63,253	53.9	6.7	39.6	35.3	35,221	21.8	39.4	11.3
22 099	St. Martin	34,180	68.3	13.2	40,382	61.3	8.9	39.2	29.8	40,342	15.7	33.6	14.4
22 101	St. Mary	35,538	68.2	10.9	42,158	57.9	14.1	35.4	34.1	40,051	19.6	34.0	12.7
22 103	St. Tammany	159,182	39.6	29.4	184,093	63.7	8.2	41.9	25.1	58,781	8.5	20.1	26.0
22 105	Tangipahoa	76,538	54.7	19.0	95,141	62.1	13.3	36.2	30.4	38,937	18.9	35.0	13.6
22 109	Terrebonne	71,701	64.7	12.8	86,234	61.0	7.4	41.3	23.6	48,548	14.0	26.3	18.6
22 111	Union	15,349	64.6	11.7	18,099	50.6	10.0	34.5	38.3	34,255	24.4	37.9	9.8
22 113	Vermilion	37,807	65.6	13.5	44,382	61.7	9.3	38.6	30.0	45,662	11.3	29.2	15.5
22 115	Vernon	31,371	51.8	19.6	39,741	63.6	6.1	50.5	23.6	47,037	9.7	22.7	13.2
22 117	Washington	31,405	63.9	10.9	36,602	50.0	16.8	27.6	42.6	31,210	21.6	42.2	8.4
22 119	Webster	27,951	63.0	12.8	32,555	53.3	12.1	32.2	37.3	35,395	18.6	36.8	10.7
22 121	West Baton Rouge	15,634	54.3	17.9	18,782	65.7	8.6	45.3	26.4	48,397	13.6	28.7	23.5

Table B-2. Counties — What: Education, Employment, and Income, 2010–2012—*Continued*

State or county code	State or county	Educational attainment			Employment status				Percent of households with no workers	Median household income (dollars)	Percent of families with income below poverty	Percent of households with income less than $25,000	Percent of households with income of $100,000 or more
		Total population 25 years and over	Percent with a high school diploma or less	Percent with a bachelor's degree or more	Total population 16 years and over	Percent in the labor force	Unemployment rate	Percent who worked full-time year-round					
	ACS table number:	C15002	C15002	C15002	B23025	B23025	B23025	C20005	C08202	B19013	C17013	C19001	C19001
	Column number:	1	2	3	4	5	6	7	8	9	10	11	12
23 000	**Maine**	942,582	43.1	27.8	1,091,925	64.4	8.1	38.8	30.7	47,344	9.3	26.0	16.2
23 001	Androscoggin	73,541	50.1	19.3	86,269	66.2	9.9	39.9	30.9	44,518	12.0	28.8	14.1
23 003	Aroostook	51,498	53.7	16.7	59,077	57.3	8.1	34.8	38.5	37,195	10.5	35.0	8.8
23 005	Cumberland	199,175	31.1	41.5	231,910	69.4	6.5	42.6	25.6	58,065	7.3	20.7	24.1
23 007	Franklin	21,245	48.7	22.6	25,530	63.5	9.4	33.7	31.5	38,973	11.1	29.3	11.0
23 009	Hancock	40,468	39.8	33.5	45,997	64.8	8.7	37.4	33.4	44,432	10.0	29.0	15.5
23 011	Kennebec	86,339	45.2	23.9	100,257	63.3	9.2	41.3	32.0	46,353	8.5	25.6	15.0
23 013	Knox	29,567	43.9	30.1	32,996	62.9	5.8	36.7	32.0	48,026	6.5	23.7	14.8
23 015	Lincoln	25,932	40.3	30.3	28,827	58.7	6.2	37.0	33.4	48,059	9.1	20.9	13.9
23 017	Oxford	41,515	55.8	18.7	47,108	61.0	11.2	34.0	34.3	40,286	12.6	31.1	10.3
23 019	Penobscot	103,943	45.6	23.3	127,672	62.2	8.4	36.3	31.3	42,334	11.0	30.4	13.3
23 023	Sagadahoc	25,681	39.2	32.1	28,691	65.6	6.4	39.8	29.0	52,248	8.2	20.9	18.1
23 025	Somerset	37,514	55.1	15.3	42,399	57.7	9.6	34.2	37.6	38,350	12.9	31.7	9.5
23 027	Waldo	27,808	46.2	28.0	31,817	62.9	8.9	36.0	32.5	40,094	10.6	31.2	10.1
23 029	Washington	23,860	51.2	19.8	27,189	55.1	11.4	28.5	40.1	36,647	14.1	34.9	7.5
23 031	York	141,386	41.0	28.6	161,690	67.8	7.4	42.2	26.9	56,104	6.4	20.0	20.2
24 000	**Maryland**	3,922,966	37.3	36.6	4,649,740	69.0	8.6	46.0	22.0	71,707	7.0	16.1	34.6
24 001	Allegany	52,012	55.9	16.5	63,040	52.4	9.5	31.0	38.4	39,166	10.4	32.6	12.1
24 003	Anne Arundel	370,153	34.6	36.6	433,543	71.3	6.7	49.6	18.9	86,454	4.1	10.8	42.4
24 005	Baltimore	552,757	37.5	35.4	655,843	67.1	8.3	44.4	24.2	64,306	6.3	16.5	28.8
24 009	Calvert	59,075	39.7	29.7	69,710	71.9	7.2	50.0	18.4	92,517	4.0	10.6	46.0
24 011	Caroline	21,866	59.9	13.9	25,666	65.1	9.6	42.5	25.3	58,006	10.4	21.5	21.4
24 013	Carroll	112,551	39.6	32.5	133,042	69.4	5.5	47.0	21.3	82,581	3.3	11.9	40.4
24 015	Cecil	67,187	49.2	21.7	79,700	66.8	10.3	43.9	24.9	64,763	7.7	19.2	28.0
24 017	Charles	97,104	39.3	26.3	115,615	71.3	8.1	53.2	17.6	91,801	5.5	11.3	44.7
24 019	Dorchester	23,102	55.2	19.6	26,616	64.5	13.3	39.0	33.6	42,885	13.2	29.3	14.3
24 021	Frederick	157,886	33.6	38.0	185,194	72.3	6.5	47.9	18.8	82,311	4.0	11.4	40.5
24 023	Garrett	21,094	56.5	18.6	24,544	60.2	7.3	37.5	31.6	44,223	9.7	27.9	14.4
24 025	Harford	166,795	37.1	32.1	194,632	70.1	7.9	46.8	20.8	78,448	6.1	13.4	36.0
24 027	Howard	197,243	19.4	59.7	229,383	73.1	5.3	51.6	14.2	106,222	3.6	7.3	53.7
24 029	Kent	14,163	46.7	27.7	17,176	57.9	8.2	35.5	35.2	53,854	6.7	25.4	20.5
24 031	Montgomery	680,294	23.3	56.8	782,928	72.5	6.6	48.8	17.7	94,767	4.6	10.5	48.0
24 033	Prince George's	567,395	41.5	29.8	692,819	73.3	10.0	49.4	16.9	72,254	6.8	12.6	33.0
24 035	Queen Anne's	33,350	38.4	34.8	38,468	69.6	7.5	45.3	21.1	85,334	5.8	12.1	40.9
24 037	St. Mary's	68,948	40.6	29.9	83,114	69.7	5.6	49.7	16.7	86,209	5.5	11.6	40.8
24 039	Somerset	17,011	62.7	15.1	22,702	39.6	7.6	26.3	35.8	37,733	14.8	34.1	9.5
24 041	Talbot	27,994	39.3	33.2	31,560	61.7	9.2	35.8	33.5	59,307	7.0	18.4	26.6
24 043	Washington	102,440	52.2	19.1	119,014	63.5	9.4	41.4	28.0	54,239	9.4	22.5	20.5
24 045	Wicomico	62,920	46.2	27.8	79,967	64.2	11.4	38.3	27.0	50,523	12.0	24.6	19.3
24 047	Worcester	38,312	44.0	26.3	43,225	60.8	10.8	36.1	34.4	58,687	6.0	18.9	24.0
24 510	Baltimore city	411,314	50.1	26.1	502,239	62.2	15.4	37.6	33.5	39,788	20.2	34.6	14.8
25 000	**Massachusetts**	4,509,799	36.7	39.2	5,368,399	67.6	9.2	40.7	26.3	65,029	8.3	20.8	31.4
25 001	Barnstable	164,317	30.7	39.2	184,239	59.2	8.7	33.2	36.6	58,751	6.8	20.7	24.9
25 003	Berkshire	93,228	42.7	30.5	108,878	62.4	9.5	33.5	34.1	46,206	9.9	27.5	17.0
25 005	Bristol	376,520	48.1	25.7	444,588	66.4	11.1	38.6	29.1	54,221	9.5	24.9	23.9
25 009	Essex	512,703	37.7	36.5	599,751	67.9	9.1	41.5	26.2	66,089	9.0	20.7	32.0
25 011	Franklin	51,966	35.9	33.0	59,543	68.4	8.3	39.0	26.2	52,308	7.7	21.2	17.5
25 013	Hampden	306,779	47.1	24.9	370,501	62.7	11.4	36.0	32.7	49,080	13.6	28.8	20.0
25 015	Hampshire	98,035	31.3	43.1	137,230	65.5	7.8	33.6	25.6	59,679	6.7	20.9	25.8
25 017	Middlesex	1,056,856	30.0	50.3	1,239,488	70.1	7.4	44.4	22.1	80,150	5.5	15.8	40.0
25 021	Norfolk	471,064	28.4	48.6	545,269	69.1	8.2	43.6	23.9	82,468	4.3	15.2	41.6
25 023	Plymouth	339,192	38.2	33.4	395,432	68.4	9.8	40.3	24.6	72,633	5.7	16.3	34.4
25 025	Suffolk	479,917	40.9	39.8	620,508	68.0	11.4	39.4	28.2	51,153	17.3	30.2	24.7
25 027	Worcester	540,001	39.2	33.7	641,401	67.6	9.7	40.9	25.6	63,687	8.2	20.4	29.2
26 000	**Michigan**	6,593,489	41.7	25.7	7,861,941	61.7	13.1	34.4	32.7	47,175	12.4	26.5	17.4
26 005	Allegan	74,208	49.5	19.8	86,706	62.4	9.2	35.9	29.1	49,394	11.3	23.1	14.9
26 007	Alpena	21,202	45.9	16.3	24,109	57.6	11.9	29.5	39.9	37,895	12.5	32.4	10.3
26 009	Antrim	17,261	43.0	25.0	19,399	56.0	14.0	27.6	40.5	43,934	10.9	26.0	12.3
26 015	Barry	40,413	46.9	18.1	46,534	62.0	10.2	36.7	29.6	52,211	7.5	19.2	16.5
26 017	Bay	74,792	46.5	18.6	86,722	60.1	11.7	35.0	35.8	45,064	10.0	26.8	13.7
26 021	Berrien	106,960	44.0	24.6	124,512	61.1	12.6	34.8	33.2	43,303	12.5	29.5	14.8
26 023	Branch	30,131	55.7	12.9	34,869	54.9	11.2	34.4	33.8	40,438	13.9	29.8	10.6
26 025	Calhoun	90,901	46.6	18.8	107,144	60.5	13.8	34.4	33.8	40,771	14.1	30.3	13.5
26 027	Cass	36,363	50.4	16.1	41,908	59.7	10.8	35.0	32.7	43,921	9.5	25.5	12.6
26 029	Charlevoix	18,711	41.4	26.1	21,246	61.1	10.3	33.4	35.1	44,756	9.5	25.6	13.7
26 031	Cheboygan	19,112	52.9	16.7	21,570	53.5	16.8	26.8	43.6	37,573	15.1	32.3	9.5
26 033	Chippewa	26,929	48.0	19.1	32,009	53.3	15.0	29.0	39.0	38,996	14.5	33.8	9.2
26 035	Clare	22,006	56.0	11.1	25,316	47.2	18.1	23.5	50.9	31,539	22.4	40.7	5.9
26 037	Clinton	49,297	35.4	26.4	59,878	64.6	8.5	38.8	28.2	58,251	6.5	19.5	21.7
26 041	Delta	26,594	47.3	17.0	30,145	58.7	11.7	31.6	38.9	39,904	11.5	33.5	8.9
26 043	Dickinson	18,900	48.2	20.6	21,309	58.4	9.7	36.4	34.5	42,468	8.3	29.2	14.1
26 045	Eaton	73,526	36.8	24.2	86,467	64.4	11.1	39.3	29.8	53,878	7.6	20.2	16.7
26 047	Emmet	22,988	34.7	31.8	26,623	64.3	10.4	34.8	32.3	50,000	7.3	23.6	17.2
26 049	Genesee	279,802	44.9	18.8	330,702	57.3	17.5	29.4	39.6	40,860	16.8	30.7	12.7

Table B-2. Counties — What: Education, Employment, and Income, 2010–2012—Continued

State or county code	State or county	Educational attainment			Employment status				Percent of households with no workers	Median household income (dollars)	Percent of families with income below poverty	Percent of households with income less than $25,000	Percent of households with income of $100,000 or more
		Total population 25 years and over	Percent with a high school diploma or less	Percent with a bachelor's degree or more	Total population 16 years and over	Percent in the labor force	Unemployment rate	Percent who worked full-time year-round					
	ACS table number:	C15002	C15002	C15002	B23025	B23025	B23025	C20005	C08202	B19013	C17013	C19001	C19001
	Column number:	1	2	3	4	5	6	7	8	9	10	11	12
	Michigan—Cont.												
26 051	Gladwin	18,862	55.7	11.9	21,210	47.1	15.1	25.2	48.4	37,137	14.8	32.3	7.3
26 055	Grand Traverse	62,179	35.7	29.6	71,337	65.2	9.1	34.6	28.8	50,275	8.4	24.6	18.8
26 057	Gratiot	28,502	53.1	13.8	34,327	53.2	11.9	31.7	33.9	40,486	14.8	30.9	10.6
26 059	Hillsdale	31,103	54.6	15.0	37,073	57.5	13.1	32.5	35.8	41,260	14.0	28.0	9.8
26 061	Houghton	21,678	44.3	27.7	29,838	55.8	10.1	27.2	38.1	35,323	13.4	36.2	8.9
26 063	Huron	24,007	58.5	14.1	26,980	56.8	10.5	32.4	40.6	39,925	10.4	29.6	8.6
26 065	Ingham	167,939	31.3	35.6	230,193	63.2	10.9	32.4	29.3	43,971	14.7	30.4	16.6
26 067	Ionia	42,445	51.2	13.8	49,609	60.1	12.5	33.9	30.9	47,392	13.0	26.0	11.9
26 069	Iosco	19,566	51.7	14.0	21,795	47.1	15.7	23.5	52.4	34,989	13.0	32.4	7.4
26 073	Isabella	35,676	43.9	25.1	59,600	61.5	13.8	25.1	31.3	35,536	15.7	37.9	11.3
26 075	Jackson	108,710	45.2	18.5	127,783	58.2	13.1	32.9	34.6	44,071	13.5	28.9	13.3
26 077	Kalamazoo	157,001	31.8	34.3	202,630	65.5	11.5	35.7	30.4	45,453	11.9	28.0	17.4
26 081	Kent	387,362	37.7	31.3	467,811	68.9	10.3	39.7	25.2	50,940	11.2	23.0	17.8
26 087	Lapeer	60,406	48.1	16.0	70,342	60.2	13.6	32.7	32.3	51,435	8.8	20.6	16.1
26 089	Leelanau	16,443	28.9	39.8	18,288	56.6	7.9	29.8	37.5	53,512	6.7	20.8	20.1
26 091	Lenawee	67,133	47.0	19.2	79,535	60.1	11.9	33.1	32.2	46,608	9.1	25.6	12.8
26 093	Livingston	123,745	32.8	32.0	142,924	67.6	8.7	39.9	23.8	71,039	4.8	13.7	30.1
26 099	Macomb	581,469	43.4	22.4	676,281	64.5	12.9	37.1	30.6	51,971	10.4	22.5	19.8
26 101	Manistee	18,240	47.6	19.1	20,710	51.1	14.0	28.0	41.5	39,485	12.0	31.3	8.9
26 103	Marquette	45,100	39.8	28.6	56,571	58.2	8.4	31.5	34.9	44,528	9.0	29.6	14.4
26 105	Mason	20,453	45.1	20.0	23,385	60.7	12.4	31.8	34.8	41,174	11.2	30.6	12.4
26 107	Mecosta	25,579	46.6	20.9	35,709	56.6	17.8	26.0	39.0	38,597	12.5	31.4	10.0
26 109	Menominee	17,463	51.9	15.2	19,699	59.0	11.8	33.5	37.9	40,047	10.3	29.7	6.5
26 111	Midland	56,704	35.7	32.0	67,131	60.4	9.1	36.2	30.8	52,352	8.6	22.7	21.4
26 115	Monroe	102,789	47.0	18.0	120,269	62.8	11.3	36.2	30.8	52,227	9.0	22.0	18.1
26 117	Montcalm	42,947	52.5	14.1	50,210	55.1	13.7	32.4	36.0	39,926	14.0	29.7	9.5
26 121	Muskegon	113,262	47.0	17.2	134,058	59.5	15.5	31.7	35.3	40,158	16.6	31.8	11.7
26 123	Newaygo	32,668	54.8	12.7	38,069	55.9	14.6	30.5	36.9	42,084	14.3	29.2	9.7
26 125	Oakland	838,677	28.1	42.7	967,417	66.9	10.9	40.5	26.3	63,205	7.8	18.7	29.3
26 127	Oceana	17,984	52.1	15.1	20,870	55.0	10.3	28.1	36.1	38,289	14.2	31.5	8.5
26 129	Ogemaw	15,813	57.1	11.5	17,910	48.0	13.8	25.2	48.8	35,379	14.6	35.9	6.7
26 133	Osceola	15,919	56.0	14.5	18,539	53.8	12.3	30.0	38.8	36,879	15.6	32.9	6.5
26 137	Otsego	16,902	46.0	20.4	19,435	59.8	12.6	33.8	34.7	47,821	9.3	21.4	12.0
26 139	Ottawa	164,292	39.7	29.6	205,743	68.1	8.7	38.4	23.5	55,568	7.1	18.5	19.8
26 143	Roscommon	19,126	52.9	13.7	21,078	41.4	15.6	18.9	56.1	33,743	13.1	36.4	7.5
26 145	Saginaw	132,076	48.0	18.8	158,536	58.3	13.8	31.9	37.9	41,793	13.5	29.1	13.0
26 147	St. Clair	111,156	47.5	16.0	129,382	60.9	14.9	31.4	35.2	46,055	11.0	25.3	14.4
26 149	St. Joseph	40,514	54.5	14.6	47,125	59.9	14.1	35.8	32.2	42,677	14.1	27.9	9.9
26 151	Sanilac	29,588	59.5	11.5	34,071	56.7	14.7	33.2	39.3	40,034	10.6	29.7	9.1
26 155	Shiawassee	47,475	48.5	14.3	55,815	60.3	11.7	35.4	33.0	46,717	11.6	25.0	13.0
26 157	Tuscola	38,183	53.7	12.9	44,204	57.8	13.3	31.4	36.2	43,247	11.6	25.4	11.1
26 159	Van Buren	50,965	49.2	17.7	59,345	60.6	10.7	34.3	31.7	45,077	14.6	28.2	13.5
26 161	Washtenaw	216,676	22.7	50.4	286,134	65.6	9.6	37.2	25.8	57,548	8.0	21.8	27.6
26 163	Wayne	1,175,532	46.6	21.1	1,410,759	58.7	19.0	31.0	37.7	40,123	20.0	33.6	14.8
26 165	Wexford	22,505	51.1	16.3	25,664	58.4	14.9	31.3	37.7	38,608	13.2	30.7	8.9
27 000	**Minnesota**	3,562,974	34.7	32.6	4,212,521	70.3	7.4	43.1	24.1	58,434	7.6	20.0	23.8
27 003	Anoka	221,474	36.2	26.5	258,904	73.8	8.4	46.7	19.5	67,469	5.8	13.9	27.9
27 005	Becker	22,549	44.9	21.3	25,662	64.6	5.5	39.8	29.1	48,996	9.8	25.9	14.4
27 007	Beltrami	27,343	36.1	28.5	35,215	65.4	11.0	36.6	29.3	44,186	13.3	27.6	12.9
27 009	Benton	25,400	41.0	21.2	30,239	72.9	8.9	43.2	25.1	52,604	7.4	23.8	16.0
27 013	Blue Earth	37,598	34.4	30.8	53,433	71.8	6.5	39.7	23.5	48,982	8.1	24.6	16.3
27 015	Brown	17,645	47.7	21.2	20,773	69.5	5.3	42.0	27.0	46,779	5.0	22.0	14.2
27 017	Carlton	24,394	42.2	22.1	28,127	61.7	7.3	37.6	30.9	50,566	8.6	24.9	15.4
27 019	Carver	59,292	26.1	43.7	68,701	75.9	6.2	50.9	16.0	83,903	3.3	10.4	39.9
27 021	Cass	20,616	45.8	19.5	23,103	57.8	10.2	32.7	38.6	43,083	13.5	27.1	12.2
27 025	Chisago	36,196	41.9	20.4	41,965	69.2	6.7	41.6	23.0	65,922	4.9	15.1	25.2
27 027	Clay	35,893	35.4	29.6	47,270	73.0	5.7	44.7	23.3	53,404	7.0	24.1	17.3
27 035	Crow Wing	43,768	39.0	21.7	50,196	62.6	9.2	35.9	34.3	47,663	8.5	25.0	13.7
27 037	Dakota	266,996	27.3	38.7	310,361	74.6	7.1	48.0	19.3	72,037	4.8	13.3	32.8
27 039	Dodge	12,915	40.3	24.1	15,089	74.2	4.5	49.6	22.4	64,971	4.8	18.1	24.4
27 041	Douglas	25,675	37.4	24.2	29,474	66.2	6.3	40.6	28.0	51,630	4.9	22.9	17.0
27 045	Fillmore	14,466	49.1	18.5	16,434	66.9	5.6	42.5	28.9	49,034	7.5	23.0	15.2
27 047	Freeborn	22,028	49.3	15.0	25,046	63.7	5.7	40.1	31.9	43,788	9.0	27.4	14.2
27 049	Goodhue	32,171	42.0	22.0	36,550	68.1	6.7	43.3	27.1	55,047	6.2	21.6	21.5
27 053	Hennepin	793,606	26.1	45.8	933,732	72.2	8.0	44.7	22.3	62,448	8.9	19.4	29.0
27 057	Hubbard	14,802	39.7	23.2	16,613	59.2	6.3	35.0	35.6	43,547	7.3	25.4	12.4
27 059	Isanti	25,427	45.7	16.3	29,614	70.9	9.4	41.0	20.4	57,609	5.3	16.4	18.8
27 061	Itasca	32,275	42.3	21.4	36,589	58.7	10.0	29.9	37.0	45,599	8.7	25.4	12.2
27 067	Kandiyohi	28,222	41.4	21.6	33,494	69.2	7.7	41.6	26.5	48,446	8.9	23.2	15.9
27 079	Le Sueur	18,831	44.2	22.6	21,520	72.3	6.6	44.9	24.9	57,346	6.8	17.3	19.4
27 083	Lyon	16,101	42.7	27.6	20,086	73.5	5.2	46.6	23.5	49,321	7.3	25.4	18.2
27 085	McLeod	24,631	45.6	19.0	28,327	70.2	6.1	45.4	26.6	54,327	5.7	19.2	18.4
27 091	Martin	14,792	50.4	17.6	16,659	65.3	4.3	40.8	30.4	51,375	6.9	23.7	14.8
27 093	Meeker	15,798	48.7	17.6	17,995	67.4	7.2	40.9	27.4	51,239	7.0	21.1	13.3
27 095	Mille Lacs	17,635	48.9	14.6	20,182	62.9	9.2	36.1	30.8	45,153	10.5	26.7	13.8
27 097	Morrison	22,700	50.2	16.3	26,077	68.2	8.5	41.3	29.3	45,459	7.3	26.1	11.6
27 099	Mower	25,950	45.7	17.6	30,569	68.0	7.0	40.3	30.6	45,518	11.5	28.9	14.4

Table B-2. Counties — What: Education, Employment, and Income, 2010–2012—Continued

State or county code	State or county	Educational attainment			Employment status			Percent who worked full-time year-round	Percent of households with no workers	Median household income (dollars)	Percent of families with income below poverty	Percent of households with income less than $25,000	Percent of households with income of $100,000 or more
		Total population 25 years and over	Percent with a high school diploma or less	Percent with a bachelor's degree or more	Total population 16 years and over	Percent in the labor force	Unemployment rate						
	ACS table number:	C15002	C15002	C15002	B23025	B23025	B23025	C20005	C08202	E19013	C17013	C19001	C19001
	Column number:	1	2	3	4	5	6	7	8	9	10	11	12
	Minnesota—Cont.												
27 103	Nicollet	20,708	32.3	34.4	26,433	74.3	4.8	46.4	21.2	58,189	5.4	16.5	19.3
27 105	Nobles	13,975	54.1	15.4	16,527	67.2	5.8	44.3	29.0	44,917	12.3	27.6	14.3
27 109	Olmsted	98,229	28.4	39.1	113,103	72.7	3.9	47.4	19.5	64,877	4.3	16.9	27.4
27 111	Otter Tail	41,179	41.4	22.8	46,599	63.2	5.6	38.6	32.3	49,550	7.5	24.4	15.3
27 115	Pine	21,185	55.4	13.1	24,004	60.9	9.7	35.0	32.2	44,586	10.5	26.1	11.1
27 119	Polk	20,980	41.9	21.5	24,935	66.5	5.8	40.4	27.3	50,396	8.5	25.8	17.6
27 123	Ramsey	334,598	33.4	38.5	408,734	68.6	9.0	40.0	25.5	52,834	12.1	23.3	21.5
27 131	Rice	39,913	42.3	28.3	51,753	69.1	7.1	37.0	23.4	60,036	7.9	20.1	22.7
27 137	St. Louis	135,885	36.7	25.7	166,150	61.9	9.5	33.2	33.3	44,969	10.3	28.7	14.7
27 139	Scott	84,519	29.2	39.0	97,644	77.7	6.2	51.6	14.0	82,867	3.7	10.4	39.0
27 141	Sherburne	56,114	33.0	24.5	66,443	74.3	7.7	45.5	17.3	69,769	5.7	12.7	24.9
27 145	Stearns	92,807	39.3	24.7	120,074	71.6	7.2	41.6	23.2	53,541	7.2	21.2	18.5
27 147	Steele	24,256	44.0	25.2	27,972	71.2	6.8	45.6	26.7	54,952	6.4	20.7	18.1
27 153	Todd	16,797	50.9	14.0	19,480	63.2	7.3	38.6	31.5	44,765	10.6	28.0	10.9
27 157	Wabasha	14,948	45.3	20.3	17,006	69.4	5.8	46.8	26.2	54,629	5.6	19.0	20.1
27 163	Washington	160,650	26.5	41.2	185,987	72.6	5.8	46.6	19.6	80,537	4.4	11.5	37.2
27 169	Winona	30,689	41.7	26.0	42,865	71.2	8.8	37.7	24.7	45,809	5.8	27.9	15.8
27 171	Wright	80,410	36.3	28.0	92,479	76.3	7.0	49.3	17.8	70,586	4.4	12.7	30.0
28 000	**Mississippi**	1,914,622	49.0	20.0	2,311,888	58.5	11.6	37.3	31.9	37,792	18.2	34.7	12.4
28 001	Adams	22,629	57.0	16.2	26,122	46.4	10.0	30.9	39.1	25,829	24.8	48.6	7.8
28 003	Alcorn	24,917	54.8	18.1	28,945	58.2	12.2	34.7	38.9	32,142	13.8	36.8	11.5
28 011	Bolivar	21,111	51.1	20.5	26,255	57.4	17.6	32.5	37.5	28,619	28.8	44.4	8.9
28 025	Clay	13,365	52.4	20.3	15,922	56.4	18.9	31.5	35.3	29,935	23.5	41.9	11.0
28 027	Coahoma	15,537	52.1	16.9	19,188	54.3	19.6	30.3	41.3	25,328	32.9	49.2	5.7
28 029	Copiah	18,705	55.3	13.3	22,621	54.7	15.3	35.1	35.5	34,131	21.5	39.9	9.9
28 031	Covington	13,166	59.5	14.4	15,594	52.4	13.0	32.3	39.6	31,508	22.6	41.8	8.6
28 033	DeSoto	104,960	41.8	21.2	123,179	69.5	8.6	48.4	19.3	56,942	7.9	18.3	20.6
28 035	Forrest	45,610	45.1	26.1	59,878	61.0	12.6	33.3	30.6	31,885	24.3	41.5	9.9
28 039	George	14,615	64.9	10.3	17,348	54.6	12.9	32.4	37.4	44,941	17.3	29.9	12.3
28 043	Grenada	14,067	54.2	13.6	17,065	54.4	10.3	32.6	37.1	35,460	15.8	40.2	10.9
28 045	Hancock	30,468	44.8	23.0	35,952	57.6	13.2	33.6	35.5	40,203	20.9	32.7	14.2
28 047	Harrison	123,995	43.4	20.8	149,627	65.3	9.8	40.6	26.9	41,283	16.4	29.4	13.5
28 049	Hinds	153,481	39.7	26.9	190,571	61.4	11.9	39.6	28.6	36,681	19.9	34.8	12.6
28 057	Itawamba	15,493	54.4	14.1	18,778	55.7	8.6	37.8	33.0	35,858	10.4	33.9	6.1
28 059	Jackson	92,124	44.8	20.1	108,871	60.6	10.8	39.1	28.6	47,068	11.8	26.2	15.8
28 067	Jones	44,017	50.2	16.4	52,634	55.2	7.5	37.0	33.2	37,938	17.4	34.1	11.3
28 071	Lafayette	26,336	33.8	38.4	40,335	57.3	12.8	31.6	26.8	43,254	10.4	31.6	16.9
28 073	Lamar	35,831	36.4	30.6	43,953	66.7	8.1	42.7	22.4	47,910	11.3	29.7	16.3
28 075	Lauderdale	52,397	45.3	18.7	62,682	58.5	11.6	38.9	31.0	36,022	20.6	36.6	14.1
28 079	Leake	13,950	58.4	11.8	17,171	53.2	13.2	34.2	35.6	29,870	23.4	41.4	9.2
28 081	Lee	54,659	45.9	20.4	64,491	62.6	7.0	42.1	26.0	41,654	17.4	31.4	12.7
28 083	Leflore	19,247	56.7	18.4	24,019	48.7	19.7	29.0	41.6	24,035	33.0	51.1	6.2
28 085	Lincoln	22,519	52.3	17.0	26,805	54.5	6.7	35.8	32.5	37,454	19.5	34.1	9.3
28 087	Lowndes	38,415	49.3	19.7	46,504	63.0	15.2	37.2	32.1	34,879	23.4	39.8	11.5
28 089	Madison	62,959	27.1	46.6	74,535	66.5	6.3	49.4	21.7	57,861	11.2	21.7	26.1
28 091	Marion	17,673	59.5	12.8	20,664	49.0	11.8	30.3	40.3	29,378	21.3	42.6	9.4
28 093	Marshall	24,743	62.6	9.8	29,177	53.9	13.9	33.2	36.0	34,831	20.4	34.7	9.0
28 095	Monroe	24,521	59.6	13.6	28,838	53.3	12.1	33.2	39.2	35,450	18.0	36.4	8.0
28 099	Neshoba	18,639	53.5	12.5	22,107	60.4	13.2	38.9	30.3	35,845	20.3	34.7	11.6
28 101	Newton	13,911	46.6	16.6	16,762	57.8	11.1	37.8	32.5	34,058	18.8	35.2	8.8
28 105	Oktibbeha	24,186	31.0	43.8	40,156	58.2	15.4	29.8	35.8	31,181	21.6	42.6	12.3
28 107	Panola	22,038	55.3	14.5	26,287	55.1	15.2	36.1	38.1	36,948	18.3	36.8	8.7
28 109	Pearl River	36,836	53.7	14.4	43,682	53.1	11.7	34.8	38.3	37,989	20.7	36.6	11.2
28 113	Pike	25,836	53.0	15.2	30,405	51.4	10.2	31.4	40.4	33,555	20.6	39.6	8.6
28 115	Pontotoc	19,721	59.6	13.3	23,119	57.8	8.5	38.5	31.7	39,468	11.5	29.2	8.0
28 117	Prentiss	16,506	63.7	10.2	19,998	54.3	13.5	33.7	38.0	32,986	21.0	39.5	7.7
28 121	Rankin	96,464	40.5	27.5	112,073	65.0	6.7	47.8	22.0	57,250	8.4	20.5	23.0
28 123	Scott	17,728	62.1	10.8	21,580	57.7	8.7	38.1	28.9	36,962	16.4	32.0	6.7
28 127	Simpson	17,784	58.9	14.7	20,927	57.4	9.8	38.8	30.9	36,753	15.2	33.9	10.6
28 133	Sunflower	18,200	59.3	13.4	22,404	48.7	23.2	24.4	38.6	26,589	35.3	46.6	5.7
28 137	Tate	18,017	47.4	16.4	22,023	61.3	10.6	40.4	29.3	44,569	13.0	29.9	13.3
28 139	Tippah	14,583	63.9	9.5	17,314	53.1	11.9	34.5	42.8	32,603	20.9	41.0	7.9
28 145	Union	18,026	56.9	14.0	21,067	58.7	11.2	36.4	32.6	35,933	20.2	36.8	9.9
28 149	Warren	31,943	45.3	24.1	37,237	58.1	8.5	40.8	31.8	38,066	20.0	36.8	13.3
28 151	Washington	31,444	53.4	19.0	38,046	58.8	24.2	32.1	38.2	27,251	33.8	47.4	8.4
28 153	Wayne	13,367	64.4	9.8	15,907	55.1	11.2	33.1	38.4	29,299	25.0	46.2	10.3
28 163	Yazoo	18,539	61.6	11.9	22,012	51.9	22.9	30.5	38.3	25,980	30.9	48.7	7.7
29 000	**Missouri**	4,005,241	44.1	26.1	4,758,971	64.2	9.2	40.4	28.7	46,068	11.2	26.5	16.6
29 001	Adair	14,022	47.9	26.9	21,266	55.5	8.3	32.2	33.9	33,336	10.8	39.8	11.7
29 007	Audrain	17,310	61.4	12.7	20,347	56.0	8.8	38.8	31.8	42,155	11.8	28.0	7.9
29 009	Barry	24,560	58.7	14.5	28,054	58.4	11.9	35.0	36.7	37,576	13.8	29.3	8.6
29 019	Boone	96,111	26.2	49.0	134,956	68.3	7.0	40.6	22.3	45,381	8.9	28.9	18.1
29 021	Buchanan	58,488	51.1	20.3	70,855	64.0	9.5	38.5	29.2	42,881	12.6	30.2	12.0
29 023	Butler	29,548	57.6	12.5	34,206	59.4	9.1	38.6	37.0	35,297	14.2	36.2	8.4

Table B-2. Counties — What: Education, Employment, and Income, 2010–2012—*Continued*

State or county code	State or county	Educational attainment			Employment status				Percent of households with no workers	Median household income (dollars)	Percent of families with income below poverty	Percent of households with income less than $25,000	Percent of households with income of $100,000 or more
		Total population 25 years and over	Percent with a high school diploma or less	Percent with a bachelor's degree or more	Total population 16 years and over	Percent in the labor force	Unemployment rate	Percent who worked full-time year-round					
	ACS table number:	C15002	C15002	C15002	B23025	B23025	B23025	C20005	C08202	B19013	C17013	C19001	C19001
	Column number:	1	2	3	4	5	6	7	8	9	10	11	12
	Missouri—Cont.												
29 027	Callaway..................	29,507	50.9	21.4	35,761	61.2	6.5	43.2	27.9	46,053	11.9	27.4	13.0
29 029	Camden..................	32,700	45.6	21.8	36,479	55.1	8.2	32.5	37.9	42,670	9.5	26.7	10.3
29 031	Cape Girardeau	49,676	46.2	26.9	61,408	65.0	8.0	40.6	27.9	45,171	10.0	26.2	14.2
29 037	Cass......................	66,488	43.5	23.4	76,792	67.6	7.9	43.3	23.6	57,921	6.9	16.1	21.0
29 043	Christian.................	51,394	39.6	25.2	59,656	66.6	7.2	44.3	23.5	51,592	8.0	20.2	16.9
29 047	Clay......................	149,433	35.5	31.0	174,064	71.5	7.9	47.8	21.2	59,095	6.9	16.4	23.5
29 049	Clinton	14,138	50.3	16.1	16,342	64.6	9.4	40.0	25.4	52,936	6.4	19.0	17.2
29 051	Cole......................	51,516	39.6	31.2	60,610	63.9	4.6	46.6	24.8	53,997	9.1	21.0	19.2
29 055	Crawford.................	16,871	59.9	13.3	19,472	56.3	11.3	32.4	36.1	35,122	17.6	36.4	8.2
29 069	Dunklin..................	21,044	69.8	10.4	24,755	51.7	10.6	35.9	40.2	30,269	20.3	41.7	9.4
29 071	Franklin..................	68,385	49.9	17.1	79,515	64.9	9.6	40.6	29.1	44,963	9.5	24.4	14.2
29 077	Greene	180,865	37.4	28.4	225,891	64.1	8.7	38.3	28.2	40,452	13.0	30.2	11.6
29 083	Henry	15,633	52.4	16.1	17,817	59.4	9.0	37.6	36.6	40,518	13.7	29.7	10.5
29 091	Howell	27,178	54.9	16.9	31,542	54.8	9.0	35.0	40.3	32,926	16.4	40.8	6.3
29 095	Jackson	448,810	41.5	27.3	529,001	66.7	10.1	42.2	27.6	45,577	13.8	27.6	16.4
29 097	Jasper	74,988	50.2	20.5	90,060	65.2	8.1	41.5	28.5	38,861	12.4	32.1	11.5
29 099	Jefferson	146,800	47.4	16.9	171,830	68.6	10.3	41.1	24.7	53,212	9.4	19.3	17.0
29 101	Johnson	30,681	39.5	23.9	42,936	64.4	6.9	40.9	21.5	48,495	9.7	27.3	13.6
29 105	Laclede	23,870	62.5	13.6	27,805	60.2	9.3	38.5	31.3	40,391	13.3	27.5	10.1
29 107	Lafayette.................	22,479	55.0	17.0	26,238	63.8	7.8	42.8	29.7	50,423	8.5	23.5	13.3
29 109	Lawrence	25,425	57.7	16.3	29,584	59.5	9.4	38.7	31.3	39,280	14.2	32.1	8.9
29 113	Lincoln...................	34,189	55.8	14.4	40,037	67.3	12.6	38.6	25.3	51,420	11.0	21.8	14.6
29 119	McDonald................	14,630	58.3	12.0	17,318	61.7	11.4	38.8	33.7	35,614	18.2	35.6	9.9
29 127	Marion...................	19,216	56.0	17.0	22,593	59.6	6.1	39.2	29.1	39,217	12.2	30.8	8.2
29 131	Miller	16,877	56.8	14.5	19,462	57.8	10.6	33.2	35.7	33,970	17.8	35.7	8.9
29 141	Morgan	14,583	59.3	14.3	16,479	49.9	16.2	27.7	48.0	33,877	16.7	36.0	6.7
29 145	Newton	38,800	47.4	19.5	45,514	61.4	7.7	37.6	30.4	42,100	10.6	29.2	10.9
29 147	Nodaway	12,625	52.5	23.4	19,776	63.0	6.9	30.4	23.6	36,239	11.5	36.1	8.8
29 159	Pettis....................	27,719	51.6	15.9	32,650	62.5	6.6	40.0	30.8	36,702	13.6	33.6	10.6
29 161	Phelps...................	27,573	47.8	26.5	36,457	56.2	9.5	33.1	31.5	41,596	12.2	29.7	12.0
29 165	Platte....................	61,838	29.0	38.8	71,333	72.6	6.6	50.8	20.0	66,331	5.1	15.7	30.4
29 167	Polk	20,031	57.5	15.0	24,450	55.6	10.7	33.9	34.2	38,443	15.4	32.1	8.7
29 169	Pulaski	28,218	41.4	21.5	41,531	73.8	8.0	43.0	23.9	47,671	10.8	21.6	12.5
29 175	Randolph................	17,149	55.7	13.1	20,101	53.7	9.5	33.8	32.1	38,245	11.7	30.6	7.8
29 177	Ray	15,860	57.1	13.6	18,272	59.7	10.2	39.3	31.8	49,783	8.4	21.3	13.4
29 183	St. Charles	241,403	33.3	35.2	282,747	71.8	7.0	48.1	20.5	68,935	4.8	12.7	30.2
29 187	St. Francois	45,557	51.4	15.0	53,210	52.1	10.2	32.4	34.2	34,950	14.7	33.3	10.1
29 189	St. Louis.................	681,956	30.8	40.3	798,490	66.7	9.2	42.5	26.0	56,803	8.4	20.6	26.1
29 195	Saline....................	15,255	57.3	15.3	18,803	59.2	7.6	36.9	32.0	37,567	15.5	34.1	8.5
29 201	Scott.....................	26,317	61.1	15.3	30,635	63.1	7.1	41.5	31.6	36,746	14.7	34.8	11.3
29 207	Stoddard.................	20,805	62.7	13.1	24,044	55.5	8.5	37.0	36.5	39,447	9.0	31.2	11.5
29 209	Stone....................	24,113	56.9	14.0	26,741	51.9	11.9	29.9	44.7	39,681	12.9	28.7	6.8
29 213	Taney....................	35,629	51.8	18.4	42,236	59.9	13.6	31.6	36.7	37,371	13.0	30.9	9.3
29 215	Texas....................	17,706	64.8	10.2	20,846	50.0	8.5	30.7	39.0	34,605	13.7	37.4	6.6
29 217	Vernon	13,958	58.7	14.2	16,374	60.7	6.9	40.7	32.1	40,820	13.5	32.4	9.6
29 219	Warren	22,346	50.2	16.9	25,613	67.1	11.3	39.7	28.6	48,073	12.1	21.3	16.5
29 221	Washington	17,103	67.1	8.2	19,769	51.8	15.6	27.1	40.8	31,722	17.5	39.3	7.9
29 225	Webster..................	23,621	56.1	15.5	27,741	56.3	9.6	36.5	32.2	43,301	10.0	24.8	9.5
29 510	St. Louis city............	213,457	42.8	29.1	258,781	65.3	15.9	38.0	32.7	33,299	22.2	39.2	11.1
30 000	**Montana**	678,572	37.8	28.8	800,999	64.7	7.6	38.9	28.3	45,072	10.0	26.9	14.5
30 013	Cascade..................	54,859	40.8	22.4	65,197	63.4	5.6	39.9	28.4	44,116	11.7	25.8	13.4
30 029	Flathead..................	63,092	38.3	29.0	72,682	64.7	10.5	33.9	30.7	44,734	8.7	26.8	13.2
30 031	Gallatin..................	57,701	23.9	46.4	74,205	71.2	6.8	40.2	19.8	51,911	6.8	21.9	18.7
30 047	Lake.....................	19,358	40.8	25.0	22,554	58.6	12.2	30.4	37.2	36,138	17.1	35.4	10.2
30 049	Lewis and Clark	44,216	28.1	38.7	51,287	68.3	6.7	45.9	26.1	54,139	7.7	19.1	17.2
30 063	Missoula.................	71,798	27.9	39.4	91,061	70.2	9.8	37.1	24.5	45,054	9.2	27.5	15.9
30 081	Ravalli...................	29,273	42.6	24.6	32,788	57.6	9.8	30.6	38.2	38,110	11.5	32.0	11.6
30 093	Silver Bow................	23,526	45.7	23.2	28,103	61.6	7.6	36.4	34.1	38,417	12.9	32.8	11.6
30 111	Yellowstone	101,476	38.4	28.8	118,581	68.5	5.3	43.6	24.0	50,000	8.9	23.8	17.5
31 000	**Nebraska**................	1,196,710	37.7	28.5	1,431,553	70.8	6.1	46.8	23.0	50,957	8.9	22.9	17.8
31 001	Adams....................	20,198	43.8	20.9	24,646	68.6	5.6	46.3	24.7	45,879	8.3	24.9	12.8
31 019	Buffalo...................	27,952	34.1	32.4	36,629	73.8	4.4	47.0	18.7	50,927	6.9	23.4	19.0
31 025	Cass......................	17,181	38.0	24.1	19,718	69.0	5.7	47.1	24.1	61,515	4.4	14.5	22.3
31 043	Dakota...................	12,548	60.4	10.1	15,652	73.6	5.1	51.7	15.4	47,389	14.4	23.4	13.1
31 047	Dawson..................	15,243	57.1	16.8	18,249	70.1	6.4	48.3	21.3	46,840	9.1	22.2	9.2
31 053	Dodge	25,038	51.8	18.8	28,754	68.7	7.5	43.8	25.6	44,454	8.7	24.7	11.6
31 055	Douglas..................	335,637	32.7	36.5	402,000	72.2	7.3	46.8	22.2	52,428	10.6	23.2	21.1
31 067	Gage	15,434	45.8	20.5	17,456	66.0	6.0	43.9	29.5	48,338	9.2	26.7	13.7
31 079	Hall	38,327	50.3	17.1	45,268	73.1	6.5	49.3	22.9	46,345	12.0	24.0	12.8
31 109	Lancaster	180,064	29.6	35.8	230,041	72.6	6.9	45.2	21.4	50,585	9.3	23.2	18.8
31 111	Lincoln...................	24,534	43.8	17.7	28,216	66.5	4.8	43.8	26.6	47,633	8.4	26.5	14.4
31 119	Madison..................	22,568	39.9	22.5	27,121	70.4	4.8	45.7	24.4	45,904	10.4	27.6	14.8
31 141	Platte....................	21,159	40.7	18.9	24,864	74.4	4.9	50.6	19.1	53,582	6.6	16.8	15.3

Table B-2. Counties — What: Education, Employment, and Income, 2010–2012—*Continued*

State or county code	State or county	Educational attainment			Employment status				Percent of households with no workers	Median household income (dollars)	Percent of families with income below poverty	Percent of households with income less than $25,000	Percent of households with income of $100,000 or more
		Total population 25 years and over	Percent with a high school diploma or less	Percent with a bachelor's degree or more	Total population 16 years and over	Percent in the labor force	Unemployment rate	Percent who worked full-time year-round					
	ACS table number:	C15002	C15002	C15002	B23025	B23025	B23025	C20005	C08202	B19013	C17013	C19001	C19001
	Column number:	1	2	3	4	5	6	7	8	9	10	11	12
	Nebraska—Cont.												
31 153	Sarpy	102,127	28.5	35.6	121,066	76.4	5.7	53.5	16.6	67,694	5.9	12.6	27.3
31 155	Saunders	14,192	41.3	22.9	16,066	68.0	4.1	48.2	25.1	56,978	5.1	20.8	20.8
31 157	Scotts Bluff	24,471	43.2	21.6	28,850	68.5	7.3	44.4	24.6	43,003	10.6	28.1	10.7
31 177	Washington	13,595	39.0	30.4	15,828	69.5	2.4	47.5	22.3	71,505	4.2	15.9	28.3
32 000	**Nevada**	1,813,077	44.7	22.2	2,139,247	65.6	13.0	39.6	26.3	50,949	11.9	22.6	19.0
32 001	Churchill	16,499	45.7	13.8	19,509	63.3	12.5	37.8	27.2	48,604	11.5	20.7	17.4
32 003	Clark	1,304,095	45.8	22.0	1,539,701	66.4	13.2	40.4	25.1	50,943	12.3	22.2	18.6
32 005	Douglas	34,892	33.3	26.6	38,856	59.7	11.6	34.1	35.2	57,455	8.4	18.8	24.3
32 007	Elko	30,723	47.3	15.3	37,128	70.8	5.7	46.0	15.0	68,380	7.3	16.0	27.4
32 019	Lyon	35,295	45.6	15.0	40,747	56.4	18.7	30.7	33.6	44,186	14.5	24.4	11.6
32 023	Nye	32,077	51.9	13.9	35,873	46.8	17.1	27.1	46.8	40,022	14.4	31.3	13.0
32 031	Washoe	282,492	38.8	27.3	337,953	66.5	11.9	39.6	26.4	50,916	11.3	23.9	20.7
32 510	Carson City	38,648	42.9	20.3	44,857	62.1	16.5	34.1	34.7	52,436	11.0	23.2	16.0
33 000	**New Hampshire**	913,752	37.9	33.7	1,073,282	69.2	7.0	43.7	23.7	63,962	5.9	17.2	27.9
33 001	Belknap	43,614	39.7	29.0	49,631	65.7	6.3	42.5	28.3	58,047	7.3	20.8	21.9
33 003	Carroll	36,299	39.4	29.7	40,216	60.7	5.1	36.5	33.7	50,335	6.6	19.3	17.0
33 005	Cheshire	51,842	44.2	29.8	63,818	67.4	9.0	38.1	25.6	54,921	5.6	20.7	20.8
33 007	Coos	24,430	54.1	16.1	27,453	59.1	8.7	34.3	36.0	39,246	8.5	32.0	9.1
33 009	Grafton	60,507	38.2	37.5	74,911	63.5	5.9	38.8	26.1	52,839	6.1	20.1	22.3
33 011	Hillsborough	274,777	36.5	35.5	320,843	71.7	7.4	46.9	21.8	69,395	5.9	15.9	31.8
33 013	Merrimack	102,286	37.6	32.6	119,446	67.7	6.8	43.4	23.5	63,357	6.2	18.2	25.7
33 015	Rockingham	209,038	34.4	37.2	239,537	72.7	6.2	46.8	20.1	77,813	3.8	12.1	36.4
33 017	Strafford	79,492	38.2	31.1	101,679	69.1	8.0	40.0	24.5	55,196	8.6	19.9	22.2
33 019	Sullivan	31,467	46.2	27.2	35,748	66.3	6.9	43.2	26.4	55,173	6.8	20.4	20.7
34 000	**New Jersey**	6,013,231	41.0	35.8	7,033,377	66.5	10.6	42.2	24.8	70,062	7.9	17.7	34.2
34 001	Atlantic	186,048	49.4	24.0	219,793	66.9	13.9	36.7	27.9	53,019	11.0	23.3	22.6
34 003	Bergen	640,848	33.5	45.9	734,437	65.8	7.9	45.2	22.5	81,560	5.6	15.0	41.2
34 005	Burlington	309,816	38.5	34.7	360,776	67.8	9.5	43.7	23.2	76,426	4.0	12.3	36.2
34 007	Camden	343,896	44.6	28.9	404,825	67.2	12.9	40.3	27.5	60,186	10.4	21.4	26.9
34 009	Cape May	71,167	46.0	28.7	81,108	60.4	10.9	34.0	35.7	55,867	7.2	20.3	24.8
34 011	Cumberland	104,725	63.0	13.9	123,961	58.8	14.3	35.3	31.6	51,130	14.1	25.6	19.6
34 013	Essex	517,921	45.2	32.2	614,593	65.9	14.5	40.7	27.5	53,381	14.2	26.3	26.7
34 015	Gloucester	193,064	43.2	28.4	228,232	68.3	10.7	41.5	24.0	74,012	5.1	14.5	33.8
34 017	Hudson	449,243	44.0	36.4	527,395	69.0	11.4	46.4	21.5	57,672	14.2	23.7	27.4
34 019	Hunterdon	89,366	29.3	47.7	102,450	69.9	8.3	44.3	19.6	103,461	2.7	9.6	51.4
34 021	Mercer	244,828	39.4	38.3	295,609	66.5	11.1	41.5	25.0	72,143	7.8	17.7	36.0
34 023	Middlesex	549,088	38.1	40.4	654,127	66.4	9.1	43.5	21.0	77,877	6.0	14.2	37.3
34 025	Monmouth	432,864	34.2	40.9	501,884	66.7	9.3	41.6	24.2	82,460	5.1	14.5	41.8
34 027	Morris	343,646	30.3	49.0	394,569	69.2	8.0	45.5	20.6	94,415	3.3	10.4	47.1
34 029	Ocean	400,449	47.7	25.6	458,366	58.8	10.9	33.6	36.8	59,793	7.7	19.4	26.2
34 031	Passaic	326,769	52.4	25.9	393,299	64.5	11.3	41.8	26.2	56,763	13.0	23.5	27.7
34 033	Salem	45,046	52.6	20.0	52,673	63.0	13.9	35.5	32.1	57,280	9.4	22.3	24.7
34 035	Somerset	224,187	28.9	51.0	255,757	69.7	7.3	47.4	19.2	98,091	3.6	9.5	49.1
34 037	Sussex	102,597	38.3	32.7	118,766	70.6	10.7	42.5	20.1	85,562	4.3	11.3	40.8
34 039	Union	362,993	45.0	31.6	424,229	69.1	11.9	43.8	23.5	67,932	8.7	17.5	33.1
34 041	Warren	74,670	46.6	29.4	86,528	67.6	9.3	43.4	23.6	69,882	5.4	15.4	31.3
35 000	**New Mexico**	1,353,059	42.8	25.7	1,617,544	60.7	10.2	38.0	29.6	43,518	16.4	29.5	16.4
35 001	Bernalillo	441,578	36.3	31.9	527,945	64.6	9.1	41.6	26.8	47,128	14.8	26.9	18.7
35 005	Chaves	40,791	48.3	17.7	49,523	59.6	7.7	38.5	28.2	39,076	17.2	29.2	12.5
35 006	Cibola	18,305	61.6	11.4	21,083	55.6	15.6	33.2	31.5	36,974	25.7	34.1	8.7
35 009	Curry	30,042	44.2	20.6	36,997	63.9	8.2	43.1	27.6	38,373	16.3	32.8	11.7
35 013	Dona Ana	128,702	44.5	25.9	162,572	62.0	13.4	36.0	28.1	36,782	22.7	36.2	12.2
35 015	Eddy	35,451	50.7	16.9	41,661	63.1	8.4	42.9	28.6	46,965	9.4	25.7	19.4
35 017	Grant	20,830	44.1	25.5	23,727	53.9	10.7	30.6	38.4	36,879	13.2	36.3	10.1
35 025	Lea	39,609	60.1	12.1	47,871	61.1	7.9	40.5	22.8	48,434	14.1	24.0	19.0
35 027	Lincoln	15,433	42.2	22.7	17,039	56.2	10.6	32.4	39.5	41,667	10.4	29.3	12.6
35 029	Luna	16,252	62.8	14.5	19,108	55.1	16.0	29.2	41.3	29,481	20.1	43.7	5.0
35 031	McKinley	41,370	58.7	12.5	53,022	49.6	11.6	29.6	34.5	30,188	30.7	42.2	9.6
35 035	Otero	42,087	45.8	16.9	51,043	54.9	12.2	32.9	37.2	37,217	18.5	33.3	10.7
35 039	Rio Arriba	27,092	52.5	15.0	31,716	59.8	15.1	35.8	34.9	39,004	16.4	32.4	11.7
35 041	Roosevelt	10,977	46.2	20.9	15,569	63.6	7.7	37.4	25.1	37,161	19.1	33.1	5.3
35 043	Sandoval	88,348	35.8	28.2	103,012	61.2	9.2	40.6	26.9	55,587	11.9	20.8	22.0
35 045	San Juan	79,434	50.6	15.8	96,114	58.8	8.5	38.9	24.3	47,897	17.2	25.8	18.1
35 047	San Miguel	19,669	47.9	20.9	23,652	46.9	8.0	32.0	42.4	30,118	20.7	43.6	8.7
35 049	Santa Fe	104,263	33.8	39.2	119,170	65.1	10.3	37.7	29.0	50,826	13.4	25.6	21.1
35 055	Taos	23,979	38.4	29.1	27,041	61.4	14.7	33.1	35.7	32,274	17.4	39.2	10.0
35 061	Valencia	50,106	49.6	16.6	59,240	54.9	14.6	33.6	35.1	41,254	20.7	31.7	13.1
36 000	**New York**	13,205,241	42.3	33.0	15,724,512	63.4	9.5	40.5	27.4	56,657	12.0	23.6	26.4
36 001	Albany	203,836	34.0	38.4	252,858	65.2	7.3	41.5	27.0	58,585	8.9	21.5	25.5
36 003	Allegany	30,568	53.0	18.7	39,878	57.6	10.1	30.9	35.5	42,102	12.2	28.5	10.7
36 005	Bronx	865,413	58.5	17.6	1,073,639	59.3	15.9	36.0	33.7	33,064	28.0	40.5	11.2
36 007	Broome	133,902	43.4	26.2	164,670	59.7	9.5	34.5	33.3	45,452	11.9	28.0	16.1
36 009	Cattaraugus	53,710	53.8	17.2	63,656	59.8	9.3	35.3	32.7	42,285	12.0	29.2	10.8
36 011	Cayuga	55,685	49.6	19.0	65,287	61.7	9.4	36.9	31.6	50,782	7.8	23.0	15.9
36 013	Chautauqua	90,034	47.9	21.0	109,173	58.6	8.5	33.7	35.1	41,922	14.9	30.5	11.6
36 015	Chemung	60,925	46.8	21.1	71,560	58.7	6.6	35.9	31.1	48,754	12.0	27.8	17.7
36 017	Chenango	35,268	53.7	16.8	40,574	58.0	8.9	35.2	35.3	42,391	10.5	28.2	11.1

Table B-2. Counties — What: Education, Employment, and Income, 2010–2012—Continued

State or county code	State or county	Educational attainment			Employment status						Percent of families with income below poverty	Percent of households with income less than $25,000	Percent of households with income of $100,000 or more
		Total population 25 years and over	Percent with a high school diploma or less	Percent with a bachelor's degree or more	Total population 16 years and over	Percent in the labor force	Unemployment rate	Percent who worked full-time year-round	Percent of households with no workers	Median household income (dollars)			
	ACS table number:	C15002	C15002	C15002	B23025	B23025	B23025	C20005	C08202	B19013	C17013	C19001	C19001
	Column number:	1	2	3	4	5	6	7	8	9	10	11	12
	New York—Cont.												
36 019	Clinton	55,762	51.5	21.7	68,427	56.9	7.9	36.1	33.2	49,891	10.2	25.7	17.6
36 021	Columbia	45,418	42.5	28.2	52,042	62.6	9.4	38.7	28.1	57,491	6.4	18.4	23.9
36 023	Cortland	30,369	46.3	22.5	40,246	61.0	8.4	37.8	28.7	47,310	8.6	25.4	15.5
36 025	Delaware	33,512	52.1	20.3	39,622	56.8	10.8	32.2	38.0	40,949	9.6	30.1	11.7
36 027	Dutchess	200,305	37.9	32.7	242,683	64.8	10.2	40.1	25.9	70,359	5.5	16.5	32.2
36 029	Erie	626,357	39.2	30.7	748,994	63.4	8.9	38.0	31.7	49,603	10.9	26.4	18.9
36 031	Essex	28,925	47.9	21.7	32,951	57.8	9.7	34.1	33.6	46,434	9.7	24.3	13.2
36 033	Franklin	35,776	52.4	18.3	42,360	52.7	9.4	33.0	34.6	45,078	13.3	28.6	13.1
36 035	Fulton	38,810	53.8	15.1	44,902	59.4	10.0	38.3	32.4	45,868	11.6	26.0	13.3
36 037	Genesee	41,724	47.0	20.1	48,832	66.9	7.8	41.4	25.9	50,617	9.0	22.5	15.8
36 039	Greene	35,075	52.2	18.8	41,068	53.8	10.4	33.8	35.9	47,112	10.0	24.9	15.9
36 043	Herkimer	44,738	46.3	21.6	52,237	61.5	9.8	37.7	33.6	44,304	11.6	27.9	12.5
36 045	Jefferson	73,488	47.8	19.8	91,243	65.3	10.5	42.9	28.4	45,884	12.2	25.3	12.7
36 047	Kings	1,676,663	49.3	30.0	2,006,348	62.2	11.3	40.1	27.0	44,340	20.3	31.1	19.6
36 049	Lewis	18,410	58.3	14.1	21,430	61.4	7.8	38.9	32.5	44,680	9.7	24.6	13.1
36 051	Livingston	42,558	44.0	26.0	53,662	61.2	5.8	37.0	27.0	53,260	9.1	21.9	17.0
36 053	Madison	47,602	43.6	26.4	59,598	58.2	5.3	38.8	29.6	51,504	6.8	21.2	17.2
36 055	Monroe	496,162	35.4	35.6	601,302	64.1	8.5	38.9	29.9	51,459	11.3	24.6	20.4
36 057	Montgomery	34,513	54.2	16.5	39,924	60.6	12.0	37.5	33.9	42,109	15.2	29.7	14.0
36 059	Nassau	922,055	34.8	41.4	1,078,150	65.1	7.7	43.2	22.1	94,273	4.5	11.2	47.5
36 061	New York	1,194,350	27.1	58.3	1,392,324	67.2	9.0	44.7	26.7	67,291	14.2	24.1	36.7
36 063	Niagara	149,965	45.1	22.9	175,934	61.7	8.2	37.7	33.5	47,544	10.2	26.0	17.7
36 065	Oneida	160,147	45.0	23.5	189,859	59.8	8.6	37.0	33.2	48,703	11.6	25.9	17.9
36 067	Onondaga	309,669	37.9	32.7	374,654	63.3	7.6	40.5	29.2	53,545	10.1	24.6	21.8
36 069	Ontario	74,663	37.4	30.9	87,653	64.8	6.9	40.0	26.0	53,817	6.9	19.5	21.2
36 071	Orange	236,350	41.9	29.0	286,538	66.3	8.5	42.3	23.8	68,329	8.7	17.8	32.4
36 073	Orleans	29,544	55.8	15.3	34,803	57.1	11.7	35.1	32.0	49,665	11.0	23.7	13.6
36 075	Oswego	79,269	55.1	16.7	98,169	59.6	10.1	34.6	31.3	46,655	12.1	25.6	15.7
36 077	Otsego	40,447	45.3	26.2	52,620	58.8	8.7	33.3	32.5	47,071	8.3	26.2	14.5
36 079	Putnam	69,188	33.8	39.5	79,804	68.1	8.8	42.7	20.8	93,150	3.4	11.5	46.5
36 081	Queens	1,574,531	47.4	29.9	1,845,097	64.3	10.2	42.4	23.6	54,948	12.7	22.9	23.4
36 083	Rensselaer	107,353	39.7	28.6	130,266	67.9	9.3	42.7	27.5	58,542	9.8	21.2	24.0
36 085	Richmond	318,019	44.1	29.8	375,837	59.4	8.2	41.3	26.1	72,060	9.3	18.6	34.1
36 087	Rockland	199,160	36.4	40.2	237,537	65.5	8.3	41.2	21.6	84,752	9.3	15.0	42.1
36 089	St. Lawrence	71,682	48.6	21.5	91,647	55.8	11.8	31.1	36.0	42,551	13.8	29.4	13.5
36 091	Saratoga	154,298	32.6	36.9	178,094	68.1	6.7	45.1	24.5	66,581	3.7	14.9	29.8
36 093	Schenectady	104,954	41.5	28.9	124,322	65.6	8.6	41.7	29.5	54,590	9.1	23.3	21.6
36 095	Schoharie	22,396	50.3	19.2	27,045	62.1	12.8	35.5	32.7	52,121	8.6	24.4	17.0
36 099	Seneca	24,815	49.3	20.6	28,933	55.9	6.2	37.8	32.0	49,377	8.9	26.9	15.7
36 101	Steuben	68,408	48.1	20.3	79,106	60.5	9.4	37.4	33.9	46,065	11.6	25.3	15.1
36 103	Suffolk	1,013,103	40.4	33.0	1,191,931	65.7	7.7	42.8	22.6	85,931	4.5	12.2	42.4
36 105	Sullivan	53,312	50.0	21.2	62,056	60.4	12.9	35.8	33.6	47,537	14.1	27.8	16.7
36 107	Tioga	35,527	46.8	23.2	40,979	64.9	9.0	40.6	28.3	55,306	6.3	22.4	18.9
36 109	Tompkins	58,167	24.9	51.3	88,117	59.5	5.8	32.7	30.0	52,070	7.5	26.6	22.6
36 111	Ulster	127,941	40.7	29.9	151,431	62.9	10.8	36.7	29.4	56,642	7.6	22.5	23.8
36 113	Warren	47,389	42.1	29.1	54,287	62.3	7.5	39.9	32.6	55,442	8.9	21.6	20.4
36 115	Washington	44,668	56.9	17.5	51,838	62.2	10.6	38.3	29.8	50,958	10.0	22.6	14.1
36 117	Wayne	64,410	47.8	20.3	74,411	65.0	7.7	41.7	27.6	52,458	7.4	20.4	17.0
36 119	Westchester	650,295	34.2	45.1	757,766	65.4	8.4	42.1	23.7	79,887	6.9	16.1	41.2
36 121	Wyoming	30,254	53.1	15.1	34,682	58.9	8.8	38.3	29.0	50,216	6.5	21.9	13.6
36 123	Yates	16,494	51.0	23.6	20,042	62.4	6.4	38.7	29.1	49,094	11.9	23.0	13.4
37 000	**North Carolina**	6,409,433	42.4	27.0	7,624,214	63.5	11.5	39.0	28.8	45,215	13.3	27.3	16.4
37 001	Alamance	101,070	47.0	20.6	121,266	63.5	10.9	38.7	29.7	41,650	13.7	29.5	13.3
37 003	Alexander	25,968	61.8	11.4	29,947	60.2	11.4	37.2	31.4	38,884	14.1	32.7	9.1
37 007	Anson	18,415	62.0	10.7	21,400	56.8	18.6	33.1	35.4	33,333	16.2	37.2	8.1
37 009	Ashe	20,079	53.3	17.1	22,509	57.0	10.1	32.4	39.3	33,656	14.0	38.3	7.4
37 013	Beaufort	33,637	49.8	19.3	38,385	55.8	13.9	32.1	39.3	39,186	16.6	32.7	10.6
37 015	Bertie	14,894	63.4	11.5	17,259	52.0	15.3	31.0	42.0	29,525	15.7	41.7	8.5
37 017	Bladen	24,133	56.4	11.0	28,081	55.6	13.1	35.7	40.7	27,313	21.6	45.5	8.4
37 019	Brunswick	83,467	42.2	25.6	91,851	53.2	14.5	28.4	42.5	45,797	13.1	27.4	15.3
37 021	Buncombe	171,832	36.4	33.5	198,688	63.2	9.5	36.3	30.9	43,177	12.9	27.6	14.4
37 023	Burke	62,383	52.6	17.5	73,786	58.1	13.8	34.3	34.5	37,952	14.3	33.1	9.5
37 025	Cabarrus	118,021	42.9	24.3	138,048	66.4	12.3	41.4	24.9	51,887	10.1	21.8	19.1
37 027	Caldwell	57,310	59.0	12.4	66,869	56.8	15.4	32.8	39.5	33,183	16.9	39.7	6.9
37 031	Carteret	49,600	39.4	25.6	56,184	62.2	10.9	35.5	31.1	45,684	11.7	24.2	16.1
37 033	Caswell	17,026	57.9	10.1	19,416	53.2	12.0	32.0	38.0	38,866	15.1	33.9	8.5
37 035	Catawba	105,167	47.4	21.5	121,860	63.3	9.8	39.9	28.0	43,286	11.2	26.0	13.2
37 037	Chatham	47,108	39.0	35.6	52,591	62.0	12.0	38.0	32.0	55,225	8.7	22.3	22.6
37 039	Cherokee	20,333	48.8	16.2	22,826	45.3	9.4	25.8	43.7	32,759	12.2	35.8	5.2
37 045	Cleveland	66,030	52.7	16.2	77,272	59.5	14.5	35.3	36.2	38,062	15.7	36.1	10.2
37 047	Columbus	39,341	52.3	11.7	46,170	50.2	12.6	33.0	39.2	32,651	17.8	39.2	10.9
37 049	Craven	67,517	40.7	22.0	82,993	63.0	12.8	38.5	32.3	48,371	11.3	24.1	14.4
37 051	Cumberland	195,966	37.8	22.6	245,708	66.4	12.0	44.4	26.1	44,694	14.6	26.0	14.0
37 053	Currituck	16,600	46.7	19.4	18,978	66.6	7.8	41.6	22.2	57,531	7.3	17.5	21.0

Table B-2. Counties — What: Education, Employment, and Income, 2010–2012—*Continued*

State or county code	State or county	Educational attainment			Employment status				Percent of households with no workers	Median household income (dollars)	Percent of families with income below poverty	Percent of households with income less than $25,000	Percent of households with income of $100,000 or more
		Total population 25 years and over	Percent with a high school diploma or less	Percent with a bachelor's degree or more	Total population 16 years and over	Percent in the labor force	Unemployment rate	Percent who worked full-time year-round					
	ACS table number:	C15002	C15002	C15002	B23025	B23025	B23025	C20005	C08202	B19013	C17013	C19001	C19001
	Column number:	1	2	3	4	5	6	7	8	9	10	11	12
	North Carolina—Cont.												
37 055	Dare	25,374	32.3	29.4	28,271	71.2	7.5	42.5	25.8	55,620	7.6	18.0	20.4
37 057	Davidson	112,604	53.7	17.3	129,435	63.6	13.8	39.0	31.4	41,920	11.6	28.2	11.3
37 059	Davie	28,959	48.5	26.2	33,033	60.1	7.4	38.9	31.4	49,062	8.6	24.9	16.8
37 061	Duplin	39,141	57.3	10.9	45,873	61.3	14.0	35.2	34.0	33,172	18.9	39.4	5.8
37 063	Durham	180,467	31.4	44.0	217,868	67.3	8.9	43.1	23.1	49,066	13.7	25.0	20.1
37 065	Edgecombe	37,648	59.1	10.4	44,575	60.9	19.1	34.0	36.4	34,153	19.6	35.1	7.3
37 067	Forsyth	233,395	40.2	31.6	279,239	63.3	10.8	38.7	28.2	44,038	13.5	27.3	16.9
37 069	Franklin	41,359	52.7	16.5	48,197	63.0	13.6	38.5	30.1	41,190	13.2	28.8	13.5
37 071	Gaston	140,168	48.0	17.8	163,847	63.3	14.8	37.8	30.9	41,092	14.4	30.9	13.0
37 077	Granville	41,229	54.4	15.6	48,589	56.1	12.3	39.0	29.1	48,009	14.2	24.9	15.9
37 079	Greene	14,549	56.5	11.4	17,054	57.7	12.0	32.9	32.0	36,760	15.9	32.9	8.6
37 081	Guilford	323,001	38.4	33.0	393,382	65.7	11.7	39.3	26.5	43,827	13.3	27.4	16.5
37 083	Halifax	37,254	57.9	12.0	43,655	53.6	18.5	31.1	42.1	31,374	21.8	41.9	8.5
37 085	Harnett	73,721	46.4	18.0	89,328	62.1	11.4	39.0	27.2	42,080	12.8	27.8	13.2
37 087	Haywood	43,229	44.2	22.3	49,243	55.7	9.6	35.0	38.9	41,471	12.3	27.8	11.8
37 089	Henderson	78,904	39.0	27.6	88,279	55.9	10.3	32.7	37.2	45,585	10.2	24.7	14.4
37 091	Hertford	16,945	53.4	14.3	20,031	51.2	20.0	28.3	42.7	30,509	21.8	43.7	8.9
37 093	Hoke	29,776	44.1	18.3	35,755	62.5	10.7	41.2	22.2	44,433	15.2	26.9	12.4
37 097	Iredell	107,684	43.5	23.9	125,868	63.6	12.7	38.8	27.6	49,886	10.6	24.7	18.6
37 099	Jackson	25,439	42.7	27.2	33,980	54.8	9.0	31.2	34.5	35,671	10.6	34.5	10.2
37 101	Johnston	111,386	47.1	19.8	130,096	67.6	10.5	43.7	24.5	48,656	12.4	25.7	15.3
37 105	Lee	38,530	49.1	19.0	45,122	63.7	13.4	40.3	30.1	41,367	17.3	30.0	12.5
37 107	Lenoir	40,381	53.7	14.0	46,878	60.4	14.3	35.0	36.2	35,715	20.5	36.3	9.1
37 109	Lincoln	54,668	46.3	20.1	62,857	64.7	12.9	39.6	28.8	47,918	10.3	23.4	18.3
37 111	McDowell	32,090	58.5	13.5	36,276	54.7	14.8	30.6	40.2	34,306	15.4	39.0	7.2
37 113	Macon	25,259	43.5	23.9	28,255	50.1	11.4	28.3	44.5	37,665	12.4	32.7	9.7
37 115	Madison	14,647	52.5	19.0	17,205	54.8	8.2	33.9	36.9	36,961	12.1	33.4	9.6
37 117	Martin	17,006	54.5	12.3	19,661	55.1	18.3	34.0	42.7	35,891	20.0	35.9	6.1
37 119	Mecklenburg	617,419	31.3	40.4	731,426	71.7	11.1	44.9	20.3	54,417	12.4	21.6	24.0
37 123	Montgomery	18,899	55.2	15.1	21,878	53.6	15.6	27.7	41.7	31,878	24.0	40.6	12.3
37 125	Moore	64,396	35.9	30.6	72,479	54.3	10.4	33.6	38.3	48,648	13.7	27.8	18.8
37 127	Nash	65,104	51.5	18.0	76,210	62.2	14.0	37.7	31.4	42,928	14.0	29.3	13.0
37 129	New Hanover	139,281	31.0	36.8	169,770	65.5	10.8	38.2	28.2	49,530	10.4	24.8	20.0
37 131	Northampton	15,570	61.6	8.8	17,941	52.5	17.3	31.0	42.6	30,949	20.4	37.8	8.9
37 133	Onslow	94,956	38.8	18.1	138,538	69.8	9.0	47.2	22.0	44,611	11.3	22.4	10.1
37 135	Orange	82,721	25.0	55.0	111,508	64.8	7.6	36.7	24.0	52,439	11.4	25.3	28.8
37 139	Pasquotank	26,249	47.0	20.1	32,536	64.2	15.5	34.5	27.3	45,283	16.9	28.5	13.3
37 141	Pender	37,020	46.4	21.4	42,780	59.8	10.8	35.4	33.2	43,686	11.2	26.8	14.9
37 145	Person	27,219	53.3	14.3	31,403	60.6	11.1	37.5	30.9	41,732	11.7	30.5	11.1
37 147	Pitt	100,557	39.1	29.1	136,569	67.2	12.3	38.2	25.7	40,454	15.2	33.6	15.0
37 149	Polk	15,172	42.4	27.1	17,161	52.3	16.6	30.2	43.6	43,926	10.4	26.4	14.0
37 151	Randolph	96,112	55.3	13.7	111,354	63.3	11.2	38.5	30.3	40,688	14.5	28.7	10.4
37 153	Richmond	30,914	56.5	12.2	36,635	54.6	18.0	31.3	40.8	32,072	19.3	40.0	7.1
37 155	Robeson	83,933	59.7	12.5	102,669	53.1	12.8	31.7	35.1	30,370	25.8	42.4	7.2
37 157	Rockingham	65,598	56.9	12.5	75,583	57.9	14.9	35.1	38.6	37,164	13.6	32.3	10.3
37 159	Rowan	93,400	52.3	16.3	109,385	58.7	12.5	34.2	32.5	39,681	14.9	30.8	10.3
37 161	Rutherford	47,602	50.1	15.9	54,669	54.2	16.1	31.3	39.7	35,256	16.4	35.4	8.2
37 163	Sampson	42,399	59.8	13.0	49,419	61.5	12.5	38.4	31.5	36,594	18.1	33.2	10.3
37 165	Scotland	23,789	58.4	14.6	28,466	45.3	16.8	27.8	45.5	30,757	25.4	42.5	8.3
37 167	Stanly	41,287	52.2	15.7	48,239	60.8	15.4	35.6	34.5	41,103	11.4	32.7	10.3
37 169	Stokes	33,370	58.3	12.6	38,378	59.1	11.5	34.7	34.0	40,306	16.2	32.7	10.7
37 171	Surry	51,104	54.6	15.1	58,480	58.7	10.2	36.1	35.9	35,391	14.8	35.2	10.6
37 175	Transylvania	24,782	38.6	29.6	28,425	52.8	8.6	29.4	39.8	42,873	8.3	24.7	11.8
37 179	Union	128,403	39.9	30.7	151,026	68.2	10.0	44.0	19.3	63,717	8.0	16.7	27.1
37 181	Vance	29,534	60.2	13.1	35,114	56.1	11.6	35.5	34.8	34,421	18.8	37.8	8.7
37 183	Wake	600,584	25.7	46.9	714,752	70.9	8.2	46.7	18.2	63,882	8.4	16.1	29.7
37 185	Warren	14,838	60.8	14.5	17,096	47.1	10.2	27.0	44.7	34,007	17.9	40.3	10.9
37 189	Watauga	28,180	32.0	36.5	45,374	61.6	10.6	26.7	29.9	33,148	11.9	41.3	11.5
37 191	Wayne	80,606	48.6	15.1	96,479	64.1	12.8	40.0	29.5	40,406	17.2	32.4	10.7
37 193	Wilkes	48,961	57.9	12.0	55,842	55.9	16.1	31.0	38.9	31,847	18.8	39.8	7.3
37 195	Wilson	54,461	54.8	17.8	63,860	61.4	14.5	37.1	33.4	36,867	18.6	33.4	10.1
37 197	Yadkin	26,544	58.0	11.8	30,709	60.0	10.6	39.4	33.0	39,013	15.0	33.5	11.7
38 000	**North Dakota**	450,055	36.3	27.3	551,175	70.5	3.4	47.4	22.2	52,427	7.6	22.7	19.3
38 015	Burleigh	56,122	30.9	33.0	66,944	72.5	3.7	50.5	20.7	60,214	4.7	18.3	23.8
38 017	Cass	95,492	24.7	37.9	123,235	77.4	4.0	50.3	17.3	52,416	6.6	21.7	20.3
38 035	Grand Forks	38,732	32.1	33.4	55,370	71.4	3.9	44.0	19.5	44,707	7.9	26.5	16.7
38 059	Morton	19,107	40.6	25.0	22,065	73.7	3.5	51.6	21.8	56,241	7.3	19.4	20.4
38 089	Stark	16,768	42.5	24.4	20,301	73.5	1.9	52.0	20.6	59,899	4.4	19.3	24.7
38 093	Stutsman	14,584	50.5	21.9	17,299	66.9	4.5	46.1	26.2	48,881	8.7	24.7	16.0
38 101	Ward	39,389	35.5	25.6	50,385	73.0	2.8	50.8	19.2	54,324	7.0	19.4	17.0
38 105	Williams	16,470	38.8	18.7	19,498	71.0	1.0	50.6	17.2	76,206	4.9	16.3	34.0
39 000	**Ohio**	7,744,886	46.4	24.9	9,165,238	63.7	10.2	38.9	29.9	47,030	11.8	26.5	17.1
39 001	Adams	19,222	66.8	9.1	22,206	55.3	18.5	29.2	40.1	33,893	17.3	40.7	7.6
39 003	Allen	68,808	52.6	17.2	83,587	62.0	12.0	34.2	33.2	42,025	15.2	30.4	12.7
39 005	Ashland	35,010	56.5	20.1	42,197	63.0	13.5	36.7	30.4	43,368	13.3	26.9	9.3
39 007	Ashtabula	69,610	60.2	13.3	80,210	58.4	11.4	34.4	34.2	39,245	13.6	33.5	10.4
39 009	Athens	33,913	43.2	27.8	55,678	54.6	11.2	27.1	35.0	34,705	16.7	39.5	10.0
39 011	Auglaize	31,025	52.2	17.6	35,859	67.2	8.6	40.6	29.4	50,821	7.0	21.1	14.7

Table B-2. Counties — What: Education, Employment, and Income, 2010–2012—Continued

State or county code	State or county	Total population 25 years and over	Percent with a high school diploma or less	Percent with a bachelor's degree or more	Total population 16 years and over	Percent in the labor force	Unemployment rate	Percent who worked full-time year-round	Percent of households with no workers	Median household income (dollars)	Percent of families with income below poverty	Percent of households with income less than $25,000	Percent of households with income of $100,000 or more
	ACS table number:	C15002	C15002	C15002	B23025	B23025	B23025	C20005	C08202	B19013	C17013	C19001	C19001
	Column number:	1	2	3	4	5	6	7	8	9	10	11	12
	Ohio—Cont.												
39 013	Belmont	50,898	56.7	14.1	58,268	56.8	9.3	36.5	34.4	42,254	10.5	29.0	11.1
39 015	Brown	30,182	66.0	11.0	35,034	58.6	13.8	35.6	33.1	43,439	11.6	26.8	9.9
39 017	Butler	236,498	45.3	27.2	288,073	66.5	9.2	41.8	25.6	55,895	9.6	21.4	22.6
39 019	Carroll	20,279	66.2	11.1	23,178	58.1	9.4	34.3	32.4	41,790	13.4	27.1	10.7
39 021	Champaign	26,745	56.8	15.8	31,298	62.1	12.7	38.3	30.9	47,947	9.9	23.4	14.5
39 023	Clark	93,111	51.5	17.7	109,340	59.7	12.0	34.6	34.8	41,235	14.3	30.4	12.1
39 025	Clermont	132,632	47.5	25.3	154,377	66.4	7.7	43.7	24.7	56,530	7.9	20.0	23.2
39 027	Clinton	27,696	57.4	13.7	32,865	62.9	14.0	36.5	33.4	42,269	14.2	28.8	11.1
39 029	Columbiana	76,128	60.3	13.2	86,897	59.4	11.1	35.6	32.6	41,930	12.4	28.8	10.5
39 031	Coshocton	25,235	65.4	10.4	29,321	58.0	9.3	34.3	33.4	41,125	15.3	29.8	9.8
39 033	Crawford	30,111	58.7	11.3	34,516	56.4	9.1	35.4	36.9	41,288	13.2	29.1	9.7
39 035	Cuyahoga	874,069	41.4	29.4	1,023,490	63.5	12.1	38.1	32.6	42,500	14.4	30.7	16.5
39 037	Darke	35,749	62.9	11.7	41,023	62.7	9.8	39.1	31.3	43,010	10.2	26.7	11.1
39 039	Defiance	25,980	53.6	16.3	30,748	64.6	10.0	35.5	29.8	46,467	11.4	24.6	13.5
39 041	Delaware	115,792	24.5	50.3	132,712	70.7	4.8	49.8	17.3	87,890	3.6	12.0	43.0
39 043	Erie	54,275	51.2	20.0	61,917	63.3	9.9	35.1	32.3	45,870	8.0	25.2	15.0
39 045	Fairfield	97,461	43.4	26.0	114,245	66.2	8.2	42.7	25.2	60,375	8.0	19.3	23.2
39 047	Fayette	19,619	61.2	13.3	22,865	61.5	12.8	36.1	30.6	37,753	15.6	30.3	8.1
39 049	Franklin	761,493	36.3	35.8	927,248	69.3	9.3	44.0	23.8	49,670	13.6	25.3	19.6
39 051	Fulton	28,566	52.1	16.6	33,188	67.2	9.9	39.9	27.8	51,644	9.1	19.9	13.9
39 053	Gallia	20,779	58.7	14.5	24,381	52.6	9.8	31.9	36.3	37,830	13.9	33.0	12.8
39 055	Geauga	63,356	38.0	35.0	73,033	66.8	5.7	42.2	23.2	66,469	4.4	15.0	30.9
39 057	Greene	104,315	34.8	35.4	132,725	62.7	8.5	38.0	28.9	55,153	10.0	22.3	23.7
39 059	Guernsey	27,320	58.8	12.7	31,699	58.1	13.0	33.9	36.2	38,102	13.9	31.7	9.3
39 061	Hamilton	530,519	38.6	33.4	634,640	66.0	10.5	40.0	29.3	47,643	14.0	28.7	20.4
39 063	Hancock	49,879	46.5	23.6	59,923	67.8	10.0	40.8	27.8	49,400	10.6	25.5	16.3
39 065	Hardin	19,563	64.3	13.8	25,172	60.3	11.6	32.6	33.5	41,367	12.0	28.9	9.9
39 069	Henry	19,082	54.5	13.8	22,081	65.0	8.8	40.6	30.2	48,576	10.6	23.3	13.9
39 071	Highland	29,062	60.4	11.4	33,663	58.3	16.4	34.3	35.8	38,198	14.7	31.2	7.3
39 073	Hocking	20,176	59.4	13.4	23,448	58.0	10.6	34.6	33.8	40,981	14.0	30.9	13.0
39 075	Holmes	24,043	77.3	8.1	29,842	63.3	6.1	39.5	23.0	42,934	13.3	23.1	10.0
39 077	Huron	39,428	59.9	13.0	45,721	65.0	9.3	40.1	30.0	48,448	10.5	23.5	13.8
39 079	Jackson	22,273	61.2	16.5	25,888	56.6	10.6	33.5	37.5	36,714	17.4	37.5	8.8
39 081	Jefferson	48,489	54.7	15.8	56,865	55.2	8.5	33.3	38.1	41,095	11.8	30.7	11.6
39 083	Knox	39,282	53.5	20.1	48,243	61.7	7.7	39.2	28.5	50,325	11.9	24.3	15.2
39 085	Lake	162,461	42.9	25.1	186,299	67.6	8.5	42.3	26.9	54,873	6.7	20.5	19.8
39 087	Lawrence	42,758	59.1	15.1	49,802	53.4	10.1	35.0	40.5	40,232	13.0	31.5	10.8
39 089	Licking	111,982	48.0	22.0	131,194	66.7	8.0	42.1	26.8	53,984	9.6	22.6	19.5
39 091	Logan	30,875	62.5	15.8	35,695	61.7	9.6	37.6	31.5	44,853	12.9	25.9	14.3
39 093	Lorain	204,881	46.1	21.6	239,005	63.3	10.6	38.4	29.7	50,230	11.3	23.1	18.6
39 095	Lucas	287,958	44.2	23.4	347,114	63.8	14.1	35.6	33.1	40,416	16.8	32.4	14.0
39 097	Madison	29,876	52.9	16.7	34,906	58.9	6.9	37.2	28.3	55,121	6.2	19.2	20.5
39 099	Mahoning	166,571	50.9	21.1	193,536	59.2	12.2	33.1	36.6	40,005	13.2	32.1	12.3
39 101	Marion	46,452	58.7	11.2	54,199	53.4	9.9	33.7	33.3	41,222	14.7	28.9	10.4
39 103	Medina	118,187	39.3	29.2	135,826	68.3	6.8	43.1	23.2	63,609	5.9	15.6	24.9
39 105	Meigs	16,533	61.0	12.7	18,941	51.9	15.9	28.7	43.1	32,683	19.5	40.6	8.6
39 107	Mercer	27,104	57.7	15.6	31,488	68.8	7.1	43.2	27.2	49,300	7.3	22.1	12.5
39 109	Miami	70,599	49.8	20.0	81,206	65.1	9.9	40.6	28.7	50,594	11.0	23.2	15.7
39 113	Montgomery	362,103	42.0	24.2	426,745	61.6	11.1	36.6	33.4	42,100	13.6	29.9	14.1
39 117	Morrow	23,467	58.9	12.8	26,888	63.7	9.6	40.9	26.1	51,623	10.2	20.6	14.2
39 119	Muskingum	57,819	58.1	13.7	68,181	61.0	10.4	36.4	34.0	39,829	13.9	32.7	9.9
39 123	Ottawa	30,461	48.9	20.8	34,199	60.7	7.0	37.7	33.7	52,366	7.1	21.9	20.1
39 127	Perry	23,848	62.2	10.6	28,128	60.7	13.5	36.9	34.1	39,669	15.6	31.1	9.1
39 129	Pickaway	37,937	57.3	17.4	44,476	58.7	7.6	38.1	28.2	54,294	10.0	19.8	18.1
39 131	Pike	19,218	68.9	11.0	22,419	54.0	20.1	32.0	43.8	35,939	19.5	35.9	10.7
39 133	Portage	102,953	47.8	25.1	133,171	67.0	10.9	37.5	27.4	51,201	10.7	24.0	17.9
39 135	Preble	28,765	58.6	12.1	33,121	64.3	8.3	39.5	27.4	47,757	8.0	22.2	12.5
39 137	Putnam	22,781	50.9	20.6	26,325	70.1	5.0	45.9	25.5	60,205	3.4	15.7	18.3
39 139	Richland	85,824	54.6	15.3	99,220	57.7	10.5	34.8	33.6	41,697	12.5	27.5	11.5
39 141	Ross	54,350	57.3	14.8	62,361	55.4	15.3	33.4	36.1	43,089	14.0	28.3	14.8
39 143	Sandusky	41,255	52.7	13.0	47,994	63.5	8.7	39.5	30.6	44,576	9.3	24.7	12.2
39 145	Scioto	53,481	57.7	13.1	63,461	50.0	12.9	29.1	41.0	35,269	17.1	37.9	10.4
39 147	Seneca	37,019	56.3	14.6	44,804	63.4	11.1	38.3	30.5	41,872	13.0	27.4	10.9
39 149	Shelby	32,357	57.9	14.6	37,782	65.2	7.7	43.3	26.2	51,145	8.5	21.2	15.6
39 151	Stark	257,156	49.6	20.8	300,889	63.5	11.0	37.4	31.2	44,333	10.9	26.6	14.2
39 153	Summit	370,051	42.2	29.3	434,709	64.9	10.8	40.3	30.0	48,252	11.4	25.8	18.1
39 155	Trumbull	146,609	57.0	16.7	168,864	56.7	9.4	33.7	36.8	41,671	13.2	29.1	11.0
39 157	Tuscarawas	63,565	61.7	15.4	73,142	63.0	8.8	37.8	30.5	42,636	10.5	26.5	11.1
39 159	Union	34,673	44.9	25.6	40,154	65.0	6.0	45.4	19.5	62,622	5.0	15.1	27.0
39 161	Van Wert	19,528	58.7	14.8	22,449	64.0	11.2	39.7	35.3	44,893	9.2	26.1	11.8
39 165	Warren	142,776	36.3	37.1	163,588	68.1	7.3	46.0	20.1	71,134	4.2	12.6	31.7
39 167	Washington	43,456	54.9	16.1	50,385	57.4	10.4	35.7	35.0	42,834	10.5	28.4	14.5
39 169	Wayne	74,213	56.7	20.8	89,212	64.5	7.1	39.0	25.9	47,795	8.7	22.9	14.4
39 171	Williams	25,946	56.7	13.6	29,844	61.8	12.8	37.1	34.0	40,593	10.1	28.6	11.1
39 173	Wood	78,390	37.1	29.4	103,335	67.1	10.0	38.6	25.9	50,284	9.0	24.1	19.7
39 175	Wyandot	15,584	62.3	12.4	17,906	67.7	8.9	42.0	26.7	45,483	5.5	25.5	10.2

Table B-2. Counties — What: Education, Employment, and Income, 2010–2012—Continued

State or county code	State or county	Educational attainment			Employment status				Percent of households with no workers	Median household income (dollars)	Percent of families with income below poverty	Percent of households with income less than $25,000	Percent of households with income of $100,000 or more
		Total population 25 years and over	Percent with a high school diploma or less	Percent with a bachelor's degree or more	Total population 16 years and over	Percent in the labor force	Unemployment rate	Percent who worked full-time year-round					
	ACS table number:	C15002	C15002	C15002	B23025	B23025	B23025	C20005	C08202	B19013	C17003	C19001	C19001
	Column number:	1	2	3	4	5	6	7	8	9	10	11	12
40 000	**Oklahoma**	2,467,328	45.3	23.5	2,953,243	62.1	7.4	41.5	28.3	44,239	12.8	27.8	15.1
40 001	Adair......................	14,406	64.0	11.9	17,029	54.9	9.1	39.4	33.0	33,900	21.0	39.0	6.3
40 009	Beckham.................	14,484	55.2	16.2	17,554	55.1	1.7	39.4	26.1	48,847	10.4	26.5	19.0
40 013	Bryan	28,036	49.9	20.6	33,812	61.2	10.3	37.1	31.5	37,663	12.6	33.9	10.3
40 015	Caddo	19,631	56.9	13.8	23,001	52.8	9.9	35.0	34.5	38,741	14.0	32.5	8.9
40 017	Canadian................	78,172	36.6	25.7	91,166	68.3	5.8	49.6	20.9	60,978	5.7	14.9	23.7
40 019	Carter	31,831	58.4	16.8	36,759	60.0	7.5	44.1	29.0	40,994	10.1	28.6	10.4
40 021	Cherokee................	29,511	43.1	24.7	37,727	53.9	8.1	34.1	33.6	35,584	15.7	37.0	9.5
40 027	Cleveland................	163,535	35.6	31.8	208,018	65.9	5.6	44.7	21.4	53,247	8.9	21.1	20.8
40 031	Comanche..............	77,544	45.2	19.9	97,538	65.6	7.8	43.2	25.0	45,850	13.6	25.5	14.0
40 037	Creek	47,506	52.3	16.2	55,245	58.5	9.6	37.9	32.0	41,962	12.3	27.6	13.6
40 039	Custer....................	16,619	50.3	25.2	22,157	63.7	6.5	37.7	23.9	43,303	13.5	29.6	13.9
40 041	Delaware................	29,342	54.3	16.3	33,304	52.6	9.9	32.8	39.6	36,084	16.5	35.8	9.8
40 047	Garfield..................	40,192	50.7	21.6	47,433	65.4	6.2	44.8	25.3	44,585	9.5	22.7	11.9
40 049	Garvin....................	18,529	59.2	15.9	21,566	55.5	6.8	40.2	32.9	37,054	15.3	34.8	10.4
40 051	Grady	34,826	51.1	17.3	41,213	59.4	5.4	41.8	28.0	48,318	10.2	26.7	14.8
40 065	Jackson	16,661	46.9	19.8	19,900	66.5	8.2	47.3	25.3	40,623	10.9	26.4	12.8
40 071	Kay	30,658	47.3	19.3	35,818	61.0	9.4	37.9	34.1	40,097	13.1	30.6	11.8
40 079	Le Flore	33,378	56.3	12.3	39,458	52.4	12.0	31.9	40.0	34,650	17.4	37.1	8.5
40 081	Lincoln...................	23,203	55.2	13.2	26,764	59.0	10.1	40.3	32.3	40,915	13.1	30.7	13.2
40 083	Logan	28,267	43.1	25.2	33,745	60.7	6.8	40.5	23.9	53,032	9.8	22.6	21.9
40 087	McClain..................	23,283	48.8	19.9	26,946	63.0	3.2	46.9	24.0	53,638	9.2	22.3	22.1
40 089	McCurtain..............	21,881	60.8	13.6	25,638	53.3	12.6	30.9	39.8	31,130	22.7	41.4	7.9
40 091	McIntosh................	14,789	56.6	13.0	16,691	45.4	11.0	28.5	45.4	35,032	17.9	37.4	8.6
40 097	Mayes	27,356	52.7	16.0	32,045	57.6	10.7	35.1	34.7	40,547	15.0	31.1	8.9
40 101	Muskogee...............	46,782	49.6	17.7	55,189	54.8	9.8	36.4	36.9	38,156	18.1	35.3	9.0
40 109	Oklahoma...............	471,307	39.7	29.5	564,483	65.8	7.1	43.3	26.1	44,271	14.8	27.9	16.7
40 111	Okmulgee...............	26,293	50.5	13.6	31,109	54.9	11.2	35.9	41.2	37,617	14.0	34.1	10.3
40 113	Osage	32,722	55.4	15.2	37,745	55.5	8.5	38.5	36.1	40,477	12.8	30.7	11.7
40 115	Ottawa	20,963	52.0	13.7	25,010	58.3	10.6	38.4	35.3	35,507	17.9	36.5	8.5
40 119	Payne	41,946	35.5	37.0	64,597	62.8	6.2	33.4	25.1	36,542	13.2	35.3	12.0
40 121	Pittsburg................	31,843	52.0	15.6	36,678	53.5	5.7	38.3	34.9	40,689	15.0	30.6	12.3
40 123	Pontotoc................	24,063	45.7	27.4	29,831	63.9	8.0	43.3	28.7	41,820	13.4	30.2	10.5
40 125	Pottawatomie..........	45,784	51.0	17.0	54,655	58.4	6.6	39.8	29.9	41,584	14.8	30.9	12.5
40 131	Rogers	57,627	41.5	24.1	67,905	64.4	6.5	46.0	23.7	57,466	6.9	18.6	20.3
40 133	Seminole................	16,686	55.2	13.4	19,742	54.8	9.4	37.0	37.2	34,016	16.4	36.6	9.1
40 135	Sequoyah...............	28,033	59.0	13.0	32,664	55.8	11.2	36.0	36.4	38,020	13.9	33.7	9.4
40 137	Stephens................	30,717	54.0	17.7	35,410	58.3	7.7	40.0	33.1	43,790	10.9	28.6	13.3
40 139	Texas.....................	12,708	55.4	21.0	15,690	70.2	7.6	49.1	18.2	46,805	8.2	23.2	14.0
40 143	Tulsa	395,189	37.8	29.5	470,140	67.0	7.6	44.5	24.6	46,893	12.1	25.6	17.9
40 145	Wagoner................	49,015	45.8	22.4	57,135	63.6	6.6	43.4	26.4	54,805	8.3	20.2	18.8
40 147	Washington	35,102	43.6	26.2	40,644	59.2	8.3	40.6	33.0	49,086	12.0	25.0	18.1
40 153	Woodward	13,531	51.2	20.1	15,704	63.8	4.0	45.5	25.3	51,162	8.4	24.0	17.6
41 000	**Oregon**	2,643,922	35.7	29.3	3,104,852	62.9	11.9	35.0	30.8	48,525	11.7	25.2	17.9
41 003	Benton...................	51,215	21.7	49.0	72,896	59.3	8.7	28.8	32.1	46,238	10.2	30.6	21.8
41 005	Clackamas..............	262,405	31.9	31.0	303,623	65.1	11.0	39.1	27.3	61,682	6.7	17.4	26.5
41 007	Clatsop...................	26,593	37.2	21.3	30,665	62.1	9.8	30.8	32.6	45,691	12.4	26.3	12.5
41 009	Columbia................	34,141	47.1	16.4	39,287	58.6	12.9	33.9	34.1	52,739	10.2	23.6	17.5
41 011	Coos......................	46,252	44.2	18.1	52,484	52.0	12.7	28.2	44.7	37,345	11.6	33.1	8.6
41 013	Crook	15,145	53.5	12.7	16,921	53.3	20.5	28.2	44.9	35,052	16.5	35.3	7.5
41 015	Curry	17,447	39.9	21.9	19,246	47.7	18.3	24.7	53.0	38,017	8.4	34.5	10.1
41 017	Deschutes...............	112,271	30.1	30.8	128,212	62.4	13.9	32.2	34.8	47,265	11.1	24.9	17.3
41 019	Douglas..................	77,926	45.7	15.7	88,652	52.0	14.4	27.1	42.2	38,974	14.7	30.4	9.7
41 027	Hood River..............	15,082	43.5	29.3	17,283	69.9	7.8	40.3	24.7	58,344	7.4	18.0	18.3
41 029	Jackson...................	143,357	39.1	24.1	165,847	60.0	14.4	30.9	36.2	42,424	13.0	28.9	13.1
41 031	Jefferson.................	14,326	47.5	16.3	16,826	59.0	18.0	33.3	31.0	45,069	14.8	21.6	12.8
41 033	Josephine...............	60,191	42.4	17.2	68,424	49.0	15.8	24.8	48.2	36,102	14.0	33.8	9.0
41 035	Klamath.................	45,510	43.4	19.6	53,130	58.2	14.5	30.0	37.0	37,903	13.9	33.1	9.7
41 039	Lane	238,255	34.7	27.5	292,515	59.8	12.7	30.1	34.5	41,465	12.7	30.2	13.6
41 041	Lincoln...................	35,108	39.9	24.6	39,021	56.8	11.4	32.0	40.7	42,342	11.0	29.3	11.9
41 043	Linn	79,774	42.2	16.5	92,575	57.7	10.9	33.2	34.7	44,296	14.1	28.3	10.4
41 045	Malheur..................	20,123	50.2	13.9	24,058	51.4	13.3	28.0	33.4	36,318	16.7	37.2	8.9
41 047	Marion....................	203,907	43.9	21.1	244,073	62.5	15.0	34.2	30.2	45,405	15.4	25.5	13.9
41 051	Multnomah..............	526,036	29.9	39.3	611,844	68.7	11.1	38.0	26.4	50,185	13.4	25.5	20.6
41 053	Polk.......................	48,260	36.0	28.5	59,721	59.4	12.6	33.1	33.3	50,178	11.9	24.9	18.4
41 057	Tillamook................	18,670	47.9	19.6	21,075	54.5	10.7	31.3	37.7	42,957	9.9	27.8	8.1
41 059	Umatilla.................	49,090	47.1	14.6	58,541	62.3	10.0	36.5	28.8	46,305	12.3	27.3	12.9
41 061	Union	17,069	43.3	22.2	20,687	55.7	9.4	30.2	36.3	41,462	10.6	33.3	11.1
41 065	Wasco....................	17,443	42.3	19.3	20,239	58.4	11.2	31.7	34.1	42,080	9.8	23.3	12.6
41 067	Washington	358,641	28.3	39.6	417,929	69.8	9.7	42.9	20.9	63,224	8.5	16.7	27.0
41 071	Yamhill...................	64,753	46.8	21.5	78,304	62.8	10.0	35.2	29.2	51,055	10.6	21.4	17.9
42 000	**Pennsylvania**	8,708,982	48.6	27.3	10,320,759	62.8	9.2	39.2	29.8	51,402	9.5	24.2	20.4
42 001	Adams....................	69,406	56.2	20.1	82,436	65.9	5.7	42.5	25.8	57,285	6.7	20.0	20.0
42 003	Allegheny...............	865,053	38.2	35.7	1,017,820	63.9	8.1	41.0	30.2	50,693	8.9	25.5	20.6
42 005	Armstrong...............	50,000	61.7	14.6	56,589	59.2	8.9	37.3	35.6	43,734	10.0	26.8	11.8
42 007	Beaver	122,307	48.9	21.8	140,111	60.9	7.5	39.1	33.5	48,417	9.7	25.4	16.2
42 009	Bedford	35,444	65.0	13.0	40,228	59.1	7.8	37.2	34.1	40,605	10.2	30.6	10.8
42 011	Berks	273,725	54.2	22.9	328,147	65.7	9.9	40.4	27.9	53,882	10.3	21.9	20.3
42 013	Blair	88,695	59.9	17.3	103,580	59.7	7.5	38.7	33.0	42,785	8.2	28.1	12.0

Table B-2. Counties — What: Education, Employment, and Income, 2010–2012—*Continued*

State or county code	State or county	Educational attainment			Employment status				Percent of households with no workers	Median household income (dollars)	Percent of families with income below poverty	Percent of households with income less than $25,000	Percent of households with income of $100,000 or more
		Total population 25 years and over	Percent with a high school diploma or less	Percent with a bachelor's degree or more	Total population 16 years and over	Percent in the labor force	Unemployment rate	Percent who worked full-time year-round					
	ACS table number:	C15002	C15002	C15002	B23025	B23025	B23025	C20005	C08202	B19013	C17013	C19001	C19001
	Column number:	1	2	3	4	5	6	7	8	9	10	11	12
	Pennsylvania—Cont.												
42 015	Bradford	44,086	61.0	16.5	50,535	57.5	5.9	37.6	33.2	46,070	9.7	25.2	13.6
42 017	Bucks	437,593	38.6	35.5	503,452	68.9	8.2	40.2	22.7	74,375	4.3	13.6	35.5
42 019	Butler	126,855	43.3	30.3	149,058	64.8	7.3	40.9	27.2	56,524	6.0	19.3	23.8
42 021	Cambria	101,389	58.3	18.2	118,308	55.2	8.9	34.5	37.1	41,208	9.3	29.9	10.8
42 025	Carbon	47,051	57.3	15.8	53,437	58.9	10.3	36.1	34.2	49,491	6.7	24.2	14.1
42 027	Centre	85,974	39.5	40.1	133,463	58.2	6.0	33.8	27.0	47,596	7.0	27.6	19.3
42 029	Chester	335,304	31.1	48.1	394,912	69.3	6.8	45.5	20.4	83,501	4.3	12.2	41.5
42 031	Clarion	25,850	59.7	17.7	33,128	56.8	9.2	34.8	35.7	41,750	9.9	30.8	11.1
42 033	Clearfield	59,007	63.7	13.5	67,593	56.5	9.0	35.3	35.0	41,612	10.6	30.5	10.6
42 035	Clinton	25,212	58.4	17.3	32,348	57.3	7.7	35.9	32.6	41,001	10.7	30.6	10.5
42 037	Columbia	43,705	57.8	21.2	56,321	58.8	6.2	37.1	31.6	43,997	7.8	28.6	14.3
42 039	Crawford	59,961	59.2	18.8	71,322	57.6	9.1	33.6	35.2	41,299	12.8	30.1	10.1
42 041	Cumberland	163,151	44.1	32.1	194,534	65.7	6.5	42.9	26.1	58,845	6.2	17.2	23.3
42 043	Dauphin	184,234	47.1	27.4	214,697	66.5	8.0	44.3	26.8	53,041	9.8	21.4	20.4
42 045	Delaware	371,836	40.5	34.8	447,207	65.2	9.2	41.2	25.6	61,760	7.6	18.6	29.2
42 047	Elk	23,429	61.1	14.8	26,426	60.4	6.3	41.5	34.3	45,353	8.2	22.3	11.0
42 049	Erie	184,842	50.7	24.4	225,735	62.4	9.6	36.7	31.0	44,475	12.2	28.6	14.5
42 051	Fayette	98,222	63.6	13.8	112,385	52.7	10.5	32.7	40.2	38,494	13.8	33.0	9.5
42 055	Franklin	102,894	58.1	19.5	119,243	63.8	7.6	41.5	28.8	51,608	7.8	20.0	17.2
42 059	Greene	27,033	61.5	16.8	32,007	50.3	6.4	33.7	31.6	44,100	9.9	27.0	15.2
42 061	Huntingdon	32,517	63.4	14.9	38,115	53.3	8.3	33.0	34.8	43,504	9.3	26.5	10.8
42 063	Indiana	56,607	56.1	22.6	73,980	57.2	8.7	33.6	33.3	43,632	10.3	29.6	13.4
42 065	Jefferson	31,710	64.6	13.1	36,620	57.7	8.3	37.0	35.4	40,215	10.8	30.0	8.8
42 067	Juniata	17,095	69.7	11.6	19,618	62.2	7.7	39.4	30.8	45,105	7.7	24.7	10.8
42 069	Lackawanna	149,400	49.2	25.4	176,457	60.8	8.3	38.5	32.3	44,117	9.5	27.3	16.4
42 071	Lancaster	344,048	55.1	23.5	410,062	66.5	7.4	41.2	24.8	54,704	7.9	20.1	19.2
42 073	Lawrence	64,128	56.4	19.8	73,880	58.6	8.2	35.9	34.9	42,112	12.3	30.1	12.7
42 075	Lebanon	92,104	59.9	19.4	107,319	65.4	8.4	41.5	28.5	53,791	8.0	20.0	17.1
42 077	Lehigh	239,152	47.5	27.6	280,286	65.8	10.6	40.2	28.1	53,201	9.7	22.6	20.7
42 079	Luzerne	226,643	52.1	20.6	265,456	60.1	9.0	37.5	33.5	43,536	12.4	29.4	14.8
42 081	Lycoming	79,922	56.0	18.6	95,550	61.9	9.3	37.8	30.5	44,214	10.6	27.3	11.8
42 083	McKean	30,264	60.3	15.4	35,434	55.5	11.9	35.3	36.3	40,871	12.5	29.5	8.5
42 085	Mercer	80,349	55.1	20.4	95,166	56.7	8.6	34.1	34.4	42,246	9.6	27.6	12.1
42 087	Mifflin	32,705	69.5	11.7	37,357	56.4	8.4	33.6	37.3	37,890	11.7	31.5	7.5
42 089	Monroe	112,658	47.0	23.2	136,099	64.7	14.9	37.2	27.5	56,735	9.8	20.3	21.3
42 091	Montgomery...............	560,194	32.1	45.5	645,495	68.8	7.3	45.5	22.1	77,813	4.0	13.7	37.8
42 095	Northampton	204,425	46.4	26.5	243,045	63.3	8.8	39.5	28.2	58,225	8.0	19.8	24.3
42 097	Northumberland	68,273	65.7	14.3	78,180	58.0	9.6	38.3	34.4	40,403	9.7	29.1	11.3
42 099	Perry	31,727	59.3	16.2	36,845	66.0	8.9	44.8	26.4	55,769	7.6	19.1	16.4
42 101	Philadelphia	992,077	54.0	23.5	1,232,442	58.4	16.0	34.0	36.8	35,581	21.8	37.6	12.6
42 103	Pike	40,301	45.8	22.4	46,512	59.6	14.6	34.1	35.5	56,052	7.4	18.9	20.5
42 107	Schuylkill....................	107,862	62.5	14.3	122,232	57.8	9.9	36.8	34.1	45,255	9.4	27.5	12.4
42 109	Snyder	26,070	63.7	16.6	32,073	61.9	5.6	39.0	28.2	46,370	7.2	21.3	13.2
42 111	Somerset	56,834	65.0	14.1	64,468	56.0	8.2	36.6	34.7	42,743	8.5	27.8	11.7
42 115	Susquehanna	30,965	58.8	16.7	35,260	60.7	9.0	37.5	32.0	47,606	8.5	24.2	14.2
42 117	Tioga	29,038	56.7	18.2	34,772	57.0	8.4	36.6	34.8	42,963	10.6	28.1	11.3
42 119	Union	30,472	57.1	21.3	37,697	49.6	8.2	32.7	32.5	46,450	9.2	25.7	14.6
42 121	Venango	38,989	59.8	15.4	44,560	59.0	7.4	36.6	35.7	41,009	12.1	30.0	8.9
42 123	Warren	30,202	57.5	18.2	34,159	58.2	7.6	38.1	34.4	43,318	8.5	27.5	12.2
42 125	Washington	147,182	49.9	25.4	171,154	62.6	7.9	38.9	31.3	52,771	7.4	23.3	19.9
42 127	Wayne	38,813	54.1	19.1	43,987	53.5	8.6	32.7	35.1	47,605	9.7	25.1	13.7
42 129	Westmoreland	264,902	47.7	25.2	302,463	61.1	7.1	39.1	32.9	48,250	7.3	25.2	18.6
42 131	Wyoming...................	19,642	57.9	17.3	22,994	61.4	8.5	39.2	30.1	49,288	7.9	23.5	16.2
42 133	York..........................	299,171	53.8	22.0	348,053	67.8	9.3	42.8	26.0	57,247	7.3	18.8	21.8
44 000	**Rhode Island**............	710,902	42.3	31.0	858,819	66.0	10.2	39.1	28.8	54,900	9.7	24.2	23.9
44 001	Bristol	33,774	33.7	43.2	40,805	65.2	9.1	37.3	27.0	66,288	5.6	18.3	33.9
44 003	Kent	119,516	40.5	29.4	136,213	69.0	10.2	41.3	27.9	59,707	6.2	20.0	24.4
44 005	Newport	58,499	30.9	43.3	68,407	67.4	7.4	41.9	26.2	70,723	5.9	17.6	32.6
44 007	Providence	414,578	47.6	26.2	508,467	64.8	11.3	38.1	30.0	48,225	12.9	28.9	19.7
44 009	Washington	84,535	30.6	43.3	104,927	67.3	7.1	39.9	26.6	70,411	4.0	14.8	33.1
45 000	**South Carolina**..........	3,115,808	46.0	24.6	3,719,118	61.4	11.8	37.8	30.8	43,490	14.1	29.2	15.4
45 001	Abbeville...................	16,915	59.2	11.1	20,259	53.4	13.7	33.4	41.0	35,335	15.5	36.8	6.7
45 003	Aiken........................	110,551	46.3	24.0	129,429	57.1	9.9	37.1	33.5	43,555	15.1	28.5	16.7
45 007	Anderson...................	127,667	51.8	18.5	148,769	58.7	11.1	36.1	33.7	40,044	13.7	30.9	13.8
45 011	Barnwell	14,479	58.0	11.6	17,401	56.5	18.2	35.0	38.4	35,189	24.9	38.2	10.4
45 013	Beaufort	114,176	35.3	36.5	134,597	58.5	9.2	34.8	34.7	56,369	8.8	18.1	22.4
45 015	Berkeley	118,781	45.8	21.2	142,779	65.9	12.4	43.1	24.1	50,680	12.1	22.7	15.5
45 019	Charleston.................	242,052	33.3	38.7	290,900	65.7	10.1	41.8	25.9	49,914	13.4	26.6	21.0
45 021	Cherokee	36,169	61.8	12.6	43,371	57.1	15.1	32.3	36.6	33,030	18.5	39.5	8.0
45 023	Chester......................	22,193	61.4	11.3	25,865	55.9	17.3	33.9	36.4	31,867	22.5	39.7	8.2
45 025	Chesterfield	31,141	65.4	11.5	36,713	56.2	12.4	35.8	38.6	30,979	18.2	41.5	8.6
45 027	Clarendon.................	23,538	59.8	13.0	27,998	50.4	20.1	27.5	43.3	32,331	20.2	39.3	8.2
45 029	Colleton....................	25,694	60.2	13.4	30,245	54.3	16.6	31.5	39.2	30,357	18.6	39.5	6.9
45 031	Darlington	45,649	57.2	15.8	54,052	57.2	16.1	33.3	36.4	35,225	20.0	37.2	10.7

Table B-2. Counties — What: Education, Employment, and Income, 2010–2012—*Continued*

State or county code	State or county	Educational attainment			Employment status				Percent of households with no workers	Median household income (dollars)	Percent of families with income below poverty	Percent of households with income less than $25,000	Percent of households with income of $100,000 or more
		Total population 25 years and over	Percent with a high school diploma or less	Percent with a bachelor's degree or more	Total population 16 years and over	Percent in the labor force	Unemployment rate	Percent who worked full-time year-round					
	ACS table number:	C15002	C15002	C15002	B23025	B23025	B23025	C20005	C08202	B19013	C17013	C19001	C19001
	Column number:	1	2	3	4	5	6	7	8	9	10	11	12
	South Carolina—Cont.												
45 033	Dillon....................	20,639	67.9	6.4	24,700	53.1	17.6	28.7	39.5	26,063	27.8	48.0	5.7
45 035	Dorchester............	90,590	41.4	23.8	106,749	66.6	11.1	43.5	23.4	52,177	9.1	21.5	20.0
45 037	Edgefield	18,939	55.0	16.6	21,801	51.4	11.3	33.6	33.6	44,651	16.1	29.3	14.8
45 039	Fairfield................	16,291	60.2	14.4	19,130	55.5	13.1	34.8	39.1	33,508	20.5	40.0	7.8
45 041	Florence................	90,190	50.2	21.1	107,377	61.6	13.7	38.9	30.4	41,147	16.2	29.1	14.2
45 043	Georgetown	43,060	48.0	22.4	49,138	51.9	14.1	30.7	42.9	38,985	15.4	33.4	14.4
45 045	Greenville	305,964	40.5	30.9	361,452	64.3	9.6	40.4	26.7	48,076	12.2	26.8	19.3
45 047	Greenwood	46,032	51.8	22.7	55,451	58.3	15.0	33.8	37.8	35,165	17.1	37.9	12.2
45 049	Hampton	13,950	64.2	11.7	16,638	56.3	16.5	35.4	38.1	35,734	20.2	38.2	9.6
45 051	Horry...................	194,743	45.2	22.9	227,104	60.8	11.2	33.5	34.0	40,655	14.5	29.2	11.9
45 053	Jasper..................	16,438	67.4	11.1	19,875	65.8	10.3	37.8	24.5	35,741	15.1	33.7	5.8
45 055	Kershaw...............	42,156	49.1	18.7	48,961	61.0	12.7	37.1	31.7	41,343	14.0	31.0	13.9
45 057	Lancaster	53,785	50.5	19.1	61,808	56.8	14.2	34.3	36.4	41,845	17.1	31.8	10.9
45 059	Laurens	44,418	59.6	13.7	53,098	58.1	13.4	34.4	33.5	36,887	16.0	34.7	9.4
45 063	Lexington	179,201	40.2	27.8	209,997	67.5	9.9	44.6	24.6	52,911	10.9	21.9	19.2
45 067	Marion..................	22,081	63.0	12.1	25,952	55.1	18.1	30.9	39.2	28,171	22.0	44.5	8.0
45 069	Marlboro...............	19,710	67.1	10.1	23,254	46.8	15.3	29.1	42.1	27,648	26.6	46.4	6.6
45 071	Newberry	25,086	55.5	18.9	29,939	59.9	11.0	38.4	34.9	41,439	14.1	29.5	13.3
45 073	Oconee.................	52,624	50.6	21.7	60,575	53.9	13.7	33.2	39.1	42,254	12.1	30.8	12.3
45 075	Orangeburg............	59,588	56.7	18.3	73,243	54.3	15.8	31.8	37.9	32,687	20.9	38.6	8.0
45 077	Pickens	73,294	49.3	22.0	98,159	57.7	12.8	32.1	32.6	40,244	11.2	31.5	12.2
45 079	Richland................	243,209	33.1	35.5	311,921	67.5	10.7	41.2	24.4	47,147	12.1	26.3	18.0
45 083	Spartanburg...........	188,789	49.3	20.8	225,373	61.6	11.5	37.2	31.0	42,243	14.4	29.5	14.2
45 085	Sumter..................	68,936	48.9	17.7	83,214	60.2	13.5	38.3	31.0	40,280	14.8	30.0	10.6
45 087	Union	19,814	60.2	13.2	23,009	54.8	15.9	33.4	42.2	33,186	15.8	39.0	8.2
45 089	Williamsburg	23,274	62.6	12.6	27,065	45.6	11.6	27.7	42.9	25,169	24.3	49.8	6.0
45 091	York.....................	151,312	40.6	28.9	178,718	67.3	12.2	42.1	24.8	51,542	10.9	24.0	21.5
46 000	**South Dakota**	538,464	41.6	26.4	644,256	69.0	5.3	46.8	24.1	48,900	9.1	23.9	15.7
46 011	Brookings	16,942	33.7	40.0	26,957	70.3	4.4	38.0	19.6	45,991	7.8	28.3	15.0
46 013	Brown..................	24,415	42.8	26.3	29,230	71.6	3.4	50.4	21.9	51,047	3.4	23.6	16.6
46 029	Codington	18,080	46.0	23.0	21,431	72.0	4.9	49.5	24.0	46,720	7.5	26.1	10.9
46 081	Lawrence	16,427	39.0	29.1	20,216	65.9	4.9	44.2	26.8	44,042	8.2	29.9	14.9
46 083	Lincoln.................	30,060	30.1	38.0	34,355	77.1	1.6	61.4	14.5	74,288	3.1	11.9	30.5
46 093	Meade..................	16,507	40.1	21.1	20,190	70.9	4.0	49.5	23.6	52,312	6.9	19.1	15.9
46 099	Minnehaha	112,471	39.9	28.8	134,116	74.0	5.1	51.9	20.0	50,604	8.9	20.8	16.4
46 103	Pennington	67,975	37.2	27.8	80,382	69.2	6.3	44.7	25.0	49,637	7.8	22.2	16.4
46 135	Yankton.................	15,818	47.0	26.0	18,210	64.8	3.6	43.1	25.8	52,445	8.2	24.9	14.9
47 000	**Tennessee**	4,294,543	49.0	23.7	5,077,947	61.5	10.4	38.7	30.1	42,959	13.6	29.0	15.0
47 001	Anderson...............	53,068	49.8	22.7	60,882	57.1	8.9	36.9	36.4	42,304	13.5	29.2	16.1
47 003	Bedford.................	29,254	65.6	12.0	34,578	59.3	10.8	39.2	32.2	40,203	15.7	31.3	11.5
47 009	Blount..................	86,609	49.4	20.7	99,928	60.0	9.8	37.5	32.2	45,204	11.4	26.1	12.9
47 011	Bradley.................	66,731	51.9	17.8	79,744	60.1	12.7	35.1	32.2	38,823	15.2	32.5	11.5
47 013	Campbell	28,644	71.4	8.3	32,968	46.9	14.1	28.6	45.6	30,555	19.6	43.1	4.5
47 017	Carroll	19,523	63.0	14.8	22,973	53.7	13.6	32.8	40.1	35,073	13.0	35.0	9.2
47 019	Carter	40,741	57.0	16.6	47,460	55.2	9.5	33.5	38.1	32,847	18.6	38.0	6.0
47 021	Cheatham	26,461	54.9	18.1	30,562	65.0	9.3	41.1	24.0	49,703	12.4	20.4	15.7
47 025	Claiborne...............	22,398	67.8	13.8	26,233	49.4	8.5	34.1	40.6	32,525	19.8	39.1	7.0
47 029	Cocke...................	25,318	71.4	8.6	28,864	53.8	16.3	27.4	45.1	28,509	24.1	45.6	6.4
47 031	Coffee...................	35,980	59.5	17.7	41,746	58.0	14.0	34.6	35.2	34,885	18.2	35.1	8.6
47 035	Cumberland............	42,033	58.0	16.4	47,067	46.5	10.1	27.1	48.3	36,957	11.1	34.6	7.6
47 037	Davidson................	426,209	38.8	35.3	511,368	68.3	9.3	42.9	23.6	45,147	14.7	27.2	16.8
47 043	Dickson.................	33,783	61.1	12.9	39,429	61.1	9.2	40.4	28.5	43,448	12.7	28.4	11.3
47 045	Dyer....................	25,894	58.4	18.5	30,213	58.7	10.4	39.4	30.7	36,931	14.2	31.3	11.3
47 047	Fayette.................	27,197	50.9	21.0	30,784	60.8	9.3	40.2	30.0	55,005	10.8	22.1	22.4
47 051	Franklin................	27,705	55.7	18.0	33,334	55.0	12.5	32.9	38.1	41,548	10.7	29.3	11.2
47 053	Gibson..................	33,816	56.3	14.4	38,905	57.9	13.6	36.8	34.6	36,493	14.9	34.3	9.2
47 055	Giles	20,313	62.3	14.2	23,762	56.8	13.9	33.9	36.8	37,027	13.1	34.3	7.6
47 057	Grainger	15,998	68.4	10.8	18,438	53.3	12.8	32.3	39.6	33,969	17.1	38.3	8.1
47 059	Greene	48,754	60.1	16.5	56,170	54.5	9.9	34.0	38.7	34,797	19.7	37.1	7.4
47 063	Hamblen................	43,045	60.3	15.9	49,757	58.8	12.8	37.0	36.3	37,293	17.0	35.5	9.2
47 065	Hamilton................	233,657	41.4	27.2	275,972	63.4	10.0	39.6	29.1	46,068	11.9	27.3	17.5
47 069	Hardeman..............	18,628	68.9	8.2	21,895	46.4	21.9	27.4	43.2	27,641	21.1	45.4	8.3
47 071	Hardin..................	18,214	67.1	12.0	20,929	52.3	19.0	30.0	42.7	31,035	17.1	41.9	8.2
47 073	Hawkins.................	40,364	62.6	12.2	45,486	55.4	10.0	36.1	36.8	37,660	9.9	29.9	9.8
47 077	Henderson..............	18,961	59.7	12.7	22,030	57.1	11.1	36.5	35.8	36,387	14.5	30.1	9.8
47 079	Henry...................	23,011	61.4	16.7	25,959	55.5	13.9	35.4	37.0	37,398	14.1	32.9	8.7
47 081	Hickman................	16,979	67.2	11.3	19,608	54.3	10.7	30.7	37.4	40,166	12.1	31.2	9.5
47 089	Jefferson................	35,289	60.0	13.0	42,051	60.2	13.0	35.9	33.8	38,872	13.0	30.0	10.4
47 093	Knox....................	290,630	36.3	34.0	352,558	64.3	7.1	41.8	26.8	45,761	9.5	26.6	17.4
47 097	Lauderdale.............	18,511	68.6	10.5	21,797	49.4	14.3	30.3	38.0	31,465	25.9	40.9	6.4
47 099	Lawrence...............	28,103	65.1	12.0	32,478	59.8	12.0	35.1	34.8	36,607	13.0	32.5	7.2
47 103	Lincoln.................	23,108	58.9	14.2	26,688	59.6	8.1	36.4	33.7	40,981	12.4	27.7	10.8
47 105	Loudon.................	36,118	47.1	24.9	40,576	55.0	12.1	34.1	37.5	47,096	9.7	23.2	16.9
47 107	McMinn.................	36,171	59.1	14.4	42,010	54.4	10.2	32.3	35.7	38,585	15.0	35.4	10.5
47 109	McNairy.................	18,167	66.1	11.5	20,639	51.1	14.7	31.2	44.1	30,926	15.3	39.6	6.6

Table B-2. Counties — What: Education, Employment, and Income, 2010–2012—Continued

State or county code	State or county	Educational attainment			Employment status				Percent of households with no workers	Median household income (dollars)	Percent of families with income below poverty	Percent of households with income less than $25,000	Percent of households with income of $100,000 or more
		Total population 25 years and over	Percent with a high school diploma or less	Percent with a bachelor's degree or more	Total population 16 years and over	Percent in the labor force	Unemployment rate	Percent who worked full-time year-round					
	ACS table number:	C15002	C15002	C15002	B23025	B23025	B23025	C20005	C08202	B19013	C17013	C19001	C19001
	Column number:	1	2	3	4	5	6	7	8	9	10	11	12
	Tennessee—Cont.												
47 111	Macon	14,964	69.5	8.9	17,598	59.5	11.8	37.3	30.1	34,515	16.5	34.7	5.7
47 113	Madison	63,648	48.5	23.7	78,011	60.6	12.8	37.6	29.8	41,317	13.9	30.0	14.5
47 115	Marion	19,811	61.4	15.1	22,538	55.4	8.4	36.9	33.9	38,761	14.2	33.0	12.3
47 117	Marshall	20,847	62.5	13.2	24,216	62.4	12.0	37.3	31.2	38,698	11.9	30.7	12.9
47 119	Maury	54,976	51.5	18.4	63,871	64.0	9.7	39.0	30.0	43,967	12.9	29.3	12.6
47 123	Monroe	31,527	64.2	10.9	36,149	55.0	13.3	30.1	38.0	35,777	15.2	34.7	8.8
47 125	Montgomery	107,154	41.4	23.6	133,942	66.4	9.9	42.9	23.2	48,605	13.1	22.9	13.5
47 129	Morgan	15,525	70.9	7.7	17,912	43.4	10.2	28.2	38.5	36,979	15.0	33.2	9.3
47 131	Obion	21,756	60.7	15.7	25,023	56.2	13.4	33.8	37.0	40,113	14.2	32.4	9.6
47 133	Overton	15,258	66.4	12.5	17,570	52.8	11.6	34.2	39.2	32,310	18.2	39.2	5.9
47 141	Putnam	46,205	54.4	22.4	59,157	56.6	9.8	33.9	34.3	33,539	17.8	37.6	10.8
47 143	Rhea	21,510	63.9	11.7	25,232	55.1	12.8	33.1	38.6	36,499	16.7	36.7	9.2
47 145	Roane	39,081	55.0	17.5	44,141	53.5	10.6	34.1	37.5	42,357	10.4	28.9	14.7
47 147	Robertson	44,464	54.9	16.5	51,803	65.3	8.9	43.6	25.3	52,578	9.9	19.3	16.0
47 149	Rutherford	166,896	39.9	28.3	206,530	70.2	9.5	44.9	20.0	53,675	8.9	19.5	18.2
47 151	Scott	14,784	69.4	11.0	17,228	50.7	17.1	25.9	44.8	29,302	21.8	42.5	6.4
47 155	Sevier	63,825	56.6	13.7	73,616	65.8	10.1	38.7	27.5	42,883	10.6	28.6	11.0
47 157	Shelby	594,117	40.9	29.1	719,945	65.5	12.1	41.4	25.4	45,488	16.7	28.4	18.6
47 163	Sullivan	113,027	50.6	21.6	128,988	56.4	9.9	35.3	37.3	38,899	13.7	33.1	13.0
47 165	Sumner	109,823	46.4	22.9	127,533	65.1	7.5	43.6	23.6	52,996	8.3	20.2	19.7
47 167	Tipton	39,021	53.1	14.2	47,012	63.8	13.0	39.8	27.7	51,213	11.0	24.5	16.9
47 177	Warren	27,295	67.5	11.5	31,255	54.7	10.7	33.3	37.7	31,122	20.9	40.6	8.0
47 179	Washington	85,125	42.8	29.8	101,666	59.3	6.8	40.1	31.8	42,937	12.5	29.2	16.2
47 183	Weakley	21,847	54.5	20.8	28,835	59.1	12.8	33.2	34.6	35,164	13.2	36.6	10.7
47 185	White	18,043	70.2	11.6	20,820	55.7	11.4	34.1	39.6	33,913	17.4	35.8	5.4
47 187	Williamson	122,808	23.5	52.2	140,218	68.9	5.4	45.8	18.2	87,959	5.3	11.0	44.3
47 189	Wilson	79,116	45.7	26.0	91,327	64.7	8.5	44.8	24.2	58,983	8.3	18.7	23.8
48 000	**Texas**	16,080,717	44.3	26.4	19,465,219	65.0	8.4	43.4	22.2	50,776	14.1	24.4	21.2
48 001	Anderson	41,730	59.7	10.1	48,144	45.1	6.1	31.3	32.3	41,102	15.5	29.9	14.3
48 005	Angelina	56,037	53.4	14.4	65,986	58.9	10.8	37.3	30.8	40,994	13.0	28.6	11.3
48 007	Aransas	17,326	50.4	20.4	19,380	48.6	8.0	29.6	42.1	39,635	15.1	31.3	16.6
48 013	Atascosa	28,680	61.9	13.9	33,862	59.7	10.5	36.7	27.5	47,885	14.6	26.9	17.3
48 015	Austin	18,978	48.4	19.3	22,245	63.3	9.1	46.5	30.7	49,419	8.7	25.7	19.8
48 019	Bandera	15,715	39.0	20.8	17,134	53.9	7.0	35.5	35.2	47,526	5.2	21.2	16.5
48 021	Bastrop	49,665	51.6	16.5	56,975	63.9	8.7	45.7	21.9	52,251	8.8	21.7	20.0
48 025	Bee	21,568	59.6	9.1	25,973	42.6	9.6	28.5	28.9	40,201	21.5	32.7	10.5
48 027	Bell	188,311	40.0	21.3	236,380	66.1	8.2	47.2	22.9	49,643	11.4	22.5	16.5
48 029	Bexar	1,090,525	42.3	26.2	1,336,889	65.4	8.5	43.3	22.8	49,201	14.3	24.9	18.7
48 037	Bowie	62,250	47.1	19.7	73,216	56.6	9.3	38.2	32.1	42,021	15.8	31.9	14.3
48 039	Brazoria	205,329	40.9	26.7	240,769	65.1	6.6	46.6	19.3	65,308	8.6	17.3	30.4
48 041	Brazos	97,370	36.7	37.7	161,624	62.9	9.0	32.7	24.6	36,770	15.6	37.1	15.8
48 049	Brown	25,112	55.5	15.3	29,925	51.3	3.4	38.1	34.6	40,144	13.6	31.4	11.9
48 053	Burnet	30,554	49.4	21.5	34,672	56.2	7.0	37.3	34.7	47,917	11.4	24.1	12.9
48 055	Caldwell	23,849	58.2	16.7	29,778	53.8	10.7	34.6	27.8	43,290	13.7	27.9	13.8
48 057	Calhoun	14,312	53.6	15.8	16,382	60.9	10.8	39.3	32.6	45,430	17.2	28.3	17.1
48 061	Cameron	235,352	60.9	15.1	292,354	54.8	10.7	33.9	29.0	32,214	30.3	40.4	10.0
48 067	Cass	21,211	55.8	13.4	24,385	53.8	11.6	32.0	37.2	34,241	14.1	36.2	9.6
48 071	Chambers	22,844	43.0	17.9	26,572	61.4	8.2	46.9	23.9	73,143	6.2	15.9	34.9
48 073	Cherokee	32,810	58.7	13.2	39,048	54.4	7.0	34.4	31.7	35,913	21.5	36.1	10.2
48 085	Collin	522,528	22.5	48.8	607,360	72.5	5.8	52.2	13.0	82,296	6.0	11.4	40.6
48 089	Colorado	14,331	57.4	18.1	16,293	58.7	4.9	45.7	31.0	43,278	14.5	30.9	15.5
48 091	Comal	77,763	35.9	31.4	89,082	62.0	7.0	42.5	27.9	61,032	7.6	17.4	29.0
48 097	Cooke	25,348	50.5	17.0	30,172	66.4	10.5	41.7	28.8	47,665	10.8	27.3	16.3
48 099	Coryell	45,955	46.4	14.8	57,286	56.7	7.4	42.9	25.1	49,747	9.9	20.0	14.0
48 113	Dallas	1,510,506	46.0	28.3	1,819,105	68.5	9.3	46.5	19.7	48,509	15.9	24.5	19.8
48 121	Denton	429,364	26.8	39.9	520,017	74.6	7.0	50.8	14.7	71,857	5.5	13.6	34.6
48 123	DeWitt	14,231	60.9	12.1	16,189	56.1	8.3	34.9	30.6	44,863	13.3	29.0	17.0
48 135	Ector	83,783	55.5	13.0	103,493	66.3	5.4	46.0	20.9	50,474	13.5	25.4	17.3
48 139	Ellis	95,109	46.5	21.3	114,352	68.0	8.6	46.5	20.2	60,608	8.9	18.6	23.9
48 141	El Paso	480,971	49.8	20.6	602,559	60.1	9.0	39.2	23.5	39,821	20.7	32.1	13.5
48 143	Erath	22,277	46.1	25.8	31,266	65.9	5.2	39.9	24.6	39,095	11.9	34.7	11.7
48 147	Fannin	23,469	54.9	16.1	27,307	53.1	8.2	35.6	34.2	43,368	12.8	27.8	12.5
48 149	Fayette	17,746	56.6	15.3	20,028	60.8	3.0	44.8	31.2	44,447	9.0	30.0	14.3
48 157	Fort Bend	383,059	31.1	39.9	453,184	67.6	5.9	48.5	13.1	82,668	7.1	12.3	40.0
48 167	Galveston	195,444	39.0	28.3	229,638	66.1	9.2	43.3	22.6	60,597	9.6	20.1	28.2
48 171	Gillespie	18,339	41.6	31.2	20,752	59.0	7.2	38.1	37.7	53,194	5.8	23.1	20.3
48 177	Gonzales	12,775	59.2	14.8	15,091	60.4	8.9	41.9	29.8	39,450	14.6	33.5	12.9
48 179	Gray	15,412	52.1	14.8	17,645	56.8	6.1	38.2	28.0	42,691	9.8	27.1	11.4
48 181	Grayson	81,007	46.0	19.7	96,164	60.7	9.9	39.7	30.1	46,564	12.4	26.5	14.9
48 183	Gregg	78,462	45.9	19.8	94,607	62.3	7.6	40.8	27.7	43,021	15.9	28.2	14.9
48 185	Grimes	18,552	58.5	10.6	21,434	49.8	6.7	34.1	30.1	44,902	11.7	27.1	16.9
48 187	Guadalupe	87,254	43.2	25.4	103,939	68.3	7.1	46.5	21.1	61,822	7.0	15.8	24.4
48 189	Hale	21,808	61.3	13.7	27,201	59.1	8.1	40.8	24.6	39,139	20.3	32.0	10.1
48 199	Hardin	36,739	54.5	14.2	42,462	60.4	7.2	40.5	28.9	51,579	8.7	25.4	16.9
48 201	Harris	2,597,308	44.9	28.2	3,141,800	68.3	9.2	45.6	18.3	51,902	15.7	23.5	23.2
48 203	Harrison	42,997	51.0	17.8	51,789	61.5	8.2	41.4	29.4	46,113	13.1	26.5	16.3
48 209	Hays	94,870	31.2	37.6	128,032	65.8	7.3	42.0	18.8	57,495	9.2	24.0	26.3

Table B-2. Counties — What: Education, Employment, and Income, 2010–2012—Continued

State or county code	State or county	Educational attainment			Employment status				Percent of households with no workers	Median household income (dollars)	Percent of families with income below poverty	Percent of households with income less than $25,000	Percent of households with income of $100,000 or more
		Total population 25 years and over	Percent with a high school diploma or less	Percent with a bachelor's degree or more	Total population 16 years and over	Percent in the labor force	Unemployment rate	Percent who worked full-time year-round					
	ACS table number:	C15002	C15002	C15002	B23025	B23025	B23025	C20005	C08202	B19013	C17013	C19001	C19001
	Column number:	1	2	3	4	5	6	7	8	9	10	11	12
	Texas—Cont.												
48 213	Henderson	54,612	54.6	13.7	62,907	53.5	9.5	33.4	38.2	38,540	13.7	32.0	11.2
48 215	Hidalgo	434,224	61.9	16.1	550,527	58.3	11.2	34.0	25.4	33,549	31.1	39.5	10.8
48 217	Hill	23,771	52.1	13.7	27,555	58.6	10.3	38.1	30.2	39,802	14.6	31.7	11.6
48 219	Hockley	14,036	50.5	17.4	17,564	65.1	6.2	43.8	25.0	48,577	10.3	24.8	16.0
48 221	Hood	37,508	44.4	23.4	42,281	57.2	9.3	35.8	33.6	51,485	6.1	18.3	20.9
48 223	Hopkins	23,576	56.0	15.3	27,360	61.5	9.0	41.7	29.4	42,305	14.2	27.2	12.0
48 225	Houston	17,116	56.7	14.8	19,289	46.9	8.8	29.4	41.1	31,529	16.8	41.9	8.4
48 227	Howard	23,710	54.4	11.8	28,167	48.5	7.8	34.1	34.0	42,173	14.6	27.5	14.3
48 231	Hunt	56,261	51.6	17.9	67,742	60.2	13.7	37.7	32.1	44,457	15.3	27.1	16.6
48 233	Hutchinson	14,532	51.8	13.5	16,970	58.9	6.4	41.7	29.1	47,338	11.6	25.5	16.7
48 241	Jasper	24,293	58.7	10.9	28,011	52.0	13.2	34.9	40.1	38,840	14.1	34.0	11.9
48 245	Jefferson	165,337	50.2	17.8	199,550	57.9	11.2	36.7	30.9	41,465	17.8	32.1	15.6
48 249	Jim Wells	25,607	62.3	12.0	30,875	59.9	8.5	40.4	25.4	41,724	17.5	28.8	17.3
48 251	Johnson	98,150	50.1	15.7	115,692	64.2	8.5	42.9	23.6	56,579	10.2	17.8	20.1
48 253	Jones	14,689	67.2	8.8	17,192	31.5	6.8	20.9	35.7	38,052	14.7	33.9	11.1
48 257	Kaufman	66,789	48.7	17.5	78,625	67.0	10.2	46.3	21.0	60,690	10.5	19.4	24.0
48 259	Kendall	24,270	30.5	40.5	27,682	61.3	4.4	40.5	24.8	64,916	4.5	16.6	34.7
48 265	Kerr	35,806	41.1	30.1	40,880	54.3	8.3	35.0	38.5	43,199	12.8	28.6	15.7
48 273	Kleberg	18,402	50.0	25.3	25,258	60.1	11.8	33.9	28.1	37,825	20.1	33.9	13.6
48 277	Lamar	33,188	51.0	15.3	39,296	58.7	7.9	38.1	32.9	41,339	16.7	32.3	12.2
48 281	Lampasas	13,783	40.4	21.3	15,933	61.6	8.5	41.9	28.4	47,687	10.5	22.3	21.6
48 291	Liberty	49,654	61.7	8.3	59,107	55.6	14.1	35.3	26.2	48,275	13.5	26.8	18.0
48 293	Limestone	15,960	58.9	13.8	18,690	57.1	5.3	38.8	26.8	39,812	13.8	29.9	13.0
48 303	Lubbock	166,326	40.8	28.0	221,076	67.0	7.1	41.4	22.9	43,632	14.3	30.0	15.8
48 309	McLennan	143,436	45.2	22.4	184,491	61.6	8.1	39.2	27.0	40,894	15.5	30.5	14.6
48 321	Matagorda	23,315	58.3	17.4	28,201	59.8	7.5	41.6	29.2	41,618	17.5	32.9	18.8
48 323	Maverick	30,932	66.1	12.1	38,732	57.8	12.0	33.3	26.9	30,269	29.6	43.4	8.0
48 325	Medina	30,474	50.6	17.8	36,406	56.2	8.2	39.3	27.1	53,315	12.5	24.8	15.3
48 329	Midland	88,244	42.3	22.8	105,826	69.2	4.4	49.5	17.6	58,875	8.6	18.4	25.7
48 331	Milam	16,248	57.0	16.1	18,901	55.8	10.9	34.3	35.7	35,406	18.6	37.3	13.3
48 339	Montgomery	304,183	38.2	30.6	356,647	66.0	7.7	44.5	21.4	65,717	10.0	17.9	30.2
48 341	Moore	12,868	62.3	13.2	15,736	69.6	3.5	47.8	19.7	50,139	11.7	19.1	12.6
48 347	Nacogdoches	36,917	46.1	25.4	51,516	57.5	9.3	36.1	31.0	37,059	19.2	36.5	11.4
48 349	Navarro	30,621	55.0	16.7	36,487	61.8	10.1	38.9	28.5	39,944	15.8	29.3	13.0
48 355	Nueces	219,595	46.7	20.3	265,556	63.9	7.8	41.6	24.5	46,079	14.4	26.0	17.7
48 361	Orange	54,737	54.4	12.1	64,660	58.5	9.8	36.0	29.0	46,808	12.4	25.0	16.8
48 363	Palo Pinto	18,950	56.9	13.9	21,996	57.3	7.7	38.7	33.1	39,444	13.1	29.9	13.1
48 365	Panola	16,356	56.7	11.4	18,555	56.9	7.0	42.1	33.0	53,898	9.6	24.4	14.9
48 367	Parker	78,986	38.7	24.1	92,561	62.4	7.5	43.3	24.4	63,672	8.4	17.4	28.8
48 373	Polk	32,364	57.8	12.2	37,059	47.0	12.2	30.9	40.2	38,350	14.7	31.0	11.4
48 375	Potter	75,798	51.4	15.5	91,449	62.2	6.2	42.5	24.0	35,819	19.3	34.2	10.8
48 381	Randall	79,014	31.7	30.3	95,970	68.9	4.6	49.0	22.7	57,479	7.1	20.6	21.5
48 397	Rockwall	51,986	29.3	36.2	59,913	69.1	6.8	49.7	16.3	83,502	4.8	11.7	39.6
48 401	Rusk	36,109	53.3	13.2	42,584	55.6	6.2	39.8	29.2	45,822	10.2	26.7	15.9
48 407	San Jacinto	18,384	60.8	13.2	21,182	53.9	15.4	35.3	32.0	46,230	13.9	23.5	17.7
48 409	San Patricio	41,076	51.5	15.8	49,253	61.6	8.0	40.9	27.1	50,426	15.8	25.3	17.6
48 419	Shelby	16,296	58.8	14.6	19,546	58.7	7.3	40.8	31.5	36,181	17.1	32.2	12.9
48 423	Smith	135,529	40.5	24.6	164,114	63.0	8.0	40.3	26.5	45,131	12.2	26.6	17.0
48 427	Starr	34,119	74.7	9.9	43,274	53.0	12.2	27.5	31.0	24,629	40.6	50.7	6.8
48 439	Tarrant	1,158,850	39.8	29.0	1,388,492	69.5	8.9	47.0	19.4	55,222	12.4	21.1	23.1
48 441	Taylor	81,514	43.3	24.0	103,728	62.7	7.4	40.7	26.5	43,503	13.0	28.1	14.3
48 449	Titus	19,180	55.5	13.4	23,830	63.3	7.9	41.2	26.1	40,296	16.5	28.5	13.4
48 451	Tom Green	70,465	49.2	21.7	88,379	64.5	6.4	42.0	27.2	43,390	13.7	29.6	14.8
48 453	Travis	682,091	30.4	44.1	834,732	71.9	7.9	46.8	17.7	55,625	13.1	21.6	25.3
48 457	Tyler	15,436	57.3	11.1	17,918	47.0	13.7	26.6	40.9	38,767	11.7	33.7	9.2
48 459	Upshur	26,730	52.0	14.0	31,094	58.6	7.9	38.0	30.2	44,417	9.3	25.8	14.9
48 463	Uvalde	16,225	52.9	16.4	19,842	58.6	12.0	35.1	30.1	34,100	18.3	34.8	9.9
48 465	Val Verde	28,696	60.2	14.8	35,583	62.0	9.6	39.5	25.0	41,358	16.3	29.3	14.1
48 467	Van Zandt	36,082	55.5	13.7	41,403	53.0	6.7	35.2	36.0	41,521	14.3	29.7	11.7
48 469	Victoria	56,692	50.4	15.4	67,419	64.6	8.6	42.8	27.2	49,183	14.7	26.2	18.0
48 471	Walker	44,071	51.9	17.8	58,471	40.4	6.7	27.1	29.7	37,472	17.6	34.4	13.9
48 473	Waller	25,345	57.8	19.8	34,587	58.2	7.7	41.8	23.2	50,480	12.2	24.8	20.2
48 477	Washington	22,716	49.1	23.0	27,460	55.2	4.9	39.7	31.2	46,015	12.5	25.8	15.6
48 479	Webb	137,961	58.0	16.3	175,536	58.8	6.2	37.8	19.2	36,462	27.8	35.4	12.3
48 481	Wharton	26,806	60.9	13.4	31,421	64.5	8.1	44.3	27.6	37,861	16.5	34.3	12.3
48 485	Wichita	82,943	48.3	19.6	104,577	62.5	6.5	41.5	27.3	43,023	11.1	27.0	14.1
48 489	Willacy	13,621	72.1	8.8	16,962	34.0	9.3	25.6	42.9	27,627	33.5	47.8	9.4
48 491	Williamson	283,514	28.5	38.0	328,664	71.5	8.1	49.4	17.5	69,418	5.4	12.6	29.6
48 493	Wilson	29,241	49.2	18.0	34,136	64.8	5.3	45.3	22.8	65,114	9.1	18.2	27.2
48 497	Wise	39,438	54.7	15.1	46,150	63.6	10.0	42.6	25.1	53,588	9.0	19.1	20.8
48 499	Wood	30,455	51.5	17.9	34,437	49.4	7.6	30.0	41.8	42,543	10.1	25.5	13.1
49 000	**Utah**	1,612,410	33.0	30.1	2,020,550	68.5	7.9	40.9	19.7	57,255	9.9	19.0	21.0
49 003	Box Elder	29,343	42.8	21.0	35,393	64.2	6.7	40.7	24.1	53,538	7.5	15.8	14.9
49 005	Cache	58,542	29.8	35.3	82,322	70.2	7.1	37.6	17.2	48,325	11.2	23.3	15.6
49 007	Carbon	13,328	43.1	12.6	16,164	62.0	10.0	34.4	30.7	45,897	11.0	28.2	11.9
49 011	Davis	176,646	26.7	34.3	215,615	69.6	5.0	45.0	16.2	68,683	6.5	13.0	28.1
49 021	Iron	24,717	35.6	26.0	34,305	63.5	16.6	32.3	26.1	40,526	16.9	30.7	10.5

Table B-2. Counties — What: Education, Employment, and Income, 2010–2012—*Continued*

State or county code	State or county	Total population 25 years and over	Percent with a high school diploma or less	Percent with a bachelor's degree or more	Total population 16 years and over	Percent in the labor force	Unemployment rate	Percent who worked full-time year-round	Percent of households with no workers	Median household income (dollars)	Percent of families with income below poverty	Percent of households with income less than $25,000	Percent of households with income of $100,000 or more
		Educational attainment			**Employment status**						**Percent of families with income below poverty**	**Percent of households with income less than $25,000**	**Percent of households with income of $100,000 or more**
ACS table number:		C15002	C15002	C15002	B23025	B23025	B23025	C20005	C08202	B19013	C17013	C19001	C19001
Column number:		1	2	3	4	5	6	7	8	9	10	11	12
	Utah—Cont.												
49 035	Salt Lake	636,295	34.4	30.9	774,509	71.5	8.4	44.2	18.3	58,732	10.5	19.1	22.2
49 039	Sanpete	15,311	37.5	20.2	20,635	53.2	10.3	28.6	29.0	45,825	7.1	23.6	14.2
49 041	Sevier	12,592	43.4	16.6	14,904	60.1	7.9	34.3	31.8	43,378	14.0	27.7	10.2
49 043	Summit	24,533	23.4	47.9	28,258	73.2	6.2	48.3	16.6	93,030	6.4	10.9	46.0
49 045	Tooele	33,256	41.4	20.0	39,893	68.4	7.2	46.5	16.4	61,970	8.4	14.7	22.7
49 047	Uintah	19,017	49.8	16.3	23,253	66.7	5.1	39.0	19.8	60,120	9.9	18.5	18.1
49 049	Utah	259,355	24.0	36.2	361,499	67.8	7.9	35.4	15.8	58,675	10.4	18.3	21.2
49 051	Wasatch	14,434	31.5	31.3	17,054	69.1	6.3	41.9	17.3	62,716	5.9	15.1	25.6
49 053	Washington	85,922	34.5	25.9	103,244	58.0	11.2	32.1	34.5	46,936	10.5	23.3	14.1
49 057	Weber	140,443	39.6	22.9	171,569	68.0	7.9	42.6	22.0	54,334	9.7	18.5	17.8
50 000	**Vermont**	433,835	39.3	34.8	516,064	67.7	6.8	41.0	26.4	53,037	7.6	22.3	19.2
50 001	Addison	24,795	41.0	34.7	30,411	68.3	7.6	39.0	24.6	57,335	8.8	21.1	19.3
50 003	Bennington	26,188	38.2	34.3	30,646	64.7	7.8	36.2	29.2	51,223	9.8	24.1	18.2
50 005	Caledonia	21,491	46.6	26.2	25,296	65.0	8.3	36.8	29.7	42,487	10.9	29.8	14.0
50 007	Chittenden	102,023	27.7	47.5	130,849	71.1	6.1	42.3	21.5	62,204	6.0	18.8	25.9
50 011	Franklin	32,993	48.8	22.3	37,852	70.4	6.5	46.1	23.2	53,910	9.2	21.6	19.4
50 015	Lamoille	16,944	41.1	35.1	19,956	68.3	4.4	43.8	28.7	51,460	10.9	23.9	17.6
50 017	Orange	20,603	44.6	29.7	23,690	68.2	6.5	42.7	23.5	52,141	8.2	20.8	16.5
50 019	Orleans	19,439	54.4	20.8	22,298	59.3	7.6	36.5	35.3	39,802	11.9	32.6	10.4
50 021	Rutland	43,495	45.5	28.4	51,197	65.1	8.3	38.9	30.0	48,533	8.1	24.8	15.3
50 023	Washington	42,072	34.5	38.1	49,090	69.3	5.7	44.5	23.4	57,351	4.9	18.6	19.6
50 025	Windham	31,990	41.0	34.0	36,875	66.6	7.7	37.6	29.1	50,220	6.2	23.1	15.3
50 027	Windsor	41,961	40.2	34.0	46,832	65.2	6.4	41.8	31.0	51,812	6.3	22.6	19.0
51 000	**Virginia**	5,433,053	38.0	34.9	6,460,347	66.5	7.2	45.1	23.4	62,811	8.2	18.9	29.3
51 001	Accomack	23,838	62.1	16.5	27,003	59.3	6.9	42.2	36.2	38,880	14.5	35.0	11.7
51 003	Albemarle	66,732	26.1	52.2	81,582	60.3	5.2	39.8	25.9	67,159	5.2	16.9	33.0
51 009	Amherst	22,283	55.5	16.4	26,576	61.3	9.8	38.6	31.8	43,463	8.1	27.6	11.7
51 013	Arlington	161,788	16.6	71.0	184,024	79.4	3.9	60.2	13.0	101,319	5.6	9.9	50.7
51 015	Augusta	53,088	57.9	20.2	60,357	59.4	5.8	39.2	27.3	49,784	8.0	20.7	14.4
51 019	Bedford	49,583	46.4	25.1	56,024	63.1	7.4	42.2	27.9	56,611	6.3	19.0	20.3
51 023	Botetourt	23,752	46.1	24.2	26,801	63.8	5.5	44.3	26.1	65,417	3.7	14.7	24.0
51 027	Buchanan	17,686	66.2	7.2	20,161	44.0	10.3	28.0	45.7	30,226	20.0	41.3	5.9
51 031	Campbell	38,021	54.7	16.6	44,694	61.4	9.1	39.8	29.0	44,517	12.2	25.6	13.8
51 033	Caroline	19,677	56.2	17.6	22,942	66.1	12.8	44.3	28.1	54,553	7.4	20.1	23.9
51 035	Carroll	21,820	58.9	11.4	24,559	56.5	9.7	36.0	38.4	31,281	15.6	38.4	7.1
51 041	Chesterfield	210,634	34.1	36.5	249,074	68.6	7.5	46.7	20.1	71,492	4.9	11.8	32.1
51 047	Culpeper	31,671	50.3	21.4	36,851	64.0	8.4	43.5	20.1	61,297	7.9	15.9	27.0
51 053	Dinwiddie	19,259	59.5	14.6	22,690	59.9	10.4	40.4	29.6	51,684	10.1	20.6	16.4
51 059	Fairfax	752,161	22.1	57.8	867,328	73.3	5.1	52.1	14.0	107,923	4.0	7.7	54.4
51 061	Fauquier	44,706	35.8	33.2	51,872	69.1	5.8	48.1	19.6	90,657	3.5	9.7	44.2
51 065	Fluvanna	18,719	45.6	29.8	20,649	59.5	6.0	45.2	27.3	64,025	5.3	15.0	24.6
51 067	Franklin	40,186	51.1	20.1	46,277	56.9	8.6	35.6	34.6	42,175	9.9	28.4	14.4
51 069	Frederick	53,603	42.8	29.1	62,495	66.6	7.4	43.7	21.2	68,795	3.9	14.9	30.7
51 073	Gloucester	26,043	44.1	20.2	30,066	62.9	7.7	40.9	26.0	59,927	6.8	15.6	22.7
51 075	Goochland	16,167	38.1	39.6	17,678	60.9	5.5	42.3	20.5	83,977	4.3	11.7	41.7
51 083	Halifax	25,366	57.5	14.3	29,048	54.0	11.1	36.0	40.9	34,819	16.0	38.2	8.6
51 085	Hanover	67,738	36.6	35.8	79,195	67.1	5.8	44.9	21.7	73,664	3.7	13.0	33.7
51 087	Henrico	211,167	32.6	39.6	245,280	70.1	8.3	46.5	22.0	59,739	8.2	16.8	25.9
51 089	Henry	38,450	59.2	10.5	43,732	55.6	14.1	31.9	37.6	32,914	12.7	35.8	5.8
51 093	Isle of Wight	24,792	43.0	27.9	28,664	67.0	8.5	46.3	25.8	66,781	7.6	17.2	31.7
51 095	James City	49,036	29.2	45.5	55,484	59.6	5.6	40.2	31.4	76,569	4.9	12.9	33.9
51 099	King George	15,499	37.8	33.5	18,285	70.8	7.1	51.0	18.0	88,382	4.5	9.7	44.1
51 105	Lee	18,499	58.8	11.9	21,162	43.6	10.4	26.1	45.8	31,050	17.3	39.9	3.8
51 107	Loudoun	207,765	21.1	57.0	237,390	76.8	4.4	56.0	9.2	121,621	2.6	4.8	61.2
51 109	Louisa	23,839	58.2	17.1	27,141	63.0	7.4	43.5	26.8	54,649	3.3	19.4	21.2
51 117	Mecklenburg	23,623	58.3	14.2	26,739	49.4	9.0	31.2	42.6	34,524	13.5	38.3	8.4
51 121	Montgomery	50,306	32.3	43.8	81,586	59.3	6.5	34.1	26.0	43,247	9.3	33.3	17.8
51 137	Orange	23,968	50.3	23.1	27,358	60.7	12.6	38.1	28.0	61,707	9.1	19.3	22.4
51 139	Page	17,070	65.6	12.5	19,689	58.6	11.8	34.3	35.6	41,834	14.5	30.0	10.2
51 143	Pittsylvania	45,555	56.2	14.2	51,734	58.7	8.9	36.8	33.4	41,730	11.2	28.7	10.2
51 145	Powhatan	19,970	41.9	26.7	22,947	60.0	4.0	41.8	22.6	71,669	4.3	13.7	35.7
51 147	Prince Edward	13,038	54.2	22.9	19,479	46.0	12.0	26.7	33.3	36,904	15.1	32.2	11.5
51 149	Prince George	24,491	50.3	17.3	29,196	56.3	7.5	41.4	21.4	56,898	4.8	11.4	22.5
51 153	Prince William	262,896	32.9	37.2	311,677	75.2	6.0	54.3	11.5	95,427	4.9	7.8	47.4
51 155	Pulaski	25,776	52.4	15.4	29,152	57.8	9.3	37.4	34.3	42,981	9.1	28.6	11.5
51 161	Roanoke	66,249	35.1	33.0	75,483	64.7	5.3	45.0	25.1	60,155	5.8	16.7	23.1
51 163	Rockbridge	16,420	53.0	22.8	18,498	53.9	4.4	37.0	34.9	46,104	7.8	23.7	14.1
51 165	Rockingham	51,868	55.6	24.0	60,931	64.2	6.4	41.8	27.0	51,099	8.6	21.7	17.9
51 167	Russell	20,719	63.3	10.7	23,660	48.5	9.7	33.1	44.8	32,797	16.2	38.3	9.1
51 169	Scott	16,934	64.2	10.5	19,170	51.2	8.6	33.8	43.4	34,484	15.5	37.4	8.7
51 171	Shenandoah	30,141	58.8	19.0	34,035	61.4	5.1	42.2	30.7	47,968	9.9	25.1	17.5
51 173	Smyth	22,940	61.9	13.2	26,175	55.0	8.9	37.3	39.9	35,540	15.1	36.3	8.5
51 177	Spotsylvania	80,333	42.6	27.9	95,465	69.0	7.3	45.3	18.1	78,089	5.9	12.1	36.4
51 179	Stafford	82,005	33.0	35.6	99,430	71.6	5.7	51.8	14.0	97,136	4.0	8.0	47.9
51 185	Tazewell	32,328	57.4	11.4	36,795	48.2	8.1	31.8	40.3	33,810	16.7	38.1	7.7
51 187	Warren	25,727	54.0	18.1	30,099	68.5	8.1	44.5	23.5	59,644	6.0	20.1	22.5

Table B-2. Counties — What: Education, Employment, and Income, 2010–2012—*Continued*

State or county code	State or county	Educational attainment			Employment status				Percent of households with no workers	Median household income (dollars)	Percent of families with income below poverty	Percent of households with income less than $25,000	Percent of households with income of $100,000 or more
		Total population 25 years and over	Percent with a high school diploma or less	Percent with a bachelor's degree or more	Total population 16 years and over	Percent in the labor force	Unemployment rate	Percent who worked full-time year-round					
	ACS table number:	C15002	C15002	C15002	B23025	B23025	B23025	C20005	C08202	B19013	C17013	C19001	C19001
	Column number:	1	2	3	4	5	6	7	8	9	10	11	12
	Virginia—Cont.												
51 191	Washington	39,545	50.8	21.4	45,342	57.8	6.6	37.6	34.0	41,193	5.9	26.9	11.8
51 195	Wise......................	28,542	59.9	12.5	33,873	47.6	12.9	27.3	44.9	34,414	20.9	38.2	9.6
51 197	Wythe.....................	21,049	54.3	13.3	23,708	61.4	11.4	39.6	34.7	37,468	10.4	34.2	10.0
51 199	York......................	43,133	26.0	41.6	51,550	66.1	4.2	47.0	18.9	78,920	5.7	10.6	38.1
51 510	Alexandria city.........	109,114	21.3	60.5	120,655	78.8	5.0	59.9	13.0	82,438	6.0	11.1	41.5
51 540	Charlottesville city......	25,317	34.0	48.5	37,791	60.5	6.6	35.8	27.6	44,183	10.8	30.4	20.3
51 550	Chesapeake city.........	147,465	36.5	28.7	175,472	68.6	7.4	47.8	19.1	68,750	7.5	14.9	28.4
51 590	Danville city.............	29,382	51.7	16.6	34,688	56.5	16.7	31.1	41.7	31,134	22.5	41.4	7.8
51 600	Fairfax city	16,131	23.0	53.1	18,949	68.6	6.5	46.7	18.8	94,496	5.3	11.3	49.0
51 630	Fredericksburg city......	15,018	38.7	34.0	20,947	64.6	13.1	34.9	27.6	46,397	10.8	25.0	19.2
51 650	Hampton city	88,701	38.6	22.8	109,809	64.6	10.2	43.0	25.9	51,654	12.0	23.4	17.8
51 660	Harrisonburg city	22,152	44.8	36.1	42,908	52.8	7.0	28.7	25.6	37,212	11.3	33.9	9.7
51 670	Hopewell city	14,061	61.8	8.9	16,975	58.6	15.4	39.3	40.6	36,748	16.0	32.2	8.2
51 680	Lynchburg city...........	44,167	41.1	31.6	63,378	57.5	11.0	30.9	33.3	37,020	16.9	34.9	13.3
51 683	Manassas city............	24,423	44.2	27.5	29,698	73.0	7.4	50.7	14.1	67,105	11.2	14.2	32.2
51 700	Newport News city......	112,906	39.7	24.0	142,113	70.0	9.9	44.8	24.0	49,690	11.4	23.1	15.5
51 710	Norfolk city..............	145,248	41.0	25.4	198,234	69.9	10.6	46.7	25.0	43,708	14.4	27.3	14.8
51 730	Petersburg city..........	21,568	62.6	13.3	26,164	53.7	18.5	32.0	41.4	34,214	19.7	38.7	5.6
51 740	Portsmouth city...........	62,704	47.7	19.2	75,624	62.3	10.2	41.0	28.9	44,945	15.2	28.3	12.3
51 760	Richmond city............	133,104	41.6	34.3	171,277	64.4	11.3	37.6	29.5	40,001	20.9	33.7	14.3
51 770	Roanoke city..............	67,489	47.5	23.9	77,909	62.7	8.5	40.6	32.1	38,593	16.6	32.4	10.2
51 775	Salem city	16,589	37.4	31.5	20,723	61.2	6.4	35.7	28.1	47,549	12.4	25.4	17.2
51 790	Staunton city.............	16,930	45.7	30.6	19,781	60.5	6.2	40.6	31.8	40,318	12.6	33.2	11.5
51 800	Suffolk city..............	55,950	41.9	25.3	65,546	67.8	7.9	45.9	21.1	67,546	8.1	16.7	27.8
51 810	Virginia Beach city......	290,821	29.8	32.5	350,695	70.7	6.0	50.1	19.2	65,169	6.7	13.6	28.0
51 820	Waynesboro city..........	14,218	56.6	20.8	16,254	60.5	8.9	38.8	32.7	43,656	18.0	30.1	9.6
51 840	Winchester city	17,424	47.9	28.2	21,048	63.5	9.3	39.5	31.7	42,590	14.7	29.4	17.3
53 000	**Washington**	4,577,171	33.7	31.5	5,419,523	65.1	9.9	39.3	26.6	57,966	9.3	20.1	24.3
53 003	Asotin....................	15,402	44.6	16.3	17,772	55.1	9.3	32.7	39.4	41,402	9.6	29.0	10.6
53 005	Benton....................	115,078	35.5	29.5	136,869	64.1	7.2	42.0	24.4	61,244	8.5	19.1	26.8
53 007	Chelan....................	48,712	46.1	22.4	57,139	62.6	9.2	39.4	31.2	49,670	9.5	21.9	18.0
53 009	Clallam...................	53,784	35.7	25.2	60,580	50.2	11.1	27.5	46.0	45,776	7.3	26.0	13.5
53 011	Clark.....................	283,860	34.9	25.9	333,040	64.6	11.7	37.8	26.7	56,696	9.4	18.4	21.6
53 015	Cowlitz...................	69,542	43.7	15.5	80,630	56.3	15.5	30.4	37.5	44,749	14.2	28.9	14.5
53 017	Douglas...................	25,217	47.5	17.4	29,773	65.0	9.5	36.6	27.8	52,442	11.5	17.8	15.4
53 021	Franklin..................	46,260	55.0	14.7	57,401	65.2	8.5	41.9	20.2	55,291	17.6	23.1	15.8
53 025	Grant.....................	54,015	51.8	15.0	65,853	64.3	13.7	37.1	27.7	42,904	16.2	27.8	11.8
53 027	Grays Harbor	50,559	45.9	14.7	58,807	54.1	16.3	27.8	39.6	42,192	12.6	27.2	12.0
53 029	Island....................	56,136	29.2	31.5	64,662	60.9	9.1	36.8	33.4	58,876	6.6	18.3	22.4
53 031	Jefferson.................	24,021	28.7	35.8	26,131	48.5	11.1	21.3	46.3	44,907	5.1	27.2	13.6
53 033	King......................	1,374,523	25.6	45.6	1,601,168	69.7	8.2	43.7	21.7	69,346	7.6	17.0	33.7
53 035	Kitsap	171,484	30.6	28.9	204,960	63.1	9.9	39.5	28.4	59,684	7.8	17.2	23.5
53 037	Kittitas..................	24,752	38.7	30.5	34,528	60.2	11.9	29.9	32.7	40,469	13.1	32.5	13.7
53 039	Klickitat.................	14,770	45.6	19.9	16,450	51.4	7.6	30.2	38.3	41,639	13.9	26.7	8.8
53 041	Lewis.....................	51,820	45.7	14.8	60,502	55.4	14.5	28.4	40.0	42,192	9.9	27.1	12.1
53 045	Mason	44,007	41.6	17.0	49,884	52.5	15.2	28.2	43.2	45,374	11.4	26.7	13.8
53 047	Okanogan..................	28,640	48.3	17.9	32,894	56.4	12.4	32.2	39.2	39,487	15.5	32.9	11.2
53 049	Pacific...................	15,732	45.2	16.6	17,539	50.3	10.8	27.0	44.1	38,934	10.3	33.8	11.2
53 053	Pierce....................	525,634	39.0	23.6	628,767	65.9	11.2	40.8	25.2	57,837	8.8	18.6	22.3
53 057	Skagit....................	80,312	37.2	24.1	93,550	59.8	10.0	35.1	32.1	54,429	9.2	20.3	20.0
53 061	Snohomish.................	486,727	33.6	28.6	570,957	68.5	10.0	42.2	22.2	66,377	7.3	15.8	28.3
53 063	Spokane	311,397	32.5	28.8	377,411	63.1	10.6	35.9	29.8	49,059	10.2	25.4	16.5
53 065	Stevens...................	30,684	41.8	16.9	34,882	51.8	12.2	28.8	41.1	40,668	13.5	28.4	10.4
53 067	Thurston..................	173,856	29.8	32.5	204,598	64.6	9.3	39.8	27.0	61,741	7.8	18.0	23.1
53 071	Walla Walla...............	38,309	34.0	25.2	47,568	57.4	6.4	33.3	34.2	45,252	12.6	27.2	14.9
53 073	Whatcom..................	132,203	31.3	32.2	166,705	63.8	9.9	34.5	28.5	52,034	10.0	23.9	18.2
53 075	Whitman	21,720	23.4	48.9	39,548	57.8	7.4	24.5	27.1	33,677	13.4	41.6	15.2
53 077	Yakima....................	146,644	55.1	15.8	179,013	62.1	10.8	36.1	28.4	43,480	18.5	28.0	14.6
54 000	**West Virginia**...........	1,297,393	57.1	18.3	1,513,935	54.4	8.6	35.4	37.0	40,151	13.1	32.7	12.5
54 003	Berkeley..................	71,413	51.9	19.6	82,736	65.9	12.0	41.6	26.4	52,631	9.8	22.2	19.0
54 005	Boone.....................	17,113	68.3	10.1	19,572	44.8	8.0	32.0	43.8	42,480	15.4	30.7	14.0
54 009	Brooke....................	17,095	55.3	16.7	20,039	56.1	11.0	33.7	39.1	41,028	9.6	28.4	12.2
54 011	Cabell....................	65,123	47.5	26.2	79,674	56.0	7.6	33.4	36.2	37,707	16.4	36.5	11.7
54 019	Fayette...................	32,931	64.9	10.2	37,540	45.7	10.1	30.1	43.1	32,465	16.0	37.8	6.6
54 025	Greenbrier	25,841	59.3	17.2	29,403	52.9	7.6	34.7	39.9	39,458	15.3	34.6	8.9
54 027	Hampshire	16,934	77.8	6.9	19,072	52.2	11.7	34.0	43.2	26,018	11.4	48.4	3.5
54 029	Hancock...................	22,451	56.0	16.1	24,956	58.1	8.6	36.5	33.5	36,784	14.3	31.3	10.7
54 033	Harrison..................	49,179	54.6	19.4	56,096	55.6	7.6	37.4	35.9	40,353	14.8	31.8	14.2
54 035	Jackson...................	20,535	56.8	16.4	23,475	51.8	10.7	33.8	42.9	40,007	15.8	29.2	14.4
54 037	Jefferson.................	35,797	45.8	27.5	42,729	66.8	9.0	43.2	22.5	63,563	7.6	19.3	26.4
54 039	Kanawha	137,723	50.6	24.6	157,103	60.1	7.5	41.1	33.2	44,972	10.9	28.4	15.1
54 043	Lincoln...................	15,179	69.6	8.3	17,333	44.1	11.9	28.2	41.8	33,960	21.5	36.3	5.7
54 045	Logan.....................	26,260	64.4	8.9	29,875	44.2	9.2	28.8	47.2	35,222	17.8	36.7	11.3
54 047	McDowell	15,674	78.2	5.5	17,811	32.9	13.4	22.6	58.7	22,405	29.8	53.4	5.4
54 049	Marion....................	39,364	52.9	20.7	46,556	57.8	5.3	40.3	33.0	41,238	11.7	32.0	12.9

Table B-2. Counties — What: Education, Employment, and Income, 2010–2012—*Continued*

State or county code	State or county	Educational attainment			Employment status				Percent of households with no workers	Median household income (dollars)	Percent of families with income below poverty	Percent of households with income less than $25,000	Percent of households with income of $100,000 or more
		Total population 25 years and over	Percent with a high school diploma or less	Percent with a bachelor's degree or more	Total population 16 years and over	Percent in the labor force	Unemployment rate	Percent who worked full-time year-round					
	ACS table number:	C15002	C15002	C15002	B23025	B23025	B23025	C20005	C08202	B19013	C17013	C19001	C19001
	Column number:	1	2	3	4	5	6	7	8	9	10	11	12
	West Virginia—Cont.												
54 051	Marshall....................	23,657	58.1	15.5	27,065	54.4	9.1	32.1	37.4	39,895	10.2	31.1	10.9
54 053	Mason	19,321	62.8	10.3	22,053	47.3	8.1	32.6	40.7	38,737	11.7	32.3	8.5
54 055	Mercer......................	43,944	57.1	18.4	50,920	49.2	6.4	32.6	41.1	35,124	14.2	35.6	8.4
54 057	Mineral....................	19,591	65.6	12.9	22,970	52.8	12.9	31.4	46.2	28,702	12.5	46.0	8.8
54 059	Mingo......................	18,681	67.8	10.9	21,347	43.9	12.3	28.2	49.5	37,133	17.4	35.7	12.0
54 061	Monongalia	56,696	40.3	38.4	84,670	59.6	6.5	36.8	28.4	42,698	9.7	34.1	18.0
54 067	Nicholas..................	18,772	64.3	14.6	21,532	50.5	10.9	30.4	41.4	38,098	15.4	34.8	11.8
54 069	Ohio........................	30,717	44.7	27.6	36,730	60.5	7.2	36.9	33.6	39,379	11.1	31.8	13.4
54 077	Preston....................	24,649	63.5	12.4	27,911	54.9	8.4	36.0	31.2	45,327	10.9	27.3	8.7
54 079	Putnam....................	39,441	48.6	23.7	44,482	60.1	4.7	45.8	27.9	53,661	7.6	20.5	20.9
54 081	Raleigh....................	56,120	57.7	17.8	64,433	49.2	6.5	33.3	39.0	39,757	13.1	32.6	12.7
54 083	Randolph..................	21,148	64.0	18.4	24,227	51.9	8.1	34.6	35.5	38,288	11.6	32.9	10.6
54 097	Upshur....................	16,428	64.1	16.2	19,875	50.9	7.4	34.1	35.3	40,229	15.4	33.3	10.4
54 099	Wayne......................	29,453	63.2	12.3	34,022	48.2	7.5	34.9	45.5	34,638	16.3	39.0	8.6
54 107	Wood......................	61,354	48.4	17.4	70,181	58.3	11.4	36.7	36.6	41,026	11.9	30.8	14.3
54 109	Wyoming..................	16,699	70.8	8.7	19,084	39.3	7.2	26.7	47.9	34,116	15.1	39.4	9.8
55 000	**Wisconsin**..............	3,828,580	42.4	26.7	4,538,112	67.8	8.1	41.4	26.5	51,340	9.0	22.9	18.2
55 001	Adams......................	16,226	57.2	13.0	17,856	49.1	11.6	27.3	44.2	45,431	7.9	24.1	9.6
55 005	Barron......................	32,334	52.6	16.0	36,892	64.8	8.2	39.0	32.0	44,276	8.1	25.3	10.7
55 009	Brown......................	164,315	42.1	26.4	195,752	70.0	7.5	44.0	23.7	51,975	7.9	21.6	18.6
55 015	Calumet..................	33,011	43.5	27.6	38,067	71.2	5.6	47.9	23.2	64,802	4.1	13.7	23.3
55 017	Chippewa..................	43,416	49.0	18.0	49,773	66.5	8.1	42.1	29.0	50,180	8.0	22.6	13.6
55 019	Clark........................	21,918	62.2	11.9	25,550	65.6	6.9	41.2	26.9	42,007	12.1	27.3	9.7
55 021	Columbia..................	39,782	43.2	21.9	45,266	70.2	7.5	45.7	24.0	56,892	5.7	18.0	19.9
55 025	Dane........................	324,536	25.4	46.5	400,953	73.3	5.9	45.2	19.9	61,125	7.1	18.8	25.5
55 027	Dodge......................	62,630	51.7	16.2	71,888	64.9	8.2	41.8	25.5	52,211	6.7	19.2	14.6
55 029	Door	21,304	42.9	27.5	23,621	62.6	8.2	35.0	35.6	48,140	7.8	23.2	13.7
55 031	Douglas....................	30,308	40.2	20.1	35,645	65.1	8.2	38.1	29.6	43,910	12.5	25.8	12.8
55 033	Dunn........................	26,522	44.1	23.8	36,082	66.3	6.9	35.8	26.8	47,119	8.8	24.4	13.6
55 035	Eau Claire................	61,460	34.3	31.9	81,266	69.9	6.4	38.6	24.5	46,746	8.9	28.0	16.5
55 039	Fond du Lac..............	69,855	49.5	19.4	81,602	70.0	8.3	41.9	26.3	52,999	7.4	20.4	14.9
55 043	Grant........................	31,602	48.6	20.3	41,634	64.8	5.0	38.5	26.8	46,060	7.8	25.6	11.1
55 045	Green	25,672	47.3	20.9	29,065	71.6	6.2	46.1	22.5	54,272	6.9	20.8	17.8
55 049	Iowa........................	16,591	43.1	22.2	18,756	70.7	5.4	47.1	23.0	53,516	5.3	19.7	17.5
55 053	Jackson....................	14,339	57.3	14.0	16,378	57.2	6.4	37.7	32.4	40,990	13.5	28.2	8.9
55 055	Jefferson..................	55,603	45.5	22.9	66,569	70.7	7.1	43.9	24.7	53,028	7.3	20.0	17.7
55 057	Juneau......................	18,997	57.4	11.6	21,652	60.7	10.2	38.0	33.3	43,433	10.5	30.1	10.9
55 059	Kenosha	107,986	44.6	23.6	129,939	68.1	11.6	41.2	25.4	53,931	10.3	22.2	20.2
55 061	Kewaunee	14,401	55.0	13.1	16,390	66.4	5.5	43.9	28.3	52,204	7.2	23.3	14.5
55 063	La Crosse..................	72,996	34.9	30.3	94,527	69.1	5.7	41.1	24.6	49,286	6.2	23.6	17.2
55 067	Langlade..................	14,415	58.0	12.6	16,347	60.9	7.9	33.6	35.3	41,578	9.3	28.1	8.5
55 069	Lincoln....................	20,636	52.1	15.1	23,349	63.9	7.6	40.3	31.1	48,328	6.5	22.8	10.8
55 071	Manitowoc................	57,090	51.1	19.1	65,488	66.9	7.5	41.4	29.2	48,114	6.6	23.2	14.3
55 073	Marathon	91,330	48.8	21.8	106,009	70.6	8.1	43.3	23.8	52,059	7.8	21.4	17.1
55 075	Marinette..................	30,022	53.8	13.2	34,560	58.7	10.0	33.6	38.4	40,061	8.2	31.8	9.1
55 079	Milwaukee................	608,388	43.3	27.6	741,035	66.3	11.8	39.0	28.9	42,097	17.4	31.0	14.7
55 081	Monroe	30,180	53.2	16.6	34,740	65.3	6.7	43.0	27.0	46,064	12.6	25.0	12.3
55 083	Oconto	26,954	54.7	14.8	30,412	66.8	7.4	41.5	29.8	50,394	7.0	24.5	15.1
55 085	Oneida......................	27,084	42.0	21.8	30,230	59.1	9.3	33.2	38.0	41,677	9.4	28.3	12.0
55 087	Outagamie................	118,339	40.8	26.8	139,064	71.2	5.5	45.5	22.5	57,104	5.9	18.6	20.1
55 089	Ozaukee..................	60,019	26.3	46.0	69,182	68.1	5.9	43.7	23.5	75,401	3.0	13.4	35.7
55 093	Pierce......................	25,071	36.8	26.9	33,087	71.2	6.2	42.2	21.5	57,586	6.5	18.9	23.5
55 095	Polk	30,841	47.3	19.5	35,041	66.1	9.3	38.4	29.3	47,860	8.0	22.3	15.2
55 097	Portage....................	44,074	44.6	26.7	57,347	68.4	8.6	37.7	26.6	49,022	7.1	22.9	14.9
55 101	Racine......................	131,192	44.7	22.9	152,561	65.9	10.6	41.1	28.2	52,820	10.4	22.5	19.3
55 105	Rock........................	106,908	48.4	19.3	125,337	66.5	10.8	38.6	28.7	48,164	10.9	23.8	14.9
55 109	St. Croix..................	56,308	33.6	32.7	64,443	74.3	7.0	47.7	19.0	67,098	5.5	13.7	28.4
55 111	Sauk........................	43,053	47.2	21.2	49,396	70.9	6.3	44.0	24.3	50,168	8.6	24.6	14.7
55 115	Shawano..................	29,425	58.5	14.3	33,620	63.8	8.3	39.7	28.7	44,797	8.3	24.7	10.1
55 117	Sheboygan................	78,900	47.3	22.7	91,676	68.8	7.9	41.2	25.9	51,763	7.1	20.9	16.1
55 119	Taylor......................	14,188	58.9	13.7	16,309	66.4	7.9	41.4	28.5	42,892	9.5	27.6	8.6
55 121	Trempealeau............	20,098	53.2	16.7	22,827	68.5	5.6	47.5	25.4	47,918	9.4	23.1	14.5
55 123	Vernon......................	20,208	51.3	18.7	23,036	61.8	5.9	42.1	31.7	44,938	10.5	26.8	12.0
55 125	Vilas........................	16,668	42.6	23.9	18,242	54.6	9.9	30.0	41.6	39,043	9.5	28.3	9.9
55 127	Walworth..................	66,930	43.6	25.0	81,720	69.0	8.6	41.0	22.9	53,577	9.0	20.4	17.6
55 131	Washington	91,510	38.4	27.4	104,243	72.4	6.1	46.5	22.1	65,809	4.2	14.5	27.1
55 133	Waukesha	271,399	29.2	40.3	311,239	69.9	6.2	44.6	23.9	74,014	3.7	13.2	33.7
55 135	Waupaca..................	37,191	53.9	16.3	42,246	65.0	8.3	39.6	29.9	50,086	7.8	19.6	12.6
55 137	Waushara	18,152	55.6	14.5	20,438	56.2	8.8	33.2	37.5	42,028	7.2	26.8	10.5
55 139	Winnebago................	112,630	42.8	25.4	136,048	65.8	6.7	42.0	26.2	50,515	7.8	22.7	15.7
55 141	Wood........................	52,337	48.6	17.9	59,835	64.8	7.6	40.0	30.5	45,586	7.6	25.1	12.6

Table B-2. Counties — What: Education, Employment, and Income, 2010–2012—*Continued*

State or county code	State or county	Educational attainment			Employment status				Percent of households with no workers	Median household income (dollars)	Percent of families with income below poverty	Percent of households with income less than $25,000	Percent of households with income of $100,000 or more
		Total population 25 years and over	Percent with a high school diploma or less	Percent with a bachelor's degree or more	Total population 16 years and over	Percent in the labor force	Unemployment rate	Percent who worked full-time year-round					
	ACS table number:	C15002	C15002	C15002	B23025	B23025	B23025	C20005	C08202	B19013	C17013	C19001	C19001
	Column number:	1	2	3	4	5	6	7	8	9	10	11	12
56 000	**Wyoming**...............	376,874	38.3	24.5	448,174	68.7	5.7	45.9	22.7	55,979	8.0	19.9	21.4
56 001	Albany.......................	20,061	18.5	49.1	31,449	66.7	5.8	35.3	20.7	41,095	13.6	32.6	16.1
56 005	Campbell...................	29,482	44.4	19.2	35,192	76.5	4.7	55.8	12.1	74,233	5.5	10.1	31.5
56 013	Fremont.....................	26,882	36.7	21.2	31,440	65.8	10.4	39.0	26.5	50,628	11.0	25.4	16.8
56 021	Laramie......................	61,598	35.5	25.0	73,032	68.5	5.2	48.5	22.8	54,028	7.7	20.8	21.6
56 025	Natrona.....................	51,275	37.4	21.2	60,834	70.1	6.0	45.1	23.3	54,543	7.0	19.8	21.2
56 029	Park..........................	20,033	35.4	28.6	23,012	66.9	3.7	46.8	28.1	55,425	5.4	18.1	17.7
56 033	Sheridan	20,525	35.3	26.5	23,502	65.3	4.2	44.1	27.1	54,089	4.6	19.7	19.3
56 037	Sweetwater	27,952	47.4	17.1	33,096	72.4	6.3	50.6	19.0	67,787	7.9	13.3	31.0
56 039	Teton	15,581	27.5	51.8	17,827	78.6	6.1	46.2	15.8	68,371	...	10.8	30.6
56 041	Uinta	13,118	47.1	17.5	15,444	70.2	7.0	46.4	15.9	56,507	11.2	22.1	21.0

Table B-3. Metropolitan Areas — What: Education, Employment, and Income, 2012

Metro area or division code	Area name	Educational attainment — Total population 25 years and over	Percent with a high school diploma or less	Percent with a bachelor's degree or more	Employment status — Total population 16 years and over	Percent in the labor force	Unemployment rate	Percent who worked full-time year-round	Percent of households with no workers	Median household income (dollars)	Percent of families with income below poverty	Percent of households with income less than $25,000	Percent of households with income of $100,000 or more
ACS table number:		C15002	C15002	C15002	B23025	B23025	B23025	C20005	C08202	B19013	C17013	C19001	C19001
Column number:		1	2	3	4	5	6	7	8	9	10	11	12
10180	Abilene, TX	105,670	47.3	21.2	131,931	57.2	6.6	37.6	28.4	43,407	14.1	28.4	13.8
10420	Akron, OH	474,507	43.7	28.4	570,472	64.8	9.6	40.4	29.2	49,731	11.6	25.7	18.4
10500	Albany, GA	98,344	49.5	18.4	120,203	59.7	16.0	34.8	35.8	34,469	21.6	37.4	12.4
10580	Albany–Schenectady–Troy, NY	595,301	35.8	34.1	716,559	65.5	8.0	42.2	27.8	60,625	6.7	20.5	25.1
10740	Albuquerque, NM	596,766	37.6	29.9	710,886	62.0	9.0	40.4	28.7	46,725	15.3	27.1	18.1
10780	Alexandria, LA	100,940	52.7	19.0	119,379	56.5	8.6	38.5	32.8	40,896	16.7	31.8	12.1
10900	Allentown–Bethlehem–Easton, PA–NJ	568,626	47.3	26.3	667,455	64.8	8.8	41.0	27.2	55,766	7.3	19.4	21.3
11020	Altoona, PA	89,086	60.8	17.8	103,515	59.5	7.7	37.6	34.3	41,258	8.9	28.8	12.0
11100	Amarillo, TX	160,765	42.5	21.7	195,426	63.7	4.2	44.9	23.8	46,434	13.0	28.2	16.6
11180	Ames, IA	48,121	22.6	50.8	76,765	68.1	6.8	36.0	22.6	49,489	8.8	30.6	17.0
11260	Anchorage, AK	248,743	33.5	30.9	302,392	71.6	7.1	45.2	18.0	71,494	7.1	15.0	34.2
11300	Anderson, IN	88,738	52.2	16.7	103,768	59.0	12.6	35.3	34.5	42,933	9.5	27.7	10.0
11340	Anderson, SC	128,148	50.9	19.1	149,940	58.4	11.8	37.3	34.9	39,232	15.4	31.7	13.5
11460	Ann Arbor, MI	218,395	23.6	49.7	289,962	64.9	8.2	37.8	25.4	56,330	8.5	22.0	26.1
11500	Anniston–Oxford, AL	77,984	53.3	16.9	93,505	58.5	15.3	35.1	34.6	39,169	18.4	32.9	12.4
11540	Appleton, WI	153,050	41.2	27.9	178,928	70.8	5.0	46.5	22.7	60,166	5.8	18.3	20.9
11700	Asheville, NC	311,916	39.1	30.4	357,711	59.1	8.5	35.2	34.6	43,172	11.9	27.6	13.3
12020	Athens–Clarke County, GA	112,332	41.3	35.5	158,136	59.1	8.2	33.3	29.2	38,028	14.6	34.7	16.0
12060	Atlanta–Sandy Springs–Marietta, GA	3,521,146	36.7	35.3	4,185,881	67.3	11.1	43.4	22.3	54,628	13.2	22.1	23.7
12100	Atlantic City, NJ	186,216	49.7	25.1	219,667	67.2	14.4	35.3	29.1	51,191	11.6	24.3	20.9
12220	Auburn–Opelika, AL	84,063	40.3	32.9	118,260	63.0	6.7	37.7	23.9	45,043	13.4	32.9	16.7
12260	Augusta–Richmond County, GA–SC	372,767	43.8	24.6	445,084	59.5	10.1	37.8	30.0	44,761	16.4	28.7	16.5
12420	Austin–Round Rock, TX	1,176,621	31.2	40.5	1,423,425	70.3	7.1	45.9	17.9	59,433	10.6	19.4	26.5
12540	Bakersfield, CA	503,688	53.4	15.3	627,772	59.5	14.0	34.5	27.2	45,910	20.0	27.0	17.8
12580	Baltimore–Towson, MD	1,864,017	37.4	36.4	2,206,230	67.8	8.5	44.9	24.1	66,970	7.9	18.6	32.5
12620	Bangor, ME	104,587	47.4	22.9	128,671	61.9	8.2	35.5	31.9	41,653	11.4	29.6	12.8
12700	Barnstable Town, MA	164,390	30.3	40.6	184,188	59.4	8.0	34.4	36.8	59,453	6.1	20.4	26.1
12940	Baton Rouge, LA	522,364	46.6	26.8	640,344	64.5	7.3	42.4	24.8	50,286	13.7	25.7	20.4
12980	Battle Creek, MI	91,170	44.8	20.1	107,022	61.6	11.4	35.8	33.0	39,190	13.6	30.7	11.2
13020	Bay City, MI	74,924	48.4	17.1	86,638	58.9	10.4	35.5	36.6	44,548	8.6	26.3	11.4
13140	Beaumont–Port Arthur, TX	255,961	50.1	17.1	307,298	58.2	10.5	37.7	30.9	43,421	14.8	30.6	16.6
13380	Bellingham, WA	133,716	33.4	31.0	168,727	64.2	9.9	35.2	30.1	51,458	11.8	25.6	19.1
13460	Bend, OR	114,542	31.0	32.3	129,855	60.2	11.2	31.1	34.6	47,576	14.5	27.2	17.5
13740	Billings, MT	109,803	36.9	27.0	127,546	68.1	4.8	45.0	23.5	49,255	8.6	22.7	17.9
13780	Binghamton, NY	170,209	42.1	27.6	205,544	60.9	9.0	35.7	31.9	48,140	10.4	26.9	17.2
13820	Birmingham–Hoover, AL	766,699	40.8	27.9	900,192	60.7	8.7	43.5	29.8	46,763	13.4	27.5	18.0
13900	Bismarck, ND	76,688	34.0	31.2	90,638	73.0	3.3	52.7	18.6	62,028	4.1	14.9	26.1
13980	Blacksburg–Christiansburg–Radford, VA	98,658	44.6	29.4	141,792	55.3	5.8	33.3	30.6	42,455	12.3	34.3	14.2
14020	Bloomington, IN	115,204	40.6	32.6	164,219	60.8	8.0	33.1	29.2	38,794	13.1	33.6	11.9
14060	Bloomington–Normal, IL	103,329	29.2	43.6	138,711	70.0	6.0	42.6	19.8	62,117	7.7	21.7	25.3
14260	Boise City–Nampa, ID	407,785	34.2	29.7	482,561	66.1	8.1	40.7	24.4	48,968	11.5	23.6	17.0
14460	Boston–Cambridge–Quincy, MA–NH	3,189,555	33.9	42.9	3,782,563	69.2	7.9	42.9	23.8	71,738	7.5	18.8	35.4
1446014484	•Boston–Quincy, MA Division	1,310,880	35.5	41.1	1,577,709	68.4	8.9	41.5	25.6	66,149	8.7	21.6	32.6
1446015764	•Cambridge–Newton–Framingham, MA Division	1,070,754	29.2	50.5	1,254,870	70.1	6.7	44.7	21.5	82,226	5.7	15.8	41.3
1446037764	•Peabody, MA Division	516,730	38.3	36.2	606,157	68.0	8.6	42.1	25.0	67,888	9.6	20.6	32.6
1446040484	•Rockingham County–Strafford County, NH Division	291,191	36.2	35.2	343,827	71.5	7.2	44.0	21.9	69,981	5.7	14.4	31.2
14500	Boulder, CO	196,357	18.7	57.9	250,346	70.3	6.5	41.2	19.4	66,989	5.9	19.9	34.4
14540	Bowling Green, KY	78,811	47.6	24.1	102,244	63.2	9.9	33.0	28.8	41,140	13.8	30.2	12.7
14740	Bremerton–Silverdale, WA	173,947	29.7	29.7	206,490	62.4	9.3	39.6	28.8	59,073	7.3	17.0	23.9
14860	Bridgeport–Stamford–Norwalk, CT	632,056	32.0	46.3	735,459	68.6	9.5	42.1	22.9	79,841	6.6	16.2	41.8
15180	Brownsville–Harlingen, TX	237,677	61.2	16.1	296,311	55.5	12.1	33.5	30.3	30,953	31.9	42.5	9.4
15260	Brunswick, GA	74,311	44.8	23.1	86,974	61.6	11.0	38.5	29.7	43,346	14.4	28.7	16.2
15380	Buffalo–Niagara Falls, NY	779,253	39.2	29.7	926,633	63.2	7.8	38.8	32.1	50,269	10.6	25.9	19.2
15500	Burlington, NC	101,895	46.5	19.2	122,867	61.7	8.9	33.0	29.7	39,782	14.8	30.3	12.5
15540	Burlington–South Burlington, VT	141,050	33.2	42.0	175,986	71.0	6.2	43.3	21.7	60,889	6.6	18.8	24.5
15940	Canton–Massillon, OH	277,233	49.2	20.6	325,020	62.7	9.8	33.3	30.6	45,157	11.0	26.0	13.7
15980	Cape Coral–Fort Myers, FL	472,573	44.9	24.2	535,865	53.9	12.4	31.1	40.0	46,278	10.7	24.5	16.1
16020	Cape Girardeau–Jackson, MO–IL	63,131	47.3	24.7	77,158	61.6	7.8	39.3	30.6	42,686	9.3	31.2	14.1
16180	Carson City, NV	38,658	39.0	20.4	44,058	61.5	12.8	35.8	34.9	49,779	10.69	23.3	12.4
16220	Casper, WY	52,364	35.1	23.3	61,926	71.5	4.7	45.6	21.3	54,526	9.0	22.2	22.4
16300	Cedar Rapids, IA	173,944	34.2	30.9	205,146	69.4	5.6	45.2	24.1	57,222	5.9	20.1	21.7
16580	Champaign–Urbana, IL	136,639	31.5	40.1	193,069	65.3	6.8	37.4	24.8	47,632	10.5	28.3	18.4
16620	Charleston, WV	215,809	50.7	23.0	245,501	56.4	6.0	39.5	34.4	47,610	11.0	28.4	15.3
16700	Charleston–North Charleston, SC	463,649	37.1	31.3	555,042	66.0	10.2	43.2	25.0	50,108	11.4	23.8	18.8
16740	Charlotte–Gastonia–Concord, NC–SC	1,199,248	36.4	33.4	1,415,099	68.7	10.3	43.8	22.1	52,470	11.9	22.7	22.2
16820	Charlottesville, VA	137,316	35.2	43.1	169,920	59.8	4.6	39.9	25.1	62,880	7.5	19.1	28.9
16860	Chattanooga, TN–GA	370,865	45.7	22.3	434,316	60.9	9.3	39.2	30.5	43,475	11.5	28.0	16.0
16940	Cheyenne, WY	62,201	38.5	23.7	74,873	66.7	7.3	45.0	23.5	54,192	7.3	19.5	22.1
16980	Chicago–Naperville–Joliet, IL–IN–WI	6,295,451	38.1	34.8	7,467,683	67.6	10.8	42.2	24.1	59,261	11.1	21.4	26.7
1698016974	•Chicago–Naperville–Joliet, IL Division	5,266,482	37.4	35.6	6,243,718	67.9	11.0	42.5	24.0	58,911	11.3	21.7	26.6
1698023844	•Gary, IN Division	469,167	49.8	20.6	552,348	62.3	11.0	36.9	28.9	51,478	12.9	24.3	19.6
1698029404	•Lake County–Kenosha County, IL–WI Division	559,802	34.4	39.0	671,617	69.7	8.8	44.1	20.9	69,240	7.8	16.1	33.6

Table B-3. Metropolitan Areas — What: Education, Employment, and Income, 2012—*Continued*

Metro area or division code	Area name	Educational attainment			Employment status				Percent of households with no workers	Median household income (dollars)	Percent of families with income below poverty	Percent of households with income less than $25,000	Percent of households with income of $100,000 or more
		Total population 25 years and over	Percent with a high school diploma or less	Percent with a bachelor's degree or more	Total population 16 years and over	Percent in the labor force	Unemployment rate	Percent who worked full-time year-round					
	ACS table number:	C15002	C15002	C15002	B23025	B23025	B23025	C20005	C08202	B19013	C17013	C19001	C19001
	Column number:	1	2	3	4	5	6	7	8	9	10	11	12
17020	Chico, CA............................	142,262	35.5	24.1	182,451	55.7	15.0	27.7	41.2	40,960	13.6	29.7	14.8
17140	Cincinnati–Middletown, OH–KY–IN.......	1,418,382	42.1	29.6	1,679,086	66.5	8.3	42.6	26.1	52,439	11.2	24.5	21.7
17300	Clarksville, TN–KY.................	173,752	42.4	20.7	216,342	64.1	8.8	43.5	23.9	44,392	14.3	25.4	11.4
17420	Cleveland, TN......................	80,784	53.8	16.6	96,154	57.4	15.1	32.9	34.0	38,343	14.8	32.5	10.8
17460	Cleveland–Elyria–Mentor, OH.............	1,425,156	41.4	28.5	1,658,695	63.8	9.9	39.4	31.0	46,944	12.0	27.8	18.6
17660	Coeur d'Alene, ID..................	95,429	34.8	23.6	112,420	62.6	10.4	33.5	29.5	46,870	9.3	22.6	14.1
17780	College Station–Bryan, TX...........	122,721	40.2	35.7	190,200	62.2	8.1	34.9	26.2	40,346	12.8	34.2	15.9
17820	Colorado Springs, CO...............	425,892	27.6	34.8	517,607	68.2	8.6	44.2	22.9	55,320	9.1	20.7	23.4
17860	Columbia, MO......................	103,271	25.8	47.8	144,682	67.8	7.1	41.4	20.1	43,172	7.9	29.1	18.8
17900	Columbia, SC......................	511,883	38.1	31.1	625,376	66.0	10.0	42.1	26.7	48,763	12.2	25.4	17.8
17980	Columbus, GA–AL..................	193,170	41.3	21.9	237,066	61.8	8.9	39.3	30.7	42,972	14.3	29.8	13.0
18020	Columbus, IN......................	53,120	48.5	26.5	61,635	67.2	4.9	42.9	22.9	53,671	10.2	20.8	18.6
18140	Columbus, OH.....................	1,229,535	37.8	34.1	1,468,810	67.6	7.2	44.3	23.3	53,699	10.8	22.7	21.8
18580	Corpus Christi, TX.................	283,038	47.8	18.6	339,615	63.2	6.5	42.7	25.4	49,047	12.5	25.2	18.3
18700	Corvallis, OR......................	51,918	20.2	53.1	73,167	61.8	10.1	29.6	30.8	51,133	8.5	30.0	23.9
18880	Crestview–Fort Walton Beach–Destin, FL	128,101	34.5	28.1	152,187	66.4	6.9	44.6	23.8	52,787	12.1	20.7	18.7
19060	Cumberland, MD–WV.................	70,955	56.6	15.1	85,256	54.3	10.8	32.7	40.9	35,645	9.7	38.5	9.7
19100	Dallas–Fort Worth–Arlington, TX.........	4,208,465	38.8	31.6	5,021,156	69.1	7.6	47.7	18.7	56,954	11.8	20.6	25.0
1910019124	•Dallas–Plano–Irving, TX Division.....	2,807,470	38.2	33.4	3,349,316	69.6	7.6	48.2	18.2	57,152	11.6	20.6	25.9
1910023104	•Fort Worth–Arlington, TX Division......	1,400,995	40.0	28.0	1,671,840	68.1	7.7	46.6	19.6	56,562	12.1	20.7	23.2
19140	Dalton, GA........................	90,204	61.9	11.7	108,135	63.0	14.5	40.8	27.8	32,858	18.0	35.3	9.5
19180	Danville, IL........................	54,742	52.1	14.0	63,613	58.1	13.3	37.5	37.6	40,311	13.6	30.3	11.7
19260	Danville, VA.......................	75,828	54.1	15.7	85,929	57.6	8.3	36.1	37.1	38,071	13.8	32.7	10.6
19340	Davenport–Moline–Rock Island, IA–IL.....	258,586	39.1	25.1	303,222	64.9	7.1	42.3	28.7	51,678	8.6	22.2	18.8
19380	Dayton, OH........................	566,720	41.2	26.1	674,333	62.7	9.9	38.4	31.7	45,524	12.0	27.8	16.3
19460	Decatur, AL........................	104,288	51.4	19.6	122,071	60.4	12.7	38.4	32.0	42,088	15.5	31.2	14.6
19500	Decatur, IL........................	75,411	44.8	23.3	87,453	64.9	13.1	37.9	30.2	44,533	17.2	29.8	15.3
19660	Deltona–Daytona Beach–Ormond Beach, FL	360,335	46.7	21.0	416,665	51.1	10.3	32.3	41.3	40,106	13.6	30.6	11.7
19740	Denver–Aurora, CO	1,776,101	30.6	39.9	2,066,676	71.0	7.5	46.6	20.9	61,453	9.0	18.7	27.4
19780	Des Moines–West Des Moines, IA	385,588	32.5	35.0	451,628	72.3	5.7	48.7	21.2	59,157	9.5	19.3	23.7
19820	Detroit–Warren–Livonia, MI..........	2,901,654	39.7	28.2	3,412,043	62.4	12.2	36.5	31.7	50,310	13.4	25.8	21.2
1982019804	•Detroit–Livonia–Dearborn, MI Division	1,172,581	46.3	21.2	1,405,738	57.9	16.5	31.9	37.6	39,486	21.0	34.7	14.7
1982047644	•Warren–Troy–Farmington Hills, MI Division	1,729,073	35.2	33.0	2,006,305	65.6	9.6	39.8	27.7	57,916	8.5	19.9	25.5
20020	Dothan, AL........................	100,967	53.8	18.9	116,764	57.2	8.7	39.2	34.0	37,632	15.3	34.3	13.7
20100	Dover, DE.........................	109,122	47.7	22.3	131,200	63.1	10.6	39.6	27.2	52,894	8.3	19.9	20.3
20220	Dubuque, IA.......................	63,011	42.6	29.1	75,425	68.3	3.3	45.0	25.0	49,793	9.8	23.1	15.6
20260	Duluth, MN–WI....................	190,952	37.8	25.2	230,196	62.1	8.1	35.9	33.2	46,848	9.8	26.8	13.3
20500	Durham, NC.......................	345,424	31.1	44.7	419,389	65.1	8.7	40.6	25.2	50,262	11.8	25.1	22.6
20740	Eau Claire, WI.....................	107,031	39.1	26.8	132,822	68.6	6.1	39.8	24.9	48,691	7.9	25.7	16.6
20940	El Centro, CA......................	106,011	58.9	13.0	132,810	53.3	19.3	26.9	32.6	40,200	21.4	35.7	14.1
21060	Elizabethtown, KY..................	78,846	47.3	19.3	93,938	65.9	10.3	44.1	26.3	47,323	12.3	25.5	14.6
21140	Elkhart–Goshen, IN.................	125,134	57.1	17.5	150,799	66.1	7.9	39.7	26.0	45,315	12.5	24.8	12.5
21300	Elmira, NY........................	60,601	45.5	21.5	71,450	58.9	6.3	35.8	32.8	45,974	9.5	30.0	16.8
21340	El Paso, TX........................	488,529	48.9	20.9	614,031	60.6	9.9	39.5	24.1	40,345	20.6	31.9	13.1
21500	Erie, PA...........................	185,586	48.7	25.2	225,533	62.5	9.1	38.7	30.3	46,563	11.0	27.9	13.8
21660	Eugene–Springfield, OR	239,075	35.0	27.4	294,217	58.4	12.0	29.7	35.9	40,675	13.5	31.4	13.5
21780	Evansville, IN–KY..................	243,400	44.4	22.2	286,327	64.3	7.4	41.9	28.1	44,887	10.6	26.0	15.5
21820	Fairbanks, AK......................	61,586	29.9	31.2	78,067	72.2	6.3	44.2	19.9	66,539	4.8	15.4	26.8
22020	Fargo, ND–MN.....................	134,019	27.8	37.1	173,157	75.9	4.0	50.5	18.8	51,525	5.9	20.5	19.3
22140	Farmington, NM...................	79,366	47.6	17.9	95,998	60.5	11.5	37.9	26.1	46,385	17.4	28.1	20.0
22180	Fayetteville, NC...................	228,961	38.2	21.6	284,864	65.0	11.9	43.9	25.8	44,823	13.5	26.2	11.8
22220	Fayetteville–Springdale–Rogers, AR–MO	299,335	45.7	28.1	364,365	64.8	6.6	44.5	23.5	45,611	11.7	26.3	17.0
22380	Flagstaff, AZ.......................	78,822	36.2	29.8	108,860	65.7	8.2	34.1	24.6	45,640	18.1	29.4	17.0
22420	Flint, MI..........................	278,884	44.9	19.4	329,830	56.4	14.9	30.5	39.0	40,323	16.4	29.6	12.6
22500	Florence, SC.......................	136,100	49.7	21.2	161,230	60.7	13.0	37.5	31.6	38,163	17.0	32.8	13.5
22520	Florence–Muscle Shoals, AL	101,122	51.1	21.0	119,168	55.9	9.9	35.4	37.4	41,450	14.3	32.1	14.5
22540	Fond du Lac, WI...................	69,892	47.7	19.9	81,860	68.5	6.8	43.3	26.7	53,065	5.6	18.6	15.2
22660	Fort Collins–Loveland, CO...........	201,560	23.2	44.7	254,128	69.0	7.6	38.6	21.7	55,890	7.0	22.6	22.7
22900	Fort Smith, AR–OK.................	198,892	54.0	15.8	232,244	56.6	7.4	38.1	32.2	36,061	18.0	35.2	9.6
23060	Fort Wayne, IN....................	272,097	42.3	24.4	323,523	66.9	8.2	43.4	24.9	49,301	11.1	22.6	15.2
23420	Fresno, CA........................	560,633	50.1	18.5	700,526	61.0	15.7	32.4	29.4	41,627	24.1	30.6	16.2
23460	Gadsden, AL......................	71,725	54.4	15.0	83,471	52.7	11.7	29.8	39.7	34,264	16.5	37.9	7.4
23540	Gainesville, FL....................	159,219	32.9	38.6	225,946	58.2	8.4	32.7	30.7	41,226	14.7	34.6	17.1
23580	Gainesville, GA....................	116,497	51.7	21.5	139,901	62.5	9.3	39.5	25.2	49,737	16.2	22.6	17.5
24020	Glens Falls, NY....................	92,214	48.9	24.6	106,580	63.2	10.6	38.6	31.0	53,368	8.8	21.9	17.8
24140	Goldsboro, NC....................	81,564	48.6	15.5	97,268	63.3	14.9	37.5	33.7	37,905	19.1	35.1	11.9
24220	Grand Forks, ND–MN...............	59,470	36.8	29.5	80,723	69.8	3.8	43.8	23.0	43,648	10.1	28.5	16.6
24300	Grand Junction, CO................	99,300	39.5	23.0	117,733	64.3	9.0	37.8	30.3	45,892	12.3	23.7	16.0
24340	Grand Rapids–Wyoming, MI	508,905	39.9	27.9	607,344	66.8	9.2	39.3	26.0	50,658	11.9	23.0	17.0

Table B-3. Metropolitan Areas — What: Education, Employment, and Income, 2012—Continued

Metro area or division code	Area name	Educational attainment			Employment status						Percent of families with income below poverty	Percent of households with income less than $25,000	Percent of households with income of $100,000 or more
		Total population 25 years and over	Percent with a high school diploma or less	Percent with a bachelor's degree or more	Total population 16 years and over	Percent in the labor force	Unemployment rate	Percent who worked full-time year-round	Percent of households with no workers	Median household income (dollars)			
	ACS table number:	C15002	C15002	C15002	B23025	B23025	B23025	C20005	C08202	B19013	C17013	C19001	C19001
	Column number:	1	2	3	4	5	6	7	8	9	10	11	12
24500	Great Falls, MT	55,008	44.9	21.3	65,511	61.3	6.1	38.8	30.5	41,732	14.3	29.3	14.5
24540	Greeley, CO	163,543	41.3	26.3	198,211	68.5	7.2	43.2	19.9	55,357	10.6	20.2	20.2
24580	Green Bay, WI	207,632	44.8	24.1	244,552	69.3	6.3	44.7	24.8	50,777	8.5	23.5	19.5
24660	Greensboro–High Point, NC	490,879	43.8	26.2	585,347	63.5	11.1	39.4	28.5	41,751	14.3	28.5	13.7
24780	Greenville, NC	116,177	41.1	24.5	156,812	68.1	13.1	38.0	27.1	37,759	15.0	34.0	12.8
24860	Greenville–Mauldin–Easley, SC	428,895	44.4	28.5	518,437	61.7	9.8	38.4	28.7	43,724	12.8	29.9	17.0
25060	Gulfport–Biloxi, MS	169,385	43.5	20.7	202,440	62.8	10.4	38.3	28.7	41,254	16.8	30.6	13.4
25180	Hagerstown–Martinsburg, MD–WV	188,710	52.3	17.9	217,793	62.9	9.3	41.2	28.5	51,386	11.4	23.3	19.4
25260	Hanford–Corcoran, CA	93,536	54.5	12.1	114,101	56.4	15.6	36.4	25.8	45,935	17.3	26.0	16.5
25420	Harrisburg–Carlisle, PA	382,325	46.5	28.6	448,689	66.2	7.4	44.1	26.2	54,742	9.3	20.6	20.9
25500	Harrisonburg, VA	75,731	50.8	28.8	105,393	59.2	5.9	35.7	27.7	44,971	11.6	27.8	14.3
25540	Hartford–West Hartford–East Hartford, CT	832,908	37.2	36.6	986,074	67.3	9.3	41.6	26.4	66,732	7.7	19.3	30.8
25620	Hattiesburg, MS	88,423	42.7	25.8	114,890	60.5	11.0	34.7	28.6	36,815	19.2	37.2	10.7
25860	Hickory–Lenoir–Morganton, NC	251,801	53.4	16.7	292,896	59.8	10.5	37.1	33.2	37,364	14.2	33.9	10.5
25980	Hinesville–Fort Stewart, GA	47,543	44.6	17.4	61,231	66.5	13.1	44.6	22.8	43,368	13.6	24.8	9.4
26100	Holland–Grand Haven, MI	167,622	40.6	28.7	208,737	67.8	8.0	39.3	24.1	54,323	7.2	17.4	18.5
26180	Honolulu, HI	662,195	36.2	32.2	788,881	66.2	6.1	45.0	20.6	71,404	7.0	15.5	32.2
26300	Hot Springs, AR	69,135	41.4	22.8	79,995	56.2	9.6	33.4	36.8	40,893	13.3	31.5	14.3
26380	Houma–Bayou Cane–Thibodaux, LA	135,758	63.2	15.6	162,005	61.8	7.3	42.4	25.7	48,866	11.3	26.8	18.7
26420	Houston–Sugar Land–Baytown, TX	3,909,515	42.4	29.6	4,687,028	67.2	8.4	45.7	18.6	55,910	13.0	21.4	26.3
26580	Huntington–Ashland, WV–KY–OH	197,394	52.8	19.0	231,875	53.7	8.9	33.9	39.9	39,160	12.8	33.7	12.2
26620	Huntsville, AL	289,311	33.7	36.9	341,829	64.8	8.7	43.1	25.8	54,617	8.2	22.7	24.2
26820	Idaho Falls, ID	79,020	36.3	24.6	95,107	65.9	6.4	40.7	24.5	49,200	11.2	22.0	18.1
26900	Indianapolis–Carmel, IN	1,175,144	39.9	32.1	1,383,474	68.6	8.5	44.4	22.8	51,808	10.5	22.7	21.0
26980	Iowa City, IA	95,338	25.1	47.6	129,453	71.4	2.6	43.5	18.9	52,767	6.3	25.3	22.4
27060	Ithaca, NY	58,927	22.8	51.9	88,503	55.6	5.8	31.1	32.2	49,930	4.8	26.7	23.4
27100	Jackson, MI	109,423	47.8	19.3	128,167	57.1	11.5	33.5	33.8	42,653	15.0	30.6	13.0
27140	Jackson, MS	351,182	39.0	30.3	424,365	62.4	10.4	41.8	26.1	42,604	16.4	29.5	18.2
27180	Jackson, TN	74,650	47.7	22.9	91,982	60.4	10.6	39.4	28.2	42,270	13.7	32.0	13.9
27260	Jacksonville, FL	925,289	39.9	28.0	1,093,872	63.9	11.3	40.0	28.4	48,118	12.1	25.9	18.7
27340	Jacksonville, NC	97,744	36.4	19.2	141,355	68.1	11.3	46.4	22.2	44,250	9.9	20.9	10.4
27500	Janesville, WI	107,345	47.0	19.7	125,326	64.4	10.2	39.3	29.0	45,989	11.4	25.3	13.7
27620	Jefferson City, MO	100,171	46.9	26.4	120,125	60.1	5.3	43.1	27.1	46,835	10.0	24.2	15.3
27740	Johnson City, TN	139,276	51.1	23.2	163,790	57.4	6.1	38.3	35.1	39,137	15.1	33.6	10.9
27780	Johnstown, PA	100,802	57.3	18.3	117,549	55.0	9.9	34.3	38.8	39,969	10.2	31.5	11.8
27860	Jonesboro, AR	79,093	50.8	21.2	96,584	62.5	6.8	40.7	28.5	41,551	13.1	30.2	13.3
27900	Joplin, MO	113,632	49.9	20.8	135,468	63.5	7.2	40.1	30.4	38,229	12.5	33.7	9.7
28020	Kalamazoo–Portage, MI	209,388	35.4	30.7	264,480	62.7	9.3	35.3	30.7	44,326	11.1	29.7	15.3
28100	Kankakee–Bradley, IL	73,700	48.9	16.3	88,882	63.4	9.8	39.2	27.1	51,703	14.0	24.6	20.0
28140	Kansas City, MO–KS	1,374,632	35.8	33.5	1,601,985	68.2	7.8	45.2	24.4	54,519	9.6	21.5	22.0
28420	Kennewick–Richland–Pasco, WA	165,030	39.4	24.8	198,996	65.3	7.8	42.6	23.0	57,189	11.7	20.8	24.2
28660	Killeen–Temple–Fort Hood, TX	252,990	39.1	21.0	316,161	62.2	7.1	45.0	24.8	48,633	11.6	22.9	16.3
28700	Kingsport–Bristol–Bristol, TN–VA	222,427	53.5	19.2	254,375	56.5	9.6	35.7	38.7	37,769	12.3	32.3	11.4
28740	Kingston, NY	128,840	39.8	30.7	151,264	62.9	11.8	36.5	29.4	57,566	7.7	22.4	23.5
28940	Knoxville, TN	483,523	39.9	29.6	574,516	61.2	7.5	39.9	30.7	44,766	12.1	28.2	15.8
29020	Kokomo, IN	67,807	50.6	16.6	78,379	56.7	10.1	34.9	39.7	39,885	12.6	29.2	14.8
29100	La Crosse, WI–MN	86,884	35.9	28.0	110,105	67.5	4.1	41.3	25.0	47,642	6.6	24.7	16.5
29140	Lafayette, IN	116,514	40.7	31.4	166,928	63.7	7.6	36.6	25.0	43,881	9.9	27.8	14.6
29180	Lafayette, LA	179,337	49.1	24.3	218,300	68.1	6.7	44.0	23.2	46,813	14.1	29.5	19.8
29340	Lake Charles, LA	129,775	52.8	19.6	156,731	62.1	8.1	38.8	28.7	45,102	13.4	30.1	17.0
29420	Lake Havasu City–Kingman, AZ	150,231	54.5	11.2	168,531	44.3	15.4	23.2	49.6	34,445	15.8	35.3	9.7
29460	Lakeland, FL	418,167	52.7	19.2	490,501	55.1	13.8	33.7	36.7	41,325	13.8	27.4	10.9
29540	Lancaster, PA	347,124	54.3	24.5	413,402	65.4	7.0	41.2	25.0	54,776	8.2	18.9	19.2
29620	Lansing–East Lansing, MI	290,370	32.9	32.2	378,468	63.6	10.1	34.7	29.4	48,637	13.0	27.5	17.4
29700	Laredo, TX	140,289	59.7	17.0	178,376	56.2	5.3	39.1	20.8	36,624	27.8	35.7	11.0
29740	Las Cruces, NM	130,217	43.4	27.9	164,346	63.2	13.8	35.8	26.3	37,566	21.6	34.3	11.9
29820	Las Vegas–Paradise, NV	1,327,029	45.2	22.1	1,564,705	65.9	12.6	39.7	25.4	49,546	12.6	22.6	17.4
29940	Lawrence, KS	63,950	26.7	48.0	94,136	70.0	6.1	39.2	20.3	50,184	10.4	28.3	19.3
30020	Lawton, OK	77,484	46.0	19.0	97,852	64.5	8.5	42.5	25.9	44,874	13.8	25.2	13.2
30140	Lebanon, PA	92,821	58.8	18.8	108,365	65.7	7.5	41.1	28.1	51,557	9.2	22.0	14.6
30300	Lewiston, ID–WA	42,924	39.4	21.3	49,743	60.4	9.1	34.9	32.7	44,568	6.9	25.7	12.1
30340	Lewiston–Auburn, ME	73,631	48.3	18.4	86,207	68.5	8.2	42.0	30.2	44,297	12.1	29.3	15.4
30460	Lexington–Fayette, KY	315,237	37.4	35.2	387,204	67.5	6.9	43.6	23.7	47,952	10.2	25.2	20.0
30620	Lima, OH	69,248	50.3	17.9	82,907	61.0	7.9	35.8	30.3	41,729	14.7	29.4	12.5
30700	Lincoln, NE	192,116	28.9	35.9	245,529	72.1	5.9	46.9	22.3	50,668	8.3	23.7	18.6
30780	Little Rock–North Little Rock–Conway, AR	468,720	41.4	29.4	558,905	64.6	7.7	45.1	26.9	47,845	10.3	26.2	17.0
30860	Logan, UT–ID	66,710	29.5	34.6	91,950	68.5	6.4	35.6	20.4	45,813	10.8	25.3	14.8
30980	Longview, TX	141,373	49.0	16.8	168,479	60.2	7.3	39.7	27.5	42,522	14.1	27.3	16.1
31020	Longview, WA	70,165	44.1	16.0	80,907	56.5	14.9	33.8	38.3	47,692	12.5	28.5	13.6
31100	Los Angeles–Long Beach–Santa Ana, CA	8,562,973	41.2	31.8	10,333,989	65.1	10.9	39.1	22.4	57,271	13.7	22.5	27.2
3110031084	•Los Angeles–Long Beach–Glendale, CA Division	6,525,066	43.4	30.0	7,890,145	64.6	11.6	38.7	23.0	53,001	15.2	24.4	24.7
3110042044	•Santa Ana–Anaheim–Irvine, CA Division	2,037,907	33.9	37.3	2,443,844	66.6	9.0	40.7	20.4	71,983	9.3	16.0	35.5

Table B-3. Metropolitan Areas — What: Education, Employment, and Income, 2012—Continued

Metro area or division code	Area name	Educational attainment			Employment status				Percent of households with no workers	Median household income (dollars)	Percent of families with income below poverty	Percent of households with income less than $25,000	Percent of households with income of $100,000 or more
		Total population 25 years and over	Percent with a high school diploma or less	Percent with a bachelor's degree or more	Total population 16 years and over	Percent in the labor force	Unemployment rate	Percent who worked full-time year-round					
	ACS table number:	C15002	C15002	C15002	B23025	B23025	B23025	C20005	C08202	B19013	C17013	C19001	C19001
	Column number:	1	2	3	4	5	6	7	8	9	10	11	12
31140	Louisville–Jefferson County, KY–IN	879,830	43.4	26.5	1,030,747	65.3	9.0	41.5	28.2	48,895	11.6	25.9	17.6
31180	Lubbock, TX..	171,239	40.3	27.3	228,013	66.3	7.5	40.9	24.0	41,667	15.2	29.9	15.2
31340	Lynchburg, VA......................................	170,251	46.8	23.5	209,870	59.0	7.1	38.4	30.6	43,082	12.6	27.1	15.2
31420	Macon, GA..	152,718	50.4	20.7	181,800	58.4	10.1	36.8	31.5	39,525	17.8	33.7	14.3
31460	Madera, CA...	93,341	56.4	12.5	113,528	51.8	9.8	27.3	42.9	42,039	19.0	32.0	13.4
31540	Madison, WI..	385,952	27.8	42.6	472,144	72.4	5.4	45.1	20.8	58,894	7.2	19.3	24.2
31700	Manchester–Nashua, NH.........................	277,324	35.9	37.3	323,471	70.8	6.1	48.0	21.3	69,089	7.2	16.1	31.1
31740	Manhattan, KS.......................................	71,957	32.8	33.2	107,036	70.0	3.2	47.5	17.3	46,083	4.9	22.8	12.4
31860	Mankato–North Mankato, MN..............	59,024	33.3	33.2	80,425	71.2	4.4	41.4	21.9	52,542	5.1	22.1	18.1
31900	Mansfield, OH..	85,027	54.5	15.4	98,400	57.6	9.9	33.8	34.1	41,680	14.7	30.1	10.4
32580	McAllen–Edinburg–Mission, TX.............	442,346	60.8	16.3	561,403	58.0	11.6	34.8	27.0	33,761	30.2	40.2	10.3
32780	Medford, OR..	143,813	38.6	24.9	167,107	59.1	12.0	32.5	36.0	44,810	11.5	26.8	12.5
32820	Memphis, TN–MS–AR	852,644	42.4	26.1	1,025,207	64.7	10.9	42.0	26.1	45,687	15.5	28.2	17.3
32900	Merced, CA...	149,009	59.0	12.8	190,901	60.8	17.2	33.1	27.4	43,597	20.6	29.9	15.4
33100	Miami–Fort Lauderdale–Pompano Beach, FL	4,029,471	43.3	29.4	4,695,857	63.5	11.6	39.7	27.8	46,648	13.9	27.1	19.9
3310022744	•Fort Lauderdale–Pompano Beach–Deerfield Beach, FL Division..................	1,265,045	39.7	29.8	1,469,627	67.2	11.8	41.4	25.9	49,793	11.7	24.1	20.9
3310033124	•Miami–Miami Beach–Kendall, FL Division...	1,791,575	48.6	27.3	2,108,889	62.8	11.8	40.5	25.2	41,400	17.5	31.7	17.1
3310048424	•West Palm Beach–Boca Raton–Boynton Beach, FL Division....................	972,851	38.2	32.9	1,117,341	59.8	10.6	36.2	34.6	51,278	10.4	23.6	23.2
33140	Michigan City–La Porte, IN	76,754	54.0	15.1	89,222	57.5	10.6	35.1	29.0	46,048	16.6	25.6	15.5
33260	Midland, TX...	92,166	41.5	23.6	109,538	69.7	3.5	51.4	17.4	61,331	4.3	16.3	29.0
33340	Milwaukee–Waukesha–West Allis, WI ...	1,038,932	37.6	32.5	1,231,442	67.4	8.0	42.4	26.9	52,605	11.6	24.8	21.2
33460	Minneapolis–St. Paul–Bloomington, MN–WI	2,234,124	29.2	39.5	2,622,751	72.5	6.5	46.5	21.1	66,282	7.4	17.0	29.5
33540	Missoula, MT...	72,905	27.1	42.8	92,678	70.3	8.0	36.2	22.8	45,595	7.2	27.3	16.8
33660	Mobile, AL...	271,194	48.8	21.5	323,273	58.1	11.6	36.7	32.0	39,691	17.6	33.0	12.7
33700	Modesto, CA..	321,347	51.0	16.1	393,712	62.1	17.2	32.1	27.8	46,405	16.0	25.8	17.1
33740	Monroe, LA..	113,287	50.2	22.0	136,716	57.8	8.9	39.9	29.8	34,809	21.7	36.6	12.4
33780	Monroe, MI..	103,051	47.0	18.6	120,419	62.3	9.1	37.5	31.3	50,675	8.4	23.1	16.8
33860	Montgomery, AL....................................	245,640	43.3	26.8	294,982	61.1	9.3	41.1	29.5	44,674	14.4	28.5	16.0
34060	Morgantown, WV..................................	82,679	48.2	30.9	113,629	58.6	7.3	35.9	30.6	40,177	10.3	33.8	14.5
34100	Morristown, TN.....................................	94,475	60.3	14.2	112,659	56.3	12.6	35.1	37.5	38,137	17.5	33.9	9.5
34580	Mount Vernon–Anacortes, WA	80,146	37.2	24.9	94,172	59.1	7.8	35.7	30.8	53,400	10.0	20.8	18.8
34620	Muncie, IN...	70,796	48.8	21.3	97,504	58.1	13.0	28.5	33.9	37,032	14.2	34.6	9.1
34740	Muskegon–Norton Shores, MI...............	113,659	46.6	17.3	134,568	59.6	13.3	33.7	35.4	40,535	18.1	31.3	11.3
34820	Myrtle Beach–Conway–North Myrtle Beach, SC	199,572	43.7	21.0	232,091	60.0	10.5	32.6	34.3	40,353	14.4	30.9	11.5
34900	Napa, CA...	94,818	39.0	30.3	111,683	66.8	9.6	37.8	27.6	68,553	6.3	14.9	31.7
34940	Naples–Marco Island, FL........................	245,709	41.2	31.0	277,491	53.5	8.6	32.3	43.4	54,126	7.9	20.2	23.5
34980	Nashville–Davidson–Murfreesboro–Franklin, TN	1,091,074	40.7	32.6	1,291,223	67.4	7.7	44.3	22.5	51,500	10.8	22.3	20.2
35300	New Haven–Milford, CT.........................	589,478	42.1	32.7	697,550	66.5	11.4	39.8	28.0	59,271	10.8	22.7	27.6
35380	New Orleans–Metairie–Kenner, LA	813,789	44.0	26.7	959,556	63.2	9.5	41.3	27.8	44,379	14.6	29.8	18.4
35620	New York–Northern New Jersey–Long Island, NY–NJ–PA	13,083,126	40.8	37.0	15,384,167	64.9	9.6	42.2	25.1	63,982	11.8	21.6	32.0
3562020764	•Edison, NJ Division	1,616,783	37.3	39.1	1,884,265	64.6	8.6	41.1	25.9	75,355	6.3	15.1	36.7
3562035004	•Nassau–Suffolk, NY Division	1,944,290	37.6	37.4	2,285,935	65.1	7.3	42.8	22.7	90,147	4.8	11.9	45.1
3562035084	•Newark–Union, NJ–PA Division	1,463,826	39.8	36.8	1,710,602	68.3	11.3	42.8	23.7	70,062	8.9	18.5	34.8
3562035644	•New York–White Plains–Wayne, NY–NJ Division	8,058,227	42.5	36.5	9,503,365	64.3	10.1	42.3	25.7	56,007	15.5	25.6	27.7
35660	Niles–Benton Harbor, MI	107,322	43.7	25.6	124,822	59.0	9.2	35.7	32.3	43,526	14.9	30.1	14.2
35840	North Port–Brenton–Sarasota, FL..........	545,189	39.6	29.5	609,279	53.6	10.8	31.7	43.1	47,813	9.5	24.8	17.8
35980	Norwich–New London, CT	188,543	41.3	30.9	224,650	68.3	8.4	41.9	24.2	66,603	6.8	17.0	30.9
36100	Ocala, FL...	244,540	51.0	18.0	278,972	48.1	13.5	27.9	47.0	37,098	12.7	32.0	9.4
36140	Ocean City, NJ.......................................	71,261	46.6	30.7	81,097	61.3	11.2	33.7	35.9	57,001	6.0	19.4	23.5
36220	Odessa, TX...	87,016	53.9	13.5	106,833	66.7	4.7	48.3	19.3	51,946	9.6	23.0	18.2
36260	Ogden–Clearfield, UT............................	328,533	31.7	29.4	399,864	68.5	4.6	44.9	18.0	61,834	8.0	15.9	22.4
36420	Oklahoma City, OK................................	835,652	39.5	28.4	1,007,363	65.1	5.5	44.6	25.1	48,557	11.9	24.9	18.2
36500	Olympia, WA..	176,421	29.5	29.6	206,546	65.1	9.7	40.2	26.1	58,239	7.6	18.0	22.2
36540	Omaha–Council Bluffs, NE–IA	574,033	34.5	33.7	678,967	70.9	5.9	48.3	21.6	54,158	9.6	21.3	21.2
36740	Orlando–Kissimmee, FL..........................	1,472,237	41.2	27.8	1,777,569	65.5	11.4	40.1	25.4	46,020	13.0	25.7	17.1
36780	Oshkosh–Neenah, WI............................	114,092	40.5	27.6	136,620	66.5	6.8	43.3	26.8	51,458	6.3	21.6	17.5
36980	Owensboro, KY......................................	79,578	53.7	18.3	91,720	61.4	7.5	40.3	30.6	44,032	13.9	29.5	13.3
37100	Oxnard–Thousand Oaks–Ventura, CA ...	542,924	35.5	31.6	651,101	67.6	10.0	40.3	23.6	71,517	8.9	15.3	33.6
37340	Palm Bay–Melbourne–Titusville, FL........	398,770	39.3	26.8	455,985	57.1	13.4	33.3	38.8	46,162	10.6	25.9	17.1
37380	Palm Coast, FL.......................................	72,765	46.3	23.6	82,306	46.9	12.3	28.2	46.5	42,856	12.0	26.4	14.0
37460	Panama City–Lynn Haven, FL.................	118,914	39.0	23.4	137,498	64.0	10.8	38.6	29.1	46,005	12.1	26.1	14.1
37620	Parkersburg–Marietta–Vienna, WV–OH	115,476	53.6	17.1	133,213	56.5	8.9	37.6	34.7	42,398	13.3	28.4	13.0
37700	Pascagoula, MS......................................	106,980	46.5	20.3	127,249	58.2	8.7	37.9	28.6	46,130	13.4	27.4	15.3
37860	Pensacola–Ferry Pass–Brent, FL.............	308,513	40.3	24.2	372,240	61.7	9.1	39.1	28.7	49,917	10.4	24.7	15.6
37900	Peoria, IL...	256,242	40.7	25.8	300,043	64.5	6.5	42.6	28.4	53,469	9.5	22.8	20.8

Table B-3. Metropolitan Areas — What: Education, Employment, and Income, 2012—*Continued*

Metro area or division code	Area name	Educational attainment			Employment status				Percent of households with no workers	Median household income (dollars)	Percent of families with income below poverty	Percent of households with income less than $25,000	Percent of households with income of $100,000 or more
		Total population 25 years and over	Percent with a high school diploma or less	Percent with a bachelor's degree or more	Total population 16 years and over	Percent in the labor force	Unemployment rate	Percent who worked full-time year-round					
	ACS table number:	C15002	C15002	C15002	B23025	B23025	B23025	C20005	C08202	B19013	C17013	C19001	C19001
	Column number:	1	2	3	4	5	6	7	8	9	10	11	12
37980	Philadelphia–Camden–Wilmington, PA–NJ–DE–MD	4,046,559	41.6	34.0	4,812,261	65.0	10.4	40.6	27.3	60,105	9.3	21.9	28.0
3798015804	•Camden, NJ Division	850,735	41.8	31.3	998,332	66.5	10.6	41.4	25.9	68,241	6.9	17.3	31.3
3798037964	•Philadelphia, PA Division	2,721,314	41.5	35.4	3,244,416	64.4	10.6	40.0	28.1	56,701	10.4	23.8	27.1
3798048864	•Wilmington, DE–MD–NJ Division	474,510	41.5	31.0	569,513	65.5	9.3	42.5	25.2	62,075	7.5	18.9	27.2
38060	Phoenix–Mesa–Scottsdale, AZ	2,799,426	37.3	29.2	3,339,135	62.8	8.9	40.9	26.5	51,359	12.7	22.7	20.9
38220	Pine Bluff, AR	65,800	57.9	16.5	78,169	50.6	11.6	32.4	34.7	36,127	21.1	37.9	10.8
38300	Pittsburgh, PA	1,682,175	43.0	30.5	1,956,214	62.8	7.2	40.8	31.0	50,489	8.6	24.7	19.7
38340	Pittsfield, MA	92,776	41.5	31.7	109,003	62.3	9.9	33.8	35.3	46,509	10.8	27.5	15.8
38540	Pocatello, ID	55,456	37.6	27.2	68,864	65.4	8.0	36.6	26.4	42,409	12.0	28.2	11.6
38860	Portland–South Portland–Biddeford, ME	370,250	35.4	36.5	425,641	68.1	6.2	41.4	26.3	53,701	7.7	20.5	21.1
38900	Portland–Vancouver–Beaverton, OR–WA	1,565,093	30.6	35.1	1,820,474	66.8	9.6	39.7	25.4	56,978	9.9	20.5	24.4
38940	Port St. Lucie, FL	313,413	42.6	25.2	356,245	54.6	14.5	31.1	41.3	42,316	12.3	26.8	16.3
39100	Poughkeepsie–Newburgh–Middletown, NY	437,055	39.9	29.7	532,656	65.4	9.1	40.7	25.3	66,612	7.2	18.0	31.4
39140	Prescott, AZ	159,040	36.1	26.5	179,519	51.2	10.9	27.9	44.0	44,035	10.4	25.9	12.9
39300	Providence–New Bedford–Fall River, RI–MA	1,090,589	43.7	29.4	1,307,354	65.8	9.8	39.5	29.0	54,243	9.5	24.7	23.6
39340	Provo–Orem, UT	269,350	25.4	35.8	375,945	69.8	6.7	36.8	14.8	58,218	11.3	18.2	21.1
39380	Pueblo, CO	107,016	42.6	19.9	126,913	58.5	11.2	35.8	33.3	41,262	14.3	29.1	11.1
39460	Punta Gorda, FL	131,422	43.4	21.6	143,051	43.6	11.6	23.9	52.9	45,247	8.5	25.0	10.8
39540	Racine, WI	131,278	42.2	23.4	152,633	64.9	11.3	41.2	28.1	51,904	10.6	22.3	19.0
39580	Raleigh–Cary, NC	771,983	30.3	42.0	916,145	69.3	7.4	45.9	19.3	60,319	9.3	17.9	26.6
39660	Rapid City, SD	86,205	39.5	25.7	102,990	68.6	4.4	44.9	24.0	50,383	5.3	21.1	16.0
39740	Reading, PA	274,513	54.7	22.1	329,684	65.9	9.9	40.0	27.8	52,022	10.9	22.9	19.0
39820	Redding, CA	124,220	37.8	18.2	144,489	54.9	11.8	28.0	38.6	45,442	10.8	26.9	15.8
39900	Reno–Sparks, NV	289,122	37.5	27.6	344,966	66.2	10.9	39.9	27.5	49,108	13.8	26.8	19.4
40060	Richmond, VA	861,088	39.5	32.6	1,024,651	66.1	8.3	43.4	24.2	56,769	8.2	19.9	24.3
40140	Riverside–San Bernardino–Ontario, CA	2,659,572	46.7	19.5	3,285,964	60.2	14.1	34.6	27.1	51,695	15.3	23.6	20.6
40220	Roanoke, VA	218,593	43.1	25.5	252,437	61.6	6.5	40.5	30.2	46,974	10.5	26.9	15.5
40340	Rochester, MN	126,840	30.6	35.9	146,342	72.0	3.2	47.7	19.7	63,733	5.5	17.1	25.7
40380	Rochester, NY	711,991	37.5	31.9	856,913	64.5	8.4	39.5	29.2	50,701	10.4	24.2	19.6
40420	Rockford, IL	230,497	47.0	21.6	269,120	65.4	11.8	38.9	27.1	50,647	12.8	24.9	16.7
40580	Rocky Mount, NC	100,907	56.2	15.7	119,902	60.1	16.2	33.5	33.9	37,319	19.0	35.3	10.7
40660	Rome, GA	62,888	50.8	18.3	75,253	58.6	13.8	33.0	36.8	37,841	18.2	33.5	13.8
40900	Sacramento–Arden–Arcade–Roseville, CA	1,437,996	33.7	30.3	1,731,134	63.1	13.1	35.9	28.6	56,813	12.2	21.8	25.0
40980	Saginaw–Saginaw Township North, MI	131,913	47.5	19.1	158,797	56.9	13.6	31.3	39.5	40,318	13.5	30.7	12.3
41060	St. Cloud, MN	120,560	39.4	25.1	151,356	71.3	5.4	42.9	22.3	54,573	6.6	22.8	19.0
41100	St. George, UT	87,913	34.1	24.4	106,690	56.5	9.2	31.5	34.3	43,837	11.6	26.9	14.3
41140	St. Joseph, MO–KS	85,152	51.8	20.0	103,184	61.2	7.8	38.9	28.7	43,784	11.8	28.9	12.9
41180	St. Louis, MO–IL	1,907,084	37.7	30.8	2,239,645	66.0	9.0	42.2	26.8	52,243	10.6	23.6	21.4
41420	Salem, OR	255,141	41.0	23.3	306,405	62.8	15.6	34.2	30.9	45,656	16.2	26.5	14.4
41500	Salinas, CA	265,340	49.2	24.0	324,853	63.3	9.0	34.8	23.3	58,109	13.9	19.4	24.6
41540	Salisbury, MD	81,559	47.7	25.3	103,719	59.6	9.3	37.6	28.3	49,357	13.5	26.4	18.3
41620	Salt Lake City, UT	707,291	32.9	32.4	856,376	71.6	7.4	45.4	17.9	60,061	9.5	18.5	23.6
41660	San Angelo, TX	73,609	49.5	18.5	91,783	64.1	5.7	42.2	28.2	44,910	12.9	26.3	15.3
41700	San Antonio, TX	1,418,358	41.6	26.5	1,718,686	65.1	7.9	43.4	22.6	51,486	13.7	24.0	20.3
41740	San Diego–Carlsbad–San Marcos, CA	2,079,795	33.1	34.8	2,536,682	64.8	9.2	40.0	24.7	60,330	11.5	20.4	27.8
41780	Sandusky, OH	53,653	49.1	21.3	61,810	63.0	8.8	35.4	32.9	44,694	7.4	24.0	14.3
41860	San Francisco–Oakland–Fremont, CA	3,142,686	28.7	45.0	3,631,714	66.8	8.8	41.4	24.5	74,922	8.2	17.8	38.5
4186036084	•Oakland–Fremont–Hayward, CA Division	1,788,089	30.9	41.1	2,100,699	65.8	9.6	40.0	25.0	71,931	9.0	17.9	36.7
4186041884	•San Francisco–San Mateo–Redwood City, CA Division	1,354,597	25.9	50.1	1,531,015	68.2	7.7	43.2	23.7	78,840	6.9	17.8	40.9
41940	San Jose–Sunnyvale–Santa Clara, CA	1,276,271	29.1	46.4	1,491,380	66.9	8.8	42.8	19.1	90,737	7.6	14.0	45.4
42020	San Luis Obispo–Paso Robles, CA	180,650	27.9	33.5	228,704	60.8	6.8	36.2	27.2	60,264	7.8	19.1	26.6
42060	Santa Barbara–Santa Maria–Goleta, CA	266,202	40.4	30.2	343,991	62.0	9.1	36.4	26.4	61,890	10.0	19.5	27.7
42100	Santa Cruz–Watsonville, CA	172,067	30.1	38.3	218,080	67.0	8.1	35.5	24.0	67,769	7.8	17.8	33.3
42140	Santa Fe, NM	105,733	33.0	39.5	120,055	63.5	10.0	38.9	30.1	50,720	13.8	24.0	20.2
42220	Santa Rosa–Petaluma, CA	339,841	33.9	31.8	399,578	64.7	9.4	35.2	28.5	59,941	8.4	18.8	27.7
42340	Savannah, GA	232,809	40.2	29.2	284,818	63.8	9.3	41.5	26.7	47,059	13.4	26.4	17.7
42540	Scranton–Wilkes-Barre, PA	395,863	50.8	22.3	465,547	60.4	8.8	38.3	33.2	42,883	11.4	29.7	14.5
42660	Seattle–Tacoma–Bellevue, WA	2,432,130	29.7	37.7	2,847,146	68.3	7.6	43.8	22.2	65,677	7.8	17.1	30.4
4266042644	•Seattle–Bellevue–Everett, WA Division	1,899,340	27.2	40.6	2,210,432	69.0	7.0	44.3	21.5	68,562	7.4	16.7	32.8
4266045104	•Tacoma, WA Division	532,790	38.7	23.9	636,714	65.8	9.4	41.9	24.7	57,629	9.1	18.4	21.9
42680	Sebastian–Vero Beach, FL	104,665	41.1	26.7	117,025	50.9	17.2	26.7	48.0	40,413	11.5	32.8	15.8

Table B-3. Metropolitan Areas — What: Education, Employment, and Income, 2012—*Continued*

Metro area or division code	Area name	Educational attainment			Employment status				Percent of households with no workers	Median household income (dollars)	Percent of families with income below poverty	Percent of households with income less than $25,000	Percent of households with income of $100,000 or more
		Total population 25 years and over	Percent with a high school diploma or less	Percent with a bachelor's degree or more	Total population 16 years and over	Percent in the labor force	Unemployment rate	Percent who worked full-time year-round					
ACS table number:		C15002	C15002	C15002	B23025	B23025	B23025	C20005	C08202	B19013	C17013	C19001	C19001
Column number:		1	2	3	4	5	6	7	8	9	10	11	12
43100	Sheboygan, WI	79,730	46.7	24.1	91,592	70.1	7.7	42.2	26.0	51,899	9.4	20.7	15.6
43300	Sherman–Denison, TX	81,542	41.1	20.0	96,941	60.1	9.1	41.2	30.5	47,475	12.7	25.5	15.4
43340	Shreveport–Bossier City, LA	266,090	45.7	23.4	315,823	62.3	7.5	42.2	26.6	44,118	14.6	28.1	18.4
43580	Sioux City, IA–NE–SD	91,566	49.7	19.8	110,789	68.2	5.2	46.7	23.2	44,879	12.3	26.1	13.4
43620	Sioux Falls, SD	155,254	39.3	29.2	182,479	74.2	3.7	54.4	18.6	51,745	7.4	18.7	17.7
43780	South Bend–Mishawaka, IN–MI	207,904	44.2	26.4	251,546	63.1	9.7	36.5	28.2	44,769	11.1	26.8	14.3
43900	Spartanburg, SC	190,631	50.3	20.5	227,503	59.9	10.9	37.1	31.6	40,879	15.3	30.5	12.4
44060	Spokane, WA	314,381	32.3	27.4	378,070	61.8	9.3	36.2	31.2	47,624	11.4	26.3	16.3
44100	Springfield, IL	144,789	37.3	33.1	168,121	67.1	8.0	44.4	26.9	55,621	10.4	21.5	21.6
44140	Springfield, MA	459,431	41.2	30.6	568,922	63.4	9.9	35.5	30.9	51,531	12.5	26.6	21.1
44180	Springfield, MO	290,605	41.0	25.5	353,742	63.4	8.4	39.2	27.8	42,263	12.0	28.3	11.8
44220	Springfield, OH	92,598	52.2	17.3	109,216	59.9	13.3	33.6	36.7	39,178	15.5	31.7	11.5
44300	State College, PA	87,461	39.0	39.4	133,953	56.9	5.9	34.5	27.8	50,809	8.0	26.9	21.0
44600	Steubenville–Weirton, OH	86,562	53.5	17.5	100,241	54.5	7.3	33.7	36.7	38,775	12.7	30.4	11.8
44700	Stockton, CA	427,418	47.3	18.9	523,060	61.4	16.0	32.9	28.1	50,722	14.7	25.0	21.5
44940	Sumter, SC	69,796	44.2	18.0	84,362	62.9	13.6	39.7	28.9	39,667	14.7	30.2	11.0
45060	Syracuse, NY	436,702	40.9	29.0	532,717	61.9	7.8	38.9	30.1	51,259	10.1	24.7	19.6
45220	Tallahassee, FL	228,309	34.0	37.1	312,951	63.3	10.9	36.0	25.6	44,715	11.4	29.7	17.2
45300	Tampa–St. Petersburg–Clearwater, FL	2,010,425	42.8	27.1	2,322,858	59.8	10.9	38.3	33.5	44,402	12.0	27.2	16.9
45460	Terre Haute, IN	113,750	51.4	19.3	139,822	59.9	8.4	35.0	29.3	41,039	13.6	31.5	11.9
45500	Texarkana, TX–Texarkana, AR	91,212	49.2	17.7	107,618	57.2	9.2	38.1	30.3	38,556	18.7	34.8	11.5
45780	Toledo, OH	425,144	43.6	23.7	519,847	63.9	11.7	37.5	31.8	43,334	14.5	29.8	15.4
45820	Topeka, KS	157,576	42.3	26.6	183,097	65.3	6.8	44.1	28.6	48,464	10.5	23.8	15.1
45940	Trenton–Ewing, NJ	244,580	39.7	38.2	297,053	65.8	11.5	40.8	25.6	67,991	7.2	17.8	34.9
46060	Tucson, AZ	663,098	34.3	30.2	794,157	59.4	10.3	36.0	32.6	44,762	13.6	28.1	16.9
46140	Tulsa, OK	625,553	41.4	26.2	738,134	64.1	7.5	44.2	26.0	47,969	11.7	25.6	17.1
46220	Tuscaloosa, AL	134,355	47.7	27.4	180,436	56.9	8.5	34.4	31.8	38,749	15.5	34.4	15.0
46340	Tyler, TX	136,386	40.2	24.2	165,470	62.1	6.2	39.3	24.7	46,286	13.7	25.9	17.0
46540	Utica–Rome, NY	205,882	45.1	23.4	242,056	60.6	9.4	37.2	33.6	46,633	12.0	27.6	15.1
46660	Valdosta, GA	83,959	48.6	19.4	113,386	62.9	14.6	36.0	27.8	36,456	18.3	36.3	11.7
46700	Vallejo–Fairfield, CA	279,393	36.9	24.1	334,140	64.3	13.3	36.2	26.0	62,066	10.9	19.3	27.7
47020	Victoria, TX	77,713	51.6	15.0	91,862	64.4	7.2	41.3	25.8	50,122	13.0	26.1	18.7
47220	Vineland–Millville–Bridgeton, NJ	105,487	63.3	13.9	124,633	56.8	13.9	33.7	34.1	47,072	15.6	28.8	18.0
47260	Virginia Beach–Norfolk–Newport News, VA–NC	1,101,806	35.9	28.8	1,349,610	67.5	8.2	45.8	23.2	55,997	10.4	19.9	22.8
47300	Visalia–Porterville, CA	257,393	56.7	14.7	322,615	61.1	13.6	33.9	25.9	40,302	25.6	31.9	15.1
47380	Waco, TX	144,375	44.3	22.3	186,375	60.2	7.7	38.1	27.5	40,658	12.9	30.1	15.2
47580	Warner Robins, GA	93,959	37.3	24.6	111,871	66.8	11.7	43.9	24.0	54,457	15.2	25.8	20.4
47900	Washington–Arlington–Alexandria, DC–VA–MD–WV	3,914,650	29.1	48.2	4,594,928	72.7	6.5	50.9	16.7	88,233	5.7	11.5	44.1
4790013644	•Bethesda–Gaithersburg–Frederick, MD Division	851,731	25.7	53.4	983,917	71.9	6.5	49.2	17.7	91,542	4.5	9.9	46.6
4790047894	•Washington–Arlington–Alexandria, DC–VA–MD–WV Division	3,062,919	30.1	46.7	3,611,011	73.0	6.5	51.3	16.4	87,231	6.1	12.0	43.5
47940	Waterloo–Cedar Falls, IA	107,553	44.4	27.2	135,997	67.7	7.6	42.1	28.0	50,729	6.5	20.7	15.2
48140	Wausau, WI	92,016	47.5	22.6	106,354	70.7	8.3	43.4	24.2	52,419	7.6	20.2	16.2
48300	Wenatchee, WA	74,321	46.7	21.7	87,749	62.5	9.3	37.6	30.0	47,251	10.0	22.0	18.4
48540	Wheeling, WV–OH	104,717	53.9	18.3	121,744	58.7	8.5	35.1	34.6	41,677	11.1	31.3	9.9
48620	Wichita, KS	401,390	37.8	28.1	479,472	66.5	7.2	43.7	24.8	48,509	10.4	24.0	17.1
48660	Wichita Falls, TX	96,831	46.1	20.3	120,120	62.5	5.1	43.4	25.2	46,653	10.1	26.2	15.9
48700	Williamsport, PA	80,310	54.0	19.0	95,909	63.4	9.6	39.6	29.5	45,710	8.7	26.0	13.3
48900	Wilmington, NC	264,074	36.1	31.1	310,497	61.3	10.4	36.5	32.7	49,999	11.4	23.5	17.9
49020	Winchester, VA–WV	88,320	49.2	25.4	104,472	63.8	7.6	41.3	26.0	47,850	5.8	25.8	20.7
49180	Winston-Salem, NC	325,184	43.7	28.7	384,995	61.9	11.0	38.9	29.6	42,254	15.7	30.6	16.3
49340	Worcester, MA	543,590	39.1	33.6	645,829	66.9	8.3	41.5	25.8	62,505	8.3	21.0	29.0
49420	Yakima, WA	147,642	55.0	14.7	180,206	61.8	10.8	36.1	29.3	43,942	17.6	27.7	13.8
49620	York–Hanover, PA	300,874	53.8	22.0	350,264	66.1	8.3	42.3	26.2	55,648	7.0	19.1	20.3
49660	Youngstown–Warren–Boardman, OH–PA	392,658	54.1	18.8	456,942	57.4	9.1	34.0	35.5	40,686	12.8	30.7	11.3
49700	Yuba City, CA	103,665	43.6	16.9	127,172	60.2	14.1	32.9	30.1	45,646	16.6	27.6	16.2
49740	Yuma, AZ	121,796	52.1	14.3	151,920	55.2	13.8	31.6	35.6	39,485	18.7	30.8	9.3

Table B-4. Cities — What: Education, Employment, and Income, 2010–2012

STATE and Place code	STATE city	Educational attainment			Employment status				Percent of households with no workers	Median household income (dollars)	Percent of families with income below poverty	Percent of households with ncome less than $25,000	Percent of households with income of $100,000 or more
		Total population 25 years and over	Percent with a high school diploma or less	Percent with a bachelor's degree or more	Total population 16 years and over	Percent in the labor force	Unemployment rate	Percent who worked full-time year-round					
	ACS table number:	C15002	C15002	C15002	B23025	B23025	B23025	C20005	C08202	B19013	C17013	C19001	C19001
	Column number:	1	2	3	4	5	6	7	8	9	10	11	12
00 00000	**United States**	206,597,203	42.3	28.6	246,234,513	64.1	10.1	39.8	27.3	51,771	11.6	24.1	21.6
01 00000	**Alabama**	3,192,004	48.2	22.5	3,806,456	59.3	11.0	37.7	32.4	42,054	14.8	30.7	15.3
01 00820	Alabaster city	20,416	33.0	32.3	23,291	72.0	6.1	47.2	17.2	67,891	7.5	16.1	23.7
01 00988	Albertville city	13,389	57.1	13.6	15,482	65.5	7.3	42.3	28.7	37,681	20.0	34.4	11.5
01 01852	Anniston city	16,087	49.4	21.5	18,907	55.0	15.5	30.0	40.8	34,752	18.4	38.1	10.3
01 02956	Athens city	14,940	45.3	26.6	17,809	61.8	11.8	38.5	32.5	49,251	7.5	24.3	18.6
01 03076	Auburn city	24,117	19.2	60.5	46,485	59.4	10.0	28.7	26.9	37,853	9.6	38.9	16.9
01 05980	Bessemer city	17,589	55.9	12.1	20,960	50.9	17.2	30.0	45.2	29,736	25.3	46.2	4.9
01 07000	Birmingham city	140,632	45.3	21.6	170,335	58.5	16.0	33.7	36.0	30,276	27.0	43.3	8.2
01 19648	Daphne city	14,967	23.9	40.5	17,309	65.5	7.8	41.9	25.5	61,776	4.7	18.9	29.9
01 20104	Decatur city	37,848	49.6	21.7	44,438	65.9	11.5	39.1	31.7	41,972	13.6	31.3	14.8
01 21184	Dothan city	44,783	45.7	23.4	52,797	60.7	8.6	40.7	30.5	41,417	15.7	31.4	15.8
01 24184	Enterprise city	18,008	39.2	28.8	21,335	61.3	7.9	42.2	28.7	49,828	13.9	25.4	21.6
01 26896	Florence city	25,608	44.0	27.3	32,331	56.5	8.6	33.1	37.3	34,305	18.7	38.1	11.9
01 28696	Gadsden city	25,064	54.0	13.7	29,234	48.9	15.4	26.8	48.1	25,878	25.2	48.7	6.0
01 35800	Homewood city	14,708	25.0	54.4	19,975	70.4	5.0	44.5	19.1	57,755	4.8	20.5	24.1
01 35896	Hoover city	55,369	16.9	56.8	62,767	69.7	6.2	48.3	19.9	75,606	4.5	10.2	36.4
01 37000	Huntsville city	121,241	30.8	38.6	147,333	65.7	11.6	40.9	27.4	46,821	12.4	27.9	21.5
01 45784	Madison city	28,111	17.6	56.0	33,315	71.4	7.6	49.3	13.5	92,427	5.4	9.4	46.6
01 50000	Mobile city	126,147	42.3	27.0	154,831	59.4	13.1	37.0	32.8	38,566	19.9	33.9	13.9
01 51000	Montgomery city	129,842	40.1	31.5	160,033	61.6	9.6	39.7	29.0	42,403	19.2	31.3	15.7
01 51696	Mountain Brook city	n.a.	n.a.	n.a.	14,890	64.5	2.5	44.8	18.3	133,173	0.5	4.7	63.6
01 55200	Northport city	15,468	39.4	33.9	18,171	62.8	6.4	47.6	28.6	51,478	10.5	25.5	16.0
01 57048	Opelika city	18,327	48.0	25.3	21,808	63.2	6.3	41.4	26.8	40,693	17.8	31.6	15.6
01 57576	Oxford city	14,332	53.6	15.8	16,700	63.4	11.1	42.1	27.2	50,676	7.8	20.7	18.4
01 58848	Pelham city	14,707	32.4	32.6	17,232	75.7	7.9	50.1	20.0	64,455	4.9	15.7	24.0
01 59472	Phenix City city	22,064	45.6	20.0	26,908	64.2	11.2	41.2	28.7	35,151	22.0	35.8	11.9
01 62328	Prattville city	21,319	40.7	28.8	26,099	65.0	7.9	44.2	22.8	57,323	7.9	19.6	22.6
01 62496	Prichard city	14,516	61.4	7.4	17,942	50.9	22.1	27.0	44.2	22,303	30.8	53.5	2.2
01 69120	Selma city	12,698	57.7	17.1	15,170	48.1	24.7	25.4	54.8	21,073	39.7	54.9	7.3
01 76944	Trussville city	13,796	26.6	40.7	15,613	65.9	7.6	49.3	15.9	84,656	2.6	11.3	40.7
01 77256	Tuscaloosa city	49,303	39.0	34.3	77,414	54.9	8.0	32.3	30.2	36,429	19.4	36.1	14.1
01 78552	Vestavia Hills city	23,605	12.0	68.0	26,540	62.8	3.7	44.5	26.9	78,968	3.0	13.3	42.7
02 00000	**Alaska**	457,070	35.7	27.5	555,762	70.9	8.4	42.7	20.3	68,818	7.2	15.7	30.8
02 03000	Anchorage municipality	186,778	30.9	32.5	228,921	74.1	7.1	48.6	16.1	74,648	6.2	13.0	35.2
02 05000	Badger CDP	11,502	34.7	22.1	14,765	73.8	4.5	48.7	16.8	74,548	4.6	11.2	28.3
02 24230	Fairbanks city	18,262	40.1	19.3	24,035	71.6	9.7	46.4	21.0	53,140	9.3	21.7	17.3
02 36400	Juneau city and borough	21,880	25.1	37.5	25,634	71.6	5.3	48.7	18.5	78,547	4.4	9.9	33.9
04 00000	**Arizona**	4,209,589	38.9	26.7	5,034,808	60.5	10.8	37.4	30.1	48,307	13.4	24.9	18.5
04 02430	Anthem CDP	13,267	18.9	44.0	14,807	65.9	8.7	45.5	23.1	72,677	3.0	9.3	34.2
04 02830	Apache Junction city	26,783	48.9	12.0	29,786	45.4	21.7	23.4	56.2	36,982	14.0	31.6	8.3
04 04720	Avondale city	43,673	47.0	20.2	55,101	72.3	11.9	49.6	13.6	55,513	14.3	17.1	17.8
04 07940	Buckeye city	31,244	47.9	15.7	37,451	53.9	9.9	38.4	21.1	60,503	13.8	16.9	15.8
04 08220	Bullhead City city	28,433	51.4	12.6	32,486	50.5	15.1	28.1	47.8	35,488	14.6	33.6	7.1
04 10530	Casa Grande city	31,700	43.6	18.1	37,833	55.4	13.5	33.2	36.2	44,522	10.7	22.8	13.3
04 10670	Casas Adobes CDP	48,526	28.4	35.0	55,270	64.9	9.1	39.7	28.7	52,965	7.7	19.1	20.9
04 11230	Catalina Foothills CDP	40,729	11.6	61.8	45,087	56.8	6.7	34.4	34.6	78,532	4.2	14.2	37.6
04 12000	Chandler city	153,790	26.0	39.0	182,703	73.7	7.5	50.3	15.8	69,917	6.8	13.2	31.8
04 20540	Drexel Heights CDP	17,471	56.1	11.6	20,853	62.2	14.8	37.4	24.5	43,338	17.9	26.4	9.8
04 22220	El Mirage city	18,370	47.4	13.6	22,672	65.2	8.7	39.7	22.1	47,154	16.1	21.9	9.7
04 23620	Flagstaff city	34,828	26.8	42.0	54,664	71.1	9.1	34.2	19.0	46,033	14.7	26.9	18.6
04 23760	Florence town	21,043	54.7	8.4	24,117	14.8	6.8	13.0	56.5	45,055	8.4	25.8	8.8
04 25030	Fortuna Foothills CDP	22,483	45.0	16.7	24,593	39.6	8.8	25.0	56.4	54,287	6.7	19.9	15.0
04 25300	Fountain Hills town	18,329	22.4	43.9	20,278	54.8	7.1	34.6	35.5	69,764	1.3	11.4	30.2
04 27400	Gilbert town	129,198	22.2	38.9	152,791	74.2	6.8	50.0	14.4	77,739	5.7	10.3	35.7
04 27820	Glendale city	139,765	44.2	21.7	174,661	67.0	13.2	41.4	23.4	47,129	16.1	26.2	17.6
04 28380	Goodyear city	44,648	34.0	26.0	51,581	61.2	8.5	43.0	22.9	67,206	6.3	11.4	25.7
04 29710	Green Valley CDP	21,726	28.8	39.5	22,045	17.7	4.9	8.3	79.2	43,959	2.0	22.5	15.0
04 37620	Kingman city	20,046	46.2	14.0	22,923	53.2	11.3	33.0	40.8	44,175	13.4	26.5	11.6
04 39370	Lake Havasu City city	39,638	45.3	14.1	44,391	49.6	12.0	27.8	46.5	40,364	10.7	27.0	11.3
04 44270	Marana town	24,496	22.9	40.2	27,493	66.6	8.1	44.8	24.4	70,227	1.9	9.5	25.4
04 44410	Maricopa city	28,660	32.9	26.9	31,945	68.7	9.1	49.1	15.8	62,488	2.3	11.7	17.4
04 46000	Mesa city	288,558	39.8	23.5	346,806	62.0	10.2	37.8	30.7	46,496	12.6	24.7	16.5
04 49640	Nogales city	11,763	68.8	10.7	14,892	56.2	20.4	26.4	30.5	23,864	36.7	52.0	7.1
04 51600	Oro Valley town	29,782	15.9	51.8	33,834	53.9	8.3	32.1	39.3	68,863	4.2	14.3	32.3
04 54050	Peoria city	103,705	33.0	26.7	121,519	65.4	8.4	42.6	26.1	60,953	7.9	18.0	26.0
04 55000	Phoenix city	909,881	43.7	26.0	1,105,472	66.1	10.7	42.7	22.5	44,649	18.4	27.2	17.9
04 57380	Prescott city	31,520	26.8	36.8	35,285	44.7	11.0	22.7	51.1	43,501	8.5	28.7	15.5
04 57450	Prescott Valley town	25,859	38.8	17.7	30,478	58.7	8.8	30.1	35.0	41,555	13.4	27.5	8.5
04 58150	Queen Creek town	15,045	19.3	37.8	17,735	71.1	4.6	50.9	15.8	82,458	6.3	8.6	40.1
04 62140	Sahuarita town	16,998	26.4	34.3	18,500	58.4	4.6	41.4	32.0	64,132	4.7	12.0	20.1
04 63470	San Luis city	14,006	67.4	9.9	18,677	48.7	18.7	22.5	37.1	30,581	30.4	41.6	3.3
04 64210	San Tan Valley CDP	46,223	35.6	23.3	54,343	67.9	14.0	41.8	19.6	56,784	8.7	14.3	14.7
04 65000	Scottsdale city	165,447	19.0	51.9	186,132	64.0	7.2	42.2	28.5	69,876	5.8	17.3	34.8
04 66820	Sierra Vista city	28,860	27.3	31.7	36,202	63.9	6.1	41.0	30.6	55,826	8.0	20.3	20.8
04 70320	Sun City CDP	37,526	45.6	19.6	37,798	18.6	19.7	9.7	79.8	36,519	3.5	30.2	4.7
04 70355	Sun City West CDP	25,276	31.0	36.1	25,407	10.9	10.2	...	86.2	44,789	2.2	19.2	11.8
04 71510	Surprise city	77,179	32.8	28.6	87,034	56.6	10.6	36.0	34.1	57,249	8.0	15.3	18.0
04 73000	Tempe city	94,780	26.2	40.8	139,191	68.6	11.2	38.0	22.2	46,105	14.2	26.8	18.2
04 77000	Tucson city	327,819	40.3	24.3	418,471	61.2	12.7	34.4	30.1	36,050	19.3	35.4	10.8
04 85540	Yuma city	55,358	47.3	16.6	71,074	60.7	12.1	39.0	30.1	43,147	15.9	27.4	11.9

Table B-4. Cities — What: Education, Employment, and Income, 2010–2012—*Continued*

STATE and Place code	STATE city	Educational attainment			Employment status				Percent of households with no workers	Median household income (dollars)	Percent of families with income below poverty	Percent of households with income less than $25,000	Percent of households with income of $100,000 or more
		Total population 25 years and over	Percent with a high school diploma or less	Percent with a bachelor's degree or more	Total population 16 years and over	Percent in the labor force	Unemployment rate	Percent who worked full-time year-round					
	ACS table number:	C15002	C15002	C15002	B23025	B23025	B23025	C20005	C08202	B19013	C17013	C19001	C19001
	Column number:	1	2	3	4	5	6	7	8	9	10	11	12
05 00000	**Arkansas**	1,938,675	51.3	20.2	2,302,696	59.8	9.1	38.9	31.5	40,104	14.5	31.8	13.0
05 04840	Bella Vista town	20,995	30.4	37.7	22,398	52.7	4.7	37.3	40.6	60,929	2.7	14.5	23.5
05 05290	Benton city	20,561	41.9	27.5	24,035	64.5	6.1	44.9	28.7	53,276	6.7	23.2	21.4
05 05320	Bentonville city	23,347	32.8	41.1	27,562	67.1	5.7	52.1	16.3	64,695	6.8	19.1	29.8
05 10300	Cabot city	15,169	36.7	25.1	17,768	70.1	5.8	50.0	21.1	55,912	9.0	18.7	20.4
05 15190	Conway city	33,885	34.7	36.8	48,749	68.1	7.5	41.4	21.4	46,775	10.9	29.4	19.8
05 23290	Fayetteville city	42,443	27.9	44.1	63,048	66.6	8.4	35.9	25.4	36,262	11.9	38.0	17.9
05 24550	Fort Smith city	56,295	49.8	20.4	66,897	61.5	6.7	41.7	28.7	36,792	19.9	33.1	12.7
05 33400	Hot Springs city	24,806	50.4	17.8	28,993	54.6	11.5	30.5	38.8	32,390	20.8	42.1	8.5
05 34750	Jacksonville city	17,290	49.7	17.1	21,947	62.8	6.1	43.8	25.0	38,102	15.4	26.7	9.2
05 35710	Jonesboro city	41,243	42.7	28.0	53,512	63.6	10.4	38.1	30.7	39,267	18.7	33.7	16.3
05 41000	Little Rock city	128,324	32.9	38.7	152,996	66.6	10.3	43.4	27.3	45,267	14.0	30.2	19.2
05 50450	North Little Rock city	42,576	42.2	25.2	49,211	63.2	9.6	43.0	31.0	39,871	15.3	31.8	10.3
05 53390	Paragould city	17,369	60.7	14.0	20,979	56.9	12.2	37.0	38.3	35,665	11.4	37.2	9.6
05 55310	Pine Bluff city	29,867	52.6	18.3	37,271	58.1	19.0	32.4	34.8	30,581	23.6	42.1	7.8
05 60410	Rogers city	34,359	49.9	27.5	42,286	68.1	6.5	48.6	19.5	52,308	11.0	20.0	20.1
05 61670	Russellville city	16,209	47.7	26.0	22,484	64.4	7.8	33.8	24.0	35,561	19.2	34.9	11.0
05 63020	Searcy city	12,968	42.7	30.7	19,140	57.9	7.2	33.0	28.9	42,346	13.3	29.8	13.5
05 63800	Sherwood city	20,760	38.4	30.7	23,744	68.3	4.9	51.9	19.8	53,548	11.8	21.9	20.3
05 66080	Springdale city	42,137	57.4	18.6	50,727	68.1	9.1	46.5	19.1	40,029	20.3	26.9	13.5
05 68810	Texarkana city	20,267	55.0	12.8	23,396	60.9	9.6	41.7	31.6	38,357	16.8	31.5	10.6
05 71480	Van Buren city	13,972	50.1	15.5	16,762	61.1	6.8	40.8	28.9	38,109	20.4	34.2	7.2
05 74540	West Memphis city	15,846	59.6	11.0	19,015	62.6	15.1	38.3	29.9	29,438	28.4	43.1	8.1
06 00000	**California**	24,444,584	39.7	30.5	29,523,512	64.0	12.1	37.5	25.2	59,368	12.3	21.2	27.9
06 00296	Adelanto city	15,259	58.8	7.3	20,643	47.0	24.1	26.4	34.1	34,925	35.5	37.5	6.5
06 00394	Agoura Hills city	14,073	18.9	50.0	16,333	67.3	10.6	40.7	20.4	103,894	4.3	5.1	53.5
06 00562	Alameda city	53,174	22.5	49.2	60,821	68.6	9.9	42.4	22.3	71,709	6.7	15.3	34.7
06 00884	Alhambra city	61,269	41.1	32.0	70,239	63.4	7.9	41.1	19.6	54,517	10.8	22.6	22.0
06 00947	Aliso Viejo city	32,144	15.9	57.9	36,984	77.4	8.3	53.7	10.8	97,664	3.6	6.9	49.3
06 01290	Altadena CDP	31,258	28.9	43.4	36,523	66.3	10.5	38.5	22.8	81,396	6.3	14.1	39.8
06 02000	Anaheim city	211,701	50.1	23.9	258,961	67.8	12.5	41.2	20.1	57,345	13.4	19.6	24.3
06 02210	Antelope CDP	27,639	39.8	20.5	35,779	66.1	10.2	37.9	18.5	63,399	8.7	14.2	22.7
06 02252	Antioch city	65,024	42.2	19.1	79,913	65.7	15.4	36.3	23.3	65,238	10.3	18.0	28.5
06 02364	Apple Valley town	44,005	45.7	17.1	53,681	52.0	13.9	29.1	36.9	45,440	17.1	28.8	19.9
06 02462	Arcadia city	39,663	23.4	53.6	45,553	60.2	6.4	40.7	23.6	74,814	10.0	18.1	39.9
06 02553	Arden-Arcade CDP	62,463	29.4	34.0	73,121	61.6	15.4	31.9	37.8	41,339	15.5	30.2	19.4
06 02924	Arvin city	9,722	81.0	2.6	13,345	67.2	16.8	30.0	20.8	31,462	32.2	38.9	5.2
06 02980	Ashland CDP	13,799	54.1	20.6	17,231	63.4	14.6	37.5	23.7	46,490	13.8	30.2	13.9
06 03064	Atascadero city	20,265	29.4	27.9	23,429	60.0	6.4	38.0	25.3	65,808	10.0	17.4	23.3
06 03162	Atwater city	16,654	55.7	12.4	20,548	61.1	18.4	35.3	31.0	40,265	20.8	30.7	11.8
06 03386	Azusa city	25,287	57.0	18.1	36,599	64.7	7.9	37.1	16.6	53,176	16.4	22.8	18.9
06 03526	Bakersfield city	204,502	45.7	20.4	257,350	65.1	13.3	38.5	24.2	54,422	16.4	23.9	22.6
06 03666	Baldwin Park city	45,516	68.8	11.5	57,539	63.9	15.7	34.2	16.6	50,676	16.4	20.6	15.7
06 03820	Banning city	21,585	54.2	17.0	24,852	43.4	14.2	25.3	53.7	38,880	14.5	30.1	7.5
06 04030	Barstow city	13,433	49.1	10.8	17,103	55.1	14.8	36.6	31.1	41,556	22.9	36.6	13.3
06 04415	Bay Point CDP	13,553	61.5	14.7	16,866	69.3	15.9	38.1	24.6	43,139	25.3	24.7	13.5
06 04758	Beaumont city	24,218	36.9	24.0	27,939	64.5	10.5	42.3	24.5	65,740	8.3	17.2	27.1
06 04870	Bell city	19,923	73.6	7.1	25,791	61.2	16.7	33.8	15.2	34,657	27.0	33.7	6.5
06 04982	Bellflower city	45,679	52.8	15.5	56,679	62.8	12.3	40.9	22.1	46,359	15.9	25.9	16.1
06 04996	Bell Gardens city	23,313	81.2	5.3	29,890	63.5	14.5	35.3	17.9	36,352	26.6	31.9	5.5
06 05108	Belmont city	18,736	17.2	56.4	21,068	71.1	7.9	48.1	21.8	100,037	3.9	11.4	50.0
06 05290	Benicia city	18,983	21.4	40.6	21,723	65.7	9.4	40.0	25.0	82,270	2.7	10.5	42.6
06 06000	Berkeley city	69,747	13.6	68.4	101,549	57.4	8.9	29.0	31.6	61,300	9.1	26.3	32.6
06 06308	Beverly Hills city	24,646	18.9	60.3	28,623	65.5	11.3	41.0	23.3	87,703	5.8	16.4	45.2
06 07064	Bloomington CDP	12,798	69.8	7.5	17,040	62.4	18.8	30.4	14.6	45,931	21.3	21.2	12.2
06 07218	Blythe city	14,630	59.7	7.8	17,087	42.0	21.5	22.6	31.4	47,117	20.8	30.6	17.4
06 08058	Brawley city	13,747	60.7	10.2	17,693	56.8	20.2	28.1	31.5	40,577	24.0	35.0	14.5
06 08100	Brea city	26,737	25.5	40.0	32,153	67.5	9.7	41.3	19.4	78,229	5.0	12.0	38.8
06 08142	Brentwood city	32,990	30.1	29.5	39,440	66.0	11.0	41.1	19.3	87,478	3.5	8.8	45.4
06 08786	Buena Park city	52,396	41.7	28.4	63,625	63.0	7.6	38.9	18.0	64,623	8.5	16.1	27.0
06 08954	Burbank city	75,564	30.1	36.7	85,435	67.5	9.2	43.0	23.4	64,603	6.3	20.4	29.2
06 09066	Burlingame city	21,253	18.3	54.7	23,146	68.9	6.2	43.8	22.2	77,453	6.4	13.3	39.1
06 09598	Calabasas city	15,980	16.2	61.0	18,138	64.8	8.4	43.9	20.1	120,114	4.8	9.3	57.5
06 09710	Calexico city	22,492	61.8	14.2	28,454	56.2	20.3	24.7	28.5	36,845	24.8	36.0	10.3
06 10046	Camarillo city	45,372	25.4	38.8	52,290	65.1	9.2	39.1	28.6	81,349	4.3	13.4	39.1
06 10345	Campbell city	28,439	24.0	45.8	32,968	72.6	5.6	50.5	17.0	81,108	3.3	13.4	39.0
06 11194	Carlsbad city	76,516	16.8	50.9	86,399	61.1	9.2	38.5	29.3	78,085	10.9	17.6	39.7
06 11390	Carmichael CDP	43,537	27.5	31.2	50,780	59.7	17.7	32.0	35.4	51,658	11.3	23.3	21.0
06 11530	Carson city	60,924	42.8	24.5	74,675	65.0	15.8	37.4	21.8	70,360	7.3	15.6	30.2
06 11964	Castro Valley CDP	42,452	31.2	36.3	49,084	65.2	9.8	41.6	23.3	81,879	5.4	12.4	41.3
06 12048	Cathedral City city	31,589	53.8	14.4	38,860	64.5	12.3	35.0	27.4	43,064	16.8	26.9	15.0
06 12524	Ceres city	26,843	62.7	9.6	33,931	64.7	18.6	32.5	24.0	43,884	19.7	27.2	14.3
06 12552	Cerritos city	34,581	23.1	49.5	40,662	59.8	7.7	40.6	22.7	86,977	3.4	8.0	43.7
06 13014	Chico city	49,411	26.8	32.8	72,067	63.7	13.4	29.4	31.6	41,216	13.3	31.1	16.1
06 13210	Chino city	51,889	44.3	22.7	63,431	60.3	11.2	36.4	17.8	69,066	8.8	18.0	31.2

Table B-4. Cities — What: Education, Employment, and Income, 2010–2012—*Continued*

STATE and Place code	STATE city	Educational attainment			Employment status				Percent of households with no workers	Median household income (dollars)	Percent of families with income below poverty	Percent of households with income less than $25,000	Percent of households with income of $100,000 or more
		Total population 25 years and over	Percent with a high school diploma or less	Percent with a bachelor's degree or more	Total population 16 years and over	Percent in the labor force	Unemployment rate	Percent who worked full-time year-round					
	ACS table number:	C15002	C15002	C15002	B23025	B23025	B23025	C20005	C08202	B19013	C17013	C19001	C19001
	Column number:	1	2	3	4	5	6	7	8	9	10	11	12
	California—Cont.												
06 13214	Chino Hills city	47,670	24.9	42.8	58,853	69.9	12.0	41.6	14.3	92,775	5.7	9.6	46.2
06 13392	Chula Vista city	154,469	38.8	27.4	190,269	66.1	14.0	39.7	22.1	63,769	9.0	18.3	28.1
06 13588	Citrus Heights city	57,227	38.5	19.0	67,655	66.4	15.9	35.0	28.6	51,434	10.2	19.5	15.3
06 13756	Claremont city	22,214	16.7	57.8	29,595	58.3	11.9	31.4	30.9	83,598	3.7	13.4	43.2
06 14218	Clovis city	59,431	32.3	29.6	73,612	63.8	13.4	37.6	26.4	63,305	10.1	19.6	26.2
06 14260	Coachella city	21,459	80.6	4.1	27,481	70.8	23.6	35.0	16.7	40,267	27.8	29.4	9.2
06 14890	Colton city	28,158	58.6	12.1	37,612	66.0	16.7	34.8	21.4	38,329	22.1	31.4	10.6
06 15044	Compton city	52,851	67.0	6.5	68,742	61.7	18.7	33.5	26.1	41,371	23.9	29.7	10.6
06 16000	Concord city	84,808	36.1	31.1	98,119	68.7	12.3	38.8	21.7	64,022	9.4	17.3	31.1
06 16224	Corcoran city	17,468	69.6	3.2	20,260	23.2	18.4	16.6	32.3	32,127	23.3	38.4	7.0
06 16350	Corona city	94,021	39.3	26.1	115,844	69.1	12.2	42.5	13.4	77,756	8.7	13.6	34.9
06 16378	Coronado city	15,736	12.9	59.5	19,487	64.9	4.2	46.1	27.9	86,198	5.1	13.6	42.9
06 16532	Costa Mesa city	75,407	31.2	35.4	89,381	74.2	10.1	43.7	18.1	64,136	11.5	17.7	30.0
06 16742	Covina city	30,408	37.3	23.7	36,872	67.8	15.4	37.2	22.6	61,008	11.2	18.1	26.2
06 17498	Cudahy city	12,362	82.2	3.1	16,449	64.9	15.8	36.7	18.8	37,919	32.7	32.3	4.1
06 17568	Culver City city	29,002	19.9	52.8	32,336	69.9	9.9	43.1	25.5	75,562	7.2	16.4	37.4
06 17610	Cupertino city	40,388	10.4	75.0	45,134	61.0	6.4	45.0	20.5	130,403	3.3	10.2	64.5
06 17750	Cypress city	32,461	26.8	39.2	38,854	63.9	6.7	39.9	17.7	75,491	4.5	9.3	37.1
06 17918	Daly City city	72,724	34.8	32.0	84,601	69.5	10.3	43.2	18.8	69,358	5.5	14.4	33.6
06 17946	Dana Point city	25,615	19.5	45.8	28,220	68.7	8.1	41.8	26.3	82,062	5.6	12.4	42.0
06 17988	Danville town	29,276	11.5	64.6	32,705	62.9	8.0	40.8	23.7	134,545	2.7	6.6	62.6
06 18100	Davis city	33,414	12.0	70.9	55,973	61.6	9.5	28.4	23.8	56,214	7.5	26.7	32.7
06 18394	Delano city	30,088	74.0	6.5	38,456	48.1	16.0	25.3	20.9	35,376	29.5	30.7	8.1
06 18996	Desert Hot Springs city	16,101	58.4	11.9	19,611	58.3	20.2	28.9	32.4	32,548	25.1	33.3	6.6
06 19192	Diamond Bar city	38,859	25.1	49.3	46,343	64.2	8.3	41.7	16.4	84,165	4.9	8.5	41.2
06 19318	Dinuba city	12,296	65.4	6.5	15,644	66.9	17.5	32.4	17.9	38,646	23.2	32.1	6.2
06 19766	Downey city	71,383	49.8	20.4	86,153	66.1	11.8	41.1	19.6	56,983	9.3	18.7	22.3
06 19990	Duarte city	14,982	45.0	28.2	17,387	60.5	11.6	39.0	24.2	59,196	12.0	24.0	25.1
06 20018	Dublin city	32,923	22.5	50.2	37,570	65.8	6.0	46.4	14.2	113,141	2.8	7.8	57.3
06 20802	East Los Angeles CDP	72,972	76.5	5.8	94,086	61.5	13.8	34.5	19.6	37,001	25.6	33.1	7.5
06 20956	East Palo Alto city	15,681	61.7	13.8	20,664	68.9	12.9	34.4	14.6	47,974	16.7	23.5	19.9
06 21230	Eastvale CDP	31,362	31.3	36.6	38,004	70.4	10.4	46.3	11.2	110,608	2.8	5.6	56.4
06 21712	El Cajon city	62,057	50.6	17.7	78,149	61.6	16.2	32.5	29.2	43,690	21.9	30.9	16.3
06 21782	El Centro city	25,533	52.6	16.1	31,476	60.5	18.2	32.0	29.8	41,085	22.8	35.5	15.7
06 21796	El Cerrito city	18,742	20.5	55.9	20,648	66.5	10.5	37.6	28.0	79,369	3.6	14.7	39.0
06 21880	El Dorado Hills CDP	28,170	15.2	51.4	33,049	64.6	8.8	41.4	22.6	117,896	3.0	5.4	57.9
06 22020	Elk Grove city	96,247	27.9	34.4	115,474	67.8	10.8	42.6	17.7	78,146	7.4	11.1	35.8
06 22230	El Monte city	72,363	70.2	11.6	88,242	61.4	15.7	36.0	18.4	39,260	22.3	28.6	11.9
06 22300	El Paso de Robles (Paso Robles)	20,562	38.8	20.1	23,539	65.6	9.8	38.8	24.5	54,995	10.5	16.7	23.0
06 22678	Encinitas city	44,036	20.2	53.4	49,276	66.1	8.3	38.6	23.6	88,765	6.7	15.2	44.4
06 22804	Escondido city	90,806	48.5	20.2	111,091	60.8	9.4	35.3	24.9	45,693	16.1	25.2	17.7
06 23042	Eureka city	18,797	39.3	23.8	22,874	61.2	10.8	32.5	32.8	34,825	12.0	36.3	10.3
06 23182	Fairfield city	66,424	38.8	23.3	82,293	66.9	10.3	40.8	21.5	63,389	10.2	18.0	27.8
06 23294	Fair Oaks CDP	22,945	24.7	40.4	26,310	62.0	12.7	32.9	30.1	68,721	8.6	15.9	33.4
06 23462	Fallbrook CDP	20,879	46.6	21.2	25,683	56.6	10.7	33.2	32.7	50,804	14.6	19.7	17.9
06 24477	Florence-Graham CDP	33,605	82.0	3.4	45,068	60.7	12.0	37.8	18.2	36,529	31.3	32.7	7.3
06 24498	Florin CDP	30,181	57.3	10.0	37,029	58.3	21.2	29.5	34.2	40,372	22.3	32.3	10.5
06 24638	Folsom city	48,863	24.9	44.7	56,823	64.1	10.2	39.4	19.3	93,964	2.0	9.6	47.5
06 24680	Fontana city	114,401	55.0	14.9	144,342	66.4	17.7	36.9	15.4	62,651	13.5	16.4	23.5
06 24722	Foothill Farms CDP	21,454	46.8	12.7	25,489	67.3	15.3	36.4	27.5	45,816	22.0	24.6	11.0
06 25338	Foster City city	22,919	14.8	60.9	25,006	68.3	6.1	47.5	18.6	110,374	2.7	8.0	56.4
06 25380	Fountain Valley city	40,333	28.9	37.2	46,796	62.5	9.0	38.6	25.2	80,275	4.1	13.2	37.9
06 26000	Fremont city	149,422	30.1	49.8	170,382	65.7	9.0	44.0	27.8	95,101	4.3	10.5	48.0
06 26067	French Valley CDP	15,163	33.0	24.2	17,974	65.9	9.2	43.7	14.0	82,693	1.8	5.9	34.2
06 27000	Fresno city	289,612	49.1	19.5	368,855	62.4	17.1	32.5	29.7	40,761	25.1	32.5	14.7
06 28000	Fullerton city	88,701	32.0	36.9	108,954	66.7	11.4	36.8	21.3	65,578	11.4	18.2	31.2
06 28112	Galt city	14,731	46.0	14.9	17,528	65.7	18.9	36.7	27.1	54,633	15.8	18.8	16.8
06 28168	Gardena city	41,509	46.5	25.4	47,536	64.1	10.7	41.3	25.6	50,111	9.3	24.2	19.7
06 29000	Garden Grove city	111,330	49.5	19.2	136,391	63.8	12.1	37.8	19.8	58,832	13.0	20.2	24.7
06 29504	Gilroy city	30,292	45.2	25.2	36,435	69.0	13.4	39.0	19.1	76,060	11.1	17.5	35.0
06 30000	Glendale city	139,304	35.7	37.5	160,791	61.7	12.0	35.1	26.4	51,275	10.3	25.6	24.3
06 30014	Glendora city	32,853	30.8	29.7	39,993	62.9	10.9	36.7	23.8	70,741	6.2	13.8	32.3
06 30378	Goleta city	19,895	29.3	42.1	25,065	68.5	5.8	42.1	25.8	71,367	2.3	14.6	33.2
06 30693	Granite Bay CDP	14,844	17.0	54.5	17,375	60.2	10.5	35.8	23.9	127,179	2.3	7.3	58.7
06 31596	Hacienda Heights CDP	39,843	37.1	35.0	46,225	59.8	8.8	40.2	21.7	73,546	6.3	14.1	34.0
06 31960	Hanford city	32,200	48.2	17.3	39,944	63.4	12.7	40.5	25.1	53,395	17.2	22.1	21.3
06 32548	Hawthorne city	51,626	49.8	17.9	63,699	66.3	9.6	42.1	18.9	42,518	18.1	28.5	12.8
06 33000	Hayward city	95,522	47.5	23.4	115,619	68.4	15.4	37.8	23.0	60,754	12.1	19.9	26.5
06 33182	Hemet city	52,787	52.8	12.0	61,545	46.7	21.4	23.0	52.0	31,393	19.6	40.7	8.4
06 33308	Hercules city	16,289	22.8	40.0	19,137	68.6	8.5	47.5	15.3	92,869	3.0	12.5	45.4
06 33434	Hesperia city	53,791	56.7	10.0	67,443	55.0	20.2	28.7	29.6	41,776	19.8	29.1	13.1
06 33588	Highland city	30,533	51.6	19.1	38,235	62.3	14.9	37.2	22.7	53,524	16.8	20.0	22.3
06 34120	Hollister city	21,272	52.6	15.9	26,216	69.5	15.4	36.3	19.9	62,170	9.1	19.4	22.8
06 36000	Huntington Beach city	137,319	24.5	39.7	159,330	68.4	10.2	40.8	23.7	77,945	6.2	12.8	39.0
06 36056	Huntington Park city	33,321	80.5	5.1	42,335	69.6	16.2	36.6	15.2	35,253	27.6	35.6	6.0
06 36294	Imperial Beach city	15,814	45.7	16.6	19,881	65.1	15.8	37.3	24.8	47,851	14.6	24.9	12.0

Table B-4. Cities — What: Education, Employment, and Income, 2010–2012—*Continued*

STATE and Place code	STATE city	Educational attainment			Employment status				Percent of households with no workers	Median household income (dollars)	Percent of families with income below poverty	Percent of households with income less than $25,000	Percent of households with income of $100,000 or more
		Total population 25 years and over	Percent with a high school diploma or less	Percent with a bachelor's degree or more	Total population 16 years and over	Percent in the labor force	Unemployment rate	Percent who worked full-time year-round					
	ACS table number:	C15002	C15002	C15002	B23025	B23025	B23025	C20005	C08202	B19013	C17013	C19001	C19001
	Column number:	1	2	3	4	5	6	7	8	9	10	11	12
	California—Cont.												
06 36448	Indio city	47,062	52.3	16.1	56,461	61.6	17.7	31.9	31.8	43,434	19.3	29.4	19.8
06 36546	Inglewood city	69,986	48.5	17.8	84,570	65.5	14.2	38.0	26.5	41,210	19.5	29.2	13.4
06 36770	Irvine city	140,615	12.0	65.7	178,036	65.5	7.4	42.3	17.7	91,760	6.2	14.9	46.1
06 36868	Isla Vista CDP	3,016	28.9	51.6	23,802	49.4	16.9	6.6	30.2	16,690	25.5	62.0	5.4
06 37692	Jurupa Valley city	56,164	63.3	9.4	72,102	66.0	20.8	33.9	23.0	52,296	15.9	21.4	18.0
06 39003	La Cañada Flintridge city	13,266	8.9	70.8	16,275	57.2	7.7	38.5	20.2	146,528	1.3	4.6	69.0
06 39045	La Crescenta-Montrose CDP	13,963	18.4	55.0	16,249	63.4	7.1	43.1	24.1	83,760	5.0	14.8	42.9
06 39114	Ladera Ranch CDP	...	...	...	15,913	76.6	4.9	55.1	11.1	128,153	3.7	6.5	67.9
06 39122	Lafayette city	17,038	7.7	74.7	19,453	60.9	5.6	39.0	25.0	126,266	1.1	8.3	59.0
06 39178	Laguna Beach city	18,341	9.4	63.5	19,606	66.1	7.6	40.8	27.1	89,073	3.4	13.9	45.7
06 39220	Laguna Hills city	22,225	28.6	42.3	25,489	67.8	10.1	41.7	20.1	78,564	3.3	11.5	40.9
06 39248	Laguna Niguel city	44,468	15.3	55.4	51,511	69.4	8.2	45.2	17.6	100,888	3.0	9.2	50.4
06 39290	La Habra city	38,750	47.3	21.5	46,657	65.8	10.7	41.2	20.1	57,758	12.6	18.7	24.3
06 39486	Lake Elsinore city	29,884	51.6	13.9	38,769	67.9	14.3	39.3	15.7	60,693	11.7	17.1	25.8
06 39496	Lake Forest city	52,978	22.9	44.7	61,960	72.3	7.0	47.4	16.1	90,519	4.7	9.7	46.3
06 39766	Lakeside CDP	13,484	41.8	19.3	16,262	62.4	10.8	36.1	27.0	60,476	8.2	16.9	29.1
06 39892	Lakewood city	53,877	36.2	27.0	63,628	67.7	10.2	45.8	20.1	74,933	6.0	11.3	33.9
06 40004	La Mesa city	39,406	27.0	35.5	47,193	67.3	10.3	41.1	27.1	53,339	9.2	19.8	23.1
06 40032	La Mirada city	31,551	38.2	27.2	39,747	59.5	8.8	37.2	25.5	77,206	4.2	13.8	36.6
06 40130	Lancaster city	93,776	48.6	15.1	117,191	55.8	13.4	37.3	27.6	48,990	18.6	27.7	18.7
06 40326	La Presa CDP	20,584	43.2	18.0	26,301	65.8	13.8	39.3	23.0	58,595	11.0	16.9	18.9
06 40340	La Puente city	24,451	72.1	9.2	30,646	61.6	11.1	39.6	16.5	52,212	10.3	18.7	15.4
06 40354	La Quinta city	27,203	27.4	34.6	30,920	55.0	11.4	29.6	37.8	67,033	5.4	15.1	30.0
06 40830	La Verne city	21,411	29.3	33.9	25,640	59.9	10.0	35.0	31.1	71,649	6.3	18.0	35.3
06 40886	Lawndale city	19,365	57.8	15.4	24,244	67.7	12.6	40.1	18.5	42,056	15.2	26.7	10.0
06 41124	Lemon Grove city	15,807	50.5	15.3	19,769	62.5	15.3	36.9	29.7	50,744	16.2	24.6	14.6
06 41152	Lemoore city	14,376	40.6	19.3	17,865	71.0	12.4	46.6	19.9	56,921	9.5	19.8	24.3
06 41180	Lennox CDP	12,301	79.2	4.5	15,703	62.2	8.5	30.4	10.8	35,526	34.7	38.2	6.2
06 41474	Lincoln city	31,253	24.0	33.0	34,125	53.3	10.5	32.7	42.3	68,974	7.8	15.3	29.0
06 41992	Livermore city	55,430	25.9	39.1	64,727	71.2	7.4	45.5	19.2	100,385	3.9	11.0	50.3
06 42202	Lodi city	38,703	48.4	18.4	47,211	62.1	16.0	33.4	28.7	47,399	14.4	25.4	19.3
06 42370	Loma Linda city	16,532	23.9	49.2	19,124	60.4	9.3	39.7	27.7	59,358	9.6	25.3	28.2
06 42468	Lomita city	13,880	43.4	23.9	16,317	67.7	8.6	40.3	24.7	56,683	10.6	25.3	24.8
06 42524	Lompoc city	25,937	53.8	15.1	31,856	56.9	13.8	38.0	28.1	47,938	17.4	23.2	15.9
06 43000	Long Beach city	295,380	40.0	28.7	364,218	66.7	13.2	37.6	23.4	51,623	17.1	24.9	22.4
06 43280	Los Altos city	21,149	7.8	77.0	22,910	58.1	6.8	38.8	29.8	140,162	1.2	7.8	62.9
06 44000	Los Angeles city	2,524,960	45.0	31.0	3,062,428	66.2	12.6	38.2	24.1	47,742	18.3	27.9	21.9
06 44028	Los Banos city	19,950	63.5	9.6	25,643	62.0	20.1	28.0	28.6	45,000	24.1	29.4	14.7
06 44112	Los Gatos town	21,495	7.9	70.4	23,819	62.3	6.5	42.9	23.3	125,227	2.9	8.7	55.7
06 44574	Lynwood city	38,020	75.1	5.6	50,254	58.7	14.9	34.7	18.2	41,795	22.4	29.3	11.4
06 45022	Madera city	33,035	65.2	8.6	42,498	59.3	8.3	29.5	41.0	41,469	24.3	29.7	11.3
06 45400	Manhattan Beach city	25,554	9.3	73.2	27,658	67.0	4.9	47.6	22.5	134,035	3.6	7.7	63.0
06 45484	Manteca city	42,281	50.6	15.0	50,438	68.6	17.6	38.3	23.1	57,715	8.9	17.2	20.5
06 45778	Marina city	12,968	40.6	23.1	16,176	65.3	9.6	33.5	26.0	53,233	12.3	22.4	21.7
06 46114	Martinez city	26,241	25.4	37.4	30,185	68.1	8.8	40.4	20.7	80,724	4.5	12.3	39.5
06 46492	Maywood city	14,738	80.6	4.6	19,516	64.4	11.6	38.9	14.5	36,278	28.8	34.3	7.2
06 46646	Mead Valley CDP	11,052	71.3	6.0	14,897	58.6	24.2	26.5	26.0	43,179	22.9	33.5	17.1
06 46842	Menifee city	52,734	41.5	16.8	61,289	58.6	18.1	33.5	36.3	54,417	7.2	19.0	17.6
06 46870	Menlo Park city	23,183	17.6	67.8	25,552	68.7	7.1	46.2	22.5	109,209	3.4	8.6	54.7
06 46898	Merced city	44,921	49.5	15.4	57,561	60.5	15.9	33.0	29.9	38,688	23.3	33.5	14.1
06 47486	Millbrae city	15,870	26.6	39.9	17,937	61.0	7.2	39.8	30.4	84,615	3.5	11.1	40.0
06 47766	Milpitas city	47,657	34.0	40.4	54,256	64.8	9.0	43.9	18.9	96,194	5.4	10.9	48.5
06 48256	Mission Viejo city	65,891	21.1	44.8	76,717	66.1	8.7	42.8	22.4	94,121	3.8	10.8	46.8
06 48354	Modesto city	126,719	47.9	17.9	154,888	61.4	17.0	32.2	30.3	45,405	18.0	27.0	17.8
06 48648	Monrovia city	25,679	32.9	35.1	29,542	71.2	8.9	44.9	18.3	72,489	8.3	19.6	35.8
06 48788	Montclair city	22,697	61.7	11.7	28,385	63.2	13.1	38.6	18.0	47,360	14.5	23.7	12.0
06 48816	Montebello city	41,014	58.6	15.8	49,212	56.2	8.7	39.0	28.1	46,717	11.4	25.4	17.3
06 48872	Monterey city	19,606	21.6	47.6	24,326	67.6	5.8	41.1	28.3	61,374	2.9	20.9	22.4
06 48914	Monterey Park city	43,491	48.9	26.2	50,625	58.9	11.8	36.2	26.5	54,848	10.6	23.5	22.7
06 49138	Moorpark city	22,186	26.2	37.6	26,756	73.9	6.4	46.5	11.6	100,104	3.8	9.1	50.1
06 49270	Moreno Valley city	109,689	52.4	15.5	142,643	63.0	16.0	34.4	20.7	52,947	17.5	21.2	18.5
06 49278	Morgan Hill city	24,909	29.1	39.0	29,739	68.3	12.7	38.7	18.8	91,777	9.8	15.1	46.0
06 49670	Mountain View city	54,007	20.4	61.7	60,731	73.7	8.2	48.4	18.2	90,647	6.9	14.0	46.8
06 50076	Murrieta city	64,082	31.6	28.0	78,064	67.1	11.4	41.4	21.7	72,308	6.3	12.6	31.6
06 50258	Napa city	51,866	41.3	27.7	60,559	67.4	10.4	38.2	25.3	60,357	9.6	19.2	26.5
06 50398	National City city	36,400	58.6	10.5	46,792	61.4	10.9	37.8	27.7	36,304	21.3	34.7	9.1
06 50916	Newark city	29,869	46.0	25.0	34,254	69.2	7.1	45.8	30.7	83,573	5.8	11.7	40.2
06 51182	Newport Beach city	63,901	11.7	65.0	73,071	64.8	7.9	39.0	25.5	105,505	5.9	12.5	53.0
06 51560	Norco city	18,800	47.0	17.4	22,069	53.5	10.8	31.2	20.0	79,807	7.7	11.3	36.9
06 51924	North Highlands CDP	27,066	46.9	11.8	34,068	55.1	14.0	28.4	32.6	41,056	20.6	29.3	8.9
06 52379	North Tustin CDP	18,480	14.9	57.4	21,415	59.0	6.3	36.4	24.1	121,869	2.4	6.9	61.6
06 52526	Norwalk city	65,454	53.2	15.2	80,743	64.4	12.4	41.2	18.9	58,868	12.0	17.8	21.6
06 52582	Novato city	38,322	27.1	44.4	42,531	66.7	9.1	36.7	24.9	72,017	5.1	16.4	36.7
06 52694	Oakdale city	12,843	49.1	12.8	15,624	61.6	15.5	32.2	29.2	52,038	16.8	25.2	19.0
06 53000	Oakland city	274,989	36.9	38.4	320,131	65.7	12.7	37.0	28.5	50,326	18.3	28.6	24.2
06 53070	Oakley city	22,242	46.1	13.1	27,254	67.3	11.6	38.5	20.2	70,352	6.9	17.6	33.4
06 53322	Oceanside city	109,369	38.7	24.1	134,083	64.4	9.9	39.0	26.3	59,699	9.6	18.0	24.5
06 53448	Oildale CDP	19,499	56.1	8.6	23,224	56.4	17.4	30.4	35.1	30,435	30.3	40.9	6.8
06 53896	Ontario city	98,728	58.4	12.2	125,588	67.9	15.3	36.9	17.9	54,313	14.9	18.3	17.0
06 53980	Orange city	90,117	34.8	35.1	110,762	66.5	9.9	39.6	18.4	74,976	9.1	14.8	35.0
06 54092	Orangevale CDP	23,098	32.2	25.3	26,941	63.7	16.2	35.0	32.9	56,974	6.0	17.2	23.9

Table B-4. Cities — What: Education, Employment, and Income, 2010–2012—*Continued*

STATE and Place code	STATE city	Educational attainment			Employment status				Percent of households with no workers	Median household income (dollars)	Percent of families with income below poverty	Percent of households with income less than $25,000	Percent of households with income of $100,000 or more
		Total population 25 years and over	Percent with a high school diploma or less	Percent with a bachelor's degree or more	Total population 16 years and over	Percent in the labor force	Unemployment rate	Percent who worked full-time year-round					
	ACS table number:	C15002	C15002	C15002	B23025	B23025	B23025	C20005	C08202	B19013	C17013	C19001	C19001
	Column number:	1	2	3	4	5	6	7	8	9	10	11	12
	California—Cont.												
06 54120	Orcutt CDP	20,938	32.0	24.8	23,707	57.9	8.7	36.0	32.3	68,717	5.1	13.6	32.6
06 54652	Oxnard city	118,203	56.7	15.8	148,749	68.5	10.9	38.3	19.2	60,667	13.4	18.3	24.0
06 54806	Pacifica city	27,480	22.5	41.3	31,168	69.2	7.7	47.2	20.0	95,872	3.6	9.0	47.7
06 55156	Palmdale city	84,147	50.9	15.3	109,664	59.6	16.0	33.6	21.7	52,284	18.4	23.3	20.9
06 55184	Palm Desert city	37,906	30.1	33.7	42,450	53.0	12.7	28.2	45.2	52,503	6.4	20.6	24.2
06 55254	Palm Springs city	36,880	32.7	34.9	40,217	55.5	13.1	30.2	43.0	44,544	13.5	29.0	19.9
06 55282	Palo Alto city	46,765	7.8	79.6	52,641	62.6	5.9	42.3	26.5	118,396	2.7	11.0	57.1
06 55520	Paradise town	19,974	34.8	20.0	22,609	50.2	16.1	26.2	49.2	37,107	10.0	32.3	14.4
06 55618	Paramount city	30,605	70.4	7.8	39,367	64.5	15.1	40.1	17.6	44,672	21.4	24.5	11.8
06 56000	Pasadena city	99,095	27.8	49.1	115,465	67.7	10.1	41.4	24.6	69,472	7.4	19.3	35.0
06 56112	Patterson city	11,815	58.6	11.2	14,328	61.6	13.6	32.9	22.2	51,778	13.1	18.4	20.8
06 56700	Perris city	35,886	65.5	7.5	46,660	63.4	21.7	28.8	19.7	43,767	26.5	28.0	7.9
06 56784	Petaluma city	40,381	30.4	36.9	45,793	69.9	8.2	39.9	22.0	76,032	6.4	16.0	34.4
06 56924	Pico Rivera city	39,262	63.0	11.5	48,844	61.4	12.6	37.4	21.5	53,703	12.5	18.5	19.6
06 57456	Pittsburg city	40,577	47.0	17.8	50,159	65.6	14.2	33.4	21.3	56,844	15.9	21.1	23.6
06 57526	Placentia city	32,939	34.1	33.7	39,727	67.2	11.9	39.3	19.8	74,669	9.1	15.2	35.3
06 57764	Pleasant Hill city	23,759	20.9	49.1	27,986	62.5	7.7	37.8	26.1	71,727	5.4	14.7	38.9
06 57792	Pleasanton city	47,564	19.1	55.1	55,260	67.0	8.8	43.9	21.1	115,724	3.8	10.1	58.4
06 58072	Pomona city	86,161	59.0	16.1	112,523	60.7	13.4	33.5	20.9	47,874	18.3	24.3	14.7
06 58240	Porterville city	30,414	56.5	10.5	37,745	61.4	15.5	34.6	28.2	42,796	21.5	30.5	13.4
06 58296	Port Hueneme city	13,053	48.7	17.2	16,786	65.6	13.8	37.5	27.9	49,028	18.7	25.1	14.7
06 58520	Poway city	32,836	25.1	44.0	39,064	65.3	7.0	41.2	21.2	90,768	3.3	10.5	45.3
06 59346	Ramona CDP	13,938	50.6	19.6	16,635	64.9	11.6	38.7	26.3	63,330	9.0	17.8	26.0
06 59444	Rancho Cordova city	43,184	37.7	24.9	50,982	67.6	16.2	39.2	24.9	51,084	12.9	20.5	20.0
06 59451	Rancho Cucamonga city	109,384	30.7	30.2	132,034	69.7	11.1	42.1	18.3	75,672	5.7	12.7	36.4
06 59514	Rancho Palos Verdes city	30,795	12.3	65.5	33,849	55.4	5.2	37.3	30.6	118,204	3.1	7.6	57.9
06 59550	Rancho San Diego CDP	15,822	25.3	36.4	18,870	63.7	11.3	40.3	26.4	80,244	5.3	9.5	37.0
06 59587	Rancho Santa Margarita city	30,504	19.9	47.6	36,523	74.7	6.1	51.3	12.9	101,081	2.9	8.5	51.0
06 59920	Redding city	60,261	36.4	21.9	71,902	57.8	13.0	28.3	38.0	41,717	14.7	29.8	14.8
06 59962	Redlands city	44,813	29.7	38.7	54,906	61.3	8.5	38.1	25.3	66,930	8.4	17.3	31.1
06 60018	Redondo Beach city	50,243	15.5	58.5	54,324	74.7	6.8	49.4	19.2	99,077	3.4	13.8	49.7
06 60102	Redwood City city	52,355	34.8	40.1	59,586	71.2	8.1	44.6	20.6	76,858	5.4	13.3	40.1
06 60242	Reedley city	13,664	58.5	14.6	17,291	66.2	13.1	31.7	20.5	47,445	21.1	23.6	15.0
06 60466	Rialto city	54,680	62.0	8.4	71,237	64.2	17.8	33.9	20.3	48,242	18.4	23.3	14.2
06 60620	Richmond city	68,322	44.2	25.2	81,067	65.8	12.8	37.3	26.4	51,885	16.1	24.1	20.7
06 60704	Ridgecrest city	17,879	31.3	29.4	21,441	63.6	9.2	41.2	26.6	59,707	6.5	18.1	22.9
06 61068	Riverbank city	13,123	53.5	15.0	16,575	69.8	18.7	36.3	21.6	53,651	12.1	19.0	19.1
06 62000	Riverside city	181,495	45.8	21.9	238,684	61.9	14.9	34.3	24.9	53,893	14.0	22.7	21.9
06 62364	Rocklin city	37,811	21.4	40.2	44,249	68.7	11.8	40.7	24.1	72,571	6.9	16.0	33.3
06 62546	Rohnert Park city	26,720	35.0	23.4	34,088	70.2	11.9	36.8	25.8	57,340	6.9	21.3	24.1
06 62896	Rosemead city	37,589	62.9	15.1	44,083	60.1	14.2	35.8	20.0	43,469	16.9	27.7	15.2
06 62910	Rosemont CDP	14,651	33.2	24.8	17,605	67.5	13.9	37.3	24.6	53,497	15.8	22.8	16.7
06 62938	Roseville city	80,285	25.2	35.4	94,114	66.1	9.4	41.0	25.6	72,970	5.3	14.9	35.6
06 63218	Rowland Heights CDP	35,905	36.2	37.1	42,779	58.8	6.6	38.7	20.8	61,185	7.8	16.4	28.7
06 64000	Sacramento city	303,802	38.2	28.7	368,984	64.1	15.3	35.8	29.8	48,692	18.0	27.4	18.8
06 64224	Salinas city	87,662	61.3	13.1	109,342	65.1	11.1	35.3	21.3	48,771	18.4	23.6	17.1
06 65000	San Bernardino city	118,249	59.6	11.5	152,878	56.3	19.2	30.1	31.5	37,472	27.6	35.0	10.6
06 65028	San Bruno city	30,256	29.8	36.3	34,249	71.2	7.8	44.8	20.2	80,323	6.5	11.8	37.1
06 65042	San Buenaventura (Ventura) city	74,261	29.8	33.0	86,641	67.0	10.5	39.7	26.9	62,458	7.6	19.5	28.7
06 65070	San Carlos city	20,635	15.4	58.8	22,419	72.2	7.8	44.9	18.9	114,327	2.8	7.7	54.8
06 65084	San Clemente city	43,046	17.8	46.8	49,723	66.4	8.1	41.9	23.4	86,604	5.5	11.1	44.1
06 66000	San Diego city	867,856	29.6	41.3	1,070,694	67.5	9.5	42.1	22.2	63,034	11.3	20.2	29.5
06 66070	San Dimas city	23,378	29.5	35.3	28,036	60.6	9.6	39.3	25.6	76,071	4.0	15.2	35.0
06 66140	San Fernando city	14,146	65.9	13.9	17,294	66.7	9.0	41.0	16.4	54,434	12.7	18.1	18.5
06 67000	San Francisco city	632,398	27.5	52.2	717,664	68.4	8.0	43.3	25.2	72,888	8.5	21.7	38.3
06 67042	San Gabriel city	29,136	48.7	30.3	33,611	62.8	7.2	39.6	18.7	54,295	8.1	19.2	25.5
06 67056	Sanger city	14,339	55.8	11.4	17,445	65.3	17.6	32.1	23.7	40,511	18.9	29.2	15.3
06 67112	San Jacinto city	25,765	55.4	9.6	32,058	59.0	22.8	29.1	32.1	47,000	15.9	26.8	11.8
06 68000	San Jose city	642,294	36.2	37.3	758,038	67.7	11.0	41.2	18.5	80,155	8.8	15.6	40.0
06 68028	San Juan Capistrano city	23,647	35.3	34.2	26,776	64.1	12.1	34.9	27.2	71,560	10.7	17.1	35.8
06 68084	San Leandro city	60,716	44.7	26.6	69,847	67.7	10.9	41.0	22.7	62,627	7.4	17.2	26.5
06 68112	San Lorenzo CDP	16,722	49.2	20.4	19,895	66.6	15.7	37.1	25.7	70,393	6.6	15.2	28.1
06 68154	San Luis Obispo city	23,262	19.6	50.0	40,746	63.1	10.6	30.0	27.9	45,756	8.3	31.7	20.5
06 68196	San Marcos city	54,378	36.3	27.8	65,383	56.3	8.9	34.3	30.4	49,602	14.8	23.2	20.9
06 68252	San Mateo city	70,539	29.5	42.6	80,711	71.0	8.9	45.3	23.3	82,551	3.6	11.0	40.6
06 68294	San Pablo city	18,212	63.0	11.3	22,519	63.6	19.2	28.3	29.3	39,393	20.2	31.3	10.6
06 68364	San Rafael city	41,904	28.6	44.4	47,630	68.2	8.1	39.9	26.2	71,995	8.6	16.4	34.8
06 68378	San Ramon city	46,993	12.8	62.9	53,312	73.3	6.7	49.7	11.1	125,060	2.6	5.0	63.4
06 69000	Santa Ana city	187,494	69.2	11.1	240,190	67.8	11.1	40.1	13.1	52,961	19.1	20.2	18.6
06 69070	Santa Barbara city	60,460	30.0	41.7	73,524	68.4	7.7	39.5	25.6	64,098	9.4	19.4	32.1
06 69084	Santa Clara city	78,339	23.0	52.1	92,438	67.8	9.4	43.5	20.6	90,902	5.9	14.7	45.6
06 69088	Santa Clarita city	114,023	31.3	30.9	137,789	69.5	10.6	40.8	19.6	80,723	6.2	13.0	37.4
06 69112	Santa Cruz city	33,971	21.3	49.8	53,392	62.3	7.0	28.6	25.2	62,631	6.5	22.5	28.8
06 69196	Santa Maria city	58,166	60.1	13.5	72,858	66.7	12.9	37.2	24.4	50,084	17.8	24.0	17.4

Table B-4. Cities — What: Education, Employment, and Income, 2010–2012—*Continued*

STATE and Place code	STATE city	Educational attainment			Employment status				Percent of households with no workers	Median household income (dollars)	Percent of families with income below poverty	Percent of households with income less than $25,000	Percent of households with income of $100,000 or more
		Total population 25 years and over	Percent with a high school diploma or less	Percent with a bachelor's degree or more	Total population 16 years and over	Percent in the labor force	Unemployment rate	Percent who worked full-time year-round					
	ACS table number:	C15002	C15002	C15002	B23025	B23025	B23025	C20005	C08202	B19013	C17013	C19001	C19001
	Column number:	1	2	3	4	5	6	7	8	9	10	11	12
	California—Cont.												
06 70000	Santa Monica city	69,602	14.3	64.5	79,207	70.1	10.5	40.4	28.0	69,785	5.5	21.1	36.8
06 70042	Santa Paula city	16,704	56.5	14.5	21,641	65.1	11.9	37.3	25.5	52,913	14.2	24.3	21.1
06 70098	Santa Rosa city	113,003	35.4	29.9	133,916	66.2	11.9	34.9	28.0	58,893	9.1	19.8	24.1
06 70224	Santee city	35,456	35.3	22.3	42,510	66.2	9.9	42.6	23.9	69,210	6.4	13.3	31.2
06 70280	Saratoga city	22,073	7.2	76.7	24,151	58.4	7.3	37.4	26.5	164,428	2.2	8.1	70.1
06 70686	Seal Beach city	20,286	22.1	44.4	21,641	46.9	6.8	27.5	51.9	49,052	4.4	25.7	27.0
06 70742	Seaside city	20,564	48.4	23.4	25,405	71.1	11.7	38.1	16.7	51,659	16.4	19.4	20.5
06 70882	Selma city	13,798	62.2	10.1	17,387	63.6	16.1	29.5	25.0	40,809	28.9	31.3	12.4
06 72016	Simi Valley city	83,618	30.3	32.6	98,354	72.3	9.6	44.3	18.2	87,364	4.6	9.3	43.1
06 72520	Soledad city	18,374	72.0	2.5	21,607	34.6	11.2	19.7	16.3	48,886	21.1	19.5	15.7
06 72996	South El Monte city	12,618	76.3	8.9	15,314	60.1	6.1	42.6	12.3	52,852	14.3	18.5	16.1
06 73080	South Gate city	55,681	74.7	6.2	70,773	64.3	15.8	37.2	17.8	41,102	20.6	26.9	10.8
06 73108	South Lake Tahoe city	14,293	45.6	21.1	17,460	69.4	12.9	31.0	27.2	39,148	10.8	30.3	13.9
06 73220	South Pasadena city	18,035	12.7	60.6	19,982	70.3	7.6	45.9	18.5	78,725	4.8	12.4	39.7
06 73262	South San Francisco city	45,321	40.5	29.5	52,334	67.8	9.1	43.8	23.3	71,140	5.2	15.1	34.3
06 73290	South San Jose Hills CDP	12,299	71.9	8.1	15,989	57.6	9.0	39.9	17.9	57,700	14.7	16.7	14.8
06 73430	South Whittier CDP	35,746	53.9	15.4	43,781	63.3	9.6	41.2	21.0	64,045	11.8	18.2	25.5
06 73696	Spring Valley CDP (San Diego County)	19,393	37.8	22.4	23,552	68.0	11.0	40.8	17.4	65,257	10.1	14.7	26.6
06 73962	Stanton city	24,211	57.3	20.1	29,551	68.3	13.0	40.3	19.8	46,258	16.5	23.0	17.1
06 75000	Stockton city	172,279	49.2	17.6	217,496	61.1	18.1	31.6	30.1	45,360	20.7	28.3	16.9
06 75630	Suisun City city	17,704	38.5	19.5	21,177	69.7	11.6	39.5	20.2	70,077	9.5	15.9	29.3
06 77000	Sunnyvale city	101,146	21.1	58.5	113,769	70.7	9.3	46.7	17.3	100,194	4.9	11.0	50.2
06 78120	Temecula city	61,080	30.5	29.8	75,728	65.7	11.2	39.3	19.3	75,213	8.5	14.3	34.0
06 78138	Temescal Valley CDP	15,685	32.9	28.4	18,047	63.0	11.4	44.6	24.1	83,580	7.3	13.0	40.8
06 78148	Temple City city	25,468	35.8	37.8	29,514	60.9	7.9	39.5	22.3	60,917	8.2	20.3	27.3
06 78582	Thousand Oaks city	85,849	22.6	47.9	100,323	66.8	10.0	39.6	23.2	95,362	5.3	12.1	47.9
06 80000	Torrance city	103,115	25.5	43.2	118,371	65.5	9.1	40.7	25.7	73,694	5.1	15.9	34.6
06 80238	Tracy city	50,610	44.4	22.3	60,971	69.6	15.6	37.8	15.4	71,843	7.5	13.1	35.1
06 80644	Tulare city	34,232	59.0	11.4	42,300	61.0	12.6	37.1	26.2	44,144	18.9	28.7	14.8
06 80812	Turlock city	42,712	45.8	24.3	52,804	63.9	15.9	35.1	26.5	52,530	11.8	24.5	19.3
06 80854	Tustin city	48,136	34.2	39.4	58,490	73.1	9.6	45.2	15.2	70,253	9.9	15.9	32.8
06 80994	Twentynine Palms city	11,480	42.9	17.9	19,373	71.4	7.5	54.6	22.4	40,975	9.6	21.8	11.6
06 81204	Union City city	46,816	38.6	36.7	54,792	67.0	9.9	42.8	26.2	80,195	5.4	12.2	41.2
06 81344	Upland city	49,514	33.2	29.1	59,227	64.4	10.7	39.7	22.6	61,992	11.3	19.7	26.5
06 81554	Vacaville city	62,812	37.5	21.3	74,761	62.7	10.9	38.2	21.5	72,497	7.8	14.0	31.3
06 81638	Valinda CDP	12,363	62.1	14.2	15,041	61.9	11.9	38.4	19.4	63,368	10.1	14.4	24.1
06 81666	Vallejo city	77,990	39.4	22.6	92,840	64.6	17.6	34.3	27.7	56,499	14.4	23.7	23.1
06 82590	Victorville city	64,652	53.4	10.4	83,423	54.7	16.3	32.9	26.6	50,426	21.0	26.4	15.8
06 82852	Vineyard CDP	15,614	36.3	27.7	18,819	70.7	11.7	41.5	17.1	74,717	9.7	12.6	32.8
06 82954	Visalia city	77,158	41.0	22.3	93,819	65.4	12.7	38.7	25.1	52,272	15.9	22.8	22.2
06 82996	Vista city	60,335	49.5	17.6	73,035	58.5	8.4	35.3	26.8	43,702	13.3	22.3	14.5
06 83332	Walnut city	20,503	20.5	51.6	24,697	62.6	7.4	41.4	14.4	104,506	3.6	6.6	53.2
06 83346	Walnut Creek city	50,313	13.3	61.7	55,176	60.7	6.6	36.4	35.3	77,717	2.7	12.3	39.3
06 83542	Wasco city	15,636	78.3	3.5	19,711	43.2	15.4	24.3	24.9	38,683	27.2	30.6	8.4
06 83668	Watsonville city	29,027	67.1	10.1	37,545	65.9	10.5	30.5	20.9	44,255	20.0	27.2	13.3
06 84144	West Carson CDP	14,609	41.0	32.7	16,900	63.9	11.7	40.2	26.3	55,342	9.6	18.6	25.4
06 84200	West Covina city	68,425	40.9	26.0	83,579	65.4	15.1	38.7	20.9	66,001	8.0	14.8	27.3
06 84410	West Hollywood city	30,829	17.0	57.6	33,178	74.9	10.2	44.7	27.0	53,319	6.8	26.7	25.7
06 84550	Westminster city	60,896	50.7	21.0	72,424	61.4	12.9	35.7	23.7	52,191	14.3	22.2	24.3
06 84592	Westmont CDP	17,541	56.8	8.8	21,920	55.7	16.9	29.5	39.7	27,328	35.0	45.9	8.0
06 84774	West Puente Valley CDP	14,276	71.6	8.2	18,309	60.9	14.6	36.9	15.1	61,179	9.5	10.8	16.8
06 84780	West Rancho Dominguez CDP	12,857	57.1	10.4	15,858	58.0	15.8	32.6	30.3	42,252	16.3	28.3	9.8
06 84816	West Sacramento city	31,264	44.2	22.3	37,393	65.4	14.3	36.8	29.1	49,968	17.0	27.1	20.5
06 84921	West Whittier-Los Nietos CDP	16,827	62.0	9.8	20,596	64.2	14.6	37.5	20.2	59,767	8.6	16.3	21.4
06 85292	Whittier city	54,951	41.3	23.8	67,970	64.5	9.3	40.1	22.5	64,757	10.4	17.8	30.7
06 85446	Wildomar city	20,335	40.3	16.0	24,624	66.1	15.2	33.4	25.5	58,883	11.3	19.0	23.8
06 85614	Willowbrook CDP	10,067	68.9	6.5	13,424	58.7	19.7	32.1	27.8	35,920	30.1	38.0	8.6
06 85922	Windsor town	17,477	35.2	29.4	20,738	66.5	8.8	40.9	25.2	79,425	2.7	12.5	36.7
06 85992	Winter Gardens CDP	14,333	42.0	14.1	16,921	66.8	12.8	38.9	24.5	61,921	8.9	16.8	21.2
06 86328	Woodland city	35,652	43.9	24.0	43,796	66.5	11.7	38.4	26.1	53,788	9.1	21.3	22.3
06 86832	Yorba Linda city	44,479	17.7	46.9	52,404	68.3	8.8	43.3	18.3	112,447	2.0	8.5	57.4
06 86972	Yuba City city	40,437	44.4	19.1	49,548	62.0	15.5	34.2	30.7	49,274	15.0	26.4	18.4
06 87042	Yucaipa city	33,900	42.0	18.7	40,509	60.6	14.0	33.8	29.3	57,539	11.1	19.0	24.2
06 87056	Yucca Valley town	13,507	43.9	12.9	15,842	52.3	20.3	26.8	42.4	40,057	14.5	31.5	10.5
08 00000	**Colorado**	3,388,423	32.2	36.8	4,021,332	69.1	8.9	43.0	23.0	56,837	9.2	20.8	24.6
08 03455	Arvada city	75,415	31.6	35.3	86,421	69.6	8.7	46.0	24.9	64,643	6.2	16.2	26.8
08 04000	Aurora city	210,485	39.8	26.3	251,072	72.0	11.4	44.1	20.4	51,019	12.5	21.0	17.9
08 07850	Boulder city	56,640	11.6	71.3	87,734	67.2	7.7	33.3	22.3	56,205	6.8	26.6	29.4
08 08675	Brighton city	20,955	48.3	15.9	24,620	65.5	9.1	42.1	19.5	59,960	7.1	15.8	20.8
08 09280	Broomfield city	38,048	21.3	48.0	43,931	73.7	7.1	50.7	20.0	77,239	5.7	14.6	36.7
08 12415	Castle Rock town	31,471	23.4	44.1	35,953	77.1	7.3	50.1	13.9	79,708	4.9	11.0	37.2
08 12815	Centennial city	70,141	18.0	52.2	80,220	71.0	6.5	47.2	17.7	85,952	3.7	8.8	41.5
08 15165	Clifton CDP	12,857	54.8	11.8	15,960	68.3	13.7	37.7	22.9	39,106	12.7	29.4	8.1
08 16000	Colorado Springs city	275,503	28.3	36.1	331,710	68.4	10.0	42.6	23.8	52,896	10.5	22.7	21.8

Table B-4. Cities — What: Education, Employment, and Income, 2010–2012—*Continued*

STATE and Place code	STATE city	Educational attainment			Employment status				Percent of households with no workers	Median household income (dollars)	Percent of families with income below poverty	Percent of households with income less than $25,000	Percent of households with income of $100,000 or more
		Total population 25 years and over	Percent with a high school diploma or less	Percent with a bachelor's degree or more	Total population 16 years and over	Percent in the labor force	Unemployment rate	Percent who worked full-time year-round					
	ACS table number:	C15002	C15002	C15002	B23025	B23025	B23025	C20005	C08202	B19013	C17013	C19001	C19001
	Column number:	1	2	3	4	5	6	7	8	9	10	11	12
	Colorado—Cont.												
08 16110	Columbine CDP	16,938	23.3	46.0	19,442	69.6	7.5	44.8	23.6	79,811	3.1	11.5	38.2
08 16495	Commerce City city	28,366	51.1	17.8	32,960	70.4	9.8	46.5	18.0	60,134	14.4	18.5	20.3
08 19150	Dakota Ridge CDP	22,018	26.3	36.8	25,456	76.4	5.9	53.4	14.5	78,019	3.0	10.6	31.9
08 20000	Denver city	424,886	33.4	42.8	497,431	71.1	9.4	44.7	24.1	49,049	14.7	26.5	21.5
08 24785	Englewood city	22,194	37.5	31.7	25,385	72.3	9.2	43.7	26.0	44,820	13.8	27.5	12.2
08 27425	Fort Collins city	85,376	17.8	51.9	120,197	70.4	9.0	37.4	21.0	51,830	8.1	25.3	20.7
08 27865	Fountain city	15,714	32.9	22.3	18,426	68.6	7.1	50.6	21.9	54,602	8.7	18.5	20.2
08 31660	Grand Junction city	39,710	36.4	28.6	47,729	62.8	9.4	36.0	32.7	44,446	11.7	27.3	16.8
08 32155	Greeley city	54,959	43.8	24.3	73,403	63.3	9.7	37.9	26.7	44,622	15.7	29.5	15.5
08 36410	Highlands Ranch CDP	63,245	14.2	60.0	72,345	75.2	5.1	52.4	12.9	105,245	2.5	5.3	53.2
08 40377	Ken Caryl CDP	21,538	22.7	42.0	25,344	76.3	7.8	50.4	17.0	84,617	2.1	10.5	38.5
08 41835	Lafayette city	17,125	21.2	54.4	19,779	76.9	9.9	46.1	17.1	66,736	5.7	16.6	30.4
08 43000	Lakewood city	100,823	33.6	35.9	117,921	67.4	9.6	42.7	27.0	54,556	9.4	21.1	21.9
08 45255	Littleton city	30,104	24.4	42.2	35,057	66.0	8.4	41.5	28.0	56,011	7.5	24.0	25.3
08 45970	Longmont city	56,759	33.5	37.3	67,558	69.8	8.7	40.8	20.9	56,862	11.4	19.6	24.7
08 46465	Loveland city	46,963	31.8	32.5	54,607	68.6	9.4	42.5	24.2	54,715	7.4	22.1	17.4
08 54330	Northglenn city	23,437	51.0	15.8	28,772	70.3	11.6	43.6	26.0	49,138	10.6	24.3	14.8
08 57630	Parker town	28,714	16.2	50.7	32,563	79.8	5.9	57.2	11.9	93,596	3.4	9.0	44.1
08 62000	Pueblo city	71,066	45.1	19.2	84,403	57.7	13.6	33.2	37.1	34,083	18.1	36.4	9.1
08 62220	Pueblo West CDP	19,368	33.4	26.0	22,489	64.3	8.9	41.9	26.0	65,973	6.2	15.3	19.5
08 68847	Security-Widefield CDP	21,187	34.4	18.7	24,973	66.7	9.1	43.3	23.1	56,790	7.5	15.6	18.9
08 77290	Thornton city	74,124	41.2	25.7	89,000	74.4	8.3	49.0	14.3	63,580	7.8	14.2	25.0
08 83835	Westminster city	72,865	33.6	34.8	84,805	74.0	9.3	48.1	19.8	64,329	7.9	15.9	26.0
08 84440	Wheat Ridge city	22,244	37.3	33.5	25,229	66.3	10.9	42.1	29.2	49,805	12.4	27.2	20.2
09 00000	**Connecticut**	2,446,413	38.6	36.3	2,878,893	68.0	10.2	41.1	25.3	67,544	7.7	18.6	32.4
09 08000	Bridgeport city	90,901	58.0	15.8	112,039	68.0	17.8	35.9	29.6	37,700	21.6	35.4	13.4
09 08420	Bristol city	42,955	50.0	22.7	48,916	69.8	11.3	43.8	28.2	57,179	7.9	19.3	21.1
09 18430	Danbury city	57,188	47.4	30.4	68,044	73.6	8.9	42.5	20.7	63,276	8.1	19.1	29.2
09 18920	Darien CDP	12,677	10.8	77.9	14,267	57.7	8.4	36.8	24.1	185,583	4.8	9.1	67.0
09 22700	East Hartford CDP	35,156	52.9	18.5	41,526	69.2	14.5	39.7	30.3	47,056	14.0	27.7	17.3
09 22980	East Haven CDP	21,263	56.2	18.4	24,071	67.0	11.3	42.3	23.8	61,263	9.0	17.7	23.5
09 37000	Hartford city	73,172	60.1	15.1	96,862	61.6	19.9	30.3	35.3	28,415	31.9	45.4	7.5
09 44690	Manchester CDP	21,095	40.6	26.9	25,124	70.4	11.5	40.5	26.3	53,488	10.4	22.1	18.5
09 46450	Meriden city	41,844	53.3	18.8	48,776	66.8	13.7	40.3	27.6	50,305	12.6	23.8	18.5
09 47290	Middletown city	32,310	40.6	33.2	39,949	66.8	8.3	40.5	23.4	60,066	8.3	18.5	26.2
09 47515	Milford city (balance)	37,811	35.3	38.9	42,023	70.3	9.0	45.3	24.1	77,625	3.5	15.0	36.5
09 49880	Naugatuck borough	22,032	46.1	22.9	25,302	72.4	12.5	42.5	27.1	58,393	9.2	21.7	26.6
09 50370	New Britain city	46,255	58.2	18.1	57,686	67.8	16.8	34.6	29.7	37,339	19.4	34.2	11.0
09 52000	New Haven city	80,644	48.4	31.8	104,896	65.5	16.0	33.6	31.9	36,413	23.8	36.6	14.9
09 52210	Newington CDP	22,646	37.3	35.8	25,485	68.6	9.0	42.9	26.9	75,718	2.7	13.2	30.0
09 52280	New London city	17,011	52.8	18.2	23,345	68.0	14.1	39.3	26.5	41,588	18.7	31.3	13.3
09 54940	North Haven CDP	17,824	36.6	38.4	19,634	69.4	10.1	40.3	25.4	79,090	3.4	11.0	37.7
09 55990	Norwalk city	66,235	35.5	42.5	72,674	72.4	8.4	48.2	23.6	71,400	6.0	16.1	34.3
09 56200	Norwich city	27,944	49.5	21.0	32,394	68.8	12.3	40.7	31.1	46,109	13.2	26.7	18.5
09 68100	Shelton city	29,036	35.8	37.9	33,117	67.5	9.6	42.2	24.1	85,516	3.5	11.1	42.5
09 73000	Stamford city	85,912	35.2	44.8	98,498	72.4	11.0	43.9	20.7	73,265	8.0	17.2	36.6
09 74260	Stratford CDP	37,140	43.3	28.9	42,432	67.7	12.3	39.8	27.2	64,342	4.9	15.5	29.8
09 76500	Torrington city	26,133	52.3	20.3	29,551	66.3	10.2	38.8	30.2	51,394	7.7	23.8	18.6
09 77270	Trumbull CDP	24,219	27.7	50.0	28,033	65.2	7.2	41.8	22.7	102,224	0.8	11.4	50.7
09 80000	Waterbury city	70,573	57.6	16.3	85,667	61.8	13.7	35.8	32.6	40,094	20.0	32.6	12.7
09 82660	West Hartford CDP	44,539	23.1	58.4	50,783	67.4	7.2	42.0	26.2	80,848	5.3	16.1	41.1
09 82800	West Haven city	36,948	49.0	20.3	44,552	69.7	13.2	41.0	25.4	48,111	11.7	24.4	20.5
09 83570	Westport CDP	17,804	13.1	75.3	19,945	63.0	9.2	40.6	20.5	151,908	2.8	7.9	64.9
09 84970	Wethersfield CDP	19,538	34.4	40.9	21,718	64.3	7.3	40.8	32.0	76,945	2.8	15.6	36.9
10 00000	**Delaware**	610,658	44.3	28.6	726,185	64.0	9.0	41.1	26.9	59,144	8.0	19.4	25.0
10 04130	Bear CDP	12,763	49.1	20.4	15,683	71.6	9.1	48.9	16.8	61,940	10.2	15.1	27.8
10 21200	Dover city	21,229	44.8	26.2	29,292	58.4	12.6	34.3	31.8	43,902	14.8	27.5	13.9
10 50670	Newark city	13,989	22.1	54.7	29,084	49.2	5.4	23.1	29.0	49,005	4.1	31.9	25.3
10 77580	Wilmington city	47,254	51.7	24.9	55,498	62.6	13.3	37.6	32.0	37,167	23.2	35.5	15.7
11 00000	**District of Columbia**	428,597	31.2	51.7	524,752	67.8	11.3	46.0	25.7	64,610	14.6	22.9	33.8
11 50000	Washington city	428,597	31.2	51.7	524,752	67.8	11.3	46.0	25.7	64,610	14.6	22.9	33.8
12 00000	**Florida**	13,307,799	44.1	26.2	15,562,915	59.9	12.3	36.6	32.8	45,637	12.3	26.6	17.2
12 00410	Alafaya CDP	46,959	24.7	40.9	60,181	73.2	8.9	47.5	13.7	60,827	8.9	14.5	25.5
12 00950	Altamonte Springs city	30,464	34.3	31.8	34,818	69.7	11.1	46.5	19.8	46,416	9.9	21.4	13.3
12 01700	Apopka city	27,506	38.2	27.1	33,443	67.0	10.7	44.8	20.0	58,217	14.1	20.7	21.5
12 02681	Aventura city	27,942	28.5	46.7	30,508	52.8	11.4	34.1	39.6	53,703	11.5	26.5	27.7
12 04162	Bayonet Point CDP	18,004	58.8	10.9	20,330	45.0	15.0	24.3	52.4	28,845	13.9	40.7	3.4
12 05462	Bellview CDP	14,088	43.4	16.0	16,098	64.5	12.9	43.1	28.9	46,170	6.1	20.6	10.5
12 06875	Bloomingdale CDP	14,887	31.7	33.6	16,995	67.7	11.1	39.6	19.7	67,044	3.6	11.4	33.2
12 07300	Boca Raton city	61,067	23.2	50.7	73,287	62.1	10.6	35.1	30.1	68,828	6.6	16.4	35.5
12 07525	Bonita Springs city	35,715	43.7	28.0	39,298	47.0	10.0	28.0	50.3	48,489	12.8	21.6	24.5
12 07875	Boynton Beach city	49,654	43.2	25.1	57,584	62.5	14.4	37.4	36.7	43,606	13.0	27.8	16.0
12 07950	Bradenton city	36,393	51.5	20.2	41,649	57.2	13.0	33.4	40.8	40,492	14.4	30.1	9.7
12 08150	Brandon CDP	68,817	37.8	26.5	83,956	67.1	6.7	47.0	19.8	53,534	8.5	18.2	16.8
12 08300	Brent CDP	12,242	53.8	11.8	18,358	62.3	14.5	30.3	34.0	33,171	24.1	40.8	4.9

Table B-4. Cities — What: Education, Employment, and Income, 2010–2012—*Continued*

STATE and Place code	STATE city	Educational attainment			Employment status				Percent of households with no workers	Median household income (dollars)	Percent of families with income below poverty	Percent of households with income less than $25,000	Percent of households with income of $100,000 or more
		Total population 25 years and over	Percent with a high school diploma or less	Percent with a bachelor's degree or more	Total population 16 years and over	Percent in the labor force	Unemployment rate	Percent who worked full-time year-round					
	ACS table number:	C15002	C15002	C15002	B23025	B23025	B23025	C20005	C08202	B19013	C17013	C19001	C19001
	Column number:	1	2	3	4	5	6	7	8	9	10	11	12
	Florida—Cont.												
12 09415	Buenaventura Lakes CDP	19,198	58.4	9.3	24,260	63.1	13.4	38.0	23.3	37,841	16.3	27.1	7.7
12 10275	Cape Coral city	110,663	48.9	19.5	124,868	60.3	16.0	34.0	33.3	47,586	12.1	23.0	15.4
12 10825	Carrollwood CDP	24,722	28.9	39.2	29,272	70.1	9.9	47.0	22.2	52,114	8.6	19.8	21.7
12 11050	Casselberry city	18,137	42.4	20.9	21,310	64.3	12.9	40.5	27.6	41,165	11.1	27.0	12.4
12 12425	Citrus Park CDP	15,752	36.4	32.3	18,597	70.2	11.2	44.3	20.0	55,106	9.1	19.1	20.5
12 12875	Clearwater city	79,611	42.7	27.5	90,459	59.0	10.3	37.8	36.3	40,619	11.4	31.3	16.3
12 12925	Clermont city	19,640	35.8	29.0	22,916	60.9	9.1	35.4	33.0	57,056	7.9	18.2	20.5
12 13275	Coconut Creek city	37,974	38.4	32.2	43,798	65.9	10.4	41.1	30.3	51,453	6.4	21.7	19.5
12 14125	Cooper City city	20,086	24.7	40.9	24,175	71.5	8.5	46.1	14.6	89,569	3.1	8.0	43.2
12 14250	Coral Gables city	32,327	16.8	62.7	41,527	59.1	7.7	39.8	22.5	84,118	3.5	18.3	45.0
12 14400	Coral Springs city	78,578	31.7	34.7	95,833	73.3	12.7	43.8	15.3	64,022	8.1	16.4	29.1
12 14412	Coral Terrace CDP	17,982	53.8	21.5	20,733	60.7	12.9	39.2	23.7	46,967	11.1	27.8	16.8
12 14895	Country Club CDP	29,851	41.9	28.4	35,752	69.9	8.1	52.0	14.2	49,094	17.7	23.6	10.2
12 15475	Crestview city	13,223	40.5	18.7	15,643	64.6	11.5	41.3	26.7	48,090	20.8	30.5	11.8
12 15968	Cutler Bay town	26,943	37.9	29.9	32,299	65.8	8.7	46.4	18.5	62,564	5.2	15.8	26.3
12 16335	Dania Beach city	20,893	46.3	23.8	24,389	66.9	16.5	37.6	29.0	39,684	20.7	33.1	13.9
12 16475	Davie town	61,276	37.1	30.3	74,690	70.3	10.1	43.0	20.0	56,179	9.6	21.3	27.0
12 16525	Daytona Beach city	41,168	47.8	18.2	53,142	49.4	12.7	25.4	43.6	27,593	21.7	44.5	6.2
12 16725	Deerfield Beach city	56,032	53.3	22.1	63,929	61.7	12.2	37.9	35.4	36,754	15.4	33.6	13.0
12 16875	DeLand city	17,051	46.2	21.5	21,744	48.3	13.8	29.2	45.0	36,141	17.8	36.4	9.1
12 17100	Delray Beach city	46,511	37.4	33.6	52,850	62.5	12.8	36.0	35.3	50,273	10.1	24.5	20.3
12 17200	Deltona city	56,598	52.0	14.7	66,972	58.8	11.8	38.1	30.8	44,824	10.9	24.3	12.1
12 17935	Doral city	28,747	23.0	56.0	34,090	68.1	6.6	51.3	9.4	70,157	7.4	11.3	29.8
12 18575	Dunedin city	27,570	37.2	27.5	29,917	60.8	8.0	36.5	36.8	47,661	7.4	26.4	15.2
12 19206	East Lake CDP	24,189	27.7	41.8	27,209	59.7	10.4	37.4	29.3	68,492	6.3	15.2	32.4
12 19212	East Lake-Orient Park CDP	14,056	51.1	14.6	17,449	70.1	15.9	41.2	26.0	37,533	20.8	36.8	5.8
12 19825	Edgewater city	15,928	43.2	16.7	17,828	55.8	15.9	37.4	38.7	42,203	8.6	23.5	8.8
12 20108	Egypt Lake-Leto CDP	27,080	57.5	14.7	32,436	67.8	12.1	38.8	20.2	35,028	23.5	35.9	7.9
12 20925	Ensley CDP	14,139	47.0	16.8	17,012	65.2	13.6	41.8	29.4	39,495	14.4	29.6	8.5
12 21150	Estero CDP	18,267	28.7	42.5	20,181	40.3	8.6	22.9	55.5	66,389	3.7	13.7	32.3
12 22275	Ferry Pass CDP	19,958	33.1	31.6	24,814	59.1	8.4	36.0	32.0	40,999	7.3	30.2	14.8
12 22660	Fleming Island CDP	19,786	21.5	45.7	24,484	67.9	7.0	44.6	18.5	86,598	1.4	10.2	41.8
12 24000	Fort Lauderdale city	125,788	39.0	34.4	142,159	65.6	13.5	39.6	29.3	48,561	15.1	26.9	22.9
12 24125	Fort Myers city	44,363	51.4	22.0	52,227	53.9	18.1	29.4	37.8	35,128	20.0	34.4	12.2
12 24300	Fort Pierce city	27,501	61.4	12.6	32,862	54.5	18.1	26.0	41.5	25,382	31.5	49.4	5.1
12 24475	Fort Walton Beach city	13,422	40.2	23.0	16,301	66.4	9.5	39.4	27.3	46,193	9.5	23.2	14.2
12 24562	Fountainebleau CDP	39,186	50.6	24.4	45,421	63.5	11.4	45.1	19.5	40,518	11.5	27.7	10.6
12 24581	Four Corners CDP	20,070	43.6	20.5	23,266	66.9	13.4	35.9	25.4	44,060	15.8	25.7	10.0
12 24925	Fruit Cove CDP	18,782	15.6	49.6	22,652	67.7	6.0	45.6	19.9	89,088	3.0	9.2	42.1
12 25175	Gainesville city	62,426	29.0	42.8	111,604	57.1	9.9	29.0	29.4	31,294	15.6	41.7	12.2
12 26300	Golden Gate CDP	17,043	68.2	12.6	20,882	71.0	10.0	40.4	15.6	37,592	27.1	29.4	5.2
12 26375	Golden Glades CDP	21,471	59.0	14.8	26,055	62.8	17.1	35.4	23.0	36,941	21.5	33.1	7.4
12 27322	Greenacres city	26,213	54.6	18.3	30,666	68.4	14.5	39.9	28.5	41,140	17.4	30.1	9.2
12 28400	Haines City city	12,759	60.3	15.2	14,858	59.0	10.1	32.2	34.8	32,285	20.7	35.1	6.8
12 28452	Hallandale Beach city	30,474	43.3	25.7	33,642	56.6	18.1	32.9	41.8	33,136	12.9	38.8	12.1
12 30000	Hialeah city	164,690	67.1	13.1	192,475	59.6	14.7	36.3	29.1	29,271	21.4	43.1	6.2
12 30025	Hialeah Gardens city	15,066	60.8	16.6	17,994	63.3	17.8	41.6	22.7	43,017	16.5	28.6	9.0
12 31075	Holiday CDP	15,383	59.4	9.9	17,273	48.4	19.0	28.4	49.1	33,602	15.8	35.2	3.7
12 32000	Hollywood city	101,969	43.5	27.5	116,463	67.1	14.3	38.2	27.1	44,360	12.2	27.2	17.5
12 32275	Homestead city	36,658	59.8	14.1	43,815	68.5	14.1	42.9	23.5	38,479	29.0	34.0	15.5
12 32967	Hunters Creek CDP	13,889	30.3	39.0	16,082	75.3	9.2	51.3	16.8	54,983	8.7	17.2	16.4
12 33250	Immokalee CDP	11,082	85.8	3.2	15,924	59.8	15.0	31.0	25.3	22,674	50.2	54.1	3.8
12 35000	Jacksonville city	546,909	42.3	24.7	655,147	66.3	12.3	41.7	26.1	45,577	13.9	27.2	16.4
12 35050	Jacksonville Beach city	15,950	26.9	40.7	18,200	67.5	7.0	46.1	23.6	55,148	6.7	24.2	23.3
12 35875	Jupiter town	42,382	29.3	44.9	45,860	62.0	6.0	39.8	32.0	65,274	5.2	17.7	31.3
12 36062	Kendale Lakes CDP	43,278	46.3	23.2	50,339	67.2	12.5	44.2	19.5	49,057	12.8	23.7	17.3
12 36100	Kendall CDP	56,194	30.4	44.1	64,305	66.5	8.6	44.6	22.6	55,515	6.9	20.8	27.2
12 36121	Kendall West CDP	26,133	44.6	25.8	31,934	63.9	11.7	45.6	20.2	44,456	16.2	30.1	16.5
12 36462	Keystone CDP	15,966	23.8	44.0	18,393	68.9	4.5	47.9	16.2	107,554	1.6	4.7	56.9
12 36550	Key West city	18,871	36.1	29.9	21,604	70.9	6.0	48.8	21.5	51,891	5.7	19.4	21.0
12 36950	Kissimmee city	37,553	53.4	14.5	47,189	67.2	13.3	39.2	24.5	33,779	22.6	34.9	8.2
12 38250	Lakeland city	66,006	47.7	24.1	80,125	55.6	14.4	33.0	37.7	37,833	15.3	29.7	10.9
12 38350	Lake Magdalene CDP	21,369	36.8	34.4	24,442	62.4	9.5	38.9	29.7	48,786	8.4	23.7	23.1
12 38813	Lakeside CDP	20,951	41.2	25.9	25,234	65.7	11.5	40.0	25.2	54,817	8.4	16.3	18.4
12 39075	Lake Worth city	23,386	59.7	19.4	28,160	74.2	17.2	41.7	24.6	36,827	26.7	34.1	10.8
12 39200	Land O' Lakes CDP	22,944	34.7	32.1	26,442	65.3	9.7	41.3	22.6	64,421	2.7	11.2	25.5
12 39425	Largo city	60,150	50.0	19.5	67,166	57.5	14.1	36.1	41.9	39,930	9.5	29.6	9.1
12 39525	Lauderdale Lakes city	21,762	59.6	12.2	26,287	69.8	20.2	35.5	27.6	34,095	23.8	38.4	7.1
12 39550	Lauderhill city	44,173	48.3	20.2	53,406	68.0	16.3	37.5	27.4	35,841	17.6	33.4	11.0
12 39775	Lealman CDP	15,546	69.8	8.4	17,340	55.0	19.5	31.2	46.0	30,471	22.7	42.7	4.9
12 39875	Leesburg city	13,852	46.1	21.7	16,708	52.2	16.6	28.8	45.7	31,899	14.9	40.8	4.4
12 39925	Lehigh Acres CDP	60,484	58.3	12.8	72,706	62.5	18.7	34.5	28.6	39,085	14.8	29.4	7.8
12 39950	Leisure City CDP	13,759	71.2	8.3	17,644	55.1	16.7	29.1	30.5	32,645	36.1	43.8	5.4
12 43125	Margate city	39,446	49.3	20.8	45,332	66.4	12.5	36.3	32.7	42,072	9.4	28.0	11.7
12 43800	Meadow Woods CDP	15,716	50.3	20.2	18,818	71.0	15.6	40.9	12.9	46,298	14.2	19.9	12.8
12 43975	Melbourne city	54,980	42.6	23.9	64,534	57.5	14.4	33.0	38.2	38,714	12.2	30.8	12.4
12 44275	Merritt Island CDP	26,025	34.7	32.8	29,694	59.0	12.1	36.1	35.5	58,689	8.5	21.2	25.2
12 45000	Miami city	297,156	59.5	22.4	339,935	60.6	14.5	36.6	32.1	28,935	26.7	44.7	11.5
12 45025	Miami Beach city	69,317	34.0	43.5	76,556	68.7	5.7	47.8	27.0	40,713	11.0	32.3	22.4
12 45060	Miami Gardens city	69,389	59.3	13.7	85,382	61.9	18.8	38.2	25.6	39,230	19.7	32.2	10.2
12 45100	Miami Lakes town	20,316	36.8	31.2	23,913	65.6	9.9	45.3	18.6	60,733	11.0	20.4	19.9
12 45975	Miramar city	79,671	35.8	30.7	96,599	74.1	12.8	47.9	11.5	63,608	8.4	13.7	24.3

Table B-4. Cities — What: Education, Employment, and Income, 2010–2012—*Continued*

STATE and Place code	STATE city	Educational attainment			Employment status				Percent of households with no workers	Median household income (dollars)	Percent of families with income below poverty	Percent of households with income less than $25,000	Percent of households with income of $100,000 or more
		Total population 25 years and over	Percent with a high school diploma or less	Percent with a bachelor's degree or more	Total population 16 years and over	Percent in the labor force	Unemployment rate	Percent who worked full-time year-round					
	ACS table number:	C15002	C15002	C15002	B23025	B23025	B23025	C20005	C08202	B19013	C17013	C19001	C19001
	Column number:	1	2	3	4	5	6	7	8	9	10	11	12
	Florida—Cont.												
12 47625	Naples city	17,208	21.3	51.0	18,164	39.9	6.4	23.9	54.2	77,965	3.3	16.8	40.6
12 48050	Navarre CDP	20,167	27.6	31.6	23,961	67.4	7.7	46.4	21.7	66,364	6.0	14.0	29.4
12 48625	New Smyrna Beach city	18,242	40.5	29.4	19,512	43.7	7.9	28.1	48.6	47,603	13.4	25.8	15.9
12 49260	Northdale CDP	13,639	30.0	38.2	16,279	69.0	10.7	44.5	18.3	59,378	8.9	13.8	24.8
12 49350	North Fort Myers CDP	34,097	51.1	18.6	36,568	35.8	12.7	19.7	62.8	38,683	7.2	29.7	11.1
12 49425	North Lauderdale city	24,243	60.1	14.2	30,720	73.5	14.5	41.0	15.0	42,441	17.0	25.9	9.6
12 49450	North Miami city	38,513	54.0	18.0	47,509	63.1	14.0	37.9	21.9	36,136	24.7	36.8	11.7
12 49475	North Miami Beach city	28,709	46.6	20.3	33,991	66.7	15.2	42.3	23.0	36,818	20.0	32.7	9.9
12 49675	North Port city	39,992	49.4	14.6	46,366	60.4	13.1	37.6	35.2	49,357	7.8	21.0	11.4
12 50575	Oakland Park city	29,854	43.7	21.6	34,275	74.9	14.1	42.5	22.3	43,054	18.7	27.1	13.6
12 50638	Oak Ridge CDP	13,608	64.9	8.0	16,451	72.6	11.6	44.9	18.0	28,713	22.3	42.9	3.4
12 50750	Ocala city	37,247	43.9	23.2	44,720	57.8	16.2	35.3	37.1	35,310	20.0	36.5	11.5
12 51075	Ocoee city	22,797	39.6	29.9	28,104	72.6	12.7	44.8	17.2	63,381	8.7	14.7	23.7
12 53000	Orlando city	160,591	37.1	32.1	195,250	73.2	11.5	44.4	20.9	41,266	15.8	29.7	14.1
12 53150	Ormond Beach city	29,246	34.2	30.1	32,901	49.7	9.5	27.6	44.2	44,814	9.8	26.0	17.4
12 53575	Oviedo city	21,716	23.1	45.0	25,940	70.4	9.3	44.8	13.5	84,634	3.8	9.0	38.3
12 53725	Pace CDP	13,106	38.0	22.7	15,064	65.1	7.2	43.9	24.5	59,334	4.1	13.8	19.4
12 54000	Palm Bay city	70,459	50.0	16.5	82,776	59.6	14.8	34.2	32.2	41,865	12.1	26.6	9.9
12 54075	Palm Beach Gardens city	37,752	24.0	48.5	42,096	59.1	7.0	38.8	34.3	66,246	3.7	15.7	32.6
12 54175	Palm City CDP	16,620	28.7	41.0	18,809	55.9	11.4	30.7	42.0	72,012	4.5	16.0	35.5
12 54200	Palm Coast city	55,389	45.3	22.0	62,317	49.6	12.3	30.6	43.0	45,572	11.9	25.8	12.1
12 54275	Palmetto Bay village	15,518	20.0	55.4	18,562	65.2	9.1	43.9	15.1	106,484	4.8	12.4	53.6
12 54350	Palm Harbor CDP	45,268	34.1	33.1	50,931	57.7	9.9	38.3	37.6	53,131	6.0	21.4	21.2
12 54387	Palm River-Clair Mel CDP	14,376	61.5	14.3	16,842	59.5	16.2	36.1	27.8	33,399	25.4	38.2	7.2
12 54450	Palm Springs village	13,403	59.9	12.1	15,548	72.5	15.5	37.2	24.1	34,037	21.1	34.2	4.4
12 54525	Palm Valley CDP	14,838	17.1	53.3	16,915	65.7	8.6	41.5	23.7	84,212	5.9	11.3	44.2
12 54700	Panama City city	24,513	43.0	20.2	29,096	62.1	12.8	36.8	32.6	37,449	17.2	35.6	9.8
12 55125	Parkland city	15,457	14.1	60.4	18,420	72.5	7.1	46.1	11.0	125,497	5.3	9.4	59.9
12 55775	Pembroke Pines city	110,103	35.2	32.1	126,671	67.6	10.9	43.1	25.3	59,264	6.3	20.3	25.9
12 55925	Pensacola city	37,283	34.9	31.5	43,372	65.1	10.6	40.1	31.6	43,646	10.8	27.8	16.7
12 56825	Pine Hills CDP	39,522	57.9	12.7	47,898	70.0	17.5	37.3	23.0	36,707	22.0	32.5	8.7
12 56975	Pinellas Park city	36,064	51.6	17.2	41,770	60.1	12.0	38.0	35.5	42,126	9.3	27.5	9.9
12 57425	Plantation city	62,737	28.7	39.5	70,769	70.2	9.6	45.6	19.7	64,936	7.6	14.5	28.8
12 57550	Plant City city	22,142	54.6	18.2	26,277	64.4	8.6	41.8	28.3	44,480	16.6	26.7	13.7
12 57900	Poinciana CDP	34,524	47.4	21.8	40,661	57.5	18.9	30.6	33.1	41,088	12.9	23.6	8.4
12 58050	Pompano Beach city	74,368	52.4	22.4	84,515	58.5	14.0	35.7	36.5	37,779	19.0	32.5	13.0
12 58350	Port Charlotte CDP	42,072	47.1	17.3	47,040	52.5	13.1	28.0	45.8	39,597	12.1	29.7	9.6
12 58575	Port Orange city	41,940	42.3	25.4	47,705	53.8	10.4	32.1	38.6	44,297	6.6	24.1	15.6
12 58715	Port St. Lucie city	112,049	46.8	20.3	130,567	63.5	16.3	37.3	31.4	47,401	11.8	21.3	14.6
12 58875	Princeton CDP	13,696	56.2	16.8	17,391	65.1	15.8	43.1	18.1	45,632	19.1	23.0	15.3
12 60230	Richmond West CDP	23,670	42.9	25.2	28,442	66.3	8.7	46.4	11.0	67,593	7.4	8.9	26.1
12 60950	Riverview CDP	45,781	35.7	29.0	53,285	67.9	9.3	47.1	18.4	64,953	8.7	15.2	22.1
12 60975	Riviera Beach city	20,603	50.0	20.6	25,607	65.9	20.3	35.5	30.3	37,299	21.4	32.7	12.6
12 61500	Rockledge city	17,768	32.1	28.9	20,458	65.1	13.7	40.6	30.2	57,077	6.7	18.5	21.2
12 62100	Royal Palm Beach village	22,281	37.9	27.6	26,648	69.6	12.0	44.6	19.6	67,734	7.1	17.1	29.5
12 62625	St. Cloud city	25,007	49.4	15.9	29,418	67.7	13.9	41.3	25.7	46,727	14.6	23.9	12.3
12 63000	St. Petersburg city	177,178	40.7	28.5	204,334	64.8	11.7	40.8	29.8	43,886	11.6	27.7	15.9
12 63650	Sanford city	33,900	44.3	19.6	40,911	63.6	14.9	36.0	27.5	39,717	18.7	31.2	8.9
12 64175	Sarasota city	38,682	43.6	29.1	44,771	59.3	14.0	31.9	37.2	40,370	16.1	32.5	15.7
12 64825	Sebastian city	16,545	46.8	16.4	18,346	54.3	19.6	28.3	46.4	38,055	8.6	29.0	7.9
12 67258	South Bradenton CDP	16,176	57.2	11.0	18,803	56.8	15.8	34.8	42.7	31,369	14.3	36.9	4.6
12 67575	South Miami Heights CDP	24,849	61.0	14.5	28,982	63.1	12.3	39.2	26.7	37,644	17.4	35.5	10.5
12 68350	Spring Hill CDP	71,924	53.1	14.5	81,592	49.9	19.8	27.6	48.1	40,222	12.9	30.4	7.7
12 69250	Sun City Center CDP	18,366	36.2	31.0	18,631	16.9	26.3	7.7	84.1	40,470	1.7	25.0	10.4
12 69555	Sunny Isles Beach city	17,199	28.3	46.4	18,864	56.0	6.8	40.0	40.2	43,750	13.3	33.8	21.8
12 69700	Sunrise city	61,005	44.5	25.9	69,969	69.1	10.0	44.8	25.2	48,134	11.0	26.3	17.9
12 70345	Sweetwater city	13,769	69.7	14.3	16,842	55.9	12.8	40.3	26.9	29,945	30.3	38.8	3.0
12 70600	Tallahassee city	97,090	23.9	47.8	156,334	64.9	13.0	34.7	25.6	38,865	16.8	36.1	15.6
12 70675	Tamarac city	47,817	45.2	21.8	52,516	61.5	11.5	36.8	37.9	40,960	9.9	28.8	11.2
12 70700	Tamiami CDP	39,516	53.0	25.5	46,920	62.7	10.2	43.5	17.4	48,532	12.0	24.5	18.5
12 71000	Tampa city	224,986	41.5	32.6	275,365	65.4	12.8	41.2	27.4	41,524	17.8	31.8	18.6
12 71150	Tarpon Springs city	18,664	44.3	23.1	20,405	52.0	16.4	29.5	42.3	40,738	8.1	27.2	15.5
12 71400	Temple Terrace city	16,176	30.2	39.1	20,338	67.8	10.0	39.3	28.3	43,100	12.4	27.6	13.1
12 71564	The Acreage CDP	27,494	50.4	18.0	32,440	68.9	9.7	45.6	14.7	71,107	5.9	9.5	28.0
12 71567	The Crossings CDP	17,220	30.7	39.7	19,991	68.6	10.7	46.0	15.3	59,243	12.4	18.8	29.0
12 71569	The Hammocks CDP	34,860	37.7	31.4	44,151	66.9	11.6	45.4	12.8	52,051	12.6	22.4	19.2
12 71625	The Villages CDP	53,908	33.7	32.3	53,999	17.4	11.0	5.6	79.0	53,520	3.2	16.1	13.9
12 71900	Titusville city	31,279	45.1	19.0	36,254	57.1	14.0	34.1	38.2	41,855	13.5	26.2	11.4
12 72145	Town 'n' Country CDP	56,291	46.1	24.5	66,265	69.7	13.9	42.8	22.5	47,260	10.7	22.6	15.7
12 73163	University CDP (Hillsborough County)	22,895	53.8	19.5	32,576	63.2	23.8	27.3	38.3	20,440	46.2	58.9	1.4
12 73172	University CDP (Orange County)	9,062	35.3	37.0	24,459	46.8	13.2	18.5	25.1	32,459	15.9	41.1	13.3
12 73287	University Park CDP	19,328	54.5	27.6	23,720	54.1	9.2	34.2	27.8	41,795	15.0	27.9	13.7
12 73700	Valrico CDP	24,263	35.4	32.1	28,037	61.7	8.1	43.0	28.1	69,745	6.6	14.1	31.3
12 73900	Venice city	18,871	34.5	33.9	19,563	32.8	16.6	15.9	66.4	46,892	4.4	23.6	14.0
12 74200	Vero Beach South CDP	16,169	41.0	23.7	18,096	56.6	17.0	28.6	41.2	41,145	11.3	29.9	14.9
12 75275	Wekiwa Springs CDP	17,209	22.7	49.6	20,156	63.2	9.8	39.4	23.0	73,033	4.0	12.4	36.0
12 75812	Wellington village	38,031	25.8	43.6	44,955	67.5	9.5	43.8	20.6	77,985	6.7	12.7	36.2
12 75875	Wesley Chapel CDP	28,410	28.1	35.8	32,129	74.0	7.9	52.1	17.9	72,290	5.1	12.0	25.3
12 76062	Westchase CDP	15,035	17.4	56.8	16,471	74.1	9.2	52.4	16.0	88,714	5.4	13.2	44.8
12 76075	Westchester CDP	22,181	49.9	25.4	25,511	62.5	13.0	40.9	27.5	46,868	10.7	24.9	17.0

Table B-4. Cities — What: Education, Employment, and Income, 2010–2012—Continued

STATE and Place code	STATE city	Educational attainment			Employment status						Percent of families with income below poverty	Percent of households with income less than $25,000	Percent of households with income of $100,000 or more
		Total population 25 years and over	Percent with a high school diploma or less	Percent with a bachelor's degree or more	Total population 16 years and over	Percent in the labor force	Unemployment rate	Percent who worked full-time year-round	Percent of households with no workers	Median household income (dollars)			
	ACS table number:	C15002	C15002	C15002	B23025	B23025	B23025	C20005	C08202	B19013	C17013	C19001	C19001
	Column number:	1	2	3	4	5	6	7	8	9	10	11	12
	Florida—Cont.												
12 76487	West Little River CDP	21,462	64.9	9.3	25,385	64.2	18.5	35.2	28.0	32,011	20.2	38.0	4.5
12 76582	Weston city	40,675	15.9	58.7	48,283	69.6	8.1	43.8	12.8	86,628	5.9	10.5	44.5
12 76600	West Palm Beach city	72,157	40.1	29.6	84,101	63.3	11.9	39.4	30.7	42,843	13.9	28.5	16.9
12 76675	West Pensacola CDP	13,731	59.0	9.1	16,630	58.8	22.9	29.0	36.4	29,215	32.0	41.8	3.1
12 78250	Winter Garden city	23,206	29.2	35.5	26,607	69.4	9.1	45.6	15.4	57,621	5.9	17.1	27.8
12 78275	Winter Haven city	24,000	53.6	15.1	27,299	54.3	12.2	30.7	40.8	34,849	17.6	37.2	8.8
12 78300	Winter Park city	18,961	20.5	53.0	23,972	56.8	8.5	36.9	31.3	60,111	7.4	23.1	33.0
12 78325	Winter Springs city	22,730	34.0	35.3	27,141	68.0	13.3	39.5	21.2	66,807	5.4	13.0	29.7
12 78800	Wright CDP	16,380	43.4	18.7	20,420	74.0	12.6	43.0	22.1	40,194	23.5	28.1	10.4
13 00000	**Georgia**	6,326,651	44.3	27.7	7,600,267	63.6	11.8	40.1	26.4	47,642	14.4	26.8	18.9
13 00408	Acworth city	13,113	32.7	31.7	15,594	67.9	9.8	45.4	18.5	49,014	10.8	19.3	14.2
13 01052	Albany city	47,164	50.6	16.1	59,731	57.4	19.7	31.6	39.3	27,400	31.1	46.2	7.4
13 01696	Alpharetta city	38,137	15.2	63.7	43,411	71.4	6.1	52.0	16.9	85,471	3.9	12.4	41.5
13 03440	Athens-Clarke County (balance)	61,022	36.7	40.4	98,571	56.1	9.2	29.0	30.0	32,809	21.7	41.3	12.9
13 04000	Atlanta city	288,405	32.6	46.5	359,405	65.2	14.2	39.5	28.5	44,784	21.1	32.4	22.7
13 04204	Augusta-Richmond County (balance)	123,959	46.8	20.3	153,375	60.6	11.4	37.2	30.5	38,910	20.2	34.2	11.3
13 12834	Candler-McAfee CDP	15,904	57.6	14.9	18,087	57.8	23.3	32.6	37.5	32,516	22.9	38.4	9.5
13 12988	Canton city	14,923	48.3	25.4	16,923	70.3	9.4	41.1	17.7	46,691	13.4	29.0	15.5
13 13492	Carrollton city	12,866	47.2	31.5	19,550	58.7	15.7	28.5	29.6	34,725	27.1	43.1	17.5
13 19000	Columbus city	120,815	42.9	22.4	150,605	62.5	10.7	37.7	30.4	39,113	15.9	31.8	12.9
13 21380	Dalton city	20,650	60.6	18.2	24,644	64.1	11.9	40.7	23.6	34,272	23.6	33.4	10.4
13 23900	Douglasville city	19,249	38.7	29.4	23,069	68.3	11.5	43.0	21.3	46,189	18.2	25.6	16.1
13 24600	Duluth city	18,614	34.1	41.9	21,335	68.9	9.2	46.8	21.6	52,491	15.7	22.1	21.9
13 24768	Dunwoody city	32,293	18.2	63.0	36,398	67.6	8.7	46.2	22.6	74,230	9.6	14.7	35.6
13 25720	East Point city	22,339	46.5	25.2	27,327	66.5	21.4	36.3	30.4	37,557	22.0	35.0	10.4
13 28044	Evans CDP	20,384	24.1	45.5	23,805	66.3	5.8	42.3	20.5	89,178	3.5	9.0	41.4
13 31908	Gainesville city	19,432	57.6	24.1	24,892	64.7	10.6	39.6	26.8	39,224	25.5	33.2	13.6
13 35324	Griffin city	14,896	61.1	19.0	18,154	56.0	18.5	32.1	36.8	30,019	27.9	44.6	7.8
13 38964	Hinesville city	19,088	39.0	19.1	24,795	69.7	9.9	48.2	16.1	48,428	14.0	21.8	9.8
13 42425	Johns Creek city	50,435	13.7	62.6	59,122	70.4	7.6	49.9	13.4	105,978	4.3	9.2	53.0
13 43192	Kennesaw city	19,335	31.2	33.4	23,633	76.0	11.8	47.5	15.5	57,284	9.2	17.9	21.5
13 44340	LaGrange city	17,720	55.2	21.8	22,783	58.6	16.4	37.2	35.7	30,724	27.5	43.1	8.7
13 45488	Lawrenceville city	16,765	52.0	20.9	20,606	68.5	14.6	42.5	20.8	40,516	23.3	32.9	9.5
13 48288	Mableton CDP	25,131	40.1	36.2	29,507	74.0	12.4	46.7	18.1	54,330	13.9	21.5	21.8
13 48624	McDonough city	14,240	41.5	22.8	16,627	63.0	16.0	37.2	28.1	42,787	16.3	34.0	9.5
13 49000	Macon city	55,148	57.4	16.3	69,387	53.3	16.6	29.0	37.9	24,847	33.0	50.3	7.3
13 49756	Marietta city	38,151	32.0	37.7	45,618	75.3	10.8	42.3	18.2	42,135	17.8	27.3	17.3
13 50036	Martinez CDP	24,188	34.2	34.0	28,532	69.2	7.7	48.9	18.7	61,768	7.2	16.3	23.6
13 51670	Milton city	21,752	10.8	66.8	24,295	66.5	5.3	45.9	15.2	111,250	4.9	7.8	54.0
13 55020	Newnan city	20,765	44.1	27.7	24,427	60.7	10.1	42.8	30.5	44,897	15.1	29.2	19.1
13 56000	North Atlanta CDP	26,567	35.1	50.8	31,089	77.1	4.9	54.6	15.0	58,565	16.5	22.6	30.2
13 59724	Peachtree City city	22,930	20.8	50.9	26,883	67.1	8.3	43.0	22.7	87,460	5.0	11.3	43.7
13 62104	Pooler city	12,282	30.5	40.5	14,481	69.3	4.4	57.3	13.2	69,464	4.9	11.4	26.8
13 63952	Redan CDP	20,694	35.2	24.3	25,986	72.6	20.4	42.1	18.2	43,517	14.1	24.4	9.3
13 66668	Rome city	22,749	54.1	20.9	27,919	56.8	15.8	32.4	37.2	32,226	22.4	38.8	10.7
13 67284	Roswell city	63,473	21.8	55.0	71,910	71.6	8.7	50.1	19.2	76,291	4.8	12.1	39.9
13 68516	Sandy Springs city	67,510	21.3	56.2	77,686	73.3	7.8	47.5	20.1	61,046	8.1	18.6	31.8
13 69000	Savannah city	85,929	46.9	25.1	112,065	59.8	11.7	36.7	31.0	34,832	20.6	36.9	8.8
13 71492	Smyrna city	36,127	24.9	52.2	40,922	77.3	10.3	53.4	18.7	53,605	11.3	18.9	27.8
13 73256	Statesboro city	10,662	40.9	24.3	26,086	48.5	9.8	19.0	29.4	20,358	30.9	55.9	5.8
13 73704	Stockbridge city	15,382	32.1	33.9	18,970	68.1	13.7	46.1	19.2	47,758	14.3	18.2	13.7
13 77652	Tucker CDP	20,280	29.1	46.0	22,073	71.2	11.0	45.7	20.4	67,061	10.0	17.1	31.6
13 78324	Union City city	11,582	42.6	21.0	14,117	65.1	14.9	39.9	33.1	31,878	29.0	36.0	4.8
13 78800	Valdosta city	30,423	47.2	23.1	44,881	61.7	15.2	31.5	30.7	28,397	24.7	43.6	9.2
13 80508	Warner Robins city	43,514	40.8	21.9	52,291	68.1	12.6	41.0	23.4	44,285	19.2	28.6	12.0
13 84176	Woodstock city	15,692	21.6	44.6	17,987	72.9	5.7	53.2	17.1	63,508	2.1	13.1	28.9
15 00000	**Hawaii**	941,038	38.1	29.6	1,107,535	65.8	7.1	43.3	22.9	65,087	8.1	17.4	29.2
15 06290	East Honolulu CDP	36,541	21.6	52.6	40,330	62.9	3.5	43.9	26.4	107,163	3.0	8.6	54.1
15 07470	Ewa Gentry CDP	13,692	34.7	28.6	16,994	74.3	5.4	52.7	5.9	78,483	1.3	6.4	38.0
15 14650	Hilo CDP	28,769	40.5	28.5	34,304	56.5	8.8	33.9	32.4	49,065	11.9	25.9	21.2
15 22700	Kahului CDP	18,227	56.9	15.6	21,954	63.7	12.2	38.0	23.3	58,512	9.9	18.5	26.3
15 23150	Kailua CDP (Honolulu County)	28,451	25.8	42.8	32,367	67.1	6.2	45.1	19.8	95,074	4.8	9.9	46.6
15 28250	Kaneohe CDP	24,130	36.9	33.1	27,717	66.0	4.9	46.5	21.2	79,892	4.0	11.8	36.5
15 51000	Mililani Mauka CDP	13,305	20.1	47.6	14,969	77.7	4.5	62.8	8.4	98,388		2.5	48.1
15 51050	Mililani Town CDP	20,468	30.1	34.3	24,096	66.6	5.2	46.0	18.9	93,214	3.3	6.3	44.9
15 62600	Pearl City CDP	34,187	37.8	27.5	39,545	64.1	6.0	45.8	23.0	80,766	5.1	11.7	39.0
15 71550	Urban Honolulu CDP	246,033	36.5	34.7	288,287	64.6	5.5	43.3	24.5	57,452	7.8	20.3	24.6
15 79700	Waipahu CDP	25,824	55.6	12.7	30,942	63.6	5.9	41.7	20.1	64,507	9.6	18.2	30.4
16 00000	**Idaho**	999,548	38.9	25.1	1,201,048	63.8	9.3	37.1	27.3	45,395	11.7	25.6	14.2
16 08830	Boise City city	140,353	27.6	37.5	169,360	68.5	8.9	40.7	24.3	45,985	11.0	25.0	18.5
16 12250	Caldwell city	26,717	52.7	14.6	33,922	64.7	14.2	35.3	29.1	39,101	17.5	33.9	6.0
16 16750	Coeur d'Alene city	29,435	37.9	24.1	36,164	62.4	10.6	31.7	31.8	38,262	10.1	29.6	10.0
16 23410	Eagle city	13,392	18.6	48.0	15,444	61.0	6.5	38.8	27.8	74,278	3.1	14.5	35.9
16 39700	Idaho Falls city	36,067	35.4	25.9	42,993	65.2	7.8	39.7	26.6	45,582	14.2	26.9	16.5
16 46540	Lewiston city	21,888	42.6	21.6	26,186	63.5	5.7	36.1	31.6	43,842	5.4	26.4	12.0
16 52120	Meridian city	47,487	27.6	34.0	54,697	70.2	8.7	47.8	19.3	61,990	6.5	14.4	21.2
16 54550	Moscow city	11,775	20.0	51.3	20,994	61.4	8.1	28.3	27.3	32,238	10.5	38.2	13.6
16 56260	Nampa city	47,861	46.9	18.9	58,187	63.9	12.2	34.0	28.5	39,171	19.0	30.9	8.8
16 64090	Pocatello city	32,442	35.4	30.1	42,204	66.4	8.5	35.2	27.6	39,169	13.0	32.1	10.6
16 64810	Post Falls city	18,062	33.4	20.7	20,919	71.2	10.7	40.6	24.5	49,858	10.9	21.2	13.6
16 67420	Rexburg city	8,428	14.2	36.9	20,630	59.3	10.4	20.5	18.6	26,060	30.7	47.0	7.6
16 82810	Twin Falls city	27,129	43.9	18.3	33,980	62.3	8.3	37.6	24.6	40,544	14.7	26.3	8.3

Table B-4. Cities — What: Education, Employment, and Income, 2010–2012—*Continued*

STATE and Place code	STATE city	Educational attainment			Employment status				Percent of households with no workers	Median household income (dollars)	Percent of families with income below poverty	Percent of households with income less than $25,000	Percent of households with income of $100,000 or more
		Total population 25 years and over	Percent with a high school diploma or less	Percent with a bachelor's degree or more	Total population 16 years and over	Percent in the labor force	Unemployment rate	Percent who worked full-time year-round					
	ACS table number:	C15002	C15002	C15002	B23025	B23025	B23025	C20005	C08202	B19013	C17013	C19001	C19001
	Column number:	1	2	3	4	5	6	7	8	9	10	11	12
17 00000	**Illinois**...................	8,515,161	40.1	31.2	10,130,477	66.2	10.8	40.6	26.0	55,231	10.6	22.5	23.6
17 00243	Addison village	23,962	51.1	22.9	28,052	71.9	11.6	42.9	19.3	57,012	10.0	21.1	24.0
17 00685	Algonquin village	19,445	24.2	44.1	22,807	75.3	10.8	49.2	14.1	92,545	2.0	8.3	46.7
17 01114	Alton city	18,039	44.4	16.8	21,362	59.7	13.2	34.9	35.3	33,231	17.9	38.8	6.6
17 02154	Arlington Heights village.............	53,494	24.1	54.2	61,072	66.6	6.7	42.8	24.5	75,845	2.8	13.2	37.0
17 03012	Aurora city	117,090	45.0	30.6	141,891	74.3	11.2	46.7	14.6	61,968	11.9	16.1	27.0
17 04013	Bartlett village	27,595	27.4	42.2	32,225	72.4	7.9	46.3	15.4	93,984	3.5	11.0	46.3
17 04078	Batavia city	16,794	19.9	50.5	19,519	73.6	9.9	45.5	21.1	89,815	6.1	15.0	44.9
17 04845	Belleville city	31,237	34.7	24.1	35,756	67.9	6.8	45.7	27.5	47,046	11.0	27.5	15.0
17 05092	Belvidere city	15,520	61.8	11.3	19,413	65.6	16.8	37.8	28.5	46,454	16.7	25.9	12.4
17 05573	Berwyn city	36,518	54.4	16.7	43,351	67.4	13.9	41.6	23.9	49,689	13.2	24.4	14.0
17 06587	Bloomingdale village	16,343	35.4	35.9	18,454	70.5	7.6	44.8	20.5	69,831	4.2	13.0	31.1
17 06613	Bloomington city	49,621	28.4	43.7	59,943	71.7	7.2	47.6	20.8	60,319	6.8	20.6	25.9
17 06704	Blue Island city	14,663	56.0	14.8	17,492	66.3	16.5	36.7	28.4	39,621	19.0	33.4	10.1
17 07133	Bolingbrook village	44,989	37.1	34.7	54,390	72.8	9.4	47.6	12.2	77,611	6.9	11.4	36.0
17 09447	Buffalo Grove village	29,751	16.5	61.2	33,774	73.5	6.7	50.1	17.3	92,666	1.9	9.8	45.2
17 09642	Burbank city	19,387	63.5	12.5	22,828	63.6	11.4	38.0	23.6	56,806	11.3	18.4	15.9
17 10487	Calumet City city	23,196	42.5	15.4	27,605	64.9	20.6	36.3	34.6	36,798	16.2	33.7	8.5
17 11163	Carbondale city	10,850	24.1	46.3	22,699	51.7	11.9	16.1	40.3	17,444	33.1	59.6	7.3
17 11332	Carol Stream village	26,327	30.9	37.7	31,713	78.3	10.1	49.2	17.7	71,765	7.4	13.6	31.8
17 11358	Carpentersville village	21,551	53.7	20.6	26,410	76.2	13.1	45.6	12.3	55,855	14.4	20.9	20.8
17 12385	Champaign city	44,420	23.5	49.4	69,698	63.6	8.8	34.2	25.0	40,766	12.7	34.1	17.1
17 12567	Charleston city	9,337	33.6	34.3	19,401	58.0	11.5	22.9	32.6	26,893	16.1	46.8	9.4
17 14000	Chicago city	1,787,913	42.5	33.8	2,156,150	66.2	14.2	39.9	27.0	45,483	19.3	29.9	19.9
17 14026	Chicago Heights city	18,384	56.5	13.8	22,781	64.4	20.0	35.9	29.2	44,599	22.7	28.1	12.3
17 14351	Cicero town	46,369	73.2	7.8	58,463	68.1	14.9	39.0	18.3	41,876	20.2	23.2	11.0
17 15599	Collinsville city	17,218	40.6	25.0	20,182	66.4	9.1	41.3	30.2	49,445	14.4	25.4	15.6
17 17458	Crest Hill city	15,280	43.4	18.6	16,863	58.2	7.8	39.3	28.6	46,621	8.7	23.0	12.5
17 17887	Crystal Lake city	26,097	28.0	40.7	30,917	73.2	7.1	44.8	16.3	75,688	5.7	13.5	34.9
17 18563	Danville city	21,000	53.8	15.4	25,328	53.2	13.9	31.5	40.0	35,257	27.8	40.2	9.1
17 18628	Darien city	15,931	24.7	44.3	18,214	63.3	10.3	37.9	28.0	74,606	4.7	14.5	35.7
17 18823	Decatur city	51,189	48.0	20.1	60,537	60.5	14.8	34.2	34.7	38,878	17.4	32.7	10.8
17 19161	DeKalb city	20,613	33.3	33.6	37,283	64.6	11.4	28.4	25.8	38,062	16.6	38.3	14.7
17 19642	Des Plaines city	42,936	39.4	33.9	48,406	69.2	7.5	43.8	25.1	63,313	4.0	14.8	25.0
17 20292	Dolton village	14,799	43.3	19.4	18,278	66.2	23.9	35.3	32.8	49,335	15.8	24.7	15.3
17 20591	Downers Grove village	34,469	22.7	50.4	39,776	70.1	7.3	43.8	21.7	82,490	3.0	14.3	41.3
17 22073	East Moline city	14,170	50.8	14.9	16,263	56.8	10.8	33.3	35.9	41,728	11.7	25.5	9.7
17 22164	East Peoria city	15,983	42.1	20.5	18,020	63.5	7.8	42.2	30.3	49,497	8.5	23.8	17.9
17 22255	East St. Louis city	16,156	54.2	6.8	19,927	48.3	18.6	25.1	46.7	19,225	45.0	59.0	2.4
17 22697	Edwardsville city	13,795	23.2	50.4	19,931	64.7	5.7	35.3	20.8	67,403	6.0	19.4	34.7
17 23074	Elgin city	67,988	48.4	22.8	80,770	71.0	10.9	43.2	20.0	56,920	11.8	18.8	22.0
17 23256	Elk Grove Village village	23,933	30.8	36.6	27,513	69.3	4.9	47.1	23.9	64,985	4.3	15.1	30.2
17 23620	Elmhurst city	28,647	18.6	55.7	34,079	65.5	8.5	39.1	22.5	90,944	1.8	12.0	45.9
17 23724	Elmwood Park village	17,615	46.6	28.3	20,386	68.5	11.2	40.4	22.4	55,411	6.8	20.2	22.8
17 24582	Evanston city	46,892	17.1	66.1	61,178	65.0	9.0	37.4	24.3	63,604	7.1	21.4	33.7
17 27884	Freeport city	17,614	47.8	16.5	20,286	62.8	16.3	33.5	37.7	37,163	15.6	34.8	8.7
17 28326	Galesburg city	21,886	55.3	16.4	26,557	51.9	10.5	30.0	41.8	32,212	16.8	39.6	9.3
17 28872	Geneva city	13,783	17.5	57.8	16,245	68.0	8.9	40.1	20.7	86,016	2.3	11.3	44.1
17 29730	Glendale Heights village	21,316	44.7	30.0	26,084	76.4	13.5	46.0	13.3	59,455	9.6	14.5	17.2
17 29756	Glen Ellyn village	18,022	17.7	62.0	20,664	67.9	11.0	41.6	25.7	91,583	4.5	18.4	45.7
17 29938	Glenview village	32,367	19.9	60.7	35,987	61.4	6.4	40.7	27.6	87,453	2.1	11.9	45.6
17 30926	Granite City city	20,235	61.4	13.4	23,698	58.1	11.0	35.4	35.0	43,132	15.6	31.6	12.0
17 31121	Grayslake village	12,658	22.9	52.6	15,403	76.9	4.5	51.9	16.0	97,034	3.6	12.6	48.1
17 32018	Gurnee village	20,685	26.2	46.6	24,470	73.5	10.4	46.8	15.3	83,970	2.7	12.3	42.2
17 32746	Hanover Park village	24,177	49.8	22.2	29,129	72.9	11.0	46.2	15.1	66,493	11.8	12.9	23.2
17 33383	Harvey city	14,640	63.0	10.1	17,800	60.8	28.0	30.5	39.5	27,576	26.7	45.1	8.1
17 34722	Highland Park city	20,691	11.9	70.1	23,647	65.0	6.1	41.0	25.3	109,418	3.5	10.4	55.3
17 35411	Hoffman Estates village.............	34,796	29.3	45.6	40,780	72.3	7.3	48.4	15.0	77,941	4.5	10.4	36.9
17 35835	Homer Glen village	16,659	36.0	34.3	19,102	68.2	7.4	43.9	22.2	94,931	2.2	8.8	46.0
17 36750	Huntley village	17,582	27.9	35.1	19,208	53.9	6.6	35.3	38.1	71,820	0.3	9.6	34.8
17 38570	Joliet city	88,393	45.1	24.3	107,591	70.0	12.2	42.0	20.9	60,881	9.9	18.2	23.2
17 38934	Kankakee city	16,885	57.0	11.5	20,234	57.4	15.4	32.1	36.6	31,132	27.0	41.2	7.8
17 41105	Lake Forest city	12,743	10.6	74.0	14,951	52.8	6.8	33.1	28.9	134,138	3.2	9.5	64.1
17 41183	Lake in the Hills village	18,176	38.0	27.0	21,449	77.9	11.3	50.3	12.6	84,053	5.1	9.0	38.1
17 41742	Lake Zurich village	12,568	24.5	50.5	14,867	76.3	7.7	49.2	12.9	105,694	5.7	9.5	53.3
17 42028	Lansing village	19,571	42.9	18.8	22,730	68.8	12.7	41.6	28.1	50,891	7.8	20.7	18.1
17 43250	Libertyville village	14,118	16.6	61.6	15,956	67.1	6.5	44.1	22.1	105,144	2.3	8.3	52.6
17 43939	Lisle village	15,393	16.9	53.4	18,045	72.1	7.7	47.9	19.3	69,712	4.4	13.2	34.3
17 44225	Lockport city	16,070	32.8	29.6	18,510	76.4	11.7	50.8	20.1	72,268	3.9	11.6	30.5
17 44407	Lombard village	31,051	27.2	40.7	36,389	69.3	10.1	41.9	24.9	69,524	3.2	13.8	30.9
17 45031	Loves Park city	15,887	40.8	24.8	18,355	71.3	12.0	40.3	23.3	52,590	7.4	21.4	15.3
17 45694	McHenry city	17,740	40.7	26.1	20,884	73.3	13.5	40.9	23.5	63,115	7.5	18.7	23.6
17 45726	Machesney Park village	15,388	53.2	13.4	18,355	70.9	13.6	42.3	22.3	53,726	7.4	15.3	15.1
17 47774	Maywood village	16,273	55.7	13.4	18,996	59.0	22.0	31.2	32.8	41,364	15.7	30.9	14.4
17 48242	Melrose Park village	14,981	68.3	9.4	18,641	69.1	12.0	40.2	21.6	43,428	14.2	26.4	13.4

Table B-4. Cities — What: Education, Employment, and Income, 2010–2012—*Continued*

STATE and Place code	STATE city	Educational attainment			Employment status				Percent of households with no workers	Median household income (dollars)	Percent of families with income below poverty	Percent of households with income less than $25,000	Percent of households with income of $100,000 or more
		Total population 25 years and over	Percent with a high school diploma or less	Percent with a bachelor's degree or more	Total population 16 years and over	Percent in the labor force	Unemployment rate	Percent who worked full-time year-round					
	ACS table number:	C15002	C15002	C15002	B23025	B23025	B23025		C20005	C08202	B19013	C17013	C19001	C19001
	Column number:	1	2	3	4	5	6	7	8	9	10	11	12
	Illinois—Cont.												
17 49867	Moline city	29,689	41.1	25.8	34,612	66.0	8.3	41.5	27.8	48,221	7.9	23.1	15.8
17 50647	Morton Grove village	17,563	31.4	42.9	19,334	60.2	10.8	36.2	29.8	68,550	6.6	16.0	30.9
17 51089	Mount Prospect village	37,800	36.8	35.7	43,312	69.3	7.7	45.3	21.0	66,245	2.6	11.1	28.9
17 51349	Mundelein village	20,445	36.5	40.9	24,071	75.2	10.7	46.2	15.8	76,515	4.6	9.4	37.9
17 51622	Naperville city	91,374	15.3	66.2	109,559	70.3	6.8	47.0	14.5	109,527	3.0	8.4	54.2
17 52584	New Lenox village	15,353	31.9	37.4	18,164	72.1	6.6	47.5	18.5	87,825	2.6	6.2	41.5
17 53000	Niles village	22,626	48.1	26.3	24,716	52.8	9.2	31.2	36.8	43,491	9.0	24.8	18.3
17 53234	Normal town	25,669	27.4	49.1	45,266	68.3	6.4	32.2	19.7	51,948	7.3	29.4	24.3
17 53481	Northbrook village	23,452	13.2	68.4	26,614	59.7	6.7	39.2	27.4	103,601	3.7	12.2	52.4
17 53559	North Chicago city	14,545	46.3	19.8	24,825	76.6	8.9	48.4	25.1	40,176	25.6	28.8	13.5
17 54638	Oak Forest city	18,434	39.1	27.4	22,447	72.0	14.4	39.4	21.1	67,332	5.0	14.5	30.1
17 54820	Oak Lawn village	40,102	44.7	26.5	46,376	63.6	13.5	37.3	31.3	55,275	6.4	21.2	22.1
17 54885	Oak Park village	36,158	12.3	66.4	40,330	74.3	8.9	49.1	21.1	78,022	6.2	15.8	39.3
17 55249	O'Fallon city	17,937	19.4	50.8	21,453	70.8	8.8	46.5	18.1	74,347	6.6	17.0	37.1
17 56640	Orland Park village	40,190	31.2	40.3	46,967	63.5	9.0	38.1	29.2	73,384	4.2	13.0	34.4
17 56887	Oswego village	19,457	22.6	44.0	22,389	77.2	4.1	54.4	9.5	95,205	4.0	8.1	46.2
17 57225	Palatine village	46,927	31.0	46.8	53,903	71.8	7.9	47.3	18.0	69,388	6.0	13.4	32.6
17 57732	Park Forest village	14,964	36.3	25.5	17,413	68.5	18.3	38.1	28.9	48,076	15.7	27.5	12.2
17 57875	Park Ridge city	25,942	20.4	55.8	29,839	62.9	6.0	40.8	26.0	84,747	2.8	11.0	43.8
17 58447	Pekin city	23,523	49.7	16.5	27,130	62.4	8.4	40.8	30.4	46,358	9.8	24.0	12.3
17 59000	Peoria city	72,203	39.2	31.9	89,042	63.8	10.7	37.5	29.4	44,061	18.0	29.9	16.9
17 60287	Plainfield village	23,255	22.3	49.1	27,133	74.0	6.1	52.5	8.5	109,493	3.1	7.1	54.9
17 62367	Quincy city	27,683	46.7	20.2	32,603	64.5	8.5	41.1	31.9	39,449	13.9	30.7	9.4
17 65000	Rockford city	98,279	50.7	20.3	115,900	62.2	16.5	32.9	34.5	36,870	20.5	36.2	11.2
17 65078	Rock Island city	24,473	44.8	22.1	30,795	61.2	8.1	33.2	35.3	39,752	17.1	32.9	10.5
17 65338	Rolling Meadows city	16,801	42.2	27.8	19,502	71.2	8.0	46.1	20.5	63,258	8.6	18.5	21.5
17 65442	Romeoville village	23,230	43.3	24.7	28,608	68.7	11.1	44.9	20.0	64,322	7.5	11.5	22.0
17 65806	Roselle village	15,715	29.4	35.8	18,726	75.3	9.0	46.3	17.9	74,946	3.9	12.9	31.2
17 66040	Round Lake Beach village	16,509	58.2	15.3	20,432	76.1	11.8	44.0	13.1	56,753	14.8	19.5	19.4
17 66703	St. Charles city	23,022	24.1	51.3	26,202	70.7	4.2	49.0	18.8	82,641	2.7	8.0	43.0
17 68003	Schaumburg village	53,005	29.3	43.2	60,435	71.3	7.3	48.4	20.6	68,126	5.5	13.4	27.0
17 70122	Skokie village	46,988	30.2	44.7	53,662	61.2	9.6	37.8	26.5	63,187	8.5	20.0	28.5
17 70720	South Elgin village	13,228	33.8	32.2	15,375	71.9	6.8	49.3	13.3	81,909	1.0	8.4	38.4
17 70850	South Holland village	14,724	35.7	28.0	17,499	64.1	15.5	38.1	25.9	63,950	5.7	15.9	25.1
17 72000	Springfield city	79,558	35.6	33.5	93,650	65.2	9.5	40.9	29.3	46,615	14.7	27.2	17.5
17 73157	Streamwood village	25,906	38.8	33.3	29,939	76.4	9.9	49.0	13.4	68,209	2.9	9.1	29.6
17 75484	Tinley Park village	40,159	32.8	35.2	45,585	70.2	8.9	43.4	22.5	74,037	6.1	13.5	32.9
17 77005	Urbana city	19,016	23.6	54.8	37,293	58.9	7.4	21.2	28.9	28,534	14.0	45.8	11.4
17 77694	Vernon Hills village	16,701	20.5	58.3	19,319	73.5	8.0	49.0	17.2	84,090	1.7	11.0	41.8
17 77993	Villa Park village	14,704	35.9	32.6	17,059	73.8	10.5	45.5	18.2	69,779	5.8	14.2	26.9
17 79293	Waukegan city	52,583	58.2	17.6	65,631	69.2	12.3	38.8	22.6	42,612	19.4	26.5	14.6
17 80060	West Chicago city	15,716	52.9	24.7	19,441	74.6	11.7	42.8	12.1	63,790	14.2	13.9	26.9
17 80645	Westmont village	18,628	29.9	40.0	20,942	67.2	11.8	43.6	26.6	57,165	6.3	18.4	23.0
17 81048	Wheaton city	35,017	17.0	59.6	42,560	69.1	7.8	43.1	20.1	82,420	5.6	11.2	40.7
17 81087	Wheeling village	26,496	40.9	34.9	30,092	73.2	7.7	49.3	17.5	55,429	8.6	19.6	19.0
17 82075	Wilmette village	17,757	6.5	81.8	20,488	59.7	4.6	37.5	24.6	117,465	2.3	7.3	56.7
17 83245	Woodridge village	22,743	25.5	45.5	26,972	77.5	9.1	52.0	13.1	75,469	3.6	8.3	32.7
17 83349	Woodstock city	16,241	36.6	31.8	19,073	73.4	11.9	46.3	18.8	55,146	10.3	21.8	19.9
17 84220	Zion city	14,334	49.8	14.6	17,850	69.9	15.1	38.3	28.6	51,074	11.9	29.0	15.7
18 00000	**Indiana**	4,256,342	48.2	23.1	5,099,178	64.2	9.8	39.3	27.6	47,185	11.2	25.2	15.9
18 01468	Anderson city	36,764	56.1	14.8	44,523	56.5	17.4	30.1	43.1	32,646	20.6	38.9	5.8
18 05860	Bloomington city	35,903	22.0	54.4	72,053	54.4	9.4	22.2	33.6	26,925	20.0	47.1	11.3
18 08416	Brownsburg town	14,351	33.8	38.1	16,623	69.1	3.9	48.8	23.0	62,336	3.1	15.0	21.8
18 10342	Carmel city	54,012	11.6	67.9	61,526	71.0	5.2	48.8	16.3	109,928	2.5	8.7	54.5
18 12934	Clarksville town	14,631	51.2	20.9	17,220	63.4	7.3	42.3	32.5	40,818	13.1	30.8	9.7
18 14734	Columbus city	30,016	41.8	31.2	34,855	65.4	6.9	42.4	28.8	50,523	11.0	24.1	20.9
18 16138	Crown Point city	20,330	46.0	28.9	23,322	61.0	8.6	38.5	26.4	61,300	3.4	19.4	25.9
18 19486	East Chicago city	16,651	62.7	7.1	20,771	53.7	15.4	29.5	40.7	25,428	33.5	49.2	5.5
18 20728	Elkhart city	31,197	61.0	13.8	37,453	64.1	13.9	37.5	31.7	35,249	25.0	34.7	5.3
18 22000	Evansville city	79,241	50.6	17.5	95,841	63.8	8.8	40.4	29.7	35,282	15.3	33.7	8.0
18 23278	Fishers town	49,717	16.2	59.5	56,674	77.8	5.5	55.3	8.8	87,968	1.5	6.2	41.7
18 25000	Fort Wayne city	161,133	41.4	25.3	193,816	64.9	10.8	40.9	28.0	43,673	14.5	26.6	12.7
18 25450	Franklin city	14,366	48.0	22.2	17,848	64.9	7.8	40.0	26.5	48,487	13.6	24.3	18.3
18 27000	Gary city	51,066	54.2	12.4	60,700	50.7	19.3	26.2	44.2	26,870	33.4	47.3	5.9
18 28386	Goshen city	19,861	59.1	19.2	24,119	64.1	12.7	34.7	30.1	38,155	21.1	31.6	7.3
18 28800	Granger CDP	18,577	21.8	52.0	21,458	68.6	5.2	44.8	17.9	91,985	2.6	8.2	47.1
18 29520	Greenfield city	14,058	48.6	19.1	16,669	63.6	7.3	42.9	25.6	49,090	9.7	21.0	14.3
18 29898	Greenwood city	34,722	44.1	25.6	40,173	68.8	8.5	45.7	24.1	54,029	9.7	20.0	19.9
18 31000	Hammond city	50,530	58.4	13.9	61,045	61.9	15.1	34.1	31.3	37,176	19.6	32.5	7.6
18 33466	Highland town	16,583	41.3	28.5	19,070	66.1	6.6	43.1	25.8	61,821	5.1	16.2	19.9
18 34114	Hobart city	19,802	52.0	15.1	22,770	66.4	11.8	40.5	27.4	52,136	9.0	24.2	14.3
18 36003	Indianapolis city (balance)	533,283	45.3	26.9	641,645	67.4	12.2	40.0	26.5	40,167	16.9	30.3	13.5
18 38358	Jeffersonville city	31,437	43.8	21.9	36,496	67.7	10.3	43.5	26.2	50,289	7.2	23.9	14.3
18 40392	Kokomo city	38,670	51.8	16.3	44,960	58.7	13.2	32.9	39.8	33,598	15.8	36.0	9.7
18 40788	Lafayette city	41,867	46.8	25.3	52,967	70.0	9.4	41.4	26.0	38,225	14.5	31.8	8.1
18 42246	La Porte city	14,967	57.0	14.4	17,339	63.4	15.3	35.6	32.0	35,741	15.9	35.3	5.9
18 42426	Lawrence city	29,560	36.2	32.5	34,458	75.5	10.9	45.3	18.7	50,814	12.9	21.8	17.5

Table B-4. Cities — What: Education, Employment, and Income, 2010–2012—*Continued*

STATE and Place code	STATE city	Educational attainment			Employment status				Percent of households with no workers	Median household income (dollars)	Percent of families with income below poverty	Percent of households with income less than $25,000	Percent of households with income of $100,000 or more
		Total population 25 years and over	Percent with a high school diploma or less	Percent with a bachelor's degree or more	Total population 16 years and over	Percent in the labor force	Unemployment rate	Percent who worked full-time year-round					
ACS table number:		C15002	C15002	C15002	B23025	B23025	B23025	C20005	C08202	B19013	C17013	C19001	C19001
Column number:		1	2	3	4	5	6	7	8	9	10	11	12
	Indiana—Cont.												
18 46908	Marion city	18,018	59.5	16.5	23,230	52.6	12.7	27.4	43.9	29,670	22.4	43.4	7.5
18 48528	Merrillville town	22,912	44.5	21.8	27,268	64.2	11.8	38.2	27.9	52,703	10.0	25.4	15.8
18 48798	Michigan City city	20,182	54.5	15.0	24,587	56.4	16.6	29.8	35.4	34,245	25.4	40.0	6.3
18 49932	Mishawaka city	31,312	48.5	24.6	38,654	68.4	11.8	38.7	27.2	36,008	17.6	32.7	8.4
18 51876	Muncie city	37,659	50.7	21.3	59,541	55.7	17.3	22.6	38.8	28,975	21.8	44.5	5.6
18 51912	Munster town	17,016	34.0	40.1	19,507	60.3	7.8	37.3	29.8	71,694	6.1	15.6	33.9
18 52326	New Albany city	24,073	54.1	15.2	28,953	64.0	11.8	39.1	31.7	38,624	18.4	34.4	7.9
18 54180	Noblesville city	36,293	24.9	45.8	41,176	74.3	5.3	52.7	15.3	64,420	5.4	12.5	26.5
18 60246	Plainfield town	18,571	43.4	26.5	21,543	61.4	7.7	43.3	23.4	56,883	5.6	16.5	19.6
18 61092	Portage city	24,517	53.4	15.3	28,773	61.3	11.6	38.6	30.6	48,778	10.9	26.0	16.9
18 64260	Richmond city	24,141	57.7	16.5	29,375	53.9	14.4	29.3	37.9	28,492	24.8	42.6	6.7
18 68220	Schererville town	21,042	37.8	32.6	23,705	68.0	8.5	46.8	23.4	68,643	4.0	13.1	30.0
18 71000	South Bend city	63,301	46.9	23.3	75,334	64.4	16.3	34.1	33.7	33,420	22.7	37.0	8.6
18 75428	Terre Haute city	37,685	50.2	19.6	50,389	55.3	10.4	29.4	34.3	31,989	16.9	37.8	9.0
18 78326	Valparaiso city	19,845	35.9	33.1	25,717	60.5	7.5	36.2	29.5	50,558	10.4	25.5	18.6
18 82700	Westfield town	18,683	17.9	58.0	21,852	76.4	4.0	55.6	10.9	82,410	4.6	9.0	40.6
18 82862	West Lafayette city	12,009	15.9	69.0	26,756	52.3	8.4	20.8	34.9	30,498	3.5	41.8	15.5
18 86372	Zionsville town	14,721	11.5	69.6	16,675	68.6	3.6	46.7	17.0	102,068	0.2	5.6	51.9
19 00000	**Iowa**	2,027,762	42.0	25.8	2,420,545	68.0	6.0	44.0	25.5	50,773	8.4	22.9	17.3
19 01855	Ames city	26,389	13.2	63.9	52,345	65.9	7.4	30.3	22.0	40,945	10.7	34.7	15.8
19 02305	Ankeny city	29,972	19.7	46.5	35,240	77.4	3.7	54.8	14.2	71,419	2.9	11.9	28.5
19 06355	Bettendorf city	23,221	23.7	48.3	26,187	65.3	4.2	45.0	24.8	72,139	3.8	14.8	33.1
19 09550	Burlington city	17,606	44.7	21.0	20,330	61.2	11.4	35.7	34.1	37,722	19.5	35.0	8.7
19 11755	Cedar Falls city	21,056	27.8	45.7	33,890	67.3	8.8	33.7	27.9	47,474	7.8	25.3	21.0
19 12000	Cedar Rapids city	82,840	34.1	31.4	101,317	71.2	6.2	45.5	22.7	52,455	7.0	22.1	18.0
19 14430	Clinton city	18,575	50.7	17.5	21,414	61.7	7.2	37.9	34.0	41,801	12.7	29.5	12.8
19 16860	Council Bluffs city	40,739	48.8	17.4	49,152	68.5	8.1	45.6	26.7	43,458	13.2	27.7	11.7
19 19000	Davenport city	65,632	38.8	26.0	78,916	65.4	7.8	41.0	27.2	42,451	12.5	27.2	13.5
19 21000	Des Moines city	132,365	45.0	24.9	158,866	69.8	9.2	44.1	25.1	44,292	14.6	27.0	13.1
19 22395	Dubuque city	38,716	43.2	28.8	47,441	67.2	7.0	39.9	26.8	44,737	9.3	24.4	12.1
19 28515	Fort Dodge city	16,867	44.6	19.6	20,425	59.8	13.2	34.5	34.4	36,331	14.1	34.2	11.9
19 38595	Iowa City city	35,854	18.5	57.8	59,734	67.7	4.8	33.0	22.1	41,412	12.0	35.2	18.7
19 49485	Marion city	23,567	28.9	34.3	27,000	71.8	4.6	48.4	21.0	59,993	3.8	18.3	25.7
19 49755	Marshalltown city	17,976	48.4	21.7	21,087	65.2	7.5	39.9	28.5	48,871	9.9	20.2	13.4
19 50160	Mason City city	19,142	41.0	19.0	22,539	64.7	7.3	40.3	30.5	40,318	12.2	32.0	9.6
19 55110	Muscatine city	15,342	50.6	15.3	17,708	64.5	6.0	41.0	28.7	43,439	10.7	27.1	12.0
19 60465	Ottumwa city	16,514	53.5	15.4	20,013	62.6	11.2	35.4	29.4	35,879	14.6	34.0	9.6
19 73335	Sioux City city	51,856	49.2	19.8	63,840	68.1	6.7	43.3	26.2	41,408	14.5	29.3	11.4
19 79950	Urbandale city	27,434	23.5	49.4	31,403	76.3	4.7	52.5	15.7	75,786	4.0	10.9	37.4
19 82425	Waterloo city	44,677	50.1	20.3	53,560	67.0	9.2	42.4	29.8	41,492	14.1	28.4	9.6
19 83910	West Des Moines city	38,519	20.8	51.2	45,762	76.2	4.9	54.1	17.3	68,839	5.1	13.9	29.5
20 00000	**Kansas**	1,854,150	37.8	30.1	2,225,644	67.9	7.2	44.3	24.0	50,346	9.4	23.2	18.5
20 17800	Derby city	14,704	24.2	36.4	17,792	75.2	4.7	52.7	17.3	64,247	3.7	11.2	21.8
20 18250	Dodge City city	16,088	55.2	17.9	20,362	70.8	9.3	46.9	17.9	47,416	16.4	20.0	11.8
20 21275	Emporia city	14,232	46.0	26.0	20,025	69.5	8.9	36.7	24.6	37,525	15.5	34.6	6.8
20 25325	Garden City city	15,320	56.9	16.1	19,236	72.8	3.4	49.5	14.7	44,145	12.1	19.7	12.6
20 25425	Gardner city	11,736	34.6	27.7	13,659	76.4	7.9	54.4	18.2	61,415	2.7	10.4	19.9
20 31100	Hays city	11,947	34.9	34.6	16,847	76.5	5.6	45.0	20.8	41,024	8.7	32.2	12.9
20 33625	Hutchinson city	28,084	37.8	19.6	33,295	61.0	6.9	42.2	29.9	38,232	9.0	29.7	10.8
20 35750	Junction City city	14,505	39.9	18.8	18,492	71.9	8.0	52.5	19.6	44,381	10.1	17.7	9.3
20 36000	Kansas City city	90,607	54.9	14.8	109,035	66.4	14.2	38.2	29.2	37,501	20.2	32.6	9.0
20 38900	Lawrence city	46,854	22.4	52.4	74,642	71.3	7.9	36.3	17.3	45,514	8.3	29.8	17.9
20 39000	Leavenworth city	23,087	38.9	31.4	27,221	58.0	8.2	39.7	26.0	50,211	11.1	22.9	20.7
20 39075	Leawood city	21,769	7.3	73.3	24,345	65.6	4.2	44.3	21.5	124,314	2.3	8.5	62.3
20 39350	Lenexa city	32,844	18.6	51.4	38,132	74.5	6.2	50.0	16.7	71,831	5.4	16.4	33.2
20 39825	Liberal city	11,393	65.6	10.8	14,554	69.6	10.1	48.8	19.7	47,700	14.6	23.4	11.3
20 44250	Manhattan city	25,488	19.4	52.6	46,950	66.0	4.2	36.3	20.3	42,950	5.8	29.9	14.6
20 52575	Olathe city	80,283	24.5	44.6	94,507	77.4	5.4	52.5	14.2	75,476	4.5	12.1	33.4
20 53775	Overland Park city	120,981	16.0	57.4	138,020	72.8	5.6	49.7	19.5	70,592	4.2	13.4	33.1
20 56025	Pittsburg city	10,544	32.7	33.4	16,439	63.3	7.6	35.6	27.6	31,827	16.5	40.1	10.0
20 57575	Prairie Village city	16,054	9.8	68.3	17,590	68.8	4.4	48.6	22.7	81,250	2.0	13.4	38.7
20 62700	Salina city	31,543	45.2	23.5	37,463	69.7	6.4	45.1	23.7	42,116	14.9	29.2	12.3
20 64500	Shawnee city	41,532	26.7	41.1	47,878	73.2	4.9	50.4	16.0	71,751	4.3	13.3	31.8
20 71000	Topeka city	83,809	43.4	27.2	99,376	65.1	9.4	40.1	29.6	39,118	17.5	30.2	11.4
20 79000	Wichita city	244,036	40.0	27.9	293,680	68.7	10.0	43.4	24.6	44,612	13.0	26.9	15.1
21 00000	**Kentucky**	2,922,675	51.2	21.1	3,454,206	60.0	10.2	37.5	32.8	41,782	14.6	31.1	14.3
21 02368	Ashland city	15,476	48.3	16.3	17,706	54.6	12.1	32.7	42.3	33,945	16.1	36.5	11.9
21 08902	Bowling Green city	32,721	45.3	26.5	48,764	64.7	12.6	32.4	28.7	31,272	23.4	41.3	8.7
21 17848	Covington city	26,950	51.7	18.6	32,156	61.4	13.5	35.9	32.1	34,557	22.6	38.0	7.2
21 24274	Elizabethtown city	18,689	44.0	27.2	22,807	61.9	10.5	39.0	26.9	40,306	15.1	31.9	15.0
21 27982	Florence city	20,008	43.1	25.4	23,109	65.8	7.0	43.1	26.6	48,436	12.0	26.3	13.3
21 28900	Frankfort city	18,582	48.9	25.2	22,477	61.3	10.0	37.1	30.9	38,651	20.8	29.0	11.4
21 30700	Georgetown city	18,368	44.1	23.7	22,402	71.2	10.5	46.6	24.4	54,698	10.7	21.4	17.4
21 35866	Henderson city	20,070	52.7	18.5	23,336	59.1	13.6	35.5	37.2	34,235	18.4	36.1	9.4
21 37918	Hopkinsville city	21,411	50.0	16.7	25,566	56.1	16.9	32.9	36.4	33,061	20.4	38.0	8.7
21 39142	Independence city	15,677	40.7	28.6	18,267	74.0	6.2	51.7	16.7	63,816	9.8	15.7	20.3
21 40222	Jeffersontown city	18,655	33.2	35.1	21,580	73.4	9.3	47.0	19.2	59,512	8.4	17.1	23.2
21 46027	Lexington-Fayette urban county	194,695	32.6	39.8	243,487	69.0	8.8	42.2	23.2	47,785	11.4	27.1	20.2

Table B-4. Cities — What: Education, Employment, and Income, 2010–2012—*Continued*

STATE and Place code	STATE city	Educational attainment: Total population 25 years and over	Educational attainment: Percent with a high school diploma or less	Educational attainment: Percent with a bachelor's degree or more	Employment status: Total population 16 years and over	Employment status: Percent in the labor force	Employment status: Unemployment rate	Employment status: Percent who worked full-time year-round	Percent of households with no workers	Median household income (dollars)	Percent of families with income below poverty	Percent of households with income less than $25,000	Percent of households with income of $100,000 or more
	ACS table number:	C15002	C15002	C15002	B23025	B23025	B23025	C20005	C08202	B19013	C17013	C19001	C19001
	Column number:	1	2	3	4	5	6	7	8	9	10	11	12
	Kentucky—Cont.												
21 48006	Louisville/Jefferson County metro	402,854	43.3	27.0	474,812	65.4	12.1	39.7	30.5	42,609	14.6	29.9	16.1
21 56136	Nicholasville city	18,154	50.2	18.9	21,151	68.1	10.3	43.5	23.1	42,698	18.6	30.4	11.4
21 58620	Owensboro city	38,589	52.8	18.9	45,405	59.2	8.7	37.3	35.1	37,654	16.6	34.2	10.2
21 58836	Paducah city	18,218	40.4	21.8	20,418	53.9	10.9	35.4	40.7	32,523	19.4	39.0	11.4
21 63912	Radcliff city	14,111	43.8	13.9	16,865	67.7	11.2	45.2	25.4	46,548	21.2	30.4	12.7
21 65226	Richmond city	17,014	41.6	27.3	26,666	62.5	11.9	29.0	31.9	29,213	23.2	45.3	5.6
22 00000	**Louisiana**	2,980,393	51.9	21.5	3,580,858	61.5	9.2	40.0	28.4	43,484	15.3	30.5	17.1
22 00975	Alexandria city	30,509	53.3	19.0	36,139	56.0	11.7	37.1	33.9	35,001	24.1	39.2	10.4
22 05000	Baton Rouge city	136,991	40.2	33.2	184,862	65.2	10.8	37.1	26.8	37,419	17.4	35.6	14.9
22 05210	Bayou Cane CDP	13,631	59.8	13.6	15,951	62.7	5.8	43.9	19.2	48,503	10.0	19.9	17.7
22 08920	Bossier City city	40,379	44.3	23.8	48,841	69.1	6.4	48.2	24.1	45,239	14.7	26.5	15.3
22 13960	Central city	18,728	44.9	21.0	22,078	66.6	5.8	43.3	23.3	61,455	4.3	14.9	23.0
22 32755	Hammond city	11,117	49.0	29.5	16,759	59.8	12.3	29.9	31.7	30,229	23.1	43.5	19.6
22 33245	Harvey CDP	14,160	56.8	19.3	17,360	62.0	5.4	46.4	25.5	41,250	20.5	35.1	17.1
22 36255	Houma city	21,893	58.1	16.9	26,112	62.9	6.5	42.4	26.9	45,869	13.2	28.9	17.3
22 39475	Kenner city	45,515	48.9	21.8	54,010	66.2	11.1	42.0	27.6	46,634	12.5	25.0	15.9
22 40735	Lafayette city	77,084	39.2	32.8	98,592	66.6	6.6	40.2	24.3	43,928	14.3	31.9	19.3
22 41155	Lake Charles city	46,614	47.9	22.8	57,784	61.5	11.2	32.8	30.5	33,836	18.5	37.6	13.3
22 42030	Laplace CDP	19,143	52.5	18.4	23,093	67.4	9.1	41.7	24.1	57,028	10.6	18.3	19.7
22 48785	Marrero CDP	22,627	69.0	7.0	27,118	55.5	8.1	40.2	31.2	31,622	20.9	38.3	8.9
22 50115	Metairie CDP	97,764	38.7	31.8	112,121	66.2	7.2	43.4	26.5	49,591	9.3	24.8	20.9
22 51410	Monroe city	29,406	50.6	26.1	37,458	57.1	11.3	34.8	33.3	27,122	30.9	46.4	12.0
22 54035	New Iberia city	19,052	61.0	16.2	23,058	59.8	11.8	34.8	30.2	37,751	22.3	33.6	11.5
22 55000	New Orleans city	239,521	40.3	33.0	290,873	62.0	12.8	38.2	31.9	36,004	23.2	37.8	15.6
22 62385	Prairieville CDP	15,894	33.9	34.9	19,363	73.3	3.8	51.3	15.7	89,362	4.9	10.5	45.4
22 66655	Ruston city	10,397	33.3	44.5	18,260	58.0	12.6	28.7	36.2	28,711	23.3	44.2	9.8
22 70000	Shreveport city	130,134	46.0	25.1	156,710	62.4	8.6	40.9	27.7	37,531	18.0	33.8	15.7
22 70805	Slidell city	18,586	48.2	22.9	21,459	62.4	9.4	39.6	28.3	47,410	12.3	21.7	15.3
22 73640	Sulphur city	13,561	48.8	21.4	15,551	55.8	10.5	37.1	36.1	42,719	14.2	30.5	17.0
22 75180	Terrytown CDP	14,319	50.1	17.3	17,446	73.1	8.7	47.2	19.5	45,016	18.5	27.7	14.6
23 00000	**Maine**	942,582	43.1	27.8	1,091,925	64.4	8.1	38.8	30.7	47,344	9.3	26.0	16.2
23 02060	Auburn city	15,613	43.5	24.9	18,214	64.4	9.9	38.2	32.8	42,654	9.9	29.0	13.5
23 02795	Bangor city	21,629	39.4	26.5	27,807	60.1	8.1	34.0	33.3	33,718	16.5	36.7	12.4
23 04860	Biddeford city	13,961	48.1	22.3	17,201	69.9	6.2	41.8	24.9	44,161	11.4	29.1	13.1
23 38740	Lewiston city	24,325	53.9	15.3	29,770	61.4	10.9	35.6	37.1	35,982	20.0	38.2	10.6
23 60545	Portland city	47,850	28.6	45.9	56,500	70.3	7.0	42.1	27.7	45,069	14.3	30.1	16.0
23 71990	South Portland city	17,910	30.7	39.9	20,477	72.3	4.5	47.0	23.4	54,354	7.8	20.2	19.6
24 00000	**Maryland**	3,922,966	37.3	36.6	4,649,740	69.0	8.6	46.0	22.0	71,707	7.0	16.1	34.6
24 01600	Annapolis city	27,175	33.4	41.9	31,559	72.1	6.3	49.2	22.8	71,082	8.5	18.0	33.2
24 02275	Arnold CDP	15,099	19.5	51.3	17,545	74.5	4.3	49.5	15.7	99,688	1.8	6.6	49.8
24 02825	Aspen Hill CDP	33,962	35.8	39.4	38,939	70.6	8.5	45.9	23.2	75,420	8.1	15.6	34.0
24 04000	Baltimore city	411,314	50.1	26.1	502,239	62.2	15.4	37.6	33.5	39,788	20.2	34.6	14.8
24 05825	Bel Air North CDP	19,748	30.0	43.2	23,528	70.1	4.8	47.9	17.8	95,895	2.8	7.3	47.3
24 05950	Bel Air South CDP	30,458	29.4	39.8	34,754	71.8	6.6	49.3	18.5	86,561	3.5	12.1	41.7
24 07125	Bethesda CDP	43,447	6.6	83.2	49,042	70.5	3.8	50.9	18.6	139,626	1.4	7.1	63.6
24 08775	Bowie city	37,059	24.2	46.5	43,338	75.9	7.0	54.2	14.6	105,106	1.5	5.4	53.0
24 13325	Carney CDP	19,342	40.3	30.1	21,716	68.8	5.3	48.5	29.3	58,909	4.1	15.8	22.1
24 14125	Catonsville CDP	27,353	30.4	45.3	34,636	59.9	7.9	39.6	28.4	72,106	4.4	15.8	34.6
24 16875	Chillum CDP	24,999	58.1	19.0	31,298	77.1	10.6	49.8	16.0	56,902	10.9	15.0	21.7
24 17900	Clinton CDP	25,737	40.2	26.8	30,596	69.4	10.9	50.8	17.3	97,431	3.5	8.7	48.1
24 18250	Cockeysville CDP	13,463	23.6	46.6	16,078	73.9	6.2	52.4	14.8	67,950	6.7	15.5	26.2
24 18750	College Park city	9,846	30.2	49.6	28,751	53.2	12.8	19.5	24.6	53,913	8.3	32.2	23.3
24 19125	Columbia CDP	70,770	17.4	63.1	81,899	74.0	6.7	51.1	16.0	97,731	4.3	9.0	48.9
24 20875	Crofton CDP	19,128	17.9	54.3	21,636	78.8	4.5	59.2	11.6	103,029	2.3	4.2	51.1
24 21325	Cumberland city	14,278	54.5	16.3	16,614	53.9	12.1	30.9	45.3	32,256	15.8	39.3	9.5
24 23975	Dundalk CDP	41,737	66.5	8.3	48,522	60.9	14.1	37.4	34.8	47,854	9.9	24.8	12.7
24 25150	Edgewood CDP	16,971	44.5	19.2	20,285	73.4	12.6	46.5	19.7	56,495	15.5	20.2	15.5
24 25575	Eldersburg CDP	20,424	29.5	44.4	23,875	66.7	4.3	47.4	20.0	104,416	1.4	6.9	52.4
24 26000	Ellicott City CDP	45,631	15.4	65.6	52,682	70.1	4.4	47.9	16.7	110,628	3.8	7.0	56.2
24 26600	Essex CDP	25,124	59.9	11.3	29,584	70.5	12.5	43.3	25.3	51,451	9.4	22.2	16.3
24 27250	Fairland CDP	14,682	28.0	48.6	17,434	71.4	9.8	44.1	18.2	62,487	11.4	14.9	26.2
24 29525	Fort Washington CDP	18,029	25.5	43.1	21,071	70.6	9.1	50.3	18.5	109,265	3.2	7.9	55.1
24 30325	Frederick city	44,716	35.1	37.1	52,165	74.3	8.4	47.4	20.6	65,070	7.1	15.7	29.3
24 31175	Gaithersburg city	42,219	25.3	51.3	47,623	74.2	6.0	51.8	13.9	73,996	7.5	12.7	38.5
24 32025	Germantown CDP	57,136	25.4	44.8	66,463	79.6	7.3	53.5	10.3	84,012	5.3	10.7	41.5
24 32650	Glen Burnie CDP	46,931	46.6	18.2	55,478	72.4	8.0	47.9	19.4	62,357	8.4	17.1	25.6
24 34775	Greenbelt city	15,286	33.4	40.5	18,457	77.4	6.4	51.8	14.6	57,252	11.3	14.0	21.7
24 36075	Hagerstown city	26,893	53.7	15.5	31,382	66.8	14.4	40.3	32.5	36,897	21.0	35.9	9.6
24 41475	Ilchester CDP	16,126	20.5	55.7	18,653	77.2	6.1	56.5	10.9	104,430	4.9	7.0	53.2
24 45325	Landover CDP	13,982	57.1	13.0	17,032	71.3	11.4	47.0	20.0	48,535	14.9	21.9	16.5
24 45525	Langley Park CDP	13,817	79.6	9.1	17,236	85.8	11.9	39.6	7.3	50,636	11.7	19.4	13.9
24 45900	Laurel city	17,345	39.7	38.5	19,830	78.2	7.4	56.5	14.5	65,640	9.7	14.8	29.4
24 47450	Lochearn CDP	17,622	42.7	23.7	20,321	64.3	10.1	40.0	28.2	51,880	6.7	19.7	20.1
24 52300	Middle River CDP	17,425	52.6	14.3	21,017	71.8	9.4	48.8	20.8	51,115	10.0	19.0	18.3

Table B-4. Cities — What: Education, Employment, and Income, 2010–2012—*Continued*

STATE and Place code	STATE city	Educational attainment			Employment status				Percent of households with no workers	Median household income (dollars)	Percent of families with income below poverty	Percent of households with income less than $25,000	Percent of households with income of $100,000 or more
		Total population 25 years and over	Percent with a high school diploma or less	Percent with a bachelor's degree or more	Total population 16 years and over	Percent in the labor force	Unemployment rate	Percent who worked full-time year-round					
	ACS table number:	C15002	C15002	C15002	B23025	B23025	B23025	C20005	C08202	B19013	C17013	C19001	C19001
	Column number:	1	2	3	4	5	6	7	8	9	10	11	12
	Maryland—Cont.												
24 52562	Milford Mill CDP	21,723	37.9	29.9	25,877	74.5	13.1	49.5	15.8	57,552	5.4	13.8	20.3
24 53325	Montgomery Village CDP	22,091	31.3	44.5	25,445	75.7	5.9	53.9	15.0	72,445	4.2	9.6	34.7
24 56337	North Bethesda CDP	33,714	13.6	70.9	38,060	72.6	4.8	54.0	18.1	104,520	3.9	9.9	52.9
24 56875	North Potomac CDP	15,436	10.7	75.5	18,190	70.9	6.0	49.3	11.5	144,931	1.9	5.3	69.8
24 58300	Odenton CDP	24,326	24.8	44.3	28,527	76.2	5.3	54.3	17.1	98,527	2.7	9.3	49.5
24 58900	Olney CDP	23,551	14.1	62.9	27,542	73.3	6.2	49.9	15.2	123,488	2.2	5.2	61.5
24 59425	Owings Mills CDP	21,532	21.6	48.4	26,539	76.7	6.1	56.2	13.7	73,621	5.8	7.9	31.9
24 60275	Parkville CDP	21,663	46.9	24.2	26,079	72.0	7.9	49.9	20.9	52,666	8.1	19.7	16.5
24 60475	Pasadena CDP	15,865	46.0	25.8	18,904	74.6	6.3	52.0	13.7	94,023	1.7	5.2	43.1
24 60975	Perry Hall CDP	20,332	32.9	39.7	23,792	71.3	5.7	49.2	17.8	74,313	2.0	10.5	33.5
24 61400	Pikesville CDP	24,302	24.7	54.6	26,539	63.2	6.4	41.6	31.3	72,216	6.5	17.6	36.5
24 63300	Potomac CDP	32,366	10.4	79.5	36,639	64.2	4.9	44.3	19.9	175,267	1.6	5.9	73.5
24 64950	Randallstown CDP	20,833	35.3	33.6	24,361	68.4	8.9	44.7	24.6	69,044	7.7	16.7	30.7
24 65600	Reisterstown CDP	17,813	35.7	37.4	21,339	74.4	7.0	46.3	17.4	53,933	12.2	19.3	20.6
24 67675	Rockville city	45,060	21.1	61.4	50,478	72.3	5.2	50.3	19.0	96,650	3.7	9.2	48.3
24 69925	Salisbury city	17,536	45.0	27.7	24,923	57.9	15.7	32.5	32.1	36,674	20.7	35.6	9.6
24 71150	Severn CDP	29,677	36.0	33.4	34,336	73.0	6.8	53.1	15.1	87,181	5.7	10.3	43.3
24 71200	Severna Park CDP	24,992	23.0	56.3	28,933	70.0	9.1	47.1	20.7	118,690	2.4	8.5	58.2
24 72450	Silver Spring CDP	52,731	28.2	53.5	61,222	80.1	8.0	51.2	15.8	69,996	8.7	16.2	32.2
24 73650	South Laurel CDP	16,590	34.8	36.2	19,323	77.1	7.5	54.3	12.4	62,783	5.6	10.9	26.1
24 75725	Suitland CDP	14,564	48.4	14.6	18,374	74.0	12.7	49.8	19.2	54,300	9.9	17.9	15.5
24 78425	Towson CDP	34,944	21.0	61.6	48,153	56.1	5.7	35.6	28.8	69,512	4.7	18.3	34.8
24 81175	Waldorf CDP	44,797	37.1	26.6	54,092	75.8	9.9	55.8	14.4	83,571	7.4	12.6	39.2
24 83775	Wheaton CDP	33,099	45.4	32.7	38,885	79.7	8.7	46.6	13.8	76,761	9.2	11.8	35.1
24 86475	Woodlawn CDP (Baltimore County)	25,729	34.0	33.8	29,722	70.0	11.3	45.7	25.2	61,477	7.1	18.4	21.4
25 00000	**Massachusetts**	4,509,799	36.7	39.2	5,368,399	67.6	9.2	40.7	26.3	65,029	8.3	20.8	31.4
25 00840	Agawam Town city	20,234	40.0	27.6	23,264	69.8	7.0	43.4	27.5	68,140	7.0	18.3	28.9
25 01640	Arlington CDP	32,267	19.9	64.8	35,042	72.6	7.1	49.3	22.7	85,978	1.5	13.8	42.0
25 02690	Attleboro city	30,431	42.7	29.9	34,940	70.5	10.3	44.5	24.9	62,558	6.3	21.4	26.7
25 03690	Barnstable Town city	34,136	32.3	37.5	37,683	60.6	8.3	35.5	34.6	56,381	8.1	23.6	22.8
25 05105	Belmont CDP	17,327	13.0	72.0	19,561	67.1	5.1	45.0	21.3	106,731	4.3	11.1	53.6
25 05595	Beverly city	27,088	29.0	43.3	33,483	68.7	7.0	41.4	26.8	70,504	5.5	19.6	34.3
25 07000	Boston city	405,173	37.9	43.4	534,765	67.9	11.4	39.2	28.4	51,452	17.4	30.8	25.7
25 07740	Braintree Town city	24,967	35.3	35.3	28,988	70.2	8.5	43.8	22.7	84,910	5.4	14.2	38.6
25 09000	Brockton city	59,638	54.6	18.3	73,066	65.7	15.6	36.3	29.8	47,277	16.4	28.5	15.7
25 09210	Brookline CDP	40,613	12.2	78.5	49,366	65.5	5.9	43.9	28.9	81,776	3.2	21.5	43.3
25 09875	Burlington CDP	18,013	29.8	46.4	20,422	69.1	8.1	44.5	22.7	92,786	3.7	12.3	46.5
25 11000	Cambridge city	72,807	15.6	74.3	94,874	67.2	5.8	41.3	26.0	70,757	9.9	19.9	35.5
25 13205	Chelsea city	23,235	68.1	15.2	27,845	71.1	13.7	39.8	25.8	45,319	21.3	31.1	15.9
25 13660	Chicopee city	38,686	54.0	17.8	45,509	62.3	11.0	37.1	35.3	46,396	10.0	26.9	13.0
25 16285	Danvers CDP	19,153	32.0	39.4	21,485	69.6	9.2	44.5	26.6	76,003	3.8	11.0	35.1
25 16530	Dedham CDP	17,922	26.7	48.5	20,386	66.2	7.2	43.0	25.2	88,218	2.0	12.4	42.7
25 21990	Everett city	29,712	59.2	15.4	35,382	73.5	10.5	45.4	23.3	49,717	9.6	22.8	18.3
25 23000	Fall River city	61,779	59.4	14.8	71,811	60.0	16.8	32.5	40.3	32,305	20.4	40.2	8.7
25 23875	Fitchburg city	26,060	50.3	19.6	32,709	64.1	14.9	32.9	31.3	44,742	15.2	30.3	15.0
25 24960	Framingham CDP	48,760	34.8	46.0	56,301	71.1	8.1	43.9	22.7	69,221	6.9	19.8	34.9
25 25172	Franklin Town city	20,237	26.4	51.0	24,211	74.0	7.4	45.3	18.4	100,352	3.6	11.8	50.1
25 25485	Gardner city	14,370	51.4	16.5	16,529	58.6	12.8	32.5	34.4	45,567	12.9	29.8	12.9
25 26150	Gloucester city	21,753	43.0	29.9	24,296	65.9	11.3	34.6	30.3	56,992	6.2	21.9	23.7
25 29405	Haverhill city	42,358	40.6	28.6	49,074	69.5	10.0	43.4	25.0	58,974	10.2	21.9	26.4
25 30840	Holyoke city	25,824	52.3	20.3	30,834	58.1	14.6	30.4	40.3	33,438	30.8	42.9	11.1
25 34550	Lawrence city	44,900	63.7	11.5	56,982	62.0	14.0	34.0	30.6	31,147	29.6	43.0	10.2
25 35075	Leominster city	29,524	45.3	25.6	33,907	70.3	12.3	40.3	28.1	58,244	8.1	23.2	21.8
25 35250	Lexington CDP	22,049	12.3	75.7	24,599	63.0	6.0	41.9	23.3	131,990	4.2	10.1	63.2
25 37000	Lowell city	70,375	53.7	21.4	86,238	67.1	11.5	38.5	28.1	50,599	15.1	26.1	16.7
25 37490	Lynn city	58,684	56.0	18.7	71,301	67.1	13.0	40.6	30.7	43,949	18.9	31.6	18.4
25 37875	Malden city	41,389	47.3	29.2	49,248	71.8	13.1	41.5	24.1	51,614	13.8	25.0	21.2
25 38435	Marblehead CDP	13,826	13.6	69.5	15,295	69.5	5.7	43.4	18.2	105,866	3.9	9.4	53.3
25 38715	Marlborough city	27,114	39.2	41.4	32,105	76.4	6.8	49.2	18.7	69,992	4.9	14.9	33.6
25 39835	Medford city	41,365	34.4	44.5	49,038	70.1	7.1	45.9	21.4	75,366	6.5	14.2	35.3
25 40115	Melrose city	20,061	23.8	50.2	22,254	72.3	4.7	47.8	22.5	84,731	0.8	14.6	41.4
25 40710	Methuen Town city	32,879	43.1	28.5	37,904	68.7	8.4	42.7	27.6	66,670	6.8	19.4	29.0
25 41200	Milford city	17,509	43.0	32.1	20,031	70.3	10.1	41.6	22.9	59,882	11.9	19.9	29.1
25 41725	Milton CDP	16,962	19.5	61.1	21,249	66.5	7.5	41.9	23.6	105,805	3.0	13.5	53.7
25 44140	Needham CDP	19,758	11.8	73.5	22,361	68.0	6.0	43.0	21.6	123,523	1.4	9.3	59.1
25 45000	New Bedford city	64,558	61.6	14.8	75,701	62.5	12.3	33.9	34.9	36,449	18.1	35.7	11.3
25 45560	Newton city	56,214	13.3	75.5	69,253	67.4	5.9	42.8	22.6	117,188	3.9	12.3	56.8
25 46330	Northampton city	19,602	25.3	56.0	24,625	68.4	8.8	35.7	23.7	54,105	8.8	22.9	25.1
25 50285	Norwood CDP	20,516	32.2	40.7	22,969	69.6	5.9	44.3	22.1	76,928	6.6	13.9	35.8
25 52490	Peabody city	37,852	42.4	29.4	42,190	65.5	6.3	42.7	31.3	63,672	4.6	18.0	27.5
25 53960	Pittsfield city	31,662	45.8	24.5	36,244	63.1	10.8	32.9	36.5	39,053	15.3	32.5	11.4

Table B-4. Cities — What: Education, Employment, and Income, 2010–2012—*Continued*

STATE and Place code	STATE city	Educational attainment			Employment status				Percent of households with no workers	Median household income (dollars)	Percent of families with inccme below poverty	Percent of households with income less than $25,000	Percent of households with income of $100,000 or more
		Total population 25 years and over	Percent with a high school diploma or less	Percent with a bachelor's degree or more	Total population 16 years and over	Percent in the labor force	Unemployment rate	Percent who worked full-time year-round					
	ACS table number:	C15002	C15002	C15002	B23025	B23025	B23025	C20005	C08202	B19013	C17013	C19001	C19001
	Column number:	1	2	3	4	5	6	7	8	9	10	11	12
	Massachusetts—Cont.												
25 55745	Quincy city	69,711	37.9	38.7	79,098	71.1	10.5	43.7	24.5	59,332	8.4	20.6	25.5
25 55990	Randolph CDP	22,629	43.0	28.6	26,463	70.4	12.7	40.5	24.9	61,319	11.4	22.7	27.3
25 56165	Reading CDP	17,002	20.5	55.0	19,142	69.9	6.6	45.1	20.1	100,025	1.5	7.6	50.0
25 56585	Revere city	37,955	59.5	18.4	43,031	67.4	11.3	40.2	28.3	49,360	16.4	27.0	17.4
25 59105	Salem city	28,532	33.3	37.6	35,675	70.6	11.0	42.2	28.1	57,644	11.2	25.6	21.7
25 60050	Saugus CDP	20,612	47.3	26.1	22,948	66.7	9.4	41.4	26.4	74,802	3.6	15.9	34.9
25 62535	Somerville city	54,189	32.2	54.1	66,595	74.3	6.9	46.5	19.6	61,306	11.4	22.5	27.6
25 67000	Springfield city	91,879	55.1	17.6	117,425	58.3	16.3	30.3	37.6	34,175	24.4	39.8	10.1
25 67700	Stoneham CDP	15,794	32.9	38.9	17,800	71.0	7.7	43.1	25.8	70,057	3.0	15.6	35.4
25 69170	Taunton city	39,016	55.0	19.3	45,705	66.6	12.9	39.0	30.1	50,971	10.8	24.7	19.1
25 72250	Wakefield CDP	17,889	30.1	44.0	20,326	74.4	7.0	50.4	19.4	83,158	2.7	13.4	40.3
25 72600	Waltham city	41,732	36.4	47.0	53,185	68.2	5.5	41.9	22.0	72,205	7.0	19.1	31.2
25 73440	Watertown Town city	25,059	26.3	56.0	28,106	75.1	7.6	52.1	19.8	84,149	3.1	14.0	40.8
25 74210	Wellesley CDP	16,063	9.0	82.7	21,923	59.7	5.9	34.8	22.7	157,083	2.0	8.1	67.5
25 76030	Westfield city	26,415	40.0	28.1	33,926	64.6	8.5	38.2	28.4	60,674	5.2	23.4	25.7
25 77890	West Springfield Town city	19,716	42.7	27.3	23,188	65.6	11.5	40.2	29.2	52,549	9.1	25.7	20.4
25 78972	Weymouth Town city	39,653	38.6	30.6	44,682	71.0	11.4	43.0	27.2	67,253	4.9	15.1	31.7
25 80195	Wilmington CDP	15,178	36.6	36.8	17,425	73.6	7.8	44.3	16.4	94,463	1.7	8.0	45.4
25 80545	Winchester CDP	14,304	16.4	68.3	15,890	66.3	6.3	45.1	19.3	125,606	1.6	4.0	58.9
25 81035	Woburn city	28,680	43.1	32.2	31,643	71.9	7.1	45.2	23.0	71,692	5.9	15.6	35.1
25 82000	Worcester city	115,536	44.6	29.9	147,054	62.6	11.6	36.6	30.5	43,999	16.9	31.3	17.5
26 00000	**Michigan**	6,593,489	41.7	25.7	7,861,941	61.7	13.1	34.4	32.7	47,175	12.4	26.5	17.4
26 00440	Adrian city	12,624	55.5	20.0	16,761	56.9	18.5	23.9	41.4	28,219	24.1	45.2	8.0
26 01380	Allen Park city	19,378	44.8	22.1	22,973	61.6	13.9	34.4	34.7	54,147	5.6	20.0	18.1
26 03000	Ann Arbor city	65,631	12.5	69.3	101,468	61.6	7.7	31.6	28.2	53,351	6.6	25.0	25.9
26 04105	Auburn Hills city	13,812	30.8	38.9	17,591	69.3	10.7	40.3	21.3	51,636	8.5	21.0	16.4
26 05920	Battle Creek city	34,268	43.9	21.6	40,115	60.0	15.6	33.1	36.3	36,051	19.5	35.8	11.3
26 06020	Bay City city	22,843	51.8	16.5	27,198	61.3	14.1	32.5	37.6	35,845	16.3	36.0	8.2
26 08640	Birmingham city	n.a.	n.a.	n.a.	15,714	67.3	4.6	47.1	19.6	95,521	2.2	10.3	48.2
26 12060	Burton city	20,217	49.0	14.3	23,525	60.1	18.2	32.3	36.4	42,440	14.7	29.2	9.1
26 21000	Dearborn city	58,997	41.5	27.4	71,241	53.7	13.3	30.3	34.1	44,468	24.3	30.5	16.7
26 21020	Dearborn Heights city	38,017	48.7	18.9	44,373	57.0	16.0	31.0	36.0	40,929	16.2	30.4	11.6
26 22000	Detroit city	439,221	55.5	12.7	546,899	53.3	29.8	23.6	47.2	25,576	35.0	49.2	6.0
26 24120	East Lansing city	15,038	10.8	68.8	45,177	50.0	8.3	15.3	29.7	29,696	10.2	46.3	17.3
26 24290	Eastpointe city	20,689	50.5	12.0	24,841	64.0	19.7	31.9	38.5	36,706	21.8	34.8	7.6
26 27440	Farmington Hills city	57,201	22.5	52.2	65,348	65.1	7.5	41.5	25.5	67,526	5.5	18.6	29.1
26 27880	Ferndale city	14,572	30.0	39.8	16,914	74.9	14.0	46.7	24.9	46,673	14.7	22.8	16.4
26 29000	Flint city	62,896	54.4	11.1	77,597	50.8	28.1	21.1	51.2	24,758	35.6	50.4	4.1
26 29580	Forest Hills CDP	17,249	12.3	64.4	19,953	68.9	5.0	42.3	17.7	112,861	1.3	5.5	55.6
26 31420	Garden City city	18,936	52.8	13.2	21,879	66.2	14.2	35.8	29.8	50,239	8.4	20.5	13.3
26 34000	Grand Rapids city	114,675	41.2	28.9	146,609	67.0	13.8	34.9	30.3	37,791	20.9	33.4	10.3
26 36280	Hamtramck city	11,992	68.5	11.5	15,531	50.6	21.8	23.7	38.2	25,385	38.9	49.2	5.2
26 37100	Haslett CDP	13,845	17.1	56.1	17,145	64.7	8.6	36.2	28.9	53,638	10.4	26.5	24.0
26 38640	Holland city	18,798	45.6	29.7	25,886	61.7	8.7	31.9	28.4	40,260	14.3	27.8	12.3
26 38780	Holt CDP	16,347	29.0	33.1	18,327	69.7	8.4	45.1	23.7	58,787	8.6	15.7	27.0
26 40680	Inkster city	14,734	51.9	11.4	18,214	55.1	26.4	24.5	45.6	26,181	33.9	48.3	4.5
26 41420	Jackson city	20,197	49.0	14.1	24,523	59.8	21.2	28.1	41.0	26,586	32.9	46.9	5.2
26 42160	Kalamazoo city	38,972	31.9	32.1	61,277	63.8	14.4	27.8	33.4	31,109	24.2	41.6	10.1
26 42820	Kentwood city	32,142	38.9	31.0	39,172	69.5	10.0	42.0	24.9	47,275	11.2	24.7	14.2
26 46000	Lansing city	71,951	39.7	24.0	89,952	66.3	14.9	32.6	32.5	34,420	23.9	36.9	6.3
26 47800	Lincoln Park city	24,889	60.1	8.1	29,296	58.2	14.6	30.8	33.6	37,135	17.6	30.4	7.0
26 49000	Livonia city	69,351	31.4	35.0	79,383	63.4	9.0	38.0	29.5	67,767	4.5	14.0	28.1
26 50560	Madison Heights city	21,405	46.5	20.7	24,730	65.0	15.3	34.9	32.9	37,624	14.5	30.5	9.6
26 51900	Marquette city	12,282	34.8	36.2	19,132	56.3	8.5	27.4	33.2	36,016	12.4	38.9	13.4
26 53780	Midland city	28,139	28.6	42.0	33,767	60.4	8.1	34.8	32.4	50,216	9.6	26.3	23.3
26 55020	Monroe city	13,502	47.7	18.3	16,092	59.7	9.2	33.8	30.9	43,311	15.9	29.2	11.1
26 56020	Mount Pleasant city	9,391	30.2	41.0	23,744	56.0	13.0	18.2	29.2	27,969	20.5	48.0	11.1
26 56320	Muskegon city	24,824	57.6	11.5	29,996	52.2	24.5	23.4	43.3	25,531	29.9	49.3	4.8
26 59140	Norton Shores city	16,428	35.1	29.3	19,718	61.2	11.6	36.2	33.9	49,469	5.6	22.4	17.8
26 59440	Novi city	38,390	20.0	54.1	44,018	70.2	6.8	47.7	22.9	76,462	4.6	11.9	37.7
26 59920	Oak Park city	18,971	33.7	28.1	23,209	63.7	17.5	33.8	29.0	45,481	16.9	28.8	13.8
26 60340	Okemos CDP	13,420	11.1	67.5	17,067	66.2	6.8	38.6	24.3	69,375	6.1	21.6	34.2
26 65440	Pontiac city	36,679	55.6	12.6	45,565	60.3	21.9	27.2	38.6	26,584	32.0	47.8	5.0
26 65560	Portage city	31,190	26.5	39.8	36,648	68.2	9.9	41.9	28.3	54,186	8.6	22.2	21.1
26 65820	Port Huron city	19,314	48.6	14.1	23,231	59.8	19.3	28.1	39.2	31,527	23.2	43.0	7.2
26 69035	Rochester Hills city	50,092	21.5	49.0	56,976	67.4	8.4	42.0	24.8	75,419	5.1	14.4	36.8
26 69420	Romulus city	15,598	52.2	9.7	18,326	61.4	17.2	33.3	31.5	42,634	16.3	30.4	8.3
26 69800	Roseville city	32,586	55.5	10.1	37,684	64.8	15.5	34.9	34.5	39,288	13.7	30.6	6.5
26 70040	Royal Oak city	44,273	23.1	48.3	49,816	74.6	7.4	49.7	23.6	61,138	4.2	18.8	26.8
26 70520	Saginaw city	31,158	59.3	10.5	39,019	55.4	24.7	26.0	44.5	27,630	33.1	46.3	4.7

Table B-4. Cities — What: Education, Employment, and Income, 2010–2012—*Continued*

STATE and Place code	STATE city	Educational attainment			Employment status				Percent of households with no workers	Median household income (dollars)	Percent of families with income below poverty	Percent of households with income less than $25,000	Percent of households with income of $100,000 or more
		Total population 25 years and over	Percent with a high school diploma or less	Percent with a bachelor's degree or more	Total population 16 years and over	Percent in the labor force	Unemployment rate	Percent who worked full-time year-round					
	ACS table number:	C15002	C15002	C15002	B23025	B23025	B23025	C20005	C08202	B19013	C17013	C19001	C19001
	Column number:	1	2	3	4	5	6	7	8	9	10	11	12
	Michigan—Cont.												
26 70760	St. Clair Shores city	44,365	40.2	22.5	49,628	64.3	12.0	37.7	34.6	50,988	8.8	22.8	16.0
26 74900	Southfield city	51,308	27.9	36.9	59,196	60.1	15.4	35.7	35.3	47,744	12.4	25.1	17.2
26 74960	Southgate city	21,051	48.6	16.5	25,172	60.6	12.7	35.3	36.0	45,242	8.3	24.1	15.3
26 76460	Sterling Heights city	90,862	43.1	25.2	105,999	63.8	12.2	37.4	28.2	55,033	10.2	20.3	22.0
26 79000	Taylor city	41,443	56.4	9.3	49,087	61.8	19.8	30.9	35.6	40,324	19.5	30.3	8.0
26 80700	Troy city	56,549	21.9	55.9	65,268	64.9	9.1	40.4	23.2	81,070	5.9	14.4	37.4
26 82960	Walker city	15,925	35.1	28.3	19,148	70.3	8.3	44.5	23.7	50,335	8.7	24.5	15.6
26 84000	Warren city	90,380	52.5	16.6	107,082	61.2	15.2	34.2	35.3	42,671	16.4	29.1	11.2
26 84800	Waverly CDP	17,174	27.8	35.3	20,291	63.8	10.6	40.5	33.5	52,495	6.7	21.3	15.7
26 86000	Westland city	57,241	46.9	17.0	67,622	63.8	14.4	35.9	33.3	42,808	12.4	29.8	13.4
26 88900	Wyandotte city	18,360	50.2	15.3	20,993	65.2	12.2	37.3	33.5	49,661	9.3	26.9	15.1
26 88940	Wyoming city	46,110	50.2	18.3	55,455	73.2	11.4	42.6	22.6	44,287	13.2	23.4	9.7
26 89140	Ypsilanti city	9,797	34.9	29.1	16,901	63.6	15.3	25.9	34.0	30,551	27.1	45.4	9.0
27 00000	**Minnesota**	3,562,974	34.7	32.6	4,212,521	70.3	7.4	43.1	24.1	58,434	7.6	20.0	23.8
27 01486	Andover city	19,060	29.0	33.0	22,880	77.1	6.9	48.5	12.2	85,527	3.9	7.5	39.9
27 01900	Apple Valley city	33,014	21.2	45.5	38,509	75.9	7.3	49.0	17.6	74,635	3.6	10.9	35.2
27 02908	Austin city	15,918	45.8	18.7	19,304	66.9	8.8	37.0	33.4	37,417	15.2	34.5	11.9
27 06382	Blaine city	39,039	32.2	30.1	44,568	76.0	8.1	48.4	17.4	69,938	3.4	10.6	29.5
27 06616	Bloomington city	61,552	29.2	39.8	69,764	68.5	8.4	41.2	26.8	59,637	6.4	16.5	25.0
27 07948	Brooklyn Center city	19,641	48.6	19.0	23,118	67.0	11.3	40.6	26.0	45,166	18.9	26.3	10.3
27 07966	Brooklyn Park city	46,698	34.0	31.6	56,525	73.9	9.3	46.4	17.0	58,549	11.3	16.8	26.0
27 08794	Burnsville city	41,398	28.8	34.5	48,585	73.3	8.3	45.1	21.4	60,806	7.7	17.1	23.5
27 10846	Champlin city	16,090	26.8	34.2	18,585	80.3	4.2	54.1	14.3	80,077	1.9	10.7	35.6
27 10918	Chanhassen city	15,352	14.2	59.2	17,321	75.3	5.5	53.9	14.2	104,244	1.1	6.5	52.8
27 10972	Chaska city	15,498	25.9	41.2	17,841	76.7	5.1	50.7	15.9	69,213	4.4	12.4	30.9
27 13114	Coon Rapids city	40,727	35.6	25.0	48,311	74.2	9.1	46.7	21.2	62,102	7.2	15.4	23.8
27 13456	Cottage Grove city	21,993	30.8	34.5	25,629	78.4	5.5	51.6	15.1	79,421	5.5	9.1	34.4
27 14158	Crystal city	16,316	36.3	28.7	17,960	70.3	5.1	48.6	22.8	58,217	5.4	15.6	18.1
27 17000	Duluth city	53,222	32.2	31.9	72,407	64.9	9.8	32.4	30.0	40,606	13.3	32.3	14.6
27 17288	Eagan city	43,182	19.8	49.8	50,093	77.6	6.1	52.9	16.7	78,093	4.9	11.4	37.9
27 18116	Eden Prairie city	40,698	14.2	59.7	46,495	75.4	6.4	49.5	16.4	92,008	4.1	10.1	46.6
27 18188	Edina city	33,950	12.3	67.2	38,232	63.4	5.9	40.7	31.3	83,769	2.4	13.4	43.6
27 18674	Elk River city	14,659	30.8	30.7	17,467	75.3	7.6	46.9	15.5	70,843	4.1	8.0	28.2
27 20546	Faribault city	15,732	52.1	20.5	17,983	61.3	11.1	35.5	24.9	50,897	12.5	21.0	13.3
27 20618	Farmington city	13,337	25.1	33.6	15,045	80.7	5.3	56.6	11.2	86,309	0.3	7.4	37.7
27 22814	Fridley city	18,270	39.4	26.4	21,568	67.5	9.2	42.5	27.0	53,310	10.4	18.5	15.3
27 24308	Golden Valley city	15,430	21.5	52.2	16,773	69.9	4.4	46.0	24.8	77,782	4.4	14.1	38.8
27 27530	Hastings city	15,182	38.4	26.1	17,238	71.1	7.4	44.6	22.3	63,791	4.4	14.2	27.0
27 31076	Inver Grove Heights city	22,731	34.7	31.2	27,129	72.7	8.0	45.1	21.2	61,729	4.4	14.1	28.7
27 35180	Lakeville city	35,545	23.5	45.3	41,194	77.9	5.3	51.3	14.1	91,827	3.4	8.7	46.4
27 37322	Lino Lakes city	13,290	31.1	38.0	15,591	72.2	6.0	48.0	11.4	98,989	3.4	9.1	48.8
27 39878	Mankato city	20,630	30.1	35.4	34,021	71.0	7.6	34.5	25.2	40,309	12.1	31.7	12.5
27 40166	Maple Grove city	43,192	20.9	48.2	48,097	79.0	5.7	55.5	13.2	90,304	3.3	7.7	45.1
27 40382	Maplewood city	26,914	38.7	28.5	30,955	64.8	7.2	41.2	26.5	56,430	7.1	18.3	21.9
27 43000	Minneapolis city	252,879	28.7	46.2	316,645	73.0	10.3	41.5	23.6	48,228	16.9	28.0	21.2
27 43252	Minnetonka city	37,177	17.3	54.3	41,546	70.2	6.8	46.0	23.0	75,945	2.6	12.6	38.3
27 43864	Moorhead city	22,275	32.8	32.9	31,544	72.6	6.7	41.2	24.4	47,837	7.5	28.0	15.2
27 45430	New Brighton city	15,121	24.7	45.7	17,286	65.3	6.3	39.5	28.6	59,489	8.7	17.3	27.0
27 45628	New Hope city	14,556	36.0	30.9	16,432	66.6	7.1	40.5	26.3	52,200	8.8	22.5	17.6
27 46924	Northfield city	9,747	24.3	49.2	17,225	70.7	6.3	26.0	29.9	54,357	8.7	28.4	27.6
27 47680	Oakdale city	17,789	32.2	28.9	21,184	74.0	6.9	46.8	20.8	66,190	4.8	14.6	24.8
27 49300	Owatonna city	16,887	42.7	28.0	19,578	71.4	6.6	45.6	27.3	52,206	6.8	22.8	17.9
27 51730	Plymouth city	50,200	16.9	56.7	57,244	71.8	6.4	47.8	19.7	84,639	4.5	10.9	41.6
27 52594	Prior Lake city	14,798	22.8	43.2	17,155	77.0	5.9	51.3	17.6	93,219	5.1	13.1	46.0
27 53026	Ramsey city	15,167	30.8	24.9	17,680	80.9	7.8	53.9	12.3	80,085	2.4	8.3	33.3
27 54214	Richfield city	25,500	37.5	32.9	29,106	74.3	8.6	45.3	24.8	52,072	10.6	20.8	19.5
27 54880	Rochester city	72,554	27.7	41.0	83,747	72.3	3.9	47.0	20.0	61,547	4.9	18.9	24.9
27 55726	Rosemount city	13,683	23.2	39.6	16,047	76.9	5.4	47.7	13.8	83,142	4.8	10.7	41.1
27 55852	Roseville city	24,288	27.8	46.4	28,678	65.0	5.7	39.0	31.4	59,718	5.1	18.0	24.9
27 56896	St. Cloud city	38,385	34.0	28.2	54,503	67.1	11.2	33.2	27.1	42,140	13.8	30.8	13.2
27 57220	St. Louis Park city	32,916	19.4	54.1	37,846	74.9	5.7	49.3	19.7	63,642	7.7	15.8	25.8
27 58000	St. Paul city	175,919	36.3	37.3	223,954	70.0	10.6	39.5	24.6	45,782	18.0	28.9	17.1
27 58738	Savage city	17,139	24.3	44.7	19,958	81.5	6.8	52.9	9.1	92,224	1.8	4.6	44.7
27 59350	Shakopee city	24,267	32.2	40.0	27,997	78.9	6.6	55.2	11.1	76,916	4.6	11.8	33.2
27 59998	Shoreview city	18,472	23.7	50.5	20,590	68.2	6.2	45.5	24.7	78,184	3.5	11.7	36.1
27 61492	South St. Paul city	13,947	36.7	22.6	16,346	73.6	10.9	46.2	23.0	55,362	9.0	22.0	14.0
27 69970	White Bear Lake city	16,744	32.7	29.9	18,773	65.7	5.1	40.1	28.8	59,323	2.7	15.3	20.3
27 71032	Winona city	15,228	37.8	31.0	24,749	70.7	11.1	31.2	27.1	38,194	4.9	34.2	14.3
27 71428	Woodbury city	41,289	16.8	56.7	47,050	76.2	4.5	53.2	14.2	96,107	2.2	7.8	47.1

Table B-4. Cities — What: Education, Employment, and Income, 2010–2012—*Continued*

STATE and Place code	STATE city	Educational attainment			Employment status				Percent of households with no workers	Median household income (dollars)	Percent of families with income below poverty	Percent of households with income less than $25,000	Percent of households with income of $100,000 or more
		Total population 25 years and over	Percent with a high school diploma or less	Percent with a bachelor's degree or more	Total population 16 years and over	Percent in the labor force	Unemployment rate	Percent who worked full-time year-round					
	ACS table number:	C15002	C15002	C15002	B23025	B23025	B23025	C20005	C08202	B19013	C17013	C19001	C19001
	Column number:	1	2	3	4	5	6	7	8	9	10	11	12
28 00000	**Mississippi**	1,914,622	49.0	20.0	2,311,888	58.5	11.6	37.3	31.9	37,792	18.2	34.7	12.4
28 06220	Biloxi city	28,478	40.2	24.6	36,143	68.7	8.5	40.6	27.1	37,826	19.2	35.5	12.1
28 08300	Brandon city	15,189	32.4	38.6	17,117	65.7	5.8	49.3	18.9	71,076	7.1	12.9	34.6
28 14420	Clinton city	15,933	25.7	44.3	20,468	64.4	6.0	41.5	24.0	54,605	8.1	20.4	23.8
28 15380	Columbus city	15,542	52.1	18.9	18,806	58.3	18.3	32.2	38.8	24,749	36.6	50.3	9.0
28 29180	Greenville city	21,269	51.0	20.1	25,422	60.1	23.9	32.8	35.9	28,734	31.6	46.1	8.3
28 29700	Gulfport city	44,780	46.1	19.9	53,587	63.7	12.2	37.5	29.5	36,726	21.6	33.7	11.1
28 31020	Hattiesburg city	26,282	42.4	31.0	38,309	62.6	13.9	30.5	32.7	24,064	32.2	50.9	8.2
28 33700	Horn Lake city	15,536	50.9	10.9	18,832	71.7	11.2	47.1	19.5	45,121	14.2	25.9	9.1
28 36000	Jackson city	105,223	41.8	25.3	132,203	61.1	13.7	39.0	29.8	32,232	25.2	39.6	9.9
28 44520	Madison city	15,833	14.1	64.4	17,903	71.2	6.2	53.2	16.8	95,112	5.5	9.7	46.8
28 46640	Meridian city	26,068	44.6	21.7	31,160	57.2	14.0	36.0	34.0	28,137	30.0	45.9	11.8
28 54040	Olive Branch city	22,134	40.2	26.8	26,553	71.2	8.3	51.6	17.9	60,291	5.2	14.6	22.6
28 54840	Oxford city	9,437	23.8	53.3	16,274	55.4	11.7	26.2	32.8	30,996	15.7	43.5	14.9
28 55360	Pascagoula city	14,438	47.3	18.9	17,573	58.7	11.3	39.0	29.4	40,187	19.3	34.1	12.5
28 55760	Pearl city	16,800	45.1	17.6	20,301	65.9	9.4	48.9	22.2	40,556	8.4	25.5	13.8
28 62520	Ridgeland city	16,529	19.5	52.1	19,639	73.5	4.6	58.3	17.0	53,366	5.2	20.4	19.7
28 69280	Southaven city	31,421	39.1	21.2	36,747	69.9	8.2	49.4	19.9	55,829	7.3	19.5	19.7
28 70240	Starkville city	12,806	27.5	46.7	20,141	60.7	14.4	32.2	33.0	28,099	20.1	46.4	13.4
28 74840	Tupelo city	22,685	41.4	26.9	26,618	61.6	6.6	39.3	27.5	41,478	25.4	35.6	14.4
28 76720	Vicksburg city	15,297	49.5	20.8	18,322	52.7	10.7	34.9	39.0	24,855	30.7	50.3	7.7
29 00000	**Missouri**	4,005,241	44.1	26.1	4,758,971	64.2	9.2	40.4	28.7	46,068	11.2	26.5	16.6
29 01972	Arnold city	14,211	42.8	19.8	16,635	69.8	8.2	42.1	25.7	54,931	3.1	14.8	18.7
29 03160	Ballwin city	20,835	15.7	54.5	24,054	69.7	5.2	43.4	17.7	82,371	2.1	10.2	38.9
29 04384	Belton city	14,051	41.4	20.4	17,095	70.2	9.9	45.7	22.4	49,445	11.7	20.1	14.3
29 06652	Blue Springs city	34,314	36.6	26.8	40,577	71.0	7.6	47.2	19.9	61,870	6.7	15.6	20.8
29 11242	Cape Girardeau city	24,248	39.8	32.1	31,411	62.8	9.4	36.0	29.4	38,479	15.3	32.3	14.5
29 13600	Chesterfield city	33,807	14.0	64.4	38,160	63.6	5.6	41.4	25.5	94,406	2.7	11.4	46.9
29 15670	Columbia city	59,603	21.1	56.0	91,980	66.9	6.7	37.3	22.3	41,576	10.3	32.6	17.6
29 23986	Ferguson city	13,522	40.7	24.3	16,198	65.1	13.2	40.8	28.4	35,215	20.6	37.2	7.8
29 24778	Florissant city	34,796	42.5	20.5	41,676	68.2	11.8	42.5	27.4	49,833	6.8	21.5	12.2
29 27190	Gladstone city	18,008	39.9	25.8	20,683	66.8	9.6	41.7	29.5	50,098	8.2	21.1	16.2
29 28324	Grandview city	15,946	46.9	17.1	19,336	72.3	10.6	44.5	23.5	41,421	10.2	24.3	8.7
29 31276	Hazelwood city	16,968	38.4	24.4	19,995	71.6	11.5	48.1	24.7	42,282	11.4	23.7	13.7
29 35000	Independence city	80,470	50.8	17.2	92,830	61.2	9.7	39.8	32.6	42,825	13.9	29.8	11.7
29 37000	Jefferson City city	29,632	37.6	33.3	35,125	59.8	5.9	42.7	27.3	45,610	11.4	26.0	17.7
29 37592	Joplin city	33,348	45.8	22.0	41,589	66.3	9.9	39.8	30.5	36,348	14.5	35.4	10.6
29 38000	Kansas City city	306,325	38.4	31.3	362,639	68.9	10.6	43.6	26.1	44,277	15.5	28.6	16.8
29 39044	Kirkwood city	19,821	17.4	61.2	22,309	66.1	3.9	45.9	25.5	75,775	3.0	16.2	37.6
29 41348	Lee's Summit city	59,668	25.0	41.9	69,424	72.8	6.6	48.5	20.8	73,937	5.3	13.2	34.2
29 42032	Liberty city	19,292	34.6	36.8	23,302	66.5	10.3	43.0	25.8	61,884	5.8	13.7	24.7
29 46586	Maryland Heights city	19,497	35.9	34.6	22,584	72.7	10.0	48.6	20.4	54,895	6.5	18.3	19.3
29 47180	Mehlville CDP	21,791	47.3	22.0	25,831	65.2	9.4	38.6	28.6	45,388	10.1	25.8	14.3
29 53876	Oakville CDP	26,025	29.4	36.9	30,151	69.0	5.5	44.0	21.5	80,898	2.1	8.8	37.6
29 54074	O'Fallon city	50,328	32.8	36.9	59,150	75.7	5.7	52.9	16.9	74,960	4.4	11.9	32.6
29 54352	Old Jamestown CDP	13,514	32.5	35.2	15,743	65.6	6.8	44.9	20.9	72,883	2.3	11.9	32.3
29 60788	Raytown city	19,714	44.2	23.8	22,805	64.8	6.7	43.2	29.1	48,883	10.6	22.6	13.9
29 64082	St. Charles city	43,480	37.8	34.0	54,510	67.8	7.8	44.2	24.8	54,934	9.5	17.5	22.7
29 64550	St. Joseph city	49,897	51.0	20.7	60,989	63.5	10.0	37.6	30.1	40,742	14.0	32.3	10.8
29 65000	St. Louis city	213,457	42.8	29.1	258,781	65.3	15.9	38.0	32.7	33,299	22.2	39.2	11.1
29 65126	St. Peters city	36,622	31.1	34.4	42,669	73.3	6.9	50.0	19.6	67,647	1.8	11.5	26.3
29 66440	Sedalia city	13,855	50.8	15.8	16,517	61.3	7.5	39.2	35.2	28,980	19.6	44.5	8.5
29 69266	Spanish Lake CDP	11,758	47.4	17.7	13,720	63.8	20.5	33.8	35.8	30,437	27.1	40.6	9.6
29 70000	Springfield city	100,815	39.8	26.4	134,873	63.5	10.5	34.8	30.4	32,359	17.9	38.4	7.5
29 75220	University City city	24,856	23.5	51.8	29,266	65.9	10.8	43.3	30.2	52,708	14.1	26.5	24.9
29 78154	Webster Groves city	15,649	12.8	66.0	18,052	68.8	4.2	48.1	23.8	86,506	2.3	15.4	40.7
29 78442	Wentzville city	18,886	30.9	32.2	21,409	75.1	5.3	52.1	13.2	67,591	3.4	10.1	29.3
29 79820	Wildwood city	23,130	12.5	64.8	26,480	70.6	3.9	48.9	13.8	121,258	2.8	6.5	61.2
30 00000	**Montana**	678,572	37.8	28.8	800,999	64.7	7.6	38.9	28.3	45,072	10.0	26.9	14.5
30 06550	Billings city	71,525	36.9	30.8	83,980	67.6	5.3	42.3	25.1	46,655	10.6	26.0	16.3
30 08950	Bozeman city	21,188	14.8	55.4	32,935	71.9	8.2	38.0	18.1	44,106	7.2	28.5	15.7
30 11397	Butte-Silver Bow (balance)	22,933	45.6	23.4	27,369	61.4	7.1	36.5	34.2	38,507	12.6	32.8	11.7
30 32800	Great Falls city	39,760	40.6	22.2	46,958	63.4	5.8	38.9	29.4	42,171	13.4	27.5	11.7
30 35600	Helena city	19,944	23.2	47.3	23,826	66.7	5.3	43.5	28.3	49,635	8.5	23.8	17.4
30 40075	Kalispell city	12,913	34.8	27.9	15,445	66.6	11.8	39.1	32.3	38,340	12.0	33.5	8.5
30 50200	Missoula city	42,400	23.6	44.8	56,698	70.7	9.5	35.8	24.2	40,369	9.9	32.0	13.1
31 00000	**Nebraska**	1,196,710	37.7	28.5	1,431,553	70.8	6.1	46.8	23.0	50,957	8.9	22.9	17.8
31 03950	Bellevue city	33,558	35.6	27.1	39,719	71.4	8.7	46.9	23.2	57,882	9.7	18.0	18.0
31 10110	Columbus city	14,754	38.8	20.2	17,044	73.9	5.5	49.4	20.5	50,029	6.7	17.7	13.4
31 17670	Fremont city	17,655	50.3	20.2	20,461	68.8	7.7	43.7	25.3	43,271	11.1	25.6	10.5
31 19595	Grand Island city	31,658	51.6	16.7	37,498	72.7	7.0	48.9	23.5	43,249	13.7	26.2	11.5
31 21415	Hastings city	16,134	45.3	19.5	19,587	69.0	5.8	45.7	25.3	42,089	9.3	27.9	11.4
31 25055	Kearney city	17,679	30.3	36.0	24,863	75.0	5.1	45.1	17.7	46,046	8.2	25.3	18.4
31 28000	Lincoln city	161,699	29.7	35.8	208,839	72.3	7.3	44.2	21.9	48,295	10.2	24.5	17.2

STATE and Place code	STATE city	Educational attainment			Employment status				Percent of households with no workers	Median household income (dollars)	Percent of families with income below poverty	Percent of households with income less than $25,000	Percent of households with income of $100,000 or more
		Total population 25 years and over	Percent with a high school diploma or less	Percent with a bachelor's degree or more	Total population 16 years and over	Percent in the labor force	Unemployment rate	Percent who worked full-time year-round					
	ACS table number:	C15002	C15002	C15002	B23025	B23025	B23025	C20005	C08202	B19013	C17013	C19001	C19001
	Column number:	1	2	3	4	5	6	7	8	9	10	11	12
	Nebraska—Cont.												
31 34615	Norfolk city	14,844	37.6	25.0	18,483	71.2	5.7	44.3	24.9	39,626	13.2	31.6	13.0
31 35000	North Platte city	16,323	46.1	15.6	18,912	67.3	4.9	42.4	27.8	42,264	10.3	31.2	11.6
31 37000	Omaha city	267,113	35.9	32.8	323,389	70.9	8.4	44.7	24.1	46,202	12.6	26.5	16.8
31 38295	Papillion city	12,807	26.7	39.7	15,157	72.6	4.7	50.8	18.5	72,605	2.4	11.9	33.2
32 00000	**Nevada**	1,813,077	44.7	22.2	2,139,247	65.6	13.0	39.6	26.3	50,949	11.9	22.6	19.0
32 09700	Carson City	38,648	42.9	20.3	44,857	62.1	16.5	34.1	34.7	52,436	11.0	23.2	16.0
32 23770	Enterprise CDP	80,564	36.6	31.2	93,663	74.9	9.4	49.7	13.0	67,185	7.3	12.9	26.4
32 31900	Henderson city	181,566	34.7	30.8	208,637	65.5	11.3	41.8	25.3	62,720	7.1	15.8	27.5
32 40000	Las Vegas city	389,374	46.8	21.4	459,099	64.8	13.9	38.5	27.4	49,726	13.3	23.9	18.0
32 51800	North Las Vegas city	128,765	52.9	15.1	158,051	66.5	12.6	42.9	20.6	51,836	14.6	20.9	16.4
32 53800	Pahrump CDP	25,953	51.0	13.9	28,924	43.1	20.6	22.9	50.4	39,812	14.6	30.7	11.4
32 54600	Paradise CDP	150,355	48.3	20.3	177,356	68.7	13.7	40.5	25.6	44,362	13.3	27.0	13.7
32 60600	Reno city	147,155	38.7	28.4	180,759	66.5	11.9	38.4	27.2	44,318	14.3	28.4	17.0
32 68400	Sparks city	61,117	43.8	21.2	71,687	68.9	11.3	42.9	24.6	50,925	10.7	21.0	19.5
32 68585	Spring Valley CDP	126,922	42.3	23.8	149,790	70.9	12.1	42.6	21.6	49,956	10.5	20.3	16.8
32 70900	Summerlin South CDP	17,970	25.9	45.6	19,571	62.9	10.5	40.2	29.4	88,512	3.3	10.2	43.5
32 71400	Sunrise Manor CDP	110,693	62.0	9.5	136,820	65.0	18.3	35.3	28.5	37,796	21.6	31.3	9.3
32 83800	Whitney CDP	25,778	49.7	18.0	30,094	71.8	15.7	43.9	20.4	44,802	12.7	20.3	12.1
32 84600	Winchester CDP	19,830	61.4	16.3	23,128	61.9	17.8	32.6	34.3	34,967	22.1	33.4	10.9
33 00000	**New Hampshire**	913,752	37.9	33.7	1,073,282	69.2	7.0	43.7	23.7	63,962	5.9	17.2	27.9
33 14200	Concord city	30,213	33.5	33.7	34,862	65.8	7.7	42.5	24.8	52,310	6.8	21.1	20.2
33 17860	Derry CDP	15,089	43.5	26.7	17,500	74.7	6.4	45.2	20.8	51,392	9.3	23.4	20.9
33 18820	Dover city	20,236	28.9	38.2	24,901	74.5	7.9	45.0	21.0	54,361	5.5	17.3	23.1
33 39300	Keene city	14,218	38.6	37.0	20,141	62.8	12.4	33.4	31.4	50,483	6.6	25.4	18.3
33 45140	Manchester city	75,383	46.6	26.2	89,161	70.8	8.9	46.1	25.2	54,122	10.7	22.1	19.7
33 50260	Nashua city	59,540	36.0	35.9	69,682	71.5	8.4	45.6	23.9	65,955	7.1	20.0	29.5
33 62900	Portsmouth city	16,353	24.1	53.1	18,173	73.4	4.6	48.7	23.4	66,526	3.9	16.8	30.2
33 65140	Rochester city	21,285	51.5	18.9	24,747	65.2	7.8	41.2	31.7	46,458	12.8	23.5	13.3
34 00000	**New Jersey**	6,013,231	41.0	35.8	7,033,377	66.5	10.6	42.2	24.8	70,062	7.9	17.7	34.2
34 02080	Atlantic City city	25,847	65.5	14.6	30,215	62.1	17.8	31.9	39.1	28,997	28.7	44.6	8.2
34 03580	Bayonne city	45,155	49.6	30.5	52,093	64.5	8.8	46.2	26.8	55,971	12.1	22.2	23.6
34 05170	Bergenfield borough	18,876	37.8	38.6	21,973	68.7	7.7	46.5	20.9	74,658	8.4	17.7	36.3
34 07600	Bridgeton city	15,781	76.5	5.8	19,532	50.1	16.9	28.1	33.3	39,890	32.2	36.6	13.0
34 10000	Camden city	43,620	68.0	8.3	55,645	57.1	24.8	29.4	42.6	25,366	36.6	49.5	7.4
34 10750	Carteret borough	15,481	51.7	21.1	18,511	69.3	16.3	36.4	24.7	60,642	12.3	21.5	18.2
34 13570	Cliffside Park borough	18,280	43.2	37.6	20,177	60.2	10.7	42.4	32.4	48,810	12.1	28.1	25.2
34 13690	Clifton city	56,858	45.0	29.8	67,260	67.8	9.1	46.2	22.7	62,664	7.4	18.3	28.4
34 19390	East Orange city	42,431	52.8	15.7	50,536	65.8	20.3	36.6	35.9	35,948	18.8	37.2	11.6
34 21000	Elizabeth city	78,376	67.2	11.5	94,416	71.5	13.3	44.0	22.8	43,070	17.9	27.3	14.0
34 21480	Englewood city	19,461	36.3	46.4	22,125	68.4	7.8	47.3	24.7	70,658	7.3	19.8	37.1
34 22470	Fair Lawn borough	22,962	26.0	52.0	26,019	69.7	9.2	48.1	20.9	99,804	3.1	13.5	49.9
34 24420	Fort Lee borough	27,839	29.1	52.1	30,495	61.1	7.9	42.9	30.8	64,272	6.4	20.0	32.6
34 25770	Garfield city	20,747	60.1	18.7	24,673	65.2	10.7	44.5	24.1	43,923	10.0	27.2	15.0
34 28680	Hackensack city	31,663	45.8	32.0	36,299	67.2	8.1	51.0	22.7	54,968	14.8	22.5	24.4
34 32250	Hoboken city	38,332	16.8	73.9	44,532	78.2	3.5	63.2	14.4	103,617	10.7	13.9	52.3
34 34470	Iselin CDP	13,987	40.7	40.2	16,119	66.3	8.1	43.3	19.5	76,707	4.7	9.9	37.3
34 36000	Jersey City city	174,786	38.8	42.1	205,250	66.9	11.4	46.9	20.4	57,274	16.0	25.2	28.1
34 36510	Kearny town	27,436	56.0	19.9	32,470	69.5	14.4	48.6	20.1	64,030	7.4	15.0	26.1
34 38580	Lakewood CDP	19,986	48.1	25.6	27,799	56.3	7.5	21.6	23.4	37,915	33.2	35.0	11.7
34 40350	Linden city	28,603	58.1	17.4	33,534	69.0	12.9	45.4	25.9	59,922	6.9	19.3	23.4
34 41100	Lodi borough	16,658	48.5	25.4	19,574	66.9	9.3	43.8	23.7	48,391	9.5	21.0	19.4
34 41310	Long Branch city	20,734	51.8	26.7	24,394	69.9	13.7	35.6	28.1	46,919	15.2	28.3	19.4
34 46680	Millville city	18,574	59.4	15.0	22,133	66.7	14.7	38.9	32.4	49,657	14.6	26.8	18.9
34 51000	Newark city	173,215	64.1	13.2	213,625	62.9	21.1	34.0	33.0	32,385	27.6	40.0	9.3
34 51210	New Brunswick city	25,419	64.5	20.4	44,714	61.1	10.2	33.9	22.9	36,705	24.1	33.7	11.5
34 53280	North Plainfield borough	14,516	49.7	23.0	16,940	79.7	7.4	49.0	15.0	62,767	12.0	13.9	26.8
34 54690	Old Bridge CDP	16,277	37.6	33.8	19,093	68.0	8.7	41.3	22.7	98,927	1.5	10.4	49.4
34 55950	Paramus borough	19,663	30.7	48.6	21,931	59.5	6.7	39.5	25.8	98,162	2.0	8.7	49.3
34 56550	Passaic city	40,002	71.0	13.2	50,478	59.8	12.7	37.2	28.3	30,237	27.9	41.7	9.4
34 57000	Paterson city	88,576	68.5	10.9	109,935	57.7	13.7	40.0	32.4	32,969	24.7	37.7	10.5
34 58200	Perth Amboy city	32,183	66.4	15.8	39,062	59.2	7.1	42.9	23.8	42,065	20.1	31.7	14.8
34 59190	Plainfield city	32,703	57.5	18.2	39,664	75.8	14.7	44.4	22.1	51,453	19.3	24.7	22.2
34 59640	Pleasantville city	12,779	64.7	10.5	15,638	71.4	20.7	34.1	24.8	38,343	20.9	30.7	12.2
34 61530	Rahway city	19,454	45.8	25.6	22,159	69.4	12.3	45.2	26.2	56,957	9.1	19.6	24.7
34 63000	Ridgewood village	16,276	10.6	74.1	18,514	64.7	6.4	45.0	18.7	131,578	1.9	7.9	62.3
34 64620	Roselle borough	14,568	50.3	19.8	16,770	62.2	14.6	40.7	30.6	42,100	13.1	28.1	14.8
34 65790	Sayreville borough	29,935	39.1	33.3	34,934	67.2	8.6	43.4	18.8	78,182	5.2	11.9	34.8
34 68370	Somerset CDP	17,837	25.2	53.2	19,557	67.5	7.7	50.1	20.8	92,034	1.9	9.2	46.5
34 69390	South Plainfield borough	16,972	41.3	37.1	19,164	71.3	10.3	46.6	19.7	87,056	2.7	9.3	40.4

Table B-4. Cities — What: Education, Employment, and Income, 2010–2012—*Continued*

STATE and Place code	STATE city	Educational attainment			Employment status				Percent of households with no workers	Median household income (dollars)	Percent of families with income below poverty	Percent of households with income less than $25,000	Percent of households with income of $100,000 or more
		Total population 25 years and over	Percent with a high school diploma or less	Percent with a bachelor's degree or more	Total population 16 years and over	Percent in the labor force	Unemployment rate	Percent who worked full-time year-round					
	ACS table number:	C15002	C15002	C15002	B23025	B23025	B23025	C20005	C08202	B19013	C17013	C19001	C19001
	Column number:	1	2	3	4	5	6	7	8	9	10	11	12
	New Jersey—Cont.												
34 71430	Summit city....................	14,465	15.4	70.1	16,116	65.6	7.4	45.9	21.4	121,008	4.4	9.7	57.9
34 73110	Toms River CDP............	62,819	43.7	29.9	72,932	65.7	9.2	39.7	27.1	71,521	5.4	14.7	34.0
34 74000	Trenton city...................	53,260	68.1	10.3	65,048	61.9	20.0	34.5	36.2	34,768	24.8	38.3	9.6
34 74630	Union City city..............	44,165	63.9	15.8	53,664	67.0	14.9	40.1	23.0	39,510	22.7	33.0	12.2
34 76070	Vineland city.................	39,174	58.7	17.3	46,539	64.7	13.8	39.2	28.4	51,710	12.6	25.4	20.3
34 79040	Westfield town..............	19,930	18.3	65.3	22,829	68.2	8.9	42.4	18.3	127,177	1.5	8.2	60.7
34 79610	West New York town.....	35,688	56.5	25.1	41,347	71.0	14.9	42.0	22.8	44,888	17.3	27.5	17.5
34 81950	Woodbridge CDP...........	13,650	37.6	40.1	15,252	70.8	8.2	48.2	16.8	85,005	3.6	12.1	39.0
35 00000	**New Mexico**................	1,353,059	42.8	25.7	1,617,544	60.7	10.2	38.0	29.6	43,518	16.4	29.5	16.4
35 01780	Alamogordo city...........	21,185	44.4	15.9	24,740	56.1	8.9	34.6	35.6	40,189	15.4	29.8	11.3
35 02000	Albuquerque city..........	363,808	34.4	32.9	434,787	65.7	9.1	42.2	27.0	46,060	14.7	27.4	17.9
35 12150	Carlsbad city.................	17,210	50.3	18.4	20,331	61.9	6.1	42.9	30.2	43,730	8.4	29.4	16.3
35 16420	Clovis city.....................	24,079	44.8	20.3	29,036	63.2	8.9	41.9	29.2	38,404	16.8	33.5	11.4
35 25800	Farmington city............	28,603	43.9	21.0	34,111	63.0	6.3	39.8	20.3	53,778	13.5	22.8	22.3
35 28460	Gallup city....................	12,682	51.0	21.7	15,722	57.9	5.6	37.8	24.2	46,250	20.9	31.7	15.9
35 32520	Hobbs city....................	20,839	56.9	15.1	25,007	61.3	7.1	38.7	20.8	47,030	16.0	24.3	18.8
35 39380	Las Cruces city..............	61,279	34.7	31.4	77,554	61.7	13.5	35.4	30.3	39,319	17.9	35.4	12.2
35 63460	Rio Rancho city.............	57,491	32.2	27.6	66,958	63.8	7.7	43.4	24.8	56,891	9.7	19.0	21.4
35 64930	Roswell city..................	29,943	46.6	17.8	36,401	60.8	8.2	38.6	28.3	37,424	19.3	31.1	11.3
35 70500	Santa Fe city.................	50,415	31.0	43.1	56,815	65.2	10.3	38.7	32.9	47,105	14.2	26.9	17.9
35 74520	South Valley CDP..........	26,851	63.1	12.7	32,558	59.7	11.5	38.2	26.3	39,694	19.4	31.2	11.2
36 00000	**New York**....................	13,205,241	42.3	33.0	15,724,512	63.4	9.5	40.5	27.4	56,657	12.0	23.6	26.4
36 01000	Albany city....................	59,856	38.0	35.5	82,802	61.1	10.6	35.5	31.5	40,404	18.6	34.2	14.7
36 03078	Auburn city...................	19,261	53.0	15.9	22,965	58.0	12.6	30.4	39.0	38,526	12.4	34.6	9.8
36 04143	Baldwin CDP..................	16,024	36.9	41.4	19,865	73.0	6.8	47.2	17.3	90,820	8.6	10.7	41.4
36 04935	Bay Shore CDP...............	18,369	49.2	25.7	22,030	69.2	11.3	43.3	25.9	61,538	6.1	21.2	26.8
36 06607	Binghamton city............	30,372	48.1	23.6	38,912	53.8	11.8	28.0	41.3	31,098	24.5	42.8	9.9
36 08026	Brentwood CDP.............	36,975	66.6	12.7	44,468	70.7	11.0	46.7	14.9	68,394	8.1	13.7	29.3
36 08257	Brighton CDP.................	25,674	17.5	59.9	30,445	61.9	6.0	40.3	27.9	62,323	4.4	16.8	28.0
36 11000	Buffalo city...................	164,812	46.6	24.2	208,662	59.7	14.3	31.5	37.5	29,891	26.3	43.6	9.1
36 13376	Centereach CDP.............	21,961	42.7	26.4	26,216	68.7	6.3	46.5	15.7	95,336	4.2	9.4	46.2
36 13552	Central Islip CDP...........	23,929	64.0	14.8	29,347	69.4	10.0	47.0	22.5	62,321	14.3	19.4	28.4
36 15000	Cheektowaga CDP.........	53,970	47.6	20.2	63,129	64.7	7.8	41.7	31.6	48,035	7.8	22.6	12.6
36 17530	Commack CDP................	23,889	27.0	48.4	27,223	65.7	7.2	42.4	20.6	107,067	2.0	7.7	52.8
36 18146	Copiague CDP...............	15,024	54.6	20.9	17,658	69.4	9.3	47.2	20.9	71,008	7.2	13.9	31.9
36 18157	Coram CDP....................	26,374	36.5	33.1	29,960	70.2	7.4	47.4	20.3	80,147	4.9	12.1	37.8
36 19972	Deer Park CDP...............	17,844	42.7	27.8	20,068	69.2	7.1	45.0	22.3	81,631	3.2	13.2	41.6
36 20687	Dix Hills CDP.................	18,469	21.7	57.4	21,921	64.3	5.9	41.4	16.7	134,771	1.9	7.1	63.7
36 22502	East Meadow CDP..........	27,257	36.6	35.5	32,278	59.0	6.6	40.6	22.9	94,305	2.2	12.2	47.5
36 22612	East Northport CDP........	14,004	24.5	47.1	16,177	69.6	9.0	41.3	21.8	105,825	4.1	11.1	53.1
36 22733	East Patchogue CDP.......	17,137	51.6	21.6	19,344	63.3	7.5	44.0	28.2	69,491	8.6	19.9	33.4
36 24229	Elmira city....................	18,013	56.3	14.0	22,792	51.1	9.2	28.4	36.0	29,028	24.6	40.4	9.3
36 24273	Elmont CDP...................	24,257	40.2	29.2	29,860	70.5	9.5	46.5	14.6	88,326	5.6	11.0	42.8
36 27309	Franklin Square CDP.......	20,945	47.1	29.2	24,024	64.7	7.8	42.5	22.7	86,991	3.8	10.9	44.0
36 27485	Freeport village............	29,913	51.5	23.2	34,450	70.1	9.8	44.7	22.3	69,377	12.5	19.5	33.6
36 28178	Garden City village........	14,563	18.0	64.7	17,593	60.3	5.0	41.5	25.9	147,643	5.0	7.5	66.4
36 29113	Glen Cove city...............	19,008	47.4	33.1	21,852	61.6	5.8	42.0	23.5	60,368	11.2	19.4	30.6
36 32402	Harrison village............	16,129	31.0	48.0	22,218	60.8	7.2	35.6	20.0	101,958	6.1	13.0	50.8
36 32732	Hauppauge CDP............	14,338	32.3	40.4	16,317	65.1	6.3	42.9	22.4	96,285	1.6	7.6	47.4
36 33139	Hempstead village.........	34,564	59.4	15.8	41,905	68.3	12.6	42.2	24.3	51,059	16.7	25.1	21.1
36 34374	Hicksville CDP...............	30,473	38.4	34.1	35,100	65.2	8.2	44.2	19.7	88,497	3.3	9.0	44.6
36 35056	Holbrook CDP................	18,520	41.2	26.3	21,156	70.2	8.1	46.8	16.5	91,241	3.9	7.4	45.2
36 35254	Holtsville CDP...............	13,186	37.5	27.7	16,055	64.6	4.7	44.2	21.2	86,883	4.2	12.1	41.8
36 37044	Huntington Station CDP..	20,901	48.8	26.6	25,178	67.7	10.9	43.4	22.3	66,535	10.7	16.4	34.1
36 37737	Irondequoit CDP............	36,881	35.5	33.7	42,273	64.7	8.1	42.1	31.8	52,872	9.5	21.4	18.2
36 38077	Ithaca city....................	10,763	18.1	67.7	28,401	48.8	7.7	16.6	42.7	27,331	13.0	47.6	13.2
36 38264	Jamestown city..............	20,224	50.1	17.7	24,102	60.0	14.3	32.3	39.2	30,240	24.6	41.1	7.4
36 39727	Kingston city.................	16,087	48.0	19.9	19,105	60.3	11.1	34.9	35.6	39,507	16.4	32.7	12.4
36 39853	Kiryas Joel village.........	5,691	78.4	7.3	8,502	50.9	7.5	25.8	12.8	24,579	51.6	51.0	8.7
36 40838	Lake Ronkonkoma CDP...	13,523	41.6	30.3	15,994	64.8	6.8	42.2	16.1	87,273	2.5	14.6	43.2
36 42081	Levittown CDP...............	36,944	40.3	29.3	43,040	67.8	7.7	47.4	18.7	95,039	1.1	5.8	47.4
36 42554	Lindenhurst village........	19,109	47.3	25.1	22,474	67.9	7.6	42.0	20.4	86,250	3.0	12.0	40.8
36 43082	Lockport city.................	14,609	49.0	20.4	16,947	60.1	10.6	35.1	36.3	39,864	18.0	32.1	10.7
36 43335	Long Beach city.............	25,217	30.4	44.0	28,737	67.6	5.5	49.6	23.3	82,769	7.4	16.7	40.9
36 45986	Massapequa CDP...........	14,740	31.4	42.4	17,209	66.8	6.1	42.2	18.3	120,114	0.5	6.2	55.8
36 46404	Medford CDP.................	16,826	48.3	21.7	20,260	65.4	7.0	44.3	18.6	86,970	4.2	11.8	40.1
36 46514	Melville CDP..................	14,066	26.9	52.3	16,554	56.7	6.2	36.8	29.1	107,416	3.9	8.5	54.2
36 46668	Merrick CDP..................	14,517	22.2	57.4	17,258	65.8	6.1	44.5	17.5	121,646	2.0	5.1	64.0
36 47042	Middletown city............	17,339	51.2	19.5	21,377	69.4	14.3	40.3	26.7	52,440	13.8	23.8	17.2
36 49121	Mount Vernon city.........	45,742	45.6	26.2	53,727	67.9	14.6	43.3	26.7	49,050	11.9	27.0	20.0
36 50034	Newburgh city...............	15,623	69.8	9.9	20,633	60.3	10.8	38.9	31.0	32,263	32.6	38.2	13.4

Table B-4. Cities — What: Education, Employment, and Income, 2010–2012—*Continued*

STATE and Place code	STATE city	Educational attainment			Employment status				Percent of households with no workers	Median household income (dollars)	Percent of families with income below poverty	Percent of households with income less than $25,000	Percent of households with income of $100,000 or more
		Total population 25 years and over	Percent with a high school diploma or less	Percent with a bachelor's degree or more	Total population 16 years and over	Percent in the labor force	Unemployment rate	Percent who worked full-time year-round					
	ACS table number:	C15002	C15002	C15002	B23025	B23025	B23025	C20005	C08202	B19013	C17013	C19001	C19001
	Column number:	1	2	3	4	5	6	7	8	9	10	11	12
	New York—Cont.												
36 50100	New City CDP	23,797	22.9	54.6	27,600	67.1	7.6	43.7	18.7	117,378	2.7	6.8	60.3
36 50617	New Rochelle city	51,850	39.7	40.4	62,290	64.9	8.3	41.5	23.1	65,251	8.4	19.1	34.1
36 51000	New York city	5,628,982	45.2	34.0	6,693,245	63.2	11.0	41.1	27.1	50,711	17.7	28.1	24.2
36 51055	Niagara Falls city	33,790	51.8	16.1	40,287	57.0	11.1	33.2	41.1	32,041	21.1	40.0	9.1
36 51495	North Bay Shore CDP	12,141	59.0	11.2	15,264	72.5	9.0	47.6	13.8	66,563	7.1	12.6	34.8
36 51517	North Bellmore CDP	14,588	36.8	39.1	16,364	64.5	7.4	43.8	17.0	96,344	2.4	2.0	46.8
36 53682	North Tonawanda city	22,635	43.1	24.8	26,394	65.7	8.1	41.8	31.2	46,427	7.6	24.0	17.5
36 54441	Oceanside CDP	22,869	32.1	44.8	26,628	65.6	6.7	43.8	21.7	94,768	3.7	11.5	47.6
36 55530	Ossining village	17,828	55.9	28.1	20,426	70.1	10.3	41.1	18.1	65,208	17.7	19.2	31.1
36 56979	Peekskill city	16,620	49.6	24.3	19,277	72.9	13.2	40.6	27.8	54,958	9.2	24.5	25.5
36 58442	Plainview CDP	18,989	24.7	55.1	21,640	63.6	5.1	40.9	24.1	117,110	1.9	9.1	59.8
36 59223	Port Chester village	19,638	58.3	22.4	23,394	76.6	9.9	42.1	16.9	55,521	11.2	20.4	21.8
36 59641	Poughkeepsie city	20,433	48.7	23.6	24,191	62.0	14.1	36.7	34.7	38,189	19.6	35.8	15.6
36 63000	Rochester city	130,152	47.9	25.0	164,584	61.4	14.2	33.2	35.4	29,942	30.4	43.1	7.2
36 63264	Rockville Centre village	16,304	21.7	61.1	19,069	64.4	6.5	43.5	26.4	110,192	5.4	14.8	52.9
36 63418	Rome city	23,259	49.5	18.7	27,327	54.7	6.8	36.7	34.3	44,942	11.2	25.9	15.1
36 63473	Ronkonkoma CDP	13,553	40.8	26.4	15,731	68.7	7.2	43.1	15.1	83,843	1.6	9.0	38.7
36 63924	Rotterdam CDP	15,184	42.5	19.6	17,580	64.8	8.2	43.0	27.8	57,344	3.3	17.2	19.0
36 65255	Saratoga Springs city	18,929	25.5	47.7	22,830	65.2	6.8	39.1	28.9	63,740	1.3	19.9	28.3
36 65508	Schenectady city	41,619	52.9	18.0	51,694	64.4	12.5	38.1	32.8	36,225	20.4	35.6	8.0
36 66212	Selden CDP	13,396	44.8	27.5	16,673	68.9	5.4	41.5	16.7	84,676	3.6	11.7	35.3
36 67070	Shirley CDP	17,695	59.2	14.4	20,752	69.9	6.5	47.4	15.6	79,044	7.0	14.1	35.9
36 67851	Smithtown CDP	17,779	29.7	41.4	21,062	66.1	8.4	41.1	20.6	108,946	5.0	8.9	59.2
36 70420	Spring Valley village	18,557	55.2	18.8	22,945	72.4	12.3	41.6	19.5	49,850	21.9	24.9	15.0
36 72554	Syosset CDP	12,955	18.6	64.5	14,782	62.6	4.2	43.5	22.6	123,288	3.4	7.6	57.9
36 73000	Syracuse city	82,963	48.6	25.4	114,911	55.3	12.7	30.5	37.7	30,299	28.3	43.5	10.2
36 74183	Tonawanda CDP	41,851	36.8	31.7	48,603	64.4	6.4	39.5	32.9	54,356	8.6	22.9	16.9
36 75484	Troy city	29,016	46.0	24.4	40,764	62.8	13.3	34.2	33.4	36,234	24.9	34.2	11.5
36 76089	Uniondale CDP	14,379	53.4	20.0	18,356	66.1	9.5	41.5	18.8	75,000	6.9	16.3	35.1
36 76540	Utica city	38,646	52.9	17.0	48,086	57.1	13.5	30.6	40.5	30,457	26.9	42.6	8.1
36 76705	Valley Stream village	25,154	43.3	30.6	29,816	69.4	12.3	41.4	23.6	82,947	8.4	14.0	41.4
36 78608	Watertown city	17,233	48.8	21.1	21,321	62.9	12.4	38.8	34.3	37,229	17.3	35.6	8.5
36 79246	West Babylon CDP	30,406	51.9	21.2	35,775	66.0	8.9	44.7	23.2	83,750	2.4	11.8	39.6
36 80302	West Islip CDP	18,240	36.5	35.2	21,773	67.1	5.1	43.9	19.8	102,644	2.4	7.6	51.9
36 80907	West Seneca CDP	31,673	40.9	26.0	36,631	66.9	8.2	41.9	30.2	57,555	4.7	19.9	20.3
36 81677	White Plains city	41,310	36.1	45.6	46,864	70.3	6.1	45.1	21.5	77,319	6.5	14.7	40.2
36 84000	Yonkers city	135,322	46.7	29.7	157,931	62.4	9.3	42.0	27.4	57,132	13.0	24.2	25.9
37 00000	**North Carolina**	6,409,433	42.4	27.0	7,624,214	63.5	11.5	39.0	28.8	45,215	13.3	27.3	16.4
37 01520	Apex town	23,864	12.3	59.6	27,327	79.4	7.4	53.3	11.0	90,008	1.9	5.8	45.0
37 02080	Asheboro city	15,701	56.4	16.1	18,756	61.3	12.3	34.7	34.1	31,818	23.3	36.7	5.8
37 02140	Asheville city	60,191	29.9	42.5	70,219	64.5	9.6	36.4	32.2	42,419	13.6	30.2	13.3
37 09060	Burlington city	34,406	47.1	22.6	40,429	63.8	12.8	36.5	32.7	36,111	18.0	33.5	10.9
37 10620	Carrboro town	13,134	20.8	64.3	15,788	81.5	5.0	46.2	18.9	42,363	13.3	31.2	22.1
37 10740	Cary town	92,731	17.8	60.4	106,799	72.5	5.4	50.5	14.8	89,139	5.1	10.4	45.1
37 11800	Chapel Hill town	28,875	12.6	74.0	49,028	56.4	7.7	28.5	28.4	60,159	9.7	26.0	32.7
37 12000	Charlotte city	490,751	32.1	39.8	585,547	71.8	11.7	44.6	20.6	51,209	14.2	23.3	21.9
37 14100	Concord city	52,355	39.4	27.2	61,714	66.6	13.5	41.4	24.4	50,779	9.6	20.7	20.5
37 14700	Cornelius town	17,490	25.3	49.3	19,949	73.8	7.9	50.6	19.2	76,944	4.2	9.6	38.4
37 19000	Durham city	151,273	29.9	45.9	185,329	68.4	9.1	42.6	23.1	46,924	15.0	26.8	19.2
37 22920	Fayetteville city	121,646	34.8	25.0	155,404	66.2	11.9	45.0	26.0	44,472	15.7	25.2	12.6
37 25480	Garner town	17,502	28.1	36.6	20,197	72.3	9.3	46.4	20.5	55,242	8.1	17.6	20.9
37 25580	Gastonia city	45,353	46.6	21.4	54,704	63.2	15.9	35.5	29.7	39,598	19.3	33.3	13.0
37 26880	Goldsboro city	23,794	44.5	18.2	28,648	58.3	17.8	35.5	36.4	34,445	22.3	37.8	10.4
37 28000	Greensboro city	174,262	36.3	35.6	218,989	65.8	11.7	38.6	26.4	40,323	15.0	30.4	14.4
37 28080	Greenville city	45,067	32.5	37.2	71,171	67.5	13.3	35.6	25.0	33,439	17.9	39.8	14.0
37 30120	Havelock city	9,698	33.3	12.9	15,808	75.2	6.6	55.2	20.7	47,440	13.2	19.0	10.7
37 31060	Hickory city	26,689	39.7	31.8	31,912	61.8	7.9	40.2	28.8	40,075	14.2	30.5	17.2
37 31400	High Point city	68,256	40.0	28.9	81,551	67.0	13.6	38.8	27.4	41,980	18.1	29.9	13.7
37 32260	Holly Springs town	15,990	17.2	53.5	17,550	73.1	7.5	51.9	12.5	84,974	1.4	6.9	38.7
37 33120	Huntersville town	32,222	21.2	52.3	36,116	75.6	8.1	52.1	15.5	84,524	3.0	12.2	43.6
37 33560	Indian Trail town	20,581	33.0	34.4	24,437	73.4	10.0	47.7	13.4	64,675	5.0	9.0	25.0
37 34200	Jacksonville city	31,038	32.7	22.7	53,886	74.7	6.8	53.8	18.8	42,122	10.7	21.9	9.8
37 35200	Kannapolis city	28,024	52.7	16.2	32,795	63.4	12.9	38.8	30.7	37,578	15.1	32.2	9.5
37 35600	Kernersville town	16,359	38.9	28.7	18,796	65.5	8.7	41.2	24.3	46,578	8.8	26.4	16.5
37 35920	Kinston city	14,532	53.4	15.0	16,714	55.4	20.5	29.6	44.4	28,454	27.4	45.2	6.9
37 39700	Lumberton city	14,400	53.6	18.8	16,924	48.5	8.9	32.5	38.2	33,905	23.8	40.1	10.9
37 41960	Matthews town	18,692	21.2	45.5	21,780	71.3	8.9	43.5	20.8	69,946	6.1	13.5	30.5
37 43480	Mint Hill town	16,457	32.8	32.7	18,119	66.7	8.4	43.7	24.8	66,735	3.4	13.1	29.7
37 43920	Monroe city	20,929	62.3	15.7	24,514	66.0	13.4	43.1	26.0	43,742	19.4	30.3	12.4
37 44220	Mooresville town	20,979	30.9	30.0	25,033	68.6	13.6	42.7	24.4	59,967	6.9	22.6	23.9
37 44520	Morrisville town	13,287	14.3	64.2	14,680	77.4	4.4	59.3	5.6	79,933	2.4	8.0	38.9
37 46340	New Bern city	19,438	43.1	25.2	23,221	64.6	18.7	33.3	36.8	40,707	17.7	32.5	11.1
37 55000	Raleigh city	261,155	26.4	45.9	327,845	70.1	9.3	45.6	19.8	52,709	12.6	20.9	21.7
37 57500	Rocky Mount city	38,498	50.0	19.5	45,704	59.3	17.4	34.3	35.6	37,901	18.5	34.3	10.7
37 58860	Salisbury city	21,467	45.0	23.0	26,251	50.0	14.6	27.6	38.9	33,083	23.8	38.7	8.9
37 59280	Sanford city	17,606	54.3	18.3	21,140	65.7	16.4	39.6	30.3	35,606	23.6	35.4	12.0
37 61200	Shelby city	14,006	49.9	21.3	15,937	54.9	18.7	32.3	42.4	30,358	22.8	43.8	11.5
37 64740	Statesville city	15,802	49.8	19.0	19,149	62.3	18.3	34.2	34.4	30,561	28.7	42.4	8.4

Table B-4. Cities — What: Education, Employment, and Income, 2010–2012—*Continued*

STATE and Place code	STATE city	Educational attainment			Employment status				Percent of households with no workers	Median household income (dollars)	Percent of families with income below poverty	Percent of households with income less than $25,000	Percent of households with income of $100,000 or more
		Total population 25 years and over	Percent with a high school diploma or less	Percent with a bachelor's degree or more	Total population 16 years and over	Percent in the labor force	Unemployment rate	Percent who worked full-time year-round					
	ACS table number:	C15002	C15002	C15002	B23025	B23025	B23025	C20005	C08202	B19013	C17013	C19001	C19001
	Column number:	1	2	3	4	5	6	7	8	9	10	11	12
	North Carolina—Cont.												
37 67420	Thomasville city	17,062	56.9	13.5	20,235	65.4	19.1	35.2	32.5	33,131	23.8	40.3	4.0
37 70540	Wake Forest town	19,614	22.6	48.2	22,219	71.4	4.6	44.8	17.1	71,204	7.1	13.0	33.6
37 74440	Wilmington city	70,278	30.7	39.8	90,301	65.1	12.5	34.2	30.7	41,554	15.3	31.8	17.8
37 74540	Wilson city	31,702	51.5	22.8	37,869	60.5	16.8	35.8	35.2	34,952	22.8	37.3	10.5
37 75000	Winston-Salem city	147,124	41.2	32.0	181,133	63.1	12.5	36.9	29.7	39,170	17.9	31.5	14.7
38 00000	**North Dakota**	450,055	36.3	27.3	551,175	70.5	3.4	47.4	22.2	52,427	7.6	22.7	19.3
38 07200	Bismarck city	43,123	31.3	33.1	51,137	71.1	3.5	49.5	22.8	54,099	5.4	21.0	20.3
38 25700	Fargo city	66,212	23.9	39.2	89,022	76.8	4.7	48.1	17.8	45,644	8.5	25.0	17.7
38 32060	Grand Forks city	30,167	31.4	35.1	45,084	71.4	4.3	41.4	19.7	41,444	9.1	29.0	15.0
38 53380	Minot city	27,012	35.2	26.8	34,553	71.9	3.1	48.7	20.9	50,201	8.5	21.5	15.4
38 84780	West Fargo city	17,044	27.2	35.8	20,301	79.9	2.5	56.5	15.9	64,708	4.3	15.6	23.9
39 00000	**Ohio**	7,744,886	46.4	24.9	9,165,238	63.7	10.2	38.9	29.9	47,030	11.8	26.5	17.1
39 01000	Akron city	127,867	49.2	20.2	158,104	62.7	16.3	34.9	35.2	32,565	22.2	39.1	8.3
39 01420	Alliance city	13,871	65.3	10.6	18,261	56.9	18.5	29.5	39.8	27,957	24.2	46.3	6.4
39 02568	Ashland city	13,245	50.1	28.7	16,801	62.6	14.7	34.8	35.9	38,519	12.6	32.5	10.6
39 02736	Athens city	6,478	18.4	60.6	22,318	49.2	10.8	14.3	35.2	17,986	18.1	57.4	10.9
39 03184	Austintown CDP	21,599	49.4	19.9	24,561	61.8	12.1	36.2	36.3	40,783	9.5	27.5	9.6
39 03352	Avon city	14,500	27.9	49.8	15,924	65.0	4.9	45.4	27.3	77,970	4.2	13.6	40.1
39 03464	Avon Lake city	15,317	22.9	51.4	17,227	66.6	5.3	46.5	24.1	82,406	3.2	12.1	39.6
39 03828	Barberton city	18,221	64.9	11.3	21,026	63.5	12.4	36.7	34.6	36,184	14.6	35.2	6.7
39 04720	Beavercreek city	31,265	23.4	48.5	37,210	63.8	5.5	43.5	24.8	72,610	3.0	12.4	32.8
39 07454	Boardman CDP	25,246	39.8	27.8	28,885	66.8	7.2	39.6	28.5	45,075	7.0	26.1	13.8
39 07972	Bowling Green city	13,590	32.7	42.1	27,408	66.3	14.0	27.3	22.3	35,353	15.1	36.6	14.9
39 09680	Brunswick city	23,133	44.9	20.1	27,489	72.4	7.2	43.7	20.7	60,219	5.7	15.6	17.8
39 12000	Canton city	48,038	56.0	13.7	55,952	62.5	15.6	32.7	36.0	30,296	24.0	41.1	6.1
39 13190	Centerville city	17,534	24.4	46.0	19,616	58.5	8.4	38.8	35.2	52,655	4.9	19.6	22.8
39 14184	Chillicothe city	15,520	52.2	20.3	17,697	55.8	17.8	30.1	42.2	37,805	15.8	33.3	10.2
39 15000	Cincinnati city	187,416	41.8	31.3	237,546	63.9	14.0	36.1	34.0	32,591	25.3	41.4	13.0
39 16000	Cleveland city	257,373	56.3	14.3	311,641	58.8	19.9	30.8	40.9	25,819	30.7	48.7	5.6
39 16014	Cleveland Heights city	29,877	22.2	50.3	36,269	66.4	10.5	40.9	27.5	47,441	15.5	29.2	20.0
39 18000	Columbus city	507,380	38.4	32.4	630,501	69.6	10.4	43.5	24.3	42,491	17.5	29.5	13.7
39 19778	Cuyahoga Falls city	35,258	40.5	29.3	40,122	67.4	7.9	45.1	27.5	47,247	9.6	24.2	13.2
39 21000	Dayton city	87,807	51.1	15.8	113,847	57.7	16.8	27.6	41.2	27,278	28.9	46.7	5.4
39 21434	Delaware city	22,513	36.5	31.9	27,841	67.8	5.5	45.9	21.8	56,060	7.9	23.0	22.4
39 22694	Dublin city	27,231	8.5	73.1	30,520	72.4	4.2	52.5	12.1	112,273	2.2	4.5	60.1
39 25256	Elyria city	36,698	50.8	14.5	43,663	65.9	11.5	38.0	31.2	41,459	16.1	29.0	10.1
39 25704	Euclid city	32,954	45.6	19.5	38,453	62.1	14.9	37.0	35.3	35,107	14.0	35.6	9.4
39 25914	Fairborn city	19,634	44.0	23.4	26,441	64.1	10.4	34.4	30.6	38,928	22.3	36.6	10.7
39 25970	Fairfield city	29,740	41.4	25.2	34,258	72.2	10.2	46.9	21.9	54,555	7.7	17.1	19.2
39 27048	Findlay city	27,474	44.1	25.1	34,062	66.5	12.4	37.3	30.9	42,715	16.1	31.8	14.3
39 29106	Gahanna city	22,382	25.4	46.5	27,271	71.5	6.7	47.7	20.8	72,486	2.0	13.4	34.9
39 29428	Garfield Heights city	18,969	55.5	14.6	22,234	64.9	12.7	39.8	29.7	41,680	12.7	28.4	9.3
39 31860	Green city	18,008	38.2	32.2	20,994	66.3	6.2	44.0	27.7	55,953	4.4	15.3	21.8
39 32592	Grove City city	24,693	37.8	28.4	28,770	67.0	5.5	46.5	24.6	63,402	7.4	16.2	25.3
39 33012	Hamilton city	41,660	60.4	15.0	48,234	61.5	12.9	38.0	33.3	39,111	18.3	32.8	9.3
39 35476	Hilliard city	18,113	28.6	43.1	21,194	74.5	7.8	50.9	16.9	82,432	5.7	10.5	40.1
39 36610	Huber Heights city	25,603	40.0	21.4	29,936	61.9	9.7	39.9	29.4	48,527	8.9	22.6	14.3
39 36651	Hudson city	14,586	12.9	68.7	16,966	64.3	5.3	45.7	19.7	117,253	2.7	7.2	58.2
39 39872	Kent city	13,210	28.8	45.5	25,361	66.3	14.0	26.3	27.8	30,435	21.9	44.0	12.5
39 40040	Kettering city	40,083	32.9	30.5	45,375	65.4	7.9	40.7	30.4	48,010	8.8	24.6	15.5
39 41664	Lakewood city	35,786	30.5	40.4	42,626	73.4	9.5	46.0	24.1	42,327	14.5	29.7	12.7
39 41720	Lancaster city	25,640	54.4	14.8	30,189	60.3	10.7	35.1	36.6	37,754	15.5	32.9	8.9
39 42364	Lebanon city	12,664	37.2	30.3	15,086	72.7	10.4	45.2	21.8	60,947	9.4	17.8	22.5
39 43554	Lima city	22,961	58.0	11.2	29,311	58.0	19.6	27.2	37.9	26,736	31.6	47.5	5.2
39 44856	Lorain city	41,375	55.4	12.1	48,561	60.2	17.1	33.1	38.5	34,926	24.9	38.1	9.9
39 47138	Mansfield city	33,455	57.0	13.4	38,587	49.8	14.9	27.2	39.5	31,717	22.6	38.9	8.0
39 47306	Maple Heights city	15,775	51.6	11.8	18,780	64.5	19.0	35.0	37.8	34,810	19.7	35.6	6.5
39 47754	Marion city	26,046	63.6	8.0	31,162	47.4	12.3	27.9	35.9	32,238	24.2	39.6	6.0
39 48160	Marysville city	14,790	46.3	24.7	17,636	59.4	6.7	40.7	18.4	54,996	5.3	18.1	22.3
39 48188	Mason city	19,452	25.6	53.5	22,663	70.9	7.5	48.0	15.3	80,849	2.5	9.8	38.7
39 48244	Massillon city	22,040	56.1	15.0	26,060	61.3	13.2	33.8	37.4	36,846	13.4	33.1	7.7
39 48790	Medina city	17,070	38.3	34.4	20,058	65.3	6.8	40.4	28.2	53,550	12.6	22.9	19.3
39 49056	Mentor city	34,261	36.4	30.0	38,414	68.7	6.8	45.6	24.3	64,476	5.5	14.9	25.2
39 49434	Miamisburg city	14,303	46.6	21.3	15,763	60.6	7.3	42.2	31.7	52,445	9.6	26.0	20.1
39 49840	Middletown city	32,198	61.2	14.5	37,816	60.8	15.0	34.2	37.2	34,934	21.2	36.2	8.4
39 54040	Newark city	31,992	53.9	16.3	37,266	63.3	10.1	37.3	33.0	36,664	17.9	35.6	10.0
39 56882	North Olmsted city	24,070	34.2	29.4	27,068	67.7	8.2	42.8	27.4	57,933	5.1	15.8	21.3
39 56966	North Ridgeville city	21,558	39.6	24.6	23,954	68.5	10.3	42.6	24.7	65,216	3.9	12.2	23.4
39 57008	North Royalton city	22,348	34.8	34.9	25,527	68.3	6.4	45.5	24.8	66,096	3.4	13.6	27.4
39 57386	Norwood city	12,295	53.1	22.1	15,617	70.7	8.3	41.7	23.8	33,868	13.1	36.5	9.9
39 58730	Oregon city	14,301	49.4	16.8	16,766	62.1	10.9	36.2	33.8	50,784	5.8	25.5	18.9
39 59234	Oxford city	5,784	24.1	62.7	19,763	50.3	5.7	15.9	29.2	28,929	12.4	47.7	14.8
39 61000	Parma city	57,197	49.4	18.6	66,688	65.1	8.6	39.2	29.4	47,729	9.3	23.7	13.3
39 61028	Parma Heights city	14,754	49.3	17.6	16,507	63.0	7.4	37.3	34.9	41,831	13.1	32.2	10.7
39 62148	Perrysburg city	14,387	21.0	46.4	16,292	71.2	6.1	46.9	21.4	70,780	2.3	19.0	33.9
39 62848	Piqua city	13,662	61.5	8.8	16,079	63.4	15.6	35.8	33.1	31,911	24.3	39.8	8.0

Table B-4. Cities — What: Education, Employment, and Income, 2010–2012—*Continued*

STATE and Place code	STATE city	Educational attainment			Employment status						Percent of families with income below poverty	Percent of households with income less than $25,000	Percent of households with income of $100,000 or more
		Total population 25 years and over	Percent with a high school diploma or less	Percent with a bachelor's degree or more	Total population 16 years and over	Percent in the labor force	Unemployment rate	Percent who worked full-time year-round	Percent of households with no workers	Median household income (dollars)			
	ACS table number:	C15002	C15002	C15002	B23025	B23025	B23025	C20005	C08202	B19013	C17013	C19001	C19001
	Column number:	1	2	3	4	5	6	7	8	9	10	11	12
	Ohio—Cont.												
39 64304	Portsmouth city	13,839	54.5	15.5	17,109	47.9	11.6	25.3	45.7	26,684	18.8	47.0	7.9
39 66390	Reynoldsburg city	23,190	38.1	31.2	27,584	73.0	8.3	47.9	23.0	57,842	10.1	18.5	22.9
39 67468	Riverside city	16,458	47.5	16.0	19,690	62.8	13.8	38.0	34.8	39,714	13.8	28.3	11.1
39 68056	Rocky River city	14,674	20.7	58.8	16,190	64.0	6.5	40.3	33.8	62,816	2.2	17.8	31.0
39 70380	Sandusky city	17,701	58.3	13.7	20,530	62.5	13.6	33.3	35.6	32,882	15.4	39.7	9.1
39 71682	Shaker Heights city	19,524	13.4	64.8	22,001	66.7	6.2	44.3	24.0	71,242	5.6	19.2	37.2
39 72424	Sidney city	14,364	59.6	12.6	16,792	62.2	8.6	40.5	29.7	44,188	13.5	27.5	10.1
39 72928	Solon city	15,669	20.6	53.4	17,662	66.9	7.4	46.1	24.8	90,404	2.9	11.0	43.9
39 73264	South Euclid city	14,667	30.5	39.7	18,137	70.3	10.9	43.1	23.1	56,260	7.3	18.7	19.1
39 74118	Springfield city	38,598	57.1	15.2	47,035	57.1	15.0	31.1	39.1	30,375	25.4	42.0	7.9
39 74944	Stow city	24,095	31.5	37.3	28,027	67.8	6.3	47.4	23.3	62,984	4.8	13.7	25.3
39 75098	Strongsville city	31,418	30.6	41.5	35,850	68.8	7.3	44.4	22.4	74,362	3.1	13.7	35.4
39 77000	Toledo city	181,523	49.5	17.3	224,946	63.2	17.2	32.5	36.0	32,351	23.1	39.8	7.0
39 77504	Trotwood city	16,800	48.5	14.4	19,759	56.7	11.8	31.7	36.7	37,334	17.1	35.2	9.1
39 77588	Troy city	16,711	48.9	21.4	19,281	66.8	7.9	43.9	26.1	47,410	13.7	24.6	11.7
39 79002	Upper Arlington city	23,468	10.5	72.8	26,345	66.5	4.4	45.5	22.8	96,134	2.3	9.9	48.5
39 80304	Wadsworth city	14,523	35.9	30.6	16,550	66.6	7.7	44.3	28.0	53,490	5.3	17.8	18.5
39 80892	Warren city	27,363	63.0	11.1	32,175	49.2	13.0	27.7	44.7	28,965	24.9	43.5	5.1
39 83342	Westerville city	24,277	23.0	52.6	29,695	68.3	4.7	43.2	17.9	80,693	4.8	12.5	38.4
39 83622	Westlake city	23,719	23.0	53.3	26,307	64.8	6.3	44.0	25.3	73,639	3.0	11.2	36.2
39 84812	White Oak CDP	13,980	42.0	28.2	15,884	67.9	6.8	43.1	25.9	62,013	8.3	21.0	24.7
39 85484	Willoughby city	16,355	39.9	28.4	18,851	67.5	7.5	43.1	28.2	49,930	3.4	18.9	15.1
39 86548	Wooster city	16,476	46.3	30.5	21,550	62.0	7.2	33.7	30.3	40,638	12.3	28.3	13.1
39 86772	Xenia city	17,045	51.1	17.8	19,935	58.2	12.8	34.5	38.2	37,028	19.2	32.9	10.2
39 88000	Youngstown city	44,043	61.6	10.9	53,411	50.1	21.4	23.4	45.7	23,752	29.2	52.7	3.6
39 88084	Zanesville city	16,684	63.9	11.2	19,503	53.2	13.0	28.6	42.3	26,219	27.0	48.5	4.4
40 00000	**Oklahoma**	2,467,328	45.3	23.5	2,953,243	62.1	7.4	41.5	28.3	44,239	12.8	27.8	15.1
40 02600	Ardmore city	16,206	53.7	20.0	18,677	62.9	8.6	45.2	28.2	40,490	11.1	29.1	9.9
40 04450	Bartlesville city	24,584	40.0	29.8	28,559	59.1	7.2	40.6	33.8	48,566	12.7	25.2	18.4
40 06400	Bixby city	13,982	25.5	38.3	15,633	66.8	5.0	48.1	21.4	65,727	5.0	16.6	30.8
40 09050	Broken Arrow city	65,062	32.4	30.6	76,801	71.0	6.3	49.3	18.0	62,841	5.8	13.8	24.1
40 19900	Del City city	12,784	52.0	11.7	15,946	62.2	8.5	39.4	33.0	38,577	17.3	33.2	6.2
40 21900	Duncan city	15,904	52.4	20.3	18,255	59.1	8.0	40.6	32.3	42,404	12.0	30.6	11.8
40 23200	Edmond city	51,816	20.9	50.9	65,171	67.5	6.1	44.1	21.2	69,431	6.0	18.0	31.4
40 23950	Enid city	32,728	51.6	21.0	38,823	64.5	6.5	43.2	26.4	42,370	10.0	24.1	11.3
40 41850	Lawton city	59,674	45.6	19.2	75,816	66.0	7.9	43.4	24.6	43,779	15.2	26.6	11.7
40 48350	Midwest City city	36,882	40.6	19.9	43,272	64.2	6.6	43.2	29.1	43,208	12.6	27.1	11.2
40 49200	Moore city	35,890	41.2	23.0	42,601	70.5	6.7	50.1	18.8	56,903	9.5	17.6	17.8
40 50050	Muskogee city	24,901	49.9	18.6	29,977	56.9	9.8	36.0	38.1	33,360	23.6	38.2	7.3
40 52500	Norman city	67,193	27.1	44.5	94,025	64.8	6.2	41.1	23.8	48,388	11.3	27.0	21.2
40 55000	Oklahoma City city	382,692	40.5	28.1	454,620	67.0	7.1	44.6	24.8	44,519	14.6	27.1	16.5
40 56650	Owasso city	19,001	33.3	30.1	22,778	73.9	5.6	50.7	14.3	65,838	5.4	13.4	24.8
40 59850	Ponca City city	16,582	45.9	20.9	19,301	60.0	10.8	37.7	36.6	36,968	15.2	33.6	10.8
40 65400	Sapulpa city	13,991	46.4	20.3	16,705	56.6	10.9	35.8	35.5	39,848	13.4	29.3	13.8
40 66800	Shawnee city	18,583	47.0	22.0	23,163	61.9	8.0	39.3	30.5	36,173	20.3	36.0	10.5
40 70300	Stillwater city	21,277	23.7	48.0	39,789	62.8	6.0	28.4	25.8	32,567	15.1	40.8	11.2
40 75000	Tulsa city	255,091	39.1	29.6	306,857	65.5	8.4	42.5	27.0	40,359	16.1	30.3	15.1
40 82950	Yukon city	15,806	38.0	27.4	18,089	65.9	6.2	45.9	27.3	58,682	6.7	19.0	20.8
41 00000	**Oregon**	2,643,922	35.7	29.3	3,104,852	62.9	11.9	35.0	30.8	48,525	11.7	25.2	17.9
41 01000	Albany city	33,534	35.3	21.5	39,197	62.3	12.4	34.8	32.4	44,730	17.4	28.9	13.1
41 01650	Aloha CDP	32,647	36.4	26.8	38,019	75.2	10.1	45.9	14.8	60,854	9.9	15.1	17.6
41 03050	Ashland city	13,996	14.0	57.9	17,246	61.2	11.5	27.1	37.3	43,858	10.9	29.8	19.1
41 05350	Beaverton city	61,094	25.3	43.9	72,048	70.0	10.4	41.5	21.7	54,929	11.9	20.1	22.4
41 05800	Bend city	54,317	23.5	37.8	61,782	66.1	11.4	35.6	32.0	49,576	8.9	23.9	17.4
41 05950	Bethany CDP	12,988	10.0	69.5	15,148	65.7	7.2	43.5	18.1	101,155	2.2	8.0	51.1
41 15800	Corvallis city	28,748	16.8	55.3	47,255	58.6	8.3	25.1	31.9	37,382	13.1	38.0	18.0
41 23850	Eugene city	98,744	25.0	39.4	133,278	60.0	11.3	28.6	33.4	40,435	12.5	32.4	15.9
41 26200	Forest Grove city	13,714	45.5	21.4	17,066	62.8	11.3	35.3	31.9	46,915	13.0	29.4	16.9
41 30550	Grants Pass city	23,286	42.6	14.6	27,341	52.8	14.3	28.4	45.9	32,267	17.6	37.1	8.6
41 31250	Gresham city	69,285	45.7	18.6	83,621	65.3	13.7	35.0	29.0	45,595	17.0	26.5	14.3
41 34100	Hillsboro city	59,424	34.1	32.5	70,711	71.1	9.3	45.0	17.3	65,220	10.0	16.1	25.1
41 38500	Keizer city	23,990	38.6	23.8	28,128	64.9	10.9	38.8	25.9	49,937	12.0	21.1	14.5
41 39700	Klamath Falls city	13,874	42.5	21.5	17,036	60.2	15.1	27.1	36.3	29,753	20.1	43.9	7.5
41 40550	Lake Oswego city	27,010	12.0	65.7	29,940	65.5	11.1	38.2	28.7	81,296	4.8	13.4	40.4
41 45000	McMinnville city	20,325	48.7	19.8	25,534	61.4	11.3	32.7	33.9	40,869	14.1	27.1	11.9
41 47000	Medford city	50,710	41.7	22.4	60,256	62.6	15.0	32.0	34.2	41,589	16.1	29.7	12.1
41 48650	Milwaukie city	14,364	33.7	24.5	16,520	67.2	12.4	43.0	26.0	51,395	11.2	23.4	12.5
41 52100	Newberg city	13,023	45.6	26.3	17,429	67.4	8.1	35.3	23.4	49,522	10.4	16.7	18.4
41 55200	Oregon City city	21,527	35.7	22.3	25,077	65.4	12.8	38.8	28.1	55,477	9.8	19.6	17.8
41 59000	Portland city	425,214	27.2	43.2	491,902	69.4	10.5	38.6	26.0	49,958	12.9	26.1	21.3
41 61200	Redmond city	16,547	39.2	18.0	20,153	63.7	20.1	29.7	37.6	37,204	20.9	32.0	7.8
41 63650	Roseburg city	16,233	40.1	19.2	18,108	54.7	16.1	33.1	40.7	42,094	12.8	30.4	11.2
41 64900	Salem city	101,156	38.1	26.9	120,827	61.9	15.1	34.4	31.1	45,215	15.5	26.4	14.8
41 69600	Springfield city	38,556	45.2	14.6	46,724	64.7	13.9	33.4	29.9	37,658	18.4	33.6	7.2
41 73650	Tigard city	33,919	24.3	40.4	39,645	71.2	8.8	41.8	21.4	59,852	6.9	17.4	27.3
41 74950	Tualatin city	17,255	28.8	40.2	20,547	73.9	10.1	46.5	18.7	62,828	7.9	17.9	29.9
41 80150	West Linn city	17,261	13.9	56.0	20,343	64.7	9.0	36.4	21.7	85,792	4.4	11.7	42.5
41 82800	Wilsonville city	13,647	31.1	36.1	15,709	63.3	8.5	41.0	29.5	56,462	4.4	18.5	25.9
41 83750	Woodburn city	14,633	60.6	13.2	18,231	61.0	17.5	32.5	33.1	41,941	20.5	30.3	10.5

Table B-4. Cities — What: Education, Employment, and Income, 2010–2012—*Continued*

STATE and Place code	STATE city	Educational attainment			Employment status				Percent of households with no workers	Median household income (dollars)	Percent of families with income below poverty	Percent of households with income less than $25,000	Percent of households with income of $100,000 or more
		Total population 25 years and over	Percent with a high school diploma or less	Percent with a bachelor's degree or more	Total population 16 years and over	Percent in the labor force	Unemployment rate	Percent who worked full-time year-round					
	ACS table number:	C15002	C15002	C15002	B23025	B23025	B23025	C20005	C08202	B19013	C17013	C19001	C19001
	Column number:	1	2	3	4	5	6	7	8	9	10	11	12
42 00000	**Pennsylvania**	8,708,982	48.6	27.3	10,320,759	62.8	9.2	39.2	29.8	51,402	9.5	24.2	20.4
42 02000	Allentown city	72,834	59.3	16.4	90,988	62.6	15.3	34.5	32.6	34,289	21.5	36.0	7.7
42 02056	Allison Park CDP	15,194	27.2	48.0	17,901	65.1	5.1	41.5	27.3	77,721	2.1	14.1	34.3
42 02184	Altoona city	31,351	61.3	14.6	36,757	58.0	10.6	34.9	36.0	35,572	13.3	35.7	7.6
42 06064	Bethel Park municipality	23,489	31.8	44.0	26,251	65.9	7.8	42.1	26.6	68,139	2.3	13.5	28.7
42 06088	Bethlehem city	47,861	46.2	27.2	62,095	57.9	10.6	33.5	34.9	44,876	18.2	29.9	13.7
42 12536	Chambersburg borough	13,150	57.6	21.1	15,834	57.2	7.7	35.6	36.1	40,278	17.5	33.2	10.6
42 13208	Chester city	20,778	66.9	9.9	27,366	53.5	18.3	29.6	38.7	28,716	25.1	42.8	5.0
42 19920	Drexel Hill CDP	19,937	36.5	38.2	22,958	72.1	10.0	46.5	23.7	62,832	4.2	18.6	27.6
42 21648	Easton city	16,583	59.9	16.4	22,193	54.4	11.8	32.3	30.7	37,713	21.1	34.8	11.1
42 24000	Erie city	64,366	56.0	20.3	80,146	60.8	11.7	33.8	35.2	31,838	22.7	40.3	7.3
42 32800	Harrisburg city	30,442	57.3	18.9	37,338	63.4	16.4	37.8	32.3	33,080	29.2	39.0	7.8
42 33408	Hazleton city	16,065	65.7	11.2	19,806	60.8	15.1	33.2	36.3	30,205	21.8	36.7	8.0
42 38288	Johnstown city	14,753	64.6	10.6	16,715	51.9	14.0	27.6	49.1	27,274	26.2	47.2	2.8
42 41216	Lancaster city	36,444	59.0	17.4	46,624	62.0	15.8	33.8	31.4	31,462	24.5	41.1	6.4
42 42168	Lebanon city	16,222	72.4	10.7	19,595	65.4	16.4	36.4	37.9	31,678	26.6	42.4	6.4
42 42928	Levittown CDP	36,468	52.7	15.4	42,279	68.4	9.8	35.2	22.8	64,962	7.5	15.1	22.4
42 46256	McKeesport city	13,930	57.1	13.1	16,206	55.5	11.9	31.5	39.1	26,501	22.5	46.3	6.6
42 50528	Monroeville municipality	21,472	35.9	37.1	23,569	59.0	5.6	39.2	32.4	56,603	4.4	19.7	23.4
42 52432	Murrysville municipality	14,797	27.7	48.6	16,819	67.3	5.4	44.2	26.7	82,468	2.5	12.6	41.4
42 53368	New Castle city	15,732	62.7	15.0	18,266	52.5	11.8	31.9	43.2	28,119	24.1	44.9	5.9
42 54656	Norristown borough	22,936	59.9	17.1	27,194	69.6	13.4	42.7	25.4	40,596	19.7	31.9	9.5
42 60000	Philadelphia city	992,077	54.0	23.5	1,232,442	58.4	16.0	34.0	36.8	35,581	21.8	37.6	12.6
42 61000	Pittsburgh city	200,833	39.6	35.4	262,311	61.4	10.4	36.5	33.4	37,280	16.3	35.9	14.3
42 61536	Plum borough	19,052	35.4	34.1	21,986	68.0	7.4	43.8	26.5	64,476	3.9	16.6	23.7
42 62416	Pottstown borough	15,319	57.8	17.0	17,510	69.6	10.2	42.8	27.6	43,050	11.3	28.4	15.0
42 63624	Reading city	50,066	72.9	8.3	64,058	58.5	20.8	29.0	39.8	25,753	38.1	48.8	3.7
42 69000	Scranton city	49,185	54.2	20.6	62,388	57.6	9.8	34.9	35.4	36,149	16.4	35.2	10.1
42 73808	State College borough	10,511	16.4	65.8	40,413	43.5	7.7	15.9	31.2	23,092	14.6	52.4	11.3
42 83512	West Mifflin borough	14,793	44.1	20.1	17,260	63.3	8.5	40.8	31.3	48,813	8.5	25.2	13.0
42 85152	Wilkes-Barre city	25,782	57.4	15.3	33,742	55.7	9.1	31.6	36.4	31,133	23.5	41.5	7.2
42 85312	Williamsport city	17,213	54.9	17.2	23,931	61.4	13.5	30.3	31.7	31,452	23.6	41.3	6.7
42 87048	York city	25,941	73.2	9.5	32,533	60.3	25.6	28.6	40.6	29,469	35.0	44.0	4.5
44 00000	**Rhode Island**	710,902	42.3	31.0	858,819	66.0	10.2	39.1	28.8	54,900	9.7	24.2	23.9
44 19180	Cranston city	56,293	44.6	29.5	66,716	64.2	11.4	39.0	26.8	57,463	6.9	21.3	24.9
44 22960	East Providence city	33,582	48.8	25.3	37,800	64.4	10.8	39.1	35.0	47,983	8.2	29.2	17.5
44 49960	Newport city	16,987	26.5	47.9	21,081	69.7	6.8	43.3	25.6	58,180	7.3	20.2	28.5
44 54640	Pawtucket city	48,569	55.5	16.9	56,866	65.7	12.9	38.9	32.9	38,324	15.1	33.7	10.4
44 59000	Providence city	101,132	50.7	27.9	143,234	63.7	15.0	33.2	30.2	37,654	24.6	37.6	14.2
44 74300	Warwick city	60,894	39.6	29.8	68,942	69.4	9.7	43.5	28.0	58,886	4.8	19.7	22.9
44 80780	Woonsocket city	27,526	56.0	14.6	31,869	58.1	8.2	37.0	36.1	34,518	19.9	37.5	13.2
45 00000	**South Carolina**	3,115,808	46.0	24.6	3,719,118	61.4	11.8	37.8	30.8	43,490	14.1	29.2	15.4
45 00550	Aiken city	20,156	29.5	41.0	24,570	53.5	7.9	35.4	36.6	52,771	9.7	24.8	25.2
45 01360	Anderson city	17,341	54.2	18.2	21,166	56.5	14.8	29.9	41.2	28,231	24.6	44.7	10.6
45 13330	Charleston city	81,611	26.0	48.2	103,651	66.5	8.6	42.9	25.1	50,602	14.7	27.5	22.2
45 16000	Columbia city	74,595	33.9	39.2	110,445	64.8	11.2	35.6	26.9	40,501	17.1	32.5	15.5
45 21985	Easley city	13,775	47.9	20.9	15,576	59.5	10.8	37.4	33.4	38,915	11.9	28.4	12.7
45 25810	Florence city	24,685	40.4	28.8	28,637	65.0	12.1	41.2	30.2	41,660	15.8	30.5	15.7
45 29815	Goose Creek city	21,768	35.5	27.3	28,694	72.7	8.6	51.7	16.4	59,654	9.5	15.9	19.0
45 30850	Greenville city	39,662	35.4	40.5	48,614	66.5	11.8	37.8	28.4	39,308	17.8	33.4	19.0
45 30895	Greenwood city	14,869	56.7	19.0	18,219	54.9	19.0	29.2	46.3	23,016	24.8	53.5	7.7
45 30985	Greer city	16,900	43.9	27.3	19,665	69.1	9.1	43.3	23.4	42,341	17.7	31.5	16.5
45 34045	Hilton Head Island town	29,534	27.8	46.4	32,359	56.0	7.3	31.8	38.8	69,622	4.2	13.2	30.8
45 45115	Mauldin city	15,683	33.8	31.9	18,026	68.2	5.6	48.5	20.7	54,095	5.5	17.6	17.6
45 48535	Mount Pleasant town	47,725	15.4	58.6	53,800	70.9	6.8	48.0	20.0	71,521	6.6	14.4	35.8
45 49075	Myrtle Beach city	19,957	44.7	27.6	23,123	63.6	13.6	32.9	32.2	33,537	23.0	39.9	12.2
45 50695	North Augusta city	15,070	34.9	34.4	17,200	58.4	8.4	40.2	32.4	50,323	8.5	22.6	19.6
45 50875	North Charleston city	62,217	50.0	18.2	77,120	67.7	12.7	42.9	24.0	38,444	18.8	33.1	10.8
45 61405	Rock Hill city	41,698	42.0	27.8	53,461	69.3	13.1	40.7	25.9	40,551	13.2	31.0	12.3
45 62395	St. Andrews CDP	12,648	37.6	26.9	15,547	71.3	13.0	40.3	28.7	31,222	21.1	41.1	5.9
45 67390	Socastee CDP	13,491	41.9	17.5	16,077	66.6	10.9	32.9	26.1	36,868	17.9	25.6	4.4
45 68290	Spartanburg city	23,834	44.8	26.9	30,199	57.7	15.7	29.7	39.1	32,104	25.2	42.7	9.2
45 70270	Summerville town	28,724	34.4	30.4	33,875	67.5	11.3	43.1	25.5	50,665	11.8	21.2	18.7
45 70405	Sumter city	25,865	41.0	22.5	31,387	62.1	13.3	39.7	32.1	39,061	17.1	31.0	13.0
45 71395	Taylors CDP	15,872	37.2	25.7	18,073	68.1	8.1	43.6	25.0	47,685	10.4	23.6	13.5
46 00000	**South Dakota**	538,464	41.6	26.4	644,256	69.0	5.3	46.8	24.1	48,900	9.1	23.9	15.7
46 00100	Aberdeen city	16,945	43.6	26.2	20,647	71.8	4.2	47.9	23.3	47,910	3.9	27.3	14.0
46 07580	Brookings city	10,555	28.8	46.2	19,059	69.3	4.3	32.6	18.7	39,835	10.0	32.5	12.4
46 52980	Rapid City city	45,534	36.5	29.1	54,030	67.9	7.3	42.2	27.1	44,382	9.5	25.9	13.6
46 59020	Sioux Falls city	102,985	38.1	31.9	122,411	73.9	4.9	52.6	20.1	50,295	9.2	21.4	17.5
46 69300	Watertown city	14,611	44.1	24.3	17,497	71.1	4.7	48.7	24.7	44,655	8.3	28.8	10.0

Table B-4. Cities — What: Education, Employment, and Income, 2010–2012—*Continued*

STATE and Place code	STATE city	Educational attainment			Employment status				Percent of households with no workers	Median household income (dollars)	Percent of families with income below poverty	Percent of households with income less than $25,000	Percent of households with income of $100,000 or more
		Total population 25 years and over	Percent with a high school diploma or less	Percent with a bachelor's degree or more	Total population 16 years and over	Percent in the labor force	Unemployment rate	Percent who worked full-time year-round					
	ACS table number:	C15002	C15002	C15002	B23025	B23025	B23025	C20005	C08202	B19013	C17013	C19001	C19001
	Column number:	1	2	3	4	5	6	7	8	9	10	11	12
47 00000	**Tennessee**	4,294,543	49.0	23.7	5,077,947	61.5	10.4	38.7	30.1	42,959	13.6	29.0	15.0
47 03440	Bartlett city	37,039	31.8	34.2	43,130	69.2	7.2	47.6	17.7	75,308	2.3	6.9	33.2
47 08280	Brentwood city	24,102	11.5	68.3	28,117	65.4	4.4	43.1	13.7	133,450	1.8	4.0	65.7
47 08540	Bristol city	18,411	48.1	21.9	22,039	56.0	10.0	36.0	37.8	33,147	16.1	39.1	9.3
47 14000	Chattanooga city	114,232	44.8	25.2	137,436	61.6	12.5	37.1	33.2	37,140	17.6	34.2	12.6
47 15160	Clarksville city	79,728	39.5	23.9	102,894	67.1	10.7	43.2	22.9	44,760	15.0	24.4	11.6
47 15400	Cleveland city	26,351	46.4	23.4	33,423	58.3	11.2	32.4	31.4	33,065	19.3	38.3	10.8
47 16420	Collierville town	28,855	21.0	51.9	34,445	69.5	6.7	46.4	14.0	100,839	3.0	7.3	50.4
47 16540	Columbia city	22,163	53.1	15.4	25,795	60.8	13.4	36.2	34.7	30,637	21.2	41.3	8.7
47 16920	Cookeville city	17,809	48.8	27.2	25,500	52.7	13.0	28.5	38.7	28,212	26.7	45.6	10.7
47 22720	East Ridge city	14,952	46.6	19.3	17,017	61.8	9.3	43.1	32.3	37,755	9.9	33.4	5.9
47 25760	Farragut town	13,599	16.9	57.5	16,047	61.4	5.6	36.7	24.3	96,034	3.5	9.9	48.7
47 27740	Franklin city	43,643	21.4	53.5	49,598	70.9	5.3	47.8	19.5	78,536	6.6	14.8	39.6
47 28540	Gallatin city	20,733	47.7	19.8	24,088	63.2	6.9	43.1	28.3	44,516	12.9	24.8	16.3
47 28960	Germantown city	27,406	11.5	65.3	31,123	63.1	4.7	44.1	22.6	113,294	2.0	7.0	56.3
47 33280	Hendersonville city	34,103	38.2	31.9	39,830	68.5	6.4	46.7	20.9	59,602	7.9	20.0	24.9
47 37640	Jackson city	41,440	46.7	26.6	52,427	60.2	15.3	35.2	30.8	36,838	16.6	34.5	14.0
47 38320	Johnson City city	41,639	35.6	37.5	52,661	59.0	6.3	37.6	32.0	38,198	16.2	34.0	18.1
47 39560	Kingsport city	36,997	46.0	26.0	41,765	56.5	10.9	35.0	39.6	39,619	13.7	33.5	14.5
47 40000	Knoxville city	118,957	39.5	30.5	151,996	60.9	7.8	37.9	31.7	32,632	14.5	36.7	9.0
47 41200	La Vergne city	20,520	50.5	19.2	23,629	72.3	9.4	51.5	13.2	52,583	8.3	13.8	13.0
47 41520	Lebanon city	18,061	57.1	19.6	21,117	58.6	12.3	35.4	34.5	43,727	13.4	29.3	14.4
47 46380	Maryville city	18,666	34.7	35.1	22,271	58.3	6.7	36.8	31.5	52,846	8.3	23.8	17.5
47 48000	Memphis city	410,597	47.0	23.7	505,640	63.6	14.4	38.2	28.6	36,062	22.7	35.5	11.6
47 50280	Morristown city	19,245	60.4	16.1	22,918	55.4	12.5	33.0	38.8	28,929	25.8	44.7	5.7
47 50780	Mount Juliet city	17,083	31.0	33.5	19,548	68.9	7.4	50.0	17.9	68,083	7.5	13.2	27.4
47 51560	Murfreesboro city	65,946	31.1	35.7	87,926	69.3	10.0	41.3	22.7	47,405	11.3	24.1	18.2
47 52006	Nashville-Davidson (balance)	410,027	39.2	34.5	492,803	68.5	9.3	43.0	23.7	44,271	15.1	27.7	15.9
47 55120	Oak Ridge city	20,722	30.7	41.0	23,614	60.8	9.4	39.9	33.0	53,826	11.5	25.8	24.6
47 67760	Shelbyville city	12,388	75.7	4.7	14,791	54.5	10.6	34.5	36.2	26,633	27.2	46.0	3.1
47 69420	Smyrna town	25,813	42.4	24.4	30,239	72.5	6.0	50.2	19.8	51,323	10.2	21.4	15.0
47 70580	Spring Hill city	18,854	27.1	41.8	20,846	78.7	3.8	54.9	11.9	76,408	4.8	5.3	32.0
48 00000	**Texas**	16,080,717	44.3	26.4	19,465,219	65.0	8.4	43.4	22.2	50,776	14.1	24.4	21.2
48 01000	Abilene city	74,162	45.9	22.1	95,887	58.5	7.6	37.5	26.3	41,460	14.2	29.6	12.6
48 01924	Allen city	54,428	16.8	52.5	63,362	75.3	6.1	52.3	9.4	99,950	4.6	8.2	50.0
48 02272	Alvin city	15,261	46.9	17.3	18,506	61.9	8.9	41.3	24.0	42,521	16.4	29.8	18.6
48 03000	Amarillo city	121,653	41.9	22.7	146,350	67.9	5.8	47.6	22.9	45,350	13.5	27.3	15.0
48 04000	Arlington city	226,938	39.4	28.6	282,325	71.9	9.8	46.7	17.5	51,787	14.1	21.4	19.6
48 04462	Atascocita CDP	43,674	28.9	32.2	52,125	69.3	6.3	50.1	10.7	77,908	4.7	6.6	37.6
48 05000	Austin city	524,914	30.4	44.9	654,595	73.1	8.0	47.0	17.8	51,668	14.5	23.4	22.7
48 05372	Balch Springs city	12,646	63.5	11.6	16,558	61.0	9.3	45.1	24.2	51,749	24.2	32.8	6.9
48 06128	Baytown city	43,617	52.2	12.7	52,960	61.8	12.1	39.1	24.7	46,730	18.1	24.5	15.3
48 07000	Beaumont city	75,128	46.7	22.5	92,492	60.2	12.2	37.0	31.9	37,343	19.6	35.7	14.4
48 07132	Bedford city	34,174	27.0	33.3	39,055	70.9	5.8	50.8	20.0	58,935	7.4	16.4	24.8
48 07552	Benbrook city	15,482	30.5	32.9	17,623	65.2	6.0	46.1	27.7	60,153	6.5	19.3	27.5
48 08236	Big Spring city	18,515	55.1	12.2	22,108	46.7	8.4	32.4	32.4	40,943	15.3	27.6	14.0
48 10768	Brownsville city	99,124	59.2	16.2	124,425	58.4	12.0	34.9	25.2	31,246	31.3	41.4	10.2
48 10897	Brushy Creek CDP	14,113	18.6	51.2	16,078	77.0	8.7	53.4	10.2	97,482	. . .	4.1	49.1
48 10912	Bryan city	44,852	50.7	24.9	60,214	66.1	10.9	36.2	27.6	36,235	18.9	36.7	11.8
48 11428	Burleson city	23,665	36.6	24.3	27,710	74.6	7.2	50.6	19.1	70,948	5.8	11.4	25.8
48 12580	Canyon Lake CDP	15,220	37.5	26.2	16,708	57.5	10.1	38.7	39.1	52,059	4.8	16.6	20.7
48 13024	Carrollton city	80,804	33.9	35.4	95,068	76.3	6.5	52.9	12.4	69,045	6.9	10.7	31.8
48 13492	Cedar Hill city	27,957	31.2	30.1	33,351	73.6	8.4	50.8	16.5	63,664	7.8	14.0	26.0
48 13552	Cedar Park city	34,392	20.9	43.3	40,412	72.8	7.6	49.2	13.8	75,578	5.6	11.3	34.7
48 14236	Channelview CDP	20,297	61.6	12.0	26,493	67.4	13.5	41.8	18.1	43,235	20.9	25.5	14.4
48 15364	Cleburne city	17,878	54.8	14.3	21,919	63.3	7.9	41.3	27.2	46,835	14.2	25.1	13.0
48 15628	Cloverleaf CDP	12,589	72.7	8.0	16,786	64.2	14.4	37.9	21.2	35,880	25.8	28.7	11.6
48 15976	College Station city	37,309	19.0	55.6	82,948	59.8	8.2	27.2	23.6	30,980	14.7	42.6	16.3
48 15988	Colleyville city	15,391	11.4	66.5	18,101	66.7	4.5	45.2	13.1	147,399	1.2	2.6	68.4
48 16432	Conroe city	36,865	52.4	18.0	44,032	64.3	6.2	40.5	23.7	41,952	19.2	31.1	15.3
48 16612	Coppell city	25,716	14.7	62.3	29,559	71.9	4.2	51.6	11.3	104,486	3.4	7.5	53.9
48 16624	Copperas Cove city	20,166	37.1	18.8	23,991	63.1	9.7	47.0	24.1	51,719	9.0	17.8	16.8
48 16696	Corinth city	12,585	23.0	41.3	14,910	75.5	8.4	54.1	16.2	89,033	7.3	11.4	43.8
48 17000	Corpus Christi city	196,313	45.9	20.9	238,236	64.4	7.7	42.1	24.1	46,470	14.3	25.5	17.8
48 17060	Corsicana city	14,762	57.3	17.1	17,943	62.8	10.5	39.6	27.7	38,370	18.6	30.2	9.5
48 19000	Dallas city	774,823	48.6	29.2	931,275	67.6	9.7	45.1	21.7	41,745	20.7	29.3	17.6
48 19624	Deer Park city	20,249	42.9	19.4	24,492	69.1	7.1	48.3	18.9	72,603	4.5	13.5	33.0
48 19792	Del Rio city	21,525	60.7	15.7	25,887	61.4	11.7	37.8	27.4	40,307	16.3	31.2	13.0
48 19900	Denison city	15,321	51.7	16.2	17,832	57.2	10.5	36.7	35.2	36,260	17.0	34.6	8.9
48 19972	Denton city	64,730	27.8	38.4	96,907	69.0	10.7	36.9	21.6	47,695	9.4	26.9	17.4
48 20092	DeSoto city	33,127	30.4	29.3	39,447	67.4	9.7	47.2	24.0	56,886	8.0	20.2	22.7
48 21628	Duncanville city	24,704	41.4	28.0	29,452	67.7	6.5	46.9	21.2	52,814	8.8	17.2	17.0
48 21892	Eagle Pass city	15,972	59.4	18.1	19,197	57.6	10.4	35.7	30.3	33,643	24.3	40.2	10.0

Table B-4. Cities — What: Education, Employment, and Income, 2010–2012—*Continued*

STATE and Place code	STATE city	Educational attainment			Employment status				Percent of households with no workers	Median household income (dollars)	Percent of families with income below poverty	Percent of households with income less than $25,000	Percent of households with income of $100,000 or more
		Total population 25 years and over	Percent with a high school diploma or less	Percent with a bachelor's degree or more	Total population 16 years and over	Percent in the labor force	Unemployment rate	Percent who worked full-time year-round					
	ACS table number:	C15002	C15002	C15002	B23025	B23025	B23025	C20005	C08202	B19013	C17013	C19001	C19001
	Column number:	1	2	3	4	5	6	7	8	9	10	11	12
	Texas—Cont.												
48 22660	Edinburg city..............	44,239	45.1	26.4	57,087	66.2	11.7	40.5	18.8	40,726	23.8	34.1	13.5
48 24000	El Paso city...............	399,688	47.2	22.6	496,467	60.4	8.6	39.5	24.0	40,920	18.7	31.2	14.7
48 24768	Euless city................	34,194	34.4	32.4	40,219	74.3	9.5	51.2	16.6	52,629	11.1	17.6	18.7
48 25452	Farmers Branch city.......	18,764	43.3	32.0	22,512	70.0	8.7	43.9	18.8	56,554	9.1	18.5	21.8
48 26232	Flower Mound town	41,529	14.7	55.9	48,939	74.1	4.9	53.6	12.2	120,740	2.0	4.3	61.0
48 26736	Fort Hood CDP............	...	...	...	22,685	74.9	4.7	62.2	10.2	41,563	13.7	17.3	5.1
48 27000	Fort Worth city...........	465,297	44.8	25.9	560,034	67.9	9.8	45.7	20.7	50,129	15.5	25.2	18.5
48 27648	Friendswood city..........	24,000	21.0	47.7	28,641	65.7	6.0	46.2	16.7	100,954	1.7	7.3	50.8
48 27684	Frisco city................	74,648	14.3	58.7	85,176	78.4	5.1	57.1	9.4	108,088	3.8	6.4	54.1
48 28068	Galveston city............	31,512	47.4	26.2	39,106	61.1	11.5	34.8	31.0	36,232	18.1	36.5	14.7
48 29000	Garland city..............	140,649	47.9	21.6	170,318	72.5	10.3	48.2	17.1	52,084	12.8	18.3	18.6
48 29336	Georgetown city..........	34,100	30.1	41.1	38,850	52.6	9.9	36.2	42.1	60,687	7.9	17.2	23.0
48 30464	Grand Prairie city........	106,364	47.6	21.4	128,520	71.9	10.8	49.3	16.8	51,638	14.0	21.3	18.1
48 30644	Grapevine city............	31,322	27.8	43.9	36,237	76.4	4.1	53.8	13.3	72,070	9.5	14.6	34.4
48 30920	Greenville city...........	16,513	52.6	19.0	19,773	58.0	12.7	37.3	33.5	34,934	20.6	31.7	12.4
48 31928	Haltom City city..........	26,523	60.2	12.4	32,507	67.2	7.8	46.6	21.4	42,511	16.0	26.1	11.0
48 32312	Harker Heights city.......	16,001	34.4	28.3	20,121	65.0	7.3	46.6	21.7	63,857	12.6	18.1	28.1
48 32372	Harlingen city............	40,384	53.6	19.6	47,992	48.6	7.5	35.1	34.5	32,937	26.4	38.9	11.7
48 35000	Houston city..............	1,355,026	47.2	28.9	1,639,571	67.8	10.0	43.9	20.7	43,792	20.1	29.0	19.1
48 35528	Huntsville city...........	22,992	51.4	18.6	34,541	34.6	10.5	18.3	31.1	27,134	27.8	47.8	10.2
48 35576	Hurst city................	25,591	41.6	26.7	29,931	65.4	8.1	44.6	23.3	50,404	11.9	21.3	22.8
48 37000	Irving city...............	140,876	41.9	33.2	166,367	73.2	8.7	51.3	14.3	49,407	13.7	22.2	19.3
48 38632	Keller city...............	26,092	14.6	56.6	30,411	68.0	5.5	47.8	16.6	113,025	3.7	9.3	56.6
48 39040	Kerrville city............	15,880	45.3	28.7	18,349	51.8	9.0	31.7	40.9	35,943	16.5	34.4	12.8
48 39148	Killeen city..............	73,709	36.1	17.0	94,188	70.5	11.2	48.2	18.8	45,360	13.8	24.0	10.6
48 39352	Kingsville city...........	14,283	49.1	26.4	19,814	59.9	11.5	33.8	29.3	36,419	22.4	36.2	11.8
48 39952	Kyle city.................	17,791	33.6	26.7	20,542	75.6	6.1	57.4	7.7	78,731	3.6	9.7	31.9
48 40588	Lake Jackson city.........	17,380	25.9	32.4	21,411	65.4	6.2	45.5	18.3	70,571	3.8	12.2	30.8
48 41212	Lancaster city............	23,038	45.6	19.3	27,283	66.4	10.5	50.9	21.4	51,570	12.2	23.6	16.4
48 41440	La Porte city.............	21,885	49.4	12.9	26,598	69.4	10.2	44.6	19.1	64,249	8.6	17.7	29.3
48 41464	Laredo city...............	130,885	57.0	16.8	166,153	59.2	6.2	38.4	19.0	36,957	27.3	34.8	12.7
48 41980	League City city..........	56,651	25.4	41.8	64,635	73.2	5.6	53.6	14.4	84,013	3.1	8.6	41.0
48 42016	Leander city..............	17,017	31.0	31.9	19,154	76.7	8.1	52.9	9.6	73,502	5.7	9.5	34.5
48 42508	Lewisville city...........	63,383	34.6	29.9	74,880	78.2	6.9	54.2	14.4	56,020	8.6	15.6	20.9
48 43012	Little Elm city...........	16,462	34.2	26.0	18,492	77.4	9.1	56.7	9.6	75,235	5.3	10.6	34.4
48 43888	Longview city.............	51,981	45.3	20.4	62,615	61.6	8.0	40.0	28.5	41,550	15.8	28.8	13.2
48 45000	Lubbock city..............	134,661	39.1	29.5	183,944	67.3	7.0	41.1	23.3	42,139	14.6	31.1	14.7
48 45072	Lufkin city...............	22,272	53.3	18.3	27,163	60.0	11.9	36.0	33.3	37,455	16.4	31.9	12.1
48 45384	McAllen city..............	81,473	46.6	26.7	99,939	61.8	7.7	39.9	22.6	41,375	23.6	32.5	17.3
48 45744	McKinney city.............	84,267	25.3	45.8	98,792	70.4	3.8	52.1	13.1	81,204	7.5	12.2	39.3
48 46452	Mansfield city............	35,047	26.2	40.8	41,311	75.2	6.7	50.4	15.2	87,352	6.4	13.4	44.8
48 46776	Marshall city.............	14,167	52.1	20.7	18,438	59.7	9.6	37.6	32.8	30,652	23.1	39.4	8.8
48 47892	Mesquite city.............	84,687	47.5	18.0	104,267	70.4	8.1	49.5	16.2	48,329	14.2	22.8	15.7
48 48072	Midland city..............	71,394	41.3	23.2	85,940	69.1	4.6	49.9	18.1	59,336	9.9	19.3	25.7
48 48768	Mission city..............	44,031	51.3	24.9	54,621	58.7	8.0	38.1	24.7	41,978	22.4	31.7	16.3
48 48772	Mission Bend CDP..........	21,181	49.6	23.2	26,551	68.0	6.9	45.7	10.1	55,367	11.2	12.7	18.0
48 48804	Missouri City city........	44,357	26.2	40.3	52,467	69.6	6.2	50.8	14.8	77,944	5.2	10.2	36.6
48 50256	Nacogdoches city..........	16,725	41.0	30.7	27,276	57.1	11.7	32.9	31.0	30,059	22.9	43.8	9.3
48 50820	New Braunfels city........	37,836	38.4	25.8	44,341	66.4	7.5	44.8	25.2	53,221	9.1	19.1	19.0
48 52356	North Richland Hills city ..	42,963	33.1	29.6	51,306	71.4	6.8	49.9	18.7	60,849	6.5	15.8	24.5
48 53388	Odessa city...............	61,857	52.4	15.5	76,540	67.2	5.2	47.2	20.7	50,731	13.3	25.3	18.0
48 55080	Paris city................	16,635	51.7	14.7	19,827	58.1	10.0	35.8	35.9	32,918	23.9	39.7	8.2
48 56000	Pasadena city.............	89,700	59.8	13.5	111,431	63.3	11.8	41.1	22.9	45,684	17.9	27.3	16.3
48 56348	Pearland city.............	59,012	27.0	44.6	68,815	74.3	5.4	55.2	11.7	87,519	3.7	9.1	44.0
48 57176	Pflugerville city.........	31,641	28.3	34.5	36,921	73.8	5.0	54.5	14.1	72,948	8.2	13.9	30.8
48 57200	Pharr city................	39,161	66.1	12.5	48,723	56.5	12.6	32.1	29.5	29,664	34.2	44.6	8.2
48 57980	Plainview city............	12,683	59.7	14.6	16,230	65.1	8.9	44.0	22.6	40,208	22.1	33.3	9.7
48 58016	Plano city................	179,327	21.0	52.7	206,554	72.1	6.2	52.3	14.4	81,339	5.7	11.3	40.3
48 58820	Port Arthur city..........	34,213	58.7	10.9	41,111	61.3	14.0	35.6	33.8	32,219	25.3	40.1	10.4
48 61796	Richardson city...........	67,519	25.5	49.2	82,358	69.1	7.8	46.7	18.6	68,518	5.6	17.0	31.1
48 62828	Rockwall city.............	25,411	26.5	38.5	28,889	69.5	5.5	50.8	17.6	82,762	3.5	11.5	39.2
48 63284	Rosenberg city............	18,766	64.9	9.3	23,109	63.9	6.5	45.3	20.6	40,661	18.2	28.4	15.0
48 63500	Round Rock city...........	63,328	29.3	38.0	75,789	74.4	7.7	52.2	11.2	67,856	6.4	11.8	29.8
48 63572	Rowlett city..............	37,486	34.1	32.1	45,597	71.3	8.0	50.9	11.9	83,088	3.8	8.5	36.0
48 64064	Sachse city...............	14,234	30.7	31.9	16,391	73.6	6.3	51.4	11.0	85,914	3.4	5.7	39.7
48 64112	Saginaw city..............	12,985	43.9	21.3	15,663	74.9	8.6	51.6	15.5	70,254	4.2	11.8	25.8
48 64472	San Angelo city...........	58,411	49.7	21.7	74,726	65.0	6.9	41.3	27.8	41,357	14.9	31.6	13.6
48 65000	San Antonio city..........	845,750	44.7	24.3	1,040,155	64.7	8.9	42.3	23.9	45,074	16.3	27.7	16.0
48 65036	San Benito city...........	14,267	68.1	7.7	16,983	53.5	13.7	30.2	37.1	27,083	32.6	46.2	6.7
48 65516	San Juan city.............	18,733	72.4	7.2	23,139	60.4	9.5	36.1	25.6	33,427	28.8	35.8	6.8
48 65600	San Marcos city...........	19,930	37.1	30.8	41,122	60.3	9.8	27.9	24.1	27,055	16.0	45.4	6.3
48 66128	Schertz city..............	22,208	33.2	31.2	25,527	70.0	7.1	49.6	21.1	69,286	3.9	10.7	29.4
48 66644	Seguin city...............	16,209	58.8	14.3	19,942	63.5	11.1	38.5	28.0	39,421	18.4	34.0	10.3
48 67496	Sherman city..............	24,248	46.8	19.8	30,456	63.0	12.3	39.6	28.0	41,809	16.7	29.9	12.5
48 68636	Socorro city..............	18,189	69.6	6.7	23,318	59.5	14.2	33.0	24.6	29,858	31.2	39.5	4.3
48 69032	Southlake city............	16,922	9.9	68.5	19,384	63.8	5.1	44.7	14.8	167,060	3.0	8.5	72.7

Table B-4. Cities — What: Education, Employment, and Income, 2010–2012—*Continued*

STATE and Place code	STATE city	Educational attainment			Employment status				Percent of households with no workers	Median household income (dollars)	Percent of families with income below poverty	Percent of households with income less than $25,000	Percent of households with income of $100,000 or more
		Total population 25 years and over	Percent with a high school diploma or less	Percent with a bachelor's degree or more	Total population 16 years and over	Percent in the labor force	Unemployment rate	Percent who worked full-time year-round					
	ACS table number:	C15002	C15002	C15002	B23025	B23025	B23025	C20005	C08202	B19013	C17013	C19001	C19001
	Column number:	1	2	3	4	5	6	7	8	9	10	11	12
	Texas—Cont.												
48 69596	Spring CDP	34,494	43.1	19.3	41,165	71.3	8.6	52.1	13.6	64,556	7.3	10.8	23.2
48 70808	Sugar Land city	54,939	20.0	52.8	64,640	65.9	5.4	47.1	12.8	105,338	3.6	7.1	53.4
48 72176	Temple city	45,954	44.6	25.0	52,363	60.1	5.7	44.6	29.7	47,672	9.2	24.5	17.1
48 72368	Texarkana city	23,980	39.7	28.2	29,025	58.0	12.0	35.9	34.1	37,679	18.6	36.3	12.9
48 72392	Texas City city	29,058	49.8	12.4	34,159	61.3	13.3	38.0	28.8	44,559	17.1	28.7	14.9
48 72530	The Colony city	23,927	30.0	32.6	28,475	80.8	7.9	58.4	10.5	71,090	3.5	9.1	32.8
48 72656	The Woodlands CDP	65,486	15.6	58.9	75,233	65.7	5.4	46.3	18.1	102,458	4.8	11.5	51.5
48 73057	Timberwood Park CDP	17,360	22.0	48.3	19,900	72.0	5.3	53.1	9.6	102,157	2.2	4.5	51.3
48 74144	Tyler city	61,253	36.8	30.2	77,774	63.9	7.3	39.4	26.8	41,348	13.9	30.1	16.4
48 74492	University Park city	...	...	...	17,503	61.8	7.3	36.2	17.1	172,404	1.8	9.8	69.8
48 75428	Victoria city	40,044	49.6	16.1	48,659	65.2	9.4	42.0	27.8	44,978	17.0	29.0	15.6
48 76000	Waco city	70,796	48.4	21.7	98,325	59.1	9.7	34.3	28.8	32,353	21.6	38.9	9.9
48 76672	Watauga city	15,280	43.4	18.0	17,963	74.4	9.5	50.5	14.3	59,487	4.3	15.5	18.2
48 76816	Waxahachie city	18,839	42.7	24.4	23,389	67.1	9.0	44.0	22.0	54,036	10.0	21.0	17.8
48 76864	Weatherford city	16,355	36.2	24.9	19,582	62.9	8.3	42.8	27.9	50,569	9.3	21.7	16.6
48 77272	Weslaco city	22,011	58.9	17.4	26,402	55.0	12.7	32.3	36.7	36,734	25.7	35.7	10.3
48 77728	West Odessa CDP	12,874	63.8	6.6	15,989	62.6	6.9	41.9	20.7	49,346	14.5	26.5	13.2
48 79000	Wichita Falls city	64,105	48.4	21.0	83,037	62.4	7.0	40.6	27.6	42,305	13.0	28.4	13.4
48 80356	Wylie city	25,288	29.7	34.9	30,352	75.7	5.9	54.8	11.0	79,794	3.8	8.1	35.3
49 00000	**Utah**	1,612,410	33.0	30.1	2,020,550	68.5	7.9	40.9	19.7	57,255	9.9	19.0	21.0
49 01310	American Fork city	13,693	23.8	33.3	17,296	64.4	6.7	39.5	18.3	65,499	10.0	17.5	23.7
49 07690	Bountiful city	26,223	21.9	40.7	31,563	62.8	6.2	39.0	24.6	64,252	6.6	13.8	26.2
49 11320	Cedar City city	14,586	30.0	32.6	21,990	65.3	17.6	31.3	24.6	39,391	19.0	32.9	10.2
49 13850	Clearfield city	16,317	41.7	19.2	20,331	72.9	6.6	48.2	18.0	46,454	11.9	22.4	13.3
49 14290	Clinton city	11,372	31.9	23.2	13,677	73.1	4.3	49.7	12.3	68,217	2.6	6.9	22.2
49 16270	Cottonwood Heights city	22,602	20.0	45.5	26,787	69.4	7.9	43.5	17.6	70,620	4.2	8.4	28.3
49 20120	Draper city	25,821	22.5	36.4	30,605	64.0	5.6	43.1	9.2	86,517	3.1	8.0	42.9
49 20810	Eagle Mountain city	9,993	21.8	32.2	12,542	73.3	7.2	49.2	8.3	66,505	6.9	8.2	20.0
49 24740	Farmington city	10,793	15.2	44.9	13,095	68.7	3.0	44.7	9.9	80,540	5.1	4.8	37.1
49 34970	Herriman city	10,789	27.6	27.6	13,431	73.2	3.6	49.1	8.8	64,766	9.1	13.4	28.3
49 36070	Holladay city	18,028	14.6	55.3	20,814	64.0	6.3	38.6	27.4	64,005	4.9	18.0	34.8
49 40360	Kaysville city	14,972	21.0	41.5	18,391	69.2	4.1	43.1	17.3	80,373	8.1	16.8	39.7
49 40470	Kearns CDP	18,903	54.8	10.6	23,157	73.2	9.4	46.5	14.7	53,277	11.3	13.7	10.6
49 43660	Layton city	38,842	27.3	32.1	48,142	67.7	4.6	44.9	16.1	65,312	8.3	14.9	25.2
49 44320	Lehi city	23,739	20.8	38.6	29,272	70.0	8.5	42.2	14.2	67,160	5.9	10.7	26.2
49 45860	Logan city	22,176	30.0	37.0	37,775	70.7	8.4	32.1	15.8	33,437	19.5	36.4	9.0
49 47290	Magna CDP	15,921	55.2	8.8	19,549	72.7	10.7	47.6	13.2	55,990	12.1	14.7	14.2
49 49710	Midvale city	18,515	44.9	21.6	22,744	72.8	10.2	44.6	19.6	46,029	13.5	24.0	9.8
49 50150	Millcreek CDP	42,842	26.4	41.6	50,163	67.2	5.9	42.3	23.7	59,891	6.9	18.9	24.7
49 53230	Murray city	31,058	31.0	31.1	37,313	70.5	7.7	44.9	23.8	53,261	9.1	20.6	19.3
49 55980	Ogden city	48,826	48.6	18.0	61,690	66.1	11.0	36.8	24.2	40,878	19.1	28.1	9.6
49 57300	Orem city	48,027	25.8	35.3	65,273	67.1	8.3	36.0	17.9	53,058	12.6	21.6	18.1
49 60930	Pleasant Grove city	17,376	24.2	35.5	22,627	67.7	7.2	39.2	14.6	60,380	8.6	16.0	20.3
49 62470	Provo city	48,755	24.5	38.3	91,395	69.2	8.2	23.6	17.9	38,338	22.9	33.2	11.5
49 64340	Riverton city	21,711	23.9	32.8	25,983	77.1	3.9	52.7	8.6	80,160	1.4	5.3	32.5
49 65110	Roy city	22,093	41.4	19.2	26,249	70.0	6.2	46.7	20.9	58,922	7.8	14.8	16.1
49 65330	St. George city	44,843	34.2	25.1	55,060	57.6	12.5	31.9	35.4	44,793	9.7	25.5	13.8
49 67000	Salt Lake City city	120,108	31.6	40.8	149,536	70.8	9.6	40.9	23.5	42,267	15.7	30.5	16.9
49 67440	Sandy city	55,455	26.3	38.3	66,314	70.3	7.3	43.7	16.8	73,458	6.6	12.1	33.1
49 67825	Saratoga Springs city	9,015	15.9	44.4	10,782	70.8	5.2	45.4	8.7	72,197	2.3	3.4	27.5
49 70850	South Jordan city	30,214	21.9	36.8	36,911	70.6	6.2	44.7	13.4	85,997	3.6	6.2	41.0
49 71070	South Salt Lake city	14,850	47.0	22.1	18,604	65.8	10.3	38.4	23.3	35,547	27.1	38.2	4.9
49 71290	Spanish Fork city	17,742	32.8	26.6	22,620	68.4	8.5	39.2	13.4	59,261	4.1	12.0	14.0
49 72280	Springville city	15,523	26.9	36.0	19,943	70.3	5.9	41.9	15.2	58,907	5.9	14.4	18.2
49 74810	Syracuse city	12,745	24.2	37.2	15,656	76.8	4.1	50.4	9.5	85,671	2.8	3.7	37.2
49 75360	Taylorsville city	36,910	40.0	20.2	44,474	73.5	9.1	44.0	19.4	55,579	9.9	19.6	18.0
49 76680	Tooele city	18,249	42.8	16.8	21,844	67.2	8.8	44.0	18.2	54,391	9.3	15.7	16.4
49 81960	Washington city	12,269	36.0	25.4	14,387	63.9	8.6	37.5	32.0	46,168	12.2	20.4	13.4
49 82950	West Jordan city	59,442	36.6	24.3	74,409	77.2	8.4	49.4	11.0	67,217	8.1	12.7	24.2
49 83470	West Valley City city	75,002	54.5	12.7	91,960	74.2	11.1	45.5	15.7	50,445	19.4	20.8	12.3
50 00000	**Vermont**	433,835	39.3	34.8	516,064	67.7	6.8	41.0	26.4	53,037	7.6	22.3	19.2
50 10675	Burlington city	23,134	29.3	48.8	37,947	64.8	9.6	32.0	26.8	41,387	12.0	32.3	14.5
51 00000	**Virginia**	5,433,053	38.0	34.9	6,460,347	66.5	7.2	45.1	23.4	62,811	8.2	18.9	29.3
51 01000	Alexandria city	109,114	21.3	60.5	120,655	78.8	5.0	59.9	13.0	82,438	6.0	11.1	41.5
51 01912	Annandale CDP	29,248	38.1	38.9	33,613	71.8	5.8	46.8	19.0	76,747	8.6	12.1	35.5
51 03000	Arlington CDP	161,788	16.6	71.0	184,024	79.4	3.9	60.2	13.0	101,319	5.6	9.9	50.7
51 03320	Ashburn CDP	30,105	16.5	60.5	34,064	76.3	4.4	56.8	11.6	118,524	2.3	4.1	61.4
51 04088	Bailey's Crossroads CDP	16,356	44.1	39.2	19,318	70.5	7.7	48.7	19.3	66,503	17.9	22.2	29.3
51 07784	Blacksburg town	13,853	14.2	70.3	38,871	50.7	9.8	22.2	27.8	27,078	12.2	47.9	16.8
51 11464	Burke CDP	27,176	17.7	60.3	31,539	70.9	3.4	50.7	13.3	130,537	1.3	2.7	65.2
51 13720	Cave Spring CDP	18,807	20.1	47.4	21,836	67.4	6.0	45.1	25.4	62,598	6.2	16.5	26.3
51 14440	Centreville CDP	47,640	21.3	52.7	56,838	78.6	5.9	54.4	6.3	99,494	4.4	5.2	49.6
51 14744	Chantilly CDP	13,875	28.0	50.3	16,266	76.3	6.5	56.7	11.0	113,622	7.1	9.6	56.1

Table B-4. Cities — What: Education, Employment, and Income, 2010–2012—*Continued*

STATE and Place code	STATE city	Educational attainment: Total population 25 years and over	Educational attainment: Percent with a high school diploma or less	Educational attainment: Percent with a bachelor's degree or more	Employment status: Total population 16 years and over	Employment status: Percent in the labor force	Employment status: Unemployment rate	Percent who worked full-time year-round	Percent of households with no workers	Median household income (dollars)	Percent of families with income below poverty	Percent of households with income less than $25,000	Percent of households with income of $100,000 or more
	ACS table number:	C15002	C15002	C15002	B23025	B23025	B23025	C20005	C08202	B19013	C17013	C19001	C19001
	Column number:	1	2	3	4	5	6	7	8	9	10	11	12
	Virginia—Cont.												
51 14968	Charlottesville city	25,317	34.0	48.5	37,791	60.5	6.6	35.8	27.6	44,183	10.8	30.4	20.3
51 16000	Chesapeake city	147,465	36.5	28.7	175,472	68.6	7.4	47.8	19.1	68,750	7.5	14.9	28.4
51 16096	Chester CDP	14,955	43.8	26.8	18,214	66.0	9.3	45.1	20.3	58,950	6.4	13.4	19.4
51 16608	Christiansburg town	14,106	32.8	37.3	16,674	70.3	4.1	45.7	22.2	48,649	11.9	23.3	14.0
51 21088	Dale City CDP	41,828	40.5	24.6	50,679	74.3	7.8	50.4	12.0	82,338	5.8	9.6	38.6
51 21344	Danville city	29,382	51.7	16.6	34,688	56.5	16.7	31.1	41.7	31,134	22.5	41.4	7.8
51 26496	Fairfax city	16,131	23.0	53.1	18,949	68.6	6.5	46.7	18.8	94,496	5.3	11.3	49.0
51 26875	Fair Oaks CDP	21,838	13.5	65.5	25,822	82.9	4.7	60.1	9.3	94,599	5.6	8.5	46.6
51 29628	Franklin Farm CDP	...	...	...	15,139	74.2	3.1	54.3	6.4	166,134	4.1	4.6	82.1
51 29744	Fredericksburg city	15,018	38.7	34.0	20,947	64.6	13.1	34.9	27.6	46,397	10.8	25.0	19.2
51 35000	Hampton city	88,701	38.6	22.8	109,809	64.6	10.2	43.0	25.9	51,654	12.0	23.4	17.8
51 35624	Harrisonburg city	22,152	44.8	36.1	42,908	52.8	7.0	28.7	25.6	37,212	11.3	33.9	9.7
51 36648	Herndon town	16,208	34.7	45.6	18,567	81.3	4.6	57.9	8.5	95,811	2.4	5.6	45.9
51 38424	Hopewell city	14,061	61.8	8.9	16,975	58.6	15.4	39.3	40.6	36,748	16.0	32.2	8.2
51 43432	Lake Ridge CDP	28,167	24.3	45.0	32,941	74.7	5.9	54.6	11.8	102,988	2.1	4.0	52.3
51 44984	Leesburg town	27,788	30.3	47.6	32,375	77.4	5.4	55.3	7.7	95,104	5.4	7.4	47.1
51 45784	Lincolnia CDP	15,769	35.5	43.7	18,190	75.8	5.2	56.3	13.1	87,364	12.4	11.1	43.3
51 45957	Linton Hall CDP	23,369	16.6	50.1	26,390	82.6	2.9	61.4	5.5	127,897	0.6	2.4	71.9
51 47672	Lynchburg city	44,167	41.1	31.6	63,378	57.5	11.0	30.9	33.3	37,020	16.9	34.9	13.3
51 48376	McLean CDP	32,532	7.5	80.5	37,421	61.6	4.6	43.4	22.4	182,138	1.4	5.5	76.2
51 48450	McNair CDP	13,942	15.4	65.3	16,147	83.2	3.4	70.1	6.0	104,741	3.5	4.7	54.7
51 48952	Manassas city	24,423	44.2	27.5	29,698	73.0	7.4	50.7	14.1	67,105	11.2	14.2	32.2
51 49792	Marumsco CDP	24,443	57.8	19.5	28,932	76.6	8.3	54.5	11.7	69,469	11.1	12.6	27.9
51 50856	Mechanicsville CDP	25,276	36.0	32.7	28,766	67.1	5.8	47.1	22.4	67,379	3.0	12.5	28.1
51 52658	Montclair CDP	12,740	20.3	53.0	15,153	74.4	6.3	54.4	14.8	114,875	3.9	5.3	61.0
51 56000	Newport News city	112,906	39.7	24.0	142,113	70.0	9.9	44.8	24.0	49,690	11.4	23.1	15.5
51 57000	Norfolk city	145,248	41.0	25.4	198,234	69.9	10.6	46.7	25.0	43,708	14.4	27.3	14.8
51 58472	Oakton CDP	26,649	19.9	66.1	29,154	72.6	4.4	51.1	14.5	117,500	3.8	7.6	55.8
51 61832	Petersburg city	21,568	62.6	13.3	26,164	53.7	18.5	32.0	41.4	34,214	19.7	38.7	5.6
51 64000	Portsmouth city	62,704	47.7	19.2	75,624	62.3	10.2	41.0	28.9	44,945	15.2	28.3	12.3
51 66672	Reston CDP	42,429	14.6	66.7	46,907	76.9	5.5	55.8	12.8	108,087	3.9	8.9	54.0
51 67000	Richmond city	133,104	41.6	34.3	171,277	64.4	11.3	37.6	29.5	40,001	20.9	33.7	14.3
51 68000	Roanoke city	67,489	47.5	23.9	77,909	62.7	8.5	40.6	32.1	38,593	16.6	32.4	10.2
51 70000	Salem city	16,589	37.4	31.5	20,723	61.2	6.4	35.7	28.1	47,549	12.4	25.4	17.2
51 72272	Short Pump CDP	16,874	11.0	69.3	19,690	74.2	4.1	52.0	12.2	106,961	3.0	6.2	54.9
51 74100	South Riding CDP	14,443	14.2	66.3	16,171	77.3	5.5	57.8	6.9	140,548	2.9	2.5	71.9
51 74592	Springfield CDP	22,543	42.8	36.9	25,782	67.4	6.7	47.4	28.0	86,061	5.8	10.0	41.2
51 75216	Staunton city	16,930	45.7	30.6	19,781	60.5	6.2	40.6	31.8	40,318	12.6	33.2	11.5
51 75376	Sterling CDP	17,276	43.1	34.9	20,835	78.7	4.9	53.6	10.9	87,617	4.9	9.3	40.7
51 76432	Suffolk city	55,950	41.9	25.3	65,546	67.8	7.9	45.9	21.1	67,546	8.1	16.7	27.8
51 79560	Tuckahoe CDP	30,615	24.8	52.7	35,597	66.5	6.7	44.5	25.4	63,333	7.7	16.9	29.6
51 79952	Tysons Corner CDP	16,110	11.9	73.7	17,588	75.6	6.0	57.5	14.2	103,811	5.8	10.8	52.9
51 82000	Virginia Beach city	290,821	29.8	32.5	350,695	70.7	6.0	50.1	19.2	65,169	6.7	13.6	28.0
51 83680	Waynesboro city	14,218	56.6	20.8	16,254	60.5	8.9	38.8	32.7	43,656	18.0	30.1	9.6
51 84368	West Falls Church CDP	19,679	34.3	45.6	22,089	76.0	5.5	52.9	16.6	86,636	4.7	10.0	43.8
51 84976	West Springfield CDP	16,842	21.7	56.0	19,425	71.1	4.9	50.8	15.5	115,341	1.3	4.1	57.9
51 86720	Winchester city	17,424	47.9	28.2	21,048	63.5	9.3	39.5	31.7	42,590	14.7	29.4	17.3
53 00000	**Washington**	4,577,171	33.7	31.5	5,419,523	65.1	9.9	39.3	26.6	57,966	9.3	20.1	24.3
53 03180	Auburn city	46,507	42.3	21.8	56,552	65.7	10.6	39.9	26.2	53,058	11.3	20.6	21.0
53 03736	Bainbridge Island city	16,960	12.4	65.0	18,803	60.4	9.7	35.2	30.6	90,446	3.4	12.1	44.7
53 05210	Bellevue city	89,257	16.2	61.1	102,806	66.7	7.6	43.6	20.5	86,695	5.6	12.2	42.8
53 05280	Bellingham city	49,112	25.4	39.4	70,420	64.7	11.2	31.3	28.7	41,594	13.0	30.3	13.6
53 07380	Bothell city	24,417	24.9	42.4	27,583	69.6	8.9	43.5	23.2	72,379	6.7	15.7	35.4
53 07695	Bremerton city	24,005	34.8	19.7	31,816	65.3	10.9	42.5	33.1	41,376	15.6	29.9	10.7
53 08850	Burien city	32,987	43.4	22.9	38,509	65.0	10.4	38.8	26.8	49,821	14.9	26.9	18.0
53 09480	Camas city	12,757	23.4	39.5	14,603	66.3	7.3	43.6	19.2	78,558	3.2	10.3	39.2
53 14940	Cottage Lake CDP	14,906	13.3	58.3	17,210	68.5	5.0	45.5	12.3	130,988	0.7	5.1	67.3
53 17635	Des Moines city	20,579	44.0	19.9	23,999	63.8	9.1	39.6	26.7	58,345	11.8	18.8	21.1
53 19630	Eastmont CDP	13,103	27.6	33.6	15,265	71.8	7.2	48.6	15.9	84,227	3.2	9.0	38.2
53 20750	Edmonds city	29,497	19.4	44.5	33,594	61.5	7.7	38.4	29.4	70,052	5.3	15.4	33.1
53 22640	Everett city	69,673	40.7	19.4	83,096	68.4	12.4	39.6	26.1	45,553	13.2	26.1	15.3
53 23160	Fairwood CDP (King County)	13,411	22.2	41.6	15,813	70.3	7.6	42.1	23.3	85,962	3.3	9.6	38.5
53 23515	Federal Way city	58,660	38.2	26.1	71,098	66.5	9.7	40.6	23.3	52,444	13.3	23.3	22.0
53 24188	Five Corners CDP	12,225	42.1	17.4	14,765	68.6	14.7	37.4	19.8	65,092	12.3	13.4	16.0
53 27785	Graham CDP	15,747	39.4	18.6	18,123	72.6	7.5	46.5	16.9	68,680	6.1	11.7	26.1
53 33380	Inglewood-Finn Hill CDP	16,792	18.2	47.6	18,771	72.8	7.1	46.4	14.5	84,141	4.6	9.3	39.8
53 33805	Issaquah city	23,222	12.6	58.5	25,294	70.0	5.9	46.4	25.9	82,859	1.0	10.4	42.5
53 35170	Kenmore city	14,341	20.6	49.1	15,935	67.8	8.2	44.1	21.5	90,625	4.6	15.1	42.1
53 35275	Kennewick city	46,286	42.1	22.1	56,200	64.3	6.7	41.6	24.7	50,681	11.5	24.1	19.4
53 35415	Kent city	75,934	43.0	24.0	92,473	67.3	10.5	41.0	21.4	55,244	14.9	21.3	21.9
53 35940	Kirkland city	36,251	16.1	57.3	41,041	73.1	7.6	49.0	18.8	87,005	3.7	11.6	42.5
53 36745	Lacey city	28,805	31.0	30.7	33,773	60.3	9.5	39.5	29.1	58,617	8.1	15.5	16.1
53 37900	Lake Stevens city	18,031	33.9	21.8	21,208	72.0	10.3	43.0	20.6	68,652	7.3	14.3	26.6
53 38038	Lakewood city	40,222	40.0	22.2	47,601	60.0	13.9	34.7	32.8	43,801	12.7	28.2	13.8
53 40245	Longview city	25,824	42.6	15.8	29,193	53.5	17.3	27.8	42.6	36,172	20.1	38.4	12.3

Table B-4. Cities — What: Education, Employment, and Income, 2010–2012—*Continued*

STATE and Place code	STATE city	Educational attainment			Employment status				Percent of households with no workers	Median household income (dollars)	Percent of families with income below poverty	Percent of households with income less than $25,000	Percent of households with income of $100,000 or more
		Total population 25 years and over	Percent with a high school diploma or less	Percent with a bachelor's degree or more	Total population 16 years and over	Percent in the labor force	Unemployment rate	Percent who worked full-time year-round					
	ACS table number:	C15002	C15002	C15002	B23025	B23025	B23025	C20005	C08202	B19013	C17013	C19001	C19001
	Column number:	1	2	3	4	5	6	7	8	9	10	11	12
	Washington—Cont.												
53 40840	Lynnwood city	24,904	38.1	27.9	29,938	66.1	9.1	38.1	29.8	50,656	10.7	22.8	18.9
53 43150	Maple Valley city	14,749	26.1	33.5	17,066	74.2	8.5	49.0	13.6	93,493	4.5	8.5	45.9
53 43955	Marysville city	39,163	40.3	17.6	46,595	69.8	10.6	42.7	23.3	64,103	6.8	17.4	24.2
53 45005	Mercer Island city	16,676	8.9	74.8	18,211	58.4	4.7	38.4	29.1	124,597	2.4	7.2	59.3
53 47245	Moses Lake city	12,769	42.7	19.8	15,110	66.0	11.6	39.5	24.2	43,065	11.1	26.3	10.7
53 47490	Mountlake Terrace city	14,836	36.4	25.3	16,700	72.9	8.1	43.6	20.0	60,272	5.5	13.7	21.7
53 47560	Mount Vernon city	19,038	43.4	20.5	23,629	60.8	11.5	34.6	29.8	42,808	15.8	25.9	16.3
53 47735	Mukilteo city	14,200	19.9	48.4	16,860	70.3	8.0	43.5	17.2	82,900	5.4	8.4	42.6
53 50360	Oak Harbor city	13,862	34.7	23.4	16,458	68.7	8.3	42.3	25.5	48,594	8.2	22.0	9.8
53 51300	Olympia city	32,684	27.2	41.0	39,043	66.6	9.2	39.0	28.8	50,934	9.2	24.9	20.1
53 51795	Orchards CDP	12,232	39.7	19.6	14,839	72.6	11.6	42.4	18.6	55,005	9.2	15.8	17.1
53 53335	Parkland CDP	21,387	48.7	13.3	28,412	64.2	13.9	36.4	26.9	47,148	14.7	24.9	10.0
53 53545	Pasco city	34,426	57.1	13.9	42,874	66.4	8.8	41.4	21.7	53,775	18.6	24.6	14.3
53 56625	Pullman city	10,685	13.1	67.4	27,319	56.8	8.8	17.3	25.2	23,285	17.7	53.1	14.6
53 56695	Puyallup city	25,008	40.8	22.6	30,553	67.4	11.1	41.3	24.3	62,010	4.7	16.3	25.3
53 57535	Redmond city	39,852	15.8	59.9	44,470	72.1	6.7	50.3	16.9	95,249	4.4	10.2	47.0
53 57745	Renton city	64,603	39.8	27.5	74,320	72.3	8.5	48.6	21.7	62,859	9.8	19.0	24.6
53 58235	Richland city	33,910	23.0	44.9	39,314	64.9	6.1	44.1	24.8	71,739	6.3	16.6	34.0
53 61000	Salmon Creek CDP	14,380	28.6	31.2	16,698	64.5	16.9	33.9	30.1	63,228	10.7	18.4	25.3
53 61115	Sammamish city	29,780	8.3	73.0	34,258	69.9	5.2	48.5	11.1	137,949	2.1	4.2	72.1
53 62288	SeaTac city	18,213	50.4	17.5	21,986	65.5	13.3	38.1	22.0	47,904	16.6	21.5	13.8
53 63000	Seattle city	455,349	18.9	56.6	533,899	72.6	7.4	44.2	22.2	62,617	7.6	20.2	30.4
53 63960	Shoreline city	38,703	26.5	41.4	45,184	64.4	12.1	36.6	27.9	60,518	6.0	19.0	26.9
53 64365	Silverdale CDP	13,180	29.3	28.0	16,449	63.5	11.4	41.9	27.7	55,749	9.5	16.1	23.9
53 64380	Silver Firs CDP	13,291	19.5	42.0	15,410	74.2	6.8	49.8	11.0	101,865	2.0	5.3	50.7
53 65922	South Hill CDP	33,718	39.4	23.8	40,889	70.3	10.7	43.0	18.8	69,857	6.3	12.6	25.8
53 66255	Spanaway CDP	17,288	50.8	10.1	20,478	63.0	7.6	41.9	23.1	61,804	8.0	16.5	18.2
53 67000	Spokane city	137,818	33.4	28.7	168,020	63.0	11.2	35.2	31.5	41,593	13.3	30.1	12.4
53 67167	Spokane Valley city	60,218	37.9	20.6	71,223	64.3	12.8	35.7	31.3	47,499	11.9	25.1	12.6
53 70000	Tacoma city	131,919	41.2	24.8	159,178	65.3	12.8	39.2	28.2	49,556	13.6	24.6	18.4
53 73465	University Place city	20,462	25.9	33.0	24,775	69.1	13.8	42.6	24.1	59,896	5.7	19.3	28.3
53 74060	Vancouver city	110,017	38.3	24.2	130,003	64.6	13.0	37.0	28.8	48,273	13.0	23.4	15.2
53 75775	Walla Walla city	21,254	35.2	22.1	26,362	54.3	8.4	30.7	37.0	41,681	12.2	31.5	11.9
53 77105	Wenatchee city	20,693	46.3	22.5	24,582	62.6	6.8	41.7	28.7	47,558	10.3	22.2	17.3
53 80010	Yakima city	58,035	53.0	17.9	69,816	62.1	12.0	35.7	31.6	40,104	19.1	32.1	13.7
54 00000	**West Virginia**	1,297,393	57.1	18.3	1,513,935	54.4	8.6	35.4	37.0	40,151	13.1	32.7	12.5
54 14600	Charleston city	36,594	37.9	39.6	42,053	61.6	7.4	41.1	32.8	47,864	14.4	30.0	20.0
54 39460	Huntington city	32,493	44.6	27.1	41,789	54.3	8.6	30.9	39.1	28,201	22.6	46.2	7.8
54 55756	Morgantown city	14,426	30.1	46.9	28,387	54.4	8.9	24.8	33.4	31,883	10.1	45.5	14.0
54 62140	Parkersburg city	22,121	53.9	13.5	25,545	55.6	12.7	33.3	42.6	31,989	16.0	40.1	8.6
54 86452	Wheeling city	20,221	45.2	27.2	23,325	57.6	7.3	35.5	38.2	34,433	13.0	36.2	11.2
55 00000	**Wisconsin**	3,828,580	42.4	26.7	4,538,112	67.8	8.1	41.4	26.5	51,340	9.0	22.9	18.2
55 02375	Appleton city	47,599	36.2	31.9	57,234	68.6	5.6	42.6	23.0	51,674	9.4	21.1	16.8
55 06500	Beloit city	22,707	58.7	13.7	28,586	64.7	16.6	31.8	33.4	35,605	20.7	34.3	8.7
55 10025	Brookfield city	26,677	20.3	55.4	30,230	61.8	6.4	39.3	29.7	86,038	3.6	11.0	41.8
55 11950	Caledonia village	18,059	34.5	32.5	20,123	66.0	7.9	44.4	26.8	64,675	4.6	13.2	31.4
55 19775	De Pere city	14,299	35.9	32.4	18,719	70.4	7.7	42.9	22.6	52,659	6.8	21.5	15.8
55 22300	Eau Claire city	38,591	30.9	34.0	54,635	71.4	6.8	37.4	23.6	42,508	10.0	30.7	14.4
55 25950	Fitchburg city	16,987	30.8	45.9	19,829	72.1	5.9	47.8	17.2	66,044	12.0	19.6	27.2
55 26275	Fond du Lac city	29,192	47.5	20.8	34,275	67.9	10.7	39.1	29.0	44,740	11.6	25.7	12.1
55 27300	Franklin city	25,155	34.5	32.5	28,546	63.8	5.7	43.1	24.1	73,821	4.8	13.4	35.3
55 31000	Green Bay city	67,252	46.4	22.4	81,584	67.3	9.1	40.8	27.2	41,404	13.2	28.7	11.6
55 31175	Greenfield city	28,258	43.9	25.0	31,603	63.1	7.7	40.5	32.4	49,680	5.3	22.3	15.6
55 37825	Janesville city	42,134	45.0	20.7	49,016	66.9	10.6	38.7	29.3	47,040	12.6	24.8	13.8
55 39225	Kenosha city	62,793	45.8	22.9	76,798	67.8	12.9	39.5	27.0	48,063	14.3	26.8	15.9
55 40775	La Crosse city	29,235	36.4	29.4	44,437	65.4	6.5	31.6	26.9	38,440	9.2	32.1	8.9
55 48000	Madison city	146,792	21.3	54.0	198,425	72.4	6.6	41.0	20.5	52,599	10.5	24.2	20.8
55 48500	Manitowoc city	23,784	50.3	21.2	27,272	64.0	9.3	38.6	32.3	40,098	9.1	28.7	12.5
55 51000	Menomonee Falls village	25,675	32.5	40.8	28,902	67.5	5.3	43.9	26.7	73,787	1.7	14.7	32.4
55 51150	Mequon city	16,646	15.8	62.5	18,638	60.8	6.4	39.1	26.0	107,382	1.7	8.5	53.1
55 53000	Milwaukee city	356,629	49.7	21.9	454,218	65.2	14.8	35.9	30.3	34,439	25.3	37.8	9.3
55 54875	Mount Pleasant village	18,638	38.5	31.6	21,343	66.1	8.4	43.1	27.2	59,003	4.4	15.8	25.6
55 55275	Muskego city	16,739	36.3	31.5	19,182	75.1	4.8	46.7	18.8	87,750	2.2	7.9	39.5
55 55775	Neenah city	17,292	39.3	28.1	19,743	69.3	6.7	46.9	25.4	50,599	7.4	20.3	15.5
55 56375	New Berlin city	28,957	28.0	40.4	32,421	67.9	6.6	44.8	26.8	72,107	3.5	11.8	33.6
55 58800	Oak Creek city	23,836	37.9	28.0	27,544	74.0	7.7	49.7	21.0	65,948	3.9	16.5	26.7
55 60500	Oshkosh city	40,939	47.5	22.9	55,128	61.8	7.4	36.6	26.3	41,842	11.5	29.9	10.5
55 63300	Pleasant Prairie village	12,826	36.6	32.6	15,474	67.2	10.8	43.8	25.7	72,777	2.8	12.9	31.0
55 66000	Racine city	48,967	51.5	16.4	58,623	64.4	14.7	38.0	32.8	37,397	20.4	34.3	10.2
55 72975	Sheboygan city	32,457	52.1	19.8	38,331	69.5	9.8	38.7	28.0	41,792	11.9	26.5	9.7
55 75125	South Milwaukee city	14,333	46.8	19.0	16,855	66.5	10.3	40.7	27.9	50,214	7.4	23.6	16.6
55 77200	Stevens Point city	13,991	35.7	31.3	22,504	66.9	10.7	29.4	28.9	39,174	10.7	32.0	10.1

Table B-4. Cities — What: Education, Employment, and Income, 2010–2012—*Continued*

STATE and Place code	STATE city	Educational attainment			Employment status				Percent of households with no workers	Median household income (dollars)	Percent of families with income below poverty	Percent of households with income less than $25,000	Percent of households with income of $100,000 or more
		Total population 25 years and over	Percent with a high school diploma or less	Percent with a bachelor's degree or more	Total population 16 years and over	Percent in the labor force	Unemployment rate	Percent who worked full-time year-round					
	ACS table number:	C15002	C15002	C15002	B23025	B23025	B23025	C20005	C08202	B19013	C17013	C19001	C19001
	Column number:	1	2	3	4	5	6	7	8	9	10	11	12
	Wisconsin—Cont.												
55 78600	Sun Prairie city............................	19,708	24.3	42.8	22,543	78.9	5.1	53.1	15.6	67,294	4.5	11.6	27.5
55 78650	Superior city................................	17,955	39.1	20.1	21,980	66.7	8.1	37.7	28.6	38,135	17.9	30.9	11.6
55 83975	Watertown city............................	15,645	47.3	23.2	18,504	70.7	12.8	40.3	27.1	48,958	8.7	24.7	13.3
55 84250	Waukesha city..............................	46,706	33.4	33.9	56,325	73.0	6.8	46.0	24.1	55,863	8.2	20.2	19.0
55 84475	Wausau city..................................	26,496	45.4	24.6	31,223	66.4	11.4	35.4	27.8	40,115	15.8	32.7	13.4
55 84675	Wauwatosa city............................	33,160	18.7	52.8	37,357	71.1	5.8	48.5	25.5	68,077	2.4	15.6	28.3
55 85300	West Allis city...............................	42,963	44.8	22.4	48,880	69.5	8.4	42.9	27.3	43,890	10.1	29.1	10.8
55 85350	West Bend city..............................	21,576	37.2	25.6	24,361	70.4	7.9	43.4	27.0	56,089	6.3	20.0	17.0
56 00000	**Wyoming**...................................	376,874	38.3	24.5	448,174	68.7	5.7	45.9	22.7	55,979	8.0	19.9	21.4
56 13150	Casper city...................................	37,297	35.2	22.8	44,770	69.7	5.3	45.2	24.4	54,618	6.3	18.6	20.1
56 13900	Cheyenne city..............................	39,904	35.1	24.8	47,501	68.3	6.0	46.7	23.5	50,420	8.8	22.2	18.4
56 31855	Gillette city..................................	18,648	44.4	18.4	22,575	75.7	4.9	56.1	14.0	70,843	7.6	13.7	29.0
56 45050	Laramie city.................................	16,466	17.1	51.1	27,260	67.0	6.3	34.1	19.5	36,540	15.4	35.1	13.7
56 67235	Rock Springs city..........................	14,701	46.6	17.5	17,595	72.8	6.2	51.1	19.6	63,235	9.3	14.5	27.9

Where
Migration, Housing, and Transportation

Where: Migration, Housing, and Transportation

Migration

An important question that the ACS can help to answer is how many people have moved recently, and from where to where. Nationally, 85 percent of Americans lived in the same home as they did one year earlier. However, there was much variation among the smaller geographic areas. About one-third of those people who moved stayed in the same city or town, and just one in five moved to a new state.

Among the states, Nevada had the highest proportion of movers (22.8 percent) and New Jersey had the lowest proportion (9.6 percent). Hawaii and the District of Columbia had the highest percentages of residents who moved from abroad—about 1.5 percent. The District of Columbia (8.6 percent), North Dakota, and Wyoming (both 5.5 percent) had the highest proportions of movers from other states. California (1.3 percent), Michigan, and New York (both 1.4 percent) had the lowest proportion of movers from out of state.

In six metropolitan areas, about 90 percent of the residents had not moved in the past year. Most of these were smaller metropolitan areas, but among them was New York—the metropolitan area with the largest population. In two metropolitan areas, less than 70 percent of the population had lived in the same house—both of them with large student populations: Ames, Iowa; and Lawrence, Kansas. Five metropolitan areas with large college and military populations were also areas where 15 percent to 20 percent of the population had moved into the metropolitan area within one year. In sixteen metropolitan areas, less than 3 percent of the population was new to the area. Brownsville–Harlingen, Texas, had the lowest level of in-migration (1.9 percent). Other metropolitan areas with few new residents included New York, Detroit, and Chicago.

In four counties, more than 20 percent of the population had moved into the county within the past year. the highest proportion was in Pulaski County, Missouri, home of a large military base. Among larger counties, 11.6 percent of the residents of Denver County, Colorado, had moved into the county within the past year, and more than eight percent of the population of Suffolk County, Massachusetts (Boston), Cobb and Fulton counties, Georgia (Atlanta), and the District of Columbia were new residents in the 2010–2012 time period. Most of the counties with low levels of new residents had very small populations, with the exception of New York City. Only .9 percent of the residents of Richmond County (Staten Island) had moved there within the

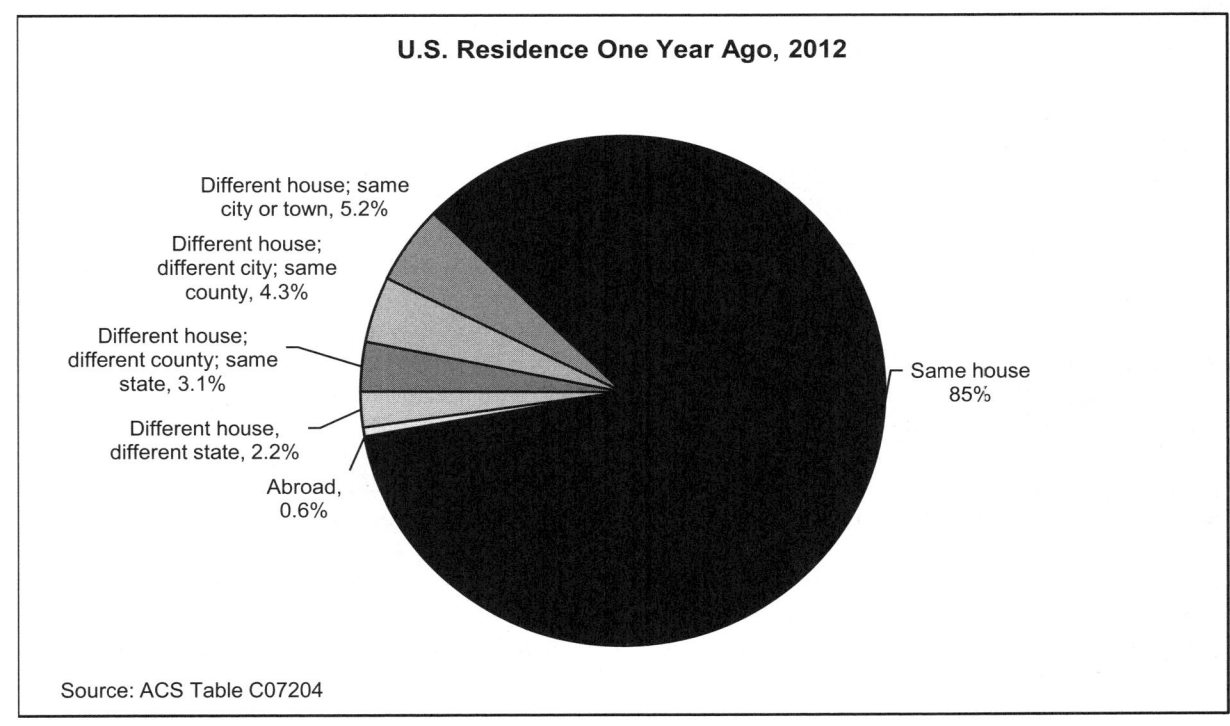

U.S. Residence One Year Ago, 2012

Different house; same city or town, 5.2%
Different house; different city; same county, 4.3%
Different house; different county; same state, 3.1%
Different house, different state, 2.2%
Abroad, 0.6%
Same house 85%

Source: ACS Table C07204

year, and Kings (Brooklyn), Bronx, and Queens, counties all had in-migration levels less than 2 percent.

In 17 cities, more than 95 percent of the residents lived in the same house they had lived in one year earlier. All were relatively small cities. At the other extreme, less than half of the population in seven cities lived in the same house a year earlier. These were also small cities, all with universities. Among larger cities, in-migrants within the past year included more than 10 percent of the residents of Denver, Seattle, Las Vegas, Boston, and Austin. Only 3.2 percent of New York's residents were new to the city.

Owning and Renting

Home ownership in the United States reached record high levels in the last decade before beginning to decline in 2008. In 2012, owners occupied 63.9 percent of American housing units. West Virginia had the highest rate of ownership at 72 percent, followed by seven states where more than 70 percent of households owned their homes: Iowa, Minnesota, Maine, Michigan, Vermont, New Hampshire, and Delaware. The states with the smallest proportion of owner-occupied units were New York and California, both about 54 percent. The District of Columbia (41.5 percent) had a lower rate than any of the states. However, the District of Columbia's home-ownership rate was higher than cities like Los Angeles, San Francisco, Boston, New York, and Miami, all below 40 percent. New York City's relatively low home-ownership rate of 31.7 percent brought down the state's overall rate.

Home-ownership rates vary considerably by race of householder. Nationally, 71.5 percent of non-Hispanic White households lived in a home they owned, while fewer than half of Black and Hispanic householders were home owners. Six states—led by Mississippi with 54 percent—had 50 percent or more of Black householders residing in owner-occupied units. More than 50 percent of Hispanic households were home owners in 15 states—including Texas and Florida, both with large Hispanic populations. About 57 percent of Asian-headed households were home owners.

Home ownership varied even more by age of householder. For all householders age 25 to 44, 49.1 percent owned their own homes, compared with 73 percent of 45- to 64-year-olds, and 78.7 percent of householders 65 years old and over. Iowa had the highest proportion of younger home owners, with 62.9 percent of 25- to 44-year-olds, while South Carolina had the highest home-ownership rate among householders 65 and older, with 83.5 percent.

Nearly 80 percent of married-couple family households were home owners, while only 45 percent of female-headed family households owned their homes. The home-ownership rate of nonfamily households was slightly higher, at 50 percent. In Mississippi, 59 percent of nonfamily households owned their homes. About 88 percent of married-couple families in Minnesota and Iowa owned their homes.

In the Barnstable Town, Massachusetts, metropolitan area, 81.6 percent of housing units were owner-occupied. Punta Gorda, Florida; and Holland–Grand Haven, Michigan; also had home-ownership rates above 78 percent. The metropolitan area with the lowest home-ownership rate (48.4 percent) was Los Angeles. Three small metropolitan areas had rates below 50 percent, and the rate for the New York metropolitan area was also low, at 51.4 percent.

More than 150 counties had home-ownership rates higher than 80 percent, most of them counties with populations between 20,000 and 100,000. But Nassau County, New York, with nearly half a million households, had a rate of 80.4 percent. The three lowest home-ownership rates in the country were in the New York City boroughs of Bronx County at 19 percent, New York County (Manhattan) at 22 percent, and Kings County (Brooklyn) at 29.5 percent.

Thirty-eight cities had home-ownership rates higher than 90 percent, and thirty were below 30 percent. New York City's overall home-ownership rate was just under one-third, and Miami, Boston, San Francisco, and Los Angeles, were all below 40 percent. Very few of the largest cities exceeded home-ownership rates of 60 percent.

In 2012, American households had an average size of 2.64 persons per household. Owner-occupied households tended to be slightly larger (2.70) than renter-occupied households (2.53). Only Utah and Hawaii exceeded three persons per household. Housing quality is sometimes measured by crowding (more than one person per room is considered crowded) and lack of complete plumbing (which consists of hot and cold piped water, a flush toilet, and a bathtub or shower). Nationally, 3.6 percent of housing units were considered substandard by this definition, but 10 percent of housing units in Alaska, 9.4 percent in Hawaii, and 8.6 percent in California did not meet these standards.

Housing Value and Costs

The median value of owner-occupied housing units in the United States was $171,900. Hawaii and the District of Columbia had the most expensive houses, with median values of $496,600 and $446,600, respectively. California's median housing value of $349,400 ranks third, about 39 percent below its 2006 level when it had the highest median value in the nation.[1] The median value was under $100,000 in Mississippi,

---

1. Source: 2012 and 2009 American Community Survey 1-year Estimates, Comparison Table CP04.

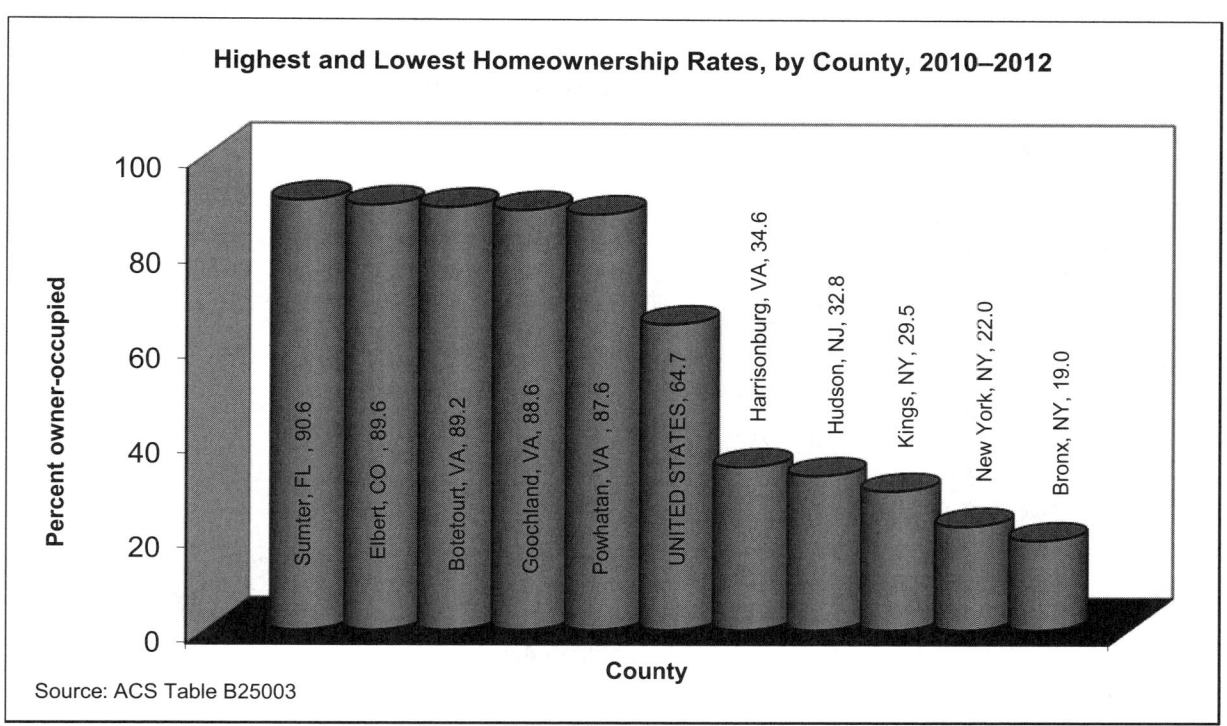

Highest and Lowest Homeownership Rates, by County, 2010–2012

Percent owner-occupied

- Sumter, FL , 90.6
- Elbert, CO , 89.6
- Botetourt, VA, 89.2
- Goochland, VA, 88.6
- Powhatan, VA , 87.6
- UNITED STATES, 64.7
- Harrisonburg, VA, 34.6
- Hudson, NJ, 32.8
- Kings, NY, 29.5
- New York, NY, 22.0
- Bronx, NY, 19.0

County

Source: ACS Table B25003

and West Virginia's median was $100,400. In four metropolitan areas—all in California and Hawaii—the median value was higher than $500,000, with the San Jose metropolitan area topping the list at $624,200. Thirty-two metropolitan areas had median housing values below $100,000, the lowest being the Brownsville–Harlingen, Texas, metropolitan area with a median value estimated at $75,700. Housing values topped $800,000 in New York County (Manhattan), while four California counties and Teton County, Wyoming, had median values above $700,000. McDowell County, West Virginia, had an estimated median value just below $40,000. Eight additional counties had values between $50,000 and $60,000. The disparities become more pronounced at the city level, with 13 California cities and Darien, Connecticut, having median values above the million dollar level. Eight cities had median values below $50,000.

Almost two-thirds of owner-occupants held mortgages on their homes. More than 75 percent of home owners in the District of Columbia, Maryland, and Colorado, held mortgages, while less than 50 percent of West Virginia's home owners did. More than 12 percent of all owner-occupants held a second mortgage and/or a home equity loan. Seventeen percent or more of home owners in Connecticut, Maryland, and the District of Columbia, held these mortgages, while fewer than 5 percent had them in Arkansas and Texas.

For all Americans, the median monthly housing cost was $971. For owners, this included mortgages, real estate taxes, insurance, utilities, fuel, and condominium fees,

where appropriate. For renters, this included the contract rent, utilities, and fuels if paid by the renter. Median housing costs were highest in New Jersey, Hawaii, and the District of Columbia (more than $1,400) and lowest in West Virginia (less than $600).

On average, renters devoted a relatively high share of their monthly income to rent: a median of more than 31 percent. Even owners with a mortgage spent relatively less on their housing—23.7 percent of monthly household income. (Those with no mortgage spent 12.3 percent.)

Among the states, renters in Florida paid the highest proportion of their incomes for their rental costs—34.7 percent—while renters in North and South Dakota paid only 24 percent and 26 percent of their incomes, respectively. Median gross rents were highest in Hawaii, the District of Columbia, and California,—all $1,200 or more. The lowest median gross rent was $607 in West Virginia. Three Virginia counties, suburbs of Washington, DC, had median rents above $1,600. Five more counties in California, Virginia, and Maryland had median gross rents higher than $1,500. Twenty-three counties had median gross rents under $500. Among the cities, 12 had median rents of $1,900 or more, 6 of them in California.

Hawaii homeowners with mortgages paid 29.3 percent of their incomes for owner costs, while those in North Dakota paid only 18.9 percent. In seven metropolitan areas—three in Florida and two each in New Jersey and

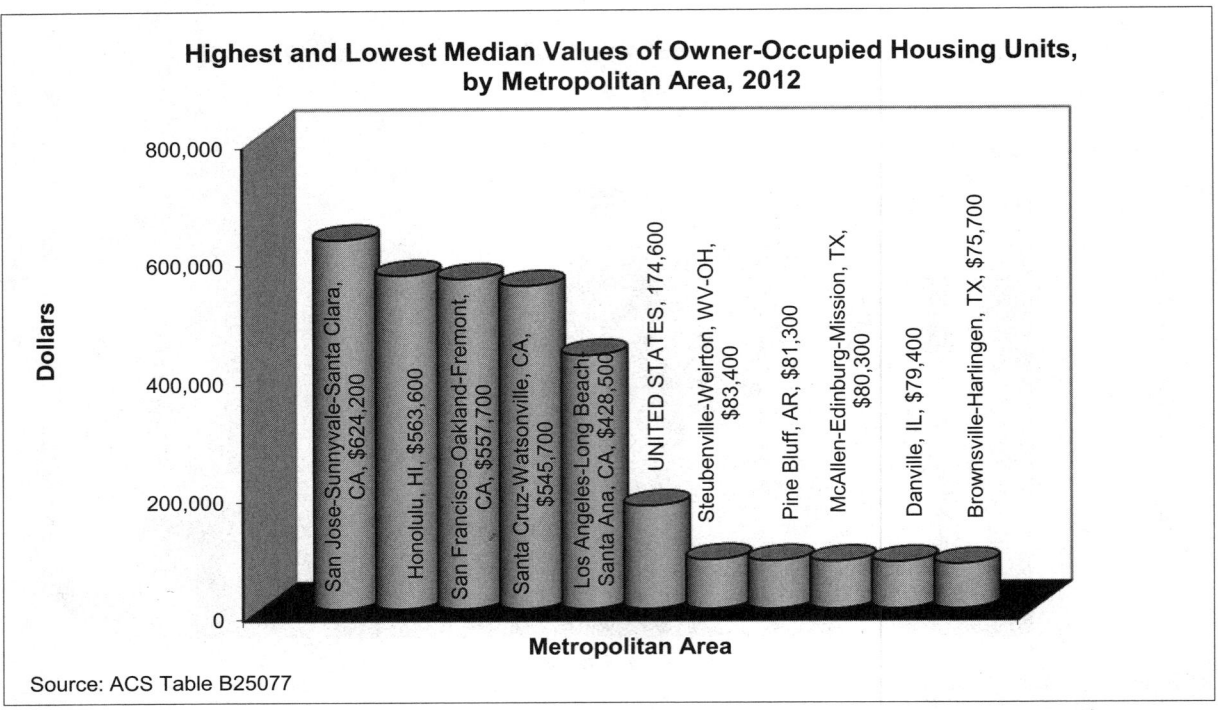

Highest and Lowest Median Values of Owner-Occupied Housing Units, by Metropolitan Area, 2012

Dollars

Metropolitan Area

San Jose-Sunnyvale-Santa Clara, CA, $624,200
Honolulu, HI, $563,600
San Francisco-Oakland-Fremont, CA, $557,700
Santa Cruz-Watsonville, CA, $545,700
Los Angeles-Long Beach-Santa Ana, CA, $428,500
UNITED STATES, 174,600
Steubenville-Weirton, WV-OH, $83,400
Pine Bluff, AR, $81,300
McAllen-Edinburg-Mission, TX, $80,300
Danville, IL, $79,400
Brownsville-Harlingen, TX, $75,700

Source: ACS Table B25077

California—homeowners with a mortgage paid 30 percent or more of their incomes for monthly owner costs. In twelve cities, the median monthly owner costs for mortgaged housing units were more than 40 percent of income. Eight of these were in New Jersey. Median owner costs for mortgaged properties in New Jersey, the District of Columbia, Hawaii, California, Connecticut, and Massachusetts, were more than $2,000. In West Virginia and Arkansas, median monthly owner costs for households with a mortgage were lower than $1,000.

Property taxes vary widely from the national median of $2,075. New Jersey residents pay a median of $7,183 per year, with Connecticut, New Hampshire, and New York, all paying more than $4,000. The median is below $1,000 in seven states, with Alabama and West Virginia both paying less than $600 per year.

Transportation

More than 90 percent of housing units had at least one vehicle. More than half had two or more vehicles, and the share of housing units with three or more vehicles was more than double the share without any at all. In the New York metropolitan area, 31.5 percent of households had no vehicle, nearly double the proportion of any other metropolitan area. In New York County (Manhattan), 78.8 percent of households had no vehicle, while well over half of the residents of Bronx and Kings (Brooklyn) counties also had no cars. More than 30 percent of residents of Queens County, New York; the District of Columbia; Suffolk County, Massachusetts (Boston); Philadelphia County, Pennsylvania; Hudson County, New Jersey; Baltimore City, Maryland; and San Francisco County, California, had no vehicles. The level was 30 percent in Holmes County, Ohio, with a large Amish population.

More than three out of four Americans drove their cars to work alone, and one-tenth car pooled. Less than 5 percent took public transportation, and about the same number walked, bicycled, or used "other means." Americans' average commute (excluding those who worked at home) was 25 minutes. This ranged from 16.7 minutes in South Dakota to 31.9 minutes in Maryland. Nationally, commuting by public transportation averaged nearly twice as long as commuting by car, but car trips ranged from an average of 17 minutes in South Dakota to 30.2 minutes in Maryland. Public transportation ranged from 27 minutes in Iowa to 64.9 minutes in New Hampshire.

Commuting patterns are influenced by local conditions, so broad national averages are not very revealing. Walking or biking are generally more popular in a climate with good weather, and the presence or absence of public transport obviously determines how many people use it. For instance, 38.6 percent of people who lived in the District of Columbia took public transportation to work, as did 27.3 percent in New York state, 10.6 percent in New Jersey, and more than 8 percent in Massachusetts, Maryland, and Illinois—not many other Americans have this option.

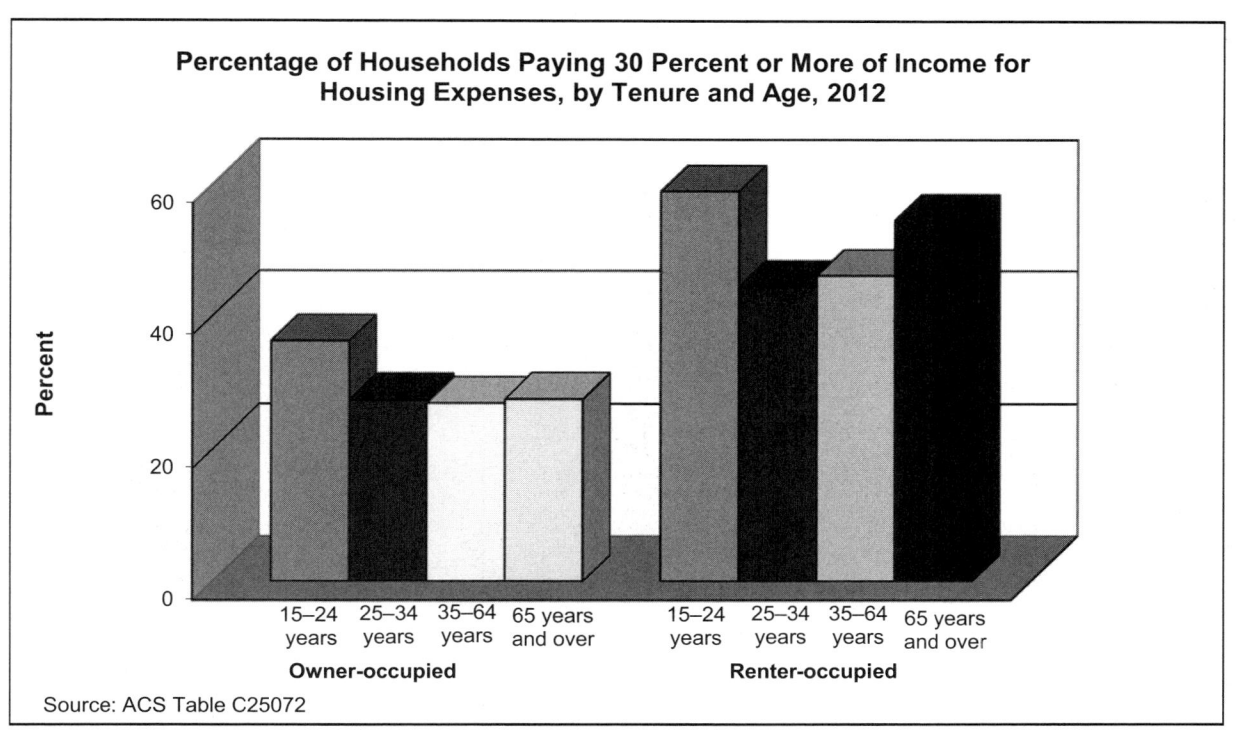

Percentage of Households Paying 30 Percent or More of Income for Housing Expenses, by Tenure and Age, 2012

Source: ACS Table C25072

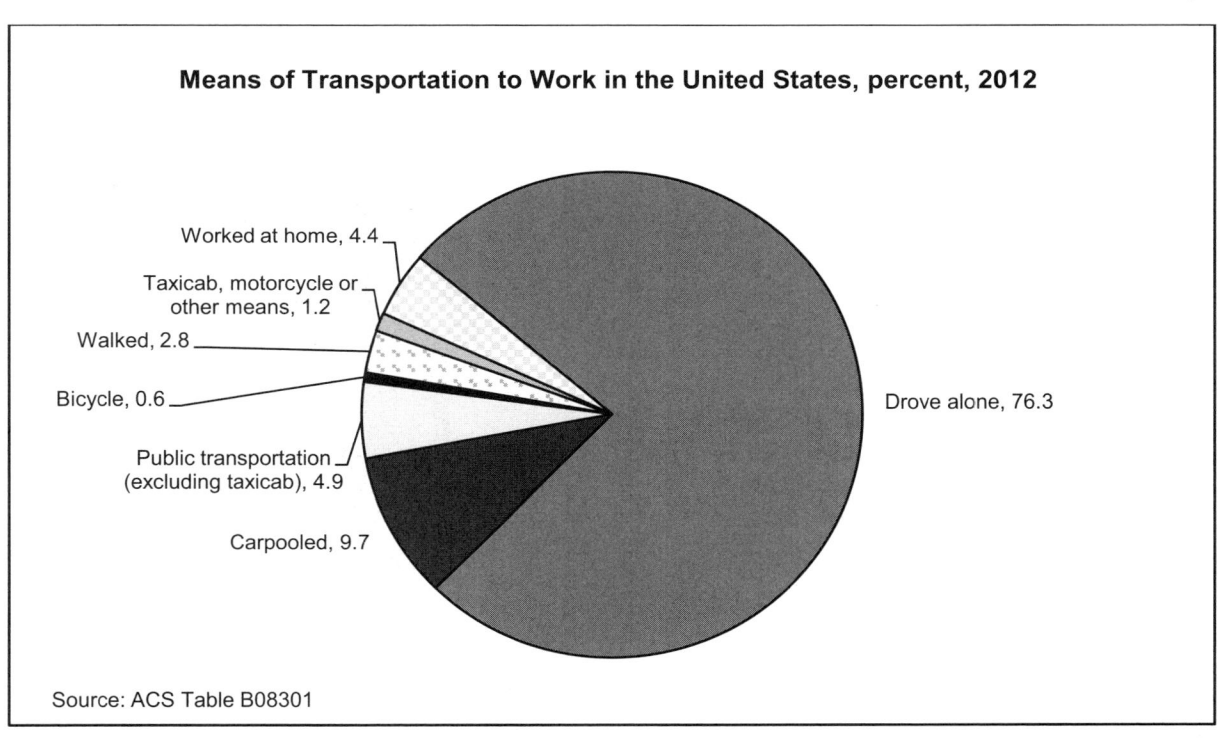

Means of Transportation to Work in the United States, percent, 2012

Worked at home, 4.4

Taxicab, motorcycle or other means, 1.2

Walked, 2.8

Bicycle, 0.6

Public transportation (excluding taxicab), 4.9

Carpooled, 9.7

Drove alone, 76.3

Source: ACS Table B08301

State Rankings, 2012
Selected Rankings

Lived in the same house one year ago rank	State	Percent who lived in the same house one year ago [C-1, col. 2]	Did not live in the state one year ago rank	State	Percent who did not live in the state one year ago [C-1, cols. 6 + 7]	Owner-occupied housing unit rank	State	Percent of owner-occupied housing units [C-1, col. 9]
	United States	85.0		United States	2.9		United States	63.9
1	New Jersey	90.4	1	District of Columbia	10.0	1	West Virginia	72.0
2	New York	88.9	2	North Dakota	6.0	2	Iowa	71.9
3	Pennsylvania	87.9	3	Wyoming	5.8	3	Minnesota	71.4
4	West Virginia	87.8	4	Hawaii	5.5	3	Maine	71.4
5	Connecticut	87.6	5	Alaska	5.3	5	Michigan	71.1
6	Massachusetts	87.4	6	Nevada	5.1	6	Vermont	71.0
7	Maryland	87.1	7	Colorado	4.7	7	New Hampshire	70.9
8	Illinois	86.5	8	New Hampshire	4.3	8	Delaware	70.8
8	Rhode Island	86.5	8	Vermont	4.3	9	Utah	69.6
10	Delaware	86.3	10	Delaware	4.2	10	Indiana	69.4
11	New Hampshire	86.1	10	Arizona	4.2	11	Wyoming	69.0
11	Maine	86.1	10	Idaho	4.2	12	Pennsylvania	68.9
11	Louisiana	86.1	13	Montana	4.0	13	Alabama	68.8
14	New Mexico	85.9	14	Virginia	3.9	14	Idaho	68.4
15	Vermont	85.8	14	Washington	3.9	15	Mississippi	68.2
15	Mississippi	85.8	16	Utah	3.8	16	South Carolina	68.1
17	Wisconsin	85.7	16	Rhode Island	3.8	17	New Mexico	67.7
18	Minnesota	85.3	18	South Carolina	3.7	18	Missouri	67.5
18	Ohio	85.3	18	Kansas	3.7	19	Wisconsin	67.3
20	Michigan	85.2	18	Florida	3.7	20	South Dakota	67.1
20	Iowa	85.2	18	South Dakota	3.7	20	Montana	67.1
22	Alabama	85.1	22	Oregon	3.6	22	Kentucky	67.0
22	Indiana	85.1	23	Maryland	3.4	23	Connecticut	66.9
24	Kentucky	84.9	23	Georgia	3.4	24	Tennessee	66.7
25	Virginia	84.8	23	North Carolina	3.4	25	Illinois	66.6
26	North Carolina	84.7	26	Oklahoma	3.3	26	Maryland	66.5
26	Hawaii	84.7	27	New Mexico	3.2	27	Oklahoma	66.4
28	Tennessee	84.6	28	Missouri	3.1	27	Kansas	66.4
28	California	84.6	28	Tennessee	3.1	29	Nebraska	66.3
30	Arkansas	84.2	28	Massachusetts	3.1	29	Ohio	66.3
30	Nebraska	84.2	31	Kentucky	3.0	31	Arkansas	66.2
30	South Carolina	84.2	31	Connecticut	3.0	31	Virginia	66.2
33	Georgia	84.0	31	Arkansas	3.0	33	Louisiana	65.7
34	Florida	83.9	34	Iowa	2.9	34	Florida	65.6
35	Missouri	83.4	35	Nebraska	2.8	35	North Carolina	65.4
36	Montana	83.3	36	Texas	2.7	36	New Jersey	65.1
37	Texas	83.1	36	West Virginia	2.7	37	North Dakota	65.0
38	Kansas	82.9	36	Mississippi	2.7	38	Colorado	64.0
38	Washington	82.9	39	Alabama	2.5	39	Georgia	63.7
40	Utah	82.8	39	Indiana	2.5	40	Alaska	63.4
41	Oklahoma	82.6	41	Maine	2.4	41	Arizona	62.6
42	Idaho	82.5	41	Minnesota	2.4	42	Washington	62.3
43	South Dakota	82.3	43	Louisiana	2.3	42	Texas	62.3
44	Alaska	82.2	44	New York	2.2	44	Massachusetts	62.2
45	Oregon	81.9	44	Illinois	2.2	45	Oregon	61.6
46	North Dakota	81.8	46	Pennsylvania	2.1	46	Rhode Island	60.0
47	Arizona	81.0	46	New Jersey	2.1	47	Hawaii	56.9
48	Colorado	80.6	46	Ohio	2.1	48	Nevada	54.9
48	Wyoming	80.6	46	Wisconsin	2.1	49	California	54.0
50	District of Columbia	80.1	50	California	2.0	50	New York	53.7
51	Nevada	77.2	51	Michigan	1.8	51	District of Columbia	41.5

State Rankings, 2012—*Continued*
Selected Rankings

Median value of owner-occupied housing units rank	State	Median value of owner-occupied housing units (dollars) [C-1, col. 45]	Mean travel time to work rank	State	Mean travel time to work (minutes) [C-1, col. 78]	Median selected monthly owner (with a mortgage) costs as a percentage of household income rank	State	Median selected monthly owner (with a mortgage) costs as a percentage of household income [C-1, col. 59]
	United States	171,900		United States	25.7		United States	23.7
1	Hawaii	496,600	1	Maryland	31.9	1	Hawaii	29.3
2	District of Columbia	460,700	2	New York	31.8	2	California	28.4
3	California	349,400	3	New Jersey	30.7	3	New Jersey	27.7
4	Massachusetts	323,800	4	District of Columbia	29.9	4	Florida	27.1
5	New Jersey	311,600	5	Massachusetts	28.3	5	New Hampshire	25.8
6	New York	280,900	6	Illinois	28.0	6	Oregon	25.6
7	Maryland	279,900	7	Virginia	27.9	7	Connecticut	25.5
8	Connecticut	267,800	8	California	27.5	8	Nevada	25.4
9	Alaska	245,100	9	Georgia	26.9	8	Rhode Island	25.4
10	Washington	243,000	10	New Hampshire	26.3	10	New York	25.3
11	Virginia	237,800	11	Florida	26.2	11	Washington	25.0
12	New Hampshire	236,000	12	Pennsylvania	26.1	12	Vermont	24.8
13	Colorado	234,900	13	Hawaii	26.0	13	Massachusetts	24.4
14	Rhode Island	234,600	13	Washington	26.0	14	Illinois	24.2
15	Delaware	226,900	15	Delaware	25.8	15	Delaware	23.8
16	Oregon	223,900	16	Texas	25.3	15	Maine	23.8
17	Vermont	216,900	17	West Virginia	25.2	15	Maryland	23.8
18	Utah	199,700	17	Louisiana	25.2	18	Arizona	23.6
19	Wyoming	187,400	19	Connecticut	24.8	18	Idaho	23.6
20	Montana	184,800	20	Arizona	24.6	20	Colorado	23.5
21	Minnesota	178,400	21	Colorado	24.5	20	Utah	23.5
22	Maine	172,300	21	Alabama	24.5	22	Alaska	23.3
23	Illinois	170,600	23	Tennessee	24.4	22	District of Columbia	23.3
24	Wisconsin	165,200	23	Rhode Island	24.4	24	Georgia	23.1
25	Pennsylvania	163,800	25	Nevada	24.0	24	New Mexico	23.1
26	New Mexico	157,500	25	Michigan	24.0	24	Virginia	23.1
27	Idaho	154,500	25	Mississippi	24.0	27	Wisconsin	23.0
28	Arizona	151,500	28	North Carolina	23.7	28	Montana	22.9
29	Nevada	150,700	29	South Carolina	23.5	29	Tennessee	22.7
30	North Carolina	150,100	29	Maine	23.5	30	Pennsylvania	22.6
31	Florida	148,200	29	Indiana	23.5	31	Michigan	22.4
32	North Dakota	142,500	32	Ohio	23.2	31	Mississippi	22.4
33	Georgia	142,300	33	Missouri	23.1	33	North Carolina	22.3
34	Louisiana	139,500	33	Vermont	23.1	34	Minnesota	22.1
35	Tennessee	137,800	35	Minnesota	22.9	34	South Carolina	22.1
36	South Carolina	135,500	35	Kentucky	22.9	34	Texas	22.1
37	Missouri	135,000	37	Oregon	22.7	37	Ohio	21.7
38	South Dakota	134,300	38	Utah	22.0	38	Missouri	21.6
39	Kansas	130,100	39	Wisconsin	21.8	39	Alabama	21.3
40	Texas	129,200	40	New Mexico	21.4	40	Kentucky	21.1
41	Nebraska	128,300	40	Arkansas	21.4	41	Louisiana	20.9
42	Ohio	127,600	42	Oklahoma	21.1	41	South Dakota	20.9
43	Iowa	126,300	43	Idaho	20.2	43	Kansas	20.8
44	Alabama	123,200	44	Arkansas	19.6	43	Oklahoma	20.8
45	Indiana	122,700	45	Kansas	19.0	45	Nebraska	20.7
46	Kentucky	120,800	46	Iowa	18.8	46	Wyoming	20.6
47	Michigan	115,700	47	Montana	18.4	47	Arkansas	20.2
48	Oklahoma	114,300	48	Nebraska	18.2	48	Indiana	20.0
49	Arkansas	107,600	49	Wyoming	18.1	48	Iowa	20.0
50	West Virginia	100,400	50	North Dakota	17.4	50	West Virginia	19.2
51	Mississippi	99,800	51	South Dakota	16.7	51	North Dakota	18.9

County Rankings, 2010–2012
Selected Rankings

Lived in the same house one year ago rank	County	Percent who lived in the same house one year ago [C-2, col. 1]	Did not live in the county one year ago rank	County	Percent who did not live in the county one year ago [C-2, col. 2]	Mean travel time to work rank	County	Mean travel time to work (minutes) [C-2. col. 11]
	United States	84.8		United States	5.3		United States	25.5
1	St. James Parish, LA	95.0	1	Pulaski County, MO	31.5	1	Pike County, PA	42.6
2	McDowell County, WV	94.8	2	Fredericksburg city, VA	23.5	2	San Jacinto County, TX	42.5
3	Butler County, AL	94.6	2	Lassen County, CA	20.9	2	Bronx County, NY	42.5
3	Putnam County, NY	94.6	4	Harrisonburg city, VA	20.6	4	Charles County, MD	42.1
3	Holmes County, OH	94.6	5	Madison County, ID	19.4	5	Queens County, NY	41.6
3	Putnam County, WV	94.6	6	Whitman County, WA	18.8	6	Warren County, VA	41.3
7	Wilkes County, NC	94.5	7	Jones County, TX	18.0	7	Kings County, NY	41.0
8	Geauga County, OH	94.4	8	Brookings County, SD	17.9	8	Richmond County, NY	40.8
9	McNairy County, TN	94.2	9	Lafayette County, MS	17.8	9	Fauquier County, VA	40.5
9	Colorado County, TX	94.2	10	Winchester city, VA	17.0	9	Jefferson County, WV	40.5
11	Kewaunee County, WI	94.1	11	Albany County, WY	16.8	11	Elbert County, CO	40.3
12	Richmond County, NY	94.0	12	Bee County, TX	16.7	12	Bandera County, TX	39.9
13	De Soto Parish, LA	93.9	13	Charlottesville city, VA	16.6	13	Prince William County, VA	39.8
13	Wayne County, WV	93.9	14	Watauga County, NC	15.8	14	Stafford County, VA	39.7
15	Toombs County, GA	93.8	15	Prince George County, VA	15.4	14	Monroe County, PA	39.7
15	Union Parish, LA	93.8	16	Nodaway County, MO	15.2	16	Calvert County, MD	39.1
15	Carroll County, MD	93.8	17	McDonough County, IL	14.9	17	Hickman County, TN	38.9
15	Dinwiddie County, VA	93.8	18	Prince Edward County, VA	14.6	18	Orange County, VA	38.8
19	Accomack County, VA	93.7	18	Liberty County, GA	14.6	18	Hampshire County, WV	38.8
19	Goochland County, VA	93.7	18	Story County, IA	14.6	20	Putnam County, NY	38.6
21	Morehouse Parish, LA	93.6	21	Lynchburg city, VA	14.4	21	Spotsylvania County, VA	37.9
21	Colleton County, SC	93.6	21	Oktibbeha County, MS	14.4	21	Sussex County, NJ	37.9
21	Botetourt County, VA	93.6	21	Payne County, OK	14.4	23	Paulding County, GA	36.7
24	Nassau County, NY	93.5	24	Broomfield County, CO	14.2	24	Perry County, OH	36.6
24	Elk County, PA	93.5	24	Rowan County, KY	14.2	25	Caroline County, VA	36.5
26	Escambia County, AL	93.4	24	Logan County, IL	14.2	25	Marion County, MS	36.5
26	Ashe County, NC	93.4	24	Wakulla County, FL	14.2	27	Caroline County, MD	36.0
26	Buchanan County, VA	93.4	24	Comanche County, OK	14.2	28	King George County, VA	35.9
26	Wyoming County, WV	93.4	29	Riley County, KS	14.0	28	Calaveras County, CA	35.9
30	Manitowoc County, WI	93.3	29	Montgomery County, VA	14.0	28	Leake County, MS	35.9
31	Beaufort County, NC	93.2	31	Monroe County, IN	13.9	31	Prince George's County, MD	35.8
31	Calumet County, WI	93.2	32	Caldwell County, TX	13.8	32	Frederick County, MD	35.4
31	Oconto County, WI	93.2	32	Tattnall County, GA	13.8	33	Lincoln County, MO	35.2
34	Elbert County, GA	93.1	32	Vernon Parish, LA	13.8	33	Louisa County, VA	35.2
34	Ohio County, KY	93.1	35	Walker County, TX	13.7	35	George County, MS	35.0
34	Yadkin County, NC	93.1	36	Hockley County, TX	13.6	35	Carroll County, MD	35.0
34	Marion County, SC	93.1	37	Leavenworth County, KS	13.3	37	Barrow County, GA	34.9
34	Williamsburg County, SC	93.1	37	Onslow County, NC	13.3	37	Lincoln County, WV	34.9
34	Fluvanna County, VA	93.1	37	Adair County, MO	13.3	39	Livingston Parish, LA	34.8
40	Suffolk County, NY	93.0	37	Isabella County, MI	13.3	40	Warren County, NJ	34.7
41	Cass County, MI	92.9	41	Sanpete County, UT	13.2	41	Wyoming County, WV	34.6
41	Davie County, NC	92.9	41	Christian County, KY	13.2	42	Manassas city, VA	34.4
43	Benton County, IA	92.8	43	Liberty County, TX	13.1	42	Pearl River County, MS	34.4
44	Clarke County, AL	92.7	43	Meade County, SD	13.1	44	Chambers County, TX	34.3
44	Franklin County, GA	92.7	43	Centre County, PA	13.1	44	Montgomery County, MD	34.3
44	Rio Arriba County, NM	92.7	46	Latah County, ID	13.0	46	Washington County, MO	34.2
44	Adair County, OK	92.7	46	Brazos County, TX	13.0	46	Culpeper County, VA	34.2
44	Lincoln County, WV	92.7	48	Dale County, AL	12.9	48	Queen Anne's County, MD	34.1
49	Letcher County, KY	92.6	49	Newport News city, VA	12.7	49	Page County, VA	34.0
49	Bergen County, NJ	92.6	49	Muscogee County, GA	12.7	49	Monmouth County, NJ	34.0
49	Somerset County, NJ	92.6	49	Tompkins County, NY	12.7	51	Meade County, KY	33.9
49	Warren County, NJ	92.6	52	Hale County, TX	12.6	51	Hudson County, NJ	33.9
49	McKinley County, NM	92.6	52	Arlington County, VA	12.6	51	Gloucester County, VA	33.9
49	Rockland County, NY	92.6	52	Johnson County, MO	12.6	51	Van Zandt County, TX	33.9
49	Putnam County, OH	92.6	52	Athens County, OH	12.6	55	McHenry County, IL	33.8
49	Bucks County, PA	92.6	56	Rusk County, TX	12.5	55	Nassau County, NY	33.8
57	Madison County, GA	92.5	56	Clarke County, GA	12.5	57	Grimes County, TX	33.7
57	White County, GA	92.5	56	Geary County, KS	12.5	57	Brown County, OH	33.7
59	Sussex County, NJ	92.4	56	Tom Green County, TX	12.5	59	Caswell County, NC	33.5
59	Augusta County, VA	92.4	60	Summit County, CO	12.4	60	Liberty County, TX	33.4
61	Marshall County, KY	92.3	61	Somerset County, MD	12.3	60	Simpson County, MS	33.4
61	Lewis County, NY	92.3	61	Lamar County, MS	12.3	60	Orange County, NY	33.4
61	Vance County, NC	92.3	61	Alexandria city, VA	12.3	63	Currituck County, NC	33.3
61	Chester County, SC	92.3	61	Phelps County, MO	12.3	63	Hunterdon County, NJ	33.3
61	Wharton County, TX	92.3	65	Hardin County, KY	12.2	63	Contra Costa County, CA	33.3
66	Adams County, MS	92.2	66	Montgomery County, IL	12.1	66	Rockdale County, GA	33.2
66	Panola County, MS	92.2	66	Montgomery County, TN	12.1	66	Henry County, GA	33.2
66	Bedford County, VA	92.2	68	Aransas County, TX	12.0	66	Loudoun County, VA	33.2
66	Clark County, WI	92.2	68	Ellis County, KS	12.0	69	Cheatham County, TN	33.1
70	Whiteside County, IL	92.1	70	Albemarle County, VA	11.9	70	Hood County, TX	33.0
70	Antrim County, MI	92.1	71	Fairfax city, VA	11.8	70	Fluvanna County, VA	33.0
70	Wabasha County, MN	92.1	71	Hays County, TX	11.8	72	Dawson County, GA	32.9
70	Copiah County, MS	92.1	71	Orange County, NC	11.8	73	Kendall County, IL	32.8
70	Warren County, MS	92.1	74	Jasper County, SC	11.7	73	Will County, IL	32.8
70	Wayne County, MS	92.1	74	Clark County, AR	11.7	73	Colleton County, SC	32.8
70	Juniata County, PA	92.1						
70	Somerset County, PA	92.1						
70	Hardeman County, TN	92.1						
70	Shelby County, TX	92.1						
70	Russell County, VA	92.1						

Median value of owner-occupied housing units rank	County	Median value of owner-occupied housing units (dollars) [C-2, col. 5]	Median selected monthly owner (with a mortgage) costs as a percentage of household income rank	County	Median selected monthly owner (with a mortgage) costs as a percentage of household income [C-2, col. 6]	Median gross rent as a percentage of household income rank	County	Median gross rent as a percentage of household income [C-2, col. 9]
	United States	174,600		United States	24.5		United States	31.5
1	New York County, NY	812,300	1	Monroe County, FL	35.7	1	Watauga County, NC	50.0
2	Marin County, CA	759,300	2	Kings County, NY..................	33.8	2	Whitman County, WA............	48.8
3	San Francisco County, CA	737,700	3	Miami-Dade County, FL...........	33.7	3	Brazos County, TX.................	45.1
4	San Mateo County, CA	710,100	4	Maui County, HI	33.5	4	Conway County, AR..............	44.4
5	Teton County, WY	705,600	5	Mendocino County, CA...........	33.3	5	Kittitas County, WA	43.9
6	Santa Clara County, CA	634,000	6	Bronx County, NY	32.9	6	George County, MS	43.5
7	Arlington County, VA	584,500	7	Kauai County, HI	32.8	7	Somerset County, MD	43.2
8	Honolulu County, HI..............	556,400	7	Nevada County, CA	32.8	7	Yazoo County, MS	43.2
9	Kings County, NY	556,300	9	Queens County, NY................	32.7	9	Decatur County, GA..............	43.0
10	Santa Cruz County, CA	549,800	9	San Benito County, CA............	32.7	10	Cheatham County, TN............	42.7
11	Maui County, HI....................	532,100	9	Lake County, CA....................	32.7	11	Taos County, NM	42.6
12	Westchester County, NY	516,600	12	Hudson County, NJ	32.2	11	Miami County, KS	42.6
13	Orange County, CA...............	509,500	13	Crook County, OR..................	31.8	13	Columbia County, AR............	42.4
14	Alexandria city, VA	491,500	14	Los Angeles County, CA..........	31.7	14	Jackson County, IL................	42.3
15	Summit County, UT...............	488,700	14	Passaic County, NJ................	31.7	15	Baldwin County, GA..............	42.2
16	Alameda County, CA	484,200	14	Collier County, FL.................	31.7	16	Buchanan County, VA............	42.1
17	Kauai County, HI...................	477,400	17	Plumas County, CA	31.5	16	McDonough County, IL	42.1
18	Fairfax County, VA	474,700	18	Osceola County, FL................	31.4	18	Monroe County, IN	41.9
19	Eagle County, CO.................	469,800	19	Atlantic County, NJ	31.1	19	Montgomery County, VA	41.8
20	Nassau County, NY	452,200	19	Charlotte County, FL	31.1	20	Athens County, OH...............	41.6
21	Fairfax city, VA	450,900	21	Hawaii County, HI	31.0	21	Madison County, ID	41.4
22	Bergen County, NJ	448,100	22	Tuolumne County, CA.............	30.9	22	Oktibbeha County, MS...........	41.2
23	Queens County, NY...............	447,500	22	Klickitat County, WA	30.9	22	De Soto Parish, LA	41.2
24	Montgomery County, MD	444,100	22	Siskiyou County, CA...............	30.9	24	Isabella County, MI................	41.1
25	Summit County, CO	442,800	25	Essex County, NJ	30.8	25	Marion County, MS	40.7
25	Richmond County, NY...........	442,800	25	Blaine County, ID	30.8	26	Hempstead County, AR...........	40.5
27	District of Columbia..............	436,000	27	Riverside County, CA..............	30.7	27	Antrim County, MI	40.2
28	Santa Barbara County, CA.....	434,700	27	Broward County, FL...............	30.7	27	Newton County, GA...............	40.2
29	Ventura County, CA	433,300	27	Hardee County, FL.................	30.7	27	Bulloch County, GA...............	40.2
30	Loudoun County, VA.............	433,100	30	Santa Cruz County, CA	30.6	30	Hays County, TX...................	40.1
31	Rockland County, NY	430,400	30	Amador County, CA...............	30.6	30	Benton County, OR	40.1
32	Fairfield County, CT.............	429,400	30	Madera County, CA...............	30.6	32	Grady County, GA.................	40.0
33	Morris County, NJ	428,600	33	Palm Beach County, FL...........	30.5	32	Walker County, TX................	40.0
34	Howard County, MD..............	417,700	33	St. Lucie County, FL................	30.5	34	Crisp County, GA..................	39.8
35	Los Angeles County, CA	414,100	35	Calaveras County, CA	30.4	35	Monroe County, FL	39.6
36	San Luis Obispo County, CA..	410,500	36	Monterey County, CA	30.2	36	Wakulla County, FL	39.5
37	Napa County, CA..................	403,600	36	Curry County, OR	30.2	37	Miami-Dade County, FL..........	39.4
38	Hunterdon County, NJ...........	398,600	36	Flagler County, FL.................	30.2	37	Sussex County, NJ	39.4
39	Somerset County, NJ............	398,000	36	Hardeman County, TN............	30.2	37	Russell County, VA	39.4
40	San Diego County, CA	396,500	40	Nassau County, NY	30.1	40	Centre County, PA	39.3
41	Middlesex County, MA..........	396,400	40	San Luis Obispo County, CA....	30.1	41	St. Lucie County, FL...............	39.1
42	Sonoma County, CA	396,300	40	Georgetown County, SC	30.1	42	Willacy County, TX................	39.0
43	Contra Costa County, CA......	392,900	43	Okeechobee County, FL	30.0	43	Natchitoches Parish, LA..........	38.9
44	Norfolk County, MA..............	389,100	44	Suffolk County, NY	29.9	44	Mason County, WA...............	38.8
45	Monmouth County, NJ...........	387,700	44	Somerset County, MD	29.9	44	Leon County, FL	38.8
46	Routt County, CO	387,400	46	San Diego County, CA	29.8	44	Alachua County, FL	38.8
47	Suffolk County, NY	383,000	46	Glenn County, CA.................	29.8	44	Lafayette County, MS............	38.8
48	Monroe County, FL	380,000	48	San Francisco County, CA	29.7	48	Ocean County, NJ	38.7
49	Bronx County, NY	373,500	48	Summit County, CO	29.7	48	Chesterfield County, SC	38.7
50	King County, WA	369,000	48	Union County, NJ	29.7	50	Washington County, MS	38.5
51	Essex County, NJ	365,800	48	Humboldt County, CA.............	29.7	50	Clarke County, GA................	38.5
52	Barnstable County, MA	364,500	52	Sonoma County, CA	29.6	52	Amador County, CA..............	38.1
53	Putnam County, NY	364,300	52	Clatsop County, OR................	29.6	53	Lake County, CA...................	38.0
54	Blaine County, ID	362,200	54	Marin County, CA	29.5	53	Bibb County, GA...................	38.0
55	Union County, NJ	360,400	54	Bergen County, NJ	29.5	53	Bertie County, NC	38.0
56	Goochland County, VA..........	357,400	54	Ocean County, NJ	29.5	56	Ogemaw County, MI.............	37.9
57	Suffolk County, MA	355,300	54	Tehama County, CA...............	29.5	56	Gadsden County, FL..............	37.9
58	Newport County, RI..............	354,400	54	Jasper County, SC	29.5	58	Siskiyou County, CA..............	37.8
59	Boulder County, CO..............	353,800	59	San Mateo County, CA	29.4	58	Macon County, NC	37.8
60	El Dorado County, CA...........	350,300	59	Bonner County, ID.................	29.4	58	Orleans Parish, LA	37.8
61	Calvert County, MD	349,900	61	Orange County, CA...............	29.3	58	DeKalb County, IL	37.8
62	Passaic County, NJ...............	348,700	61	Napa County, CA..................	29.3	58	Salem city, VA	37.8
63	Essex County, MA	346,700	61	Routt County, CO	29.3	58	Forrest County, MS	37.8
64	Queen Anne's County, MD....	346,100	61	Barnstable County, MA	29.3	64	Hardeman County, TN............	37.6
65	Nevada County, CA...............	345,300	61	El Dorado County, CA............	29.3	64	Walton County, FL................	37.6
66	Monterey County, CA	344,200	66	Flathead County, MT..............	29.2	64	Jackson County, OR	37.6
67	Fauquier County, VA	343,400	66	Martin County, FL.................	29.2	64	Teller County, CO.................	37.6
68	Hudson County, NJ	342,000	66	Stanislaus County, CA............	29.2	64	Payne County, OK................	37.6
69	La Plata County, CO.............	334,400	69	Eagle County, CO.................	29.1	69	Nevada County, CA...............	37.5
70	San Benito County, CA..........	332,900	69	Richmond County, NY............	29.1	69	Wayne County, MI	37.5
71	Anne Arundel County, MD....	332,300	69	Santa Barbara County, CA.......	29.1	69	Dallas County, AL.................	37.5
72	Williamson County, TN..........	332,000	69	Cape May County, NJ............	29.1	69	Delaware County, IN	37.5
73	Middlesex County, NJ...........	330,300	69	Garfield County, CO..............	29.1	73	Mendocino County, CA..........	37.4
74	Douglas County, CO	330,100	69	San Bernardino County, CA.....	29.1	73	Albany County, WY...............	37.4
75	Plymouth County, MA...........	328,800	69	Washington County, UT..........	29.1	75	Thomas County, GA..............	37.3
			69	Walton County, FL	29.1	75	Wasco County, OR	37.3
			69	Coahoma County, MS............	29.1			

Metropolitan Area Rankings, 2012
Selected Rankings

Lived in the same house one year ago rank	Area name	Percent who lived in the same house one year ago [C-3, col. 1]	Did not live in this MSA one year ago rank	Area name	Percent who did not live in this MSA one year ago [C-3, col. 2]
	United States	85.0		United States	4.5
1	Wenatchee-East Wenatchee, WA	91.7	1	Ames, IA	17.8
2	Pine Bluff, AR	90.7	2	Jacksonville, NC	15.4
2	Johnstown, PA	90.7	3	Lawton, OK	15.3
4	Brownsville-Harlingen, TX	90.6	3	Ithaca, NY	15.3
5	New York-Northern New Jersey-Long Island, NY-NJ-PA	90.4	5	Hinesville-Fort Stewart, GA	15.0
6	Barnstable Town, MA	90.2	6	State College, PA	14.0
7	Poughkeepsie-Newburgh-Middletown, NY	89.8	7	San Angelo, TX	13.2
7	Bay City, MI	89.8	8	Manhattan, KS	13.0
9	Kankakee-Bradley, IL	89.7	9	Lawrence, KS	12.5
9	Appleton, WI	89.7	10	Elizabethtown, KY	12.1
9	Parkersburg-Marietta-Vienna, WV-OH	89.7	11	Fairbanks, AK	12.0
12	Racine, WI	89.6	12	Bloomington, IN	11.8
13	Lancaster, PA	89.5	13	Corvallis, OR	11.5
14	York-Hanover, PA	89.2	14	Auburn-Opelika, AL	11.2
14	Monroe, MI	89.2	14	College Station-Bryan, TX	11.2
16	Worcester, MA	89.1	16	Columbus, GA-AL	11.1
17	Madera-Chowchilla, CA	89.0	17	Gainesville, FL	10.9
18	Farmington, NM	88.9	18	Hanford-Corcoran, CA	10.6
19	Vineland-Millville-Bridgeton, NJ	88.8	18	Ann Arbor, MI	10.6
19	Atlantic City-Hammonton, NJ	88.8	20	Blacksburg-Christiansburg-Radford, VA	10.5
19	Ocean City, NJ	88.8	20	Lafayette, IN	10.5
22	Morristown, TN	88.7	20	Champaign-Urbana, IL	10.5
22	Sheboygan, WI	88.7	20	Lake Havasu City-Kingman, AZ	10.5
22	Altoona, PA	88.7	20	Clarksville, TN-KY	10.5
22	Philadelphia-Camden-Wilmington, PA-NJ-DE-MD	88.7	25	Boulder, CO	10.4
26	Hickory-Lenoir-Morganton, NC	88.5	25	Fayetteville, NC	10.4
27	Palm Coast, FL	88.4	25	Flagstaff, AZ	10.4
28	Steubenville-Weirton, WV-OH	88.3	28	Wichita Falls, TX	10.3
29	Baltimore-Towson, MD	88.1	29	Columbia, MO	10.2
29	Winchester, VA-WV	88.1	30	Tallahassee, FL	10.1
29	Gainesville, GA	88.1	30	Midland, TX	10.1
32	Jackson, TN	88.0	30	Mankato-North Mankato, MN	10.1
32	Youngstown-Warren-Boardman, OH-PA	88.0	33	Colorado Springs, CO	10.0
32	Pittsburgh, PA	88.0	33	Athens-Clarke County, GA	10.0
32	Kingston, NY	88.0	35	Logan, UT-ID	9.8
36	Pittsfield, MA	87.9	36	Muncie, IN	9.7
36	Napa, CA	87.9	36	Tyler, TX	9.7
36	Warner Robins, GA	87.9	38	Coeur d'Alene, ID	9.5
39	Utica-Rome, NY	87.7	38	Bowling Green, KY	9.5
39	Fort Wayne, IN	87.7	38	Killeen-Temple-Fort Hood, TX	9.5
39	Hartford-West Hartford-East Hartford, CT	87.7	41	Grand Forks, ND-MN	9.4
39	Providence-New Bedford-Fall River, RI-MA	87.7	42	Bloomington-Normal, IL	9.3
39	Buffalo-Niagara Falls, NY	87.7	43	Greeley, CO	9.2
39	Green Bay, WI	87.7	44	Durham-Chapel Hill, NC	9.1
39	Waterloo-Cedar Falls, IA	87.7	45	Greenville, NC	9.0
39	New Haven-Milford, CT	87.7	45	Crestview-Fort Walton Beach-Destin, FL	9.0
39	Glens Falls, NY	87.7	45	Lubbock, TX	9.0
48	Saginaw-Saginaw Township North, MI	87.6	45	Valdosta, GA	9.0
48	Trenton-Ewing, NJ	87.6	45	Panama City-Lynn Haven-Panama City Beach, FL	9.0
48	Florence, SC	87.6	50	Iowa City, IA	8.9
48	Monroe, LA	87.6	50	Morgantown, WV	8.9
48	Scranton–Wilkes-Barre, PA	87.6	50	San Luis Obispo-Paso Robles, CA	8.9
53	Oxnard-Thousand Oaks-Ventura, CA	87.5	50	Missoula, MT	8.9
53	Akron, OH	87.5	50	Fort Collins-Loveland, CO	8.9
53	Albany-Schenectady-Troy, NY	87.5	55	Hot Springs, AR	8.8
56	Wausau, WI	87.4	55	Hattiesburg, MS	8.8
56	Dubuque, IA	87.4	57	Harrisonburg, VA	8.7
56	Alexandria, LA	87.4	57	Abilene, TX	8.7
59	Pascagoula, MS	87.3	59	St. Cloud, MN	8.5
60	Canton-Massillon, OH	87.2	59	Olympia, WA	8.5
60	Bridgeport-Stamford-Norwalk, CT	87.2	59	Tuscaloosa, AL	8.5
60	Wheeling, WV-OH	87.2	59	Charlottesville, VA	8.5
60	Danville, VA	87.2	63	Cape Coral-Fort Myers, FL	8.4
64	Laredo, TX	87.1	63	Fargo, ND-MN	8.4
64	Huntington-Ashland, WV-KY-OH	87.1	63	Gulfport-Biloxi, MS	8.4
66	Allentown-Bethlehem-Easton, PA-NJ	87.0	66	Columbus, IN	8.3
66	Lynchburg, VA	87.0	66	Provo-Orem, UT	8.3
66	Chicago-Joliet-Naperville, IL-IN-WI	87.0	66	Waco, TX	8.3
69	Florence-Muscle Shoals, AL	86.9	69	Carson City, NV	8.2
69	Punta Gorda, FL	86.9	70	Salisbury, MD	8.0
71	Dover, DE	86.8	70	Prescott, AZ	8.0
71	Shreveport-Bossier City, LA	86.8	70	Battle Creek, MI	8.0
71	Anderson, SC	86.8	73	St. Joseph, MO-KS	7.9
71	Charleston, WV	86.8	73	Michigan City-La Porte, IN	7.9
71	Manchester-Nashua, NH	86.8	75	Bremerton-Silverdale, WA	7.8
			75	Holland-Grand Haven, MI	7.8

Mean travel time to work rank	Area name	Mean travel time to work (minutes) [C-3, col. 11]	Median value of owner-occupied housing units rank	Area name	Median value of owner-occupied housing units (dollars) [C-3, col. 5]
	United States	25.7		United States	171,900
1	New York-Northern New Jersey-Long Island, NY-NJ-PA	35.2	1	San Jose-Sunnyvale-Santa Clara, CA	624,200
2	Washington-Arlington-Alexandria, DC-VA-MD-WV	34.0	2	Honolulu, HI	563,600
3	Poughkeepsie-Newburgh-Middletown, NY.........................	32.6	3	San Francisco-Oakland-Fremont, CA	557,700
4	Riverside-San Bernardino-Ontario, CA	31.2	4	Santa Cruz-Watsonville, CA	545,700
5	Chicago-Joliet-Naperville, IL-IN-WI...........................	30.6	5	Los Angeles-Long Beach-Santa Ana, CA..........	428,500
6	San Francisco-Oakland-Fremont, CA	30.4	6	Oxnard-Thousand Oaks-Ventura, CA	413,100
7	Bremerton-Silverdale, WA	30.0	7	San Luis Obispo-Paso Robles, CA	410,900
7	Baltimore-Towson, MD.......................................	30.0	8	Santa Barbara-Santa Maria-Goleta, CA	409,700
7	Atlanta-Sandy Springs-Marietta, GA...........................	30.0	9	Bridgeport-Stamford-Norwalk, CT	403,400
10	Stockton, CA	29.7	10	New York-Northern New Jersey-Long Island, NY-NJ-PA	400,000
11	Boston-Cambridge-Quincy, MA-NH...........................	29.5	11	Napa, CA	396,500
12	Winchester, VA-WV...	29.2	12	San Diego-Carlsbad-San Marcos, CA...........	386,400
12	Hagerstown-Martinsburg, MD-WV.............................	29.2	13	Santa Rosa-Petaluma, CA	380,100
14	Los Angeles-Long Beach-Santa Ana, CA.........................	28.9	14	Washington-Arlington-Alexandria, DC-VA-MD-WV	367,600
15	Houston-Sugar Land-Baytown, TX.............................	28.6	15	Boulder, CO	364,100
15	Philadelphia-Camden-Wilmington, PA-NJ-DE-MD.................	28.6	16	Barnstable Town, MA.........................	361,500
17	Seattle-Tacoma-Bellevue, WA................................	28.5	17	Boston-Cambridge-Quincy, MA-NH.............	358,400
17	Worcester, MA...	28.5	18	Salinas, CA	318,200
19	Vallejo-Fairfield, CA..	28.2	19	Ocean City, NJ..............................	305,900
20	Bridgeport-Stamford-Norwalk, CT............................	28.1	20	Seattle-Tacoma-Bellevue, WA.................	293,700
21	Miami-Fort Lauderdale-Pompano Beach, FL.....................	28.0	21	Corvallis, OR	275,500
22	Cape Coral-Fort Myers, FL...................................	27.7	22	Trenton-Ewing, NJ...........................	272,900
22	Trenton-Ewing, NJ..	27.7	23	Baltimore-Towson, MD.......................	271,100
24	Allentown-Bethlehem-Easton, PA-NJ...........................	27.6	24	Santa Fe, NM...............................	270,200
25	Kingston, NY..	27.5	25	Poughkeepsie-Newburgh-Middletown, NY........	269,900
26	Orlando-Kissimmee-Sanford, FL	27.3	26	Charlottesville, VA..........................	269,500
26	Yuba City, CA..	27.3	27	Anchorage, AK..............................	266,700
28	Dallas-Fort Worth-Arlington, TX..............................	27.1	28	Bremerton-Silverdale, WA....................	255,600
28	York-Hanover, PA...	27.1	29	Bellingham, WA.............................	255,500
30	Honolulu, HI...	27.0	30	Sacramento–Arden-Arcade–Roseville, CA........	250,000
30	Palm Coast, FL...	27.0	31	Burlington-South Burlington, VT..............	249,700
32	Modesto, CA...	26.9	32	Portland-Vancouver-Hillsboro, OR-WA..........	249,300
32	Denver-Aurora-Broomfield, CO................................	26.9	33	Norwich-New London, CT.....................	248,200
34	Baton Rouge, LA..	26.7	34	Denver-Aurora-Broomfield, CO................	246,900
35	Pittsburgh, PA...	26.5	35	Worcester, MA..............................	246,500
35	Merced, CA..	26.5	35	Providence-New Bedford-Fall River, RI-MA......	246,500
37	Manchester-Nashua, NH......................................	26.4	37	Hartford-West Hartford-East Hartford, CT......	243,800
37	Port St. Lucie, FL...	26.4	38	Fort Collins-Loveland, CO....................	243,600
39	Nashville-Davidson—Murfreesboro—Franklin, TN	26.3	39	Mount Vernon-Anacortes, WA.................	242,600
40	Detroit-Warren-Livonia, MI..................................	26.2	40	Manchester-Nashua, NH......................	242,300
40	Morristown, TN..	26.2	41	New Haven-Milford, CT......................	242,100
40	Lakeland-Winter Haven, FL...................................	26.2	42	Bend, OR	235,300
40	Gainesville, GA..	26.2	43	Philadelphia-Camden-Wilmington, PA-NJ-DE-MD......	235,100
44	Greeley, CO...	26.1	44	Vallejo-Fairfield, CA.........................	234,900
44	Alexandria, LA...	26.1	45	Naples-Marco Island, FL.....................	233,500
46	Tampa-St. Petersburg-Clearwater, FL..........................	25.9	46	Virginia Beach-Norfolk-Newport News, VA-NC....	233,300
46	Steubenville-Weirton, WV-OH................................	25.9	47	Portland-South Portland-Biddeford, ME.........	232,000
48	Phoenix-Mesa-Glendale, AZ..................................	25.8	48	Olympia, WA...............................	228,300
48	Birmingham-Hoover, AL......................................	25.8	49	Atlantic City-Hammonton, NJ.................	226,800
50	Santa Cruz-Watsonville, CA..................................	25.7	50	Salt Lake City, UT...........................	221,100
50	San Jose-Sunnyvale-Santa Clara, CA	25.7	51	Missoula, MT...............................	220,700
50	Santa Rosa-Petaluma, CA....................................	25.7	52	Kingston, NY...............................	220,600
53	Dover, DE...	25.6	53	Wenatchee-East Wenatchee, WA..............	219,500
53	Charlotte-Gastonia-Rock Hill, NC-SC..........................	25.6	54	Madison, WI...............................	217,600
55	Mount Vernon-Anacortes, WA................................	25.5	55	Colorado Springs, CO........................	216,000
55	Austin-Round Rock-San Marcos, TX...........................	25.5	56	Fairbanks, AK..............................	214,500
55	Providence-New Bedford-Fall River, RI-MA......................	25.5	57	Flagstaff, AZ...............................	214,300
58	New Orleans-Metairie-Kenner, LA.............................	25.4	58	Riverside-San Bernardino-Ontario, CA..........	214,100
58	Sacramento–Arden-Arcade–Roseville, CA.......................	25.4	59	Springfield, MA.............................	210,500
58	St. Louis, MO-IL..	25.4	60	Provo-Orem, UT.............................	207,800
58	Jacksonville, NC..	25.4	61	Richmond, VA..............................	207,400
62	Anderson, IN...	25.3	62	Chicago-Joliet-Naperville, IL-IN-WI...........	207,100
63	Houma-Bayou Cane-Thibodaux, LA............................	25.2	63	Eugene-Springfield, OR.......................	206,600
63	Jacksonville, FL..	25.2	64	Pittsfield, MA..............................	206,400
65	Indianapolis-Carmel, IN.....................................	25.1	65	Minneapolis-St. Paul-Bloomington, MN-WI......	203,700
65	Flint, MI..	25.1	66	Raleigh-Cary, NC...........................	203,600
65	Deltona-Daytona Beach-Ormond Beach, FL......................	25.1	67	Chico, CA	203,100
65	Portland-Vancouver-Hillsboro, OR-WA.........................	25.1	68	Redding, CA...............................	202,500
69	Richmond, VA..	25.0	69	Winchester, VA-WV..........................	199,600
69	Madera-Chowchilla, CA......................................	25.0	70	Medford, OR...............................	199,400
71	San Antonio-New Braunfels, TX..............................	24.9	71	Harrisonburg, VA...........................	198,200
71	Reading, PA...	24.9	72	Grand Junction, CO.........................	197,700
71	Pascagoula, MS..	24.9	73	Dover, DE.................................	197,500
71	Minneapolis-St. Paul-Bloomington, MN-WI......................	24.9	74	Albany-Schenectady-Troy, NY.................	197,000
75	Pensacola-Ferry Pass-Brent, FL...............................	24.7	75	Allentown-Bethlehem-Easton, PA-NJ...........	196,400

Metropolitan Area Rankings, 2012—*Continued*
Selected Rankings

Median selected monthly owner (with a mortgage) costs as a percentage of household income rank	Area name	Median selected monthly owner (with a mortgage) costs as a percentage of household income [C-3, col. 6]	Median gross rent as a percentage of household income rank	Area name	Median gross rent as a percentage of household income [C-3, col. 9]
	United States	23.7		United States	31.1
1	Palm Coast, FL............................	31.9	1	Corvallis, OR...............................	42.0
2	Ocean City, NJ.............................	30.9	2	Muskegon-Norton Shores, MI........	41.7
3	Atlantic City-Hammonton, NJ.........	30.7	3	College Station-Bryan, TX.............	39.8
4	Miami-Fort Lauderdale-Pompano Beach, FL................	30.3	4	Sebastian-Vero Beach, FL..............	39.2
5	Punta Gorda, FL...........................	30.2	5	Port St. Lucie, FL.........................	39.1
6	Madera-Chowchilla, CA..................	30.0	5	Gainesville, FL.............................	39.1
7	Los Angeles-Long Beach-Santa Ana, CA...................	29.9	7	Tallahassee, FL.............................	38.7
7	Naples-Marco Island, FL................	29.9	8	Vineland-Millville-Bridgeton, NJ......	38.6
9	San Luis Obispo-Paso Robles, CA	29.4	8	Bloomington, IN...........................	38.6
10	Salinas, CA..................................	29.2	10	Muncie, IN..................................	38.5
11	San Diego-Carlsbad-San Marcos, CA............	29.1	11	Atlantic City-Hammonton, NJ.........	38.0
12	Santa Cruz-Watsonville, CA	29.0	12	Chico, CA...................................	37.5
13	New York-Northern New Jersey-Long Island, NY-NJ-PA	28.8	12	Ames, IA....................................	37.5
14	Riverside-San Bernardino-Ontario, CA...........	28.7	14	St. George, UT............................	37.4
15	Honolulu, HI................................	28.6	15	Madera-Chowchilla, CA..................	37.3
16	St. George, UT.............................	28.5	15	Laredo, TX..................................	37.3
17	Bend, OR....................................	28.4	17	Lafayette, IN...............................	37.2
18	Santa Rosa-Petaluma, CA...............	28.3	18	Miami-Fort Lauderdale-Pompano Beach, FL............	37.0
18	Barnstable Town, MA.....................	28.3	19	Lima, OH....................................	36.9
20	Oxnard-Thousand Oaks-Ventura, CA.........	28.1	20	Oxnard-Thousand Oaks-Ventura, CA.........	36.8
20	Napa, CA....................................	28.1	20	State College, PA.........................	36.8
22	Deltona-Daytona Beach-Ormond Beach, FL...............	28.0	22	Myrtle Beach-North Myrtle Beach-Conway, SC	36.7
23	Santa Barbara-Santa Maria-Goleta, CA	27.9	23	Modesto, CA...............................	36.4
24	Modesto, CA...............................	27.8	24	Boulder, CO................................	36.3
25	Poughkeepsie-Newburgh-Middletown, NY.................	27.6	24	Auburn-Opelika, AL......................	36.3
26	San Francisco-Oakland-Fremont, CA......	27.4	26	Deltona-Daytona Beach-Ormond Beach, FL............	36.2
26	Medford, OR...............................	27.4	26	Macon, GA.................................	36.2
26	Port St. Lucie, FL.........................	27.4	28	Riverside-San Bernardino-Ontario, CA........	36.1
29	Bridgeport-Stamford-Norwalk, CT....	27.2	29	Hattiesburg, MS...........................	36.0
30	Sebastian-Vero Beach, FL...............	27.1	30	Blacksburg-Christiansburg-Radford, VA........	35.9
30	El Centro, CA...............................	27.1	31	Kokomo, IN................................	35.7
32	Eugene-Springfield, OR..................	27.0	32	Pascagoula, MS............................	35.5
32	Visalia-Porterville, CA...................	27.0	33	Niles-Benton Harbor, MI................	35.4
34	Chico, CA...................................	26.9	34	Poughkeepsie-Newburgh-Middletown, NY............	35.3
34	Fresno, CA..................................	26.9	34	Redding, CA................................	35.3
34	Orlando-Kissimmee-Sanford, FL	26.9	34	Ocala, FL....................................	35.3
34	Hinesville-Fort Stewart, GA............	26.9	37	Fresno, CA..................................	35.2
38	Sacramento–Arden-Arcade–Roseville, CA.............	26.8	37	Burlington, NC.............................	35.2
38	Stockton, CA...............................	26.8	39	Los Angeles-Long Beach-Santa Ana, CA........	35.1
40	San Jose-Sunnyvale-Santa Clara, CA	26.7	39	Pine Bluff, AR..............................	35.1
40	Vallejo-Fairfield, CA......................	26.7	41	Stockton, CA...............................	35.0
40	Wenatchee-East Wenatchee, WA.....	26.7	42	Orlando-Kissimmee-Sanford, FL	34.9
40	Reno-Sparks, NV..........................	26.7	42	Salisbury, MD..............................	34.9
40	Vineland-Millville-Bridgeton, NJ......	26.7	44	Lansing-East Lansing, MI................	34.8
40	North Port-Bradenton-Sarasota, FL..	26.7	45	Barnstable Town, MA....................	34.7
46	Yuba City, CA..............................	26.6	45	Visalia-Porterville, CA...................	34.7
47	Prescott, AZ................................	26.5	45	Columbia, MO.............................	34.7
48	New Haven-Milford, CT..................	26.4	48	Santa Barbara-Santa Maria-Goleta, CA	34.6
49	Kingston, NY...............................	26.3	48	Kingston, NY...............................	34.6
49	Fairbanks, AK..............................	26.3	50	Flint, MI.....................................	34.5
49	Salem, OR..................................	26.3	50	Ann Arbor, MI.............................	34.5
49	Carson City, NV...........................	26.3	50	Mankato-North Mankato, MN	34.5
49	Brownsville-Harlingen, TX...............	26.3	53	El Centro, CA..............................	34.4
54	Redding, CA................................	26.2	53	Vallejo-Fairfield, CA......................	34.4
55	Cape Coral-Fort Myers, FL..............	26.1	53	Yuba City, CA..............................	34.4
55	Ocala, FL....................................	26.1	56	Santa Rosa-Petaluma, CA...............	34.2
57	Santa Fe, NM..............................	26.0	56	Eugene-Springfield, OR..................	34.2
57	Bremerton-Silverdale, WA..............	26.0	56	Lubbock, TX................................	34.2
57	Mount Vernon-Anacortes, WA	26.0	59	Naples-Marco Island, FL................	34.1
57	Myrtle Beach-North Myrtle Beach-Conway, SC	26.0	59	Sacramento–Arden-Arcade–Roseville, CA.........	34.1
61	Trenton-Ewing, NJ........................	25.9	59	New Haven-Milford, CT..................	34.1
61	Hanford-Corcoran, CA...................	25.9	59	Savannah, GA..............................	34.1
63	Chicago-Joliet-Naperville, IL-IN-WI...	25.8	63	San Diego-Carlsbad-San Marcos, CA..........	34.0
64	Seattle-Tacoma-Bellevue, WA.........	25.7	63	Medford, OR...............................	34.0
64	Manchester-Nashua, NH.................	25.7	63	Yuma, AZ...................................	34.0
64	Tampa-St. Petersburg-Clearwater, FL..	25.7	63	Tuscaloosa, AL.............................	34.0
67	Grand Junction, CO.......................	25.6	63	Lawrence, KS...............................	34.0
68	Olympia, WA...............................	25.5	68	Jackson, MI.................................	33.9
68	Las Vegas-Paradise, NV	25.5	68	Albany, GA.................................	33.9
68	Laredo, TX..................................	25.5	70	Jacksonville, FL............................	33.8
71	Providence-New Bedford-Fall River, RI-MA..	25.4	70	Las Cruces, NM...........................	33.8
71	Palm Bay-Melbourne-Titusville, FL ...	25.4	70	Fort Collins-Loveland, CO..............	33.8
73	Brunswick, GA.............................	25.3	70	Jackson, TN................................	33.8
74	Virginia Beach-Norfolk-Newport News, VA-NC	25.2	70	Greenville, NC.............................	33.8
74	Flagstaff, AZ...............................	25.2	70	Terre Haute, IN...........................	33.8
74	Bakersfield-Delano, CA..................	25.2			
74	Merced, CA.................................	25.2			
74	Lakeland-Winter Haven, FL.............	25.2			

City Rankings, 2010–2012
Selected Rankings

Lived in the same house one year ago rank	City	Percent who lived in the same house one year ago [C-4, col. 1]	Did not live in the city one year ago rank	City	Percent who did not live in the city one year ago [C-4, col. 2]	Mean travel time to work rank	City	Mean travel time to work (minutes) [C-4, col. 11]
	United States	84.8		United States	10.1		United States	25.5
1	Oceanside CDP, NY	96.9	1	Isla Vista CDP, CA	49.3	1	Temescal Valley CDP, CA	47.7
2	Merrick CDP, NY	96.1	2	Fort Hood CDP, TX	39.7	2	Bainbridge Island city, WA	44.7
3	Plainview CDP, NY	95.9	3	State College borough, PA	38.1	3	Waldorf CDP, MD	43.1
4	Homer Glen village, IL	95.7	4	North Chicago city, IL	36.5	4	Fort Washington CDP, MD	42.3
4	Franklin Square CDP, NY	95.7	5	University CDP (Orange County), FL	36.3	5	Los Banos city, CA	42.2
6	Dix Hills CDP, NY	95.6	6	Oxford city, OH	34.8	6	Poinciana CDP, FL	42.1
7	Garfield city, NJ	95.5	7	East Lansing city, MI	34.5	7	Linton Hall CDP, VA	41.9
7	Passaic city, NJ	95.5	7	Ypsilanti city, MI	34.5	8	Lake Elsinore city, CA	41.7
7	Holtsville CDP, NY	95.5	9	Florence town, AZ	32.9	9	Fairland CDP, MD	41.6
7	West Islip CDP, NY	95.5	10	College Park city, MD	32.2	10	Dale City CDP, VA	41.1
11	Country Club CDP, FL	95.4	11	Rexburg city, ID	31.4	10	Eastvale city, CA	41.1
11	Paramus borough, NJ	95.4	12	Mount Pleasant city, MI	30.4	10	Montclair CDP, VA	41.1
11	New City CDP, NY	95.4	13	Twentynine Palms city, CA	29.9	13	Long Beach city, NY	41.0
14	Rotterdam CDP, NY	95.3	14	Newark city, DE	29.5	14	Tracy city, CA	40.9
15	Walnut city, CA	95.2	14	Urbana city, IL	29.5	15	Lake Ridge CDP, VA	40.8
15	Old Bridge CDP, NJ	95.2	14	West Lafayette city, IN	29.5	15	Patterson city, CA	40.8
15	Commack CDP, NY	95.2	17	Oxford city, MS	29.3	17	French Valley CDP, CA	40.3
18	Deer Park CDP, NY	95.0	18	Ithaca city, NY	29.0	18	Clinton CDP, MD	40.2
19	West Babylon CDP, NY	94.9	19	South Salt Lake city, UT	28.9	18	Syosset CDP, NY	40.2
20	West Whittier-Los Nietos CDP, CA	94.7	20	Athens city, OH	28.8	20	San Tan Valley CDP, AZ	39.9
20	Hicksville CDP, NY	94.7	21	University CDP (Hillsborough County), FL	28.3	20	Brentwood city, CA	39.9
22	Granger CDP, IN	94.6	22	Pullman city, WA	27.2	22	Richmond West CDP, FL	39.8
22	Smithtown CDP, NY	94.6	22	Morgantown city, West VA	27.2	23	Oakley city, CA	39.5
22	Southlake city, TX	94.6	24	Leavenworth city, KS	26.9	24	Palmdale city, CA	39.4
25	Sayreville borough, NJ	94.5	24	Havelock city, NC	26.9	25	Antioch city, CA	39.2
26	Levittown CDP, PA	94.4	26	Jacksonville city, NC	26.1	26	Langley Park CDP, MD	39.0
27	South Plainfield borough, NJ	94.3	27	Fairbanks city, AK	26.0	26	South Riding CDP, VA	39.0
28	Eldersburg CDP, MD	94.2	27	Monterey city, CA	26.0	26	New York city, NY	39.0
28	Lindenhurst village, NY	94.2	29	Bloomington city, IN	25.8	29	Hoboken city, NJ	38.9
28	Mission Bend CDP, TX	94.2	29	Blacksburg town, VA	25.8	29	Huntley village, IL	38.9
31	Marrero CDP, LA	94.1	31	San Marcos city, TX	25.6	31	Maple Valley city, WA	38.3
31	Hauppauge CDP, NY	94.1	32	Adelanto city, CA	25.5	32	Hercules city, CA	38.2
33	Lockport city, IL	94.0	33	St. Andrews CDP, SC	25.3	33	Westport CDP, CT	38.1
33	Allen Park city, MI	94.0	34	Columbia city, SC	25.2	34	Menifee city, CA	37.9
33	Bayonne city, NJ	94.0	35	Statesboro city, GA	24.9	34	Elmont CDP, NY	37.9
33	Lake Ronkonkoma CDP, NY	94.0	36	Bowling Green city, OH	24.7	34	Plainfield village, IL	37.9
33	Levittown CDP, NY	94.0	37	Brookings city, SD	24.6	37	Montgomery Village CDP, MD	37.7
33	Melville CDP, NY	94.0	38	Fredericksburg city, VA	24.2	38	Ridgewood village, NJ	37.4
39	Miami Lakes town, FL	93.9	39	Spanish Lake CDP, MO	24.0	39	Algonquin village, IL	37.3
39	Fair Lawn borough, NJ	93.9	39	Kent city, OH	24.0	40	Hesperia city, CA	37.0
39	Syosset CDP, NY	93.9	41	Radcliff city, KY	23.7	41	Graham CDP, WA	36.9
39	Caledonia village, WI	93.9	42	Tysons Corner CDP, VA	23.5	42	Dolton village, IL	36.8
43	Wethersfield CDP, CT	93.8	43	College Station city, TX	23.4	43	Coram CDP, NY	36.7
43	Plainfield village, IL	93.8	44	Ruston city, LA	23.1	44	Germantown CDP, MD	36.6
43	Colleyville city, TX	93.8	44	Winchester CDP, NV	23.1	44	Chino Hills city, CA	36.6
46	Cerritos city, CA	93.7	46	Enterprise CDP, NV	22.9	44	Massapequa CDP, NY	36.6
46	Rockville Centre village, NY	93.7	46	Provo city, UT	22.9	47	San Jacinto city, CA	36.3
48	Old Jamestown CDP, MO	93.6	48	Tempe city, AZ	22.8	48	Romeoville village, IL	36.2
48	Uniondale CDP, NY	93.6	49	Ames city, IA	22.7	48	Hacienda Heights CDP, CA	36.2
50	Westport CDP, CT	93.5	49	Bozeman city, MT	22.7	50	Holtsville CDP, NY	36.1
50	Darien city, IL	93.5	51	Chapel Hill town, NC	22.5	50	Merrick CDP, NY	36.1
50	Saugus CDP, MA	93.5	52	Stillwater city, OK	22.4	52	Fair Oaks CDP, VA	36.0
50	Forest Hills CDP, MI	93.5	53	South Bradenton CDP, FL	22.3	52	South Laurel CDP, MD	36.0
50	Cottage Grove city, MN	93.5	53	Harrisonburg city, VA	22.3	54	The Hammocks CDP, FL	35.9
50	Holbrook CDP, NY	93.5	55	Goose Creek city, SC	21.9	54	Aspen Hill CDP, MD	35.9
50	Murrysville municipality, PA	93.5	56	San Tan Valley CDP, AZ	21.6	56	Marumsco CDP, VA	35.8
57	Lake Zurich village, IL	93.4	56	North Bethesda CDP, MD	21.6	56	Wheaton CDP, MD	35.8
57	Lodi borough, NJ	93.4	58	Homewood city, AL	21.5	58	Chillum CDP, MD	35.7
57	Baldwin CDP, NY	93.4	58	Fair Oaks CDP, VA	21.5	58	Redan CDP, GA	35.7
60	Clifton city, NJ	93.3	60	Carbondale city, IL	21.3	58	Acworth city, GA	35.7
61	Bartlett village, IL	93.2	61	Wilsonville city, OR	21.2	61	Laurel city, MD	35.6
61	Bolingbrook village, IL	93.2	62	Charleston city, IL	21.1	61	Lake in the Hills village, IL	35.6
61	Olney CDP, MD	93.2	63	Sandy Springs city, GA	21.0	61	Rockville Centre village, NY	35.6
61	Randallstown CDP, MD	93.2	63	Chillum CDP, MD	21.0	61	Olney CDP, MD	35.6
61	Chantilly CDP, VA	93.2	63	Cambridge city, MA	21.0	61	Summit city, NJ	35.6
66	Darien CDP, CT	93.1	66	Douglasville city, GA	20.9	66	South Miami Heights CDP, FL	35.5
66	Central city, LA	93.1	66	University Park city, TX	20.9	66	Bowie city, MD	35.5
66	Summit city, NJ	93.1	68	Boulder city, CO	20.8	68	Canyon Lake CDP, TX	35.4
66	Garden City village, NY	93.1	68	Smyrna city, GA	20.8	68	Somerset CDP, NJ	35.4
66	Glen Cove city, NY	93.1	70	Auburn city, AL	20.7	68	The Acreage CDP, FL	35.4
66	Selden CDP, NY	93.1	70	Carrboro town, NC	20.7	68	Dix Hills CDP, NY	35.4
72	Stratford CDP, CT	93.0	70	Huntsville city, TX	20.7	72	Kendall West CDP, FL	35.3
73	Miami Gardens city, FL	92.9	70	Laramie city, WY	20.7	72	Cutler Bay town, FL	35.3
73	Oak Forest city, IL	92.9	74	West Hollywood city, CA	20.6	72	North Potomac CDP, MD	35.3
73	Munster town, IN	92.9	74	Auburn Hills city, MI	20.6	72	Old Bridge CDP, NJ	35.3
73	Wilmington CDP, MA	92.9						
73	Green city, OH	92.9						
73	North Royalton city, OH	92.9						

City Rankings, 2010–2012—*Continued*
Selected Rankings

Median value of owner-occupied housing units rank	City	Median value of owner-occupied housing units (dollars)[1] [C-4, col. 5]
	United States	174,600
1	Beverly Hills city, CA	1,000,000
1	Burlingame city, CA	1,000,000
1	Coronado city, CA	1,000,000
1	Cupertino city, CA	1,000,000
1	La Cañada Flintridge city, CA	1,000,000
1	Laguna Beach city, CA	1,000,000
1	Los Altos city, CA	1,000,000
1	Los Gatos town, CA	1,000,000
1	Manhattan Beach city, CA	1,000,000
1	Menlo Park city, CA	1,000,000
1	Newport Beach city, CA	1,000,000
1	Palo Alto city, CA	1,000,000
1	Saratoga city, CA	1,000,000
1	Darien CDP, CT	1,000,000
15	Santa Monica city, CA	983,800
16	Westport CDP, CT	969,600
17	Lafayette city, CA	960,900
18	Rancho Palos Verdes city, CA	958,500
19	University Park city, TX	922,600
20	McLean CDP, VA	908,000
21	San Carlos city, CA	906,200
22	Wellesley CDP, MA	897,400
23	Millbrae city, CA	877,700
24	Belmont city, CA	876,900
25	Calabasas city, CA	872,400
26	Potomac CDP, MD	867,100
27	Mercer Island city, WA	860,400
28	Santa Barbara city, CA	846,500
29	Lake Forest city, IL	837,600
30	South Pasadena city, CA	836,300
31	Danville town, CA	826,300
32	Foster City city, CA	823,800
33	Harrison village, NY	819,200
34	Bethesda CDP, MD	807,300
35	Arcadia city, CA	805,400
36	Kailua CDP (Honolulu County), HI	788,900
37	Garden City village, NY	780,800
38	East Honolulu CDP, HI	764,200
39	North Tustin CDP, CA	760,800
40	Redwood City city, CA	750,400
41	Summit city, NJ	749,800
42	Mountain View city, CA	749,200
43	San Francisco city, CA	737,700
44	Naples city, FL	722,100
45	Sunnyvale city, CA	713,200
46	Dix Hills CDP, NY	709,500
47	Redondo Beach city, CA	708,900
48	Ridgewood village, NJ	703,300
49	San Mateo city, CA	698,000
50	Pleasanton city, CA	696,600
51	San Clemente city, CA	696,200
52	Berkeley city, CA	695,200
53	Encinitas city, CA	692,800
54	Lexington CDP, MA	692,000
55	Brookline CDP, MA	689,400
56	San Rafael city, CA	687,600
57	San Ramon city, CA	686,100
58	Newton city, MA	685,900
59	Dana Point city, CA	684,600
60	Winchester CDP, MA	677,000
61	Yorba Linda city, CA	675,500
62	Melville CDP, NY	666,300
63	Agoura Hills city, CA	660,700
64	Laguna Niguel city, CA	652,500
65	Needham CDP, MA	648,000
66	Irvine city, CA	646,500
67	Campbell city, CA	645,400
68	Santa Cruz city, CA	636,400
69	Belmont CDP, MA	631,900
70	Walnut city, CA	630,600
71	Westfield town, NJ	628,600
72	Huntington Beach city, CA	616,700
73	Kaneohe CDP, HI	614,100
74	Rockville Centre village, NY	613,900
75	Alameda city, CA	613,300

Median selected monthly owner (with a mortgage) costs as a percentage of household income rank	City	Median selected monthly owner (with a mortgage) costs as a percentage of household income[2] [C-4, col. 6]
	United States	24.5
1	Paterson city, NJ	46.6
1	Sunny Isles Beach city, FL	46.6
3	Garfield city, NJ	44.3
4	Lakewood CDP, NJ	43.7
5	Roselle borough, NJ	43.5
6	East St. Louis city, IL	42.8
7	Lodi borough, NJ	42.6
8	Newark city, NJ	41.0
9	Passaic city, NJ	40.3
9	Leisure City CDP, FL	40.3
11	Key West city, FL	40.1
11	Atlantic City city, NJ	40.1
13	East Orange city, NJ	39.9
14	Huntington Park city, CA	39.1
15	Union City city, NJ	38.9
15	Aventura city, FL	38.9
17	Uniondale CDP, NY	38.3
18	Bell city, CA	38.0
18	Miami city, FL	38.0
20	Kiryas Joel village, NY	37.9
21	Cicero town, IL	37.7
22	Lauderdale Lakes city, FL	37.5
23	Rosemead city, CA	37.1
24	Lennox CDP, CA	37.0
25	Beverly Hills city, CA	36.9
26	East Palo Alto city, CA	36.8
26	South Gate city, CA	36.8
26	Willowbrook CDP, CA	36.8
29	Hempstead village, NY	36.7
29	Pleasantville city, NJ	36.7
31	Spring Valley village, NY	36.6
31	Kendall West CDP, FL	36.6
31	North Chicago city, IL	36.6
31	Sweetwater city, FL	36.6
35	West Rancho Dominguez CDP, CA	36.5
36	Everett city, MA	36.4
37	Tamiami CDP, FL	36.3
38	Naples city, FL	36.2
39	Golden Glades CDP, FL	36.1
39	Meadow Woods CDP, FL	36.1
41	North Miami city, FL	35.9
41	Miami Gardens city, FL	35.9
43	Lynwood city, CA	35.8
44	Inglewood city, CA	35.7
45	Miami Lakes town, FL	35.6
45	University Park CDP, FL	35.6
45	Cudahy city, CA	35.6
45	Hialeah city, FL	35.6
49	South Lake Tahoe city, CA	35.5
50	Bayonne city, NJ	35.4
50	Rahway city, NJ	35.4
50	Central Islip CDP, NY	35.4
50	Wildomar city, CA	35.4
50	North Miami Beach city, FL	35.4
55	Ashland CDP, CA	35.2
55	San Pablo city, CA	35.2
55	Socastee CDP, SC	35.2
55	Hallandale Beach city, FL	35.2
55	South Miami Heights CDP, FL	35.2
60	West Little River CDP, FL	35.1
61	Glen Cove city, NY	35.0
61	Elizabeth city, NJ	35.0
61	National City city, CA	35.0
64	Lawndale city, CA	34.9
64	Buenaventura Lakes CDP, FL	34.9
66	Florence-Graham CDP, CA	34.8
67	Cliffside Park borough, NJ	34.7
68	East Los Angeles CDP, CA	34.6
68	South San Jose Hills CDP, CA	34.6
68	Perris city, CA	34.6
71	Brentwood CDP, NY	34.5
71	Palm Springs village, FL	34.5
73	Revere city, MA	34.4
73	Port Hueneme city, CA	34.4
73	Maywood city, CA	34.4
73	Bloomington CDP, CA	34.4

Median gross rent as a percentage of household income rank	City	Median gross rent as a percentage of household income[2] [C-4, col. 9]
	United States	31.5
1	Isla Vista CDP, CA	50.0
1	Westmont CDP, CA	50.0
1	Sun City Center CDP, FL	50.0
1	Carbondale city, IL	50.0
1	College Park city, MD	50.0
1	East Lansing city, MI	50.0
1	Eastpointe city, MI	50.0
1	Paramus borough, NJ	50.0
1	Garden City village, NY	50.0
1	Kiryas Joel village, NY	50.0
1	Athens city, OH	50.0
1	Oxford city, OH	50.0
1	State College borough, PA	50.0
1	College Station city, TX	50.0
1	Colleyville city, TX	50.0
1	Corinth city, TX	50.0
1	Blacksburg town, VA	50.0
1	Pullman city, WA	50.0
19	University CDP (Orange County), FL	49.5
20	Flint city, MI	49.3
21	Charleston city, IL	49.1
22	Agoura Hills city, CA	48.8
23	Sun City West CDP, AZ	48.6
23	Madison city, MS	48.6
25	Tamiami CDP, FL	48.5
26	Poinciana CDP, FL	48.4
27	Lakewood CDP, NJ	48.1
27	West Lafayette city, IN	48.1
29	Shirley CDP, NY	47.9
30	Bloomington city, IN	47.1
31	Sweetwater city, FL	46.8
32	San Juan Capistrano city, CA	46.7
32	San Marcos city, TX	46.7
34	Rosemead city, CA	46.6
34	University Park CDP, FL	46.6
34	Niles village, IL	46.6
37	South Holland village, IL	46.4
37	Statesboro city, GA	46.4
39	Davis city, CA	46.0
40	Adelanto city, CA	45.9
41	Miami Gardens city, FL	45.6
41	University CDP (Hillsborough County), FL	45.6
43	Camden city, NJ	45.4
43	Saginaw city, MI	45.4
45	Kent city, OH	45.2
46	Hialeah city, FL	45.1
47	Kendall West CDP, FL	45.0
47	Perris city, CA	45.0
47	Prichard city, AL	45.0
50	Detroit city, MI	44.9
51	Hemet city, CA	44.8
52	Dolton village, IL	44.7
53	Fort Pierce city, FL	44.6
54	Shelby city, NC	44.5
55	The Hammocks CDP, FL	44.3
56	Huntsville city, TX	44.2
57	DeKalb city, IL	44.0
58	West Rancho Dominguez CDP, CA	43.9
59	North Miami city, FL	43.8
60	Iowa City city, IA	43.7
61	Sun City CDP, AZ	43.6
62	Riviera Beach city, FL	43.5
62	Palm River-Clair Mel CDP, FL	43.5
62	Corvallis city, OR	43.5
65	Florence-Graham CDP, CA	43.2
65	Auburn city, AL	43.2
65	Rexburg city, ID	43.2
68	Maywood village, IL	43.1
68	Klamath Falls city, OR	43.1
70	Lauderdale Lakes city, FL	43.0
70	Bella Vista town, AR	43.0
72	Newburgh city, NY	42.8
72	Canton city, GA	42.8
74	Dania Beach city, FL	42.7
75	Roselle borough, NJ	42.6
75	Leisure City CDP, FL	42.6
75	Myrtle Beach city, SC	42.6
75	Bridgeton city, NJ	42.6

[1]The top code 1,000,000 symbolizes a median value of more than 1 million dollars.
[2]The top code 50.0 symbolizes a median gross rent as a percentage of household income of 50 percent or more.

Table C-1. States — Where: Migration, Housing, and Transportation, 2012

State code	STATE	Total population 1 year and over	Residence 1 year ago						Total occupied housing units (households)	Percent owner occupied
			Same house	Different house; same city or town	Different house; different city; same county	Different house; different county; same state	Different house; different state	Abroad		
	ACS table number:	C07204	C07204	C07204	C07204	C07204	C07204	C07204	B25003	B25003
	Column number:	1	2	3	4	5	6	7	8	9

Table C-1. States — Where: Migration, Housing, and Transportation, 2012—*Continued*

State code	STATE	Homeownership by race and Hispanic origin of householder									
		Non-Hispanic White		Black		American Indian and Alaska Native		Asian, Hawaiian, and Pacific Islander		Hispanic or Latino	
		Number of householders	Percent owners	Number of householders	Percent owners	Number of householders	Percent owners	Number of householders	Percent owners	Number of householders	Percent owners
	ACS table number:	B25003H	B25003H	B25003B	B25003B	B25003C	B25003C	B25003D+ B25003E	B25003D + B25003E	B25003I	B25003I
	Column number:	10	11	12	13	14	15	16	17	18	19

Table C-1. States — Where: Migration, Housing, and Transportation, 2012—*Continued*

State code	STATE	Homeownership by age of householder							
		15 to 24 years		25 to 44 years		45 to 64 years		65 years and over	
		Number of householders	Percent owners	Number of householders	Percent owners	Number of householders	Percent owners	Number of householders	Percent owners
	ACS table number:	B25007	B25007	B25007	B25007	B25007	B25007	B25007	B25007
	Column number:	20	21	22	23	24	25	26	27

Table C-1. States — Where: Migration, Housing, and Transportation, 2012—*Continued*

State code	STATE	Homeownership by household type								Average household size		
		Married-couple family households		Male householder families, no wife present		Female householder families, no husband present		Nonfamily households		All house-holds	Owner-occupied households	Renter-occupied households
		Number of householders	Percent owners	Number of householders	Percent owners	Number of householders	Percent owners	Number of householders	Percent owners			
	ACS table number:	C25115	C25115	C25115	C25115	C25115	C25115	C25115	C25115	B25010	B25010	B25010
	Column number:	28	29	30	31	32	33	34	35	36	37	38

Table C-1. States — Where: Migration, Housing, and Transportation, 2012—*Continued*

State code	STATE	Percent of housing units that are crowded or lacking complete plumbing	Median household income in the past 12 months (in 2012 inflation-adjusted dollars)					Median housing value (owner estimated)			Owner occupied housing units		
			All house-holds	Owner-occupied households			Renter-occupied house-holds	All owner-occupied households	Households with a mortgage	House-holds without a mortgage	Total owner-occupied housing units	Percent with a mort-gage	Percent with a second mortgage, or a home equity loan, or both
				All owner-occupied households	House-holds with a mort-gage	House-holds without a mortgage							
	ACS table number:	C25016	B25119	B25099	B25099	B25099	B25119	B25097	B25097	B25097	B25081	B25081	B25081
	Column number:	39	40	41	42	43	44	45	46	47	48	49	50

Table C-1. States — Where: Migration, Housing, and Transportation, 2012—*Continued*

State code	STATE	Median monthly housing costs for all housing units with costs (dollars)	Gross rent for renter-occupied housing units		Median selected monthly owner costs for owner-occupied housing units			Median annual real estate taxes paid by owner-occupied housing units (dollars)	Median selected monthly owner costs as a percentage of household income		
			Median gross rent (dollars)	As a percentage of household income	All owner-occupied households	Households with a mortgage	Households without a mortgage		All owner-occupied households	Households with a mortgage	Households without a mortgage[1]
	ACS table number:	B25105	B25064	B25071	B25088	B25088	B25088	B25103	B25092	B25092	B25092
	Column number:	51	52	53	54	55	56	57	58	59	60

Table C-1. States — Where: Migration, Housing, and Transportation, 2012—*Continued*

State code	STATE	Households who pay 30 percent or more of income for housing expenses by tenure and age of householder (percent)								Total number of workers 16 years and over
		Owner-occupied households				Renter-occupied households				
		15 to 24 years	25 to 34 years	35 to 64 years	65 years and over	15 to 24 years	25 to 34 years	35 to 64 years	65 years and over	
	ACS table number:	C25093	C25093	C25093	C25093	C25072	C25072	C25072	C25072	B08301
	Column number:	61	62	63	64	65	66	67	68	69

Table C-1. States — Where: Migration, Housing, and Transportation, 2012—*Continued*

State code	STATE	Means of transportation to work (percent)							Number of workers who did not work at home
		Car, truck, or van		Public transportation (excluding taxicab)	Bicycle	Walked	Taxicab, motorcycle, or other means	Worked at home	
		Drove alone	Car-pooled						
	ACS table number:	B08301	B08301	B08301	B08301	B08301	B08301	B08301	B08301
	Column number:	70	71	72	73	74	75	76	77

Table C-1. States — Where: Migration, Housing, and Transportation, 2012—*Continued*

State code	STATE	Mean travel time to work (minutes)				Vehicles available (percent of households)					Average vehicles per household
		All workers who did not work at home	By car, truck, or van	Public transportation	Taxicab, motorcycle, bicycle, walked, or by other means	Number of households	No vehicles	One vehicle	Two vehicles	Three or more vehicles	
	ACS table number:	C08136/ B08301	C08136/ B08301	C08136/ B08301	C08136/ B08301	B08201	B08201	B08201	B08201	B08201	B25046/ B08201
	Column number:	78	79	80	81	82	83	84	85	86	87

Table C-2. Counties — Where: Migration, Housing, and Transportation, 2010–2012

STATE and county code	STATE or county	Percent who lived in the same house one year ago	Percent who did not live in the same county one year ago	Total occupied housing units	Percent owner-occupied housing units	Median value of owner-occupied housing units (dollars)	Median selected monthly owner costs as a percentage of household income		Median gross rent (dollars)	Median gross rent as a percentage of household income[1]	Percent of workers who drove alone to work	Mean travel time to work (minutes)	Percent of occupied housing units with no vehicle available
							With a mortgage	Without a mortgage[1]					
	ACS table number:	C07204	C07204	B25003	B25003	B25077	B25092	B25092	B25064	B25071	C08301	B08013/ B08012	C25045
	Column number:	1	2	3	4	5	6	7	8	9	10	11	12

Table C-3. Metropolitan Areas — Where: Migration, Housing, and Transportation, 2012

Metro area or division code	Area name	Percent who lived in the same house one year ago	Percent who did not live in this MSA one year ago	Total occupied housing units	Percent owner-occupied housing units	Median value of owner-occupied housing units (dollars)	Median selected monthly owner costs as a percentage of household income		Median gross rent (dollars)	Median gross rent as a percentage of household income	Percent of workers who drove alone to work	Mean travel time to work (minutes)	Percent of occupied housing units with no vehicle available
							With a mortgage	Without a mortgage					
	ACS table number:	C07201	C07201	B25003	B25003	B25077	B25092	B25092	B25064	B25071	C08301	B08013/ B08012	C25045
	Column number:	1	2	3	4	5	6	7	8	9	10	11	12

Table C-4. Cities — Where: Migration, Housing, and Transportation, 2010–2012

STATE and place code	STATE or city	Percent who lived in the same house one year ago	Percent who did not live in the same city one year ago	Total occupied housing units	Percent owner-occupied housing units	Median value of owner-occupied housing units (dollars)[1]	Median selected monthly owner costs as a percentage of household income[2]		Median gross rent (dollars)[3]	Median gross rent as a percentage of household income[4]	Percent of workers who drove alone to work	Mean travel time to work (minutes)	Percent of occupied housing units with no vehicle available
							With a mortgage	Without a mortgage[2]					
	ACS table number:	C07204	C07204	B25003	B25003	B25077	B25092	B25092	B25064	B25071	C08301	B08013/ C08012	C25045
	Column number:	1	2	3	4	5	6	7	8	9	10	11	12

Table C-1. States — Where: Migration, Housing, and Transportation, 2012

State code	STATE	Total population 1 year and over	Residence 1 year ago						Total occupied housing units (households)	Percent owner occupied
			Same house	Different house; same city or town	Different house; different city; same county	Different house; different county; same state	Different house; different state	Abroad		
	ACS table number:	C07204	C07204	C07204	C07204	C07204	C07204	C07204	B25003	B25003
	Column number:	1	2	3	4	5	6	7	8	9
00	United States	310,212,755	85.0	4.9	4.2	3.1	2.3	0.6	115,969.540	63.9
01	Alabama..........................	4,764,428	85.1	4.4	4.6	3.4	2.2	0.3	1,845.169	68.8
02	Alaska.............................	721,186	82.2	7.7	2.4	2.4	4.6	0.6	251.651	63.4
04	Arizona...........................	6,468,907	81.0	7.8	5.2	1.8	3.6	0.6	2,392.168	62.6
05	Arkansas.........................	2,912,680	84.2	5.4	4.1	3.4	2.6	0.3	1,143.859	66.2
06	California........................	37,572,738	84.6	6.0	4.7	2.8	1.3	0.7	12,552.658	54.0
08	Colorado	5,123,944	80.6	6.4	3.3	4.9	4.0	0.7	1,996.088	64.0
09	Connecticut.....................	3,555,319	87.6	3.8	3.9	1.8	2.3	0.7	1,357.812	66.9
10	Delaware.........................	906,576	86.3	2.1	6.5	0.9	3.8	0.4	340.308	70.8
11	District of Columbia..........	624,847	80.1	9.9	0.0	0.0	8.6	1.4	266.662	41.5
12	Florida	19,114,620	83.9	3.9	5.6	3.0	2.8	0.9	7,197.943	65.6
13	Georgia	9,796,547	84.0	2.8	5.1	4.7	2.8	0.5	3,532.908	63.7
15	Hawaii............................	1,374,852	84.7	3.8	5.5	0.5	4.0	1.5	447.748	56.9
16	Idaho.............................	1,573,036	82.5	5.6	4.1	3.6	3.8	0.4	583.106	68.4
17	Illinois............................	12,725,119	86.5	5.2	3.6	2.5	1.6	0.5	4,770.194	66.6
18	Indiana...........................	6,457,067	85.1	5.2	3.7	3.5	2.1	0.4	2,480.077	69.4
19	Iowa..............................	3,035,469	85.2	5.8	2.9	3.3	2.5	0.4	1,227.048	71.9
20	Kansas............................	2,848,708	82.9	6.9	2.8	3.7	3.1	0.6	1,113.911	66.4
21	Kentucky.........................	4,328,626	84.9	4.4	4.2	3.5	2.6	0.4	1,707.004	67.0
22	Louisiana.........................	4,545,914	86.1	4.4	3.9	3.3	2.0	0.3	1,719.473	65.7
23	Maine.............................	1,315,586	86.1	2.7	6.0	2.8	2.1	0.3	554.543	71.4
24	Maryland	5,816,472	87.1	3.0	3.9	2.6	2.7	0.7	2,157.717	66.5
25	Massachusetts	6,580,641	87.4	3.9	3.2	2.4	2.2	0.9	2,522.394	62.2
26	Michigan	9,778,980	85.2	3.7	5.6	3.6	1.4	0.5	3,819.068	71.1
27	Minnesota	5,315,228	85.3	4.5	3.4	4.3	1.9	0.5	2,111.943	71.4
28	Mississippi.......................	2,947,696	85.8	3.9	3.9	3.7	2.5	0.2	1,090.521	68.2
29	Missouri..........................	5,951,913	83.4	4.8	4.6	4.0	2.7	0.4	2,359.135	67.5
30	Montana..........................	995,544	83.3	5.5	3.7	3.5	3.8	0.2	408.938	67.1
31	Nebraska	1,829,420	84.2	7.8	1.9	3.3	2.4	0.4	733.570	66.3
32	Nevada	2,725,280	77.2	8.8	8.0	0.9	4.6	0.5	1,006.605	54.9
33	New Hampshire	1,309,203	86.1	3.0	4.1	2.4	3.9	0.5	519.137	70.9
34	New Jersey......................	8,772,744	90.4	2.2	3.2	2.0	1.5	0.7	3,198.799	65.1
35	New Mexico.....................	2,060,595	85.9	6.1	2.5	2.3	2.7	0.5	764.996	67.7
36	New York........................	19,352,153	88.9	4.9	2.3	1.7	1.4	0.8	7,238.922	53.7
37	North Carolina	9,640,490	84.7	4.5	3.9	3.4	2.8	0.5	3,731.325	65.4
38	North Dakota...................	689,838	81.8	6.0	2.4	3.8	5.5	0.5	290.944	65.0
39	Ohio..............................	11,414,635	85.3	4.8	4.6	3.2	1.7	0.4	4,554.672	66.3
40	Oklahoma.......................	3,762,311	82.6	6.8	3.2	4.1	2.9	0.4	1,446.667	66.4
41	Oregon...........................	3,857,465	81.9	6.3	4.8	3.4	3.1	0.5	1,516.957	61.6
42	Pennsylvania	12,630,082	87.9	3.2	4.1	2.6	1.7	0.4	4,958.249	68.9
44	Rhode Island....................	1,040,527	86.5	4.2	3.5	2.0	3.2	0.6	413.083	60.0
45	South Carolina.................	4,668,886	84.2	2.7	6.0	3.4	3.4	0.4	1,787.340	68.1
46	South Dakota...................	821,669	82.3	6.7	3.0	4.4	3.2	0.5	323.765	67.1
47	Tennessee	6,378,278	84.6	5.4	3.8	3.1	2.8	0.3	2,480.090	66.7
48	Texas.............................	25,711,791	83.1	6.7	3.7	3.8	2.0	0.8	8,970.959	62.3
49	Utah..............................	2,805,440	82.8	4.8	5.5	3.1	3.1	0.7	895.691	69.6
50	Vermont	620,224	85.8	2.2	5.8	1.9	3.9	0.4	258.520	71.0
51	Virginia	8,085,389	84.8	3.9	2.7	4.7	3.1	0.8	3,038.967	66.2
53	Washington	6,815,763	82.9	4.8	5.8	2.7	3.2	0.7	2,636.817	62.3
54	West Virginia	1,837,518	87.8	2.1	4.7	2.7	2.6	0.2	741.544	72.0
55	Wisconsin	5,660,677	85.7	5.4	3.6	3.3	1.8	0.3	2,288.362	67.3
56	Wyoming.........................	569,734	80.6	7.3	3.7	2.5	5.5	0.4	223,513	69.0

Table C-1. States — Where: Migration, Housing, and Transportation, 2012—*Continued*

State code	STATE	Homeownership by race and Hispanic origin of householder									
		Non-Hispanic White		Black		American Indian and Alaska Native		Asian, Hawaiian, and Pacific Islander		Hispanic or Latino	
		Number of householders	Percent owners	Number of householders	Percent owners	Number of householders	Percent owners	Number of householders	Percent owners	Number of householders	Percent owners
	ACS table number:	B25003H	B25003H	B25003B	B25003B	B25003C	B25003C	B25003D+ B25003E	B25003D + B25003E	B25003I	B25003I
	Column number:	10	11	12	13	14	15	16	17	18	19
00	United States	80,890,895	71.5	14,051,208	42.5	824,949	54.0	4,973,619	56.7	14,005,690	45.7
01	Alabama.......................	1,285,879	75.7	469,229	52.7	10,026	74.1	19,188	51.5	44,830	46.3
02	Alaska..........................	181,112	68.5	9,490	21.4	27,408	62.5	11,074	45.9	12,160	44.0
04	Arizona........................	1,609,065	68.8	100,066	33.7	76,843	57.5	66,008	53.7	521,581	51.1
05	Arkansas......................	885,537	71.7	172,697	44.5	7,772	54.2	13,468	52.2	50,783	50.6
06	California.....................	6,325,940	63.0	819,829	34.7	91,250	44.2	1,623,308	56.3	3,504,293	41.8
08	Colorado......................	1,532,181	68.8	72,416	40.2	15,410	49.2	47,838	64.3	307,342	47.0
09	Connecticut..................	1,018,149	76.1	130,674	38.4	3,154	55.3	44,987	54.3	150,939	33.8
10	Delaware	239,952	79.1	67,325	50.6	1,311	78.8	8,915	58.7	19,698	45.8
11	District of Columbia.......	108,213	48.0	124,481	37.5	1,121	19.1	9,195	47.7	20,748	31.4
12	Florida.........................	4,668,029	73.6	984,074	45.6	18,256	51.8	154,424	67.1	1,328,169	52.5
13	Georgia........................	2,118,331	74.0	1,060,959	47.4	8,603	48.9	99,917	62.4	221,261	43.5
15	Hawaii.........................	140,124	51.9	10,013	18.7	1,664	24.6	209,864	66.1	32,646	32.8
16	Idaho..........................	515,695	70.3	2,898	29.2	6,517	56.4	6,014	61.3	44,979	51.7
17	Illinois.........................	3,330,225	75.1	660,432	39.4	9,340	54.8	202,963	58.0	526,736	52.0
18	Indiana........................	2,089,412	74.1	222,791	38.2	5,846	56.4	37,224	53.1	104,739	51.3
19	Iowa............................	1,125,920	74.4	31,585	29.8	2,528	26.5	16,835	48.8	40,398	51.6
20	Kansas.........................	924,451	70.0	64,124	38.7	8,388	55.5	22,415	56.7	78,362	52.8
21	Kentucky	1,499,234	70.7	134,957	36.3	3,250	66.4	16,891	51.4	35,992	39.4
22	Louisiana	1,093,376	74.8	514,717	49.7	9,376	66.3	23,460	54.8	61,528	44.3
23	Maine	531,368	72.5	3,859	24.2	3,550	32.6	4,642	55.6	5,178	49.7
24	Maryland	1,272,487	76.0	623,453	50.6	6,755	56.4	105,182	67.3	123,041	48.9
25	Massachusetts	2,019,619	69.3	152,906	31.5	5,448	40.6	119,960	48.7	198,367	24.4
26	Michigan	3,040,408	77.1	512,840	42.8	20,749	62.7	77,619	58.5	122,621	53.4
27	Minnesota	1,846,088	76.2	98,152	21.3	19,219	47.1	61,316	53.1	65,332	45.1
28	Mississippi....................	675,004	76.9	379,939	54.0	3,962	59.4	7,389	64.1	18,156	46.2
29	Missouri	1,966,401	72.3	264,065	39.5	10,468	53.4	32,885	54.7	58,621	47.2
30	Montana	369,323	69.0	878	51.8	19,967	45.1	2,748	58.3	9,888	50.1
31	Nebraska	635,093	70.1	30,423	32.6	5,059	36.2	11,031	49.5	45,782	47.0
32	Nevada	633,447	62.1	81,628	32.2	10,625	53.9	68,756	54.3	195,853	42.1
33	New Hampshire	487,802	72.2	4,700	43.3	1,231	73.7	9,981	56.6	10,748	41.8
34	New Jersey....................	2,046,769	77.4	422,205	40.2	7,063	51.0	238,148	61.8	471,544	35.3
35	New Mexico..................	377,281	71.0	15,032	44.4	49,371	65.1	8,088	66.4	310,136	65.4
36	New York......................	4,604,281	66.4	1,059,063	30.9	25,087	47.4	468,583	45.4	1,055,634	23.1
37	North Carolina..............	2,597,371	73.1	781,013	47.3	39,982	60.1	73,240	58.4	207,630	43.2
38	North Dakota................	267,111	67.5	3,284	4.2	11,400	46.3	2,397	28.7	4,565	39.2
39	Ohio............................	3,778,132	71.8	547,832	36.3	10,299	44.6	68,242	54.5	104,091	41.0
40	Oklahoma.....................	1,071,748	71.1	103,262	42.9	91,206	62.0	20,674	56.5	88,501	48.9
41	Oregon........................	1,281,206	64.7	24,408	29.8	15,768	53.4	51,546	53.5	114,726	41.0
42	Pennsylvania	4,100,066	73.9	494,004	43.3	7,084	46.1	113,910	57.0	217,328	41.1
44	Rhode Island.................	336,366	66.1	23,472	32.2	1,926	16.7	10,215	47.1	38,833	25.4
45	South Carolina..............	1,219,587	75.5	465,419	52.8	5,770	55.5	18,671	61.1	63,368	42.4
46	South Dakota................	290,682	70.7	4,110	18.5	17,807	41.1	2,066	25.3	6,004	35.2
47	Tennessee	1,946,968	72.6	390,511	45.4	6,354	42.0	32,785	56.4	77,593	37.5
48	Texas...........................	4,729,010	70.5	1,093,934	42.2	45,930	59.8	336,833	58.9	2,695,186	56.9
49	Utah............................	756,388	72.8	9,399	39.2	9,288	55.3	23,850	55.3	90,798	54.0
50	Vermont	248,294	72.3	1,702	11.5	1,053	22.0	2,200	42.4	2,703	41.9
51	Virginia	2,110,521	73.1	567,721	48.4	8,459	56.4	139,216	64.6	175,098	44.1
53	Washington	2,063,488	66.9	90,730	30.5	32,398	43.8	180,374	58.2	208,017	40.2
54	West Virginia	698,943	73.3	22,252	39.4	887	58.3	4,383	60.5	6,562	62.9
55	Wisconsin	1,999,959	72.0	124,942	27.8	19,312	48.2	37,660	41.6	90,310	37.2
56	Wyoming......................	198,859	70.9	1,292	14.1	3,389	54.9	1,494	51.7	16,292	57.4

Table C-1. States — Where: Migration, Housing, and Transportation, 2012—*Continued*

State code	STATE	Homeownership by age of householder							
		15 to 24 years		25 to 44 years		45 to 64 years		65 years and over	
		Number of householders	Percent owners	Number of householders	Percent owners	Number of householders	Percent owners	Number of householders	Percent owners
	ACS table number:	B25007	B25007	B25007	B25007	B25007	B25007	B25007	B25007
	Column number:	20	21	22	23	24	25	26	27
00	United States	4,639,337	12.5	38,663,120	49.1	46,139,863	73.0	26,527,220	78.7
01	Alabama..................	79,361	15.4	588,343	54.3	730,642	77.2	446,823	83.4
02	Alaska....................	12,234	16.1	94,961	47.7	108,329	76.2	36,127	81.8
04	Arizona...................	108,794	14.5	807,935	45.2	882,669	71.2	592,770	82.2
05	Arkansas.................	60,360	15.6	363,426	52.8	442,295	74.7	277,778	81.4
06	California.................	430,554	9.0	4,466,619	36.4	5,028,934	63.4	2,626,551	73.5
08	Colorado	101,935	11.2	720,177	50.3	792,590	75.4	381,386	80.3
09	Connecticut..............	32,022	11.4	414,476	51.2	584,589	75.8	326,725	76.3
10	Delaware	11,469	6.8	104,221	56.7	138,445	78.7	86,173	83.8
11	District of Columbia...	12,482	2.8	115,720	30.1	88,743	49.9	49,717	62.7
12	Florida	233,096	12.9	2,095,723	45.3	2,774,200	72.4	2,094,924	82.8
13	Georgia	149,345	12.4	1,284,221	48.5	1,404,293	74.3	695,049	81.1
15	Hawaii	15,899	7.4	139,488	34.0	178,829	66.1	113,532	77.6
16	Idaho	36,746	15.2	194,286	55.3	217,019	80.5	135,055	82.3
17	Illinois	172,088	13.4	1,641,775	53.2	1,893,530	75.8	1,062,801	79.6
18	Indiana	118,863	14.4	820,958	58.1	983,182	77.7	557,074	83.0
19	Iowa	71,622	17.7	391,346	62.9	468,969	81.3	295,111	82.3
20	Kansas...................	64,864	15.2	370,494	55.0	429,173	76.3	249,380	79.5
21	Kentucky	77,571	15.3	554,869	54.5	682,446	74.9	392,118	81.4
22	Louisiana	80,764	18.3	579,042	51.5	682,408	73.7	377,259	83.2
23	Maine	18,419	14.7	156,367	58.1	237,857	79.6	141,900	79.8
24	Maryland	60,243	12.8	725,547	51.3	903,818	76.0	468,109	78.5
25	Massachusetts	68,289	5.9	805,420	47.9	1,055,915	71.8	592,770	71.2
26	Michigan	156,183	16.9	1,153,471	58.0	1,580,287	79.1	929,127	82.7
27	Minnesota	93,237	15.2	716,211	61.7	841,671	81.8	460,824	79.0
28	Mississippi	43,623	17.4	353,568	53.3	434,197	75.7	259,133	84.5
29	Missouri	113,105	14.9	758,295	55.6	927,282	75.8	560,453	80.4
30	Montana..................	21,731	12.0	119,021	51.5	169,055	77.7	99,131	79.5
31	Nebraska	43,092	13.2	249,767	56.1	276,816	76.4	163,895	78.8
32	Nevada	41,109	15.1	365,620	39.4	386,534	62.5	213,342	75.1
33	New Hampshire	15,476	12.0	152,054	57.1	233,343	80.3	118,264	77.7
34	New Jersey..............	60,326	10.7	1,021,937	49.6	1,363,446	72.6	753,090	76.8
35	New Mexico..............	34,905	13.2	241,172	51.3	303,836	77.0	185,083	84.2
36	New York.................	205,010	7.9	2,368,614	38.3	2,983,987	62.3	1,681,311	65.5
37	North Carolina	162,201	11.1	1,279,581	51.1	1,440,357	74.8	849,186	81.4
38	North Dakota............	25,232	14.0	93,937	59.5	107,734	76.4	64,041	74.0
39	Ohio	186,300	11.9	1,433,683	52.4	1,838,860	74.6	1,095,829	79.8
40	Oklahoma.................	81,095	15.7	480,553	53.1	544,924	75.7	340,095	82.3
41	Oregon	71,864	7.7	495,550	45.5	585,055	72.3	364,488	76.8
42	Pennsylvania	161,314	12.5	1,490,039	56.1	2,028,476	77.7	1,278,420	77.0
44	Rhode Island.............	16,608	7.6	124,244	47.1	171,837	68.3	100,394	70.4
45	South Carolina..........	74,509	14.7	571,672	52.8	707,906	75.2	433,253	86.0
46	South Dakota............	18,797	16.8	105,136	55.9	123,653	79.2	76,179	75.3
47	Tennessee	107,705	13.9	818,354	52.7	978,762	74.5	575,269	83.1
48	Texas.....................	441,489	11.1	3,413,911	48.5	3,414,460	73.6	1,701,099	80.6
49	Utah	57,220	18.5	364,348	61.6	306,968	80.5	167,155	84.5
50	Vermont	9,624	8.3	72,777	57.1	112,567	80.1	63,552	80.3
51	Virginia	112,248	12.4	1,048,865	50.3	1,220,602	76.5	657,252	81.5
53	Washington	117,463	9.0	912,820	47.0	1,040,123	73.7	566,411	77.1
54	West Virginia	30,325	18.6	209,279	59.9	300,910	77.6	201,030	84.3
55	Wisconsin	107,505	11.3	739,162	55.8	918,701	77.5	522,994	77.1
56	Wyoming.................	13,021	21.3	74,065	56.9	88,639	78.2	47,788	83.7

Table C-1. States — Where: Migration, Housing, and Transportation, 2012—*Continued*

State code	STATE	Married-couple family households Number of householders	Percent owners	Male householder families, no wife present Number of householders	Percent owners	Female householder families, no husband present Number of householders	Percent owners	Nonfamily households Number of householders	Percent owners	Average household size All households	Owner-occupied households	Renter-occupied households
	ACS table number:	C25115	C25115	C25115	C25115	C25115	C25115	C25115	C25115	B25010	B25010	B25010
	Column number:	28	29	30	31	32	33	34	35	36	37	38
00	United States	55,754,450	79.9	5,578,212	53.8	15,176,600	45.1	39,460,278	50.1	2.64	2.70	2.53
01	Alabama....................	883,291	83.6	73,078	61.4	277,568	49.5	611,232	57.0	2.55	2.58	2.49
02	Alaska......................	123,248	76.4	13,531	61.3	29,621	45.6	85,251	51.0	2.80	2.91	2.62
04	Arizona....................	1,122,884	76.6	129,258	51.4	308,545	44.7	831,481	52.0	2.68	2.66	2.70
05	Arkansas..................	557,982	81.2	50,353	55.0	150,266	44.8	385,258	54.4	2.51	2.53	2.46
06	California.................	6,104,099	67.6	759,288	42.9	1,722,400	38.3	3,966,871	42.1	2.97	3.00	2.93
08	Colorado	975,070	79.7	92,296	52.2	210,898	46.7	717,824	49.3	2.54	2.59	2.45
09	Connecticut.............	660,876	83.8	63,217	61.3	178,276	44.3	455,443	52.0	2.56	2.68	2.31
10	Delaware	163,460	85.9	16,261	64.7	45,872	52.3	114,715	57.6	2.62	2.64	2.57
11	District of Columbia ...	62,149	66.5	9,378	44.5	40,966	31.8	154,169	33.8	2.22	2.31	2.16
12	Florida	3,319,620	78.8	323,901	54.3	954,701	47.6	2,599,721	56.9	2.62	2.61	2.66
13	Georgia	1,693,386	79.4	166,418	53.0	546,422	44.3	1,126,682	50.9	2.73	2.77	2.68
15	Hawaii	229,027	65.4	23,569	57.9	56,569	50.0	138,583	45.5	3.01	3.15	2.83
16	Idaho	322,225	80.4	24,334	52.0	59,349	46.6	177,198	56.1	2.69	2.71	2.63
17	Illinois	2,289,429	83.9	220,129	58.4	611,462	46.4	1,649,174	51.2	2.64	2.73	2.45
18	Indiana	1,229,106	85.6	114,772	57.7	304,294	48.1	831,905	54.8	2.56	2.64	2.39
19	Iowa	625,952	87.9	49,737	59.8	121,055	53.0	430,304	55.4	2.42	2.51	2.20
20	Kansas	563,407	82.7	50,269	53.9	113,495	48.6	386,740	49.4	2.52	2.62	2.32
21	Kentucky	834,642	83.0	81,133	57.4	224,996	46.0	566,233	53.2	2.49	2.56	2.36
22	Louisiana	744,806	83.6	90,302	62.1	290,551	47.7	593,814	52.7	2.60	2.65	2.51
23	Maine	270,568	86.9	23,220	66.1	53,162	55.3	207,593	55.9	2.33	2.43	2.09
24	Maryland	1,018,129	82.4	106,455	57.1	312,529	48.9	720,604	52.9	2.66	2.75	2.49
25	Massachusetts	1,173,287	81.8	103,712	56.7	321,868	43.0	923,527	44.8	2.54	2.71	2.26
26	Michigan	1,821,915	87.3	167,036	62.9	493,661	50.9	1,336,456	57.4	2.53	2.60	2.34
27	Minnesota	1,079,809	88.3	89,887	63.2	204,740	48.4	737,507	54.1	2.48	2.59	2.21
28	Mississippi................	481,032	83.8	56,977	60.6	209,611	49.3	342,901	59.0	2.65	2.65	2.66
29	Missouri	1,124,203	84.7	100,724	59.6	292,304	46.9	841,904	52.5	2.48	2.57	2.29
30	Montana...................	205,584	81.4	19,373	58.4	34,693	49.1	149,288	52.5	2.39	2.44	2.28
31	Nebraska	369,338	84.0	31,736	54.2	73,490	44.2	259,006	48.9	2.46	2.56	2.26
32	Nevada	445,312	68.6	65,513	44.1	140,008	37.9	355,772	46.3	2.70	2.67	2.74
33	New Hampshire	269,048	85.3	21,686	64.1	50,984	53.8	177,419	54.7	2.47	2.57	2.22
34	New Jersey................	1,626,018	80.5	154,115	50.8	431,509	45.4	987,157	50.4	2.71	2.82	2.52
35	New Mexico..............	347,070	80.9	43,701	59.9	110,650	53.4	263,575	57.7	2.67	2.71	2.58
36	New York.................	3,147,912	72.7	369,635	45.6	1,070,310	35.7	2,651,065	39.4	2.62	2.76	2.47
37	North Carolina..........	1,795,932	81.0	171,133	56.7	505,165	45.8	1,259,095	52.4	2.55	2.58	2.48
38	North Dakota............	139,907	84.8	12,000	57.6	23,464	49.0	115,564	45.1	2.32	2.51	1.96
39	Ohio........................	2,131,425	84.7	203,016	57.5	578,871	43.6	1,641,360	51.4	2.47	2.55	2.29
40	Oklahoma.................	702,265	81.5	73,544	56.6	181,258	47.6	489,600	53.1	2.56	2.59	2.49
41	Oregon	729,381	78.2	69,058	47.5	166,453	41.0	552,065	47.6	2.51	2.55	2.46
42	Pennsylvania	2,386,165	86.5	215,049	61.2	600,875	51.4	1,756,160	51.9	2.49	2.60	2.24
44	Rhode Island.............	180,454	82.3	18,936	51.0	58,029	42.0	155,664	41.9	2.44	2.59	2.22
45	South Carolina..........	839,168	83.5	86,504	61.0	278,369	48.4	583,299	56.5	2.57	2.58	2.54
46	South Dakota............	159,567	85.2	13,925	59.3	33,176	41.3	117,097	50.6	2.47	2.56	2.28
47	Tennessee	1,200,647	82.3	110,534	57.1	330,484	46.9	838,425	53.4	2.54	2.59	2.44
48	Texas.......................	4,492,603	77.8	465,881	52.5	1,280,711	46.2	2,731,764	46.0	2.84	2.95	2.66
49	Utah........................	542,587	80.4	38,021	56.6	86,053	53.6	229,030	52.2	3.14	3.24	2.89
50	Vermont	126,519	87.4	10,128	59.9	24,231	53.6	97,642	55.3	2.32	2.41	2.11
51	Virginia....................	1,541,185	80.8	127,036	55.3	376,201	46.5	994,545	52.4	2.61	2.67	2.51
53	Washington	1,301,823	78.1	115,931	49.2	270,032	43.7	949,031	47.6	2.56	2.65	2.42
54	West Virginia	358,666	87.2	31,782	63.1	81,088	55.6	270,008	57.8	2.44	2.51	2.23
55	Wisconsin	1,126,874	87.0	100,452	57.7	234,247	42.5	826,789	48.6	2.44	2.56	2.19
56	Wyoming..................	115,398	82.7	10,279	60.6	21,068	45.6	76,768	56.0	2.52	2.53	2.48

State code	STATE	Percent of housing units that are crowded or lacking complete plumbing	Median household income in the past 12 months (in 2012 inflation-adjusted dollars)					Median housing value (owner estimated)			Owner occupied housing units		
			All households	Owner-occupied households			Renter-occupied households	All owner-occupied households	Households with a mortgage	Households without a mortgage	Total owner-occupied housing units	Percent with a mortgage	Percent with a second mortgage, or a home equity loan, or both
				All owner-occupied households	Households with a mortgage	Households without a mortgage							
ACS table number:		C25016	B25119	B25099	B25099	B25099	B25119	B25097	B25097	B25097	B25081	B25081	B25081
Column number:		39	40	41	42	43	44	45	46	47	48	49	50
00	United States	3.6	51,371	65,514	77,199	44,005	31,888	171,900	187,600	143,100	74,119,256	65.7	12.2
01	Alabama	2.3	41,574	52,124	65,297	36,367	23,587	123,200	142,600	91,500	1,268,565	58.3	8.5
02	Alaska	10.0	67,712	83,746	94,352	59,081	46,691	245,100	260,400	206,500	159,427	65.2	6.5
04	Arizona	5.2	47,826	59,103	69,604	40,231	32,777	151,500	159,700	125,800	1,496,650	66.2	10.9
05	Arkansas	2.9	40,112	50,674	61,204	35,970	23,827	107,600	121,300	87,100	757,722	57.6	4.6
06	California	8.6	58,328	79,895	91,024	50,240	39,687	349,400	358,100	318,800	6,781,817	73.9	16.3
08	Colorado	2.9	56,765	73,460	81,304	48,052	35,218	234,900	240,500	216,500	1,278,158	73.9	15.4
09	Connecticut	1.9	67,276	87,742	97,646	60,615	34,226	267,800	270,900	260,400	908,452	70.7	17.6
10	Delaware	2.0	58,415	70,117	79,610	46,372	35,035	226,900	233,500	206,800	241,050	69.7	15.1
11	District of Columbia	3.9	66,583	109,266	119,398	68,904	43,655	460,700	464,200	444,600	110,681	78.7	17.2
12	Florida	3.1	45,040	54,530	64,414	40,419	31,244	148,200	156,700	124,900	4,724,428	61.1	12.0
13	Georgia	2.8	47,209	61,696	71,353	40,736	28,569	142,300	152,300	111,500	2,248,702	69.4	12.6
15	Hawaii	9.4	66,259	83,364	94,565	60,250	48,354	496,600	496,200	497,600	254,770	67.8	15.4
16	Idaho	3.2	45,489	55,787	62,118	40,582	28,674	154,500	158,400	143,900	398,671	67.8	12.2
17	Illinois	2.8	55,137	70,553	80,948	47,808	31,313	170,600	180,200	152,800	3,177,104	67.8	13.4
18	Indiana	2.0	46,974	58,913	66,792	41,030	26,684	122,700	129,600	105,800	1,720,780	68.0	11.5
19	Iowa	1.8	50,957	61,361	71,360	44,336	27,581	126,300	137,000	109,700	882,584	61.8	9.8
20	Kansas	2.5	50,241	63,240	74,497	44,882	31,027	130,100	144,800	98,600	739,191	62.5	9.0
21	Kentucky	2.1	41,724	53,515	66,183	35,847	24,173	120,800	135,800	90,400	1,144,309	60.8	10.9
22	Louisiana	2.8	42,944	55,122	70,674	38,456	25,951	139,500	158,300	104,900	1,130,134	55.5	6.1
23	Maine	2.4	46,709	57,048	66,223	40,500	27,051	172,300	180,200	157,800	396,014	63.9	13.3
24	Maryland	2.2	71,122	90,577	101,171	56,317	43,742	279,900	286,500	255,900	1,433,937	75.2	17.2
25	Massachusetts	2.0	65,339	87,959	100,244	56,002	35,901	323,800	326,600	316,300	1,570,055	71.5	16.7
26	Michigan	1.9	46,859	57,610	68,744	40,325	25,349	115,700	125,500	96,800	2,713,964	63.6	13.4
27	Minnesota	2.3	58,906	72,214	82,353	49,510	31,307	178,400	186,100	163,700	1,508,810	68.7	16.0
28	Mississippi	3.2	37,095	46,564	59,737	34,216	21,570	99,800	121,000	79,700	743,611	52.9	5.5
29	Missouri	2.0	45,321	57,374	67,990	39,699	25,971	135,000	145,500	111,700	1,591,686	64.1	9.9
30	Montana	2.4	45,076	56,854	68,103	40,036	27,933	184,800	199,600	160,700	274,196	57.9	7.2
31	Nebraska	2.2	50,723	64,508	74,121	47,092	30,574	128,300	138,000	110,100	486,642	63.1	9.1
32	Nevada	5.0	49,760	63,800	71,022	44,863	36,558	150,700	153,400	137,900	552,324	71.7	12.1
33	New Hampshire	1.6	63,280	78,025	88,490	51,942	36,322	236,000	241,300	222,700	367,863	68.5	14.6
34	New Jersey	3.5	69,667	90,728	101,703	59,786	38,718	311,600	318,400	295,200	2,081,481	70.1	15.2
35	New Mexico	4.1	42,558	53,243	65,215	37,338	27,672	157,500	171,400	122,100	518,106	58.4	7.5
36	New York	5.3	56,448	77,305	90,924	53,541	36,450	280,900	299,700	240,600	3,883,893	64.4	12.6
37	North Carolina	2.8	45,150	56,762	67,875	37,031	28,712	150,100	162,100	117,100	2,441,626	66.0	13.1
38	North Dakota	1.5	53,585	69,274	81,730	53,272	32,552	142,500	161,600	110,800	189,193	53.5	7.4
39	Ohio	1.5	46,829	60,664	70,849	41,713	25,912	127,600	135,700	112,600	3,019,382	65.9	14.4
40	Oklahoma	3.1	44,312	55,779	67,288	40,281	27,527	114,300	127,200	92,300	960,369	57.8	5.5
41	Oregon	3.5	49,161	63,307	73,328	42,945	30,377	223,900	231,500	201,900	933,775	68.3	14.0
42	Pennsylvania	1.7	51,230	63,951	77,138	43,475	29,162	163,800	176,700	138,700	3,416,499	62.1	13.1
44	Rhode Island	2.0	54,554	75,410	84,818	49,802	30,344	234,600	236,400	229,300	247,790	71.5	16.8
45	South Carolina	2.1	43,107	53,488	65,791	35,852	26,304	135,500	153,000	99,400	1,217,692	61.1	10.1
46	South Dakota	2.8	48,362	61,013	69,582	48,153	29,962	134,300	149,700	101,300	217,200	57.4	7.3
47	Tennessee	2.2	42,764	54,078	62,902	39,733	26,220	137,800	145,800	119,800	1,654,001	61.9	8.8
48	Texas	5.4	50,740	65,502	78,895	45,470	32,834	129,200	145,400	98,600	5,586,856	61.1	4.9
49	Utah	4.1	57,049	69,046	74,120	52,525	34,072	199,700	202,200	193,500	623,589	72.9	13.0
50	Vermont	1.6	52,977	63,804	73,468	44,285	31,309	216,900	225,300	197,900	183,563	65.6	13.9
51	Virginia	2.2	61,741	76,792	90,004	46,747	40,076	237,800	257,400	182,600	2,010,442	71.4	15.7
53	Washington	3.2	57,573	73,475	83,287	49,781	36,825	243,000	249,300	223,800	1,643,637	70.8	14.2
54	West Virginia	1.9	40,196	48,367	62,698	35,767	21,958	100,400	119,900	81,100	533,758	48.3	6.4
55	Wisconsin	2.1	51,059	65,242	74,471	46,282	29,021	165,200	169,500	156,500	1,539,778	66.4	14.3
56	Wyoming	2.5	54,901	67,540	79,938	49,010	34,578	187,400	195,700	171,900	154,329	57.5	7.1

Table C-1. States — Where: Migration, Housing, and Transportation, 2012—*Continued*

State code	STATE	Median monthly housing costs for all housing units with costs (dollars)	Gross rent for renter-occupied housing units		Median selected monthly owner costs for owner-occupied housing units			Median annual real estate taxes paid by owner-occupied housing units (dollars)	Median selected monthly owner costs as a percentage of household income		
			Median gross rent (dollars)	As a percentage of household income	All owner-occupied households	Households with a mortgage	Households without a mortgage		All owner-occupied households	Households with a mortgage	Households without a mortgage[1]
	ACS table number:	B25105	B25064	B25071	B25088	B25088	B25088	B25103	B25092	B25092	B25092
	Column number:	51	52	53	54	55	56	57	58	59	60
00	United States	971	884	31.1	1,066	1,460	434	2,075	20.0	23.7	12.3
01	Alabama	706	689	29.9	725	1,104	326	535	17.4	21.3	11.1
02	Alaska......................	1,239	1,120	29.0	1,364	1,831	549	2,904	19.6	23.3	11.3
04	Arizona	925	888	30.8	969	1,320	370	1,327	19.7	23.6	10.9
05	Arkansas..................	642	640	29.4	647	975	309	671	16.6	20.2	10.7
06	California..................	1,375	1,200	34.1	1,682	2,119	478	2,945	24.5	28.4	11.7
08	Colorado	1,110	934	30.5	1,281	1,551	400	1,478	20.6	23.5	10.1
09	Connecticut..............	1,352	1,019	31.7	1,668	2,027	806	5,075	23.4	25.5	16.5
10	Delaware	1,101	960	29.5	1,215	1,517	419	1,191	20.3	23.8	10.9
11	District of Columbia	1,431	1,235	29.3	1,925	2,262	542	2,635	21.0	23.3	10.0
12	Florida	972	954	34.7	992	1,425	447	1,643	21.8	27.1	13.2
13	Georgia	927	837	31.7	1,039	1,331	375	1,390	19.8	23.1	11.4
15	Hawaii	1,494	1,379	32.7	1,646	2,244	513	1,377	23.9	29.3	10.0
16	Idaho	808	702	30.0	913	1,174	323	1,194	19.4	23.6	10.0
17	Illinois	1,031	868	30.4	1,215	1,618	545	3,939	21.1	24.2	13.6
18	Indiana	777	715	29.7	834	1,069	353	1,053	17.5	20.0	10.6
19	Iowa	742	661	27.5	817	1,140	403	1,834	17.3	20.0	11.5
20	Kansas.....................	799	711	27.9	892	1,250	423	1,805	17.8	20.8	11.8
21	Kentucky	681	636	29.2	732	1,084	311	1,015	17.4	21.1	10.5
22	Louisiana	721	747	31.5	689	1,148	296	653	16.0	20.9	10.0
23	Maine......................	852	744	30.9	933	1,300	456	2,127	20.4	23.8	13.6
24	Maryland	1,388	1,170	30.3	1,589	1,918	556	3,066	21.5	23.8	12.3
25	Massachusetts	1,313	1,036	29.8	1,621	2,010	681	3,821	22.4	24.4	14.9
26	Michigan	834	748	32.5	902	1,233	441	2,114	19.4	22.4	13.3
27	Minnesota	982	813	29.2	1,130	1,465	450	2,186	19.2	22.1	11.3
28	Mississippi................	644	666	32.4	625	1,031	317	771	17.5	22.4	11.7
29	Missouri	779	706	30.5	861	1,176	376	1,359	18.3	21.6	11.8
30	Montana...................	734	681	28.8	804	1,233	371	1,609	18.4	22.9	11.6
31	Nebraska	798	692	27.1	918	1,229	449	2,399	17.9	20.7	12.0
32	Nevada	1,030	944	30.7	1,159	1,433	397	1,460	21.7	25.4	10.7
33	New Hampshire	1,244	967	29.6	1,466	1,828	716	4,987	23.4	25.8	16.7
34	New Jersey................	1,479	1,148	32.4	1,884	2,342	930	7,183	25.3	27.7	18.6
35	New Mexico..............	755	753	30.8	760	1,193	311	1,163	17.9	23.1	10.0
36	New York..................	1,192	1,079	31.9	1,371	1,967	683	4,402	22.2	25.3	15.1
37	North Carolina...........	826	756	29.8	903	1,209	351	1,286	19.0	22.3	11.7
38	North Dakota.............	668	644	24.0	708	1,205	394	1,737	14.8	18.9	10.0
39	Ohio	804	700	29.7	925	1,215	417	1,979	18.8	21.7	12.4
40	Oklahoma.................	712	686	28.9	742	1,111	348	982	17.0	20.8	10.7
41	Oregon	989	862	32.1	1,193	1,544	449	2,474	22.0	25.6	12.7
42	Pennsylvania	887	798	30.0	971	1,382	474	2,448	19.4	22.6	13.5
44	Rhode Island	1,124	878	30.3	1,500	1,774	657	3,842	23.3	25.4	16.2
45	South Carolina...........	778	754	31.5	801	1,155	318	765	18.1	22.1	11.2
46	South Dakota.............	712	651	26.0	778	1,174	399	1,797	17.3	20.9	10.5
47	Tennessee	766	730	30.6	807	1,143	338	1,018	18.5	22.7	10.7
48	Texas.......................	897	831	29.2	988	1,374	432	2,473	18.4	22.1	11.8
49	Utah	1,029	851	29.8	1,156	1,396	372	1,431	20.1	23.5	10.0
50	Vermont	1,031	860	30.3	1,159	1,478	619	3,652	22.7	24.8	16.8
51	Virginia	1,178	1,068	30.1	1,273	1,670	396	1,884	19.9	23.1	10.6
53	Washington	1,137	954	30.4	1,356	1,715	493	2,759	21.8	25.0	12.1
54	West Virginia	543	607	29.1	494	931	278	587	14.3	19.2	10.0
55	Wisconsin	885	743	29.4	1,060	1,376	507	3,223	20.3	23.0	13.6
56	Wyoming..................	787	742	27.4	839	1,297	365	1,149	16.6	20.6	10.0

[1]A value of 10.0 represents 10 percent or less.

Table C-1. States — Where: Migration, Housing, and Transportation, 2012—*Continued*

State code	STATE	Households who pay 30 percent or more of income for housing expenses by tenure and age of householder (percent)								Total number of workers 16 years and over
		Owner-occupied households				Renter-occupied households				
		15 to 24 years	25 to 34 years	35 to 64 years	65 years and over	15 to 24 years	25 to 34 years	35 to 64 years	65 years and over	
	ACS table number:	C25093	C25093	C25093	C25093	C25072	C25072	C25072	C25072	B08301
	Column number:	61	62	63	64	65	66	67	68	69
00	United States	36.2	27.4	26.9	27.5	59.0	44.5	46.1	54.6	140,862,960
01	Alabama..................	38.2	22.0	21.4	21.2	53.5	43.4	39.8	42.1	1,970,822
02	Alaska.....................	59.6	27.7	24.0	27.9	48.3	49.3	39.2	51.9	356,567
04	Arizona...................	33.4	25.7	26.9	25.2	61.9	44.3	44.4	57.4	2,721,795
05	Arkansas.................	36.3	20.7	18.4	18.5	52.8	43.2	39.3	43.0	1,233,150
06	California.................	50.0	42.1	39.1	32.9	67.2	51.1	53.0	62.9	16,432,358
08	Colorado	40.1	26.8	26.7	26.4	65.2	44.1	45.1	56.9	2,538,793
09	Connecticut.............	51.5	33.4	32.3	39.1	60.2	45.3	48.7	54.7	1,728,325
10	Delaware.................	33.7	29.7	27.3	26.0	55.8	45.4	43.1	47.5	421,883
11	District of Columbia...	91.5	28.3	26.5	31.6	69.7	41.0	44.1	49.8	326,143
12	Florida	40.8	33.1	34.3	30.4	63.7	51.7	52.4	59.4	8,161,313
13	Georgia	42.2	26.4	26.2	26.7	60.7	46.5	45.3	50.6	4,213,128
15	Hawaii....................	73.9	52.5	39.2	29.0	60.1	55.2	47.9	44.6	670,355
16	Idaho.....................	38.8	27.9	25.4	23.5	52.6	44.5	41.6	53.6	697,765
17	Illinois	33.5	31.3	28.5	29.4	59.2	42.6	44.5	56.5	5,927,604
18	Indiana...................	30.0	18.8	18.9	20.9	56.7	42.8	42.0	51.4	2,954,205
19	Iowa......................	25.1	19.2	16.8	19.4	55.7	35.4	36.7	48.9	1,530,289
20	Kansas....................	28.8	20.3	19.1	20.8	53.0	36.5	37.3	48.7	1,388,601
21	Kentucky	22.4	18.2	20.1	21.0	54.8	40.4	40.6	44.2	1,845,659
22	Louisiana	30.6	23.4	20.4	18.7	58.5	44.4	43.3	47.0	1,965,689
23	Maine.....................	44.3	28.5	26.7	29.9	51.0	48.2	45.8	47.6	631,826
24	Maryland	42.1	32.1	28.0	29.6	61.9	45.8	44.7	57.0	2,909,794
25	Massachusetts	56.1	31.5	29.2	36.2	58.3	39.4	47.1	52.0	3,273,690
26	Michigan	35.6	25.0	24.2	26.9	61.5	46.5	46.9	55.5	4,190,898
27	Minnesota	27.7	21.3	21.4	26.0	55.7	36.4	43.1	58.6	2,737,424
28	Mississippi..............	35.0	23.6	23.6	22.0	52.5	46.0	44.0	42.4	1,178,427
29	Missouri.................	32.0	22.7	21.6	22.7	57.6	43.1	43.6	51.9	2,734,275
30	Montana..................	25.2	25.1	24.5	20.6	56.3	34.2	41.2	46.6	475,299
31	Nebraska	40.3	20.3	18.1	21.1	49.9	34.8	36.1	47.5	946,684
32	Nevada	38.7	30.0	32.1	30.4	56.1	47.1	46.2	57.8	1,216,345
33	New Hampshire	59.2	35.7	30.7	37.1	52.2	41.8	45.3	50.9	677,232
34	New Jersey...............	49.2	40.3	37.2	43.0	62.3	45.1	50.9	58.9	4,113,910
35	New Mexico.............	30.5	32.9	23.8	22.4	57.0	45.0	43.4	47.5	865,474
36	New York.................	42.8	30.8	32.4	35.7	62.0	46.1	48.8	57.5	8,916,499
37	North Carolina..........	38.7	23.0	23.6	26.3	58.2	43.5	41.9	47.6	4,263,889
38	North Dakota...........	27.1	13.9	11.7	15.3	45.5	20.0	24.7	47.7	376,246
39	Ohio	24.7	21.1	21.4	24.3	57.7	41.3	42.9	52.5	5,183,203
40	Oklahoma................	27.1	20.7	19.2	19.5	52.1	37.8	39.7	51.2	1,682,277
41	Oregon...................	26.5	30.7	31.6	28.0	59.0	46.7	47.4	57.5	1,700,679
42	Pennsylvania	37.0	24.0	23.7	27.0	56.0	41.8	44.3	50.7	5,810,858
44	Rhode Island............	28.4	35.4	31.8	35.5	60.1	43.5	46.5	50.4	503,788
45	South Carolina..........	32.6	22.2	22.4	24.2	56.7	43.6	45.1	47.5	1,999,706
46	South Dakota............	25.5	16.5	16.8	18.6	49.9	27.7	34.0	45.6	421,018
47	Tennessee	37.4	24.3	23.4	22.5	56.3	42.9	44.0	45.6	2,777,627
48	Texas......................	35.0	25.3	22.4	22.6	56.5	41.4	41.9	53.0	11,608,001
49	Utah	33.6	31.5	25.4	21.6	56.3	38.4	46.9	52.5	1,296,763
50	Vermont	79.3	26.7	29.7	36.7	54.9	48.3	43.4	48.5	318,829
51	Virginia	37.4	27.4	25.5	25.7	62.5	43.1	43.8	52.4	3,967,188
53	Washington	47.0	35.0	29.3	29.2	61.7	42.3	44.4	59.9	3,181,100
54	West Virginia	31.0	15.3	15.9	14.1	45.5	37.6	37.9	39.2	733,687
55	Wisconsin	32.3	24.2	24.0	27.4	58.0	39.6	42.3	56.9	2,799,940
56	Wyoming.................	22.7	23.5	17.4	19.0	45.7	38.1	37.8	35.5	285,940

Table C-1. States — Where: Migration, Housing, and Transportation, 2012—*Continued*

State code	STATE	Means of transportation to work (percent)							Number of workers who did not work at home
		Car, truck, or van		Public transportation (excluding taxicab)	Bicycle	Walked	Taxicab, motorcycle, or other means	Worked at home	
		Drove alone	Car-pooled						
	ACS table number:	B08301	B08301	B08301	B08301	B08301	B08301	B08301	B08301
	Column number:	70	71	72	73	74	75	76	77
00	United States	76.3	9.7	5.0	0.6	2.8	1.2	4.4	134,719,017
01	Alabama..........................	85.3	9.5	0.4	0.1	1.2	0.9	2.6	1,919,867
02	Alaska.............................	66.2	13.3	1.6	1.1	7.4	4.8	5.6	336,668
04	Arizona...........................	76.7	11.0	2.0	0.9	2.0	1.9	5.4	2,573,491
05	Arkansas.........................	82.2	11.2	0.5	0.1	1.6	1.0	3.5	1,190,483
06	California........................	73.4	11.1	5.2	1.1	2.7	1.3	5.3	15,567,196
08	Colorado.........................	74.4	9.7	3.2	1.5	3.4	1.2	6.6	2,370,579
09	Connecticut....................	78.6	8.2	4.8	0.3	3.0	1.0	4.1	1,656,785
10	Delaware.........................	81.5	8.1	2.5	0.3	2.3	0.9	4.4	403,316
11	District of Columbia........	34.1	5.6	38.6	4.1	11.9	1.0	4.6	311,014
12	Florida	79.3	9.7	2.2	0.7	1.6	1.6	5.0	7,757,026
13	Georgia	79.6	10.4	2.0	0.2	1.7	1.3	4.8	4,011,658
15	Hawaii	65.2	15.3	6.7	1.2	4.7	2.4	4.4	640,879
16	Idaho	77.8	10.1	0.8	1.0	2.9	1.5	5.9	656,748
17	Illinois	73.6	8.9	8.5	0.7	3.1	1.0	4.1	5,683,562
18	Indiana	82.4	9.4	1.1	0.5	2.2	1.0	3.3	2,855,891
19	Iowa	79.9	9.0	1.1	0.5	3.6	1.1	4.7	1,458,360
20	Kansas............................	82.2	9.7	0.6	0.3	2.2	1.0	4.1	1,332,275
21	Kentucky	82.7	9.8	1.0	0.2	2.3	0.9	3.1	1,789,062
22	Louisiana	82.5	9.9	1.2	0.4	1.9	1.7	2.4	1,918,744
23	Maine	76.9	11.0	0.6	0.4	4.3	1.4	5.3	598,598
24	Maryland	73.4	9.8	8.9	0.4	2.5	0.9	4.2	2,787,912
25	Massachusetts	71.9	7.8	9.4	0.8	4.9	0.9	4.2	3,136,643
26	Michigan	82.5	9.0	1.3	0.5	2.2	0.8	3.7	4,036,961
27	Minnesota	78.0	8.9	3.3	0.8	2.8	0.8	5.3	2,591,196
28	Mississippi	83.5	10.7	0.4	0.1	1.7	1.1	2.4	1,150,196
29	Missouri	81.3	9.7	1.3	0.3	1.9	1.1	4.4	2,614,036
30	Montana.........................	74.4	10.7	1.0	1.6	4.8	1.0	6.5	444,232
31	Nebraska	80.2	10.0	0.6	0.7	2.8	0.8	4.9	900,483
32	Nevada	78.0	10.9	3.6	0.4	2.3	1.7	3.1	1,178,781
33	New Hampshire	81.9	7.2	0.7	0.3	3.1	1.0	5.8	637,747
34	New Jersey......................	72.0	8.3	10.6	0.4	3.0	1.6	4.1	3,945,265
35	New Mexico.....................	78.9	11.3	1.1	0.5	2.3	1.3	4.5	826,180
36	New York........................	53.7	6.9	27.3	0.6	6.4	1.3	3.9	8,566,966
37	North Carolina	80.6	10.5	1.1	0.3	1.9	1.1	4.5	4,072,520
38	North Dakota..................	79.5	9.7	0.4	0.4	3.8	0.6	5.6	355,264
39	Ohio	83.3	8.1	1.6	0.3	2.4	0.9	3.4	5,004,577
40	Oklahoma.......................	82.3	10.4	0.4	0.2	2.0	1.3	3.3	1,626,405
41	Oregon	71.2	10.4	4.1	2.5	4.6	1.0	6.2	1,595,991
42	Pennsylvania	76.5	8.9	5.4	0.5	3.8	0.9	3.9	5,584,155
44	Rhode Island..................	78.8	8.9	3.1	0.4	3.6	1.5	3.6	485,623
45	South Carolina................	82.9	9.3	0.5	0.4	2.2	1.3	3.4	1,931,496
46	South Dakota..................	78.7	9.1	0.5	0.8	3.9	1.1	5.8	396,728
47	Tennessee.......................	83.6	9.4	0.8	0.1	1.3	1.1	3.7	2,676,009
48	Texas..............................	80.1	11.0	1.6	0.3	1.6	1.5	3.9	11,152,347
49	Utah	75.7	12.2	2.5	1.0	2.6	1.3	4.8	1,234,950
50	Vermont..........................	73.5	10.2	1.2	1.0	6.1	0.7	7.3	295,636
51	Virginia...........................	77.3	9.9	4.4	0.4	2.2	1.0	4.7	3,779,438
53	Washington	72.2	10.7	5.8	0.9	3.6	1.2	5.5	3,005,863
54	West Virginia..................	81.7	10.6	0.7	0.1	3.2	0.9	2.9	712,516
55	Wisconsin	80.2	8.9	1.8	0.9	3.3	1.0	3.9	2,690,547
56	Wyoming.........................	75.7	11.6	1.5	1.2	3.2	1.2	5.5	270,152

Table C-1. States — Where: Migration, Housing, and Transportation, 2012—*Continued*

State code	STATE	Mean travel time to work (minutes)					Vehicles available (percent of households)				
		All workers who did not work at home	By car, truck, or van	Public transportation	Taxicab, motorcycle, bicycle, walked, or by other means	Number of households	No vehicles	One vehicle	Two vehicles	Three or more vehicles	Average vehicles per household
	ACS table number:	C08136/ B08301	C08136/ B08301	C08136/ B08301	C08136/ B08301	B08201	B08201	B08201	B08201	B08201	B25046/ B08201
	Column number:	78	79	80	81	82	83	84	85	86	87
00	United States	25.7	24.8	48.2	18.2	115,969,540	9.2	34.1	37.3	19.3	1.75
01	Alabama	24.5	24.5	33.5	21.1	1,845,169	6.7	33.4	36.8	23.1	1.86
02	Alaska..........................	19.6	18.3	51.2	23.9	251,651	9.5	33.5	36.6	20.3	1.78
04	Arizona........................	24.6	24.3	47.6	20.7	2,392,168	7.0	38.4	38.2	16.4	1.70
05	Arkansas......................	21.4	21.6	29.0	13.7	1,143,859	6.6	34.6	38.7	20.1	1.80
06	California......................	27.5	26.8	48.3	19.5	12,552,658	7.9	32.6	37.6	21.9	1.84
08	Colorado......................	24.5	24.1	45.8	19.1	1,996,088	5.7	31.9	39.9	22.5	1.88
09	Connecticut..................	24.8	23.7	53.8	15.2	1,357,812	9.1	32.8	38.5	19.6	1.76
10	Delaware......................	25.8	25.4	54.7	14.9	340,308	6.3	33.0	40.8	19.9	1.82
11	District of Columbia	29.9	27.0	37.6	19.3	266,662	37.9	43.7	14.4	3.9	0.86
12	Florida	26.2	25.8	48.4	23.1	7,197,943	7.4	42.2	37.4	13.0	1.60
13	Georgia	26.9	26.7	48.3	20.3	3,532,908	6.9	34.6	38.3	20.2	1.79
15	Hawaii	26.0	25.1	45.8	18.2	447,748	8.4	35.8	35.1	20.8	1.79
16	Idaho	20.2	20.0	61.8	16.1	583,106	4.4	27.5	40.1	28.0	2.04
17	Illinois	28.0	26.4	48.7	18.2	4,770,194	11.0	35.1	36.9	17.0	1.66
18	Indiana	23.5	23.5	43.4	17.7	2,480,077	7.1	32.8	38.9	21.2	1.83
19	Iowa	18.8	19.1	27.0	12.9	1,227,048	5.6	30.2	40.0	24.2	1.94
20	Kansas.........................	19.0	19.1	33.9	15.6	1,113,911	5.4	31.1	39.3	24.2	1.93
21	Kentucky	22.9	23.0	38.8	14.0	1,707,004	7.7	34.0	37.8	20.5	1.79
22	Louisiana	25.2	25.1	40.0	22.9	1,719,473	8.3	38.2	37.5	16.0	1.66
23	Maine	23.5	24.0	43.5	14.6	554,543	7.1	34.6	40.3	18.0	1.76
24	Maryland	31.9	30.2	53.6	18.6	2,157,717	9.6	33.3	36.2	20.9	1.77
25	Massachusetts	28.3	27.2	45.4	17.3	2,522,394	12.7	36.2	36.7	14.4	1.58
26	Michigan	24.0	24.0	42.1	17.4	3,819,068	8.1	35.3	38.2	18.4	1.74
27	Minnesota	22.9	22.8	38.2	14.4	2,111,943	6.9	30.3	40.7	22.1	1.88
28	Mississippi....................	24.0	24.0	42.6	19.9	1,090,521	6.9	34.8	36.9	21.4	1.81
29	Missouri.......................	23.1	23.0	45.6	17.8	2,359,135	7.8	33.7	38.0	20.6	1.80
30	Montana......................	18.4	18.5	37.1	14.9	408,938	5.5	29.2	37.1	28.2	2.03
31	Nebraska	18.2	18.3	39.3	12.0	733,570	5.9	29.8	40.0	24.4	1.95
32	Nevada	24.0	22.9	55.0	21.4	1,006,605	8.2	36.5	38.1	17.2	1.71
33	New Hampshire	26.3	26.4	64.9	17.4	519,137	5.5	31.1	42.3	21.1	1.88
34	New Jersey....................	30.7	28.0	57.3	17.6	3,198,799	11.9	34.7	36.4	17.1	1.65
35	New Mexico..................	21.4	21.3	43.9	16.8	764,996	5.7	34.0	37.5	22.8	1.87
36	New York......................	31.8	26.0	49.3	16.6	7,238,922	29.8	32.8	26.1	11.4	1.23
37	North Carolina	23.7	23.7	38.2	18.7	3,731,325	6.7	33.1	38.4	21.8	1.84
38	North Dakota................	17.4	17.7	27.0	11.6	290,944	5.3	28.6	38.3	27.8	2.04
39	Ohio	23.2	23.0	44.9	16.6	4,554,672	8.4	34.6	37.3	19.7	1.76
40	Oklahoma	21.1	21.2	28.0	16.3	1,446,667	5.8	33.7	39.5	21.0	1.85
41	Oregon	22.7	22.1	43.7	18.4	1,516,957	8.3	32.6	38.3	20.9	1.81
42	Pennsylvania	26.1	25.5	45.1	15.7	4,958,249	11.6	34.4	36.4	17.7	1.67
44	Rhode Island................	24.4	24.1	47.1	17.1	413,083	10.0	37.4	36.3	16.3	1.65
45	South Carolina..............	23.5	23.6	43.8	17.4	1,787,340	7.1	34.8	38.4	19.7	1.78
46	South Dakota................	16.7	17.0	35.9	10.1	323,765	4.6	30.2	37.5	27.8	2.03
47	Tennessee	24.4	24.4	44.7	20.6	2,480,090	6.4	33.4	38.0	22.2	1.85
48	Texas...........................	25.3	25.0	47.9	20.7	8,970,959	5.8	34.6	40.3	19.3	1.80
49	Utah	22.0	21.4	48.0	19.5	895,691	4.6	26.8	41.3	27.2	2.04
50	Vermont	23.1	23.7	35.0	14.0	258,520	6.6	33.0	41.8	18.6	1.80
51	Virginia	27.9	27.3	46.3	19.5	3,038,967	6.4	30.5	38.0	25.1	1.93
53	Washington	26.0	25.0	44.4	21.0	2,636,817	6.9	31.3	38.0	23.8	1.90
54	West Virginia	25.2	25.5	43.5	15.1	741,544	8.8	36.6	36.8	17.8	1.70
55	Wisconsin	21.8	21.9	39.9	14.1	2,288,362	7.2	32.4	40.6	19.7	1.81
56	Wyoming......................	18.1	18.5	28.9	10.2	223,513	3.2	28.0	38.4	30.4	2.14

Table C-2. Counties — Where: Migration, Housing, and Transportation, 2010–2012

STATE and county code	STATE or county	Percent who lived in the same house one year ago	Percent who did not live in the same county one year ago	Total occupied housing units	Percent owner-occupied housing units	Median value of owner-occupied housing units (dollars)	Median selected monthly owner costs as a percentage of household income — With a mortgage	Without a mortgage[1]	Median gross rent (dollars)	Median gross rent as a percentage of household income[1]	Percent of workers who drove alone to work	Mean travel time to work (minutes)	Percent of occupied housing units with no vehicle available
ACS table number:		C07204	C07204	B25003	B25003	B25077	B25092	B25092	B25064	B25071	C08301	B08013/B08012	C25045
Column number:		1	2	3	4	5	6	7	8	9	10	11	12
00 000	**United States**	84.8	5.3	115,241,776	64.7	174,600	24.5	12.7	889	31.5	76.4	25.5	9.2
01 000	**Alabama**	84.7	5.6	1,837,823	69.6	123,400	22.3	11.8	698	31.4	84.8	24.2	6.5
01 001	Autauga	87.9	7.7	20,001	77.8	132,900	20.8	10.0	837	30.1	89.1	26.1	5.7
01 003	Baldwin	81.5	7.1	73,210	70.7	170,000	23.2	11.3	887	31.1	82.4	26.1	3.4
01 005	Barbour	83.3	9.0	9,292	66.2	89,600	22.3	13.3	591	29.5	83.6	25.1	9.4
01 007	Bibb	84.0	7.6	7,107	77.0	97,400	27.1	13.5	570	31.9	81.5	26.9	3.3
01 009	Blount	87.3	5.6	21,192	79.0	114,300	22.3	11.9	582	26.6	83.2	32.2	3.7
01 013	Butler	94.6	1.8	8,177	70.5	73,900	24.1	14.6	569	33.0	88.1	24.0	10.5
01 015	Calhoun	83.8	6.2	45,553	67.9	103,700	21.4	10.5	632	30.5	85.5	22.2	5.9
01 017	Chambers	83.1	4.8	13,688	66.4	81,900	22.5	14.0	644	36.3	81.9	25.8	9.6
01 019	Cherokee	88.6	4.9	11,999	74.2	96,800	23.9	15.8	629	26.7	82.8	27.4	4.0
01 021	Chilton	89.6	3.3	16,262	75.7	100,600	23.0	11.4	550	29.0	82.5	31.3	6.3
01 025	Clarke	92.7	1.4	9,840	75.5	89,200	20.4	14.1	509	32.3	86.1	24.7	10.4
01 031	Coffee	84.9	8.1	19,108	71.2	124,900	21.4	10.6	647	25.5	84.4	21.0	5.9
01 033	Colbert	87.7	5.2	22,302	71.1	99,100	22.7	12.6	650	30.4	90.1	23.5	5.2
01 039	Covington	85.0	4.4	14,934	74.3	86,800	22.2	13.1	560	31.7	81.4	23.7	6.5
01 043	Cullman	84.3	4.6	31,222	74.9	103,800	22.8	12.4	604	33.1	82.0	26.1	5.4
01 045	Dale	79.1	12.9	19,732	61.3	100,800	19.7	10.0	607	26.0	85.0	19.8	5.6
01 047	Dallas	85.7	3.1	16,153	60.3	76,600	24.5	15.9	515	37.5	79.0	23.2	15.2
01 049	DeKalb	90.0	3.2	25,160	77.5	94,200	23.7	11.7	526	26.8	85.0	22.9	4.3
01 051	Elmore	84.0	9.7	28,370	77.1	142,400	22.0	10.8	770	26.7	86.0	28.5	3.9
01 053	Escambia	93.4	3.0	13,787	71.3	81,000	22.0	14.5	567	36.6	84.8	22.0	8.1
01 055	Etowah	84.8	4.7	39,881	71.6	94,300	23.1	13.1	608	32.8	87.5	23.8	6.9
01 059	Franklin	88.5	6.0	12,417	71.5	84,100	22.1	14.1	529	23.6	82.6	27.6	5.0
01 061	Geneva	81.8	9.2	11,004	70.9	77,500	21.0	10.9	570	29.1	83.0	25.3	4.8
01 069	Houston	85.8	5.3	39,172	64.8	123,500	20.6	10.6	654	29.4	88.0	20.4	6.4
01 071	Jackson	91.1	2.7	21,097	76.2	89,300	20.8	11.8	517	26.0	88.9	25.8	4.3
01 073	Jefferson	83.4	4.8	257,586	64.5	141,900	23.3	12.3	782	33.0	84.8	23.4	8.4
01 077	Lauderdale	86.5	4.6	38,524	71.1	114,700	21.5	10.0	586	32.3	86.7	25.3	6.1
01 079	Lawrence	89.4	5.2	13,325	81.0	91,200	21.7	12.9	570	27.8	92.4	27.8	5.7
01 081	Lee	74.8	11.4	55,655	61.7	154,700	22.4	11.7	762	36.0	81.9	21.9	4.8
01 083	Limestone	87.8	5.9	31,807	76.8	138,200	20.5	10.4	624	27.9	87.9	26.2	4.1
01 087	Macon	83.8	7.7	8,055	67.4	74,900	27.2	14.6	587	32.3	75.8	23.6	13.0
01 089	Madison	85.4	5.1	132,631	69.5	165,200	19.4	10.0	732	29.1	86.0	20.7	5.0
01 091	Marengo	87.9	4.9	8,536	70.1	95,900	20.9	12.9	465	33.4	83.3	21.5	14.7
01 093	Marion	85.4	4.5	12,538	74.8	77,000	22.9	13.0	470	28.7	82.8	25.5	4.8
01 095	Marshall	85.8	5.2	34,253	72.5	114,000	21.4	11.3	590	27.2	79.5	24.5	4.9
01 097	Mobile	85.4	3.0	156,085	66.6	126,500	23.4	12.6	739	34.3	84.6	23.7	7.4
01 099	Monroe	90.8	2.0	8,487	77.1	78,200	23.1	12.0	539	31.9	89.1	23.8	10.9
01 101	Montgomery	78.1	7.4	88,569	60.1	122,900	22.6	10.4	789	33.9	85.2	19.3	8.3
01 103	Morgan	87.5	4.4	45,753	71.8	123,400	20.0	10.0	591	27.2	86.4	23.2	5.3
01 109	Pike	80.8	9.1	13,053	57.1	106,200	23.5	10.8	608	36.4	84.5	19.4	9.7
01 111	Randolph	86.0	4.5	9,173	72.4	94,100	25.3	11.2	630	31.4	77.1	27.6	6.1
01 113	Russell	81.5	7.9	21,376	60.4	110,500	23.9	13.1	696	32.8	84.1	23.5	8.0
01 115	St. Clair	86.9	5.6	31,323	80.8	137,300	22.2	12.4	746	24.5	88.3	29.4	2.6
01 117	Shelby	86.3	6.9	74,187	78.9	190,600	21.7	10.0	904	27.5	85.4	29.8	2.6
01 121	Talladega	84.2	7.7	31,346	69.0	93,500	24.4	13.6	592	30.9	85.1	23.9	7.9
01 123	Tallapoosa	87.1	4.5	16,172	72.7	92,500	23.5	11.5	593	29.7	81.2	24.2	7.4
01 125	Tuscaloosa	80.4	7.3	67,244	64.6	154,700	22.9	11.2	754	33.3	85.0	21.6	6.6
01 127	Walker	84.6	4.6	25,624	74.8	81,400	21.3	12.0	586	28.7	82.3	29.3	5.7
01 133	Winston	85.3	5.4	9,686	74.7	83,800	23.4	13.5	471	25.0	82.6	30.0	6.3
02 000	**Alaska**	80.8	7.7	253,718	63.5	241,400	23.2	11.3	1,080	28.3	67.1	19.0	9.9
02 020	Anchorage	79.8	7.4	105,688	60.0	282,800	23.1	11.5	1,110	29.1	74.5	19.6	6.3
02 090	Fairbanks North Star	73.5	11.0	36,499	58.8	210,900	25.8	12.6	1,213	30.3	73.2	19.5	6.3
02 110	Juneau	82.0	6.1	12,314	63.9	309,500	24.8	11.8	1,188	26.9	66.2	15.3	7.0
02 122	Kenai Peninsula	85.9	6.3	21,561	75.3	207,400	22.5	10.0	867	27.7	69.1	19.7	5.4
02 170	Matanuska-Susitna	84.6	7.2	31,383	76.2	217,400	23.0	11.4	1,039	29.5	72.3	32.1	3.6
04 000	**Arizona**	80.2	5.5	2,357,799	63.9	158,100	25.0	11.2	878	31.1	76.3	24.6	7.0
04 001	Apache	91.7	4.6	19,445	76.4	78,100	22.9	10.0	548	19.2	75.4	31.2	11.2
04 003	Cochise	81.1	9.2	49,533	68.0	142,500	23.7	10.7	768	28.3	76.3	18.7	6.6
04 005	Coconino	79.9	9.0	44,949	60.3	220,000	25.2	10.0	957	33.7	65.8	17.9	6.4
04 007	Gila	88.2	5.8	19,980	75.1	124,800	25.8	12.2	708	31.5	76.4	22.3	8.5
04 009	Graham	84.2	5.8	10,563	77.1	127,100	23.4	10.1	648	26.3	71.5	20.6	6.7
04 012	La Paz	86.0	7.4	9,913	75.2	95,600	24.5	10.0	613	27.8	78.6	12.0	6.6
04 013	Maricopa	79.7	4.5	1,404,105	61.7	167,100	24.8	11.1	921	30.9	76.4	25.4	6.9
04 015	Mohave	78.8	8.8	80,346	68.5	127,000	27.5	12.4	798	31.9	77.1	19.3	5.6
04 017	Navajo	85.9	5.1	34,107	71.9	110,200	23.9	10.0	666	28.6	73.0	22.6	9.1
04 019	Pima	79.5	5.2	381,827	62.1	164,800	24.8	12.0	788	32.3	77.1	24.0	8.6
04 021	Pinal	80.2	10.1	122,490	75.6	112,100	25.9	11.9	965	30.8	78.8	30.9	4.7
04 023	Santa Cruz	87.2	4.5	15,371	64.0	136,800	24.6	10.7	634	33.3	80.3	19.8	6.7
04 025	Yavapai	81.0	8.3	91,813	69.4	176,200	27.5	11.8	799	33.0	74.4	22.3	5.3
04 027	Yuma	81.5	6.3	70,062	69.8	116,900	26.5	11.1	827	31.2	77.4	19.0	5.7

[1] 10.0 represents 10 percent or less; 50.0 represents 50 percent or higher.

Table C-2. Counties — Where: Migration, Housing, and Transportation, 2010–2012—*Continued*

STATE and county code	STATE or county	Percent who lived in the same house one year ago	Percent who did not live in the same county one year ago	Total occupied housing units	Percent owner-occupied housing units	Median value of owner-occupied housing units (dollars)	Median selected monthly owner costs as a percentage of household income With a mortgage	Without a mortgage[1]	Median gross rent (dollars)	Median gross rent as a percentage of household income[1]	Percent of workers who drove alone to work	Mean travel time to work (minutes)	Percent of occupied housing units with no vehicle available
	ACS table number:	C07204	C07204	B25003	B25003	B25077	B25092	B25092	B25064	B25071	C08301	B08013/B08012	C25045
	Column number:	1	2	3	4	5	6	7	8	9	10	11	12
05 000	**Arkansas**	83.5	6.2	1,129,845	66.9	106,900	20.9	10.9	653	30.0	82.3	21.3	6.5
05 003	Ashley	87.1	3.2	8,684	76.9	62,100	19.0	10.7	547	29.8	86.9	18.7	5.7
05 005	Baxter	86.8	4.9	17,741	78.1	117,500	23.9	12.4	590	33.8	83.9	16.2	4.3
05 007	Benton	82.1	6.3	81,141	67.4	147,900	20.3	10.0	757	25.6	82.9	20.0	3.7
05 009	Boone	84.8	5.7	15,163	71.6	108,200	22.7	10.2	553	29.1	88.3	21.8	5.6
05 015	Carroll	78.4	8.3	11,372	72.7	110,200	25.1	12.5	654	26.4	78.0	19.5	5.2
05 019	Clark	80.2	11.7	8,079	64.2	91,000	21.2	13.1	557	32.6	77.6	19.3	5.5
05 023	Cleburne	87.0	7.3	10,018	77.7	123,300	22.1	11.2	602	29.3	83.3	24.3	3.7
05 027	Columbia	83.5	5.4	9,526	69.7	84,100	20.3	11.0	560	42.4	83.2	18.2	8.1
05 029	Conway	85.8	6.6	8,331	74.0	85,500	21.5	10.1	603	44.4	84.5	20.9	5.5
05 031	Craighead	74.9	8.1	37,834	60.0	122,800	19.3	10.4	639	30.7	84.9	17.6	6.3
05 033	Crawford	84.2	7.9	23,333	74.1	105,900	23.2	10.6	600	29.0	86.8	23.0	4.2
05 035	Crittenden	79.8	5.9	18,302	58.4	98,600	22.9	11.1	650	34.0	82.6	21.0	10.5
05 045	Faulkner	82.2	7.6	43,040	63.8	137,800	20.3	10.0	692	28.8	83.5	23.7	5.3
05 051	Garland	81.1	7.0	38,910	69.0	134,900	24.3	10.5	726	29.8	79.7	21.4	7.4
05 055	Greene	81.5	4.7	16,660	62.3	95,000	21.3	12.0	635	28.7	87.6	19.4	3.9
05 057	Hempstead	85.7	5.5	8,513	68.0	76,900	21.6	10.3	591	40.5	78.3	19.6	6.1
05 059	Hot Spring	87.8	6.5	12,291	70.2	83,100	20.0	10.4	645	30.1	85.1	28.6	5.4
05 063	Independence	84.7	7.2	14,425	70.2	85,500	22.0	11.7	584	36.0	85.3	19.6	4.6
05 069	Jefferson	83.3	6.0	28,592	63.2	81,800	19.6	12.4	646	30.7	84.3	20.5	7.7
05 071	Johnson	86.9	4.9	10,051	69.6	86,300	19.8	10.0	609	33.7	83.1	20.8	5.3
05 083	Logan	87.4	4.7	8,442	76.0	81,200	19.5	10.0	504	31.8	79.7	26.5	5.2
05 085	Lonoke	86.6	6.3	25,274	73.3	117,400	19.6	10.0	685	26.3	81.8	25.6	4.3
05 091	Miller	79.3	6.4	16,746	66.0	87,500	20.5	10.7	662	29.6	87.0	21.2	9.7
05 093	Mississippi	82.3	6.4	16,962	60.3	81,500	18.0	13.1	599	30.4	80.6	18.6	10.4
05 103	Ouachita	89.5	3.3	10,745	67.1	71,900	19.6	11.8	561	28.5	83.0	22.9	9.1
05 107	Phillips	85.7	4.8	8,396	53.0	59,800	22.7	10.0	605	36.6	84.4	19.4	11.9
05 111	Poinsett	78.5	6.4	9,056	59.2	66,000	20.8	13.1	521	29.7	82.1	22.9	9.3
05 113	Polk	92.0	2.8	8,118	75.9	85,300	21.4	10.1	501	30.8	80.1	20.7	5.8
05 115	Pope	82.6	6.9	22,558	71.7	111,300	22.0	10.0	606	29.6	82.6	18.6	5.2
05 119	Pulaski	83.0	5.3	154,268	60.4	143,300	21.6	11.2	759	31.1	85.8	19.6	7.5
05 123	St. Francis	81.7	7.1	9,528	55.8	67,400	17.7	13.1	590	30.1	79.2	20.5	11.7
05 125	Saline	88.4	5.9	41,717	79.1	137,100	20.7	10.2	781	29.3	85.2	25.4	4.5
05 131	Sebastian	84.7	5.2	49,165	62.8	112,100	19.6	10.7	614	29.2	83.6	17.4	7.1
05 139	Union	87.1	3.2	16,706	69.9	74,600	18.6	10.8	603	29.4	85.4	17.6	6.9
05 143	Washington	75.2	8.8	79,464	56.8	143,400	21.9	10.4	685	31.2	75.2	20.7	5.9
05 145	White	86.7	5.7	29,702	69.8	97,000	19.7	10.0	600	29.8	81.2	22.8	6.1
05 149	Yell	89.7	3.9	7,739	68.6	103,700	19.4	10.2	519	33.7	76.2	21.2	7.5
06 000	**California**	84.0	4.1	12,474,950	54.9	358,800	29.5	11.6	1,205	34.0	73.3	27.2	7.9
06 001	Alameda	83.8	5.2	543,175	52.8	484,200	28.2	10.4	1,262	31.7	65.3	28.6	10.5
06 005	Amador	84.5	6.8	14,146	74.7	250,000	30.6	13.7	983	38.1	78.4	29.6	4.8
06 007	Butte	78.3	5.1	84,421	59.3	219,600	28.0	13.0	885	35.4	73.7	20.3	6.7
06 009	Calaveras	88.4	5.3	18,819	79.3	251,400	30.4	13.8	1,055	30.7	77.5	35.9	3.9
06 011	Colusa	83.1	2.5	6,882	61.3	172,000	27.1	10.1	839	28.8	74.8	21.6	6.1
06 013	Contra Costa	85.0	4.8	374,552	65.1	392,900	28.8	12.0	1,329	33.1	69.9	33.3	5.9
06 015	Del Norte	76.2	10.7	9,474	61.6	202,000	26.8	14.4	868	34.0	77.8	12.3	7.4
06 017	El Dorado	85.7	4.9	67,209	73.4	350,300	29.3	13.5	1,067	31.8	76.5	28.6	4.4
06 019	Fresno	83.3	3.2	288,016	53.6	190,400	27.2	11.6	865	34.7	77.0	22.3	9.2
06 021	Glenn	83.6	6.6	9,577	63.0	230,300	29.8	13.4	716	28.3	77.7	21.2	7.2
06 023	Humboldt	81.5	6.4	52,621	55.2	292,400	29.7	12.1	876	36.5	72.4	17.3	7.1
06 025	Imperial	83.2	4.1	47,828	56.6	141,800	27.6	12.4	742	34.6	78.4	22.0	9.3
06 029	Kern	80.1	4.8	254,255	57.8	156,400	26.2	11.3	861	33.2	76.0	23.9	7.3
06 031	Kings	81.4	7.9	40,684	52.2	171,100	26.5	10.0	870	30.8	77.2	20.7	6.1
06 033	Lake	81.5	7.7	26,261	60.8	173,400	32.7	15.1	877	38.0	75.1	29.3	6.5
06 035	Lassen	71.0	20.9	10,206	64.5	182,000	23.6	10.0	853	31.6	76.9	18.0	6.9
06 037	Los Angeles	86.1	2.2	3,211,482	46.4	414,100	31.7	11.6	1,186	35.5	72.4	29.3	9.9
06 039	Madera	87.4	5.5	41,702	60.8	174,000	30.6	11.5	866	31.8	76.3	25.4	6.4
06 041	Marin	84.8	6.4	102,286	62.0	759,300	29.5	11.6	1,577	34.0	66.3	28.4	4.9
06 045	Mendocino	82.6	5.2	33,791	56.2	316,100	33.3	13.0	988	37.4	71.6	18.1	7.2
06 047	Merced	81.6	4.6	74,958	53.2	143,000	26.7	11.3	845	33.8	78.6	25.8	7.4
06 053	Monterey	83.5	5.3	124,727	49.2	344,200	30.2	10.5	1,194	33.6	71.0	22.3	5.7
06 055	Napa	86.8	4.7	49,517	59.4	403,600	29.3	12.3	1,315	32.7	75.9	23.7	4.9
06 057	Nevada	85.3	5.5	41,707	70.9	345,300	32.8	14.5	1,088	37.5	76.1	25.0	4.5
06 059	Orange	84.5	3.7	992,242	58.3	509,500	29.3	10.4	1,465	33.8	78.0	26.3	4.9
06 061	Placer	85.6	5.9	132,525	70.4	328,000	28.7	13.9	1,220	32.8	78.4	26.8	3.9
06 063	Plumas	86.0	4.9	8,412	71.7	237,100	31.5	14.7	848	27.6	71.0	22.0	5.2
06 065	Riverside	82.5	5.5	679,014	66.3	223,700	30.7	13.9	1,145	36.4	77.9	31.7	5.1
06 067	Sacramento	79.8	4.6	513,594	56.3	224,800	28.0	10.9	1,004	34.2	75.4	25.7	7.8
06 069	San Benito	81.8	7.2	16,893	63.9	332,900	32.7	13.3	1,267	33.4	75.9	29.2	2.8
06 071	San Bernardino	82.7	5.4	601,327	61.8	211,700	29.1	12.0	1,081	36.2	75.8	30.0	5.9
06 073	San Diego	83.9	4.0	1,067,043	53.6	396,500	29.8	11.1	1,277	34.3	76.3	24.3	6.2
06 075	San Francisco	83.8	6.2	341,721	36.4	737,700	29.7	11.0	1,463	28.6	36.6	30.5	30.7
06 077	San Joaquin	81.0	4.7	214,808	57.4	201,000	28.6	11.8	1,002	34.7	76.6	28.7	7.2
06 079	San Luis Obispo	78.4	7.8	100,767	57.2	410,500	30.1	11.9	1,195	35.2	74.1	21.1	4.2
06 081	San Mateo	87.2	5.3	257,529	58.6	710,100	29.4	10.8	1,559	30.6	70.5	25.2	5.9
06 083	Santa Barbara	79.3	5.8	141,196	52.1	434,700	29.1	11.0	1,326	34.0	66.4	19.5	6.8
06 085	Santa Clara	84.2	3.9	607,217	56.9	634,000	27.9	10.0	1,510	28.9	76.8	24.9	5.2

[1]10.0 represents 10 percent or less; 50.0 represents 50 percent or higher.

Table C-2. Counties — Where: Migration, Housing, and Transportation, 2010–2012—*Continued*

STATE and county code	STATE or county	Percent who lived in the same house one year ago	Percent who did not live in the same county one year ago	Total occupied housing units	Percent owner-occupied housing units	Median value of owner-occupied housing units (dollars)	Median selected monthly owner costs as a percentage of household income		Median gross rent (dollars)	Median gross rent as a percentage of household income[1]	Percent of workers who drove alone to work	Mean travel time to work (minutes)	Percent of occupied housing units with no vehicle available
							With a mortgage	Without a mortgage[1]					
ACS table number:		C07204	C07204	B25003	B25003	B25077	B25092	B25092	B25064	B25071	C08301	B08013/B08012	C25045
Column number:		1	2	3	4	5	6	7	8	9	10	11	12
	California—Cont.												
06 087	Santa Cruz..................	83.7	6.7	92,834	57.8	549,800	30.6	12.0	1,403	34.1	70.8	25.5	5.1
06 089	Shasta........................	81.9	5.6	68,408	64.2	211,200	28.4	13.3	918	37.2	80.9	20.4	7.1
06 093	Siskiyou.....................	82.0	5.3	19,500	62.2	193,100	30.9	14.2	786	37.8	71.9	18.2	8.4
06 095	Solano........................	81.4	5.3	140,669	61.1	250,900	28.4	10.0	1,244	33.6	76.4	28.4	5.9
06 097	Sonoma......................	85.3	3.4	183,773	59.8	396,300	29.6	12.5	1,241	34.1	76.3	25.4	5.3
06 099	Stanislaus...................	80.1	4.4	166,948	57.6	166,600	29.2	12.5	978	36.4	79.4	26.7	7.2
06 101	Sutter	81.9	5.6	31,620	59.8	182,000	26.6	11.6	863	31.9	75.4	27.7	6.6
06 103	Tehama......................	83.2	6.5	23,441	65.5	167,000	29.5	12.3	835	31.0	70.7	23.5	5.6
06 107	Tulare........................	84.1	3.5	131,426	58.2	158,300	27.6	11.7	804	33.1	75.1	21.6	7.2
06 109	Tuolumne..................	86.0	7.5	21,733	68.8	261,100	30.9	14.3	877	35.0	79.1	26.0	5.1
06 111	Ventura......................	86.1	4.2	266,414	64.6	433,300	28.8	11.5	1,430	34.2	75.7	24.5	4.8
06 113	Yolo...........................	76.4	9.7	70,114	53.3	299,500	25.9	10.0	1,060	36.4	68.5	22.2	8.1
06 115	Yuba..........................	76.5	10.5	24,060	58.5	168,200	27.8	12.6	851	32.8	76.7	29.3	6.2
08 000	**Colorado**	80.6	8.8	1,977,737	64.9	235,000	24.3	10.6	920	30.9	75.1	24.4	5.8
08 001	Adams........................	81.9	8.2	152,332	64.8	184,600	25.5	11.6	965	31.5	77.3	28.3	5.5
08 005	Arapahoe...................	80.1	9.6	225,471	62.5	228,200	24.1	10.1	964	31.2	78.7	26.8	5.3
08 013	Boulder......................	76.5	9.4	120,203	63.0	353,800	22.9	10.0	1,082	35.1	65.1	22.3	5.3
08 014	Broomfield.................	82.8	14.2	21,553	68.7	276,000	22.4	10.0	1,137	26.5	77.5	26.0	4.3
08 029	Delta..........................	84.2	7.1	12,424	75.2	194,200	28.3	13.6	790	30.9	70.3	24.3	3.8
08 031	Denver........................	76.4	11.6	266,248	49.0	249,700	23.5	10.8	863	29.8	69.7	24.2	12.3
08 035	Douglas......................	85.4	7.7	103,574	80.2	330,100	23.1	10.0	1,237	26.5	80.0	27.6	1.9
08 037	Eagle..........................	88.2	5.9	18,390	63.6	469,800	29.1	13.5	1,171	28.8	69.1	19.9	1.1
08 039	Elbert........................	87.4	9.3	8,180	89.6	325,400	27.4	10.0	1,049	27.8	75.4	40.3	1.8
08 041	El Paso.......................	77.4	8.9	237,258	63.4	214,400	24.2	10.0	887	30.2	77.8	21.6	4.9
08 043	Fremont.....................	83.2	7.2	16,909	71.1	158,800	26.4	11.8	698	30.2	76.1	22.8	5.1
08 045	Garfield......................	78.5	7.2	20,188	64.2	290,300	29.1	12.5	1,112	33.3	66.9	26.9	4.2
08 059	Jefferson....................	84.1	8.1	218,728	70.2	259,500	23.6	10.2	955	30.8	78.3	26.3	4.6
08 067	La Plata.....................	79.5	8.5	20,956	67.4	334,400	25.0	10.0	984	31.1	70.1	20.7	3.3
08 069	Larimer......................	79.1	8.9	121,183	65.2	243,700	24.2	10.0	955	33.0	76.1	22.9	4.4
08 075	Logan.........................	80.3	9.6	7,845	69.9	124,600	21.8	12.3	593	24.3	76.4	17.3	5.4
08 077	Mesa..........................	82.0	6.5	58,652	71.6	206,100	24.9	10.2	821	32.6	79.5	21.3	5.8
08 083	Montezuma................	82.1	7.2	11,040	69.5	175,200	27.5	11.7	652	31.9	75.6	21.4	5.9
08 085	Montrose....................	83.3	8.2	16,977	71.5	197,700	27.9	11.8	812	29.6	73.7	21.5	6.0
08 087	Morgan	79.5	6.9	10,467	62.8	136,900	24.6	12.9	679	27.8	76.2	17.4	6.5
08 101	Pueblo	82.2	4.4	62,260	65.5	136,400	24.6	12.1	722	34.0	79.8	20.3	8.2
08 107	Routt.........................	81.5	6.0	9,705	72.7	387,400	29.3	12.0	1,145	28.4	67.0	16.1	2.3
08 117	Summit......................	78.4	12.4	12,103	65.4	442,800	29.7	11.6	1,117	28.3	61.0	16.5	3.3
08 119	Teller.........................	89.8	5.9	9,493	81.5	229,100	24.5	10.0	867	37.6	74.8	32.2	2.3
08 123	Weld..........................	81.5	8.4	90,830	69.2	191,600	24.6	11.1	835	32.6	78.6	26.4	4.4
09 000	**Connecticut**..............	87.9	4.0	1,355,973	67.6	278,600	26.2	17.1	1,036	32.2	78.9	24.8	9.1
09 001	Fairfield......................	88.5	3.4	331,766	68.6	429,400	28.2	18.3	1,272	33.1	73.9	28.0	8.6
09 003	Hartford.....................	87.2	3.6	348,446	65.1	242,200	24.8	16.3	952	31.5	80.3	22.1	10.8
09 005	Litchfield...................	91.1	3.2	75,801	78.1	264,100	27.0	17.2	925	30.2	83.2	26.6	5.1
09 007	Middlesex..................	89.9	4.9	65,962	75.6	293,100	25.7	16.7	1,026	28.4	82.8	25.0	4.5
09 009	New Haven.................	88.0	3.4	328,434	63.7	255,600	27.0	18.5	1,042	34.0	79.5	24.2	11.5
09 011	New London	85.6	6.3	106,959	67.6	252,600	24.8	15.0	974	30.2	79.2	22.6	7.6
09 013	Tolland	86.2	8.7	54,537	74.9	253,300	23.9	14.2	1,015	30.9	81.7	25.9	2.7
09 015	Windham	87.6	5.4	44,068	70.8	212,500	26.0	17.4	848	30.3	83.6	26.6	7.0
10 000	**Delaware**	86.1	4.6	334,228	71.7	235,900	24.2	11.2	980	31.1	80.9	25.1	6.4
10 001	Kent	86.5	5.7	57,023	71.9	202,500	24.7	11.7	962	33.2	83.9	25.7	6.3
10 003	New Castle.................	85.1	4.7	201,107	69.0	245,300	23.6	10.8	995	30.4	79.8	25.1	7.3
10 005	Sussex........................	88.6	3.4	76,098	78.8	235,900	26.0	11.7	924	31.5	81.4	24.8	4.3
11 000	**District of Columbia**...	79.7	8.3	261,567	41.6	436,000	24.1	10.3	1,236	29.7	34.0	29.8	37.2
11 001	District of Columbia.....	79.7	8.3	261,567	41.6	436,000	24.1	10.3	1,236	29.7	34.0	29.8	37.2
12 000	**Florida**	83.6	5.6	7,120,273	66.9	154,900	28.4	13.9	971	35.3	79.6	25.8	7.2
12 001	Alachua	74.7	9.8	94,455	54.0	168,900	23.7	11.5	877	38.8	72.4	20.0	8.4
12 003	Baker.........................	86.9	7.6	8,596	77.7	116,000	22.8	12.1	708	36.0	82.3	29.9	4.5
12 005	Bay............................	78.6	7.5	68,622	61.5	158,400	25.7	12.2	926	32.0	83.6	21.8	6.3
12 007	Bradford	85.0	9.8	8,828	74.7	105,500	24.0	13.0	591	33.0	78.8	27.7	8.9
12 009	Brevard......................	84.7	5.1	219,293	73.8	135,700	26.0	12.6	883	32.6	82.6	24.2	4.8
12 011	Broward.....................	82.9	4.8	664,337	65.4	170,800	30.7	17.6	1,145	36.1	79.5	27.3	7.8
12 015	Charlotte	84.1	7.7	70,035	78.4	138,300	31.1	13.5	904	31.1	79.9	23.0	5.7
12 017	Citrus........................	88.8	5.0	59,783	82.2	114,200	25.6	12.5	775	34.5	83.8	25.7	4.9
12 019	Clay...........................	85.3	6.7	66,626	75.3	156,500	24.1	10.0	1,008	29.9	83.9	31.2	4.0
12 021	Collier	85.5	5.3	121,788	73.9	245,300	31.7	14.0	974	33.3	74.2	24.1	5.9
12 023	Columbia	79.0	9.4	23,472	70.5	109,900	27.2	11.1	751	28.8	83.5	21.7	5.7
12 027	DeSoto	81.1	8.1	10,595	71.9	88,700	26.9	11.8	703	32.7	62.4	26.2	7.1
12 031	Duval.........................	81.3	5.4	329,194	61.6	146,700	26.5	12.8	919	33.5	80.7	23.2	8.1
12 033	Escambia	80.9	8.6	110,981	63.9	125,700	25.1	11.9	859	32.6	76.8	21.7	7.8
12 035	Flagler.......................	88.1	6.3	35,363	78.7	162,500	30.2	13.3	993	32.1	83.3	26.7	4.1
12 039	Gadsden.....................	91.7	4.2	16,847	72.7	106,300	25.3	11.9	674	37.9	78.9	28.5	12.5
12 049	Hardee.......................	86.9	6.2	7,687	73.2	84,400	30.7	12.6	633	31.0	61.4	24.9	7.8

[1]10.0 represents 10 percent or less; 50.0 represents 50 percent or higher.

Table C-2. Counties — Where: Migration, Housing, and Transportation, 2010–2012—*Continued*

STATE and county code	STATE or county	Percent who lived in the same house one year ago	Percent who did not live in the same county one year ago	Total occupied housing units	Percent owner-occupied housing units	Median value of owner-occupied housing units (dollars)	Median selected monthly owner costs as a percentage of household income — With a mortgage	Without a mortgage[1]	Median gross rent (dollars)	Median gross rent as a percentage of household income[1]	Percent of workers who drove alone to work	Mean travel time to work (minutes)	Percent of occupied housing units with no vehicle available
ACS table number:		C07204	C07204	B25003	B25003	B25077	B25092	B25092	B25064	B25071	C08301	B08013/ B08012	C25045
Column number:		1	2	3	4	5	6	7	8	9	10	11	12
	Florida—Cont.												
12 051	Hendry..................	82.8	7.1	10,809	70.0	73,900	25.8	12.9	748	35.2	63.6	26.4	5.5
12 053	Hernando.............	86.2	7.1	70,046	80.1	113,100	28.5	13.0	863	36.6	83.2	30.2	5.6
12 055	Highlands	85.5	5.8	39,466	77.3	92,400	26.9	13.0	734	34.9	77.4	21.5	7.1
12 057	Hillsborough.........	82.2	5.2	467,397	59.8	154,900	26.2	13.0	925	34.2	79.5	25.7	7.1
12 061	Indian River..........	86.0	5.9	57,183	75.6	152,400	26.8	13.8	819	36.8	83.0	21.6	5.7
12 063	Jackson.................	86.6	7.7	15,148	76.6	87,800	22.5	14.0	593	31.2	86.6	23.2	6.2
12 069	Lake......................	84.8	6.3	114,640	75.2	138,900	26.9	14.0	979	36.1	80.7	27.6	5.1
12 071	Lee	80.1	7.0	238,476	70.1	137,300	27.8	14.0	909	33.4	76.6	27.2	5.3
12 073	Leon	72.2	9.6	109,003	54.4	184,000	24.2	11.5	925	38.8	81.9	20.1	7.0
12 075	Levy	84.0	8.2	16,180	79.5	97,700	25.5	12.4	649	35.7	76.6	28.8	7.3
12 081	Manatee................	82.5	7.2	131,255	70.5	159,600	28.0	13.7	892	33.7	79.4	23.4	5.4
12 083	Marion..................	85.1	6.0	132,975	76.1	114,800	28.4	13.2	807	35.9	79.3	24.6	6.4
12 085	Martin...................	85.7	7.1	59,741	75.5	188,100	29.2	13.4	907	36.2	78.9	23.9	5.2
12 086	Miami-Dade...........	86.8	2.2	822,746	55.7	188,400	33.7	16.4	1,063	39.4	76.8	29.2	11.5
12 087	Monroe.................	84.1	8.7	28,341	60.7	380,000	35.7	14.4	1,387	39.6	66.2	18.9	7.8
12 089	Nassau..................	87.3	5.9	27,937	78.8	181,800	26.7	11.0	938	28.2	79.0	28.8	3.0
12 091	Okaloosa	80.2	8.6	72,695	65.5	179,900	25.4	11.0	988	31.8	82.9	22.9	4.7
12 093	Okeechobee	89.0	5.0	13,413	71.6	101,400	30.0	13.0	716	32.7	74.2	23.4	4.8
12 095	Orange..................	79.4	6.8	414,460	57.3	161,000	28.7	13.7	996	36.6	80.3	26.1	6.3
12 097	Osceola.................	85.4	5.9	90,945	62.3	119,100	31.4	14.5	988	36.2	79.9	30.3	6.7
12 099	Palm Beach	84.7	4.5	520,971	71.0	190,500	30.5	16.3	1,130	36.1	79.3	24.4	6.5
12 101	Pasco....................	86.1	5.7	181,324	76.8	115,600	27.7	13.2	897	34.6	81.0	29.4	5.5
12 103	Pinellas	84.0	5.1	399,785	66.2	147,800	28.0	15.6	928	33.8	80.7	23.2	9.4
12 105	Polk......................	83.2	4.9	220,874	69.6	109,000	26.2	13.1	854	34.0	82.0	26.0	7.0
12 107	Putnam.................	87.8	4.7	28,634	75.3	90,000	27.3	11.6	644	34.3	83.9	27.6	7.4
12 109	St. Johns...............	82.8	8.1	75,762	75.3	237,100	27.1	12.4	1,078	30.2	82.0	25.1	4.4
12 111	St. Lucie...............	82.7	7.2	106,641	73.8	118,200	30.5	14.4	956	39.1	79.9	27.7	6.1
12 113	Santa Rosa............	82.2	9.5	57,180	73.9	162,200	24.5	11.4	976	29.9	83.7	26.8	3.0
12 115	Sarasota................	83.6	6.6	169,819	74.2	168,700	28.9	14.0	987	32.7	82.4	22.1	6.2
12 117	Seminole...............	86.6	6.2	145,481	70.5	177,200	27.0	12.1	1,025	33.2	84.9	26.3	4.0
12 119	Sumter..................	86.3	8.6	43,178	90.6	187,600	26.1	12.7	747	27.6	72.9	24.4	4.1
12 121	Suwannee..............	88.7	7.5	15,697	70.2	94,800	24.7	11.2	671	33.5	77.8	27.2	8.0
12 123	Taylor...................	86.3	7.7	7,776	76.7	88,600	23.8	11.4	616	35.2	...	20.1	8.1
12 127	Volusia..................	85.5	6.4	193,177	72.4	137,200	28.6	14.0	891	35.7	82.5	25.3	7.4
12 129	Wakulla.................	77.7	14.2	10,577	77.7	133,200	24.0	10.8	886	39.5	85.1	31.4	3.2
12 131	Walton..................	84.0	8.9	22,138	72.3	157,100	29.1	12.2	970	37.6	82.2	25.0	5.1
12 133	Washington	87.3	9.2	8,310	76.2	86,000	24.8	12.5	546	29.5	79.0	28.5	6.7
13 000	**Georgia**	83.7	7.5	3,504,888	64.9	149,300	24.3	12.1	849	32.2	79.4	27.0	6.8
13 009	Baldwin.................	79.0	7.7	16,159	56.1	101,000	24.6	12.4	691	42.2	81.6	20.1	9.2
13 013	Barrow..................	86.6	7.1	23,190	78.9	127,100	24.3	12.2	890	32.1	84.2	34.9	3.6
13 015	Bartow..................	81.7	5.7	34,714	67.2	123,400	24.9	11.4	769	31.5	84.3	29.1	4.7
13 021	Bibb......................	82.7	5.9	56,393	55.1	124,400	24.1	12.6	721	38.0	84.4	20.7	11.6
13 029	Bryan....................	81.7	9.4	10,956	69.7	188,400	23.5	10.6	937	31.0	83.3	29.8	3.2
13 031	Bulloch.................	78.4	10.7	25,786	51.1	131,700	23.3	10.8	719	40.2	78.1	20.5	5.5
13 033	Burke....................	91.8	4.3	7,892	72.2	79,800	23.9	14.9	555	32.0	86.7	25.9	9.5
13 035	Butts.....................	85.8	11.5	7,785	73.6	121,100	24.5	10.9	731	29.8	80.6	29.4	3.7
13 039	Camden.................	81.3	9.9	18,998	63.7	156,500	26.5	10.0	884	27.3	84.9	22.5	4.0
13 045	Carroll	81.3	8.0	39,392	66.7	116,900	23.4	10.9	758	35.7	82.8	28.4	5.4
13 047	Catoosa................	87.0	7.7	23,630	76.0	127,300	21.7	10.8	677	29.0	87.4	21.6	4.1
13 051	Chatham	85.6	6.5	102,502	57.2	171,100	25.8	13.3	922	33.6	80.7	21.3	8.2
13 055	Chattooga.............	85.8	3.6	9,510	70.2	67,600	24.0	13.4	606	28.9	88.3	23.0	6.6
13 057	Cherokee...............	86.6	6.6	76,576	79.7	187,400	23.6	10.7	970	29.5	81.3	31.9	2.5
13 059	Clarke...................	76.3	12.5	40,529	46.0	157,000	23.5	11.0	756	38.5	72.6	18.9	7.8
13 063	Clayton.................	79.3	10.2	85,801	55.0	95,300	26.9	12.6	858	37.0	77.9	29.9	7.9
13 067	Cobb.....................	81.0	9.0	260,646	65.9	194,400	23.1	10.0	956	30.4	79.6	29.5	4.2
13 069	Coffee...................	87.6	4.6	14,748	65.8	79,800	25.1	10.6	605	30.5	82.4	19.4	6.9
13 071	Colquitt................	82.2	6.6	15,874	68.1	78,700	25.3	12.6	584	33.4	74.6	20.3	9.0
13 073	Columbia...............	86.5	8.3	45,271	77.1	167,900	22.3	10.0	1,007	26.8	86.4	24.3	2.4
13 077	Coweta..................	83.6	9.4	46,706	72.3	175,800	24.3	11.3	901	29.2	81.8	30.4	4.4
13 081	Crisp.....................	91.4	2.5	8,792	61.5	89,900	23.6	12.2	542	39.8	...	18.5	9.0
13 085	Dawson.................	85.7	5.6	8,138	74.1	173,200	28.3	11.4	1,088	32.6	79.6	32.9	4.2
13 087	Decatur.................	89.0	6.2	10,458	63.8	93,900	23.6	13.8	623	43.0	80.5	23.1	10.5
13 089	DeKalb..................	81.9	7.8	260,968	56.5	167,100	25.8	12.8	959	33.8	71.7	30.8	9.7
13 091	Dodge...................	89.2	5.3	8,097	68.4	70,800	23.1	12.6	571	27.5	85.9	22.9	8.2
13 095	Dougherty	83.2	5.8	36,084	46.4	100,500	24.7	13.7	690	36.6	76.5	17.6	12.2
13 097	Douglas.................	83.0	9.1	46,335	69.1	131,400	25.4	10.6	901	31.5	80.4	31.8	3.8
13 103	Effingham..............	86.6	4.4	17,871	76.6	155,000	22.0	10.4	898	29.4	84.6	29.8	3.7
13 105	Elbert....................	93.1	3.6	7,784	66.5	83,000	23.3	12.8	604	28.9	85.5	21.5	9.0
13 107	Emanuel................	84.2	5.1	7,863	66.3	68,700	25.7	16.0	599	31.5	76.6	25.2	10.3
13 111	Fannin	86.6	4.7	9,683	80.2	155,300	28.2	12.5	599	31.3	78.3	25.7	5.1
13 113	Fayette..................	89.2	6.9	37,817	83.5	224,900	23.5	10.0	1,072	27.1	81.6	30.4	2.6
13 115	Floyd.....................	85.6	4.8	34,961	64.8	109,800	23.7	12.6	701	32.0	81.4	21.8	7.9
13 117	Forsyth..................	90.7	4.8	54,017	85.4	255,300	23.4	10.1	1,122	33.1	81.5	30.0	2.8
13 119	Franklin.................	92.7	3.3	8,766	70.1	122,900	24.0	13.9	574	28.3	80.3	24.3	9.9
13 121	Fulton...................	79.8	8.6	365,494	53.2	235,600	24.2	12.9	954	31.2	72.5	26.7	11.7
13 123	Gilmer...................	81.2	8.9	10,768	74.2	145,800	26.4	11.9	768	31.7	82.1	28.1	5.3

[1]10.0 represents 10 percent or less; 50.0 represents 50 percent or higher.

Table C-2. Counties — Where: Migration, Housing, and Transportation, 2010–2012—*Continued*

STATE and county code	STATE or county	Percent who lived in the same house one year ago	Percent who did not live in the same county one year ago	Total occupied housing units	Percent owner-occupied housing units	Median value of owner-occupied housing units (dollars)	Median selected monthly owner costs as a percentage of household income - With a mortgage	Median selected monthly owner costs as a percentage of household income - Without a mortgage[1]	Median gross rent (dollars)	Median gross rent as a percentage of household income[1]	Percent of workers who drove alone to work	Mean travel time to work (minutes)	Percent of occupied housing units with no vehicle available
ACS table number:		C07204	C07204	B25003	B25003	B25077	B25092	B25092	B25064	B25071	C08301	B08013/B08012	C25045
Column number:		1	2	3	4	5	6	7	8	9	10	11	12
	Georgia—Cont.												
13 127	Glynn	80.7	5.7	31,392	63.0	157,400	25.6	11.2	814	29.1	81.7	19.0	5.2
13 129	Gordon	85.5	4.1	19,128	66.8	116,700	24.6	12.4	645	30.3	80.7	22.7	6.2
13 131	Grady	91.2	5.1	9,614	61.8	113,500	24.9	14.5	702	40.0	83.1	25.4	11.4
13 135	Gwinnett	85.7	5.5	267,526	67.6	169,000	24.8	11.2	976	32.9	79.6	31.4	2.8
13 137	Habersham	91.2	5.5	14,317	76.4	133,300	25.6	12.7	635	28.8	84.5	23.7	4.6
13 139	Hall	86.1	5.3	60,520	68.1	164,100	26.0	10.9	826	30.5	79.1	25.4	6.5
13 143	Haralson	84.0	6.4	10,711	70.5	102,700	23.1	15.9	696	28.3	82.4	28.0	5.3
13 145	Harris	90.7	6.3	11,570	87.3	215,100	21.8	12.0	900	32.2	86.3	27.7	1.5
13 147	Hart	85.4	7.8	10,508	73.6	108,900	27.2	12.4	561	35.4	83.5	24.4	6.2
13 151	Henry	85.5	7.7	69,233	73.7	145,400	24.7	11.6	1054	30.6	82.5	33.2	2.7
13 153	Houston	84.7	7.1	52,077	67.4	133,900	19.8	10.1	813	28.2	85.3	20.6	4.4
13 157	Jackson	88.0	6.1	21,146	77.3	158,600	25.5	12.0	744	30.2	84.1	30.0	4.7
13 169	Jones	83.8	6.9	10,494	76.1	137,500	23.0	11.3	821	30.8	89.7	27.5	4.6
13 175	Laurens	87.4	3.0	17,667	65.9	85,900	22.5	12.2	598	30.7	87.2	24.0	8.1
13 177	Lee	84.1	9.9	9,873	73.5	163,900	21.1	13.2	962	31.1	84.1	22.1	3.0
13 179	Liberty	75.6	14.6	22,967	52.7	129,200	25.2	10.4	928	29.9	84.2	19.0	4.7
13 185	Lowndes	77.1	9.2	39,481	53.0	137,200	24.4	10.8	780	33.1	82.5	18.6	6.9
13 187	Lumpkin	81.6	11.2	10,406	70.2	160,800	27.9	11.0	860	37.2	79.9	30.8	3.5
13 189	McDuffie	89.3	5.3	8,403	67.4	108,900	28.2	12.5	623	34.4	81.9	25.7	9.6
13 195	Madison	92.5	3.1	9,515	74.6	120,900	23.0	10.8	649	31.0	83.0	25.6	4.8
13 199	Meriwether	84.0	9.6	7,792	70.8	93,100	27.1	15.8	677	31.1	80.6	31.1	6.6
13 205	Mitchell	88.1	6.0	8,291	61.4	79,600	25.3	14.7	593	33.6	75.5	20.2	13.4
13 207	Monroe	86.4	10.4	9,551	75.5	144,300	23.2	11.7	712	36.9	87.7	27.0	4.8
13 213	Murray	87.5	4.5	13,923	70.2	88,200	25.1	12.1	641	31.2	86.8	25.1	2.9
13 215	Muscogee	75.2	12.7	71,509	52.5	131,000	23.7	11.6	791	31.4	76.9	19.1	10.2
13 217	Newton	81.5	8.4	34,208	73.8	124,800	26.9	11.5	921	40.2	81.8	31.9	4.3
13 219	Oconee	91.5	6.1	11,268	78.1	239,000	21.3	10.0	880	26.6	85.4	24.4	3.0
13 223	Paulding	86.3	7.7	47,751	80.1	131,800	23.6	11.4	975	30.2	80.9	36.7	2.7
13 225	Peach	86.0	8.3	9,700	64.3	122,500	22.9	10.0	632	29.1	80.6	21.9	10.0
13 227	Pickens	87.7	4.5	10,993	78.4	162,500	26.6	11.4	764	34.2	76.8	29.3	2.5
13 233	Polk	85.8	3.6	14,711	70.8	104,900	26.5	14.8	639	32.0	81.8	26.3	8.1
13 237	Putnam	87.9	8.0	8,814	79.2	117,000	24.9	12.4	649	30.4	76.0	29.5	4.7
13 245	Richmond	78.8	9.7	71,826	54.6	103,100	23.4	12.6	769	32.9	81.8	20.2	9.1
13 247	Rockdale	81.7	10.0	29,104	70.4	149,000	24.4	10.0	928	31.9	76.1	33.2	4.4
13 255	Spalding	81.5	7.9	22,519	60.2	116,300	25.2	13.6	771	36.2	78.7	28.8	8.1
13 257	Stephens	89.8	4.4	9,112	79.3	97,400	24.1	12.9	597	27.8	77.8	21.6	5.4
13 261	Sumter	86.3	6.8	11,384	60.0	91,600	23.3	13.3	575	28.1	79.1	18.9	12.4
13 267	Tattnall	80.4	13.8	8,090	69.3	89,700	27.9	13.1	523	23.5	78.9	23.0	9.1
13 275	Thomas	90.5	4.2	17,256	54.0	123,700	25.8	14.3	665	37.3	81.1	20.9	12.1
13 277	Tift	87.8	6.0	13,492	63.2	118,500	22.7	12.5	616	30.7	79.3	18.1	8.2
13 279	Toombs	93.8	2.0	10,368	61.1	90,700	21.7	11.3	541	36.2	86.1	21.5	8.9
13 285	Troup	81.7	7.6	24,738	62.6	120,500	24.2	12.2	730	34.7	84.8	20.7	10.8
13 291	Union	91.3	3.5	8,926	77.9	169,500	24.4	12.8	591	31.3	...	27.2	6.7
13 293	Upson	82.7	4.3	9,992	65.1	87,300	24.0	13.8	677	33.4	79.5	22.0	9.6
13 295	Walker	83.1	6.7	26,323	71.7	104,100	22.5	11.9	631	31.6	85.6	26.2	5.8
13 297	Walton	86.9	6.9	29,261	75.7	157,400	24.4	12.8	792	35.7	81.6	31.5	5.0
13 299	Ware	78.0	8.3	13,271	66.0	91,800	24.1	12.5	642	32.8	83.5	18.6	10.8
13 303	Washington	92.0	5.0	6,809	74.3	80,300	24.6	12.7	484	36.4	85.7	21.7	13.7
13 305	Wayne	83.7	6.2	10,133	72.7	80,200	23.4	12.9	675	25.0	83.6	24.5	8.0
13 311	White	92.5	5.4	11,402	74.3	179,900	27.4	13.6	763	36.3	81.3	32.1	5.7
13 313	Whitfield	84.7	4.6	34,409	64.6	120,600	24.4	10.7	690	29.7	82.6	20.1	5.5
13 321	Worth	87.5	7.5	8,089	79.0	68,600	24.6	13.0	660	29.9	84.9	27.2	7.8
15 000	**Hawaii**	85.0	4.6	447,566	57.3	503,100	29.7	10.0	1353	33.4	66.4	25.7	8.8
15 001	Hawaii	86.6	3.9	63,897	65.1	304,900	31.0	10.0	1002	34.2	71.5	25.2	4.8
15 003	Honolulu	84.8	4.9	308,906	55.3	556,400	28.9	10.3	1443	33.5	64.4	26.8	10.5
15 007	Kauai	88.3	3.2	22,565	62.2	477,400	32.8	11.7	1297	31.6	74.9	21.6	3.6
15 009	Maui	83.2	4.5	52,158	57.4	532,100	33.5	10.0	1232	33.0	70.1	20.7	5.7
16 000	**Idaho**	82.5	7.2	580,280	69.0	160,000	24.3	10.2	710	30.3	77.5	20.1	4.5
16 001	Ada	82.9	6.6	151,822	66.3	176,900	23.7	10.0	800	30.4	79.0	20.0	4.8
16 005	Bannock	79.6	8.0	30,098	67.9	146,400	23.4	10.5	601	31.3	78.6	19.5	6.0
16 011	Bingham	88.0	5.7	14,885	75.3	135,300	21.6	10.0	601	21.9	78.8	20.9	4.9
16 013	Blaine	84.5	4.9	9,290	71.1	362,200	30.8	13.2	899	27.3	72.0	16.7	2.5
16 017	Bonner	86.0	4.7	17,643	71.0	219,300	29.4	11.3	731	29.2	76.0	23.6	5.1
16 019	Bonneville	84.5	5.4	36,010	74.0	154,200	21.7	10.0	675	30.6	78.7	19.0	4.8
16 027	Canyon	80.6	7.9	63,130	69.3	119,900	25.8	11.3	714	31.9	80.1	23.2	5.1
16 031	Cassia	80.1	8.8	7,637	69.5	129,000	23.8	10.2	508	26.6	78.8	17.1	5.0
16 039	Elmore	79.6	8.6	9,847	63.1	136,800	26.0	10.8	701	26.4	76.4	17.9	2.1
16 051	Jefferson	90.8	4.2	8,143	82.9	156,200	24.1	10.6	631	22.7	76.6	22.8	2.3
16 053	Jerome	86.5	5.6	7,856	62.9	139,700	24.9	11.9	667	29.2	82.9	19.3	3.7
16 055	Kootenai	81.5	6.8	55,713	69.3	186,900	25.7	10.5	795	33.1	80.8	20.7	3.6
16 057	Latah	71.3	13.0	14,871	53.8	188,500	21.5	10.0	653	35.4	65.7	18.0	5.1
16 065	Madison	59.8	19.4	9,982	51.3	170,400	23.2	10.0	626	41.4	61.3	16.8	2.5
16 067	Minidoka	87.7	6.1	6,989	71.1	107,900	19.2	10.0	555	26.4	78.6	16.2	3.4
16 069	Nez Perce	85.8	6.6	16,050	69.2	167,300	22.4	11.4	642	26.7	80.3	17.0	6.4

[1]10.0 represents 10 percent or less; 50.0 represents 50 percent or higher.

Table C-2. Counties — Where: Migration, Housing, and Transportation, 2010–2012—*Continued*

STATE and county code	STATE or county	Percent who lived in the same house one year ago	Percent who did not live in the same county one year ago	Total occupied housing units	Percent owner-occupied housing units	Median value of owner-occupied housing units (dollars)	Median selected monthly owner costs as a percentage of household income With a mortgage	Without a mortgage[1]	Median gross rent (dollars)	Median gross rent as a percentage of household income[1]	Percent of workers who drove alone to work	Mean travel time to work (minutes)	Percent of occupied housing units with no vehicle available
	ACS table number:	C07204	C07204	B25003	B25003	B25077	B25092	B25092	B25064	B25071	C08301	B08013/ B08012	C25045
	Column number:	1	2	3	4	5	6	7	8	9	10	11	12
	Idaho—Cont.												
16 075	Payette	86.1	5.3	8,172	75.5	125,800	27.5	12.4	643	30.7	78.9	18.4	3.8
16 083	Twin Falls	79.1	8.1	28,129	65.4	149,700	25.1	10.0	686	28.0	80.7	16.8	4.3
17 000	**Illinois**	86.8	4.1	4,759,131	67.3	179,900	25.1	13.8	877	31.2	73.5	28.0	10.8
17 001	Adams	88.2	3.4	26,517	72.0	103,700	20.9	10.5	615	29.5	83.4	16.4	6.3
17 007	Boone	89.6	4.2	17,755	85.6	152,400	25.0	12.9	678	32.0	82.2	29.2	3.9
17 011	Bureau	91.1	3.9	14,181	75.3	102,500	21.5	12.9	623	27.3	80.8	20.9	5.4
17 019	Champaign	72.9	8.4	79,246	53.8	150,800	21.2	11.0	782	36.0	68.4	17.4	11.4
17 021	Christian	89.4	5.0	14,333	71.4	84,300	20.6	11.3	613	27.7	81.8	24.7	5.9
17 027	Clinton	90.6	5.3	14,048	82.1	131,000	20.4	12.7	686	22.9	84.1	25.4	3.8
17 029	Coles	76.9	9.9	20,932	63.6	90,100	21.5	12.6	613	36.3	74.7	17.7	8.0
17 031	Cook	86.4	2.7	1,927,303	57.9	227,400	28.4	16.0	949	32.1	62.4	31.6	17.9
17 037	DeKalb	78.8	9.1	37,386	61.3	171,700	25.9	16.2	827	37.8	78.6	25.7	7.5
17 043	DuPage	87.9	5.2	334,764	74.5	283,100	26.1	14.6	1,071	29.5	78.2	28.9	4.1
17 049	Effingham	90.1	3.0	13,761	78.3	114,600	20.4	11.3	548	20.7	83.7	18.2	5.0
17 051	Fayette	87.9	7.2	8,156	80.8	80,200	19.8	10.3	512	24.2	79.2	22.4	5.1
17 055	Franklin	87.3	4.0	16,112	76.9	66,300	20.4	12.4	565	27.6	86.4	23.2	7.5
17 057	Fulton	88.1	4.5	14,557	75.7	80,000	20.2	13.1	586	30.6	83.3	28.3	5.6
17 063	Grundy	88.7	5.2	18,051	74.4	177,900	25.7	13.1	887	31.7	85.3	28.6	4.3
17 073	Henry	90.2	4.3	20,143	78.0	107,100	19.8	13.1	636	25.6	82.3	23.1	5.2
17 075	Iroquois	89.2	3.8	11,889	75.8	98,400	22.0	12.2	632	29.6	78.8	24.5	5.2
17 077	Jackson	75.2	11.1	23,189	53.5	97,500	21.4	12.4	651	42.3	77.9	17.5	12.5
17 081	Jefferson	83.7	6.5	15,185	71.9	83,100	19.9	12.5	577	26.6	84.4	19.9	8.3
17 083	Jersey	92.0	2.6	8,742	82.1	117,900	21.1	11.0	671	25.7	86.6	29.3	4.7
17 085	Jo Daviess	90.4	4.7	9,532	77.9	140,000	23.6	13.8	656	23.1	81.4	21.8	5.9
17 089	Kane	86.9	5.0	169,535	75.3	219,900	26.8	15.1	983	33.4	80.1	29.2	4.8
17 091	Kankakee	87.4	3.9	41,515	68.5	149,500	24.5	13.8	771	31.5	81.1	23.8	6.8
17 093	Kendall	89.8	5.3	38,486	84.7	209,300	27.4	15.2	1,136	28.2	83.8	32.8	2.0
17 095	Knox	88.0	5.7	21,592	66.8	79,400	19.8	12.6	589	30.0	82.3	18.9	9.0
17 097	Lake	87.7	4.9	240,273	76.3	252,100	26.6	15.3	1,001	30.9	77.0	29.5	5.0
17 099	LaSalle	89.1	3.5	44,023	75.1	124,000	23.1	12.9	678	28.5	84.5	22.2	6.4
17 103	Lee	85.8	6.2	13,591	72.8	112,200	22.0	11.3	659	25.5	85.2	22.3	5.4
17 105	Livingston	85.5	8.2	14,351	74.1	110,800	21.6	12.3	631	24.4	83.7	22.2	6.0
17 107	Logan	78.7	14.2	10,338	70.5	97,800	19.0	11.9	579	30.1	82.5	20.5	6.1
17 109	McDonough	71.1	14.9	12,697	61.5	86,300	19.2	12.1	661	42.1	77.9	16.0	7.8
17 111	McHenry	91.2	4.2	108,995	82.8	218,400	27.0	15.6	1,018	32.7	82.5	33.8	3.1
17 113	McLean	80.2	8.0	63,314	66.8	156,800	20.1	11.7	737	28.3	79.9	17.8	6.4
17 115	Macon	84.0	4.9	45,580	68.5	92,700	19.5	12.0	661	29.3	85.7	18.8	9.5
17 117	Macoupin	88.3	4.1	19,647	75.4	96,300	20.9	11.6	615	26.8	82.7	27.0	4.7
17 119	Madison	86.8	4.6	107,047	73.1	124,600	21.8	12.2	761	32.4	85.2	24.3	6.1
17 121	Marion	85.6	4.0	15,748	75.2	70,700	20.7	13.3	615	33.0	81.7	21.7	7.7
17 133	Monroe	89.4	6.8	12,443	84.6	201,200	22.7	13.8	793	27.1	86.3	30.5	2.9
17 135	Montgomery	82.2	12.1	10,750	77.7	79,200	20.3	11.7	617	27.8	82.0	24.0	5.5
17 137	Morgan	82.4	8.2	13,738	69.4	91,300	19.5	10.3	605	28.4	79.8	18.5	6.0
17 141	Ogle	90.9	3.3	20,812	75.6	144,900	22.1	14.4	682	23.6	84.4	22.8	4.4
17 143	Peoria	83.9	5.3	76,007	66.0	124,400	20.9	11.7	681	29.0	84.1	19.5	9.6
17 145	Perry	87.3	7.7	8,030	77.5	78,400	21.3	12.6	503	28.4	83.8	28.1	4.7
17 157	Randolph	90.3	5.1	12,072	76.6	92,100	19.5	11.4	648	27.5	83.6	23.1	5.3
17 161	Rock Island	86.2	4.2	60,758	70.6	113,200	21.8	12.2	648	29.0	82.0	19.1	9.5
17 163	St. Clair	87.5	4.5	101,778	66.8	124,000	22.3	13.1	788	32.5	81.7	23.6	8.7
17 165	Saline	84.8	5.4	10,170	72.4	73,900	21.2	13.2	609	30.9	86.2	22.8	9.2
17 167	Sangamon	83.6	5.1	82,927	69.6	125,600	19.8	11.4	714	31.0	81.4	19.1	7.4
17 173	Shelby	90.2	5.8	8,915	81.3	85,900	21.3	11.4	642	23.5	83.5	22.8	6.1
17 177	Stephenson	87.3	4.4	19,420	72.9	102,100	22.1	13.5	595	32.9	80.7	20.3	9.9
17 179	Tazewell	88.3	4.2	54,302	76.1	134,000	21.1	11.6	653	27.2	86.3	20.4	5.0
17 183	Vermilion	87.8	3.3	31,486	70.2	77,600	20.8	11.8	628	29.7	82.8	20.6	9.7
17 195	Whiteside	92.1	2.2	22,878	76.8	100,400	21.3	13.2	623	30.3	81.7	19.6	6.4
17 197	Will	91.5	3.6	222,401	82.4	216,200	26.8	14.4	991	31.2	82.6	32.8	4.1
17 199	Williamson	86.9	5.5	26,383	71.4	95,500	19.9	12.5	619	28.8	84.8	20.8	7.0
17 201	Winnebago	86.9	3.2	112,594	67.2	124,600	23.6	13.7	735	31.2	84.5	21.7	8.1
17 203	Woodford	87.6	6.9	14,276	81.5	160,000	20.4	10.6	643	25.9	83.1	23.0	3.4
18 000	**Indiana**	85.0	5.5	2,474,926	69.9	122,600	20.9	11.0	717	30.4	83.3	23.4	6.8
18 001	Adams	90.9	2.2	12,097	78.3	111,400	20.9	10.0	555	25.5	77.3	21.2	11.9
18 003	Allen	87.4	3.1	137,586	69.6	112,500	19.6	10.0	653	27.0	86.0	20.2	7.3
18 005	Bartholomew	83.4	6.7	29,929	70.6	138,900	20.2	11.8	792	27.3	84.3	19.6	5.0
18 011	Boone	89.2	5.3	21,799	76.1	183,000	20.0	12.3	798	29.5	86.0	24.8	4.7
18 015	Carroll	88.2	7.3	7,990	79.6	105,900	20.6	10.6	645	28.2	80.8	25.6	3.2
18 017	Cass	86.1	4.7	14,857	74.9	80,300	21.9	11.0	585	28.6	85.0	19.8	6.9
18 019	Clark	89.5	3.9	42,689	71.0	131,200	21.8	11.3	714	28.9	87.0	24.5	5.9
18 021	Clay	86.5	5.8	9,919	76.8	89,700	19.3	12.4	663	29.0	82.8	26.6	5.3
18 023	Clinton	84.6	5.5	11,724	70.3	95,700	20.2	10.4	703	27.1	77.4	23.0	5.3
18 027	Daviess	89.7	3.1	11,258	76.4	100,900	19.7	10.0	589	24.0	73.5	21.8	11.2

[1]10.0 represents 10 percent or less; 50.0 represents 50 percent or higher.

Table C-2. Counties — Where: Migration, Housing, and Transportation, 2010–2012—*Continued*

STATE and county code	STATE or county	Percent who lived in the same house one year ago	Percent who did not live in the same county one year ago	Total occupied housing units	Percent owner-occupied housing units	Median value of owner-occupied housing units (dollars)	Median selected monthly owner costs as a percentage of household income — With a mortgage	Without a mortgage[1]	Median gross rent (dollars)	Median gross rent as a percentage of household income[1]	Percent of workers who drove alone to work	Mean travel time to work (minutes)	Percent of occupied housing units with no vehicle available
	ACS table number:	C07204	C07204	B25003	B25003	B25077	B25092	B25092	B25064	B25071	C08301	B08013/ B08012	C25045
	Column number:	1	2	3	4	5	6	7	8	9	10	11	12
	Indiana—Cont.												
18 029	Dearborn	89.3	3.7	18,454	78.5	159,200	21.6	11.1	681	31.8	83.2	30.8	5.1
18 031	Decatur	84.7	3.7	9,655	72.9	108,100	22.8	10.7	729	26.3	87.6	22.8	3.9
18 033	DeKalb	86.3	5.5	16,343	77.9	106,500	22.1	10.1	610	26.8	84.5	21.3	5.9
18 035	Delaware	72.5	10.5	46,179	62.6	90,700	19.7	12.1	653	37.5	79.6	19.9	8.3
18 037	Dubois	89.1	3.7	15,854	78.0	131,500	19.7	10.1	621	24.1	85.3	20.0	2.8
18 039	Elkhart	84.0	4.4	69,984	71.2	122,700	21.6	10.6	703	29.8	79.3	19.8	8.4
18 041	Fayette	84.4	3.3	9,466	70.2	79,700	22.5	13.7	615	35.6	83.0	26.1	8.5
18 043	Floyd	86.2	7.0	28,844	71.9	150,600	21.8	11.6	696	29.8	86.9	23.5	7.3
18 047	Franklin	90.0	5.4	8,491	82.7	151,000	22.3	11.9	668	28.6	84.1	30.3	4.1
18 049	Fulton	81.4	7.2	8,248	73.4	93,300	20.7	11.5	613	29.5	82.0	24.2	6.4
18 051	Gibson	87.7	4.9	12,949	78.7	103,400	19.7	10.3	609	27.4	85.5	21.6	4.4
18 053	Grant	85.6	4.7	27,158	71.1	79,200	20.6	11.4	598	28.0	81.1	19.1	6.7
18 055	Greene	88.0	5.1	13,065	78.4	88,600	18.9	12.0	554	28.1	82.9	29.6	4.8
18 057	Hamilton	86.7	7.1	103,033	79.5	213,100	20.3	10.0	915	24.2	85.6	27.0	2.8
18 059	Hancock	88.3	6.8	25,968	80.6	156,200	21.5	10.0	822	29.3	86.4	26.9	3.0
18 061	Harrison	90.9	4.0	14,487	81.9	124,000	21.1	10.0	713	31.1	86.0	30.8	4.7
18 063	Hendricks	89.1	5.8	52,743	82.5	162,200	20.7	11.0	895	27.9	87.9	25.7	2.8
18 065	Henry	84.5	6.5	18,164	73.8	93,200	21.6	11.8	606	28.7	85.6	26.3	7.2
18 067	Howard	84.3	4.9	34,446	70.3	94,800	19.7	10.2	622	35.4	84.6	19.8	9.1
18 069	Huntington	86.4	4.5	14,269	76.7	96,500	20.7	11.8	649	27.6	82.8	20.8	5.4
18 071	Jackson	84.6	4.5	16,374	74.4	117,000	20.5	11.2	684	26.7	84.3	20.7	4.6
18 073	Jasper	88.5	5.8	12,131	77.8	145,800	20.4	10.0	632	26.9	84.9	27.8	5.7
18 075	Jay	89.6	3.0	8,131	77.1	78,600	18.9	13.0	548	26.5	84.3	22.1	5.4
18 077	Jefferson	86.1	5.8	12,664	71.7	112,100	22.4	11.4	660	31.6	82.6	22.7	6.8
18 079	Jennings	87.8	6.0	10,534	77.4	96,700	22.1	12.5	668	26.9	85.0	26.4	2.3
18 081	Johnson	84.8	7.6	52,464	73.3	143,500	19.9	10.3	831	30.8	85.1	26.3	3.7
18 083	Knox	81.2	8.6	14,591	67.2	82,200	19.1	11.6	588	29.8	86.2	20.9	9.1
18 085	Kosciusko	87.0	4.6	29,284	77.4	128,500	19.8	10.3	693	24.7	80.6	21.8	5.1
18 087	LaGrange	90.3	6.2	11,713	79.7	156,300	26.5	11.2	647	25.5	51.8	22.8	25.7
18 089	Lake	88.2	3.5	181,174	69.2	137,700	22.5	11.8	778	32.9	85.7	27.8	8.7
18 091	LaPorte	85.0	6.7	42,715	72.4	122,300	20.8	10.0	692	31.8	86.7	23.2	6.6
18 093	Lawrence	89.7	3.4	18,974	78.1	99,500	21.4	13.1	603	30.9	86.0	25.8	5.0
18 095	Madison	84.7	4.3	49,973	70.1	91,500	20.2	11.9	672	31.8	83.7	25.5	8.6
18 097	Marion	82.7	4.5	358,923	55.6	117,300	21.6	11.9	750	32.6	82.1	22.7	9.3
18 099	Marshall	88.7	4.1	17,788	77.5	124,000	22.1	12.3	645	25.7	80.8	20.5	7.6
18 103	Miami	87.1	7.4	13,160	74.1	85,500	19.6	11.8	606	28.1	83.2	24.2	4.3
18 105	Monroe	68.0	13.9	53,551	55.2	158,400	21.0	10.6	782	41.9	70.4	18.3	8.9
18 107	Montgomery	85.6	5.8	14,667	70.8	105,800	21.1	10.0	661	29.1	81.6	21.2	5.8
18 109	Morgan	85.0	6.0	25,501	77.2	145,500	21.0	10.0	765	27.8	83.6	29.5	3.0
18 113	Noble	83.3	6.0	17,522	76.9	112,600	22.2	10.0	639	26.4	81.4	23.8	5.5
18 119	Owen	87.2	7.1	8,738	77.7	110,200	24.3	12.4	668	30.2	74.2	31.5	4.6
18 127	Porter	88.2	5.8	61,297	77.5	164,700	20.3	10.5	820	28.2	86.7	26.7	4.4
18 129	Posey	89.1	4.3	10,201	82.6	124,000	18.9	10.7	704	27.3	88.6	23.1	3.3
18 133	Putnam	82.6	10.0	12,484	78.8	124,200	23.3	12.1	637	26.3	80.0	29.7	5.5
18 135	Randolph	86.7	5.3	10,497	73.7	77,500	19.8	11.3	596	28.2	83.5	22.4	5.6
18 137	Ripley	90.9	4.0	10,643	77.2	134,100	21.5	12.1	649	24.0	81.8	26.8	5.9
18 141	St. Joseph	83.1	5.4	101,171	68.8	116,500	20.3	10.0	707	30.6	82.3	20.3	6.9
18 143	Scott	85.1	4.6	8,932	69.5	98,900	23.2	12.6	639	32.1	87.6	25.6	6.1
18 145	Shelby	86.9	6.4	17,104	70.5	121,000	22.0	11.9	700	27.5	85.0	24.7	5.6
18 147	Spencer	91.4	4.4	7,945	83.3	117,200	18.9	11.5	572	23.4	85.6	25.9	2.3
18 149	Starke	86.7	6.3	9,087	78.3	101,000	24.6	11.3	672	28.1	81.3	29.0	4.9
18 151	Steuben	84.3	7.0	13,317	79.5	122,200	22.0	11.0	633	26.5	87.0	22.1	3.1
18 153	Sullivan	87.8	8.2	7,728	71.6	76,100	17.0	11.6	644	32.8	86.9	24.4	8.1
18 157	Tippecanoe	71.5	10.1	66,464	54.5	129,700	19.8	10.0	766	36.2	76.5	17.6	7.1
18 163	Vanderburgh	83.5	5.3	74,271	64.4	112,900	20.9	11.9	703	30.6	83.6	19.0	8.5
18 167	Vigo	84.9	5.7	39,326	64.6	94,200	19.1	10.7	651	31.8	85.1	20.2	6.9
18 169	Wabash	84.2	6.1	12,584	74.5	94,400	19.0	10.0	612	30.5	84.7	19.0	7.7
18 173	Warrick	90.8	5.2	22,380	83.1	140,400	21.0	10.1	775	31.2	88.9	22.4	3.4
18 175	Washington	88.6	5.3	10,591	81.3	101,200	23.4	11.9	639	28.9	83.1	30.2	5.7
18 177	Wayne	80.8	6.2	28,230	67.3	91,100	22.2	12.0	614	31.7	83.0	20.2	9.6
18 179	Wells	85.5	5.0	10,888	77.1	109,700	18.3	10.0	592	28.6	86.2	21.9	5.1
18 181	White	86.2	5.9	9,441	74.7	107,200	19.2	11.6	670	26.3	81.9	24.1	3.2
18 183	Whitley	90.9	4.9	13,136	84.0	129,900	22.6	10.0	654	29.3	80.6	24.7	2.7
19 000	**Iowa**	85.0	6.0	1,224,399	72.3	124,300	20.7	11.7	660	28.1	79.9	18.8	5.8
19 011	Benton	92.8	3.1	10,204	81.9	131,900	21.0	10.6	580	23.8	79.4	24.0	3.8
19 013	Black Hawk	82.9	5.4	51,852	67.7	124,000	19.4	10.6	658	31.7	83.0	16.0	6.7
19 015	Boone	84.4	7.5	10,328	76.3	117,300	21.8	13.0	671	25.0	80.5	21.6	4.4
19 017	Bremer	88.7	5.9	9,232	80.0	142,200	19.8	10.3	577	24.2	81.5	18.7	2.8
19 019	Buchanan	91.0	3.5	8,225	78.5	118,500	19.7	10.6	611	24.4	81.4	20.3	6.2
19 021	Buena Vista	80.4	5.6	7,638	71.4	97,600	21.1	10.3	575	23.6	67.7	13.5	6.4
19 027	Carroll	88.6	3.9	8,470	77.6	105,400	19.7	10.0	517	27.7	80.8	13.9	5.6
19 033	Cerro Gordo	86.9	5.2	20,034	71.7	112,100	20.7	12.2	555	28.1	81.1	16.3	7.3
19 045	Clinton	88.1	4.4	19,677	74.2	112,100	20.5	13.0	589	28.0	85.0	19.8	5.8
19 049	Dallas	85.8	8.6	26,221	78.2	175,600	21.5	11.7	841	24.6	86.9	20.8	2.5

[1]10.0 represents 10 percent or less; 50.0 represents 50 percent or higher.

Table C-2. Counties — Where: Migration, Housing, and Transportation, 2010–2012—*Continued*

STATE and county code	STATE or county	Percent who lived in the same house one year ago	Percent who did not live in the same county one year ago	Total occupied housing units	Percent owner-occupied housing units	Median value of owner-occupied housing units (dollars)	Median selected monthly owner costs as a percentage of household income		Median gross rent (dollars)	Median gross rent as a percentage of household income[1]	Percent of workers who drove alone to work	Mean travel time to work (minutes)	Percent of occupied housing units with no vehicle available
							With a mortgage	Without a mortgage[1]					
	ACS table number:	C07204	C07204	B25003	B25003	B25077	B25092	B25092	B25064	B25071	C08301	B08013/ B08012	C25045
	Column number:	1	2	3	4	5	6	7	8	9	10	11	12
	Iowa—Cont.												
19 057	Des Moines........	87.5	4.6	16,934	73.7	92,700	21.9	13.3	619	28.0	80.8	17.0	7.5
19 061	Dubuque	87.2	5.1	37,548	72.9	146,500	20.6	12.8	668	29.9	81.7	16.8	6.5
19 065	Fayette...............	85.7	5.9	8,601	76.3	85,800	20.0	12.1	512	23.1	74.3	21.1	4.6
19 087	Henry..................	90.3	4.9	7,497	75.2	100,000	21.7	12.9	590	28.3	82.8	18.7	4.8
19 097	Jackson...............	87.7	5.6	8,368	73.8	104,800	22.2	11.7	571	28.8	79.3	23.1	7.1
19 099	Jasper	87.8	5.1	14,781	72.2	114,700	23.3	11.8	634	27.5	81.0	21.9	6.8
19 103	Johnson..............	72.4	11.4	54,073	59.7	186,400	21.8	11.3	823	35.0	67.3	18.1	6.6
19 105	Jones..................	86.0	7.7	8,265	80.3	124,600	21.0	12.5	579	26.7	81.3	25.0	4.7
19 111	Lee.....................	89.5	3.5	14,194	75.2	83,900	19.9	11.9	558	25.5	85.0	18.3	6.1
19 113	Linn....................	84.6	5.1	85,889	73.1	144,000	20.4	11.9	662	26.7	81.3	18.8	6.7
19 123	Mahaska.............	83.0	5.4	9,030	71.2	101,900	20.0	11.1	570	24.9	77.9	17.1	7.6
19 125	Marion................	85.8	6.2	12,780	77.8	135,600	20.4	11.6	638	24.7	79.3	21.2	3.6
19 127	Marshall..............	85.6	4.9	15,316	74.6	106,100	20.5	12.9	622	24.3	76.3	16.7	7.2
19 139	Muscatine...........	86.7	5.5	16,445	74.4	120,700	21.3	13.6	726	31.3	81.7	17.6	5.7
19 149	Plymouth	89.6	5.2	10,008	79.4	127,100	18.3	10.5	593	22.7	77.5	17.1	3.7
19 153	Polk...................	82.6	5.6	171,697	69.3	153,300	21.3	11.9	762	28.9	82.7	18.7	6.1
19 155	Pottawattamie	85.3	5.2	36,440	71.1	126,100	21.7	11.9	723	29.4	84.3	20.9	6.8
19 163	Scott	85.5	5.6	66,945	69.0	144,400	20.8	11.4	682	29.0	86.5	17.7	5.6
19 167	Sioux	86.6	3.9	11,614	77.7	135,500	19.8	10.0	580	19.8	71.8	12.7	3.3
19 169	Story	68.3	14.6	35,314	54.6	162,000	20.9	10.4	718	35.3	72.4	18.3	5.7
19 179	Wapello..............	85.0	4.3	14,572	72.8	77,200	20.7	13.3	609	30.4	81.4	17.5	7.4
19 181	Warren................	84.4	8.4	17,335	79.7	155,000	21.0	11.4	732	25.1	82.3	25.3	3.0
19 183	Washington	87.8	5.2	9,213	73.9	115,300	22.1	11.6	649	27.0	75.9	21.8	6.3
19 187	Webster..............	83.7	7.8	15,483	66.5	85,700	18.7	10.5	522	26.1	83.6	15.3	7.6
19 191	Winneshiek	88.2	5.9	8,078	78.1	152,900	22.9	11.2	571	23.3	64.9	15.8	3.7
19 193	Woodbury	83.4	5.3	38,737	66.9	97,700	20.6	11.8	627	30.0	81.3	17.5	8.5
20 000	**Kansas**............	83.2	6.6	1,106,960	67.4	128,500	21.5	12.1	718	28.3	82.0	19.0	5.3
20 009	Barton	85.4	5.5	11,293	72.1	77,300	18.2	11.3	573	26.4	83.9	16.8	4.9
20 015	Butler.................	83.6	8.3	23,995	77.3	127,100	20.8	12.5	711	27.3	87.7	22.0	4.5
20 021	Cherokee............	88.1	3.7	8,166	76.0	71,600	20.7	13.2	553	27.3	85.0	21.2	7.6
20 035	Cowley...............	77.3	9.2	13,804	69.4	77,800	19.9	12.3	586	30.0	80.2	18.1	5.0
20 037	Crawford............	80.0	7.3	15,490	61.2	84,000	20.6	13.8	658	33.1	86.4	15.7	5.0
20 045	Douglas..............	70.6	10.3	43,566	49.8	180,000	22.7	12.2	850	33.3	75.6	20.1	4.3
20 051	Ellis...................	75.0	12.0	11,941	63.5	149,500	22.9	12.4	580	31.1	83.9	12.5	5.0
20 055	Finney................	83.7	6.0	12,521	62.0	114,500	22.6	12.1	657	24.3	79.2	15.6	3.9
20 057	Ford...................	86.3	4.8	10,976	61.6	88,400	21.5	11.5	595	22.1	83.6	14.7	4.2
20 059	Franklin..............	83.7	7.1	10,047	69.6	120,900	23.8	13.5	714	29.4	82.7	24.8	4.9
20 061	Geary.................	75.2	12.5	12,775	45.9	132,600	22.4	12.1	917	26.9	77.9	16.8	5.4
20 079	Harvey	84.8	8.4	13,089	73.8	107,800	20.6	11.3	660	31.5	82.3	15.6	4.6
20 091	Johnson..............	85.7	6.0	215,199	70.5	208,100	21.5	10.9	897	27.1	85.1	20.8	3.5
20 099	Labette	86.9	5.4	8,639	70.2	67,000	21.0	13.1	558	26.1	83.3	16.8	4.4
20 103	Leavenworth........	78.9	13.3	26,103	65.7	166,000	22.1	11.8	881	25.9	82.3	21.7	3.9
20 111	Lyon	76.1	8.5	12,984	61.0	95,800	20.9	12.2	562	29.4	78.0	16.0	7.0
20 113	McPherson..........	84.7	5.4	11,567	77.4	121,400	20.6	10.0	606	21.8	78.5	14.1	3.4
20 121	Miami.................	88.6	6.5	12,033	81.7	166,400	24.3	13.8	757	42.6	82.0	28.1	3.1
20 125	Montgomery........	82.6	6.9	13,876	70.5	72,100	19.5	11.9	565	30.8	82.5	17.0	10.8
20 149	Pottawatomie	91.5	5.9	8,000	78.3	151,300	20.4	12.0	717	25.1	82.0	22.4	2.5
20 155	Reno..................	79.5	5.9	25,770	67.7	89,600	21.3	12.1	618	27.0	81.5	18.1	5.2
20 161	Riley..................	75.1	14.0	25,831	42.4	167,200	21.8	10.4	841	31.4	70.1	16.5	5.2
20 169	Saline................	83.1	5.9	22,480	65.7	118,800	22.1	12.3	651	28.9	82.3	15.4	5.4
20 173	Sedgwick............	83.1	4.1	191,191	64.7	123,800	21.6	12.2	701	28.9	85.3	18.2	6.2
20 175	Seward...............	82.8	6.2	7,367	65.2	88,200	20.0	10.5	669	23.7	66.9	17.6	5.8
20 177	Shawnee.............	82.4	4.6	72,189	64.0	120,400	21.4	11.8	692	29.9	82.1	17.3	8.0
20 191	Sumner...............	83.5	7.6	9,241	78.2	84,100	22.8	12.0	606	25.0	80.7	23.6	5.3
20 209	Wyandotte...........	82.0	7.5	56,817	60.9	93,100	24.9	16.2	721	32.1	82.9	21.0	9.8
21 000	**Kentucky**..........	85.0	6.0	1,690,132	68.1	120,800	21.7	11.1	640	29.8	82.7	22.9	7.8
21 003	Allen..................	83.5	8.9	8,144	73.9	91,800	22.6	10.4	552	26.7	78.7	25.8	9.2
21 005	Anderson............	87.2	5.8	8,446	74.5	130,600	23.0	11.8	707	22.6	82.7	25.6	3.6
21 009	Barren................	85.6	5.9	16,616	69.5	96,900	19.8	12.2	535	35.0	82.9	20.1	6.3
21 013	Bell....................	91.2	4.7	11,056	66.5	65,400	21.6	11.6	482	34.1	82.2	22.6	13.2
21 015	Boone................	88.3	6.2	42,680	75.8	170,600	22.0	11.5	848	28.2	86.2	24.8	4.0
21 019	Boyd..................	87.1	5.8	19,097	69.1	97,800	18.8	10.9	595	30.0	85.3	20.0	9.6
21 021	Boyle.................	79.2	9.9	11,190	63.3	131,100	23.2	11.3	635	30.1	77.4	19.0	6.2
21 027	Breckinridge........	90.7	4.1	7,510	82.4	81,600	21.2	10.0	501	30.1	78.6	26.2	8.1
21 029	Bullitt.................	87.1	7.0	28,109	79.9	145,800	22.7	11.9	754	24.7	85.8	26.6	3.4
21 035	Calloway.............	79.9	9.0	14,656	67.4	117,400	20.8	10.9	524	32.1	87.5	18.1	6.4
21 037	Campbell............	85.0	7.8	35,254	68.3	145,700	20.8	12.0	706	29.3	83.0	21.9	7.9
21 043	Carter................	89.1	4.3	10,398	78.7	76,300	19.0	10.2	560	33.0	77.8	31.5	7.2
21 047	Christian............	76.5	13.2	25,828	52.2	102,800	22.8	10.1	742	30.0	75.5	18.7	7.8
21 049	Clark..................	79.9	7.2	14,559	65.9	148,100	20.6	12.1	666	30.2	82.6	24.0	8.4
21 051	Clay...................	91.8	3.7	7,479	74.3	58,500	21.5	14.0	460	30.6	82.7	30.5	14.4
21 059	Daviess	88.0	3.6	37,435	70.6	109,800	20.3	10.0	618	28.8	85.8	18.4	5.9
21 067	Fayette...............	75.8	8.7	122,046	55.8	164,400	21.1	10.0	737	31.2	79.8	19.4	8.4
21 071	Floyd..................	87.4	4.2	15,522	68.9	71,100	24.3	11.1	551	33.7	82.2	25.5	10.2

[1]10.0 represents 10 percent or less; 50.0 represents 50 percent or higher.

STATE and county code	STATE or county	Percent who lived in the same house one year ago	Percent who did not live in the same county one year ago	Total occupied housing units	Percent owner-occupied housing units (dollars)	Median value of owner-occupied housing units (dollars)	Median selected monthly owner costs as a percentage of household income		Median gross rent (dollars)	Median gross rent as a percentage of household income[1]	Percent of workers who drove alone to work	Mean travel time to work (minutes)	Percent of occupied housing units with no vehicle available
							With a mortgage	Without a mortgage[1]					
ACS table number:		C07204	C07204	B25003	B25003	B25077	B25092	B25092	B25064	B25071	C08301	B08013/ B08012	C25045
Column number:		1	2	3	4	5	6	7	8	9	10	11	12
	Kentucky—Cont.												
21 073	Franklin	80.9	7.8	21,237	62.1	142,600	22.5	10.0	685	32.6	80.9	17.9	5.0
21 081	Grant	88.4	4.5	8,506	72.5	128,500	22.9	13.0	678	28.7	86.0	28.0	3.1
21 083	Graves	90.4	3.7	14,517	74.7	82,600	21.2	10.5	557	33.7	81.7	22.1	8.2
21 085	Grayson	83.0	7.3	9,944	71.9	92,700	23.4	11.8	511	28.9	79.6	25.1	5.8
21 089	Greenup	91.1	4.4	14,208	77.4	91,300	20.3	10.3	605	31.7	87.5	24.7	7.6
21 093	Hardin	76.8	12.2	39,246	63.1	140,800	20.8	10.0	721	27.5	80.9	22.1	4.8
21 095	Harlan	91.4	2.7	11,066	70.8	50,500	19.6	10.9	491	28.3	77.7	23.2	13.5
21 101	Henderson	83.9	4.9	18,826	65.7	100,700	21.7	10.8	580	30.6	86.6	21.5	10.0
21 107	Hopkins	86.3	4.0	18,257	71.4	85,500	19.4	12.2	585	25.3	87.8	21.4	6.7
21 111	Jefferson	85.6	3.9	303,988	62.4	148,800	21.8	11.6	707	29.6	82.2	22.0	10.2
21 113	Jessamine	80.4	8.4	18,112	66.4	152,600	24.3	11.8	711	28.4	83.5	24.2	4.7
21 115	Johnson	90.0	3.2	9,263	78.4	79,100	22.2	12.9	470	24.3	84.9	29.5	7.4
21 117	Kenton	85.3	6.8	61,671	67.3	144,200	21.7	11.5	724	29.1	85.7	23.2	7.7
21 121	Knox	86.7	5.9	12,762	62.9	77,700	21.8	12.9	513	33.5	87.5	18.3	14.0
21 125	Laurel	84.4	5.3	23,280	70.6	97,000	22.1	11.6	556	29.0	83.9	21.7	7.0
21 133	Letcher	92.6	1.8	9,157	76.7	56,900	20.7	10.0	483	29.8	83.7	28.4	13.6
21 137	Lincoln	87.4	7.0	9,602	73.3	88,400	21.7	12.5	497	34.5	84.7	27.7	7.6
21 141	Logan	84.4	6.6	10,801	70.2	90,400	23.9	11.2	549	30.2	84.4	23.3	6.0
21 145	McCracken	86.9	4.7	27,159	67.9	119,100	19.4	10.3	582	25.5	86.5	17.5	7.5
21 151	Madison	79.9	8.1	31,085	60.2	146,100	22.0	11.7	612	31.0	78.3	22.1	5.7
21 155	Marion	91.8	4.6	7,369	76.0	100,900	23.6	12.8	533	32.2	79.0	20.2	9.9
21 157	Marshall	92.3	3.0	12,119	82.1	104,100	21.6	10.0	580	27.6	83.8	21.5	4.3
21 163	Meade	82.1	8.5	10,282	73.6	117,500	21.8	10.0	765	27.4	87.9	33.9	4.9
21 167	Mercer	83.8	7.7	8,647	75.3	128,900	19.4	11.7	519	35.2	87.9	23.9	5.7
21 173	Montgomery	82.6	5.3	10,131	66.5	111,000	24.0	11.5	602	24.8	...	25.1	8.8
21 177	Muhlenberg	85.9	4.6	11,839	79.6	79,200	21.4	10.5	502	27.5	86.3	21.6	5.3
21 179	Nelson	87.0	5.0	16,470	75.0	118,700	23.0	10.0	671	32.2	84.5	26.0	5.3
21 183	Ohio	93.1	1.5	8,439	82.3	79,800	21.0	10.7	530	29.9	82.1	24.9	5.4
21 185	Oldham	87.7	8.9	19,533	85.2	243,900	22.7	10.1	841	28.6	84.1	25.8	2.9
21 193	Perry	86.2	4.4	11,176	70.6	65,000	22.1	10.0	521	32.3	84.2	20.0	12.0
21 195	Pike	88.7	3.6	26,492	70.6	64,800	21.1	11.2	584	30.3	85.5	24.0	9.8
21 199	Pulaski	85.9	3.9	26,135	69.9	106,400	21.9	11.8	578	35.1	84.2	20.3	7.1
21 205	Rowan	79.2	14.2	8,143	65.7	104,800	19.4	10.6	628	29.0	81.5	21.0	6.9
21 209	Scott	82.5	6.8	17,881	72.2	159,900	20.2	10.0	706	29.1	83.6	22.6	6.5
21 211	Shelby	86.6	7.1	15,394	71.2	162,800	22.7	10.0	763	28.4	78.6	25.3	3.7
21 217	Taylor	86.8	5.4	9,439	70.7	97,800	21.2	10.6	550	26.8	80.4	18.3	7.5
21 227	Warren	76.9	9.6	44,378	57.7	141,000	21.2	10.2	650	33.2	83.1	18.4	6.8
21 231	Wayne	88.3	5.5	8,176	69.1	77,400	26.1	11.4	465	29.8	79.7	23.5	7.4
21 235	Whitley	80.7	7.3	13,308	68.8	74,100	24.9	11.4	556	28.5	84.0	21.0	9.7
21 239	Woodford	90.6	4.2	9,506	69.8	182,800	20.4	10.0	719	25.0	80.5	21.9	4.0
22 000	**Louisiana**	85.6	5.5	1,706,091	66.7	138,800	21.4	10.0	760	32.3	82.1	24.8	8.6
22 001	Acadia	85.3	4.2	22,508	67.3	87,900	19.7	10.0	540	28.7	79.8	28.0	9.0
22 003	Allen	85.2	5.9	8,205	68.7	77,900	18.5	10.0	558	25.9	86.7	27.5	11.2
22 005	Ascension	86.7	4.2	37,877	80.3	165,100	19.2	10.0	821	34.1	86.4	28.6	4.4
22 007	Assumption	91.3	2.3	8,857	80.3	101,400	17.7	10.0	590	29.8	82.1	32.1	11.3
22 009	Avoyelles	85.7	4.8	15,277	71.2	85,800	20.9	11.1	578	32.8	75.4	30.2	8.2
22 011	Beauregard	85.6	8.1	13,040	76.3	92,400	18.6	10.0	610	27.2	80.0	29.8	5.5
22 015	Bossier	83.3	8.4	45,632	66.2	147,700	20.7	10.0	815	29.7	86.7	21.5	7.1
22 017	Caddo	84.1	4.9	98,582	61.5	124,000	20.8	10.3	722	31.4	83.7	20.5	10.8
22 019	Calcasieu	83.2	4.5	73,614	70.9	120,500	20.0	10.0	724	31.4	84.8	20.6	6.8
22 029	Concordia	81.7	6.9	7,940	63.3	78,800	21.8	11.5	477	28.8	78.8	27.0	11.7
22 031	De Soto	93.9	2.9	10,254	74.8	88,600	19.0	10.6	569	41.2	81.9	27.6	13.1
22 033	East Baton Rouge	84.2	5.0	167,220	61.1	167,600	22.0	10.0	815	33.7	82.4	22.7	7.0
22 037	East Feliciana	87.1	7.2	6,901	77.9	123,800	21.0	10.0	552	29.3	90.0	30.6	7.5
22 039	Evangeline	90.2	4.8	12,172	69.0	76,500	18.4	10.1	526	37.1	78.6	28.7	11.4
22 041	Franklin	84.8	7.1	7,692	73.0	77,900	19.9	10.0	512	31.5	80.0	26.6	11.5
22 043	Grant	87.9	8.8	7,199	78.6	75,100	19.5	11.8	591	24.3	88.0	31.4	8.6
22 045	Iberia	86.2	4.1	26,463	72.0	98,800	19.8	10.0	663	28.4	82.4	23.4	9.1
22 047	Iberville	85.3	10.3	11,101	74.9	88,200	18.9	10.2	595	31.8	86.2	24.5	9.8
22 051	Jefferson	87.1	4.9	166,467	62.9	171,400	24.2	11.0	875	31.8	81.0	23.7	8.0
22 053	Jefferson Davis	86.7	6.8	11,816	75.5	87,200	17.8	10.2	565	29.8	80.9	32.6	7.3
22 055	Lafayette	84.1	5.6	86,632	64.2	163,900	20.0	10.0	740	29.7	82.3	22.2	6.7
22 057	Lafourche	88.7	3.8	35,360	77.5	128,500	19.0	10.0	686	30.7	80.2	24.8	7.8
22 061	Lincoln	74.3	9.8	16,886	54.5	113,400	20.9	10.0	643	35.6	80.7	21.0	8.7
22 063	Livingston	89.4	5.0	46,185	81.5	152,100	21.3	10.0	753	29.3	84.8	34.8	3.4
22 067	Morehouse	93.6	2.7	10,559	64.4	76,500	22.5	12.4	526	29.4	86.0	26.3	11.3
22 069	Natchitoches	87.0	5.7	15,013	60.3	100,800	19.9	10.2	590	38.9	78.1	22.0	10.4
22 071	Orleans	81.2	7.1	146,018	47.4	179,500	26.7	14.1	901	37.8	70.1	23.0	18.7
22 073	Ouachita	85.3	4.6	57,825	59.1	117,600	19.5	10.0	664	32.9	87.8	19.9	9.1
22 075	Plaquemines	89.4	7.9	8,823	74.8	172,300	23.7	10.0	1099	24.7	83.7	27.7	3.9
22 077	Pointe Coupee	90.0	2.0	9,121	76.7	119,200	19.9	10.0	554	28.1	83.1	30.0	9.8
22 079	Rapides	87.5	4.0	47,148	66.2	119,000	22.0	10.2	675	33.3	83.8	23.0	7.7

[1]10.0 represents 10 percent or less; 50.0 represents 50 percent or higher.

Table C-2. Counties — Where: Migration, Housing, and Transportation, 2010–2012—*Continued*

STATE and county code	STATE or county	Percent who lived in the same house one year ago	Percent who did not live in the same county one year ago	Total occupied housing units	Percent owner-occupied housing units	Median value of owner-occupied housing units (dollars)	Median selected monthly owner costs as a percentage of household income — With a mortgage	Without a mortgage[1]	Median gross rent (dollars)	Median gross rent as a percentage of household income[1]	Percent of workers who drove alone to work	Mean travel time to work (minutes)	Percent of occupied housing units with no vehicle available
ACS table number:		C07204	C07204	B25003	B25003	B25077	B25092	B25092	B25064	B25071	C08301	B08013/B08012	C25045
Column number:		1	2	3	4	5	6	7	8	9	10	11	12
	Louisiana—Cont.												
22 083	Richland	87.9	5.2	7,566	68.7	80,400	19.7	10.0	496	24.3	90.4	21.6	10.0
22 085	Sabine	91.6	2.1	9,246	77.7	79,100	18.9	10.4	450	26.1	81.0	30.3	7.1
22 087	St. Bernard	84.6	7.2	13,694	70.0	121,700	22.0	10.0	787	36.8	87.1	26.0	6.0
22 089	St. Charles	90.7	5.1	18,267	81.5	184,600	22.9	10.8	926	31.9	89.0	26.1	4.0
22 093	St. James	95.0	2.5	7,710	84.4	124,000	19.6	10.0	723	35.8	87.0	24.8	7.9
22 095	St. John the Baptist	89.7	4.7	15,467	77.1	148,700	22.1	10.3	875	29.0	85.5	26.9	7.5
22 097	St. Landry	91.2	3.3	30,940	70.3	87,000	19.7	10.0	563	31.6	86.9	25.8	11.0
22 099	St. Martin	91.4	3.6	18,672	79.8	96,800	19.1	10.0	626	28.4	83.8	27.4	8.9
22 101	St. Mary	86.0	4.8	20,095	69.1	92,900	20.9	11.0	651	27.8	79.6	23.1	11.3
22 103	St. Tammany	86.0	6.2	87,583	76.0	197,600	23.1	11.0	991	32.8	82.5	31.7	3.8
22 105	Tangipahoa	84.0	5.4	44,111	67.1	133,600	22.3	10.0	733	34.6	79.0	28.5	7.8
22 109	Terrebonne	83.6	5.3	39,436	71.9	132,600	20.0	10.0	796	28.1	82.6	24.1	7.4
22 111	Union	93.8	3.6	8,376	78.1	79,600	18.6	10.0	531	37.1	89.4	28.3	7.7
22 113	Vermilion	88.4	4.4	21,659	77.4	99,300	19.5	10.0	588	26.9	83.3	28.3	5.7
22 115	Vernon	78.9	13.8	18,437	55.7	88,300	17.7	10.0	853	24.1	81.3	20.8	4.5
22 117	Washington	86.7	4.9	17,756	72.2	82,500	21.7	11.8	568	33.8	80.0	29.9	10.5
22 119	Webster	84.4	5.8	16,226	70.2	81,700	19.7	10.9	588	31.7	84.0	25.3	9.1
22 121	West Baton Rouge	86.2	9.5	9,016	71.9	147,700	20.0	10.0	756	28.6	83.5	22.8	4.8
23 000	**Maine**	86.0	5.3	552,963	71.6	173,900	24.1	14.0	748	31.0	78.7	23.4	7.4
23 001	Androscoggin	84.6	5.3	44,502	65.3	155,100	23.8	16.1	692	29.3	77.8	23.0	10.7
23 003	Aroostook	87.5	3.4	30,763	71.7	93,600	21.2	13.1	536	28.9	79.9	17.0	7.8
23 005	Cumberland	83.5	6.1	117,068	68.5	241,500	24.7	14.5	927	30.7	78.3	22.4	8.1
23 007	Franklin	88.2	5.1	12,198	78.6	128,000	23.0	11.6	628	34.5	73.1	24.1	5.8
23 009	Hancock	87.7	5.4	24,248	73.8	192,100	24.2	13.9	751	31.9	68.4	23.3	6.9
23 011	Kennebec	86.0	4.6	51,509	70.5	151,900	22.3	13.0	688	31.7	81.2	23.3	7.7
23 013	Knox	89.1	4.3	17,060	79.2	198,200	27.0	14.8	765	30.6	73.4	19.3	5.5
23 015	Lincoln	90.8	3.4	14,846	82.2	203,600	26.1	13.3	825	27.7	80.5	25.2	2.4
23 017	Oxford	86.9	5.3	23,321	77.1	137,500	24.6	14.5	592	34.1	80.5	26.8	6.6
23 019	Penobscot	83.7	6.3	62,186	66.2	137,300	22.7	13.2	709	33.7	81.2	21.7	8.7
23 023	Sagadahoc	89.6	6.6	14,854	75.6	185,500	23.9	13.1	747	35.8	80.4	22.8	7.1
23 025	Somerset	88.3	4.5	21,860	79.5	111,800	23.6	13.8	650	32.0	79.4	25.0	6.3
23 027	Waldo	87.6	5.6	16,604	76.8	155,100	25.2	14.8	713	32.8	75.5	26.8	5.5
23 029	Washington	86.7	4.7	14,115	75.4	103,000	24.4	14.2	551	27.4	75.8	19.1	9.2
23 031	York	86.8	5.4	80,414	72.0	229,100	25.4	14.8	859	30.2	80.5	27.6	5.5
24 000	**Maryland**	86.8	5.3	2,141,086	67.1	289,300	24.7	12.7	1,177	31.0	73.2	32.0	9.6
24 001	Allegany	85.5	6.0	28,829	69.0	122,700	21.5	13.8	612	32.4	81.7	22.1	9.3
24 003	Anne Arundel	87.3	6.0	199,577	74.0	332,300	24.2	11.7	1,421	29.2	80.4	29.8	4.1
24 005	Baltimore	88.5	4.5	313,195	65.8	254,300	24.0	12.7	1,120	30.4	78.8	28.7	8.3
24 009	Calvert	89.4	5.3	30,780	80.7	349,900	23.9	10.8	1,411	34.4	80.0	39.1	3.7
24 011	Caroline	89.3	5.6	11,983	71.2	203,300	27.7	14.8	862	25.4	79.6	36.0	4.7
24 013	Carroll	93.8	3.1	59,373	83.4	324,100	24.9	13.5	1,047	31.4	83.2	35.0	4.2
24 015	Cecil	86.7	5.4	35,997	71.2	251,500	24.6	14.4	971	32.3	82.8	29.6	5.1
24 017	Charles	89.4	5.3	51,274	77.3	292,900	24.6	11.1	1,448	34.4	78.3	42.1	4.1
24 019	Dorchester	89.3	4.8	13,827	66.3	192,900	27.5	16.4	814	32.7	79.4	26.0	10.7
24 021	Frederick	87.8	4.4	85,862	75.0	298,400	24.0	12.7	1,226	30.2	75.8	35.4	4.7
24 023	Garrett	89.5	3.8	12,144	75.4	169,600	24.3	12.2	646	30.1	76.4	21.8	7.7
24 025	Harford	90.9	4.3	90,302	79.1	281,400	24.1	12.9	1,096	29.7	82.9	31.2	4.6
24 027	Howard	88.9	5.8	106,284	73.6	417,700	23.3	10.0	1,450	29.3	81.0	30.4	3.6
24 029	Kent	89.4	6.0	7,779	70.5	254,000	24.6	15.2	785	25.3	72.8	27.1	9.1
24 031	Montgomery	85.9	5.0	359,995	66.5	444,100	24.1	11.4	1,550	31.0	65.1	34.3	7.9
24 033	Prince George's	84.7	5.9	302,436	62.6	263,700	28.1	12.3	1,224	31.1	64.5	35.8	9.9
24 035	Queen Anne's	91.3	4.4	17,107	85.8	346,100	25.0	13.8	1,120	32.6	81.7	34.1	2.5
24 037	St. Mary's	87.7	5.4	37,772	71.5	304,600	22.5	11.9	1,273	24.6	84.3	28.5	5.6
24 039	Somerset	83.1	12.3	8,470	68.9	157,900	29.9	16.5	639	43.2	77.6	23.0	7.8
24 041	Talbot	89.4	5.8	16,033	71.8	325,900	25.4	13.1	946	33.1	80.2	25.2	6.3
24 043	Washington	84.4	5.8	55,790	65.9	200,600	24.6	12.8	827	29.2	81.7	27.7	8.0
24 045	Wicomico	81.3	8.1	36,019	63.5	178,100	23.7	13.4	945	34.9	81.4	21.9	7.1
24 047	Worcester	87.5	6.0	19,683	78.7	247,000	26.7	14.5	924	32.9	82.4	22.2	5.0
24 510	Baltimore city	83.0	5.3	240,575	47.1	156,800	26.0	15.4	900	32.9	59.8	30.1	31.1
25 000	**Massachusetts**	86.8	4.8	2,524,028	62.3	328,300	25.4	15.4	1,050	30.3	72.3	28.0	12.8
25 001	Barnstable	90.4	4.0	93,426	78.6	364,500	29.3	15.9	1,124	35.1	83.7	24.7	5.5
25 003	Berkshire	87.8	3.6	55,573	68.3	205,600	25.0	16.0	738	30.7	79.9	20.5	11.2
25 005	Bristol	89.1	3.3	209,314	62.5	277,800	26.3	15.8	795	30.4	82.4	26.8	10.6
25 009	Essex	87.7	3.4	285,412	63.2	346,700	26.0	15.8	1,018	31.5	76.4	27.7	11.0
25 011	Franklin	86.6	5.1	30,159	67.8	220,000	24.6	14.6	824	28.5	77.9	24.3	7.2
25 013	Hampden	87.3	2.9	177,900	62.0	198,100	23.9	15.3	777	32.3	82.9	22.7	13.9
25 015	Hampshire	83.5	8.6	58,670	66.4	263,000	24.8	13.6	896	31.5	70.9	23.7	7.9
25 017	Middlesex	86.2	5.3	580,358	62.5	396,400	24.7	14.9	1,260	28.5	69.8	28.5	10.6
25 021	Norfolk	89.1	5.7	257,153	69.1	389,100	24.7	15.6	1,237	29.7	71.9	31.3	9.5
25 023	Plymouth	89.8	4.0	179,835	76.6	328,800	26.6	16.7	1,105	32.8	81.1	32.5	6.7
25 025	Suffolk	78.7	8.3	288,162	34.7	355,300	26.9	15.6	1,240	31.1	40.3	29.0	34.8
25 027	Worcester	88.0	3.4	298,224	65.4	258,400	24.4	14.5	895	29.7	82.0	27.9	9.2

[1]10.0 represents 10 percent or less; 50.0 represents 50 percent or higher.

Table C-2. Counties — Where: Migration, Housing, and Transportation, 2010–2012—*Continued*

STATE and county code	STATE or county	Percent who lived in the same house one year ago	Percent who did not live in the same county one year ago	Total occupied housing units	Percent owner-occupied housing units	Median value of owner-occupied housing units (dollars)	Median selected monthly owner costs as a percentage of household income With a mortgage	Without a mortgage[1]	Median gross rent (dollars)	Median gross rent as a percentage of household income[1]	Percent of workers who drove alone to work	Mean travel time to work (minutes)	Percent of occupied housing units with no vehicle available
ACS table number:		C07204	C07204	B25003	B25003	B25077	B25092	B25092	B25064	B25071	C08301	B08013/ B08012	C25045
Column number:		1	2	3	4	5	6	7	8	9	10	11	12
26 000	**Michigan**	85.2	5.0	3,805,261	71.9	119,200	23.6	13.7	755	33.0	82.8	24.0	7.9
26 005	Allegan	86.4	5.8	41,881	81.1	136,400	23.6	13.2	725	29.8	84.9	23.5	4.3
26 007	Alpena	85.9	3.4	12,862	78.4	97,900	22.9	12.7	529	28.4	83.5	16.1	7.7
26 009	Antrim	92.1	3.7	9,536	86.9	137,800	26.9	13.1	701	40.2	76.9	24.0	3.4
26 015	Barry	90.5	3.9	22,355	85.0	131,800	23.6	13.0	700	30.9	85.3	26.9	3.9
26 017	Bay	88.5	4.0	43,793	77.9	92,400	21.8	12.9	633	32.3	85.9	20.7	7.7
26 021	Berrien	87.3	3.5	59,373	73.3	131,300	22.6	13.1	638	33.0	82.9	20.0	8.9
26 023	Branch	90.2	4.8	15,640	78.8	97,800	23.6	12.5	676	34.0	79.0	24.8	7.0
26 025	Calhoun	85.1	5.5	52,569	69.5	98,600	23.5	14.0	648	31.4	81.0	19.9	8.1
26 027	Cass	92.9	3.7	19,742	84.4	128,300	25.1	13.5	718	29.7	86.8	25.0	4.8
26 029	Charlevoix	89.6	5.0	10,191	83.5	146,400	25.1	13.8	614	31.6	81.6	18.5	6.4
26 031	Cheboygan	86.6	6.3	11,201	81.9	115,300	24.6	13.8	566	31.2	80.7	26.0	5.1
26 033	Chippewa	82.5	7.6	14,597	69.8	101,000	21.8	13.3	594	33.2	77.1	16.3	8.9
26 035	Clare	85.9	5.1	13,436	79.1	80,500	28.0	13.9	572	35.6	81.9	26.5	8.6
26 037	Clinton	86.4	8.6	28,521	80.9	151,200	22.3	12.2	760	31.9	82.1	23.3	2.9
26 041	Delta	88.0	4.7	15,973	76.6	99,300	23.7	12.6	538	31.6	82.6	18.8	7.8
26 043	Dickinson	88.7	6.5	11,405	81.5	83,500	22.4	13.8	589	31.8	85.7	15.4	4.9
26 045	Eaton	86.2	6.8	42,981	72.7	134,800	22.8	12.8	746	29.8	85.0	23.1	5.4
26 047	Emmet	87.0	5.4	13,140	78.2	164,600	24.3	12.2	725	31.3	75.5	19.6	4.4
26 049	Genesee	84.8	3.3	165,651	69.9	89,000	24.3	14.3	695	37.2	85.5	25.7	8.7
26 051	Gladwin	89.7	4.7	10,721	85.1	101,400	26.0	13.8	538	34.2	83.4	30.0	6.1
26 055	Grand Traverse	86.0	7.1	34,555	75.8	167,100	23.9	13.3	821	34.3	81.2	21.0	5.0
26 057	Gratiot	82.7	7.7	14,754	76.2	85,600	22.1	13.3	590	32.3	80.4	21.6	6.9
26 059	Hillsdale	87.8	4.7	17,784	79.1	103,000	24.7	13.2	611	29.9	80.7	24.3	6.4
26 061	Houghton	83.9	6.1	13,987	70.5	86,100	20.8	13.0	595	33.6	73.2	14.4	7.3
26 063	Huron	90.9	3.4	13,957	80.7	92,300	24.2	12.8	586	29.2	80.4	20.5	5.8
26 065	Ingham	75.6	9.6	108,326	58.6	118,300	23.0	13.7	755	35.4	76.3	19.9	8.5
26 067	Ionia	85.3	6.8	22,464	77.5	111,000	24.0	13.0	682	34.2	83.5	26.4	5.2
26 069	Iosco	87.3	5.8	11,256	82.4	85,800	24.2	12.4	579	31.0	83.4	20.0	4.8
26 073	Isabella	66.4	13.3	24,456	58.6	117,500	23.4	12.4	666	41.1	76.8	18.0	6.8
26 075	Jackson	82.5	5.4	59,781	72.5	109,300	23.7	13.2	723	33.2	82.8	23.0	8.3
26 077	Kalamazoo	78.8	7.5	99,085	64.8	138,000	22.2	13.1	706	35.1	83.4	20.1	7.9
26 081	Kent	84.0	4.5	229,328	69.3	136,000	22.7	13.0	737	30.4	82.5	21.0	8.0
26 087	Lapeer	88.8	5.1	32,426	84.1	129,500	24.7	13.6	775	31.6	83.4	32.5	4.6
26 089	Leelanau	91.0	5.4	9,267	85.6	233,100	28.1	11.2	788	36.0	76.0	21.9	3.3
26 091	Lenawee	85.0	5.1	37,498	77.4	113,700	24.3	13.6	693	32.1	84.4	27.2	5.4
26 093	Livingston	90.3	4.4	67,112	84.7	179,500	24.0	12.9	899	28.5	85.0	31.4	2.9
26 099	Macomb	88.5	4.0	331,023	75.1	118,900	23.6	14.6	811	31.7	87.3	26.9	6.8
26 101	Manistee	85.2	6.9	10,729	77.2	105,000	25.0	13.9	649	29.8	79.7	19.3	7.7
26 103	Marquette	83.0	5.6	27,180	70.2	125,300	19.9	12.1	599	31.5	81.4	18.1	5.5
26 105	Mason	86.2	5.6	12,242	73.4	120,400	24.5	13.1	652	29.1	81.8	18.1	8.3
26 107	Mecosta	81.5	9.0	15,376	73.2	109,500	23.8	12.4	639	35.0	77.7	23.3	6.6
26 109	Menominee	89.9	3.9	10,622	80.9	93,900	23.1	11.9	521	27.7	81.4	21.7	6.6
26 111	Midland	84.8	8.4	33,552	74.9	130,300	20.9	11.7	720	29.4	86.0	20.0	4.6
26 115	Monroe	88.4	3.9	57,876	78.2	136,800	23.4	13.4	797	29.7	86.9	24.5	5.4
26 117	Montcalm	88.7	5.4	23,285	79.5	93,000	24.4	13.2	670	31.3	81.8	29.5	5.3
26 121	Muskegon	83.9	5.3	64,394	74.6	99,400	23.1	13.4	649	34.6	83.9	21.4	9.0
26 123	Newaygo	89.9	4.5	18,074	83.9	103,000	24.2	14.1	672	33.6	82.2	28.4	5.9
26 125	Oakland	85.5	5.2	485,367	71.1	165,300	23.3	14.0	904	29.5	85.7	26.0	5.9
26 127	Oceana	89.0	5.8	9,466	81.2	104,700	25.0	14.0	667	34.0	73.3	23.4	4.4
26 129	Ogemaw	85.5	6.8	9,031	82.3	91,200	26.4	13.9	624	37.9	84.8	23.2	5.6
26 133	Osceola	86.8	6.4	8,877	77.3	90,400	23.3	13.4	565	30.0	78.7	24.8	8.0
26 137	Otsego	82.6	8.1	9,803	79.1	118,300	22.5	11.7	662	31.0	83.4	20.6	5.9
26 139	Ottawa	84.9	6.8	94,154	78.3	152,500	22.4	11.8	743	31.2	84.3	20.1	3.9
26 143	Roscommon	86.4	6.3	11,723	82.5	93,000	28.7	12.7	657	34.4	75.7	23.8	4.9
26 145	Saginaw	86.6	4.4	77,081	72.7	96,500	23.1	13.5	703	32.9	85.8	22.1	8.1
26 147	St. Clair	85.4	4.3	64,291	76.9	118,600	25.0	14.3	709	32.9	81.4	28.0	7.3
26 149	St. Joseph	91.4	2.5	22,577	77.1	107,500	23.0	12.3	629	30.7	81.6	23.7	6.1
26 151	Sanilac	92.0	2.7	16,011	80.6	95,000	24.5	14.1	611	29.9	77.9	28.2	5.4
26 155	Shiawassee	86.5	5.7	27,183	77.8	105,500	23.7	13.0	653	29.4	82.9	28.4	5.8
26 157	Tuscola	86.9	5.6	21,180	82.0	95,200	25.0	13.3	643	32.7	83.4	30.6	4.7
26 159	Van Buren	90.4	4.5	27,952	78.9	119,800	24.2	13.1	646	32.8	83.0	24.4	5.3
26 161	Washtenaw	76.6	9.3	134,570	60.5	193,000	23.4	13.4	893	32.3	73.0	22.8	8.7
26 163	Wayne	85.4	2.8	667,145	64.3	83,800	24.5	15.5	781	37.5	81.2	25.0	13.9
26 165	Wexford	84.5	6.3	12,271	74.1	98,800	25.4	13.3	649	31.6	80.7	21.4	9.2
27 000	**Minnesota**	85.4	6.3	2,102,761	72.4	185,800	23.2	11.8	804	29.9	78.0	22.9	7.2
27 003	Anoka	87.9	6.1	122,793	81.2	187,500	23.9	11.7	945	31.4	81.8	27.9	4.8
27 005	Becker	89.4	5.0	13,347	79.9	172,500	24.1	13.2	616	27.7	77.1	23.4	6.0
27 007	Beltrami	85.5	6.9	16,677	70.4	149,900	23.7	12.3	705	29.3	75.0	19.8	6.3
27 009	Benton	85.0	7.5	15,390	70.3	158,300	23.8	11.3	661	32.1	82.5	21.4	7.1
27 013	Blue Earth	81.6	10.5	24,573	66.2	156,900	22.0	10.0	699	34.2	81.7	17.3	5.9
27 015	Brown	91.4	4.2	10,688	78.6	118,500	21.9	10.5	596	27.3	78.1	15.0	5.2
27 017	Carlton	90.7	5.4	13,621	78.3	160,000	24.3	12.5	685	31.7	84.0	21.7	5.7
27 019	Carver	88.2	7.4	33,166	81.0	261,400	23.6	11.0	893	30.0	83.5	25.0	3.9
27 021	Cass	90.4	5.3	13,009	81.8	175,000	25.0	12.7	638	30.6	75.7	22.3	5.4

[1] 10.0 represents 10 percent or less; 50.0 represents 50 percent or higher.

Table C-2. Counties — Where: Migration, Housing, and Transportation, 2010–2012—*Continued*

STATE and county code	STATE or county	Percent who lived in the same house one year ago	Percent who did not live in the same county one year ago	Total occupied housing units	Percent owner-occupied housing units	Median value of owner-occupied housing units (dollars)	Median selected monthly owner costs as a percentage of household income — With a mortgage	Median selected monthly owner costs as a percentage of household income — Without a mortgage[1]	Median gross rent (dollars)	Median gross rent as a percentage of household income[1]	Percent of workers who drove alone to work	Mean travel time to work (minutes)	Percent of occupied housing units with no vehicle available
ACS table number:		C07204	C07204	B25003	B25003	B25077	B25092	B25092	B25064	B25071	C08301	B08013/E08012	C25045
Column number:		1	2	3	4	5	6	7	8	9	10	11	12
	Minnesota—Cont.												
27 025	Chisago	87.4	9.2	19,807	84.6	194,700	26.5	11.1	786	32.2	84.0	32.1	4.2
27 027	Clay	83.4	8.7	22,352	70.2	153,900	21.8	12.0	661	33.4	79.3	19.1	6.5
27 035	Crow Wing	85.9	5.4	26,793	75.1	180,000	23.9	11.6	709	29.8	78.8	21.6	6.4
27 037	Dakota	87.1	5.7	153,554	75.4	219,500	23.0	11.1	917	29.1	82.6	24.2	4.6
27 039	Dodge	90.2	4.7	7,414	84.6	159,700	21.7	12.5	658	33.8	82.2	23.5	3.5
27 041	Douglas	85.0	5.4	15,609	76.2	189,000	24.0	12.1	624	29.9	81.7	18.8	6.2
27 045	Fillmore	90.3	3.5	8,349	79.2	134,200	23.3	12.9	590	27.0	70.5	25.8	7.7
27 047	Freeborn	88.7	3.5	13,249	76.2	104,600	22.2	11.9	539	26.4	81.5	18.6	7.6
27 049	Goodhue	89.3	5.2	18,623	77.3	182,700	24.8	12.6	730	31.7	78.9	23.0	6.5
27 053	Hennepin	82.0	6.2	478,538	63.5	228,100	23.4	12.5	894	29.7	73.6	22.9	10.4
27 057	Hubbard	91.4	5.1	8,506	82.5	175,000	27.0	13.1	658	28.3	80.0	23.3	3.7
27 059	Isanti	89.6	6.4	13,771	83.5	174,600	25.5	12.2	798	29.6	81.5	32.2	3.6
27 061	Itasca	86.9	5.2	18,341	81.4	151,800	24.8	11.8	596	28.7	81.0	23.1	7.1
27 067	Kandiyohi	88.0	4.8	17,154	73.9	159,400	23.4	11.5	626	31.9	80.3	17.2	7.6
27 079	Le Sueur	89.1	4.9	11,098	80.0	178,400	25.0	11.7	738	28.9	81.9	24.7	3.1
27 083	Lyon	82.7	7.2	10,030	67.7	141,100	20.0	10.0	628	25.4	72.9	15.1	7.0
27 085	McLeod	89.1	3.7	14,802	76.0	153,200	23.3	13.1	645	24.2	81.1	22.7	3.9
27 091	Martin	90.2	3.6	8,884	75.7	105,800	19.6	10.0	617	26.3	79.9	15.7	7.4
27 093	Meeker	90.3	4.4	9,493	80.3	156,700	25.4	12.9	682	30.2	81.2	25.3	4.3
27 095	Mille Lacs	85.2	6.6	10,356	74.8	144,000	25.8	15.5	655	28.9	79.9	28.6	7.1
27 097	Morrison	88.9	5.5	13,496	79.9	154,100	26.1	13.0	621	28.6	75.3	25.1	6.7
27 099	Mower	86.3	5.2	15,748	73.0	107,500	19.8	10.8	690	32.7	78.6	17.6	6.6
27 103	Nicollet	82.6	9.2	12,240	74.3	168,400	23.4	11.6	719	28.6	74.0	15.9	3.6
27 105	Nobles	84.5	3.4	7,877	72.0	104,900	21.4	12.3	582	26.6	74.4	15.6	6.2
27 109	Olmsted	85.7	5.2	57,073	74.4	169,700	21.6	10.0	771	29.5	76.6	17.2	6.1
27 111	Otter Tail	88.5	4.3	24,350	78.5	163,500	23.0	11.5	603	28.7	76.1	21.0	5.4
27 115	Pine	87.9	5.8	12,008	80.3	142,700	26.7	13.7	718	27.6	79.1	29.5	5.7
27 119	Polk	83.1	7.7	12,682	71.0	124,100	19.5	11.6	652	29.4	80.4	16.7	6.8
27 123	Ramsey	80.4	7.9	204,535	59.4	194,600	23.1	12.1	826	31.3	74.6	22.6	11.3
27 131	Rice	83.5	8.5	22,321	74.6	190,700	24.1	12.3	750	28.8	70.6	23.0	6.4
27 137	St. Louis	83.0	5.7	84,519	71.0	135,800	22.4	11.7	650	32.7	77.8	19.5	9.7
27 139	Scott	89.8	6.7	45,770	84.7	243,400	23.8	10.5	970	28.2	83.7	26.1	3.3
27 141	Sherburne	86.0	9.0	30,356	80.7	188,600	24.9	10.8	874	30.2	82.4	31.6	2.9
27 145	Stearns	79.6	9.3	56,182	72.4	167,900	22.7	11.9	721	30.3	77.8	20.6	5.3
27 147	Steele	86.1	4.9	14,448	76.3	154,900	23.2	11.1	686	30.2	84.3	17.8	7.6
27 153	Todd	91.2	3.5	10,118	82.5	127,100	25.3	13.1	530	27.3	74.5	23.0	6.3
27 157	Wabasha	92.1	3.4	8,845	83.7	159,100	23.3	12.1	661	29.4	74.1	22.7	3.9
27 163	Washington	90.2	5.3	89,096	80.8	237,900	22.7	10.1	1074	28.5	83.0	25.2	3.6
27 169	Winona	84.0	6.9	18,998	70.3	156,600	24.0	10.9	617	31.9	75.6	17.4	7.2
27 171	Wright	88.8	5.3	45,213	84.1	192,100	24.0	11.9	873	31.1	84.7	30.2	3.0
28 000	**Mississippi**	85.9	6.1	1,085,563	69.2	100,000	23.1	12.0	692	32.8	83.7	23.9	6.9
28 001	Adams	92.2	3.8	12,237	69.2	84,900	26.9	14.0	550	34.6	88.9	18.8	8.3
28 003	Alcorn	86.8	5.1	14,389	72.1	85,100	23.5	12.4	588	31.0	87.8	21.9	6.1
28 011	Bolivar	86.0	4.5	12,257	55.3	84,700	22.3	12.8	563	31.8	83.1	16.4	13.7
28 025	Clay	89.7	2.9	7,947	70.9	80,700	28.3	14.3	617	35.2	86.3	22.0	10.2
28 027	Coahoma	84.8	6.1	9,396	52.5	54,400	29.1	14.6	536	28.5	73.4	18.9	15.3
28 029	Copiah	92.1	4.3	10,027	73.3	67,200	22.4	12.0	606	30.0	86.9	23.8	9.2
28 031	Covington	91.6	6.0	7,267	83.1	74,100	25.7	13.2	538	30.4	83.8	28.6	6.1
28 033	DeSoto	86.4	6.3	57,912	75.1	151,100	22.4	10.2	941	29.7	86.5	25.5	2.9
28 035	Forrest	78.0	10.0	27,608	55.4	117,700	23.7	13.2	680	37.8	80.0	20.3	8.4
28 039	George	85.4	5.3	7,740	83.1	94,700	19.6	10.0	848	43.5	74.9	35.0	7.4
28 043	Grenada	86.6	4.6	8,102	72.4	91,700	24.3	10.9	531	33.9	78.0	23.7	8.5
28 045	Hancock	84.1	10.1	18,131	75.6	135,900	25.9	13.7	732	32.2	82.1	27.7	3.6
28 047	Harrison	79.1	9.0	72,134	61.1	140,000	25.2	11.4	838	33.3	81.4	21.1	5.0
28 049	Hinds	85.5	4.4	87,736	60.1	108,800	22.9	10.4	759	36.8	84.5	21.2	7.4
28 057	Itawamba	86.6	8.9	8,945	78.5	81,400	20.7	10.8	611	31.5	88.7	23.8	3.1
28 059	Jackson	85.0	5.4	50,558	71.3	121,600	23.1	11.4	832	32.7	81.7	23.4	3.8
28 067	Jones	86.1	6.5	24,560	72.8	84,100	22.5	11.9	644	28.1	85.9	22.4	5.8
28 071	Lafayette	71.1	17.8	14,428	61.8	156,100	21.9	12.0	802	38.8	84.1	18.8	4.5
28 073	Lamar	80.6	12.3	21,665	64.6	150,800	22.7	10.4	787	32.8	85.4	24.9	4.8
28 075	Lauderdale	86.5	6.5	29,458	66.3	89,500	22.9	11.5	607	32.0	85.2	20.8	7.4
28 079	Leake	89.8	3.9	8,175	73.4	73,400	21.4	15.4	551	28.7	78.6	35.9	9.4
28 081	Lee	88.1	4.9	31,534	69.0	104,100	22.1	11.1	645	29.5	89.2	19.0	5.1
28 083	Leflore	91.5	3.5	10,896	51.1	68,300	24.1	13.7	568	33.7	85.9	17.2	11.2
28 085	Lincoln	91.9	3.4	13,170	74.5	83,200	21.2	12.3	578	28.8	89.1	27.0	3.8
28 087	Lowndes	84.2	6.3	23,518	61.5	107,800	24.8	10.7	681	35.3	85.2	20.8	9.1
28 089	Madison	89.1	5.3	36,617	70.3	197,600	21.7	10.0	845	27.8	87.2	22.6	4.5
28 091	Marion	88.7	3.6	9,902	76.9	82,400	22.7	14.2	520	40.7	79.7	36.5	9.8
28 093	Marshall	85.7	5.6	13,041	77.6	90,300	26.1	15.3	709	34.7	82.1	30.2	7.4
28 095	Monroe	88.0	3.1	13,790	76.5	77,200	22.9	12.7	551	24.8	85.2	22.0	7.5
28 099	Neshoba	88.9	4.5	10,587	74.3	79,300	22.8	12.2	609	24.3	77.3	23.7	5.6
28 101	Newton	87.8	5.7	8,053	76.9	67,100	21.5	12.2	604	25.2	81.2	26.3	5.2
28 105	Oktibbeha	72.1	14.4	18,499	50.4	131,000	21.8	12.3	685	41.2	81.2	18.4	7.3
28 107	Panola	92.2	3.1	11,525	76.1	81,900	20.8	13.2	667	35.2	87.5	23.9	9.6
28 109	Pearl River	86.6	5.6	20,344	75.9	109,400	24.1	13.9	783	34.5	84.0	34.4	6.0

[1]10.0 represents 10 percent or less; 50.0 represents 50 percent or higher.

Table C-2. Counties — Where: Migration, Housing, and Transportation, 2010–2012—*Continued*

STATE and county code	STATE or county	Percent who lived in the same house one year ago	Percent who did not live in the same county one year ago	Total occupied housing units	Percent owner-occupied housing units (dollars)	Median value of owner-occupied housing units (dollars)	Median selected monthly owner costs as a percentage of household income — With a mortgage	Without a mortgage[1]	Median gross rent (dollars)	Median gross rent as a percentage of household income[1]	Percent of workers who drove alone to work	Mean travel time to work (minutes)	Percent of occupied housing units with no vehicle available
	ACS table number:	C07204	C07204	B25003	B25003	B25077	B25092	B25092	B25064	B25071	C08301	B08013/B08012	C25045
	Column number:	1	2	3	4	5	6	7	8	9	10	11	12
	Mississippi—Cont.												
28 113	Pike	82.6	4.4	14,686	68.3	77,000	23.8	12.3	630	32.7	80.2	23.9	10.7
28 115	Pontotoc	89.8	3.8	9,769	78.1	81,300	22.0	11.5	598	24.7	81.2	25.4	4.3
28 117	Prentiss	84.7	5.6	9,711	74.5	72,600	23.3	11.9	503	34.1	79.9	23.7	8.7
28 121	Rankin	84.0	7.2	52,875	74.5	148,000	20.5	10.0	840	29.1	87.3	25.2	3.0
28 123	Scott	84.3	5.2	9,753	79.4	67,800	23.7	11.1	543	25.0	76.4	24.1	8.0
28 127	Simpson	88.4	4.6	9,883	77.5	73,100	21.4	10.7	539	26.4	76.0	33.4	5.4
28 133	Sunflower	83.1	9.2	8,285	57.2	70,100	26.7	11.7	523	33.4	79.9	18.0	14.7
28 137	Tate	89.4	5.7	9,967	71.7	122,000	23.7	11.0	701	36.6	86.8	29.5	3.0
28 139	Tippah	87.8	4.5	8,318	76.4	73,500	27.2	10.7	543	29.9	83.8	23.9	7.1
28 145	Union	88.1	4.9	10,234	71.7	80,000	22.9	10.0	662	32.4	79.4	24.4	5.4
28 149	Warren	92.1	2.7	18,508	65.2	103,000	21.5	11.1	651	34.8	88.3	19.0	9.0
28 151	Washington	79.3	6.2	18,301	54.4	74,000	23.6	14.0	596	38.5	78.0	18.1	14.7
28 153	Wayne	92.1	3.4	8,192	83.4	68,700	24.5	15.5	562	30.9	78.4	29.8	6.5
28 163	Yazoo	86.4	5.2	8,515	58.8	64,800	25.2	15.0	601	43.2	83.1	27.8	12.7
29 000	**Missouri**	83.7	6.7	2,354,106	68.4	137,100	22.2	11.9	714	30.1	81.5	23.0	7.4
29 001	Adair	72.2	13.3	9,512	61.2	100,200	17.8	12.2	510	36.2	77.6	15.6	9.9
29 007	Audrain	84.2	9.9	9,337	72.8	89,400	20.0	11.6	624	24.7	81.3	18.5	7.3
29 009	Barry	84.5	5.2	13,477	75.0	109,100	23.4	10.9	580	25.7	77.9	20.7	3.2
29 019	Boone	73.2	10.1	64,944	57.1	160,500	20.5	10.0	769	33.5	79.2	18.6	5.2
29 021	Buchanan	79.3	8.6	33,578	63.8	108,200	20.3	12.0	640	31.9	82.2	16.9	8.6
29 023	Butler	82.8	4.5	16,894	68.5	86,800	20.2	11.7	576	30.7	86.5	16.1	7.2
29 027	Callaway	81.3	9.1	16,904	76.0	133,400	22.7	10.0	624	27.5	85.2	20.3	3.9
29 029	Camden	86.2	6.6	17,642	79.8	172,900	24.4	11.1	621	29.2	79.2	21.8	3.5
29 031	Cape Girardeau	80.9	8.7	29,489	65.0	135,300	19.9	10.5	673	29.8	82.7	18.1	7.1
29 037	Cass	87.4	5.4	37,183	78.0	155,700	24.0	12.5	890	28.7	82.8	27.2	2.8
29 043	Christian	82.7	8.6	29,537	73.7	139,300	21.9	12.2	744	28.8	81.0	25.3	3.3
29 047	Clay	84.7	6.1	86,466	72.1	152,800	22.2	12.7	794	27.6	84.6	23.1	4.2
29 049	Clinton	82.3	9.1	8,059	72.2	143,300	22.3	12.2	721	23.9	81.7	27.6	3.2
29 051	Cole	83.9	7.0	29,288	66.9	145,600	19.1	10.0	579	26.0	83.4	17.1	7.5
29 055	Crawford	83.8	6.5	9,580	74.8	105,500	23.2	13.0	582	32.2	77.5	27.4	7.6
29 069	Dunklin	84.2	6.3	12,635	62.2	71,300	20.5	12.6	488	31.4	86.1	19.8	10.7
29 071	Franklin	89.3	3.4	39,448	76.5	146,800	24.0	11.6	624	26.2	82.3	27.9	4.9
29 077	Greene	78.5	8.1	115,196	59.6	129,100	21.9	10.4	664	31.5	83.3	18.9	6.7
29 083	Henry	82.1	6.5	9,500	72.4	101,500	22.7	13.0	627	27.9	82.5	22.2	4.7
29 091	Howell	86.7	3.6	15,921	68.2	107,600	22.4	10.0	511	32.8	85.7	18.8	8.9
29 095	Jackson	83.2	5.0	269,581	61.0	126,900	22.9	13.4	783	32.4	81.9	22.7	10.1
29 097	Jasper	82.9	5.2	45,262	65.0	98,800	20.8	13.3	637	30.2	84.4	18.0	7.9
29 099	Jefferson	89.0	4.3	81,076	81.7	153,200	22.7	11.9	729	29.8	84.8	30.1	4.3
29 101	Johnson	74.1	12.6	20,139	62.0	141,800	21.9	12.0	713	31.6	82.9	22.0	4.0
29 105	Laclede	83.8	6.9	14,064	72.0	96,100	22.5	11.1	584	24.3	80.4	21.7	5.1
29 107	Lafayette	83.6	8.4	13,050	75.4	117,900	19.4	11.8	632	31.4	77.6	26.3	5.0
29 109	Lawrence	83.8	6.1	14,665	74.0	94,800	24.0	11.8	591	25.4	78.4	21.8	5.9
29 113	Lincoln	86.4	5.4	19,009	79.3	148,500	23.6	11.9	666	29.8	80.9	35.2	4.5
29 119	McDonald	83.1	10.6	8,249	68.1	81,700	22.1	11.2	575	27.3	74.3	28.1	5.9
29 127	Marion	86.0	4.8	11,206	67.0	104,500	20.0	11.0	549	27.8	79.4	18.5	7.5
29 131	Miller	88.5	4.1	9,891	74.5	110,500	22.2	11.2	566	29.9	76.5	30.5	5.8
29 141	Morgan	90.5	4.6	7,945	82.7	114,000	28.3	12.4	549	28.7	71.2	23.6	7.7
29 145	Newton	82.4	6.8	22,205	74.2	103,100	22.4	11.2	595	27.9	79.4	19.9	6.5
29 147	Nodaway	70.9	15.2	8,563	57.0	109,700	21.7	11.2	593	35.4	77.7	15.1	7.3
29 159	Pettis	81.9	8.2	16,256	68.4	98,500	21.5	11.5	674	36.7	76.5	19.2	8.1
29 161	Phelps	75.2	12.3	16,861	62.1	110,500	21.1	10.0	613	30.9	78.8	18.4	8.3
29 165	Platte	83.0	8.2	36,355	64.6	181,100	20.9	12.0	838	27.0	83.3	23.0	4.9
29 167	Polk	86.3	7.1	11,727	68.7	115,700	21.7	11.6	638	30.9	82.8	23.6	3.9
29 169	Pulaski	58.0	31.5	15,610	54.2	121,900	20.6	10.4	912	25.3	53.3	18.1	5.3
29 175	Randolph	83.7	8.9	8,767	69.4	87,300	21.6	12.3	608	26.8	81.1	21.7	6.4
29 177	Ray	84.6	5.5	9,040	75.0	114,400	22.6	12.1	753	29.2	79.3	30.0	7.5
29 183	St. Charles	89.2	5.0	135,386	80.4	188,900	21.8	11.9	855	27.9	87.3	24.9	3.4
29 187	St. Francois	77.0	9.4	24,934	64.5	100,700	21.9	10.7	600	29.9	82.6	24.3	8.3
29 189	St. Louis	85.7	5.4	402,680	70.8	174,100	22.2	12.6	838	30.1	84.0	23.4	7.2
29 195	Saline	82.5	6.8	8,848	66.2	82,500	21.8	12.7	545	27.2	78.1	19.5	9.9
29 201	Scott	85.4	4.2	15,335	66.8	96,400	19.3	11.1	584	30.3	79.5	18.5	7.2
29 207	Stoddard	85.8	4.3	12,179	71.9	87,700	19.0	10.3	506	25.5	84.4	20.0	6.7
29 209	Stone	85.7	7.9	12,934	79.9	145,600	23.2	11.8	693	29.8	76.1	28.8	3.4
29 213	Taney	77.4	8.6	19,933	63.7	136,700	26.1	11.3	667	30.4	75.2	20.3	3.2
29 215	Texas	84.7	6.2	9,564	72.1	99,900	21.1	11.8	488	31.0	84.6	26.9	5.5
29 217	Vernon	86.0	6.1	8,078	72.3	85,500	21.3	10.4	590	28.1	76.5	17.5	7.3
29 219	Warren	87.4	5.8	12,766	78.5	148,500	22.5	12.3	673	28.3	82.3	32.0	5.5
29 221	Washington	88.8	7.1	9,114	73.7	73,300	20.8	11.2	510	27.1	81.4	34.2	8.0
29 225	Webster	85.1	7.1	12,481	76.3	116,800	22.4	10.0	602	26.7	79.0	32.7	8.2
29 510	St. Louis city	77.9	8.7	138,981	44.6	120,600	23.8	14.2	719	33.7	71.3	23.7	22.1

[1]10.0 represents 10 percent or less; 50.0 represents 50 percent or higher.

Table C-2. Counties — Where: Migration, Housing, and Transportation, 2010–2012—*Continued*

STATE and county code	STATE or county	Percent who lived in the same house one year ago	Percent who did not live in the same county one year ago	Total occupied housing units	Percent owner-occupied housing units	Median value of owner-occupied housing units (dollars)	Median selected monthly owner costs as a percentage of household income — With a mortgage	Without a mortgage[1]	Median gross rent (dollars)	Median gross rent as a percentage of household income[1]	Percent of workers who drove alone to work	Mean travel time to work (minutes)	Percent of occupied housing units with no vehicle available
ACS table number:		C07204	C07204	B25003	B25003	B25077	B25092	B25092	B25064	B25071	C08301	B08013/B08012	C25045
Column number:		1	2	3	4	5	6	7	8	9	10	11	12
30 000	**Montana**	83.7	7.1	404,990	68.2	183,600	23.9	11.7	672	28.5	75.4	18.3	5.2
30 013	Cascade	81.5	7.5	32,982	64.6	158,000	22.3	11.3	616	26.2	79.0	16.6	7.2
30 029	Flathead	90.8	3.3	36,950	69.9	226,900	29.2	12.7	749	30.8	77.3	19.4	4.2
30 031	Gallatin	75.1	11.0	36,704	60.9	260,000	26.6	11.3	823	29.2	72.4	17.1	4.4
30 047	Lake	83.0	7.4	12,094	70.9	222,600	27.8	13.2	596	30.0	69.5	22.4	4.1
30 049	Lewis and Clark	84.7	5.8	26,502	72.4	203,500	24.2	10.0	692	26.3	79.6	17.4	5.1
30 063	Missoula	76.9	8.6	45,413	59.2	232,900	24.9	12.4	743	32.7	72.8	16.8	5.7
30 081	Ravalli	85.4	7.8	17,026	72.3	237,100	28.4	12.9	662	34.4	75.4	28.0	2.5
30 093	Silver Bow	81.0	8.7	14,874	65.3	129,500	19.6	11.6	585	28.7	81.8	15.6	8.9
30 111	Yellowstone	83.7	6.3	60,814	69.6	180,200	22.2	11.5	696	28.5	80.2	19.3	5.4
31 000	**Nebraska**	83.2	6.3	726,422	66.8	127,800	21.0	12.4	694	27.2	80.8	18.2	5.7
31 001	Adams	80.5	10.5	12,721	69.4	99,200	19.8	11.4	609	23.3	81.7	15.1	4.8
31 019	Buffalo	78.9	8.8	17,615	64.1	142,000	19.7	10.8	649	28.4	78.9	15.6	4.9
31 025	Cass	91.1	5.1	9,689	79.2	148,600	23.1	13.0	722	27.6	81.0	27.3	3.9
31 043	Dakota	85.8	3.5	7,308	65.0	104,500	19.9	12.7	710	28.0	81.5	15.8	4.4
31 047	Dawson	87.5	4.3	8,706	68.4	85,000	20.1	12.9	603	21.3	77.9	15.8	3.1
31 053	Dodge	83.9	4.8	15,282	67.9	109,800	19.7	12.9	644	26.1	84.1	17.9	5.2
31 055	Douglas	81.9	5.1	203,592	62.6	143,100	21.7	13.2	780	29.4	82.5	18.9	7.9
31 067	Gage	89.4	4.9	9,028	73.2	106,300	20.7	12.4	552	24.5	82.3	21.0	6.1
31 079	Hall	82.1	6.3	22,366	65.2	112,100	21.7	13.2	626	25.8	82.5	15.0	6.7
31 109	Lancaster	77.7	6.4	114,964	59.2	148,300	21.1	11.0	699	29.0	80.6	18.6	6.6
31 111	Lincoln	86.4	5.2	15,104	70.3	107,800	21.1	14.2	572	25.2	82.2	13.9	5.3
31 119	Madison	83.1	7.4	14,050	65.2	110,400	19.0	12.7	602	27.2	83.5	14.6	4.9
31 141	Platte	88.5	5.3	12,547	70.7	118,900	19.5	10.6	606	21.5	82.7	15.3	3.3
31 153	Sarpy	82.8	8.7	59,930	69.6	162,200	21.3	11.9	843	26.0	86.8	20.1	2.7
31 155	Saunders	87.5	6.3	8,282	77.4	144,800	23.0	13.9	675	23.7	79.9	25.6	4.8
31 157	Scotts Bluff	84.4	6.5	14,906	66.9	99,300	21.9	15.1	638	28.9	81.3	15.1	5.0
31 177	Washington	91.1	4.0	7,721	81.7	174,000	22.2	12.2	703	20.0	83.9	21.9	4.8
32 000	**Nevada**	76.9	5.1	992,757	56.2	161,300	26.9	11.7	966	31.2	78.3	23.8	7.9
32 001	Churchill	78.7	9.3	9,597	62.1	150,000	23.8	10.0	844	25.8	82.7	18.1	3.1
32 003	Clark	75.7	4.4	703,972	53.8	156,500	27.3	11.6	992	31.4	78.8	24.2	8.4
32 005	Douglas	87.0	6.0	19,429	72.1	272,200	29.0	12.5	1,011	29.1	76.6	24.8	2.8
32 007	Elko	84.3	6.0	17,425	72.2	175,400	19.4	10.0	895	22.6	66.0	28.0	2.7
32 019	Lyon	79.8	10.9	19,504	68.5	132,900	27.1	12.7	922	31.0	84.1	30.6	3.5
32 023	Nye	81.9	7.6	18,431	70.3	97,600	28.8	12.9	880	32.9	78.6	26.6	5.2
32 031	Washoe	78.3	5.7	162,452	57.0	190,600	27.2	12.2	893	32.2	77.7	21.5	8.6
32 510	Carson City	78.3	9.2	21,212	58.5	198,100	25.1	12.0	838	28.8	83.7	16.8	8.1
33 000	**New Hampshire**	86.4	5.6	518,009	71.4	239,100	26.2	16.8	969	30.2	81.4	26.4	5.2
33 001	Belknap	89.4	5.8	25,422	75.3	218,000	26.5	16.7	889	28.6	85.3	26.9	5.9
33 003	Carroll	88.8	5.0	21,192	80.7	223,000	27.4	14.7	905	32.4	81.5	25.5	3.8
33 005	Cheshire	83.4	7.7	30,405	70.1	198,800	26.1	19.2	943	33.1	80.6	21.7	5.6
33 007	Coos	86.4	4.9	14,515	70.3	132,000	26.3	17.1	650	28.8	79.5	21.9	8.6
33 009	Grafton	84.5	8.4	35,102	69.4	211,500	24.5	16.2	892	28.3	73.8	22.4	6.1
33 011	Hillsborough	86.4	4.2	153,838	67.3	249,100	25.6	16.6	1,028	29.9	82.1	26.9	6.1
33 013	Merrimack	86.6	5.9	57,387	71.7	230,200	27.2	17.7	899	32.1	81.9	26.1	5.9
33 015	Rockingham	89.7	4.6	116,143	76.9	279,600	26.4	15.7	1,062	28.7	84.0	29.1	2.8
33 017	Strafford	79.1	8.9	46,300	65.3	220,000	27.6	18.3	943	33.1	77.6	25.3	5.9
33 019	Sullivan	87.6	4.9	17,705	75.5	172,500	24.7	17.0	860	30.0	76.3	25.5	5.3
34 000	**New Jersey**	90.1	3.6	3,181,881	65.6	325,800	28.4	18.9	1,156	32.4	72.0	30.5	11.8
34 001	Atlantic	88.9	3.3	99,782	68.1	235,300	31.1	19.8	1,025	34.8	75.5	23.4	14.1
34 003	Bergen	92.6	2.7	333,711	65.7	448,100	29.5	19.7	1,306	31.4	70.2	31.0	8.5
34 005	Burlington	90.9	4.0	164,889	77.7	250,200	25.9	17.1	1,165	32.2	82.4	28.8	4.9
34 007	Camden	88.4	4.0	187,178	67.7	210,800	27.5	19.6	963	35.8	77.2	28.0	12.0
34 009	Cape May	89.5	4.3	41,459	74.6	315,500	29.1	18.3	1,029	34.4	77.2	21.7	9.8
34 011	Cumberland	86.6	4.6	49,981	67.6	168,600	26.5	17.9	968	36.2	80.2	23.9	10.4
34 013	Essex	89.2	3.1	276,592	45.7	365,800	30.8	20.6	1,041	33.7	61.6	32.4	23.5
34 015	Gloucester	91.8	3.6	104,568	80.7	225,200	26.6	18.5	1,012	33.2	86.1	28.4	5.7
34 017	Hudson	85.5	4.3	243,675	32.8	342,000	32.2	21.8	1,156	28.7	39.4	33.9	32.7
34 019	Hunterdon	91.6	5.1	47,306	84.1	398,600	26.3	16.0	1,268	30.9	82.2	33.3	3.2
34 021	Mercer	87.1	5.3	131,315	65.6	283,000	26.0	16.5	1,111	31.9	71.3	27.2	11.8
34 023	Middlesex	88.5	4.1	280,599	66.0	330,300	28.0	18.3	1,244	29.2	72.9	32.4	8.1
34 025	Monmouth	91.5	3.0	234,366	75.5	387,700	28.2	18.4	1,221	34.6	75.1	34.0	7.9
34 027	Morris	91.9	3.8	179,946	75.4	428,600	27.4	16.8	1,326	29.0	79.6	29.9	4.9
34 029	Ocean	91.5	3.0	222,796	81.3	268,000	29.5	20.3	1,309	38.7	82.1	31.1	6.5
34 031	Passaic	92.0	2.2	162,615	53.8	348,700	31.7	22.0	1,130	36.9	72.1	25.9	16.7
34 033	Salem	88.7	4.1	24,817	70.0	192,100	25.1	18.7	980	36.8	86.2	26.7	9.5
34 035	Somerset	92.6	3.4	115,709	78.2	398,000	26.8	17.5	1,371	30.0	78.9	31.8	5.7
34 037	Sussex	92.4	3.7	54,274	84.4	282,900	27.9	18.6	1,187	39.4	84.4	37.9	3.2
34 039	Union	89.2	4.0	184,721	60.2	360,400	29.7	20.1	1,148	32.6	69.3	29.5	11.4
34 041	Warren	92.6	3.5	41,582	75.2	267,200	28.4	19.4	954	31.3	80.3	34.7	6.0

[1] 10.0 represents 10 percent or less; 50.0 represents 50 percent or higher.

Table C-2. Counties — Where: Migration, Housing, and Transportation, 2010–2012—*Continued*

STATE and county code	STATE or county	Percent who lived in the same house one year ago	Percent who did not live in the same county one year ago	Total occupied housing units	Percent owner-occupied housing units	Median value of owner-occupied housing units (dollars)	Median selected monthly owner costs as a percentage of household income — With a mortgage	Without a mortgage[1]	Median gross rent (dollars)	Median gross rent as a percentage of household income[1]	Percent of workers who drove alone to work	Mean travel time to work (minutes)	Percent of occupied housing units with no vehicle available
ACS table number:		C07204	C07204	B25003	B25003	B25077	B25092	B25092	B25064	B25071	C08301	B08013/ B08012	C25045
Column number:		1	2	3	4	5	6	7	8	9	10	11	12
35 000	**New Mexico**	85.4	5.4	765,306	68.1	159,300	23.6	10.0	744	30.4	79.2	21.7	5.8
35 001	Bernalillo	83.9	5.3	264,592	62.5	186,400	24.2	10.0	768	30.6	80.0	21.7	6.6
35 005	Chaves	83.4	5.8	23,386	66.1	95,400	20.0	10.0	621	28.5	83.1	17.3	4.2
35 006	Cibola	89.3	4.9	8,056	74.5	81,800	19.1	10.0	582	24.8	75.9	22.0	7.1
35 009	Curry	82.7	5.9	18,058	60.3	122,600	21.0	10.0	634	29.7	84.9	15.3	6.9
35 013	Dona Ana	81.3	6.1	73,889	64.8	137,300	23.7	11.0	680	34.8	81.5	20.3	5.5
35 015	Eddy	85.8	6.0	19,860	73.7	108,200	17.4	10.0	725	24.4	81.1	18.3	3.0
35 017	Grant	90.8	3.1	12,226	74.4	128,000	22.8	10.0	590	37.2	76.6	21.4	4.1
35 025	Lea	88.5	4.4	20,396	69.8	94,900	17.9	10.0	734	26.6	83.1	16.9	3.5
35 027	Lincoln	87.1	7.9	8,644	78.9	157,600	23.8	12.8	743	26.6	69.8	19.9	3.7
35 029	Luna	82.6	7.4	9,329	67.9	85,700	25.5	10.0	592	26.9	73.1	20.9	6.5
35 031	McKinley	92.6	2.9	17,642	71.2	75,200	20.1	10.0	531	21.8	71.1	22.8	12.5
35 035	Otero	80.8	7.8	24,463	65.5	100,800	22.9	11.1	706	27.1	76.8	21.3	5.5
35 039	Rio Arriba	92.7	2.6	15,029	78.1	127,700	21.6	10.2	643	26.0	77.7	25.1	6.7
35 041	Roosevelt	77.5	10.7	7,188	57.2	117,500	20.1	10.0	654	32.9	77.7	14.4	5.1
35 043	Sandoval	90.2	5.4	47,339	81.2	176,800	25.4	10.0	974	30.8	80.9	29.3	3.6
35 045	San Juan	88.1	3.7	41,128	73.7	152,500	21.2	10.0	737	27.6	84.2	24.6	5.4
35 047	San Miguel	89.8	3.4	11,614	71.2	111,500	27.1	12.6	641	34.0	77.8	21.5	5.3
35 049	Santa Fe	84.0	5.8	61,371	67.9	280,100	27.4	10.0	899	32.4	72.2	21.4	5.0
35 055	Taos	88.7	3.4	13,534	71.7	208,900	24.5	10.8	754	42.6	71.4	20.7	6.2
35 061	Valencia	85.6	6.6	27,290	79.1	136,200	25.5	10.0	752	36.5	82.4	28.7	4.4
36 000	**New York**	88.7	3.1	7,210,095	53.9	286,700	25.9	15.3	1,076	32.1	54.0	31.5	29.4
36 001	Albany	85.8	5.9	121,548	59.2	209,100	22.5	13.3	893	29.0	77.8	19.9	12.7
36 003	Allegany	85.0	7.5	18,572	72.7	68,100	20.8	14.3	592	31.6	72.9	21.2	7.8
36 005	Bronx	87.9	1.4	471,665	19.0	373,500	32.9	14.4	1,022	35.2	22.7	42.5	61.2
36 007	Broome	85.8	4.8	80,214	66.3	108,300	20.7	13.1	685	32.1	79.5	18.5	11.6
36 009	Cattaraugus	87.4	4.2	32,114	71.9	79,800	21.6	13.8	608	27.8	79.0	21.8	10.0
36 011	Cayuga	86.5	4.9	30,819	73.0	103,700	20.7	13.0	639	27.7	32.2	21.2	8.9
36 013	Chautauqua	85.5	4.8	54,688	69.6	83,700	19.9	13.8	597	30.3	79.5	18.1	11.1
36 015	Chemung	84.8	5.3	35,240	67.5	94,400	18.3	12.8	679	29.8	34.8	19.1	11.6
36 017	Chenango	90.9	3.5	19,371	75.9	92,000	21.7	13.8	579	30.2	74.2	23.1	6.8
36 019	Clinton	84.2	6.8	31,901	66.6	124,900	21.0	12.2	713	30.8	77.4	20.6	10.0
36 021	Columbia	89.8	4.4	24,953	72.9	219,300	26.2	14.8	855	27.7	77.4	25.7	6.6
36 023	Cortland	86.2	5.2	17,923	68.5	104,200	22.2	14.3	660	28.0	76.9	21.3	9.3
36 025	Delaware	88.2	5.0	19,887	73.8	132,000	24.8	14.5	639	28.8	74.2	24.0	8.8
36 027	Dutchess	87.9	4.5	107,134	69.6	288,400	28.1	17.0	1,090	32.2	76.5	31.1	8.6
36 029	Erie	87.2	2.9	379,140	65.0	125,100	21.2	13.5	707	30.3	81.5	21.0	13.8
36 031	Essex	86.5	8.0	16,523	70.5	147,900	23.6	14.2	776	34.4	74.1	21.2	9.4
36 033	Franklin	82.7	8.3	19,184	71.8	97,600	20.9	13.5	650	30.7	78.0	19.7	10.8
36 035	Fulton	86.4	4.8	22,665	68.4	106,600	23.1	13.4	701	29.6	82.4	22.3	8.9
36 037	Genesee	89.4	3.8	23,840	73.3	105,700	21.4	15.0	677	29.1	83.7	20.9	5.8
36 039	Greene	91.6	5.0	18,569	74.0	171,900	25.5	19.8	821	34.8	81.3	27.0	7.9
36 043	Herkimer	88.5	3.7	26,951	70.5	93,600	20.0	13.9	608	29.5	80.5	23.2	9.9
36 045	Jefferson	74.3	11.1	45,679	56.6	128,600	22.1	14.1	909	30.0	76.9	18.4	9.7
36 047	Kings	90.4	1.3	908,959	29.5	556,300	33.8	17.9	1,135	33.0	19.1	41.0	57.7
36 049	Lewis	92.3	3.6	10,885	76.2	108,700	21.2	13.2	657	32.4	82.8	23.6	7.7
36 051	Livingston	85.9	8.0	24,065	75.0	118,800	22.7	14.3	687	32.2	81.2	24.0	5.6
36 053	Madison	89.1	6.2	26,523	76.4	121,200	23.1	14.4	713	27.4	81.9	22.9	6.0
36 055	Monroe	84.9	3.5	296,800	64.8	135,700	22.2	13.6	797	33.8	82.4	19.7	11.7
36 057	Montgomery	86.0	5.2	19,701	67.5	101,900	22.1	16.6	693	31.2	79.6	23.2	13.3
36 059	Nassau	93.5	2.5	441,906	80.4	452,200	30.1	19.6	1,484	33.5	69.6	33.8	7.6
36 061	New York	83.3	4.8	733,765	22.0	812,300	20.9	10.9	1,418	28.5	6.6	30.5	78.8
36 063	Niagara	90.8	3.3	88,432	70.1	106,500	21.2	14.5	643	29.6	85.4	20.9	9.9
36 065	Oneida	86.2	4.8	90,538	67.3	110,600	20.5	12.8	684	30.0	82.4	20.0	12.2
36 067	Onondaga	84.6	4.4	184,224	65.3	133,500	21.5	13.2	751	30.6	80.5	19.5	12.7
36 069	Ontario	85.0	6.4	44,113	73.0	135,100	21.8	14.7	765	30.2	81.0	23.1	7.7
36 071	Orange	90.5	3.7	125,338	69.4	275,700	28.5	18.4	1,139	35.6	72.3	33.4	10.0
36 073	Orleans	84.7	6.9	15,849	77.7	90,300	23.4	16.8	644	31.3	85.2	26.7	7.4
36 075	Oswego	85.8	5.0	44,893	72.5	93,900	21.6	13.8	715	32.8	80.6	23.8	7.3
36 077	Otsego	84.4	8.3	23,875	72.3	139,500	22.5	14.0	754	35.8	68.8	22.9	9.3
36 079	Putnam	94.6	2.9	34,855	83.1	364,300	28.0	17.7	1,201	37.0	78.5	38.6	5.0
36 081	Queens	89.8	1.5	773,822	43.3	447,500	32.7	15.4	1,303	33.8	31.8	41.6	38.0
36 083	Rensselaer	86.4	6.6	63,991	65.9	179,800	23.4	14.4	836	29.3	80.2	22.1	10.5
36 085	Richmond	94.0	0.9	162,916	68.4	442,800	29.1	15.7	1,144	31.9	56.7	40.8	16.7
36 087	Rockland	92.6	2.4	97,943	69.3	430,400	29.0	18.1	1,326	35.2	71.6	29.9	10.6
36 089	St. Lawrence	82.1	6.9	42,055	71.1	87,000	21.6	14.1	679	32.0	75.7	20.3	10.2
36 091	Saratoga	88.5	5.2	89,371	71.7	229,000	23.1	13.0	937	27.5	83.9	25.1	5.2
36 093	Schenectady	90.8	4.0	58,120	66.0	168,800	23.4	14.5	819	31.7	81.5	22.3	11.9
36 095	Schoharie	84.8	6.8	12,942	76.0	141,500	23.2	14.0	709	32.9	79.0	29.5	8.0
36 099	Seneca	85.8	8.6	13,321	73.4	96,800	21.4	13.5	660	29.3	83.7	23.4	6.4
36 101	Steuben	87.8	3.8	41,422	70.0	87,000	20.8	12.6	626	25.4	80.3	21.8	8.7
36 103	Suffolk	93.0	1.8	496,396	78.9	383,000	29.9	19.6	1,459	34.3	79.1	30.7	5.3
36 105	Sullivan	85.4	6.5	29,768	66.7	173,000	27.9	15.8	837	33.2	76.5	29.1	10.3
36 107	Tioga	91.0	3.8	20,135	79.8	109,100	20.0	12.6	615	26.7	85.8	24.1	6.4
36 109	Tompkins	71.0	12.7	38,530	55.5	169,700	21.8	12.4	946	32.9	59.7	19.4	14.6

[1] 10.0 represents 10 percent or less; 50.0 represents 50 percent or higher.

Table C-2. Counties — Where: Migration, Housing, and Transportation, 2010–2012—*Continued*

STATE and county code	STATE or county	Percent who lived in the same house one year ago	Percent who did not live in the same county one year ago	Total occupied housing units	Percent owner-occupied housing units	Median value of owner-occupied housing units (dollars)	Median selected monthly owner costs as a percentage of household income		Median gross rent (dollars)	Median gross rent as a percentage of household income[1]	Percent of workers who drove alone to work	Mean travel time to work (minutes)	Percent of occupied housing units with no vehicle available
							With a mortgage	Without a mortgage[1]					
	ACS table number:	C07204	C07204	B25003	B25003	B25077	B25092	B25092	B25064	B25071	C08301	B08013/E08012	C25045
	Column number:	1	2	3	4	5	6	7	8	9	10	11	12
	New York—Cont.												
36 111	Ulster	87.6	4.8	69,477	69.2	232,300	27.2	18.5	988	34.8	77.4	27.1	7.6
36 113	Warren	88.4	4.8	28,195	69.8	192,400	23.3	14.0	833	32.2	83.0	22.9	8.1
36 115	Washington	85.5	6.9	24,242	75.3	147,900	24.8	14.1	804	31.6	79.0	26.2	6.3
36 117	Wayne	87.5	4.9	36,872	77.7	105,700	20.7	14.6	668	28.5	85.7	23.7	5.5
36 119	Westchester	89.6	3.4	342,568	62.1	516,600	27.8	19.2	1,302	33.3	60.2	31.9	14.6
36 121	Wyoming	88.3	7.2	15,716	74.9	101,000	21.2	12.6	589	29.6	80.4	26.1	5.6
36 123	Yates	88.5	6.4	9,466	79.3	116,500	22.7	12.8	617	28.9	72.3	21.7	11.0
37 000	**North Carolina**	84.6	6.2	3,699,308	66.3	152,800	23.3	12.2	761	30.9	81.2	23.5	6.7
37 001	Alamance	84.8	5.3	60,459	66.4	135,900	23.3	12.0	699	31.3	80.9	23.6	7.0
37 003	Alexander	90.2	4.3	13,949	76.1	116,000	21.7	10.0	563	27.8	84.2	24.5	4.6
37 007	Anson	85.7	6.8	9,592	72.6	80,800	23.5	14.3	637	32.3	81.5	23.9	9.9
37 009	Ashe	93.4	2.8	11,646	77.3	148,500	28.9	11.1	610	33.0	75.9	27.2	6.7
37 013	Beaufort	93.2	3.0	19,218	70.0	120,300	25.6	14.7	615	33.9	83.9	22.2	8.5
37 015	Bertie	90.3	6.0	7,661	73.4	83,700	23.8	14.5	618	38.0	83.5	25.4	9.7
37 017	Bladen	91.2	4.2	14,362	69.0	84,000	24.1	17.7	593	32.9	82.2	23.8	9.9
37 019	Brunswick	86.2	6.1	47,114	74.9	179,100	27.2	12.8	818	34.3	80.1	23.1	5.0
37 021	Buncombe	82.9	7.0	100,782	63.9	187,700	24.4	11.7	789	31.0	78.8	20.7	7.7
37 023	Burke	87.9	4.7	34,563	72.5	110,700	21.9	11.0	614	30.0	85.0	21.0	7.0
37 025	Cabarrus	87.6	5.0	64,386	73.2	163,500	23.7	12.3	774	28.9	83.2	25.8	5.1
37 027	Caldwell	88.5	3.8	31,899	71.0	104,600	23.0	12.5	593	36.7	86.0	22.5	5.6
37 031	Carteret	82.2	7.3	28,481	67.5	204,200	24.3	13.2	738	28.4	82.3	23.2	5.6
37 033	Caswell	85.4	10.6	8,623	73.6	99,100	21.3	12.3	576	34.2	81.2	33.5	8.0
37 035	Catawba	88.7	4.5	58,281	71.0	128,500	21.8	11.1	677	28.4	87.8	22.8	5.4
37 037	Chatham	87.6	6.1	25,834	80.3	204,600	24.5	12.4	791	29.0	75.8	26.4	5.5
37 039	Cherokee	90.6	4.1	10,916	84.2	142,000	27.3	11.6	598	32.3	85.8	22.3	5.7
37 045	Cleveland	88.0	4.6	36,958	67.6	106,500	22.3	11.8	637	34.1	86.3	23.6	8.1
37 047	Columbus	88.2	6.1	21,790	70.9	82,200	27.1	13.0	583	35.3	85.7	22.7	7.5
37 049	Craven	81.7	9.4	39,932	64.2	151,800	23.1	12.6	839	29.2	77.1	20.9	8.0
37 051	Cumberland	76.8	9.1	120,577	55.1	129,300	23.3	11.4	851	29.0	82.4	22.1	6.4
37 053	Currituck	91.9	5.2	9,093	80.2	229,600	26.4	12.0	999	34.6	86.1	33.3	1.7
37 055	Dare	86.4	6.0	14,722	70.5	291,800	28.7	12.3	991	28.8	78.8	19.0	3.4
37 057	Davidson	88.0	3.9	64,482	72.0	131,500	22.6	11.5	611	27.8	85.7	23.4	5.6
37 059	Davie	92.9	4.2	16,750	80.0	156,000	21.1	11.9	650	26.8	82.0	26.1	4.7
37 061	Duplin	87.0	5.7	22,586	66.8	85,600	24.0	14.0	598	33.4	81.3	23.3	9.0
37 063	Durham	76.6	9.6	110,642	54.3	177,100	22.4	11.5	834	31.3	75.6	21.4	9.4
37 065	Edgecombe	86.0	5.1	20,673	63.5	80,100	23.1	16.6	624	32.0	82.2	22.1	11.5
37 067	Forsyth	85.2	5.0	139,085	63.4	152,100	22.4	11.3	705	31.5	83.7	20.8	8.0
37 069	Franklin	89.5	5.0	23,417	75.4	124,800	24.9	13.9	708	29.9	82.4	29.1	5.2
37 071	Gaston	86.7	3.8	79,259	67.5	125,300	23.7	12.1	707	32.5	85.8	24.2	6.0
37 077	Granville	88.1	6.7	19,493	74.5	134,100	23.8	14.1	740	27.0	85.5	28.1	5.9
37 079	Greene	85.3	10.3	7,039	67.9	87,200	23.5	15.1	582	26.3	82.4	23.3	7.7
37 081	Guilford	84.7	5.6	196,171	61.3	155,100	23.8	11.6	736	30.3	82.2	20.9	7.6
37 083	Halifax	86.6	3.2	21,914	62.1	85,700	24.1	15.9	648	36.9	83.3	21.2	12.7
37 085	Harnett	84.5	8.9	40,352	67.3	133,100	24.1	13.2	738	30.6	84.8	27.7	4.6
37 087	Haywood	87.5	5.2	26,240	73.3	152,300	24.6	11.2	690	30.1	83.1	23.2	4.2
37 089	Henderson	87.2	5.9	44,465	75.3	185,000	23.6	10.1	714	31.9	81.1	21.3	5.6
37 091	Hertford	85.3	8.5	8,637	62.2	80,900	23.9	15.3	600	31.7	83.9	24.4	12.5
37 093	Hoke	81.5	11.3	15,958	68.8	142,800	24.6	12.2	801	31.6	84.7	24.7	6.3
37 097	Iredell	87.8	5.6	59,408	73.3	168,600	23.4	11.4	762	31.5	84.1	23.4	4.6
37 099	Jackson	84.3	9.4	15,620	69.1	171,800	25.1	10.0	595	35.8	79.6	17.9	5.7
37 101	Johnston	90.0	4.8	60,552	71.7	143,100	22.9	11.9	750	34.8	82.5	28.7	4.6
37 105	Lee	83.7	6.4	21,191	66.9	124,400	22.2	13.5	678	28.8	84.2	22.9	7.9
37 107	Lenoir	86.4	3.7	24,032	60.4	96,900	22.6	15.0	628	32.7	79.1	22.9	10.8
37 109	Lincoln	88.0	6.6	29,724	78.5	151,100	21.6	10.8	664	30.7	82.4	29.5	4.5
37 111	McDowell	88.6	4.5	16,791	70.5	98,400	22.0	11.3	560	29.7	80.1	23.9	6.8
37 113	Macon	89.1	3.8	15,750	72.8	173,800	27.0	10.0	768	37.8	81.0	19.9	6.6
37 115	Madison	89.4	7.5	8,511	72.2	155,100	27.4	10.0	622	26.1	82.7	29.0	6.1
37 117	Martin	91.1	3.6	9,562	70.4	88,200	24.0	15.7	584	27.7	85.7	24.3	9.8
37 119	Mecklenburg	80.5	6.6	362,469	59.9	181,600	23.0	11.6	876	30.4	77.5	24.8	7.0
37 123	Montgomery	90.3	3.3	10,315	72.7	84,200	23.9	11.4	527	30.5	82.0	25.5	8.9
37 125	Moore	89.5	5.0	37,021	75.2	194,700	23.0	11.7	687	30.7	86.3	25.4	6.4
37 127	Nash	88.0	4.6	37,210	64.4	117,400	23.1	13.6	764	31.4	84.7	21.0	7.8
37 129	New Hanover	80.4	8.1	85,918	58.4	215,100	24.6	12.8	886	32.1	79.8	20.2	5.9
37 131	Northampton	87.5	7.6	8,738	72.7	81,300	22.9	17.9	620	34.7	82.2	25.1	11.8
37 133	Onslow	73.7	13.3	60,656	55.2	152,200	25.0	12.4	957	31.9	73.0	24.2	4.7
37 135	Orange	77.0	11.8	51,372	59.5	266,500	22.5	11.2	862	33.9	67.3	22.9	7.3
37 139	Pasquotank	80.1	8.9	14,416	65.1	168,900	27.2	15.8	869	31.8	78.2	23.5	10.3
37 141	Pender	84.9	9.6	19,598	76.7	154,000	24.7	14.0	789	29.0	77.4	28.5	6.9
37 145	Person	88.2	4.2	15,228	72.4	117,400	24.1	11.0	643	29.8	84.1	30.4	6.4
37 147	Pitt	78.8	8.9	65,837	54.8	136,600	22.4	14.2	704	33.9	82.1	19.7	7.8
37 149	Polk	91.6	4.5	8,871	75.2	167,000	24.7	10.0	649	29.6	78.5	26.7	5.8
37 151	Randolph	90.4	3.3	54,744	74.7	120,100	24.1	12.5	650	29.9	86.5	23.1	5.4
37 153	Richmond	84.0	4.2	18,304	63.7	76,600	22.6	13.4	597	32.8	79.7	19.2	10.4

[1]10.0 represents 10 percent or less; 50.0 represents 50 percent or higher.

STATE and county code	STATE or county	Percent who lived in the same house one year ago	Percent who did not live in the same county one year ago	Total occupied housing units	Percent owner-occupied housing units (dollars)	Median value of owner-occupied housing units (dollars)	Median selected monthly owner costs as a percentage of household income — With a mortgage	Without a mortgage[1]	Median gross rent (dollars)	Median gross rent as a percentage of household income[1]	Percent of workers who drove alone to work	Mean travel time to work (minutes)	Percent of occupied housing units with no vehicle available
ACS table number:		C07204	C07204	B25003	B25003	B25077	B25092	B25092	B25064	B25071	C08301	B08013/B08012	C25045
Column number:		1	2	3	4	5	6	7	8	9	10	11	12
	North Carolina—Cont.												
37 155	Robeson	88.7	4.5	44,706	64.3	68,500	23.7	14.0	584	32.9	83.9	23.5	9.2
37 157	Rockingham	88.1	4.1	37,496	70.8	103,300	22.9	11.7	608	32.6	83.4	25.7	5.9
37 159	Rowan	86.4	5.2	52,290	68.2	127,100	23.7	12.2	688	30.4	84.1	23.1	6.0
37 161	Rutherford	86.2	4.0	27,024	71.6	107,100	22.5	13.3	586	29.0	83.5	22.4	6.2
37 163	Sampson	85.9	6.0	23,504	68.9	87,700	23.3	13.4	563	27.3	78.3	24.9	7.9
37 165	Scotland	87.3	5.4	12,934	66.3	76,100	24.3	14.9	614	34.8	84.7	21.0	10.0
37 167	Stanly	88.0	5.1	23,246	74.3	127,300	23.4	13.2	631	33.7	83.8	26.3	6.6
37 169	Stokes	89.4	5.7	19,141	78.7	118,300	22.0	10.1	586	28.6	84.7	28.5	4.1
37 171	Surry	89.8	3.5	30,026	71.9	111,600	23.2	12.5	576	29.3	84.7	25.7	6.4
37 175	Transylvania	88.4	5.6	13,790	76.2	174,200	24.2	10.0	701	31.8	83.0	23.0	6.1
37 179	Union	87.8	6.0	67,769	81.6	190,700	22.6	11.5	800	32.5	30.7	29.4	3.3
37 181	Vance	92.3	3.7	15,934	64.9	106,000	23.7	13.0	669	35.6	36.5	23.3	11.8
37 183	Wake	83.0	6.2	346,096	65.3	228,800	21.6	10.0	886	28.2	30.7	23.5	4.8
37 185	Warren	91.2	6.2	7,426	67.8	106,800	26.3	17.2	743	37.2	32.7	27.7	8.8
37 189	Watauga	71.7	15.8	20,354	55.8	223,400	24.0	11.1	780	50.0	74.0	18.9	6.4
37 191	Wayne	82.8	6.3	48,016	61.6	103,000	22.9	12.3	655	30.5	32.0	21.9	9.5
37 193	Wilkes	94.5	1.4	27,575	74.8	111,200	25.5	12.4	582	33.9	33.4	24.3	7.2
37 195	Wilson	81.2	6.0	31,853	59.7	112,200	25.4	15.3	720	34.0	31.4	19.7	9.7
37 197	Yadkin	93.1	2.7	14,847	76.9	116,200	23.5	12.2	599	29.6	35.6	27.5	4.6
38 000	**North Dakota**	82.5	8.5	285,639	65.7	130,500	19.3	10.0	632	25.2	79.6	16.8	5.5
38 015	Burleigh	83.6	7.7	34,391	71.0	168,700	20.0	10.8	663	23.8	79.7	19.4	4.6
38 017	Cass	77.1	9.8	65,568	53.2	158,400	20.7	10.5	657	25.6	33.3	16.5	6.4
38 035	Grand Forks	77.1	10.9	27,483	52.0	151,500	20.7	10.4	671	29.5	79.9	13.6	7.2
38 059	Morton	85.3	8.4	11,371	77.6	140,300	21.0	11.7	678	24.6	30.1	19.7	3.9
38 089	Stark	83.4	8.4	10,238	69.4	166,000	18.1	10.0	706	24.9	30.1	16.8	5.6
38 093	Stutsman	86.2	6.0	8,736	69.5	99,900	18.3	10.6	543	24.4	34.9	12.0	4.9
38 101	Ward	77.5	9.6	24,834	62.5	153,800	20.5	10.0	688	26.0	31.9	16.2	5.5
38 105	Williams	78.3	11.3	9,974	68.8	155,000	14.5	10.0	669	19.7	82.7	16.6	5.1
39 000	**Ohio**	85.5	4.8	4,542,141	67.3	130,600	22.7	12.9	708	30.5	83.4	23.0	8.3
39 001	Adams	87.7	3.6	10,870	73.7	88,900	27.7	13.2	530	32.0	79.7	32.4	6.2
39 003	Allen	82.8	5.3	40,398	68.7	105,600	20.9	12.5	646	33.8	86.9	19.3	7.5
39 005	Ashland	86.2	5.5	20,261	72.6	119,600	23.4	13.0	659	26.4	81.7	22.5	6.4
39 007	Ashtabula	87.3	3.8	39,103	72.6	110,900	23.6	14.3	623	34.5	82.7	24.6	8.1
39 009	Athens	69.2	12.6	22,023	58.1	118,300	22.2	11.9	675	41.6	68.1	19.7	10.1
39 011	Auglaize	88.4	4.3	18,418	73.2	131,200	20.8	11.6	638	24.5	87.0	20.9	4.0
39 013	Belmont	89.2	4.4	28,383	74.5	90,600	20.3	11.1	520	26.0	86.8	24.0	7.9
39 015	Brown	88.8	6.4	16,501	76.2	116,100	26.0	14.4	666	27.7	82.4	33.7	5.5
39 017	Butler	85.0	5.6	134,423	71.7	156,100	22.6	12.8	789	32.0	85.0	23.5	5.5
39 019	Carroll	89.1	3.7	11,226	75.3	114,600	23.3	12.2	566	31.1	83.0	31.4	6.1
39 021	Champaign	84.2	5.4	15,075	73.9	118,700	22.0	12.3	660	29.8	85.5	25.7	4.9
39 023	Clark	85.1	4.5	54,969	66.0	104,400	22.2	12.0	658	30.8	82.5	21.8	8.9
39 025	Clermont	89.5	4.9	74,067	74.4	152,000	22.3	12.9	759	29.1	86.1	27.4	4.7
39 027	Clinton	85.1	5.3	16,000	66.2	116,100	23.8	13.7	668	29.9	84.0	25.8	8.6
39 029	Columbiana	87.0	4.3	42,471	70.9	96,800	21.4	10.8	583	26.6	84.7	24.5	7.8
39 031	Coshocton	88.1	3.1	14,568	73.4	94,400	22.7	11.5	571	26.3	80.3	23.6	7.9
39 033	Crawford	86.1	3.8	17,367	71.3	88,200	21.8	11.8	633	29.1	85.8	22.3	5.2
39 035	Cuyahoga	85.3	3.2	531,045	60.7	125,700	24.2	14.6	722	31.7	79.9	23.9	13.5
39 037	Darke	85.9	4.2	21,016	73.3	107,700	22.0	11.9	576	27.0	84.5	22.7	6.3
39 039	Defiance	85.4	5.2	15,322	75.1	108,000	21.1	11.9	637	29.7	86.7	19.8	5.7
39 041	Delaware	88.3	7.0	64,360	82.0	245,900	22.8	12.6	858	27.9	84.8	25.5	2.5
39 043	Erie	86.3	4.9	31,908	68.0	136,600	22.5	13.6	686	26.4	83.1	20.9	6.3
39 045	Fairfield	85.1	5.6	54,138	73.1	165,600	22.1	11.1	773	30.2	84.6	26.4	4.6
39 047	Fayette	84.8	5.7	11,451	61.5	106,900	24.4	12.8	698	32.5	82.8	21.6	7.1
39 049	Franklin	80.0	5.6	467,314	54.3	151,200	23.0	12.9	800	30.0	81.6	21.5	8.6
39 051	Fulton	88.3	3.0	16,272	79.7	129,300	22.7	13.2	671	27.6	88.7	21.9	3.3
39 053	Gallia	88.4	3.2	11,497	73.9	91,900	23.2	12.6	584	26.4	84.9	24.3	7.6
39 055	Geauga	94.4	2.4	34,527	86.4	220,600	24.0	13.6	738	27.5	84.0	28.0	6.9
39 057	Greene	86.2	7.2	62,924	67.2	157,700	22.0	12.8	825	30.5	85.5	20.3	5.0
39 059	Guernsey	87.9	5.8	15,348	74.8	95,200	23.7	11.1	576	30.4	85.2	22.6	6.1
39 061	Hamilton	83.3	3.9	323,398	60.0	144,700	22.7	13.4	692	32.4	79.8	22.6	12.2
39 063	Hancock	84.2	6.1	29,974	71.1	125,900	20.9	10.8	659	28.3	83.4	17.3	5.2
39 065	Hardin	84.2	6.0	11,655	70.8	96,800	22.0	11.8	628	29.1	78.5	22.5	7.4
39 069	Henry	89.8	3.7	11,163	78.9	111,700	22.4	13.3	669	27.3	85.4	21.4	4.0
39 071	Highland	84.3	6.1	17,062	69.3	97,700	24.4	12.6	611	30.1	80.8	30.1	6.7
39 073	Hocking	88.3	6.3	11,413	76.2	110,600	22.4	12.3	555	29.6	83.2	30.0	5.9
39 075	Holmes	94.6	2.4	12,392	75.4	149,700	23.4	10.1	552	22.7	51.4	24.0	30.0
39 077	Huron	86.3	4.1	22,350	73.8	118,800	21.7	11.8	600	27.2	85.0	21.6	5.9
39 079	Jackson	85.8	4.1	13,421	67.6	92,600	22.8	14.5	615	32.0	81.0	27.5	10.0
39 081	Jefferson	90.6	3.9	28,224	72.7	87,200	19.7	11.5	600	29.2	83.2	24.7	8.6
39 083	Knox	85.2	6.2	22,311	70.3	134,200	22.2	12.4	666	27.8	79.3	27.2	8.1
39 085	Lake	89.0	3.7	94,137	74.8	149,500	23.0	13.6	775	29.8	88.3	23.1	6.1
39 087	Lawrence	87.7	4.7	23,408	74.5	96,300	21.6	12.1	620	29.5	90.3	24.1	6.4
39 089	Licking	86.6	4.9	63,875	73.3	150,100	22.8	12.7	728	29.8	81.7	25.4	5.6
39 091	Logan	86.6	5.1	18,377	73.3	116,900	22.0	14.2	676	28.2	81.0	23.1	7.4

[1]10.0 represents 10 percent or less; 50.0 represents 50 percent or higher.

Table C-2. Counties — Where: Migration, Housing, and Transportation, 2010–2012—*Continued*

STATE and county code	STATE or county	Percent who lived in the same house one year ago	Percent who did not live in the same county one year ago	Total occupied housing units	Percent owner-occupied housing units (dollars)	Median value of owner-occupied housing units (dollars)	Median selected monthly owner costs as a percentage of household income — With a mortgage	Median selected monthly owner costs as a percentage of household income — Without a mortgage[1]	Median gross rent (dollars)	Median gross rent as a percentage of household income[1]	Percent of workers who drove alone to work	Mean travel time to work (minutes)	Percent of occupied housing units with no vehicle available
ACS table number:		C07204	C07204	B25003	B25003	B25077	B25092	B25092	B25064	B25071	C08301	B08013/ E08012	C25045
Column number:		1	2	3	4	5	6	7	8	9	10	11	12
	Ohio—Cont.												
39 093	Lorain	86.1	4.3	116,604	72.5	140,100	22.9	12.8	726	31.4	85.1	24.7	6.3
39 095	Lucas	83.2	4.2	177,384	61.8	108,400	22.8	13.9	646	32.3	84.7	20.0	10.8
39 097	Madison	85.8	9.0	14,720	71.7	149,100	22.0	13.3	736	26.5	82.8	22.9	5.9
39 099	Mahoning	89.0	4.0	97,457	69.1	97,100	22.3	13.1	619	31.6	86.1	21.6	8.7
39 101	Marion	80.8	7.2	24,839	66.0	99,400	22.0	12.3	688	30.0	85.7	22.5	8.0
39 103	Medina	89.8	5.2	65,591	79.5	180,300	22.8	12.3	813	29.6	86.4	27.8	4.2
39 105	Meigs	89.2	5.6	9,469	79.4	84,500	21.6	13.3	544	32.9	86.6	28.7	6.3
39 107	Mercer	91.2	3.2	15,910	77.6	121,900	21.5	11.5	661	28.9	83.7	18.8	5.0
39 109	Miami	85.1	4.8	40,994	70.8	137,900	21.8	11.9	700	28.3	85.1	20.5	4.9
39 113	Montgomery	82.3	5.2	222,279	61.6	112,300	23.5	14.3	710	32.4	81.5	21.3	10.0
39 117	Morrow	89.5	4.3	12,629	81.3	134,700	24.3	13.4	698	28.0	85.1	30.5	5.3
39 119	Muskingum	86.2	3.9	33,947	68.7	107,000	21.6	13.2	622	31.2	85.7	24.5	8.2
39 123	Ottawa	89.0	5.1	17,495	79.5	136,000	22.9	12.8	731	29.1	84.6	22.6	5.3
39 127	Perry	87.1	4.0	13,656	73.3	88,700	21.5	12.1	550	29.2	83.3	36.6	7.8
39 129	Pickaway	84.0	8.5	19,307	75.7	146,100	23.0	12.2	722	30.7	83.9	27.5	5.9
39 131	Pike	85.4	5.0	10,865	70.6	97,600	25.5	12.1	652	35.1	84.5	29.3	9.9
39 133	Portage	83.2	7.4	60,143	68.9	152,000	22.3	13.0	775	31.9	83.5	24.3	5.5
39 135	Preble	86.8	4.2	16,360	77.6	116,700	23.2	14.3	713	28.3	85.3	25.5	3.5
39 137	Putnam	92.6	2.0	12,982	84.2	132,400	19.8	10.0	646	21.4	85.3	23.1	3.7
39 139	Richland	85.3	5.5	48,336	69.6	102,600	22.7	11.6	614	26.5	86.8	20.6	8.3
39 141	Ross	86.0	5.9	28,074	71.6	113,700	20.9	12.7	648	29.5	86.3	26.0	6.5
39 143	Sandusky	89.0	4.2	23,907	75.7	108,700	21.2	12.3	585	28.4	85.5	18.6	5.6
39 145	Scioto	87.6	4.8	29,339	69.4	89,500	20.9	13.1	547	32.8	85.4	23.9	7.9
39 147	Seneca	86.4	5.2	21,792	71.2	99,400	20.1	12.3	602	29.2	85.8	20.4	7.4
39 149	Shelby	89.0	3.5	18,508	74.5	121,100	21.4	12.5	685	26.2	89.4	18.9	4.0
39 151	Stark	87.4	3.6	149,275	70.1	121,600	22.1	12.3	662	29.7	85.1	21.7	7.3
39 153	Summit	88.8	3.7	219,302	68.0	134,600	22.2	13.1	730	31.3	87.4	22.6	9.0
39 155	Trumbull	88.8	3.4	86,233	71.4	96,800	21.9	12.2	612	31.5	87.8	22.1	7.2
39 157	Tuscarawas	89.3	3.6	36,140	73.2	110,000	21.1	12.3	627	28.6	84.5	20.6	5.6
39 159	Union	84.8	8.4	18,208	76.7	171,100	23.3	14.3	757	27.5	87.8	24.4	5.3
39 161	Van Wert	87.1	5.8	11,331	78.1	88,600	20.9	11.0	582	29.4	85.2	19.3	4.7
39 165	Warren	87.8	6.5	76,331	77.5	187,300	22.6	12.3	895	28.0	87.7	24.3	2.2
39 167	Washington	88.2	4.2	24,652	76.7	108,100	20.9	11.0	570	30.1	85.8	22.7	6.3
39 169	Wayne	87.2	4.4	42,023	73.9	136,300	22.9	10.7	657	27.6	78.4	20.6	8.5
39 171	Williams	82.2	6.0	14,741	74.1	102,900	21.9	13.4	600	30.5	83.4	19.8	4.7
39 173	Wood	79.7	9.3	48,870	68.1	146,300	22.2	13.2	706	28.7	83.3	20.1	4.8
39 175	Wyandot	87.5	5.1	9,408	71.0	105,200	19.9	10.4	589	27.1	84.0	23.7	3.8
40 000	**Oklahoma**	82.6	6.9	1,441,163	67.1	112,900	21.5	11.1	690	29.1	81.8	21.1	5.6
40 001	Adair	92.7	2.8	7,863	70.5	74,300	21.8	11.1	514	26.7	77.2	23.5	7.1
40 009	Beckham	83.0	11.3	7,727	64.1	98,000	20.6	10.0	609	18.2	84.7	19.0	5.4
40 013	Bryan	80.6	7.9	16,563	63.1	88,700	19.7	11.4	637	27.9	76.7	19.8	7.1
40 015	Caddo	83.6	7.0	10,215	72.9	76,500	19.4	10.3	506	23.8	83.9	21.1	6.1
40 017	Canadian	84.6	6.5	42,386	77.1	138,000	21.7	10.4	805	26.6	85.0	22.9	3.6
40 019	Carter	90.4	3.2	17,125	70.0	89,300	20.4	10.8	651	26.0	81.3	17.6	4.8
40 021	Cherokee	86.9	5.6	17,256	66.4	104,200	22.6	10.6	591	30.4	78.3	22.9	6.8
40 027	Cleveland	80.1	8.2	96,150	67.8	139,900	21.3	11.2	799	31.3	83.5	22.4	3.5
40 031	Comanche	71.4	14.2	44,614	56.4	114,400	21.2	10.3	749	27.3	73.1	16.8	6.7
40 037	Creek	88.9	6.8	26,476	74.6	108,400	22.4	11.6	643	28.2	83.6	23.2	4.2
40 039	Custer	81.4	10.0	10,369	59.3	113,900	20.4	11.6	562	25.4	83.6	19.4	4.1
40 041	Delaware	85.3	6.7	16,891	78.8	106,300	26.1	11.9	586	27.1	76.6	27.7	3.9
40 047	Garfield	78.5	7.2	23,745	66.1	91,700	20.7	10.0	631	23.0	82.6	15.9	5.0
40 049	Garvin	91.1	3.6	10,294	73.0	82,100	21.6	12.1	598	24.8	85.8	23.5	6.0
40 051	Grady	85.9	6.8	19,711	75.3	107,700	22.0	10.0	630	24.8	83.6	26.1	3.9
40 065	Jackson	84.6	6.9	10,503	60.8	85,700	18.5	11.4	650	24.4	81.9	14.6	3.6
40 071	Kay	80.2	6.5	18,387	69.5	76,800	19.6	11.3	597	26.7	81.2	16.9	6.3
40 079	Le Flore	87.2	5.3	18,255	73.8	76,800	23.1	11.7	549	29.2	80.3	20.3	5.6
40 081	Lincoln	88.5	6.1	13,234	74.4	93,500	20.1	10.0	551	30.2	79.5	28.8	4.6
40 083	Logan	84.2	10.7	14,997	77.6	141,100	21.2	10.0	643	26.0	82.6	28.8	4.2
40 087	McClain	87.5	6.9	12,863	81.9	143,300	21.7	10.6	673	27.9	82.7	28.1	2.4
40 089	McCurtain	88.3	6.2	12,849	70.1	71,100	23.5	11.5	531	27.7	77.2	23.2	8.0
40 091	McIntosh	90.8	3.1	8,078	79.3	82,400	23.1	11.4	561	32.4	83.2	24.6	4.7
40 097	Mayes	84.5	6.3	16,036	72.5	100,800	22.5	11.0	603	26.5	82.5	24.5	6.3
40 101	Muskogee	84.8	6.0	26,604	67.2	88,000	22.3	11.5	613	32.8	79.9	20.8	8.6
40 109	Oklahoma	79.8	5.9	282,883	60.0	126,500	22.3	11.9	744	31.3	82.1	20.2	6.8
40 111	Okmulgee	81.5	5.4	15,000	69.6	77,600	21.1	11.8	591	25.7	78.3	25.8	8.4
40 113	Osage	89.5	5.9	18,507	77.3	87,900	21.0	12.3	578	28.6	84.5	24.0	5.9
40 115	Ottawa	84.7	7.2	12,050	72.8	81,000	21.6	11.7	594	29.7	85.5	21.1	5.3
40 119	Payne	68.6	14.4	30,218	51.0	133,400	22.8	10.9	700	37.6	75.1	17.8	5.4
40 121	Pittsburg	84.5	5.5	19,100	71.3	86,200	19.1	10.0	655	28.9	84.8	20.0	6.3
40 123	Pontotoc	81.4	5.9	14,680	68.1	97,200	22.7	10.0	612	29.9	82.8	17.7	7.1
40 125	Pottawatomie	85.5	6.1	26,043	71.9	98,400	20.2	10.9	656	28.6	83.8	23.6	5.8
40 131	Rogers	85.9	7.6	32,902	79.0	143,900	21.6	10.0	780	26.7	85.9	24.9	3.4
40 133	Seminole	86.7	5.9	9,501	75.2	72,200	21.6	10.3	511	26.9	82.1	21.6	6.6
40 135	Sequoyah	83.9	5.3	15,542	72.1	86,200	19.6	11.6	616	28.1	81.7	23.9	5.4

[1]10.0 represents 10 percent or less; 50.0 represents 50 percent or higher.

STATE and county code	STATE or county	Percent who lived in the same house one year ago	Percent who did not live in the same county one year ago	Total occupied housing units	Percent owner-occupied housing units	Median value of owner-occupied housing units (dollars)	Median selected monthly owner costs as a percentage of household income — With a mortgage	Without a mortgage[1]	Median gross rent (dollars)	Median gross rent as a percentage of household income[1]	Percent of workers who drove alone to work	Mean travel time to work (minutes)	Percent of occupied housing units with no vehicle available
ACS table number:		C07204	C07204	B25003	B25003	B25077	B25092	B25092	B25064	B25071	C08301	B08013/ B08012	C25045
Column number:		1	2	3	4	5	6	7	8	9	10	11	12
	Oklahoma—Cont.												
40 137	Stephens..............	80.0	6.9	17,875	70.0	91,000	20.5	11.0	620	25.7	83.0	19.4	5.1
40 139	Texas..................	83.0	8.3	7,177	64.7	84,500	19.5	10.0	632	21.7	70.2	16.5	2.1
40 143	Tulsa..................	82.1	5.4	240,665	61.3	134,400	21.9	11.7	736	29.7	82.6	19.6	6.3
40 145	Wagoner...............	88.0	8.3	26,749	81.9	136,900	21.4	11.4	747	29.9	84.9	24.2	3.1
40 147	Washington	84.4	7.3	21,242	74.6	110,200	19.6	10.6	646	28.0	81.9	17.4	4.9
40 153	Woodward	87.2	6.3	7,203	72.6	105,000	17.0	10.4	620	22.2	89.2	18.5	2.4
41 000	**Oregon**	81.8	6.6	1,513,005	61.6	233,900	26.6	12.9	855	32.5	71.7	22.5	8.1
41 003	Benton................	81.0	9.9	32,925	57.8	263,500	23.5	10.7	790	40.1	64.1	18.3	8.3
41 005	Clackamas.............	85.2	6.8	145,555	68.8	294,200	27.4	13.4	958	29.9	77.4	26.9	5.8
41 007	Clatsop...............	80.4	9.7	15,357	65.2	251,800	29.6	12.6	778	31.2	70.1	19.2	8.6
41 009	Columbia..............	87.5	6.0	18,901	75.5	213,500	24.7	12.2	759	36.1	80.2	30.8	4.5
41 011	Coos..................	81.1	5.7	25,910	67.4	175,300	26.5	13.6	690	33.9	75.1	20.2	6.5
41 013	Crook.................	80.6	7.3	8,923	69.6	172,700	31.8	11.9	724	36.2	84.1	21.3	5.9
41 015	Curry.................	87.7	7.2	10,132	66.5	242,000	30.2	12.1	731	32.2	75.3	13.6	5.5
41 017	Deschutes.............	80.2	6.7	64,982	64.6	236,100	29.0	13.2	906	33.8	77.7	19.6	5.0
41 019	Douglas...............	82.2	5.5	43,654	68.8	171,900	27.1	12.4	755	31.3	74.8	20.2	5.4
41 027	Hood River............	89.2	4.8	7,802	67.6	324,100	25.4	12.5	846	28.2	73.5	16.4	2.8
41 029	Jackson...............	81.1	5.8	82,524	62.0	222,900	28.6	14.2	854	37.6	76.6	19.6	6.6
41 031	Jefferson.............	80.4	11.0	8,032	62.1	161,600	27.0	10.3	737	26.5	75.2	22.3	4.9
41 033	Josephine.............	85.3	4.9	34,151	64.5	217,200	28.0	12.5	782	36.0	81.2	19.6	6.4
41 035	Klamath...............	82.4	6.9	27,789	65.8	157,300	25.9	11.5	708	36.4	72.8	18.4	7.4
41 039	Lane..................	77.0	6.0	145,265	58.7	216,500	27.1	12.9	827	34.6	71.1	19.7	8.5
41 041	Lincoln...............	83.7	6.4	20,979	65.7	227,400	27.0	13.5	809	31.9	71.8	18.1	6.3
41 043	Linn..................	86.0	5.2	44,926	65.1	171,200	26.3	12.2	766	31.8	77.9	22.8	6.0
41 045	Malheur...............	83.6	6.9	10,125	64.2	133,200	22.1	12.2	582	35.5	68.6	16.9	7.7
41 047	Marion................	81.3	5.0	113,116	59.8	190,500	27.0	12.9	780	33.4	73.8	21.7	8.1
41 051	Multnomah.............	79.8	7.3	305,069	53.5	264,500	26.6	14.3	886	33.2	61.0	24.6	14.5
41 053	Polk..................	80.7	7.5	28,501	65.2	222,800	25.8	12.4	786	31.3	75.5	24.7	5.1
41 057	Tillamook.............	88.2	4.7	10,367	72.7	223,300	28.5	13.0	814	30.7	78.1	21.4	3.8
41 059	Umatilla..............	81.1	6.4	26,867	63.4	145,400	22.3	11.6	658	27.1	78.9	16.8	6.0
41 061	Union.................	83.0	6.2	10,185	62.7	153,300	22.2	11.7	638	34.5	67.5	16.4	6.7
41 065	Wasco.................	85.6	7.0	9,693	63.5	174,500	24.1	11.6	748	37.3	70.4	15.9	9.3
41 067	Washington	82.9	6.6	201,111	61.0	276,700	25.4	12.5	965	29.2	74.8	24.2	5.8
41 071	Yamhill...............	84.4	6.8	33,574	68.0	216,700	26.7	12.7	862	32.6	73.3	23.5	6.5
42 000	**Pennsylvania**	87.9	4.4	4,949,494	69.6	164,700	23.3	13.7	800	30.4	76.7	26.0	11.7
42 001	Adams.................	86.6	5.0	37,919	76.7	196,200	25.3	13.4	802	32.1	81.8	27.7	4.4
42 003	Allegheny.............	86.8	3.9	522,238	65.2	121,200	20.6	13.4	740	28.8	71.6	26.1	14.4
42 005	Armstrong.............	90.6	3.5	28,735	76.4	92,800	20.8	12.2	579	28.8	82.2	28.5	8.1
42 007	Beaver	89.6	4.0	70,787	73.0	114,400	21.2	13.0	622	28.0	83.1	25.3	9.5
42 009	Bedford	91.6	2.3	20,570	78.9	117,400	22.5	13.3	595	28.7	82.0	27.4	7.3
42 011	Berks	85.7	4.1	154,092	71.4	170,900	24.3	15.0	825	32.2	80.3	24.4	9.7
42 013	Blair.................	88.9	3.1	50,990	72.2	104,800	20.6	12.3	618	28.9	82.9	19.2	8.7
42 015	Bradford	90.6	3.4	24,103	75.5	116,400	21.5	12.7	613	27.0	78.8	22.5	6.1
42 017	Bucks.................	92.6	3.2	230,384	77.9	309,400	25.6	15.6	1,103	31.5	82.2	28.4	4.4
42 019	Butler................	88.4	4.9	73,147	76.1	169,500	21.6	12.1	738	29.0	83.6	26.7	5.9
42 021	Cambria...............	89.5	4.3	58,197	73.8	86,300	20.0	13.5	555	27.9	82.9	23.0	9.9
42 025	Carbon................	90.7	4.0	25,919	78.7	147,400	25.8	14.0	687	30.4	79.8	31.8	9.9
42 027	Centre	73.3	13.1	57,266	59.2	190,500	22.1	11.9	870	39.3	67.5	20.0	10.0
42 029	Chester	89.9	4.6	184,364	75.1	324,100	24.3	14.2	1,150	28.1	80.9	27.4	4.9
42 031	Clarion...............	83.7	6.8	16,027	71.1	107,800	19.9	10.8	573	32.7	78.9	23.0	9.1
42 033	Clearfield............	89.2	4.8	32,158	77.3	87,700	21.7	14.2	565	28.3	81.9	24.6	7.5
42 035	Clinton	82.6	8.0	15,287	71.3	107,500	23.0	15.3	643	28.0	79.0	24.0	8.2
42 037	Columbia..............	88.5	6.1	26,188	70.5	139,800	21.6	13.9	659	30.6	81.6	20.8	8.0
42 039	Crawford..............	87.7	5.2	35,042	73.4	103,900	22.4	12.9	572	28.2	76.4	22.1	9.2
42 041	Cumberland............	85.3	7.0	95,126	71.4	183,500	22.7	12.5	841	28.1	82.6	21.0	6.2
42 043	Dauphin...............	84.5	5.3	107,891	64.2	158,600	22.4	13.1	830	28.0	81.5	21.3	9.7
42 045	Delaware..............	90.2	3.9	205,185	70.0	236,300	25.0	15.5	948	33.6	75.2	27.8	11.3
42 047	Elk...................	93.5	1.5	13,596	79.8	93,300	20.3	11.5	549	25.9	82.3	17.0	6.2
42 049	Erie..................	85.3	4.4	109,522	66.3	115,600	21.0	12.2	651	31.3	81.2	18.9	11.6
42 051	Fayette...............	91.4	2.6	54,372	72.0	84,400	21.2	12.8	585	27.9	84.7	25.3	8.6
42 055	Franklin..............	86.7	4.9	57,739	72.8	177,300	24.2	12.2	779	28.8	82.2	23.3	4.9
42 059	Greene	84.8	7.7	14,222	71.2	88,800	18.8	10.7	606	29.8	84.2	26.8	8.6
42 061	Huntingdon	88.2	6.7	16,992	76.5	116,200	21.7	12.5	554	28.5	77.4	28.1	7.4
42 063	Indiana	83.5	7.5	34,652	71.9	108,900	20.7	12.1	637	32.5	79.6	23.1	9.0
42 065	Jefferson.............	88.4	4.1	18,637	73.9	87,200	21.2	11.4	563	27.2	81.6	21.3	9.7
42 067	Juniata...............	92.1	1.4	9,321	77.2	139,600	24.2	12.2	582	28.3	73.8	29.9	7.0
42 069	Lackawanna............	88.0	4.3	85,721	66.0	145,500	23.1	14.9	677	28.2	79.1	20.3	10.1
42 071	Lancaster.............	89.2	2.9	193,931	69.8	187,100	24.3	13.2	861	31.6	79.8	22.5	9.7
42 073	Lawrence..............	91.8	2.5	36,752	74.1	98,400	22.1	13.3	619	31.6	85.3	22.3	8.2
42 075	Lebanon...............	88.5	4.3	51,807	72.1	163,200	23.3	12.7	727	28.6	81.5	23.1	8.0
42 077	Lehigh................	85.3	4.9	133,322	66.9	197,400	24.6	14.7	892	33.2	80.8	24.2	10.6

[1]10.0 represents 10 percent or less; 50.0 represents 50 percent or higher.

Table C-2. Counties — Where: Migration, Housing, and Transportation, 2010–2012—*Continued*

STATE and county code	STATE or county	Percent who lived in the same house one year ago	Percent who did not live in the same county one year ago	Total occupied housing units	Percent owner-occupied housing units	Median value of owner-occupied housing units (dollars)	Median selected monthly owner costs as a percentage of household income — With a mortgage	Median selected monthly owner costs as a percentage of household income — Without a mortgage[1]	Median gross rent (dollars)	Median gross rent as a percentage of household income[1]	Percent of workers who drove alone to work	Mean travel time to work (minutes)	Percent of occupied housing units with no vehicle available
	ACS table number:	C07204	C07204	B25003	B25003	B25077	B25092	B25092	B25064	B25071	C08301	B08013/ E08012	C25045
	Column number:	1	2	3	4	5	6	7	8	9	10	11	12
	Pennsylvania—Cont.												
42 079	Luzerne......................	87.2	4.2	130,097	66.9	120,700	22.4	14.6	647	28.9	80.3	22.2	10.7
42 081	Lycoming...................	87.3	4.7	45,933	68.8	131,700	23.1	13.8	669	29.2	80.8	20.4	8.7
42 083	McKean.....................	87.7	4.1	17,373	72.5	70,800	19.9	12.0	601	30.7	82.1	20.9	9.1
42 085	Mercer......................	88.7	4.4	46,345	74.0	102,600	21.4	12.9	596	29.6	82.5	20.8	9.2
42 087	Mifflin......................	91.1	2.2	18,947	73.6	97,600	23.7	14.2	577	27.6	77.2	22.0	12.0
42 089	Monroe......................	90.0	5.1	58,173	80.3	191,400	28.9	16.7	960	33.8	79.4	39.7	5.2
42 091	Montgomery..............	90.1	4.8	307,618	72.6	291,600	24.0	14.5	1,118	29.2	79.2	27.4	6.4
42 095	Northampton..............	86.8	5.4	112,120	72.7	212,700	24.8	15.4	916	32.7	83.8	27.3	8.5
42 097	Northumberland	90.1	4.2	39,109	71.3	98,500	21.2	13.5	592	26.3	82.3	23.8	10.4
42 099	Perry	88.8	4.6	18,231	79.4	159,100	23.4	13.1	692	27.4	79.0	31.9	5.5
42 101	Philadelphia	85.6	3.7	576,889	53.4	142,300	25.6	15.6	874	34.9	49.9	31.9	34.2
42 103	Pike	89.2	5.3	21,759	82.9	193,900	27.4	15.2	1,126	35.7	81.6	42.6	5.1
42 107	Schuylkill..................	89.9	3.3	59,689	75.5	93,700	22.0	14.5	605	26.7	81.4	26.2	8.9
42 109	Snyder	89.7	4.9	14,481	76.6	138,500	22.7	12.2	656	26.5	78.4	23.7	5.9
42 111	Somerset	92.1	3.4	29,626	78.0	96,800	21.7	13.3	533	25.3	81.8	23.6	7.5
42 115	Susquehanna	90.9	3.4	17,001	77.9	141,000	23.0	14.3	672	28.0	82.0	27.3	5.0
42 117	Tioga	88.5	4.9	17,039	74.9	114,100	21.5	14.0	676	31.1	77.8	23.9	5.8
42 119	Union	82.9	9.7	15,295	71.5	153,700	24.1	13.3	697	31.0	75.2	21.4	6.6
42 121	Venango	86.1	4.7	22,956	75.7	80,400	20.5	11.3	571	29.3	79.3	21.6	7.3
42 123	Warren	90.2	3.4	17,046	77.0	88,500	20.9	12.2	564	26.6	78.7	20.4	6.9
42 125	Washington	87.9	5.0	83,920	76.5	145,200	19.7	11.6	618	27.6	82.3	25.9	7.7
42 127	Wayne	88.6	7.7	19,521	79.1	180,400	28.0	13.6	719	32.7	81.7	30.0	5.3
42 129	Westmoreland	91.1	3.6	152,022	74.9	134,400	20.9	12.8	638	27.4	83.7	26.7	7.5
42 131	Wyoming	89.7	5.0	10,852	78.2	156,700	23.4	14.0	673	27.6	81.1	26.4	5.0
42 133	York	88.1	4.0	168,566	75.2	174,600	24.3	14.7	808	29.5	84.8	26.7	6.5
44 000	**Rhode Island**..............	86.5	4.7	409,308	60.3	245,300	26.7	16.3	891	30.5	79.9	23.6	9.9
44 001	Bristol	88.3	6.0	19,241	71.8	326,700	26.6	18.7	893	34.1	81.5	24.4	8.0
44 003	Kent	90.3	4.6	68,271	69.6	219,300	26.3	17.0	968	31.2	86.6	23.8	6.1
44 005	Newport	85.3	8.0	34,364	62.2	354,400	26.1	14.1	1,113	27.9	78.0	21.3	7.1
44 007	Providence	85.4	3.8	237,634	53.6	221,700	27.1	16.4	857	30.9	77.3	23.2	12.5
44 009	Washington	86.9	6.3	49,798	74.0	317,300	25.8	15.2	1,003	29.2	83.3	26.2	5.2
45 000	**South Carolina**..........	84.3	6.6	1,774,128	68.8	136,300	23.1	11.7	758	32.0	82.7	23.6	7.2
45 001	Abbeville..................	89.7	5.0	9,716	77.7	88,400	22.6	12.7	549	33.7	88.0	27.9	6.6
45 003	Aiken	86.9	5.2	63,373	71.7	126,300	21.6	10.4	708	30.7	85.9	25.8	7.1
45 007	Anderson	86.4	4.2	72,891	72.7	122,100	21.8	10.8	658	33.6	86.9	23.9	6.1
45 011	Barnwell	91.9	1.9	8,284	79.3	71,600	23.2	13.6	640	34.8	85.2	27.4	10.2
45 013	Beaufort	81.2	9.8	63,600	71.0	272,800	28.5	12.0	995	31.8	74.6	21.2	5.6
45 015	Berkeley	82.5	10.2	65,396	70.5	148,900	24.0	12.0	952	32.2	83.3	25.8	4.5
45 019	Charleston	79.5	8.0	142,536	61.2	234,800	26.8	13.5	940	34.9	78.2	22.6	8.8
45 021	Cherokee	84.7	5.3	21,096	65.4	81,100	22.4	12.3	641	29.1	83.7	20.7	8.8
45 023	Chester	92.3	3.7	12,348	74.0	83,400	22.4	12.7	590	33.9	79.8	30.3	9.6
45 025	Chesterfield	90.8	3.3	17,471	69.9	79,200	22.3	11.3	606	38.7	85.8	23.6	9.4
45 027	Clarendon.................	88.8	5.9	12,044	72.3	87,300	24.8	11.1	598	30.4	78.5	27.6	11.7
45 029	Colleton	93.6	2.4	14,808	75.1	89,800	27.9	15.8	693	35.4	84.7	32.8	9.7
45 031	Darlington	87.9	3.8	26,568	69.2	88,300	20.4	11.8	587	31.6	86.0	23.1	9.7
45 033	Dillon	88.0	4.1	11,875	64.0	66,500	24.5	15.3	548	28.3	76.0	22.9	12.0
45 035	Dorchester	83.3	8.3	50,323	69.5	164,300	24.8	12.5	955	32.3	82.7	28.2	5.7
45 037	Edgefield	87.3	6.5	8,908	80.1	108,600	19.8	12.0	560	29.5	79.5	25.3	5.2
45 039	Fairfield	87.8	4.7	9,869	67.1	94,100	25.3	13.4	638	32.2	84.6	27.8	14.2
45 041	Florence	85.4	5.0	51,477	66.3	112,800	21.1	10.8	655	30.2	84.6	21.9	8.5
45 043	Georgetown	88.9	5.2	23,229	78.4	149,700	30.1	13.6	790	32.6	83.5	24.5	6.6
45 045	Greenville	84.2	6.1	175,023	66.7	152,400	21.8	10.3	740	29.3	84.4	21.4	7.0
45 047	Greenwood	83.4	6.3	26,354	65.5	100,400	20.5	11.7	656	33.6	88.6	21.2	9.4
45 049	Hampton	88.4	3.9	7,507	75.6	76,700	19.9	16.6	631	28.7	77.6	30.2	8.4
45 051	Horry	82.6	6.8	113,314	68.7	158,900	27.0	11.9	822	36.0	82.4	21.0	5.9
45 053	Jasper	81.9	11.7	8,537	71.1	187,100	29.5	13.2	754	33.8	76.1	26.3	8.3
45 055	Kershaw	84.4	7.5	24,020	76.3	111,300	24.2	11.4	681	28.2	82.1	27.3	6.0
45 057	Lancaster	87.2	3.4	29,268	74.7	137,100	23.5	10.8	611	32.1	84.3	27.0	6.3
45 059	Laurens	88.2	5.3	24,783	70.1	78,300	20.6	10.6	673	32.0	85.0	24.3	7.1
45 063	Lexington	85.1	6.7	103,724	73.9	138,200	20.7	10.3	803	29.6	84.9	25.4	4.9
45 067	Marion.....................	93.1	2.2	12,010	64.6	79,100	22.5	14.0	523	37.0	80.6	27.4	16.0
45 069	Marlboro	89.3	6.3	9,697	69.7	59,900	21.1	13.6	562	31.6	82.0	23.2	12.6
45 071	Newberry	86.8	6.4	13,875	72.1	109,600	22.4	11.3	599	31.6	84.8	24.7	8.3
45 073	Oconee....................	82.7	6.7	30,082	74.8	134,200	22.9	10.0	680	30.0	83.1	23.8	6.1
45 075	Orangeburg	89.9	3.9	34,266	67.7	83,500	23.6	13.5	666	33.4	85.0	24.6	9.5
45 077	Pickens	81.0	8.9	43,553	68.6	123,400	21.4	10.8	690	34.1	86.1	23.8	4.6
45 079	Richland...................	77.8	11.0	142,881	60.7	148,100	22.8	11.2	833	33.1	78.8	20.7	6.9
45 083	Spartanburg..............	84.4	4.8	106,734	69.1	122,500	21.7	10.0	679	30.9	85.8	21.9	6.9
45 085	Sumter.....................	86.3	4.8	39,766	63.8	104,900	21.7	12.2	710	28.3	82.5	22.3	9.8
45 087	Union	87.9	4.9	11,734	72.0	76,500	20.4	13.0	601	33.9	86.0	27.7	9.9
45 089	Williamsburg	93.1	3.4	11,823	73.1	65,300	26.6	14.1	575	32.5	81.6	29.3	14.4
45 091	York.......................	86.0	5.5	86,271	71.4	159,300	22.3	10.3	782	29.7	81.9	25.3	5.4

[1]10.0 represents 10 percent or less; 50.0 represents 50 percent or higher.

Table C-2. Counties — Where: Migration, Housing, and Transportation, 2010–2012—*Continued*

STATE and county code	STATE or county	Percent who lived in the same house one year ago	Percent who did not live in the same county one year ago	Total occupied housing units	Percent owner-occupied housing units	Median value of owner-occupied housing units (dollars)	Median selected monthly owner costs as a percentage of household income — With a mortgage	Without a mortgage[1]	Median gross rent (dollars)	Median gross rent as a percentage of household income[1]	Percent of workers who drove alone to work	Mean travel time to work (minutes)	Percent of occupied housing units with no vehicle available
ACS table number:		C07204	C07204	B25003	B25003	B25077	B25092	B25092	B25064	B25071	C08301	B08013/ B08012	C25045
Column number:		1	2	3	4	5	6	7	8	9	10	11	12
46 000	**South Dakota**	83.9	7.0	322,005	68.0	131,600	21.5	10.9	629	26.2	78.1	16.8	5.6
46 011	Brookings	66.0	17.9	12,275	56.6	146,900	22.7	10.3	662	28.4	74.2	14.2	3.7
46 013	Brown	84.2	5.6	15,593	70.9	137,500	20.6	12.3	558	24.7	81.3	13.6	6.2
46 029	Codington	86.9	4.6	11,519	71.2	135,800	21.5	11.2	579	26.4	80.5	14.5	6.1
46 081	Lawrence	83.1	8.4	10,445	65.3	170,700	24.5	11.5	576	27.4	72.5	19.4	5.7
46 083	Lincoln	86.3	5.8	17,269	76.4	184,500	20.9	10.0	834	24.3	86.2	18.6	2.6
46 093	Meade	79.8	13.1	9,911	68.0	159,000	23.2	12.1	799	28.0	78.7	19.0	3.1
46 099	Minnehaha	83.8	5.2	67,205	63.5	149,800	21.9	10.0	691	27.0	83.9	17.5	5.8
46 103	Pennington	80.2	6.0	40,606	65.4	153,600	23.0	12.2	753	27.9	83.8	17.5	5.8
46 135	Yankton	84.1	9.7	8,512	72.3	119,600	19.5	10.3	524	25.5	79.0	14.7	6.6
47 000	**Tennessee**	84.5	5.7	2,466,659	67.5	138,400	23.3	11.3	731	31.2	83.8	24.3	6.4
47 001	Anderson	84.5	6.0	30,638	69.5	131,900	22.0	10.7	665	28.7	87.6	23.0	5.8
47 003	Bedford	87.4	4.6	16,290	68.9	117,800	21.7	12.0	636	30.1	82.5	25.2	5.6
47 009	Blount	84.7	6.5	48,349	72.7	163,800	23.7	10.1	715	29.3	86.4	24.1	5.2
47 011	Bradley	82.9	5.2	37,747	66.1	138,400	23.3	11.1	690	33.8	83.9	21.6	6.8
47 013	Campbell	86.2	2.5	15,880	70.6	90,000	22.9	13.3	538	33.0	87.7	25.4	7.7
47 017	Carroll	89.2	3.7	10,705	77.9	80,700	21.9	11.6	520	30.4	85.8	26.4	8.9
47 019	Carter	86.4	5.1	23,940	72.9	100,700	22.5	12.3	525	29.7	83.5	22.8	5.5
47 021	Cheatham	89.1	6.6	14,476	80.8	150,800	24.4	11.3	893	42.7	80.8	33.1	2.9
47 025	Claiborne	88.2	6.1	12,679	73.9	99,600	22.6	11.0	517	30.7	84.2	25.8	4.7
47 029	Cocke	84.0	4.9	14,680	68.3	97,500	24.9	11.7	527	32.4	84.8	26.3	9.2
47 031	Coffee	85.7	5.9	21,064	65.4	117,500	24.1	11.6	635	33.2	88.5	21.8	5.8
47 035	Cumberland	87.7	4.9	23,243	79.5	143,200	25.1	10.4	591	31.0	85.7	22.9	4.5
47 037	Davidson	78.6	7.6	254,917	53.8	167,200	24.5	11.7	814	31.1	79.4	23.1	8.0
47 043	Dickson	86.8	4.1	18,526	73.5	143,100	23.5	11.5	744	33.1	82.9	31.1	5.0
47 045	Dyer	83.4	4.7	14,825	64.1	98,200	22.2	13.4	613	30.5	90.9	19.0	7.8
47 047	Fayette	90.7	6.0	14,578	80.2	177,500	23.2	10.0	596	24.1	85.9	31.3	3.9
47 051	Franklin	87.7	5.0	15,927	76.0	106,300	23.3	10.5	587	25.3	82.1	23.4	5.6
47 053	Gibson	87.4	3.5	19,064	74.7	87,300	24.6	12.3	573	29.1	89.4	24.9	6.4
47 055	Giles	89.8	3.5	11,541	72.8	93,800	23.1	11.5	550	34.4	87.2	25.4	6.7
47 057	Grainger	90.3	5.5	8,831	83.5	91,800	22.5	12.8	526	28.7	85.0	32.5	5.6
47 059	Greene	87.2	4.4	29,192	71.5	108,000	23.7	10.0	566	30.2	85.7	23.1	4.1
47 063	Hamblen	86.6	5.8	24,200	69.5	120,500	23.0	11.7	638	33.4	85.2	20.8	5.8
47 065	Hamilton	83.8	5.4	135,018	64.9	155,300	22.2	11.1	731	29.9	83.8	21.7	8.1
47 069	Hardeman	92.1	4.1	8,762	72.7	85,400	30.2	13.1	520	37.6	89.4	28.5	10.6
47 071	Hardin	88.7	4.1	9,817	77.4	101,000	26.0	12.6	484	29.9	87.3	22.2	6.0
47 073	Hawkins	87.9	5.9	23,495	77.4	110,600	22.0	11.3	577	28.1	90.1	24.6	4.8
47 077	Henderson	91.1	4.6	11,073	77.5	99,900	22.5	12.4	578	23.9	87.6	24.0	6.0
47 079	Henry	83.2	4.7	13,298	73.0	93,300	21.5	10.4	588	26.4	84.6	22.3	7.6
47 081	Hickman	88.0	7.0	8,741	80.1	101,000	23.4	10.1	624	34.8	76.1	38.9	6.9
47 089	Jefferson	84.8	7.4	19,742	74.6	118,900	22.7	12.2	618	25.2	82.3	26.5	4.2
47 093	Knox	86.5	4.9	181,578	64.6	154,600	22.3	10.9	757	30.4	85.8	21.6	6.1
47 097	Lauderdale	78.3	8.2	9,932	63.5	80,500	25.0	13.7	610	29.0	89.5	23.5	8.2
47 099	Lawrence	89.6	3.1	15,953	74.4	99,000	22.9	11.9	586	29.2	83.2	24.8	6.4
47 103	Lincoln	87.3	4.7	13,517	74.4	100,900	23.8	11.4	612	26.3	83.2	28.3	5.4
47 105	Loudon	87.7	7.4	19,921	77.2	178,500	22.9	10.0	682	26.3	85.0	24.7	4.7
47 107	McMinn	84.4	4.9	20,418	73.5	111,500	22.8	11.4	567	31.2	85.7	21.2	5.1
47 109	McNairy	94.2	1.7	9,736	70.6	88,600	24.1	13.5	532	30.1	87.2	22.9	6.3
47 111	Macon	85.2	3.9	8,319	71.7	89,000	23.3	11.0	534	26.2	83.7	28.9	6.4
47 113	Madison	87.2	5.0	35,185	65.0	113,900	22.8	11.3	721	36.5	84.2	18.8	6.4
47 115	Marion	91.8	4.8	11,078	74.6	120,400	23.2	11.1	548	29.3	81.6	28.4	6.7
47 117	Marshall	86.6	7.0	11,857	73.8	104,600	21.8	12.4	657	30.1	83.6	28.2	5.2
47 119	Maury	85.3	6.6	31,800	69.5	136,600	23.7	11.8	667	31.1	81.4	29.5	6.3
47 123	Monroe	81.8	7.9	17,767	71.7	117,400	23.2	12.6	602	29.4	86.8	27.0	5.5
47 125	Montgomery	74.8	12.1	64,010	61.1	142,500	22.5	10.9	827	29.0	85.0	23.5	4.4
47 129	Morgan	84.1	11.5	7,416	80.7	95,400	21.9	12.2	572	25.9	82.0	31.6	5.3
47 131	Obion	86.4	5.1	12,205	69.0	93,900	20.5	11.9	577	32.7	89.6	19.2	7.1
47 133	Overton	89.7	2.8	8,826	77.6	87,400	22.4	11.5	553	30.1	85.4	29.3	6.6
47 141	Putnam	84.2	5.6	28,829	63.9	134,800	23.2	11.1	571	36.8	90.3	22.9	3.6
47 143	Rhea	81.9	8.6	12,051	69.9	106,500	23.0	10.9	552	31.8	82.7	24.7	5.5
47 145	Roane	89.5	4.1	22,041	74.7	119,600	22.3	11.5	663	29.9	85.2	25.5	4.5
47 147	Robertson	87.9	5.7	24,302	77.1	150,500	24.2	11.4	805	24.9	82.5	30.4	4.9
47 149	Rutherford	82.5	6.3	95,363	68.3	157,000	22.8	10.0	848	31.0	86.4	27.2	3.3
47 151	Scott	88.3	3.5	8,226	79.2	80,200	24.2	12.8	530	36.6	83.5	26.0	7.8
47 155	Sevier	83.5	6.0	36,333	66.7	158,400	23.8	10.0	702	27.5	76.2	26.4	3.3
47 157	Shelby	82.7	3.5	342,124	58.6	132,500	24.5	12.7	837	34.7	82.3	22.2	9.6
47 163	Sullivan	85.4	4.7	66,038	73.4	122,100	21.0	10.6	594	30.0	86.9	21.8	6.0
47 165	Sumner	84.3	6.5	60,301	71.4	174,900	24.5	10.3	820	28.8	82.1	27.6	4.5
47 167	Tipton	85.0	7.4	21,350	74.1	137,300	22.2	10.9	672	31.2	83.7	31.8	4.0
47 177	Warren	90.4	3.7	15,223	69.5	89,900	23.0	11.7	556	29.9	83.1	23.0	6.2
47 179	Washington	84.3	5.8	52,066	67.1	148,500	22.6	10.0	668	29.8	86.5	21.1	5.7
47 183	Weakley	78.4	10.3	13,741	64.9	91,300	19.2	11.4	561	33.0	87.1	21.6	5.5
47 185	White	86.4	6.6	9,907	76.9	101,400	25.2	11.6	561	34.2	84.0	25.4	8.2
47 187	Williamson	87.5	7.4	66,153	80.3	332,000	22.6	10.0	1,061	30.6	80.4	26.9	2.3
47 189	Wilson	86.5	6.4	42,697	80.0	185,400	23.1	10.8	844	33.0	87.1	28.3	2.8

[1]10.0 represents 10 percent or less; 50.0 represents 50 percent or higher.

Table C-2. Counties — Where: Migration, Housing, and Transportation, 2010–2012—*Continued*

STATE and county code	STATE or county	Percent who lived in the same house one year ago	Percent who did not live in the same county one year ago	Total occupied housing units	Percent owner-occupied housing units	Median value of owner-occupied housing units (dollars)	Median selected monthly owner costs as a percentage of household income — With a mortgage	Without a mortgage[1]	Median gross rent (dollars)	Median gross rent as a percentage of household income[1]	Percent of workers who drove alone to work	Mean travel time to work (minutes)	Percent of occupied housing units with no vehicle available
ACS table number:		C07204	C07204	B25003	B25003	B25077	B25092	B25092	B25064	B25071	C08301	B08013/E08012	C25045
Column number:		1	2	3	4	5	6	7	8	9	10	11	12
48 000	**Texas**	82.8	5.8	8,852,441	63.0	128,400	22.8	12.3	834	29.8	79.9	24.9	6.0
48 001	Anderson	80.5	9.7	16,738	72.9	78,800	19.8	13.1	716	30.8	84.9	21.4	7.1
48 005	Angelina	81.7	5.0	31,055	66.4	85,400	21.9	11.6	717	30.4	81.9	17.5	4.8
48 007	Aransas	79.9	12.0	9,516	76.2	109,200	28.4	14.5	824	30.2	78.4	20.5	5.2
48 013	Atascosa	87.3	6.2	15,107	75.8	84,900	22.4	12.2	702	23.8	79.9	28.9	4.9
48 015	Austin	90.7	4.4	10,855	76.5	154,900	24.6	14.0	785	27.4	83.0	27.8	5.0
48 019	Bandera	89.3	5.9	8,687	77.0	142,600	21.4	13.0	781	26.7	82.2	39.9	2.3
48 021	Bastrop	86.7	5.7	25,097	79.2	119,900	23.4	12.9	869	31.1	77.8	32.7	4.3
48 025	Bee	76.9	16.7	8,940	64.8	77,900	19.4	13.6	716	25.4	78.9	23.4	7.5
48 027	Bell	76.5	10.3	103,230	56.2	120,300	21.7	11.0	850	28.9	83.3	19.3	5.1
48 029	Bexar	80.9	4.9	602,654	59.2	123,500	22.4	11.5	823	29.6	79.1	24.0	8.2
48 037	Bowie	85.7	6.3	34,013	66.6	96,100	20.4	11.5	690	30.7	82.6	17.0	6.6
48 039	Brazoria	87.1	5.8	107,526	73.3	147,400	21.9	10.7	861	26.2	85.5	28.3	3.3
48 041	Brazos	67.2	13.0	69,824	46.8	150,600	22.8	11.2	838	45.1	75.5	18.3	7.1
48 049	Brown	90.4	4.5	13,004	70.0	87,900	22.1	12.0	647	32.0	86.7	16.2	6.5
48 053	Burnet	84.6	6.9	16,567	71.2	147,900	25.2	13.9	795	28.2	78.0	27.2	4.8
48 055	Caldwell	80.6	13.8	11,766	65.0	103,100	24.3	12.8	727	31.1	76.5	30.3	6.7
48 057	Calhoun	84.9	4.5	7,906	71.4	96,300	19.2	10.6	712	36.4	78.3	21.3	4.8
48 061	Cameron	89.6	1.8	118,445	66.1	76,500	25.8	13.2	636	32.8	80.1	19.7	9.1
48 067	Cass	88.9	4.4	11,776	73.4	74,900	20.8	12.1	514	30.3	84.2	26.6	8.8
48 071	Chambers	86.4	6.8	12,115	83.3	142,200	19.2	11.9	901	22.2	87.1	34.3	2.0
48 073	Cherokee	83.7	7.0	17,455	71.0	73,600	23.7	12.5	650	32.2	86.3	23.2	7.1
48 085	Collin	86.0	6.2	287,166	68.2	205,000	22.1	11.3	1,028	26.7	81.6	27.5	2.7
48 089	Colorado	94.2	3.8	7,883	76.2	112,600	22.5	12.2	618	22.8	80.9	22.7	3.9
48 091	Comal	84.2	8.6	42,043	75.1	204,200	22.4	10.8	924	30.9	79.1	30.1	4.0
48 097	Cooke	84.3	7.4	14,409	70.5	108,400	21.6	13.3	735	27.8	76.4	25.3	5.6
48 099	Coryell	81.2	11.3	19,793	57.2	97,300	20.0	10.0	890	25.7	75.2	19.8	4.4
48 113	Dallas	82.8	4.2	854,403	52.5	128,000	24.6	13.4	864	29.4	79.2	25.9	7.2
48 121	Denton	80.8	8.6	242,679	64.9	181,000	22.3	12.3	917	28.5	80.4	27.2	2.8
48 123	DeWitt	84.1	7.1	6,840	73.8	79,200	18.5	10.4	577	26.7	83.6	23.0	8.5
48 135	Ector	82.3	6.0	49,495	66.5	92,200	19.6	10.1	741	25.7	80.5	20.6	5.4
48 139	Ellis	84.5	5.7	50,850	72.4	138,500	22.4	12.8	871	30.1	82.0	28.5	3.5
48 141	El Paso	84.0	4.3	256,148	61.8	112,200	23.6	11.5	718	30.8	79.1	23.1	7.9
48 143	Erath	79.3	10.0	14,340	57.9	114,500	23.2	11.0	654	34.0	82.1	17.6	4.0
48 147	Fannin	82.6	10.8	11,943	74.3	100,600	22.0	13.3	669	33.1	80.9	30.3	4.3
48 149	Fayette	92.0	4.4	10,079	74.6	127,500	20.6	12.3	672	27.4	78.6	22.2	3.4
48 157	Fort Bend	89.6	5.1	189,865	78.3	181,300	23.0	11.9	1,124	27.6	82.6	29.9	2.6
48 167	Galveston	82.6	6.7	109,510	68.8	146,800	22.4	11.9	887	31.9	80.5	26.8	6.1
48 171	Gillespie	84.1	5.5	10,496	75.6	211,300	26.4	11.9	829	32.6	72.4	18.3	2.5
48 177	Gonzales	...	...	6,453	72.3	82,000	22.0	13.0	545	21.7	77.3	22.4	7.6
48 179	Gray	83.8	10.9	8,398	74.9	71,100	21.1	11.6	617	27.6	81.0	18.3	2.4
48 181	Grayson	80.0	5.4	46,349	67.3	105,800	22.2	13.3	775	28.4	81.0	24.7	5.3
48 183	Gregg	80.9	6.5	44,819	62.8	119,000	21.6	11.8	759	29.5	83.0	20.4	6.6
48 185	Grimes	84.7	9.1	8,816	74.5	93,700	19.2	12.6	718	25.0	82.2	33.7	5.5
48 187	Guadalupe	87.3	6.6	46,485	78.6	155,600	21.7	11.2	832	26.1	82.3	24.9	3.6
48 189	Hale	77.7	12.6	11,616	63.5	66,500	19.4	10.4	579	26.6	83.3	15.2	5.2
48 199	Hardin	90.0	3.8	20,608	79.4	99,400	18.9	11.0	766	27.5	89.4	27.2	4.6
48 201	Harris	82.0	3.8	1,419,274	56.3	131,000	23.4	12.2	863	30.1	79.0	27.2	7.2
48 203	Harrison	83.9	7.2	23,670	74.1	113,100	21.7	10.6	662	26.6	82.0	23.3	5.4
48 209	Hays	78.7	11.8	56,282	66.4	173,200	24.5	12.3	913	40.1	75.9	28.9	2.4
48 213	Henderson	85.2	7.5	29,673	75.0	86,300	24.6	14.6	657	31.5	76.5	28.6	5.0
48 215	Hidalgo	86.6	2.5	217,706	67.9	79,100	24.4	13.2	629	33.7	78.4	21.7	6.5
48 217	Hill	85.2	6.3	13,501	69.7	82,500	22.5	13.7	626	28.3	79.0	28.1	5.9
48 219	Hockley	78.3	13.6	8,033	69.5	78,900	17.9	10.7	718	25.3	76.3	20.4	5.3
48 221	Hood	84.0	6.8	20,783	78.6	144,000	22.9	11.9	865	29.7	83.1	33.0	3.0
48 223	Hopkins	84.8	6.5	13,468	71.7	92,100	22.8	12.6	650	29.4	76.8	20.7	5.8
48 225	Houston	85.2	7.2	7,847	70.8	71,600	22.7	14.6	627	34.8	77.0	22.4	7.2
48 227	Howard	78.5	9.4	10,869	67.1	67,700	18.7	11.0	658	25.0	79.6	16.3	9.3
48 231	Hunt	83.2	7.3	30,939	69.9	91,800	22.2	12.7	718	32.9	81.4	28.5	5.9
48 233	Hutchinson	87.4	6.7	8,336	76.2	70,100	17.0	10.0	668	22.6	80.7	19.5	5.1
48 241	Jasper	88.5	4.1	13,369	77.6	81,300	19.7	10.9	623	34.7	77.9	29.7	7.8
48 245	Jefferson	83.2	6.2	92,508	64.1	97,800	22.2	12.3	736	32.0	82.1	19.3	8.8
48 249	Jim Wells	88.4	4.7	13,118	73.6	66,500	20.5	12.2	686	25.4	80.5	24.1	7.2
48 251	Johnson	86.0	6.1	52,243	73.4	115,300	21.4	12.3	851	26.2	86.6	30.0	2.6
48 253	Jones	79.0	18.0	5,436	76.5	65,500	20.9	13.5	514	23.3	83.3	19.7	9.6
48 257	Kaufman	83.7	7.8	35,181	78.4	124,900	23.8	12.9	864	32.6	82.9	32.7	4.1
48 259	Kendall	84.3	8.0	12,987	71.6	279,300	25.1	12.1	991	31.0	74.8	25.1	2.5
48 265	Kerr	82.6	7.4	20,656	70.6	152,400	24.2	12.9	772	28.5	80.2	19.2	3.3
48 273	Kleberg	81.6	7.5	11,081	52.8	74,100	25.4	10.0	696	29.8	73.1	18.2	10.0
48 277	Lamar	82.7	6.0	19,008	67.6	85,800	19.6	13.1	636	31.7	82.6	18.6	8.9
48 281	Lampasas	81.0	7.6	7,639	75.0	125,900	19.7	14.1	692	30.3	74.4	28.8	4.5
48 291	Liberty	80.3	13.1	24,813	78.7	87,900	21.8	12.1	711	27.3	81.4	33.4	4.4
48 293	Limestone	84.8	5.8	8,245	74.4	86,000	20.3	13.4	700	28.5	76.0	20.1	4.5
48 303	Lubbock	75.0	9.3	105,477	57.7	109,300	21.3	12.1	783	33.9	82.2	16.2	5.2
48 309	McLennan	80.1	6.6	84,399	60.6	108,700	22.8	13.3	749	32.3	81.1	18.7	7.2
48 321	Matagorda	90.0	3.8	13,278	70.5	93,700	20.7	13.2	645	26.1	81.2	23.4	5.8

[1] 10.0 represents 10 percent or less; 50.0 represents 50 percent or higher.

Table C-2. Counties — Where: Migration, Housing, and Transportation, 2010–2012—*Continued*

STATE and county code	STATE or county	Percent who lived in the same house one year ago	Percent who did not live in the same county one year ago	Total occupied housing units	Percent owner-occupied housing units	Median value of owner-occupied housing units (dollars)	Median selected monthly owner costs as a percentage of household income — With a mortgage	Without a mortgage[1]	Median gross rent (dollars)	Med an gross rent as a percentage of household income[1]	Percent of workers who drove alone to work	Mean travel time to work (minutes)	Percent of occupied housing units with no vehicle available
ACS table number:		C07204	C07204	B25003	B25003	B25077	B25092	B25092	B25064	B25071	C08301	B08013/ B08012	C25045
Column number:		1	2	3	4	5	6	7	8	9	10	11	12
	Texas—Cont.												
48 323	Maverick	90.0	1.6	15,843	69.7	84,300	28.2	15.5	585	29.4	78.8	19.8	8.2
48 325	Medina	91.0	6.0	15,349	77.6	107,700	21.6	11.7	691	24.9	83.5	30.2	3.6
48 329	Midland	83.2	7.3	50,251	67.8	146,600	20.7	10.8	923	26.9	84.3	19.2	4.1
48 331	Milam	88.5	6.3	9,304	67.7	83,000	22.6	12.5	650	30.0	74.9	26.0	8.5
48 339	Montgomery	83.5	7.5	163,842	72.6	165,100	22.2	12.1	939	27.7	79.4	31.3	3.5
48 341	Moore	76.8	7.9	6,797	74.4	86,400	20.9	10.0	643	27.2	71.1	17.2	5.7
48 347	Nacogdoches	77.2	10.4	23,627	56.6	102,800	21.4	11.3	682	32.3	80.2	18.4	8.5
48 349	Navarro	85.1	6.1	17,627	67.7	77,500	23.2	13.3	662	28.1	82.2	24.9	7.8
48 355	Nueces	80.6	6.3	122,839	58.1	111,300	23.2	13.0	831	30.6	77.8	19.4	8.4
48 361	Orange	87.5	5.0	30,401	77.5	89,000	21.0	10.8	745	26.4	88.1	22.9	4.4
48 363	Palo Pinto	86.2	6.6	10,385	72.4	80,900	22.4	13.0	734	29.8	80.8	22.8	4.4
48 365	Panola	87.7	5.4	8,965	76.8	89,400	19.5	10.2	678	25.3	82.8	24.3	5.3
48 367	Parker	86.4	8.2	42,457	79.2	150,100	21.5	11.9	879	27.8	83.7	30.9	3.6
48 373	Polk	84.9	8.2	17,292	79.8	80,600	22.4	12.4	627	29.2	71.7	25.1	3.5
48 375	Potter	79.5	5.7	42,670	57.9	85,600	23.2	11.7	688	31.5	74.1	18.6	8.0
48 381	Randall	82.9	5.5	48,617	68.0	140,200	20.1	11.7	750	28.2	84.1	19.2	4.2
48 397	Rockwall	89.5	6.4	27,108	81.1	188,900	23.1	13.8	1284	26.3	81.2	30.7	2.2
48 401	Rusk	81.5	12.5	17,780	78.0	91,900	19.0	10.0	643	25.7	88.2	25.6	4.7
48 407	San Jacinto	86.6	9.4	9,300	81.6	88,700	25.1	10.9	700	22.5	75.0	42.5	5.9
48 409	San Patricio	83.1	8.3	22,121	67.2	88,700	21.5	12.5	804	27.1	81.3	22.2	7.9
48 419	Shelby	92.1	3.6	9,884	73.4	66,300	20.1	10.4	529	32.2	75.5	21.9	8.4
48 423	Smith	79.7	8.1	79,299	66.2	120,500	22.8	12.3	812	31.4	82.3	21.7	6.1
48 427	Starr	87.9	2.6	15,783	77.1	67,600	27.2	14.5	481	34.6	73.7	23.3	10.6
48 439	Tarrant	82.5	5.2	657,094	61.4	135,100	22.9	12.8	867	29.9	82.9	25.9	4.7
48 441	Taylor	77.3	7.0	49,159	60.7	94,500	21.0	11.9	759	31.2	80.5	16.0	6.3
48 449	Titus	88.6	5.5	10,474	71.5	94,200	22.0	12.1	606	29.0	80.8	17.3	6.7
48 451	Tom Green	74.1	12.5	41,907	63.7	98,800	21.2	11.8	687	29.9	79.1	16.9	5.6
48 453	Travis	75.6	7.8	409,351	51.2	215,700	23.9	12.8	964	31.3	73.1	24.1	6.2
48 457	Tyler	89.0	8.8	8,249	81.5	73,900	19.6	11.8	583	26.7	75.7	31.2	6.0
48 459	Upshur	87.9	6.8	14,387	81.2	88,200	19.8	10.9	692	26.1	80.7	28.0	4.2
48 463	Uvalde	86.9	5.4	8,503	70.2	71,100	21.5	12.6	630	28.9	78.8	19.2	8.1
48 465	Val Verde	84.4	6.5	14,960	67.9	93,500	22.2	13.3	661	28.0	77.2	18.7	5.8
48 467	Van Zandt	90.9	3.7	19,093	77.5	99,700	21.8	12.7	671	32.7	82.6	33.9	4.4
48 469	Victoria	82.2	6.2	31,967	65.0	111,100	21.1	12.6	712	30.0	80.3	20.1	7.3
48 471	Walker	80.0	13.7	20,601	57.3	112,200	21.1	11.1	737	40.0	83.8	23.9	5.6
48 473	Waller	88.6	8.0	13,482	69.6	131,500	24.8	12.2	746	28.2	83.8	31.0	5.9
48 477	Washington	87.0	5.5	11,718	71.5	136,400	24.3	12.8	761	29.0	76.5	20.5	6.2
48 479	Webb	82.8	2.1	67,572	61.5	107,500	27.6	14.7	726	35.9	77.3	21.6	8.9
48 481	Wharton	92.3	3.0	14,653	68.5	91,600	21.8	13.9	647	32.9	78.4	23.7	6.5
48 485	Wichita	80.9	9.4	47,266	62.6	88,500	21.8	13.3	700	28.2	81.7	15.3	5.5
48 489	Willacy	88.8	8.2	5,396	77.4	54,700	20.8	13.7	555	39.0	90.6	18.7	7.6
48 491	Williamson	80.8	9.7	154,373	66.5	176,100	23.3	12.0	1033	27.5	80.5	26.0	2.9
48 493	Wilson	91.0	6.3	15,593	85.2	153,800	21.5	11.5	716	25.8	78.9	31.6	3.1
48 497	Wise	86.2	6.0	20,404	78.6	121,200	22.2	12.6	826	28.3	84.1	30.9	2.4
48 499	Wood	85.9	8.3	16,015	79.9	107,400	24.1	12.5	724	30.2	78.9	27.4	4.1
49 000	**Utah**	82.6	6.0	886,032	69.7	209,000	24.3	10.0	841	29.9	76.6	21.6	4.7
49 003	Box Elder	88.6	5.4	16,012	79.7	163,900	22.9	10.0	619	24.0	77.8	23.1	4.0
49 005	Cache	79.3	7.9	35,449	64.9	188,200	24.2	10.0	651	29.3	74.9	16.7	4.0
49 007	Carbon	84.7	6.6	7,625	70.8	124,300	20.8	10.0	572	26.2	79.3	15.8	6.6
49 011	Davis	86.1	6.6	95,457	77.2	218,900	22.8	10.0	858	28.6	80.3	22.6	3.3
49 021	Iron	87.0	6.4	15,500	60.7	160,500	28.7	10.0	665	31.6	78.4	19.4	5.4
49 035	Salt Lake	82.4	4.7	344,171	66.7	228,300	24.7	10.0	878	30.9	76.6	22.4	6.1
49 039	Sanpete	79.5	13.2	7,933	73.4	165,300	23.4	10.0	586	23.6	69.1	19.8	2.8
49 041	Sevier	84.1	6.0	7,060	76.6	148,200	24.3	10.0	633	24.8	80.4	15.5	5.3
49 043	Summit	86.2	8.3	12,367	78.2	488,700	24.7	10.0	1198	26.6	77.9	24.6	2.3
49 045	Tooele	85.3	6.8	18,102	75.1	172,700	22.5	10.0	869	27.5	67.3	29.5	4.5
49 047	Uintah	84.2	7.1	10,829	72.5	182,800	22.3	10.0	898	23.0	81.5	20.4	4.4
49 049	Utah	77.9	7.4	142,724	67.6	217,400	24.7	10.0	843	31.7	73.0	21.2	3.0
49 051	Wasatch	85.1	7.0	7,515	74.9	291,500	26.4	10.0	945	35.4	75.7	26.4	3.3
49 053	Washington	82.4	5.8	47,115	68.6	205,700	29.1	10.0	935	32.7	80.5	18.0	3.5
49 057	Weber	85.0	5.4	79,718	71.4	169,200	23.6	10.0	782	28.0	79.1	21.3	5.1
50 000	**Vermont**	86.2	5.7	257,887	70.9	215,700	25.4	16.6	859	31.2	74.4	22.2	6.7
50 001	Addison	86.3	6.7	14,106	74.7	235,000	26.6	17.7	871	29.8	69.5	24.7	4.3
50 003	Bennington	87.7	4.9	15,389	72.0	217,000	26.2	17.1	844	34.8	77.7	19.4	7.0
50 005	Caledonia	87.6	4.9	12,635	72.5	161,200	24.6	16.9	659	33.3	75.6	21.5	9.4
50 007	Chittenden	80.3	7.3	62,699	64.4	268,500	24.3	14.3	991	32.4	71.4	19.8	8.0
50 011	Franklin	89.3	3.8	18,800	75.7	202,900	25.1	15.4	863	34.1	75.5	27.2	5.9
50 015	Lamoille	87.1	6.9	9,899	72.2	215,800	27.9	16.7	861	31.4	78.5	25.7	4.1
50 017	Orange	91.9	5.0	11,794	81.0	181,100	24.3	15.4	809	34.2	75.8	26.1	6.2
50 019	Orleans	87.4	4.7	11,342	76.8	153,800	26.5	18.8	670	32.4	79.2	22.7	4.9
50 021	Rutland	86.3	4.7	26,070	69.5	174,000	25.8	17.1	802	31.0	79.6	20.9	6.4

[1]10.0 represents 10 percent or less; 50.0 represents 50 percent or higher.

Table C-2. Counties — Where: Migration, Housing, and Transportation, 2010–2012—*Continued*

STATE and county code	STATE or county	Percent who lived in the same house one year ago	Percent who did not live in the same county one year ago	Total occupied housing units	Percent owner-occupied housing units (dollars)	Median value of owner-occupied housing units (dollars)	Median selected monthly owner costs as a percentage of household income		Median gross rent (dollars)	Median gross rent as a percentage of household income[1]	Percent of workers who drove alone to work	Mean travel time to work (minutes)	Percent of occupied housing units with no vehicle available
							With a mortgage	Without a mortgage[1]					
ACS table number:		C07204	C07204	B25003	B25003	B25077	B25092	B25092	B25064	B25071	C08301	B08013/ B08012	C25045
Column number:		1	2	3	4	5	6	7	8	9	10	11	12
	Vermont—Cont.												
50 023	Washington	89.5	4.6	24,956	72.8	201,500	24.4	16.7	837	28.5	72.4	22.0	6.2
50 025	Windham	88.2	5.0	19,142	70.3	211,800	28.2	18.6	802	28.7	74.0	21.5	7.0
50 027	Windsor	87.6	6.4	25,171	69.3	213,800	26.0	18.6	823	28.7	75.7	21.9	7.2
51 000	**Virginia**	85.0	7.8	3,007,690	67.1	243,100	23.9	11.1	1,075	30.2	77.4	27.8	6.3
51 001	Accomack	93.7	2.6	14,483	69.1	156,900	23.4	12.9	709	25.4	78.5	20.7	10.2
51 003	Albemarle	82.5	11.9	37,788	65.7	319,100	22.4	11.0	1083	29.5	79.7	22.7	5.1
51 009	Amherst	90.2	4.7	12,624	75.4	152,700	22.9	10.6	647	23.4	81.4	23.5	6.9
51 013	Arlington	77.6	12.6	93,236	44.3	584,500	22.2	10.2	1,701	26.3	53.8	27.4	11.9
51 015	Augusta	92.4	3.4	28,281	81.8	197,100	23.4	11.5	763	27.8	87.9	24.7	3.9
51 019	Bedford	92.2	4.8	27,146	84.7	197,200	22.2	10.0	738	32.1	83.6	28.2	3.9
51 023	Botetourt	93.6	4.4	12,663	89.2	210,200	22.7	10.0	710	23.2	90.5	25.6	3.0
51 027	Buchanan	93.4	2.9	9,411	80.9	68,500	22.3	10.0	608	42.1	90.9	29.6	7.4
51 031	Campbell	90.2	6.2	21,452	77.0	148,700	23.0	10.0	717	27.9	83.4	21.9	6.1
51 033	Caroline	85.2	8.2	10,686	83.6	191,500	24.7	12.2	958	36.8	79.5	36.5	3.5
51 035	Carroll	91.7	3.0	12,720	77.1	106,200	22.9	11.9	510	32.2	84.7	26.2	6.9
51 041	Chesterfield	88.5	5.4	112,630	76.9	225,500	23.3	10.5	1,055	29.4	84.8	25.5	3.2
51 047	Culpeper	87.9	5.9	16,175	72.3	245,000	24.6	10.0	978	32.2	83.6	34.2	3.9
51 053	Dinwiddie	93.8	3.7	9,736	75.9	164,500	25.4	10.2	864	27.1	84.7	27.1	2.3
51 059	Fairfax	86.2	5.8	390,130	68.3	474,700	22.6	10.0	1,631	28.3	72.2	32.3	4.4
51 061	Fauquier	89.6	6.6	22,768	79.8	343,400	23.8	10.8	1,119	27.2	80.3	40.5	3.4
51 065	Fluvanna	93.1	4.8	9,582	85.7	222,900	23.7	11.6	1,076	30.0	77.1	33.0	3.6
51 067	Franklin	85.7	6.6	23,022	77.3	162,700	24.9	10.0	626	30.3	78.4	29.6	5.5
51 069	Frederick	88.1	5.6	28,866	78.6	224,200	22.6	11.5	1,055	29.2	84.9	30.4	3.5
51 073	Gloucester	89.0	3.9	13,685	83.5	230,800	27.3	10.0	841	26.1	82.7	33.9	3.1
51 075	Goochland	93.7	4.1	8,037	88.6	357,400	23.6	10.0	862	31.0	85.1	30.1	1.5
51 083	Halifax	89.9	2.3	14,558	74.3	108,200	21.8	12.7	557	36.2	82.7	24.2	8.7
51 085	Hanover	90.3	6.0	36,329	84.2	258,000	23.4	10.8	961	30.8	86.3	25.5	1.8
51 087	Henrico	82.5	8.6	123,131	64.7	219,600	23.6	10.8	989	29.1	82.9	21.6	5.2
51 089	Henry	88.0	4.6	22,522	74.0	93,900	23.9	11.2	576	29.1	88.0	24.3	8.1
51 093	Isle of Wight	91.3	5.6	13,353	82.0	247,900	24.8	11.9	988	26.9	85.4	28.1	4.0
51 095	James City	90.3	6.2	26,836	76.0	326,800	23.9	10.0	1,159	31.4	85.5	24.1	3.5
51 099	King George	86.9	9.8	8,023	77.5	277,400	21.8	10.0	1,100	25.5	83.2	35.9	2.0
51 105	Lee	89.5	4.2	9,799	71.9	76,600	24.2	10.2	475	32.5	83.5	28.7	7.9
51 107	Loudoun	88.7	5.5	106,027	77.9	433,100	24.6	10.0	1,612	27.8	78.5	33.2	2.5
51 109	Louisa	91.5	4.0	12,728	83.5	191,400	23.9	10.1	949	29.1	77.5	35.2	3.6
51 117	Mecklenburg	91.5	4.0	13,132	71.0	123,800	25.5	13.6	632	33.3	77.4	25.2	9.9
51 121	Montgomery	71.4	14.0	34,718	54.5	205,000	21.6	10.0	810	41.8	76.1	17.9	5.7
51 137	Orange	86.5	9.2	12,239	77.5	223,700	23.9	10.0	859	28.2	80.4	38.8	4.6
51 139	Page	89.5	3.4	9,584	73.6	176,600	24.1	12.7	698	35.2	81.9	34.0	2.6
51 143	Pittsylvania	91.1	4.8	25,845	79.8	109,200	22.1	11.7	592	27.5	83.8	26.0	5.5
51 145	Powhatan	89.6	8.4	9,405	87.6	267,000	23.3	10.7	958	31.8	83.1	32.3	2.4
51 147	Prince Edward	81.6	14.6	7,238	69.2	154,200	24.5	10.0	761	35.7	71.3	23.7	9.0
51 149	Prince George	80.2	15.4	10,595	70.8	190,800	23.4	10.0	1,178	28.1	82.7	21.7	4.2
51 153	Prince William	85.9	8.2	132,261	71.2	310,400	23.6	10.0	1,467	30.2	73.1	39.8	2.9
51 155	Pulaski	89.3	4.9	15,275	74.3	128,900	23.1	10.8	597	30.6	83.0	23.5	6.4
51 161	Roanoke	88.1	6.7	38,024	76.7	196,000	23.2	10.1	820	26.2	87.3	20.3	4.2
51 163	Rockbridge	91.3	3.6	9,181	75.0	181,200	26.8	10.8	692	27.4	86.0	21.6	4.8
51 165	Rockingham	89.4	5.9	29,063	77.3	193,200	24.3	10.0	786	28.5	80.5	21.7	4.6
51 167	Russell	92.1	2.9	10,824	77.7	94,200	23.2	11.0	502	39.4	84.2	29.9	9.3
51 169	Scott	90.3	4.0	9,392	78.8	89,800	20.0	10.4	477	26.9	87.0	28.3	10.4
51 171	Shenandoah	84.9	7.3	16,780	72.5	206,600	25.3	10.6	810	31.2	80.8	30.2	4.3
51 173	Smyth	86.3	4.6	12,550	69.4	97,000	21.2	11.2	540	28.9	86.6	20.7	9.5
51 177	Spotsylvania	87.1	6.9	41,892	76.1	241,800	23.8	10.7	1,303	29.0	79.7	37.9	3.2
51 179	Stafford	85.1	9.4	41,760	77.4	294,400	23.3	10.3	1,399	30.9	72.3	39.7	2.6
51 185	Tazewell	89.3	3.8	18,308	70.5	89,100	22.1	11.6	547	29.3	82.9	26.2	8.7
51 187	Warren	87.9	6.6	14,334	73.9	211,300	24.1	12.4	953	31.5	75.5	41.3	4.0
51 191	Washington	87.1	6.4	22,879	76.2	135,900	22.4	11.5	619	27.5	86.0	23.2	6.5
51 195	Wise	87.1	5.6	15,539	69.3	86,500	18.9	11.4	605	36.9	82.0	21.8	10.4
51 197	Wythe	91.9	2.5	11,807	71.7	107,700	22.2	10.0	611	27.4	85.5	21.3	7.7
51 199	York	84.8	9.5	23,983	74.6	303,800	22.7	10.0	1,324	32.2	83.2	21.4	2.4
51 510	Alexandria city	79.2	12.3	64,754	42.3	491,500	22.7	11.8	1,449	28.3	59.7	30.2	9.2
51 540	Charlottesville city	72.4	16.6	17,142	41.3	283,900	22.0	14.0	988	32.5	60.5	17.3	10.8
51 550	Chesapeake city	85.3	9.3	78,867	72.2	254,700	26.4	13.3	1,141	31.4	86.6	24.6	4.2
51 590	Danville city	82.6	8.1	18,481	55.0	86,700	22.9	12.1	591	34.4	80.0	19.4	15.7
51 600	Fairfax city	81.5	11.8	8,358	71.0	450,900	21.5	10.1	1,538	31.4	71.9	31.8	6.0
51 630	Fredericksburg city	70.6	23.5	9,629	35.5	307,300	22.1	11.9	1,044	33.9	71.8	25.2	9.5
51 650	Hampton city	86.1	6.6	51,699	61.6	196,700	25.5	13.2	976	35.6	82.3	21.7	8.3
51 660	Harrisonburg city	69.1	20.6	15,268	34.6	209,600	22.2	11.2	832	34.2	74.7	15.9	9.3
51 670	Hopewell city	91.8	4.6	8,593	51.6	135,700	26.7	11.0	780	31.7	86.6	20.4	10.6
51 680	Lynchburg city	74.8	14.4	28,363	52.8	145,300	23.9	12.5	709	33.3	77.7	16.8	14.8
51 683	Manassas city	84.5	9.3	12,204	65.4	234,600	23.9	15.5	1,317	35.1	78.5	34.4	7.0
51 700	Newport News city	75.4	12.7	69,003	50.3	200,200	25.1	12.9	980	31.6	77.2	22.3	9.2
51 710	Norfolk city	77.7	11.0	85,626	44.6	201,500	28.3	14.1	942	33.6	70.4	21.8	12.2
51 730	Petersburg city	85.6	7.1	12,031	44.3	113,800	24.5	13.1	812	33.5	76.4	21.4	16.9

[1]10.0 represents 10 percent or less; 50.0 represents 50 percent or higher.

Table C-2. Counties — Where: Migration, Housing, and Transportation, 2010–2012—*Continued*

STATE and county code	STATE or county	Percent who lived in the same house one year ago	Percent who did not live in the same county one year ago	Total occupied housing units	Percent owner-occupied housing units (dollars)	Median value of owner-occupied housing units (dollars)	Median selected monthly owner costs as a percentage of household income		Median gross rent (dollars)	Median gross rent as a percentage of household income[1]	Percent of workers who drove alone to work	Mean travel time to work (minutes)	Percent of occupied housing units with no vehicle available
							With a mortgage	Without a mortgage[1]					
ACS table number:		C07204	C07204	B25003	B25003	B25077	B25092	B25092	B25064	B25071	C08301	B08013/ B08012	C25045
Column number:		1	2	3	4	5	6	7	8	9	10	11	12
	Virginia—Cont.												
51 740	Portsmouth city	81.5	8.2	36,752	56.8	177,700	28.9	15.6	940	33.5	79.4	25.5	11.2
51 760	Richmond city	76.6	10.6	83,747	43.9	193,700	27.0	15.7	870	33.6	71.9	21.4	17.0
51 770	Roanoke city	82.0	7.5	41,819	55.6	135,700	25.6	13.9	671	28.5	30.5	18.8	12.8
51 775	Salem city	79.8	9.8	9,820	68.2	172,400	24.8	12.4	786	37.8	82.8	16.9	6.7
51 790	Staunton city	83.2	10.9	10,809	56.6	170,300	23.1	12.4	724	36.3	79.3	19.8	10.4
51 800	Suffolk city	85.7	6.6	30,657	72.5	243,400	25.9	12.1	979	33.6	86.9	28.6	4.7
51 810	Virginia Beach city	82.0	8.1	164,066	64.3	266,200	26.5	12.5	1,224	31.9	81.7	22.7	3.6
51 820	Waynesboro city	83.9	7.8	8,592	57.6	164,700	23.8	12.5	741	31.0	85.3	19.1	10.2
51 840	Winchester city	76.3	17.0	10,668	49.4	226,900	24.2	13.3	890	36.2	74.2	21.9	9.2
53 000	**Washington**	82.5	5.9	2,624,689	62.8	256,500	25.9	12.3	953	30.4	72.9	25.6	6.9
53 003	Asotin	82.4	8.6	9,298	67.3	175,200	23.3	10.9	661	29.4	78.9	16.8	5.8
53 005	Benton	84.5	6.4	65,278	69.2	180,400	19.5	10.0	782	27.7	78.7	21.7	4.7
53 007	Chelan	89.3	4.5	26,915	65.3	254,600	26.6	10.1	751	26.7	78.4	17.9	7.1
53 009	Clallam	84.9	6.6	30,750	69.9	224,000	26.7	11.4	817	31.7	76.0	21.2	6.9
53 011	Clark	83.4	5.7	158,539	65.0	225,200	26.2	12.1	923	31.2	79.1	24.8	5.5
53 015	Cowlitz	82.8	4.3	39,823	65.0	175,500	25.5	13.1	725	36.6	80.3	24.4	7.0
53 017	Douglas	87.6	8.6	14,207	72.2	198,300	24.1	11.4	760	26.6	79.0	20.2	2.6
53 021	Franklin	83.6	8.4	23,466	65.7	160,600	22.7	10.0	714	27.7	75.3	20.9	6.1
53 025	Grant	85.2	4.6	30,367	59.3	160,000	24.5	10.7	648	25.7	75.7	18.8	5.5
53 027	Grays Harbor	84.1	5.4	27,582	70.6	156,100	26.2	11.4	685	29.5	75.0	25.1	6.6
53 029	Island	83.6	9.0	32,698	68.8	290,900	27.9	12.0	1,035	29.3	75.6	27.7	4.0
53 031	Jefferson	85.7	7.6	13,826	74.1	279,300	28.4	14.2	785	30.8	70.8	21.8	5.6
53 033	King	81.4	5.3	796,640	57.4	369,000	25.9	13.3	1,096	29.3	65.4	26.8	9.6
53 035	Kitsap	82.5	6.9	98,682	66.1	262,600	25.7	12.3	1,001	30.9	69.0	29.5	5.3
53 037	Kittitas	72.5	11.0	16,490	56.9	252,600	27.6	12.1	764	43.9	73.5	21.4	6.4
53 039	Klickitat	91.7	4.0	8,209	67.3	197,900	30.9	11.8	808	28.4	75.0	20.8	2.7
53 041	Lewis	83.1	6.6	29,391	68.3	187,100	24.8	12.0	742	32.0	77.7	26.1	5.5
53 045	Mason	87.8	6.6	23,565	78.6	210,000	27.3	11.6	853	38.8	77.3	30.9	4.3
53 047	Okanogan	87.0	4.4	16,415	65.7	166,800	24.2	10.0	620	31.2	74.6	18.6	5.6
53 049	Pacific	84.2	6.4	9,358	72.7	158,100	23.8	13.6	691	30.0	79.4	21.4	5.4
53 053	Pierce	81.8	6.0	299,514	61.4	235,700	27.3	13.3	987	31.4	78.7	28.6	5.6
53 057	Skagit	83.9	5.2	45,207	67.7	256,200	27.5	12.6	930	31.6	80.3	25.0	4.9
53 061	Snohomish	83.1	5.9	268,565	66.4	286,800	27.9	13.4	1,076	30.5	75.2	29.2	5.0
53 063	Spokane	81.6	5.6	187,863	63.6	183,500	24.2	11.2	750	32.4	76.4	21.1	7.6
53 065	Stevens	87.3	4.9	17,858	77.4	173,200	28.1	11.2	654	30.1	74.5	28.8	5.3
53 067	Thurston	81.4	7.4	101,296	66.7	240,300	26.1	12.4	996	29.3	77.8	24.9	4.9
53 071	Walla Walla	82.4	9.2	21,572	62.2	199,100	23.9	12.6	668	29.8	71.8	15.8	8.8
53 073	Whatcom	81.9	6.0	79,643	63.1	269,900	26.6	12.3	889	32.9	74.7	21.1	7.3
53 075	Whitman	63.9	18.8	16,865	45.7	182,300	21.3	10.0	680	48.8	55.7	15.2	8.1
53 077	Yakima	84.2	3.3	79,396	61.4	157,900	23.0	11.3	742	32.7	79.8	19.9	5.6
54 000	**West Virginia**	88.1	5.0	741,661	72.9	98,300	19.7	10.0	606	29.6	82.3	25.5	8.6
54 003	Berkeley	84.5	6.8	40,297	74.2	164,000	23.6	10.0	800	30.3	84.3	31.0	7.6
54 005	Boone	87.9	5.4	9,506	77.8	78,400	18.7	10.0	531	24.8	88.0	27.5	9.7
54 009	Brooke	90.8	4.9	10,008	77.2	81,300	17.1	10.0	568	25.7	81.5	26.6	9.9
54 011	Cabell	81.3	7.9	39,766	60.7	110,300	19.5	10.0	619	33.3	81.8	20.1	13.4
54 019	Fayette	90.6	3.3	17,267	75.7	71,100	19.2	11.1	560	27.0	80.3	24.6	9.4
54 025	Greenbrier	88.4	4.1	15,206	74.4	98,000	21.4	10.0	622	31.0	85.7	24.2	6.9
54 027	Hampshire	91.8	5.0	10,829	51.4	122,000	23.8	11.4	493	31.3	83.1	38.8	8.7
54 029	Hancock	85.4	6.9	12,978	75.5	84,400	19.2	10.2	606	28.9	83.4	24.8	5.4
54 033	Harrison	89.5	4.3	27,904	73.6	93,400	18.2	10.5	608	30.8	82.6	22.0	9.4
54 035	Jackson	89.3	5.5	11,428	78.1	106,500	18.0	10.0	550	31.3	83.2	30.2	6.1
54 037	Jefferson	85.4	5.9	19,681	77.4	208,300	24.2	12.1	838	32.6	73.2	40.5	3.2
54 039	Kanawha	87.4	4.1	83,146	69.9	98,800	18.7	10.0	667	25.9	80.1	21.6	10.1
54 043	Lincoln	92.7	3.6	8,298	80.4	76,500	19.7	10.0	548	28.6	79.2	34.9	8.0
54 045	Logan	87.8	3.5	14,656	74.4	74,400	18.4	10.0	540	25.8	90.2	26.0	10.4
54 047	McDowell	94.8	2.6	8,489	76.2	39,900	19.2	11.3	484	34.6	86.9	27.0	15.1
54 049	Marion	91.6	4.0	22,750	77.1	91,400	17.5	11.8	640	31.2	83.7	25.6	6.6
54 051	Marshall	89.9	3.7	14,113	76.0	83,700	18.8	10.0	498	24.6	84.1	21.8	7.6
54 053	Mason	89.6	4.0	10,304	82.1	85,800	19.5	10.4	504	26.4	85.2	27.1	9.8
54 055	Mercer	89.0	3.9	26,117	73.2	81,500	20.0	10.0	548	29.7	84.0	21.2	7.9
54 057	Mineral	90.9	4.2	11,053	59.1	116,600	20.7	11.1	514	33.6	79.9	26.1	15.8
54 059	Mingo	89.1	3.3	10,751	77.5	68,300	19.2	10.0	514	26.8	84.7	29.8	8.2
54 061	Monongalia	80.1	9.6	36,183	55.8	163,300	18.0	10.0	704	32.5	77.0	20.3	6.9
54 067	Nicholas	88.9	5.3	10,398	79.7	74,600	19.0	10.0	522	31.0	87.6	27.1	7.8
54 069	Ohio	87.3	5.7	18,437	67.9	98,800	18.9	10.0	537	31.1	82.3	20.2	12.3
54 077	Preston	85.1	6.5	12,652	78.9	114,000	19.5	10.3	547	27.1	78.8	30.7	6.6
54 079	Putnam	94.6	2.7	21,176	85.1	143,500	19.6	10.0	699	30.0	86.8	25.5	4.6
54 081	Raleigh	86.4	5.4	31,384	73.2	95,100	19.0	10.9	620	25.5	83.9	24.2	8.3
54 083	Randolph	90.5	4.5	11,129	74.8	103,300	20.1	10.0	538	35.5	82.4	21.5	9.3
54 097	Upshur	85.8	7.0	8,990	75.3	103,600	21.5	10.0	535	26.8	84.0	25.3	6.4
54 099	Wayne	93.9	2.7	16,708	77.5	80,400	18.7	10.0	543	35.9	91.4	23.8	9.4
54 107	Wood	89.4	3.7	35,302	73.3	104,800	20.5	10.0	586	31.2	83.4	18.9	7.9
54 109	Wyoming	93.4	2.8	9,068	81.4	59,400	14.9	10.0	528	27.9	87.9	34.6	9.7

[1]10.0 represents 10 percent or less; 50.0 represents 50 percent or higher.

Table C-2. Counties — Where: Migration, Housing, and Transportation, 2010–2012—*Continued*

STATE and county code	STATE or county	Percent who lived in the same house one year ago	Percent who did not live in the same county one year ago	Total occupied housing units	Percent owner-occupied housing units	Median value of owner-occupied housing units (dollars)	Median selected monthly owner costs as a percentage of household income — With a mortgage	Without a mortgage[1]	Median gross rent (dollars)	Median gross rent as a percentage of household income[1]	Percent of workers who drove alone to work	Mean travel time to work (minutes)	Percent of occupied housing units with no vehicle available
ACS table number:		C07204	C07204	B25003	B25003	B25077	B25092	B25092	B25064	B25071	C08301	B08013/ B08012	C25045
Column number:		1	2	3	4	5	6	7	8	9	10	11	12
55 000	**Wisconsin**	85.8	5.0	2,282,454	68.0	167,200	23.9	13.9	747	29.6	80.3	21.8	7.2
55 001	Adams	87.4	7.3	8,244	84.3	135,500	25.9	17.2	675	28.0	80.3	27.7	3.1
55 005	Barron	86.9	5.2	18,660	75.0	133,400	25.1	14.4	599	29.0	81.0	20.2	6.3
55 009	Brown	85.8	4.1	98,677	66.2	158,600	22.7	12.8	682	26.9	83.3	18.4	5.5
55 015	Calumet	93.2	4.6	18,211	83.0	162,500	21.5	13.4	652	24.8	84.2	19.8	3.4
55 017	Chippewa	87.3	6.2	24,398	71.1	146,200	23.1	12.2	681	29.3	81.5	21.4	5.7
55 019	Clark	92.2	3.4	12,990	77.7	111,500	23.5	13.8	544	25.7	72.7	21.1	8.8
55 021	Columbia	87.0	5.9	22,743	75.1	173,900	24.3	13.5	723	28.3	80.8	25.6	4.4
55 025	Dane	79.6	6.8	205,451	59.7	228,500	24.2	12.4	880	31.0	73.1	20.8	8.6
55 027	Dodge	87.5	5.7	33,293	74.3	155,400	25.0	14.9	752	26.6	83.9	22.0	3.6
55 029	Door	91.9	3.4	13,345	76.6	187,800	25.7	14.7	680	26.0	77.7	18.9	5.7
55 031	Douglas	85.4	6.1	18,955	67.7	127,600	22.8	12.5	662	32.8	80.7	20.7	8.2
55 033	Dunn	78.0	10.5	16,457	66.5	157,200	24.7	14.1	683	28.4	77.9	21.5	3.9
55 035	Eau Claire	81.4	7.4	39,957	63.6	147,800	22.6	13.1	694	31.6	81.0	17.4	6.5
55 039	Fond du Lac	86.9	3.9	41,025	70.6	146,400	23.5	13.5	676	25.9	80.9	20.2	5.9
55 043	Grant	81.2	8.6	19,538	71.7	128,400	22.1	13.4	645	29.0	77.4	21.1	4.0
55 045	Green	90.0	4.1	14,674	75.1	157,600	24.3	14.6	644	28.5	79.4	22.6	4.9
55 049	Iowa	88.7	4.9	9,630	76.0	160,500	25.5	14.7	672	25.7	74.9	26.1	5.0
55 053	Jackson	88.2	7.1	8,133	74.1	125,000	26.8	16.1	598	29.8	81.4	21.8	6.2
55 055	Jefferson	87.5	4.8	32,115	71.8	179,600	24.9	14.8	745	28.5	81.1	23.1	5.0
55 057	Juneau	89.2	6.8	10,658	74.8	115,800	25.8	15.3	653	29.0	82.3	22.5	4.8
55 059	Kenosha	85.6	5.4	62,408	67.1	168,400	25.2	14.6	829	31.2	84.5	25.6	6.1
55 061	Kewaunee	94.1	3.9	7,984	81.5	146,600	23.8	14.3	613	29.9	79.2	21.6	4.1
55 063	La Crosse	81.3	6.8	46,174	64.9	154,300	22.0	13.2	719	30.1	80.3	18.5	6.4
55 067	Langlade	86.3	5.4	8,727	74.8	112,800	22.0	13.2	550	31.5	79.9	19.3	6.7
55 069	Lincoln	90.6	2.7	12,474	76.0	129,400	22.5	13.3	591	27.0	81.8	23.2	5.1
55 071	Manitowoc	93.3	1.7	34,062	75.8	124,600	22.7	13.4	589	24.9	83.8	19.7	6.5
55 073	Marathon	87.4	3.5	52,515	73.1	142,100	22.3	12.4	690	29.2	81.5	18.6	4.9
55 075	Marinette	90.0	3.5	18,386	78.0	107,200	23.9	14.3	567	28.9	83.2	21.2	4.8
55 079	Milwaukee	81.1	3.7	379,601	51.0	158,700	25.2	16.0	777	33.1	75.8	21.9	14.6
55 081	Monroe	84.7	5.7	17,450	67.6	135,500	23.7	13.5	722	27.7	79.1	19.8	6.3
55 083	Oconto	93.2	2.8	15,641	83.0	147,300	24.3	14.4	602	28.7	81.6	26.1	3.0
55 085	Oneida	89.0	5.2	15,884	81.9	163,500	26.3	15.0	686	35.1	81.5	19.6	5.4
55 087	Outagamie	88.9	5.0	69,255	72.6	156,600	22.8	13.1	703	26.1	83.9	19.5	4.6
55 089	Ozaukee	90.4	4.9	34,281	78.2	252,900	22.7	13.0	807	26.2	84.8	23.4	2.9
55 093	Pierce	82.9	10.8	15,190	72.6	187,200	24.2	13.7	752	29.7	76.5	27.1	4.5
55 095	Polk	90.2	3.2	18,239	77.1	158,100	27.2	14.9	702	28.2	80.4	29.1	4.1
55 097	Portage	80.9	6.7	28,189	68.8	143,400	22.1	12.2	659	29.7	79.7	19.5	5.6
55 101	Racine	89.7	3.6	75,450	68.3	170,100	24.2	14.7	751	30.1	84.2	23.3	8.2
55 105	Rock	85.6	4.2	63,114	70.2	132,700	24.1	13.7	724	32.8	80.9	23.7	5.7
55 109	St. Croix	87.5	5.9	32,023	78.3	204,300	23.5	13.3	860	29.6	82.3	28.1	4.0
55 111	Sauk	89.1	3.8	25,547	69.5	169,200	24.2	14.7	727	29.3	79.9	21.8	5.6
55 115	Shawano	88.7	4.5	17,007	75.2	131,500	24.1	14.7	606	27.0	78.8	22.9	4.5
55 117	Sheboygan	87.4	3.9	46,072	71.1	154,200	22.8	14.1	642	26.0	84.0	18.7	6.4
55 119	Taylor	90.1	3.8	8,788	77.7	127,500	25.1	13.9	517	25.7	76.7	20.8	5.9
55 121	Trempealeau	91.7	3.1	11,802	74.1	133,900	23.1	14.7	602	25.7	79.6	20.6	4.7
55 123	Vernon	91.4	3.5	11,657	79.5	140,500	24.6	13.5	606	27.5	75.4	24.0	8.4
55 125	Vilas	91.1	3.2	10,589	76.6	183,900	28.7	14.8	695	30.6	80.7	19.2	4.1
55 127	Walworth	82.9	6.7	39,455	67.9	194,000	25.7	13.9	814	30.2	81.4	24.9	4.9
55 131	Washington	90.7	4.2	51,759	78.1	223,200	23.9	14.1	802	28.0	85.0	24.3	4.3
55 133	Waukesha	88.9	5.2	152,574	76.7	250,000	23.2	13.5	914	28.2	86.0	24.0	4.7
55 135	Waupaca	87.0	5.3	21,218	76.1	137,000	23.4	14.3	636	23.9	83.1	21.2	4.3
55 137	Waushara	88.5	6.4	9,759	81.8	137,500	24.2	15.0	631	29.5	79.0	27.8	5.9
55 139	Winnebago	85.2	6.5	67,750	66.9	141,400	22.4	13.5	646	26.0	84.2	19.0	5.9
55 141	Wood	89.9	3.8	31,949	74.7	118,500	21.7	12.1	577	29.1	83.1	18.3	6.3
56 000	**Wyoming**	80.8	8.2	222,558	70.0	183,200	21.5	10.0	741	26.1	76.2	18.3	3.5
56 001	Albany	66.1	16.8	15,246	51.6	196,800	23.2	10.3	699	37.4	63.4	12.2	3.8
56 005	Campbell	79.4	7.6	17,240	75.0	199,500	19.6	10.0	893	24.4	81.4	19.2	2.8
56 013	Fremont	83.5	6.2	15,375	72.3	183,100	21.9	10.0	662	26.6	73.8	18.4	4.8
56 021	Laramie	80.9	5.9	37,119	67.5	179,200	22.2	10.0	734	26.3	83.6	15.1	4.9
56 025	Natrona	79.1	7.6	31,080	69.6	173,700	21.3	10.0	805	27.8	81.4	18.4	3.2
56 029	Park	82.5	8.6	11,909	73.2	214,300	22.7	11.8	670	20.0	75.2	15.5	1.6
56 033	Sheridan	84.0	8.3	12,247	70.0	216,500	22.8	11.4	744	27.5	77.9	15.7	6.5
56 037	Sweetwater	79.3	8.9	16,480	70.4	174,500	19.6	10.0	865	22.9	76.3	21.9	3.2
56 039	Teton	86.3	3.7	7,224	59.3	705,600	25.4	10.0	1,087	30.2	61.7	16.0	2.1
56 041	Uinta	80.2	9.1	7,263	73.6	175,200	21.3	10.0	657	25.6	76.3	24.5	2.2

[1] 10.0 represents 10 percent or less; 50.0 represents 50 percent or higher.

Table C-3. Metropolitan Areas — Where: Migration, Housing, and Transportation, 2012

Metro area or division code	Area name	Percent who lived in the same house one year ago	Percent who did not live in this MSA one year ago	Total occupied housing units	Percent owner-occupied housing units	Median value of owner-occupied housing units (dollars)	Median selected monthly owner costs as a percentage of household income		Median gross rent (dollars)	Median gross rent as a percentage of household income	Percent of workers who drove alone to work	Mean travel time to work (minutes)	Percent of occupied housing units with no vehicle available
							With a mortgage	Without a mortgage					
ACS table number:		C07201	C07201	B25003	B25003	B25077	B25092	B25092	B25064	B25071	C08301	B08013/ B08012	C25045
Column number:		1	2	3	4	5	6	7	8	9	10	11	12
10180	Abilene, TX	76.9	8.7	60,066	59.9	94,600	20.0	10.2	748	28.9	80.3	17.8	5.4
10420	Akron, OH	87.5	4.5	280,887	67.0	131,800	21.0	12.0	741	30.7	86.1	23.1	8.5
10500	Albany, GA	84.0	6.3	57,699	56.6	107,300	22.4	13.0	660	33.9	79.5	20.7	9.6
10580	Albany–Schenectady–Troy, NY	87.5	4.3	342,705	64.5	197,000	22.2	13.5	864	28.0	79.6	22.5	10.1
10740	Albuquerque, NM	84.9	4.7	344,869	66.8	175,600	24.1	10.0	781	31.6	80.2	23.0	6.1
10780	Alexandria, LA	87.4	3.2	57,277	66.4	118,100	21.4	10.0	667	30.4	82.3	26.1	7.4
10900	Allentown–Bethlehem–Easton, PA–NJ	87.0	4.1	314,173	69.7	196,400	24.7	15.1	904	32.3	82.0	27.6	8.8
11020	Altoona, PA	88.7	3.9	50,098	70.4	105,300	19.6	12.1	627	30.1	81.4	19.2	9.4
11100	Amarillo, TX	82.4	4.6	94,559	63.8	118,000	20.1	12.4	733	29.6	79.5	19.0	4.8
11180	Ames, IA	65.7	17.8	35,541	55.9	165,800	20.7	10.0	711	37.5	70.9	17.2	5.9
11260	Anchorage, AK	82.2	6.1	137,052	63.5	266,700	23.0	11.4	1,164	29.9	72.4	22.8	5.0
11300	Anderson, IN	82.3	3.9	49,124	69.4	88,500	20.1	10.0	669	31.5	82.1	25.3	8.3
11340	Anderson, SC	86.8	5.0	72,363	74.2	125,400	22.1	10.9	623	32.5	88.6	22.7	5.9
11460	Ann Arbor, MI	76.2	10.6	137,565	58.6	191,000	22.2	12.9	921	34.5	72.9	22.5	8.4
11500	Anniston–Oxford, AL	84.5	5.7	45,986	68.4	105,800	19.6	10.0	651	28.5	84.3	22.7	5.8
11540	Appleton, WI	89.7	5.0	87,010	74.2	156,400	21.0	12.1	696	26.6	85.5	19.4	4.2
11700	Asheville, NC	84.3	5.8	178,131	68.9	177,100	23.1	10.8	782	31.1	79.8	21.5	7.0
12020	Athens–Clarke County, GA	79.2	10.0	67,610	56.1	159,500	22.7	11.4	771	33.4	80.1	22.8	6.4
12060	Atlanta–Sandy Springs–Marietta, GA	83.4	4.2	1,923,727	63.8	160,800	23.0	11.0	929	32.1	78.0	30.0	6.2
12100	Atlantic City–Hammonton, NJ	88.8	3.7	100,065	64.9	226,800	30.7	18.8	1,033	38.0	75.6	22.7	16.0
12220	Auburn–Opelika, AL	74.2	11.2	55,520	62.2	155,400	20.9	10.2	779	36.3	83.4	23.3	4.5
12260	Augusta–Richmond County, GA–SC	85.7	5.6	204,147	66.3	127,900	21.3	10.2	752	31.4	84.7	23.2	6.3
12420	Austin–Round Rock–San Marcos, TX	77.7	7.4	665,027	57.7	191,600	23.2	12.7	978	30.1	76.0	25.5	4.7
12540	Bakersfield–Delano, CA	81.0	5.1	255,967	57.8	150,200	25.2	11.6	872	33.5	77.1	24.2	6.8
12580	Baltimore–Towson, MD	88.1	3.6	1,034,914	65.9	271,100	23.4	12.5	1,089	29.8	76.5	30.0	11.9
12620	Bangor, ME	82.1	6.3	63,171	65.1	135,100	22.4	13.8	716	31.1	80.0	21.2	9.5
12700	Barnstable Town, MA	90.2	5.8	89,766	81.6	361,500	28.3	15.7	1,016	34.7	81.6	24.3	6.3
12940	Baton Rouge, LA	86.2	3.5	298,690	67.6	160,400	20.2	10.0	788	32.5	85.4	26.7	5.3
12980	Battle Creek, MI	80.8	8.0	53,182	67.6	96,000	22.6	12.9	643	31.0	83.4	19.5	8.4
13020	Bay City, MI	89.8	3.7	43,967	77.5	90,800	21.9	12.2	674	31.0	84.0	21.2	6.8
13140	Beaumont–Port Arthur, TX	84.6	5.0	143,663	69.6	96,900	21.1	10.8	696	31.2	87.2	21.1	7.0
13380	Bellingham, WA	82.3	6.8	79,029	62.3	255,500	24.8	11.7	878	33.4	72.7	20.9	8.7
13460	Bend, OR	77.6	6.2	66,086	64.1	235,300	28.4	13.4	863	32.8	75.8	20.2	3.9
13740	Billings, MT	82.1	7.1	65,215	68.9	186,300	21.3	12.0	712	27.5	79.8	20.9	4.8
13780	Binghamton, NY	85.5	4.5	101,258	69.0	108,600	19.6	11.7	676	30.5	80.6	20.7	10.3
13820	Birmingham–Hoover, AL	85.5	3.6	437,667	69.4	142,600	21.3	10.9	758	30.1	85.7	25.8	7.0
13900	Bismarck, ND	83.6	7.6	46,991	72.6	169,300	19.2	10.4	716	23.2	78.9	20.0	3.7
13980	Blacksburg–Christiansburg–Radford, VA	74.8	10.5	63,346	58.2	159,000	20.6	10.0	700	35.9	78.3	19.6	6.6
14020	Bloomington, IN	71.6	11.8	76,163	60.5	132,200	19.7	11.4	786	38.6	71.4	21.7	6.1
14060	Bloomington–Normal, IL	79.4	9.3	65,744	65.9	155,300	19.5	10.5	770	29.3	81.0	17.9	6.4
14260	Boise City–Nampa, ID	83.0	5.5	231,388	66.1	153,400	23.2	10.0	775	29.6	79.0	21.2	4.6
14460	Boston–Cambridge–Quincy, MA–NH	86.6	4.0	1,757,711	61.3	358,400	24.5	15.1	1,162	29.5	68.6	29.5	13.2
1446014484	•Boston–Quincy, MA Division	86.2	4.1	728,639	57.6	356,500	24.9	15.8	1,189	30.3	51.3	31.1	18.6
1446015764	•Cambridge–Newton–Framingham, MA Division	86.7	4.3	582,405	62.7	394,800	23.5	14.6	1,252	28.0	69.6	28.9	10.1
1446037764	•Peabody, MA Division	88.0	2.5	283,543	62.1	347,800	24.6	14.9	1,040	30.8	76.5	27.6	10.8
1446040484	•Rockingham County–Strafford County, NH Division	85.2	4.7	163,124	71.3	265,200	26.5	15.6	987	29.4	83.1	28.2	3.9
14500	Boulder, CO	76.7	10.4	121,743	61.3	364,100	21.8	10.0	1,108	36.3	65.4	22.4	5.5
14540	Bowling Green, KY	81.0	9.5	50,137	57.0	136,400	20.4	12.1	641	31.3	83.9	18.9	8.2
14740	Bremerton–Silverdale, WA	82.3	7.8	97,027	68.4	255,600	26.0	12.7	1,010	30.5	68.5	30.0	5.5
14860	Bridgeport–Stamford–Norwalk, CT	87.2	4.8	334,255	68.3	403,400	27.2	17.4	1,266	31.9	73.1	28.1	8.5
15180	Brownsville–Harlingen, TX	90.6	1.9	121,179	64.3	75,700	26.3	13.1	610	32.2	82.4	19.9	9.9
15260	Brunswick, GA	81.8	7.3	41,858	67.1	131,000	25.3	10.1	713	30.0	80.7	22.7	4.7
15380	Buffalo–Niagara Falls, NY	87.7	2.8	468,089	65.9	123,100	20.3	13.2	692	29.5	82.9	20.9	12.6
15500	Burlington, NC	85.4	5.6	59,520	63.9	143,600	22.6	12.4	695	35.2	83.3	23.1	5.0
15540	Burlington–South Burlington, VT	82.8	6.0	84,977	67.6	249,700	24.2	15.3	953	29.5	70.8	22.8	7.1
15940	Canton–Massillon, OH	87.2	4.2	161,763	69.2	118,300	21.2	12.2	654	26.8	85.8	23.2	7.1
15980	Cape Coral–Fort Myers, FL	82.2	8.4	245,100	68.1	137,600	26.1	13.5	905	31.6	77.5	27.7	5.9
16020	Cape Girardeau–Jackson, MO–IL	83.7	7.7	37,612	68.8	120,500	19.3	11.4	629	28.7	83.6	20.7	8.3
16180	Carson City, NV	75.7	8.2	21,494	53.3	158,800	26.3	11.2	807	25.4	84.5	17.3	8.4
16220	Casper, WY	80.4	7.7	32,065	68.6	178,600	19.8	10.0	806	28.2	80.5	17.9	2.3
16300	Cedar Rapids, IA	86.3	4.3	102,818	74.3	146,700	19.6	12.1	668	25.4	80.5	19.7	6.2
16580	Champaign–Urbana, IL	75.4	10.5	92,073	58.6	138,200	20.5	11.2	748	33.1	71.8	18.6	11.3
16620	Charleston, WV	86.8	3.7	127,153	74.2	103,700	18.6	10.0	654	25.6	80.8	23.9	8.4
16700	Charleston–North Charleston–Summerville, SC	80.7	6.7	262,131	63.4	182,500	24.3	12.5	958	33.0	81.4	24.2	7.2
16740	Charlotte–Gastonia–Rock Hill, NC–SC	83.6	5.4	675,362	64.3	164,700	21.7	11.4	834	29.3	78.8	25.6	6.2
16820	Charlottesville, VA	83.4	8.5	77,795	64.1	269,500	22.0	10.0	964	28.0	74.4	24.5	5.2
16860	Chattanooga, TN–GA	84.4	4.9	207,794	66.7	142,800	21.8	10.8	708	29.9	83.4	23.2	7.2
16940	Cheyenne, WY	80.3	6.1	35,245	67.4	181,800	21.0	11.6	763	27.7	82.1	15.5	4.3
16980	Chicago–Joliet–Naperville, IL–IN–WI	87.0	2.5	3,426,426	64.8	207,100	25.8	14.8	941	31.1	70.9	30.6	12.6
1698016974	•Chicago–Joliet–Naperville, IL Division	87.1	2.4	2,864,963	63.3	215,100	26.5	15.5	952	31.2	68.9	31.1	13.8

Table C-3. Metropolitan Areas — Where: Migration, Housing, and Transportation, 2012—*Continued*

Metro area or division code	Area name	Percent who lived in the same house one year ago	Percent who did not live in this MSA one year ago	Total occupied housing units	Percent owner-occupied housing units	Median value of owner-occupied housing units (dollars)	Median selected monthly owner costs as a percentage of household income — With a mortgage	Median selected monthly owner costs as a percentage of household income — Without a mortgage	Median gross rent (dollars)	Median gross rent as a percentage of household income	Percent of workers who drove alone to work	Mean travel time to work (minutes)	Percent of occupied housing units with no vehicle available
ACS table number:		C07201	C07201	B25003	B25003	B25077	B25092	B25092	B25064	B25071	C08301	B08013/B08012	C25045
Column number:		1	2	3	4	5	6	7	8	9	10	11	12
1698023844	•Gary, IN Division	87.9	2.1	256,947	72.0	144,500	20.8	10.7	779	31.1	84.1	28.0	8.1
1698029404	•Lake County–Kenosha County, IL–WI Division	86.0	3.6	304,516	72.9	217,300	25.1	15.0	965	29.4	79.1	28.8	5.1
17020	Chico, CA	79.6	6.0	85,388	59.4	203,100	26.9	11.6	891	37.5	74.9	19.2	6.1
17140	Cincinnati–Middletown, OH–KY–IN	85.6	2.9	825,221	66.5	151,800	21.1	12.1	723	30.5	83.5	24.2	8.3
17300	Clarksville, TN–KY	77.3	10.5	101,067	59.5	134,100	22.5	10.0	798	30.0	81.9	22.0	4.9
17420	Cleveland, TN	85.2	5.5	46,079	65.7	129,800	23.1	10.0	672	29.9	83.3	22.6	7.6
17460	Cleveland–Elyria–Mentor, OH	86.5	3.1	839,838	65.2	139,400	22.7	13.5	720	31.1	82.3	24.6	11.3
17660	Coeur d'Alene, ID	79.4	9.5	55,848	68.9	177,500	24.4	10.0	828	32.9	82.8	21.1	3.3
17780	College Station–Bryan, TX	72.8	11.2	82,134	51.1	146,100	22.3	10.6	793	39.8	75.6	19.2	6.6
17820	Colorado Springs, CO	77.5	10.0	247,950	63.8	216,000	23.7	10.0	899	30.9	77.3	21.8	4.3
17860	Columbia, MO	73.9	10.2	69,963	57.0	155,700	19.8	10.0	774	34.7	79.7	17.9	4.9
17900	Columbia, SC	82.4	7.7	294,039	68.0	139,800	20.9	10.2	792	30.5	81.7	22.7	5.7
17980	Columbus, GA–AL	78.2	11.1	110,334	57.4	129,700	22.9	11.9	770	29.0	79.5	20.9	10.1
18020	Columbus, IN	85.0	8.3	29,640	71.3	136,900	20.3	10.8	788	26.6	83.4	18.2	5.2
18140	Columbus, OH	82.8	4.8	719,081	61.1	157,300	22.2	12.5	791	29.1	82.1	22.8	6.9
18580	Corpus Christi, TX	82.0	5.9	156,182	60.9	108,600	22.5	12.4	832	28.3	79.7	21.5	7.4
18700	Corvallis, OR	80.0	11.5	33,395	57.6	275,500	22.2	11.4	815	42.0	63.2	18.0	7.7
18880	Crestview–Fort Walton Beach–Destin, FL	81.1	9.0	75,099	62.2	175,400	24.6	11.0	985	29.5	83.9	23.4	5.0
19060	Cumberland, MD–WV	86.6	5.3	39,475	63.5	118,200	21.7	14.0	581	30.6	83.5	22.2	11.8
19100	Dallas–Fort Worth–Arlington, TX	83.5	4.0	2,337,076	59.5	149,600	22.2	12.2	877	28.6	80.9	27.1	5.1
1910019124	•Dallas–Plano–Irving, TX Division	83.6	4.0	1,555,596	58.2	158,200	22.5	12.5	886	28.3	79.6	27.3	5.5
1910023104	•Fort Worth–Arlington, TX Division	83.2	4.1	781,480	62.3	135,100	21.6	11.7	857	29.2	83.3	26.8	4.3
19140	Dalton, GA	86.5	3.3	48,205	64.1	106,000	23.1	10.6	610	32.6	84.4	21.8	6.0
19180	Danville, IL	86.4	3.3	31,714	69.9	79,400	19.7	12.1	609	28.3	87.2	19.9	8.7
19260	Danville, VA	87.2	6.1	45,216	68.9	104,400	20.6	10.0	595	27.3	82.3	23.8	11.6
19340	Davenport–Moline–Rock Island, IA–IL	85.9	4.5	155,726	70.3	125,000	19.6	11.4	668	28.3	84.6	19.5	6.9
19380	Dayton, OH	82.7	4.9	341,240	63.6	119,500	22.0	13.2	714	30.2	82.6	21.3	8.2
19460	Decatur, AL	85.6	3.8	59,790	71.4	116,800	19.8	10.0	558	28.7	89.0	24.5	4.1
19500	Decatur, IL	80.0	5.3	46,336	67.8	91,100	19.3	12.1	656	30.7	84.5	19.6	10.7
19660	Deltona–Daytona Beach–Ormond Beach, FL	84.3	7.7	197,599	70.4	130,000	28.0	13.4	868	36.2	82.1	25.1	7.0
19740	Denver–Aurora–Broomfield, CO	81.2	5.6	1,021,036	62.4	246,900	23.1	10.0	961	29.7	75.6	26.9	6.4
19780	Des Moines–West Des Moines, IA	83.3	5.5	230,228	71.0	158,900	20.5	11.9	774	27.6	83.4	19.7	5.3
19820	Detroit–Warren–Livonia, MI	86.5	2.2	1,645,835	69.0	116,200	22.4	14.0	813	32.6	83.7	26.2	9.7
1982019804	•Detroit–Livonia–Dearborn, MI Division	85.8	2.0	660,724	62.9	77,200	22.9	14.7	772	36.4	80.9	24.6	14.8
1982047644	•Warren–Troy–Farmington Hills, MI Division	87.1	2.4	985,111	73.2	144,100	22.2	13.5	850	29.6	85.4	27.2	6.3
20020	Dothan, AL	86.4	4.3	56,259	68.5	99,400	20.4	10.3	620	30.2	88.1	23.3	5.8
20100	Dover, DE	86.8	5.8	59,499	71.6	197,500	24.2	10.0	936	32.1	86.1	25.6	5.2
20220	Dubuque, IA	87.4	4.3	37,726	72.2	144,700	20.7	12.9	690	31.7	79.5	17.1	6.2
20260	Duluth, MN–WI	83.7	5.2	116,531	70.7	137,100	22.1	11.6	671	32.3	78.4	19.7	8.4
20500	Durham–Chapel Hill, NC	78.3	9.1	207,572	59.4	188,500	22.1	11.3	828	29.9	73.6	23.6	8.7
20740	Eau Claire, WI	83.7	5.8	64,765	66.1	148,700	22.0	12.6	709	30.8	79.9	18.9	5.2
20940	El Centro, CA	83.0	4.9	46,747	56.7	133,800	27.1	13.3	726	34.4	76.6	21.9	8.8
21060	Elizabethtown, KY	77.9	12.1	44,998	62.5	140,000	20.5	10.0	704	24.5	80.8	21.4	5.0
21140	Elkhart–Goshen, IN	86.2	3.5	70,857	67.3	120,700	20.4	10.0	708	27.3	76.6	20.0	9.0
21300	Elmira, NY	86.3	5.8	34,867	70.2	95,500	18.3	14.7	647	32.3	83.7	19.0	11.7
21340	El Paso, TX	85.7	5.4	260,645	60.9	113,200	22.9	11.5	726	30.4	79.4	23.5	8.1
21500	Erie, PA	84.2	5.5	109,973	65.4	115,200	19.2	12.1	656	30.7	81.6	18.9	10.3
21660	Eugene–Springfield, OR	75.9	7.1	146,327	58.7	206,600	27.0	12.7	821	34.2	68.6	19.2	8.7
21780	Evansville, IN–KY	83.9	4.3	145,212	69.3	115,600	19.6	11.0	666	30.1	85.0	20.5	6.8
21820	Fairbanks, AK	75.2	12.0	35,944	59.7	214,500	26.3	13.2	1,222	31.9	72.5	20.3	5.8
22020	Fargo, ND–MN	79.5	8.4	89,002	57.6	160,000	20.9	10.7	665	25.5	82.7	17.3	6.7
22140	Farmington, NM	88.9	3.0	40,025	74.5	145,700	20.4	10.0	699	28.6	80.5	22.8	6.1
22180	Fayetteville, NC	76.6	10.4	139,404	55.3	127,500	23.0	11.4	855	29.6	82.5	22.1	6.3
22220	Fayetteville–Springdale–Rogers, AR–MO	79.3	6.0	179,264	62.6	137,200	20.2	10.1	689	28.1	80.1	21.1	5.0
22380	Flagstaff, AZ	78.7	10.4	46,366	60.2	214,300	25.2	10.0	979	31.9	65.5	17.0	6.2
22420	Flint, MI	84.8	3.2	166,225	69.5	84,100	23.2	13.8	680	34.5	85.0	25.1	8.6
22500	Florence, SC	87.6	2.6	77,878	67.0	102,700	20.1	10.8	620	29.2	85.0	22.2	8.8
22520	Florence–Muscle Shoals, AL	86.9	3.5	58,960	69.5	113,400	20.0	10.0	587	29.8	86.9	24.5	5.6
22540	Fond du Lac, WI	84.7	4.2	41,191	70.7	141,700	22.7	13.0	709	25.0	79.6	19.6	5.2
22660	Fort Collins–Loveland, CO	78.8	8.9	124,031	63.7	243,600	22.5	10.5	966	33.8	73.9	22.8	4.5
22900	Fort Smith, AR–OK	84.7	3.6	116,089	68.3	98,600	21.3	10.5	582	30.5	82.1	21.2	6.9
23060	Fort Wayne, IN	87.7	3.2	162,645	71.1	114,800	18.9	10.0	645	27.2	83.6	20.5	7.0
23420	Fresno, CA	82.8	3.8	292,280	51.4	174,200	26.9	12.0	858	35.2	75.2	22.8	9.5
23460	Gadsden, AL	83.5	5.2	39,031	67.0	90,500	21.2	12.3	570	31.8	87.9	23.8	5.7
23540	Gainesville, FL	76.6	10.9	99,542	56.9	162,000	23.2	10.7	842	39.1	74.2	20.6	8.7
23580	Gainesville, GA	88.1	5.5	60,500	66.0	152,400	24.1	10.0	811	29.0	76.4	26.2	5.9
24020	Glens Falls, NY	87.7	4.2	51,781	73.4	168,600	23.9	13.6	840	31.2	81.1	24.4	6.8
24140	Goldsboro, NC	84.1	6.3	47,554	59.3	105,300	21.7	12.4	628	30.3	77.8	22.7	10.8

Metro area or division code	Area name	Percent who lived in the same house one year ago	Percent who did not live in this MSA one year ago	Total occupied housing units	Percent owner-occupied housing units	Median value of owner-occupied housing units (dollars)	Median selected monthly owner costs as a percentage of household income — With a mortgage	Without a mortgage	Median gross rent (dollars)	Median gross rent as a percentage of household income	Percent of workers who drove alone to work	Mean travel time to work (minutes)	Percent of occupied housing units with no vehicle available
	ACS table number:	C07201	C07201	B25003	B25003	B25077	B25092	B25092	B25064	B25071	C08301	B08013/ B08012	C25045
	Column number:	1	2	3	4	5	6	7	8	9	10	11	12
24220	Grand Forks, ND–MN	80.7	9.4	40,954	56.0	150,000	19.5	10.5	662	30.7	80.4	15.2	6.2
24300	Grand Junction, CO	83.5	7.2	58,779	71.0	197,700	25.6	10.0	791	30.5	77.3	21.8	6.7
24340	Grand Rapids–Wyoming, MI	84.1	4.7	294,081	71.3	125,700	21.6	12.9	730	29.8	82.7	22.4	7.4
24500	Great Falls, MT	82.8	6.8	33,471	61.0	162,400	21.6	10.3	611	28.9	81.1	16.5	9.4
24540	Greeley, CO	81.3	9.2	92,447	67.8	194,400	24.2	11.2	895	30.4	79.1	26.1	4.5
24580	Green Bay, WI	87.7	3.7	122,718	68.0	156,300	21.8	13.2	682	28.1	82.1	19.8	5.4
24660	Greensboro–High Point, NC	86.6	4.7	292,421	64.2	133,800	22.9	11.2	703	29.2	83.2	21.7	7.2
24780	Greenville, NC	78.1	9.0	76,461	53.3	124,700	21.1	12.6	686	33.8	81.3	19.3	7.8
24860	Greenville–Mauldin–Easley, SC	85.1	5.6	245,906	65.8	142,200	20.0	10.5	724	30.1	84.8	22.3	6.4
25060	Gulfport–Biloxi, MS	80.4	8.4	100,195	61.4	134,500	23.8	11.4	796	33.5	81.2	22.2	4.6
25180	Hagerstown–Martinsburg, MD–WV	83.6	7.1	104,765	67.1	170,800	23.1	11.3	841	28.3	82.0	29.2	6.7
25260	Hanford–Corcoran, CA	77.7	10.6	40,376	49.0	161,200	25.9	10.0	795	29.5	72.5	20.8	7.3
25420	Harrisburg–Carlisle, PA	86.2	4.8	220,146	67.9	170,500	22.1	12.5	810	28.5	82.5	22.0	8.2
25500	Harrisonburg, VA	82.1	8.7	45,298	63.0	198,200	23.3	10.0	849	32.1	78.7	19.0	8.3
25540	Hartford–West Hartford–East Hartford, CT	87.7	3.8	468,942	66.7	243,800	24.3	15.6	948	30.3	81.4	23.4	9.1
25620	Hattiesburg, MS	78.4	8.8	53,480	58.6	129,400	22.8	12.1	717	36.0	81.2	23.5	7.0
25860	Hickory–Lenoir–Morganton, NC	88.5	3.3	140,419	69.7	116,900	21.2	11.2	587	29.0	87.6	23.3	5.7
25980	Hinesville–Fort Stewart, GA	77.4	15.0	28,309	52.8	116,500	26.9	10.0	929	29.8	85.3	20.6	4.7
26100	Holland–Grand Haven, MI	83.5	7.8	95,048	78.3	147,700	22.0	10.8	709	29.8	83.5	20.0	4.3
26180	Honolulu, HI	84.4	6.4	308,072	54.4	563,600	28.6	10.3	1,483	33.1	62.9	27.0	10.3
26300	Hot Springs, AR	79.3	8.8	40,656	68.2	144,300	22.6	10.0	723	30.1	75.9	19.7	8.2
26380	Houma–Bayou Cane–Thibodaux, LA	85.3	3.2	74,435	76.4	130,500	19.2	10.0	777	26.4	82.6	25.2	5.9
26420	Houston–Sugar Land–Baytown, TX	83.3	3.8	2,099,897	61.4	141,400	22.3	11.5	873	29.2	79.6	28.6	6.0
26580	Huntington–Ashland, WV–KY–OH	87.1	4.3	112,510	71.1	97,200	19.1	10.0	586	31.7	84.4	21.9	9.8
26620	Huntsville, AL	86.0	5.6	167,556	70.1	160,600	19.3	10.0	710	27.3	86.7	21.8	5.1
26820	Idaho Falls, ID	86.1	4.1	43,620	76.2	153,400	21.2	10.0	665	30.4	79.8	18.9	4.8
26900	Indianapolis–Carmel, IN	85.4	4.2	682,276	64.8	145,700	20.0	11.1	773	29.5	82.6	25.1	6.8
26980	Iowa City, IA	77.9	8.9	64,540	61.4	174,200	21.1	10.9	781	32.7	67.8	19.1	6.2
27060	Ithaca, NY	74.4	15.3	38,269	55.4	174,600	22.0	13.4	976	29.6	62.5	18.4	13.9
27100	Jackson, MI	80.8	5.6	60,420	71.5	103,300	22.9	12.6	692	33.9	80.2	23.1	7.5
27140	Jackson, MS	85.4	3.8	196,282	66.4	133,900	21.2	10.0	748	32.0	85.5	23.1	5.8
27180	Jackson, TN	88.0	4.3	43,040	64.7	108,900	21.6	11.6	715	33.8	85.4	20.1	6.0
27260	Jacksonville, FL	82.3	5.5	508,977	65.0	147,400	25.1	11.5	912	33.8	80.7	25.2	7.2
27340	Jacksonville, NC	74.3	15.4	61,842	53.8	154,200	24.4	12.9	926	30.0	70.1	25.4	3.4
27500	Janesville, WI	84.6	5.7	63,287	67.9	129,300	23.5	13.7	710	31.3	80.4	23.0	6.5
27620	Jefferson City, MO	84.8	5.6	57,934	72.2	139,000	20.1	10.0	550	25.8	82.9	19.8	6.1
27740	Johnson City, TN	85.0	4.9	83,530	69.3	128,400	21.5	10.0	634	30.2	84.1	22.9	6.8
27780	Johnstown, PA	90.7	3.0	58,228	75.8	85,400	19.4	13.6	543	28.1	83.5	23.2	10.0
27860	Jonesboro, AR	76.5	7.2	47,481	60.1	112,600	18.9	10.5	634	28.8	82.8	19.2	6.5
27900	Joplin, MO	81.1	5.2	68,745	65.9	101,600	19.6	13.3	611	33.3	81.8	19.1	8.8
28020	Kalamazoo–Portage, MI	82.0	6.5	128,529	67.3	131,900	22.4	13.1	672	33.3	82.8	20.4	7.6
28100	Kankakee–Bradley, IL	89.7	3.6	41,267	69.3	148,800	23.3	13.5	775	29.1	85.0	24.2	6.1
28140	Kansas City, MO–KS	84.9	3.9	801,060	65.8	156,000	21.6	12.4	804	29.2	83.2	22.7	6.7
28420	Kennewick–Pasco–Richland, WA	84.2	4.6	90,215	68.0	176,100	20.1	10.0	773	27.9	80.3	19.9	6.1
28660	Killeen–Temple–Fort Hood, TX	81.5	9.5	133,995	57.9	118,600	20.2	10.9	827	28.9	82.1	20.7	5.0
28700	Kingsport–Bristol–Bristol, TN–VA	85.7	4.7	127,704	73.7	115,900	20.3	10.4	593	29.4	85.8	22.7	5.8
28740	Kingston, NY	88.0	4.9	70,353	69.6	220,600	26.3	17.6	969	34.6	77.5	27.5	7.9
28940	Knoxville, TN	85.9	4.5	290,393	67.1	157,200	22.1	10.2	734	29.5	84.9	22.8	5.7
29020	Kokomo, IN	85.9	5.0	40,571	71.3	86,900	18.9	10.4	650	35.7	82.6	19.7	8.7
29100	La Crosse, WI–MN	82.0	6.3	54,799	66.3	156,900	21.9	12.6	705	28.7	78.6	18.2	5.9
29140	Lafayette, IN	74.3	10.5	79,034	58.6	121,100	19.3	10.0	757	37.2	78.3	19.2	7.5
29180	Lafayette, LA	84.3	5.3	106,842	66.6	154,200	20.0	10.0	725	31.1	80.4	23.5	7.0
29340	Lake Charles, LA	83.8	5.8	77,201	71.1	119,400	19.3	10.0	683	31.1	84.1	21.7	7.5
29420	Lake Havasu City–Kingman, AZ	75.6	10.5	79,239	64.3	118,400	24.8	13.0	792	31.0	75.9	18.6	6.9
29460	Lakeland–Winter Haven, FL	84.0	5.4	223,507	67.8	96,900	25.2	12.6	838	32.0	83.0	26.2	7.4
29540	Lancaster, PA	89.5	2.6	194,198	69.0	188,800	23.5	12.8	877	32.1	80.4	22.5	9.3
29620	Lansing–East Lansing, MI	80.1	7.6	181,262	65.1	124,900	21.3	13.3	740	34.8	79.5	21.4	6.3
29700	Laredo, TX	87.1	3.4	68,980	63.3	106,600	25.5	14.0	701	37.3	78.8	21.8	8.8
29740	Las Cruces, NM	83.4	5.0	73,717	65.2	132,900	23.9	10.0	704	33.8	80.1	20.6	5.5
29820	Las Vegas–Paradise, NV	75.9	5.5	715,837	52.5	145,200	25.5	11.0	974	30.7	78.5	24.1	8.6
29940	Lawrence, KS	67.5	12.5	43,992	51.0	177,700	21.6	11.3	812	34.0	77.2	20.6	6.6
30020	Lawton, OK	71.4	15.3	43,470	58.2	111,900	21.6	10.0	759	26.2	74.4	17.0	6.9
30140	Lebanon, PA	85.1	7.2	52,424	70.3	162,700	23.5	12.8	724	28.0	77.3	22.7	8.2
30300	Lewiston, ID–WA	83.8	6.3	25,325	61.9	168,100	21.5	10.0	639	24.2	78.0	16.8	6.2
30340	Lewiston–Auburn, ME	83.9	6.0	44,641	64.5	152,500	22.6	15.5	691	28.5	72.4	23.0	10.0
30460	Lexington–Fayette, KY	80.5	6.4	191,487	59.1	163,600	20.0	10.5	718	29.2	81.1	20.7	7.5
30620	Lima, OH	81.9	7.3	40,366	68.3	103,500	20.1	11.3	646	36.9	85.4	19.7	4.9
30700	Lincoln, NE	78.4	6.0	121,906	59.1	148,000	20.7	10.6	683	28.7	80.3	18.5	7.3
30780	Little Rock–North Little Rock–Conway, AR	86.6	3.5	277,026	65.4	135,600	20.2	10.1	712	29.3	85.1	22.6	6.6
30860	Logan, UT–ID	79.1	9.8	39,798	68.3	186,200	24.5	10.0	675	29.9	73.6	17.1	3.6

Table C-3. Metropolitan Areas — Where: Migration, Housing, and Transportation, 2012—*Continued*

Metro area or division code	Area name	Percent who lived in the same house one year ago	Percent who did not live in this MSA one year ago	Total occupied housing units	Percent owner-occupied housing units	Median value of owner-occupied housing units (dollars)	Median selected monthly owner costs as a percentage of household income — With a mortgage	Without a mortgage	Median gross rent (dollars)	Median gross rent as a percentage of household income	Percent of workers who drove alone to work	Mean travel time to work (minutes)	Percent of occupied housing units with no vehicle available
	ACS table number:	C07201	C07201	B25003	B25003	B25077	B25092	B25092	B25064	B25071	C08301	B08013/B08012	C25045
	Column number:	1	2	3	4	5	6	7	8	9	10	11	12
30980	Longview, TX	81.3	7.1	75,315	69.2	100,500	20.2	10.7	700	27.6	83.5	22.2	5.6
31020	Longview, WA	81.7	4.2	38,834	63.9	169,800	24.6	12.8	750	33.2	81.1	21.5	7.1
31100	Los Angeles–Long Beach–Santa Ana, CA	86.3	2.7	4,227,028	48.4	428,500	29.9	11.4	1,233	35.1	74.1	28.9	8.8
3110031084	•Los Angeles–Long Beach–Glendale, CA Division	86.6	2.6	3,231,660	45.8	399,500	30.7	11.7	1,175	35.5	72.9	29.6	10.0
3110042044	•Santa Ana–Anaheim–Irvine, CA Division	85.2	3.0	995,368	56.9	492,200	28.1	10.3	1,465	33.9	77.7	26.7	5.0
31140	Louisville–Jefferson County, KY–IN	86.2	3.7	510,269	67.2	147,300	21.4	10.7	710	29.5	82.9	23.7	8.1
31180	Lubbock, TX	75.7	9.0	108,426	57.0	108,000	21.6	11.6	791	34.2	82.6	16.5	5.8
31340	Lynchburg, VA	87.0	5.2	99,273	71.9	159,600	22.1	10.0	676	30.2	82.4	23.2	8.0
31420	Macon, GA	82.6	5.6	84,022	61.4	121,100	23.0	10.8	697	36.2	85.1	23.0	9.8
31460	Madera–Chowchilla, CA	89.0	2.8	41,035	59.8	168,800	30.0	11.4	883	37.3	78.5	25.0	7.5
31540	Madison, WI	79.6	7.2	239,964	61.0	217,600	23.5	12.9	850	29.8	73.9	21.4	7.8
31700	Manchester–Nashua, NH	86.8	5.3	155,260	67.5	242,300	25.7	15.5	1,027	29.2	82.6	26.4	6.2
31740	Manhattan, KS	78.4	13.0	47,675	49.4	156,500	22.7	12.3	834	29.1	71.8	18.0	4.7
31860	Mankato–North Mankato, MN	80.6	10.1	36,476	69.5	163,500	21.3	10.0	708	34.5	77.6	17.1	5.6
31900	Mansfield, OH	84.5	6.5	48,529	70.5	96,800	21.7	11.7	616	29.4	85.9	20.3	7.4
32580	McAllen–Edinburg–Mission, TX	86.7	3.6	222,849	67.3	80,300	24.0	13.0	621	33.2	79.0	21.8	6.6
32780	Medford, OR	82.9	5.2	80,957	64.8	199,400	27.4	13.5	842	34.0	75.5	19.5	5.9
32820	Memphis, TN–MS–AR	83.6	3.5	484,923	62.2	131,100	23.3	12.0	825	33.5	83.0	23.5	8.4
32900	Merced, CA	82.4	4.9	76,451	53.5	138,100	25.2	11.8	834	33.7	76.5	26.5	7.3
33100	Miami–Fort Lauderdale–Pompano Beach, FL	85.5	4.0	2,024,878	62.0	175,500	30.3	15.7	1,093	37.0	77.6	28.0	9.2
3310022744	•Fort Lauderdale–Pompano Beach–Deerfield Beach, FL Division	83.3	4.2	663,905	65.6	165,600	29.4	16.4	1,135	34.8	78.6	27.6	8.0
3310033124	•Miami–Miami Beach–Kendall, FL Division	87.2	3.3	838,772	54.3	181,500	32.0	15.4	1,057	39.1	76.4	29.5	11.6
3310048424	•West Palm Beach–Boca Raton–Boynton Beach, FL Division	85.0	4.9	522,201	69.9	184,400	29.3	15.2	1,116	35.1	78.6	25.3	6.9
33140	Michigan City–La Porte, IN	84.9	7.9	43,468	69.9	121,700	20.2	10.0	650	28.9	86.7	24.1	9.4
33260	Midland, TX	83.5	10.1	51,216	66.6	148,900	19.0	10.0	941	27.0	82.9	19.3	2.8
33340	Milwaukee–Waukesha–West Allis, WI	84.8	3.1	623,682	59.9	192,900	23.1	14.2	789	31.9	80.2	23.1	11.0
33460	Minneapolis–St. Paul–Bloomington, MN–WI	84.8	3.5	1,296,603	69.4	203,700	22.2	11.5	895	29.5	78.2	24.9	7.4
33540	Missoula, MT	77.9	8.9	46,384	58.2	220,700	23.3	12.2	729	31.9	70.9	16.4	5.8
33660	Mobile, AL	84.5	3.4	156,755	64.2	125,500	22.3	12.2	725	33.0	85.6	24.1	7.8
33700	Modesto, CA	81.7	4.8	167,497	55.6	159,800	27.8	11.9	959	36.4	79.1	26.9	6.5
33740	Monroe, LA	87.6	4.6	67,742	62.4	113,600	19.6	10.0	606	31.6	90.2	22.0	9.1
33780	Monroe, MI	89.2	5.5	57,506	77.1	128,100	22.2	13.6	803	28.8	87.1	23.8	5.0
33860	Montgomery, AL	82.6	6.0	142,926	65.5	123,900	21.7	10.8	785	31.2	85.3	22.9	7.0
34060	Morgantown, WV	81.8	8.9	49,069	60.1	148,400	17.5	10.0	645	30.2	74.5	22.6	8.1
34100	Morristown, TN	88.7	4.2	52,341	75.4	114,000	23.5	10.6	591	30.6	82.0	26.2	4.4
34580	Mount Vernon–Anacortes, WA	83.1	6.4	44,671	68.0	242,600	26.0	12.6	951	32.1	79.1	25.5	5.1
34620	Muncie, IN	75.6	9.7	46,572	62.2	86,200	18.2	12.4	633	38.5	78.9	20.8	7.8
34740	Muskegon–Norton Shores, MI	83.5	5.9	63,860	74.1	99,900	22.5	13.1	622	41.7	85.1	22.0	10.5
34820	Myrtle Beach–North Myrtle Beach–Conway, SC	82.9	7.4	118,092	66.9	154,100	26.0	11.2	815	36.7	82.3	21.7	6.6
34900	Napa, CA	87.9	4.6	48,224	60.6	396,500	28.1	13.0	1,276	30.7	76.4	23.9	3.7
34940	Naples–Marco Island, FL	86.1	6.1	123,714	74.2	233,500	29.9	13.4	1,031	34.1	71.4	24.4	5.6
34980	Nashville-Davidson–Murfreesboro–Franklin, TN	83.1	4.7	616,606	64.6	172,300	23.1	10.0	828	29.6	82.4	26.3	5.5
35300	New Haven–Milford, CT	87.7	4.3	330,054	63.4	242,100	26.4	18.3	1,030	34.1	78.8	23.9	11.3
35380	New Orleans–Metairie–Kenner, LA	86.0	4.2	463,402	60.6	172,400	23.7	11.0	876	33.7	79.2	25.4	10.1
35620	New York–Northern New Jersey–Long Island, NY–NJ–PA	90.4	2.1	6,872,526	51.4	400,000	28.8	18.0	1,209	32.3	49.8	35.2	31.5
3562020764	•Edison, NJ Division	91.1	1.9	860,223	74.2	324,000	27.4	18.6	1,246	32.5	75.7	32.7	7.4
3562035004	•Nassau–Suffolk, NY Division	93.7	1.1	938,085	79.6	404,500	29.4	19.4	1,473	33.0	73.7	32.7	6.3
3562035084	•Newark–Union, NJ–PA Division	90.2	1.9	766,727	61.9	356,700	28.0	17.9	1,101	33.2	72.2	31.8	12.9
3562035644	•New York–White Plains–Wayne, NY–NJ Division	89.5	2.4	4,307,491	38.8	450,300	29.5	17.2	1,203	32.1	34.4	37.0	45.1
35660	Niles–Benton Harbor, MI	85.2	4.5	60,223	72.2	131,000	21.8	12.2	654	35.4	82.8	20.4	9.2
35840	North Port–Bradenton–Sarasota, FL	83.1	7.0	303,355	71.8	160,100	26.7	13.1	936	33.0	80.3	23.3	6.0
35980	Norwich–New London, CT	86.4	6.2	105,801	65.5	248,200	23.9	14.2	958	31.3	78.1	21.8	7.5
36100	Ocala, FL	83.6	7.6	133,910	74.5	113,200	26.1	12.4	772	35.3	79.5	24.3	5.9
36140	Ocean City, NJ	88.8	6.3	40,470	73.4	305,900	30.9	16.8	979	33.5	77.8	21.4	11.1
36220	Odessa, TX	81.4	7.6	49,382	69.0	95,500	18.0	10.0	800	25.4	85.9	21.6	4.2
36260	Ogden–Clearfield, UT	86.1	5.0	179,915	74.8	190,400	22.8	10.0	805	28.5	79.0	22.2	4.7
36420	Oklahoma City, OK	81.6	4.8	484,733	64.3	131,300	21.2	11.0	740	30.7	82.9	22.0	6.0
36500	Olympia, WA	81.9	8.5	102,335	66.1	228,300	25.5	11.2	988	32.7	75.5	24.3	5.0
36540	Omaha–Council Bluffs, NE–IA	84.2	3.5	341,740	65.6	144,700	21.3	12.8	777	28.2	83.1	20.0	6.5
36740	Orlando–Kissimmee–Sanford, FL	83.2	5.9	778,593	61.4	143,200	26.9	13.3	980	34.9	80.8	27.3	5.8
36780	Oshkosh–Neenah, WI	85.7	5.9	67,627	67.1	144,200	21.5	13.2	639	24.6	84.4	19.3	5.6
36980	Owensboro, KY	86.3	3.0	46,026	71.2	109,600	19.3	10.0	616	31.9	83.9	20.4	6.2
37100	Oxnard–Thousand Oaks–Ventura, CA	87.5	4.2	267,877	64.2	413,100	28.1	10.8	1,438	36.8	76.3	24.5	4.4
37340	Palm Bay–Melbourne–Titusville, FL	85.1	5.3	218,094	72.9	126,000	25.4	12.5	873	32.0	82.8	23.7	5.4
37380	Palm Coast, FL	88.4	5.5	36,358	75.9	151,900	31.9	12.0	939	28.9	80.0	27.0	3.5

Table C-3. Metropolitan Areas — Where: Migration, Housing, and Transportation, 2012—*Continued*

Metro area or division code	Area name	Percent who lived in the same house one year ago	Percent who did not live in this MSA one year ago	Total occupied housing units	Percent owner-occupied housing units	Median value of owner-occupied housing units (dollars)	Median selected monthly owner costs as a percentage of household income — With a mortgage	Median selected monthly owner costs as a percentage of household income — Without a mortgage	Median gross rent (dollars)	Median gross rent as a percentage of household income	Percent of workers who drove alone to work	Mean travel time to work (minutes)	Percent of occupied housing units with no vehicle available
	ACS table number:	C07201	C07201	B25003	B25003	B25077	B25092	B25092	B25064	B25071	C08301	B08013/ B08012	C25045
	Column number:	1	2	3	4	5	6	7	8	9	10	11	12
37460	Panama City–Lynn Haven–Panama City Beach, FL	77.5	9.0	68,653	59.9	156,600	24.6	11.8	901	32.3	82.7	23.8	6.5
37620	Parkersburg–Marietta–Vienna, WV–OH	89.7	2.9	66,271	74.2	103,300	19.5	10.0	567	29.1	85.9	20.4	6.5
37700	Pascagoula, MS................	87.3	4.4	58,424	73.7	113,400	21.5	10.0	829	35.5	79.5	24.9	4.8
37860	Pensacola–Ferry Pass–Brent, FL............	81.5	7.4	172,413	64.1	132,100	22.7	11.0	901	29.7	80.3	24.7	5.2
37900	Peoria, IL................	85.8	3.8	152,743	70.4	134,800	20.5	11.1	669	27.8	82.0	20.9	7.1
37980	Philadelphia–Camden–Wilmington, PA–NJ–DE–MD	88.7	2.8	2,227,140	67.5	235,100	24.4	15.2	968	32.0	73.3	28.6	13.9
3798015804	•Camden, NJ Division	90.2	2.7	454,987	74.3	217,100	25.8	18.2	1,033	33.9	80.8	28.6	7.9
3798037964	•Philadelphia, PA Division	88.7	2.7	1,508,981	65.3	244,000	24.1	15.1	955	32.1	69.6	29.1	16.9
3798048864	•Wilmington, DE–MD–NJ Division	85.6	3.8	263,172	68.5	233,000	23.7	11.8	973	29.6	80.7	25.8	7.2
38060	Phoenix–Mesa–Glendale, AZ................	81.2	4.8	1,551,267	61.6	156,100	23.4	10.9	936	30.4	77.3	25.8	6.6
38220	Pine Bluff, AR................	90.7	2.9	35,581	64.9	81,300	18.8	11.7	645	35.1	81.5	21.9	7.5
38300	Pittsburgh, PA	88.0	3.0	990,931	69.4	124,300	19.9	12.4	700	27.8	77.3	26.5	10.9
38340	Pittsfield, MA	87.9	4.6	55,420	67.2	206,400	24.7	15.1	748	33.2	76.0	20.9	12.0
38540	Pocatello, ID................	79.3	6.1	33,239	67.3	147,300	22.8	10.0	572	32.4	78.1	19.2	4.9
38860	Portland–South Portland–Biddeford, ME	85.9	4.3	213,459	69.8	232,000	25.1	14.0	891	31.7	77.7	24.4	6.1
38900	Portland–Vancouver–Hillsboro, OR–WA................	83.1	4.4	872,878	60.5	249,300	25.0	12.6	934	31.0	70.8	25.1	8.8
38940	Port St. Lucie, FL	83.4	7.0	170,309	72.4	133,600	27.4	13.8	927	39.1	78.6	26.4	6.3
39100	Poughkeepsie–Newburgh–Middletown, NY	89.8	4.6	232,334	69.2	269,900	27.6	18.3	1,086	35.3	75.1	32.6	9.4
39140	Prescott, AZ................	81.0	8.0	93,697	67.8	177,900	26.5	11.3	844	31.4	74.6	21.8	4.9
39300	Providence–New Bedford–Fall River, RI–MA	87.7	3.2	622,066	60.6	246,500	25.4	15.9	848	30.0	80.4	25.5	10.6
39340	Provo–Orem, UT................	78.7	8.3	147,329	67.0	207,800	23.7	10.0	852	31.3	72.6	21.7	2.3
39380	Pueblo, CO	83.1	4.3	62,388	63.9	131,300	24.1	11.9	755	33.0	78.5	20.9	8.0
39460	Punta Gorda, FL	86.9	7.5	71,811	79.8	131,900	30.2	12.9	840	29.4	81.0	22.6	5.6
39540	Racine, WI	89.6	3.9	75,752	68.4	162,100	23.1	14.8	734	30.3	84.1	23.3	7.3
39580	Raleigh–Cary, NC	84.8	6.2	441,987	64.9	203,600	20.7	10.0	877	27.8	80.3	24.5	4.6
39660	Rapid City, SD	79.1	7.0	50,646	65.8	161,600	22.6	11.9	781	28.1	80.8	18.0	4.6
39740	Reading, PA	86.6	4.2	151,291	70.5	166,500	23.9	15.6	817	31.6	79.2	24.9	10.0
39820	Redding, CA	83.8	5.6	68,165	62.0	202,500	26.2	13.5	913	35.3	82.7	19.9	6.3
39900	Reno–Sparks, NV	81.3	5.9	165,964	57.4	177,400	26.7	11.4	870	33.3	77.7	22.4	9.3
40060	Richmond, VA	84.5	4.9	476,759	67.2	207,400	22.8	10.9	939	30.8	81.5	25.0	6.9
40140	Riverside–San Bernardino–Ontario, CA................	83.8	4.5	1,285,948	62.4	214,100	28.7	13.5	1,094	36.1	77.7	31.2	5.5
40220	Roanoke, VA	83.7	4.4	129,023	69.5	165,700	23.5	10.5	710	28.0	83.5	21.4	7.8
40340	Rochester, MN	85.8	5.3	73,900	75.4	167,100	21.1	10.0	749	30.1	77.2	18.6	5.9
40380	Rochester, NY	84.5	3.8	419,798	66.8	130,100	21.5	13.8	774	32.3	82.4	21.1	10.7
40420	Rockford, IL	86.1	2.7	130,401	68.0	122,100	22.9	12.7	705	28.2	84.4	22.8	7.8
40580	Rocky Mount, NC	85.9	3.9	55,868	64.8	96,400	22.8	13.9	651	32.2	84.4	20.3	9.5
40660	Rome, GA	85.5	6.4	34,373	65.9	111,000	23.7	12.4	682	31.2	81.8	22.2	8.5
40900	Sacramento–Arden–Arcade–Roseville, CA................	81.4	4.3	786,864	59.1	250,000	26.8	11.3	1,022	34.1	75.5	25.4	6.8
40980	Saginaw–Saginaw Township North, MI................	87.6	4.7	78,010	73.1	92,200	22.4	13.7	669	33.5	85.3	22.0	8.3
41060	St. Cloud, MN	79.9	8.5	71,971	71.9	161,600	21.6	12.0	677	31.6	78.8	20.7	5.2
41100	St. George, UT................	80.7	6.5	48,186	68.2	182,200	28.5	10.0	951	37.4	78.2	20.2	2.7
41140	St. Joseph, MO–KS................	82.0	7.9	47,656	64.7	111,100	20.4	11.3	652	31.0	82.8	18.9	7.2
41180	St. Louis, MO–IL................	86.0	2.8	1,108,723	69.7	155,200	21.7	12.2	767	31.1	82.4	25.4	8.6
41420	Salem, OR................	82.0	5.8	142,746	62.5	189,100	26.3	12.9	780	32.9	73.7	22.9	8.2
41500	Salinas, CA	85.8	5.3	124,171	48.8	318,200	29.2	11.0	1,185	33.4	71.4	22.8	5.1
41540	Salisbury, MD	83.6	8.0	44,623	64.3	171,200	23.7	12.6	895	34.9	78.6	23.1	5.8
41620	Salt Lake City, UT	83.2	5.3	380,362	67.0	221,100	23.6	10.0	894	29.9	75.0	23.2	6.2
41660	San Angelo, TX	73.1	13.2	43,104	58.9	103,500	19.8	11.3	684	25.6	84.0	16.3	4.8
41700	San Antonio–New Braunfels, TX..........	82.9	4.8	766,963	62.4	132,100	21.5	11.1	828	28.9	79.7	24.9	6.8
41740	San Diego–Carlsbad–San Marcos, CA ..	84.3	5.0	1,079,653	53.1	386,400	29.1	11.4	1,253	34.0	76.2	24.6	6.2
41780	Sandusky, OH................	84.5	6.6	31,739	68.9	138,600	21.6	13.2	668	24.2	83.4	21.5	6.7
41860	San Francisco–Oakland–Fremont, CA ...	85.2	4.7	1,636,828	53.0	557,700	27.4	11.3	1,399	31.1	60.4	30.4	12.8
4186036084	•Oakland–Fremont–Hayward, CA Division	84.9	4.1	928,671	57.1	435,800	26.9	11.3	1,289	32.1	65.8	31.5	8.7
4186041884	•San Francisco–San Mateo–Redwood City, CA Division................	85.6	5.6	708,157	47.6	719,800	28.4	11.2	1,545	29.9	53.8	29.0	18.2
41940	San Jose–Sunnyvale–Santa Clara, CA ...	84.9	5.4	630,849	56.4	624,200	26.7	10.0	1,560	29.2	76.5	25.7	5.4
42020	San Luis Obispo–Paso Robles, CA........	78.3	8.9	101,897	55.1	410,900	29.4	11.2	1,183	32.6	73.1	22.1	4.5
42060	Santa Barbara–Santa Maria–Goleta, CA................	78.2	6.6	141,639	51.7	409,700	27.9	10.9	1,324	34.6	67.3	18.7	7.1
42100	Santa Cruz–Watsonville, CA................	82.7	7.4	93,253	56.7	545,700	29.0	10.8	1,474	32.4	70.1	25.7	4.8
42140	Santa Fe, NM	85.5	5.8	62,311	67.5	270,200	26.0	10.0	881	32.2	74.0	21.6	3.9
42220	Santa Rosa–Petaluma, CA................	85.7	3.4	184,348	59.9	380,100	28.3	11.9	1,251	34.2	75.4	25.7	5.1
42340	Savannah, GA	86.0	6.2	132,868	60.0	171,700	24.1	13.7	890	34.1	80.9	23.4	7.4
42540	Scranton–Wilkes-Barre, PA	87.6	3.7	225,527	65.6	133,300	21.9	14.4	644	28.7	79.3	21.3	10.3

Table C-3. Metropolitan Areas — Where: Migration, Housing, and Transportation, 2012—*Continued*

Metro area or division code	Area name	Percent who lived in the same house one year ago	Percent who did not live in this MSA one year ago	Total occupied housing units	Percent owner-occupied housing units	Median value of owner-occupied housing units (dollars)	Median selected monthly owner costs as a percentage of household income		Median gross rent (dollars)	Median gross rent as a percentage of household income	Percent of workers who drove alone to work	Mean travel time to work (minutes)	Percent of occupied housing units with no vehicle available
							With a mortgage	Without a mortgage					
ACS table number:		C07201	C07201	B25003	B25003	B25077	B25092	B25092	B25064	B25071	C08301	B08013/ B08012	C25045
Column number:		1	2	3	4	5	6	7	8	9	10	11	12
42660	Seattle–Tacoma–Bellevue, WA	82.2	5.4	1,375,184	59.5	293,700	25.7	13.1	1,079	29.5	69.6	28.5	7.7
4266042644	•Seattle–Bellevue–Everett, WA Division	82.2	5.5	1,074,630	59.2	325,200	25.5	13.2	1,103	29.2	67.3	28.3	8.3
4266045104	•Tacoma, WA Division	82.2	5.1	300,554	60.7	218,000	26.4	12.9	986	31.0	78.2	29.1	5.6
42680	Sebastian–Vero Beach, FL	84.9	6.6	58,950	74.6	139,500	27.1	13.4	771	39.2	82.4	23.1	7.0
43100	Sheboygan, WI	88.7	5.4	46,653	70.3	145,700	21.4	12.7	636	27.0	84.9	18.1	6.2
43300	Sherman–Denison, TX	79.1	6.6	47,770	69.2	105,100	20.1	12.4	761	28.0	81.8	24.4	5.8
43340	Shreveport–Bossier City, LA	86.8	3.9	153,275	62.3	128,600	20.2	10.0	732	29.6	86.2	21.8	9.8
43580	Sioux City, IA–NE–SD	84.7	4.6	53,573	67.8	98,500	20.3	11.0	708	28.6	84.4	17.7	5.2
43620	Sioux Falls, SD	82.5	4.9	90,466	64.6	154,500	21.3	10.3	718	25.8	84.4	17.7	3.5
43780	South Bend–Mishawaka, IN–MI	86.0	5.1	121,241	71.9	118,700	20.5	10.0	698	28.9	82.1	21.2	7.5
43900	Spartanburg, SC	82.4	6.6	108,569	67.7	114,800	20.3	10.3	682	30.1	82.3	22.2	7.4
44060	Spokane, WA	82.4	5.7	189,004	63.0	174,900	24.0	11.4	754	33.1	75.7	20.8	7.8
44100	Springfield, IL	84.8	4.6	87,490	71.1	126,600	19.0	11.0	704	31.6	81.5	19.2	6.9
44140	Springfield, MA	86.3	4.6	263,453	64.1	210,500	23.4	14.2	798	31.9	79.4	22.8	11.9
44180	Springfield, MO	80.9	6.5	176,987	63.5	129,700	21.5	10.0	660	30.8	80.8	21.5	6.2
44220	Springfield, OH	83.4	4.5	54,288	64.7	101,300	22.1	12.0	647	31.1	83.3	23.0	8.5
44300	State College, PA	75.7	14.0	56,980	60.5	196,100	22.6	11.1	912	36.8	68.0	20.7	8.7
44600	Steubenville–Weirton, WV–OH	88.3	3.4	50,663	71.0	83,400	18.8	11.0	612	28.7	84.3	25.9	9.1
44700	Stockton, CA	82.6	5.1	215,761	56.5	190,600	26.8	11.8	986	35.0	78.2	29.7	7.2
44940	Sumter, SC	85.0	6.1	40,321	63.9	107,700	20.3	10.0	698	27.6	82.4	22.1	8.4
45060	Syracuse, NY	85.3	4.6	257,456	67.2	124,400	21.1	13.3	729	30.2	80.2	20.3	11.9
45220	Tallahassee, FL	74.1	10.1	140,759	58.7	164,900	23.2	11.3	871	38.7	82.7	22.2	7.6
45300	Tampa–St. Petersburg–Clearwater, FL	83.9	5.0	1,131,949	64.3	132,400	25.7	12.9	892	33.5	80.0	25.9	7.7
45460	Terre Haute, IN	84.0	5.6	65,165	67.2	90,300	19.1	10.9	633	33.8	87.4	20.9	8.0
45500	Texarkana, TX–Texarkana, AR	82.6	6.0	53,337	62.8	91,400	19.8	12.2	643	29.7	87.2	18.5	6.5
45780	Toledo, OH	83.4	4.1	260,332	64.8	114,900	21.3	13.2	630	30.3	85.3	20.7	9.8
45820	Topeka, KS	82.5	4.3	93,196	67.0	117,100	20.8	12.1	687	28.1	81.9	19.0	7.2
45940	Trenton–Ewing, NJ	87.6	6.0	132,004	65.2	272,900	25.9	16.1	1,085	33.6	73.5	27.7	12.5
46060	Tucson, AZ	80.3	5.4	386,104	61.6	153,500	23.7	11.0	784	33.1	76.7	24.1	9.3
46140	Tulsa, OK	83.5	4.6	369,404	65.9	128,400	21.0	10.8	725	28.9	83.3	21.0	5.8
46220	Tuscaloosa, AL	81.4	8.5	77,713	65.3	150,200	22.6	11.7	670	34.0	83.7	22.6	9.3
46340	Tyler, TX	80.4	9.7	78,290	64.0	121,100	21.3	11.7	772	28.4	81.9	21.8	5.0
46540	Utica–Rome, NY	87.7	4.0	118,135	67.0	110,000	19.8	12.9	654	29.9	80.0	20.9	12.7
46660	Valdosta, GA	75.0	9.0	51,065	53.4	126,500	22.3	11.8	775	33.4	79.0	20.1	6.9
46700	Vallejo–Fairfield, CA	80.1	6.4	141,139	59.1	234,900	26.7	10.0	1,244	34.4	77.9	28.2	6.3
47020	Victoria, TX	83.9	6.8	42,565	65.6	109,200	18.2	11.4	708	28.1	75.4	22.6	8.1
47220	Vineland–Millville–Bridgeton, NJ	88.8	5.6	50,068	67.9	165,300	26.7	19.9	962	38.6	80.1	22.9	11.0
47260	Virginia Beach–Norfolk–Newport News, VA–NC	82.3	5.3	623,964	60.8	233,300	25.2	12.1	1,047	32.8	80.9	24.0	6.4
47300	Visalia–Porterville, CA	85.6	4.1	132,614	56.6	155,100	27.0	11.8	810	34.7	77.6	21.8	6.1
47380	Waco, TX	79.2	8.3	85,171	62.4	104,600	21.9	13.6	752	30.3	82.2	18.8	8.0
47580	Warner Robins, GA	87.9	5.4	52,832	68.3	137,300	19.4	10.0	850	30.5	87.5	20.6	4.0
47900	Washington–Arlington–Alexandria, DC–VA–MD–WV	85.2	5.0	2,085,494	62.9	367,600	23.3	10.2	1,424	29.6	65.8	34.0	10.4
4790013644	•Bethesda–Rockville–Frederick, MD Division	86.5	4.4	447,608	68.2	394,300	23.3	11.2	1,491	30.5	67.2	34.2	6.7
4790047894	•Washington–Arlington–Alexandria, DC–VA–MD–WV Division	84.9	5.1	1,637,886	61.4	359,300	23.4	10.0	1,408	29.4	65.4	33.9	11.4
47940	Waterloo–Cedar Falls, IA	87.7	3.9	66,320	71.5	129,200	19.1	10.4	640	28.6	83.1	15.1	5.8
48140	Wausau, WI	87.4	3.5	52,147	73.4	143,700	22.3	12.4	702	27.4	78.6	18.7	5.6
48300	Wenatchee–East Wenatchee, WA	91.7	3.1	41,750	67.1	219,500	26.7	10.0	743	26.7	78.1	19.4	6.4
48540	Wheeling, WV–OH	87.2	4.8	61,627	69.2	97,100	19.4	10.0	522	28.9	82.8	22.7	10.1
48620	Wichita, KS	82.8	4.4	239,925	65.3	123,000	21.0	12.0	687	28.2	85.0	18.8	5.7
48660	Wichita Falls, TX	82.4	10.3	56,261	61.9	92,300	19.4	11.8	726	27.5	82.2	17.2	4.7
48700	Williamsport, PA	85.1	4.0	45,595	70.5	130,500	22.0	13.4	711	27.1	81.3	20.6	8.1
48900	Wilmington, NC	82.7	7.6	152,292	66.3	183,900	24.8	12.7	881	29.5	78.7	22.5	5.0
49020	Winchester, VA–WV	88.1	4.2	50,815	66.4	199,600	22.3	10.9	801	30.5	82.7	29.2	6.0
49180	Winston–Salem, NC	86.5	4.5	193,105	65.2	147,100	21.6	11.0	669	31.0	82.8	22.9	6.9
49340	Worcester, MA	89.1	3.7	300,308	64.3	246,500	23.9	14.5	892	29.3	82.3	28.5	8.8
49420	Yakima, WA	84.9	2.7	78,472	62.1	157,900	23.7	10.5	728	30.9	76.3	20.6	4.9
49620	York–Hanover, PA	89.2	4.3	168,508	74.4	167,400	23.8	14.7	795	29.5	84.1	27.1	6.0
49660	Youngstown–Warren–Boardman, OH–PA	88.0	3.7	229,328	69.6	97,600	20.9	12.3	616	29.7	84.4	21.9	8.1
49700	Yuba City, CA	79.8	6.2	56,101	59.2	169,000	26.6	12.2	862	34.4	74.9	27.3	6.3
49740	Yuma, AZ	81.0	7.3	70,895	67.6	109,200	24.8	11.5	842	34.0	79.3	18.4	4.7

Table C-4. Cities — Where: Migration, Housing, and Transportation, 2010–2012

STATE and place code	STATE or city	Percent who lived in the same house one year ago	Percent who did not live in the same city one year ago	Total occupied housing units	Percent owner-occupied housing units	Median value of owner-occupied housing units (dollars)[1]	Median selected monthly owner costs as a percentage of household income[2] — With a mortgage	Without a mortgage	Median gross rent (dollars)[2]	Median gross rent as a percentage of household income[4]	Percent of workers who drove alone to work	Mean travel time to work (minutes)	Percent of occupied housing units with no vehicle available
	ACS table number:	C07204	C07204	B25003	B25003	B25077	B25092	B25092	B25064	B25071	CC8301	B08013/C08012	C25045
	Column number:	1	2	3	4	5	6	7	8	9	10	11	12
00 00000	**United States**	84.8	10.1	115,241,776	64.7	174,600	24.5	12.7	889	31.5	76.4	25.5	9.2
01 00000	**Alabama**	84.7	10.6	1,837,823	69.6	123,400	22.3	11.8	698	31.4	84.8	24.2	6.5
01 00820	Alabaster city	89.3	8.8	10,708	84.8	162,100	21.9	10.7	1,021	30.7	84.9	30.2	1.1
01 00988	Albertville city	80.4	10.9	7,297	62.7	102,600	21.9	10.0	593	27.3	81.3	18.3	5.2
01 01852	Anniston city	79.6	11.1	9,561	57.2	108,900	24.3	11.0	620	27.8	87.9	18.9	11.1
01 02956	Athens city	86.8	8.2	8,914	66.3	146,800	20.1	10.6	646	29.4	. . .	25.4	5.1
01 03076	Auburn city	62.2	20.7	20,700	44.1	218,600	22.6	10.4	769	43.2	77.1	18.5	3.8
01 05980	Bessemer city	85.1	8.4	10,378	56.9	89,300	29.4	15.1	675	35.0	84.1	24.7	16.3
01 07000	Birmingham city	78.2	9.3	87,407	49.5	86,800	27.0	14.4	698	36.5	81.7	21.9	15.4
01 19648	Daphne city	80.0	15.7	8,403	70.1	177,800	24.4	13.0	1,032	26.8	86.4	25.6	1.2
01 20104	Decatur city	87.1	6.0	22,076	63.0	126,700	20.8	10.0	575	27.5	84.1	20.3	7.1
01 21184	Dothan city	83.7	7.7	25,799	59.2	138,000	20.8	10.0	657	29.6	88.9	17.9	7.1
01 24184	Enterprise city	81.5	15.0	10,075	64.8	161,800	20.8	10.0	718	25.4	84.7	18.4	6.7
01 26896	Florence city	81.9	8.8	17,508	58.4	119,000	22.3	10.0	575	33.9	84.8	17.5	6.7
01 28696	Gadsden city	81.9	9.3	14,823	60.0	70,800	25.2	14.3	572	33.3	85.7	21.2	10.8
01 35800	Homewood city	73.5	21.5	9,144	52.7	268,100	22.8	10.7	863	27.7	79.0	17.3	3.2
01 35896	Hoover city	83.0	12.1	31,316	66.9	261,000	21.5	10.0	918	28.1	84.9	23.9	2.8
01 37000	Huntsville city	81.9	8.6	75,373	60.1	158,000	20.4	10.0	705	31.1	84.7	18.2	7.0
01 45784	Madison city	84.8	12.6	15,986	73.4	236,900	17.0	10.0	872	24.0	90.5	18.3	1.8
01 50000	Mobile city	83.8	6.2	76,621	57.9	127,200	24.6	12.4	738	34.4	84.2	20.6	10.0
01 51000	Montgomery city	77.2	8.5	79,764	57.5	119,100	22.6	10.2	789	34.0	85.4	18.6	8.6
01 51696	Mountain Brook city	92.1	6.1	7,294	85.2	567,200	19.9	10.0	1,011	26.4	. . .	16.0	0.3
01 55200	Northport city	78.6	15.3	8,758	65.9	165,600	23.2	10.0	798	27.7	90.7	19.3	5.1
01 57048	Opelika city	82.2	9.3	11,055	64.2	145,700	20.2	12.0	705	33.1	82.6	19.6	9.6
01 57576	Oxford city	83.5	15.1	7,564	67.7	120,300	21.9	10.0	783	20.8	. . .	18.1	3.8
01 58848	Pelham city	88.6	9.4	8,466	82.8	162,900	21.7	10.0	1,030	25.5	86.6	28.3	1.7
01 59472	Phenix City city	76.5	13.5	14,105	51.2	120,500	23.2	12.9	715	31.8	85.0	21.6	8.2
01 62328	Prattville city	81.9	14.4	12,092	68.9	152,100	19.5	10.0	867	29.6	89.4	22.8	4.7
01 62496	Prichard city	85.1	11.3	8,650	54.9	66,000	31.0	16.0	672	45.0	84.4	24.2	18.9
01 69120	Selma city	85.6	6.0	7,743	48.8	87,800	23.4	15.6	488	38.5	80.2	18.0	20.9
01 76944	Trussville city	89.4	8.9	7,116	87.6	228,900	21.8	10.0	1,231	25.2	86.8	26.0	1.0
01 77256	Tuscaloosa city	73.0	13.9	30,979	49.6	162,600	24.1	11.9	738	36.3	81.0	18.2	10.0
01 78552	Vestavia Hills city	86.6	11.3	13,797	73.6	331,700	20.9	10.7	1,066	32.4	87.9	20.7	6.7
02 00000	**Alaska**	80.8	11.2	253,718	63.5	241,400	23.2	11.3	1,080	28.3	67.1	19.0	9.9
02 03000	Anchorage municipality	79.8	8.2	105,688	60.0	282,800	23.1	11.5	1,110	29.1	74.5	19.6	6.3
02 05000	Badger CDP	78.1	17.0	6,988	76.3	199,200	25.2	13.1	1,416	28.9	81.6	23.6	2.9
02 24230	Fairbanks city	64.9	26.0	11,811	36.2	194,800	31.4	13.7	1,227	33.1	68.8	14.0	11.3
02 36400	Juneau city and borough	82.0	6.5	12,314	63.9	309,500	24.8	11.8	1,188	26.9	66.2	15.3	7.0
04 00000	**Arizona**	80.2	11.5	2,357,799	63.9	158,100	25.0	11.2	878	31.1	76.3	24.6	7.0
04 02430	Anthem CDP	76.2	11.4	7,652	69.3	208,800	27.7	10.0	1,428	27.7	. . .	28.6	1.9
04 02830	Apache Junction city	85.4	8.3	14,525	80.5	86,500	28.3	12.0	737	29.4	81.2	28.1	8.0
04 04720	Avondale city	78.2	15.9	22,330	60.4	117,000	24.8	12.5	1,051	25.3	80.0	25.3	4.2
04 07940	Buckeye town	78.5	15.8	14,454	65.5	126,400	23.8	10.0	1,081	33.2	81.5	33.9	3.0
04 08220	Bullhead City city	71.8	13.4	16,569	61.8	99,500	28.4	12.0	797	33.2	79.6	17.8	6.3
04 10530	Casa Grande city	81.1	8.7	16,716	70.8	105,600	25.9	14.6	885	29.9	81.5	20.0	5.9
04 10670	Casas Adobes CDP	80.3	16.2	27,904	65.5	176,900	23.7	12.3	946	31.7	81.4	23.2	5.9
04 11230	Catalina Foothills CDP	83.7	13.3	24,046	72.0	394,900	24.2	10.3	922	22.9	78.1	22.6	4.1
04 12000	Chandler city	80.2	12.6	86,507	63.4	203,400	22.7	10.0	1,058	26.7	78.1	23.8	3.3
04 20540	Drexel Heights CDP	86.9	9.6	8,663	76.8	108,600	28.4	12.7	826	37.4	82.5	27.6	5.7
04 22220	El Mirage city	85.8	10.5	10,005	65.0	89,100	26.8	11.7	1,058	32.3	75.7	33.8	3.9
04 23620	Flagstaff city	70.0	16.3	22,385	44.9	263,300	23.8	10.0	1,001	35.8	62.3	15.2	6.7
04 23760	Florence town	63.1	32.9	5,273	70.1	103,600	22.7	10.2	860	29.4	. . .	0.0	6.0
04 25030	Fortuna Foothills CDP	85.2	13.5	12,932	85.9	118,100	21.8	10.0	1,304	27.2	83.4	21.5	1.8
04 25300	Fountain Hills town	86.8	7.2	10,215	84.2	327,000	27.8	10.0	1,117	26.4	79.2	26.7	1.3
04 27400	Gilbert town	78.8	14.4	69,703	70.4	212,000	23.3	10.0	1,261	26.5	77.0	26.7	2.2
04 27820	Glendale city	80.7	13.7	78,437	56.7	133,800	24.1	12.6	830	33.2	73.6	26.6	8.9
04 28380	Goodyear city	81.3	14.5	22,141	70.0	169,300	23.6	10.5	1,206	28.0	83.9	29.1	4.3
04 29710	Green Valley CDP	87.4	9.8	13,144	84.1	173,300	24.0	10.0	916	33.3	. . .	18.6	5.3
04 37620	Kingman city	70.7	12.1	10,880	63.3	110,700	22.5	11.5	847	24.7	75.7	16.9	10.1
04 39370	Lake Havasu City city	82.1	8.2	22,977	69.3	193,600	28.9	13.8	835	32.4	78.7	16.2	5.3
04 44270	Marana town	79.2	14.0	13,128	75.6	202,300	24.7	11.4	1,254	26.5	82.5	27.4	2.0
04 44440	Maricopa city	84.8	7.3	14,469	77.8	118,200	25.0	13.0	1,247	32.0	71.8	33.7	1.4
04 46000	Mesa city	78.6	11.4	165,344	60.6	140,500	24.4	11.0	852	31.7	77.5	24.8	7.7
04 49640	Nogales city	84.2	7.8	6,332	48.9	116,900	26.2	12.2	556	35.8	78.1	16.1	12.9
04 51600	Oro Valley town	83.3	11.5	16,684	71.9	284,500	23.8	10.0	1,019	27.5	78.6	26.4	3.8
04 54050	Peoria city	85.3	9.4	56,220	70.5	168,500	24.7	11.2	1,048	30.8	79.5	27.7	5.5
04 55000	Phoenix city	78.7	8.2	516,383	54.8	146,400	25.7	12.2	850	31.9	75.0	24.4	9.1
04 57380	Prescott city	77.7	13.9	19,284	63.2	261,500	27.6	12.3	775	34.5	73.8	18.3	9.0
04 57450	Prescott Valley town	77.6	15.9	15,177	58.7	160,900	26.2	10.1	799	33.7	80.1	22.0	6.0
04 58150	Queen Creek town	78.3	16.3	7,982	82.5	220,900	26.8	10.0	1,349	34.0	78.5	32.1	0.7
04 62140	Sahuarita town	84.6	7.5	9,417	79.4	188,300	24.3	12.2	1,195	27.6	77.4	27.4	1.8

1. A median value of $1,000,000 or more is represented as $1,000,000.
2. Median selected monthly owner costs of 10 percent or less as a percenage of household income is represented as 10.0
3. A median gross rent of $2,000 or more is represented as $2,000.
4. A median gross rent of 50 percent or more as a percentage of household income is represented as 50.0.

Table C-4. Cities — Where: Migration, Housing, and Transportation, 2010–2012—*Continued*

STATE and place code	STATE or city	Percent who lived in the same house one year ago	Percent who did not live in the same city one year ago	Total occupied housing units	Percent owner-occupied housing units	Median value of owner-occupied housing units (dollars)[1]	Median selected monthly owner costs as a percentage of household income[2] With a mortgage	Without a mortgage	Median gross rent (dollars)[2]	Median gross rent as a percentage of household income[4]	Percent of workers who drove alone to work	Mean travel time to work (minutes)	Percent of occupied housing units with no vehicle available
	ACS table number:	C07204	C07204	B25003	B25003	B25077	B25092	B25092	B25064	B25071	C08301	B08013/C08012	C25045
	Column number:	1	2	3	4	5	6	7	8	9	10	11	12
	Arizona—Cont.												
04 63470	San Luis city	89.9	9.0	6,866	77.7	113,000	30.2	15.3	480	32.9	73.4	23.7	10.1
04 64210	San Tan Valley CDP	74.1	21.6	23,627	71.9	118,100	26.5	10.0	1,150	29.8	81.0	39.9	2.0
04 65000	Scottsdale city	80.7	11.8	99,734	66.8	360,100	26.2	11.9	1,104	27.6	77.5	22.2	4.9
04 66820	Sierra Vista city	72.3	20.0	17,691	53.7	182,600	19.5	10.0	926	27.1	75.4	15.7	6.4
04 70320	Sun City CDP	86.2	11.0	22,943	79.9	113,600	26.5	11.0	934	43.6	82.5	27.5	8.0
04 70355	Sun City West CDP	91.1	6.5	14,922	88.6	177,100	24.5	10.0	1,070	48.6	. . .	24.1	7.0
04 71510	Surprise city	83.8	11.2	42,029	74.4	162,900	24.8	11.2	1,180	29.2	81.7	33.2	2.6
04 73000	Tempe city	66.3	22.8	63,328	44.2	189,500	23.5	10.0	890	32.2	72.1	20.4	10.0
04 77000	Tucson city	75.9	9.1	200,627	50.4	137,300	25.1	12.7	726	34.2	74.5	21.8	12.1
04 85540	Yuma city	74.1	12.2	33,492	60.1	129,500	26.2	11.9	874	32.4	76.4	16.1	6.4
05 00000	**Arkansas**	83.5	10.6	1,129,845	66.9	106,900	20.9	10.9	653	30.0	82.3	21.3	6.5
05 04840	Bella Vista town	84.6	10.7	11,423	87.5	148,100	18.8	10.2	991	43.0	. . .	25.1	1.9
05 05290	Benton city	84.1	10.6	11,794	71.4	137,400	20.9	11.5	728	28.6	83.4	24.9	8.0
05 05320	Bentonville city	72.6	20.3	13,779	56.9	158,300	18.9	10.0	702	24.9	82.6	16.4	5.8
05 10300	Cabot city	85.2	9.5	9,043	70.1	139,500	20.5	10.0	695	25.0	82.4	24.2	4.0
05 15190	Conway city	77.0	12.4	23,046	50.6	155,200	20.5	10.0	693	29.8	82.2	18.9	6.7
05 23290	Fayetteville city	65.1	20.0	32,050	42.0	174,200	21.0	10.0	685	34.0	70.9	17.9	7.8
05 24550	Fort Smith city	82.8	6.9	34,062	55.6	107,900	19.8	10.7	605	29.1	82.6	14.7	8.8
05 33400	Hot Springs city	76.8	10.9	14,791	54.3	120,000	27.0	11.5	655	32.6	76.1	16.9	14.6
05 34750	Jacksonville city	76.9	15.1	10,734	53.8	113,900	24.6	11.6	729	28.1	85.3	19.3	8.6
05 35710	Jonesboro city	70.5	12.2	26,359	55.1	135,800	19.6	10.3	641	32.4	86.7	15.8	7.9
05 41000	Little Rock city	82.7	6.5	79,047	57.1	151,900	21.9	11.7	758	31.7	84.2	17.8	7.6
05 50450	North Little Rock city	78.9	13.7	25,763	51.9	122,100	21.3	11.0	768	32.2	87.3	18.7	12.1
05 53390	Paragould city	74.8	9.9	10,627	53.5	97,900	21.9	11.3	637	29.7	86.5	16.9	5.2
05 55310	Pine Bluff city	80.2	7.0	18,107	54.0	70,300	20.7	13.9	641	34.5	82.3	18.5	10.1
05 60410	Rogers city	79.8	11.8	19,280	59.6	145,100	21.5	10.3	798	24.9	81.7	16.8	5.0
05 61670	Russellville city	77.6	14.6	9,723	58.5	124,200	22.7	10.0	632	34.8	79.2	14.0	7.0
05 63020	Searcy city	71.5	17.2	8,348	53.2	127,800	19.0	10.0	616	29.1	80.0	17.5	9.2
05 63800	Sherwood city	83.7	12.9	12,006	67.9	147,700	20.1	10.1	786	28.1	88.9	20.4	3.2
05 66080	Springdale city	76.6	11.8	24,286	53.8	124,400	21.8	11.1	693	29.3	76.9	18.0	6.2
05 68810	Texarkana city	74.3	11.3	11,887	59.6	93,700	20.6	11.2	673	29.8	87.2	18.6	10.3
05 71480	Van Buren city	78.3	14.3	8,549	66.2	112,100	23.0	10.1	624	30.2	83.2	18.9	4.9
05 74540	West Memphis city	72.0	9.8	9,505	47.6	87,500	23.0	11.6	665	39.1	80.7	18.1	14.3
06 00000	**California**	84.0	9.7	12,474,950	54.9	358,800	29.5	11.6	1,205	34.0	73.3	27.2	7.9
06 00296	Adelanto city	71.1	25.5	7,371	58.0	92,000	32.6	13.2	1,046	45.9	. . .	34.7	3.8
06 00394	Agoura Hills city	91.4	7.2	7,086	76.1	660,700	29.0	10.0	1,861	48.8	79.9	28.6	4.8
06 00562	Alameda city	81.8	12.5	29,709	47.7	613,300	27.8	10.0	1,309	29.4	61.5	28.1	9.3
06 00884	Alhambra city	86.7	10.0	29,065	39.5	476,000	30.3	10.6	1,173	32.2	79.7	30.2	8.0
06 00947	Aliso Viejo city	81.2	14.9	18,269	63.6	447,200	28.3	10.0	1,753	29.8	80.2	25.9	2.7
06 01290	Altadena CDP	90.5	8.8	15,025	71.7	549,000	27.6	10.0	1,380	32.7	78.7	26.6	4.5
06 02000	Anaheim city	83.3	9.7	98,137	47.2	392,300	30.0	10.0	1,322	36.9	75.6	26.6	7.5
06 02210	Antelope CDP	85.1	10.8	14,369	66.7	201,600	30.2	14.1	1,386	34.5	77.3	29.0	3.5
06 02252	Antioch city	79.9	9.3	32,064	61.8	222,200	29.8	10.5	1,310	37.3	73.1	39.2	6.5
06 02364	Apple Valley town	81.6	10.3	23,656	67.5	162,900	27.3	14.2	958	41.5	67.2	28.3	5.4
06 02462	Arcadia city	88.4	8.3	19,036	60.6	805,400	31.7	12.5	1,438	31.9	80.1	29.3	5.5
06 02553	Arden-Arcade CDP	75.6	17.0	40,088	44.8	268,400	26.8	10.2	856	36.0	76.1	22.2	11.3
06 02924	Arvin city	. . .	. . .	4,555	43.6	94,500	33.1	10.0	785	32.8	65.0	24.4	4.8
06 02980	Ashland CDP	82.6	14.7	7,606	31.9	260,700	35.2	11.0	1,103	35.1	70.6	33.1	11.4
06 03064	Atascadero city	85.0	12.6	11,077	61.9	375,900	29.3	10.0	1,109	33.2	79.7	20.8	4.5
06 03162	Atwater city	79.5	10.7	8,643	49.6	121,800	25.0	11.3	878	34.0	84.6	21.2	9.1
06 03386	Azusa city	82.5	12.9	11,286	50.0	296,200	30.2	10.9	1,177	35.3	68.5	27.4	8.3
06 03526	Bakersfield city	79.5	7.5	110,198	57.8	171,400	26.5	11.1	961	33.3	79.4	23.1	6.9
06 03666	Baldwin Park city	88.8	8.2	16,846	59.5	275,800	33.7	10.0	1,187	34.6	71.0	32.5	7.0
06 03820	Banning city	85.0	11.5	12,272	69.5	157,300	28.2	13.9	899	37.5	74.7	24.7	8.5
06 04030	Barstow city	79.3	5.4	8,094	49.2	96,900	20.3	10.0	746	32.4	67.7	25.4	14.3
06 04415	Bay Point CDP	87.6	11.2	6,695	50.6	145,800	30.0	10.0	1,145	39.7	69.2	34.2	5.8
06 04758	Beaumont city	88.0	6.9	12,821	78.7	198,400	31.2	11.3	1,037	40.6	84.1	29.7	3.3
06 04870	Bell city	90.0	8.2	8,844	29.0	270,200	38.0	10.8	988	39.3	72.5	30.1	10.6
06 04982	Bellflower city	86.7	8.6	23,088	37.3	337,300	32.0	10.8	1,155	37.4	77.9	28.9	8.2
06 04996	Bell Gardens city	90.0	5.4	9,868	22.6	263,200	32.3	10.0	1,085	38.1	71.7	28.6	10.9
06 05108	Belmont city	86.4	10.8	10,349	58.3	876,900	27.2	10.0	1,463	28.5	74.7	25.7	4.9
06 05290	Benicia city	82.3	10.1	10,412	70.2	399,200	25.4	10.0	1,346	29.7	75.6	28.6	3.1
06 06000	Berkeley city	69.1	19.9	44,826	41.7	695,200	25.9	11.5	1,267	34.9	38.0	26.6	21.7
06 06308	Beverly Hills city	86.2	10.4	14,252	40.4	1,000,000	36.9	14.6	1,880	30.8	72.0	24.9	8.2
06 07064	Bloomington CDP	. . .	. . .	5,007	76.7	165,300	34.4	10.0	1,109	36.8	74.2	31.3	1.9
06 07218	Blythe city	76.5	17.3	5,316	52.2	127,400	23.2	10.0	681	31.0	78.2	13.7	11.6
06 08058	Brawley city	82.7	4.5	7,307	57.0	129,400	27.7	14.3	692	33.1	80.9	19.7	9.9
06 08100	Brea city	85.2	12.2	13,856	62.4	518,200	28.7	10.0	1,450	31.4	80.8	27.9	3.7
06 08142	Brentwood city	84.5	9.8	16,342	71.9	338,800	30.1	17.9	1,822	31.0	76.0	39.9	1.7
06 08786	Buena Park city	86.3	11.0	22,947	57.1	380,600	28.7	10.3	1,348	35.8	74.3	29.6	5.1

1. A median value of $1,000,000 or more is represented as $1,000,000.
2. Median selected monthly owner costs of 10 percent or less as a percentage of household income is represented as 10.0
3. A median gross rent of $2,000 or more is represented as $2,000.
4. A median gross rent of 50 percent or more as a percentage of household income is represented as 50.0.

Table C-4. Cities — Where: Migration, Housing, and Transportation, 2010–2012—Continued

STATE and place code		STATE or city	Percent who lived in the same house one year ago	Percent who did not live in the same city one year ago	Total occupied housing units	Percent owner-occupied housing units	Median value of owner-occupied housing units (dollars)[1]	Median selected monthly owner costs as a percentage of household income[2]		Median gross rent (dollars)[2]	Median gross rent as a percentage of household income[4]	Percent of workers who drove alone to work	Mean travel time to work (minutes)	Percent of occupied housing units with no vehicle available
								With a mortgage	Without a mortgage					
		ACS table number:	C07204	C07204	B25003	B25003	B25077	B25092	B25092	B25064	B25071	C08301	B08013/ C08012	C25045
		Column number:	1	2	3	4	5	6	7	8	9	10	11	12
		California—Cont.												
06	08954	Burbank city	86.5	8.7	40,962	43.0	542,700	31.4	10.0	1,313	31.7	77.2	25.0	8.9
06	09066	Burlingame city	84.7	12.8	12,677	46.0	1,000,000	31.8	11.2	1,499	29.9	71.6	26.4	7.6
06	09598	Calabasas city	88.5	10.1	8,751	73.1	872,400	30.5	13.1	1,909	39.5	. . .	32.2	0.6
06	09710	Calexico city	89.1	3.2	9,139	53.8	150,200	30.6	11.2	801	37.7	73.3	26.2	11.8
06	10046	Camarillo city	85.3	8.6	23,854	70.5	446,500	27.2	10.6	1,550	33.9	83.8	22.8	4.9
06	10345	Campbell city	84.7	12.4	16,017	50.9	645,400	29.3	10.5	1,399	28.9	78.5	23.5	6.3
06	11194	Carlsbad city	85.3	11.7	42,299	61.3	606,100	28.6	10.8	1,612	33.3	78.7	28.6	3.3
06	11390	Carmichael CDP	81.9	12.9	25,430	55.1	270,300	27.3	10.0	912	35.9	79.2	24.4	9.9
06	11530	Carson city	87.2	9.7	24,849	75.0	337,000	30.1	10.0	1,308	31.9	79.5	27.1	5.0
06	11964	Castro Valley CDP	87.1	9.0	22,055	65.2	527,700	26.1	10.0	1,380	31.8	76.0	30.2	4.3
06	12048	Cathedral City city	81.5	8.1	16,141	61.6	172,300	33.8	18.1	1,115	34.8	72.7	20.4	5.9
06	12524	Ceres city	78.1	13.6	13,145	59.5	148,300	31.6	13.1	923	39.6	78.7	27.9	5.8
06	12552	Cerritos city	93.7	4.6	14,954	80.4	591,200	27.8	10.0	1,936	35.3	82.1	30.8	3.3
06	13014	Chico city	67.3	12.2	33,516	43.7	259,600	27.5	12.6	909	34.8	68.9	17.3	8.5
06	13210	Chino city	79.7	16.9	21,625	70.4	323,800	31.5	10.0	1,247	34.7	81.5	33.1	4.5
06	13214	Chino Hills city	88.8	7.9	22,897	81.1	474,100	29.4	10.0	1,763	35.1	77.2	36.6	3.4
06	13392	Chula Vista city	88.9	6.7	76,159	58.4	345,700	31.8	10.0	1,234	36.7	79.6	26.9	5.2
06	13588	Citrus Heights city	78.4	15.6	32,472	55.1	184,500	29.2	11.0	1,003	30.5	78.0	25.8	6.1
06	13756	Claremont city	84.4	13.5	11,865	65.5	532,800	26.6	10.8	1,245	30.1	66.2	28.8	7.0
06	14218	Clovis city	85.6	9.8	33,284	61.3	240,100	27.4	12.1	1,018	33.3	84.8	20.5	5.8
06	14260	Coachella city	88.4	6.5	9,000	65.7	137,400	32.1	17.7	863	40.0	79.3	21.5	3.9
06	14890	Colton city	81.6	12.3	14,485	50.9	156,600	29.8	12.5	962	39.7	79.9	27.2	8.2
06	15044	Compton city	87.0	8.4	23,387	53.7	233,100	34.0	14.4	1,037	40.4	68.1	27.7	8.6
06	16000	Concord city	84.5	9.0	44,492	59.8	348,700	28.8	12.0	1,248	33.5	70.2	30.3	6.5
06	16224	Corcoran city	78.5	17.6	3,610	42.6	116,500	27.6	10.9	774	31.8	79.2	17.9	9.7
06	16350	Corona city	87.7	8.2	44,071	66.7	316,800	28.6	12.5	1,302	33.4	78.1	35.0	3.8
06	16378	Coronado city	78.4	17.9	8,983	45.0	1,000,000	33.9	12.8	1,938	30.5	64.2	19.4	4.9
06	16532	Costa Mesa city	83.4	10.8	40,576	39.4	570,800	30.2	10.0	1,480	32.9	76.8	22.3	5.2
06	16742	Covina city	84.7	13.6	15,418	57.9	364,500	31.4	10.9	1,207	35.6	76.0	31.4	4.9
06	17498	Cudahy city	. . .	. . .	5,671	17.0	210,400	35.6	11.7	1,121	36.9	64.7	31.8	10.1
06	17568	Culver City city	84.9	12.5	16,613	54.5	610,100	29.3	10.8	1,562	29.4	78.6	24.9	6.6
06	17610	Cupertino city	83.9	12.0	20,868	64.2	1,000,000	26.6	10.0	2,000	21.8	79.7	24.7	3.5
06	17750	Cypress city	87.9	9.8	15,633	65.1	485,800	27.8	10.0	1,566	32.2	80.9	28.7	3.6
06	17918	Daly City city	87.1	9.0	30,731	55.2	545,900	32.5	10.2	1,482	34.2	61.6	27.7	8.2
06	17946	Dana Point city	79.9	14.3	14,521	56.4	684,600	28.8	12.2	1,736	34.2	75.0	27.4	3.6
06	17988	Danville town	90.9	6.4	15,796	85.0	826,300	28.4	12.4	2,000	32.1	76.0	31.2	3.3
06	18100	Davis city	67.7	17.2	23,693	45.0	530,800	22.8	10.0	1,227	46.0	57.5	20.8	9.7
06	18394	Delano city	77.6	12.7	10,335	52.5	128,800	31.6	15.1	752	33.7	69.3	21.2	5.3
06	18996	Desert Hot Springs city	70.9	13.7	8,799	44.3	127,500	31.8	13.9	891	38.8	74.5	32.2	9.0
06	19192	Diamond Bar city	87.9	8.9	17,275	80.1	507,900	29.6	11.3	1,722	34.4	78.3	34.7	2.5
06	19318	Dinuba city	83.3	8.6	5,864	53.4	139,300	31.4	14.7	770	30.6	70.6	23.5	12.0
06	19766	Downey city	87.1	7.5	33,044	49.5	403,800	31.9	10.0	1,201	35.4	83.3	27.7	4.6
06	19990	Duarte city	91.2	7.9	7,058	65.0	348,400	31.7	10.0	1,171	32.9	79.3	28.8	6.4
06	20018	Dublin city	78.8	17.0	15,349	63.0	536,900	28.1	10.6	1,743	25.6	73.1	29.1	4.4
06	20802	East Los Angeles CDP	91.7	6.2	30,816	34.0	283,900	34.6	10.0	951	36.0	65.2	28.5	14.2
06	20956	East Palo Alto city	81.9	13.8	6,808	39.8	350,100	36.8	13.3	1,204	38.7	69.5	23.6	6.3
06	21230	Eastvale CDP	86.5	11.1	12,454	80.9	380,200	31.9	14.6	2,000	29.9	77.8	41.1	2.2
06	21712	El Cajon city	80.3	13.3	31,995	37.5	309,200	28.8	12.9	1,070	38.3	80.2	23.5	9.7
06	21782	El Centro city	80.8	7.4	12,774	52.7	140,800	24.8	12.3	732	37.4	79.1	20.3	11.2
06	21796	El Cerrito city	86.2	11.7	10,210	59.8	580,000	27.3	10.0	1,406	32.5	52.5	32.0	8.7
06	21880	El Dorado Hills CDP	90.8	6.1	14,122	85.3	449,400	28.2	13.6	1,781	28.7	78.2	30.7	1.9
06	22020	Elk Grove city	83.8	8.0	47,132	72.1	250,000	27.1	11.2	1,442	31.6	75.1	30.3	2.9
06	22230	El Monte city	90.3	5.8	28,995	40.5	341,400	33.4	11.1	1,063	39.8	72.3	30.6	9.7
06	22300	El Paso de Robles (Paso Robles)	76.5	13.0	11,495	52.9	340,800	31.4	13.0	1,117	32.3	78.7	22.7	3.5
06	22678	Encinitas city	86.1	10.0	22,544	65.1	692,800	29.3	10.1	1,694	31.6	74.6	24.1	2.2
06	22804	Escondido city	87.3	6.4	44,581	49.0	321,200	31.6	12.7	1,160	40.1	78.9	24.5	7.4
06	23042	Eureka city	76.7	13.7	10,914	44.5	253,800	29.5	10.0	786	36.5	74.7	14.0	11.6
06	23182	Fairfield city	80.4	10.4	34,199	58.7	248,200	30.2	10.2	1,268	33.6	74.4	27.1	4.9
06	23294	Fair Oaks CDP	83.7	13.3	13,021	65.1	350,300	26.7	10.0	1,046	36.4	78.4	26.0	2.3
06	23462	Fallbrook CDP	84.3	11.5	10,885	55.3	365,900	34.3	12.2	1,026	33.6	69.3	27.0	7.4
06	24477	Florence-Graham CDP	89.9	8.2	14,181	37.4	232,600	34.8	10.2	969	43.2	68.1	31.4	15.4
06	24498	Florin CDP	79.5	17.0	14,986	52.7	136,500	28.2	14.5	973	37.4	73.7	26.1	9.4
06	24638	Folsom city	84.8	10.5	24,700	67.4	364,800	25.7	12.3	1,355	26.2	78.8	24.0	3.8
06	24680	Fontana city	85.5	8.7	48,176	68.4	236,800	30.4	10.7	1,079	38.5	77.7	32.7	4.2
06	24722	Foothill Farms CDP	75.6	18.7	12,189	54.3	154,400	30.1	13.1	998	36.3	77.7	27.6	6.2
06	25338	Foster City city	82.7	11.6	12,012	59.3	823,800	27.8	12.4	2,000	25.3	75.6	25.6	3.4
06	25380	Fountain Valley city	89.5	8.5	18,581	71.9	598,900	26.9	10.0	1,532	34.6	83.1	24.6	5.7
06	26000	Fremont city	86.6	7.7	70,645	63.1	586,300	26.7	10.0	1,538	26.4	74.4	29.4	4.2
06	26067	French Valley CDP	. . .	. . .	7,247	73.7	265,000	34.3	17.5	2,000	29.2	81.8	40.3	1.0
06	27000	Fresno city	80.3	5.9	157,154	47.7	174,000	27.4	11.5	874	36.8	77.5	21.7	11.3
06	28000	Fullerton city	79.5	13.5	43,938	54.7	476,300	29.5	10.0	1,320	34.9	76.8	28.7	4.1

1. A median value of $1,000,000 or more is represented as $1,000,000.
2. Median selected monthly owner costs of 10 percent or less as a percentage of household income is represented as 10.0
3. A median gross rent of $2,000 or more is represented as $2,000.
4. A median gross rent of 50 percent or more as a percentage of household income is represented as 50.0.

Table C-4. Cities — Where: Migration, Housing, and Transportation, 2010–2012—*Continued*

STATE and place code		STATE or city	Percent who lived in the same house one year ago	Percent who did not live in the same city one year ago	Total occupied housing units	Percent owner-occupied housing units	Median value of owner-occupied housing units (dollars)[1]	Median selected monthly owner costs as a percentage of household income[2]		Median gross rent (dollars)[2]	Median gross rent as a percentage of household income[4]	Percent of workers who drove alone to work	Mean travel time to work (minutes)	Percent of occupied housing units with no vehicle available
								With a mortgage	Without a mortgage				B08013/ C08012	
		ACS table number:	C07204	C07204	B25003	B25003	B25077	B25092	B25092	B25064	B25071	C08301		C25045
		Column number:	1	2	3	4	5	6	7	8	9	10	11	12
		California—Cont.												
06	28112	Galt city	83.7	6.5	7,447	69.1	183,400	29.9	10.2	960	32.3	78.9	28.9	4.5
06	28168	Gardena city	89.0	9.8	21,004	50.3	331,300	31.2	11.8	1,101	32.2	81.0	26.1	8.6
06	29000	Garden Grove city	88.2	7.9	46,227	55.7	389,400	29.8	10.0	1,311	34.8	78.3	26.6	5.8
06	29504	Gilroy city	85.7	7.3	14,694	59.4	421,100	30.0	12.7	1,305	32.7	71.6	29.1	6.7
06	30000	Glendale city	87.7	7.6	69,678	37.9	582,000	33.5	11.3	1,262	39.6	74.9	26.7	12.3
06	30014	Glendora city	89.5	7.7	16,358	68.9	456,200	31.9	10.5	1,400	33.0	82.1	30.5	4.5
06	30378	Goleta city	83.0	12.7	11,056	53.1	598,100	28.9	10.1	1,530	30.3	70.1	16.8	5.4
06	30693	Granite Bay CDP	. . .	. . .	7,529	90.5	579,500	29.8	16.8	1,881	32.2	81.5	27.1	1.9
06	31596	Hacienda Heights CDP	92.8	6.2	16,243	78.7	449,100	29.8	11.2	1,594	36.6	79.6	36.2	3.4
06	31960	Hanford city	84.2	5.8	16,812	57.6	168,800	25.5	10.5	937	31.0	79.9	20.1	6.8
06	32548	Hawthorne city	84.1	10.6	28,451	26.3	383,500	32.8	10.0	1,006	34.9	77.5	28.0	10.3
06	33000	Hayward city	82.7	10.7	44,815	53.5	316,200	30.2	10.3	1,244	35.5	73.2	28.8	6.8
06	33182	Hemet city	75.1	15.5	30,500	58.4	109,700	29.5	14.9	913	44.8	78.3	30.0	12.4
06	33308	Hercules city	84.6	12.9	8,013	77.9	350,600	29.1	10.3	1,409	40.2	68.3	38.2	3.1
06	33434	Hesperia city	82.6	11.1	26,419	62.3	137,200	28.7	12.5	985	39.7	67.6	37.0	6.2
06	33588	Highland city	82.1	11.7	14,716	61.8	228,200	27.5	11.9	958	37.1	80.5	25.5	6.9
06	34120	Hollister city	79.4	9.8	10,036	58.6	276,600	32.9	11.0	1,290	34.3	72.8	29.7	3.5
06	36000	Huntington Beach city	86.4	8.0	73,787	58.4	616,700	28.9	10.7	1,521	31.5	82.2	27.1	4.0
06	36056	Huntington Park city	88.2	7.3	14,668	26.3	275,000	39.1	10.0	913	38.3	60.8	29.9	17.5
06	36294	Imperial Beach city	77.3	17.7	8,571	31.5	332,200	29.5	10.0	1,146	33.9	74.6	26.3	11.5
06	36448	Indio city	77.3	11.2	23,282	63.5	187,600	30.9	13.8	925	37.6	78.5	22.4	6.5
06	36546	Inglewood city	87.4	9.0	36,350	35.1	316,200	35.7	11.9	1,068	38.1	73.9	28.3	10.0
06	36770	Irvine city	78.2	14.4	79,235	48.9	646,500	27.4	10.0	1,809	29.2	79.4	23.5	3.5
06	36868	Isla Vista CDP	27.3	49.3	5,186	1.8	368,300	. . .	. . .	1,366	50.0	30.2	14.1	14.2
06	37692	Jurupa Valley city	85.2	10.7	24,054	63.8	211,900	30.1	13.1	1,085	35.5	78.0	30.4	5.4
06	39003	La Cañada Flintridge city	. . .	. . .	6,746	90.2	1,000,000	29.4	10.2	1,986	31.0	80.2	26.8	0.6
06	39045	La Crescenta-Montrose CDP	. . .	. . .	7,071	65.4	608,700	32.0	10.0	1,280	26.9	81.3	28.4	5.1
06	39114	Ladera Ranch CDP	88.1	8.7	7,445	70.2	602,100	29.1	11.6	1,935	30.7	. . .	29.7	2.6
06	39122	Lafayette city	92.4	5.7	9,315	74.4	960,900	27.5	10.3	1,563	27.3	66.9	29.4	2.7
06	39178	Laguna Beach city	87.8	8.6	11,289	62.4	1,000,000	29.9	11.8	1,827	32.4	75.7	27.9	2.8
06	39220	Laguna Hills city	85.3	13.2	10,808	72.4	555,400	29.4	10.4	1,774	40.4	77.6	25.2	5.8
06	39248	Laguna Niguel city	86.2	10.8	23,951	72.0	652,500	29.1	10.0	1,761	34.5	78.6	28.4	2.8
06	39290	La Habra city	86.7	7.7	18,677	55.5	367,200	29.2	11.4	1,246	37.1	77.9	28.6	5.2
06	39486	Lake Elsinore city	80.4	11.8	13,959	66.6	196,800	30.6	14.5	1,230	34.5	75.9	41.7	4.2
06	39496	Lake Forest city	88.8	9.0	27,440	71.0	480,500	27.5	11.2	1,637	30.0	83.5	25.6	2.8
06	39766	Lakeside CDP	88.9	9.2	7,144	73.6	317,300	29.8	16.1	1,090	29.4	86.4	27.0	4.0
06	39892	Lakewood city	88.3	10.1	26,665	70.9	409,400	28.0	10.0	1,455	32.6	81.6	27.1	3.6
06	40004	La Mesa city	76.0	18.8	23,220	45.8	365,800	27.4	10.9	1,213	35.7	80.9	23.4	8.8
06	40032	La Mirada city	89.9	8.5	14,042	78.6	390,000	29.3	10.1	1,505	34.3	81.7	29.5	2.7
06	40130	Lancaster city	86.7	8.0	47,311	59.2	155,800	28.4	14.5	1,012	36.9	82.5	29.7	7.3
06	40326	La Presa CDP	92.2	6.3	10,118	61.8	265,400	31.2	10.0	1,203	33.9	80.4	26.9	5.9
06	40340	La Puente city	88.1	9.9	9,206	56.7	271,100	31.6	10.0	1,224	33.9	74.8	32.5	7.4
06	40354	La Quinta city	88.4	7.7	15,157	73.2	328,600	32.5	17.0	1,343	33.5	79.8	23.6	4.4
06	40830	La Verne city	88.2	9.6	10,876	73.0	429,200	27.5	13.5	1,231	32.1	76.6	29.5	4.9
06	40886	Lawndale city	. . .	. . .	9,496	31.6	341,400	34.9	14.0	1,304	37.4	77.5	23.4	6.7
06	41124	Lemon Grove city	92.0	6.3	7,959	52.5	286,900	33.2	11.8	1,122	36.3	78.8	26.3	6.9
06	41152	Lemoore city	80.6	13.7	8,020	53.9	199,700	26.7	10.0	859	29.0	82.4	21.8	5.6
06	41180	Lennox CDP	. . .	. . .	5,259	29.4	292,900	37.0	11.8	956	38.9	67.9	26.4	10.6
06	41474	Lincoln city	88.5	8.9	16,683	78.0	307,800	32.5	12.9	1,514	31.8	79.8	28.3	2.6
06	41992	Livermore city	86.8	8.0	28,999	69.2	464,200	26.8	10.0	1,424	28.5	79.7	27.8	4.0
06	42202	Lodi city	80.3	6.8	21,871	51.2	223,500	26.2	13.6	987	34.4	78.0	22.2	7.6
06	42370	Loma Linda city	82.6	13.8	8,657	39.3	272,000	26.4	10.0	1,088	29.0	81.3	18.9	6.6
06	42468	Lomita city	81.8	15.4	7,763	41.2	455,000	29.5	10.4	1,209	30.0	73.9	23.2	7.7
06	42524	Lompoc city	81.6	9.3	13,375	47.6	228,700	29.2	10.6	941	32.5	66.4	25.5	10.3
06	43000	Long Beach city	80.6	8.9	159,984	40.1	421,300	29.7	10.0	1,086	33.8	73.1	28.4	10.7
06	43280	Los Altos city	91.6	7.7	11,250	84.5	1,000,000	27.7	10.0	2,000	26.9	78.1	22.7	3.3
06	44000	Los Angeles city	84.8	5.6	1,317,210	37.0	437,600	34.2	13.5	1,159	36.8	67.0	29.3	13.5
06	44028	Los Banos city	77.4	10.5	10,098	52.4	139,900	27.5	14.0	1,062	35.4	76.7	42.2	5.6
06	44112	Los Gatos town	85.7	9.7	12,148	62.2	1,000,000	26.5	10.0	1,689	26.3	81.1	24.3	2.8
06	44574	Lynwood city	90.6	7.0	14,836	47.5	263,800	35.8	13.0	1,012	41.1	70.9	28.5	8.0
06	45022	Madera city	87.6	3.9	16,067	50.1	153,900	31.3	10.0	839	32.4	73.8	23.1	11.2
06	45400	Manhattan Beach city	88.9	7.6	14,463	67.3	1,000,000	25.9	10.0	1,885	24.9	79.2	27.5	2.1
06	45484	Manteca city	81.3	11.3	22,128	58.8	204,200	29.5	12.8	1,183	33.6	80.5	31.2	3.8
06	45778	Marina city	79.5	15.9	6,612	45.9	349,400	31.0	11.0	1,110	31.7	75.3	23.6	6.4
06	46114	Martinez city	88.5	9.1	13,791	66.7	385,800	27.7	10.0	1,361	30.3	78.5	27.7	2.4
06	46492	Maywood city	. . .	. . .	6,283	26.4	279,000	34.4	10.0	996	36.7	67.5	27.3	12.1
06	46646	Mead Valley CDP	84.9	9.7	4,433	63.2	159,600	28.4	13.8	1,109	42.3	72.6	34.7	4.4
06	46842	Menifee city	80.9	12.4	26,686	77.4	187,500	30.8	13.8	1,305	39.7	76.1	37.9	3.9
06	46870	Menlo Park city	86.1	12.3	12,483	53.0	1,000,000	27.4	10.0	1,712	25.1	74.0	20.8	4.8
06	46898	Merced city	81.1	6.9	24,542	45.1	138,100	25.2	10.9	811	35.0	79.8	21.7	10.0
06	47486	Millbrae city	90.4	7.2	7,863	64.3	877,700	32.1	12.6	1,646	30.6	69.9	27.9	7.0
06	47766	Milpitas city	84.6	11.0	19,280	64.5	509,700	28.6	10.0	1,690	28.4	81.1	23.5	3.5

1. A median value of $1,000,000 or more is represented as $1,000,000.
2. Median selected monthly owner costs of 10 percent or less as a percentage of household income is represented as 10.0.
3. A median gross rent of $2,000 or more is represented as $2,000.
4. A median gross rent of 50 percent or more as a percentage of household income is represented as 50.0.

Table C-4. Cities — Where: Migration, Housing, and Transportation, 2010–2012—*Continued*

STATE and place code		STATE or city	Percent who lived in the same house one year ago	Percent who did not live in the same city one year ago	Total occupied housing units	Percent owner-occupied housing units	Median value of owner-occupied housing units (dollars)[1]	Median selected monthly owner costs as a percentage of household income[2] With a mortgage	Without a mortgage	Median gross rent (dollars)[2]	Median gross rent as a percentage of household income[4]	Percent of workers who drove alone to work	Mean travel time to work (minutes)	Percent of occupied housing units with no vehicle available
		ACS table number:	C07204	C07204	B25003	B25003	B25077	B25092	B25092	B25064	B25071	C08301	B08013/ C08012	C25045
		Column number:	1	2	3	4	5	6	7	8	9	10	11	12
		California—Cont.												
06	48256	Mission Viejo city	88.4	9.1	33,255	75.5	536,600	28.2	10.0	1,815	34.0	80.3	26.7	4.1
06	48354	Modesto city	78.5	9.3	68,814	53.0	161,600	28.2	11.5	990	37.0	81.2	25.6	8.7
06	48648	Monrovia city	85.6	11.3	13,318	50.4	534,200	29.4	13.3	1,314	29.2	80.0	27.9	4.9
06	48788	Montclair city	89.6	9.3	9,980	59.5	240,700	33.7	12.5	1,056	34.6	82.0	31.0	8.2
06	48816	Montebello city	89.8	7.7	19,133	44.4	376,500	32.5	10.8	1,102	34.7	76.2	34.7	12.3
06	48872	Monterey city	69.4	26.0	11,812	32.1	593,200	28.2	10.0	1,336	31.9	58.8	16.4	6.3
06	48914	Monterey Park city	88.2	8.0	18,426	50.9	473,000	30.5	10.6	1,233	32.7	77.6	28.8	8.4
06	49138	Moorpark city	89.0	8.1	10,475	75.4	522,000	29.0	12.5	1,730	37.4	81.4	25.4	2.1
06	49270	Moreno Valley city	79.7	10.1	50,180	60.8	171,000	31.0	12.4	1,250	39.4	81.2	33.7	5.1
06	49278	Morgan Hill city	86.5	9.2	12,455	71.5	568,100	28.5	11.8	1,537	36.9	72.9	31.6	3.3
06	49670	Mountain View city	80.4	15.0	31,736	40.7	749,200	24.5	10.1	1,551	25.2	72.4	20.6	6.8
06	50076	Murrieta city	77.8	15.9	32,215	67.7	267,700	30.2	13.7	1,542	33.0	80.7	34.3	2.3
06	50258	Napa city	86.0	5.5	28,315	55.1	380,600	29.9	12.5	1,254	33.5	77.9	21.5	6.1
06	50398	National City city	89.1	7.3	16,004	34.5	264,200	35.0	10.0	924	35.5	67.1	24.0	14.1
06	50916	Newark city	92.1	5.9	13,086	67.1	418,500	29.1	10.0	1,476	28.9	77.6	26.0	3.2
06	51182	Newport Beach city	80.8	13.2	38,093	55.2	1,000,000	32.0	10.8	1,885	28.3	80.9	23.6	2.7
06	51560	Norco city	86.1	11.5	7,127	77.9	369,800	31.3	10.5	1,760	33.2	76.7	35.2	4.2
06	51924	North Highlands CDP	75.6	17.5	14,772	48.9	142,300	27.8	11.7	957	39.2	74.3	27.6	9.5
06	52379	North Tustin CDP	90.9	8.5	8,937	89.9	760,800	26.7	10.0	2,000	24.8	82.2	24.9	2.0
06	52526	Norwalk city	89.8	5.9	26,703	65.0	306,300	30.3	10.0	1,227	33.9	79.8	28.2	6.6
06	52582	Novato city	86.3	9.2	20,743	66.3	515,700	33.3	12.1	1,597	34.0	70.9	27.6	3.7
06	52694	Oakdale city	73.4	13.1	7,130	54.4	191,700	29.6	10.2	1,101	32.1	84.9	25.5	6.3
06	53000	Oakland city	83.2	8.1	154,737	40.0	420,400	30.4	12.7	1,068	33.1	55.3	28.3	18.2
06	53070	Oakley city	91.7	7.5	11,089	74.8	222,100	29.3	12.6	1,306	38.3	77.2	39.5	4.8
06	53322	Oceanside city	81.8	10.8	57,210	57.0	339,600	30.4	11.8	1,394	34.9	77.8	27.9	5.3
06	53448	Oildale CDP	70.3	17.2	11,507	44.1	119,800	27.8	14.2	797	38.7	80.4	23.0	12.2
06	53896	Ontario city	85.1	9.4	44,255	54.2	239,800	33.0	12.1	1,223	34.3	76.7	29.3	4.3
06	53980	Orange city	82.7	11.6	43,294	58.3	496,000	29.2	10.0	1,456	34.2	79.6	25.2	4.5
06	54092	Orangevale CDP	85.4	11.8	12,607	72.5	241,700	30.6	12.2	1,191	37.8	81.6	25.0	2.6
06	54120	Orcutt CDP	88.7	7.0	10,973	76.0	318,900	27.2	15.1	1,589	31.3	84.6	22.1	3.3
06	54652	Oxnard city	87.1	4.7	50,022	54.4	317,100	29.8	11.5	1,272	35.8	71.5	22.7	5.5
06	54806	Pacifica city	90.0	6.9	14,169	69.4	598,800	28.8	10.0	1,722	27.5	74.6	28.3	3.6
06	55156	Palmdale city	82.8	8.8	40,762	62.7	167,600	30.2	13.2	1,159	41.8	73.9	39.4	6.2
06	55184	Palm Desert city	82.8	13.8	23,489	65.8	291,900	30.6	17.9	1,094	32.5	74.8	19.8	7.5
06	55254	Palm Springs city	80.1	12.1	22,648	56.9	267,200	30.6	18.6	953	35.2	72.6	21.1	7.5
06	55282	Palo Alto city	82.7	13.0	26,426	55.7	1,000,000	24.6	10.0	1,897	26.4	63.8	22.4	6.4
06	55520	Paradise town	87.6	7.5	11,657	69.5	196,600	29.3	15.3	858	40.8	79.6	20.4	6.1
06	55618	Paramount city	86.5	9.0	13,378	41.0	257,500	33.6	10.0	1,163	37.6	76.3	26.8	6.4
06	56000	Pasadena city	81.2	13.3	54,371	44.1	609,000	28.6	12.3	1,337	29.5	71.8	25.8	10.8
06	56112	Patterson city	85.4	7.6	5,624	66.4	156,400	32.5	12.9	1,330	32.2	75.5	40.8	3.0
06	56700	Perris city	82.9	10.2	15,842	62.8	144,700	34.6	11.1	1,193	45.0	78.2	35.0	4.0
06	56784	Petaluma city	86.9	6.8	21,318	64.7	419,000	27.5	12.6	1,423	32.8	72.6	29.7	5.3
06	56924	Pico Rivera city	89.4	8.4	16,262	67.2	320,600	31.2	10.0	1,262	35.7	79.8	28.0	7.6
06	57456	Pittsburg city	82.1	10.8	19,267	58.1	209,400	29.3	13.2	1,270	37.3	66.3	34.8	5.6
06	57526	Placentia city	85.6	11.2	15,579	65.1	493,000	30.1	10.2	1,447	36.8	79.7	27.1	4.6
06	57764	Pleasant Hill city	83.7	13.9	13,712	57.1	485,000	27.4	11.8	1,414	30.7	69.9	30.3	8.5
06	57792	Pleasanton city	87.6	8.9	24,715	69.9	696,600	27.0	10.0	1,612	28.5	72.4	29.4	2.6
06	58072	Pomona city	84.3	10.3	37,883	53.6	247,100	33.7	12.7	1,094	39.0	72.4	29.1	7.1
06	58240	Porterville city	86.8	5.0	15,749	59.3	142,700	27.1	13.1	770	33.1	78.5	22.3	6.5
06	58296	Port Hueneme city	79.2	16.2	7,032	42.0	286,500	34.4	17.1	1,382	37.4	65.7	24.3	6.8
06	58520	Poway city	88.4	7.5	15,675	75.4	479,600	26.7	11.6	1,436	31.6	82.5	24.5	5.6
06	59346	Ramona CDP	85.4	11.0	6,387	62.8	355,200	31.5	15.5	1,103	34.4	77.3	30.7	3.9
06	59444	Rancho Cordova city	77.2	13.1	23,679	57.0	182,800	27.8	10.9	930	32.9	76.6	24.5	6.8
06	59451	Rancho Cucamonga city	82.0	11.9	54,680	65.4	348,900	28.8	12.3	1,394	33.5	79.1	30.0	3.9
06	59514	Rancho Palos Verdes city	91.0	8.1	15,535	80.7	958,500	25.3	10.0	2,000	36.9	81.5	32.4	2.2
06	59550	Rancho San Diego CDP	85.1	12.3	8,358	71.3	476,400	32.2	10.3	1,564	41.1	82.3	24.9	4.5
06	59587	Rancho Santa Margarita city	86.8	9.2	16,759	71.7	480,500	27.7	16.8	1,677	31.3	84.4	27.8	3.9
06	59920	Redding city	76.7	10.4	34,623	53.0	218,100	27.8	14.0	943	37.5	82.6	17.7	9.4
06	59962	Redlands city	82.6	13.0	24,485	60.5	279,800	26.3	10.0	1,099	30.2	80.4	23.2	5.2
06	60018	Redondo Beach city	85.0	9.5	28,666	51.9	708,900	28.1	10.0	1,641	29.1	81.9	26.8	4.6
06	60102	Redwood City city	86.5	8.3	27,731	51.3	750,400	29.7	12.2	1,462	33.5	75.0	23.3	5.3
06	60242	Reedley city	87.0	8.6	6,291	60.6	165,700	22.2	11.1	851	33.4	70.3	21.9	7.3
06	60466	Rialto city	82.4	10.2	24,269	62.9	169,400	31.1	12.6	1,065	38.3	78.4	31.5	5.7
06	60620	Richmond city	82.4	11.8	36,317	49.2	258,200	31.0	10.4	1,153	34.6	62.8	31.1	10.2
06	60704	Ridgecrest city	82.0	7.0	10,856	58.2	180,900	19.2	10.0	804	27.4	79.1	14.7	6.2
06	61068	Riverbank city	88.5	6.0	6,526	66.9	162,600	29.5	13.7	1,035	35.2	80.9	24.6	4.1
06	62000	Riverside city	81.3	9.9	89,588	55.9	226,500	28.6	10.0	1,097	37.3	77.1	29.0	5.7
06	62364	Rocklin city	83.5	11.9	21,467	66.0	308,200	28.1	15.0	1,272	35.2	82.7	27.6	4.0
06	62546	Rohnert Park city	81.6	13.0	15,875	51.9	299,600	30.6	12.7	1,183	34.5	80.7	28.6	5.4

1. A median value of $1,000,000 or more is represented as $1,000,000.
2. Median selected monthly owner costs of 10 percent or less as a percenage of household income is represented as 10.0
3. A median gross rent of $2,000 or more is represented as $2,000.
4. A median gross rent of 50 percent or more as a percentage of household income is represented as 50.0.

STATE and place code		STATE or city	Percent who lived in the same house one year ago	Percent who did not live in the same city one year ago	Total occupied housing units	Percent owner-occupied housing units	Median value of owner-occupied housing units (dollars)[1]	Median selected monthly owner costs as a percentage of household income[2] With a mortgage	Without a mortgage	Median gross rent (dollars)[2]	Median gross rent as a percentage of household income[4]	Percent of workers who drove alone to work	Mean travel time to work (minutes)	Percent of occupied housing units with no vehicle available
		ACS table number:	C07204	C07204	B25003	B25003	B25077	B25092	B25092	B25064	B25071	C08301	B08013/ C08012	C25045
		Column number:	1	2	3	4	5	6	7	8	9	10	11	12
		California—Cont.												
06	62896	Rosemead city	90.5	6.4	14,271	46.7	429,600	37.1	10.0	1,164	46.6	77.3	28.1	6.7
06	62910	Rosemont CDP	80.0	19.0	8,610	58.8	178,800	26.8	10.1	997	38.5	76.0	25.9	8.0
06	62938	Roseville city	82.5	10.1	45,049	64.6	300,200	26.7	13.7	1,211	32.1	79.3	26.0	4.4
06	63218	Rowland Heights CDP	88.7	8.0	14,408	67.4	477,900	31.5	12.8	1,276	36.5	73.3	32.9	4.8
06	64000	Sacramento city	77.6	10.6	175,723	48.2	218,200	28.3	10.1	978	33.9	72.6	24.0	10.6
06	64224	Salinas city	85.7	3.8	40,959	42.6	247,200	32.5	10.0	1,098	34.7	70.7	23.0	7.1
06	65000	San Bernardino city	78.1	11.2	57,865	49.3	141,800	28.8	11.6	910	39.9	74.1	27.2	11.9
06	65028	San Bruno city	89.5	7.8	14,672	56.7	605,500	29.9	10.5	1,606	29.1	71.6	24.3	5.1
06	65042	San Buenaventura (Ventura) city	86.1	6.7	41,174	54.4	414,400	27.2	10.9	1,317	32.9	75.6	22.2	6.0
06	65070	San Carlos city	90.2	8.3	11,413	71.0	906,200	27.2	11.6	1,488	28.1	77.8	25.4	3.3
06	65084	San Clemente city	81.1	11.0	24,286	63.9	696,200	31.6	10.0	1,652	33.3	73.0	30.6	3.0
06	66000	San Diego city	81.4	8.7	469,700	47.9	434,500	28.9	10.0	1,309	32.9	74.9	22.4	7.4
06	66070	San Dimas city	83.8	13.8	11,698	72.6	414,600	28.7	10.3	1,500	35.7	78.4	32.9	6.0
06	66140	San Fernando city	92.6	5.3	6,187	59.7	274,200	33.1	10.0	1,026	38.8	76.3	26.2	8.4
06	67000	San Francisco city	83.8	7.8	341,721	36.4	737,700	29.7	11.0	1,463	28.6	36.6	30.5	30.7
06	67042	San Gabriel city	85.9	10.4	12,174	48.7	549,400	28.8	13.2	1,250	35.2	75.7	27.7	9.2
06	67056	Sanger city	. . .	. . .	6,998	54.2	157,800	27.3	13.7	942	36.5	76.4	24.1	10.2
06	67112	San Jacinto city	83.5	13.2	13,113	67.2	135,000	29.2	12.9	1,005	41.7	80.2	36.3	6.7
06	68000	San Jose city	85.1	6.5	305,787	57.2	546,300	28.5	10.4	1,441	31.5	78.4	25.9	5.5
06	68028	San Juan Capistrano city	85.5	8.3	11,538	73.4	500,400	33.6	14.2	1,692	46.7	70.8	24.0	5.7
06	68084	San Leandro city	86.7	7.2	30,496	55.4	360,000	28.9	10.0	1,234	30.1	71.9	28.3	6.8
06	68112	San Lorenzo CDP	89.1	9.8	7,362	73.7	337,200	29.5	10.0	1,427	29.3	73.0	29.0	6.3
06	68154	San Luis Obispo city	62.9	17.8	17,774	36.8	493,800	28.8	10.1	1,227	41.2	71.0	15.0	7.2
06	68196	San Marcos city	88.6	8.0	27,752	59.7	360,100	33.6	14.0	1,281	35.1	80.5	24.0	3.3
06	68252	San Mateo city	84.5	10.1	37,364	51.4	698,000	29.4	11.1	1,626	29.5	68.4	24.6	6.6
06	68294	San Pablo city	81.8	11.8	8,875	45.4	176,900	35.2	13.5	1,017	40.9	58.3	30.6	15.6
06	68364	San Rafael city	84.4	10.0	22,782	51.5	687,600	29.0	10.9	1,436	35.4	62.5	25.4	9.1
06	68378	San Ramon city	86.7	10.6	25,013	67.7	686,100	27.4	11.3	1,676	28.8	75.9	32.1	3.1
06	69000	Santa Ana city	84.1	6.5	71,584	46.3	329,500	31.9	10.0	1,268	36.0	71.2	24.4	6.0
06	69070	Santa Barbara city	80.1	10.2	33,667	40.8	846,500	31.3	10.7	1,500	33.9	62.1	16.8	9.7
06	69084	Santa Clara city	81.8	14.0	41,942	45.7	606,600	26.8	10.0	1,541	27.4	76.1	21.6	5.2
06	69088	Santa Clarita city	83.4	9.9	58,865	68.9	367,300	29.0	12.6	1,488	33.3	76.2	32.4	4.9
06	69112	Santa Cruz city	71.0	19.5	20,865	43.4	636,400	28.9	10.0	1,563	38.6	57.3	22.1	7.7
06	69196	Santa Maria city	81.4	6.3	27,417	49.5	250,200	29.1	12.7	1,134	33.6	67.0	21.1	7.8
06	70000	Santa Monica city	80.5	14.4	45,805	27.9	983,800	28.9	11.6	1,500	29.9	68.9	26.0	10.9
06	70042	Santa Paula city	85.7	6.7	8,411	57.7	307,200	30.7	11.6	1,106	37.0	68.7	26.0	9.4
06	70098	Santa Rosa city	81.9	8.1	62,249	54.0	355,400	28.5	12.2	1,217	33.9	78.6	22.6	6.8
06	70224	Santee city	85.5	11.3	18,790	70.4	326,700	28.8	10.3	1,236	31.1	84.8	24.3	4.1
06	70280	Saratoga city	91.8	7.3	10,823	86.4	1,000,000	27.4	10.0	2,000	28.1	82.2	27.2	2.4
06	70686	Seal Beach city	84.3	13.8	12,704	75.2	297,500	32.1	12.1	1,480	35.3	82.4	28.8	11.5
06	70742	Seaside city	79.4	16.0	10,318	37.5	336,900	30.2	10.0	1,383	33.8	68.3	18.9	6.5
06	70882	Selma city	83.7	9.5	6,595	57.3	155,300	30.8	11.9	782	38.1	67.1	25.0	11.6
06	72016	Simi Valley city	86.9	5.9	41,388	73.6	422,200	28.1	10.7	1,663	31.4	79.9	28.8	4.0
06	72520	Soledad city	76.5	17.8	3,759	56.3	197,400	29.7	10.0	1,007	37.2	72.9	25.8	4.6
06	72996	South El Monte city	91.2	6.4	4,585	53.8	323,100	29.8	10.0	1,097	35.2	68.4	31.3	7.9
06	73080	South Gate city	87.0	8.2	23,294	46.6	286,100	36.8	10.0	974	38.4	74.0	28.4	7.4
06	73108	South Lake Tahoe city	79.5	9.1	8,580	46.4	308,600	35.5	14.3	848	33.7	62.2	15.1	9.3
06	73220	South Pasadena city	83.5	12.5	10,245	43.5	836,300	27.4	10.0	1,407	27.4	76.3	27.8	3.5
06	73262	South San Francisco city	89.6	7.3	21,631	57.3	584,000	29.4	10.8	1,488	33.2	66.0	24.5	9.6
06	73290	South San Jose Hills CDP	. . .	. . .	4,183	75.2	256,400	34.6	10.0	1,350	30.5	65.8	35.1	6.3
06	73430	South Whittier CDP	89.1	7.1	15,398	63.0	333,200	28.6	10.0	1,202	38.5	81.4	29.0	6.0
06	73696	Spring Valley CDP (San Diego County)	92.5	6.7	9,440	59.6	334,200	28.7	12.0	1,393	32.9	83.6	25.5	2.9
06	73962	Stanton city	86.8	10.2	12,032	49.1	275,300	32.0	13.8	1,249	38.2	72.5	27.1	10.7
06	75000	Stockton city	79.0	7.0	90,318	50.9	162,000	28.4	11.1	935	37.1	75.2	26.1	10.1
06	75630	Suisun City city	82.2	14.3	8,450	66.5	205,500	27.9	10.0	1,521	40.5	75.1	31.7	5.2
06	77000	Sunnyvale city	80.4	14.4	54,071	46.6	713,200	24.9	10.0	1,530	22.4	77.0	22.4	4.2
06	78120	Temecula city	81.6	13.1	31,409	65.7	289,800	30.2	13.3	1,462	35.4	79.0	33.5	3.2
06	78138	Temescal Valley CDP	89.5	9.9	7,641	87.7	307,400	33.0	15.9	2,000	30.3	78.1	47.7	1.0
06	78148	Temple City city	87.3	9.4	11,683	63.9	572,700	32.9	10.7	1,325	39.5	78.7	29.3	4.2
06	78582	Thousand Oaks city	85.6	9.4	44,969	72.8	590,500	28.3	12.5	1,829	34.1	77.3	24.0	4.2
06	80000	Torrance city	87.0	7.5	54,894	57.1	605,900	29.9	10.0	1,407	29.8	83.0	25.3	4.7
06	80238	Tracy city	82.2	8.7	24,014	65.4	252,800	29.0	12.4	1,345	32.6	77.9	40.9	4.9
06	80644	Tulare city	85.6	3.9	17,865	59.8	155,800	25.4	13.9	912	35.9	83.9	19.6	5.8
06	80812	Turlock city	78.5	9.0	23,266	55.8	187,800	28.0	13.3	946	33.6	81.6	23.3	8.2
06	80854	Tustin city	80.6	14.1	24,902	50.9	486,600	31.2	11.4	1,459	35.6	78.4	23.8	4.2
06	80994	Twentynine Palms city	56.0	29.9	8,057	30.5	129,300	23.7	11.0	932	31.1	60.0	15.0	7.8
06	81204	Union City city	90.1	7.5	20,574	66.3	463,600	28.5	11.3	1,390	32.4	76.9	29.5	6.0
06	81344	Upland city	84.8	12.0	26,009	57.4	400,100	27.9	10.0	1,165	35.1	82.5	29.2	5.7
06	81554	Vacaville city	82.4	8.5	30,946	60.6	259,900	27.4	10.0	1,340	30.0	82.9	24.3	4.9
06	81638	Valinda CDP	. . .	. . .	4,447	78.3	314,700	31.3	10.0	1,254	38.0	82.2	32.6	3.9
06	81666	Vallejo city	80.7	8.3	39,574	56.5	212,900	29.8	10.0	1,157	36.5	72.4	33.0	8.8

1. A median value of $1,000,000 or more is represented as $1,000,000.
2. Median selected monthly owner costs of 10 percent or less as a percenage of household income is represented as 10.0
3. A median gross rent of $2,000 or more is represented as $2,000.
4. A median gross rent of 50 percent or more as a percentage of household income is represented as 50.0.

Table C-4. Cities — Where: Migration, Housing, and Transportation, 2010–2012—*Continued*

STATE and place code	STATE or city	Percent who lived in the same house one year ago	Percent who did not live in the same city one year ago	Total occupied housing units	Percent owner-occupied housing units	Median value of owner-occupied housing units (dollars)[1]	Median selected monthly owner costs as a percentage of household income[2] — With a mortgage	Median selected monthly owner costs as a percentage of household income[2] — Without a mortgage	Median gross rent (dollars)[2]	Median gross rent as a percentage of household income[4]	Percent of workers who drove alone to work	Mean travel time to work (minutes)	Percent of occupied housing units with no vehicle available
	ACS table number:	C07204	C07204	B25003	B25003	B25077	B25092	B25092	B25064	B25071	C08301	B08013/ C08012	C25045
	Column number:	1	2	3	4	5	6	7	8	9	10	11	12
	California—Cont.												
06 82590	Victorville city	81.6	10.8	30,780	61.7	131,900	27.0	13.3	1,082	40.4	60.8	34.7	5.6
06 82852	Vineyard CDP	82.5	14.8	7,630	76.2	241,700	31.4	10.0	1,580	39.4	77.9	27.3	1.2
06 82954	Visalia city	80.6	7.8	41,823	60.1	169,300	27.3	10.9	937	33.2	77.5	19.8	8.0
06 82996	Vista city	88.9	8.0	30,058	48.8	336,400	33.4	13.4	1,192	38.1	78.2	23.5	4.0
06 83332	Walnut city	95.2	3.7	8,115	89.4	630,600	29.0	10.1	1,920	31.1	81.3	35.0	0.9
06 83346	Walnut Creek city	81.6	14.7	29,685	64.8	562,300	25.9	17.6	1,392	28.7	65.1	32.2	8.3
06 83542	Wasco city	71.1	18.9	5,239	55.2	119,600	26.4	10.0	627	29.5	73.0	25.8	8.3
06 83668	Watsonville city	89.5	4.2	13,587	40.6	307,400	33.7	11.3	1,162	35.6	67.9	21.5	8.6
06 84144	West Carson CDP	89.9	8.9	7,083	72.2	360,600	33.3	11.5	1,062	29.6	73.8	26.4	4.7
06 84200	West Covina city	83.7	11.9	30,643	63.6	370,500	30.5	10.0	1,348	33.6	76.8	34.4	5.0
06 84410	West Hollywood city	76.6	20.6	22,070	20.6	589,400	29.3	22.2	1,340	33.3	75.2	26.0	15.2
06 84550	Westminster city	86.1	10.3	27,123	54.6	439,300	31.0	10.1	1,311	38.6	80.2	26.0	6.5
06 84592	Westmont CDP	87.9	10.6	9,888	32.2	296,200	34.2	11.5	990	50.0	68.6	33.6	20.9
06 84774	West Puente Valley CDP	. . .	. . .	5,059	78.3	286,800	31.4	10.0	1,363	38.5	83.0	31.9	5.3
06 84780	West Rancho Dominguez CDP	. . .	. . .	6,246	62.1	237,800	36.5	11.2	1,021	43.9	75.4	30.5	6.8
06 84816	West Sacramento city	82.5	10.0	17,184	56.8	222,000	27.6	10.0	871	34.8	74.0	23.5	8.5
06 84921	West Whittier-Los Nietos CDP	94.7	4.8	6,484	75.3	310,600	32.9	10.8	1,218	28.6	80.8	30.3	6.6
06 85292	Whittier city	87.7	8.2	27,212	55.9	416,300	28.9	10.0	1,145	32.9	79.5	29.3	5.8
06 85446	Wildomar city	82.9	13.1	9,909	74.0	222,600	35.4	12.5	1,326	34.9	77.4	34.6	2.3
06 85614	Willowbrook CDP	. . .	. . .	4,672	40.0	212,100	36.8	12.2	997	42.0	59.5	28.1	14.1
06 85922	Windsor town	90.9	4.1	9,333	75.5	358,900	29.6	15.0	1,567	32.0	83.0	23.8	5.1
06 85992	Winter Gardens CDP	86.7	12.2	7,093	54.7	287,400	30.0	14.2	1,143	33.2	81.6	25.3	3.7
06 86328	Woodland city	83.4	7.0	19,363	55.9	240,900	27.9	10.0	923	32.4	77.1	21.8	7.9
06 86832	Yorba Linda city	89.5	7.8	21,943	83.5	675,500	28.5	10.0	1,665	39.4	81.0	31.0	3.7
06 86972	Yuba City city	82.7	5.9	21,679	57.2	180,700	27.0	12.5	870	32.5	77.7	26.6	7.9
06 87042	Yucaipa city	85.1	7.9	17,478	71.7	206,700	27.6	12.7	1,136	31.4	77.2	29.1	4.6
06 87056	Yucca Valley town	77.8	14.0	7,498	59.0	141,200	27.5	15.7	850	33.3	72.3	26.8	9.0
08 00000	**Colorado**	80.6	12.8	1,977,737	64.9	235,000	24.3	10.6	920	30.9	75.1	24.4	5.8
08 03455	Arvada city	85.3	10.7	43,522	74.8	239,400	24.2	10.9	951	29.9	81.9	25.8	4.7
08 04000	Aurora city	76.3	12.8	121,540	58.1	174,800	25.4	10.8	926	33.2	76.2	28.3	6.6
08 07850	Boulder city	62.6	20.8	40,913	48.7	492,900	23.4	10.0	1,145	40.9	52.0	19.4	8.7
08 08675	Brighton city	88.1	9.6	10,520	71.1	192,300	25.2	10.4	961	29.5	80.1	26.6	5.7
08 09280	Broomfield city	82.8	14.4	21,553	68.7	276,000	22.4	10.0	1,137	26.5	77.5	26.0	4.3
08 12415	Castle Rock town	81.8	9.6	17,449	74.7	270,000	24.2	13.6	1,155	32.9	80.3	28.9	2.7
08 12815	Centennial city	85.7	12.5	37,985	81.9	288,000	22.5	10.0	1,331	28.3	81.5	25.7	2.5
08 15165	Clifton CDP	81.9	14.9	7,799	68.6	139,700	25.3	11.2	791	29.4	73.5	25.2	5.1
08 16000	Colorado Springs city	75.6	12.1	167,862	58.4	210,100	23.9	10.0	845	30.1	79.9	20.6	6.0
08 16110	Columbine CDP	92.4	7.0	9,671	90.0	268,600	23.2	10.0	1,569	28.2	77.2	26.2	3.4
08 16495	Commerce City city	82.5	13.7	14,634	73.0	178,600	26.5	12.3	917	32.3	76.3	28.9	4.7
08 19150	Dakota Ridge CDP	88.5	9.8	12,588	78.9	245,900	24.2	10.0	1,158	27.5	82.0	26.6	2.0
08 20000	Denver city	76.4	12.5	266,248	49.0	249,700	23.5	10.8	863	29.8	69.7	24.2	12.3
08 24785	Englewood city	78.1	18.0	14,288	47.0	209,600	24.3	11.5	785	29.5	76.0	25.6	11.0
08 27425	Fort Collins city	71.9	14.8	56,319	55.0	244,300	24.4	10.0	981	35.0	72.9	19.7	5.2
08 27865	Fountain city	76.8	19.9	9,100	64.0	174,100	23.8	10.0	1,136	33.9	82.2	24.2	3.5
08 31660	Grand Junction city	74.8	13.5	24,778	61.5	220,800	24.8	10.9	812	32.6	79.4	16.2	8.2
08 32155	Greeley city	74.5	13.5	33,494	55.3	163,800	24.0	11.0	722	32.1	77.4	21.4	7.1
08 36410	Highlands Ranch CDP	86.2	10.2	34,763	80.7	330,400	22.0	10.0	1,485	25.0	80.4	25.9	1.5
08 40377	Ken Caryl CDP	89.2	8.8	12,620	84.0	247,500	23.4	11.7	1,123	24.0	82.4	28.0	1.5
08 41835	Lafayette city	80.8	14.9	10,228	70.9	249,800	22.7	10.7	1,169	31.8	74.0	24.8	1.9
08 43000	Lakewood city	78.5	14.5	60,712	57.6	237,600	24.0	10.2	910	30.8	78.3	25.1	6.8
08 45255	Littleton city	79.7	15.8	18,420	61.5	262,500	24.2	10.2	871	31.3	77.4	25.3	7.2
08 45970	Longmont city	80.0	10.0	33,527	61.3	238,400	23.1	10.0	948	32.3	73.1	23.0	5.6
08 46465	Loveland city	83.1	11.5	28,384	63.3	211,300	23.6	10.0	923	30.1	80.9	25.1	5.2
08 54330	Northglenn city	82.5	15.7	13,715	56.0	179,100	25.8	14.1	979	34.7	80.6	27.2	7.9
08 57630	Parker town	82.8	10.4	16,372	77.5	280,500	23.6	10.0	1,136	26.0	80.3	28.7	2.1
08 62000	Pueblo city	79.4	7.5	42,981	58.0	113,700	24.8	12.5	687	36.1	78.0	17.8	10.6
08 62220	Pueblo West CDP	88.6	6.5	10,508	81.4	177,200	23.7	11.7	896	24.7	89.5	25.3	3.8
08 68847	Security-Widefield CDP	85.7	11.3	11,570	81.4	167,100	23.6	10.0	1,034	30.9	82.2	22.0	2.4
08 77290	Thornton city	84.6	11.3	40,547	69.4	202,700	24.3	11.2	1,062	31.0	81.5	28.9	3.7
08 83835	Westminster city	81.9	14.1	41,399	63.7	223,600	23.4	10.0	1,018	29.9	76.0	27.0	4.0
08 84440	Wheat Ridge city	80.1	16.2	13,243	54.8	234,800	22.3	10.9	789	35.3	75.5	25.3	11.0
09 00000	**Connecticut**	87.9	8.5	1,355,973	67.6	278,600	26.2	17.1	1,036	32.2	78.9	24.8	9.1
09 08000	Bridgeport city	82.7	6.3	49,928	41.8	188,300	33.6	25.3	1,053	38.2	68.1	26.5	22.0
09 08420	Bristol city	89.2	5.1	25,087	65.4	207,300	26.8	17.5	891	28.3	82.8	23.7	6.7
09 18430	Danbury city	84.7	8.8	29,268	59.5	304,800	30.5	17.3	1,203	32.0	75.6	25.4	10.2
09 18920	Darien CDP	93.1	4.8	6,553	88.5	1,000,000	22.2	15.1	1,936	29.8	60.9	34.6	2.0
09 22700	East Hartford CDP	84.7	9.9	20,085	57.0	174,700	27.8	17.5	863	32.4	71.9	22.6	14.1
09 22980	East Haven CDP	89.7	7.1	11,300	75.8	220,200	28.9	18.6	1,085	30.9	87.6	23.5	5.5
09 37000	Hartford city	78.3	9.9	45,739	22.6	168,000	32.7	16.5	852	35.7	55.8	21.4	35.2
09 44690	Manchester CDP	86.5	9.8	12,864	55.6	181,100	25.6	17.0	1,017	35.4	81.2	21.1	9.6
09 46450	Meriden city	84.6	7.6	23,361	60.3	189,200	29.1	17.1	920	33.8	82.1	22.4	11.2

1. A median value of $1,000,000 or more is represented as $1,000,000.
2. Median selected monthly owner costs of 10 percent or less as a percenage of household income is represented as 10.0.
3. A median gross rent of $2,000 or more is represented as $2,000.
4. A median gross rent of 50 percent or more as a percentage of household income is represented as 50.0.

Table C-4. Cities — Where: Migration, Housing, and Transportation, 2010–2012—*Continued*

STATE and place code	STATE or city	Percent who lived in the same house one year ago	Percent who did not live in the same city one year ago	Total occupied housing units	Percent owner-occupied housing units	Median value of owner-occupied housing units (dollars)[1]	Median selected monthly owner costs as a percentage of household income[2] With a mortgage	Without a mortgage	Median gross rent (dollars)[2]	Median gross rent as a percentage of household income[4]	Percent of workers who drove alone to work	Mean travel time to work (minutes)	Percent of occupied housing units with no vehicle available
	ACS table number:	C07204	C07204	B25003	B25003	B25077	B25092	B25092	B25064	B25071	C08301	B08013/ C08012	C25045
	Column number:	1	2	3	4	5	6	7	8	9	10	11	12
	Connecticut—Cont.												
09 47290	Middletown city	83.0	10.6	19,065	53.6	235,200	24.5	17.2	986	28.3	77.8	22.1	9.4
09 47515	Milford city (balance)	89.1	6.4	20,427	78.0	301,600	26.7	21.6	1,327	29.6	82.9	25.7	4.7
09 49880	Naugatuck borough	92.1	4.8	12,588	65.8	198,000	24.7	19.9	957	27.0	85.3	27.2	6.9
09 50370	New Britain city	81.9	8.7	27,540	39.3	166,100	28.1	18.8	862	34.4	77.0	20.2	18.1
09 52000	New Haven city	80.3	10.3	49,680	30.7	206,300	30.6	18.9	1,075	36.8	58.1	21.7	27.8
09 52210	Newington CDP	90.0	7.8	12,818	82.1	233,600	25.3	16.2	1,101	26.9	87.8	20.4	3.6
09 52280	New London city	71.5	17.5	10,293	36.6	194,400	28.0	16.3	845	32.0	57.2	20.1	21.2
09 54940	North Haven CDP	92.7	5.4	8,838	85.0	296,200	28.0	17.6	1,171	29.8	87.0	21.3	4.3
09 55990	Norwalk city	88.9	6.4	37,882	63.7	412,300	33.3	19.1	1,308	30.6	75.0	24.8	9.9
09 56200	Norwich city	86.6	7.5	16,930	54.0	187,200	26.4	18.6	915	31.7	78.0	21.3	12.4
09 68100	Shelton city	92.0	5.5	14,878	80.2	350,100	27.1	16.9	1,117	24.3	88.7	24.8	4.2
09 73000	Stamford city	86.5	7.0	44,854	54.4	514,900	28.7	18.2	1,490	35.2	68.4	24.8	11.7
09 74260	Stratford CDP	93.0	4.2	19,942	80.0	263,700	30.3	22.9	1,120	34.1	81.3	26.5	5.4
09 76500	Torrington city	89.0	4.3	15,067	67.5	174,100	27.5	18.8	844	30.2	82.5	24.8	8.3
09 77270	Trumbull CDP	92.8	5.9	11,821	88.9	402,600	25.8	22.6	2,000	34.3	82.6	28.7	3.8
09 80000	Waterbury city	87.5	4.5	41,419	47.9	149,000	29.3	22.1	889	35.7	80.2	23.8	18.7
09 82660	West Hartford CDP	88.7	7.4	24,960	72.6	301,100	23.5	15.8	1,175	28.8	84.6	19.5	8.5
09 82800	West Haven city	87.7	7.4	21,341	52.9	214,800	30.9	22.1	1,053	35.4	78.3	22.8	14.1
09 83570	Westport CDP	93.5	4.7	9,309	85.8	969,600	25.7	17.9	1,698	26.4	62.5	38.1	1.9
09 84970	Wethersfield CDP	93.8	4.6	10,919	79.4	257,700	23.9	16.0	958	26.4	85.8	19.4	8.0
10 00000	**Delaware**	86.1	11.8	334,228	71.7	235,900	24.2	11.2	980	31.1	80.9	25.1	6.4
10 04130	Bear CDP	80.8	18.3	6,862	68.3	182,600	26.3	18.0	1,363	25.4	84.3	27.6	4.3
10 21200	Dover city	76.3	16.8	12,398	52.6	182,800	24.3	12.1	928	32.2	79.8	20.3	11.7
10 50670	Newark city	59.1	29.5	10,039	52.5	273,900	21.6	10.0	912	41.5	64.1	21.5	9.3
10 77580	Wilmington city	77.6	11.8	29,045	46.0	175,900	24.7	14.0	871	33.9	68.4	20.9	22.7
11 00000	**District of Columbia**	79.7	9.6	261,567	41.6	436,000	24.1	10.3	1,236	29.7	34.0	29.8	37.2
11 50000	Washington city	79.7	9.6	261,567	41.6	436,000	24.1	10.3	1,236	29.7	34.0	29.8	37.2
12 00000	**Florida**	83.6	12.2	7,120,273	66.9	154,900	28.4	13.9	971	35.3	79.6	25.8	7.2
12 00410	Alafaya CDP	81.0	16.5	26,938	63.6	185,100	26.6	14.3	1,157	36.2	82.7	29.7	3.1
12 00950	Altamonte Springs city	80.2	13.8	15,734	50.1	135,100	29.5	15.0	946	29.4	84.1	24.5	5.4
12 01700	Apopka city	86.4	10.3	14,071	79.6	155,600	27.8	15.7	1,041	37.0	83.9	30.6	4.3
12 02681	Aventura city	77.3	18.0	17,266	64.6	265,200	38.9	25.4	1,602	39.9	76.3	29.7	8.4
12 04162	Bayonet Point CDP	84.6	11.3	10,287	75.2	67,900	32.0	15.1	891	35.2	82.4	29.1	6.8
12 05462	Bellview CDP	87.6	9.6	7,955	75.3	99,100	24.3	12.9	976	30.8	82.9	21.8	5.2
12 06875	Bloomingdale CDP	88.1	10.7	7,159	78.9	184,900	25.5	13.0	1,508	35.5	76.3	32.0	4.0
12 07300	Boca Raton city	82.4	12.2	35,304	68.4	346,300	28.9	15.1	1,406	37.7	78.2	19.9	4.2
12 07525	Bonita Springs city	81.9	12.5	17,871	72.8	232,800	28.2	13.8	994	37.5	72.2	24.7	2.7
12 07875	Boynton Beach city	82.5	13.9	27,852	66.2	136,000	30.1	17.6	1,189	36.6	82.1	22.5	8.2
12 07950	Bradenton city	77.0	13.0	20,698	54.5	122,500	26.1	14.5	886	37.0	78.0	22.2	9.4
12 08150	Brandon CDP	80.9	13.8	38,860	57.0	140,900	25.2	11.7	1,024	30.2	83.7	25.1	4.6
12 08300	Brent CDP	81.4	15.7	6,553	57.5	84,700	23.9	13.7	853	35.2	57.9	18.6	10.8
12 09415	Buenaventura Lakes CDP	89.9	7.4	8,992	68.1	98,900	34.9	15.6	1,148	39.1	82.8	28.7	5.2
12 10275	Cape Coral city	80.1	11.1	55,406	70.1	130,000	29.1	15.2	1,014	36.0	83.7	27.7	3.7
12 10825	Carrollwood CDP	85.7	12.6	14,316	66.4	174,000	28.3	14.0	967	30.4	84.3	25.5	3.8
12 11050	Casselberry city	86.4	8.8	9,737	64.3	115,500	31.0	14.2	888	34.2	84.2	28.3	4.7
12 12425	Citrus Park CDP	88.5	9.2	8,571	69.2	168,600	26.5	12.6	1,121	39.3	78.0	27.0	4.0
12 12875	Clearwater city	84.0	10.6	47,178	59.4	152,800	29.6	17.3	928	37.6	76.2	21.7	12.8
12 12925	Clermont city	87.2	8.5	10,362	71.8	173,100	26.8	13.1	1,090	37.3	82.4	28.5	2.7
12 13275	Coconut Creek city	84.1	11.1	22,223	68.7	122,800	26.6	25.3	1,284	31.9	82.6	25.0	5.2
12 14125	Cooper City city	90.8	8.5	9,868	87.7	274,800	28.1	13.3	1,675	31.3	82.9	26.7	1.1
12 14250	Coral Gables city	78.5	16.7	17,731	63.5	586,300	29.4	14.6	1,312	36.0	74.8	21.4	5.3
12 14400	Coral Springs city	83.3	10.6	40,511	64.3	262,000	29.6	13.8	1,309	35.1	82.3	27.1	5.2
12 14412	Coral Terrace CDP	88.4	8.7	7,334	63.2	226,500	29.6	17.1	1,261	42.5	87.2	24.5	6.6
12 14895	Country Club CDP	95.4	3.0	14,987	54.5	141,900	32.4	16.5	1,145	33.6	88.0	26.5	4.1
12 15475	Crestview city	75.1	17.8	7,489	59.2	154,200	25.6	12.0	1,036	32.4	80.5	28.0	7.8
12 15968	Cutler Bay town	90.9	7.2	12,811	77.0	173,100	30.6	11.0	1,220	33.5	79.8	35.3	4.7
12 16335	Dania Beach city	80.9	16.9	12,040	54.2	148,600	28.4	18.8	1,107	42.7	76.1	23.5	9.2
12 16475	Davie town	82.7	13.3	32,146	71.9	200,200	27.7	18.3	1,196	36.6	83.5	26.8	5.3
12 16525	Daytona Beach city	79.8	13.5	25,186	48.1	116,300	30.2	15.4	722	35.8	75.3	19.1	18.1
12 16725	Deerfield Beach city	82.9	13.6	31,277	64.8	103,200	34.1	20.5	1,120	35.6	78.9	24.1	11.4
12 16875	DeLand city	81.2	16.4	9,475	57.9	147,500	26.7	16.8	907	38.3	77.7	24.0	14.7
12 17100	Delray Beach city	83.6	12.6	26,128	63.8	169,000	33.8	16.1	1,253	33.5	74.7	22.5	6.7
12 17200	Deltona city	89.1	9.0	27,727	81.4	118,200	28.0	13.4	1,085	35.5	85.0	30.7	3.5
12 17935	Doral city	79.0	14.5	13,682	57.4	280,200	33.2	14.8	1,672	36.1	84.9	27.3	2.4
12 18575	Dunedin city	82.5	12.0	15,803	62.3	158,300	27.1	16.8	926	35.3	80.2	25.3	10.8
12 19206	East Lake CDP	84.7	13.4	13,544	77.3	266,000	27.5	14.5	1,115	30.3	82.2	31.1	1.9
12 19212	East Lake-Orient Park CDP	80.9	15.8	8,801	51.6	90,200	28.8	13.1	882	40.1	81.5	22.1	13.3

1. A median value of $1,000,000 or more is represented as $1,000,000.
2. Median selected monthly owner costs of 10 percent or less as a percenage of household income is represented as 10.0
3. A median gross rent of $2,000 or more is represented as $2,000.
4. A median gross rent of 50 percent or more as a percentage of household income is represented as 50.0.

Table C-4. Cities — Where: Migration, Housing, and Transportation, 2010–2012—*Continued*

STATE and place code	STATE or city	Percent who lived in the same house one year ago	Percent who did not live in the same city one year ago	Total occupied housing units	Percent owner-occupied housing units	Median value of owner-occupied housing units (dollars)[1]	Median selected monthly owner costs as a percentage of household income[2] With a mortgage	Without a mortgage	Median gross rent (dollars)[2]	Median gross rent as a percentage of household income[4]	Percent of workers who drove alone to work	Mean travel time to work (minutes)	Percent of occupied housing units with no vehicle available
	ACS table number:	C07204	C07204	B25003	B25003	B25077	B25092	B25092	B25064	B25071	C08301	B08013/ C08012	C25045
	Column number:	1	2	3	4	5	6	7	8	9	10	11	12
	Florida—Cont.												
12 19825	Edgewater city	86.5	10.1	8,545	82.7	128,700	28.3	12.4	893	37.1	84.7	25.8	3.8
12 20108	Egypt Lake-Leto CDP	77.1	19.2	13,770	41.9	109,100	33.5	10.5	850	36.4	77.1	22.5	5.4
12 20925	Ensley CDP	81.8	13.7	8,130	59.7	112,200	28.2	11.3	937	28.7	83.7	19.3	7.0
12 21150	Estero CDP	88.4	9.4	10,244	83.9	238,300	27.9	13.0	1,210	30.5	. . .	21.9	2.3
12 22275	Ferry Pass CDP	76.6	19.4	12,369	50.3	138,700	25.3	10.3	844	35.8	81.2	22.2	10.2
12 22660	Fleming Island CDP	82.6	12.2	10,645	78.7	224,900	25.5	10.0	1,460	27.4	80.7	29.2	1.7
12 24000	Fort Lauderdale city	79.2	13.3	72,479	53.1	233,400	31.1	17.0	1,029	34.0	71.5	24.7	9.9
12 24125	Fort Myers city	73.8	15.9	22,967	45.9	112,600	25.7	12.1	783	35.6	70.0	25.8	12.8
12 24300	Fort Pierce city	81.3	12.2	15,765	43.1	80,800	32.3	20.8	804	44.6	70.6	23.0	17.1
12 24475	Fort Walton Beach city	81.9	12.1	7,957	62.2	154,000	26.2	11.1	984	29.7	81.9	18.0	4.9
12 24562	Fountainebleau CDP	85.2	11.2	17,780	54.9	125,700	33.2	17.2	1,221	37.6	84.2	28.2	5.7
12 24581	Four Corners CDP	74.7	15.5	10,225	52.2	137,000	26.4	13.4	1,003	36.2	80.1	25.5	5.7
12 24925	Fruit Cove CDP	. . .	. . .	9,702	86.5	290,900	24.4	12.6	1,959	35.2	87.1	28.0	3.3
12 25175	Gainesville city	65.0	17.8	46,374	37.7	153,200	23.2	11.5	845	41.5	63.4	16.2	12.0
12 26300	Golden Gate CDP	81.4	13.2	6,734	52.1	123,400	32.3	14.7	891	40.0	66.9	26.4	9.6
12 26375	Golden Glades CDP	85.2	11.8	9,222	57.7	137,100	36.1	16.5	928	36.2	78.5	29.5	11.2
12 27322	Greenacres city	82.2	15.2	12,971	67.3	96,100	31.2	17.1	1,135	38.0	73.8	27.0	5.8
12 28400	Haines City city	85.1	9.0	6,948	60.0	89,200	29.8	19.2	798	32.5	73.5	31.7	8.9
12 28452	Hallandale Beach city	77.5	17.3	18,047	61.4	136,300	35.2	21.3	992	38.0	76.9	31.4	12.6
12 30000	Hialeah city	92.7	3.3	68,760	50.1	152,000	35.6	17.1	977	45.1	77.2	24.7	13.5
12 30025	Hialeah Gardens city	. . .	. . .	5,933	65.0	158,800	31.3	14.2	1,122	35.2	85.0	26.3	5.5
12 31075	Holiday CDP	89.9	8.0	8,602	69.6	75,600	28.6	12.1	876	42.0	80.6	27.5	7.6
12 32000	Hollywood city	84.0	10.3	54,825	60.5	169,900	32.1	15.6	981	38.1	77.7	28.7	8.1
12 32275	Homestead city	77.3	12.6	19,165	41.7	104,000	26.3	14.5	997	41.1	66.7	32.2	14.2
12 32967	Hunters Creek CDP	88.1	10.7	7,251	52.5	228,200	33.2	15.4	1,238	34.7	. . .	25.7	1.1
12 33250	Immokalee CDP	. . .	. . .	4,081	41.6	74,000	33.8	21.5	622	32.7	44.5	32.8	27.2
12 35000	Jacksonville city	81.3	6.2	310,528	61.8	142,000	26.4	12.8	909	33.7	80.6	23.2	8.3
12 35050	Jacksonville Beach city	81.0	15.7	9,616	55.1	243,500	28.7	12.9	1,109	32.8	81.3	21.6	5.5
12 35875	Jupiter town	87.6	8.7	24,036	71.7	256,200	30.8	13.6	1,359	31.8	83.3	22.4	4.4
12 36062	Kendale Lakes CDP	90.2	8.0	17,903	72.9	160,200	31.4	15.6	1,321	39.1	83.0	34.0	4.4
12 36100	Kendall CDP	87.2	9.5	28,328	64.1	286,500	28.5	14.8	1,224	35.9	79.7	30.4	6.7
12 36121	Kendall West CDP	88.9	9.3	11,184	63.5	167,100	36.6	17.9	1,176	45.0	84.5	35.3	5.6
12 36462	Keystone CDP	91.7	7.4	8,098	93.6	309,300	24.2	10.0	2,000	25.7	80.1	31.7	1.1
12 36550	Key West city	79.1	12.1	9,412	45.7	435,300	40.1	14.3	1,586	39.9	51.8	15.0	15.0
12 36950	Kissimmee city	83.7	12.2	20,514	43.3	105,700	29.8	14.0	898	42.1	77.6	28.2	11.4
12 38250	Lakeland city	78.2	12.7	39,776	54.0	111,900	24.2	13.7	850	33.3	82.7	20.5	11.1
12 38350	Lake Magdalene CDP	86.6	12.3	11,715	71.2	162,900	24.9	15.2	848	35.3	79.2	25.6	6.2
12 38813	Lakeside CDP	83.4	13.2	11,066	73.7	152,800	23.9	10.0	1,002	28.7	89.2	29.6	5.4
12 39075	Lake Worth city	77.1	12.4	11,363	50.2	118,500	30.1	18.5	944	38.9	57.2	27.1	15.1
12 39200	Land O' Lakes CDP	83.7	13.5	11,544	81.2	167,100	27.9	11.3	1,241	28.9	82.8	29.0	0.7
12 39425	Largo city	80.5	15.6	35,622	57.7	94,100	25.0	15.6	894	32.1	80.2	20.9	11.4
12 39525	Lauderdale Lakes city	87.5	11.1	11,309	61.8	84,700	37.5	22.3	993	43.0	73.2	29.1	13.2
12 39550	Lauderhill city	80.5	13.9	23,973	58.2	101,500	32.9	20.4	953	40.8	78.1	28.8	12.7
12 39775	Lealman CDP	78.2	19.9	8,894	58.2	64,500	27.1	17.1	817	34.3	78.0	18.1	17.1
12 39875	Leesburg city	74.4	16.7	8,280	53.0	112,900	23.5	14.3	861	39.9	80.5	17.5	12.0
12 39925	Lehigh Acres CDP	69.5	19.7	29,024	62.4	75,700	25.7	10.9	870	33.1	71.9	35.0	5.5
12 39950	Leisure City CDP	80.1	14.3	6,073	62.4	86,700	40.3	18.4	1,006	42.6	71.3	29.6	9.2
12 43125	Margate city	88.2	10.0	21,026	78.6	104,400	31.3	17.9	1,149	36.8	81.9	30.9	10.5
12 43800	Meadow Woods CDP	87.0	12.5	7,440	66.4	134,600	36.1	10.0	1,182	35.0	82.7	28.9	6.7
12 43975	Melbourne city	83.1	12.5	32,235	62.1	111,300	26.9	13.3	804	31.7	83.7	21.3	6.8
12 44275	Merritt Island CDP	85.5	10.0	14,127	77.9	169,300	24.2	12.7	863	32.8	84.3	24.7	4.0
12 45000	Miami city	82.1	8.3	149,591	32.1	202,100	38.0	17.4	922	40.0	69.4	26.3	21.1
12 45025	Miami Beach city	73.6	14.6	42,859	36.3	327,900	33.2	23.4	1,090	35.6	50.0	25.4	26.9
12 45060	Miami Gardens city	92.9	5.1	30,757	67.4	127,500	35.9	13.6	1,063	45.6	79.9	29.6	7.6
12 45100	Miami Lakes town	93.9	5.5	9,906	65.8	287,700	35.6	14.6	1,341	37.1	81.4	27.7	3.8
12 45975	Miramar city	86.5	9.0	37,820	74.7	173,900	33.5	16.5	1,408	35.6	81.4	30.1	3.1
12 47625	Naples city	85.9	8.2	9,712	79.2	722,100	36.2	16.9	1,141	31.8	66.2	19.1	6.5
12 48050	Navarre CDP	80.1	16.2	11,523	69.4	196,800	25.4	12.2	1,204	32.0	85.5	27.2	3.1
12 48625	New Smyrna Beach city	79.7	15.2	10,443	68.2	210,100	29.1	13.9	1,038	34.7	80.2	25.8	5.8
12 49260	Northdale CDP	83.7	15.0	7,665	72.5	175,800	26.5	14.9	1,010	30.1	85.6	28.4	1.6
12 49350	North Fort Myers CDP	89.2	8.8	18,810	85.0	66,300	27.2	16.1	705	28.8	79.2	26.8	3.3
12 49425	North Lauderdale city	80.2	16.6	11,607	56.8	100,000	33.8	17.0	1,144	41.2	72.6	27.0	7.9
12 49450	North Miami city	85.0	11.4	17,550	52.1	129,000	35.9	17.6	918	43.8	73.2	30.5	10.8
12 49475	North Miami Beach city	87.4	10.0	13,829	57.4	140,300	35.4	19.3	984	41.9	72.5	31.3	11.5
12 49675	North Port city	83.7	9.3	21,768	77.6	117,100	25.7	13.6	915	29.4	90.3	27.9	4.2
12 50575	Oakland Park city	79.9	15.9	17,469	56.0	149,300	32.4	11.4	1,035	38.7	76.9	23.6	8.5
12 50638	Oak Ridge CDP	81.9	14.8	7,213	34.5	89,000	32.3	15.5	844	41.5	71.8	25.0	14.2
12 50750	Ocala city	76.5	13.0	21,767	50.9	126,100	25.1	15.7	785	35.0	78.1	19.1	11.6
12 51075	Ocoee city	84.1	13.8	11,188	75.4	169,500	28.4	11.6	1,159	27.4	81.6	28.9	4.0

1. A median value of $1,000,000 or more is represented as $1,000,000.
2. Median selected monthly owner costs of 10 percent or less as a percenage of household income is represented as 10.0
3. A median gross rent of $2,000 or more is represented as $2,000.
4. A median gross rent of 50 percent or more as a percentage of household income is represented as 50.0.

Table C-4. Cities — Where: Migration, Housing, and Transportation, 2010–2012—*Continued*

STATE and place code	STATE or city	Percent who lived in the same house one year ago	Percent who did not live in the same city one year ago	Total occupied housing units	Percent owner-occupied housing units	Median value of owner-occupied housing units (dollars)[1]	Median selected monthly owner costs as a percentage of household income[2]		Median gross rent (dollars)[2]	Median gross rent as a percentage of household income[4]	Percent of workers who drove alone to work	Mean travel time to work (minutes)	Percent of occupied housing units with no vehicle available
							With a mortgage	Without a mortgage					
ACS table number:		C07204	C07204	B25003	B25003	B25077	B25092	B25092	B25064	B25071	C08301	B08013/ C08012	C25045
Column number:		1	2	3	4	5	6	7	8	9	10	11	12
	Florida—Cont.												
12 53000	Orlando city	71.6	15.4	98,916	38.7	159,700	28.9	14.5	958	35.1	78.7	24.6	8.6
12 53150	Ormond Beach city	89.6	8.9	15,829	79.1	163,800	28.5	14.0	973	37.9	83.8	22.2	6.0
12 53575	Oviedo city	89.6	8.8	9,982	81.6	210,700	24.8	10.8	1,333	32.6	84.9	30.6	1.7
12 53725	Pace CDP	80.6	14.1	7,049	81.7	156,800	24.3	12.2	948	29.1	85.0	27.4	1.7
12 54000	Palm Bay city	83.0	9.4	36,939	74.8	100,600	28.0	11.3	909	39.2	83.0	27.6	4.0
12 54075	Palm Beach Gardens city	84.9	11.0	21,936	74.7	283,700	27.2	14.4	1,314	33.9	81.9	21.0	3.6
12 54175	Palm City CDP	88.7	7.0	8,799	84.0	250,600	27.2	14.0	1,243	29.1	83.7	26.4	1.5
12 54200	Palm Coast city	87.4	7.9	27,054	79.0	156,400	31.1	13.2	1,032	34.1	83.1	27.7	3.6
12 54275	Palmetto Bay village	89.8	8.9	7,444	80.5	420,300	25.2	12.5	1,124	42.4	78.1	33.6	2.2
12 54350	Palm Harbor CDP	82.3	14.0	26,189	73.4	167,000	26.5	15.0	1,072	35.6	85.2	25.8	5.9
12 54387	Palm River-Clair Mel CDP	82.6	14.5	7,265	62.4	105,400	28.8	11.7	876	43.5	83.7	23.2	6.9
12 54450	Palm Springs village	81.1	14.2	7,169	57.7	78,700	34.5	20.4	993	35.9	73.7	26.0	7.4
12 54525	Palm Valley CDP	84.5	13.7	8,080	75.1	363,000	25.8	11.2	1,166	26.9	82.2	24.5	2.0
12 54700	Panama City city	75.4	15.4	15,219	49.3	129,400	24.8	14.7	853	35.5	83.1	19.5	13.2
12 55125	Parkland city	84.2	14.9	7,486	82.5	482,500	30.9	10.0	1,927	34.1	79.8	27.7	1.2
12 55775	Pembroke Pines city	85.2	10.5	56,871	72.6	194,900	29.1	19.9	1,356	37.3	83.9	29.2	7.7
12 55925	Pensacola city	81.7	12.2	22,416	60.1	147,500	24.5	12.5	814	31.0	81.4	19.2	9.5
12 56825	Pine Hills CDP	77.7	16.1	19,833	58.3	92,000	32.0	13.0	1,003	40.4	78.6	30.2	10.4
12 56975	Pinellas Park city	86.9	9.8	20,236	68.5	109,100	27.3	15.6	938	32.7	80.1	21.4	10.1
12 57425	Plantation city	82.0	13.5	33,427	67.6	239,000	28.0	15.6	1,323	30.6	84.4	25.7	3.4
12 57550	Plant City city	82.5	8.6	12,147	57.6	132,000	25.0	12.3	812	34.4	82.8	24.2	4.4
12 57900	Poinciana CDP	81.7	15.8	17,236	77.4	100,200	31.7	14.2	1,088	48.4	82.5	42.1	4.5
12 58050	Pompano Beach city	79.3	14.3	41,231	56.5	154,400	31.3	16.6	1,022	41.3	74.1	24.1	12.2
12 58350	Port Charlotte CDP	86.9	6.8	22,864	77.8	109,500	31.7	13.4	942	36.3	80.7	21.6	6.7
12 58575	Port Orange city	87.0	9.3	22,707	77.2	144,200	26.6	14.9	961	30.1	86.3	22.6	4.0
12 58715	Port St. Lucie city	81.1	11.1	58,095	78.4	127,500	31.0	14.5	1,137	36.6	82.1	30.1	3.3
12 58975	Princeton CDP	82.0	12.1	5,888	68.1	122,000	33.7	10.0	1,302	34.7	79.3	34.3	4.0
12 60230	Richmond West CDP	90.7	8.7	9,073	90.1	187,700	33.4	10.1	1,627	22.6	78.2	39.8	0.7
12 60950	Riverview CDP	85.3	10.6	23,683	75.7	152,200	24.3	12.6	1,174	33.2	85.1	31.9	1.1
12 60975	Riviera Beach city	84.9	8.6	11,602	56.1	134,200	31.2	14.2	1,037	43.5	83.4	18.8	12.2
12 61500	Rockledge city	90.5	6.9	9,841	81.2	135,900	23.1	13.8	900	32.9	87.0	23.1	2.3
12 62100	Royal Palm Beach village	88.2	8.9	11,246	81.2	175,600	27.3	13.0	1,340	34.7	84.1	28.9	3.9
12 62625	St. Cloud city	85.2	10.4	13,323	66.5	112,700	28.8	16.0	1,009	30.3	81.4	29.3	5.3
12 63000	St. Petersburg city	83.0	8.2	104,131	59.5	139,800	27.9	14.6	887	33.2	80.1	21.6	10.7
12 63650	Sanford city	84.6	10.2	17,693	56.1	111,800	28.7	12.4	904	38.4	86.7	26.7	8.0
12 64175	Sarasota city	75.8	14.8	22,018	54.5	145,600	31.6	15.0	890	32.0	73.4	19.1	13.3
12 64825	Sebastian city	87.4	8.9	9,205	80.8	141,800	29.0	14.8	854	33.5	. . .	24.1	5.1
12 67258	South Bradenton CDP	72.7	22.3	10,188	53.0	63,600	29.1	10.1	792	31.7	82.0	19.0	8.2
12 67575	South Miami Heights CDP	86.6	11.1	10,400	56.8	131,400	35.2	13.6	876	36.0	78.7	35.5	10.7
12 68350	Spring Hill CDP	86.3	8.4	38,976	79.6	115,100	28.4	12.9	892	38.0	84.0	29.8	4.7
12 69250	Sun City Center CDP	89.1	9.2	11,215	83.1	129,300	26.6	15.6	1,937	50.0	. . .	29.1	9.3
12 69555	Sunny Isles Beach city	83.5	14.8	11,352	52.3	270,300	46.6	27.6	1,316	31.1	76.5	30.0	14.6
12 69700	Sunrise city	85.2	12.0	31,170	71.6	135,500	31.3	21.5	1,201	33.7	83.7	27.9	8.2
12 70345	Sweetwater city	80.0	16.5	5,646	43.3	103,200	36.6	17.7	1,102	46.8	80.1	32.8	11.2
12 70600	Tallahassee city	64.3	15.6	72,525	41.6	179,600	24.3	11.6	923	40.6	81.0	18.2	8.9
12 70675	Tamarac city	82.3	13.7	27,172	73.5	111,500	31.6	18.5	1,087	35.4	83.7	28.0	8.4
12 70700	Tamiami CDP	91.7	7.4	15,503	78.5	211,000	36.3	15.9	1,342	48.5	84.1	31.2	2.1
12 71000	Tampa city	78.0	11.1	135,990	49.9	157,000	27.0	13.4	922	34.0	76.5	22.9	11.6
12 71150	Tarpon Springs city	79.7	12.3	9,862	74.0	162,700	28.8	18.4	835	32.5	81.3	31.9	7.6
12 71400	Temple Terrace city	82.5	15.5	10,337	56.0	159,600	25.9	12.9	967	39.2	83.9	23.0	4.8
12 71564	The Acreage CDP	91.9	6.9	11,969	89.0	209,900	28.9	20.7	1,544	34.1	89.2	35.4	1.6
12 71567	The Crossings CDP	88.9	10.3	8,195	78.6	212,300	31.1	13.6	1,380	28.9	83.7	32.5	1.6
12 71569	The Hammocks CDP	85.1	13.2	16,375	62.5	209,900	32.4	11.9	1,229	44.3	84.8	35.9	3.7
12 71625	The Villages CDP	90.6	7.3	29,690	97.0	209,700	26.0	12.3	1,236	. . .	62.0	22.2	3.0
12 71900	Titusville city	81.8	9.5	17,742	68.9	92,600	24.6	10.9	814	32.4	81.0	23.4	6.9
12 72145	Town 'n' Country CDP	84.7	12.0	29,746	59.3	129,300	28.1	14.1	941	29.2	78.2	23.9	4.3
12 73163	University CDP (Hillsborough County)	65.3	28.3	16,096	13.4	84,300	28.8	15.9	754	45.6	64.0	22.7	24.8
12 73172	University CDP (Orange County)	60.6	36.3	5,958	48.6	129,100	28.4	13.4	899	49.5	65.5	23.9	5.8
12 73287	University Park CDP	83.8	14.5	8,181	63.6	232,600	35.6	21.6	1,181	46.6	84.4	27.3	6.9
12 73700	Valrico CDP	88.0	10.4	12,320	84.7	191,700	24.1	14.2	1,285	35.3	81.8	32.5	2.1
12 73900	Venice city	86.7	9.5	11,177	74.2	174,700	31.6	15.0	946	32.1	80.0	21.1	8.7
12 74200	Vero Beach South CDP	87.1	12.3	9,045	73.6	135,000	24.3	12.7	847	39.7	89.1	18.0	6.1
12 75725	Wekiwa Springs CDP	90.3	7.4	8,647	83.0	230,000	24.2	11.3	1,338	30.2	84.8	28.8	2.8
12 75812	Wellington village	88.6	8.9	19,195	82.1	282,100	28.2	15.2	1,380	37.3	83.2	28.5	2.5
12 75875	Wesley Chapel CDP	84.1	10.3	15,129	78.4	142,500	24.1	11.0	1,280	24.6	81.8	32.6	3.6
12 76062	Westchase CDP	81.1	18.6	8,165	66.7	277,500	21.4	11.1	1,203	28.0	. . .	28.1	3.2
12 76075	Westchester CDP	92.8	6.2	9,141	66.6	228,600	32.5	18.7	1,138	37.5	80.2	28.9	9.0
12 76487	West Little River CDP	91.4	6.5	9,306	63.4	111,700	35.1	14.3	764	39.8	77.2	29.0	16.6
12 76582	Weston city	81.7	11.8	20,818	72.5	364,000	27.9	17.1	1,860	32.5	81.9	30.1	2.2
12 76600	West Palm Beach city	79.5	11.6	41,680	52.2	162,400	30.8	16.4	1,007	34.5	76.2	22.4	10.1
12 76675	West Pensacola CDP	83.7	11.4	7,796	52.8	75,400	27.7	12.7	803	37.2	78.2	19.8	15.4

1. A median value of $1,000,000 or more is represented as $1,000,000.
2. Median selected monthly owner costs of 10 percent or less as a percenage of household income is represented as 10.0
3. A median gross rent of $2,000 or more is represented as $2,000.
4. A median gross rent of 50 percent or more as a percentage of household income is represented as 50.0.

Table C-4. Cities — Where: Migration, Housing, and Transportation—*Continued*

STATE and place code		STATE or city	Percent who lived in the same house one year ago	Percent who did not live in the same city one year ago	Total occupied housing units	Percent owner-occupied housing units	Median value of owner-occupied housing units (dollars)[1]	Median selected monthly owner costs as a percentage of household income[2]		Median gross rent (dollars)[2]	Median gross rent as a percentage of household income[4]	Percent of workers who drove alone to work	Mean travel time to work (minutes)	Percent of occupied housing units with no vehicle available
								With a mortgage	Without a mortgage					
		ACS table number:	C07204	C07204	B25003	B25003	B25077	B25092	B25092	B25064	B25071	C08301	B08013/ C08012	C25045
		Column number:	1	2	3	4	5	6	7	8	9	10	11	12
		Florida—Cont.												
12	78250	Winter Garden city..................	83.4	11.1	11,891	69.6	196,700	28.5	13.4	967	30.5	80.8	25.8	4.7
12	78275	Winter Haven city	79.7	14.3	13,501	58.8	104,000	27.6	13.9	756	37.9	83.4	23.6	10.9
12	78300	Winter Park city	80.1	15.9	11,331	63.9	319,000	23.8	13.1	1,033	32.9	79.8	21.1	6.4
12	78325	Winter Springs city..................	88.6	9.1	11,301	79.9	181,800	24.0	10.7	1,129	30.8	87.4	26.1	2.4
12	78800	Wright CDP	75.4	16.2	10,563	47.3	162,100	28.6	10.0	883	32.4	83.1	20.1	9.4
13	00000	**Georgia**...............................	83.7	13.2	3,504,888	64.9	149,300	24.3	12.1	849	32.2	79.4	27.0	6.8
13	00408	Acworth city...........................	82.6	15.0	7,908	68.6	153,400	26.7	10.7	843	29.1	. . .	35.7	5.8
13	01052	Albany city..............................	81.9	7.4	29,538	39.9	96,100	24.8	14.0	685	36.8	75.0	17.0	14.1
13	01696	Alpharetta city	86.1	11.5	22,175	65.6	310,100	21.4	13.0	1,110	23.7	80.3	25.8	4.3
13	03440	Athens-Clarke County (balance)....	76.2	13.1	40,003	45.5	157,100	23.5	11.0	755	38.4	72.5	18.8	7.8
13	04000	Atlanta city	75.6	12.3	177,215	44.3	204,800	25.3	14.8	935	32.4	67.4	25.1	17.4
13	04204	Augusta-Richmond County (balance)	78.8	10.8	70,152	54.2	103,500	23.4	12.6	766	32.7	81.8	20.0	9.2
13	12834	Candler-McAfee CDP................	85.9	10.6	7,563	60.1	97,100	31.6	14.7	842	40.9	62.2	32.1	15.9
13	12988	Canton city..............................	79.4	15.4	8,031	59.4	155,300	26.2	10.1	796	42.8	82.3	29.1	6.7
13	13492	Carrollton city	73.6	16.6	8,257	42.1	142,900	20.9	11.5	693	40.5	82.0	19.4	10.1
13	19000	Columbus city..........................	75.2	13.4	71,509	52.5	131,000	23.7	11.6	791	31.4	76.9	19.1	10.2
13	21380	Dalton city...............................	75.8	11.1	11,464	43.8	121,100	24.4	10.9	698	30.6	81.9	17.2	10.3
13	23900	Douglasville city	71.7	20.9	11,446	47.5	148,300	27.9	10.0	912	29.4	85.3	30.0	5.8
13	24600	Duluth city...............................	87.8	10.5	10,470	54.7	172,700	23.6	10.0	946	29.0	82.1	28.6	1.5
13	24768	Dunwoody city..........................	83.2	14.1	19,066	53.8	349,800	23.6	13.0	1,132	28.1	76.5	25.0	4.1
13	25720	East Point city	77.0	17.6	12,578	45.4	104,300	26.1	16.0	856	37.5	61.4	29.2	19.3
13	28044	Evans CDP	84.5	12.3	10,253	84.4	228,000	22.4	10.0	1,436	26.5	88.8	27.7	1.2
13	31908	Gainesville city	77.4	12.3	11,118	40.4	155,800	27.1	12.7	783	30.5	69.8	21.3	16.9
13	35324	Griffin city	76.2	8.5	8,557	41.5	114,600	23.7	15.2	769	37.4	77.8	24.6	14.6
13	38964	Hinesville city	77.0	18.2	12,581	51.3	132,400	25.4	10.0	852	28.3	89.6	18.0	4.8
13	42425	Johns Creek city	89.6	9.2	25,886	80.4	319,900	21.5	11.9	1,276	25.5	76.8	29.9	1.7
13	43192	Kennesaw city...........................	81.5	14.3	11,515	63.2	164,600	24.5	10.8	1,051	28.6	83.8	29.1	3.8
13	44340	LaGrange city	75.4	12.7	11,395	42.5	114,200	28.3	13.4	720	34.3	78.3	19.4	16.8
13	45488	Lawrenceville city	82.3	14.3	9,475	54.9	120,900	24.5	16.2	857	42.0	77.3	30.4	6.5
13	48288	Mableton CDP	82.0	13.9	14,001	71.1	152,700	24.6	11.5	935	30.9	76.2	29.1	4.8
13	48624	McDonough city	77.8	17.8	7,775	46.8	132,200	24.0	12.6	975	33.6	78.5	33.1	7.1
13	49000	Macon city...............................	79.1	8.3	33,184	43.5	86,200	26.7	14.4	680	41.8	80.3	20.1	17.5
13	49756	Marietta city	74.3	17.2	23,034	45.2	203,500	24.5	11.2	859	32.0	71.5	26.6	9.9
13	50036	Martinez CDP	88.4	11.2	13,522	69.3	148,200	22.1	10.0	980	24.4	85.4	21.1	3.1
13	51670	Milton city...............................	90.0	9.1	11,813	71.6	466,700	20.6	10.0	1,167	26.0	. . .	30.7	1.2
13	55020	Newnan city.............................	75.6	16.5	12,424	48.2	178,300	25.0	10.0	934	29.9	. . .	28.0	9.0
13	56000	North Atlanta CDP.....................	83.1	14.3	15,514	42.0	371,400	23.9	12.6	1,008	28.6	62.9	28.7	13.4
13	59724	Peachtree City city	87.9	9.1	12,443	74.8	270,100	22.9	10.0	1,127	22.7	79.5	28.2	2.9
13	62104	Pooler city................................	86.0	12.2	7,169	67.2	173,700	26.8	10.7	1,159	20.0	. . .	21.9	2.3
13	63952	Redan CDP	80.4	15.4	11,080	62.4	102,300	27.5	12.5	1,110	37.1	69.9	35.7	7.9
13	66668	Rome city.................................	81.0	8.4	13,400	49.1	116,600	26.7	15.3	712	33.6	77.8	17.1	15.4
13	67284	Roswell city..............................	88.9	8.0	34,440	67.2	284,700	21.8	10.1	978	31.1	78.1	27.0	5.2
13	68516	Sandy Springs city....................	75.1	21.0	40,833	46.5	409,900	22.5	11.1	960	28.0	74.1	24.2	6.2
13	69000	Savannah city...........................	82.6	9.8	51,445	45.8	142,300	27.7	13.7	875	35.9	75.8	19.7	13.4
13	71492	Smyrna city..............................	74.6	20.8	22,946	52.3	209,000	21.4	13.5	896	30.8	82.3	27.3	3.9
13	73256	Statesboro city	66.8	24.9	9,985	25.2	118,200	20.6	13.2	690	46.4	75.9	15.7	7.6
13	73704	Stockbridge city	83.7	14.7	9,413	57.2	126,800	26.2	13.1	985	27.7	. . .	31.0	1.7
13	77652	Tucker CDP	84.7	12.1	10,631	69.8	219,500	23.5	10.0	934	34.7	75.7	28.0	3.4
13	78324	Union City city..........................	79.1	19.5	7,748	43.2	102,800	30.0	14.3	798	34.2	75.0	31.7	12.1
13	78800	Valdosta city	72.1	12.0	21,259	38.6	137,100	26.7	12.4	776	36.1	79.0	15.8	9.2
13	80508	Warner Robins city....................	82.2	11.8	26,128	57.4	110,000	20.7	11.3	810	29.5	83.0	20.3	5.3
13	84176	Woodstock city	83.4	12.3	9,611	68.7	174,800	22.4	12.5	1,021	27.7	82.4	32.9	3.3
15	00000	**Hawaii**.................................	85.0	11.2	447,566	57.3	503,100	29.7	10.0	1,353	33.4	66.4	25.7	8.8
15	06290	East Honolulu CDP....................	91.2	6.0	17,069	81.0	764,200	29.3	10.8	2,000	30.9	72.4	29.7	5.1
15	07470	Ewa Gentry CDP	79.0	18.9	6,561	70.1	396,700	32.8	10.0	1,693	37.8	72.8	34.1	3.5
15	14650	Hilo CDP...................................	88.9	5.4	14,352	64.8	304,000	24.4	10.0	799	34.8	77.8	18.5	6.9
15	22700	Kahului CDP	82.7	10.4	6,730	53.1	520,100	31.3	10.0	1,030	29.1	62.5	20.1	7.8
15	23150	Kailua CDP (Honolulu County)	90.1	6.5	12,949	72.6	788,900	28.7	11.8	2,000	31.5	74.3	26.7	3.8
15	28250	Kaneohe CDP	88.9	8.5	10,905	67.2	614,100	28.3	10.0	1,670	32.4	69.1	27.8	4.5
15	51000	Mililani Mauka CDP	83.5	14.8	6,770	82.4	568,700	29.1	10.0	1,812	32.4	76.8	32.1	2.4
15	51050	Mililani Town CDP.....................	92.1	6.0	9,316	80.2	544,100	25.8	10.0	1,807	33.9	77.0	30.8	2.8
15	62600	Pearl City CDP...........................	87.9	11.2	14,410	73.0	578,200	24.5	10.0	1,643	33.4	68.5	26.9	5.6
15	71550	Urban Honolulu CDP..................	84.8	8.2	127,145	42.6	567,000	29.0	12.0	1,229	32.0	57.5	22.0	18.4
15	79700	Waipahu CDP............................	91.2	6.3	8,273	57.2	488,000	27.5	10.3	1,176	32.9	55.1	32.6	11.0
16	00000	**Idaho**..................................	82.5	11.5	580,280	69.0	160,000	24.3	10.2	710	30.3	77.5	20.1	4.5
16	08830	Boise City city	79.6	9.4	86,763	58.6	172,800	23.0	10.0	761	29.8	78.5	17.9	6.6
16	12250	Caldwell city	80.4	11.2	15,979	64.1	98,100	25.8	11.1	698	31.7	85.5	22.5	6.4
16	16750	Coeur d'Alene city	76.0	13.2	19,137	56.0	172,300	24.8	10.8	763	37.3	79.0	17.7	6.3
16	23410	Eagle city.................................	91.7	7.4	7,408	79.3	280,500	24.5	10.0	1,088	29.4	75.3	21.1	2.1

1. A median value of $1,000,000 or more is represented as $1,000,000.
2. Median selected monthly owner costs of 10 percent or less as a percentage of household income is represented as 10.0.
3. A median gross rent of $2,000 or more is represented as $2,000.
4. A median gross rent of 50 percent or more as a percentage of household income is represented as 50.0.

Table C-4. Cities — Where: Migration, Housing, and Transportation—*Continued*

STATE and place code		STATE or city	Percent who lived in the same house one year ago	Percent who did not live in the same city one year ago	Total occupied housing units	Percent owner-occupied housing units	Median value of owner-occupied housing units (dollars)[1]	Median selected monthly owner costs as a percentage of household income[2]		Median gross rent (dollars)[3]	Median gross rent as a percentage of household income[4]	Percent of workers who drove alone to work	Mean travel time to work (minutes)	Percent of occupied housing units with no vehicle available
								With a mortgage	Without a mortgage					
		ACS table number:	C07204	C07204	B25003	B25003	B25077	B25092	B25092	B25064	B25071	C08301	B08013/ C08012	C25045
		Column number:	1	2	3	4	5	6	7	8	9	10	11	12
		Idaho—Cont.												
16	39700	Idaho Falls city	83.2	8.7	20,948	68.2	142,800	21.4	10.0	654	30.5	80.4	16.8	5.8
16	46540	Lewiston city	85.8	7.2	13,279	67.5	168,000	22.7	12.9	634	26.8	80.9	15.3	6.7
16	52120	Meridian city	86.0	9.6	26,876	73.6	183,300	23.6	10.0	975	31.5	82.5	23.3	3.3
16	54550	Moscow city	63.0	20.2	9,596	38.5	201,600	21.0	10.0	645	37.2	59.5	13.6	6.6
16	56260	Nampa city	77.0	13.7	27,068	63.6	107,500	25.8	12.0	728	33.5	78.2	22.5	6.6
16	64090	Pocatello city	75.4	11.6	20,539	62.3	134,200	23.0	10.4	608	32.1	78.3	16.8	6.6
16	64810	Post Falls city	80.4	10.3	10,941	66.6	165,200	23.6	10.0	780	28.4	. . .	20.3	1.9
16	67420	Rexburg city	46.0	31.4	6,726	35.5	171,600	22.4	10.0	627	43.2	53.2	15.6	3.5
16	82810	Twin Falls city	75.4	12.6	16,037	57.3	140,800	25.5	10.0	677	27.7	81.0	14.9	4.6
17	00000	**Illinois**	86.8	7.9	4,759,131	67.3	179,900	25.1	13.8	877	31.2	73.5	28.0	10.8
17	00243	Addison village	84.5	8.2	12,062	69.5	241,600	28.3	18.5	900	30.5	81.0	27.7	3.9
17	00685	Algonquin village	90.9	7.7	10,467	88.4	238,700	24.1	15.0	1,489	30.6	81.2	37.3	1.7
17	01114	Alton city	85.2	8.6	11,609	58.5	83,300	24.3	12.8	713	32.6	81.3	22.7	9.2
17	02154	Arlington Heights village	90.1	7.8	30,144	76.5	317,200	26.2	14.9	1,138	28.1	81.5	28.7	6.4
17	03012	Aurora city	85.0	8.0	61,135	68.5	182,100	27.0	13.9	1,011	33.1	77.2	28.9	5.4
17	04013	Bartlett village	93.2	4.5	13,937	87.2	268,200	27.9	14.9	1,221	36.2	82.6	34.1	3.7
17	04078	Batavia city	89.3	8.7	9,278	76.5	275,100	23.7	11.0	1,019	30.1	80.7	28.1	4.9
17	04845	Belleville city	87.2	8.8	18,473	61.7	103,100	21.8	13.4	754	32.0	81.4	22.8	7.4
17	05092	Belvidere city	86.7	5.3	8,437	77.0	118,000	26.7	14.4	672	31.7	79.2	28.4	6.9
17	05573	Berwyn city	89.4	6.7	18,734	61.4	180,900	32.1	18.6	897	31.8	69.7	29.3	11.6
17	06587	Bloomingdale village	86.2	11.3	8,682	73.1	273,700	28.9	16.1	1,106	30.3	87.4	28.1	3.7
17	06613	Bloomington city	81.7	10.4	30,397	62.5	160,700	20.6	12.6	728	25.6	80.7	15.8	8.6
17	06704	Blue Island city	91.7	6.9	7,917	55.8	132,600	31.6	16.1	823	37.5	72.9	29.3	11.5
17	07133	Bolingbrook village	93.2	5.1	21,861	84.0	211,500	27.0	14.1	1,107	39.9	82.3	32.9	3.5
17	09447	Buffalo Grove village	90.6	8.3	16,511	82.4	297,500	25.7	15.7	1,243	25.8	84.4	30.2	4.2
17	09642	Burbank city	. . .	. . .	9,023	78.5	191,700	28.2	17.3	1,000	25.8	79.8	30.4	7.4
17	10487	Calumet City city	88.3	9.4	14,352	57.9	109,300	32.9	16.9	881	34.5	73.9	32.5	16.3
17	11163	Carbondale city	59.6	21.3	9,137	24.5	111,000	20.9	12.5	678	50.0	66.2	11.5	20.0
17	11332	Carol Stream village	88.6	8.5	14,478	68.0	235,900	25.0	13.8	977	31.1	81.3	29.1	5.3
17	11358	Carpentersville village	84.1	8.7	10,854	72.8	158,300	29.3	13.9	1,014	40.0	81.6	30.4	4.9
17	12385	Champaign city	68.9	17.5	32,331	47.8	150,500	20.8	11.0	820	38.3	65.3	15.5	12.5
17	12567	Charleston city	60.7	21.1	7,616	48.8	98,400	22.8	11.3	631	49.1	67.0	17.2	10.6
17	14000	Chicago city	83.5	5.0	1,023,839	44.9	229,200	28.7	16.0	932	32.3	50.1	33.3	27.2
17	14026	Chicago Heights city	89.1	8.2	9,893	63.2	120,100	23.6	14.9	842	35.4	79.8	27.3	13.0
17	14351	Cicero town	88.9	4.6	21,284	51.8	153,500	37.7	15.0	835	30.3	64.7	30.5	10.8
17	15599	Collinsville city	86.6	9.3	10,995	61.3	122,300	21.5	12.4	783	31.5	86.3	25.0	8.1
17	17458	Crest Hill city	87.8	10.1	8,097	65.6	162,300	27.4	17.9	1,015	32.3	89.8	31.3	5.7
17	17887	Crystal Lake city	91.6	5.6	14,216	77.9	209,400	24.4	17.2	1,117	29.7	81.6	32.5	3.9
17	18563	Danville city	85.2	6.2	12,488	57.8	68,500	21.1	11.9	661	37.4	76.7	14.4	16.0
17	18628	Darien city	93.5	4.4	8,681	83.7	304,100	26.6	15.2	1,008	38.1	83.2	29.2	2.7
17	18823	Decatur city	80.9	7.3	31,973	60.7	80,000	19.8	12.5	654	30.2	84.0	17.3	12.6
17	19161	DeKalb city	68.9	17.5	15,029	45.7	166,100	25.3	14.5	804	44.0	71.5	19.6	11.0
17	19642	Des Plaines city	92.5	5.0	22,763	79.2	241,100	27.9	16.5	948	30.3	78.7	27.4	6.8
17	20292	Dolton village	89.5	10.0	7,821	71.9	114,000	29.4	17.7	1,075	44.7	68.5	36.8	11.6
17	20591	Downers Grove village	91.0	7.6	18,951	78.1	327,000	24.2	13.8	1,081	28.7	74.7	28.5	6.2
17	22073	East Moline city	82.8	12.6	8,119	63.0	112,000	23.5	11.3	587	26.9	81.6	20.5	13.9
17	22164	East Peoria city	90.2	5.7	9,356	74.9	134,300	22.5	13.0	628	31.6	86.2	17.6	7.8
17	22255	East St. Louis city	84.6	7.8	9,997	46.2	57,700	42.8	16.5	542	35.1	63.9	23.6	28.8
17	22697	Edwardsville city	76.9	15.3	8,675	72.2	187,800	20.5	12.8	871	35.7	85.5	22.8	2.7
17	23074	Elgin city	86.6	5.0	34,322	70.0	176,200	28.0	15.1	911	34.9	80.4	28.3	5.4
17	23256	Elk Grove Village village	92.6	6.2	13,406	75.8	264,600	27.7	15.5	947	29.1	83.3	25.0	7.1
17	23620	Elmhurst city	91.6	6.9	15,425	81.5	365,000	27.5	13.6	1,329	28.4	75.2	27.4	5.1
17	23724	Elmwood Park village	89.1	8.3	9,005	66.7	219,600	29.6	15.8	908	29.7	75.5	33.5	7.5
17	24582	Evanston city	77.1	15.1	28,790	54.0	352,700	25.9	16.5	1,137	34.5	48.5	28.1	14.8
17	27884	Freeport city	83.3	6.6	10,705	65.2	77,200	21.5	14.2	595	33.6	77.7	15.9	15.8
17	28326	Galesburg city	85.5	8.4	13,036	58.2	73,300	20.3	13.4	588	31.8	79.1	14.8	12.6
17	28872	Geneva city	91.1	5.4	7,750	81.6	312,200	26.5	14.8	1,127	31.5	76.6	28.9	3.7
17	29730	Glendale Heights village	84.2	10.3	11,295	70.7	176,000	32.0	15.9	966	32.8	82.1	27.5	4.7
17	29756	Glen Ellyn village	87.1	11.1	10,370	73.0	382,700	24.5	15.3	949	30.6	71.9	27.9	7.0
17	29938	Glenview village	91.2	6.6	16,916	81.0	463,300	25.7	16.1	1,604	35.0	72.6	30.5	6.5
17	30926	Granite City city	86.9	5.9	11,959	69.6	81,500	19.4	12.6	609	33.3	82.8	21.5	9.4
17	31121	Grayslake village	90.5	7.6	7,351	74.7	226,400	23.3	11.8	937	28.2	76.6	32.6	4.1
17	32018	Gurnee village	89.3	9.5	11,354	74.9	259,700	24.5	14.2	1,103	30.0	80.4	29.2	4.0
17	32746	Hanover Park village	88.1	9.5	11,001	79.2	185,500	27.7	14.4	997	30.0	76.2	29.2	2.6
17	33383	Harvey city	87.1	7.7	7,416	48.3	89,000	33.0	19.4	891	38.9	71.5	29.3	20.1
17	34722	Highland Park city	91.3	6.0	11,618	81.7	494,200	25.6	15.6	1,363	30.1	69.3	28.5	3.1
17	35411	Hoffman Estates village	87.6	10.6	17,880	74.8	260,700	25.4	14.0	1,048	29.0	82.0	29.5	3.8
17	35835	Homer Glen village	95.7	3.8	7,958	92.3	321,300	27.1	15.1	1,694	39.5	84.6	33.3	4.3
17	36750	Huntley village	88.4	10.0	9,832	95.3	228,000	27.3	17.6	1,495	35.9	86.4	38.9	2.9
17	38570	Joliet city	88.0	6.0	46,586	72.4	170,600	27.3	14.5	858	31.6	83.3	29.6	7.2
17	38934	Kankakee city	82.1	8.8	9,426	48.8	101,600	27.5	14.5	690	38.4	77.1	19.0	15.8

1. A median value of $1,000,000 or more is represented as $1,000,000.
2. Median selected monthly owner costs of 10 percent or less as a percenage of household income is represented as 10.0.
3. A median gross rent of $2,000 or more is represented as $2,000.
4. A median gross rent of 50 percent or more as a percentage of household income is represented as 50.0.

Table C-4. Cities — Where: Migration, Housing, and Transportation, 2010–2012—*Continued*

STATE and place code		STATE or city	Percent who lived in the same house one year ago	Percent who did not live in the same city one year ago	Total occupied housing units	Percent owner-occupied housing units	Median value of owner-occupied housing units (dollars)[1]	Median selected monthly owner costs as a percentage of household income[2] With a mortgage	Without a mortgage	Median gross rent (dollars)[2]	Median gross rent as a percentage of household income[4]	Percent of workers who drove alone to work	Mean travel time to work (minutes)	Percent of occupied housing units with no vehicle available
		ACS table number:	C07204	C07204	B25003	B25003	B25077	B25092	B25092	B25064	B25071	C08301	B08013/ C08012	C25045
		Column number:	1	2	3	4	5	6	7	8	9	10	11	12
		Illinois—Cont.												
17	41105	Lake Forest city	89.1	9.1	6,592	88.9	837,600	28.6	13.8	1,259	28.0	63.6	30.7	1.3
17	41183	Lake in the Hills village	91.7	7.8	9,632	93.2	202,500	26.3	18.6	1,528	23.9	85.1	35.6	0.8
17	41742	Lake Zurich village	93.4	5.2	6,405	88.7	316,300	23.9	11.7	1,233	29.7	82.0	29.5	2.0
17	42028	Lansing village	91.7	6.8	11,158	73.0	137,600	28.7	14.5	918	28.9	77.3	30.8	4.6
17	43250	Libertyville village	89.7	8.2	7,602	76.9	400,600	22.7	14.0	1,117	28.7	77.4	26.0	7.1
17	43939	Lisle village	80.9	16.8	9,165	59.4	313,800	25.5	11.8	1,078	32.3	77.5	27.0	6.3
17	44225	Lockport city	94.0	5.4	9,107	88.4	212,000	27.8	20.4	896	26.4	85.7	34.4	3.6
17	44407	Lombard village	88.5	9.3	17,610	73.2	240,500	26.8	14.3	1,163	28.2	82.6	26.5	4.6
17	45031	Loves Park city	92.3	6.3	9,192	73.3	119,000	23.9	13.1	791	27.5	90.1	21.0	3.6
17	45694	McHenry city	90.4	8.4	9,800	76.9	182,300	26.5	14.8	985	41.7	81.2	30.1	6.6
17	45726	Machesney Park village	90.4	7.4	8,425	78.3	123,100	22.3	13.7	854	27.1	86.6	24.3	4.5
17	47774	Maywood village	87.9	6.1	7,772	61.2	153,400	33.2	15.2	865	43.1	78.9	27.9	14.4
17	48242	Melrose Park village	85.1	10.4	7,539	54.0	184,600	32.6	17.1	870	32.2	70.5	25.1	10.5
17	49867	Moline city	86.7	7.8	18,300	68.6	111,800	21.4	12.1	672	27.3	82.8	17.6	8.0
17	50647	Morton Grove village	90.8	8.4	8,512	89.2	300,300	29.2	17.1	1,433	27.9	75.9	27.0	5.7
17	51089	Mount Prospect village	89.5	7.0	19,911	72.8	297,100	27.9	16.7	950	27.9	77.5	27.6	4.6
17	51349	Mundelein village	90.4	5.9	10,521	77.7	232,900	26.7	16.7	1,041	26.6	81.3	28.6	2.7
17	51622	Naperville city	88.4	7.8	48,897	76.6	376,000	23.9	12.2	1,228	26.1	74.7	33.7	2.8
17	52584	New Lenox village	89.2	9.5	7,990	83.2	274,400	24.6	14.8	977	23.2	81.0	34.4	2.5
17	53000	Niles village	91.6	5.7	11,385	75.0	267,900	32.6	17.8	1,009	46.6	76.6	29.2	11.5
17	53234	Normal town	69.3	19.7	18,039	57.2	160,600	20.0	10.0	769	38.4	74.8	16.8	5.9
17	53481	Northbrook village	90.0	7.5	12,246	85.5	515,800	25.6	15.7	1,785	37.5	69.0	27.5	3.9
17	53559	North Chicago city	58.7	36.5	6,771	39.2	127,700	36.6	18.0	1,002	30.9	35.9	14.9	11.3
17	54638	Oak Forest city	92.9	4.4	9,766	79.6	196,100	25.6	13.9	942	28.4	81.9	29.4	4.4
17	54820	Oak Lawn village	92.8	5.5	21,794	81.2	199,600	29.0	17.6	949	37.3	80.1	32.0	7.9
17	54885	Oak Park village	87.2	9.3	21,605	62.4	354,500	26.0	13.9	993	29.3	57.1	31.7	11.8
17	55249	O'Fallon city	84.4	12.6	10,456	67.9	205,900	19.9	12.5	1,065	33.9	86.1	22.4	4.0
17	56640	Orland Park village	92.5	6.6	21,451	88.5	279,600	26.9	17.7	1,009	28.0	81.8	33.5	3.6
17	56887	Oswego village	91.4	5.6	10,310	86.3	230,500	26.9	16.4	1,741	26.2	82.5	32.7	1.2
17	57225	Palatine village	86.1	8.9	25,646	69.1	274,400	26.2	15.0	1,100	29.5	80.2	27.5	3.9
17	57732	Park Forest village	91.2	8.2	8,556	66.7	90,500	27.5	13.1	1,059	37.2	75.2	31.1	10.4
17	57993	Park Ridge city	92.8	4.7	14,182	83.4	400,500	27.2	16.6	1,136	26.6	71.7	28.3	4.0
17	58447	Pekin city	83.8	8.2	13,939	70.1	100,200	20.8	11.2	620	25.5	85.5	18.1	7.5
17	59000	Peoria city	79.7	9.2	47,114	56.1	122,500	21.3	12.0	687	30.3	81.3	17.4	13.7
17	60287	Plainfield village	93.8	5.2	11,459	88.9	287,200	25.7	13.0	1,390	23.9	83.4	37.9	2.9
17	62367	Quincy city	85.3	5.6	16,650	63.7	97,100	21.5	10.4	623	31.1	81.8	13.8	8.7
17	65000	Rockford city	83.6	6.5	58,379	56.2	101,700	24.2	14.3	709	33.4	80.3	19.9	12.2
17	65078	Rock Island city	83.1	9.2	15,531	65.8	99,100	21.4	14.4	662	33.5	75.1	17.7	14.6
17	65338	Rolling Meadows city	89.8	6.0	8,931	69.7	230,800	28.2	16.3	1,093	34.2	75.3	22.9	6.7
17	65442	Romeoville village	90.9	7.7	12,022	83.5	170,200	30.2	13.9	1,268	34.2	84.8	36.2	2.6
17	65806	Roselle village	88.5	7.9	8,834	77.5	249,100	26.8	13.7	1,050	29.7	83.7	28.9	2.6
17	66040	Round Lake Beach village	91.8	6.0	8,203	81.6	138,400	28.2	14.7	980	37.1	80.9	31.0	3.1
17	66703	St. Charles city	83.9	9.7	12,503	73.5	279,300	23.6	16.0	1,132	28.1	83.1	30.4	4.5
17	68003	Schaumburg village	83.7	12.8	29,885	63.6	245,800	28.0	13.8	1,170	26.6	83.8	27.5	5.9
17	70122	Skokie village	91.8	5.0	23,176	72.1	285,600	31.1	17.8	1,103	37.6	72.6	29.9	8.8
17	70720	South Elgin village	. . .	. . .	6,739	88.5	203,900	27.5	18.9	1,191	30.5	80.9	31.9	2.1
17	70850	South Holland village	. . .	. . .	7,150	88.9	154,900	29.9	13.9	1,680	46.4	77.7	33.5	7.1
17	72000	Springfield city	80.6	10.3	51,264	63.0	116,000	19.8	11.8	704	31.4	78.6	17.4	10.0
17	73157	Streamwood village	91.3	7.6	12,802	86.6	187,800	28.3	11.9	1,444	34.9	79.4	30.6	1.9
17	75484	Tinley Park village	91.4	6.7	21,517	84.5	230,700	25.8	16.6	989	29.9	80.6	34.6	2.6
17	77005	Urbana city	57.2	29.5	16,068	31.3	151,000	20.8	10.7	766	38.7	47.5	14.3	22.7
17	77694	Vernon Hills village	88.3	9.8	9,415	72.8	307,800	26.2	16.2	1,244	33.8	83.8	27.3	8.9
17	77993	Villa Park village	88.4	7.0	7,608	71.2	234,600	26.4	14.2	992	31.1	80.8	27.3	3.7
17	79293	Waukegan city	84.6	7.3	28,829	52.9	140,900	29.8	16.3	838	31.5	71.9	26.4	10.4
17	80060	West Chicago city	89.7	5.9	7,595	67.0	223,200	28.6	13.9	872	33.7	71.4	25.0	3.9
17	80645	Westmont village	81.1	14.6	10,810	50.6	269,400	27.3	16.6	943	28.7	75.5	28.6	8.6
17	81048	Wheaton city	82.3	12.4	18,973	70.3	338,500	23.9	13.3	1,143	28.9	72.9	26.7	4.2
17	81087	Wheeling village	87.9	10.1	14,163	63.9	185,000	30.2	15.5	990	31.2	80.6	26.5	6.4
17	82075	Wilmette village	90.0	7.6	9,479	82.6	610,100	27.0	14.8	1,683	25.0	58.5	33.5	3.9
17	83245	Woodridge village	87.4	10.1	12,793	66.4	254,100	27.1	13.4	1,084	25.9	76.8	30.6	4.0
17	83349	Woodstock city	87.7	8.4	9,470	68.1	175,100	28.8	18.0	903	32.4	84.2	28.3	6.7
17	84220	Zion city	85.3	11.2	8,099	55.5	142,900	28.9	14.0	897	34.5	84.8	26.2	13.7
18	00000	**Indiana**	85.0	9.4	2,474,926	69.9	122,600	20.9	11.0	717	30.4	83.3	23.4	6.8
18	01468	Anderson city	79.7	7.0	22,481	59.0	73,600	21.6	13.6	659	35.4	80.1	23.2	14.1
18	05860	Bloomington city	52.6	25.8	29,534	34.4	180,400	20.6	10.2	765	47.1	59.8	15.2	13.4
18	08416	Brownsburg town	89.4	8.8	8,510	78.6	145,800	19.2	13.9	898	30.4	. . .	25.6	3.3
18	10342	Carmel city	84.8	11.0	29,769	78.0	291,900	18.2	10.0	1,063	22.6	85.5	25.0	3.2
18	12934	Clarksville town	88.6	6.1	8,868	60.7	117,800	20.5	12.6	719	30.8	90.4	19.9	8.3
18	14734	Columbus city	80.1	9.5	17,840	62.3	143,300	19.3	11.7	804	27.7	84.3	17.1	7.1
18	16138	Crown Point city	86.2	10.6	10,746	75.2	170,600	21.4	12.0	896	25.0	89.2	27.8	3.9

1. A median value of $1,000,000 or more is represented as $1,000,000.
2. Median selected monthly owner costs of 10 percent or less as a percenage of household income is represented as 10.0
3. A median gross rent of $2,000 or more is represented as $2,000.
4. A median gross rent of 50 percent or more as a percentage of household income is represented as 50.0

Table C-4. Cities — Where: Migration, Housing, and Transportation, 2010–2012—*Continued*

STATE and place code		STATE or city	Percent who lived in the same house one year ago	Percent who did not live in the same city one year ago	Total occupied housing units	Percent owner-occupied housing units	Median value of owner-occupied housing units (dollars)[1]	Median selected monthly owner costs as a percentage of household income[2]		Median gross rent (dollars)[2]	Median gross rent as a percentage of household income[4]	Percent of workers who drove alone to work	Mean travel time to work (minutes)	Percent of occupied housing units with no vehicle available
								With a mortgage	Without a mortgage					
		ACS table number:	C07204	C07204	B25003	B25003	B25077	B25092	B25092	B25064	B25071	C08301	308013/ C08012	C25045
		Column number:	1	2	3	4	5	6	7	8	9	10	11	12
		Indiana—Cont.												
18	19486	East Chicago city	82.3	10.1	9,660	42.8	83,400	25.6	13.7	651	36.3	81.0	21.5	20.7
18	20728	Elkhart city	75.5	11.3	19,025	53.8	84,300	21.3	13.5	668	30.2	77.2	20.8	11.9
18	22000	Evansville city	80.9	7.1	51,410	54.6	90,500	21.7	13.0	683	30.8	80.7	18.3	11.6
18	23278	Fishers town	89.0	9.1	27,620	84.3	205,300	20.8	10.0	975	22.8	85.6	27.7	1.0
18	25000	Fort Wayne city	85.8	4.5	100,418	63.5	99,900	19.6	10.0	640	27.5	85.4	19.6	8.5
18	25450	Franklin city	80.5	12.4	8,333	59.2	111,800	20.7	10.9	856	30.8	79.5	23.9	4.9
18	27000	Gary city	85.5	5.3	30,229	51.1	64,500	24.4	13.3	696	40.1	82.5	25.0	18.8
18	28386	Goshen city	76.1	13.6	11,413	58.3	111,200	23.0	13.0	703	31.9	75.0	17.8	9.8
18	28800	Granger CDP	94.6	4.0	9,676	95.7	190,700	17.8	10.0	1,057	19.0	89.2	22.4	1.0
18	29520	Greenfield city	86.6	8.1	7,927	68.7	117,400	21.1	10.0	781	26.7	85.9	24.9	4.4
18	29898	Greenwood city	81.5	12.9	20,736	61.7	129,100	19.5	10.6	809	30.4	87.5	26.4	4.8
18	31000	Hammond city	87.4	7.2	28,565	62.5	91,300	22.8	12.9	791	33.7	82.4	26.9	10.4
18	33466	Highland town	91.2	6.0	9,565	78.0	152,900	21.1	10.0	926	25.7	89.5	25.2	2.8
18	34114	Hobart city	90.6	6.5	11,124	71.5	132,600	21.8	14.2	799	30.5	86.9	25.6	5.9
18	36003	Indianapolis city (balance)	82.4	5.7	325,624	54.9	117,200	21.7	11.8	754	32.9	81.9	22.5	9.6
18	38358	Jeffersonville city	90.2	5.7	17,660	66.9	129,600	21.1	12.1	709	28.6	85.4	22.6	6.7
18	40392	Kokomo city	80.4	7.4	24,785	64.0	80,500	19.9	11.3	625	35.9	83.2	19.0	11.6
18	40788	Lafayette city	75.6	12.2	28,474	50.5	103,100	19.7	10.0	716	32.3	79.4	16.1	8.6
18	42246	La Porte city	81.9	10.1	9,016	62.2	91,500	22.4	11.6	669	29.7	87.6	19.8	8.6
18	42426	Lawrence city	87.3	10.5	16,994	69.7	124,000	22.0	14.5	787	26.9	83.7	25.2	4.0
18	46908	Marion city	81.5	8.3	11,402	60.1	63,700	22.2	12.5	552	29.0	78.5	16.1	11.3
18	48528	Merrillville town	85.0	12.9	12,789	65.5	130,800	25.0	10.0	901	32.4	85.7	27.9	8.0
18	48798	Michigan City city	80.5	10.8	12,309	53.8	93,700	21.7	13.1	687	36.4	83.0	19.8	12.2
18	49932	Mishawaka city	77.1	15.4	20,738	49.0	95,400	21.2	12.1	705	29.2	83.7	19.7	7.9
18	51876	Muncie city	62.5	17.6	27,611	49.4	72,300	20.7	13.0	650	40.6	74.1	16.9	11.4
18	51912	Munster town	92.9	5.9	8,588	86.4	200,800	22.7	10.0	889	30.8	83.2	25.9	5.0
18	52326	New Albany city	79.8	11.2	14,931	55.7	114,200	23.7	12.0	676	30.2	83.2	20.9	12.4
18	54180	Noblesville city	85.3	10.6	21,030	73.1	169,700	21.9	11.3	835	26.8	86.3	28.5	2.9
18	60246	Plainfield town	81.1	14.6	9,559	75.0	146,200	21.1	13.3	869	28.6	. . .	24.2	2.7
18	61092	Portage city	86.5	7.4	13,731	72.4	138,000	20.0	13.9	777	29.5	88.3	27.0	4.2
18	64260	Richmond city	75.5	11.1	15,489	55.7	80,300	21.9	12.0	584	32.4	81.7	16.2	14.6
18	68220	Schererville town	92.2	6.5	11,759	75.0	215,200	22.2	10.7	794	26.0	87.8	31.5	4.5
18	71000	South Bend city	79.1	9.5	39,167	59.6	85,400	22.1	11.0	683	33.2	79.5	19.1	11.6
18	75428	Terre Haute city	82.3	9.9	21,585	56.8	78,000	19.7	11.4	639	33.2	82.1	18.4	9.7
18	78326	Valparaiso city	81.7	12.5	11,897	59.3	162,500	20.2	10.5	803	28.8	80.7	22.2	10.5
18	82700	Westfield town	88.1	9.4	11,083	82.9	211,200	20.2	10.7	830	20.8	85.4	27.4	6.1
18	82862	West Lafayette city	56.6	29.5	12,073	32.9	172,100	17.5	10.0	836	48.1	59.6	15.2	12.5
18	86372	Zionsville town	92.3	4.7	8,224	81.4	331,600	19.3	10.6	1,189	28.1	. . .	24.7	2.9
19	00000	**Iowa**	85.0	9.1	1,224,399	72.3	124,300	20.7	11.7	660	28.1	79.9	18.8	5.8
19	01855	Ames city	58.4	22.7	22,838	41.6	172,100	20.0	10.0	734	38.8	67.4	16.7	7.0
19	02305	Ankeny city	83.7	10.5	18,328	76.5	171,900	21.2	11.7	743	24.7	87.3	20.9	3.8
19	06355	Bettendorf city	86.0	10.4	13,221	77.1	173,600	19.8	10.0	766	27.6	87.0	17.9	3.8
19	09550	Burlington city	85.9	7.1	10,909	68.6	80,800	22.9	13.8	638	29.4	79.0	15.6	10.1
19	11755	Cedar Falls city	77.2	14.0	14,369	63.8	164,100	19.1	10.0	724	37.6	79.2	14.1	5.7
19	12000	Cedar Rapids city	82.3	8.6	52,438	69.6	132,600	20.9	12.2	690	27.7	80.3	17.6	8.0
19	14430	Clinton city	85.1	5.3	11,107	67.2	93,800	20.7	13.3	595	29.5	82.9	15.9	9.0
19	16860	Council Bluffs city	81.9	7.5	24,673	64.5	111,300	22.2	12.6	720	30.6	83.6	18.8	8.7
19	19000	Davenport city	83.0	7.8	40,894	61.7	120,400	22.0	12.4	672	29.8	85.8	16.5	7.3
19	21000	Des Moines city	78.5	9.2	81,018	62.8	118,500	22.7	13.2	730	32.0	79.1	18.4	9.1
19	22395	Dubuque city	83.8	8.4	24,051	64.6	130,800	19.9	13.1	668	30.4	80.3	15.0	9.1
19	28515	Fort Dodge city	80.4	11.1	10,429	60.4	81,500	19.6	10.4	518	27.7	85.4	12.6	10.5
19	38595	Iowa City city	60.6	19.9	28,050	48.3	183,700	21.6	11.5	822	43.7	56.8	16.2	9.6
19	49485	Marion city	85.0	10.6	14,235	74.1	144,700	20.2	12.1	589	25.6	86.0	19.2	6.1
19	49755	Marshalltown city	82.8	7.3	9,963	68.1	100,600	20.5	13.2	611	24.7	74.3	13.1	9.5
19	50160	Mason City city	84.8	6.3	13,015	67.5	97,900	21.2	13.1	559	30.3	81.4	14.2	9.6
19	55110	Muscatine city	84.6	8.4	9,303	66.6	104,900	21.2	14.5	734	30.4	82.5	15.2	8.3
19	60465	Ottumwa city	82.6	5.1	10,379	67.9	70,300	19.8	13.5	610	30.5	79.0	14.7	8.9
19	73335	Sioux City city	81.7	6.9	31,350	63.3	94,100	21.3	12.0	632	30.8	81.0	16.7	9.9
19	79950	Urbandale city	89.1	9.5	16,355	81.1	190,900	20.0	10.0	785	27.9	86.6	17.9	2.7
19	82425	Waterloo city	83.4	7.1	28,283	64.8	100,300	20.3	11.6	639	31.0	84.0	15.8	8.1
19	83910	West Des Moines city	79.2	15.9	24,068	61.9	181,800	19.9	10.9	850	24.2	87.0	16.3	3.2
20	00000	**Kansas**	83.2	9.7	1,106,960	67.4	128,500	21.5	12.1	718	28.3	82.0	19.0	5.3
20	17800	Derby city	84.7	8.8	9,155	68.7	151,700	22.5	10.9	849	23.7	87.7	18.8	3.8
20	18250	Dodge City city	85.3	6.3	8,784	57.7	86,300	22.0	11.8	596	22.5	83.0	13.7	4.2
20	21275	Emporia city	71.5	12.8	9,594	52.8	93,000	21.0	11.6	554	29.9	77.2	13.8	8.9
20	25325	Garden City city	82.7	8.8	9,257	58.5	111,700	24.0	12.9	671	24.7	77.5	15.0	5.1
20	25425	Gardner city	88.5	5.7	6,841	70.5	159,600	24.3	20.3	861	23.5	. . .	24.7	2.1
20	31100	Hays city	70.3	18.4	8,569	56.2	157,800	22.3	12.6	593	31.6	84.9	10.2	6.6
20	33625	Hutchinson city	76.2	11.0	17,286	60.6	88,200	21.8	12.6	619	27.5	82.3	15.8	6.0
20	35750	Junction City city	76.4	14.5	9,456	50.4	131,800	22.8	12.9	830	26.5	78.1	16.4	6.9

1. A median value of $1,000,000 or more is represented as $1,000,000.
2. Median selected monthly owner costs of 10 percent or less as a percentage of household income is represented as 10.0.
3. A median gross rent of $2,000 or more is represented as $2,000.
4. A median gross rent of 50 percent or more as a percentage of household income is represented as 50.0.

Table C-4. Cities — Where: Migration, Housing, and Transportation, 2010–2012—Continued

STATE and place code	STATE or city	Percent who lived in the same house one year ago	Percent who did not live in the same city one year ago	Total occupied housing units	Percent owner-occupied housing units	Median value of owner-occupied housing units (dollars)[1]	Median selected monthly owner costs as a percentage of household income[2] With a mortgage	Without a mortgage	Median gross rent (dollars)[2]	Median gross rent as a percentage of household income[4]	Percent of workers who drove alone to work	Mean travel time to work (minutes)	Percent of occupied housing units with no vehicle available
	ACS table number:	C07204	C07204	B25003	B25003	B25077	B25092	B25092	B25064	B25071	C08301	B08013/ C08012	C25045
	Column number:	1	2	3	4	5	6	7	8	9	10	11	12
	Kansas—Cont.												
20 36000	Kansas City city	81.9	8.4	52,447	60.2	89,300	24.8	16.2	719	32.4	82.3	20.9	10.2
20 38900	Lawrence city	66.2	14.0	34,574	43.7	178,000	22.3	12.1	846	33.8	74.0	18.6	4.7
20 39000	Leavenworth city	66.1	26.9	12,184	47.1	119,900	20.8	12.4	836	25.5	79.2	17.0	6.1
20 39075	Leawood city	89.9	8.8	12,044	92.5	385,400	20.5	11.0	2,000	27.2	85.8	19.8	2.9
20 39350	Lenexa city	81.3	15.5	19,563	60.2	215,900	21.0	10.3	928	27.8	86.2	19.6	5.6
20 39825	Liberal city	82.3	6.8	6,577	63.0	84,600	20.1	10.0	659	23.6	65.5	17.2	6.4
20 44250	Manhattan city	73.4	16.5	20,118	38.8	174,800	21.9	10.8	825	32.1	73.3	15.8	6.5
20 52575	Olathe city	85.8	8.5	45,072	73.2	193,000	21.7	10.0	876	28.7	83.5	21.1	3.1
20 53775	Overland Park city	84.5	10.0	72,431	66.0	222,400	21.5	10.3	927	26.2	84.6	20.6	3.7
20 56025	Pittsburg city	72.7	12.8	7,945	46.7	81,400	19.3	12.7	657	33.9	85.3	13.7	6.9
20 57575	Prairie Village city	87.3	11.9	9,724	80.0	204,300	19.8	10.8	1,140	23.8	88.1	20.3	4.2
20 62700	Salina city	82.5	7.5	19,503	62.6	113,200	22.5	12.3	649	29.3	83.0	14.7	5.8
20 64500	Shawnee city	87.8	9.9	23,731	71.8	191,600	21.7	12.2	780	28.2	87.3	21.2	3.1
20 71000	Topeka city	79.1	6.9	53,366	56.0	94,700	21.7	12.6	674	29.8	80.9	16.0	10.3
20 79000	Wichita city	81.8	5.8	149,703	60.6	117,600	21.7	12.2	682	29.3	84.6	17.5	7.1
21 00000	**Kentucky**	85.0	10.4	1,690,132	68.1	120,800	21.7	11.1	640	29.8	82.7	22.9	7.8
21 02368	Ashland city	86.0	7.7	9,299	61.7	97,200	17.7	10.3	567	30.4	78.2	16.0	13.3
21 08902	Bowling Green city	65.3	19.5	23,219	36.7	134,400	22.9	11.8	637	33.4	79.9	14.9	10.8
21 17848	Covington city	77.7	13.0	16,696	48.3	104,100	23.7	12.2	678	34.3	79.7	22.2	16.9
21 24274	Elizabethtown city	78.0	14.8	11,458	49.2	149,700	20.2	10.0	677	28.7	83.6	19.9	8.1
21 27982	Florence city	81.7	14.0	12,415	52.8	136,100	23.3	10.0	802	28.7	81.9	21.4	9.3
21 28900	Frankfort city	75.8	11.3	12,233	48.0	133,300	22.7	10.0	668	31.6	77.6	15.7	6.8
21 30700	Georgetown city	77.0	13.3	10,997	63.4	149,400	19.7	10.0	714	29.0	82.4	19.5	8.2
21 35866	Henderson city	83.6	7.3	12,310	55.3	95,000	22.7	10.0	577	32.1	85.1	18.5	12.9
21 37918	Hopkinsville city	80.4	11.1	12,969	51.2	111,100	23.2	10.9	589	29.3	84.7	17.4	10.4
21 39142	Independence city	89.7	7.7	8,690	80.7	155,900	21.5	12.4	867	28.9	. . .	26.2	2.8
21 40222	Jeffersontown city	81.5	15.3	10,363	65.8	162,900	20.1	10.0	811	26.7	83.3	21.5	2.2
21 46027	Lexington-Fayette urban county	75.8	9.7	122,046	55.8	164,400	21.1	10.0	737	31.2	79.8	19.4	8.4
21 48006	Louisville/Jefferson County (balance)	85.7	5.3	242,395	61.0	139,400	22.1	11.7	683	30.2	81.6	22.5	11.4
21 56136	Nicholasville city	75.4	12.6	10,669	57.8	137,700	23.5	12.5	744	29.2	88.5	24.6	5.8
21 58620	Owensboro city	84.7	6.5	23,387	60.2	101,900	21.7	10.6	616	28.6	84.2	15.3	8.0
21 58836	Paducah city	80.8	9.5	11,429	50.5	95,300	19.5	12.1	555	26.4	85.1	14.9	14.0
21 63912	Radcliff city	68.9	23.7	8,536	48.9	127,100	21.9	10.0	650	26.8	83.9	21.0	4.9
21 65226	Richmond city	69.5	16.2	12,385	40.8	135,100	24.4	14.6	579	32.5	75.4	20.7	7.3
22 00000	**Louisiana**	85.6	9.8	1,706,091	66.7	138,800	21.4	10.0	760	32.3	82.1	24.8	8.6
22 00975	Alexandria city	84.7	6.5	16,587	55.1	124,400	25.2	11.4	728	38.8	82.7	17.4	13.3
22 05000	Baton Rouge city	80.3	9.1	87,336	50.9	155,100	22.6	10.5	774	35.6	78.1	20.3	9.9
22 05210	Bayou Cane CDP	77.3	18.2	7,616	61.1	147,500	19.9	11.2	882	27.0	84.4	21.8	4.5
22 08920	Bossier City city	80.9	12.2	25,021	54.5	141,800	20.8	10.0	788	30.2	85.7	17.8	9.0
22 13960	Central city	93.1	5.3	10,278	83.7	173,000	21.1	10.0	743	32.1	88.4	28.7	3.1
22 32755	Hammond city	72.1	18.1	6,885	48.0	156,900	20.2	13.3	792	39.2	76.4	21.9	9.3
22 33245	Harvey CDP	86.5	11.3	7,900	61.4	150,300	22.7	10.0	921	39.1	83.7	26.6	8.7
22 36255	Houma city	84.2	8.4	12,750	65.7	149,700	21.6	10.3	725	26.7	81.1	22.5	11.0
22 39475	Kenner city	89.1	7.2	24,270	60.2	175,400	24.2	10.6	925	33.2	80.2	24.7	7.3
22 40735	Lafayette city	81.4	8.9	49,438	57.9	172,300	22.5	11.2	758	32.1	80.0	19.7	8.0
22 41155	Lake Charles city	77.4	11.1	29,568	56.0	123,200	22.3	10.5	711	32.4	81.3	17.6	10.8
22 42030	Laplace CDP	87.3	6.2	10,274	76.4	159,800	23.7	10.0	894	27.4	84.5	26.9	6.6
22 48785	Marrero CDP	94.1	4.2	12,597	62.9	128,800	26.4	10.0	750	41.2	82.0	24.5	12.8
22 50115	Metairie CDP	83.8	10.1	57,040	60.5	209,400	23.8	11.7	854	29.5	81.0	20.8	7.1
22 51410	Monroe city	84.2	6.2	18,695	45.6	123,900	21.9	11.8	573	36.1	84.1	15.4	15.7
22 54035	New Iberia city	83.1	8.6	11,391	62.3	103,800	21.6	10.0	668	28.6	78.8	19.9	14.2
22 55000	New Orleans city	81.2	7.8	146,018	47.4	179,500	26.7	14.1	901	37.8	70.1	23.0	18.7
22 62385	Prairieville CDP	91.1	7.5	8,808	90.7	209,000	18.9	10.0	903	. . .	86.9	30.9	2.7
22 66655	Ruston city	66.3	23.1	8,282	41.8	127,000	21.8	12.3	661	36.5	79.7	14.0	9.2
22 70000	Shreveport city	82.1	6.8	78,212	55.8	124,500	21.1	10.4	739	32.1	82.5	18.8	12.1
22 70805	Slidell city	82.1	10.6	9,979	68.8	153,300	23.7	12.4	1,052	33.6	81.3	27.3	4.6
22 73640	Sulphur city	81.4	12.4	7,832	71.5	119,700	17.9	10.9	750	29.7	89.9	15.5	6.9
22 75180	Terrytown CDP	85.8	12.3	8,225	52.6	160,000	23.2	10.0	912	33.4	78.8	26.1	10.5
23 00000	**Maine**	86.0	11.3	552,963	71.6	173,900	24.1	14.0	748	31.0	78.7	23.4	7.4
23 02060	Auburn city	80.5	12.2	9,798	59.0	159,800	23.6	16.5	688	28.6	76.8	19.6	11.7
23 02795	Bangor city	75.4	17.0	14,258	42.2	142,800	22.9	15.1	726	35.1	77.1	14.9	16.1
23 04860	Biddeford city	79.6	13.5	8,987	46.1	223,000	25.4	13.4	791	32.1	76.4	23.2	12.1
23 38740	Lewiston city	80.6	11.2	15,535	49.4	148,000	25.0	18.0	665	31.6	73.0	19.4	17.4
23 60545	Portland city	74.3	14.1	30,846	44.4	234,500	26.7	14.1	900	31.1	69.0	17.6	18.5
23 71990	South Portland city	81.6	13.7	10,994	61.6	219,400	26.0	14.9	996	29.7	82.2	19.1	5.8
24 00000	**Maryland**	86.8	10.1	2,141,086	67.1	289,300	24.7	12.7	1,177	31.0	73.2	32.0	9.6
24 01600	Annapolis city	83.5	12.1	16,136	53.1	363,900	24.4	11.8	1,338	28.9	68.1	25.9	11.9
24 02275	Arnold CDP	90.1	8.0	8,131	84.7	376,500	23.8	10.3	1,679	29.7	88.0	29.9	1.0
24 02825	Aspen Hill CDP	85.3	12.7	17,050	62.6	389,500	24.4	11.5	1,414	33.7	66.5	35.9	8.0
24 04000	Baltimore city	83.0	5.9	240,575	47.1	156,800	26.0	15.4	900	32.9	59.8	30.1	31.1

1. A median value of $1,000,000 or more is represented as $1,000,000.
2. Median selected monthly owner costs of 10 percent or less as a percenage of household income is represented as 10.0.
3. A median gross rent of $2,000 or more is represented as $2,000.
4. A median gross rent of 50 percent or more as a percentage of household income is represented as 50.0.

Table C-4. Cities — Where: Migration, Housing, and Transportation, 2010–2012—*Continued*

STATE and place code		STATE or city	Percent who lived in the same house one year ago	Percent who did not live in the same city one year ago	Total occupied housing units	Percent owner-occupied housing units	Median value of owner-occupied housing units (dollars)[1]	Median selected monthly owner costs as a percentage of household income[2] With a mortgage	Median selected monthly owner costs as a percentage of household income[2] Without a mortgage	Median gross rent (dollars)[2]	Median gross rent as a percentage of household income[4]	Percent of workers who drove alone to work	Mean travel time to work (minutes)	Percent of occupied housing units with no vehicle available
		ACS table number:	C07204	C07204	B25003	B25003	B25077	B25092	B25092	B25064	B25071	C08301	B08013/ C08012	C25045
		Column number:	1	2	3	4	5	6	7	8	9	10	11	12
		Maryland—Cont.												
24	05825	Bel Air North CDP	91.8	6.4	10,175	89.7	312,900	23.5	11.1	1,562	36.6	. . .	34.6	2.4
24	05950	Bel Air South CDP	90.6	7.0	17,035	81.1	278,400	22.6	10.9	1,141	27.0	86.1	31.1	4.8
24	07125	Bethesda CDP	85.7	11.1	25,000	66.7	807,300	21.0	12.1	1,856	26.5	58.8	29.2	7.3
24	08775	Bowie city	91.0	8.2	19,068	86.7	297,700	25.4	10.5	1,757	27.9	73.8	35.5	3.8
24	13325	Carney CDP	87.1	11.1	11,903	54.5	231,100	22.4	10.0	1,196	32.5	79.7	27.1	11.7
24	14125	Catonsville CDP	90.8	7.7	14,999	68.6	314,400	22.6	10.7	1,273	32.9	84.3	25.4	11.0
24	16875	Chillum CDP	75.3	21.0	11,593	38.3	220,000	26.5	12.8	1,240	30.2	54.0	35.7	13.8
24	17900	Clinton CDP	91.7	7.6	12,629	85.2	286,900	27.5	13.7	1,745	36.3	70.9	40.2	4.1
24	18250	Cockeysville CDP	82.9	15.5	8,817	37.8	329,200	23.1	10.0	1,049	24.9	82.8	25.3	7.1
24	18750	College Park city	60.6	32.2	6,307	44.4	253,100	26.1	11.9	1,333	50.0	46.9	26.8	9.0
24	19125	Columbia CDP	87.1	9.5	40,526	66.0	360,900	23.8	10.0	1,474	29.6	80.9	29.9	5.1
24	20875	Crofton CDP	87.1	8.3	10,988	75.8	370,600	22.9	10.0	1,485	21.8	85.3	34.4	2.0
24	21325	Cumberland city	84.8	6.5	8,956	58.6	97,200	22.1	17.4	582	32.6	83.2	15.5	16.2
24	23975	Dundalk CDP	85.3	7.9	23,501	66.8	153,600	23.2	13.5	944	31.8	75.6	25.9	11.9
24	25150	Edgewood CDP	92.0	6.6	9,705	65.0	187,900	26.4	18.8	1,070	31.8	73.1	30.8	9.4
24	25575	Eldersburg CDP	94.2	4.7	10,274	90.3	367,200	22.1	13.3	1,126	27.1	87.2	34.6	2.4
24	26000	Ellicott City CDP	87.9	9.5	24,413	75.9	495,800	22.9	10.0	1,402	28.6	82.5	29.7	2.5
24	26600	Essex CDP	86.7	9.8	14,486	55.8	191,100	25.5	13.4	877	29.5	73.4	28.7	14.5
24	27250	Fairland CDP	84.5	13.8	8,434	49.5	312,500	26.5	10.0	1,446	36.7	71.0	41.6	8.6
24	29525	Fort Washington CDP	. . .		8,672	88.1	327,700	27.5	11.5	1,669	27.4	74.4	42.3	2.6
24	30325	Frederick city	78.5	11.5	26,038	55.0	241,200	25.1	16.3	1,198	30.9	67.9	33.9	8.9
24	31175	Gaithersburg city	83.6	12.4	22,526	56.6	354,300	24.4	11.1	1,439	32.5	65.9	31.2	7.4
24	32025	Germantown CDP	84.1	9.2	30,942	66.7	304,500	26.2	10.0	1,590	32.0	73.4	36.6	5.8
24	32650	Glen Burnie CDP	84.8	10.6	26,283	60.6	242,400	25.5	12.3	1,126	30.6	82.5	27.2	6.9
24	34775	Greenbelt city	81.3	14.9	9,317	45.4	211,700	23.9	10.0	1,278	30.5	61.1	30.3	9.7
24	36075	Hagerstown city	76.0	13.2	16,293	41.5	152,000	24.9	15.6	807	31.8	76.8	22.8	17.1
24	41475	Ilchester CDP	91.3	7.8	9,047	78.1	363,900	22.7	12.9	1,502	27.5	87.3	28.5	3.1
24	45325	Landover CDP	83.5	15.5	7,907	46.9	176,600	32.4	17.2	1,182	33.9	57.4	33.2	18.6
24	45525	Langley Park CDP	85.3	12.6	5,188	23.5	207,300	34.1	13.1	1,156	33.1	30.1	39.0	25.2
24	45900	Laurel city	81.1	13.3	9,639	49.2	236,000	28.8	10.8	1,332	29.9	70.9	35.6	9.9
24	47450	Lochearn CDP	91.5	7.0	9,526	67.6	209,200	27.2	15.0	1,051	33.3	73.4	31.2	8.8
24	52300	Middle River CDP	87.5	11.2	9,931	57.8	171,200	24.8	14.8	1,070	31.3	77.1	30.7	10.4
24	52562	Milford Mill CDP	88.4	10.4	12,339	49.8	222,000	24.7	11.9	1,186	29.6	79.4	29.4	7.7
24	53325	Montgomery Village CDP	86.0	12.4	11,871	73.6	257,900	27.9	10.0	1,388	32.4	68.3	37.7	7.4
24	56337	North Bethesda CDP	75.3	21.6	20,448	52.2	504,200	23.4	11.4	1,775	26.8	56.8	31.1	9.4
24	56875	North Potomac CDP	92.3	6.4	7,701	81.4	612,400	22.9	10.0	2,000	27.6	74.4	35.3	3.6
24	58300	Odenton CDP	81.0	16.5	14,296	68.4	305,000	22.9	10.0	1,756	27.8	82.0	29.1	1.0
24	58900	Olney CDP	93.2	5.6	11,881	86.3	486,900	24.0	10.0	1,493	30.7	76.8	35.6	2.3
24	59425	Owings Mills CDP	83.4	11.1	13,305	42.9	270,100	22.9	13.3	1,280	25.4	74.0	33.9	5.7
24	60275	Parkville CDP	87.5	9.8	12,894	62.8	197,400	24.3	12.4	1,045	33.3	73.6	27.8	11.4
24	60475	Pasadena CDP	89.3	10.1	8,233	86.4	275,100	25.0	11.3	1,603	38.8	85.0	28.8	1.6
24	60975	Perry Hall CDP	90.1	7.8	11,472	79.9	256,700	23.7	12.5	1,298	29.2	84.4	29.1	3.0
24	61400	Pikesville CDP	89.0	8.2	14,127	65.3	299,500	23.2	15.2	1,195	29.8	73.7	25.4	9.5
24	63300	Potomac CDP	88.7	10.1	15,991	87.9	867,100	23.0	10.4	2,000	29.0	72.8	31.5	1.8
24	64950	Randallstown CDP	93.2	5.9	11,277	72.6	240,000	26.4	12.2	1,006	31.6	77.2	33.9	8.5
24	65600	Reisterstown CDP	87.7	10.5	10,413	53.9	239,700	24.8	11.7	1,099	34.2	68.3	33.3	8.4
24	67675	Rockville city	85.5	11.5	24,375	58.5	485,500	23.5	10.9	1,746	28.8	59.9	30.9	9.2
24	69525	Salisbury city	68.6	18.3	11,541	36.9	152,000	25.8	13.3	950	35.5	72.2	20.4	14.7
24	71150	Severn CDP	89.2	10.1	15,909	72.8	318,900	25.1	12.7	1,340	32.3	82.2	30.0	4.5
24	71200	Severna Park CDP	92.6	6.4	12,730	91.8	470,800	22.5	11.1	1,405	35.3	86.5	29.9	2.5
24	72450	Silver Spring CDP	78.9	15.7	30,566	37.3	440,400	22.8	12.7	1,397	31.3	52.8	34.0	17.7
24	73650	South Laurel CDP	83.4	13.9	9,551	41.8	313,300	29.4	10.0	1,248	29.3	69.1	36.0	6.9
24	75725	Suitland CDP	81.8	15.0	9,699	41.7	199,600	30.0	14.2	1,104	31.0	59.2	34.4	16.1
24	78425	Towson CDP	82.0	13.7	20,991	57.4	324,900	22.3	11.8	1,244	32.6	77.3	24.9	9.2
24	81175	Waldorf CDP	88.4	7.3	24,821	68.2	261,200	24.8	10.0	1,491	33.8	77.0	43.1	4.6
24	83775	Wheaton CDP	82.8	14.4	14,708	64.5	325,200	26.4	11.3	1,594	35.6	57.1	35.8	8.0
24	86475	Woodlawn CDP (Baltimore County)	87.0	11.2	14,960	60.4	210,400	24.7	11.0	1,141	28.1	84.3	28.5	9.9
25	00000	**Massachusetts**	86.8	9.0	2,524,028	62.3	328,300	25.4	15.4	1,050	30.3	72.3	28.0	12.8
25	00840	Agawam Town city	92.8	6.0	11,253	76.9	236,100	23.3	14.1	833	29.0	90.4	22.3	5.1
25	01640	Arlington CDP	89.2	8.0	18,915	59.0	489,900	23.4	16.8	1,345	24.4	67.4	29.5	9.4
25	02690	Attleboro city	88.0	7.3	16,580	64.8	276,900	26.1	15.7	916	28.8	82.6	30.0	6.6
25	03690	Barnstable Town city	91.5	5.2	19,369	74.8	345,700	29.7	17.6	1,112	34.4	83.9	22.6	8.9
25	05105	Belmont CDP	85.9	10.2	9,016	63.2	631,900	23.9	15.2	1,599	24.6	64.6	27.5	5.6
25	05595	Beverly city	86.8	10.0	15,406	62.6	362,500	25.7	15.8	1,023	30.7	75.3	26.3	10.4
25	07000	Boston city	77.4	11.3	248,738	33.2	368,600	26.0	14.5	1,260	30.9	38.1	28.9	36.9
25	07740	Braintree Town city	90.7	6.4	12,955	72.2	365,000	25.6	14.4	1,291	32.6	75.1	29.8	6.3
25	09000	Brockton city	85.6	6.6	33,057	57.2	226,200	29.4	18.1	1,009	37.3	77.9	29.3	17.0

1. A median value of $1,000,000 or more is represented as $1,000,000.
2. Median selected monthly owner costs of 10 percent or less as a percentage of household income is represented as 10.0.
3. A median gross rent of $2,000 or more is represented as $2,000.
4. A median gross rent of 50 percent or more as a percentage of household income is represented as 50.0.

STATE and place code		STATE or city	Percent who lived in the same house one year ago	Percent who did not live in the same city one year ago	Total occupied housing units	Percent owner-occupied housing units	Median value of owner-occupied housing units (dollars)[1]	Median selected monthly owner costs as a percentage of household income[2] With a mortgage	Without a mortgage	Median gross rent (dollars)[2]	Median gross rent as a percentage of household income[4]	Percent of workers who drove alone to work	Mean travel time to work (minutes)	Percent of occupied housing units with no vehicle available
		ACS table number:	C07204	C07204	B25003	B25003	B25077	B25092	B25092	B25064	B25071	C08301	B08013/C08012	C25045
		Column number:	1	2	3	4	5	6	7	8	9	10	11	12
		Massachusetts—Cont.												
25	09210	Brookline CDP	81.4	14.4	25,897	48.3	689,400	24.1	15.2	1,722	33.0	41.5	28.7	25.1
25	09875	Burlington CDP	87.6	9.7	9,434	70.3	405,600	24.2	14.0	1,639	29.0	81.7	27.2	5.5
25	11000	Cambridge city	71.2	21.0	44,598	36.3	526,200	22.5	13.0	1,591	29.4	29.3	25.2	31.2
25	13205	Chelsea city	86.1	7.7	11,927	29.5	246,800	29.4	20.3	1,114	32.0	45.9	29.2	30.8
25	13660	Chicopee city	86.7	8.0	23,123	57.3	174,000	24.2	16.2	786	28.4	86.1	20.7	11.6
25	16285	Danvers CDP	90.6	8.2	10,314	65.8	354,800	25.7	16.7	1,290	26.5	84.9	26.2	6.0
25	16530	Dedham CDP	87.9	9.9	9,580	71.6	374,200	25.4	17.5	1,491	29.1	76.8	29.6	5.9
25	21990	Everett city	87.8	10.1	15,611	39.5	311,400	36.4	14.9	1,185	33.0	58.0	31.6	17.6
25	23000	Fall River city	83.6	7.0	38,292	35.1	237,700	28.4	17.0	705	31.6	82.0	22.6	19.6
25	23875	Fitchburg city	82.6	9.8	14,680	55.9	189,300	25.1	18.1	828	30.6	79.8	25.6	12.8
25	24960	Framingham CDP	83.0	11.7	26,682	55.5	342,900	25.5	14.3	1,080	28.5	76.8	26.9	10.7
25	25172	Franklin Town city	92.2	6.5	11,063	79.8	377,800	23.4	14.5	1,056	25.6	75.6	34.5	5.7
25	25485	Gardner city	79.9	10.5	7,913	53.7	173,300	28.6	16.5	697	28.0	76.1	25.8	13.2
25	26150	Gloucester city	89.5	5.8	12,099	62.0	364,200	30.4	19.6	931	28.3	75.1	25.5	8.8
25	29405	Haverhill city	86.3	6.8	23,923	63.3	259,700	26.5	14.5	976	33.5	79.3	29.1	9.1
25	30840	Holyoke city	84.1	8.2	15,760	40.8	190,500	25.6	13.7	648	32.8	77.3	20.4	25.9
25	34550	Lawrence city	82.1	6.2	26,606	28.3	213,900	31.3	12.5	953	36.2	64.9	23.0	25.8
25	35075	Leominster city	86.2	7.7	16,870	53.3	233,600	25.1	14.3	889	28.4	84.6	25.9	10.4
25	35250	Lexington CDP	92.1	5.5	11,627	82.7	692,000	23.0	14.3	1,814	36.8	74.8	29.8	5.1
25	37000	Lowell city	84.7	7.8	38,913	45.5	228,300	27.3	13.8	969	29.8	74.3	25.7	15.4
25	37490	Lynn city	83.8	7.0	32,900	46.0	248,800	28.8	18.7	935	32.8	67.2	27.6	22.6
25	37875	Malden city	82.0	13.5	22,565	42.6	327,000	29.8	14.9	1,189	30.1	51.9	33.1	19.2
25	38435	Marblehead CDP	89.7	6.3	7,618	80.4	544,400	25.2	14.0	1,159	27.4	73.2	28.6	3.3
25	38715	Marlborough city	83.8	10.4	15,726	58.4	307,100	24.5	15.4	1,082	27.3	79.9	27.7	8.1
25	39835	Medford city	84.2	12.3	22,448	58.0	386,700	29.0	17.0	1,390	26.9	64.7	28.7	9.4
25	40115	Melrose city	89.6	7.3	11,422	66.0	419,400	24.1	14.7	1,012	25.6	62.9	30.8	8.9
25	40710	Methuen Town city	90.5	6.5	17,885	71.8	278,000	24.4	15.4	919	31.3	85.3	24.4	9.1
25	41200	Milford CDP	86.2	6.6	9,562	63.9	285,400	24.3	18.7	1,075	32.3	78.2	29.9	9.3
25	41725	Milton CDP	89.7	8.8	8,937	79.4	495,600	24.6	17.8	1,120	31.6	71.9	31.2	8.1
25	44140	Needham CDP	90.4	7.7	10,449	83.2	648,000	24.0	13.9	1,329	27.4	72.3	29.6	4.6
25	45000	New Bedford city	85.7	4.3	38,851	43.6	218,600	30.3	18.5	753	30.6	75.5	23.6	18.7
25	45560	Newton city	85.1	11.1	30,484	70.9	685,900	23.2	13.9	1,611	28.1	62.6	26.3	6.7
25	46330	Northampton city	83.0	12.0	11,628	58.7	273,400	25.7	15.3	910	30.1	64.2	21.5	10.5
25	50285	Norwood CDP	89.4	7.8	11,296	59.0	373,900	23.8	14.8	1,169	25.3	78.0	27.8	7.6
25	52490	Peabody city	90.4	5.5	21,564	62.6	329,500	26.4	15.6	1,202	31.9	85.0	25.7	10.7
25	53960	Pittsfield city	86.4	6.0	19,905	59.2	171,500	25.0	17.9	727	31.3	81.2	17.7	15.8
25	55745	Quincy city	81.7	11.8	39,414	48.1	341,200	27.9	17.5	1,184	29.1	61.4	32.6	16.1
25	55990	Randolph CDP	90.0	6.8	11,580	70.5	261,300	28.9	13.6	1,208	35.4	74.5	34.7	10.0
25	56165	Reading CDP	90.2	7.9	9,122	80.9	439,100	26.8	14.6	1,285	22.1	81.2	28.6	5.0
25	56585	Revere city	85.5	9.0	19,757	49.8	307,000	34.4	21.2	1,154	34.4	56.4	29.9	19.5
25	59105	Salem city	81.6	11.0	18,150	48.9	304,900	27.2	21.0	1,066	30.0	66.0	29.2	16.2
25	60050	Saugus CDP	93.5	4.7	10,433	78.8	341,200	27.9	17.6	967	28.5	81.4	27.5	3.8
25	62535	Somerville city	77.3	15.8	31,630	33.4	425,000	28.0	18.7	1,374	28.3	43.0	28.3	25.0
25	67000	Springfield city	83.8	6.7	55,911	48.5	149,500	26.3	17.8	771	35.8	76.2	21.5	22.3
25	67700	Stoneham CDP	90.5	6.2	8,899	64.3	394,300	25.6	15.8	1,232	32.7	86.6	24.4	9.9
25	69170	Taunton city	91.0	4.6	21,594	63.1	243,400	27.4	16.0	878	31.5	84.6	28.1	10.1
25	72250	Wakefield CDP	91.3	6.4	9,730	74.8	408,600	25.4	13.7	1,117	26.5	80.1	28.2	5.4
25	72600	Waltham city	80.1	15.2	23,488	49.5	406,000	26.1	16.2	1,298	29.0	70.0	24.6	10.6
25	73440	Watertown Town city	82.5	14.1	14,093	51.8	429,600	26.6	16.9	1,448	23.2	67.1	26.6	10.3
25	74210	Wellesley CDP	88.2	9.7	8,561	82.9	897,400	22.5	15.7	1,498	23.8	61.4	25.9	2.7
25	76030	Westfield city	85.7	9.4	15,299	66.3	223,400	22.2	14.9	800	33.1	82.9	24.1	8.3
25	77890	West Springfield Town city	86.2	11.6	11,585	61.5	201,800	25.4	15.9	820	26.9	87.0	19.7	9.3
25	78972	Weymouth Town city	92.1	5.8	22,672	67.2	312,500	26.2	17.7	1,092	29.3	78.8	31.3	9.0
25	80195	Wilmington CDP	92.9	6.1	7,555	87.9	370,300	23.7	16.0	1,585	27.0	90.1	28.4	2.6
25	80545	Winchester CDP	92.7	6.2	7,516	84.5	677,000	23.1	15.8	1,437	29.0	74.2	27.3	4.1
25	81035	Woburn city	86.7	8.5	15,140	59.3	361,300	26.0	16.2	1,245	27.6	82.6	24.2	6.9
25	82000	Worcester city	84.4	7.6	68,665	44.4	214,800	26.2	14.9	903	31.9	74.7	23.2	18.4
26	00000	**Michigan**	85.2	11.1	3,805,261	71.9	119,200	23.6	13.7	755	33.0	82.8	24.0	7.9
26	00440	Adrian city	68.9	18.9	7,836	52.0	75,700	25.9	18.0	680	41.6	76.7	17.0	14.1
26	01380	Allen Park city	94.0	5.2	10,858	85.5	93,900	21.5	13.8	833	33.1	85.8	22.4	4.8
26	03000	Ann Arbor city	64.1	20.3	45,974	45.2	225,100	23.0	13.1	976	32.4	58.4	18.9	12.4
26	04105	Auburn Hills city	75.0	20.6	8,746	47.0	110,900	22.9	16.1	889	25.1	82.9	22.1	5.1
26	05920	Battle Creek city	81.2	9.4	20,745	60.8	83,900	24.2	14.4	650	34.3	77.7	17.8	11.7
26	06020	Bay City city	83.3	7.8	14,339	68.6	68,100	23.4	14.8	519	33.8	85.2	18.9	13.0
26	08640	Birmingham city	82.9	12.4	8,658	72.4	346,300	26.3	14.0	1,193	21.6	86.9	22.2	3.0
26	12060	Burton city	88.3	7.1	11,404	76.0	68,200	24.7	13.9	749	39.3	85.4	23.4	7.1
26	21000	Dearborn city	85.2	6.7	31,824	68.2	99,800	26.2	15.2	962	38.5	83.0	21.7	8.4
26	21020	Dearborn Heights city	87.4	8.4	20,931	75.0	82,800	25.9	15.2	962	39.2	86.3	22.4	7.3
26	22000	Detroit city	84.0	4.2	253,968	51.6	48,000	29.7	18.0	745	44.9	69.7	26.7	24.5
26	24120	East Lansing city	47.9	34.5	13,473	35.3	172,400	22.1	11.1	829	50.0	52.0	16.0	10.0

1. A median value of $1,000,000 or more is represented as $1,000,000.
2. Median selected monthly owner costs of 10 percent or less as a percenage of household income is represented as 10.0
3. A median gross rent of $2,000 or more is represented as $2,000.
4. A median gross rent of 50 percent or more as a percentage of household income is represented as 50.0.

Table C-4. Cities — Where: Migration, Housing, and Transportation, 2010–2012—Continued

STATE and place code		STATE or city	Percent who lived in the same house one year ago	Percent who did not live in the same city one year ago	Total occupied housing units	Percent owner-occupied housing units	Median value of owner-occupied housing units (dollars)[1]	Median selected monthly owner costs as a percentage of household income[2] With a mortgage	Median selected monthly owner costs as a percentage of household income[2] Without a mortgage	Median gross rent (dollars)[2]	Median gross rent as a percentage of household income[4]	Percent of workers who drove alone to work	Mean travel time to work (minutes)	Percent of occupied housing units with no vehicle available
		ACS table number:	C07204	C07204	B25003	B25003	B25077	B25092	B25092	B25064	B25071	C08301	B08013/ C08012	C25045
		Column number:	1	2	3	4	5	6	7	8	9	10	11	12
		Michigan—Cont.												
26	24290	Eastpointe city	80.9	17.6	12,513	73.3	58,100	26.9	17.4	971	50.0	83.9	22.5	6.5
26	27440	Farmington Hills city	82.7	14.4	33,932	62.3	192,200	23.2	13.5	955	28.3	85.2	24.0	5.4
26	27880	Ferndale city	80.7	13.9	9,383	59.9	88,900	23.3	16.2	835	27.6	82.6	21.9	8.2
26	29000	Flint city	77.7	7.8	40,853	56.1	41,600	26.5	15.9	670	49.3	79.3	21.7	18.0
26	29580	Forest Hills CDP	93.5	5.4	9,028	94.2	248,800	19.4	10.9	1,317	26.1	89.3	20.3	1.3
26	31420	Garden City city	87.4	10.5	10,149	78.8	79,200	22.7	14.5	979	34.6	86.4	23.3	5.7
26	34000	Grand Rapids city	76.6	11.3	72,868	54.9	108,800	23.0	13.0	746	34.3	74.9	19.4	14.0
26	36280	Hamtramck city	84.7	10.4	6,046	49.3	39,700	28.6	20.4	611	33.4	75.6	27.0	19.2
26	37100	Haslett CDP	83.0	15.0	8,908	56.2	172,000	23.7	12.7	744	28.9	81.6	20.0	5.4
26	38640	Holland city	71.5	17.7	11,302	65.3	118,300	23.2	14.2	746	37.7	75.9	16.3	8.4
26	38780	Holt CDP	84.8	11.3	9,513	72.9	147,400	22.1	14.3	867	28.4	89.2	20.3	3.5
26	40680	Inkster city	77.1	18.0	9,272	49.1	54,200	27.7	17.5	707	40.7	84.7	23.6	15.5
26	41420	Jackson city	73.6	11.2	12,679	51.4	68,400	23.6	14.8	610	34.9	76.3	18.7	18.7
26	42160	Kalamazoo city	64.9	20.0	27,568	45.9	99,200	23.2	15.7	704	38.3	78.1	17.9	14.6
26	42820	Kentwood city	81.5	14.4	19,820	61.4	125,000	22.9	15.7	763	27.1	83.6	18.6	10.1
26	46000	Lansing city	76.6	12.2	47,522	52.4	83,100	24.3	15.0	714	35.2	78.1	19.0	12.2
26	47800	Lincoln Park city	83.5	12.1	14,252	71.6	58,200	24.4	15.3	779	32.9	82.4	23.2	7.2
26	49000	Livonia city	91.4	5.7	37,094	85.4	148,900	22.1	12.5	918	26.7	88.5	23.8	3.7
26	50560	Madison Heights city	83.6	11.5	12,751	63.6	83,800	23.6	14.4	725	34.5	82.6	22.7	12.7
26	51900	Marquette city	70.9	16.5	8,082	47.8	160,000	19.8	10.7	643	34.2	71.3	11.3	7.4
26	53780	Midland city	79.0	14.7	17,650	64.0	142,000	19.7	11.6	719	29.5	85.7	15.6	6.5
26	55020	Monroe city	81.9	11.5	8,145	59.2	105,800	22.0	12.0	776	28.9	82.8	21.5	11.1
26	56020	Mount Pleasant city	47.6	30.4	8,217	35.0	122,100	20.8	11.2	656	40.3	66.8	13.1	14.2
26	56320	Muskegon city	74.3	14.8	14,207	50.1	66,000	24.5	13.8	597	38.9	76.6	18.9	18.8
26	59140	Norton Shores city	88.1	10.5	9,570	85.5	118,500	22.2	14.1	773	25.3	88.4	18.4	3.3
26	59440	Novi city	85.2	12.6	23,254	64.6	224,800	21.4	13.7	988	24.6	90.2	26.4	4.0
26	59920	Oak Park city	85.0	11.3	11,195	57.2	79,600	24.1	14.1	1,029	37.4	77.8	23.1	11.5
26	60340	Okemos CDP	82.9	13.8	8,399	65.6	187,700	21.4	12.1	786	30.8	80.5	19.9	4.9
26	65440	Pontiac city	75.0	10.6	23,223	48.1	57,000	27.3	17.2	690	39.6	78.6	21.8	19.4
26	65560	Portage city	84.0	11.1	19,348	68.6	148,600	21.5	13.4	700	31.3	88.0	20.0	4.9
26	65820	Port Huron city	79.2	10.5	12,072	56.8	79,600	26.7	15.8	630	33.4	75.3	18.3	16.3
26	69035	Rochester Hills city	87.8	9.5	27,546	76.7	203,300	22.6	12.6	1,051	27.6	87.5	26.7	4.5
26	69420	Romulus city	81.4	16.3	8,954	68.6	69,200	26.1	15.7	774	31.1	83.4	23.8	9.2
26	69800	Roseville city	86.9	9.6	19,990	67.6	64,000	26.4	15.0	821	34.4	83.8	24.9	9.5
26	70040	Royal Oak city	82.6	12.2	28,485	67.8	150,800	21.3	15.1	855	24.1	87.1	22.6	5.1
26	70520	Saginaw city	82.3	8.3	19,247	60.3	49,100	24.5	15.9	653	45.4	77.3	19.2	16.6
26	70760	St. Clair Shores city	89.3	7.9	26,492	79.2	88,500	22.1	14.8	845	30.0	87.6	26.7	6.5
26	74900	Southfield city	79.8	14.1	31,386	49.7	104,500	24.4	16.3	944	33.4	83.4	24.0	10.9
26	74960	Southgate city	88.0	9.8	12,772	65.8	85,300	22.4	14.4	780	27.5	90.9	23.1	5.5
26	76460	Sterling Heights city	88.4	8.5	49,577	74.5	138,000	23.4	13.3	838	31.4	89.3	25.8	5.6
26	79000	Taylor city	82.7	13.1	23,573	65.6	74,200	24.6	14.0	763	33.6	84.3	22.7	8.5
26	80700	Troy city	86.8	10.9	30,382	72.8	208,300	22.2	12.2	1,016	25.2	86.8	24.4	4.7
26	82960	Walker city	83.3	12.8	10,141	61.5	143,300	21.9	13.3	683	24.8	87.5	19.7	7.1
26	84000	Warren city	86.4	9.5	52,377	73.0	85,800	23.7	16.5	818	35.5	85.7	23.9	9.5
26	84800	Waverly CDP	80.4	16.0	11,130	56.4	139,800	21.9	14.2	761	27.6	84.7	19.2	7.3
26	86000	Westland city	82.0	13.9	33,798	60.8	86,600	22.3	13.6	779	35.1	87.6	24.9	9.3
26	88900	Wyandotte city	88.3	8.3	10,453	73.5	84,000	21.9	14.9	711	34.7	82.9	22.4	8.4
26	88940	Wyoming city	84.3	12.0	26,908	64.7	100,800	23.6	12.3	694	28.4	86.1	19.4	7.2
26	89140	Ypsilanti city	57.6	34.5	7,573	32.0	108,100	25.9	16.1	693	36.5	64.2	21.0	19.5
27	00000	**Minnesota**	85.4	10.1	2,102,761	72.4	185,800	23.2	11.8	804	29.9	78.0	22.9	7.2
27	01486	Andover city	91.7	7.3	10,095	93.0	227,700	24.0	10.0	1,216	38.4	81.9	29.4	2.7
27	01900	Apple Valley city	86.1	9.6	19,067	78.3	216,600	22.4	11.0	1,160	30.0	80.4	23.9	4.0
27	02908	Austin city	83.2	7.3	9,992	65.6	91,600	19.0	10.4	715	33.5	78.5	13.4	8.9
27	06382	Blaine city	89.2	7.8	21,737	86.4	180,700	22.9	12.9	1,056	29.3	84.1	26.4	3.6
27	06616	Bloomington city	86.5	9.1	35,940	69.3	218,700	23.5	12.0	898	30.1	78.4	21.2	6.5
27	07948	Brooklyn Center city	83.9	14.7	11,124	60.8	136,400	26.2	13.7	881	40.7	72.8	26.5	10.0
27	07966	Brooklyn Park city	83.7	13.3	26,100	69.2	183,000	24.8	11.4	827	34.8	79.2	25.4	7.8
27	08794	Burnsville city	83.3	12.0	24,737	65.0	208,700	24.0	12.5	937	28.9	82.5	23.4	6.5
27	10846	Champlin city	90.3	8.8	8,951	85.3	199,200	25.0	10.8	997	31.7	87.1	26.6	3.1
27	10918	Chanhassen city	89.4	9.2	8,408	86.5	332,000	21.9	10.4	1,025	31.8	86.0	23.3	1.2
27	10972	Chaska city	86.5	10.0	9,234	67.0	220,300	23.3	10.0	926	28.4	85.0	24.0	5.0
27	13114	Coon Rapids city	86.6	9.9	23,411	76.9	168,000	23.2	11.5	994	31.4	83.4	25.7	5.1
27	13456	Cottage Grove city	93.5	4.6	11,989	89.0	205,900	23.0	11.1	1,088	28.5	83.8	25.5	1.5
27	14158	Crystal city	89.5	8.7	9,212	73.8	165,500	23.9	12.0	844	31.8	81.4	22.8	6.5
27	17000	Duluth city	75.8	10.8	35,340	59.5	144,700	22.4	12.3	695	35.5	74.8	16.8	13.5
27	17288	Eagan city	85.2	10.4	25,433	71.0	247,000	20.9	10.0	930	25.9	83.7	23.7	4.7
27	18116	Eden Prairie city	87.0	10.0	23,427	72.9	306,400	21.8	10.0	1,097	24.4	82.2	21.8	2.5
27	18188	Edina city	87.1	11.4	20,398	73.0	385,900	23.0	13.3	1,121	25.8	76.0	21.7	6.7
27	18674	Elk River city	86.4	11.3	8,163	79.8	193,000	25.4	10.3	823	24.7	82.5	28.6	2.7

1. A median value of $1,000,000 or more is represented as $1,000,000.
2. Median selected monthly owner costs of 10 percent or less as a percentage of household income is represented as 10.0
3. A median gross rent of $2,000 or more is represented as $2,000.
4. A median gross rent of 50 percent or more as a percentage of household income is represented as 50.0.

Table C-4. Cities — Where: Migration, Housing, and Transportation, 2010–2012—*Continued*

STATE and place code		STATE or city	Percent who lived in the same house one year ago	Percent who did not live in the same city one year ago	Total occupied housing units	Percent owner-occupied housing units	Median value of owner-occupied housing units (dollars)[1]	Median selected monthly owner costs as a percentage of household income[2]		Median gross rent (dollars)[2]	Median gross rent as a percentage of household income[4]	Percent of workers who drove alone to work	Mean travel time to work (minutes)	Percent of occupied housing units with no vehicle available
								With a mortgage	Without a mortgage					
		ACS table number:	C07204	C07204	B25003	B25003	B25077	B25092	B25092	B25064	B25071	C08301	B08013/ C08012	C25045
		Column number:	1	2	3	4	5	6	7	8	9	10	11	12
		Minnesota—Cont.												
27	20546	Faribault city	78.8	14.2	8,200	67.8	148,800	23.2	12.7	794	29.1	78.0	19.5	9.6
27	20618	Farmington city	91.0	8.1	7,379	88.1	195,300	23.5	10.3	806	23.5	85.0	30.4	2.1
27	22814	Fridley city	81.2	13.9	11,083	66.3	171,300	24.1	12.7	852	28.4	74.2	22.2	7.7
27	24308	Golden Valley city	85.8	13.4	8,773	78.2	260,700	21.4	14.3	987	26.4	76.8	19.9	5.5
27	27530	Hastings city	85.2	6.2	8,538	75.4	176,100	22.3	12.1	788	30.7	85.0	24.1	4.5
27	31076	Inver Grove Heights city	87.1	9.8	13,549	71.5	200,100	25.0	10.9	938	29.5	81.3	21.7	3.8
27	35180	Lakeville city	89.9	8.2	18,816	87.2	244,000	22.8	10.0	1,066	29.0	84.5	25.9	1.7
27	37322	Lino Lakes city	89.5	9.7	6,400	90.6	258,200	22.3	10.0	1,084	37.4	85.8	27.2	2.2
27	39878	Mankato city	75.4	15.5	15,230	54.5	147,400	22.2	10.3	702	37.3	82.1	14.8	8.3
27	40166	Maple Grove city	90.4	7.8	23,778	86.2	244,300	21.8	10.0	1,161	29.2	84.4	25.1	2.5
27	40382	Maplewood city	85.9	12.6	15,278	72.0	186,200	24.9	12.4	868	33.7	80.5	22.8	8.7
27	43000	Minneapolis city	73.9	12.9	165,018	49.2	205,100	24.2	13.9	809	30.8	61.5	22.4	18.7
27	43252	Minnetonka city	86.5	11.6	21,880	74.3	285,000	22.8	13.8	1,068	25.8	83.1	21.0	4.7
27	43864	Moorhead city	77.1	14.1	14,567	62.3	151,800	21.8	12.2	660	34.0	79.4	16.7	8.1
27	45430	New Brighton city	81.6	16.7	8,977	65.1	215,200	20.9	13.7	812	26.1	82.2	22.3	9.5
27	45628	New Hope city	84.8	13.1	8,600	56.0	188,300	24.1	10.7	855	32.9	80.8	22.1	9.8
27	46924	Northfield city	80.8	10.9	6,207	67.0	200,500	21.8	11.8	678	31.2	52.4	20.7	8.0
27	47680	Oakdale city	89.3	7.9	10,551	75.5	190,900	23.1	10.0	943	31.0	83.9	23.4	5.7
27	49300	Owatonna city	83.4	6.3	10,366	72.0	149,800	22.8	10.0	697	31.7	85.1	15.6	9.4
27	51730	Plymouth city	86.5	11.1	28,748	72.5	282,300	21.2	10.0	1,080	26.8	79.5	22.4	2.9
27	52594	Prior Lake city	87.8	11.0	8,495	82.7	261,300	23.7	10.7	1,155	33.0	88.9	26.4	4.9
27	53026	Ramsey city	90.9	8.0	7,966	92.0	205,400	25.7	10.0	1,377	29.0	79.4	31.7	0.9
27	54214	Richfield city	83.6	12.2	14,566	62.3	188,400	22.9	13.5	826	31.3	68.0	21.5	8.9
27	54880	Rochester city	83.8	7.6	43,055	70.4	161,900	21.4	10.0	763	29.8	75.1	16.0	7.3
27	55726	Rosemount city	92.2	6.3	7,405	88.2	232,700	23.1	14.6	962	30.7	86.2	27.1	4.0
27	55852	Roseville city	84.7	12.9	14,847	64.8	215,100	21.6	11.2	891	26.8	78.6	20.8	7.6
27	56896	St. Cloud city	69.4	16.9	25,211	53.6	148,100	23.3	11.4	700	34.4	78.9	18.2	8.2
27	57220	St. Louis Park city	81.0	14.8	21,441	57.4	232,700	23.1	12.5	937	25.5	78.9	20.4	7.6
27	58000	St. Paul city	76.2	11.6	111,521	49.4	176,200	23.6	12.1	797	31.8	70.1	22.5	15.1
27	58738	Savage city	92.2	7.2	9,066	89.5	246,000	22.8	10.0	1,192	32.7	82.6	25.0	1.9
27	59350	Shakopee city	87.4	9.1	13,285	77.9	208,700	23.1	10.0	962	28.2	82.1	25.0	3.4
27	59998	Shoreview city	89.7	9.2	10,663	82.3	234,300	21.0	12.6	968	27.8	84.1	25.0	3.4
27	61492	South St. Paul city	83.0	12.1	8,454	68.2	165,800	24.4	12.0	780	29.7	78.4	20.8	8.7
27	69970	White Bear Lake city	88.3	8.6	10,158	72.1	191,500	23.8	12.0	972	30.3	84.1	24.1	5.7
27	71032	Winona city	76.9	12.1	10,431	61.9	138,800	25.0	10.0	612	34.1	73.1	14.1	10.0
27	71428	Woodbury city	90.0	8.2	23,195	78.7	257,600	21.2	10.3	1,214	24.9	83.4	24.5	2.4
28	00000	**Mississippi**	85.9	10.3	1,085,563	69.2	100,000	23.1	12.0	692	32.8	83.7	23.9	6.9
28	06220	Biloxi city	76.0	17.6	17,821	48.4	141,200	23.7	11.3	825	32.6	74.2	18.8	7.5
28	08300	Brandon city	83.8	9.9	7,835	79.0	164,800	18.4	10.0	863	22.5	89.3	23.5	2.0
28	14420	Clinton city	89.4	7.2	9,123	71.6	152,000	19.9	10.0	869	31.3	85.6	21.4	3.9
28	15380	Columbus city	84.2	6.0	9,729	48.6	90,600	31.4	12.1	629	36.6	80.7	18.3	13.4
28	29180	Greenville city	78.4	8.2	12,168	52.6	76,900	22.0	13.4	608	38.5	77.4	16.1	16.1
28	29700	Gulfport city	75.0	14.2	26,288	55.2	122,700	25.6	12.6	815	35.4	81.8	19.7	6.1
28	31020	Hattiesburg city	71.2	14.9	18,225	34.9	114,600	24.4	12.2	657	38.1	77.9	17.1	11.6
28	33700	Horn Lake city	84.3	11.7	8,659	66.3	96,600	20.9	12.1	942	35.6	80.6	25.2	3.8
28	36000	Jackson city	83.5	5.3	61,612	52.9	89,800	23.5	11.4	741	37.7	84.3	19.6	9.1
28	44520	Madison city	90.0	6.3	8,473	92.3	229,300	19.5	10.0	1,422	48.6	88.2	22.1	1.2
28	46640	Meridian city	84.6	6.4	15,855	52.5	84,100	23.5	12.7	596	33.1	84.7	18.2	11.4
28	54040	Olive Branch city	86.9	8.6	12,548	77.3	162,500	24.4	10.6	1,036	24.3	85.6	25.5	3.0
28	54840	Oxford city	59.4	29.3	6,707	38.6	243,900	27.1	11.3	807	41.0	84.4	0.0	6.2
28	55360	Pascagoula city	77.9	12.4	8,342	56.5	107,300	23.7	10.9	712	33.8	79.1	17.3	7.3
28	55760	Pearl city	80.3	12.9	9,964	62.2	109,200	20.8	10.0	754	30.4	87.6	20.8	3.0
28	62520	Ridgeland city	85.7	10.7	10,969	46.7	164,200	20.4	10.0	920	25.4	88.5	18.8	6.6
28	69280	Southaven city	83.8	11.2	18,143	68.1	142,700	22.0	10.0	926	29.0	89.1	23.5	2.3
28	70240	Starkville city	73.1	18.1	10,402	37.9	155,400	19.8	10.0	656	36.3	80.6	17.6	8.9
28	74840	Tupelo city	86.9	8.5	13,438	61.4	113,600	22.9	10.4	681	33.4	89.3	15.9	7.3
28	76720	Vicksburg city	91.4	4.4	9,276	54.8	92,600	26.2	13.7	600	38.8	85.6	16.2	13.6
29	00000	**Missouri**	83.7	11.3	2,354,106	68.4	137,100	22.2	11.9	714	30.1	81.5	23.0	7.4
29	01972	Arnold city	88.1	9.6	8,127	81.6	149,800	22.3	11.3	796	27.9	89.2	26.6	3.3
29	03160	Ballwin city	86.8	10.7	11,328	80.0	243,200	20.0	11.3	961	28.1	36.1	24.2	1.0
29	04384	Belton city	84.8	11.6	8,417	68.9	124,300	23.9	19.1	945	28.1	31.1	23.6	2.1
29	06652	Blue Springs city	86.6	7.5	19,207	69.2	143,200	23.2	11.7	912	28.9	33.8	24.7	2.2
29	11242	Cape Girardeau city	75.9	14.5	15,062	55.0	129,700	19.7	11.6	655	32.2	30.3	13.6	9.0
29	13600	Chesterfield city	88.4	8.5	18,813	78.9	327,100	20.7	12.6	1,003	29.8	36.1	22.9	3.1
29	15670	Columbia city	66.3	17.1	43,348	47.3	168,700	20.9	10.0	777	34.2	77.4	16.8	7.2
29	23986	Ferguson city	87.3	11.9	8,863	58.8	94,300	25.7	12.1	780	42.2	78.5	29.0	18.4
29	24778	Florissant city	85.5	11.1	20,827	73.1	104,300	22.2	12.9	867	28.5	85.9	25.0	5.4
29	27190	Gladstone city	84.0	11.7	10,693	70.6	128,300	24.1	13.8	782	28.7	83.2	22.4	4.7
29	28324	Grandview city	75.1	20.2	9,603	61.7	100,500	23.5	11.8	719	32.3	80.7	21.3	6.8
29	31276	Hazelwood city	82.5	16.0	11,089	59.4	112,200	25.3	12.6	733	30.6	84.7	23.1	9.5
29	35000	Independence city	88.6	6.6	47,939	66.1	101,400	22.8	13.5	754	33.2	86.2	22.6	7.4
29	37000	Jefferson City city	78.7	10.7	17,033	57.8	138,100	18.2	10.0	553	27.1	83.1	15.1	10.4

1. A median value of $1,000,000 or more is represented as $1,000,000.
2. Median selected monthly owner costs of 10 percent or less as a percentage of household income is represented as 10.0
3. A median gross rent of $2,000 or more is represented as $2,000.
4. A median gross rent of 50 percent or more as a percentage of household income is represented as 50.0.

Table C-4. Cities — Where: Migration, Housing, and Transportation, 2010–2012—Continued

STATE and place code	STATE or city	Percent who lived in the same house one year ago	Percent who did not live in the same city one year ago	Total occupied housing units	Percent owner-occupied housing units	Median value of owner-occupied housing units (dollars)[1]	Median selected monthly owner costs as a percentage of household income[2]		Median gross rent (dollars)[2]	Median gross rent as a percentage of household income[4]	Percent of workers who drove alone to work	Mean travel time to work (minutes)	Percent of occupied housing units with no vehicle available
							With a mortgage	Without a mortgage					
	ACS table number:	C07204	C07204	B25003	B25003	B25077	B25092	B25092	B25064	B25071	C08301	B08013/ C08012	C25045
	Column number:	1	2	3	4	5	6	7	8	9	10	11	12
	Missouri—Cont.												
29 37592	Joplin city	77.7	10.4	21,193	57.3	100,500	22.2	13.2	655	30.2	82.8	15.3	10.6
29 38000	Kansas City city	80.0	9.3	190,467	55.9	135,000	22.7	13.7	774	31.4	80.5	21.5	11.7
29 39044	Kirkwood city	90.1	7.5	11,866	77.6	239,400	20.6	11.8	1,012	30.0	87.0	20.5	4.6
29 41348	Lee's Summit city	88.1	8.2	33,846	74.2	186,300	21.3	11.1	1,001	31.3	85.8	24.0	5.6
29 42032	Liberty city	82.7	13.7	10,813	75.3	165,600	21.9	13.3	749	28.7	82.7	21.5	4.5
29 46586	Maryland Heights city	79.8	16.7	11,666	57.3	154,400	21.2	12.3	819	24.5	88.1	21.5	4.2
29 47180	Mehlville CDP	85.3	11.7	13,435	63.6	154,800	22.4	12.5	746	26.9	83.9	23.3	7.0
29 53876	Oakville CDP	90.9	6.6	13,783	86.6	205,300	20.9	11.6	807	23.9	87.7	26.8	1.3
29 54074	O'Fallon city	88.3	9.0	28,697	80.4	193,600	21.7	11.7	911	30.1	89.0	26.4	4.0
29 54352	Old Jamestown CDP	93.6	6.0	7,290	94.3	168,100	24.3	16.2	1,123	29.3	84.3	28.5	0.9
29 60788	Raytown city	87.0	10.9	11,730	67.9	101,000	22.9	13.3	862	27.9	88.6	22.9	6.2
29 64082	St. Charles city	83.0	12.0	26,344	64.7	172,300	20.4	13.4	799	28.7	86.8	20.9	5.0
29 64550	St. Joseph city	77.3	10.0	29,005	60.3	101,400	20.1	12.2	639	32.1	81.3	15.7	9.8
29 65000	St. Louis city	77.9	9.4	138,981	44.6	120,600	23.8	14.2	719	33.7	71.3	23.7	22.1
29 65126	St. Peters city	91.9	7.0	21,017	81.8	169,300	22.2	10.4	807	23.0	86.2	23.9	4.2
29 66440	Sedalia city	77.6	11.1	8,972	57.7	86,900	23.1	12.7	680	41.9	76.0	16.2	10.9
29 69266	Spanish Lake CDP	72.2	24.0	7,616	46.7	107,200	27.5	12.2	735	36.1	85.1	27.7	16.8
29 70000	Springfield city	73.2	12.8	70,120	47.7	107,800	21.9	10.4	638	32.4	81.9	17.0	9.1
29 75220	University City city	81.5	15.1	15,963	58.7	188,000	22.6	15.4	912	33.1	78.0	19.8	14.1
29 78154	Webster Groves city	87.9	8.2	9,241	81.3	244,600	19.8	12.1	1,090	40.1	83.3	20.8	7.1
29 78442	Wentzville city	90.4	6.9	10,305	85.9	190,200	24.3	11.0	953	29.3	87.9	27.7	3.4
29 79820	Wildwood city	91.2	6.2	12,185	91.5	346,500	21.1	10.0	1,110	22.9	82.4	28.1	1.3
30 00000	**Montana**	83.7	11.0	404,990	68.2	183,600	23.9	11.7	672	28.5	75.4	18.3	5.2
30 06550	Billings city	81.9	9.0	43,926	63.7	181,300	21.9	11.1	696	28.7	78.8	17.6	6.6
30 08950	Bozeman city	63.2	22.7	15,360	45.6	249,700	26.7	10.0	813	29.7	69.6	13.5	6.7
30 11397	Butte-Silver Bow (balance)	80.8	9.0	14,500	64.8	131,500	19.6	11.6	586	28.6	81.7	15.5	9.0
30 32800	Great Falls city	80.8	9.0	24,535	61.9	157,000	22.6	10.5	602	27.5	80.1	14.9	8.5
30 35600	Helena city	79.1	10.8	12,799	56.8	196,800	21.2	10.0	672	26.9	76.8	13.6	8.2
30 40075	Kalispell city	85.1	9.7	8,388	53.3	178,700	30.8	12.1	716	33.0	76.8	15.0	8.8
30 50200	Missoula city	72.6	13.7	28,776	47.6	232,600	24.4	12.7	734	32.9	68.9	14.9	7.6
31 00000	**Nebraska**	83.2	8.8	726,422	66.8	127,800	21.0	12.4	694	27.2	80.8	18.2	5.7
31 03950	Bellevue city	79.7	13.6	19,517	67.1	134,300	20.7	12.5	835	28.1	85.1	19.6	3.9
31 10110	Columbus city	87.1	5.5	8,881	66.1	115,500	19.9	11.0	623	22.5	86.2	13.0	4.3
31 17670	Fremont city	82.1	6.8	10,829	61.2	114,500	19.0	14.3	652	26.2	84.0	16.7	6.7
31 19595	Grand Island city	80.2	8.0	18,702	62.4	108,100	22.1	13.3	625	26.5	83.1	14.4	7.6
31 21415	Hastings city	78.0	13.1	10,416	66.2	93,600	19.9	11.5	606	24.0	82.0	14.0	5.6
31 25055	Kearney city	72.8	12.5	11,999	57.4	141,900	19.2	10.0	653	29.0	78.8	13.9	5.3
31 28000	Lincoln city	76.1	8.2	105,019	56.6	143,100	21.0	11.2	699	29.0	80.7	18.1	7.1
31 34615	Norfolk city	80.1	12.2	9,833	58.8	114,700	19.7	13.5	608	27.6	85.8	13.9	6.1
31 35000	North Platte city	82.8	7.5	10,384	65.1	96,700	20.7	15.5	550	25.6	83.9	11.2	7.3
31 37000	Omaha city	80.4	7.0	164,695	57.8	132,300	22.0	13.3	768	29.8	81.8	18.2	9.2
31 38295	Papillion city	88.4	8.5	7,495	69.2	167,200	19.7	10.0	734	26.3	87.4	20.6	4.5
32 00000	**Nevada**	76.9	14.1	992,757	56.2	161,300	26.9	11.7	966	31.2	78.3	23.8	7.9
32 09700	Carson City	78.3	9.4	21,212	58.5	198,100	25.1	12.0	838	28.8	83.7	16.8	8.1
32 23770	Enterprise CDP	73.3	22.9	41,666	57.1	188,800	26.6	11.7	1,331	29.0	84.0	22.1	2.5
32 31900	Henderson city	81.9	10.3	98,623	62.9	201,200	27.0	10.3	1,141	28.3	81.2	23.2	3.7
32 40000	Las Vegas city	74.7	11.4	210,927	53.3	153,700	27.1	11.8	967	31.5	78.1	25.2	9.9
32 51800	North Las Vegas city	73.5	15.6	67,222	56.7	129,600	27.5	10.0	1,101	34.3	82.9	26.8	6.5
32 53800	Pahrump CDP	80.3	9.0	14,962	73.2	108,800	31.1	13.2	960	37.3	80.3	31.9	5.0
32 54600	Paradise CDP	73.9	18.3	87,162	41.0	142,900	26.8	12.9	862	31.3	72.3	21.6	15.1
32 60600	Reno city	75.8	10.7	89,155	46.2	191,500	26.3	12.5	850	32.7	76.7	19.7	11.3
32 68400	Sparks city	75.0	15.5	34,330	58.2	165,500	28.0	12.1	952	31.2	78.7	22.0	8.5
32 68585	Spring Valley CDP	74.3	17.9	69,215	46.8	157,900	28.5	11.8	1,070	31.2	79.2	22.2	7.2
32 70900	Summerlin South CDP	80.2	18.5	10,146	64.3	340,200	23.2	11.7	1,463	29.0	. . .	23.7	3.8
32 71400	Sunrise Manor CDP	74.0	17.4	58,720	52.1	95,000	29.5	13.1	855	36.4	75.9	26.7	11.0
32 83800	Whitney CDP	80.5	17.4	13,598	57.9	101,000	27.8	11.4	997	31.8	76.4	27.4	6.0
32 84600	Winchester CDP	71.6	23.1	10,793	35.6	105,900	30.5	14.6	877	32.5	73.5	24.1	17.2
33 00000	**New Hampshire**	86.4	10.2	518,009	71.4	239,100	26.2	16.8	969	30.2	81.4	26.4	5.2
33 14200	Concord city	81.5	10.4	17,318	54.1	217,200	25.8	18.8	926	30.9	79.8	22.7	10.3
33 17860	Derry CDP	87.5	9.4	9,059	54.7	208,300	29.2	27.7	1,034	32.4	84.9	30.5	4.0
33 18820	Dover city	77.0	14.0	12,484	49.3	244,000	28.0	15.1	953	31.8	76.2	21.5	5.9
33 39300	Keene city	73.2	18.8	9,080	55.7	192,700	26.9	21.1	1,024	34.3	78.6	15.7	10.5
33 45140	Manchester city	79.4	8.2	44,629	48.3	215,100	27.4	15.6	980	30.3	81.0	23.0	9.3
33 50260	Nashua city	83.6	8.7	34,600	58.4	235,100	24.7	17.0	1,068	29.6	80.9	25.2	8.9
33 62900	Portsmouth city	83.2	12.3	10,425	54.5	333,700	24.8	19.3	1,077	28.2	76.5	20.7	6.0
33 65140	Rochester city	81.6	10.4	12,782	65.3	170,500	27.2	21.5	893	34.3	80.8	25.3	6.0
34 00000	**New Jersey**	90.1	7.6	3,181,881	65.6	325,800	28.4	18.9	1,156	32.4	72.0	30.5	11.8
34 02080	Atlantic City city	85.3	7.2	15,721	30.8	207,900	40.1	20.9	811	36.1	39.4	19.4	45.0
34 03580	Bayonne city	94.0	4.1	25,933	38.5	332,600	35.4	21.6	1,084	27.1	54.9	32.0	23.1
34 05170	Bergenfield borough	90.7	5.7	9,219	69.5	339,300	33.6	18.5	1,151	34.7	74.7	31.2	12.2
34 07600	Bridgeton city	79.6	12.6	5,784	42.8	110,400	25.2	19.4	1,028	42.6	60.5	27.3	18.4

1. A median value of $1,000,000 or more is represented as $1,000,000.
2. Median selected monthly owner costs of 10 percent or less as a percentage of household income is represented as 10.0.
3. A median gross rent of $2,000 or more is represented as $2,000.
4. A median gross rent of 50 percent or more as a percentage of household income is represented as 50.0.

Table C-4. Cities — Where: Migration, Housing, and Transportation, 2010–2012—Continued

STATE and place code	STATE or city	Percent who lived in the same house one year ago	Percent who did not live in the same city one year ago	Total occupied housing units	Percent owner-occupied housing units	Median value of owner-occupied housing units (dollars)[1]	Median selected monthly owner costs as a percentage of household income[2] With a mortgage	Without a mortgage	Median gross rent (dollars)[2]	Median gross rent as a percentage of household income[4]	Percent of workers who drove alone to work	Mean travel time to work (minutes)	Percent of occupied housing units with no vehicle available
	ACS table number:	C07204	C07204	B25003	B25003	B25077	B25092	B25092	B25064	B25071	C08301	B08013/C08012	C25045
	Column number:	1	2	3	4	5	6	7	8	9	10	11	12
	New Jersey—Cont.												
34 10000	Camden city	82.0	6.2	24,739	38.8	87,700	29.3	16.8	825	45.4	62.4	24.3	33.4
34 10750	Carteret borough	89.0	5.6	7,549	58.6	245,900	32.2	16.7	1,233	36.1	73.8	29.7	8.9
34 13570	Cliffside Park borough	91.6	6.2	10,174	46.6	384,800	34.7	29.9	1,241	34.6	59.4	32.0	14.0
34 13690	Clifton city	93.3	4.6	28,383	61.2	343,000	32.0	24.4	1,208	35.0	77.1	26.0	10.3
34 19390	East Orange city	84.7	8.1	25,239	26.7	229,600	39.9	20.5	964	33.8	57.9	32.0	33.6
34 21000	Elizabeth city	82.5	8.5	38,814	27.3	276,000	35.0	24.7	1,042	33.4	52.8	26.3	25.2
34 21480	Englewood city	89.5	7.4	10,602	54.5	392,100	33.2	22.1	1,275	33.9	62.8	31.9	13.8
34 22470	Fair Lawn borough	93.9	4.7	11,516	76.7	389,700	28.0	18.6	1,385	27.5	69.1	31.2	6.2
34 24420	Fort Lee borough	92.7	6.0	16,871	59.1	325,800	28.3	17.6	1,455	31.7	60.7	33.7	13.4
34 25770	Garfield city	95.5	3.5	10,763	38.1	335,100	44.3	25.6	1,146	36.8	70.9	25.0	13.8
34 28680	Hackensack city	85.9	9.4	17,644	36.2	290,500	34.0	21.3	1,225	30.9	63.7	28.1	14.8
34 32250	Hoboken city	75.4	15.8	24,487	31.1	532,400	23.7	20.4	1,702	23.1	27.7	38.9	35.3
34 34470	Iselin CDP	86.2	10.7	6,325	62.9	306,100	28.7	15.1	1,507	24.3	67.9	32.6	10.0
34 36000	Jersey City city	85.5	6.8	95,560	30.3	323,700	31.9	21.2	1,165	28.9	33.2	34.9	38.2
34 36510	Kearny town	87.8	7.4	13,373	46.3	317,800	32.7	20.0	1,176	29.2	71.0	29.9	13.4
34 38580	Lakewood CDP	89.1	6.3	9,956	36.1	404,700	43.7	25.2	1,300	48.1	53.9	21.7	14.4
34 40350	Linden city	89.2	6.8	14,698	57.4	277,800	32.5	24.0	1,113	29.3	75.8	26.5	9.1
34 41100	Lodi borough	93.4	4.4	9,262	37.3	347,200	42.6	23.2	1,157	31.7	75.1	26.4	10.5
34 41310	Long Branch city	82.7	8.0	12,157	39.4	342,900	33.4	18.0	1,223	37.0	59.7	31.1	14.7
34 46680	Millville city	84.1	7.8	10,169	62.8	170,100	28.1	16.5	858	34.4	83.9	23.2	12.8
34 51000	Newark city	86.3	5.5	91,552	22.4	246,100	41.0	22.9	964	34.5	48.5	32.6	40.3
34 51210	New Brunswick city	69.0	15.7	14,153	22.4	240,600	32.9	17.7	1,322	41.9	37.9	24.1	33.6
34 53280	North Plainfield borough	90.3	6.9	7,190	56.1	283,900	32.2	21.2	1,150	33.3	71.4	27.8	9.7
34 54690	Old Bridge CDP	95.2	3.5	7,643	86.1	349,400	26.5	14.7	785	33.0	77.5	35.3	5.1
34 55950	Paramus borough	95.4	4.4	8,533	89.1	561,500	28.2	16.5	1,812	50.0	73.8	31.0	5.6
34 56550	Passaic city	95.5	2.2	20,530	22.9	312,700	40.3	23.1	1,009	39.1	47.4	26.7	38.7
34 57000	Paterson city	89.2	3.2	43,618	26.7	277,700	46.6	22.4	1,083	42.1	60.5	22.2	29.7
34 58200	Perth Amboy city	92.6	4.7	16,750	34.1	248,000	31.9	28.3	1,095	37.8	74.2	24.4	23.6
34 59190	Plainfield city	83.8	6.8	14,096	49.4	259,600	33.3	21.3	1,139	38.9	52.8	29.4	16.6
34 59640	Pleasantville city	85.5	9.5	6,248	54.3	155,900	36.7	20.7	1,104	34.8	67.7	18.9	21.6
34 61530	Rahway city	92.3	4.8	10,508	58.3	296,900	35.4	23.4	1,108	31.6	76.6	28.4	14.2
34 63000	Ridgewood village	92.4	6.5	8,223	78.3	703,300	26.5	19.7	1,713	27.6	59.8	37.4	4.2
34 64620	Roselle borough	87.3	8.3	8,439	55.4	234,500	43.5	23.4	1,080	42.6	78.9	31.0	13.8
34 65790	Sayreville borough	94.5	4.2	15,509	68.9	309,900	28.4	21.3	1,126	25.6	77.0	34.1	6.3
34 68370	Somerset CDP	90.5	7.0	8,816	75.1	311,800	25.0	18.4	1,297	21.2	81.1	35.4	7.0
34 69390	South Plainfield borough	94.3	3.9	8,113	86.1	326,100	29.1	19.0	1,356	29.3	83.2	29.6	3.2
34 71430	Summit city	93.1	3.8	7,871	70.0	749,800	25.3	18.0	1,558	24.6	59.5	35.6	6.7
34 73110	Toms River CDP	91.4	6.2	33,512	80.9	290,900	28.1	17.6	1,294	35.4	83.6	30.1	5.5
34 74000	Trenton city	82.9	8.6	28,218	39.1	115,700	27.3	18.6	975	38.1	60.3	22.7	31.7
34 74630	Union City city	83.3	8.7	22,440	18.6	313,100	38.9	28.8	1,039	33.3	30.9	31.3	43.7
34 76070	Vineland city	90.1	4.2	20,577	66.8	173,500	25.8	16.9	1,006	35.2	82.5	22.7	10.8
34 79040	Westfield town	92.1	5.7	10,236	79.9	628,600	25.4	19.7	1,593	27.3	74.3	33.5	4.1
34 79610	West New York town	83.1	9.6	18,859	20.0	303,800	33.3	26.4	1,123	31.0	31.7	33.9	37.0
34 81950	Woodbridge CDP	85.4	11.1	6,933	61.6	273,600	26.2	19.3	1,583	24.6	71.2	34.8	5.6
35 00000	**New Mexico**	85.4	8.6	765,306	68.1	159,300	23.6	10.0	744	30.4	79.2	21.7	5.8
35 01780	Alamogordo city	80.0	11.5	12,398	59.3	112,000	21.8	10.0	633	27.1	76.4	17.8	5.5
35 02000	Albuquerque city	83.0	6.7	224,766	59.4	187,000	24.1	10.3	764	30.6	80.4	21.4	7.2
35 12150	Carlsbad city	83.5	9.0	10,019	71.0	96,500	17.6	10.7	724	24.8	82.0	18.2	3.8
35 16420	Clovis city	83.1	6.4	14,373	63.2	127,600	20.7	10.1	618	30.4	83.8	15.3	8.3
35 25800	Farmington city	82.1	12.5	15,696	67.4	185,600	22.2	10.0	736	29.3	82.2	18.2	5.3
35 28460	Gallup city	85.8	9.6	6,108	59.5	142,300	21.3	10.0	590	23.8	70.9	20.9	10.1
35 32520	Hobbs city	86.4	8.3	10,621	65.9	97,800	18.3	10.0	788	27.2	82.2	15.2	2.7
35 39380	Las Cruces city	74.2	10.8	37,828	56.9	151,800	23.4	10.0	705	36.2	82.8	19.2	6.4
35 63460	Rio Rancho city	88.6	6.8	32,137	78.9	172,700	26.0	10.0	997	31.4	85.0	29.8	2.9
35 64930	Roswell city	82.4	8.3	17,714	62.8	91,600	19.8	10.0	643	29.6	83.8	15.9	4.9
35 70500	Santa Fe city	79.3	9.5	31,570	59.1	283,600	29.2	10.0	910	33.3	71.1	18.1	6.9
35 74520	South Valley CDP	89.7	8.6	12,956	76.2	138,900	25.9	10.0	666	33.2	77.9	23.3	3.9
36 00000	**New York**	88.7	6.3	7,210,095	53.9	286,700	25.9	15.3	1,076	32.1	54.0	31.5	29.4
36 01000	Albany city	80.0	11.1	38,841	39.9	181,500	23.4	14.1	823	32.6	64.2	18.8	25.5
36 03078	Auburn city	79.1	10.3	11,159	49.6	95,900	19.3	14.0	607	28.1	77.5	15.9	18.7
36 04143	Baldwin CDP	93.4	5.4	7,627	77.6	352,200	32.5	13.9	1,572	33.9	65.5	34.7	6.5
36 04935	Bay Shore CDP	88.2	9.5	9,217	55.1	309,000	33.4	22.9	1,240	34.0	73.9	30.9	12.9
36 06607	Binghamton city	79.1	12.1	20,327	46.5	86,200	22.8	15.1	643	37.5	70.7	18.0	23.0
36 08026	Brentwood CDP	92.7	4.1	14,024	69.8	284,700	34.5	20.6	1,336	33.9	67.4	26.6	9.6
36 08257	Brighton CDP	80.4	16.3	15,535	56.4	169,800	21.1	11.7	920	28.6	80.3	15.7	7.9
36 11000	Buffalo city	80.5	8.2	111,275	41.3	66,000	21.8	13.3	664	34.9	66.9	20.6	30.4
36 13376	Centereach CDP	91.9	6.9	9,979	85.1	347,200	30.9	17.9	2,000	33.3	85.3	30.9	4.9
36 13552	Central Islip CDP	91.5	5.7	10,062	65.4	274,300	35.4	18.5	1,355	38.3	65.2	26.9	10.5
36 15000	Cheektowaga CDP	90.0	5.9	32,306	70.8	96,900	21.3	15.3	748	26.3	86.6	19.4	9.9
36 17530	Commack CDP	95.2	4.2	11,685	92.4	468,700	29.3	21.5	1,575	36.7	82.5	33.2	3.9

1. A median value of $1,000,000 or more is represented as $1,000,000.
2. Median selected monthly owner costs of 10 percent or less as a percenage of household income is represented as 10.0
3. A median gross rent of $2,000 or more is represented as $2,000.
4. A median gross rent of 50 percent or more as a percentage of household income is represented as 50.0.

Table C-4. Cities — Where: Migration, Housing, and Transportation, 2010–2012—*Continued*

STATE and place code		STATE or city	Percent who lived in the same house one year ago	Percent who did not live in the same city one year ago	Total occupied housing units	Percent owner-occupied housing units	Median value of owner-occupied housing units (dollars)[1]	Median selected monthly owner costs as a percentage of household income[2] With a mortgage	Median selected monthly owner costs as a percentage of household income[2] Without a mortgage	Median gross rent (dollars)[2]	Median gross rent as a percentage of household income[4]	Percent of workers who drove alone to work	Mean travel time to work (minutes)	Percent of occupied housing units with no vehicle available
		ACS table number:	C07204	C07204	B25003	B25003	B25077	B25092	B25092	B25064	B25071	C08301	B08013/C08012	C25045
		Column number:	1	2	3	4	5	6	7	8	9	10	11	12
		New York—Cont.												
36	18146	Copiague CDP	92.3	3.7	7,236	69.7	335,400	30.9	23.1	1,408	34.9	71.3	25.9	8.2
36	18157	Coram CDP	90.2	7.4	14,007	65.0	318,300	29.6	25.8	1,666	34.4	83.5	36.7	4.3
36	19972	Deer Park CDP	95.0	2.7	8,969	82.1	357,700	30.5	22.2	1,192	30.9	79.3	31.8	4.7
36	20687	Dix Hills CDP	95.6	3.2	8,550	91.8	709,500	28.5	21.8	1,453	25.6	77.2	35.4	2.6
36	22502	East Meadow CDP	91.1	8.6	12,640	87.6	391,200	29.5	18.3	1,783	34.1	74.8	34.2	6.6
36	22612	East Northport CDP	92.1	5.2	7,193	85.5	434,300	26.6	17.9	1,342	37.4	81.3	32.5	5.4
36	22733	East Patchogue CDP	92.4	6.0	8,696	63.3	323,900	30.7	16.6	1,353	36.0	84.0	25.4	5.1
36	24229	Elmira city	75.9	12.8	10,569	45.2	66,300	19.0	14.1	606	29.7	75.5	16.9	24.2
36	24273	Elmont CDP	91.6	6.4	9,594	80.9	375,900	33.7	20.6	1,305	27.8	65.2	37.9	9.9
36	27309	Franklin Square CDP	95.7	3.5	9,829	81.8	428,600	34.3	23.0	1,361	34.9	80.6	31.8	5.5
36	27485	Freeport village	92.2	5.4	13,663	65.8	330,200	34.2	18.0	1,277	39.5	61.1	31.7	15.5
36	28178	Garden City village	93.1	5.8	7,489	95.5	780,800	26.6	18.9	1,983	50.0	64.8	33.7	4.4
36	29113	Glen Cove city	93.1	4.7	9,431	54.2	477,800	35.0	23.6	1,485	36.3	73.7	25.2	12.5
36	32402	Harrison village	82.8	12.5	8,525	64.2	819,200	32.1	18.4	1,780	33.3	60.5	25.2	6.5
36	32732	Hauppauge CDP	94.1	5.2	7,045	84.6	463,800	28.0	18.0	1,734	30.6	81.7	28.9	2.7
36	33139	Hempstead village	87.9	8.1	16,240	42.6	327,800	36.7	20.2	1,269	38.3	53.6	31.7	28.0
36	34374	Hicksville CDP	94.7	4.8	13,665	82.4	395,000	31.0	17.8	1,636	29.5	73.1	30.8	5.4
36	35056	Holbrook CDP	93.5	5.4	8,902	75.4	363,800	27.2	19.1	1,718	33.5	87.8	33.3	2.1
36	35254	Holtsville CDP	95.5	4.0	6,641	83.7	346,300	28.8	22.9	1,612	35.2	79.1	36.1	5.1
36	37044	Huntington Station CDP	. . .	. . .	10,453	66.8	369,400	30.3	20.9	1,349	34.8	76.6	26.4	5.5
36	37737	Irondequoit CDP	91.8	6.0	22,050	78.1	116,200	22.8	14.7	766	30.6	87.8	20.0	9.0
36	38077	Ithaca city	51.0	29.0	9,910	26.4	203,400	23.0	13.2	957	41.2	28.6	15.0	32.6
36	38264	Jamestown city	80.8	10.5	13,476	50.8	64,200	20.6	13.2	588	34.4	74.9	15.3	21.0
36	39727	Kingston city	79.1	10.3	9,720	44.6	185,800	27.8	19.6	945	37.0	71.3	21.1	21.9
36	39853	Kiryas Joel village	. . .	. . .	3,726	34.9	346,300	37.9	46.9	1,185	50.0	25.8	24.2	56.3
36	40838	Lake Ronkonkoma CDP	94.0	6.0	6,782	73.1	347,500	29.3	17.1	1,323	33.3	87.0	30.9	8.3
36	42081	Levittown CDP	94.0	4.2	16,571	91.1	365,700	31.2	18.5	1,878	31.9	81.2	32.2	3.9
36	42554	Lindenhurst village	94.2	5.0	8,979	79.4	349,400	31.5	19.3	1,387	31.5	74.0	33.6	7.4
36	43082	Lockport city	83.8	11.4	8,928	56.6	78,600	22.4	13.0	644	32.0	80.0	20.3	15.4
36	43335	Long Beach city	88.9	6.8	14,477	54.1	476,300	29.8	17.3	1,614	30.2	59.2	41.0	14.0
36	45986	Massapequa CDP	. . .	. . .	7,086	94.4	485,500	27.0	23.8	1,446	34.9	74.4	36.6	4.1
36	46404	Medford CDP	. . .	. . .	7,766	86.5	296,800	29.8	24.7	1,682	29.9	84.7	29.5	4.2
36	46514	Melville CDP	94.0	5.2	7,141	85.6	666,300	26.2	17.2	2,000	25.5	. . .	30.6	2.9
36	46668	Merrick CDP	96.1	2.5	7,105	95.6	517,300	29.9	18.2	1,886	31.8	72.0	36.1	3.5
36	47042	Middletown city	82.4	9.3	9,453	47.9	212,700	32.2	15.0	1,123	36.3	61.4	29.6	20.8
36	49121	Mount Vernon city	90.0	4.7	26,283	38.2	377,900	31.8	25.5	1,152	35.9	60.8	31.5	27.2
36	50034	Newburgh city	83.9	6.6	8,907	31.5	174,500	31.0	18.9	988	42.8	50.8	23.5	33.1
36	50100	New City CDP	95.4	3.4	10,962	89.8	487,100	26.0	16.7	1,420	32.8	78.6	32.4	3.0
36	50617	New Rochelle city	86.4	6.8	27,785	50.5	553,400	29.5	19.9	1,303	35.0	58.4	29.3	17.8
36	51000	New York city	88.6	3.2	3,051,127	31.7	490,400	30.5	15.2	1,187	32.2	22.4	39.0	56.1
36	51055	Niagara Falls city	90.7	3.8	21,503	55.4	69,800	20.9	15.6	633	32.9	80.3	17.5	19.1
36	51495	North Bay Shore CDP	. . .	. . .	4,882	71.9	281,700	33.8	14.9	1,289	32.2	71.8	25.4	9.2
36	51517	North Bellmore CDP	92.6	5.0	6,723	89.3	429,700	30.1	19.5	1,782	33.1	75.1	30.0	6.0
36	53682	North Tonawanda city	87.9	6.1	13,946	66.8	102,900	19.9	14.4	647	28.9	85.4	20.0	7.1
36	54441	Oceanside CDP	96.9	1.9	11,240	88.2	442,700	29.5	23.6	1,368	29.3	73.0	33.7	4.3
36	55530	Ossining village	91.4	5.1	7,449	48.8	398,700	32.9	17.0	1,408	37.5	56.8	28.1	14.1
36	56979	Peekskill city	86.4	8.1	8,691	52.3	318,000	28.5	22.9	1,225	38.6	61.0	31.0	16.8
36	58442	Plainview CDP	95.9	3.6	9,330	94.6	489,400	27.8	19.8	. . .	28.9	75.1	34.8	4.8
36	59223	Port Chester village	80.3	9.0	9,536	43.0	437,000	34.1	19.8	1,402	34.8	53.9	23.2	20.6
36	59641	Poughkeepsie city	82.0	7.3	12,192	40.8	223,500	29.6	23.3	954	38.3	66.4	23.4	27.1
36	63000	Rochester city	75.2	8.6	86,273	38.4	75,200	23.4	13.9	743	38.1	71.3	18.8	26.2
36	63264	Rockville Centre village	93.7	6.2	9,100	73.1	613,900	24.2	18.0	1,259	34.3	60.6	35.6	11.5
36	63418	Rome city	83.1	9.8	13,002	57.3	87,700	19.9	13.2	681	24.9	82.4	18.2	13.7
36	63473	Ronkonkoma CDP	. . .	. . .	6,528	79.4	344,200	29.8	24.3	1,480	28.5	85.1	29.4	2.4
36	63924	Rotterdam CDP	95.3	4.0	7,942	80.8	158,300	22.6	14.7	793	32.9	90.5	20.0	5.9
36	65255	Saratoga Springs city	79.9	14.3	11,530	54.3	310,500	24.8	12.5	957	27.9	74.6	22.1	9.6
36	65508	Schenectady city	87.9	7.4	24,486	45.9	115,500	25.4	16.8	790	31.9	72.8	22.8	21.0
36	66212	Selden CDP	93.1	6.2	6,414	79.5	307,500	31.8	18.7	1,446	30.2	80.8	31.4	4.8
36	67070	Shirley CDP	. . .	. . .	7,973	86.2	258,500	31.1	16.2	1,645	47.9	84.1	32.0	3.8
36	67851	Smithtown CDP	94.6	4.9	8,561	86.4	476,800	26.6	18.0	1,141	30.9	84.4	30.3	4.3
36	70420	Spring Valley village	84.7	7.8	9,021	31.5	257,100	36.6	15.7	1,135	36.2	55.3	24.2	19.4
36	72554	Syosset CDP	93.9	4.7	6,445	91.8	609,700	29.2	21.9	1,750	33.0	65.5	40.2	2.8
36	73000	Syracuse city	72.7	12.6	54,577	39.4	87,500	21.9	13.8	699	35.9	65.2	17.3	28.2
36	74183	Tonawanda CDP	89.0	7.7	25,202	72.8	115,600	19.3	13.6	744	25.6	84.2	19.2	8.0
36	75484	Troy city	75.5	12.8	19,869	38.4	143,200	22.8	14.7	810	32.7	67.0	19.6	23.8
36	76089	Uniondale CDP	93.6	4.5	5,348	74.6	319,200	38.3	15.6	1,380	42.0	67.9	30.1	10.5
36	76540	Utica city	80.0	9.0	23,888	47.5	90,300	22.0	14.3	642	34.3	72.8	16.8	25.0
36	76705	Valley Stream village	92.7	5.8	11,197	78.1	374,600	32.1	21.8	1,485	33.4	68.9	35.2	6.6
36	78608	Watertown city	69.2	19.8	11,853	41.4	111,900	20.1	13.6	747	30.6	77.6	15.6	20.3
36	79246	West Babylon CDP	94.9	3.5	14,286	78.0	345,500	31.9	19.0	1,389	38.2	83.3	29.6	6.1
36	80302	West Islip CDP	95.5	3.6	8,899	93.3	420,600	29.5	23.8	1,163	24.7	82.8	30.9	2.6

1. A median value of $1,000,000 or more is represented as $1,000,000.
2. Median selected monthly owner costs of 10 percent or less as a percentage of household income is represented as 10.0
3. A median gross rent of $2,000 or more is represented as $2,000.
4. A median gross rent of 50 percent or more as a percentage of household income is represented as 50.0

Table C-4. Cities — Where: Migration, Housing, and Transportation, 2010–2012—Continued

STATE and place code	STATE or city	Percent who lived in the same house one year ago	Percent who did not live in the same city one year ago	Total occupied housing units	Percent owner-occupied housing units	Median value of owner-occupied housing units (dollars)[1]	Median selected monthly owner costs as a percentage of household income[2] With a mortgage	Without a mortgage	Median gross rent (dollars)[2]	Median gross rent as a percentage of household income[4]	Percent of workers who drove alone to work	Mean travel time to work (minutes)	Percent of occupied housing units with no vehicle available
	ACS table number:	C07204	C07204	B25003	B25003	B25077	B25092	B25092	B25064	B25071	C08301	B08013/C08012	C25045
	Column number:	1	2	3	4	5	6	7	8	9	10	11	12
	New York—Cont.												
36 80907	West Seneca CDP	91.1	6.7	18,518	77.1	127,800	20.9	13.3	700	30.6	86.0	19.9	7.7
36 81677	White Plains city	88.0	7.0	22,070	53.3	517,000	26.3	18.5	1,412	33.9	55.5	25.5	16.6
36 84000	Yonkers city	89.7	5.0	73,077	47.6	411,800	28.7	20.8	1,161	33.0	57.6	32.0	25.5
37 00000	**North Carolina**	84.6	10.8	3,699,308	66.3	152,800	23.3	12.2	761	30.9	81.2	23.5	6.7
37 01520	Apex town	83.0	14.9	13,193	71.9	258,000	19.0	10.0	998	23.0	79.5	22.9	2.3
37 02080	Asheboro city	76.7	12.3	9,729	50.9	117,400	25.0	13.7	646	30.8	86.8	20.7	9.9
37 02140	Asheville city	76.0	14.3	36,896	52.1	190,400	25.6	13.2	817	29.1	73.6	17.9	11.2
37 09060	Burlington city	80.0	11.4	21,922	55.8	127,000	23.2	12.6	697	35.0	81.9	21.6	8.3
37 10620	Carrboro town	71.5	20.7	8,980	33.1	329,400	22.1	10.0	805	30.3	59.1	21.7	10.5
37 10740	Cary town	83.2	11.8	51,021	69.1	305,600	19.6	10.0	944	24.9	79.3	22.5	2.4
37 11800	Chapel Hill town	64.8	22.5	19,756	49.0	377,900	22.2	10.0	904	37.6	58.0	20.2	10.7
37 12000	Charlotte city	79.4	7.9	292,501	56.8	170,500	23.3	11.8	868	30.7	76.8	24.4	8.0
37 14100	Concord city	83.1	10.0	29,364	69.2	163,800	23.8	12.1	769	29.9	83.2	25.6	5.5
37 14700	Cornelius town	78.9	14.8	10,130	66.7	246,400	22.0	10.0	977	24.3	74.7	27.9	5.0
37 19000	Durham city	75.1	12.0	95,863	49.8	177,200	22.7	11.3	825	31.5	74.8	21.1	10.4
37 22920	Fayetteville city	73.5	15.8	76,398	50.3	127,400	23.7	11.7	867	28.6	80.5	20.4	6.4
37 25480	Garner town	86.1	13.3	10,671	65.3	165,600	22.9	11.7	880	28.6	78.4	25.6	4.3
37 25580	Gastonia city	82.9	7.1	26,141	55.8	137,800	25.0	11.8	751	34.6	83.8	23.3	7.8
37 26880	Goldsboro city	73.5	16.7	14,349	39.2	115,000	24.2	13.7	674	30.6	78.7	18.0	19.1
37 28000	Greensboro city	82.7	8.3	111,765	53.5	146,900	23.8	12.2	723	30.3	81.2	19.9	8.3
37 28080	Greenville city	67.9	17.7	34,263	37.7	153,100	21.9	12.9	711	36.2	81.5	17.2	10.5
37 30120	Havelock city	65.5	26.9	6,811	44.3	138,300	23.0	10.0	1,063	28.5	64.7	16.6	4.3
37 31060	Hickory city	83.5	8.5	16,140	52.3	153,000	22.2	11.2	647	28.5	87.3	19.6	8.0
37 31400	High Point city	82.9	8.2	40,848	57.6	143,500	25.8	12.8	760	31.5	81.3	20.7	10.6
37 32260	Holly Springs town	86.5	10.7	8,665	86.4	232,700	22.3	10.0	1,181	19.3	81.7	27.4	1.6
37 33120	Huntersville town	84.6	11.4	17,647	74.1	247,600	20.0	12.8	983	24.1	80.6	26.3	2.4
37 33560	Indian Trail town	87.7	9.8	11,119	85.5	172,600	23.2	10.7	1,034	30.4	81.0	29.7	0.6
37 34200	Jacksonville city	66.3	26.1	20,720	38.0	160,100	23.9	12.0	1,026	33.6	62.3	20.5	6.7
37 35200	Kannapolis city	86.7	6.9	15,666	60.9	120,200	26.2	15.6	712	29.9	82.6	23.1	7.6
37 35600	Kernersville town	83.7	12.2	9,904	55.3	174,500	22.6	13.9	724	28.5	86.5	21.9	6.5
37 35920	Kinston city	78.4	9.2	9,009	42.8	106,400	28.4	17.2	602	34.4	70.8	19.2	22.7
37 39700	Lumberton city	85.6	8.9	7,480	54.2	99,300	23.6	15.7	662	33.7	82.0	17.8	10.6
37 41960	Matthews town	85.1	12.9	10,614	72.8	214,500	20.4	10.6	912	37.5	83.0	24.7	3.4
37 43480	Mint Hill town	92.1	7.5	8,598	77.6	200,000	21.8	10.0	800	27.0	. . .	28.3	1.7
37 43920	Monroe city	85.1	8.5	10,932	59.0	146,700	23.4	13.3	749	35.4	74.5	28.3	9.7
37 44220	Mooresville town	83.0	9.5	11,899	68.1	179,400	23.5	12.5	875	24.6	86.6	21.9	3.6
37 44520	Morrisville town	77.7	18.3	7,598	50.9	267,700	19.4	10.0	978	19.0	82.4	20.0	1.4
37 46340	New Bern city	83.6	12.1	12,358	52.9	143,000	24.7	17.0	762	30.9	74.1	20.2	16.2
37 55000	Raleigh city	78.8	10.8	161,309	53.5	204,800	22.4	10.0	873	29.9	80.7	21.0	6.6
37 57500	Rocky Mount city	83.4	6.7	22,942	55.2	108,200	23.5	16.3	756	33.1	85.9	19.0	11.7
37 58860	Salisbury city	77.1	16.3	12,109	49.7	119,000	24.8	13.1	685	32.9	79.3	20.8	11.1
37 59280	Sanford city	77.4	9.8	9,980	52.6	121,400	21.8	13.3	666	29.7	82.1	20.6	13.4
37 61200	Shelby city	81.8	8.0	8,267	52.4	120,000	23.1	11.5	650	44.5	89.6	18.8	14.7
37 64740	Statesville city	82.1	10.5	9,663	48.1	125,900	22.9	15.0	699	35.5	79.0	19.6	11.9
37 67420	Thomasville city	81.6	8.7	10,804	57.5	107,500	23.9	13.2	586	35.0	81.6	21.0	8.9
37 70540	Wake Forest town	84.5	11.7	10,832	75.6	252,200	23.0	10.0	913	24.8	82.0	28.9	4.7
37 74440	Wilmington city	74.6	13.3	46,561	45.9	218,100	25.1	13.8	843	33.5	78.2	17.5	8.9
37 74540	Wilson city	77.2	8.6	19,168	49.6	133,600	27.0	16.9	733	35.0	82.0	18.2	13.1
37 75000	Winston-Salem city	82.0	7.1	90,752	56.0	140,400	23.2	11.7	694	32.2	81.9	19.4	10.2
38 00000	**North Dakota**	82.5	11.1	285,639	65.7	130,500	19.3	10.0	632	25.2	79.6	16.8	5.5
38 07200	Bismarck city	82.6	9.0	27,576	65.7	160,000	19.8	11.2	662	23.7	79.6	18.6	5.3
38 25700	Fargo city	72.2	14.8	47,991	44.8	158,300	20.5	10.6	650	25.8	82.5	15.5	7.9
38 32060	Grand Forks city	74.0	14.1	22,518	47.6	154,100	21.1	10.5	673	30.0	80.0	12.7	8.0
38 53380	Minot city	75.0	11.4	17,698	60.3	152,300	21.0	10.0	680	26.3	82.3	15.3	7.2
38 84780	West Fargo city	85.7	12.1	10,741	70.3	152,700	21.5	12.2	695	25.6	86.8	17.2	3.3
39 00000	**Ohio**	85.5	9.5	4,542,141	67.3	130,600	22.7	12.9	708	30.5	83.4	23.0	8.3
39 01000	Akron city	84.7	6.8	82,276	54.4	84,900	23.2	13.9	667	34.7	83.1	20.1	15.8
39 01420	Alliance city	78.2	11.4	8,633	54.8	83,000	24.6	13.6	593	32.1	80.4	17.7	12.0
39 02568	Ashland city	79.0	9.3	8,235	60.0	103,400	21.1	15.2	647	26.0	79.2	17.9	8.6
39 02736	Athens city	46.5	28.8	6,377	33.7	161,100	24.8	10.0	726	50.0	46.1	13.9	15.0
39 03184	Austintown CDP	89.0	6.7	12,888	68.7	91,900	21.7	12.9	573	26.8	. . .	19.4	4.6
39 03352	Avon city	. . .	. . .	7,829	77.6	244,200	19.6	16.5	1,073	33.2	. . .	26.5	2.8
39 03464	Avon Lake city	91.8	4.5	8,837	81.3	211,100	21.3	10.2	972	27.0	88.2	26.1	4.5
39 03828	Barberton city	89.2	6.2	10,920	63.7	83,900	23.0	14.8	653	30.8	86.5	22.5	12.7
39 04720	Beavercreek city	87.2	10.2	17,974	73.3	174,400	20.6	13.0	1,072	25.9	87.5	18.4	3.2
39 07454	Boardman CDP	90.3	6.1	15,760	63.8	112,300	22.4	12.1	618	29.1	89.3	20.6	7.0
39 07972	Bowling Green city	54.2	24.7	10,776	41.8	154,700	20.0	11.2	625	34.6	70.0	15.6	9.5
39 09680	Brunswick city	90.0	5.6	13,100	74.1	157,100	22.1	10.9	782	28.5	88.0	28.3	3.9

1. A median value of $1,000,000 or more is represented as $1,000,000.
2. Median selected monthly owner costs of 10 percent or less as a percenage of household income is represented as 10.0
3. A median gross rent of $2,000 or more is represented as $2,000.
4. A median gross rent of 50 percent or more as a percentage of household income is represented as 50.0.

Table C-4. Cities — Where: Migration, Housing, and Transportation, 2010–2012—Continued

STATE and place code		STATE or city	Percent who lived in the same house one year ago	Percent who did not live in the same city one year ago	Total occupied housing units	Percent owner-occupied housing units	Median value of owner-occupied housing units (dollars)[1]	Median selected monthly owner costs as a percentage of household income[2]		Median gross rent (dollars)[2]	Median gross rent as a percentage of household income[4]	Percent of workers who drove alone to work	Mean travel time to work (minutes)	Percent of occupied housing units with no vehicle available
								With a mortgage	Without a mortgage					
		ACS table number:	C07204	C07204	B25003	B25003	B25077	B25092	B25092	B25064	B25071	C08301	B08013/ C08012	C25045
		Column number:	1	2	3	4	5	6	7	8	9	10	11	12
		Ohio—Cont.												
39	12000	Canton city............................	82.4	8.5	29,928	54.2	76,200	23.2	11.9	596	33.2	79.4	18.8	15.5
39	13190	Centerville city.......................	86.5	10.7	10,829	69.5	167,200	23.3	16.1	840	27.1	89.4	21.8	4.6
39	14184	Chillicothe city.......................	81.4	10.7	9,196	57.9	98,200	21.2	12.2	620	28.4	83.8	22.0	11.8
39	15000	Cincinnati city........................	75.2	9.4	127,708	40.7	123,900	23.7	13.9	632	33.1	72.1	22.6	21.0
39	16000	Cleveland city.........................	80.5	7.2	165,887	44.5	76,700	27.0	15.1	656	35.9	70.2	24.0	24.9
39	16014	Cleveland Heights city............	81.2	14.8	19,155	56.5	128,900	24.5	14.0	813	32.3	73.8	22.3	13.4
39	18000	Columbus city.........................	76.7	10.0	324,641	46.0	131,200	23.6	12.8	792	30.3	80.3	21.3	10.3
39	19778	Cuyahoga Falls city.................	91.2	6.4	21,794	61.6	117,900	21.4	12.6	742	27.1	91.6	22.0	7.0
39	21000	Dayton city.............................	73.8	11.9	56,385	48.3	69,400	24.2	15.0	630	37.6	71.0	20.0	20.4
39	21434	Delaware city..........................	82.2	11.4	13,496	62.2	157,200	21.9	12.8	793	29.4	83.5	25.8	6.0
39	22694	Dublin city..............................	88.8	8.1	14,908	79.9	332,200	22.4	10.3	1,152	19.7	85.2	22.4	2.2
39	25256	Elyria city...............................	82.6	8.6	23,118	61.5	99,100	22.5	13.6	695	29.4	82.4	22.8	9.5
39	25704	Euclid city...............................	81.7	11.2	21,550	51.6	89,900	23.8	14.5	718	34.4	82.3	23.7	14.9
39	25914	Fairborn city...........................	84.1	10.1	14,138	45.7	104,700	22.8	11.4	744	31.6	86.5	20.0	7.1
39	25970	Fairfield city...........................	83.5	12.6	17,187	65.3	145,600	21.8	11.4	851	27.1	90.0	23.3	2.2
39	27048	Findlay city.............................	79.5	10.6	17,279	61.8	122,900	20.2	11.1	630	31.3	82.4	14.8	7.4
39	29106	Gahanna city..........................	87.5	8.6	12,853	74.3	183,900	21.9	13.4	929	30.3	83.9	21.6	5.8
39	29428	Garfield Heights city...............	87.1	9.9	11,247	70.8	86,100	25.1	15.4	748	32.4	82.3	23.4	10.5
39	31860	Green city...............................	92.9	5.7	10,421	77.7	174,200	23.5	11.2	810	26.4	. . .	21.7	2.4
39	32592	Grove City city........................	86.9	9.4	14,175	70.0	159,000	21.6	14.9	829	28.1	86.0	21.3	3.7
39	33012	Hamilton city..........................	83.4	8.7	24,149	56.6	99,200	22.9	12.3	701	32.2	81.2	23.4	12.0
39	35476	Hilliard city.............................	87.5	9.0	9,991	75.2	210,500	22.2	14.3	927	28.9	86.6	21.8	3.9
39	36610	Huber Heights city..................	85.8	8.9	15,071	72.1	107,600	22.7	13.3	842	34.3	84.1	22.4	5.7
39	36651	Hudson city.............................	89.3	9.8	7,512	87.6	284,900	18.6	11.1	1,218	24.1	84.2	29.6	1.5
39	39872	Kent city.................................	61.9	24.0	10,104	39.0	143,900	18.9	11.6	689	45.2	70.1	20.5	9.0
39	40040	Kettering city..........................	84.5	10.3	25,560	60.8	132,800	22.2	13.3	707	29.3	84.0	20.1	6.8
39	41664	Lakewood city.........................	79.2	12.3	24,362	43.7	127,300	23.7	14.5	695	28.0	78.2	24.7	13.5
39	41720	Lancaster city..........................	81.1	8.2	15,919	54.6	117,300	23.3	11.0	710	33.2	81.9	23.9	10.5
39	42364	Lebanon city...........................	81.8	10.6	7,146	60.2	157,100	20.0	11.1	775	23.2	84.6	24.2	3.4
39	43554	Lima city.................................	74.2	13.2	14,460	46.2	71,400	20.8	14.7	612	35.9	84.2	19.0	13.6
39	44856	Lorain city...............................	83.6	8.0	25,243	59.5	94,000	22.9	12.8	645	34.5	85.0	24.3	11.5
39	47138	Mansfield city.........................	79.5	9.7	18,422	55.7	79,400	24.5	12.8	577	28.5	83.6	16.8	14.0
39	47306	Maple Heights city..................	90.2	7.9	9,510	69.9	82,700	25.3	14.7	683	36.8	80.8	22.2	10.5
39	47754	Marion city.............................	73.4	13.6	13,154	55.7	76,100	23.1	12.0	664	35.3	83.5	19.8	12.5
39	48160	Marysville city.........................	74.8	16.4	7,393	60.3	160,600	22.5	16.6	842	29.1	87.5	22.4	9.3
39	48188	Mason city..............................	90.4	6.5	10,651	81.9	214,100	22.4	12.4	1,052	30.0	89.2	23.3	1.5
39	48244	Massillon city..........................	86.0	9.6	13,108	66.7	98,200	22.5	14.1	605	29.8	85.9	21.4	10.4
39	48790	Medina city.............................	87.0	8.3	10,328	67.5	160,200	21.7	10.9	809	34.0	85.5	25.7	9.0
39	49056	Mentor city.............................	91.8	6.6	19,015	84.9	166,800	21.6	12.9	857	33.3	88.3	23.9	5.2
39	49434	Miamisburg city......................	86.9	10.1	8,205	69.3	141,600	22.0	14.7	677	34.3	84.5	21.9	10.2
39	49840	Middletown city......................	82.8	8.1	19,650	58.2	99,700	25.1	14.9	748	36.2	85.4	20.9	9.1
39	54040	Newark city.............................	78.5	9.9	19,655	56.3	112,000	20.5	12.2	670	34.1	82.2	21.6	10.7
39	56882	North Olmsted city..................	91.5	6.8	13,667	77.9	147,600	24.0	15.1	842	25.8	83.7	22.9	4.0
39	56966	North Ridgeville city................	90.4	6.1	12,031	85.4	162,700	22.9	12.5	698	32.8	85.6	26.5	3.1
39	57008	North Royalton city.................	92.9	5.4	12,275	71.1	194,800	22.8	14.8	740	22.0	85.9	26.3	4.3
39	57386	Norwood city..........................	80.4	11.9	8,222	46.8	118,800	23.7	17.2	629	33.1	78.8	18.1	15.3
39	58730	Oregon city.............................	88.2	6.6	8,406	70.9	133,500	22.0	13.7	634	27.1	88.8	19.9	5.6
39	59234	Oxford city.............................	43.9	34.8	5,710	33.3	196,700	18.6	10.0	719	50.0	49.7	14.1	8.6
39	61000	Parma city..............................	88.5	7.9	32,925	73.7	116,200	22.6	14.3	715	30.0	87.3	23.9	6.7
39	61028	Parma Heights city..................	74.8	19.9	8,922	55.5	118,300	23.3	15.8	748	31.5	89.0	25.4	9.5
39	62148	Perrysburg city........................	91.2	7.4	8,609	68.8	189,300	20.8	11.8	867	22.8	89.6	20.5	4.6
39	62848	Piqua city...............................	80.5	5.6	8,604	60.3	87,000	23.4	13.3	652	35.6	84.6	16.9	7.5
39	64304	Portsmouth city.......................	82.2	10.4	8,083	51.5	74,500	19.8	11.6	516	31.7	80.3	17.7	13.3
39	66390	Reynoldsburg city....................	83.6	10.7	13,889	59.9	144,800	22.3	13.1	822	30.3	81.2	22.9	5.7
39	67468	Riverside city..........................	80.5	15.8	9,989	56.4	94,400	22.5	13.7	697	26.5	88.7	17.8	6.7
39	68056	Rocky River city.......................	91.9	6.1	8,754	75.6	205,500	21.8	17.2	790	26.4	84.0	23.9	7.2
39	70380	Sandusky city..........................	80.6	7.1	11,420	51.4	86,400	22.3	14.1	594	28.6	79.4	17.6	13.1
39	71682	Shaker Heights city..................	90.8	6.9	11,595	62.0	216,600	22.5	15.3	907	30.0	75.C	22.4	7.5
39	72424	Sidney city..............................	83.9	6.8	8,581	63.3	98,700	21.8	13.2	665	28.1	91.C	16.4	6.4
39	72928	Solon city...............................	92.6	5.7	8,289	84.4	259,900	22.3	12.7	997	28.9	89.8	26.3	4.1
39	73264	South Euclid city.....................	92.5	6.3	8,918	84.0	109,800	24.5	16.8	1,045	35.6	83.0	23.2	4.0
39	74118	Springfield city........................	78.6	8.4	24,184	51.2	81,600	22.3	12.0	629	33.5	77.4	19.4	14.5
39	74944	Stow city................................	92.0	6.2	13,733	69.6	167,400	21.3	12.1	860	26.1	90.4	25.0	5.3
39	75098	Strongsville city......................	91.3	7.4	17,163	80.3	192,500	22.0	13.6	797	26.2	86.9	27.0	4.2
39	77000	Toledo city.............................	81.0	6.0	117,071	54.8	83,000	23.6	14.2	625	34.0	82.1	19.2	13.9
39	77504	Trotwood city.........................	82.8	12.9	10,280	57.3	79,500	25.5	15.0	686	34.9	80.0	24.8	12.7
39	77588	Troy city.................................	80.0	11.1	10,058	58.8	128,400	20.2	11.2	692	27.6	83.6	17.9	6.5
39	79002	Upper Arlington city................	90.5	7.3	13,326	83.6	300,200	22.0	13.3	973	26.1	85.7	19.4	3.7
39	80304	Wadsworth city.......................	84.2	9.5	8,611	70.0	154,600	22.3	15.0	789	28.3	88.0	21.8	7.8
39	80892	Warren city.............................	83.2	6.9	17,110	53.7	62,200	22.1	15.1	580	33.6	88.7	19.2	12.8

1. A median value of $1,000,000 or more is represented as $1,000,000.
2. Median selected monthly owner costs of 10 percent or less as a percenage of household income is represented as 10.0
3. A median gross rent of $2,000 or more is represented as $2,000.
4. A median gross rent of 50 percent or more as a percentage of household income is represented as 50.0.

Table C-4. Cities — Where: Migration, Housing, and Transportation, 2010–2012—*Continued*

STATE and place code	STATE or city	Percent who lived in the same house one year ago	Percent who did not live in the same city one year ago	Total occupied housing units	Percent owner-occupied housing units	Median value of owner-occupied housing units (dollars)[1]	Median selected monthly owner costs as a percentage of household income[2]		Median gross rent (dollars)[2]	Median gross rent as a percentage of household income[4]	Percent of workers who drove alone to work	Mean travel time to work (minutes)	Percent of occupied housing units with no vehicle available
							With a mortgage	Without a mortgage					
	ACS table number:	C07204	C07204	B25003	B25003	B25077	B25092	B25092	B25064	B25071	C08301	B08013/ C08012	C25045
	Column number:	1	2	3	4	5	6	7	8	9	10	11	12
	Ohio—Cont.												
39 83342	Westerville city	84.1	13.1	13,291	73.4	209,100	20.2	10.0	950	27.8	84.1	20.4	3.3
39 83622	Westlake city	88.8	9.6	13,392	75.6	228,300	21.7	12.3	965	24.0	84.5	24.4	7.1
39 84812	White Oak CDP	87.5	10.7	7,871	73.5	131,100	21.5	10.8	606	33.8	87.6	22.4	6.9
39 85484	Willoughby city	86.4	11.1	10,398	60.4	147,600	22.8	13.2	821	27.1	89.1	20.8	6.0
39 86548	Wooster city	76.4	11.8	10,403	60.8	124,200	22.4	10.5	641	28.9	74.6	17.0	8.9
39 86772	Xenia city	86.7	8.1	10,539	63.9	97,400	23.6	13.4	667	34.5	85.3	21.6	10.1
39 88000	Youngstown city	83.9	8.3	26,165	58.1	47,000	24.0	13.8	584	40.6	79.8	20.7	17.5
39 88084	Zanesville city	78.7	9.2	10,535	43.5	76,500	22.4	14.3	587	35.0	77.1	20.4	18.3
40 00000	**Oklahoma**	82.6	10.5	1,441,163	67.1	112,900	21.5	11.1	690	29.1	81.8	21.1	5.6
40 02600	Ardmore city	87.5	6.8	8,918	61.3	94,300	20.7	11.3	669	26.5	79.1	13.9	5.8
40 04450	Bartlesville city	83.7	8.8	15,191	70.0	108,700	19.4	10.5	641	28.3	81.2	15.4	6.3
40 06400	Bixby city	85.8	11.9	7,660	81.3	186,900	22.1	12.0	819	32.1	86.1	23.3	4.3
40 09050	Broken Arrow city	87.9	8.6	36,180	78.8	149,400	21.8	10.8	925	27.8	84.6	20.2	2.6
40 19900	Del City city	76.3	15.1	8,280	62.2	79,500	21.0	12.6	760	29.9	80.9	18.1	6.3
40 21900	Duncan city	73.7	12.2	9,668	65.4	99,000	22.2	11.6	642	27.9	83.6	17.0	5.8
40 23200	Edmond city	82.0	12.8	30,704	69.3	196,600	21.5	10.0	868	29.9	84.3	21.0	4.0
40 23950	Enid city	75.5	11.1	19,457	62.2	91,100	20.9	10.0	637	23.4	83.3	14.7	5.7
40 41850	Lawton city	68.0	18.1	35,159	49.3	108,100	21.0	10.4	750	27.7	72.0	14.7	7.7
40 48350	Midwest City city	84.1	10.7	22,702	61.9	99,700	21.9	12.0	737	29.4	87.8	21.6	5.6
40 49200	Moore city	85.0	9.8	20,427	75.2	118,000	21.1	12.8	862	33.1	87.6	22.0	3.1
40 50050	Muskogee city	81.8	7.7	15,203	57.4	80,700	21.7	11.1	611	34.1	78.3	16.2	12.8
40 52500	Norman city	74.3	12.5	44,382	57.3	150,800	20.7	10.0	767	33.6	79.1	21.5	5.1
40 55000	Oklahoma City city	79.4	9.1	226,306	59.4	132,100	22.8	12.1	745	31.1	81.9	20.2	6.8
40 56650	Owasso city	84.4	11.3	10,979	68.6	151,600	20.4	11.2	799	29.8	85.2	19.7	3.3
40 59850	Ponca City city	77.6	8.6	10,230	66.6	81,400	19.4	12.9	626	29.0	82.0	15.4	7.2
40 65400	Sapulpa city	87.7	9.3	8,179	64.3	108,500	23.1	13.9	701	31.3	87.3	18.7	6.2
40 66800	Shawnee city	80.5	10.6	11,774	58.8	91,900	21.7	12.6	665	28.7	80.1	19.8	8.9
40 70300	Stillwater city	59.4	22.4	18,187	37.9	150,400	25.5	10.2	709	39.3	71.7	15.4	6.0
40 75000	Tulsa city	79.7	7.5	162,791	53.5	122,600	22.5	12.0	712	30.2	81.5	18.5	7.9
40 82950	Yukon city	83.4	10.1	8,709	76.8	122,700	21.6	10.0	697	27.0	83.0	21.4	5.8
41 00000	**Oregon**	81.8	12.0	1,513,005	61.6	233,900	26.6	12.9	855	32.5	71.7	22.5	8.1
41 01000	Albany city	83.6	8.6	19,681	59.2	173,700	25.5	12.6	747	33.9	80.8	19.0	9.1
41 01650	Aloha CDP	82.5	14.4	16,733	60.8	222,700	26.3	11.5	1,062	29.7	73.1	26.9	4.8
41 03050	Ashland city	76.1	14.0	9,069	56.0	350,000	31.3	13.6	863	38.4	56.5	17.4	5.6
41 05350	Beaverton city	77.7	16.0	35,730	49.1	278,200	24.9	14.0	928	30.0	71.5	24.0	8.0
41 05800	Bend city	77.2	9.8	32,633	58.7	239,200	27.6	13.9	918	31.7	76.3	16.2	6.2
41 05950	Bethany CDP	83.5	11.9	7,468	80.5	385,800	22.9	10.0	1,113	33.7	81.0	22.8	2.8
41 15800	Corvallis city	74.4	16.6	20,821	44.4	255,500	22.5	10.3	790	43.5	57.1	16.6	11.6
41 23850	Eugene city	70.4	13.5	65,952	49.0	237,500	25.8	13.5	836	37.7	66.1	17.1	11.4
41 26200	Forest Grove city	79.0	13.6	7,819	59.5	221,900	26.3	15.9	743	41.4	68.9	24.1	14.0
41 30550	Grants Pass city	78.2	10.7	14,471	46.9	181,200	26.5	13.5	771	36.1	82.5	15.6	11.0
41 31250	Gresham city	80.9	12.9	39,011	52.6	213,700	27.1	13.8	856	34.9	72.2	26.8	10.6
41 34100	Hillsboro city	80.5	12.5	32,267	54.9	236,500	26.1	12.3	1,057	27.3	73.3	25.5	6.6
41 38500	Keizer city	80.8	14.9	13,919	59.0	200,300	26.4	13.9	799	30.7	78.2	20.6	7.4
41 39700	Klamath Falls city	76.1	14.0	9,377	49.3	144,200	26.3	14.3	703	43.1	75.6	14.7	12.2
41 40550	Lake Oswego city	82.5	11.9	16,039	68.8	462,700	24.3	12.9	1,205	31.9	77.2	23.1	6.0
41 45000	McMinnville city	82.3	9.8	11,550	57.2	188,100	24.2	13.8	824	33.8	73.0	20.2	10.0
41 47000	Medford city	78.2	10.9	29,771	50.8	201,200	27.4	13.7	851	37.6	79.7	16.5	9.5
41 48650	Milwaukie city	82.2	14.7	8,430	59.1	222,700	28.5	13.9	882	26.7	72.7	23.7	7.3
41 52100	Newberg city	78.3	12.6	7,165	61.8	210,200	29.1	13.6	884	35.4	68.6	21.4	7.7
41 55200	Oregon City city	82.6	9.7	12,216	59.2	247,900	27.5	13.2	986	33.0	78.5	27.1	8.0
41 59000	Portland city	79.1	9.7	248,701	52.5	278,000	26.5	14.5	889	32.9	58.3	24.3	15.8
41 61200	Redmond city	75.2	13.4	10,049	56.3	147,100	32.5	12.8	814	36.4	79.8	21.2	7.4
41 63650	Roseburg city	84.5	10.2	9,658	58.5	168,600	24.0	11.3	804	32.8	74.4	13.6	8.2
41 64900	Salem city	78.0	11.7	57,838	55.0	186,400	25.9	13.2	776	33.3	74.7	20.6	9.1
41 69600	Springfield city	73.6	14.4	23,495	52.2	165,900	28.6	16.8	786	31.7	72.6	18.6	8.1
41 73650	Tigard city	85.3	12.2	19,427	60.8	291,600	26.0	11.4	919	30.1	76.7	22.1	4.6
41 74950	Tualatin city	89.7	8.7	10,532	54.5	297,000	23.7	10.0	958	27.9	79.9	22.2	6.5
41 80150	West Linn city	86.0	11.2	9,448	79.7	380,400	27.2	10.0	1,149	30.7	80.5	23.2	3.4
41 82800	Wilsonville city	72.9	21.2	7,776	48.0	336,800	26.0	14.3	946	27.5	79.5	23.2	8.3
41 83750	Woodburn city	86.6	6.8	7,926	55.7	150,400	27.7	14.3	735	30.4	72.0	23.1	10.2
42 00000	**Pennsylvania**	87.9	8.9	4,949,494	69.6	164,700	23.3	13.7	800	30.4	76.7	26.0	11.7
42 02000	Allentown city	76.4	10.7	42,457	46.3	134,100	27.7	16.3	861	37.7	68.1	23.2	21.6
42 02056	Allison Park CDP	90.5	6.5	8,494	81.7	196,300	21.4	12.9	881	33.3	84.5	24.4	5.9
42 02184	Altoona city	86.5	4.7	18,954	66.5	82,400	20.9	12.5	556	30.8	79.6	17.5	13.0
42 06064	Bethel Park municipality	92.3	6.8	12,865	79.1	156,000	19.9	13.4	893	28.2	74.3	30.4	5.1
42 06088	Bethlehem city	78.1	11.5	29,528	51.1	175,300	25.2	14.4	875	32.8	78.3	22.1	15.1
42 12536	Chambersburg borough	81.0	11.2	7,985	49.3	155,900	20.7	12.2	737	31.0	78.4	19.8	12.0
42 13208	Chester city	84.3	9.1	12,131	40.0	69,800	25.3	13.8	774	35.5	60.7	22.5	33.8
42 19920	Drexel Hill CDP	89.1	8.9	11,455	68.7	196,800	25.3	19.7	874	35.1	77.7	30.2	8.3
42 21648	Easton city	69.6	16.6	9,294	50.3	130,100	27.0	15.4	848	33.0	73.4	27.7	20.7
42 24000	Erie city	81.1	8.1	41,214	50.7	83,800	21.8	13.7	610	33.0	75.7	16.4	20.2

1. A median value of $1,000,000 or more is represented as $1,000,000.
2. Median selected monthly owner costs of 10 percent or less as a percenage of household income is represented as 10.0
3. A median gross rent of $2,000 or more is represented as $2,000.
4. A median gross rent of 50 percent or more as a percentage of household income is represented as 50.0.

Table C-4. Cities — Where: Migration, Housing, and Transportation, 2010–2012—*Continued*

STATE and place code	STATE or city	Percent who lived in the same house one year ago	Percent who did not live in the same city one year ago	Total occupied housing units	Percent owner-occupied housing units	Median value of owner-occupied housing units (dollars)[1]	Median selected monthly owner costs as a percentage of household income[2] — With a mortgage	Without a mortgage	Median gross rent (dollars)[2]	Median gross rent as a percentage of household income[4]	Percent of workers who drove alone to work	Mean travel time to work (minutes)	Percent of occupied housing units with no vehicle available
	ACS table number:	C07204	C07204	B25003	B25003	B25077	B25092	B25092	B25064	B25071	C08301	B08013/C08012	C25045
	Column number:	1	2	3	4	5	6	7	8	9	10	11	12
	Pennsylvania—Cont.												
42 32800	Harrisburg city	78.2	10.1	20,640	39.1	85,300	23.4	15.2	760	33.0	65.1	19.4	25.5
42 33408	Hazleton city	80.1	8.9	9,494	49.4	86,900	26.3	17.4	661	29.5	72.2	20.5	18.9
42 38288	Johnstown city	85.5	8.0	9,806	53.2	43,700	21.5	14.1	467	31.1	72.6	21.2	27.9
42 41216	Lancaster city	81.8	11.1	22,420	45.3	104,500	25.8	13.4	752	36.4	70.5	19.6	21.3
42 42168	Lebanon city	81.4	7.2	10,344	45.4	92,300	21.0	13.5	657	34.2	71.5	21.1	22.4
42 42928	Levittown CDP	94.4	4.3	18,312	85.1	229,800	27.5	17.5	1,094	33.5	86.1	23.5	3.7
42 46256	McKeesport city	84.0	7.5	8,763	55.6	47,100	21.9	13.5	549	32.4	64.4	30.4	30.0
42 50528	Monroeville municipality	88.4	9.4	12,229	66.0	132,200	20.1	11.8	873	27.5	78.6	27.3	5.7
42 52432	Murrysville municipality	93.5	5.2	7,877	87.2	209,500	21.3	10.0	805	26.5	80.6	30.3	3.5
42 53368	New Castle city	86.7	5.0	9,578	59.8	58,700	22.7	14.0	529	34.2	83.8	19.9	15.4
42 54656	Norristown borough	90.2	6.2	13,058	41.1	153,000	27.2	16.6	968	38.5	64.8	22.7	25.3
42 60000	Philadelphia city	85.6	4.6	576,889	53.4	142,300	25.6	15.6	874	34.9	49.9	31.9	34.2
42 61000	Pittsburgh city	78.7	11.5	131,719	48.4	88,200	19.9	13.9	746	30.3	54.1	23.1	25.5
42 61536	Plum borough	91.8	6.0	10,663	80.3	136,100	20.0	12.3	854	28.0	83.7	27.1	5.2
42 62416	Pottstown borough	87.3	7.0	9,612	58.5	135,100	26.3	20.3	780	34.7	76.4	26.3	16.2
42 63624	Reading city	75.4	9.0	30,896	42.4	68,200	28.1	14.6	697	39.6	57.5	24.3	30.3
42 69000	Scranton city	83.0	9.0	29,585	50.8	109,800	23.1	16.6	676	29.3	70.8	18.7	15.0
42 73808	State College borough	42.3	38.1	12,471	18.2	274,700	20.7	10.0	897	50.0	41.4	15.3	20.6
42 83512	West Mifflin borough	91.1	5.3	8,604	76.2	87,400	20.5	13.3	601	23.9	77.9	29.2	10.1
42 85152	Wilkes-Barre city	77.8	13.7	16,027	49.2	80,700	23.0	13.7	617	30.5	70.5	18.4	20.2
42 85312	Williamsport city	74.9	13.2	11,121	38.0	101,200	23.4	14.6	642	32.3	72.4	17.7	18.5
42 87048	York city	74.1	10.7	15,861	41.3	86,500	26.6	17.8	685	36.9	72.5	21.2	27.7
44 00000	**Rhode Island**	86.5	9.5	409,308	60.3	245,300	26.7	16.3	891	30.5	79.9	23.6	9.9
44 19180	Cranston city	89.0	7.9	30,200	65.9	220,500	26.9	19.3	957	30.7	84.1	21.6	6.2
44 22960	East Providence city	86.6	6.6	19,829	55.7	224,000	27.7	17.7	845	28.4	86.7	20.5	10.5
44 49960	Newport city	78.7	15.1	10,746	45.1	382,500	27.4	13.5	1,065	26.6	65.4	17.5	11.5
44 54640	Pawtucket city	85.4	8.1	29,164	43.3	183,000	29.8	18.0	790	30.5	76.9	23.6	17.7
44 59000	Providence city	76.9	11.5	60,526	35.7	191,800	29.3	15.2	888	32.6	58.8	21.6	19.4
44 74300	Warwick city	91.2	4.6	35,097	71.4	208,300	26.4	16.5	1,017	32.6	87.1	23.0	6.5
44 80780	Woonsocket city	90.0	3.7	16,714	38.8	184,400	29.0	16.6	762	29.7	82.1	24.7	17.5
45 00000	**South Carolina**	84.3	13.0	1,774,128	68.8	136,300	23.1	11.7	758	32.0	82.7	23.6	7.2
45 00550	Aiken city	82.3	12.9	12,379	66.3	179,200	21.0	10.0	842	32.0	84.6	20.8	9.7
45 01360	Anderson city	73.5	15.9	10,609	50.3	123,100	23.6	10.3	628	35.1	83.6	19.2	14.8
45 13330	Charleston city	75.7	14.8	52,182	53.1	249,300	25.7	13.2	958	34.7	76.4	21.7	10.4
45 16000	Columbia city	65.4	25.2	44,324	47.6	160,700	22.2	11.7	797	33.9	66.4	16.0	11.6
45 21985	Easley city	80.0	8.6	7,961	62.8	137,800	21.8	12.1	750	36.1	89.9	22.9	8.0
45 25810	Florence city	84.0	8.0	14,680	60.3	144,900	21.4	10.0	655	32.4	83.7	19.0	11.2
45 29815	Goose Creek city	74.0	21.9	12,281	66.0	170,500	23.1	10.0	1,003	35.2	77.5	22.7	2.6
45 30850	Greenville city	75.8	17.8	25,539	45.2	201,200	22.2	11.7	746	29.3	81.1	17.6	11.0
45 30895	Greenwood city	77.1	12.6	8,659	46.8	89,000	22.2	16.6	657	38.3	. . .	20.9	17.6
45 30985	Greer city	78.2	15.2	9,622	56.9	133,200	23.4	12.4	737	26.9	87.9	21.5	6.5
45 34045	Hilton Head Island town	85.1	9.9	16,390	72.5	449,300	31.8	11.7	1,002	31.5	73.0	18.1	5.1
45 45115	Mauldin city	83.6	12.9	9,073	64.2	152,400	21.5	10.0	838	27.0	. . .	18.8	7.3
45 48535	Mount Pleasant town	78.9	10.5	27,718	71.9	338,300	26.5	11.2	1,267	34.0	82.8	22.0	3.4
45 49075	Myrtle Beach city	83.1	11.5	11,875	51.1	171,400	29.9	10.0	826	42.6	73.7	16.2	12.4
45 50695	North Augusta city	86.2	9.8	8,854	68.9	153,500	22.1	10.0	688	29.1	86.7	26.9	8.8
45 50875	North Charleston city	74.5	16.9	35,889	48.9	138,600	27.1	14.9	842	33.3	75.4	22.2	11.9
45 61405	Rock Hill city	78.1	11.1	26,257	51.3	132,000	23.4	14.0	756	32.2	79.6	22.3	9.0
45 62395	St. Andrews CDP	69.6	25.3	9,211	35.3	108,500	25.0	12.2	717	34.8	79.4	18.7	11.7
45 67390	Socastee CDP	78.7	18.4	7,632	59.1	149,400	35.2	11.8	800	31.8	80.5	18.7	3.9
45 68290	Spartanburg city	80.3	11.8	15,763	50.9	122,200	23.1	12.0	644	33.1	81.2	18.8	16.7
45 70270	Summerville town	76.4	18.6	17,022	59.4	176,000	23.7	13.0	953	33.0	84.0	27.7	6.6
45 70405	Sumter city	80.3	13.5	15,818	50.8	124,500	21.8	11.4	708	29.3	78.6	19.2	14.3
45 71395	Taylors CDP	85.9	11.3	8,471	70.4	137,500	21.5	10.1	734	34.4	83.6	20.0	4.7
46 00000	**South Dakota**	83.9	9.6	322,005	68.0	131,600	21.5	10.9	629	26.2	78.1	16.8	5.6
46 00100	Aberdeen city	80.9	9.8	11,130	64.5	136,800	21.0	13.9	546	24.9	81.9	11.3	8.0
46 07580	Brookings city	56.8	24.6	8,422	46.3	143,600	22.7	10.0	675	29.4	71.9	12.9	5.0
46 52980	Rapid City city	77.3	9.0	28,016	56.6	151,600	23.4	12.7	754	28.3	82.8	15.1	7.4
46 59020	Sioux Falls city	82.1	7.0	62,651	60.5	152,500	21.6	10.0	705	27.3	84.3	16.4	6.4
46 69300	Watertown city	85.2	5.4	9,442	67.4	137,700	21.7	11.7	580	26.4	81.8	13.1	6.9
47 00000	**Tennessee**	84.5	10.1	2,466,659	67.5	138,400	23.3	11.3	731	31.2	83.8	24.3	6.4
47 03440	Bartlett city	91.7	6.3	18,861	82.3	170,200	22.2	10.5	1,146	30.3	89.6	23.9	2.5
47 08280	Brentwood city	91.5	5.8	12,305	92.5	488,000	21.7	10.0	2,000	27.2	83.4	23.2	1.8
47 08540	Bristol city	80.2	11.7	11,426	67.0	103,100	23.2	14.2	605	30.5	88.3	20.7	6.5
47 14000	Chattanooga city	79.9	9.9	69,721	53.9	141,300	23.5	12.9	719	30.2	80.7	18.7	12.3
47 15160	Clarksville city	70.6	17.8	49,635	54.6	135,700	22.7	11.3	824	29.0	84.8	21.8	4.9
47 15400	Cleveland city	73.9	12.4	15,964	48.0	155,200	23.6	11.9	694	34.5	78.9	18.0	11.0
47 16420	Collierville town	88.1	9.6	14,590	86.2	276,700	23.4	10.0	1,077	26.3	87.9	24.4	1.1
47 16540	Columbia city	81.3	9.3	13,813	56.8	114,200	25.9	14.7	642	33.4	81.6	24.5	9.1
47 16920	Cookeville city	77.5	11.9	12,246	44.6	165,600	23.1	11.1	576	36.8	91.6	19.3	4.2
47 22720	East Ridge city	82.3	11.7	9,109	54.6	120,400	22.9	11.3	726	32.6	. . .	18.4	7.6

1. A median value of $1,000,000 or more is represented as $1,000,000.
2. Median selected monthly owner costs of 10 percent or less as a percenage of household income is represented as 10.0
3. A median gross rent of $2,000 or more is represented as $2,000.
4. A median gross rent of 50 percent or more as a percentage of household income is represented as 50.0.

Table C-4. Cities — Where: Migration, Housing, and Transportation, 2010–2012—*Continued*

STATE and place code		STATE or city	Percent who lived in the same house one year ago	Percent who did not live in the same city one year ago	Total occupied housing units	Percent owner-occupied housing units	Median value of owner-occupied housing units (dollars)[1]	Median selected monthly owner costs as a percentage of household income[2]: With a mortgage	Median selected monthly owner costs as a percentage of household income[2]: Without a mortgage	Median gross rent (dollars)[3]	Median gross rent as a percentage of household income[4]	Percent of workers who crove alone to work	Mean travel time to work (minutes)	Percent of occupied housing units with no vehicle available
		ACS table number:	C07204	C07204	B25003	B25003	B25077	B25092	B25092	B25064	B25071	C08301	B08013/ C08012	C25045
		Column number:	1	2	3	4	5	6	7	8	9	10	11	12
		Tennessee—Cont.												
47	25760	Farragut town	84.3	14.0	7,140	89.0	313,100	20.8	10.0	1,120	30.2	86.4	24.5	3.7
47	27740	Franklin city	81.2	13.0	25,281	67.2	298,900	23.0	10.5	1,023	28.9	80.7	23.4	3.4
47	28540	Gallatin city	78.2	13.7	11,952	55.2	164,800	23.2	11.5	819	27.1	. . .	24.9	7.0
47	28960	Germantown city	91.2	7.6	14,138	87.1	283,100	21.4	10.6	1,408	26.5	90.8	19.6	2.2
47	33280	Hendersonville city	84.2	10.7	19,476	70.9	197,700	23.5	10.0	858	31.3	83.1	25.8	3.8
47	37640	Jackson city	84.0	7.6	23,764	56.8	117,900	23.3	13.0	727	37.9	85.8	17.0	8.4
47	38320	Johnson City city	80.2	10.6	27,008	56.3	156,000	21.3	10.0	650	32.1	84.5	18.4	7.6
47	39560	Kingsport city	83.1	10.1	22,462	64.4	138,200	19.6	10.0	557	29.8	86.0	18.0	9.3
47	40000	Knoxville city	85.1	6.7	84,221	50.0	114,100	23.9	13.5	725	31.9	83.6	19.9	9.8
47	41200	La Vergne city	87.8	8.2	10,636	79.4	128,200	23.9	10.0	1,015	29.8	87.6	30.0	1.1
47	41520	Lebanon city	77.5	16.0	10,191	60.0	168,900	23.4	12.1	778	34.1	89.8	22.8	7.3
47	46380	Maryville city	81.4	13.2	10,595	63.8	185,000	22.6	10.0	761	27.9	83.7	21.3	6.4
47	48000	Memphis city	80.0	5.3	244,775	50.5	96,800	25.9	13.7	806	36.1	79.0	21.3	12.6
47	50280	Morristown city	81.9	10.8	11,058	52.5	111,500	23.0	15.2	640	36.0	81.5	20.8	9.4
47	50780	Mount Juliet city	88.2	9.9	9,365	82.8	195,100	22.0	10.0	959	34.9	. . .	28.4	1.6
47	51560	Murfreesboro city	73.2	14.5	41,261	52.5	178,000	23.0	10.5	818	31.6	87.2	25.8	5.1
47	52006	Nashville-Davidson (balance)	78.2	8.6	246,103	53.2	164,900	24.5	11.8	812	31.2	79.2	23.2	8.2
47	55120	Oak Ridge city	81.6	10.9	12,571	61.4	146,700	19.2	10.0	727	29.6	85.0	20.5	7.4
47	67760	Shelbyville city	81.9	7.4	7,171	46.0	94,500	26.3	14.1	649	30.9	. . .	20.1	9.8
47	69420	Smyrna town	81.7	13.4	15,186	67.4	146,500	23.1	10.2	846	29.8	83.7	26.2	4.1
47	70580	Spring Hill city	87.1	10.6	9,743	77.6	197,700	21.8	10.0	1,069	28.3	. . .	31.1	2.1
48	00000	**Texas**	82.8	10.3	8,852,441	63.0	128,400	22.8	12.3	834	29.8	79.9	24.9	6.0
48	01000	Abilene city	75.9	10.4	42,110	56.5	91,800	20.9	12.0	761	31.5	80.3	14.9	7.0
48	01924	Allen city	87.1	9.6	28,556	76.5	196,700	21.1	10.0	1,160	25.5	81.4	27.6	1.5
48	02272	Alvin city	81.0	13.2	8,335	54.1	108,200	21.4	10.0	756	32.9	82.7	27.4	4.6
48	03000	Amarillo city	80.6	6.0	73,908	61.2	113,300	21.4	12.1	720	29.5	78.9	17.9	6.6
48	04000	Arlington city	79.1	9.5	132,177	57.5	128,900	23.5	11.8	831	31.4	81.2	25.6	4.4
48	04462	Atascocita CDP	84.5	13.6	21,985	79.1	151,300	22.3	12.8	1,175	24.4	86.3	31.3	1.1
48	05000	Austin city	72.6	10.9	327,971	44.4	218,800	24.0	12.8	954	31.0	72.4	22.8	7.0
48	05372	Balch Springs city	86.9	11.1	7,016	57.6	84,300	29.6	14.5	893	36.7	82.2	29.5	7.2
48	06128	Baytown city	80.4	8.0	23,866	61.1	95,600	22.7	13.0	828	30.9	79.8	23.4	7.7
48	07000	Beaumont city	82.2	6.8	45,417	57.7	98,600	22.8	13.0	751	34.4	80.0	18.7	10.9
48	07132	Bedford city	84.1	12.4	20,756	55.7	160,400	21.8	10.8	859	28.4	87.6	23.1	4.9
48	07552	Benbrook city	88.1	9.9	9,349	67.2	134,500	19.7	12.5	848	30.9	87.9	23.9	3.2
48	08236	Big Spring city	76.1	13.9	8,017	59.2	69,300	17.6	11.9	658	24.6	80.5	16.2	10.2
48	10768	Brownsville city	87.5	4.3	50,159	61.6	81,800	27.0	14.1	611	33.0	78.0	19.0	11.2
48	10897	Brushy Creek CDP	83.3	11.2	7,325	75.6	216,000	22.7	11.8	1,299	23.6	. . .	27.8	1.1
48	10912	Bryan city	71.6	17.9	27,502	48.7	109,700	23.5	12.6	759	35.0	73.7	17.3	10.5
48	11428	Burleson city	83.0	9.7	13,244	71.2	123,700	20.0	11.7	1,053	26.6	85.4	26.4	2.7
48	12580	Canyon Lake CDP	87.4	8.4	8,461	82.4	163,000	26.7	11.6	1,028	30.5	. . .	35.4	0.4
48	13024	Carrollton city	84.2	9.0	42,972	62.5	165,200	22.0	12.5	954	26.8	81.2	23.9	2.7
48	13492	Cedar Hill city	90.0	8.0	15,647	72.5	129,900	24.0	12.6	1,053	31.5	83.3	30.3	4.5
48	13552	Cedar Park city	83.0	13.8	18,499	69.2	192,500	24.5	12.3	1,044	28.9	84.2	25.2	1.3
48	14236	Channelview CDP	83.0	10.0	10,926	69.6	91,700	27.5	14.7	964	37.9	82.3	24.8	4.2
48	15364	Cleburne city	77.0	13.6	10,391	57.3	97,300	21.5	14.4	792	27.5	85.9	23.0	4.3
48	15628	Cloverleaf CDP	81.7	15.1	6,787	58.3	99,000	24.6	13.6	728	33.2	74.9	25.3	3.3
48	15976	College Station city	58.2	23.4	33,540	35.3	174,200	22.3	10.3	899	50.0	74.4	17.8	5.8
48	15988	Colleyville city	93.8	5.5	7,968	96.1	421,100	23.7	11.2	1,823	50.0	85.4	26.0	
48	16432	Conroe city	79.1	12.0	20,149	50.0	127,300	24.6	14.5	817	30.9	72.4	25.3	6.6
48	16612	Coppell city	85.9	11.1	14,375	70.8	284,700	20.8	11.8	1,147	23.6	82.4	24.1	1.4
48	16624	Copperas Cove city	82.4	12.6	10,601	59.1	99,600	20.1	10.9	847	25.3	87.9	22.6	4.3
48	16696	Corinth city	87.2	12.8	7,108	87.0	169,200	21.9	12.5	886	50.0	87.3	30.0	2.2
48	17000	Corpus Christi city	79.6	7.4	110,803	56.6	113,400	23.1	12.9	836	30.5	78.3	19.1	8.7
48	17060	Corsicana city	79.2	10.0	8,765	55.8	76,200	22.0	13.1	670	28.5	80.8	19.2	10.7
48	19000	Dallas city	80.5	8.0	456,781	43.3	130,000	25.1	14.1	816	29.2	77.7	25.2	9.9
48	19624	Deer Park city	86.1	10.9	10,900	72.3	132,100	19.5	11.0	968	28.4	88.4	22.6	4.1
48	19792	Del Rio city	84.1	8.7	11,169	65.9	92,000	22.4	13.3	603	26.8	78.3	16.3	6.8
48	19900	Denison city	75.3	9.1	8,770	59.5	75,000	23.0	13.5	741	30.9	81.4	20.8	8.0
48	19972	Denton city	68.6	18.7	41,474	48.1	146,100	23.7	12.9	836	36.1	72.6	23.1	5.3
48	20092	DeSoto city	89.5	7.9	18,673	64.9	139,800	26.7	13.5	909	33.5	83.4	31.8	5.8
48	21628	Duncanville city	92.2	6.5	14,027	67.6	112,100	24.7	12.4	927	27.3	85.7	27.0	4.8
48	21892	Eagle Pass city	88.8	5.6	8,477	62.1	103,600	27.6	15.1	530	27.4	77.1	16.6	11.3
48	22660	Edinburg city	77.7	11.7	24,104	55.2	100,300	22.7	13.6	653	29.2	79.3	18.8	5.6
48	24000	El Paso city	83.7	6.6	216,792	59.2	117,600	23.1	11.5	723	30.6	79.5	22.5	8.4
48	24768	Euless city	78.3	16.0	20,862	42.9	144,500	21.9	10.0	933	26.4	82.8	22.7	3.3
48	25452	Farmers Branch city	81.8	14.2	10,643	60.9	142,500	22.9	13.8	998	25.8	79.9	19.8	2.0
48	26232	Flower Mound town	90.6	6.5	21,264	91.0	267,900	21.0	10.0	1,520	23.6	80.7	28.8	1.0
48	26736	Fort Hood CDP	57.8	39.7	5,913	0.8	43,500	. . .	. . .	1,123	32.6	53.8	11.0	0.6
48	27000	Fort Worth city	81.9	8.9	264,584	57.9	120,000	23.1	13.6	839	30.5	82.0	25.8	6.5
48	27648	Friendswood city	87.3	9.5	12,522	82.2	217,700	20.7	12.1	1,172	26.9	83.6	31.5	2.5
48	27684	Frisco city	86.2	10.1	41,055	75.8	245,200	20.8	11.3	1,188	25.8	80.6	27.5	1.4

1. A median value of $1,000,000 or more is represented as $1,000,000.
2. Median selected monthly owner costs of 10 percent or less as a percenage of household income is represented as 10.0
3. A median gross rent of $2,000 or more is represented as $2,000.
4. A median gross rent of 50 percent or more as a percentage of household income is represented as 50.0.

Table C-4. Cities — Where: Migration, Housing, and Transportation, 2010–2012—*Continued*

STATE and place code	STATE or city	Percent who lived in the same house one year ago	Percent who did not live in the same city one year ago	Total occupied housing units	Percent owner-occupied housing units	Median value of owner-occupied housing units (dollars)[1]	Median selected monthly owner costs as a percentage of household income[2] — With a mortgage	Median selected monthly owner costs as a percentage of household income[2] — Without a mortgage	Median gross rent (dollars)[2]	Median gross rent as a percentage of household income[4]	Percent of workers who drove alone to work	Mean travel time to work (minutes)	Percent of occupied housing units with no vehicle available
	ACS table number:	C07204	C07204	B25003	B25003	B25077	B25092	B25092	B25064	B25071	C08301	B08013/ C08012	C25045
	Column number:	1	2	3	4	5	6	7	8	9	10	11	12
	Texas—Cont.												
48 28068	Galveston city	70.6	15.5	19,805	46.8	143,000	24.8	12.3	808	37.9	69.8	18.9	14.9
48 29000	Garland city	84.7	8.0	72,934	65.5	115,300	24.3	12.9	926	31.3	78.7	27.4	4.4
48 29336	Georgetown city	83.0	10.8	19,304	69.0	180,200	24.5	12.0	999	29.9	80.8	24.2	5.3
48 30464	Grand Prairie city	85.3	9.8	57,572	61.1	124,300	25.3	12.7	877	31.8	83.3	27.0	4.3
48 30644	Grapevine city	80.8	10.8	18,165	58.8	227,500	21.2	11.7	1,019	27.1	84.3	22.8	3.2
48 30920	Greenville city	79.9	10.9	9,957	53.9	81,900	23.8	12.7	706	33.4	81.1	18.1	9.4
48 31928	Haltom City city	80.8	16.0	14,892	54.8	87,500	22.0	12.5	779	27.0	83.2	23.7	3.3
48 32312	Harker Heights city	73.9	17.0	8,169	62.8	173,600	21.5	10.2	772	28.2	. . .	19.8	2.7
48 32372	Harlingen city	91.4	4.7	20,829	56.6	76,800	24.0	14.1	703	31.0	84.5	17.4	10.0
48 35000	Houston city	79.0	7.5	770,098	45.1	123,900	23.7	12.8	830	30.0	75.8	25.7	10.2
48 35528	Huntsville city	71.7	20.7	10,376	36.1	126,900	19.5	13.4	725	44.2	81.7	19.6	9.1
48 35576	Hurst city	86.7	10.5	14,714	67.1	138,600	21.9	14.3	793	31.6	86.0	24.1	2.3
48 37000	Irving city	77.9	10.4	82,382	39.3	138,100	24.3	12.0	876	27.1	79.2	22.5	5.6
48 38632	Keller city	87.6	9.8	13,876	83.9	283,800	21.9	12.8	1,140	25.9	85.0	31.0	1.1
48 39040	Kerrville city	77.9	11.8	9,596	60.6	130,600	24.6	14.2	772	31.7	82.2	13.5	6.4
48 39148	Killeen city	69.3	18.7	44,085	49.1	110,900	24.0	10.1	846	28.9	86.0	20.3	5.4
48 39352	Kingsville city	80.1	8.5	9,007	47.2	72,900	26.1	10.6	693	30.6	74.8	17.2	10.5
48 39952	Kyle city	84.8	12.7	9,090	81.6	146,300	22.3	11.8	1,186	26.0	76.1	31.6	2.1
48 40588	Lake Jackson city	79.8	12.3	9,781	68.1	146,300	19.8	10.5	842	27.0	89.7	22.3	3.9
48 41212	Lancaster city	91.7	6.3	13,277	67.0	99,500	26.4	12.9	905	33.6	86.8	34.1	4.3
48 41440	La Porte city	86.6	9.5	11,295	76.2	118,900	20.3	12.0	997	31.6	86.1	24.2	4.1
48 41464	Laredo city	82.5	3.6	64,115	60.7	111,000	27.4	14.9	730	36.0	77.9	21.2	9.0
48 41980	League City city	85.8	10.4	31,114	74.4	172,000	21.8	11.8	1,108	25.5	85.8	29.6	2.3
48 42016	Leander city	78.6	15.9	8,811	76.0	148,500	23.0	12.3	1,301	28.8	81.4	30.6	2.3
48 42508	Lewisville city	72.8	16.9	38,392	44.3	154,400	22.0	11.8	910	27.2	81.0	24.8	3.4
48 43012	Little Elm city	. . .	. . .	8,288	81.2	148,400	26.9	10.0	1,501	27.2	82.7	33.0	0.8
48 43888	Longview city	79.3	9.3	29,841	56.6	125,500	22.1	12.0	765	30.0	83.4	19.0	7.3
48 45000	Lubbock city	72.7	11.9	88,762	53.7	112,100	21.3	12.5	787	34.5	82.2	15.3	5.3
48 45072	Lufkin city	77.3	10.9	13,120	53.2	97,200	21.6	13.0	752	34.1	82.9	13.4	6.0
48 45384	McAllen city	85.1	7.4	42,241	60.3	108,800	22.7	12.8	708	30.0	75.4	19.8	6.2
48 45744	McKinney city	83.3	10.4	44,732	69.1	185,600	22.3	13.8	1,075	29.7	79.8	28.2	3.1
48 46452	Mansfield city	86.7	10.3	19,193	76.5	174,200	22.4	13.0	1,143	31.8	86.3	29.8	2.4
48 46776	Marshall city	79.7	8.5	8,202	57.8	87,200	23.2	12.7	638	31.1	76.6	17.8	9.8
48 47892	Mesquite city	83.8	10.6	48,321	59.5	108,500	23.8	12.0	934	30.9	82.6	28.5	4.6
48 48072	Midland city	82.4	8.4	40,862	64.7	152,600	21.2	11.0	939	26.8	83.9	18.3	4.8
48 48768	Mission city	90.5	6.7	22,664	72.6	97,500	22.8	12.3	702	33.1	79.8	24.6	6.0
48 48772	Mission Bend CDP	94.2	5.5	10,093	83.5	112,600	26.9	12.3	1,260	34.9	83.8	32.9	1.5
48 48804	Missouri City city	92.5	6.0	22,382	86.1	155,100	23.3	12.8	1,331	27.1	81.5	28.9	1.8
48 50256	Nacogdoches city	67.4	16.0	12,039	39.8	126,200	22.4	13.3	699	35.6	81.4	14.9	11.5
48 50820	New Braunfels city	79.4	12.7	21,531	63.7	164,800	22.1	12.2	950	32.0	78.2	24.0	5.2
48 52356	North Richland Hills city	86.6	9.4	24,745	63.1	142,300	21.8	13.2	877	30.8	84.9	26.3	4.6
48 53388	Odessa city	80.4	8.7	37,223	61.9	102,000	19.5	11.3	764	25.2	82.0	17.9	5.7
48 55080	Paris city	75.0	9.7	10,026	53.4	76,300	19.5	14.7	639	31.5	81.7	15.4	13.8
48 56000	Pasadena city	80.9	9.8	48,255	56.3	101,900	23.4	11.7	759	29.5	80.3	25.2	6.0
48 56348	Pearland city	89.7	8.8	32,096	79.7	179,700	23.3	10.6	1,131	25.9	85.9	29.4	2.1
48 57176	Pflugerville city	89.9	8.0	17,303	77.0	164,600	22.8	11.0	1,051	33.4	80.9	25.3	4.1
48 57200	Pharr city	85.3	10.4	19,993	59.4	73,600	26.4	13.7	632	35.7	82.2	20.4	7.0
48 57980	Plainview city	79.4	10.1	7,424	60.9	69,400	19.9	10.9	598	28.0	83.9	13.9	6.5
48 58016	Plano city	86.6	8.8	99,888	63.5	216,900	21.9	10.6	1,058	26.4	81.9	25.5	3.7
48 58820	Port Arthur city	83.1	7.6	19,967	59.0	70,200	23.2	11.8	659	31.7	78.2	19.8	12.7
48 61796	Richardson city	83.8	11.1	38,786	61.4	184,200	21.4	12.9	1,026	27.0	76.6	24.2	3.2
48 62828	Rockwall city	86.7	9.5	13,409	74.3	192,000	21.0	14.6	1,210	27.9	80.5	29.6	3.6
48 63284	Rosenberg city	82.4	10.9	9,928	46.7	108,600	25.6	12.8	853	33.1	81.4	25.1	7.4
48 63500	Round Rock city	75.7	18.9	34,847	56.4	167,700	22.1	10.0	1,021	27.0	79.9	24.1	3.0
48 63572	Rowlett city	92.1	6.6	18,552	84.2	162,000	23.5	12.9	1,373	27.3	83.6	31.2	1.0
48 64064	Sachse city	84.2	11.6	7,181	86.4	185,900	24.1	14.2	1,541	29.9	83.0	29.9	0.2
48 64112	Saginaw city	88.1	10.3	7,031	79.8	122,400	21.5	14.8	959	24.7	87.2	26.9	1.4
48 64472	San Angelo city	71.7	15.5	35,375	59.9	97,100	21.5	12.3	678	30.0	78.4	15.7	6.1
48 65000	San Antonio city	80.5	6.4	476,131	55.3	113,400	22.5	12.0	801	29.9	79.3	23.2	9.5
48 65036	San Benito city	91.5	3.6	7,052	65.3	58,800	28.2	12.1	532	35.1	75.7	18.0	14.3
48 65516	San Juan city	88.2	8.4	9,017	74.4	78,700	30.1	13.2	560	33.5	83.8	20.3	8.0
48 65600	San Marcos city	57.1	25.6	17,030	27.2	129,300	26.0	15.4	887	46.7	77.4	20.2	5.1
48 66128	Schertz city	86.4	11.4	12,151	77.1	162,000	20.6	11.0	959	23.4	87.0	24.8	1.6
48 66644	Seguin city	83.9	7.0	8,733	62.4	100,600	22.2	13.7	702	29.0	76.0	19.7	10.3
48 67496	Sherman city	73.3	13.5	14,571	52.0	99,100	21.2	13.5	803	29.3	80.8	19.4	7.2
48 68636	Socorro city	91.3	7.5	8,812	77.3	79,500	29.6	12.6	615	34.3	81.8	26.9	6.0
48 69032	Southlake city	94.6	4.1	8,661	92.4	504,300	24.0	12.2	. . .	. . .	80.0	29.6	1.8
48 69596	Spring CDP	86.0	10.4	17,728	76.3	109,100	23.4	11.4	1,182	26.8	86.1	30.5	2.1
48 70808	Sugar Land city	90.4	7.6	26,237	81.0	256,600	21.9	10.0	1,437	25.2	80.6	28.5	1.6
48 72176	Temple city	86.8	7.8	24,155	58.3	116,300	19.4	11.9	785	29.1	85.2	15.7	7.8
48 72368	Texarkana city	84.6	9.7	13,925	56.3	93,000	22.1	12.4	663	30.5	83.4	15.2	11.6
48 72392	Texas City city	76.3	11.7	16,019	57.5	99,800	23.0	11.2	855	35.2	80.1	22.2	7.7

1. A median value of $1,000,000 or more is represented as $1,000,000.
2. Median selected monthly owner costs of 10 percent or less as a percenage of household income is represented as 10.0
3. A median gross rent of $2,000 or more is represented as $2,000.
4. A median gross rent of 50 percent or more as a percentage of household income is represented as 50.0.

Table C-4. Cities — Where: Migration, Housing, and Transportation, 2010–2012—*Continued*

STATE and place code	STATE or city	Percent who lived in the same house one year ago	Percent who did not live in the same city one year ago	Total occupied housing units	Percent owner-occupied housing units	Median value of owner-occupied housing units (dollars)[1]	Median selected monthly owner costs as a percentage of household income[2] With a mortgage	Median selected monthly owner costs as a percentage of household income[2] Without a mortgage	Median gross rent (dollars)[2]	Median gross rent as a percentage of household income[4]	Percent of workers who drove alone to work	Mean travel time to work (minutes)	Percent of occupied housing units with no vehicle available
ACS table number:		C07204	C07204	B25003	B25003	B25077	B25092	B25092	B25064	B25071	C08301	B08013/ C08012	C25045
Column number:		1	2	3	4	5	6	7	8	9	10	11	12
	Texas—Cont.												
48 72530	The Colony city........................	84.2	12.7	13,572	64.9	138,800	21.7	10.0	1,101	27.6	85.2	28.8	1.0
48 72656	The Woodlands CDP..................	80.9	12.6	36,759	74.0	269,000	22.2	10.9	1,120	25.5	80.6	30.5	3.4
48 73057	Timberwood Park CDP...............	83.5	14.8	8,699	78.0	272,500	21.3	10.0	1,296	28.9	83.6	33.0	0.5
48 74144	Tyler city................................	74.3	14.0	38,832	53.4	128,100	22.9	12.2	800	32.5	81.6	18.2	8.3
48 74492	University Park city...................	74.4	20.9	7,144	75.5	922,600	26.9	12.2	1,900	31.6	73.8	16.2	1.6
48 75428	Victoria city............................	79.9	8.9	23,833	58.5	110,600	21.7	13.3	722	31.3	77.5	17.2	8.9
48 76000	Waco city................................	74.3	12.2	45,326	47.7	94,700	24.2	13.6	727	33.8	78.6	16.6	10.3
48 76672	Watauga city...........................	86.3	11.9	8,070	79.0	105,000	23.8	11.6	1,146	28.5	80.5	28.9	0.8
48 76816	Waxahachie city.......................	75.0	12.0	10,405	57.6	130,200	23.0	13.6	941	31.8	85.0	23.5	7.3
48 76864	Weatherford city......................	80.8	12.1	9,821	64.4	131,800	22.8	12.1	865	28.8	81.3	22.3	8.0
48 77272	Weslaco city............................	83.7	10.4	11,342	61.3	73,900	23.7	12.8	601	29.1	78.1	21.0	9.0
48 77728	West Odessa CDP......................	87.3	8.5	7,364	80.5	67,100	21.5	10.0	669	37.2	74.9	29.5	5.2
48 79000	Wichita Falls city.....................	79.6	12.4	36,659	57.9	90,900	21.9	13.3	696	28.8	80.1	14.0	6.5
48 80356	Wylie city...............................	87.3	10.2	13,645	87.0	156,300	23.3	17.5	990	28.8	85.4	32.0	0.9
49 00000	**Utah**...................................	82.6	12.5	886,032	69.7	209,000	24.3	10.0	841	29.9	76.6	21.6	4.7
49 01310	American Fork city....................	85.8	13.1	7,185	73.2	215,300	24.8	10.0	999	33.2	78.4	21.2	2.4
49 07690	Bountiful city..........................	84.8	11.7	13,871	73.3	234,900	23.2	10.0	852	25.9	81.3	19.8	3.7
49 11320	Cedar City city........................	81.8	10.8	9,933	50.5	165,700	28.0	10.0	642	30.1	77.3	17.8	6.1
49 13850	Clearfield city.........................	82.9	14.2	9,648	54.1	150,700	23.7	10.0	884	31.8	78.9	19.3	6.3
49 14290	Clinton city............................	89.0	10.4	6,087	83.8	178,100	21.9	10.0	1,212	27.2	83.1	24.3	2.5
49 16270	Cottonwood Heights city...........	85.9	11.6	12,078	72.3	298,000	22.7	10.0	958	24.5	81.3	21.4	1.4
49 20120	Draper city.............................	82.9	12.8	11,995	78.8	362,100	25.5	10.0	1,152	28.0	79.2	25.7	2.2
49 20810	Eagle Mountain city..................	84.1	10.8	5,319	88.5	185,400	25.2	10.0	1,263	29.7	73.3	34.0	1.7
49 24740	Farmington city........................	87.0	10.1	5,624	83.6	269,900	23.8	10.0	784	22.3	75.3	26.2	0.5
49 34970	Herriman city..........................	82.8	13.8	5,809	80.3	266,700	31.4	11.3	1,362	33.2	78.0	29.2	0.8
49 36070	Holladay city...........................	86.4	11.4	10,370	74.2	338,500	24.3	10.0	946	27.5	80.6	20.3	2.4
49 40360	Kaysville city...........................	89.5	8.1	7,938	83.7	259,300	23.2	10.0	663	28.7	76.7	22.8	3.6
49 40470	Kearns CDP.............................	88.0	10.3	9,274	82.3	152,100	27.0	10.0	1,244	27.1	78.6	26.5	3.6
49 43660	Layton city.............................	83.7	12.7	21,561	74.9	198,900	21.8	10.0	819	29.9	81.7	23.7	4.7
49 44320	Lehi city.................................	84.9	12.0	12,477	81.4	239,700	24.8	10.0	1,191	34.0	76.4	22.5	2.1
49 45860	Logan city...............................	65.8	19.2	15,855	42.5	170,300	27.4	10.0	628	30.8	70.8	14.4	5.3
49 47290	Magna CDP..............................	87.3	7.5	7,826	78.6	149,500	25.2	10.8	974	27.4	79.8	21.9	3.7
49 49710	Midvale city............................	78.9	16.9	10,958	46.5	193,500	27.5	10.8	911	29.3	75.9	21.7	8.8
49 50150	Millcreek CDP..........................	80.0	17.4	24,499	62.5	271,700	24.1	10.0	870	28.2	79.1	21.1	5.1
49 53230	Murray city.............................	82.5	15.2	18,413	64.6	227,200	23.6	10.2	880	32.2	79.5	20.6	6.9
49 55980	Ogden city..............................	77.3	12.7	28,687	55.7	132,300	24.4	10.0	726	30.0	73.1	19.4	8.8
49 57300	Orem city................................	79.7	13.8	26,071	62.5	196,900	23.9	10.0	845	32.5	77.5	17.8	3.6
49 60930	Pleasant Grove city..................	79.8	17.0	9,617	67.1	217,300	23.9	10.0	1,000	31.7	77.1	21.3	3.5
49 62470	Provo city...............................	59.1	22.9	31,937	41.5	198,300	24.5	10.0	713	33.1	60.8	17.0	4.3
49 64340	Riverton city...........................	89.5	8.2	10,995	88.0	262,900	24.9	10.0	986	23.6	81.7	25.7	1.8
49 65110	Roy city..................................	88.6	9.7	12,250	83.4	158,600	23.2	10.0	882	21.8	81.4	22.2	1.8
49 65330	St. George city.........................	82.2	10.0	25,259	64.6	204,100	28.1	10.0	857	32.9	80.7	15.0	4.1
49 67000	Salt Lake City city....................	77.2	12.9	74,037	48.3	231,300	24.3	10.4	765	31.0	67.9	19.4	13.3
49 67440	Sandy city...............................	86.6	9.8	28,158	78.6	269,000	23.3	10.0	1,045	29.5	80.6	23.3	3.3
49 67825	Saratoga Springs city................	78.2	16.8	4,723	80.3	238,100	28.4	10.0	1,470	26.7	84.8	31.3	0.3
49 70850	South Jordan city.....................	81.5	16.1	14,302	79.9	310,800	24.4	10.0	1,404	28.5	80.1	24.2	3.0
49 71070	South Salt Lake city..................	66.6	28.9	8,504	40.5	173,000	27.4	10.0	734	34.5	71.1	21.8	14.7
49 71290	Spanish Fork city.....................	84.4	11.4	9,179	77.3	188,800	25.8	10.0	963	27.6	80.3	21.9	1.4
49 72280	Springville city........................	83.2	12.3	8,751	72.0	189,800	25.8	10.0	898	27.0	76.9	21.1	3.2
49 74810	Syracuse city...........................	91.5	7.7	6,605	91.3	242,600	23.4	10.0	1,394	28.4	84.4	28.0	0.5
49 75360	Taylorsville city.......................	83.0	13.6	19,633	69.3	183,900	23.2	10.0	870	33.3	78.6	20.3	5.1
49 76680	Tooele city..............................	85.7	7.1	10,218	72.8	159,700	23.2	10.2	918	29.8	67.0	28.8	5.0
49 81960	Washington city.......................	81.4	14.3	6,770	69.7	221,800	29.5	10.6	1,132	36.8	. . .	16.5	3.8
49 82950	West Jordan city......................	87.1	10.3	30,840	76.7	215,200	24.7	10.0	985	31.7	79.6	24.5	2.5
49 83470	West Valley City city.................	79.8	13.6	37,418	68.1	168,800	26.6	10.0	884	36.4	75.0	22.7	4.7
50 00000	**Vermont**..............................	86.2	11.6	257,887	70.9	215,700	25.4	16.6	859	31.2	74.4	22.2	6.7
50 10675	Burlington city.........................	65.6	20.2	16,744	40.5	256,500	26.2	15.1	949	36.6	54.4	16.8	15.8
51 00000	**Virginia**..............................	85.0	11.2	3,007,690	67.1	243,100	23.9	11.1	1,075	30.2	77.4	27.8	6.3
51 01000	Alexandria city........................	79.2	15.0	64,754	42.3	491,500	22.7	11.8	1,449	28.3	59.7	30.2	9.2
51 01912	Annandale CDP........................	87.2	9.4	13,746	57.6	407,600	25.2	11.4	1,454	32.9	75.6	31.8	6.4
51 03000	Arlington CDP..........................	77.6	14.4	93,236	44.3	584,500	22.2	10.2	1,701	26.3	53.8	27.4	11.9
51 03320	Ashburn CDP...........................	87.3	9.0	15,475	72.6	398,600	22.8	10.0	1,673	30.1	82.9	31.8	3.9
51 04088	Bailey's Crossroads CDP............	85.5	12.2	8,922	38.9	308,100	25.1	14.9	1,393	32.6	61.2	29.7	12.2
51 07784	Blacksburg town.......................	54.9	25.8	13,327	29.5	265,100	19.3	10.0	841	50.0	61.2	14.8	7.0
51 11464	Burke CDP...............................	90.4	8.5	13,207	85.4	472,800	19.8	10.0	2,000	27.9	72.6	33.7	1.1
51 13720	Cave Spring CDP......................	86.9	9.1	11,742	67.3	215,000	22.3	10.0	836	26.6	88.2	18.8	4.9
51 14440	Centreville CDP........................	81.9	13.2	24,536	70.3	371,100	24.1	10.0	1,585	28.8	78.8	35.1	2.6
51 14744	Chantilly CDP..........................	93.2	6.2	6,795	81.1	424,700	23.1	10.0	1,568	42.1	80.1	31.7	3.8

1. A median value of $1,000,000 or more is represented as $1,000,000.
2. Median selected monthly owner costs of 10 percent or less as a percentage of household income is represented as 10.0
3. A median gross rent of $2,000 or more is represented as $2,000.
4. A median gross rent of 50 percent or more as a percentage of household income is represented as 50.0.

Table C-4. Cities — Where: Migration, Housing, and Transportation, 2010–2012—*Continued*

STATE and place code		STATE or city	Percent who lived in the same house one year ago	Percent who did not live in the same city one year ago	Total occupied housing units	Percent owner-occupied housing units	Median value of owner-occupied housing units (dollars)[1]	Median selected monthly owner costs as a percentage of household income[2] With a mortgage	Median selected monthly owner costs as a percentage of household income[2] Without a mortgage	Median gross rent (dollars)[2]	Median gross rent as a percentage of household income[4]	Percent of workers who drove alone to work	Mean travel time to work (minutes)	Percent of occupied housing units with no vehicle available
		ACS table number:	C07204	C07204	B25003	B25003	B25077	B25092	B25092	B25064	B25071	C08301	B08013/ C08012	C25045
		Column number:	1	2	3	4	5	6	7	8	9	10	11	12
		Virginia—Cont.												
51	14968	Charlottesville city	72.4	18.5	17,142	41.3	283,900	22.0	14.0	988	32.5	60.5	17.3	10.8
51	16000	Chesapeake city	85.3	9.6	78,867	72.2	254,700	26.4	13.3	1,141	31.4	86.6	24.6	4.2
51	16096	Chester CDP	87.6	9.2	8,461	62.7	211,500	24.1	10.5	924	29.4	81.7	22.2	4.3
51	16608	Christiansburg town	79.1	14.1	8,838	60.2	173,700	21.6	11.3	804	29.8	86.7	17.4	4.6
51	21088	Dale City CDP	85.7	11.6	20,269	70.3	244,100	24.9	10.0	1,553	32.1	69.9	41.1	3.7
51	21344	Danville city	82.6	8.4	18,481	55.0	86,700	22.9	12.1	591	34.4	80.0	19.4	15.7
51	26496	Fairfax city	81.5	14.2	8,358	71.0	450,900	21.5	10.1	1,538	31.4	71.9	31.8	6.0
51	26875	Fair Oaks CDP	73.5	21.5	13,939	49.6	405,800	24.2	10.0	1,677	28.3	76.8	36.0	3.1
51	29628	Franklin Farm CDP	. . .	. . .	6,260	94.6	568,400	19.5	10.0	2,000	26.4	79.7	33.0	. . .
51	29744	Fredericksburg city	70.6	24.2	9,629	35.5	307,300	22.1	11.9	1,044	33.9	71.8	25.2	9.5
51	35000	Hampton city	86.1	6.9	51,699	61.6	196,700	25.5	13.2	976	35.6	82.3	21.7	8.3
51	35624	Harrisonburg city	69.1	22.3	15,268	34.6	209,600	22.2	11.2	832	34.2	74.7	15.9	9.3
51	36648	Herndon town	90.0	7.5	7,575	60.8	358,200	22.9	16.8	1,615	28.8	72.6	27.3	2.7
51	38424	Hopewell city	91.8	4.6	8,593	51.6	135,700	26.7	11.0	780	31.7	86.6	20.4	10.6
51	43432	Lake Ridge CDP	84.0	13.4	14,319	72.9	275,900	21.6	10.0	1,671	26.2	72.8	40.8	2.3
51	44984	Leesburg town	86.6	10.2	14,162	68.7	366,200	24.9	10.0	1,339	30.2	74.1	31.2	3.2
51	45784	Lincolnia CDP	85.4	11.3	7,795	51.5	419,200	22.2	10.0	1,642	31.5	60.1	31.5	5.4
51	45957	Linton Hall CDP	88.7	9.3	11,306	85.9	357,100	23.8	10.0	2,000	29.9	80.1	41.9	2.0
51	47672	Lynchburg city	74.8	14.9	28,363	52.8	145,300	23.9	12.5	709	33.3	77.7	16.8	14.8
51	48376	McLean CDP	91.9	6.6	16,746	86.9	908,000	19.9	10.0	2,000	27.7	70.3	28.3	3.4
51	48450	McNair CDP	73.9	18.3	8,103	29.3	370,500	22.2	10.0	1,636	22.8	73.6	27.9	4.0
51	48952	Manassas city	84.5	9.4	12,204	65.4	234,600	23.9	15.5	1,317	35.1	78.5	34.4	7.0
51	49792	Marumsco CDP	81.1	17.0	11,812	50.5	187,800	24.2	10.0	1,347	29.1	65.2	35.8	3.6
51	50856	Mechanicsville CDP	89.3	9.2	13,627	83.4	228,000	24.0	10.7	970	31.7	89.5	23.0	2.1
51	52658	Montclair CDP	89.8	9.3	6,584	88.5	338,100	23.5	11.8	1,955	27.6	71.7	41.1	1.1
51	56000	Newport News city	75.4	13.6	69,003	50.3	200,200	25.1	12.9	980	31.6	77.2	22.3	9.2
51	57000	Norfolk city	77.7	11.5	85,626	44.6	201,500	28.3	14.1	942	33.6	70.4	21.8	12.2
51	58472	Oakton CDP	86.5	12.3	13,392	61.8	536,500	21.2	10.0	1,767	26.0	59.7	34.4	4.2
51	61832	Petersburg city	85.6	7.2	12,031	44.3	113,800	24.5	13.1	812	33.5	76.4	21.4	16.9
51	64000	Portsmouth city	81.5	8.4	36,752	56.8	177,700	28.9	15.6	940	33.5	79.4	25.5	11.2
51	66672	Reston CDP	83.2	13.6	25,214	60.4	438,000	21.9	10.0	1,508	24.9	75.5	30.1	5.0
51	67000	Richmond city	76.6	11.2	83,747	43.9	193,700	27.0	15.7	870	33.6	71.9	21.4	17.0
51	68000	Roanoke city	82.0	7.8	41,819	55.6	135,700	25.6	13.9	671	28.5	80.5	18.8	12.8
51	70000	Salem city	79.8	12.4	9,820	68.2	172,400	24.8	12.4	786	37.8	82.8	16.9	6.7
51	72272	Short Pump CDP	80.2	15.7	9,346	64.1	359,500	19.8	10.0	1,274	19.6	. . .	20.7	2.1
51	74100	South Riding CDP	90.0	9.7	7,037	86.4	534,900	24.8	10.0	2,000	23.8	79.7	39.0	1.0
51	74592	Springfield CDP	91.7	7.5	10,104	64.8	368,900	26.0	10.0	1,766	32.8	60.8	29.8	11.0
51	75216	Staunton city	83.2	11.3	10,890	56.6	170,300	23.1	12.4	724	36.3	79.3	19.8	10.4
51	75376	Sterling CDP	88.1	10.3	8,699	72.8	287,500	25.1	10.6	1,551	29.1	79.9	28.1	4.5
51	76432	Suffolk city	85.7	7.1	30,657	72.5	243,400	25.9	12.1	979	33.6	86.9	28.6	4.7
51	79560	Tuckahoe CDP	82.1	14.1	18,052	63.7	271,100	22.7	10.3	976	28.2	77.8	21.0	6.2
51	79952	Tysons Corner CDP	75.0	23.5	9,814	43.7	464,000	24.6	13.4	1,734	22.6	73.1	27.9	5.1
51	82000	Virginia Beach city	82.0	8.9	164,066	64.3	266,200	26.5	12.5	1,224	31.9	81.7	22.7	3.6
51	83680	Waynesboro city	83.9	7.8	8,592	57.6	164,700	23.8	12.5	741	31.0	85.3	19.1	10.2
51	84368	West Falls Church CDP	89.9	9.0	9,919	67.7	406,900	24.7	11.9	1,452	31.1	68.7	31.1	7.8
51	84976	West Springfield CDP	90.4	8.3	8,352	80.0	415,300	21.8	10.0	1,883	26.5	73.4	31.4	2.7
51	86720	Winchester city	76.3	17.5	10,668	49.4	226,900	24.2	13.3	890	36.2	74.2	21.9	9.2
53	00000	**Washington**	82.5	12.5	2,624,689	62.8	256,500	25.9	12.3	953	30.4	72.9	25.6	6.9
53	03180	Auburn city	81.9	12.3	27,345	59.7	231,600	26.4	14.9	956	34.6	75.5	29.4	8.1
53	03736	Bainbridge Island city	87.3	7.3	9,338	75.7	544,600	26.7	13.7	1,121	26.8	42.3	44.7	5.0
53	05210	Bellevue city	78.5	14.5	51,064	54.6	517,000	24.8	12.7	1,352	23.9	65.8	22.3	6.7
53	05280	Bellingham city	74.3	14.2	33,873	46.4	271,600	26.1	11.4	880	33.5	71.0	17.6	11.3
53	07380	Bothell city	84.3	12.6	13,884	65.6	336,500	24.5	18.0	1,218	32.4	71.4	27.2	4.6
53	07695	Bremerton city	71.1	18.2	14,677	41.4	194,700	26.6	11.2	862	33.1	57.3	24.2	13.3
53	08850	Burien city	81.7	14.5	18,199	52.7	271,400	28.7	12.3	944	34.0	73.6	24.7	9.3
53	09480	Camas city	83.9	14.4	6,741	78.7	286,800	24.6	11.2	886	28.9	78.6	29.0	2.6
53	14940	Cottage Lake CDP	90.7	9.0	7,750	92.1	516,300	23.5	12.2	1,598	28.4	78.7	28.5	1.0
53	17635	Des Moines city	86.0	10.9	11,161	61.2	250,100	28.5	14.3	1,029	29.2	73.8	24.8	5.9
53	19630	Eastmont CDP	82.5	17.5	6,820	83.4	297,800	28.4	11.6	1,445	28.3	76.6	26.7	2.8
53	20750	Edmonds city	87.0	10.6	17,263	68.8	380,600	27.4	14.0	995	29.5	70.0	27.2	4.8
53	22640	Everett city	75.3	16.5	41,699	44.5	229,500	28.3	14.8	915	31.4	71.0	25.0	11.9
53	23160	Fairwood CDP (King County)	83.0	13.5	7,301	73.2	314,800	23.9	11.6	1,150	33.1	72.9	30.6	3.8
53	23515	Federal Way city	78.6	12.6	33,638	54.5	242,000	27.3	13.5	977	33.9	76.0	29.8	9.0
53	24188	Five Corners CDP	81.6	17.9	5,808	69.5	202,800	27.9	10.0	1,176	28.5	79.1	22.5	2.0
53	27785	Graham CDP	91.4	7.8	8,304	84.6	222,700	28.2	11.3	1,255	28.5	83.8	36.9	1.7
53	33380	Inglewood-Finn Hill CDP	82.0	15.9	8,841	74.8	377,300	27.6	13.9	1,245	29.4	72.2	27.3	2.6
53	33805	Issaquah city	77.9	18.4	13,688	58.8	432,100	26.0	13.4	1,426	27.3	71.1	28.5	6.0
53	35170	Kenmore city	88.0	11.6	7,670	78.0	382,600	26.2	15.5	1,249	28.3	71.5	30.6	4.0
53	35275	Kennewick city	80.2	12.6	26,974	63.7	166,700	20.4	10.5	751	29.8	77.8	21.8	6.1
53	35415	Kent city	80.3	13.1	41,854	52.0	251,400	27.0	12.9	970	34.0	73.2	29.1	7.8

1. A median value of $1,000,000 or more is represented as $1,000,000.
2. Median selected monthly owner costs of 10 percent or less as a percentage of household income is represented as 10.0
3. A median gross rent of $2,000 or more is represented as $2,000.
4. A median gross rent of 50 percent or more as a percentage of household income is represented as 50.0.

Table C-4. Cities — Where: Migration, Housing, and Transportation, 2010–2012—*Continued*

STATE and place code	STATE or city	Percent who lived in the same house one year ago	Percent who did not live in the same city one year ago	Total occupied housing units	Percent owner-occupied housing units	Median value of owner-occupied housing units (dollars)[1]	Median selected monthly owner costs as a percentage of household income[2] — With a mortgage	Median selected monthly owner costs as a percentage of household income[2] — Without a mortgage	Median gross rent (dollars)[2]	Median gross rent as a percentage of household income[4]	Percent of workers who drove alone to work	Mean travel time to work (minutes)	Percent of occupied housing units with no vehicle available
	ACS table number:	C07204	C07204	B25003	B25003	B25077	B25092	B25092	B25064	B25071	C08301	B08013/ C08012	C25045
	Column number:	1	2	3	4	5	6	7	8	9	10	11	12
	Washington—Cont.												
53 35940	Kirkland city	81.5	14.4	22,018	57.6	449,400	26.1	14.0	1,375	25.9	74.5	22.6	3.7
53 36745	Lacey city	78.1	18.3	16,724	56.2	219,800	26.8	12.7	1,065	29.8	80.0	23.5	5.3
53 37900	Lake Stevens city	84.1	11.5	9,942	71.6	238,800	28.3	16.8	1,259	28.3	81.0	31.3	2.7
53 38038	Lakewood city	77.3	17.1	24,085	45.1	223,800	26.9	12.6	826	34.5	78.8	23.8	9.4
53 40245	Longview city	78.6	9.4	15,149	54.9	172,700	26.1	12.8	680	38.6	78.1	19.9	14.2
53 40840	Lynnwood city	83.9	11.6	14,052	51.1	273,100	27.7	13.0	977	34.2	67.5	28.0	9.5
53 43150	Maple Valley city	84.6	10.3	8,125	80.8	283,900	26.3	10.0	1,359	29.6	81.7	38.3	3.1
53 43955	Marysville city	82.9	12.6	21,744	69.4	227,000	27.1	13.6	1,098	31.2	77.1	31.1	3.3
53 45005	Mercer Island city	89.9	8.2	9,427	74.9	860,400	26.4	11.6	1,536	25.6	68.5	23.0	3.7
53 47245	Moses Lake city	79.8	13.3	7,984	54.0	163,000	24.6	10.5	686	24.8	75.9	17.3	7.3
53 47490	Mountlake Terrace city	82.7	16.2	8,364	60.6	252,100	28.8	10.0	1,106	31.0	73.1	26.8	3.2
53 47560	Mount Vernon city	81.1	11.8	11,271	54.1	222,200	27.4	12.7	902	34.0	76.5	22.7	5.8
53 47735	Mukilteo city	84.6	11.0	7,934	68.0	441,700	25.5	10.0	1,277	27.9	75.1	25.8	2.7
53 50360	Oak Harbor city	73.4	18.9	8,881	45.6	222,700	30.6	14.0	1,056	29.6	83.7	18.6	6.5
53 51300	Olympia city	77.3	16.2	20,549	52.0	236,400	23.9	13.6	893	32.1	71.4	21.2	10.4
53 51795	Orchards CDP	87.0	12.6	6,865	64.6	181,800	25.6	11.2	997	37.5	80.0	24.0	4.2
53 53335	Parkland CDP	79.3	18.0	13,127	48.7	182,100	27.8	12.2	863	31.9	77.7	27.0	7.9
53 53545	Pasco city	82.8	9.3	17,711	63.8	153,400	22.9	10.0	705	27.5	74.5	20.4	7.2
53 56625	Pullman city	52.8	27.2	10,346	29.0	217,600	20.9	10.0	684	50.0	47.1	12.3	10.7
53 56695	Puyallup city	76.9	17.5	14,841	51.4	252,300	26.0	12.2	995	29.3	81.4	26.4	8.3
53 57535	Redmond city	76.5	17.9	23,650	51.8	442,300	22.2	11.2	1,356	22.3	72.2	20.1	5.9
53 57745	Renton city	79.7	13.2	36,182	54.3	278,800	28.3	14.1	1,086	29.8	70.8	28.2	7.8
53 58235	Richland city	83.3	12.8	19,964	66.9	202,400	18.3	10.0	893	26.6	79.4	19.9	4.7
53 61000	Salmon Creek CDP	77.2	17.1	7,569	69.6	229,800	25.8	10.7	893	30.0	75.3	25.4	6.0
53 61115	Sammamish city	91.0	7.0	15,581	88.1	564,200	23.2	10.7	1,664	23.0	72.1	28.7	1.0
53 62288	SeaTac city	80.6	14.6	10,022	53.8	220,300	30.5	15.8	881	30.3	73.4	26.5	7.5
53 63000	Seattle city	77.4	11.0	284,559	46.1	426,600	25.3	13.6	1,053	29.1	52.0	25.3	16.2
53 63960	Shoreline city	84.8	12.8	21,269	62.9	325,500	27.7	13.8	1,066	31.9	67.1	28.3	8.7
53 64365	Silverdale CDP	75.1	19.2	8,057	50.5	283,500	22.9	11.7	1,080	31.7	78.8	23.6	6.9
53 64380	Silver Firs CDP	. . .	. . .	6,677	91.8	344,700	27.4	12.1	1,737	26.0	77.7	33.6	0.8
53 65922	South Hill CDP	82.4	15.1	18,545	71.9	233,900	26.6	15.9	1,248	32.3	80.1	32.2	3.3
53 66255	Spanaway CDP	84.2	14.6	9,535	68.0	189,600	27.8	14.1	1,184	26.3	84.8	33.6	3.0
53 67000	Spokane city	80.7	8.8	88,184	56.8	158,100	24.4	12.4	717	33.3	75.6	19.5	10.7
53 67167	Spokane Valley city	81.7	11.8	36,143	61.5	173,000	25.7	10.6	760	32.2	80.5	19.2	6.8
53 70000	Tacoma city	79.4	11.4	77,704	51.1	211,500	27.3	13.9	909	32.0	77.2	25.4	9.1
53 73465	University Place city	85.3	12.3	12,665	55.3	281,200	24.2	12.5	936	30.4	83.1	26.1	4.2
53 74060	Vancouver city	79.9	11.2	65,449	50.7	196,200	26.3	12.0	880	31.5	77.4	21.9	8.0
53 75775	Walla Walla city	80.7	10.7	11,760	59.9	178,500	24.5	13.7	690	32.9	68.4	13.3	12.0
53 77105	Wenatchee city	84.7	7.9	11,596	56.3	203,400	25.9	10.0	746	28.1	75.1	15.3	9.9
53 80010	Yakima city	79.5	8.7	33,020	53.8	157,800	22.1	11.4	757	34.5	79.6	18.2	8.5
54 00000	**West Virginia**	88.1	9.8	741,661	72.9	98,300	19.7	10.0	606	29.6	82.3	25.5	8.6
54 14600	Charleston city	82.4	9.5	23,454	59.9	139,600	18.7	10.0	664	26.2	76.9	17.3	15.9
54 39460	Huntington city	78.4	11.6	21,353	50.6	85,900	21.2	11.3	578	35.8	79.3	16.7	18.7
54 55756	Morgantown city	60.8	27.2	10,200	38.3	166,900	16.1	10.0	662	40.5	65.3	16.4	13.7
54 62140	Parkersburg city	87.2	8.0	13,274	61.2	88,000	20.2	12.0	584	34.5	79.4	16.5	12.8
54 86452	Wheeling city	86.5	7.2	12,621	61.5	94,200	18.3	10.0	531	31.3	79.7	18.5	16.7
55 00000	**Wisconsin**	85.8	8.7	2,282,454	68.0	167,200	23.9	13.9	747	29.6	80.3	21.8	7.2
55 02375	Appleton city	85.7	10.4	28,620	70.0	138,100	22.9	14.0	653	26.9	82.9	17.5	5.9
55 06500	Beloit city	83.5	7.5	14,277	59.9	86,300	24.4	15.1	688	35.1	74.3	22.5	8.7
55 10025	Brookfield city	91.8	6.3	14,524	87.6	278,000	22.4	13.9	1,267	32.3	86.6	21.0	2.6
55 11950	Caledonia village	93.9	4.8	10,018	80.9	203,800	24.1	13.7	788	29.3	88.5	25.4	4.1
55 19775	De Pere city	77.6	15.2	9,197	59.4	168,100	23.9	14.3	749	25.0	84.0	17.0	6.4
55 22300	Eau Claire city	76.5	10.8	26,837	55.7	137,300	22.0	12.6	708	33.3	79.9	15.6	7.2
55 25950	Fitchburg city	76.8	19.2	10,109	53.3	267,200	23.4	11.8	863	30.6	75.8	20.8	7.9
55 26275	Fond du Lac city	81.9	7.5	17,982	56.9	127,500	22.6	14.4	665	26.8	78.9	17.5	9.5
55 27300	Franklin city	84.8	13.6	12,820	76.1	234,800	23.4	13.8	890	28.4	86.4	24.4	3.0
55 31000	Green Bay city	83.4	8.3	42,755	57.9	129,900	23.5	13.1	635	28.2	81.0	18.1	8.2
55 31175	Greenfield city	87.9	8.6	16,783	59.6	179,400	24.0	19.4	816	27.7	85.6	23.4	6.3
55 37825	Janesville city	82.4	6.8	25,325	66.3	129,600	23.8	12.6	734	35.1	81.9	21.9	6.5
55 39225	Kenosha city	81.7	7.7	37,653	58.3	149,100	25.3	14.3	785	32.4	83.6	23.0	8.1
55 40775	La Crosse city	71.9	14.2	20,740	50.4	127,400	22.9	14.6	692	34.1	75.7	15.4	9.4
55 48000	Madison city	71.9	13.8	101,354	49.3	212,100	24.4	11.7	885	33.2	63.6	19.3	13.1
55 48500	Manitowoc city	91.7	3.2	15,018	65.5	108,200	22.4	13.5	595	25.6	81.0	15.6	8.7
55 51000	Menomonee Falls village	91.3	6.9	14,444	75.6	227,700	22.3	14.3	890	30.3	87.6	20.5	5.0
55 51150	Mequon city	91.4	6.6	9,164	87.6	343,600	20.9	11.1	1,382	28.6	84.2	22.5	2.2
55 53000	Milwaukee city	77.6	5.9	228,852	43.2	128,200	27.0	17.1	757	35.9	70.5	21.7	18.7

1. A median value of $1,000,000 or more is represented as $1,000,000.
2. Median selected monthly owner costs of 10 percent or less as a percentage of household income is represented as 10.0.
3. A median gross rent of $2,000 or more is represented as $2,000.
4. A median gross rent of 50 percent or more as a percentage of household income is represented as 50.0.

Table C-4. Cities — Where: Migration, Housing, and Transportation, 2010–2012—*Continued*

STATE and place code		STATE or city	Percent who lived in the same house one year ago	Percent who did not live in the same city one year ago	Total occupied housing units	Percent owner-occupied housing units	Median value of owner-occupied housing units (dollars)[1]	Median selected monthly owner costs as a percentage of household income[2]		Median gross rent (dollars)[2]	Median gross rent as a percentage of household income[4]	Percent of workers who drove alone to work	Mean travel time to work (minutes)	Percent of occupied housing units with no vehicle available
								With a mortgage	Without a mortgage					
		ACS table number:	C07204	C07204	B25003	B25003	B25077	B25092	B25092	B25064	B25071	C08301	B08013/ C08012	C25045
		Column number:	1	2	3	4	5	6	7	8	9	10	11	12
		Wisconsin—Cont.												
55	54875	Mount Pleasant village	90.2	7.8	10,762	76.1	183,300	23.6	15.5	755	24.2	87.1	21.5	4.4
55	55275	Muskego city	91.2	6.0	8,988	86.4	275,900	24.5	13.5	972	32.1	91.0	25.6	3.3
55	55750	Neenah city	82.2	9.2	10,619	67.9	132,200	21.9	12.6	639	24.6	84.6	18.2	6.6
55	56375	New Berlin city	90.8	8.6	16,384	77.4	237,000	22.9	14.2	1,031	28.8	89.2	23.4	3.9
55	58800	Oak Creek city	86.5	11.3	13,900	61.0	215,500	23.0	13.9	941	26.0	87.9	24.0	3.6
55	60500	Oshkosh city	78.9	11.8	25,344	54.8	115,300	22.2	14.2	637	28.4	81.9	17.4	8.5
55	63300	Pleasant Prairie village	92.0	6.9	7,031	80.1	216,200	23.1	15.1	1,137	26.8	. . .	26.0	4.0
55	66000	Racine city	86.8	4.4	30,358	53.9	119,600	24.3	15.9	715	32.9	79.1	20.5	14.2
55	72975	Sheboygan city	84.2	5.4	20,028	62.3	114,100	22.1	14.9	604	26.7	83.2	17.2	10.2
55	75125	South Milwaukee city	89.6	7.3	8,181	62.9	159,600	25.4	14.2	720	30.4	79.5	22.1	9.0
55	77200	Stevens Point city	69.0	17.0	10,611	49.8	111,500	22.7	12.8	666	33.8	72.7	16.3	8.2
55	78600	Sun Prairie city	86.2	8.8	11,628	61.7	201,600	23.8	12.7	961	26.7	83.8	21.1	4.7
55	78650	Superior city	82.2	9.3	11,960	55.5	110,300	22.3	11.2	653	33.2	81.2	14.7	11.7
55	83975	Watertown city	86.3	6.6	9,280	64.1	157,100	26.1	14.8	735	29.0	80.3	20.3	9.8
55	84250	Waukesha city	81.5	10.8	28,645	58.5	197,700	24.5	14.7	826	28.3	80.7	22.1	8.5
55	84475	Wausau city	78.1	8.5	16,353	57.9	115,300	22.8	13.0	642	32.0	78.6	15.1	9.1
55	84675	Wauwatosa city	87.5	8.9	20,283	66.1	224,000	23.1	12.4	892	28.0	83.7	20.2	8.1
55	85300	West Allis city	85.4	10.6	27,253	56.2	149,800	26.4	17.8	747	30.7	82.6	21.3	12.4
55	85350	West Bend city	87.9	6.4	12,810	65.1	173,200	23.0	16.5	755	27.8	83.7	24.1	8.1
56	00000	**Wyoming**	80.8	12.2	222,558	70.0	183,200	21.5	10.0	741	26.1	76.2	18.3	3.5
56	13150	Casper city	79.7	9.7	23,191	67.1	174,000	21.5	10.0	804	27.6	82.3	17.3	3.8
56	13900	Cheyenne city	76.9	12.0	24,849	61.4	172,600	22.1	10.0	718	26.4	84.0	12.8	6.4
56	31855	Gillette city	74.8	11.2	11,358	68.7	191,600	20.1	10.0	888	26.1	81.4	17.4	4.0
56	45050	Laramie city	63.3	20.7	13,081	46.1	183,700	24.1	10.6	700	38.0	61.9	11.2	4.1
56	67235	Rock Springs city	75.0	12.9	9,081	65.5	171,600	20.1	10.0	855	24.4	75.0	18.8	3.6

1. A median value of $1,000,000 or more is represented as $1,000,000.
2. Median selected monthly owner costs of 10 percent or less as a percenage of household income is represented as 10.0
3. A median gross rent of $2,000 or more is represented as $2,000.
4. A median gross rent of 50 percent or more as a percentage of household income is represented as 50.0.

Appendixes

Appendixes

APPENDIX A:
GLOSSARY

Accuracy. One of four key dimensions of survey quality. Accuracy refers to the difference between the survey estimate and the true (unknown) value. Attributes are measured in terms of sources of error (for example, coverage, sampling, nonresponse, measurement, and processing).

American FactFinder (AFF). An electronic system for access to and dissemination of Census Bureau data on the Internet. AFF offers prepackaged data products and user-selected data tables and maps from Census 2000, the 1990 Census of Population and Housing, the 1997 and 2002 Economic Censuses, the Population Estimates Program, annual economic surveys, and the ACS.

Balance. A consolidated city results from the merger of a county with its principal incorporated place. The "balance" is that portion of a consolidated city minus the semi-independent places that remain.

Block group. A subdivision of a census tract (or, prior to 2000, a block numbering area), a block group is a cluster of blocks having the same first digit of their four-digit identifying number within a census tract.

Census geography. A collective term referring to the types of geographic areas used by the Census Bureau in its data collection and tabulation operations, including their structure, designations, and relationships to one another. See www.census.gov/geo/www/index.html .

Census tract. A small, relatively permanent statistical subdivision of a county delineated by a local committee of census data users for the purpose of presenting data. Census tract boundaries normally follow visible features, but may follow governmental unit boundaries and other nonvisible features; they always nest within counties. Designed to be relatively homogeneous units with respect to population characteristics, economic status, and living conditions at the time of establishment, census tracts average about 4,000 inhabitants.

Coefficient of variation (CV). The ratio of the standard error (square root of the variance) to the value being estimated, usually expressed in terms of a percentage (also known as the relative standard deviation). The lower the CV, the higher the relative reliability of the estimate.

Comparison profile. Comparison profiles are available from the American Community Survey for 1-year estimates beginning in 2007. These tables are available for the United States, the 50 states, the District of Columbia, and geographic areas with a population of more than 65,000.

Confidence interval. The sample estimate and its standard error permit the construction of a confidence interval that represents the degree of uncertainty about the estimate. A 90-percent confidence interval can be interpreted roughly as providing 90 percent certainty that the interval defined by the upper and lower bounds contains the true value of the characteristic.

Confidentiality. The guarantee made by law (Title 13, United States Code) to individuals who provide census information, regarding nondisclosure of that information to others.

Consolidated city. The U.S. Census Bureau refers to a governmental unit for which the functions of an incorporated place and its county or minor civil division have merged as a consolidated government. If one or more other incorporated places continue to function as separate governmental units even though they are part of a consolidated government, the Census Bureau refers to the primary incorporated place as a consolidated city.

Consumer Price Index (CPI). The CPI program of the Bureau of Labor Statistics produces monthly data on changes in the prices paid by urban consumers for a representative basket of goods and services.

Controlled. During the ACS weighting process, the intercensal population and housing estimates are used as survey controls. Weights are adjusted so that ACS estimates conform to these controls.

Current Population Survey (CPS). The CPS is a monthly survey of about 50,000 households conducted by the Census Bureau for the Bureau of Labor Statistics. The CPS is the primary source of information on the labor force characteristics of the U.S. population.

Current residence. The concept used in the ACS to determine who should be considered a resident of a sample address. Everyone who is currently living or staying at a sample address is considered a resident of that address, except people staying there for 2 months or less. People who have established residence at the sample unit and are away for only a short period of time are also considered to be current residents.

Custom tabulations. The Census Bureau offers a wide variety of general purpose data products from the ACS. These products are designed to meet the needs of the majority of data users and contain predefined sets of data for standard census geographic areas, including both political and statistical geography. These products are available on the American FactFinder and the ACS Web site. For users with data needs not met through the general purpose products, the Census Bureau offers "custom" tabulations on a cost-reimbursable basis, with the American Community Survey Custom Tabulation program. Custom tabulations are created by tabulating data from ACS microdata files. They vary in size, complexity, and cost depending on the needs of the sponsoring client.

Data profiles. Detailed tables that provide summaries by social, economic, and housing characteristics. There is a new ACS demographic and housing units profile that should be used if official estimates from the Population Estimates Program are not available.

Detailed tables. Approximately 1,200 different tables that contain basic distributions of characteristics. These tables provide the most detailed data and are the basis for other ACS products.

Disclosure avoidance (DA). Statistical methods used in the tabulation of data prior to releasing data products to ensure the confidentiality of responses. See Confidentiality.

Estimates. Numerical values obtained from a statistical sample and assigned to a population parameter. Data produced from the ACS interviews are collected from samples of housing units. These data are used to produce estimates of the actual figures that would have been obtained by interviewing the entire population using the same methodology.

File Transfer Protocol (FTP) site. A Web site that allows data files to be downloaded from the Census Bureau Web site.

Five-year estimates. Estimates based on 5 years of ACS data. These estimates reflect the characteristics of a geographic area over the entire 5-year period and will be published for all geographic areas down to the census block group level.

Geographic comparison tables. More than 80 single-variable tables comparing key indicators for geographies other than states.

Geographic summary level. A geographic summary level specifies the content and the hierarchical relationships of the geographic elements that are required to tabulate and summarize data. For example, the county summary level specifies the state-county hierarchy. Thus, both the state code and the county code are required to uniquely identify a county in the United States or Puerto Rico.

Group quarters (GQ) facilities. A GQ facility is a place where people live or stay that is normally owned or managed by an entity or organization providing housing and/or services for the residents. These services may include custodial or medical care, as well as other types of assistance. Residency is commonly restricted to those receiving these services. People living in GQ facilities are usually not related to each other. The ACS collects data from people living in both housing units and GQ facilities.

Group quarters (GQ) population. The number of persons residing in GQ facilities.

Institutionalized population. People under formally authorized, supervised care or custody in institutions at the time of enumeration. Generally restricted to the institution under the care of supervision of trained staff, and classified as "patients" or "inmates."

Item allocation rates. Allocation is a method of imputation used when values for missing or inconsistent items cannot be derived from the existing response record. In these cases, the imputation must be based on other techniques such as using answers from other people in the household, other responding housing units, or people believed to have similar characteristics. Such donors are reflected in a table referred to as an allocation matrix. The rate is the percentage of times this method is used.

Margin of error (MOE). Some ACS products provide an MOE instead of confidence intervals. An MOE is the difference between an estimate and its upper or lower confidence bounds. Confidence bounds can be created by adding the margin of error to the estimate (for the upper bound) and subtracting the margin of error from the estimate (for the lower bound). All published ACS margins of error are based on a 90-percent confidence level.

Multiyear estimates. Three- and five-year estimates based on multiple years of ACS data. Three-year estimates will be published for geographic areas with a population of 20,000 or more. Five-year estimates will be published for all geographic areas down to the census block group level.

Narrative profile. A data product that includes easy-to-read descriptions for a particular geography.

Non-institutionalized population. People who live in group quarters other than institutions; for example college dormitories, rooming houses, religious group homes, communes, and halfway houses.

Nonsampling error. Total survey error can be classified into two categories—sampling error and nonsampling error. Nonsampling error includes measurement errors due to interviewers, respondents, instruments, and mode; nonresponse error; coverage error; and processing error.

Period estimates. An estimate based on information collected over a period of time. For ACS the period is either 1 year, 3 years, or 5 years.

Point-in-time estimates. An estimate based on one point in time. The decennial census long-form estimates for Census 2000 were based on information collected as of April 1, 2000.

Population Estimates Program. Official Census Bureau estimates of the population of the United States, states, metropolitan areas, cities and towns, and counties; also official Census Bureau estimates of housing units.

Public Use Microdata Area (PUMA). An area that defines the extent of territory for which the Census Bureau releases Public Use Microdata Sample (PUMS) records.

Public Use Microdata Sample (PUMS) files. Computerized files that contain a sample of individual records, with identifying information removed, showing the population and housing characteristics of the units, and people included on those forms.

Puerto Rico Community Survey (PRCS). The counterpart to the ACS that is conducted in Puerto Rico.

Quality measures. Statistics that provide information about the quality of the ACS data. The ACS releases four different quality measures with the annual data release: (1) initial sample size and final interviews, (2) coverage rates, (3) response rates, and (4) item allocation rates for all collected variables. The ACS Quality Measures website http://www.census.gov/acs/www/methodology/sample_size_and_data_quality/ provides these statistics each year. In addition, the coverage rates are also available for males and females separately.

Reference period. Time interval to which survey responses refer. For example, many ACS questions refer to the day of the interview; others refer to "the past 12 months" or "last week."

Residence rules. The series of rules that define who (if anyone) is considered to be a resident of a sample address for purposes of the survey or census.

Sampling error. Errors that occur because only part of the population is directly contacted. With any sample, differences are likely to exist between the characteristics of the sampled population and the larger group from which the sample was chosen.

Sampling variability. Variation that occurs by chance because a sample is surveyed rather than the entire population.

Selected population profiles. An ACS data product that provides certain characteristics for a specific race or ethnic group (for example, Alaska Natives) or other population subgroup (for example, people aged 60 years and over). This data product is produced directly from the sample microdata (that is, not a derived product).

Single-year estimates. Estimates based on the set of ACS interviews conducted from January through December of a given calendar year. These estimates are published each year for geographic areas with a population of 65,000 or more.

Standard error. The standard error is a measure of the deviation of a sample estimate from the average of all possible samples.

Statistical significance. The determination of whether the difference between two estimates is not likely to be from random chance (sampling error) alone. This determination is based on both the estimates themselves and their standard errors. For ACS data, two estimates are "significantly different at the 90 percent level" if their difference is large enough to infer that there was a less than 10 percent chance that the difference came entirely from random variation.

Subject tables. Data products organized by subject area that present an overview of the information that analysts most often receive requests for from data users.

Summary files. Consist of detailed tables of all social, economic, and housing characteristics compiled from the ACS sample. An alternative to American Fact Finder for advanced users.

Thematic maps. Display geographic variation in map format from the geographic ranking tables.

Three-year estimates. Estimates based on 3 years of ACS data. These estimates are meant to reflect the characteristics of a geographic area over the entire 3-year period. These estimates will be published for geographic areas with a population of 20,000 or more.

APPENDIX B:
SOURCE NOTES AND EXPLANATIONS

With one exception, all data in this book are from the American Community Survey (ACS). The state and metropolitan area data are 1-year estimates from the 2012 ACS and the county and city data are 3-year estimates from the 2010–2012 ACS. The sole exception is the population change between 2010 and 2012 for counties and cities, which comes from the Census Bureau's Population Estimates Program and is included here as an indicator of the level of growth of each geographic area.

This section of source notes is generally excerpted from: www.census.gov/acs/www/Downloads/data_documentation/ SubjectDefinitions/2012_ACSSubjectDefinitions.pdf .

The data were assembled from the ACS detailed tables and the following notes reference the numbers of those detailed tables. Also included with each table number and title is the table's universe, which is the total number of units (e.g., individuals, households, businesses, in the population of interest). Many of the data items can also be found in ACS profiles, subject tables, geographic comparison tables, and other formats available on the ACS website.

Symbols

A "..." in a cell indicates that either there were no sample cases or the number of sample cases was too small.

In several categories, including median value of owner-occupied housing units and median gross rent as a percentage of household income, top codes are used. In this publication, these codes are only present in Tables C-2 and C-4.

Part A — WHO

Table A-1. Who — Age, Race/Ethnicity, and Household Structure

Table A-1 presents 61 items for the United States as a whole and for each individual state and the District of Columbia

POPULATION AND POPULATION CHANGE, Items 1 and 2
Source: Table B01003. Total Population
Universe: Total Population

In the 2012 1-year ACS, the total population for states is the official estimate from the Population Estimates Program. The 2010 1-year ACS used the total population from the 2010 census.

RACE, Items 3–8, 10–11
Sources: Table B02001. Race; Table B02008. White Alone or in Combination with One or More Other Races; Table B02009. Black or African American Alone or in Combination with One or More Other Races; Table B02010. American Indian and Alaska Native alone or in Combination with One or More Other Races; Table B02011. Asian Alone or in Combination with One or More Other Races; Table B02012. Native Hawaiian and Other Pacific Islander Alone or in Combination with One or More Other Races; Table B02013. Some Other Race Alone or in Combination with One or More Other Races; and Table B01001H. Sex by Age (White Alone, not Hispanic or Latino)
Universe: Total Population

The concept of race, as used by the Census Bureau, reflects self-identification by people according to the race or races with which they most closely identify. These categories are socio-political constructs and should not be interpreted as being scientific or anthropological in nature. Furthermore, the race categories include both racial and national-origin groups. The racial classifications used by the Census Bureau adhere to the October 30, 1997, *Federal Register Notice* entitled, "Revisions to the Standards for the Classification of Federal Data on Race and Ethnicity," issued by the Office of Management and Budget (OMB). These standards govern the categories used to collect and present federal data on race and ethnicity. The OMB requires five minimum categories (White, Black or African American, American Indian or Alaska Native, Asian, and Native Hawaiian or Other Pacific Islander) for race. The race categories are described below with a sixth category, "Some other race," added with OMB approval.

In addition to the five race groups, the OMB also states that respondents should be offered the option of selecting one or more races.

The **White** population includes persons having origins in any of the original peoples of Europe, the Middle East, or North Africa. It includes people who indicate their race as "White" or report entries such as Irish, German, Italian, Lebanese, Near Easterner, Arab, or Polish.

Black population includes persons having origins in any of the Black racial groups of Africa. It includes people who indicate their race as "Black, African American, or Negro," or provide written entries such as African American, Afro-American, Kenyan, Nigerian, or Haitian.

The **American Indian or Alaska Native** population includes persons having origins in any of the original peoples of North and South America (including Central America) and who maintain tribal affiliation or community attachment. It includes people who classified themselves as Canadian Indian, French-American Indian, Spanish-American Indian, Eskimo, Aleut, Alaska Indian, or any of the American Indian or Alaska Native tribes.

The **Asian** population includes persons having origins in any of the original peoples of the Far East, Southeast Asia, or the Indian subcontinent including, for example, Cambodia, China, India, Japan, Korea, Malaysia, Pakistan, the Philippine Islands, Thailand, and Vietnam. It includes Asian Indian, Chinese, Filipino, Korean, Japanese, Vietnamese, and Other Asian.

The **Native Hawaiian or Other Pacific Islander** population includes persons having origins in any of the original peoples of Hawaii, Guam, Samoa, or other Pacific Islands. It includes people who indicate their race as Native Hawaiian, Guamanian or Chamorro, Samoan, and Other Pacific Islander.

Some Other Race includes all other responses not included in the "White," "Black or African American," "American Indian or Alaska Native," "Asian," and "Native Hawaiian or Other Pacific Islander" race categories described above. Respondents providing write-in entries such as multiracial, mixed, interracial, or a Hispanic/Latino group (for example, Mexican, Puerto Rican, or Cuban) in the "Some other race" write-in space are included in this category.

Two or More Races. People may have chosen to provide two or more races either by checking two or more race response check boxes, by providing multiple write-in responses, or by some combination of check boxes and write-in responses.

HISPANIC ORIGIN, Item 9
Source: Table C03002. Hispanic or Latino by Race
Universe: Total Population

The data on the **Hispanic or Latino** population was asked of all people. The terms "Spanish," "Hispanic," and "Latino" are used interchangeably. Some respondents identify with all three terms, while others may identify with only one of these three specific terms. Hispanics or Latinos who identify with the terms "Spanish," "Hispanic," or "Latino" are those who classify themselves in one of the specific Hispanic or Latino categories listed on the questionnaire—"Mexican," "Puerto Rican," or "Cuban"—as well as those who indicate that they are "other Spanish/Hispanic/Latino." People who do not identify with one of the specific origins listed on the questionnaire but indicate that they are "other Spanish/Hispanic/Latino" are those whose origins are from Spain, the Spanish-speaking countries of Central or South America, the Dominican Republic, or people identifying themselves generally as Spanish, Spanish-American, Hispanic, Hispano, Latino, and so on.

AGE, Items 12–21, 23–31
Sources: Table B01001. Sex by Age; Table B01002. Median Age by Sex; Table B01002H. Median Age by Sex (White Alone, not Hispanic or Latino); Table B01002B. Median Age by Sex (Black or African American Alone); Table B01002C. Median Age by Sex (American Indian and Alaska Native); Table B01002D. Median Age by Sex (Asian Alone); Table B01002E. Median Age by Sex (Native Hawaiian and Other Pacific Islander Alone); Table B01002F. Median Age by Sex (Some Other Race Alone); Table B01002G. Median Age by Sex (Two or More Races); and Table B01002I. Median Age by Sex (Hispanic or Latino)
Universe: Total Population

The age classification is based on the age of the person in complete years at the time of interview. Both age and date of birth are used in combination to calculate the most accurate age at the time of the interview. Inconsistently reported and missing values are assigned or imputed based on the values of other variables for that person, from other people in the household, or from people in other households ("hot deck" imputation). Data on age are used to determine the applicability of other questions for a particular individual and to classify other characteristics in tabulations. Age data are needed to interpret most social and economic characteristics used to plan and analyze programs and policies. Therefore, age data are tabulated by many different age groupings, such as 5-year age groups.

The median age is the age that divides the population into two equal-size groups. Half of the population is older than the median age and half is younger. Median age is based on a standard distribution of the population by single years of age and is shown to the nearest tenth of a year.

PERCENT FEMALE, Item 22
Source: Table B01001. Sex by Age
Universe: Total Population

The female population is shown as a percentage of the total population.

MARITAL STATUS, Items 32–36
Source: Table B12001. Sex by Marital Status for the Population 15 Years and Over
Universe: Population 15 Years and Over

The **marital status** classification refers to the status at the time of interview. Data on marital status are tabulated only for people 15 years old and over. All people were asked whether they were "now married," "widowed," "divorced," "separated," or "never married." Couples who live together (unmarried people, people in common-law marriages) were allowed to report the marital status they considered the most appropriate. When marital status was not reported, it was imputed according to the relationship to the householder and sex and age of the person. Differences in the number of currently married males and females occur because there is no step in the weighting process to equalize the weighted estimates of husbands and wives.

Never married includes all people who have never been married, including people whose only marriage(s) was annulled.

Now married includes all people whose current marriage has not ended by widowhood or divorce. This category includes people defined as "separated" and "spouse absent." The category may also include couples who live together or people in common-law marriages if they consider this category the most appropriate. "Now married" does not include same-sex married people even if the marriage was performed in a state issuing marriage certificates for same-sex couples.

Widowed includes widows and widowers who have not remarried.

Divorced includes people who are legally divorced and who have not remarried.

Differences between the number of currently married males and the number of currently married females occur because of reporting differences, because some husbands and wives have their usual residence in different areas,

and because husbands and wives do not have the same weights. By definition, the numbers would be the same.

FOREIGN BORN, Item 37
Source: Table C05002. Place of Birth by Citizenship Status
Universe: Total Population

The **foreign-born** population includes anyone who was not a U.S. citizen or a U.S. national at birth. This includes respondents who indicated they were a U.S. citizen by naturalization or not a U.S. citizen.

LANGUAGES SPOKEN, Items 38–41
Source: Table B16002. Household Language by Linguistic Isolation
Universe: Households

Language Spoken at Home. Questions on language spoken at home were asked only of persons 5 years of age and older. Instructions mailed with the American Community Survey questionnaire instructed respondents to mark "Yes" if they sometimes or always spoke a language other than English at home, and "No" if a language was spoken only at school—or if speaking was limited to a few expressions or slang. Respondents printed the name of the non-English language they spoke at home. If the person spoke more than one non-English language, they reported the language spoken most often. If the language spoken most frequently could not be determined, the respondent reported the language learned first.

The questions referred to languages spoken at home in an effort to measure the current use of languages other than English. This category excluded respondents who spoke a language other than English exclusively outside of the home.

Most respondents who reported speaking a language other than English also spoke English. The questions did not permit a determination of the primary language of persons who spoke both English and another language.

Household Language. In households where one or more people spoke a language other than English, the household language assigned to all household members was the non-English language spoken by the first person with a non-English language. This assignment scheme ranked household members in the following order: householder, spouse, parent, sibling, child, grandchild, other relative, stepchild, unmarried partner, housemate or roommate, and other nonrelatives. Therefore, a person who spoke only English may have had a non-English household language assigned during tabulations by household language.

Ability to Speak English. Respondents who reported speaking a language other than English were asked to indicate their English ability based on one of the following categories: "Very well," "Well," "Not well," or "Not at all." Ideally, the data on ability to speak English represented a person's perception of their own ability. However, because one household member usually completes American Community Survey questionnaires, the responses may have represented the perception of another household member.

Linguistic Isolation. A linguistically isolated household was one in which all adults had some limitation in communicating English. A household was classified as "linguistically isolated" if, (1) No household member age 14 years and over spoke only English, and (2) No household member age 14 years and over who spoke another language spoke English "Very well." All members of a linguistically isolated household were tabulated as linguistically isolated, including members under 14 years old who may have spoken only English.

HOUSEHOLDS AND HOUSEHOLD TYPE, Item 42–61
Sources: Table B11001. Household Type (Including Living Alone); Table B11006. Households by Presence of People 60 Years and Over by Household Type; Table B11009. Unmarried-Partner Households by Sex of Partner; B11010. Nonfamily Households by Sex of Householder by Living Alone by Age of Householder; Table C11005. Households by Presence of People Under 18 Years by Household Type; and Table B25010. Average Household Size of Occupied-Housing Units by Tenure
Universe: Households

A **household** includes all the people who occupy a housing unit. (People not living in households are classified as living in group quarters.) A housing unit is a house, an apartment, a mobile home, a group of rooms, or a single room that is occupied (or if vacant, is intended for occupancy) as separate living quarters. Separate living quarters are those in which the occupants live separately from any other people in the building and which have direct access from the outside of the building or through a common hall. The occupants may be a single family, one person living alone, two or more families living together, or any other group of related or unrelated people who share living arrangements.

A **family household** consists of a householder and one or more other people living in the same household who are related to the householder by birth, marriage, or adoption. All people in a household who are related to the householder are regarded as members of his or her family. A family household may contain people not related to the householder, but those people are not included as part of the householder's family in tabulations. Thus, the number

of family households is equal to the number of families, but family households may include more members than do families. A household can contain only one family for purposes of tabulations.

A **married-couple family** is one in which the householder and his or her spouse are listed as members of the same household.

The category **male family households** includes only male-headed family households with no spouse present. Similarly, the category **female family households** includes only female-headed family households with no spouse present.

A **nonfamily household** consists of a group of unrelated people or of one person living alone.

An **unmarried-partner household** is a household other than a "married-couple household" that includes a householder and an "unmarried partner." An "unmarried partner" can be of the same sex or of the opposite sex as the householder. An "unmarried partner" in an "unmarried-partner household" is an adult who is unrelated to the householder, but shares living quarters and has a close personal relationship with the householder. An unmarried-partner household also may be a family household or a nonfamily household, depending on the presence or absence of another person in the household who is related to the householder. There may be only one unmarried partner per household, and an unmarried partner may not be included in a married-couple household, as the householder cannot have both a spouse and an unmarried partner. Same-sex married couples are included in the count of unmarried-partner households for tabulations purposes and for public use data files.

Tables A-2, A-3, and A-4. Who—Age, Race/Ethnicity, and Household Structure

Table A-2 presents 24 items for the United States as a whole, each individual state and the District of Columbia, and 1,846 counties, county equivalents, and independent cities with a 2012 population of 20,000 or more.

Table A-3 presents 24 items for 366 Metropolitan Statistical Areas and 29 Metropolitan Divisions within the 12 largest Metropolitan Statistical Areas.

Table A-4 presents 24 items for 2,143 cities, Census Designated Places, and the principal portions of consolidated cities with a 2012 population of 20,000 or more.

POPULATION, Item 1
Source: Table B01003. Total Population
Universe: Total Population

In the 2012, 3-year ACS, the total population is based on the official estimate from the Population Estimates Program adjusted to reflect the 3-year time period 2010 through 2012. In Table A-3, the 1-year ACS total population is based on the official estimate of the Population Estimates Program.

POPULATION CHANGE, Item 2
Source: U.S. Census Bureau—Population Estimates for Tables A-2 and A-4; ACS Comparison Table CP05. ACS Demographic and Housing Estimates for Table A-3

In Tables A-2 and A-4, The population change data for 2010 through 2012 are from the official estimates of the Population Estimates Program which estimates the population as of July 1 each year. These are used because the ACS does not release 1-year data for many of the counties and cities. In Table A-3, the population change is derived from the ACS population totals which are based on the Population Estimates Program.

AGE, Items 3–9
Sources: Table B01001. Sex by Age and Table B01002. Median Age by Sex
Universe: Total Population

The age classification is based on the age of the person in complete years at the time of interview. Both age and date of birth are used in combination to calculate the most accurate age at the time of the interview. Inconsistently reported and missing values are assigned or imputed based on the values of other variables for that person, from other people in the household, or from people in other households ("hot deck" imputation). Data on age are used to determine the applicability of other questions for a particular individual and to classify other characteristics in tabulations. Age data are needed to interpret most social and economic characteristics used to plan and analyze programs and policies. Therefore, age data are tabulated by many different age groupings, such as 5-year age groups.

The median age is the age that divides the population into two equal-size groups. Half of the population is older than the median age and half is younger. Median age is based on a standard distribution of the population by single years of age and is shown to the nearest tenth of a year.

RACE, Items 10–13
Sources: Table B02008. White Alone or in Combination with One or More Other Races; Table B02009. Black or African American Alone or in Combination with One or More Other Races; Table B02010. American Indian and Alaska Native alone or in Combination with One or More Other Races; Table B02011. Asian Alone or in Combination with One or More Other Races; Table B02012. Native

Hawaiian and Other Pacific Islander Alone or in Combination with One or More Other Races; and Table B02013. Some Other Race Alone or in Combination with One or More Other Races
Universe: Total Population

The concept of race, as used by the Census Bureau, reflects self-identification by people according to the race or races with which they most closely identify. These categories are socio-political constructs and should not be interpreted as being scientific or anthropological in nature. Furthermore, the race categories include both racial and national-origin groups. The racial classifications used by the Census Bureau adhere to the October 30, 1997, *Federal Register Notice* entitled, "Revisions to the Standards for the Classification of Federal Data on Race and Ethnicity," issued by the Office of Management and Budget (OMB). These standards govern the categories used to collect and present federal data on race and ethnicity. The OMB requires five minimum categories (White, Black or African American, American Indian or Alaska Native, Asian, and Native Hawaiian or Other Pacific Islander) for race. The race categories are described below with a sixth category, "Some other race," added with OMB approval. In addition to the five race groups, the OMB also states that respondents should be offered the option of selecting one or more races.

The **White** population includes persons having origins in any of the original peoples of Europe, the Middle East, or North Africa. It includes people who indicate their race as "White" or report entries such as Irish, German, Italian, Lebanese, Near Easterner, Arab, or Polish.

Black population includes persons having origins in any of the Black racial groups of Africa. It includes people who indicate their race as "Black, African American, or Negro," or provide written entries such as African American, Afro-American, Kenyan, Nigerian, or Haitian.

The **American Indian or Alaska Native** population includes persons having origins in any of the original peoples of North and South America (including Central America) and who maintain tribal affiliation or community attachment. It includes people who classified themselves as Canadian Indian, French-American Indian, Spanish-American Indian, Eskimo, Aleut, Alaska Indian, or any of the American Indian or Alaska Native tribes.

The **Asian and Pacific Islander** population combines two census groupings: Asian and Native Hawaiian or Other Pacific Islander. The **Asian** population includes persons having origins in any of the original peoples of the Far East, Southeast Asia, or the Indian subcontinent including, for example, Cambodia, China, India, Japan, Korea,

Malaysia, Pakistan, the Philippine Islands, Thailand, and Vietnam. It includes Asian Indian, Chinese, Filipino, Korean, Japanese, Vietnamese, and Other Asian. The **Native Hawaiian or Other Pacific Islander** population includes persons having origins in any of the original peoples of Hawaii, Guam, Samoa, or other Pacific Islands. It includes people who indicate their race as Native Hawaiian, Guamanian or Chamorro, Samoan, and Other Pacific Islander. While the groups are combined in Tables A-2, A-3, and A-4, the **Asian** alone or in combination population is shown in Table A-1, States.

Some Other Race. Includes all other responses not included in the "White," "Black or African American," "American Indian or Alaska Native," "Asian," and "Native Hawaiian or Other Pacific Islander" race categories described above. Respondents reporting entries such as multiracial, mixed, interracial, or a Hispanic, Latino, or Spanish group (for example, Mexican, Puerto Rican, Cuban, or Spanish) in response to the race question are included in this category. In Tables A-2 through A-4, this group is combined with the **American Indian or Alaska Native** group. The **Some Other Race** alone or in combination is shown separately in Table A-1, States.

HISPANIC ORIGIN, Item 14
Source: Table B03003. Hispanic or Latino Origin
Universe: Total Population

The data on the **Hispanic or Latino** population was asked of all people. The terms "Spanish," "Hispanic," and "Latino" are used interchangeably. Some respondents identify with all three terms, while others may identify with only one of these three specific terms. Hispanics or Latinos who identify with the terms "Spanish," "Hispanic," or "Latino" are those who classify themselves in one of the specific Hispanic or Latino categories listed on the questionnaire – "Mexican," "Puerto Rican," or "Cuban"—as well as those who indicate that they are "other Spanish/Hispanic/Latino." People who do not identify with one of the specific origins listed on the questionnaire but indicate that they are "other Spanish/Hispanic/Latino" are those whose origins are from Spain, the Spanish-speaking countries of Central or South America, the Dominican Republic, or people identifying themselves generally as Spanish, Spanish-American, Hispanic, Hispano, Latino, and so on.

FOREIGN-BORN, Item 15
Source: Table C05003. Sex by Age by Nativity
Universe: Total Population

The **foreign-born** population includes anyone who was not a U.S. citizen or a U.S. national at birth. This includes respondents who indicated they were a U.S. citizen by naturalization or not a U.S. citizen.

HOUSEHOLDS AND HOUSEHOLD TYPE, Items 16–24
Sources: Table B11001. Household Type (Including Living Alone); Table B11006. Households by Presence of People 60 Years and Over by Household Type; and Table B11005. Households by Presence of People Under 18 Years by Household Type
Universe: Households

A **household** includes all the people who occupy a housing unit. (People not living in households are classified as living in group quarters.) A housing unit is a house, an apartment, a mobile home, a group of rooms, or a single room that is occupied (or if vacant, is intended for occupancy) as separate living quarters. Separate living quarters are those in which the occupants live separately from any other people in the building and which have direct access from the outside of the building or through a common hall. The occupants may be a single family, one person living alone, two or more families living together, or any other group of related or unrelated people who share living arrangements.

A **family household** consists of a householder and one or more other people living in the same household who are related to the householder by birth, marriage, or adoption. All people in a household who are related to the householder are regarded as members of his or her family. A family household may contain people not related to the householder, but those people are not included as part of the householder's family in tabulations. Thus, the number of family households is equal to the number of families, but family households may include more members than do families. A household can contain only one family for purposes of tabulations.

A **married-couple family** is one in which the householder and his or her spouse are listed as members of the same household.

The category **male family households** includes only male-headed family households with no spouse present. Similarly, the category **female family households** includes only female-headed family households with no spouse present.

A **nonfamily household** consists of a group of unrelated people or of one person living alone.

Part B — WHAT

Table B-1. What — Education, Employment, and Income

Table B-1 presents 158 items for the United States as a whole and for each individual state and the District of Columbia.

EDUCATIONAL ATTAINMENT, Items 1–6
Source: Table C15002. Sex by Educational Attainment for the Population 25 Years and Over
Universe: Population 25 Years and Over

Data on **educational attainment** were derived from a question that asked respondents for the highest level of school completed or the highest degree received. Persons currently enrolled in school are instructed to report the level of the previous grade attended or the highest degree received. Persons who had passed a high school equivalency examination were considered high school graduates. Schooling received in foreign schools was to be reported as the equivalent grade or years in the regular American school system.

Specifically excluded are vocational and technical training, such as barber school training; business, trade, technical, and vocational schools; or other training for a specific trade.

No high school diploma includes all persons who have not received a high school diploma.

High school graduate includes persons whose highest degree was a high school diploma or its equivalent, including those who passed a high school equivalency examination.

Some college or associates degree includes people who attended college but did not receive a degree or received an associates degree.

Bachelors degree includes persons who have received bachelors degrees.

Graduate or professional degree includes persons who have received masters degrees, professional school degrees (such as law school or medical school degrees), or doctoral degrees.

SCHOOL ENROLLMENT, Items 7–17
Source: Table C14002. School Enrollment by Level of School by Type of School by for the Population 3 Years and Over
Universe: Population 3 Years and Over

People were classified as **enrolled in school** if they were attending a "regular" public or private school or college at any time during the 3 months prior to the time of interview. The question included instructions to "include only nursery or preschool, kindergarten, elementary school, and schooling that leads to a high school diploma, or a college degree" as regular school or college. Respondents who did not answer the enrollment question were assigned the enrollment status and type of school of a person with the same age, sex, race, and Hispanic or Latino origin whose residence was in the same or nearby area.

A regular school advances a person toward an elementary school certificate, a high school diploma, or a college, university, or professional school (such as law or medicine) degree. Tutoring or correspondence schools are included if credit can be obtained in a "regular school." People enrolled in "vocational, technical, or business school" were not reported as enrolled in regular school. Field interviewers were instructed to classify individuals who were home schooled as enrolled in private school. The guide sent out with the mail questionnaire does not include explicit instructions for how to classify home schoolers.

Enrolled in public and private school includes people who attended school in the reference period and indicated they were enrolled by marking one of the questionnaire categories for "public school, public college," or "private school, private college." The instruction guide defines a public school as "any school or college controlled and supported primarily by a local, county, state, or federal government." Private schools are defined as schools supported and controlled primarily by religious organizations or other private groups. Respondents who marked both the "public" and "private" boxes are edited to the first entry, "public."

Grade in which enrolled. Since 1999, in the American Community Survey, people reported to be enrolled in "public school, public college" or "private school, private college" were classified by grade or level according to responses to the question "What grade or level was this person attending?" Seven levels were identified: **nursery school, preschool**; **kindergarten**; **elementary grade 1 to grade 4** or **grade 5 to grade 8**; **high school grade 9 to grade 12**; **college undergraduate** years (freshman to senior); and **graduate or professional school** (for example: medical, dental, or law school).

EMPLOYMENT STATUS, Items 18–40
Sources: Table C20005. Sex by Work Experience in the Past 12 Months by Earnings in the Past 12 Months (in 2012 Inflation-Adjusted Dollars) for the Population 16 Years and Over; and Table C23001. Sex by Age by Employment status for the Population 16 Years and Over
Universe: Population 16 Years and Over
Table B23006. Educational Attainment by Employment Status for the Population 25 to 64 Years
Universe: Population 25 to 64 Years
Table C14005. Sex by School Enrollment by Educational Attainment by Employment Status for the Population 16 to 19 Years
Universe: Population 16 to 19 Years
Table C08202. Household Size by Number of Workers in Household
Universe: Households

Total employment includes all civilians 16 years old and over who were either (1) "at work"—those who did any work at all during the reference week as paid employees, worked in either their own business or profession, worked on their own farm, or worked 15 hours or more as unpaid workers in a family farm or business; or were (2) "with a job, but not at work"—those who had a job but were not at work that week due to illness, weather, industrial dispute, vacation, or other personal reasons.

The **labor force** consists of all persons 16 years old and over who are either employed or unemployed, including those in the armed forces.

The **unemployment rate** represents the number of unemployed people as a percentage of the labor force.

Unemployment includes all persons who did not work during the survey week, made specific efforts to find a job during the previous four weeks, and were available for work during the survey week (except for temporary illness). Persons waiting to be called back to a job from which they had been laid off and those waiting to report to a new job within the next 30 days are included in unemployment figures.

Full-time, year-round includes all persons 16 years old and over who usually worked 35 hours or more per week for 50 to 52 weeks in the past 12 months.

Households with no worker. The term "worker" as used here refers to work status in the past 12 months.

Not enrolled, not high school graduate. This category includes people of compulsory school attendance age or above (ages 16 to 19) who were not enrolled in school and were not high school graduates. These people may be referred to as "high school dropouts." There is no restriction on when they "dropped out" of school; therefore, they may have dropped out before high school and never attended high school.

CHILDREN IN FAMILIES BY LIVING ARRANGEMENTS AND EMPLOYMENT STATUS OF PARENTS, Items 41–60

Sources: Table C23008. Age of Own Children Under 18 Years in Families and Subfamilies by Living Arrangements by Employment Status of Parents
Universe: Own Children Under 18 Years in Families and Subfamilies
Table C23007. Presence of Own Children Under 18 Years by Family Type by Employment Status
Universe: Families
Table B23003. Presence of Own Children Under 18 Years by Age of Own children Under 18 Years by Employment Status for Females 20 to 64 Years
Universe: Females 20 to 64 Years in Households

An **own child** is a never-married child under 18 years who is a son or daughter by birth, a stepchild, or an adopted child of the householder. Own children are further classified as living with two parents or with one parent only. Own children of the householder living with two parents are by definition found only in married-couple families. In the employment status tabulations in this book, own child refers to a never married child under the age of 18 in a family or a subfamily who is a son or daughter, by birth, marriage, or adoption, of a member of the householder's family, but not necessarily of the householder.

CLASS OF WORKER, Items 61–64

Source: Table C24080. Sex by Class of Worker for the Civilian Employed Population 16 Years and Over
Universe: Civilian Employed Population 16 Years and Over

For employed people, the data on **class of worker** refer to the person's job during the previous week. For those who worked two or more jobs, the data refer to the job where the person worked the greatest number of hours. For unemployed people, the data refer to their last job. The information on **class of worker** refers to the same job as a respondent's industry and occupation and categorizes people according to the type of ownership of the employing organization. The class of worker categories are defined as follows:

Private wage and salary workers includes people who worked for wages, salary, commission, tips, pay-in-kind, or piece rates for a private for-profit employer or a private not-for-profit, tax-exempt or charitable organization. Self-employed people whose business was incorporated are included with private wage and salary workers because they are paid employees of their own companies.

Government workers includes people who were employees of any local, state, or federal governmental unit, regardless of the activity of the particular agency. Employees of foreign governments, the United Nations, or other formal international organizations controlled by governments were classified as "federal government workers." The class of worker government categories includes all government workers, though government workers may work in different industries. For example, people who work in a public elementary or secondary school are coded as local government class of workers.

Self-employed includes people who worked for profit or fees in their own unincorporated business, profession, or trade, or who operated a farm.

Unpaid family workers includes people who worked 15 hours or more a week without pay in a business or on a farm operated by a relative.

OCCUPATION, Items 65–71
Source: Table B24060. Occupation by Class of Worker for the Civilian Employed Population 16 Years and Over
Universe: Civilian Employed Population 16 Years and Over

For employed people, the data on **occupation** refer to the person's job during the previous week. For those who worked two or more jobs, the data refer to the job where the person worked the greatest number of hours. For unemployed people, the data refer to their last job.

Written responses to the occupation questions are coded using the occupational classification system developed for the 2000 census and modified in 2010. This system consists of 509 specific occupational categories, including military, for employed people, arranged into 23 major occupational groups. This classification was developed based on the *Standard Occupational Classification (SOC) Manual: 2010*, published by the Executive Office of the President, Office of Management and Budget.

INDUSTRY, Items 72–84
Source: Table C24070. Industry by Class of Worker for Civilian Employed Population 16 Years and Over
Universe: Civilian Employed Population 16 Years and Over

For employed people, the data on **industry** refer to the person's job during the previous week. For those who worked two or more jobs, the data refer to the job where the person worked the greatest number of hours. For unemployed people, the data refer to their last job.

Written responses to the industry questions are coded using the industry classification system developed for Census 2000 and modified in 2002 and again in 2007. This system consists of 269 categories for employed people, including military, classified into 20 sectors. The modified 2007 census industry classification was developed from the 2007 North American Industry Classification System (NAICS) published by the Executive Office of the President, Office of Management and Budget. The NAICS was developed to increase comparability in industry definitions between the United States, Mexico, and Canada. It provides industry classifications that group establishments into industries based on the activities in which they are primarily engaged. The NAICS was created for establishment designations and provides detail about the smallest operating establishment, while the American Community Survey data are collected from households and differ in detail and nature from those obtained from establishment surveys. Because of disclosure issues, ACS data cannot be released in great detail, and the industry classification system, while defined in NAICS terms, cannot reflect the full detail for all categories.

The industry category, "Public administration," is limited to regular government functions such as legislative, judicial, administrative, and regulatory activities. Other government organizations such as public schools, public hospitals, liquor stores, and bus lines are classified by industry according to the activity in which they are engaged.

VETERAN STATUS, Item 85
Source: Table B21001. Sex by Age by Veteran Status for the Civilian Population 18 Years and Over
Universe: Civilian Population 18 Years and Over

A "civilian veteran" is a person 18 years old or over who has served (even for a short time), but is not now serving, on active duty in the U.S. Army, Navy, Air Force, Marine Corps, or the Coast Guard, or who served in the U.S. Merchant Marines during World War II. People who served in the National Guard or military Reserves are classified as veterans only if they were ever called or ordered to active duty, not counting the 4–6 months for initial training or yearly summer camps. All other civilians 18 years old and over are classified as nonveterans.

HOUSEHOLD INCOME, Items 86–99, 113–138
Sources: Table B19049. Median Household Income in the Past 12 Months (in 2012 Inflation -Adjusted Dollars) By Age of Householder; Table B19013A through B19013I Median Household Income in the Past 12 Months (in 2012 Inflation-Adjusted Dollars) for 9 Race and Hispanic Origin Groups; Table B19052. Wage or Salary Income in the Past 12 Months for Households; Table B19053. Self-Employed Income in the Past 12 Months for Households; Table B19054. Interest, Dividends, or Net Rental Income in the Past 12 Months for Households; Table B19055. Social Security Income in the Past 12 Months for Households; Table B19056. Supplemental Security Income (SSI) in the Past 12 Months for Households; Table B19057. Public Assistance Income in the Past 12 Months for Households; Table B19058. Public Assistance Income or Food Stamps in the Past 12 Months for Households; Table B19059. Retirement Income in the Past 12 Months for Households; Table B19060. Other Types of Income in the Past 12 Months for Households; Table C19001. Household Income in the Past 12 Months (in 2012 Inflation-Adjusted Dollars); and Table C19037. Age of Householder by Household Income in the Past 12 Months (in 2012 Inflation-Adjusted Dollars)
Universe: Households

Income of households includes the income of the householder and all other individuals 15 years old and over in the household, whether they are related to the householder or not. Because many households consist of only one person, average household income is usually less than average family income. Although the household income statistics cover the past 12 months, the characteristics of individuals and the composition of households refer to the time of interview. Thus, the income of the household does not include amounts received by individuals who were members of the household during all or part of the past 12 months if these individuals no longer resided in the household at the time of interview. Similarly, income amounts reported by individuals who did not reside in the household during the past 12 months but who were members of the household at the time of interview are included. However, the composition of most households was the same during the past 12 months as at the time of interview.

Income components were reported for the 12 months preceding the interview month. Monthly Consumer Price Indices (CPI) factors were used to inflation-adjust these components to a reference calendar year (January through December). For example, a household interviewed in March 2012 reports their income for March 2011 through February 2012. Their income is adjusted to the 2012 reference calendar year by multiplying their reported income by 2012 average annual CPI (January–December 2012) and then dividing by the average CPI for March 2011–February 2012.

In order to inflate income amounts from previous years, the dollar values on individual records are inflated to the latest year's dollar values by multiplying by a factor equal to the average annual CPI-U-RS factor for the current year, divided by the average annual CPI-U-RS factor for the earlier/earliest year.

Median income divides the income distribution into two equal parts, with half of all cases below the median income level and half of all cases above the median income level. For households and families, the median income is based on the distribution of the total number of households and families, including those with no income. Median income for households is computed on the basis of a standard distribution with a minimum value of less than $2,500 and a maximum value of $250,000 or more and is rounded to the nearest whole dollar.

The eight types of income reported in the American Community Survey are defined as follows:

1. **Wage or salary income:** Wage or salary income includes total money earnings received for work performed as an employee during the past 12 months. It includes wages, salary, armed forces pay, commissions, tips, piece-rate payments, and cash bonuses earned before deductions were made for taxes, bonds, pensions, union dues, etc.

2. **Self-employment income:** Self-employment income includes both farm and non-farm self-employment income.

Farm self-employment income includes net money income (gross receipts minus operating expenses) from the operation of a farm by a person on his or her own account, as an owner, renter, or sharecropper. Gross receipts include the value of all products sold, government farm programs, money received from the rental of farm equipment to others, and incidental receipts from the sale of wood, sand, gravel, etc. Operating expenses include cost of feed, fertilizer, seed, and other farming supplies, cash wages paid to farmhands, depreciation charges, cash rent, interest on farm mortgages, farm building repairs, farm taxes (not state and federal personal income taxes), etc. The value of fuel, food, or other farm products used for family living is not included as part of net income.

Non-farm self-employment income includes net money income (gross receipts minus expenses) from one's own business, professional enterprise, or partnership. Gross receipts include the value of all goods sold and services rendered. Expenses include costs of goods purchased, rent, heat, light, power, depreciation charges, wages and salaries paid, business taxes (not personal income taxes), etc.

3. **Interest, dividends, or net rental income:** Interest, dividends, or net rental income includes interest on savings or bonds, dividends from stockholdings or membership in associations, net income from rental of property to others and receipts from boarders or lodgers, net royalties, and periodic payments from an estate or trust fund.

4. **Social Security income:** Social Security income includes Social Security pensions and survivor benefits, permanent disability insurance payments made by the Social Security Administration prior to deductions for medical insurance, and railroad retirement insurance checks from the U.S. government. Medicare reimbursements are not included.

5. **Supplemental Security Income (SSI):** Supplemental Security Income (SSI) is a nationwide U.S. assistance program administered by the Social Security Administration that guarantees a minimum level of income for needy aged, blind, or disabled individuals.

6. **Public assistance income:** Public assistance income includes general assistance and Temporary Assistance to Needy Families (TANF). Separate payments received for hospital or other medical care, (vendor payments) are excluded. This does not include Supplemental Security Income (SSI) or noncash benefits such as Food Stamps. The terms "public assistance income" and "cash public assistance" are used interchangeably in the 2012 ACS data products.

7. **Retirement, survivor, or disability income:** Retirement income includes: (1) retirement pensions and survivor benefits from a former employer; labor union; or federal, state, or local government; and the U.S. military; (2) disability income from companies or unions; federal, state, or local government; and the U.S. military; (3) periodic receipts from annuities and insurance; and (4) regular income from IRA and Keogh plans. This does not include Social Security income.

8. **All other income:** All other income includes unemployment compensation, Veterans' Administration (VA) payments, alimony and child support, contributions received periodically from people not living in the household, military family allotments, and other kinds of periodic income other than earnings.

Receipts from the following sources are not included as income: capital gains, money received from the sale of property (unless the recipient was engaged in the business of selling such property); the value of income "in kind" from food stamps, public housing subsidies, medical care, employer contributions for individuals, etc.; withdrawal of bank deposits; money borrowed; tax refunds; exchange of money between relatives living in the same household; gifts and lump-sum inheritances, insurance payments, and other types of lump-sum receipts.

Although receipt of **food stamps** is included in an income table, the data on Food Stamp benefits were obtained from a Housing Question in the 2012 American Community Survey. The Food Stamp Act of 1977 defines this federally-funded program as one intended to "permit low-income households to obtain a more nutritious diet" (from Title XIII of Public Law 95-113, The Food Stamp Act of 1977, declaration of policy). Food purchasing power is increased by providing eligible households with coupons or cards that can be used to purchase food. The Food and Nutrition Service (FNS) of the U.S. Department of Agriculture (USDA) administers the Food Stamp Program through state and local welfare offices. The Food Stamp Program is the major national income support program to which all low-income and low-resource households, regardless of household characteristics, are eligible. In 2008, the Federal Food Stamp program was renamed SNAP (Supplemental Nutrition Assistance Program). Respondents were asked if one or more of the current members received food stamps or a food stamp benefit card during the past 12 months. Respondents were also asked to include benefits from the Supplemental Nutrition Assistance Program (SNAP) in order to incorporate the program name change.

The questions on participation in the Food Stamp Program were designed to identify households in which one or more of the current members received food stamps during the past 12 months. Once a food stamp household was identified, a question was asked about the total value of all food stamps received for the household during that 12-month period.

FAMILY INCOME, Items 100–106
Source: Table B19126. Median Family Income in the Past 12 Months (in 2012 Inflation-Adjusted Dollars) by Family Type by Presence of Own Children Under 18 Years Universe: Families

In compiling statistics on **family income**, the incomes of all members 15 years old and over related to the householder are summed and treated as a single amount. Although the family income statistics cover the past 12 months, the characteristics of individuals and the composition of families refer to the time of interview. Thus, the income of the family does not include amounts received by individuals who were members of the family during all or part of the past 12 months if these individuals no longer resided with the family at the time of interview. Similarly, income amounts reported by individuals who did not reside with the family during the past 12 months but who were members of the family at the time of interview are included. However, the composition of most families was the same during the past 12 months as at the time of interview.

NONFAMILY HOUSEHOLD INCOME, Items 107–109
Source: Table B19215. Median Nonfamily Household Income in the Past 12 Months (in 2012 Inflation-Adjusted Dollars) by Sex of Householder by Living Alone by Age of Householder Universe: Nonfamily Households

Nonfamily household income includes the income of the householder and all other individuals 15 years old and over in the nonfamily household. Although the household income statistics cover the past 12 months, the characteristics of individuals and the composition of households refer to the time of interview. Thus, the income of the household does not include amounts received by individuals who were members of the household during all or part of the past 12 months if these individuals no longer resided in the household at the time of interview. Similarly, income amounts reported by individuals who did not reside in the household during the past 12 months but who were members of the household at the time of interview are included. However, the composition of most households was the same during the past 12 months as at the time of interview.

INCOME OF INDIVIDUALS, Items 110–111
Source: Table B19326. Median Income in the Past 12 Months (in 2012 Inflation-Adjusted Dollars) by Sex by

Work Experience in the Past 12 Months for the Population 15 Years and Over with Income
Universe: Population 15 Years and Over with Income in the Past 12 Months

Income of individuals. Income for individuals is obtained by summing the eight types of income for each person 15 years old and over. The characteristics of individuals are based on the time of interview even though the amounts are for the past 12 months.

PER CAPITA INCOME, Item 112
Source: Table B19301. Per Capita Income in the Past 12 Months (in 2012 Inflation-Adjusted Dollars)
Universe: Total Population

Per capita income is the mean income computed for every man, woman, and child in a particular group including those living in group quarters. It is derived by dividing the aggregate income of a particular group by the total population in that group. Per capita income is rounded to the nearest whole dollar.

POVERTY STATUS, Items 139–154
Sources: Table C17017. Poverty Status in the Past 12 Months by Household Type
Universe: Households
Table C17001. Poverty Status in the Past 12 Months by Sex by Age
Universe: Population for Whom Poverty Status is Determined

The **poverty status** data were derived from data collected on the number of persons in the household, from questionnaire item 3, which provides data on each person's relationship to the householder, and items 47 and 48, the same questions used to derive the income data. The Social Security Administration (SSA) developed the original poverty definition in 1964, which federal interagency committees subsequently revised in 1969 and 1980. The Office of Management and Budget's (OMB) *Directive 14* prescribes the SSA's definition as the official poverty measure for federal agencies to use in their statistical work. Poverty statistics presented in American Community Survey products adhere to the standards defined by OMB in *Directive 14*.

The poverty thresholds vary depending on three criteria: size of family, number of children, and, for one- and two-person families, age of householder. In determining the poverty status of families and unrelated individuals, the Census Bureau uses thresholds (income cutoffs) arranged in a two-dimensional matrix. The matrix consists of family size (from one person to nine or more persons), cross-classified by presence and number of family members under

18 years old (from no children present to eight or more children present). Unrelated individuals and two-person families are further differentiated by age of reference person (under 65 years old and 65 years old and over). To determine a person's poverty status, the person's total family income in the last 12 months is compared to the poverty threshold appropriate for that person's family size and composition. If the total income of that person's family is less than the threshold appropriate for that family, then the person is considered poor or "below the poverty level," together with every member of his or her family. If a person is not living with anyone related by birth, marriage, or adoption, then the person's own income is compared with his or her poverty threshold. The average poverty threshold for a four-person family was $23,492 in 2012.

Since ACS is a continuous survey, people respond throughout the year. Because the income questions specify a period covering the last 12 months, the appropriate poverty thresholds are determined by multiplying the base-year poverty thresholds (1982) by the average of the monthly inflation factors for the 12 months preceding the data collection.

HEALTH INSURANCE, Items 155–159
Source: Table C27010. Types of Health Insurance Coverage by Age
Universe: Civilian Non-institutionalized Population

In 2012, respondents were instructed to report their current health insurance coverage and to mark "yes" or "no" for each of the eight types listed:
a. Insurance through a current or former employer or union (of this person or another family member)
b. Insurance purchased directly from an insurance company (by this person or another family member)
c. Medicare, for people 65 and older, or people with certain disabilities
d. Medicaid, Medical Assistance, or any kind of government-assistance plan for those with low incomes or a disability
e. TRICARE or other military health care
f. VA (including those who have ever used or enrolled for VA health care)
g. Indian Health Service
h. Any other type of health insurance or health coverage plan (Respondents who answered "yes" were asked to provide their other type of coverage type in a write-in field.)

Health insurance coverage in the ACS and other Census Bureau surveys define coverage to include plans and programs that provide comprehensive health coverage. Plans that provide insurance for specific conditions or situations such as cancer and long-term care policies are not considered coverage. Likewise, other types of insurance like dental, vision, life, and disability insurance are not considered health insurance coverage.

In defining types of coverage, write-in responses were reclassified into one of the first seven types of coverage or determined not to be a coverage type. Write-in responses that referenced the coverage of a family member were edited to assign coverage based on responses from other family members. As a result, only the first seven types of health coverage are included in the four categories in this table.

An eligibility edit was applied to give Medicaid, Medicare, and TRICARE coverage to individuals based on program eligibility rules. TRICARE or other military health care was given to active-duty military personnel and their spouses and children. Medicaid or other means-tested public coverage was given to foster children, certain individuals receiving Supplementary Security Income or Public Assistance, and the spouses and children of certain Medicaid beneficiaries. Medicare coverage was given to people 65 and older who received Social Security or Medicaid benefits.

People were considered insured if they reported at least one "yes". People who had no reported health coverage, or those whose only health coverage was Indian Health Service, were considered uninsured. For reporting purposes, the Census Bureau broadly classifies health insurance coverage as private health insurance or public coverage. Private health insurance is a plan provided through an employer or union, a plan purchased by an individual from a private company, or TRICARE or other military health care. Respondents reporting a "yes" to the types listed in parts a, b, or e were considered to have private health insurance. Public health coverage includes the federal programs Medicare, Medicaid, and VA Health Care (provided through the Department of Veterans Affairs); the Children's Health Insurance Program (CHIP); and individual state health plans. Respondents reporting a "yes" to the types listed in c, d, or f were considered to have public coverage. The types of health insurance are not mutually exclusive; people may be covered by more than one at the same time.

Tables B-2, B-3, and B-4. What — Education, Employment, and Income

Table B-2 presents 12 items for the United States as a whole, each individual state and the District of Columbia, and 1,846 counties, county equivalents, and independent cities with a 2012 population of 20,000 or more.

Table B-3 presents 12 items for 366 Metropolitan Statistical Areas and 29 Metropolitan Divisions within the 12 largest Metropolitan Statistical Areas.

Table B-4 presents 12 items for 2,143 cities, Census Designated Places, and the principal portions of consolidated cities with a 2012 population of 20,000 or more.

EDUCATIONAL ATTAINMENT, Items 1–3
Source: Table C15002. Sex by Educational Attainment for the Population 25 Years and Over
Universe: Population 25 Years and Over

Data on **educational attainment** were derived from a question that asked respondents for the highest level of school completed or the highest degree received. Persons currently enrolled in school are instructed to report the level of the previous grade attended or the highest degree received. Persons who had passed a high school equivalency examination were considered high school graduates. Schooling received in foreign schools was to be reported as the equivalent grade or years in the regular American school system.

Specifically excluded are vocational and technical training, such as barber school training; business, trade, technical, and vocational schools; or other training for a specific trade.

High school diploma or less. This category includes persons whose highest degree was a high school diploma or its equivalent, and those who reported any level lower than a high school diploma.

Bachelors degree or more. This category includes persons who have received bachelors degrees, masters degrees, professional school degrees (such as law school or medical school degrees), or doctoral degrees.

EMPLOYMENT STATUS, Items 4–8
Sources: Table C20005. Sex by Work Experience in the Past 12 Months by Earnings in the Past 12 Months (in 2012 Inflation-Adjusted Dollars) for the Population 16 Years and Over; and Table B23025. Employment Status for the Population 16 Years and Over
Universe: Population 16 Years and Over
Table C08202. Household Size by Number of Workers in Household
Universe: Households

Total employment includes all persons 16 years old and over who were either (1) "at work"—those who did any work at all during the reference week as paid employees, worked in either their own business or profession, worked on their own farm, or worked 15 hours or more as unpaid workers in a family farm or business; or were (2) "with a job, but not at work"—those who had a job but were not at work that week due to illness, weather, industrial dispute, vacation, or other personal reasons.

The **labor force** consists of all persons 16 years old and over who are either employed or unemployed, including those in the armed forces.

The **unemployment rate** represents the number of unemployed people as a percentage of the labor force.

Unemployment includes all persons who did not work during the survey week, made specific efforts to find a job during the previous four weeks, and were available for work during the survey week (except for temporary illness). Persons waiting to be called back to a job from which they had been laid off and those waiting to report to a new job within the next 30 days are included in unemployment figures.

Full-time, year-round includes all persons 16 years old and over who usually worked 35 hours or more per week for 50 to 52 weeks in the past 12 months.

Households with no worker. The term "worker" as used here refers to work status in the past 12 months.

INCOME, Items 9–12

Sources: Table B19013. Median Household Income in the Past 12 Months (in 2012 Inflation-Adjusted Dollars); Table C17013. Poverty Status in the Past 12 Months of Families by Number of Persons in Family. C19001. Household Income in the Past 12 Months (in 2012 Inflation-Adjusted Dollars)
Universe: Households

Household income includes the income of the householder and all other individuals 15 years old and over in the household, whether or not they are related to the householder. Since many households consist of only one person, average household income is usually less than average family income. Although the household income statistics cover the past 12 months, the characteristics of individuals and the composition of households refer to the time of enumeration. Thus, the income of the household does not include amounts received by individuals who were members of the household during all or part of the past 12 months if these individuals no longer resided in the household at the time of enumeration. Similarly, income amounts reported by individuals who did not reside in the household during the past 12 months but who were members of the household at the time of enumeration are included. However, the composition of most households was the same during the past 12 months as at the time of enumeration.

Median income divides the income distribution into two equal parts, with half of all cases below the median income level and half of all cases above the median income level.

For households and families, the median income is based on the distribution of the total number of households and families, including those with no income. Median income for households is computed on the basis of a standard distribution with a minimum value of less than $2,500 and a maximum value of $250,000 or more and is rounded to the nearest whole dollar.

For **family income**, the incomes of all household members 15 years old and over related to the householder are summed and treated as a single amount. Although the family income statistics cover the past 12 months, the characteristics of individuals and the composition of families refer to the time of enumeration. Thus, the income of the family does not include amounts received by individuals who were members of the family during all of part of the past 12 months if these individuals no longer resided with the family at the time of enumeration. Similarly, income amounts reported by individuals who did not reside with the family during the past 12 months but who were members of the family at the time of enumeration are included. However, the composition of most families was the same during the past 12 months as at the time of enumeration.

Income in the American Community Survey is for the past 12 months as opposed to a single reference year.

The **poverty status** data were derived from data collected on the number of persons in the household, from questionnaire item 3, which provides data on each person's relationship to the householder, and items 41 and 42, the same questions used to derive the income data. The Social Security Administration (SSA) developed the original poverty definition in 1964, which federal interagency committees subsequently revised in 1969 and 1980. The Office of Management and Budget's (OMB) *Directive 14* prescribes the SSA's definition as the official poverty measure for federal agencies to use in their statistical work. Poverty statistics presented in American Community Survey products adhere to the standards defined by OMB in *Directive 14*.

The poverty thresholds vary depending on three criteria: size of family, number of children, and, for one- and two-person families, age of householder. In determining the poverty status of families and unrelated individuals, the Census Bureau uses thresholds (income cutoffs) arranged in a two-dimensional matrix. The matrix consists of family size (from one person to nine or more persons), cross-classified by presence and number of family members under 18 years old (from no children present to eight or more children present). Unrelated individuals and two-person families are further differentiated by age of reference person (under 65 years old and 65 years old and over). To determine a person's poverty status, the person's total family income in the last 12 months is compared to the poverty threshold appropriate for that person's family size and composition. If the total income of that person's family is less than the threshold appropriate for that family, then the person is considered poor or "below the poverty level," together with every member of his or her family. If a person is not living with anyone related by birth, marriage, or adoption, then the person's own income is compared with his or her poverty threshold. The average poverty threshold for a four-person family was $23,492 in 2012.

Since ACS is a continuous survey, people respond throughout the year. Because the income questions specify a period covering the last 12 months, the appropriate poverty thresholds are determined by multiplying the base-year poverty thresholds (1982) by the average of the monthly inflation factors for the 12 months preceding the data collection.

Part C — WHERE

Table C-1. Where — Migration, Housing, and Transportation

Table C-1 presents 88 items for the United States as a whole and for each individual state and the District of Columbia.

PLACE OF RESIDENCE, Items 1–7

Source: Table C07204. Geographical Mobility in the Past Year for Current Residence—State, County, and Place Level in the United States
Universe: Population 1 Year and Over in the United States

Residence one year ago is used in conjunction with location of current residence to determine the extent of residential mobility of the population and the resulting redistribution of the population across the various states, metropolitan areas, and regions of the country.

Same house includes all people 1 year and over who did not move during the 1 year as well as those who had moved and returned to their residence 1 year ago.

Different house in the United States includes people who lived in the United States 1 year ago but in a different house or apartment from the one they occupied at the time of interview. These movers are then further subdivided according to the type of move. Movers within the U.S. are divided into groups according to their previous residence: **Different house, same city or town; Different house, different city, same county; Different house, different county, same state; and Different state.**

Abroad includes those whose previous residence was in a foreign country, Puerto Rico, American Samoa, Guam, the

Northern Marianas, or the U.S. Virgin Islands, including members of the armed forces and their dependents.

HOME-OWNERSHIP BY RACE, HISPANIC ORIGIN, AGE OF HOUSEHOLDER, AND HOUSEHOLD TYPE, Items 8–35

Sources: Table B25003. Tenure; Table B25003H. Tenure (White alone, Not Hispanic or Latino Householder); Table B25003B. Tenure (Black or African American Alone Householder); Table B25003C. Tenure (American Indian and Alaska Native Alone Householder); Table B25003D. Tenure (Asian Alone Householder); Table B25003E. Tenure (Native Hawaiian and Other Pacific Islander Alone Householder); Table B25003I. Tenure (Hispanic or Latino Householder); Table B25007. Tenure by Age of Householder; and Table C25115. Tenure by Household Type
Universe: Occupied Housing Units

A **housing unit** is a house, apartment, mobile home or trailer, group of rooms, or single room occupied or, if vacant, intended for occupancy as separate living quarters. Separate living quarters are those in which the occupants do not live and eat with any other person in the structure and which have direct access from the outside of the building or through a common hall. For vacant units, the criteria of separateness and direct access are applied to the intended occupants whenever possible. If that information cannot be obtained, the criteria are applied to the previous occupants.

The occupants of a housing unit may be a single family, one person living alone, two or more families living together, or any other group of related or unrelated persons who share living arrangements. Both occupied and vacant housing units are included in the housing inventory, although recreational vehicles, tents, caves, boats, railroad cars, and the like are included only if they are occupied as a person's usual place of residence.

Occupied housing units are classified as either owner occupied or renter occupied. A housing unit is classified as occupied if it is the usual place of residence of the person or group of persons living in it at the time of enumeration, or if the occupants are only temporarily absent from the residence for two months or less, that is, away on vacation or a business trip. If all the people staying in the unit at the time of the interview are staying there for two months or less, the unit is considered to be temporarily occupied and classified as "vacant."

A housing unit is **owner occupied** if the owner or co-owner lives in the unit even if it is mortgaged or not fully paid for. The owner or co-owner must live in the unit and usually is Person 1 on the questionnaire. The unit is "Owned by you or someone in this household with a mortgage or loan" if it is being purchased with a mortgage or some other debt arrangement such as a deed of trust, trust deed, contract to purchase, land contract, or purchase agreement. The unit also is considered owned with a mortgage if it is built on leased land and there is a mortgage on the unit. Mobile homes occupied by owners with installment loan balances also are included in this category.

All occupied housing units which are not owner occupied, whether they are rented for cash rent or occupied without payment of cash rent, are classified as **renter occupied**. "No cash rent" units are separately identified in the rent tabulations. Such units are generally provided free by friends or relatives or in exchange for services such as resident manager, caretaker, minister, or tenant farmer. Housing units on military bases also are classified in the "No cash rent" category. "Rented for cash rent" includes units in continuing care, sometimes called life care arrangements. These arrangements usually involve a contract between one or more individuals and a health services provider guaranteeing the individual shelter, usually a house or apartment, and services, such as meals or transportation to shopping or recreation.

HOUSEHOLD SIZE, Items 36–38
Source: Table B25010. Average Household Size of Occupied Housing Units by Tenure
Universe: Occupied Housing Units

Household size is based on the count of people in occupied housing units. All people occupying the housing unit are counted, including the householder, occupants related to the householder, and lodgers, roomers, boarders, and so forth.

Average household size of occupied units is obtained by dividing the number of people living in occupied housing units by the total number of occupied housing units. This measure is rounded to the nearest hundredth.

Average household size of owner-occupied units is obtained by dividing the number of people living in owner-occupied housing units by the total number of owner-occupied housing units. This measure is rounded to the nearest hundredth.

Average household size of renter-occupied units is obtained by dividing the number of people living in renter-occupied housing units by the total number of renter-occupied housing units. This measure is rounded to the nearest hundredth.

UNITS THAT ARE CROWDED OR LACKING COMPLETE PLUMBING, Item 39
Source: Table C25016. Tenure by Plumbing Facilities by Occupants per Room
Universe: Occupied Housing Units

Item 39 shows the percentage of housing units in the state that are **crowded** or **lacking complete plumbing facilities.**

Occupants per room is obtained by dividing the number of people in each occupied housing unit by the number of rooms in the unit. Although the Census Bureau has no official definition of **crowded** units, many users consider units with more than one occupant per room to be crowded, the measure used in this item.

The question on plumbing facilities was asked at both occupied and vacant housing units. Complete plumbing facilities include: (1) hot and cold piped water, (2) a flush toilet, and (3) a bathtub or shower. All three facilities must be located inside the house, apartment, or mobile home, but not necessarily in the same room. Housing units are classified as **lacking complete plumbing facilities** when any of the three facilities is not present.

MEDIAN HOUSEHOLD INCOME IN THE PAST 12 MONTHS, Items 40–44
Sources: Table B25119. Median Household Income the Past 12 Months (in 2012 Inflation-Adjusted Dollars) by Tenure
Universe: Occupied Housing Units
Table B25099. Mortgage Status by Median Household Income in the Past 12 Months (in 2012 Inflation-Adjusted Dollars)
Universe: Owner-Occupied Housing Units

The data on **mortgage status** were obtained from questions that were asked at owner-occupied units. The category **with a mortgage** refers to all forms of debt where the property is pledged as security for repayment of the debt, including deeds of trust; trust deeds; contracts to purchase; land contracts; junior mortgages; and home equity loans.

The category **without a mortgage** comprises housing units owned free and clear of debt.

HOUSING VALUES AND COSTS, Items 45–51, 54–64
Sources: Table B25097. Mortgage Status by Median Value (Dollars); Table B25081. Mortgage Status; Table B25092. Median Selected Monthly Owner Costs as a Percentage of Household Income in the Past 12 Months; Table B25088. Median Selected Monthly Owner Costs (Dollars) by Mortgage Status; Table B25103. Mortgage Status by Median Real Estate Taxes Paid (Dollars); and Table C25093. Age of Householder by Selected Monthly Owner costs as a Percentage of Household Income in the Past 12 Months
Universe: Owner-Occupied Housing Units
Table: B25105. Median Monthly Housing Costs (Dollars)
Universe: Occupied Housing Units with Monthly Housing Cost

Median value is the dollar amount that divides the distribution of specified owner-occupied housing units into two equal parts, with half of all units below the median value and half above the median value. Value is defined as the respondent's estimate of what the house would sell for if it were for sale. If the house or mobile home was owned or being bought, but the land on which it sits was not, the respondent was asked to estimate the combined value of the house or mobile home and the land. For vacant units, value was the price asked for the property. Value was tabulated separately for all owner-occupied and vacant-for-sale housing units, as well as owner-occupied and vacant-for-sale mobile homes.

Since value is the only dollar amount captured on the questionnaire in specified intervals (checkboxes), the category boundaries for previous years are not adjusted for inflation. However, the median value is adjusted for inflation by multiplying a factor equal to the average annual CPI-U-RS factor for the current year, divided by the average annual CPI-U-RS factor for the earlier/earliest year.

Housing cost, as a percentage of income, is shown separately for owners with mortgages, owners without mortgages, and renters. Selected owner costs include utilities and fuels, mortgage payments, insurance, taxes, etc. In each case, the ratio of housing cost to income is computed separately for each housing unit. The housing cost ratios for half of all units are above the median shown in this book, and half are below the median shown in the book.

The data for monthly housing costs in item 51 are developed from a distribution of **Selected monthly owner costs** for owner-occupied units and **gross rent** for renter-occupied units.

Selected monthly owner costs are the sum of payments for mortgages, deeds of trust, contracts to purchase, or similar debts on the property (including payments for the first mortgage, second mortgages, home equity loans, and other junior mortgages); real estate taxes; fire, hazard, and flood insurance on the property; utilities (electricity, gas, and water and sewer); and fuels (oil, coal, kerosene, wood, etc.). It also includes, where appropriate, the monthly condominium fee for condominiums and mobile home costs (installment loan payments, personal property taxes, site rent, registration fees, and license fees). Selected monthly owner costs were tabulated for all owner-occupied units, and usually are shown separately for units "with a mortgage" and for units "not mortgaged."

Real estate taxes include state, local, and all other real estate taxes even if delinquent, unpaid, or paid by someone who is not a member of the household. However, taxes due from prior years are not included. If taxes are paid on other than a yearly basis, the payments are converted to a yearly basis.

RENT, Items 52–53, 65–68
Sources: Table B25064. Median Gross Rent (Dollars); and Table B25071. Median Gross Rent as a Percentage of Household Income in the Past 12 Months (Dollars)
Universe: Renter-Occupied Housing Units Paying Cash Rent
Table C25072. Age of Householder by Gross Rent as a Percentage of Household Income in the Past 12 Months
Universe: Renter-Occupied Housing Units

Median gross rent divides the distribution of renter-occupied housing units into two equal parts: one-half of the cases falling below the median gross rent and one-half above the median.

Gross rent is the **contract rent** plus the estimated average monthly cost of **utilities** (electricity, gas, and water and sewer) and fuels (oil, coal, kerosene, wood, etc.) if these are paid by the renter (or paid for the renter by someone else). Gross rent is intended to eliminate differentials that result from varying practices with respect to the inclusion of utilities and fuels as part of the rental payment. The estimated costs of water and sewer, and fuels are reported on a 12-month basis but are converted to monthly figures for the tabulations. Renter units occupied without payment of cash rent are not included in the tabulations.

To inflate gross rent amounts from previous years, the dollar values are inflated to the latest year's dollar values by multiplying by a factor equal to the average annual Consumer Price Index (CPI-U-RS) factor for the current year, divided by the average annual CPI-U-RS factor for the earlier/earliest year.

Gross rent as a percentage of household income is a computed ratio of monthly gross rent to monthly household income (total household income divided by 12). Median gross rent divides the gross rent as a percentage of household income distribution into two equal parts: one-half of the cases falling below the median gross rent as a percentage of household income and one-half above the median.

MEANS OF TRANSPORTATION TO WORK, ITEMS 69–76
Source: Table B08301. Means of Transportation to Work
Universe: Workers 16 Years and Over

Means of transportation to work refers to the principal mode of travel or type of conveyance that the worker usually used to get from home to work during the reference week. People who used different means of transportation on different days of the week were asked to specify the one they used most often, that is, the greatest number of days. People who used more than one means of transportation to get to work each day were asked to report the one used for the longest distance during the work trip.

The category, **car, truck, or van**, includes workers using a car (including company cars but excluding taxicabs), a truck of one-ton capacity or less, or a van. A question on vehicle occupancy was asked of people who indicated that they worked at some time during the reference week and who reported that their means of transportation to work was **car, truck, or van**. The category, **drove alone**, includes people who usually drove alone to work as well as people who were driven to work by someone who then drove back home or to a nonwork destination. The category, **carpooled**, includes workers who reported that two or more people usually rode to work in the vehicle during the reference week.

The category, **public transportation**, includes workers who used a bus or trolley bus, streetcar or trolley car, subway or elevated, railroad, or ferryboat, even if each mode is not shown separately in the tabulation. The category, "Other means," includes workers who used a mode of travel that is not identified separately within the data distribution.

MEAN TRAVEL TIME TO WORK, Items 77–82
Sources: Table B08301. Means of Transportation to Work
Universe: Workers 16 Years and Over
Table C08136. Aggregate Travel Time to Work (in Minutes) of Workers by Means of Transportation to Work
Universe: Workers 16 Years and Over Whom Did Not Work at Home

Travel time to work refers to the total number of minutes that it usually took the worker to get from home to work during the reference week. The elapsed time includes time spent waiting for public transportation, picking up passengers in carpools, and time spent in other activities related to getting to work.

Mean travel time to work (in minutes) is the average travel time that workers usually took to get from home to work (one way) during the reference week. This measure is obtained by dividing the total number of minutes taken to get from home to work (the aggregate travel time) by the number of workers 16 years old and over who did not work at home.

VEHICLES AVAILABLE, Items 83–88
Sources: Table B08201 Household Size by Vehicles Available; and Table B25046 Aggregate Number of Vehicles Available by Tenure
Universe: Occupied Housing Units

The data on vehicles available show the number of passenger cars, vans, and pickup or panel trucks of one-ton capacity or less kept at home and available for the use of household members. Vehicles rented or leased for one

month or more, company vehicles, and police and government vehicles are included if kept at home and used for non-business purposes. Dismantled or immobile vehicles are excluded. Vehicles kept at home but used only for business purposes also are excluded

Tables C-2, C-3, and C-4. Where — Migration, Housing, and Transportation

Table C-2 presents 12 items for the United States as a whole, each individual state and the District of Columbia, and 1,846 counties, county equivalents, and independent cities with a 2012 population of 20,000 or more.

Table C-3 presents 12 items for 366 Metropolitan Statistical Areas and 29 Metropolitan Divisions within the 12 largest Metropolitan Statistical Areas.

Table C-4 presents 12 items for 2,143 cities, Census Designated Places, and the principal portions of consolidated cities with a 2012 population of 20,000 or more.

PLACE OF RESIDENCE, Items 1 and 2
Sources: Table C07204. Geographical Mobility in the Past Year for Current Residence—State, County and Place Level in the United States (for states, counties, and cities)
Universe: Population 1 Year and Over in the United States
Table C07201. Geographical Mobility in the Past Year for Current Residence—Metropolitan Statistical Area Level in the United States (for Metropolitan Areas)
Universe: Population 1 Year and Over Living in a Metropolitan Statistical Area in the United States

Residence one year ago is used in conjunction with location of current residence to determine the extent of residential mobility of the population and the resulting redistribution of the population across the various states, metropolitan areas, and regions of the country. **Same house** includes all people 1 year old and over who, a year earlier, lived in the same house or apartment that they occupied at the time of interview.

Did not live in county/city/metropolitan area one year ago includes all persons who did not live in the listed county, city, or metropolitan area 1 year ago, whether their previous residence was in the same state, a different state, Puerto Rico, or abroad.

OCCUPIED HOUSING UNITS, Items 3–4
Source: Table B25003. Tenure
Universe: Occupied Housing Units

A **housing unit** is a house, apartment, mobile home or trailer, group of rooms, or single room occupied or, if vacant, intended for occupancy as separate living quarters. Separate living quarters are those in which the occupants do not live and eat with any other person in the structure and which have direct access from the outside of the building or through a common hall. For vacant units, the criteria of separateness and direct access are applied to the intended occupants whenever possible. If that information cannot be obtained, the criteria are applied to the previous occupants.

The occupants of a housing unit may be a single family, one person living alone, two or more families living together, or any other group of related or unrelated persons who share living arrangements. Both occupied and vacant housing units are included in the housing inventory, although recreational vehicles, tents, caves, boats, railroad cars, and the like are included only if they are occupied as a person's usual place of residence.

Occupied housing units are classified as either owner occupied or renter occupied. A housing unit is classified as occupied if it is the usual place of residence of the person or group of persons living in it at the time of enumeration, or if the occupants are only temporarily absent from the residence for two months or less, that is, away on vacation or a business trip. If all the people staying in the unit at the time of the interview are staying there for two months or less, the unit is considered to be temporarily occupied and classified as "vacant."

A housing unit is **owner occupied** if the owner or co-owner lives in the unit even if it is mortgaged or not fully paid for. The owner or co-owner must live in the unit and usually is Person 1 on the questionnaire. The unit is "Owned by you or someone in this household with a mortgage or loan" if it is being purchased with a mortgage or some other debt arrangement such as a deed of trust, trust deed, contract to purchase, land contract, or purchase agreement. The unit also is considered owned with a mortgage if it is built on leased land and there is a mortgage on the unit. Mobile homes occupied by owners with installment loan balances also are included in this category.

All occupied housing units that are not owner occupied, whether they are rented for cash rent or occupied without payment of cash rent, are classified as **renter occupied**. "No cash rent" units are separately identified in the rent tabulations. Such units are generally provided free by friends or relatives or in exchange for services such as resident manager, caretaker, minister, or tenant farmer. Housing units on military bases also are classified in the "No cash rent" category. "Rented for cash rent" includes units in continuing care, sometimes called life care arrangements. These arrangements usually involve a contract between one or more individuals and a health services provider guaranteeing the individual shelter, usually a house or apartment, and services, such as meals or transportation to shopping or recreation.

HOUSING VALUES AND COSTS, Items 5–7
Sources: Table B25077. Median Value (Dollars) and Table B25092. Median Selected Monthly Owner Costs as a Percentage of Household Income in the Past 12 Months
Universe: Owner-Occupied Housing Units

Median value is the dollar amount that divides the distribution of specified owner-occupied housing units into two equal parts, with half of all units below the median value and half above the median value. Value is defined as the respondent's estimate of what the house would sell for if it were for sale. If the house or mobile home was owned or being bought, but the land on which it sits was not, the respondent was asked to estimate the combined value of the house or mobile home and the land. For vacant units, value was the price asked for the property. Value was tabulated separately for all owner-occupied and vacant-for-sale housing units, as well as owner-occupied and vacant-for-sale mobile homes. The top code symbolizing a median value over one million dollars is $1,000,000.

Since value is the only dollar amount captured on the questionnaire in specified intervals (checkboxes), the category boundaries for previous years are not adjusted for inflation. However, the median value is adjusted for inflation by multiplying a factor equal to the average annual CPI-U-RS factor for the current year, divided by the average annual CPI-U-RS factor for the earlier/earliest year.

Housing cost, as a percentage of income, is shown separately for owners with mortgages and owners without mortgages. Selected owner costs include utilities and fuels, mortgage payments, insurance, taxes, etc. In each case, the ratio of housing cost to income is computed separately for each housing unit. The housing cost ratios for half of all units are above the median shown in this book, and half are below the median shown in the book.

RENT, Items 8–9
Source: Table B25064. Median Gross Rent (Dollars) and Table B25071. Median Gross Rent as a Percentage of Household Income in the Past 12 Months (Dollars)
Universe: Renter-Occupied Housing Units Paying Cash Rent

Median gross rent divides the distribution of renter-occupied housing units into two equal parts: one-half of the cases falling below the median gross rent and one-half above the median.

Gross rent is the **contract rent** plus the estimated average monthly cost of **utilities** (electricity, gas, and water and sewer) and fuels (oil, coal, kerosene, wood, etc.) if these are paid by the renter (or paid for the renter by someone else). Gross rent is intended to eliminate differentials that result from varying practices with respect to the inclusion of utilities and fuels as part of the rental payment. The estimated costs of water and sewer, and fuels are reported on a 12-month basis but are converted to monthly figures for the tabulations. Renter units occupied without payment of cash rent are not included in the tabulations. The top code, symbolizing a rent of $2,000 or more is $2,000.

To inflate gross rent amounts from previous years, the dollar values are inflated to the latest year's dollar values by multiplying by a factor equal to the average annual Consumer Price Index (CPI-U-RS) factor for the current year, divided by the average annual CPI-U-RS factor for the earlier/earliest year.

Gross rent as a percentage of household income is a computed ratio of monthly gross rent to monthly household income (total household income divided by 12). Median gross rent divides the gross rent as a percentage of household income distribution into two equal parts: one-half of the cases falling below the median gross rent as a percentage of household income and one-half above the median. The top code symbolizing a median gross rent as a percentage of household income of 50.0 percent or more is 50.0.

MEANS OF TRANSPORTATION TO WORK, Item 10
Source: Table C08301. Means of Transportation to Work
Universe: Workers 16 Years and Over

Means of transportation to work refers to the principal mode of travel or type of conveyance that the worker usually used to get from home to work during the reference week. People who used different means of transportation on different days of the week were asked to specify the one they used most often, that is, the greatest number of days. People who used more than one means of transportation to get to work each day were asked to report the one used for the longest distance during the work trip.

Item 10 shows the percentage of workers who drove alone to work. Other means of transportation include carpooling, public transportation, walking, taking a taxicab, motorcycling, bicycling, other means, or working at home.

MEAN TRAVEL TIME TO WORK, Item 11
Sources: Table B08013. Aggregate Travel Time to Work (in Minutes) of Workers by Sex; and Table B08012. Sex of Workers by Travel Time to Work
Universe: Workers 16 Years and Over Who Did Not Work at Home

Travel time to work refers to the total number of minutes that it usually took the worker to get from home to work during the reference week. The elapsed time includes time spent waiting for public transportation, picking up passengers in carpools, and time spent in other activities related to getting to work.

Mean travel time to work (in minutes) is the average travel time that workers usually took to get from home to work (one way) during the reference week. This measure is obtained by dividing the total number of minutes taken to get from home to work (the aggregate travel time) by the number of workers 16 years old and over who did not work at home.

VEHICLES AVAILABLE, Item 12
Source: Table C25045. Tenure by Vehicles Available
Universe: Occupied Housing Units

The data on vehicles available show the number of passenger cars, vans, and pickup or panel trucks of one-ton capacity or less kept at home and available for the use of household members. Vehicles rented or leased for one month or more, company vehicles, and police and government vehicles are included if kept at home and used for non-business purposes. Dismantled or immobile vehicles are excluded. Vehicles kept at home but used only for business purposes also are excluded.

APPENDIX C:
GEOGRAPHIC CONCEPTS AND CODES

GEOGRAPHIC AREAS COVERED

The Who, What, and Where of America presents American Community Survey (ACS) data for the United States, all states, all metropolitan areas, counties with populations of 20,000 or more, and cities with populations of 20,000 or more. ACS population sizes are based on the most recent population estimates from the Census Bureau's Population Estimates Program, except in census years. A few counties and cities show populations below 20,000. If a geographic area met the threshold for a previous period but dropped below the threshold for the current period, it will continue to be published as long as the population does not drop more than 5 percent below the threshold. All estimates are based on the geographic boundaries as they existed on January 1 of the sample year or, in the case of multiyear data products, at the beginning of the final year of data collection.

STATES AND COUNTIES

Data are presented for each of the 50 states, the District of Columbia, and the United States as a whole. The states are arranged alphabetically and counties are arranged alphabetically within each state. Data are presented for 1,846 counties and county equivalents with populations of 20,000 or more.

County equivalents

In Louisiana, the primary divisions of the state are known as parishes rather than counties. In Alaska, the county equivalents are the organized boroughs, together with the census areas that were developed for general statistical purposes by the state of Alaska and the U.S. Census Bureau. Four states—Maryland, Missouri, Nevada, and Virginia—have one or more incorporated places that are legally independent of any county and thus constitute primary divisions of their states. Within each state, independent cities are listed alphabetically following the list of counties. The District of Columbia is not divided into counties or county equivalents—data for the entire district are presented as a county equivalent. New York City contains five counties: Bronx, Kings, New York, Queens, and Richmond.

METROPOLITAN AREAS

Data are included for all 366 metropolitan statistical areas and 29 metropolitan divisions, which are located within the 11 largest metropolitan statistical areas. The metropolitan statistical areas are listed alphabetically, and the metropolitan divisions are listed alphabetically under the metropolitan statistical area of which they are components.

The U.S. Office of Management and Budget (OMB) defines metropolitan and micropolitan statistical areas according to published standards. The major purpose of defining these areas is to enable all U.S. government agencies to use the same geographic definitions in tabulating and publishing data. The general concept of a metropolitan or micropolitan statistical area is that of a core area containing a substantial population nucleus, together with adjacent communities that have a high degree of economic and social integration with the core. The standards for delineating the areas are reviewed and revised once every ten years, prior to each decennial census. Generally, the areas are delineated using the most recent set of standards following each decennial census. Between censuses, the delineations are updated annually to reflect the most recent Census Bureau population estimates. The metropolitan statistical areas in this book are based on application of the 2000 standards to 2000 decennial census data, updated each year according to the most recent population estimates, most recently effective December 1, 2009. Areas based on the 2010 standards and Census Bureau data were delineated in February of 2013. The ACS will begin using those new delineations with the 2013 data to be released in 2014.

Standard definitions of metropolitan areas were first issued in 1949 by the Bureau of the Budget (the predecessor of the OMB), under the designation "standard metropolitan area" (SMA). The term was changed to "standard metropolitan statistical area" (SMSA) in 1959, and to "metropolitan statistical area" (MSA) in 1983. The term "metropolitan area" (MA) was adopted in 1990 and refers collectively to metropolitan statistical areas (MSAs), consolidated metropolitan statistical areas (CMSAs), and primary metropolitan statistical areas (PMSAs). The term "core based statistical area" (CBSA) became effective in

2000 and refers collectively to metropolitan and micropolitan statistical areas.

The standards implemented in 2000 provide that each CBSA must contain at least one urban area of 10,000 or more population. Each metropolitan statistical area must have at least one urbanized area of 50,000 or more inhabitants. Each micropolitan statistical area must have at least one urban cluster of at least 10,000, but less than 50,000, people.

Under the standards, the county (or counties) in which at least 50 percent of the population resides within urban areas of 10,000 or more population, or that contain at least 5,000 people residing within a single urban area of 10,000 or more population, is identified as a "central county" (counties). Additional "outlying counties" are included in the CBSA if they meet specified requirements of commuting to or from the central counties. Counties or equivalent entities form the geographic "building blocks" for metropolitan and micropolitan statistical areas throughout the United States.

If specified criteria are met, a metropolitan statistical area containing a single core with a population of 2.5 million or more may be subdivided to form smaller groupings of counties referred to as "metropolitan divisions."

The largest city in each metropolitan statistical area is designated a "principal city." Additional cities qualify if specified requirements are met concerning population size and employment. The title of each metropolitan statistical area consists of the names of up to three of its principal cities and the name of each state into which the metropolitan statistical area extends. Titles of metropolitan divisions also typically are based on principal city names, but in certain cases consist of county names. The principal city need not be an incorporated place if it meets the requirements of population size and employment. Usually such a principal city is a Census designated place.

In view of the importance of cities and town in New England, the standards implemented in 2000 also provide for a set of geographic areas that are defined using cities and towns in the six New England states. These New England city and town areas (NECTAs) are not included in this volume.

CITIES

This book presents data for 2,143 cities with estimated populations of 20,000 or more in 2012. Corresponding data for states are also provided. The states are arranged alphabetically and the cities are ordered alphabetically within each state.

As used in this volume, the term *city* refers to *places* as defined by the Census Bureau. These include places that have been incorporated as cities, boroughs, towns, or villages under the laws of their respective states, as well as Census designated places (CDPs). CDPs are delineated by the Census Bureau, in cooperation with states and localities, as statistical counterparts of incorporated places for purposes of the decennial census and the ACS. CDPs comprise densely settled concentrations of population that are identifiable by name but are not legally incorporated places.

Included with the incorporated cities are the principal portions of seven consolidated cities. A consolidated city is an incorporated place that has combined its government functions with a county or subcounty entity but contains one or more other semi-independent incorporated places that continue to function as local governments within the consolidated government. Consolidated cities are not included in this book, but the "consolidated city (balance)" portions are treated as incorporated places in the ACS data. Consolidated city (balance) portions included in this volume are Milford, Connecticut; Athens-Clarke County, Georgia Augusta-Richmond County, Georgia; Indianapolis, Indiana; Louisville-Jefferson County, Kentucky; Butte-Silver Bow, Montana; and Nashville-Davidson, Tennessee.

Towns in the New England states and New York are treated as minor civil divisions (MCDs) and are not included in this book.

GEOGRAPHIC CODES

The tables in this book provide a geographic code or codes for each area.

For counties, a five-digit state and county code is given for each state and county. The first two digits indicate the state; the remaining three represent the county. Within each state, the counties are listed in order, beginning with 001, with even numbers usually omitted. Independent cities follow the counties and begin with the number 510. In the state-level tables, a two-digit state code is provided. The state code is a sequential numbering, with some gaps, of the states and the District of Columbia in alphabetical order from Alabama (01) to Wyoming (56).

These codes have been established by the U.S. government as Federal Information Processing Standards and are often referred to as *FIPS codes*. They are used by U.S. government agencies and many other organizations for data presentation. The codes are provided in this volume for use in matching the data given here with other data sources in which counties are identified by FIPS code.

The metropolitan area tables provide metro area codes for each metropolitan area, as well as metropolitan division codes where appropriate.

For cities, a seven-digit state and place code is included. The first two digits identify the state and are the same as the FIPS codes described above. The remaining five digits are the place FIPS codes established by the U.S. government.

INDEPENDENT CITIES

The following independent cities are not included in any county; their data are presented separately in this volume.

MARYLAND
Baltimore (separate from Baltimore County)

MISSOURI
St. Louis (separate from St. Louis County)

NEVADA
Carson City

VIRGINIA

Alexandria	Norfolk
Charlottesville	Petersburg
Chesapeake	Portsmouth
Danville	Richmond
Fairfax	Roanoke
Fredericksburg	Salem
Hampton	Staunton
Harrisonburg	Suffolk
Hopewell	Virginia Beach
Lynchburg	Waynesboro
Manassas	Winchester
Newport News	